Dear West Customer:

West Academic Publishing has changed the look of its American Casebook Series®.

In keeping with our efforts to promote sustainability, we have replaced our former covers with book covers that are more environmentally friendly. Our casebooks will now be covered in a 100% renewable natural fiber. In addition, we have migrated to an ink supplier that favors vegetable-based materials, such as soy.

Using soy inks and natural fibers to print our textbooks reduces VOC emissions. Moreover, our primary paper supplier is certified by the Forest Stewardship Council, which is testament to our commitment to conservation and responsible business management.

The new cover design has migrated from the long-standing brown cover to a contemporary charcoal fabric cover with silver-stamped lettering and black accents. Please know that inside the cover, our books continue to provide the same trusted content that you've come to expect from West.

We've retained the ample margins that you have told us you appreciate in our texts while moving to a new, larger font, improving readability. We hope that you will find these books a pleasing addition to your bookshelf.

Another visible change is that you will no longer see the brand name Thomson West on our print products. With the recent merger of Thomson and Reuters, I am pleased to announce that books published under the West Academic Publishing imprint will once again display the West brand.

It will likely be several years before all of our casebooks are published with the new cover and interior design. We ask for your patience as the new covers are rolled out on new and revised books knowing that behind both the new and old covers, you will find the finest in legal education materials for teaching and learning.

Thank you for your continued patronage of the West brand, which is both rooted in history and forward looking towards future innovations in legal education. We invite you to be a part of our next evolution.

Best regards,

Louis H. Higgins
Editor in Chief, West Academic Publishing

INTERNATIONAL LAW
CASES AND MATERIALS

Fifth Edition

■ ■ ■

By

Lori Fisler Damrosch

*Henry L. Moses Professor of Law
and International Organization,
Columbia University, School of Law*

Louis Henkin

*University Professor Emeritus,
Columbia University, School of Law*

Sean D. Murphy

*Patricia Roberts Harris Research Professor of Law,
George Washington University Law School*

Hans Smit

*Stanley H. Fuld Professor of Law,
Columbia University, School of Law*

AMERICAN CASEBOOK SERIES®

WEST®
A Thomson Reuters business

Mat #40736800

American Casebook Series is a trademark registered in the U.S. Patent and Trademark Office.

COPYRIGHT © 1980, 1987, 1993 WEST PUBLISHING CO.
© West, a Thomson business, 2001
© 2009 Thomson Reuters

  610 Opperman Drive
  St. Paul, MN 55123
  1–800–313–9378

Printed in the United States of America

ISBN: 978–0–314–19128–1

This book is dedicated to our predecessors in international law at Columbia University
Philip C. Jessup
Wolfgang G. Friedmann
Oliver J. Lissitzyn
Oscar Schachter

*

PREFACE TO THE FIFTH EDITION

This edition renews and enriches a "classical" casebook on international law. It reflects our aspiration to enable teaching international law in essential continuity with the great traditions of the discipline, yet with fresh appreciation and even some radical change.

International law in the twenty-first century is being invigorated with ideas and energy from peoples around the world. Grass-roots movements, transnational networks, and non-governmental organizations have focused attention on issues where international law can make notable contributions to solution of problems affecting all humanity. New standards of conduct have been elaborated in fields as diverse as human rights, trade, the environment, and disarmament; and new institutions are emerging to realize ambitious goals through law. While the nation state remains a central player, international law is no longer the specialized preserve of states, governments, or diplomats: it is now put to use by activists around the globe.

The transformations in the hitherto largely state-centered nature of our discipline are a major theme of the present edition. Along with emphasizing the centrality of human rights in contemporary international law, we have given enhanced attention to non-state actors and their influence on the theory, content, and implementation of international law, illustrated by developments since the last edition, such as the responses to the attacks of September 11, 2001 and the establishment of the International Criminal Court.

The electronic revolution continues to work changes in the ways that we teach, research, and practice international law. Informational resources that were formerly the province of experts in international law (with access to specialized research libraries) are now instantly available around the world. In view of the ephemeral nature of many Internet resources and the quickly-changing landscape of electronic addresses and search techniques, we have retained print-based citations to standard sources, such as treaty collections, national digests of practice, and case reports, while also indicating as appropriate the main resources of the World Wide Web for contemporary international law research. The exigencies of print production have imposed a closing date of early 2009 for taking account of recent developments.

The editors have compiled a collection of basic documents published as a supplement to the present volume, which provides a convenient reference to the main primary sources discussed in the casebook. Of course, such instruments are also available in original sources, other collections, or electronic databases.

v

We welcome to our editorial team another colleague in the Columbia Law School tradition, Professor Sean D. Murphy (Columbia J.D. 1985). The result, we believe, is a casebook fit for a new generation.

L.F.D.
L.H.
S.D.M.
H.S.

ABBREVIATIONS

A.F.D.I. or Ann. Français — Annuaire Français de Droit International

A.J.I.L. — American Journal of International Law

Ann. de l'Institut de Droit Int. — Annuaire de l'Institut de Droit International

Ann. Dig. — Annual Digest

A.S.I.L. Proc. — American Society of International Law Proceedings

Brit. Y.B.I.L. or Brit. Y.B. Int'l Law — British Yearbook of International Law

E.J.I.L. — European Journal of International Law

E.S.C. Res. — Economic and Social Council Resolution

E.S.C.O.R. — United Nations Economic and Social Council Official Records

E.T.S. — European Treaty Series

G.A.O.R. — United Nations General Assembly Official Records

G.A. Res. — United Nations General Assembly Resolution

Gr. Brit. T.S. — Great Britain Treaty Series

Hackworth — Hackworth, Digest of International Law (1940–44)

Hyde — Hyde, International Law Chiefly as Interpreted and Applied by the United States (2d ed. 1945)

Hudson — Hudson, International Legislation

I.C.J. — International Court of Justice Reports

I.C.L.Q. — International and Comparative Law Quarterly

I.C.T.R. — International Criminal Tribunal for Rwanda

I.C.T.Y. — International Criminal Tribunal for the Former Yugoslavia

I.L.C. — International Law Commission

I.L.C.Rep. — International Law Commission Reports

I.L.M. or Int'l Leg. Mat'ls — International Legal Materials

I.L.R. — International Law Reports

L.N.T.S. — League of Nations Treaty Series

Malloy — Malloy, Treaties, Conventions, International Acts, Protocols and Agreements Between the United States of America and Other Powers (1910–38)

O'Connell ---------------------------------- O'Connell, International Law (2nd ed. 1970)

Oppenheim -------------------------------- Oppenheim, International Law, vol. 1 (9th ed. Jennings and Watts 1992), vol. 2 (7th ed. Lauterpacht 1952)

P.C.I.J. -------------------------------------- Permanent Court of International Justice Reports

Rec. des Cours ------------------------------ Recueil des Cours, Académie de Droit International

Restatement (Third) ------------------------ Restatement of the Law (Third), The Foreign Relations Law of the United States (1987)

S.C.O.R. ------------------------------------- United Nations Security Council Official Records

S.C. Res. ------------------------------------ United Nations Security Council Resolution

State Dept. Bull. --------------------------- State Department Bulletin

Stat. --- Statutes at Large, United States

T.I.A.S. -------------------------------------- Treaty and Other International Act Series

U.N.C.I.O. ---------------------------------- United Nations Conference on International Organization

U.N.Doc. ------------------------------------ United Nations Document

U.N.R.I.A.A. or U.N. Rep. Int'l Arb.
  Awards ------------------------------------ United Nations Reports of International Arbitration Awards

U.N.T.S. ------------------------------------- United Nations Treaty Series

U.S.C.A. ------------------------------------- United States Code Annotated

U.S.G.A.O. ---------------------------------- United States General Accounting Office

U.S.T. -- United States Treaties and Other International Agreements

Whiteman ----------------------------------- Whiteman, Digest of International Law (1963–73)

Yb.I.L.C. ------------------------------------ Yearbook of the International Law Commission

ACKNOWLEDGMENTS

We acknowledge and are indebted to a large number of individuals who generously contributed their time and effort to make the Fifth Edition possible. We naturally include those people who assisted in the previous editions. We are grateful to our present and former colleagues in international law and related fields at Columbia and George Washington Universities, where we benefit from exceptionally stimulating environments for teaching and research. We also thank the users of the previous editions who gave us comments and suggestions for improvement, and many present and former students.

The editors of the Fifth Edition would like to acknowledge in particular their great debt to Richard Crawford Pugh, formerly of the Columbia Law School faculty and in recent years Distinguished Professor of Law at the University of San Diego School of Law. His involvement goes back to the predecessor casebook published in 1969 of which he was a co-editor (together with Wolfgang Friedmann and Oliver Lissitzyn), as well as the previous four editions of the present work. His influence pervades the book and we thank him for his many contributions.

In the preparation of this edition we would like to extend our appreciation to Joie Chowdhury, Columbia LL.M. 2009; Jeffrey Brundage, Erin Creegan of the George Washington University J.D. class of 2010; Kelly Dunn, George Washington University J.D. 2009; Amara Levy–Moore, Columbia M.I.A. 2009; and Neelanjan Maitra of the Columbia J.D. class of 2010. Yahaira Alonzo provided valuable support.

We extend our warm thanks for reference assistance readily and frequently given by the staff of the Arthur W. Diamond Law Library at Columbia University and of the Jacob Burns Law Library at George Washington University.

Finally, we acknowledge our indebtedness to the following authors and publishers who granted us permission to reprint copyrighted material:

American Law Institute, for permission to reprint from the Restatement of the Law (Third), The Foreign Relations Law of the United States (1987).

American Society of International Law, for permission to reprint from the following articles appearing in the American Journal of International Law and the Proceedings of the American Society of International Law, © The American Society of International Law: Abbott, International Relations Theory, International Law, and the Regime Governing Internal Conflicts, 93 A.J.I.L. 361, 361–67 (1999); Acheson, Remarks on the Cuban Quarantine, 57 A.S.I.L. Proc. 9, 14 (1963); Ben–Naftali, The Extraterritorial Application of Human Rights to Occupied Territories, 100 A.S.I.L. Proc. 90, 92–94 (2006); Buergenthal, The Evolving International Human Rights System, 100 A.J.I.L. 783 (2006); Caron, The ILC Articles on State Responsibility: The Paradoxical

Relationship Between Form and Authority, 96 A.J.I.L. 857, 858 (2002); Charlesworth, Chinkin & Wright, Feminist Approaches to International Law, 85 A.J.I.L. 613, 615, 621–23, 625 (1991); Charnovitz, Nongovernmental Organizations and International Law, 100 A.J.I.L. 348, 350–68 (2006); Dennis, Application of Human Rights Treaties Extraterritorially During Times of Armed Conflict, 100 A.S.I.L. Proc. 90, 92–94 (2006); Dunoff & Trachtman, The Law and Economics of Humanitarian Law Violations in Internal Conflict, 93 A.J.I.L. 394, 395, 397 (1999); Friedmann, United States Policy and the Crisis of International Law, 59 A.J.I.L. 857 (1965); Joyner, Reflections on the Lawfulness of Invasion, 78 A.J.I.L. 131 (1984); Kearney & Dalton, The Treaty on Treaties, 64 A.J.I.L. 495 (1970); McDougal, The Hydrogen Bomb Tests, 49 A.J.I.L. 357 (1955); Meeker, Defensive Quarantine and the Law, 57 A.J.I.L. 523 (1963); Moore, Grenada and the International Double Standard, 78 A.J.I.L. 145 (1984); Oxman, The 1994 Agreement and the Convention, 88 A.J.I.L. 687, 688–95 (1994); Ratner, Drawing a Better Line: *Uti Possidetis* and the Borders of New States, 90 A.J.I.L. 590, 591 (1996); Reisman, Coercion and Self–Determination: Construing Charter Article 2(4), 78 A.J.I.L. 642 (1984); Reisman, International Law After the Cold War, 84 A.J.I.L. 859, 860–62 (1990); Schachter, The Legality of Pro–Democratic Invasion, 78 A.J.I.L. 645 (1984); Schachter, The Twilight Existence of Nonbinding International Agreements, 71 A.J.I.L. 296 (1977); Schachter, United Nations Law in the Gulf Conflict, 85 A.J.I.L. 542 (1991); Shelton, Normative Hierarchy in International Law, 100 A.J.I.L. 291, 297–99, 302–03, 305–07 (2006); Simma & Paulus, The Responsibility of Individuals for Human Rights Abuses in Internal Conflicts: A Positivist View, 93 A.J.I.L. 302, 303–05 (1999); Taft & Buchwald, Preemption, Iraq, and International Law, 97 A.J.I.L. 557 (2003); Talmon, The Security Council as World Legislature, 99 A.J.I.L. 175, 179, 182–86 (2005); Vagts, Hegemonic International Law, 95 A.J.I.L. 843, 843–48 (2001); Weil, Towards Relative Normativity in International Law?, 77 A.J.I.L. 413, 421 (1983); Wiessner & Willard, Policy–Oriented Jurisprudence and Human Rights Abuses in Internal Conflict: Toward a World Public Order of Human Dignity, 93 A.J.I.L. 316, 318–20 (1999). Reproduced with permission from The American Society of International Law, © The American Society of International Law.

American Society of International Law, for permission to reprint from the following articles from Law and Force in the New International Order (Damrosch & Scheffer eds. 1991): Chayes, The Use of Force in the Persian Gulf; Gardner, Commentary on the Law of Self–Defense; Schachter, Authorized Uses of Force by the United Nations and Regional Organizations; Scheffer, Commentary on Collective Security. Copyright © 1991 The American Society of International Law.

American Society of International Law, for permission to reprint the international arbitral award in Texaco Overseas Petroleum, et al. v. Libyan Arab Republic, 17 I.L.M. 1 (1978); and the introductory note by Schreuer to the Brčko arbitral award, 38 I.L.M. 534 (1999).

American Society of International Law, for permission to reprint from U.S. Policy Toward the International Criminal Court: Furthering Positive

Engagement, Report of an Independent Task Force (March 2009). Copyright © 2009 The American Society of International Law.

Arizona Law Review, for permission to reprint from Wyman, The Property Rights Challenge in Marine Fisheries, 50 Ariz. L. Rev. 511, 515–25 (2008).

Cambridge University Press, for permission to reprint from Murphy, Democratic Legitimacy and the Recognition of States and Governments, 48 I.C.L.Q. 545, 566–79 (1999).

Canadian Institute of International Affairs, for permission to reprint from Friedmann, The Role of International Law in the Conduct of International Affairs, 20 International Journal 158 (1965).

Carnegie Corporation of New York and Rowman & Littlefield, Publishers, Inc., for permission to reprint from Words Over War: Mediation and Arbitration to Prevent Deadly Conflict (Greenberg, Barton & McGuinness, eds., 2000).

Case Western Reserve Journal of International Law, for permission to reprint from Smith, Note, Sovereignty over Unoccupied Territories—The Western Sahara Decision, 9 Case W. Res. J. Int'l L. 135, 140–41 (1977).

Columbia Journal of Transnational Law, for permission to reprint from Henkin, The Invasion of Panama Under International Law: A Gross Violation, 29 Colum. J. Transnat. L. 293 (1991); and Murphy, Taking Multinational Corporate Codes of Conduct to the Next Level, 43 Columbia J. Transnat'l L. 389 (2005).

Columbia University Press, for permission to reprint from Friedmann, The Changing Structure of International Law © 1964 Columbia University Press; Henkin, The Age of Rights 74, 76–77 © 1990 Columbia University Press; and The International Bill of Rights: The Covenant on Civil and Political Rights, Introduction, 21–22 (Henkin ed. 1981).

Council on Foreign Relations, Inc., and Foreign Affairs, for permission to reprint from Boutros–Ghali, Empowering the United Nations, 71 Foreign Affairs 89, 98–99 (Winter 1992/93). Reprinted by permission of Foreign Affairs. Copyright 1993 by the Council on Foreign Relations, Inc.

Council on Foreign Relations Press, for permission to reprint from Acevedo, The Haitian Crisis and the OAS Response: A Test of Effectiveness in Protecting Democracy, in Enforcing Restraint: Collective Intervention in Internal Conflicts (Damrosch ed. 1993); Henkin, How Nations Behave (2d ed.1979); and Henkin, The Use of Force: Law and U.S. Policy, in Right v. Might: International Law and the Use of Force (2d ed. 1991).

Energy Law Journal, for permission to reprint from Dernbach & Kakade, Climate Change Law: An Introduction, 29 Energy L.J. 1, 8–9, 29–30 (2008).

European Journal of International Law and Oxford University Press, for permission to reprint from Krisch & Kingsbury, Global Governance and Global Administrative Law in the International Legal Order, 17 E.J.I.L. 1, 2–5, 12–13 (2006).

Foundation Press, for permission to reprint from Human Rights 334, 358, 370, 396, 598 (Henkin, Neuman, Orentlicher & Leebron, eds, 1999).

Thomas M. Franck, for permission to reprint from Franck, The Power of Legitimacy Among Nations (1990).

Hague Academy of International Law, for permission to reprint from Baxter, Treaties and Custom, 129 Rec. des Cours 25 (1970–I); Damrosch, Enforcing International Law Through Non–Forcible Measures, 269 Rec. des Cours 9 (1997); Henkin, International Law: Politics, Values and Functions, 216 Rec. des Cours 9, 22, 24–28 (1989–IV); Jiménez de Aréchaga, International Law in the Past Third of a Century, 159 Rec. des Cours 9 (1978–I); Schachter, International Law in Theory and Practice, 178 Rec. des Cours 21 (1982–V); Waldock, General Course on Public International Law, 106 Rec. des Cours 1 (1962–II).

Harvard Law Review Association, for permission to reprint from Henkin, The Constitution and United States Sovereignty: A Century of Chinese Exclusion and Its Progeny, 100 Harv. L. Rev. 853 (1987).

Louis Henkin, for permission to reprint from Foreign Affairs and the United States Constitution, 2d edition, Oxford University Press, 1996, © Louis Henkin 1996; International Law: Politics and Values (1995).

Holt, Rinehart & Winston, for permission to reprint from Kelsen, Principles of International Law 252, 438–39, 450–452 (2d rev. ed. Tucker ed. 1966).

Kluwer Law International/Kluwer Academic Publishers/Martinus Nijhoff Publishers, for permission to reprint from Henkin, International Law: Politics and Values (1995); Schachter, International Law in Theory and Practice (1991), with the kind permission of Kluwer Law International/Kluwer Academic Publishers.

Macmillan (U.S.)/Simon and Schuster, for permission to reprint from Philip Jessup, A Modern Law of Nations (1948).

Manchester University Press and Sir Ian M. Sinclair, for permission to reprint from Sinclair, The Vienna Convention on the Law of Treaties (2d ed. 1984).

Estate of the late Dr. F.A. Mann, for permission to reprint from Mann, Reflections on a Commercial Law of Nations, 33 Brit. Y.B.I.L. 20, 34–39 (1957); and Mann, State Contracts and International Arbitration, 42 Brit. Y.B.I.L. 1, 27–28 (1967).

Michigan Law Review, for permission to reprint from Henkin, International Law as Law in the United States, 82 Mich. L. Rev. 1555 (1984); and from Schachter, The Right of States to Use Armed Force, 82 Mich. L. Rev. 1620 (1984).

New York University Journal of International Law and Politics, for permission to reprint from Oxman, The Duty to Respect Generally Accepted International Standards, 24 N.Y.U. J. Int'l L. & Pol. 143 (1991).

Oxford University Press, for permission to reprint from Brierly, The Law of Nations (6th ed. Waldock 1963); Hart, The Concept of Law 227–30 (2d ed.

1994); Xue, Chinese Observations on International Law, 6 Chinese J. Int'l L. 83, 85–86 (2007).

Pearson Education, for permission to reprint from Oppenheim, International Law 7–8 (9th ed. Jennings & Watts eds. 1992). Reprinted by permission of Pearson Education Limited © Longman Group Ltd.

W.   Michael Reisman, for permission to reprint from McDougal & Feliciano, Law and Minimum World Public Order (1961).

Royal Institute of International Affairs, for permission to reprint from Bowett, Reservations to Non–Restricted Multilateral Treaties, 48 Brit. Y.B.I.L. 88–90 (1976–77); Rama–Montaldo, International Legal Personality and Implied Powers of International Organizations, 44 Brit. Y.B.I.L. 111, 123–124 (1970).

Sweet & Maxwell, Ltd., for permission to reprint from Lauterpacht, International Law and Human Rights 27–29 (1973); 1 O'Connell, International Law 108–09 (2d ed. 1970).

Yale Law Journal, for permission to reprint from Koh, Why Do Nations Obey International Law?, 106 Yale L.J. 2364, 2646, 2651–55 (1997).

*

INTRODUCTION TO THE STUDY
OF INTERNATIONAL LAW

Traditionally, international law was seen as the law of the international community of states, the basic units in the world political system from the Peace of Westphalia (1648) forward. At least from the mid-twentieth century, however, international law has increasingly dealt also with other entities, notably including the individual as bearer of human rights.

That international law has been understood as the law made by states to govern relations among them implies an important frame for the conception of the subject-matter, and accordingly for the presentation of material in a casebook for a course in the field. Conceptually, if international law is state-to-state in its origin and application, other entities would be governed by international law only to the extent that states have accepted to include them in the functioning of what would remain fundamentally an interstate system. Under this view, intergovernmental or non-governmental organizations come within the framework of international law by virtue of decisions made through interstate processes; multinational corporations or other enterprises would not participate directly in the international legal system; and the rights and obligations of individuals would flow from processes in which states were the fundamental actors.

From some perspectives, no doubt, these distinctions are artificial. A more inclusive view maintains that contemporary international relations consist of much more than official relations between states or their governments; that even these relations cannot be understood in isolation from other relations involving other actors; and that the law of intergovernmental relations cannot be seen independently of other law governing other transnational relations. For these reasons, some prefer a more comprehensive perspective that includes all the law—national, international, or mixed—that applies to all actors whose activities or influences cross state lines. The term "transnational law" was coined to express this more capacious conception—a broader one than we can cover comprehensively in the present casebook.

Certainly, beginning already in the first half of the twentieth century and accelerating in the second half, international law came to govern not only relations between states, but also the status, rights, and duties of individuals and of certain kinds of organizations and corporations. Ever-growing numbers of international organizations have acquired existence, personality, rights and duties, and their competences extend across all spheres of human activity. States have conferred ever more expansive authorities on certain intergovernmental organizations, such as the European Union. The influence of the international human rights movement on the system of international law has been profound, to the point that it is no longer accurate to think of international law as strictly an interstate system. International law protects the rights of individuals against their own states and even accords them independent status and standing before some international bodies. International law also imposes duties on individuals and may bring them to international trial and punishment.

For purposes of study and analysis, there are convincing reasons to maintain a focus on interstate relations and institutions, even while recognizing that one must attend to all the other rings in the world circus as well. International law is a conceptually distinct system, independent of the national systems with which it interacts. It deals with relations which individual states do not effectively govern. International law is thus to be distinguished from national law that governs foreign and other transnational transactions and relations: each state has its own constitutional foreign relations law, and various intersecting bodies of law address the different sorts of commercial and economic relationships that cross national boundaries. For example, the treaty-making powers of the President-and-Senate, and limitations on those powers in favor of rights of individuals or states of the United States, are questions of U.S. foreign relations law that may have important international significance and even some international legal relevance, without being (strictly speaking) questions of international law. (The relation of international law to national law is a question with which each state must struggle in different ways. See Chapter 10.)

While international law can profitably be studied without too many excursions into other domains, the study of international law can also benefit from broader perspectives. The governance and the law of the international political order merit study with attention to insights about law more generally. One can, and should, ask the same questions, *mutatis mutandis*, from the same variety of perspectives about international law as about other forms of law, even though the answers might be very different. Feminist analysis, critical theories of law, and law-and-economics are among the approaches offering new ways to think about international law.

International law is not a "course"; it is a curriculum. One can find in it the basic concepts of any legal system—property and tort, injury and remedy, status and contract. It has its own law-making and law-applying procedures. There is law governing "public lands" and common environments, as in outer space and the deep sea. The "public law" of the international legal system is not yet vast, as was true of the national law of even developed states until quite recently; nonetheless, it might well fill several courses in any comprehensive curriculum of international law, including international counterparts of constitutional law, administrative law, legislation, and judicial process.

Philosophers and other scholars of law can also ask questions about the international legal system from the vantage point of their discipline. There is a jurisprudence and a sociology of international law, and the beginnings of a criminology. The student of political science can—and should—consider the character of the international political system, its premises and assumption, and how it is governed; he or she might ask whether there are legislative, executive, and judicial functions, and how they are exercised. One might ask why and how law is made; whether law is enforced and what mechanisms are used to induce compliance with it; by what institutions is law interpreted, applied, developed; how are disputes settled; what is its system of administrative regulation, law and procedure.

Analogies and nomenclature from domestic law are, of course, deceptive, for there are profound differences between domestic societies and international society (itself a metaphor), and between national and international law. But the concepts, the perspectives, even the terminology and categories of domestic law, when used with caution and with awareness of the differences, can be directed at the international system as well. A comprehensive perspective on international law like that which is commonly applied to domestic law can thus benefit the student of international law.

*

HISTORICAL INTRODUCTION [1]

Human history has long known tribes and peoples, inhabiting defined territories, governed by chiefs or princes, and interacting with each other in a manner requiring primitive forms of diplomatic relations and covenants of peace or alliances for war. These relations between peoples or princes, however, were not governed by any agreed, authoritative principles or rules. At various times, moreover, most of the peoples of the known world were part of large empires; and relations between them were subject to an imperial, "domestic" government and law. Empire, actual or potential, was also sometimes supported by an ideology that claimed universal authority over all peoples, or otherwise rejected the independence and equality of nations or any principles governing relations between them other than imperial law.

Thus, classical Chinese philosophy, as formulated by Confucius in the 6th century B.C.E., regarded the ruler of China as the "Son of Heaven," who governs the universe as a righteous ruler. From this conception—often greatlyat variance with the division of China into many rival kingdoms and factions—developed a notion that frequently shaped Chinese attitudes toward international relations: that Chinese rulers were culturally superior "fathers" or "elder brothers" of other nations or states. This notion served to legitimate conquest and subjugation of others.

Ancient Judaism, ideologically committed to monotheism, did not in principle accept the equality of polytheistic nations. But Judaism has not been the ideology of a politically independent people for 2000 years until our own day, and Judaism did not develop a universalist political ideology comparable to that of Christianity or Islam.

In medieval Christianity, the Holy Roman Empire claimed universal authority for the Pope as the spiritual head, and for the Emperor as the temporal head, of the Christian nations of Europe. Thus, religious and political goals coalesced to legitimatize European efforts to conquer—and then convert—non-Christian peoples around the world. Even among the nations of Europe, as long as the concept of universal authority was ascendant, there was little need to develop rules concerning diplomatic intercourse between sovereign states, principles of territorial sovereignty, jurisdiction, treatymaking, state responsibility, and other aspects of interstate relations that form the bulk of the modern law of nations.

Similarly, Islam, like Christianity in its formative phase, sought to extend the religion's reach and therefore held back from recognizing the equality and respecting the integrity of non-Islamic nations. For Moslem jurists, the world

---

1. See generally Nussbaum, A Concise History of the Law of Nations (rev. ed. 1954); Verzijl, et al., International Law in Historical Perspective, 11 vols. (1968–1992); History of the Law of Nations, 7 Encyclopedia of Public International Law 126–173 (1984). Compare also Onuma, When Was the Law of International Society Born? An Inquiry of the History of International Law from an Intercivilizational Perspective, 2 J. Hist. Int'l L. 1 (2000).

was divided into countries under Moslem rule (*dar al Islam*) and the rest of the world (*dar al Harb*).

Universalist ideologies and approaches to international relations were modified in recent centuries. Nation-states of different religions increasingly came into contact with each other and were compelled to deal with each other on a basis of equality and mutual respect for sovereignty. The structure and development of the modern law of nations is intimately connected with the era of sovereign national states dealing with each other as independent units. In a strict sense, therefore, the history of the modern law of nations begins with the emergence of independent nation-states from the ruins of the medieval Holy Roman Empire, and is commonly dated from the Peace of Westphalia (1648).

Origins of International Law in the Western World before Grotius

Before the Macedonian conquest, the Greek states never achieved unity; they alternated between peace and war. As a result, the Greeks, in their classical period, developed rules governing relations between the various Greek city-states, rules that more closely parallel the modern system of international law than those of any other early civilization. Any reader of Thucydides' *History of the Peloponnesian War* will detect a modern ring in the reasoning and techniques used by the Greek city-states in diplomatic practices, in treaties of alliance and in certain elementary rules of war. Disputes were sometimes submitted to arbitration. However, relations between Greeks and non-Greeks were not regulated in the same way; the latter were regarded by the Greeks as barbarians, and not as moral or legal equals.

The Roman Empire, which at its height comprised hundreds of different races, tribes and religions, could not acknowledge an international legal system in the modern sense, within the borders of an empire that comprised almost the entire civilized world. Although there were always wars at the borders of the Roman Empire, they gave rise to very few rules or usages. The significance of the Roman contribution to international law lies not in the development of any modern system of interstate legal relations, but rather in the development of *jus gentium*, a system of legal rules governing the relations between Roman citizens and foreigners. The *jus gentium* contained many principles of general equity and "natural law," some of which are similar to certain "general principles of law recognized by civilized nations"— one of the sources of contemporary international law listed in Article 38 of the Statute of the International Court of Justice. But the *jus gentium* was strictly a municipal system of law administered by a Roman magistrate, the *Praetor peregrinus*, as a system parallel to the *jus civile* applicable to relations between Roman citizens.

The Rise of the National State and the Evolution of International Law

As the medieval Holy Roman Empire disintegrated, the void was filled by a growing number of separate states, ranging from large nation-states such as England and France to hundreds of smaller kingdoms, dukedoms, principalities and city republics, especially in Germany and Italy. This multiplicity of independent political units spurred the development of a system of interstate relations.

Frederick III, German emperor from 1440 to 1493, was the last of the emperors crowned in Rome by the Pope, but at that time Europe was already divided into a large number of independent states. The collapse of the political, legal and moral authority of the emperors, and the weakening of the ecclesiastical authority of the Pope—greatly accelerated by the Reformation—made it necessary for the newly emerging independent states to develop a system of rules that could govern their mutual relations. For these legal relations, they drew predominantly upon Roman law and canon law. The professional clerks who ran the chancelleries of the newly emerging states and city republics received their training largely in universities such as Bologna, Padua or Paris, where the Renaissance had revived the study of classical civilization and, in particular, the study of Roman law. The system of the Roman law, as codified in Justinian's *Corpus Juris*, dominated the teaching of the so-called "Glossators" at these universities. Justinian's code thus spread its influence over the entire European continent, except for the Scandinavian countries. England remained largely free from the influence of Roman law both in the structure and in the substantive principles of its legal system. Although the legal systems of most of the states of continental Europe were progressively codified and modernized during the 19th and 20th centuries, they are still heavily influenced by Roman law. Some concepts of Roman law have strongly influenced international legal rules, such as those governing the acquisition of title over territory.

However, the division between the civil law world—comprising most of continental Europe, and a large number of non-European states—and the English-speaking, common law world is of relatively little significance in international legal relations. In the first place, canon law, with its essentially Romanistic conceptual framework, had an important influence on many aspects of English law. Second, the growth of international trade from the 8th century onwards led to the development of an international law merchant and, in particular, to various compilations of maritime law which gained increasing international recognition. The most famous of these are the Rhodian laws, a collection of maritime laws probably compiled between the 7th and 9th centuries, and the *Consolato del Mare,* a private collection of rules and customs of maritime law published in Barcelona during the 14th century.

The Foundations of the Modern Law of Nations

The several centuries that preceded the Thirty Years' War (1618–1648) were marked in Europe by an intensification of international trade, improvements in navigation and military techniques, and the discovery of many distant lands. These events stimulated the further development of international practices and the emergence of modern conceptions of a law of nations. In northern Europe, the Hanseatic League, founded in the 13th century by certain German city-states and comprising at its height in the early 15th century over 150 trading cities and centers, established a network of commercial and diplomatic relations which contributed substantially to the growth of international usages and customs. In Italy, city-republics, such as Venice,

Genoa and Florence, developed the practice of sending resident ambassadors to the capitals of other states, thus giving rise to legal principles governing diplomatic relations and, in particular, the immunities of ambassadors and their staffs. The growth of trade led to an increasing number of commercial treaties. The discovery and subjugation of distant lands and peoples by European explorers and conquerors produced conflicting claims of sovereignty, jurisdiction and rights of trade and navigation, as well as problems of relations with indigenous populations. These difficulties stimulated juristic thought, encouraged resort to Roman law for helpful norms or analogies, and ultimately led to new practices and principles.

By the beginning of the 17th century, the growing complexity of international customs and treaties had given rise to a need for compilation and systematization. At the same time, the growing disorders and sufferings of war, especially of the Thirty Years' War, which laid waste hundreds of towns and villages and inflicted great suffering and privation on peasants and city dwellers, urgently called for some further rules governing the conduct of war. The preoccupation with war is demonstrated by the titles of the two most important treatises of the period: De Jure Belli Libri Tres (*De Jure Belli*) (1598) by Alberico Gentili (1552–1608), the Italian-born Professor of Civil Law at Oxford, and the classic treatise of Hugo Grotius, De Jure Belli Ac Pacis Libri Tres (*De Jure Belli Ac Pacis*) (1623–1624), which is generally regarded as the foundation of modern international law.

Although the relative importance of the laws of war and the laws of peace has greatly shifted since the time of Grotius, the latter being by far the more important part of the contemporary law of nations, the importance of these classical treatises, and others, lay in their attempts to systematize the growing number of customs, usages and state practices that had developed over the previous centuries. The details of their systems are not of much contemporary importance, except for the history of international law. However, it is of interest and not without importance or reward to survey the basic ideas underlying the evolution of international law, and of the principal phases of development from the time of Grotius to the present.

Natural Law Philosophy and the Principles of International Law

Hugo Grotius (1583–1645), a Dutch jurist, historian, theologian and diplomat, who for the last ten years of his life was the ambassador of Sweden in Paris, is the best known of an important school of international jurists guided by the philosophy of natural law. Among his predecessors in this approach are the Spanish theologians Francisco de Vitoria (probably 1486–1546) and Francisco Suárez (1548–1617). The most important of the later natural law philosophers in international law is the German, Samuel Pufendorf (1632–1694), who occupied a chair for the law of nature and nations at the University of Heidelberg and whose most important work is *De Jure Naturae et Gentium* (1672). Vitoria and Suárez closely follow the natural law philosophy of St. Thomas Aquinas (1225–1274). Aquinas believed that all human laws derive from, and are subordinate to, the law of God. This law is partly reflected in the law of nature, a body of permanent principles grounded in the Divine Order, and partly revealed in the Scripture. By contrast, Grotius is a rationalist who derives the principles of the law of nature from universal reason rather than from divine authority.

Natural law adherents have been divided, throughout the ages, over the positive meaning of the laws of nature in the world of human institutions and actions. Two of the most important principles of the law of nature in Grotius' system of the law of nations are (1) that restitution must be made for a harm done by one party to another, and (2) that promises given, through signature to treaties or otherwise, must be kept (*pacta sunt servanda*). These two principles have been preserved and developed—though with many variations and modifications—throughout subsequent phases of international law, even without the doctrinal support of natural law philosophy. Another basic principle of natural law for Grotius is the freedom of the seas, a thesis expounded in an early work published in 1609, *Mare Liberum*. On this issue, he was strongly opposed by the Englishman John Selden (1584–1654), who in 1635 published a defense of the closed sea: Mare Clausum Sive De Dominio Maris (*Mare Clausum*). The opposing theses illustrate the difficulties of agreement on the concrete applications of natural law where opposing political, economic or social interests are involved. The rejection of the freedom of the seas by Selden corresponded to the interests of England, at that time navally inferior to Holland. The work of Grotius served to vindicate the interests of the Netherlands as a rising maritime and colonial power not only against England, but also against Spain and Portugal, states which claimed the right to control navigation on distant oceans and trade with the East Indies. Later, when England became dominant at sea, it also became an ardent champion of the freedom of the seas—at least in times of peace.[2]

The Turn to Positivism

No less important than the emphasis on the law of nature as a basis of the law of nations is the distinction made by Grotius between the *jus naturale*—to which Grotius devotes his main attention—and the *jus gentium*, the customary law of nations (also called *jus voluntarium*, i.e., a body of law formed by the conduct and will of nations).

This latter aspect of the law of nations gained increasing significance as adherence to natural law philosophy declined and positivist philosophy gained. Although positivism has a number of different meanings and nuances,[3] its essential meaning in the theory and development of international law is reliance on the practice of states and the conduct of international relations as evidenced by customs or treaties, as against the derivation of norms from basic metaphysical principles. The rise of positivism in Western political and legal theory, especially from the latter part of the 18th century to the early part of the 20th century, corresponds to the steady rise of the national state and its increasingly absolute claims to legal and political supremacy. In the theory of the law of nations the shift from natural law to positivism came gradually, through increasing emphasis on the voluntary law of nations built

2. In times of war, belligerent naval powers—like Britain in the two world wars of the 20th century—sought to restrict the freedom of the seas, especially neutral trade, to the utmost. Neutral powers stressed the freedom of the seas.

3. See Friedmann, Legal Theory, ch. 21 (5th ed. 1967).

up by state practice and custom. The most influential exponents of this turn toward positivism were the Englishman Richard Zouche (1590–1660), Professor of Civil Law at Oxford and a Judge of the Admiralty Court, and the Swiss lawyer Emerich de Vattel (1714–1767). Zouche's work, *Juris et Iudicii Fecialis, sive Juris inter Gentes* (1650), has been called the first manual of international law. Without denying the existence of the law of nature, it emphasizes the customary law of nations which he calls *jus inter gentes*. The relegation of natural law to a secondary position is made explicit by Vattel, whose treatise dominated the philosophy of international law from the middle of the 18th century to the end of the First World War. Vattel's treatise, *Le Droit des Gens, ou Principes de la Loi Naturelle, appliqués à la Conduite et aux Affaires des Nations et des Souverains* (1758), although including the *principes de la loi naturelle* in the title, distinguishes between the internal law of nations (law of conscience) and the external law (law of action). While Vattel acknowledges natural law with the assertion that "the law of nations is originally no other than the law of nature applied to nations," he considers all effective international law to have been derived from the will of nations, a presumed consent expressing itself in treaties or customs.

There is an interesting parallel between this theory and Hindu doctrine which distinguishes between *dharmasastras* (principles of right conduct) and *arthasastras* (manuals of international politics). The former corresponds to Vattel's "law of conscience" and the latter to his "law of action." As an Indian scholar has observed, "Hindu conditions presented a comparable picture to that of modern international law."[4] This approach to international law, in part foreshadowed by the German philosopher, Christian Wolff (1679–1754), in effect expresses the philosophy of the modern national state, which recognizes no international obligations other than those to which it has voluntarily agreed through practice hardening into custom, or through specific written consent expressed in treaties or other international agreements.[5]

The period between the publication of Vattel's treatise and the outbreak of the First World War in 1914 was one of phenomenal growth of international law as the diplomatic and commercial relations between nations—almost all of which were Western—multiplied and intensified. The physical volume of international law increased through a continuous growth of custom and treaties, and very few writers continued to assert the supremacy of the law of nature. The bulk of legal and political theory discussed the sovereignty of the state. It was impossible to justify international law under the state sovereignty theory, except as norms voluntarily accepted by sovereign states. Among the best known treatises reconciling the validity of international law with the concept of sovereignty are those of Georg Jellinek (1851–1911), *Allgemeine Rechtslehre* (1905), Heinrich Triepel (1868–1946), *Völkerrecht und Landesrecht* (1899), and Giorgio del Vecchio (1878–1970), *Lezioni di Filosofia del*

4. Chacko, India's Contribution to the Field of International Law Concepts, 93 Rec. des Cours 122 (1958).

5. Among other 18th century exponents of the positivist philosophy of international law are the Dutch jurist, Cornelius van Bynkershoek (1673–1743), the German jurist, Johann Jakob Moser (1701–1785), and Georg Friedrich von Martens (1756–1821).

Diritto (1929). These writers of the early 20th century sought to reconcile the sovereignty of the state with the binding nature of international law in a number of ways: by developing a doctrine of "self-limitation" of the state (Jellinek); by merging agreements made by states into an objective body of conventions which then becomes binding upon states (Triepel); or by half-heartedly reviving the natural law principle that reason demands the mutual recognition of states as equals (del Vecchio). Other positivists rejected this compromise. The English jurist, John Austin (1790–1859), whose *Province of Jurisprudence Determined* (1832) dominated jurisprudential thinking in the common law world in the 19th century, regarded a command emanating from a definite superior and punitive sanction enforcing the command as indispensable elements of law. He therefore relegated international law to the status of "positive morality." On the other hand, ideological approaches to international law were dominated by nationalist philosophy. The most influential of the nationalist philosophers, the German Georg Wilhelm Friedrich Hegel (1770–1831), in his *Philosophy of Law and State*, constructed an elaborate dialectic system, culminating in the glorification of the national (monarchic) state and denying the validity of international law (for which he substituted "The Passing of the State into World History").

From a different point of departure, Marxist doctrine challenged the national state and its legal system as an instrument of exploitation of the working class by the capitalist bourgeoisie, and called for revolution by the working classes of the world. This, of course, was incompatible with the structure of the law of nations, built on a system of sovereign national states. This philosophy influenced Soviet Communism and was proclaimed by Maoist China, but ceased to be heard in the last half of the 20th century, long before the demise of Soviet Communism.

The League of Nations and the Evolution of International Law

The most important aspect of the era of positivism and the supremacy of the national state was the freedom of the state to choose between war and peace. The Hague and Geneva Conventions of the 20th century formulated a number of rules of conduct in warfare, as distinct from principles governing the rightness or wrongness of war. Any state had the legal right to pursue its aims by means of war. This freedom meant the denial of any legally relevant distinction between just and unjust wars. A major break in this orientation came with the establishment of the League of Nations following the First World War.

In condemning "external aggression" against "the territorial integrity and existing political independence" of League members, and in providing for economic and even military sanctions to be imposed by the international community against a state violating its obligations, the League Covenant limited the legal freedom of the sovereign state to pursue war as the ultimate instrument of national policy.

The era of the League of Nations, i.e., the interwar period, was marked by another significant departure in the development of international law. The constitution of the International Labour Organisation (ILO), in association with the League of Nations, signals the end of an era in which international law was, with few exceptions, confined to the regulation of relations between states. The ILO was the first permanent international organization concerned with the improvement of labor conditions and social welfare on a world-wide scale. At the same time the establishment of the Permanent Court of International Justice—a counterpart to the limitation on the unrestricted right of states to seek solutions to international disputes by force—was a major attempt to substitute organic methods of peaceful and legal settlement of disputes for the use of force in international affairs. Parallel to the establishment of the Permanent Court, there was a significant growth in the number of bilateral treaties requiring arbitration and other methods of peaceful settlement for disputes between states.

The noble attempt to substitute international authority for national use of force collapsed because of inadequate support from the major nations in times of crises—notably on the occasion of the Italian invasion of Abyssinia (Ethiopia) in 1935. The efforts of the ILO to achieve international standards for labor and social welfare remained severely limited by continuing divergencies in national standards. The Permanent Court of International Justice played only a marginal role in the affairs of nations. But the world did not return to the pre–1914 state of affairs. It did not return to a system in which international law included no control in the use of force; nor did it abandon its halting efforts to develop an international organization of mankind for purposes of cooperation.

The interwar period also brought the first major threat to the universality of the system of international law, as it had gradually developed since the time of Grotius. The original family of nations, consisting of the older European states, was, at the end of the 18th century, enlarged by the accession of the United States and, a few decades later, by the newly independent states of Latin America. Only a small number of relatively impotent non-Western states joined the family of nations. With the success of the Bolshevik Revolution and the establishment of the Soviet Union, differences of political and social ideology began to challenge the universality of the system in international law. The Soviet Union established itself in place of the old Russian empire as a single major state with a radically different political and social philosophy, but it was compelled to co-exist with other states. To that extent, the Soviet challenge to the traditional system of international law was mitigated. In fact, it was the aggression-minded, fascist states of Germany, Italy and Japan that challenged the whole system of international law more immediately than did the Soviet Union.

The impact of ideological and other structural divergencies between states on the universality of the law of nations was to become a matter of major importance in the reorganization and development of international law following the end of World War II.

International Law After the Second World War

The creation of the United Nations Organization was a major development in the international political system. The attempt in the United Nations

Charter to reintroduce a system of collective security against aggression was, historically and ideologically, essentially a resumption of the League of Nations effort. However, three major developments following the end of the Second World War signaled a new departure in the evolution of international law. The first was the massive expansion of international organization for cooperative purposes, of which the ILO had been a forerunner. The United Nations, its specialized agencies and other international organizations, some on a universal and others on a regional level, marked the transition of international law from the traditional system of formal rules of mutual respect and abstention to an incipient system of organized, cooperative efforts. Organizations were formed to address a broad range of ills plaguing the world community. Most of these organizations lack executive powers and make only limited encroachments upon the traditional prerogatives of national sovereignty, but their creation confirmed a new pattern of international conduct. Their concerns include international peace and security; monetary control; international development aid; food production and distribution; universal standards of health; international communication and transport; protection of the environment; outer space and the ocean bed; and the international promotion and protection of human rights. This phase reflects the needs of an international society where ready communication and increased interdependence, the threat of nuclear annihilation, the growth of population and the increasing threat of exhaustion of the resources of the earth no longer permit an international attitude of laissez-faire. Consequently, international law is no longer predominantly a system of interstate diplomatic norms. It has deeply penetrated the economic and social fabrics of national life.

A second major development has been the growing importance of states representing non-Western civilizations as members of the family of nations. This development raised the question of the compatibility of the basic cultural values and institutions of these non-Western societies with the system of international law developed by a relatively small group of Western nations. The experience with the new states of Asia and Africa has shown that this development did not fundamentally affect the system of interstate relations. Since their accession to United Nations membership, states such as India (with a long Hindu cultural tradition), Indonesia (with a Moslem background) and the new African nations (most of them emerging from tribal societies), have not diverged in essence from the attitudes of Western countries in their approaches to interstate relations. The new states have generally accepted the traditional norms of customary law, participated in international treaties and joined a variety of international organizations. For new states, the necessity of collaboration—to face the problems of statehood and sovereignty in a divided world, the issues of war and peace, the conflicts of political and economic aspirations and the tensions between competition and cooperation in the affairs of mankind—prevailed over the diversity of cultural traditions.

A third development has been the growing gap between the economically developed and the economically less developed countries, which resulted in the creation of new types of international organization specifically designed to deal with the problems arising from the co-existence of rich and poor nations.

Included among such bodies are the International Bank for Reconstruction and Development (World Bank), the International Monetary Fund, and the United Nations Conference on Trade and Development (UNCTAD). The division between developed and developing states intensified challenges to certain norms of international law developed by the economically advanced and capital-exporting states of the West, notably for the protection of the economic interests of foreign investors. It created demands for a New International Economic Order. It led to new arrangements in international law favored by Third World states—such as key elements in a new law of the sea; and for some forms of cooperation for economic development. But the Third World did not succeed in obtaining significant steps towards a new international economic order. Insufficient commitment by the states of the Third World, and the competition for their favor by East and West, had the unhappy effect of politicizing and hampering various international programs—as in the protection of human rights.

Even in a divided world living in the ever-present shadow of possible nuclear destruction, the dramatic increase in the number of new states and the appearance of many problems in the economic and the social spheres have accounted for many important new developments in international law, and greatly increased both its scope and complexity. But in a larger historical context this is the continuation and intensification of an evolution that has accompanied the entire history of international law. Many norms of international law, such as the freedom of the seas, the extent of territorial waters and the principles of state responsibility, have always been the product of an adjustment between conflicting national interests.

Perhaps the most significant development of the postwar period, the addition of a new field of international cooperation and organization to the traditional system of the law of nations, has not fulfilled all its promises. But the law of nations has passed from the phase in which it was primarily an international law of co-existence—which characterized it from its birth in the early 17th century to mid–20th century—to a phase in which the nations of the world must develop new forms of cooperation and organization to supplement the traditional rules of interstate relations.

International Law After the Cold War

During more than four decades following the end of the Second World War, international law reflected and was shaped by ideological conflict and Cold War between nuclear superpowers, as well as the end of colonialism, the multiplication of new nations, and the emergence of the "Third World." Ideological conflict, together with divergent interests between developed and developing states ("North and South"), hampered the growth of international law and frustrated the development of international institutions—notably the United Nations Security Council and the International Court of Justice. Traditional approaches to international law were maintained, uncomfortably, alongside special attitudes of the Soviet Union, Communist China, and groupings of new states. New developments in the law, such as the birth of the law of human rights, had to paper over fundamental differences; institutions to induce compliance with the law were reduced to a very low common denominator.

The end of the Cold War, the demise of international Communism, the dissolution of the Soviet Empire and the fragmentation of the Soviet Union itself, led to a radically changed world order with new opportunities and challenges for international law. The law of collective security and the authority of the U.N. Security Council were revisited, revived and extended, at least for a time. Civil wars and ethnic hostilities have suggested the need to reexamine the traditional conceptions of state sovereignty and to enlarge the scope of permissible collective intervention for humanitarian assistance and protection of human rights. Political change revived aspirations for the International Court of Justice; while alongside that venerable body, a whole constellation of new tribunals has increasingly significant jurisdiction. New needs and new perceptions have enhanced efforts to develop new norms and new institutions to protect the global environment and to reorder economic relations. Regional arrangements that once responded in part to East–West rivalry have broadened their membership and created new functions, as seen in the Organization for Security and Cooperation in Europe (OSCE) and the North Atlantic Treaty Organization (NATO). The European Community became the European Union and continues its quest for political integration even while expanding to include much of the former East bloc.

International Law in the Era of Globalization and Non–State Terrorism

The international system of the 21st century is in many senses a borderless world, yet one in which the nation-state retains much of its traditional significance for the processes of international law. Communications flow instantaneously without regard to international boundaries, and the Internet facilitates new modes of social interaction. Many barriers to the transborder movement of goods and services have been removed or drastically reduced. Economies are increasingly integrated across national lines. Individuals maintain significant ties not only with the states of their birth or parentage but also where they have studied, worked or formed other community connections. Environmental challenges such as global climate change require urgent attention, not only within existing structures for policy coordination but also through new modes of cooperation.

The attacks of September 11, 2001 struck at symbols of these forces of globalization, as well as of the state power of the United States. The deployment by non-state actors of violence on a scale hitherto monopolized by states brought home the nature of systemic changes and called into question the continuing viability of existing structures for the maintenance of international security. The multileveled responses to the attacks—through states in the exercise of individual and collective self-defense, through regional and international institutions, through the adoption of national and international measures to suppress terrorist financing and activities, as well as new border controls and other restrictions—illustrate both the persistence of the state as the locus for the first line of defense against security threats and the inexorability of global trends apart from traditional state-centered forms of organization.

The problems facing the international community in the early 21st century are many and acute. New international law will surely be an essential tool to give effect to new solutions to new and old human problems.

SUMMARY OF CONTENTS

TABLE OF CONTENTS

_____

*

TABLE OF CASES

The principal cases are in bold type. Cases cited or discussed in the text are in roman type. References are to pages. Cases cited in principal cases and within other quoted materials arc not included.

INTERNATIONAL LAW
CASES AND MATERIALS

Fifth Edition

*

PART 1

STRUCTURE OF INTERNATIONAL LAW

■ ■ ■

CHAPTER 1

NATURE OF INTERNATIONAL LAW

■ ■ ■

SECTION 1. INTERNATIONAL LAW AS BINDING LAW

The field of international law is concerned with law that principally operates among sovereign countries (or "states"), arising from sources such as treaties and the customary practice of states. The sources of international law will be considered in depth in Chapters 2, 3 and 4. While states are the primary actors that create, interpret, comply with, and enforce international law, other actors are also important in this field, including: international organizations, non-governmental organizations, corporations, and individuals. Indeed, while many of the readings in this chapter speak exclusively about "states" as the salient actors in the field of international law, non-state actors are increasingly significant subjects and objects of international law, with substantive rights that, at times, they may directly enforce before national and international fora. These various actors are considered in Chapters 5, 6, and 7.

Since international law is not created, interpreted, and enforced through the kinds of institutions that operate in national legal systems, it has over the centuries had to justify its legitimacy and reality. This chapter, therefore, is concerned with the nature of international law.

A. IS IT LAW?

International law's title to "law" has been challenged on the ground that, by hypothesis and definition, there can be no law governing sovereign states. Skeptics have argued that there can be no international law since there is no international legislature to make it, no effective international judiciary to interpret and develop it, or to resolve disputes about it, and no international executive to enforce it. International law, it has been said, is not "real law" since it is commonly disregarded, states obeying it only when they wish to, or when it is in their interest to do so. At best it is a series of moral or political standards that states generally try to live by, but that have no legally binding effect. The classical denial of the legal character of international law was expressed early in the 19th century by John Austin and continues to be heard today.

The jurisprudence of international law, however, has rejected the narrow definitions and unfounded assumptions implied in these challenges. The great English legal philosopher H.L.A. Hart saw something more in international law than just a series of moral rules, given the social structure of international law. International lawyers, such as Louis Henkin, acknowledged the inescapable political dimension to international law, but saw that dimension, as well as the purposes sought by international law, as comparable to national law.

As you read the following excerpts, consider whether you think international law is properly regarded as "law." If not, then what is it?

AUSTIN, THE PROVINCE OF JURISPRUDENCE DETERMINED

Originally published in 1832
117–18, 171 (1995 ed. Rumble ed.)

Laws properly so called are a species of *commands*. But, being a *command*, every law properly so called flows from a *determinate* source * * *. * * * [W]henever a *command* is expressed or intimated, one party signifies a wish that another shall do or forbear: and the latter is obnoxious to an evil which the former intends to inflict in case the wish be disregarded. * * * Every sanction properly so called is an eventual evil *annexed to a command.* * * *

* * *

And hence it inevitably follows, that the law obtaining between nations is not positive law: for every positive law is set by a given sovereign to a person or persons in a state of subjection to its author. As I have already intimated, the law obtaining between nations is law (improperly so called) set by general opinion. The duties which it imposes are enforced by moral sanctions: by fear on the part of nations, or by fear on the part of sovereigns, of provoking general hostility, and incurring its probable evils, in case they shall violate maxims generally received and respected.

HART, THE CONCEPT OF LAW

227–30 (2d ed. 1994)

Sometimes insistence that the rules governing the relations between states are only moral rules, is inspired by the old dogmatism, that any form of social structure that is not reducible to orders backed by threats can only be a form of 'morality'. It is, of course, possible to use the word 'morality' in this very comprehensive way; so used, it provides a conceptual wastepaper basket into which will go the rules of games, clubs, etiquette, the fundamental provisions of constitutional law and international law, together with rules and principles which we ordinarily think of as moral ones, such as the common prohibitions of cruelty, dishonesty, or lying. The objection to this procedure is that between what is thus classed together as 'morality' there are such important differences of both form and social function, that no conceivable purpose, practical or theoretical, could be served by so crude a classification. Within the category of morality thus artificially widened, we should have to mark out afresh the old distinctions which it blurs.

In the particular case of international law there are a number of different reasons for resisting the classification of its rules as 'morality'. The first is that states often reproach each other for immoral conduct or praise themselves or others for living up to the standard of international morality. No doubt *one* of the virtues which states may show or fail to show is that of abiding by international law, but that does not mean that that law is morality. In fact the appraisal of states' conduct in terms of morality is recognizably different from the formulation of claims, demands, and the acknowledgements of rights and obligations under the rules of international law. * * * [C]ertain features * * * might be taken as defining characteristics of social morality: among them * * * the distinctive form of moral pressure by which moral rules are primarily supported. This consists not of appeals to fear or threats of retaliation or demands for compensation, but of appeals to conscience, made in the expectation that once the person addressed is reminded of the moral principle at stake, he may be led by guilt or shame to respect it and make amends.

Claims under international law are not couched in such terms though of course, as in municipal law, they may be joined with a moral appeal. What predominate in the arguments, often technical, which states address to each other over disputed matters of international law, are references to precedents, treaties, and juristic writings; often no mention is made of moral right or wrong, good or bad. Hence the claim that the Peking Government has or has not a right under international law to expel the Nationalist forces from Formosa is very different from the question whether this is fair, just, or a morally good or bad thing to do, and is backed by characteristically different arguments. No doubt in the relations between states there are halfway houses between what is clearly law and what is clearly morality, analogous to the standards of politeness and courtesy recognized in private life. Such is the sphere of international 'comity' exemplified in the privilege extended to diplomatic envoys of receiving goods intended for personal use free of duty.

A more important ground of distinction is the following. The rules of international law, like those of municipal law, are often morally quite indifferent. A rule may exist because it is convenient or necessary to have some clear fixed rule about the subjects with which it is concerned, but not because any moral importance is attached to the particular rule. It may well be but one of a large number of possible rules, any one of which would have done equally well. Hence legal rules, municipal and international, commonly contain much specific detail, and draw arbitrary distinctions, which would be unintelligible as elements in moral rules or principles. * * * Law, however, though it also contains much that is of moral importance, can and does contain just such rules, and the arbitrary distinctions, formalities, and highly specific detail which would be most difficult to understand as part of morality, are consequently natural and easily comprehensible features of law. For one of the typical functions of law, unlike morality, is to introduce just these elements in order to maximize certainty and predictability and to facilitate the proof or assessments of claims. Regard for forms and detail carried to excess, has earned for law the reproaches of 'formalism' and 'legalism'; yet it is important to remember that these vices are exaggerations of some of the law's distinctive qualities.

It is for this reason that just as we expect a municipal legal system, but not morality, to tell us how many witnesses a validly executed will must have, so we expect international law, but not morality, to tell us such things as the number of days a belligerent vessel may stay for refueling or repairs in a neutral port; the width of territorial waters; the methods to be used in their measurement. All these things are necessary and desirable provisions for *legal rules* to make, but so long as the sense is retained that such rules may equally well take any of several forms, or are important only as one among many possible means to specific ends, they remain distinct from rules which have the status in individual or social life characteristic of morality. Of course not all the rules of international law are of this formal, or arbitrary, or morally neutral kind. The point is only that legal rules *can* and moral rules *cannot* be of this kind.

The difference in character between international law and anything which we naturally think of as morality has another aspect. Though the effect of a law requiring or proscribing certain practices might ultimately be to bring about changes in the morality of a group, the notion of a legislature making or repealing moral rules is * * * an absurd one. A legislature cannot introduce a new rule and give it the status of a moral rule by its *fiat*, just as it cannot, by the same means, give a rule the status of a tradition, though the reasons why this is so may not be the same in the two cases. Accordingly morality does not merely lack or happen not to have a legislature; the very idea of change by human legislative *fiat* is repugnant to the idea of morality. This is so because we conceive of morality as the ultimate standard by which human actions (legislative or otherwise) are evaluated. The contrast with international law is clear. There is nothing in the nature or function of international law which is similarly inconsistent with the idea that the rules might be subject to legislative change; the lack of a legislature is just a lack which many think of as a defect one day to be repaired.

HENKIN, INTERNATIONAL LAW: POLITICS AND VALUES
4–5 (1995) (footnotes omitted)

First, law is politics. Students of law as well as students of politics are taught to distinguish law from politics. Law is normative and binding, and failure to abide by legal obligations invites legal remedies and brings other legal responses; politics suggests freedom of choice, diplomacy, bargaining, accommodation. In fact, however, the distinction between law and politics is only a part-truth. In a larger, deeper sense, law *is* politics. Law is made by political actors, through political procedures, for political ends. The law that emerges is the resultant of political forces; the influences of law on state behaviour are also determined by political forces.

* * *

[Second, international] law is the normative expression of the international political system. To appreciate the character of international law and its relation to the international political system, it is helpful to invoke (though with caution) domestic law as an analogue. Domestic (national) law, such as the law of the Netherlands, of the United States, or of Nigeria, is an expression of a domestic political system in a domestic (national) society. A domestic society consists of people, human beings, though in developed societies law has also created artificial juristic persons (e.g., companies, associations). Domestic law is a construct of norms, standards, principles, institutions and procedures that serve the purposes of the society. Law serves, notably, to establish and maintain order and enhance the reliability of expectations; to protect persons, their property and other interests; to promote the welfare of individuals (or of some of them), and to further other societal values—justice, the good life, the good society.

Similarly, analogously, international law is the product of its particular "society," its political system. International law, too, is a construct of norms, standards, principles, institutions and procedures. The purposes of international law, like those of domestic law, are to establish and maintain order and enhance reliable expectations, to protect "persons," their property and other interests, to further other values. But the constituency of the international society is different. The "persons" constituting international society are not individual human beings but political entities, "states," and the society is an inter-state system, a system of states.

NOTES

1. *An Empty Debate?* Professor Glanville Williams insisted that jurisprudential debate over the reality of international law is merely a debate about words. Williams, International Law and the Controversy Concerning the Word "Law," 22 Brit. Y.B.I.L. 146, 159–62 (1945). For Williams, if one does not like the term "international law," then perhaps different words could be chosen, but the same assessment would follow as to how the field operates in creating,

interpreting, and enforcing norms to which states generally comply. See also Brownlie, The Reality and Efficacy of International Law, 52 Brit. Y.B.I.L. 1 (1981).

2.   *The Lack of Resort to Courts.* As will be discussed in greater depth in Chapter 9, states are not generally compelled to appear before international courts or tribunals when violations of international law are said to occur; they are only so compelled when they consent in advance or at the time of a dispute. In the absence of general compulsory jurisdiction for an international court or tribunal, can it be said that there exists a rule of law in international relations? Judge Dillard of the International Court of Justice opined: "Law and what is legally permitted may be determined by what a court decides, but they are not only what a court decides. Law 'goes on' every day without adjudication of any kind." *Legal Consequences for States of the Continued Presence of South Africa in Namibia (South West Africa) notwithstanding Security Council Resolution 276 (1970)*, Advisory Opinion, 1971 I.C.J. 150, 168 (Separate Opinion of Judge Dillard). Do you agree?

3.   *Objections to the Legalistic–Moralistic Approach.* "Realists" of international relations theory, who are inclined to see international law as simply a set of moral rules, object to the efforts of others to elevate the field to a higher status, as well as the imposition of "do-gooder" sentiments on the conduct of states operating in a dangerous world. Consequently, there is an old but recurrent controversy as to the applicability of moral principles to the behavior of states and governments. For a rejection of the "legalistic-moralistic approach to international problems," see Kennan, American Diplomacy 95 (1984); see also Kennan, Morality and Foreign Policy, 64 Foreign Aff. 205 (Winter 1985–86). For a different view see Henkin, How Nations Behave 335–37 (2d ed. 1979). What is the proper and practical role for international law in the creation of a better-ordered world community?

B.   IS IT BINDING LAW?

HENKIN, HOW NATIONS BEHAVE

25–26 (2d ed. 1979) (footnotes omitted)

[T]o many an observer, governments seem largely free to decide whether to agree to new law, whether to accept another nation's view of existing law, whether to comply with agreed law. International law, then, is voluntary and only hortatory. It must always yield to national interest. Surely, no nation will submit to law any questions involving its security or independence, even its power, prestige, influence. Inevitably, a diplomat holding these views will be reluctant to build policy on law he deems ineffective. He will think it unrealistic and dangerous to enact laws which will not be observed, to build institutions which will not be used, to base his government's policy on the expectation that other governments will observe law or agreement. Since other nations do not attend to law except when it is in their interest, the diplomat might not see why his government should do so at the sacrifice of important interests. He might be impatient with his lawyers who tell him that the government may not do what he would like to see done.

* * * [D]espite inadequacies in legislative method, international law has grown and developed and changed. If international law is difficult to make, yet it is made; if its growth is slow, yet it grows. If there is no judiciary as effective as in some developed national systems, there is an International Court of Justice whose judgments and opinions, while few, are respected. The inadequacies of the judicial system are in some measure supplied by other bodies: international disputes are resolved and law is developed through a network of arbitrations by continuing or *ad hoc* tribunals. National courts help importantly to determine, clarify, develop international law. Political bodies like the Security Council and the General Assembly of the United Nations also apply law, their actions and resolutions interpret and develop the law, their judgments help to deter violations in some measure. If there is no international executive to enforce international law, the United Nations has some enforcement powers and there is "horizontal enforcement" in the reactions of other nations. The gaps in substantive law are real and many and require continuing effort to fill them, but they do not vitiate the force and effect of the law that exists, in the international society that is.

Above all, the lawyer will insist, critics of international law ask and answer the wrong questions. What matters is not whether the international system has legislative, judicial, or executive branches, corresponding to those we have become accustomed to seek in a domestic society; what matters is whether international law is reflected in the policies of nations and in relations between nations. The question is not whether there is an effective legislature; it is whether there is law that responds and corresponds to the changing needs of a changing society. The question is not whether there is an effective judiciary, but whether disputes are resolved in an orderly fashion in accordance with international law. Most important, the question is not whether law is enforceable or even effectively enforced; rather, whether law is observed, whether it governs or influences behavior, whether international behavior reflects stability and order. The fact is, lawyers insist, that nations have accepted important limitations on their sovereignty, that they have observed these norms and undertakings, that the result has been substantial order in international relations.

NOTES

1. *Can a Sovereign State Bind Itself?* At one time, the idea of a "sovereign state" being bound by a higher law was challenged as an oxymoron—how can a sovereign state submit to law? The argument was disposed of in the first contentious case of the Permanent Court of International Justice, where the Court said: "The Court declines to see in the conclusion of any treaty by which a State undertakes to perform or refrain from performing a particular act an abandonment of its sovereignty. No doubt any convention creating an obligation of this kind places a restriction upon the exercise of the sovereign rights of the State, in the sense that it requires them to be exercised

in a certain way. But the right of entering into international engagements is an attribute of State sovereignty." *S.S. Wimbledon Case*, 1923 P.C.I.J. (ser. A.) No. 1, at 25.

2. *The Restatement (Third)*. The Introductory Note to Chapter 1 of The Restatement of the Law (Third): Foreign Relations Law of the United States (1987) states:

> *International law as law.* The absence of central legislative and executive institutions has led to skepticism about the legal quality of international law. Many observers consider international law to be only a series of precepts of morality or etiquette, of cautions and admonitions lacking in both specificity and binding quality. Governments, it is sometimes assumed, commonly disregard international law and observe it only when they deem it to be in their interest to do so.

> These impressions are mistaken. International law is law like other law, promoting order, guiding, restraining, regulating behavior. States, the principal addressees of international law, treat it as law, consider themselves bound by it, attend to it with a sense of legal obligation and with concern for the consequences of violation. Some states refer to international law in their constitutions; many incorporate it into their domestic legal systems; all take account of it in their governmental institutional arrangements and in their international relations. There is reference to the "Law of Nations" in the Constitution of the United States (Article 1, Section 8). It is part of the law of the United States, respected by Presidents and Congresses, and by the States, and given effect by the courts.

3. *Scholarly Commentary*. Earlier writers stressed that the authority of international law resides in the fact that the states which constitute international society recognize it as binding, and the system treats them as bound, irrespective of their individual will. See, e.g., Brierly, The Basis of Obligation in International Law (Lauterpacht & Waldock eds. 1958); Brierly, The Law of Nations 55–56 (6th ed. Waldock ed. 1963); Fitzmaurice, The Foundations of the Authority of International Law and the Problem of Enforcement, 19 Mod. L. Rev. 1 (1956); Manning, The Nature of International Society 106–07 (1962). For a more recent assessment, see 1 Oppenheim at 8–13.

C. COMPLIANCE WITH INTERNATIONAL LAW

Inquiry into the "reality" of international law has been largely concerned with whether international law works—whether states act in conformity with the law. That inquiry has sometimes reflected skepticism—how can it be that states obey the law when there is no effective means of enforcing it? As noted below, Professor Louis Henkin famously declared: "It is probably the case that *almost all nations observe almost all principles of international law and almost all of their obligations almost all of the time.*" Henkin, How Nations Behave 47 (2d ed. 1979). Is this a correct statement? If so, how does one explain such widespread compliance? Consider the following possibilities: states are compelled to adhere

by external sanctions; states see it in their long-term self-interest to comply with international law, knowing that non-compliance will provoke reciprocal non-compliance by other states; states comply because their leaders wish to maintain a good reputation for themselves and their states; states comply simply out of habit, following the "path of least resistance"; states are drawn to the moral legitimacy of international rules, when they are formed in accordance with agreed upon processes, are clear, and are coherent; states are responding to being embedded in complex, necessary and efficient treaty regimes; or states are constrained by the internalization of international law into domestic law. Do you favor some or all of these explanations?

HENKIN, HOW NATIONS BEHAVE

47, 49–50, 92–95, 97–98 (2d ed. 1979) (footnotes omitted)

Violations of law attract attention and the occasional important violation is dramatic; the daily, sober loyalty of nations to the law and their obligations is hardly noted. It is probably the case that *almost all nations observe almost all principles of international law and almost all of their obligations almost all of the time*. Every day nations respect the borders of other nations, treat foreign diplomats and citizens and property as required by law, observe thousands of treaties with more than a hundred countries. * * *

* * *

The impression that nations commonly violate international norms and undertakings may be due not only to incomplete observation, but also to erroneous *a priori* assumptions about how nations behave. Much is made, in particular, of the lack of executive authority to enforce international law and the lack of effective "sanctions" against the violator. The assumption seems to be that since laws and agreements limit the freedom of nations, governments will not observe these obligations, unless they are compelled by external authority and power. In fact, we know—although effective "sanctions," as that term is commonly used, are indeed lacking— that nations do generally observe laws and obligations. The preoccupation with "sanctions," then, seems largely misplaced. The threat of such sanctions is not the principal inducement to observe international obligations. At least, the absence of sanctions does not necessarily make it likely that nations will violate law. There are other forces which induce nations to observe law.

A more sophisticated suggestion has it that since there is no body to enforce the law, nations will comply with international law only if it is in their interest to do so; they will disregard law or obligation if the advantages of violation outweigh the advantages of observance. Of course, if national interest and advantage are defined broadly enough, this formula may be true and may indeed be a truism. The cynic's formula, if I may call it that, is, however, out of focus. The fact is that law observance, not violation, is the common way of nations. It usually requires an expectation of important countervailing advantage to tempt a nation to violate law. Observance, one may conclude, appears to be generally "more advantageous" than violation; indeed, nations seem to see advantage in law observance "in principle." At least, then, one would have to revise the judgment to state that barring an infrequent non-rational act, nations will observe international obligations unless violation promises an important balance of advantage over cost. Moreover, there are domestic as well as external costs of violation, and observance will be importantly affected also by internal forces and impulsions not strictly related to national cost or advantage.

To adopt some formula like that suggested is, of course, the beginning of the inquiry, not the end of it. We must attempt to discover what are the costs and advantages nations consider in their international relations, what weights they might assign to different advantages and costs at different times. We may ask which norms or agreements, in what circumstances, are particularly observed; which are more likely to be violated. And we may ask how these considerations of international advantage or disadvantage are modified by domestic facts and forces.

* * *

* * * The fact is that, in domestic society, individuals observe law principally from fear of consequences, and there are "extralegal" consequences that are often enough to deter violation, even were official punishment lacking. (Where law enforcement is deficient, such consequences may be particularly material.) In the mainstreams of domestic society, an illegal action tends to bring social opprobrium and other extra-legal "costs" of violation. This merely emphasizes that law often coincides so clearly with the interests of the society that its members react to antisocial behavior in ways additional to those prescribed by law. In international society, law observance must depend more heavily on these extra-legal sanctions, which means that law observance will depend more closely on the law's current acceptability and on the community's—especially the victim's—current interest in vindicating it. It does not mean that law is not law, or that its observance is less law observance.

There are several mistakes in the related impression that nations do pursuant to law only what they would do anyhow. In part, the criticism misconceives the purpose of law. Law is generally not designed to keep individuals from doing what they are eager to do. Much of law, and the most successful part, is a codification of existing mores, of how people behave and feel they ought to behave. To that extent law reflects, rather than imposes, existing order. If there were no law against homicide, most individuals in contemporary societies would still refrain from murder. Were that not so, the law could hardly survive and be effective. To say that nations act pursuant to law only as they would act anyhow may indicate not that the law is irrelevant, but rather that it is sound and viable, reflecting the true interests and attitudes of nations, and that it is likely to be maintained.

At the same time much law (particularly tort law and "white collar crimes") is observed because it is law and because its violation would have undesirable consequences. The effective legal system, it should be clear, is not the one which punishes the most violators, but rather that which has few violations to punish because the law deters potential violators. He who does violate is punished, principally, to reaffirm the standard of behavior and to deter others. This suggests that the law does not address itself principally to "criminal elements" on the one hand or to "saints" on the other. The "criminal elements" are difficult to deter; the "saint" is not commonly tempted to commit violations, and it is not law or fear of punishment that deters him. The law is aimed principally at the mass in between—at those who, while generally law-abiding, may yet be tempted to some violations by immediate self-interest. In international society, too, law is not effective against the Hitlers, and is not needed for that nation which is content with its lot and has few temptations. International law aims at nations which are in principle law-abiding but which might be tempted to commit a violation if there were no threat of undesirable consequences. In international society, too, the reactions to a violation—as in Korea in 1950 or at Suez in 1956—reaffirm the law and strengthen its deterrent effect for the future.

In many respects, the suggestion that nations would act the same way if there were no law is a superficial impression. The deterrent influence of law is there, though it is not always apparent, even to the actor himself. The criticism overlooks also the educative roles of law, which causes persons and nations to feel that what is unlawful is wrong and should not be done. The government which does not even consider certain actions because they are "not done" or because they are not its "style" may be reflecting attitudes acquired because law has forbidden these actions.

In large part, however, the argument that nations do pursuant to law only what they would do anyhow is plain error. The fact that particular behavior is required by law brings into play those ultimate advantages in law observance that suppress temptations and override the apparent immediate advantages from acting otherwise. In many areas, the law at least achieves a common standard or rule and clarity as to what is agreed. The law of the territorial sea established a standard and made it universal. In the absence of law, a foreign vessel would not have thought of observing precisely a twelve-mile territorial sea (assuming that to be the rule), nor would it have respected the territorial sea of weaker nations which had no shore batteries. In regard to treaties, surely, it is not the case that nations act pursuant to agreement as they would have acted if there were none, or if it were not established that agreements shall be observed. Nations do not give tariff concessions, or extradite persons, or give relief from double taxation, except for some *quid pro quo* pursuant to an agreement which they expect to be kept.* * *

* * *

The most common deprecation of international law, finally, insists that no government will observe international law "in the crunch, when it really hurts." If the implication is that nations observe law only when it does not matter, it is grossly mistaken. Indeed, one might as well urge the very opposite: violations in "small matters" sometimes occur because the actor knows that the victim's response will be slight; serious violations are avoided because they might bring serious reactions. The most serious violation—the resort to war—generally does not occur, although it is only when major interests are at stake that nations would even be tempted to this violation. On the other hand, if the suggestion is that when it costs too much to observe international law nations will violate it, the charge is no doubt true. But the implications are less devastating than might appear, since a nation's perception of "when it really hurts" to observe law must take into account its interests in law and in its observance, and the costs of violation. * * *

* * *

Whether, in the total, there is an effective "international order" is a question of perspective and definition. Order is not measurable, and no purpose is served by attempts to "grade" it in a rough impressionistic way. How much of that order is attributable to law is a question that cannot be answered in theory or in general, only in time and context. Law is one force—an important one among the forces that govern international relations at any time; the deficiencies of international society make law more dependent on other forces to render the advantages of observance high, the costs of violation prohibitive.

KOH, WHY DO NATIONS OBEY INTERNATIONAL LAW?

106 Yale L.J. 2634, 2646, 2651–55 (1997) (footnotes omitted)

The short answer to the question, "Why do nations obey international law?" is not simply: "interest"; "identity"; "identity-formation"; and/or "international society." A complete answer must also account for the importance of *interaction* within the transnational legal process, *interpretation* of international norms, and domestic *internalization* of those norms as determinants of why nations obey. What is missing, in brief, is a modern version of the fourth historical strand of compliance theory—the strand based on *transnational legal process*.

* * *

* * * [S]uch a process can be viewed as having three phases. One or more transnational actors provokes an *interaction* (or series of interactions) with another, which forces an *interpretation* or enunciation of the global norm applicable to the situation. By so doing, the moving party seeks not simply to coerce the other party, but to *internalize* the new interpretation of the international norm into the other party's internal normative system. The aim is to "bind" that other party to obey the interpretation as part of its internal value set. Such a transnational legal

process is normative, dynamic, and constitutive. The transaction generates a legal rule which will guide future transnational interactions between the parties; future transactions will further internalize those norms; and eventually, repeated participation in the process will help to reconstitute the interests and even the identities of the participants in the process."

* * *

* * * As governmental and nongovernmental transnational actors repeatedly interact within the transnational legal process, they generate and interpret international norms and then seek to internalize those norms domestically. To the extent that those norms are successfully internalized, they become future determinants of why nations obey. The international society theorists seem to recognize that this process occurs, but have given little close study to the "transmission belt," whereby norms created by international society infiltrate into *domestic* society.

These explanations can be used together as complementary conceptual lenses to give a richer explanation of why compliance with international law does or does not occur in particular cases. Take, for example, a recent episode in the evolving Middle East peace process: the signing of the 1997 Hebron disengagement agreement. As opposition leader of Israel's right-wing Likud party, Benjamin Netanyahu had pledged never to meet Palestinian Authority leader Yasser Arafat. Netanyahu declared himself unalterably opposed to the extension of Palestinian sovereignty and ran for and won the Prime Ministership on a platform opposing any negotiation with the Palestinians. In particular, he denounced as "failed" the so-called Oslo Accords, a series of peace agreements signed by the Labor government starting in 1993. Even after those accords were concluded, Netanyahu urged their abrogation and even led street protests against the signing of further Oslo agreements. Yet remarkably, as Prime Minister of Israel in January 1997, Netanyahu completed and implemented an agreement with Arafat and the Palestinian Authority called for by the Oslo accords: to redeploy Israeli troops from the Arab sections of the West Bank town of Hebron. Netanyahu's staunchest supporters ferociously condemned the redeployment and key members of his governing coalition resigned in protest. Yet under Netanyahu's leadership, a Likud-led coalition of religious and nationalist conservatives acquiesced in a process that they had fiercely resisted for nearly four years.

Why did Israel choose to obey the Oslo accords? Interest, identity, and international society each provide parts of the explanation. Before becoming Prime Minister, Netanyahu had expressed his doubts as to whether continued extension of power to the Palestinian authority served any Israeli interest. Yet Oslo brought economic benefits to Israel in the form of foreign investment and improved relations with Europe and moderate Arab states. Once the Oslo process began, it came to involve other actors besides Israel and the Palestinians, most significantly the United States, Jordan, and Egypt. These countries developed strong expectations that Oslo provided the only framework within which peace could be achieved and greeted Netanyahu's early attempts to back away from Oslo with strong pressure and criticism. Thus, Israel's entry into an "international society," not just with the Palestinians, but with other nations committed to the peace process, helped to reshape and reconstitute its national interests.

Once this interest-shaping process began, the relative openness of Israel's liberal democratic society created multiple channels to spur it forward: through public opinion, the news media, and other mechanisms of public accountability faced daily by Netanyahu and his party. As important, the transnational legal process set in motion under the Oslo accords called for and established a negotiation mechanism and structure that committed the parties to interact with each other repeatedly over many months. The repeated interaction of the parties against the shadow of the future *interpreted* the core norms of the Oslo accords, which came to frame the relationship between the parties. Israel and Palestine began repeatedly to invoke the terms of the accords against one another, and thus became further bound to obey the core interpretation. A third step came when the Israeli Parliament (the Knesset) formally approved Oslo under the predecessor Rabin government, thereby legislatively internalizing the norms required under the Oslo agreement. This legal internalization had the effect of making Oslo a *fait accompli*, dramatically raising the domestic costs of Netanyahu's noncompliance. These factors worked together to impel Netanyahu to sign the Hebron deal with Arafat, which forced the Likud party effectively to "take ownership" of Oslo. The Hebron deal made it even more difficult for Israel to attack frontally a process with which it had become so tightly enmeshed. In short, an interactive process linking state interest, national identity, international society and internalization worked to override the vehement political opposition that Netanyahu had initially voiced against Oslo. The episode shows the power of transnational legal process to promote interaction, generate and reinforce norms, and to embed those norms into domestic legal systems.

Process is not panacea, of course, and at this writing, the future of the Mideast peace process remains shaky. But even if the Oslo process ultimately collapses, the Hebron incident still illustrates how international norms and transnational process can permeate and influence domestic policy. As transnational actors interact, they create patterns of behavior that ripen into institutions, regimes, and transnational networks. Their interactions generate both general norms of external conduct (such as treaties) and specific interpretation of those norms in particular circumstances * * *, which they in turn internalize into their domestic legal and political structures through executive action, legislation, and judicial decisions. Legal ideologies prevail among domestic decisionmakers and cause them to be affected by perceptions that their actions are, or will be seen as, unlawful. Domestic decisionmaking becomes "enmeshed" with international legal norms, as institutional arrangements for the making and maintenance of an international commitment become entrenched in domestic legal and political processes. Domestic institutions adopt symbolic structures, standard operating procedures, and other internal mechanisms to maintain habitual compliance with the internalized norms.

These institutions become "carriers of history," and evolve in path-dependent routes that avoid conflict with the internalized norms. These institutional habits lead nations into default patterns of compliance. Thus, in Henkin's words, "almost all nations observe almost all principles of international law ... almost all of the time." When a nation deviates from that pattern of presumptive compliance, frictions are created. To avoid such frictions in a nation's continuing interactions, national leaders may shift over time from a policy of violation to one of compliance. It is through this transnational legal process, this repeated cycle of interaction, interpretation, and internalization, that international law acquires its "stickiness," that nation-states acquire their identity, and that nations come to "obey" international law out of perceived self-interest. In tracing the move from the external to the internal, from one-time grudging compliance with an external norm to habitual internalized obedience, the key factor is repeated participation in the transnational legal-process. That participation helps to reconstitute national interests, to establish the identity of actors as ones who obey the law, and to develop the norms that become part of the fabric of emerging international society.

NOTES

1. *Compliance Due to Self–Interest.* Most scholars view the self-interest of states as a primary motivator for complying with international rules to which they have previously consented. "Realist" political scientists, such as Professor Hans Morgenthau, go so far as to declare that is it the "iron law of international politics, that legal obligations must yield to the national interest." Morgenthau, In Defense of the National Interest 144 (1951); see also, Morgenthau, Positivism, Functionalism, and International Law, 34 A.J.I.L. 260 (1940). For an extended argument that "international law emerges from states acting rationally to maximize their interests, given their perceptions of the interests of other states and the distribution of state power," see Goldsmith & Posner, The Limits of International Law 3 (2005). Goldsmith and Posner's thesis has been controversial in the academy, in that it posits that international law *only* results from states relentlessly pursuing their interests and does not play any independent or exogenous role in constraining state behavior. For critiques of this thesis, see Berman, Seeing Beyond the Limits of International Law, 84 Tex. L. Rev. 1265 (2006); Steinberg & Zasloff, Power and International Law, 100 A.J.I.L. 64 (2006); Swaine, Restoring (and Risking) Interest in International Law, 100 A.J.I.L. 259 (2006); Symposium, The Limits of International Law, 34 Ga. J. Int'l & Comp. L. 253 (2006).

Do you think compliance with international law is solely a function of states pursuing their self-interest? If so, do you distinguish between short-term self-interest (i.e., complying with rules that are consistent with the state's immediate interests) and long-term self-interest (i.e., complying with a system that in the long-term benefits the state, even if it requires adherence to certain rules that, in the short-term, harm the state)? At some point, does one end up expanding the meaning of "self-interest" to a point where it becomes unhelpful in explaining why states do what they do? Presumably in gauging self-interest, it is necessary to weigh the benefits versus the costs of compliance, as suggested in the excerpt above by Henkin. How would you define the "costs" of non-compliance? See Guzman, How International Law Works: A Rational Choice Theory 33 (2008) ("three costs—reputation, reciprocity, and retaliation, which I refer to as the Three Rs of Compliance—are the keys to understanding why states comply with international obligations").

2. *Compliance Due to Acculturation.* If one were to explain why states comply with international law beyond simply their self-interest, what further factors might be identified? Compliance with international law also has been explained by reference to a "culture" of compliance, whereby states operate in accordance with international rules because they have been socialized to do so—in essence, they have adopted the beliefs and behavioral patterns of the culture that surrounds them. See Goodman & Jinks, How to Influence States: Socialization and International Human Rights Law, 54 Duke L.J. 621 (2004). If this is true, what influences do you think helped build such a culture, and how it can be purposefully promoted? Note that if a culture of compliance suggests that attitudes of compliance are contagious, violations may be contagious as well.

3. *Compliance Pull toward Legitimate Rules.* Is there something inherent in the rules of international law themselves that helps "pull" states into compliance? Professor Thomas Franck argues that states are likely to obey norms of international law that have a high degree of "legitimacy." Franck defines legitimacy as "a property of a rule or rulemaking institution which itself exerts a pull toward compliance on those addressed normatively because those addressed believe that the rule or institution has come into being and operates in accordance with generally accepted principles of right process." Franck, The Power of Legitimacy Among Nations 24 (1990) (emphasis omitted).

Franck identifies four indicators of legitimacy: "determinacy"—the ability of a rule to convey a clear message; "symbolic validation"—a ritual or signal of "pedigree" that induces compliance by communicating the authority of the rule or of its originator; "coherence"—the extent to which application of a rule is consistent and also justifiable in principled terms; "adherence"—the nexus between a "primary rule of obligation" and a "hierarchy of secondary rules" that defines how rules are to be made, interpreted and applied. Franck concludes that "to the extent a rule, or rule process, exhibits these four properties it will exert a strong pull on states to comply. To the extent these properties are not present, the institution will be easier to ignore and the rule easier to avoid by a state tempted to pursue its short-term self-interest." Id. at 49. In context, "[i]t is the community which invests legitimacy with meaning; it is in the community that legitimacy exerts its pull to rule-compliance. It is because states constitute a community that legitimacy has the power to influence their conduct." Id. at 205. See also Franck's earlier article, Legitimacy in the International System, 82 A.J.I.L. 705 (1988). For a critique of Franck's concept of "legitimacy" in international law, see Alvarez,

The Quest for Legitimacy: An Examination of The Power of Legitimacy Among Nations by Thomas M. Franck, 24 N.Y.U. J. Int'l L. & Pol. 199 (1991).

4. *Compliance under Complex Treaty Regimes.* In their book entitled *The New Sovereignty*, Abram and Antonia Chayes set forth a model to explain how international regulation is accomplished through treaty regimes. They posit that three factors—national interest, efficiency, and regime norms— contribute to the general compliance of states with treaty rules. Occasional non-compliance stems not from willful disregard of norms, but from the lack of capacity of parties to carry out their undertakings, and from the ambiguity and indeterminacy of treaty language. The Chayeses present a model of international compliance based on "management," to induce compliance not through coercion, but through interactive processes of justification, discourse, and persuasion. Compliance therefore may be understood as stemming not from a state's fear of coercive sanctions but, rather, from processes to ensure transparency, resolve ambiguities, and strengthen states' capacity to comply with international undertakings. See Chayes & Chayes, The New Sovereignty: Compliance with International Regulatory Agreements (1995). For other commentary on compliance with treaty regimes, see Weiss & Jacobson, Engaging Countries (1998); Downs, Danish, & Barsoom, The Transformational Model of International Regime Design, 38 Colum. J. Transnat'l L. 465 (2000).

5. *Transnational Legal Process.* Dean Harold Koh of the Yale Law School has set forth his views on transnational legal process in further works. See Koh, The 1998 Frankel Lecture: Bringing International Law Home, 35 Hous. L. Rev. 623 (1998); Koh, Transnational Legal Process, 75 Neb. L. Rev. 181 (1996); see also Downs, Rocke, & Barsoom, Is the Good News about Compliance Good News about Cooperation?, 50 Int'l Org. 379 (1996). Koh's work suggests that compliance theory should take account of both international and national pressures toward compliance, and should focus on the role of both state actors and non-state actors in the creation, interpretation, and monitoring of international law, since non-state actors are pressuring states to adhere to international norms. See Keane, Global Civil Society? (2003). For a discussion of why even state actors should be understood as a series of government networks (i.e., loose, cooperative arrangements across borders by like-minded bureaucrats), see Slaughter, A New World Order (2004). For an argument that the rights of states are derivative of the rights and interests of persons who live within them, and that international law and domestic justice are fundamentally connected, see Tesón, The Kantian Theory of International Law, 92 Colum. L. Rev. 53 (1992); see also Buchanan, Justice, Legitimacy, and Self–Determination: Moral Foundations for International Law (2004).

6. *The Role of Courts and Tribunals.* The need to improve procedures to deter or remedy violations of international law has placed increased emphasis on the development of international courts, quasi-judicial commissions, and alternative means of dispute resolution. See Chapter 9. The development of new norms often depends on accompanying arrangements for dispute resolution—states are more likely to agree to a norm or a particular expression of a norm if means are in place for resolving disputes as to its meaning or application, but even this is no guarantee. See, e.g., Convention on the Law of the Sea, pt. XV, arts. 279–99. As Koh indicates, national courts can also play a

role. Falk has observed that "the decentralized quality of international law places a special burden upon all legal institutions at the national level," not least domestic courts. See Falk, The Role of Domestic Courts in the International Legal Order 65 (1964); see also Mann, The Consequences of an International Wrong in International and National Law, 48 Brit. Y.B.I.L. 1 (1976–77). Yet Professor Friedmann noted the "great temptation for national courts—to which they have yielded mostly—to arrive at and justify a decision that favors their own nationals." Friedmann, National Courts and the International Legal Order: Projections on the Implications of the Sabbatino Case, 34 Geo. Wash. L. Rev. 443, 453 (1966).

7. *The Problem of Essential Security Interests.* As Henkin notes, often the issue of whether states comply with international law is discussed in the context of the most extreme circumstances, where a state is reacting to what it deems a serious threat to its national security. Thus, questions about the efficacy of international law may lead to reflections on the U.S. invasion of Iraq in 2003 or Israeli incursions into Lebanon, the West Bank, or the Gaza strip. Is compliance with international law best analyzed in the context of those extreme circumstances?

In considering whether international law has a role to play in such circumstances, consider the Cuban Missile Crisis. In October 1962, with the Cold War at perhaps its most intense, many saw the United States and the U.S.S.R. on the verge of nuclear war as a result of the emplacement of Soviet nuclear missiles in Cuba. The United States responded with a quarantine of vessels headed for Cuba. While the U.S. response was approved by a resolution of the Organization of American States, the U.N. Charter is generally viewed as not according to regional organizations the power to authorize the use of military force (that power is reserved for the U.N. Security Council). See Chapter 15. Reflecting upon the crisis, former Secretary of State Dean Acheson stated:

> I must conclude that the propriety of the Cuban quarantine is not a legal issue. The power, position and prestige of the United States had been challenged by another state; and law simply does not deal with such questions of ultimate power—power that comes close to the sources of sovereignty. I cannot believe that there are principles of law that say we must accept destruction of our way of life. One would be surprised if practical men, trained in legal history and thought, had devised and brought to a state of general acceptance a principle condemnatory of an action so essential to the continuation of pre-eminent power as that taken by the United States last October. Such a principle would be as harmful to the development of restraining procedures as it would be futile. No law can destroy the state creating the law. The survival of states is not a matter of law.

> However, in the action taken in the Cuban quarantine, one can see the influence of accepted legal principles. These principles are procedural devices designed to reduce the severity of a possible clash. Those devices cause wise delay before drastic action, create a "cooling off" period, permit the consideration of others' views. The importance of the Organization of American States was also procedural, and emphasized the

desirability of collective action, thus creating a common denominator of action. Some of these desirable consequences are familiar to us in the domestic industrial area.

The Cuban Quarantine, Remarks by the Honorable Dean Acheson, 57 A.S.I.L. Proc. 13, 14 (1963). In response to these remarks, Professor Wolfgang Friedmann stated:

> The basic defect of the Acheson thesis does not so much lie in its analysis of the present situation as in the implication that the present state of affairs should be recognized as the only "realistic" approach to the conduct of international relations. * * *

> * * *

> * * * Just as the jet plane and the long-range missile move at speeds hundreds or thousands of times greater than that of the horse and buggy, so the need to create organized alternatives to mutual destruction * * * cannot be met with the means of earlier ages. "Co-operate or perish" is a stark fact, not an evangelistic aspiration.

Friedmann, The Role of International Law in the Conduct of International Affairs, 20 Int'l J. 158, 168–69 (1965). Henkin has said that persons conversant with the deliberations suggested that the constrictions of international law influenced the final decision to avoid (or mitigate) a violation of international law by implementing a quarantine rather than resorting to bombing of Cuban territory. See Henkin, How Nations Behave 286–90 (2d ed. 1979); see also Chayes, The Cuban Missile Crisis: International Crises and the Role of Law (2d ed. 1987).

D. ENFORCEMENT OF INTERNATIONAL LAW

Even if states largely comply with international law without compulsion, there will still be situations where a state decides not to comply. That, in turn, has encouraged inquiry as to the means of enforcing international law. Is international law only enforced when powerful states insist upon it? Or are there other forms of sanction that can be deployed to enforce the law?

DAMROSCH, ENFORCING LAW THROUGH NON–FORCIBLE MEASURES
269 Rec. des Cours 9, 19–22, 24 (1997)

A fundamental (and frequent) criticism of international law is the weakness of mechanisms for enforcement. For the skeptics and the critics of international law, a system so woefully deficient in means for compelling compliance can hardly qualify as "law", at least in the sense in which that term is used in domestic systems.

A variety of responses may be made to these objections, including along the following lines:

(1) There is much more *voluntary compliance* with international law than the critics would acknowledge. This is the argument of Louis Henkin

in *How Nations Behave*: "almost all nations observe almost all principles of international law and almost all of their obligations almost all of the time". Others, notably Thomas Franck in *The Power of Legitimacy among Nations*, have shown how rules of international law differ in the extent to which they exert a normative "pull" towards compliance: actors are more likely to comply voluntarily with some kinds of rules than others, and if we understand the forces that motivate voluntary compliance, then perhaps we can improve the content of the rules, or improve the system for making rules, so that a greater portion of the system will exert a greater pull towards compliance.

(2) There are more sanctions for disobedience than is generally realized, although some of those sanctions are relatively soft. Under this heading belong claims that the force of public opinion and the "mobilization of shame" are non-trivial kinds of enforcement mechanisms. We would also include under this heading the role of non-governmental organizations (such as human rights monitoring groups) in bringing the glare of publicity on violations of international law, to mobilize public pressure for compliance.

(3) There are more *coercive* sanctions for disobedience than the critics would admit, although those sanctions are largely decentralized and non-forcible. Victims of breaches of international law can affirm their rights and obtain at least rudimentary remedies through self-help mechanisms like countermeasures and economic sanctions. For example, a State that is a victim of a material breach of a treaty can generally suspend or terminate the treaty; and the threat that it would do so serves as a deterrent to breaches, as a sanction against breaches, and to some extent as remedial mechanism. * * *

(4) There may be non-forcible remedies available in *national* courts. These could relate to the kinds of economic remedies mentioned above: for example, a victim State might use its own courts or other domestic tribunals to adjudicate claims of its nationals against the breaching State. Alternatively, it may be possible to invoke judicial remedies in third countries (wholly uninvolved in the breach) for violations of international obligations. * * *

(5) There are some *forcible* measures which provide even stronger forms of compulsion. If one State violates the rule prohibiting use of force against another's territorial integrity or political independence, then the victim State can respond with individual or collective self-defense (within limits, which are themselves regulated by law). This is a form of enforcement of the primary rule against use of force, although the method of enforcement is largely decentralized.

(6) There are embryonic *centralized* enforcement mechanisms, both non-forcible and forcible. The primary source for these is Chapter VII of the United Nations Charter, which went virtually unused until 1990 but has witnessed a significant revival. Pursuant to decisions of the Security Council under its compulsory powers, centralized coercion has been

brought to bear in a number of recent situations involving violations of
international law. Collective economic sanctions have been applied, both
under the authority of regional organizations and in application of the
compulsory powers of the United Nations Security Council, for enforcement of international legal rules against use of force (e.g., Iraq's invasion
of Kuwait), war crimes and humanitarian law (former Yugoslavia), terrorism (Libya), and serious violations of human rights (e.g. Haiti), among
other instances. In several instances collective economic sanctions have
laid the groundwork for the subsequent authorization by the Security
Council of the use of multilateral military force for enforcement purposes,
as in the cases of Iraq, Haiti and former Yugoslavia, among others.

(7) Additionally, some centralized organs now exist for the enforcement of international criminal law against individuals. The *ad hoc* International Criminal Tribunals for the Former Yugoslavia and for Rwanda
have been created through the authority of the Security Council under
Chapter VII of the United Nations Charter; and substantial progress has
been made toward the establishment of a standing international criminal
court. These bodies can supplement national criminal enforcement of
international law.

NOTES

1. *Law Enforcement by the United Nations.* The United Nations does not
and was not designed to enforce all international law. While the U.N. Security
Council is accorded considerable power to address threats to the peace,
neither the Council nor any other U.N. organ was conceived of as a body that
would police and enforce international law generally. Even when threats to
the peace emerge in violation of international law, the Security Council's
enforcement role is not always applied. Due to tensions between the East and
West, the Council's ability to act was largely frustrated during the Cold War.
With the end of the Cold War in 1989, the role conceived for the Security
Council was reawakened, as during the 1990–1991 Gulf War, when the
Security Council authorized states cooperating with Kuwait to repel Iraq's
unlawful invasion (although even here, the Security Council acted not by
deploying U.N. forces, but by authorizing the use of force by member states).
Yet even since the end of the Cold War, the Security Council has not assumed
a police power to enforce or induce compliance with international law generally. Unless there has been an egregious violation of international law, the
Security Council typically does not act.

2. *Horizontal or Decentralized Enforcement.* Given the lack of centralized enforcement, the main sanctions of international law have thus operated
horizontally between states. Breaches of international law entail the possibility of reciprocal suspension of obligations owed to the breaching state, and
other forms of retaliation. A state that fails to respect international law may
find that other states treat it as a lawbreaker and refuse to carry on normal
relations with it. For example, a state that violates its obligations toward
foreign diplomats may be excluded from regular diplomatic interactions with
other states. States generally want to be perceived by other states and by

public opinion as law-abiding, and therefore are generally responsive to pressures from other states to bring their conduct into compliance with international law.

3. *Countermeasures.* Measures taken by a state that, standing alone, would be internationally unlawful nevertheless might be lawful when taken in response to a violation of law by another state. Such a "countermeasure" is defined as a non-forcible act that would normally be contrary to the international obligations of a state, but that is deemed permissible when taken in response to the wrongful act of another state and in order to induce cessation of, and reparation for, that act. For further treatment, see Chapter 8, section 6.

4. *Authoritative Decision–Makers, Coercion, and Reciprocity.* Some international relations theorists speak of states as akin to "billiard balls" bouncing against each other on the international plane. See Waltz, Man, the State, and War (1959). But other theorists note that when states act, they do so through the conduct of *persons*, and those persons are cognizant that their conduct today may have repercussions tomorrow. As such, the fear of future enforcement against them may induce compliant behavior. Indeed, McDougal and Feliciano object to the fact that the participants in the international sanctioning process "are customarily and summarily described as the attacking and target states and their respective allies." They argue that "[f]or purposes of precision in description * * * as well as for the application of certain sanctioning procedures such as those providing for criminal liability, one must frequently go behind the institutional abstraction "state" and refer to the effective decision-makers * * *." McDougal & Feliciano, Law and Minimum World Public Order 12–13 (1961).

SECTION 2. DYNAMIC CHANGE IN INTERNATIONAL LAW

Any inquiry into the character and development of international law must take into account the character of international society and of the law *at given times.* In the international system of states, as in national counterparts, politics will turn to law to achieve desired ends and to promote the values of its members. Different actors, faced with different problems at different times, may desire different objectives, and both politics and the law will differ as well. To cite several examples, both law and society looked different after the Peace of Westphalia established the modern secular state and the society of such states; after the birth of international institutions, mostly since 1918; after the enactment of the U.N. Charter and the advent of nuclear weapons; after the end of colonialism and the consequent proliferation of nation-states; after post-Cold War globalization and a revised world order; and after the dramatic terrorist attacks of 9/11. This section considers important ways in which international law has changed and is changing.

A. CHANGING DIMENSIONS OF SOVEREIGNTY

One value common to international and national systems throughout political history has been maintaining orderly relations among members. International law fosters the security and autonomy of states, paramount values in a "liberal" system of states; to that end, the law prohibits the threat or use of force by any state against the territorial integrity or political independence of any other state. Increasingly, the law has pursued those values through intergovernmental organizations and collective action.

Of course, an international (inter-state) system assumes a conception and a definition of a "state." Which entities are properly seen as states normally is not problematic. Other states know a state when they "see" one and deal with it through diplomatic intercourse with its government. Extraordinarily, defining what constitutes a "state" and applying facts to an entity claiming statehood becomes a matter of political interest and controversy, such as exists today with respect to Kosovo or Palestine. See Chapter 5.

Once a recognized state exists, it has been assumed that states are "sovereign," though there is sometimes confusion as to whether sovereignty was a characteristic, an implication, a consequence, or a definition of statehood. At one time, some states would habitually object to any exposure of their internal conduct to external scrutiny, on grounds that such scrutiny was offensive to their "sovereign rights." Article 2(7) of the U.N. Charter itself states: "Nothing contained in the present Charter shall authorize the United Nations to intervene in matters which are essentially within the domestic jurisdiction of any state or shall require the Members to submit such matters to settlement under the present Charter; but this principle shall not prejudice the application of enforcement measures under Chapter VII."

Such a sacrosanct conception of sovereign autonomy has come into serious question, buffeted by the frequent and insistent effects of globalization, the world market, cyberspace, and the human rights movement. International institutions have proven to be important instruments for enhancing cooperation in areas of interdependence, such as on international environmental protection and in trade, finance, and other economic matters. For more than a half of a century, the international system has shown commitment to values that transcend purely "state values," notably to human rights. These changing values and new means for promoting them inevitably influence the traditional axioms and assumptions of the state system. Most notably, the concept of state "sovereignty," which was commonly noted as an implicit, axiomatic characteristic of statehood, has been increasingly challenged as outdated and exaggerated. Do you agree?

HENKIN, INTERNATIONAL LAW:
POLITICS AND VALUES

8–11 (1995) (some footnotes omitted)

States are commonly described as "sovereign," and "sovereignty" is commonly noted as an implicit, axiomatic characteristic of statehood. The pervasiveness of that term is unfortunate, rooted in mistake, unfortunate mistake. Sovereignty is a bad word, not only because it has served terrible national mythologies; in international relations, and even in international law, it is often a catchword, a substitute for thinking and precision. It means many things, some essential, some insignificant; some agreed, some controversial; some that are not warranted and should not be accepted. Once there was serious debate as to whether there is, or can be, a law of nations since, it was argued, a sovereign state cannot be subject to any other authority, even to agreements of its own making or to law which it helped make or to which it consented. If today such arguments are no longer heard, states continue to argue that certain kinds of law or agreements, certain kinds of institutions, are impossible or inappropriate for "sovereign states," inconsistent with their sovereignty.[1]

* * *

For legal purposes at least, we might do well to relegate the term sovereignty to the shelf of history as a relic from an earlier era. To this end, it is necessary to analyze, "decompose," the concept; to identify the elements that have been deemed to be inherent in, or to derive from, "sovereignty"; and to determine which of them are appropriate and desirable for a "state" in a system of states at the turn of the twenty-first century. As applied to a state, elements long identified with "sovereignty" are inevitably only metaphors, fictions, fictions upon fictions; some of them, however, do constitute essential characteristics and indicia of statehood today. These include principally: independence, equality, autonomy, "personhood," territorial authority, integrity and inviolability, impermeability and "privacy."

* * *

The essential quality of statehood in a state system is the autonomy of each state. State autonomy suggests that a state is not subject to any external authority unless it has voluntarily consented to such authority. The state has a "will," moral authority, the power to consent, to enter into relations, to conclude agreements, to form associations. By their

---

1. States sometimes dare even to invoke their "sovereignty" to preclude scrutiny and judgment when they are charged with violating international law and their international obligations, notably in respect of human rights. * * *

The banner of "sovereignty" also continues to frustrate the system in smaller but significant ways. For example, the International Court of Justice continues to struggle with inadequate * * * procedures because to modernize them even in modest respects, such as imposing limitations on the number of pages in a memorial or on the number of hours of oral argument, would be unthinkable since the parties are "sovereign states."

ability to consent, to have relations and conclude agreements, states have in effect created the international political system, by a kind of international "social contract." By their ability to consent to external authority and to conclude agreements, they have created norms and institutions to govern these relations, the international law of the system. Only states can make law for the system but nothing suggests that they can make law only for themselves. States can make law for entities they create (e.g. international organizations), for entities created by individual states (e.g. companies), and for human individuals.

XUE, CHINESE OBSERVATIONS ON INTERNATIONAL LAW

6 Chinese J. Int'l L. 83, 85–86 (2007) (footnotes omitted)

8.   From the viewpoint of the developing countries, * * * international law is based on a foreign legacy. After their independence from colonial rule, mostly after WWII, these new states accepted international law as the normative framework to conduct their international relations. They did so not only because as a condition for recognition they had to, but also because they did consider fundamental principles of the legal system as enshrined in the UN Charter reflected certain values they had been fighting for: sovereignty, equality, democracy and self-determination. International law entitled them to maintain political independence and territorial integrity, and empowered them to establish the political system of their own choice, which are of fundamental importance to these new nations.

9.   Today, when the sovereignty issue may be a matter of little concern in the West, it still relates to almost everything under the agenda of the developing countries, from foreign policy to internal development plan[s]. It should be noted that either during or after the Cold War, controversy over the principles of sovereignty and non-intervention often occurs between countries of different ideology, political system, religious belief or cultural background, particularly, in the areas where [W]estern liberalism and values dominate. More often than not, international law provides the last resort for the developing countries to defend their political system, economic policy or social stability. Of course, this does not mean that international law is perfect. On the contrary, the legal system in practice often fails to live up to the expectations of states. As is analysed, "sovereignty is a concept to describe a pre-existing reality, a scheme of interpretation, used to organize and structure our understanding of political life". [The international] legal system was not and cannot be designed; it is only the result of international reality. If we understand that such political life is built upon the diversity of autonomous political communities, the concept of sovereignty is not only meaningful but also essential. If, however, we come to understand that such political life should exist only in one single social model, the notion then becomes pointless and irrelevant.

10.   As a developing country, China attaches great importance to the role of international law and believes that international law will contribute to peace, stability and development. In its international relations, China strongly upholds the principle of sovereignty, because it believes in diversity and mutual respect in international political life. This position rests both upon its historical past as well as its vision of the future world order. * * *

11.   Today, international law has definitely undergone profound changes, but given what [has] happened in Asia and in Africa in the past 15 years, we have to admit that the role of the state remains at the centre for any success of economic development and social progress. I think that the current change is mainly two-fold, namely, multiplicity of international actors and fragmentation of international law. * * *

12.   On the multiplicity of actors, we agree that the business sector with transnational corporations in particular and the civil society with NGOs as the main forces have directly entered the world stage. * * * However, to what extent such influence has changed the basis of decision-making is questionable. What we have seen is that national interests remain a determining factor for international cooperation. This is even true for the most integrated region, for example, the EU, where the communal interests of the Union are greatly substantiated, but, if I understand it correctly, national interests in the final analysis are still decisive in the policy-making of the Union. Globalized economic relations and the cross-border civil actions have enormously intensified contacts and interactions between states, but not fundamentally changed the state-centric pattern of international politics. The legal system reflects this fact.

NOTES

1.   *Sovereignty and Globalization.* The concept of "globalization," loosely defined, includes the expanding reaches, economic power, and influence of multinational companies, some that are wealthier, more powerful, and more influential than many of the states in which they invest and conduct operations. Globalization has been enhanced by the demise of communism with its extremely centralized form of government, by "privatization" of functions once exercised by governments, by the expanding world market making borders increasingly porous to goods, services, and people, and by the emergence of free flows of information across cyberspace and the Internet. At the same time, numerous international organizations and tribunals have emerged, exercising legal authority of varying kinds over their members. Non-governmental organizations have also emerged as important new actors, their existence and activities being recognized by states and by international bodies. For an overall assessment, see Governance and International Legal Theory (Dekker & Werner eds. 2004).

Is the sovereign state withering away? Professor Schachter presented a thesis of such decline under four headings: (1) The Impact of Global Capitalism on State Authority; (2) The Enhanced Roles of Civil and Uncivil Society;

(3) The Resurgence of Particularism (the political theory that sub-state political or ethnic groups have a right to promote their interest over those of the larger state—particularly, independence); and (4) Failed States, Illegal Regimes, and Popular Sovereignty. At the same time, Schachter concluded his article with a fifth section entitled "The Resilience of the State System." Schachter, The Decline of the Nation–State and its Implications for International Law, 36 Colum. J. Transnat'l L. 7 (1997). What do you think of the supposed resilience of state sovereignty?

2. *Sovereignty and Cultural Diversity.* Is there a tension between maintaining a system of sovereign states with diverse cultures and traditions, while pursuing uniform rules within that system and common institutions? In the Preamble to the U.N. Charter, the peoples of the United Nations, apparently in recognition of diversity among states and cultures, dedicate themselves "to practice tolerance and live together with one another as good neighbors." Do you think that a universal culture or ideology is a prerequisite for the existence or growth of international law? Or do you think that, in its essentials, international law responds to interests and needs common to diverse states? See Human Rights, Culture and Context: Anthropological Perspectives (Wilson ed. 1997).

3. *Sovereignty and the State's Responsibility to Its People.* Certain subject matter areas of international law, such as human rights and international environmental law, appear to be eroding traditional notions of state sovereignty, by asserting that even practices occurring largely within a single state are nevertheless the legitimate concern of other states and of international institutions. See, e.g., Meron, The Humanization of International Law (2006) (examining the effects that human rights and humanitarian law have had on other fields of public international law, including the law of war and the law of treaties). For further commentary, see Secretary–General Presents His Annual Report to General Assembly, U.N. Doc. SG/SM/7136, GA/9596 (Sept. 20, 1999) ("The State is now widely understood to be the servant of its people, and not vice versa."); Allott, The Concept of International Law, 10 E.J.I.L. 31, 37 (1999) ("International law is the self-constituting of all-humanity through law. It is the actualizing through law of the common interest of international society, the society of all societies. The legal relations of international law organize the potential willing and acting of all human beings and all human societies, including the forms of society conventionally known as 'states'."); U.N. Secretary–General Boutros–Ghali, Empowering the United Nations, 71 Foreign Aff. 89, 98–99 (Winter 1992–93) ("While respect for the fundamental sovereignty and integrity of the state remains central, it is undeniable that the centuries-old doctrine of absolute and exclusive sovereignty no longer stands, and was in fact never so absolute as it was conceived to be in theory."); Lillich, Sovereignty and Humanity: Can They Converge?, in The Spirit of Uppsala 406, 406–07 (Grahl–Madsen & Toman eds. 1984) ("the concept of sovereignty in international law is an idea whose time has come and gone. * * * 'humanity'—is the *raison d'être* of any legal system. It goes without saying, one would think, but it needs saying nevertheless.").

B. CHANGING HISTORICAL CONTEXTS

In understanding the nature of international law, it is important to keep an eye on wide-ranging historical shifts, since they can assist in understanding why international law emerged at certain times, whether older precedents remain of relevance today, and where international law is headed in the future.

As noted in the Historical Introduction, one particularly important historic milestone for international law occurred after the Second World War, with the establishment of the United Nations, the rise of other international organizations covering an array of fields, and the acceleration through those organizations of multilateral treaty-making. Yet progress towards the realization of U.N. goals was frustrated early with the emergence of Cold War tensions. For its first forty years under the U.N. Charter, the international system suffered ideological conflict between two superpowers and their respective allies, armed with increasingly destructive nuclear weapons. The Cold War, punctuated by only brief periods of détente, put into serious question whether there was any common *bona fide* commitment to U.N. purposes. The Cold War also underscored ideological differences in attitude towards international law generally, preventing or curtailing the development of new norms, institutions, and procedures, and rendering others the subject of only specious agreement or of minimal value.

The decades after the Second World War also saw the transformation of the international system by the end of colonialism and the proliferation of new, mostly poor, less-developed nations, soon emerging as the "Third World." In general, these new states declared themselves ideologically "non-aligned" in the Cold War between East and West, but many of them frequently joined with the Communist bloc, both in pressing for normative change that the West resisted and in resisting developments pursued by the West. These new states also pressed their own agenda to establish principles of "economic self-determination," economic and social development, and a new international economic order.

The Cold War and "Third World non-alignment" did not prevent significant development of international law. Some new areas of law and new norms that developed during the past fifty years are now firmly established, such as: human rights law, international environmental law, and the law governing outer space. But the norms and institutions developed during this period often reflected only the lowest common denominator of agreement, or concealed differences with minimal success. The heralded "New Economic Order" that would have shifted significant economic resources to developing states did not come to pass, but a new economic order has been continually in process, an order made up of discrete steps, some small, some larger—some preferences in trade, some debt relief, some financial assistance—within the present liberal free-market system. Ten years of negotiation produced a new Convention on the Law of the Sea in 1982, which came into force in 1994 (though as of early 2009, the United States still has not become a party to it). See Chapter 17.

In the late 1980s and 1990s the political cast of the international system once again changed dramatically. The end of the Cold War, the collapse of the Soviet empire, the splintering of the U.S.S.R., the demise of international communism, and a spreading commitment to democracy and to the market economy, relaxed large-scale international tensions and reordered political and economic alignments. These developments have brought and promise further important changes in international law and institutions, such as treaties establishing an International Criminal Court or addressing key problems such as ozone depletion, climate change, and loss of biological diversity.

Unfortunately, fragmentation of the U.S.S.R. and Yugoslavia, and realignment of multiethnic states, also fueled rivalries leading to repression and erupting into civil wars, revealing inadequacies in the laws of war, in humanitarian law, and in the law of human rights, especially in the protection of the rights of minorities. Resulting disorder has challenged established legal norms and the traditional commitment to state autonomy. The desperate plight of the populations in war-torn Somalia, in the Great Lakes region of Africa, and in the Darfur region of Sudan evoked clamor for new forms of collective action for humanitarian assistance and forms of collective intervention. Concern with global terrorism exploded in the aftermath of 9/11, spawning U.S.-led interventions in Afghanistan and Iraq, and a renewed interest in methods of countering terrorism through treaties and international institutions.

Political transformations have freed nations to attend to crying needs—the urgency of controlling the proliferation of weapons of mass destruction and trade in weapons generally; the threat of environmental catastrophe, such as climate change and related causes; the causes of incessant flows of and the rights of refugees; the continuing population explosion; chaos in financial and economic relations; regulation of the movement of people, goods, capital, and ideas; and control of drug smuggling, terrorism, and other transnational crimes. Political change with important implications for international law continues in different regions, notably in the development of the European Union, the emergence of the African Union, the continuing role and expansion of NATO (the North Atlantic Treaty Organization), and the continuing evolution of myriad human rights regimes.

In the twenty-first century, is the international community now in a better position to tackle global problems or will political dynamics in the years to come continue to inhibit the effective pursuit of a just world order?

REISMAN, INTERNATIONAL LAW
AFTER THE COLD WAR

84 A.J.I.L. 859, 860–62, 866 (1990) (footnotes omitted)

The Cold War deformed the traditional international law that had developed over centuries to facilitate and regulate political, economic and other human relationships across national boundaries. It could hardly have been otherwise. For almost half a century, the world lived in a state of neither war nor peace. The independence and rights of choice of smaller states were restricted by larger neighbors in their own interest and, it was often avowed, in the interest of systemic security. The slow effort to centralize authoritative coercive force and to restrict the freedom of unilateral action, the hallmark of civilized political arrangements and the major acknowledged defect of international law, was impeded by an international security system that accorded a veto power to each of the major protagonists. That insured its ineffectiveness. Even the freedom of the oceans, one of the most venerable struts of the international system, which had reserved five-sevenths of the planet as a public highway for exchange, was attenuated to facilitate weapons development. As soon as outer space became accessible, it, too, became part of the military arena.

* * *

Some of the traditional norms and practices of international law that were suppressed during the Cold War can now be revived. As between the two blocs, the distinction between war and peace, each with its own legal regime, will be reinstated. As a consequence, there should be reduced tolerance for, hence conduct of, covert activities. There should be less international tolerance, but not necessarily less national public support, for interventions in so-called critical defense zones under rubrics such as the Brezhnev and Reagan Doctrines. * * * Nevertheless, in terms of a pre-Cold War baseline, one should expect some revival of the norm of national political autonomy.

But national political autonomy will not mean a revival of the older notion of sovereignty in its entirety. Radical changes in conceptions of the legitimacy of national authority, deriving from the international human rights program, have supplanted the older absolute notions. There is much more room for the operation of human rights norms, for the global communications system means that all of the inhabitants of the globe live in a state of electronic simultaneity, if not physical proximity. Instantaneous communication has extended the basis for symbolic, and perhaps physical, interventions into domestic processes in which gross violations of international norms are occurring. But because such humanitarian interventions, as exercises of power, are perforce reflections of the world power process, the arena of their operation will continue to be the internal affairs of smaller and weaker states.

* * *

* * * The international political system is at the threshold of a time of hope. The ending of the Cold War is a major achievement * * *. * * * The need for international law after the Cold War will be more urgent than it was during the conflict. In many ways, what is expected of international law will be greater.

* * * The challenge to international lawyers and scholars must be to clarify continuously the common interests of this ever-changing community, drawing on historic policies but bearing in mind that the constitutive and institutional arrangements that were devised to achieve them may be no longer pertinent or effective.

VAGTS, HEGEMONIC INTERNATIONAL LAW

95 A.J.I.L. 843, 843–48 (2001) (footnotes omitted)

One increasingly sees the United States designated as the hegemonic (or indispensable, dominant, or preeminent) power. Those employing this terminology include former officials of high rank as well as widely read publicists. The French, for their part, use the term "hyper-power." A passage by Charles Krauthammer in *Time* best captures the spirit: "America is no mere international citizen. It is the dominant power in the world, more dominant than any since Rome. Accordingly, America is in a position to reshape norms, alter expectations and create new realities. How? By unapologetic and implacable demonstrations of will."

The idea of hegemony has begun to work its way into the world of international law to the point where a session of the annual meeting of the American Society of International Law in 2000 was dedicated to "the single superpower." A new undersecretary of state, John Bolton, while still at the American Enterprise Institute, wrote in an article entitled *Is There Really "Law" in International Affairs?* that we "should be unashamed, unapologetic, uncompromising American constitutional hegemonists." Since the terrorist attacks of September 11, 2001, the shapers of American foreign policy are showing some signs of second thoughts about the U.S. hegemonic position or at least of thinking of hegemony as a form of leadership rather than command. But it is still appropriate to ask whether there is such a thing as hegemonic international law (HIL) and what it would look like. Bolton answers in the negative, but this Editorial maintains that there can be, and has been, such a thing as HIL. It does not take a position as to whether the United States is or should be a hegemon but merely addresses the lawyer's question of what the legal implications would be if it is.

* * *

II. *HIL as Normative*

The received body of international law is based on the idea of the equality of states. The United Nations Charter in Article 2 (1) proclaims that it is "based on the principle of the sovereign equality of all its

Members." In 1979 the General Assembly reinforced that idea by passing a resolution entitled "Inadmissibility of the Policy of Hegemonism in International Relations" (which the United States and three other members opposed). To get to HIL, one must discard or seriously modify this principle. Note that equality is questioned by another influential body of international law thinking, the one that asserts that a different law prevails among liberal democracies than in the rest of the world. HIL advocates would also say that norms cannot stray too far from reality and must therefore recognize inequalities of power. Schmitt spoke in terms of concrete order thinking and sought to move thinking on both German constitutional law and international law to focus on where power was located and what followed from that, including inequality between states. Even classical publicists of international law acknowledged the role that power, and disparities in power, played in their subject. In the scholarship of international relations, power has been a central object of study ever since the work of Hans Morgenthau.

One might thus conclude that no law graces the hegemon's universe and this is what Bolton seems to say. But the historical record shows that it can be convenient for the hegemon to have a body of law to work with, provided that it is suitably adapted. Moreover, those subject to its domination may need clear indications of what is expected of them. The hegemon is also a trading party and the world of trade needs rules. While Bolton's national security world may be rather free of rules, his colleague, Special Trade Representative Robert Zoellick, has to operate in the highly legalized universe of the World Trade Organization.

III. HIL and Intervention

A shift to HIL most specially requires setting aside the norm of nonintervention into the internal affairs of states. Indeed, Bolton's objection to international law centers particularly on its attempted use to hamper unilateral intervention by the United States. German thinking about hegemony centered on defending the legitimacy of German intervention within Europe for such purposes as protecting persons of German origin and attacking the appropriateness of intervention by nations outside the continent. The United States, as all students of history know, openly asserted through the Monroe Doctrine the right to exclude other powers from the Western Hemisphere. It is less generally remembered that the United States also assumed for itself the right to intervene militarily within that territory. In earlier years that assumption was quite overt and legalized. Schmitt hailed Article III of the 1903 Treaty on Relations with Cuba as a piece of hegemonic drafting. It stated:

> The Government of Cuba consents that the United States may exercise the right to intervene for the preservation of Cuban independence, the maintenance of a government adequate for the protection of life, property, and individual liberty, and for discharging the obligations with respect to Cuba imposed by the Treaty of Paris on

the United States, now to be assumed and undertaken by the Government of Cuba.

An early fan of indeterminacy, Schmitt noted that indeterminacy in this agreement gave the key to the hegemonic power, which had the right to interpret the law, a doctrine he labeled "decisionism." Since President Franklin D. Roosevelt withdrew the marines from Haiti and Nicaragua, we have been more circumspect about intervention but have not ceased the practice. Indeed, even without United Nations blessings we have projected military force into areas outside Latin America such as Sudan, Afghanistan, Libya, and the former Yugoslavia. A true hegemon would have reverted to the practice of overt intervention and would have demonstrated its unapologetic and implacable will by not canceling air cover for the Bay of Pigs invasion. Whatever changes that would require in international law would have been made.

IV. HIL and Treaties

Treaties, since they represent constraints at some level on unilateral action by the parties, irritate hegemonists. In particular, they would avoid agreements creating international regimes or organizations that might enable lesser powers to form coalitions that might frustrate the hegemon. Of course, a hegemon can use an international organization to magnify its authority by a judicious combination of voting power and leadership, as the United States has often done. A dominant power can minimize the problem by refusing to enter into treaties it finds inconvenient; one need not call the roll of these agreements, starting with the Law of the Sea Convention and the Vienna Convention on the Law of Treaties and running to the convention on land mines. The hegemon can pronounce as customary law those portions of such a convention that suit its interests while ignoring the rest. Bent on ridding itself of an existing obligation, a power can resort to the *clausula rebus sic stantibus* [the doctrine that a treaty may become inapplicable due to a fundamental change of circumstances], even if others have difficulty finding those circumstances. German international lawyers paid special attention to this doctrine. Of course, a hegemon must set aside the rule enshrined in the Vienna Convention that treaties obtained through coercion are invalid. The Reich's prevailing on Czechoslovakia to agree to the protectorate in 1939 exemplifies what the drafters of that rule had in mind.

United States thinkers have increasingly chosen the route of declaring that treaties do not have legally binding effect. The American hegemonist school of thought specializes in resorting to the later-in-time rule, which puts internal laws above international law as a matter of American constitutional doctrine. According to Bolton, treaties are thus left with only political and moral standing. * * *

V. HIL and Customary International Law

A hegemon confronts customary international law differently from other countries. In terms of the formation of customary law, such a power can by its abstention prevent the emerging rule from becoming part of custom. It is disputed how nearly unanimous the acceptance of a rule must be for it to meet the requirement of Article 38 of the Statute of the International Court of Justice that it be "general practice." Abstention by a hegemonic power does seem to be enough to keep it from being general. For example, the dissenters from the ruling in *The Paquete Habana* that fishing boats were exempt from capture said that "[i]t is difficult to conceive of a law of the sea of universal obligation to which Great Britain has not acceded." By the same token, a customary rule against executing those who commit crimes while under eighteen cannot be confirmed if it is not joined in by the United States—not to mention its sympathizers, such as Iran and Iraq. This implies that, whereas a lesser state might find itself bound by custom even if it failed to sign a treaty that had gained overwhelming assent, a hegemon could safely abstain. If a custom has crystallized, the hegemon can disregard it more safely than a treaty rule and have its action hailed as creative. * * *

VI.   *Conclusion*

This brief survey sketches what HIL might become if international relations move in that direction. Hegemony can obviously vary in degree, ranging from empire to first among equals. The process of adapting present international law to a move toward hegemony would be technically manageable but would highlight features of the hegemonic order that many would find unattractive. Moreover, it would force people who do find the idea of American hegemony attractive to confront its implications in a concrete way.

NOTES

1.   *Communist Influences on International Law.* Though the Cold War is over, there is an ~~enduring~~ influence of Cold War thinking in the structure, content, and institutions (e.g., NATO) of international law. For Soviet attitudes that influenced the theory and content of international law, see Tunkin, Theory of International Law (Butler trans. 1974); Grzybowski, Soviet Public International Law: Doctrines and Diplomatic Practice (1970), The Soviet Impact on International Law (Baade ed. 1965). Since the end of the Cold War, writers of the former U.S.S.R. have stressed the need for cooperation in international law. See Damrosch, Danilenko & Müllerson, Beyond Confrontation: International Law for the Post–Cold War Era (1995) (confirming major commonalities in East-West views on international law, even during the Cold War). Early attitudes of the People's Republic of China were dismissive of international law. See Chiu, Communist China's Attitude Toward International Law, 60 A.J.I.L. 245 (1966); Chiu & Edwards, Communist China's Attitude Toward the United Nations, 62 A.J.I.L. 20 (1968); Cohen & Chiu, People's China and International Law (1974). Following the removal of the "Gang of Four" in the late 1970s, the People's Republic of China displayed renewed interest in international law. See Chen, The People's Republic of China and Public International Law, 8 Dalhousie L.J. 3 (1984); Wang,

Teaching and Research of International Law in Present Day China, 22 Colum. J. Transnat'l L. 77 (1983); Wang, International Law in China, 221 Rec. des Cours 195 (1990–II).

2. *"Third World" Influences on International Law.* Four decades of Cold War, the end of colonialism and the emergence of the "Third World," also left marks on international law. The literature exploring the effects of colonialism and the influence of "new states" includes: Anand, International Law and the Developing Countries: Confrontation or Cooperation? (1987); Anghie, Imperialism, Sovereignty and the Making of International Law (2005); Chimni, International Law and World Order: A Critique of Contemporary Approaches (1993); Elias, Africa and the Development of International Law (2d ed. 1988); Garcia–Amador, Current Attempts to Revise International Law—A Comparative Analysis, 77 A.J.I.L. 286 (1983); International Law and the Developing World: A Millennial Analysis (Symposium Issue), 41 Harv. Int'l L.J. 263 (2000); Moore–Gilbert, Postcolonial Theory: Contexts, Practices, Politics (1997); Okafor, Re-Defining Legitimate Statehood: International Law and State Fragmentation in Africa (2000); Third World Attitudes Toward International Law: An Introduction (Snyder & Sathirathai eds. 1987); Rajagopal, International Law From Below (2003).

3. *Pax Americana?* The title of Detlev Vagts' article might lead a reader to think that international law at present simply serves the will of the hegemon; is that what Vagts is saying? For a collection of essays on the effects of the U.S. "hyper-power" on international law, see United States Hegemony and the Foundations of International Law (Byers & Nolte eds. 2003); see also Alvarez, Hegemonic International Law Revisited, 97 A.J.I.L. 873 (2003); Krisch, International Law in Times of Hegemony: Unequal Power and the Shaping of the International Legal Order, 16 E.J.I.L. 369 (2005); Schoenbaum, International Relations: The Path Not Taken—Using International Law to Promote World Peace and Security (2006); Weller, The Future of International Law (2003); Glennon, American Hegemony in an Unplanned World Order, 5 J. Conflict & Sec. L. 3 (2000); Nye, The Paradox of American Power: Why the World's Only Superpower Can't Go It Alone (2002). For a broader thesis that international law for some two hundred years has been formally based on sovereign equality, but has concomitantly accommodated the prerogatives of great powers while disfavoring rogue or "outlaw" states, see Simpson, Great Powers and Outlaw States: Unequal Sovereigns in the International Legal Order (2004).

C. FRAGMENTATION OF INTERNATIONAL LAW

One aspect of change in international law has been the extraordinary diversification of fields of international law, the depth of activity in those fields, and the potential for conflicts when issues arise relating to more than one field. Overlaps may occur on both the relevant substantive law and the relevant institution or tribunal for addressing a particular problem. In 2006, a study group of the International Law Commission (a group of esteemed legal experts convened under U.N. auspices to seek to codify and progressively develop international law) issued a report on the problem and prospects for such "fragmentation" of international law. Do you think fragmentation will be a significant problem for international law in the years to come, such that efforts should be made to "universalize" it across disciplines? See Weeramantry, Universalizing International Law (2004).

FRAGMENTATION OF INTERNATIONAL LAW: DIFFICULTIES ARISING FROM THE DIVERSIFICATION AND EXPANSION OF INTERNATIONAL LAW

Report of the Study Group of the International Law Commission
Finalized by Koskenniemi
U.N. Doc. A/CN.4/L.682 (2006) (some footnotes omitted)

5.   The background of fragmentation was sketched already half a century ago by Wilfred Jenks, drawing attention in particular to two phenomena. On the one hand, the international world lacked a general legislative body. Thus:

> ... law-making treaties are tending to develop in a number of historical, functional and regional groups which are separate from each other and whose mutual relationships are in some respects analogous to those of separate systems of municipal law.[8]

6.   Very presciently, Jenks envisaged the need for a close analogy with conflicts of laws to deal with this type of fragmentation. This would be a law regulating not conflicts between territorial legal systems, but conflicts between treaty regimes. A second reason for the phenomenon he found within the law itself.

> One of the most serious sources of conflict between law-making treaties is the important development of the law governing the revision of multilateral instruments and defining the legal effects of revision.[9]

7.   There is little to be added to that analysis today. Of course, the volume of multilateral—"legislative"—treaty activity has grown manifold in the past fifty years. It has also been accompanied by various more or less formal regulatory regimes not all of which share the public law orientation of multilateral diplomacy. One of the features of late international modernity has been what sociologists have called "functional differentiation", the increasing specialization of parts of society and the related autonomization of those parts. This takes place nationally as well as internationally. It is a well-known paradox of globalization that while it has led to increasing uniformization of social life around the world, it has also [led] to its increasing fragmentation—that is, to the emergence of specialized and relatively autonomous spheres of social action and structure.

---

8.   C. Wilfried Jenks, "The Conflict of Law–Making Treaties", BYBIL vol. 30, (1953) p. 403.

9.   Ibid.

8.   The fragmentation of the international social world has attained legal significance especially as it has been accompanied by the emergence of specialized and (relatively) autonomous rules or rule-complexes, legal institutions and spheres of legal practice. What once appeared to be governed by "general international law" has become the field of operation for such specialist systems as "trade law", "human rights law", "environmental law", "law of the sea", "European law" and even such exotic and highly specialized knowledges as "investment law" or "international refugee law" etc.—each possessing their own principles and institutions. The problem, as lawyers have seen it, is that specialized law-making and institution-building tends to take place with relative ignorance of legislative and institutional activities in the adjoining fields and of the general principles and practices of international law. The result is conflicts between rules or rule-systems, deviating institutional practices and, possibly, the loss of an overall perspective on the law.

9.   While the reality and importance of fragmentation, both in its legislative and institutional form, cannot be doubted, international lawyers have been divided in their assessment of the phenomenon. Some commentators have been highly critical of what they have seen as the erosion of general international law, emergence of conflicting jurisprudence, forum-shopping and loss of legal security. Others have seen here a merely technical problem that has emerged naturally with the increase of international legal activity [and] may be controlled by the use of technical streamlining and coordination.

10.   Without going into details of the sociological or political background that has led to the emergence of special or specialist rule-systems and institutions, the nature of the legal problem may perhaps best be illustrated by reference to a practical example. The question of the possible environment effects [upon Ireland] of the operation of the "MOX Plant" nuclear facility at Sellafield, United Kingdom, has recently been raised at three different institutional procedures: an Arbitral Tribunal set up under Annex VII of the United Nations Convention on the Law of the Sea (UNCLOS), the compulsory dispute settlement procedure under the Convention on the Protection of the Marine Environment of the North–East Atlantic (OSPAR Convention) as well as under the European Community and Euratom Treaties within the European Court of Justice (ECJ). Three rule-complexes all appear to address the same facts: the (universal) rules of the UNCLOS, the (regional) rules of the OSPAR Convention, and the (regional) rules of EC/EURATOM. Which should be determinative? Is the problem principally about the law of the sea, about (possible) pollution of the North Sea, or about inter-EC relationships? Already to pose such questions points to the difficulty of providing an answer. How do such rule-complexes link to each other, if at all? What principles should be used in order to decide a potential conflict between them?

11.   Yet the problem is even more difficult. Discussing the British objection to its jurisdiction on account of the same matter being also

pending before an OSPAR arbitral tribunal and the ECJ, the Arbitral Tribunal set up under Annex VII UNCLOS observed:

> even if the OSPAR Convention, the EC Treaty and the Euratom treaty contain rights or obligations similar to or identical with the rights set out in [the UNCLOS], the rights and obligations under these agreements have a separate existence from those under [the UNCLOS].

12. The Tribunal held that the application of even the same rules by different institutions might be different owing to the "differences in the respective context, object and purpose, subsequent practice of parties and *travaux préparatoires*" [the treaty's negotiating record]. The UNCLOS Arbitral tribunal recognized that the meaning of legal rules and principles is dependent on the context in which they are applied. If the context, including the normative environment, is different, then even identical provisions may appear differently. But what does this do to the objective of legal certainty and equality of legal subjects?

13. The previous paragraph raises both institutional and substantive problems. The former have to do with the competence of various institutions applying international legal rules and their hierarchical relations *inter se*. The Commission decided to leave this question aside. The issue of institutional competencies is best dealt with by the institutions themselves. The Commission has instead wished to focus on the substantive question—the splitting up of the law into highly specialized "boxes" that claim relative autonomy from each other and from general law. What are the substantive effects of such specialization? How should the relationship between such "boxes" be conceived? In the terms of the above example: what is the relationship between the UNCLOS, an environmental treaty, and a regional integration instrument?

14. The Commission has understood the subject to have both positive and negatives sides, as attested to by its reformulation of the title of the topic: "Fragmentation of international law: Difficulties arising from the diversification and expansion of international law". On the one hand, fragmentation does create the danger of conflicting and incompatible rules, principles, rule-systems and institutional practices. On the other hand, it reflects the rapid expansion of international legal activities into various new fields and the diversification of its objects and techniques. The title seems to suggest that although there are "problems", they are neither altogether new nor of such nature that they could not be dealt with through techniques international lawyers have used to deal with the normative conflicts that may have arisen in the past.

15. The rationale for the Commission's treatment of fragmentation is that the emergence of new and special types of law, "self-contained regimes" and geographically or functionally limited treaty-systems creates problems of coherence in international law. New types of specialized law do not emerge accidentally but seek to respond to new technical and functional requirements. The emergence of "environmental law" is a

response to growing concern over the state of the international environment. "Trade law" develops as an instrument to regulate international economic relations. "Human rights law" aims to protect the interest of individuals and "international criminal law" gives legal expression to the "fight against impunity". Each rule-complex or "regime" comes with its own principles, its own form of expertise and its own "ethos", not necessarily identical to the ethos of neighbouring specialization. "Trade law" and "environmental law", for example, have highly specific objectives and rely on principles that may often point in different directions. In order for the new law to be efficient, it often includes new types of treaty clauses or practices that may not be compatible with old general law or the law of some other specialized branch. Very often new rules or regimes develop precisely in order to deviate from what was earlier provided by the general law. When such deviations * * * become general and frequent, the unity of the law suffers.

16. Such deviations should not be understood as legal-technical "mistakes". They reflect the differing pursuits and preferences that actors in a pluralistic (global) society have. In conditions of social complexity, it is pointless to insist on formal unity. A law that would fail to articulate the experienced differences between fact-situations or between the interest or values that appear relevant in particular problem-areas would seem altogether unacceptable, utopian and authoritarian simultaneously. * * *

17. The starting-point of this report is that it is desirable to provide a conceptual frame within which what is perhaps inevitable can be grasped, assessed, and managed in a legal-professional way. That frame is provided by the Vienna Convention on the Law of Treaties of 1969 (VCLT). One aspect that does seem to unite most of the new regimes is that they claim binding force from and are understood by their practitioners to be covered by the law of treaties. As the organ that had once prepared the Vienna Convention, the Commission is in a position to analyse international law's alleged fragmentation from that perspective. It is useful to note what is implicated here. * * * [A]lthough, sociologically speaking, present fragmentation contains many new features, and its intensity differs from analogous phenomena in the past, it is nevertheless an incident of the diversity of the international social world—a quality that has always marked the international system, contrasting it to (relatively) more homogenous domestic context. The fragmentation of the international legal system into technical "regimes", when examined from the point of view of the law of treaties, is not different from its traditional fragmentation into more or less autonomous territorial regimes called "national legal systems".

18. This is why it is useful to have regard to the wealth of techniques in the traditional law for dealing with tensions or conflicts between legal rules and principles. What is common to these techniques is that they seek to establish meaningful relationships between such rules and principles so as to determine how they should be used in any particular

dispute or conflict. [There are] four types of relationships that lawyers have traditionally understood to be implicated in normative conflicts;

(a) Relations between special and general law * * *;

(b) Relations between prior and subsequent law * * *;

(c) Relations between laws at different hierarchical levels * * *; and

(d) Relations of law to its "normative environment" more generally * * *.

19.   Such relations may be conceived in varying ways. At one end of the spectrum is the case where one law (norm, rule, principle, rule-complex) simply invalidates the other law. This takes place only in hierarchical relations involving *jus cogens* [a peremptory norm of international law from which no deviation is permitted]. Much more often, priority is "relative". The "other law" is set aside only temporarily and may often be allowed to influence "from the background" the interpretation and application of the prioritized law. Then there is the case where the two norms are held to act concurrently, mutually supporting each other. And at this end of the spectrum is the case where, finally, there appears to be no conflict or divergence at all. The laws are in harmony.

20.   * * * [I]nternational law's traditional "fragmentation" has already equipped practitioners with techniques to deal with rules and rule-systems that point in different directions. This does not mean to cancel out the importance of the recent push towards functional specialization of regulatory regimes. But it does suggest that these factual developments are of relatively minor significance to the operation of legal reasoning. In an important sense, "fragmentation" and "coherence" are not aspects of the world but lie in the eye of the beholder. What is new and unfamiliar will (by definition) challenge accustomed ways of thinking and organizing the world. Novelty presents itself as "fragmentation" of the old world. In such case, it is the task of reasoning to make the unfamiliar familiar by integrating it into received patterns of thought or by amending those patterns so that the new phenomenon can be accommodated. Of course, there will always remain some "cognitive dissonance" between the familiar conceptual system and the new information we receive from the world. The problems of coherence raised by the MOX plant case, for example, have not *already* been resolved in some juristic heaven so that the only task would be to try to find that pre-existing solution. But the fact that the potential overlap or conflict between the rules of the UNCLOS, the OSPAR Convention and EC law cannot be immediately resolved does not mean that it could not be brought under familiar patterns of legal reasoning.

NOTE

Creating Cohesiveness. One avenue for addressing fragmentation is to identify and promote ways that international regimes and tribunals engage in informal dialogues and coordination across subject matter areas. See Speech by Judge Rosalyn Higgins, President of the International Court of Justice, Meeting of Legal Advisers of the Ministries of Foreign Affairs 3–5 (Oct. 29, 2007), available at www.icj-cij.org (asserting that fragmentation is "best avoided by regular dialogue between courts and exchanges of information"); see also Shany, The Competing Jurisdictions of International Courts and Tribunals (2003); Martinez, Towards an International Judicial System, 56 Stan. L. Rev. 429 (2003).

SECTION 3.   DIFFERING METHODOLOGICAL APPROACHES

A discerning student of international law should be aware that different observers will approach the field from different perspectives and may employ different methodologies in identifying and analyzing international law. Hence, disagreements about international law may arise not from erroneous factual understanding or analytical reasoning, but from fundamentally different approaches in how one perceives the law and its function.

Such perspectives or methodologies could reflect philosophical or theoretical differences about the law—for example, whether international law is seen as natural law or as positive law. Further, international law has not escaped contemporary movements addressing law generally, e.g. feminist perspectives, the critical legal studies movement, or the analytical tools of law and economics. Some writing on international law reflects perceived differences between national and international law, such as the character of international law as a political system deriving from relations among states, as opposed to national law grounded in sovereign power backed by effective sanctions.

Seven perspectives or methods were set forth in a symposium in the American Journal of International Law in April 1999, several of which are excerpted below: (1) legal positivism; (2) the New Haven School; (3) international legal process; (4) critical legal studies; (5) international law and international relations; (6) feminist jurisprudence; and (7) law and economics. The symposium was ultimately turned into a book, with some changes, including the addition of a perspective from two "Third World" scholars. See Anghie & Chimni, Third World Approaches to International Law and Individual Responsibility in Internal Conflict, in The Methods of International Law (Ratner & Slaughter eds. 2004). As you read these excerpts, consider whether you think any of them reflect your own perspective on or methodological approach to law, and whether there are ways of reconciling, or at least learning from, these different approaches.

A. LEGAL POSITIVISM

SIMMA & PAULUS, THE RESPONSIBILITY OF INDIVIDUALS FOR HUMAN RIGHTS ABUSES IN INTERNAL CONFLICTS: A POSITIVIST VIEW

93 A.J.I.L. 302, 303–05 (1999) (footnotes omitted)

The main characteristic of the classic view [of positivism] is the association of law with an emanation of state will (voluntarism). Voluntarism requires the deduction of all norms from acts of state will: states create international norms by reaching consent on the content of a rule. If a state later changes its mind, there must be another—this time nonconsensual—rule that prevents the state from unilaterally withdrawing its consent. The German positivist Heinrich Triepel thus based international law on the "collective will" of states instead of the individual will of each and every one of them. The combination of positivism and voluntarism found its classic expression in the famous *Lotus* judgment of the Permanent Court of International Justice:

> International law governs relations between independent States. The rules of law binding upon States therefore emanate from their own free will as expressed in conventions or by usages generally accepted as expressing principles of law and established in order to regulate the relations between these co-existing independent communities or with a view to the achievement of common aims. Restrictions upon the independence of States cannot therefore be presumed.

From this viewpoint, the role of the lawyer is limited to interpreting the authentic will of the states concerned.

But one need not necessarily associate positivism with state voluntarism. Positivism can also be understood as the strict separation of the law in force, as derived from formal sources that are part of a unified system of law, from nonlegal factors such as natural reason, moral principles and political ideologies. For the modern representatives of analytical positivism, the unity of the legal system, embodied by the *Grundnorm* (basic norm) or the "unity of primary and secondary sources," is more important than the emanation of law from concrete acts of will.

Let us then summarize the classic positivist perspective on law as follows: Law is regarded as a unified system of rules that, according to most variants, emanate from state will. This system of rules is an "objective" reality and needs to be distinguished from law "as it should be." Classic positivism demands rigorous tests for legal validity. Extralegal arguments, e.g., arguments that have no textual, systemic or historical basis, are deemed irrelevant to legal analysis; there is only hard law, no soft law. For some, the unity of the legal system will provide one correct answer for any legal problem; for others, even if law is "open-textured," it still provides determinate guidance for officials and individuals.

For international law, this implies that all norms derive their pedigree from one of the traditional sources of international law, custom and treaty. Treaties embody the *express* consent of states, custom nothing but their *tacit* consent. The only relevant conduct is that of states seen as unitary actors. Treaties, including so-called *lawmaking treaties*—e.g., those creating new rules or changing old ones—are binding upon the contracting parties only. Whether habitual conduct of states amounts to legally binding custom is a question of objective determination of fact.

B. THE NEW HAVEN SCHOOL

WIESSNER & WILLARD, POLICY–ORIENTED JURISPRUDENCE AND HUMAN RIGHTS ABUSES IN INTERNAL CONFLICT: TOWARD A WORLD PUBLIC ORDER OF HUMAN DIGNITY

93 A.J.I.L. 316, 318–20 (1999) (footnotes omitted)

On the basis of historical and anthropological research, Professors [Harold] Lasswell and [Myres] McDougal, the founders of policy-oriented jurisprudence, developed a classification to inventory human desires or wants, i.e., what people value; hence the term "values." All people value power, enlightenment, wealth, well-being, skill, affection, respect and rectitude. Although the approach defines each of these terms, it is important to emphasize that these eight value categories, as with all of the conceptual categories that are a part of policy-oriented jurisprudence, are logically exhaustive, but empirically open. For example, the specification of each value, the relative importance of particular values, and how values are and should be shaped and shared will vary from context to context, depending on the configuration and interstimulation of many factors, including the culture, class, interests and personalities of those involved. The ways that the world community addresses these issues and the outcomes of its deliberations largely make up the international human rights program. Large-scale incidents of violence, in particular, constitute major violations of values such as well-being, respect, affection and rectitude.

For policy-oriented jurisprudence, "law" is the process through which members of a community seek to clarify and secure their common interest. Human rights are established, maintained and changed through the action of this process and refer to the way law in any community authoritatively protects and empowers individual human beings in their ongoing efforts to shape and share each of the eight values. When the community in question is the world community, the process through which such protection and empowerment are established, maintained and changed is the empirical phenomenon referred to by the term "international law of human rights."

Among the distinctive aspects of policy-oriented jurisprudence, a few might benefit from elaboration in this context. First, law is conceived of as an ongoing process of authoritative and controlling decision. It is a human artifact, established, maintained and changed by the decisions of the politically relevant actors. In particular, law is not equated with a "body of rules" that enforce themselves. Rules always require for their implementation the "conveyor belt of human action," which is powered in large measure by human decision within particular communities. It is critical to understand that decision and law are not synonyms. For policy-oriented jurisprudence, only those decisions, i.e., communications with *policy*, or prescriptive, *content*, that are taken from community wide perspectives of *authority* and backed up by *control intent*, are characterized as law. These are decisions that are made by the persons who are expected to make them, in accordance with criteria expected by community members, in established structures of authority, with sufficient bases in effective power to secure consequential control, and by authorized procedures. Compliance with the policy content of authoritative decision promises and/or generates significant benefits or indulgences in terms of any or all values; noncompliance is sanctioned by the threat and/or imposition of severe deprivations, again, in terms of any or all values.

The jurisprudence of positivism provides the counterimage to this empirical, dynamic conception of law. Its common focus on "existing" rules, emanating solely from entities deemed equally "sovereign," does not properly reflect the reality of how law is made, applied and changed. Positivism remains fixated on the past, trying to reap from words laid down, irrespective of the context in which they were written, the solution to a problem that arises today or tomorrow in very different circumstances. Without identifying the conditioning factors of the past decisions they rely on—such as the personality, political inclinations, gender and cultural background of the decision makers, as well as the mood of the times, and other societal factors—positivists try hard, in an ultimately futile quest for "certainty" of law, to predict future decisions. But, as they do not take into account changing and changed contexts (e.g., different legislators, judges, shifts in public opinion), their predictions are unlikely to be precise; they may even be inaccurate. Moreover, positivists gain no help from their theory when asked what the law "should" be. Indeed, their theory eschews any creative or prescriptive function. Conversely, Bruno Simma and Andreas Paulus's charge against the "New Haven School" as "conflating law, political science and politics" is not backed up by reference to any of its proponents' works; more important, it is unfounded. As detailed above, law is not to be equated with processes of power. It is a process of authoritative and controlling decision, a very discrete part of the social process at large.

C. INTERNATIONAL LEGAL PROCESS

The international legal process approach to international law arose from a lawyering methodology associated with Harvard Law School and the work of Professors Abram Chayes, Thomas Ehrlich, and Andreas

Lowenfeld. Like the New Haven School, this approach maintains that transnational actors' compliance with transnational law can be explained through reference to the process by which such actors operate in public and private fora. Here the emphasis is on process as *policy constraint* rather than the New Haven School's emphasis on process as *policy justification*. An excellent example of this approach is the excerpt from Harold Koh's article on Why Do Nations Obey International Law, *supra* this chapter at Section 1(C).

D. CRITICAL LEGAL STUDIES

The critical legal studies (CLS) movement asserts that the logic and structure of law arises from power relationships within society. The law is not a value-free system emanating from broadly democratic processes; rather, it supports the interests of particular groups (or classes) that form the law at the expense of the broader population. Hence, law is best seen as a system of prejudices that legitimize societal injustices, and such hierarchical structures of domination should be studied and perhaps overturned. The CLS movement has helped spawn various further movements, such as feminist legal theory and critical race theory. See generally Kelman, A Guide to Critical Legal Studies (1987); Ungar, The Critical Legal Studies Movement (1983).

In international law, the CLS movement has had various influences. One observer has identified four lines of reasoning.

> Contemporary international law scholars [associated with CLS or the "New Stream" movement] have maintained (1) that the logic of liberalism in international law is internally incoherent; (2) that international legal discourse operates within a constrained structure; (3) that international legal analysis is indeterminate; and, (4) that whatever authority international law may have is self-validated. These criticisms parallel claims made by CLS scholars outside the area of international law, but only rarely have they been systematically discussed as a unified theory of international legal analysis.

Purvis, Critical Legal Studies and International Law, 32 Harv. Int'l L.J. 81, 92 (1991). Like their counterparts focused on national law, "crits" of international law study the language, structure, and institutions of the international legal system in an effort to demonstrate that some of the dominant conceptions of international law advanced by positivists and others are internally incoherent, and to reveal the manner in which powerful constituencies have embedded in international law, under the guise of "neutral" rules, various norms that sustain that constituency's privileged position.

E. INTERNATIONAL LAW AND INTERNATIONAL RELATIONS

ABBOTT, INTERNATIONAL RELATIONS THEORY, INTERNATIONAL LAW AND THE REGIME GOVERNING ATROCITIES IN INTERNAL CONFLICTS

93 A.J.I.L. 361, 361–67 (1999) (footnotes omitted)

Over the last ten years, international relations (IR) theory, a branch of political science, has animated some of the most exciting scholarship in international law. If a true joint discipline has not yet emerged, scholars in both fields have clearly established the value of interdisciplinary cross-fertilization. Yet IR—like international law—comprises several distinct theoretical approaches or "methods." * * *

IR theory is most helpful in performing three different, though equally significant, intellectual tasks: *description, explanation* and *institutional design*. First, while lawyers *describe* rules and institutions all the time, we inevitably—and often subconsciously—use some intellectual template (frequently a positivist one) to determine which elements of these complex phenomena to emphasize, which to omit. The carefully constructed models of social interaction underlying IR theory remind us to choose these templates carefully, in light of our purpose. More specifically, IR helps us describe legal institutions richly, incorporating the political factors which shape the law: the interests, power, and governance structures of states and other actors; the information, ideas and understandings in which they operate; the institutions within which they interact.

IR scholars are primarily concerned with *explaining* political behavior—recently, at least, including law-related behavior. Especially within those schools that favor rationalist approaches, scholars seek to identify the actors relevant to an issue, the factors (material or subjective) that affect their behavior or otherwise influence events, and the "causal pathways" by which those factors have effect. These elements are typically incorporated in a model that singles out particular factors for study. In designing research, scholars look for ways to test explanatory hypotheses, using case studies or data analysis. * * *

A scholar applying IR theory might treat legal rules and institutions as phenomena to be explained ("dependent variables"). * * * Alternatively, IR might analyze legal rules and institutions—including the processes of legal decision making—as explanatory factors ("independent variables"). One might ask, has the existence of the International Criminal Tribunal for the former Yugoslavia (ICTY), or the way it has handled cases, affected the behavior of governments and other actors in the Balkans? If so, by what means?

Why should a lawyer care about questions like these? Analyses treating law as a dependent variable are valuable in many settings, for they help us understand the functions, origin and meaning of rules and institutions. Analyses treating law as an independent variable are also valuable (though unfortunately less common): they help us assess the workings and effectiveness of legal arrangements in the real world. Both forms of explanation, then, are valuable in their own rights. But explanation is at least as important for its forward-looking applications: predicting future developments and *designing institutions* capable of affecting behavior in desirable ways. It is here—constructing law-based options for the future * * *—that lawyers can play their greatest role and IR can make its most significant contribution.

* * *

Four visions of international politics are prominent in IR scholarship today. Within IR, each school views itself as foundational. Yet in studying complex phenomena * * *, they frequently overlap, with each providing important insights. * * *

Realist theory has dominated IR since before World War II. Realists treat states as the principal actors in international politics. States interact in an environment of anarchy, defined as the absence of any central government able to keep peace or enforce agreements. Security is their overriding goal, and self-help their guiding principle. Under these conditions, differences in power are usually sufficient to explain important events. Realists concentrate on interactions among major powers and on matters of war and peace. Other issues—even related issues like war crimes—are secondary.

* * *

Many *institutionalist* scholars start from a similar model of decentralized state interaction. Some share with realists a conviction that states are "real" actors with clearly specified national interests. Most, however, view states as legal fictions that aggregate the interests and preferences of their citizens; these scholars rely on state-centric analysis rather than true "methodological individualism" because it allows for more parsimonious explanation. In either case, these theorists acknowledge a broad spectrum of interests, from wealth to a cleaner environment, that depend on cooperation. Drawing on game theory, economics and other disciplines, institutionalists identify conditions that prevent states from realizing potential gains from cooperation—"market failures," in economic terms— and analyze how rules and other institutions can overcome those obstacles. Regime theory, a more expansive vein of institutionalist scholarship, incorporates information and ideas as well as power and interests, and acknowledges significant roles for private and supranational actors and domestic politics.

* * *

Various forms of *liberal* IR theory have been influential for many years, but this approach has recently been given new vitality. Liberals insist on methodological individualism, viewing individuals and private groups as the fundamental actors in international (and domestic) politics. States are not insignificant, but their preferences are determined by domestic politics rather than assumed interests or material factors like relative power. This approach implies that interstate politics are more complex and fluid than realists and institutionalists assume: national preferences can vary widely and change unpredictably. It calls for careful attention to the domestic politics and constitutional structures of individual states—a daunting prospect for analysts of international relations.

* * *

Constructivist theory differs fundamentally from these rationalist accounts. Constructivists reject the notion that states or other actors have objectively determined interests that they can pursue by selecting appropriate strategies and designing effective institutions. Rather, international actors operate within a social context of shared subjective understandings and norms, which constitute their identities and roles and define appropriate forms of conduct. Even fundamental notions like the state, sovereignty and national interests are socially constructed. They are not objectively true, but subjective; their meaning is not fixed, but contingent. Hilary Charlesworth's analysis of the construction of international law on a gendered basis disadvantageous to women is a telling example. Even anarchy, the central concept of realism, "is what states make of it."

F. FEMINIST JURISPRUDENCE

CHARLESWORTH, CHINKIN, & WRIGHT, FEMINIST APPROACHES TO INTERNATIONAL LAW

85 A.J.I.L. 613, 615, 621–23, 625 (1991) (footnotes omitted)

THE ORGANIZATIONAL STRUCTURE OF INTERNATIONAL LAW

The structure of the international legal order reflects a male perspective and ensures its continued dominance. The primary subjects of international law are states and, increasingly, international organizations. In both states and international organizations the invisibility of women is striking. Power structures within governments are overwhelmingly masculine: women have significant positions of power in very few states, and in those where they do, their numbers are minuscule. Women are either unrepresented or underrepresented in the national and global decision-making processes.

States are patriarchal structures not only because they exclude women from elite positions and decision-making roles, but also because they are based on the concentration of power in, and control by, an elite and the domestic legitimation of a monopoly over the use of force to maintain that control. This foundation is reinforced by international legal principles of sovereign equality, political independence and territorial integrity and the legitimation of force to defend those attributes.

International organizations are functional extensions of states that allow them to act collectively to achieve their objectives. Not surprisingly, their structures replicate those of states, restricting women to insignificant and subordinate roles. Thus, in the United Nations itself, where the achievement of nearly universal membership is regarded as a major success of the international community, this universality does not apply to women.

* * *

Why is it significant that all the major institutions of the international legal order are peopled by men? Long-term domination of all bodies wielding political power nationally and internationally means that issues traditionally of concern to men become seen as human concerns, while "women's concerns" are relegated to a special, limited category. * * * The orthodox face of international law and politics would change dramatically if their institutions were truly human in composition: their horizons would widen to include issues previously regarded as domestic—in the two senses of the word. * * *

The Normative Structure of International Law

* * * International jurisprudence assumes that international law norms directed at individuals within states are universally applicable and neutral. It is not recognized, however, that such principles may impinge differently on men and women; consequently, women's experiences of the operation of these laws tend to be silenced or discounted.

The normative structure of international law has allowed issues of particular concern to women to be either ignored or undermined.

G. LAW AND ECONOMICS

DUNOFF & TRACHTMAN, THE LAW AND ECONOMICS OF HUMANITARIAN LAW VIOLATIONS IN INTERNAL CONFLICT

93 A.J.I.L. 394, 395, 397 (1999) (footnotes omitted)

Economics is the study of rational choice under conditions of limited resources. Rational choice assumes that individual actors seek to maximize their preferences. The goal of [law and economics (or L&E)] analysis is to identify the legal implications of this maximizing behavior, both in and out of markets, and for markets and other institutions. While the first generation of L&E scholarship often employed cost-benefit analyses to address these issues, our focus is not just on cost-benefit analysis, but also on transaction cost analysis and game theory, and the application of these methodologies to political contexts through public choice theory.

In many respects these techniques formalize, extend and contextualize insights that are familiar to most international lawyers. But this formalization is important—it allows us to focus on relevant variables, generate hypotheses, and, to some extent, empirically test these hypotheses. Furthermore, it provides a firmer and less subjective basis for argumentation than traditional international law analysis. It is less subjective insofar as it eschews simple natural law or epithet-based argumentation, and provides the capacity to render transparent the distributive consequences of legal rules. Perhaps most important to scholars, it furnishes a basis for a progressive research program built on shared foundations, one that will seek to answer research questions and move on, rather than endlessly address the same tired questions.

* * *

* * * [L&E analysis] is premised upon a normatively determined approach termed "methodological individualism." Under this approach, no particular outcome or norm is a priori deemed desirable; rather, individual choice, sometimes called "consumer sovereignty," is the ultimate source of values. The assumption that individuals are the ultimate source of norms sharply distinguishes L&E analysis from other approaches to international law, such as natural law theories.

When extended to the international realm, the commitment to methodological individualism has substantial normative implications. For example, given the emphasis on individual choice, L&E methods will tend to favor more, rather than less, representative institutions. Moreover, methodological individualism views the state not as a player in its own right with its own normative value, but as a mediating institution with only derivative normative value. Thus, while L&E rejects state-centered positivism, it would rehabilitate the state as an institution, just as it would validate the corporation as an institution: as a vehicle for individuals to work together more productively. Finally, the L&E approach is consistent with the legal positivism that respects the law as written because—and to the extent that—it is the product of legislative processes that reflect individual preferences better than the alternative preference-revealing mechanisms.

NOTES

1. *Legal Positivism*. Positivism appears to be the dominant approach to international law from the 19th through the early 21st centuries. The student of international law in the 21st century can best appreciate positivism through an examination of classical doctrines of sources of international law, which will be the subject-matter of Chapters 2, 3, and part of 4.

2. *The New Haven School*. The "New Haven School" approach has also been referred to "law, science and policy," "configurative jurisprudence," and "policy-oriented jurisprudence." For an important two-volume statement of the jurisprudence, see Lasswell & McDougal, Jurisprudence for a Free Society: Studies in Law, Science and Policy (1992); see also Lasswell, World Politics and Personal Insecurity (1965); Lasswell & Kaplan, Power and Society: a Framework for Political Inquiry (1950); Reisman & Schreiber, Jurisprudence: Understanding and Shaping Law (1987).

3. *International Legal Process*. For examples of this approach, see Chayes, The Cuban Missile Crisis: International Crises and the Role of Law (1974); Chayes, An Inquiry Into the Workings of Arms Control Agreements, 85 Harv. L. Rev. 905 (1972); Fisher, Bringing Law to Bear on Governments, 74 Harv. L. Rev. 1130 (1961); Katz & Brewster, Law of International Transactions and Relations (1960); Lowenfeld, International Economic Law (1981) (six vols.). For an assessment of "new" international legal process, see O'Connell, New International Legal Process, 93 A.J.I.L. 334 (1999).

4. *Critical Legal Studies*. Critical legal scholars have argued that much, if not all, of international law, is merely an ideological construct intended to secure the observance of international norms by convincing states and people that the law is politically neutral and just. For examples of the scholarship, see Boyle, Ideals and Things: International Legal Scholarship and the Prison-house of Language, 26 Harv. Int'l L.J. 327 (1985); Carty, Critical International Law: Recent Trends in the Theory of International Law, 2 E.J.I.L. 66 (1991); Carty, The Decay of International Law?: A Reappraisal of the Limits of Legal Imagination in International Affairs (1986); Cass, Navigating the Newstream: Recent Critical Scholarship in International Law, 65 Nordic J. Int'l L. 341 (1996); Kennedy, A New Stream of International Law Scholarship, 7 Wis. Int'l L.J. 1 (1988); Kennedy, International Legal Structures 107 (1987); Kennedy, Theses about International Legal Discourse, 23 German Y.B.I.L. 353 (1980); International Law (Koskenniemi ed. 1992); Koskenniemi, From Apology to Utopia: The Structure of International Legal Argument (2005). For a survey of the literature, see Trimble, International Law, World Order, and Critical Legal Studies, 42 Stan. L. Rev. 811 (1990). For representation of a variety of critical perspectives on international law, see 93 A.S.I.L. Proc. 291 (1999).

5. *International Law and International Relations*. For a bibliography of interdisciplinary scholarship on IR theory and its reciprocal influence on the study of international law, see Slaughter, Tulumello, & Wood, International Law and International Relations Theory: A New Generation of Interdisciplinary Scholarship, 92 A.J.I.L. 367, 393–97 (1998); see also Steinberg & Zasloff, Power and International Law, 100 A.J.I.L. 64 (2006); Goldsmith, Sovereignty, International Relations Theory, and International Law, 52 Stan. L. Rev. 959 (2000); Keohane, International Relations and International Law: Two Optics, 38 Harv. Int'l L.J. 487 (1997); Slaughter Burley, International Law and International Relations Theory: A Dual Agenda, 87 A.J.I.L. 205 (1993). For compendia of IL/IR articles, see International Law and International Relations (Simmons & Steinberg eds. 2007); Foundations of International Law and Politics (Hathaway & Koh eds. 2005). For an IR perspective on fundamental problems in international law-making, see Byers, Custom, Power and the Power of Rules: International Relations and Customary International Law (1999). For applications in context, such as the use of force, see International Rules: Approaches from International Law and International Relations (Beck, Arend, & Lugt eds. 1996).

6. *Feminist Jurisprudence*. Professor Charlesworth also contributed an essay to the American Journal's symposium issue. See Charlesworth, Feminist Methods in International Law, 93 A.J.I.L. 379, 392–93 (1999); see also Charlesworth & Chinkin, The Boundaries of International Law: A Feminist

Analysis (2000); International Law: Modern Feminist Approaches (Buss & Manji eds. 2005); Reconceiving Reality: Women and International Law (Dallmeyer ed. 1993); Knop, Re/Statements: Feminism and State Sovereignty in International Law, 3 Transnat'l L. & Contemp. Probs. 293 (1993); Symposium, 12 Australian Y.B.I.L. 177 (1992). For a critique, see Tesón, Feminism and International Law: A Reply, 33 Va. J. Int'l L. 647 (1993).

7. *Law and Economics.* For a comprehensive law and economics (L&E) perspective on the discipline and the study of international law, see Dunoff & Trachtman, Economic Analysis of International Law, 24 Yale J. Int'l L. 1 (1999); see also Scott & Stephan, The Limits of Leviathan: Contract Theory and the Enforcement of International Law (2006); Bhandari & Sykes, Economic Dimensions in International Law (1997). L&E methods, such as game theory, have been deployed to critique traditional concepts of international law. For example, game-theoretic models (such as the prisoner's dilemma) can be used to question conventional wisdom about whether customary international law affects state behavior. See Norman & Trachtman, The CIL Game, 99 A.J.I.L. 541 (2005); Goldsmith & Posner, A Theory of Customary International Law, 66 U. Chi. L. Rev. 1113 (1999); Goldsmith & Posner, The Limits of International Law (2005). Along with other approaches in international relations theory, game theory has also been applied to the international law of treaties. See Setear, An Iterative Perspective on Treaties: A Synthesis of International Relations Theory and International Law, 37 Harv. Int'l L.J. 139 (1996); Setear, Responses to Breach of a Treaty and Rationalist International Relations Theory, 83 Va. L. Rev. 1 (1997). For applications of public choice theory to contemporary transnational problems, and an examination of aspects of international law that arguably bolster the influence of interest groups across national boundaries, see Benvenisti, Exit and Voice in the Age of Globalization, 98 Mich. L. Rev. 167 (1999).

8. *Other Voices.* Recent scholarship has emphasized "different voices," not only of developing states, but also of groups and persons within states who have been historically excluded from participation in the processes of international law. Colonial and postcolonial domination, lack of voting rights and political power on the part of indigenous or minority groups, and other forms of exclusion had given traditional international law a relatively narrow participatory base. With increasing democratization of politics at both the domestic and the international levels, these barriers are being overcome (or at least their salience is increasingly recognized), thereby opening up new possibilities for transforming the foundations of international law. For reflections on these possibilities, see International Law and Its Others (Orford ed. 2006); Knop, Diversity and Self–Determination in International Law (2002); Otto, Subalternity and International Law: The Problems of Global Community and the Incommensurability of Difference, 5 Soc. & Legal Studs. 337 (1996); Peoples and Minorities in International Law (Brölmann, Lefeber, & Zieck eds. 1993); Thornberry, International Law and the Rights of Minorities (1991).

9. *Further Reading.* In 1999, the American Society of International Law devoted much of its annual meeting to these new approaches. For the results, see 93 A.S.I.L. Proc. 291 (1999). Several of these approaches were treated

nearly twenty years earlier in a series of essays on international legal theory in The Structure and Process of International Law: Essays in Legal Philosophy, Doctrine, and Theory (Macdonald & Johnston eds. 1983). On intellectual influences giving rise to new approaches to international law in recent decades, see Kennedy, The Disciplines of International Law and Policy, 12 Leiden J. Int'l L. 9 (1999).

CHAPTER 2

SOURCES: CUSTOMARY INTERNATIONAL
LAW

■ ■ ■

SECTION 1. SOURCES AND EVIDENCE OF INTERNATIONAL LAW GENERALLY

STATUTE OF THE INTERNATIONAL COURT OF JUSTICE

Signed June 26, 1945
59 Stat. 1055, T.S. 993

Article 38

1. The Court, whose function is to decide in accordance with international law such disputes as are submitted to it, shall apply:

　　a. international conventions, whether general or particular, establishing rules expressly recognized by the contesting states;

　　b. international custom, as evidence of a general practice accepted as law;

　　c. the general principles of law recognized by civilized nations;

　　d. subject to the provisions of Article 59, judicial decisions and the teachings of the most highly qualified publicists of the various nations, as subsidiary means for the determination of rules of law.

2. This provision shall not prejudice the power of the Court to decide a case *ex aequo et bono,* if the parties agree thereto.

SCHACHTER, INTERNATIONAL LAW IN THEORY AND PRACTICE

35–37 (1991)

The principal intellectual instrument in the last century for providing objective standards of legal validation has been the doctrine of sources. That doctrine which became dominant in the nineteenth century and continues to prevail today lays down verifiable conditions for ascertaining and validating legal prescriptions. The conditions are the observable manifestations of the "wills" of States as revealed in the *processes* by

55

which norms are formed—namely, treaty and State practice accepted as law. (These are the principal processes; Article 38 of the Statute of the Court expands them to include general principles of law.) The emphasis in this doctrine on criteria of law applied solely on the basis of observable "positive" facts can be linked to those intellectual currents of the nineteenth century that extolled inductive science. It has been suggested that the sociological positivism of Comte was especially influential on juristic thinking. Not surprisingly, the conception of a positive science of law had a strong attraction in the prevailing intellectual climate.

Moreover, within the field of international law itself, the competing ideas of natural law based on moral and philosophic conceptions were increasingly perceived as irrelevant to the political order of sovereign States. It had become evident to international lawyers as it had to others that States, which made and applied law, were not governed by morality or "natural reason;" they acted for reasons of power and interest. It followed that law could only be ascertained and determined through the actual methods used by States to give effect to their "political wills." In this way, the powerful ideas of positive science and State sovereignty were harnessed to create a doctrine for removing subjectivism and morality from the "science" of international law. It was intended to make international law realistic and definite. It satisfied those concerned with the realities of State power and the importance of sovereignty. It also met the intellectual requirements of the analytical theorists of law who sought to place jurisprudence on scientific foundations. Interestingly, the doctrine of sources became acceptable to the Marxist–Leninist legal theorists despite Marxist objections to philosophical positivism. From their standpoint, the doctrine of sources properly recognized the will of sovereign States as decisive. The Soviet jurists saw international law as the product of the "coordination of wills" of the sovereign States manifested in treaties and practice *accepted* by them as law.

The doctrine of sources was more than a grand theoretical conception. It also provided the stimulus for a methodology of international law that called for detailed "inductive" methods for ascertaining and validating law. If sources were to be used objectively and scientifically, it was necessary to examine in full detail the practice and related legal convictions *(opinio juris)* of States. * * * The favored instruments of the positivist methodology were the national digests of State practice prepared by, or in close association with the government of the State concerned. * * * They were mainly systematic collections of legal conclusions and relevant facts expressed in diplomatic correspondence and in governmental officials' legal opinions * * *. It would be possible for an arbiter to conclude whether a particular decision came within the rule evidenced by the precedents in the digest. * * * However, a closer look * * * indicates that there were significant deviations from the doctrine and its methodology. These deviations suggest that the idea of an inductive, factual positive science of international law may be characterized more as myth than reality.

NOTES

1. *Voluntarism and Positivism.* These two terms are often used in the writings on international law relating to sources. They conceptualize theories of international law that have been widely accepted and also strongly criticized. Their significance goes beyond legal theory; they reflect conceptions of international order that influence political and legal decisions.

"Voluntarism" is the classic doctrine of state sovereignty applied to the formation of international law. It holds that international legal rules emanate exclusively from the free will of states as expressed in conventions or by usages generally accepted as law. (See the *Lotus Case* decision on p. 68.) "Positivism" as used in this context emphasizes the obligatory nature of legal norms and the fixed authoritative character of the formal sources. It also tends to consider that to be "law," the international norm must be capable, in principle, of application by a judicial body. Recall the overview of positivist methodology presented in Chapter 1.

The political significance of "positivist voluntarism" is brought out in the following comment by a contemporary proponent:

> This means that states are at once the creators and addressees of the norms of international law and that there can be no question today, any more than yesterday, of some "international democracy" in which a majority or representative proportion of states is considered to speak in the name of all and thus be entitled to impose its will on other states. Absent voluntarism, international law would no longer be performing its function.

Weil, Towards Relative Normativity in International Law?, 77 A.J.I.L. 413, 420 (1983).

> Supporters of "voluntarism" emphasize its necessity for a heterogeneous, pluralistic world society. Moreover, they stress the importance of maintaining a clear distinction between existing law *(lex lata)* and law in formation *(lex ferenda)*. In Weil's words, the legal system must be "perceived as a self-contained, self-sufficient world." Id. at 421. Legal normativity cannot be a matter of more or less.

The material in this chapter will present questions that bear on the voluntarist thesis. Is it realistic to consider that actual legal rules are the product of state "will" or consent in a meaningful sense? Are there basic and axiomatic norms that are recognized as such independently of consent? Does "general acceptance" of *new* law require verifiable expressions of "will" by all states? What are the advantages and disadvantages of considering the international legal system as a "self-contained, self-sufficient world" of "positive" rules? What legal significance should be given to various types of norms and standards that do not meet the criteria of Article 38 but influence state conduct and accountability (sometimes called "soft law," as addressed in Chapter 4)?

Is international law moving toward gradations in the legal force of its rules? Do recent tendencies give greater importance to the "general will of the international community" and less to the "sovereign equality" of states in the formation of law? What processes for determining the community "will" would support legal development in the common interest? All of these questions are implicitly raised by recent trends relating to "sources." They are not easily answered, but they merit reflection in studying the material that follows.

2. *Restatement on Sources of International Law.* The Restatement (Third) § 102, offers the following formulation on sources:

> (1) A rule of international law is one that has been accepted as such by the international community of states
>
> (a) in the form of customary law;
>
> (b) by international agreement; or
>
> (c) by derivation from general principles common to the major legal systems of the world.
>
> (2) Customary international law results from a general and consistent practice of states followed by them from a sense of legal obligation.
>
> (3) International agreements create law for the states parties thereto and may lead to the creation of customary international law when such agreements are intended for adherence by states generally and are in fact widely accepted.
>
> (4) General principles common to the major legal systems, even if not incorporated or reflected in customary law or international agreement, may be invoked as supplementary rules of international law where appropriate.

Do you discern any significant differences between Article 38 of the I.C.J. Statute and the Restatement's treatment of sources? On the authority of the Restatement, see Chapter 4.

3. *Sources and Evidence.* Article 38 of the Statute refers to judicial decisions and to teachings of the most highly qualified publicists as "subsidiary means for the determination of rules of law." The Restatement (Third) § 103 characterizes judicial decisions and the "writings of scholars" as "evidence" of whether a rule has become international law. It also includes as evidence the pronouncements by states that undertake to state a rule of international law when such pronouncements are not seriously challenged by other states. The Restatement notes in Comment *c* to § 103 that such pronouncements include declaratory resolutions of international organizations. See Chapter 4.

The present chapter deals mainly with the first two categories referred to in Article 38 of the I.C.J. Statute and § 102 of the Restatement—custom and treaties. We take a more detailed look at treaties as sources of law in Chapter 3. Other sources—including resolutions of international organizations, judicial decisions, views of scholars, transnational regulation, and "soft law"—are addressed in Chapter 4.

SECTION 2. CUSTOMARY INTERNATIONAL LAW

Article 38(1)(b) refers to "international custom, as evidence of a general practice accepted as law." Some writers have found this formulation curious, since it is the practice which is evidence of the emergence of a custom. However, the order of words makes little difference. What is clear is that the definition of custom comprises two distinct elements: (1) "general practice" and (2) its acceptance as law.

Clear as it may seem, this definition gives rise to a number of questions, many of which are highly controversial. In reading the material that follows, you should bear in mind the following questions:

(1) What constitutes state practice?

(a) Are claims or assertions of states in themselves practice or must they be accompanied by physical acts? Would assertions *in abstracto* constitute practice or must they be made in the context of particular situations? Are votes for general declarations of law in international bodies manifestations of practice?

(b) Is state practice made only by organs competent to bind or speak for states in international affairs? May national laws, municipal court judgments, or executive acts of an internal character constitute practice? Are there circumstances in which actions of non-official entities may be regarded as state practice? Are omissions and absence of action a form of practice?

(2) How much practice is required?

(a) Is repetition required or may a single act be sufficient to constitute general practice? What if a large number of states participate in a single act (e.g., a decision of a conference)? What if there is no practice contradicting the rule asserted in regard to a single act?

(b) How much time is required? What if no precedents can be found against the rule?

(c) How many states are needed? Is it necessary that there be "a very widespread and representative participation in the practice"? (International Court of Justice in *North Sea Continental Shelf Cases*, p. 90 *infra*). Must it include states specially affected? Is there a significant difference in the numbers required when there is conflicting practice or the absence of conflict? Is a greater number required to overturn an existing rule of law?

(d) Is the practice of some states more important than the practice of others? How much weight should be given to the non-participation of states with special interests?

(3) How much consistency is required?

(a) Are minor inconsistencies sufficient to negate a custom?

(b) Can one resolve apparent inconsistencies on the basis of new conditions and attitudes, as with the changes that have occurred between the 19th and 21st centuries?

(4) Are dissenting and non-participating States bound by custom?

(a) May a state be bound if it has no practice and if the precedents did not involve it? Can a state prevent a rule of customary law from becoming binding on it? At what time must it express opposition?

(b) Are new states bound by established custom in which they had no opportunity to participate? How may they change rules to which they are opposed?

(5) What evidence is required for *opinio juris*, the requirement that practice be accepted as law?

(a) Must states "believe" that something is law before it can become law?

(b) Can one presume *opinio juris* from consistent practice when there are no negative statements (or disclaimers) as to legal obligations?

(c) Can the requirement of *opinio juris* be met by a finding that the practice was socially necessary or suited to international needs?

(d) Is it necessary that the belief as to legal requirement be accompanied by statements that the conduct in question is obligatory? May the context provide evidence of belief in the absence of such statements? Are such statements or positive indication required to prove an obligation to act, but not required to support a permissive rule (the freedom to act)?

(e) What significance do protests and acquiescence have for *opinio juris?* Are isolated protests enough to prevent customary law on the basis of substantial practice? Would protest by a single state carry decisive weight if that state was the only one seriously affected? Is failure to protest against an abstract assertion of law less significant than failure to protest concrete application of the purported rule? May protests override practice arising from physical acts (e.g., seizures) by states?

(6) May treaties be invoked as evidence of customary law? May they create customary law?

(a) Should decisive weight be given to statements in a treaty or in preparatory work to the effect that some or all provisions are declaratory of existing law?

(b) May one infer that a treaty is not declaratory of international law from the fact that it provides for withdrawal, revision, or reservations?

(c) Under what circumstances are treaty rules which are not initially declaratory likely to become part of customary law by subsequent practice?

(d) Would bilateral treaties which have similar rules and are widely adhered to constitute evidence of state practice accepted as law or of custom?

(e) What effect would a resolution of the General Assembly or of an expert body (such as the U.N. International Law Commission or as professional organization like the *Institut de droit international)* have on the recognition of a treaty or the draft of a treaty as customary law?

(7) Is there a normative hierarchy in customary law?

(a) Are some principles accepted as postulates of the state system (e.g., territorial integrity of a state, autonomy, obligation to perform agreements), irrespective of consent?

(b) Do certain principles enjoy a higher status, such that they prevail over "ordinary" custom or treaties?

(8) Would declarations of law adopted (without dissent or by a substantial majority) by the U.N. General Assembly constitute presumptive evidence of accepted international law, irrespective of actual state practice?

All these questions have arisen in cases or in exchanges of views among states. They have often given rise to controversy. The material that follows will provide answers to, or at least throw light on, these questions. For further exploration, see International Law Association (I.L.A.), Final Report of the Committee on Formation of Customary (General) International Law (Statement of Principles Applicable to the Formation of General Customary International Law), adopted at the I.L.A. London Conference (2000) (hereinafter cited as I.L.A. Customary International Law Report).

A.   GENERAL PRACTICE

THE PAQUETE HABANA

Supreme Court of the United States, 1900
175 U.S. 677

MR. JUSTICE GRAY delivered the opinion of the court:

These are two appeals from decrees of the district court of the United States for the southern district of Florida, condemning two fishing vessels and their cargoes as prize of war.

Each vessel was a fishing smack, running in and out of Havana, and regularly engaged in fishing on the coast of Cuba; sailed under the Spanish flag; was owned by a Spanish subject of Cuban birth, living in the city of Havana; was commanded by a subject of Spain, also residing in

Havana. * * * Her cargo consisted of fresh fish, caught by her crew from the sea, put on board as they were caught, and kept and sold alive. Until stopped by the blockading squadron she had no knowledge of the existence of the war or of any blockade. She had no arms or ammunition on board, and made no attempt to run the blockade after she knew of its existence, nor any resistance at the time of the capture. * * *

We are then brought to the consideration of the question whether, upon the facts appearing in these records, the fishing smacks were subject to capture by the armed vessels of the United States during the recent war with Spain.

By an ancient usage among civilized nations, beginning centuries ago, and gradually ripening into a rule of international law, coast fishing vessels, pursuing their vocation of catching and bringing in fresh fish, have been recognized as exempt, with their cargoes and crews, from capture as prize of war. * * *

[The Court then describes the earliest known acts protecting foreign fishermen in time of war. In 1403 and 1406, Henry IV of England issued orders protecting fishermen of foreign states. The order of 1406 placed all fishermen of France, Flanders and Brittany, with their fishing vessels and boats and equipment, everywhere on the sea, under his special protection. As long as they were coming or going from fishing activities in good conduct, they were not to be hindered by His Majesty's officers. This practice, based upon prior agreement with the French King for reciprocal treatment, was followed in a treaty made October 2, 1521 between the Emperor Charles V and Francis I of France. In 1536, Dutch edicts permitted herring fishing in time of war. Early French practice even permitted admirals to accord fishing truces in time of war. In ordinances passed in 1681 and 1692, France curtailed this practice, apparently because of the failure of her enemies to accord reciprocal treatment.]

The doctrine which exempts coast fishermen, with their vessels and cargoes, from capture as prize of war, has been familiar to the United States from the time of the War of Independence.

On June 5, 1779, Louis XVI, our ally in that war, addressed a letter to his admiral, informing him that the wish he had always had of alleviating, as far as he could, the hardships of war, had directed his attention to that class of his subjects which devoted itself to the trade of fishing, and had no other means of livelihood; that he had thought that the example which he should give to his enemies * * * would determine them to allow to fishermen the same facilities which he should consent to grant; and that he had therefore given orders to the commanders of all his ships not to disturb English fishermen, nor to arrest their vessels laden with fresh fish * * *; provided they had no offensive arms, and were not proved to have made any signals creating a suspicion of intelligence with the enemy; and the admiral was directed to communicate the King's intentions to all officers under his control. By a royal order in council of November 6, 1780, the former orders were confirmed; and the capture and ransom, by a

French cruiser, of *The John and Sarah,* an English vessel, coming from Holland, laden with fresh fish, were pronounced to be illegal. 2 Code des Prises (ed. 1784) 721, 901, 903.

Among the standing orders made by Sir James Marriott, Judge of the English High Court of Admiralty, was one of April 11, 1780, by which it was "ordered that all causes of prize of fishing boats or vessels taken from the enemy may be consolidated in one monition, and one sentence or interlocutory, if under 50 tons burthen, and not more than 6 in number." Marriott's Formulary, 4. But by the statements of his successor, and of both French and English writers, it appears that England, as well as France, during the American Revolutionary War, abstained from interfering with the coast fisheries. The Young Jacob and Johanna, 1 C.Rob. 20; 2 Ortolan, 53; Hall, § 148.

In the treaty of 1785 between the United States and Prussia, article 23 (which was proposed by the American Commissioners, John Adams, Benjamin Franklin, and Thomas Jefferson, and is said to have been drawn up by Franklin), provided that, if war should arise between the contracting parties, "all women and children, scholars of every faculty, cultivators of the earth, artisans, manufacturers, and fishermen, unarmed and inhabiting unfortified towns, villages, or places, and in general all others whose occupations are for the common subsistence and benefit of mankind, shall be allowed to continue their respective employments, and shall not be molested in their persons, nor shall their houses or goods be burnt or otherwise destroyed, nor their fields wasted by the armed force of the enemy, into whose power, by the events of war, they may happen to fall; but if anything is necessary to be taken from them for the use of such armed force, the same shall be paid for at a reasonable price." 8 Star. at L. 96; 1 Kent, Com. 91, note; Wheaton, History of the Law of Nations, 306, 308. Here was the clearest exemption from hostile molestation or seizure of the persons, occupations, houses, and goods of unarmed fishermen inhabiting unfortified places. The article was repeated in the later treaties between the United States and Prussia of 1799 and 1828. 8 Star. at L. 174, 384. And Dana, in a note to his edition of Wheaton's International Laws, says: "In many treaties and decrees, fishermen catching fish as an article of food are added to the class of persons whose occupation is not to be disturbed in war." Wheaton, International Law (8th ed.) § 345, note 168.

Since the United States became a nation, the only serious interruptions, so far as we are informed, of the general recognition of the exemption of coast fishing vessels from hostile capture, arose out of the mutual suspicions and recriminations of England and France during the wars of the French Revolution.

[The Court then surveys the measures and countermeasures taken by both governments.

[On May 23, 1806, the British government "ordered in council, that all fishing vessels under Prussian and other colors, and engaged for the purpose of catching fish * * * shall not be molested * * *'' An order in council of May 2, 1810 directing the capture of certain vessels, specifically excepted "vessels employed in catching and conveying fish fresh to market * * *."]

In the war with Mexico, in 1846, the United States recognized the exemption of coast fishing boats from capture. * * *

[I]t appears that Commodore Conner, commanding the Horne Squadron blockading the east coast of Mexico, on May 14, 1846, wrote a letter * * * to Mr. Bancroft, the Secretary of the Navy, inclosing a copy of the commodore's "instructions to the commanders of the vessels of the Home Squadron, showing the principles to be observed in the blockade of the Mexican ports," one of which was that "Mexican boats engaged in fishing on any part of the coast will be allowed to pursue their labors unmolested;" and that on June 10, 1846, those instructions were approved by the Navy Department. * * *

In the treaty of peace between the United States and Mexico, in 1848, were inserted the very words of the earlier treaties with Prussia, already quoted, forbidding the hostile molestation or seizure in time of war of the persons, occupations, houses, or goods of fishermen. 9 Stat. at L. 939, 940. * * *

[The Court then notes that France had forbidden the molestation of enemy coastal fisheries during the Crimean, Italian and Prussian wars, and that England had justified destruction by her cruisers of fisheries on the Sea of Azof during the Crimean War on the ground that these were on a large scale and intended directly for the support of the Russian army.]

Since the English orders in council of 1806 and 1810, before quoted, in favor of fishing vessels employed in catching and bringing to market fresh fish, no instance has been found in which the exemption from capture of private coast fishing vessels honestly pursuing their peaceful industry has been denied by England or by any other nation. And the Empire of Japan (the last state admitted into the rank of civilized nations), by an ordinance promulgated at the beginning of its war with China in August, 1894, established prize courts, and ordained that "the following enemy's vessels are exempt from detention," including in the exemption "boats engaged in coast fisheries," as well as "ships engaged exclusively on a voyage of scientific discovery, philanthropy, or religious mission." Takahashi, International Law, 11, 178.

International law is part of our law, and must be ascertained and administered by the courts of justice of appropriate jurisdiction as often as questions of right depending upon it are duly presented for their determination. For this purpose, where there is no treaty and no controlling executive or legislative act or judicial decision, resort must be had to the customs and usages of civilized nations, and, as evidence of these, to the works of jurists and commentators who by years of labor, research, and experience have made themselves peculiarly well acquainted with the subjects of which they treat. Such works are resorted to by judicial tribunals, not for the speculations of their authors concerning what the law ought to be, but for trustworthy evidence of what the law really is. Hilton v. Guyot, 159 U.S. 113, 163, 164, 214, 215.

Wheaton places, among the principal sources of international law, "text-writers of authority, showing what is the approved usage of nations, or the general opinion respecting their mutual conduct, with the definitions and modifications introduced by general consent." As to these he forcibly observes: "Without wishing to exaggerate the importance of these writers, or to substitute, in any case, their authority for the principles of reason, it may be affirmed that they are generally impartial in their judgment. They are witnesses of the sentiments and usages of civilized nations, and the weight of their testimony increases every time that their authority is invoked by statesmen, and every year that passes without the rules laid down in their works being impugned by the avowal of contrary principles." Wheaton, International Law (8th ed.), § 15.

Chancellor Kent says: "In the absence of higher and more authoritative sanctions, the ordinances of foreign states, the opinions of eminent statesmen, and the writings of distinguished jurists, are regarded as of great consideration on questions not settled by conventional law. In cases where the principal jurists agree, the presumption will be very great in favor of the solidity of their maxims; and no civilized nation that does not arrogantly set all ordinary law and justice at defiance will venture to disregard the uniform sense of the established writers on international law." 1 Kent, Com. 18.

[The Court then discusses the views of French, Argentine, German, Dutch, English, Austrian, Spanish, Portuguese, and Italian writers on international law, and concludes:]

This review of the precedents and authorities on the subject appears to us abundantly to demonstrate that at the present day, by the general consent of the civilized nations of the world, and independently of any express treaty or other public act, it is an established rule of international law, founded on considerations of humanity to a poor and industrious order of men, and of the mutual convenience of belligerent states, that coast fishing vessels, with their implements and supplies, cargoes and crews, unarmed and honestly pursuing their peaceful calling of catching and bringing in fresh fish, are exempt from capture as prize of war. * * *

This rule of international law is one which prize courts administering the law of nations are bound to take judicial notice of, and to give effect to, in the absence of any treaty or other public act of their own government in relation to the matter. * * *

[Finding no express intention on the part of the United States to enforce the 1898 blockade of Cuba against coastal fishermen peacefully pursuing their calling, the Court ordered the reversal of the District Court decree and the payment to the claimants of the proceeds of the sale of the vessels and cargo, together with damages and costs.

[Chief Justice Fuller argued in a dissenting opinion, in which Harlan and McKenna, JJ., concurred, that the captured vessels were of such size and range as not to fall within the exemption, and that the exemption in any case had not become a customary rule of international law but was only "an act of grace" that had not been authorized by the President.]

NOTES

1. *Consistency and Representativeness of Practice.* Did not the Supreme Court find inconsistencies in the practice of states in respect of the alleged rule? How many states did it refer to in support of the practice? Consider the rather small number of states in the world during the time covered. Would such support meet the requirement of a "very widespread and representative participation" as required by the International Court of Justice in the *North Sea Continental Shelf Cases* (p. 90 *infra*)? Does the case show that a small number of states create a rule of customary law, if there is no practice which conflicts with the rule and no protests? Is it necessary (and realistic) to assume the acquiescence of the large majority of non-participating and silent states? Would the inconsistent conduct of one or two states be sufficient to prevent the creation of a general custom; if so, in what circumstances? See discussion of Non–Consenting States *infra* pp. 100–05; see also I.L.A. Customary International Law Report, 20–26.

2. *Evidence of Official Practice.* What evidence did the Court consider in arriving at its conclusions concerning the alleged "ancient usage among civilized nations"? Note the wide range of evidence of custom considered by the Court. It includes national law, executive decrees, and acts of military commanders, as well as judgments of national tribunals. Is every official act of a state officer an element of state practice? Are executive pronouncements, legislative acts, and municipal court decisions of equal weight in "committing" a state to a given practice? Should the conduct of military officers and other subordinate officials constitute state practice? What significance should be attached to the acts of military commanders, acting independently in the field? See Akehurst, Custom as a Source of International Law, 47 Brit. Y.B.I.L. 8–10 (1974–75); Wolfke, Custom in Present International Law (1964); Waldock, General Course on Public International Law, 106 Rec. des Cours, 1, 42–43 (1962–II) and sources cited; I.L.A. Customary International Law Report, 13–18.

3. *Scholarly Treatises.* Note the weight given by the Supreme Court to writers on international law and the quotation from Chancellor Kent that "no civilized nation will venture to disregard the uniform sense of the established writers on international law." For further comment on the role of international law scholars, see Chapter 4.

4. *Claims and Responses.* Myres S. McDougal has described customary law "as a process of continuous interaction, of continuous demand and response, in which the decision-makers of particular nation-states unilaterally put forward claims of the most diverse and conflicting character * * * and in which other decision-makers, external to the demanding state * * * weigh and appraise these competing claims * * * and ultimately accept or reject

them." In this process, McDougal observes, state officials honor each other's unilateral claims "by mutual tolerances expressed in countless decisions in foreign offices, national courts, and national legislatures—which create expectations that effective power will be restrained and exercised in certain uniformities of pattern." He adds that it is "the reciprocal tolerances of the external decision-makers which create the expectations of pattern and uniformity in decision, of practice in accord with rule, commonly regarded as law." McDougal emphasizes that states are influenced by "reasonableness" in their claims and reactions; in the process, values are clarified and "perceptions of common interest" realized. McDougal, The Hydrogen Bomb Tests, 49 A.J.I.L. 357–58 (1955). Under the jurisprudential approach formulated by McDougal and associates in influential writings, a "world constitutive process of authoritative decision" includes a broader frame of reference than traditional diplomacy. See McDougal & Lasswell, Jurisprudence for a Free Society: Studies in Law, Science and Policy (1992).

5. *Practice of Non–State Actors.* Under the classical theory of international law, it is "state" practice that generates customary international law. Does the conduct of persons without official state capacity count in any way toward the formation of custom (or the disintegration of customary rules previously formed in the traditional way)? The I.L.A. Customary International Law Report maintained the traditional state-centered perspective as recently as 2000, saying (at 16) that while acts of individuals, corporations, and other non-governmental bodies can contribute to practice in an *extended* sense (e.g., by encouraging adoption of certain behavior by governments), they do not constitute state practice as such. Others have proposed conceptualizing the domain of customary law formation to include non-state actors, at least in the domains in which international law has evolved to accord rights and responsibilities to "persons" other than states. See Mertus, Considering Nonstate Actors in the New Millennium: Toward Expanded Participation in Norm Generation and Norm Application, 32 N.Y.U. J. Int'l L. & Pol. 537 (2000); Paust, The Reality of Private Rights, Duties, and Participation in the International Legal Process, 25 Mich. J. Int'l L. 1229 (2004); Ochoa, The Individual and Customary International Law Formation, 48 Va. J. Int'l L. 119 (2007).

Should the practice of insurgent forces or other non-traditional armed groups "count" in establishing the customary law of armed conflict? Should the positions of non-governmental organizations (such as those affiliated with the Red Cross movement) factor into the analysis? On such questions, see the multivolume study prepared under the auspices of the International Committee of the Red Cross, Customary International Humanitarian Law (Henckaerts & Doswald-Beck eds. 2005) (hereinafter I.C.R.C. study) and the spirited debate over methodological issues in its aftermath, as addressed more fully in Chapter 15.

6. *Methodology of International Tribunals Applying Customary Law.* Theodor Meron, in a comment prompted by issuance of the I.C.R.C. study in 2005, has observed that international criminal tribunals applying the customary law of war have had to be rigorous in their methodology, in light of the principle of legality—that a defendant may be convicted only on the basis of rules that were clearly established when the crime was committed. In seeking to ascertain international custom relevant to internal conflicts, such tribunals

have cast a wide net. In the *Tadić* case, for example (discussed further in Chapters 4, 6, and 16), the International Criminal Tribunal for the Former Yugoslavia reviewed (among other sources) written instructions given by Mao Tse-tung to the Chinese "People's Liberation Army," agreement of parties to the 1967 conflict in Yemen, a statement of the rebel army in El Salvador, and I.C.R.C. principles concerning internal conflicts. Meron, Revival of Customary Humanitarian Law, 99 A.J.I.L. 817, 827–28 (2005). On what theory should the quest for custom expand beyond the practice of official state organs?

7. *Custom and Multilateral Treaty–Making Compared.* Would states be more likely to realize common interests by negotiating multilateral law-making treaties to meet perceived needs than by relying on the step-by-step gradualism of customary law? Is customary law more responsive to disparities in power and interest and therefore more "realistic" than law-making by international conferences in which all states take part on an equal footing? Which form of law-making is more "democratic"? See the comments on Relationship Between Custom and Treaties, Section 3 below, and further attention to whether customary law enjoys sufficient democratic validation in Chapter 10 on application of customary international law in domestic legal systems.

8. *Obligation or Interest?* A recent reexamination of *Paquete Habana* takes a revisionist point of view, arguing that the Supreme Court offered unconvincing evidence for the proposition that states had acted out of a sense of legal obligation in refraining from seizing coastal fishing vessels. The authors contend that states so refrained only when it suited their national interests. Goldsmith & Posner, Understanding the Resemblance Between Modern and Traditional Customary International Law, 40 Va. J. Int'l L. 639 (2000); see also Goldsmith & Posner, The Limits of International Law 66–78 (2005). For rebuttal, see Vagts, International Relations Looks at Customary International Law: A Traditionalist Defense, 13 E.J.I.L. 1031, 1032–33 (2004).

9. *Further Reading.* For a readable account locating the principal case in the context of the Spanish–American War and explaining the motivations of the actors involved, see Dodge, The Paquete Habana, in International Law Stories 175 (Noyes, Dickinson & Janis eds. 2007).

THE CASE OF THE S.S. LOTUS (FRANCE v. TURKEY)

Permanent Court of International Justice, 1927
P.C.I.J. (ser. A) No. 10

[A collision on the high seas in 1926 between a French steamer, the Lotus, and a Turkish steamer, the Boz–Kourt, resulted in the sinking of the Turkish vessel and the death of eight Turkish nationals. When the French ship reached Constantinople (Istanbul) the Turkish authorities instituted criminal proceedings against the French officer on watch-duty at the time of the collision (Lieutenant Demons). The Turkish Court overruled Demons' objection that Turkey had no jurisdiction and after a trial sentenced him to 80 days imprisonment and a fine of twenty-two pounds. The French Government challenged Turkey's action as a violation of international law and demanded reparation. Following negotiations, the two states by special agreement submitted the dispute to the Permanent Court of International Justice. The arguments put forward by the two parties related exclusively to whether according to principles of international law Turkey had or had not jurisdiction to prosecute the case. Both parties recognized the applicability of the Convention of Lausanne of 1923 which provided in Article 15: "Subject to the provisions of Article 16, all questions of jurisdiction as between Turkey and the other contracting parties shall be decided in accordance with the principles of international law."]

The Court, having to consider whether there are any rules of international law which may have been violated by the prosecution in pursuance of Turkish law of Lieutenant Demons, is confronted in the first place by a question of principle which, in the written and oral arguments of the two Parties, has proved to be a fundamental one. The French Government contends that the Turkish Courts, in order to have jurisdiction, should be able to point to some title to jurisdiction recognized by international law in favour of Turkey. On the other hand, the Turkish Government takes the view that Article 15 allows Turkey jurisdiction whenever such jurisdiction does not come into conflict with a principle of international law.

The latter view seems to be in conformity with the special agreement itself, No. 1 of which asks the Court to say whether Turkey has acted contrary to the principles of international law and, if so, what principles. According to the special agreement, therefore, it is not a question of stating principles which would permit Turkey to take criminal proceedings, but of formulating the principles, if any, which might have been violated by such proceedings.

This way of stating the question is also dictated by the very nature and existing conditions of international law.

International law governs relations between independent States. The rules of law binding upon States therefore emanate from their own free will as expressed in conventions or by usages generally accepted as expressing principles of law and established in order to regulate the relations between these co-existing independent communities or with a view to the achievement of common aims. Restrictions upon the independence of States cannot therefore be presumed.

Now the first and foremost restriction imposed by international law upon a State is that—failing the existence of a permissive rule to the contrary—it may not exercise its power in any form in the territory of another State. In this sense jurisdiction is certainly territorial; it cannot be exercised by a State outside its territory except by virtue of a permissive rule derived from international custom or from a convention.

It does not, however, follow that international law prohibits a State from exercising jurisdiction in its own territory, in respect of any case which relates to acts which have taken place abroad, and in which it cannot rely on some permissive rule of international law. Such a view would only be tenable if international law contained a general prohibition to States to extend the application of their laws and the jurisdiction of their courts to persons, property and acts outside their territory, and if, as an exception to this general prohibition, it allowed States to do so in certain specific cases. But this is certainly not the case under international law as it stands at present. Far from laying down a general prohibition to the effect that States may not extend the application of their laws and the jurisdiction of their courts to persons, property and acts outside their territory, it leaves them in this respect a wide measure of discretion which is only limited in certain cases by prohibitive rules; as regards other cases, every State remains free to adopt the principles which it regards as best and most suitable.

* * *

In these circumstances, all that can be required of a State is that it should not overstep the limits which international law places upon its jurisdiction; within these limits, its title to exercise jurisdiction rests in its sovereignty.

It follows from the foregoing that the contention of the French Government to the effect that Turkey must in each case be able to cite a rule of international law authorizing her to exercise jurisdiction, is opposed to the generally accepted international law to which Article 15 of the Convention of Lausanne refers. Having regard to the terms of Article 15 and to the construction which the Court has just placed upon it, this contention would apply in regard to civil as well as to criminal cases, and would be applicable on conditions of absolute reciprocity as between Turkey and the other contracting Parties; in practice, it would therefore in many cases result in paralyzing the action of the courts, owing to the impossibility of citing a universally accepted rule on which to support the exercise of their jurisdiction.

* * *

Nevertheless, it has to be seen whether the foregoing considerations really apply as regards criminal jurisdiction, or whether this jurisdiction is governed by a different principle: this might be the outcome of the close connection which for a long time existed between the conception of supreme criminal jurisdiction and that of a State, and also by the especial importance of criminal jurisdiction from the point of view of the individual.

Though it is true that in all systems of law the principle of the territorial character of criminal law is fundamental, it is equally true that all or nearly all these systems of law extend their action to offences committed outside the territory of the State which adopts them, and they do so in ways which vary from State to State. The territoriality of criminal law, therefore, is not an absolute principle of international law and by no means coincides with territorial sovereignty.

* * *

The Court therefore must, in any event, ascertain whether or not there exists a rule of international law limiting the freedom of States to extend the criminal jurisdiction of their courts to a situation uniting the circumstances of the present case.

* * *

The arguments advanced by the French Government, other than those considered above, are, in substance, the three following:

(1) International law does not allow a State to take proceedings with regard to offences committed by foreigners abroad, simply by reason of the nationality of the victim; and such is the situation in the present case because the offence must be regarded as having been committed on board the French vessel.

(2) International law recognizes the exclusive jurisdiction of the State whose flag is flown as regards everything which occurs on board a ship on the high seas.

(3) Lastly, this principle is especially applicable in a collision case.

* * *

As has already been observed, the characteristic features of the situation of fact are as follows: there has been a collision on the high seas between two vessels flying different flags, on one of which was one of the persons alleged to be guilty of the offence, whilst the victims were on board the other.

This being so, the Court does not think it necessary to consider the contention that a State cannot punish offences committed abroad by a foreigner simply by reason of the nationality of the victim. For this contention only relates to the case where the nationality of the victim is the only criterion on which the criminal jurisdiction of the State is based. Even if that argument were correct generally speaking—and in regard to this the Court reserves its opinion—it could only be used in the present case if international law forbade Turkey to take into consideration the fact that the offence produced its effects on the Turkish vessel and consequently in a place assimilated to Turkish territory in which the application of Turkish criminal law cannot be challenged, even in regard to offences committed there by foreigners. But no such rule of international law exists. No argument has come to the knowledge of the Court from which it could be deduced that States recognize themselves to be under an obligation towards each other only to have regard to the place where the author of the offence happens to be at the time of the offence. On the contrary, it is certain that the courts of many countries, even of countries which have given their criminal legislation a strictly territorial character, interpret criminal law in the sense that offences, the authors of which at the moment of commission are in the territory of another State, are nevertheless to be regarded as having been committed in the national territory, if one of the constituent elements of the offence, and more especially its effects, have taken place there. French courts have, in regard to a variety of situations, given decisions sanctioning this way of interpreting the territorial principle. Again, the Court does not know of any cases in which governments have protested against the fact that the criminal law of some country contained a rule to this effect or that the courts of a country construed their criminal law in this sense. Consequently, once it is admitted that the effects of the offence were produced on the Turkish vessel, it becomes impossible to hold that there is a rule of international law which prohibits Turkey from prosecuting Lieutenant Demons because of the fact that the author of the offence was on board the French ship. Since, as has already been observed, the special agreement does not deal with the provision of Turkish law under which the prosecution was instituted, but only with the question whether the prosecution should be regarded as contrary to the principles of international law, there is no reason preventing the Court from confining itself to observing that, in this case, a prosecution may also be justified from the point of view of the so-called territorial principle.

* * *

The second argument put forward by the French Government is the principle that the State whose flag is flown has exclusive jurisdiction over everything which occurs on board a merchant ship on the high seas.

It is certainly true that—apart from certain special cases which are defined by international law—vessels on the high seas are subject to no authority except that of the State whose flag they fly. In virtue of the principle of the freedom of the seas, that is to say, the absence of any territorial sovereignty upon the high seas, no State may exercise any kind of jurisdiction over foreign vessels upon them. Thus, if a war vessel, happening to be at the spot where a collision occurs between a vessel flying its flag and a foreign vessel, were to send on board the latter an officer to make investigations or to take evidence, such an act would undoubtedly be contrary to international law.

But it by no means follows that a State can never in its own territory exercise jurisdiction over acts which have occurred on board a foreign ship on the high seas. A corollary of the principle of the freedom of the seas is that a ship on the high seas is assimilated to the territory of the State the flag of which it flies, for, just as in its own territory, that State exercises its authority upon it, and no other State may do so. All that can be said is that by virtue of the principle of the freedom of the seas, a ship is placed in the same position as national territory; but there is nothing to support the claim according to which the rights of the State under whose flag the vessel sails may go farther than the rights which it exercises within its territory properly so called. It follows that what occurs on board a vessel on the high seas must be regarded as if it occurred on the territory of the State whose flag the ship flies. If, therefore, a guilty act committed on the high seas produces its effects on a vessel flying another flag or in foreign territory, the same principles must be applied as if the territories of two different States were concerned, and the conclusion must therefore be drawn that there is no rule of international law prohibiting the State to which the ship on which the effects of the offence have taken place belongs, from regarding the offence as having been committed in its territory and prosecuting, accordingly, the delinquent.

This conclusion could only be overcome if it were shown that there was a rule of customary international law which, going further than the principle stated above, established the exclusive jurisdiction of the State whose flag was flown. The French Government has endeavoured to prove the existence of such a rule, having recourse for this purpose to the teachings of publicists, to decisions of municipal and international tribunals, and especially to conventions which, whilst creating exceptions to the principle of the freedom of the seas by permitting the war and police vessels of a State to exercise a more or less extensive control over the merchant vessels of another State, reserve jurisdiction to the courts of the country whose flag is flown by the vessel proceeded against.

In the Court's opinion, the existence of such a rule has not been conclusively proved.

In the first place, as regards teachings of publicists, and apart from the question as to what their value may be from the point of view of establishing the existence of a rule of customary law, it is no doubt true that all or nearly all writers teach that ships on the high seas are subject exclusively to the jurisdiction of the State whose flag they fly. But the important point is the significance attached by them to this principle; now it does not appear that in general, writers bestow upon this principle a scope differing from or wider than that explained above and which is equivalent to saying that the jurisdiction of a State over vessels on the high seas is the same in extent as its jurisdiction in its own territory. On the other hand, there is no lack of writers who, upon a close study of the special question whether a State can prosecute for offences committed on board a foreign ship on the high seas, definitely come to the conclusion that such offences must be regarded as if they had been committed in the territory of the State whose flag the ship flies, and that consequently the general rules of each legal system in regard to offences committed abroad are applicable.

In regard to precedents, it should first be observed that, leaving aside the collision cases which will be alluded to later, none of them relates to offences affecting two ships flying the flags of two different countries, and that consequently they are not of much importance in the case before the Court. The case of the *Costa Rica Packet* is no exception, for the prauw on which the alleged depredations took place was adrift without flag or crew, and this circumstance certainly influenced, perhaps decisively, the conclusion arrived at by the arbitrator.

On the other hand, there is no lack of cases in which the State has claimed a right to prosecute for an offence, committed on board a foreign ship, which it regarded as punishable under its legislation. Thus Great Britain refused the request of the United States for the extradition of John Anderson, a British seaman who had committed homicide on board an American vessel, stating that she did not dispute the jurisdiction of the United States but that she was entitled to exercise hers concurrently. This case, to which others might be added, is relevant in spite of Anderson's British nationality, in order to show that the principle of the exclusive jurisdiction of the country whose flag the vessel flies is not universally accepted.

The cases in which the exclusive jurisdiction of the State whose flag was flown has been recognized would seem rather to have been cases in which the foreign State was interested only by reason of the nationality of the victim, and in which, according to the legislation of that State itself or the practice of its courts, that ground was not regarded as sufficient to authorize prosecution for an offence committed abroad by a foreigner.

Finally, as regards conventions expressly reserving jurisdiction exclusively to the State whose flag is flown, it is not absolutely certain that this stipulation is to be regarded as expressing a general principle of law rather than as corresponding to the extraordinary jurisdiction which these conventions confer on the state-owned ships of a particular country in respect of ships of another country on the high seas. Apart from that, it should be observed that these conventions relate to matters of a particular kind, closely connected with the policing of the seas, such as the slave trade, damage to submarine cables, fisheries, etc., and not to common-law offences. Above all it should be pointed out that the offences contemplated by the conventions in question only concern a single ship; it is impossible therefore to make any deduction from them in regard to matters which concern two ships and consequently the jurisdiction to two different States.

The Court therefore has arrived at the conclusion that the second argument put forward by the French Government does not, any more than the first, establish the existence of a rule of international law prohibiting Turkey from prosecuting Lieutenant Demons.

[The Court then addressed itself to the third argument advanced by France that, according to international law, criminal proceedings arising from collisions are within the exclusive jurisdiction of the state whose flag is flown. In offering this view, the French Agent pointed out that questions of jurisdiction in collision cases, which frequently arise before civil courts, rarely are presented to criminal courts. This fact led him to conclude that prosecutions only occur before the courts of the state whose flag is flown, which was proof of a tacit adherence by states to the rule of positive international law barring prosecutions by other states.

[The Court rejected this argument, explaining that even if the facts alleged were true, they would merely show that states had often abstained from instituting criminal proceedings, not that they felt obligated to do so. The Court observed that there were no decisions of international tribunals in the matter and that, of the four municipal court decisions cited by the parties, two supported the exclusive jurisdiction of the flag state and two supported the opposite contention. The Court pointed out that "as municipal jurisprudence is thus divided, it is hardly possible to see in it an indication of the existence of the restrictive rule of international law which alone could serve as a basis for the contention of the French Government." On the other hand, the Court stressed the fact that the French and German governments had failed to protest against the exercise of criminal jurisdiction by states whose flag was not being flown in the two cases cited by Turkey, and observed that the French and German governments would hardly have failed to protest if they "had really thought that this was a violation of international law."]

The conclusion at which the Court has therefore arrived is that there is no rule of international law in regard to collision cases to the effect that criminal proceedings are exclusively within the jurisdiction of the State whose flag is flown.

* * *

* * * Neither the exclusive jurisdiction of either State, nor the limitations of the jurisdiction of each to the occurrences which took place on the respective ships would appear calculated to satisfy the requirements of justice and effectively to protect the interests of the two States. It is only natural that each should be able to exercise jurisdiction and to do so in respect of the incident as a whole. It is therefore a case of concurrent jurisdiction.

* * *

FOR THESE REASONS, the Court, having heard both Parties, gives, by the President's casting vote—the votes being equally divided—judgment to the effect

(1) that, following the collision which occurred on August 2nd, 1926, on the high seas between the French steamship *Lotus* and the Turkish steamship *Boz–Kourt,* and upon the arrival of the French ship at Stamboul, and in consequence of the loss of the *Boz–Kourt* having involved the death of eight Turkish nationals, Turkey, by instituting criminal proceedings in pursuance of Turkish law against Lieutenant Demons, officer of the watch on board the *Lotus* at the time of the collision, has not acted in conflict with the principles of international law, contrary to Article 15 of the Convention of Lausanne of July 24th, 1923, respecting conditions of residence and business and jurisdiction;

(2) that, consequently, there is no occasion to give judgment on the question of the pecuniary reparation which might have been due to Lieutenant Demons if Turkey, by prosecuting him as above stated, had acted in a manner contrary to the principles of international law.

[The six dissenting judges disagreed with the proposition that France had the burden of showing a customary law rule that prohibited Turkey's exercise of jurisdiction. They took issue with the basic premise of the judgment that "restrictions upon the freedom of states cannot be presumed" and its implicit corollary that international law permits all that it does not forbid. In their view, the question was whether international law authorized Turkey to exercise jurisdiction in the particular circumstances and they concluded that customary law did not authorize a state to exercise criminal jurisdiction over a foreigner for an act committed in a foreign country or in a vessel of another state on the high seas.]

NOTES

1. *Positivism and Its Critics.* The *Lotus Case* has been strongly criticized for its "extreme positivism" and especially for asserting that restrictions on the freedom of states cannot be presumed. Was this principle necessary for the Court to rule on the French contention that Turkey was not permitted under customary law to prosecute the French officer? Note that the Court's jurisdiction rested on a special agreement of the parties that asked it to decide whether Turkey acted contrary to principles of international law. Did this formulation make it reasonable for the Court to impose the burden of proof on France to show that Turkey's action violated international law rather than requiring Turkey to prove its legal right to do so?

2. *Is International Law a Complete System?* If the Court found no specific customary law that either permitted or prohibited criminal jurisdiction in the given circumstances, should it have declined to decide the case? Is it necessary to assume the formal completeness of the international legal system so that there is no gap in the system? Kelsen wrote: "If there is no norm of conventional or customary international law imposing * * * the obligation to behave in a certain way, the subject is, under international law, legally free to behave as it pleases; and by a decision to this effect existing international law is applied." Kelsen, Principles of International Law 438–39 (2d rev. ed. Tucker ed. 1966). Some writers who agree that international law must be formally complete (i.e., every dispute must be capable of legal determination) reject the residual principle of state freedom expressed in the *Lotus Case.* They consider that every case can be decided either by existing legal rules or by deriving such rules from general principles and concepts within the legal system. See Oppenheim, International Law 12–13 (9th ed. Jennings & Watts ed. 1992). This position expressed most influentially by Sir Hersch Lauterpacht (as a scholar and when a judge in the International Court) relies heavily on general principles and analogy to solve hard cases in order to ensure the coherence and effectiveness of the international legal system. On that view, judges cannot refuse to decide on the ground that the law is unclear (the Latin term *non liquet,* meaning "it is not clear," is sometimes used in such situations), nor can they resort to residual principles such as sovereignty. For such writers (if not for states) the system must be seen as materially (and not only formally) complete.

Other writers move beyond decisions limited to legal rules and principles. They would turn to "purposes" and "policies" of the international community for determining criteria in a balancing process. See Schachter, International Law in Theory and Practice 18–31 (1991); McDougal & Reisman, International Law in Policy–Oriented Perspective, in The Structure and Process of International Law 103–29 (Macdonald & Johnston eds. 1983); McDougal & Lasswell, Jurisprudence for a Free Society: Studies in Law, Science and Policy (1992).

Can a good argument be made that an international court should decline to decide a case if the law is not clear enough *(non liquet)*? For that view, see Stone, *Non Liquet* and the Function of Law in the International Community, 35 Brit. Y.B.I.L. 124 (1959). For more on these questions, see the notes following the excerpt from the I.C.J.'s *Nuclear Weapons* advisory opinion, p. 86, and on equity as a general principle of law in Chapter 4.

3. *Relevance of Legislation and Judicial Practice.* Referring again to the *Lotus Case,* does it seem unreasonable or unjust that Turkey should have the right to try a French captain of a French vessel for his acts outside of Turkish jurisdiction because Turkish nationals were injured in a collision between the French and Turkish vessels? Is it significant that the national courts in many countries apply their criminal law to acts committed outside the country if such acts have effects in the country? Do such municipal law cases constitute state practice? Can it be shown that they are accompanied by a belief that their acts are permissible under international law when that question does *not* arise? Is the absence of protests in such cases supportive of customary law? Suppose, as the Court says, most countries recognize the exclusive jurisdiction of the flag state even if the victims of an accident are non-nationals but a few states do not? Should exceptions weigh decisively against a customary rule of exclusive jurisdiction?

4. *Restraint in Asserting Jurisdiction.* Why did France fail in its argument that abstention of states from exercising jurisdiction over foreign vessels or nationals involved in high seas collisions showed that there was a rule of international law restricting such jurisdiction to the flag state? What would satisfy the Court that such abstention was followed because of a conviction that it was required by international law? When does practice consisting of *omissions* give rise to *opinio juris?* See Section 2.D below on *opinio juris.*

In *Arrest Warrant of 11 April 2000* (Democratic Republic of the Congo v. Belgium), 2002 I.C.J. 3, the International Court concluded that customary international law requires the grant of immunity from prosecution in third states to sitting foreign ministers. Although the Court said that it had considered state practice, national legislation, and court decisions (para. 58), it did not specify the evidence that enabled it to reach this conclusion. What form of evidence might be adduced to demonstrate that states have *refrained*, out of a sense of *legal obligation*, from prosecuting high-level officials of other states? On jurisdictional restraint and international custom as regards jurisdictional immunities, see Chapters 11 and 12.

5. *Protests.* As the *Lotus Case* indicates, protests and acquiescence are critical factors in the formation of customary law. The Court envisaged verbal protests such as those made in diplomatic correspondence or in international

conferences, which have often been regarded as effective expressions of a state's objection to an asserted rule. See, for example, *North Sea Continental Shelf Case (infra)* and *Fisheries Jurisdiction Case* (United Kingdom v. Iceland), 1974 I.C.J. 3. In *Fisheries Jurisdiction*, several judges emphasized the existence of protests as refuting the claim of Iceland to an exclusive fishing zone exceeding twelve miles; other judges disagreed by noting that many interested states had not protested. 1974 I.C.J. at 47, 58, 161. How much weight is to be given isolated protests or the failure to protest? Judge Dillard's separate opinion (1974 I.C.J. 53 at 58) notes the importance of protest by states specially affected. Conversely, the lack of protests by non-interested states does not imply that they necessarily acquiesce in the legal theory of the claims.

6. *Protests versus Physical Acts.* States sometimes consider it necessary to back their protests by physical action, as by seizing allegedly trespassing ships or sending their vessels into waters claimed by other states. For example, the U.S. rejection of the Canadian claim of competence to exclude vessels from certain Arctic waters has been emphasized by sending in U.S. vessels without Canadian authorization. Are there good reasons to require physical acts to demonstrate the "seriousness" of the protest? Would such requirement increase the danger of armed conflict and give advantages to great powers? See conflicting views in Akehurst, Custom as a Source of International Law, 47 Brit. Y.B.I.L. 1, 39–42 (1974–75), and D'Amato, The Concept of Custom in International Law 88–89 (1971).

In 2000, the I.L.A. Customary International Law Report (at 14–15) affirmed that verbal acts as well as physical acts can constitute state practice—a proposition which it found consistent with voluntarist theories of international law and with the relative frequency of verbal as contrasted to physical acts. Since not all states are in a position to register protests through forceful acts such as arrests or seizures, allowing verbal acts to count as state practice maintains the juridical equality of states. Even so, strong states like the United States continue to register protests against what they perceive as unwarranted claims by others, not only verbally but through physical manifestation of their own claims of right. The United States through its freedom of navigation program regularly challenges other states' claims by sending vessels (even warships) or aircraft into disputed zones.

Disputed claims in the Arctic illustrate different approaches to registering positions on differing views of the customary law regime prevailing there. For an account of an accelerated race by several states to back up their positions on rights in the Arctic through tangible (even forcible) action, see Graff, Who Owns the Arctic? Fight for the Top of the World, Time Magazine, Oct. 1, 2007, at 28, 34–36.

7. *Subsequent History.* After the *Lotus Case*, many governments adopted a treaty provision which reversed the Court's ruling and prohibited a state other than the flag state from exercising criminal jurisdiction against a non-national in case of a collision or accident on the high seas. Article 97 of the U.N. Convention on the Law of the Sea now regulates the matter and may be considered reflective of modern customary law. See Chapter 17. If custom has changed since *Lotus*, how did that change come about?

LEGALITY OF THE THREAT OR USE
OF NUCLEAR WEAPONS

International Court of Justice, Advisory Opinion, 1996
1996 I.C.J 226

[The U.N. General Assembly asked the I.C.J. for an advisory opinion, pursuant to Article 96(1) of the U.N. Charter, on the following question: "Is the threat or use of nuclear weapons in any circumstance permitted under international law?" The Court determined that it had jurisdiction to give a reply to the request, and likewise concluded that there were no "compelling reasons" to exercise a discretionary power to decline to answer the question.

[The Court turned to arguments pressed by some states in reliance on the *Lotus* case, including contentions that restrictions on states' freedom of action cannot be found in international law in the absence of positive law emanating from state consent. The Court also considered claims advanced by some nuclear-weapons states, to the effect that states specially affected by a purported rule of customary international law could not be presumed to be bound by such a rule without their consent and over their objections. On these points the Court said:]

21. The use of the word "permitted" in the question put by the General Assembly was criticized before the Court by certain States on the ground that this implied that the threat or the use of nuclear weapons would only be permissible if authorization could be found in a treaty provision or in customary international law. Such a starting point, those States submitted, was incompatible with the very basis of international law, which rests upon the principles of sovereignty and consent; accordingly, and contrary to what was implied by use of the word "permitted", States are free to threaten or use nuclear weapons unless it can be shown that they are bound not to do so by reference to a prohibition in either treaty law or customary international law. Support for this contention was found in dicta of the Permanent Court of International Justice in the "*Lotus*" case that "restrictions upon the independence of States cannot ... be presumed" and that international law leaves to States "a wide measure of discretion which is only limited in certain cases by prohibitive rules" * * *. Reliance was also placed on the dictum of the present Court in the case concerning *Military and Paramilitary Activities in and Against Nicaragua (Nicaragua v. United States of America)* that:

> "in international law there are no rules, other than such rules as may be accepted by the State concerned, by treaty or otherwise, whereby the level of armaments of a sovereign State can be limited" (*I.C.J. Reports 1986*, p. 135, para. 269).

For other States, the invocation of these dicta in the "*Lotus*" case was inapposite; their status in contemporary international law and applicability in the very different circumstances of the present case were challenged. It was also contended that the above-mentioned dictum of the present

Court was directed to the *possession* of armaments and was irrelevant to the threat or use of nuclear weapons. * * *

22. The Court notes that the nuclear-weapon States appearing before it either accepted, or did not dispute, that their independence to act was indeed restricted by the principles and rules of international law, more particularly humanitarian law * * *, as did the other States which took part in the proceedings.

Hence, the argument concerning the legal conclusions to be drawn from the use of the word "permitted", and the questions of burden of proof to which it was said to give rise, are without particular significance for the disposition of the issues before the Court. * * *

[Turning to possible sources of law, the Court surveyed various treaties and other instruments potentially bearing on the question. It addressed customary law, and the interaction between treaties and custom, in the following passages:]

52. The Court notes by way of introduction that international customary and treaty law does not contain any specific prescription authorizing the threat or use of nuclear weapons or any other weapon in general or in certain circumstances, in particular those of the exercise of legitimate self-defence. Nor, however, is there any principle or rule of international law which would make the legality of the threat or use of nuclear weapons or of any other weapons dependent on a specific authorization. State practice shows that the illegality of the use of certain weapons as such does not result from an absence of authorization but, on the contrary, is formulated in terms of prohibition. * * *

* * *

60. Those States that believe that recourse to nuclear weapons is illegal stress that the conventions that include various rules providing for the limitation or elimination of nuclear weapons in certain areas (such as the Antarctic Treaty of 1959 which prohibits the deployment of nuclear weapons in the Antarctic, or the Treaty of Tlatelolco of 1967 which creates a nuclear-weapon-free zone in Latin America), or the conventions that apply certain measures of control and limitation to the existence of nuclear weapons (such as the 1963 Partial Test–Ban Treaty or the Treaty on the Non–Proliferation of Nuclear Weapons) all set limits to the use of nuclear weapons. In their view, these treaties bear witness, in their own way, to the emergence of a rule of complete legal prohibition of all uses of nuclear weapons.

61. Those States who defend the position that recourse to nuclear weapons is legal in certain circumstances see a logical contradiction in reaching such a conclusion. According to them, those Treaties, such as the Treaty on the Non–Proliferation of Nuclear Weapons, as well as Security Council resolutions 255 (1968) and 984 (1995) which take note of the security assurances given by the nuclear-weapon States to the non-nuclear-weapon States in relation to any nuclear aggression against the

latter, cannot be understood as prohibiting the use of nuclear weapons, and such a claim is contrary to the very text of those instruments. For those who support the legality in certain circumstances of recourse to nuclear weapons, there is no absolute prohibition against the use of such weapons. The very logic and construction of the Treaty on the Non–Proliferation of Nuclear Weapons, they assert, confirm this. This Treaty, whereby, they contend, the possession of nuclear weapons by the five nuclear-weapon States has been accepted, cannot be seen as a treaty banning their use by those States; to accept the fact that those States possess nuclear weapons is tantamount to recognizing that such weapons may be used in certain circumstances. Nor, they contend, could the security assurances given by the nuclear-weapon States in 1968, and more recently in connection with the Review and Extension Conference of the Parties to the Treaty on the Non–Proliferation of Nuclear Weapons in 1995, have been conceived without its being supposed that there were circumstances in which nuclear weapons could be used in a lawful manner. For those who defend the legality of the use, in certain circumstances, of nuclear weapons, the acceptance of those instruments by the different non-nuclear-weapon States confirms and reinforces the evident logic upon which those instruments are based.

62.   The Court notes that the treaties dealing exclusively with acquisition, manufacture, possession, deployment and testing of nuclear weapons, without specifically addressing their threat or use, certainly point to an increasing concern in the international community with these weapons; the Court concludes from this that these treaties could therefore be seen as foreshadowing a future general prohibition of the use of such weapons, but they do not constitute such a prohibition by themselves. As to the treaties of Tlatelolco and Rarotonga and their Protocols, and also the declarations made in connection with the indefinite extension of the Treaty on the Non–Proliferation of Nuclear Weapons, it emerges from these instruments that:

(a) a number of States have undertaken not to use nuclear weapons in specific zones (Latin America; the South Pacific) or against certain other States (non-nuclear-weapon States which are parties to the Treaty on the Non–Proliferation of Nuclear Weapons);

(b) nevertheless, even within this framework, the nuclear-weapon States have reserved the right to use nuclear weapons in certain circumstances; and

(c) these reservations met with no objection from the parties to the Tlatelolco or Rarotonga Treaties or from the Security Council.

63.   These two treaties, the security assurances given in 1995 by the nuclear-weapon States and the fact that the Security Council took note of them with satisfaction, testify to a growing awareness of the need to liberate the community of States and the international public from the dangers resulting from the existence of nuclear weapons. The Court moreover notes the signing, even more recently, on 15 December 1995, at

Bangkok, of a Treaty on the Southeast Asia Nuclear–Weapon–Free Zone, and on 11 April 1996, at Cairo, of a treaty on the creation of a nuclear-weapons-free zone in Africa. It does not, however, view these elements as amounting to a comprehensive and universal conventional prohibition on the use, or the threat of use, of those weapons as such.

* * *

64. The Court will now turn to an examination of customary international law to determine whether a prohibition of the threat or use of nuclear weapons as such flows from that source of law. As the Court has stated, the substance of that law must be "looked for primarily in the actual practice and *opinio juris* of States" * * *

65. States which hold the view that the use of nuclear weapons is illegal have endeavoured to demonstrate the existence of a customary rule prohibiting this use. They refer to a consistent practice of non-utilization of nuclear weapons by States since 1945 and they would see in that practice the expression of an *opinio juris* on the part of those who possess such weapons.

66. Some other States, which assert the legality of the threat and use of nuclear weapons in certain circumstances, invoked the doctrine and practice of deterrence in support of their argument. They recall that they have always, in concert with certain other States, reserved the right to use those weapons in the exercise of the right to self-defence against an armed attack threatening their vital security interests. In their view, if nuclear weapons have not been used since 1945, it is not on account of an existing or nascent custom but merely because circumstances that might justify their use have fortunately not arisen.

67. The Court does not intend to pronounce here upon the practice known as the "policy of deterrence." It notes that it is a fact that a number of States adhered to that practice during the greater part of the Cold War and continue to adhere to it. Furthermore, the Members of the international community are profoundly divided on the matter of whether non-recourse to nuclear weapons over the past fifty years constitutes the expression of an *opinio juris*. Under these circumstances the Court does not consider itself able to find that there is such an *opinio juris*.

68. According to certain States, the important series of General Assembly resolutions, beginning with resolution 1653 (XVI) of 24 November 1961, that deal with nuclear weapons and that affirm, with consistent regularity, the illegality of nuclear weapons, signify the existence of a rule of international customary law which prohibits recourse to those weapons. According to other States, however, the resolutions in question have no binding character on their own account and are not declaratory of any customary rule of prohibition of nuclear weapons; some of these States have also pointed out that this series of resolutions not only did not meet with the approval of all of the nuclear-weapon States but of many other States as well.

69. States which consider that the use of nuclear weapons is illegal indicated that those resolutions did not claim to create any new rules, but were confined to a confirmation of customary law relating to the prohibition of means or methods of warfare which, by their use, overstepped the bounds of what is permissible in the conduct of hostilities. In their view, the resolutions in question did no more than apply to nuclear weapons the existing rules of international law applicable in armed conflict; they were no more than the "envelope" or *instrumentum* containing certain pre-existing customary rules of international law. For those States it is accordingly of little importance that the *instrumentum* should have occasioned negative votes, which cannot have the effect of obliterating those customary rules which have been confirmed by treaty law.

70. The Court notes that General Assembly resolutions, even if they are not binding, may sometimes have normative value. They can, in certain circumstances, provide evidence important for establishing the existence of a rule or the emergence of an *opinio juris*. To establish whether this is true of a given General Assembly resolution, it is necessary to look at its content and the conditions of its adoption; it is also necessary to see whether an *opinio juris* exists as to its normative character. Or a series of resolutions may show the gradual evolution of the *opinio juris* required for the establishment of a new rule.

71. Examined in their totality, the General Assembly resolutions put before the Court declare that the use of nuclear weapons would be "a direct violation of the Charter of the United Nations"; and in certain formulations that such use "should be prohibited". The focus of these resolutions has sometimes shifted to diverse related matters; however, several of the resolutions under consideration in the present case have been adopted with substantial numbers of negative votes and abstentions; thus, although those resolutions are a clear sign of deep concern regarding the problem of nuclear weapons, they still fall short of establishing the existence of an *opinio juris* on the illegality of the use of such weapons.

72. The Court further notes that the first of the resolutions of the General Assembly expressly proclaiming the illegality of the use of nuclear weapons, resolution 1653 (XVI) of 24 November 1961 (mentioned in subsequent resolutions), after referring to certain international declarations and binding agreements, from the Declaration of St. Petersburg of 1868 to the Geneva Protocol of 1925, proceeded to qualify the legal nature of nuclear weapons, determine their effects, and apply general rules of customary international law to nuclear weapons in particular. That application by the General Assembly of general rules of customary law to the particular case of nuclear weapons indicates that, in its view, there was no specific rule of customary law which prohibited the use of nuclear weapons; if such a rule had existed, the General Assembly could simply have referred to it and would not have needed to undertake such an exercise of legal qualification.

73. Having said this, the Court points out that the adoption each year by the General Assembly, by a large majority, of resolutions recalling the content of resolution 1653 (XVI), and requesting the member States to conclude a convention prohibiting the use of nuclear weapons in any circumstance, reveals the desire of a very large section of the international community to take, by a specific and express prohibition of the use of nuclear weapons, a significant step forward along the road to complete nuclear disarmament. The emergence, as *lex lata,* of a customary rule specifically prohibiting the use of nuclear weapons as such is hampered by the continuing tensions between the nascent *opinio juris* on the one hand, and the still strong adherence to the practice of deterrence on the other.

* * *

74. The Court not having found a conventional rule of general scope, nor a customary rule specifically proscribing the threat or use of nuclear weapons *per se,* it will now deal with the question whether recourse to nuclear weapons must be considered as illegal in the light of the principles and rules of international humanitarian law applicable in armed conflict and of the law of neutrality.

[In the next segment of the opinion, the Court identified two "cardinal principles" of international humanitarian law, which require states to refrain from using weapons that are incapable of distinguishing between civilian and military targets or which would inflict useless suffering. (These humanitarian principles are addressed in Chapter 15.) The Court found that the threat or use of nuclear weapons, because of their inherently destructive nature, would generally violate those principles. At the same time, the Court went on to assert that it was unable to conclude definitively that in *all* circumstances the threat or use of nuclear weapons was unlawful.]

95. Nor can the Court make a determination on the validity of the view that the recourse to nuclear weapons would be illegal in any circumstance owing to their inherent and total incompatibility with the law applicable in armed conflict. Certainly, as the Court has already indicated, the principles and rules of law applicable in armed conflict—at the heart of which is the overriding consideration of humanity—make the conduct of armed hostilities subject to a number of strict requirements. Thus, methods and means of warfare, which would preclude any distinction between civilian and military targets, or which would result in unnecessary suffering to combatants, are prohibited. In view of the unique characteristics of nuclear weapons, to which the Court has referred above, the use of such weapons in fact seems scarcely reconcilable with respect for such requirements. Nevertheless, the Court considers that it does not have sufficient elements to enable it to conclude with certainty that the use of nuclear weapons would necessarily be at variance with the principles and rules of law applicable in armed conflict in any circumstance.

96. Furthermore, the Court cannot lose sight of the fundamental right of every State to survival, and thus its right to resort to self-defence, in accordance with Article 51 of the Charter, when its survival is at stake.

Nor can it ignore the practice referred to as "policy of deterrence", to which an appreciable section of the international community adhered for many years. The Court also notes the reservations which certain nuclear-weapon States have appended to the undertakings they have given, notably under the Protocols to the Treaties of Tlatelolco and Rarotonga, and also under the declarations made by them in connection with the extension of the Treaty on the Non–Proliferation of Nuclear Weapons, not to resort to such weapons.

97. Accordingly, in view of the present state of international law viewed as a whole, as examined above by the Court, and of the elements of fact at its disposal, the Court is led to observe that it cannot reach a definitive conclusion as to the legality or illegality of use of nuclear weapons by a State in an extreme circumstance of self-defence, in which its very survival would be at stake.

[The Court then addressed the claim of an obligation expressed in Article VI of the Non–Proliferation Treaty to negotiate in good faith toward the objective of nuclear disarmament, and affirmed (paragraph 103) that "it remains without doubt an objective of vital importance to the whole of the international community today."

[In paragraph (2) of the operative portion of its judgment, the Court replied as follows to the question put by the General Assembly:]

A. Unanimously,

There is in neither customary nor conventional international law any specific authorization of the threat or use of nuclear weapons;

B. By eleven votes to three,

There is in neither customary nor conventional international law any comprehensive and universal prohibition of the threat or use of nuclear weapons as such, * * *

C. Unanimously,

A threat or use of force by means of nuclear weapons that is contrary to Article 2, paragraph 4, of the United Nations Charter and that fails to meet all the requirements of Article 51, is unlawful;

D. Unanimously,

A threat or use of nuclear weapons should also be compatible with the requirements of the international law applicable in armed conflict, particularly those of the principles and rules of international humanitarian law, as well as with specific obligations under treaties and other undertakings which expressly deal with nuclear weapons;

E.   By seven votes to seven, by the President's casting vote,

It follows from the above-mentioned requirements that the threat or use of nuclear weapons would generally be contrary to the rules of international law applicable in armed conflicts, and in particular the principles and rules of humanitarian law;

However, in view of the current state of international law, and of the elements of fact at its disposal, the Court cannot conclude definitively whether the threat or use of nuclear weapons would be lawful or unlawful in an extreme circumstance of self-defence, in which the very survival of a State would be at stake; * * *

F.   Unanimously,

There exists an obligation to pursue in good faith and bring to a conclusion negotiations leading to nuclear disarmament in all its aspects under strict and effective international control.

NOTES

1.   *Judicial Realism?* The seven judges voting in favor of operative paragraph 2E were: President Bedjaoui (Algeria), who cast the tie-breaking vote, Judges Ranjeva (Madagascar), Herczegh (Hungary), Shi (China), Fleischhauer (Germany), Vereshchetin (Russian Federation), and Ferrari Bravo (Italy). The seven judges voting against were: Vice–President Schwebel (United States), Judges Oda (Japan), Guillaume (France), Shahabuddeen (Guyana), Weeramantry (Sri Lanka), Koroma (Sierra Leone), and Higgins (United Kingdom). Note that the judges from nuclear-weapons states were to be found on both sides of this curiously worded paragraph.

2.   *Voluntarism: Separate and Dissenting Views.* Each member of the Court took advantage of the opportunity to append a declaration or a separate or dissenting opinion to the advisory opinion, in which they clarified their views on various issues. Several of these individual opinions dealt at length with the fundamental issues of international legal theory posed in the *Lotus* case, including whether international law embodies a residual principle of state freedom, whether rules of international law derive in principle from the free will of states, and if so, how acceptance of a prohibitory rule is to be proved or inferred, as well as with the problem of states claiming to be specially affected by an allegedly emergent new rule. For other questions addressed in the *Nuclear Weapons* advisory opinion, see Chapter 4 on the legal effects of General Assembly resolutions and Chapter 15 on the use of force.

3.   *"Sovereignty" versus Human Survival.* In an extended critique of arguments based on the *Lotus* case, Judge Shahabuddeen wrote in his dissenting opinion in *Nuclear Weapons* (1996 I.C.J. at 375, 395–96):

The notions of sovereignty and independence which the *"Lotus"* Court had in mind did not evolve in a context which visualized the possibility that a single State could possess the capability of wiping out the practical existence both of itself and of all other States. The Court was dealing with a case of collision at sea and the criminal jurisdiction of

States in relation thereto—scarcely an earth-shaking issue. Had its mind been directed to the possibility of the planet being destroyed by a minority of warring States, it is not likely that it would have left the position which it took without qualification. * * *

* * * Whichever way the issue in *"Lotus"* was determined, the Court's determination could be accommodated within the framework of an international society consisting of "co-existing independent communities". Not so as regards the issue whether there is a right to use nuclear weapons. Were the Court to uphold such a right, it would be upholding a right which could be used to destroy that framework and which could not therefore be accommodated within it. However extensive might be the powers available to a State, there is not any basis for supposing that the Permanent Court of International Justice considered that, in the absence of a prohibition, they included powers the exercise of which could extinguish civilization and annihilate mankind and thus destroy the framework of the international community; powers of this kind were not in issue. To the extent that a course of action could be followed by so apocalyptic a consequence, the case is distinguishable; it does not stand in the way of this Court holding that States do not have a right to embark on such a course of action unless, which is improbable, it can be shown that the action is authorized under international law.

Judge Weeramantry's dissent elaborated additional reasons for a skeptical approach to the implications of *Lotus* (1996 I.C.J. 429, 495):

It is implicit in *"Lotus"* that the sovereignty of other States should be respected. One of the characteristics of nuclear weapons is that they violate the sovereignty of other countries who have in no way consented to the intrusion upon their fundamental sovereign rights, which is implicit in the use of the nuclear weapon. It would be an interpretation totally out of context that the *"Lotus"* decision formulated a theory, equally applicable in peace and war, to the effect that a State could do whatever it pleased so long as it had not bound itself to the contrary. Such an interpretation of *"Lotus"* would cast a baneful spell on the progressive development of international law.

4　*Nuclear–Weapons States as "Specially Affected."* The argument was proffered in the *Nuclear Weapons* advisory opinion (on behalf of several of the declared nuclear weapons states) that emergence of a rule of customary international law requires the consent or acquiescence of specially affected states, that the nuclear weapons states would be "specially affected" by any purported restriction on such weapons, and that those states had strenuously and consistently maintained the lawfulness of the potential use of these weapons for deterrence of an attack (against themselves or against states under their protection). Vice–President Schwebel dissented from the Court's refusal to hold that use in extraordinary self-defense would be lawful (1996 I.C.J. at 311, 312):

State practice demonstrates that nuclear weapons have been manufactured and deployed by States for some 50 years; that in that deployment inheres a threat of possible use; and that the international community, by treaty and through action of the United Nations Security

Council, has, far from proscribing the threat or use of nuclear weapons in all circumstances, recognized in effect or in terms that in certain circumstances nuclear weapons may be used or their use threatened.

Not only have the nuclear Powers avowedly and for decades, with vast effort and expense, manufactured, maintained and deployed nuclear weapons. They have affirmed that they are legally entitled to use nuclear weapons in certain circumstances and to threaten their use. They have threatened their use by the hard facts and inexorable implications of the possession and deployment of nuclear weapons; by a posture of readiness to launch nuclear weapons 365 days a year, 24 hours of every day; by the military plans, strategic and tactical, developed and sometimes publicly revealed by them; and in a very few international crises, by threatening the use of nuclear weapons. In the very doctrine and practice of deterrence, the threat of the possible use of nuclear weapons inheres.

This nuclear practice is not a practice of a lone and secondary persistent objector. This is not a practice of a pariah Government crying out in the wilderness of otherwise adverse international opinion. This is the practice of five of the world's major Powers, of the permanent Members of the Security Council, significantly supported for almost 50 years by their allies and other States sheltering under their nuclear umbrellas. That is to say, it is the practice of States—and a practice supported by a large and weighty number of other States—that together represent the bulk of the world's military and economic and financial and technological power and a very large proportion of its population. This practice has been recognized, accommodated and in some measure accepted by the international community. That measure of acceptance is ambiguous but not meaningless. It is obvious that the alliance structures that have been predicated upon the deployment of nuclear weapons accept the legality of their use in certain circumstances. * * *

Other judges, who dissented for the opposite reason (because they thought that the Court should have found the weapons unambiguously unlawful), rejected the proposition that nuclear weapons states were "specially affected." Judge Shahabuddeen wrote that "[w]here what is in issue is the lawfulness of the use of a weapon which could annihilate mankind and so destroy all States, the test of which States are specially affected turns not on the ownership of the weapon, but on the consequences of its use. From this point of view, all States are equally affected, for, like the people who inhabit them, they all have an equal right to exist." 1996 I.C.J. 375, 414 (Dissenting Opinion of Judge Shahabuddeen); see also 1996 I.C.J. 429, 535–36 (Dissenting Opinion of Judge Weeramantry) ("A balanced view of the matter is that no one group of nations—nuclear or non-nuclear—can say that its interests are most specially affected. Every nation in the world is specially affected by nuclear weapons, for when matters of survival are involved, this is a matter of universal concern.").

5. *Multicultural Roots of International Custom.* Judge Weeramantry devoted a heading of his dissent to the "Multicultural Background to the Humanitarian Laws of War," tracing the evolution of efforts to limit the destructive effects of warfare in Hindu, Buddhist, Chinese, Christian, Islamic

and traditional African cultures: "These cultures have all given expression to a variety of limitations on the extent to which any means can be used for the purposes of fighting one's enemy. * * * The multicultural traditions that exist on this important matter cannot be ignored in the Court's consideration of this question, for to do so would be to deprive its conclusions of that plenitude of universal authority which is available to give it added strength— the strength resulting from the depth of the tradition's historical roots and the width of its geographical spread." 1996 I.C.J. 429, 478. See also Weeramantry, Nuclear Weapons and Scientific Responsibility 341 (1999); Lombardi, Islamic Law in the Jurisprudence of the International Court of Justice: An Analysis, 8 Chi. J. Int'l L. 85, 109–11 (2007).

6. *Lacunae.* Another provocative issue addressed in several individual opinions in *Nuclear Weapons* is the problem of *non liquet*, or what the international judge should do when the evidence at hand does not clearly resolve whether a rule of customary international law governs the conduct at issue. In his declaration appended to the *Nuclear Weapons* advisory opinion, Judge Vereshchetin wrote that in an advisory proceeding the Court should "refuse to assume the burden of law-creation, which in general should not be the function of the Court. In advisory procedure, where the Court finds a lacuna in the law or finds the law to be imperfect, it ought merely to state this without trying to fill the lacuna or improve the law by way of judicial legislation. The Court cannot be blamed for indecisiveness or evasiveness where the law, upon which it is called to pronounce, is itself inconclusive." 1996 I.C.J. 279, 280.

Judge Rosalyn Higgins regretted that the Court had effectively chosen to pronounce a *non liquet*, for even if the case were one involving an "antimony" between clashing elements in the law, "the judge's role is precisely to decide which of two or more competing norms is applicable in the particular circumstances. The corpus of international law is frequently made up of norms that, taken in isolation, appear to pull in different directions—for example, States may not use force/States may use force in self-defence * * *. It is the role of the judge to resolve, in context, and on grounds that should be articulated, why the application of one norm rather than another is to be preferred in the particular case. As these norms indubitably exist, and the difficulties that face the Court relate to their application, there can be no question of judicial legislation." 1996 I.C.J. 583, 592.

7. *Alternative Explanations for Patterns of Restraint.* The Court in *Nuclear Weapons* searched for relevant *opinio juris,* as discussed in paragraphs 64–72 of the excerpts reprinted above and in several of the separate and dissenting opinions. Could the allegation that states had refrained after August 1945 from using nuclear weapons be explained in terms of a subjective belief that they were obliged under customary international law so to refrain?

8. *Multilateral Treaty–Making and Customary Law.* A few months after the *Nuclear Weapons* advisory opinion, the U.N. General Assembly approved a Comprehensive Test Ban Treaty which was promptly signed by many states but is not yet in force. (By its terms—see Documents Supplement—ratifications on the part of forty-four identified states are preconditions to entry into force.) On the occasion of the signing, President Clinton asserted that the

signatures of the declared nuclear powers, along with those of the vast majority of countries, "will immediately create an international norm against nuclear testing even before the treaty formally enters into force." See Mitchell, Clinton, at U.N., Signs Treaty Banning All Nuclear Testing, N.Y. Times, Sept. 25, 1996, at A1. Could signatures of a large number of states, not necessarily followed by ratifications, create a kind of "instant custom"? Could they provide evidence of *opinio juris* accompanying an alleged custom of refraining from nuclear tests? Compare the materials below on the interaction of treaties and custom.

Two states that neither signed nor ratified the Comprehensive Test Ban Treaty—Pakistan and India—exploded nuclear devices in May and June 1998. These states denied the existence of any rule of customary international law restricting their freedom of action in nuclear matters. Could a customary rule have come into being without their consent? Over their objection? Compare p. 100 *infra* on the "persistent objector" principle. Could their actions be justified in terms of the concepts elaborated in the I.C.J.'s advisory opinion (for example, an implicit exception in light of the Court's inability to reach a definitive conclusion on extreme self-defense)?

9. *Further Reading.* For a range of perspectives on the *Nuclear Weapons* advisory opinion, see International Law, the International Court of Justice and Nuclear Weapons (Boisson de Chazournes & Sands eds. 1999); Nanda & Krieger, Nuclear Weapons and the World Court (1998); Symposium: Nuclear Weapons, the World Court, and Global Security, 7 Transnat. L. & Contemp. Probs. 313–457 (1997); Falk, Nuclear Weapons, International Law and the World Court: A Historic Encounter, 91 A.J.I.L. 64 (1997); Matheson, The Opinions of the International Court of Justice on the Threat or Use of Nuclear Weapons, 91 A.J.I.L. 417 (1997). These pieces make diverse predictions on whether the advisory opinion would be likely to affect state practice henceforth. More than a decade after its issuance, how would you evaluate its effects? On that question, see Damrosch, Codification and Legal Issues, in The United Nations and Nuclear Orders (Boulden, Thakur, & Weiss eds. forthcoming 2009). On the legal effects of advisory opinions generally, see Chapter 9.

B.   PRACTICE ACCEPTED AS LAW (*OPINIO JURIS*)

NORTH SEA CONTINENTAL SHELF CASES (FEDERAL REPUBLIC OF GERMANY v. DENMARK; FEDERAL REPUBLIC OF GERMANY v. NETHERLANDS)

International Court of Justice, 1969
1969 I.C.J. 3

[The cases involved a dispute over the delimitation of the continental shelf shared by Denmark, the Netherlands and the Federal Republic of Germany. Denmark and the Netherlands claimed that the dispute should be decided in accordance with the principle of equidistance under Article 6 of the Geneva Convention of 1958 on the Continental Shelf, which provides in paragraph 2: "In the absence of agreement, and unless another boundary line is justified by special circumstances, the boundary shall be determined by application of the principle of equidistance * * *." The Court rejected the application of the Convention to which Germany was not a party. However, Denmark and the Netherlands also maintained that the principle in Article 6 of the Convention is part of the corpus of general international law, and in particular of customary law. The Court rejected this contention by a vote of 11 to 6 for the reasons given below.]

70.   * * * [Denmark and the Netherlands argue] that even if there was at the date of the Geneva Convention no rule of customary international law in favour of the equidistance principle, and no such rule was crystallized in Article 6 of the Convention, nevertheless such a rule has come into being since the Convention, partly because of its own impact, partly on the basis of subsequent State practice * * *

71.   In so far as this contention is based on the view that Article 6 of the Convention has had the influence, and has produced the effect described, it clearly involves treating that Article as a norm-creating provision which has constituted the foundation of, or has generated a rule which, while only conventional or contractual in its origin, has since passed into the general *corpus* of international law, and is now accepted as such by the *opinio juris,* so as to have become binding even for countries which have never, and do not, become parties to the Convention. There is no doubt that this process is a perfectly possible one and does from time to time occur: it constitutes indeed one of the recognized methods by which new rules of customary international law may be formed. At the same time this result is not lightly to be regarded as having been attained.

72.   It would in the first place be necessary that the provision concerned should, at all events potentially, be of a fundamentally norm-creating character such as could be regarded as forming the basis of a general rule of law. Considered *in abstracto* the equidistance principle might be said to fulfill this requirement. Yet in the particular form in which it is embodied in Article 6 of the Geneva Convention, and having regard to the relationship of that Article to other provisions of the Convention, this must be open to some doubt. In the first place, Article 6 is so framed as to put second the obligation to make use of the equidistance method, causing it to come after a primary obligation to effect delimitation by agreement. Such a primary obligation constitutes an unusual preface to what is claimed to be a potential general rule of law. * * * Secondly the part played by the notion of special circumstances relative to the principle of equidistance as embodied in Article 6, and the very considerable, still unresolved controversies as to the exact meaning and scope of this notion, must raise further doubts as to the potentially norm-creating character of the rule. Finally, the faculty of making reservations to Article 6, while it might not of itself prevent the equidistance principle being eventually received as general law, does add considerably to the difficulty of regarding this result as having been brought about (or being potentially possible) on the basis of the Convention: for so long as

this faculty continues to exist, * * * it is the Convention itself which would, for the reasons already indicated, seem to deny to the provisions of Article 6 the same norm-creating character as, for instance, Articles 1 and 2 possess.

73.   With respect to the other elements usually regarded as necessary before a conventional rule can be considered to have become a general rule of international law, it might be that, even without the passage of any considerable period of time, a very widespread and representative participation in the convention might suffice of itself, provided it included that of States whose interests were specially affected. In the present case however, the Court notes that, even if allowance is made for the existence of a number of States to whom participation in the Geneva Convention is not open, or which, by reason for instance of being land-locked States, would have no interest in becoming parties to it, the number of ratifications and accessions so far secured is, though respectable, hardly sufficient. That nonratification may sometimes be due to factors other than active disapproval of the convention concerned can hardly constitute a basis on which positive acceptance of its principles can be implied. The reasons are speculative, but the facts remain.

74.   As regards the time element, the Court notes that it is over ten years since the Convention was signed, but that it is even now less than five since it came into force in June 1964 * * *. Although the passage of only a short period of time is not necessarily, or of itself, a bar to the formation of a new rule of customary international law on the basis of what was originally a purely conventional rule, an indispensable requirement would be that within the period in question, short though it might be, State practice, including that of States whose interests are specially affected, should have been both extensive and virtually uniform in the sense of the provision invoked;—and should moreover have occurred in such a way as to show a general recognition that a rule of law or legal obligation is involved.

75.   The Court must now consider whether State practice in the matter of continental shelf delimitation has, subsequent to the Geneva Convention, been of such a kind as to satisfy this requirement. * * * [S]ome fifteen cases have been cited in the course of the present proceedings, occurring mostly since the signature of the 1958 Geneva Convention, in which continental shelf boundaries have been delimited according to the equidistance principle—in the majority of the cases by agreement, in a few others unilaterally—or else the delimitation was foreshadowed but has not yet been carried out. But even if these various cases constituted more than a very small proportion of those potentially calling for delimitation in the world as a whole, the Court would not think it necessary to enumerate or evaluate them separately, since there are, *a priori,* several grounds which deprive them of weight as precedents in the present context.

* * *

77. The essential point in this connection—and it seems necessary to stress it—is that even if these instances of action by nonparties to the Convention were much more numerous than they in fact are, they would not, even in the aggregate, suffice in themselves to constitute the *opinio juris;*—for, in order to achieve this result, two conditions must be fulfilled. Not only must the acts concerned amount to a settled practice, but they must also be such, or be carried out in such a way, as to be evidence of a belief that this practice is rendered obligatory by the existence of a rule of law requiring it. The need for such a belief, i.e., the existence of a subjective element, is implicit in the very notion of the *opinio juris sive necessitatis.* The States concerned must therefore feel that they are conforming to what amounts to a legal obligation. The frequency, or even habitual character of the acts is not in itself enough. There are many international acts, e.g., in the field of ceremonial and protocol, which are performed almost invariably, but which are motivated only by considerations of courtesy, convenience or tradition, and not by any sense of legal duty.

78. In this respect the Court follows the view adopted by the Permanent Court of International Justice in the *Lotus* case * * * [T]he position is simply that in certain cases—not a great number—the States concerned agreed to draw or did draw the boundaries concerned according to the principle of equidistance. There is no evidence that they so acted because they felt legally compelled to draw them in this way by reason of a rule of customary law obliging them to do so—especially considering that they might have been motivated by other obvious factors.

[In a dissenting opinion, Judge Lachs took issue with the Court's conclusion regarding *opinio juris.* He said, in part, 1969 I.C.J. 219, 228–31:]

All this leads to the conclusion that the principles and rules enshrined in the Convention, and in particular the equidistance rule, have been accepted not only by those States which are parties to the Convention on the Continental Shelf, but also by those which have subsequently followed it in agreements, or in their legislation, or have acquiesced in it when faced with legislative acts of other States affecting them. This can be viewed as evidence of a practice widespread enough to satisfy the criteria for a general rule of law.

* * *

Can the practice above summarized be considered as having been accepted as law, having regard to the subjective element required? The process leading to this effect is necessarily complex. There are certain areas of State activity and international law which by their very character may only with great difficulty engender general law, but there are others, both old and new, which may do so with greater ease. Where Continental Shelf law is concerned, some States have at first probably accepted the rules in question, as States usually do, because they found them convenient and useful, the best possible solution for the problems involved.

Others may also have been convinced that the instrument elaborated within the framework of the United Nations was intended to become and would in due course become general law (the teleological element is of no small importance in the formation of law). Many States have followed suit under the conviction that it was law.

Thus at the successive stages in the development of the rule the motives which have prompted States to accept it have varied from case to case. It could not be otherwise. At all events, to postulate that all States, even those which initiate a given practice, believe themselves to be acting under a legal obligation is to resort to a fiction—and in fact to deny the possibility of developing such rules. For the path may indeed start from voluntary, unilateral acts relying on the confident expectation that they will find acquiescence or be emulated; alternatively the starting-point may consist of a treaty to which more and more States accede and which is followed by unilateral acceptance. It is only at a later stage that, by the combined effect of individual or joint action, response and interaction in the field concerned, i.e., of that reciprocity so essential in international legal relations, there develops the chain-reaction productive of international consensus.

* * *

In sum, the general practice of States should be recognized as prima facie evidence that it is accepted as law. Such evidence may, of course, be controverted—even on the test of practice itself, if it shows "much uncertainty and contradiction" (Asylum, Judgment, I.C.J. Reports 1950, p. 277). It may also be controverted on the test of *opinio juris* with regard to "the States in question" or the parties to the case.

NOTES

1. *Lack of Protest.* What evidence would satisfy the requirement of *opinio juris* under the majority opinion in the *North Sea* cases? Some writers maintain that an inference of *opinio juris* can only be supported by the statements of states as to legal right or obligation. On the other hand, as Judge Lachs points out, individual governments often act for convenience or utility even though their legal right to do so is unclear or non-existent. If other governments do not object and take similar actions, the general practice is recognized as a legal rule. Thus, a nascent period of formation of a rule would not exhibit the *opinio juris generalis* but with repeated instances, states come to treat the practice as law. A much cited example is the Truman Proclamation in 1945 of exclusive jurisdiction over the continental shelf adjacent to the United States, discussed further at p. 104 note 8 and in Chapter 17, which was a novel position unsupported by existing law when first announced but became recognized as general customary law when other coastal states followed the U.S. action and none objected to it.

2. *Inference from Conduct.* Kelsen points out that "in practice it appears that the *opinio juris* is commonly inferred from the constancy and uniformity of state conduct. But to the extent that it is so inferred, it is this conduct and

not the state of mind that is decisive." He notes that in a period of stability, this creates no great concern. However, at a time of pervasive and rapid change, and "the equivocal nature of much state practice today," the uncertainties of law-creation through custom are much greater than in the past. Kelsen, Principles of International Law 450–52 (2d rev. ed. Tucker ed. 1966).

3. *"Instant Custom."* Has custom become less important in this time of pervasive change (as Kelsen suggests) or has its character changed in response to rapidly changing demands? Today some writers refer to "instant custom" or to "custom on demand." Instead of emphasis on uniformities of conduct (the material element), more importance is accorded to the subjective element of *opinio juris,* particularly when declared by states collectively with reasonable expectation of future conduct conforming to the new principle. Henkin comments: "Such efforts to create new customary law by purposeful activity have included * * * resolutions adopted by international organizations * * * to promote, declare or confirm principles of law by overwhelming majorities or by consensus resolutions which discourage dissent." Henkin, International Law: Politics, Values and Functions, 216 Rec. des Cours 58 (1989–IV). On the legal effects of U.N. resolutions, see Chapter 4.

4. Opinio Juris *without Practice?* The tendency to "find" new customary law based mainly on *opinio juris* (i.e., statements that a legal rule has now been recognized) without demonstrating uniform conduct among states in general is especially evident in regard to human rights, environmental protection, and economic development. Is this attempt to put new wine into old bottles legitimized by the felt necessity to extend law to meet social objectives, when neither treaties nor uniform practice serve that function? For varied views, see following articles in 12 Australian Y.B.I.L. (1992): Schachter, Recent Trends in International Law–Making 1–15; Pellet, The Normative Dilemma: Will and Consent in International Law–Making, 22–53; Simma & Alston, The Sources of Human Rights Law: Custom, Jus Cogens and General Principles, 82–108. See also Roberts, Traditional and Modern Approaches to Customary International Law: A Reconciliation, 95 A.J.I.L. 757, 758–59 (2001); Meron, Human Rights and Humanitarian Norms as Customary Law 92–97, 134 (1989); Meron, Revival of Customary Humanitarian Law, 99 A.J.I.L. 817, 819 (2005). The contradictory tendencies are emphasized by Koskenniemi, From Apology to Utopia 342–421 (2d ed. 2005).

MILITARY AND PARAMILITARY ACTIVITIES IN AND AGAINST NICARAGUA (NICARAGUA v. UNITED STATES)

International Court of Justice, 1986
1986 I.C.J. 14

[In 1984 Nicaragua instituted proceedings against the United States in the International Court of Justice, alleging unlawful military and paramilitary acts by the United States in Nicaragua (for the substance see Chapter 15). The United States contested the jurisdiction of the Court on several grounds, including a reservation it had made in accepting the Court's jurisdiction that its acceptance would not apply to certain disputes arising under multilateral treaties—in this case, the U.N. Charter. Nicaragua responded that its claim was based on rules of customary law which were similar in content to the Charter. The Court accepted the Nicaraguan contention for the reasons given in the following extract.]

183.   * * * [T]he Court has next to consider what are the rules of customary international law applicable to the present dispute. For this purpose, it has to direct its attention to the practice and *opinio juris* of States; as the Court recently observed,

> "It is of course axiomatic that the material of customary international law is to be looked for primarily in the actual practice and *opinio juris* of States, even though multilateral conventions may have an important role to play in recording and defining rules deriving from custom, or indeed in developing them." *(Continental Shelf (Libyan Arab Jamahiriya/Malta), I.C.J. Reports 1985*, pp. 29–30, para. 27.)

In this respect the Court must not lose sight of the Charter of the United Nations and that of the Organization of American States, notwithstanding the operation of the multilateral treaty reservation. Although the Court has no jurisdiction to determine whether the conduct of the United States constitutes a breach of those conventions, it can and must take them into account in ascertaining the content of the customary international law which the United States is also alleged to have infringed.

184.   The Court notes that there is in fact evidence, to be examined below, of a considerable degree of agreement between the Parties as to the content of the customary international law relating to the non-use of force and non-intervention. This concurrence of their views does not however dispense the Court from having itself to ascertain what rules of customary international law are applicable. The mere fact that States declare their recognition of certain rules is not sufficient for the Court to consider these as being part of customary international law, and as applicable as such to those States. Bound as it is by Article 38 of its Statute to apply, *inter alia,* international custom "as evidence of a general practice accepted as law", the Court may not disregard the essential role played by general practice. Where two States agree to incorporate a particular rule in a treaty, their agreement suffices to make that rule a legal one, binding upon them; but in the field of customary international law, the shared view of the Parties as to the content of what they regard as the rule is not enough. The Court must satisfy itself that the existence of the rule in the *opinio juris* of States is confirmed by practice.

185.   In the present dispute, the Court, while exercising its jurisdiction only in respect of the application of the customary rules of non-use of force and non-intervention, cannot disregard the fact that the Parties are bound by these rules as a matter of treaty law and of customary international law. Furthermore, in the present case, apart from the treaty commitments binding the Parties to the rules in question, there are various instances of their having expressed recognition of the validity thereof as customary international law in other ways. It is therefore in the

light of this "subjective element"—the expression used by the Court in its 1969 Judgment in the *North Sea Continental Shelf* cases *(I.C.J. Reports 1969,* p. 44)—that the Court has to appraise the relevant practice.

186. It is not to be expected that in the practice of States the application of the rules in question should have been perfect, in the sense that States should have refrained, with complete consistency, from the use of force or from intervention in each other's internal affairs. The Court does not consider that, for a rule to be established as customary, the corresponding practice must be in absolutely rigorous conformity with the rule. In order to deduce the existence of customary rules, the Court deems it sufficient that the conduct of States should, in general, be consistent with such rules, and that instances of State conduct inconsistent with a given rule should generally have been treated as breaches of that rule, not as indications of the recognition of a new rule. If a State acts in a way prima facie incompatible with a recognized rule, but defends its conduct by appealing to exceptions or justifications contained within the rule itself, then whether or not the State's conduct is in fact justifiable on that basis, the significance of that attitude is to confirm rather than to weaken the rule.

187. The Court must therefore determine, first, the substance of the customary rules relating to the use of force in international relations, applicable to the dispute submitted to it. The United States has argued that, on this crucial question of the lawfulness of the use of force in inter-State relations, the rules of general and customary international law, and those of the United Nations Charter, are in fact identical. In its view this identity is so complete that, as explained above (paragraph 173), it constitutes an argument to prevent the Court from applying this customary law, because it is indistinguishable from the multilateral treaty law which it may not apply. In its Counter–Memorial on jurisdiction and admissibility the United States asserts that "Article 2(4) of the Charter *is* customary and general international law". It quotes with approval an observation by the International Law Commission to the effect that

> "the great majority of international lawyers today unhesitatingly hold that Article 2, paragraph 4, together with other provisions of the Charter, authoritatively declares the modern customary law regarding the threat or use of force" *(ILC Yearbook,* 1966, Vol. II, p. 247).

The United States points out that Nicaragua has endorsed this view, since one of its counsel asserted that "indeed it is generally considered by publicists that Article 2, paragraph 4, of the United Nations Charter is in this respect an embodiment of existing general principles of international law". And the United States concludes:

> "In sum, the provisions of Article 2(4) with respect to the lawfulness of the use of force *are* 'modern customary law' (International Law Commission, *loc. cit.)* and the 'embodiment of general principles of international law' (counsel for Nicaragua, Hearing of 25

April 1984, morning, *loc. cit.*). There is no other 'customary and general international law' on which Nicaragua can rest its claims."

"It is, in short, inconceivable that this Court could consider the lawfulness of an alleged use of armed force without referring to the principal source of the relevant international law—Article 2(4) of the United Nations Charter."

As for Nicaragua, the only noteworthy shade of difference in its view lies in Nicaragua's belief that

"in certain cases the rule of customary law will not necessarily be identical in content and mode of application to the conventional rule".

188.   The Court thus finds that both Parties take the view that the principles as to the use of force incorporated in the United Nations Charter correspond, in essentials, to those found in customary international law. The Parties thus both take the view that the fundamental principle in this area is expressed in the terms employed in Article 2, paragraph 4, of the United Nations Charter. They therefore accept a treaty-law obligation to refrain in their international relations from the threat or use of force against the territorial integrity or political independence of any State, or in any other manner inconsistent with the purposes of the United Nations. The Court has however to be satisfied that there exists in customary international law an *opinio juris* as to the binding character of such abstention. This *opinio juris* may, though with all due caution, be deduced from, *inter alia,* the attitude of the Parties and the attitude of States towards certain General Assembly resolutions, and particularly resolution 2625 (XXV) entitled "Declaration on Principles of International Law concerning Friendly Relations and Co-operation among States in accordance with the Charter of the United Nations". The effect of consent to the text of such resolutions cannot be understood as merely that of a "reiteration or elucidation" of the treaty commitment undertaken in the Charter. On the contrary, it may be understood as an acceptance of the validity of the rule or set of rules declared by the resolution by themselves. The principle of non-use of force, for example, may thus be regarded as a principle of customary international law, not as such conditioned by provisions relating to collective security, or to the facilities or armed contingents to be provided under Article 43 of the Charter. It would therefore seem apparent that the attitude referred to expresses an *opinio juris* respecting such rule (or set of rules), to be thenceforth treated separately from the provisions, especially those of an institutional kind, to which it is subject on the treaty-law plane of the Charter.

* * *

190.   A further confirmation of the validity as customary international law of the principle of the prohibition of the use of force expressed in Article 2, paragraph 4, of the Charter of the United Nations may be found in the fact that it is frequently referred to in statements by State representatives as being not only a principle of customary international

law but also a fundamental or cardinal principle of such law. The International Law Commission * * * expressed the view that "the law of the Charter concerning the prohibition of the use of force in itself constitutes a conspicuous example of a rule in international law having the character of *jus cogens*" * * *. * * * The United States, in its Counter–Memorial on the questions of jurisdiction and admissibility, found it material to quote the views of scholars that this principle is a "universal norm," a "universal international law," a "universally recognized principle of international law," and a "principle of *jus cogens*."

NOTES

1. *Dispensing With Proof of Practice?* Note how the Court related *opinio juris* to evidence of practice. It found (para. 184) "a considerable degree of agreement between the parties as to the content of the customary international law." In this light, the Court referred only generally to the relevant practice. One scholar concludes that "if there exist concordant views as to the existence of an applicable rule, less stringent proof is required to establish existence of a settled practice and *opinio juris*. * * * Where concordant views exist, the dispute * * * will above all concern * * * the facts * * *." Rijpkema, Customary International Law in the Nicaragua Case, 20 Neth. Y.B.I.L. 91, 96–97 (1989). Compare this conclusion to the Court's decision in both the *Lotus* and the *North Sea Continental Shelf* cases where one of the parties denied the existence of an applicable customary law norm. In those cases the Court looked to see if practice was accepted as law (i.e., *opinio juris*). In the *Nicaragua* case, *opinio juris* was not disputed and the Court states (para. 185) that it will "appraise the relevant practice" in the light of the "subjective element." Thus, *opinio juris* is established prior to appraising practice in contrast to the *Lotus* and *North Sea* judgments.

2. *Higher–Order Norms?* Is the question of state practice of less importance when the norms in question are recognized as "fundamental"? The Court refers (para. 190) to the fact that the non-use of force is frequently referred to as a fundamental or cardinal principle and as a principle of *jus cogens* (peremptory norm). Is this a good reason for the Court to be less stringent in requiring proof of a general practice in conformity with the norm? See Schachter, Entangled Treaty and Custom, in International Law at a Time of Perplexity 717, 733–34 (Dinstein ed. 1989), noting that the "higher normativity" of the rule against aggression justifies maintaining the rule even in the face of inconsistent practice. For discussion of peremptory norms, see p. 105 and Chapter 3, p. 194.

3. *Treaty Codification Superseding Custom.* After the invasion of Panama in 1989, the State Department Legal Adviser, in justifying the legality of the U.S. action, argued for a "common law approach to use of force rules" that "would take account of the circumstance of each case and avoid a mechanical application of the rules." Sofaer, The Legality of the United States Invasion of Panama, 29 Colum. J. Transnat'l Law 281, 282 n. 10 (1991). Henkin, in response, wrote:

Customary international law indeed has important similarities to the common law but there are essential differences between them * * *.

If the invasion of Panama, and the legal arguments to justify it, were designed to erode or modify established law, they have been rejected by the large majority of the states and of the legal communities—"the judges" of the "international common law." Indeed, the history of the common law rejects its use as an analogy to justify the U.S. invasion of Panama. When the common law proved inadequate, when society could not tolerate the law's ambiguities and uncertainties and its dependence on imperfect institutions, the law was codified, made more clear, more firm, leaving less room for violators and for reliance on an imperfect judiciary * * * Because the "common law" on the use of force failed, the law was codified, establishing clearer, firmer prohibitions, designed to leave few loopholes and little room for distortion.

Henkin, The Invasion of Panama and International Law: A Gross Violation, 29 Colum. J. Transnat'l L. 293, 311–12 (1991).

C. THE POSITION OF "NON–CONSENTING" STATES

WALDOCK, GENERAL COURSE ON PUBLIC INTERNATIONAL LAW

106 Rec. des Cours 1, 49–53 (1962–II) (some footnotes omitted)

The view of most international lawyers is that customary law is not a form of tacit treaty but an independent form of law; and that, when a custom satisfying the definition in Article 38 is established, it constitutes a general rule of international law which, subject to one reservation, applies to every State. The reservation concerns the case of a State which, while the custom is in process of formation, unambiguously and persistently registers its objection to the recognition of the practice as law. Thus, in the *Anglo–Norwegian Fisheries* case the Court, having rejected the so-called ten-mile rule for bays, said:

> "In any event, the ten-mile rule would appear to be inapplicable as against Norway, inasmuch as she has always opposed any attempt to apply it to the Norwegian coast."

Similarly, in the *Asylum* case it said:

> "Even if it could be supposed that such a custom existed between certain Latin–American States only, it could not be invoked against Peru, which, far from having by its attitude adhered to it, has on the contrary repudiated it."

These pronouncements seem clearly to indicate that a customary rule may arise notwithstanding the opposition of one State, or even perhaps a few States, provided that otherwise the necessary degree of generality is reached. But they also seem to lay down that the rule so created will not bind the objectors; in other words, that in international law there is no majority rule even with respect to the formation of customary law.

On the other hand, it is no less clear that, if a custom becomes established as a general rule of international law, it binds all States which have not opposed it, whether or not they themselves played an active part in its formation. This means that in order to invoke a custom against a State it is not necessary to show specifically the *acceptance* of the custom as law by that State; its acceptance of the custom will be presumed so that it will be bound unless it can adduce evidence of its actual opposition to the practice in question. The Court in applying a general custom may well refer to the practice, if any, of the parties to the litigation in regard to the custom; but it has never yet treated evidence of their acceptance of the practice as a *sine qua non* of applying the custom to them. * * *

An aspect of this question of the legal basis of custom which is of particular importance to-day is the position of the new-born State with regard to existing general rules of customary law. We know that, generally speaking, a new State begins with a clean slate in regard to treaties, although often of its own choice it takes over many of the treaty obligations formerly applicable to the territory. Logically enough on the treaty theory of custom, Communist writers maintain that the same is true for customary law; and they have strong things to say about "European" or "Western" States trying to impose norms of general international law upon the new States of Asia and Africa.

This doctrine has not been without its attraction for new States emerging from colonial régimes. But, quite apart from any theoretical difficulty about the nature of customary law, the fundamental objection to it is that it really denies the existence of a general international legal order and the new States have at least as much to lose as anyone else from a denial of the validity of existing international law. If consent is so far the basis of customary law that a new State may reject any customary rule it chooses, how can it be said that an older State is not free, vis-à-vis the new State, to reject any customary rule that it may choose? Either there is an international legal order or there is not. * * *

* * * The new States have every right to a full and equal voice both in resolving the existing controversies and in shaping the new customary law; but surely that right will itself be meaningless if it is not founded upon and given expression through a stable legal order. At any rate, it is an encouraging sign that, when controversial points in customary law are debated in the [U.N.] International Law Commission and the Sixth [Legal] Committee [of the U.N. General Assembly], a large measure of common agreement is often reached and the divisions of opinion when they occur are on other lines than the differences between new and old States.

NOTES

1. *Time for Registering Objection.* The Restatement (Third) agrees that "in principle a dissenting state which indicates its dissent from a practice

while the law is still in a state of development is not bound by that rule of law even after it matures" (§ 102, Comment *d*). Presumably, a state that is silent during the period of formation would be bound by the rule when it comes into force as would a new state. Is it reasonable to apply this principle to states that had no interest in or knowledge of the conduct that developed the rule?

2. *Scarcity of Instances.* Judicial expression of a "persistent objector" rule is found in just a handful of cases, including the *Asylum* and *Fisheries* cases mentioned by Waldock. States have rarely claimed or been granted an exemption on the basis of the persistent objector principle. For a compilation of judicial decisions and state practice, see I.L.A. Customary International Law Report, 27–29. See also Charney, The Persistent Objector Rule and the Development of Customary International Law, 56 Brit. Y.B.I.L. 1 (1985); Stein, The Approach of the Different Drummer: The Principle of the Persistent Objector in International Law, 26 Harv. Int'l L.J. 457, 459–60 (1985). Notwithstanding the paucity of practice, Stein concludes that the principle of the persistent dissenter will increasingly be used to claim exemption from new principles of customary law developed by the majority of states. He points to the trend toward formation of new principles of customary law as a consequence of majority positions adopted in international conferences and in United Nations organs. He anticipates that the states opposing such rules will increasingly have recourse to the persistent objector principle to claim exemption. Id. at 463–69.

3. *Relation to U.N. Declaratory Resolutions.* Is the "persistent objector" rule likely to be asserted more often because of declarations by international conferences or U.N. bodies that purport to state international legal rules? Henkin comments that "efforts to make new law purposefully by custom (in effect, circumventing the multilateral treaty which requires individual consent) has given the persistent objector principle new vitality, perhaps its first real life." 216 Rec. des Cours 59 (1989–IV). Would this new "vitality" be significantly different from the traditional requirement of *opinio juris* required of states generally and especially of those particularly affected by the rule in question? Is the critical factor the effective power of the objecting state vis-à-vis the majority of states? See p. 95 note 3 *supra* (on "instant custom") and Chapter 4 (on General Assembly resolutions).

4. *Overcoming Persistent Objections.* The Restatement (Third) gives only one example of the application of the "persistent dissenter" principle. It states that the United States would not be bound by a customary law rule that prohibited deep seabed mining outside the regime established by the 1982 Convention on the Law of the Sea. It notes in § 523 that the U.S. rejected those principles as binding on states not parties to the Convention. See Chapter 17.

Charney, in contrast, observes that "[n]o case is cited in which the objector effectively maintained its status after the rule became well accepted in international law. * * * This is certainly the plight that befell the United States, the United Kingdom, and Japan in the law of the sea. Their objections to expanded coastal state jurisdiction were ultimately to no avail, and they have been forced to accede to 12–mile territorial seas and 200–mile exclusive economic zones." Charney, *supra*, at 24. Does this mean that the persistent objector "rule" is of no significance? Charney suggests that it gives an objecting state "a tool it may use over the short term with direct and indirect negotiations with the proponents of a new rule. * * * As a particularly affected state, it will have leverage in determining the evolution of the applicable rule of law and will have the theoretical advantage of invoking the persistent objector rule. * * * When the rule does settle, * * * a few states may continue to maintain their objection to a new rule of law. If they are few, they will not be able to block a finding that the new rule represents international law." Id. at 23–24. Charney has elsewhere written of the demands on the international legal system to produce universally binding international law—especially in response to universal problems, such as threats to the peace and the global environment—with no enduring exemptions for objecting states. Charney, Universal International Law, 87 A.J.I.L. 529, 538–42, 551 (1993); cf. Charney & Danilenko, Consent and the Creation of International Law, in Beyond Confrontation 23, 47–50 (Damrosch, Danilenko, & Mullerson eds, 1995); compare Danilenko, Law–Making in the International Community (1993). On the pressures tending to overcome persistent objection in practice, see also Byers, Custom, Power, and the Power of Rules 102–05, 152, 177–78, 180–83 (1999).

    5. *Apartheid.* Should South Africa during the period of apartheid have been considered exempt from the customary law rule prohibiting systematic racial discrimination because it persistently dissented from that rule during the time the rule was being developed? The United Kingdom, in its pleadings in the *Anglo–Norwegian Fisheries Case,* questioned the right of a persistent dissenter to an exemption from a rule of law of fundamental importance. *Fisheries Case,* 1949–1951 I.C.J. Pleadings, Oral Arguments, 428–30. The Restatement (Third) implies that the persistent objector rule may not apply to peremptory norms *(jus cogens)* that permit no derogation, and it indicates that the rule against apartheid falls into the class of peremptory norms. Restatement (Third) § 102, Comment *k* and Reporters' Note 6; § 702, Comments *i* and *n* and Reporters' Note 11. Charney has analyzed the difference of views on whether South Africa could invoke the persistent objector rule (and on whether persistent objection could ever apply in the case of *jus cogens)* and has concluded that ultimately South Africa was compelled to abide by the obligation. Charney, Universal International Law, 87 A.J.I.L. 529, 539–41 (1993); see also Byers, Custom, Power, and the Power of Rules 177–78, 194–95 (1999). On peremptory norms, see Chapter 3.

    6. *Nuclear Weapons.* In the *Nuclear Weapons* advisory opinion, *supra,* the significance of lack of consent (especially from the nuclear weapons states) was vigorously debated and addressed in several of the separate and dissenting opinions. As noted above (note 4 on pp. 87–88), Judge Schwebel considered the posture of the nuclear weapons states as a fundamental obstacle to any putative new rule, not by virtue of a "persistent objector" exception, but because of the formidable array of states opposed to such a prohibition. On this distinction, see I.L.A. Customary International Law Report, 27.

    7. *Death Penalty.* Some assert that a customary international law rule may be in the process of emerging to restrict certain applications of the death penalty, e.g., as against persons under age 18 at the time of commission of the crime. If so, how would states register objections ("persistent" or otherwise)

to such an emergent rule? The United States has carefully worded its acceptance of human rights obligations, notably in the form of reservations to human rights treaties, to preserve the legal position that capital punishment could be applied now or in the future by the federal or state governments. See Chapters 3 and 13. Would such reservations qualify the United States as a persistent objector to a rule in formation?

In 2005, the U.S. Supreme Court revisited the juvenile death penalty and overruled a 1989 decision that had allowed the penalty for those who were ages 16 or 17 at the time of the crime. In contrast to the earlier decision, which had rejected arguments derived from international sources, the Court referred to international authorities and foreign law in concluding that the juvenile death penalty was no longer compatible with "evolving standards of decency" and therefore had become cruel and unusual punishment prohibited under the Eighth Amendment of the U.S. Constitution. *Roper v. Simmons*, 543 U.S. 551, 561 (2005), excerpted in Chapter 10. Although the Court did not rest its decision on customary international law as such, it observed that "it is fair to say that the United States now stands alone in a world that has turned its face against the juvenile death penalty." Would it be plausible to infer from this juridical episode that the United States is no longer in "persistent objection" to a customary law norm against the juvenile death penalty?

8. *Withdrawal of Consent through Changing Practice.* What is the consequence of a large number of states departing from an existing rule of law? Such departures are, in their inception, clearly violations of law. However, such violations carried out by a number of states may—and often have—resulted in new customary law. This development occurred dramatically after the 1945 Truman Proclamation as states by practice eroded the existing principle of the freedom of the seas by extending their jurisdiction over adjacent waters up to 200 miles and over the continental shelf. See Chapter 17. To determine when such new law has repealed the old rule, it is necessary to consider the same elements that are involved in creating customary law— namely, (1) the extent, consistency and frequency of the departures from old law, (2) the relation of the states concerned (both those departing and those adhering) to the subject matter of the rule, and (3) the duration of the process. *Opinio juris* must also be considered. At some point, a large number of "representative states" may conclude that their infringements have become new law, and that they will not be charged with violating existing law. Presumably, the new rule will not be opposable to states that have openly manifested their opposition to it from the start. But such states, if few, cannot prevent the adoption of a new rule.

9. *Objections by New States.* May a state that was not in existence at the time a customary rule was formed object to the rule when it emerges as an independent state? Many new states have objected to particular rules of international law, in regard to state responsibility, some rules of treaty law (in particular, relating to unequal treaties), and some aspects of the law of the sea. See Anand, New States and International Law 62 (1972); Abi–Saab, The Newly–Independent States and the Rules of International Law, 8 Howard L.J. 95 (1962); Guha Roy, Is the Law of Responsibility of States a Part of Universal International Law, 55 A.J.I.L. 866 (1961); Bokor–Szego, New States and International Law (1970). These states did not reject existing customary

law in its entirety. Nor did they maintain that their consent was required for every rule to be binding upon them. Their basic position was that a rule of customary law should no longer be considered as a general rule valid for all states when most (or many) states rejected it as law. Thus the question was not whether a new state may reject a rule it did not like but rather whether the objection by a large number of states (often a majority) to a general rule must mean that that rule is no longer valid (if it ever was) for the entire international community.

Does this position mean that a number of new states may terminate any rule of customary international law they do not like? May they do this by resolution adopted by majority votes in the General Assembly? May they accomplish that goal by collectively disregarding the old rule and asserting that it is no longer law? Would they have to establish a new customary rule by general and consistent practice accompanied by *opinio juris* which other states would recognize? Would a minority of the older states be able to prevent such changes?

D. NORMATIVE HIERARCHY: *JUS COGENS* (PEREMPTORY NORMS)

Neither Article 38 of the I.C.J. Statute nor positivist doctrine draws hierarchical distinctions among customary norms. However, international tribunals and writers have done so under various headings. The International Court of Justice has sometimes referred to "fundamental principles" (or "cardinal" or "intransgressible" rules) as a category differentiated from ordinary custom or treaty norms. See *Nicaragua*, para. 190; *Nuclear Weapons*, *supra*, paras. 74ff. Scholars have elaborated theories under which certain principles considered essential to international public order would take precedence over other rules derived from custom or treaty.

Some writers have described principles such as sovereign equality, political independence, and territorial integrity as axiomatic or constitutional in character. Henkin, for example, refers to assumptions of state autonomy, *pacta sunt servanda*, and the concept of nationality as "implicit, inherent in Statehood in a State System" (Henkin, General Course, 216 Rec. des Cours 52 (1989–IV)) and thus not derived from or dependent on practice. Schachter refers to principles of this kind as "authoritative by virtue of the inherent necessities of a pluralist society." Such "rules of necessity" are considered as akin to "entrenched" constitutional rules that cannot be set aside by majorities whether through practice or agreements. Their emphasis on autonomy and equality as basic rights is not unlike the declarations of individual rights that reflect Western political thought. See Schachter, International Law in Theory and Practice 30–31 (1991). Although described as "implicit" and "unwritten," they have been expressed in the Principles of Chapter I of the U.N. Charter, as well as in various declarations of basic rights of states prepared by international legal bodies and in U.N. declarations. See, for example, the Declaration of Rights and Duties of States, prepared by the U.N. International Law Commission and adopted by the General Assembly in 1949, G.A. Res. 375 (IV) (Dec. 6, 1949). The much cited Declaration of Principles of International Law adopted by the U.N. General Assembly in 1970 (without dissent) is also a statement of basic principles that are mostly postulates of the state system. See Documents Supp. Although they may be described as higher law and as axiomatic, this does not mean that their content is fixed, beyond influence of state practice and agreements.

Another category of "higher norms" is found in Article 103 of the U.N. Charter which declares that:

> In the event of a conflict between the obligations of Members of the United Nations under the present Charter and their obligations under any other international agreement, their obligations under the present Charter shall prevail.

The I.C.J. has made reference to this article several times, including in the jurisdictional phase of *Nicaragua* (see note 6 on p. 112), and in the *Lockerbie* case addressed in Chapter 9.

With the assertion by the U.N. Security Council in recent years of authority to impose obligations on members under Chapter VII of the Charter, addressed in Chapters 4, 6, and 15, new questions of constitutional character have arisen. Is there a "higher law" constraining the Council in the exercise of its powers, and if so, what would be its source and how might its limits be ascertained and applied?

The following extracts and notes introduce some of the debates over the concept of hierarchically superior law in the international legal system, using alternatively the terms *jus cogens* (compelling law) or peremptory norms to express the idea of principles from which no deviation is permitted. We will return for a closer look at peremptory norms in the next chapter in the law of treaties.

WEIL, TOWARDS RELATIVE NORMATIVITY IN INTERNATIONAL LAW?

77 A.J.I.L. 413, 421 (1983)

There is now a trend towards the replacement of the monolithically conceived normativity of the past by graduated normativity. While it has always been difficult to locate the threshold beyond which a legal norm existed, at least there used to be no problem once the threshold could be pronounced crossed: the norm created legal rights and obligations; it was binding, its violation sanctioned with international responsibility. There was no distinction on that score to be made between one legal norm and another. But the theory of *jus cogens,* with its distinction between peremptory and merely binding norms, and the theory of international crimes and delicts, with its distinction between norms creating obligations essential for the preservation of fundamental interests and norms creating obligations of a less essential kind, are both leading to the fission of this unity. Normativity is becoming a question of "more or less": some norms are now held to be of greater specific gravity than others, to be more binding than others. Thus, the scale of normativity is reemerging in a new guise, its gradations no longer plotted merely between norms and non-norms, but also among those norms most undeniably situated on the positive side of the normativity threshold. Having taken its rise in the subnormative domain, the scale of normativity has now been projected and protracted into the normative domain itself, so that, henceforth, there are "norms and norms."

OPPENHEIM, INTERNATIONAL LAW

7–8 (9th ed. Jennings & Watts eds. 1992)

§ *2 Ius cogens* States may, by and within the limits of agreement between themselves, vary or even dispense altogether with most rules of international law. There are, however, a few rules from which no derogation is permissible. The latter—rules of *ius cogens,* or peremptory norms of general international law—have been defined in Article 53 of the Vienna Convention on the Law of Treaties 1969 (and for the purpose of that Convention) as norms 'accepted and recognised by the international community of states as a whole as a norm from which no derogation is permitted and which can be modified only by a subsequent norm of general international law having the same character'; and Article 64 contemplates the emergence of new rules of *ius cogens* in the future.

Such a category of rules of *ius cogens* is a comparatively recent development and there is no general agreement as to which rules have this character. The International Law Commission regarded the law of the Charter concerning the prohibition of the use of force as a conspicuous example of such a rule. Although the Commission refrained from giving in its draft Articles on the Law of Treaties any examples of rules of *ius cogens,* it did record that in this context mention had additionally been made of the prohibition of criminal acts under international law, and of acts such as trade in slaves, piracy or genocide, in the suppression of which every state is called upon to cooperate; the observance of human rights, the equality of states and the principle of self-determination. The full content of the category of *ius cogens* remains to be worked out in the practice of states and in the jurisprudence of international tribunals.* * *

The operation and effect of rules of *ius cogens* in areas other than that of treaties are similarly unclear. Presumably no act done contrary to such a rule can be legitimated by means of consent, acquiescence or recognition; nor is a protest necessary to preserve rights affected by such an act; nor can such an act be justified as a reprisal against a prior illegal act; nor can a rule of customary international law which conflicts with a rule of *ius cogens* continue to exist or subsequently be created (unless it has the character of *ius cogens,* a possibility which raises questions—to which no firm answer can yet be given—of the relationship between rules of *ius cogens,* and of the legitimacy of an act done in reliance on one rule of *ius cogens* but resulting in a violation of another such rule).

SHELTON, NORMATIVE HIERARCHY
IN INTERNATIONAL LAW

100 A.J.I.L. 291, 297–99, 302–03, 305–07 (2006) (footnotes omitted)

The theory of *jus cogens* or peremptory norms posits the existence of rules of international law that admit of no derogation and that can be amended only by a new general norm of international law of the same value. It is a concept that lacks both an agreed content and consensus in state practice. In most instances it is also an unnecessary concept because, as discussed further below, the derogating act violates treaty or custom and thus contravenes international law without the need to label the norm peremptory.

Development of jus cogens. The notion of *jus cogens* originated solely as a limitation on international freedom of contract. It was discussed at length for the first time by Verdross in 1937. Even prior to this, however, Quincy Wright had noted the problem of "illegal" treaties, based on a 1916 judgment of the Central American Court of Justice denying the capacity of Nicaragua to conclude the 1914 Bryan–Chamorro Treaty with the United States. * * *

* * *

In the considerable literature that has materialized since the appearance of Verdross's article, the concept of *jus cogens* has received widespread support, without any agreement or clarity about its source, content, or impact.

Sources of peremptory norms. Verdross viewed the source of peremptory norms as residing in general principles of law recognized by all legal systems. Others believe peremptory norms arise from consent, natural law (*jus necessarium pro omnium*), international public order, or constitutional principles. A strictly voluntarist view of international law rejects the notion that a state may be bound by an international legal rule without its consent and thus does not recognize a collective interest that is capable of overriding the will of an individual member of the society. * * *

The only references to peremptory norms in international texts are found in the Vienna conventions on the law of treaties and they can be read largely to support a voluntarist basis for *jus cogens*. * * *

* * *

The content of jus cogens. Neither the International Law Commission nor the Vienna Conference on the Law of Treaties developed an accepted list of peremptory norms, although both made reference in commentaries and discussion to the norms against genocide, slave trading, and use of force other than in self-defense. Some developing countries referred to permanent sovereignty over natural resources as a peremptory norm. The different theories as to the source of peremptory norms affect the contents; those who adhere to the voluntarist approach generally see the content as limited to a few rules that states have recognized as not being subject to derogation, reservation, or denunciation. Natural law proponents would subscribe to an even stricter list of immutable principles of justice. In contrast, theories based on community values result in a longer list of evolving norms. Eduardo Jiménez de Aréchaga posits that "[t]he substantive contents of *jus cogens* are likely to be constantly changing in accordance with the progress and development of international law and international morality."

Since the adoption of the Vienna Convention, the literature has abounded in claims that additional international norms constitute *jus cogens*. Proponents have argued for the inclusion of all human rights, all humanitarian norms (human rights and the laws of war), or singly, the duty not to cause transboundary environmental harm, freedom from torture, the duty to assassinate dictators, the right to life of animals, self-determination, the right to development, free trade, and territorial sovereignty (despite legions of treaties transferring territory from one state to another). * * * In most instances, little evidence has been presented to demonstrate how and why the preferred norm has become *jus cogens*. * * *

* * *

The concept of *jus cogens* has been invoked largely outside its original context in the law of treaties and with only limited impact. At the International Court of Justice, until early 2006, the term appeared only in separate or dissenting opinions or when the Court was quoting other sources. Previously, states rarely raised the issue, and when they did the Court seemed to take pains to avoid any pronouncement on it.

The 1986 *Nicaragua* decision, most often cited for the Court's recognition of *jus cogens*, did not in fact approve either the concept or the content of such norms. In the subsequent advisory opinion on nuclear weapons, the ICJ utilized descriptive phrases that could be taken to refer to peremptory norms, although the language is unclear. The Court called some rules of international humanitarian law so fundamental to respect for the human person and "elementary considerations of humanity" that "they constitute intransgressible principles of international customary law." Whether "intransgressible" means the rules are peremptory or was used simply to emphasize the binding nature of the customary norms is uncertain, but the former reading may be more plausible.

The first occasion on which the International Court gave support to the existence of *jus cogens* was in the February 3, 2006, Judgment on Preliminary Objections in *Armed Activities on the Territory of the Congo* [Democratic Republic of the Congo v. Rwanda]. * * *

The Court for the first time explicitly and overwhelmingly recognized the existence of *jus cogens* in its analysis of the validity of Rwanda's reservations to the Genocide and Racial Discrimination Conventions. With respect to the Genocide Convention, the Court reaffirmed that the rights and obligations contained therein are rights and obligations *erga omnes*, then pronounced the prohibition of genocide to be "assuredly" a peremptory norm of general international law. In making this straightforward statement, the Court did not offer any reference, evidence, or analysis that might help to establish criteria for identifying other peremptory norms or the consequences of such a characterization.

As in most other cases where peremptory norms have been recognized, the legal consequences of this classification were essentially imperceptible. The Court held by 15–2 that it lacked jurisdiction over the dispute, reaffirming that "[u]nder the Court's Statute that jurisdiction is always based on the consent of the parties." Concerning the Rwandan reservations [excluding the Court's jurisdiction under the treaties invoked by the Congo], the Court held that a reservation to ICJ jurisdiction cannot be judged invalid on the ground that it withholds jurisdiction over *jus cogens* violations. * * * [The reservation was meant to exclude one method of dispute settlement and not to affect] substantive obligations relating to acts of genocide themselves. It was therefore valid, there being no peremptory norm of international law requiring a state to consent to ICJ jurisdiction in a case involving genocide.

NOTES

1. *Prohibition on Use of Force as a Peremptory Norm.* In its 1986 Judgment (Merits) in the *Nicaragua* case, *supra*, the I.C.J. observed that the International Law Commission had referred to the rule against the use of force as "a conspicuous example of a rule in international law having the character of *jus cogens*." 1986 I.C.J. 14, 100, para. 190. Shelton, in the extract above, gives a restrictive interpretation to this passage from *Nicaragua*, observing (in an omitted footnote) that the Court merely cited the International Law Commission's assertion to this effect as evidence of the rule's customary status. Alexander Orakhelashvili disagrees with Shelton and understands the I.C.J. in *Nicaragua* to have lent its imprimatur both to the concept of peremptory norms and to the prohibition on the use of force as belonging to that category. Orakhelashvili, Peremptory Norms in International Law 41–42 (2006). How would you read the passage in question (p. 98–99 *supra*)?

2. *Catalogue of Peremptory Norms.* The peremptory norms mentioned in the above extracts are examples of rules to which no state would claim exceptions, e.g., the prohibition of genocide, slavery, aggression. Would the "international community as a whole" (the phrase from Article 53 of the Vienna Convention on the Law of Treaties, addressed in Chapter 3) be likely to determine that past acts which some states have engaged in by mutual consent or without objection (e.g., environmental pollution) have now become illegal under newly created *jus cogens?* Does Shelton's enumeration of possibly exaggerated claims of *jus cogens* status cast doubt on the entire category? Orakhelashvili's monograph (cited in the previous note) devotes a chapter (at 36–66) to the identification of peremptory norms, with attention to non-use of

force, self-determination, human rights and humanitarian law, and environmental law.

    3. *"International Community as a Whole."* Should the expression "the international community as a whole" meet a qualitative as well as a quantitative standard? Some suggest a "very large majority" is sufficient; others would require that the large majority include "essential" or "important" states. Would the latter rule (asserted by the United States and other major powers) mean that peremptory rules would not be recognized unless accepted as such by all major powers and countries from all regions of the world? During the conference on the Law of the Sea Convention, a large majority of states declared that a peremptory norm of customary law had evolved to the effect that the sea bed beyond national jurisdiction was the common heritage of mankind and not open to exploitation by individual states except when carried out under the international regime contemplated by the 1982 Convention. The fact that important industrial states including the United States opposed this position was not considered by its proponents as sufficient to negate the new principle. A similar effort has also been made in United Nations bodies to establish the principle of "permanent sovereignty over resources" as part of *jus cogens,* in spite of the opposition of several large industrial states. Neither of these efforts has thus far resulted in acceptance of the new rules by dissenting states. Considering these examples a recent study by a Russian scholar concludes that "the emergence of effective international peremptory norms obviously requires the achievement of a genuine consensus among all essential components of the modern international community. * * * [O]pposition to a proposed norm on the part of at least one important element of the international community, whatever its numerical strength, would undermine any claim that such norm is a general peremptory rule * * *." Danilenko, International Jus Cogens, 2 E.J.I.L. 42, 65 (1991); see also Charney & Danilenko, Consent and the Creation of International Law, in Beyond Confrontation 46–50 (Damrosch, Danilenko, & Mullerson eds. 1995).

    4. *Persistent Objection and Peremptory Norms.* Macdonald has suggested that it is inherent in the conception of peremptory norm that it applies against states that have not accepted the norm. See Macdonald, Fundamental Norms in Contemporary International Law, 25 Can. Y.B.I.L. 115, 131 (1987). See also Alexidze, Legal Nature of Jus Cogens in Contemporary International Law, 172 Rec. des Cours 219, 246–47, 258 (1981–III); Restatement (Third) § 102, Comments *d* and *k*; Byers, Custom, Power and the Power of Rules 183–203 (1999), and references in notes 4–5 on pp. 102–103 on (non)applicability of the persistent objector principle to *jus cogens.* Orakhelashvili maintains that in principle, a norm can become binding on a state as a peremptory norm without that state's consent. Orakhelashvili, *supra,* at 105. Shelton, by contrast, elaborates a voluntarist conception.

    5. *Consequences of Violation of Peremptory Norms.* Chapter 3 deals with the invalidity of treaties where violations of peremptory norms are at issue. What other consequences might attach to such violations? As Shelton notes, the I.C.J. has maintained a consensual approach to its own jurisdiction and thus has not invalidated reservations that states have interposed to the dispute settlement clauses of treaties whose substance deals with peremptory norms. Might other international tribunals, or perhaps even national courts,

be more assertive in their approach? For surveys of judicial invocations of the concept through 2006, taking different approaches and reaching different conclusions, compare the treatments by Shelton and Orakhelashvili cited above.

6. *U.N. Charter in Normative Hierarchy.* The I.C.J. referred to Article 103 in its 1984 Judgment on Jurisdiction in *Nicaragua*, pointing out that "all regional, bilateral and even unilateral arrangements that the parties have made * * * must be made always subject to the provisions of Article 103." 1984 I.C.J. 440, para. 107. Some commentators consider that treaties contrary to the Charter are null and void. McNair, The Law of Treaties 222 (1961). Others maintain that Article 103 only requires suspension or modification of an incompatible treaty obligation. See Czaplinski & Danilenko, Conflicts of Norms in International Law 21 Neth. Y.B.I.L. 14–15 (1990). For more on the problem of potential conflicts between Security Council resolutions and *jus cogens*, see Orakhelashvili, *supra*, 413–85; Shelton, 100 A.J.I.L. at 311–13.

In *Kadi v. Council*, the Court of First Instance of the European Union considered that it was "empowered to check, indirectly, the lawfulness of the resolutions of the Security Council in question with regard to *jus cogens*, understood as a body of higher rules of public international law binding on all subjects of international law, including the bodies of the United Nations, and from which no derogation is possible." It did not, however, find any violation of *jus cogens* in the application of European Community measures implementing U.N. Security Council sanctions against alleged terrorists. On appeal, the Grand Chamber of the European Court of Justice considered that the role of the judicial organ of the Community was to evaluate the contested European regulation in the light of fundamental rights forming part of general European law, rather than to review the legality of a Security Council resolution as such. It therefore found it unnecessary to examine the claim invoking *jus cogens*. *Kadi & Al Barakat International Foundation v. Council of the European Union* Case T–315/01 (Eur. Ct. Justice, C.F.I., Sept. 21, 2005; Grand Chamber, Sept. 3, 2008), addressed further in Chapter 10, p. 749.

SECTION 3. THE RELATIONSHIP OF CUSTOM AND TREATIES

A. TREATIES AND CUSTOM COMPARED

Article 38 of the I.C.J. Statute, in its list of sources according to which disputes are to be decided, gives first place to "international conventions, whether general or particular, establishing rules expressly recognized by the contracting States." Although Article 38 does not provide for a hierarchy among sources, the priority of position given to treaties reflects the understanding of states and of international lawyers that, in Lauterpacht's words:

The rights and duties of States are determined in the first instance, by their agreement as expressed in treaties—just as in the case of individuals their rights are specifically determined by any contract which is binding upon them. When a controversy arises between two or more States with regard to a matter regulated by a treaty, it is natural that the parties should invoke and that the adjudicating agency should apply, in the first instance, the provisions of the treaty in question.

1 Lauterpacht, International Law: Collected Papers, 86–87 (1970).

That it may be "natural" to apply a treaty in the first instance should not be taken to mean that a treaty provision necessarily prevails over a customary rule. The maxim, *lex specialis derogat generali, the specific prevails over the general, is an accepted* guide; it may give priority either to treaty or custom. The intentions of the parties are of paramount importance. They may show a common intent to replace a treaty with a customary rule; a treaty may become a dead-letter terminated by desuetude. When neither specificity nor intentions provide sufficient guidance, treaty and custom have equal weight with priority to the later in time, subject however to certain presumptions of interpretation. These presumptions operate in both directions. It is presumed that a treaty is not terminated or altered by subsequent custom in the absence of evidence that the parties had that intention. On the other hand, there is support for a general presumption that treaties are not intended to derogate from general custom. The complex interaction of treaty and custom is dealt with below and also in the next chapter.

International agreements—the *lex scripta* of the society of states—have proliferated since the end of World War Two and now address virtually every aspect of social life. Many multilateral treaties lay down broad rules of conduct for states generally and are in that respect somewhat like legislation . Among these are general treaties (open to all states) establishing rules of behavior which in the I.C.J.'s words are of a fundamentally norm-creating character such as could be regarded as forming the basis of a general rule of law *(North Sea Continental Shelf Case,* p. 90). These general normative treaties are to be distinguished from those establishing regimes for institutionalized cooperation or administrative regulation, as addressed further in Chapter 4.

By far the largest number of treaties are bilateral agreements, which are typically drafted in contractual terms of mutual exchange of rights and obligations and in that respect are different from the multilateral treaties that have a more legislative form. The bilateral treaties differ widely in scope and subject matter. Some do establish general norms as, for example, certain treaties of friendship, commerce and navigation as discussed in Chapter 14. It is not uncommon to find standardized provisions for particular subjects, which establish similar rights and duties for a large group of states. Many such agreements on extradition, air transport, rivers and foreign investment may create networks of obligation that are virtually general international law. However, whether they may be considered as evidence of custom and therefore binding for non-parties is another matter. On this aspect see pp. 118 and 121 note 6 below.

NOTES

1. *Advantages of Treaties.* Are treaties superior to custom for international law-making? Richard Baxter wrote in 1970:

> As one looks at the present state of international law and attempts to see into the future, it should be quite clear that treaty law will increasingly gain paramountcy over customary international law. The treaty-making process is a rational and orderly one, permitting participation in the creation of law by all States on a basis of equity. Newly independent States, otherwise subject to a body of customary international law in the making of which they played no part, can influence the progressive development of the law or help to "codify" it in such a way as to make it more responsive to their needs and ideals. For the more established States, the codification process provides a welcome opportunity to secure widespread agreement upon norms which have hitherto been the subject of doubt or controversy or have been rejected by other States.

> Even in those cases in which customary international law is already clear and generally agreed upon, the treaty will strengthen that rule and simplify its application. Article 1 of the Chicago Convention confirms what is already agreed to be a State's sovereign right to exclude foreign aircraft from its airspace. The presence in bilateral treaties of a requirement of exhaustion of local remedies reminds us that the well-understood rule of customary international law has not lost its validity.

Baxter, Treaties and Custom, 129 Rec. des Cours 25, 101 (1970–I) (footnotes omitted). The leading Soviet theorist, G.I. Tunkin, maintained that treaties are the dominant and "basic source" of international law. Theory of International Law 133–36 (Butler trans. 1974).

2. *Advantages of Custom.* What are the advantages of custom over treaty for developing law to meet new needs? Is custom more responsive to concrete situations and more malleable than multilateral treaties? Does it give more weight to power? For comment on "competition" between treaty and custom, see Schachter, Entangled Treaty and Custom, in International Law at a Time of Perplexity 717, 720–22 (Dinstein ed. 1989).

B. TREATIES OF CODIFICATION AND PROGRESSIVE DEVELOPMENT

SCHACHTER, INTERNATIONAL LAW IN THEORY AND PRACTICE
66–69, 71–72 (1991)

The rationalist belief in the development of law through deliberate, carefully considered and well designed instruments finds expression in two closely related processes: codification and "progressive development" through multilateral law-making treaties. Both aim at achieving an international *lex scripta* through the international equivalent of a legislative process. It is easy to see advantages of that process. In place of the uncertain and slow process of custom, built upon instances that are necessarily contingent and limited, governments negotiate and collaborate in formulating rules and principles to meet perceived needs of the entire community of states. The texts bring clarity and precision where there had been obscurity and doubt. Moreover, all governments have the opportunity to take part in the legislative process and to express their consent or objection in accordance with their constitutional procedures. Neither of these opportunities was clearly available to all states in the creation of customary law.

* * *

Codification is distinct, in principle, from the so-called law-making treaty that comes within "progressive development." The Statute of the U.N. International Law Commission defined codification as "the more precise formulation and systematization of rules of international law in fields where there already has been extensive state practice, precedent and doctrine." There is almost a deceptive simplicity about this definition, as indeed there is about the act of codification.

* * *

Before the United Nations began its work in the early nineteen-fifties, sharp differences had been expressed on whether codification should be a scientific or political task. The debate on this issue reflected, in some degree, the differences concerning positivism, voluntarism, and state sovereignty. Those who saw codification as essentially scientific considered as Cecil Hurst did that its task was to "ascertain" and "declare the existing rule of international law, irrespective of any question as to whether the rule is satisfactory or unsatisfactory, obsolete or still adequate to modern conditions, just or unjust in the eyes of those who formulate it." That task could be carried out, it was assumed, solely on the basis of state practice and precedent. It was in its essence an inductive process that could and should be entrusted to independent jurists, not governments. * * *

* * *

The idea of a truly scientific, non-governmental restatement of international law did not find the requisite support in the United Nations. Nor was it generally supported by international lawyers, though there were notable exceptions. The objection to scientific, non-official codification had several grounds. There was a basic difficulty with the idea implicit in the I.L.C. definition (referred to earlier) that "extensive state practice, precedent and doctrine" would yield a rule of law. Hersch Lauterpacht commented that the absence of state practice could show the non-existence of a rule but that the converse did not hold because, in his view, the area of agreement that would be revealed by state practice "is small in the extreme." Others went further, pointing out that any attempt to formulate an explicit and clear rule, or systematizing rules based on precedent, involved elements of novelty. It assumes agreement where none may exist.

* * *

The experience of the last 25 years showed that the skepticism about the practicality of universal codification * * * was excessive. For one thing, the governments in the United Nations and the International Law Commission quickly recognized that codification involved "new law" to some degree but that it was possible and desirable to distinguish codification that had a substantial foundation in customary law from treaties that sought to formulate new principles and rules for matters previously unregulated by international law. In the former category, the drafts prepared by the Commission were mainly based on practice and precedent but often filled in lacunae and removed inconsistencies found in State practice. These elements of "progressive development" were identified in the reports of the Commission and in the *travaux préparatoires* leading to adoption by the conference of States. Since such new law generally did not involve significant conflicts of interest between States, it was regarded as essentially technical ("lawyers' law") and therefore appropriate in a codification. The fact that the codifications were drafted as treaties and passed upon in detail by conferences which included nearly all States was perceived as "settling" rather than unsettling customary law (except for the few provisions that were identified as new law in the *travaux*).

* * *

The anticipated difficulties proved less of an obstacle than had been predicted. Governments were not deterred by the fact that in reducing the unwritten law of precedents to written, generalized rules they were performing a "legislative" act that was in some measure "progressive development." They realized (as did the I.L.C.) that the customary law that they were ostensibly declaring was also being supplemented and, in a degree, modified in the light of present conditions and attitudes. Inevitably this reflected current political views and some bargaining in the negotiations at the conference. But the apprehension that codification would not be acceptable to the States "wedded to uncompromising maintenance of sovereignty" was not borne out. A considerable measure of support by all groups of States was in fact achieved in the two-stage procedure of Commission and conference. In the Commission, the draft conventions were adopted by consensus. The Commission was informed of the governmental views in the course of its work through written comments and the discussions in the Legal Committee of the General Assembly. In the conferences, most decisions were taken by consensus and compromises were reached to avoid any significant defections.

What is noteworthy is that although these texts were in the form of conventions requiring ratification or accession, they have been widely accepted as generally declaratory of existing law and therefore actually given legal effect even prior to their formal entry into force, and, when in force, applied by non-parties as well as by parties to the treaties. In this way, the old issue of "restatement" versus convention was rendered academic since the conventions were in fact regarded and used as if they were restatements except where there was persuasive evidence that a particular provision was intended to be *de lege ferenda* * * *.

* * *

There is a practical side to this conclusion that merits mention here. This relates to what might be called the bureaucratic factor in the codification process. The legal advisers and other government officials concerned with the application of law play a major part in codification. They do so mainly by way of comments on the drafts in the preparatory stages and at the conference of plenipotentiaries at which the final text is adopted. Officials who subsequently have to ascertain and invoke law naturally look to the product of the process in which they or their colleagues took part. The text is, so to speak, "their" law. Moreover, the adopted text has the great advantage for busy officials of providing "black letter" law in an instrument that has been adopted by nearly all States of the world. The law is declared in a concise and definitive form that is highly convenient for lawyers and officials. In most cases there is little reason for them to search for the precedents that might underlie the rule; it is in any case difficult to challenge the validity of a rule that had received the support of their own government as well as of others. These practical and bureaucratic factors help to increase the use made of the adopted texts (whether or not the instrument has entered into force or has been ratified by the state invoking its authority). The consequences over time are two-fold: (1) the instrument generally accumulates more authority as declaratory of customary law and (2), in cases where the declaratory nature of a particular provision is shown to be contrary to the understanding of the drafters (as in the *North Sea Continental Shelf Cases),* the tendency to apply that provision will in time result in custom "grafted" upon the treaty. This latter process was described by the Court in the *North Sea Continental Shelf Cases* although the majority did not find that a customary rule had actually developed.

In suggesting that the generally accepted codification conventions tend to prevail over competing customary law I do not mean to suggest that they entirely replace customary law in the field covered. Custom may still apply to fill in the gaps that always occur or the treaty itself may recognize that exceptions to its rules are permissible in accordance with special custom. * * * In other words, a codification convention, authoritative as it may seem because of its universal (or nearly universal) acceptance, cannot entirely freeze the development of law. Changing conditions and new perceptions of interests and aims continue to operate. The existence of written codified law may impede the pace of change but it cannot prevent it.

NOTE

Codification and Progressive Development. A substantial part of customary international law has been codified in multilateral conventions prepared by the International Law Commission, approved by the General Assembly, and adopted by international plenipotentiary conferences. Among the most notable are those on the law of treaties (Chapter 3), diplomatic and consular immunities (Chapter 12), and law of the sea (Chapter 17).

A large number of general multilateral treaties are appropriately considered as "progressive development" or "law-making" rather than as codification of existing customary law. These treaties may be based to some degree on prior practice but by and large they are perceived as expressing new law required by states for political, social or technical reasons. Most of them have been prepared and negotiated by United Nations bodies, generally expert or specialized committees broadly representative of the main political and geographical groups in the United Nations. The subject matter of the treaties is diverse; it includes matters such as outer space, dispute settlement, narcotics, status of women, refugees, human rights of various kinds, arms control, transportation, environmental protection and telecommunication. Other related United Nations bodies have also produced hundreds of treaties. There are for example, dozens of such treaties relating to intellectual property, many on education, nearly 190 conventions on labor, and numerous treaties on civil aviation, shipping and broadcasting. Regional and functional organizations have also generated numerous treaties in their respective fields. These treaties are the product, together with the more general codification treaties, of an "international legislative process" that operates through many different organizations and conferences. That process has resulted in a dense, intricate body of rules and practices followed by governments.

C. ENTANGLED TREATY AND CUSTOM

As already indicated, treaty rules may be accepted as customary law and therefore be binding on states not parties to the treaty in question. The International Court of Justice has noted that this would occur when one of the following conditions exist:

1. Where the treaty rule is declaratory of pre-existing custom;

2. Where the treaty rule is found to have crystallized customary law in process of formation;

3. Where the treaty rule is found to have generated new customary law subsequent to its adoption.

The leading I.C.J. cases enunciating these conditions are the *North Sea Continental Shelf* cases and the 1986 judgment in the *Nicaragua* case. As the extracts above indicate, the Court has declared that a treaty provision of a norm-creating character could generate a rule "which, while only conventional or contractual in its origin, has since passed into the general corpus of international law and is now accepted as such by the *opinio juris,* so as to become binding even for countries which have never and do not, become parties to the Convention." (*North Sea*, 1969 I.C.J. at 41.) In *Nicaragua*, the Court used a different justification to support its conclusion that Articles 2(4) and 51 of the U.N. Charter were customary law. It declared (1986 I.C.J. 14, paras. 178, 181):

[E]ven if two norms belonging to two sources of international law appear identical in content, and even if the States in question are bound by these rules both on the level of treaty-law and on that of customary international law, these norms retain a separate existence. * * *

* * *

[T]he Charter gave expression in this field to principles already present in customary international law, and that law has in the subsequent four decades developed under the influence of the Charter, to such an extent that a number of rules have acquired a status independent of it.

Finding customary law identical with the Charter provisions enabled the Court to avoid the effect of a U.S. reservation that excluded from its acceptance of compulsory jurisdiction all cases involving multilateral treaties unless all treaty parties agreed to jurisdiction.

NOTES

1. *Universal Treaties.* If virtually all states are parties to a treaty—as is the case for the U.N. Charter and the Geneva Conventions on the Law of Armed Conflict—does it make any difference whether the rules are also customary as well as treaty law? Theodor Meron suggests some advantages of recognizing customary law parallel to treaty law: (1) states are not free to withdraw from customary law obligations as they might be under treaty law; (2) in many states, customary law is part of domestic law whereas treaty rules do not become domestic law unless the legislature so decides; (3) customary law—or general international law—has more weight than contractual obligations and may be a basis for the *"erga omnes"* character of the rules, allowing all states to have a legal interest in their compliance. Meron, Human Rights and Humanitarian Norms as Customary Law 3–10, 114–35, 192–95 (1989); see also Meron, Revival of Customary Humanitarian Law, 99 A.J.I.L. 817, 821 (2003).

2. *Non–Parties to Widely Ratified Treaties.* In the North Sea case, p. 90, the Court suggests that a treaty rule might be considered a customary rule of international law if the treaty has a "widespread and representative participation * * * [including] States whose interests were specially affected." 1969 I.C.J. 43, para. 73. Would this conclusion, if applied, mean that non-parties would be subject to obligations of a treaty whenever many states have become parties? Would it not be necessary to show practice and *opinio juris* on the part of non-parties as well as parties to conclude that the non-parties are subject to the treaty rules in question? Is a convention designed to codify existing custom presumptive evidence that its rules are customary, hence applicable to all states? As an illustration, the Eritrea Ethiopia Claims Commission has considered the Geneva Conventions presumptively declaratory of customary law when Eritrea was not party to the relevant treaty at the time of the conflict. See references in Meron, 99 A.J.I.L. 817 at 818 n. 9, 819 n. 19 (2005).

3. *Norms versus Bargains.* Consider the difference between multilateral conventions that proclaim a rule of law that virtually all states accept in principle even if they do not become parties to the treaty (for example, a treaty against torture or air hijacking) and a treaty that involves bargained-for compromise solutions such as a trade treaty or the law of the sea treaty. It has been suggested that in the former case, an inference of *opinio juris* may be made, based on statements of the governments even if actual practice is slight. However, in the latter case, an attempt to transport into customary law the substantive rules, disregarding the "deals" and compromises, may be difficult to justify. See Schachter, Recent Trends in International Law–Making, 12 Australian Y.B.I.L. 1, 7 (1992).

4. *"Package Deal?"* If states not parties to a general multilateral treaty declare that some but not all of its provisions are accepted as customary law (even if of recent origin), can they claim such rights vis-à-vis parties to the treaty? The United States, which has not become party to the comprehensive 1982 U.N. Convention on the Law of the Sea, declared in 1983 that it regards the provisions of the convention as existing customary law, with the exception of provisions on the deep seabed and on dispute settlement and administration. It announced it will assert its rights based on the customary law provisions and reciprocally recognize such rights of others. However, other states (and commentators) question the right of non-parties to pick the provisions they like and disregard what they do not like inasmuch as the Convention contains interlinked provisions, involving a "package deal" of compromises. Should this preclude non-parties from relying on prior custom reflected in the treaty or on new rules accepted as customary during the period the treaty was negotiated? See Caminos & Molitor, Progressive Development of International Law and the Package Deal, 79 A.J.I.L. 871 (1985) and Chapter 17.

Whether the United States can securely rely as a non-party on the position that the U.N. Convention on the Law of the Sea embodies customary law has been a lively subject of debate in connection with renewed efforts to obtain the Senate's approval of the treaty in 2007–2008. See Chapter 17. In September 2007, Deputy Secretary of State John Negroponte testified that full participation in the treaty would provide a firmer legal foundation for the exercise of navigational freedoms and other rights than continued reliance on customary law, stating:

> Customary international law is not universally accepted and, in any event, changes over time—in this case, potentially to the detriment of our interests. There are increasing pressures from coastal States around the world to evolve the law of the sea in ways that would unacceptably alter the balance of interests struck in the Convention. Operational challenges are inherently risky and resource-intensive. Joining the Convention would put the navigational rights reflected in the Convention on the firmest legal footing. We would have treaty rights rather than have to rely solely upon the acceptance of customary international law rights by other states or upon the threat or use of force. Securing these treaty rights, and obtaining a seat at the table in treaty-based institutions, would provide a safeguard against changes in State practice that could cause customary law to drift in an unfavorable direction.

See Crook, Contemporary Practice of the United States, 102 A.J.I.L. 155, 169 (2008).

5. *Custom Superseding Treaty.* May treaty-based rules be supplanted by changes in practice leading to new customary law? The 1958 Conventions on the Continental Shelf and on the High Seas were changed in important ways by the extension of jurisdiction by coastal states without any formal change in those treaties. Did President Reagan place the United States in breach of obligations under those treaties (to which it was a party) when he proclaimed that the United States accepted as customary law many of the provisions of the 1982 Convention which the U.S. did not sign or ratify? See Chapter 17.

6. *Bilateral Treaties and Custom.* Many bilateral treaties include common provisions on legal rights and obligations. Examples are found in treaties on extradition, air transport, rivers, compensation for expropriation, and commercial trade. As the treaties constitute state practice, can one infer that the common provisions in many treaties are evidence of customary law? May one distinguish between those bilateral treaties which deal with matters which are clearly recognized as within the discretion of the states and those which deal with matters generally regulated by international law? In the first category, one would include extradition and aviation on the premises that states are under no customary duty to grant the rights given in the bilateral treaties. In such cases, the treaties, numerous as they may be, would not have the *opinio juris* necessary to establish customary law. In the other category, an example would be treaties on riparian rights reflecting requirements of customary law about riparian states' duties toward others. May one conclude that such bilateral treaties are accompanied by *opinio juris*? A more controversial issue is whether agreements to pay compensation for expropriated property are evidence of customary law. See Chapter 14.

7. *International Criminal Law.* A recent treaty with high potential to contribute to the development of general international law, not merely among formal parties to the treaty, is the 1998 Rome Statute for an International Criminal Court, which entered into force in 2002. Even before entry into force, it had already been cited by international tribunals in rulings on unresolved points of international law. For an example, see the *Tadić* decision of the International Criminal Tribunal for Former Yugoslavia, Case No. IT–94–1–AR72, Appeal from Judgment of Conviction, para. 223 (July 1999) (citing the trial chamber's *Furundzija* ruling for the proposition that the Rome Statute has "significant legal value" even prior to entry into force, e.g. with respect to determining *opinio juris*). On the need for the I.C.C. to consider interactions between the Rome Statute and the parallel body of customary law, see Meron, Revival of Customary Humanitarian Law, 99 A.J.I.L. 817, 832 (2005).

CHAPTER 3

THE LAW OF TREATIES

■ ■ ■

SECTION 1. DEFINITION AND
GOVERNING LAW

Treaties, as noted in Chapter 2, are a principal source of obligation in international law. The term "treaty" is used generally to cover the binding agreements between subjects of international law that are governed by international law. In addition to the term "treaty," a number of other appellations are used to apply to international agreements. Some of the more common are convention, pact, protocol, charter, covenant, and declaration, as well as the words treaty or international agreement. Other terms are act, statute, *modus vivendi,* exchange of notes, memorandum of understanding, and on occasion, communiqué or agreed statement. The particular appellation given to an agreement has in itself no legal effect. Some of the terms used follow habitual uses; others are used to denote solemnity (e.g., covenant or charter) or the supplementary character of the agreement (e.g., protocol). The U.N. Charter in Article 102 requires the registration of "every treaty and every international agreement entered into by a Member of the United Nations." This applies whatever the form or descriptive name used for the agreement.

The phrase "international agreement" is sometimes used here as an alternative to "treaty." In the domestic practice of some states, the term "treaty" connotes an especially formal kind of agreement; in U.S. usage, for example, "treaty" typically signifies an agreement approved by the Senate under Article II of the Constitution, as contrasted to congressional-executive or sole executive agreements. In international usage, "treaty" is a generic term not limited by domestic particularities.

In concluding what purports or appears to be a treaty, the states concerned may sometimes intend to create only political or moral, as opposed to legal, commitments. Such "nonbinding agreements" are referred to in some cases as "gentlemen's agreements" and in other contexts as political or moral undertakings. Whether they are intended to be nonbinding in a legal sense is not always clear. Nor is it always clear what legal consequences flow from such agreements. On the other hand, states may sometimes intend to create legal commitments through unilateral acts rather than through exchanges of promises in treaty form. Questions pertaining to legally nonbinding agreements and to binding unilateral acts will be considered in Chapter 4.

A. THE VIENNA CONVENTION ON THE LAW OF TREATIES: GENERAL CONSIDERATIONS

The Vienna Convention on the Law of Treaties, May 23, 1969, 1155 U.N.T.S. 331, is the principal authoritative source of the law of treaties, and it will therefore be the focus of this chapter. The Convention is regarded as in large part (but not entirely) declaratory of existing law. Some of its provisions went beyond existing law or altered previously established rules. These provisions are generally characterized as "progressive development" in keeping with the terms used in Article 13 of the U.N. Charter and the Statute of the International Law Commission, G.A. Res. 174 (II) (Nov. 21, 1947). As we shall see, the distinction between the declaratory and the "new" law of the Convention is not readily apparent from the text and is sometimes subject to conflicting assessments.

The Convention entered into force on January 27, 1980 upon ratification by the thirty-fifth state and had 108 parties in 2009. The Convention had not been ratified by the United States as of 2009. However, the Department of State, in submitting the Convention to the Senate, stated that the Convention "is already recognized as the authoritative guide to current treaty law and practice." S. Exec. Doc. L., 92–1 (1971). Many subsequent statements of the Department of State have confirmed this view, including in U.S. briefs filed with international tribunals.

Work on the Vienna Convention was first undertaken by the International Law Commission in 1949. From its outset, it was assumed that the task was primarily that of codification and that draft articles would eventually form an international treaty. The Convention was concluded in 1969 in two sessions of a plenipotentiary conference of states held under U.N. auspices in Vienna. During the twenty-year period of preparation, numerous drafts and commentaries were prepared by special rapporteurs of the International Law Commission and considered in detail by the Commission and by the Legal Committee of the U.N. General Assembly. The four special rapporteurs were the leading British international lawyers of the period: James Brierly, Sir Hersch Lauterpacht, Sir Gerald Fitzmaurice and Sir Humphrey Waldock (the latter three were elected successively as judges on the International Court). The detailed reports by these rapporteurs and the summary records of the International Law Commission are a voluminous and valuable collection of the *travaux préparatoires* essential for understanding and interpretation. They have been published in the annual Yearbooks of the International Law Commission. The records of the Vienna conferences at which the treaty was finally concluded are also essential for interpretation. They have been published as U.N. documents of the United Nations Conference on the Law of

Treaties, Official Records, First (and Second) Session. A useful guide to these records is contained in Rosenne, The Law of Treaties: Guide to the Legislative History of the Vienna Convention (1970). Substantive studies dealing with the legislative history of the treaty include: Sinclair, The Vienna Convention on the Law of Treaties (2d ed. 1984); Elias, The Modern Law of Treaties (1974); Haraszti, Some Fundamental Problems of the Law of Treaties (1973); Kearney & Dalton, The Treaty on Treaties, 64 A.J.I.L. 495 (1970). More recent treatises on the law of treaties deal with applications of the concepts embodied in the Convention and the parallel body of customary law, in the practice of both parties and non-parties. See, e.g., Aust, Modern Treaty Law and Practice (2d ed. 2007); Les Conventions de Vienne sur le droit des traités: Commentaire article par article (Corten & Klein eds. 2006; Eng. ed. forthcoming 2009).

The Convention is limited to treaties concluded between states (Article 1). It does not cover treaties between states and international organizations or between international organizations themselves, which are the subject of another Vienna convention concluded in 1986 in terms largely similar to the 1969 treaty.

The Vienna Convention applies only to agreements in written form. It expressly recognizes, however, that this limitation is without prejudice to the legal force of non-written agreements or to the application to them of any of the rules set forth in the Convention to which they would be subject under international law independently of the Convention (Article 3).

The Convention declares that it is non-retroactive (Article 4). However, in this connection also it is said that the principle is "without prejudice to the application of any rules set forth in the present Convention to which treaties would be subject under international law independently of the Convention."

These latter two provisions both acknowledge the continued application of customary law and, where relevant, of general principles of law to treaties, whether covered or not by the Convention. A clause in the preamble to the Convention affirms that rules of customary international law will continue to govern questions not regulated by the Convention.

B. THE VIENNA CONVENTION AS CUSTOMARY INTERNATIONAL LAW

On the basis that the Vienna Convention was largely declaratory of customary international law, it has been invoked and applied by tribunals and by states even prior to its entry into force in 1980 and in regard to nonparties as well as parties. For example, in the *Fisheries Jurisdiction Case* (United Kingdom v. Iceland), 1974 I.C.J. 3, 18, the I.C.J. found that the principle of suspending or terminating a treaty because of a fundamental change of circumstances, as articulated in Article 62 of the Convention, along with the conditions and exceptions specified therein, "may in many respects be considered as a codification of existing customary law on the subject of the termination of a treaty relationship on account of change of circumstances." Similarly, in the Advisory Opinion on Namibia, 1971 I.C.J. 16, 47, the Court treated the rules laid down in Article 60(3) concerning termination on account of breach as a codification of existing customary law. To the same effect is the *Gabčíkovo–Nagymaros Project* (Hungary/Slovakia), 1997 I.C.J. 7, paras. 46, 99, where the Court reaffirmed the customary character of the rules of Articles 60–62 and applied them to a dispute over a treaty concluded before the Vienna Convention had entered into force.

The principles of interpretation set forth in Articles 31 to 33 have guided many international tribunals. In *Golder v. United Kingdom*, Eur. Ct. H.R. (ser. A) No. 18 (1975), the European Court of Human Rights explained that even though the Convention was not then in force (and Article 4 specifies that it is not retroactive), its articles on interpretation "enunciate in essence generally accepted principles of international law." In *Kasikili/Sedudu Island* (Botswana v. Namibia), 1999 I.C.J. 1045, the I.C.J. noted that neither Botswana nor Namibia were parties to the Vienna Convention but that both of them considered Article 31 applicable "inasmuch as it reflects customary international law" (para. 18). See also *Certain Questions of Mutual Assistance in Criminal Matters* (Djibouti v. France), 2008 I.C.J. No. 136, para. 112. The World Trade Organization's Dispute Settlement Body has likewise treated these rules as having attained the status of customary international law. See Mavroidis, No Outsourcing of Law? WTO Law as Practiced by WTO Courts, 102 A.J.I.L. 421, 443–62, 469–74 (2008).

The distinction between those rules of the Convention which are customary law (or general international law) and those provisions which are extensions or changes of existing law can be made only on the basis of a particular examination of the provision in question and its relationship to existing law. In most cases where this question has arisen the answer cannot easily be given. Ian Sinclair, a leading participant and commentator, has said that: "It is only in rare cases, and then by implication rather than by express pronouncement, that one can determine where the Commission has put forward a proposal by way of progressive development rather than by way of codification" (Sinclair, *supra*, at 14).

It is perhaps more significant that states tend to refer to all of the provisions of the Convention as an authoritative source of law, thus gradually transforming its innovative features into customary law through such application. It is natural that a Convention which was concluded with virtually unanimous approval of the international community, after some two decades of study and deliberation, should be applied by legal advisors and courts as the primary source of law. It still remains possible for a nonparty state to challenge a particular provision on the ground that it goes beyond existing law and has not become part of general international law since its inclusion. However, the tendency of states and tribunals to turn to the Convention for authority makes it highly likely that it will be regarded in its entirety as having become part of general international law (except as regards its specifically procedural features, such as dispute settlement).

SECTION 2.   CONCLUSION AND ENTRY INTO FORCE

A.   EXISTENCE OF A TREATY

States often conclude treaties through well-understood and formal processes, which can include public adoption at a multilateral conference or simultaneous signatures of foreign ministers at an event that could draw extensive media coverage. Yet the definition of "treaty" in Article 2 of the Vienna Convention does not require a particular method or level of formality and does not necessarily require signature. Are there myriad ways that a state might bind itself to an international agreement? If so, how does one know when such an agreement has come into existence?

MARITIME DELIMITATION AND TERRITORIAL QUESTIONS (QATAR v. BAHRAIN)

International Court of Justice, 1994
1994 I.C.J. 112

[Qatar invoked the jurisdiction of the I.C.J. on the basis of exchanges of letters dated December 1987 subscribed by the Amirs of Qatar and Bahrain through the mediation of the King of Saudi Arabia, and a document headed "Minutes" which had been signed at Doha, Qatar, on December 25, 1990 by the Ministers of Foreign Affairs of Bahrain, Qatar, and Saudi Arabia. Qatar claimed these documents to be international agreements creating rights and obligations for Qatar and Bahrain—specifically, an obligation to submit to the I.C.J. the whole of their dispute involving sovereignty over certain islands, sovereign rights over certain shoals, and delimitation of a maritime boundary. Bahrain denied that the instruments in question constituted international agreements establishing a jurisdictional basis for Qatar to bring a unilateral application to the Court.

[The Court first had to determine whether the 1987 exchange and the 1990 Minutes were international agreements, as a prerequisite for establishing the Court's jurisdiction under Article 36(1) of its Statute. In a judgment of July 1, 1994, the Court found both the 1987 exchange and the 1990 Minutes to be international agreements. Its judgment of February 15, 1995 was addressed to resolving differences between the parties on how the agreements should be interpreted. Its judgment of March 16, 2001 dealt with the merits of the dispute. The excerpts below concern the establishment of the existence of international agreements binding the parties to submit their dispute to the Court. For other aspects, see 1995 I.C.J. 6; 2001 I.C.J. 40.]

[The Court begins its 1994 judgment by summarizing the efforts of the parties over two decades to seek a solution to their dispute. Those efforts included "good offices" by King Fahd of Saudi Arabia, who on December 19, 1987 sent each side a letter with new proposals, which the Heads of State of Qatar and Bahrain accepted in letters respectively dated December 21 and 26, 1987. The first proposal read:

> All the disputed matters shall be referred to the International Court of Justice, at The Hague, for a final ruling binding upon both parties, who shall have to execute its terms.

Under the King's third proposal, a Tripartite Committee was to be constituted, consisting of representatives of Qatar, Bahrain, and Saudi Arabia, "for the purpose of approaching the International Court of Justice and satisfying the necessary requirements to have the dispute submitted to the Court in accordance with its regulations and instructions so that a final ruling, binding on both parties, be issued." The Committee met several times but was unable to produce an agreement satisfactory to both sides on the specific terms for submitting the dispute to the Court. Efforts toward this end resumed in December 1990, resulting in the "Minutes" which reaffirmed the previous undertakings and specified that the good offices of the Saudi King would continue until May 1991, after which time the parties "may" submit the dispute to the I.C.J.]

21. The Court will first enquire into the nature of the texts upon which Qatar relies before turning to an analysis of the content of those texts.

22. The Parties agree that the exchanges of letters of December 1987 constitute an international agreement with binding force in their mutual relations. Bahrain however maintains that the Minutes of 25 December 1990 were no more than a simple record of negotiations, similar in nature to the Minutes of the Tripartite Committee; that accordingly they did not rank as an international agreement and could not, therefore, serve as a basis for the jurisdiction of the Court.

23. The Court would observe, in the first place, that international agreements may take a number of forms and be given a diversity of names. Article 2, paragraph (1) (a), of the Vienna Convention on the Law of Treaties of 23 May 1969 provides that for the purposes of that Convention,

> " 'treaty' means an international agreement concluded between States in written form and governed by international law, whether embodied in a single instrument or in two or more related instruments and whatever its particular designation."

Furthermore, as the Court said, in a case concerning a joint communiqué,

> "it knows of no rule of international law which might preclude a joint communiqué from constituting an international agreement to submit a dispute to arbitration or judicial settlement" (*Aegean Sea Continental Shelf, Judgment, I.C.J. Reports 1978*, p. 39, para. 96).

In order to ascertain whether an agreement of that kind has been concluded, "the Court must have regard above all to its actual terms and to the particular circumstances in which it was drawn up" (*ibid.*).

24. The 1990 Minutes refer to the consultations between the two Foreign Ministers of Bahrain and Qatar, in the presence of the Foreign Minister of Saudi Arabia, and state what had been "agreed" between the Parties. * * * The circumstances are addressed under which the dispute may subsequently [after May 1991] be submitted to the Court. * * *

25. Thus the 1990 Minutes include a reaffirmation of obligations previously entered into; they entrust King Fahd with the task of attempting to find a solution to the dispute during a period of six months; and, lastly, they address the circumstances under which the Court could be seised after May 1991.

Accordingly, and contrary to the contentions of Bahrain, the Minutes are not a simple record of a meeting, similar to those drawn up within the framework of the Tripartite Committee; they do not merely give an account of discussions and summarize points of agreement and disagreement. They enumerate the commitments to which the Parties have consented. They thus create rights and obligations in international law for the Parties. They constitute an international agreement.

26. Bahrain however maintains that the signatories of the Minutes never intended to conclude an agreement of this kind. It submitted a statement made by the Foreign Minister of Bahrain and dated 21 May 1992, in which he states that "at no time did I consider that in signing the Minutes I was committing Bahrain to a legally binding agreement." He goes on to say that, according to the Constitution of Bahrain, "treaties 'concerning the territory of the State' can come into effect only after their positive enactment as a law." The Minister indicates that he would therefore not have been permitted to sign an international agreement taking effect at the time of the signature. He was aware of that situation, and was prepared to subscribe to a statement recording a political understanding, but not to sign a legally binding agreement."

27. The Court does not find it necessary to consider what might have been the intentions of the Foreign Minister of Bahrain or, for that matter, those of the Foreign Minister of Qatar. The two Ministers signed a text recording commitments accepted by their Governments, some of which were to be given immediate application. Having signed such a text, the Foreign Minister of Bahrain is not in a position subsequently to say that he intended to subscribe only to a "statement recording a political understanding," and not to an international agreement.

28. Bahrain however bases its contention, that no international agreement was concluded, also upon another argument. It maintains that the subsequent conduct of the Parties showed that they never considered the 1990 Minutes to be an agreement of this kind; and that not only was this the position of Bahrain, but it was also that of Qatar. Bahrain points out that Qatar waited until June 1991 before it applied to the United

Nations Secretariat to register the Minutes of December 1990 under Article 102 of the Charter; and moreover that Bahrain objected to such registration. * * * [N]or did [Qatar] follow the procedures required by its own Constitution for the conclusion of treaties. This conduct showed that Qatar, like Bahrain, never considered the 1990 Minutes to be an international agreement.

29. The Court would observe that an international agreement or treaty that has not been registered with the Secretariat of the United Nations may not, according to the provisions of Article 102 of the Charter, be invoked by the parties before any organ of the United Nations. Non-registration or late registration, on the other hand, does not have any consequence for the actual validity of the agreement, which remains no less binding upon the parties. * * * Nor is there anything in the material before the Court which would justify deducing from any disregard by Qatar of its constitutional rules relating to the conclusion of treaties that it did not intend to conclude, and did not consider that it had concluded, an instrument of that kind; nor could any such intention, even if shown to exist, prevail over the actual terms of the instrument in question. Accordingly Bahrain's argument on these points also cannot be accepted.

30. The Court concludes that the Minutes of 25 December 1990, like the exchanges of letters of December 1987, constitute an international agreement creating rights and obligations for the Parties.

JIMÉNEZ DE ARÉCHAGA, INTERNATIONAL LAW IN THE PAST THIRD OF A CENTURY

159 Rec. des Cours 35–37 (1978–I) (footnotes omitted)

Although the definition of an international treaty seems at first sight to be a purely academic question, judicial experience shows that the determination of whether a certain instrument constitutes a treaty has important practical consequences.

For instance, in two cases before the International Court of Justice the question whether an instrument was a treaty had decisive significance for the establishment of the Court's jurisdiction with respect to the dispute.

In the *Anglo–Iranian Oil Co.* case the jurisdiction of the court was invoked on the basis of Iran's acceptance of the optional clause, dating from 1932, which referred to disputes "relating to the application of treaties or conventions accepted by Persia and subsequent to the ratification of this declaration."

The United Kingdom invoked as a treaty subsequent to 1932 a concession contract of 1933, signed between the Government of Iran and the Anglo–Persian Oil Company, contending that this agreement had:

"a double character, the character of being at once a concessionary contract between the Iranian Government and the Company and a treaty between the two Governments."

The Court could not, however,

"accept the view that the contract signed between the Iranian Government and the Anglo–Persian Oil Company has a double character. It is nothing more than a concessionary contract between a government and a foreign corporation. The United Kingdom Government is not a party to the contract; there is no privity of contract between the Government of Iran and the Government of the United Kingdom."

From this pronouncement of the Court it results that an agreement between a State and a private company, even a multinational one, even if it is (as Anglo–Iranian was then) half-owned by a government, cannot be considered as a treaty in international law, but only as a contract. The Court's dictum implies that a treaty requires that two or more States become bound *vis-à-vis* each other.

* * *

The definition of a treaty as an agreement between subjects of international law is not in itself sufficient. There may be agreements between States which do not constitute international treaties. McNair gives the example of a purchase by the United Kingdom Government of one thousand tons of chilled beef from the Government of the Argentine Republic upon the basis of a standard form of contract used in the meat trade.

Another example of an interstate contract and not a treaty could be the purchase of a building or a piece of land for a legation, when this transaction is subject to the municipal law of one of the parties or to that of a third State. A third instance, involving an international organization, would be a loan or a guarantee agreement between the World Bank and a State, which, as has occurred in the past, is made subject to the laws of the State of New York. This is the reason why the codification in the Vienna Convention adds a requirement to the definition of a treaty: the agreement must be "governed by international law."

When is an agreement governed by international law? Is this a matter of choice or of intention of the parties? In principle, the intention of the parties, express or implied, would appear to be controlling. However, there are cases in which the nature and object of the agreement make it impossible to subject it to any system of municipal law; such an agreement must be governed by international law, whatever the intention of parties. A case in point is the cession of a small piece of land by France to Switzerland to permit the enlargement of Geneva Airport. Despite the comparatively trivial importance of this agreement, it had to be embodied in a treaty since it involved the transfer of sovereignty over State territory.

NOTES

1. *"Governed by International Law."* The Commission's Special Rapporteur, Sir Humphrey Waldock, commented upon the phrase "governed by international law," as follows:

[T]he element of subjection to international law is so essential a part of an international agreement that it should be expressly mentioned in the definition. There may be agreements between States, such as agreements for the acquisition of premises for a diplomatic mission or for some purely commercial transaction, the incidents of which are regulated by the local law of one of the parties or by a private law system determined by reference to conflict of laws principles. Whether in such cases the two States are *internationally* accountable to each other at all may be a nice question; but even if that were held to be so, it would not follow that the basis of their international accountability was a *treaty* obligation. At any rate, the Commission was clear that it ought to confine the notion of an "international agreement" for the purposes of the law of treaties to one the whole formation and execution of which (as well as the *obligation* to execute) is governed by international law.

[1962] II Yb.I.L.C. 32.

The Commission concluded that the element of intention is embraced in the phrase "governed by international law" and therefore it was not necessary to refer to intention in the definition.

2. *Intention to Apply International Law.* How is one to know when international law applies and when it does not? A clear case for the application of international law could be an agreement whose subject-matter entails high politics between states, e.g., a treaty of alliance or cession of territory. In other cases, it has been suggested that "it is in reality the intention of the parties that determines the application of private law or of public international law. In the absence of express stipulation, that intention is to be deduced by methods similar to those employed by the private international lawyer who ascertains the 'proper law' of a contract: it depends on all the material circumstances of the case. Very clear evidence will have to be required before it can be assumed that sovereign states have contracted on the basis of private law * * *. On the other hand, it would probably not be justified to speak of a presumption that public international law applies." Mann, The Law Governing State Contracts, 21 Brit. Y.B.I.L. 11, 28 (1944). Is it possible to draw up a list of "material" circumstances that will suggest that an agreement is governed by international law? Might it be material that an agreement had been concluded by "two organs of government not empowered to conduct foreign relations"?

3. *Non–State Signatories.* Agreements sharing some of the features of those covered by Article 2 of the Vienna Convention are increasingly subscribed by non-state actors, such as insurgent groups or warring factions in internal conflicts. Article 3 of the Convention contemplates the possibility that the rules set forth in the Convention, even if not directly applicable as part of the law of treaties, might nonetheless be relevant (at least by analogy) to agreements with "other subjects of international law." The applicability of this concept to armed opposition groups, indigenous peoples, or secessionist movements needs to be considered with reference to the treatment of subjects of international law in Chapter 5. For analysis of the difficulties in categorizing contemporary peace agreements in view of their hybrid subject-matter and typical mix of state and non-state participants, see Bell, Peace Agreements:

Their Nature and Legal Status, 100 A.J.I.L. 373, 379–87 (2006); see also Bell, On the Law of Peace: Legal Aspects of Peace Agreements (2008).

B. CAPACITY

RESTATEMENT OF THE LAW (THIRD)
THE FOREIGN RELATIONS LAW OF THE
UNITED STATES § 311 (1987)

§ 311 Capacity and Authority to Conclude International Agreements

(1) Every state has capacity to conclude international agreements.

(2) A person is authorized to represent a state for purposes of concluding an international agreement if (a) he produces full powers or (b) such authority clearly appears from the circumstances.

(3) A state may not invoke a violation of its internal law to vitiate its consent to be bound unless the violation was manifest and concerned a rule of fundamental importance.

Source Note:

Subsection (1) follows Article 6 of the Vienna Convention, and Subsections (2) and (3) are adapted from Articles 7(1) and 46 respectively.

NOTES

1. *Component States of Federal Unions.* Many of the most important members of the modern community of nations are federal states; i.e., single international persons made up of entities having some degree of autonomy or sovereignty in domestic affairs. Among these are Australia, Brazil, Canada, Germany, India, Mexico, Russia, Switzerland, and the United States. The question may arise whether a constituent state of such a union, e.g., New York, has the capacity to enter into an agreement with another state. It may safely be assumed, first of all, that the capacity of one constituent state to enter into an agreement with another constituent state belonging to the same federal union is a question solely of the constitutional law of that union. The constituent states of Germany and Switzerland, for example, retain the right to conclude treaties among themselves without the consent of the central government (1 Oppenheim at 176–77), while the states of the United States must receive the approval of Congress before entering into "any Agreement or Compact" (U.S. Const., art. I, § 10). On the other hand, it is not clear whether the capacity of constituent states to enter into agreements with foreign states is regulated only by the union's constitutional law. Where the constituent state is authorized by the union's constitution to enter into agreements with foreign states, does the constituent state on that basis alone have capacity under international law to enter into an agreement? Under what circumstances might the answer to this question be of practical importance? Of what significance would it be that the constitutional law of the

federal union required (as in Germany and the United States) that the federal legislature or executive approve agreements proposed to be concluded between constituent and foreign states, and that this procedure was followed?

It sometimes occurs that not only does the constitutional law of the federal union expressly permit constituent states to enter into agreements with foreign states, but that foreign states also recognize some degree of international legal personality in those states. See Triska & Slusser, The Theory, Law, and Policy of Soviet Treaties 63–64, 158–59, 427 (1962); 1 Whiteman 406–13. But see Dolan, The Member–Republics of the U.S.S.R. as Subjects of the Law of Nations, 4 I.C.L.Q. 629 (1955).

2. *Constitutions of Federal States.* The International Law Commission had proposed that the article on capacity include a second paragraph providing that members of a federal union have treaty-making capacity if and to the extent provided in the federal constitution. France regarded the provision as in accord with existing practice. Strong opposition came from Canada on several grounds, in particular that it could lead to interpretation by international bodies of the constitutions of federal states. In the final stages, the paragraph was deleted. See Kearney & Dalton at 506–08.

3. *Self–Governing Territories.* What is the treaty-making capacity of political entities that have never been states and whose international relations are exercised by a dominant state, but which are more or less self-governing in respect of internal affairs? India, for example, beginning with the Treaty of Versailles in 1919, became a separate party to numerous international agreements, as did many other members of the British Commonwealth. The Philippine Commonwealth, before attaining independence, became a party to international agreements, as did Southern Rhodesia. See Lissitzyn, Territorial Entities Other Than Independent States in the Law of Treaties, 125 Rec. des Cours 5 (1968–III).

Sir Humphrey Waldock concluded that the parties to agreements with the territories do not and cannot "legally look upon the self-governing territory as a distinct juridical person and a responsible party to the treaty entirely separate from the parent State." First Report on the Law of Treaties, [1962] II Yb.I.L.C. 27, 37. Compare the following conclusions.

It may, indeed, be doubted that international law contains any objective criteria of international personality or treaty-making capacity. The very act or practice of entering into international agreements is sometimes the only test that can be applied to determine whether an entity has such personality or capacity, or, indeed, "statehood." * * * Perhaps the only limitation on the possession and exercise of treaty-making capacity by a political subdivision is lack of consent to the exercise of such capacity by the dominant (or "sovereign") entity to which the subdivision is subordinate. Once such consent has been given, the capacity comes into being or is exercised whenever another entity is willing and able to enter into an agreement with the subdivision that is intended to be governed by international law. The very exercise of treaty-making capacity by a subordinate entity endows it with legal personality under international law. It makes little sense, therefore, to make possession of such personality a prerequisite to the conclusion of treaties. * * *

Lissitzyn, Efforts to Codify or Restate the Law of Treaties, 62 Colum. L. Rev. 1166, 1183–84 (1962). What are the essential elements of the process of consent described above?

4. *Law of the Sea Convention.* Article 305 of the 1982 Convention on the Law of the Sea provides that the Convention is open for signature to various entities (other than states) and international organizations, provided that they have competence over matters governed by the Convention and to enter treaties in respect of these matters. Articles 306 and 307 provide that the entities referred to in Article 305 may ratify or accede to the convention in the same way as states. Do the foregoing provisions alter Waldock's conclusion that the parties to the treaty cannot "legally look upon the self-governing territory as a distinct juridical person and a responsible party to the treaty entirely separate from the parent state"?

5. *World Trade Organization.* The arrangements for the General Agreement on Tariffs and Trade (1947, 1994) and the World Trade Organization allow accession by a "separate customs territory possessing full autonomy in the conduct of its external commercial relations and of the other matters provided for" in the agreements. On this basis, Hong Kong and Macao became parties in their own names while under the colonial administration of the United Kingdom and Portugal respectively. They remained parties even after their colonial status ended and they became formally part of the People's Republic of China, which was not at the time a GATT contracting party or W.T.O. member. In December 2001, China joined the W.T.O. and on January 1, 2002 Taiwan also joined as a "separate customs territory" under the name of "Chinese Taipei." To what extent are these arrangements for Hong Kong, Macao, and Taiwan unique to their particular circumstances, and to what extent do they reflect general considerations of treaty-making capacity under customary international law? See Sun, International Legal Personality of the Hong Kong Special Administrative Region, 7 Chinese J. Int'l L. 339 (2008).

6. *Geneva Conventions and Protocols; Non–State Actors.* The four Geneva Conventions of 1949 on the law of armed conflict (and the 1977 Additional Protocols thereto, excerpted in the Documents Supplement), are open for adherence by "Powers," understood as states. In denying the applicability of the Geneva Conventions to the global struggle with Al Qaeda following September 11, 2001, the U.S. government asserted that since Al Qaeda was not a state and had not accepted to be governed by the rules set forth in these treaties, its affiliates could not invoke their protections. The Supreme Court later rejected this position and found that at a minimum, Article 3 common to the Geneva Conventions does apply to the conflict with Al Qaeda. *Hamdan v. Rumsfeld*, 548 U.S. 557, 630–31 (2006). What mechanisms are available under international humanitarian law for "Parties to the conflict" (who may or may not be states parties to the treaties) to agree to comply with substantive norms specified in the treaty? See Chapter 15.

C. EXPRESSION OF CONSENT TO BE BOUND

1. Full Powers; Inherent Capacity or Apparent Authority

SINCLAIR, THE VIENNA CONVENTION ON THE LAW OF TREATIES

29–33 (2d ed. 1984) (footnotes omitted)

The first stage in the treaty-making process is to establish the authority of the representatives of the negotiating State or States concerned to perform the necessary formal acts involved in the drawing up of the text of a treaty or in the conclusion of a treaty. This authority is in principle determined by the issuance of a formal document entitled a "full power" which designates a named individual or individuals to represent the State for the purpose of negotiating and concluding a treaty. * * *

Article 7 of the Vienna Convention * * * sets out the general rule that a person is considered as representing a State for the purpose of adopting or authenticating the text of a treaty or for the purpose of expressing the consent of the State to be bound by a treaty if:

(a) he produces full powers; or

(b) it appears from the practice of the States concerned or from other circumstances that their intention was to consider that person as representing the State for such purposes and to dispense with full powers.

Thus the general rule is expressed in suitably flexible terms. Subparagraph (b) is intended to preserve the modern practice of States to dispense with full powers in the case of agreements in simplified form.

* * * Implicitly the Commission recognized that the non-production of full powers might involve a certain risk for one or other of the States concerned, in the sense that it might be subsequently claimed that an act relating to the conclusion of a treaty had been performed without authority. Partly to guard against this risk and also to respect accepted international practice, paragraph 2 of Article 7 of the Convention establishes that, "in virtue of their functions and without having to produce full powers", Heads of State, Heads of Government and Ministers for Foreign Affairs are considered as representing their State for the purpose of all acts relating to the conclusion of a treaty. Heads of diplomatic missions are likewise considered as representing their State *ex officio* and without the need to produce full powers, but only for the purpose of adopting the text of a treaty between the accrediting State and the State to which they are accredited. Finally, representatives accredited by States to an international conference or to an international organisation or one of its organs enjoy similar powers, but only for the purpose of adopting the text of a treaty in that conference, organisation or organ. * * *

An interesting point which was raised at the conference is the relationship between this rule about inherent capacity to perform certain acts relating to the conclusion of treaties and the rule set out in Article 46 of the Convention concerning the violation of provisions of internal law regarding competence to conclude treaties. It will be recalled that Article 46 establishes the principle that a State may not invoke the fact that its consent to be bound by a treaty has been expressed in violation of a provision of its internal law regarding competence to conclude treaties unless that violation was manifest and concerned a rule of its internal law of fundamental importance. The question is: does paragraph 2 of Article 7 raise an incontestable presumption as a matter of international law that the designated office-holders are *ex officio* entitled to perform the specified acts without the need to produce full powers notwithstanding that, as a matter of internal law, they are not empowered to do so? It would seem that the presumption is incontestable. * * *

NOTES

1. *Apparent Authority.* Is a state bound by apparent authority to conclude agreements? Two decisions of the Permanent Court of International Justice indicate that a state is bound when it is not evident to the other party that the official acting for the state has exceeded his authority. See *Legal Status of Eastern Greenland*, 1933 P.C.I.J. (ser. A/B) No. 53, at 71, in Chapter 4 below; *Free Zones Case*, 1932 P.C.I.J. (ser. A/B) No. 46. See also discussion in Section 5.B below relating to invalidity under Article 46 of the Vienna Convention.

2. *Authority of Heads of State and Government and Foreign Ministers.* Recall the treatment in the *Qatar–Bahrain Maritime Delimitation Case*, above, of the authority of the foreign ministers of Bahrain and Qatar to commit their states without going through the approval procedures said to be required by their respective constitutions. Do the provisions of Article 7(2)(a) shed light on this problem? See also Article 46, Section 5.B below.

2. Methods of Expressing Consent

Articles 11 to 17 of the Convention deal with the ways in which states express their consent to be bound by a treaty. Article 11 lists the various means of expressing consent as signature, exchange of instruments constituting a treaty, ratification, acceptance, approval or accession. It adds to this list "any other means if so agreed," which could include unsigned *notes verbales*.

It is important to clarify that "signature" under some circumstances (those set forth in Article 12) can express consent to be bound, but in other circumstances (see Article 14) requires confirmation through a step called ratification. The word "ratification" as used here and throughout the Convention refers only to ratification on the international plane. It is distinct and separate from the procedural act of "ratification" under municipal law such as parliamentary ratification or approval. "Accession"

(Article 15) is the method by which a state becomes party to a treaty which it has not signed. Party status lists for treaties will sometimes use the abbreviations "S," "R," or "A" to indicate whether a state has signed (but not ratified), ratified, or acceded to a treaty.

NOTES

1. *Entry into Force after Ratifications.* A common provision for multilateral agreements is: "This treaty shall come into force upon the receipt by the depositary of instruments of ratification of [a specified number of] states." A variation is found in the Rome Statute of the International Criminal Court (see Documents Supplement), which provides in Article 126 that the treaty "shall enter into force on the first day of the month after the 60th day following the date of the deposit of the 60th instrument of ratification." The 60th instrument of ratification was deposited with the U.N. Secretary–General on April 11, 2002, and the Rome Statute accordingly entered into force on July 1, 2002. See also note 3 below and Chapter 16.

2. *Depositary Functions.* The U.N. Secretary–General serves as depositary for many multilateral treaties. Treaty actions for such treaties are recorded in Multilateral Treaties Deposited with the Secretary–General, Status as at 31 December [year] (annual publication, most recently issued in 2006), U.N. Doc. ST/LEG/SER.E/[number] (most recently numbered 25) and made available online at the U.N. Treaty Collection website, http://treaties.un.org. See Summary of Practice of the Secretary–General as Depositary of Multilateral Treaties, U.N. Doc. ST/LEG/7/Rev. 1 (1999)). Other international or regional organizations can likewise be designated to perform depositary functions for treaties falling within their terms of reference. Sometimes the depositary is a specified state or states: the Nuclear Non–Proliferation Treaty, for example, specifies the United Kingdom, United States, and U.S.S.R. as its depositaries. For illustrations of policy questions in connection with depositary functions, see Kohona, Some Notable Developments in the Practice of the UN Secretary–General as Depositary of Multilateral Treaties: Reservations and Declarations, 99 A.J.I.L. 433 (2005).

3. *Signing and "Unsigning": The Rome Statute of the I.C.C.* The Statute of the International Criminal Court, approved at a diplomatic conference in Rome in July 1998, was open for signature pursuant to its Article 125(1) between July 17, 1998 and December 31, 2000. 2187 U.N.T.S. 3. (See Documents Supplement.) On December 31, 2000, the United States signed the treaty, but President Bill Clinton issued a statement that "I will not, and do not recommend that my successor, submit the treaty to the Senate for advice and consent until our fundamental concerns are satisfied." (On the nature of those concerns, see Chapter 16.)

On May 6, 2002, shortly before the Rome Statute was to enter into force (see note 1 above), the administration of President George W. Bush sent the following letter to the U.N. Secretary–General:

> This is to inform you, in connection with the Rome Statute of the International Criminal Court adopted on July 17, 1998, that the United States does not intend to become a party to the treaty. Accordingly, the

United States has no legal obligations arising from its signature on December 31, 2000. The United States requests that its intention not to become a party, as expressed in this letter, be reflected in the depositary's status lists relating to this treaty.

The document was circulated by the depositary to all signatories of the Rome Statute, and a footnote to the U.S. signature date on the U.N. treaty website records the U.S. notice. See Murphy, Contemporary Practice of the United States, 96 A.J.I.L. 724 (2002).

What factors (political or legal) might have motivated the United States to sign the treaty at a time when the outgoing administration was not prepared to recommend that the Senate approve it? Would there have been any disadvantages to refraining from signature while attempting to resolve the "fundamental concerns" at issue, with the possibility of becoming party by accession at a subsequent date? Compare Article 125(2) of the Rome Statute, which provides the procedure for ratification, acceptance or approval by signatory states (i.e., those that signed prior to December 31, 2000), and Article 125(3), which provides for accession by any state (including those that had not signed); please also examine those provisions with reference to Articles 14–15 of the Vienna Convention. On the import of the U.S. statement that it "has no legal obligations arising from its signature," see note 4 on p. 140. See also, Swaine, Unsigning, 55 Stan.L.Rev. 2061 (2003).

D. OBLIGATION NOT TO DEFEAT THE OBJECT OF A TREATY

What are the obligations of a state which has signed a treaty subject to ratification but which has not yet ratified the treaty? The Permanent Court of International Justice appears to have taken the position that, if ratification takes place, a signatory state's misuse of its rights prior to ratification may amount to a violation of its treaty obligations. *Case of Certain German Settlers in Polish Upper Silesia,* 1926 P.C.I.J. (ser. A) No. 7, at 30. The International Law Commission considered that this obligation begins when a state agrees to enter into negotiations for the conclusion of a treaty. *A fortiori,* it would attach also to a state which has actually ratified, acceded, or accepted a treaty if there is an interval before the treaty enters into force.

At the Conference, the Commission proposal was criticized for imposing a duty on states which had undertaken to negotiate. It was acknowledged that this was not an existing rule. Moreover, it was suggested that the object of a treaty could not easily be determined when it was still in negotiation. States might be discouraged from entering negotiations if they were then under a vague obligation. The proposal relating to negotiations was then defeated. See Vienna Convention Article 18 for the final formulation.

Whether Article 18 as it now stands is declaratory of prior customary law has given rise to debate. There is some authority for that conclusion (see McNair, The Law of Treaties 199, 204 (1961)), but the matter is not free from doubt. It may be expected, nonetheless, that Article 18 will be invoked from time to time against states which have signed but not ratified and against states which have consented to be bound in the interval prior to entry into force. It should be noted that the two paragraphs have limitations. Where the state has not yet consented to be bound, the obligation continues "until it has made its intention clear not to become a party to the treaty." In the case of a state which has consented to be bound but the treaty has not yet entered into force, the obligation is made conditional on the absence of undue delay in entry into force.

NOTES

1. *"Object and Purpose."* How easy is it to determine either the "object and purpose" of a treaty or actions that would "defeat" it in the sense of Article 18? We will encounter other issues concerning "object and purpose" in connection with permissibility of reservations (Article 19(c)), interpretation (Article 31), and breach (Article 60(3)(b)). See Sections 3, 4.B, and 6.C.

2. *Arms Control Treaties.* The United States and the former U.S.S.R. signed the Strategic Arms Limitation Treaty II in 1979 but did not ratify it. Each accused the other from time to time of violating terms of the unratified treaty which imposed limits on the number of missiles. In April 1986, the President ordered the elimination of two nuclear submarines in order to keep within the terms of the unratified treaty. Is the principle of Article 18 applicable to such actions or are they motivated by a mutual intent to comply with the treaty even if it has not entered into force legally? Would a failure to dismantle a missile scheduled to be eliminated defeat the object of the treaty if it could later be dismantled?

Consider Restatement (Third) § 312, Comment *i*:

> *Obligations prior to entry into force.* Under Subsection (3) [based on Vienna Convention Article 18], a state that has signed an agreement is obligated to refrain from acts that would defeat the object and purpose of the agreement. It is often unclear what actions would have such effect. The application of that principle has raised issues with regard to the Second Strategic Arms Limitation Treaty signed in 1979 but not ratified. Testing a weapon in contravention of a clause prohibiting such a test might violate the purpose of the agreement, since the consequences of the test might be irreversible. Failing to dismantle a weapon scheduled to be dismantled under the treaty might not defeat its object, since the dismantling could be effected later. The obligation under Subsection (3) continues until the state has made clear its intention not to become a party or if it appears that entry into force will be unduly delayed.

3. *Temporal Dimension.* When is the obligation expressed in Article 18 extinguished? The Comprehensive Test Ban Treaty (CTBT), Sept. 24, 1996, U.N. Doc. A/50/1027, was opened for signature in 1996 subject to ratification, and requires ratification on the part of forty-four specified states before it will enter into force. In 1999, the U.S. Senate took a vote on a resolution of advice and consent to the CTBT, but the constitutionally required two-thirds majori-

ty was not obtained. The United States has not evidently "made its intention clear not to become party to the treaty" within the meaning of Article 18(a); indeed, President Clinton and other leaders indicated that the treaty might be brought to the Senate again at a more propitious time. (There is no constitutional prohibition on requesting another vote after political conditions have changed.) As of 2009, the CTBT remains on the treaty calendar of the Senate Foreign Relations Committee; through the end of the Bush administration it was categorized as a treaty on which the Executive Branch "does not support Senate action at this time." See Treaty Priority List (2007) excerpted in Crook, Contemporary Practice of the United States, 101 A.J.I.L. 869, 872–73 (2007).

In the case of a state that had duly ratified the CTBT, would an indefinite delay in obtaining the specified forty-four ratifications required for entry into force (e.g., because of non-ratification on the part of the United States) relieve that state eventually of its Article 18 obligation?

The docket of treaties pending with the U.S. Senate in 2007–2008 included dozens of treaties transmitted by successive administrations over many years but not yet acted upon. The oldest of approximately forty previously-submitted treaties identified on the 2007 Treaty Priority List (a convention on freedom of association prepared by the International Labor Organization) had been submitted by the Truman Administration in 1949. For more on the role of the Senate and possible explanations for difficulties in securing its advice and consent, see Chapter 10 on U.S. practice concerning international agreements.

4. *"Unsigning" the Rome Statute.* Recall the U.S. actions to sign and "unsign" the Rome Statute for the International Criminal Court on December 31, 2000 and May 6, 2002 (pp. 137–38, note 3 above). In light of Article 18 of the Vienna Convention, what obligations might have applied to the United States during the period it was in signatory status? Was an instrument with the formality of the May 6, 2002 letter the proper way to extinguish any such obligations? On this episode at the intersection of international and domestic law and politics, see Bradley, Unratified Treaties, Domestic Politics, and the U.S. Constitution, 48 Harv. Int'l L. J. 307 (2007).

SECTION 3. RESERVATIONS

A. WHAT IS A RESERVATION?

A reservation is "a unilateral statement, however phrased or named, made by a State, when signing, ratifying, accepting, approving or acceding to a treaty, whereby it purports to exclude or to modify the legal effect of certain provisions of the treaty in their application to that State." Article 2(1)(d). In the context of bilateral agreements, a reservation is closely analogous to a counter-offer by the reserving state, and the legal situation is clear, whether the reservation is accepted or rejected by the other state. The most difficult problems concerning reservations, however, have arisen when one or more parties to a multilateral treaty attempts to become a party subject to one or more reservations, which may or may not elicit objections.

NOTES

1. *Reservations versus Interpretive Statements.* The International Law Commission, in its commentary on Article 2(d), noted that "States not infrequently make declarations as to their understanding of some matter or as to their interpretation of a particular provision. Such a declaration may be a mere clarification of the State's position or it may amount to a reservation, according as it does or does not vary or exclude the application of the terms of the treaty as adopted." [1966] II Yb.I.L.C. 189–90.

2. *Positions of Other Parties.* Suppose a state attaches an "interpretative statement" to its ratification which by its terms indicates that the state will become a party only if that interpretation is accepted. If the interpretation appears inconsistent with the treaty provisions, do other parties have to consider it to be a reservation and to reject it if they disagree? See Bowett, Reservations to Non–Restricted Multilateral Treaties, 48 Brit. Y.B.I.L. 69 (1976–77).

3. *Procedure.* Is a state obliged to include declarations of understanding in its instrument of ratification? Strictly speaking there is no such requirement since the other party or parties need not accept understandings that are not reservations. However, states often communicate such interpretive understandings to make their position clear. For bilateral treaties, the United States does this as a rule in a protocol of exchange of instruments of ratification. See Restatement (Third) § 314, Reporters' Note 1.

4. *"Reservation" Addressed to Domestic Implementation.* The United States and Canada concluded a treaty concerning the Niagara River which provided for the allocation of hydroelectric power. The U.S. Senate in its resolution of advice and consent included a "reservation" that the United States reserves the right to provide by legislation for the use of the U.S. share of electric power and that no project for the use of that share should be undertaken until specifically authorized by Congress. Canada did not express any objection to the reservation, saying it was none of its concern. The N.Y. Power Authority requested a license for a project to use the U.S. share of the power, but the Federal Power Commission found that Congress had not legislated and therefore the project was contrary to the reservation incorporated into the treaty. See *Power Auth. of N.Y. v. Federal Power Comm'n*, 247 F.2d 538 (D.C.Cir. 1957), vacated as moot, 355 U.S. 64 (1957). For critical comment, see Henkin, The Treaty Makers and the Law Makers: The Niagara Power Reservation, 56 Colum. L. Rev. 1151 (1956); see also Henkin, Foreign Affairs and the U.S. Constitution 451–52 (2d ed. 1996).

5. *Rome Statute.* In ratifying the Rome Statute of the International Criminal Court in 2000, France attached a statement to the effect that the treaty had no application to nuclear weapons. Was this statement a "reservation"?

B. IMPORTANCE OF RESERVATIONS

How important are reservations in the overall treaty relations among states? One statistical survey found, surprisingly, that 85% of the 1164 multilateral conventions that entered into force between 1919 and 1971 had no reservations at all. Even fewer reservations were found in the conventions (839) that were limited to certain states because of subject or geography; 92% had no reservations. Gamble, Reservations to Multilateral Treaties: A Macroscopic View of State Practice, 74 A.J.I.L. 372, 379 (1980). Most reservations did not deal with the substantive provisions of the treaties. They related to dispute settlement, nonrecognition of other parties, compatibility with specific domestic laws, and colonial territories. Of the substantive reservations, the greater number were adjudged to be minor.

Although reservations are relatively infrequent to treaties generally, reservations may be significant in enabling states to join certain kinds of multilateral treaties, especially human rights treaties. Many states have conditioned their ratifications of human rights treaties with reservations of highly substantive character. Some such reservations are addressed to specific and/or minor provisions of the treaties, but some (formulated more broadly) appear to go to the very heart of the treaty and raise questions about whether the reserving state intends in good faith to accept any international obligations at all.

Examples of apparently general reservations are those that qualify the state's treaty commitment by reference to its own domestic law, as the United States did in its ratification of the Genocide Convention with the following reservation:

> That nothing in the Convention requires or authorizes legislation or other action by the United States of America prohibited by the Constitution of the United States as interpreted by the United States.

A number of states registered objections to this U.S. reservation as incompatible with the object and purpose of the Genocide Convention, as vague, and as an improper attempt to circumvent the requirement of the law of treaties (see p. 163 below) that internal law may not be invoked to justify non-performance of a treaty obligation. Yet none of these states objected to the entry into force of the Genocide Convention for the United States or said that they would not consider the United States a party to the treaty.

Another common type of reservation to human rights treaties is a qualification in terms of principles of Islamic law or the Islamic Shari'a. Many Islamic countries have entered such reservations, either in general terms or in respect of specific provisions, when ratifying treaties such as the International Covenants or the Convention on the Elimination of Discrimination Against Women (CEDAW) Dec. 18, 1979, 1249 U.N.T.S. 13. Examples include:

- The Government of the Republic of Maldives will comply with the provisions of the Convention, except those which the Government may consider contrary to the principles of the Islamic Sharia upon which the laws and traditions of the Maldives are founded.

- The Arab Republic of Egypt is willing to comply with the content of this article [Article 2 of CEDAW], provided that such compliance does not run counter to the Islamic Sharia.

- It is clear that the child's acquisition of his father's nationality is the procedure most suitable for the child and that this does not infringe upon the principle of equality since it is customary for a woman to agree that the children shall be of the father's nationality. [Egypt's reservation to Article 9 of CEDAW]

- The Hashemite Kingdom of Jordan hereby registers its reservation and does not consider itself bound by the provisions of Article 9, paragraph 2, article 15 paragraph 4 (a woman's residence and domicile are with her husband).

For discussion of these and other examples, see Chinkin, Reservations and Objections to CEDAW, in Chinkin et al., Human Rights as General Norms and a State's Right to Opt Out: Reservations and Objections to Human Rights Conventions 64–84 (Gardner ed. 1997); Schabas, Reservations to CEDAW and the Convention on the Rights of the Child, 3 Wm. & Mary J. of Women & L. 79 (1997); Sucharipa–Behrmann, The Legal Effects of Reservations to Multilateral Treaties, 1 Austrian Rev. Int'l & Eur. L. 67, 81 (1996); Cook, Reservations to CEDAW, 30 Va. J. Int'l L. 643 (1990).

Such reservations have elicited some formal objections from states parties, as well as intense criticism from human rights groups and women's advocacy organizations. Yet the substantive import of such reservations is far from clear, since Islamic authorities have diverse views on the implications of Islamic law for particular human rights norms, especially those regarding women. It is also unclear whether such reservations are incompatible with the object and purpose of the treaty in question, and what is the status of treaty relations as between reserving and objecting states, where those states hold different views on validity of the reservation.

The materials that follow aim to shed light on the legal effects of such reservations, with or without objections from other states.

C. PERMISSIBILITY OF RESERVATIONS; OBJECTIONS

RESERVATIONS TO THE CONVENTION ON GENOCIDE

International Court of Justice, Advisory Opinion, 1951
1951 I.C.J. 15

[After a dispute had arisen concerning the legal effect of reservations made by several states to the Genocide Convention of 1948 (78 U.N.T.S.

277), the General Assembly adopted a resolution on November 16, 1950, G.A. Res. 478 (V) (Nov. 16, 1950), asking the International Court of Justice for an advisory opinion on the questions, *inter alia:*

[In so far as concerns the Convention on the Prevention and Punishment of the Crime of Genocide in the event of a State ratifying or acceding to the Convention subject to a reservation made either on ratification or on accession, or on signature followed by ratification:

    I. Can the reserving State be regarded as being a party to the Convention while still maintaining its reservation, if the reservation is objected to by one or more of the parties to the Convention but not by others?

    II. If the answer to Question I is in the affirmative, what is the effect of the reservation as between the reserving State and:

(a) The parties which object to the reservation?

(b) Those which accept it?

In answering these questions, the Court stated:]

It is well established that in its treaty relations a State cannot be bound without its consent, and that consequently no reservation can be effective against any State without its agreement thereto. It is also a generally recognized principle that a multilateral convention is the result of an agreement freely concluded upon its clauses and that consequently none of the contracting parties is entitled to frustrate or impair, by means of unilateral decisions or particular agreements, the purpose and *raison d'être* of the convention. To this principle was linked the notion of the integrity of the convention as adopted, a notion which in its traditional concept involved the proposition that no reservation was valid unless it was accepted by all the contracting parties without exception, as would have been the case if it had been stated during the negotiations.

This concept, which is directly inspired by the notion of contract, is of undisputed value as a principle. However, as regards the Genocide Convention, it is proper to refer to a variety of circumstances which would lead to a more flexible application of this principle. Among these circumstances may be noted the clearly universal character of the United Nations under whose auspices the Convention was concluded, and the very wide degree of participation envisaged by Article XI of the Convention. Extensive participation in conventions of this type has already given rise to greater flexibility in the international practice concerning multilateral conventions. More general resort to reservations, very great allowance made for tacit assent to reservations, the existence of practices which go so far as to admit that the author of reservations which have been rejected by certain contracting parties is nevertheless to be regarded as a party to the convention in relation to those contracting parties that have accepted the reservations—all these factors are manifestations of a new need for flexibility in the operation of multilateral conventions.

It must also be pointed out that although the Genocide Convention was finally approved unanimously, it is nevertheless the result of a series of majority votes. The majority principle, while facilitating the conclusion of multilateral conventions, may also make it necessary for certain States to make reservations. This observation is confirmed by the great number of reservations which have been made of recent years to multilateral conventions.

* * *

The Court * * * must now determine what kind of reservations may be made and what kind of objections may be taken to them.

The solution of these problems must be found in the special characteristics of the Genocide Convention. * * * The Genocide Convention was * * * intended by the General Assembly and by the contracting parties to be definitely universal in scope. It was in fact approved on December 9th, 1948, by a resolution which was unanimously adopted by fifty-six States.

The objects of such a convention must also be considered. The Convention was manifestly adopted for a purely humanitarian and civilizing purpose. It is indeed difficult to imagine a convention that might have this dual character to a greater degree, since its object on the one hand is to safeguard the very existence of certain human groups and on the other to confirm and endorse the most elementary principles of morality. In such a convention the contracting States do not have any interests of their own; they merely have, one and all, a common interest, namely, the accomplishment of those high purposes which are the *raison d'être* of the convention. Consequently, in a convention of this type one cannot speak of individual advantages or disadvantages to States, or of the maintenance of a perfect contractual balance between rights and duties. The high ideals which inspired the Convention provide, by virtue of the common will of the parties, the foundation and measure of all its provisions.

* * *

The object and purpose of the Genocide Convention imply that it was the intention of the General Assembly and of the States which adopted it that as many States as possible should participate. The complete exclusion from the Convention of one or more States would not only restrict the scope of its application, but would detract from the authority of the moral and humanitarian principles which are its basis. It is inconceivable that the contracting parties readily contemplated that an objection to a minor reservation should produce such a result. But even less could the contracting parties have intended to sacrifice the very object of the Convention in favour of a vain desire to secure as many participants as possible. The object and purpose of the Convention thus limit both the freedom of making reservations and that of objecting to them. It follows that it is the compatibility of a reservation with the object and purpose of the Convention that must furnish the criterion for the attitude of a State in making the reservation on accession as well as for the appraisal by a State in objecting to the reservation.

Any other view would lead either to the acceptance of reservations which frustrate the purposes which the General Assembly and the contracting parties had in mind, or to recognition that the parties to the Convention have the power of excluding from it the author of a reservation, even a minor one, which may be quite compatible with those purposes.

It has nevertheless been argued that any State entitled to become a party to the Genocide Convention may do so while making any reservation it chooses by virtue of its sovereignty. The Court cannot share this view. It is obvious that so extreme an application of the idea of State sovereignty could lead to a complete disregard of the object and purpose of the Convention.

On the other hand, it has been argued that there exists a rule of international law subjecting the effect of a reservation to the express or tacit assent of all the contracting parties. This theory rests essentially on a contractual conception of the absolute integrity of the convention as adopted. This view, however, cannot prevail if, having regard to the character of the convention, its purpose and its mode of adoption, it can be established that the parties intended to derogate from that rule by admitting the faculty to make reservations thereto.

It does not appear, moreover, that the conception of the absolute integrity of a convention has been transformed into a rule of international law. The considerable part which tacit assent has always played in estimating the effect which is to be given to reservations scarcely permits one to state that such a rule exists, determining with sufficient precision the effect of objections made to reservations. In fact, the examples of objections made to reservations appear to be too rare in international practice to have given rise to such a rule. * * *

* * *

It results from the foregoing considerations that Question I, on account of its abstract character, cannot be given an absolute answer. The appraisal of a reservation and the effect of objections that might be made to it depend upon the particular circumstances of each individual case.

Having replied to Question I, the Court will now examine Question II * * *.

[E]ach State which is a party to the Convention is entitled to appraise the validity of the reservation, and it exercises this right individually and from its own standpoint. As no State can be bound by a reservation to which it has not consented, it necessarily follows that each State objecting to it will or will not, on the basis of its individual appraisal within the limits of the criterion of the object and purpose stated above, consider the reserving State to be a party to the Convention. * * *

The disadvantages which result from this possible divergence of views—which an article concerning the making of reservations could have obviated—are real; they are mitigated by the common duty of the contracting States to be guided in their judgment by the compatibility or incompatibility of the reservation with the object and purpose of the Convention. It must clearly be assumed that the contracting States are desirous of preserving intact at least what is essential to the object of the Convention; should this desire be absent, it is quite clear that the Convention itself would be impaired both in its principle and in its application.

It may be that the divergence of views between parties as to the admissibility of a reservation will not in fact have any consequences. On the other hand, it may be that certain parties who consider that the assent given by other parties to a reservation is incompatible with the purpose of the Convention, will decide to adopt a position on the jurisdictional plane in respect of this divergence and to settle the dispute which thus arises either by special agreement or by the procedure laid down in Article IX of the Convention.

Finally, it may be that a State, whilst not claiming that a reservation is incompatible with the object and purpose of the Convention, will nevertheless object to it, but that an understanding between that State and the reserving State will have the effect that the Convention will enter into force between them, except for the clauses affected by the reservation.

Such being the situation, the task of the Secretary–General would be simplified and would be confined to receiving reservations and objections and notifying them.

* * *

For these reasons,

THE COURT IS OF OPINION,

In so far as concerns the Convention on the Prevention and Punishment of the Crime of Genocide, in the event of a State ratifying or acceding to the Convention subject to a reservation made either on ratification or on accession, or on signature followed by ratification,

On Question I:

by seven votes to five,

that a State which has made and maintained a reservation which has been objected to by one or more of the parties to the Convention but not by others, can be regarded as being a party to the Convention, if the reservation is compatible with the object and purpose of the Convention; otherwise, that State cannot be regarded as being a party to the Convention.

On Question II:

by seven votes to five,

(a) that if a party to the Convention objects to a reservation which it considers to be incompatible with the object and purpose of the Convention, it can in fact consider that the reserving State is not a party to the Convention;

(b) that if, on the other hand, a party accepts the reservation as being compatible with the object and purpose of the Convention, it can in fact consider that the reserving State is a party to the Convention * * *.

NOTES

1. *Dissenting Opinion.* Vice President Guerrero, and McNair, Read, and Hsu Mo, JJ., joined in a dissenting opinion which argued that Question I should have been answered in the negative; i.e., that if a party to the Convention objected to a reservation made by another state, the reserving state could not be considered a party to the Convention. The dissenters also criticized the Court's distinction between "compatible" and "incompatible" reservations on the grounds that it represented an innovation in the law of treaties and that the subjective nature of the distinction made it unworkable. The joint dissenting opinion concluded that "the integrity of the terms of the Convention [was] of greater importance than mere universality in its acceptance," and expressed skepticism that the effect of the majority opinion could be limited to the Genocide Convention, as opposed to "humanitarian" conventions generally. Id. at 46, 47.

2. *Governmental Reaction.* The Advisory Opinion on Reservations to the Genocide Convention was widely endorsed by governments. It gave impetus to the adoption of the flexible system for reservations to multilateral conventions adopted in the Vienna Convention, in particular Article 20(4). The Court's opinion also emphasized the legislative character of many new multilateral conventions and especially those intended to benefit individuals. In these cases, it was deemed desirable to encourage the widest participation and therefore to allow states to participate even though they were not prepared to accept every provision. See Restatement (Third) § 313, Reporters' Note 1.

3. *Limits on Permissibility of Reservations.* At the same time, both the Advisory Opinion and the Vienna Convention set limits to the permissibility of reservations. In particular, a reservation could not be accepted if it was incompatible with the object and purpose of the Convention. See Article 19 of the Vienna Convention. But query whether this test of permissibility can be maintained in the absence of an authoritative means of determining whether the reservation is compatible with object and purpose? If each state is free to make that determination, and there is no agreed means of compulsory judicial settlement or collective decision procedure, does not the test of impermissibility lose its practical significance? Judge Ruda believes it does. See Ruda, Reservations to Multilateral Conventions, 146 Rec. des Cours 95, 190 (1975–III). Bowett in contrast lays stress on the requirement of permissibility as a matter of treaty interpretation that is not dependent on the reactions of the states parties. See his comments below. Whether this is meaningful in practice would seem to depend on the readiness of states to have recourse to the Court or to other third party determinations to settle differences of views

as to compatibility. States' reluctant attitudes in this regard are brought out in their practice concerning reservations to human rights treaties, discussed further below.

4. *Possible Regimes.* The I.C.J. Advisory Opinion highlights the character and object of the Genocide Convention. By implication it suggests that some multilateral conventions should have a different regime for reservations. What other regimes are possible? Consider the following:

(1) the "classical rule" requiring consent of every contracting state;

(2) the exclusion of all reservations;

(3) the acceptance of reservations by a decision of a collective body or by the approval of a qualified majority of parties;

(4) the rejection of reservations if a qualified majority (e.g., two thirds) of the parties object to it;

Does the Vienna Convention allow for these alternative regimes? Does it require any of them in particular treaties?

5. *Types of Treaties Requiring Uniform Application.* Can one identify certain multilateral conventions which by their character and purpose require that the treaty be applied in its entirety by all parties? See Article 20(2) of the Vienna Convention. Should this hold true only for treaties with a small number of parties? Would it apply to an arms control treaty? Is it especially applicable to economic integration treaties such as the treaties establishing common markets? See Ruda, *supra*, at 186.

6. *Constitutions of International Organizations.* Reservations have been made on several occasions by states adhering to treaties that were constituent instruments of international organizations. In all these cases the practice has been to refer the reservation to the body of the organization in question. The Vienna Convention now expresses this as a rule unless the treaty provides otherwise. For prior debate, see Schachter, The Question of Treaty Reservation at the 1959 General Assembly, 54 A.J.I.L. 372 (1960).

7 *Human Rights Treaties.* Reservations are most commonly made to multilateral treaties on human rights. Is a permissive flexible system desirable in these cases? See the further readings concerning reservations to human rights treaties below. Is it desirable to exclude incompatible reservations to human rights treaties by providing for the rejection of reservations if two thirds of the contracting states object to the reservation? A clause to this effect is included in the U.N. Convention on the Elimination of All Forms of Racial Discrimination, Mar. 7, 1966, 660 U.N.T.S. 195, Article 20(2).

8. *Reservations to Genocide Convention Revisited.* The principal case was an advisory opinion under Article 65 to the I.C.J. Statute, rather than a dispute between states. Recently the I.C.J. has revisited the issue in the context of contentious cases. For example, in a series of cases that Yugoslavia (Serbia) sought to bring against NATO states for their military intervention in Kosovo, the Court's judgments treated reservations to the Genocide Convention's dispute settlement article as legally effective to bar unilateral applications against non-consenting states. See *Legality of Use of Force* (Yugoslavia v. United States), 1999 I.C.J. 916; see also Chapter 9.

The Democratic Republic of the Congo invoked the Genocide Convention in an application against Rwanda, despite the latter's having registered the same type of reservation to the dispute settlement article of the Convention on which the I.C.J. had opined in 1951. In upholding Rwanda's jurisdictional objection, the Court maintained its views expressed in 1951 concerning the possibility of reservations to the Convention, as well as its consistent jurisprudence on the consensual nature of its own jurisdiction, and observed that Congo had not objected to Rwanda's reservation when it was made. *Armed Activities on the Territory of the Congo* (New Application: 2002) (Dem. Rep. Congo v. Rwanda), Jurisdiction and Admissibility, 2006 I.C.J. 27, paras. 66–68. In a separate opinion, Judges Higgins, Kooijmans, Elaraby, Owada, and Simma wrote (para. 29) that it is "not self-evident that a reservation to Article IX could not be regarded as incompatible with the object and purpose of the Convention and * * * this is a matter that the Court should revisit for further consideration."

D. EXCLUSION OF RESERVATIONS

Are there reasons why some general multilateral conventions of a "legislative" character should not allow any reservations at all, irrespective of compatibility? Consider the reservations clause and the accompanying clause on declarations included in the 1982 U.N. Convention on the Law of the Sea:

Article 309

No reservations or exceptions may be made to this Convention unless expressly permitted by other articles of this Convention.

Article 310

Article 309 does not preclude a State, when signing, ratifying or acceding to this Convention, from making declarations or statements, however phrased or named, with a view, *inter alia*, to the harmonization of its laws and regulations with the provisions of this Convention, provided that such declarations or statements do not purport to exclude or to modify the legal effect of the provisions of this Convention in their application to that State.

NOTES

1. *"Package Deal" on Law of the Sea.* Why have reservations to the Law of the Sea Convention generally been prohibited? Is the element of complete reciprocity more important in this case than in other multilateral legislative treaties? Will it result in the nonparticipation of states that object only to one or two provisions? A Report of the U.S. delegation in 1980 said:

> Since the Convention is an overall "package deal" reflecting different priorities of different states, to permit reservations would inevitably permit one State to eliminate the "quid" of another State's "quo". Thus there was general agreement in the Conference that in principle reservations could not be permitted.

Reports of the United States Delegation to the Third United Nations Conference on the Law of the Sea 83 (Nordquist & Park eds. 1983).

In supporting Senatorial advice and consent to ratification (not yet secured as of early 2009), the U.S. Executive Branch has proposed a detailed set of interpretive understandings and declarations aimed at clarifying obligations under the Convention and the interaction of its provisions with U.S. domestic law. See Sen. Exec. Rep. No. 10 (2004). These are intended to be compatible with the Convention's prohibition on reservations.

2. *International Criminal Court.* Article 121 of the 1998 Rome Statute on the International Criminal Court likewise prohibits reservations. Yet some states have said that reservations to certain provisions may be necessary because of requirements of their domestic constitutional law, or that the possibility of making some modest reservations might facilitate a decision to join the treaty. Is it advisable to put such states to an all-or-nothing choice by precluding reservations? See Chapter 16.

E. PERMISSIBILITY VERSUS OPPOSABILITY OF RESERVATIONS

BOWETT, RESERVATIONS TO NON–RESTRICTED MULTILATERAL TREATIES

48 Brit. Y.B.I.L. 67, 88–90 (1976–77)

An examination of recent State practice on reservations suggests that there is considerable uncertainty over the operation of the rules now embodied in the Vienna Convention.

The primary source of uncertainty is the failure to perceive the difference between the issue of the "permissibility" of a reservation and the issue of the "opposability" of a reservation to a particular Party.

The issue of "permissibility" is the preliminary issue. It must be resolved by reference to the treaty and is essentially an issue of treaty interpretation; it has nothing to do with the question of whether, as a matter of policy, other Parties find the reservation acceptable or not. The consequence of finding a reservation "impermissible" may be either that the reservation alone is a nullity (which means that the reservation cannot be accepted by a Party holding it to be impermissible) or that the impermissible reservation nullifies the State's acceptance of the treaty as a whole.

The issue of "opposability" is the secondary issue and presupposes that the reservation is permissible. Whether a Party chooses to accept the reservation, or object to the reservation, or object to both the reservation and the entry into force of the treaty as between the reserving and the objecting State, is a matter for a policy decision and, as such, not subject to the criteria governing permissibility and not subject to judicial review.

It therefore follows that State practice would be clearer, and more logical, if objections to reservations stated whether the objection was based on the view that the reservation was impermissible or not. This would enable the reserving State to argue the matter of permissibility, if this were the ground of objection, whereas it cannot argue with a policy objection. It should also be incumbent upon a State objecting on the ground of impermissibility to state whether, in its view, the effect is to nullify the reservation or to nullify the acceptance of the treaty by the reserving State. Without such a statement of the legal consequences which a Party attaches to its objection on the ground of impermissibility, it is impossible to determine whether there is a treaty relationship or not.

Where the objection is not on the ground of impermissibility the matter is simpler, since Articles 20 and 21 of the Vienna Convention effectively indicate what legal consequences flow from acceptance, objection, or objection to both the reservation and any treaty relationship.

If this analysis is correct, it seems possible to formulate the following propositions which might provide useful guidance to States:

1. The test of a true reservation is whether it seeks to exclude or modify the legal effect of the provisions of the treaty to which the reservation is attached, and by this test a reservation must be distinguished from declarations or other interpretative statements however named. The latter, whilst not reservations, need not be accepted and raise an issue of treaty interpretation.

2. The permissibility of reservations under contemporary law is governed by the rules set out in Article 19 of the Vienna Convention; in essence, these rules assume the general permissibility of reservations to the non-restricted multilateral treaty except where reservations are expressly or impliedly prohibited or are incompatible with the object and purpose of the treaty. The criterion of "compatibility" does not apply to reservations which are prohibited, expressly or impliedly, or to a reservation which is expressly permitted.

3. A reservation which is expressly permitted and which requires no subsequent acceptance is one the legal effect of which is capable of being deduced from the treaty itself. Thus, a reservations clause permitting reservations to an article in general terms does not mean that all reservations to that article are *ipso facto* permissible and require no subsequent acceptance, although a reservation excluding the article *in toto* might be of this nature.

4. Therefore, in relation to reservations to an article to which reservations are allowed, the permissibility of any particular reservation will depend upon its fulfilling certain criteria, namely:

(i) that it is a true reservation;

(ii) that it is a reservation to that article and does not seek to modify the effect of some other article to which reservations are not allowed;

(iii) that it does not seek to modify rules of law which derive from some other treaty or from customary international law;

(iv) that it is not incompatible with the object and purpose of the treaty.

5. When a reservation is "impermissible" according to the rules set out in conclusions 2, 3 and 4 above, the inconsistency in the reserving State's expression of a will to be bound by the treaty and the formulation of an impermissible reservation must be resolved as a matter of construction of what the State really intended. It is suggested that the following is the proper test:

(i) a reservation not incompatible with the object and purpose of the treaty may be severed and should be disregarded as a nullity;

(ii) a reservation incompatible with the object and purpose of the treaty and not severable invalidates the State's acceptance of the treaty.

6. The question of "permissibility" is always a question to be resolved as a matter of construction of the treaty and does *not* depend on the reactions of the Parties. Therefore, though each Party may have to determine whether it regards a reservation as permissible, in the absence of any "collegiate" system it must do so on the basis of whether the treaty permits such a reservation. The issue of "permissibility" is thus entirely separate from the issue of "opposability", that is to say whether a Party accepts or does not accept a reservation which is permissible.

7. Parties may not accept an impermissible reservation.

8. As to permissible reservations, with non-restricted multilateral treaties, a reservation which is expressly authorized in the sense of conclusion 3 above requires no acceptance and takes effect with the reserving State's acceptance of the treaty. That apart, permissible reservations may meet with the following three reactions from other Parties:

(i) acceptance of the reservation: the effect is that the treaty is in force and the reservation takes full effect between the reserving and accepting States, on a reciprocal basis;

(ii) objection to the reservation: the effect is that the treaty is in force, but *minus* the provision affected by the reservation *to the extent of the reservation*. The reservation is not "opposable" to the objecting State;

(iii) objection to the reservation and an express objection to the treaty's entering into force: the effect is that the reserving and objecting States are not in any treaty relationship. Neither the treaty nor the reservation is "opposable" to the objecting State.

9. The objecting State, exercising either of the last two options set out in conclusion 8 above, is free to object on any ground: that is to say, its objection is not confined to the ground of "incompatibility" with the object and purpose of the treaty.

10. Both reservations and objections may be withdrawn in writing, taking effect on communication to the objecting or reserving State, as the case may be. The effect of withdrawal is to restore the original treaty text in the case of the withdrawal of a reservation. In the case of the

withdrawal of an objection, this is equivalent to an acceptance of the reservation.

NOTES

1. *Effect of Acceptance or Objection.* Bowett's point 8(ii) above restates Article 21(3) of the Vienna Convention. Does this rule mean that the legal effect is precisely the same for a state that accepts the reservation and for a state that objects to the reservation but does not object to the treaty coming into force between it and the reserving state?

2. *Advantages of Flexible Approach.* What motivates states to take positions on other states' reservations? Do states (whether objecting or not) benefit from the policy signals sent by the entry of a reservation? For a law-and-economics approach contending that a flexible reservations regime promotes valuable exchange of information, see Swaine, Reserving, 31 Yale J. Int'l L. 307 (2006).

F.　RESERVATIONS TO HUMAN RIGHTS TREATIES

Increasing attention has focused in recent years on issues concerning reservations that had not been anticipated when the Vienna Convention was drafted. Several of the human rights treaty bodies undertook studies of the problem of reservations in the 1990s, notably the U.N. Human Rights Committee which in 1994 produced a General Comment on the matter, as excerpted below, and the CEDAW Committee which also issued general recommendations on reservations (cited and discussed in Chinkin, p. 143 *supra*). At about the same time, the International Law Commission undertook a general study of reservations practice, for the first time since it had completed its work on the Vienna Convention in the 1960s. As of 2009, the I.L.C. study is still in progress; after more than a decade of work it has produced thirteen valuable reports by its Special Rapporteur on Reservations to Treaties, Alain Pellet (with comprehensive bibliography), as well as draft guidelines on treaty reservations practice with commentary. All of these documents are available on the I.LC. website, http://www.un.org./law/ilc. For a summary of the work so far and bibliographic references, see Report of the International Law Commission on its 60th Session, U.N. Doc. A/63/10 (2008).

In its Preliminary Conclusions on Reservations to Normative Multilateral Treaties Including Human Rights Treaties, adopted in 1997, the I.L.C. reaffirmed the Vienna Convention regime for reservations (Articles 19–23 of the Vienna Convention) and reiterated "that, in particular, the object and purpose of the treaty is the most important of the criteria for determining the admissibility of reservations." The Commission considered that, "because of its flexibility, this regime is suited to the requirements of all treaties, of whatever object or nature, and achieves a satisfactory balance between the objectives of preservation of the integrity of the text of the treaty and universality of participation in the treaty." The Commission went on to state its view that the general rules of the Vienna Convention apply equally to human rights treaties, but it acknowledged that new legal questions had arisen in view of the establishment of monitoring bodies under human rights treaties. See Report of the International Law Commission on its 49th Session, U.N. Doc. A/52/10, at 126–27 (1997). The Commission's work program adopted for its 2001–2006 and 2006–2011 cycles has proceeded on the assumption that the Vienna Convention regime remains essentially sound and that the Commission's most valuable contribution can be to clarify areas not addressed or left unclear by the Vienna Convention, which it has done through the formulation of a set of draft guidelines on reservations practice.

At the same time and somewhat in dialectical tension with the I.L.C. exercise, some of the human rights treaty bodies have staked out their own approaches to problems of reservations and have asserted authority to scrutinize reservations of parties for conformity to the object and purpose of the treaty in question. The most far-reaching of these assertions came from the Human Rights Committee in its General Comment No. 24 of 1994, set forth below, to which some states had a strongly negative reaction, as indicated by the observations of the United States excerpted immediately after the General Comment.

UNITED NATIONS HUMAN RIGHTS COMMITTEE, GENERAL COMMENT 24 ON ISSUES RELATING TO RESERVATIONS MADE TO THE ICCPR

U.N. Doc. CCPR/C/21/Rev.1/Add.6 (Nov. 11, 1994)
reprinted in 34 I.L.M. 839 (1995) (footnotes omitted)

1. As of 1 November 1994, 46 of the 127 States parties to the International Covenant on Civil and Political Rights had, between them, entered 150 reservations of varying significance to their acceptance of the obligations of the Covenant. Some of these reservations exclude the duty to provide and guarantee particular rights in the Covenant. Others are couched in more general terms, often directed to ensuring the continued paramountcy of certain domestic legal provisions. Still others are directed at the competence of the Committee. The number of reservations, their content and their scope may undermine the effective implementation of the Covenant and tend to weaken respect for the obligations of States Parties. * * *

* * *

5. The Covenant neither prohibits reservations nor mentions any type of permitted reservation. The same is true of the first Optional Protocol. * * *

6. The absence of a prohibition on reservations does not mean that any reservation is permitted. The matter of reservations under the Covenant and the first Optional Protocol is governed by international law.

Article 19(3) of the Vienna Convention on the Law of Treaties provides relevant guidance. It stipulates that where a reservation is not prohibited by the treaty or falls within the specified permitted categories, a State may make a reservation provided it is not incompatible with the object and purpose of the treaty. Even though, unlike some other human rights treaties, the Covenant does not incorporate a specific reference to the object and purpose test, that test governs the matter of interpretation and acceptability of reservations.

7.   In an instrument which articulates very many civil and political rights, each of the many articles, and indeed their interplay, secures the objectives of the Covenant. The object and purpose of the Covenant is to create legally binding standards for human rights by defining certain civil and political rights and placing them in a framework of obligations which are legally binding for those States which ratify; and to provide an efficacious supervisory machinery for the obligations undertaken.

8.   Reservations that offend peremptory norms would not be compatible with the object and purpose of the Covenant. Although treaties that are mere exchanges of obligations between States allow them to reserve *inter se* application of rules of general international law, it is otherwise in human rights treaties, which are for the benefit of persons within their jurisdiction. Accordingly, provisions in the Covenant that represent customary international law (and *a fortiori* when they have the character of peremptory norms) may not be the subject of reservations. [For the Committee's views on which provisions of the Covenant represent customary international law, see additional excerpts in Chapter 13 at p. 1017 below.]

* * *

10.   The Committee has further examined whether categories of reservations may offend the "object and purpose" test. In particular, it falls for consideration as to whether reservations to the non-derogable provisions of the Covenant are compatible with its object and purpose. While there is no hierarchy of importance of rights under the Covenant, the operation of certain rights may not be suspended, even in times of national emergency. This underlines the great importance of non-derogable rights. But not all rights of profound importance, such as articles 9 and 27 of the Covenant, have in fact been made non-derogable. * * * While there is no automatic correlation between reservations to non-derogable provisions, and reservations which offend against the object and purpose of the Covenant, a State has a heavy onus to justify such a reservation. * * *

* * *

12.   * * * Reservations often reveal a tendency of States not to want to change a particular law. And sometimes that tendency is elevated to a general policy. Of particular concern are widely formulated reservations which essentially render ineffective all Covenant rights which would

require any change in national law to ensure compliance with Covenant obligations. No real international rights or obligations have thus been accepted. And when there is an absence of provisions to ensure that Covenant rights may be sued on in domestic courts, and, further, a failure to allow individual complaints to be brought to the Committee under the first Optional Protocol, all the essential elements of the Covenant guarantees have been removed.

* * *

16. The Committee finds it important to address which body has the legal authority to make determinations as to whether specific reservations are compatible with the object and purpose of the Covenant. [Here the Committee restates the rules of the I.C.J.'s 1951 *Genocide Convention* advisory opinion and Articles 20–21 of the Vienna Convention, on objections to reservations and the legal effect of objections.]

17. As indicated above, it is the Vienna Convention on the Law of Treaties that provides the definition of reservations and also the application of the object and purpose test in the absence of other specific provisions. But the Committee believes that its provisions on the role of State objections in relation to reservations are inappropriate to address the problem of reservations to human rights treaties. Such treaties, and the Covenant specifically, are not a web of inter-State exchanges of mutual obligations. They concern the endowment of individuals with rights. The principle of inter-State reciprocity has no place * * *. And, because the operation of the classic rules on reservations is so inadequate for the Covenant, States have often not seen any legal interest in or need to object to reservations. The absence of protest by States cannot imply that a reservation is either compatible or incompatible with the object and purpose of the Covenant. * * *

18. It necessarily falls to the Committee to determine whether a specific reservation is compatible with the object and purpose of the Covenant. This is in part because, as indicated above, it is an inappropriate task for States parties in relation to human rights treaties, and in part because it is a task that the Committee cannot avoid in the performance of its functions. * * * Because of the special character of a human rights treaty, the compatibility of a reservation with the object and purpose of the Covenant must be established objectively, by reference to legal principles, and the Committee is particularly well placed to perform this task. The normal consequence of an unacceptable reservation is not that the Covenant will not be in effect at all for a reserving party. Rather, such a reservation will generally be severable, in the sense that the Covenant will be operative for the reserving party without benefit of the reservation.

19. Reservations must be specific and transparent, so that the Committee, those under the jurisdiction of the reserving State and other States parties may be clear as to what obligations of human rights compliance have or have not been undertaken. Reservations may thus not be general, but must refer to a particular provision of the Covenant and indicate in

precise terms its scope in relation thereto. * * * States should not enter so many reservations that they are in effect accepting a limited number of human rights obligations, and not the Covenant as such. So that reservations do not lead to a perpetual non-attainment of international human rights standards, reservations should not systematically reduce the obligations undertaken only to those presently existing in less demanding standards of domestic law. Nor should interpretative declarations or reservations seek to remove an autonomous meaning to Covenant obligations, by pronouncing them to be identical, or to be accepted only insofar as they are identical, with existing provisions of domestic law. * * *

20. States should institute procedures to ensure that each and every reservation is compatible with the object and purpose of the Covenant. It is desirable for a State entering a reservation to indicate in precise terms the domestic legislation or practices which it believes to be incompatible with the Covenant obligation reserved; and to explain the time period it requires to render its own laws and practices compatible with the Covenant, or why it is unable to render its own laws and practices compatible with the Covenant. States should also ensure that the necessity for maintaining reservations is periodically reviewed, taking into account any observations and recommendations made by the Committee during examination of their reports. Reservations should be withdrawn at the earliest possible moment. * * *

OBSERVATIONS BY THE UNITED STATES OF AMERICA ON GENERAL COMMENT NO. 24

U.N. Doc. A/50/40, annex VI, at 131–32, 135–59 (1995)

2. *Acceptability of Reservations: Governing Legal Principles*

* * *

It is clear that a State cannot exempt itself from a peremptory norm of international law by making a reservation to the Covenant. It is not at all clear that a State cannot choose to exclude one means of enforcement of particular norms by reserving against inclusion of those norms in its Covenant obligations.

The proposition that any reservation which contravenes a norm of customary international law is *per se* incompatible with the object and purpose of this or any other convention, however, is a much more significant and sweeping premise. It is, moreover, wholly unsupported by and is in fact contrary to international law. * * *

With respect to the actual object and purpose of this Covenant, there appears to be a misunderstanding. The object and purpose was to protect human rights, with an understanding that there need not be immediate, universal implementation of all terms of the treaty. * * *

* * * In fact, a primary object and purpose of the Covenant was to secure the widest possible adherence, with the clear understanding that a relatively liberal regime on the permissibility of reservations should therefore be required.

* * *

5. Effect of Invalidity of Reservations

It seems unlikely that one can misunderstand the concluding point of this General Comment, in paragraph 18 * * *. Since this conclusion is so completely at odds with established legal practice and principles and even the express and clear terms of adherence by many States, it would be welcome if some helpful clarification could be made.

The reservations contained in the United States' instrument of ratification are integral parts of its consent to be bound by the Covenant and are not severable. If it were to be determined that any one or more of them were ineffective, the ratification as a whole could thereby be nullified. * * *

* * *

The general view of the academic literature is that reservations are an essential part of a State's consent to be bound. They cannot simply be erased. This reflects the fundamental principle of the law of treaties: obligation is based on consent. A State which does not consent to a treaty is not bound by that treaty. A State which expressly withholds its consent from a provision cannot be presumed, on the basis of some legal fiction, to be bound by it. It is regrettable that General Comment 24 appears to suggest to the contrary.

NOTES

1. *Governmental Reactions to Human Rights Committee's Comment.* Both the United States and the United Kingdom challenged the Human Rights Committee's claim of authority to determine the validity of reservations and the legal effects of supposedly impermissible reservations. See Observations of the United States of America and of the United Kingdom on General Comment No. 24, U.N. Doc. A/50/40, annex VI, at 131–32, 135–59 (1995), reprinted in 16 Hum. Rts. L.J. 422, 424 (1995) The U.S. observations criticized the Committee for "appear[ing] to reject the established rules * * * as set forth in the Vienna Convention on the Law of Treaties" and for giving the Committee a greater role than states parties themselves in determining the meaning of the Covenant and of their own reservations.

2. *Adequacy of Vienna Convention Regime.* Was the Committee correct in its assessment that the Vienna Convention rules on objections to reservations may be "inappropriate" or "inadequate" for human rights treaties (paras. 17–18)? For comments that the Vienna Convention provisions "operate unsatisfactorily in human rights treaties," see, e.g., Higgins, The United Nations: Still a Force for Peace, 52 Mod. L. Rev. 1, 11 (1989). Professor (now

Judge) Higgins served on the Human Rights Committee when General Comment No. 24 was drafted. She has explained that the point is not to create a different legal regime for human rights treaties, but rather to address issues that were simply never considered or resolved in the Vienna Convention. These issues include how to apply the substantive standard of Article 19 of the Vienna Convention—incompatibility with object and purpose—in a given procedural context: namely, the existence of a monitoring body that can resolve questions of compatibility, irrespective of whether states choose to exercise their prerogative of registering objections. See Higgins, Introduction, in Chinkin et al., Human Rights as General Norms, *supra*, at xv–xxv.

3.   *I.L.C. Views.* The International Law Commission also responded to the claim by the Human Rights Committee that the Committee is vested with the authority to determine the validity of a reservation. In its Preliminary Conclusions on Reservations to Treaties (cited pp. 154–155 *supra*), the I.L.C. said:

> 5.   The Commission also considers that where these treaties are silent on the subject, the monitoring bodies established thereby are competent to comment upon and express recommendations with regard, *inter alia,* to the admissibility of reservations by States, in order to carry out the functions assigned to them;

> 6.   The Commission stresses that this competence of the monitoring bodies does not exclude or otherwise affect the traditional modalities of control by the contracting parties

> * * *

> 8.   The Commission notes that the legal force of the findings made by monitoring bodies in the exercise of their power to deal with reservations cannot exceed that resulting from the powers given to them for the performance of their general monitoring role.

4.   *U.S. Reservations to Genocide Convention.* The U.S. ratification of the Genocide Convention contained two paragraphs denominated "reservations" and other paragraphs with interpretive statements. Is it plausible in light of U.S. constitutional law to consider that the "reservation" quoted at p. 142 above may not be a reservation within the meaning of the Vienna Convention definition (if nothing in the U.S. Constitution would prevent the United States from carrying out the obligations of the treaty)?

A similar constitutional statement has been adopted by the U.S. Senate in connection with the resolutions of ratification of other human rights treaties; but in contrast to the Genocide Convention, the other statements have not been called "reservations" and have been circulated to states parties to the treaties separately from the instrument of ratification. Do these procedural differences have any significance under the Vienna Convention?

The other U.S. reservation to the Genocide Convention was addressed to the dispute settlement article (Article IX) and requires specific U.S. consent in the particular case to the submission of any disputes about the Convention to the International Court of Justice. This reservation is substantially similar to those of the Soviet bloc countries that led to the General Assembly's request for the advisory opinion on *Reservations to the Genocide Convention* (1951) p.

143 *supra*. The I.C.J. has given effect to this and similar reservations by other states. See Chapter 9, pp. 588–90.

5. *U.S. Reservations to Human Rights Treaties.* For excerpts from and discussion of other U.S. reservations to several human rights treaties, see Chapter 13, pp. 1014–1021 *infra*.

6. *Inter–American Human Rights Bodies.* Regional human rights organs had considered issues of reservations even before the developments in the U.N. human rights treaty bodies and the I.L.C. described above. The Inter–American Court of Human Rights in the *Advisory Opinion on Reservations*, Inter–Am. Ct. H.R. (ser. A) No. 2 (1982) addressed the legal effect of ratifications with reservations in the one-year period during which other states parties can object to reservations (Vienna Convention, Article 20(5)). The Court emphasized that requirements of acceptance and reciprocity were not appropriate for a human rights treaty which must be seen "for what in reality it is: a multilateral legal instrument or framework enabling states to make binding unilateral commitments not to violate the human rights of individuals within their jurisdiction." Advisory Opinion, para. 33. On this theory, reciprocity loses its relevance and reservations may be considered as authorized by the treaty provided they are not incompatible with the object and purpose of the treaty. Consequently states which ratified with reservations should be considered as legally bound from the date of their ratification.

In the *Advisory Opinion on Restrictions to the Death Penalty*, Adv. Op. No. OC–3 (1983) (ser. A) No. 3, 23 I.L.M. 320 (1984), the Inter–American Court of Human Rights examined Guatemala's reservation to Article 4(4) of the American Convention on Human Rights, which prohibits application of the death penalty for "political offenses or related common crimes." In its reasoning, the Court emphasized the fact that derogations from Article 4 were not permitted by the Convention: "It would follow therefrom that a reservation which was designed to enable a State to suspend any of the non-derogable fundamental rights must be deemed to be incompatible with the object and purpose of the Convention and consequently not permitted by it. The situation would be different if the reservation sought merely to restrict certain aspects of a non-derogable right without depriving the right as a whole of its basic purpose." Id. at para. 61. The Court then interpreted the reservation in a manner "most consistent with the object and purpose of the Convention," so that rather than invalidating the reservation, it gave it a limited scope.

For comments on these advisory opinions and on the linkage between non-derogability and incompatibility, see Buergenthal, The Advisory Practice of the Inter–American Human Rights Court, 79 A.J.I.L. 1, 20–33 (1985).

7. *European Court of Human Rights.* The European Court of Human Rights has also had several occasions to consider problems concerning reservations. In *Belilos v. Switzerland*, 132 Eur. Ct. H.R. (ser. A) (1988), the Court in effect determined that a state's attempted qualification of an obligation under the regional treaty was invalid as incompatible with the object and purpose of the treaty and could be disregarded: in other words, the state would remain a party to the treaty but without the benefit of the challenged restriction. See also *Loizidou v. Turkey*, 310 Eur. Ct. H.R. (ser. A) (1995).

Some of the states that disagreed with the Human Rights Committee's General Comment No. 24, e.g. in relation to its treatment of questions of severability, considered that the U.N. treaty body overstepped its authority by following the general approach of regional organs, without accounting for significant differences between regional and universal systems. Is this criticism persuasive?

8. *Further Reading.* For additional bibliography, see Horn, Reservations and Interpretive Declarations to Multilateral Treaties (1988); Clark, The Vienna Convention Regime and CEDAW, 85 A.J.I.L. 281 (1991); Lijnzaad, Reservations to UN Human Rights Treaties: Ratify and Ruin? (1995); Redgwell, Reservations to Treaties and Human Rights Committee General Comment No. 24, 46 I.C.L.Q. 390 (1997). See also Zemanek, General Course, 266 Rec. des Cours 175–92 (1997).

SECTION 4. OBSERVANCE, APPLICATION, AND INTERPRETATION

A. OBSERVANCE

1. *Pacta Sunt Servanda* and Good Faith (Article 26)

Lord McNair, The Law of Treaties 493 (1961) prefaces his discussion of the binding effect of treaties with the following remarks:

>
> In every uncodified legal system there are certain elementary and universally agreed principles for which it is almost impossible to find specific authority. In the Common Law of England and the United States of America, where can you find specific authority for the principle that a man must perform his contracts? Yet almost every decision on a contract presupposes the existence of that principle. The same is true of international law. No Government would decline to accept the principle *pacta sunt servanda,* and the very fact that Governments find it necessary to spend so much effort in explaining in a particular case that the *pactum* has ceased to exist, or that the act complained of is not a breach of it, either by reason of an implied term or for some other reason, is the best acknowledgment of that principle. * * *

The I.L.C. commentary on what became Article 26 explains that the principle of good faith is a legal principle which forms an integral part of the rule *pacta sunt servanda.* [1966] II Y.B.I.L.C. 211.

NOTES

1. *Good Faith.* In *Gabčíkovo–Nagymaros Project* (Hungary/Slovakia), 1997 I.C.J. 7, excerpted at p. 225, the I.C.J. determined that a 1977 bilateral treaty was still in force and that both parties continued to be "under a legal obligation * * * to consider, within the context of the 1977 Treaty, in what way the multiple objectives of the Treaty can best be served, keeping in mind

that all of them should be fulfilled" (para. 139). The Court elaborated on the parties' obligations as follows:

> 142.   What is required in the present case by the rule *pacta sunt servanda,* as reflected in Article 26 of the Vienna Convention of 1969 on the Law of Treaties, is that the Parties find an agreed solution within the co-operative context of the Treaty.

Article 26 combines two elements, which are of equal importance. It provides that "Every treaty in force is binding upon the parties to it and must be performed by them in good faith." This latter element, in the Court's view, implies that, in this case, it is the purpose of the Treaty, and the intentions of the parties in concluding it, which should prevail over its literal application. The principle of good faith obliges the Parties to apply it in a reasonable way and in such a manner that its purpose can be realized.

2.   *Good Faith Revisited.* In *Certain Questions of Mutual Assistance in Criminal Matters* (Djibouti v. France), 2008 I.C.J. No. 136, the Court construed an agreement that contained some level of discretion to a state in whether to execute a letter rogatory, stating:

> 145.   The Court begins its examination of Article 2 of the 1986 Convention by observing that, while it is correct, as France claims, that the terms of Article 2 provide a State to which a request for assistance has been made with a very considerable discretion, this exercise of discretion is still subject to the obligation of good faith codified in Article 26 of the 1969 Vienna Convention on the Law of Treaties [citations omitted] * * *. This requires it to be shown that the reasons for refusal to execute the letter rogatory fell within those allowed for in Article 2. Further, the Convention requires (in Art. 3) that the decision not to execute the letter must have been taken by those with the authority so to decide under the law of the requested State. The Court will examine all of these elements.

Does this passage suggest that "good faith" constrains the independence of states in carrying out their treaty commitments?

2.   Internal Law and Treaty Observance (Article 27)

The Vienna Convention restates in Article 27 the long-accepted rule of customary law that a state may not invoke its internal law as a justification for its failure to perform a treaty. See *Treatment of Polish Nationals and Other Persons of Polish Origin in Danzig Territory,* Advisory Opinion, 1932 P.C.I.J. (ser. A/B) No. 44, at 22. Where a state has a domestic rule of law that a later statute supersedes an earlier treaty (as is the case in the United States) a domestic court will apply the statute rather than the treaty. However, the state remains internationally bound by the treaty and responsible if it violates its provisions. Of importance in this connection is the principle widely accepted in national legal systems that domestic law should be construed insofar as possible to avoid violating a state's international obligation. See Chapter 10, pp. 691, 721–22.

A constitutional provision has no higher status in international law than any other provision of internal law except in one respect. A state may invoke the fact that its consent to be bound by a treaty was expressed "in violation of a provision of its internal law regarding competence to conclude treaties" if (and only if) the violation was "manifest and concerned a rule of its internal law of fundamental importance." Vienna Convention, Article 46. This aspect of the problem is dealt with at Section 5.B, pp. 186–87 *infra*.

NOTE

Compliance with Domestic Procedural Rules for Asserting International Law Claims. In *Breard v. Greene,* 523 U.S. 371 (1998), the U.S. Supreme Court was asked to stay the execution of a death sentence of a Paraguayan national, pending resolution of a dispute over consequences of non-compliance with a treaty (the Vienna Convention on Consular Relations). The dispute had been brought to the International Court of Justice upon application of Paraguay, in parallel to the habeas corpus proceedings brought by the prisoner in U.S. courts. The United States government conceded in both forums that there had been a breach of the treaty, but the government's position was that neither court could accord a remedy for the breach since the petitioner had failed to raise the treaty question in the courts of the state of Virginia at the time of his trial and subsequent appeals. On this point the Supreme Court said:

> First, while we should give respectful consideration to the interpretation of an international treaty rendered by an international court with jurisdiction to interpret such, it has been recognized in international law that, absent a clear and express statement to the contrary, the procedural rules of the forum State govern the implementation of the treaty in that State. [citations to three U.S. cases omitted] This proposition is embodied in the Vienna Convention [on Consular Relations] itself, which provides that the rights expressed in the Convention "shall be exercised in conformity with the laws and regulations of the receiving State," provided that "said laws and regulations must enable full effect to be given to the purposes for which the rights accorded under this Article are intended." Article 36(2), [1970] U.S.T., at 101. It is the rule in this country that assertions of error in criminal proceedings must first be raised in state court in order to form the basis for relief in habeas. *Wainwright v. Sykes,* 433 U.S. 72 (1977). Claims not so raised are considered defaulted. Ibid. By not asserting his Vienna Convention claim in state court, Breard failed to exercise his rights under the Vienna Convention in conformity with the laws of the United States and the Commonwealth of Virginia. Having failed to do so, he cannot raise a claim of violation of those rights now on federal habeas review.

Similar issues (concerning the relevance in international law of domestic procedural prerequisites for asserting and preserving treaty claims) were raised in cases brought by Germany involving death sentences for two of its nationals, Karl and Walter LaGrand, *Vienna Convention on Consular Relations* (Germany v. U.S.), 1999 I.C.J. 9 (Provisional Measures); 2001 I.C.J. 466

(Merits), and by Mexico involving fifty-one of its nationals. *Avena and Other Mexican Nationals* (Mexico v. United States), 2004 I.C.J. 12. In addressing the petition of one of the fifty-one Mexican nationals covered by the I.C.J.'s *Avena* judgment, the U.S. Supreme Court agreed that the judgment "constitutes an *international* law obligation on the part of the United States." A majority of the Court held, however, that "not all international law obligations automatically constitute binding federal law enforceable in United States courts." *Medellin v. Texas*, 128 S.Ct. 1346, 1356 (2008). This series of cases is addressed more fully in Chapter 9 on dispute settlement and Chapter 10 on the relationship between international and domestic law.

B. INTERPRETATION OF TREATIES

1. Problems and Methods of Treaty Interpretation (Articles 31–32)

As noted above, the I.C.J., other international tribunals, and states have treated the methodology embodied in Articles 31–32 of the Vienna Convention as declaratory of the customary international law of treaty interpretation. Those articles themselves (reprinted immediately below for convenience) require interpretation, however. How is the interpreter to determine the "object and purpose" of a treaty? (Compare the corresponding problems concerning "object and purpose" in relation to reservations, Section 3 above.) Does the reference to "purpose" imply a teleological (purposive) process, under which the interpreter may seek to advance the goals of the treaty beyond its literal terms? What elements are to be taken into account as the "context"? Are they limited to the items specified in Article 31(2)? Is "dynamic" interpretation implicit, e.g. in Article 31(3)'s reference to "any subsequent practice"? Is the use of "supplementary means" under Article 32 limited to the circumstances specified in that article? These and comparable problems are grist for the mill of international tribunals, which regularly deal with problems of treaty interpretation.

VIENNA CONVENTION ON THE LAW OF TREATIES
May 23, 1969, 1155 U.N.T.S. 331

Article 31. General rule of interpretation

1. A treaty shall be interpreted in good faith in accordance with the ordinary meaning to be given to the terms of the treaty in their context and in the light of its object and purpose.

2. The context for the purpose of the interpretation of a treaty shall comprise, in addition to the text, including its preamble and annexes:

(a) any agreement relating to the treaty which was made between all the parties in connection with the conclusion of the treaty;

(b) any instrument which was made by one or more parties in connection with the conclusion of the treaty and accepted by the other parties as an instrument related to the treaty.

3.   There shall be taken into account, together with the context:

(a) any subsequent agreement between the parties regarding the interpretation of the treaty or the application of its provisions;

(b) any subsequent practice in the application of the treaty which establishes the agreement of the parties regarding its interpretation;

(c) any relevant rules of international law applicable in the relations between the parties.

4.   A special meaning shall be given to a term if it is established that the parties so intended.

Article 32. Supplementary means of interpretation

Recourse may be had to supplementary means of interpretation, including the preparatory work of the treaty and the circumstances of its conclusion, in order to confirm the meaning resulting from the application of article 31, or to determine the meaning when the interpretation according to article 31:

(a) leaves the meaning ambiguous or obscure; or

(b) leads to a result which is manifestly absurd or unreasonable.

APPLICATION OF THE CONVENTION ON THE PREVENTION AND PUNISHMENT OF THE CRIME OF GENOCIDE (BOSNIA AND HERZEGOVINA v. SERBIA AND MONTENEGRO)

International Court of Justice, 2007
2007 I.C.J. 191

[The Republic of Bosnia and Herzegovina initiated suit in 1993 against the Federal Republic of Yugoslavia (Serbia and Montenegro) under the Genocide Convention, claiming that Serbia–Montenegro (later the Republic of Serbia) was responsible for numerous breaches of the Convention in relation to protected groups in Bosnia, in particular its Muslim population. After lengthy proceedings addressed to jurisdictional and procedural issues and ultimately the merits, the I.C.J. rendered final judgment in 2007. In the dispositive paragraphs of the judgment, the Court found that Serbia had not committed genocide, conspired to commit genocide, incited the commission of genocide, or been complicit in genocide within the meaning of the relevant articles of the Convention. It did, however, find violations of Serbia's responsibility under the Convention to prevent the crime of genocide (specifically with respect to genocide committed in Srebrenica in July 1995), and also violations of the obligations to punish genocide (specifically by failing to transfer an indictee on genocide charges, Ratko Mladić, to the International Criminal Tribunal for the Former Yugoslavia and otherwise failing to cooperate with the I.C.T.Y.). In order to reach these conclusions, the I.C.J. had to interpret provisions of the Genocide Convention, including the undertaking to "prevent and punish" genocide in Article I, the definition of genocide in Article II, and the phrase "responsibility of a State for genocide" in Article IX.

[The excerpts below concern the Court's interpretive task. For other aspects, see p. 503.]

160. The Court observes that what obligations the Convention imposes upon the parties to it depends on the ordinary meaning of the terms of the Convention read in their context and in the light of its object and purpose. To confirm the meaning resulting from that process or to remove ambiguity or obscurity or a manifestly absurd or unreasonable result, the supplementary means of interpretation to which recourse may be had include the preparatory work of the Convention and the circumstances of its conclusion. Those propositions, reflected in Articles 31 and 32 of the Vienna Convention on the Law of Treaties, are well recognized as part of customary international law [citations omitted].

161. To determine what are the obligations of the Contracting Parties under the Genocide Convention, the Court will begin with the terms of its Article I. It contains two propositions. The first is the affirmation that genocide is a crime under international law. * * * The affirmation recognizes the existing requirements of customary international law, a matter emphasized by the Court in 1951:

> [Here the Court quotes from its advisory opinion on Reservations to the Genocide Convention, including the paragraph on the objects of the Convention and its "humanitarian and civilizing purpose" excerpted on p. 145 above.]

Later in that Opinion, the Court referred to the "moral and humanitarian principles which are its basis" (*ibid.*, p. 24). The Court reaffirmed [these] statements in its Judgment of 3 February 2006 in the case concerning *Armed Activities on the Territory of the Congo (New Application 2002) (Democratic Republic of the Congo v. Rwanda)*, paragraph 64, when it added that the norm prohibiting genocide was assuredly a peremptory norm of international law (*jus cogens*).

162. Those characterizations of the prohibition on genocide and the purpose of the Convention are significant for the interpretation of the second proposition stated in Article I—the undertaking by the Contracting Parties to prevent and punish the crime of genocide, and particularly in this context the undertaking to prevent. Several features of that undertaking are significant. The ordinary meaning of the word "undertake" is to give a formal promise, to bind or engage oneself, to give a pledge or promise, to agree, to accept an obligation. It is a word regularly used in treaties setting out the obligations of the Contracting Parties [examples from other human rights treaties omitted]. It is not merely hortatory or purposive. The undertaking is unqualified (a matter considered later in relation to the scope of the obligation of prevention); and it is not to be read merely as an introduction to later express references to legislation, prosecution and extradition. Those features support the conclusion that Article I, in particular its undertaking to prevent, creates obligations

distinct from those which appear in the subsequent Articles. That conclusion is also supported by the purely humanitarian and civilizing purpose of the Convention.

163.   This conclusion is confirmed by two aspects of the preparatory work of the Convention and the circumstances of its conclusion as referred to in Article 32 of the Vienna Convention. In 1947 the United Nations General Assembly, in requesting the Economic and Social Council to submit a report and a draft convention on genocide to the Third Session of the Assembly, declared that "genocide is an international crime entailing national and international responsibility on the part of individuals and States" (A/RES/180 (II)). That duality of responsibilities is also to be seen in two other associated resolutions adopted on the same day, both directed to the newly established International Law Commission (hereinafter "the ILC"): the first on the formulation of the Nuremberg principles, concerned with the rights (Principle V) and duties of individuals, and the second on the draft declaration on the rights and duties of States * * *.

164.   The second feature of the drafting history emphasizes the operative and non-preambular character of Article I. [Here the Court examines the original draft of the Convention prepared by the Ad Hoc Committee on Genocide for the General Assembly and considers the proposals advanced by several states in order to make it more effective, inter alia by transferring the language with the undertaking to prevent and punish from the preamble to Article I of the Convention, and related drafting changes.]

165.   For the Court both changes—the movement of the undertaking from the Preamble to the first operative Article and the removal of the linking clause ("in accordance with the following articles")—confirm that Article I does impose distinct obligations over and above those imposed by other Articles of the Convention. In particular, the Contracting Parties have a direct obligation to prevent genocide.

166.   The Court next considers whether the Parties are also under an obligation, by virtue of the Convention, not to commit genocide themselves. It must be observed at the outset that such an obligation is not expressly imposed by the actual terms of the Convention. The Applicant has however advanced as its main argument that such an obligation is imposed by Article IX, which confers on the Court jurisdiction over disputes "including those relating to the responsibility of a State for genocide or any of the other acts enumerated in Article III." * * * Under Article I the States parties are bound to prevent such an act, which it describes as "a crime under international law," being committed. The Article does not *expressis verbis* require States to refrain from themselves committing genocide. However, in the view of the Court, taking into account the established purpose of the Convention, the effect of Article I is to prohibit States from themselves committing genocide. Such a prohibition follows, first, from the fact that the Article categorizes genocide as "a crime under international law": by agreeing to such a categorization, the

States parties must logically be undertaking not to commit the act so described. Secondly, it follows from the expressly stated obligation to prevent the commission of acts of genocide. * * * It would be paradoxical if States were thus under an obligation to prevent, so far as within their power, commission of genocide by persons over whom they have a certain influence, but were not forbidden to commit such acts through their own organs, or persons over whom they have such firm control that their conduct is attributable to the State concerned under international law. In short, the obligation to prevent genocide necessarily implies the prohibition of the commission of genocide.

167. The Court accordingly concludes that Contracting Parties to the Convention are bound not to commit genocide, through the actions of their organs or persons or groups whose acts are attributable to them. That conclusion must also apply to the other acts enumerated in Article III. * * *

* * *

[The Court turns to three arguments advanced by respondent to contradict the proposition that parties have a duty not to commit genocide and the other acts enumerated in Article III. The first is that international law does not recognize the criminal responsibility of states, as to which the Court observes (para. 170) that the obligations of states under the Convention and the responsibilities arising from their breach would not be of a criminal nature. The second is that the Convention is a standard international criminal law convention focused essentially on the prosecution and punishment of individuals—an argument which the Court rejects with reference to the "duality of responsibility" on which it had previously commented (in para. 163) (paras. 171–74).]

175. The third and final argument of the Respondent against the proposition that the Contracting Parties are bound by the Convention not to commit genocide is based on the preparatory work of the Convention and particularly of Article IX. The Court has already used part of that work to confirm the operative significance of the undertaking in Article I (see paragraphs 164 and 165 above), an interpretation already determined from the terms of the Convention, its context and purpose.

176. The Respondent, claiming that the Convention and in particular Article IX is ambiguous, submits that the drafting history of the Convention, in the Sixth Committee of the General Assembly, shows that "there was no question of direct responsibility of the State for acts of genocide." It claims that the responsibility of the State was related to the "key provisions" of Articles IV–VI: the Convention is about the criminal responsibility of individuals supported by the civil responsibility of States to prevent and punish. This argument against any wider responsibility for the Contracting Parties is based on the records of the discussion in the Sixth Committee, and is, it is contended, supported by the rejection of United Kingdom amendments to what became Articles IV and VI. [The history of these amendments is then reviewed.]

177. At a later stage a Belgium/United Kingdom/United States proposal which would have replaced the disputed phrase * * * was ruled by the Chairman of the Sixth Committee as a change of substance and the Committee did not adopt the motion (which required a two-thirds majority) for reconsideration (A/C.6/305). The Chairman gave the following reason for his ruling which was not challenged:

> "it was provided in article IX that those disputes, among others, which concerned the responsibility of a State for genocide or for any of the acts enumerated in article III, should be submitted to the International Court of Justice. According to the joint amendment, on the other hand, the disputes would not be those which concerned the responsibility of the State but those which resulted from an accusation to the effect that the crime had been committed in the territory of one of the contracting parties." (United Nations, *Official Records of the General Assembly, Third Session, Part I, Sixth Committee, Summary Records of the 131st meeting*, p. 690.)

By that time in the deliberations of the Sixth Committee it was clear that only individuals could be held criminally responsible under the draft Convention for genocide. The Chairman was plainly of the view that the Article IX, as it had been modified, provided for State responsibility for genocide.

178. In the view of the Court, two points may be drawn from the drafting history just reviewed. The first is that much of it was concerned with proposals supporting the criminal responsibility of States; but those proposals were *not* adopted. The second is that the amendment which was adopted—to Article IX—is about jurisdiction in respect of the responsibility of States *simpliciter*. Consequently, the drafting history may be seen as supporting the conclusion reached by the Court in paragraph 167 above.

179. Accordingly, having considered the various arguments, the Court affirms that the Contracting Parties are bound by the obligation under the Convention not to commit, through their organs or persons or groups whose conduct is attributable to them, genocide and the other acts enumerated in Article III. Thus if an organ of the State, or a person or group whose acts are legally attributable to the State, commits any of the acts proscribed by Article III of the Convention, the international responsibility of that State is incurred.

NOTES

1. *"Ordinary Meaning."* Notice how the Court finds an "ordinary meaning" in the term "undertake" (para. 162). As the Court observes, this term is frequently used in the sense of formal legal obligation. Compare Article 94(1) of the U.N. Charter, which provides that each U.N. member "undertakes to comply with the decision" of the I.C.J. in any case to which it is a party. The U.S. Supreme Court offered its interpretation of the Charter term "undertakes" in *Medellín v. Texas*, 128 S.Ct. 1346, 1358–59, 1373, 1376, 1383–84

(2008), excerpted in Chapter 10 at p. 699. Could a term such as "undertake" have different meanings in different treaties? Could it have one meaning at the level of international obligation and another meaning in connection with domestic implementation? Cf. Vázquez, Treaties as Law of the Land: The Supremacy Clause and Judicial Enforcement of Treaties, 122 Harv. L. Rev. 599, 661–62 (2008) ("undertaking" in international law entails hard obligation and should also entail a presumption of giving full force to the obligation to the extent permissible in domestic law).

2.   *"Context."* Consider the term "context" as explained in Article 31(2) of the Vienna Convention. Is that specification exclusive? What elements of "context" did the Court consider? Of what significance is the fact that a particular provision appears in the operative articles of a treaty as contrasted to its preamble (or vice versa)?

3.   *"Object and Purpose."* What work does the "humanitarian and civilizing purpose" of the Convention do in the Court's interpretation? Can the purpose of a treaty fill a gap, in the absence of express terms of obligation? What should be the limits of purposive interpretation?

4.   *Preparatory Work.* Is respondent correct that the Convention's terms are ambiguous? What use does the Court make of preparatory work? Is the Court resolving a genuine ambiguity or simply confirming a result reached through other interpretive techniques?

5.   *"Relevant Rules of International Law."* Does Article 31(3)(c) allow an interpreter to import into an international agreement a wide array of international legal rules external to the agreement, whenever needed to assist in interpretation? If so, when an international court is granted jurisdiction to interpret the meaning of a given treaty, does Article 31(3)(c) open the door for a court to go well outside the four corners of that treaty, perhaps even to explicate international legal rules as to which the court would otherwise lack jurisdiction?

In *Oil Platforms* (Iran v. United States), 2003 I.C.J. 161, Iran invoked a Treaty of Amity, Economic Relations, and Consular Rights, Aug. 15, 1955, 8 U.S.T. 899 in claiming that U.S. attacks on Iranian oil platforms during the 1987–88 Iran–Iraq war had violated treaty-based freedom of navigation. Article XX(1)(d) of the treaty excluded from the treaty's scope "measures necessary to protect [a party's] essential security interests." In arguing that Article XX(1)(d) foreclosed Iran's claim, the United States maintained that so long as the U.S. actions fell within the scope of the article, the Court could proceed no further and specifically should not analyze whether the U.S. conduct violated general rules of international law on the use of force. The Court, however, disagreed, stating:

> [U]nder the general rules of treaty interpretation as reflected in the 1969 Vienna Convention on the Law of Treaties, interpretation must take into account "any relevant rules of international law applicable in the relations between the parties" (Article 31, paragraph 3(c)). The Court cannot accept that Article XX, paragraph 1(d) of the 1955 Treaty was intended to operate wholly independently of the relevant rules of international law on the use of force, so as to be capable of being successfully invoked, even in the limited context of a claim for breach of the Treaty, in relation to an

unlawful use of force. The application of the relevant rules of international law relating to this question thus forms an integral part of the task of interpretation entrusted to the Court by [the jurisdictional article] of the 1955 Treaty.

Id. at para. 41. The Court then proceeded to analyze why the U.S. conduct violated norms contained in a different treaty, the U.N. Charter. As discussed in Chapter 9 (*Nicaragua* case), the United States had not consented to I.C.J. jurisdiction to interpret the Charter rules as such and as of 1986 had terminated its consent to jurisdiction concerning the parallel body of customary international law. Do you think the Court should have refrained from introducing Charter-based considerations into its interpretation of a security clause in a bilateral treaty?

For uses by the World Trade Organization of extra-W.T.O. materials in interpreting trade agreements, see Mavroidis, No Outsourcing of Law? WTO Law as Practiced by WTO Courts, 102 A.J.I.L. 421 (2008).

JIMÉNEZ DE ARÉCHAGA, INTERNATIONAL LAW IN THE PAST THIRD OF A CENTURY

159 Rec. des Cours 42–48 (1978–I) (footnotes omitted)

There is a fundamental opposition between two schools of thought: the first one asserts that the primary task in the interpretation of treaties is to ascertain the common or real intention of the parties; the second school defines as the objective of treaty interpretation the determination of the meaning of a text. According to the first approach, "the prime, indeed, the only legitimate object, is to ascertain and give effect to the intentions or presumed intentions of the parties"; according to the second, the fundamental objective is "to establish what the text means according to the ordinary or apparent signification of its terms; its approach is therefore through the study and analysis of the text." The test which distinguishes at the practical level one approach from the other is the position assigned to the *travaux préparatoires* of the treaty. The first school places on the same level the text of the treaty and its *travaux préparatoires,* since both serve to determine the real intention of the parties; the second school considers the text above all as the basic material for interpretation and the *travaux préparatoires* are only taken into account as a secondary or supplementary means of interpretation.

The proposals submitted to the Vienna Conference by the International Law Commission were inspired by the textual approach; primacy was accorded to the text of the treaty as the basis for its interpretation. The Commission said in its commentary that its proposal "is based on the view that the text must be presumed to be the authentic expression of the intentions of the parties; and that, in consequence, the starting point of interpretation is the elucidation of the meaning of the text, not an investigation *ab initio* into the intentions of the parties."

* * *

According to [Article 31], the interpretation of a treaty is to be carried out on the basis of what may be described as intrinsic materials, that is to say, texts and related instruments which have been agreed to by the parties. The process of interpretation must begin with an analysis of the specific provisions of the treaty concerning the question in dispute; it goes on to consider the context, that is to say, other provisions of the treaty, including its preamble, annexes and related instruments made in connection with the conclusion of the treaty, taking particularly into account the object and purpose of the treaty, as it appears from these intrinsic materials. It is important to remark that "the object and purpose of the treaty" is mentioned not as an independent element * * * but at the end of paragraph 1. This was done deliberately, in order to make clear that "object and purpose" are part of the context, the most important one, but not an autonomous element in interpretation, independent of and on the same level as the text, as is advocated by the partisans of the teleological method of interpretation. * * *

Paragraph 3 of Article 31 then proceeds to indicate further intrinsic materials to be taken into account together with the context, and these have also been the object of the express or implied consent or consensus of the parties: subsequent agreements, subsequent practice and relevant rules of international law. This is a process of interpretation which has been aptly described by Max Huber as one of *encerclement progressif* of an agreed text: the text is departed from only gradually, in concentric circles, proceeding from the central to the peripheral. * * *

On the other hand, * * * the extrinsic materials, that is to say, those which have not been the object of the specific agreement of the parties, such as the preparatory work of the treaty and the circumstances of its conclusion, are described as "supplementary means of interpretation" and are governed by a separate article. [Quotation of Article 32 omitted.]

The separation between Articles 31 and 32 is not to be viewed as establishing two distinct and successive phases in the process of interpretation, nor as providing that *travaux préparatoires* are to be only examined when, after exhausting the intrinsic materials of Article 31, an ambiguity or obscurity remains or the result is manifestly absurd or unreasonable. In the task of analysis, there need be no such succession in time and the process is largely a simultaneous one. As Sir Humphrey Waldock said in his commentary on the Article, "all the various elements, as they were present in any given case, would be thrown into the crucible and their interaction would give the legally relevant interpretation." * * *

Consequently, preparatory work is frequently examined and often taken into account. It may be difficult in practice to establish the borderline between confirming a view previously reached and actually forming it, since this belongs to the mental processes of the interpreter. In any case, the importance of *travaux préparatoires* is not to be underestimated and their relevance is difficult to deny, since the question whether a text can be said to be clear is in some degree subjective. On the other hand, the separation between Articles 31 and 32 and the restrictions contained in the latter provision constitute a necessary safeguard which strengthens the textual approach and discourages any attempt to resort to preparatory work in order to dispute an interpretation resulting from the intrinsic materials set out in Article 31.

NOTES

1. *Clarity versus Ambiguity.* In one of its first opinions, the International Court of Justice declined to "deviate from the consistent practice of the Permanent Court of International Justice, according to which there is no occasion to resort to preparatory work if the text of a convention is sufficiently clear in itself." *Conditions of Admission of a State to Membership in the United Nations*, Advisory Opinion, 1948 I.C.J. 57, 63. In a number of other cases as well, the Court displayed a readiness to assume that a treaty was clear, and consequently to dispense with preparatory work. See Lauterpacht at 121–24; Fitzmaurice, The Law and Procedure of the International Court of Justice: Treaty Interpretation and Certain Other Treaty Points, 28 Brit. Y.B.I.L. 1, 6 (1951). It is not entirely clear whether the Court has modified its attitude so as to display a greater readiness to resort to preparatory work. As the *Bosnian Genocide* case suggests, litigants are likely to draw to the Court's attention any aspects of the preparatory work supportive of their own positions; the Court may well refer to such material, without necessarily making clear whether it considers itself to be resolving an ambiguity or confirming its conclusion reached on other grounds.

2. *Questions about Authority of Preparatory Work.* Is preparatory work really of any significant value in ascertaining the true intentions of the contracting parties? While the texts of many treaties often contain accidental and even deliberate ambiguities and omissions, the records of international conferences are also sometimes less than successful in depicting the true course of negotiations. See the comments by Sir Eric Beckett upon Lauterpacht's report to the Institute of International Law on the interpretation of treaties, [1950] 1 Ann. de l'Institut de Droit Int. 435, 442–44, and Lauterpacht's reply in [1952] 1 Ann. De l'Institut de Droit Int. 197, 214–16. Haraszti, a Hungarian jurist, emphasizes that the preparatory work has interpretative value only where it throws light on the "joint intention of the parties" and relates to the text actually agreed upon. Haraszti, Some Fundamental Problems of the Law of Treaties 122–25 (1973).

3. *Admissibility in Relation to Parties That Did Not Participate in Negotiations.* Should the consideration of *travaux préparatoires* be barred by the fact that not all the parties to a dispute participated in the conference or negotiations that led to the conclusion of the treaty? In *Jurisdiction of the International Commission of the River Oder,* 1929 P.C.I.J. (ser. A) No. 23, the Permanent Court of International Justice ruled that preparatory work relevant to the interpretation of disputed articles of the Treaty of Versailles was inadmissible because three of the states involved in the proceeding had not taken part in the Conference which prepared the treaty. Should the admissibility of preparatory work against a non-participating state be influenced by the fact that the materials had been published or were otherwise available for

study? The rule in the *River Oder Case* is probably no longer followed by the International Court of Justice, and it has been rejected by the International Law Commission. See Rosenne, *Travaux Préparatoires*, 12 I.C.L.Q. 1378, 1380–81 (1963); International Law Commission, Commentary, [1964] II Yb. I.L.C. 205.

4. *Unilateral or Classified Negotiating Records.* Disagreements over interpretation of the 1972 Anti–Ballistic Missile Treaty, U.S.-U.S.S.R., May 26, 1972, 23 U.S.T. 3435. surfaced in the 1980s and persisted in a somewhat different form during the life-span of the treaty (through 2002), in relation to aspects of the Strategic Defense Initiative (colloquially known as "Star Wars") that would use exotic technologies to intercept incoming missiles. One aspect of the dispute involved the weight (if any) to be given to materials ancillary to the treaty that might favor a restrictive rather than permissive interpretation. The restrictive interpretation was supported by statements made by certain executive branch representatives to the Senate at the time of the debate on advice and consent to ratification. (Compare pp. 177–78 note 2 on the Intermediate Nuclear Forces Treaty.) A more permissive interpretation was said to be supported by the classified record of the U.S.-Soviet negotiations, in which restrictive proposals had been put forward but rejected. In terms of the methodology of the Vienna Convention, which (if any) of these materials should be taken into account? If U.S. constitutional considerations require a different interpretive methodology (perhaps because of the constitutional role of the Senate in deciding whether to approve treaty obligations), is it possible to have divergent international and domestic interpretations of a treaty? On this controversy, see Henkin, Foreign Affairs and the U.S. Constitution 182–84, 206 (2d ed. 1996) and references therein. On the relevance (if any) of materials considered by the U.S. Senate but not by the treaty partner, compare *United States v. Stuart*, 489 U.S. 353 (1989) (Scalia, J., concurring).

5. *Further Reading.* For more on problems and methods of treaty interpretation, see Aust, Modern Treaty Law and Practice (2d ed. 2007); Gardiner, Treaty Interpretation (2008).

2.   Organs of Interpretation and Interpretation by the Parties

JESSE LEWIS (THE DAVID J. ADAMS) CLAIM (UNITED STATES v. GREAT BRITAIN)

Claims Arbitration under the Special Agreement
of August 18, 1910, 1921, Nielsen Rep. 526
6 U.N. Rep. Int'l Arb. Awards 85

[By the Treaty of London of 1818, 8 Stat. 248, the United States renounced for its nationals the right to fish in Canadian waters, with the proviso that American fishermen should be permitted to enter Canadian bays and harbors "for the purpose of shelter and of repairing damages therein, of purchasing wood, and of obtaining water, and for no other purpose whatever." In 1886, the American fishing schooner *David J. Adams,* having entered Canadian waters for the purpose of purchasing fresh bait, was seized by Canadian authorities for alleged violations of the

Treaty of 1818 and of the applicable Canadian legislation. A Canadian court condemned the vessel, finding that it had violated the Treaty and legislation. On behalf of the vessel's owner, the United States subsequently claimed damages from the British Government on the ground, *inter alia,* that the seizure and condemnation were wrongful because based on an erroneous interpretation of the Treaty. The British agent argued, *inter alia,* that the Arbitral Tribunal was not competent to re-examine the Canadian court's interpretation.]

THE TRIBUNAL * * * Great Britain and Canada, acting in the full exercise of their sovereignty and by such proper legislative authority as was established by their municipal public law, had enacted and were entitled to enact such legislative provisions as they considered necessary or expedient to secure observance of the said Treaty; and, so far as they are not inconsistent with the said Treaty, those provisions are binding as municipal public law of the country on any person within the limits of British jurisdiction. At the time of the seizure of the *David J. Adams* such legislation was embodied in the British Act of 1819 (59 George III, C. 38), and the Canadian Acts of 1868 (31 Vict. 61), 1871 (34 Vict., C. 23).

Great Britain and Canada, acting by such proper judicial authority as was established by their municipal law, were fully entitled to interpret and apply such legislation and to pronounce and impose such penalty as was provided by the same, but such judicial action had the same limits as the aforesaid legislative action, that is to say so far as it was not inconsistent with the said Treaty.

In this case the question is not and cannot be to ascertain whether or not British law has been justly applied by said judicial authorities, nor to consider, revise, reverse, or affirm a decision given in that respect by British Courts. On the contrary, any such decision must be taken as the authorized expression of the position assumed by Great Britain in the subject matter, and, so far as such decision implies an interpretation of said treaty, it must be taken as the authorized expression of the British interpretation.

The fundamental principle of the juridical equality of States is opposed to placing one State under the jurisdiction of another State. It is opposed to the subjection of one State to an interpretation of a Treaty asserted by another State. There is no reason why one more than the other should impose such an unilateral interpretation of a contract which is essentially bilateral. The fact that this interpretation is given by the legislative or judicial or any other authority of one of the Parties does not make that interpretation binding upon the other Party. Far from contesting that principle, the British Government did not fail to recognize it. * * *

For that reason the mere fact that a British Court, whatever be the respect and high authority it carries, interpreted the treaty in such a way as to declare the *David J. Adams* had contravened it, cannot be accepted by this Tribunal as a conclusive interpretation binding upon the United

States Government. Such a decision is conclusive from the national British point of view; it is not from the national United States point of view. * * * [T]he duty of this international Tribunal is to determine, from the international point of view, how the provisions of the treaty are to be interpreted and applied to the facts, and consequently whether the loss resulting from the forfeiture of the vessel gives rise to an indemnity. * * *

[The Tribunal then held that the Canadian court's interpretation and application of the Treaty had not been erroneous.]

NOTES

1. *Acquiescence in Unilateral Interpretation.* A unilateral interpretation of an international agreement, whether made by the executive, legislative, or judicial organs of one of the contracting states, is not binding upon other contracting states. See McNair, The Law of Treaties 345–50 (1961); Hyde at 1460–61; Degan, L'Interprétation des accords en droit international 17–18 (1963); 1 Juris–Classeur de Droit International, Fasc. 12–C, para. 7. Would it nevertheless be prudent for contracting states to protest what they believe to be an erroneous interpretation or application of a treaty by the government or courts of another contracting state? In *Temple of Preah Vihear* (Cambodia v. Thailand), 1962 I.C.J. 6, the contending states each claimed sovereignty over a small area of frontier territory in which the ruins of the ancient Temple of Preah Vihear were located. Cambodia relied on a 1907 map which showed the Temple area to be a part of French Indochina, now Cambodia. Thailand (formerly Siam) argued that the map was erroneous because it had not been drawn in accordance with a 1904 Siamese–French treaty. The Court emphasized, in holding for Cambodia, that the map had been produced by the French at Siamese request, and that the Siamese had never protested the alleged error; this was enough, the Court concluded, to amount to Siamese acquiescence in the map as drawn.

In connection with the interpretation of the Hay–Pauncefote treaty of 1901 between the United States and Great Britain, the Counselor of the Department of State (Lansing) referred in a memorandum of 1913 to a treaty concluded between the United States and Panama in 1903. The Panama Treaty was "a matter of common knowledge and a subject of public discussion," he wrote, pointing out that Great Britain had made no protest or criticism of provisions exempting Panamanian ships from canal tolls until 1912. "It may fairly be urged," concluded the Counselor, "that the Panama Treaty was a contemporaneous interpretation of the Hay–Pauncefote Treaty, and that Great Britain gave assent to the interpretation by permitting the Governments of the United States and of Panama to act under its provisions without interposing any objections." 5 Hackworth 253–54. See generally de Visscher, Problèmes d'Interprétation Judiciaire en Droit International Public 168–81 (1963); MacGibbon, The Scope of Acquiescence in International Law, 31 Brit. Y.B.I.L. 143, 146–47 (1954).

2. *Positions of Domestic Organs within a State.* In 1988, the Senate included in its resolution ratifying the Intermediate Nuclear Forces Treaty between the United States and the Soviet Union a condition making executive

branch statements to the Senate the main source for interpreting the agreement after the text itself. In a letter to the Senate, President Reagan registered strong disapproval of this condition, maintaining that the Senate had no power to alter the traditional principles of treaty interpretation by subordinating sources such as the intent of the parties, the negotiating record, and subsequent practices to the unilateral declarations of the United States. "[T]he principles of treaty interpretation recognized and repeatedly invoked by the courts may not be limited or changed by the Senate alone, and those principles will govern any future disputes over the interpretation of this treaty," concluded the President. 27 I.L.M. 1413 (1988).

3. *Agreed Interpretation.* What is the legal effect of an interpretation made by the parties to an international agreement? See *Ste. Ruegger et Boutet v. Ste. Weber et Howard*, [1933–34] Ann. Dig. Pub. Int'l L. Cases (McNair & Lauterpacht), No. 179 (Trib. civ. de la Seine, France), in which the court held itself bound by an interpretation recorded by exchange of notes between the French Minister of Foreign Affairs and the British Ambassador, of a treaty between the two countries. The Court said that although a "unilateral" interpretation had only an "advisory effect," an interpretation agreed upon by both governments had the effect of adding an additional clause to the treaty. Should *interpretation* by the parties to a bilateral treaty be regarded as an *amendment* of the treaty? What practical results might depend upon the distinction? An interpretation agreed upon by all the parties to a treaty is commonly called an "authentic," as distinct from a "unilateral," interpretation. See Degan, *supra*, at 18–19; de Visscher, Problèmes d'Interprétation Judiciare en Droit International Public 20–21 (1963). Article 31(3)(a) of the Vienna Convention addresses the situation of subsequent agreement of the parties concerning interpretation.

4. *Interpretation of Multilateral Treaty by Fewer than All Parties.* In the case of a multilateral treaty, it is ordinarily impractical to obtain the assent of every party to a given interpretation. What is the legal effect of an interpretation made by fewer than all the parties? Should nonparticipating states be bound by the interpretation made by the other contracting states if the former do not protest within a reasonable time? Should an interpretation reached by fewer than all the contracting states be given greater weight than a "unilateral" interpretation? In *Philippson v. Imperial Airways, Ltd.*, [1939] A.C. 332, the House of Lords held that the term "High Contracting Party" as used in the Warsaw Convention on International Air Transportation, 1929, 49 Stat. 3000, 137 L.N.T.S. 11, included a state that had signed the treaty but had not yet ratified it. The British Embassy in the United States informed the Secretary of State of the decision, and stated that the British Government's interpretation of "High Contracting Party" was that the term included only states that were finally bound by the treaty's provisions. The Secretary of State expressed his agreement with the British Government's position. 4 Hackworth at 373; 5 Hackworth at 199, 250–51. Could either the United States or the United Kingdom thereafter assert against the other a different interpretation of "High Contracting Party"? Would other parties to the Warsaw Convention be bound by the U.S.–U.K. interpretation if they did not protest within a reasonable time? What would be reasonable time? Would states subsequently acceding to the Convention be bound by the U.S.–U.K.

interpretation if, upon accession, they did not reserve their position on that question?

5. *Subsequent Practice.* May the subsequent conduct of the parties to the Treaty determine the meaning of provisions that were ambiguous? See Article 31(3)(b) of the Vienna Convention. United States courts have often relied on subsequent conduct as evidence of the intent of the parties. See *Sumitomo Shoji America v. Avagliano*, 457 U.S. 176 (1982). Subsequent conduct was relied on by a federal court to find that the term "accident" as used in the Warsaw Convention on liability for aviation accidents included "hijackings." *Husserl v. Swiss Air Transport Co., Ltd.*, 351 F.Supp. 702 (S.D.N.Y. 1972). See also *Day v. Trans World Airlines, Inc.*, 528 F.2d 31 (2d Cir. 1975); Restatement (Third) § 325, Reporters' Note 5. But cf. *United States v. Alvarez–Machain*, 504 U.S. 655 (1992) (Supreme Court purported to confirm its interpretation of U.S.–Mexican extradition treaty by reference to "the history of negotiation and practice under the Treaty," while the dissent, at note 4, criticized the majority for offering no evidence from the negotiating record, ratification process, or later communications with Mexico in support of its interpretation).

6. *Subsequent Practice and Subsequent Agreement: Decolonization.* Interesting problems of interpretation—in some respects typical, in other respects novel—were raised in *Kasikili/Sedudu Island*, 1999 I.C.J. 1045, in which the I.C.J. was asked to determine a boundary line between Botswana and Namibia, on the basis of a 1890 treaty between Great Britain and Germany delimiting their respective spheres of influence in Africa. The parties disagreed on the consequences to be drawn from the facts of the case, including the significance (if any) of certain reports and correspondence prepared by their colonial predecessors. On these points, the Court said:

> 55. The Court shares [Namibia's] view that the Eason Report [a document prepared by a British captain in 1912] and its surrounding circumstances cannot be regarded as representing "subsequent practice in the application of the treaty" of 1890, within the meaning of Article 31, paragraph 3(b) of the Vienna Convention. It notes that the Report appears never to have been made known to Germany [Namibia's predecessor in interest] and to have remained at all times an internal document. The Court observes, moreover, that the British Government itself never took the Report any further * * *.

Later, after control of South–West Africa (in the territory that later became Namibia) had passed from Germany to South Africa, British and South African authorities had exchanges of correspondence concerning the disputed area. Each party relied on those documents as tending to show "subsequent practice" under the 1890 treaty, but drew opposite inferences from the evidence. The Court, after recounting these differences, observed:

> 63. From all of the foregoing, the Court concludes that the above-mentioned events, which occurred between 1947 and 1951, demonstrate the absence of agreement between South Africa and Bechuanaland with regard to the location of the boundary around Kasikili/Sedudu Island and the status of the Island. Those events cannot therefore constitute "subsequent practice in the application of the treaty [of 1890] which establishes

the agreement of the parties regarding its interpretation" (1969 Vienna Convention on the Law of Treaties, Art. 31, para. 3(b)). *A fortiori,* they cannot have given rise to an "agreement between the parties regarding the interpretation of the treaty or the application of its provisions" (*ibid.,* Art. 31, para. 3(a)).

Still later, after the U.N. General Assembly had revoked South Africa's mandate to administer South–West Africa:

> 64.   In October 1984 an incident during which shots were fired took place between members of the Botswana Defence Force and South African soldiers who were travelling by boat in the Chobe's southern channel. At a meeting held in Pretoria on 19 December 1984 between representatives of various South African and Botswanan ministries, it emerged that the incident had arisen out of differences of interpretation as to the precise location of the boundary around Kasikili/Sedudu Island. At this meeting, reference was made to the terms of the 1890 Treaty and it was agreed "that a joint survey should take place as a matter of urgency to determine whether the main Channel of the Chobe River is located to the north or the south of the Sidudu/Kasikili Island."

The joint survey was carried out at the beginning of July 1985, by a team of technical experts. Thereafter Botswana and South Africa exchanged diplomatic notes concerning the joint survey, in which Botswana insisted that the matter had been resolved in Botswana's favor and the South African authorities proposed further discussions. The I.C.J. judgment continues:

> 67.   In these proceedings, Botswana contends that the decision taken in December 1984 to carry out a joint survey, and all the documents relating to that decision—including the survey of July 1985 itself— constitute an "intergovernmental agreement ... between the parties regarding ... the application" of the 1890 Treaty * * *. Botswana points out *inter alia* that "general international law do[es] not require any particular formality for the conclusion of an international agreement" and that "[t]he only criterion is the intention of the parties to conclude a binding agreement and this can be inferred from the circumstances."

> Namibia categorically denies that the discussions conducted between the Botswana and South African authorities in 1984–1985 led to an agreement on the boundary; it stresses in this connection that the July 1985 joint survey was not "self-executing" and was devoid of any legally binding status unless the parties concerned took the appropriate measures to confer such status upon it. Namibia points out that, once the United Nations General Assembly had terminated South Africa's mandate over South West Africa in 1966, neither South Africa nor Botswana could in any case conclude any kind of agreement on the boundaries of this territory.

> 68.   Having examined the documents referred to above, the Court cannot conclude therefrom that in 1984–1985 South Africa and Botswana had agreed on anything more than the despatch of the joint team of experts. In particular, the Court cannot conclude that the two States agreed in some fashion or other to recognize themselves as legally bound by the results of the joint survey carried out in July 1985. * * *

69.   The Court has reached the conclusion that there was no agreement between South Africa and Botswana "regarding the . . . application of the [1890 Treaty]." This is in itself sufficient to dispose of the matter. It is unnecessary to add that in 1984 and 1985 the two States had no competence to conclude such an agreement, since at that time the United Nations General Assembly had already terminated South Africa's Mandate over South West Africa * * *.

Several of the separate and dissenting opinions discussed the principles of interpretation involved in this case at great length.

7.   *Interpretation by Courts of Parties.* Interpretive questions frequently arise in the domestic courts of states parties to treaties, for example in cases brought by private litigants invoking rights under treaties such as the Warsaw Convention. Do such courts engage in a common interpretive enterprise? Do they follow the same methodology? Should they give precedential weight to each other's decisions, notwithstanding the absence of a formal doctrine of *stare decisis* in international law? In one such case that reached the U.S. Supreme Court, involving a question under the Warsaw Convention that several intermediate courts in other states parties had previously decided, the majority of the justices examined the issue *de novo*, while the dissent thought that more deference should have been paid to the previous decisions in other countries, in the interests of achieving a uniform interpretation among the parties (whether or not that interpretation would have been the one that the Supreme Court might have reached if it had been the first to consider the matter). *Olympic Airways v. Husain*, 540 U.S. 644, 660–61 (2004) (Scalia, J., dissenting).

8.   *Interpretation by Courts of Third States.* May a court in a third state interpret a treaty at the request of private litigants? Would such judicial determinations contravene sovereign rights of the states that are parties to the treaty? See *Occidental of Umm v. A Certain Cargo of Petroleum*, 577 F.2d 1196 (5th Cir. 1978), cert. denied, 442 U.S. 928 (1979); *Buttes Gas & Oil Co. v. Hammer* (House of Lords) 1982 A.C. 888, reprinted in 21 I.L.M. 92 (1982).

9.   *Interpretation by International Organizations.* Which organ or organs are responsible for the interpretation of international agreements, such as the Charter of the United Nations, that serve as constitutions for international organizations? The San Francisco Conference failed to include in the Charter any specific provisions relating to the Charter's interpretation, instead leaving to the organs and member-states of the United Nations the freedom to determine for themselves the meaning of Charter provisions. The Committee on Legal Problems offered the following suggestions, which were subsequently approved by the Conference:

> In the course of the operations from day to day of the various organs of the Organization, it is inevitable that each organ will interpret such parts of the Charter as are applicable to its particular functions. This process is inherent in the functioning of any body which operates under an instrument defining its functions and powers. It will be manifested in the functioning of such a body as the General Assembly, the Security Council, or the International Court of Justice. Accordingly, it is not

necessary to include in the Charter a provision either authorizing or approving the normal operation of this principle.

Difficulties may conceivably arise in the event that there should be a difference of opinion among the organs of the Organization concerning the correct interpretation of a provision of the Charter. Thus, two organs may conceivably hold and may express or even act upon different views. Under unitary forms of national government the final determination of such a question may be vested in the highest court or in some other national authority. However, the nature of the Organization and of its operation would not seem to be such as to invite the inclusion in the Charter of any provision of this nature. If two Member States are at variance concerning the correct interpretation of the Charter, they are of course free to submit the dispute to the International Court of Justice as in the case of any other treaty. Similarly, it would always be open to the General Assembly or to the Security Council, in appropriate circumstances, to ask the International Court of Justice for an advisory opinion concerning the meaning of a provision of the Charter. Should the General Assembly or the Security Council prefer another course, an *ad hoc* committee of jurists might be set up to examine the question and report its views, or recourse might be had to a joint conference. In brief, the members or the organs of the Organization might have recourse to various expedients in order to obtain an appropriate interpretation. It would appear neither necessary nor desirable to list or to describe in the Charter the various possible expedients.

It is to be understood, of course, that if an interpretation made by any organ of the Organization or by a committee of jurists is not generally acceptable it will be without binding force. In such circumstances, or in cases where it is desired to establish an authoritative interpretation as a precedent for the future, it may be necessary to embody the interpretation in an amendment to the Charter. This may always be accomplished by recourse to the procedure provided for amendments.

13 U.N.C.I.O. Docs. 709. What difficulties might be expected to arise under the above "process" of interpretation? Does the availability of an advisory opinion by the International Court of Justice mitigate the danger of deadlock?

10. *Constitutive Instruments.* To what extent, if at all, ought special rules to be applied in the interpretation of such international agreements as the Charter of the United Nations and other constitutive instruments of international organizations, or of multilateral conventions concerned with the regulation of matters of social or humanitarian significance? Consider the following statement of Judge Azevedo, dissenting from the Advisory Opinion in *Competence of the General Assembly for the Admission of a State to the United Nations*, 1950 I.C.J. 4, 23:

[T]he interpretation of the San Francisco instruments will always have to present a teleological character if they are to meet the requirements of world peace, co-operation between men, individual freedom and social progress. The Charter is a means and not an end. To comply with its aims one must seek the methods of interpretation most likely to serve the natural evolution of the needs of mankind.

Even more than in the applications of municipal law, the meaning and the scope of international texts must continually be perfected, even if the terms remain unchanged.

Are the original intentions of the parties, assuming that these can be discovered, any longer relevant to an interpretation based on the "teleological" approach, or would it be more important to discover the "emergent purpose" of the treaty, i.e., the objects or purposes revealed by the operation and practical application of the treaty? Consider the statement of the European Court of Human Rights that the European Convention on Human Rights should be construed "in the light of modern-day conditions obtaining in the democratic societies of the Contracting States and not solely according to what might be presumed to have been in the minds of the drafters of the Convention." *Deumeland Case*, 86 I.L.R. 376, 408 (1986). See generally Fitzmaurice, The Law and Procedure of the International Court of Justice 1951–4: Treaty Interpretation and Other Treaty Points, 33 Brit. Y.B.I.L. 203, 207–09 (1957); Gordon, The World Court and the Interpretation of Constitutive Treaties, 59 A.J.I.L. 794 (1965); McDougal, Lasswell, & Miller, The Interpretation of Agreements and World Public Order (1967); Schachter, Interpretation of the Charter in the Political Organs of the United Nations, in Law, State and International Legal Order (Engel & Metall eds. 1964).

11. *Interpretation by International and National Courts of the Same Treaty.* Many modern treaties contain clauses providing that disputes concerning the interpretation or application of the treaty shall be settled by an independent and impartial authority such as an *ad hoc* arbitral tribunal or by a permanent body such as the International Court of Justice. In the 1998 *Breard* case noted above, the U.S. Supreme Court said that it should give "respectful" consideration to an interpretation rendered by an international court with jurisdiction to interpret an international treaty. If the case had arisen in a different procedural posture (without the problem of procedural default that barred Breard's federal habeas claim, and at a time when an authoritative international ruling might already be in hand before the deadline for domestic action), should the Supreme Court have considered the international court's interpretation binding? In subsequent decisions, the Supreme Court gave a negative answer and reached its own interpretation at odds with the I.C.J.'s view. *Sanchez–Llamas v. Oregon*, 548 U.S. 331 (2006); *Medellín v. Texas*, 128 S.Ct. 1346 (2008). See further discussion in Chapter 10.

12. *Interpretation by World Trade Organization.* The dispute settlement organs of the W.T.O. (panels and Appellate Body) have embraced Articles 31–32 of the Vienna Convention as authoritative on the methodology for interpreting the GATT/W.T.O. agreements. See Palmeter & Mavroidis, The WTO Legal System: Sources of Law, 92 A.J.I.L. 398, 406, 409 (1998). For a close examination of the various elements of Vienna Convention analysis in W.T.O. rulings, see Mavroidis, No Outsourcing of Law? WTO Law as Practiced by WTO Courts, 102 A.J.I.L. 421 (2008).

In addressing a dispute between the European Union and the United States, the panel said:

7.21 * * * Article 3.2 of the [Dispute Settlement Understanding] directs panels to clarify WTO provisions "in accordance with customary rules of interpretation of public international law". Articles 31 and 32 of the Vienna Convention on the Law of Treaties ("Vienna Convention") have attained the status of rules of customary international law. In recent years, the jurisprudence of the Appellate Body and WTO panels has become one of the richest sources from which to receive guidance on their application. * * *

7.22 Text, context and object-and-purpose correspond to well established textual, systemic and teleological methodologies of treaty interpretation, all of which typically come into play when interpreting complex provisions in multilateral treaties. For pragmatic reasons the normal usage, and we will follow this usage, is to start the interpretation from the ordinary meaning of the "raw" text of the relevant treaty provisions and then seek to construe it in its context and in light of the treaty's object and purpose. However, the elements referred to in Article 31—text, context and object-and-purpose as well as good faith—are to be viewed as one holistic rule of interpretation rather than a sequence of separate tests to be applied in a hierarchical order. Context and object-and-purpose may often appear simply to confirm an interpretation seemingly derived from the "raw" text. In reality it is always some context, even if unstated, that determines which meaning is to be taken as "ordinary" and frequently it is impossible to give meaning, even "ordinary meaning", without looking also at object-and-purpose.

United States—Sections 301–310 of the Trade Act of 1974, Report of the Panel, WTO Doc. WT/DS152/R (1999), reprinted in 39 I.L.M. 452, 464 (2000). For the panel's application of the Vienna Convention criteria in interpreting the W.T.O. obligations of the United States, see id. at paras. 7.58–7.94. Among the intriguing features is the panel's position that the relevant context for interpreting W.T.O. commitments includes "systemic" considerations, that is, potential effects on the W.T.O. system as a whole from the construction of a given article of one of the agreements.

SECTION 5. INVALIDITY OF TREATIES

A. GENERAL PROVISIONS RELATING TO INVALIDITY

The International Law Commission considered it important to provide that the validity of a treaty may be impeached only through the application of the Vienna Convention (Article 42). Prior to the Vienna Convention, there was some doubt whether an invalid provision of a treaty may be struck out without declaring the entire treaty invalid. The Commission favored separability provided that it did not materially upset the balance of interests on the basis of which the parties consented to be bound. This is made clear in Article 44(3). In cases where the treaty is absolutely void (as in cases of coercion or conflict with *jus cogens*) there is no separability; the treaty is entirely null and void (Article 44(5)).

The Commission was aware that provisions on invalidity involved possible abuse. A party may become aware of a ground for invalidity but "continue with the treaty and only raise the matter at a much later date when it desires for quite other reasons to put an end to its obligations under the treaty." [1966] II Yb.I.L.C. 239. Article 45 seeks to meet that situation. A state is prohibited from claiming invalidity if after becoming aware of the facts it has agreed that the treaty remains in force or by reason of its conduct must be considered to have acquiesced in the validity of the treaty or its continuation in force. This rule does not apply where the treaty is absolutely void as in cases of coercion or *jus cogens*.

The principle of acquiescence has played a role in several cases before the International Court of Justice, including *Arbitral Award Made by the King of Spain on 23 December 1906*, 1960 I.C.J. 192, 213–14, *Temple of Preah Vihear*, 1962 I.C.J. 6, 23–32, and *Territorial and Maritime Dispute between Nicaragua and Colombia*, 2007 I.C.J. No. 124. The latter judgment is excerpted below (p. 187 note 1).

NOTE

Exclusivity of Grounds for Invalidity, Suspension or Termination. In the *Gabčíkovo–Nagymaros Project* (Hungary/Slovakia), 1997 I.C.J. 7, excerpted at p. 225, Hungary argued that a 1977 treaty was not in force between the two states. Hungary put forward a number of grounds for considering that the treaty was without legal effect. Some of those grounds were based in the law of treaties as codified in the Vienna Convention (material breach in Article 60; supervening impossibility in Article 61; fundamental change of circumstances in Article 62). Other grounds were claimed outside the framework of the Vienna Convention—notably, Hungary's arguments that a "state of ecological necessity" justified suspension or termination of obligations under the treaty, and that new norms of international environmental law had developed since the treaty's conclusion. The Court evaluated certain of Hungary's claims not under the law of treaties but rather under another body of law, the law of state responsibility that pertains to the consequences of wrongful acts. (See Chapter 8.) In respect of the proposition that grounds for invalidating, suspending or terminating a treaty as such could be found in addition to those specified in the Vienna Convention, the Court said:

> 47. * * * [T]he Vienna Convention of 1969 on the Law of Treaties confines itself to defining—in a limitative manner—the conditions in which a treaty may lawfully be denounced or suspended; while the effects of a denunciation or suspension seen as not meeting those conditions are, on the contrary, expressly excluded from the scope of the Convention by operation of Article 73.

Later the Court stressed that the "stability of treaty relations" requires that the grounds specified in the Vienna Convention be applied in accordance with their strict conditions, and that it "would set a precedent with disturbing implications for treaty relations and the integrity of the rule *pacta sunt servanda*" if a party could unilaterally set aside a treaty on grounds other than those so specified. Thus, the treaty could be terminated "only on the limited grounds enumerated in the Vienna Convention." See paras. 100, 104, 114.

B. ULTRA VIRES TREATIES

As we saw earlier, a state may not invoke its internal law as justification for failure to perform a treaty. This general principle is qualified, however, by the rule stated in Article 46 of the Vienna Convention. That provision permits a state to assert as a ground of invalidity of a treaty the fact that its consent to be bound was expressed in violation of a provision of its internal law concerning the competence to conclude treaties. A state may invoke that fact only if "the violation was manifest and concerned a rule of internal law of fundamental importance." Article 46. Accordingly, in the special circumstances stated, the question of constitutional competence to conclude a treaty—a matter of internal law— becomes internationally relevant. The rule, it should be noted, may be relied upon only by the state whose consent was expressed in contravention of its own constitutional provision or other rule of fundamental importance.

The requirement that the violation must be "manifest" is of particular interest. Article 46(2) says that "a violation is manifest if it would be objectively evident to any State dealing with the matter in accordance with normal practice and good faith." Article 46(2). It is conceivable that a head of state might enter into a treaty in contravention of an unequivocal and well-known fundamental principle of his national law. But such cases are rare. See [1966] II Yb.I.L.C. 241–42. Normally when a head of state or government ratifies or accedes to a treaty, a strong presumption exists that he or she has acted within constitutional authority. Even if doubts were expressed in that respect, it is unlikely that another state would find a violation "manifest" or objectively evident.

Studies of treaty practice have confirmed that constitutional incompetence has not actually resulted in invalidating treaties. Hans Blix, in a study prior to the Vienna Convention, concluded that in fact "no treaty has been found that has been admitted to be invalid or held by an international tribunal to be invalid, because concluded by a constitutionally incompetent authority or in an unconstitutional manner * * *. Furthermore, there is no lack of treaties made in violation of constitutions, or by constitutionally incompetent authorities, and yet admitted to be valid in international law." Blix, Treaty–Making Power 373–74 (1960). A similar conclusion was reached by a later study. See Wildhaber, Treaty–Making Power and Constitutions 146–82 (1971). The latter also observes on the basis of an comparative analysis that the constitutional competences to enter into treaties "are almost never really clear." Id. at 181.

The provision in the United States Constitution that the President may not enter into a "treaty" without the advice and consent of the Senate is of particular interest. McNair commented that that requirement possesses "an international notoriety so that other states cannot hold a State bound by a treaty when in fact there has been no compliance with constitutional requirements of this type." McNair, The Law of Treaties 63 (1961). A different conclusion is drawn by Henkin in the following comment:

> But the power of the President to make many agreements without the Senate casts some doubt on "the fundamental importance" of Senate consent; in any event, failure to obtain such consent cannot be a "manifest" violation of the Constitution since no one can say with certainty when it is required.

Henkin, Foreign Affairs and the U.S. Constitution 500 (2d ed. 1996).

The Restatement (Third) contains the following comment on this point:

> Some agreements such as the U.N. Charter or the agreement creating NATO are of sufficient dignity, formality and importance that, in the unlikely event that the President attempted to make such an agreement on his own authority, his lack of authority might be regarded as "manifest".

Restatement (Third) § 311, Comment c.

NOTES

1. *Failure to Claim Invalidity.* Article 46 has only rarely been invoked before international tribunals as a basis for a claim of invalidity. In *Territorial and Maritime Dispute* (Nicaragua v. Colombia), 2007 I.C.J. No. 124, Colombia raised a jurisdictional objection in reliance on a 1928 treaty on territorial questions, which it claimed had definitively settled the matters that Nicaragua said were in dispute. Nicaragua contended that the 1928 treaty was invalid because it was "concluded in manifest violation of the Nicaraguan constitution" at a time when Nicaragua was under military occupation by the United States. In addressing this point, the Court recalled (para. 79):

> Nicaragua advanced "the nullity and lack of validity" of the 1928 Treaty for the first time in an official declaration and White Paper published on 4 February 1980. * * * The Court thus notes that, for more than 50 years, Nicaragua has treated the 1928 Treaty as valid and never contended that it was not bound by the Treaty, even after the withdrawal of the last United States troops at the beginning of 1933. At no time in those 50 years, even after it became a member of the United Nations in 1948, did Nicaragua contend that the Treaty was invalid for whatever reason, including that it had been concluded in violation of its Constitution or under foreign coercion. On the contrary, Nicaragua has, in significant ways, acted as if the 1928 Treaty was valid. * * *
>
> The Court thus finds that Nicaragua cannot today be heard to assert that the 1928 Treaty was not in force in 1948 [the date of another treaty relevant to the jurisdictional claim in the case].

2. *Invocations in Parliamentary Approval Procedures.* Article 46 was invoked in the U.S. Senate in connection with two bilateral agreements to which the United States adhered. One was an agreement between the United States and Israel in 1975 connected with the withdrawal of Israel from the Sinai peninsula, which involved a number of commitments by the United States with respect to meeting Israeli's supply needs and defense requirements. The Legislative Counsel to the Senate took the position that since the agreement was concluded without the advice and consent of the Senate, it was without force under domestic law. Moreover, since it violated in that respect a rule of fundamental importance and since Israel should reasonably have known of this constitutional defect, the agreement was without force in international law. The State Department rejected that position and no action was taken by the Senate. The Department of State memorandum is reproduced in 15 I.L.M. 198 (1976). For an analysis of the issues, see Meron, Article 46 of the Vienna Convention on the Law of Treaties (*ultra vires* treaties), 49 Brit. Y.B.I.L. 175–99 (1978).

The question of constitutional competence was also raised in the Senate in regard to the agreement between the United States and Panama concluded in 1977 with respect to the Panama Canal. In this case, the issue related to an alleged violation by Panama of its constitutional requirements for entering into an agreement of the character of the Canal treaty. A group of U.S. Senators contended that the Panama constitution clearly required a plebiscite to approve a treaty. They asserted that the plebiscite conducted prior to ratification did not meet that requirement because subsequently the United States, on the advice of the Senate, included a number of reservations, conditions and understandings in the instruments of ratification. While these were accepted by the President of Panama, they were not submitted to a second plebiscite. Several Senators argued that the violation was "manifest" and concerned a rule of fundamental importance. They maintained that unless this was corrected by renegotiation, Panama would be able in the future to claim invalidity because of the constitutional defect. Sen. Exec. Rep. 95–12 (1978); see also 71 A.J.I.L. 635–43 (1978). The Government of Panama responded that under Panamanian law, a second plebiscite was not required. Panama had accepted the Senate's conditions, reservations and understandings but regarded them as interpretations of the treaties, not as alterations or amendments. The Executive Branch of the U.S. Government considered the legal position of Panama as "reasonable." They did not see any violation of Panamanian law and certainly no manifest violations within the meaning of Article 46. Meron, *supra*, at 190. Would there be a basis for a future Panamanian Government to seek to invalidate the agreements on the ground of Article 46? Would Article 45 apply in that event?

3. *Authority of Foreign Minister.* The reluctance of tribunals to look behind the ostensible authority of a foreign minister to commit his state was evidenced in the *Legal Status of Eastern Greenland Case*, Denmark v. Norway, 1933 P.C.I.J. (ser. A/B) No. 53, decided by the Permanent Court of International Justice in 1933. The case involved a dispute between Norway and Denmark regarding Norwegian occupation of parts of Greenland. The Norwegian Foreign Minister had informed Denmark orally that the "Norwegian Government would not make any difficulty in the settlement of this

question." Norway contended that under its constitution the foreign minister could not enter into a binding international agreement on "matters of importance" without approval of the "King in Council." The Court rejected Norway's claim that this constitutional limitation invalidated the commitment of the foreign minister, finding it sufficient that the foreign minister acted "within his province" in replying to an inquiry of the Danish Government. See also Chapter 4, Section 6 on Unilateral Acts of States and the *Maritime Delimitation Case* (Qatar v. Bahrain), pp. 126, 128, paras. 26–27.

C. COERCION

The Commission considered coercion of a representative of such gravity that the consent of a state so obtained shall be without any legal effect. It referred to a case of "third-degree methods of pressure" against the President and Foreign Minister of Czechoslovakia in 1939 to extract their signatures to a treaty creating a German protectorate over Bohemia and Moravia. It also referred generally to instances in which members of legislatures were coerced to procure ratification of a treaty. Id. at 246. Coercion was also used to include a threat to ruin the career of a representative by exposing a private indiscretion as well as a threat to injure a member of his family.

The Commission considered that the principle of ~~invalidity~~ by virtue of a prohibited use or threat of force was established law. It said:

> (1) ~~The traditional doctrine prior to the~~ Covenant of the League of Nations was that the validity of a treaty was not affected by the fact that it had been brought about by the threat or use of force. However, this doctrine was simply a reflection of the general attitude of international law during that era towards the legality of the use of force for the settlement of international disputes. With the Covenant and the Pact of Paris there began to develop a strong body of opinion which held that such treaties should no longer be recognized as legally valid. The endorsement of the criminality of aggressive war in the Charters of the Allied Military Tribunals for the trial of the Axis war criminals, the clear-cut prohibition of the threat or use of force in Article 2(4) of the Charter of the United Nations, together with the practice of the United Nations itself, have reinforced and consolidated this development in the law. The Commission considers that these developments justify the conclusion that the invalidity of a treaty procured by the illegal threat or use of force is a principle which is *lex lata* in the international law of to-day.
>
> (2) Some jurists, it is true, while not disputing the moral value of the principle, have hesitated to accept it as a legal rule. They fear that to recognize the principle as a legal rule may open the door to the evasion of treaties by encouraging unfounded assertions of coercion, and that the rule will be ineffective because the same threat or compulsion that procured the conclusion of the treaty will also procure its execution, whether the law regards it as valid or invalid.

These objections do not appear to the Commission to be of such a kind as to call for the omission from the present articles of a ground of invalidity springing from the most fundamental provisions of the Charter, the relevance of which in the law of treaties as in other branches of international law cannot today be regarded as open to question.

Id. at 246.

The proposed article led to a major confrontation at the Vienna Conference when a number of states proposed an amendment to define "force" to include "economic or political pressure" (referred to as the nineteen-state amendment). An account by the U.S. representative to the Vienna Conference and his colleague follows:

The proponents of the amendment made it quite clear in the committee of the whole that their amendment was directed toward "economic needs." The representative of Tanzania described "the withdrawal of economic aid or of promises of aid [and] the recall of economic experts" as the type of conduct which should be prohibited. The Algerian representative advanced the thesis:

[T]he era of the colonial treaty was past or disappearing, but there was no overlooking the fact that some countries had resorted to new and more insidious methods, suited to the present state of international relations, in an attempt to maintain and perpetuate bonds of subjection. Economic pressure, which was a characteristic of neo-colonialism, was becoming increasingly common in relations between certain countries and the newly independent States.

Political independence could not be an end in itself; it was even illusory if it was not backed by genuine economic independence. That was why some countries had chosen the political, economic and social system they regarded as best calculated to overcome under-development as quickly as possible. That choice provoked intense opposition from certain interests which saw their privileges threatened and then sought through economic pressure to abolish or at least restrict the right of peoples to self-determination. Such neo-colonialist practices, which affected more than two-thirds of the world's population and were retarding or nullifying all efforts to overcome under-development, should therefore be denounced with the utmost rigour.

Statements of this character reinforced the already deep misgivings as to the effect of the amendment held by the states concerned with the stability of treaties.

The scope of the phrase "threat or use of force" in Article 2, paragraph 4, of the United Nations Charter, as is well known, has been for many years the source of acrimonious dispute. The legislative history of the San Francisco Conference is clear as to its original intent. The Chilean delegate made that point:

> The Brazilian delegation to the 1945 San Francisco Conference had proposed the inclusion of an express reference to the prohibition of economic pressure, and its proposal had been rejected. Consequently, any reference to the principles of the Charter in that respect must be a reference to the kind of force which all the Member States had agreed to prohibit, namely, physical or armed force.

The discussions were complicated by the fact that the United Nations Special Committee on Principles of International Law concerning Friendly Relations and Cooperation Among States had been studying the "threat or use of force" issue since 1964, and action by the Conference could only cut across the deliberations of that body. The question was also raised whether the conference was attempting to amend the United Nations Charter. The basic problem was well summed up by the Dutch representative:

> In itself, the rule stated in article [52] was perfectly clear and precise. He supported the principle underlying the article, namely, the principle that an aggressor State should not, in law, benefit from a treaty it had forced its victim to accept. Nevertheless, it must be borne in mind that there was a fundamental difference of opinion as to the meaning of the words 'threat or use of force' in Article 2, paragraph 4, of the United Nations Charter. If those words could be interpreted as including all forms of pressure exerted by one State on another, and not just the threat or use of armed force, the scope of article [52] would be so wide as to make it a serious danger to the stability of treaty relations.

The course of the debate had made it clear that if the amendment were put to the vote it would carry by quite a substantial majority. On the other hand, in private discussions it had been made quite clear to the proponents that adoption could wreck the conference because states concerned with the stability of treaties found the proposal intolerable.

> To reduce tension, discussion of the article was adjourned and private negotiations resorted to. A compromise solution was reached after some days of cooling off. The amendment was withdrawn. In its place, a draft declaration condemning threat or use of pressure in any form by a state to coerce any other state to conclude a treaty was unanimously adopted by the committee. Although at one point during the plenary it appeared that the compromise might be unraveling, it was adhered to by both sides. The declaration finally approved by the conference in 1969 is annexed to the Final Act.

Kearney & Dalton, 64 A.J.I.L. at 533–35 (footnotes omitted).

The International Law Commission also considered that a treaty imposed by illegal force should be void, as opposed to voidable. It said in this connection:

> Even if it were conceivable that after being liberated from the influence of a threat or of a use of force a State might wish to allow a treaty procured from it by such means, the Commission considered it essential that the treaty should be regarded in law as void *ab initio*. This would enable the State concerned to take its decision in regard to the maintenance of the treaty in a position of full legal equality with the other State. If, therefore, the treaty were maintained in force, it would in effect be by the conclusion of a new treaty and not by the recognition of the validity of a treaty procured by means contrary to the most fundamental principles of the Charter of the United Nations.

[1966] II Yb.I.L.C. 247.

The question of the time element in the application of the article was dealt with by the Commission in the following comments:

> The Commission considered that there is no question of the article having retroactive effects on the validity of treaties concluded prior to the establishment of the modern law. "A juridical fact must be appreciated in the light of the law contemporary with it." The present article concerns the conditions for the valid conclusion of a treaty—the conditions, that is, for the *creation* of a legal relation by treaty. An evolution of the law governing the conditions for the carrying out of a legal act does not operate to deprive of validity a legal act already accomplished in conformity with the law previously in force. The rule codified in the present article cannot therefore be properly understood as depriving of validity *ab initio* a peace treaty or other treaty procured by coercion prior to the establishment of the modern law regarding the threat or use of force.
>
> (8) As to the date from which the modern law should be considered as in force for the purposes of the present article, the Commission considered that it would be illogical and unacceptable to formulate the rule as one applicable only from the date of the conclusion of a convention on the law of treaties. As pointed out in paragraph (1) above, the invalidity of a treaty procured by the illegal threat or use of force is a principle which is *lex lata*. Moreover, whatever differences of opinion there may be about the state of the law prior to the establishment of the United Nations, the great majority of international lawyers to-day unhesitatingly hold that article 2, paragraph 4, together with other provisions of the Charter, authoritatively declares the modern customary law regarding the threat or use of force. The present article, by its formulation, recognizes by implication that the rule which it lays down is applicable at any rate to all treaties concluded since the entry into force of the Charter. On the other hand, the Commission did not think that it was part of its function, in

codifying the modern law of treaties, to specify on what precise date in the past an existing general rule in another branch of international law came to be established as such. Accordingly, it did not feel that it should go beyond the temporal indication given by the reference in the article to "the principles of the Charter of the United Nations."

Id.

NOTES

1. *Coercion through Hostage–Taking.* Would the seizure of hostages for the purpose of coercing their government to grant certain concessions and benefits to the state that seized the hostages constitute a use of force or threat of force against the political independence of the state whose nationals were seized? Would an agreement granting the benefits demanded be void under Article 52?

2. *Iran–U.S. Settlement Agreement.* When the United States and Iran reached agreements (known as the Algiers Accords) in 1980 that called for the release of U.S. diplomats and other U.S. nationals who had been held hostage in Iran, were those agreements void under Article 52 because they were procured by the use of force against the United States? Could either side have refused to perform on the ground that the treaty was void *ab initio?* The main provisions of the agreement provided for the release of the hostages plus a declaration of nonintervention by the U.S. and the unblocking of Iranian assets frozen in the U.S. in response to the seizure. The United States gave nothing to Iran beyond releasing Iranian assets. In fact Iran received back less than its assets, since a part was placed in escrow to pay creditors and other claimants of United States nationality. See Chapter 8, p. 549 and Chapter 9, p. 575. Can one say that an arrangement of this kind was "procured by" the use of threat of force, even if force was initially used against the United States? See Schachter, International Law in the Hostage Crisis, in American Hostages in Iran 325, 369–73 (Christopher et al., 1985).

3. *Kosovo.* In the aftermath of the Kosovo crisis of 1999, some critics who viewed the NATO intervention as a use of force in violation of the U.N. Charter also thought that the subsequent arrangements to settle the situation might have been tainted, and that Yugoslavia could potentially have invoked the Vienna Convention's coercion provision to impeach the validity of the settlement. See, e.g., Nambiar, India, in Kosovo and the Challenge of Humanitarian Intervention 260, 265 (Schnabel & Thakur eds. 2000). See Chapter 15. Does the Security Council's approval of the Kosovo arrangements in Resolution 1244 (1999) render moot the issue of whether Yugoslavia was "coerced" for purposes of the law of treaties?

4. *Agreement Concluded During Military Occupation.* In *Territorial and Maritime Dispute* (Nicaragua v. Colombia), 2007 I.C.J. No. 124, Nicaragua claimed that it had been coerced in entering into a 1928 Treaty on Territorial Questions with Colombia, because "at the time the Treaty was concluded, Nicaragua was under military occupation by the United States and was precluded from concluding treaties that ran contrary to the interests of the United States and from rejecting the conclusion of treaties that the United

States demanded it to conclude" (para. 75). The Court rejected Nicaragua's claim of invalidity on this ground (see passage excerpted at p. 187 note 1 above under heading of Ultra Vires Treaties). In dissent, Vice–President Al–Khasawneh pointed out that the Court had never previously ruled on an allegation of coercion in the conclusion of a treaty. The Court did not address either Article 45(b) of the Vienna Convention (on loss of right to impeach validity) or Article 52 as such. Should it have done so? Does the result suggest a preference for maintaining stability of treaty relations?

D.　CONFLICT WITH A PEREMPTORY NORM (*JUS COGENS*)

REPORT OF THE INTERNATIONAL LAW COMMISSION

[1966] II Yb.I.L.C. 169, 247–49

(1) The view that in the last analysis there is no rule of international law from which States cannot at their own free will contract out has become increasingly difficult to sustain, although some jurists deny the existence of any rules of *jus cogens* in international law, since in their view even the most general rules still fall short of being universal. The Commission pointed out that the law of the Charter concerning the prohibition of the use of force in itself constitutes a conspicuous example of a rule in international law having the character of *jus cogens*. Moreover, if some Governments in their comments have expressed doubts as to the advisability of this article unless it is accompanied by provision for independent adjudication, only one questioned the existence of rules of *jus cogens* in the international law of today. Accordingly, the Commission concluded that in codifying the law of treaties it must start from the basis that to-day there are certain rules from which States are not competent to derogate at all by a treaty arrangement, and which may be changed only by another rule of the same character.

(2) The formulation of the article is not free from difficulty, since there is no simple criterion by which to identify a general rule of international law as having the character of *jus cogens*. Moreover, the majority of the general rules of international law do not have that character, and States may contract out of them by treaty. It would therefore be going much too far to state that a treaty is void if its provisions conflict with a rule of general international law. Nor would it be correct to say that a provision in a treaty possesses the character of *jus cogens* merely because the parties have stipulated that no derogation from that provision is to be permitted, so that another treaty which conflicted with that provision would be void. Such a stipulation may be inserted in any treaty with respect to any subject-matter for any reasons which may seem good to the parties. The conclusion by a party of a later treaty derogating from such a stipulation may, of course, engage its responsibility for a breach of the earlier treaty. But the breach of the stipulation does not, simply as such, render the treaty void (see article 26). It is not the form of a general rule of international law but the particular nature of the

subject-matter with which it deals that may, in the opinion of the Commission, give it the character of *jus cogens*.

(3) The emergence of rules having the character of *jus cogens* is comparatively recent, while international law is in process of rapid development. The Commission considered the right course to be to provide in general terms that a treaty is void if it conflicts with a rule of *jus cogens* and to leave the full content of this rule to be worked out in State practice and in the jurisprudence of international tribunals. Some members of the Commission felt that there might be advantage in specifying, by way of illustration, some of the most obvious and best settled rules of *jus cogens* in order to indicate by these examples the general nature and scope of the rule contained in the article. Examples suggested included (a) a treaty contemplating an unlawful use of force contrary to the principles of the Charter, (b) a treaty contemplating the performance of any other act criminal under international law, and (c) a treaty contemplating or conniving at the commission of acts, such as trade in slaves, piracy or genocide, in the suppression of which every State is called upon to co-operate. Other members expressed the view that, if examples were given, it would be undesirable to appear to limit the scope of the article to cases involving acts which constitute crimes under international law; treaties violating human rights, the equality of States or the principle of self-determination were mentioned as other possible examples. The Commission decided against including any examples of rules of *jus cogens* in the article for two reasons. First, the mention of some cases of treaties void for conflict with a rule of *jus cogens* might, even with the most careful drafting, lead to misunderstanding as to the position concerning other cases not mentioned in the article. Secondly, if the Commission were to attempt to draw up, even on a selective basis, a list of the rules of international law which are to be regarded as having the character of *jus cogens*, it might find itself engaged in a prolonged study of matters which fall outside the scope of the present articles.

* * *

(6) The second matter is the non-retroactive character of the rule in the present article. The article has to be read in conjunction with article [64] (Emergence of a new rule of *jus cogens*), and in the view of the Commission, there is no question of the present article having retroactive effects. It concerns cases where a treaty is void *at the time of its conclusion* by reason of the fact that its provisions are in conflict with an already existing rule of *jus cogens*. The treaty is wholly void because its actual conclusion conflicts with a peremptory norm of general international law from which no States may derogate even by mutual consent. Article [64], on the other hand, concerns cases where a treaty, valid when concluded, becomes void and terminates by reason of the subsequent establishment of a new rule of *jus cogens* with which its provisions are in conflict. The words *"becomes* void and *terminates"* make it quite clear, the Commission considered, that the emergence of a new rule of *jus cogens* is not to have

retroactive effects on the validity of a treaty. The invalidity is to attach only as from the time of the establishment of the new rule of *jus cogens*. The non-retroactive character of the rules in articles [53] and [64] is further underlined in article [71], paragraph 2 of which provides in the most express manner that the *termination* of a treaty as a result of the emergence of a new rule of *jus cogens* is not to have retroactive effects.

NOTES

1. *Disputes over Peremptory Norms.* Although the draft article on per-emptory norms generated much controversy at the Vienna conference, a revised draft was adopted by a vote of 72 in favor, 3 against, and 18 abstentions. Three changes were made to meet objections:

- The words "at the time of its conclusion" were added to make clear the non-retroactive character of the rule.

- It was made explicit that the peremptory norms were the norms recognized by the international community as a whole as those from which no derogation was permitted.

- It was agreed that a party to a dispute involving *jus cogens* may submit it to the International Court for a decision in all cases in which the procedures for settlement (indicated in Article 65) have failed to produce a solution within twelve months.

The adoption of this compulsory jurisdiction clause made it possible for states apprehensive over the possible destabilizing effect of the *jus cogens* article to support adoption. For detailed accounts, see Sinclair, The Vienna Convention on the Law of Treaties 203–26 (2d ed. 1984); Elias, The Modern Law of Treaties 177–87, 192–94 (1974); Sztucki, *Jus Cogens* and the Vienna Convention (1974).

2. *Content of* Jus Cogens. What are the rules of *jus cogens* today? A former President of the International Court of Justice has suggested the following answer:

> The substantive contents of *jus cogens* are likely to be constantly changing in accordance with the progress and development of international law and international morality. *Jus cogens* is not an immutable natural law but an evolving concept: the last phrase in the definition envisages the modification of *jus cogens* by the same process which led to its establishment.

> Such subsequent rules may originate in a treaty whose norms become generally accepted. A treaty of this nature, containing a new rule of *jus cogens,* would not be void, even if some of its provisions conflicted with an established rule of *jus cogens:* the new rules of *jus cogens* would simply modify or replace the old ones. Otherwise, international society would be deprived of the necessary means of development of its notions of public policy through processes of international legislation. For instance, the traditional definition of piracy may be extended to cover hijacking of aeroplanes or the opium and drug conventions expanded to include synthetic drugs.

Jiménez de Aréchaga, 159 Rec. des Cours 9, 64–67 (1978–I). See Chapter 2, *supra*, pp. 105–12.

SINCLAIR, THE VIENNA CONVENTION ON THE LAW OF TREATIES

222–24 (2d ed. 1984) (footnotes omitted)

Whatever their doctrinal point of departure, the majority of jurists would no doubt willingly concede to the sceptics that there is little or no evidence in positive international law for the concept that nullity attaches to a treaty concluded in violation of *jus cogens*. But they would be constrained to admit that the validity of a treaty between two States to wage a war of aggression against a third State or to engage in acts of physical or armed force against a third State could not be upheld; and, having made this admission, they may be taken to have accepted the principle that there may exist norms of international law so fundamental to the maintenance of an international legal order that a treaty concluded in violation of them is a nullity.

Some (among whom may be counted your author) would be prepared to go this far, but would immediately wish to qualify this acceptance of the principle involved by sketching out the limits within which it may be operative in present-day international law. In the first place, they would insist that, in the present state of international society, the concept of an "international legal order" of hierarchically superior norms binding all States is only just beginning to emerge. Ideological differences and disparities of wealth between the individual nation States which make up the international community, combined with the contrasts between the objectives sought by them, hinder the development of an over-arching community consensus upon the content of *jus cogens*. Indeed, it is the existence of these very differences and disparities which constitute the principal danger implicit in an unqualified recognition of *jus cogens;* for it would be only too easy to postulate as a norm of *jus cogens* a principle which happened neatly to serve a particular ideological or economic goal. In the second place, they would test any assertion that a particular rule constitutes a norm of *jus cogens* by reference to the evidence for its acceptance as such by the international community as a whole, and they would require that the burden of proof should be discharged by those who allege the *jus cogens* character of the rule. Applying this test, and leaving aside the highly theoretical case of a treaty purporting to deny the application of the principle *pacta sunt servanda,* it would seem that sufficient evidence for ascribing the character of *jus cogens* to a rule of international law exists in relation to the rule which requires States to refrain in their international relations from the threat of force against the territorial integrity or political independence of any other State. There is ample evidence for the proposition that, subject to the necessary exceptions about the use of force in self-defence or under the authority of a competent organ of the United Nations or a regional agency acting in accordance with the Charter, the use of armed or physical force against the territorial integrity or political independence of any State is now prohibited. This proposition is so central to the existence of any international legal order of individual nation States (however nascent that international legal order may be) that it must be taken to have the character of *jus cogens*. Just as national legal systems begin to discard, at an early stage of their development, such concepts as "trial by battle," so also must the international legal order be assumed now to deny any cover of legality to violations of the fundamental rule embodied in Article 2(4) of the Charter.

Beyond this, uncertainty begins, and one must tread with considerable caution. The dictates of logic, and overriding considerations of morality, would appear to require that one should characterise as *jus cogens* those rules which prohibit the slave trade and genocide; but the evidence is ambivalent, since the treaties which embody these prohibitions contain normal denunciation clauses. Of course, it may be argued that the presence or absence of normal denunciation clauses should not be taken as being decisive; denunciation clauses are regularly embodied in treaties for traditional, rather than practical, reasons. In any event, it is likely that the prohibitions may now be taken to form part of general international law binding all States regardless of whether they are parties to the treaties embodying them. The unenforceability of any treaty contemplating genocide or the slave trade is further assured by the fact that such a treaty would contravene the Charter of the United Nations, which prevails in the event of conflict.

To sum up, there is a place for the concept of *jus cogens* in international law. Its growth and development will parallel the growth and development of an international legal order expressive of the consensus of the international community as a whole. Such an international legal order is, at present, inchoate, unformed and only just discernible. *Jus cogens* is neither Dr. Jekyll nor Mr. Hyde; but it has the potentialities of both. If it is invoked indiscriminately and to serve short-term political purposes, it could rapidly be destructive of confidence in the security of treaties; if it is developed with wisdom and restraint in the overall interest of the international community it could constitute a useful check upon the unbridled will of individual States.

NOTES

1. *"International Community."* Recall Chapter 2, p. 105 *supra*, for an overview of *jus cogens*. What is meant by "international community of states" in Article 53?

2. *Case Law.* Although Article 66 of the Vienna Convention provides for compulsory adjudication of disputes concerning the application of Articles 53 and 64, there is little case-law involving invocation of *jus cogens* to impeach the validity of a treaty. For a comprehensive survey of cases in which such claims were or could have been raised, see Orakhelashvili, Peremptory Norms (2006); see also Shelton, Normative Hierarchy in Internationational Law, 100 A.J.I.L. 291, 297–319 (2006).

3. *Self–Determination.* Is the principle of self-determination a *jus cogens* norm? If so, could a third state obtain judicial invalidation of a treaty between two other states on a claim that the treaty conflicted with a people's right to self-determination? The *East Timor Case* (Portugal v. Australia), 1995 I.C.J. 90, 272–73, discussed in Chapter 5, pp. 327–29, involved issues along these lines. Portugal, on behalf of East Timor, claimed that a treaty between Australia and Indonesia concerning offshore resources in the so-called Timor Gap violated the right to self-determination of the people of East Timor. The Court dismissed the case on a threshold ground (absence of Indonesia as an indispensable party), without reaching the merits. If that jurisdictional problem had been surmountable, what reasoning might have been used to resolve the *jus cogens* issue under the Vienna Convention standard? See Cassese, Self–Determination: A Legal Reappraisal 133–40 (1995).

4. *Dispute Settlement.* Would the compulsory adjudication clause of Article 66 of the Vienna Convention significantly reduce the risk that Articles 53 and 64 would "destroy the security of treaties"? Would it restrain governments from attacking treaties regarded by them as unjust? Could they not use Article 66 to impugn treaties which are alleged to be contrary to such Charter principles as sovereign equality, or such "fundamental principles" as the non-acquisition of territory by the threat or use of force? (See Chapter 5, Section 5.A.2.) Would the International Court now have wide latitude to declare treaties to be void on the basis of such principles?

5. *Emergence of New Rule.* Article 64 deals with the emergence of a new rule of *jus cogens.* The treaty becomes void but, as stated in Article 71, the termination does not affect any right, obligation, or legal situation created through the execution of the treaty "provided that those rights, obligations or situations may thereafter be maintained only to the extent that their maintenance is not in itself in conflict with the new peremptory norm of general international law." Does this proviso throw doubt on executed settlements? The International Law Commission suggested that any alteration of a rule of *jus cogens* would probably be effected by conclusion of a general multilateral treaty. But would not such a treaty when concluded contravene unlawfully the rule of *jus cogens* it purports to alter? Does this make the idea of *jus cogens* almost meaningless in that context?

6. *Restatement.* The Restatement (Third) accepts the provisions of Articles 53 and 64 as customary law. However, it adds that inasmuch as the United States is not a party to the Convention and therefore the judicial safeguards do not apply to it, "the United States is likely to take a particularly restrictive view of these doctrines, and they can be applied as international law accepted by the United States only with caution." § 331, Reporters' Note 4. The Restatement also declares in § 331, Comment *e,* that in view of the uncertainty as to the scope of *jus cogens,* there is a particularly strong need "for an impartial determination of its applicability."

SECTION 6. TERMINATION OR SUSPENSION OF TREATIES

A. TERMINATION OR WITHDRAWAL UNDER THE TERMS OF A TREATY OR BY CONSENT

Most treaties today contain clauses specifying (a) their duration, or (b) the date of termination, or (c) an event or condition to bring about termination, or (d) a right to denounce or withdraw from the treaty. The clauses themselves are varied. Whether they apply in a particular case is a matter of interpretation. Article 54 of the Vienna Convention contains the self-evident rule that a treaty may be terminated in accordance with its own provisions. It also provides that a treaty may be terminated at any time by consent of all its parties.

NOTES

1. *Competence to Terminate.* Who has the right to act for a state in terminating a treaty? In principle, this is left to municipal law just as is the competence to express consent to be bound. But suppose the termination of the treaty is declared by an organ of the state lacking constitutional authority to take such action definitively. The Vienna Convention does not deal with this question. In Article 67, it mentions only the state officials who do not have to produce full powers for acts of termination; it follows in this respect the general principle of Article 7. Article 46 deals with the violation of domestic law regarding competence to conclude a treaty. It has been suggested that a similar rule should be applied in case of termination. See Haraszti, Some Fundamental Problems of the Law of Treaties 251–53 (1973). Haraszti (a Hungarian) cites as an instance of unlawful termination the denunciation of the Warsaw Pact by Hungary "at the time of the counter-revolution of 1956." In 1979, when President Carter terminated the Mutual Defense Treaty with the Republic of China (Taiwan) by giving one year's notice in accordance with the terms of the treaty, his right to do so without obtaining the advice and consent of the Senate was challenged by a Senator who brought a judicial proceeding. However, the Supreme Court dismissed the case without reaching the merits of the constitutional claim, so that the notice of termination took effect. See *Goldwater v. Carter*, 444 U.S. 996 (1979), p. 725.

2. *Partial Termination.* Does a clause providing for unilateral termination of a treaty give a party a right to terminate one or more clauses of the treaty without abrogating the rest of the treaty? When the other party or parties refused to accept such partial termination, termination of the entire agreement was necessitated. See 5 Hackworth 309–14; McNair, The Law of Treaties 476–78 (1961).

3. *Special Circumstances.* Many agreements have special provisions for withdrawal or release under particular circumstances. These are often preferred to general unilateral withdrawal provisions because they indicate an awareness of contingencies under which release from obligations would be

acceptable. In some cases they provide for special procedures under which a party can seek to be released from some or all of its obligations. See General Agreement on Tariffs and Trade (GATT) Articles XXV(5), XXVIII. When agreements identify the circumstances that would trigger release, the determination whether those circumstances have occurred may be left to the party itself or referred to an international organ authorized to grant a waiver to the party. The latter type is found in the International Monetary Fund Agreement and various commodity agreements. For a general review of such provisions in international agreements, see Bilder, Managing the Risks of International Agreement 52–55, 98–104 (1981).

4. *Revocation of Notice of Withdrawal.* May a denunciation or withdrawal be revoked before the end of the period when it would take effect? Article 68 of the Vienna Convention answers in the affirmative. In proposing this rule, the International Law Commission commented that the right to revoke the notice is implicit in the rule that it is not to become effective until a certain date and other parties should take that into account. Accordingly, there would be no grounds for requiring consent of the other parties.

5. *North Korea and Non–Proliferation Treaty.* In 1993–1994 and again from 2002 forward, disputes arose over the compliance of the Democratic People's Republic of Korea (North Korea) with a safeguards agreement under the Nuclear Non–Proliferation Treaty (NPT). Article X, paragraph 1 of the NPT has a withdrawal clause (similar to that in other arms control agreements, such as the Anti–Ballistic Missile Treaty between the United States and the Soviet Union, which the United States terminated on notice in 2002), as follows:

> Each Party shall in exercising its national sovereignty have the right to withdraw from the Treaty if it decides that extraordinary events, related to the subject matter of this Treaty, have jeopardized the supreme interests of its country. It shall give notice of such withdrawal to all other Parties to the Treaty and to the United Nations Security Council three months in advance. Such notice shall include a statement of the extraordinary events it regards as having jeopardized its supreme interests.

On March 12, 1993, North Korea gave three months' notice of withdrawal under Article X. In the same month, the Director–General of the International Atomic Energy Agency (IAEA) reported North Korea's continuing noncompliance with the safeguards agreement. Within the three-month period, the U.N. Security Council adopted a resolution calling on North Korea to comply with the agreement. S.C. Res. 825 (May 11, 1993). Security Council members stepped up pressure to keep North Korea within the NPT framework. Following high-level talks between North Korea and the United States held June 2–11, 1993, North Korea announced that it had suspended its notice of withdrawal and would consider itself in "special status" under the NPT. The crisis eased (at least temporarily) when former President Carter negotiated a formula for resolution of North Korea's concerns, later embodied in an "Agreed Framework" between the United States and North Korea announced Oct. 21, 1994 (reprinted at 34 I.L.M. 603).

By 2002, another crisis over allegations of noncompliance was in full swing. In January 2003, North Korea announced that it would withdraw from the NPT with immediate effect. It appears, however, that the parties to the NPT and the U.N. Security Council have not accepted North Korea's position on withdrawal. North Korea has been continuously carried as a party to the NPT on status lists maintained by the United States which is one of the official depositaries of the treaty, as well as in the lists carried on the records of the U.N. Department of Disarmament Affairs and the IAEA. The Security Council in several resolutions has "deplor[ed] the DPRK's announcement of withdrawal" from the NPT, and acting in its enforcement capacity under Chapter VII of the UN Charter has "[d]emand[ed] that the DPRK immediately retract its announcement of withdrawal" and "return to the Treaty on the Non–Proliferation of Nuclear Weapons and [IAEA] safeguards." S.C. Res. 1695, preamble (July 15, 2006); S.C. Res. 1718, preamble (Oct. 14, 2006). It has acted under Article 41 of the UN Charter to impose economic sanctions to induce the DPRK to do so. Is there a clear answer to whether North Korea remains in party status?

B. DENUNCIATION OR WITHDRAWAL FROM A TREATY WHICH CONTAINS NO PROVISION REGARDING TERMINATION

Article 56 of the Vienna Convention contains a provision permitting denunciation or withdrawal where such a right "may be implied by the nature of the treaty." Examples sometimes given of such cases are treaties of alliance and of commerce. Conversely, the nature of other categories of treaties is clearly perpetual, such as those for territorial cession or settlement of a boundary. See International Law Commission, Commentary, [1966] II Yb.I.L.C. 169, 250–51; Sinclair, Vienna Convention, *supra*, at 102.

Some human rights treaties have no termination clause. Should they be considered denunciable or not? The Human Rights Committee dealt with this issue in General Comment No. 26 adopted in 1997:

UNITED NATIONS HUMAN RIGHTS COMMITTEE, GENERAL COMMENT NO. 26 ON ISSUES RELATING TO THE CONTINUITY OF OBLIGATIONS TO THE INTERNATIONAL COVENANT ON CIVIL AND POLITICAL RIGHTS

Adopted October 29, 1997
U.N. Doc. CCPR/C/21/Rev.1/Add.8/Rev.1

1.   The International Covenant on Civil and Political Rights does not contain any provision regarding its termination and does not provide for denunciation or withdrawal. Consequently, the possibility of termination, denunciation or withdrawal must be considered in the light of applicable rules of customary international law which are reflected in the Vienna Convention on the Law of Treaties. On this basis, the Covenant is not subject to denunciation or withdrawal unless it is established that the

parties intended to admit the possibility of denunciation or withdrawal or a right to do so is implied from the nature of the treaty.

2.   That the parties to the Covenant did not admit the possibility of denunciation and that it was not a mere oversight on their part to omit reference to denunciation is demonstrated by the fact that article 41(2) of the Covenant does permit a State party to withdraw its acceptance of the competence of the Committee to examine inter-State communications by filing an appropriate notice to that effect while there is no such provision for denunciation of or withdrawal from the Covenant itself. Moreover, the Optional Protocol to the Covenant, negotiated and adopted contemporaneously with it, permits States parties to denounce it. Additionally, by way of comparison, the International Convention on the Elimination of All Forms of Racial Discrimination, which was adopted one year prior to the Covenant, expressly permits denunciation. It can therefore be concluded that the drafters of the Covenant deliberately intended to exclude the possibility of denunciation. The same conclusion applies to the Second Optional Protocol in the drafting of which a denunciation clause was deliberately omitted.

3.   Furthermore, it is clear that the Covenant is not the type of treaty which, by its nature, implies a right of denunciation. Together with the simultaneously prepared and adopted International Covenant on Economic, Social and Cultural Rights, the Covenant codifies in treaty form the universal human rights enshrined in the Universal Declaration of Human Rights, the three instruments together often being referred to as the International Bill of Human Rights. As such, the Covenant does not have a temporary character typical of treaties where a right of denunciation is deemed to be admitted, notwithstanding the absence of a specific provision to that effect.

4.   The rights enshrined in the Covenant belong to the people living in the territory of the State party. The Human Rights Committee has consistently taken the view, as evidenced by its long-standing practice, that once the people are accorded the protection of the rights under the Covenant, such protection devolves with territory and continues to belong to them, notwithstanding change in government of the State party, including dismemberment in more than one State or State succession or any subsequent action of the State party designed to divest them of the rights guaranteed by the Covenant.

5.   The Committee is therefore firmly of the view that international law does not permit a State which has ratified or acceded or succeeded to the Covenant to denounce it or withdraw from it.

NOTES

1.   *North Korea's Party Status Under International Covenant.* The background to General Comment No. 26 includes the following facts, as summarized in the U.S. Department of State's Report on Human Rights Practices for 1997 (Country Report on Democratic People's Republic of Korea):

On August 22 [1997], the U.N. Subcommission on Prevention of Discrimination and Protection of Minorities adopted a resolution criticizing the DPRK for its human rights practices. On August 27, the DPRK announced that it would withdraw from the International Covenant on Civil and Political Rights (ICCPR), calling the resolution an attack on its sovereignty. On October 29 [1997], the U.N. Human Rights Committee, during its 61st session, issued a statement criticizing the attempt by North Korea to withdraw from the ICCPR.

See also U.N. Blocks Rights Move by North Korea, N.Y. Times, Oct. 31, 1997.

The U.N. Secretary–General, as depositary for the Covenant, had to determine how to exercise depositary functions in view of the DPRK's notice of withdrawal. The matter was handled as follows:

On 25 August 1997, the Secretary–General received from the Government of the Democratic People's Republic of Korea a notification of withdrawal from the Covenant, dated 23 August 1997.

As the Covenant does not contain a withdrawal provision, the Secretariat of the United Nations forwarded on 23 September 1997 an aide-mémoire to the Government of the Democratic People's Republic of Korea explaining the legal position arising from the above notification.

As elaborated in this aide-mémoire, the Secretary–General is of the opinion that a withdrawal from the Covenant would not appear possible unless all States Parties to the Covenant agree with such a withdrawal.

The above notification of withdrawal and the aide-mémoire were duly circulated to all States Parties under cover of C.N.467.TREATIES–10 of 12 November 1997.

As of 2009, the DPRK continues to be treated as a party to the Covenant, both by the Secretary–General as depositary (see Status of Multilateral Treaties Maintained by the Secretary–General) and by the Human Rights Committee. Indeed, the DPRK seems to have accepted the U.N. position, as it did file a report under the Covenant in 2000. See U.N. Doc. CCPR/ C/PRK/2000/2 (May 4, 2000).

2. *Infrastructural Improvements.* In the *Gabčíkovo–Nagymaros Project* (Hungary/Slovakia), 1997 I.C.J. 7, p. 225 *infra*, Hungary attempted to terminate a bilateral treaty without the other party's consent. The subject-matter of the treaty was construction of works for navigation, flood control, and hydroelectric power along the Danube River. After unsuccessful efforts between 1989 and early 1992 to renegotiate the plans for the works and other developments, Hungary gave a notice of termination on May 19, 1992 with purported effect as of May 25, 1992. In holding that Hungary could not terminate the treaty in this manner, the I.C.J. said:

100.   The 1977 Treaty does not contain any provision regarding its termination. Nor is there any indication that the parties intended to admit the possibility of denunciation or withdrawal. On the contrary, the Treaty establishes a long-standing and durable régime of joint investment and joint operation. Consequently, the parties not having agreed other-

wise, the Treaty could be terminated only on the limited grounds enumerated in the Vienna Convention.

* * *

109.   In this regard, it should be noted that, according to Hungary's Declaration of 19 May 1992, the termination of the 1977 Treaty was to take effect as from 25 May 1992, that is only six days later. Both Parties agree that Articles 65 to 67 of the Vienna Convention on the Law of Treaties, if not codifying customary law, at least generally reflect customary international law and contain certain procedural principles which are based on an obligation to act in good faith. * * *

The termination of the Treaty by Hungary was to take effect six days after its notification. On neither of these dates had Hungary suffered injury from acts of Czechoslovakia. The Court must therefore confirm its conclusion that Hungary's termination of the Treaty was premature.

UNITED NATIONS CONFERENCE ON INTERNATIONAL ORGANIZATION, COMMISSION I: COMMENTARY ON WITHDRAWAL

Adopted in San Francisco, 1945
1 U.N.C.I.O. Docs. 616–17

The Committee adopts the view that the Charter should not make express provision either to permit or to prohibit withdrawal from the Organization. The Committee deems that the highest duty of the nations which will become Members is to continue their cooperation within the Organization, for the preservation of international peace and security. If, however, a Member because of exceptional circumstances feels constrained to withdraw, and leave the burden of maintaining international peace and security on the other Members, it is not the purpose of the Organization to compel that member to continue its cooperation in the Organization.

It is obvious, however, that withdrawal or some other forms of dissolution of the Organization would become inevitable if, deceiving the hope of humanity, the Organization was revealed to be unable to maintain peace or could do so only at the expense of law and justice.

Nor would it be the purpose of the Organization to compel a Member to remain in the Organization if its rights and obligations as such were changed by Charter amendment in which it has not concurred and which it finds itself unable to accept, or if an amendment duly accepted by the necessary majority in the Assembly or in a general conference fails to secure the ratification necessary to bring such amendment into effect.

It is for these considerations that the Committee has decided to abstain from recommending insertion in the Charter of a formal clause specifically forbidding or permitting withdrawal.

NOTES

1. *Right to Withdraw from an International Organization?* Commission I's Rapporteur stated on June 23, 1945 that "the absence of * * * [a withdrawal] clause is not intended to impair the right of withdrawal, which each state possesses on the basis of the principle of the sovereign equality of the members. The Commission would deplore any reckless or wanton exercise of the right of withdrawal but recognizes that, under certain exceptional circumstances, a state may feel itself compelled to exercise this right." 6 U.N.C.I.O. Doc. 5, 149. The Plenary Session of the Conference approved the Report. The sole objection was raised by the Soviet delegate, who interpreted the Commentary as "condemn[ing] beforehand the grounds on which any state may find it necessary to exercise its right of withdrawal from the Organization. Such right is an expression of state sovereignty and should not be reviled, in advance, by the International Organization." 1 U.N.C.I.O. 619–20. What weight should be assigned to the above statements, as well as to the Commentary on Withdrawal, in the interpretation of the Charter? See Kelsen, The Law of the United Nations 127 (1950). For a discussion of contemporaneous United States views on the problem of withdrawal, see id. at 129 n. 1. See, in general, Feinberg, Unilateral Withdrawal from an International Organization, 39 Brit. Y.B.I.L. 189 (1963).

On Indonesia's withdrawal from the United Nations in 1965 and its return in 1966, see 4 I.L.M. 364 (1965); Livingstone, Withdrawal from the United Nations—Indonesia, 14 I.C.L.Q. 637 (1965); Schwelb, Withdrawal from the United Nations: The Indonesian Intermezzo, 61 A.J.I.L. 661 (1967).

2. *Disputed Withdrawals from World Health Organization.* In recommending acceptance by the United States of the Constitution of the World Health Organization, Congress included in its Joint Resolution a reservation to the effect that, "in the absence of any provision * * * for withdrawal from the Organization, the United States reserves its right to withdraw from the Organization on a one-year notice * * * " 62 Stat. 441–42. See 19 Dep't St. Bull. 310 (1948). The World Health Assembly unanimously accepted the United States reservation by a Resolution of July 2, 1948. See Feinberg, *supra*, at 202–03. In 1949 and 1950, a number of states of the Soviet bloc announced their withdrawal from WHO, but their notifications to the Director–General were rejected on the ground that the WHO Constitution made no provision for withdrawal. The Organization continued to regard the absent states as members, and when the Soviet Union and the other "inactive members" began to resume full participation in 1957, it was agreed that the Organization would accept a token payment of five percent in settlement of the absentee states' financial obligations for the intervening years. See generally id. at 202–08, and sources cited. After a number of states had withdrawn from and then returned to UNESCO, the Organization's Constitution was amended in 1954 to provide specifically for withdrawal. Id. at 209–11. In all the remaining Specialized Agencies of the United Nations, withdrawal is specifically authorized under the conditions stated.

3. *U.S. Withdrawals.* The United States gave notice of withdrawal from the International Labour Organisation in 1975 and returned in 1980. It

withdrew from UNESCO in 1984 and rejoined in 2003. See 1980 Digest of
U.S. Practice in Int'l L. 76–78; 84 Dep't St. Bull. 2083, 41 (1984); Murphy,
Contemporary Practice of the United States: U.S. Return to UNESCO, 97
A.J.I.L. 977 (2003).

4. *Distinction between Normative and Institutional Features of a Treaty.*
Consider the Human Rights Committee's position on non-terminability of
human rights treaties in light of the distinction between the substantive
norms of the treaties and their implementation within an institutional setting. Do the foregoing materials on withdrawal from international institutions
support drawing such a distinction in the case of human rights bodies? Should
parties to institutional treaties be considered to have an implied right of
withdrawal, or would some institutions be perpetual and their membership
likewise locked in to indefinite participation? What reasons might a state have
for wishing to withdraw from an institutional treaty? What reasons might
there be for discouraging unilateral withdrawal? Compare Hirschman, Exit,
Voice and Loyalty (1970). Do human rights institutions have special features
compared to other institutions as to which a right of withdrawal has been
explicitly granted or considered implicit?

5. *European Community/Union.* The Treaty of Rome that established
the European Economic Community had no provision on withdrawal, and
differing legal positions were developed as to its potential denunciability. See,
e.g., Weiler, Alternatives to Withdrawal from an International Organization:
The Case of the EEC, 20 Israel L. Rev. 282 (1985). From time to time,
dissatisfaction in some member states with the operation of European institutions has made the possibility of unilateral withdrawal seem more than a
hypothetical question. Does the more tightly integrated European Union
suggest a negative answer to whether a right of denunciation "may be implied
by the nature of the treaty" within the meaning of Vienna Convention Article
56(1)(b)?

C. TERMINATION OF A TREATY AS
A CONSEQUENCE OF BREACH

REPORT OF THE INTERNATIONAL LAW COMMISSION

[1966] II Yb. I.L.C. 169, 253–55

(1) The great majority of jurists recognize that a violation of a treaty
by one party may give rise to a right in the other party to abrogate the
treaty or to suspend the performance of its own obligations under the
treaty. A violation of a treaty obligation, as of any other obligation, may
give rise to a right in the other party to take nonforcible reprisals, and
these reprisals may properly relate to the defaulting party's rights under
the treaty. Opinion differs, however, as to the extent of the right to
abrogate the treaty and the conditions under which it may be exercised.
Some jurists, in the absence of effective international machinery for
securing the observance of treaties, are more impressed with the innocent
party's need to have this right as a sanction for the violation of the treaty.
They tend to formulate the right in unqualified terms, giving the innocent

party a general right to abrogate the treaty in the event of a breach. Other jurists are more impressed with the risk that a State may allege a trivial or even fictitious breach simply to furnish a pretext for denouncing a treaty which it now finds embarrassing. These jurists tend to restrict the right of denunciation to "material" or "fundamental" breaches and also to subject the exercise of the right to procedural conditions.

* * *

(5) The Commission was agreed that a breach of a treaty, however serious, does not *ipso facto* put an end to the treaty, and also that it is not open to a State simply to allege a violation of the treaty and pronounce the treaty at an end. On the other hand, it considered that within certain limits and subject to certain safeguards the right of a party to invoke the breach of a treaty as a ground for terminating it or suspending its operation must be recognized. Some members considered that it would be dangerous for the Commission to endorse such a right, unless its exercise were to be made subject to control by compulsory reference to the International Court of Justice. The Commission, while recognizing the importance of providing proper safeguards against arbitrary denunciation of a treaty on the ground of an alleged breach, concluded that the question of providing safeguards against arbitrary action was a general one which affected several articles. It, therefore, decided to formulate in the present article the substantive conditions under which a treaty may be terminated or its operation suspended in consequence of a breach, and to deal with the question of the procedural safeguards in article [65].

(6) *Paragraph 1* provides that a "material" breach of a bilateral treaty by one party entitles the other to *invoke* the breach as a ground for terminating the treaty or suspending its operation in whole or in part. The formula "invoke as a ground" is intended to underline that the right arising under the article is not a right arbitrarily to pronounce the treaty terminated. If the other party contests the breach or its character as a "material" breach, there will be a "difference" between the parties with regard to which the normal obligations incumbent upon the parties under the Charter and under general international law to seek a solution of the question through pacific means will apply. The Commission considered that the action open to the other party in the case of a material breach is to invoke either the termination or the suspension of the operation of the treaty, in whole or in part. The right to take this action arises under the law of treaties independently of any right of reprisal, the principle being that a party cannot be called upon to fulfill its obligations under a treaty when the other party fails to fulfil those which it undertook under the same treaty. This right would, of course, be without prejudice to the injured party's right to present an international claim for reparation on the basis of the other party's responsibility with respect to the breach.

(7) *Paragraph 2* deals with a material breach of a multilateral treaty, and here the Commission considered it necessary to distinguish between the right of the other parties to react jointly to the breach and the right of

an individual party specially affected by the breach to react alone. Subparagraph (a) provides that the other parties may, by a unanimous agreement, suspend the operation of the treaty or terminate it and may do so either only in their relations with the defaulting State or altogether as between all the parties. When an individual party reacts alone the Commission considered that its position is similar to that in the case of a bilateral treaty, but that its right should be limited to suspending the operation of the treaty in whole or in part as between itself and the defaulting State. In the case of a multilateral treaty the interests of the other parties have to be taken into account and a right of suspension normally provides adequate protection to the State specially affected by the breach. Moreover, the limitation of the right of the individual party to a right of suspension seemed to the Commission to be particularly necessary in the case of general multilateral treaties of a law-making character. Indeed, a question was raised as to whether even suspension would be admissible in the case of lawmaking treaties. The Commission felt, however, that it would be inequitable to allow a defaulting State to continue to enforce the treaty against the injured party, whilst itself violating its obligations towards that State under the treaty. Moreover, even such treaties as the Genocide Convention and the Geneva Conventions on the treatment of prisoners of war, sick and wounded allowed an express right of denunciation independently of any breach of the convention. The Commission concluded that general lawmaking treaties should not, simply as such, be dealt with differently from other multilateral treaties in the present connexion. Accordingly, subparagraph (b) lays down that on a material breach of a multilateral treaty any party specially affected by the breach may *invoke* it as a *ground* for suspending the operation of the treaty in whole or in part *in the relations between itself and the defaulting State.*

(8) *Paragraph 2(c)* is designed to deal with the problem raised in the comments of Governments of special types of treaty, e.g. disarmament treaties, where a breach by one party tends to undermine the whole régime of the treaty as between all the parties. In the case of a material breach of such a treaty the interests of an individual party may not be adequately protected by the rules contained in paragraphs 2(a) and (b). It could not suspend the performance of its own obligations under the treaty vis-à-vis the defaulting State without at the same time violating its obligations to the other parties. Yet, unless it does so, it may be unable to protect itself against the threat resulting from the arming of the defaulting State. In these cases, where a material breach of the treaty by one party radically changes the position of every party with respect to the further performance of its obligations, the Commission considered that any party must be permitted without first obtaining the agreement of the other parties to suspend the operation of the treaty with respect to itself generally in its relations with all the other parties. Paragraph 2(c) accordingly so provides.

(9) *Paragraph 3* defines the kind of breach which may give rise to a right to terminate or suspend the treaty. Some authorities have in the past seemed to assume that any breach of any provision would suffice to justify the denunciation of the treaty. The Commission, however, was unanimous that the right to terminate or suspend must be limited to cases where the breach is of a serious character. It preferred the term "material" to "fundamental" to express the kind of breach which is required. The word "fundamental" might be understood as meaning that only the violation of a provision directly touching the *central* purposes of the treaty can ever justify the other party in terminating the treaty. But other provisions considered by a party to be essential to the effective execution of the treaty may have been very material in inducing it to enter into the treaty at all, even though these provisions may be of an ancillary character. Clearly, an unjustified repudiation of the treaty—a repudiation not sanctioned by any of the provisions of the present articles—would automatically constitute a material breach of the treaty; and this is provided for in sub-paragraph (a) of the definition. The other and more general form of material breach is that in sub-paragraph (b), and is there defined as a violation of a provision essential to the accomplishment of any object or purpose of the treaty.

NOTES

1. *Humanitarian Treaties.* At the Vienna conference, paragraph 5 was added to the draft, with the objective of ensuring that the rules providing for termination as a consequence of breach would not cause the termination or suspension of the many conventions of a humanitarian character which protect the "human person." Reference was made to the Geneva Conventions for the Protection of Victims of War and to conventions relating to refugees and human rights. It was considered desirable to make it clear that a material breach in these cases should not lead to abrogation or suspension of the treaty. The general view is that such treaties are essentially for the benefit of individuals and they involve obligations which should not be dependent on reciprocal performance. Compare the reasoning of the International Court in its Advisory Opinion, *Reservations to the Convention on Genocide,* p. 143 *supra.*

2. *Overlooking Breach.* A state may choose to ignore a violation by another state of a treaty to which both are parties. See *Charlton v. Kelly,* 229 U.S. 447 (1913), where the Supreme Court held that inasmuch as the executive branch of government had waived its "right to free itself from the obligation to deliver up its own citizens" pursuant to an extradition treaty with Italy that had been interpreted by Italian authorities as excluding the extradition from Italy of Italian citizens, the courts were compelled to recognize the treaty as binding and in full force.

3. *Relationship to Rules of State Responsibility for Breach of Obligations.* In *Rainbow Warrior* (New Zealand v. France), 82 I.L.R. 499 (1990), a French–New Zealand Arbitration Tribunal addressed the question of whether a state can justify breach of treaty obligations by referring to exceptions

within the law of state responsibility, such as *force majeure*, distress, and necessity. (The topic of circumstances precluding wrongfulness in the law of state responsibility is treated in Chapter 8.) The Tribunal answered this question in the affirmative, holding that both the customary law of treaties and the customary law of state responsibility were relevant in ascertaining the consequences, if any, of a breach of treaty:

> The reason is that the general principles of International Law concerning State responsibility are equally applicable in the case of breach of treaty obligation, since in the international law field there is no distinction between contractual and tortious responsibility, so that any violation by a State of any obligation, of whatever origin, gives rise to State responsibility and consequently, to the duty of reparation.

Id. at 551. To similar effect on the relationship between the law of treaties and the law of state responsibility, see *Gabčíkovo–Nagymaros Project* (Hungary/Slovakia), 1997 I.C.J. 7, at paras. 47–48 (see excerpts and fuller discussion at p. 225).

4. *Loss of Right to Terminate for Breach.* In the *Gabčíkovo–Nagymaros Project* case, Hungary's contentions included an allegation of material breach by the other party, as Slovakia had put into place a variant of the Danube River plans to which Hungary had not consented. The Court concluded that even if Slovakia had thereby breached the underlying treaty, it had done so in response to Hungary's prior wrongful actions:

> 110. * * * Hungary, by its own conduct, had prejudiced its right to terminate the Treaty; this would still have been the case even if Czechoslovakia, by the time of the purported termination, had violated a provision essential to the accomplishment of the object or purpose of the Treaty.

5. *Cease–Fire Agreements.* Does a violation by one party of a single article or group of articles of an agreement justify another party in regarding itself as freed of all obligations under the agreement? In his report to the Security Council on problems concerning the Armistice Agreements concluded between Israel and various Arab states in 1949, the Secretary–General stated:

> 16. As a matter of course, each party considers its compliance with the stipulations of an armistice agreement as conditioned by compliance of the other party to the agreement. Should such a stand be given the interpretation that any one infringement of the provisions of the agreement by one party justifies reactions by the other party which, in their turn, are breaches of the armistice agreement, without any limitation as to the field within which reciprocity is considered to prevail, it would in fact mean that the armistice regime could be nullified by a single infringement by one of the parties. Although such an interpretation has never been given from responsible quarters, it appears to me that a lack of clarity has prevailed. From no side has it been said that a breach of an armistice agreement, to whatever clause it may refer, gives the other party a free hand concerning the agreement as a whole, but a tendency to regard the agreements, including the cease-fire clauses, as entities may explain a feeling that in fact, due to infringements of this or that clause, the obligations are no longer in a strict sense fully binding, and specifical-

ly that a breach of one of the clauses, other than the cease-fire clause, may justify action in contravention of that clause.

* * *

18.   The very logic of the armistice agreements shows that infringements of other articles cannot serve as a justification for an infringement of the cease-fire article. If that were not recognized, it would mean that any one of such infringements might not only nullify the armistice régime, but in fact put in jeopardy the cease-fire itself. For that reason alone, it is clear that compliance with the said article can be conditioned only by similar compliance of the other party.

U.N. Doc. S/3596, at 6–7 (1956). See the International Law Commission's comment on the separability of treaty provisions, [1966] II Yb.I.L.C. 237–39 (Article 41).

6.   *Cease–Fire with Iraq, 1991–2003.* Among the disputed legal issues concerning the renewal of military operations against Iraq in March 2003 was whether Iraq was in "material breach" of the terms of the cease-fire that had ended the 1991 Gulf War. In 1998–1999, and again in 2002–2003, issues of material breach in the context of a cease-fire agreement were given prominence when Iraq refused to comply with obligations concerning verification of elimination of its capabilities for weapons of mass destruction, in accordance with the framework established at the conclusion of the 1991 Persian Gulf war by Security Council Resolution 687 (1991). Among the claimed justifications for use of force was that Iraq's material violation of the cease-fire terms revived the legal situation of collective self-defense of Kuwait that had prevailed prior to Resolution 687. To what extent should one party's breach of a cease-fire agreement warrant a legal conclusion that another party can treat the cease-fire as suspended or terminated? For discussion, see Wedgwood, The Enforcement of Security Council Resolution 687: The Threat of Force Against Iraq's Weapons of Mass Destruction, 92 A.J.I.L. 724 (1998); see also the different points of view on material breach of the cease-fire in Agora: Future Implications of the Iraq Conflict, 97 A.J.I.L. 553 (2003). These issues are addressed further in Chapter 15.

ADVISORY OPINION ON NAMIBIA

International Court of Justice, Advisory Opinion, 1971
1971 I.C.J. 16*

[In 1966, the General Assembly adopted a resolution in which, *inter alia,* it decided that South Africa's Mandate from the League of Nations to what became known as Namibia (South West Africa) was terminated. G.A. Res. 2145 (XXI) (Oct. 27, 1966). This resolution was predicated on the General Assembly's assessment that South Africa had breached the Mandate by introducing the system of *apartheid* into South West Africa. When the General Assembly's action did not succeed in inducing South Africa to

---

* The complete title of this opinion is: Legal Consequences for States of the Continued Presence of South Africa in Namibia (South West Africa), notwithstanding Security Council Resolution 276 (1970).

terminate or relax its control of the territory or to abandon *apartheid* in South West Africa, the situation was put on the agenda of the Security Council, which on January 30, 1970, reaffirmed the General Assembly resolution and declared, *inter alia,* "that the continued presence of the South African authorities in Namibia is illegal and that consequently all acts taken by the Government of South Africa on behalf of or concerning Namibia after the termination of the Mandate are illegal and invalid." S.C. Res. 276 (Jan. 30, 1970), U.N. Doc. S/INF/25, at 1. South Africa remained adamant and refused to cooperate with the U.N. Council for Namibia which had been set up by the General Assembly in 1967 and which had begun to issue Travel Documents and Identity Certificates for inhabitants of Namibia. On July 29, 1970, the Security Council adopted a resolution submitting to the International Court of Justice for an advisory opinion the following question: "What are the legal consequences for States of the continued presence of South Africa in Namibia, notwithstanding Security Council resolution 276 (1970)?" S.C. Res. 284 (July 29, 1970).

[On June 21, 1971, the Court answered this question as follows:

by 13 votes to 2,

(1) that, the continued presence of South Africa in Namibia being illegal, South Africa is under obligation to withdraw its administration from Namibia immediately and thus put an end to its occupation of the Territory;

by 11 votes to 4,

(2) that States Members of the United Nations are under obligation to recognize the illegality of South Africa's presence in Namibia and the invalidity of its acts on behalf of or concerning Namibia, and to refrain from any acts and in particular any dealings with the Government of South Africa implying recognition of the legality of, or lending support or assistance to, such presence and administration;

(3) that it is incumbent upon States which are not Members of the United Nations to give assistance, within the scope of subparagraph (2) above, in the action which has been taken by the United Nations with regard to Namibia.

1971 I.C.J. 16, at 58.]

93. In paragraph 3 of the operative part of the resolution the General Assembly *"Declares* that South Africa has failed to fulfil its obligations in respect of the administration of the Mandated Territory and to ensure the moral and material well-being and security of the indigenous inhabitants of South West Africa and has, in fact, disavowed the Mandate". In paragraph 4 the decision is reached, as a consequence of the previous declaration "that the Mandate conferred upon His Britannic Majesty to be exercised on his behalf by the Government of the Union of South Africa is *therefore* terminated * * * ". (Emphasis added.) It is this part of the resolution which is relevant in the present proceedings.

94.   In examining this action of the General Assembly it is appropriate to have regard to the general principles of international law regulating termination of a treaty relationship on account of breach. For even if the mandate is viewed as having the character of an institution, as is maintained, it depends on those international agreements which created the system and regulated its application. As the Court indicated in 1962 "this Mandate, like practically all other similar Mandates" was "a special type of instrument composite in nature and instituting a novel international régime. It incorporates a definite agreement * * * " (I.C.J. Reports 1962, p. 331). The Court stated conclusively in that Judgment that the Mandate " * * * in fact and in law, is an international agreement having the character of a treaty or convention" (I.C.J. Reports 1962, p. 330). The rules laid down by the Vienna Convention on the Law of Treaties concerning termination of a treaty relationship on account of breach (adopted without a dissenting vote) may in many respects be considered as a codification of existing customary law on the subject. In the light of these rules, only a material breach of a treaty justifies termination, such breach being defined as:

(a) a repudiation of the treaty not sanctioned by the present Convention; or

(b) the violation of a provision essential to the accomplishment of the object or purpose of the treaty (Art. 60, para. 3).

95.   General Assembly resolution 2145 (XXI) determines that both forms of material breach had occurred in this case. By stressing that South Africa "has, in fact, disavowed the Mandate", the General Assembly declared in fact that it had repudiated it. The resolution in question is therefore to be viewed as the exercise of the right to terminate a relationship in case of a deliberate and persistent violation of obligations which destroys the very object and purpose of that relationship. * * *

96.   It has been contended that the Covenant of the League of Nations did not confer on the Council of the League power to terminate a mandate for misconduct of the Mandatory and that no such power could therefore be exercised by the United Nations, since it could not derive from the League greater powers than the latter itself had. For this objection to prevail it would be necessary to show that the mandates system, as established under the League, excluded the application of the general principle of law that a right of termination on account of breach must be presumed to exist in respect of all treaties, except as regards provisions relating to the protection of the human person contained in treaties of a humanitarian character (as indicated in Art. 60, para. 5, of the Vienna Convention). The silence of a treaty as to the existence of such a right cannot be interpreted as implying the exclusion of a right which has its source outside of the treaty, in general international law, and is dependent on the occurrence of circumstances which are not normally envisaged when a treaty is concluded.

* * *

101.   It has been suggested that, even if the Council of the League had possessed the power of revocation of the Mandate in an extreme case, it could not have been exercised unilaterally but only in cooperation with the mandatory Power. However, revocation could only result from a situation in which the Mandatory had committed a serious breach of the obligations it had undertaken. To contend, on the basis of the principle of unanimity which applied in the League of Nations, that in this case revocation could only take place with the concurrence of the Mandatory, would not only run contrary to the general principle of law governing termination on account of breach, but also postulate an impossibility. For obvious reasons, the consent of the wrongdoer to such a form of termination cannot be required.

Note

Source of Right to Terminate. Was the Court correct in saying that there is a general principle of law that a right of termination on account of breach must be presumed to exist in respect of all treaties? Briggs has noted that the Court produces no evidence in support. Moreover, he finds that Article 60 does not recognize that proposition. In the case of multilateral treaties, a material breach may be invoked only *as a ground for termination or suspension* under paragraph 2(a). Paragraphs 2(b) and 2(c) permit invocation of a material breach only as a ground for suspension, not termination. Briggs points out that the International Law Commission stated that "a breach of a treaty, however serious, does not *ipso facto* put an end to the treaty and * * * it is not open to a State simply to allege a violation of the treaty and pronounce the treaty at an end * * *." (See [1966] II Yb.I.L.C. at 253–55 quoted *supra*, p. 208.) The statement of the Court, according to Briggs, is *obiter dicta* since the *Namibia Case* did not involve a claim by a state of a unilateral right to terminate a treaty for breach. The analogy should have been with the collective right of termination set forth in paragraph 2(a) of Article 60. See Briggs, Unilateral Denunciation of Treaties, 68 A.J.I.L. 51, 56–57 (1974).

APPEAL RELATING TO THE JURISDICTION OF THE ICAO COUNCIL (INDIA v. PAKISTAN)

International Court of Justice, 1972
1972 I.C.J. 46

[Pakistan had brought a complaint against India before the Council of the International Civil Aviation Organization (ICAO) on the ground that India had violated provisions of the 1944 Chicago Convention on International Civil Aviation and the International Air Services Transport Agreement. The basis for the complaint was that India had unilaterally suspended flights of Pakistan aircraft over Indian territory. The ICAO Council assumed jurisdiction on the basis of the jurisdictional clauses in the treaties. India appealed to the International Court of Justice charging that the treaties had been suspended by India on ground of a breach by

Pakistan (in particular, the hijacking of an Indian plane, allegedly with compliance of Pakistan). Therefore, it claimed the ICAO Council had no jurisdiction.

[Pakistan objected to the Court's taking jurisdiction on the ground that India's contention that the treaties were not in force or in operation meant that India did not have standing to bring a case on the basis of the treaty jurisdictional clauses. The Court rejected the Pakistan challenge and in so doing declared:]

Nor in any case could a merely unilateral suspension per se render jurisdictional clauses inoperative, since one of their purposes might be, precisely, to enable the validity of the suspension to be tested. If a mere allegation, as yet unestablished, that a treaty was no longer operative could be used to defeat its jurisdictional clauses, all such clauses would become potentially a dead letter, even in cases like the present, where one of the very questions at issue on the merits, and as yet undecided, is whether or not the treaty is operative i.e., whether it has been validly terminated or suspended. The result would be that means of defeating jurisdictional clauses would never be wanting.

[With respect to the jurisdiction of the ICAO Council, India claimed that its right to unilateral termination or suspension for material breach had been properly exercised and accordingly the treaties no longer were in force. It followed that the ICAO Council could not have jurisdiction. India's conduct in suspending Pakistan flights was therefore outside of, not under, the treaties. In regard to this, the Court stated:]

[I]t involves a point of principle of great general importance for the jurisdictional aspects of this—or of any—case. This contention is to the effect that since India, in suspending overflights in February 1971, was not invoking any right that might be afforded by the Treaties, but was acting outside them on the basis of a general principle of international law, "therefore" the Council, whose jurisdiction was derived from the Treaties, and which was entitled to deal only with matters arising under them, must be incompetent. Exactly the same attitude has been evinced in regard to the contention that the Treaties were suspended in 1965 and never revived, or were replaced by a special régime. The Court considers however, that for precisely the same order of reason as has already been noticed in the case of its own jurisdiction in the present case, a mere unilateral affirmation of these contentions—contested by the other party—cannot be utilized so as to negative the Council's jurisdiction. The point is not that these contentions are necessarily wrong but that their validity has not yet been determined. Since therefore the Parties are in disagreement as to whether the Treaties ever were (validly) suspended or replaced by something else; as to whether they are in force between the Parties or not; and as to whether India's action in relation to Pakistan overflights was such as not to involve the Treaties, but to be justifiable *aliter et aliunde*;—these very questions are in issue before the Council, and no conclusions as to jurisdiction can be drawn from them, at least at this stage, so as to exclude *ipso facto* and *a priori* the competence of the Council.

32. To put the matter in another way, these contentions are essentially in the nature of replies to the charge that India is in breach of the Treaties: the Treaties were at the material times suspended or not operative, or replaced,—hence they cannot have been infringed. India has not of course claimed that, in consequence, such a matter can never be tested by any form of judicial recourse. This contention, if it were put forward, would be equivalent to saying that questions that prima facie may involve a given treaty, and if so would be within the scope of its jurisdictional clause, could be removed therefrom at a stroke by a unilateral declaration that the treaty was no longer operative. The acceptance of such a proposition would be tantamount to opening the way to a wholesale nullification of the practical value of jurisdictional clauses by allowing a party first to purport to terminate, or suspend the operation of a treaty, and then to declare that the treaty being now terminated or suspended, its jurisdictional clauses were in consequence void, and could not be invoked for the purpose of contesting the validity of the termination or suspension,—whereas of course it may be precisely one of the objects of such a clause to enable that matter to be adjudicated upon. Such a result, destructive of the whole object of adjudicability, would be unacceptable.

NOTES

1. *Are Jurisdictional Treaties Special?* Briggs commented on the decision as follows:

> The court properly confined itself to upholding its own jurisdiction and that of the ICAO Council; but it may be noted that much of the rationale advanced by the Court to restrict claims of a unilateral right under general international law to terminate or suspend jurisdictional treaties for breach would appear to have cogency in relation to all treaties, whether or not they contain jurisdictional clauses.

Briggs, Unilateral Denunciation of Treaties: The Vienna Convention and the International Court of Justice, 68 A.J.I.L. 60–61 (1974).

2. *Requirements during Pendency of Dispute Over Termination for Breach.* Is a party affected by a breach obliged to continue performance of a treaty which the other party is violating during the period when the required process of dispute settlement is in progress? Is the aggrieved party restricted in taking counter-measures (including non-compliance) when the treaty itself provides for negotiation, arbitration or other means of settlement? These questions were considered by an arbitral tribunal in a dispute between France and the United States concerning an Air Services Agreement. The tribunal held that the aggrieved state (the United States) was entitled to take counter-measures including suspension of its performance under the treaty when such measures were not disproportionate to the breach, notwithstanding the agreement for arbitration. *Air Services Agreement between France and the United States*, 18 U.N. Rep. Int'l Arb. Awards 417 (1978). The decision is dealt with

below in Chapter 8, Section 6 on countermeasures, p. 535 note 1. See also Damrosch, Retaliation or Arbitration—or Both?, 74 A.J.I.L. 785 (1980).

D. FUNDAMENTAL CHANGE OF CIRCUMSTANCES

REPORT OF THE INTERNATIONAL LAW COMMISSION

[1966] II Yb.I.L.C. 169, 256–58

(1) Almost all modern jurists, however reluctantly, admit the existence in international law of the principle with which this article is concerned and which is commonly spoken of as the doctrine of *rebus sic stantibus*. Just as many systems of municipal law recognize that, quite apart from any actual *impossibility* of performance, contracts may become inapplicable through a fundamental change of circumstances, so also treaties may become inapplicable for the same reason. Most jurists, however, at the same time enter a strong *caveat* as to the need to confine the scope of the doctrine within narrow limits and to regulate strictly the conditions under which it may be invoked; for the risks to the security of treaties which this doctrine presents in the absence of any general system of compulsory jurisdiction are obvious. The circumstances of international life are always changing and it is easy to allege that the changes render the treaty inapplicable.

* * *

(6) The Commission concluded that the principle, if its application were carefully delimited and regulated, should find a place in the modern law of treaties. A treaty may remain in force for a long time and its stipulations come to place an undue burden on one of the parties as a result of a fundamental change of circumstances. Then, if the other party were obdurate in opposing any change, the fact that international law recognized no legal means of terminating or modifying the treaty otherwise than through a further agreement between the same parties might impose a serious strain on the relations between the States concerned; and the dissatisfied State might ultimately be driven to take action outside the law. The number of cases calling for the application of the rule is likely to be comparatively small. As pointed out in the commentary to article [54], the majority of modern treaties are expressed to be of short duration, or are entered into for recurrent terms of years with a right to denounce the treaty at the end of each term, or are expressly or implicitly terminable upon notice. In all these cases either the treaty expires automatically or each party, having the power to terminate the treaty, has the power also to apply pressure upon the other party to revise its provisions. Nevertheless, there may remain a residue of cases in which, failing any agreement, one party may be left powerless under the treaty to obtain any legal relief from outmoded and burdensome provisions. It is in these cases that the *rebus sic stantibus* doctrine could serve a purpose as a lever to induce a spirit of compromise in the other party. Moreover, despite the strong

reservations often expressed with regard to it, the evidence of the acceptance of the doctrine in international law is so considerable that it seems to indicate a recognition of a need for this safety-valve in the law of treaties.

(7) In the past the principle has almost always been presented in the guise of a tacit condition implied in every "perpetual" treaty that would dissolve it in the event of a fundamental change of circumstances. The Commission noted, however, that the tendency to-day was to regard the implied term as only a fiction by which it was attempted to reconcile the principle of the dissolution of treaties in consequence of a fundamental change of circumstances with the rule *pacta sunt servanda*. In most cases the parties gave no thought to the possibility of a change of circumstances and, if they had done so, would probably have provided for it in a different manner. Furthermore, the Commission considered the fiction to be an undesirable one since it increased the risk of subjective interpretations and abuse. For this reason, the Commission was agreed that the theory of an implied term must be rejected and the doctrine formulated as an objective rule of law by which, on grounds of equity and justice, a fundamental change of circumstances may, under certain conditions, be invoked by a party as a ground for terminating the treaty. It further decided that, in order to emphasize the objective character of the rule, it would be better not to use the term *"rebus sic stantibus"* either in the text of the article or even in the title, and so avoid the doctrinal implication of that term.

NOTES

1. *Conditions for Invoking Fundamental Change.* Consider the five conditions that have to be met under Article 62 before a "fundamental change of circumstances" can be invoked as a ground of termination:

- The change must have been of a fundamental character.

- The change must have been unforeseen (if the treaty contains provisions for certain contingencies, e.g., economic hardships, the condition is not unforeseen).

- The circumstances which have changed must have been "an essential basis of the consent to be bound by the treaty."

- The effect of the change must be to transform radically the extent of the obligations of the party invoking the change as a ground of termination.

- The obligations in question are "still to be performed under the treaty" (hence, the article does not apply to treaties whose provisions have been fully executed).

For a detailed treatment of doctrine and state practice prior to the Vienna Convention, see Haraszti, Treaties and the Fundamental Change of Circumstances, 146 Rec. des Cours I (1975–III).

2. *Territorial Treaties*. Would the principle of Article 62 apply to settlements of a territorial nature? Note the explicit exclusion of a treaty if it "establishes a boundary." The International Law Commission rejected suggestions that the exception for boundary treaties might be inconsistent with the principle of self-determination. It considered that if a boundary treaty were not excepted, the rule "might become a source of dangerous friction." But the Commission also said: "By excepting treaties establishing a boundary from its scope, the present article would not exclude the operation of the principle of self-determination in any case where the conditions for its legitimate operation existed." [1966] II Yb.I.L.C. 259. A territorial settlement need not establish a boundary, e.g., it may transfer an island or a zone such as the Panama Canal Zone. Since these actions would not establish a boundary, the issue would be whether the treaty was fully executed or whether in some respects it is executory. In the *Free Zones Case* (1932 P.C.I.J. (ser. A/B) No. 46), Switzerland claimed that *rebus sic stantibus* did not apply to the territorial clauses which had been executed. France, however, noted that certain personal rights were created and that France, for example, had a continuing obligation to abstain from levying customs duties on individuals. The Court did not find it necessary to pass on this point but it exemplifies the case of a continuing obligation as part of a territorial settlement.

3. *Self–Generated Changes*. May a state invoke a fundamental change which has resulted from its own acts? An example mentioned in the International Law Commission was whether a state which had transformed itself from an agricultural to an industrial country could claim that change as a ground for terminating a treaty which was based on the previous agricultural character of the country. Since it could not be said that industrialization was a breach of the treaty, the exception in paragraph 2(b) of Article 62 would not apply. However, when a change is the result of a breach by a party, that party cannot invoke the change as a ground for termination.

4. *Durational Element*. Does Article 62 apply to treaties which have a fixed duration? Under customary international law, *rebus sic stantibus* was considered inapplicable to treaties containing a fixed term, however long the duration. See Jiménez de Aréchaga, 159 Rec. des Cours at 48. But the Commission considered that a fundamental change of circumstances may occur when a treaty has a fixed term and that it was desirable to apply the rule to such treaties wherever the necessary conditions were met. Is Article 62 in that respect *de lege ferenda?*

5. *Procedure for Invocation*. Does Article 62 permit an automatic extinction of a treaty? Does it provide for an unchallengeable unilateral right to terminate? By its terms, Article 62 confers a right to call for termination. Procedural requirements are laid down for this, as for other grounds of termination, in Articles 65 and 66. These provisions come into play if the claim to termination is disputed. They require that negotiation or other procedures of settlement be used as agreed by the parties. If no solution is reached, a compulsory conciliation procedure may be instituted by any party to the dispute; however, the Conciliation Commission's conclusions are not binding on the parties (Annex V of Vienna Convention). Accordingly, it remains open to a party to maintain its right to terminate on grounds of Article 62, provided that it has complied with the notification and procedural

requirements. How effective this will prove in limiting claims based on fundamental change remains to be seen. The Vienna Convention does, however, exclude the right to an absolutely unlimited right to unilateral termination, such as was apparently asserted by the United States in 1941 when the President suspended the operation of the International Load Line Convention of 1930 on grounds of changed shipping conditions brought about by the war in Europe. See 5 Hackworth at 355–56; Briggs, The Attorney–General Invokes Rebus Sic Stantibus, 36 A.J.I.L. 89 (1942).

6. *Invocation by Private Parties.* May a private party invoke the doctrine of changed circumstances to defeat the application of a treaty? A claimant in a suit against an airline for loss of cargo argued that the limits on liability of the Warsaw Convention of 1929 did not apply because fundamental changes of circumstances had occurred since its conclusion. The U.S. Supreme Court recognized that a party to a treaty might invoke changed circumstances as an excuse for terminating its treaty obligations. However, when the states parties continue to assert the vitality of the treaty, a private person who finds the continued existence of the treaty inconvenient may not invoke the doctrine of changed circumstances. *Trans World Airlines, Inc. v. Franklin Mint*, 466 U.S. 243 (1984).

7. *Exceptional Conditions Rarely Satisfied.* International tribunals, while recognizing the principle of *rebus sic stantibus,* have generally avoided terminating treaties on this ground, usually by finding that it did not apply on the facts of the case. This is borne out by the cases most often cited in this connection, including the *Free Zones Case* between France and Switzerland decided by the P.C.I.J. in 1932 (note 2 above), in which the Court found that the circumstances which had changed were not those on the basis of which the parties entered into the treaty. In the 1973 *Fisheries Jurisdiction Case* between the United Kingdom and Iceland and the 1997 *Gabčíkovo–Nagymaros Project* between Hungary and Slovakia, both excerpted immediately below, the Court considered the applicability of the principle of fundamental change of circumstances in the light of the Vienna Convention. In both cases it found that the conditions for invocation of the doctrine were not satisfied.

FISHERIES JURISDICTION
(UNITED KINGDOM v. ICELAND)

International Court of Justice, 1973
1973 I.C.J. 3

[The United Kingdom challenged the proposed extension of Iceland's exclusive fisheries jurisdiction from twelve to fifty miles around its shores. The United Kingdom founded the Court's jurisdiction on Article 36, paragraph 1, of the Court's Statute and a March 11, 1961, Exchange of Notes between the two countries under which the United Kingdom recognized Iceland's claim to a twelve-mile fisheries limit in return for Iceland's agreement that any dispute as to the extension of Icelandic fisheries jurisdiction beyond the twelve-mile limit "shall, at the request of either party, be referred to the International Court of Justice." In a letter to the Registrar of the Court, Iceland asserted that because of changed circumstances the 1961 Exchange of Notes was no longer applicable. Concerning fundamental change of circumstances, the Court said:]

31.   * * * The argument of Iceland appears * * * to be that, because of the general trend of development of international law on the subject of fishery limits during the last ten years, the right of exclusive fisheries jurisdiction to a distance of 12 miles from the baselines of the territorial sea has been increasingly recognized and claimed by States, including the applicant State itself. It would then appear to be contended that the compromissory clause was the price paid by Iceland for the recognition at that time of the 12–mile fishery limit by the other party. It is consequently asserted that if today the 12–mile fishery limit is generally recognized, there would be a failure of consideration relieving Iceland of its commitment because of the changed legal circumstances. * * *

32.   While changes in the law may under certain conditions constitute valid grounds for invoking a change of circumstances affecting the duration of a treaty, the Icelandic contention is not relevant to the present case. The motive which induced Iceland to enter into the 1961 Exchange of Notes may well have been the interest of obtaining an immediate recognition of an exclusive fisheries jurisdiction to a distance of 12 miles in the waters around its territory. It may also be that this interest has in the meantime disappeared, since a 12–mile fishery zone is now asserted by the other contracting party in respect of its own fisheries jurisdiction. But in the present case, the object and purpose of the 1961 Exchange of Notes, and therefore the circumstances which constituted an essential basis of the consent of both parties to be bound by the agreement embodied therein, had a much wider scope. That object and purpose was not merely to decide upon the Icelandic claim to fisheries jurisdiction up to 12 miles, but also to provide a means whereby the parties might resolve the question of the validity of any further claims. This follows not only from the text of the agreement but also from the history of the negotiations, that is to say, from the whole set of circumstances which must be taken into account in determining what induced both parties to agree to the 1961 Exchange of Notes.

* * *

34.   It is possible that today Iceland may find that some of the motives which induced it to enter into the 1961 Exchange of Notes have become less compelling or have disappeared altogether. But this is not a ground justifying the repudiation of those parts of the agreement the object and purpose of which have remained unchanged. Iceland has derived benefits from the executed provisions of the agreement, such as the recognition by the United Kingdom since 1961 of a 12–mile exclusive fisheries jurisdiction, the acceptance by the United Kingdom of the baselines established by Iceland and the relinquishment in a period of three years of the preexisting traditional fishing by vessels registered in the United Kingdom. Clearly it then becomes incumbent on Iceland to comply with its side of the bargain, which is to accept the testing before the Court

of the validity of its further claims to extended jurisdiction. Moreover, in the case of a treaty which is in part executed and in part executory, in which one of the parties has already benefited from the executed provisions of the treaty, it would be particularly inadmissible to allow that party to put an end to obligations which were accepted under the treaty by way of *quid pro quo* for the provisions which the other party has already executed.

* * *

35.   In his letter of 29 May 1972 to the Registrar, the Minister for Foreign Affairs of Iceland refers to "the changed circumstances resulting from the ever-increasing exploitation of the fishery resources in the seas surrounding Iceland." * * *

* * *

37.   One of the basic requirements embodied in [Article 62 of the Vienna Convention, which the Court considers customary law] is that the change of circumstances must have been a fundamental one. In this respect the Government of Iceland has, with regard to developments in fishing techniques, referred in an official publication on *Fisheries Jurisdiction in Iceland,* enclosed with the Foreign Minister's letter of 29 May 1972 to the Registrar, to the increased exploitation of the fishery resources in the seas surrounding Iceland and to the danger of still further exploitation because of an increase in the catching capacity of fishing fleets. The Icelandic statements recall the exceptional dependence of that country on its fishing for its existence and economic development. * * *

* * *

39.   The Applicant, for its part, contends that the alterations and progress in fishing techniques have not produced in the waters around Iceland the consequences apprehended by Iceland and therefore that the changes are not of a fundamental or vital character. In its Memorial, it points out that, as regards the capacity of fishing fleets, increases in the efficiency of individual trawlers have been counter-balanced by the reduction in total numbers of vessels in national fleets fishing in the waters around Iceland, and that the statistics show that the total annual catch of demersal species has varied to no great extent since 1960.

40.   The Court, at the present stage of the proceedings, does not need to pronounce on this question of fact, as to which there appears to be a serious divergence of views between the two Governments. If, as contended by Iceland, there have been any fundamental changes in fishing techniques in the waters around Iceland, those changes might be relevant for the decision on the merits of the dispute, and the Court might need to examine the contention at that stage, together with any other arguments that Iceland might advance in support of the validity of the extension of its fisheries jurisdiction beyond what was agreed to in the 1961 Exchange of Notes. But the alleged changes could not affect in the least the

obligation to submit to the Court's jurisdiction, which is the only issue at the present stage of the proceedings. It follows that the apprehended dangers for the vital interests of Iceland, resulting from changes in fishing techniques, cannot constitute a fundamental change with respect to the lapse or subsistence of the compromissory clause establishing the Court's jurisdiction.

* * *

43.   Moreover, in order that a change of circumstances may give rise to a ground for invoking the termination of a treaty it is also necessary that it should have resulted in a radical transformation of the extent of the obligations still to be performed. The change must have increased the burden of the obligations to be executed to the extent of rendering the performance something essentially different from that originally undertaken. In respect of the obligation with which the Court is here concerned, this condition is wholly unsatisfied; the change of circumstances alleged by Iceland cannot be said to have transformed radically the extent of the jurisdictional obligation which is imposed in the 1961 Exchange of Notes. The compromissory clause enabled either of the parties to submit to the Court any dispute between them relating to an extension of Icelandic fisheries jurisdiction in the waters above its continental shelf beyond the 12–mile limit. The present dispute is exactly of the character anticipated in the compromissory clause of the Exchange of Notes. Not only has the jurisdictional obligation not been radically transformed in its extent; it has remained precisely what it was in 1961.

* * *

44.   In the United Kingdom Memorial it is asserted that there is a flaw in the Icelandic contention of change of circumstances: that the doctrine never operates so as to extinguish a treaty automatically or to allow an unchallengeable unilateral denunciation by one party; it only operates to confer a right to call for termination and, if that call is disputed, to submit the dispute to some organ or body with power to determine whether the conditions for the operation of the doctrine are present. In this connection the Applicant alludes to Articles 65 and 66 of the Vienna Convention on the Law of Treaties. Those Articles provide that where the parties to a treaty have failed within 12 months to achieve a settlement of a dispute by the means indicated in Article 33 of the United Nations Charter (which means include reference to judicial settlement) any one of the parties may submit the dispute to the procedure for conciliation provided in the Annex to the Convention.

45.   In the present case, the procedural complement to the doctrine of changed circumstances is already provided for in the 1961 Exchange of Notes, which specifically calls upon the parties to have recourse to the Court in the event of a dispute relating to Iceland's extension of fisheries jurisdiction. * * *

GABČÍKOVO–NAGYMAROS PROJECT
(HUNGARY/SLOVAKIA)

International Court of Justice, 1997
1997 I.C.J. 7

[In 1977, when both Hungary and Czechoslovakia were under Communist rule, the two countries concluded a treaty for the construction and operation of a system of locks on the Danube River, comprising *inter alia* a reservoir, dam, bypass canal, hydroelectric power plants, and navigational and flood control improvements. The Danube forms the border between the two countries for a stretch affected by these works and elsewhere flows through their respective territories. Both were expected to benefit from the project. Construction began in 1978 but was not completed.

[Beginning in 1989, major transformations took place in the political and economic systems of both countries. Along with these came a heightened environmental consciousness and awareness of potential risks from carrying through with the plans. New political leadership in the two countries expressed objections to the project as originally conceived: the Hungarian government said it was a "mistake" and the Czechoslovak President called it a "totalitarian, gigomaniac monument which is against nature" but emphasized that it was already partly built.

[In response to increased criticism of the project among its public, Hungary first suspended its parts of the works in 1989 and later abandoned them. Negotiations between the parties for a mutually satisfactory solution were unsuccessful. Czechoslovakia began work in 1991 on an alternative to the original plan, known as Variant C. This variant was unacceptable to Hungary, which in May 1992 gave notice of termination of the treaty; see pp. 204–05 note 2 *supra*.

[Effective January 1, 1993, Czechoslovakia dissolved into two states; Slovakia became independent. Later in 1993, Hungary and Slovakia asked the I.C.J. to decide on the basis of international law several questions, including whether Hungary was entitled to suspend and subsequently abandon its part of the works.

[Among Hungary's claimed grounds for termination was changed circumstances, as well as an argument of impossibility. The portions of the Court's judgment dealing with those issues follow.]

102. Hungary also relied on the principle of the impossibility of performance as reflected in Article 61 of the Vienna Convention on the Law of Treaties. Hungary's interpretation of the wording of Article 61 is, however, not in conformity with the terms of that Article, nor with the intention of the Diplomatic Conference which adopted the Convention.
* * *

103. Hungary contended that the essential object of the Treaty—an economic joint investment which was consistent with environmental protection and which was operated by the two contracting parties jointly—

had permanently disappeared and that the Treaty had thus become impossible to perform. It is not necessary for the Court to determine whether the term "object" in Article 61 can also be understood to embrace a legal régime as in any event, even if that were the case, it would have to conclude that in this instance that régime had not definitively ceased to exist. The 1977 Treaty * * * actually made available to the parties the necessary means to proceed at any time, by negotiation, to the required readjustments between economic imperatives and ecological imperatives. The Court would add that, if the joint exploitation of the investment was no longer possible, this was originally because Hungary did not carry out most of the works for which it was responsible under the 1977 Treaty; Article 61, paragraph 2 of the Vienna Convention expressly provides that impossibility of performance may not be invoked for the termination of a treaty by a party to that treaty when it results from that party's own breach of an obligation flowing from the treaty.

* * *

104.   Hungary further argued that it was entitled to invoke a number of events which, cumulatively, would have constituted a fundamental change of circumstances. In this respect it specified profound changes of a political nature, the Project's diminishing economic viability, the progress of environmental knowledge and the development of new norms and prescriptions of international environmental law.

The Court recalls that, in the *Fisheries Jurisdiction* case (*I.C.J. Reports 1973*, p. 63, para. 36), it stated that,

"Article 62 of the Vienna Convention on the Law of Treaties ... may in many respects be considered as a codification of existing customary law on the subject of the termination of a treaty relationship on account of change of circumstances."

The prevailing political situation was certainly relevant for the conclusion of the 1977 Treaty. But the Court will recall that the Treaty provided for a joint investment programme for the production of energy, the control of floods and the improvement of navigation on the Danube. In the Court's view, the prevalent political conditions were thus not so closely linked to the object and purpose of the Treaty that they constituted an essential basis of the consent of the parties and, in changing, radically altered the extent of the obligations still to be performed. The same holds good for the economic system in force at the time of the conclusion of the 1977 Treaty. Besides, even though the estimated profitability of the Project might have appeared less in 1992 than in 1977, it does not appear from the record before the Court that it was bound to diminish to such an extent that the treaty obligations of the parties would have been radically transformed as a result.

The Court does not consider that new developments in the state of environmental knowledge and of environmental law can be said to have been completely unforeseen. What is more, the formulation of [the treaty articles] designed to accommodate change, made it possible for the parties to take account of such developments and to apply them when implementing those treaty provisions.

The changed circumstances advanced by Hungary are, in the Court's view, not of such a nature, either individually or collectively, that their effect would radically transform the extent of the obligations still to be performed in order to accomplish the Project. A fundamental change of circumstances must have been unforeseen; the existence of the circumstances at the time of the Treaty's conclusion must have constituted an essential basis of the consent of the parties to be bound by the Treaty. The negative and conditional wording of Article 62 of the Vienna Convention on the Law of Treaties is a clear indication moreover that the stability of treaty relations requires that the plea of fundamental change of circumstances be applied only in exceptional cases.

E. WAR BETWEEN CONTRACTING PARTIES

The Vienna Convention does not contain any provision concerning the effect of the outbreak of hostilities upon treaties. (Compare Article 73, that the Convention "shall not prejudge any question" arising from the outbreak of hostilities.) The International Law Commission explained that it:

> Considered that the study of this topic would inevitably involve a consideration of the effect of the provisions of the Charter concerning the threat or use of force upon the legality of the recourse to the particular hostilities in question; and it did not feel that this question could conveniently be dealt with in the context of its present work upon the law of treaties.

[1966] II Yb.I.L.C. 176, para. 29. Case-law and scholars have, however, dealt with such questions, and the I.LC. returned to it in 2005.

TECHT v. HUGHES

Court of Appeals of New York, 1920
229 N.Y. 222, 128 N.E 185, cert. denied, 254 U.S. 643

[An American citizen died intestate in New York, where he owned real property, on December 27, 1917, twenty days after the outbreak of war between the United States and Austria–Hungary. One of the decedent's daughters, Mrs. Techt, had previously married a citizen of Austria–Hungary and had, under Federal legislation then in force, thereby lost her United States citizenship and acquired that of her husband. The New York statute allowed citizens and "alien friends" to take and hold real property. Mrs. Techt's sister claimed the whole property on the ground that Mrs. Techt was an "alien enemy." Mrs. Techt relied on the Treaty of 1848 between the United States and Austria, 9 Stat. 944, which provided that nationals of either state could take real property by descent. The

Court of Appeals decided that Mrs. Techt was not an alien friend and not entitled to the statute's protection. Her claim therefore depended entirely upon the continuing effectiveness, despite the state of war, of the Treaty of 1848.]

CARDOZO, J. * * * The support of the statute failing, there remains the question of the treaty. The treaty, if in force, is the supreme law of the land (Const. U.S. art. 6) and supersedes all local laws inconsistent with its terms * * *. The plaintiff has an estate of inheritance, if the treaty is in force.

The effect of war upon the existing treaties of belligerents is one of the unsettled problems of the law. The older writers sometimes said that treaties ended ipso facto when war came. 3 Phillimore, Int. L. 794. The writers of our own time reject these sweeping statements. 2 Oppenheim, Int. L. § 99; Hall, Int. L. 398, 401; Fiore, Int.L. (Borchard's Transl.) § 845. International law to-day does not preserve treaties or annul them, regardless of the effects produced. It deals with such problems pragmatically, preserving or annulling as the necessities of war exact. It establishes standards, but it does not fetter itself with rules. When it attempts to do more, it finds that there is neither unanimity of opinion nor uniformity of practice. "The whole question remains as yet unsettled." Oppenheim, supra. This does not mean, of course, that there are not some classes of treaties about which there is general agreement. Treaties of alliance fall. Treaties of boundary or cession, "dispositive" or "transitory" conventions, survive. Hall, Int.L. pp. 398, 401; 2 Westlake, Int.L. 34; Oppenheim, supra. So, of course, do treaties which regulate the conduct of hostilities. Hall, supra; 5 Moore, Dig. Int. L. 372; Society for Propagation of the Gospel v. Town of New Haven, 8 Wheat. 464, 494.

Intention in such circumstances is clear. These instances do not represent distinct and final principles. They are illustrations of the same principle. They are applications of a standard. When I ask what that principle or standard is, and endeavor to extract it from the long chapters in the books, I get this, and nothing more: That provisions compatible with a state of hostilities, unless expressly terminated, will be enforced, and those incompatible rejected.

> Treaties lose their efficacy in war only if their execution is incompatible with war. Les traités ne perdent leur efficacité en temps de guerre que si leur exécution est incompatible avec la guerre elle-même.

Bluntschli, Droit International Codifié, sec. 538.

That in substance was Kent's view, here as often in advance of the thought of his day:

> All those duties, of which the exercise is not necessarily suspended by the war, subsist in their full force. The obligation of keeping faith is so far from ceasing in time of war that its efficacy becomes increased, from the increased necessity of it.

1 Kent, Comm. p. 176.

* * *

This, I think, is the principle which must guide the judicial department of the government when called upon to determine during the progress of a war whether a treaty shall be observed, in the absence of some declaration by the political departments of the government that it has been suspended or annulled. A treaty has a two-fold aspect. In its primary operation, it is a compact between independent states. In its secondary operation, it is a source of private rights for individuals within states. Head Money Cases, 112 U.S. 580, 598. Granting that the termination of the compact involves the termination of the rights, it does not follow, because there is a privilege to rescind, that the privilege has been exercised. The question is not what states may do after war has supervened, and this without breach of their duty as members of the society of nations. The question is what courts are to presume that they have done. * * *

President and Senate may denounce the treaty, and thus terminate its life. Congress may enact an inconsistent rule, which will control the action of the courts. * * * The treaty of peace itself may set up new relations, and terminate earlier compacts, either tacitly or expressly. The proposed treaties with Germany and Austria give the victorious powers the privilege of choosing the treaties which are to be kept in force or abrogated. But until some one of these things is done, until some one of these events occurs, while war is still flagrant, and the will of the political departments of the government unrevealed, the courts, as I view their function, play a humbler and more cautious part. It is not for them to denounce treaties generally en bloc. Their part it is, as one provision or another is involved in some actual controversy before them, to determine whether, alone or by force of connection with an inseparable scheme, the provision is inconsistent with the policy or safety of the nation in the emergency of war, and hence presumably intended to be limited to times of peace. The mere fact that other portions of the treaty are suspended, or even abrogated, is not conclusive. The treaty does not fall in its entirety unless it has the character of an indivisible act. * * *

To determine whether it has this character, it is not enough to consider its name or label. No general formula suffices. We must consult in each case the nature and purpose of the specific articles involved. * * *

I find nothing incompatible with the policy of the government, with the safety of the nation, or with the maintenance of the war in the enforcement of this treaty, so as to sustain the plaintiff's title. We do not confiscate the lands or goods of the stranger within our gates. If we permit him to remain, he is free during good behavior to buy property and sell it. Trading with Enemy Act Oct. 6, 1917, 40 Stat. 411, c. 106. * * * A public policy not outraged by purchase will not be outraged by inheritance.

The plaintiff is a resident; but even if she were a nonresident, and were within the hostile territory, the policy of the nation would not divest her of the title whether acquired before the war or later. Custody would then be assumed by the Alien Property Custodian. The proceeds of the property, in the event of sale, would be kept within the jurisdiction. * * *

I do not overlook the statements which may be found here and there in the works of authors of distinction (Hall, supra; Halleck, Int. L. [4th Ed.] 314; Wheaton, Int. L. [5th Ed.] 377) that treaties of commerce and navigation are to be ranked in the class of treaties which war abrogates or at least suspends. Commerce is friendly intercourse. Friendly intercourse between nations is impossible in war. Therefore treaties regulating such intercourse are not operative in war. But stipulations do not touch commerce because they happen to be embodied in a treaty which is styled one to regulate or encourage commerce. We must be on our guard against being misled by labels. Bluntschli's warning, already quoted, reminds us that the nature and not the name of covenants determines whether they shall be disregarded or observed. * * *

Restrictions upon ownership of land by aliens have a history all their own, unrelated altogether to restrictions upon trade. * * * When removed, they cease to exist for enemies as well as friends, unless the statute removing them enforces a distinction. * * * More than that, the removal, when effected by treaty, gives reciprocal privileges to the subjects of each state, and is thus of value to one side as much as to the other. For this reason, the inference is a strong one, as was pointed out by the Master of the Rolls in Sutton v. Sutton, 1 Russ. & M. 664, 675, that the privileges, unless expressly revoked are intended to endure. Cf. 2 Westlake, p. 33; also Halleck, Int. L., supra. There, as in Society for Propagation of the Gospel v. Town of New Haven, 8 Wheat. 464, 494, the treaty of 1794 between the United States and England, protecting the citizens of each in the enjoyment of their landed property, was held not to have been abrogated by the war of 1812. Undoubtedly there is a distinction between those cases and this, in that there the rights had become vested before the outbreak of the war. None the less, alike in reasoning and in conclusion, they have their value and significance. If stipulations governing the tenure of land survive the stress of war, though contained in a treaty which is described as one of amity, it is not perceived why they may not also survive, though contained in a treaty which is described as one of commerce. In preserving the right of inheritance for citizens of Austria when the land inherited is here we preserve the same right for our citizens when the land inherited is there. * * * Congress has not yet commanded us, and the exigencies of war, as I view them, do not constrain us, to throw these benefits away.

No one can study the vague and wavering statements of treaties and decision in this field of international law with any feeling of assurance at the end that he has chosen the right path. One looks in vain either for uniformity of doctrine or for scientific accuracy of exposition. There are wise cautions for the statesmen. There are few precepts for the judge. All the more, in this uncertainty, I am impelled to the belief that, until the political departments have acted, the courts, in refusing to give effect to treaties, should limit their refusal to the needs of the occasion; that they are not bound by any rigid formula to nullify the whole or nothing; and that, in determining whether this treaty survived the coming of war, they are free to make choice of the conclusion which shall seem the most in keeping with the traditions of the law, the policy of the statutes, the dictates of fair dealing, and the honor of the nation.

Judgment affirmed.

NOTES

1. *"Compatibility."* What did the court mean by its reference to the "compatibility" of the treaty with "the policy or safety of the nation in the emergency of war"? How is this "compatibility" related to the intentions of the parties? What standards of "compatibility" did the court have in mind, and to what sources of policy did it look? Would the following statement of Secretary of State Lansing, if it had been brought to the court's attention, have required a different result? "[I]n view of the present state of war between the United States and Austria–Hungary and Germany, the Department does not regard these provisions [relating to inheritance of real property] as now in operation." Letter to the Alien Property Custodian, September 10, 1918, 5 Hackworth at 379. The Supreme Court stated in *Clark v. Allen*, 331 U.S. 503, 513 (1947), that "[w]here the relevant historical sources and the instrument itself give no plain indication that it is to become inoperative in whole or in part on the outbreak of war, we are left to determine as *Techt v. Hughes,* supra, indicates, whether the provision under which rights are asserted is incompatible with national policy in time of war." The court held that a treaty provision similar to that involved in *Techt v. Hughes* was not incompatible with national policy. Compare *Karnuth v. United States ex rel. Arbro*, 279 U.S. 231 (1929), in which Article III of the Jay Treaty of 1794, 8 Stat. 116, which provided for the free passage and repassage of British and United States citizens across the Canadian border, was held to have been abrogated by the war of 1812. The Court pointed out that the treaty provision was "wholly promissory and prospective and necessarily ceases to operate in a state of war, since the passing and repassing of citizens or subjects of one sovereignty into the territory of another is inconsistent with the condition of hostility." The Court held that the "provision belongs to the class of treaties which does not survive war" between the parties. 279 U.S. at 240.

2. *Studies by Expert Bodies.* In 1985 the Institut de Droit International adopted a resolution on The Effects of Armed Conflicts on Treaties, which followed several years of study and discussion. For reports and comments see 59–I Ann. de l'Institut de Droit Int. 201–84 (1981); 59–II Ann. de l'Institut de Droit Int. 175–244 (1981); 61–I Ann. de l'Institut de Droit Int. 1–25 (1985); 61–II Ann. de l'Institut de Droit Int. (1986). The resolution states in Article 2 that the outbreak of an armed conflict "does not *ipso facto* terminate or suspend the operation of treaties in force between the parties to the armed conflict." Article 3 deals with treaties which expressly provide or which by reason of their nature or purpose are to be regarded as operative during

armed conflict and Article 4 with treaties relating to the protection of the human person. Other articles deal with procedural aspects and with the relationship to self-defense under the U.N. Charter and the actions of U.N. organs.

In 2005, the International Law Commission took up the topic of Effects of Armed Conflicts on Treaties, turning in the first instance to reports and a set of draft articles prepared by Special Rapporteur Ian Brownlie. The proposed articles would encourage continuity of treaty obligations to the extent feasible during armed conflict, would identify considerations potentially bearing on interruption of those obligations, and would specify conditions and procedural requirements for invoking suspension or termination on the part of states engaged in armed conflict. This work was still in progress in 2009. See Report of the International Law Commission on its 60th Session, U.N. Doc. A/63/10 (2008).

CHAPTER 4

OTHER SOURCES OF LAW

■ ■ ■

SECTION 1. GENERAL PRINCIPLES OF LAW AND EQUITY

A. GENERAL PRINCIPLES OF LAW

PROSECUTOR v. TADIĆ

International Criminal Tribunal for the Former Yugoslavia,
Decision on Interlocutory Appeal on Jurisdiction, 1995
Appeals Chamber, Case No. IT–94–1–AR72, 35 I.L.M. 32 (1996) (footnotes omitted)

[The first individual to be tried by the International Criminal Tribunal for the Former Yugoslavia (I.C.T.Y.) was Dusko Tadić. The trial was noteworthy as the first war crimes trial before an international tribunal since the Nuremberg and Tokyo trials after World War II. Tadić was accused of committing atrocities at the Serb-run Omarska concentration camp in northwestern Bosnia–Herzegovina in 1992. The initial contention of Tadić's defense was that the I.C.T.Y. was without jurisdiction to try him because the Tribunal had been unlawfully established. Tadić objected to the fact that the Tribunal had been created subsequent to the acts of which he was accused, by a 1993 decision of the U.N. Security Council (a body consisting of just fifteen states, without participation or consent by any of the states of the former Yugoslavia). A portion of Appeals Chamber's decision on the jurisdictional issues is set forth below; for other excerpts, see Chapter 16.]

Before: JUDGE CASSESE, PRESIDING; JUDGES LI, DESCHENES, ABI-SAAB, and SIDHWA.

* * *

4. Was The Establishment Of The International Tribunal Contrary To The General Principle Whereby Courts Must Be "Established By Law"?

41. Appellant challenges the establishment of the International Tribunal by contending that it has not been established by law. The entitlement of an individual to have a criminal charge against him determined by a tribunal which has been established by law is provided in Article 14,

paragraph 1, of the International Covenant on Civil and Political Rights. It provides:

> "In the determination of any criminal charge against him, or of his rights and obligations in a suit at law, everyone shall be entitled to a fair and public hearing by a competent, independent and impartial tribunal established by law." (ICCPR, art. 14, para. 1.)

Similar provisions can be found in Article 6(1) of the European Convention on Human Rights * * * and in Article 8(1) of the American Convention on Human Rights. * * *

Appellant argues that the right to have a criminal charge determined by a tribunal established by law is one which forms part of international law as a "general principle of law recognized by civilized nations," one of the sources of international law in Article 38 of the Statute of the International Court of Justice. In support of this assertion, Appellant emphasises the fundamental nature of the "fair trial" or "due process" guarantees afforded in the International Covenant on Civil and Political Rights, the European Convention on Human Rights and the American Convention on Human Rights. Appellant asserts that they are minimum requirements in international law for the administration of criminal justice.

42.   For the reasons outlined below, Appellant has not satisfied this Chamber that the requirements laid down in these three conventions must apply not only in the context of national legal systems but also with respect to proceedings conducted before an international court. This Chamber is, however, satisfied that the principle that a tribunal must be established by law, as explained below, is a general principle of law imposing an international obligation which only applies to the administration of criminal justice in a municipal setting. It follows from this principle that it is incumbent on all States to organize their system of criminal justice in such a way as to ensure that all individuals are guaranteed the right to have a criminal charge determined by a tribunal established by law. This does not mean, however, that, by contrast, an international criminal court could be set up at the mere whim of a group of governments. Such a court ought to be rooted in the rule of law and offer all guarantees embodied in the relevant international instruments. Then the court may be said to be "established by law."

43.   Indeed, there are three possible interpretations of the term "established by law." First, as Appellant argues, "established by law" could mean established by a legislature. Appellant claims that the International Tribunal is the product of a "mere executive order" and not of a "decision making process under democratic control, necessary to create a judicial organisation in a democratic society." Therefore Appellant maintains that the International Tribunal not been "established by law." (Defence Appeal Brief, at para. 5.4.)

The case law applying the words "established by law" in the European Convention on Human Rights has favoured this interpretation of the expression. This case law bears out the view that the relevant provision is intended to ensure that tribunals in a democratic society must not depend on the discretion of the executive; rather they should be regulated by law emanating from Parliament. * * *

Or, put another way, the guarantee is intended to ensure that the administration of justice is not a matter of executive discretion, but is regulated by laws made by the legislature.

It is clear that the legislative, executive and judicial division of powers which is largely followed in most municipal systems does not apply to the international setting nor, more specifically, to the setting of an international organization such as the United Nations. Among the principal organs of the United Nations the divisions between judicial, executive and legislative functions are not clear cut. Regarding the judicial function, the International Court of Justice is clearly the "principal judicial organ" (see United Nations Charter, art. 92). There is, however, no legislature, in the technical sense of the term, in the United Nations system and, more generally, no Parliament in the world community. That is to say, there exists no corporate organ formally empowered to enact laws directly binding on international legal subjects.

It is clearly impossible to classify the organs of the United Nations into the above-discussed divisions which exist in the national law of States. Indeed, Appellant has agreed that the constitutional structure of the United Nations does not follow the division of powers often found in national constitutions. Consequently the separation of powers element of the requirement that a tribunal be "established by law" finds no application in an international law setting. The aforementioned principle can only impose an obligation on States concerning the functioning of their own national systems.

44. A second possible interpretation is that the words "established by law" refer to establishment of international courts by a body which, though not a Parliament, has a limited power to take binding decisions. In our view, one such body is the Security Council when, acting under Chapter VII of the United Nations Charter, it makes decisions binding by virtue of Article 25 of the Charter.

According to Appellant, however, there must be something more for a tribunal to be "established by law." Appellant takes the position that, given the differences between the United Nations system and national division of powers, discussed above, the conclusion must be that the United Nations system is not capable of creating the International Tribunal unless there is an amendment to the United Nations Charter. We disagree. It does not follow from the fact that the United Nations has no legislature that the Security Council is not empowered to set up this International Tribunal if it is acting pursuant to an authority found within its constitution, the United Nations Charter. * * * [W]e are of the view that the Security Council was endowed with the power to create this

International Tribunal as a measure under Chapter VII in the light of its determination that there exists a threat to the peace.

In addition, the establishment of the International Tribunal has been repeatedly approved and endorsed by the "representative" organ of the United Nations, the General Assembly: this body not only participated in its setting up, by electing the Judges and approving the budget, but also expressed its satisfaction with, and encouragement of the activities of the International Tribunal in various resolutions. * * *

45. The third possible interpretation of the requirement that the International Tribunal be "established by law" is that its establishment must be in accordance with the rule of law. This appears to be the most sensible and most likely meaning of the term in the context of international law. For a tribunal such as this one to be established according to the rule of law, it must be established in accordance with the proper international standards; it must provide all the guarantees of fairness, justice and even-handedness, in full conformity with internationally recognized human rights instruments.

* * *

46. An examination of the Statute of the International Tribunal, and of the Rules of Procedure and Evidence adopted pursuant to that Statute leads to the conclusion that it has been established in accordance with the rule of law. The fair trial guarantees in Article 14 of the International Covenant on Civil and Political Rights have been adopted almost verbatim in Article 21 of the Statute. Other fair trial guarantees appear in the Statute and the Rules of Procedure and Evidence. For example, Article 13, paragraph 1, of the Statute ensures the high moral character, impartiality, integrity and competence of the Judges of the International Tribunal, while various other provisions in the Rules ensure equality of arms and fair trial.

47. In conclusion, the Appeals Chamber finds that the International Tribunal has been established in accordance with the appropriate procedures under the United Nations Charter and provides all the necessary safeguards of a fair trial. It is thus "established by law."

48. The first ground of appeal: unlawful establishment of the International Tribunal, is accordingly dismissed.

NOTES

1. *General Principles in International Criminal Tribunals.* The Appeals Chamber in *Tadić* made reference to several human rights treaties but was not applying them directly as treaty law. The I.C.T.Y. itself is a subsidiary organ of the U.N. Security Council and not a party to any of these treaties; thus, if the norms embodied in the treaties were to be applied by the I.C.T.Y, it would have to be as a matter of general principles.

In their subsequent rulings, the International Criminal Tribunals for the Former Yugoslavia and for Rwanda have carried out intensive examinations of national criminal laws and procedures, to try to discern "general principles of law" that might guide the tribunals in resolving disputed points, in the absence of treaty-based sources. In a later phase of the *Tadić* case, after the defendant had been convicted, he again appealed to "general principles" as part of his arguments concerning the substantive standards required to convict him of a crime under international law, in particular as regards the conditions under which an individual could be held criminally responsible for acts of others. The Appeals Chamber consulted national legislation and case law relevant to participants in a common purpose, but did not find any controlling general principle because of a divergence in approaches among countries and major legal systems. Case No. IT–94–1–AR72, Judgment on Appeal from Conviction, paras. 224–25 (July 15 1999).

The Rome Statute of the International Criminal Court (see Documents Supplement) provides in its Article 21(1) that the Court shall apply (a) its own Statute (and related instruments adopted in connection with it); (b) applicable treaties and the principles and rules of international law, including the law of armed conflict; and "(c) Failing that, general principles of law derived by the Court from national laws of legal systems of the world including, as appropriate, the national laws of States that would normally exercise jurisdiction over the crime, provided that those principles are not inconsistent with this Statute and with international law and internationally recognized norms and standards." For discussion of the relationship between the I.C.C. and national legal systems, see Chapter 16.

2. *Generality across Common–Law and Civil–Law Traditions.* In the *Erdemović* case, Case No. IT–96–22–A, Judgment on Appeal (Oct. 7, 1997), the tribunal looked in detail at national legislation from common-law and civil-law jurisdictions and at national judicial precedents, both with respect to the substantive question of whether duress can be a complete defense to a homicide and with respect to procedural points, viz., whether the defendant could withdraw a plea of guilty made with inadequate knowledge of its consequences. On the specific questions before the tribunal in *Erdemović*, common-law and civil-law traditions seemed to differ markedly, so that no truly "general" principles could emerge. Yet, as some of the judges separately explained, "general principles of law recognized by civilized nations" might well serve as a residuum of authoritative guidance in appropriate cases. Compare the Joint Separate Opinion of Judges McDonald & Vohrah, paras. 56ff, with the Separate and Dissenting Opinion of Judge Cassese, para. 1ff. (national concepts cannot be automatically transposed to the international level).

3. *Transposing Practices Found Across Many Legal Systems.* In the *Blaskić* case, the Appeals Chamber considered whether national practice as to subpoenas, contempt of court, and other procedures claimed to be "inherent powers" of a judicial organ could be transposed to the international level, in order to fill a gap in authority that had not been explicitly conferred in the Tribunal's Statute. The Chamber observed that "domestic judicial views or approaches should be handled with the greatest caution at the international level, lest one should fail to make due allowance for the unique characteristics of international criminal procedures. * * * [T]he transposition onto the international community of legal institutions, constructs or approaches pre-

vailing in national law may be a source of great confusion and misapprehension." Case No. IT–95–14–AR108*bis*, Judgment on the Request of the Republic of Croatia for Review of Decision on the Issuance of *Subpoenae Duces Tecum*, paras. 23–24, 40 (Oct. 29, 1997).

SCHACHTER, INTERNATIONAL LAW IN THEORY AND PRACTICE

50–55 (1991)

We can distinguish five categories of general principles that have been invoked and applied in international law discourse and cases. Each has a different basis for its authority and validity as law. They are

(1) The principles of municipal law "recognized by civilized nations".

(2) General principles of law "derived from the specific nature of the international community".

(3) Principles "intrinsic to the idea of law and basic to all legal systems".

(4) Principles "valid through all kinds of societies in relationships of hierarchy and co-ordination".

(5) Principles of justice founded on "the very nature of man as a rational and social being".

Although these five categories are analytically distinct, it is not unusual for a particular general principle to fall into more than one of the categories. For example, the principle that no one shall be a judge in his own cause or that a victim of a legal wrong is entitled to reparation are considered part of most, if not all, systems of municipal law and as intrinsic to the basic idea of law.

Our first category, general principles of municipal law, has given rise to a considerable body of writing and much controversy. Article 38(1)(c) of the Statute of the Court does not expressly refer to principles of national law but rather general principles "recognized by civilized nations". The travaux préparatoires reveal an interesting variety of views about this subparagraph during the drafting stage. Some of the participants had in mind equity and principles recognized "by the legal conscience of civilized nations". (The notion of "legal conscience" was a familiar concept to European international lawyers in the nineteenth and early part of the twentieth century.) Elihu Root, the American member of the drafting committee, prepared the text finally adopted and it seemed clear that his amendment was intended to refer to principles "actually recognized and applied in national legal systems". The fact that the subparagraph was distinct from those on treaty and custom indicated an intent to treat general principles as an independent source of law, and not as a subsidiary source. As an independent source, it did not appear to require any separate proof that such principles of national law had been "received" into international law.

However, a significant minority of jurists holds that national law principles, even if generally found in most legal systems, cannot *ipso facto* be international law. One view is that they must receive the *imprimatur* of State consent through custom or treaty in order to become international law. The strict positivist school adheres to that view. A somewhat modified version is adopted by others to the effect that rules of municipal law cannot be considered as recognized by civilized nations unless there is evidence of the concurrence of States on their status as international law. Such concurrence may occur through treaty, custom or other evidence of recognition. This would allow for some principles, such as *res judicata*, which are not customary law but are generally accepted in international law. * * *

Several influential international legal scholars have considered municipal law an important means for developing international law and extending it into new areas of international concern. For example, Wilfred Jenks and Wolfgang Friedmann have looked to a "common law of mankind" to meet problems raised by humanitarian concerns, environmental threats and economic relations. In this respect they followed the lead of Hersch Lauterpacht suggested in his classic work, *Private Law Sources and Analogies of International Law*. The growth of transnational commercial and financial transactions has also been perceived as a fruitful area for the application of national law rules to create a "commercial law of nations", referred to as a "vast *terra incognita*".

Despite the eloquent arguments made for using national law principles as an independent source of international law, it cannot be said that either courts or the political organs of States have significantly drawn on municipal law principles as an autonomous and distinct ground for binding rules of conduct. It is true that the International Court and its predecessor the Permanent Court of International Justice have made reference on a number of occasions to "generally accepted practice" or "all systems of law" as a basis for its approval of a legal rule. (But curiously the Court has done so without explicit reference to its own statutory authority in Article 38(1)(c).) Those references to national law have most often been to highly general ideas of legal liability or precepts of judicial administration. In the former category, we find the much-quoted principles of the *Chorzów Factory* case that "every violation of an engagement involves an obligation to make reparation" and that "a party cannot take advantage of his own wrong". These maxims and certain maxims of legal interpretation, as for example, *lex specialis derogat generalis,* and "no one may transfer more than he has", are also regarded as notions intrinsic to the idea of law and legal reasoning. As such they can be (and have been) accepted not as municipal law, but as general postulates of international law, even if not customary law in the specific sense of that concept.

The use of municipal law rules for international judicial and arbitral procedure has been more common and more specific than any other type of application. For example, the International Court has accepted *res judicata* as applicable to international litigation; it has allowed recourse to indirect evidence (i.e., inferences of fact and circumstantial evidence) and it has approved the principle that legal remedies against a judgment are equally open to either party. Arbitral tribunals have applied the principle of prescription (or laches) to international litigation relying on analogies from municipal law. Lauterpacht's *Private Law Sources and Analogies of International Law,* written in 1927, still remains a valuable repository of examples, as does Bin Cheng's later work on *General Principles as Applied by International Courts and Tribunals.*

But considerable caution is still required in inferring international law from municipal law, even where the principles of national law are found in many "representative" legal systems. The international cases show such use in a limited degree, nearly always as a supplement to fill in gaps left by the primary sources of treaty and custom. * * * The most important limitation on the use of municipal law principles arises from the requirement that the principle be appropriate for application on the international level. Thus, the universally accepted common crimes—murder, theft, assault, incest—that apply to individuals are not crimes under international law by virtue of their ubiquity. In the *Right of Passage over Indian Territory* case (India v. Portugal), the Court rejected arguments that the municipal law of easements found in most legal systems were appropriate principles for determining rights of transit over State territory. Similarly, a contention that the law of trusts could be used to interpret the mandate of South Africa over South West Africa (Namibia) did not win approval as international law but it may possibly have had an indirect influence on the Court's reasoning in its advisory opinions. Lord McNair, in an individual opinion, in the 1950 Advisory Opinion on the *International Status of South West Africa,* expressed a balanced conclusion on the subject of analogies from private law that merits quotation here.

> "International law has recruited and continues to recruit many of its rules and institutions from private systems of law * * * The way in which international law borrows from the source is not by means of importing private law institutions 'lock, stock and barrel', ready-made and fully equipped with a set of rules * * * In my opinion the true view of the duty of international tribunals in this matter is to regard any features or terminology which are reminiscent of the rules and institutions of private law as an indication of policy and principles rather than as directly importing these rules and institutions".

I would subscribe to this general formulation and stress the requirement that the use of municipal law must be appropriate for international relations.

At the same time, I would suggest a somewhat more positive approach for the emergent international law concerned with the individual, business companies, environmental dangers and shared resources. Inasmuch as these areas have become the concern of international law, national law principles will often be suitable for international application. This does not mean importing municipal rules "lock, stock and barrel", but it suggests that domestic law rules applicable to such matters as individual rights, contractual remedies, liability for extra hazardous activities, or restraints on use of common property, have now become pertinent for recruitment into international law. In these areas, we may look to representative legal systems not only for the highly abstract principles of the kind referred to earlier but to more specific rules that are sufficiently widespread as to be considered "recognized by civilized nations". It is likely that such rules will enter into international law largely through international treaties or particular arrangements accepted by the parties. But such treaties and arrangements still require supplementing their general provisions and such filling-in can often be achieved by recourse to commonly accepted national law rules. The case-law under the European Convention on Human Rights exemplifies this process. The fact that treaties and customary law now pervade most of the fields mentioned above means that the use of municipal law for specific application will normally fall within an existing frame of established international law. It would be rare that an international tribunal or organ or States themselves would be faced with the necessity of finding a specific rule in an area unregulated by international law. But there still may be such areas where injury and claims of redress by States occur in fields hitherto untouched by international regulation. Weather modification, acid rain, resource-satellites are possible examples. In these cases, municipal law analogies may provide acceptable solutions for the States concerned or for a tribunal empowered to settle a dispute.

The second category of general principles included in our list comprises principles derived from the specific character of the international community. The most obvious candidates for this category of principles are * * * the necessary principles of coexistence. They include the principles of *pacta sunt servanda,* non-intervention, territorial integrity, self-defence and the legal equality of States. Some of these principles are in the United Nations Charter and therefore part of treaty law, but others might appropriately be treated as principles required by the specific character of a society of sovereign independent members.

Our third category is even more abstract but not infrequently cited: principles "intrinsic to the idea of law and basic to all legal systems". As stated it includes an empirical element—namely, the ascertainment of principles found in "all" legal systems. It also includes a conceptual criterion—"intrinsic to the idea of law". Most of the principles cited in World Court and arbitral decisions as common in municipal law are also referred to as "basic" to all law. In this way, the tribunals move from a purely empirical municipal law basis to "necessary" principles based on the logic of the law. They thus afford a reason for acceptance by those who hesitate to accept municipal law *per se* as international law but are prepared to adopt juridical notions that are seen as intrinsic to the idea of law. Some of the examples that fall under this heading would seem to be analytical (or tautologous) propositions. *Pacta sunt servanda,* and *nemo plus iuris transfere potest quam ipse habet* (no one can transfer more rights than he possesses) are good examples. (Expressing tautologies in Latin apparently adds to their weight in judicial reasoning.) Several other maxims (also commonly expressed in Latin phrases), considered as intrinsic to all representative legal systems, are sometimes described as juridical "postulates", or as essential elements of legal reasoning. Some principles of interpretation fall in this category: for example, the *lex specialis* rule and the maxim *lex posterior derogat priori* (the later supersedes the earlier law, if both have the same source). These are not tautologies, but can be considered as "legal logic". A similar sense of lawyers' logic supports certain postulates of judicial proceedings: for example, *res judicata* and the equality of parties before a tribunal. The latter suggests that reciprocity on a more general basis may be considered as an intrinsic element of legal relations among members of a community considered equal under the law.

These various examples lend support to the theory that the general principles of law form a kind of substratum of legal postulates. In Bin Cheng's words, "They belong to no particular system of law but are common to them all * * * Their existence bears witness to the fundamental unity of law". In actual practice those postulates are established by "logic" or a process of reasoning, with illustrative examples added. The underlying and sometimes unstated premise is that they are generally accepted. They may be used "against" a State in a case because they are established law. However, if a particular principle or postulate becomes a subject of dispute regarding its general acceptance, it is likely to lose its persuasive force as an intrinsic principle. Hence, in the last analysis, these principles, however "intrinsic" they seem to be to the idea of law, rest on an implied consensus of the relevant community.

The foregoing comments are also pertinent to the next two categories of general principles. The idea of principles *"jus rationale"* "valid through all kinds of human societies" (in Judge Tanaka's words) is associated with traditional natural law doctrine. At the present time its theological links are mainly historical as far as international law is concerned, but its principal justification does not depart too far from the classic natural law emphasis on the nature of "man", that is, on the human person as a rational and social creature.

The universalist implication of this theory—the idea of the unity of the human species—has had a powerful impetus in the present era. This is evidenced in at least three significant political and legal developments. The first is the global movements against discrimination on grounds of race, colour and sex. The second is the move toward general acceptance of human rights. The third is the increased fear of nuclear annihilation. These three developments strongly reinforce the universalistic values inherent in natural law doctrine. They have found expression in numerous international and constitutional law instruments as well as in popular movements throughout the world directed to humanitarian ends. Clearly, they are a "material source" of much of the new international law manifested in treaties and customary rules.

In so far as they are recognized as general principles of law, many tend to fall within our fifth category—the principles of natural justice. This concept is well known in many municipal law systems (although identified in diverse ways). "Natural justice" in its international legal manifestation has two aspects. One refers to the minimal standards of decency and respect for the individual human being that are largely spelled out in the human rights instruments. We can say that in this aspect, "natural justice" has been largely subsumed as a source of general principles by the human rights instruments. The second aspect of "natural justice" tends to be absorbed into the related concept of equity which includes such elements of "natural justice" as fairness, reciprocity, and consideration of the particular circumstances of a case. The fact that equity and human rights have come to the forefront in contemporary international law has tended to minimize reference to "natural justice" as an operative concept, but much of its substantive content continues to influence international decisions under those other headings. Judge Sir Gerald Fitzmaurice was not far from the mark when he concluded in 1973 that there was a "strong current of opinion holding that international law must give effect to principles of natural justice" and "that this is a requirement that natural law in the international field imposes *a priori* upon States, irrespective of their individual wills or consents".

NOTES

1. *What Kinds of Principles Qualify?* The use of analogies drawn from municipal legal systems to develop or supplement international law is as old as international law itself. International tribunals have frequently employed such analogies in deciding disputes between states. Substantive principles applied as "general" principles by such tribunals have included clean hands, acquiescence, estoppel, elementary principles of humanity, duty to make reparations, equity, equality, protection of legitimate expectations, and proportionality. For references to recent decisions by a variety of international tribunals resorting to general principles as a sources of international law, see Charney, Is International Law Threatened by Multiple International Tribunals?, 271 Rec. des Cours 115, 190, 196, 200–10 (1998) (citing decisions of I.C.J., Iran–U.S. Claims Tribunal and European Court of Justice, among others).

Is it necessary to show that many states have recognized a principle of municipal law as appropriate to interstate relations in order to apply it in international law? Tunkin, a leading Soviet authority, argued that this was a requirement that could only be met by showing that the rule in question had been accepted by custom or treaty. Tunkin, op. cit. 200–01. Consider Schachter's comment that the rule must be appropriate for interstate relations and Judge McNair's even more cautious view that private law rules may be regarded as "indications of policy and principles rather than directly importing them into international law." 1950 I.C.J. 148.

2. *Necessity and Other Claims.* A provocative illustration of potential uses in international jurisprudence of claims of general principles is the

Gabčíkovo–Nagymaros Project (Hungary/Slovakia), 1997 I.C.J. 7, a dispute over the viability of a treaty dating from the socialist era to construct certain works on the Danube River. (For background and excerpts, see p. 225.) Hungary contended that the environmental risks of the project had become so grave as to create a state of "ecological necessity," such that its refusal to carry out its part of the treaty should not be viewed as wrongful. The Court's opinion takes note of a range of concepts which one or both parties had invoked as being found in legal systems in general: these included contentions that "the notion of state of necessity is ... deeply rooted in general legal thinking" (para. 50); that a party cannot be permitted to profit from its own wrongful act (*ex injuria jus non oritur*) (paras. 57, 110, 113); that an aggrieved party has a duty to mitigate damage from another's unlawful action (paras. 68, 80–81); that if an instrument cannot be applied literally, it should be applied to approximate its primary object (paras. 75–76, citing Judge Sir Hersch Lauterpacht); and that a countermeasure to a wrongful act must be proportional to the injury suffered (paras. 83–87). The Court paraphrased the parties' reliance on general principles of law but did not specifically endorse these lines of argument, typically finding that it was unnecessary to resolve the points (e.g., para. 76) or resting its own reasoning on another source of law, such as custom (e.g., para. 52).

3.   *Principles Intrinsic to Law: Res Judicata? Burdens of Proof? Duties to Produce Evidence?* As Schachter observes, the I.C.J. has applied concepts such as *res judicata* and has addressed various questions of judicial practice along lines comparable to the approaches of municipal legal systems. A recent illustration is the Bosnian *Genocide* case (excerpted in Chapter 3), 2007 I.C.J. No. 91. There the Court had to consider the import of the principle of *res judicata,* in relation to a complex sequence of developments at the Court and in the United Nations which respondent Serbia claimed had cast doubt on the correctness of the Court's previous dismissal of respondent's jurisdictional objections. After reviewing this history and probing into the purposes underlying the doctrine of *res judicata* "internationally as well as nationally" (para. 116), the Court accepted Bosnia–Herzegovina's view that the jurisdictional holding was *res judicata* and could not be reopened at a later phase of the case. Id. at paras. 80–140. In the same case—the first genocide case ever brought against a state in an international tribunal—the Court dealt with questions of first impression concerning burdens of proof, standards of proof, and methods of proof (paras. 202–30). Applicant urged the Court to draw negative inferences from respondent's withholding of certain documents that were said to contain national security information. In its treatment of this matter (paras. 204–06), would it have been appropriate for the Court to resort to "general principles," in supplementation of its power under Article 49 of its Statute to take "formal note" of any refusal to produce evidence?

4.   *General Principles and Human Rights.* Some writers consider custom a relatively weak ground for human rights, in view of violations and lack of uniform practice; they thus contend that "general principles" can be a more appropriate source, based on the support of human rights in international declarations and national constitutions. Simma & Alston, The Sources of Human Rights Law: Custom, Jus Cogens and General Principles, 12 Austra-

lian Y.B.I.L. 82 (1002). How would such principles be discerned? How much "generality" should be required?

MANN, REFLECTIONS ON A COMMERCIAL LAW OF NATIONS

33 Brit. Y.B.I.L. 20, 34–39 (1957) (footnotes omitted)

The general principles as a whole and the commercial law of nations in particular are determined and defined by comparative law, i.e., by the process of comparing municipal systems of law. Although publicists rarely refer in terms to comparative law as a "source" of international law, the great majority is likely to agree. This is so for the obvious reason that since the elimination of the direct influence of Roman law there does not exist any system or branch of law, other than comparative law, which could develop general principles. * * *

* * * In a sense it is quite true that all law and all legal systems incorporate and are based upon some such maxims as find expression in the maxims of English equity, in Article 1134 of the French or in s. 242 of the German Civil Code or in similar provisions of codified law. Many, if not most, of the specific rules and provisions accepted in the systems of municipal law can be said to be manifestations or applications of such maxims. Yet "general clauses," as they have been called, have been proved to be an unsatisfactory guide and dangerous to legal development. While no legal system has found it possible to do without them none has found it possible to work with them alone. They leave much room for a subjective approach by the court. They leave the result unpredictable. They lack that minimum degree of precision without which every legal decision would be wholly uncertain. They may, on occasions, be useful to fill a gap but in essence they are too elementary, too obvious and even too platitudinous to permit detached evaluation of conflicting interests, the specifically legal appreciation of the implications of a given situation. In short they are frequently apt to let discretion prevail over justice. For these reasons they cannot be the sole source of a sound and workable commercial law of nations. * * *

A principle of law is a general one if it is being applied by the most representative systems of municipal law.

That universality of application is not a prerequisite of a general principle of law is emphasized by almost all authors. It should be equally clear that a single system of municipal law cannot provide a general principle within the meaning of Article 38. What is usually required is that the principle pervades the municipal law of nations in general. * * *

A principle of law is a general one even though the constituent rules of the representative systems of law are similar rather than identical. * * *

NOTES

1. *Principles Common to National Legal Systems: Investment Agreements.* Disputes between states and foreign companies involving concession agreements or development contracts have involved references to principles of law common to the national legal systems of the countries involved or in a more general way to principles of law. In a well known arbitration, involving nationalization of an oil company, the sole arbitrator considered that a provision of that kind in a concession agreement brought that agreement within the domain of international law and required reference to the rules of international law, more particularly the international law of contracts. *Arbitration between Libya and Texaco Overseas Petroleum Company et al. (TOPCO)*, Award of January 19, 1977, 17 I.L.M. 1 (1978), especially paragraphs 46–51. On nationalization disputes, see Chapter 14.

2. *Principles Common to National and International Law.* In another arbitration involving the nationalization and termination of an oil concession, the relevant agreements indicated that the applicable law included both the law common to the territorial state and the home state of the company and principles of law prevailing in the modern world. The arbitral tribunal noted that the law of the territorial state (Kuwait) also incorporated international law. However, instead of declaring that the applicable law was international law, the tribunal concluded that three sources of law—municipal law of the state concerned, general principles, and international public law—should be considered as a common body of law. See *Kuwait and American Independent Oil Company (Aminoil)*, Award of Sept. 26, 1977, 21 I.L.M. 976, paras. 6–10 (1982).

3. *Generality of Concepts.* The tribunals that have applied "general principles" have not considered it necessary to carry out a detailed examination of the main (or "representative") systems of national law to determine whether the principles pervade "the municipal law of nations in general" (Mann, *supra*). They have at most referred to highly general concepts such as *pacta sunt servanda,* good faith, legitimate expectations of the parties, the equilibrium of the contract. See Schlesinger, Research on the General Principles of Law Recognized by Civilized Nations, 51 A.J.I.L. 734 (1957); Friedmann, The Uses of "General Principles" in the Development of International Law, 57 A.J.I.L. 279 (1963). The Iran–U.S. Claims Tribunal has applied a large number of general principles of law, including unjust enrichment, force majeure, changed circumstances, and other doctrines. See Crook, Applicable Law in International Arbitration: The Iran–U.S. Claims Tribunal Experience, 83 A.J.I.L. 278, 292–99 (1989).

4. *Administrative Tribunals.* General principles of municipal law have also been relied on by the administrative tribunals established by the United Nations and other international organizations to adjudicate disputes between the organization and members of its staff. In some cases such general principles of law have been held to limit the power of the governing bodies of the international organization to alter the conditions of employment of staff members. See *de Merede et al. v. The World Bank*, Decision No. 1, World Bank Admin. Trib. Rep (1981). For commentary see Amerasinghe, The Law of the

International Civil Service 151–58 (2d ed. 1994); Moron, The United Nations Secretariat, The Rules and Practice (1977). But compare the views of one eminent international law scholar, Suzanne Bastid (for many years the President of the U.N. Administrative Tribunal), who has written:

> These rules are undoubtedly inspired by the internal law of certain states, but it does not appear that they are being applied as general principles of law. "Here again one may consider that a custom is being established, which has not been contested, notably by the organs which could have recourse to the International Court of Justice against the judgments which apply the custom."

Bastid, Have the U.N. Administrative Tribunals Contributed to the Development of International Law, in Transnational Law in a Changing Society 298, 311 (Friedmann, Henkin, & Lissitzyn eds. 1972).

B. CONSIDERATIONS OF EQUITY, PROPORTIONALITY, AND HUMANITY

As the foregoing materials indicate, substantive principles applied as "general principles of law" by international tribunals have included equity, proportionality, and humanity. As you read further below about those principles, consider whether you think their use provides a useful and inevitable means for tribunals and states to fill in the gaps of the international legal system—or might they afford too much discretion for imposing norms on states to which they did not affirmatively consent?

1. Equity and Good Faith

The concept of equity is used in a variety of ways by tribunals and governments. Consider, for example, the following five uses of equity distinguished by Schachter:

> (1) Equity as a basis for "individualized" justice tempering the rigours of strict law.

> (2) Equity as consideration of fairness, reasonableness and good faith.

> (3) Equity as a basis for certain specific principles of legal reasoning associated with fairness and reasonableness: to wit, estoppel, unjust enrichment, and abuse of rights.

> (4) Equitable standards for the allocation and sharing of resources and benefits (notably, in boundary delimitation).

> (5) Equity as a broad synonym for distributive justice used to justify demands for economic and social arrangements and redistribution of wealth.

Schachter, International Law in Theory and Practice 55–56 (1991). The following materials illustrate some of its diverse applications.

FRIEDMANN, THE CHANGING STRUCTURE OF INTERNATIONAL LAW

197 (1964) (footnotes omitted)

Probably the most widely used and cited "principle" of international law is the principle of general equity in the interpretation of legal documents and relations. There has been considerable discussion on the question of whether equity is part of the law to be applied, or whether it is an antithesis to law, in the sense in which *"ex aequo et bono"* is used in Article 38, paragraph 2, of the Statute of the International Court of Justice. A strict distinction must of course be made between, on the one hand, the Roman *aequitas* and the English equity, both separate systems of judicial administration designed to correct the insufficiencies and rigidities of the existing civil or common law, and, on the other hand, the function of equity as a principle of interpretation. In the latter sense, it is beyond doubt an essential and all-pervading principle of interpretation in all modern civil codifications, and it is equally important in the modern common law systems, under a variety of terminologies such as "reasonable," "fair" or occasionally even in the guise of "natural justice." There is thus overwhelming justification for the view developed by Lauterpacht, Manley Hudson, De Visscher, and Dahm, that equity is part and parcel of any modern system of administration of justice. * * *

THE DIVERSION OF WATER FROM THE MEUSE (NETHERLANDS v. BELGIUM)

Permanent Court of International Justice, 1937
P.C.I.J. (ser. A/B) No. 70, 76–78

[The case concerned a complaint by the Netherlands that construction of certain canals by Belgium was in violation of an agreement of 1863 in that the construction would alter the water level and rate of flow of the Meuse River. The Court rejected the Netherlands claim and a Belgian counter-claim based on the construction of a lock by the Netherlands at an earlier time. Judge Hudson, in an individual concurring opinion said:]

The Court has not been expressly authorized by its Statute to apply equity as distinguished from law. Nor, indeed, does the Statute expressly direct its application of international law, though as has been said on several occasions the Court is "a tribunal of international law". Series A, No. 7, p. 19; Series A, Nos. 20/21, p. 124. Article 38 of the Statute expressly directs the application of "general principles of law recognized by civilized nations", and in more than one nation principles of equity have an established place in the legal system. The Court's recognition of equity as a part of international law is in no way restricted by the special power conferred upon it "to decide a case *ex aequo et bono,* if the parties agree thereto". [Citations omitted.] It must be concluded, therefore, that under Article 38 of the Statute, if not independently of that Article, the Court has some freedom to consider principles of equity as part of the international law which it must apply.

It would seem to be an important principle of equity that where two parties have assumed an identical or a reciprocal obligation, one party which is engaged in a continuing non-performance of that obligation should not be permitted to take advantage of a similar non-performance of that obligation by the other party. The principle finds expression in the so-called maxims of equity which exercised great influence in the creative period of the development of the Anglo–American law. Some of these maxims are, "Equality is equity"; "He who seeks equity must do equity". It is in line with such maxims that "a court of equity refuses relief to a plaintiff whose conduct in regard to the subject-matter of the litigation has been improper". 13 Halsbury's Laws of England (2nd ed., 1934), p. 87. A very similar principle was received into Roman Law. The obligations of a vendor and a vendee being concurrent, "neither could compel the other to perform unless he had done, or tendered, his own part".

NOTES

1. *Equity as Contextual Justice.* The use of equity to "individualize" decisions and to escape the rigors of rules is akin (as Schachter notes) to the practice of tribunals to distinguish prior cases in terms of the particular facts. In doing this they attribute weight to individual circumstances and thereby allow for exceptions to general rules. Treaty clauses that refer to equitable principles similarly permit exceptions on grounds of the particular facts. As Judge Jiménez de Aréchaga remarked in the 1982 Tunisia–Libya *Continental Shelf* case in the International Court:

> [T]he judicial application of equitable principles means that a court should render justice in the concrete case, by means of a decision shaped by and adjusted to the relevant "factual matrix" of that case.

1982 I.C.J. 18, para. 24. In that case, the International Court emphasized "equitable solutions" and the "particular circumstances," declaring (1982 I.C.J. at para. 132):

> Clearly each continental shelf case in dispute should be considered and judged on its own merits, having regard to its peculiar circumstances; therefore no attempt should be made to overconceptualize the application of the principles and rules.

Similar emphasis on the specific circumstances can be found in the judgment of a Chamber of the Court in the *Gulf of Maine* case between Canada and the United States. 1984 I.C.J. 246, 300.

Criticism of such "individualization" by dissenting judges and by commentators may have influenced the International Court to adopt a more "legal" view of equity. In 1985, it declared "[E]ven though [equity] looks with particularity to the peculiar circumstances of an instant case, it also looks beyond it to principles of more general application * * * having a more general validity and hence expressible in general terms." *Continental Shelf* (Libya/Malta), 1985 I.C.J. 13, para. 45.

2. *Equity Inside, Outside, or Against the Law.* In discussing exceptions to rules on equitable grounds, international lawyers (especially in Europe)

often refer to decisions *infra legem* (within the law), *praeter legem* (outside the law) and *contra legem* (against the law). A decision on equitable grounds that is *infra legem* typically occurs when a rule leaves a margin of discretion to a state or law-applying organ. Exercising such discretion on equitable grounds is clearly within the law. A decision that is *contra legem* would not normally be justifiable on grounds of equity, unless the tribunal had been authorized to act *ex aequo et bono*. See *Continental Shelf* (Tunisia/Libya), 1982 I.C.J. 18, 60, para. 71. In exceptional circumstances, a tribunal may feel it necessary to disregard a rule of law on grounds that it is unreasonable or unfair in the circumstances.

The question of whether equity may be used to support a decision *praeter legem* arises when an issue is not covered by a relevant rule and the law appears to have a lacuna in that situation. In one view, a tribunal should hold, in that event, that it cannot decide the issue in accordance with law and therefore refrain from judgment. This distinction is designated as *non liquet* (the law is not clear enough for a decision). See discussion of the 1996 Nuclear Weapons Advisory Opinion, p. 89 note 6. A contrary view maintains that no court may refrain from judgment because the law is silent or obscure. Lauterpacht has argued that the principle prohibiting *non liquet* is itself a general principle of law recognized by civilized nations. Lauterpacht, The Function of Law in the International Community 67 (1933). If that position is adopted, a tribunal may be allowed to use equitable principles as a basis for decisions *praeter legem*.

3. *Substantive Equity.* Substantive concepts of equity such as estoppel, unjust enrichment and abuse of rights have been treated as general principles of law. On estoppel, see *The Temple of Preah Vihear* (Cambodia v. Thailand), 1962 I.C.J. 6, 31, 32, 39–51, 61–65; *Arbitral Award Made by the King of Spain on 23 December 1906* (Honduras v. Nicaragua) 1960 I.C.J. 192. On unjust enrichment, see Friedmann, The Changing Structure of International Law 206–10 (1964). On abuse of rights, see Bin Cheng, General Principles of Law Applied by International Courts 121–36 (1953). See also Schwarzenberger, "Equity in International Law" 26 Y.B. World Aff. 362 (1972). Litigants before international tribunals frequent assert a "clean hands" doctrine in reliance on *Diversion of Water From the Meuse* and other cases, but are not always able to persuade the tribunal that the facts warrant application of the doctrine. For a recent example, see *Oil Platforms* (Iran v. United States), 2003 I.C.J. 161, paras. 27–30 (U.S. request for dismissal of Iran's claim because of wrongful Iranian conduct in the 1987–1988 naval war in Persian Gulf did not dissuade the Court from considering the claim on the merits).

4. *Equity in Contract and Property Claims.* Equity and "equitable doctrine" are also invoked in cases of international claims for breach of contract or taking of property by a government. The Iran–U.S. Claims Tribunal has had occasion to refer to equity as a basis for a general principle of law and also in some cases as a ground for departing from law. It declared, for example, that the concept of "unjust enrichment" has been recognized in the great majority of municipal legal systems and "assimilated into the catalogue of general principles available to be applied by international tribunals * * * Its equitable foundation makes it necessary to take into account all the

circumstances of each specific situation." *Sea-land Services v. Iran*, 6 Iran–U.S. Cl. Trib. Rep. 149, 168 (1984)

In another case, the Claims Tribunal was faced with a claim of a U.S. company that shares in an Iranian company belonged to the claimant although they were registered in the name of a third party. Iran, the respondent, argued that under Iranian law the nominal registration was conclusive as to ownership. However, the tribunal majority did not accept the Iranian argument, noting that the nominal owner had acted on the basis that the shares belonged to the claimant. The tribunal concluded that a contrary result would "be both illogical and inequitable." *Foremost Tehran v. Iran*, 10 Iran–U.S. Cl. Trib. Rep. 228, 240 (1986). Was this a use of equity *contra legem?* Would the tribunal have been able to rely on a generally accepted principle such as beneficial ownership or estoppel to reach the same result?

5. *Equity and Avoidance of Environmental Harm.* Are there situations in which equity would be appropriate to allow a tribunal (or the governments concerned) to take account of circumstances that would not be germane in a purely legal adjudication? It has been suggested that this might be the case where new international law is emerging as, for example, in regard to transborder environmental damage or access to common resources. See Lowe, The Role of Equity in International Law, 12 Australian Y.B.I.L. 54, 69 (1992). As an alternative, would it be more acceptable to rely on concepts that have been accepted as general principles of law as, for example, the obligation of a state "not to allow knowingly its territory to be used for acts contrary to the rights of other states"? (*Corfu Channel Case*, United Kingdom v. Albania, 1949 I.C.J. 4, 22.) The Latin version of this principle, *"sic utere tuo ut alienum non laedas"* (i.e., use your own so as not to injure another) is often mentioned in international legal writing and judicial decisions. See Chapter 18 on Environmental Law.

6. *Equity in Boundary Delimitations.* Equitable principles and equitable solutions have become key concepts in the law governing the delimitation of maritime boundaries between states. The International Court of Justice and *ad hoc* arbitral tribunals have adjudicated a number of delimitation disputes based on the principle enunciated by the Court in the *North Sea Continental Shelf Cases* (p. 90) that "it is precisely a rule of law that calls for an application of equitable principles." The opinion added, "there is no legal limit to the considerations which states may take account of for the purpose of making sure that they apply equitable procedures and more often than not it is the balancing-up of all such considerations that will produce this result rather than reliance on one to the exclusion of others." 1969 I.C.J. 3, 50.

Equitable principles have also been considered as part of the law applicable to land frontier disputes. The tribunal in the *Rann of Kutch* arbitration between India and Pakistan held that the parties were free to rely on principles of equity in their arguments. 50 I.L.R. 2 (1968). However, some arbitral tribunals have considered that they could not apply equity where the *compromis* (the special agreement setting up the arbitration) required a decision based on law. See Carlston, The Process of International Arbitration 158 (1946); Feller, The Mexican Claims Commissions 223 ff. (1935). For general discussion, see de Visscher, De L'Equité dans le Règlement Arbitral ou Judiciaire des Litiges de Droit International Public (1972); Lapidoth, Equity in International Law, 81 A.S.I.L. Proc. 138–47 (1987).

7. *Reasonableness.* For discussion of "reasonableness" in the jurisprudence of international courts, see Corten, L'Utilisation du "Raisonnable" par le Juge international (1997).

2. Proportionality

The idea of "proportionality" has often been referred to as an equitable criterion. It has also been called a general principle of law. See, e.g., Cannizzaro, Il Principio della Proporzionalita Nell'Ordinamento Internationale 481 (2000) (English summary).

Proportionality has been applied in various contexts by international tribunals. A recent study by Thomas Franck surveys the application of the principle across many fields of international law—evaluation of lawfulness of resort to military force and conduct of warfare; international criminal responsibility in war crimes cases; nonmilitary countermeasures; trade; human rights—and shows that tribunals provide "second opinions" on whether states have acted disproportionately in their responses to the actions of other states or in relation to the assertion of state interests against claims of individual right. Franck, On Proportionality of Countermeasures in International Law, 102 A.J.I.L. 715 (2008).

As an example, in *Oil Platforms* (Iran v. United States), 2003 I.C.J. 161, Iran complained that the United States had violated Iran's rights under a treaty providing for freedom of navigation when it attacked several oil platforms in the Persian Gulf during the Iran–Iraq war. The United States maintained that it had acted in justifiable self-defense in response to previous attacks by Iran against U.S.-flagged vessels engaged in neutral shipping. The Court found that the conditions for self-defense were not met, because the United States had failed to respect the principle of proportionality:

> [T]he Court cannot assess in isolation the proportionality of that action to the attack to which it was said to be a response; it cannot close its eyes to the scale of the whole operation, which involved, *inter alia*, the destruction of two Iranian frigates and a number of other naval vessels and aircraft. As a response to the mining, by an unidentified agency, of a single United States warship, which was severely damaged but not sunk, and without loss of life, neither [the operation as a whole, nor the destruction of the platforms] can be regarded, in the circumstances of this case, as a proportionate use of force in self-defence.

Id. at paras. 76–77.

In the *Gabčíkovo–Nagymaros Project* (Hungary/Slovakia), 1997 I.C.J. 7, 56 paras. 85–87, the I.C.J. ruled that proportionality was a condition of the legality of countermeasures taken against a wrongful act, and that Slovakia's countermeasures against Hungary were unlawful because they had failed to respect proportionality. The dispute settlement organs of the

General Agreement on Tariffs and Trade/World Trade Organization have
applied a similar principle of proportionality, as well as other general
principles of law (such as the equitable principle of estoppel). See Palmeter & Mavroidis, The WTO Legal System: Sources of Law, 92 A.J.I.L. 398,
408 (1998); Mavroidis, No Outsourcing of Law? WTO Law as Practiced by
WTO Courts, 102 A.J.I.L. 421 (2007).

In maritime boundary delimitation cases, proportionality has been
generally construed to refer to the ratio between the lengths of the coasts
of each state that border the marine area to be delimited. The state with
the longer coastline would get the proportionally larger share of the area
delimited. The case-law has distinguished between proportionality as an
"operative" criterion and its application as a test (or corrective) of a
solution reached by other criteria. The latter position was adopted by the
International Court in the Libya–Malta *Continental Shelf* case of 1985. It
was followed in the *Gulf of Maine* case between Canada and the United
States and in the 1992 decision of the Court of Arbitration established by
Canada and France to delimit the marine areas between the French
islands of St. Pierre and Miquelon and the opposite and adjacent coasts of
Canada (31 I.L.M. 1145–1219 (1992)). It was also recently followed in the
September 2007 maritime boundary delimitation between Suriname and
Guyana by an arbitration tribunal convened under the U.N. Convention
on the Law of the Sea (47 I.L.M. 164, para. 392 (2008)).

3. Humanitarian Principles

**CORFU CHANNEL CASE
(UNITED KINGDOM v. ALBANIA)**

International Court of Justice, 1949
1949 I.C.J. 4, 22

[The case involved the explosion of mines in Albanian waters which
damaged British warships and caused loss of life of British naval personnel on those vessels. The United Kingdom claimed Albania was internationally responsible and under a duty to pay damages. In regard to the
obligations of Albania, the Court stated:]

> The obligations incumbent upon the Albanian authorities consist-
> ed in notifying, for the benefit of shipping in general, the existence of
> a minefield in Albanian territorial waters and in warning the ap-
> proaching British warships of the imminent danger to which the
> minefields exposed them. Such obligations are based, not on the
> Hague Convention of 1907, No. VIII which is applicable in time of
> war, but on certain general and well-recognized principles, namely:
> elementary considerations of humanity, even more exacting in peace
> than in war; the principle of the freedom of maritime communication
> and every State's obligation not to allow knowingly its territory to be
> used for acts contrary to the rights of other States.

NOTES

1. *Treaties Expressing Principles of Humanity.* "Elementary considerations of humanity" may also be based today on the provisions of the U.N. Charter on human rights, the Universal Declaration of Human Rights, and the various human rights conventions. See the advisory opinion of the International Court in the *Namibia* case, 1971 I.C.J. 16, 57, p. 212, also discussed in note 2 on p. 270 and in note 4 on p. 272. In its earlier decision in the 1966 *South West Africa* case (2d Phase), the majority of the court declared that humanitarian considerations were not decisive and that moral principles could be considered only insofar as they are given "a sufficient expression in legal form." 1966 I.C.J. at 34.

2. *Humanitarian and Moral Dimension of International Law.* Contemporary jurists who have placed high value on the role of humanitarian and moral factors in international law include such representative scholars as Hersch Lauterpacht, Myres McDougal, Hermann Mosler, and Georg Schwarzenberger. For a recent treatment, see Meron, The Humanization of International Law (2006).

3. *Community Values.* The I.C.J.'s invocation of "elementary considerations of humanity" in the *Corfu Channel* case has been followed in, e.g., the *Nicaragua* case, 1986 I.C.J. 14 at 113–14, 129. Professor Meron in his treatment of the *Nicaragua* judgment has written that "[e]lementary considerations of humanity reflect basic community values whether already crystallized as binding norms of international law or not." Meron, Human Rights and Humanitarian Norms as Customary Law 35 (1989). In its *Nuclear Weapons* advisory opinion, 1996 I.C.J. at para. 79, the I.C.J. wrote:

> It is undoubtedly because a great many rules of humanitarian law applicable in armed conflict are so fundamental to the respect of the human person and "elementary considerations of humanity" as the Court put it in its Judgment of 9 April 1949 in the *Corfu Channel* case (*I.C.J. Reports 1949,* p. 22), that the Hague and Geneva Conventions have enjoyed a broad accession. Further these fundamental rules are to be observed by all States whether or not they have ratified the conventions that contain them, because they constitute intransgressible principles of international customary law.

Does the use of terms such as "fundamental" and "intransgressible" place "elementary considerations of humanity" in the category of hierarchically superior law?

SECTION 2. JUDICIAL DECISIONS AND PUBLICISTS

A. JUDICIAL DECISIONS

1. International Court of Justice

Article 38 of the I.C.J. Statute in its paragraph 1(d) directs the Court to apply judicial decisions as "subsidiary means for the determination of rules of law." It is expressly made subject to Article 59 which states that "the decision of the Court has no binding force except between the parties and in respect of that particular case." Hence the principle of *stare decisis* is not meant to apply to decisions of the International Court. That qualification and the relegation of judicial decisions generally to a "subsidiary" status reflect the reluctance of states to accord courts—and the International Court in particular—a law-making role. The Court's decisions are supposed to be declaratory of the law laid down by the states in conventions and customary rules. In addition, the stated objection to *stare decisis* reflects a perception of international disputes as especially individual, each distinguished by particular features and circumstances.

Despite these qualifications, I.C.J. decisions are, on the whole, regarded by international lawyers as highly persuasive authority of existing international law. The very fact that state practices are often divergent or unclear adds to the authority of the Court. Its decisions often produce a degree of certainty where previously confusion and obscurity existed. A much-quoted dictum of Justice Cardozo reflects the attraction of judicial authority, especially to lawyers in the common law tradition:

> International law or the law that governs between States, has at times, like the common law within States, a twilight existence during which it is hardly distinguishable from morality or justice, till at length the imprimatur of a court attests to its jural quality.

New Jersey v. Delaware, 291 U.S. 361 (1934).

A decision of the International Court is generally accepted as the "imprimatur of jural quality" when the Court speaks with one voice or with the support of most judges. Not infrequently, the separate opinions of dissenting judges or other individual opinions contain cogent reasoning that influences subsequent doctrine more than the decision of the majority. Judgments and advisory opinions by a significantly divided court have diminished authority. This is especially true when the issues are perceived as highly political and the judges seem to reflect the positions of the states from which they come. Notable examples are the 1966 decision of the Court in the *South West Africa Cases* and the 1984 decision on jurisdiction and admissibility in the case brought by Nicaragua against the United States. The fact that the key paragraph in the 1996 advisory opinion on *Nuclear Weapons* (excerpted in Chapter 2) was decided by the president's tie-breaking vote left many commentators convinced that the judgment had done little to clarify a contested area of the law and would have little real-world impact.

Judgments and advisory opinions are not always compelling to states. Governments respond in various ways to decisions they consider unfounded or unwise. For example, after the *Lotus Case* (*supra*), many governments adopted a treaty provision which reversed the Court's ruling. See p. 78 note 7. Individual states have also reacted to unfavorable decisions by altering or withdrawing their consent to jurisdiction, as the United States did after the *Nicaragua* case (see Chapter 9). After the *Nuclear Weapons* advisory opinion, U.S. officials noted that some aspects of the opinion confirmed U.S. position and that no change in U.S. nuclear policies could be expected. See references in note 9 on p. 90.

Notwithstanding these reactions, the Court's pronouncements, especially in non-political matters, are a primary source for international lawyers. Every judgment or advisory opinion is closely examined, dissected, quoted and pondered for its implications. They are generally lengthy and learned analyses of relevant principles and practices and particular cases include opinions often amounting to more than 200–300 pages. After nine decades the case-law and associated opinions of the two "World Courts" constitute a substantial *corpus juris* relevant to many questions of international relations.

A complex problem concerns the role of the Court in "developing" international law and reaching decisions that go beyond declarations of existing law. It is clear that states, by and large, do not expect or wish the Court to "create" new law. Yet as Brierly observed, "the act of the Court is a creative act in spite of our conspiracy to represent it as something else." The Basis of Obligation in International Law 98 (Waldock ed. 1958). Both states and judges are aware "of the discretionary elements in the art of judging: the selection of 'relevant' facts, the need to give specific meaning to broad undefined concepts, the subtle process of generalizing from past cases, the uses of analogy and metaphor, the inevitable choices between competing rules and principles." Schachter, International Law in Theory and Practice 41 (1991). These discretionary elements are more evident in international law than in most areas of domestic law. The fragmentary character of much international law and the generality of its concepts and principles leave ample room for "creative" judicial application. On the other hand, the judges are well aware of the dangers of appearing to be "legislating" and of their precarious consensual jurisdiction (see Chapter 9). One way to meet the problem is to place emphasis on the particular facts of the case to avoid the appearance of creating new law. But there is also a pull in the opposite direction. The Court needs to show that its decisions are principled and in accord with the agreed basic concepts of international law. This requirement leads to reliance on broad doctrinal concepts and precepts taken from treatises and prior case-law. When applied to new situations, the abstractions of basic doctrine create new law. Though many governments hesitate to accept or recognize this, international lawyers acknowledge the formative role of the Court while recognizing the political necessity for the Court to appear solely as an organ for declaring and clarifying the existing law.

NOTES

1. *Composition of I.C.J.* The 15 judges of the International Court are elected for nine-year terms by majority votes of political bodies, namely the Security Council and the General Assembly of the United Nations. (Statute of the Court, Articles 3–18). They are required to have the qualifications required in their respective countries for appointment to the highest judicial

office or to be "jurisconsults of recognized competence in international law." (Id. art. 2.) They are supposed to represent the "main forms of civilization and of the principal legal systems of the world." (Id. art. 9.) This requirement is considered to be met by a geographical and political distribution of seats among the main regions of the world. Many of the judges have been well known legal scholars. In recent years, most have had prior service in their national governments, as legal advisors to the foreign office or as representatives to international bodies.

2. *Representative Qualities of International Judges.* Does the fact that the judges are elected by political bodies and are considered likely to reflect the views of their own governments impugn or reduce "the jural quality" of their decisions? Is it legally justifiable to minimize a judicial decision as a source of law because many of the judges have taken the same position as their own governments? How can parties to cases before the Court seek to reduce the effect of ideological or national bias, assuming they wish to do so? See Suh, Voting Behaviors of National Judges in International Courts, 63 A.J.I.L. 224 (1969); Rosenne, The Composition of the Court, in The Future of the International Court of Justice 377 (Gross ed. 1976); Weiss, Judicial Independence and Impartiality: A Preliminary Inquiry, in The International Court of Justice at a Crossroads 123–54 (Damrosch ed. 1987); Schachter, *supra*, at 69–73 (1991).

2. Decisions of Other International Tribunals

International decisions also embrace the numerous judgments of arbitral tribunals established by international agreement for individual disputes or for categories of disputes. Though they are not in a strict sense judicial bodies, they are generally required to decide in accordance with law and their decisions are considered an appropriate subsidiary means of determining international law. Governments and tribunals refer to such decisions as persuasive evidence of law. The International Court only occasionally identifies specific arbitral awards as precedents but it has also referred generally to the jurisprudence and consistent practice of arbitral tribunals. Governments do not hesitate to cite international arbitral decisions in support of their legal positions. Such decisions may be distinguished on the basis of the agreements establishing the tribunal or other special circumstances but in many cases they have been accepted as declaratory of existing international law

Decisions of arbitral tribunals are published in the U.N.'s Reports of International Arbitral Awards (U.N. Rep. Int'l Arb. Awards), International Law Reports (Lauterpacht ed.), and International Legal Materials (published by the American Society of International Law). The Iran–U.S. Claims Tribunal, with now almost three decades of jurisprudence, has many volumes of published decisions. For further discussion of arbitration as a means of dispute settlement see Chapter 9.

Two European courts—the European Court of Justice (located in Luxembourg, with competence over questions arising within the framework of the European Communities/European Union) and the European

Court of Human Rights (an organ of the Council of Europe, located in Strasbourg) also hand down many decisions that express or interpret principles and rules of international law. The Inter–American Court of Human Rights has a growing body of case law. The decisions of these regional courts are relevant not only to their specialized subject-matter (e.g., economic integration or human rights), but also to more general problems of international law, such as the law of treaties or of state responsibility.

The 1990s and 2000s have witnessed the creation of new international tribunals of specialized subject-matter jurisdiction, with growing potential to contribute to general international law. These include the International Criminal Tribunals for the Former Yugoslavia and for Rwanda, the International Tribunal for the Law of the Sea, and the dispute settlement body of the World Trade Organization, as well as the permanent International Criminal Court established in 2002. These will be dealt with in subsequent chapters, both as regards the substantive law that they apply (e.g., Chapters 16–17) and as regards general considerations of international judicial jurisdiction (Chapter 9). For present purposes it is sufficient to draw attention to two main themes relevant to the problem of sources: (1) whether these new tribunals can be expected to apply a methodology of sources similar to that indicated in Article 38 of the Statute of the I.C.J., and (2) whether their decisions will be treated by the I.C.J. and other law-applying bodies as "subsidiary means" under Article 38(1)(d) of the I.C.J. Statute, comparably to the I.C.J.'s own judgments. Commentators evaluating the early years of operation of such tribunals have ventured an affirmative answer to the first question, and have likewise predicted the inevitable influence of such tribunals on other courts, including the I.C.J. See, e.g., Charney, Is International Law Threatened by Multiple International Tribunals? in 271 Rec. des Cours 101, 189–236 (1998); Charney, The Impact on the International Legal System of the Growth of International Courts and Tribunals, 31 N.Y.U. J. Int'l L. & Politics 697 (1999) and related symposium articles; Palmeter & Mavroidis, The WTO Legal System: Sources of Law, 92 A.J.I.L. 398 (1998) (finding that W.T.O. dispute settlement practice on sources is similar to that of I.C.J. Statute Art. 38, and discerning other parallels, e.g. in tendency to refer to prior rulings of the dispute settlement body as authoritative even though not formally binding); Mavroidis, No Outsourcing of Law? WTO Law as Practiced by WTO Courts, 102 A.J.I.L. 422 (2007).

The I.C.J. is not in a hierarchical relationship with such tribunals. Though I.C.J. judgments continue to have great influence, other bodies have felt free to differ with the I.C.J. when presented with similar (albeit not identical) questions. The result can be a productive dialogue. For example, the Appeals Chamber of the International Criminal Tribunal for the Former Yugoslavia explicitly disagreed with an aspect of the I.C.J.'s *Nicaragua* judgment, finding its reasoning "unconvincing." *Tadić, Case No. IT*–94–1–AR72, Appeal from Judgment of Conviction, para. 115ff. (July 15, 1999). When the I.C.J. later returned to related questions in the

Bosnian *Genocide* case, 2007 I.C.J. No. 91 at paras. 402–07, it explained in some detail the basis for the disagreement between the two tribunals and its reasons for adhering to its own "settled jurisprudence" in resolving the questions before it. It also relied significantly on the I.C.T.Y.'s findings of fact in cases involving individual criminal responsibility for genocide.

Other international organs perform some functions analogous to those of courts, but by virtue of their restricted competence, their authority as potential "sources" or "subsidiary means" is uncertain or disputed. As an example, the U.N. Human Rights Committee (the implementing body for the International Covenant on Civil and Political Rights) has aroused controversy for its pronouncements concerning reservations to human rights treaties; in the view of some governments, the Committee exceeded its competence in purporting to opine on the legal effects of such reservations and thus those governments contend that the Committee's opinion (expressed in the form of a "general comment") lacks authority. This controversy is addressed in Chapter 3 on the law of treaties and Chapter 13 on human rights. It is mentioned here as an illustration of the widening domain of bodies applying rules of international law, whose output might arguably (though contestedly) contribute to the sources of international law. For more on problems of interaction among international courts and tribunals, see the I.L.C.'s Fragmentation Study (Chapter 1).

3.   Precedents in International Tribunals

The fact that Article 59 of the I.C.J. Statute excludes *stare decisis* has not meant that the Court's case-law ignores precedent. The Court cites its earlier decisions and often incorporates their reasoning by reference, thereby creating a consistent jurisprudence. When the Court seems to depart from precedent, it generally distinguishes the cases and explains the reasons for the different views. See cases cited in 3 Rosenne, The Law and Practice of the International Court, 1920–2005, at 1552–58 (4th ed. 2006); Shahabuddeen, Precedent in the World Court (1996).

Most other international tribunals likewise appear be following their own precedents even though their constitutive instruments do not provide for them to do so, and also to be paying attention to what the I.C.J. and other tribunals are doing. For detailed examination of the role of prior decisions in the dispute settlement organs of the world trade system, see Mavroidis, No Outsourcing of Law? WTO Law as Practiced by WTO Courts, 102 A.J.I.L. 422 (2007); see also Bhala, The Myth About Stare Decisis and International Trade Law, 14 Am. U. Int'l L. Rev. 845 (1999); Bhala, The Precedent Setters: De Facto Stare Decisis in WTO Adjudication, 9 Fla. State U. J. Transnat'l. L. & Pol. 1 (1999); Bhala, The Power of the Past: Towards De Jure Stare Decisis in WTO Adjudication, 33 Geo. Wash. Int'l L. Rev. 873 (2001). In the context of international criminal law, a former president of the I.C.T.Y. has written that "one can discern perhaps the outlines of an informal *stare decisis* principle, as courts and governments rely on precedent rather than repeatedly engage in detailed analysis of the customary status of the same principles." Meron, Revival of Customary Humanitarian Law, 99 A.J.I.L. 817, 819–20 (2005).

NOTE

The U.S. Supreme Court's View of I.C.J. Jurisprudence. In *Sanchez–Llamas v. Oregon*, 548 U.S. 331 (2006), the U.S. Supreme Court declined to follow the interpretation of an international treaty rendered by the I.C.J. in a case brought by Mexico against the United States, *Avena and Other Mexican Nationals*, 2004 I.C.J. 12. The Supreme Court stated that "[n]othing in the structure or purpose of the ICJ suggests that its interpretations were intended to be conclusive on our courts." With reference to Article 59 of the I.C.J. Statute, the Court said: "Any interpretation of law the ICJ renders in the course of resolving particular disputes is thus not binding precedent *even as to the ICJ itself*; there is accordingly little reason to think that such interpretations were intended to be controlling on our courts." 548 U.S. 331, 355 (emphasis in original). While an interpretation by an international court may be entitled to "respectful consideration," the Supreme Court felt free to reach a different conclusion on the matter before it. See also *Medellin v. Texas*, 128 S.Ct. 1346 (2008), discussed further in Chapter 9.

4. Decisions of Municipal Courts

The opinions in *Paquete Habana* and the *Lotus Case* (Chapter 2, pp. 61, 68) cite municipal court decisions as evidence of customary law. Such municipal decisions are indicative of state practice and *opinio juris* of the state in question. However, inasmuch as national courts in many countries also apply principles and rules of international law, their decisions may be treated as a subsidiary source independently of their relation to state practice. While the authority of a national court would as a rule be less than that of an international court or arbitral body, particular decisions of the higher national courts may be the only case-law on a subject or the reasoning and learning in the decisions may be particularly persuasive. Decisions of the U.S. Supreme Court and other high courts have been relied on by arbitral bodies and have been cited by states in support of their claims. In some areas of law such as state responsibility and sovereign immunity, national court decisions have had a prominent role. See Chapters 8 and 12; see also Nollkaemper, Internationally Wrongful Acts in Domestic Courts, 101 A.J.I.L. 760 (2007).

The International Criminal Tribunal for the Former Yugoslavia (I.C.T.Y.) has referred extensively to municipal decisions, especially those applying the international laws of war. For examples, see Meron, Revival of Customary Humanitarian Law, 99 A.J.I.L. 817, 824, 826 (2005). Some judges of the I.C.T.Y. have asserted that relatively greater attention should be given to the rulings of national authorities that were sitting in the capacity of an international tribunal and applying international law (e.g., the Allied military tribunals in occupied Germany after World War II) than to national courts that were merely applying local law. See the joint separate opinion of Judges McDonald and Vohrah in *Erdemović, Case*

No. IT–96–22–A, Judgment on Appeal, paras. 42ff (Oct. 7, 1997). In the *Nuclear Weapons* advisory opinion, a Japanese court decision was noted in some of the separate and dissenting opinions as a relevant subsidiary source under Article 38(1)(d). See, e.g., 1996 I.C.J., 375, 397 (Dissenting Opinion of Judge Shahabuddeen, citing *Shimoda v. State* (Tokyo Dist. Ct. 1963)).

B. THE TEACHINGS OF THE MOST HIGHLY QUALIFIED PUBLICISTS OF THE VARIOUS NATIONS

The place of the writer in international law has always been more important than in municipal legal systems. The basic systematization of international law is largely the work of publicists, from Grotius and Gentili onwards. In many cases of first impression only the opinions of writers can be referred to in support of one or the other of the opposing contentions of the parties. The extent to which writers are referred to as "subsidiary" authorities differs often according to the tradition of the court and the individual judge. Here the practice of national as well as of international courts is relevant. As a corollary to the position of precedent in common law jurisdictions, there has traditionally been judicial reluctance, more marked in the British jurisdictions than in the United States, to refer to writers. In the civilian systems reference to textbook writers and commentators ("doctrine" in continental terminology, referring to scholarship) is a normal practice, as the perusal of any collection of decisions of the German, Swiss or other European Supreme Courts will show. In France the notes appended by jurists to important decisions published in the *Recueil Dalloz* and *Recueil Sirey* enjoy high authority and often influence later decisions. A prominent example of reliance on writers in a common law court is the decision of the U.S. Supreme Court in the *Paquete Habana* case (see p. 61).

The practice of the International Court of Justice and of its predecessor has typically been to refer to scholarly writings only in very general terms. Lauterpacht, The Development of International Law by the International Court 24 (1958). Lauterpacht suggests as a reason for the Court's reluctance to refer to writers: "There is no doubt that the availability of official records of the practice of States and of collections of treaties has substantially reduced the necessity for recourse to writings of publicists as evidence of custom. Moreover, the divergence of view among writers on many subjects as well as apparent national bias may often render citations from them unhelpful. On the other hand, in cases—admittedly rare—in which it is possible to establish the existence of a unanimous or practically unanimous interpretation, on the part of writers, of governmental or judicial practice, reliance on such evidence may add to the weight of the Judgments and Opinions of the Court." Id.

Although the Court itself has been reluctant to identify writers in its judgments and advisory opinions, it is evident from the pleadings and from the references in the separate and dissenting opinions of the judges that the opinions of authorities on international law have been brought to the attention of the Court and have often been taken into account by some of the judges. For a broad historical survey of the role and influence of "teachings" in the development of international law, see lectures by Judge Manfred Lachs, Teachings and Teaching of International Law, 151 Rec. des Cours 163–252 (1976–III).

The major treatises of international law usually cited by states and tribunals were generally produced by jurists of Western Europe. The citations in those treatises referred to state practice and judicial decisions in only a few countries. Most writers also relied heavily on quotations and paraphrases of statements by earlier writers. These highly selective tendencies, presented in support of broad conclusions of law, were far from consistent with the prevailing doctrine of sources based on state practice accepted by law by states generally. Moreover, many of the well known treatises were written from the standpoint of national concerns and perceptions. Schachter has commented that:

> [M]any of the legal scholars had close links with their official communities and there were often pressures on them, sometimes obvious and sometimes subtle, to conform to the official point of view. Even apart from such pressures, we recognize that social perspectives and values are generally shared by those in the same political and cultural community. * * * That a degree of bias is inescapable is recognized by the common assumption that more credible judgments on controversial issues of international law were more likely if made by a broadly representative body than by persons (however expert) from a single country or a particular political outlook.

Schachter, International Law in Theory and Practice 38–39 (1991). Schachter also suggests that "the selective tendency of the writers to quote the generalities of other writers, meant that their statements were steps removed from the ideal of an inductive approach." Id. at 38.

International bodies of "publicists" include the International Law Commission, an organ of the United Nations composed of 34 individuals elected by the U.N. General Assembly on the basis of government nominations and criteria of wide geographical representation. See Statute of the I.L.C., G.A. Res. 174 (II), art. 2 (Nov. 21, 1947). The I.L.C. is concerned, as indicated in Chapters 2 and 3, with the preparation of codification conventions and other draft treaties. However, in the course of its work, and in its reports, positions are expressed by the Commission as a whole on existing rules of law. The I.C.J. has drawn on such reports for authority even before completion of the I.L.C. study in question. See, e.g., *Gabčíkovo–Nagymaros Project*, 1997 I.C.J. 7, para. 83 (citing Draft Articles on State Responsibility, adopted by I.L.C. on first reading in 1996 and not finally approved until 2001; see Chapter 8).

A non-official body, the Institut de Droit International, established in 1873, is composed of about 120 members and associate members elected by the Institut on the basis of individual merit and published works. Its resolutions setting forth principles and rules of existing law and, on occasion, proposed rules, have often been cited by tribunals, states and writers. The biennial Annuaire de l'Institut contains its resolutions and the lengthy reports and records of discussion that preceded the resolution. For an account of its contribution from 1873 to 1973, see its centenary volume, Livre du Centenaire, Annuaire de l'Institut de Droit International (1973), particularly articles by Charles de Visscher and H. Battifol. See also Koskenniemi, The Gentle Civilizer of Nations (2003).

Another unofficial body, the International Law Association, (also founded in 1873), is organized in national branches in many countries. Resolutions adopted by majority votes at conferences of the Association are based on reports and studies of international committees. The multinational character of the Association adds weight to those of its resolutions that are adopted by consensus or large majorities representative of different regions and political systems. The biennial reports of the I.L.A. contain the resolutions and committee reports.

Another category of the writings of publicists is the Restatement of the Foreign Relations Law of the United States, prepared by recognized legal scholars and adopted after discussion by the American Law Institute, a non-official professional body. The first restatement appeared in 1965 designated curiously as the Restatement Second. A revised Restatement Third was published in 1987. The Restatement contains rules of international law as it applies to the United States in relations with other states and also rules of U.S. domestic law with substantial significance for U.S. foreign relations. Although prepared by a U.S. professional society, it does not purport to state rules that the U.S. government would put forward or support in all cases. As stated in its introduction, "the Restatement in stating rules of international law represents the opinion of the American Law Institute as to the rules that an international tribunal would apply if charged with deciding a controversy in accordance with international law." In considering what a hypothetical international court would decide is an applicable rule, the A.L.I. adopts a standard that aims at an objective determination of general international law. Each section consists of a statement of the "black letter law," followed by comments and reporters' notes. The latter are particularly useful because of their careful analysis of and citations to international law authorities. Unlike the comments, the reporters' notes state the views of the reporters only; their substance is not endorsed as such by the A.L.I.

In general, U.S. courts have viewed the Restatement as the most authoritative U.S. scholarly statement of contemporary international law. Some courts, however, have disagreed (occasionally in emphatic terms) with positions adopted in the Restatement and have criticized the disciplinary stance of international law embodied in Article 38(1)(d) of the I.C.J. Statute for according unwarranted deference to the opinions of scholars. See, e.g., *United States v. Yousef*, 327 F.3d 56, 98–104 (2d Cir. 2003).

Writings of authoritative international law scholars are published annually by the Hague Academy of International Law in its Collected Courses, often referred to by its French title, Recueil des Cours de l'Académie de Droit International (Rec. des Cours). The scholars are selected by the international curatorium of the Academy on a broad geographical basis, with increasing participation of scholars and practitioners from outside Europe and with diverse points of view. In addition to discussion of particular topics, the Recueil includes an annual General Course by a well-known publicist.

NOTES

1. *"Invisible College."* If "the most highly qualified publicists" are generally influenced by the interests and policies of their own states (and by their legal cultures), is their authority open to question on that ground? Would a tribunal look for majority opinions, "representative" views or "objective" data? Is there a shared disciplinary culture in the profession of international law? Schachter has described the "invisible college of international lawyers" as engaged in a continuous process of communication and collaboration across national lines. Schachter, The Invisible College of International Lawyers, 72 Nw. Univ. L. Rev. 217 (1977). For a revisiting of Schachter's idea 25 years later, see the proceedings of the annual meeting of the American Society of International Law on the theme of "The Visible College of International Law," 95 A.S.I.L. Proc. (2001).

2. *Dual Roles of Scholars as Advisers to Governments.* Since the "leading" publicists are often engaged or consulted by their own governments, they influence state conduct and are in turn influenced by their governments. What advantages and drawbacks are likely in this dual role? Can the legal advisers of foreign offices meet the sometimes conflicting demands of their "clients" and the obligation to ascertain the law objectively? Do they have the double function of applying the law in the national interest and supporting the international legal system? See Report of a Joint Committee on The Role of the Legal Adviser of the State Department, 85 A.J.I.L. 358 (1991). See also the different views expressed at the panel on Scholars in the Construction and Critique of International Law, 94 A.S.I.L. Proc. 317–20 (2000).

3. *Specialization.* The vast increase in international law has naturally led to specialization. It is no longer possible for international lawyers to claim expertise on the subject as a whole. It is even difficult to keep abreast of developments in any one of the main specialized areas. (In 2009, the American Society of International Law had more than twenty "interest groups.") Has this reduced the role of general international law? See Vagts, Are There No International Lawyers Anymore? 75 A.J.I.L. 134–37 (1981). Schachter argues for maintaining international law as a unified discipline. "The Invisible College," *supra*, at 221–23. See also Franck, Review Essay—The Case of the Vanishing Treaties, 81 A.J.I.L. 763 (1987).

SECTION 3.   U.N. DECLARATIONS AND RESOLUTIONS

The international legal system has no organ directly comparable to a national legislature with power to make law by majority vote. The powers of the U.N. General Assembly under the U.N. Charter (arts. 13–14) are basically recommendatory. The U.N. Security Council has certain compulsory powers when acting under Chapter VII of the Charter, but only extraordinarily would it exercise these powers to prescribe rules of conduct in legislative fashion. Assertion of Security Council authority to maintain peace in particular contexts (e.g., to elaborate obligations in the wake of the Iraq conflict, or to apply humanitarian law in the context of former Yugoslavia or Rwanda) will be addressed in Chapters 15 and 16.

Pressures to fill what some perceive as a vacuum in international law-making have led to a variety of attempts at proclaiming, clarifying, or codifying standards of conduct, whether on the part of states or of other actors. Some of these modes, and the controversies surrounding them, are addressed in this section and the next sections. We begin with the General Assembly and Security Council and then turn to modes of law-making in other arenas, which may be informal networks as well as formal institutions and may produce commitments at various points along a spectrum between "political" or "moral" and "legal."

A.   GENERAL ASSEMBLY DECLARATIONS AND RESOLUTIONS

The legal effect of General Assembly resolutions and other decisions has been a subject of much scholarly discussion and diverse views of governments. Article 38 of the I.C.J. Statute does not mention resolutions or decisions of international organs as either a principal "source" or subsidiary means of determining applicable international law. Moreover, the U.N. Charter does not confer on the General Assembly power to enact binding rules of conduct. In contrast to the Security Council, it does not have authority to adopt binding decisions, except for certain organizational actions (such as admission of members and credentials). Such decisions can have "dispositive force and effect," as the International Court noted in *Certain Expenses of the United Nations*, Advisory Opinion, 1962 I.C.J. 151, 163.

The more general problem of legal effect is raised by General Assembly resolutions and decisions that express or clearly imply legal principles or specific rules of law. The General Assembly has adopted thousands of resolutions and numerous other decisions from 1946 to 2009. Some— probably fewer than a hundred—express general rules of conduct for states (as the Declaration against Torture in the *Filartiga* case, below). They are usually formulated as "declarations" or "affirmations" of law. In many cases, they were the product of study and debate over many years and were adopted by consensus (without a vote) or by near-unanimity.

General Assembly resolutions, declarations or decisions may be considered by governments and by courts or arbitral tribunals as evidence of international custom or as expressing (and evidencing) a general principle of law. They may also serve to set forth principles for a future treaty, as has been the case for the Declaration against Torture and a number of other declarations in the field of human rights. The fact that a law-declaring resolution has been adopted without a negative vote or abstention is usually regarded as strong presumptive evidence that it contains a correct statement of law. A resolution that has less than unanimous support is more questionable. The size and composition of the majority, the intent and expectations of states, the political factors and other contextual elements are pertinent in judging the effect.

At the San Francisco Conference of 1945 at which the U.N. Charter was drafted, a committee report noted that the General Assembly was competent to interpret the Charter, as such competence is "inherent in the functioning of any body which operates under an instrument defining its functions and powers." It then added that an interpretation of the Charter by the General Assembly would be binding on the member states if that interpretation "was generally accepted." Does this mean that the adoption of an interpretive resolution by unanimous vote (or near-unanimity) would be legally binding on the members? Would the question arise whether the Charter was being interpreted or in effect amended? If such resolutions involve a significant modification of the rights and duties of members, should they not be required to follow the amendment procedure which involves ratification? When such broad principles as self-determination, equality of states, human rights, and political independence are construed and given more specific meaning, is there not inevitably a "legislative" component inherent in the interpretation?

General Assembly resolutions illustrating some of these issues are found in the Documents Supplement, including the Universal Declaration on Human Rights (1948), the Declaration on Principles of International Law Concerning Friendly Relations Between States (1970), the Definition of Aggression Resolution (1974), and others at various times concerning permanent sovereignty over natural resources and economic rights and duties, areas beyond national jurisdiction as the common heritage of mankind, and diverse aspects of human rights. Their legal significance as evidence of custom or of the authoritative interpretation of the U.N. Charter will be addressed in the chapters concerning the subject-matters to which they pertain. Similar questions about legal effects can be asked about resolutions or other statements adopted within the framework of the United Nations or other global institutions, such as the Millennium Declaration of 2000 or the World Summit Outcome Document of 2005, approved by heads of state and government assembled in New York.

As you read the materials below, consider the different theories of the legal force of General Assembly resolutions in the context of litigation alleging violations of international law.

FILARTIGA v. PENA–IRALA

United States Court of Appeals for the Second Circuit, 1980
630 F.2d 876

[A wrongful death action was brought in federal district court by two nationals of Paraguay, the father and sister of a 17–year old Paraguayan, who, it was alleged, was tortured to death in Paraguay by the defendant Pena–Irala who at the time was Inspector–General of the police. Jurisdiction was claimed principally on the basis of the Alien Tort Statute (28 U.S.C. § 1350) which provides: "The district courts shall have original jurisdiction of any civil action by an alien for a tort only, committed in violation of the law of nations or a treaty of the United States."

[The plaintiffs claimed that the conduct resulting in the wrongful death constituted torture which they contended violated the "law of nations"—that is, international customary law. On appeal, the Second Circuit Court of Appeals held that deliberate torture under the color of official authority violated the universal rules of international law. In reaching the conclusion that the prohibition of torture has become part of customary international law, the Court referred as evidence to the Universal Declaration of Human Rights and a 1975 U.N. General Assembly Declaration on the Protection of all Persons from Torture.

[Relevant portions of the Court's opinion follow:]

The Declaration [Against Torture] goes on to provide that "[w]here it is proved that an act of torture or other cruel, inhuman or degrading treatment or punishment has been committed by or at the instigation of a public official, the victim shall be afforded redress and compensation, in accordance with national law." This Declaration, like the [Universal] Declaration of Human Rights before it, was adopted without dissent by the General Assembly.

These U.N. declarations are significant because they specify with great precision the obligations of member nations under the Charter. Since their adoption, "[m]embers can no longer contend that they do not know what human rights they promised in the Charter to promote." Moreover, a U.N. Declaration is, according to one authoritative definition, "a formal and solemn instrument, suitable for rare occasions when principles of great and lasting importance are being enunciated." 34 U.N. ESCOR, Supp. (No. 8) 15, U.N.Doc. E/cn. 4/1/610 (1962) (memorandum of Office of Legal Affairs, U.N. Secretariat). Accordingly, it has been observed that the Universal Declaration of Human Rights "no longer fits into the dichotomy of 'binding treaty' against 'non-binding pronouncement,' but is rather an authoritative statement of the international community." E. Schwelb, Human Rights and the International Community 70 (1964). Thus, a Declaration creates an expectation of adherence, and "insofar as the expectation is gradually justified by State practice, a declaration may by custom become recognized as laying down rules binding upon the States." 34 U.N. ESCOR, supra. Indeed, several commentators have concluded that the Universal Declaration has become, *in toto,* a part of binding, customary international law.

Turning to the act of torture, we have little difficulty discerning its universal renunciation in the modern usage and practice of nations. [United States v.] Smith, supra, 18 U.S. (5 Wheat.) at 160–61. The international consensus surrounding torture has found expression in numerous international treaties and accords. E.g., American Convention on Human Rights, Art. 5, OAS Treaty Series No. 36 at 1, OAS Off. Rec. OEA/Ser 4 v/II 23, doc. 21, rev. 2 (English ed., 1975) ("No one shall be subjected to torture or to cruel, inhuman or degrading punishment or treatment"); International Covenant on Civil and Political Rights, U.N. General Assembly Res. 2200 (XXI)A, U.N. Doc. A/6316 (Dec. 16, 1966) (identical language); European Convention for the Protection of Human Rights and Fundamental Freedoms, Art. 3, Council of Europe, European Treaty Series No. 5 (1968), 213 U.N.T.S. 211 *(semble).* The substance of these international agreements is reflected in modern municipal—i.e. national—law as well. Although torture was once a routine concomitant of criminal interrogations in many nations, during the modern and hopefully more enlightened era it has been universally renounced. According to one survey, torture is prohibited, expressly or implicitly, by the constitutions of over fifty-five nations, including both the United States and Paraguay. Our State Department reports a general recognition of this principle:

> There now exists an international consensus that recognizes basic human rights and obligations owed by all governments to their citizens * * *. There is no doubt that these rights are often violated; but virtually all governments acknowledge their validity.

NOTES

1. *Subsequent History.* After the *Filartiga* case was remanded to the district court, a default judgment was granted (defendants having been deported to Paraguay) and compensatory damages plus punitive damages of $5,000,000 to each plaintiff were assessed. *Filartiga v. Pena–Irala,* 577 F.Supp. 860 (E.D.N.Y. 1984). The district court on remand also cited the General Assembly Declaration, particularly noting that it declared that the victim shall be afforded redress and compensation "in accordance with national law." Id. These damage awards have not been collected, in the absence of assets of the defendants against which execution could be had.

The *Filartiga* case has been widely cited for the proposition that certain human rights principles are customary law and therefore part of the law of the United States. See Chapter 13. For more on the history of the case and its aftermath, see Koh, *Filartiga v. Pena–Irala*: Judicial Internalization into Domestic Law of the Customary International Law Norm Against Torture, in International Law Stories 45–76 (Noyes, Dickinson & Janis eds., 2007); Aceves, The Anatomy of Torture: A Documentary History of *Filartiga v. Pena–Irala* (2007).

2. *Declarations versus Ordinary Resolutions.* Did the Court's reliance on the General Assembly Declaration as evidence of a binding rule against

torture have the effect of conferring on the Assembly a degree of law-making authority inconsistent with the U.N. Charter? Does a "declaration" of a legal principle by the General Assembly have more weight than a resolution of a recommendatory character?

3. *Universal Declaration of Human Rights.* Does the Court's reference to the Universal Declaration as an "authoritative statement of the international community" imply a new "source" of international law other than treaty or custom? Would a declaration have obligatory force because it specified "with great precision" the obligations of member states under the Charter? If so, is there any reason to declare that the Declaration is customary law?

4. *General Assembly Votes as Evidence of Custom or General Principles.* The Court refers to the "universal renunciation" of torture in usage and practice. However, reports of Amnesty International regularly show that torture is employed in many countries under color of official authority. Does that rebut a finding of "state practice" sufficiently consistent and general to support a finding of custom? Is "state practice" the laws prohibiting torture or the acts of torture by state officials? Would the problem of inconsistent practice be avoided by treating the prohibition of torture as a general principle of law recognized in the law of all countries? Does the declaration provide that evidence?

Should a declaration by the General Assembly of a general principle of law be regarded as a definitive finding if adopted without dissent? Would the rules stated in a General Assembly declaration be binding on a state that claimed it voted for the declaration on the understanding that the General Assembly had only the authority to make recommendations?

General Assembly resolutions have been cited by national courts in many countries as evidence (or definitive proof) that a proposition of law expressed or implied by the resolution is binding international law. See Schreuer, Decisions of International Institutions before Domestic Courts (1981); Henkin, Resolutions of International Organizations in American Courts, in Essays on the Development of the International Legal Order (Kalshoven, Kuyper, & Lammers eds. 1980).

SOSA v. ALVAREZ–MACHAIN

Supreme Court of the United States, 2004
542 U.S. 692

[The Supreme Court first considered the Alien Tort Statute involved in *Filartiga* in *Sosa v. Alvarez–Machain*, which is discussed in Chapter 13. The case concerned allegations that Alvarez–Machain had been involuntarily detained without legal authority by bounty-hunters operating as U.S. agents who captured him in Mexico and brought him to the United States. U.N. resolutions (including the Universal Declaration) and other U.N. sources were drawn to the Court's attention in an effort to establish that such a detention violated the law of nations. The Court lent its imprimatur to much of *Filartiga*'s approach to the Alien Tort Statute but was unpersuaded that the brief detention constituted a violation of specific obligations of the United States under the relatively strict test that it found appropriate for construing the statute. Its analysis addressed whether the instruments invoked by Alvarez–Machain, including General Assembly declarations, established an applicable rule of law.]

* * * Alvarez cites two well-known international agreements that, despite their moral authority, have little utility under the standard set out in this opinion. He says that his abduction by Sosa was an "arbitrary arrest" within the meaning of the Universal Declaration of Human Rights (Declaration), G. A. Res. 217A (III), U. N. Doc. A/810 (1948). And he traces the rule against arbitrary arrest not only to the Declaration, but also to article nine of the International Covenant on Civil and Political Rights (Covenant), Dec. 19, 1966, 999 U. N. T. S. 171, to which the United States is a party, and to various other conventions to which it is not. But the Declaration does not of its own force impose obligations as a matter of international law. See Humphrey, The UN Charter and the Universal Declaration of Human Rights, in The International Protection of Human Rights 39, 50 (E. Luard ed. 1967) (quoting Eleanor Roosevelt calling the Declaration " 'a statement of principles . . . setting up a common standard of achievement for all peoples and all nations' " and " 'not a treaty or international agreement . . . impos[ing] legal obligations' "). And, although the Covenant does bind the United States as a matter of international law, the United States ratified the Covenant on the express understanding that it was not self-executing and so did not itself create obligations enforceable in the federal courts. * * * Accordingly, Alvarez cannot say that the Declaration and Covenant themselves establish the relevant and applicable rule of international law.

NOTES

1. *Eleanor Roosevelt and the Universal Declaration on Human Rights.* The *Sosa* Court quotes the statement made by Mrs. Roosevelt at the time of the General Assembly vote on the Universal Declaration, in her capacity representing the United States. For more on the debates over the legal influence of the Declaration despite its formally non-binding quality, as well as Mrs. Roosevelt's personal positions and contributions, see Glendon, A World Made New: Eleanor Roosevelt and the Universal Declaration of Human Rights 71–72, 84–87, 166–71, 235–38 (2002), and further discussion in Chapter 13.

2. *Self–Determination.* In several advisory opinions, the International Court of Justice has referred to the General Assembly declarations on self-determination and independence of peoples in territories that have not yet attained independence as having legal effect, and as "enriching the *corpus juris gentium." Namibia*, 1971 I.C.J. 16, 31; *Western Sahara*, 1975 I.C.J. 12; *Legal Consequences of the Construction of a Wall in the Occupied Palestinian Territory*, 2004 I.C.J. 136. May these "declarations" be regarded as "authentic" interpretation of the principles of the Charter that already bind the member states and therefore as obligatory or legally authoritative for all members? Could it be plausibly argued that when such broad principles as

self-determination and human rights are given more specific meaning in General Assembly declarations, they would go beyond "recommendations" and have a legislative effect beyond that authorized by the Charter? Can one assume that the governments voting in favor of such law-declaring resolutions intend to accept them as binding, rather than recommendatory? If they do not all have that intention, can the declaration be properly regarded as a binding interpretation of the Charter? For a critique of the I.C.J.'s tendency to endorse pronouncements of the General Assembly as "law" even contrary to principled positions of affected states, see Pomerance, The ICJ's Advisory Jurisdiction and the Crumbling Wall Between the Political and the Judicial, 99 A.J.I.L. 26 (2005).

3. *Nuclear Weapons.* In the 1996 advisory opinion on *Nuclear Weapons*, p. 79 *supra*, at paras. 68–73, the I.C.J. examined a series of resolutions in which the General Assembly by large majority votes condemned nuclear weapons and characterized them as illegal. Yet the Court found that those resolutions fell short of establishing a rule of international law. What theories did the Court apply in assessing the potential legal significance of these resolutions?

Several of the separate and dissenting opinions addressed the problematic significance of General Assembly resolutions. Judge Schwebel wrote in dissent:

> In its opinion, the Court concludes that the succession of resolutions of the General Assembly on nuclear weapons "still fall short of establishing the existence of an *opinio juris* on the illegality of the use of such weapons". In my view, they do not begin to do so. * * * The continuing opposition, consisting as it does of States that bring together much of the world's military and economic power and a significant percentage of its population, more than suffices to deprive the resolutions in question of legal authority.
>
> The General Assembly has no authority to enact international law. None of the General Assembly's resolutions on nuclear weapons are declaratory of existing international law. The General Assembly can adopt resolutions declaratory of international law only if those resolutions truly reflect what international law is. If a resolution purports to be declaratory of international law, if it is adopted unanimously (or virtually so, qualitatively as well as quantitatively) or by consensus, and if it corresponds to State practice, it may be declaratory of international law. The resolutions of which resolution 1653 is the exemplar conspicuously fail to meet these criteria. While purporting to be declaratory of international law (yet calling for consultations about the possibility of concluding a treaty prohibition of what is so declared), they not only do not reflect State practice, they are in conflict with it, as shown above. Forty-six States voted against or abstained upon the resolution, including the majority of the nuclear Powers. It is wholly unconvincing to argue that a majority of the Members of the General Assembly can "declare" international law in opposition to such a body of State practice and over the opposition of such a body of States. Nor are these resolutions authentic interpretations of principles or provisions of the United Nations Charter.

The Charter contains not a word about particular weapons, about nuclear weapons, about *jus in bello*. To declare the use of nuclear weapons a violation of the Charter is an innovative interpretation of it, which cannot be treated as an authentic interpretation of Charter principles or provisions giving rise to obligations binding on States under international law. Finally, the repetition of resolutions of the General Assembly in this vein, far from giving rise, in the words of the Court, to "the nascent *opinio juris*", rather demonstrates what the law is not. When faced with continuing and significant opposition, the repetition of General Assembly resolutions is a mark of ineffectuality in law formation as it is in practical effect.

4. *Specific Determinations.* Does the General Assembly have law-making power when it makes a determination in specific cases? The International Court, in its 1971 advisory opinion on *Namibia* commented on the authority of the General Assembly to assume functions under the Mandate for South West Africa as follows: "For it would not be correct to assume that because the General Assembly is in principle vested with recommendatory powers, it is debarred from adopting in specific cases within the framework of its competence, resolutions which make determinations or have operative design." 1971 I.C.J. 16, 50. Does this not mean that if an international body is given authority (i.e., competence to make decisions) such decisions when made by the requisite majority are binding? Would this include resolutions which recognize particular entities as states for purposes of participation in that body? Would it also include resolutions that treat items as within the competence of that body and as outside the exclusively domestic jurisdiction of a State?

5. *Recent Declarations: Human Cloning; Indigenous Peoples.* Among the most recent General Assembly declarations with potential (though contested) law-generative effects are a Declaration on Human Cloning, U.N. Doc. A/RES/59/280, annex, adopted in March 2005 by a vote of 84 to 34, with 37 abstentions; and a Declaration on the Rights of Indigenous Peoples, U.N. Doc. A/RES/61/295, adopted in September 2007 by a vote of 143 to 4 (Australia, Canada, New Zealand, United States voting against), with 11 abstentions and 34 absent. What is the significance of the vote distributions on these resolutions for their import as authoritative declarations of law? In explaining its negative vote on the Indigenous People's Declaration, New Zealand observed that "the history of the negotiations on the Declaration and the divided manner in which it had been adopted demonstrated that the text did not state propositions that were reflected in State practice, or which would be recognized as general principles of law." For the voting breakdown and analysis of the Cloning resolution, see Arsanjani, Negotiating the UN Declaration on Human Cloning, 100 A.J.I.L. 164 (2006).

6. *Further Reading.* Writings on this subject include Higgins, The Development of International Law Through the Political Organs of the United Nations (1963); Schachter, International Law in Theory and Practice 85–94 (1991); Oberg, The Legal Effects of Resolutions of the U.N. Security Council and General Assembly in the Jurisprudence of the International Court of Justice, 17 E.J.I.L. 879 (2005); Alvarez, International Organizations as Law–Makers 159–69, 259–60 (2005).

B. SECURITY COUNCIL "LAW-MAKING"

The Security Council differs from the General Assembly in that the U.N. Charter confers on the Council power to take compulsory measures under Chapter VII (Articles 39–51) of the Charter, which U.N. members are legally bound to implement under Articles 24 and 25. Please examine those provisions (in the Documents Supplement). What kinds of powers do you think they confer? Until the Security Council began exercising its compulsory powers actively at the end of the Cold War, questions about the scope of (and limits on) its legal authority were largely hypothetical. Starting in 1990, however, the Council has acted with respect to a wide range of specific international and internal conflicts (some of which are discussed in Chapter 15), mostly by imposing economic sanctions and mandating other nonforcible measures under Article 41. As we will see, these actions have raised novel questions of constitutional character and have spurred a tremendous amount of controversy in diplomatic circles and in scholarship.

Beginning in the 1990s and accelerating in the 2000s, the Security Council has embarked upon certain exercises of authority that have been characterized as law-making in character. These began in the context of specific conflicts but then reached more broadly across the global agenda of threats to peace and security. In increments in the initial phases of the Iraq conflict (1990–1991) and the conflict in former Yugoslavia (1991–1995), the Council adopted resolutions "affirming" or "declaring" certain propositions of law which were widely accepted but perhaps not entirely beyond dispute at the time of their pronouncement. For example, it laid the groundwork for future proceedings to obtain reparations from Iraq and to establish responsibility for violations of international humanitarian law in ex-Yugoslavia through resolutions affirming that states and individuals committing violations could be held responsible in international law. See, e.g., S.C. Res. 674 (Oct. 29, 1990) (Iraq); S.C. Res. 764 (July 13, 1992) (Yugoslavia). In S.C. Res. 687 (Apr. 3, 1991) which established the terms of cease-fire at the end of the Iraq–Kuwait war, it imposed obligations on Iraq that were markedly more stringent than Iraq's obligations under its existing treaties or customary law and also established mechanisms for demarcating the boundary between Iraq and Kuwait and determining compensation to be paid by Iraq. To enforce that new regime, the Council maintained in place a comprehensive program of economic sanctions which affected not only Iraq but all states that would otherwise have had dealings with Iraq. On these developments, see Chapter 15.

In the decade between 1991 and 2001, the Council asserted itself in various ways with respect to global threats from terrorism, weapons of mass destruction, and serious violations of human rights and humanitarian law. Most of the novel steps in this decade were taken with respect to specific targets in order to achieve precisely defined objectives. Libya, for example, was put under sanctions for its role in the explosion of Pan Am

Flight 103 over Lockerbie, Scotland; Iraq was subjected to a unique program of supervised demilitarization and disarmament; and Haiti, Somalia, Rwanda, Sierra Leone, and other countries were placed under Chapter VII measures in order to bring extreme violence under control there. In 1999 the Council placed Taliban-controlled Afghanistan under a sanctions regime with the primary objective of ending its support for international terrorism. See Chapter 15.

Then, just days after the attacks of September 11, 2001, the Council embarked upon one of its most ambitious initiatives to date. In Resolution 1373 (Sept. 28, 2001), it required states to take a variety of obligatory measures to combat terrorism, including the enactment of criminal legislation to prevent terrorist acts and the freezing of assets. This resolution is widely perceived as a landmark in the evolution of Security Council activity, not only for its political and economic import in the global counterterrorist struggle, but also for having broken new ground in international law-making. Other Security Council resolutions that have been characterized as legislative in character include Resolutions 1422 (July 22, 2002) and 1487 (July 12, 2003) on the International Criminal Court (see Chapter 16), and perhaps most important, Resolution 1540 (Apr. 28, 2004) on weapons of mass destruction. Such resolutions, some of which are reprinted in the Documents Supplement, share the features of prescribing obligations of a general character, rather than dealing with a particular state or conflict.

Many states and commentators have welcomed the Security Council's "legislative phase," but others have been critical both on policy grounds and for legal-constitutional reasons. It is said that the Council was intended to be an executive, not legislative, organ, and that its forays into law-making may exceed its powers under the U.N. Charter. Concerns have been expressed about the Security Council's perceived "democratic deficit," in that its membership is restricted to fifteen states, of whom five— the permanent members—have a veto and thus carry disproportionate weight in deliberations over the content of obligations to be imposed on the U.N. community as a whole. In many quarters, "hegemony" of the strongest permanent member is unwelcome. Resistance to law-making by the Security Council is bound up with the long-running controversy over reforming the Council's structure to make it more representative and responsive to diverse constituencies. The debate over these questions at the intersection of U.N. constitutional law and global politics has been intense, as the following excerpt illustrates.

TALMON, THE SECURITY COUNCIL AS WORLD LEGISLATURE

99 A.J.I.L. 175, 179, 182–86 (2005) (footnotes omitted)

Several general objections may be raised to Security Council legislation. First, a patently unrepresentative and undemocratic body such as the Council is arguably unsuitable for international lawmaking. However, this objection, although valid, could also be made to any other Council action. It can hardly be maintained that authorizing the use of force requires less democratic legitimacy than imposing an obligation to prevent and suppress the financing of terrorist acts. Second, it may be argued that the International Court of Justice (ICJ) does not know of legislative resolutions as a source of international law. This contention does not take into account that Council resolutions are legally based in the United Nations Charter, an international convention in the sense of Article 38(1)(a) of the ICJ Statute, which makes them classifiable as "secondary treaty (or Charter) law." The fact that the ICJ has been able to apply resolutions of the Council without remarking upon the incompleteness of Article 38 strongly suggests that binding Council resolutions, both of a general and of a particular character, are still properly regarded as coming within the scope of the traditional sources of international law. This quality would change only if the Council expressly purported to legislate outside the Charter framework, that is to say, for nonmembers of the United Nations. Third, Council practice may be criticized as contrary to the basic structure of international law as a consent-based legal order. This view overlooks the nature of all binding decisions of the Council as, according to Article 25 of the UN Charter, based on the consent of the member states. Finally, the assumption of legislative powers by the Council may be said to be difficult to reconcile with its general role under the Charter as a "policeman" rather than a legislature or jury. Yet the powers of the Council are to be determined not by reference to its general role but on the basis of the provisions of the UN Charter.

* * *

Although the Security Council has a wide margin of discretion in deciding when and where a threat to the peace exists and what measures member states should take to maintain or restore international peace and security, its power is not legally unfettered. This part examines three possible legal limits to Council legislation: restrictions deriving from the text of the UN Charter, the principle of proportionality, and the concept of the integrity of treaties.

Restrictions Deriving from the Text of the UN Charter

The Council enjoys powers only insofar as they are conferred on it or implied in the UN Charter. Only resolutions that are *intra vires* the UN Charter acquire binding force in terms of Article 25, which speaks of "decisions of the Security Council in accordance with the present Charter." The Council's legislative powers are thus limited by the jurisdiction of the United Nations at large, as well as by the attribution and division of competences within the organization.

According to Article 39, the Council may take action under Chapter VII only to "maintain or restore international peace and security." The basic restriction of the Council's legislative power is that it must be exercised in a manner that is conducive to the maintenance of international peace and security. The Charter does not establish the Council as an omnipotent world legislator but, rather, as a single-issue legislator. This restriction is confirmed by the fact that the Charter allocates to the General Assembly the task of making recommendations for the purpose of progressively developing and codifying international law. Most international issues, especially those of an administrative or technical nature, will remain outside the ambit of Security Council legislation. For example, the Council cannot lay down general rules on the breadth of the territorial sea or the drawing of straight baselines in the law of the sea, although it may find that a particular improper or excessive territorial sea claim constitutes a threat to international peace and security. * * * [I]n all cases there must be a genuine link between the general obligations imposed and the maintenance of international peace and security. Thus, the Council cannot regulate financial transactions in general but only transactions that may be linked to a threat to the peace; that is, to terrorist acts, the proliferation of weapons of mass destruction, and possibly transnational organized crime, the illegal arms trade, and drug trafficking.

Another restriction of Council legislation may be derived from provisions in the Charter that provide for only recommendatory powers of the Council. According to Article 26, the Council "shall be responsible for formulating ... plans to be submitted to the Members of the United Nations for the establishment of a system for the regulation of armaments." Such plans are not binding on member states, not least because of their implications for national security and the right to self-defense. The term "regulation of armaments" is to be understood in the sense of "arms control," including the reduction, limitation, or elimination of arms and armed forces, as well as the production and possession of and trade in armaments. While certain types of armaments (such as nuclear, chemical, and biological weapons) or the excessive stockpiling of armaments might per se constitute a threat to the peace, the Council cannot impose general disarmament obligations on states, for example, by prohibiting the development, production, or possession of a particular type of weaponry. The Council also cannot mandate participation in the UN Register for Conventional Arms, established on a voluntary basis by the General Assembly in 1992, or limit the military budgets of states. Article 26, however, does not preclude the Council from imposing disarmament obligations on a particular state, if that state's possession of certain weapons, judged on the basis of its previous conduct, constitutes a threat to international peace and security.

* * *

The Principle of Proportionality

Even though the Security Council, when acting under Chapter VII, is not bound to respect international law apart from the Charter, the Charter itself indicates in several provisions that the Council's actions are subject to the principle of proportionality. These provisions indicate that Council legislation must be necessary in order to maintain international peace and security, meaning that the usual ways to create obligations of an abstract and general character (the conclusion of treaties and the development of customary international law) must be inadequate to achieve that aim. Council legislation is always emergency legislation. In the Council's open debate on April 22, 2004, the Swiss representative seized upon this point, stating: "It is acceptable for the Security Council to assume such a legislative role only ... in response to an urgent need." This sense of urgency was emphasized by several other delegations, as well as by the president of the Council, who stated with regard to Resolution 1540 that

> there was a gap in international law pertaining to non-State actors. So, either new international law should be created, either waiting for customary international law to develop, or by negotiating a treaty or convention. Both took a long time, and everyone felt that there was an "imminent threat", which had to be addressed and which could not wait for the usual way.

A gap or lacuna in the legal framework is not required to signal an urgent need for Council legislation, as is shown by Resolution 1373, some of whose provisions were based on the Convention for the Suppression of the Financing of Terrorism. In that case, the need for Council legislation arose because, at the time, only four states were parties to the Convention, making it a long way from coming into force.

The character of Council legislation as emergency legislation does not mean that the general obligations imposed are provisional or temporary and must be replaced by a multilaterally negotiated treaty that allows all interested states to participate, on an equal footing, in defining their obligations. Calls by several states for the early conclusion of a binding international legal instrument on the subject matter of the resolution were not included in Resolution 1540. This does not exclude the possibility that a treaty will subsequently be concluded on that subject matter. However, in the event of a conflict between the obligations under the resolution and those under a subsequent treaty, the obligations under the resolution will prevail. If the treaty were intended to replace the resolution, the Council would either have to abrogate the resolution or, at least, endorse the treaty in another resolution or a statement by the president.

In practice, the principle of proportionality will have little limiting effect on Council legislation, as the Charter allows the Council a broad margin of appreciation with respect to the proportionality of its action. Legislation would therefore violate the Charter only if its impact on the member states were manifestly out of proportion to the objective pursued, the maintenance of international peace and security. As with other *ultra vires* decisions of the Council, there is no procedure for reviewing the legality of legislation. The resulting problems are far from being resolved, and in any case are not susceptible of resolution by means of simplified formulations.

The Concept of Integrity of International Treaties

Several states have argued that the Council does not have the power to take decisions under Chapter VII to amend international treaties. For example, the representative of Pakistan declared: "Pakistan strongly adheres to the position that the Security Council, despite its wide authority and responsibilities, is not empowered to unilaterally amend or abrogate international treaties and agreements freely entered into by sovereign States." South Africa asserted that "the Council's mandate leaves no room either to reinterpret or even to amend treaties that have been negotiated and agreed by the rest of the United Nations membership." These statements must be seen in the context of the discussion about the legality of Resolutions 1422 and 1487, which turned on the interpretation of Article 16 of the Rome Statute of the International Criminal Court. The states in question argued that the provision allowed the Council to request the deferral of investigations or prosecutions only in specific cases. A general request, they argued, would amount to an amendment of the treaty. The discussion was apparently influenced more by the attitude of states toward the International Criminal Court than by the general question of the Council's authority under Chapter VII. But even had Article 16 of the Rome Statute not foreseen a general request, that could not prevent the Council from making such a request if it was necessary for the maintenance of international peace and security. According to Article 103 of the Charter, in the event of a conflict between a request and the Rome Statute, the request would prevail. The ICJ held in the *Lockerbie* case that obligations imposed by the Council take precedence over obligations under international treaties. A precondition, however, is that the Council may impose the obligation in the first instance. A decision by the Council that states shall not exercise their right under the Nuclear Non–Proliferation Treaty to withdraw from that treaty would contravene Article 26 of the UN Charter, which gives the Council only recommendatory powers in the area of regulation of armaments. A valid legislative resolution whose application is not limited in time, owing to the continuing character of the threat addressed, may have the effect of a *de facto* amendment to existing treaties, that is to say, an alteration of the treaty without altering its text.

Whether the Council may impose existing treaties upon the member states, either by obliging them to become parties or by making the treaty mandatory, is a different question. So far the Council has not done so, although several writers have advocated this practice. In Resolution 1373 the Council only called upon states in a nonbinding provision to "become parties as soon as possible to the relevant international conventions and protocols relating to terrorism." While the Council may impose certain treaty obligations on states, as in Resolution 1373, it cannot, as a rule, impose whole treaties, since they contain not just substantive obligations, but also purely technical or administrative provisions whose imposition will not be necessary to address a threat to international peace and security.

NOTES

1. *Review of Security Council Law–Making?* Article 103 of the U.N. Charter provides for Charter obligations to prevail over other obligations. Because Security Council resolutions adopted under Chapter VII of the Charter enjoy this higher status, those affected by such resolutions may well be concerned that the Council itself should act in a lawful manner, both in relation to the Charter as an international constitution and in relation to peremptory norms of international law reflecting the interests of the international community as a whole. As indicated in Chapter 2 on normative hierarchy, legal challenges to Security Council authority have been brought in a variety of national, regional, and international tribunals and those challenges are continuing. Ian Johnstone has identified at least fifteen such challenges, several of which assert that the Council has acted in violation of *jus cogens*. See Johnstone, Legislation and Adjudication in the UN Security Council: Bringing Down the Deliberative Deficit, 102 A.J.I.L. 275 (2008); see also the excerpt from the *Kadi* decision of the European Court of Justice in Chapter 10. While there have been some decisions relevant to appreciating the powers of the Security Council (including by the I.C.J. in the *Lockerbie* case where Article 103 was invoked), the legislative dimension of the Council's authority as asserted in the post–9/11 era has not yet been fully tested or settled. Given the decentralized nature of the international legal system, it is not likely that there will be a definitive answer to the questions about Security Council legislation any time soon.

2. *Further Reading.* For additional perspectives on the Security Council's law-making initiatives, see Szasz, The Security Council Starts Legislating, 96 A.J.I.L. 901 (2002); Alvarez, International Organizations as Law–Makers 184–217 (2005). For more on the debate over potential external review of Security Council law-making and other Council actions, see De Wet, The Chapter VII Powers of the United Nations Security Council (2004); Orakhelashvili, The Impact of Peremptory Norms on the Interpretation and Application of U.N. Security Council Resolutions, 16 E.J.I.L. 88 (2005); Sarooshi, International Organizations and Their Exercise of Sovereign Powers (2007).

SECTION 4. TRANSNATIONAL PUBLIC REGULATION

KRISCH & KINGSBURY, INTRODUCTION: GLOBAL GOVERNANCE AND GLOBAL ADMINISTRATIVE LAW IN THE INTERNATIONAL LEGAL ORDER

17 E.J.I.L. 1, 2–5, 12–13 (2006) (footnotes omitted)

The concept of global administrative law begins from the twin ideas that much global governance can be understood as administration, and that such administration is often organized and shaped by principles of an administrative law character. With the expansion of global governance, many administrative and regulatory functions are now performed in a global rather than national context, yet through a great number of different forms, ranging from binding decisions of international organizations to non-binding agreements in intergovernmental networks and to domestic administrative action in the context of global regimes. Examples include UN Security Council decisions on individual sanctions; World Bank rule-making for developing countries; the setting of standards on money laundering by the Financial Action Task Force; or domestic administrative decisions on market access of foreign products as part of the WTO regime. Many regulatory functions in global governance are also performed outside such formally public, governmental structures, namely by hybrid private-public or purely private institutions, such as ICANN, the Internet Corporation for Assigned Names and Numbers, or the International Organization for Standardization (ISO).

Despite these widely varying forms and institutions, we can observe in all these examples the exercise of recognizably administrative and regulatory functions: the setting and application of rules by bodies that are not legislative or primarily adjudicative in character. If similar actions were performed by a state agency, there would be little doubt as to their administrative character * * *. Classically, however, regarding them as administrative would have been difficult because of their international nature; the term 'administration' was closely tied to the state framework and could, at most, point to the domestic implementation of international norms. This categorical distinction, however, has today become problematic: too interwoven are the domestic and international elements in these processes of regulation. This is most obvious for government networks in which domestic officials are engaged in both the rule-making on a global scale and the implementation on the domestic level, often without any intervening act. * * * It is this interwovenness of the different spheres that leads us to regard the conglomerate of regulatory forms as part of one very variegated but recognizable 'global' administrative space.

* * *

* * * In many areas of global governance, and in highly variegated forms, mechanisms are emerging that seek to enhance [participation in] the accountability of global regulatory decision-making. The structural similarities between many of these disparate phenomena are striking: they testify to a growing trend of building mechanisms analogous to domestic administrative law systems to the global level; transparency, participation, and review are central among them. This trend is reflected, for instance, in the Inspection Panel set up by the World Bank to ensure its compliance with internal policies; in notice-and-comment procedures adopted by international standard-setters such as the [Organization for Economic Cooperation and Development]; in the inclusion of [non-governmental organizations] in regulatory bodies like the Codex Alimentarius Commission; or in rules about foreign participation in domestic administrative procedures as set out in the Aarhus Convention [on Access to Information, Public Participation in Decision–Making and Access to Justice in Environmental

Matters, June 25, 1998, 2161 U.N.T.S. 447]. We argue that this is a general trend of practice toward a global administrative law.

* * * [G]lobal administrative law as we understand it encompasses the legal mechanisms, principles and practices, along with supporting social understandings, that promote or otherwise affect the accountability of global administrative bodies, in particular by ensuring these bodies meet adequate standards of transparency, consultation, participation, rationality and legality, and by providing effective review of the rules and decisions these bodies make. We describe this field of law as 'global' rather than 'international' to reflect the enmeshment of domestic and international regulation, the inclusion of a large array of informal institutional arrangements (many involving prominent roles for non-state actors), and the foundation of the field in normative practices, and normative sources, that are not fully encompassed within standard conceptions of international law.

* * *

* * * International law doctrines of sources centred on Article 38 of the International Court of Justice Statute do not address these forms very well. In rare cases, practices may be widespread enough to form the basis of general principles of law, but in most instances, international lawyers will regard them as falling outside international law. But as such non-standard forms of rule-making become so influential, and indeed prevalent in some areas, it is unsatisfactory to have no better analysis of them than 'non-law'. At the same time, many questions about their status emerge: Can they be encompassed in a refurbished modern concept of *jus gentium*? Does it matter that they may have a weaker basis of legitimacy because of their weaker roots in domestic procedures and their frequent lack of general acceptance? Likewise, what status should be accorded to the *mélange* of actors producing such norms? This can hardly be confined to a formal discussion of their personality in international law; nor can they be consigned simply [to] the unexplored realm of the informal, relevant only to sociology, political science or economics.

Towards a global public law? Given these challenges, it is improbable that a traditional vision of international law as essentially a contractual order of equal states is even theoretically operable * * *. Given the diversity of forms of law and processes of rule-making, the importance of various sorts of institutions in them, and the increasingly blurred line between the domestic and the international, it is necessary to inquire whether a new global public law is emerging. * * *

NOTES

1. *Global Administrative Law as an Emerging Construct.* The ideas in the preceding extract have been further developed by its authors and colleagues in the symposium issue of the European Journal of International Law in which their introductory article appears, and in several other symposia.

See, e.g., Kingsbury, Krisch, & Stewart, The Emergence of Global Administrative Law, 68 L. & Contemp. Probs. 15 (Summer/Autumn 2005) and related symposium articles; see also the symposium articles on the same topic in 37 N.Y.U. J. Int'l L. & Pol. 799, 869 (2005).

On transnational networks among government regulators, see Slaughter, A New World Order (2004). See also Alvarez, International Organizations as Law–Makers 217–73 (2005).

2. *Standard–Setting through Intergovernmental Institutions.* Some international regulatory activity takes place within the framework of specialized international organizations, whose output may or may not be formally binding. (As discussed further in the following notes and in Section 5 below, a distinction between "hard" and "soft" law is not always significant in such contexts.) For example, the International Civil Aviation Organization (ICAO) develops international standards and recommended practices under the Chicago Convention on Civil Aviation (Articles 37–42). Member states are then expected to comply with those standards and practices or else to notify ICAO of any discrepancies. It would be up to each member to determine how to adjust its domestic regulations or other relevant laws and practices in order to come into compliance with the international standards. (In the United States, for example, the Federal Aviation Administration could promulgate a rule which would be published in the Code of Federal Regulations.) On the wide range of standard-setting activity that goes on within the ICAO framework (covering many aspects of airworthiness, safety and security, property and liability issues, crimes committed on board and against aircraft, and travel documents and entry procedures for passengers), see Alvarez, International Organizations as Law–Makers 223–24, 253–55 (2005).

3. *"Generally Accepted International Standards."* The conception of "generally accepted international standards" emerged in treaties on the law of the sea and has spread to other fields, particularly the law of the environment. Such standards may be adopted in a treaty or by international organizations pursuant to a treaty. With respect to marine safety and related matters, the Restatement (Third) states that "once a standard has been generally accepted, a state is obligated in particular to apply it to all ships flying its flag and to adopt any necessary laws or regulations" (section 502, Comment *c*). This obligation is said to apply to all states whether or not parties to the convention by virtue of customary law. See also Restatement (Third) § 601 and Comment *b*.

Oxman writes:

The duty entails a legally binding obligation to observe generally accepted standards. This obligation, however, is created by general acceptance of a standard in fact, rather than by the procedure by which the standard was articulated. Thus, it creates a useful bridge between so-called "soft law" and "hard law." This, indeed, was part of its original function. Where appropriate, standards (or guidelines) can be developed in a somewhat more relaxed procedural environment which is not specifically designed to generate legally binding obligations as such; yet those same standards can become legally binding if they become generally accepted.

The effect of the duty under discussion is to impose a legal obligation on a state to respect a standard which it would not otherwise be legally bound to respect. The consensual requirements of international law for the imposition of legal obligations are not offended by this proposition; those requirements have previously been satisfied through acceptance of the general duty either by treaty or by customary international law. It is unnecessary to restrict the scope of the duty itself to conform to such requirements.

Oxman, The Duty to Respect Generally Accepted International Standards, 24 N.Y.U. J. Int'l L. & Pol. 143–44 (1991).

4. *Other Codes and Standards.* International organizations have adopted a variety of texts, called "codes of conduct" or "guidelines," which prescribe norms for state conduct and, in some cases, for conduct of non-state entities. Such texts could be considered "non-binding," in that they are usually drafted in hortatory rather than obligatory language. However, it is clear that the states voting for such non-binding codes or guidelines intend them to be followed in practice. In many cases, the texts provide for reports by governments and for periodic review by an international organ. In some cases, specific cases of non-compliance may be brought to the attention of the competent international organ. Examples of such codes or guidelines are mainly found in economic and social fields. Foreign investment and transnational corporations have been the subject of several such texts, such as the U.N. Code on Restrictive Business Practices, 19 I.L.M. 813 (1981), and the World Bank Guidelines on the Treatment of Foreign Direct Investment, 31 I.L.M. 1363 (1992). The United Nations engaged for many years unsuccessfully in work on a comprehensive code of conduct for transnational corporations. See Chapter 7.

5. *Food Standards.* The specialized agencies of the United Nations have relied on nominally voluntary codes for important areas of international regulation. For example, the World Health Organization has adopted an International Code for the Marketing of Breast Milk Substitutes, 20 I.L.M. 1004 (1981), and the Food and Agriculture Organization jointly with the W.H.O. has promulgated the Codex Alimentarius for the codification of food standards. As Alvarez suggests (in International Organizations as Law–Makers, *supra*, at 217–35), the formal status of such standards in legal terms is less important than the fact that they have achieved widespread acceptance by the relevant actors (private parties operating in the market as well as governments) and that their terms do in fact achieve almost uniform adherence.

The W.H.O. Code on Breast Milk Substitutes was adopted by the World Health Assembly in 1981 with near-unanimity, the only dissenting vote cast by the United States. The Code's main object is to prohibit certain marketing and promotional activities that foster inappropriate and dangerous use of infant milk substitutes in poor countries with inadequate sanitation and clean water. The Code was legally a W.H.O. recommendation, not a binding set of rules. It is addressed to governments, to private firms, to institutions (such as hospitals), and to the medical and nursing professions. Some countries enacted the Code as a whole into domestic law; a considerable number have given legal effect to major parts of the Code. Some principal producers of the milk-substitutes at first resisted the Code, notably Nestlé, the largest producer. In reaction, a group of non-governmental organizations instituted an international boycott of Nestlé which resulted in major changes by the company in its marketing and promotional activities. See Zelman, The Nestlé Infant Formula Controversy: Restricting the Marketing Practices of Multinational Corporation in the Third World, 3 Transnat'l Law. 697 (1990); Alvarez, *supra*, at 234–35.

The Codex Alimentarius (a joint project of the F.A.O. and the W.H.O.) provides an institutional framework for the codification of food standards that are necessary for "protecting the health of consumers and ensuring fair practices in the food trade." Statutes, Article 1, Codex Alimentarius Commission Procedural Manual 5 (17th ed. 2007). Established in 1962, the Codex covers "all principal foods, whether processed, semi-processed or raw, for distribution to the consumer. * * * It also includes provisions of an advisory nature in the form of codes of practice, guidelines and other recommended measures." Id. at 23. Governments may respond to new standards proposed by the Codex Alimentarius Commission in one of four ways: full acceptance, target acceptance, acceptance with specific deviations, or no acceptance. Governments that refuse to accept a standard, or that prefer target acceptance, must provide an explanation of the way their own food requirements differ from the proposed ones, and must indicate whether they will allow the distribution within their borders of a product complying with the standard. The success of the Codex is not only to be measured by the number of acceptances for the standards, as the Codex also has exerted a powerful influence on non-accepting states, as well as food growers, packagers, transporters, and preparers. The Codex has been recognized in the W.T.O.'s Agreement on Sanitary and Phytosanitary Measures with a presumption favoring measures that comply with its standards. On the legal status of the code and, more significantly, its practical effects, see Alvarez, *supra*, at 222–23.

6. *International Rules of Non-Governmental Bodies.* International non-governmental organization in various fields adopt rules and standards in their respective fields of activity, many of which are given effect by official agencies, courts, and international organizations. Technical and scientific bodies in particular are authoritative sources of norms that are incorporated by reference or explicitly into rules observed by states and public agencies. Examples include the International Organization for Standardization of Weights and Measures and the International Air Transportation Association.

A striking example of an international non-governmental legal regime is the Olympic Movement. The Olympic Charter vests "supreme authority in the International Olympic Committee (IOC)" and provides that "any person or organization belonging in any capacity to the Olympic Movement is bound by the provisions of the Charter and shall abide by the decisions of the W.I.O.C." The rules, by-laws and decisions of the IOC constitute an autonomous regime governing the relevant sports world and are given effect as such by governments. A study by a European scholar in 1988 noted that "the sui generis law of the Olympic Movement is accepted, respected and applied as a State-independent body of legal rules in a growing number of municipal court decisions." Simma, quoted in Nafziger, *International Sports Law*, 86 A.J.I.L. 489, 492 (1992). When Olympic arrangements were challenged in the United States, the Ninth Circuit declared that "[t]he Olympic Games are organized and conducted under the terms of an international agreement—the Olympic Charter. We are extremely hesitant * * * to alter an event that is staged * * * under the terms of that agreement." *Martin v. IOC*, 740 F.2d 670, 677 (9th Cir. 1984). See also *Behagen v. Amateur Basketball Ass'n of U.S.*, 884 F.2d 524, 527 (10th Cir. 1989) (noting the centrality of the IOC in "governing structures for * * * American involvement in international amateur sports"). The decision of the IOC to exclude South African athletes from international competition between 1964 and 1991 for violating its rule against apartheid laws was effectively observed. IOC rules on substance abuse and "doping" have been accepted as binding on all, though in practice supervision has been inconsistent and sometimes haphazard (Nafziger, *supra*, at 503).

At the opening of the 21st century, the challenges of cyberspace raise new versions of problems of standard-setting in a global context. A variety of regulatory and self-regulatory functions are being handled by private bodies, such as the Internet Corporation for Assigned Names and Numbers, a non-profit corporation. A Memorandum of Understanding on the Generic Top Level Domain Name Space of the Internet Domain Name System has been signed by some 200 mainly non-governmental entities and deposited with the International Telecommunications Union (cited in Spiro, Globalization, International Law, and the Academy, 32 N.Y.U. J. Int'l L. & Politics 567, 571 n. 6 (2000)). On ICANN, see Goldsmith & Wu, Who Controls the Internet? 168–71 (2006).

SECTION 5. "SOFT LAW"

A. "SOFT LAW" AS A CONTESTABLE CATEGORY

The global administrative law discussed in the prior section includes some forms of law-making arising from non-legally binding instruments. When normative standards are embodied in an instrument other than a binding treaty, they are sometimes referred to as "soft law," a form of "international law-making that is designed, in whole or part, not to be enforceable." See Reisman, The Supervisory Jurisdiction of the International Court of Justice, 258 Rec. des Cours 9, 180–82 (1996); Reisman, The Concept and Functions of Soft Law in International Politics, in 1 Essays in Honor of Judge T.O. Elias 135 (Omotola ed. 1992). Yet soft law may entail some legal effects, and may well elicit compliance even in the absence of direct mechanisms for enforcement. In still another usage, "soft law" could refer to vague, weak, or hortatory terms of an international instrument.

Some question the coherence or even the existence of the category of "soft law." For the critics, there is either legal obligation or there is not; obligation cannot or should not be a matter of degree. To this effect, see the much-noted article by Prosper Weil excerpted in Chapter 2; see also Raustiala, Form and Substance in International Agreements, 99 A.J.I.L.

581, 586–91 (2005). On the other hand, as a descriptive matter one can discern processes through which norms that were initially formulated in non-binding form have gradually accrued greater authority through non-coercive means. Just as General Assembly resolutions, which are formally non-binding, can contribute to the crystallization of legal norms, normative development can likewise occur in multiple arenas in which the initial norm-formulation is not intended to establish binding law. For a review of the issues involving "soft law" and references to relevant literature, see Shelton, Normative Hierarchy in International Law, 100 A.J.I.L. 291, 319–22 (2006).

A collaborative project of the American Society of International Law seeks to understand the uses of soft law and to identify factors that may make soft law effective in influencing international behavior. The project takes up case studies in diverse areas: environment and natural resources (General Assembly ban on driftnet fishing, codes of conduct on pesticides and chemicals, agreed measures concerning Antarctica); trade and finance (e.g., money laundering); human rights (protection of minorities, labor standards, principles for corporate investment in repressive societies such as South Africa under apartheid); and multilateral arms control (missile control technology regime, physical protection of nuclear materials, and land mines). The contributors also consider whether there is a conceptual distinction between binding and non-binding norms or rather a continuum. See Commitment and Compliance: The Role of Non–Binding Norms in the International Legal System (Shelton ed. 2000). See also Alvarez, International Organizations as Law–Makers 248–57 (2005).

B. AGREEMENTS NOT INTENDED TO BE LEGALLY BINDING

SCHACHTER, THE TWILIGHT EXISTENCE OF NONBINDING INTERNATIONAL AGREEMENTS

71 A.J.I.L. 296 (1977) (some footnotes omitted)

International lawyers generally agree that an international agreement is not legally binding unless the parties intend it to be. Put more formally, a treaty or international agreement is said to require an intention by the parties to create legal rights and obligations or to establish relations governed by international law. If that intention does not exist, an agreement is considered to be without legal effect ("sans portée juridique"). States are, of course, free to enter into such nonbinding agreements, whatever the subject matter of the agreement. However, questions have often arisen as to the intention of the parties in this regard. The main reason for this is that governments tend to be reluctant (as in the case of the Helsinki Final Act) to state explicitly in an agreement that it is nonbinding or lacks legal force. Consequently inferences as to such intent have to be drawn from the language of the instrument and the attendant circumstances of its conclusion and adoption. Emphasis is often placed on the lack of precision and generality of the terms of the agreement. Statements of general aims and broad declarations of principles are considered too indefinite to create enforceable obligations and therefore agreements which do not go beyond that should be presumed to be nonbinding.[9] It is also said, not implausibly, that mere statements of intention or of common purposes are grounds for concluding that a legally binding agreement was not intended. Experience has shown that these criteria are not easy to apply especially in situations where the parties wish to convey that their declarations and undertakings are to be taken seriously, even if stated in somewhat general or "programmatic" language. Thus, conflicting inferences were drawn as to the intent of the parties in regard to some of the well-known political agreements during the Second World War, notably the Cairo, Yalta, and Potsdam agreements.[10] No doubt there was a calculated ambiguity about the obligatory force of these instruments at least in regard to some of their provisions and this was reflected in the way the governments dealt with them.[11] After all, imprecision and generalities are not unknown in treaties of unquestioned legal force. If one were to apply strict requirements of definiteness and specificity to all treaties, many of them would have all or most of their provisions considered as without legal effect. Examples of such treaties may be found particularly among agreements for cultural cooperation and often in agreements of friendship and trade which express common aims and intentions in broad language. Yet there is no doubt that they are regarded as binding treaties by the parties and that they furnish authoritative guidance to the administrative officials charged with implementation. Other examples of highly general formulas can be found in the

---

9. O'Connell, [International Law, (2d ed. 1970)] at 199–200. But other jurists have noted that vague and ill-defined provisions appear in agreements which do not lose their binding character because of such indefiniteness. See P. Reuter, Introduction au Droit des Traités 44 (1972); G.G. Fitzmaurice, Report on the Law of Treaties to the International Law Commission. [1956] 2 Y.B.Int. Law Comm. 117, UN Doc. A/CN.4/101 (1956). The latter commented that "it seems difficult to refuse the designation of treaty to an instrument—such as, for instance, a treaty of peace and amity, or of alliance even if it only establishes a bare relationship and leaves the consequences to rest on the basis of an implication as to the rights and obligations involved, without these being expressed in any definite articles." Id.

10. Statements by officials of the British and U.S. Governments indicated that they did not consider the Yalta and Potsdam agreements as binding. * * * A contrary point of view was expressed in 1969 by a representative of the USSR at the Vienna Conference on the Law of Treaties. He declared that the Yalta and Potsdam agreements as well as the Atlantic Charter provided for "rights and obligations" and laid down "very important rules of international law." UN Doc. A/Conf. 39/11 Add. 1, at 226 (para. 22). Sir Hersch Lauterpacht considered that the Yalta and Potsdam agreements "incorporated definite rules of conduct which may be regarded as legally binding on the States in question." 1 Oppenheim, International Law 788 (7th ed. H. Lauterpacht, ed. 1948). On the other hand, Professor Briggs suggested that the Yalta agreement on the Far Eastern territories may be considered only as "the personal agreement of the three leaders." Briggs, The Leaders' Agreement of Yalta, 40 AJIL 376, at 382 (1946).

11. The Yalta Agreement was published by the State Department in the Executive Agreements Series (No. 498) and was also published in U.S. Treaties in Force (1963). However, in 1956 the State Department stated to the Japanese Government in an aide-mémoire that "the United States regards the so-called Yalta Agreement as simply a statement of common purposes by the heads of the participating governments and * * * not as of any legal effect in transferring territories." 35 Dept. State Bull. 484 (1956). But see Briggs, supra note 10, for statements by the U.S. Secretary of State that an agreement was concluded by the leaders.

UN Charter and similar "constitutional" instruments the abstract principles of which have been given determinate meaning by the international organs (as, for example, has been done in regard to Articles 55 and 56 of the Charter). These cases indicate that caution is required in drawing inferences of nonbinding intention from general and imprecise undertakings in agreements which are otherwise treated as binding. However, if the text or circumstances leave the intention uncertain, it is reasonable to consider vague language and mere declarations of purpose as indicative of an intention to avoid legal effect. Other indications may be found in the way the instrument is dealt with after its conclusion—for example, whether it is listed or published in national treaty collections, whether it is registered under Article 102 of the Charter, whether it is described as a treaty or international agreement of a legal character in submissions to national parliaments or courts.[12] None of these acts can be considered as decisive evidence but together with the language of the instruments they are relevant. The level and authority of the governmental representatives who have signed or otherwise approved the agreement may also be relevant but here too, some caution is necessary in weighing the evidentiary value. Chiefs of state and foreign ministers do enter into nonbinding arrangements and lower officials may, if authorized, act for a state in incurring legally binding obligations. If a lower official, without authority, purports to conclude an agreement, the supposed agreement may be entirely void and without any effect. It would, in consequence, have to be distinguished from the kind of nonbinding agreement which is treated by the parties as an authorized and legitimate mutual engagement.

We should bear in mind that not all nonbinding agreements are general and indefinite. Governments may enter into precise and definite engagements as to future conduct with a clear understanding shared by the parties that the agreements are not legally binding. The so-called "gentlemen's agreements" fall into this category. They may be made by heads of state or governments or by ministers of foreign affairs and, if authorized, by other officials. In these cases the parties assume a commitment to perform certain acts or refrain from them. The nature of the commitment is regarded as "nonlegal" and not binding. There is nonetheless an expectation of, and reliance on, compliance by the parties. An example is the agreement made in 1908 by the United States and Japan, through their foreign ministers, relating to immigration which was observed for nearly two decades, although probably not considered binding. On the multilateral level, some gentlemen's agreements have been made by governments with regard to their activities in international organizations, particularly on voting for members of representative bodies which have to reflect an appropriate distribution of seats among various groups of states (as for instance, the London agreement of 1946 on the distribu-

---

12. The appellation of an instrument has but little evidentiary value as to its legal effect in view of the wide variety of terms used to designate binding treaties and the accepted rule that form and designation are immaterial in determining their binding effect. Thirty-nine different appellations for treaties are listed in Myers, The Names and Scope of Treaties, 51 AJIL 574 (1957).

tion of seats in the Security Council). It has been suggested that a gentlemen's agreement is not binding on the states because it is deemed to have been concluded by the representatives in their personal names and not in the name of their governments. This reasoning is rather strained in the case of agreements which are intended to apply to government action irrespective of the individual who originally represented the government. It seems more satisfactory to take the position, in keeping with well-established practice, simply that it is legitimate for governments to enter into gentlemen's agreements recognizing that they are without legal effect.

This still leaves us with questions as to the nature of the commitment accepted by the parties in a nonbinding agreement and what precisely is meant by stating that the agreement is without legal effect. We shall begin with the latter point.

It would probably be generally agreed that a nonbinding agreement, however seriously taken by the parties, does not engage their legal responsibility. What this means simply is that noncompliance by a party would not be a ground for a claim for reparation or for judicial remedies. This point, it should be noted, is quite different from stating that the agreement need not be observed or that the parties are free to act as if there were no such agreement. As we shall indicate below, it is possible and reasonable to conclude that states may regard a nonbinding undertaking as controlling even though they reject legal responsibility and sanctions. * * *

A second proposition that would command general (though not unanimous) agreement is that nonbinding agreements are not "governed by international law." Exclusion from the Vienna Convention on the Law of Treaties follows from the conclusion that such agreements are not governed by international law, a requirement laid down in the definition in Article 2(a). * * * The *travaux préparatoires* of the Vienna Convention on the Law of Treaties confirm the conclusion that nonbinding agreements were intended to be excluded from the Convention on the ground that they are not governed by international law.

The conclusion that nonbinding agreements are not governed by international law does not however remove them entirely from having legal implications. Consider the following situations. Let us suppose governments in conformity with a nonbinding agreement follow a course of conduct which results in a new situation. Would a government party to the agreement be precluded from challenging the legality of the course of conduct or the validity of the situation created by it? A concrete case could arise if a government which was a party to a gentlemen's agreement on the distribution of seats in an international body sought to challenge the validity of the election. In a case of this kind, the competent organ might reasonably conclude that the challenging government was subject to estoppel in view of the gentlemen's agreement and the reliance of the parties on that agreement.

Still another kind of legal question may arise in regard to nonbinding agreements. What principles or rules are applicable to issues of interpretation and application of such agreements? As we have already seen, customary law and the Vienna Convention do not "govern" the agreements. But if the parties (or even a third party such as an international organ) seek authoritative guidance on such issues, it would be convenient and reasonable to have recourse to rules and standards generally applicable to treaties and international agreements insofar as their applicability is not at variance with the nonbinding nature of these agreements. For example, questions as to territorial scope, nonretroactivity, application of successive agreements, or criteria for interpretation could be appropriately dealt with by reference to the Vienna Convention even though that Convention does not in terms govern the agreements. * * * It may be useful, however, to indicate what may reasonably be meant by an understanding that an agreement entails a political or moral obligation and what expectations are created by that understanding.

Two aspects may be noted. One is internal in the sense that the commitment of the state is "internalized" as an instruction to its officials to act accordingly. Thus, when a government has entered into a gentlemen's agreement on voting in the United Nations, it is expected that its officials will cast their ballots in conformity with the agreement though no legal sanction is applicable. Or when governments have agreed, as in the Helsinki Act, on economic cooperation or human rights, the understanding and expectation is that national practices will be modified, if necessary, to conform to those understandings. The political commitment implies, and should give rise to, an internal legislative or administrative response. These are often specific and determinate acts.

The second aspect is "external" in the sense that it refers to the reaction of a party to the conduct of another party. The fact that the states have entered into mutual engagements confers an entitlement on each party to make representations to the others on the execution of those engagements. It becomes immaterial whether the conduct in question was previously regarded as entirely discretionary or within the reserved domain of domestic jurisdiction. By entering into an international pact with other states, a party may be presumed to have agreed that the matters covered are no longer exclusively within its concern. When other parties make representations or offer criticism about conduct at variance with the undertakings in the agreement, the idea of a commitment is reinforced, even if it is labelled as political or moral.

* * *

The fact that nonbinding agreements may be terminated more easily than binding treaties should not obscure the role of the agreements which remain operative. De Gaulle is reported to have remarked at the signing of an important agreement between France and Germany that international agreements "are like roses and young girls; they last while they last." As long as they do last, even nonbinding agreements can be authoritative and controlling for the parties. There is no *a priori* reason to assume that the undertakings are illusory because they are not legal. To minimize their value would exemplify the old adage that "the best is the enemy of the good." It would seem wiser to recognize that nonbinding agreements may be attainable when binding treaties are not and to seek to reinforce their moral and political commitments when they serve ends we value.

NOTES

1. *Helsinki Final Act.* Schachter refers to the Helsinki Final Act as an example of a "nonbinding" agreement. The states that endorsed it in 1975 shared that view. See Russell, The Helsinki Declaration: Brobdingnag or Lilliput?, 70 A.J.I.L. 242 (1976). The Helsinki Final Act is reprinted in the Documents Supplement and it may be interesting to examine its terms in light of Schachter's criteria, and also to compare it to admittedly binding treaties covering similar subject matter, such as the International Covenant on Civil and Political Rights.

2. *Evolution of Nonbinding Pledges into Hard(er) Obligations.* Is it possible that an agreement that was "nonbinding" at its inception could attain binding force through later developments? Consider in this regard the evolution of the processes begun at Helsinki in 1975, when the Conference on Security and Co-operation in Europe was initiated and its Final Act was adopted: these processes led some fifteen years later to the establishment of the Organization for Security and Co-operation in Europe, with its complex institutions created in the 1990s and its increasingly "legal" functions. Could such developments alter the normative quality of the original Helsinki Final Act?

3. *Dimensions of Agreement Design.* Kal Raustiala has identified three dimensions of the design of international agreements: (1) legality, meaning the choice between legally binding and non-legally binding accords; (2) substance, meaning the degree of deviation from the status quo that an agreement demands (which may be shallow or deep); and (3) structure, referring to mechanisms for monitoring and enforcement. The trade-offs between these elements can help illuminate the choices involved in negotiating and implementing interstate bargains. Raustiala, Form and Substance in International Agreements, 99 A.J.I.L. 581, 586–91 (2005). See also Guzman, The Design of International Agreements, 16 E.J.I.L. 579 (2005).

C. POLITICAL DECLARATIONS AND CONCERTED ACTS

Governments engage in concerted acts of various kinds that express common understandings and positions but which are not recognized as treaties or customary law. Such acts may be expressed informally, as in a communiqué after an exchange of views. On occasion they are expressed in formal instruments, such as the Final Act of the Helsinki Conference in 1975. Political declarations have been used instead of treaties in processes of settling major disputes. For example, at the end of the Second World

War, the most important understandings relating to territorial disposition and post-war organization were expressed in declarations at the Yalta, Potsdam and Cairo Conferences.

It has been suggested that the so-called purely political instruments may have legal consequences. Schachter considers that as such instruments are official acts of states, they are evidence of the positions taken by states and "it is appropriate to draw inferences that the States concerned have recognized the principles, rules, status and rights acknowledged. This does not mean that 'new law' or a new obligation is created. However, where the points of law are not entirely clear and are disputed the evidence of official positions drawn from these instruments can be significant." Schachter, International Law in Theory and Practice, *supra*, at 129. A non-legal text may also over time become customary law on the basis of state practice and *opinio juris*. That consequence does not depend on the original intent of the parties to the instrument.

What are the implications of non-compliance with a non-legal declaration? Schachter suggests:

> States entering into a non-legal commitment generally view it as a political (or moral) obligation and intend to carry it out in good faith. Other parties and other States concerned have reason to expect such compliance and to rely on it. What we must deduce from this, I submit, is that the political texts which express commitments and positions of one kind or another are governed by the general principle of good faith. Moreover, since good faith is an accepted general principle of international law, it is appropriate and even necessary to apply it in its legal sense.

Id. at 130.

A significant practical consequence of the "good faith" principle is that a party which committed itself in good faith to a course of conduct or to recognition of a legal situation would be estopped from acting inconsistently with its commitment or adopted position when the circumstances showed that other parties reasonably relied on that undertaking or position.

These problems were considered by the Institut de Droit International in 1983. See Reports of 7th Commission (Virally, rapporteur) and Comments of Members. 60–I Ann. de l'Institut de Droit Int. 166–374 (1983) and 60–II Ann. de l'Institut de Droit Int. 117–54. (1984). See also Schachter, "Non–Conventional Concerted Acts" in International Law, Achievements and Prospects 265–69 (Bedjaoui ed. 1991).

SECTION 6.   UNILATERAL ACTS

Although the Vienna Convention on the Law of Treaties applies to agreements "between States" (Article 1)—that is, between two or more of them—unilateral declarations of states can also form the basis for obligations on the plane of international law. The legal consequences of unilateral statements have been considered by the I.C.J. and other international tribunals in several cases.

LEGAL STATUS OF EASTERN GREENLAND
(NORWAY v. DENMARK)

Permanent Court of International Justice, 1933
1933 P.C.I.J. (ser. A/B) No. 53, at 71

[For background on this territorial dispute see discussion at pp. 377–78 in Chapter 5.]

What Denmark desired to obtain from Norway was that the latter should do nothing to obstruct the Danish plans in regard to Greenland. The declaration which the Minister for Foreign Affairs gave on July 22nd, 1919, on behalf of the Norwegian Government, was definitely affirmative: "I told the Danish Minister to-day that the Norwegian Government would not make any difficulty in the settlement of this question".

The Court considers it beyond all dispute that a reply of this nature given by the Minister for Foreign Affairs on behalf of his Government in response to a request by the diplomatic representative of a foreign Power, in regard to a question falling within his province, is binding upon the country to which the Minister belongs.

NUCLEAR TESTS CASE
(AUSTRALIA & NEW ZEALAND v. FRANCE)

International Court of Justice, 1974
1974 I.C.J. 253, 457

[Australia and New Zealand brought applications to the I.C.J. demanding cessation of atmospheric nuclear tests being carried out by France in the South Pacific. While the case was pending, the French government announced that it had completed its series of tests and did not plan more tests. In deciding to dismiss the applications, the Court considered the relevance of the statements by the French authorities.]

43.   It is well recognized that declarations made by way of unilateral acts, concerning legal or factual situations, may have the effect of creating legal obligations. Declarations of this kind may be, and often are, very specific. When it is the intention of the State making the declaration that it should become bound according to its terms, that intention confers on the declaration the character of a legal undertaking, the State being thenceforth legally required to follow a course of conduct consistent with the declaration. An undertaking of this kind, if given publicly, and with an intent to be bound, even though not made within the context of international negotiations, is binding. In these circumstances, nothing in the nature of a *quid pro quo* nor any subsequent acceptance of the declaration, nor even any reply or reaction from other States, is required for the declaration to take effect, since such a requirement would be inconsistent

with the strictly unilateral nature of the juridical act by which the pronouncement by the State was made.

44.   Of course, not all unilateral acts imply obligation; but a State may choose to take up a certain position in relation to a particular matter with the intention of being bound—the intention is to be ascertained by interpretation of the act. When States make statements by which their freedom of action is to be limited, a restrictive interpretation is called for.

45.   With regard to the question of form, it should be observed that this is not a domain in which international law imposes any special or strict requirements. Whether a statement is made orally or in writing makes no essential difference, for such statements made in particular circumstances may create commitments in international law, which does not require that they should be couched in written form. Thus the question of form is not decisive. As the Court said in its Judgment on the preliminary objections in the case concerning the *Temple of Preah Vihear:*

> Where * * * as is generally the case in international law, which places the principal emphasis on the intentions of the parties, the law prescribes no particular form, parties are free to choose what form they please provided their intention clearly results from it. (*ICJ Reports 1961,* p. 31.)

The Court further stated in the same case: " * * * the sole relevant question is whether the language employed in any given declaration does reveal a clear intention * * * " (*ibid.,* p. 32).

46.   One of the basic principles governing the creation and performance of legal obligations, whatever their source, is the principle of good faith. Trust and confidence are inherent in international co-operation, in particular in an age when this co-operation in many fields is becoming increasingly essential. Just as the very rule of *pacta sunt servanda* in the law of treaties is based on good faith, so also is the binding character of an international obligation assumed by unilateral declaration. Thus interested States may take cognizance of unilateral declarations and place confidence in them, and are entitled to require that the obligation thus created be respected.

* * * The Court must however form its own view of the meaning and scope intended by the author of a unilateral declaration which may create a legal obligation, and cannot in this respect be bound by the view expressed by another State which is in no way a party to the text.

* * *

49.   Of the statements by the French Government now before the Court, the most essential are clearly those made by the President of the Republic. There can be no doubt, in view of his functions, that his public communications or statements, oral or written, as Head of State, are in international relations acts of the French State. His statements, and those of members of the French Government acting under his authority, up to the last statement made by the Minister of Defence (of 11 October 1974),

constitute a whole. Thus, in whatever form these statements were expressed, they must be held to constitute an engagement of the State, having regard to their intention and to the circumstances in which they were made.

50. The unilateral statements of the French authorities were made outside the Court, publicly and *erga omnes,* even though the first of them was communicated to the Government of Australia. As was observed above, to have legal effect, there was no need for these statements to be addressed to a particular State, nor was acceptance by any other State required. The general nature and characteristics of these statements are decisive for the evaluation of the legal implications, and it is to the interpretation of the statements that the Court must now proceed. The Court is entitled to presume, at the outset, that these statements were not made *in vacuo,* but in relation to the tests which constitute the very object of the present proceedings, although France has not appeared in the case.

FRONTIER DISPUTE CASE (BURKINA FASO/MALI)

International Court of Justice, 1986
1986 I.C.J. 554

39. The statement of Mali's Head of State on 11 April 1975 was not made during negotiations or talks between the two Parties; at most, it took the form of a unilateral act by the Government of Mali. Such declarations "concerning legal or factual situations" may indeed "have the effect of creating legal obligations" for the State on whose behalf they are made, as the Court observed in the *Nuclear Tests Cases (ICJ Reports 1974,* pp. 267, 472). But the Court also made clear in those cases that it is only "when it is the intention of the State making the declaration that it should become bound according to its terms" that "that intention confers on the declaration the character of a legal undertaking" *(ibid.).* Thus it all depends on the intention of the State in question, and the Court emphasized that it is for the Court to "form its own view of the meaning and scope intended by the author of a unilateral declaration which may create a legal obligation" *(ibid.,* pp. 269, 474). In the case concerning *Military and Paramilitary Activities in and against Nicaragua (Nicaragua v. United States of America, Merits 1986),* the Court examined a communication transmitted by the Junta of National Reconstruction of Nicaragua to the Organization of American States, in which the Junta listed its objectives; but the Court was unable to find anything in that communication "from which it can be inferred that any legal undertaking was intended to exist" *(ICJ Reports 1986,* p. 132, para. 261). The Chamber considers that it has a duty to show even greater caution when it is a question of a unilateral declaration not directed to any particular recipient.

40. In order to assess the intentions of the author of a unilateral act, account must be taken of all the factual circumstances in which the act occurred. For example, in the *Nuclear Tests Cases,* the Court took the view that since the applicant States were not the only ones concerned at

the possible continuance of atmospheric testing by the French Government, that Government's unilateral declarations had "conveyed to the world at large, including the Applicant, its intention effectively to terminate these tests" (*ICJ Reports 1974*, p. 269, para. 51; p. 474, para. 53). In the particular circumstances of those cases, the French Government could not express an intention to be bound otherwise than by unilateral declarations. It is difficult to see how it could have accepted the terms of a negotiated solution with each of the applicants without thereby jeopardizing its contention that its conduct was lawful. The circumstances of the present case are radically different. Here, there was nothing to hinder the Parties from manifesting an intention to accept the binding character of the conclusions of the Organization of African Unity Mediation Commission by the normal method: a formal agreement on the basis of reciprocity. Since no agreement of this kind was concluded between the Parties, the Chamber finds that there are no grounds to interpret the declaration made by Mali's Head of State on 11 April 1975 as a unilateral act with legal implications in regard to the present case.

NOTES

1. *I.L.C. Study.* In 1997 the International Law Commission initiated a study on unilateral acts of states, with a view toward codification and progressive development. In 2006, its working group on that subject recommended a set of "Guiding Principles applicable to unilateral declarations of States capable of creating legal obligations," which in a preambular paragraph specifies its applicability "only to unilateral acts *stricto sensu*, i.e. those taking the form of formal declarations formulated by a State with the intent to produce obligations under international law." Among the principles are:

> 1. Declarations publicly made and manifesting the will to be bound may have the effect of creating legal obligations. When the conditions for this are met, the binding character of such declarations is based on good faith; interested States may then take them into consideration and rely on them; such States are entitled to require that such obligations be respected.

* * *

> 3. To determine the legal effects of such declarations, it is necessary to take account of their content, of all the factual circumstances in which they were made, and of the reactions to which they gave rise.

> 4. A unilateral declaration binds the State internationally only if it is made by an authority vested with the power to do so. By virtue of their functions, heads of State, heads of Government and ministers for foreign affairs have the capacity to formulate such declarations. Other persons representing the State in specified areas may be authorized to bind it, through their declarations, in areas falling within their competence.

* * *

7. A unilateral declaration entails obligations for the formulating State only if it is stated in clear and specific terms. In the case of doubt as to the scope of the obligations resulting from such a declaration, such obligations must be interpreted in a restrictive manner. In interpreting the content of such obligations, weight shall be given first and foremost to the text of the declaration, together with the context and the circumstances in which it was formulated.

8. A unilateral declaration which is in conflict with a peremptory norm of general international law is void.

The Commission grappled with how to distinguish between "legal" acts and those of "political" character: for example, would security assurances given by nuclear-weapons states to non-nuclear-weapons states outside the framework of an international agreement entail any obligation on the plane of international law? The Commission's special rapporteur concluded that declarations made in 1995 by the five nuclear-weapons states parties to the Nuclear Non–Proliferation Treaty were "mainly political statements which are not legally binding upon their authors." U.N. Doc. A/CN.4/557, at 20–21, para. 112 (2005), cited in Matheson, The Fifty–Eighth Session of the International Law Commission, 101 A.J.I.L. 407, 422 n. 65 (2007).

2. *Statements Concerning W.T.O. Commitments.* A dispute settlement panel of the World Trade Organization addressed the legal significance of unilateral statements made by U.S. representatives, in connection with a complaint initiated by the European Union claiming that certain U.S. legislation was incompatible with GATT–W.T.O. commitments. The relevant U.S. administrative authority (the U.S. Trade Representative) had issued statements concerning the official U.S. policy to implement the challenged legislation in a manner consistent with W.T.O. obligations, and had reaffirmed that policy before the panel. The panel said:

7.118 Attributing international legal significance to unilateral statements made by a State should not be done lightly and should be subject to strict conditions. Although the legal effects we are ascribing to the US statements made to the DSB [Dispute Settlement Body] through this Panel are of a more narrow and limited nature and reach compared to other internationally relevant instances in which legal effect was given to unilateral declarations, we have conditioned even these limited effects on the fulfilment of the most stringent criteria. A sovereign State should normally not find itself legally affected on the international plane by the casual statement of any of the numerous representatives speaking on its behalf in today's highly interactive and inter-dependent world [citing Nuclear Test Case, excerpted above, para. 43, and other authorities] nor by a representation made in the heat of legal argument on a State's behalf. This, however, is very far from the case before us.

* * *

7.121 The statements made by the US before this Panel were a reflection of official US policy, intended to express US understanding of its international obligations as incorporated in domestic US law. The statements did not represent a new US policy or undertaking but the bringing of a pre-existing US policy and undertaking made in a domestic setting into an international forum.

7.122 The representations and statements by the representatives of the US appearing before us were solemnly made, in a deliberative manner, for the record, repeated in writing and confirmed in the Panel's second hearing. There was nothing casual about these statements nor were they made in the heat of argument. There was ample opportunity to retract. Rather than retract, the US even sought to deepen its legal commitment in this respect.

7.123 We are satisfied that the representatives appearing before us had full powers to make such legal representations and that they were acting within the authority bestowed on them. * * *

United States—Sections 301–310 of the Trade Act of 1974, Report of the Panel, WTO Doc. WT/DS152/R (1999) (citations omitted).

CHAPTER 5

STATES

■ ■ ■

Subjects of international law include entities and persons capable of possessing international rights and duties under international law and endowed with the capacity to take certain types of action on the international plane, such as concluding treaties or joining an international organization. The term "international legal person" is commonly used in referring to such persons and entities.

States are, of course, the principal examples of international persons. Indeed, at one time the generally held view was that only fully sovereign states could be persons in international law. The realities, however, were more complex and over time many different kinds of entities have been considered as capable of having international rights and duties and the capacity to act on the international plane. Even individuals and corporations or other juridical entities can be persons under or subjects of international law when they are accorded rights, duties, and other aspects of legal personality under customary international law or an international agreement. As in any legal system, not all subjects of international law are identical in their nature or their rights, and one must constantly be aware of the relativity of the concept of international legal person.

The widening of the concept of international legal personality beyond the state is one of the more significant features of contemporary international law. This broadening is particularly evident in the case of public international organizations, supranational entities such as the European Union, and insurgent communities and movements of national liberation. But these developments should not obscure the primary and predominant role of the state as the subject of international law. To quote Wolfgang Friedmann:

> The states are the repositories of legitimated authority over peoples and territories. It is only in terms of state powers, prerogatives, jurisdictional limits and law-making capabilities that territorial limits and jurisdiction, responsibility for official actions, and a host of other questions of coexistence between nations can be determined. It is by virtue of their law-making power and monopoly that states enter into

bilateral and multilateral compacts, that wars can be started or terminated, that individuals can be punished or extradited.

* * *

At present, far from witnessing the gradual absorption of national sovereignties and legal systems in a world legal system and authority, we are faced with an opposite development: the proliferation of sovereignties * * *.

Friedmann, The Changing Structure of International Law 213–14 (1964).

This chapter explores key legal concepts relating to statehood, beginning in Section 1 with traditional and contemporary criteria used for determining whether an entity should be "recognized" as a state. Section 2 considers the relevance of the principle of "self-determination" to the recognition of states, while Section 3 identifies several entities that international law accommodates through special status. Section 4 discusses the separate issue of recognition of governments. Finally, Section 5 considers the legal principles applied for acquiring and delimiting boundaries between states, an issue that remains of considerable importance for contemporary interstate disputes. The difficult legal issues of whether a newly formed state "succeeds" to the rights and obligations of previously existing states, also an issue of considerable importance when states break apart, is addressed in Chapter 19.

SECTION 1. THE DETERMINATION OF STATEHOOD

The term "recognition" is used to describe an "authoritative statement issued by competent foreign policy decision-makers in a country. Through it, those decision-makers signal the willingness of their state to treat with a new state or government or to accept that consequences, either factual or legal, flow from a new situation." Grant, The Recognition of States: Law and Practice in Debate and Evolution xix (1999). This section considers the issue of recognition of states, while Section 4 considers the issue of recognition of governments.

When should an entity be recognized as a "state"? The salience of that question is evident in considering events such as Russia's August 2008 deployment of air and ground forces into the Georgian regions of South Ossetia and Abkhazia, which were thereafter recognized by Russia as independent states. In that instance, Russia's recognition of new states was condemned by the Presidency of the Council of the European Union, the Organization for Security and Cooperation in Europe, the United States, and other nations. In fact, whether an entity should be recognized as a state can arise as a result of extraordinary political changes or circumstances in a variety of situations, such as:

1. Cases involving the break-up of an existing state into a number of states, as occurred in the break-up of the former U.S.S.R., the former Yugoslavia, and Czechoslovakia in the 1990s.

2.   Cases involving devolution or secession by part of a territory of an existing state, such as occurred when Eritrea separated from Ethiopia in 1993 or Kosovo declared independence from Serbia in 2008.

3.   Cases in which foreign control is exercised over the affairs of a state, whether by treaty, unilateral imposition or delegation of authority, such as the United States control over external affairs of the island of Palau in the Pacific Ocean until Palau's independence in 1994.

4.   Cases in which states have merged or formed a union, such as occurred when Germany reunified in 1990 or when Egypt and Syria merged in 1958 to form the United Arab Republic (Syria then seceded from the UAR in 1961 and Egypt ultimately renamed itself Egypt).

5.   Claims by constituent units of a union or federation to the attributes of statehood, such as separatist claims in Quebec.

6.   Territorial or non-territorial communities which have a special international status by virtue of treaty or customary law and which claim state-like attributes of statehood for certain purposes, such as Palestine's status as an observer at the United Nations or Taiwan's membership in certain treaties.

When these circumstances arise, what legal criteria are applied for determining that a particular entity is now a "state" or is entitled to certain attributes of statehood? What are the risks either in allowing entities to readily obtain statehood or in denying statehood to an entity that *de facto* is operating as one? Is this solely a legal question or one that is imbued with political concerns?

A.   THE TRADITIONAL REQUIREMENTS

The standard starting point for legally determining whether an entity qualifies as a "state" is the 1933 Montevideo Convention, particularly Article 1. Although only about twenty Western Hemispheric states joined the Montevideo Convention (including the United States), many states, tribunals, and scholars have regarded its terms as reflecting accepted customary international law, and it has influenced subsequent tribunals (such as the Badinter Commission concerning the former Yugoslavia, discussed below) and scholarship. See Crawford, The Creation of States in International Law 37–95 (2d ed. 2006); Restatement (Third) § 201.

MONTEVIDEO CONVENTION ON THE
RIGHTS AND DUTIES OF STATES

Signed Dec. 26, 1933
49 Stat. 3097, 165 L.N.T.S. 19

Article 1

The state as a person of international law should possess the following qualifications: (*a*) a permanent population; (*b*) a defined territory; (*c*) government; and (*d*) capacity to enter into relations with other states.

Article 2

The federal state shall constitute a sole person in the eyes of international law.

Article 3

The political existence of the state is independent of recognition by the other states. Even before recognition the state has the right to defend its integrity and independence, to provide for its conservation and prosperity, and consequently to organize itself as it sees fit, to legislate upon its interests, administer its services, and to define the jurisdiction and competence of its courts.

The exercise of these rights has no other limitation than the exercise of the rights of other states according to international law.

NOTES

1. *The Benefits of Statehood.* What exactly is gained by being declared a "state" within the meaning of international law? The Restatement (Third) § 206 maintains that the capacities, rights, and duties of states include the following:

(a) sovereignty over its territory and general authority over its nationals;

(b) status as a legal person, with capacity to own, acquire, and transfer property, to make contracts and enter into international agreements, to become a member of international organizations, and to pursue, and be subject to, legal remedies;

(c) capacity to join with other states to make international law, as customary law or by international agreement.

Sovereignty over "territory" should be understood more comprehensively than just control of the "land." With respect to maritime areas, the 1982 U.N. Convention on the Law of the Sea (UNCLOS), Dec. 10, 1982, 1833 U.N.T.S. 3, provides in Article 2:

1. The sovereignty of a coastal State extends, beyond its land territory and internal waters and, in the case of an archipelagic State, its archipelagic waters, to an adjacent belt of sea, described as the territorial sea.

2. This sovereignty extends to the air space over the territorial sea as well as to its bed and subsoil.

As discussed further in Chapter 17, the maximum breadth of the territorial sea is twelve nautical miles, and the coastal state has certain important rights to living and non-living resources in areas even outside its territorial sea.

With respect to airspace over land territory, the Chicago Convention on International Civil Aviation, Dec. 7, 1944, 61 Stat. 1180, 15 U.N.T.S. 295, provides in Article 1 that: "The contracting States recognize that every State has complete and exclusive sovereignty over the airspace above its territory." A state's authority over airspace above its territory was traditionally said to extend *usque ad coelum* (up to the sky). As space became exploitable, efforts have been made to define more precise limits and, specifically, to determine where airspace ends and outer space begins. See Gorove & Kamenetskaya, Tensions in the Development of the Law of Outer Space, in Beyond Confrontation: International Law for the Post–Cold War Era (Damrosch, Danilenko, & Müllerson eds. 1995).

With respect to subsoil resources, a state may have less than absolute authority over resources below the surface of its territory. For example, prevailing authority supports the rule that a state may not draw more from liquid resources below the surface that straddle national boundaries than its proportional share of the common pool. See generally Lagoni, Oil and Gas Deposits across National Frontiers, 73 A.J.I.L. 215 (1979).

2. *Triggering Events on the International Level.* On the international level, the issue of statehood is likely to arise when the entity whose status is in controversy seeks admission or the right of participation in an international body that is open to states alone. Issues of statehood have therefore frequently arisen in connection with applications for membership in the United Nations or its affiliated organizations, or in international conferences convened under its auspices. These issues are normally decided by the international body concerned. Questions of statehood have also arisen in regard to the rights of entities to become parties to multilateral treaties or agreements that are open only to states. In some, but not all, of the cases involving treaties, the issue may be resolved by a collective decision. The collective decision does not entail any obligation for other members to make a formal acknowledgment of recognition, nor to enter into any form of diplomatic or other bilateral relations with the newly admitted state. But such a collective act does indicate the international community's acceptance that the criteria for statehood are satisfied, and does require all member states to treat the new entrant in accordance with the principles embodied in the U.N. Charter. See Mosler, The International Society as a Legal Community, 140 Rec. des Cours 1, 60 (1974–IV); Dugard, Recognition and the United Nations (1987).

3. *Triggering Events in National Policy and Law.* National governments may also have to determine whether an entity is a state for purposes of bilateral relations. Normally this determination is made by the executive branch by recognition of the entity as a state. Such recognition may be explicit and formal or it may be implied in the initiation of diplomatic relations or from conclusion of a bilateral treaty. Questions of statehood also

arise in national courts, particularly with respect to entities which have not been recognized as states by the executive branch. Courts may have to decide whether an unrecognized entity should be regarded as a state for purposes of determining claims to property, issues of nationality, the right to sue, the validity of official acts, immunity from suit, and various other questions linked to statehood.

4. *The Separate Issue of Recognition of a New Government*. The question of whether an entity is or is not a state is distinct from the issue of whether a particular regime or authority is the government of that state. While the existence of an independent government is a requirement of statehood, once a state clearly exists, it is still the case that governments change and conflicting claims of governmental authority may arise. In these cases, foreign governments and international organizations may have to decide which government should be considered the legitimate authority of the state in question. These issues are not the same as those involved in determining statehood and are therefore treated separately in Section 4 below.

5. *Declarative Theory versus Constitutive Theory*. The question of whether an entity is a state and should be so treated has given rise to two opposing theories.

Declarative Theory: One theory is that the existence of a state depends on the facts and on whether those facts meet the criteria of statehood laid down in international law. Accordingly, a state may exist without being recognized by other states. Such recognition is merely "declaratory" of an already existing statehood. The primary function of recognition is to acknowledge the fact of the state's political existence and to declare the recognizing state's willingness to treat the entity as an international person, with the rights and obligations of a state.

Constitutive theory: The opposing position is that the act of recognition by other states itself confers international personality on an entity purporting to be a state. In effect, the other states by their recognition "constitute" or create the new state. On this "constitutive" theory an observer or a court need only look at the acts of recognition (or lack thereof) to decide whether an entity is a state.

The weight of authority and state practice support the declaratory position. This view was adopted in Article 3 of the Montevideo Convention, reprinted above, and repeated in Article 13 of the Charter of the Organization of American States, Apr. 30, 1948, 2 U.S.T. 2416, 119 U.N.T.S. 3, as amended by Protocols of 1967–93. As stated in 1936 by the prominent group of lawyers and academics who form the Institut de Droit International: "The existence of a new State with all the legal consequences attaching to this existence is not affected by the refusal of recognition by one or more states." [1936] 2 Ann. de l'Institut de Droit Int. 300 (translation). Similarly, the Badinter Commission concerning the former Yugoslavia opined that "the existence or disappearance of the State is a question of fact; that the effects of recognition by other States are purely declaratory." Conference on Yugoslavia Arbitration Commission Opinion No. 1, 31 I.L.M. 1494 (1992).

Nevertheless, some distinguished jurists and judicial authorities have supported the constitutive theory. Sir Hersch Lauterpacht, who later served as a judge on the International Court of Justice, adopted the "constitutive" theory, though he also contended that states have an obligation to recognize an entity that meets the qualifications of statehood. Lauterpacht, Recognition in International Law 12–40 (1947).

What legal policy rationales might underlie the existence of both theories? In support of the constitutive theory, it might be noted that, in order to determine whether an entity is a state, it must be ascertained whether it meets the criteria of international law. But such application may call for the determination of difficult questions of fact and law. Is there a government with the capacity to enter into relations with other states? Is it, in that sense, independent? In ascertaining these "facts," especially when they are in dispute, states and international bodies will generally give weight to recognition *vel non* by other states. Consequently, acts of recognition or refusals to recognize may have a significant and, at times, decisive role in determining controversial situations. See Crawford, The Creation of States in International Law 17–26 (2d ed. 2006).

In support of the declaratory theory, it is clear that an entity that *de facto* meets the conditions of statehood cannot, because of the lack of recognition, be denied certain fundamental rights or escape certain fundamental obligations. "Its territory cannot be considered to be no-man's-land; there is no right to overfly without permission; ships flying its flag cannot be considered stateless, and so on." Mugerwa, Subjects of International Law, in Manual of Public International Law 249, 269 (Sørensen ed. 1968). Nor can such a non-recognized entity evade the duties of states under international law. In fact, non-recognized states are often charged with violations of international law and are the object of international claims by the very states refusing recognition. For example, the United States charged North Korea, which it did not recognize as a state, with illegal action when North Korea seized a United States naval vessel, the *Pueblo*, in 1968. See 58 Dep't St. Bull. 196–97 (1968).

For this reason, the theoretical gap between the declaratory and constitutive views may be rather less in practice than in theory. Section 202(1) of the Restatement (Third) asserts that, "a state is not required to accord formal recognition to any other state but is required to treat as a state an entity that meets the requirements of [statehood, listed in] § 201." A state is obligated "not to recognize or treat as a state an entity that has attained the qualifications for statehood as a result of a threat or use of force in violation of the United Nations Charter." Restatement (Third) § 202(2). The Reporters' Notes show that the position reflected in § 202 is closer to the declaratory than the constitutive view, but that the practical differences between the two have diminished:

> Even for the declaratory theory, whether an entity satisfies the requirements for statehood is, as a practical matter, determined by other states. * * * On the other hand, the constitutive theory lost much of its significance when it was accepted that states had the obligation * * * to treat as a state any entity that had the characteristics set forth in § 201. * * * Delays in recognizing or accepting statehood have generally reflected uncertainty as to the viability of the new state, * * * or the view that it was created in violation of international law * * *.

Restatement (Third) § 202, Reporters' Note 1. As Professor Brownlie has written,

> Recognition, *as a public act of state,* is an optional and political act and there is no legal duty in this regard. However, in a deeper sense, if an entity bears the marks of statehood, other states put themselves at risk legally if they ignore the basic obligations of state relations. Few would take the view that the Arab neighbours of Israel can afford to treat her as a non-entity: the responsible United Nations organs and individual states have taken the view that Israel is protected, and bound, by the principles of the United Nations Charter governing the use of force. In this context of state *conduct* there is a duty to accept and apply certain fundamental rules of international law: there is a legal duty to 'recognize' for certain purposes at least, but no duty to make an express, public, and political determination of the question or to declare readiness to enter into diplomatic relations by means of recognition. This latter type of recognition remains political and discretionary. Even recognition is not determinant of diplomatic relations, and absence of diplomatic relations is not in itself non-recognition of the state.

Brownlie, Principles of Public International Law 89–90 (6th ed. 2003) (footnotes omitted); see also Grant, The Recognition of States: Law and Practice in Debate and Evolution 1–45 (1999).

1. Requirement of a Permanent Population and Defined Territory

In 1947, the United Nations approved the partition of the British Mandate of Palestine into two states, one that would be Jewish and the other Arab. The Arab League of States rejected the plan. In May 1948, however, Israel declared its independence and sought admission to the United Nations as a member state. Some states resisted admission of Israel on legal grounds, arguing principally that its territory was not definitively determined since its borders were contested. Philip C. Jessup, at that time the U.S. representative to the Security Council and later a judge on the International Court of Justice, advocated the admission of Israel to the United Nations.

STATEMENT OF U.S. REPRESENTATIVE PHILIP JESSUP TO THE U.N. SECURITY COUNCIL REGARDING THE ADMISSION OF ISRAEL TO THE UNITED NATIONS

U.N. Doc. S/PV.383, at 9–11 (Dec. 2, 1948)

The consideration of the application requires an examination of * * * the question of whether Israel is a State duly qualified for membership. Article 4 of the Charter of the United Nations specifies the following:

"Membership in the United Nations is open to...peace-loving States which accept the obligations contained in the present Charter and, in the judgment of the Organization, are able and willing to carry out these obligations."

* * * My Government considers that the State of Israel meets these Charter requirements.

The first question which may be raised in analyzing Article 4 of the Charter and its applicability to the membership of the State of Israel, is the question of whether Israel is a State, as that term is used in Article 4 of the Charter. It is common knowledge that, while there are traditional definitions of a State in international law, the term has been used in many different ways. We are all aware that, under the traditional definition of a State in international law, all the great writers have pointed to four qualifications: first, there must be a people; second, there must be a territory; third, there must be a government; and, fourth, there must be capacity to enter into relations with other States of the world.

In so far as the question of capacity to enter into relations with other States of the world is concerned, * * * I believe that there would be unanimity that Israel exercises complete independence of judgment and of will in forming and in executing its foreign policy. * * *

When we look at the other classic attributes of a State, we find insistence that it must also have a Government. No one doubts that Israel has a Government. * * *

According to the same classic definition, we are told that a State must have a people and a territory. Nobody questions the fact that the State of Israel has a people. * * *

The argument seems chiefly to arise in connection with territory. One does not find in the general classic treatment of this subject any insistence that the territory of a State must be exactly fixed by definite frontiers. We all know that, historically, many States have begun their existence with their frontiers unsettled. Let me take as one example, my own country, the United States of America. Like the State of Israel in its origin, it had certain territory along the seacoast. It had various indeterminate claims to an extended territory westward. But, in the case of the United States, that land had not even been explored, and no one knew just where the American claims ended and where French and British and Spanish claims began. To the North, the exact delimitation of the frontier with the territories of Great Britain was not settled until many years later. And yet, I maintain that, in the light of history and in the light of the practice and acceptance by other States, the existence of the United States of America was not in question before its final boundaries were determined.

The formulae in the classic treatises somewhat vary, one from the other, but both reason and history demonstrate that the concept of territory does not necessarily include precise delimitation of the boundaries of that territory. The reason for the rule that one of the necessary attributes of a State is that it shall possess territory is that one cannot contemplate a State as a kind of disembodied spirit. Historically, the concept is one of insistence that there must be some portion of the earth's surface which its people inhabit and over which its Government exercises authority. No one can deny that the State of Israel responds to this requirement.

NOTES

1. *Israel's Ascension to Statehood.* In 1949, Israel was admitted to the United Nations as its 59th member. Do you agree with Jessup's arguments? Would similar reasoning apply to the issue of statehood if the governing authorities of Palestine sought admission to the United Nations? For more background, see Brown, The Recognition of Israel, 42 A.J.I.L. 620 (1948).

2. *How Permanent Must Population Be?* The requirement for a permanent population would presumably prevent qualification of Antarctica as a state, as might other factors. See generally Rothwell, The Polar Regions and the Development of International Law (1996). How many people does a "permanent population" imply? Liechtenstein with 34,000 people became a U.N. member state in 1990, as did Nauru with just 14,000 people in 1999. Indeed, the Vatican City, which has been treated as a state (though is not a member of the United Nations), has a population of about 400 citizens and 800 residents. It has entered into treaties that have a specific territorial application to the Vatican City (e.g., telecommunications). The proliferation of very small "mini-states"—Andorra, Kiribati, Marshall Islands, Micronesia, Monaco, Palau, San Marino, Tonga—appears to confirm that no minimum number has been set. See Duursma, Fragmentation and the International Relations of Micro-states (1996).

3. *Is New Nationality Conferred on the Population?* When a new state is established in a territory, the inhabitants generally become nationals of that state, though they may also be allowed to retain a prior nationality. See *Case Concerning the Acquisition of Polish Nationality*, 1923 P.C.I.J. (ser. B) No. 7, at 15. See also Chapter 19 (on succession of states in relation to nationality).

4. *How Large Must the Territory Be?* With regard to territory, no rule prescribes a minimum. Monaco, for example, is only 1.95 square kilometers in size. One might speculate on whether an artificial installation on the sea-bed beyond national jurisdiction could have a territorial basis for a claim of statehood. Indeed, consider the saga of the "Principality of Sealand." During the Second World War, the United Kingdom built a fort on a sandbar six miles off its coast in what was then considered international waters. Abandoned in the mid–1950s, the fort was then occupied in the mid–1960s by persons claiming to have established a sovereign state of Sealand, complete with a constitution, national anthem, currency, and passports. Sealand, however, never gained recognition from the international community. See Menefee, "Republics of the Reefs:" Nation–Building on the Continental Shelf and in the World's Oceans, 25 Cal. W. Int'l L.J. 81, 106–11 (1994–95). Should it have been regarded as a state? Note that Article 60(8) of the 1982 U.N. Convention on the Law of the Sea provides that artificial structures do not possess the status of islands. See Chapter 17.

5. *What if Territory Is Purportedly Annexed by Another State?* A state does not cease to be a state because it is occupied and purportedly annexed by a foreign power. Restatement (Third) § 201, Comment *b*. Thus, Kuwait

remained a state notwithstanding its occupation and putative annexation by
Iraq in 1990–1991. Similarly, the United States never recognized the incorpo
ration of Estonia, Latvia and Lithuania into the U.S.S.R. throughout the Cold
War. Treaties between the United States and those countries remained in
force and their diplomatic representatives were regarded as duly accredited.
When these countries regained their independence in 1991, the United States
simply resumed full diplomatic relations. President Announces Recognition of
Baltic States, Sept. 2, 2 Foreign Pol'y Bull. 33 (Sept.–Oct. 1991).

6. *Must Territory Be Contiguous?* There is no requirement that a state's
territory be connected or contiguous. For example, the territory of the United
States consists of the forty-eight states and District of Columbia, but also
Alaska and Hawaii. Further, U.S. territory includes certain other territories:
American Samoa, Guam, Northern Mariana Islands, Puerto Rico, and the U.S.
Virgin Islands. The United States also comprises a series of minor outlying
islands, atolls, or banks, such as Johnston Atoll and Midway Islands.

2. Requirement of a Government

REPORT OF THE INTERNATIONAL COMMITTEE OF JURISTS ENTRUSTED BY THE COUNCIL OF THE LEAGUE OF NATIONS WITH THE TASK OF GIVING AN ADVISORY OPINION UPON THE LEGAL ASPECTS OF THE AALAND ISLANDS QUESTION

League of Nations O.J., Spec. Supp. 3, at 8–9 (1920)

[A Commission of Jurists appointed by the League of Nations in 1920
to address certain aspects of a dispute concerning the Aaland Islands
considered at what point Finland attained statehood after the civil war of
1917–1918 in that country. The Jurists concluded that Finland did not
attain statehood until an effective government was established. In their
opinion they stated that:]

[F]or a considerable time, the conditions required for the formation of a
sovereign State did not exist.

In the midst of revolution and anarchy, certain elements essential to
the existence of a State, even some elements of fact, were lacking for a
fairly considerable period. Political and social life was disorganised; the
authorities were not strong enough to assert themselves; civil war was
rife; further, the Diet, the legality of which had been disputed by a large
section of the people, had been dispersed by the revolutionary party, and
the Government had been chased from the capital and forcibly prevented
from carrying out its duties; the armed camps and the police were divided
into two opposing forces, and Russian troops, and after a time Germans
also, took part in the civil war * * *.

It is, therefore, difficult to say at what exact date the Finnish
Republic, in the legal sense of the term, actually became a definitely
constituted sovereign State. This certainly did not take place until a stable

political organisation had been created, and until the public authorities had become strong enough to assert themselves throughout the territories of the State without the assistance of foreign troops. It would appear that it was in May 1918, that the civil war ended and that the foreign troops began to leave the country, so that from that time onward it was possible to re-establish order and normal political and social life, little by little.

NOTES

1. *Wielding Effective Power.* The *ad hoc* Arbitration Commission established by the E.C.-sponsored Conference on Yugoslavia (see *infra* this Section at sub-section C) was asked by the Chairman of the Conference, Lord Carrington of the United Kingdom, to give its opinion on whether the Socialist Federal Republic of Yugoslavia continued to exist as a state. In concluding that the S.F.R.Y. was in the process of dissolution, the Commission commented that "in the case of a federal-type State, which embraces communities that possess a degree of autonomy and, moreover, participate in the exercise of political power within the framework of institutions common to the Federation, the existence of the State implies that the federal organs represent the components of the Federation and wield effective power * * *." It then expressed its opinion that the "composition and workings of the essential organs of the Federation, be they the Federal Presidency, the Federal Council, the Council of the Republics and the Provinces, the Federal Executive Council, the Constitutional Court or the Federal Army, no longer meet the criteria of participation and representativeness inherent in a federal State * * *." Conference on Yugoslavia Arbitration Commission Opinion No. 1, 31 I.L.M. 1494, 1495–96 (1992).

2. *Relevance of "Parent" State's Consent.* Should the standard of effective government be less stringent when a territory is granted independence by a former sovereign? No one questioned that the former Belgian Congo (later Zaire and now the Democratic Republic of Congo) was a state when it became independent in 1960 though, like Finland in 1917, it was in a state of civil war and virtual anarchy. The same could be said of Burundi and Rwanda, both granted independence when they were without an effective government. See Higgins, Development of International Law through the Political Organs of the United Nations 20–25 (1963). In contrast, Finland was engaged in a war of secession. Consider the following comment:

> A new State formed by secession from a metropolitan State will have to demonstrate substantial independence, both formal and real, before it will be regarded as definitively created. On the other hand, the independence of an existing State is protected by international law rules against illegal invasion and annexation, so that the State may, even for a considerable time, continue to exist as a legal entity despite lack of effectiveness. But where a new State is formed by grant of power from the previous sovereign * * *, considerations of pre-existing rights are no longer relevant and independence is treated as a predominantly formal criterion.

Crawford, The Criteria for Statehood in International Law, 48 Brit. Y.B.I.L. 93, 120 (1976–77); see also Crawford, The Creation of States in International

Law 55–61 (2d ed. 2006). Can a parent state block other states from recognizing an attempted secession? According to Hyde at 152–53 (footnotes omitted):

> When recognition by foreign States precedes that accorded by the parent State, complaint on the part of the latter is to be anticipated. Nevertheless, the opinion has long prevailed in the United States that the propriety of recognition is not necessarily dependent upon the approval of such State. In harmony with the theory early advocated by Jefferson respecting the recognition of new governments, it has long been the accepted American doctrine that the right to accord recognition depends solely on the circumstance of whether a new State has in fact come into being, and that the test of the existence of that fact is whether the conflict with the parent State has been substantially won.

3. *Relapse.* Once a state has been established, it is generally accepted that the state does not cease to exist when a previously functioning government becomes ineffective or defunct. A case in point is Somalia, the government of which no longer functioned effectively after the 1991 ouster of President Siad Barre by combined Northern and Southern clan-based forces. No state considered Somalia to no longer exist as a state once its government ceased functioning.

3. Requirement of Capacity to Engage in Relations With Other States

Does the requirement that the entity have the capacity to enter into foreign relations mean that it must actually exercise that capacity? In the past, there have been examples of states transferring control over foreign relations to another state. For instance, Liechtenstein transferred control of its foreign relations to Switzerland, but was nevertheless admitted as a party to the Statute of the International Court of Justice, for which only states qualify, and participated in the *Nottebohm Case* (Liechtenstein v. Guatemala), 1955 I.C.J. 4. The establishment of the European Community did not terminate the statehood of the member states or vest the Community with statehood, even though the Community assumed international responsibility for certain matters, such as establishing uniform external tariffs, which were previously controlled by the member states. What purpose, then, does this requirement serve? Does it help distinguish between an entity, such as the United States, that can constitutionally engage in foreign relations and an entity, such as Virginia, that cannot?

"Protectorates" or "protected states," predominantly from the colonial era, involved agreements by local rulers that conferred authority over foreign affairs or other matters on an external state, usually an "imperial power." Although "protectorates" have virtually disappeared as a distinct legal category, small or weak states may still be subject to varying degrees of foreign control of a military, economic, or political character. At one time—especially during the 1950s—foreign control was cited as a ground for excluding applicants from membership in the United Nations. This was clearly bound up with political and ideological factors. In recent decades a large number of newly "independent" states have been admitted without question, although they have often been heavily dependent in actuality on other powers for security and economic viability. The notable exceptions have been those "states" which have been regarded as "illegal" in the sense that their establishment was contrary to the principles of international law, for example, Southern Rhodesia and Transkei (see *infra* Section D).

B. ADDITIONAL CONTEMPORARY REQUIREMENTS?

The European Community and the United States appeared to herald a new approach to the recognition of states in late 1991, in connection with the disintegration of the Union of Soviet Socialist Republics (U.S.S.R.) and the Socialist Federal Republic of Yugoslavia (S.F.R.Y.). In what way does the declaration below go beyond the traditional legal requirements for the establishment of a state? Do you view these criteria as new legal conditions for statehood or as a statement of political conditions imposed by the European Community as the price for their recognition of new states in this particular region of the world? Does it matter if these are legal or political conditions? See also Testimony of Ralph Johnson, Deputy Assistant Secretary of State for European and Canadian Affairs, October 17, 2 Foreign Pol'y Bull. 39, 42 (Nov.–Dec. 1991).

EUROPEAN COMMUNITY DECLARATION ON THE "GUIDELINES ON THE RECOGNITION OF NEW STATES IN EASTERN EUROPE AND IN THE SOVIET UNION"

Issued Dec. 16, 1991
31 I.L.M. 1486 (1992), 4 E.J.I.L. 72 (1993)

In compliance with the European Council's request, Ministers have assessed developments in Eastern Europe and in the Soviet Union with a view to elaborating an approach regarding relations with new states.

In this connection they have adopted the following guidelines on the formal recognition of new states in Eastern Europe and in the Soviet Union:

> "The Community and its Member States confirm their attachment to the principles of the Helsinki Final Act and the Charter of Paris, in particular the principle of self-determination. They affirm their readiness to recognize, subject to the normal standards of international practice and the political realities in each case, those new States which, following the historic changes in the region, have constituted themselves on a democratic basis, have accepted the appropriate international obligations and have committed themselves in good faith to a peaceful process and to negotiations."

Therefore, they adopt a common position on the process of recognition of these new states, which requires:

— respect for the provisions of the Charter of the United Nations and the commitments subscribed to in the Final Act of Helsinki and in the Charter of Paris, especially with regard to the rule of law, democracy and human rights;

— guarantees for the rights of ethnic and national groups and minorities in accordance with the commitments subscribed to in the framework of the CSCE;

— respect for the inviolability of all frontiers which can only be changed by peaceful means and by common agreement;

— acceptance of all relevant commitments with regard to disarmament and nuclear non-proliferation as well as to security and regional stability;

— commitment to settle by agreement, including where appropriate by recourse to arbitration, all questions concerning State succession and regional disputes.

The Community and its Member States will not recognise entities which are the result of aggression. They would take account of the effects of recognition on neighbouring States.

The [commitment] to these principles opens the way to recognition by the Community and its Member States and to the establishment of diplomatic relations. It could be laid down in agreements.

NOTES

1. *Interpreting the Yugoslav Incident.* The E.C. Guidelines appear to go well beyond the traditional qualifications for statehood under customary international law and appear to imply that recognition of statehood must be "earned" by meeting the standards articulated. One commentator has observed as follows:

> This extensive catalog of criteria, far in excess of traditional standards for recognition of statehood, confirms that the Community was not applying general international law in the determination of its position. Although some of the requirements reflected objective criteria that must be fulfilled if there is to be a well-founded claim to statehood, the more specific conditions were hand tailored to fit EC interests.

Weller, The International Response to the Dissolution of the Socialist Federal Republic of Yugoslavia, 86 A.J.I.L. 569, 588 (1992) (footnotes omitted). Do you agree?

2. *U.S. Recognition of Former Soviet Republics.* On December 25, 1991, a week after the Commonwealth of Independent States was formed to replace the former Soviet Union, President George H.W. Bush made the following announcement:

> And so today, based on commitments and assurances given to us by some of these states, concerning nuclear safety, democracy, and free

markets, I am announcing some important steps designed to begin this process.

First, the United States recognizes and welcomes the emergence of a free, independent, and democratic Russia, led by its courageous President, Boris Yeltsin. Our Embassy in Moscow will remain there as our Embassy to Russia. We will support Russia's assumption of the U.S.S.R.'s seat as a Permanent Member of the United Nations Security Council. * * *

Second, the United States also recognizes the independence of Ukraine, Armenia, Kazakhstan, Belarus, and Kirgizstan—all states that have made specific commitments to us. We will move quickly to establish diplomatic relations with these states and build new ties to them. We will sponsor membership in the United Nations for those not already members.

Third, the United States also recognizes today as independent states the remaining six former Soviet Republics—Moldova, Turkmenistan, Azerbaijan, Tajikistan, Georgia, and Uzbekistan. We will establish diplomatic relations with them when we are satisfied that they have made commitments to responsible security policies and democratic principles, as have the other states we recognize today.

President Bush Welcomes Commonwealth of Independent States, Dec. 25, 1992, 2 Foreign Pol'y Bull. 12 (Jan.–Apr. 1992).

C. CASE STUDY: DISSOLUTION OF THE FORMER YUGOSLAVIA

Prior to its dissolution, the former Socialist Federal Republic of Yugoslavia consisted of six republics (Bosnia–Herzegovina, Croatia, Serbia, Slovenia, Macedonia, and Montenegro) and two autonomous regions within Serbia (Kosovo and Vojvodina). These republics and regions each had their own local governments, but a federal government existed for the entire state directed by a collective presidency whose chairmanship rotated among the heads of the republics and autonomous regions.

In late 1990, Slovenia and Croatia proclaimed that federal law would no longer be supreme in their republics and, after conducting referenda in which their peoples voted for independence, both republics declared independence in 1991.Those declarations prompted the Serb-dominated federal armed forces to move against militias in both republics. After Bosnia–Herzegovina and Macedonia also sought independence, the Balkans descended into a brutal armed conflict that lasted until the Dayton Peace Accords in 1995.

The Council of Ministers of the European Community convened a peace conference on Yugoslavia in August 1991, which established an arbitration commission that could be asked for legal advice on issues arising from the break-up of Yugoslavia. The arbitration commission consisted of the Presidents of the Constitutional Courts of Belgium, France, Germany, Italy and Spain. The President of the French Constitutional Court (Conseil Constitutionnel), Judge Robert Badinter, was chosen to act as Chairman, and hence the Arbitration Commission is often referred to as the "Badinter Commission."

Consider the following materials concerning the process by which the states of Bosnia–Herzegovina, Croatia, Macedonia, and Slovenia became recognized. Do these materials help in identifying the conditions under which recognition should be granted? Recall that many efforts by entities to be recognized as a state have failed, including: Tibet (from China), Katanga (Congo), Biafra (Nigeria), Kashmir (India), Tamil Elam (Sri Lanka), Kurdistan (Iraq/Turkey), Chechnya (Russian Federation), and Nagorno–Karabakh (Azerbaijan).

EUROPEAN COMMUNITY DECLARATION ON YUGOSLAVIA AND ON THE GUIDELINES ON THE RECOGNITION OF NEW STATES

Issued Dec. 16, 1991
31 I.L.M. 1485 (1992), 4 E.J.I.L. 73 (1993)

The European Community and its member States discussed the situation in Yugoslavia in the light of their guidelines on the recognition of new states in Eastern Europe and in the Soviet Union. They adopted a common position with regard to the recognition of Yugoslav Republics. In this connection they concluded the following:

The Community and its member States agree to recognise the independence of all the Yugoslav Republics fulfilling all the conditions set out below. The implementation of this decision will take place on January 15, 1992.

They are therefore inviting all Yugoslav Republics to state by 23 December whether:

— they wish to be recognised as independent States;

— they accept the commitments contained in the above-mentioned guidelines;

— they accept the provisions laid down in the draft Convention— especially those in Chapter II on human rights and rights of national or ethnic groups—under consideration by the Conference on Yugoslavia;

— they continue to support

     — the efforts of the Secretary General and the Security Council of the United Nations, and

     — the continuation of the Conference on Yugoslavia.

The applications of those Republics which reply positively will be submitted through the Chair of the Conference to the Arbitration Commission for advice before the implementation date.

In the meantime, the Community and its member States request the UN Secretary General and the UN Security Council to continue their efforts to establish an effective cease-fire and promote a peaceful and negotiated outcome to the conflict. They continue to attach the greatest importance to the early deployment of a UN peace-keeping force referred to in UN Security Council Resolution 724.

The Community and its member States also require a Yugoslav Republic to commit itself, prior to recognition, to adopt constitutional and political guarantees ensuring that it has no territorial claims towards a neighbouring Community State and that it will conduct no hostile propaganda activities versus a neighbouring Community State, including the use of a denomination which implies territorial claims.

CONFERENCE ON YUGOSLAVIA ARBITRATION COMMISSION OPINION NO. 4 ON INTERNATIONAL RECOGNITION OF THE SOCIALIST REPUBLIC OF BOSNIA–HERZEGOVINA BY THE EUROPEAN COMMUNITY AND ITS MEMBER STATES

Issued Jan. 11, 1992
31 I.L.M. 1501 (1992), 4 E.J.I.L. 74 (1993)

In a letter dated 20 December 1991 to the President of the Council of the European Communities, the Minister of Foreign Affairs of the Socialist Republic of Bosnia–Herzegovina asked the Member States of the Community to recognize the Republic.

The Arbitration Commission proceeded to consider this application in accordance with the Declaration on Yugoslavia and the Guidelines on the Recognition of New States in Eastern Europe and in the Soviet Union adopted by the Council on 16 December 1991 and with the rules of procedure adopted by the Arbitration Commission on 22 December.

* * *

Having regard to the information before it, and having heard the Rapporteur, the Arbitration Commission delivers the following opinion:

1. By an instrument adopted separately by the Presidency and the Government of Bosnia–Herzegovina on 20 December 1991 and published in the *Official Journal* of the Republic on 23 December these authorities accepted all the commitments indicated in the Declaration and the Guidelines of 16 December 1991.

In that instrument the authorities in question emphasized that Bosnia–Herzegovina accepted the draft Convention produced by the Hague Conference on 4 November 1991, notably the provisions in Chapter II on human rights and the rights of national or ethnic groups.

By a Decision of 8 January 1992 the Government of the SRBH accepted and undertook to apply the United Nations Charter, the Helsinki Final Act, the Charter of Paris, the Universal Declaration of Human

Rights, the International Covenant on Civil and Political Rights and all other international instruments guaranteeing human rights and freedoms and to abide by the commitments previously entered into by the SFRY concerning disarmament and arms control.

The current Constitution of the SRBH guarantees equal rights for "the nations of Bosnia–Herzegovina—Muslims, Serbs and Croats—and the members of the other nations and ethnic groups living on its territory".

The current Constitution of the SRBH guarantees respect for human rights, and the authorities of Bosnia–Herzegovina have sent the Commission a list of the laws in force giving effect to those principles; they also gave the Commission assurances that the new Constitution now being framed would provide full guarantees for individual human rights and freedoms.

The authorities gave the Commission an assurance that the Republic of Bosnia–Herzegovina had no territorial claims on neighbouring countries and was willing to guarantee their territorial integrity.

They also reaffirmed their support for the peace efforts of the United Nations Secretary–General and Security Council in Yugoslavia and their willingness to continue participating in the Conference on Yugoslavia in a spirit of constructive cooperation.

2.   The Commission also noted that on 24 October 1991 the Assembly of the SRBH adopted a "platform" on future arrangements for the Yugoslav Community. According to this document the SRBH is prepared to become a member of a new Yugoslav Community on two conditions:

(i) the new Community must include Serbia and Croatia at least; and

(ii) a convention must be signed at the same time recognizing the sovereignty of the SRBH within its present borders; the Presidency of the SRBH has informed the Commission that this in no way affects its application for recognition of its sovereignty and independence.

3.   The Commission notes:

(a) that the declarations and undertakings above were given by the Presidency and the Government of the Socialist Republic of Bosnia–Herzegovina, but that the Serbian members of the Presidency did not associate themselves with those declarations and undertakings; and

(b) that under the Constitution of Bosnia–Herzegovina as amended by Amendment LXVII, the citizens exercise their powers through a representative Assembly or by referendum.

In the eyes of the Presidency and the Government of the SRBH the legal basis for the application for recognition is Amendment LX, added to the Constitution on 31 July 1990. This states that the Republic of Bosnia–Herzegovina is a "sovereign democratic State of equal citizens, comprising the peoples of Bosnia–Herzegovina—Muslims, Serbs and Croats—and members of other peoples and other nationalities living on its territory". This statement is essentially the same as Article 1 of the 1974 Constitution and makes no significant change in the law.

Outside the institutional framework of the SRBH, on 10 November 1991 the "Serbian people of Bosnia–Herzegovina" voted in a plebiscite for a "common Yugoslav State". On 21 December 1991 an "Assembly of the Serbian people of Bosnia–Herzegovina" passed a resolution calling for the formation of a "Serbian Republic of Bosnia–Herzegovina" in a federal Yugoslav State if the Muslim and Croat communities of Bosnia–Herzegovina decided to "change their attitude towards Yugoslavia". On 9 January 1992 this Assembly proclaimed the independence of a "Serbian Republic of Bosnia–Herzegovina".

4. In these circumstances the Arbitration Commission is of the opinion that the will of the peoples of Bosnia–Herzegovina to constitute the SRBH as a sovereign and independent State cannot be held to have been fully established.

This assessment could be reviewed if appropriate guarantees were provided by the Republic applying for recognition, possibly by means of a referendum of all the citizens of the SRBH without distinction, carried out under international supervision.

NOTES

1. *E.C. Recognition.* After receiving this opinion of the Badinter Commission, as well as Opinion No. 5 on Croatia, Opinion No. 6 on Macedonia, and Opinion No. 7 on Slovenia, the European Community proceeded to take decisions on recognition of these entities as states:

- *Bosnia–Herzegovina*: In light of the Badinter Commission's finding that no popular will for independence had been established in Bosnia–Herzegovina, that republic proceeded to hold a referendum in March 1992, in which an overwhelming majority opted for independence. The European Community then granted recognition in April 1992.

- *Croatia*: Recognition of Croatia by the European Community was reportedly jeopardized at the last minute by release of Opinion No. 5, which indicated that Croatia had not yet provided all of the constitutional guarantees of the rights of minority groups called for in the E.C. Guidelines on recognition, but had otherwise met the conditions of the Guidelines. Nevertheless, the European Community recognized Croatia in January 1992. Thus, it is unclear that the European Community followed its own guidelines in according recognition in this instance.

- *Macedonia.* Although Macedonia appeared to have met the traditional criteria of statehood for some time, and was found by the Badinter Commission to have met the E.C. guidelines, formal acceptance of its status as a state was deferred because of objections by Greece (a region of which is called Macedonia). It was ultimately admitted to the United

Nations in April 1993 under the "provisional" name of "The Former Yugoslav Republic of Macedonia."

- *Slovenia.* The European Community recognized Slovenia in January 1992.

- *Serbia and Montenegro.* The federal Yugoslav authorities, seeing that continuation of the prior republic was no longer feasible, announced the existence of a "Federal Republic of Yugoslavia" (F.R.Y.) consisting of Serbia and Montenegro. The European Community stated that recognition of this new state was contingent on its compliance with various conditions, including withdrawal of federal military forces from Bosnia–Herzegovina, the facilitation of humanitarian relief, and respect for human rights and the rights of minorities. See Declaration on Bosnia and Herzegovina, U.N. Doc. S/23906, annex (May 12, 1992). After F.R.Y. President Sloboban Milošević lost power in 2000, the F.R.Y. was admitted to the United Nations as a new member state. On the F.R.Y.'s assertion under Milošević that it was the sole successor state to the rights and obligations of the former Yugoslavia, see Chapter 19. In 2003, the F.R.Y. renamed itself as "Serbia and Montenegro." In May 2006, Montenegrins decided by referendum to become independent, leading to the termination of the union of Serbia and Montenegro, and Montenegro's admission to the United Nations.

Thus, what was previously the Socialist Federal Republic of Yugoslavia by 2006 became six separate states: Bosnia–Herzegovina, Croatia, Macedonia, Montenegro, Serbia, and Slovenia. For discussions, see Radan, The Break-up of Yugoslavia and International Law 160–203 (2002); Grant, The Recognition of States: Law and Practice in Debate and Evolution 149–211 (1999).

2. *Intervention in Kosovo.* In 1999, NATO states intervened militarily in Serbia to protect ethnic Albanians living in the autonomous province of Kosovo. In the aftermath of NATO's intervention, the Security Council adopted a resolution (see Chapter 15), reaffirming "the commitment of all Member States to the sovereignty and territorial integrity of the Federal Republic of Yugoslavia"; yet it also required the removal of all F.R.Y. military and police forces from Kosovo, and it endorsed "substantial autonomy and meaningful self-administration for Kosovo," until a political settlement of Kosovo's future status. See S.C. Res. 1244, preamble, para. 11, & annex 2 (June 10, 1999); Symposium: Final Status for Kosovo: Untying the Gordian Knot, 80 Chi. Kent L. Rev. 305 (2005). In 2008, Kosovo declared its independence from Serbia, 47 I.L.M. 467 (2008) and was recognized by more than fifty states. Yet some states, such as Serbia and Russia, dispute Kosovo's statehood and, as of early 2009, it had not been admitted to the United Nations. Further, in October 2008, the General Assembly requested an advisory opinion from the International Court regarding the legality of Kosovo's declaration.

3. *U.S. Recognition.* The United States initially declined to follow the E.C. lead on the ground that the parties to the Yugoslav conflict first had to reach a peaceful settlement through negotiation and with firm protections for minorities. The then-Secretary-General of the United Nations, Javier Pérez de Cuéllar, on the recommendation of his personal envoy Cyrus Vance, had

warned that "any early, selective recognition could widen the present conflict and fuel an explosive situation." Report of the Secretary-General Pursuant to Security Council Resolution 721 (1991), U.N. Doc. S/23280, para. 25 & annex IV (Dec. 11, 1991), approved by the Security Council in S.C. Res. 724 (Dec. 15, 1991). By contrast, the European states hoped that a formal grant of recognition to Croatia would dissuade the Serbian-dominated F.R.Y. from continuing to project armed force across the Serbian-Croatian frontier (by transforming that frontier from an internal to an international boundary). To what extent were legal and political considerations intertwined in these recognition decisions?

Despite its reservations, the United States recognized Bosnia–Herzegovina, Croatia and Slovenia in April 1992. See U.S. Recognition of Former Yugoslav Republics, 3 Dep't St. Dispatch 287 (Apr. 13, 1992). Further, the United States supported Macedonia's admission to the United Nations in 1993 and, in February 2004, the United States announced that it had decided to refer to Macedonia as the "Republic of Macedonia." See 2 Murphy, United States Practice in International Law, 18–19 (2006). In 2000, after the fall of Serb President Milošević, the United States resumed diplomatic relations with the F.R.Y. In August 2006, the United States entered into diplomatic relations with the newly-established state of Montenegro. In 2008, the United States recognized Kosovo as an independent state. See Dep't St. Press Release, Statement by Secretary Condoleezza Rice, U.S. Recognizes Kosovo as an Independent State (Feb. 18, 2008) ("The United States has today formally recognized Kosovo as a sovereign and independent state.").

4. *The Badinter Commission*. Through December 1992, the Badinter Commission issued ten opinions and an interlocutory decision of July 4, 1992, upholding its authority to judge its own competence in the face of a challenge thereto by Serbia and Montenegro. Opinions 1–3 and 8–10 were in response to specific questions formulated by the Chairman of the Peace Conference. Opinions 4–7 considered the applications for international recognition submitted by four of the republics of the former Socialist Federal Republic of Yugoslavia. The interaction between the opinions of the Commission and the political decisions of the E.C. and its member states has been complex. See Radan, The Break-up of Yugoslavia and International Law 204–43 (2002); Terrett, The Dissolution of Yugoslavia and the Badinter Arbitration Commission (2000).

D. PROHIBITIONS ON RECOGNIZING STATEHOOD

A duty *not* to recognize an entity as a new state may be applicable, not just when an entity fails to satisfy relevant criteria for statehood under international law, but also when it has come into existence in violation of fundamental principles of international law. Consider the situation that arose in 1965 with respect to the British colony of Southern Rhodesia, situated north of the Limpopo River (known today as Zimbabwe). Amidst considerable turmoil in decolonization efforts, Southern Rhodesia unilaterally declared itself independent in 1965 under a white-dominated government. Various states were considering whether to recognize this entity as a new state when the Security Council decided to act.

QUESTION CONCERNING THE SITUATION IN SOUTHERN RHODESIA

S.C. Res. 217 (May 6, 1965)

The Security Council,

Deeply concerned about the situation in Southern Rhodesia,

Considering that the illegal authorities in Southern Rhodesia have proclaimed independence and that the Government of the United Kingdom of Great Britain and Northern Ireland, as the administering Power, looks upon this as an act of rebellion,

* * *

1. *Determines* that the situation resulting from the proclamation of independence by the illegal authorities in Southern Rhodesia is extremely grave, that the Government of the United Kingdom of Great Britain and Northern Ireland should put an end to it and that its continuance in time constitutes a threat to international peace and security;

* * *

3. *Condemns* the usurpation of power by a racist settler minority in Southern Rhodesia and regards the declaration of independence by it as having no legal validity;

4. *Calls upon* the Government of the United Kingdom to quell this rebellion of the racist minority;

5. *Further calls upon* the Government of the United Kingdom to take all other appropriate measures which would prove effective in eliminating the authority of the usurpers and in bringing the minority régime in Southern Rhodesia to an immediate end;

6. *Calls upon* all States not to recognize this illegal authority and not to entertain any diplomatic or other relations with it;

7. *Calls upon* the Government of the United Kingdom, as the working of the Constitution of 1961 has broken down, to take immediate measures in order to allow the people of Southern Rhodesia to determine their own future consistent with the objectives of General Assembly resolution 1514(XV);

8. *Calls upon* all States to refrain from any action which would assist and encourage the illegal régime and, in particular, to desist from providing it with arms, equipment and military material, and to do their utmost in order to break all economic relations with Southern Rhodesia, including an embargo on oil and petroleum products;

9. *Calls upon* the Government of the United Kingdom to enforce urgently and with vigour all the measures it has announced, as well as those mentioned in paragraph 8 above;

10. *Calls upon* the Organization of African Unity to do all in its power to assist in the implementation of the present resolution, in conformity with Chapter VIII of the Charter of the United Nations;

11. *Decides* to keep the question under review in order to examine what other measures it may deem it necessary to take.

NOTES

1. *Assessing the Rhodesia Incident.* At the time the above resolution was adopted, Rhodesia would have met the traditional criteria of statehood. Its government was clearly the effective authority over a discrete territory and permanent population, and had capacity to enter into foreign relations. Nonetheless, the Security Council resolution and previous General Assembly resolutions were accepted as definitive and Rhodesia was not recognized as a state by any government or treated as a state by any international organization. Does the decision in regard to Rhodesia confirm that a new requirement of statehood has been introduced—that a new state will not be recognized if it is controlled by a "minority regime" which violates the principle of self-determination? One commentator concluded that a new state must meet the requirement that "it shall not be based upon a systematic denial in its territory of certain civil and political rights, including in particular the right of every citizen to participate in the government of his country, directly or through representatives elected by regular, equal and secret suffrage." Fawcett, Security Council Resolutions on Rhodesia, 41 Brit. Y.B.I.L. 103, 112 (1965–66) (footnotes omitted). Do you agree? How can one justify a requirement for new states that does not apply to existing states? After several years of civil war between the white government and two African guerrilla organizations, the warring factions agreed in the Lancaster House Agreement upon the terms of a constitution for a new state. After U.K.-monitored elections for a new government, the United Kingdom granted Rhodesia independence in 1980, whereupon it became Zimbabwe. See generally Gowlland–Debbas, Collective Responses to Illegal Acts in International Law: United Nations Action in the Question of Southern Rhodesia (1990); Nkala, The United Nations, International Law, and the Rhodesian Independence Crisis (1985).

2. *Rejection of a Putative State Called Transkei.* During the period of apartheid, South Africa sought to establish a new country "Transkei" as a homeland for part of the South African black population. The U.N. General Assembly responded by adopting a resolution asserting both that Transkei's "independence" was a sham and that the creation of Transkei was to consolidate apartheid and perpetuate white minority domination. See G.A. Res. 31/6 (Oct. 26, 1976). The latter point suggests that even if an independent state were created, it would be denied recognition in accordance with United Nations resolutions if its establishment was considered a means to violate basic human rights. Compare this incident with the decisions of the General Assembly and the Security Council calling on states to recognize the

illegality of South Africa's presence in Namibia (South West Africa) and to refrain from any acts and any dealings with South Africa implying recognition of the legality of the presence and administration of South Africa in Namibia. See *Legal Consequences for States of the Continued Presence of South Africa in Namibia (South West Africa) notwithstanding Security Council Resolution 276 (1970)*, Advisory Opinion, 1971 I.C.J. 16.

3. *Rejection of a New State Established by Military Force.* After the Turkish invasion of Cyprus in 1974, a so-called Turkish Republic of Northern Cyprus was established on the northern part of the island several years later, which has not been recognized as a state by any state other than Turkey. The Security Council called upon all states "not to recognize any Cypriot State other than the Republic of Cyprus." S.C. Res. 541, para. 7 (Nov. 18, 1983); S.C. Res. 550 (May 11, 1984). Does the denial of recognition illustrate the general propositions about recognition elaborated in this section?

4. *Using Military Force to Absorb an Existing State.* Under international law states may not recognize a "territorial acquisition resulting from the threat or use of force." Declaration on Principles of International Law concerning Friendly Relations and Co-operation among States in accordance with the Charter of the United Nations, G.A. Res. 2625 (XXV), preamble (Oct. 24, 1970); 65 A.J.I.L. 243, 246–47 (1971). Thus, when following its invasion of Kuwait in August of 1990, Iraq announced a "comprehensive and eternal merger" with Kuwait, the U.N. Security Council unanimously adopted Resolution 662, calling upon "all States, international organizations and specialized agencies not to recognize that annexation, and to refrain from any action or dealing that might be interpreted as indirect recognition of the annexation." S.C. Res. 662 (Aug. 9, 1990).

5. *Weighing the Policy Concerns.* What policies favor or do not favor non-recognition? On the one hand, non-recognition seems a potentially useful means for helping vindicate the law. Lauterpacht has suggested that non-recognition "is the minimum of resistance which an insufficiently organized but law-abiding community offers to illegality; it is a continuous challenge to a legal wrong." Lauterpacht, Recognition in International Law 431 (1947). On the other hand, non-recognition might have the consequence of thwarting the application of law to the non-recognized entity. For instance, in litigation in the United States against the president of the self-proclaimed Bosnian Serb republic in Bosnia–Herzegovina, the Second Circuit observed:

> The customary international law of human rights, such as the proscription of official torture, applies to states without distinction between recognized and unrecognized states. *See Restatement (Third)* §§ 207, 702. It would be anomalous indeed if non-recognition by the United States, which typically reflects disfavor with a foreign regime— sometimes due to human rights abuses—had the perverse effect of shielding officials of the unrecognized regime from liability for those violations of international law norms that apply only to state actors.

> Appellants' allegations entitle them to prove that Karadžić's regime satisfies the criteria for a state, for purposes of those international law violations requiring state action. * * * Moreover, it is likely that the state action concept, where applicable to some violations like "official" torture,

requires merely the semblance of official authority. The inquiry, after all, is whether a person purporting to wield official power has exceeded internationally recognized standards of civilized conduct, not whether statehood in all its formal aspects exists.

Kadic v. Karadžić, 70 F.3d 232, 245 (2d Cir. 1995). Does this highlight how the failure to recognize *de facto* states may make it more difficult to hold them accountable for their actions? See Schoiswohl, Status and (Human Rights) Obligations of Non–Recognized De Facto Regimes in International Law (2004).

SECTION 2. THE PRINCIPLE OF SELF–DETERMINATION OF "PEOPLES"

As some of the materials in Section 1 *supra* suggest, one element in state formation concerns the will of the people in a particular territory to determine whether they should be constituted as a state. What does the concept of "self-determination" mean and is it a legal principle that can be applied in appropriate situations of state formation?

A. THE CONCEPT OF SELF–DETERMINATION

The pedigree of the principle of "self-determination" as an international political idea is often traced to Woodrow Wilson's program for the establishment of peace after World War I, or to Lenin's revolutionary theses published in 1916 (though there are earlier antecedents, going back at least to the core idea of the American and French revolutions that sovereignty belongs to the people). See Cassese, Self-determination of Peoples: A Legal Reappraisal 14–23 (1995). But the Versailles Treaty and related aspects of the peace settlement did not implement a coherent theory of self-determination, nor was there a legal expression of the concept in the Covenant of the League of Nations. As Cassese concludes, "on the whole, self-determination was deemed irrelevant where the people's will was certain to run counter to the victors' geopolitical, economic, and strategic interests." Id. at 25.

Not until the adoption of the U.N. Charter in 1945 was self-determination embraced as a "principle." See U.N. Charter, art. 1(2). In due course, this principle became accepted as an element of customary as well as treaty law. In the context of customary practice, the main application of self-determination in the first half-century of the U.N. Charter period was in the decolonization of non-self-governing territories. A list of criteria for determining non-self-governing territories under Article 11 of the Charter may be found in the Annex to General Assembly Resolution 742 (VIII). G.A. Res. 742 (VIII), annex (Nov. 27, 1953).

Self-determination also has been treated as a principle of international law in many treaty and non-treaty instruments, e.g., the two International Covenants on Human Rights (Article 1 of the International Covenant on Civil and Political Rights and of the International Covenant on

Economic, Social and Cultural Rights) and the U.N. General Assembly Declaration on Principles of International Law concerning Friendly Relations and Co-operation among States in accordance With the Charter of the United Nations, G.A. Res. 2625 (XXV), (Oct. 24, 1970).

Legal issues concerning self-determination have been raised in several cases at the International Court of Justice, including *Legal Consequences for States of the Continued Presence of South Africa in Namibia (South West Africa) notwithstanding Security Council Resolution 276 (1970)*, Advisory Opinion, 1971 I.C.J. 16, 31; *Western Sahara*, Advisory Opinion, 1975 I.C.J. 12, 31–35; and *East Timor* (Portugal v. Australia), 1995 I.C.J. 90. In *Legal Consequences of the Construction of a Wall in the Occupied Palestinian Territory*, Advisory Opinion, 2004 I.C.J. 136, the Court stated:

88. The Court * * * notes that the principle of self-determination of peoples has been enshrined in the United Nations Charter and reaffirmed by the General Assembly in resolution 2625 (XXV) * * *, pursuant to which "Every state has the duty to refrain from any forcible action which deprives peoples referred to [in that resolution] ... of their right to self-determination." Article 1 common to the International Covenant on Economic, Social and Cultural Rights and the International Covenant on Civil and Political Rights reaffirms the right of all peoples to self-determination, and lays upon the States parties the obligation to promote the realization of that right and to respect it, in conformity with the provisions of the United Nations Charter.

The Court would recall that in 1971 it emphasized that current developments in "international law in regard to non-self-governing territories, as enshrined in the Charter of the United Nations, made the principle of self-determination applicable to all [such territories]". The Court went on to state that "These developments leave little doubt that the ultimate objective of the sacred trust" referred to in Article 22, paragraph 1, of the Covenant of the League of Nations "was the self-determination ... of the peoples concerned" (*Legal Consequences for States of the Continued Presence of South Africa in Namibia (South West Africa) notwithstanding Security Council Resolution 276 (1970), Advisory Opinion, I.C.J. Reports*, 1971, p. 31, paras. 52–53). The Court has referred to this principle on a number of occasions in its jurisprudence (*ibid.*; see also *Western Sahara, Advisory Opinion, I.C.J. Reports 1975*, p. 68, para. 162). The Court indeed made it clear that the right of peoples to self-determination is today a right *erga omnes* (see *East Timor (Portugal v. Australia, Judgment, I.C.J. Reports 1995*, p. 102, para. 29).

Legal Consequences of the Construction of a Wall in the Occupied Palestinian Territory, Advisory Opinion, 2004 I.C.J. 136. The Court found that Israel's construction of a barrier enclosing portions of the West Bank with Israel posed a risk of altering the demographic composition of "Occupied

Palestinian Territory," by contributing "to the departure of Palestinian populations from certain areas. That construction ... severely impedes the exercise by the Palestinian people of its right to self-determination, and is therefore a breach of Israel's obligation to respect that right." *Id.* at para. 122. The International Court linked the violation with violations of both ICCPR Article 17(1) ("No one shall be subjected to arbitrary or unlawful interference with his privacy, family, home or correspondence, nor to unlawful attacks on his honour and reputation") and Article 12(1) ("Everyone lawfully within the territory of a State shall, within that territory, have the right to liberty of movement and freedom to choose his residence"). Id. at 128. For essays on the Court's opinion, see Agora: ICJ Advisory Opinion on Construction of a Wall in the Occupied Palestinian Territory, 99 A.J.I.L. 1 (2005).

The principle of self-determination also arose in the opinions of the Badinter Commission on Yugoslavia, *supra* Section 1(C); see Pellet, The Opinions of the Badinter Arbitration Committee: A Second Breath for the Self–Determination of Peoples, 3 E.J.I.L. 178 (1992).

In the eyes of some jurists and judges, the principle of self-determination is not only a binding rule of international law, but even enjoys the status of a peremptory norm (*jus cogens*). For discussion of the legal quality of the self-determination principle, and diverse points of view on the *jus cogens* issue, see Cassese, *supra*, at 133–40; but see Hanauer, The Irrelevance of Self–Determination Law to Ethno-National Conflict: A New Look at the Western Sahara Case, 9 Emory Int'l L. Rev. 133 (1995).

Notwithstanding its treatment in legal documents and decisions, the concept of self-determination remains fraught with uncertainty and stands in apparent tension with other equally prominent principles of international order. If the "right" of self-determination for "peoples" had a fairly well-understood meaning during most of the second half of the 20th century—that is, as a right of the people in non-self-governing territories (i.e., colonies) freely to determine their political status—its application in the post-Cold War period was highly contested. With the winding-down of U.N.-supervised decolonization has come a resurgence of claims of self-determination on the part of ethnic minorities and other groups, which seek to control territory, to exercise autonomy, and ultimately to enjoy all the prerogatives of statehood. Whether such groups qualify as "peoples" entitled to self-determination, what a "right" of self-determination would entail (which need not mean full-fledged statehood), and how such a "right" is to be reconciled with competing principles, are among the most difficult problems for the international political and legal system in the current period. See Crawford, The Creation of States in International Law 107–48 (2d ed. 2006); McWhinney, The United Nations and A New World Order for a New Millennium: Self–Determination, State Succession, and Humanitarian Intervention (2000).

The rhetoric of self-determination has been deployed in attempts to align statehood with "nationalism," that is, with ethnically-based and exclusionary conceptions of community. It is fair to ask whether state-centered concepts of classical international law have contributed to the analytical confusion about self-determination and perhaps to some pernicious interpretations. It is also fair to ask about the trajectory of development of the international law of self-determination, and whether it will be adequate to the needs of the 21st century.

The international instruments referring to a right of self-determination of "peoples" do not make clear whether the right applies outside the decolonization context, and if so, how to define "peoples" entitled to exercise the right. Sir Gerald Fitzmaurice, writing in 1973 after his retirement as a judge of the International Court, insisted that "juridically, the notion of a legal right of self-determination is nonsense, for how can an as yet juridically non-existent entity be the possessor of a legal right?" Fitzmaurice, The Future of Public International Law, in Livre du Centenaire, [1973] Ann. de l'Institut de Droit Int. 233 n. 85. Thomas Franck notes the "incoherence" of the proclaimed right since the U.N. declarations accord the right "to all peoples" but at the same time assert that the right shall not authorize or encourage action which would impair "totally or in part, the territorial integrity or political unity" of states. Franck concludes that for the right of self-determination to be seen as legitimate, the rule must make a persuasive distinction between "peoples" entitled and not entitled to self-determination. Franck, The Power of Legitimacy Among Nations 163–65 (1990); but see Cassese, *supra*, at 327 (terms such as "peoples," even if not formally defined, can be inferred and are "sufficiently clear").

Are the difficulties with a legal norm of self-determination alleviated if the norm is interpreted to comprehend degrees of autonomy and/or political participation within an existing state? Legal writers have endeavored to clarify an analytical distinction between self-determination on the one hand, and separatism or secession on the other. Compare Franck, The Emerging Right to Democratic Governance, 86 A.J.I.L. 46 (1992) (examining "internal" as well as "external" self-determination and asserting that the content of the self-determination norm outside the decolonization context does not imply a right to secede). For discussion of approaches other than separate statehood, see Lapidoth, Autonomy: Flexible Solutions to Ethnic Conflicts (1997); Hannum, Autonomy, Sovereignty and Self–Determination: The Accommodation of Conflicting Rights (rev. ed. 1996); Gottlieb, Nation Against State: A New Approach to Ethnic Conflicts and the Decline of Sovereignty (1993).

B.   THE CASE OF EAST TIMOR

An example of a long-unsettled decolonization is that of East Timor. East Timor had been a non-self-governing territory of Portugal which had not achieved self-determination when, in late 1975, Portuguese authorities withdrew from the territory and the armed forces of Indonesia intervened and occupied it. In Security Council Resolution 384, the Security Council called upon "all States to respect the territorial integrity of East Timor as well as the inalienable right of its people to self-determination"; called upon Indonesia to "withdraw without delay all its forces from the Territory"; and called upon "the Government of Portugal as administering Power to co-operate fully with the United Nations so as to enable the people of East Timor to exercise freely their right to self-determination." S.C. Res. 384 (Dec. 22, 1975). The exhortations for Indonesian withdrawal and respect for the right of self-determination of the people of East Timor were reiterated by the Security Council the following year, and by eight General Assembly resolutions between 1975 and 1982, without effect. The issue remained on the General Assembly's agenda and East Timor was maintained on the U.N. list of non-self-governing territories until after the developments of 1999 (see below).

Proceedings at the International Court of Justice (I.C.J.) were initiated in 1991 by Portugal as administering power for East Timor (a capacity that had never been formally extinguished) against Australia, which had entered into a treaty with Indonesia concerning exploration and exploitation of the continental shelf in the area known as the Timor Gap. Portugal claimed that Australia had breached the principle of self-determination by dealing with Indonesia in relation to resources belonging to East Timor. For jurisdictional reasons (see Chapter 9), Indonesia could not be made a party before the Court without its consent. In 1995, the I.C.J. dismissed Portugal's suit against Australia on the threshold ground that in the absence of Indonesia, the Court could not adjudicate a dispute over the lawfulness of Indonesia's exercise of authority in and on behalf of East Timor. *East Timor* (Portugal v. Australia), 1995 I.C.J. 90. Thus, the Court left unresolved the import of the self-determination principle regarding authority over East Timor's offshore resources.

Though the Court affirmed (paras. 31 and 37) that "for the two Parties" East Timor remained a non-self-governing territory and that its people had the right to self-determination, it declined Portugal's request to give effect to the self-determination principle as against a non-party to the suit, saying (para. 31):

> The Court notes that the argument of Portugal under consideration rests on the premise that the United Nations resolutions, and in particular those of the Security Council, can be read as imposing an obligation on States not to recognize any authority on the part of Indonesia over the Territory and, where the latter is concerned, to deal only with Portugal. The Court is not persuaded, however, that the relevant resolutions went so far.

East Timor (Portugal v. Australia), 1995 I.C.J. 90. Does this dictum purport to decide the substantive meaning of the resolutions, even though the Court had determined that it could not exercise jurisdiction on the merits? Does it imply anything one way or the other about whether self-determination is a right opposable *erga omnes*? Compare this discussion with the discussion of *erga omnes* obligations in Chapter 8 *infra*.

Developments concerning self-determination for East Timor came to a head in 1999, in the aftermath of a domestic political crisis in Indonesia. In May 1999, Portugal and Indonesia asked the U.N. Secretary–General to organize and conduct a "popular consultation" to determine whether the East Timorese people accepted or rejected a special autonomy for East Timor within Indonesia. In June 1999 the U.N. Security Council established a U.N. Mission in East Timor (UNAMET) to carry out this consultation. In a ballot in which about 98% of the registered East Timorese participated, 78.5% of the voters rejected the proposed special autonomy, thereby expressing their wish for independence. Following outbreaks of violence, the Security Council, in Resolution 1264, authorized a multinational force to restore peace and security. S.C. Res. 1264 (Sept. 15, 1999); see Chapter 15. In October 1999, Indonesia formally recognized the results of the popular consultation, and the Security Council, in Resolution 1272, set up a U.N. Transitional Administration in East Timor (UNTAET) to oversee the territory for a temporary period, pending implementation of the separation from Indonesia. S.C. Res. 1272 (Oct. 25, 1999). In May 2002, East Timor was admitted as a new member state of the United Nations, and is now known as Timor-L'Este.

C. THE CASE OF QUEBEC

The controversy over self-determination in relation to separatist aspirations became the subject-matter of an important opinion of the Supreme Court of Canada concerning Quebec:

REFERENCE RE SECESSION OF QUEBEC

Supreme Court of Canada, 1998
[1998] 2 S.C.R. 217 (Can.), 37 I.L.M. 1340 (1998)

[The Governor in Council referred the following three questions for the Supreme Court's advisory opinion:

1. Under the Constitution of Canada, can the National Assembly, legislature or government of Quebec effect the secession of Quebec from Canada unilaterally?

2. Does international law give the National Assembly, legislature or government of Quebec the right to effect the secession of Quebec from Canada unilaterally? In this regard, is there a right to self-determination under international law that would give the National Assembly, legislature or government of Quebec the right to effect the secession of Quebec from Canada unilaterally?

3. In the event of a conflict between domestic and international law on the right of the National Assembly, legislature or government of Quebec to effect the secession of Quebec from Canada unilaterally, which would take precedence in Canada?

After determining the justiciability of the questions, the Supreme Court answered Question 1 in the negative, finding that the constitutional framework would require negotiations addressing "the interests of the federal government, of Quebec and the other provinces, and other participants, as well as the rights of all Canadians both within and outside Quebec," including the rights of minorities (para. 92). It also answered Question 2 in the negative, with a detailed essay on the international law of self-determination excerpted below. In view of the negative answers to both Questions 1 and 2, the answer given to Question 3 was that there was no conflict between domestic and international law to be addressed.]

Question 2

* * *

110.   The argument before the Court on Question 2 has focused largely on determining whether, under international law, a positive legal right to unilateral secession exists in the factual circumstances assumed for the purpose of our response to Question 1. Arguments were also advanced to the effect that, regardless of the existence or non-existence of a positive right to unilateral secession, international law will in the end recognize effective political realities—including the emergence of a new state—as facts. While our response to Question 2 will address considerations raised by this alternative argument of "effectivity", it should first be noted that the existence of a positive legal entitlement is quite different from a prediction that the law will respond after the fact to a then existing political reality. These two concepts examine different points in time. The questions posed to the Court address legal rights in advance of a unilateral act of purported secession. While we touch below on the practice governing the international recognition of emerging states, the Court is as wary of entertaining speculation about the possible future conduct of sovereign states on the international level as it was under Question 1 to speculate about the possible future course of political negotiations among the participants in the Canadian federation. In both cases, the Reference questions are directed only to the *legal* framework within which the political actors discharge their various mandates.

(1) *Secession at International Law*

111.   It is clear that international law does not specifically grant component parts of sovereign states the legal right to secede unilaterally from their "parent" state. This is acknowledged by the experts who provided their opinions on behalf of both the *amicus curiae* and the Attorney General of Canada. Given the lack of specific authorization for unilateral secession, proponents of the existence of such a right at international law are therefore left to attempt to found their argument (i) on the proposition that unilateral secession is not specifically prohibited and that what is not specifically prohibited is inferentially permitted; or (ii) on the implied duty of states to recognize the legitimacy of secession brought about by the exercise of the well-established international law right of "a people" to self-determination.* * *

(a) *Absence of a Specific Prohibition*

112.   International law contains neither a right of unilateral secession nor the explicit denial of such a right, although such a denial is, to some extent, implicit in the exceptional circumstances required for secession to be permitted under the right of a people to self-determination, e.g., the right of secession that arises in the exceptional situation of an oppressed or colonial people, discussed below. As will be seen, international law places great importance on the territorial integrity of nation states and, by and large, leaves the creation of a new state to be determined by the domestic law of the existing state of which the seceding entity presently forms a part (R.Y. Jennings, *The Acquisition of Territory in International Law* (1963), at pp. 8–9). Where, as here, unilateral secession would be incompatible with the domestic Constitution, international law is likely to accept that conclusion subject to the right of peoples to self-determination, a topic to which we now turn.

(b) *The Right of a People to Self-determination*

113.   While international law generally regulates the conduct of nation states, it does, in some specific circumstances, also recognize the "rights" of entities other than nation states—such as the right of a *people* to self-determination.

114.   The existence of the right of a people to self-determination is now so widely recognized in international conventions that the principle has acquired a status beyond "convention" and is considered a general principle of international law (A. Cassese, *Self-determination of peoples: A legal reappraisal* (1995), at pp. 171–72; K. Doehring, "Self–Determination", in B. Simma, ed., *The Charter of the United Nations: A Commentary* (1994), at p. 70).

* * *

117.   This basic principle of self-determination has been carried forward and addressed in so many U.N. conventions and resolutions that, as noted by Doehring, *supra,* at p. 60:

> The sheer number of resolutions concerning the right of self-determination makes their enumeration impossible.

* * *

122.   As will be seen, international law expects that the right to self determination will be exercised by peoples within the framework of existing sovereign states and consistently with the maintenance of the territorial integrity of those states. Where this is not possible, in the exceptional circumstances discussed below, a right of secession may arise.

(i) Defining "Peoples"

123.   International law grants the right to self-determination to "peoples". Accordingly, access to the right requires the threshold step of characterizing as a people the group seeking self-determination. However, as the right to self-determination has developed by virtue of a combination of international agreements and conventions, coupled with state practice,

with little formal elaboration of the definition of "peoples", the result has been that the precise meaning of the term "people" remains somewhat uncertain.

124.   It is clear that "a people" may include only a portion of the population of an existing state. The right to self-determination has developed largely as a human right, and is generally used in documents that simultaneously contain references to "nation" and "state". The juxtaposition of these terms is indicative that the reference to "people" does not necessarily mean the entirety of a state's population. To restrict the definition of the term to the population of existing states would render the granting of a right to self-determination largely duplicative, given the parallel emphasis within the majority of the source documents on the need to protect the territorial integrity of existing states, and would frustrate its remedial purpose.

125.   While much of the Quebec population certainly shares many of the characteristics (such as a common language and culture) that would be considered in determining whether a specific group is a "people", as do other groups within Quebec and/or Canada, it is not necessary to explore this legal characterization to resolve Question 2 appropriately. Similarly, it is not necessary for the Court to determine whether, should a Quebec people exist within the definition of public international law, such a people encompasses the entirety of the provincial population or just a portion thereof. Nor is it necessary to examine the position of the aboriginal population within Quebec. As the following discussion of the scope of the right to self-determination will make clear, whatever be the correct application of the definition of people(s) in this context, their right of self-determination cannot in the present circumstances be said to ground a right to unilateral secession.

(ii) Scope of the Right to Self-determination.

126.   The recognized sources of international law establish that the right to self-determination of a people is normally fulfilled through *internal* self-determination—a people's pursuit of its political, economic, social and cultural development within the framework of an existing state. A right to *external* self-determination (which in this case potentially takes the form of the assertion of a right to unilateral secession) arises in only the most extreme of cases and, even then, under carefully defined circumstances. * * *

127.   The international law principle of self-determination has evolved within a framework of respect for the territorial integrity of existing states. The various international documents that support the existence of a people's right to self-determination also contain parallel statements supportive of the conclusion that the exercise of such a right must be sufficiently limited to prevent threats to an existing state's territorial integrity or the stability of relations between sovereign states.

[The Court then addressed the treatment of territorial integrity in the Friendly Relations Declaration, the Helsinki Final Act, and a variety of other international instruments.]

* * *

130.   * * * There is no necessary incompatibility between the maintenance of the territorial integrity of existing states, including Canada, and the right of a "people" to achieve a full measure of self-determination. A state whose government represents the whole of the people or peoples resident within its territory, on a basis of equality and without discrimination, and respects the principles of self-determination in its own internal arrangements, is entitled to the protection under international law of its territorial integrity.

(iii) Colonial and Oppressed Peoples

131.   Accordingly, the general state of international law with respect to the right to self-determination is that the right operates with the overriding protection granted to the territorial integrity of "parent" states. However, as noted by Cassese, *supra,* at p. 334, there are certain defined contexts within which the right to the self-determination of peoples does allow that right to be exercised "externally", which, in the context of this Reference, would potentially mean secession:

> ... the right to external self-determination, which entails the possibility of choosing (or restoring) independence, has only been bestowed upon two classes of peoples (those under colonial rule or foreign occupation), based upon the assumption that both classes make up entities that are inherently distinct from the colonialist Power and the occupant Power and that their 'territorial integrity', all but destroyed by the colonialist or occupying Power, should be fully restored...

132.   The right of colonial peoples to exercise their right to self-determination by breaking away from the "imperial" power is now undisputed, but is irrelevant to this Reference.

133.   The other clear case where a right to external self-determination accrues is where a people is subject to alien subjugation, domination or exploitation outside a colonial context. This recognition finds its roots in the *Declaration on Friendly Relations:* [quotations from Friendly Relations Declaration omitted].

134.   A number of commentators have further asserted that the right to self-determination may ground a right to unilateral secession in a third circumstance. Although this third circumstance has been described in several ways, the underlying proposition is that, when a people is blocked from the meaningful exercise of its right to self-determination internally, it is entitled, as a last resort, to exercise it by secession. * * *

135.   Clearly, such a circumstance parallels the other two recognized situations in that the ability of a people to exercise its right to self-

determination internally is somehow being totally frustrated. While it remains unclear whether this third proposition actually reflects an established international law standard, it is unnecessary for present purposes to make that determination. Even assuming that the third circumstance is sufficient to create a right to unilateral secession under international law, the current Quebec context cannot be said to approach such a threshold. As stated by the *amicus curiae* [citation omitted]:

[TRANSLATION] 15. The Quebec people is not the victim of attacks on its physical existence or integrity, or of a massive violation of its fundamental rights. The Quebec people is manifestly not, in the opinion of the *amicus curiae,* an oppressed people.

16. For close to 40 of the last 50 years, the Prime Minister of Canada has been a Quebecer. During this period, Quebecers have held from time to time all the most important positions in the federal Cabinet. During the 8 years prior to June 1997, the Prime Minister and the Leader of the Official Opposition in the House of Commons were both Quebecers. At present, the Prime Minister of Canada, the Right Honourable Chief Justice and two other members of the Court, the Chief of Staff of the Canadian Armed Forces and the Canadian ambassador to the United States, not to mention the Deputy Secretary–General of the United Nations, are all Quebecers. * * *

136. The population of Quebec cannot plausibly be said to be denied access to government. Quebecers occupy prominent positions within the government of Canada. Residents of the province freely make political choices and pursue economic, social and cultural development within Quebec, across Canada, and throughout the world. The population of Quebec is equitably represented in legislative, executive and judicial institutions. In short, to reflect the phraseology of the international documents that address the right to self-determination of peoples, Canada is a "sovereign and independent state conducting itself in compliance with the principle of equal rights and self-determination of peoples and thus possessed of a government representing the whole people belonging to the territory without distinction".

* * *

138. In summary, the international law right to self-determination only generates, at best, a right to external self-determination in situations of former colonies; where a people is oppressed, as for example under foreign military occupation; or where a definable group is denied meaningful access to government to pursue their political, economic, social and cultural development. In all three situations, the people in question are entitled to a right to external self-determination because they have been denied the ability to exert internally their right to self-determination. Such exceptional circumstances are manifestly inapplicable to Quebec under existing conditions. Accordingly, neither the population of the province of Quebec, even if characterized in terms of "people" or "peoples", nor its representative institutions, the National Assembly, the

legislature or government of Quebec, possess a right, under international law, to secede unilaterally from Canada.

139.   We would not wish to leave this aspect of our answer to Question 2 without acknowledging the importance of the submissions made to us respecting the rights and concerns of aboriginal peoples in the event of a unilateral secession, as well as the appropriate means of defining the boundaries of a seceding Quebec with particular regard to the northern lands occupied largely by aboriginal peoples. However, the concern of aboriginal peoples is precipitated by the asserted right of Quebec to unilateral secession. In light of our finding that there is no such right applicable to the population of Quebec, either under the Constitution of Canada or at international law, but that on the contrary a clear democratic expression of support for secession would lead under the Constitution to negotiations in which aboriginal interests would be taken into account, it becomes unnecessary to explore further the concerns of the aboriginal peoples in this Reference.

(2) *Recognition of a Factual/Political Reality: the "Effectivity" Principle*

140.   As stated, an argument advanced by the *amicus curiae* on this branch of the Reference was that, while international law may not ground a positive right to unilateral secession in the context of Quebec, international law equally does not prohibit secession and, in fact, international recognition would be conferred on such a political reality if it emerged, for example, via effective control of the territory of what is now the province of Quebec.

141.   It is true that international law may well, depending on the circumstances, adapt to recognize a political and/or factual reality, regardless of the legality of the steps leading to its creation. However, as mentioned at the outset, effectivity, as such, does not have any real applicability to Question 2, which asks whether a *right* to unilateral secession exists.

142.   No one doubts that legal consequences may flow from political facts, and that "sovereignty is a political fact for which no purely legal authority can be constituted ...", H.W.R. Wade, "The Basis of Legal Sovereignty", [1955] *Camb. L.J.* 172, at p. 196. Secession of a province from Canada, if successful in the streets, might well lead to the creation of a new state. Although recognition by other states is not, at least as a matter of theory, necessary to achieve statehood, the viability of a would-be state in the international community depends, as a practical matter, upon recognition by other states. That process of recognition is guided by legal norms. However, international recognition is not alone constitutive of statehood and, critically, does not relate back to the date of secession to serve retroactively as a source of a "legal" right to secede in the first place. Recognition occurs only after a territorial unit has been successful, as a political fact, in achieving secession.

143.   As indicated in responding to Question 1, one of the legal norms which may be recognized by states in granting or withholding recognition of emergent states is the legitimacy of the process by which the *de facto* secession is, or was, being pursued. The process of recognition, once considered to be an exercise of pure sovereign discretion, has come to be associated with legal norms. See, e.g., European Community Declaration on the *Guidelines on the Recognition of New States in Eastern Europe and in the Soviet Union,* 31 I.L.M. 148[5] (1992), at p. 1487. While national interest and perceived political advantage to the recognizing state obviously play an important role, foreign states may also take into account their view as to the existence of a right to self-determination on the part of the population of the putative state, and a counterpart domestic evaluation, namely, an examination of the legality of the secession according to the law of the state from which the territorial unit purports to have seceded. As we indicated in our answer to Question 1, an emergent state that has disregarded legitimate obligations arising out of its previous situation can potentially expect to be hindered by that disregard in achieving international recognition, at least with respect to the timing of that recognition. On the other hand, compliance by the seceding province with such legitimate obligations would weigh in favour of international recognition. The notion that what is not explicitly prohibited is implicitly permitted has little relevance where (as here) international law refers the legality of secession to the domestic law of the seceding state and the law of that state holds unilateral secession to be unconstitutional.

144.   As a court of law, we are ultimately concerned only with legal claims. If the principle of "effectivity" is no more than that "successful revolution begets its own legality" [citation omitted], it necessarily means that legality follows and does not precede the successful revolution. *Ex hypothesi,* the successful revolution took place outside the constitutional framework of the predecessor state, otherwise it would not be characterized as "a revolution". It may be that a unilateral secession by Quebec would eventually be accorded legal status by Canada and other states, and thus give rise to legal consequences; but this does not support the more radical contention that subsequent recognition of a state of affairs brought about by a unilateral declaration of independence could be taken to mean that secession was achieved under colour of a legal right.

* * *

146.   The principle of effectivity * * * proclaims that an illegal act may eventually acquire legal status if, as a matter of empirical fact, it is recognized on the international plane. Our law has long recognized that through a combination of acquiescence and prescription, an illegal act may at some later point be accorded some form of legal status. In the law of property, for example, it is well-known that a squatter on land may ultimately become the owner if the true owner sleeps on his or her right to repossess the land. In this way, a change in the factual circumstances may subsequently be reflected in a change in legal status. It is, however, quite

another matter to suggest that a subsequent condonation of an initially illegal act retroactively creates a legal right to engage in the act in the first place. The broader contention is not supported by the international principle of effectivity or otherwise and must be rejected.

NOTES

1. *Secession as a Last Resort.* The opinion in *Reference re Secession of Quebec* leaves open the possibility that the international law right of self-determination could entail secession as a "last resort" in the case of especially severe oppression that had "totally frustrated" other channels for exercising internal self-determination. For what kinds of situations might unilateral secession be viewed as a legitimate outcome?

2. *International Forums for Litigating the Principle.* In what international forum (or forums) might the content of the international law right to self-determination be adjudicated? Although Article 1 of the International Covenant on Civil and Political Rights affirms a right of self-determination of peoples, the implementing body for the Covenant (the U.N. Human Rights Committee) has not admitted petitions on behalf of groups seeking to vindicate that right, on the theory that the procedure under the Optional Protocol to the Covenant applies only to the rights of individuals and not of groups. See Mikmaq Tribal People v. Canada, Communication No. 205/1986, U.N. Doc. CCPR/C/43/D/205/1986 (Dec. 3, 1991); Lubicon Lake Band v. Canada, Communication No. 167/1984, U.N. Doc. CCPR/C/38/D/167/1984 (Feb. 15, 1984).

3. *Yugoslavia Revisited.* In the 1990s, separatist interpretations of self-determination were asserted by certain sub-groups during the disintegration of the former Yugoslavia. When Croatia and Bosnia–Herzegovina declared independence and achieved international recognition, substantial minority populations within those new states questioned whether they too could invoke self-determination, so that (for example) territories with high concentrations of Serbs might try either to form their own state or to unite with Serbia. Compare Opinion 2 of the Arbitration Commission on Yugoslavia, 31 I.L.M. 1497, 1498 (1992) (rejecting such an interpretation, on the rationale that "the right of self-determination must not involve changes to existing frontiers . . . except where the States concerned agree otherwise"). For discussion and critique, see Craven, The European Community Arbitration Commission on Yugoslavia, 66 Brit. Y.B.I.L. 333 (1995); Frowein, Self–Determination as a Limit to Obligations under International Law, in Modern Law of Self–Determination 241 (Tomuschat ed. 1993).

For example, Serbs in eastern Bosnia–Herzegovina declared the existence of a new state, the Republika Srpska, but that entity did not attain international recognition. See S.C. Res. 787, para. 3 (Nov. 16, 1992). In the 1995 Dayton Peace Agreement, Republika Srpska was acknowledged as one of two "entities" within the state of Bosnia–Herzegovina (the other being the Federation of Bosnia and Herzegovina, comprising the Muslim and Croat communities), and the external boundaries of the state of Bosnia–Herzegovina were left

intact. See General Framework Agreement for Peace in Bosnia and Herzegovina, Dec. 14, 1995, 35 I.L.M. 75 (1996).

4. *Additional Reading.* Do the materials in this section persuade you
that claims of self-determination can be resolved within the discourse of
international law? Is it necessary to rethink the foundations of the system of
international law for a more inclusive approach to such questions? A voluminous literature addresses the claims of various kinds of self-determination
movements and explores alternative approaches (other than statehood) for
ethnic groups, indigenous populations, and other minorities to exercise self-
government and perpetuate their cultures. See Summers, Peoples and International Law: How Nationalism and Self–Determination Shape a Contemporary Law of Nations (2007); Secession and Self–Determination (Macedo &
Buchanan eds. 2003); Knop, Diversity and Self–Determination in International Law (2002) (containing extensive bibliographic references); Raic, Statehood
and the Law of Self–Determination (2002); Castellino, International Law and
Self–Determination: The Interplay of the Politics of Territorial Possession
with Formulations of Post–Colonial National Identity (2000). Other literature
focuses on the unique circumstances of particular claims for self-determination. See, e.g., Sloane, The Changing Face of Recognition in International
Law: A Case Study of Tibet, 16 Emory Int'l L. Rev. 107 (2002).

SECTION 3. ENTITIES WITH SPECIAL STATUS

Our focus in this sub-section is on the practical treatment of certain
entities whose status has provoked recent and important political-legal
controversy. These entities have been accorded a *sui generis* status,
meaning that they are not viewed as traditional states, but as something
different and unique to their particular situation. Does the existence of
these entities suggest that in some circumstances it is not a binary choice
of statehood or non-statehood but, rather, a spectrum of possible sovereign
statuses which international law seeks to accommodate?

A. THE STATE OF THE VATICAN CITY AND THE HOLY SEE

The State of the Vatican City has been treated as a state and has
entered into treaties having a specific territorial application to the Vatican. More generally, the Holy See—the central administration of the
Roman Catholic Church—has engaged in international relations across a
broad range of issues. The Holy See has been admitted as a full member of
such specialized agencies of the United Nations as UNESCO, the World
Health Organization, and the International Labour Organization, which
under their constituent treaties are open only to states. Moreover, the
Holy See has become a party to many of the major multinational conventions which are open to states alone. Diplomats (from many states) are
accredited to the Holy See rather than to the State of Vatican City. See

Crawford, The Creation of States in International Law 221–33 (2d ed. 2006); Araujo, The International Personality and Sovereignty of the Holy See, 50 Cath. U. L. Rev. 291 (2001).

Yet, unlike other states, it has been the position of the Holy See that its international personality is based on its religious and spiritual authority and not its territorial enclave in Rome. The United Nations and other international organizations have taken no decision on that issue (though they use the name Holy See rather than the State of the Vatican City). To acknowledge that international personality rested on the Holy See's religious authority might give rise to similar claims by other religions, an issue that governments are not inclined to welcome. The problem has been avoided because of the ambiguity created by the fact that there is a territory, however small (and however modest its permanent population), which has been recognized by Italy as constituting the State of the Vatican City under the sovereignty of the Holy See. While no distinction is drawn by international organizations between the State of the Vatican City and the Holy See for purposes of membership or adherence to treaties, legal doctrine tends to regard them as two distinct legal persons. Consider the following comment by Hans Kelsen:

> The Head of the Church [i.e. the Holy See] is at the same time the Head of the State of the Vatican City. * * * But the State of the Vatican City, limited to a certain territory, must not be identified with the Church, which is tied to no limited territory. That means the territorial sphere of validity of the State of the Vatican City is limited, as every state territory is, whereas the territorial sphere of validity of the Roman Catholic Church is not limited.

Kelsen, Principles of International Law 252 (2d rev. ed. Tucker ed. 1966). See also Ehler, The Recent Concordats, 104 Rec. des Cours 7 (1961–III).

The Holy See has been an active participant in many international meetings and negotiations, including the 1994 Cairo conference on population, the 1995 Beijing conference on women, and the 1998 Rome conference on the International Criminal Court. Its access to U.N.-sponsored events follows from the status of "Non–Member State Permanent Observer" as it has been designated for U.N. purposes. In recent years, some have questioned whether this status accords a kind of privilege not available to other religions or to other non-governmental entities. On legal aspects of this controversy, see Abdullah, Note, The Holy See at United Nations Conferences: State or Church?, 96 Colum. L. Rev. 1835 (1996).

B. PALESTINE

The "Six–Day War" in 1967 between Israel and its neighbors ended with Israel having seized control of the West Bank from Jordan, the Gaza Strip and Sinai Peninsula from Egypt, and the Golan Heights from Syria. Thereafter, the Palestine Liberation Organization (or P.L.O., which had been established in 1964), became the leading force in seeking the creation of a Palestinian state.

Specific resolutions by the U.N. General Assembly and international conferences accorded observer status to the Palestine Liberation Organization. See G.A. Res. 3237 (XXIX) (Nov. 22, 1974). The United Kingdom representative in opposing the resolution said:

> The United Nations had always been regarded as an organization of sovereign, independent States. Observer status had heretofore been confined to non-Member States and to regional organizations. The PLO was not the government of a State, was not recognized as such by anyone and "does not purport to be one". Yet, under the draft resolution, it was being treated like a Member State except for the right to vote. That situation seemed to bring into question the nature of the United Nations.

11 U.N. Monthly Chron. 36, 39 (Dec. 1974). Despite such views, over time the P.L.O. gained widespread acceptance as the representative of the Palestinian people. See G.A. Res. 3236 (XXIX), at 4 (Nov. 22, 1974) (calling for the invitation of the P.L.O. to participate in all efforts, deliberations and conferences on the Middle East held under U.N. auspices). With General Assembly Resolution 52/250 the P.L.O.'s capacity to participate in General Assembly activities was upgraded to include some privileges ordinarily reserved for states. G.A. Res. 52/250 (July 12, 1998); see Kirgis, Admission of "Palestine" as a Member of a Specialized Agency and Withholding the Payment of Assessments in Response, 84 A.J.I.L. 218 (1990).

In November 1988, the P.L.O. declared Palestine an independent state. See Palestinian Declaration of Independence, 27 I.L.M. 1668 (1988). More than one hundred states have now accorded recognition and full diplomatic status to the P.L.O. Nevertheless, Palestine has not been admitted to the United Nations as a member state, due to the opposition of some key members, such as the United States, who consider that acceptance of Palestinian statehood requires an overall framework in which Israel's security is assured.

In a Declaration of Principles signed in Oslo in September 1993, 32 I.L.M. 1525 (1993), Israel and the P.L.O. agreed on a framework in which to negotiate their differences. In light of a letter from P.L.O. Chairman Yasser Arafat making explicit commitments—*inter alia* that the "P.L.O. recognizes the right of the State of Israel to exist in peace and security"— Prime Minister Yitzhak Rabin of Israel confirmed that "the Government of Israel has decided to recognize the P.L.O. as the representative of the Palestinian people." See Watson, The Oslo Accords International Law and the Israeli–Palestinian Peace Agreements 313 (2000). A transitional period for interim self-government arrangements began with Israel's withdrawal from the Gaza Strip and Jericho area in 1994. In 1994, the Palestinian National Authority was formed as a five-year interim body during which final status negotiations between the two parties were to take place. Technically, the Palestinian Authority is a subsidiary agency of the P.L.O. and it is the P.L.O. that enjoys international recognition as the organiza-

tion representing the Palestinian people. Significant stages in the negotiations were consummated with further agreements in 1995, 36 I.L.M. 551
(1997), and 1998, 37 I.L.M. 1251 (1998), but thereafter the process stalled,
especially with the Palestinian intifada (or rebellion) that commenced in
2000. As noted in the prior section, in an advisory opinion provided to the
U.N. General Assembly in 2004, the International Court of Justice found
that Israel's construction of a barrier that enclosed portions of the West
Bank with Israel violated Palestinian rights of self-determination. *Legal
Consequences of the Construction of a Wall in the Occupied Palestinian
Territory*, Advisory Opinion, 2004 I.C.J. 136.

C. TAIWAN

One Country/Two Systems. The issue of Taiwan has typically been
treated in international law textbooks as a problem of recognition of
governments rather than of statehood. See Section 4 below. The government of the Republic of China (R.O.C.) had authority over both mainland
China and Taiwan prior to the Communist revolution of October 1949. At
that time, however, the government of the People's Republic of China
(P.R.C.) was established on the mainland in Beijing and the R.O.C.
government retreated to the island of Taiwan, where it continued to assert
that it was the legitimate government of all of China. For decades, the
R.O.C. and the P.R.C. each insisted that there was only one China, that
Taiwan was part of China, and that their own government was the only
government of all of China. The two governments vied for international
recognition, for acceptance in international organizations, and for exclusion of the rival government from corresponding prerogatives. During the
1950s, 1960s, and 1970s, their competing and mutually exclusive positions
were intensively debated in legal as well as political terms, under the
international law of recognition of governments.

The practical and political significance of those debates seemed to
wane when the P.R.C. won the right to represent China in the United
Nations in 1971, see G.A. Res. 2758 (XXVI) (Oct. 25, 1971), and when
most major states (by the end of the 1970s) shifted their formal recognition from the R.O.C. to the P.R.C. In the aftermath of that development,
the P.R.C. government has maintained that cross-straits differences have
to be resolved on the basis of a one China policy, but have proposed that
Taiwan could retain a high degree of autonomy after reunification and
could preserve its capitalist economic system. This "one country, two
systems" approach would have some overlaps with the resolution of the
status of Hong Kong, as discussed below.

Sorting out Taiwan's Status. In the meantime, states and international organizations have grappled with how to deal with Taiwan as a *de facto*
entity with considerable economic presence (for example, total U.S.–
Taiwan trade in 2002 was $50.6 billion, making Taiwan the eighth largest
U.S. trading partner), albeit one not recognized as a state. The R.O.C. has
been seeking for some years to gain admission (or readmission) to interna-

tional organizations in parallel to the P.R.C., and has already been participating on its own behalf in some bodies dealing with economic and financial matters. Pragmatic legal solutions to the dilemma of membership in organizations reserved for "states" (such as the United Nations) have been proffered to preserve the aspiration for eventual reunification. Admission of the P.R.C. to the World Trade Organization in December 2001 paralleled admission for Taiwan in January 2002 under the official name of "Separate customs territory of Taiwan, Penghu, Kinmen, and Matsu" (unofficially referred to as "Chinese Taipei"). Similarly, fishing treaties have granted participation not just to states but also to Taiwan as a "fishing entity," by which it receives virtually all the rights and obligations of a state under the fishing regime. See, e.g., Convention on the Conservation and Management of the Highly Migratory Fish Stocks in the Western and Central Pacific Ocean, Sept. 5, 2000, art. 9(2), annex 1, S. Treaty Doc. No. 109–1. For commentary, see Attix, Between the Devil and the Deep Blue Sea: Are Taiwan's Trading Partners Implying Recognition of Taiwanese Statehood?, 25 Cal. W. Int'l L.J. 357 (1995); Crawford, The Creation of States in International Law 198–221 (2d ed. 2006).

Similarly, states have found creative ways to maintain informal bilateral ties with the R.O.C. The United States, for example, formally recognized the P.R.C. with effect from January 1, 1979 (the 1972 Shanghai Communique had prefigured the eventual formal shift). Yet at the same time, the U.S. executive branch and Congress developed a framework for maintaining unofficial relationships with Taiwan, which was elaborated in the 1979 Taiwan Relations Act, 22 U.S.C. 3301 et seq. (2000). Among other things, section 4(c) of that Act provides:

> For all purposes, including actions in any court in the United States, the Congress approves the continuation in force of all treaties and other international agreements, including multilateral conventions, entered into by the United States and the governing authorities on Taiwan recognized by the United States as the Republic of China prior to January 1, 1979, and in force between them on December 31, 1978, unless and until terminated in accordance with law.

Further, the Act provides in section 6(a) that "[p]rograms, transactions, and other relations conducted or carried out by the President or any agency of the United States Government with respect to Taiwan shall, in the manner and to the extent directed by the President, be conducted and carried out by or through * * * [t]he American Institute in Taiwan, a nonprofit corporation * * *." From Taiwan's side, unofficial commercial and cultural relations with the United States are maintained through an unofficial Taiwanese instrumentality, the Taipei Economic and Cultural Representative Office (T.E.C.R.O.), with offices in Taipei and in Washington, D.C.

Looking Ahead. Throughout the 1980s and 1990s, the basic "one China" concept persisted on both sides of the Taiwan straits and continued to set the terms of relationships with third states. In general, the

Taiwan question was understood to entail the aspiration of the people on both sides of the straits for eventual rapprochement and potential reunification. Texts and treatises on international law (including the previous editions of this casebook) avoided the troublesome topic of "self-determination" in relation to Taiwan by observing that the authorities on Taiwan had made no claim of the existence of separate statehood for that entity.

By the end of the 20th century, however, domestic political developments on Taiwan had altered the international calculus. In 1996, the Nationalist (Kuomintang or KMT) government that had ruled the R.O.C. from before the 1949 schism faced its first serious challenge from a political party identified with the cause of Taiwanese independence. The P.R.C. threatened military action if an independence program were to be pursued, and tensions mounted in the period before the March 1996 election when the Nationalist government under President Lee Teng-hui was returned to power for the next four years.

In 2000 a significant change of government on Taiwan took place with the election of President Chen Shui-bian of the Democratic Progressive Party (a party with strong sympathy for Taiwanese independence). A head-on clash with Beijing was deflected by virtue of President Chen's cautious inaugural address, in which he pledged that unless the mainland attacked Taiwan, he would not declare independence or take other overt steps to establish Taiwan's formal independence. See Huang, The Modern Concept of Sovereignty, Statehood, and Recognition: A Case Study of Taiwan, 16 N.Y. Int'l L. Rev. 99 (2003).

In September 2007, the Democratic Progressive Party approved a resolution asserting separate identity from China and called for the enactment of a new constitution for a "normal country." It also called for general use of "Taiwan" as the island's name, without abolishing its formal name, the Republic of China. The Chen administration also pushed for referendums on national defense and on seeking entry to the United Nations in the 2004 and 2008 elections, which failed due to voter turnout below the legally-required threshold of 50% of all registered voters. Moreover, in 2008, the KMT increased its majority in the Legislative Yuan and its nominee Ma Ying-jeou won the presidency, having campaigned on a platform of better ties with the mainland under a policy of "mutual nondenial." As such, the likelihood of Taiwan seeking independence appears to have diminished.

Can Taiwan properly be viewed as a self-determination unit? Some proponents of a separate Taiwanese identity argue that the issue should be viewed in the framework of decolonization. They observe that Taiwan was ceded to Japan by the Treaty of Shimonoseki of 1895 at the conclusion of a war Japan initiated against China, was ruled from Japan through World War II, and was restored to China only with the San Francisco Peace Treaty in 1945. They point out that except for the years from 1945 to 1949, Taiwan and mainland China have had entirely different political and economic systems; there are also ethnic, linguistic, and cultural differences between the populations on the island and the mainland. What relevance should these factors have for Taiwan's status?

For different points of view on Taiwan's situation, see Symposium, Bridging the Taiwan Strait–Problems and Prospects for China's Reunification or Taiwan's Independence, 32 New Eng. L. Rev. 661 (1998); Chiang, State, Sovereignty and Taiwan, 23 Fordham Int'l L.J. 959 (2000); Su, Some Reflections on the One–China Principle, 23 Fordham Int'l L.J. 1169 (2000).

D. HONG KONG AND MACAO

The situations of Hong Kong and Macao have their own peculiar features but in some ways resemble each other. Hong Kong had been a British colony and Macao a Portuguese colony, both leased from China, until their respective returns to China in 1997 and 1999. At the request of the P.R.C., the United Nations determined in 1972 that Hong Kong and Macao were part of Chinese territory occupied respectively by the British and Portuguese authorities, so that their return to China upon the expiration of the British and Portuguese leases would take place outside the framework of U.N. processes for non-self-governing territories. See Cassese, Self-determination of Peoples: A Legal Reappraisal 79–80 (1995).

Prior to reunion with China, and continuing thereafter, they have each enjoyed a measure of international legal personality, in that they have been treated as having capacity to participate on their own behalf in certain multilateral treaty regimes and treaty-based institutions. Notably, before their return to China, both had become members (in their own names) of the General Agreement on Tariffs and Trade and World Trade Organization, under provisions of the GATT/WTO agreements allowing participation by separate customs territories, and both have continued their participation in GATT/WTO arrangements subsequent to reunification with China. Their situation in respect of international human rights treaties has also been treated as functionally equivalent to continuing membership, even though China has not ratified the treaties. A report submitted by the P.R.C. on behalf of Hong Kong under the International Covenant on Civil and Political Rights was accepted and considered by the U.N. Human Rights Committee in November 1999. See U.N. Doc. CCPR/C/HKSAR/99/1 (June 16, 1999); see also Chan, State Succession to Human Rights Treaties: Hong Kong and the International Covenant on Civil and Political Rights, 45 I.C.L.Q. 928 (1996).

Certain aspects of the post-unification status of Hong Kong and Macao are governed by the terms negotiated with China by the United Kingdom and Portugal, respectively. For example, the Joint Declaration on the Question of Hong Kong (United Kingdom–China), Sept. 26, 23 I.L.M. 1366, 1371 (1984), provides in Article 3(2) that after restoration to China the territory is to "enjoy a high degree of autonomy, except in foreign and defence affairs, which are the responsibilities of the Central People's Government." In accordance with the Joint Declaration, Hong

Kong has been designated a "Special Administrative Region" pursuant to the P.R.C. Constitution, with its own Basic Law and its own Court of Final Appeal. The Basic Law provides that Hong Kong will maintain its distinct political, economic, and legal systems for at least fifty years. See Crawford, The Creation of States in International Law 244–54 (2d ed. 2006).

Sorting out the relationship between China and Hong Kong or Macao has involved some tensions. For example, in 1999, Hong Kong's Court of Final Appeal considered a Hong Kong ordinance regulating immigration, which raised delicate constitutional questions concerning the relationship of Hong Kong law to the mainland authorities. See *Ng Ka Ling v. Director of Immigration* (Hong Kong), 38 I.L.M. 551 (C.F.A. 1999). For discussion of the controversy surrounding the Court's decision and subsequent developments, as well as other aspects of the relationship, see Mushkat, One Country, Two International Legal Personalities: The Case of Hong Kong (1997); Sun, International Legal Personality of the Hong Kong Special Administrative Region, 7 Chinese J. Int'l L. 339 (2008).

U.S. policy toward Hong Kong is reflected in, *inter alia*, 22 U.S.C. 5712–13 and 5722 (2000), which express the sense of the U.S. Congress that the United States "should respect Hong Kong's status as a separate customs territory" and "should treat Hong Kong as a territory which is fully autonomous from the People's Republic of China with respect to economic and trade matters," while allowing the President to suspend U.S. laws with respect to Hong Kong if he "determines that Hong Kong is not sufficiently autonomous to justify treatment under a particular law of the United States." In *Cheung v. United States*, 213 F.3d 82 (2d Cir. 2000), the court of appeals gave effect to an extradition agreement between the United States and the Hong Kong Special Administrative Region, which had been approved by the U.S. Senate as a treaty in October 1997, after Hong Kong's reversion to China.

E. OTHER TYPES OF *SUI GENERIS* ENTITIES

Certain other types of entities that are not states (or not generally recognized as states), or whose status is disputed or unresolved, may nonetheless enjoy attributes of international personality, at least for certain purposes. Some such entities may satisfy most of the traditional criteria for statehood—a defined territory with a population under control of a government—but their capacity to engage in independent external relations may be qualified or questionable. Others may lack one or more of the "objective" criteria, such as a given territorial base. Yet some such entities participate in at least some forms of international treaties, have been (or could be) received as participants in certain international organizations, and engage in other state-like functions. By the same token, national liberation movements speaking on behalf of populations without statehood also can have international personality. See Lissitzyn, Territorial Entities Other than Independent States in the Law of Treaties, 125 Rec. des Cours 5, 9–15, 81–82 (1968–III).

Self-governing Colonies. Although colonies were not generally considered to have international personality, they were allowed to become parties to many multilateral treaties. The Covenant of the League allowed a "fully self-governing * * * Dominion or Colony" to become a member of the League. League of Nations Covenant art. 1, para. 2. India did so when its foreign affairs were, in law and in fact, under British control. Before independence in 1947, India became a party to other treaties which, by their terms, were open only to states, such as the Chicago Convention on Civil Aviation. India was an original member of the United Nations and of the specialized agencies before independence. The Philippine Commonwealth was in much the same position.

League Mandates, U.N. Trusteeships. The Mandate system was established at the end of World War I by the Allied and Associated Powers under Article 22 of the Covenant of the League of Nations. There were in all 15 mandated territories, which had been relinquished by Germany and the Ottoman Empire. Those in the Middle East eventually became independent states, and the others in the Pacific and Africa (except for South West Africa) were transferred after World War II to the U.N. trusteeship system, which was established under Chapter XII of the U.N. Charter. The U.N. trusteeship system had the same general aims as the Mandate system—namely, to promote the well-being of the people and their progressive development towards self-government or independence. U.N. Charter art. 76(b).

Trust and mandated territories were administered by an administering authority or mandatory under agreements which provided for supervision by the United Nations Trusteeship Council (see U.N. Charter Chapter XIII), or, in the case of the mandates, a League of Nations Permanent Mandates Commission. These territories did not become part of the territory of the administering power, nor did the inhabitants acquire the nationality of the administering state. Sovereignty was considered to be vested in the people of the territory, but exercised, within strict limits of the agreements, by the administering power. See Crawford, The Creation of States in International Law 565–601, 741–45 (2d ed. 2006).

For example, the islands of Micronesia formerly comprised the Trust Territory of the Pacific Islands (Micronesia) established by the United Nations after World War II, with the United States as the administering authority. Negotiations between the United States and the islands' indigenous peoples resulted in a decision by the Marianas Islands not to seek independence, but to forge closer ties with the United States by entering into a commonwealth status in 1975. By contrast, in the 1970s the Marshall Islands, the Federated States of Micronesia, and Palau decided to enter into free association with the United States. Under the compacts of free association, the associated states were self-governing and had the capacity to conduct foreign affairs, including the capacity to enter into international agreements. The Marshall Islands and Federated States of

Micronesia became members of the United Nations in 1991 and Palau in 1994.

The U.N. Trusteeship Council suspended operation in November 1994 after the independence of Palau, the last remaining U.N. trust territory. By a resolution adopted in May 1994, the Council amended its rules of procedure to drop the obligation to meet annually and agreed to meet as occasion required. Although the mandate and trust systems have disappeared, the principles of international accountability and surveillance used in the mandate and trusteeship arrangements may have application in the future. Problems of collapse of governance within existing states has led periodically to suggestions for possible revival of something like a trusteeship system, for temporary conservatorship of "failed states" or governance by international administrators. See Gordon, Some Legal Problems with Trusteeship, 28 Cornell Int'l L.J. 301 (1995); Richardson, "Failed States," Self–Determination, and Preventive Diplomacy: Colonialist Nostalgia and Democratic Expectations, 10 Temp. Int'l & Comp. L.J. 1 (1996); Fox, Humanitarian Occupation (2008).

Non–Self–Governing Territories. Although the process of decolonization has in the great majority of cases resulted in the creation of fully independent states, some territories assumed the status of non-self-governing territories on the way to full independence, and a few continue to retain that status even today. This status is captured in Chapter XI of the U.N. Charter (Articles 73–74). Typically, a non-self-governing territory elects to combine internal independence with continued dependence upon another state in matters of foreign affairs and defense. Examples of states that have passed through the status of non-self-governing territory to become independent states are the Bahamas, Dominica, Malta, and Sierra Leone, which were administered by the United Kingdom. As of early 2009, the remaining non-self-governing territories are: American Samoa, Anguilla, Bermuda, the British Virgin Islands, the Cayman Islands, the Falkland Islands, Gibraltar, Guam, Montserrat, New Caledonia, the Pitcairn Islands, St. Helena, Tokelau, the Turks and Caicos Islands, the U.S. Virgin Islands, and Western Sahara. See Crawford, The Creation of States in International Law 602–47, 746–56 (2d ed. 2006).

National Liberation Movements as Representatives of Peoples. An especially controversial aspect of international involvement in the exercise of self-determination has been granting national liberation movements access to international fora, particularly the United Nations and international conferences of states. The General Assembly adopted as a general criterion in respect of such invitations that full participation as observers should be accorded to representatives of movements recognized by the Organization of African Unity. G.A. Res. 3280 (XXIX) (Dec. 10, 1974); G.A. Res. 31/30 (Nov. 29 1976). On this basis, African liberation movements have participated in U.N. bodies, in the specialized agencies and in international conferences on multilateral treaties convened by the United

Nations. They also participated in the Diplomatic Conference on Humanitarian Law in Armed Conflicts.

Cassese has identified two bases for elevating a liberation movement to the rank of international legal subject: first, that its goals fall within the scope of the principle of self-determination (i.e., that the movement is fighting a colonial power, foreign occupier, or racist regime, with the aim of acquiring effective control over a population in a given territory), and second, that the movement is "a legitimate representative of the oppressed people," by virtue of having broad-based support among those it claims to represent. It is the attitudes of states and organizations that determine whether to accord recognition as international legal subjects to such movements (and to withhold comparable recognition from insurgencies with other kinds of objectives or without a representative base). Cassese, *supra*, at 166–69 (1995).

SECTION 4. RECOGNITION OF GOVERNMENTS

A. CRITERIA FOR RECOGNIZING GOVERNMENTS

Recognition of a state is not the same as recognition of its government, although they often go together in the case of new states. Within existing states, governments come and go through standard processes, and normally the changes raise no question of recognition by other states. Yet in some circumstances, the issue of foreign recognition of a government will arise, such as when an existing government is toppled in a military coup, a rebel insurgency defeats the military forces of an existing government, or an existing government refuses to allow a democratically elected opposition to assume control. For example, in August 2008, army commanders in Mauritania ousted and arrested that country's democratically elected president, an act widely condemned in the international community, including by the African Union, the European Union, and the United States. Often such extraordinary circumstances will result in two competing factions: (1) a *de facto* government that is in fact controlling all or most of the country; and (2) a *de jure* government that has a legitimate claim to governance but is either in exile or controls only a portion of the country.

When these extraordinary circumstances occur, foreign governments must decide which entity, if any, they will regard as the government of the state. Are there legal standards upon which that decision should be based? Should it be based on which entity objectively controls the territory of the state? On which entity can be said to genuinely represent the people of that state? Whatever criteria are used, do you regard them as *legal* criteria or as elements of case-by-case political decisions?

MEMORANDUM FROM THE SECRETARY-GENERAL TO THE PRESIDENT OF THE SECURITY COUNCIL ON THE LEGAL ASPECTS OF THE PROBLEM OF REPRESENTATION IN THE UNITED NATIONS

U.N. Doc. S/1466 (Mar. 9, 1950)

The Chinese case is unique in the history of the United Nations, not because it involves a revolutionary change of government, but because it is the first in which two rival governments exist. It is quite possible that such a situation will occur again in the future and it is highly desirable to see what principle can be followed in choosing between the rivals. It has been demonstrated that the principle of numerical preponderance of recognition is inappropriate and legally incorrect. Is any other principle possible?

It is submitted that the proper principle can be derived by analogy from Article 4 of the Charter. This Article requires that an applicant for membership must be able and willing to carry out the obligations of membership. The obligations of membership can be carried out only by governments which in fact possess the power to do so. Where a revolutionary government presents itself as representing a State, in rivalry to an existing government, the question at issue should be which of these two governments in fact is in a position to employ the resources and direct the people of the State in fulfillment of the obligations of membership. In essence, this means an inquiry as to whether the new government exercises effective authority within the territory of the State and is habitually obeyed by the bulk of the population.

If so, it would seem to be appropriate for the United Nations organs, through their collective action, to accord it the right to represent the State in the Organization, even though individual Members of the Organization refuse, and may continue to refuse, to accord it recognition as the lawful government for reasons which are valid under their national policies.

CONFERENCE ON SECURITY AND COOPERATION IN EUROPE (CSCE), DOCUMENT OF THE MOSCOW MEETING ON THE HUMAN DIMENSION

Issued Oct. 3, 1991
30 I.L.M. 1670 (1991)

(17) The participating States:

(17.1) —   condemn unreservedly forces which seek to take power from a representative government of a participating State against the will of the people as expressed in free and fair elections and contrary to justly established constitutional order;

(17.2) —   will support vigorously, in accordance with the Charter of the United Nations, in case of overthrow or attempted overthrow of a legitimately elected government of a participating State by

undemocratic means, the legitimate organs of that State upholding human rights, democracy and the rule of law, recognizing
their common commitment to countering any attempt to curb
these basic values;

(17.3) —   recognize the need to make further peaceful efforts concerning
human rights, democracy and the rule of law within the context
of security and cooperation in Europe, individually and collectively, to make democratic advances irreversible * * * .

ACEVEDO, THE HAITIAN CRISIS AND THE OAS RESPONSE: A TEST OF EFFECTIVENESS IN PROTECTING DEMOCRACY

Enforcing Restraint: Collective Intervention in Internal Conflicts
119–20, 123, 132–33 (Damrosch ed. 1993) (footnotes omitted)

In February 1991, Father Jean–Bertrand Aristide took office as the
first president in the history of Haiti who had won a free and fair election.
He carried with him the hopes of his supporters—an overwhelming
majority of Haiti's desperately poor people—for an end to decades of
abusive authoritarian rule and the beginning of a new era founded on
principles of democracy and social justice.

Less than eight months later, on September 30, those hopes were
dashed when President Aristide was overthrown in a military coup whose
perpetrators defied not only the will of the Haitian majority but also a
commitment to representative democracy undertaken on a hemisphere-
wide basis through the Organization of American States (OAS). In fact,
observers from the OAS, the United Nations, and nongovernmental organizations had monitored the election that resulted in Aristide's victory.
Thus the international community had established a baseline of expectations both legitimizing Aristide's government and supporting its continuation.

* * *

The [OAS's] concern for the effective exercise of representative democracy took a quantum leap with approval in [June] 1991 of the
Santiago Commitment to Democracy and the Renewal of the Inter–
American System and a resolution on representative democracy. The
latter calls for an automatic meeting of the OAS Permanent Council

... in the event of any occurrences giving rise to the sudden or
irregular interruption of the democratic political institutional process
or of the legitimate exercise of power by the democratically elected
government in any of the Organization's member states, in order,
within the framework of the Charter, [to convene an urgent meeting].

It further states that the purpose of any such meeting should be "to look
into the events collectively and adopt any decisions deemed appropriate, in
accordance with the Charter and international law."

Less than four months after their approval, the new procedures would be put to their first test, when the constitutional president of Haiti was forced from office and expelled from the country.

* * *

Immediately after the coup, the OAS Permanent Council held an emergency meeting on September 30 and condemned the events that occurred in Haiti. The Council demanded adherence to the constitution and respect for the government legitimately established through the free expression of the popular will.

The ad hoc Meeting of Consultation of Ministers of Foreign Affairs, which the Permanent Council convoked in response to the situation created by the coup, condemned the disruption of the democratic process in Haiti, calling it a violation of the Haitian people's right to self-determination. The ministers demanded "full restoration of the rule of law and of the constitutional regime, and the immediate reinstatement of President Jean–Bertrand Aristide in the exercise of his legitimate authority."

The resolution the ministers of foreign affairs adopted also provided that the Organization would recognize as legitimate only representatives designated by the constitutional government of President Aristide * * *. Furthermore, the resolution recommended action to bring about the diplomatic isolation of those who held de facto power in Haiti, and the suspension, by all states, of their economic, financial, and commercial ties with Haiti, except aid for strictly humanitarian purposes. * * *

When the de facto government of Haiti refused to comply with the OAS request that President Aristide be immediately reinstated, the Meeting of Consultation passed another resolution on October 8, 1991, which strongly condemned the use of violence and military coercion, as well as the decision to illegally replace the constitutional president of Haiti. The ministers also declared that "no government that may result from this illegal situation" would be accepted and that no representative of such a government would be recognized. * * *

On October [11], 1991, the U.N. General Assembly "strongly condemn[ed] both the illegal replacement of the constitutional President of Haiti and the use of violence, military coercion and the violation of human rights" in Haiti, and urged U.N. member states "to consider the adoption of measures in keeping with those agreed on by the Organization of American States."

[Thereafter, various diplomatic initiatives were pursued, including the conclusion in 1993 of an agreement signed at Governors Island in New York by Aristide and the military leader of the coup, General Raoul Cédras. The Governors Island Agreement provided for the restoration of Aristide to power, the stepping aside of and amnesty for those who undertook the coup, and the deployment to Haiti of U.N. forces (UNMIH) to assist in the transition. Cédras, however, failed to comply with the agreement. The U.N. Security Council adopted a set of compulsory economic sanctions against Haiti, S.C. Res. 841 (June 16, 1993), and then adopted a resolution authorizing "Member States to form a multinational force under unified command and control and, in this framework, to use all necessary means to facilitate the departure from Haiti of the military leadership, consistent with the Governors Island Agreement, the prompt return of the legitimately elected President and the restoration of the legitimate authorities of the Government of Haiti * * * ". S.C. Res. 940 (July 31, 1994). With U.S. forces on the verge of invading the island, the coup leaders agreed in 1994 to relinquish power, and Aristide returned to Haiti to serve as its president.]

MURPHY, DEMOCRATIC LEGITIMACY AND THE RECOGNITION OF STATES AND GOVERNMENTS

48 I.C.L.Q. 545, 566–79 (1999) (footnotes omitted)

The central (and often determinative) issue for a State when deciding whether to recognise a newly formed government has been whether the new government is in "effective control" of its State (sometimes referred to as the "*de facto* control test"). "Effective control" has largely been measured by the degree to which the government commands the obedience of the people within the State. Although in a given case there may be extremely complicated facts concerning what factions control what portions of a territory, the "effective control" test is a relatively simple one, and allows States to proceed pragmatically in their relations with the new government.

The decision by States to recognise a new government, however, has not always been dictated simply by whether the new government passes the effective control test. For instance, capital-exporting States, such as the United States, at one time found relevant whether the new government had declared its willingness to honour the international obligations of its predecessor, including debt obligations, before granting recognition, even if the new government was effectively in control of its State. Further, States often refused to recognise a government's authority over territory that the government had acquired through aggression. And, * * * historically, States have also found relevant the political nature of the new government, including the degree to which it is democratic.

* * *

B.   Past Practice

* * * [State] practice concerning recognition of governments at times has concerned itself with issues of democratic governance. This is particularly apparent in the recognition practice in Europe as democracies emerged there and US recognition practice with respect to democracies that emerged in the Western Hemisphere.

European monarchies in the late seventeenth and eighteenth centuries made it their policy not to recognise democratic revolutionary governments, because such governments represented a threat to the status quo. Initially prompted by the French Revolution, this reactionary policy was one of the driving purposes of the Holy Alliance after the Congress of Vienna in 1815.

Over time, monarchical views fell into disfavour, displaced by Kantian notions of republican government, and this had an effect on the manner in which at least democratic States regarded other States. In the United States Thomas Jefferson declared: "It accords with our principles to acknowledge any Government to be rightful which is formed by the will of the nation, substantially declared." Yet, for Jefferson, the "will of the nation" was not necessarily expressed through democracy; he accepted that States may engage in foreign relations through a monarchy. Consequently, State practice during this period, including US practice, regarded "the will of the people" as present simply by a population's tacit acquiescence in a government in effective control of a State.

The first part of the twentieth century did not see radical inroads for notions of democracy in the practice of recognising governments, although exceptions did occur. However, as in many areas of his foreign policy, US President Woodrow Wilson injected some notions of democracy into US recognition practice. The Mexican Revolution, which began in 1911, pitted urban middle classes and agrarians, led by Francisco Madero, against the country's wealth[y] elite. Madero succeeded in ousting Mexico's dictator, Porfirio Diaz, but the Mexican military, led by General Victoriano Huerta, staged a coup d'état and executed Madero. While the European powers recognised the new government of Huerta, Wilson was appalled and refused to do so, not only imposing economic sanctions but ultimately occupying Veracruz with military forces. Wilson's support allowed the revolutionary forces to gain strength. Huerta was forced from power in 1914 and the revolution resumed its course. In 1917 Venustiano Carranza was installed as president under a new constitution, which was built upon agrarian, land, church and oil reforms of the Mexican revolution. In that regard, it is important to note that US and British firms at this time controlled 90 per cent of the Mexico oil industry and virtually all of Mexico's railroads, yet Wilson eschewed recognition of a military regime whose control of the country offered security for those investments in favour of a radical revolution, explaining: "I am willing to get anything for an American that money and enterprise can obtain, except the suppression of the rights of other men."

Wilson's distaste for military suppression of the constitutional democracies that had emerged in Latin and South America led him to endorse the 1907 Tobar Doctrine, named for Ecuador's foreign minister Carlos Tobar. Under the Tobar Doctrine, States of the Western Hemisphere should deny recognition to governments that come to power pursuant to non-constitutional means. Wilson applied the doctrine when considering recognition of new governments in the Dominican Republic, Ecuador, Haiti, Cuba, Portugal and the Soviet Union.

However, the Tobar Doctrine proved difficult to maintain in practice; by definition, the issue of recognition of a new government arises only in situations where non-constitutional change has occurred, and in those situations the new regime establishes a new constitution that purports to (and may even in terms of democracy) legitimise its existence. Consequently, Wilson's approach did not have an enduring effect on US government practice or that of other States. In the famous 1923 *Tinoco Arbitration* US Chief Justice (and former President) William Howard Taft found that international obligations incurred by a non-recognised government that had assumed power unconstitutionally were nevertheless binding on its successor, an acknowledgement that the existence of such governments could not be denied by other States.

During the Cold War era, notions of democracy in recognition practice gained special importance for many governments in the West. Having overcome the onslaught of fascism that prompted the Second World War, the foreign policy of Western States was built upon expanding liberal democracies as a bulwark against the new threat, the spread of communism. To that end, the Federal Republic of Germany, Italy and Japan were provided with extensive assistance in establishing democratic governments, as were South Korea and South Vietnam. Conversely, the West sought to isolate, often through a practice of non-recognition, communist governments, such as those in China, North Korea and North Vietnam. The United States even backed this up, at times, with military intervention, such as occurred against the purported communist subversion in the Dominican Republic in 1965 and in Grenada in 1983. It made no difference that these communist-oriented governments exercised extensive, sometimes complete, control over the population of their State. Western policy, however, was often more "anti-communist" than it was "pro-democratic", in that many anti-communist regimes qualified for support regardless of their democratic pedigree (for example, the nationalist government of China, holed up on the island of Taiwan, held no elections throughout the decades it was recognised by the West as the legitimate government of China). The most extreme version of Western attitudes is found in the Reagan Doctrine, named for US President Ronald Reagan, which favoured support for insurgencies seeking to establish a democratic government against a non-democratic regime.

While some Western States advanced these notions of democracy in their recognition practice, most other States (and in particular non-democratic States, such as the Soviet Union and China and their allied States) rejected such notions. Soviet efforts to crush democratic movements in Hungary in 1956 and Czechoslovakia in 1968 culminated in the articulation of the Brezhnev Doctrine, named for Soviet President Leonid Brezhnev, which denied the legitimacy of any government that ousted a "socialist" (i.e. communist) government. The refusal to accept Western notions of democracy meant that recognition practice at international organisations (e.g. the practice of the UN Credentials Committee), and international law more generally, declined to adopt democracy as a linch-pin of governmental legitimacy. Indeed, dozens of non-democratic governments were fully represented at the various conferences that spawned the human rights treaties now pointed to as evidencing an emerging right of democratic governance.

C. Contemporary Practice

As has been fully documented elsewhere, the international community in recent years has been significantly involved in ending civil conflict within States through a process of national reconciliation that includes UN-monitored elections. Once elections occur, recognition of the new government by other States is virtually automatic.

However, as is the case regarding recognition of States, the international community does not refuse to recognise governments simply by virtue of their being non-democratic. China is the premier example of a state whose non-democratic, communist government is fully recognised within the international community, to the point of its representatives participating not just in the work of the United Nations generally but also as a permanent member of the Security Council. Yet there are dozens of other non-democratic States that are also generally recognised by the international community—mostly in Africa and the Middle East—and that participate fully in the work of international organisations. Even the United States, which in recent years has emphasised the importance of democracy in its foreign policy, recognises and maintains diplomatic relations with several non-democratic States. Understandably, the many non-democratic governments that continue to exist globally do not conduct their recognition practice so as to disfavour non-democratic States.

The continuing recognition of non-democratic governments by democratic governments cannot be explained as vestiges of history anomalously "grandfathered in" amid contemporary pro-democratic practice. Consider, for instance, the case of China. From its assumption of effective control of the Chinese mainland in 1949 until 1979, the Beijing-based communist government was not generally recognised as the government of China outside the communist bloc States. Rather, the Taiwan-based (also non-democratic) nationalist government was recognised by most States as the government of China. General recognition of the Beijing-based government occurred only * * * when representatives of the communist Chinese government were (at the expense of the now de-recognised Taiwan authorities) permitted to participate in the work of the United Nations on behalf of China. Thus, the international community has in recent years affirmatively recognised the non-democratic government in Beijing as the legitimate government of China.

Even more recently, the international community fully accepted the transfer of governance of the democratically governed Hong Kong from the democratic United Kingdom to non-democratic China on 1 July 1997. On its first day in power, the Beijing-appointed legislature voted to restrict public demonstrations, prompting activists to take to the streets demanding free and fair legislative elections immediately, and within days established a new electoral system that was expected to limit sharply the ability to elect pro-democracy candidates.

China is not the only example of contemporary recognition of non-democratic governments. After its reunification of Vietnam in July 1976, the communist government of the Socialist Republic of Vietnam gradually gained widespread global recognition, although it experienced some set-backs when it invaded Cambodia in 1978. * * *

In short, in determining whether to recognise another government, States do not find the democratic quality of the government as decisive; other factors are taken into consideration as well. The stated reason for recognising the government may be that the transition to democracy is better achieved by engaging in relations with the non-democratic government, rather than isolating it. Indeed, the willingness to recognise a non-democratic government is not necessarily detrimental to the best interests of its people; respectable arguments are made by respectable commentators that a democratic form of government is not the best form for some States depending on their stage of economic and political development. At the same time, such recognition may be for non-altruistic reasons, such as seeking trade opportunities.

Actions by a non-democratic government against the flowering of democracy also do not trigger non-recognition of that government. Chinese treatment of dissidents seeking democratic change, including the treatment of student protestors in Tianenman Square, has not led to non-recognition of the Chinese government. More recently, the violent crushing of pro-democracy demonstrations in Kenya in July 1997 led to no significant reaction by the international community in terms of non-recognition.

US efforts to direct sanctions against the non-democratic government of Cuba through the Helms–Burton Act was roundly condemned by the international community as an effort by the United States to dictate its foreign policy to other States. Yet that foreign policy, on its face, was an effort to pressure a non-democratic government by inhibiting ''trafficking'' in property owned by US nationals that was confiscated by the government, *until such time as the government transitioned toward democracy*. * * *

* * *

If there is an emphasis on democratic legitimacy in the recognition of governments, it arises primarily in situations where a democratic government is internally overthrown by non-democratic (often military) authorities. * * * Haiti is an important potential precedent for an emerging norm of democratic governance. The 1990 election of President Aristide was usurped by Haitian military and police authorities in 1991, but, despite the complete control of the new regime, the international community rallied around Aristide, refusing to recognise the legitimacy of the *de facto* government in Haiti, and instead gradually increasing sanctions until Aristide was restored to power in 1994. Arguably, this is the first step in the creation of a new international legal norm of non-recognition of governments that overthrow democratic governments. Similar co-ordinated action by States, albeit on a much less dramatic scale, has occurred since that time, such as the reaction to the threat to democracy in Sao Tome and Principe in August 1995, in Niger in January 1996 and in Paraguay in April 1996. The 1991 Moscow Meeting of the Conference on the Human Dimension of the CSCE issued a statement affirming that participating States "will support vigorously, in accordance with the Charter of the United Nations, in case of overthrow or attempted overthrow of a legitimately elected government of a participating State by undemocratic means, the legitimate organs of that State upholding human rights, democracy and the rule of law".

However, it is difficult to see that the international community has taken the second step of crystallising this notion as a legal norm, or is even over time moving toward such a legal norm. Some situations that might help support the emergenc[e] of such a norm are clouded by the complexity of their circumstances; often the reaction of the international community is in the nature of a withdrawal of economic benefits, or perhaps the imposition of economic sanctions, but not a refusal to recognise the new government. Rather than isolate the *de facto* government through a comprehensive process of non-recognition, often the reaction is to maintain diplomatic relations with the new government, but with a policy that seeks to promote re-establishment of democratic rule.

Consider the case of Cambodia. Hun Sen's Cambodian People's Party ran Cambodia as a communist one-party State throughout the 1980s. In 1993 elections were held in Cambodia under UN supervision, resulting in a coalition government, headed by First Prime Minister Norodom Ranariddh (the son of the head of State, King Norodom Sihanouk) and Second Prime Minister Hun Sen. In July 1997 Prince Ranariddh was deposed by Hun Sen, who then appointed Ung Huot as First Prime Minister. The initial reaction by the international community to the coup was negative, but also somewhat muted. In September 1997 the UN Credentials Committee refused to accept credentials signed by King Sihanouk (presenting a delegation headed by Hun Sen and Ung Huot), but also refused to accept the credentials of Prince Ranariddh (in exile in France, presenting a delegation headed by himself). On the one hand, most donor States suspended non-humanitarian aid, the World Bank pulled back from starting new projects, and the Association of South East Asian Nations (ASEAN) suspended Cambodia's application for admission. On the other hand, States did not impose comprehensive economic sanctions and continued to maintain diplomatic relations with the new government through their embassies in Phnom Penh. The Hun Sen regime allowed internationally monitored elections in July 1998, but the regime's victory was the product of its control over the election infrastructure, the national media and local administration.

Consider also the recent situation in West Africa with respect to Nigeria, Sierra Leone and Liberia. A several-year process of transition to civilian rule in Nigeria was to culminate in the election of a civilian president in June 1993. The election was held and it appeared that Chief M. K. O. Abiola won, but before the formal results could be announced the existing military-backed government annulled the election. By November the military's strong man, General Sani Abacha, formally assumed control of the country, and proceeded to engage in significant human rights abuses, including executions of dissidents. Exactly one year after the elections were annulled, General Abacha placed the apparent winner, Chief Abiola, in a "detention" that would last until his death. In response to this military suppression of democracy, however, most States did not sever diplomatic relations with the Nigerian government or refuse to recognise the Abacha government. The United States terminated most economic and military aid to Nigeria, but other than withdrawing its military attaché from the US Embassy in Abuja, it took no steps to downgrade diplomatic relations with the new government. In 1995 Nigeria was suspended from the 54–nation British Commonwealth, but was not expelled, nor did the Commonwealth impose comprehensive economic sanctions let alone threaten intervention. Why a different result from that in Haiti? Nigeria has a population of 100 million, is a major oil exporter globally, and has an enormous army capable not only of defending Nigeria but also of projecting considerable force throughout the region. As is the case of the treatment of China * * *, one might say that practicalities in recognition practice at times trump principle.

In May 1997 Sierra Leone's army ousted the democratically elected President, Ahmad Tejan Kabbah. The Organisation of African Unity Council of (Foreign) Ministers condemned the coup and called on all African countries, and the international community at large, to refrain from recognising the new regime. However, the primary means by which the international community assisted the ousted government was through an intervention led by none other than the non-democratic, military regime of Nigeria. Nigeria's motivation for intervening appears to lie less in its attraction to democracy, and more in either its desire for stability in Western Africa (achievable through either democratic or non-democratic governments, depending on the government) or, worse, its effort to extend Nigerian dominance throughout the region.

That desire to dominate may be seen in a similar Nigerian-led intervention in Liberia in 1990. That intervention checked the forces of Charles Taylor, who had ousted the non-democratic regime of Samuel Doe and seized control of the vast majority of Liberia. While the intervention probably prevented widespread human rights atrocities by Taylor's forces in Monrovia, it could not definitively end the Liberian civil war. Seven years and 150,000 lives later, the exhausted competing factions submitted to internationally monitored elections. Ironically, with 85 per cent of the people voting, Taylor was elected president with 75 per cent of the vote and his party achieved a majority in Liberia's parliament. In situations such as these, the international community as a whole appears to favour the maintenance or establishment of a democratic government, but the fundamental motivations of the most relevant actor(s) are far less clear.

Thus, the precedent for recognition practice in situations involving the ouster of democratic governments in Cambodia and in West Africa were far more equivocal than in Haiti. * * *

The failure of the international community to deny recognition to authoritarian governments that suppress democracy is particularly significant given that the international community can act when it so chooses. In this sense, Haiti helps disprove the existence of an emerging norm of non-recognition of non-democratic governments, for similar action could be repeated elsewhere but is not. At the same time, the international community has denied recognition to advance values other than democracy, most notably to punish transnational uses of force, whether or not the victim State is democratic. To that end, the Security Council called upon States not to recognise any regime set up by Iraq, which invaded and *de facto* controlled non-democratic Kuwait from August 1990 to January 1991. Similarly, to punish Serbian aggression against Croatia and Bosnia, the Security Council ordered States to reduce the level of their staff at diplomatic missions and consular posts in Serbia and Montenegro, to prevent persons of those States from participating in international sporting events, and to suspend scientific and technical co-operation and cultural exchanges and visits with those States. These instances of non-recognition (or at least diplomatic isolation) were triggered by an effort to suppress armed conflict; similar non-recognition by the Security Council or by regional organisations apparently is not uniformly triggered by the simple ouster of a democratic government by a non-democratic one, notwithstanding the reaction with respect to Haiti.

NOTES

1. *The "Effective Control Test."* The Secretary–General's 1950 memorandum is an expression of support for the "effective control" test for recognizing a government. Do you find the reasons in support of that approach persuasive? When the General Assembly considered the question of criteria for choosing between rival governments, the majority of governments rejected adoption of an "effective control" test. Instead it recommended that, "whenever more than one authority claims to be the government entitled to represent a Member State in the United Nations, and this question becomes a subject of controversy in the United Nations, the question should be considered in the light of the Purposes and Principles of the Charter and the circumstances of each case." G.A. Res. 396 (V) (Dec. 14, 1950). This resolution no doubt was influenced by the attitude toward the communist government in Beijing (the People's Republic of China or P.R.C.), which effectively controlled the vast majority of China, but which was engaged in armed hostilities against

the U.N. Forces in Korea. At the same time, the reluctance to adopt a purely factual test likely reflects a conception of "recognition" as involving value judgments. Such value judgments may be based on national interest in the specific sense of national policies and alliances. They may also be based on more general principles such as observance of human rights. The very broad formula adopted by the General Assembly left room for these conceptions. See Schachter, Problems of Law and Justice, in Annual Review of United Nations Affairs 1951, 190, 200–04 (Eagleton & Swift eds. 1952).

2. *The "Legitimacy" Test.* If the effective control test is not required, then by what standards do, or should states recognize governments? Does it matter whether the government's assumption of control occurred from interruption of constitutional governance, denial of fundamental human rights, or violation of other international norms? The 1991 CSCE Declaration suggests that legitimacy does matter, as does the international response to the coup in Haiti. Can it now be regarded as unlawful under international law to recognize an illegitimate government? If so, what are the standards for determining "legitimacy"? Is it important that such non-recognition only be undertaken by a wide-range of states (collective non-recognition)? Are states entitled to react to the presence of an illegitimate government through measures that would otherwise be lawful, such as by imposing economic sanctions that would otherwise violate trade treaties or by taking military action that would otherwise violate Article 2(4) of the U.N. Charter? For analyses, see Peterson, Recognition of Governments, Legal Doctrine and State Practice, 1815–1995, 56–68 (1997).

3. *Regime that Ousts a Democratic Government: The Haitian Incident.* How should one read the Haitian incident? Should the collective non-recognition in the Haitian case be limited to that case, be generalized to other cases of overthrow of elected governments, or be generalized even further to all instances of interference with legitimate authority, such as President Mugabe's interference in Zimbabwe's elections in 2008? What was the relevance, in the Haitian situation, of the fact that the international community had monitored President Aristide's election? Should a comparable factor (international supervision of an electoral process) have played a role in the international reaction in 1997 to the ouster of one of two Cambodian co-prime ministers in the government formed in 1993 as a result of U.N.-supervised elections? Would non-recognition of an irregular change of government be feasible or meaningful in such circumstances? See Clark, Legitimacy in International Society (2005); Roth, Governmental Illegitimacy in International Law (1999) Damrosch, Enforcing International Law through Non–Forcible Measures, 269 Rec. des Cours 9, 151–53 (1997).

4. *Regime that Violates Human Rights: The Taliban.* In 1996, the Islamic movement known as the Taliban captured the capital of Afghanistan and consolidated its control over more than 90% of Afghan territory. Though a comparable degree of territorial control might well satisfy an effective control test for recognition of a government, only three states recognized the Taliban as the government of Afghanistan. The U.N. General Assembly's credentials committee did not accept the Taliban as the government of Afghanistan; instead, an alliance of opposition groups holding almost no Afghan territory continued to be accredited for U.N. purposes and held the

Afghan seat in the General Assembly until a U.S.-led invasion of Afghanistan toppled the Taliban regime in 2001. The Taliban's governance included measures of extreme repression and discrimination (including prohibitions on employment of women, even by international organizations and humanitarian relief groups operating in Afghan territory). Were foreign attitudes concerning recognition of the Taliban shaped by the Taliban's failure to uphold internationally protected human rights and fundamental freedoms? Can withholding recognition from a government that imposes such policies meaningfully advance international protection of human rights and fundamental freedoms? After the attacks of 9/11, the United States invaded Afghanistan and ousted the Taliban from power. The Taliban, however, continues to have a presence in parts of Afghanistan and remains a threat to the current Afghan government.

5. *Role of the Security Council.* To the extent that there is uncertainty about whether a new government should be recognized, is the Security Council an appropriate organ for addressing the matter? The U.S.-led invasion of Iraq in March 2003 toppled the government of Saddam Hussein and led in June 2004 to a U.S. announcement that full sovereignty was transferred back to a new Iraqi interim government. Various Security Council resolutions during this period accepted the transfer of sovereign authority from the former Iraqi government to the new regime. See S.C. Res. 1483 (2003); S.C. Res. 1511 (2003); S.C. Res.1546 (2004). Is that a proper exercise of the Security Council's role? See Wheatley, The Security Council, Democratic Legitimacy, and Regime Change in Iraq, 17 E.J.I.L. 531 (2006).

6. *Governments–In–Exile.* In contrast to *de facto* governments, governments-in-exile have been accorded *de jure* recognition, but lack effective control over the territory of the state. In the past, most governments-in-exile based their claim to authority on continuity with a government that had formerly been in effective control of the state. States that continued to recognize such governments generally did so on the premise that the territory had been illegally occupied and that the legitimate government would be restored to power in the foreseeable future. Several countries occupied by German forces in World War II had exile governments recognized by the United States and the United Kingdom. See Brown, Sovereignty in Exile, 35 A.J.I.L. 666 (1941). The wartime governments-in-exile took part in many international conferences and signed international agreements on behalf of their states. See Marek, Identity and Continuity of States in Public International Law 93–94, 439–40 (1968). On the legal status of governments in exile that continue to be recognized, see Talmon, Recognition of Governments in International Law: With Particular Reference to Governments in Exile (1998).

Some governments-in-exile have also been formed by movements seeking independence. They have often designated themselves as "provisional governments" and have been accorded recognition as such by sympathetic governments and by international bodies. An early example was the revolutionary "provisional government" of Algeria established in 1958, some years before it achieved control of Algeria. See Fraleigh, The Algerian Revolution as a Case Study in International Law, in The International Law of Civil War 179 (Falk ed. 1971); Bedjaoui, Law and the Algerian Revolution 180 (1961). In 1970, Prince Sihanouk, who had been ousted as head of state in Cambodia, formed a government-in-exile in Peking which was immediately recognized by China and by North Vietnam. For an argument in favor of such recognition, see Barnes, United States Recognition Policy and Cambodia, in 3 The Vietnam War and International Law 148, 149, 156 (Falk ed. 1972).

Do you think recognizing governments-in-exile could be a means to promote basic political, civil and other human rights? Two commentators have suggested that the institution of governments-in-exile "provides dissident groups with an opportunity to organize, to seek international scrutiny of the conditions within a state, and to provide alternative symbols for individuals within the state to identify with. * * * [I]t provides repositories of responsibility for the acts of regular or irregular forces of the exile government. * * * We suggest that claims for recognition * * * be granted in all those cases in which aspirant status within the state in question is denied or in which real political activity is severely sanctioned." Reisman & Suzuki, Recognition and Social Change in International Law, in Toward World Order and Human Dignity 403 (Reisman & Weston eds. 1976). Does past experience show that such exile governments can serve the aims listed? What problems would such recognition by foreign states create?

The legal consequences of such *de jure* recognition of governments-in-exile included recognition in municipal law of the control by the exile government of assets in the recognizing state. The recognizing governments also acknowledged the authority of the government-in-exile over its nationals abroad. It was also acknowledged that certain decrees of the government-in-exile applicable to events in the occupied territory would be given effect in the municipal courts of the recognizing states. In a case concerning a wartime decree of the Netherlands government-in-exile to protective possession over securities confiscated by the Nazis in Netherlands, the United States Circuit Court of Appeals upheld the validity of the decree in its application to occupied territory. *State of the Netherlands v. Federal Reserve Bank of New York*, 201 F.2d 455 (2d Cir. 1953).

The decrees of the governments-in-exile were not deprived of legal effect by subsequent *de jure* recognition of another government. In this connection see *Boguslawski v. Gdynia Ameryka Linie*, [1950] 1 K.B. 157, affirmed [1951] 1 K.B. 162 (C.A.), affirmed *sub nom. Gdynia Ameryka Linie Zeglugowe Spolka Akcyjna v. Boguslawski*, [1953] A.C. 11, in which the plaintiff seamen sought to recover severance pay promised to them on July 3, 1945 by a minister of the Polish government-in-exile in London. The Foreign Secretary certified to the court that the British government had recognized the Polish government-in-exile in London as the government of Poland until midnight, July 5–6, 1945, and thereafter had recognized the new Provisional Government of National Unity (Lublin Government), which had been established June 28, 1945, as the government of Poland. The court held that the recognition of the Lublin Government by England did not operate retroactively to deprive of legal effect acts done in England by the exile government while it was still recognized by England. The court relied in part on the fact that the Polish merchant fleet, including defendant's vessels, was under the effective control of the exile government at the time the promise was made.

7. *Recognition of the Communist Government of China.* In 1971, the General Assembly decided to accept the P.R.C. as the government with authority to represent China in the United Nations. This decision has been followed throughout the U.N. system and by other international bodies, but it did not preclude member states from maintaining a different stance in their own recognition practice. At the time of the U.N. decision, the majority of U.N. member states had already shifted their own recognition from the R.O.C. government to the P.R.C. government; but a significant minority (including the United States until 1979) continued to recognize the R.O.C.

As of early 2009, twenty-three states still recognize the non-communist Republic of China (R.O.C.) based in Taiwan, rather than the P.R.C., as the government of China. The P.R.C. does not maintain diplomatic relations with any state that recognizes the R.O.C. The P.R.C.'s sensitivities over some states' recognition of the R.O.C. may have injected an extraneous negative factor into developments far removed from China. For example, shortly before the Kosovo conflict of 1999, the Former Yugoslav Republic of Macedonia's recognition of the R.O.C. was apparently a factor when the P.R.C. vetoed the renewal of the U.N. peacekeeping force that had been stationed in Macedonia in a preventive capacity. See Press Release, Security Council, Security Council Fails to Extend Mandate of United Nations Preventative Deployment Force in Former Yugoslav Republic of Macedonia, U.N. Doc. SC/6648 (Feb. 25, 1999).

8. *U.S. Recognition Practice.* Does Jefferson's "straightforward" statement on recognition mean that "effective power" alone is the prerequisite to recognition or is there a different standard in his reference to a government "formed by the will of the nation substantially declared"? Consider the following statement of a State Department deputy legal adviser:

> I think our present policy is more concerned with the acquiescence rather than the declaration of the will of the people. * * * We have not generally concerned ourselves with asking, would the people, if given a free plebiscite, endorse that change of government.

United States Recognition of Foreign Government: Hearings on S. Res. 205 Before the S. Comm. on Foreign Relations, 91st Cong. 10 (1969) (statement of George Aldrich, Acting Legal Adviser, Department of State).

9. *New Government's Adherence to International Commitments.* During the periods in which the United States refused to recognize the U.S.S.R. (1917–1933) and the People's Republic of China (1949–1978), it asserted as a condition of recognition that governments in effective control must be able and willing to live up to their international commitments. Both governments mentioned were charged with failures to observe international obligations. In retrospect, most observers would regard the United States' objections as based on ideological and political grounds. Is the requirement, as stated, legally meaningful? Does *ability* to live up to international commitments simply mean effective power to do so? Is *willingness* more than *pro forma* since no government would deny such willingness? On the other hand, does it leave room for states to deny recognition to internationally "lawless" regimes and therefore to apply sanctions against such behavior? See Peterson, Recognition of Governments: Legal Doctrine and State Practice, 1815–1995, 68–71 (1997).

10. *Recognition versus Maintenance of Diplomatic Relations*. There is a significant distinction between recognition of a government and maintaining diplomatic relations with it. For example, for decades the United States has recognized the communist government of the Republic of Cuba, yet has chosen not to engage in formal diplomatic relations with that government. Restatement (Third) § 203, Comment *d* states as follows:

> Recognition of a government is often effected by sending and receiving diplomatic representatives, but one government may recognize another yet refrain from assuming diplomatic relations with it. Similarly, breaking off relations does not constitute derecognition of the government. Some governments refrain from maintaining relations or terminate relations with each other in order to express disapproval, or from practical considerations, such as the absence of sufficient interests to warrant such relations, a lack of necessary personnel, or a desire to save the cost. Sometimes it is judged desirable to withdraw diplomatic personnel because of concern for their safety. When relations are not maintained directly they may be carried on through diplomatic channels provided by another government. Thus, the United States terminated relations with Cuba in 1961, but is represented in Cuba by the Swiss embassy in Havana, and Cuba is represented by the Czechoslovak embassy in Washington.

B. IS RECOGNITION REALLY NECESSARY?

STATEMENT OF SECRETARY OF FOREIGN RELATIONS OF MEXICO ESTRADA

Remarks made Sept. 27, 1930
2 Whiteman, Digest of International Law 85 (1963)

It is a well-known fact that some years ago Mexico suffered, as few nations have, from the consequences of that doctrine, which allows foreign governments to pass upon the legitimacy or illegitimacy of the régime existing in another country, with the result that situations arise in which the legal qualifications or national status of governments or authorities are apparently made subject to the opinion of foreigners.

Ever since the Great War, the doctrine of so-called 'recognitions' has been applied in particular to the nations of this continent, although in well-known cases of change of régime occurring in European countries the governments of the nations have not made express declarations of recognition; consequently, the system has been changing into a special practice applicable to the Latin American Republics.

After a very careful study of the subject, the Government of Mexico has transmitted instructions to its Ministers or Chargés d'Affaires in the countries affected by the recent political crises, informing them that the Mexican Government is issuing no declarations in the sense of grants of recognition, since that nation considers that such a course is an insulting practice and one which, in addition to the fact that it offends the sovereignty of other nations, implies that judgment of some sort may be passed upon the internal affairs of those nations by other governments, inasmuch as the latter assume, in effect, an attitude of criticism, when they decide, favorably or unfavorably, as to the legal qualifications of foreign régimes.

NOTES

1. *The Meaning of the Estrada Doctrine.* The Estrada Doctrine is generally understood to mean that recognition of the *government* is unnecessary once the *state* has been recognized. Is the Estrada Doctrine construed more accurately as proposing (a) the sole criterion of effective control for deciding when to deal with a new government and (b) the avoidance of explicit and formal acts of recognition? If so, what international policies would be served by this approach?

2. *The Traction of the Estrada Doctrine.* Richard Baxter, who served as a judge on the International Court of Justice, suggested that recognition is an "institution of law that causes more problems than it solves" and therefore should be rejected. "The partial withdrawal of law from this area of international relations will facilitate the maintenance of relations with states in which extraconstitutional changes of government are taking place, and in itself that is a good thing." Baxter, Foreword to Galloway, Recognizing Foreign Governments: The Practice of the United States xi (1978).

Yet according to a 1969 U.S. State Department survey, only thirty-one states indicated that they had abandoned traditional recognition policies and substituted the Estrada Doctrine or some equivalent by which they accepted whatever government was in effective control without raising the issue of recognition." Galloway, *supra*, at 10 & app. A. Mexico was among those countries, yet Mexico, the source of the Estrada Doctrine, refused relations with the Franco government of Spain for over three decades. Why are so many states unprepared to abandon the institution of recognition as a political tool? Indeed, why did the People's Republic of China insist in 1979 on recognition by the United States as a condition of "normalization of relations"? Does that suggest that recognition cannot simply be replaced by the maintenance of diplomatic relations or a liaison office?

For the point of view that the institution of recognition of governments should be preserved but governed by an "effective control" rule, see Peterson, Recognition of Governments Should Not Be Abolished, 77 A.J.I.L. 31 (1983); see also Peterson, Recognition of Governments: Legal Doctrine and State Practice, 1815–1995 (1997). For a general defense of the use of recognition to further international aims, see Reisman & Suzuki, Recognition and Social Change in International Law, in Toward World Order and Human Dignity 403 (Reisman & Weston eds. 1976).

3. *The Feasibility of the Estrada Doctrine.* Can the Estrada Doctrine be applied when there are rival claimants to power? Don't other states have to make a formal choice as between the rivals? Or should foreign governments simply deal with both sets of officials regarding problems in areas where they respectively have *de facto* control until the conflict is resolved? See Jessup, A Modern Law of Nations 62–63 (1948), who observed that the Estrada Doctrine

will not always save foreign governments from the necessity of choosing between rival claimants.

4. *U.S. Efforts to Deemphasize Formal Recognition.* According to the Restatement (Third) § 203, Reporters' Note 1:

> Since 1970 the United States has moved away from its older recognition practice. "In recent years, U.S. practice has been to deemphasize and avoid the use of recognition in cases of changes of governments and to concern ourselves with the question of whether we wish to have diplomatic relations with the new governments." [1977] Digest of U.S. Practice in Int'l L. 19–21. Repeatedly, the State Department has responded to inquiries with the statement: "The question of recognition does not arise: we are conducting our relations with the new government." [1974] *Id.* at 13: [1975] *Id.* at 34. In some situations, however, the question cannot be avoided, for example, where two regimes are contending for power, and particularly where legal consequences within the United States depend on which regime is recognized or accepted.

5. *U.K. Efforts to Deemphasize Formal Recognition.* In April 1980, a change in the British policy concerning recognition of governments was announced by Lord Carrington to the House of Lords as follows:

> [W]e have decided that we shall no longer accord recognition to Governments. The British Government recognise States in accordance with common international doctrine.
>
> Where an unconstitutional change of régime takes place in a recognised State, Governments of other States must necessarily consider what dealings, if any, they should have with the new régime, and whether and to what extent it qualifies to be treated as the Government of the State concerned. * * *
>
> We have * * * concluded that there are practical advantages in following the policy of many other countries in not according recognition to Governments. Like them, we shall continue to decide the nature of our dealings with régimes which come to power unconstitutionally in the light of our assessment of whether they are able of themselves to exercise effective control of the territory of the State concerned, and seem likely to do so.

408 Parl. Deb., H.L. (5th ser.) (1980) 1121–22. As a result, the question of whether a regime qualifies in the eyes of the United Kingdom as a government "will be left to be inferred from the nature of the dealings, if any, which [the UK Government] may have with it, and in particular on whether [the UK Government] are dealing with it on a normal Government to Government basis." 985 Parl. Deb., H.C. (5th ser.) (1980) 385. See Dixon, Recent Developments in United Kingdom Practice Concerning the Recognition of States and Governments, 22 Int'l Law. 555 (1988).

C. UNRECOGNIZED GOVERNMENTS

The lack of recognition of an entity as the government of a state has important collateral consequences. Can that entity undertake any acts that bind the state in question and that must be honored by the recognized government of that state?

1. Capacity of Unrecognized Governments to Bind the State

TINOCO CLAIMS ARBITRATION
(GREAT BRITAIN v. COSTA RICA)

Opinion and Award of William H. Taft, Sole Arbitrator
1 U.N. Rep. Int'l Arb. Awards 369 (1923)

[This case involved claims by Great Britain against Costa Rica for acts of a preceding Costa Rican regime (the Tinoco regime), which had come to power in 1917 by a coup and maintained itself in control for two years. The Tinoco regime was recognized by some governments, but not by many leading powers (including Great Britain and the United States). When the Tinoco regime fell in 1919, the restored Costa Rican government nullified all of the contracts concluded by the Tinoco government, including an oil concession to a British company. Great Britain argued that the Tinoco Government was the only government in Costa Rica when the liabilities were created and that its acts could not be repudiated. Costa Rica argued that the Tinoco regime was not a recognized government capable of entering into contracts on behalf of the state. Moreover, Costa Rica argued that that Great Britain was estopped from claiming that the Tinoco government could confer rights on British subjects given Britain's own non-recognition of the Tinoco government. The matter was placed before arbitration by a March 1923 treaty between the two states. In discussing the issue of recognition, the Arbitrator, United States Chief Justice William H. Taft, stated:]

The non-recognition by other nations of a government claiming to be a national personality, is usually appropriate evidence that it has not attained the independence and control entitling it by international law to be classed as such. But when recognition *vel non* of a government is by such nations determined by inquiry, not into its *de facto* sovereignty and complete governmental control, but into its illegitimacy or irregularity of origin, their non-recognition loses something of evidential weight on the issue with which those applying the rules of international law are alone concerned. What is true of the non-recognition of the United States in its bearing upon the existence of a *de facto* government under Tinoco for thirty months is probably in a measure true of the non-recognition by her Allies in the European War. Such non-recognition for any reason, however, cannot outweigh the evidence disclosed by this record before me as to the *de facto* character of Tinoco's government, according to the standard set by international law.

Second. It is ably and earnestly argued on behalf of Costa Rica that the Tinoco government cannot be considered a *de facto* government, because it was not established and maintained in accord with the constitution of Costa Rica of 1871. To hold that a government which establishes itself and maintains a peaceful administration, with the acquiescence of the people for a substantial period of time, does not become a *de facto* government unless it conforms to a previous constitution would be to hold that within the rules of international law a revolution contrary to the fundamental law of the existing government cannot establish a new government. This cannot be, and is not, true.

[The Arbitrator rejected the claim of estoppel because Great Britain by non-recognition did not dispute the *de facto* existence of the Tinoco regime and because the successor government had not been led by British non-recognition to change its position.]

NOTES

1. *The Basic Outcome.* Do you think the outcome in the *Tinoco* case makes sense? Weren't those who contracted with the *de facto* government on notice that there were doubts about the ability of the Tinoco government to represent the state of Costa Rica? Why shouldn't they bear the risk of that dubious status? Why should the legitimate government bear the burdens of decisions taken by a non-recognized government?

2. *Potential Significance.* In the *Tinoco* case, the *de facto* regime exercised authority throughout the country for an extended period of time. Would the legal situation be different in respect of a *de facto* regime which controlled only a part of the country or which controlled all of the country for only a short period of time? The United States–Italian Claims Commission held that Yugoslavia was not liable for acts of the wartime state of Croatia, because Croatia was a puppet regime under German–Italian control and also because it was only a local authority with limited territorial control. See *Re Dues for Reply Coupons Issued in Croatia,* 1954 I.L.R. 55; *Re Transit Charge for Mails from Occupied Yugoslavia,* 1956 I.L.R. 591.

2. Capacity of an Insurgent Authority in Control of Specific Territory

The category of *de facto* governments may also include organized insurgent groups which exercise governmental authority for a time over part of the territory of a state. Such groups may be regarded as "parastatal entities recognized as possessing a definite if limited form of international personality." Fitzmaurice, [1958] II Yb.I.L.C. 24.

Four specific attributes of such "personality" are indicated by state practice. First, the insurgent group may be recognized as a belligerent and therefore as imposing neutrality on other states. See Lauterpacht, Recognition in International Law 187 (1947). Second, an insurgent group may be recognized as possessing certain rights and obligations concerning the conduct of the armed conflict. See Protocol I to the 1949 Geneva Conventions, arts. 1(4) & 44, June 8, 1977, 1125 U.N.T.S. 3; Protocol II to the 1949 Geneva Conventions, art. 1, June 8, 1977, 1125 U.N.T.S. 609. Third, insurgent authorities in control of specific territory have also entered into agreements with governments and have therefore been considered to have treaty-making capacity. See [1958] II Yb.I.L.C. 24. For example, the Geneva Agreement of 1954 on the cessation of hostilities in Laos and Cambodia was signed by representatives of insurgent forces in control of some parts of the countries concerned although they were not recognized as *de jure* governments. For a contrasting view, see Lukashuk, Parties to Treaties—The Right of Participation, 135 Rec. des Cours 231, 280–81 (1972–I) (arguing that such an insurgency only secures treaty-making rights in certain circumstances of both *de facto* control and ultimate legitimacy). Fourth, an insurgent authority with limited territorial control may perform ordinary governmental functions in the area under its authority. It was held by a United States–Mexican Claims Commission in 1926 that the state of Mexico was liable for the conduct of a local insurrectionary regime when the latter engaged in routine governmental acts—in that particular case, the sale of money orders. The Commission indicated that other, less routine acts by an insurrectionary regime would not subject the state to liability unless the *de facto* authority extended over a major portion of the territory of the state and over a majority of its people. *Hopkins v. United Mexican States*, 4 U.N. Rep. Int'l Arb. Awards 41, 44 (1926). Is there sufficient reason to attribute to the state the responsibility for acts of a local revolutionary group which are of a routine administrative character? Is it justifiable to exclude from such attribution other "governmental acts" by the insurgents such as a contract for munitions or a large concession agreement?

The distinction between recognition of *de facto* and *de jure* governments is more than a matter of form; it has significant political and legal consequences. In Lauterpacht's words: "So long as the lawful government offers resistance which is not ostensibly hopeless or purely nominal, the *de jure* recognition of the revolutionary party as a government constitutes premature recognition which the lawful government is entitled to regard as an act of intervention contrary to international law. * * * [It] constitutes a drastic interference with the independence of the State concerned." Lauterpacht, Recognition in International Law 94–95 (1947). Suppose that the recognizing state simply acknowledges that the insurgent authority exercises *de facto* control over some territory. Apparently such recognition of an insurgent authority has been considered as sufficient to support (as a matter of international law) sovereign immunity of the *de facto* government in the courts of the state granting such recognition. *Government of the Republic of Spain v. S.S. "Arantzazu Mendi"* [1939] A.C. 256.

3. Unrecognized Governments in Municipal Law

SALIMOFF & CO. v. STANDARD OIL

New York Court of Appeals, 1933
262 N.Y. 220, 186 N.E. 679

POUND, CH. J. The Soviet government, by a nationalization decree, confiscated all oil lands in Russia and sold oil extracted therefrom to defendants. The former owners of the property, Russian nationals, join in an equitable action for an accounting on the ground that the confiscatory decrees of the unrecognized Soviet government and the seizure of oil lands thereunder have no other effect in law on the rights of the parties than seizure by bandits. (Luther v. Sagor & Co., [1921] 1 K.B. 456; s.c., 3 K.B. 532; cited in Sokoloff v. National City Bank, 239 N.Y. 158, 164, 145 N.E. 917.) The complaints have been dismissed.

The question is as to the effect on the title of a purchaser from the unrecognized confiscating Soviet Russian government. Does title pass or is the Soviet government no better than a thief, stealing the property of its nationals and giving only a robber's title to stolen property? Plaintiffs contend that the Soviet decrees of confiscation did not divest them of title.

* * *

* * * The oil property confiscated was taken in Russia from Russian nationals. A recovery in conversion is dependent upon the laws of Russia. (Riley v. Pierce Oil Corp., 245 N.Y. 152, 154, 156 N.E. 647.) When no right of action is created at the place of wrong, no recovery in tort can be had in any other State on account of the wrong. The United States government recognizes that the Soviet government has functioned as a de facto or quasi government since 1917, ruling within its borders. It has recognized its existence as a fact although it has refused diplomatic recognition as one might refuse to recognize an objectionable relative although his actual existence could not be denied. It tells us that it has no disposition to ignore the fact that such government is exercising control and power in territory of the former Russian empire. As was said by this court in Sokoloff v. National City Bank (supra, p. 165): "Juridically, a government that is unrecognized may be viewed as no government at all, if the power withholding recognition chooses thus to view it. In practice, however, since juridical conceptions are seldom, if ever, carried to the limit of their logic, the equivalence is not absolute, but is subject to self-imposed limitations of common sense and fairness, as we learned in litigations following our Civil War."

As a juristic conception, what is Soviet Russia? A band of robbers or a government? We all know that it is a government. The State Department knows it, the courts, the nations and the man on the street. If it is a government in fact, its decrees have force within its borders and over its nationals. "Recognition does not create the state." (Wulfsohn v. Russian S.F.S. Republic, 234 N.Y. 372, 375, 138 N.E. 24, 25.) It simply gives to a de facto state international status. Must the courts say that Soviet Russia is an outlaw and that the Provisional government of Russia as the successor of the Russian Imperial government is still the lawful government of Russia although it is long since dead? * * * The courts may not recognize the Soviet government as the de jure government until the State Department gives the word. They may, however, say that it is a government, maintaining internal peace and order, providing for national defense and the general welfare, carrying on relations with our own government and others. To refuse to recognize that Soviet Russia is a government regulating the internal affairs of the country, is to give to fictions an air of reality which they do not deserve.

NATIONAL PETROCHEMICAL CO. OF IRAN v. M/T STOLT SHEAF

860 F.2d 551 (2d Cir. 1988)

[In this case, a corporation wholly owned by Iran brought suit as a plaintiff in a U.S. federal court. The district court dismissed the claim on the ground that the United States had never extended recognition to the government of the Islamic Republic of Iran and that an entity wholly owned by an unrecognized government is not entitled to bring suit in U.S. courts. On appeal, the U.S. government entered the case as amicus curiae, urging that plaintiff be granted access to the court. In accepting the U.S. government's position, the court of appeals held that "the absence of formal recognition does not necessarily result in a foreign government being barred from access to United States courts." The court continued as follows.]

Two reasons support this holding. First, as this century draws to a close, the practice of extending formal recognition to new governments has altered: The United States Department of State has sometimes refrained from announcing recognition of a new government because grants of recognition have been misinterpreted as pronouncements of approval. *See 77 State Dep't Bull.* 462–63 (Oct. 10, 1977) ("In recent years, U.S. practice has been to deemphasize and avoid the use of recognition in cases of changes of governments..."); *Restatement* 3d § 203, reporter's note 1 (commenting on recent deemphasis of formal recognition). As a result, the absence of formal recognition cannot serve as the touchstone for determining whether the Executive Branch has "recognized" a foreign nation for the purpose of granting that government access to United States courts.

Second, the power to deal with foreign nations outside the bounds of formal recognition is essential to a president's implied power to maintain international relations. *Cf. United States v. Curtiss–Wright Export Corp.,* 299 U.S. 304, 318–20, 57 S.Ct. 216, 220–21, 81 L.Ed. 255 (1936). As part of this power, the Executive Branch must have the latitude to permit a foreign nation access to U.S. courts, even if that nation is not formally recognized by the U.S. government. This is because the president alone— as the constitutional guardian of foreign policy—knows what action is necessary to effectuate American relations with foreign governments. *Cf. Sabbatino*, 376 U.S. at 411 n. 12, 84 S.Ct. at 931 n. 12 (citing criticisms of any policy which would mandate formal recognition before a foreign nation could sue in U.S. courts).

This case serves as an excellent example. Relations between the United States and Iran over the past eight years have been less than friendly. Yet, the status of that relationship has not been unchanging. There have been periods of improvement, for example, release of the embassy hostages, and periods of worsening relations, most recently occasioned by the unfortunate downing of an Iranian civilian airliner by the U.S.S. Vincennes. It is evident that in today's topsy-turvy world governments can topple and relationships can change in a moment. The Executive Branch must therefore have broad, unfettered discretion in matters involving such sensitive, fast-changing, and complex foreign relationships. *See Guaranty Trust*, 304 U.S. at 137, 58 S.Ct. at 791 ("What government is to be regarded here as representative of a foreign sovereign state is a political rather than a judicial question, and is to be determined by the political department of the government."); *Sabbatino*, 376 U.S. at 410, 84 S.Ct. at 931 ("This Court would hardly be competent to undertake assessments of varying degrees of friendliness or its absence..."); *Curtiss–Wright*, 299 U.S. at 319 ("In this vast external realm, with its important, complicated, delicate and manifold problems, the President alone has the power to speak or listen as a representative of the nation.").

NOTES

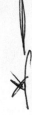

1. *Coping with the "Band of Robbers".* In *Salimoff,* neither the plaintiff nor the defendant was the unrecognized government. The issue, therefore, was whether the acts of the unrecognized government (the government of the Soviet Union) should be given effect by the U.S. court. Do you think the outcome in the case makes sense? The Restatement (Third) § 205(3) states that "courts in the United States ordinarily give effect to acts * * * of a regime not recognized as the government of a state, if those acts apply to territory under the control of that regime and relate to domestic matters only."

By contrast, English courts have generally refused to give effect to legislative acts of unrecognized governments and to legal acts pursuant to such laws. They have, for example, declined to recognize Rhodesian divorce decrees emanating from courts under the non-recognized Southern Rhodesia regime of Ian Smith. See *Adams v. Adams* [1970] 3 All E.R. 572. However in *Luther v. Sagor,* the English Court of Appeal gave effect to a Soviet confiscation decree of 1918 after receiving a letter from the Foreign Office stating that the British Government recognized the Soviet Government as the "de facto Government of Russia." The Court did not regard the distinction between *de facto* and *de jure* recognition as crucial, saying that since the British Government recognized the Soviet Government "as the Government really in possession of the powers of sovereignty in Russia, the acts of that Government must be treated by the Courts of this country with all the respect due to the acts of a duly recognized foreign sovereign state." [1921] 3 K.B. 532, 543.

2. *Access to National Courts for Unrecognized Government*. In *National Petrochemical Co. of Iran*, one of the parties (the plaintiff) was a government for which there had been no formal statement of recognition by the United States. Do you favor the outcome reached by the court?

The traditional rule generally applied by United States courts had been that an entity not recognized as a state or a regime not recognized as a government of a state cannot institute proceedings in the courts of a foreign state. The U.S. Supreme Court in 1938 explained the principle of denial of access to a non-recognized government by stating that what government is to be regarded as the recognized representative of a foreign sovereign state is a political rather than a judicial question and is to be determined by the political department whose action in recognizing a foreign government is conclusive on all domestic courts. *Guaranty Trust Co. of New York v. United States*, 304 U.S. 126 (1938).

In the *Sabbatino* case, however, the Supreme Court observed that the doctrine that non-recognition precluded suit by a foreign government had been much criticized and pointed out that since the precise question was not presented in the case (since Cuba was recognized, though diplomatic relations had been broken), the Court would intimate "no view on the possibility of access by an unrecognized government to United States courts." The severance of diplomatic relations did not imply the withdrawal of recognition and therefore did not preclude access: "It is the refusal to recognize which has a unique legal aspect, signifying this country's unwillingness to acknowledge that the government in question speaks as the sovereign authority for the territory it controls." The Court referred to the "possible incongruity" that would occur if a foreign power not recognized by the executive branch were accorded judicial recognition. See *Banco Nacional de Cuba v. Sabbatino*, 376 U.S. 398 (1964) excerpted at p. 670; see also West & Murphy, The Impact on U.S. Litigation of Non–Recognition of Foreign Governments, 26 Stan. J. Int'l L. 435 (1990).

An unrecognized government cannot bring suit in a U.K. court. See Brownlie, Principles of Public International Law 95–96 (6th ed. 2003). However, in a few cases appearances by the unrecognized government have been allowed on the theory that the case involved private rather than public law. Civil law countries also generally deny *locus standi* to unrecognized governments.

3. *Effect of Loss of Recognition*. Loss of recognition may prevent a government from maintaining an action already commenced. See *Government of France v. Isbrandtsen–Moller*, 48 F.Supp. 631 (S.D.N.Y. 1943). In *Republic of Vietnam v. Pfizer, Inc.*, 556 F.2d 892 (8th Cir. 1977), the court of appeals affirmed the dismissal of an antitrust suit that had been filed in 1970 by the Republic of Vietnam against several American drug companies. Although the Republic of [South] Vietnam was recognized when the suit was initiated, in 1975 the Republic surrendered to North Vietnam; and in 1976 the territory of the Republic was joined to that of North Vietnam to form a new state, the Socialist Republic of Vietnam. At the time in 1976, the United States

recognized no government as the sovereign authority in the territory formerly known as South Vietnam. The District Court dismissed the action on ground that the plaintiff no longer existed. The Court of Appeals affirmed, noting that the trial court has discretion in deciding whether to suspend or dismiss a suit by a plaintiff whose recognition has been lost.

4. *Suits against Unrecognized Governments.* Whether a non-recognized government may be a defendant typically arises in the context of whether they can claim sovereign immunity. United States courts have taken the position that *de facto* governments in control of a state are entitled to claim sovereign immunity on behalf of the state. See *Wulfsohn v. Russian Socialist Federated Soviet Republic*, 138 N.E. 24, 234 N.Y. 372 (1923).

5. *Unrecognized Entities in Other Contexts.* Courts sometimes have to determine how to treat an unrecognized entity for purposes of laws referring generally to foreign states, governments, or countries. Particular legislation may clarify the matter, as with the Taiwan Relations Act (discussed *supra* this Chapter, Section 3) which specifies that lack of recognition does not affect Taiwan's eligibility to sue and be sued or to participate in various programs and benefits. Or the executive branch may have made a determination on a matter falling within the President's competence, to which the courts may defer. Where the legislative or executive position is unclear, however, courts may have to resolve the ambiguity.

In *Matimak Trading Co. v. Khalily*, 118 F.3d 76 (2d Cir. 1997), the issue was whether a Hong Kong company qualified as a foreign corporation for purposes of alienage jurisdiction under the federal diversity statute, 28 U.S.C. § 1332(a)(2) (2000), which confers jurisdiction over suits between U.S. nationals and citizens or subjects of foreign states. The court had to interpret the jurisdictional statute in light of the fact that the U.S. government had not recognized Hong Kong; it concluded that in the absence of executive branch recognition, diversity jurisdiction was unavailable.

In *People's Mojahedin Organization of Iran v. Albright*, 182 F.3d 17 (D.C. Cir. 1999), two groups—the People's Mojahedin Organization of Iran and the Liberation Tigers of Tamil Eelam (LTTE)—invoked statutory procedures to challenge their designation by the Secretary of State as foreign organizations engaging in terrorist activities. One of the organizations, LTTE, claimed that it was not a "foreign organization" within the meaning of the Antiterrorism Act of 1996 but rather was a foreign government. The court observed:

> In any event, the United States replies that a court cannot make the determination the LTTE wants because recognizing foreign states is solely entrusted to the political branches, and the United States has not recognized the LTTE. "Who is the sovereign, *de jure* or *de facto*, of a territory, is not a judicial, but a political question, the determination of which by the legislative and executive departments of any government conclusively binds the judges, as well as all other officers, citizens, and subjects of that government." *Jones v. United States*, 137 U.S. 202, 212–13, 11 S.Ct. 80, 34 L.Ed. 691 (1890). Here, the Secretary determined that the LTTE was a foreign organization and, in the words of the statute, there is "substantial support" for her finding in the materials she has furnished us as an "administrative record."

182 F.3d at 24. For subsequent litigation, see National Council of Resistance of Iran v. Department of State, 251 F.3d 192 (D.C. Cir. 2001), People's Mojahedin Organization of Iran v. Department of State, 327 F.3d 1238 (D.C. Cir. 2003) (finding that the Secretary acted fully in accordance with U.S. law).

In *Kadic v. Karadžić*, 70 F.3d 232 (2d Cir. 1995), defendant was described as "the President of a three-man presidency of the self-proclaimed Bosnian–Serb republic within Bosnia–Herzegovina, sometimes referred to as 'Srpska'." One issue in the case was whether Karadžić should be treated as a head of state who might be immune from judicial jurisdiction (see Chapter 12). The court of appeals concluded that the speculative possibility of future recognition should not create the functional equivalent of immunity from jurisdiction, when the U.S. government had not recognized a Bosnian Serb government or acknowledged Karadžić as a governmental official entitled to any sort of immunity.

4. Termination of Recognition

STATEMENT OF THE UNITED STATES:
U.S. NORMALIZES RELATIONS WITH
PEOPLE'S REPUBLIC OF CHINA

79 Dep't St. Bull. 26 (Jan. 1979)

As of January 1, 1979, the United States of America recognizes the People's Republic of China as the sole legal government of China. On the same date, the People's Republic of China accords similar recognition to the United States of America. The United States thereby establishes diplomatic relations with the People's Republic of China.

On that same date, January 1, 1979, the United States of America will notify Taiwan that it is terminating diplomatic relations and that the Mutual Defense Treaty between the United States and the Republic of China is being terminated in accordance with the provisions of the Treaty. The United States also states that it will be withdrawing its remaining military personnel from Taiwan within four months.

In the future, the American people and the people of Taiwan will maintain commercial, cultural, and other relations without official government representation and without diplomatic relations.

The Administration will seek adjustments to our laws and regulations to permit the maintenance of commercial, cultural, and other nongovernmental relationships in the new circumstances that will exist after normalization.

NOTES

1. *Disappearance of the State.* If an entity ceases to possess the qualifications of statehood, is derecognition of the government unnecessary? Derecognition of the government of the German Democratic Republic was viewed as unnecessary when that state was absorbed into the Federal Republic of

Germany by accession to the Basic Law of the Federal Republic in October 1990. For a discussion, see Crawford, The Creation of States in International Law 452–66 (2d ed. 2006).

2. *Termination without Transferring Recognition.* If a state terminates its recognition of a government of another state, must it recognize some other entity as the government? Between 1975 and 1979, the Cambodian government under the Khmer Rouge regime of Pol Pot carried out a reign of terror that resulted in the deaths of some one million Cambodians. In 1979, Vietnam invaded Cambodia and set up a Vietnamese-dominated government. The United Nations refused to accept the credentials of the Vietnamese-installed government, and the U.N. seat was for some years held by representatives affiliated with the previous regime. Some states (e.g. Australia) reacted to this situation by derecognizing the Pol Pot regime and refusing to recognize any Cambodian government. See 8 Australian Y.B.I.L. 273 (1980).

SECTION 5. ACQUISITION AND DELIMITATION OF TERRITORY

As discussed in Section 1, in order to qualify as a state, an entity must have a defined territory. Sovereignty over a specific territorial area is therefore an essential element of statehood. How do states acquire territory? Once acquired, how do states resolve disputes over the possession and delimitation of territory?

A. ACQUISITION OF TERRITORY

Legal precedent on acquisition of uninhabited territory is of more historical than contemporary significance. Nonetheless scores of controversies as to sovereignty over territory remain, including issues as to what state should be regarded as exercising sovereignty over certain islands, land areas subject to boundary disputes, and polar regions. For example, there has been a dispute between Iran and the United Arab Emirates over the islands of Abu Musa and Greater and Lesser Tunb near the Strait of Hormuz at the entrance to the Persian Gulf through which 20% of the world's oil is transported. Sovereignty over the northern Kurile Islands seized by the Soviet Union at the end of World War II remains in dispute between Russia and Japan. Pursuant to one of the conditions of the U.N. Security Council-supervised cease-fire ending the 1991 Persian Gulf War, the demarcation of the land frontier between Iraq and Kuwait under a 1963 agreement was handled by an *ad hoc* boundary commission in the 1990s.

Unfortunately, long running disputes over territorial sovereignty have frequently escalated into armed conflict, as with the Falklands War between Argentina and the United Kingdom in 1982, the Ecuador–Peru conflict that erupted in 1995, and the fighting between Eritrea and

Ethiopia in 1998–2000. Conversely, settlement of territorial disputes on the basis of law can help the parties toward peaceful solutions.

Many international arbitrations and adjudications have applied international legal principles governing the acquisition of sovereignty over territory. Usually, such principles are discussed in the context of whether a state has title to territory, which may be said to exist due to one of several possible bases, as discussed below. When it is impossible to determine the existence of an original title, it is common to undertake an assessment of *effectivités* (exercises of sovereign acts over the territory) to determine sovereignty. For seminal works, see Kohen, Possession Contestée et Souveraineté Territoriale (1997); Jennings, The Acquisition of Territory in International Law (1963); Sharma, Territorial Acquisition, Disputes and International Law (1997).

1. Title by Discovering or Occupying *Terra Nullius*

At one time, territory was acquired internationally based on the Roman law concept of *terra nullius* (nobody's land). For the international law that emerged in Europe after 1648, *terra nullius* did not refer only to territory in which no persons were present; rather, it referred to territory that was discovered by a European power and that was unclaimed by any other sovereign state recognized by European powers. Thus, the early European powers in North America (France, Netherlands, Spain) largely staked their claims based on this concept.

Since recognized states have now acquired sovereignty over the great bulk of the earth's habitable territory, *terra nullius* is rarely invoked as a basis for title to territory. Certain uninhabited Pacific Islands continue to be claimed by states such as the Philippines and China based on a concept of discovery centuries ago when they were *terra nullius*. Some states maintain sovereign claims to portions of Antarctica based on the concept. Yet generally the concept appears to be falling into desuetude.

For example, Norway occupied and claimed parts of (then uninhabited) Eastern Greenland in the 1920s, claiming that it constituted *terra nullius* rather than Danish territory. Denmark sued before the Permanent Court of International Justice in *Legal Status of Eastern Greenland* (Denmark v. Norway), 1933 P.C.I.J. (ser. A/B) No. 53. Though the Court discussed the meaning of *terra nullius*, the Court held, as separate and independent grounds for its conclusion, that: (1) Norway had "debarred herself from contesting Danish sovereignty over the whole of Greenland" by becoming a party to various bilateral and multilateral agreements in which Greenland had been described as Danish or in which Denmark had excluded Greenland from the operation of the agreement, and (2) Norway had given express undertakings to the Danish government by which it promised not to contest Danish sovereignty over the whole of Greenland. For comment on the *Legal Status of Eastern Greenland Case*, see Preuss, The Dispute Between Denmark and Norway Over the Sovereignty of East

Greenland, 26 A.J.I.L. 469 (1932); Hyde, The Case Concerning the Legal Status of Greenland, 27 A.J.I.L. 732 (1933).

When the General Assembly asked the International Court of Justice for an advisory opinion on whether sparsely populated land in the Western Sahara region (Rio de Oro and Sakiet El Hamra) was *terra nullius* at the time of its colonization by Spain, the Court responded in the negative. See *Western Sahara,* Advisory Opinion, 1975 I.C.J. 12, 38–39. Moreover, in doing so the Court cast doubt upon the viability of the concept when persons are present in a territory operating under some form of social structure. The Court stated:

79. * * * The expression *"terra nullius"* was a legal term of art employed in connection with "occupation" as one of the accepted legal methods of acquiring sovereignty over territory. "Occupation" being legally an original means of peaceably acquiring sovereignty over territory otherwise than by cession or succession, it was a cardinal condition of a valid "occupation" that the territory should be *terra nullius*—a territory belonging to no-one at the time of the act alleged to constitute the "occupation" (*cf. Legal Status of Eastern Greenland, P.C.I.J., Series A/B, No. 53*, pp. 44 f. and 63 f.). In the view of the Court, therefore, a determination that Western Sahara was a *"terra nullius"* at the time of colonization by Spain would be possible only if it were established that at that time the territory belonged to no-one in the sense that it was then open to acquisition through the legal process of "occupation".

80. Whatever differences of opinion there may have been among jurists, the State practice of the relevant period indicates that territories inhabited by tribes or peoples having a social and political organization were not regarded as *terra nullius*. It shows that in the case of such territories the acquisition of sovereignty was not generally considered as effected unilaterally through "occupation" of *terra nullius* by original title but through agreements concluded with local rulers. On occasion, it is true, the word "occupation" was used in a non-technical sense denoting simply acquisition of sovereignty; but that did not signify that the acquisition of sovereignty through such agreements with authorities of the country was regarded as an "occupation" of a *"terra nullius"* in the proper sense of these terms. On the contrary, such agreements with local rulers, whether or not considered as an actual "cession" of the territory, were regarded as derivative roots of title, and not original titles obtained by occupation of *terra nullius*.

81. In the present instance, the information furnished to the Court shows that at the time of colonization Western Sahara was inhabited by peoples which, if nomadic, were socially and politically organized in tribes and under chiefs competent to represent them.

2. Title by Military Conquest

Before international law prohibited the use of force in international relations, territorial changes often came about by virtue of conquest. For example, after invading Mexico and occupying Mexico City in the Mexican–American War of 1846–1848, the United States secured in the Treaty of Guadalupe Hidalgo the cession of territory that would ultimately become Arizona, California, Nevada, Utah, and parts of Colorado, New Mexico, and Wyoming. Efforts in the 20th century to delegitimize aggression included the 1928 Kellogg–Briand Pact, the "Stimson Doctrine" of 1932 (a U.S. policy not to recognize the validity of territorial acquisitions brought about by force used in violation of the Pact), and the prohibition on the use of force in Article 2(4) of the U.N. Charter (see Chapter 15, Section 1). To what extent is title by military conquest now forbidden by international law?

DECLARATION ON PRINCIPLES OF INTERNATIONAL LAW CONCERNING FRIENDLY RELATIONS AND CO-OPERATION AMONG STATES IN ACCORDANCE WITH THE CHARTER OF THE UNITED NATIONS

G.A. Res. 2625 (XXV), preamble & annex (Oct. 24, 1970)

The General Assembly,

Having considered the principles of international law relating to friendly relations and co-operation among States,

    1. *Solemnly proclaims* the following principles:

* * *

Every State has the duty to refrain in its international relations from the threat or use of force against the territorial integrity or political independence of any State, or in any other manner inconsistent with the purposes of the United Nations. Such a threat or use of force constitutes a violation of international law and the Charter of the United Nations and shall never be employed as a means of settling international issues.

* * *

The territory of a State shall not be the object of military occupation resulting from the use of force in contravention of the provisions of the Charter. The territory of a State shall not be the object of acquisition by another State resulting from the threat or use of force. No territorial acquisition resulting from the threat or use of force shall be recognized as legal. Nothing in the foregoing shall be construed as affecting:

    (*a*) Provisions of the Charter or any international agreement prior to the Charter régime and valid under international law; or

    (*b*) The powers of the Security Council under the Charter.

SECURITY COUNCIL RESOLUTION CONCERNING IRAQ'S ATTEMPTED ANNEXATION OF KUWAIT

S.C. Res. 662 (Aug. 9, 1990)

[On August 1, 1990, the armed forces of Iraq invaded and occupied Kuwait. On August 2, the U.N. Security Council unanimously condemned the invasion and demanded that Iraq withdraw all forces immediately and unconditionally. S.C. Res. 660 (Aug. 2, 1990). Iraq then announced that it was annexing Kuwait, prompting the Security Council to adopt unanimously the following resolution.]

Gravely alarmed by the declaration by Iraq of a "comprehensive and eternal merger" with Kuwait,

Demanding once again, that Iraq withdraw immediately and unconditionally all its forces to the positions in which they were located on 1 August 1990,

Determined to bring the occupation of Kuwait by Iraq to an end and to restore the sovereignty, independence and territorial integrity to Kuwait,

Determined also to restore the authority of the legitimate Government of Kuwait,

1. *Decides* that annexation of Kuwait by Iraq under any form and whatever pretext has no legal validity, and is considered null and void;

2. *Calls upon* all States, international organizations and specialized agencies not to recognize that annexation, and to refrain from any action or dealing that might be interpreted as an indirect recognition of the annexation;

3. *Demands* that Iraq rescind its actions purporting to annex Kuwait
* * *.

NOTES

1. *The U.N. Charter Era.* In the U.N. Charter era, efforts to acquire territory through military force have declined considerably from prior times. See Zacher, The Territorial Integrity Norm: International Boundaries and the Use of Force, 55 Int'l Org. 215 (2001). In *Military and Paramilitary Activities in and against Nicaragua* (Nicaragua v. United States), 1986 I.C.J. 14, para. 190, the I.C.J. held that the principles of the U.N. Charter relating to the threat or use of force were part of customary international law with the character of *jus cogens.* Does this holding require U.N. members not to recognize any territorial acquisitions achieved by means of conquest? If a non-member makes such a conquest, does a member-state of the United Nations violate its obligations under the Charter by recognition of a change of sovereignty? See U.N. Charter, art. 2(6); Jennings, The Acquisition of Territory in International Law 53–55 (1963); see also Chapter 3, Section 5(D)). For an interesting counter-example, note that the Portuguese enclave of Goa on

the west coast of India was successfully conquered and annexed by India in 1961. See Wright, The Goa Incident, 56 A.J.I.L. 617 (1962). Will permissibility of such action depend in part on whether the prior possessor's title is regarded as legitimate (e.g., Portugal as a colonial power)? See Jennings, *supra*, at 61–65; see also Milano, Unlawful Territorial Situations in International Law (2006).

2. *Revisionism?* If international law no longer permits a state to gain title to territory by resorting to war, what is the present status of territory conquered and annexed at a time when international law did recognize such a title as valid? On a theory of intertemporal law, should states be able to question title secured yesterday based on a method deemed impermissible today? For example, should aboriginal natives in Australia be able to claim back the Australian continent on grounds that it was unlawfully taken from them by force? Should states be able to challenge contemporary borders that were the product of military conquests of the past? Note that Article 62(2)(a) of the Vienna Convention on the Law of Treaties, May 23, 1969, 1155 U.N.T.S. 331, expressly precludes reliance on changed circumstances to challenge a border treaty.

3. *Coercing an Agreement.* Is the conquering state's position in any way improved by forcing the conquered state to agree to a treaty of cession, such as The Treaty of Guadalupe Hidalgo? Article 52 of the Vienna Convention on the Law of Treaties states that a treaty (including presumably a treaty of cession) is void "if its conclusion has been procured by the threat or use of force in violation of the principles of international law embodied in the Charter of the United Nations." See Chapter 3, Section 5(C).

4. *Conquest through Lawful Defense.* Article 51 of the U.N. Charter allows a state to engage in self-defense against an armed attack. If in defending itself, a state finds it necessary to enter and occupy a portion of the territory of the attacking state, is there any basis for concluding that such occupation can give rise to a valid title to territory? See Schwebel, What Weight to Conquest?, 64 A.J.I.L. 344, 344–47 (1970).

The question is not academic. In the Arab–Israeli war in June 1967, Israeli armed forces occupied Gaza, the West Bank, Sinai, and the Golan Heights. In 1968, Israel began establishing civilian settlements in these territories. Was this permitted under international law? See Letter from State Department Legal Adviser concerning the Legality of Israeli Settlements in the Occupied Territories, Apr. 21, 1978, 1978, 17 I.L.M. 777 (1978) (reaching the conclusion that, as a belligerent occupant, Israel had no right to establish such settlements); G.A. Res. 32/5 (Oct. 18, 1977) (to the same effect by vote of 131 to 1, with the abstentions of Costa Rica, Fiji, Guatemala, Malawi, Nicaragua, Papua, New Guinea, and United States). On whether Israel had the right to develop new oil fields in Sinai and the Gulf of Suez, see Department of State Memorandum of Law on Israel's Right to Develop New Oil Fields in Sinai and the Gulf of Suez, Oct. 1, 1976, 16 I.L.M. 733 (1977) (reaching a negative answer), and the response of the Israeli Ministry of Foreign Affairs Memorandum of Law on the Right to Develop New Oil Fields in Sinai and the Gulf of Suez, Aug. 1, 1977, 17 I.L.M. 432 (1978) (giving an affirmative answer).

In *Legal Consequences of the Construction of a Wall in the Occupied Palestinian Territory*, Advisory Opinion, 2004 I.C.J. 136, the International Court of Justice was not sympathetic to Israel's argument that its inherent right of self-defense justified building a barrier enclosing portions of the West Bank, finding instead that the construction violated various norms of human rights and international humanitarian law. For a contrasting view, see Wedgwood, The ICJ Advisory Opinion on the Israeli Security Fence and the Limits of Self–Defense, 99 A.J.I.L. 52, 61 (2005) (noting that the various accords of the Middle East peace process, as endorsed by the Security Council, envisage the possibility of changes in the "Green Line" boundary between Israel and an independent Palestine to accommodate Israeli settlements and hence, in the interim, Israel should be afforded means for the protection of noncombatants in such areas).

3. Title by Treaty of Cession

An important way for a state to establish its title to certain territory is to prove that it lawfully received the territory from a prior sovereign, sometimes by purchase or as a concession in exchange for some other benefit. For example, the United States purchased the Louisiana territory from France in 1803, consummated the Gadsden Purchase of southern Arizona from Mexico in 1854 (to allow for the construction of a southern route for a transcontinental railroad), and purchased Alaska from Russia in 1867. In 1819, by terms of the Adams–Onís Treaty, Spain ceded Florida to the United States in exchange for U.S. renunciation of any claims on Texas and $5 million. The border between the United States and British North America in the northwest was defined peacefully in 1846 by the Oregon Treaty (setting the border at the 49th parallel).

In recent years, several cases have been resolved by the International Court of Justice based on interpretations of treaties by which territory was divided. See, e.g., *Territorial Dispute* (Libya/Chad), 1994 I.C.J. 6; *Kasikili/Sedudu Island* (Botswana/Namibia), 1999 I.C.J. 1045; *Sovereignty over Pulau Ligitan and Pulau Sipadan* (Indonesia/Malaysia), 2002 I.C.J. 625.

4. Title by State Succession

Another way for a state to establish its title to territory is to demonstrate that it "succeeded" to the territory when a predecessor state dissolved or disappeared, or when a new state broke away from an existing state. State formation in the latter context can occur by the new state being granted independence by a previous sovereign (devolution), such as Britain's grants of independence to India and Pakistan in 1947, or by the new state forcibly seizing independence (secession), such as Bangladesh's forcible secession from Pakistan in 1971. See Crawford, The Creation of States in International Law 329–448 (2d ed. 2006).

Issues concerning how succession of states relates to membership in international organizations, allocation of debts and assets, and other issues, are addressed in Chapter 19. For present purposes, it is simply noted that a situation of succession does not alter border treaties that exist between the territory in question and neighboring states. See Vienna Convention on the Succession of States in Respect of Treaties, Aug. 23, 1978, art. 11, 1946 U.N.T.S. 3.

5. Title Based on Longstanding Effective and Peaceful Possession (Prescription)

Assume that one state obtains title to certain territory. Assume a second state then enters into the territory and effectively and peacefully administers it for an extended period of time. Does international law recognize the transfer of sovereignty based on a concept of prescription, a concept analogous to the common law doctrine of adverse possession?

ISLAND OF PALMAS CASE
(UNITED STATES v. THE NETHERLANDS)

Permanent Court of Arbitration, 1928
2 U.N. Rep. Int'l Arb. Awards 829

[Palmas (also known as Miangas) is an isolated island of less than two square miles in area, lying about half way between Mindanao in the Philippine Islands and the most northerly of the Nanusa group in the former Dutch East Indies. It lies within the boundaries of the Philippines as ceded by Spain to the United States in 1898 by the Treaty of Paris. U.S. authorities learned in 1906 that the island was considered by the Netherlands to form a part of the Dutch possessions in that part of the world. After diplomatic correspondence, the United States and the Netherlands agreed in 1925 to submit to a member of the Permanent Court of Arbitration the question "whether the Island of Palmas (or Miangas) in its entirety forms a part of territory belonging to the United States of America or of Netherlands territory." The parties designated as sole arbitrator the Swiss jurist, Max Huber, who delivered his award on April 4, 1928.]

The *United States,* as successor to the rights of Spain over the Philippines, bases its title in the first place on discovery. * * *

* * *

The *Netherlands* Government's main argument endeavours to show that the Netherlands, represented for this purpose in the first period of colonization by the East India Company, have possessed and exercised rights of sovereignty from 1677, or probably from a date prior even to 1648, to the present day. * * *

* * *

* * * [A]n element which is essential for the constitution of sovereignty should not be lacking in its continuation. So true is this, that practice, as well as doctrine, recognizes—though under different legal formulae and with certain differences as to the conditions required—that

the continuous and peaceful display of territorial sovereignty (peaceful in relation to other States) is as good as a title. The growing insistence with which international law, ever since the middle of the 18th century, has demanded that the occupation shall be effective would be inconceivable, if effectiveness were required only for the act of acquisition and not equally for the maintenance of the right. If the effectiveness has above all been insisted on in regard to occupation, this is because the question rarely arises in connection with territories in which there is already an established order of things. * * *

Territorial sovereignty, as has already been said, involves the exclusive right to display the activities of a State. This right has as corollary a duty: the obligation to protect within the territory the rights of other States, in particular their right to integrity and inviolability in peace and in war, together with the rights which each State may claim for its nationals in foreign territory. Without manifesting its territorial sovereignty in a manner corresponding to circumstances, the State cannot fulfill this duty. Territorial sovereignty cannot limit itself to its negative side, i.e. to excluding the activities of other States; for it serves to divide between nations the space upon which human activities are employed, in order to assure them at all points the minimum of protection of which international law is the guardian.

* * *

Manifestations of territorial sovereignty assume, it is true, different forms, according to conditions of time and place. Although continuous in principle, sovereignty cannot be exercised in fact at every moment on every point of a territory. The intermittence and discontinuity compatible with the maintenance of the right necessarily differ according as inhabited or uninhabited regions are involved, or regions enclosed within territories in which sovereignty is incontestably displayed or again regions accessible from, for instance, the high seas. * * *

* * *

It is admitted by both sides that international law underwent profound modifications between the end of the Middle–Ages and the end of the 19th century, as regards the rights of discovery and acquisition of uninhabited regions or regions inhabited by savages or semi-civilised peoples. Both Parties are also agreed that a juridical fact must be appreciated in the light of the law contemporary with it, and not of the law in force at the time when a dispute in regard to it arises or fails to be settled. The effect of discovery by Spain is therefore to be determined by the rules of international law in force in the first half of the 16th century * * *.

If the view most favourable to the American arguments is adopted— with every reservation as to the soundness of such view—that is to say, if we consider as positive law at the period in question the rule that discovery as such, i.e. the mere fact of seeing land, without any act, even symbolical, of taking possession, involved *ipso jure* territorial sovereignty and not merely an "inchoate title", a *jus ad rem*, to be completed eventually by an actual and durable taking of possession within a reasonable time, the question arises whether sovereignty yet existed at the critical date, i.e. the moment of conclusion and coming into force of the Treaty of Paris.

As regards the question which of different legal systems prevailing at successive periods is to be applied in a particular case (the so-called intertemporal law), a distinction must be made between the creation of rights and the existence of rights. The same principle which [subjects] the act creative of a right to the law in force at the time the right arises, demands that the existence of the right, in other words its continued manifestation, shall follow the conditions required by the evolution of law. International law in the 19th century, having regard to the fact that most parts of the globe were under the sovereignty of States members of the community of nations, and that territories without a master had become relatively few, took account of a tendency already existing and especially developed since the middle of the 18th century, and laid down the principle that occupation, to constitute a claim to territorial sovereignty, must be effective, that is, offer certain guarantees to other States and their nationals. It seems therefore incompatible with this rule of positive law that there should be regions which are neither under the effective sovereignty of a State, nor without a master, but which are reserved for the exclusive influence of one State, in virtue solely of a title of acquisition which is no longer recognized by existing law, even if such a title ever conferred territorial sovereignty. For these reasons, discovery alone, without any subsequent act, cannot at the present time suffice to prove sovereignty over the Island of Palmas (or Miangas); and in so far as there is no sovereignty, the question of an abandonment properly speaking of sovereignty by one State in order that the sovereignty of another may take its place does not arise.

If on the other hand the view is adopted that discovery does not create a definitive title of sovereignty, but only an "inchoate" title, such a title exists, it is true, without external manifestation. However, according to the view that has prevailed at any rate since the 19th century, an inchoate title of discovery must be completed within a reasonable period by the effective occupation of the region claimed to be discovered. This principle must be applied in the present case, for the reasons given above in regard to the rules determining which of successive legal systems is to be applied (the so-called intertemporal law). Now, no act of occupation nor, except as to a recent period, any exercise of sovereignty at Palmas by Spain has been alleged. But even admitting that the Spanish title still existed as inchoate in 1898 and must be considered as included in the cession under Article III of the Treaty of Paris, an inchoate title could not prevail over the continuous and peaceful display of authority by another

State; for such display may prevail even over a prior, definitive title put forward by another State. * * *

* * *

In the last place there remains to be considered *title arising out of contiguity*. Although States have in certain circumstances maintained that islands relatively close to their shores belonged to them in virtue of their geographical situation, it is impossible to show the existence of a rule of positive international law to the effect that islands situated outside territorial waters should belong to a State from the mere fact that its territory forms the *terra firma* (nearest continent or island of considerable size). * * *

* * *

The Netherlands' arguments contend that the East India Company established Dutch sovereignty over the Island of Palmas (or Miangas) as early as the 17th century, by means of conventions with the princes of Tabukan (Taboekan) and Taruna (Taroena), two native chieftains of the Island of Sangi (Groot Sangihe), the principal island of the Talautse Isles (Sangi Islands), and that sovereignty has been displayed during the past two centuries.

* * *

* * * The questions to be solved in the present case are the following:

Was the island of Palmas (or Miangas) in 1898 *a part of territory under Netherlands' sovereignty?*

Did this sovereignty actually exist in 1898 *in regard to Palmas (or Miangas)* and are the facts proved which were alleged on this subject? * * *

* * *

* * * Since the contract of 1885 with Taruna and that of 1899 with Kandahar–Taruna comprise Palmas (or Miangas) within the territories of a native State under the suzerainty of the Netherlands and since it has been established that in 1906 on the said island a state of things existed showing at least certain traces of display of Netherlands sovereignty, it is now necessary to examine what is the nature of the facts invoked as proving such sovereignty, and to what periods such facts relate. This examination will show whether or not the Netherlands have displayed sovereignty over the Island of Palmas (or Miangas) in an effective continuous and peaceful manner at a period at which such exercise may have excluded the acquisition of sovereignty, or a title to such acquisition, by the United States of America. * * *

[After a detailed examination of the acts of the Dutch East India Company and the Netherlands State tending to establish a display of sovereignty over the Island of Palmas, the arbitrator continued:]

The claim of the United States to sovereignty over the Island of Palmas (or Miangas) is derived from Spain by way of cession under the Treaty of Paris. The latter Treaty, though it comprises the island in dispute within the limits of cession, and in spite of the absence of any reserves or protest by the Netherlands as to these limits, has not created in favour of the United States any title of sovereignty such as was not already vested in Spain. The essential point is therefore to decide whether Spain had sovereignty over Palmas (or Miangas) at the time of the coming into force of the Treaty of Paris.

* * *

The acts of indirect or direct display of Netherlands sovereignty at Palmas (or Miangas), especially in the 18th and early 19th centuries are not numerous, and there are considerable gaps in the evidence of continuous display. But apart from the consideration that the manifestations of sovereignty over a small and distant island, inhabited only by natives, cannot be expected to be frequent, it is not necessary that the display of sovereignty should go back to a very far distant period. It may suffice that such display existed in 1898, and had already existed as continuous and peaceful before that date long enough to enable any Power who might have considered herself as possessing sovereignty over the island, or having a claim to sovereignty, to have, according to local conditions, a reasonable possibility for ascertaining the existence of a state of things contrary to her real or alleged rights.

It is not necessary that the display of sovereignty should be established as having begun at a precise epoch; it suffices that it had existed at the critical period preceding the year 1898. It is quite natural that the establishment of sovereignty may be the outcome of a slow evolution, of a progressive intensification of State control. This is particularly the case, if sovereignty is acquired by the establishment of the suzerainty of a colonial Power over a native State, and in regard to outlying possessions of such a vassal State.

Now the evidence relating to the period after the middle of the 19th century makes it clear that the Netherlands Indian Government considered the island distinctly as a part of its possessions and that, in the years immediately preceding 1898, an intensification of display of sovereignty took place.

Since the moment when the Spaniards, in withdrawing from the Moluccas in 1666, made express reservations as to the maintenance of their sovereign rights, up to the contestation made by the United States in 1906, no contestation or other action whatever or protest against the exercise of territorial rights by the Netherlands over the Talautse (Sangi) Isles and their dependencies (Miangas included) has been recorded. The peaceful character of the display of Netherlands sovereignty for the entire period to which the evidence concerning acts of display relates (1700–1906) must be admitted.

* * *

The conditions of acquisition of sovereignty by the Netherlands are therefore to be considered as fulfilled. It remains now to be seen whether the United States as successors of Spain are in a position to bring forward an equivalent or stronger title. This is to be answered in the negative.

The title of discovery, if it had not been already disposed of by the Treaties of Münster and Utrecht would, under the most favourable and most extensive interpretation, exist only as an inchoate title, as a claim to establish sovereignty by effective occupation. An inchoate title however cannot prevail over a definite title founded on continuous and peaceful display of sovereignty.

The title of contiguity, understood as a basis of territorial sovereignty, has no foundation in international law.

* * *

The Netherlands title of sovereignty, acquired by continuous and peaceful display of State authority during a long period of time going probably back beyond the year 1700, therefore holds good.

NOTES

1. *Protesting Possession.* An analysis of whether title has passed from one sovereign to another through prescription appears to invite analysis of not just the conduct of the state claiming peaceful possession, but also the conduct of the state that has arguably been dispossessed. Has the latter protested or acquiesced to the former's conduct? Brierly writes:

> The principle of extinctive prescription under which the passage of time operates ultimately to bar the right of a prior owner to pursue his claim against one who, having wrongfully displaced him, has continued for a long time in adverse possession is recognized in almost all systems of municipal law and it appears equally to be admitted by international law. * * * It is a nice question as to exactly how far diplomatic and other paper forms of protest by the dispossessed state suffice to 'disturb' the possession of the interloper so as to prevent the latter from acquiring a title by prescription. * * * Thus it was largely for the purpose of avoiding any risk of the extinguishment of its claims by prescription that in 1955 the United Kingdom filed a unilateral application with the International Court challenging alleged encroachments by Argentina and Chile on the Falkland Islands Dependencies.

Brierly, The Law of Nations 167–71 (6th ed. Waldock 1963).

2. *How Effective Must the Possession Be?* How "effective" does the Dutch occupation of Palmas seem to have been? Could it be said that "effectiveness was established negatively from the absence of any competing manifestations of sovereignty, and that it was only because the Netherlands had taken more interest in the Island than Spain that it was adjudged entitled?" O'Connell at 472. In *Clipperton Island*, 2 U.N. Rep. Int'l Arb. Awards 1105, 26 A.J.I.L. 390 (1932), France was held entitled to sovereignty over a small unpopulated guano island situated in the Pacific Ocean, about

670 miles southwest of Mexico. The French claim was based on the fact that a French naval officer had, in 1858, cruised to the island, proclaimed French sovereignty, made detailed geographic notes, and landed some members of his crew. The party left no sign of sovereignty on the island, but notified French and Hawaiian officials in Honolulu, and had a declaration of sovereignty published in a Honolulu journal. No further action was taken by France or any other state until 1897, when France protested to the United States the presence on the island of three persons who had raised an American flag at the approach of a French vessel. The United States disclaimed, in 1898, any interest in the island, but meanwhile Mexico had sent a gunboat to the island and had had the Mexican flag raised. Mexico claimed that it had always enjoyed sovereignty over Clipperton by virtue of Spanish discovery, or in the alternative, that the French "occupation" from 1858 to 1897 had been ineffective and that the island was in 1897 *terra nullius*. The Arbitrator held that Spanish discovery had not been proved, nor had Spanish exercise of sovereign rights; the island was therefore capable of appropriation in 1858. Turning to the question whether France had effectively occupied the island, the Arbitrator held that although the exercise of effective, exclusive authority ordinarily required the establishment of an administration capable of securing respect for the sovereign's rights, this was not necessary in the case of uninhabited territory which is at the occupying state's absolute and undisputed disposition from the latter's first appearance. Should the *Clipperton Island* case be limited to situations closely paralleling its facts; i.e., small unpopulated islands?

3. *Acts* à Titre de Souverain. When considering whether a state has effective possession, courts will sometimes refer to acts *à titre de souverain*, meaning acts consistent with sovereignty. In *Kasikili/Sedudu Island* (Botswana v. Namibia), 1999 I.C.J. 1045, Botswana and Namibia asked the I.C.J. to determine the legal status of a small island in the Chobe River, long used by Masubia tribespeople. According to Namibia, four conditions had to be fulfilled to enable possession by a state to mature into a prescriptive title: (1) the possession of the state must be exercised *à titre de souverain*; (2) the possession must be peaceful and uninterrupted; (3) the possession must be public; and (4) the possession must endure for a certain length of time (para. 94). Botswana concurred in those conditions (para. 95). The Court stated:

> 97.   For present purposes, the Court need not concern itself with the status of acquisitive prescription in international law or with the conditions for acquiring title to territory by prescription. It considers, for the reasons set out below, that the conditions cited by Namibia itself are not satisfied in this case and that Namibia's argument on acquisitive prescription therefore cannot be accepted.

> 98.   * * * [T]he evidence shows that the Masubia used the Island intermittently, according to the seasons and their needs, for exclusively agricultural purposes; this use, which began prior to the establishment of any colonial administration in the Caprivi Strip, seems to have subsequently continued without being linked to territorial claims on the part of the Authority administering the Caprivi. [The Court also concluded that as soon as Namibia's predecessor officially claimed title, Botswana's

predecessor "did not accept that claim, which precluded acquiescence on its part."]

99. In the Court's view, Namibia has not established with the necessary degree of precision and certainty that acts of State authority capable of providing alternative justification for prescriptive title, in accordance with the conditions set out by Namibia, were carried out by its predecessors or by itself with regard to Kasikili/Sedudu Island. * * *

By contrast, in *Sovereignty over Pedra Branca/Pulau Batu Puteh, Middle Rocks and South Ledge* (Malaysia/Singapore), 2008 I.C.J. ___, the Court found that Malaysia (or its predecessor) had original title to a granite island called Pedra Branca/Pulau Batu Puteh based on a continuous and peaceful display of sovereignty. However, in the 1950s correspondence between Malaysia and Singapore demonstrated that Malaysia did not view itself as sovereign over the island, while Singapore began handling shipwrecks that occurred at the island, granting permission to Malaysia to conduct surveys of the adjacent waters, flying the Singapore ensign and installing military equipment on the island, and performing other acts *à titre de souverain*. Given that Malaysia failed to protest such acts, the court concluded that sovereignty over the island had passed from Malaysia to Singapore.

3. *Problem of Intertemporal Law.* The Arbitrator in *Island of Palmas* referred to the problem of "intertemporal law." That problem wrestles with how to handle a legal concept that has changed in meaning over time. Assume that two parties agree, in year one, that rule X shall apply between them. Assume further that, in year fifty, rule X has mutated in the practice of states to have a different meaning, referred to as rule Y. Is the relevant rule governing the two parties X or Y? In other words, should the concept be interpreted as understood at the time it was adopted or at the time of its application?

The International Court of Justice faced this issue in its *Legal Consequences for States of the Continued Presence of South Africa in Namibia (South West Africa) notwithstanding Security Council Resolution 276 (1970)*, Advisory Opinion, 1971 I.C.J. 16, when it had to interpret terms of the Covenant of the League of Nations, with respect to the League's establishment of Southwest Africa as a mandate entrusted to South Africa. The relevant terms in the Covenant included "sacred trust," and "well-being and development" of the indigenous inhabitants. The opinion of the Court included the following conclusions relating to this problem:

> Mindful as it is of the primary necessity of interpreting an instrument in accordance with the intentions of the parties at the time of its conclusion, the Court is bound to take into account the fact that the concepts embodied in Article 22 of the Covenant * * * were not static, but were by definition evolutionary, as also, therefore, was the concept of the sacred trust. The parties to the Covenant must consequently be deemed to have accepted them as such.

Id. at 31. The Court consequently reached the following conclusion: "That is why, viewing the institutions of 1919, the Court must take into consideration the changes which have occurred in the supervening half-century, and its interpretation cannot remain unaffected by the subsequent development of law, through the Charter of the United Nations and by way of customary law." Id. The Court further added: "Moreover, an international instrument has to be interpreted and applied within the framework of the entire legal system prevailing at the time of interpretation." Id.

In the context of title to territory, however, should the Court's approach in the *Namibia* advisory opinion hold true? If so, would it require every state constantly to examine its title to each portion of its territory "in order to determine whether a change in the law had necessitated, as it were, a reacquisition"? Jessup, The Palmas Island Arbitration, 22 A.J.I.L. 735, 740 (1928). See also de Visscher, Theory and Reality in Public International Law 209–12 (rev. ed. Corbett trans. 1968). In *Island of Palmas*, the arbitrator decided (and both parties agreed) that the juridical fact of legal possession of territory "must be appreciated in the light of the law contemporary with it, and not of the law in force at the time when a dispute in regard to it arises or fails to be settled." Do you agree with that approach?

In the boundary dispute between Botswana and Namibia referred to in the prior note, the International Court of Justice had to interpret a term in a 1890 treaty between Germany and Great Britain, which delineated their spheres of influence with reference to the "main channel" of the Chobe River. The Court focused on the legal meaning of "main channel" in 1890, though it stated that in "order to illuminate the meaning of words agreed upon in 1890, there is nothing that prevents the Court from taking into account the present-day state of scientific knowledge, as reflected in the documentary material submitted to it by the Parties * * *." *Kasikili/Sedudu Island* (Botswana/Namibia), 1999 I.C.J. 1045, para. 20. In her separate declaration, Judge Higgins clarified her position on the intertemporal issues:

1. At paragraph 28 of its Judgment, the Court states that it is interpreting words in a treaty to give them their ordinary meaning; and that this is what it is doing in determining the meaning of "main channel" by "reference to the most commonly used criteria in international law." I find this somewhat fanciful. * * * [N]o "ordinary meaning" of this term exists, either in international law or in hydrology, which allows the Court to suppose that it is engaging in such an exercise. * * * The Court is really doing something rather different. It is applying a somewhat general term, decided upon by the Parties in 1890, to a geographic and hydrographic situation much better understood today.

2. The term "the main channel" is not a "generic term" * * *— that is to say, a known legal term, whose content the parties expected would change through time. * * *

3. The Court is indeed, for this particular task, entitled to look at all the criteria the Parties have suggested as relevant. This is not to discover a mythical "ordinary meaning" within the Treaty, but rather because the general terminology chosen long ago falls to be decided today. To use contemporary knowledge and scientific data to assist in fulfilling that task is not at all inconsistent with the intertemporal rule in the *Island of Palmas* Award, which was concerned with the legal rules applicable to title to territory and not with identification, through the legal technique of evaluating evidence, of a chosen term.

Id. 1999 I.C.J. 1113 (declaration of Judge Higgins); see Castellino & Allen, Title to Territory in International Law: A Temporal Analysis (2003).

4. *Squaring* Palmas *with* Western Sahara. Can the Court's view that the Western Sahara was not *terra nullius* because it was inhabited by socially and politically organized tribes be squared with the conclusion in the *Island of Palmas* case that the Netherlands could acquire sovereignty over Palmas by "occupation," given that Palmas was inhabited by natives who presumably were also to some extent socially and politically organized? Consider the following comment:

> If a territory is not *terra nullius,* the result is that some politically organized group must be exercising traditional acts of sovereignty in relation to it. If those traditional acts include, as the court in the *Island of Palmas* case indicates, the right to exclude the activities of other States, as well as the ability to protect the rights of other nationals in the territory, then the Western Sahara Court would be hard-pressed to name the party displaying these acts of sovereignty in Western Sahara. * * * [T]he Court in the *Island of Palmas* case defines sovereignty in such a way as to disqualify all of the parties with an interest in Western Sahara. * * * Indeed, Morocco and Mauritania are disqualified because of the Court's determination later in the opinion that they lacked sufficient ties of territorial sovereignty to Western Sahara. The burden similarly cannot be placed on the tribes of Western Sahara simply because they were incapable of exercising the acts of sovereignty required by the *Palmas* decision over the vast majority of the territory. Thus, the Court's conclusion that Western Sahara was not *terra nullius* in 1884 is not consistent with the fact that there was no country or group of individuals in a position to occupy the territory at that time.

Smith, Note, Sovereignty Over Unoccupied Territories—The Western Sahara Decision, 9 Case W. Res. J. Int'l L. 135, 140–41 (1977).

5. *Laying Claim to Antarctica.* On April 2, 1924, Secretary of State Hughes wrote to the Norwegian Minister, H.H. Bryn, in regard to the legal effect of Roald Amundsen's explorations in the Antarctic:

> In the penultimate paragraph of your letter you state that, in order to avoid any misunderstanding, you would add that possession of all the land which Mr. Amundsen may discover will, of course, be taken in the name of His Majesty, the King of Norway. In my opinion rights similar to those which in earlier centuries were based upon the acts of a discoverer, followed by occupation or settlement consummated at long and uncertain periods thereafter, are not capable of being acquired at the present time. Today, if an explorer is able to ascertain the existence of lands still unknown to civilization, his act of so-called discovery, coupled with a formal taking of possession, would have no significance, save as he might herald the advent of the settler; and where for climatic or other reasons actual settlement would be an impossibility, as in the case of the Polar regions, such conduct on his part would afford frail support for a reasonable claim of sovereignty.

The Norwegian Minister replied on November 12, 1924, that the Norwegian Government did not intend "to invoke a possible discovery of new land as a basis for a claim to sovereignty. It only meant that the Norwegian Government claimed the right to priority in acquiring subsequently the sovereignty by settlement or by other procedure sanctioned by International Law." Both notes are quoted in 1 Hackworth at 399–400.

6. *Island Spats.* Disputes have arisen over the sovereignty to various small islands dotting the oceans. Although sovereignty over many has not been claimed, strategic location and possible oil and mineral reserves especially in adjacent maritime areas enhance their current attractiveness. Recent cases before the International Court of this type include *Maritime Delimitation and Territorial Questions* (Qatar v. Bahrain), 2001 I.C.J. 40.

The Spratly and Paracel Islands in the South China Sea have been claimed by China, the Philippines, and Vietnam. For analysis of these claims, see Clagett, Competing Claims of Vietnam and China in the Vanguard Bank and Blue Dragon Areas of the South China Sea, 13 Oil & Gas L. & Tax'n Rev. 375 (1995); Park, The South China Sea Disputes: Who Owns the Islands and the Natural Resources?, 5 Ocean Dev. & Int'l L.J. 27 (1978). Similarly, Japan and China dispute the sovereignty over the Senkaku Islands in the East China Sea, while Japan and Russia dispute sovereignty over the southernmost Kuril Islands. See Schoenbaum, Peace in Northeast Asia: Resolving Japan's Territorial and Maritime Disputes with China, Korea and the Russian Federation (2008); Maritime Boundary Issues and Islands Disputes in the East Asian Region (Kim ed. 1998).

On when and how sovereignty can be claimed over newly emerged islands, see Dingley, Note, Eruptions in International Law: Emerging Volcanic Islands and the Law of Territorial Acquisition, 11 Cornell Int'l L.J. 121 (1978). On sovereignty over uninhabitable islands in relation to delimitation of maritime zones, see Charney, Rocks That Cannot Sustain Human Habitation, 93 A.J.I.L. 863 (1999).

B. DELIMITING BOUNDARIES: THE PRINCIPLE OF *UTI POSSIDETIS JURIS*

FRONTIER DISPUTE (BURKINA FASO/MALI)

International Court of Justice, 1986
1986 I.C.J. 554

[Burkina Faso (previously Republic of Upper Volta) and the Republic of Mali submitted to a Chamber of the I.C.J. pursuant to a special agreement the question "[w]hat is the line of the frontier" of the Upper Volta and the Republic of Mali in "a band of territory extending from the sector Koro (Mali) Djibo (Upper Volta) up to and including the region of Béli." Prior to analyzing the evidence and drawing the line of the frontier, the Chamber (Judges Lachs, Ruda, Bedjaoui, Luchaire, Abi–Saab) commented as follows on the principle of *uti possidetis* (literally, "as you possess"), a principle originating in Roman law that territory and other property remains with its possessor at the end of a period of change, unless otherwise provided by agreement. Here the Court uses the principle when establishing the frontiers of two newly independent states following decolonization.]

19. The characteristic feature of the legal context of the frontier determination to be undertaken by the Chamber is that both States involved derive their existence from the process of decolonization which has been unfolding in Africa during the past 30 years. Their territories, and that of Niger, were formerly part of the French colonies which were grouped together under the name of French West Africa (AOF). Considering only the situation which prevailed immediately before the accession to independence of the two States, and disregarding previous administrative changes, it can be said that Burkina Faso corresponds to the colony of Upper Volta, and the Republic of Mali to the colony of Sudan (formerly French Sudan). It is to be supposed that the Parties drew inspiration from the principle expressly stated in the well-known resolution (AGH/Res. 16 (I)), adopted at the first session of the Conference of African Heads of State and Government, meeting in Cairo in 1964, whereby the Conference solemnly declared that all member States of the Organization of African Unity "solemnly ... pledge themselves to respect the frontiers existing on their achievement of national independence", inasmuch as, in the preamble to their Special Agreement, they stated that the settlement of the dispute by the Chamber must be "based in particular on respect for the principle of the intangibility of frontiers inherited from colonization". It is clear from this text, and from the pleadings and oral arguments of the Parties, that they are in agreement as regards both the applicable law and the starting-point for the legal reasoning which is to lead to the determination of the frontier between their territories in the disputed area.

20. Since the two Parties have, as noted above, expressly requested the Chamber to resolve their dispute on the basis, in particular, of the "principle of the intangibility of frontiers inherited from colonization", the Chamber cannot disregard the principle of *uti possidetis juris,* the application of which gives rise to this respect for intangibility of frontiers. Although there is no need, for the purposes of the present case, to show that this is a firmly established principle of international law where decolonization is concerned, the Chamber nonetheless wishes to emphasize its general scope, in view of its exceptional importance for the African continent and for the two Parties. In this connection it should be noted that the principle of *uti possidetis* seems to have been first invoked and applied in Spanish America, inasmuch as this was the continent which first witnessed the phenomenon of decolonization involving the formation of a number of sovereign States on territory formerly belonging to a single metropolitan State. Nevertheless the principle is not a special rule which pertains solely to one specific system of international law. It is a general principle, which is logically connected with the phenomenon of the obtaining of independence, wherever it occurs. Its obvious purpose is to prevent the independence and stability of new States being endangered by fratricidal struggles provoked by the changing of frontiers following the withdrawal of the administering power.

21. It was for this reason that, as soon as the phenomenon of decolonization characteristic of the situation in Spanish America in the 19th century subsequently appeared in Africa in the 20th century, the principle of *uti possidetis,* in the sense described above, fell to be applied. The fact that the new African States have respected the administrative boundaries and frontiers established by the colonial powers must be seen not as a mere practice contributing to the gradual emergence of a principle of customary international law, limited in its impact to the African continent as it had previously been to Spanish America, but as the application in Africa of a rule of general scope.

22. The elements of *uti possidetis* were latent in the many declarations made by African leaders in the dawn of independence. These declarations confirmed the maintenance of the territorial status quo at the time of independence, and stated the principle of respect both for the frontiers deriving from international agreements, and for those resulting from mere internal administrative divisions. The Charter of the Organization of African Unity did not ignore the principle of *uti possidetis,* but made only indirect reference to it in Article 3, according to which member States solemnly affirm the principle of respect for the sovereignty and territorial integrity of every State. However, at their first summit conference after the creation of the Organization of African Unity, the African Heads of State, in their Resolution mentioned above (AGH/Res. 16(I)), adopted in Cairo in July 1964, deliberately defined and stressed the principle of *uti possidetis juris* contained only in an implicit sense in the Charter of their organization.

23. There are several different aspects to this principle, in its well-known application in Spanish America. The first aspect, emphasized by the Latin genitive *juris,* is found in the pre-eminence accorded to legal title over effective possession as a basis of sovereignty. Its purpose, at the time of the achievement of independence by the former Spanish colonies of America, was to scotch any designs which non-American colonizing powers might have on regions which had been assigned by the former metropolitan State to one division or another, but which were still uninhabited or unexplored. However, there is more to the principle of *uti possidetis* than this particular aspect. The essence of the principle lies in its primary aim of securing respect for the territorial boundaries at the moment when independence is achieved. Such territorial boundaries might be no more than delimitations between different administrative divisions or colonies all subject to the same sovereign. In that case, the application of the principle of *uti possidetis* resulted in administrative boundaries being transformed into international frontiers in the full sense of the term. This is true both of the States which took shape in the regions of South America which were dependent on the Spanish Crown, and of the States Parties to the present case, which took shape within the vast territories of French West Africa. *Uti possidetis,* as a principle which upgraded former administrative delimitations, established during the colonial period, to international frontiers, is therefore a principle of a general

kind which is logically connected with this form of decolonization wherever it occurs.

24.   The territorial boundaries which have to be respected may also derive from international frontiers which previously divided a colony of one State from a colony of another, or indeed a colonial territory from the territory of an independent State, or one which was under protectorate, but had retained its international personality. There is no doubt that the obligation to respect pre-existing international frontiers in the event of a State succession derives from a general rule of international law, whether or not the rule is expressed in the formula *uti possidetis*. Hence the numerous solemn affirmations of the intangibility of the frontiers existing at the time of the independence of African States, whether made by senior African statesmen or by organs of the Organization of African Unity itself, are evidently declaratory rather than constitutive: they recognize and confirm an existing principle, and do not seek to consecrate a new principle or the extension to Africa of a rule previously applied only in another continent.

25.   However, it may be wondered how the time-hallowed principle has been able to withstand the new approaches to international law as expressed in Africa, where the successive attainment of independence and the emergence of new States have been accompanied by a certain questioning of traditional international law. At first sight this principle conflicts outright with another one, the right of peoples to self-determination. In fact, however, the maintenance of the territorial status quo in Africa is often seen as the wisest course, to preserve what has been achieved by peoples who have struggled for their independence, and to avoid a disruption which would deprive the continent of the gains achieved by much sacrifice. The essential requirement of stability in order to survive, to develop and gradually to consolidate their independence in all fields, has induced African States judiciously to consent to the respecting of colonial frontiers, and to take account of it in the interpretation of the principle of self-determination of peoples.

26.   Thus the principle of *uti possidetis* has kept its place among the most important legal principles, despite the apparent contradiction which explained its coexistence alongside the new norms. Indeed it was by deliberate choice that African States selected, among all the classic principles, that of *uti possidetis*. This remains an undeniable fact. In the light of the foregoing remarks, it is clear that the applicability of *uti possidetis* in the present case cannot be challenged merely because in 1960, the year when Mali and Burkina Faso achieved independence, the Organization of African Unity which was to proclaim this principle did not yet exist, and the above-mentioned resolution calling for respect for the pre-existing frontiers dates only from 1964.

NOTES

1. *Applying the Uti Possidetis Principle.* The International Court referred to the Chamber's decision in the above *Frontier Dispute* case when it decided *Territorial and Maritime Dispute in the Caribbean Sea* (Nicaragua v. Honduras), 2007 I.C.J. __, at paras. 151–53. In that case, when applying the *uti possidetis* principle, the Court analyzed first whether the colonial power (Spain) had allocated the disputed territory to one or the other of its colonial provinces. Finding that it had not, the Court went on to analyze whether there was evidence of colonial *effectivités*, meaning conduct of the administrative authorities in the colonial period demonstrating allocation of the territory to one or the other province. Finding that no such evidence existed, the Court then sought to identify any post-colonial *effectivités*, and concluded that Honduras had exercised a "modest but real display of authority" over the territory in question, id. at para. 208, such as by enforcing its criminal and civil law, and regulating immigration and fisheries activities. As such, the Court concluded that the disputed territory was Honduran.

2. *Badinter Commission.* In the context of the break-up of the former Yugoslavia, the Badinter Commission considered whether *internal* boundaries of the republics of that country should serve as the boundaries of newly emerged states. In answering in the affirmative, the Commission stated:

> Except where otherwise agreed, the former boundaries become frontiers protected by international law. This conclusion follows from the principle of respect for the territorial *status quo* and, in particular, from the principle of *uti possidetis*. *Uti possidetis*, though initially applied in settling decolonization issues in America and Africa, is today recognized as a general principle, as stated by the International Court of Justice in its Judgment of 22 December 1986 in the case between Burkina Faso and Mali (*Frontier Dispute* * * *).

Conference on Yugoslavia Arbitration Commission Opinion No. 3 (Jan. 11, 1992), 31 I.L.M. 1499 (1992), 3 E.J.I.L. 184 (1992).

3. *Improving on Uti Possidetis?* Is it appropriate to automatically apply the *uti possidetis* doctrine in situations like the breakup of former Yugoslavia, so as to transform internal administrative borders into international boundaries? Consider the following assessment:

> Reliance on *uti possidetis* during the post-Cold War breakups has stemmed from three arguments or assumptions. First, *uti possidetis* reduces the prospects of armed conflict by providing the only clear outcome in such situations. Absent such a policy, all borders would be open to dispute, and new states would fall prey to irredentist neighbors or internal secessionist claimants. Second, because a cosmopolitan democratic state can function within any borders, the conversion of administrative borders to international borders is as sensible as any other approach and far simpler. Third, and buttressing the other two, *uti possidetis* is asserted as a default rule of international law mandating the conversion of all administrative boundaries into international borders. This rule emerged during the decolonization of Latin America and Africa but would

apply by logical extension to the breakup of states today. The most significant elaboration of this extension came from the commission chaired by Judge Robert Badinter advising the European Community on legal questions associated with the breakup of Yugoslavia.

These views seem compelling; yet the easy embrace by governments of *uti possidetis* and the suggestion that it is now a general rule of international law to govern the breakup of states lead to two distinct, yet opposite, spillover effects that endanger global order at this time of ethnic conflict. First, a policy or rule that transforms all administrative borders of modern states into international boundaries creates a significant hazard in the name of simplicity—namely, the temptation of ethnic separatists to divide the world further along administrative lines. If the Republic of Georgia's new borders must coincide with those of the former Georgian Soviet Socialist Republic, are not the future Republic of Abhazia's just as clearly those of the former Abhaz Autonomous Soviet Socialist Republic? Would the Québecois consider secession so readily if the new state had different borders from those established by Canada and the United Kingdom for the purpose of integrating Quebec into the Dominion?

Second, the extension of *uti possidetis* to modern breakups leads to genuine injustices and instability by leaving significant populations both unsatisfied with their status in new states and uncertain of political participation there. By hiding behind inflated notions of *uti possidetis,* state leaders avoid engaging the issue of territorial adjustments—even minor ones—which is central to the process of self-determination. In the case of Yugoslavia, for instance, although *uti possidetis* hardly caused the eruption of armed conflict, the assumption by states of its applicability from the outset prevented any debate over the adjustment of boundaries and limited the universe of possible borders to one—leaving those people on the "wrong" side of the border ripe for "ethnic cleansing." * * *

It is thus time to reexamine this oft-invoked principle of international law and relations. For application of *uti possidetis* to the breakup of states today both ignores critical distinctions between internal lines and international boundaries and, more important, is profoundly at odds with current trends in international law and politics. Many internal borders do merit transformation into international boundaries based on historical and other characteristics; but the assumption that all such borders must be so transformed is unwarranted.

Ratner, Drawing a Better Line: *Uti Possidetis* and the Borders of New States, 90 A.J.I.L. 590, 591 (1996) (footnotes omitted); see LaLonde, Determining Boundaries in a Conflicted World: The Role of Uti Possidetis Juris (2002). Do you agree?

C. DELIMITING BOUNDARIES: METHODS OF DISPUTE SETTLEMENT

1. Bilateral Negotiation

Most disputes over territory are not resolved through courts or tribunals. Of some 348 territorial disputes from 1919 to 1995, only thirty were addressed through judicial or arbitral means. See Allee & Huth, Legitimizing Dispute Settlement: International Legal Rulings as Domestic Political Cover, 100 Am. Pol. Sci. Rev. 219 (2006). Instead, two states will often resolve a boundary dispute through bilateral negotiation leading to an international agreement that delimits the boundary. See Ratner, Land Feuds and Their Solutions: Finding International Law Beyond the Tribunal Chamber, 100 A.J.I.L. 808 (2006).

2.   Third Party Mediation or Arbitration

When bilateral negotiations are at an impasse, states have frequently sought the aid of third parties in resolving such disputes through mediation. For example, in October 1998, the Congresses of Peru and Ecuador agreed to ask Argentina, Brazil, Chile, and the United States to mediate a definitive solution to resolve the long-standing forty-nine-mile border dispute between Peru and Ecuador. The border dispute had twice previously provoked armed conflict and a significant arms race between the two nations. After mediation efforts, the presidents of Peru and Ecuador signed an agreement that resolved the border conflict. The agreement (1) reaffirmed a 1942 protocol that declared most of the disputed territory as part of Peru; (2) permitted Ecuador to exercise control over a small enclave in Peruvian territory where Ecuador will build a monument to its war dead; (3) demilitarized a fifty-mile stretch of the border; and (4) provided for a transition in the border area from monitoring by peacekeepers of the four guarantor nations to monitoring by police and park rangers in two national parks on each side of the border. In addition, the two countries signed commercial treaties granting Ecuador trade and navigational access to economically important shipping routes in Peru's Amazon territory. See Treaty of Trade and Navigation between the Governments of the Republic of Peru and the Republic of Ecuador, Peru–Ecuador, Oct. 26, 1998, 38 I.L.M. 266 (1999); see also Simmons, Territorial Disputes and Their Resolution: The Case of Ecuador and Peru, Peaceworks No. 27, U.S. Institute of Peace (1999). On May 13, 1999, Ecuador and Peru completed the demarcation of their common border, with Presidents Fujimori and Mahuad dedicating the last border marker. In doing so, the comprehensive peace agreement was brought fully into force.

Third-party mediation, however, is not always successful. The Falkland Islands, or Islas Malvinas, are the subject of a longstanding dispute between Argentina and the United Kingdom. The islands have been under British control since 1833, by virtue of successful military conquest, but Argentina has never given up its claims to territorial sovereignty. After Argentina attempted to change the status quo by sending armed forces to the islands in 1982, the countries turned to third-party mediation by the United States and the United Nations. That mediation failed to resolve the dispute, leading to a U.K. military response that resulted in a decisive victory. The islands remain under U.K. control. See Franck, Dulce et Decorum Est: The Strategic Role of Legal Principles in the Falklands War,

77 A.J.I.L. 109 (1983); Beck, The Falkland Islands as an International Problem (1988).

A third party country can also serve as an arbitrator, conducting a formal proceeding where the views of both sides are heard, and then issuing an arbitral award. For example, the Beagle Channel Islands (specifically Lennox, Nueva, and Picton Islands, located between the Atlantic and Pacific oceans at the southern tip of South America) were in dispute between Argentina and Chile from 1905 to 1984. Although both countries agreed in 1971 that the British Government should arbitrate their dispute, 10 I.L.M. 1182 (1971), the award of the islands to Chile, 17 I.L.M. 632 (1978), was not honored by Argentina. With war looming, Chile and Argentina then agreed to mediation by the Pope, 18 I.L.M. 1 (1979), who also urged that Argentina recognize Chile's claim. Ultimately, the dispute was resolved in favor of that outcome in a treaty signed at the Vatican on November 29, 1984, 24 I.L.M. 11 (1985). For discussion of the factors that rendered the Beagle Channel dispute so difficult to solve, including the reasons why Argentina did not accept the arbitral award but was willing to entertain the solution offered through papal mediation, see Laudy, The Vatican Mediation of the Beagle Channel Dispute: Crisis Intervention and Forum Building, in Words Over War: Mediation and Arbitration to Prevent Deadly Conflict 293 (Greenberg, Barton, & McGuinness eds. 2000).

3. *Ad Hoc* Arbitral Panel

Sometimes an *ad hoc* international arbitral panel of experts (rather than a third country) is constituted to decide a boundary dispute on the basis of international law.

For example, Egypt and Israel established an arbitration tribunal to determine a boundary dispute along their border at the town of Taba. The dispute concerned the location of nearly 100 "pillars" of demarcation originally erected in 1906 and 1907. The 1979 Israel–Egypt Treaty of Peace established that the permanent international boundary between Egypt and Israel is "the recognized international boundary between Egypt and the former mandated territory of Palestine." A joint Israeli–Egyptian Commission was established for the purpose, *inter alia*, of "organiz[ing] the demarcation of the international boundary." When this commission failed to agree on the location of the pillars demarcating the boundary line, the issues were submitted to arbitration. In the course of its award, the tribunal indicated the importance of adhering to any previously agreed demarcation by the two disputants:

> If a boundary line is once demarcated jointly by the parties concerned, the demarcation is considered as an authentic interpretation of the boundary agreement even if deviations may have occurred or if there are some inconsistencies with maps. This has been confirmed in practice and legal doctrine, especially for the case that a long time has elapsed since demarcation.

Egypt–Israel Arbitration Tribunal, Award in Boundary Dispute Concerning the Taba Area, Sept. 29, 1988, 27 I.L.M. 1421, 1430, 1482 (1988); see also Kaikobad, Some Observations on the Doctrine of Continuity and Finality of Boundaries, 54 Brit. Y.B.I.L. 119 (1983) (suggesting that the principle of finality and stability in various manifestations constitutes one of the more fundamental and important precepts in the law of international boundaries).

More recently, Ethiopia and Eritrea concluded a provision in the December 2000 Peace Agreement ending their armed conflict that established a boundary commission to delimit their boundary. See Peace Agreement, Ethiopia–Eritrea, Dec. 12, 2001, art. 4, 40 I.L.M. 260 (2001). After receiving extensive written and oral pleadings from the two parties, the Commission in April 2002 issued a delimitation decision which sets forth the principal features of the boundary line, accompanied by a list of coordinates through which the boundary runs. See Decision Regarding Delimitation of the Border between the State of Eritrea and the Federal Democratic Republic of Ethiopia, Jan. 1, 2002, 41 I.L.M. 1057 (2002). Both parties announced their acceptance of the decision, but subsequent efforts to demarcate the boundary on the ground through the emplacement of boundary pillars was not accomplished. Ethiopia contended that the demarcation should be undertaken in a manner that adjusts the line to eliminate situations in which villages were divided or roads were cut by the boundary, whereas Eritrea maintained that the line should be demarcated without any change. The Commission maintained that, absent agreement of the parties, it lacked the authority to vary the delimited boundary line except in cases of manifest impracticality. See Eritrea–Ethiopia Boundary Commission, Statement by the Commission, para. 7, Nov. 27, 2006, 46 I.L.M. 155 (2007); see also Shaw, Title, Control, and Closure? The Experience of the Eritrea–Ethiopia Boundary Commission, 56 I.C.L.Q. 755 (2007).

4. Delimitation by the International Court of Justice

Land (and maritime) boundary delimitation has been a particularly active component of the docket of the International Court of Justice, as the cases noted above demonstrate. Cases on the Court's docket as of publication of this casebook include: *Territorial and Maritime Dispute* (Nicaragua v. Colombia); and *Maritime Dispute* (Peru v. Chile). To check on the status of these and other delimitation cases at the Court, visit http://www.icj-cij.org.

5. Security Council Delimitation

Exceptionally, the Security Council has addressed situations where territorial disputes threaten international peace and security. After the 1991 Iraq–Kuwait war, respect for the inviolability of the international boundary as set out in a 1963 agreement between Iraq and Kuwait was one condition of the Security Council's "cease-fire" resolution. See S.C.

Res. 687, paras. 2–4 (Apr. 3, 1991). The same resolution called upon the U.N. Secretary–General "to lend his assistance to make arrangements with Iraq and Kuwait to demarcate the boundary between Iraq and Kuwait." The Secretary–General then constituted a five-member Iraq–Kuwait Boundary Demarcation Commission, which over the course of two years proceeded to demarcate the boundary between the two states by the emplacement of 106 boundary pillars along a 240–kilometer border. For the final report of the Commission, see Letter Dated 21 May 1993 from the Secretary–General Addressed to the President of the Security Council, U.N. Doc. S/25811, app. (May 21, 1993).

During the course of the demarcation, the Security Council adopted a resolution making clear the source and sanctity of the boundary:

> *Recalling* in this connection that through the demarcation process the Commission is not reallocating territory between Kuwait and Iraq, but it is simply carrying out the technical task necessary to demarcate for the first time the precise coordinates of the boundary set out in the Agreed Minutes between the State of Kuwait and the Republic of Iraq regarding the restoration of Friendly Relations, Recognition and Related Matters signed by them on 4 October 1963, and that this task is being carried out in the special circumstances following Iraq's invasion of Kuwait and pursuant to resolution 687 (1991) * * *.

> * * *

> 4. *Underlines* its guarantee of the inviolability of the above-mentioned international boundary and its decision to take as appropriate all necessary measures to that end in accordance with the Charter, as provided for in paragraph 4 of resolution 687 (1991) * * *.

S.C. Res. 773 (Aug. 26, 1992).

CHAPTER 6

INTERNATIONAL & NON-GOVERNMENTAL ORGANIZATIONS

■ ■ ■

This chapter concerns the legal status and capacity in international law of public international organizations and of non-governmental organizations. (Chapter 7 takes up the position of the individual in international law, as well as transnational corporations and other private entities.)

Organizations for purposes of the present chapter are either intergovernmental or non-governmental, a basic distinction for legal purposes. Within these categories, organizations exhibit remarkable diversity in function, structure, and effect. In international law, the term "international organization" is generally used to refer to organizations composed entirely or mainly of states and usually established by treaty, which serves as the organization's constituent instrument. Non-governmental organizations (commonly known as NGOs) are not the creations of states but, rather, are formed under national law by individuals or private groups sharing a common non-profit objective. They include worldwide organizations involved in humanitarian, health, human rights, and environmental matters; professional and scientific associations; federations and international unions made up of national associations representing labor or employers; religious bodies; scientific academies; and so on. NGOs provide vehicles through which transnational "civil society" can influence the decisions and actions of states and of international organizations, and indeed the attitudes and conduct of diverse actors.

In considering the materials in this chapter, the reader should bear in mind the questions posed earlier in this casebook, concerning the extent to which international law has been mainly a state-centered system and the more diffuse influences that now shape that system. If international organizations came into being as the creatures of states, in what sense might they now be understood as having autonomous authority? Are non-governmental organizations able to transcend the state system and participate directly in the making and enforcement of international law?

SECTION 1. INTERNATIONAL ORGANIZATIONS

International organizations are often tersely defined as simply "intergovernmental organizations," though it is not always clear whether that definition is referring to the type of constituent instrument that creates the organization, to the actual membership of the organization, or to the purposes served by the organization. Moreover, the definition is not entirely accurate, in that some entities that are widely accepted as international organizations were created not by states, but by other international organizations. Some members of international organizations are not states, and some states are represented at international organizations by entities other than governments. For example, the World Tourism Organisation, a specialized agency of the United Nations, includes 153 states as "full members," but also has "territories or groups of territories" as "associate members" and "international bodies, both intergovernmental and non-governmental" as "affiliate members." See Statutes of the World Tourism Organization, Sept. 27, 1970, 985 U.N.T.S. 339. In the course of its current study of the "responsibility of international organizations," the International Law Commission has tentatively and more cautiously defined an "international organization" to be "an organization which includes States among its members insofar as it exercises in its own capacity certain governmental functions." See Report of the International Law Commission, 55th Sess., U.N. Doc. A/58/10, at 33 (2003).

However defined, international organizations have existed since the 19th century, but became an especially notable feature during the period following World War II, with the creation of the United Nations, the World Bank, the International Monetary Fund, and many other U.N. "specialized agencies." See Armstrong, Lloyd, & Redmond, From Versailles to Maastricht: International Organisation in the Twentieth Century (1996). Several foundational cases and legal precedents emerged during the early post-war period as international law sought to understand and accommodate the presence of these new entities on the international stage. Those cases and precedents continue to undergird contemporary legal analyses of the powers, functions, membership and status of international organizations. Indeed, the law of international organizations is generally regarded as a subdivision of international law with its own series of rules and anomalies, just as corporate law is a specialty area of law in most national legal systems. See Restatement (Third), Part II, Chapter 2, Introductory Note.

In what is generally regarded as the most advanced international organization, twenty-seven European states have delegated certain national powers to the European Union as a means of achieving goals that they view as in their collective interest. At the most general level, the European Union is organized into three "pillars," or areas of cooperation. Under the first pillar, the European Community (E.C.) pursues the economic integration of the national economics of its member states. This is achieved principally by eliminating trade barriers between member states and by adopting a common economic policy, including customs duties, in relation to non-member states. The second pillar establishes a common foreign and security policy, while the third pillar creates a justice and home affairs policy. For the official consolidated text of the Treaty on European Union and the European Community Treaty, see [2006] O.J. C 321.

As of the 21st century, the numbers, ambition and range of activities of such organizations have increased markedly, with hundreds of international organizations now in existence. The United Nations counts as members nearly all the states of the world; indeed, an entity can solidify its status as a "state" by obtaining admission to the United Nations. Linked to the United Nations are the autonomous "specialized agencies," for example the Food and Agriculture Organization (FAO) based in Rome, the World Health Organization (WHO) based in Geneva, and the International Civil Aviation Organization (ICAO) based in Montreal. Many international organizations are regional bodies, either broad in scope or specialized, such as the Organization of American States (OAS) based in Washington, D.C., or the African Union (AU) based in Addis Ababa. Still others are concerned with a particular commodity or with an activity in a particular area, such as the Organization for the Prohibition of Chemical Weapons (OPCW) based in The Hague, or the World Trade Organization (WTO) based in Geneva.

Some states have also created entities of an international character to conduct financial or commercial activities, or have formed associations for economic purposes. Indeed, a number of similar organizations have been established by intergovernmental agreement of states engaged in the production of primary commodities. Examples have included producers of bauxite, copper, iron ore, and of agricultural commodities such as coffee, cocoa, bananas, and sisal. Their main objective is to secure fair (i.e., higher) prices for their product and to coordinate national action so as to increase the return to producers and to promote national control over the industry concerned. The associations engage in joint price fixing sometimes backed by export limits, production quotas, and market allocations. The developed market-economy countries have criticized such intergovernmental associations as cartel-like attempts to raise costs artificially and impose restraints on international trade.

Some entities may be established by treaty but also function to an extent under national law. For example, the Bank of International Settlements (B.I.S.) was established by a 1930 Convention of six states, but operates under a Swiss charter and is governed by Swiss law to the extent not inconsistent with the Convention. Several multinational public enterprises operate as consortia in the fields of aviation and shipping, such as Scandinavian Air Lines and Air Afrique. It is not always clear whether such entities act independently of their members, thus raising questions about their true legal nature.

For any given international organization, the first step in understanding its legal nature entails reading the organization's constituent instrument, which is usually a *sui generis* multilateral treaty, but can also take the form of a resolution adopted by a "parent" international organization. Typically, the constituent instrument expressly provides for a plenary organ in which all member states are represented, a smaller organ entrusted with certain important decisions (e.g., an executive committee or council), and a secretariat or staff to carry out administrative, representative, advisory, and technical functions.

The 1945 U.N. Charter established six principal organs:

- General Assembly (all 192 member states are represented)
- Security Council (fifteen member states are represented, including five permanent members—China, France, Russia, United Kingdom, United States—who can "veto" substantive resolutions, and ten non-permanent members elected by the General Assembly for two-year terms)
- Economic and Social Council (fifty-four members elected by the General Assembly for three-year terms)
- Trusteeship Council (suspended operations in 1994 with the independence of Palau, the last remaining United Nations trust territory)
- International Court of Justice (fifteen judges elected by the General Assembly and Security Council to serve nine-year terms)
- Secretariat (a staff of approximately 8,900 persons from about 170 countries, headed by a Secretary–General who is appointed by the General Assembly on the recommendation of the Security Council for a five-year, renewable term)

Large international organizations also have subsidiary bodies such as commissions and agencies which are under the authority of the principal organs, but which often have considerable authority delegated to them. The United Nations has well over a hundred such subsidiary bodies performing executive, advisory, rule-making, and even judicial functions, including the U.N. Development Program and the U.N. High Commissioner for Refugees.

The second step for understanding an international organization's legal nature is to study the practice of the relevant organs since their inception, especially the rules of procedure they adopt, precedents they set in the course of their decision-making, opinions issued by legal counsel at the organization, and, where available, judicial or arbitral decisions rendered by competent dispute settlers that interpret the meaning of the constituent instrument. While the constituent instrument is the core "constitution" of the organization, the subsequent practice of its organs provides an important gloss on the meaning of the constitution and crystalizes expectations about what the organization is implicitly empowered to do, or how it can do it.

A third step involves studying the broader field of international organizations law, by reviewing the basic legal norms and practices that seem to guide all or most international organizations. One reason the "early" post-war cases on the United Nations (such as the *Reparation for Injuries* case below) continue to be studied today is that they influenced the way lawyers think about not just the United Nations as a legal entity, but all international organizations.

Finally, while the law of international organizations has its own special rules, it remains a subset of the broader field of international law, such that the norms considered throughout this casebook provide a backdrop for understanding international organizations law. Thus, while there is a special Vienna Convention on the Law of Treaties between States and International Organizations or between International Organizations, Mar. 21, 1986, 25 I.L.M. 543 (1986), the provisions of that treaty (which has not yet entered into force) closely parallel those of the Vienna Convention on the Law of Treaties, the better-known treaty that sets forth rules governing treaties solely between states. Hence, knowing the broader field informs an understanding of the specialized area.

Legal issues about international organizations arise on a daily basis for lawyers working at those organizations or their member states, on matters such as the express and implied powers of the organs, the privileges and immunities of the organization and its staff from national jurisdiction, the admission, suspension, or expulsion of members, or rules on internal hiring, firing, or sanctioning of staff members. A good source of information on such issues at the United Nations and related international organizations is the *U.N. Juridical Yearbook*, which has been published on an annual basis since 1963, and is available at http://www.un.org/law/UNJuridicalYearbook/index.htm. The following sections explore some of the most rudimentary aspects of the law of international organizations.

A. INTERNATIONAL LEGAL PERSONALITY

It has long been accepted under international law that a state may bring a claim against another state for an internationally wrongful act. The rules on state responsibility for wrongful acts will be explored in Chapter 8 and the means for litigating an inter-state dispute will be discussed in Chapter 9. Can an international organization bring a claim against a state? What if that state is not a member of the international organization? Conversely, can a state bring a claim against an international organization for a wrongful act of that organization? In short, are international organizations just like states when it comes to their rights and obligations under international law?

Such questions have often evoked discussion about whether international organizations have a legal "personality" separate from their member states, meaning that they have a distinct legal status akin to what exists for states themselves. Attribution of international legal personality signals a capacity to perform legal acts on the international plane, rather than just within a national law system, as would be the case for a corporation.

When international organizations emerged as a major feature of the international landscape after World War II, questions about their legal "personality" became more than academic. International organizations were involved in major diplomatic initiatives, in movement of billions of dollars of capital in grants and loans, in inspections of nuclear facilities worldwide, and in other extremely important and sensitive actions. Determining whether they were independent, accountable entities or were simply empty shells through which states acted became very significant. In thinking through exactly what these entities were, various questions arose:

(1) Is international personality an inherent (or objective) attribute of international organization or does it depend on the constituent instrument and the powers expressly or impliedly granted to it?

(2) If international personality does exist for a specific international organization, is there a precise category of legal rights and duties that flow from that personality? Or do the rights and duties still depend on the powers and functions expressly granted by states to the international organization?

(3) If the member states deny international personality to their international organization does that mean the entity cannot be regarded as an international organization under international law?

A seminal case for answering some of those questions was the 1949 *Reparation for Injuries* advisory opinion issued by the International Court of Justice. Count Folke Bernadotte was a Swedish diplomat chosen to be the U.N. Security Council's mediator in the Arab–Israeli conflict of 1947–1948. Bernadotte was assassinated in Jerusalem in September 1948, at a time when Israel had declared its independence but was not yet a U.N. member state. See S.C. Res. 57 (Sept. 18, 1948). If Israel was responsible, could the United Nations bring a claim against Israel under international law for attacking one of its agents? Could the U.N. claim encompass both injury to the United Nations itself (for interfering with its work) and personal injury to Bernadotte (hence vindicating interests of Bernadotte's heirs), or should the latter type of injury be left to Sweden to vindicate if it chose to do so? Did it matter that Israel was not yet a U.N. member state and hence had no formal legal connection to the United Nations? In December 1948, the General Assembly put these questions to the International Court of Justice for an advisory opinion.

REPARATION FOR INJURIES SUFFERED IN THE SERVICE OF THE UNITED NATIONS

International Court of Justice, Advisory Opinion, 1949
1949 I.C.J. 174

The first question asked of the Court is as follows:

"In the event of an agent of the United Nations in the performance of his duties suffering injury in circumstances involving the responsibility of a State, has the United Nations, as an Organization, the capacity to bring an international claim against the responsible *de jure* or *de facto* government with a view to obtaining the reparation due in respect of the damage caused (*a*) to the United Nations, (*b*) to the victim or to persons entitled through him?"

* * *

Competence to bring an international claim is, for those possessing it, the capacity to resort to the customary methods recognized by international law for the establishment, the presentation and the settlement of claims. Among these methods may be mentioned protest, request for an enquiry, negotiation, and request for submission to an arbitral tribunal or to the Court in so far as this may be authorized by the Statute.

This capacity certainly belongs to the State; a State can bring an international claim against another State. Such a claim takes the form of a claim between two political entities, equal in law, similar in form, and both the direct subjects of international law. It is dealt with by means of negotiation, and cannot, in the present state of the law as to international jurisdiction, be submitted to a tribunal, except with the consent of the States concerned.

When the Organization brings a claim against one of its Members, this claim will be presented in the same manner, and regulated by the same procedure. It may, when necessary, be supported by the political means at the disposal of the Organization. In these ways the Organization would find a method for securing the observance of its rights by the Member against which it has a claim.

But, in the international sphere, has the Organization such a nature as involves the capacity to bring an international claim? In order to answer this question, the Court must first enquire whether the Charter has given the Organization such a position that it possesses, in regard to its Members, rights which it is entitled to ask them to respect. In other words, does the Organization possess international personality? This is no doubt a doctrinal expression, which has sometimes given rise to controversy. But it will be used here to mean that if the Organization is recognized as having that personality, it is an entity capable of availing itself of obligations incumbent upon its Members.

To answer this question, which is not settled by the actual terms of the Charter, we must consider what characteristics it was intended thereby to give to the Organization.

The subjects of law in any legal system are not necessarily identical in their nature or in the extent of their rights, and their nature depends upon the needs of the community. Throughout its history, the development of international law has been influenced by the requirements of international life, and the progressive increase in the collective activities of States has already given rise to instances of action upon the international plane by certain entities which are not States. This development culminated in the establishment in June 1945 of an international organization whose purposes and principles are specified in the Charter of the United Nations. But to achieve these ends the attribution of international personality is indispensable.

The Charter has not been content to make the Organization created by it merely a centre "for harmonizing the actions of nations in the attainment of these common ends" (Article 1, para. 4). It has equipped that centre with organs, and has given it special tasks. It has defined the position of the Members in relation to the Organization by requiring them to give it every assistance in any action undertaken by it (Article 2, para. 5), and to accept and carry out the decisions of the Security Council; by authorizing the General Assembly to make recommendations to the Members; by giving the Organization legal capacity and privileges and immunities in the territory of each of its Members; and by providing for the conclusion of agreements between the Organization and its Members. Practice—in particular the conclusion of conventions to which the Organization is a party—has confirmed this character of the Organization, which occupies a position in certain respects in detachment from its Members, and which is under a duty to remind them, if need be, of certain obligations. It must be added that the Organization is a political body, charged with political tasks of an important character, and covering a wide field namely, the maintenance of international peace and security, the development of friendly relations among nations, and the achievement of international co-operation in the solution of problems of an economic, social, cultural or humanitarian character (Article 1); and in dealing with its Members it employs political means. The "Convention on the Privileges and Immunities of the United Nations" of 1946 creates rights and duties between each of the signatories and the Organization (see, in particular, Section 35). It is difficult to see how such a convention could operate except upon the international plane and as between parties possessing international personality.

In the opinion of the Court, the Organization was intended to exercise and enjoy, and is in fact exercising and enjoying, functions and rights which can only be explained on the basis of the possession of a large measure of international personality and the capacity to operate upon an international plane. It is at present the supreme type of international organization, and it could not carry out the intentions of its founders if it was devoid of international personality. It must be acknowledged that its Members, by entrusting certain functions to it, with the attendant duties and responsibilities, have clothed it with the competence required to enable those functions to be effectively discharged.

Accordingly, the Court has come to the conclusion that the Organization is an international person. That is not the same thing as saying that it is a State, which it certainly is not, or that its legal personality and rights and duties are the same as those of a State. Still less is it the same thing as saying that it is "a super-State", whatever that expression may mean. It does not even imply that all its rights and duties must be upon the international plane, any more than all the rights and duties of a State must be upon that plane. What it does mean is that it is a subject of international law and capable of possessing international rights and duties, and that it has capacity to maintain its rights by bringing international claims.

The next question is whether the sum of the international rights of the Organization comprises the right to bring the kind of international claim described in the Request for this Opinion. That is a claim against a State to obtain reparation in respect of the damage caused by the injury of an agent of the Organization in the course of the performance of his duties. Whereas a State possesses the totality of international rights and duties recognized by international law, the rights and duties of an entity such as the Organization must depend upon its purposes and functions as specified or implied in its constituent documents and developed in practice. The functions of the Organization are of such a character that they could not be effectively discharged if they involved the concurrent action, on the international plane, of fifty-eight or more Foreign Offices, and the Court concludes that the Members have endowed the Organization with capacity to bring international claims when necessitated by the discharge of its functions.

[With respect to Question I (a), the Court continued:]

* * * It cannot be doubted that the Organization has the capacity to bring an international claim against one of its Members which has caused injury to it by a breach of its international obligations towards it. The damage specified in Question I(a) means exclusively damage caused to the interests of the Organization itself, to its administrative machine, to its property and assets and to the interests of which it is the guardian. It is clear that the Organization has the capacity to bring a claim for this damage. As the claim is based on the breach of an international obligation on the part of the Member held responsible by the Organization, the Member cannot contend that this obligation is governed by municipal law, and the Organization is justified in giving its claim the character of an international claim.

When the Organization has sustained damage resulting from a breach by a Member of its international obligations, it is impossible to see how it can obtain reparation unless it possesses capacity to bring an international claim. It cannot be supposed that in such an event all the Members of the

Organization, save the defendant State, must combine to bring a claim against the defendant for the damage suffered by the Organization.

The Court is not called upon to determine the precise extent of the reparation which the Organization would be entitled to recover. It may, however, be said that the measure of the reparation should depend upon the amount of the damage which the Organization has suffered as the result of the wrongful act or omission of the defendant State and should be calculated in accordance with the rules of international law. * * *

[With respect to Question I (*b*), the Court stated:]

* * *

The Court is here faced with a new situation. The questions to which it gives rise can only be solved by realizing that the situation is dominated by the provisions of the Charter considered in the light of the principles of international law.

The question * * * presupposes that the injury for which the reparation is demanded arises from a breach of an obligation designed to help an agent of the Organization in the performance of his duties. It is not a case in which the wrongful act or omission would merely constitute a breach of the general obligations of a State concerning the position of aliens; claims made under this head would be within the competence of the national State and not, as a general rule, within that of the Organization.

The Charter does not expressly confer upon the Organization the capacity to include, in its claim for reparation, damage caused to the victim or to persons entitled through him. The Court must therefore begin by enquiring whether the provisions of the Charter concerning the functions of the Organization, and the part played by its agents in the performance of those functions, imply for the Organization power to afford its agents the limited protection that would consist in the bringing of a claim on their behalf for reparation for damage suffered in such circumstances. Under international law, the Organization must be deemed to have those powers which, though not expressly provided in the Charter, are conferred upon it by necessary implication as being essential to the performance of its duties. This principle of law was applied by the Permanent Court of International Justice to the International Labour Organization in its Advisory Opinion No. 13 of July 23rd, 1926 (Series B., No. 13, p. 18), and must be applied to the United Nations.

Having regard to its purposes and functions already referred to, the Organization may find it necessary, and has in fact found it necessary, to entrust its agents with important missions to be performed in disturbed parts of the world. Many missions, from their very nature, involve the agents in unusual dangers to which ordinary persons are not exposed. For the same reason, the injuries suffered by its agents in these circumstances will sometimes have occurred in such a manner that their national State would not be justified in bringing a claim for reparation on the ground of diplomatic protection, or, at any rate, would not feel disposed to do so.

Both to ensure the efficient and independent performance of these missions and to afford effective support to its agents, the Organization must provide them with adequate protection.

* * *

* * * For that purpose, it is necessary that, when an infringement occurs, the Organization should be able to call upon the responsible State to remedy its default, and, in particular, to obtain from the State reparation for the damage that the default may have caused to its agent.

In order that the agent may perform his duties satisfactorily, he must feel that this protection is assured to him by the Organization, and that he may count on it. To ensure the independence of the agent, and, consequently, the independent action of the Organization itself, it is essential that in performing his duties he need not have to rely on any other protection than that of the Organization (save of course for the more direct and immediate protection due from the State in whose territory he may be). In particular, he should not have to rely on the protection of his own State. If he had to rely on that State, his independence might well be compromised, contrary to the principle applied by Article 100 of the Charter. And lastly, it is essential that—whether the agent belongs to a powerful or to a weak State; to one more affected or less affected by the complications of international life; to one in sympathy or not in sympathy with the mission of the agent—he should know that in the performance of his duties he is under the protection of the Organization. This assurance is even more necessary when the agent is stateless.

Upon examination of the character of the functions entrusted to the Organization and of the nature of the missions of its agents, it becomes clear that the capacity of the Organization to exercise a measure of functional protection of its agents arises by necessary intendment out of the Charter.

The obligations entered into by States to enable the agents of the Organization to perform their duties are undertaken not in the interest of the agents, but in that of the Organization. When it claims redress for a breach of these obligations, the Organization is invoking its own right, the right that the obligations due to it should be respected. On this ground, it asks for reparation of the injury suffered, for "it is a principle of international law that the breach of an engagement involves an obligation to make reparation in an adequate form"; as was stated by the Permanent Court in its Judgment No. 8 of July 26th, 1927 (Series A., No. 9, p. 21). In claiming reparation based on the injury suffered by its agent, the Organization does not represent the agent, but is asserting its own right, the right to secure respect for undertakings entered into towards the Organization.

Having regard to the foregoing considerations, and to the undeniable right of the Organization to demand that its Members shall fulfill the obligations entered into by them in the interest of the good working of the

Organization, the Court is of the opinion that, in the case of a breach of these obligations, the Organization has the capacity to claim adequate reparation, and that in assessing this reparation it is authorized to include the damage suffered by the victim or by persons entitled through him.

The question remains whether the Organization has "the capacity to bring an international claim against the responsible *de jure* or *de facto* government with a view to obtaining the reparation due in respect of the damage caused (*a*) to the United Nations, (*b*) to the victim or to persons entitled through him" when the defendant State is not a member of the Organization.

In considering this aspect of Questions I (*a*) and (*b*), it is necessary to keep in mind the reasons which have led the Court to give an affirmative answer to it when the defendant State is a Member of the Organization. It has now been established that the Organization has capacity to bring claims on the international plane, and that it possesses a right of functional protection in respect of its agents. Here again the Court is authorized to assume that the damage suffered involves the responsibility of a State, and it is not called upon to express an opinion upon the various ways in which that responsibility might be engaged. Accordingly the question is whether the Organization has capacity to bring a claim against the defendant State to recover reparation in respect of that damage or whether, on the contrary, the defendant State, not being a member, is justified in raising the objection that the Organization lacks the capacity to bring an international claim. On this point, the Court's opinion is that fifty States, representing the vast majority of the members of the international community, had the power, in conformity with international law, to bring into being an entity possessing objective international personality, and not merely personality recognized by them alone, together with capacity to bring international claims.

Accordingly, the Court arrives at the conclusion that an affirmative answer should be given to Questions I (*a*) and (*b*) whether or not the defendant State is a Member of the United Nations.

Question II is as follows:

"In the event of an affirmative reply on point I (*b*), how is action by the United Nations to be reconciled with such rights as may be possessed by the State of which the victim is a national?"

* * * When the victim has a nationality, cases can clearly occur in which the injury suffered by him may engage the interest both of his national State and of the Organization. In such an event, competition between the State's right of diplomatic protection and the Organization's right of functional protection might arise, and this is the only case with which the Court is invited to deal.

In such a case, there is no rule of law which assigns priority to the one or to the other, or which compels either the State or the Organization to refrain from bringing an international claim. The Court sees no reason why the parties concerned should not find solutions inspired by goodwill and common sense, and as between the Organization and its Members it draws attention to their duty to render "every assistance" provided by Article 2, paragraph 5, of the Charter.

Although the bases of the two claims are different, that does not mean that the defendant State can be compelled to pay the reparation due in respect of the damage twice over. International tribunals are already familiar with the problem of a claim in which two or more national States are interested, and they know how to protect the defendant State in such a case.

* * *

The question of reconciling action by the Organization with the rights of a national State may arise in another way; that is to say, when the agent bears the nationality of the defendant State.

The ordinary practice whereby a State does not exercise protection on behalf of one of its nationals against a State which regards him as its own national, does not constitute a precedent which is relevant here. The action of the Organization is in fact based not upon the nationality of the victim, but upon his status as agent of the Organization. Therefore it does not matter whether or not the State to which the claim is addressed regards him as its own national, because the question of nationality is not pertinent to the admissibility of the claim.

NOTES

1. *Two Doctrinal Approaches: Inherent Powers Due to Legal "Personality" versus Implied Powers Due to Constituent Instrument.* Does the opinion of the Court rest upon the finding of international personality in the objective characteristics of the organization ("objective international personality")? Or does the Court base its conclusion on the "implied powers doctrine" as many writers have assumed? What difference does it make? Consider the following comment:

> If all these activities have their legal basis in the personality of the organization, it is sufficient that an organization should possess international personality for it to have the legal capacity to perform them. On the other hand, if they have their basis in implied powers the question will be posed in different terms for each organization. Likewise, member States will in each case possess the right to claim that certain activity of the organization does not conform to, or goes beyond, the purposes and functions expressed or implied in the constitutional provisions and therefore to refuse to collaborate financially or otherwise * * *.

Rama–Montaldo, International Legal Personality and Implied Powers of International Organizations, 44 Brit. Y.B.I.L. 111, 123–24 (1970) (footnotes omitted).

2. *A Switch–Hitting Court.* A close reading of the Court's *Reparation for Injuries* opinion suggests that it followed both doctrinal approaches, but used each for different conclusions. It referred to the "characteristics" of the organization and to activities that "can only be based on a large measure of international personality and the capacity to operate upon an international plane." It concluded, on that basis, that the organization had the capacity to maintain its rights by international claims that is, "to negotiate, to conclude a special agreement and to prosecute a claim before an international tribunal." But after the Court reached this conclusion, it turned to a different question: whether the general right to bring a claim "comprises the right to bring the kind of international claim described in the Request for this Opinion." In answering this question, the Court did not rely on inherent legal personality; it said the answer depended on the "purposes and functions as specified or implied in its constituent documents and developed in practice." This led the Court to consider the powers of the Organization to protect its agents as relevant to the particular claim.

Do you think the Court reached the correct conclusions? The Court was unanimous in finding that Israel's lack of membership in the United Nations did not effect the outcome; do you agree? When suing a non-member, should it make any difference if the international organization in question has a much smaller membership? The Court split by a vote of 11–4 over whether the United Nations could advance a diplomatic claim on behalf of the Count himself (or his heirs). In a dissent, Judge Hackworth opined that only states had previously been regarded as competent to advance such claims, not international organizations.

> Certainly there is no specific provision in the Charter, nor is there provision in any other agreement of which I am aware, conferring upon the Organization authority to assume the rôle of a State, and to represent its agents in the espousal of diplomatic claims on their behalf. I am equally convinced that there is no implied power to be drawn upon for this purpose.

1949 I.C.J. 174, 197–98. Do you find Judge Hackworth's position compelling? More broadly, do you think that this ability to read powers into an international organization based on legal personality or as a matter of implication is a useful technique for letting international organizations evolve over time? Or does this technique give courts and international organizations themselves too much discretion for deviating from the original intent of the member states? If so, are there ways states can contract around that problem if they wish to deny the organization unintended powers?

3. *Why Implied Powers Doctrine Tends to Dominate.* Some scholars have argued that international organizations that meet certain criteria (e.g., are not under the jurisdiction of any state) have, in law and practice, "objective legal personality" and may therefore perform any international act which they are in a practical position to perform, subject only to the following legal limitations: (1) constitutional provisions forbidding acts for certain purposes or procedures; (2) the principle that the acts do not impose obligations on member states unless they have so agreed or on third parties without a special legal basis. See Seyersted, Objective International Personality of Intergovern-

mental Organizations (1963); see also Fitzmaurice, The Law and Procedure of the International Court of Justice: International Organizations and Tribunals, 29 Brit. Y.B.I.L. 1, 2–6 (1952). One difficulty in demonstrating that this position has been followed is that acts carried out by international organizations are virtually always said to be legally justified on the basis of constitutional powers and functions rather than on grounds of inherent powers. Consequently the acts, if challenged, are regarded as valid or invalid in terms of the delegated or implied purposes and competence of the organization. This has been evident in the cases brought before the International Court of Justice involving challenges to the legal authority of the United Nations. See, for example, *Effects of Awards of Compensation Made by the United Nations Administrative Tribunal*, Advisory Opinion, 1954 I.C.J. 47; *Certain Expenses of the United Nations*, Advisory Opinion, 1962 I.C.J. 151, discussed below in Chapter 15, Section 3; *Legal Consequences for States of the Continued Presence of South Africa in Namibia (South West Africa) notwithstanding Security Council Resolution 276 (1970)*, Advisory Opinion, 1971 I.C.J. 16, Chapter 3, p. 212. There is little reason to expect that any international organization will assert a general inherent legal power to perform "sovereign" international acts on grounds of its objective legal personality irrespective of the constitutional definition of its functions and powers.

4. *Contemporary International Legal Capacity of International Organizations*. The International Court has maintained a relatively liberal reading of international organizations as "subjects" of international law, albeit ones with more limited competence than that of states. See *Legality of the Use by a State of Nuclear Weapons in Armed Conflict*, Advisory Opinion, 1996 I.C.J. 66, para. 25 ("The Court need hardly point out that international organizations are subjects of international law which do not, unlike States, possess a general competence."). As it turns out, international organizations have exercised international legal capacity in a wide variety of ways, including by concluding treaties with states, sending and receiving ambassadors, flagging vessels for use on the high seas, and even occupying territory with civil and military personnel. For a discussion of the latter phenomenon, see Fox, Humanitarian Occupation (2008) (discussing in depth Security Council-backed international administration of Bosnia, East Timor, Eastern Slavonia, and Kosovo).

In exercising international legal capacity and, correlatively, in assuming international responsibility for their acts, international organizations draw a distinction in terms of legal powers and obligations between the organization and its member states. That distinction also requires that the organization possess organs capable of exercising such legal capacity and responsibilities on the international plane. Standing conferences of states under multilateral conventions or loose associations such as the British Commonwealth lack such organs and consequently do not exercise the attributes of international personality. An international organization may also have been denied such international personality by its constituent instrument or decisions of its members.

5. *Capacity to Resort to International Tribunals*. Assuming that the international organization has the capacity to bring an international claim against a state (or perhaps against another international organization), does that mean it can file the claim before an international tribunal? Only states

appear as parties before the principal international judicial organ, the International Court of Justice, though advisory opinions may be requested from the Court by the U.N. General Assembly and the Security Council, and, when so authorized by the General Assembly, other U.N. organs and specialized agencies (Article 96 of the Charter). An indirect method for overcoming the barrier to *locus standi* for international organizations before the Court is found in section 30 of the Convention on the Privileges and Immunities of the United Nations, Feb. 13, 1946, 21 U.S.T. 1418, 1 U.N.T.S. 15. That section provides that if a difference arises between the United Nations and a member state in regard to the interpretation or application of the Convention, a request shall be made for an advisory opinion in accordance with the Charter. Moreover, the opinion of the Court shall be accepted as decisive. Thus, a dispute between the United Nations and a state can be the subject of a *binding* decision by the Court on the basis of a proceeding which, in substance, would be akin to a contentious proceeding. For further discussion on the I.C.J.'s advisory and contentious jurisdiction, see Chapter 9.

Proposals have been made to expand the possibility for international organizations to be parties to cases at the I.C.J. and other tribunals. Such proposals would equalize the legal position of states and international organizations, and would correspond more closely to the acceptance of international organizations as subjects of international law for most purposes. They might also provide a forum for resolution of disputes that currently lack a place for authoritative settlement—for example, over monetary obligations owed by states to international organizations. On the pros and cons of such proposals, see Szasz, Granting International Organizations *Ius Standi* in the International Court of Justice, in The International Court of Justice 169 (Muller, Raič, & Thuránszky eds. 1997). Further, it should be noted that international organizations may be parties to arbitration proceedings in disputes with states. The Agreement between the United Nations and the United States of America Regarding the Headquarters of the United Nations, June 26, 1947, 61 Stat. 3416, 11 U.N.T.S. 11, provides for arbitration in case of disputes under that agreement. Many similar arbitration clauses have been placed in agreements between international organizations and states.

6. *Treaty–Making Capacity*. International organizations have long assumed a capacity to enter into agreements with states, irrespective of whether that power could be found expressed or implied in its constituent instrument. Fitzmaurice, usually cautious, concluded as far back as 1953 that: "the necessary attribute of international personality, is the power to enter, directly or mediately, into relationship (by treaty or otherwise) with other international persons." Fitzmaurice, The Law and Procedure of the International Court of Justice, 1951–54: General Principles and Sources of Law, 30 Brit. Y.B.I.L. 1, 2 (1953). However, attributing treaty-making capacity to international personality does not answer whether negotiation of a particular treaty falls within the purposes and competence of the international organization. For that question, one must look to the constitution and the powers granted or implied by it; it is not determined by the existence of international personality. Thus, the 1986 Convention on Treaties Concluded between States and International Organizations or between Two or More International Organizations provides in Article 6: "The capacity of an international organization to

conclude treaties is governed by the relevant rules of that organization." For Commentary on that article, see Report of the International Law Commission on the Work of Its Thirty–Third Session, U.N. Doc A/36/10, at 127 (1981); Gaja, A 'New' Vienna Convention on Treaties Between States and International Organizations or Between International Organizations: A Critical Commentary, 58 Brit. Y.B.I.L. 253 (1987).

7. *Relevance of IO Status under National Law.* If an international organization is granted a status under national law, such as immunity from national jurisdiction, does that necessarily demonstrate its status on the international plane? Note that Article 104 of the U.N. Charter provides: "The Organization shall enjoy in the territory of each of its Members such legal capacity as may be necessary for the exercise of its functions and the fulfillment of its purposes." Though such a provision imposes upon member states an obligation to accord the United Nations a special status, the International Court did not point to Article 104 as evidence of an international legal personality. Rather, the Court stated that the question of such personality was "not settled by the actual terms of the Charter." It would appear that the issue of the organization's status under international law and its status under national law are separate issues. Regardless of the international organization's status in the international sphere, national law may require that the international organization's status be determined based on a bilateral agreement between the host state and the organization (a "headquarters agreement") or by a national statute. At the same time, the absence of special status under national law is not relevant to the organization's status under international law. See The Charter of the United Nations 1302–06 (2d ed. Simma ed. 2002); Muller, International Organizations and Their Host States (1995); Reinisch, International Organizations before National Courts (2000).

8. *Disabling of the Member States?* Assuming that an international organization is deemed to have a legal personality, may its member states act only through the organization and not independently on matters covered by the functions of the organization? This question arose in a foundational case involving the European Community (EC), where the relevant issue was whether a treaty on European road transport (ERTA) could be negotiated by the Community. The EC Court of Justice referred to the powers of the Community and said:

> This Community authority excludes the possibility of a concurrent authority on the part of Member States, since any initiative taken outside the framework of the common institutions would be incompatible with the unity of the Common Market and the uniform application of Community law.

ERTA Case, 47 I.L.R. 278, 305 (1971). Would this conclusion be appropriate for the United Nations or one of its specialized agencies?

9. *Post–Script.* The Swedish government initially believed that Israeli government agents had assassinated Bernadotte, but later it was revealed that the assassins were members of an underground Zionist group called Lehi. Lehi was forcibly disarmed by Israel and many of its members were arrested, but no one was charged with Count Bernadotte's death. Bernadotte's princi-

pal aide, the U.S. diplomat Ralph Bunche, succeeded Bernadotte as U.N. mediator. Bunche arranged the 1949 Armistice Agreements between Israel and its neighbors, for which he received the 1950 Nobel Peace Prize. After conclusion of the armistice, Israel was admitted to the United Nations as a member state in May 1949. In 1950, Israel admitted that it was lax in its investigation of the Bernadotte assassination and paid to the United Nations $54,628 in compensation. For further background on the assassination, see Marton, A Death in Jerusalem (1994); Ilan, Bernadotte in Palestine, 1948 (1989); Stanger, A Haunting Legacy: The Assassination of Count Bernadotte, 42 Middle E.J. 260 (1988); Persson, Mediation & Assassination: Count Bernadotte's Mission to Palestine, 1948 (1979); Bell, Assassination in International Politics, 16 Int'l Stud. Q. 59 (1972).

10. *Further Reading.* Several treatises seek to explore the nature of international organizations and the basic rules that guide them. See Alvarez, International Organizations as Law-makers (2005); Amerasinghe, Principles of the Institutional Law of International Organizations (2d rev. ed. 2005); Archer, International Organizations (3d ed. 2001); Dupuy, A Handbook on International Organizations (1998); Klabbers, An Introduction to International Institutional Law (2002); International Institutions (Martin & Simmons eds. 2001); Louis–Jacques & Korman, Introduction to International Organizations (1996); Sands & Klein, Bowett's Law of International Institutions (5th ed. 2001); Schermers & Blokker, International Institutional Law: Unity Within Diversity (3d ed. 1995); The United Nations at Age Fifty: A Legal Perspective (Tomuschat ed. 1995); White, The Law of International Organisations (2d ed. 2005).

B. INTERPRETING THE POWERS OF THE INTERNATIONAL ORGANIZATION

The constituent instrument of each international organization prescribes the powers and functions of the organization and also identifies the organs entitled to exercise the powers granted to the organization. As indicated in the *Reparation for Injuries* case, it will often be important to show that an organization has been given, expressly or by implication, the power to perform the acts in question. In demonstrating that such a power exists or does not exist, what elements of a legal analysis should be included? Should the focus be solely on a specific provision of the constituent instrument? On related provisions found elsewhere in the instrument? On the negotiating history of the instrument? On the practice of the organs of the international organization subsequent to their creation? On the general purposes for which the organization was created? Suppose a particular power is accorded to one organ, but a different organ then exercises the power. Is that action to be considered a lawful act of the organization or is it legally ineffective?

These questions were considered in an advisory opinion of the International Court of Justice concerning *Certain Expenses of the United Nations*, Advisory Opinion, 1962 I.C.J. 151. The "expenses" referred to were incurred by the United Nations for two U.N. peacekeeping operations in the Sinai Peninsula and the Congo (later Zaire and presently the Democratic Republic of the Congo or D.R.C.). Though the Security Council had some involvement in the early stages of resolving those conflicts, the peacekeeping operations were principally undertaken pursuant to resolutions of the General Assembly. Moreover, the General Assembly included the costs of the operations in the U.N. budget as "expenses" within the meaning of U.N. Charter Article 17(2), which meant that all member states were obliged to pay the expenses based on an allocation decided by the General Assembly. The legality of that decision was questioned by several member states—principally, the U.S.S.R. and France, who both refused to pay their share of the expenses. Those states argued that the only expenses that states were obliged to pay concerned U.N. administrative expenses, meaning the costs of the day-to-day running of the United Nations, not special programs. Alternatively, they claimed that since the underlying actions concerned matters of peace and security, and since those actions were not authorized by the proper organ of the United Nations (the Security Council), then the actions were not lawfully incurred. Faced with a constitutional crisis, the General Assembly once again turned to the International Court for advice.

CERTAIN EXPENSES OF THE UNITED NATIONS

International Court of Justice, 1962
1962 I.C.J. 151, 167–68

* * * In determining whether the actual expenditures authorized constitute "expenses of the Organization within the meaning of Article 17, paragraph 2, of the Charter", the Court agrees that such expenditures must be tested by their relationship to the purposes of the United Nations in the sense that if an expenditure were made for a purpose which is not one of the purposes of the United Nations, it could not be considered an "expense of the Organization".

The purposes of the United Nations are set forth in Article 1 of the Charter. The first two purposes as stated in paragraphs 1 and 2, may be summarily described as pointing to the goal of international peace and security and friendly relations. The third purpose is the achievement of economic, social, cultural and humanitarian goals and respect of human rights. The fourth and last purpose is: "To be a center for harmonizing the actions of nations in the attainment of these common ends."

The primary place ascribed to international peace and security is natural, since the fulfilment of the other purposes will be dependent upon the attainment of that basic condition. These purposes are broad indeed, but neither they nor the powers conferred to effectuate them are unlimited. Save as they have entrusted the Organization with the attainment of these common ends, the Member States retain their freedom of action. But when the Organization takes action which warrants the assertion that it was appropriate for the fulfillment of one of the stated purposes of the

United Nations, the presumption is that such action is not *ultra vires* the Organization.

If it is agreed that the action in question is within the scope of the functions of the Organization but it is alleged that it has been initiated or carried out in a manner not in conformity with the division of functions among the several organs which the Charter prescribes, one moves to the internal plane, to the internal structure of the Organization. If the action was taken by the wrong organ, it was irregular as a matter of the internal structure, but this would not necessarily mean that the expense incurred was not an expense of the Organization. Both national and international law contemplate cases in which the body corporate or politic may be bound, as to third parties, by an *ultra vires* act of an agent.

[The Court then analyzed the operations and financing of ONUC and UNEF. The Court found that, in both instances, the peacekeeping operations were not coercive in nature, since the peacekeepers were not authorized to use coercive action, and Congo and Egypt respectively consented to the U.N. deployments. As such, the two operations fell within the scope of permissible General Assembly recommended "measures" in U.N. Charter Article 14 and were not enforcement actions that fell exclusively to the Security Council under U.N. Charter Chapter VII. Further, the Court found that in both instances the deployments were for the purpose of promoting and maintaining peace. As such, the Court concluded that the costs of such operations properly fell within the scope of "expenses" of the United Nations in Article 17.]

NOTES

1. *Implying a Peacekeeping Power.* The U.N. Charter contains no express power for the General Assembly to authorize deployment of a peacekeeping operation. (Indeed, the word "peacekeeping" appears nowhere in the Charter.) When France and the Soviet Union ratified the Charter, it is unlikely that they were aware that such a power existed. In light of that, did the Court reach the wrong conclusion? To what extent do you think the Court was attracted to a teleological interpretation of the U.N. Charter, meaning an interpretation that focuses less on the express text of the Charter and more on the purposes for which the United Nations was created? In a 1996 advisory opinion, the Court stated: "International organizations are governed by the 'principle of speciality', that is to say, they are invested by the States which create them with powers, the limits of which are a function of the common interests whose promotion those State entrust to them." *Legality of the Use by a State of Nuclear Weapons in Armed Conflict*, Advisory Opinion, 1996 I.C.J. 66, para. 25.

2. *Effect of an* Ultra Vires *Action.* In the final paragraph of the extracted part of the case, the Court states that even if the action was taken by the wrong organ, this might still not prevent the expenses from being lawfully incurred. Although this excerpt refers to the action as binding in respect of third parties, the opinion also supports the conclusion that the Assembly's action is binding on its members. Yet one of the Court's judges, Sir Gerald

Fitzmaurice, thought that this point should "not be pressed too far." He considered that the United Nations may be bound by *ultra vires* acts toward parties outside the United Nations, but he doubted that the same principle could apply as between the United Nations and the member states *inter se*. See *Certain Expenses of the United Nations*, Advisory Opinion, 1962 I.C.J. 151, 199–200.

3. *Judicial Review of an* Ultra Vires *Act?* When a dispute arises over whether a given international organization has exceeded its powers, there may not be a ready forum for authoritative resolution of the dispute. Several cases at the I.C.J. and other tribunals have presented variants on this problem. In the *Lockerbie* cases brought by Libya against the United States and the United Kingdom, Libya sought orders to enjoin those two countries from taking coercive action against Libya in the Security Council, where those states were pressing for economic sanctions aimed at inducing Libya to surrender two individuals charged with causing a bomb to be placed on Pan Am Flight 103 that exploded over Lockerbie, Scotland. Libya's contentions included the argument that the Security Council would exceed or abuse its powers by adopting the sanctions in question. While the case was pending, the Security Council mandated the sanctions against Libya. S.C. Res. 748 (Mar. 31, 1992). In its order denying Libya's request for provisional measures against the United Kingdom, the I.C.J. said in part:

> Whereas both Libya and the United Kingdom, as Members of the United Nations, are obliged to accept and carry out the decisions of the Security Council in accordance with Article 25 of the Charter; whereas the Court, which is at the stage of proceedings on provisional measures, considers that prima facie this obligation extends to the decision contained in resolution 748 (1992); and whereas, in accordance with Article 103 of the Charter, the obligations of the Parties in that respect prevail over their obligations under any other international agreement, including the Montreal Convention; * * *.

Questions of Interpretation and Application of the 1971 Montreal Convention arising from the Aerial Incident at Lockerbie (Libya v. United Kingdom), 1992 I.C.J. 3, para. 39; see also *Questions of Interpretation and Application of the 1971 Montreal Convention arising from the Aerial Incident at Lockerbie* (Libya v. United States) 1992 I.C.J. 114. In the aftermath of this decision, legal commentators expounded diverse points of view on whether the I.C.J. had authority under the U.N. Charter to engage in constitutional review of actions of the Security Council as a coordinate principal organ of the United Nations, and whether the I.C.J. had in effect reviewed and affirmed the constitutionality of the Security Council's exercise of authority in the Libyan case. See Petculescu, The Review of the United Nations Security Council Decisions by the International Court of Justice, 52 Neth. Int'l L. Rev. 167 (2005), and literature cited therein.

A similar issue arose in the case brought by Bosnia–Herzegovina against the Federal Republic of Yugoslavia (Serbia and Montenegro) under the Genocide Convention. In its Application initiating the case, Bosnia–Herzegovina maintained that, among other things, the arms embargo that the Security Council had mandated in respect of all of the former Yugoslavia was illegal in its application to Bosnia, as an excess of the Security Council's powers under the Charter and a derogation from Bosnia's inherent right to defend itself against aggression and genocide. The provisional measures order entered in that case was limited to an exhortation not to commit genocide and did not address the underlying questions of the scope of the Security Council's powers. See *Application of the Convention on the Prevention and Punishment of the Crime of Genocide* (Bosnia–Herzegovina v. Yugoslavia), 1993 I.C.J. 3 & 1993 I.C.J. 325. In subsequent written pleadings, Bosnia–Herzegovina refocused its case solely on the conduct of Serbia, and the Court's 1996 judgment on jurisdiction and 2007 judgment on the merits did not pass upon this issue.

While the I.C.J. has not squarely confronted its authority to rule on the legality of actions taken by another principal organ of the United Nations, a sub-organ of the Security Council, the International Criminal Tribunal for the former Yugoslavia, has passed upon whether the Security Council was empowered to create that sub-organ.

PROSECUTOR v. TADIĆ

Appeals Chamber, International Criminal Tribunal for the former Yugoslavia, 1992
Case No. IT–94–1–AR72, 35 I.L.M. 32 (1996)

[Dušan Tadić was the first defendant brought for trial before the International Criminal Tribunal for the former Yugoslavia (I.C.T.Y.). Tadić challenged the jurisdiction of the Tribunal on the ground, *inter alia*, that the Security Council had exceeded its powers under Chapter VII of the U.N. Charter by establishing a criminal tribunal. The Appeals Chamber thus was confronted with the question of its authority to rule on the legality of the Security Council's decision to create the I.C.T.Y. As a threshold matter, the Appeals Chamber determined that every tribunal has an inherent power to resolve challenges to its own jurisdiction: "It is a necessary component in the exercise of the judicial function and does not need to be expressly provided for in the constitutive documents of those tribunals, although this is often done * * * ." (para. 18). This inherent or incidental jurisdiction would extend to a power to determine the validity of the Tribunal's own establishment by the Security Council. Proceeding to the substance of defendant's jurisdictional challenge, the Tribunal addressed the issue of the scope of the Security Council's powers in the following excerpts, under the heading "The Issue of Constitutionality".]

26. Many arguments have been put forward by Appellant in support of the contention that the establishment of the International Tribunal is invalid under the Charter of the United Nations or that it was not duly established by law. * * *

27. * * * These arguments raise a series of constitutional issues which all turn on the limits of the power of the Security Council under Chapter VII of the Charter of the United Nations and determining what action or measures can be taken under this Chapter, particularly the establishment of an international criminal tribunal. Put in the interrogative, they can be formulated as follows:

1. was there really a threat to the peace justifying the invocation of Chapter VII as a legal basis for the establishment of the International Tribunal?

2. assuming such a threat existed, was the Security Council authorized, with a view to restoring or maintaining peace, to take any measures at its own discretion, or was it bound to choose among those expressly provided for in Articles 41 and 42 (and possibly Article 40 as well)?

3. in the latter case, how can the establishment of an international criminal tribunal be justified, as it does not figure among the ones mentioned in those Articles, and is of a different nature?

1.   *The Power Of The Security Council To Invoke Chapter VII*

28.   Article 39 opens Chapter VII of the Charter of the United Nations and determines the conditions of application of this Chapter. It provides:

> "The Security Council shall determine the existence of any threat to the peace, breach of the peace, or act of aggression and shall make recommendations, or decide what measures shall be taken in accordance with Articles 41 and 42, to maintain or restore international peace and security." (United Nations Charter, 26 June 1945, Art. 39.)

It is clear from this text that the Security Council plays a pivotal role and exercises a very wide discretion under this Article. But this does not mean that its powers are unlimited. The Security Council is an organ of an international organization, established by a treaty which serves as a constitutional framework for that organization. The Security Council is thus subjected to certain constitutional limitations, however broad its powers under the constitution may be. Those powers cannot, in any case, go beyond the limits of the jurisdiction of the Organization at large, not to mention other specific limitations or those which may derive from the internal division of power within the Organization. In any case, neither the text nor the spirit of the Charter conceives of the Security Council as *legibus solutus* (unbound by law).

In particular, Article 24, after declaring, in paragraph 1, that the Members of the United Nations "confer on the Security Council primary responsibility for the maintenance of international peace and security", imposes on it, in paragraph 3, the obligation to report annually (or more frequently) to the General Assembly, and provides, more importantly, in paragraph 2, that:

> "In discharging these duties the Security Council shall act in accordance with the Purposes and Principles of the United Nations. The specific powers granted to the Security Council for the discharge of these duties are laid down in Chapters VI, VII, VIII, and XII." (*Id.*, Art. 24(2).)

The Charter thus speaks the language of specific powers, not of absolute fiat.

29.   What is the extent of the powers of the Security Council under Article 39 and the limits thereon, if any?

The Security Council plays the central role in the application of both parts of the Article. It is the Security Council that makes the *determination* that there exists one of the situations justifying the use of the "exceptional powers" of Chapter VII. And it is also the Security Council that chooses the reaction to such a situation: it either makes *recommendations* (*i.e.*, opts not to use the exceptional powers but to continue to operate under Chapter VI) or decides to use the exceptional powers by ordering *measures* to be taken in accordance with Articles 41 and 42 with a view to maintaining or restoring international peace and security.

The situations justifying resort to the powers provided for in Chapter VII are a "threat to the peace", a "breach of the peace" or an "act of aggression." While the "act of aggression" is more amenable to a legal determination, the "threat to the peace" is more of a political concept. But the determination that there exists such a threat is not a totally unfettered discretion, as it has to remain, at the very least, within the limits of the Purposes and Principles of the Charter.

30.   It is not necessary for the purposes of the present decision to examine any further the question of the limits of the discretion of the Security Council in determining the existence of a "threat to the peace", for two reasons.

The first is that an armed conflict (or a series of armed conflicts) has been taking place in the territory of the former Yugoslavia since long before the decision of the Security Council to establish this International Tribunal. If it is considered an international armed conflict, there is no doubt that it falls within the literal sense of the words "breach of the peace" (between the parties or, at the very least, as a "threat to the peace" of others).

But even if it were considered merely as an "internal armed conflict", it would still constitute a "threat to the peace" according to the settled practice of the Security Council and the common understanding of the United Nations membership in general. Indeed, the practice of the Security Council is rich with cases of civil war or internal strife which it classified as a "threat to the peace" and dealt with under Chapter VII, with the encouragement or even at the behest of the General Assembly, such as the Congo crisis at the beginning of the 1960s and, more recently, Liberia and Somalia. It can thus be said that there is a common understanding, manifested by the "subsequent practice" of the membership of the United Nations at large, that the "threat to the peace" of Article 39 may include, as one of its species, internal armed conflicts.

The second reason, which is more particular to the case at hand, is that Appellant * * * no longer contests the Security Council's power to determine whether the situation in the former Yugoslavia constituted a threat to the peace, nor the determination itself. * * * But he continues to contest the legality and appropriateness of the measures chosen by the Security Council to that end.

2. *The Range of Measures Envisaged Under Chapter VII*

31. Once the Security Council determines that a particular situation poses a threat to the peace or that there exists a breach of the peace or an act of aggression, it enjoys a wide margin of discretion in choosing the course of action: as noted above (see para. 29) it can either continue, in spite of its determination, to act via recommendations, *i.e.*, as if it were still within Chapter VI (*"Pacific Settlement of Disputes"*) or it can exercise its exceptional powers under Chapter VII. In the words of Article 39, it would then "decide what measures shall be taken in accordance with Articles 41 and 42, to maintain or restore international peace and security." (United Nations Charter, art. 39.)

A question arises in this respect as to whether the choice of the Security Council is limited to the measures provided for in Articles 41 and 42 of the Charter (as the language of Article 39 suggests), or whether it has even larger discretion in the form of general powers to maintain and restore international peace and security under Chapter VII at large. In the latter case, one of course does not have to locate every measure decided by the Security Council under Chapter VII within the confines of Articles 41 and 42, or possibly Article 40. In any case, under both interpretations, the Security Council has a broad discretion in deciding on the course of action and evaluating the appropriateness of the measures to be taken. The language of Article 39 is quite clear as to the channelling of the very broad and exceptional powers of the Security Council under Chapter VII through Articles 41 and 42. These two Articles leave to the Security Council such a wide choice as not to warrant searching, on functional or other grounds, for even wider and more general powers than those already expressly provided for in the Charter.

These powers are *coercive vis-à-vis* the culprit State or entity. But they are also *mandatory vis-à-vis* the other Member States, who are under an obligation to cooperate with the Organization (Article 2, paragraph 5, Articles 25, 48) and with one another (Articles 49), in the implementation of the action or measures decided by the Security Council.

3. *The Establishment Of The International Tribunal As A Measure Under Chapter VII*

32. As with the determination of the existence of a threat to the peace, a breach of the peace or an act of aggression, the Security Council has a very wide margin of discretion under Article 39 to choose the appropriate course of action and to evaluate the suitability of the measures chosen, as well as their potential contribution to the restoration or maintenance of peace. But here again, this discretion is not unfettered; moreover, it is limited to the measures provided for in Articles 41 and 42.

[The Appeals Chamber then concluded that although the establishment of an international criminal tribunal is not expressly mentioned in Articles 41 and 42, the measures set out there are merely illustrative examples that do not exclude other measures. After rejecting appellant's other objections, it held that the Tribunal had been lawfully established as a measure under Chapter VII of the Charter.]

NOTES

1. *Parsing Tadić.* Does the *Tadić* ruling clarify how to determine "inherent" powers of an international organization (such as the power of a judicial body to resolve challenges to its own jurisdiction? Is an analysis distinguishing among explicit, implicit, and inherent powers useful? If the Security Council's powers are not "unfettered" but indeed bounded by law, where might the limits of those powers be discerned?

2. *Building upon Tadić.* In addition to "inherent" power to rule on jurisdictional objections, what other powers not expressly conferred in its founding instrument might be available to an international organ such as a criminal tribunal? In *Prosecutor v. Blaskić*, Case No. IT–95–14–AR108bis, Judgment on the Request of Croatia (Oct. 29, 1997), the I.C.T.Y.'s Appeals Chamber addressed a set of questions concerning judicial powers with respect to ordering production of evidence. Croatia had requested review of a "subpoena" issued by a trial chamber, which purported to order Croatia to produce a variety of documents for inspection. The Appeals Chamber began with a clarification of terms:

> 25.   The Appeals Chamber holds the view that the term "subpoena" (in the sense of injunction accompanied by threat of penalty) cannot be applied or addressed to States. This finding rests on two grounds.

> First of all, the International Tribunal does not possess any power to take enforcement measures against States. Had the drafters of the [I.C.T.Y.'s] Statute intended to vest the International Tribunal with such a power, they would have expressly provided for it. In the case of an international judicial body, this is not a power that can be regarded as inherent in its functions. * * *

> Secondly, * * * [u]nder present international law it is clear that States, by definition, cannot be the subject of criminal sanctions akin to those provided for in national criminal systems.

However, the Appeals Chamber did find a power to issue "binding orders" to states, which it derived from the obligation on all states to cooperate with the Tribunal, as laid down in Article 29 of the I.C.T.Y.'s Statute promulgated by the Security Council and restated in a mandatory resolution of the Council. In the event of a state's non-compliance with such a binding order, the Appeals Chamber said:

> 33.   * * * As stated above, the International Tribunal is not vested with any enforcement or sanctionary power *vis-à-vis* States. It is primarily for its parent body, the Security Council, to impose sanctions, if any, against a recalcitrant State, under the conditions provided for in Chapter

VII of the United Nations Charter. However, the International Tribunal
is endowed with the inherent power to make a judicial finding concerning
a State's failure to observe the provisions of the Statute or the Rules. It
also has the power to report this judicial finding to the Security Council.

The power to make this judicial finding is an inherent power: the
International Tribunal must possess the power to make all those judicial
determinations that are necessary for the exercise of its primary jurisdiction.
This inherent power inures to the benefit of the International
Tribunal in order that its basic judicial function may be fully discharged
and its judicial role safeguarded. The International Tribunal's power to
report to the Security Council is derived from the relationship between
the two institutions. The Security Council established the International
Tribunal pursuant to Chapter VII of the United Nations Charter for the
purpose of the prosecution of persons responsible for serious violations of
international humanitarian law committed in the territory of the former
Yugoslavia. A logical corollary of this is that any time a State fails to fulfil
its obligation under Article 29, thereby preventing the International
Tribunal from discharging the mission entrusted to it by the Security
Council, the International Tribunal is entitled to report this non-observance
to the Security Council.

For more on the I.C.T.Y.'s powers and jurisprudence, see Chapter 16.

3. *Further Reading.* For treatises on the law of the United Nations, see
The United Nations: Law and Practice (Cede & Sucharipa–Behrmann eds.
2001); Conforti, The Law and Practice of the United Nations (3d rev. ed.
2005); Cot & Pellet, La Charte des Nations Unies: Commentaire article par
article (2d ed. 1991); Goodrich, Hambro, & Simons, Charter of the United
Nations (3d rev. ed. 1969); Global Governance and the United Nations System
(Rittberger ed. 2001); United Nations Legal Order (Schachter & Joyner eds.
1995) (2 vols.); The Charter of the United Nations: A Commentary (2d ed.
Simma ed. 2002) (2 vols.); International Organizations and International
Dispute Settlement: Trends and Prospects (Boisson de Chazournes, Romano,
& Mackenzie eds. 2002); United Nations: Law, Policies, and Practice (Wolf-
rum ed. 1995) (2 vols.).

C. RESPONSIBILITY OF INTERNATIONAL ORGANIZATIONS

Chapter 8 will discuss the basic rules of international law on the
responsibility of states for their wrongful acts; do similar rules apply to
international organizations as well?

The International Court has stated that "[i]nternational organizations
are subjects of international law and, as such, are bound by any
obligations incumbent upon them under general rules of international law,
under their constitutions or under international agreements to which they
are parties." *Interpretation of the Agreement of 25 March 1951 between the
WHO and Egypt*, Advisory Opinion, 1980 I.C.J. 73, para. 37. Similarly,
"the Court wishes to point out that the question of immunity from legal

process is distinct from the issue of compensation for any damages incurred as a result of acts performed by the United Nations or by its agents acting in their official capacity * * *. The United Nations may be required to bear responsibility for the damage arising from such acts." *Difference Relating to Immunity from Legal Process of a Special Rapporteur of the Commission on Human Rights*, Advisory Opinion, 1999 I.C.J. 62, para. 66. The U.N. Secretary–General has stated that "the principle of State responsibility—widely accepted to be applicable to international organizations—that damage caused in breach of an international obligation and which is attributable to the State (or to the Organization) entails the international responsibility of the State (or the Organization) * * *." Report of the Secretary–General, U.N. Doc. A/51/389 para. 6 (Sept. 20, 1996) (reproduced in 37 I.L.M. 700 (1998)).

Thus, while an international organization can be a "plaintiff" on the international plane, it can also be a "defendant" when it fails to uphold the obligations to which it is bound, and the issue of whether immunity may exist from national jurisdiction is separate from whether it bears international responsibility for wrongful acts. The International Law Commission is currently embarked on a project to study and codify rules concerning the responsibility of international organizations. The Commission has tentatively adopted an Article 3 on "General principles" that provides:

> 1. Every internationally wrongful act of an international organization entails the international responsibility of the international organization.
>
> 2. There is an internationally wrongful act of an international organization when conduct consisting of an action or omission:
>
>> (a) Is attributed to the international organization under international law; and
>>
>> (b) Constitutes a breach of an international obligation of that international organization.

Report of the International Law Commission, 55th Sess., U.N. Doc. A/58/10, at 45 (2003). That rule and others being developed by the Commission closely parallel rules developed by the Commission on the responsibility of states.

In practice, international organizations have long accepted responsibility for tortious acts of its officials, agents, and others (such as troops) acting under their control. Most international organizations have also assumed financial responsibility for contractual obligations *vis-à-vis* states. The contractual responsibilities of international organizations *vis-à-vis* private persons have generated a substantial body of law and practice, especially with respect to applicable law, terms of contracts, and settlement of disputes.

Questions of responsibility of international organizations have arisen most conspicuously in connection with the peacekeeping activities of the

United Nations. These include complex legal and political questions as to the financial costs incurred and the obligation of member states to bear these costs when they regard the actions as *ultra vires*, such as the questions considered by the International Court in its advisory opinion on *Certain Expenses of the United Nations*, Advisory Opinion, 1962 I.C.J. 151. Responsibility for wrongful damage and personal injuries by military forces provided by member states, but acting under the authority of the United Nations, are normally accepted by the United Nations. Agreements with the governments that contribute troops and with the host (i.e., territorial) governments set forth the terms of financial responsibility and the procedures for settling particular cases. For a U.N. report on sexual abuse and exploitation by U.N. peacekeepers, and the possibilities for organization, managerial, and command accountability, as well as individual disciplinary, financial and criminal responsibility, see U.N. Doc. A/59/710 (Mar. 24, 2005).

Can international organizations commit acts that directly implicate the responsibility of member states? In other words, is it possible to "pierce through" the international organization so as to reach those states that created it? It is well accepted that conduct of an organ or personnel of an international organization created by several member states cannot, by reason of that fact alone, be attributed to those states. This principle is often recognized in agreements concluded by the organizations with their host states. Further, the member states of an organization do not, as a general matter, incur direct responsibility for the acts or engagements of the organization, unless the constituent instrument so provides. Member states may, nevertheless, bear the costs incurred by the international organization from wrongful acts since the states are typically obliged to pay for the financial expenses of the organization. See the Institut de Droit International's 1995 Lisbon Resolution, The Legal Consequences for Member States of the Non-fulfilment by International Organizations of their Obligations toward Third Parties, [1996] Ann. de l'Institut de Droit Int. 445; see also Stumer, Liability of Member States for Acts of International Organizations: Reconsidering the Policy Objections, 48 Harv. Int'l L.J. 553 (2007).

What if the international organization essentially goes bankrupt, leaving debts to third parties? Can the member states of an international organization then be secondarily or concurrently liable for those debts? This issue was the focus of decisions by the English Court of Appeals in *Maclaine Watson & Co. Ltd. v. Department of Trade & Indus.*, [1988] 3 All E.R. 257, and by the House of Lords in *J.H. Rayner Ltd. v. Department of Trade & Indus.*, [1990] 2 A.C. 418 (H.L.), which arose out of the defaults by the International Tin Council (I.T.C.) on contracts to purchase tin and on bank loans entered into as a part of its efforts to support the price of tin through maintenance of a buffer stock. The I.T.C. was an international organization established with "international legal personality" by the Sixth International Tin Agreement to which more than twenty states and the European Community were parties. The Court of Appeals rejected secondary or concurrent liability of the member states, and the House of Lords affirmed.

On the basis of an examination of these English cases, the principal textual authorities, and state practice, Amerasinghe concludes that:

> [T]he better view is that there is no presumption, when the constituent instrument does not indicate such an intention, that members of an international organization are concurrently or secondarily liable for its obligations. The presumption is thus the reverse. However, though there is no evidence of this in the sources, policy reasons also suggest the need to limit this rule on the basis of estoppel: the presumption of nonliability could be displaced by evidence that members (some or all of them) or the organization with the approval of members gave creditors reason to assume that members (some or all of them) would accept concurrent or secondary liability even without an express or implied intention to that effect in the constituent instrument.

Amerasinghe, Liability to Third Parties of Member States of International Organizations: Practice, Principle and Judicial Precedent, 85 A.J.I.L. 259, 280 (1991).

D. IMMUNITIES OF INTERNATIONAL ORGANIZATIONS

Internal Operations. Normally, international organizations are absolutely immune from suits arising out of their internal operations, including their relations with their employees. See, e.g., *Mendaro v. World Bank*, 717 F.2d 610 (D.C. Cir. 1983). The internal autonomy of international organizations has been extensively considered in decisions of international tribunals and national courts. See *Effect of Awards of Compensation Made by the United Nations Administrative Tribunal*, Advisory Opinion, 1954 I.C.J. 4; *Judgments of the Administrative Tribunal of the International Labour Organization upon Complaints Made against UNESCO*, Advisory Opinion, 1956 I.C.J. 77; *Application for Review of Judgment No. 158 of the United Nations Administrative Tribunal*, Advisory Opinion, 1973 I.C.J. 166; see also Reinisch, The Immunity of International Organizations and the Jurisdiction of their Administrative Tribunals, 7 Chinese J. Int'l L. 285 (2008). One can discern in these analyses a tension between the legal principle of internal autonomy of the organization and the inescapable political pressures by member states that seek to intrude upon that autonomy.

Since national courts are not available for resolution of internal personnel disputes, judicial tribunals have been established within international organizations to adjudicate disputes between the organization and its staff members. The U.N. Administrative Tribunal includes within its jurisdiction not only the United Nations, but also some of the specialized agencies. The Administrative Tribunal of the International Labour

Organisation (I.L.O.) similarly has an extended jurisdiction beyond itself, including, by special agreement, several of the specialized agencies located in Europe (e.g., UNESCO, FAO, and WHO). The European Communities did not have to create a special tribunal, since its Court of Justice had jurisdiction with respect to complaints of staff members. A considerable body of case-law has been developed by the several tribunals concerning the rights and obligations of international organizations *vis-à-vis* international officials. In particular, procedural rights analogous to due process have been defined in a great variety of situations of international employment.

External Operations. On the issue of whether absolute immunity is applicable for suits arising out of the external operations of international organizations, see Reinisch, International Organizations Before National Courts (2000); Oparil, Immunity of International Organizations in United States Courts: Absolute or Restrictive?, 24 Vand. J. Transnat'l L. 689 (1991). Regardless of the general rule, the organization's charter may expressly waive immunity. Thus, Article VII, Section 3 of the World Bank's Articles of Agreement has been held to constitute a waiver of immunity from suits "arising out of the Bank's *external* relations with its debtors and creditors." *Mendaro v. World Bank, supra,* at 618. Immunity may also be expressly waived by an appropriate organ or officer of the organization, and may be done through a contract or lease agreement. Such organ or officer may also waive the immunity of the organization in a particular case after a dispute has arisen and may further agree to arbitration. As a general matter, however, a separate express waiver must exist to overcome immunity from execution against assets of the international organization. For further discussion of the immunities of international organizations and their staffs, see Chapter 12, Section 5.

E. MEMBERSHIP AND REPRESENTATION IN INTERNATIONAL ORGANIZATIONS

Membership in international organizations is generally limited to states, but in some cases other entities have also been admitted to membership where permitted by the constituent instrument. States become members by: (1) becoming parties to the constituent treaty establishing the organization; (2) admission through votes of one or more of the principal organs; or (3) succession by a new state to the membership held by a predecessor state, in accordance with the rules of the organization.

In the United Nations, an applicant state must first receive the recommendation of the Security Council, including the concurring vote of the five permanent members, and then receive the affirmative vote of two-thirds of the General Assembly. See U.N. Charter, art. 4(2). Early in the life of the United Nations, Cold War ideologies resulted in stalemates within the Security Council on the admission of new states, with the West opposing new applicants from the Soviet orbit and the East opposing new applicants aligned with the West. Since Western states dominated the

General Assembly in the 1950s, some argued that an affirmative Security Council resolution was not actually necessary; that it was enough for an unfavorable recommendation to issue, which the General Assembly could then simply take into account when reaching a decision on whether to admit. The General Assembly asked the International Court of Justice for its advice on the matter, and the Court responded that:

> To hold that the General Assembly has power to admit a State to membership in the absence of a recommendation of the Security Council would be to deprive the Security Council of an important power which has been entrusted to it by the Charter. It would almost nullify the role of the Security Council in the exercise of one of the essential functions of the Organisation. It would mean that the Security Council would have merely to study the case, present a report, give advice, and express an opinion. This is not what Article 4, paragraph 2, says.

See *Competence of the General Assembly for the Admission of a State to the United Nations*, Advisory Opinion, 1950 I.C.J. 4. In the aftermath of the Court's advisory opinion, the stalemate at the Security Council continued for five years, until a package deal could be agreed upon for admission of a group of new states spanning the East/West alignments. In December 1955, the following states were simultaneously admitted: Albania, Austria, Bulgaria, Cambodia, Finland, Hungary, Ireland, Italy, Jordan, Lao People's Democratic Republic, Libyan Arab Jamahiriya, Nepal, Portugal, Romania, Spain, and Sri Lanka.

As for the substantive qualifications for admission, the constituent instrument of the international organization may set requirements that must be met by states before admission. Many organizations are open to all states so long as they accept the obligations imposed by the constituent instrument. Regional organizations, however, limit membership to states within a defined region. The constituent instrument may impose other qualifications. For example, the U.N. Charter declares (art. 4) that membership is open only to an entity that is a "state," is "peace-loving," and is "able and willing to carry out" the obligations of the Charter. Whether such qualifications are actually met is left to each existing member state to decide in the course of casting its vote. In its very first advisory opinion, the International Court made clear that a member's decision on admission should turn solely on whether the qualifications set forth in the Charter have been met, and not on other matters. See *Conditions of Admission of a State to Membership in the United Nations (Article 4 of the Charter)*, Advisory Opinion, 1948 48 I.C.J. 57. That opinion obviously did not avoid Cold War politics intruding upon admission decisions. Further, whether an applicant was truly an independent and viable "state" has been vigorously debated in several cases. In recent years, many mini-states, including some associated states that do not conduct their own foreign relations or defense, have been admitted to U.N. membership even though it appeared that they were dependent politically and economically on other states.

Once admitted to the international organization, the state may appoint persons to serve as its representatives or delegates to the organization. Changes in regime or form of government do not affect the rights or obligations of a member. In a number of instances, competing authorities have claimed to be the government with the right to represent the state. The decision as to which competing authority has the right to appoint representatives is made by the organization, generally by accepting or rejecting credentials submitted by the competitors. Many states have argued that the decision should be taken on "objective" criteria, in particular, which competitor is in effective control of the territory of the state and able to employ the resources and direct the people in fulfillment of the obligations of membership. Others have maintained that even if a regime is not in effective control of its territory, the willingness of a regime to fulfill the purposes of the Organization and to abide by its principles is sufficient. See Chapter 5, Section 4, on the recognition of governments.

The credentials of a delegation were rejected in some instances because the government in question was considered to be "unrepresentative" or to have violated principles of the constituent instrument. South Africa was denied participation in the U.N. General Assembly on these grounds during its apartheid era. Objection to that action as illegal was registered by the United States on the ground that it was an indirect suspension of the rights of membership without conforming to the Charter's condition for such suspension, in particular, an affirmative vote by the Security Council. On suspension of membership rights or exclusion from an organization as a sanction for violation of the obligations of membership, see Chayes & Chayes, The New Sovereignty 68–87 (1995).

While it is normally the case that a state is known to either be or not be a member of an international organization, in unusual circumstances an ambiguous status may exist that only becomes clear over time. Such ambiguity may exist intentionally as the international organization seeks to leave open options for handing a transitory situation. For example, in the early 1990s, the Socialist Federal Republic of Yugoslavia (S.F.R.Y.)—consisting of Bosnia–Herzegovina, Croatia, Macedonia, Montenegro, Serbia, and Slovenia—began to break up into several new states. Whereas most of the republics sought admission to the United Nations as new members, Serbia and Montenegro declared themselves to be the "Federal Republic of Yugoslavia" (F.R.Y.) and asserted that they succeeded to the membership in the United Nations of the S.F.R.Y. As such, the F.R.Y. claimed that it was already a member state. The Security Council and General Assembly rejected that position, but left somewhat vague the exact status of the F.R.Y. See S.C. Res. 757, pmbl. (May 30, 1992); S.C. Res. 777, pmbl. (Sept. 25, 1992); G.A. Res. 47/1 (Sept. 26, 1992). The Secretary–General and the U.N. Legal Counsel then opined that the F.R.Y. could not *participate* in the work of the General Assembly and its subsidiary organs, or in their conferences and meetings, but that the General Assembly had neither suspended nor terminated the *membership* of "Yugoslavia" in the United Nations, and the seat, nameplate, and flag of the S.F.R.Y. would continue to be present at the U.N. headquarters. See U.N. Doc. A/47/485, annex (Sept. 30, 1992). Years later, the International Court of Justice opined on the issue in the context of determining whether the F.R.Y. was a party to the Statute of the Court during the 1990s, which would only be the case if it was at that time a U.N. member state. If the F.R.Y. were not a party to the Court's Statute, then the Court would have no jurisdiction to hear a case filed at the Court in 1999 by the F.R.Y. against various NATO states, including the United Kingdom.

LEGALITY OF USE OF FORCE
(SERBIA & MONTENEGRO v. UNITED KINGDOM)

International Court of Justice, 2004
2004 I.C.J. 1307, 1332–38, 1352

62.   * * * [T]he legal position of the Federal Republic of Yugoslavia within the United Nations and vis-à-vis that Organization remained highly complex during the period 1992–2000. In fact, it is the view of the Court that the legal situation that obtained within the United Nations during that eight-year period concerning the status of the Federal Republic of Yugoslavia, after the break-up of the Socialist Federal Republic of Yugoslavia, remained ambiguous and open to different assessments. This was due, *inter alia*, to the absence of an authoritative determination by the competent organs of the United Nations defining clearly the legal status of the Federal Republic of Yugoslavia vis-à-vis the United Nations.

63.   Within the United Nations, three different positions were taken on the issue of the legal status of the Federal Republic of Yugoslavia. In the first place, there was the position taken by the two political organs concerned. The Security Council, as an organ of the United Nations which under the Charter is vested with powers and responsibilities as regards membership, stated in its resolution 777 (1992) of 19 September 1992 that it "consider[ed] that the state formerly known as the Socialist Federal Republic of Yugoslavia has ceased to exist" and that it "[c]onsider[ed] that the Federal Republic of Yugoslavia (Serbia and Montenegro) cannot continue automatically the membership of the Socialist Federal Republic of Yugoslavia in the United Nations".

64.   The other organ which under the Charter is vested with powers and responsibilities as regards membership in the United Nations is the General Assembly. In the wake of this Security Council resolution, and especially in light of its recommendation to the General Assembly that "it decide that the Federal Republic of Yugoslavia (Serbia and Montenegro) should apply for membership in the United Nations", the Assembly took the position in resolution 47/1 of 22 September 1992 that it "[c]onsider[ed] that the Federal Republic of Yugoslavia (Serbia and Montenegro) cannot continue automatically the membership of the former Socialist Federal Republic of Yugoslavia in the United Nations". On that basis, it "decide[d] that the Federal Republic of Yugoslavia (Serbia and Montenegro) should apply for membership in the United Nations".

65.   While it is clear from the voting figures * * * that these resolutions reflected a position endorsed by the vast majority of the Members of the United Nations, they cannot be construed as conveying an authoritative determination of the legal status of the Federal Republic of Yugoslavia within, or vis-à-vis, the United Nations. The uncertainty surrounding the question is evidenced, *inter alia*, by the practice of the General Assembly in budgetary matters during the years following the break-up of the Socialist Federal Republic of Yugoslavia.

[The Court first recounted how the F.R.Y. was assessed annual contributions to the United Nations throughout the 1990s. Second, the Court noted that the F.R.Y. maintained its claim that it continued the legal personality of the S.F.R.Y.].

68.   Thirdly, another organ that came to be involved in this problem was the Secretariat of the United Nations. In the absence of any authoritative determination on the legal status of the Federal Republic of Yugoslavia within, or vis-à-vis, the United Nations, the Secretariat, as the administrative organ of the Organization, simply continued to keep to the practice of the *status quo ante* that had prevailed up to the break-up of the Socialist Federal Republic of Yugoslavia in 1992, pending such a determination. This is illustrated by the practice of the Secretariat in its role in the preparation of the budget of the Organization for consideration and approval by the General Assembly. * * *

* * *

71.   To sum up, all these events testify to the rather confused and complex state of affairs that obtained within the United Nations surrounding the issue of the legal status of the Federal Republic of Yugoslavia in the Organization during this period. * * *

* * *

73.   This situation, however, came to an end with a new development in 2000. On 24 September 2000, Mr. Koštunica was elected President of the Federal Republic of Yugoslavia. In that capacity, on 27 October 2000 he sent a letter to the Secretary–General requesting admission of the Federal Republic of Yugoslavia to membership in the United Nations * * *.

74.   Acting upon this application by the Federal Republic of Yugoslavia for membership in the United Nations, the Security Council on 31 October 2000 "*recommend[ed]* to the General Assembly that the Federal Republic of Yugoslavia be admitted to membership in the United Nations" (United Nations doc. S/RES/1326). On 1 November 2000, the General Assembly, by resolution 55/12, "*[h]aving considered* the application for membership of the Federal Republic of Yugoslavia", decided to "admit the Federal Republic of Yugoslavia to membership in the United Nations".

* * *

76. This new development effectively put to an end the *sui generis* position of the Federal Republic of Yugoslavia within the United Nations.
* * *

77. * * * [F]rom the vantage point from which the Court now looks at the legal situation, and in light of the legal consequences of the new development since 1 November 2000, the Court is led to the conclusion that Serbia and Montenegro was not a Member of the United Nations, and in that capacity a State party to the Statute of the International Court of Justice, at the time of filing its Application to institute the present proceedings before the Court on 29 April 1999.

* * *

115. For these reasons,

THE COURT,

Unanimously,

Finds that it has no jurisdiction to entertain the claims made in the Application filed by Serbia and Montenegro on 29 April 1999.

NOTES

1. *Bosnia-Herzegovina v. F.R.Y. Genocide Case.* The International Court also addressed this issue in a case brought by Bosnia-Herzegovina against the F.R.Y. in 1993 for alleged acts of genocide in Bosnia-Herzegovina in the early 1990s. At the preliminary objections stage in 1996, the Court was not called upon to address the F.R.Y.'s membership in the United Nations, since the F.R.Y. at that time maintained it was a member and Bosnia-Herzegovina, as the applicant, had no desire to cast doubt upon its ability to sue the F.R.Y. before the Court. After the F.R.Y. gave up its claim to be the continuator of the S.F.R.Y., and instead sought and received admission to the United Nations, the F.R.Y. requested that the Court revisit whether it had jurisdiction over Bosnia-Herzegovina's case, since it was now known that the F.R.Y. was not a member of the United Nations when the case was filed. The Court, however, declined to revisit its prior decision, since a "revision" of a prior judgment is only justified if a "new fact" comes to light that was unknown when the judgment was issued. See I.C.J. Statute, art. 61(1). According to the Court, the F.R.Y.'s admission to the United Nations in 2000 was not such a fact. *Application for Revision of the Judgment of 11 July 1996 in the Case Concerning Application of the Convention on the Prevention and Punishment of the Crime of Genocide* (Yugoslavia v. Bosnia–Herzegovina), 2003 I.C.J. 7, 31. When the Court reached the merits of Bosnia-Herzegovina's case in 2007, it stated that the F.R.Y.'s "capacity to appear before the Court in accordance with the Statute was an element in the reasoning of the 1996 Judgment which can—and indeed must—be read into the Judgment as a matter of logical construction. That element is not one which can at any time be reopened and re-examined. . . ." *Application of the Convention on the Prevention and Punishment of the Crime of Genocide* (Bosnia–Herzegovina v. Serbia & Montenegro), 2007 I.C.J. 191, para. 135.

2. *Squaring the Circle.* Do you find it unusual that the Court would find in 2004 that Serbia & Montenegro could not sue the United Kingdom in 1999 because it was not a member of the United Nations in the 1990s, whereas in 2007 the Court reached the merits of a case filed by Bosnia-Herzegovina against Serbia (or more precisely, Serbia's predecessor state, the F.R.Y.) in 1993? For analysis, see Blum, Was Yugoslavia a Member of the United Nations in the Years 1992–2000?, 101 A.J.I.L. 800 (2007).

SECTION 2.   NON–GOVERNMENTAL ORGANIZATIONS

Non-governmental organizations (NGOs) play an active role on the international scene and in some cases have a recognized legal status under treaties and other international arrangements. Article 71 of the U.N. Charter provides for consultative arrangements between the Economic and Social Council and NGOs, and hundreds of NGOs have consultative status under that provision. Similar arrangements exist in other international organizations. The numerous international NGOs range over the entire array of human activity, including humanitarian, health, human rights and environmental matters; professional and scientific associations; federations and international unions made up of national associations representing labor or employers; religious bodies; scientific academies; and so on.

International NGOs are like international organizations in that they are legal persons operating transnationally and are organized to pursue public purposes. At the same time, NGOs are created under national law, not international law, and are the product of cooperation among individuals not states. Should NGOs be accorded the full status of international legal persons, akin to the status accorded international organizations? Exactly what kinds of access do they have in the realm of international law and what functions do they serve? Can they be said to have affected international law in significant ways? Given that NGOs are not formed by states or through some form of democratic process, are they really a legitimate voice within international law?

CHARNOVITZ, NONGOVERNMENTAL ORGANIZATIONS AND INTERNATIONAL LAW
100 A.J.I.L. 348, 350–68 (2006) (footnotes omitted)

I.   WHO NGOS ARE AND WHAT THEY DO

The Identity of NGOs

The NGOs that are the subject of this article are groups of persons or of societies, freely created by private initiative, that pursue an interest in matters that cross or transcend national borders and are not profit seeking. Such NGOs are usually international in the sense of drawing members from more than one country. Although profit-seeking business entities are not NGOs, associations of business entities can be, such as the International Chamber of Commerce.

Everything about nongovernmental organizations is contested, including the meaning of the term. In his 1963 treatise on NGOs, J. J. Lador-Lederer observed that the semantic negation neglects the most significant part of the organizations, which is that their strength comes from "their capacity at continuous existence and development." Recently, Philip Alston took note of the widespread use of "nongovernmental organization" and "nonstate actor," and remarked that the insistence upon defining actors "in terms of what they are not combines impeccable purism in terms of traditional international legal analysis with an unparalleled capacity to marginalize a significant part of the international human rights regime." During the past two decades, the term "civil society organization" has gained popularity in some circles as an alternative to "NGO." Recognizing the longtime usage of the NGO acronym, some commentators have suggested keeping it, but changing its meaning to "Necessary to Governance Organization." That clever wordplay has not caught on.

The UN system continues to use the term "NGO," and the chief reason for doing so may be because Article 71 of the UN Charter states, "The Economic and Social Council may make suitable arrangements for consultation with non-governmental organizations which are concerned with matters within its competence." The Charter, however, does not define NGO.

* * *

NGO Functions in International Law

* * * NGOs contribute to the development, interpretation, judicial application, and enforcement of international law.

NGOs may be most prolific when new fields of law are initiated or new treaties drafted. An early example concerns the rights of women. In 1928, after women's groups journeyed to the sixth Pan–American Conference, the governments agreed to hold a plenary session to hear the women's representatives, and accepted their proposal to create the Inter-American Commission of Women. Another major milestone occurred when NGOs advanced language on human rights for the UN Charter and then aided the diplomats drafting the Universal Declaration of Human Rights. Advocacy by NGOs and indigenous groups has been similarly instrumental in achieving new international protections for indigenous peoples. In recent years, networks of NGOs worked to inspire negotiations for the International Criminal Court.

Another function engaged in by NGOs is the interpretation of international law. For example, NGOs helped to develop the "Siracusa Principles" in 1984, on the meaning and scope of the derogation and limitation provisions of the International Covenant on Civil and Political Rights. Theodor Meron has noted that by championing a broad construction of the

Fourth Geneva Convention, the International Committee of the Red Cross (ICRC) clarified that rape is a crime under international humanitarian law.

NGOs seek to contribute to international adjudication by making friend-of-the-court submissions to tribunals. Typically, an NGO initiates action by requesting leave from a court to submit a brief. In an authoritative study of NGO participation, Dinah Shelton found that major international tribunals, except the International Court of Justice (ICJ), had developed procedures to enable NGOs to submit information or statements on pending cases. Since the publication of Shelton's study in 1994, the trends she documented have continued apace. For example, organs of the International Criminal Tribunal for the Former Yugoslavia and the International Criminal Tribunal for Rwanda have requested amicus submissions in some cases and received them from individual jurists and NGOs. On the other hand, NGOs have not yet sought to submit an amicus brief to the International Tribunal for the Law of the Sea.

* * *

In contrast to their participation as amici, the ability of NGOs to initiate cases is less extensive. One tribunal that has been open to NGOs is the African Commission on Human and Peoples' Rights, which has allowed states, individuals, and NGOs with observer status to submit communications alleging a violation of the African Charter. The European Court of Human Rights permits an NGO to bring a case if the NGO itself claims to be a victim. Other opportunities present themselves in international administrative entities that permit NGOs to bring complaints. For example, the World Bank Inspection Panel entertains requests for inspection from an organization, association, society, or other grouping of two or more individuals that believes it is likely to be adversely affected as a result of the Bank's violation of its own policies and procedures.

NGOs are now often engaged in the review and promotion of state compliance with international obligations. Oscar Schachter, a keen observer, detected this budding development in 1960, and in the following decades, the NGO role flowered in the monitoring of human rights, humanitarian, and environmental law. In their 1995 book *The New Sovereignty*, Abram Chayes and Antonia Chayes devoted a chapter to the impact of NGOs on treaty compliance, and pointed out that, "[i]n a real sense, [NGOs] supply the personnel and resources for managing compliance that states have become increasingly reluctant to provide." In the decade since that book was published, the NGO role has continued to expand. For example, the parties to the Aarhus Convention agreed to allow NGOs with observer status to nominate candidates for the Convention's Compliance Committee. NGOs can also play an important role within a domestic political system in pressing the government to meet its obligations under a ratified treaty.

The last NGO function to be noted is assistance to collective enforcement efforts. For example, in a 1992 resolution regarding the former

Yugoslavia, the UN Security Council called on states "and, as appropriate, international humanitarian organizations to collate substantiated information" relating to violations of humanitarian law. In a 2003 resolution regarding Sierra Leone, the Security Council called on "States, international organizations and non-governmental organizations to continue to support the National Recovery Strategy of the Government of Sierra Leone."

II.   LEGAL STATUS OF NGOs
* * *

NGO Personality

Legal personality is a key factor in determining the rights and immunities of an NGO and its standing before courts. In general, an NGO enjoys legal personality only in municipal law, not in international law. Yet because NGOs so often operate in more than one country, they face potential problems of being subject to conflicting laws and of inability to carry their legal status from one country to another. Aware that this situation could prove problematic for internationally active NGOs, both the Institut de droit international (Institut) and the International Law Association began in 1910 to promote consideration of a convention to grant legal personality to international NGOs. Almost a century later, advocates have not made much progress toward that goal.

* * *

Transnational NGOs have learned how to maneuver without formal international personality. In some instances, the crucial role that an NGO plays has led governments to accord rights to it that are typically granted only to IOs. For example, the ICRC and the International Federation of Red Cross and Red Crescent Societies have signed headquarters agreements with numerous states that provide for certain privileges and immunities.

Over the years, the efforts to achieve an international legal personality for NGOs have exposed some unresolved tensions. On the one hand, providing such recognition may help prevent interstate conflicts * * * and may further "the general interest of the international community to encourage the development of non profit-making international associations." On the other hand, states have worried that granting international recognition to NGOs may reduce governmental control over them, and NGOs have worried that such recognition might entail a loss of autonomy. With the increased attention to NGO (mis)behavior in recent years, a new treaty would more likely impose regulation on NGOs than facilitate freedom of association.

NGOs as Consultation Partners

In the absence of international NGO law as such, Article 71 of the UN Charter has served de facto as a charter for NGO activities. The legal capacity of the NGO under Article 71 might be termed a consultation partner. Although Article 71 establishes consultative opportunities for the NGOs granted status by the UN Economic and Social Council (ECOSOC), an individual NGO does not have a treaty-based right to be consulted in a particular situation.

* * *

* * * Article 71 soon took on an importance far broader than its own text and, for that reason, the status attained by NGOs through Article 71 became a foundation stone for their efforts to strengthen international law. Even though Article 71 refers only to ECOSOC, a consultative role for NGOs gradually became an established practice throughout the UN system. Article 71 was implemented comprehensively by ECOSOC in 1950 (the 1950 NGO Rule) in a resolution that was superseded by a new resolution in 1968, and then again in 1996 by the resolution now in place (the 1996 NGO Rule).

Although many of these ECOSOC rules have remained constant, some have changed significantly. First, the 1950 NGO Rule required that an NGO be of "recognized standing" *and* that it "represent a substantial proportion of the organized persons within the particular field in which it operates." By contrast, the 1996 Rule dispenses with this two-part requirement. Now the NGO must "be of recognized standing within the particular field of its competence *or* of a representative character." Second, the preference in the 1950 Rule for international, rather than national, NGOs has now been eliminated. Third, the 1996 Rule adds a requirement that an NGO given status "have a democratically adopted constitution" and that it "have a representative structure and possess appropriate mechanisms of accountability to its members, who shall exercise effective control over its policies and actions through the exercise of voting rights or other appropriate democratic and transparent decision-making processes." This attention to internal NGO governance reflects the growing concerns in the early 1990s about the legitimacy and accountability of NGOs.

* * *

In the early twenty-first century, NGOs are pervasive. No policy issues are off-limits for government-NGO consultations. As Alexandre Kiss and Dinah Shelton have observed, "Today, purely inter-state development of norms is probably non-existent in most fields of international law." This circumstance has been appreciated by the U.S. Congress, which in a November 2005 appropriation defined an "international conference" as a "conference attended by representatives of the United States Government and representatives of foreign governments, international organizations, or nongovernmental organizations."

Nᴏᴛᴇs

1. *International Legal Personality for NGOs.* In the *LaGrand Case*, the International Court of Justice made clear that, in addition to states, individuals can have rights under international law. *LaGrand Case* (Germany v. United States), 2001 I.C.J. 466, para. 77. If that is true, then do you think that NGOs can also have rights and obligations under international law as well? Can they achieve a status that approximates the status accorded to international organizations? Should they?

2. *Consultative Status through the U.N. ECOSOC.* Professor Charnovitz observes that Article 71 of the U.N. Charter establishes consultative opportunities for NGOs when they are granted status by the U.N. Economic and Social Council (ECOSOC). Article 71 provides:

> The Economic and Social Council may make suitable arrangements for consultation with non-governmental organizations which are concerned with matters within its competence. Such arrangements may be made with international organizations and, where appropriate, with national organizations after consultation with the Member of the United Nations concerned.

ECOSOC's "Arrangements for Consultation with Non–Governmental Organizations," as revised in 1996, are embodied in E.S.C. Res. 1996/31. The Arrangements are implemented through ECOSOC's Committee on NGOs (the "Committee") and the NGOs Section of the U.N. Secretariat. NGOs in consultative relationships with ECOSOC include those at international, regional, subregional, or national levels. The Committee is instructed to "ensure, to the extent possible, participation of non-governmental organizations from all regions, and particularly from developing countries, in order to help achieve a just, balanced, effective and genuine involvement of non-governmental organizations from all regions and areas of the world" (para. 5). Where an applicant is a national NGO, the Committee is to take account of the views of the member state concerned and the response to such views from the NGO. The Arrangements contain provisions aimed at ascertaining that an NGO is representative of its members and has a governance structure with transparent decision-making.

The nature of consultative relationships preserves what the Arrangements characterize as a "fundamental" distinction between privileges accorded to states and international organizations on the one hand, and NGOs on the other (para. 18). The purpose of consultative status (para. 20) is to enable ECOSOC organs "to secure expert information or advice from organizations having special competence in the subjects for which consultative arrangements are made, and, on the other hand, to enable international, regional, subregional and national organizations that represent important elements of public opinion to express their views." NGOs concerned with a wide range of activities and "broadly representative of major segments of society in a large number of countries in different regions of the world" may be admitted to general consultative status, while those with more specialized scope are in special consultative status or are listed on a roster indicating their availability

for consultation (paras. 21–26). The Arrangements specify the various privileges available to the respective statuses (e.g., attendance at meetings; information exchange), as well as the guidelines for NGO participation in international conferences convened by the United Nations. Provisions for suspension
and withdrawal of consultative status are also specified (paras. 55–57), as
where an organization "clearly abuses its status by engaging in a pattern of
acts contrary to the purposes and principles of the Charter of the United
Nations including unsubstantiated or politically motivated acts against Member States of the United Nations incompatible with those purposes and
principles" (para. 57(a)).

Under the ECOSOC Arrangements, more than a hundred groups have
been admitted to general consultative status and more than a thousand to
special consultative status as of 2009. Still, the formulation of the principles
leaves room for dispute over eligibility of particular groups, as well as over
whether states could prevail upon the Committee on NGOs to block admission
of groups whose message they dislike. In the case of NGOs with a national
rather than international base, the views of the member state concerned are
one factor that the Committee considers, so that negative views of an
influential state could present a significant obstacle.

3. *NGO Standing Before International Tribunals.* As will be discussed in
Chapter 9 on dispute settlement, NGOs typically would not have standing to
be direct parties in international courts or tribunals. The jurisdiction of the
I.C.J. is limited to states in contentious cases and to international organizations for advisory jurisdiction, the statutes of other bodies (such as the
Dispute Settlement Understanding of the WTO) limit formal participation in
dispute procedures to member states, and other systems have vested the
function of initiating cases in a specialized organ such as an executive
commission. Nonetheless, as Professor Charnovitz notes, NGOs have contributed vibrantly to the jurisprudence of international tribunals, even of quintessentially state-centered tribunals.

4. *Bypassing States Entirely.* NGO activities can seek to affect decisions
of states (or organizations of states) or affect other segments of society. Can
NGOs be said to participate directly in the processes of international law, if
some of their endeavors to set standards or induce compliance bypass state
organs? Compare Thakur & Maley, The Ottawa Convention on Landmines: A
Landmark Humanitarian Treaty in Arms Control?, 5 Global Governance 273
(1999) (noting NGO efforts to establish an inter-state treaty regime), with
Wapner, Politics Beyond the State: Environmental Activism and World Civic
Politics, 47 World Pol. 311 (1995) (noting NGO efforts to change conditions
without directly pressuring states).

5. *Future Reforms?* While NGO influence is not limited to their impact
on states or state-created international organizations, much of their effectiveness nevertheless stems from gaining access to arenas in which states deliberate, negotiate, decide on, and apply international standards. Through such
access NGOs can participate (indirectly if not directly) in agenda-setting,
information exchange, publicity, and other processes bearing on the content
and implementation of international law. It is thus important for international lawyers to be aware of the procedural framework in which NGOs partici-

pate in (or are formally excluded from) the work of intergovernmental organizations. By the same token, since NGOs generally cannot be direct parties to cases in international tribunals, it is necessary to look beneath the surface to understand how they can communicate views to courts and other panels that determine substantive questions of international law. Thus, in connection with several U.N.-sponsored World Conferences (such as the 1995 World Conference on Women held in Beijing), parallel NGO events provided an alternative forum for airing a diversity of viewpoints.

Some NGOs (or, more broadly, members of civil society whether or not acting through organized groups) complain about the closed procedures of certain international organizations, the lack of transparency surrounding their activities, and the difficulty of gaining access to their processes. Such frustrations were part of the motivation for street protests in recent years at meetings of the World Trade Organization, the World Bank, and the International Monetary Fund in Washington. What procedural opportunities might respond to these concerns?

6. *Further Reading.* For additional readings addressed to these themes, see Lindblom, Non–Governmental Organizations in International Law (2005); O'Brien, et al., Contesting Global Governance: Multilateral Economic Institutions and Global Social Movements (2000); Non–State Actors as New Subjects of International Law–From the Traditional State Order Towards the Law of the Global Community (Hofmann & Geissler eds., 1999).

CHAPTER 7

INDIVIDUALS AND CORPORATIONS

■ ■ ■

While the preceding chapters have demonstrated the significant role played by states in the international legal system, natural and legal persons are increasingly important actors within the system of international law, in many instances directly possessing rights and obligations, in addition to being beneficiaries of international obligations imposed upon states. As you read the materials in this chapter, as well as other chapters such as Chapter 12 (immunities), Chapter 13 (human rights), Chapter 14 (injury to aliens and foreign investors), and Chapter 16 (international criminal law), note the myriad ways individuals have become features of the international law landscape. For example, individuals from one North American Free Trade Agreement (NAFTA) country who invest in another NAFTA country can directly bring a claim against the host state before an international arbitral tribunal. Individual experts serve in their personal capacity on important international institutions, such as the International Law Commission, or on the various human rights committees established under human rights treaties. Individuals now have a wide array of rights not just as aliens in a foreign country but as against their own govern-ment in their own country, which in some instances can be vindicated by bringing individual petitions before a human rights court (e.g., the European Court of Human Rights) or one of the human rights committees. Conversely, individuals can be prosecuted for violating international law before the International Criminal Court or the various *ad hoc* war crimes tribunals relating to specific countries. As noted below, the person has always been a feature of international law, but the focus of international law on the individual dramatically accelerated in the twentieth century and continues apace in our century.

SECTION 1. STATUS, RIGHTS, AND OBLIGATIONS OF THE INDIVIDUAL IN INTERNATIONAL LAW

A. THE STATUS OF THE INDIVIDUAL

As pointed out in the Historical Introduction, during its early development following the Peace of Westphalia in 1648, the law of nations was rooted in natural law. When natural law principles were looked to as its primary source, the law of nations could readily encompass individuals as well as nation-states. Thus, in 1765, Blackstone could write:

> The law of nations is a system of rules, deducible by natural reason, and established by universal consent among the civilized inhabitants of the world; in order to decide all disputes, to regulate all ceremonies and civilities, and to ensure the observance of justice and good faith, in that intercourse which must frequently occur between two or more independent states, *and the individuals belonging to each.*

4 Blackstone, Commentaries on the Laws of England 66 (1st ed. 1765–69) (footnotes omitted) (emphasis added). Yet as positivism rose to prominence in legal discourse, the law of nations came to be seen as largely denoting law applicable to nation-states in their relations with one another, which in turn encouraged the development of a dichotomy between public international law governing the relations between the states and "private" international law, or, to use Justice Story's term, the "conflict of laws," governing international transactions of private parties. Story, Commentaries on the Conflict of Laws, Foreign and Domestic (1st ed. 1834). Defining international law as law for states alone, however, proved to be unrealistically narrow. In fact, individuals were implicated in a number of areas of international law even after positivist theories became ascendant.

First, there were crimes under customary international law for which individuals could be tried and punished by national courts. Two leading, early examples were piracy and slave trading. In some states, including the United States, trial and conviction of such crimes in a national court were conditional on enactment of legislation making the customary international crime a crime under municipal law.

Second, there have been many instances of forceful intervention by a state to protect its own nationals from mistreatment in another state, as well as some interventions to protect the nationals of the targeted state, an act referred to as "humanitarian intervention." On the justifications for such uses of force, see Chapter 15.

Third, individuals (and private juridical entities such as corporations) have long been implicated under the customary international law of state responsibility, as discussed in Chapters 8 and 14. Under this regime, if an alien individual is injured by a wrongful act or omission by, or attributable to, a state and if the individual is unable to obtain redress under the legal system of that state, the state of which the injured individual is a national may intercede and assert a claim against the offending state. In this way, what begins as an injury to an individual or juridical entity may be elevated to the level of a state-to-state claim in which the claimant state seeks reparation from the offending state. This was the position adopted by the Permanent Court of International Justice in *Mavrommatis Palestine Concessions* (Greece v. Great Britain), 1924 P.C.I.J. (ser. A.) No. 2.

The Greek Government brought a suit against Great Britain arising out of the alleged refusal of the Palestine Government, then under the sovereignty of Great Britain, to recognize rights acquired by Mavrommatis, a Greek national, under agreements concluded with him by the authorities of the Ottoman Empire, the predecessor sovereign in Palestine. The British Government filed a preliminary objection to the jurisdiction of the Court. In upholding its jurisdiction, the Court stated as follows, at 12:

> In the case of the Mavrommatis concessions it is true that the dispute was at first between a private person and a State—i.e. between M. Mavrommatis and Great Britain. Subsequently, the Greek Government took up the case. The dispute then entered upon a new phase; it entered the domain of international law, and became a dispute between two States. * * *

> * * * It is an elementary principle of international law that a State is entitled to protect its subjects, when injured by acts contrary to international law committed by another State, from whom they have been unable to obtain satisfaction through the ordinary channels. By taking up the case of one of its subjects and by resorting to diplomatic action or international judicial proceedings on his behalf, a State is in reality asserting its own rights—its right to ensure, in the person of its subjects, respect for the rules of international law.

See Leigh, Nationality and Diplomatic Protection, 20 I.C.L.Q. 453 (1971).

Fourth, not infrequently international agreements created rights in individuals and juridical entities against foreign states. For example, treaties of friendship, commerce, and navigation sometimes encompassed the right of a national of one contracting state doing business in the other to be free from discriminatory treatment and from having business property expropriated without compensation. In some cases, the rights created by treaty could be enforced against the offending state directly by the injured private party. More often, however, those rights could be enforced only by the state of which the injured individual or juridical entity was a national.

Fifth, a large body of international agreements, international custom, and national law has long governed transnational transactions involving private parties. Much of this was subsumed under the rubric of private international law because the rights and duties were those of private parties, not states.

Given these ways in which individuals have played a role in the field of international law, how exactly would you characterize their status? Are individuals principally "objects" of international law, meaning that states decide whether and how to protect individuals, in the same way that property interests might be protected? Or are individuals "subjects" of international law, capable of advancing certain international rights and of being held to certain international obligations, even if those rights and obligations are more circumscribed than those placed upon states? Do you think it matters how one conceives of the individual in international law?

LAUTERPACHT, INTERNATIONAL
LAW AND HUMAN RIGHTS

27–29 (1973) (footnotes omitted)

The position of the individual as a subject of international law has often been obscured by the failure to observe the distinction between the recognition, in an international instrument, of rights enuring to the benefit of the individual and the enforceability of these rights at his instance. The fact that the beneficiary of rights is not authorised to take independent steps in his own name to enforce them does not signify that he is not a subject of the law or that the rights in question are vested exclusively in the agency which possesses the capacity to enforce them. Thus, in relation to the current view that the rights of the alien within foreign territory are the rights of his State and not his own, the correct way of stating the legal position is not that the State asserts its own exclusive right but that it enforces, in substance, the right of the individual who, as the law now stands, is incapable of asserting it in the international sphere. Conversely, there seems to be no warrant for the disposition to allow the question of enforceability of rights to be influenced by the doctrine that individuals cannot be subjects of international law. The question whether individuals in any given case are subjects of international law and whether that quality extends to the capacity of enforcement must be answered pragmatically by reference to the given situation and to the relevant international instrument. That instrument may make them subjects of the law without conferring upon them procedural capacity; it may aim at, and achieve, both these objects.

The legal position in the matter is well illustrated by the question whether individuals can acquire rights directly by treaty independently of municipal legislation. Prior to the Advisory Opinion of the Permanent Court of International Justice in the case concerning the Jurisdiction of the Courts of Danzig in the matter of Danzig railway officials, that question was generally answered in the negative—though even then some caution would have been indicated having regard to the law of some countries, such as the United States, in which [certain] duly ratified treaties are a self-executing part of municipal law. Similarly, there had already existed treaties—such as that establishing the Central American Court of Justice, the provisions relating to the Mixed Arbitral Tribunals in the Peace Treaties of 1919, and the Polish–German Upper Silesian Convention—which conferred upon individuals direct rights of international action. However, it was the Advisory Opinion, given in 1928, in the case concerning the Jurisdiction of the Courts of Danzig, which dealt a decisive blow to the dogma of the impenetrable barrier separating individuals from international law. In that case Poland contended that the agreement between her and Danzig regulating the conditions of employment of Danzig officials whom she had taken over into her railway service was an international treaty which created rights and obligations as between

Poland and Danzig only, that as that agreement had not been incorporated into Polish municipal law it did not create rights and obligations for individuals; that Poland's responsibility was limited to that owed to Danzig; and that therefore Danzig courts, before which the officials had brought an action in the matter, had no jurisdiction. The Court rejected this contention. It said:

> 'It may be readily admitted that, according to a well established principle of international law, the *Beamtenabkommen*, being an international agreement, cannot, as such, create direct rights and obligations for private individuals. But it cannot be disputed that the very object of an international agreement, according to the intention of the contracting Parties, may be the adoption by the parties of some definite rules creating individual rights and obligations and enforceable by the national courts. That there is such an intention in the present case can be established by reference to the terms of the *Beamtenabkommen*.'

This pronouncement is among the most important rendered by the Court. On the first occasion on which it was directly confronted with the traditional argument, it rejected it * * *. It laid down, in effect, that no considerations of theory can prevent the individual from becoming the subject of international rights if States so wish. That affirmation by the Permanent Court of International Justice of the right of individuals to acquire rights directly under treaties was not an isolated event. It was followed—and the coincidence is significant—by other judicial decisions pointing in the same direction.

O'CONNELL, INTERNATIONAL LAW

108–09 (2d ed. 1970) (footnotes omitted)

The individual as the end of community is a *member* of the community, and a member has status: he is not an object. It is not a sufficient answer to assert that the State is the medium between international law and its own nationals, for the law has often fractured this link when it failed in its purpose. For example, in the areas of black and white slavery, human rights and protection of minorities, international law has selected the individual as a member of the international community for rights and duties, even against the national State. * * *

Theory and practice establish that the individual has legally protected interests, can perform legally prescribed acts, can enjoy rights and be the subject of duties under municipal law deriving from international law; and if personality is no more than a sum of capacities, then he is a person in international law, though his capacities may be different from and less in number and substance than the capacities of States. An individual, for example, cannot acquire territory, he cannot make treaties and he cannot have belligerent rights. But he can commit war crimes, and piracy, and crimes against humanity and foreign sovereigns, and he can own property which international law protects, and he can have claims to compensation for acts arising *ex contractu* or ex *delicto*. He may not be able to pursue his claims and take action to protect his property without the intervention of his own State, but it is still his claim and still his interest which the machinery of enforcement is designed to facilitate.

The statements of doctrine of the International Court on this matter have tended to reflect the object theory which was current when they were made. The Court in the *Mavrommatis* case said that only when the national State takes up the complaint of its subject does the matter enter "the domain of international law." What, then, was the nature of the dispute before it became one between two States? It certainly was not a dispute in municipal law, because there was no municipal law on the subject. The Court would have to say that the dispute was not a legal one at all, and became such only when taken up by the Greek Government. This would be an unacceptable answer when Mavrommatis' whole position was based on the assertion that international law regulated his rights and property. In many similar instances the law officers would advise their governments that Mr. X should be compensated or his claim acknowledged, and their advice is surely in reference to law. The contention that X's claim is no claim in law at all until X's government takes it up is based upon the theory that States alone have capacity in international law and that the "object" of the law has no claim in law. The *Mavrommatis* approach on these lines demonstrates how artificial is the supposed distinction between the claim when it was a non-legal one and the claim when it became a legal one; it was still the same claim based upon the same legal propositions; the only difference was a change in the formal identity of the claimant.

Even if international law does directly create rights and duties in the individual it would not follow that the national State of the individual is no more than a technique for securing recognition of them. International law endows the national State with discretion to act in relation to these rights and duties, and if discretion to act is legal competence then it is true to say that the national State has capacity over and above the capacity of the individual.

NOTES

1. *The Status of the Individual.* In light of the above readings, what status do you accord to the individual in international law? Concluding that the individual has no status seems quite wrong, but equally it appears that individuals do not have the panoply of rights and obligations possessed by states in the international law system, nor even those possessed by international organizations, such as in the area of privileges and immunities. If the individual falls somewhere in between those two extremes, will one's attitude about the significance of the individual as an actor on the international plane make a difference in close cases, where questions arise as to whether international law accords to an individual personal rights?

2. *Further Reading.* For additional reading, see Orakhelashvili, The Position of the Individual in International Law, 31 Cal. W. Int'l L.J. 241

(2001); see also Nijman, The Concept of International Legal Personality (2004); Ochoa, The Individual and Customary International Law Formation, 48 Va. J. Int'l L. 119 (2007); Jackson, World Habeas Corpus, 91 Cornell L. Rev. 303 (2006).

B. RIGHTS OF THE INDIVIDUAL

LAGRAND CASE (GERMANY v. UNITED STATES)

International Court of Justice, 2001
2001 I.C.J. 466

[From 1998 to 2004, the International Court of Justice considered three cases filed against the United States by Paraguay (the *Vienna Convention on Consular Relations [Breard]* case), Germany (the *LaGrand* case), and Mexico (the *Avena* case) concerning the treatment of aliens on death row in the United States. A central issue in these cases was that U.S. law enforcement personnel repeatedly failed to advise aliens upon their arrest of the right to have their consulate notified, a right contained in Article 36 of the Vienna Convention on Consular Relations, Apr. 24, 1963, 21 U.S.T. 77, 596 U.N.T.S. 261 (VCCR). A further issue was whether, as a remedy for violation of the VCCR, state courts should review and reconsider the death sentences, to determine whether the lack of consular access prejudiced the aliens (i.e., whether the inability to have consular assistance impaired the alien from undertaking a strong defense). VCCR Article 36(1)(b) provides in part that the "receiving State" must inform an alien of "his rights" to have his consular authorities informed of the arrest.

In its judgment on the merits, the Court found that by not immediately informing LaGrand (and his brother who was executed prior to the I.C.J.'s provisional-measures order) of the right of consular notification, the United States breached its obligations to Germany under the Vienna Convention. The U.S. failure to provide judicial review of the conviction and sentence in light of the lack of notification constituted a further breach to Germany. The Court also considered whether these actions could also be said to violate *individual rights* held by the LaGrand brothers under international law (i.e., not just rights held by Germany).]

75. Germany further contends that "the breach of Article 36 by the United States did not only infringe upon the rights of Germany as a State party to the [Vienna] Convention but also entailed a violation of the individual rights of the LaGrand brothers". Invoking its right of diplomatic protection, Germany also seeks relief against the United States on this ground.

Germany maintains that the right to be informed of the rights under Article 36, paragraph 1 *(b)*, of the Vienna Convention, is an individual right of every national of a State party to the Convention who enters the territory of another State party. It submits that this view is supported by the ordinary meaning of the terms of Article 36, paragraph 1 (b), of the

Vienna Convention, since the last sentence of that provision speaks of the "rights" under this subparagraph of "the person concerned", i.e., of the foreign national arrested or detained. Germany adds that the provision in Article 36, paragraph 1 *(b)*, according to which it is for the arrested person to decide whether consular notification is to be provided, has the effect of conferring an individual right upon the foreign national concerned. In its view, the context of Article 36 supports this conclusion since it relates to both the concerns of the sending and receiving States and to those of individuals. According to Germany, the *travaux préparatoires* of the Vienna Convention lend further support to this interpretation. In addition, Germany submits that the "United Nations Declaration on the human rights of individuals who are not nationals of the country in which they live", adopted by General Assembly resolution 40/144 on 13 December 1985, confirms the view that the right of access to the consulate of the home State, as well as the information on this right, constitute individual rights of foreign nationals and are to be regarded as human rights of aliens.

76. The United States questions what this additional claim of diplomatic protection contributes to the case * * *.

The United States contends, furthermore, that rights of consular notification and access under the Vienna Convention are rights of States, and not of individuals, even though these rights may benefit individuals by permitting States to offer them consular assistance. It maintains that the treatment due to individuals under the Convention is inextricably linked to and derived from the right of the State, acting through its consular officer, to communicate with its nationals, and does not constitute a fundamental right or a human right. * * * The *travaux préparatoires* of the Vienna Convention, according to the United States, do not reflect a consensus that Article 36 was addressing immutable individual rights, as opposed to rights derivative of the rights of States.

77. The Court notes that Article 36, paragraph 1 *(b)*, spells out the obligations the receiving State has towards the detained person and the sending State. It provides that, at the request of the detained person, the receiving State must inform the consular post of the sending State of the individual's detention "without delay". It provides further that any communication by the detained person addressed to the consular post of the sending State must be forwarded to it by authorities of the receiving State "without delay". Significantly, this subparagraph ends with the following language: "The said authorities shall inform the person concerned without delay of *his rights* under this subparagraph" (emphasis added). Moreover, under Article 36, paragraph 1 *(c)*, the sending State's right to provide consular assistance to the detained person may not be exercised "if he expressly opposes such action". The clarity of these provisions, viewed in their context, admits of no doubt. It follows, as has been held on a number of occasions, that the Court must apply these as they stand * * *. Based on the text of these provisions, the Court concludes that Article 36, paragraph 1, creates individual rights, which * * * may be invoked in this

Court by the national State of the detained person. These rights were violated in the present case.

NOTES

1. *LaGrand Aftermath.* The International Court in *LaGrand* also found that "should nationals of the Federal Republic of Germany nonetheless be sentenced to severe penalties" without their right to consular notification having been respected, the United States, "by means of its own choosing, shall allow the review and reconsideration of the conviction and sentence by taking account of the violation of the rights set forth" in the Vienna Convention. *LaGrand Case* (Germany v. United States), 2001 I.C.J. 466, para. 128(7). After a similar case before the Court involving Mexican nationals, *Avena and Other Mexican Nationals* (Mexico v. United States), 2004 I.C.J. 12, litigation was brought in U.S. courts to attempt to obtain review and reconsideration of the imposition of the death penalty based on the Court's decisions. In *Medellín v. Texas*, 128 S.Ct. 1346 (2008), the U.S. Supreme Court declined to give effect to the Court's decision, finding that the *Avena* judgment did not give rise to self-executing obligations under U.S. law. For further discussion, see Chapter 10, Section 3.

2. *Individuals in the E.C. System.* In the field of international law, the European Community system is perhaps the most advanced in recognizing the status of the individual. There are three levels of law that may confer rights on individuals enforceable against E.C. institutions (E.C. Council or Commission) or against a member state. The first are treaty provisions that create rights and obligations between member states themselves. These provisions can confer enforceable rights on individuals only indirectly as a consequence of the adoption of national implementing measures. A second group of treaty provisions require E.C. institutions to adopt implementing measures to achieve E.C. objectives. These fall broadly into two categories: (1) regulations applicable directly to individuals and (2) directives addressed to member states that affect individuals only if and when further implemented by the member state. In the latter case, the individual may recover damages against her home state for its failure to implement a directive. In Cases C/6/90 & 9/90, *Francovich v. Italy*, 1991 E.C.R. I–5357, the E.C.J. held that a member state is obligated to make good losses suffered by individuals as a result of a failure of a member state to adopt a law implementing a directive. The third category of provisions were initially directed to and created obligations only for member states in the area of intergovernmental cooperation, but were held by the E.C.J. in the *Van Gend en Loos* case to be of such a character as to produce direct effects applicable to individuals (the "direct effects" doctrine) and to confer on them rights that may override national law of a member state. For discussion, see Smith, Remedies for Breaches of EU Law in National Courts: Legal Variation and Selection, in The Evolution of EU Law 287 (Craig & de Búrca eds. 1999).

C. OBLIGATIONS OF THE INDIVIDUAL

If a state violates international law thereby causing injury to another state, claims for such violation are properly addressed by the government of the injured state to that of the state responsible for the violation. Ordinarily, the officials or other persons who committed the act constituting the violation are not held personally responsible for it under international law. See Chapter 8.

In a growing number of circumstances, however, international law has recognized *individual* responsibility for conduct labeled as criminal under international law. There are many references, for example, to individuals committing "an offense against the law of nations." A prominent historical example is individual responsibility for acts of piracy, which, although crimes under customary international law, have been prosecuted in national courts in the absence of an international court with jurisdiction. See, e.g., United States v. Smith, 18 U.S. (5 Wheat.) 153, 161–62, (1820). The U.S. Constitution vests power in the U.S. Congress to define and punish "Piracies and Felonies committed on the High Seas, and Offenses against the Law of Nations." U.S. Const. art. 1, § 8(10). Thus, U.S. courts can punish pirates only pursuant to statute. Under the universal principle of jurisdiction, international law permits any state to apply its national law to punish piracy even when the accused is not a national of the state and the act of piracy was not committed in that state's territorial waters or against one of its vessels. See the discussion of permissible bases for the exercise of legislative jurisdiction in Chapter 11. For the provision on piracy in the U.N. Convention on the Law of the Sea, see Chapter 17.

As discussed in greater depth in Chapter 16, individuals accused of violations of the laws of war may be punished by the country of which they are nationals, by the enemy or by "international authorities." Ex parte Quirin, 317 U.S. 1 (1942). The four 1949 Geneva Conventions regulate the conduct of war by requiring humane treatment of sick, wounded and shipwrecked persons in the armed forces, prisoners of war and civilians. Any person who commits a grave breach under the Conventions, that is, commits one of the more serious crimes proscribed by them, is subject to trial and punishment by any state party, regardless of the nationality of the accused and the location of the crime. E.g., Geneva Convention Relative to the Protection of Civilian Persons in Time of War, Aug. 12, 1949, art. 147, 6 U.S.T. 3516, 75 U.N.T.S. 287.

Provisions in the anti-terrorism conventions, such as the conventions relating to the suppression of aircraft hijacking and sabotage, frequently require any state party to make the offense punishable by severe penalties and either (1) to investigate and prosecute, if appropriate, an alleged offender in its custody or (2) to extradite the individual to another party having jurisdiction under the convention. E.g., Hague Convention for the Suppression of Unlawful Seizure of Aircraft, December 16, 1970, Art. 2, 22

U.S.T. 1641, T.I.A.S. No. 7192; Montreal Convention for Suppression of Unlawful Acts Against the Safety of Civilian Aviation, September 23, 1971, arts. 3 and 7, 24 U.S.T. 564, T.I.A.S. No. 7570. See Chapter 16, Section 2.

The first instances in modern times of the trial of individuals by an international tribunal for crimes under international law were the trials of Nazi and Japanese war criminals after World War II by the multinational military tribunals in Nuremberg and Tokyo. The International Military Tribunal (IMT) at Nuremberg was established by the London Agreement of August 8, 1945 between the four victor states: France, the United Kingdom, the United States and the U.S.S.R. A Charter annexed to the agreement defined the constitution, jurisdiction, and functions of the IMT. The Tribunal was comprised of four judges, one from each of the victorious powers.

The Charter was based on the premise that major Nazi war criminals were to be held criminally responsible as individuals for:

(a) crimes against peace (planning, preparation, initiation of a war of aggression or in violation of international treaties);

(b) war crimes (violations of the laws of war);

(c) crimes against humanity; and

(d) conspiracy to commit any of the foregoing crimes.

Counsel for the accused argued, inter alia, (1) that international law is concerned only with actions of states and does not encompass punishment of individuals and (2) when the conduct is an act of state, individuals who carry it out are not responsible. The Tribunal's Judgment rejected these arguments, stating:

> * * * In the opinion of the Tribunal, both these submissions must be rejected. That international law imposes duties and liabilities upon individuals as well as upon States has long been recognized. In the recent case of Ex parte Quirin (1942, 317 U.S. 1), before the Supreme Court of the United States, persons were charged during the war with landing in the United States for purposes of spying and sabotage. The late Chief Justice Stone, speaking for the Court, said:

>> From the very beginning of history this Court has applied the law of war as including that part of the law of nations which prescribes for the conduct of war, the status, rights, and duties of enemy nations as well as enemy individuals.

> He went on to give a list of cases tried by the Courts, where individual offenders were charged with offenses against the laws of nations, and particularly the laws of war. Many other authorities could be cited, but enough has been said to show that individuals can be punished for violations of international law. Crimes against international law are committed by men, not by abstract entities, and only by punishing individuals who commit such crimes can the provisions of international law be enforced.

International Military Tribunal (Nuremberg) Judgment and Sentences, 41 A.J.I.L. 220–21 (1947).

SECTION 2. NATIONALITY OF INDIVIDUALS

A. SIGNIFICANCE OF NATIONALITY

An individual's nationality is significant under international law at a number of points. International law recognizes the right of a state to enact laws that regulate its nationals, even when they are engaging in conduct outside its territory; by contrast, a state's right to enact laws that regulate aliens outside its territory is much more circumscribed. See Chapter 11. Further, when a state's national travels abroad and is harmed due to a violation of international law, international law recognizes the state's ability to pursue a claim on behalf of its national, an act referred to as "diplomatic protection of nationals." See Chapter 8, Section 7(D) and Chapter 14. By contrast, a state may intercede diplomatically on behalf of an alien only under very special circumstances, for example, when human rights violations under a treaty or customary international law are involved. See Chapter 13. Treaty regimes will often identify rights or protections for individuals based on nationality. Thus, a bilateral investment treaty will typically protect the interests of nationals of a sending state when they travel to a host state, but will not protect all aliens in the host state nor protect the nationals of the host state in their own country. Extradition treaties may generally obligate a state to extradite persons when requested, but will often provide that a state need not extradite its own nationals. See Chapter 11. Hence, whenever international law is being construed as it relates to individuals, a threshold issue will be to ascertain the nationality of the individuals in question.

How though, does an individual acquire nationality? Does a person always have a right to have a nationality or can a state in its discretion strip a person of their nationality? Must a state have a genuine connection to a person before bestowing nationality upon him or her? Can a person possess multiple nationalities and, if so, how does that affect their international rights? The following materials address some of those constraints.

B. ACQUISITION AND DENIAL OF NATIONALITY

In the first instance, for any given state, one must usually look to its national law to ascertain how persons may acquire that state's nationality. Those laws might accord nationality to children who are born within that state (*jus soli*), to children born to parents who are already nationals of that state (*jus sanguinis*), and/or to persons who apply for nationality and meet specified conditions (naturalization). Since the national laws of different states are not usually coordinated, it becomes possible for persons to acquire nationality of two states (dual nationals) or even multiple states, though some states seek to avoid this by providing in their nationality law that a person loses an initial nationality upon acquisition of a second nationality. See Citizenship Today: Global Perspectives and Practices (Aleinikoff & Klusmeyer eds. 2001).

Does international law impose any constraints on states in this regard? In *Tunis and Morocco Nationality Decrees,* 1923 P.C.I.J. (ser. B.) No. 4, the Permanent Court of International Justice held that whether a state treated an individual as its national was a matter within its exclusive domestic jurisdiction. Yet, at the same time, the 1930 Hague Convention on Certain Questions Relating to the Conflict of Nationality Laws, Apr. 12, 1930, 179 L.N.T.S. 89, 5 Hudson 359, stated in Article 1: "It is for each State to determine under its own law who are its nationals. This law shall be recognized by other States *in so far as it is consistent with international conventions, international custom, and the principles of law generally recognised with regard to nationality*" (emphasis added). Over the years, international law norms have emerged that constrain an untrammeled power of a state to confer its nationality on an individual or to withdraw it.

For example, European states have adopted certain treaties in an effort to regulate nationality laws within their region. The 1963 Convention on Reduction of Cases of Multiple Nationality and Military Obligations in Cases of Multiple Nationality, May 6, 1963, E.T.S. No. 43, was based on the then-widely-accepted position that multiple nationality was undesirable and prohibited parties from enacting national laws that allowed for multiple nationality. Subsequent developments, however, caused the Council of Europe to reconsider the policy of avoiding multiple nationality: labor migrations resulting in substantial immigrant populations, the growing number of marriages between spouses of different nationalities and freedom of movement among European Union member states. Further, the principle of equality of sexes meant that men and women should be able to acquire the nationality of their spouse under the same conditions and that both spouses should be free to transfer their nationality to their children. In 1993, the Second Protocol to the 1963 Convention on Reduction of Cases of Multiple Nationality withdrew the prohibition on national laws that allowed multiple nationality. Feb. 2, 1993, E.T.S. No. 149.

In 1997, the Council of Europe adopted the European Convention on Nationality, Nov. 6, 1997, E.T.S. No. 166, 37 I.L.M. 44 (1998). Unlike the 1963 Convention, the 1997 Convention deals with all major aspects of nationality: principles, acquisition, retention, loss, recovery, procedural rights, multiple nationality, nationality in the context of state succession, military obligations, and cooperation between the parties. As of early 2009, the Convention is in force for sixteen states: Albania, Austria, Bulgaria, the Czech Republic, Denmark, Germany, Hungary, Iceland, Macedonia, Moldova, the Netherlands, Portugal, Romania, Slovakia, Sweden, and Ukraine. Further, the convention has been signed but not yet ratified by Bosnia–Herzegovina, Croatia, Finland, France, Greece, Italy,

Latvia, Malta, Norway, Poland, and Russia. See Citizenship and Nationality Status in the New Europe 220–54 (O'Leary & Tiilikainen eds. 1998).

Assuming that the convention reflects either binding treaty law or customary international law in Europe, what constraints does it impose on the discretion of a state to accord or deny nationality to an individual? See European Convention on Nationality, Articles 4–6.

NOTES

1. *Statelessness*. A focus of considerable attention has been whether the individual has a right to a nationality. One aspect of this is the right to be protected from statelessness, meaning the absence of a nationality of any state. A stateless individual has no right to invoke the diplomatic protection of any state. If expelled by the country of residence, no state is required to accept him or her. Another aspect of a right to nationality concerns whether an individual has a right to change his or her nationality. See Weis, Nationality and Statelessness in International Law (2d ed. 1979).

Various instruments and treaties address the issue of a right to nationality. Article 15 of the 1948 Universal Declaration of Human Rights, G.A. Res. 217 (III) (Dec. 10, 1948), provides that "[e]veryone has the right to a nationality" and that "[n]o one shall be arbitrarily deprived of his nationality nor denied the right to change his nationality." Article 24(3) of the 1966 International Covenant on Civil and Political Rights, Dec. 19, 1966, 999 U.N.T.S. 171, 6 I.L.M. 368 (1967), expresses in treaty form a more limited right, providing that "[e]very child has the right to acquire a nationality." The 1954 U.N. Convention relating to the Status of Stateless Persons, Sept. 28, 1954, 360 U.N.T.S. 117, provides certain minimal protections to persons already rendered stateless. The 1961 U.N. Convention on the reduction of statelessness, Aug. 30, 1961, 989 U.N.T.S. 175, prohibits denationalization, except for serious acts of disloyalty, if it would render the individual stateless, and it prohibits denationalization based on marriage to a foreign national if the result would be statelessness. The 1967 Protocol relating to the Status of Refugees, Jan. 31, 1967, 19 U.S.T. 6223, 606 U.N.T.S. 267, accords protection under certain circumstances to stateless refugees. For commentary, see Chan, The Right to a Nationality as a Human Right, 12 Hum. Rts. L.J. 1 (1991); Restatement (Third) § 211, Comment *e*.

2. *Nationality and the Baltic States*. The International Law Commission's Articles on Nationality in Relation to the Succession of States, cited and discussed in Chapter 19, Sections 1 & 7, emphasize a state's positive legal obligation to protect inhabitants from statelessness in the event of state succession. See Blackman, State Successions and Statelessness: The Emerging Right to an Effective Nationality under International Law, 19 Mich. J. Int'l L. 1141 (1998). The problem that arises in such circumstances may be illustrated by the nationality policies in the Baltic Republics after their separation from the Soviet Union.

While most former Soviet republics at the time of independence in 1991 granted citizenship to all those living permanently within their territory, the Baltic states of Estonia and Latvia faced a more complicated transition. The immigration of ethnic Russians to Estonia and Latvia over the fifty years of Soviet rule (1940–1991) made non-Baltic people a large percentage of the populations in these countries. In 1989, one year before regaining independence, ethnic Estonians made up 61.5% of the population and ethnic Latvians made up 52% of the population in their respective countries. Upon achieving independence, these states enacted citizenship laws with an ethnic bias. Estonia automatically granted citizenship to ethnic Estonians, while requiring non-ethnic Estonians who had migrated during the Soviet occupation to meet residency requirements and pass a test on the Estonian language and Constitution before becoming naturalized. Latvia required non-ethnic residents to pass a test on the Latvian language and Constitution, meet a residency requirement of sixteen years, take an oath of loyalty and renounce any other citizenship. The resulting loss of nationality for the large population of non-ethnic residents attracted international criticism and threatened Latvia's membership in the Council of Europe. Article 2(a) of the 1997 European Convention on Nationality, Nov. 6, 1997, E.T.S. No. 166, discourages ethnic origin as a basis for citizenship by stating that nationality is "the legal bond between a person and a State and does not indicate the person's ethnic origin." See Kalvaitis, Citizenship and National Identity in the Baltic States, 16 B.U. Int'l L.J. 231 (1998); Visek, Creating the Ethnic Electorate through Legal Restorationism: Citizenship Rights in Estonia, 38 Harv. Int'l L.J. 315 (1997); Barrington, The Making of Citizenship Policy in the Baltic States, 13 Geo. Immigr. L.J. 159 (1999).

3. *The Inter–American System.* The American Convention on Human Rights, which was adopted by the Organization of American States and entered force in 1978, provides:

1. Every person has the right to a nationality.
2. Every person has the right to the nationality of the State in whose territory he was born if he does not have the right to any other nationality.
3. No one shall be arbitrarily deprived of his nationality or of the right to change it.

American Convention on Human Rights, art. 20, Nov. 22, 1969, 1144 U.N.T.S. 123. In an advisory opinion on whether proposed amendments to the Costa Rica Constitution violated Article 20 of the American Convention on Human Rights, the Inter–American Court of Human Rights opined that nationality is an inherent right of all human beings and that a state's regulation of nationality is subject to a state's obligations to protect the human rights of individuals. *Amendments to the Naturalization Provisions of the Constitution of Costa Rica*, Advisory Opinion of the Inter–American Commission on Human Rights, OC–4/84, reported in 5 Hum. Rts. L.J. 161 (1984).

C. LIMITS ON THE CONFERRING OF NATIONALITY

What limits do "international custom" and "the principles of law generally recognised with regard to nationality" impose on the power of states to confer nationality? A Harvard research project suggested a rule in 1929 that the power of a state to confer its nationality was not unlimited, observing that although it might be difficult to specify the limitations imposed by international law on such power, "it is obvious that some limitations do exist." The Law of Nationality, art. 2, 23 A.J.I.L. Spec. Supp. 11, 24–27 (1929). The Hague Codification Conference of 1930 was unable to agree upon a more precise formulation, but a number of participating governments asserted that states were not obligated under international law to recognize nationality conferred upon a person in the absence of some generally recognized relationship or connection between the person and the state claiming him as its national. The German government, for example, stated:

> * * * [A] State has no power, by means of a law or administrative act, to confer its nationality on all the inhabitants of another State or on all foreigners entering [its] territory. Further, if the State confers its nationality on the subjects of other States without their request, when the persons in question are not attached to it by any particular bond, as, for instance, origin, domicile or birth, the States concerned will not be bound to recognise such naturalization.

Conference for the Codification of International Law, Bases of Discussion, Nationality, League of Nations Doc. C.73.M.38.1929.V I, at 13 (1929). Similarly, the United States was of the opinion that there were "certain grounds generally recognised by civilised States upon which a State may properly clothe individuals with its nationality at or after birth, but * * * no State is free to extend the application of its laws of nationality in such a way as to reach out and claim the allegiance of whomsoever it pleases. The scope of municipal laws governing nationality must be regarded as limited by consideration of the rights and obligations of individuals and of other States." Id. at 145–46. Although certain governments participating in the Conference questioned the existence of rules of international law, other than those laid down in treaties, that limited a state's freedom in matters of nationality, the text of Article 1 of the Convention on Certain Questions Relating to the Conflict of Nationality Laws was adopted by an overwhelming majority (see p. 459).

In his well-regarded treatise on international law, Charles Cheney Hyde stated:

> In a broad sense international law limits the right of a State to impress its national character upon an individual, or to prevent that character from being lost or transferred. The freedom of action of each member of the family of nations is, however, wide. That circumstance, as well as the modern practice of States to declare by statute what persons are deemed to be nationals by birth, and how nationality may be acquired or lost, serves to obscure from view the final test of the reasonableness of the local law.

Hyde at 1066. If that is correct, what circumstances make it "reasonable" for a state to confer its nationality upon an individual?

NOTTEBOIIM CASE
(LIECHTENSTEIN v. GUATEMALA)

International Court of Justice, 1955
1955 I.C.J. 4

[Nottebohm had been a German national from his birth in Germany in 1881 until his naturalization in Liechtenstein in 1939, shortly after the outbreak of war in Europe. In 1905, he had taken up residence in Guatemala and engaged in substantial business dealings in that country. Thereafter, he sometimes went to Germany on business, to other countries on holidays, and to Liechtenstein in order to visit a brother who lived there after 1931. In early 1939, Nottebohm went to Europe and eventually applied for naturalization in Liechtenstein on October 9, 1939. Nottebohm sought and received dispensation from residence requirements, paid his fees and gave security for the payment of taxes, and completed the naturalization process by taking an oath of allegiance on October 20, 1939. He obtained a Liechtenstein passport, had it endorsed by the Guatemalan consul in Zurich, and returned to Guatemala to resume his business activities. At his request, Guatemalan authorities made appropriate changes regarding Nottebohm's nationality in the Register of Aliens and in his identity document.

On July 17, 1941, the United States blacklisted Nottebohm and froze his assets in the United States. War broke out between the United States and Germany, and between Guatemala and Germany, on December 11, 1941. Nottebohm was arrested by Guatemalan authorities in 1943 and deported to the United States, where he was interned until 1946 as an enemy alien. He applied upon his release for readmission to Guatemala, but his application was refused. Nottebohm then took up residence in Liechtenstein, but Guatemala had in the meantime taken measures against his properties in that country, culminating in confiscatory legislation of 1949.

Liechtenstein exercised the right of diplomatic protection on behalf of Nottebohm whom it regarded as its national, pursuant to principles of state responsibility discussed in Chapter 8, Section 7(D) and Chapter 14. Liechtenstein instituted proceedings against Guatemala in the International Court of Justice, asking the Court to declare that Guatemala had violated international law "in arresting, detaining, expelling and refusing to readmit Mr. Nottebohm and in seizing and retaining his property," and consequently was obligated to pay compensation as reparation. Guatemala's principal argument in reply was that the Liechtenstein claim was inadmissible on grounds of the claimant's nationality.

The Court rejected Liechtenstein's argument that Guatemala was precluded from contesting Nottebohm's nationality because Guatemala had on several occasions acknowledged Nottebohm's claim of Liechtenstein nationality. The Court then continued:]

Since no proof has been adduced that Guatemala has recognized the title to the exercise of protection relied upon by Liechtenstein as being derived from the naturalization which it granted to Nottebohm, the Court must consider whether such an act of granting nationality by Liechtenstein directly entails an obligation on the part of Guatemala to recognize its effect, namely, Liechtenstein's right to exercise its protection. In other words, it must be determined whether that unilateral act by Liechtenstein is one which can be relied upon against Guatemala in regard to the exercise of protection. The Court will deal with this question without considering that of the validity of Nottebohm's naturalization according to the law of Liechtenstein.

* * *

* * * [T]he issue which the Court must decide is not one which pertains to the legal system of Liechtenstein. It does not depend on the law or on the decision of Liechtenstein whether that State is entitled to exercise its protection, in the case under consideration. To exercise protection, to apply to the Court, is to place oneself on the plane of international law. It is international law which determines whether a State is entitled to exercise protection and to seise the Court.

* * *

The practice of certain States which refrain from exercising protection in favour of a naturalized person when the latter has in fact, by his prolonged absence, severed his links with what is no longer for him anything but his nominal country, manifests the view of these States that, in order to be capable of being invoked against another State, nationality must correspond with the factual situation. * * *

The character thus recognized on the international level as pertaining to nationality is in no way inconsistent with the fact that international law leaves it to each State to lay down the rules governing the grant of its own nationality. The reason for this is that the diversity of demographic conditions has thus far made it impossible for any general agreement to be reached on the rules relating to nationality, although the latter by its very nature affects international relations. It has been considered that the best way of making such rules accord with the varying demographic conditions in different countries is to leave the fixing of such rules to the competence of each State. On the other hand, a State cannot claim that the rules it has thus laid down are entitled to recognition by another State unless it has acted in conformity with this general aim of making the legal bond of nationality accord with the individual's genuine connection with the State which assumes the defence of its citizens by means of protection as against other States.

* * *

According to the practice of States, to arbitral and judicial decisions and to the opinions of writers, nationality is a legal bond having as its basis a social fact of attachment, a genuine connection of existence, interests and sentiments, together with the existence of reciprocal rights and duties. It may be said to constitute the juridical expression of the fact that the individual upon whom it is conferred, either directly by the law or as the result of an act of the authorities is in fact more closely connected with the population of the State conferring nationality than with that of any other State. Conferred by a State, it only entitles that State to exercise protection vis-à-vis another State, if it constitutes a translation into juridical terms of the individual's connection with the State which has made him its national.

* * *

Since this is the character which nationality must present when it is invoked to furnish the State which has granted it with a title to the exercise of protection and to the institution of international judicial proceedings, the Court must ascertain whether the nationality granted to Nottebohm by means of naturalization is of this character or, in other words, whether the factual connection between Nottebohm and Liechtenstein in the period preceding, contemporaneous with and following his naturalization appears to be sufficiently close, so preponderant in relation to any connection which may have existed between him and any other State, that it is possible to regard the nationality conferred upon him as real and effective, as the exact juridical expression of a social fact of a connection which existed previously or came into existence thereafter.

Naturalization is not a matter to be taken lightly. * * * In order to appraise its international effect, it is impossible to disregard the circumstances in which it was conferred, the serious character which attaches to it, the real and effective, and not merely the verbal preference of the individual seeking it for the country which grants it to him.

At the time of his naturalization does Nottebohm appear to have been more closely attached by his tradition, his establishment, his interests, his activities, his family ties, his intentions for the near future to Liechtenstein than to any other State?

* * *

At the date when he applied for naturalization Nottebohm had been a German national from the time of his birth. He had always retained his connections with members of his family who had remained in Germany and he had always had business connections with that country. His country had been at war for more than a month, and there is nothing to indicate that the application for naturalization then made by Nottebohm was motivated by any desire to dissociate himself from the Government of his country.

He had been settled in Guatemala for 34 years. He had carried on his activities there. It was the main seat of his interests. He returned there shortly after his naturalization, and it remained the centre of his interests and of his business activities. He stayed there until his removal as a result of war measures in 1943. He subsequently attempted to return there, and he now complains of Guatemala's refusal to admit him. There, too, were several members of his family who sought to safeguard his interests.

In contrast, his actual connections with Liechtenstein were extremely tenuous. No settled abode, no prolonged residence in that country at the time of his application for naturalization: the application indicates that he was paying a visit there and confirms the transient character of this visit by its request that the naturalization proceedings should be initiated and concluded without delay. No intention of settling there was shown at that time or realized in the ensuing weeks, months or years—on the contrary, he returned to Guatemala very shortly after his naturalization and showed every intention of remaining there. If Nottebohm went to Liechtenstein in 1946, this was because of the refusal of Guatemala to admit him. No indication is given of the grounds warranting the waiver of the condition of residence, required by the 1934 Nationality Law, which waiver was implicitly granted to him. There is no allegation of any economic interests or of any activities exercised or to be exercised in Liechtenstein, and no manifestation of any intention whatsoever to transfer all or some of his interests and his business activities to Liechtenstein. It is unnecessary in this connection to attribute much importance to the promise to pay the taxes levied at the time of his naturalization. The only links to be discovered between the Principality and Nottebohm are the short sojourns already referred to and the presence in Vaduz of one of his brothers: but his brother's presence is referred to in his application for naturalization only as a reference to his good conduct. Furthermore, other members of his family have asserted Nottebohm's desire to spend his old age in Guatemala.

These facts clearly establish, on the one hand, the absence of any bond of attachment between Nottebohm and Liechtenstein and, on the other hand, the existence of a long-standing and close connection between him and Guatemala, a link which his naturalization in no way weakened. That naturalization was not based on any real prior connection with Liechtenstein, nor did it in any way alter the manner of life of the person upon whom it was conferred in exceptional circumstances of speed and accommodation. In both respects, it was lacking in the genuineness requisite to an act of such importance, if it is to be entitled to be respected by a State in the position of Guatemala. It was granted without regard to the concept of nationality adopted in international relations.

Naturalization was asked for not so much for the purpose of obtaining a legal recognition of Nottebohm's membership in fact in the population of Liechtenstein, as it was to enable him to substitute for his status as a national of a belligerent State that of a national of a neutral State, with the sole aim of thus coming within the protection of Liechtenstein but not of becoming wedded to its traditions, its interests, its way of life or of assuming the obligations—other than fiscal obligations—and exercising the rights pertaining to the status thus acquired.

Guatemala is under no obligation to recognize a nationality granted in such circumstances. Liechtenstein consequently is not entitled to extend its protection to Nottebohm vis-à-vis Guatemala and its claim must, for this reason, be held to be inadmissible.

For these reasons, THE COURT, by eleven votes to three, holds that the claim submitted by the Government of the Principality of Liechtenstein is inadmissible.

NOTES

1. *The "Genuine Link" Concept.* Do you think *Nottebohm* was correctly decided? Given that Guatemala had deported Nottebohm and then confiscated his property, why shouldn't the state of Nottebohm's nationality be able to pursue a claim against Guatemala? Note that from the time the claim was presented to the International Court through the date of its decision, Nottebohm was residing in Liechtenstein. Relying on the *Nottebohm* case, the Restatement takes the position that states need not accept nationality conferred on an individual by another state when it is not based on a "genuine link" between the conferring state and the individual. Restatement (Third) § 211. Comment *c* notes as follows:

> The precise contours of this concept, however, are not clear. Laws that confer nationality on grounds of birth in a state's territory (*ius soli*) or birth to parents who are nationals (*ius sanguinis*) are universally accepted as based on genuine links. Voluntary naturalization is generally recognized by other states but may be questioned when there are no other ties to the state, *e.g.,* a period of residence in the state. The comparative "genuineness" and strength of links between a state and an individual are relevant also for resolving competing claims between two states asserting nationality, or between such states and a third state.

See also Sloane, Breaking the Genuine Link: The International Legal Regulation of Nationality, 50 Harv. Int'l L.J. 1 (forthcoming 2009); Brownlie, Principles of Public International Law 396–406 (6th ed. 2003). For implications of the *Nottebohm* decision in the context of investor-state disputes, see Chapter 14, Section 4(E).

2. *Forcible Imposition of Nationality.* The imposition by a state of its nationality on an individual against his or her will, or if that nationality has been renounced, may violate international law. A state is not required to recognize a nationality imposed by another state on an individual against that individual's will on the basis of a link such as marriage to a national, a specified period of residence, acquisition of real property in the state's territory, bearing of a child there or having a particular ethnic or national origin. Another state is not required to recognize a nationality that the individual has renounced. Restatement (Third) § 211, Comment *d*. Additionally, as Restatement (Third) § 211, Reporters' Note 2 states:

> [L]egislation that operates only prospectively and gives the alien a reasonable opportunity to avoid the imposition of nationality would probably not violate international law. Laws that provide that a woman automatically acquires her husband's nationality upon marriage are questionable if the

woman objects, under the principle of gender equality now internationally recognized, *e.g.*, in the Convention on the Nationality of Women, 49 Stat. 2957, T.S. No. 875 (1934), and in the Universal Declaration of Human Rights and the principal human rights covenants.

D. DUAL NATIONALITY

If an individual is born with or acquires a second nationality without losing the first nationality, he or she becomes a "dual national." In the normal course of events, possession of dual nationality does not pose any particular impediment to the person or the states whose nationality he or she holds. Yet in one area, the possession of dual nationality has proved of importance: the ability of the state of one nationality to bring a diplomatic claim on behalf of the person against the state of the second nationality. One the one hand, the "plaintiff" state normally would be able to pursue a diplomatic claim on behalf of someone who possesses its nationality. One the other hand, normally a state cannot pursue a diplomatic claim against another state for a wrongful act undertaken by that other state against its own national.

IRAN–UNITED STATES CLAIMS
TRIBUNAL, CASE NO. A/18

Dec. No. 32–A/18–FT, 5 Iran–U.S. Cl. Trib. Rep. 251 (1984–I) (footnotes omitted)

[In 1979, after the Iranian revolution, Iranian militants seized U.S. diplomatic and consular personnel, and other U.S. nationals, in Iran as hostages. The United States responded by blocking Iranian assets in the United States and undertaking a rescue mission that ultimately failed. Several U.S. companies and persons with claims against Iran filed suit in U.S. courts and levied attachments against the blocked Iranian assets. In January 1981, the government of Algeria succeeded in mediating a solution to the crisis through adoption of the "Algiers Accords," a series of declarations and agreements accepted by both states, including a Claims Settlement Declaration. Among other things, the Algiers Accords resulted in the release of the hostages, the creation of an arbitral tribunal in The Hague to hear claims by the nationals of either state against the government of the other state (as well as claims between the two governments), and the return of Iranian assets to Iran, except for a portion sent to The Hague for use in paying awards issued against Iran by the tribunal. After establishment of the tribunal, several claims were filed by dual U.S.– Iranian nationals against Iran.]

The question now before the Tribunal is whether the Claims Settlement Declaration grants the Tribunal jurisdiction over claims against Iran filed by persons who, during the relevant period which is from the date the claim arose until 19 January 1981, were Iranian citizens under the law of Iran and United States citizens under the law of the United States.

The relevant provisions of the Claims Settlement Declaration which the Tribunal must interpret are Article II, paragraph 1, and Article VII, paragraph 1(a).

Article II, paragraph 1, states:

An international tribunal (the Iran–United States Claims Tribunal) is hereby established for the purpose of deciding claims of nationals of the United States against Iran and claims of nationals of Iran against the United States . . .

Article VII, paragraph 1 (a), states:

A "national" of Iran or of the United States, as the case may be, means (a) a natural person who is a citizen of Iran or the United States; . . .

* * *

Iran takes the position that persons, who under Iranian law are Iranian citizens, may not bring before this Tribunal claims against Iran, irrespective of whether they may also be United States citizens. * * *

* * *

The United States takes the position that by the express terms of the Claims Settlement Declaration the Tribunal has jurisdiction over claims of a United States citizen against Iran whether or not that person is also a citizen of Iran. * * *

* * *

Neither of these arguments can be accepted. The Tribunal cannot agree that the text is so clear and unambiguous as to make further analysis unnecessary. * * *

* * * There is a considerable body of law and legal literature, analyzed herein, which leads the Tribunal to the conclusion that the applicable rule of international law is that of dominant and effective nationality.

1. *The 1930 Hague Convention*

On 12 April 1930, a convention was concluded at The Hague "Concerning Certain Questions Relating to the Conflict of Nationality Laws" (the "Hague Convention"). As Article 1 of that Convention makes plain, a determination by one State as to who are its nationals will be respected by another State "in so far as it is consistent" with international law governing nationality. International law, then, does not determine who is a national, but rather sets forth the conditions under which that determination must be recognized by other States.

Article 4 of the Convention provides: "A State may not afford diplomatic protection to one of its nationals against a State whose nationality such person also possesses." But this provision must be interpreted very cautiously. Not only is it more than 50 years old and found in a treaty to which only 20 States are parties, but great changes have occurred since then in the concept of diplomatic protection, which concept has been expanded. *See* Siorat, *Juris–Classeur Droit International,* La Protection Diplomatique, Fasc. 250–B., No. 20 (1965); Kiss, *Répertoire de Droit International,* Dalloz, Protection Diplomatique No.14. This concept continues to be in a process of transformation, and it is necessary to distinguish between different types of protection, whether consular or claims-related.

* * *

2. *Precedents*

In this field, there is a considerable number of relevant judicial and arbitral decisions, most of them prior to the Second World War, supplemented and interpreted by the writings of scholars. The writing of at least one scholar, Professor E.B. Borchard, apparently had a considerable effect, not only because of the later writers who have echoed his views which favored the rule of non-responsibility [of a state of nationality], but also because of his influence on the Hague Conference that adopted the 1930 Convention discussed above. In fact, the precedents on which Borchard relied did not generally support his conclusion, and the Parties in the present case have acknowledged that the law prior to 1930 was uncertain. Iran, however, considers the conclusion of the 1930 Convention a decisive turning point that crystallized the rule of non-responsibility. The United States, on the other hand, points to the limited number of parties to that Convention and the practice of States, particularly in the conclusion and interpretation of claims settlement agreements since the Second World War. The Tribunal, having had the benefit of extensive written and oral argument of these issues by eminent counsel, does not believe it would be worthwhile for it to recite and comment upon the many precedents cited by the Parties, for the Tribunal is satisfied that, whatever the state of the law prior to 1945, the better rule at the time the Algiers Declarations were concluded and today is the rule of dominant and effective nationality.

The two most important decisions on the subject in the years following the Second World War have had a decisive effect. First, the International Court of Justice, in the *Nottebohm Case,* on 6 April 1955, stated the following:

> International arbitrators have ... given their preference to the real and effective nationality, that which accorded with the facts, [and] that [demonstrates] stronger factual ties between the person concerned and one of the States whose nationality is involved. Different factors are taken into consideration, and their importance will vary from one case to the next: the habitual residence of the individual concerned is an important factor, but there are other factors such as the centre of his interests, his family ties, his participation in public life, attachment shown by him for a given country and inculcated in his children, etc.
>
> Similarly, the courts of third States, when they have before them an individual whom two other States hold to be their national, seek to

resolve the conflict by having recourse to international criteria and their prevailing tendency is to prefer the real and effective nationality.

While *Nottebohm* itself did not involve a claim against a State of which Nottebohm was a national, it demonstrated the acceptance and approval by the International Court of Justice of the search for the real and effective nationality based on the facts of a case, instead of an approach relying on more formalistic criteria. The effects of the *Nottebohm* decision have radiated throughout the international law of nationality.

A few months later, on 10 June 1955, the Italian–United States Conciliation Commission set up by application of the Peace Treaty of 1947, decided in the *Mergé Case* that the principle "... based on the sovereign equality of States, which excludes diplomatic protection in the case of dual nationality, must yield before the principle of effective nationality whenever such nationality is that of the claiming State". *Mergé Case* (United States v. Italy) 14 R.I.A.A. 236, 247 (1955). The Commission then applied this same analysis in numerous other similar cases involving dual nationals. The Franco–Italian Conciliation Commission also decided several claims of dual nationals according to the "link theory". *See Rambaldi Claim* (France v. Italy)13 R.I.A.A. 786 (1957); *Menghi Claim* (France v. Italy) 13 R.I.A.A. 801 (1958); *Lombroso Claim* (France v. Italy) 13 R.I.A.A. 804 (1958).

3. *Legal Literature*

Support for the principles applied in these cases is shared by some of the most competent international lawyers. Basdevant wrote that effective nationality must prevail, because nationality is the juridical translation of a social fact. Maury in "L'Arrêt Nottebohm et la Condition de Nationalité Effective" 23 *Rabels Zeitschrift* 515 (1958), expressed his doubts about the alleged rule forbidding a State to act against another State in cases of dual nationality, and concluded that the *Nottebohm* decision has a general scope. * * *

* * *

This trend toward modification of the Hague Convention rule of non-responsibility by search for the dominant and effective nationality is scarcely surprising as it is consistent with the contemporaneous development of international law to accord legal protections to individuals, even against the State of which they are nationals. Moreover, * * * many of the relevant decisions, even in the 19th century, reflected similar concerns by giving weight to domicile.

Thus, the relevant rule of international law which the Tribunal may take into account for purposes of interpretation, as directed by Article 31, paragraph 3(c), of the Vienna Convention, is the rule that flows from the *dictum* of *Nottebohm,* the rule of real and effective nationality, and the search for "stronger factual ties between the person concerned and one of the States whose nationality is involved". In view of the pervasive effect of this rule since the *Nottebohm* decision, the Tribunal concludes that the references to "national" and "nationals" in the Algiers Declarations must be understood as consistent with that rule unless an exception is clearly stated. * * * [T]he Tribunal does not find that the text of the Algiers Declarations provides such a clear exception.

For the reasons stated above, the Tribunal holds that it has jurisdiction over claims against Iran by dual Iran–United States nationals when the dominant and effective nationality of the claimant during the relevant period from the date the claim arose until 19 January 1981 was that of the United States. In determining the dominant and effective nationality, the Tribunal will consider all relevant factors, including habitual residence, center of interests, family ties, participation in public life and other evidence of attachment.

NOTES

1. *Dominant and Effective Nationality Doctrine.* The Iran–U.S. Claims Tribunal proceeded to use the dominant and effective nationality doctrine to dispose of numerous cases brought before the Tribunal by dual nationals, sometimes allowing the claim and sometimes not. Those decisions help define the contours of when a nationality is dominantly and effectively that of one state rather than another. For detailed discussion of the case law, see Aldrich, The Jurisprudence of the Iran–United States Claims Tribunal 54–79 (1996); Brower & Brueschke, The Iran–United States Claims Tribunal 32–42, 288–322 (1998). For more general discussion of dual nationality, see Bol, Multiple Nationality and International Law (2007); Rights and Duties of Dual Nationals: Evolution and Prospects (Martin & Hailbronner eds. 2002); Rode, Dual Nationals and the Doctrine of Dominant Nationality, 53 A.J.I.L. 139 (1959).

2. *Setting Aside the Doctrine: Diplomatic Claims against Third States.* Can the state of the less dominant nationality bring a claim against a third state or does that claim have to be brought by the state of the more dominant nationality? The Eritrea Ethiopia Claims Commission confronted this issue when Eritrea advanced claims against Ethiopia on behalf of dual nationals who possessed both Eritrean nationality and the nationality of a state other than Ethiopia. Ethiopia argued that Eritrea must demonstrate that the Eritrean nationality was the dominant and effective nationality. Eritrea argued that the dominant and effective nationality doctrine was not relevant in such a circumstance. The Commission found:

> 10. Doctrine is rather divided on this matter. Some authors consider that the notion of dominant and effective nationality has general application, and is not confined to situations involving persons holding the nationality of the two disputing parties. Other authorities believe its application is limited to such situations.

> 11. Following the latter approach, the Commission believes that a dominant and effective nationality test must be restrictively applied, and limited to cases where a claimant holds the nationality of the two disputing States. This is because international dispute settlement traditionally requires an international element that is absent if the claim

involves a person with the nationality of the defendant State. The test only makes sense as a means to assess whether a claim in an international forum has this predominantly international character. This reasoning also explains why diplomatic protection for claims related to persons with nationality of both the claimant and the respondent State can only be granted when the first nationality is the most effective and dominant.

Partial Award on Loss of Property in Ethiopia by Non–Residents (Eritrea's Claim 24), Eritrea Ethiopia Claims Commission (2005), http://www.pca-cpa. org/showpage.asp?pag_id=1151 (footnotes omitted).

3. *Setting Aside the Doctrine: U.N. Compensation Commission*. The U.N. Compensation Commission established by the Security Council to supervise the compensation of victims of international law violations by Iraq in connection with its 1990–1991 invasion of Kuwait decided that Iraqi nationals could file claims if they "have bona fide nationality of any other state," without having to demonstrate that the other nationality is the dominant and effective one. See Governing Council Decision 1, U.N. Doc. S/AC.26/1991/1, para. 17 (Aug. 2, 1991); see also Brower, International Law: On the Edge of Credibility in the Wake of Iraq's Invasion and Occupation of Kuwait, 86 A.S.I.L. Proc. 478, 480 (1992). The panel addressing claims concerning departures from Iraq or Kuwait (Category "A" claims), which were filed on an expedited basis because of the urgent needs of the persons at issue, interpreted and applied this decision as follows:

    27.   Governing Council Decision 1 established that "[c]laims will not be considered on behalf of Iraqi nationals who do not have bona fide nationality of any other State" * * *. As a result, unless Iraqi nationals have a second nationality they are not eligible to claim compensation before the Commission. This also means that, to be entitled to claim compensation, the second nationality must be possessed in good faith.

    28.   Neither the Rules nor other Governing Council decisions define the term "bona fide nationality". Therefore the Panel had to establish the criteria to be met in order for an Iraqi dual national to be considered a bona fide holder of a second nationality.

    29.   In adopting a method to deal with this issue, the Panel was mindful of two considerations: (1) that the claims in connection with which this issue arose were "urgent claims" for the compensation of which "expedited procedures" had been prescribed by the Governing Council (Decision 1); and (2) that the issue to be determined was whether the second nationality was acquired bona fide in the context of eligibility to be able to claim compensation before the Commission. Neither consideration involved the more complex issue of the effectiveness of nationality. The Panel, therefore, aimed for a method of evaluating the bona fide nationality of these claimants that could be applied without having to resort to lengthy procedures that are incompatible with an expedited approach.

    30.   The logic of the method approved by the Panel is based on the object of the determination that is to be made, namely, whether an Iraqi dual national had acquired his or her second nationality mainly or solely for the purpose of becoming eligible to claim compensation before the

Commission. Applying this logic, it seemed reasonable to hold that an Iraqi dual national would not be considered to have applied for or acquired a second nationality in bad faith if he or she had applied for the second nationality before the eligibility criteria for claims had been established by the Governing Council in Decision 1 * * * .

31.   * * * [T]he records show that no Iraqi dual national who had submitted a claim had applied for or acquired a second nationality after the relevant date. The Panel, therefore, holds that all Iraqi dual nationals who filed claims with the Commission were holders in good faith of their second nationality.

Report and Recommendations Made by the Panel of Commissioners Concerning the Sixth Instalment of Claims for Departure from Iraq or Kuwait (Category "A" Claims), U.N. Doc. S/AC.26/1996/3, paras. 27–30 (Oct. 16, 1996), reprinted in 109 I.L.R. 99, 106–07 (1998) (footnotes omitted).

4. *International Law Commission Efforts to Clarify.* The International Law Commission is currently embarked on a project to clarify the rules on the "diplomatic protection of nationals," which is discussed further in Chapter 8, Section 7(D) and Chapter 14. Among other things, the I.L.C. is discussing the treatment of claims made by states on behalf of dual nationals. See Report of the International Law Commission, Fifty-eighth Session, U.N. Doc. A/61/10, at 24 (2006).

5. *Additional Reading.* For additional reading, see Dual Nationality, Social Rights and Federal Citizenship in the U.S. and Europe (Hansen & Weil eds., 2002); Rights and Duties of Dual Nationals: Evolution and Prospects (Martin & Hailbronner eds., 2003).

E. DENATIONALIZATION

When, if ever, can a state take away the nationality of one of its nationals? The materials in Section B above suggest that a state cannot render a person stateless, nor arbitrarily strip a person of his or her nationality. What would constitute arbitrarily taking away someone's nationality? For example, suppose a state feels threatened by having some of its nationals in possession of a second nationality, since that second nationality happens to be of an enemy state. Can the state strip the dual national of their first nationality? For one approach, see European Convention on Nationality, arts. 7–8, E.T.S. No. 166, 37 I.L.M. 44 (1998).

ERITREA ETHIOPIA CLAIMS COMMISSION, PARTIAL AWARD, CIVILIAN CLAIMS, ERITREA'S CLAIMS 15, 16, 23 & 27–32
Decided Dec. 17, 2004
44 I.L.M. 601 (2005) (footnotes omitted)

[In April 1993, a U.N.-monitored referendum was held in which persons of Eritrean origin could vote on whether they wished to see a new state of Eritrea established from a portion of Ethiopia. Persons who obtained an Eritrean "national identity card" were permitted to vote in the referendum and thousands did so, with an overwhelming majority favoring an independent Eritrea. The new state of Eritrea was then admitted to the United Nations in May 1993. In 1998, war broke out between Eritrea and Ethiopia. Some 66,000 persons who voted in the referendum were living outside the Eritrean region of the former Ethiopian state before separation and remained in Ethiopia after creation of the new state of Eritrea. Ethiopia asserted that because they voted in the referendum, these persons were Eritrean nationals, and thus could be expelled to Eritrea under international law as "enemy nationals." Eritrea maintained that these persons had never relinquished their Ethiopian nationality and were being unlawfully denationalized and expelled. A bilateral claims commission, set up pursuant to the December 2000 peace agreement that ended the war, concluded that these persons were dual nationals; by voting in the referendum they had acquired Eritrean nationality, but by continuing to reside in Ethiopia and receiving the benefits of Ethiopian nationality (e.g., passports) they had retained their Ethiopian nationality. The commission then turned to whether, in time of war, Ethiopia could denationalize these persons, given that their second nationality was that of an enemy state.]

57. Neither international humanitarian law nor any treaty applicable between the Parties during the war addresses the loss of nationality or the situation of dual nationals in wartime. With respect to customary international law, Ethiopia contended that customary international law gives a State discretion to deprive its nationals of its nationality if they acquire a second nationality. For its part, Eritrea emphasized everyone's right to a nationality, as expressed in Article 15 of the Universal Declaration of Human Rights, particularly the right not to be arbitrarily deprived of one's nationality. Eritrea maintained that those expelled had not acquired Eritrean nationality, and so were unlawfully rendered stateless by Ethiopia's actions.

58. The Commission agrees with both Parties regarding the relevance of the customary law rules they cited. The problem remains, however, to apply them in the circumstances here. The question before the Commission is whether Ethiopia's actions were unlawful in the unusual circumstances of the creation of the new State of Eritrea followed by the outbreak of war between Eritrea and Ethiopia.

59. With respect to Ethiopia's contention, the Commission recognizes that some States permit their nationals to possess another nationality while others do not. International law prohibits neither position. Accordingly, international law would have allowed Ethiopia to take appropriate measures to implement its 1930 nationality law at the time of the 1993 Referendum as to persons who acquired Eritrean nationality then. For reasons that appear to have been quite commendable, Ethiopia did not do so. It instead allowed Ethiopians who had also acquired Eritrean nationality to continue to exercise their Ethiopian nationality, while agreeing with Eritrea that these people would have to choose one national-

ity or the other at some future time. The war came before these matters were resolved.

60.   With respect to Eritrea's contention, the Commission also recognizes that international law limits States' power to deprive persons of their nationality. In this regard, the Commission attaches particular importance to the principle expressed in Article 15, paragraph 2, of the Universal Declaration of Human Rights, that "no one shall be arbitrarily deprived of his nationality." In assessing whether deprivation of nationality was arbitrary, the Commission considered several factors, including whether the action had a basis in law; whether it resulted in persons being rendered stateless; and whether there were legitimate reasons for it to be taken given the totality of the circumstances.

61.   As to the legal basis of Ethiopia's action, there was no proclamation or similar document in the record recording the decision to terminate the affected persons' Ethiopian nationality, but counsel indicated that this was done pursuant to Ethiopia's 1930 nationality law, a law of long standing comparable to laws of many other countries, which provides that Ethiopian nationality is lost when an Ethiopian acquires another nationality. Neither Party has pointed to any other Ethiopian law that could have been a basis for the termination by Ethiopia of the nationality of any Ethiopians. Consequently, the Commission accepts that all terminations for Ethiopian nationality for which Eritrea is claiming were made on the basis of that law.

62.   If Ethiopia's nationality law were properly implemented in accordance with its terms, only dual nationals could be affected, and that law, by itself, could not result in making any person stateless. Given the fact, however, that Ethiopia did not implement that law until sometime in 1998 with respect to its nationals who had acquired Eritrean nationality between 1993 and 1998, the possibility could not be excluded that some persons who had acquired Eritrean nationality had subsequently lost it and thus were made stateless by Ethiopia's action. Perhaps more likely, statelessness would result if Ethiopia erroneously determined that one of its nationals had acquired Eritrean nationality when, in fact, he or she had not done so. Such an unfortunate result might be most likely to occur with respect to Ethiopian nationals not resident in Ethiopia, but it could occur even with respect to Ethiopians resident in Ethiopia. The evidence indicates that Ethiopia appears to have made at least a few errors in this process. While Eritrea cannot claim for the loss suffered by the persons who were the victims of those errors, Ethiopia is liable to Eritrea for any damages caused to it by those errors.

63.   It remains for the Commission to consider the grounds for Ethiopia's actions as they affected dual nationals in light of the factual circumstances of the emergence of the new State of Eritrea and of the armed conflict between the two. Ethiopia contended that it cannot be arbitrary and unlawful in time of war for it to have terminated the Ethiopian nationality of anyone who, within the past five years, had

chosen to obtain the nationality of the enemy State. Eritrea contended that those deprived of their Ethiopian nationality had not been shown to threaten Ethiopia's security, and that it was arbitrary for Ethiopia, which had encouraged people to participate in the Referendum without notice of the potential impact on their Ethiopian nationality, to deprive them of Ethiopian nationality for doing so.

64. The Commission will examine separately Eritrea's claims regarding several groups deprived of their Ethiopian nationality.

65. *Dual Nationals Deprived of their Ethiopian Nationality and Expelled for Security Reasons.* Ethiopia contended that when the war broke out, its duration and extent could not be foreseen. Ethiopian security officials were said to be deeply concerned about the potential security threats posed by over 66,000 Ethiopian residents who had shown a significant attachment to the now-enemy State by acquiring Eritrean nationality in order to register for the Referendum or otherwise.

66. Ethiopia insisted that it did not view Eritrean nationality alone as sufficient to deem anyone a security threat subject to loss of nationality and expulsion. For that, additional ties or actions indicating a possible threat to Ethiopia's security were required. The principal indicators were raising money on behalf of Eritrea or participating in organizations promoting Eritrean Government interests or encouraging closer links between expatriate Eritreans and Eritrea. Involvement in two organizations drew particular scrutiny.

67. The first was the Popular Front for Democracy and Justice ("PFDJ"). The evidence showed that the PFDJ was the ruling political party in Eritrea, but it was more than a western-style political party. It was more akin to a national movement, constituting a significant element in Eritrea's machinery of government. The evidence showed that the PFDJ maintained a structure of local groups at numerous locations in Ethiopia, which were used to promote the interests of Eritrea.

68. Ethiopia's screening process also focused on persons active in the Eritrean Community Associations. The Community Associations were less overtly political than the PFDJ. Nevertheless, the evidence showed that they raised funds to support Eritrea and promoted nationalistic solidarity among their members.

69. The evidence indicated that the overall structure and direction of the security effort was the responsibility of Ethiopia's national security agency, "SIRAA." Persons were identified through a decentralized structure implementing guidance from the central authorities. Ethiopia's evidence portrayed a complex process by which a tier of security committees, including committees at the wereda, tabia and kebele level, identified persons meeting the criteria as potential security threats. SIRAA officials apparently reviewed recommendations and controlled this process.

70. Persons identified through this process were then individually detained, brought to collection centers and then expelled, usually within a

few days. Expellees' passports and other documents indicating Ethiopian nationality were confiscated, and Ethiopia subsequently treated them as having lost their Ethiopian nationality. Eritrea's evidence was consistent with Ethiopia's claim that the process involved deliberation and selection of individuals. Eritrean witnesses regularly described Ethiopian security personnel coming to their residences or places of work seeking them individually by name.

71.   Deprivation of nationality is a serious matter with important and lasting consequences for those affected. In principle, it should follow procedures in which affected persons are adequately informed regarding the proceedings, can present their cases to an objective decision maker, and can seek objective outside review. Ethiopia's process often fell short of this. The process was hurried. Detainees received no written notification, and some claimed they were never told what was happening. Ethiopia contended that detainees could orally apply to security officials seeking release. The record includes some declarations of persons who were released, but it also includes senior Ethiopian witnesses' statements suggesting that there were few appeals. Some declarants claim that they were deprived of Ethiopian nationality and expelled even though they did not qualify to vote in the Referendum or meet Ethiopia's other selection criteria.

72.   Notwithstanding the limitations of the process, the record also shows that Ethiopia faced an exceptional situation. It was at war with Eritrea. Thousands of Ethiopians with personal and ethnic ties to Eritrea had taken steps to acquire Eritrean nationality. Some of these participated in groups that supported the Eritrean Government and often acted on its behalf. In response, Ethiopia devised and implemented a system applying reasonable criteria to identify individual dual nationals thought to pose threats to its wartime security. Given the exceptional wartime circumstances, the Commission, finds that the loss of Ethiopian nationality after being identified though this process was not arbitrary and contrary to international law. Eritrea's claims in the regard are rejected.

73.   *Dual Nationals Who Chose to Leave Ethiopia and Go to Eritrea.* There were many dual nationals who decided to leave Ethiopia during the war and go to Eritrea. The total number is uncertain. Ethiopia counted 21,905 family members who accompanied those who were expelled for security reasons. Others left by aircraft or other means. While many, but not all, of these were relatives of those who were expelled for security reasons, the Commission recognizes that, whatever their individual motives may have been, it was a serious act that could not be without consequences for any dual national of two hostile belligerents to choose to leave one for the other while they were at war with each other. The Commission decides that the termination of the Ethiopian nationality of these persons was not arbitrary and was not in violation of international law.

74. *Dual Nationals Remaining in Ethiopia: "Yellow–Card People."*
It is undisputed that a considerable number of other dual nationals
remained in Ethiopia during the war, that Ethiopia deprived them of their
Ethiopian nationality and, in August 1999, required them to present
themselves and register as aliens and obtain a residence permit. The
August 1999 call for registration ordered that "any Eritrean of eighteen
years of age and over, who has acquired Eritrean nationality [by] taking
part in the Eritrean independence referendum or thereafter" must report
and be registered. Those who did not comply "will be considered an illegal
person who has unlawfully entered the country and shall be treated as
such according to the law."

75.   Those who registered received distinctive yellow alien identity
cards, and were referred to at the hearing as "yellow-card people." The
numbers affected were disputed. Counsel for Eritrea estimated that about
50,000 persons were affected. Ethiopia stated that a much smaller group—
about 24,000 persons—registered and obtained the yellow identity cards.
Eritrea contended that persons in this group were wrongly deprived of
their Ethiopian nationality. Whatever the numbers affected, there was no
evidence indicating that the dual nationals in this group threatened
Ethiopian security or suggesting other reasons for taking away their
Ethiopian nationality. There was no process to identify individuals warranting special consideration and no apparent possibility of review or
appeal. Considering that rights to such benefits as land ownership and
business licenses, as well as passports and other travel documents were at
stake, the Commission finds that this wide-scale deprivation of Ethiopian
nationality of persons remaining in Ethiopia was, under the circumstances, arbitrary and contrary to international law.

76.   *Dual Nationals Who Were in Third Countries or Who Left
Ethiopia To Go to Third Countries.* Eritrea also contended that an
undetermined number of the persons found by the Commission to have
been dual nationals were present in other countries when Ethiopia determined that they would no longer be accepted as Ethiopian nationals. As
with the "yellow-card people," there is no evidence indicating that these
people, by their mere presence in third countries could reasonably be
presumed to be security threats or that they were found to be potential
threats through any individualized assessment process. Moreover, the only
means by which they could contest their treatment was to approach
Ethiopian diplomatic or consular establishments abroad, and the evidence
showed that those who did so to seek clarification or assistance were sent
away. The Commission finds that the members of this group were also
arbitrarily deprived of their Ethiopian citizenship in violation of international law.

77.   *Dual Nationals Who Were in Eritrea.* The record does not
indicate how many dual nationals were in Eritrea when the war began in
May 1998 and soon thereafter, when Ethiopia terminated the Ethiopian
nationality of Eritrea–Ethiopia dual nationals, but the Commission must
assume that some were there. While it could not fairly be assumed that

their mere presence in Eritrea was proof that such dual-nationals were security risks, the Commission finds that the evident risks and the inability to contact them under wartime conditions made such termination not arbitrary or otherwise unlawful.

78. *Dual Nationals Expelled for Other Reasons.* While Ethiopia asserted that no one was expelled except for holders of Eritrean nationality found to be security risks through the process previously described, the evidence shows that an unknown, but considerable, number of dual nationals were expelled without having been subject to this process. Particularly in smaller towns and in agricultural areas near the border, most or all dual nationals were sometimes rounded up by local authorities and forced into Eritrea for reasons that cannot be established. There is also evidence to suggest that these expulsions included some dual national relatives of persons who had been expelled as security risks and may have included some dual nationals who were expelled against their will. The Commission holds that the termination of the Ethiopian nationality of all such persons was arbitrary and unlawful.

NOTES

1. *Constitutional Sources Relating to U.S. Nationality.* The Fourteenth Amendment of the U.S. Constitution provides that "[a]ll persons born or naturalized in the United States and subject to the jurisdiction thereof, are citizens of the United States and of the State wherein they reside." U.S. Const. amend. XIV, § 1. At the same time, Congress' power "[t]o establish a uniform Rule of Naturalization," U.S. Const. art. I, § 8, cl. 4, is interpreted as including an implied power of denationalization.

2. *Bases for Loss of U.S. Nationality.* Section 349 of the U.S. Immigration and Naturalization Act (INA) provides that a U.S. national "shall lose his nationality by voluntarily performing any [one of several specified] acts with the intention of relinquishing United States nationality." 8 U.S.C.A. § 1481 (2008). Those acts include:

(1) obtaining naturalization in a foreign state upon his own application or upon an application filed by a duly authorized agent, after having attained the age of eighteen years;

(2) taking an oath or making an affirmation or other formal declaration of allegiance to a foreign state or a political subdivision thereof after having attained the age of eighteen years; or

(3) entering, or serving in, the armed forces of a foreign state if (A) such armed forces are engaged in hostilities against the United States, or (B) such person serves as a commissioned or non-commissioned officer.

3. *Limitation on Loss of U.S. Nationality.* Up until 1967, the U.S. Supreme Court generally accepted that a U.S. national could lose his or her citizenship through operation of some objective act; so long as a person voluntarily performed that act (e.g., acquisition of a foreign nationality), then the person could lose his or her U.S. citizenship. In *Afroyim v. Rusk*, 387 U.S.

253, 268 (1967), however, the Court held that relinquishment of U.S. citizenship itself had to be voluntary, stating:

> We hold that the Fourteenth Amendment was designed to, and does, protect every citizen of this Nation against a congressional forcible destruction of his citizenship, whatever his creed, color, or race. Our holding does no more than to give to this citizen that which is his own, a constitutional right to remain a citizen in a free country unless he voluntarily relinquishes that citizenship.

See also *Vance v. Terrazas*, 444 U.S. 252 (1980). Taking account of the Supreme Court's views, INA § 349 was amended to require that the act be taken "with the intention of relinquishing United States nationality." In determining whether citizenship is being relinquished "voluntarily," the U.S. Department of State has adopted an administrative standard of evidence that assumes U.S. citizens intend to retain their citizenship when they obtain naturalization in a foreign state, subscribe to routine declarations of allegiance to a foreign state, serve in the military forces of a foreign state not engaged in hostilities against the United States, or accept non-policy level employment with a foreign government. That administrative presumption, however, does not apply when an individual seeks elected public office or a policy-level position in a foreign state. See 22 C.F.R. §§ 50.40, 50.50, 50.51 (2007).

Further, the Office of Legal Counsel at the U.S. Department of Justice, with an eye to U.S. nationals who fought with the Afghanistan Taliban in the wake of the terrorist attacks of 9/11, opined that "[v]oluntary service in a foreign armed force that is engaged in hostilities against the United States has frequently been viewed as a particularly strong manifestation of an intention to abandon citizenship." Office of Legal Counsel, Memorandum for the Solicitor General on Survey of the Law of Expatriation (June 12, 2002), http://www.usdoj.gov/olc/expatriation.htm.

SECTION 3. TRANSNATIONAL CORPORATIONS UNDER INTERNATIONAL LAW

A. THE STATUS OF TRANSNATIONAL CORPORATIONS IN INTERNATIONAL LAW

In the last few decades, considerable attention has been given to the international role of private corporations that are incorporated in (and often have their headquarters in) one state and carry out operations in many countries around the world. Such transnational or multinational corporations (TNCs or MNCs) have become the focus of considerable controversy because of their economic and, in some cases, political power, the mobility and complexity of their operations, and the difficulties they create for nation states—both "home" and "host" states—which seek to exercise legal authority over them.

Such corporations are most often private, non-governmental entities; they are subject to applicable national laws and they are not international legal persons in the technical sense. That is, they are not generally subject to obligations and generally do not enjoy rights under international law. However, in some cases they have entered into agreements with governments under which the parties have agreed that principles of public international law or general principles of law, rather than national law, will govern the transaction or investment. Moreover, bilateral and multilateral treaties may confer rights on a private corporation that may be enforced against the host state in its courts or, under certain circumstances, in an international arbitral tribunal or, if the corporation's claim is espoused by the state of which it is a national, before the International Court of Justice. See, e.g., Murphy, The ELSI Case: An Investment Dispute at the International Court of Justice, 16 Yale J. Int'l L. 391 (1991).

Commentary on the nature and status of transnational corporations has been voluminous. See e.g., Regulating International Business (Picciotto & Mayne eds. 1999); Introduction to International Business Law: Legal Transactions in a Global Economy (Seer & Smolka–Day eds. 1996).

B.   NATIONALITY OF CORPORATIONS

For most purposes, private corporations are treated in international law as the nationals of a particular state, whether the state of incorporation, the state where the corporation's management is located, or the state where the corporation maintains its headquarters or registered office (*siège social*). Corporations, like individuals, must in most instances rely on the protection of the government of which they are nationals and do not have direct access to international legal proceedings to protect their rights, although there are some exceptions. If a host state harms a foreign corporation in violation of international law, must the state where the corporation is incorporated or located bring the diplomatic claim on its behalf, or can a state where a majority of the shareholders are located do so?

BARCELONA TRACTION, LIGHT AND POWER COMPANY, LTD. (BELGIUM v. SPAIN)

International Court of Justice, 1970
1970 I.C.J. 3

[Proceedings were instituted before the I.C.J. against Spain by the Government of Belgium on behalf of persons (individuals and companies) of Belgian nationality, who were shareholders of Barcelona Traction, Light and Power Company, Limited, a corporation organized under the laws of, and with its registered office in, Canada. Belgium alleged that Spain should be held responsible for acts of the Spanish Government in violation of international law that caused injury, directly, to the Canadian corporation and, indirectly, to its Belgian shareholders, the value of whose shares was effectively eliminated as a consequence of the injury to the corporation. Rejecting the claim of Belgium, the court stated, in part:]

31.   Thus the Court has to deal with a series of problems arising out of a triangular relationship involving the State whose nationals are shareholders in a company incorporated under the laws of another State, in whose territory it has its registered office; the State whose organs are alleged to have committed against the company unlawful acts prejudicial to both it and its shareholders; and the State under whose laws the company is incorporated, and in whose territory it has its registered office.

32.   In these circumstances it is logical that the Court should first address itself to what was originally presented as the subject-matter of the third preliminary objection: namely the question of the right of Belgium to exercise diplomatic protection of Belgian shareholders in a company which is a juristic entity incorporated in Canada, the measures complained of having been taken in relation not to any Belgian national but to the company itself.

33.   When a State admits into its territory foreign investments or foreign nationals, whether natural or juristic persons, it is bound to extend to them the protection of the law and assumes obligations concerning the treatment to be afforded them. * * *

* * *

35.   * * * In the present case it is therefore essential to establish whether the losses allegedly suffered by Belgian shareholders in Barcelona Traction were the consequence of the violation of obligations of which they were the beneficiaries. In other words: has a right of Belgium been violated on account of its nationals' having suffered infringement of their rights as shareholders in a company not of Belgian nationality?

36.   Thus it is the existence or absence of a right, belonging to Belgium and recognized as such by international law, which is decisive for the problem of Belgium's capacity.

> "This right is necessarily limited to intervention [by a State] on behalf of its own nationals because, in the absence of a special agreement, it is the bond of nationality between the State and the individual which alone confers upon the State the right of diplomatic protection, and it is as a part of the function of diplomatic protection that the right to take up a claim and to ensure respect for the rules of international law must be envisaged." (*Panevezys–Saldutiskis Railway, Judgment, 1939, P.C.I.J., Series A/B, No. 76,* p. 16.)

It follows that the same question is determinant in respect of Spain's responsibility towards Belgium. Responsibility is the necessary corollary of a right. In the absence of any treaty on the subject between the Parties, this essential issue has to be decided in the light of the general rules of diplomatic protection.

37.   In seeking to determine the law applicable to this case, the Court has to bear in mind the continuous evolution of international law. Diplomatic protection deals with a very sensitive area of international relations, since the interest of a foreign State in the protection of its nationals confronts the rights of the territorial sovereign, a fact of which the general law on the subject has had to take cognizance in order to prevent abuses and friction. From its origins closely linked with international commerce, diplomatic protection has sustained a particular impact from the growth of international economic relations, and at the same time from the profound transformations which have taken place in the economic life of nations. These latter changes have given birth to municipal institutions, which have transcended frontiers and have begun to exercise considerable influence on international relations. One of these phenomena which has a particular bearing on the present case is the corporate entity.

38.   In this field international law is called upon to recognize institutions of municipal law that have an important and extensive role in the international field. This does not necessarily imply drawing any analogy between its own institutions and those of municipal law, nor does it amount to making rules of international law dependent upon categories of municipal law. All it means is that international law has had to recognize the corporate entity as an institution created by States in a domain essentially within their domestic jurisdiction. This in turn requires that, whenever legal issues arise concerning the rights of States with regard to the treatment of companies and shareholders, as to which rights international law has not established its own rules, it has to refer to the relevant rules of municipal law. Consequently, in view of the relevance to the present case of the rights of the corporate entity and its shareholders under municipal law, the Court must devote attention to the nature and interrelation of those rights.

* * *

40.   There is, however, no need to investigate the many different forms of legal entity provided for by the municipal laws of States, because the Court is concerned only with that exemplified by the company involved in the present case: Barcelona Traction—a limited liability company whose capital is represented by shares. * * *

41.   Municipal law determines the legal situation not only of such limited liability companies but also of those persons who hold shares in them. Separated from the company by numerous barriers, the shareholder cannot be identified with it. The concept and structure of the company are founded on and determined by a firm distinction between the separate entity of the company and that of the shareholder, each with a distinct set of rights. The separation of property rights as between company and shareholder is an important manifestation of this distinction. So long as the company is in existence the shareholder has no right to the corporate assets.

* * *

44.   Notwithstanding the separate corporate personality, a wrong done to the company frequently causes prejudice to its shareholders. But the mere fact that damage is sustained by both company and shareholder does not imply that both are entitled to claim compensation. Thus no legal conclusion can be drawn from the fact that the same event caused damage simultaneously affecting several natural or juristic persons. Creditors do not have any right to claim compensation from a person who, by wronging their debtor, causes them loss. In such cases, no doubt, the interests of the aggrieved are affected, but not their rights. Thus whenever a shareholder's interests are harmed by an act done to the company, it is to the latter that he must look to institute appropriate action; for although two separate entities may have suffered from the same wrong, it is only one entity whose rights have been infringed.

* * *

48.   The Belgian Government claims that shareholders of Belgian nationality suffered damage in consequence of unlawful acts of the Spanish authorities and, in particular, that the Barcelona Traction shares, though they did not cease to exist, were emptied of all real economic content. It accordingly contends that the shareholders had an independent right to redress, notwithstanding the fact that the acts complained of were directed against the company as such. Thus the legal issue is reducible to the question of whether it is legitimate to identify an attack on company rights, resulting in damage to shareholders, with the violation of their direct rights.

* * *

51.   On the international plane, the Belgian Government has advanced the proposition that it is inadmissible to deny the shareholders' national State a right of diplomatic protection merely on the ground that another State possesses a corresponding right in respect of the company itself. In strict logic and law this formulation of the Belgian claim to *jus standi* assumes the existence of the very right that requires demonstration. In fact the Belgian Government has repeatedly stressed that there exists no rule of international law which would deny the national State of the shareholders the right of diplomatic protection for the purpose of seeking redress pursuant to unlawful acts committed by another State against the company in which they hold shares. This, by emphasizing the absence of any express denial of the right, conversely implies the admission that there is no rule of international law which expressly confers such a right on the shareholders' national State.

52.   International law may not, in some fields, provide specific rules in particular cases. In the concrete situation, the company against which allegedly unlawful acts were directed is expressly vested with a right, whereas no such right is specifically provided for the shareholder in respect of those acts. Thus the position of the company rests on a positive rule of both municipal and international law. As to the shareholder, while

he has certain rights expressly provided for him by municipal law * * *, appeal can, in the circumstances of the present case, only be made to the silence of international law. Such silence scarcely admits of interpretation in favour of the shareholder.

* * *

70. In allocating corporate entities to States for purposes of diplomatic protection, international law is based, but only to a limited extent, on an analogy with the rules governing the nationality of individuals. The traditional rule attributes the right of diplomatic protection of a corporate entity to the State under the laws of which it is incorporated and in whose territory it has its registered office. These two criteria have been confirmed by long practice and by numerous international instruments. This notwithstanding, further or different links are at times said to be required in order that a right of diplomatic protection should exist. Indeed, it has been the practice of some States to give a company incorporated under their law diplomatic protection solely when it has its seat *(siège social)* or management or centre of control in their territory, or when a majority or a substantial proportion of the shares has been owned by nationals of the State concerned. Only then, it has been held, does there exist between the corporation and the State in question a genuine connection of the kind familiar from other branches of international law. However, in the particular field of the diplomatic protection of corporate entities, no absolute test of the "genuine connection" has found general acceptance. Such tests as have been applied are of a relative nature, and sometimes links with one State have had to be weighed against those with another. In this connection reference has been made to the *Nottebohm* case. In fact the Parties made frequent reference to it in the course of the proceedings. However, given both the legal and factual aspects of protection in the present case the Court is of the opinion that there can be no analogy with the issues raised or the decision given in that case.

71. In the present case it is not disputed that the company was incorporated in Canada and has its registered office in that country. The incorporation of the company under the law of Canada was an act of free choice. Not only did the founders of the company seek its incorporation under Canadian law but it has remained under that law for a period of over fifty years. It has maintained in Canada its registered office, its accounts and its share registers. Board meetings were held there for many years; it has been listed in the records of the Canadian tax authorities. Thus a close and permanent connection has been established, fortified by the passage of over half a century. This connection is in no way weakened by the fact that the company engaged from the very outset in commercial activities outside Canada, for that was its declared object. Barcelona Traction's links with Canada are thus manifold.

* * *

76. * * * [T]he record shows that from 1948 onwards the Canadian Government made to the Spanish Government numerous representations which cannot be viewed otherwise than as the exercise of diplomatic protection in respect of the Barcelona Traction company. Therefore this was not a case where diplomatic protection was refused or remained in the sphere of fiction. It is also clear that over the whole period of its diplomatic activity the Canadian Government proceeded in full knowledge of the Belgian attitude and activity.

77. It is true that at a certain point the Canadian Government ceased to act on behalf of Barcelona Traction, for reasons which have not been fully revealed, though a statement made in a letter of 19 July 1955 by the Canadian Secretary of State for External Affairs suggests that it felt the matter should be settled by means of private negotiations. The Canadian Government has nonetheless retained its capacity to exercise diplomatic protection; no legal impediment has prevented it from doing so: no fact has arisen to render this protection impossible. It has discontinued its action of its own free will.

* * *

79. The State must be viewed as the sole judge to decide whether its protection will be granted, to what extent it is granted, and when it will cease. It retains in this respect a discretionary power the exercise of which may be determined by considerations of a political or other nature, unrelated to the particular case. Since the claim of the State is not identical with that of the individual or corporate person whose cause is espoused, the State enjoys complete freedom of action. Whatever the reasons for any change of attitude, the fact cannot in itself constitute a justification for the exercise of diplomatic protection by another government, unless there is some independent and otherwise valid ground for that.

* * *

81. The cessation by the Canadian Government of the diplomatic protection of Barcelona Traction cannot, then, be interpreted to mean that there is no remedy against the Spanish Government for the damage done by the allegedly unlawful acts of the Spanish authorities. It is not a hypothetical right which was vested in Canada, for there is no legal impediment preventing the Canadian Government from protecting Barcelona Traction. Therefore there is no substance in the argument that for the Belgian Government to bring a claim before the Court represented the only possibility of obtaining redress for the damage suffered by Barcelona Traction and, through it, by its shareholders.

* * *

83. The Canadian Government's right of protection in respect of the Barcelona Traction company remains unaffected by the present proceedings.

* * *

88. It follows from what has already been stated above that, where it is a question of an unlawful act committed against a company representing foreign capital, the general rule of international law authorizes the national State of the company alone to make a claim.

* * *

92. Since the general rule on the subject does not entitle the Belgian Government to put forward a claim in this case, the question remains to be considered whether nonetheless, as the Belgian Government has contended during the proceedings, considerations of equity do not require that it be held to possess a right of protection. It is quite true that it has been maintained, that, for reasons of equity, a State should be able, in certain cases, to take up the protection of its nationals, shareholders in a company which has been the victim of a violation of international law. Thus a theory has been developed to the effect that the State of the shareholders has a right of diplomatic protection when the State whose responsibility is invoked is the national State of the company. Whatever the validity of this theory may be, it is certainly not applicable to the present case, since Spain is not the national State of Barcelona Traction.

93. On the other hand, the Court considers that, in the field of diplomatic protection as in all other fields of international law, it is necessary that the law be applied reasonably. It has been suggested that if in a given case it is not possible to apply the general rule that the right of diplomatic protection of a company belongs to its national State, considerations of equity might call for the possibility of protection of the shareholders in question by their own national State. This hypothesis does not correspond to the circumstances of the present case.

94. In view, however, of the discretionary nature of diplomatic protection, considerations of equity cannot require more than the possibility for some protector State to intervene, whether it be the national State of the company, by virtue of the general rule mentioned above, or, in a secondary capacity, the national State of the shareholders who claim protection. In this connection, account should also be taken of the practical effects of deducing from considerations of equity any broader right of protection for the national State of the shareholders. It must first of all be observed that it would be difficult on an equitable basis to make distinctions according to any quantitative test: it would seem that the owner of 1 per cent. and the owner of 90 per cent. of the share-capital should have the same possibility of enjoying the benefit of diplomatic protection. The protector State may, of course, be disinclined to take up the case of the single small shareholder, but it could scarcely be denied the right to do so in the name of equitable considerations. In that field, protection by the national State of the shareholders can hardly be graduated according to the absolute or relative size of the shareholding involved.

95. The Belgian Government, it is true, has also contended that as high a proportion as 88 per cent. of the shares in Barcelona Traction belonged to natural or juristic persons of Belgian nationality, and it has

used this as an argument for the purpose not only of determining the amount of the damages which it claims, but also of establishing its right of action on behalf of the Belgian shareholders. Nevertheless, this does not alter the Belgian Government's position, as expounded in the course of the proceedings, which implies, in the last analysis, that it might be sufficient for one single share to belong to a national of a given State for the latter to be entitled to exercise its diplomatic protection.

96. The Court considers that the adoption of the theory of diplomatic protection of shareholders as such, by opening the door to competing diplomatic claims, could create an atmosphere of confusion and insecurity in international economic relations. The danger would be all the greater inasmuch as the shares of companies whose activity is international are widely scattered and frequently change hands. It might perhaps be claimed that, if the right of protection belonging to the national States of the shareholders were considered as only secondary to that of the national State of the company, there would be less danger of difficulties of the kind contemplated. However, the Court must state that the essence of a secondary right is that it only comes into existence at the time when the original right ceases to exist. As the right of protection vested in the national State of the company cannot be regarded as extinguished because it is not exercised, it is not possible to accept the proposition that in case of its non-exercise the national States of the shareholders have a right of protection secondary to that of the national State of the company. Furthermore, study of factual situations in which this theory might possibly be applied gives rise to the following observations.

97. The situations in which foreign shareholders in a company wish to have recourse to diplomatic protection by their own national State may vary. It may happen that the national State of the company simply refuses to grant it its diplomatic protection, or that it begins to exercise it (as in the present case) but does not pursue its action to the end. It may also happen that the national State of the company and the State which has committed a violation of international law with regard to the company arrive at a settlement of the matter, by agreeing on compensation for the company, but that the foreign shareholders find the compensation insufficient. Now, as a matter of principle, it would be difficult to draw a distinction between these three cases so far as the protection of foreign shareholders by their national State is concerned, since in each case they may have suffered real damage. Furthermore, the national State of the company is perfectly free to decide how far it is appropriate for it to protect the company, and is not bound to make public the reasons for its decision. To reconcile this discretionary power of the company's national State with a right of protection falling to the shareholders' national State would be particularly difficult when the former State has concluded, with the State which has contravened international law with regard to the company, an agreement granting the company compensation which the foreign shareholders find inadequate. If, after such a settlement, the national State of the foreign shareholders could in its turn put forward a

claim based on the same facts, this would be likely to introduce into the negotiation of this kind of agreement a lack of security which would be contrary to the stability which it is the object of international law to establish in international relations.

* * *

99.   It should also be observed that the promoters of a company whose operations will be international must take into account the fact that States have, with regard to their nationals, a discretionary power to grant diplomatic protection or to refuse it. When establishing a company in a foreign country, its promoters are normally impelled by particular considerations; it is often a question of tax or other advantages offered by the host State. It does not seem to be in any way inequitable that the advantages thus obtained should be balanced by the risks arising from the fact that the protection of the company and hence of its shareholders is thus entrusted to a State other than the national State of the shareholders.

100.   In the present case, it is clear from what has been said above that Barcelona Traction was never reduced to a position of impotence such that it could not have approached its national State, Canada, to ask for its diplomatic protection, and that, as far as appeared to the Court, there was nothing to prevent Canada from continuing to grant its diplomatic protection to Barcelona Traction if it had considered that it should do so.

101.   For the above reasons, the Court is not of the opinion that, in the particular circumstances of the present case, *jus standi* is conferred on the Belgian Government by considerations of equity.

* * *

103.   Accordingly,

THE COURT

rejects the Belgian Government's claim by fifteen votes to one, twelve votes of the majority being based on the reasons set out in the present Judgment.

NOTES

1.   *Nationality Based on Both Incorporation and Shareholders.* In some instances, it may be important to determine not just where the corporation is incorporated or located, but also to determine the nationality of the shareholders. The 1981 Claims Settlement Declaration that set up in the Iran–United States Claims Tribunal defined "national" of the United States to include a corporation organized under the laws of the United States *if* U.S. nationals owned directly or indirectly a 50% or greater interest in its capital stock. See *Flexi–Van Leasing, Inc. v. Iran*, 1 Iran–U.S. Cl. Trib. Rep. 455 (1982) (the same rule applied *mutatis mutandis* to Iranian corporations). Similarly, the United States is a party to a number of treaties of friendship, commerce and navigation that usually treat companies "constituted under the

applicable laws and regulations within the territories of either High Contracting Party [as] companies thereof," but that also permit each party to deny certain rights when the company is controlled by nationals of a third country. See, e.g., Convention of Establishment, United States–France, arts. XIII and XIV(5), Nov. 25, 1959, 11 U.S.T. 2398, 401 U.N.T.S. 75.

2. *Looking beyond Barcelona Traction.* The United States usually treats a corporation organized under the law of the United States or one of its constituent states as a U.S. corporation. Civil law countries generally look to the *siège social*, the place from which the corporation is managed or controlled. When national security issues are involved, however, many states, including the United States, focus on the nationality of the owners of the corporation's stock or of those who control the corporation. Further, it has been proposed that when promotion and protection of certain national interests, such as subsidizing and safeguarding technology, are at stake, a broader "economic commitment" test should be applied to identify corporations entitled to protection. The nationality (or national identity) of a corporation would be fixed by referring to structural, organizational, and operational features of the firm, such as the nature and geographic location of its principal assets, the geographic source of its earnings, and its relationships with third-party contractors. See Mabry, Multinational Corporations and U.S. Technology Policy: Rethinking the Concept of Corporate Nationality, 87 Geo. L.J. 563, 567 (1999). Would application of such a test be appropriate or feasible in the context of the issues for which the nationality of a corporation must be ascertained under international law?

3. *Protecting Foreign Shareholders' Rights in a Local Corporation.* What if the foreign shareholders own shares in a local corporation that is harmed by the host state? In that instance, do you think the state of the shareholders should be able to bring a diplomatic claim against the host state? In fact, the bulk of foreign investment is carried on by subsidiary corporations which are organized under the laws of the state where the business will be conducted and are controlled by a multinational corporation organized under the laws of another state. For that reason, many bilateral commercial or investment agreements protect both direct *and* indirect investments, allowing capital-exporting states (such as the United States), where the parent corporation is a national, to protest and pursue international claims for properties of a foreign subsidiary that have been expropriated. See, e.g., *Elettronica Sicula S.p.A. (ELSI)* (United States v. Italy), 1989 I.C.J. 15 (diplomatic claim brought by the United States on behalf of two U.S. companies who were shareholders in an Italian subsidiary, where the injury concerned Italy's requisition of the property of the subsidiary).

4. *Further Reading.* For contemporaneous commentary on *Barcelona Traction*, see Higgins, Aspects of the Case Concerning the Barcelona Traction, Light and Power Company, Ltd., 11 Va. J. Int'l L. 327 (1971); Lillich, The Rigidity of Barcelona, 65 A.J.I.L. 522 (1971); Jiménez de Aréchaga, International Responsibility of States for Acts of the Judiciary, in Transnational Law in a Changing Society 171 (Friedmann, Henkin, & Lissitzyn eds. 1972). For a contemporary effort to catalogue international rules on diplomatic protection, including in situations involving corporate and shareholder rights, see Report

of the International Law Commission, Fifty-eighth Session, U.N. Doc. A/61/10, at 24 (2006).

C. REGULATING TRANSNATIONAL CORPORATIONS

Transnational corporations can be regulated by the national laws of the state of the corporate nationality and can further be regulated by the state in which it conducts operations. Given that the "home state" may not have any direct interest in how its corporations are acting abroad, and given that the "host state" may have relatively lax requirements about treatment of workers, environmental protection, and so on, does there exist within the realm of international law some form of further normative constraints?

MURPHY, TAKING MULTINATIONAL CORPORATE CODES OF CONDUCT TO THE NEXT LEVEL

43 Colum. J. Transnat'l L. 389, 397–398, 400–02, 407–08, 422–23 (2005) (footnotes omitted)

The activities of MNCs provide significant benefits by creating wealth in the states where they operate: MNCs provide jobs, produce goods and services, introduce technologies, and develop markets. While much of the increased MNC activity of the 1990s was among states of the developed world, a portion of that activity included the movement of MNC operations to the developing world to take advantage of a cheaper supply of labor and other resources. Indeed, though the story of the 1970s and 1980s may have been one of developing countries seeking to nationalize or expropriate foreign investment as a means of stemming post-colonial economic "neo-colonization," the story of the 1990s was one of developing states realizing the great benefits of attracting foreign investment and technology, so as to develop export economies of their own.

At the same time, concerns have arisen from this increased MNC activity in the developing world. One aspect of the investment in developing countries is a greater willingness of developing countries to allow MNCs to own or manage projects in key public sectors, such as energy, telecommunications, transport, water, and sanitation. While there may be benefits from privatizing decision-making in such sectors, it means that core societal needs and natural resources are largely controlled by entities that governments may not have the capacity to hold accountable for customer service and compliance with local laws. Some observers assert that the distribution of wealth generated by MNCs when they operate in developing countries has been largely skewed in favor of the MNCs (and their shareholders) and against laborers. Moreover, the working conditions of laborers for MNCs in developing countries are often very poor: laborers have difficulty unionizing, factory conditions generally are unhealthful, and child labor is common. Environmental standards in developing states tend to be low or unenforced, often allowing relatively unchecked emissions of air pollutants and toxic materials.

* * *

In short, MNCs operating in developing countries have done what one would expect them to do in a free market: seek out the least expensive means of conducting operations so as to maximize profits. The problem is that, in doing so, they have inflicted unacceptable harm and mistreatment. As human rights, labor rights, and environmental rights continue to advance within the global consciousness, the practices of many MNCs in developing countries have been regarded as out of step with social expectations. This gap, in turn, has led to strident criticism of MNC activity, and sometimes to consumer backlash whereby MNCs are faced with demands for products certified as having been produced without adverse social consequences.

MNCs themselves recognize this divergence of MNC operations from social expectations, and consequently many have embraced the movement toward voluntary codes of conduct that inculcate key norms in the fields of labor, human rights, consumer protection, anticorruption, and the environment. To date, these codes have taken many shapes and sizes, but they generally can be characterized in the following manner. The codes are voluntary in nature; MNCs are not forced to adopt the codes but, rather, pledge themselves to the code because they see it as in their interests to do so. The codes typically consist of a series of principles, standards or guidelines, which may be broad and aspirational in nature or may be more detailed and operational in nature. The codes may draw on or refer to international law norms (particularly in the field of international labor, environmental, or human rights law), may focus on MNC adherence to local laws, and/or may call for adherence to norms articulated solely in the code itself. A code might be developed ad hoc for a specific company (sometimes referred to as an "operational" or "internal" code). Alternatively, a code might be developed for a class of companies in a particular field (e.g., the apparel or extractive industries) or for companies generally (sometimes referred to as "model" or "external" codes), which can then lead to the creation of associated operational codes. The codes might be drafted solely by private sector entities, usually bringing together a range of stakeholders such as labor, environmental, religious, and corporate groups. Alternatively, the codes might be drafted under the auspices of governments or by government representatives working through international organizations, although even then relevant stakeholders are typically a part of the drafting process. Once a code is established, typically an MNC is expected to pledge itself publicly to the code and to develop internal corporate rules or policies based on the code. MNC managers are then trained to comply with those rules or policies in corporate decision-making and operations. While the codes normally call upon the MNC to make public its decision to adhere to the code, further transparency regarding corporate adherence to the code may not be required. Different techniques of monitoring, verification, audits, or certification might be an element of a particular code, but in any event the codes often do not require such steps by an entity external to the MNC. Since the codes are voluntary, MNCs are not exposed to any criminal or civil penalties in the event that they fail to abide by them (they remain, of course, exposed to penalties if the MNC violates relevant national laws). Thus, the codes are legally unenforceable.

* * *

Since the codes are voluntary in nature, they are not written to impose constraints that MNCs would find onerous. Instead, the codes are crafted to promote conduct that, although it entails some costs to the MNC, brings greater benefits to the MNC. The costs include the basic expenses involved in altering internal corporate rules and policies, training personnel regarding the new policies, pursuing any associated internal or external monitoring, verification, audits, or certification, and internalizing costs that had previously been externalized (e.g., paying higher wages and avoiding environmental harms). The benefits to MNCs can take various forms. Arguably there will be some internal cost savings achieved, such as from more efficient use of resources (e.g., achieved when pursuing waste reduction), or from having a healthier and thus more productive work force. Cost savings may also arise if adherence to such a code allows the MNC to save on insurance premiums or have access to capital at lower rates, if insurers or lenders are concerned about possible adverse consequences of MNC activities. To the extent that the code is adopted by an MNC's competitors, then the code may assist in creating a level playing field for the MNC, so that its good corporate conduct does not put it at a competitive disadvantage. Finally, by adhering to such a code, the MNC may enjoy an enhanced public image, thus avoiding shareholder dissatisfaction with management, consumer boycotts of MNC goods or services, labor unrest, and undesirable regulation by either its host or home governments.

* * *

In the field of human rights, the UN Sub–Commission on the Promotion and Protection of Human Rights recently adopted a code on the responsibilities of transnational corporations. The [2003] code recognizes that states have the primary responsibility for the promotion and protection of human rights, but also asserts that MNCs have such obligations as well. The code then sets forth six types of rights or obligations that MNCs must observe: (1) the right to equal opportunity and non-discriminatory treatment; (2) the right to security of persons; (3) the rights of workers, such as rights against forced or child labor, to remuneration that ensures an adequate standard of living, and to collective bargaining; (4) respect for national sovereignty (e.g., refraining from bribery) and human rights (e.g., right to food and drinking water); (5) obligations with regard to consumer protection; and (6) obligations with regard to environmental protection, such as complying with relevant national and international laws.

One interesting component of this code is that it contains several provisions relating to implementation. The code states that MNCs "shall adopt . . . internal rules of operation in compliance" with the code, shall periodically report on implementation, and shall incorporate the code into their contracts with suppliers, distributors, licensees, and others. Further, the code states that MNCs shall be subject to transparent and independent monitoring and verification by the United Nations and "other international and national mechanisms already in existence or yet to be created." The code provides that states "should" establish the legal framework necessary for implementing the code. Moreover, MNCs "shall provide prompt effective and adequate reparation to those persons" adversely affected by failure to comply with the norms.

Supporters of the code have heralded it as a "landmark step" and even as the "first nonvoluntary initiative accepted at the international level." Initial enthusiasm for the code, however, has been muted. The Commission on Human Rights (which, unlike the Sub–Commission, consists of representatives of governments) took note of the code, but, in its recommendation to the UN Economic and Social Council, affirmed that the code "has not been requested by the Commission and, as a draft proposal, has no legal standing, and that the Sub–Commission should not perform any monitoring function in this regard." Major international business organizations have criticized the code as an inappropriate effort to "privatize" vague human rights standards in a manner that will invite "highly subjective, politicized claims."

* * *

Over time, if the codes remain in nature as they presently are, while demands for social and environmental justice increase, the codes may lose much of their legitimacy. Consumers, shareholders, and other stakeholders may not feel that adoption of a code has any significance and that the code is disingenuous. At best, current criticisms may persist; at worst, if demands for greater corporate responsibility increase, the notion of allowing the "fox" to guard the "hen-house" may fall into severe disrepute, such that the codes wither in meaning, if not in form.

The unease with voluntary codes of conduct has led to calls for transforming the codes into binding law, both at the international and national level. Some treaties already exist designed to rein in corporate misconduct, ranging from [International Labour Organization (ILO)] treaties and regulations (some dating to the early Twentieth Century) to recent initiatives concerning corporate bribery of officials and corporate exports of tobacco. One can imagine aggressively pursuing the transformation of the existing voluntary codes into treaty law, either on a broad scale or in selected areas, with appropriate enforcement or monitoring mechanisms. One can also imagine adopting new national "command and control" legislation codifying and developing such norms, and urging international and national courts to use the codes as though they expressed rules of law. If, over time, this is the fate of voluntary corporate codes, then as they wither away, the codes will be viewed as simply stepping stones in the crystallization of law.

There are, however, reasons to doubt that such a movement toward binding law will succeed, at least in the near term. Many of the binding treaties on issues addressing corporate conduct have secured low rates of ratification, such as several of the ILO treaties. There remain considerable differences of views among blocs of states, and not just between North and South, regarding the development of such conventions, which suggests that successes in crafting new agreements will be difficult. National legislation remains a possibility, but developed states are wary of adopting constraints on their MNCs that place them at a competitive disadvantage, while developing states will likely lack the capacity to do so. Unless the enactment of national laws can be coordinated among blocs of states, the development of such laws will likely prove problematic. Perhaps most importantly, MNCs, who remain powerful actors to whom governments pay heed, will resist such transformation into binding law. Indeed, the reason voluntary codes were adopted to begin with was because of the political obstacles and legal complications in regulating non-state entities who operate across borders, and because of a desire to preserve some level of flexibility in the regulation of such actors as well as to promote true "internalization" of values by MNCs. Those same factors will continue to make direct regulation of MNC activity problematic.

NOTES

1. *Next Steps.* Professor Murphy suggests a future focus on using government power to enhance MNC codes of conduct, not by turning them into "command-and-control" international and national laws, but by other initiatives that might address their weaknesses. He suggests governmental efforts aimed toward: bringing a wider array of stakeholders together for formation of codes, developing a "code for the codes" that outlines the kinds of provisions robust codes should contain, creating regulatory safe harbors for MNCs who adopt and adhere to a code, promoting leniency in criminal prosecution and restrictions on civil claims where robust codes have been adopted and followed, and requiring adherence to such codes as a condition of government procurement and financing. Do you think such efforts would be effective?

2. *Further Reading.* For further reading, see Liability of Multinational Corporations Under International Law (Kamminga & Zia–Zarifi eds. 2000); Branson, The Very Uncertain Prospect of "Global" Convergence in Corporate Governance, 34 Cornell Int'l L.J. 321 (2001); Kinley & Tadaki, From Talk to Walk: The Emergence of Human Rights Responsibilities for Corporations at International Law, 44 Va. J. Int'l L. 931 (2004); Muchlinski, Multinational Enterprises and the Law (2007); Ratner, Corporations and Human Rights: A Theory of Legal Responsibility, 111 Yale L.J. 443 (2001); Tully, Corporations and International Lawmaking (2007); Vázquez, Direct vs. Indirect Obligations of Corporations Under International Law, 43 Colum. J. Transnat'l L. 927

(2005); Ruggie, Business and Human Rights: The Evolving International Agenda, 101 A.J.I.L. 819 (2007).

CHAPTER 8

RULES ON STATE RESPONSIBILITY

■ ■ ■

Chapters 1–4 identified the nature and sources of international law, and Chapters 5–7 focused on the relevant actors of international law. When those actors violate or breach international law, what consequences follow?

As a general matter, if a state by its act or omission breaches an international obligation, it incurs what is commonly referred to as "international responsibility." If the consequence of the breach is an injury to another state, the delinquent state is responsible to make reparation for the breach to the injured state. Thus, when an internationally wrongful act occurs, it creates new legal relations between the states concerned. A state injured by a violation may seek redress by claims made through diplomatic channels or through a procedure of dispute settlement to which the states concerned have agreed (see Chapter 9). Under some circumstances, the injured state may take measures of self-help or countermeasures not involving use of force. This chapter addresses these various aspects of the rules on state responsibility for wrongful acts.

SECTION 1. GENERAL PRINCIPLES OF STATE RESPONSIBILITY

A. GENERAL PRINCIPLES

A fundamental principle of the rules on state responsibility is that a breach by a state of an international obligation engages the "responsibility" of the state for the consequences of that breach. In *Corfu Channel*, the International Court of Justice held Albania liable for certain omissions, in particular the absence of a warning of the danger of mines laid in her territorial waters. The International Court stated:

These grave omissions involve the international responsibility of Albania.

The Court therefore reaches the conclusion that Albania is responsible under international law for the explosions which occurred * * * and for the damage and loss of human life which resulted from them, and that there is a duty upon Albania to pay compensation to the United Kingdom.

Corfu Channel (United Kingdom v. Albania), 1949 I.C.J. 4, 23.

A second fundamental principle is that, if the breach results in an injury to another state, the injured state is entitled to reparation. There is no requirement that the particular norm being breached, such as a treaty, expressly contain within it a norm that calls for reparation. In the much quoted words of the Permanent Court of International Justice:

> It is a principle of international law that the breach of an engagement involves an obligation to make reparation in an adequate form. Reparation therefore is the indispensable complement of a failure to apply a convention and there is no necessity for this to be stated in the convention itself.

Factory at Chorzów (Germany v. Poland), 1927 P.C.I.J. (ser. A) No. 9, at 21.

A third fundamental principle is that responsibility arises whenever there is a breach of an international obligation, whatever its origin. There is no distinction in this respect between breach of a treaty and a violation of a rule of customary international law. Moreover, since any violation of an obligation resulting in injury to another state gives rise to international responsibility, the substantive grounds for such responsibility are as numerous and varied as the norms of international law. Consider the recent case in which the Democratic Republic of the Congo (D.R.C.) successfully proved to the International Court that Uganda had violated various norms of international law by its military intervention in the D.R.C. In concluding that Uganda was responsible to make full reparation for the injuries caused by its acts, the Court stated:

> The Court observes that it is well established in general international law that a State which bears responsibility for an internationally wrongful act is under an obligation to make full reparation for the injury caused by that act (see *Factory at Chorzów, Jurisdiction, 1927, P.C.I.J., Series A. No. 9*, p. 21; *Gabčíkovo–Nagymaros Project (Hungary/Slovakia), Judgment, I.C.J. Reports 1997*, p. 81, para. 152; *Avena and Other Mexican Nationals (Mexico v. United States of America), Judgment, I.C.J. Reports 2004*, p. 59, para. 119). Upon examination of the case file, given the character of the internationally wrongful acts for which Uganda has been found responsible (illegal use of force, violation of sovereignty and territorial integrity, military intervention, occupation of Ituri, violations of international human rights law and of international humanitarian law, looting, plunder and exploitation of the DRC's natural resources), the Court considers that those acts resulted in injury to the DRC and to persons on its territory. Having satisfied itself that this injury was caused to the DRC by Uganda, the Court finds that Uganda has an obligation to make reparation accordingly.

Armed Activities on the Territory of the Congo (Democratic Republic of the Congo v. Uganda), 2005 I.C.J. 168, para. 259.

These and associated rules on state responsibility establish a general framework within which can operate rules that specifically determine the legality or illegality of conduct. The latter rules—such as the obligation to allow innocent passage of ships through the territorial sea—are sometimes described as "primary" rules, the breach of which is the source of responsibility. The general rules of state responsibility do not attempt to catalogue all those primary rules; instead, the rules on state responsibility are referred to as "secondary," inasmuch as they determine the legal consequences of a failure to fulfill obligations established by the primary rules. The International Court has addressed the distinction between these two different types of rules as follows:

> Nor does the Court need to dwell upon the question of the relationship between the law of treaties and the law of State responsibility, * * * as those two branches of international law obviously have a scope that is distinct. A determination of whether a convention is or is not in force, and whether it has or has not been properly suspended or denounced, is to be made pursuant to the law of treaties. On the other hand, an evaluation of the extent to which the suspension or denunciation of a convention, seen as incompatible with the law of treaties, involves the responsibility of the State which proceeded to it, is to be made under the law of State responsibility.

Gabčíkovo–Nagymaros Project (Hungary/Slovakia), 1997 I.C.J. 3, para. 47.

The materials in this chapter deal with these framework or "secondary" rules of state responsibility, starting with the general conditions under which a state may be held to have committed an act that may give rise to international responsibility, and then moving to the consequences that an internationally wrongful act may have, such as the obligation of reparation and the procedures that may be used for redress. As you read these materials, consider as well the extent to which international law is evolving from state-centrism toward a greater emphasis on individuals as bearers of both rights and responsibilities.

B. THE 2001 INTERNATIONAL LAW COMMISSION ARTICLES ON STATE RESPONSIBILITY

One important instrument when studying the rules on state responsibility is the "Articles on State Responsibility" adopted by the International Law Commission in 2001. See Articles on Responsibility of States for Internationally Wrongful Acts, in Report of the International Law Commission, Fifty-third Session, U.N. Doc. A/56/10, at 59 (2001) (hereinafter "I.L.C. Articles") (included in the Documents Supplement). While these fifty-nine articles are not in the form of a treaty and have not been drafted or adopted by states, they are the product of an extensive study of the rules of state responsibility by the eminent scholars and practitioners who serve on the Commission. Moreover, there is an associated commentary to the articles setting forth the various cases and instruments upon which the articles are based. See Crawford, The International Law Commission's Articles on State Responsibility: Introduction, Text, and Commentaries (2002).

Proposals for codification of rules of state responsibility came before the International Law Commission starting with its first session in 1949. Work began in 1956 under a series of special rapporteurs: F.V. García–Amador (1956–1961); Roberto Ago (1963–1980); Willem Riphagen (1980–1986); Gaetano Arangio–Ruiz (1987–1995); and James Crawford (1997–2001). The special rapporteurs produced thirty-two reports among them, leading the I.L.C. to provisionally adopt portions of the articles in stages during the 1970s, 1980s, and 1990s, to provisionally adopt a complete set of articles in 1996, and to adopt a final set of articles in 2001. The various sets of articles during their drafting were the object of commentary and criticism on the part of governments and scholars. For critiques of the final articles, see Symposium: The I.L.C.'s State Responsibility Articles, 96 A.J.I.L. 773 (2002); Symposium: Assessing the Work of the International Law Commission on State Responsibility, 13 E.J.I.L. 1053 (2002); see also International Responsibility Today: Essays in Memory of Oscar Schachter (Ragazzi ed. 2005).

Even while being drafted, the I.L.C. articles had a weighty influence on the jurisprudence of international tribunals. In *Gabčíkovo–Nagymaros Project* (Hungary/Slovakia), 1997 I.C.J. 7, paras. 47–52, the International Court of Justice treated certain aspects of the draft articles as reflecting the customary international law of state responsibility. Other tribunals have likewise considered various parts of the draft articles and the I.L.C.'s commentary as authoritative expressions of customary law. See, e.g., *Prosecutor v. Blaskić*, I.C.T.Y. Case No. IT–95–14–AR108*bis*, para. 26 n. 34 (1997) (issue of who is an "injured State," with reference to Draft Article 40); and other cases referenced in this chapter. Tribunals continue to cite today to the final articles adopted in 2001. See, e.g., *Application of the Convention on the Prevention and Punishment of the Crime of Genocide* (Bosnia–Herzegovina v. Serbia & Montenegro), 2007 I.C.J. 191, para. 385 (excerpted below).

The impact of the articles on states is less certain. While the U.N. General Assembly has commended the articles to the attention of governments, see G.A. Res. 56/83, para. 3 (Dec. 12, 2001), many governments have registered strenuous objections to some aspects of the I.L.C.'s articles, especially on countermeasures. See, e.g., State Responsibility: Comments and Observations Received from Governments, U.N. Doc. A/CN.4/515 (Mar. 19, 2001). Governmental objections indicate skepticism about whether the more controversial aspects of the articles reflect state practice and/or *opinio juris*. For example, it is questionable whether any governments contemplating countermeasures against internationally wrongful acts (e.g., through economic sanctions) have believed that the limitations on countermeasures proposed in the articles reflect constraints that are already binding law (as opposed to suggestions for prospective law-making that states could accept or reject if the articles are eventually put forward in treaty form). Reflecting on the I.L.C.'s decades-long effort to adopt the articles, and their likely future influence, Professor Caron has observed that:

> [T]he articles are sometimes controversial and even more often un-clear. The basic approach to the entire project and the choices implicit in particular articles continue to trouble some states and scholars. Several, if not many, of the articles clearly involve the progressive development of the law rather than its codification. Yet they are still quite influential. It is this influence amid controversy that is paradoxical. Given that the influence took hold even while the articles were only in the form of a partial draft, it is perhaps understandable that the ILC in the recommendation accompanying their adoption suggest-ed that the United Nations General Assembly only "take note" of the articles for the time being, rather than immediately subjecting them to the unpredictable scrutiny of a diplomatic lawmaking conference. But it will be argued that the decision to eschew consideration of the articles as a treaty and to choose influence despite controversy raises fundamental questions about the ILC, arbitral decision making, and traditional images of the making of international law.

>   Three phenomena may be taking place. First, the ILC, perhaps from wisdom and perhaps from hubris, may be pushing the limits of its legitimacy to state what the law is. Second, the failure of some states to object to the General Assembly's decision not to submit the articles to a diplomatic lawmaking conference may be an indication of how dysfunctional they perceive such a conference to be. Third, the arbitrators and other decision makers to whom the articles are addressed (particularly the former) may give too much authority (and therefore influence) to the articles. * * * My experience leads me to believe that these articles will have great influence in arbitration and other adjudicatory processes. Indeed, * * * my concern is not that they will lack effect but, rather, that they will be adopted without sufficient probing by arbitral panels.

Caron, The ILC Articles on State Responsibility: The Paradoxical Relationship Between Form and Authority, 96 A.J.I.L. 857, 858 (2002) (footnotes omitted).

SECTION 2.   ATTRIBUTION OF CONDUCT TO A STATE

APPLICATION OF THE CONVENTION ON THE PREVENTION AND PUNISHMENT OF THE CRIME OF GENOCIDE (BOSNIA & HERZEGOVINA v. SERBIA & MONTENEGRO)

International Court of Justice, 2007
2007 I.C.J. 191

[In the early 1990s, the Socialist Federal Republic of Yugoslavia (S.F.R.Y.) began to break up, with the republics of Bosnia and Herzegovina, Croatia, Macedonia, and Slovenia declaring themselves to be independent states. The republics of Serbia and Montenegro first tried to hold together the S.F.R.Y. and then declared themselves—as the Federal Republic of Yugoslavia (F.R.Y.)—to be the successor state to the S.F.R.Y. See Chapter 5, Section 1. Within Bosnia and Herzegovina, armed conflict broke out during 1992–1995 between the new Bosnian government (dominated by persons of Muslim and Croat heritage) and Bosnian Serbs, who attempted to create their own republic, Republika Srpska, with their own army, the Vojska Republike Srpske (V.R.S.) headed by General Ratko Mladić. In the course of this conflict, various atrocities were committed against the civilian population, culminating in a massacre by Serbian forces of 8,000 Bosnian Muslim men of fighting age at the small mountain town of Srebrenica in July of 1995.

In 1993, Bosnia and Herzegovina brought a case against the F.R.Y. at the International Court of Justice, alleging the F.R.Y. (Serbia–Montenegro) had violated its obligations under the Convention on the Prevention and Punishment of the Crime of Genocide, Dec. 9, 1948, 78 U.N.T.S. 277. In considering whether the F.R.Y.—which later became "Serbia and Montenegro" and then "Serbia" when Montenegro declared its independence—had violated the Genocide Convention, the Court first addressed two questions on attribution of conduct: were the acts committed at Srebrenica committed by an organ of Serbia? If no, were they committed by persons acting on instructions, or under the direction or control, of Serbia?]

385.   The first of these two questions relates to the well-established rule, one of the cornerstones of the law of State responsibility, that the conduct of any State organ is to be considered an act of the State under international law, and therefore gives rise to the responsibility of the State if it constitutes a breach of an international obligation of the State. This rule, which is one of customary international law, is reflected in Article 4 of the ILC Articles on State Responsibility as follows:

"Article 4

Conduct of organs of a State

1.   The conduct of any State organ shall be considered an act of that State under international law, whether the organ exercises

legislative, executive, judicial or any other functions, whatever position it holds in the organization of the State, and whatever its character as an organ of the central Government or of a territorial unit of the State.

2.   An organ includes any person or entity which has that status in accordance with the internal law of the State."

386.   When applied to the present case, this rule first calls for a determination whether the acts of genocide committed in Srebrenica were perpetrated by "persons or entities" having the status of organs of the Federal Republic of Yugoslavia (as the Respondent was known at the time) under its internal law, as then in force. It must be said that there is nothing which could justify an affirmative response to this question. It has not been shown that the FRY army took part in the massacres, nor that the political leaders of the FRY had a hand in preparing, planning or in any way carrying out the massacres. * * * Further, neither the Republika Srpska, nor the VRS were *de jure* organs of the FRY, since none of them had the status of organ of that State under its internal law.

387.   The Applicant has however claimed that all officers in the VRS, including General Mladić, remained under FRY military administration, and that their salaries were paid from Belgrade right up to 2002, and accordingly contends that these officers "were *de jure* organs of [the FRY], intended by their superiors to serve in Bosnia and Herzegovina with the VRS". * * *

388.   The Court notes first that no evidence has been presented that either General Mladić or any of the other officers whose affairs were handled by the 30th Personnel Centre were, according to the internal law of the Respondent, officers of the army of the Respondent—a *de jure* organ of the Respondent. Nor has it been conclusively established that General Mladić was one of those officers; and even on the basis that he might have been, the Court does not consider that he would, for that reason alone, have to be treated as an organ of the FRY for the purposes of the application of the rules of State responsibility. There is no doubt that the FRY was providing substantial support, *inter alia*, financial support, to the Republika Srpska * * *, and that one of the forms that support took was payment of salaries and other benefits to some officers of the VRS, but this did not automatically make them organs of the FRY. Those officers were appointed to their commands by the President of the Republika Srpska, and were subordinated to the political leadership of the Republika Srpska. In the absence of evidence to the contrary, those officers must be taken to have received their orders from the Republika Srpska or the VRS, not from the FRY. * * *

* * *

390.   The argument of the Applicant however goes beyond mere contemplation of the status, under the Respondent's internal law, of the persons who committed the acts of genocide; it argues that Republika

Srpska and the VRS, as well as the paramilitary militias known as the "Scorpions", the "Red Berets", the "Tigers" and the "White Eagles" must be deemed, notwithstanding their apparent status, to have been "*de facto* organs" of the FRY, in particular at the time in question, so that all of their acts, and specifically the massacres at Srebrenica, must be considered attributable to the FRY, just as if they had been organs of that State under its internal law; reality must prevail over appearances. The Respondent rejects this contention, and maintains that these were not *de facto* organs of the FRY.

391. The first issue raised by this argument is whether it is possible in principle to attribute to a State conduct of persons—or groups of persons—who, while they do not have the legal status of State organs, in fact act under such strict control by the State that they must be treated as its organs for purposes of the necessary attribution leading to the State's responsibility for an internationally wrongful act. The Court has in fact already addressed this question, and given an answer to it in principle, in its Judgment of 27 June 1986 in the case concerning *Military and Paramilitary Activities in and against Nicaragua (Nicaragua v. United States of America) (Merits, Judgment, I.C.J. Reports 1986*, pp. 62–64). In paragraph 109 of that Judgment the Court stated that it had to

> "determine . . . whether or not the relationship of the *contras* to the United States Government was so much one of dependence on the one side and control on the other that it would be right to equate the *contras*, for legal purposes, with an organ of the United States Government, or as acting on behalf of that Government" (p. 62).

Then, examining the facts in the light of the information in its possession, the Court observed that "there is no clear evidence of the United States having actually exercised such a degree of control in all fields as to justify treating the *contras* as acting on its behalf" (para. 109), and went on to conclude that "the evidence available to the Court . . . is insufficient to demonstrate [the *contras'*] complete dependence on United States aid", so that the Court was "unable to determine that the *contra* force may be equated for legal purposes with the forces of the United States" (pp. 62–63, para. 110).

392. The passages quoted show that, according to the Court's jurisprudence, persons, groups of persons or entities may, for purposes of international responsibility, be equated with State organs even if that status does not follow from internal law, provided that in fact the persons, groups or entities act in "complete dependence" on the State, of which they are ultimately merely the instrument. In such a case, it is appropriate to look beyond legal status alone, in order to grasp the reality of the relationship between the person taking action, and the State to which he is so closely attached as to appear to be nothing more than its agent: any other solution would allow States to escape their international responsibility by choosing to act through persons or entities whose supposed independence would be purely fictitious.

393.   However, so to equate persons or entities with State organs when they do not have that status under internal law must be exceptional, for it requires proof of a particularly great degree of State control over them, a relationship which the Court's Judgment quoted above expressly described as "complete dependence". It remains to be determined in the present case whether, at the time in question, the persons or entities that committed the acts of genocide at Srebrenica had such ties with the FRY that they can be deemed to have been completely dependent on it; it is only if this condition is met that they can be equated with organs of the Respondent for the purposes of its international responsibility.

394.   The Court can only answer this question in the negative. At the relevant time, July 1995, neither the Republika Srpska nor the VRS could be regarded as mere instruments through which the FRY was acting, and as lacking any real autonomy. While the political, military and logistical relations between the federal authorities in Belgrade and the authorities in Pale, [and] between the Yugoslav army and the VRS, had been strong and close in previous years * * *, and these ties undoubtedly remained powerful, they were, at least at the relevant time, not such that the Bosnian Serbs' political and military organizations should be equated with organs of the FRY. It is even true that differences over strategic options emerged at the time between Yugoslav authorities and Bosnian Serb leaders; at the very least, these are evidence that the latter had some qualified, but real, margin of independence. Nor, notwithstanding the very important support given by the Respondent to the Republika Srpska, without which it could not have "conduct[ed] its crucial or most significant military and paramilitary activities" (*I.C.J. Reports 1986*, p. 63, para. 1ll), did this signify a total dependence of the Republika Srpska upon the Respondent.

395.   * * * The Court therefore finds that the acts of genocide at Srebrenica cannot be attributed to the Respondent as having been committed by its organs or by persons or entities wholly dependent upon it, and thus do not on this basis entail the Respondent's international responsibility.

* * *

398.   On [the second question] the applicable rule, which is one of customary law of international responsibility, is laid down in Article 8 of the ILC Articles on State Responsibility as follows:

"Article 8

Conduct directed or controlled by a State

The conduct of a person or group of persons shall be considered an act of a State under international law if the person or group of persons is in fact acting on the instructions of, or under the direction or control of, that State in carrying out the conduct."

399.   This provision must be understood in the light of the Court's jurisprudence on the subject, particularly that of the 1986 Judgment in the case concerning *Military and Paramilitary Activities in and against Nicaragua (Nicaragua v. United States of America)* referred to above (paragraph 391). In that Judgment the Court, as noted above, after having rejected the argument that the *contras* were to be equated with organs of the United States because they were "completely dependent" on it, added that the responsibility of the Respondent could still arise if it were proved that it had itself "directed or enforced the perpetration of the acts contrary to human rights and humanitarian law alleged by the applicant State" (*I.C.J. Reports 1986*, p. 64, para. 115); this led to the following significant conclusion:

> "For this conduct to give rise to legal responsibility of the United States, it would in principle have to be proved that that State had effective control of the military or paramilitary operations in the course of which the alleged violations were committed." (*Ibid.* p. 65.)

400.   The test thus formulated differs in two respects from the test—described above—to determine whether a person or entity may be equated with a State organ even if not having that status under internal law. First, in this context it is not necessary to show that the persons who performed the acts alleged to have violated international law were in general in a relationship of "complete dependence" on the respondent State; it has to be proved that they acted in accordance with that State's instructions or under its "effective control". It must however be shown that this "effective control" was exercised, or that the State's instructions were given, in respect of each operation in which the alleged violations occurred, not generally in respect of the overall actions taken by the persons or groups of persons having committed the violations.

* * *

402.   The Court notes however that the Applicant has * * * questioned the validity of applying, in the present case, the criterion adopted in the *Military and Paramilitary Activities* Judgment. It has drawn attention to the Judgment of the ICTY Appeals Chamber in the *Tadić* case (IT–94–1–A, Judgment, 15 July 1999). In that case the Chamber did not follow the jurisprudence of the Court in the *Military and Paramilitary Activities* case: it held that the appropriate criterion, applicable in its view both to the characterization of the armed conflict in Bosnia and Herzegovina as international, and to imputing the acts committed by Bosnian Serbs to the FRY under the law of State responsibility, was that of the "overall control" exercised over the Bosnian Serbs by the FRY; and further that that criterion was satisfied in the case * * *. In other words, the Appeals Chamber took the view that acts committed by Bosnian Serbs could give rise to international responsibility of the FRY on the basis of the overall control exercised by the FRY over the Republika Srpska and the VRS, without there being any need to prove that each operation during which

acts were committed in breach of international law was carried out on the FRY's instructions, or under its effective control.

* * *

404. * * * Insofar as the "overall control" test is employed to determine whether or not an armed conflict is international, which was the sole question which the Appeals Chamber was called upon to decide, it may well be that the test is applicable and suitable; the Court does not however think it appropriate to take a position on the point in the present case, as there is no need to resolve it for purposes of the present Judgment. On the other hand, the ICTY presented the "overall control" test as equally applicable under the law of State responsibility for the purpose of determining—as the Court is required to do in the present case—when a State is responsible for acts committed by paramilitary units, armed forces which are not among its official organs. In this context, the argument in favour of that test is unpersuasive.

405. It should first be observed that logic does not require the same test to be adopted in resolving the two issues, which are very different in nature: the degree and nature of a State's involvement in an armed conflict on another State's territory which is required for the conflict to be characterized as international, can very well, and without logical inconsistency, differ from the degree and nature of involvement required to give rise to that State's responsibility for a specific act committed in the course of the conflict.

406. It must next be noted that the "overall control" test has the major drawback of broadening the scope of State responsibility well beyond the fundamental principle governing the law of international responsibility: a State is responsible only for its own conduct, that is to say the conduct of persons acting, on whatever basis, on its behalf. That is true of acts carried out by its official organs, and also by persons or entities which are not formally recognized as official organs under internal law but which must nevertheless be equated with State organs because they are in a relationship of complete dependence on the State. Apart from these cases, a State's responsibility can be incurred for acts committed by persons or groups of persons—neither State organs nor to be equated with such organs—only if, assuming those acts to be internationally wrongful, they are attributable to it under the rule of customary international law reflected in Article 8 cited above (paragraph 398). This is so where an organ of the State gave the instructions or provided the direction pursuant to which the perpetrators of the wrongful act acted or where it exercised effective control over the action during which the wrong was committed. In this regard the "overall control" test is unsuitable, for it stretches too far, almost to breaking point, the connection which must exist between the conduct of a State's organs and its international responsibility.

407. Thus it is on the basis of its settled jurisprudence that the Court will determine whether the Respondent has incurred responsibility

under the rule of customary international law set out in Article 8 of the ILC Articles on State Responsibility.

* * *

410.   The Court was referred to * * * evidence supporting or denying the Respondent's effective control over, participation in, involvement in, or influence over the events in and around Srebrenica in July 1995. The Respondent quotes two substantial reports prepared seven years after the events, both of which are in the public domain, and readily accessible. The first, *Srebrenica—a "safe" area*, published in 2002 by the Netherlands Institute for War Documentation was prepared over a lengthy period by an expert team. The Respondent has drawn attention to the fact that this report contains no suggestion that the FRY leadership was involved in planning the attack or inciting the killing of non-Serbs; nor any hard evidence of assistance by the Yugoslav army to the armed forces of the Republika Srpska before the attack; nor any suggestion that the Belgrade Government had advance knowledge of the attack. * * *

* * *

412.   The second report is *Balkan Battlegrounds*, prepared by the United States Central Intelligence Agency, also published in 2002. The first volume under the heading "The Possibility of Yugoslav involvement" arrived at the following conclusion:

> "No basis has been established to implicate Belgrade's military or security forces in the post-Srebrenica atrocities. * * *" * * *

* * *

413.   In the light of the information available to it, the Court finds, as indicated above, that it has not been established that the massacres at Srebrenica were committed by persons or entities ranking as organs of the Respondent (see paragraph 395 above). It finds also that it has not been established that those massacres were committed on the instructions, or under the direction of organs of the Respondent State, nor that the Respondent exercised effective control over the operations in the course of which those massacres, which * * * constituted the crime of genocide, were perpetrated.

NOTES

1.   *International Law Commission Rules on Attribution.* In the case brought by Bosnia-Herzegovina, the Court cited to two of the articles adopted by the I.L.C. on state responsibility. For the entire series of articles on attribution (Articles 4–11) adopted by the I.L.C., see Report of the International Law Commission, Fifty-third Session, U.N. Doc. A/56/10, at 84–122 (2001). For a historical account in this area, see Hessbruegge, The Historical Development of the Doctrines of Attribution and Due Diligence in International Law, 36 N.Y.U. J. Int'l L. & Pol. 265 (2004).

2.   *Attribution Based on Act/Omission of a State Organ.* Acts or omissions of a state "organ" are attributable to the state. While the Court declined

to find that Serbia committed genocide at Srebrenica, either through its organs or through persons whose acts engaged its responsibility, the Court nevertheless in a portion of the decision not excerpted above found that Serbia violated the Genocide Convention by *failing to take acts to try to prevent* the massacres (given that it had influence over the Bosnian Serb forces) and by failing to transfer Ratko Mladić to the International Criminal Tribunal for the former Yugoslavia (I.C.T.Y.) for prosecution. The Court determined, however, that Serbia was not required to make reparation for its failure to try to prevent the massacres, since it was not clear that, had it tried to do so, the massacres would actually have been prevented.

3. *Acts of Minor Officials*. Does it matter at what level of government the act is committed? There is ample support in diplomatic practice and arbitral awards for attribution to the state of conduct of minor officials, whether of the national government or political subdivisions. A well known example of attribution of the act of an official is the *William T. Way Claim* (United States v. Mexico), 4 U.N. Rep. Int'l Arb. Awards 391 (1928). The United States–Mexico General Claims Commission held the state of Mexico responsible for the actions of a local mayor who had issued an invalid arrest warrant which led to the killing of a U.S. citizen by Mexican law enforcement authorities. The consistent practice of the United States has been to accept responsibility under international law for acts or omissions of agents of its political subdivisions and to require such acceptance by the national governments of foreign states. For example, the United States paid an indemnity to Italy because authorities of the City of New Orleans failed to prevent the lynching of Italian nationals being held for trial. 6 Moore, International Law Digest 837 (1906). Recall that a federal state is responsible for the fulfillment of treaty obligations in its entire territory irrespective of internal division of powers, unless a different rule is specified in the treaty or established as the intention of the parties. See Vienna Convention on the Law of Treaties, art. 29, May 23, 1969, 1155 U.N.T.S. 331. In the cases before the International Court of Justice concerning the failure of state law enforcement officials to provide consular notification to aliens, as required by the Vienna Convention on Consular Relations, the U.S. government accepted that acts of state officials were attributable to the United States as a matter of international law.

4. *Acts of Different Government Branches*. Does separation of powers within a national government affect attribution? Article 4 of the I.L.C. Articles on State Responsibility, quoted above, indicates that it makes no difference whether the organ was part of the executive, legislative, or judicial branch. Can a state be internationally accountable for officials performing entirely domestic duties, irrespective of whether their conduct had been endorsed or known to the officials charged with international matters?

5. *Attribution of Conduct Directed or Controlled by a State*. If an organ of the state did not commit the conduct in question, under what circumstances might it still be attributed to the state? Bosnia-Herzegovina argued that Serbia was responsible for the acts committed by the Bosnian Serb army—why did the Court not agree?

From the Court's decision, it should be apparent that there was tension between the Court's "effective control" test and the I.C.T.Y. Appeals Chamber's "overall control" test in the 1999 *Tadić* case. The Appeals Chamber had construed "general rules on State responsibility" in order to determine whether the Bosnian Serb Army was acting as a de facto organ of the Federal Republic of Yugoslavia (Serbia–Montenegro). See *Prosecutor v. Tadić*, I.C.T.Y. Case No. IT–94–1–AR72, Judgment of Appeal from Conviction, paras. 102–45 (1999). The Appeals Chamber discussed the international law of attribution and imputability in detail, with reference to the I.L.C. Draft Articles and further I.L.C. work through 1998. A noteworthy aspect of this discussion was the I.C.T.Y.'s critique of the judgment of the International Court in *Military and Paramilitary Activities in and against Nicaragua* (Nicaragua v. United States), 1986 I.C.J. 14, where one issue had been whether actions of the Nicaraguan counter-revolutionaries (*contras*) were attributable to the United States.

The I.C.T.Y. considered the I.C.J.'s "effective control" test enunciated in *Nicaragua* to be "unconvincing" in light of "the very logic of the entire system of international law on State responsibility," which the I.C.T.Y. thought should entail a "lower degree of control" than the *Nicaragua* test when the actors in question are organized military or paramilitary groups rather than unorganized individuals. *Prosecutor v. Tadić*, I.C.T.Y. Case No. IT–94–1–AR72, paras. 115, 124 (1999). In applying the lower standard, the Appeals Chamber concluded that the Bosnian Serb armed forces were acting under the "overall control" of and on behalf of the Federal Republic of Yugoslavia (para. 162). When the International Court of Justice revisited this issue in the 2007 *Bosnia v. Serbia* case excerpted above, it declined to follow the approach taken by the I.C.T.Y. Which tribunal do you think had the better approach? For reflections on the Court's 2007 decision by one of the judges in the *Tadić* case, see Cassese, The Nicaragua and Tadic Tests Revisited in Light of the ICJ Judgment of Genocide in Bosnia, 18 E.J.I.L. 649 (2007) (maintaining that attribution of conduct may be found whenever the state exercises "overall control" over the organized armed groups or military units); see also Milanović, State Responsibility for Genocide: A Follow–Up, 18 E.J.I.L. 669 (2007).

6. *Attribution of Conduct Adopted by the State as Its Own.* In *United States Diplomatic and Consular Staff in Tehran* (United States v. Iran), 1980 I.C.J. 3, 29–37, the Court found that certain private persons (student militants) were not acting as an organ of the state when they first seized the hostages. Nevertheless, after the initial seizure of the hostages, the responsibility of Iran for that conduct was found to exist, in part because

> expressions of approval of the take-over of the Embassy, and indeed also of the Consulates at Tabriz and Shiraz, by militants came immediately from numerous Iranian authorities, including religious, judicial, executive, police and broadcasting authorities. Above all, the Ayatollah Khomeini himself made crystal clear the endorsement by the State both of the take-over of the Embassy and Consulates and of the detention of the Embassy staff as hostages.

Id. at para. 71. Article 11 of the I.L.C. Articles on State Responsibility provides "[c]onduct which is not attributable to a State under the preceding articles shall nevertheless be considered an act of that State under international law if and to the extent that the State acknowledges and adopts the conduct in question as its own." U.N. Doc. A/56/10, at 168 (2001). For further analysis of Iranian government responsibility for acts occurring during and after the 1979 Iranian revolution, see Caron, The Basis of Responsibility: Attribution and Other Trans-substantive Rules, in The Iran–United States Claims Tribunal: Its Contribution to the Law of State Responsibility (Lillich, Magraw, & Bederman eds. 1998).

7. *Contemplating Alternative Fact Patterns.* Cases such as *Diplomatic and Consular Staff* and *Application of the Genocide Convention* help provide a conceptual framework for deciding whether conduct should be attributed to a state. Can you contemplate alternative fact patterns where the issue of attribution would be important to analyze and how you would conceptually approach the issue? Suppose a state (e.g., Afghanistan) tolerates the presence of a terrorist organization (e.g., Al Qaeda) for many years, leading up to an attack by that terrorist group on a second state (e.g., the United States). If the government of the first state (e.g., the Taliban) had no prior knowledge that the attack would take place and did not embrace the act as its own, should the attack nevertheless be attributed to the first state, thereby allowing the second state to respond in self-defense? Does it make a difference if the first state declined to hand over members of the terrorist group for prosecution? See Proulx, Babysitting Terrorists: Should States be Strictly Liable for Failing to Prevent Trans-border Attacks?, 23 Berkeley J. Int'l L. 615 (2005); Becker, Terrorism and the State: Rethinking the Rules of State Responsibility (2006). Such issues arise as well in the field of human rights. For example, when do you think a state should incur responsibility on the international plane for failing to protect citizens from "death squads" or for ignoring domestic violence that results in death or serious injury to women and children? See Chapter 13.

SECTION 3. BREACH OF AN INTERNATIONAL OBLIGATION

Article 12 of the I.L.C. Articles on State Responsibility provides: "There is a breach of an international obligation by a State when an act of that State is not in conformity with what is required of it by that obligation, regardless of its origin or character." U.N. Doc. A/56/10, at 124 (2001). This relatively straightforward proposition raises some important and difficult questions. First, in determining whether a breach has occurred, is it sufficient simply to show that the conduct violated the international norm, or is it necessary to show that a state was at fault in some sense (e.g., negligent in its conduct)? Second, does a breach occur even if another state experiences no identifiable injury, or must some cognizable harm occur?

A. FAULT

The I.L.C. Articles on State Responsibility do not establish a general rule requiring that a state be at fault before it can be said that a breach occurs; at the same time, the Articles do not establish a rule of strict liability or any other general rule. Instead, the Articles are neutral on what standard of culpability must exist for a breach to occur, leaving the issue to be addressed by the "primary rules" of the specific obligation at issue in any given case. The final I.L.C. rapporteur on this topic, James Crawford, has written:

> [D]ifferent primary rules of international law impose different standards ranging from "due diligence" to strict liability, and that breach of the correlative obligations gives rise to responsibility without any additional requirements. There does not appear to be any general principle or presumption about the role of fault in relation to any given primary rule, since it depends on the interpretation of that rule in light of its object or purpose. Nor should there be, since the functions of different areas of the law, all underpinned by State responsibility, vary so widely.

Crawford, The International Law Commission's Articles on State Responsibility: Introduction, Text and Commentaries 13 (2002) (footnotes omitted).

The element of "fault" is sometimes raised in connection with the assertion that every state has a general duty to prevent the use of its territory to cause significant harm to other states. Many lawful activities within states (e.g., operating industrial plants that emit sulfur dioxide or nitrous dioxide fumes) may adversely affect neighboring states, or common areas such as the high seas. To establish state responsibility for such harm, is it enough to show that the harm has occurred, or must some element of fault (negligence, lack of good faith, or intentional failure to comply with international standards) also be established?

State responsibility in such cases has sometimes been considered under the principles of "abuse of right" or "liability without fault." However, the trend has been to move away from these general, abstract and vague notions, and instead to define the specific conduct expected by states to prevent harm to other states. Thus, the obligation to avoid harmful environmental damage has been stated as an obligation to take such measures as may be necessary to ensure that activities within the jurisdiction or control of a state conform to international rules and standards for the protection of the environment of other states or areas beyond national jurisdiction. See Restatement (Third) § 601. More specific obligations are then set forth in treaties relating to common waters and marine areas, as well as to Antarctica and outer space. These "primary rules" of conduct determine the elements that are pertinent in deciding whether the obligation has been violated; once a violation is identified, the "secondary rules" of state responsibility determine the consequences of the violation. These matters as they relate to international environmental law are addressed in Chapter 18.

B. INJURY AND LEGAL INTEREST

Does the breach of an obligation give rise to responsibility irrespective of injury caused to another state? It is sometimes said that the answer to this question depends on the primary rule of conduct, and that in the case of some primary rules, a breach does not occur unless and until injury occurs. For example, a state has a duty under international law to protect the embassy of a foreign government, but a breach of that obligation occurs only if the embassy suffers damage; negligence in protection is not itself a breach.

However, in the case of other kinds of primary rules, state responsibility may be engaged even without tangible injury to another state. There may be situations where states claim to have suffered injury in a legal sense, even though they cannot point to specific material harm. Analytically, it is useful to distinguish between situations where harm *could* occur to a given state but remains inchoate at the time of the claim, and situations where the nature of the obligation is such that it is highly unlikely that any other state could ever be materially injured. In either instance, a breach might be found to exist.

An extended discussion of the first kind of situation was given by a dispute settlement panel of the World Trade Organization in a case brought by the European Community (EC) against the United States. The EC complained that under Sections 301–10 of the U.S. Trade Act, the U.S. Trade Representative (U.S.T.R.) is empowered to take certain unilateral actions against other countries that the EC claimed would be incompatible with obligations under the GATT/WTO agreements. The United States defended against the petition on the grounds (*inter alia*) that the EC had suffered no injury, because the U.S.T.R. had not in fact imposed measures against the EC under this section. The EC responded that the very existence of the challenged legislation violated GATT/WTO obligations, even if it had not been applied against the EC and regardless of whether the EC had suffered injury. The dispute settlement panel wrote:

> 7.80. * * * [U]nder traditional public international law, legislation under which an eventual violation could, or even would, subsequently take place, does not normally in and of itself engage State responsibility. If, say, a State undertakes not to expropriate property of foreign nationals without appropriate compensation, its State responsibility would normally be engaged only at the moment foreign property had actually been expropriated in a given instance. * * *

> 7.81. * * * In treaties which concern only the relations between States, State responsibility is incurred only when an actual violation takes place. By contrast, in a treaty the benefits of which depend in

part on the activity of individual operators the legislation itself may be construed as a breach, since the mere existence of legislation could have an appreciable "chilling effect" on the economic activities of individuals.

* * *

7.88.   * * * A law reserving the right for unilateral measures to be taken contrary to [WTO dispute settlement] rules and procedures may—as is the case here—constitute an ongoing threat and produce a "chilling effect" causing serious damage in a variety of ways. [The panel then discussed how that "chilling effect" might operate in the context of the economic decisions of individual operators.]

World Trade Organization, United States—Sections 301–310 of the Trade Act of 1974, Report of the Panel, WTO Doc. WT/DS152/R, paras. 7.80–7.81, 7.88 (1999) (footnotes omitted). The panel went on to conclude, however, that although U.S. responsibility was *prima facie* engaged by the mere existence of GATT-illegal legislation on the statute books, the would-be responsibility was discharged by firm assurances tendered by the United States that the U.S.T.R. would not exercise its statutory discretion in a GATT-incompatible manner. Id. at para. 7.126.

C. *ERGA OMNES* OBLIGATIONS

The second type of situation that implicates state responsibility even in the absence of tangible injury concerns obligations which a state owes generally to treaty partners or to the international community as a whole. Article 48(1) of the I.L.C. Articles on State Responsibility states:

1.   Any State other than an injured State is entitled to invoke the responsibility of another State * * * if:

(a) The obligation breached is owed to a group of States including that State, and is established for the protection of a collective interest of the group; or

(b) The obligation breached is owed to the international community as a whole.

U.N. Doc. A/56/10, at 318 (2001). The I.L.C. Commentary on Article 48(1) states in part:

(6) Under *subparagraph (1)(a)*, States other than the injured State may invoke responsibility if two conditions are met: first, the obligation whose breach has given rise to responsibility must have been owed to a group to which the State invoking responsibility belongs; and second, the obligation must have been established for the protection of a collective interest. The provision does not distinguish between different sources of international law; obligations protecting a collective interest of the group may derive from multilateral treaties or customary international law. Such obligations have sometimes been referred to as "obligations *erga omnes partes*".

(7) Obligations coming within the scope of paragraph (1)(a) have to be "collective obligations", i.e. they must apply between a group of States and have been established in some collective interest. They might concern, for example, the environment or security of a region (e.g., a regional nuclear free zone treaty, or a regional system for the protection of human rights). They are not limited to arrangements established only in the interest of the member States but would extend to agreements established by a group of States in some wider common interest. But in any event the arrangement must transcend the sphere of bilateral relations of the States parties. As to the requirement that the obligation in question protect a collective interest, it is not the function of the articles to provide an enumeration of such interests. If they fall within subparagraph (1)(a), their principal purpose will be to foster a common interest, over and above any interests of the States concerned individually. This would include situations in which States, attempting to set general standards of protection for a group or people, have assumed obligations protecting non-State entities.

(8) Under *subparagraph (1)(b)*, States other than the injured State may invoke responsibility if the obligation in question was owed to "the international community as a whole". The provision intends to give effect to the International Court's statement in the *Barcelona Traction* case, where the Court drew "an essential distinction" between obligations owed to particular States and those "owed towards the international community as a whole". With regard to the latter, the Court went on to state that "[i]n view of the importance of the rights involved, all States can be held to have a legal interest in their protection; they are obligations *erga omnes*".

U.N. Doc. A/56/10, at 320–21 (2001) (footnotes omitted).

As indicated in this Commentary, the International Court of Justice commented on this question in its judgment in the *Barcelona Traction* case. We have already encountered this case in Chapter 7 (on corporate nationality) and will return to it in Chapter 13 (on human rights as *erga omnes* obligations). The following excerpts from the Court's Judgment are pertinent to the issue of state responsibility:

BARCELONA TRACTION, LIGHT AND POWER COMPANY, LTD. (BELGIUM v. SPAIN)
International Court of Justice, 1970
1970 I.C.J. 3

[As noted in Chapter 7, p. 482, proceedings were instituted before the I.C.J. against Spain by the Government of Belgium on behalf of persons (individuals and companies) of Belgian nationality, who were shareholders of Barcelona Traction, Light and Power Company, Limited, a corporation organized under the laws of, and with its registered office in, Canada. Belgium alleged that Spain should be held responsible for acts in violation of international law that caused injury, directly, to the Canadian corporation and, indirectly, to its Belgian shareholders, the value of whose shares was effectively eliminated as a consequence of the injury to the corporation. The portion of the decision in Chapter 7 highlighted how the Court found that Belgium had no standing to pursue an inter-state claim based on harm to a Canadian national (the corporation). This portion of the Court's decision considers whether the alleged obligation of Spain was owed to the international community as a whole, such that Belgium would have standing derived from its membership in the international community.]

33.   When a State admits into its territory foreign investments or foreign nationals, whether natural or juristic persons, it is bound to extend to them the protection of the law and assumes obligations concerning the treatment to be afforded them. These obligations, however, are neither absolute nor unqualified. In particular, an essential distinction should be drawn between the obligations of a State towards the international community as a whole, and those arising vis-à-vis another State in the field of diplomatic protection. By their very nature the former are the concern of all States. In view of the importance of the rights involved, all States can be held to have a legal interest in their protection; they are obligations *erga omnes*.

34.   Such obligations derive, for example, in contemporary international law, from the outlawing of acts of aggression, and of genocide, as also from the principles and rules concerning the basic rights of the human person, including protection from slavery and racial discrimination. Some of the corresponding rights of protection have entered into the body of general international law (*Reservations to the Convention on the Prevention and Punishment of the Crime of Genocide, Advisory Opinion, I.C.J. Reports 1951,* p. 23); others are conferred by international instruments of a universal or quasi-universal character.

35.   Obligations the performance of which is the subject of diplomatic protection are not of the same category. It cannot be held, when one such obligation in particular is in question, in a specific case, that all States have a legal interest in its observance. In order to bring a claim in respect of the breach of such an obligation, a State must first establish its right to do so, for the rules on the subject rest on two suppositions:

> "The first is that the defendant State has broken an obligation towards the national State in respect of its nationals. The second is that only the party to whom an international obligation is due can bring a claim in respect of its breach." (*Reparation for Injuries Suffered in the Service of the United Nations, Advisory Opinion, I.C.J. Reports 1949,* pp. 181–82.)

NOTES

1. *South West Africa Cases.* Before the *Barcelona Traction* case, a similar idea had been asserted in a case brought in the International Court by

Ethiopia and Liberia against South Africa. Those two states claimed that South Africa had violated the League of Nations mandate under which it administered the territory of South West Africa. Ethiopia and Liberia asserted that, as former members of the League, they had a legal interest to vindicate the rights of that community of states in the mandate allegedly violated by South Africa. The Court rejected their claim to legal standing, finding that their claim was analogous to the *actio popularis* in Roman law under which a citizen could request the courts to protect a public interest. The Court observed that the *actio popularis* was "not known to international law as it stands at present." *South West Africa Cases* (Ethiopia v. South Africa; Liberia v. South Africa), 1966 I.C.J. 6, para. 88.

When the Court subsequently endorsed the *erga omnes* conception in the *Barcelona Traction* case, did it imply support of the right of any state to bring an action to protect a "public" or "collective" interest of the community? Such a right, if recognized, would be similar to the *actio popularis*. The concept of *erga omnes* obligations expressed by the Court was generally accepted in the international legal community, including by the Restatement (Third). See Restatement (Third) § 902.

2. *Significance of the Concept.* Notwithstanding the apparent acceptance of the *erga omnes* concept, it has not generated substantial international litigation in the years since its enunciation in the *Barcelona Traction* case, probably because claims based on violation of an *erga omnes* obligation cannot be placed before an international tribunal unless the tribunal has jurisdiction over the two states. In other words, it is not enough for a state to show that it has "standing" to bring a claim; it must also find a tribunal competent to adjudicate the claim. See Chapter 9; see also Lee, Barcelona Traction in the 21st Century: Revisiting its Customary and Policy Underpinning 35 Years Later, 42 Stan. J. Int'l L. 237 (2006).

3. *Desirability of the Concept.* Query whether it would contribute to wider law observance if every state could bring judicial action against a law violator (subject to jurisdictional requirements) for that state's infringement of collective interests. By increasing the class of potential plaintiffs, legal actions for breaches of law might become more common and thus enhance observance of norms that are in the interest of all states. On the other hand, would that very consequence make states more reluctant to submit in advance to jurisdiction of an international tribunal? See discussion in Schachter, International Law in Theory and Practice 342–45 (1991); Schwelb, The Actio Popularis and International Law, 2 Isr. Y.B. Hum. Rts. 47 (1972).

Recognition of *erga omnes* obligations has consequences beyond judicial proceedings. States considered to have a legal interest in vindicating important community or collective interests may assert that interest in relevant non-judicial arenas such as international organs. Or, more importantly, they may take countermeasures unilaterally or jointly against offending states. See Section 6 below. Would such countermeasures strengthen compliance with basic rules of conduct? Is there a danger that in the absence of judicial control every state "in the name of higher values as determined by itself * * * could appoint itself as the avenger of the international community" and thus add to international chaos? See Weil, Towards Relative Normativity in International Law?, 77 A.J.I.L. 413, 433 (1983).

SECTION 4. CIRCUMSTANCES PRECLUDING WRONGFULNESS

Normally an act of state that is not in conformity with an international obligation is an internationally wrongful act entailing responsibility on the part of the state. However, under some special circumstances wrongfulness is precluded. See I.L.C. Articles on State Responsibility, Articles 20–27. The circumstances that are generally considered to have this effect are: consent, *force majeure*, distress, and necessity. Two other categories of state conduct may also be considered to exclude wrongfulness: counter-measures and self-defense. Countermeasures are dealt with in Section 6 of this chapter. Self-defense is treated in Chapter 15 on the use of force. The present section focuses on other circumstances.

RAINBOW WARRIOR (NEW ZEALAND v. FRANCE)

France–New Zealand Arbitration Tribunal, 1990
82 I.L.R. 500, 551–64 (1990)

[Using two highly explosive devices, a team of French agents destroyed the *Rainbow Warrior,* a civilian vessel owned by Greenpeace International, at its moorings in Auckland Harbor, New Zealand, on July 10, 1985. A serious dispute ensued between France, which requested the extradition of two captured agents (Major Alain Mafart and Captain Dominique Prieur), and New Zealand, which sought reparations for the incident. Unable to reach a settlement, France and New Zealand submitted their disagreements to the Secretary–General of the United Nations for binding arbitration.

The Secretary–General's ruling, issued on July 6, 1986, required France to pay reparations of U.S. $7 million and to cease interfering in New Zealand's trade affairs with the European Economic Community. As to extradition, the Secretary–General ordered that Mafart and Prieur be transferred to a French military facility on the isolated island of Hao in French Polynesia for a three-year period. The ruling stipulated that the two agents were "prohibited from leaving the island for any reason, except with the mutual consent of the two Governments." France and New Zealand formalized their understanding of the Secretary–General's ruling in an exchange of letters described as the "1986 Agreement" or the "First Agreement."

About five months after the transfer of the two agents to Hao, France asked New Zealand for permission to transport Major Mafart to a hospital in Paris to undergo urgent medical treatment for an abdominal pain of unknown cause. In the midst of negotiations to acquire New Zealand's consent, France transferred Mafart to Paris. After voicing strong objection to France's unilateral action, New Zealand sent a physician, Dr. R.S.

Croxson, to Paris in order to examine Mafart. Although he expressed doubt as to the necessity of an emergency evacuation, Croxson confirmed that Mafart's medical condition required sophisticated tests that were unavailable in Hao. Croxson continued to observe Mafart on a regular basis; on February 12, 1988, he informed New Zealand that Mafart's medical condition no longer warranted his continued stay in Paris. Instead of returning Mafart to Hao, France declared him "repatriated for health reasons" on March 11, 1988.

A similar episode occurred with Captain Prieur. On May 3, 1988, France requested New Zealand's permission to transfer Prieur to Paris because she was pregnant. New Zealand asked to examine Prieur on Hao before consenting to the transfer. France agreed. However, when French authorities learned that Prieur's father was dying of cancer, they decided "for obvious humanitarian reasons" to fly her to Paris before arrangements to obtain New Zealand's consent were completed.

Soon thereafter, New Zealand and France again submitted their dispute to an arbitral tribunal. New Zealand demanded (1) a declaration that France had breached its obligations by failing to obtain New Zealand's consent prior to the removal of Mafart and Prieur from Hao and (2) an order that France must return the two agents to the island for the balance of their three-year sentences. France denied international responsibility on the theories of *force majeure* and distress. The Tribunal commented, with reference to draft I.L.C. Articles that were renumbered when finalized, as follows:]

Circumstances Precluding Wrongfulness

76. Under the title "Circumstances Precluding Wrongfulness" the International Law Commission proposed in Articles 29 to 35 a set of rules which include three provisions, on *force majeure* and fortuitous event (Article 31), distress (Article 32), and state of necessity (Article 33), which may be relevant to the decision on this case.

* * *

77. * * * [T]here are several reasons for excluding the applicability of the excuse of *force majeure* in this case. As pointed out in the report of the International Law Commission, Article 31 refers to "a situation facing the subject taking the action, which leads it, as it were, *despite itself*, to act in a manner not in conformity with the requirements of an international obligation incumbent on it." * * * *Force majeure* is "generally invoked to justify *involuntary*, or at least unintentional conduct"; it refers "to an irresistible force or an unforeseen external event against which it has no remedy and which makes it 'materially impossible' for it to act in conformity with the obligation," since "no person is required to do the impossible." * * *

* * *

* * * New Zealand is right in asserting that the excuse of *force majeure* is not of relevance in this case because the test of its applicability is of absolute and material impossibility, and because a circumstance rendering performance more difficult or burdensome does not constitute a case of *force majeure*. Consequently, this excuse is of no relevance in the present case.

78. Article 32 of the Articles drafted by the International Law Commission deals with another circumstance which may preclude wrongfulness in international law, namely, that of the "distress" of the author of the conduct which constitutes the act of the State whose wrongfulness is in question.

* * *

The commentary of the International Law Commission explains that " 'distress' means a situation of extreme peril in which the organ of the State which adopts that conduct has, at that particular moment, no means of saving himself or persons entrusted to his care other than to act in a manner not in conformity with the requirements of the obligation in question." * * *

* * *

The question therefore is to determine whether the circumstances of distress in a case of extreme urgency involving elementary humanitarian considerations affecting the acting organs of the State may exclude wrongfulness in this case.

79. In accordance with the previous legal considerations, three conditions would be required to justify the conduct followed by France in respect to Major Mafart and Captain Prieur:

1) the existence of very exceptional circumstances of extreme urgency involving medical or other considerations of an elementary nature, provided always that a prompt recognition of the existence of those exceptional circumstances is subsequently obtained from the other interested party or is clearly demonstrated.

2) The reestablishment of the original situation of compliance with the assignment in Hao as soon as the reasons of emergency invoked to justify the repatriation had disappeared.

3) The existence of a good faith effort to try to obtain the consent of New Zealand in terms of the 1986 Agreement.

The Case of Major Mafart

80. The New Zealand reaction to the French initiative for the removal of Major Mafart appears to have been conducted in conformity with the above considerations.

* * *

81. The sending of Dr. Croxson to examine Major Mafart the same day of the arrival of the latter in Paris [implied] that if the alleged conditions of urgency justifying the evacuation were verified, consent would very likely have been given to what was until then a unilateral removal.

* * *

* * * Dr. Croxson's first report, of 14 December 1987, accepts that Major Mafart needed "detailed investigations which were not available in Hao[.]" * * *

* * *

83. [Dr. Croxson's] sixth report, dated 12 February 1988, on the other hand, evidences that there was by that time a clear obligation of the French authorities to return Major Mafart to Hao, by reason of the disappearance of the urgent medical emergency which had determined his evacuation. This report, together with the absence of other medical reports showing the recurrence of the symptoms which determined the evacuation, demonstrates that Major Mafart should have been returned to Hao at least on 12 February 1988, and that failure to do so constituted a breach by the French Government of its obligations under the First Agreement. * * *

* * *

88. * * * Both parties recognized that the return of Major Mafart to Hao depended mainly on his state of health. Thus, the French Ministry of Foreign Affairs in its note of 30 December 1987 to the New Zealand Embassy referring to France's respect for the 1986 Agreement had said that Major Mafart will return to Hao when his state of health allowed.

Consequently, there was no valid ground for Major Mafart continuing to remain in metropolitan France and the conclusion is unavoidable that this omission constitutes a material breach by the French Government of the First Agreement.

* * *

The Case of Captain Prieur

89. As to the situation of Captain Prieur, the French authorities advised the New Zealand Government, on 3 May 1988, that she was pregnant, adding that a medical report indicated that "this pregnancy should be treated with special care..." The advice added that "the medical facilities on Hao are not equipped to carry out the necessary medical examinations and to give Mrs. Prieur the care required by her condition."

* * *

93.   The facts * * *, which are not disputed, show that New Zealand would not oppose Captain Prieur's departure, if that became necessary because of special care which might be required by her pregnancy. * * *

94.   On the other hand, it appears that during the day of 5 May the French Government suddenly decided to present the New Zealand Government with the fait accompli of Captain Prieur's hasty return for a new reason, the health of Mrs. Prieur's father, who was seriously ill, hospitalized for cancer. * * *

* * *

96.   * * * [D]uring the day of 5 May 1988, France did not seek New Zealand's approval in good faith for Captain Prieur's sudden departure; and accordingly, the return of Captain Prieur, who left Hao on Thursday, 5 May at 11:30 p.m. (French time) and arrived in Paris on Friday, 6 May, thus constituted a violation of the obligations under the 1986 Agreement. * * *

* * *

97.   Moreover, France continued to fall short of its obligations by keeping Captain Prieur in Paris after the unfortunate death of her father on 16 May 1988. * * *

* * *

99.   In summary, the circumstances of distress, of extreme urgency and the humanitarian considerations invoked by France may have been circumstances excluding responsibility for the unilateral removal of Major Mafart without obtaining New Zealand's consent, but clearly these circumstances entirely fail to justify France's responsibility for the removal of Captain Prieur and from the breach of its obligations resulting from the failure to return the two officers to Hao (in the case of Major Mafart once the reasons for their removal had disappeared). There was here a clear breach of its obligations and a breach of material character.

GABČÍKOVO–NAGYMAROS PROJECT
(HUNGARY/SLOVAKIA)

International Court of Justice, 1997
1997 I.C.J. 7

[For the background of this case, see p. 225 *supra*.]

49.   The Court will now consider the question of whether there was, in 1989, a state of necessity which would have permitted Hungary, without incurring international responsibility, to suspend and abandon works that it was committed to perform in accordance with the 1977 Treaty and related instruments.

50.   In the present case, the Parties are in agreement in considering that the existence of a state of necessity must be evaluated in the light of the criteria laid down by the International Law Commission in Article 33

of the Draft Articles on the International Responsibility of States that it adopted on first reading. * * * In its Commentary, the Commission defined the "state of necessity" as being

> "the situation of a State whose sole means of safeguarding an essential interest threatened by a grave and imminent peril is to adopt conduct not in conformity with what is required of it by an international obligation to another State" [Yb.I.L.C. 1980, Vol. II, Part 2, p. 34, para. 1].

It concluded that "the notion of state of necessity is ... deeply rooted in general legal thinking" (*ibid.*, p. 49, para. 31).

51.   The Court considers, first of all, that the state of necessity is a ground recognized by customary international law for precluding the wrongfulness of an act not in conformity with an international obligation. It observes moreover that such ground for precluding wrongfulness can only be accepted on an exceptional basis. The International Law Commission was of the same opinion when it explained that it had opted for a negative form of words in Article 33 of its Draft

> "in order to show, by this formal means also, that the case of invocation of a state of necessity as a justification must be considered as really constituting an exception—and one even more rarely admissible than is the case with the other circumstances precluding wrongfulness ..." (*ibid.*, p. 51, para. 40).

Thus, according to the Commission, the state of necessity can only be invoked under certain strictly defined conditions which must be cumulatively satisfied; and the State concerned is not the sole judge of whether those conditions have been met.

52.   In the present case, the following basic conditions set forth in Draft Article 33 are relevant: it must have been occasioned by an "essential interest" of the State which is the author of the act conflicting with one of its international obligations; that interest must have been threatened by a "grave and imminent peril"; the act being challenged must have been the "only means" of safeguarding that interest; that act must not have "seriously impair[ed] an essential interest" of the State towards which the obligation existed; and the State which is the author of that act must not have "contributed to the occurrence of the state of necessity". Those conditions reflect customary international law.

The Court will now endeavour to ascertain whether those conditions had been met at the time of the suspension and abandonment, by Hungary, of the works that it was to carry out in accordance with the 1977 Treaty.

53.   The Court has no difficulty in acknowledging that the concerns expressed by Hungary for its natural environment in the region affected by the Gabčíkovo–Nagymaros Project related to an "essential interest" of that State, within the meaning given to that expression in Article 33 of the Draft of the International Law Commission.

The Commission, in its Commentary, indicated that one should not, in that context, reduce an "essential interest" to a matter only of the "existence" of the State, and that the whole question was, ultimately, to be judged in the light of the particular case (see *Yearbook of the International Law Commission,* 1980, Vol. II, Part 2, p. 49, para. 32); at the same time, it included among the situations that could occasion a state of necessity, "a grave danger to . . . the ecological preservation of all or some of [the] territory [of a State]" (*ibid.,* p. 35, para. 3); and specified, with reference to State practice, that "It is primarily in the last two decades that safeguarding the ecological balance has come to be considered an 'essential interest' of all States." (*Ibid.,* p. 39, para. 14.)

* * *

54.   The verification of the existence, in 1989, of the "peril" invoked by Hungary, of its "grave and imminent" nature, as well as of the absence of any "means" to respond to it, other than the measures taken by Hungary to suspend and abandon the works, are all complex processes.

* * * Hungary on several occasions expressed, in 1989, its "uncertainties" as to the ecological impact of putting in place the Gabčíkovo–Nagymaros barrage system, which is why it asked insistently for new scientific studies to be carried out.

The Court considers, however, that serious though these uncertainties might have been they could not, alone, establish the objective existence of a "peril" in the sense of a component element of a state of necessity. The word "peril" certainly evokes the idea of "risk"; that is precisely what distinguishes "peril" from material damage. But a state of necessity could not exist without a "peril" duly established at the relevant point in time; the mere apprehension of a possible "peril" could not suffice in that respect. It could moreover hardly be otherwise, when the "peril" constituting the state of necessity has at the same time to be "grave" and "imminent". "Imminence" is synonymous with "immediacy" or "proximity" and goes far beyond the concept of "possibility". As the International Law Commission emphasized in its commentary, the "extremely grave and imminent" peril must "have been a threat to the interest at the actual time" (*Yearbook of the International Law Commission,* 1980, Vol. II, Part 2, p. 49, para. 33). That does not exclude, in the view of the Court, that a "peril" appearing in the long term might be held to be "imminent" as soon as it is established, at the relevant point in time, that the realization of that peril, however far off it might be, is not thereby any less certain and inevitable.

* * *

Both Parties have placed on record an impressive amount of scientific material aimed at reinforcing their respective arguments. The Court has given most careful attention to this material, in which the Parties have developed their opposing views as to the ecological consequences of the Project. It concludes, however, that, as will be shown below, it is not necessary in order to respond to the questions put to it in the Special Agreement for it to determine which of those points of view is scientifically better founded.

55. * * * The Court notes that the dangers ascribed to the upstream reservoir were mostly of a long-term nature and, above all, that they remained uncertain. * * * It follows that, even if it could have been established—which, in the Court's appreciation of the evidence before it, was not the case—that the reservoir would ultimately have constituted a "grave peril" for the environment in the area, one would be bound to conclude that the peril was not "imminent" at the time at which Hungary suspended and then abandoned the works relating to the dam.

56. * * * The Court also notes that, in these proceedings, Hungary acknowledged that, as a general rule, the quality of the Danube waters have improved over the past 20 years, even if those waters remained subject to hypertrophic conditions.

However "grave" it might have been, it would accordingly have been difficult, in the light of what is said above, to see the alleged peril as sufficiently certain and therefore "imminent" in 1989.

The Court moreover considers that Hungary could, in this context also, have resorted to other means in order to respond to the dangers that it apprehended. * * *

57. The Court concludes from the foregoing that, with respect to both Nagymaros and Gabčíkovo, the perils invoked by Hungary, without prejudging their possible gravity, were not sufficiently established in 1989, nor were they "imminent"; and that Hungary had available to it at that time means of responding to these perceived perils other than the suspension and abandonment of works with which it had been entrusted.

NOTES

1. *Consent*. Article 20 of the I.L.C. Articles on State Responsibility provides: "Valid consent by a State to the commission of a given act by another State precludes the wrongfulness of that act in relation to the former State to the extent that the act remains within the limits of that consent." Many cases recognize that, when a state entitled to observance of an obligation agrees to its nonobservance, the other state does not commit an unlawful act by such nonobservance. See *Russian Indemnity Case*, 4 U.N. Rep. Int'l Arb. Awards 421 (1912). May consent be implied or presumed? Is it truly consent if there are elements of coercion? Would implicit threats of invasion invalidate consent? Would threats of economic retaliation? See Abass, Consent Precluding State Responsibility: A Critical Analysis, 53 I.C.L.Q. 211 (2004).

2. *Consent and Military Intervention*. The entry of foreign troops into territory of another state, which would normally be unlawful, becomes lawful if it took place with the consent of that state. Many cases involving such entry of troops have occurred, a number were considered by the U.N. General

Assembly and Security Council, and the basic principle of consent as a legitimating factor was not challenged. Differences of opinion arose, however, on whether consent had been validly expressed on behalf of the state, whether rights of other states were violated, or whether a peremptory norm was infringed. Among such cases were those involving the entry of Soviet troops into Hungary (1956), Czechoslovakia (1968) and Afghanistan (1979), and the entry of U.S. troops into Lebanon (1958), Grenada (1983), and Panama (1989). Can a state consent in advance to the entry of foreign troops upon the occurrence of a condition, such as the overthrow of its democratic government? See Chapter 15.

3. *Consent and Third States or Persons.* Consent precludes the wrongfulness of an act only in relation to the state giving consent. However, the act of consent itself may be a breach toward another state. For example, consenting to the deployment of troops to one's country may involve a breach to another state (as for example where a treaty of neutrality is violated). Injury to nationals of a consenting state in violation of an international convention may also involve a breach toward other parties to the convention. The conventions on human rights are pertinent.

4. *Force Majeure.* Article 23(1) of the I.L.C. Articles on State Responsibility provides: "The wrongfulness of an act of a State not in conformity with an international obligation of that State is precluded if the act is due to *force majeure*, that is the occurrence of an irresistible force or of an unforeseen event, beyond the control of the State, making it materially impossible in the circumstances to perform the obligation." *Force majeure* is frequently invoked as a reason for excluding wrongfulness. Although the use of the term is not uniform in practice, the situations covered have one common feature: the State organs are involuntarily placed in a situation which makes it "materially impossible" for them to adopt conduct in conformity with the requirements of an international obligation incumbent on their State or to realize that the conduct they are engaging in is not of the character required.

Examples of such situations have often arisen when vessels or aircraft have entered the territory of another state without prior consent. Such entry may be due to bad weather or defects in equipment that made entry unavoidable or made it impossible for the pilot to know he had made an error. While such situations are not treated as international wrongs, disputes about them arise because facts and motives may not be verifiable. For example, the shooting down in 1983 by a Soviet military plane of a Korean passenger plane in flight over the U.S.S.R. in eastern Asia was followed by charges and counter-charges as to whether the plane had erroneously diverted from its course or had done so intentionally. If fortuitous events, such as equipment failure, had been responsible for the pilot to go off course unknowingly, then the flight would not have been wrongful. See Report of the International Civil Aviation Organization, Air Navigation Commission's Review and Council Resolution Condemning the Destruction of the Aircraft, 23 I.L.M. 1924 (1984). In some cases the state claiming *force majeure* may have contributed to the occurrence of the event. It may, for example, have failed to provide adequate guidance to an aircraft that intruded into foreign territory. It would seem doubtful in that case that the state should be able to disclaim responsibility because of *force majeure*.

5. *Force Majeure and Debt. Force majeure* has also been invoked as a ground for a state to avoid payment of its debt. Two cases that reached the Permanent Court of International Justice involved pleas by debtor states that they were unable to pay in gold as required by the loan agreement. In both cases, the defense was unsuccessful on the ground that it was not in fact impossible for the states to pay in gold or equivalent value. See *Serbian Loans* (France v. Yugoslavia), 1929 P.C.I.J. (ser. C.) No. 16–III; *Brazilian Loans* (Brazil/France), 1929 P.C.I.J. (ser. A.) No. 20/21, at 33–40. Would *force majeure* in the sense of "material impossibility" or "irresistible force" apply when the debtor state could not pay without imposing severe hardships on its inhabitants?

6. *Distress.* Article 24(1) of the I.L.C. Articles on State Responsibility provides: "The wrongfulness of an act of a State not in conformity with an international obligation of that State is precluded if the author of the act in question has no other reasonable way, in a situation of distress, of saving the author's life or the lives of other persons entrusted to the author's care." The concept of "distress" differs from *force majeure* in that, for the former, conformity with the obligation is *possible*, but would result in a loss of life. Distress has been invoked as an excuse when a frontier was violated by a vessel or aircraft to save lives in peril. See Lissitzyn, Treatment of Aerial Intruders in Recent Practice and International Law, 47 A.J.I.L. 559 (1953). Multilateral conventions on the law of the sea and marine pollution contain exculpatory provisions for both *force majeure* and distress. See U.N. Convention on the Law of the Sea, arts. 18(2) & 39(1)(e) Dec. 10, 1982, 1833 U.N.T.S. 3; International Convention for the Prevention of Pollution of the Sea by Oil, art. IV, May 12, 1954, 327 U.N.T.S. 3. Do you think the *Rainbow Warrior* case was correctly decided on this issue? See Pugh, Legal Aspects of the Rainbow Warrior Affair, 36 I.C.L.Q. 655 (1987). Would "distress" be a legitimate ground for a state to refuse to pay a debt if such payment would require so substantial a reduction in living standards as to cause starvation or higher rates of infant mortality? Leaders of some debtor countries have raised this issue.

7. *Necessity.* Necessity as a ground for precluding wrongfulness differs from *force majeure* in that the former involves a deliberate act not to conform to the obligation (whereas the latter involves material impossibility to conform with the obligation or to realize the conduct is contrary to the obligation). A state of necessity is an intentional breach, one that is considered necessary to safeguard an "essential interest" of the state against a "grave and imminent peril." See Article 25(1)(a) of the I.L.C. Articles on State Responsibility.

What are the "essential interests" of the state that justify breaking international obligations when such interests are endangered? Presumably maintaining the existence of the state itself is an essential interest. What about the maintenance of conditions in which essential services can function, the keeping of domestic peace, the survival of a portion of the state's population, or the ecological preservation of all or some of its territory? For example, may a state invoke necessity to avoid payment of a financial debt on the ground the payment would clearly entail such disruption of its public services as to jeopardize public order and economic life of the country? See

Société Commerciale de Belgique (Belgium v. Greece), 1939 P.C.I.J. (ser. A/B) No. 78, at 19 (implicitly accepting such a proposition). Would a "state of necessity" justify an incursion into foreign territory to rescue or protect endangered persons detained by hostile forces not under the control of the territorial state? In the context of the NATO intervention in Kosovo in 1999, some scholars argued that a justification on the ground of necessity was preferable to creating a new exception to the general prohibition on the use of force. Do the I.L.C. Articles provide any support for such an argument? Some treaties explicitly or implicitly exclude necessity as an excuse for non-performance. For example, the non-derogable provisions of human rights treaties cannot be infringed on grounds of necessity.

8. *Peremptory Norms*. Article 26 of the I.L.C. Articles on State Responsibility provides that none of these circumstances excuses transgression of a peremptory norm of international law. U.N. Doc. A/56/10, at 26 (2001). Hence, even freely given consent by a state would not absolve another state from responsibility where the second state's obligation was *jus cogens*. Would a government be free to consent to another state's commission of genocide against the first state's people? Or is the second state still responsible for its conduct? See pp. 108–112.

9. *Allocating the Costs*. Should a state that justifiably invokes one of the circumstances precluding wrongfulness be required nonetheless to pay compensation for material damage due to its violation of the obligation? Such payment of compensation would not be reparation for "a wrongful act", but is there any reason why it could not be a separate "primary" obligation of the state that caused injury by its own deliberate act? See I.L.C. Article 27(b).

SECTION 5. REPARATION FOR THE BREACH OF AN INTERNATIONAL OBLIGATION

If a state has committed an act that breaches an international obligation and thereby causes injury, the state is obliged to make "reparation" for the injury. "Reparation" is a generic term that covers various methods by which a state can discharge or release itself from its responsibility. See Jiménez de Aréchaga, International Law in the Past Third of a Century, 159 Rec. des Cours 285–87 (1978–I). As for the extent of reparation that is due, the Permanent Court of International Justice famously stated:

> [R]eparation must, as far as possible, wipe out all the consequences of the illegal act and re-establish the situation which would, in all probability, have existed if that act had not been committed. Restitution in kind, or, if this is not possible, payment of a sum corresponding to the value which a restitution in kind would bear; the award, if need be, of damages for loss sustained which would not be covered by restitution in kind or payment in place of it—such are the principles which should serve to determine the amount of compensation due for an act contrary to international law.

Factory at Chorzów (Germany v. Poland), 1928 P.C.I.J. (ser. A) No. 17, at 47–48. Article 34 of the I.L.C. Articles on State Responsibility asserts that "[f]ull reparation for the injury caused by the internationally wrongful act shall take the form of restitution, compensation and satisfaction, either singly or in combination, in accordance with the provisions of this chapter." According to Article 35, restitution is not the required remedy if it is not materially possible or imposes "a burden out of all proportion to the benefit deriving from restitution instead of compensation." Article 37(2) provides that "[s]atisfaction may consist in an acknowledgement of the breach, an expression of regret, a formal apology or another appropriate modality."

NOTES

1. *Restitution-in-kind or Compensation?* In the *Factory at Chorzów* case, the Permanent Court seemed to favor restitution (i.e., reestablishing the *status quo ante*) as a form of reparation, when it stated that states should make "[r]estitution in kind, or, if this is not possible, payment of a sum." In practice, however, it does not appear that restitution is always the favored remedy. In the *Avena* case before the International Court, Mexico established that the United States failed to notify numerous Mexican nationals after their arrest of their right to consular access, in violation of the Vienna Convention on Consular Relations, and that thereafter the Mexicans were convicted and sentenced to death in U.S. courts. Mexico sought a remedy that would "restore the *status quo ante*, by annulling or otherwise depriving of full force or effect the conviction and sentences" of the Mexicans. The Court declined to grant such reparation, but did order the United States to allow within its courts "review and reconsideration" of the conviction and sentence of each Mexican, taking into account the effects of the violation of the Vienna Convention. *Avena and Other Mexican Nationals* (Mexico v. U.S.), 2004 I.C.J. 12, paras. 128–34, 140–43; see also *LaGrand* (Germany v. U.S.), 2001 I.C.J. 466, para. 125.

Should restitution-in-kind be the preferred remedy when a state contracts with individuals? In *British Petroleum v. Libya*, the sole arbitrator (Judge Lagergren) extensively reviewed the authorities on reparation and decided that restitution would not be a proper remedy in case of confiscation of a rights to oil extraction in breach of the concession agreement. *British Petroleum v. Libya*, 53 I.L.R. 297, 346–48 (1979). See Buxbaum, A Legal History of International Reparations, 23 Berkeley J. Int'l L. 314 (2005); Kirgis, Restitution as a Remedy in U.S. Courts for Violations of International Law, 95 A.J.I.L. 341 (2001).

2. *Scope of Compensable Damages.* Compensation may be for both direct and indirect damages. In the context of an ongoing company, compensation has, at times, been awarded both for the direct harm to the company (sometimes referred to as *damnum emergens*, based on the Roman law concept) and for lost future profits (*lucrum cessans*). Precedents for the scope of damages may be found in myriad cases dating back more than one hundred years. For a useful compendium and categorization of such cases up until the mid-twentieth century, see Whiteman, Damages in International Law (1937) (3 vols.). More recent case law may be found in some of the important arbitral

institutions that have been set up, such as the Iran–U.S. Claims Tribunal, the U.N. Compensation Commission (whose jurisdiction, however, was limited to "direct" loss or damage; see. S.C. Res. 687, para. 16 (Apr. 3, 1991)), the Eritrea Ethiopia Claims Commission, and NAFTA and ICSID arbitrations. Even the new International Criminal Court is empowered to decide upon reparation for victims of war crimes. See Rome Statute of the International Criminal Court, art. 75, July 17, 1998, 2187 U.N.T.S. 3; see also Di Giovanni, The Prospect of ICC Reparations in the Case Concerning Northern Uganda: On a Collision Course with Incoherence?, 2 J. Int'l L. & Int'l Rel. 25 (2006) (expressing concern about awarding reparations if it conflicts with larger goals of transitional justice).

3. *Satisfaction.* One form of "satisfaction" is simply an apology or expression of regret by the wrongdoing state. See Bilder, The Role of Apology in International Law and Diplomacy, 46 Va. J. Int'l L. 433 (2006). Another is a guaranty or assurance by the wrongdoer that there will be no repetition of the wrongful act. See Tams, Recognizing Guarantees and Assurances of Non–Repetition: *LaGrand* and the Law of State Responsibility, 27 Yale J. Int'l L. 441 (2002). Yet often an international tribunal that has determined the existence of a violation of international law, but no tangible or material injury, will declare that its own finding is sufficient reparation, without requiring any further action by the wrongdoer. For example, in *Corfu Channel*, Albania felt affronted by an unlawful mine-sweeping operation by the British Navy in Albania's territorial waters. The I.C.J. said that "to ensure respect for international law, of which it is the organ, the Court must declare that the action of the British Navy constituted a violation of Albanian sovereignty. This declaration is in accordance with the request made by Albania through her Counsel, and is in itself appropriate satisfaction." *Corfu Channel* (United Kingdom v. Albania), 1949 I.C.J. 4, 35. More recently, Djibouti sued France before the International Court, claiming that France failed to execute a letter rogatory that sought information on a murder case, in violation of France's obligation under a 1986 Convention on Mutual Assistance in Criminal Matters. Djibouti asked that the Court not only determine the existence of a violation, but also order France to publish the reasons for its failure to comply. The Court agreed that France had violated Article 17 of the convention by refusing to give its reasons for not executing the letter rogatory, but rather than order France to disclose those reasons (which the Court found had already passed into the public domain), the Court decided that its finding of a violation constituted appropriate satisfaction for that violation. *Certain Questions of Mutual Assistance in Criminal Matters* (Djibouti v. France), 2008 I.C.J. ___, para. 205(2)(a). At the same time, a state that offers to make an apology, or that has already apologized, does not necessarily avoid other forms of reparation. See *LaGrand* (Germany v. U.S.), 2001 I.C.J. 466, para. 125 (finding that "an apology would not suffice in cases where the individuals concerned have been subjected to prolonged detention or convicted and sentenced to severe penalties").

4. *Specific Performance.* Since the primary obligation of the violating state is to undo the wrong and discontinue the acts that caused the violation, tribunals have occasionally issued orders directing the respondent state to take such steps. In the Iranian hostage case, the International Court of

Justice ordered Iran to release the hostages and turn over the premises and archives of the U.S. Embassy to the Protecting Power. *United States Diplomatic and Consular Staff in Tehran* (United States v. Iran), 1980 I.C.J. 3, 45. Specific performance may be especially important in cases involving continuing environmental damage, an increasingly important topic of international claims. In *Gabčíkovo–Nagymaros Project* (Hungary/Slovakia), 1997 I.C.J. 7, the parties had asked the Court to determine future conduct as well as the legal consequences of past conduct. The Court did so not by specifying the particular steps that either party would be required to take, but by instructing the parties to negotiate within the general framework of the legal principles that the Court had laid down, in order to implement a joint operational regime for the project in question. Id. at paras. 131–50.

5. *Interest*. The breaching state is obligated to pay interest on the principal sum due, from the date the sum is due until the date it is paid, if interest is appropriate for ensuring full reparation. See I.L.C. Articles on State Responsibility, art. 38. The level of interest used has varied considerably. The P.C.I.J. in the *S.S. "Wimbledon"* case awarded 6% interest, while commercial claims before the Iran–U.S. Claims Tribunal were typically (but not uniformly) awarded 12% interest. See *S.S. "Wimbledon"*, 1923 P.C.I.J. (ser. A) No. 1, at 32; Aldrich, The Jurisprudence of the Iran–United States Claims Tribunal 475–76 (1996). International law appears to accord states and tribunals considerable latitude to award a level of interest deemed appropriate for compensating the injured party. Although most international courts and tribunals have awarded simple interest, a growing number have concluded that compound interest is the only appropriate way of insuring full reparation to an injured state or national. See Tecnicas Medioambientales Tecmed S.a. ("Tecmed") v. Mexico, ICSID Case No. ARB(AF)/00/2, Award, 43 I.L.M. 133, para. 196 (2004) (and citations therein) (reproduced in Chapter 14, Section 5). For the position of the United States, see Memorial of United States, *Elettronica Sicula S.p.A. (ELSI)* (United States v. Italy), 1987 I.C.J. Pleadings 114–15 (filed May 15, 1987). For a careful assessment of the jurisprudence of the past fifty years of international courts, tribunals, and commissions, see Nevill, Awards of Interest by International Courts and Tribunals, 78 B.Y.I.L. 255 (2008).

SECTION 6.   COUNTERMEASURES

A state injured by another state's violation of an international obligation is entitled to take measures against the offending state as a means of inducing that state's compliance. Such unilateral measures are sometimes described as "self-help" or as "countermeasures." More specific legal terms are used to describe three different kinds of unilateral measures, as follows:

- *Reprisal* refers to countermeasures that would be unlawful if not for the prior illegal act of the state against which they were taken. Reprisals under traditional international law sometimes involved use of force but they also include non-forcible measures.

- *Reciprocal measures* or measures "by way of reciprocity" refer to non-performance by the injured state of its obligations toward the offending state when such obligations correspond to or are directly connected with the obligations breached.

• *Retorsion* refers to measures of the injured state against the offending state that are generally permissible in international law irrespective of the prior breach (for example, suspending diplomatic relations or bilateral aid).

The articles developed by the International Law Commission on countermeasures have proven to be among the most controversial, as they embody a series of compromises between arguably irreconcilable positions. On the one hand are those who would affirm the need for self-help measures in a world that does not yet have a central authority to deal with violations of the primary rules of international law. On the other hand are those who would emphasize the need for strict limitations on the use of self-help, in order to prevent abuses (especially by strong states against weaker ones) and to provide for procedural controls including dispute settlement.

As you read the materials in this section, consider whether you think there should be substantive or procedural limitations on the right to the resort to countermeasures. For example, as a substantive limitation, should the countermeasures be proportional to the breach? As a procedural limitation, must the state engaging in the countermeasures be willing to resolve the matter through compulsory dispute settlement?

GABČÍKOVO–NAGYMAROS PROJECT (HUNGARY/SLOVAKIA)

International Court of Justice, 1997
1997 I.C.J. 7

[For the background of this case, see p. 225. In the following excerpt, the Court considered Slovakia's contention that it was entitled to implement a significant variation from the original plan for the Danube River project, known as "Variant C," in response to Hungary's previous repudiation of the plans established by the 1977 Treaty between the parties.]

82. Although it did not invoke the plea of countermeasures as a primary argument, since it did not consider Variant C to be unlawful, Slovakia stated that "Variant C could be presented as a justified countermeasure to Hungary's illegal acts".

The Court has concluded, in paragraph 78 above, that Czechoslovakia committed an internationally wrongful act in putting Variant C into operation. Thus, it now has to determine whether such wrongfulness may be precluded on the ground that the measure so adopted was in response to Hungary's prior failure to comply with its obligations under international law.

83. In order to be justifiable, a countermeasure must meet certain conditions (see *Military and Paramilitary Activities in and against Nicaragua (Nicaragua v. United States of America), Merits, Judgment, I.C.J.*

Reports 1986, p. 127, para. 249. See also *Arbitral Award of 9 December 1978 in the case concerning the Air Services Agreement of 27 March 1946 between the United States of America and France,* United Nations, *Reports of International Arbitral Awards (RIAA),* Vol. XVIII, pp. 443 *et seq.:* also Articles 47 to 50 of the Draft Articles on State Responsibility adopted by the International Law Commission on first reading * * *.

In the first place it must be taken in response to a previous international wrongful act of another State and must be directed against that State. Although not primarily presented as a countermeasure, it is clear that Variant C was a response to Hungary's suspension and abandonment of works and that it was directed against that State; and it is equally clear, in the Court's view, that Hungary's actions were internationally wrongful.

84.   Secondly, the injured State must have called upon the State committing the wrongful act to discontinue its wrongful conduct or to make reparation for it. It is clear from the facts of the case, as recalled above by the Court (see paragraphs 61 *et seq.*) that Czechoslovakia requested Hungary to resume the performance of its treaty obligations on many occasions.

85.   In the view of the Court, an important consideration is that the effects of a countermeasure must be commensurate with the injury suffered, taking account of the rights in question.

In 1929, the Permanent Court of International Justice, with regard to navigation on the River Oder, stated as follows:

> "[the] community of interest in a navigable river becomes the basis of a common legal right, the essential features of which are the perfect equality of all riparian States in the user of the whole course of the river and the exclusion of any preferential privilege of any one riparian State in relation to the others" (*Territorial Jurisdiction of the International Commission of the River Oder, Judgment No. 16, 1929, P.C.I.J., Series A, No. 23,* p. 27).

Modern development of international law has strengthened this principle for non-navigational uses of international watercourses as well, as evidenced by the adoption of the Convention of 21 May 1997 on the Law of the Non–Navigational Uses of International Watercourses by the United Nations General Assembly.

The Court considers that Czechoslovakia, by unilaterally assuming control of a shared resource, and thereby depriving Hungary of its right to an equitable and reasonable share of the natural resources of the Danube—with the continuing effects of the diversion of these waters on the ecology of the riparian area of the Szigetköz—failed to respect the proportionality which is required by international law.

* * *

87.   The Court thus considers that the diversion of the Danube carried out by Czechoslovakia was not a lawful countermeasure because it

was not proportionate. It is therefore not required to pass upon one other condition for the lawfulness of a countermeasure, namely that its purpose must be to induce the wrongdoing State to comply with its obligations under international law, and that the measure must therefore be reversible.

NOTES

1. *Proportionality of Countermeasures*. Article 51 of the I.L.C. Articles on State Responsibility provides: "Countermeasures must be commensurate with the injury suffered, taking into account the gravity of the internationally wrongful act and the rights in question." Is proportionality a quantitative or qualitative concept? What understanding of proportionality did the I.C.J. apply in the *Gabčíkovo–Nagymaros Project* case? See Franck, On Proportionality of Countermeasures in International Law, 102 A.J.I.L. 715 (2008); Damrosch, Enforcing International Law Through Non–Forcible Measures, 269 Rec. des Cours 9, 57–60 (1997). The tribunal in the *Air Services* arbitration, referred to in the excerpt above at para. 83, said that countermeasures must have "some degree of equivalence with the breach" (para. 83). This suggests a "tit for tat" response to a breach. But is that always permissible? Would the United States have had the right to hold Iranian diplomats as hostages in 1979–1981 because the Iranians unlawfully held hostage U.S. diplomats? Are not some countermeasures, although "equivalent," impermissible because they are contrary to peremptory norms or recognized humanitarian principles? How difficult, in practice, are the concepts of "proportionality" and "equivalence" to apply? Is it always possible to weigh the equivalence of countermeasures against the wrongful act?

2. *Reversibility/Impermissibility of Countermeasures*. What is the basis for the suggestion in I.L.C. Article 49(3) that a countermeasure must be reversible? In *Gabčíkovo-Nagymaros Project*, the Court assumed the existence of such a requirement but found it unnecessary to decide whether Slovakia's diversion would have met such a test. Would such a limitation rule out measures whose effects might persist after the measure itself had been removed? Article 50 of the I.L.C. Articles on State Responsibility lists several types of acts that cannot be undertaken as countermeasures, including violations of human rights, humanitarian law, peremptory norms of general international law, and U.N. Charter norms on the use of force.

3. *Reciprocal Non-performance*. Should a distinction be made between a countermeasure in the nature of reprisal and non-performance of an obligation in response to a breach of the same or equivalent obligation by the other party? The latter has been referred to in international law jurisprudence as the principle of *inadimplenti non est adimplendum* (no performance is due to a non-performer), described by Judge Anzilotti as "so just, so equitable, so universally recognized." *The Diversion of Water from the Meuse*, 1937 P.C.I.J. (ser. A/B) No. 70, at 50 (Dissenting Opinion of Judge Anzilotti). What criteria are relevant for differentiating non-performance as a measure of reciprocity from non-performance as a measure of self-help subject to limita-

tions imposed by international law? For general discussion of reciprocity and unilateral remedies, see Zoller, Peacetime Unilateral Remedies 14–27 (1984).

4. *Relevance of an Arbitral and Judicial Forum.* Should a countermeasure generally be impermissible where an agreement between the parties provides for compulsory arbitral or judicial settlement? An affirmative answer was given by the Institut de Droit International in 1934, Resolutions votées par l'Institut, art. 5, 38 Ann. de l'Institut de Droit Int. 708, 709–10 (1934), as well as some scholars. See, e.g., Stein, Contempt, Crisis and the Court, 76 A.J.I.L. 512 (1982); Bowett, Economic Coercion and Reprisal by States, 13 Va. J. Int'l L. 1 (1972); Dumbauld, Interim Measures of Protection in International Controversies 182–84 (1932). Yet Article 52(3) of the I.L.C. Articles on State Responsibility provides: "Countermeasures may not be taken, and if already taken must be suspended without undue delay if: (*a*) the internationally wrongful act has ceased; and (*b*) the dispute is pending before a court or tribunal which has the authority to make decisions binding on the parties." Why the difference? Damrosch maintains that a victim state should not be required to "embark on lengthy and expensive litigation" before it may suspend its performance in the event of breach. Damrosch, Retaliation or Arbitration—or Both?, 74 A.J.I.L. 785, 806 (1980). The "interplay and even escalation of responses before a dispute reaches a tribunal can serve important purposes." Id. at 807. Do you agree? Is it preferable to make the exhaustion of amicable settlement procedures a parallel obligation, rather than a precondition, for resort to countermeasures—that is, the injured state could take countermeasures until such time as the wrongdoing state agreed to a dispute settlement procedure? Or would the immediate imposition of countermeasures put the injured state in an unfair position of strength in any ensuing negotiations agreed to by the wrongdoing state? Would it make a difference if you knew whether the tribunal was capable of protecting the aggrieved state from injury during the pendency of the case?

5. *Targeting Individuals.* May countermeasures against a state's wrongful conduct take the form of sanctions against individuals because they are nationals of the offending state? May the assets of individuals be frozen or seized on the ground that the state of which they are nationals has acted wrongfully? A U.S. court held such action permissible with respect to Cuban nationals in the United States, *Sardino v. Federal Reserve Bank of N.Y.*, 361 F.2d 106 (2d Cir. 1966). The court observed that "the Constitution protects the alien from arbitrary action by our government but not from reasonable response to such action by his own." Id. at 111. Does international law impose a limit? For example if the state whose nationals were affected maintains that the "freeze" of assets was disproportionate or arbitrary, an international law issue would be raised. See Restatement (Third) § 905. Would retaliatory action against individuals for the wrongs of their states raise human rights issues based on invidious discrimination or disproportionate penalties? See *Narenji v. Civiletti*, 617 F.2d 745 (D.C. Cir. 1979), upholding U.S. regulations that required Iranian students in the United States during the Iranian hostage crisis to report to the U.S. Immigration and Naturalization Service for a check on their compliance with their visas. U.S. legislation on countermeasures generally includes procedural provisions to protect individuals af-

fected from arbitrary action. See Zoller, Enforcing International Law Through U.S. Legislation 42–57 (1985).

6. *Self–Contained Regimes.* There is considerable disagreement over whether states belonging to a so-called "self-contained regime"—defined generally as an international regime creating both substantive obligations *and* special procedures in the event of a breach—may resort to countermeasures based on general international law in addition to the remedies specified by the regime's constitutive instrument. In the *United States Diplomatic and Consular Staff in Tehran* case, the International Court of Justice found that the regime of diplomatic law constituted a "self-contained regime," so that Iran's possibility of taking self-help measures against alleged breaches by U.S. personnel was limited to declaring them *personae non grata* and sending them home. 1980 I.C.J. 3, para. 86. Some commentators have found examples of "self-contained regimes" in the European Community, in certain human rights systems (such as under the European Convention on Human Rights and Fundamental Freedoms), or in trade agreements under the auspices of the World Trade Organization, all of which establish not just substantive rights but also compulsory dispute settlement procedures. See, e.g., Charnovitz, Rethinking WTO Trade Sanctions, 95 A.J.I.L. 792 (2001); Mitchell, Proportionality and Remedies in WTO Disputes, 17 E.J.I.L. 985 (2006). Other commentators, however, criticize the whole notion of "self-contained regimes." Compare Simma, Self–Contained Regimes, 16 Neth. Y.B.I.L. 111 (1985) with Zemanek, The Legal Foundations of the International System, 266 Rec. des Cours 9, 235–36, 332 (1997).

7. *Is Actual Injury Required?* Must a state show actual injury in order to resort to countermeasures or is a mere breach of international law sufficient for a state to act? I.L.C. Article 49(1) states that an "injured" state may "undertake" countermeasures. U.N. Doc. A/56/10, at 328–33 (2001). Why would the I.L.C. limit countermeasures only to states that are actually injured? A former I.L.C. special rapporteur on state responsibility, Willem Riphagen, said that the International Law Commission should "take the greatest care, in devising the conditions of lawful resort to such actions, to ensure that the factual inequalities among States do not unduly operate to the advantage of the strong and rich over the weak and needy." Report of the International Law Commission on the Work of Its Forty-third Session, U.N. Doc. A/46/10, at 327 (1991). Do you think there is an inherent risk in a liberal regime of countermeasures that a powerful nation could assume for itself a role as the "world's police" to enforce its own conception of the law, such that requiring actual injury may help contain that risk? Or does such a requirement under-mine the ability to react to important breaches of international law? See Damrosch, Enforcing International Law Through Non–Forcible Measures, 269 Rec. des Cours 9, 50–54 (1997) (on the application of the concept of "injured state" and "effects" for purposes of taking countermeasures in cases of human rights violations). Note that in 1999 the European Union interrupted air services to the Federal Republic of Yugoslavia in response to violations of human rights and humanitarian law in Kosovo. Assuming that this ban would otherwise have breached existing air services agreements in force with Yugoslavia, it could only be justified if the conditions for resort to countermeasures were met.

8. *Countermeasures to a Violation of a Multilateral Treaty.* A state injured by a breach of a multilateral treaty may suspend its performance of obligations toward the state that acted wrongfully. Article 60(2)(b) of the Vienna Convention on the Law of Treaties provides that a party "specially affected by the breach may invoke it as a ground for suspending the operation of the treaty in whole or in part in the relations between itself and the defaulting State." 1155 U.N.T.S. 331. However, certain exceptions to this broad right appear to be required under the law of treaties. First, suspending performance of the obligation toward a defaulting state may adversely affect the rights of all other parties to the multilateral treaty. In that case the countermeasure would injure third states as well as the offending state. An example is a breach of a multilateral treaty concerning pollution. If a party suspends its restraints on pollution with respect to a state guilty of violation it almost surely will also injure other states parties to the treaty. In some cases, non-performance may adversely affect a collective interest such as protection of the high seas, Antarctica or outer space. When a unilateral remedy against a violator by way of non-performance would entail damage to a collective interest, there is good reason to bar unilateral non-performance. Second, multilateral treaties may provide expressly for responses to violations by collective decisions or other procedures. Such express stipulations are generally construed to exclude other responses by injured parties. See Restatement (Third) § 905, Comment *a*.

9. *Retorsion.* As indicated at the beginning of this section, "retorsion" refers to retaliatory measures that an aggrieved state is legally free to take whether or not the offending state committed an illegal act. In practice, most retaliatory acts fall into this category. Typical examples of such retaliatory actions are the severing of diplomatic relations, cessation of trade in general or in specific items, curtailment of immigration from the offending state, and denial of benefits available to the offending government, such as foreign aid.

Whether acts of retorsion are effective in advancing their objectives depends on the particular circumstances. In many cases, economic boycotts or denial of specific benefits have not resulted in changing the policies of the offending states. This has been most evident when the target state's conduct is a manifestation of a basic political position. For example, the economic sanctions adopted by the United States against "unfriendly" regimes in Cuba, Iran, and Sudan are often considered to have failed to change the behavior of those states. See Doxey, International Sanctions in Contemporary Perspective (2d rev. ed. 1996). However, some studies show that economic sanctions have probably influenced the offending state's behavior in a number of cases, though it is difficult to say whether such sanctions were decisive in that respect. See Hufbauer et al., Economic Sanctions Reconsidered (3d ed. 2008) (analyzing more than one hundred cases of economic sanctions and their apparent effects).

10. *Legal Limits on Retorsion?* Since states are generally free to refuse to trade with others or to deny benefits and to take other action that fails under the heading of retorsion, the question of their legality does not normally arise. However, their legality may be questioned when the counter-measures are directed to an unlawful end. Consider the example of a state discontinuing trade with an offending country and imposing as a condition for

the resumption of trade a change in a lawful internal or foreign policy of the offending state. On that example, Schachter has written: "There is good reason to consider such use of retorsion as illegal because of its improper objective. One may characterize it as an abuse of rights, but it is more precise to refer to a primary rule that precludes such coercion." Schachter, International Law in Theory and Practice 199 (1991). Do you agree?

11.   *Retorsion and Proportionality.* Should acts of retorsion be subject to requirements of proportionality? Retorsion is often an "equivalent" act of retaliation in response to an unfriendly act. For example, the expulsion of a diplomat by the receiving state is commonly followed by the sending state declaring as *persona non grata* a diplomat of equivalent rank from the first state. Diplomatic or trade relations are rarely, if ever, suspended for minor or isolated offenses. While states are not legally required to maintain diplomatic or trade relations—or, in general, to be friendly—an "unfriendly act" that is disproportionate to an offense and causes substantial damage to another state may be viewed as "an abuse of rights" and therefore illegitimate. Oppenheim, International Law 345 (8th ed. Lauterpacht ed. 1955) concludes that states are legally precluded from taking measures that would otherwise be permitted if such measures would "inflict upon another State an injury which cannot be justified by a legitimate consideration of its own advantage." Is this general formulation of an "abuse of rights" principle verifiable as a rule of customary international law? If not, should it be favored as a rule *de lege ferenda?*

12.   *Collective Countermeasures.* Countermeasures against an offending state for violation of an international obligation may be taken by aggrieved states through joint or parallel action. Such actions, commonly called "collective sanctions," have typically involved severance of diplomatic relations, trade boycotts and, in some cases, cessation of air or sea traffic. These measures, if not contrary to treaty obligations, fall within the discretionary authority of states (retorsion). Where they are contrary to treaty obligations or customary law obligations, they may be legally justified as reprisals by states injured by the offending state's violation. In several cases states not directly injured have joined in collective countermeasures on the ground that the violation affected a collective interest or a common concern of the international community. While such instances might have been characterized as responses to violations of *erga omnes* obligations, the states taking the action have rarely, if ever, explicitly referred to that doctrine.

The U.N. Security Council may adopt collective sanctions of a non-forcible character under Article 41 of the U.N. Charter, in which case they are binding on all member states. Decisions of the Council under that article must be based on a determination of the existence of a threat to, or breach of, peace or an act of aggression. See U.N. Charter, art. 39. (If such measures are inadequate, the Security Council may order forcible action under Article 42; see Chapter 15.) Collective economic sanctions mandated by the U.N. Security Council have become a frequent practice since the end of the Cold War. Some of the most important sanctions episodes are:

- Almost immediately after the Iraqi invasion of Kuwait in August 1990, the Security Council imposed a sweeping trade and financial embargo on Iraq. S.C. Res. 661 (Aug. 6, 1990). As part of the terms of the cease-fire, sanctions remained in place pending Iraq's discharge of the obligations mandated by the Council, including supervised disarmament. S.C. Res. 687 (Apr. 3, 1991). Only after Iraq's president, Saddam Hussein, was toppled during the 2003 U.S.-led invasion of Iraq were the sanctions lifted. See S.C. Res. 1483 (May 22, 2003).

• In May 1992, the Security Council declared trade sanctions and an oil embargo on Yugoslavia, comprising Serbia and Montenegro, in response to the savage conflict in Bosnia and Herzegovina and violations of international humanitarian law, including "ethnic cleansing." S.C. Res. 757 (May 30, 1992). The measures were tightened the following year, and the area of Bosnia and Herzegovina under the control of Bosnian Serb forces was also made a target of sanctions. S.C. Res. 820 (Apr. 17, 1993). U.N. sanctions were suspended and eventually ended in 1995–1996 as a result of the Dayton Agreement on a peace settlement for Bosnia and Herzegovina. S.C. Res. 1021 (Nov. 22, 1995), S.C. Res. 1022 (Nov. 22, 1995), S.C. Res. 1074 (Oct. 1, 1996). In 1998, an arms embargo was re-imposed against the Federal Republic of Yugoslavia (Serbia–Montenegro), because of its repressive actions in Kosovo. S.C. Res. 1160 (Mar. 31, 1998). Those sanctions were then lifted after the fall from power of F.R.Y. President Slobodan Milošević. See S.C. Res. 1367 (Sept. 10, 2001).

• In 1992 and 1993, the Security Council mandated sanctions against Libya, to induce Libya to "demonstrate by concrete actions its renunciation of terrorism" and to surrender for trial before a United Kingdom or United States court the suspects in the 1988 explosion of Pan Am Flight 103 over Lockerbie, Scotland. S.C. Res. 731 (Jan. 21, 1992), S.C. Res. 748 (Mar. 31, 1992), S.C. Res. 883 (Nov. 11, 1993). These measures were suspended in 1999, when Libya turned over two suspects for trial in The Hague before Scottish judges, and then were lifted after Libya took various steps to renounce terrorism and compensate those it had victimized. For a discussion, see Schwartz, Dealing with a Rogue State: The Libya Precedent, 101 A.J.I.L. 553 (2007).

• In 1999, the Security Council imposed aviation and financial sanctions against the Taliban regime in Afghanistan, with the objective of ending support for international terrorists and inducing the Taliban to surrender for trial Osama bin Laden, who was under U.S. indictment for the August 1998 bombings of two U.S. embassies. S.C. Res. 1267 (Nov. 24, 1999).

• In 2004, the Security Council imposed an arms embargo on all nongovernmental forces and individuals in the Darfur region, hoping to stem the violence of an ethnic conflict that claimed as many as 400,000 lives. S.C. Res. 1556 (July 30, 2004). This embargo was expanded in 2005 in an effort to compel implementation of the N'djamena Humanitarian Ceasefire Agreement and its terms. S.C. Res. 1591 (Mar. 29, 2005). The Security Council also took measures in 2006 to freeze the assets and restrict the travel of four individuals associated with the conflict, and threatened additional, similar restrictions against any individual or group trying to block the implementation of the Darfur

Peace Agreement. S.C. Res. 1672 (Apr. 25, 2006); S.C. Res. 1679 (May 16, 2006).

- In 2006, in light of years of non-cooperation exhibiting a "pattern of concealment" concerning the development of Iran's nuclear program, the Security Council imposed restrictions on the transfer of any materials or technology that could be used to aid in the enrichment of uranium or in the development of a missile program. See Implementation of the NPT Safeguards Agreement in the Islamic Republic of Iran, IAEA Doc. GOV/2004/83, para. 112 (Nov. 15, 2004); S.C. Res. 1696 (July 31, 2006). As Iran continued to resist the monitoring attempts of the International Atomic Energy Agency (IAEA), the Security Council tightened these restrictions, specifying materials which could not be transferred to Iran and mandating that a number of Iranian nationals involved in the nuclear program be subject to a freezing of all their assets held abroad. S.C. Res. 1737 (Dec. 27, 2006); S.C. Res. 1747 (Mar. 24, 2007); S.C. Res. 1803 (Mar. 3, 2008); S.C. Res. 1835 (Sept. 27, 2008).

Some of these Security Council-organized sanctions are analyzed in Cortwright & Lopez, Sanctions and the Search for Security: Challenges to UN Action (2002); Cortwright & Lopez, The Sanctions Decade: Assessing UN Strategies in the 1990s (2000). On the adverse humanitarian impacts that frequently result from sanctions, see also Damrosch, The Civilian Impact of Economic Sanctions, in Enforcing Restraint: Collective Intervention in Internal Conflicts 274 (Damrosch ed. 1993); Gibbons, Sanctions in Haiti: Human Rights and Democracy under Assault (1999). Because of the hardships broad sanctions can inflict on the civilian population, efforts in recent years have been made to impose "smart" sanctions that target the bank accounts and travel abroad of regime elites.

In one instance, collective sanctions were apparently found to be required on the basis of a *declaratory* (not binding) resolution of the U.N. Security Council. In 1970, the Security Council affirmed a General Assembly resolution that declared South Africa's mandate over South West Africa (Namibia) terminated. The Council then declared that the presence of South African authorities in Namibia was illegal and that their acts concerning Namibia were illegal and invalid. An advisory opinion of the International Court of Justice in 1971 held that, in light of these declarations, all states were legally obliged not to recognize South Africa's administration of Namibia. *Legal Consequences for States of the Continued Presence of South Africa in Namibia (South West Africa) notwithstanding Security Council Resolution 276 (1970)*, Advisory Opinion, 1971 I.C.J. 3, 16. In light of this opinion, do all states have a duty to take appropriate measures (particularly, non-recognition of illegal acts) when an offending state has committed a serious breach of law of concern to the international community?

SECTION 7.   PROCEDURES FOR PURSUING AN INTERNATIONAL CLAIM

An injured state that is legally entitled to reparation from a state responsible for a wrongful act may bring a claim through diplomatic channels or through any procedure for dispute settlement to which the states have agreed. Diplomatic channels normally involve exchanges and negotiations between the parties. Dispute settlement procedures may be bilateral as, for example, through a commission composed of representatives of the two states. Other procedures of dispute settlement may involve third parties; either states or individuals. Dispute settlement procedures embrace a variety of arrangements provided for in existing treaties or ad hoc agreements. They include bilateral commissions, conciliation and mediation procedures, arbitration and judicial settlement. See Chapter 9. Claims and settlement procedures, although diverse in character, present a few common problems of a procedural character, which are discussed below.

A. NOTICE AND NEGOTIATION AS A PREREQUISITE

It appears to be a general rule of state responsibility that an injured state must provide notice to the state that allegedly committed the injury prior to resorting to dispute resolution procedures. See I.L.C. Articles on State Responsibility, art. 43, U.N. Doc. A/56/10, at 301 (2001). The reason for providing notice of a claim is that the state regarded in default may agree that injury has occurred and that reparation should be undertaken. Indeed, the United States has settled some important inter-state claims on the basis of ad hoc agreement, though in some instances it has done so without formal acknowledgment of liability (that is, compensation is paid on an *ex gratia* basis). For example, the United States agreed to pay China $28 million in compensation for damage to the Chinese Embassy in Belgrade from inadvertent NATO bombing during the Kosovo conflict of 1999, while China agreed to pay compensation for the ensuing protests in China that damaged U.S. consular facilities. See 1 Murphy, United States Practice in International Law 99–102 (2002).

Even if a bilateral settlement is not reached, the process of negotiation may be important for purposes of subsequently pursuing the claim. Most agreements that provide for dispute settlement before an international court or tribunal, or through conciliation or mediation, require that bilateral negotiation, consultation, or "diplomacy" be resorted to before the claim can be submitted to a tribunal or other procedure for settlement. Even when that has not been specified in an agreement, tribunals have treated negotiation as an implied condition. The Permanent Court of International Justice stated that a requirement that negotiation take place may be implied, since it was necessary to show that a dispute actually exists and that "a difference of views is in question which has not been capable of being otherwise overcome." *Factory at Chorzów* (Germany v. Poland), 1927 P.C.I.J. (ser. A) No. 13, at 10–11. The International Court of Justice in the *North Sea Continental Shelf Cases* observed that

> [T]he parties are under an obligation to enter into negotiation with a view to arriving at an agreement * * *; they are under an obligation

so to conduct themselves that the negotiations are meaningful, which will not be the case when either of them insists upon its own position without contemplating any modification of it * * *.

(Germany/Denmark; Germany/Netherlands), 1969 I.C.J. 3, para. 85. The obligation to negotiate before filing a claim, however, does not mean that the negotiation must be lengthy or even detailed. In the *Mavrommatis* case, the Permanent Court of International Justice commented:

> Negotiations do not of necessity always presuppose a more or less lengthy series of notes and despatches; it may suffice that a discussion should have been commenced, * * * a deadlock is reached, or if finally a point is reached at which one of the parties definitely declares himself unable or refuses to give way * * *.

Mavrommatis Palestine Concessions (Greece v. United Kingdom), 1924 P.C.I.J. (ser. A) No. 2, at 13. Indeed, the court or tribunal might simply consider whether the claim has not been resolved by the two states. When Iran tried to argue that the United States did not meaningfully seek to negotiate a resolution of matters underlying a U.S. counter-claim brought before the International Court, the Court focused on the requirement in the treaty establishing its jurisdiction, which provided that the claim not yet be "satisfactorily adjusted by diplomacy." In concluding that this requirement was met, the Court stated:

> It is established that a dispute has arisen between Iran and the United States over the issues raised in the counter-claim. The Court has to take note that the dispute has not been satisfactorily adjusted by diplomacy. Whether the fact that diplomatic negotiations have not been pursued is to be regarded as attributable to the conduct of the one Party or the other is irrelevant for present purposes, as is the question whether it is the Applicant or the Respondent that has asserted a *fin de non-recevoir* on this ground. As in previous cases involving virtually identical treaty provisions (see *United States Diplomatic and Consular Staff in Tehran*, I.C.J. Reports, 1980, pp. 26–28; *Military and Paramilitary Activities in and against Nicaragua (Nicaragua v. United States of America)*, I.C.J. Reports 1984, pp. 427–29), it is sufficient for the Court to satisfy itself that the dispute was not satisfactorily adjusted by diplomacy before being submitted to the Court.

Oil Platforms (Iran v. United States), 2003 I.C.J. 161, para. 107; see Chapter 9, Section 2.

As a practical matter, what criteria would an international court or tribunal employ to determine whether a party that purports to be ready to negotiate a dispute is being genuine? Is there a value in insisting upon further discussions if one state is taking positions that have no chance of acceptance by the other state? Can an international court or tribunal really satisfy itself that negotiation in that case is a sham or futile? Is it desirable as a matter of judicial efficiency to dismiss a claim based on a failure of sufficient negotiations, if the expectation is that within six months or so the claim will simply be filed again?

B. STANDING TO MAKE CLAIMS

States may present claims through diplomatic channels or to tribunals only if they have the requisite legal interest. As discussed above in Section 3, this depends on determining to whom the obligation is owed and on the meaning of "injury." Where a particular state, or one of its nationals, has been directly injured, there is little difficulty in establishing standing for that state to bring a claim. By contrast, the ability of a state to bring a claim when it has not been directly injured is problematic. Although the concept of certain *erga omnes* obligations has been recognized in principle, no judicial or arbitral proceeding has been identified where the claimant's standing was based on the *erga omnes* concept. The issue of standing to bring a claim has been considered by the International Court of Justice in the *Nottebohm Case* (Liechtenstein v. Guatemala), 1955 I.C.J. 4; *South West Africa Cases* (Ethiopia v. South Africa; Liberia v. South Africa), 1966 I.C.J. 6; and *Barcelona Traction, Light and Power Company, Ltd.* (Belgium v. Spain), 1970 I.C.J. 3. Cases concerning intervention by third parties have also considered the meaning of "legal interest." See Chapter 9.

Rather than rely on general rules of state responsibility as they relate to standing, it is possible to establish special rules for particular treaty regimes. Several international conventions allow *any* party to the convention to bring a case against another party for breach of an obligation, provided that both parties have accepted an optional protocol or clause to that effect. See, e.g., Convention on the Elimination of All Forms of Racial Discrimination, art. 22, Mar. 1, 1966, 660 U.N.T.S. 195 (allowing one party to sue another party before the I.C.J. for "any" dispute concerning "interpretation or application" of the convention).

Historically, states have brought international claims against other states in the exercise of the right of diplomatic protection of nationals under international law. In recent years, however, especially in cases where a large class of persons have been injured, and a claims commission is established to address their claims, the nationals themselves have been permitted to present and litigate the claim before the claims tribunal against the defendant state. In the period since the establishment of the Iran–U.S. Claims Tribunal, an important feature of claims settlement practice is the trend toward creating vehicles for injured individuals or companies to present their own claims, not necessarily through the intermediation of their state of nationality. The U.N. Compensation Commission (U.N.C.C.), for example, although generally requiring claims to be submitted by governments, has created special procedures for submission of claims "on behalf of persons who are not in a position to have their claims submitted by a Government" (e.g., stateless persons).

See U.N.C.C. Governing Council, Provisional Rules for Claims Procedure, U.N. Doc. S/AC.26/1992/10, annex, art. 5(2) (June 16, 1992).

C. WAIVER OR LACHES

The I.L.C. Articles on State Responsibility provide in Article 45, U.N. Doc. A/56/10, at 307 (2001), that responsibility may not be invoked if the injured state has waived the claim or "validly acquiesced in the lapse of the claim." A state can waive its right to pursue a claim for injury to itself or its nationals, either before or after the injury occurs. For example, the parties to the International Convention on the Settlement of Investment Disputes between States and Nationals of Other States, Mar. 18, 1965, 17 U.S.T. 1270, 575 U.N.T.S. 159, have agreed not to diplomatically espouse claims of their nationals in respect of disputes submitted to arbitration under the Convention.

Whether international law includes a rule of laches has arisen in several cases. An opinion of the U.S.–Mexican General Claims Commission stated that "no rule of international law put[s] a limit on * * * the presentation of an international claim to an international tribunal." *George W. Cook Claim*, 4 U.N. Rep. Int'l Arb. Awards 3, 213. Yet some tribunals have denied a remedy when the claim was brought only after a long lapse of time, on the ground that the respondent government was placed in an unfair position in making its defense. See Ralston, The Law and Procedure of International Tribunals, 375–83 (rev. ed. 1926), Supplement 185–87 (1936). The Institut de Droit International concluded in 1925 that "it is left to the unfettered discretion of the international tribunal" to determine whether there has been undue delay. 32 Ann. de l'Institut de Droit Int. 558–60 (1925). An arbitral tribunal endorsed this principle in the *Ambatielos Claim* when it denied a British contention that the claim of Greece should be rejected because of undue delay in its presentation. *Ambatielos Claim*, 12 U.N. Rep. Int'l Arb. Awards 83, 103–04 (1956).

The trend in recent claims programs has been for the agreement or instrument establishing the tribunal (or its procedural rules) to set relatively brief time limits for receipt of claims once the tribunal is functioning: e.g., one year for the Iran–U.S. Claims Tribunal or the U.N. Compensation Commission. Such time limits facilitate processing of the claims and disbursement of any funds that may have been allocated for payment.

D. PROCEDURAL RULES ON DIPLOMATIC PROTECTION OF NATIONALS

There is a further set of "Articles" currently under development by the International Law Commission on the topic of "diplomatic protection of nationals." Such terminology refers not to rules relating to diplomats, but to rules on when a state, through the exercise of international diplomacy, can protect the interests of its nationals. Draft Article 1 of the Articles on Diplomatic Protection states that:

[D]iplomatic protection consists of the invocation by a State, through diplomatic action or other means of peaceful settlement, of the responsibility of another State for an injury caused by an internationally wrongful act of that State to a natural or legal person that is a national of the former State with a view to the implementation of such responsibility.

Report of the International Law Commission, Fifty-eighth Session, U.N. Doc. A/61/10, at 13, 16 (2006). In Chapter 14, this casebook addresses the core procedural and substantive rules of international law that arise in the context of the diplomatic protection of nationals (including foreign investors), such as the exhaustion of local remedies rule, the continuous nationality rule, the national treatment standard, the fair and equitable treatment standard, and the prohibition on expropriation without compensation. Some of those rules are relevant as well to the ability of a state or of a person to advance a claim for a violation of human rights, which is the focus of Chapter 13.

E.   LUMP–SUM SETTLEMENTS AND CLAIMS COMMISSIONS

Lump–Sum Settlements. When two states are amenable to negotiating a settlement of an entire class of claims, usually involving injury to a large number of nationals of the claimant state, they will sometimes conclude a "lump-sum settlement agreement," by which the entire class of claims are settled in exchange for the payment of a lump-sum to the claimant state. After the Second World War, several lump-sum settlement agreements were made by the United States with countries in Europe and later with China. Such agreements have continued to be concluded with states whenever the United States reestablishes diplomatic relations with a foreign country after a lengthy period, such as when diplomatic relations were reestablished with Vietnam in 1995. See International Claims: Their Settlement by Lump–Sum Agreements (Lillich & Weston eds. 1975) (2 vols.); International Claims: Their Settlement by Lump–Sum Agreements, 1975–1995 (Weston, Lillich, & Bederman eds. 1999).

When the lump sum is received by the United States, the U.S. Foreign Claims Settlement Commission (a part of the U.S. Department of Justice) typically receives claims from and distributes the lump-sum funds to the U.S. nationals. 22 U.S.C. §§ 1621–27 (2000). The Commission considers each claim separately and determines its validity and amount on the basis of "principles of international law, justice and equity." 22. U.S.C. 1623(a)(2)(B); see Ratner, Regulatory Takings in Institutional Context, 102 A.J.I.L. 475, 493–96 (2008); Lillich, International Claims: Their Adjudication by National Commissions (1962). For an example of a lump-sum settlement agreement involving payment by the United States, see Partial Award on Agreed Terms, 32 Iran–U.S. Cl. Trib. Rep. 207 (1996); see also Agora: The Downing of Iran Air Flight 655, 83 A.J.I.L. 318 (1989).

If a mass of claims cannot be settled through negotiation, the states concerned might elect to submit the claims to an *ad hoc* arbitral tribunal for consideration and disposition of claims over a period of time. Sometimes these tribunals are referred to as "mixed claims commissions" if they consist of representatives from the two states as well as a "neutral" presiding arbitrator. Many claims commissions and arbitral tribunals have been established for this purpose, some of which are discussed below.

Early Commissions. In 1794, the United States and Great Britain concluded the Jay Treaty under which several hundred claims based on maritime seizures were referred to a mixed commission for arbitration. See Hyde at 1587–88. A number of arbitration cases involving the United States took place in the 19th century, one of the more notable being the U.S. claims against Great Britain for damage covered by the Confederate warship *Alabama.* See Hyde at 1592–93. Several claims commissions were established, beginning in 1868, to deal with U.S.–Mexican claims, mostly against Mexico but some against the United States The two U.S.–Mexico Claims Commissions set up in 1923 dealt with more than 6,000 claims and, in doing so, created a significant body of case law on state responsibility. See General Claims Convention, United States–Mexico, Sept. 8, 1923, 43 Stat. 1730, 4 Malloy at 4441; see also Feller, The Mexican Claims Commissions 1923–1934 (1935).

Post–World War I Commissions. Various "mixed" claims commissions were set up after the two world wars, principally to resolve claims for loss, damage, or injury incurred by nationals of the victorious states from war-related acts of the vanquished states. (It should be noted that these claims commissions were separate and distinct from the "war guilt clause" and associated Reparation Commission of the Treaty of Versailles, in the sense that they separately addressed contract and property claims through traditional arbitral tribunals.) The Franco–German arbitral tribunal adjudicated some 20,000 claims and the Anglo–German arbitral tribunal adjudicated some 10,000 claims before their dissolutions in 1930. The resolution of these claims entailed various mechanisms, including differential treatment for large and small claims, and the use of inter-party settlements where possible. See Wormser, Collection of International War Damage Claims (1944); see also Baruch, The Making of the Reparation and Economic Sections of the Treaty (1920).

The U.S.–German Mixed Claims Commission technically was not a creation of the Treaty of Versailles, since the United States did not ratify that treaty nor participate in the claims processes it established. See Berlin Treaty of Peace, United States–Germany, Aug. 25, 1921, 42 Stat. 1939; Agreement for a Mixed Claims Commission, United States–Germany, Aug. 10, 1922, 42 Stat. 2200. The jurisprudence of that Commission, however, provides important guidance in "determining the meaning of words in the treaty, such as '*directly* in consequence of hostilities,' involving the degree of proximity or remoteness of the operative cause of the damage, and of other words and phrases in the treaty." Borchard, The Opinions of the Mixed Claims Commission, United States and Germany,

19 A.J.I.L. 133, 135 (1925); see also Final Report of H. H. Martin: Acting Agent of the United States before the Mixed Claims Commission, United States and Germany (1941); Kiesselbach, Problems of the German–American Claims Commission (Zeydel trans. 1930). Both the administrative and case-specific decisions of such commissions continue to be cited today in a variety of contexts concerning general principles of state responsibility, including by the International Court of Justice, arbitral tribunals, and other sources, such as the commentary to the I.L.C. Articles on State Responsibility.

Post–World War II Reparations. The post-World War II peace treaties with Bulgaria, Finland, Hungary, Italy, and Romania all provided for the establishment of mixed commissions for the settlement of disputes. The comprehensive multilateral peace treaty with Japan after the Second World War contained provisions relating to claims and property, but did not create claims commissions. Rather, the treaty allowed for substantial Japanese assets located in the victorious states to be seized, liquidated, and used to pay compensation to persons injured by Japan's conduct during the war. See Treaty of Peace with Japan, art. 14, Sept. 8, 1951, 3 U.S.T. 3169, 136 U.N.T.S. 45.

There was no comprehensive multilateral peace treaty with Germany after the Second World War. Pursuant to the London Agreement on German External Debts, Feb. 27, 1953, 4 U.S.T. 445, 333 U.N.T.S. 3, the post-war German government agreed to assume the external debts incurred before the war by Nazi Germany, and certain arbitral bodies were created thereunder to adjudicate claims of private debtors and creditors. Further, the major powers that occupied Germany enacted laws in their respective zones to restore property confiscated by the Nazi government to the original owners. These laws, however, did not address loss other than property loss, such as physical suffering or unjust deprivation of freedom, since the Allies contemplated that a new German government would assume such responsibility.

In the 1950s, the Federal Republic of Germany enacted legislation (thereafter occasionally amended) to provide restitution for persons persecuted by the Nazi regime because of political opposition or for racial, religious, or ideological reasons. Thus, under the 1952 German Federal Compensation Law (B.E.G.), compensation was provided to residents of Germany who suffered loss of life, damage to limb or health, loss of liberty, property or possessions, or harm to vocational or economic pursuits. Foreign nationals and states wishing to appeal adverse decisions of German courts to an international arbitral body could do so under the Convention on the Settlement of Matters arising out of the War and the Occupation, May 26, 1952, 49 A.J.I.L. Supp. 69 (1955).

While these complex German restitution laws permitted recovery by many persons who were German nationals or residents, or stateless persons, during the war, or who were refugees within the meaning of the 1949 Geneva Conventions, the laws excluded many others. In the years thereafter, Germany concluded bilateral agreements with several countries to compensate persons not eligible under the German restitution laws. After German reunification in 1990, Germany expanded its program to include persons to whom the German Democratic Republic had denied relief. For an overall discussion of post-war efforts to obtain compensation for Holocaust claims, see Pross, Paying for the Past: The Struggle over Reparations for Surviving Victims of the Nazi Terror (Cooper trans. 1998); see also Ferencz, Less Than Slaves: Jewish Forced Labor and the Quest for Compensation (1979). On recent efforts to handle mass claims against companies and banks (not governments) dating from the time of the World War II Holocaust, see Bazyler & Alford, Holocaust Restitution: Perspectives on the Litigation and Its Legacy (2006).

Iran–U.S. Claims Tribunal. The Iran–United States Claims Tribunal was established by the Algiers Accords in 1980, ending the Iranian hostage crisis. As part of its efforts to obtain the release of the hostages, the Carter Administration froze assets of the Iranian Government in the United States. U.S. companies brought hundreds of lawsuits and obtained judicial attachments of assets of the Government of Iran and its agencies. Eventually, the Algiers Accords between the United States and Iran were negotiated with the Algerian Government acting as intermediary. See Settlement of the Hostage Crisis, 20 I.L.M. 223 (1981). These Accords established procedures for the release of most frozen Iranian assets in exchange for the release of the U.S. hostages, lifted judicial attachments in return for the establishment of a Claims Tribunal, and created a Security Account from a portion of the frozen assets out of which the Tribunal was authorized to pay legitimate claims brought by U.S. nationals against Iran. Established at The Hague, the Tribunal consists of nine arbitrators, three from the United States, three from Iran, and three from third countries.

The Tribunal received over 4,700 claims and as of mid-2008 had concluded 3,936 cases by award, decision, or order. Of those cases, the Tribunal has issued some 600 awards and partial awards, totaling $2,166,998,515 for U.S. claimants and $1,013,716,179 for Iran and Iranian claimants. Communiqué No. 08/2 (Apr. 25, 2008), www.iusct.org/communique_english.pdf. For background, see Aldrich, The Jurisprudence of the Iran–United States claims Tribunal (1996); Brower & Brueschke, The Iran–United States Claims Tribunal (1998); The Iran–United States Claims Tribunal and the Process of International Claims Resolution (Caron & Crook eds. 2000); The Iran–United States Claims Tribunal: Its Contribution to the Law of State Responsibility (Lillich, Magraw, & Bederman eds.1998); Khan, Iran–United States Claims Tribunal: Controversies, Cases and Contribution (1990); Westberg, International Transactions and Claims Involving Government Parties: Case Law of the Iran–United States Claims Tribunal (1991). The Tribunal is still functioning as of 2009, with the remaining cases principally concerning Iran's extensive claims against the U.S. government for losses incurred when the U.S. military sales program to Iran was shut down in 1979.

U.N. Compensation Commission. In the aftermath of Iraq's 1990–1991 invasion of Kuwait, the U.N. Security Council created the U.N. Compensation Commission to pay compensation for loss, damage or injury directly caused by the invasion and occupation of Kuwait. See S.C. Res. 692 (May 20, 1991). The Commission was charged with responsibility for dealing with a variety of complex administrative, financial, legal and policy issues, including developing procedures for receiving, evaluating, and verifying claims, determining payments for meritorious claims, and operating an account funded by Iraq for the payment of claims. See Report of the Secretary General Pursuant to Paragraph 19 of Security Council Resolution 687 (1991), U.N. Doc. S/22559 (May 2, 1991), 30 I.L.M. 1706 (1991).

Although limited to "direct" loss, the U.N.C.C. has taken a fairly broad approach to compensable damages. The U.N.C.C. Governing Council determined in Decision No. 7 that Iraq had to compensate for:

> [A]ny loss suffered as a result of: (a) Military operations or threat of military action by either side during the period 2 August to 2 March 1991; (b) Departure from or inability to leave Iraq or Kuwait (or a decision not to return) during that period; (c) Actions by officials, employees or agents of the Government of Iraq or its controlled entities during that period in connection with the invasion or occupation; (d) The breakdown of civil order in Kuwait or Iraq during that period; or (e) Hostage-taking or other illegal detention.

U.N.C.C. Governing Council Decision No. 7, U.N. Doc. S/AC.26/1991/7/ Rev.1, para. 6 (1991).

As of early 2009, the U.N.C.C. had processed more than 2.68 million claims and had awarded more than $52 billion to successful claimants. Approximately $28 billion in awards has yet to be paid. See the U.N.C.C. website at http://www2.unog.ch/uncc/status.htm.

For further discussion of the U.N.C.C., see Caron & Morris, The United Nations Compensation Commission: Practical Justice, Not Retribution, 13 E.J.I.L. 183 (2002); The United Nations Compensation Commission (Lillich ed. 1995); Crook, The United Nations Compensation Commission–A New Structure to Enforce State Responsibility, 87 A.J.I.L. 144 (1993).

Other Commissions. Various other claims commission have also been established. A claims commission with an innovative jurisdiction grounded in international law is the Commission for Real Property Claims of Displaced Persons and Refugees, established by the 1995 Dayton Agreement as part of the peace settlement for Bosnia and Herzegovina. The Eritrea Ethiopia Claims Commission was established by those states in 2000 to address claims arising from their 1998–2000 war. For an overview of developments concerning mass claims settlement, see Permanent Court of Arbitration, Redressing Injustices Through Mass Claims Processes: Innovative Responses to Unique Challenges (2006); Permanent Court of

Arbitration, Institutional and Procedural Aspects of Mass Claims Settlement Systems (2000).

F. NATIONAL PROCEDURES FOR PRIVATE PERSONS TO PURSUE INTERNATIONAL CLAIMS

Is a state required by international law to provide a remedy to injured persons in its national system for a violation of international law by that state? The Restatement (Third), § 906, provides that a "private person, whether natural or juridical, injured by a violation of an international obligation by a state, may bring a claim against that state or assert that violation as a defense," in a court or other tribunal "of that state *pursuant to its law*" or "of the injured person's state of nationality or of a third state, *pursuant to the law of such state*, subject to limitations under international law" (emphasis added). Professor Schachter observes:

> There is no general requirement in international law that States provide such remedies. By and large, international law leaves it to them to meet their obligations in such ways as the state determines. * * * However, in some cases there are obligations of means—that is, specific requirements as to the procedures and agencies that are to be used for the fulfilment of obligations of result. Such obligations of means are specified in treaties of various kinds, particularly those which are intended to benefit private persons.
>
> * * * Some treaties require that individuals have a right to a remedy by a competent authority, leaving it to the State to decide whether that authority would be executive, administrative or judicial. In other cases, treaties do not expressly confer a right to judicial remedies, but an implication to that effect can be drawn.

Schachter, International Law in Theory and Practice 240 (1991) (footnotes omitted). While certain treaties expressly or by implication may provide for access to national courts to vindicate an international wrong, the Restatement (Third) declares in § 907, Comment *a*, that: "International agreements, even those directly benefiting private persons, generally do not create private rights or provide for a private cause of action in domestic courts, but there are exceptions with respect to both rights and remedies * * *".

NOTES

1. *Express Treaty Obligation to Accord Access to National Courts*. For an example of a treaty provision expressly addressing individual remedies, see Article 2(3) of the International Covenant on Civil and Political Rights, which obliges each state party to ensure "an effective remedy" to any person whose rights have been violated. It also requires that the right to such remedy be determined by "a competent authority provided for by the legal system of the state" and that the remedies granted be enforced by the state. See Schachter,

The Obligation to Implement the Covenant in Domestic Law, in The International Bill of Rights 311 (Henkin ed. 1981).

2. *Implied Treaty Obligation to Accord Access to National Courts.* Whether a treaty that says nothing about individual rights or remedies may be interpreted as conferring such rights or remedies may be easy to determine in some cases but difficult in others. For example, in the United States, treaties concerned with rights of property by descent or inheritance have long been treated as conferring rights upon individuals. See Head Money Cases, 112 U.S. 580 (1884). Similarly, treaties according nationals of the contracting states equal treatment have been construed to give individuals judicial remedies. See Asakura v. Seattle, 128 S.Ct. 1346 (1924). In both Sanchez–Llamas v. Oregon, 548 U.S. 331 (2006) and Medellín v. Texas, 128 S.Ct. 1346 (2008), the U.S. Supreme Court assumed without deciding that the Vienna Convention on Consular Relations confers rights that are individually enforceable in U.S. courts, albeit subject to standard U.S. procedural rules. However, treaties concerned with the use of force, such as the U.N. Charter, and other treaties seen as aspirational in nature, have been interpreted as not conferring enforceable rights on individuals. See Chapter 10, Section 3(D) on self-executing treaties. On individual remedies specifically for human rights violations, see Chapter 13, Section 5.

3. *Customary International Law Obligation to Accord Access?* Does international customary law require a state to provide a judicial remedy for an alien injured by a breach of international law? See Murphy, Does International Law Obligate States to Open Their National Courts to Persons for the Invocation of Treaty Norms that Protect or Benefit Persons?, in The Role of Domestic Courts in Treaty Enforcement: A Comparative Study (Sloss ed., forthcoming 2009); Mann, The Consequences of an International Wrong in International and National Law, 48 Brit. Y.B.I.L. 1 (1975–76).

4. *Other National Law Hurdles.* Even if a potentially enforceable right is available under national law, there may still be hurdles for an individual to overcome in having that right adjudicated. In some instances relief may be barred on grounds of non-justiciability, standing, or the act of state doctrine. See Chapter 10, Section 2. Further, remedies in national courts are limited by jurisdictional requirements. The forum state must have jurisdiction to adjudicate and the substantive law must be within its legislative jurisdiction. Suits brought by foreign nationals may be limited by rules of the forum including the principle of *forum non conveniens.* See Chapter 11.

SECTION 8. PROCEDURES FOR ENFORCING AN INTER–STATE JUDGMENT OR AWARD

States have generally complied with judgments or awards of international courts and tribunals, though in some instances non-compliance occurs, usually with the defaulting state objecting to the jurisdiction of the tribunal or on other grounds of nullity. See, e.g., Schulte, Compliance with Decisions of the International Court of Justice (2004); Schachter, The Enforcement of International Judicial and Arbitral Awards, 54 A.J.I.L. 1 (1960); Chapter 9, pp. 623 and 647. In cases of non-compliance, a prevailing state may simply decide to wait until the opportunity arises to revisit the matter with the defaulting state, such when a new government comes to power in the defaulting state or political conditions otherwise change. Yet if it prefers not to wait, does a prevailing state have any international or national avenues of recourse against the defaulting state?

One avenue of recourse could be to invoke any enforcement provisions that exist in an applicable multilateral treaty. Article 94 of the U.N. Charter provides that the Security Council may take measures to give effect to a judgment of the International Court when requested to do so. No such action, however, has been taken by the Security Council as of early 2009 (Nicaragua sought enforcement of the Court's judgment against the United States in the mid–1980s, only to see the United States veto adoption of a resolution). The Convention on International Civil Aviation of 1944 also refers to possible non-compliance by a contracting state with a decision of the International Court or of an arbitral tribunal in a matter covered by the convention. The contracting states are obliged to exclude the airline of a contracting state from operating in their territory if the Council of the International Civil Aviation Organization has determined that the airline is not in compliance with the final decision of the International Court or arbitral tribunal. Convention on International Civil Aviation, art 87, Dec. 7, 1944, 61 Stat. 1180, 15 U.N.T.S. 295. See also Constitution of International Labor Organization, art. 33.

Another avenue of recourse could be for the prevailing state to demand that a third state, in which assets of the defaulting state are located, transfer those assets in payment of the international judgment or award. In *Corfu Channel* (United Kingdom v. Albania), 1949 I.C.J. 244 (Assessment of the Amount of Compensation Due from Albania), the International Court of Justice ordered Albania to pay a sum of money to the United Kingdom for damage caused to U.K. vessels as they passed through the Corfu strait. When Albania refused to pay, the United Kingdom sought to obtain the compensation from gold that the Nazi German government removed from Rome, and that then came into the custody of France, the United States, and the United Kingdom after the defeat of Nazi Germany in 1945. The United Kingdom argued that since the gold originally had been seized from Albania, and since Albania was entitled to that gold, then the gold could be used to pay the damages awarded by the International Court. The three governments were all of the opinion that the required amount of gold could be paid to the United Kingdom to satisfy the Court's award, provided that it was decided by arbitration that Albania was in fact entitled to the gold held by the three governments. Although an arbitrator did so decide, Italy filed a case before the International Court contesting the arbitrator's decision, on grounds that Italy itself had a claim to the gold that was superior to the United Kingdom's claim. Italy further argued that the International Court could not definitively resolve the rights in the gold in the absence of Albania as a party to the case. The Court agreed. See *Case of Monetary Gold Removed from Rome in 1943* (Italy v. France, United Kingdom & United States),

1954 I.C.J. 19; see also Oliver, The Monetary Gold Decision in Perspective, 49 A.J.I.L. 216 (1955). In consequence, the gold was not transferred to the United Kingdom (nor to Italy), and it took until 1996 before claims to the gold could be addressed through multilateral agreement. Though transfer of the gold to the United Kingdom was thwarted by Italy's competing claim, the reasoning underlying the position of the three fiduciary governments generally supports the proposition that a state may use funds under its control that are owned by a second state to meet the demand of a third state that is seeking to execute a binding decision of an international court or tribunal.

A third possible avenue for executing an international judgment or award could be through the domestic courts of a state where funds of the defaulting state are located. For instance, in the case of *Société Commerciale de Belgique,* a private Belgian company was awarded damages against Greece by an international arbitral tribunal. See 1939 P.C.I.J. (ser. C) No. 87; Socobelge v. Greek State and Bank of Greece, 47 A.J.I.L. 508 (1953). When Greece did not pay, the Belgian company sought to attach funds of the Greek government in Belgium. The Belgian court allowed an attachment as a conservatory action pending an *exequator* from the Belgian government certifying the validity and binding character of the arbitral award. The Belgian court also held that the funds of Greece were not entitled to immunity against execution because they were related to business done by Greece in Belgium. Can it be maintained that courts of a third state are under an obligation to recognize and enforce judgments of international tribunals that are binding on the parties in accordance with international law? Should such judgments be enforced as a matter of comity? Would the national court have to ensure that competing claims are met? See Remarks by O'Connell, 85 A.S.I.L. Proc. 439 (1991). A separate question is whether an award of an international court or tribunal is entitled to be treated as a "foreign arbitral award" for purposes of recognition and enforcement under the U.N. Convention on Recognition and Enforcement of Foreign Arbitral Awards, June 10, 1958, 21 U.S.T. 2517, 330 U.N.T.S. 38 (often referred to as the New York Convention). For an analysis, see Paulsson, Arbitration Unbound: Award Detached from the Law of its Country of Origin, 30 I.C.L.Q. 358 (1981).

An unusual arrangement to ensure payment of awards was included in the Algiers Accords between the United States and Iran, which ended the 1979–1981 hostages crisis. Under those Accords, a Security Account held at a Dutch bank was established out of a portion of the Iranian funds that had been frozen in the United States. Claims of U.S. nationals against Iran (many of which had been filed in U.S. courts) were transferred to the arbitral tribunal established in The Hague. Whenever the tribunal issued an award in favor of a U.S. national or the U.S. government, the award would be paid out of the Security Account. See Murphy, Securing Payment of the Award, in The Iran–United States Claims Tribunal and the Process of International Claims Resolution 299 (Caron & Crook eds. 2000) An earlier arrangement for a fund to pay claims may be found in the Peace Treaties of 1947, which gave the victorious states a right to retain the property of the enemy states situated in their territory and to liquidate such property for the purpose of paying claims which the government and their nationals had against the enemy country. See Mann, Enemy Property and the Paris Peace Treaties, 64 L.Q. Rev. 492 (1948).

The most complex arrangement to date for payment of claims may be found in the U.N. Compensation Commission, a subsidiary body of the Security Council which was established to address claims against Iraq arising out of its 1990–1991 invasion of Kuwait. Although comprehensive economic sanctions were maintained in Iraq after the war in an effort to promote identification and elimination of Iraq's weapons of mass destruction, the Security Council allowed Iraq to sell a certain amount of its oil and to use the proceeds to purchase food and medicine for the Iraq population (the U.N. "Oil-for-Food" program). See S.C. Res. 986 (Apr. 14, 1995); S.C. Res. 1111 (June 4, 1997); S.C. Res. 1153 (Feb. 20, 1998); S.C. Res. 1483 (May 22, 2003). A portion of the proceeds from those sales was allocated to a U.N. Compensation Fund, which was used to pay awards rendered by the U.N. Compensation Commission. As of early 2009, more than $20 billion had been awarded to claimants, the bulk of which had been paid through the Compensation Fund. Information on the UNCC may be found at http://www2.unog.ch/uncc/.

CHAPTER 9

DISPUTE SETTLEMENT

■ ■ ■

The multiplicity of international legal dispute settlement bodies in our era makes it an exciting time for the study and practice of international law. New modes of international jurisdiction make it more likely than ever before that when disputes arise, there will be a forum available for their resolution—provided that the parties have the will to use it.

The Project on International Courts and Tribunals (PICT) provides a convenient and frequently updated overview of the growing constellation of international dispute settlement arrangements. For details, see the PICT website at http://www.pict-pcti.org. PICT's synoptic chart, "The International Judiciary in Context," identifies some 125 international bodies and mechanisms, of which more than eighty are currently functioning; the remainder are extinct, dormant, or planned but not yet operational. These are divided between international judicial bodies (approximately one-third of the total, including about twenty courts in operation now) and "quasi-judicial, implementation control and other dispute settlement bodies" (approximately two-thirds of the total, of which some sixty-five are currently functioning).

"Judicial" bodies are distinguished from "quasi-judicial" in that the former satisfy the following criteria:

a) are permanent institutions;

b) are composed of independent judges;

c) adjudicate disputes between two or more entities, at least one of which is either a state or an international organization;

d) work on the basis of predetermined rules of procedure; and

e) render decisions that are binding.

The quasi-judicial, implementation control, and other bodies generally satisfy some but not all of the above criteria. For example, U.N. human rights treaty bodies such as the Human Rights Committee (discussed in more detail in Chapter 13) satisfy the first four criteria, but their decisions are not formally binding.

Of more than forty international judicial bodies whose existence is documented in PICT's display, at least twenty are active as of 2009. These include one court of general jurisdiction (the International Court of Justice, discussed further in Section 4 below); several international criminal courts and tribunals (see Chapter 16); various courts of specialized subject-matter jurisdiction open to multilateral treaty participants (for example, the International Tribunal for the Law of the Sea, addressed in Section 5 below and in Chapter 17, and the dispute settlement organs of the World Trade Organization, also in Section 5); and regional courts for Europe, the Americas, and Africa addressing economic and political integration and human rights (see Section 5 and Chapter 13). Several more such standing international tribunals are expected to come on stream in the near future, as detailed in PICT's materials.

The flourishing of international judicial activity today should not obscure the fact that most international disputes never reach any international court (or indeed any formal mode of legal settlement). Just as most disputes within domestic legal systems do not come to court at all, international disputes generally work their way through other avenues of resolution and only exceptionally arrive before a formal tribunal.

It is important to appreciate both the similarities and the differences between dispute settlement within national and international legal orders, notably including the absence in the international system of any generally available jurisdiction or comprehensive set of institutions covering all disputes. Partly for this reason, some international disputes persist without effective settlement for years or even centuries.

In the early twenty-first century, it remains generally the case that the jurisdiction of international dispute settlement bodies is grounded in consent, given either in advance or once a dispute arises. Though there may be some harbingers of alternatives to the traditional consent paradigm (for example, recent developments in collective enforcement and international criminal jurisdiction discussed in Chapters 15 and 16), there is as yet no international court with general compulsory jurisdiction or with effective power to compel reluctant parties to submit to judicial authority. Because of the patchwork character of international dispute settlement, an important part of the international lawyer's craft is knowledge of the available forums and the scope of (and limitations on) their jurisdiction.

The subject of dispute settlement presupposes a concept of "dispute," or of the kinds of disputes amenable to resolution in the eyes of international law. As we will see, the I.C.J. and other international legal bodies have developed and applied a legal definition of "dispute," which is a starting point for determining their jurisdiction. There is also extensive case law dealing with the recurrent objection that some kinds of disputes demand political rather than legal resolution.

This chapter surveys the variety of techniques available for settlement of international disputes, beginning with general considerations and moving through a spectrum of mechanisms displaying differing degrees of party control and differing requirements to abide by formal substantive and procedural rules. We begin with the framework set out in the U.N. Charter for dispute settlement "by peaceful means." We will survey a range of non-adjudicatory techniques, including negotiation, mediation, and facilities of regional and international organizations. We then turn to arbitration and adjudication, with particular attention to the I.C.J. as a classic model for adjudicatory settlement. The final section addresses the growing number of specialized tribunals, in order to shed light on cross-cutting questions of structure, procedure, and implementation.

SECTION 1.   THE OBLIGATION TO SETTLE DISPUTES BY PEACEFUL MEANS

A.   THE U.N. CHARTER AND OTHER TREATY OBLIGATIONS

Article 2(3) of the U.N. Charter obliges U.N. members to "settle their international disputes by peaceful means in such a manner that international peace and security, and justice, are not endangered." Article 33 of the Charter lists a spectrum of peaceful means, including "negotiation, enquiry, mediation, conciliation, arbitration, judicial settlement," and resort to regional agencies. The Security Council can become involved in dispute settlement as provided in Articles 33–38. Article 36(3) provides for the Council to consider "that legal disputes should as a general rule be referred by the parties to the International Court of Justice" in accordance with the I.C.J. Statute.

Please read Chapter VI of the Charter on dispute settlement and think about its provisions in relation to other aspects of the Charter, including the obligation of Article 2(4) to avoid use or threat of force and the Security Council's responsibilities for maintenance of peace under Chapter VII. Does the obligation to settle disputes by peaceful means signify more than merely refraining from resort to force? Are states obliged to settle all their disputes or only those endangering international peace (Article 33)? May the Security Council require a state or states to settle disputes that threaten peace?

Many treaties other than the Charter include dispute settlement obligations. For an overview, see Merrills, International Dispute Settlement (4th ed. 2005). A few of the most important are surveyed here:

1.   The General Act of 1928

The most notable attempt to establish obligations of peaceful settlement of all disputes was the General Act for the Pacific Settlement of International Disputes adopted by the League of Nations in 1928 (sometimes referred to as the Geneva Act). Chapter I of the Act provides for the conciliation of legal disputes if the parties so agree; if conciliation fails, Chapter II requires the submission of the dispute to arbitration or adjudication. Non-legal disputes are to be submitted to conciliation or to an arbitral tribunal for settlement under Chapter III. In 1949, the General

Assembly of the United Nations revised the Act in some minor respects, G.A. Res. 268 (III) (April 28, 1949).

The General Act was acceded to by twenty-two states but some later denounced it. The 1949 Revised General Act, Apr. 28, 1949, 71 U.N.T.S. 101, has only eight accessions as of 2009. The United States did not become a party to either of the General Acts.

Whether the 1928 General Act was still in force has been questioned in several cases, including the *Nuclear Tests Cases*, 1974 I.C.J. 253; the *Trial of Pakistani Prisoners of War Case*, 1973 I.C.J. 328; and the *Aegean Sea Continental Shelf Case*, 1978 I.C.J. 3. In the *Case Concerning the Aerial Incident of 10 August 1999* (Pakistan v. India), 2000 I.C.J. 12 (Judgment on Jurisdiction), Pakistan argued that British acceptance of the General Act in the interwar period carried over to both India and Pakistan, but the Court concluded that India had effectively rejected the General Act upon attaining independence.

2. Other Dispute Settlement Treaties

Between the two World Wars, many treaties were concluded providing for conciliation or arbitration of disputes between states. Generally, they exclude some categories of disputes such as those involving "vital interests" or domestic matters. The United States entered into about twenty bilateral treaties for conciliation and arbitration. Over 200 such treaties are reproduced in the U.N. Systematic Survey of Treaties for the Pacific Settlement of International Disputes 1928–1948 (1949).

After the United Nations Charter came into force, new treaties that dealt solely with peaceful settlement decreased sharply. This is understandable, since the Charter itself includes obligations of pacific settlement. However, regional treaties were still thought to be useful to spell out obligations of dispute settlement and their implementation. In 1957, a European Convention on the Peaceful Settlement of Disputes, 320 U.N.T.S. 243, was concluded, and in 1964 the African states concluded a Protocol on Conciliation and Arbitration to implement the general dispute settlement obligation in the Charter of African Unity. See U.N. Handbook on the Peaceful Settlement of Disputes Between States (1992). On more recent regional initiatives, see Section 5.

3. Dispute Clauses in Treaties on Other Matters

In addition to these specialized dispute settlement treaties, many treaties dealing with other matters contain broadly stated obligations to settle disputes through negotiation, conciliation, arbitration, or judicial settlement. Writing in 1976, Sohn noted that out of 17,000 treaties registered with the League of Nations or the United Nations, some 4,000 include compromissory clauses providing for the pacific settlement of disputes relating to the interpretation and application of the treaty. He writes:

They present a rich and wondrous mosaic. The methods of settlement employed range from bilateral negotiations through conciliation and various forms of arbitration to reference to the International Court of Justice or other permanent tribunals.

Some clauses take the form of a single sentence; others embody extensive codes of structural and procedural provisions, sometimes even offering alternative methods of settlement for different kinds of disputes.

Sohn, Settlement of Disputes Relating to the Interpretation and Application of Treaties, 136 Rec. des Cours 205, 259 (1976–II). Many of these clauses bind all disputants to submit to the procedure at the unilateral request of one of them. Other clauses state simply that the dispute shall be submitted to arbitration or other means of settlement.

The most common clauses in bilateral agreements provide for settlement through bilateral negotiations, consultation or other contacts of the parties. They do not involve third parties and therefore do not provide for binding decisions. Mixed commissions are often utilized, such as the Standing Consultative Commission for arms control disputes between the United States and the former Soviet Union. See Chayes & Chayes, The New Sovereignty: Compliance With International Regulatory Agreements 177, 207, 213 (1995).

Elaborate treaty provisions for dispute settlement are contained in the U.N. Convention on the Law of Sea of 1982, Dec. 10, 1982, 1833 U.N.T.S. 3 (LOS Convention). They include a variety of procedures for binding and non-binding decisions on disputes arising under the Convention and allow for considerable flexibility in the choice of procedures. However, every contracting party must signify, at the time it expresses its consent to be bound, its choice of the basic procedure or forum it is willing to accept. Part XV and Annexes V, VI, and VII of the Convention on the Law of the Sea, 1982. See Chapter 17. A major development following the entry into force of the LOS Convention in 1994 is the establishment of the International Tribunal on the Law of the Sea: its judges were elected in 1996 and it began hearing cases in 1998. See Section 5.

B.　THE MEANING OF "DISPUTE"

The obligation of peaceful settlement applies to "disputes," not to all disagreements between states. International case-law and commentary have considered the term "dispute" as a term with a special legal meaning. The failure of an applicant to show the existence of a dispute has been a ground for rejecting cases. See *Electricity Company of Sofia*, 1939 P.C.I.J. (Ser. A/B) No. 77, at 64, 83; *Northern Cameroons Case*, 1963 I.C.J. 15, 33–34; *Nuclear Tests Cases*, 1974 I.C.J. 253, 260, 270–271.

A dispute requires a degree of specificity and contestation. In the *Mavrommatis Case,* the International Court defined dispute as "a disagreement on a point of law or fact, a conflict of legal views or interests between two persons." 1924 P.C.I.J. (ser. A) No. 2, at 11–12. There is authority that a disagreement is not a dispute if its resolution would not have any practical effect on the relations of the parties. In the *Northern Cameroons Case,* the International Court was faced with a disagreement on the interpretation of a U.N. trusteeship agreement that was no longer in force where the applicant made no claim for reparation. In declining to adjudicate the claim, the Court said:

> The Court's judgment must have some practical consequence in the sense that it can affect existing legal rights or obligations of the parties, thus removing uncertainty from their legal relations. No judgment on the merits in this case could satisfy these essentials of the judicial function.

1963 I.C.J. 15 at 34.

In the *Nuclear Tests Cases* brought by Australia and New Zealand against France, the majority of the Court considered that French government statements that the tests had ceased meant that a dispute between the parties no longer existed. 1974 I.C.J. 253 at 270–71. However, four dissenting judges noted that the claims and legal grounds advanced by the applicants were rejected by the French government on legal grounds. They said: "these circumstances in themselves suffice to qualify the present dispute as a 'dispute in regard to which the parties are in conflict as to their legal rights' and as a 'legal dispute' * * *." Id. at 366. (Joint Dissenting Opinion of Judges Jiménez de Aréchaga, Dillard, Onyeama and Waldock. Compare the doctrine of "mootness" in U.S. domestic courts. For the Court's rejection of a subsequent attempt to revive these cases upon France's resumption of a different form of testing (underground rather than atmospheric), see *Request for an Examination of the Situation in the Nuclear Tests Case* (New Zealand v. France), 1995 I.C.J. 288.

Is prior negotiation necessary to determine that a dispute exists? The P.C.I.J. declared in one of the *Chorzów Cases:* "The manifestation of a dispute in a specific manner, as for instance by diplomatic negotiations, is not required." But the Court added that it is "desirable" that a State should not summon another State to appear before the Court without having endeavored to make it clear that the difference between them "has not been capable of being otherwise overcome." 1927 P.C.I.J. (Ser. A) No. 13, at 10–11.

Whether a dispute in the legal sense exists is frequently tested through threshold objections to the jurisdiction of international tribunals. A recent instance is the case brought by Georgia against the Russian Federation in August 2008 in the context of armed conflict between them. Georgia invoked the jurisdictional clause of the Convention on the Elimination of Race Discrimination (CERD) to which both states were parties, while Russia denied the existence of a legal dispute falling within the scope of CERD and accordingly asserted that the I.C.J. manifestly lacked jurisdiction. In ruling on Georgia's request for provisional measures, the Court found a disagreement between the parties concerning the applicability of Articles 2 and 5 of CERD to the events in South Ossetia and Abkhazia and concluded that this was sufficient to establish the existence of a dispute under CERD's dispute settlement article. See *Application of the International Convention on the Elimination of All Forms of Racial Discrimination* (Georgia v. Russian Federation), 2008 I.C.J. No. 140, paras. 66, 77, 81, 84–86, 95–103, 112 (Order on Request for the Indication of Provisional Measures Oct. 15), discussed further in Section 4 below.

Disputes regarding the interpretation or application of a treaty are recognized as essentially legal, even when they arise in the context of wider political disputes. See Section 4 below; see also Restatement (Third), § 903, Comment *d*.

SECTION 2.   NON–ADJUDICATORY PROCEDURES

A.   NEGOTIATION

Negotiation is the dominant mode for settling disputes, or indeed for seeking to prevent them from arising in the first place. As a method that remains completely within the control of the parties, negotiation need not (and often does not) produce an outcome favoring the side with the stronger legal position. Nonetheless, in international as well as domestic matters, parties "bargain in the shadow of the law," and legal considerations are frequently relevant to the negotiating process.

A growing number of international cases deal with negotiation in the framework of international law, rather than mere power politics. An example is the obligation of parties to negotiate in good faith. In the *North Sea Continental Shelf Case,* the International Court said:

> The parties are under an obligation to enter into negotiations with a view to arriving at an agreement * * *. [T]hey are under an obligation so to conduct themselves that the negotiations are meaningful, which will not be the case when either of the parties insists upon its own position without contemplating any modification of it.

1969 I.C.J. 3, 47–48. In the *Gabčíkovo–Nagymaros Project Case,* 1997 I.C.J. 7 at 77, para. 139, the Court found the parties to be under a legal obligation to negotiate in order to consider in what way to fulfill all the multiple objectives of their 1977 treaty concerning works on the Danube River.

In the *Nuclear Weapons Advisory Opinion*, 1996 I.C.J. 226, paras. 99–103, the Court interpreted Article VI of the Treaty on the Non–Proliferation of Nuclear Weapons, which contains an undertaking "to pursue negotiations in good faith on effective measures relating to the cessation of the nuclear arms race at an early date and to nuclear disarmament, and on a treaty on general and complete disarmament under strict and effective international control." The Court said (para. 99):

The legal import of that obligation goes beyond that of a mere obligation of conduct; the obligation involved here is an obligation to achieve a precise result—nuclear disarmament in all its aspects—by adopting a particular course of conduct, namely, the pursuit of negotiations on the matter in good faith.

In the operative portion of its judgment (para. 2(F)), the Court unanimously held that there "exists an obligation to pursue in good faith *and bring to a conclusion* negotiations leading to nuclear disarmament in all its aspects under strict and effective international control." (Emphasis added.)

Many dispute settlement clauses in international treaties apply to disputes that are "not settled by negotiation" (or "by diplomacy"), thereby indicating that negotiations would normally be the route of first resort. Much international litigation has considered the application of such clauses in situations where one party claims that the other has not shown willingness to negotiate or has not pursued negotiations in good faith. The I.C.J. and other tribunals have frequently had to address preliminary objections to their jurisdiction based on the argument that the applicant had not attempted to negotiate at all or had otherwise failed to satisfy a requirement of good-faith diplomacy as a precondition to adjudicatory jurisdiction. For a recent example, see the case brought by Georgia against the Russian Federation in August 2008, excerpted and discussed in Section 4.

NOTE

Further Reading. On negotiation in general, see Merrills, International Dispute Settlement 1–27 (4th ed. 2005) and references therein. See also Fisher & Ury, Getting to Yes: Negotiating Agreement Without Giving In (2d ed. 1991); Cohen, Negotiating Across Cultures (rev. ed. 1997).

B.   GOOD OFFICES AND MEDIATION

Good offices, inquiry, fact-finding, mediation, and conciliation all entail some form of third-party involvement in seeking a resolution of the dispute. Typically the parties to the dispute agree to receive third-party assistance but are not bound to accept the outcome of the process or the third party's proposals for a solution. Good offices are frequently provided by the U.N. Secretary–General or another international leader to help the parties toward mutually acceptable terms of settlement. Fact-finding and inquiry include procedures under which an impartial third party investigates disputed facts and renders a report with conclusions: such investigations may go forward under the auspices of ad hoc or standing institutions, sometimes under the formal title of a "commission of inquiry." Under conciliation, the third party makes an impartial examination of the dispute and attempts to define the terms of a proposed settlement which the parties are invited (but not required) to accept.

Mediation is distinguished from conciliation and fact-finding in that the mediator is expected to have a more active role by furthering negotiation and interacting with the parties in the making of proposals for settlement. Techniques of mediation have been extensively studied by political scientists, historians, and social psychologists and a large body of research findings and analysis (along with historical and anecdotal narrative) is available. Flexibility and adaptation to the particular circumstances characterize the more successful efforts. Most observers agree that little would be gained by attempting to prescribe precise procedural rules or legal structures for mediation. On the other hand, detailed rules are available for conciliation, inquiry, and other structured procedures of dispute settlement, which the parties may draw on as appropriate.

Mediators or other third-party facilitators may be individuals, committees, or institutional bodies. Heads of governments and experienced diplomats have often performed that role. In some cases, they can exercise leverage because of their ability to benefit or withhold benefits from the parties. They may have a representative role acting on behalf of the United Nations or an international regional agency. They may facilitate negotiation by providing information and ideas, by subdividing ("fractionating") issues, by offering services (such as monitoring compliance or providing resources), or even offering guarantees. Each dispute reveals its distinctive features and requires its own combination of methods.

Some of the world's most intractable conflicts have benefited from mediators' efforts, while others still elude solution even after extensive involvement of mediators. The Middle Eastern conflicts have drawn the attention of several U.S. presidents and a variety of other international actors, resulting in several durable accords (between Egypt and Israel in the 1978 Camp David accords which produced their 1979 peace treaty; between Israel and Jordan in 1994) and other processes of varying degrees of success (and failure). U.S. mediation brought about the 1993 Oslo Accords between Israel and the Palestine Liberation Organization, a process of considerable interest from the legal point of view notwithstanding its subsequent difficulties. See generally Watson, The Oslo Accords: International Law and the Israeli–Palestinian Peace Agreements (2000); Watson, The "Wall" Decisions in Legal and Political Context, 99 A.J.I.L. 6 (2005). Efforts to achieve a mediated solution to the Israeli–Palestinian conflict were drawn to the attention of the I.C.J. in 2004 in connection with the "Quartet Performance-based Roadmap to a Permanent Two–State Solution to the Israeli–Palestinian Conflict" when the I.C.J. was considering the General Assembly's request for an advisory opinion on the construction by Israel of a wall in the occupied Palestinian territory, as discussed at pp. 630, 632, 635 in Section 4 below. The Quartet consists of representatives of the United States, the European Union, the Russian Federation and the United Nations; as of 2009, its mediation was still in progress under the leadership of former U.K. prime minister Tony Blair.

As another recent and prominent example, the conflict between Georgia and Russia which erupted into war in 2008 has involved mediation in various ways. After military action began, President Nicolas Sarkozy of France formulated a set of principles for settlement which were accepted by President Dmitri Medvedev in Moscow and then carried by President Sarkozy to Tbilisi for discussion with President Mikheil Saakashvili of Georgia. Those principles (as adjusted in Sarkozy's consultations with the Georgian and Russian leaders and subsequently endorsed by leaders in South Ossetia and Abkhazia) formed the basis for cessation of hostilities, disengagement of forces, and access to humanitarian assistance. These endeavors (and related activities of the Organization for Security and Cooperation in Europe and the European Union) were noted when the I.C.J. had to consider Georgia's request for provisional measures in a case brought against Russia excerpted later in this chapter, in which Russia described itself as "an impartial mediator in the ethnic conflicts in the Caucasus." 2008 I.C.J. No. 140, para. 70.

Mediation of international disputes has frequently involved situations that for one reason or another could not be settled by resort to a legal institution or by application of international law. In a well-known example, mediation by the representative of the Pope, Cardinal Antonio Samoré, was able to bring about a definitive settlement of the dispute between Argentina and Chile concerning the Beagle Channel, after Argentina refused to accept the outcome of an arbitration that had awarded the disputed islands to Chile. The mediator could propose flexible approaches unavailable to the arbitrators, who were constrained to apply existing rules of international law to decide a boundary dispute. The mediator was able to defuse a crisis that could otherwise have led to war, by disaggregating the issues and finding a solution that respected both parties' genuine interests (separating possession of the island territories, of primary interest to Chile, from access to the maritime areas surrounding them, which was critical for Argentina). For discussion, see Laudy, The Vatican Mediation of the Beagle Channel Dispute: Crisis Intervention and Forum Building, in Words Over War: Mediation and Arbitration to Prevent Deadly Conflict 293–320 (Greenberg, Barton, & McGuinness eds. 2000).

Recent literature on international conflict resolution explores the factors conducing toward successful mediation of international disputes. In a study of mediation sponsored by the Carnegie Commission on Preventing Deadly Conflict, published as Words Over War (Greenberg, Barton, & McGuinness eds. 2000), the editors pursue the theme of "whether mediators embraced or avoided concepts of international law," or more provocatively, whether substantive rules of international law might sometimes even impede the quest for just, sensible, and durable solutions to international conflict. See Greenberg, Barton, & McGuinness, Introduction: Background and Analytical Perspectives, in Words Over War at 1, 3–4, 7. They perceive some major problems with the existing rules and principles of international law, notably "zero-sum" notions of sovereignty which seem to discourage creative and pragmatic solutions to self-determination conflicts. Id., at 13. After a review of a dozen case studies, including separatist conflicts and self-determination claims (Abkhazia,

Bosnia, Croatia, Palestine), integrative processes (Cambodia, El Salvador, Northern Ireland, Rwanda, South Africa), and non-civil conflicts (Aral Sea basin, Beagle Channel, North Korean nuclear proliferation), they conclude:

> The body of international law dealing with autonomy proved positively harmful. In those cases that confronted the intermixed questions of sovereignty, autonomy, confederation, self-determination, and independence, e.g., Abkhazia, Bosnia, Croatia, Northern Ireland, the legal debate stood in the way of effective dispute resolution. The legal concepts are too blunt to allow for political compromise; there is formally no such thing as partial sovereignty—even though, in practice, sovereignty is always limited by practical and formal international obligations and by responsibilities beyond the management of the nation-state. The absoluteness of the sovereignty concept often becomes an absolute barrier to agreement. * * *

> In other areas, international law has provided a framework, and may well have averted many disputes from ever reaching the conflict stage. Nevertheless, the technicalities of international law can create problems, as in the Beagle Channel dispute. * * * [R]esolution of the Beagle Channel dispute involved separating the treatment of rights over islands from the treatment of rights over associated exclusive economic zones in a way that was legally irrational but politically sensible. * * *

> In contrast to the performance of substantive international law, the performance of procedural international law has been excellent in essentially all the examples. Existing processes have successfully led to the availability of international mediators and a reasonable focus of discussion in almost all disputes studied. * * *

> The panel of legal experts who advised our group also pointed out the success of *emerging* principles of international law, which coincide with political science notions of democratic processes, transparency, and the right of the individual to security. Inherent in the substance of every mediated agreement were adherence to democratic procedures, fair elections, transparent governmental procedures, the primacy of the rule of law, and the promise of human rights to all individuals. Many of the agreements and subsequent implementation agreements incorporated specific international legal norms and covenants (e.g., the annexes of the Dayton Accords, the new South African constitution).

> A further surprise arises in connection with the application of international law during the follow-up to an agreement. As indicated above, we are now able (relatively) quickly and easily to incorporate international actions to assist in making an agreement work. This is exemplified by guarantees and UN forces, such as those in Cambodia and Croatia. * * *

Barton & Greenberg, Lessons of the Case Studies, in Words Over War 343, 358–59 (2000).

NOTES

1. *Non–Governmental Organizations and Private Mediation.* Third-party mediation has sometimes been carried out by non-governmental organizations and private individuals, as in the above example of papal mediation of the Beagle Channel dispute between Argentina and Chile. In 1993, a Roman Catholic lay society in Rome played a key role in bringing an end to a bloody civil war in Mozambique that had gone on for almost a decade. See Hume, The Mozambique Peace Process, in the Diplomatic Record 1993. The International Committee of the Red Cross and the Society of Friends (Quakers) have both carried out mediation efforts through "quiet diplomacy." Former heads of state and government, such as ex-U.S. President Jimmy Carter, have mediated solutions to several sensitive disputes (e.g, the 1994 dispute over North Korean compliance with non-proliferation obligations) while acting in a private capacity. See, e.g., Tang, The North Korean Nuclear Proliferation Crisis, in Words Over War 321–40 (2000).

2. *Studies of Mediation.* For other studies of interest, see Merrills, in International Dispute Settlement 28–44 (4th ed. 2005) (chapter on mediation); Zartman, Ripe for Resolution (1985); Pechota, Complementary Structures of Third Party Settlement in International Disputes (UNITAR Study), reprinted in Dispute Settlement Through the United Nations 149–220 (Raman ed. 1977); Young, The Intermediaries, Third Parties in International Crises (1967). For other examples and analysis, see Final Report of the Carnegie Commission on Prevention of Deadly Conflict (1998).

C. CONCILIATION AND INQUIRY

Conciliation is a distinct form of third-party settlement, more formal than good offices or mediation but still non-binding. Procedures for commissions of inquiry, also a distinct form of settlement, were introduced in the 1899 and 1907 Hague Conventions for the Pacific Settlement of Disputes. Fact-finding commissions under the Hague Conventions were utilized in several disputes of the early twentieth century and a number of bilateral treaties provided for commissions of inquiry (*commissions d'enquête*). See Bar–Yaacov, The Handling of International Disputes By Means of Inquiry (1974); Report of the U.N. Secretary–General on Methods of Fact–Finding, U.N. Doc. A/5694 (1965) and A/6228 (1966); Merrills at 46–63 (4th ed. 2005). Inquiries under the Hague Conventions include several episodes in which there had been exchange of fire or allegations of attack and the parties disagreed over exactly what had happened. For example, a commission of inquiry investigated the 1904 Dogger Bank incident, in which a Russian warship had fired on a British fishing fleet in the mistaken belief that a Japanese torpedo attack was underway. Upon issuance of the report which concluded that there was no justification for opening fire, Russia paid an indemnity to Britain and the matter was considered closed. See Brierly, The Law of Nations 373–76 (6th ed. Waldock, 1963); Merrills, International Dispute Settlement 47–48 (4th ed. 2005).

Conciliation for dispute settlement is provided in the Vienna Convention on the Law of Treaties and the Vienna Convention on Succession of States in respect of Treaties. In both conventions, conciliation may be requested by any party to the dispute relating to the convention. The dispute is then referred to a conciliation commission which would seek to bring about an amicable settlement. The commission may make proposals to the parties, but such proposals are not binding on the parties. See Kearney & Dalton, The Treaty on Treaties, 64 A.J.I.L. 495, 553–55 (1970); Lavalle, The Dispute Settlement Provisions of the Vienna Convention on Succession of States in Respect of Treaties, 73 A.J.I.L. 407 (1979). The U.N. Convention on the Law of the Sea of 1982 provides for compulsory (but non-binding) conciliation at the request of any party to a dispute relating to certain fisheries, scientific research and boundary questions. Article 297(3).

Conciliation procedures are also found in other multilateral treaties, including the Covenant on Civil and Political Rights (Article 42) and other human rights treaties. The objective of such procedures may be to reach an "amicable solution" or "friendly settlement" of a dispute under the treaty, without full-scale adjudication of the factual and legal issues. Compare the *Case of Denmark v. Turkey*, Friendly Settlement Judgment, European Court of Human Rights, Apr. 5, 2000, 39 I.L.M. 788 (2000) (case concerning allegations of torture of a Danish citizen in Turkey settled under art. 38(1)(b) of European Convention as amended by Protocol No. 11).

Several new mechanisms for conciliation and related procedures were introduced in the 1990s. Under U.N. auspices, a set of Model Rules for the Conciliation of Disputes Between States was approved: see U.N. Doc. A/50/33 (1995) and discussion in Merrills, International Dispute Settlement 82–83 (4th ed. 2005). The Permanent Court of Arbitration has issued Optional Conciliation Rules (1996) and Optional Rules for Fact–Finding Commissions of Inquiry (1997), reprinted in Permanent Court of Arbitration, Basic Documents: Conventions, Rules, Model Clauses and Guidelines 153–84 (1998). The Organization for Security and Cooperation in Europe (O.S.C.E.) has likewise elaborated a Dispute Settlement Mechanism with elements of both mediation and conciliation, known as the Valletta Procedure, with enhancements subsequently adopted to induce resort to the available procedures. See Decision on Peaceful Settlement of Disputes, 32 I.L.M. 551 (1993) and related instruments discussed in Merrills, at 83–87. The Stockholm Convention on Conciliation and Arbitration, Dec. 15, 1992, 1842 U.N.T.S. 151, also an O.S.C.E. instrument, came into force in 1994 with twelve European states as initial parties.

It remains to be seen whether any of these innovations will encourage greater resort to conciliation as a means of international dispute settlement. As an illustration of the relative underutilization of conciliation as a dispute settlement technique, only three of sixty-three disputes submitted to the World Bank's International Centre for Settlement of Investment Disputes (ICSID) took advantage of the Centre's conciliation facility, while the rest were arbitration cases (as reported in summary at 39 I.L.M. 966, 979 (2000)). What factors might disincline disputants toward the use of this technique?

NOTES

1. *Bryan Treaties*. Early in the twentieth century, the United States pursued a program of negotiating what became known as the "Bryan peace treaties," beginning with a 1914 treaty with Great Britain. The United States eventually concluded forty-eight "Bryan peace treaties," many of which are still in force. See 6 Hackworth at 5; Hyde at 1570–72; Report of the Secretary–General on Methods of Factfinding, U.N. Doc. A/5694, at 29–33 (May 1, 1964). The gist of the treaties was an agreement to refer "all disputes of every nature whatsoever" which could not be otherwise settled to a standing Peace Commission, consisting of one national and one non-national nominated by each party and a fifth member chosen by agreement.

The Bryan treaties lay dormant until the 1990s, when the United States and Chile agreed to submit a highly sensitive dispute to a commission constituted under the 1914 Bryan–Suárez Mujica Treaty. The dispute concerned the assassination in Washington, D.C. in 1976 of Orlando Letelier, a former Chilean Foreign minister in exile, and his American assistant. In the wake of both a domestic civil lawsuit brought by the victims' heirs against Chile, and a criminal investigation which revealed involvement of personnel of the Chilean intelligence service, the United States made an international claim against Chile. Chile denied responsibility but eventually offered to make an *ex gratia* payment corresponding to the sum that would have been payable if liability had been established. A commission was established under the Bryan treaty framework, which settled the amount of compensation to be paid. The United States and Chile accepted the outcome of this process in final settlement of their dispute over the Letelier assassination. See Chile–United States: Agreement to Settle Dispute Concerning Compensation for the Deaths of Letelier and Moffitt, 30 I.L.M. 422 (1991). For the award, see 31 I.L.M. 1 (1992); 88 I.L.R. 727.

2. *Recommendatory Nature of Conciliation*. Should the purely recommendatory character of a conciliation commission's proposals be reinforced by declaring in the rules that the parties are in no way bound or estopped by the findings of the commission? A proposal to this effect made by Fitzmaurice to the *Institut de Droit International* was not carried. See 2 Ann. de l'Institut de Droit Int. 214 (1961). If a conciliation commission (e.g., under the Vienna Convention on the Law of Treaties) should find in favor of a state claiming invalidity of a treaty, would that finding furnish a good legal basis for that state to take steps to release it from the treaty commitment? Conversely, would a finding that there was no right to terminate estop a state from taking such action? It has been suggested that in determining the obligations of a party to the conciliation, the finding of the conciliator on the law and facts

should be given weight but not treated as conclusive. Schachter, International Law in Theory and Practice 216 (1991).

3. *Level of Procedural Formality in Conciliation.* Are conciliation commissions more effective if their procedure resembles that of negotiation (e.g., a round-table conference without rules of procedure)? Or is it generally desirable to have rules of procedure of a quasi-judicial nature? Both approaches have been followed in bilateral conciliation commissions. For consideration of the approaches, see 48–I Ann. de l'Institut de Droit Int. 5 (1959), 49–II id., 214 (1961). When a commission faces a disagreement on a question of fact and seeks to interrogate witnesses or experts, should the proceedings be of a judicial nature? See Fox, Conciliation in International Disputes: The Legal Aspects, in Report of David Davies Memorial Institute 93 (1972). For general treatment of conciliation, see also Cot, International Conciliation (Eng. trans. 1972).

D. DISPUTE SETTLEMENT THROUGH INTERNATIONAL ORGANIZATIONS

Any of the foregoing procedures can be pursued under the auspices of international organizations. The United Nations provides a forum for negotiated settlement of all sorts of disputes, as do regional organizations within their regions or specialized agencies within their sphere of competence. The U.N. Secretary–General can provide good offices in his own person or can designate a Special Representative ("S.R.S.G.") for any of the numerous conflicts demanding engagement at a given time. In a substantial number of cases, the U.N. Security Council has authorized the Secretary–General to seek to facilitate settlement of internal disputes between competing factions in a country. Such peace-making efforts are increasingly associated with peacekeeping operations acting under U.N. mandate, as addressed in Chapter 15.

Regional organizations such as the Organization of American States (O.A.S.), the Organization of African Unity (O.A.U.) which was replaced by the African Union in 2002, the Arab League, the Organization for Security and Cooperation in Europe (O.S.C.E.), the Association of South–East Asian States (ASEAN), and others have also had active roles in non-adjudicatory dispute settlement. The conflicts in ex-Yugoslavia were dealt with through joint efforts of mediators appointed by the U.N. Secretary–General and the European Community/European Union. Efforts toward settlement of the civil war in El Salvador were carried out by representatives of the O.A.S. and the U.N. Secretary–General in 1991–1993, as were the efforts to restore democratic government in Haiti from 1991–1994. Several African conflicts have included initiatives of a subregional organization, the Economic Community of West African States.

It has often been suggested that regional (or subregional) machinery be used before recourse is had to the United Nations; indeed, Article 52(2) and (3) of the U.N. Charter would appear to express a preference for prior resort to dispute settlement through regional arrangements. There is little evidence that the regional bodies have been more effective in dealing with high-intensity conflicts. Even conceding that regional bodies may be better for dispute settlement involving countries of the region, it is questionable whether the idea of regional primacy should deter or delay action in other bodies when it appears that regional measures will not be taken or are inadequate.

NOTES

1. *"Honest Broker" or Not?* The role of international institutions in facilitating negotiation may be substantially reduced when the governing bodies adopt positions or express views in favor of one side. When an organization is perceived by one party as hostile, it prejudices its opportunity to act as a third-party intermediary or to have its officials perform that role. Does this imply that international bodies should renounce their role of expressing international policy or applying principles of law to particular situations? May their positions, when based on a general consensus, generate pressure for negotiation even though the organization does not act in a mediational role? These questions have been raised in major disputes brought to the United Nations when one side has been supported by large majorities in the General Assembly or Security Council.

In a report to U.N. Secretary–General Kofi Annan in August 2000, a panel commissioned to review all aspects of U.N. peacekeeping addressed this tension between organizational "impartiality" and the need to take a stand against evident violations of international law. See p. 1263 note 3, in Chapter 15.

In some cases regional bodies have been perceived by one of the parties to the conflict as partial to the other and therefore as unsuitable for a mediatory role. From that standpoint the United Nations was preferred since its larger membership provided more assurance of even-handed treatment. Regional organizations also lack the resources and experience of the United Nations, particularly in regard to peacekeeping forces and large-scale fact-finding. The experiences in regard to the conflicts in ex-Yugoslavia, Somalia, and Haiti underlined the relative weakness of the respective regional bodies and the need for United Nations involvement. See generally Enforcing Restraint: Collective Intervention in Internal Conflicts (Damrosch ed. 1993) and further discussion in Chapter 15.

2. *Post–Conflict Settlement Arrangements.* Post-conflict agreements may influence the choice of dispute settlement mechanisms. Mediators (whether governments or international organs) may contribute to the solution of the difficulties by accepting a role in security or economic arrangements to be carried out after an agreed settlement. For example, the United Nations may provide observers to supervise demilitarization. The World Bank played a key role in settling the Indus River dispute by providing development funds. Large-scale multilateral assistance is also relevant to major disputes over water management and other scarce resources. See Weinthal, Making Waves: Third Parties and International Mediation in the Aral Sea Basin, in Words Over War 263–92 (2000). Prospects for settlement of the Israeli–Palestinian

dispute depend in part on external commitments concerning economic as well as security assistance.

SECTION 3.   ARBITRATION

A.   THE NATURE AND ROLE OF INTERNATIONAL ARBITRATION

Arbitration, in contrast to conciliation or mediation, leads to a binding settlement of a dispute on the basis of law. The arbitral body is composed of judges who are normally appointed by the parties but who are not subject to their instructions. The arbitral body may be established *ad hoc* by the parties or it may be a continuing body set up to handle certain categories of disputes. Arbitration differs from judicial settlement in that the parties have competence as a rule to appoint arbitrators, to determine the procedure and, to a certain extent, to indicate the applicable law.

The history of international arbitration can be traced as far back as ancient Greece, and its use as a means of peaceful settlement was frequent even during the Middle Ages. See generally Ralston, International Arbitration from Athens to Locarno 153–89 (1929). The process fell into disuse, however, until its revival in the nineteenth century by a series of arbitrations between the United States and the United Kingdom arising out of the Jay Treaty (1794) and the Treaty of Ghent (1814). See Simpson & Fox, International Arbitration 1–4 (1959); Hyde at 1587–88. A number of other international arbitrations occurred later in the nineteenth century, one of the most important of which concerned the claims of the United States against the United Kingdom for damages arising out of the activities of the Confederate warship *Alabama*. See Simpson & Fox at 8–9; Hyde at 1592–93. A system of rules and procedures was by this time gradually receiving general acceptance and in 1875 the *Institut de Droit International* completed an influential draft code of arbitral procedure. See Projet de règlement pour la procédure arbitrale internationale, I Ann. de l'Institut de Droit Int. 126 (1877).

At the Hague Peace Conference of 1899 arbitration was one of the most important topics under discussion. The resulting Convention for the Pacific Settlement of International Disputes, July 29, 1899, 32 Stat. 1799, 2 Malloy 2016, contained, in addition to provisions on good offices, mediation, and inquiry, a number of articles on international arbitration, the object of which was stated in Article XV to be "the settlement of differences between States by judges of their own choice, and on the basis of respect for law." Article XVI set out the parties' recognition that, "[i]n questions of a legal nature, and especially in the interpretation or application of International Conventions," international arbitration was the "most effective, and at the same time the most equitable, means of settling disputes which diplomacy has failed to settle." Article XVIII specified that an agreement to arbitrate implied the legal obligation to submit to the terms of the award. The Convention did not impose any specific obligation to arbitrate; it merely attempted to set up institutions and procedures that could be utilized when and if two or more states desired to submit a dispute to arbitration. Detailed rules on arbitral procedure were set out in the 1899 and 1907 Hague Conventions, and the so-called Permanent Court of Arbitration was established.

Since World War II, states have looked with less favor on the adoption of general multilateral conventions for compulsory arbitration. However, support for arbitration as a preferred means of adjudication still finds wide support among states. States continue to have frequent recourse to arbitration on an *ad hoc* basis. In some cases, arbitration has been used even when hostilities between the parties had broken out. A successful example is the *Rann of Kutch Case* between India and Pakistan, 50 I.L.R. 2 (1968), which involved a territorial dispute. See Blum, Islands of Agreement 60–253 (2007). More recently, the parties to the Dayton Agreement for settlement of the conflict in Bosnia–Herzegovina agreed to binding arbitration concerning the disputed territory known as the Brčko corridor. See note on pp. 580–81.

The tremendous growth of international commerce after the Second World War has led to a concomitant growth in the settlement of disputes arising from such commerce through arbitration. A leading institution in this field has been the International Court of Arbitration of the International Chamber of Commerce in Paris, France. Under its auspices and rules, a steadily growing number of disputes are settled. The United Nations Commission on International Trade Law has made international arbitration one of its preoccupations. It has developed the UNCITRAL Arbitration Rules that may be used both in *ad hoc* and institutionally supervised arbitration. Many arbitration institutions, including the American Arbitration Association (AAA), will administer arbitrations, under either their own rules or the UNCITRAL Rules. See Smit, The New International Arbitration Rules of the American Arbitration Association, 2 Am. Rev. Int'l Arb. 1 (1992). UNCITRAL has also developed a Model Law on International Commercial Arbitration, which has been adopted by a number of states in the United States and abroad. Developments in the field of international arbitration are addressed in the World Arbitration Reporter (Parker School of Foreign and Comparative Law, Columbia University) and the American Review of International Arbitration.

B. EXAMPLES OF CURRENT ARBITRAL SYSTEMS

As indicated, a variety of forums and rules are now available to facilitate arbitration, whether on a state-to-state basis, or between states and non-state parties, or entirely between private parties. A vast amount of information about these institutions can be accessed through the Electronic Information System for International Law, a project of the American Society of International Law linked via the A.S.I.L. website at www.asil.org and at http://www.eisil.org (following links to International Dispute Settlement/Arbitration). These electronic resources include entry points on the Permanent Court of Arbitration in The Hague, the International Court of Arbitration in Paris, the London Court of Arbitration, the World Intellectual Property Organization, the Court of Arbitration for Sport, the International Convention on the Settlement of Investment Disputes (ICSID), arbitration under Chapter 11 of the North American Free Trade Agreement (NAFTA), and the Court of Conciliation and Arbitration within the Organization for Security and Cooperation in Europe. National arbitral institutions are also accessible through the same website.

Several important arbitral systems addressing international law questions are examined here, in order to illustrate general considerations involving arbitration as a dispute settlement technique. For related developments involving the establishment of tribunals in specialized fields of international law (including arbitration of trade disputes under the auspices of the World Trade Organization), see Section 5 of this chapter.

1. Permanent Court of Arbitration

The Permanent Court of Arbitration (P.C.A.), established under the Hague Conventions of 1899 and 1907, was in no sense a "permanent court"—it did, however, make it possible to convene a Court from among a permanent panel of arbitrators. Under the method of selection laid down by Article XLIV of the revised Convention, Oct. 18, 1907, 36 Stat. 2199, 2 Malloy 2220, each party to the Convention was eligible to nominate a maximum of four persons "of known competency in questions of international law, of the highest moral reputation, and disposed to accept the duties of Arbitrator." When two states decided to refer a dispute to the Court, they could select two arbitrators from among those nominated by the states party to the Convention. Only one of those selected could be a national or a nominee of the selecting state. The four arbitrators would then choose an umpire. Detailed provision was made for the selection of an umpire if the arbitrators were unable to agree upon a single individual. Some of the P.C.A's twentieth-century cases are classics of international law, such as the *Island of Palmas* arbitration excerpted in Chapter 5.

The P.C.A. has evolved from its early-twentieth-century conception to become a multipurpose forum for the arbitration of different kinds of disputes which need not be of state-to-state character. The P.C.A.'s website at http://www.pca-cpa.org/ provides an overview of the dispute settlement services currently offered under P.C.A. auspices. It makes these services available to states, state entities, intergovernmental organizations, and private parties, under flexible systems of rules designed to accommodate the preferences of different categories of disputants over diverse subject-matters. As of 2009, the P.C.A. was hosting a wide array of fascinating cases, including eighteen investor-state arbitrations under bilateral or multilateral investment treaties; four other arbitrations under contracts or agreements involving at least one state, state-controlled entity, or intergovernmental organization as a party; and the Eritrea Ethiopia Claims Commission. Among its significant recently concluded proceedings were the Eritrea Ethiopia Boundary Commission (2008), the MOX Plant Case between Ireland and the United Kingdom (2008), and the Guyana–Suriname Maritime Boundary Delimitation (2007).

2. The Iran–United States Claims Tribunal

The most active arbitral tribunal in recent years has been the Iran–United States Claims Tribunal established under the Declaration of Algeria. 20 I.L.M. 223 (1981). It continues to function as of 2009, having already concluded and paid awards on 3,936 claims of individuals, companies, and banks. The most significant items remaining on its docket are government-to-government claims.

The Tribunal, which has its seat at The Hague, has had jurisdiction over private claims of nationals of the United States against Iran and nationals of Iran against the United States, as well as over certain claims between the two governments. However, it may not decide claims arising under a contract which contained a forum-selection clause specifying the Iranian courts. In one of the earliest cases, the Tribunal ruled that it also has no jurisdiction over "direct" claims by one government against the nationals of the other. Case No. A/2, decision of 19 December 1981, reprinted in 21 I.L.M. 78 (1982).

The Tribunal consists of nine members, of which three are chosen by Iran, three by the U.S., and three by the six thus appointed. The arbitration rules of the United Nations Commission on International Trade Law (UNCITRAL) govern the appointment of arbitrators and the procedure of the Tribunal. See Baker & Davis, The UNCITRAL Arbitration Rules in Practice: The Experience of the Iran–United States Claims Tribunal (1992). If the parties fail to agree on any of the three arbitrators chosen jointly, according to these rules, the Secretary–General of the Permanent Court of Arbitration at The Hague shall designate an appointing authority who may exercise his discretion in appointing an arbitrator to the disputed position. UNCITRAL Arbitration Rules, art. 7(b), 15 I.L.M. 701, 705 (1976). Pursuant to this provision, the Secretary–General designated the President of the Supreme Court of the Netherlands, Judge Moons, as the appointing authority. Appointments were made by him in several cases, including the appointment of the President of the Tribunal in 1985. In 1999, upon the resignation of Judge Moons as appointing authority, Judge Sir Robert Jennings of the United Kingdom was designated as the new appointing authority. He soon had to rule on a notice of challenge filed by Iran to the president of the tribunal. See Iran–U.S. Claims Tribunal Appointing Authority, 94 A.J.I.L. 378–79 (2000). The appointing authority also has the power to rule on challenges to the continued presence of a judge who refuses to withdraw and has done so in several cases. Articles 10–12, UNCITRAL Arbitration Rules, arts. 10–12. In the 1984 decision of the Tribunal on dual nationality (see Chapter 7, p. 468) the dissenting Iranian members declared that "[t]he composition of the so-called neutral arbitrators, itself the result of the imposed mechanism of the UNCITRAL Rules, is so unbalanced as to have made the

Tribunal lose all credibility to adjudicate any dispute between the Islamic Republic of Iran * * * and the United States." Case No. A/18, decision of 6 April 1984, 5 Iran–U.S. Claims Tribunal Reports 251, 266.

All decisions and awards of the Tribunal are final and binding. They are enforceable against either government in the courts of any nation in accordance with its laws. A fund was also established in the Central Bank of the Netherlands for payment of the awards to U.S. claimants. See Chapter 8, Section 8.

The Tribunal is required to decide cases on the basis of respect for law, applying choice of law rules and principles of commercial and international law which it determines to be applicable. For a statement on the implications of this provision, see Damrosch, et al., Panel on Decisions of Iran–United States Claims Tribunal, 78 A.S.I.L. Proc. 221, 227–33 (1984). See also Khan, The Iran–United States Claims Tribunal: Controversies, Cases and Contribution (1990); Caron, The Nature of the Iran–United States Claims Tribunal and the Evolving Structure of International Dispute Resolution, 84 A.J.I.L. 104 (1990); Aldrich, The Jurisprudence of the Iran–United States Claims Tribunal (1996); The Iran–United States Claims Tribunal (Lillich, Magraw, & Bederman eds. 1998); Brower & Brueschke, The Iran–United States Claims Tribunal (1998); The Iran–United States Claims Tribunal and the Process of International Claims Resolution (Caron & Crook eds. 2000); Holtzmann & Jansdóttir, International Mass Claims Processes: Legal and Practical Perspectives (2007).

3. Investor–State Arbitration Under ICSID and NAFTA

In addition to the foregoing institutions which have served to resolve certain investment disputes along with other kinds of disputes, major arenas for resolution of disputes between foreign investors and host states are available under the International Convention for the Settlement of Investment Disputes (ICSID) and under Chapter 11 of the North American Free Trade Agreement (NAFTA). Chapter 14 provides examples of investor-state arbitrations under the auspices of ICSID and NAFTA. See also Ratner, Regulatory Takings in Institutional Context: Beyond the Fear of Fragmented International Law, 102 A.J.I.L. 475 (2008) (surveying expropriation decisions of a variety of arbitral systems).

4. Arbitration of Law of the Sea Disputes

The U.N. Convention on the Law of the Sea reflects a preference for arbitration as the means to be used in default of any other choice of settlement machinery. See Article 287 on choice of dispute settlement procedure (especially Article 287, paragraph 3, which establishes arbitration as the default mechanism) and Annexes VII and VIII containing the provisions for constituting arbitral tribunals and special arbitral tribunals.

As of 2009, although the United States had not yet ratified the Law of the Sea Convention, the Executive Branch and the Senate Foreign Relations Committee had both indicated that the U.S. election among the several forms of dispute settlement available under the Convention would be for arbitration. For more on the Convention and the institutions established and available thereunder, including the relationship between arbitration and other modes of settlement of law of the sea disputes, see Section 5 below and Chapter 17.

C. THE UNDERTAKING TO ARBITRATE AND PROBLEMS RELATING TO EFFECTIVENESS OF ARBITRATION AGREEMENTS

Generally, parties to a dispute undertake to submit the controversy to arbitration and, in the same instrument, specify the method by which the arbitral tribunal is to be constituted, the questions it is to answer, and the procedures by which it shall arrive at a decision. The undertaking to arbitrate may also appear as an independent agreement or as a part thereof. Standing by itself, the undertaking to arbitrate usually does not dispose of all the detailed questions that must be settled before arbitration actually takes place. It may, as a minimum, specify the manner in which the arbitrators are to be selected. Other questions remain to be answered by the parties in a subsequent agreement, sometimes called the *compromis d'arbitrage*. The agreement to arbitrate will frequently make reference to one of the several available comprehensive bodies of arbitral rules and procedures (see above), with such adjustments as the parties deem suitable to their circumstances.

Questions of procedure not answered in the *compromis* or in the rules to which it refers must be settled by the tribunal. The *compromis* will normally give the tribunal the express power to perform this task, although it is often maintained that such a provision is unnecessary inasmuch as any arbitral tribunal has the inherent power to determine its procedures in a way not inconsistent with the *compromis*. Precedents established by past tribunals are often of great value.

Three persistent problems are related to international arbitration agreements: (1) the severability of an arbitration clause from the remainder of a contract or treaty, (2) the claim of denial of justice by refusal to arbitrate, and (3) the authority of a truncated international arbitral tribunal. These problems arise in public international arbitration between states or between a state and a private entity and in international commercial arbitration between private parties. See Schwebel, International Arbitration: Three Salient Problems (1987).

Severability of Arbitration Clause. The issue of severability arises when a contract or treaty containing an arbitration clause is claimed to be invalid or to have been terminated or suspended. In these circumstances it has been often argued that the nullification of the contract also vitiates the arbitral obligations of the parties. If the contract is invalid or no longer in force, it is claimed that the obligation to arbitrate fails with the agreement of which it is part. The argument against severability has been generally rejected on three principal grounds. First, an arbitration clause will ordinarily be comprehensive in terms and encompass "any dispute" arising out of or relating to the contract, including disputes over the validity of the agreement. See Delaume, Transnational Contracts: Applicable Law and Settlement of Disputes 59–61 (1985); Alvarez, Autonomy of International Arbitration Process, in Pervasive Problems in International Arbitration 137 (Mistelis & Lew eds., 2006). Second, if one party could deny the other a right to arbitration by the mere allegation that the agreement lacked initial or continuing validity, then the simple expedient of declaring the agreement void would always be open to a party to avoid its arbitral obligation. *Losinger & Co. Case*, 1936 P.C.I.J. (ser. C) No. 78, at 113–16. See Schwebel, International Arbitration 4 (1987). Third, it has been legally presumed that the parties to an agreement containing an arbitral clause conclude not one but two agreements: the principal substantive agreement and a second separable agreement providing for arbitration. Id. at 5. But see Wetter, Salient Features of Swedish Arbitrations Clauses, [1983] Y.B. Arb. Inst. Stockholm Chamber of Com. 33, 35 ("such a conception is almost always very far from [the parties'] minds as well as from those of their legal advisors.").

Despite these arguments in favor of severability, it has been claimed that two situations may be inappropriate for its application. Where the issue is not whether the principal agreement is valid, but whether it was actually concluded at all, there may be room to challenge the existence of the arbitration clause. See Jennings, Nullity and Effectiveness in International Law, in Cambridge Essays in International Law 66–67 (1965). Second, where the issue is whether the agreement to arbitrate is valid, the decision of the arbitral tribunal on the matter may be reviewable in a national court. See, e.g., French Code of Civil Procedure, as amended by Decree No. 81–500 of 12 May 1981, reprinted in 20 I.L.M. 917–22 (1981).

The major international arbitration agreements recognize the severability of the principal contract and an arbitration clause. The 1976 Arbitration Rules (Article 21(2)) adopted by the United Nations Commission on International Trade Law (UNCITRAL) provide that "an arbitration clause which forms part of a contract and which provides for arbitration under these Rules shall be treated as an agreement independent of the other terms of the contract." See also the 1985 Model Law on International Commercial Arbitration (Article 16(1)) ("A decision by the arbitral tribunal that the contract is null and void shall not entail *ipso jure* the invalidity of the arbitration clause"); the Rules of the Court of Arbitration of the International Chamber of Commerce (Article 8(4)) ("the arbitrator shall not cease to have jurisdiction by reason of any claim that the contract is null and void * * * provided he upholds the validity of the agreement to arbitrate."); Resolution on Arbitration between States, State Enterprises or State Entities, and Foreign Enterprises, 63–II Ann. de l'Institut de Droit Int. 324, art. 3(a) (1990) ("Unless the arbitration agreement provides otherwise * * * [t]he arbitration agreement is separable from the legal relationship to which it refers * * * ''). See further Schwebel, International Arbitration 13–23 (1987).

Denial of Justice from Refusal to Arbitrate. The Restatement (Third) § 712, Comment *h* declares that "a state may be responsible for a denial of justice under international law * * * if, having committed itself to a special forum for dispute settlement, such as arbitration, it fails to honor such commitment. * * * " The claim of denial of justice by refusal to arbitrate has been raised by states at various times. In the arbitrations involving *Texaco Overseas Petroleum Company (TOPCO) and California Asiatic Oil Company v. the Government of the Libyan Arab Republic*, 53 I.L.R. 389 (1979); and *Libyan American Oil Company (LIAMCO) v. Government of the Libyan Arab Republic*, 62 I.L.R. 141 (1982), the United States delivered the following note of protest to Libya over its decrees affecting the interests of TOPCO and LIAMCO:

> The concession agreements governing the operations of the oil companies specifically provide * * * for arbitration of disputes not otherwise settled. * * * The United States Government understands that the companies in question have requested arbitration; it expects that the Government of the Libyan Arab Republic will respond positively to their request since failure to do so would constitute a denial of justice and an additional breach of international law.

[1975] Digest of United States Practice in International Law 490 (1976).

In *Elf Aquitaine Iran v. National Iranian Oil Company*, 11 Y.B. Com. Arb. 98 (1986), the sole arbitrator stated that "[i]t is a recognized principle of international law that a state is bound by an arbitration clause contained in an agreement * * * and cannot thereafter unilaterally set aside the access of the other party to the system envisaged by the parties in their agreement for the settlement of disputes." Id. at 104. The arbitrator concluded that "[t]he existing precedents demonstrate * * * that a government bound by an arbitration clause cannot validly free itself of this obligation by an act of its own will such as, for example, by changing its internal law, or by a unilateral cancellation of the contract or of the concession." This unpublished portion of the Preliminary Award of 1982 is reproduced in Schwebel, International Arbitration 101 (1987).

Truncated Tribunals. The problem that arises in the case of a truncated arbitral tribunal is whether the tribunal has the power to issue a binding award when an arbitrator refuses to participate in the final award on his own initiative or on the instruction of a party, or when an arbitrator withdraws and a party fails to designate a replacement. This is a problem that has arisen in interstate arbitration and in arbitrations between states and aliens. Schwebel concludes that the weight of the law supports the authority of a truncated arbitral tribunal to render a binding award, but notes that the cases and the legal opinion of scholars are divided. Schwebel, International Arbitration 153 (1987). See also the extensive comments by members of the International Law Commission and other commentators on the authority of truncated tribunals, id. at

154–180; Lew et al., Comparative International Commercial Arbitration 322–28 (2003); Schwebel, The Validity of an Arbitral Award Rendered by a Truncated Tribunal, 6 I.C.C. Bull. 19 (1995); Sohlchi, The Validity of Truncated Tribunals Proceedings and Awards, 9 Arb. Int. 303 (1993).

The Iran–United States Claim Tribunal was confronted with the purposeful absence of arbitrators appointed by Iran. For example, in Case No. 17, 1 Iran–U.S. Claim Tribunal Rep. 415 (1982), Chamber Three of the Tribunal issued an award that was signed by only two of the three judges; the third judge from Iran, Judge Sani, informed the Tribunal that he would not sign the award because he had not been notified of the deliberative session of the Chamber during which the award was decided. One of the other judges responded that the case had been heard on September 1 and 2, 1982 and that during the following four months there had been numerous deliberations. Citing the *travaux préparatoires* of the UNCITRAL Rules, which the Iran–U.S. Claims Tribunal had incorporated into its own rules, the arbitrator signing the award contended that "under international law, Judge Sani cannot frustrate the work of the Chamber or the Tribunal by wilfully absenting himself and refusing to sign an award." Id. at 425. Similar absences of Iranian Judges occurred in nine other cases, but the Tribunal or the Chambers within it proceeded to give awards. Iran initially mounted a challenge to the awards in the courts of the Netherlands, but ultimately discontinued its claims. Schwebel maintains that in view of such discontinuance, "it may be concluded that Iran has acquiesced in the validity of those awards." Schwebel, International Arbitration: Three Salient Problems 253 (1987). See also Resolution on Arbitration between States, State Enterprises, or State Entities, and Foreign Enterprises, 63–II Ann. de l'Institut de Droit Int. 324, art. 3(c) (1990) ("A Party's refusal to participate in the arbitration, whether by failing to appoint an arbitrator pursuant to the arbitration agreement, or through the withdrawal of an arbitrator, or by resorting to other obstructionist measures, neither suspends the proceedings nor prevents the rendition of a valid award.").

On these and other problems, see Petrochilos, Procedural Law in International Arbitration (2004); Pervasive Problems in International Arbitration (Mistelis & Lew eds. 2006); Contemporary Issues in International Arbitration and Mediation: The Fordham Papers 2007 (Rovine ed. 2008).

NOTE

Bosnian Tribunal. In the 1995 Dayton Accords (General Framework Agreement for Peace in Bosnia and Herzegovina, 35 I.L.M. 75 (1996)), the parties committed themselves to binding arbitration to resolve a dispute over the inter-entity boundary line between the Bosnian–Croat Federation on the one hand and the Republika Srpska on the other, in the strategically important area known as Brčko. Each of the two sides appointed an arbitrator, and (in the absence of agreement between those two on a third) a Presiding

Arbitrator, Roberts B. Owen, was chosen by the President of the International Court of Justice as appointing authority. The Dayton Accords had envisioned the contingency of the tribunal being unable to reach a majority, and had provided that in that event, the decision of the Presiding Arbitrator would be final and binding. In each of three awards rendered in 1997, 1998, and 1999 respectively, only the Presiding Arbitrator signed the award. See 36 I.L.M. 396 (1997); 38 I.L.M. 534 (1999).

The Final Award is notable for its finding of massive failure of compliance on the part of the Serb authorities to meet the requirements of the previous awards, and for its ruling that non-compliance could be a ground for transferring the contested area entirely out of the territory of the non-complying side into the exclusive control of the other side. Other innovations include a regime for demilitarizing the corridor and setting up a structure to administer the area. See Introductory Note by Schreuer at 38 I.L.M. 534–35 (1999), commenting as follows:

> The Tribunal clearly assumed a public order function in deciding this case. Traditionally, arbitration is perceived as a mandate narrowly defined by the parties' agreement. Digression beyond this parameter is sometimes threatened by nullity. The Brčko Tribunal took a much broader view of its function. Despite its seemingly narrow task to determine the Inter–Entity Boundary Line, it took it upon itself to find the optimum solution as determined by the object and purpose of the Dayton Accords. It first created an international system of supervision and then a special neutral regime for the disputed area. The Tribunal took its mandate less from the disputing parties' agreement than from its role as an agent of the international community.

D. VALIDITY AND ENFORCEMENT OF ARBITRAL AWARDS

A most important advantage of international arbitration is that its awards are recognized and enforced in a large number of countries. As of 2009, the New York Convention on the Recognition and Enforcement of Foreign Arbitral Awards of June 10, 1958, 21 U.S.T. 2517, 330 U.N.T.S. 3, had been ratified by 143 states, including nearly all major commercial nations. This feature of international arbitration offers particular advantages in relations with foreign states. An arbitration clause in a contract with a foreign state ensures not only that there will be a forum to adjudicate any dispute that may arise under the contract, but also that any award rendered in such a dispute will be enforceable virtually anywhere in the world. In this respect, awards entitled to recognition and enforcement under the New York Convention enjoy more effective enforcement than other awards or judgments, including those of the International Court of Justice.

Under Article V of the New York Convention, recognition and enforcement of an arbitral award may be refused only under very limited circumstances. (For full terms, see Documents Supplement.) The grounds specified for denial of enforcement under Article V(1) are:

(a) incapacity of the parties to enter into the arbitral agreement under the law applicable to them, or invalidity of the agreement under governing law;

(b) lack of notice of appointment of the arbitrator or of the arbitration proceedings, or inability to present a case;

(c) the award does not fall within the terms of the submission to arbitration or contains decisions on matters beyond the scope of the submission;

(d) the composition of the arbitral authority or the arbitral procedure was not in accordance with the parties' agreement (or, in the absence thereof, with the law of the country where the arbitration took place); or

(e) the award has not yet become binding on the parties or has been set aside or suspended by a competent authority of the country in which (or under the law of which) it was made.

Two other grounds for refusal of enforcement are specified in Article V(2) as follows:

(a) the subject matter of the difference is not capable of settlement by arbitration under the law of the country where enforcement is sought; or

(b) enforcement would be contrary to the public policy of that country.

A large body of case law addresses the applicability of these exceptions to enforcement within the national legal systems of the various countries in which arbitrations are regularly held or where the assets of judgment debtors may be found.

NOTE

Further Reading. On international arbitration generally, see Lowenfeld, International Litigation and Arbitration 2d ed. 2002); Born, International Commercial Arbitration (rev. ed. 2009).

SECTION 4. THE INTERNATIONAL COURT OF JUSTICE

Before turning to the materials in this Section on the I.C.J., please read Articles 92–96 of the U.N. Charter and Articles 34–38 of the I.C.J. Statute (in the Documents Supplement), which are fundamental in understanding the basic structure of the I.C.J. and the main forms of its jurisdiction. All U.N. members are *ipso facto* parties to the I.C.J. Statute, but this legal relationship needs to be carefully distinguished from whether any given state accepts the Court's jurisdiction as provided in Article 36 of the Statute.

The Court has two kinds of jurisdiction: to decide contentious cases between states and to render advisory opinions. These two forms of jurisdiction are considered respectively in Sections 4.A and 4.B.

The historical precursor of the I.C.J. was the Permanent Court of International Justice which sat in the interwar period. The present I.C.J. Statute is derived in large part from the P.C.I.J. Statute, and the jurisprudence of the two bodies is essentially continuous. Declarations of acceptance of the compulsory jurisdiction of the Permanent Court are carried over to the I.C.J. pursuant to Article 36, paragraph 5 of the latter's Statute.

There are fifteen judges on the Court elected by the Security Council and the General Assembly, each body voting separately. The judges may include no more than one national of any state. Judges serve for nine years, with five judges rotating off each three years. Judges may be reelected and often are. Nominations are made by national groups rather than by governments. See Articles 2–12 of the Statute.

A "gentlemen's agreement" among members of the United Nations generally governs the distribution of seats among the various regions of the world. A practice has also evolved (consistent with the Security Council's role in elections) under which the permanent members of the Security Council generally have judges of their nationality on the bench. Following the regular triennial elections held in November 2008 for the seats to be filled with effect from February 2009, the Court had one judge from the United States, four from "western Europe and other" (France, Germany, New Zealand, and the United Kingdom,), two from eastern Europe (Russian Federation and Slovakia), three from Asia (China, Japan, and Jordan), three from Africa (Morocco, Sierra Leone, and Somalia), and two from Latin America (Brazil and Mexico).

If a party in a case does not have a judge of its nationality on the standing bench, it may designate an *ad hoc* judge (Article 31).

The Court generally has decided cases by a full bench. It may, however, form chambers, composed of three or more judges to deal with a particular case or a category of cases (Articles 25–26). The Court also has a standing chamber of five judges to determine cases by summary procedure where speedy action is required (Article 29). In 1993 a special Environmental Chamber was established; it was discontinued in 2006.

All questions are decided by a majority vote of the judges present. In case of a tie the President has a casting vote (Article 55). The casting vote has been used in several of the Court's most controversial judgments, including the 1996 *Nuclear Weapons* advisory opinion where the judges were equally divided and President Bedjaoui (Algeria) cast the deciding vote. See p. 86 note 1.

In its first half-century (1946–1996), the Court had just about a hundred cases presented to it, of which seventy-five were under its contentious (state-to-state) jurisdiction and twenty-two were advisory opinion proceedings at the request of international organizations. It rendered sixty-two judgments, of which thirty-nine were on the merits, and twenty-two advisory opinions. It also issued 298 orders, mostly of a procedural character but including some indicating provisional measures. See I.C.J. Yb. 1996–1997, at 3.

In the last decade the number of cases brought to the Court has increased markedly, and the Court has had to cope with a docket that is growing in size, variety, complexity, and significance. At the opening of 2009, the Court had sixteen pending cases, coming from every U.N. regional group and covering a wide range of subject-matters: territorial sovereignty, maritime delimitation, armed conflict, human rights, mutual legal assistance, environmental matters, and a variety of other issues. As the outgoing president of the Court, Judge Rosalyn Higgins, informed the U.N. General Assembly in her speech surveying annual developments on October 30, 2008, the Court had just completed "the most productive year in its history."

Many of the Court's judgments and advisory opinions have been of major significance for the clarification and development of international law. Nonetheless, international lawyers and students of international relations have noted and often deplored the fact that states have not chosen to submit most of their legal disputes to the Court, for reasons summed up in the following comments:

> It is no great mystery why they are reluctant to have their disputes adjudicated. Litigation is uncertain, time consuming, troublesome. Political officials do not want to lose control of a case that they might resolve by negotiation or political pressures. Diplomats naturally prefer diplomacy; political leaders value persuasion, manoeuvre and flexibility. They often prefer to "play it by ear," making their rules fit the circumstances rather than submit to pre-existing rules. Political forums, such as the United Nations, are often more attractive, especially to those likely to get wide support for political reasons. We need only compare the large number of disputes brought to the United Nations with the few submitted to adjudication. One could go on with other reasons. States do not want to risk losing a case when the stakes are high or be troubled with litigation in minor matters. An international tribunal may not inspire confidence, especially when some judges are seen as "political" or as hostile. There is apprehension that the law is too malleable or fragmentary to sustain "true" judicial decisions. In some situations, the legal issues are viewed as but one element in a complex political situation and consequently it is considered unwise or futile to deal with them separately. Finally we note the underlying perception of many governments that law essentially supports the *status quo* and that courts are not responsive to demands for justice or change.

Schachter, International Law in Theory and Practice 218 (1991). These concerns persist, even as the number and complexity of cases brought to the Court has increased.

NOTES

1. *Nominations by National Groups.* On the practice for choosing judges, with particular reference to the role of the national groups "at one remove" from governments, see presentations by Abi–Saab and Damrosch on the topic "Ensuring the Best Bench: Ways of Selecting Judges," in Increasing the Effectiveness of the International Court of Justice 165–206 (Peck & Lee eds. 1997). On the way that the U.S. National Group has carried out consultations with professional organizations as recommended in Article 6 of the I.C.J. Statute, see Damrosch, The Election of Thomas Buergenthal to the International Court of Justice, 94 A.J.I.L. 579 (2000).

2. Ad Hoc *Judges.* Sometimes interesting issues arise concerning the use of *ad hoc* judges. For example, when the Federal Republic of Yugoslavia brought separate cases against ten NATO member states concerning legality of use of force in the 1999 Kosovo crisis, Yugoslavia named its own judge *ad hoc* but objected to designation of judges *ad hoc* by certain of the respondents, on the ground that the bench already contained five judges from NATO respondent countries (France, Germany, the Netherlands, the United Kingdom, and the United States). The Court, after deliberation, found that the nomination of judges *ad hoc* by the respective respondents in their own cases was justified at the provisional measures phase. See *Legality of Use of Force* (Yugoslavia v. Belgium), Request for the Indication of Provisional Measures, 1999 I.C.J. 124, para. 12, 38 I.L.M. 950, 954 (1999), and similar orders in the cases of Yugoslavia v. Canada, Yugoslavia v. Italy, Yugoslavia v. Spain, 38 I.L.M. at 1036, 1041 (para. 12); 1088, 1092 (para. 12); 1149, 1153 (para. 12). Portugal was sued but did not name a judge *ad hoc.* (Hungary, also a NATO member, had a judge on the bench but was not sued by Yugoslavia.)

3. *Chambers. Ad hoc* chambers have been used in a number of recent cases, including *Gulf of Maine Area Case* (Canada/United States), 1984 I.C.J. 246; *Frontier Dispute* (Burkina Faso/Mali), 1986 I.C.J. 554; *ELSI Case* (United States/Italy), 1989 I.C.J. 15; *Land, Island and Maritime Frontier Dispute* (El Salvador/Honduras; Nicaragua intervening), 1992 I.C.J. 351; and *Frontier Dispute* (Benin/Niger), 2005 I.C.J. 90. One of the controversial aspects of the use of chambers is the extent to which the parties may influence or control the selection of the judges. Judge Oda has noted that, although the jurisprudence of the Court is intended to reflect the diversity of the world's legal systems:

> In the case of all four of the ad hoc Chambers that have been constituted during recent years, consideration of "the main forms of civilization and the principal legal systems of the world" apparently was not in the minds of the parties in proposing the judges to sit on the Chamber or of the Court as a whole in electing the Chamber. * * * It may also be asked, when there are five main regions according to United Nations practice, by what criteria is the Court to choose three judges from among these five regions?

Oda, Note and Comment, Further Thoughts on the Chambers Procedure of the International Court of Justice, 82 A.J.I.L. 556, 557 (1988). Do you agree that the objectivity, neutrality, and reputation of the Court is threatened by a system that allows the parties to have their dispute heard by an ad hoc chamber because they fear that the composition of the full court may not suit their goals? Consider an opposing view in favor of the use of chambers by Judge Schwebel:

> The workings of this process to date show that it affords the Court the opportunity to settle international disputes in a fashion that meets the needs of the parties and the international community, and does not detract from the integrity of the Court. It has not "fractionalized" or "regionalized" international law in any degree. It has not thrown into question the universal character of international law. It may be that sometimes the parties may desire, or settle upon, a Chamber of regional complexion; other times they will not. That happens in ad hoc arbitration as well.

Schwebel, Ad Hoc Chambers of the International Court of Justice, 81 A.J.I.L. 831, 850 (1987).

4. *Further Reading*. Several valuable treatises survey the law and procedure of the I.C.J, including The Statute of the International Court of Justice: A Commentary (Zimmermann, Oellers–Frahm, & Tomuschat eds. 2006); Rosenne, The Law and Practice of the International Court, 1920–2004 (4th ed. 2005); Rosenne's The World Court: What It Is and How It Works (6th rev. ed. Gill ed. 2003).

A. CONTENTIOUS CASES

Only states may be parties to a contentious case, not international organizations or private persons. The jurisdiction of the Court in contentious cases is based on the consent of the parties, express or implied (Article 36 of the Statute). Consent may be given *ad hoc* or by prior agreement in a treaty (Article 36(1)) or by accepting compulsory jurisdiction under Article 36(2). In the latter case, the case must be a "legal dispute." No such limitation is imposed in Article 36(1). However, Article 38 states that the function of the Court is to "decide in accordance with international law such disputes as are submitted to it." See Restatement § 903, Comment *d*.

1. General Principles: Consent and Reciprocity

Consent and reciprocity are the two bedrock principles of the Court's contentious jurisdiction. Consent is typically established by reference to the terms of a treaty or special agreement invoked under Article 36(1) or a unilateral declaration of acceptance under Article 36(2). Additionally, even if there is no preexisting agreement or declaration, a state may indicate its consent to be sued by pleading to the merits of a claim without raising any objections to jurisdiction. This last possibility, known as the principle of *forum prorogatum*, has been applied in the jurisprudence of both the Permanent Court and the present Court, as in the *Haya de la Torre* case, 1951 I.C.J. 71, 78, where the Court observed:

The Parties have in the present case consented to the jurisdiction of the Court. All the questions submitted to it have been argued on the merits, and no objection has been made to a decision on the merits. This conduct of the Parties is sufficient to confer jurisdiction on the Court.

More recently, in *Certain Questions of Mutual Assistance in Criminal Matters* (Djibouti v. France), 2008 I.C.J. No. 136, Djibouti successfully sought to found the Court's jurisdiction upon consent to be given prospectively by the respondent. In due course, France gave consent by means of a letter specifying that its consent was "valid only for the purposes of the case, within the meaning of Article 38, paragraph 5, i.e. in respect of the dispute forming the subject of the Application and strictly within the limits of the claims formulated therein." When the parties later disagreed on the precise scope of their mutual consent, the Court had to resolve the matter by reading Djibouti's application in conjunction with France's letter in order to determine the extent of its own jurisdiction.

Reciprocity in an Article 36(1) case is usually found in the mutual obligations of the parties under the treaty invoked by the applicant. In an Article 36(2) case, however, the Court must determine whether both parties, by virtue of their unilateral declarations, have accepted "the same obligation." The Court's decisions establish that the respondent may invoke, by way of reciprocity, any material conditions that the applicant has placed on its own consent to jurisdiction. There is by now a considerable body of case law applying the principle of reciprocity. See, e.g., the *Nicaragua* case and notes at pp. 607–09 below.

2. Jurisdiction by Special Agreement

Many cases come to the I.C.J. by means of a special agreement (*compromis*), in which the parties specifically define the terms of the dispute and the questions they would like the Court to resolve. It has sometimes been suggested that cases submitted on the basis of a negotiated agreement with contemporaneous consent (that is, after the contours of a dispute are known) are positively correlated with the likelihood that the judicial proceeding will successfully resolve the underlying dispute. On questions of compliance, see Section 4.A.8, p. 623 below.

Under cases brought by special agreement, the Court is limited to the questions put by the parties. For example, in *Sovereignty over Pedra Branca/Pulau Batu Puteh, Middle Rocks and South Ledge* (Malaysia/Singapore), 2008 I.C.J. No. 130, Malaysia and Singapore had executed a special agreement to submit to the Court their dispute over Pedra Branca/Pulau Batu Puteh (a granite island), Middle Rocks (two clusters of small rocks), and South Ledge (a rock formation visible only at low tide). Article 2 of the special agreement asked the Court to determine whether sovereignty over each of these three specified maritime features belongs to Malaysia or Singapore. The Court ruled that sovereignty over the first belongs to Singapore and over the second to Malaysia, but with respect to the third, South Ledge, it found itself unable to make a specific determination. The difficulty with South Ledge concerned its status as a low-tide elevation (above water at low tide but submerged at high tide), which according to the Court's prior jurisprudence could not be considered territory in the same sense as islands. Sovereignty over a low-tide elevation located within a state's territorial waters would lie with that state. In the case of the Malaysia/Singapore dispute, however, no delimitation of their overlapping claims to territorial waters had yet been made, and the Court had not been asked to draw such a line of delimitation. Accordingly, the Court concluded (paras. 291–300) that because the special agreement did not authorize the Court to decide on the delimitation of territorial waters, the Court would have to limit itself to determining that sovereignty over South Ledge "belongs to the State in the territorial waters of which it is located," without specifying which one that would be.

3. Jurisdiction by Treaty

ARMED ACTIVITIES ON THE TERRITORY OF THE CONGO (DEMOCRATIC REPUBLIC OF THE CONGO v. RWANDA)

International Court of Justice, 2006
2006 I.C.J. No. 126

[The Democratic Republic of the Congo brought an application against Rwanda in 2002, complaining of Rwandan involvement in and support for a variety of military activities in Congo's territory. The D.R.C. sought to found the jurisdiction of the Court on nine treaties with dispute settlement clauses providing for I.C.J. jurisdiction. Rwanda contested jurisdiction, insisting that it had never bound itself to submit treaty-based disputes to the I.C.J. Two of the treaties—the Convention Against Torture and the Convention on Privileges and Immunities of the Specialized Agencies—were easily disposed of because Rwanda had never become party to the first and because the D.R.C. did not pursue any contentions concerning the latter. As for the remaining treaties, Rwanda's position was either that it had entered reservations to their dispute settlement clauses or that the treaty provisions in question did not cover the matters in dispute. In response to Rwanda's preliminary objections, the D.R.C. denied the validity or effectiveness of Rwanda's reservations to the dispute settlement clauses and endeavored to show that the dispute fell within the terms of the treaties invoked. The Court upheld Rwanda's preliminary objections and dismissed the case for lack of jurisdiction. Excerpts from its judgment follow, covering several of the treaties at issue; its analysis for other treaties was similar.]

27. The Court will examine in the following order the compromissory clauses invoked by the DRC: Article IX of the Genocide Convention; Article 22 of the Convention on Racial Discrimination; Article 29, paragraph 1, of the Convention on Discrimination against Women;

Article 75 of the [World Health Organization] Constitution, Article XIV, paragraph 2 of the Unesco Convention; Article 14, paragraph 1, of the Montreal Convention [for the Suppression of Unlawful Acts against the Safety of Civil Aviation]; Article 66 of the Vienna Convention on the Law of Treaties.

[The Court begins by quoting from Articles II, III, and IX of the Genocide Convention; for these provisions, see Documents Supplement. Rwanda contended that it had excluded the entirety of any dispute settlement obligation under the Genocide Convention by virtue of a reservation entered at the time of ratification which read: "The Rwandese Republic does not consider itself as bound by Article IX of the Convention." The D.R.C. claimed that Rwanda had withdrawn this reservation by committing itself at the time of a 1993 peace agreement (aimed at ending an internal conflict on its territory) that it would withdraw all reservations to human rights treaties, and that an internal Rwandan decree-law and public statements subsequently made by Rwanda's Minister of Justice had effectuated such a withdrawal. The Court, however, noted that Rwanda had never taken formal acts on the international plane to bring about withdrawal of the reservation:]

41.   * * * [A] clear distinction has to be drawn between a decision to withdraw a reservation to a treaty taken within a State's domestic legal order and the implementation of that decision by the competent national authorities within the international legal order, which can be effected only by notification of withdrawal of the reservation to the other States parties to the treaty in question. It is a rule of international law, deriving from the principle of legal security and well established in practice, that, subject to agreement to the contrary, the withdrawal by a contracting State of a reservation to a multilateral treaty takes effect in relation to the other contracting States only when they have received notification thereof [quoting Articles 22–23 of the Vienna Convention on the Law of Treaties on written notification of such an action].

42.   The Court observes that in this case it has not been shown that Rwanda notified the withdrawal of its reservations * * * to the States parties to the Genocide Convention. Nor has it been shown that there was any agreement whereby such withdrawal could have become operative without notification. In the Court's view, the adoption of that *décret-loi* and its publication in the Official Journal of the Rwandese Republic cannot in themselves amount to such notification. In order to have effect in international law, the withdrawal would have had to be the subject of a notice received at the international level.

43.   The Court * * * observes that this Convention is a multilateral treaty whose depositary is the Secretary–General of the United Nations, and it considers that it was normally through the latter that Rwanda should have notified withdrawal of its reservation. * * * [I]t is thus in principle through the medium of the Secretary–General that [states parties] must be informed both of the making of a reservation to the

Convention and of its withdrawal. Rwanda notified its reservation to Article IX of the Genocide Convention to the Secretary–General. However, the Court does not have any evidence that Rwanda notified the Secretary–General of the withdrawal of this reservation.

* * *

89.   The Court will now examine the conditions laid down by Article 29 of the Convention on Discrimination against Women. It will begin by considering whether in this case there exists a dispute between the Parties "concerning the interpretation or application of [that] Convention" which could not have been settled by negotiation.

90.   The Court recalls in this regard that, as long ago as 1924, the Permanent Court of International Justice stated that "a dispute is a disagreement on a point of law or fact, a conflict of legal views or interests" (*Mavrommatis Palestine Concessions, Judgment No. 2, 1924, P.C.I.J., Series A, No. 2*, p. 11).

For its part, the present Court has had occasion a number of times to state the following:

> "In order to establish the existence of a dispute, 'it must be shown that the claim of one party is positively opposed to the other' * * * and further, 'Whether there exists an international dispute is a matter for objective determination' * * *." [Citations omitted.]

91.   The Court notes that in the present case the DRC made numerous protests against Rwanda's actions in alleged violation of international human rights law, both at the bilateral level through direct contact with Rwanda and at the multilateral level within the framework of international institutions such as the United Nations Security Council and the Commission on Human and Peoples' Rights of the Organization of African Unity. In its Counter–Memorial and at the hearings the DRC presented these protests as proof that "the DRC has satisfied the preconditions to the seisin of the Court in the compromissory clauses invoked." Whatever may be the legal characterization of such protests as regards the requirement of the existence of a dispute between the DRC and Rwanda for purposes of Article 29 of the Convention, that Article requires also that any such dispute be the subject of negotiations. The evidence has not satisified the Court that the DRC in fact sought to commence negotiations in respect of the interpretation or application of the Convention.

92.   The Court further notes that the DRC has also failed to prove any attempts on its part to initiate arbitration proceedings with Rwanda under Article 29 of the Convention. The Court cannot in this regard accept the DRC's argument that the impossibility of opening or advancing in negotiations with Rwanda prevented it from contemplating having recourse to arbitration; since this is a condition formally set out in Article 29 of the Convention on Discrimination against Women, the lack of agreement between the parties as to the organization of an arbitration cannot be presumed. The existence of such disagreement can follow only

from a proposal for arbitration by the applicant, to which the respondent has made no answer or which it has expressed its intention not to accept [citations omitted]. In the present case, the Court has found nothing in the file which would enable it to conclude that the DRC made a proposal to Rwanda that arbitration proceedings should be organized, and that the latter failed to respond thereto.

93.   It follows from the foregoing that Article 29, paragraph 1, of the Convention on Discrimination against Women cannot serve to found the jurisdiction of the Court in the present case.

[The portions of the opinion dealing with the other treaties invoked by the DRC are omitted.]

125.   * * * Finally, the Court deems it necessary to recall that the mere fact that rights and obligations *erga omnes* or peremptory norms of general international law (*jus cogens*) are at issue in a dispute cannot in itself constitute an exception to the principle that its jurisdiction always depends on the consent of the parties * * *.

126.   The Court concludes from all of the foregoing considerations that it cannot accept any of the bases of jurisdiction put forward by the DRC in the present case. Since it has no jurisdiction to entertain the Application, the Court is not required to rule on its admissibility.

NOTES

1.   *Patterns of Treaty–Based Jurisdiction.* Nearly 300 treaties currently in force provide for resolution of disputes by the International Court. See the Court's Yearbook and website for details. The United States is a party to more than seventy bilateral and multilateral treaties that include compromissory clauses providing for I.C.J. jurisdiction. Morrison, Treaties as a Source of Jurisdiction Especially in U.S. Practice, in The International Court of Justice at a Crossroads 58, 61 (Damrosch ed. 1987). For a list of these treaties, see the appendix to Justice Breyer's dissent in *Medellin v. Texas*, 128 S.Ct. 1346, 1392 (2008), discussed in Chapter 10.

2.   *Multilateral Treaties.* Some general multilateral conventions provide for compulsory jurisdiction through optional protocols such as those to the Vienna Conventions on Diplomatic Relations and on Consular Relations. Other conventions have jurisdictional clauses that allow any party to bring the dispute to the Court. Some of these conventions expressly allow reservations; others are silent on reservations but have had reservations made to them, as discussed in the principal case in relation to the Genocide Convention.

3.   *Treaties of Friendship, Commerce and Navigation.* Many bilateral treaties include provisions for compulsory jurisdiction of disputes relating to the interpretation and application of the treaty. Treaties of friendship, commerce and navigation entered into by the United States with some thirty countries have such clauses. One was invoked by the United States in its case against Iran concerning the hostages in Tehran and another was invoked by

Nicaragua in its proceeding against the United States for military and paramilitary activity against Nicaragua (*infra*).

The U.S.–Iranian treaty came before the Court again in the *Oil Platforms* case, 1996 I.C.J. 803, 2003 I.C.J. 161; on that occasion Iran (which had ignored the Court in the *Tehran Hostages* case) sued the United States in relation to incidents occurring during the Iran–Iraq naval war of 1987–1988, when the U.S. military had destroyed certain Iranian oil platforms in the Persian Gulf which (according to the United States) had been used by the Iranian military to mount hostile attacks on neutral merchant shipping in the Gulf. Although Iran invoked several aspects of the bilateral treaty (known as the Treaty of Amity, Economic Relations, and Consular Rights), the Court confirmed jurisdiction only with respect to the Iranian contention that the U.S. conduct had interfered with freedom of navigation in violation of the treaty. The case is discussed further at p. 623 note 4.

4. Compulsory Jurisdiction Under the Optional Clause

Article 36(2) of the Statute provides:

> 2. The states parties to the present Statute may at any time declare that they recognize as compulsory *ipso facto* and without special agreement, in relation to any other state accepting the same obligation, the jurisdiction of the Court in all legal disputes concerning:
>
> a. the interpretation of a treaty;
>
> b. any question of international law;
>
> c. the existence of any fact which, if established, would constitute a breach of an international obligation;
>
> d. the nature or extent of the reparation to be made for the breach of an international obligation.

Article 36(3) of the Statute states:

> 3. The declarations referred to above may be made unconditionally or on condition of reciprocity on the part of several or certain states, or for a certain time.

As of 2009, sixty-six states were bound by declarations under Article 36(2). They are listed and their declarations are reprinted in the Yearbooks of the I.C.J. and also on the Court's website (www.icj-cij.org). Although for some periods of time certain groups of states (notably the Soviet bloc) had refrained from joining the optional clause system, this situation changed with the end of the Cold War, and the states accepting compulsory jurisdiction under Article 36(2) now come from all regions, including several of the post-Soviet and Eastern European states. Some declarations date from the period of the Permanent Court of International Justice: under Article 36(5) of the I.C.J. Statute, such declarations are deemed to be acceptances of the jurisdiction of the successor Court. The declarations of about a dozen more states are no longer effective, either because they have expired or have been withdrawn or terminated without being replaced. As summarized in the Restatement § 903, Reporters' Note 2:

> Some of the declarations are without limit of time; others are for a specific period (usually five or ten years), in many instances with an automatic renewal clause. Many declarations reserve the right to terminate by a notice of withdrawal effective upon receipt by the Secretary–General of the United Nations. Some declarations specify that they apply only to disputes arising after the declaration was made or concerning situations or facts subsequent to a specified date. Seventeen declarations are without any reservation; the remaining declarations are accompanied by a variety of reservations. Many states have modified their reservations, some of them several times.

> The most common reservation excludes disputes committed by the parties to other tribunals or which the parties have agreed to settle by other means of settlement. Another common reservation excludes disputes relating to matters that are "exclusively" or "essentially" within the domestic jurisdiction of the declarant state; some of these reservations provide in addition that the question whether a dispute is essentially within the domestic jurisdiction is to be determined by the declaring state (a so-called "self-judging" clause). Several declarations exclude disputes arising under a multilateral treaty "unless all parties to the treaty affected by the decision are also parties to the case before the Court" or, more broadly, "unless all parties to the treaty are also parties to the case before the Court." Some reservations exclude disputes as to a particular subject, such as territorial or maritime boundaries or other law of the sea issues.

> A few declarations, using various formulas, exclude disputes arising out of hostilities to which the declarant state is a party; the most comprehensive of these reservations is that of India which excludes "disputes relating to or connected with facts or situations of hostilities, armed conflicts, individual or collective actions taken in self-defense, resistance to aggression, fulfillment of obligations imposed by international bodies, and other similar or related acts, measures or situations in which India is, has been or may in future be involved." A reservation of the United Kingdom made in 1957 excluded disputes "relating to any question which, in the opinion of the Government of the United Kingdom, affects the national security of the United Kingdom or of any of its dependent territories"; this clause was restricted in the United Kingdom's 1958 declaration to certain past disputes and was omitted in its 1963 declaration.

> An increasing number of states have added to their declarations clauses designed to avoid surprise suits by states that accept the Court's jurisdiction and immediately bring a case against another state. For instance, some states have excluded any dispute that was brought before the Court by a party to a dispute less than 12 months

after the party had accepted the jurisdiction of the Court with respect to that category of disputes. Many states have reserved the right to modify or terminate a declaration peremptorily by means of a notification to the Secretary–General of the United Nations, with effect from the moment of that notification.

ILLUSTRATIVE DECLARATIONS RECOGNIZING COMPULSORY JURISDICTION

GUINEA–BISSAU

[Translation from the French]

7 VIII 89.

In accordance with Article 36, paragraph 2, of the Statute of the International Court of Justice, the Republic of Guinea–Bissau accepts as compulsory *ipso facto* and without special agreement, in relation to any other State accepting the same obligation, the jurisdiction of the Court in all legal disputes referred to in Article 36, paragraph 2, of the Statute thereof.

This declaration will remain in force until six months following the date on which the Government of Guinea–Bissau makes known its intention of terminating it.

New York, 7 August 1989.

(Signed) Raul A. DE MELO CABRAL,

Chargé d'affaires a.i.

UNITED KINGDOM OF GREAT BRITAIN AND NORTHERN IRELAND

5 July 2004

1. The Government of the United Kingdom of Great Britain and Northern Ireland accept as compulsory *ipso facto* and without special convention, on condition of reciprocity, the jurisdiction of the International Court of Justice, in conformity with paragraph 2 of Article 36 of the Statute of the Court, until such time as notice may be given to terminate the acceptance, over all disputes arising after 1 January 1974, with regard to situations or facts subsequent to the same date, other than:

(i) any dispute which the United Kingdom has agreed with the other Party or Parties thereto to settle by some other method of peaceful settlement;

(ii) any dispute with the government of any other country which is or has been a Member of the Commonwealth;

(iii) any dispute in respect of which any other Party to the dispute has accepted the compulsory jurisdiction of the International Court of Justice only in relation to or for the purpose of the dispute; or where the acceptance of the Court's compulsory jurisdiction on behalf of any other Party to the dispute was deposited or ratified less than twelve months prior to the filing of the application bringing the dispute before the Court.

2.   The Government of the United Kingdom also reserve the right at any time, by means of a notification addressed to the Secretary–General of the United Nations, and with effect as from the moment of such notification, either to add to, amend or withdraw any of the foregoing reservations, or any that may hereafter be added.

New York, 5 July 2004.

(Signed) Emyr JONES PARRY

Permanent Representative of the United Kingdom of Great Britain and Northern Ireland to The United Nations

UNITED STATES OF AMERICA

26 VIII 46.

I, Harry S. Truman, President of the United States of America, declare on behalf of the United States of America, under Article 36, paragraph 2, of the Statute of the International Court of Justice, and in accordance with the Resolution of 2 August 1946 of the Senate of the United States of America (two-thirds of the Senators present concurring therein), that the United States of America recognizes as compulsory *ipso facto* and without special agreement, in relation to any other State accepting the same obligation, the jurisdiction of the International Court of Justice in all legal disputes hereafter arising concerning—

(a) the interpretation of a treaty;

(b) any question of international law;

(c) the existence of any fact which, if established, would constitute a breach of an international obligation;

(d) the nature or extent of the reparation to be made for the breach of an international obligation;

Provided, that this declaration shall not apply to—

(a) disputes the solution of which the parties shall entrust to other tribunals by virtue of agreements already in existence or which may be concluded in the future; or

(b) disputes with regard to matters which are essentially within the domestic jurisdiction of the United States of America as determined by the United States of America; or

(c) disputes arising under a multilateral treaty, unless (1) all parties to the treaty affected by the decision are also parties to the case before the Court, or (2) the United States of America specially agrees to jurisdiction; and

Provided further, that this declaration shall remain in force for a period of five years and thereafter until the expiration of six months after notice may be given to terminate this declaration.

(Signed) Harry S. TRUMAN

Done at Washington this fourteenth day of August 1946.

NOTES

1. *Termination of U.S. Declaration.* The U.S. acceptance of compulsory jurisdiction was terminated by President Reagan on October 7, 1985, with effect six months from that date. The termination was linked to the decision of the International Court in November 1984 in the case brought by Nicaragua against the United States for military and paramilitary activities in and against Nicaragua, 1984 I.C.J. 392. A summary of the case is at p. 598.

In explaining the motives for the decision to terminate acceptance of the compulsory jurisdiction clause, the Legal Adviser of the State Department observed that the United States had never successfully brought another state before the Court under the compulsory jurisdiction clause although it tried to do so several times. Sofaer, Statement to Senate Foreign Relations Committee, December 4, 1985, 86:2106 Dep't. St. Bull. 67 (1986). See p. 609 below. One reason he noted was that under the principle of reciprocity the respondent state could invoke the U.S. reservation involving matters essentially within domestic jurisdiction as determined by the United States, as was done by Bulgaria in 1960 in a case brought by the United States against Bulgaria for an aerial incident injuring U.S. nationals. See Gross, Bulgaria Invokes the Connally Amendment, 56 A.J.I.L. 357 (1962).

2. *Reciprocity in the Application of Reservations.* France brought a case against Norway based on the acceptance of compulsory jurisdiction by both states. The French declaration of acceptance contained a clause similar to that in the U.S. acceptance. Norway argued it had the right to rely on the restrictions in the French declaration and claimed that the matter fell within the national jurisdiction of Norway. The Court held that, in accordance with the condition of reciprocity, "Norway, equally with France, is entitled to except from the compulsory jurisdiction of the Court disputes understood by Norway to be essentially within its national jurisdiction." The French application was therefore rejected. The Court declared that it was not called upon to examine the validity of the reservation since the question of its validity was not presented by the issues in the proceedings inasmuch as both parties relied on the reservation. *Case of Certain Norwegian Loans,* 1957 I.C.J. 9. Judge Lauterpacht in a separate opinion maintained that a self-judging reservation was invalid and, if not separable, invalidated the acceptance of compulsory jurisdiction. 1957 I.C.J. 34. Similar views were expressed by Lauterpacht and three other judges in the *Interhandel Case,* 1959 I.C.J. 6 at 95; see also 1959 I.C.J. at 54, 75, 85.

3. *Theory of Reciprocity.* Do the words of the clause in Article 36(2) that jurisdiction is accepted "in relation to any other state accepting the same obligation" mean that every acceptance impliedly includes a condition of

reciprocity? Professor Edith Brown Weiss points out in an illuminating study of reciprocity that

> The current theory of reciprocity under the Optional Clause has three primary postulates. 1. Jurisdiction exists under the Optional Clause only to the extent that both parties have accepted a common commitment. 2. Determination of reciprocity takes place only at the moment the Court is seised of a case. 3. Reciprocity applies only to the scope and substance of the commitments, not to the formal conditions of their creation, duration or extinction.

Brown Weiss, Reciprocity and the Optional Clause, in the International Court at a Crossroads 82, 84 (Damrosch ed. 1987).

4. *Temporal Dimension*. The United States argued in the 1984 *Nicaragua* case that it should benefit from an implied condition in Nicaragua's declaration permitting Nicaragua to terminate its declaration at will with immediate effect. The Court refused to apply reciprocity to such temporal conditions of termination or modification, though the Court has recognized that the temporal conditions which exclude disputes prior to a given date are covered by reciprocity.

5. *"Hit and Run."* May a state that accepted compulsory jurisdiction withdraw such acceptance when it learns that a case is about to be brought against it? May a state accept compulsory jurisdiction to bring a specific case and immediately thereafter withdraw its acceptance to avoid being sued in another matter? Would such "hit-and-run" tactics be contrary to the principle of reciprocity or good faith?

6. *Minority of States Accepting Compulsory Jurisdiction*. When the United States terminated its acceptance, its spokesmen observed that a majority of judges in 1985 came from states that had not accepted compulsory jurisdiction and that only forty-seven countries in all had such acceptances. (This was about one-third of the then-existing U.N. members—a ratio that has remained relatively stable over time as the number of states eligible to participate has increased.) In what respect do these facts bear on the desirability or not of continued acceptance? Brown Weiss concluded that "acceptance of the compulsory jurisdiction of the Court by less than one-third of the countries that are parties to the Statute of the Court has not in practice resulted in significant inequities for those states that have accepted the Optional Clause" (loc. cit at 105).

7. *Categorical Exclusions*. In *Fisheries Jurisdiction* (Spain v. Canada), 1998 I.C.J. 432, Spain complained of Canada's arrest in 1995 of a Spanish trawler on the high seas outside Canada's exclusive economic zone in the regulatory area of the Northwest Atlantic Fisheries Organization (NAFO). In determining whether it had jurisdiction by virtue of the two parties' optional clause declarations, the Court had to interpret Canada's amended declaration filed May 10, 1994, which excluded "disputes arising out of or concerning conservation and management measures taken by Canada with respect to vessels fishing in the NAFO Regulatory Area * * *." The Court affirmed its previous jurisprudence to the effect that "It is for each State, in formulating its declaration, to decide upon the limits it places upon its acceptance of the jurisdiction of the Court * * *." 1998 I.C.J. at para. 44. After close analysis of

Canada's reservation in relation to the dispute in question, the Court concluded that the reservation was applicable and that the Court lacked jurisdiction to consider the dispute.

8. *Acceptance Subsequent to Date the Dispute Arose.* On April 26, 1999 the Federal Republic of Yugoslavia (Serbia–Montenegro) deposited a declaration of acceptance of compulsory jurisdiction under Article 36(2). On April 29, 1999 it initiated suit against ten NATO members, complaining that the bombing campaign concerning Kosovo which had begun on March 24, 1999 and which was then in progress was in violation of treaty obligations and general international law. Jurisdiction was asserted against some of the respondents under both Article 36(1) and Article 36(2) of the I.C.J. Statute: Article 36(1) was invoked as to the compromissory clause (Article IX) of the Genocide Convention, to which most of the respondents were parties, and Article 36(2) was invoked in relation to those NATO members (Belgium, Canada, the Netherlands, Portugal, Spain, the United Kingdom) that had accepted jurisdiction under Article 36(2)'s optional clause. In preliminary rulings dealing in the first instance with Yugoslavia's request for provisional measures (see p. 616 note 2 below), the Court held that it lacked prima facie jurisdiction to consider the request. A principal ground for the ruling concerning jurisdiction under Article 36(2) was that the dispute had already arisen before Yugoslavia deposited its instrument of acceptance of optional clause jurisdiction. *Legality of Use of Force* (Yugoslavia v. Belgium), 1999 I.C.J. 124, 2004 I.C.J. 279, and related cases.

5. Objections to Jurisdiction or Admissibility

MILITARY AND PARAMILITARY ACTIVITIES IN AND AGAINST NICARAGUA
(NICARAGUA v. UNITED STATES)

International Court of Justice, 1984
1984 I.C.J. 392 (Jurisdiction)

[The following summary of the Court's decision on jurisdiction is taken from the Yearbook of the International Court of Justice 1984–85, at 135–47:]

On 9 April 1984 the Government of Nicaragua filed an Application instituting proceedings against the United States of America, accompanied by a request for the indication of provisional measures, in respect of a dispute concerning responsibility for military and paramilitary activities in and against Nicaragua. As basis for the jurisdiction of the Court it invoked [the] declaration[s] accepting the Court's jurisdiction deposited by the two States under Article 36 of the Statute of the Court.

* * *

Proceedings and Submissions of the Parties (paras. 1–11)

After recapitulating the various stages in the proceedings and setting out the submissions of the Parties (paras. 1–10), the Court recalls that the case concerns a dispute between the Government of the Republic of Nicaragua and the Government of the United States of America arising out of military and paramilitary activities in Nicaragua and in the waters off its coasts, responsibility for which is attributed by Nicaragua to the United States. In the present phase, the case concerns the Court's jurisdiction to entertain and pronounce upon this dispute, as well as the admissibility of Nicaragua's Application referring it to the Court (para. 11).

1. *The Question of the Jurisdiction of the Court to Entertain the Dispute (paras. 12–83)*

A. *The Declaration of Nicaragua and Article 36, Paragraph 5, of the Statute of the Court (paras. 12–51)*

To found the jurisdiction of the Court, Nicaragua relied on Article 36 of the Statute of the Court and the declarations accepting the compulsory jurisdiction of the Court made by the United States and itself.

*The Relevant Texts and the Historical Background
to Nicaragua's Declaration (paras. 12–16)*

On 6 April 1984 the Government of the United States deposited with the Secretary–General of the United Nations a notification signed by the Secretary of State, Mr. George Shultz (hereinafter referred to as "the 1984 notification"), referring to the declaration of 1946, and stating that:

"the aforesaid declaration shall not apply to disputes with any Central American State or arising out of or related to events in Central America, any of which disputes shall be settled in such manner as the parties to them may agree.

"Notwithstanding the terms of the aforesaid declaration, this proviso shall take effect immediately and shall remain in force for two years, so as to foster the continuing regional dispute settlement process which seeks a negotiated solution to the interrelated political, economic and security problems of Central America."

In order to be able to rely upon the United States declaration of 1946 to found jurisdiction in the present case, Nicaragua has to show that it is a "State accepting the same obligation" as the United States within the meaning of Article 36, paragraph 2, of the Statute.

For this purpose, it relies on a declaration made by it on 24 September 1929 pursuant to Article 36, paragraph 2, of the Statute of the Permanent Court of International Justice, the predecessor of the present Court, which provided that:

"The Members of the League of Nations and the States mentioned in the Annex to the Covenant may, either when signing or ratifying the Protocol to which the present Statute is adjoined, or at a later moment, declare that they recognize as compulsory *ipso facto* and without special agreement, in relation to any other Member or State accepting the same obligation, the jurisdiction of the Court * * *" in any of the same categories of dispute as listed in Article 36, paragraph 2, of the Statute of the present Court.

Nicaragua relies further on Article 36, paragraph 5, of the Statute of the present Court, which provides that:

> "Declarations made under Article 36 of the Statute of the Permanent Court of International Justice and which are still in force shall be deemed, as between the parties to the present Statute, to be acceptances of the compulsory jurisdiction of the International Court of Justice for the period which they still have to run and in accordance with their terms."

The Judgment recalls the circumstances in which Nicaragua made its declaration: on 14 September 1929, as a Member of the League of Nations, it signed the Protocol of Signature of the Statute of the Permanent Court of International Justice[1]: this Protocol provided that it was subject to ratification and that instruments of ratification were to be sent to the Secretary–General of the League of Nations. On 24 September 1929 Nicaragua deposited with the Secretary–General of the League a declaration under Article 36, paragraph 2, of the Statute of the Permanent Court which reads:

[Translation from the French]

> "On behalf of the Republic of Nicaragua I recognize as compulsory unconditionally the jurisdiction of the Permanent Court of International Justice.

Geneva, 24 September 1929.

(Signed) T.F. MEDINA."

The national authorities in Nicaragua authorized its ratification, and, on 29 November 1939, the Ministry of Foreign Affairs of Nicaragua sent a telegram to the Secretary–General of the League of Nations advising him of the despatch of the instrument of ratification. The files of the League, however, contain no record of an instrument of ratification ever having been received and no evidence has been adduced to show that such an instrument of ratification was ever despatched to Geneva. After the Second World War, Nicaragua became an original Member of the United Nations, having ratified the Charter on 6 September 1945; on 24 October 1945 the Statute of the International Court of Justice, which is an integral part of the Charter, came into force.

The Arguments of the Parties (paras. 17–23) and
the Reasoning of the Court (paras. 24–42)

This being the case, the United States contends that Nicaragua never became a party to the Statute of the Permanent Court and that its 1929

---

1. While a State admitted to membership of the United Nations automatically becomes a party to the Statute of the International Court of Justice, a State member of the League of Nations only became a party to that of the Permanent Court of International Justice if it so desired, and, in that case, it was required to accede to the Protocol of Signature of the Statute of the Court.

declaration was therefore not "still in force" within the meaning of the English text of Article 36, paragraph 5, of the Statute of the present Court.

In the light of the arguments of the United States and the opposing arguments of Nicaragua, the Court sought to determine whether Article 36, paragraph 5, could have applied to Nicaragua's declaration of 1929.

The Court notes that the Nicaraguan declaration was valid at the time when the question of the applicability of the new Statute, that of the International Court of Justice, arose, since under the system of the Permanent Court of International Justice a declaration was valid only on condition that it had been made by a State which had signed the Protocol of Signature of the Statute. It had not become binding under that Statute, since Nicaragua had not deposited its instrument of ratification of the Protocol of Signature and it was therefore not a party to the Statute. However, it is not disputed that the 1929 declaration could have acquired binding force. All that Nicaragua need have done was to deposit its instrument of ratification, and it could have done that at any time until the day on which the new Court came into existence. It follows that the declaration had a certain potential effect which could be maintained for many years. Having been made "unconditionally" and being valid for an unlimited period, it had retained its potential effect at the moment when Nicaragua became a party to the Statute of the new Court.

In order to reach a conclusion on the question whether the effect of a declaration which did not have binding force at the time of the Permanent Court could be transposed to the International Court of Justice through the operation of Article 36, paragraph 5, of the Statute of that body, the Court took several considerations into account.

As regards the French phrase *"pour une durée qui n'est pas encore expirée"* applying to declarations made under the former system, the Court does not consider it to imply that *"la durée non expirée"* (the unexpired period) is that of a commitment of a binding character. The deliberate choice of the expression seems to denote an intention to widen the scope of Article 36, paragraph 5, so as to cover declarations which have not acquired binding force. The English phrase "still in force" does not expressly exclude a valid declaration of unexpired duration, made by a State not party to the Protocol of Signature of the Statute of the Permanent Court, and therefore not of binding character.

With regard to the considerations governing the transfer of the powers of the former Court to the new one, the Court takes the view that the primary concern of those who drafted its Statute was to maintain the greatest possible continuity between it and the Permanent Court and that their aim was to ensure that the replacement of one Court by another should not result in a step backwards in relation to the progress accomplished towards adopting a system of compulsory jurisdiction. The logic of a general system of devolution from the old Court to the new resulted in the ratification of the new Statute having exactly the same effects as those of the ratification of the Protocol of Signature of the old Statute, i.e., in the case of Nicaragua, a transformation of a potential commitment into an effective one. Nicaragua may therefore be deemed to have given its consent to the transfer of its declaration to the International Court of Justice when it signed and ratified the Charter, thus accepting the Statute and its Article 36, paragraph 5.

Concerning the publications of the Court referred to by the Parties for opposite reasons, the Court notes that they have regularly placed Nicaragua on the list of those States that have recognized the compulsory jurisdiction of the Court by virtue of Article 36, paragraph 5, of the Statute. The attestations furnished by these publications have been entirely official and public, extremely numerous and have extended over a period of nearly 40 years. The Court draws from this testimony the conclusion that the conduct of States parties to the Statute has confirmed the interpretation of Article 36, paragraph 5, of the Statute, whereby the provisions of this Article cover the case of Nicaragua.

The Conduct of the Parties (paras. 43–51)

Nicaragua also contends that the validity of Nicaragua's recognition of the compulsory jurisdiction of the Court finds an independent basis in the conduct of the Parties. It argues that its conduct over 38 years unequivocally constitutes consent to be bound by the compulsory jurisdiction of the Court and that the conduct of the United States over the same period unequivocally constitutes its recognition of the validity of the declaration of Nicaragua of 1929 as an acceptance of the compulsory jurisdiction of the Court. The United States, however, objects that the contention of Nicaragua is inconsistent with the Statute and, in particular that compulsory jurisdiction must be based on the clearest manifestation of the State's intent to accept it. After considering Nicaragua's particular circumstances and noting that Nicaragua's situation has been wholly unique, the Court considers that, having regard to the source and generality of statements to the effect that Nicaragua was bound by its 1929 declaration, it is right to conclude that the constant acquiescence of that State in those affirmations constitutes a valid mode of manifestation of its intent to recognize the compulsory jurisdiction of the Court under Article 36, paragraph 2, of the Statute. It further considers that the estoppel on which the United States has relied and which would have barred Nicaragua from instituting proceedings against it in the Court, cannot be said to apply to it.

Finding: the Court therefore finds that the Nicaraguan declaration of 1929 is valid and that Nicaragua accordingly was, for the purposes of Article 36, paragraph 2, of the Statute of the Court, a "State accepting the same obligation" as the United States at the date of filing of the Application and could therefore rely on the United States declaration of 1946.

B. The Declaration of the United States (paras. 52–76)
The Notification of 1984 (paras. 52–66)

The acceptance of the jurisdiction of the Court by the United States on which Nicaragua relies is the result of the United States declaration of

14 August 1946. However, the United States argues that effect should be given to the letter sent to the Secretary–General of the United Nations on 6 April 1984 [see p. 599 above]. It is clear that if this notification were valid as against Nicaragua at the date of filing of the Application, the Court would not have jurisdiction under Article 36 of the Statute. After outlining the arguments of the Parties in this connection, the Court points out that the most important question relating to the effect of the 1984 notification is whether the United States was free to disregard the six months' notice clause which, freely and by its own choice, it has appended to its declaration, in spite of the obligation it has entered into vis-à-vis other States which have made such a declaration. The Court notes that the United States has argued that the Nicaraguan declaration, being of undefined duration, is liable to immediate termination, and that Nicaragua has not accepted "the same obligation" as itself and may not rely on the time-limit proviso against it. The Court does not consider that this argument entitles the United States validly to derogate from the time-limit proviso included in its 1946 declaration. In the Court's opinion, the notion of reciprocity is concerned with the scope and substance of the commitments entered into, including reservations, and not with the formal conditions of their creation, duration or extinction. Reciprocity cannot be invoked in order to excuse departure from the terms of a State's own declaration. The United States cannot rely on reciprocity since the Nicaraguan declaration contains no express restriction at all. On the contrary, Nicaragua can invoke the six months' notice against it, not on the basis of reciprocity, but because it is an undertaking which is an integral part of the instrument that contains it. The 1984 notification cannot therefore override the obligation of the United States to submit to the jurisdiction of the Court vis-à-vis Nicaragua.

The United States Multilateral Treaty Reservation (paras. 67–76)

The question remains to be resolved whether the United States declaration of 1946 constitutes the necessary consent of the United States to the jurisdiction of the Court in the present case, taking into account the reservations which were attached to the declaration. Specifically, the United States had invoked proviso (c) to that declaration, which provides that the United States acceptance of the Court's compulsory jurisdiction shall not extend to

"disputes arising under a multilateral treaty, unless (1) all parties to the treaty affected by the decision are also parties to the case before the Court, or (2) the United States of America specially agrees to jurisdiction".

This reservation will be referred to as the "multilateral treaty reservation."

The United States argues that Nicaragua relies in its Application on four multilateral treaties, and that the Court, in view of the above reservation, may exercise jurisdiction only if all treaty parties affected by a prospective decision of the Court are also parties to the case.

The Court notes that the States which, according to the United States, might be affected by the future decision of the Court, have made declarations of acceptance of the compulsory jurisdiction of the Court, and are free, any time, to come before the Court with an application instituting proceedings, or to resort to the incidental procedure of intervention. These States are therefore not defenceless against any consequences that may arise out of adjudication by the Court and they do not need the protection of the multilateral treaty reservation (in so far as they are not already protected by Article 59 of the Statute). The Court considers that obviously the question of what States may be affected is not a jurisdictional problem and that it has no choice but to declare that the objection based on the multilateral treaty reservation does not possess, in the circumstances of the case, an exclusively preliminary character.

Finding: the Court finds that, despite the United States notification of 1984, Nicaragua's Application is not excluded from the scope of the acceptance by the United States of the compulsory jurisdiction of the Court. The two declarations afford a basis for its jurisdiction.

C. *The Treaty of Friendship, Commerce and Navigation of 21 January 1956 as a Basis of Jurisdiction (paras. 77–83)*

In its Memorial, Nicaragua also relies, as a "subsidiary basis" for the Court's jurisdiction in this case, on the Treaty of Friendship, Commerce and Navigation which it concluded at Managua with the United States on 21 January 1956 and which entered into force on 24 May 1958. Article XXIV, paragraph 2, reads as follows:

> "Any dispute between the Parties as to the interpretation or application of the present Treaty, not satisfactorily adjusted by diplomacy, shall be submitted to the International Court of Justice, unless the Parties agree to settlement by some other pacific means."

Nicaragua submits that this treaty has been and is being violated by the military and paramilitary activities of the United States as described in the Application. The United States contends that, since the Application presents no claims of any violation of the treaty, there are no claims properly before the Court for adjudication, and that, since no attempt to adjust the dispute by diplomacy has been made, the compromissory clause cannot operate. The Court finds it necessary to satisfy itself as to jurisdiction under the treaty inasmuch as it has found that the objection based upon the multilateral treaty reservation in the United States declaration does not debar it from entertaining the Application. In the view of the Court, the fact that a State has not expressly referred, in negotiations with another State, to a particular treaty as having been violated by the conduct of that other State, does not debar that State from invoking a compromissory clause in that treaty. Accordingly, the Court finds that it has jurisdiction under the 1956 Treaty to entertain the claims made by Nicaragua in its Application.

II. The Question of the Admissibility of Nicaragua's Application (paras. 84–108)

The Court now turns to the question of the admissibility of Nicaragua's Application. The United States contended that it is inadmissible on five separate grounds, each of which, it is said, is sufficient to establish such inadmissibility, whether considered as a legal bar to adjudication or as "a matter requiring the exercise of prudential discretion in the interest of the integrity of the judicial function".

The *first ground of inadmissibility* (paras. 85–88) put forward by the United States is that Nicaragua has failed to bring before the Court parties whose presence and participation is necessary for the rights of those parties to be protected and for the adjudication of the issues raised in the Application. In this connection, the Court recalls that it delivers judgments with binding force as between the Parties in accordance with Article 59 of the Statute, and that States which consider they may be affected by the decision are free to institute separate proceedings or to employ the procedure of intervention. There is no trace, either in the Statute or in the practice of international tribunals, of an "indispensable parties" rule which would only be conceivable in parallel to a power, which the Court does not possess, to direct that a third State be made a party to proceedings. None of the States referred to can be regarded as being in a position such that its presence would be truly indispensable to the pursuance of the proceedings.

The *second ground of inadmissibility* (paras. 89–90) relied on by the United States is that Nicaragua is, in effect, requesting that the Court in this case determines the existence of a threat to peace, a matter falling essentially within the competence of the Security Council because it is connected with Nicaragua's complaint involving the use of force. The Court examines this ground of inadmissibility at the same time as the *third ground* (paras. 91–98) based on the position of the Court within the United Nations system, including the impact of proceedings before the Court on the exercise of the inherent right of individual or collective self-defence under Article 51 of the Charter. The Court is of the opinion that the fact that a matter is before the Security Council should not prevent it from being dealt with by the Court and that both proceedings could be pursued *pari passu*. The Council has functions of a political nature assigned to it, whereas the Court exercises purely judicial functions. Both organs can therefore perform their separate but complementary functions with respect to the same events. In the present case, the complaint of Nicaragua is not about an ongoing war [or] armed conflict between it and the United States, but about a situation demanding the peaceful settlement of disputes, a matter which is covered by Chapter VI of the Charter. Hence, it is properly brought before the principal judicial organ of the United Nations for peaceful settlement. This is not a case which can only be dealt with by the Security Council in accordance with the provisions of Chapter VII of the Charter.

With reference to Article 51 of the Charter, the Court notes that the fact that the inherent right of self-defence is referred to in the Charter as a "right" is indicative of a legal dimension, and finds that if, in the present proceedings, it became necessary for the Court to judge in this respect between the Parties, it cannot be debarred from doing so by the existence of a procedure requiring that the matter be reported to the Security Council.

A *fourth ground of inadmissibility* (paras. 99–101) put forward by the United States is the inability of the judicial function to deal with situations involving ongoing armed conflict, since the resort to force during an ongoing armed conflict lacks the attributes necessary for the application of the judicial process, namely a pattern of legally relevant facts discernible by the means available to the adjudicating tribunal. The Court observes that any judgment on the merits is limited to upholding such submissions of the Parties as has been supported by sufficient proof of relevant facts and that ultimately it is the litigant who bears the burden of proof.

The *fifth ground of inadmissibility* (paras. 102–108) put forward by the United States is based on the non-exhaustion of the established processes for the resolution of the conflicts occurring in Central America. It contends that the Nicaraguan Application is incompatible with the Contadora process to which Nicaragua is a party.

The Court recalls its earlier decisions that there is nothing to compel it to decline to take cognizance of one aspect of a dispute merely because that dispute has other aspects *(United States Diplomatic and Consular Staff in Tehran* case, *I.C.J., Reports 1980,* p. 19, para. 36), and the fact that negotiations are being actively pursued during the proceedings is not, legally, any obstacle to the exercise by the Court of its judicial function *(Aegean Sea Continental Shelf* case, I.C.J. *Reports 1978,* p. 12, para. 29). The Court is unable to accept either that there is any requirement of prior exhaustion of regional negotiating processes as a precondition to seising the Court or that the existence of the Contadora process constitutes in this case an obstacle to the examination by the Court of Nicaragua's Application.

The Court is therefore unable to declare the Application inadmissible on any of the grounds the United States has advanced.

* * *

Operative Clause (para. 113)

"For these reasons,

THE COURT,

(1)(a) *finds,* by eleven votes to five, that it has jurisdiction to entertain the Application filed by the Republic of Nicaragua on 9 April 1984, on the basis of Article 36, paragraphs 2 and 5, of the Statute of the Court;

IN FAVOUR: *President* Elias; *Vice–President* Sette–Camara; *Judges* Lachs, Morozov, Nagendra Singh, Ruda, El–Khani, de Lacharrière, Mbaye, Bedjaoui; *Judge* ad hoc Colliard;

AGAINST: *Judges* Mosler, Oda, Ago, Schwebel and Sir Robert Jennings;

(b) *finds*, by fourteen votes to two, that it has jurisdiction to entertain the Application filed by the Republic of Nicaragua on 9 April 1984, in so far as that Application relates to a dispute concerning the interpretation or application of the Treaty of Friendship, Commerce and Navigation between the United States of America and the Republic of Nicaragua signed at Managua on 21 January 1956, on the basis of Article XXIV of that Treaty;

IN FAVOUR: *President* Elias; *Vice–President* Sette–Camara; *Judges* Lachs, Morozov, Nagendra Singh, Mosler, Oda, Ago, El–Khani, Sir Robert Jennings, de Lacharrière, Mbaye, Bedjaoui; *Judge* ad hoc Colliard;

AGAINST: *Judges* Ruda and Schwebel;

(c) *finds,* by fifteen votes to one, that it has jurisdiction to entertain the case;

IN FAVOUR: *President* Elias; *Vice–President* Sette–Camara; *Judges* Lachs, Morozov, Nagendra Singh, Ruda, Mosler, Oda, Ago, El–Khani, Sir Robert Jennings, de Lacharrière, Mbaye, Bedjaoui; *Judge* ad hoc Colliard;

AGAINST: *Judge* Schwebel;

(2) *finds,* unanimously, that the said Application is admissible."

NOTES

1. *Dissenters' Position.* Five judges dissented from that part of the Court's judgment relating to Nicaragua's 1929 declaration accepting compulsory jurisdiction. The dissenting judges considered that the declaration was not an "acceptance" within the meaning of Article 36(5) of the Court's statute inasmuch as it was not "in force" because it was never ratified. 1984 I.C.J. 461, 471, 514, 533, 558. Was the Court's use of the French text of Article 36(5) helpful to resolve the question of interpretation as to what is meant by "in force"? Was Nicaragua's "subsequent conduct" indicating its belief that it was bound by the 1929 declaration a valid reason to consider it bound? Was the U.S. objection a technical one that should not have overridden Nicaragua's assertion that it was bound?

2. *Reciprocity.* Was the Court justified in denying the right of the United States to modify its acceptance on the ground that the six-month notice clause applied? Should that clause have been given effect even though Nicaragua had no similar clause in its acceptance and could have terminated it at any time? What does reciprocity mean in this connection? See opinions of dissenting Judges Ago and Jennings, 1984 I.C.J. 514, 533. See notes at pp. 596–98 on reciprocity.

3. *Treaty of Friendship, Commerce and Navigation.* Two judges dissented from the finding of the Court that it had jurisdiction on the basis of a dispute settlement clause in the Treaty of Friendship, Commerce and Navigation of 1956. Judge Ruda considered that negotiation had not taken place and that such negotiation was a pre-condition of submission to the Court. Id. at 454. Judge Schwebel declared that the bilateral treaty "is a purely commercial agreement whose terms do not relate to the use or misuse of force in international relations." He observed that the treaty expressly precluded its application to "traffic in arms" and to measures "necessary to protect the essential security interests" of a party. Id. (Dissenting Opinion of Judge Schwebel, paras. 117–29). Other judges, however, noted that Nicaragua had alleged violations of specific provisions of the bilateral treaty (for example, that mining of ports and territorial waters and attacks on airports endangered traffic and trade in violation of the treaty), and that it would be up to Nicaragua to prove such treaty violations in the proceedings on the merits. In their view, the allegations were sufficient to support a finding of jurisdiction. See, e.g., Separate Opinion of Judge Ago, para. 2.

Compare the treatment of issues under a similar bilateral treaty in the *Oil Platforms* case, 1996 I.C.J. 803 (Iran v. United States), where allegations of unlawful use of force were likewise asserted under a treaty concerned with commerce and navigation. As noted above (p. 592), the Court did not accept the applicant's most sweeping jurisdictional contentions (e.g., that a treaty of "amity" should be read to reach claims involving military hostilities) but did confirm jurisdiction limited to the treaty provisions on navigation.

4. *Multilateral Treaty Reservation.* Was the Court justified in rejecting the U.S. argument, based on its reservation excluding disputes under a multilateral treaty unless all parties to the treaty affected by the decision were also parties to the case? The pleadings showed that El Salvador, Costa Rica and Honduras were involved in the charges and counter-charges. It was not clear that Nicaragua's complaint rested on multilateral treaties alone; Nicaragua had also argued violations of customary law on use of force. If so, would the U.S. reservation apply? Was the Court warranted in holding that this issue, as well as the question of whether Nicaragua's neighbors would be affected by the decision, could not be answered until the Court dealt with the merits? Judge Schwebel contended that the Court was nullifying the jurisdictional bar inserted by the United States in its acceptance. Id. (Dissenting Opinion of Judge Schwebel, para. 71–72.) See Damrosch, Multilateral Disputes, in The International Court of Justice at a Crossroads 376 (Damrosch ed. 1987).

5. *Admissibility.* Note the distinction in the Court's decision between jurisdiction and admissibility. A similar distinction was drawn in the *Tehran Hostages Case*, 1980 I.C.J. 3. Although the United States contended in the *Nicaragua Case* that the case was "inadmissible" on five separate grounds, the Court unanimously decided that the application was admissible. Is admissibility the same as "justiciability," that is, whether the dispute is a legal dispute capable of judicial determination? If the claim presents a legal question, is the Court entitled to abstain from acting on it because political issues are also involved, or because military hostilities are under way, or because the matter has been or is before the U.N. Security Council? Should a

claim of self-defense be treated as justiciable? For a lively debate on those questions among international lawyers and public officials, see Proceedings of the American Society of International Law for 1985 and 1986.

6. *Termination of U.S. Acceptance.* About one year after the decision on jurisdiction and admissibility in the *Nicaragua Case,* the United States terminated its acceptance of compulsory jurisdiction, for reasons linked to the decision of the Court in *Nicaragua.* 24 I.L.M. at 1742–45. See also statement of the Legal Adviser of the State Department to the Senate Foreign Relations Committee, extracts from which follow.

STATEMENT OF THE LEGAL ADVISER OF THE STATE DEPARTMENT, ABRAHAM D. SOFAER, TO THE SENATE FOREIGN RELATIONS COMMITTEE

December 4, 1985
86 Dept. St. Bull. 67, 70–71 (Jan.1986)

THE NICARAGUA CASE

* * *

Even more disturbing, for the first time in its history, the Court has sought to assert jurisdiction over a controversy concerning claims related to an ongoing use of armed force. This action concerns every state. It is inconsistent with the structure of the UN system. The only prior case involving use-of-force issues—the *Corfu Channel* case—went to the Court after the disputed actions had ceased and the Security Council had determined that the matter was suitable for judicial consideration. In the Nicaragua case, the Court rejected without a soundly reasoned explanation our arguments that claims of the sort made by Nicaragua were intended by the UN Charter exclusively for resolution by political mechanisms—in particular, the Security Council and the Contadora process— and that claims to the exercise of the inherent right of individual and collective self-defense were excluded by Article 51 of the Charter from review by the Court.

I cannot predict whether the Court's approach to these fundamental Charter issues in the jurisdictional phase of the Nicaragua case will be followed in the Court's judgment on the merits. Nevertheless, the record gives us little reason for confidence. It shows a Court majority apparently prepared to act in ways profoundly inconsistent with the structure of the Charter and the Court's place in that structure. The Charter gives to the Security Council—not the Court—the responsibility for evaluating and resolving claims concerning the use of armed force and claims of self-defense under article 51. With regard to the situation in Central America, the Security Council exercised its responsibility by endorsing the Contadora process as the appropriate mechanism for resolving the inter-locking political, security, economic, and other concerns of the region.

IMPLICATIONS FOR U.S. NATIONAL SECURITY

The fact that the ICJ indicated it would hear and decide claims about the ongoing use of force made acceptance of the Court's compulsory jurisdiction an issue of strategic significance. Despite our deep reluctance to do so and the many domestic constraints that apply, we must be able to use force in our self-defense and in the defense of our friends and allies. We are a law-abiding nation, and when we submit ourselves to adjudication of a subject, we regard ourselves as obliged to abide by the result. For the United States to recognize that the ICJ has authority to define and adjudicate with respect to our right of self-defense, therefore, is effectively to surrender to that body the power to pass on our efforts to guarantee the safety and security of this nation and of its allies.

* * *

We recognize that this nation has a special obligation to support the ICJ and all other institutions that advance the rule of law in a world full of terror and disorder. Our belief in this obligation is what led us to set an example by accepting the Court's compulsory jurisdiction in 1946 and by continuing that acceptance long after it became clear that the world would not follow suit and that our acceptance failed to advance our interests in any tangible manner.

Yet, the President also is responsible to the American people and to Congress to avoid potential threats to our national security. The ICJ's decisions in the Nicaragua case created real and important additional considerations that made the continued acceptance of compulsory jurisdiction unacceptable, despite its symbolic significance. We hope that, in the long run, this action, coupled with our submission of disputes under article 36(1), will strengthen the Court in the performance of its proper role in the international system established by the UN Charter and the Court's own Statute.

NOTES

1. *Security Council's Authority.* Consider the contention in the above statement that the competence of the Security Council under Article 51 excludes adjudication by the Court of the legality of self-defense where the court has jurisdiction by virtue of a treaty provision or an acceptance under Article 36(2) rather than an agreed submission. The Council is authorized to take measures necessary to maintain peace and security. When it takes such measures, is a decision by the Council on the legality of the use of force implied? Is the Council an appropriate body to make legal determinations? Would a decision by the International Court on legality impose an obstacle (legal or political) to Council action? Suppose the Council is seized of the dispute but takes no action or does no more than request the parties to settle their dispute by peaceful means (as the Council did in the Nicaraguan case); should that decision deprive a state from seeking a judgment on the legality of the use of force by another state when that other state accepted jurisdiction in accordance with Article 36 of the statute of the Court? What if the respondent state is protected by the veto (its own or an ally's) from an adverse decision by the Council?

2. *Disputes Involving Use of Force.* If the right of self-defense is non-justiciable (as implied by the Legal Adviser's comment on the right of the United States to decide the issue for itself), does that mean in effect that there is no legal restraint on use of force? Is it consistent with the notion of a legal right to exclude determination by a competent judicial body? If states have accepted compulsory jurisdiction of the Court by treaty or a declaration under Article 36(2) without excluding issues of self-defense or cases involving use of force, should the Court abstain from adjudicating the issue of self-defense? See Schachter, 80 A.S.I.L. Proc. 210 (1986).

Is there good reason to consider that the Court cannot generally decide factual issues concerning the use of force? See Military and Paramilitary Activities (Nicaragua v. United States) (Merits), 1986 I.C.J. 14 at 97–98 (Chapter 15). Even if the Court has a limited capacity to find the truth in cases of past or ongoing hostilities, does it follow that it should hold the case to be inadmissible? Would it be appropriate for the Court to consider the merits as argued by the parties and take account of difficulties in fact-finding as it decides what form of relief (if any) might be appropriate?

3. *Judicial Objectivity.* Consider the observation of the Legal Adviser (above) that "no state" can rely on the International Court to decide questions of illegal intervention "properly and fairly." Does that assume that the judges (or most of them) are incapable of deciding such issues "fairly and properly" because of political bias? Or does it suggest that the judicial process is unable to produce answers to the issues because the issues are not answerable by "judicial standards"?

On the objectivity of the Court, and related issues, see Schachter, International Law in Theory and Practice 43–46 (1991); Brown Weiss, Judicial Independence and Impartiality: A Preliminary Inquiry, in The International Court of Justice at a Crossroads 123–54 (Damrosch ed. 1987). On the question whether the Court may and should deal with cases involving use of force, see Schachter, Disputes Involving the Use of Force, in The International Court of Justice at a Crossroads 223–41; Gill, Litigation Strategy at the International Court (1989); Bilder, Judicial Procedures Relating to the Use of Force, 31 Va. J. Int'l L. 249 (1991).

4. *Other Termination of Compulsory Jurisdiction.* The United States is not the only state to have terminated its acceptance of compulsory jurisdiction in reaction to unwelcome litigation: France also did so in the wake of the *Nuclear Tests Cases* brought by Australia and New Zealand, 1974 I.C.J. 253, 457. If the objective of Australia and New Zealand was to bring about a cessation of tests after the judgment, did the dispute cease when the French statements were made even if those statements did not amount to a legal undertaking? For a closely reasoned analysis of the meaning of "dispute" in this context, see Macdonald & Hough, The Nuclear Tests Case Revisited, 20 Germ. Y.B.I.L. 337 (1977). Other commentaries on the case include: Franck, Word Made Law, 69 A.J.I.L. 612 (1975); Lellouche, The Nuclear Tests Cases, 16 Harv. Int'l L.J. 614 (1975); McWhinney, International Law–Making and the Judicial Process: The World Court and the French Nuclear Tests Case, 3 Syracuse J. Int'l L. & Comm. 9 (1975). See also pp. 293–95 in Chapter 4.

6. Provisional Measures of Protection

The Court has the "power to indicate, if it considers the circumstances so require, any provisional measures which ought to be taken to preserve the respective rights of the parties." Article 41 of the Statute. This right is analogous to the common law interlocutory injunction under which parties may be enjoined from acting in a way to prejudice the outcome during the proceedings. The two criteria most often invoked for such provisional relief (also known as interim measures) are urgency and irreparable injury. These criteria were satisfied in the *Tehran Hostages* and *Nicaragua* cases excerpted above. In other cases, however, the Court has declined to order provisional measures. It will only do so if it is satisfied that there is a prima facie basis for jurisdiction and will not do so if the claimed injury could in principle be remedied by monetary compensation. The Court has also felt free to diverge from the specific measures requested by the applicant state and even to order restraints on the applicant itself. The case below and accompanying notes illustrate these and related problems.

APPLICATION OF THE INTERNATIONAL CONVENTION ON THE ELIMINATION OF ALL FORMS OF RACIAL DISCRIMINATION (GEORGIA v. RUSSIAN FEDERATION)

International Court of Justice, 2008 Order on Request
for the Indication of Provisional Measures.
2008 I.C.J. No. 140

[Georgia instituted proceedings against the Russian Federation for alleged violation of the Convention on Elimination of Racial Discrimination (CERD) in respect of ethnic conflict in South Ossetia and Abkhazia and neighboring parts of Georgia. Georgia contended that Russia sought to consolidate changes in the ethnic composition of these two regions which had formed part of the Republic of Georgia since the dissolution of the former Soviet Union, including by forcible displacement of persons of Georgian ethnicity from these areas and by undermining Georgia's capacity to exercise jurisdiction in this part of territory falling within the internationally accepted borders of Georgia. Georgia traced a history of Russian conduct between 1990 and 2008 involving support for secessionist forces in the two regions and implementation of racially discriminatory policies under cover of a peacekeeping operation therein, as well as the conferral of Russian citizenship upon the non-ethnic Georgian population in the two regions and the harassment of Georgians who sought to remain there. Georgia further claimed that Russian forces had invaded Georgian territory on August 8, 2008 and in that connection had perpetrated widespread and systematic discrimination against South Ossetia's and Abkhazia's ethnic Georgian population and had committed numerous other discriminations against Georgians in the context of the ensuing military conflict. Russia disputed all these allegations. In connection with

Georgia's request for an order requiring Russia to refrain from any discriminatory violations of the rights of ethnic Georgians and related measures, the Court said:]

118.   Whereas the power of the Court to indicate provisional measures under Article 41 of the Statute of the Court has as its object the preservation of the respective rights of the parties pending the decision of the Court, in order to ensure that irreparable prejudice shall not be caused to rights which are the subject of dispute in judicial proceedings; and whereas it follows that the Court must be concerned to preserve by such measures the rights which may subsequently be adjudged by the Court to belong either to the Applicant or to the Respondent [citations omitted]; whereas a link must therefore be established between the alleged rights the protection of which is the subject of the provisional measures being sought, and the subject of the proceedings before the Court on the merits of the case;

* * *

141.   Whereas the Court is not called upon, for the purpose of its decision on the Request for the indication of provisional measures, to establish the existence of breaches of CERD, but to determine whether the circumstances require the indication of provisional measures for the protection of rights under CERD; whereas it cannot at this stage make definitive findings of fact, nor finding of attribution; and whereas the right of each Party to submit arguments in respect of the merits remains unaffected by the Court's decision on the Request for the indication of provisional measures;

142.   Whereas, nevertheless, the rights in question in these proceedings, in particular those stipulated in Article 5, paragraphs (b) and (d)(i) of CERD, are of such a nature that prejudice to them could be irreparable; whereas the Court considers that violations of the right to security of persons and of the right to protection by the State against violence or bodily harm (Article 5, paragraph (b)) could involve potential loss of life or bodily injury and could therefore cause irreparable prejudice; whereas the Court further considers that violations of the right to freedom of movement and residence within a State's borders (Article 5, paragraph (d)(i)) could also cause irreparable prejudice in situations where the persons concerned are exposed to privation, hardship, anguish and even danger to life and health; and whereas the Court finds that individuals forced to leave their own place of residence and deprived of their right of return could, depending on the circumstances, be subject to a serious risk of irreparable prejudice;

143.   Whereas the Court is aware of the exceptional and complex situation on the ground in South Ossetia, Abkhazia and adjacent areas and takes note of the continuing uncertainties as to where lines of authority lie; whereas, based on the information before it in the case file, the Court is of the opinion that the ethnic Georgian population in the areas affected by the recent conflict remains vulnerable;

Whereas the situation in South Ossetia, Abkhazia and adjacent areas in Georgia is unstable and could rapidly change; whereas, given the ongoing tension and the absence of an overall settlement to the conflict in this region, the Court considers that the ethnic Ossetian and Abkhazian populations also remain vulnerable;

Whereas, while the problems of refugees and internally displaced persons in this region are currently being addressed, they have not yet been resolved in their entirety;

Whereas, in light of the foregoing, with regard to these above-mentioned ethnic groups of the population, there exists an imminent risk that the rights at issue in this case mentioned in the previous paragraph may suffer irreparable prejudice;

144.   Whereas States parties to CERD "condemn racial discrimination and undertake to pursue by all appropriate means and without delay a policy of eliminating racial discrimination in all its forms;" whereas in the view of the Court, in the circumstances brought to its attention in which there is a serious risk of acts of racial discrimination being committed, Georgia and the Russian Federation, whether or not any such acts in the past may be legally attributable to them, are under a clear obligation to do all in their power to ensure that any such acts are not committed in the future;

145.   Whereas the Court is satisfied that the indication of measures is required for the protection of rights under CERD which form the subject-matter of the dispute; and whereas the Court has the power, under its Statute, when a request for provisional measures has been made, to indicate measures that are in whole or in part other than those requested, or measures that are addressed to the party which has itself made the request; whereas Article 75, paragraph 2, of the Rules of Court specifically refers to this power of the Court; and whereas the Court has already exercised this power on several occasions in the past [citations omitted];

146.   Whereas the Court, having found that the indication of provisional measures is required in the current proceedings, has considered the terms of the provisional measures requested by Georgia; whereas the Court does not find that, in the circumstances of the case, the measures to be indicated are to be identical to those requested by Georgia; whereas the Court, having considered the material before it, considers it appropriate to indicate measures addressed to both Parties;

147.   Whereas the Court's "orders on provisional measures under Article 41 [of the Statute] have binding effect" (*LaGrand (Germany v. United States of America), Judgment, I.C.J. Reports 2001*, p. 506, para. 109) and thus create international legal obligations which both Parties are required to comply with (*Armed Activities on the Territory of the Congo (Democratic Republic of the Congo v. Uganda), Judgment, I.C.J. Reports 2005*, p. 258, para. 263);

148.   Whereas the decision given in the present proceedings in no way prejudges the question of the jurisdiction of the Court to deal with the merits of the case or any questions relating to the admissibility of the Application, or relating to the merits themselves; and whereas it leaves unaffected the right of the Governments of Georgia and the Russian Federation to submit arguments in respect of those questions;

149.   For these reasons,

THE COURT, reminding the Parties of their duty to comply with their obligations under the International Convention on the Elimination of All Forms of Racial Discrimination,

Indicates the following provisional measures:

A.   By eight votes to seven,

Both Parties, within South Ossetia and Abkhazia and adjacent areas in Georgia, shall

(1) refrain from any act of racial discrimination against persons, groups of persons or institutions;

(2) abstain from sponsoring, defending or supporting racial discrimination by any persons or organizations;

(3) do all in their power, whenever and wherever possible, to ensure, without distinction as to national or ethnic origin,

   (i) security of persons;

   (ii) the right of persons to freedom of movement and residence within the border of the State;

   (iii) the protection of the property of displaced persons and of refugees;

(4) do all in their power to ensure that public authorities and public institutions under their control or influence do not engage in acts of racial discrimination against persons, group of persons or institutions;

IN FAVOUR: *President* Higgins; *Judges* Buergenthal, Owada, Simma, Abraham, Keith, Sepúlveda–Amor, *Judge* ad hoc Gaja;
AGAINST: *Vice–President* Al–Khasawneh; *Judges* Ranjeva, Shi, Koroma, Tomka, Bennouna, Skotnikov;

B.   By eight votes to seven,

Both Parties shall facilitate, and refrain from placing any impediment to, humanitarian assistance in support of the rights to which the local population are entitled under the International Convention on the Elimination of All Forces of Racial Discrimination; [List of judges voting for and against is the same as above.]

C.   By eight votes to seven,

Each Party shall refrain from any action which might prejudice the rights of the other Party in respect of whatever judgment the Court may render in the case, or which might aggravate or extend the dispute before the Court or make it more difficult to resolve; [List of judges voting for and against is the same as above.]

D.   By eight votes to seven,

Each Party shall inform the Court as to its compliance with the above provisional measures [List of judges voting for and against is the same above].

NOTES

1.   *Dissenting Views.* The seven dissenting judges appended a joint dissenting opinion, in which they questioned the existence of a dispute between the parties concerning the interpretation or application of CERD and the other preconditions for establishing the Court's jurisdiction under Article 22 of CERD (providing for I.C.J. settlement of a dispute "which is not settled by negotiation or by the other procedures expressly provided for by this Convention"). In the dissenters' view, in the absence of any evidence of efforts to resolve the dispute by negotiation or by CERD's own procedures, Georgia had not made out a case of prima facie jurisdiction as required under the Court's jurisprudence. (See note 2 below.) Nor were the conditions of irreparable injury and urgency established under the circumstances, in light of the conclusion of a cease-fire agreement and the commencement of progressive return of displaced persons to their homes. Do you think that the Court's treatment of these issues is persuasive? Did the Court act properly in entering measures addressed to both parties (and the same measures at that)?

2.   *Requirement of Prima Facie Jurisdiction.* To what extent must the Court be satisfied as to its jurisdiction before imposing provisional measures? In the *Fisheries Jurisdiction Case*, the Court declared:

> On a request for provisional measures, the Court need not, before indicating them, finally satisfy itself that it has jurisdiction on the merits of the case, yet it ought not to act under Article 41 of the Statute of the Court if the absence of jurisdiction on the merits is manifest.

1972 I.C.J. at 15–16. As Judge Jiménez de Aréchaga said in the *Aegean Sea Case*, 1976 I.C.J. 3 at 15: "In cases where there is no reasonable probability, prima facie ascertained by the Court, of jurisdiction on the merits it would be devoid of sense to indicate provisional measures to ensure the execution of a judgment the Court will never render."

The Court's provisional measures jurisprudence requires applicant to show a prima facie basis for jurisdiction. Where jurisdiction cannot be established even prima facie, provisional measures will be denied, no matter how urgent the matter or how serious the allegation of likely irreparable harm to applicant. Thus in the Kosovo cases of 1999, provisional measures were denied since applicant was not able to show a prima facie case for jurisdiction. *Legality of Use of Force* (Yugoslavia v. Belgium) and related cases, 1999 I.C.J. 124.

3.   *Subsequent Determination of Lack of Jurisdiction.* The possibility that the Court might find prima facie jurisdiction sufficient to sustain a provisional

measures order, and then later determine that objections to jurisdiction were persuasive, has happened on occasion, including in the *Anglo–Iranian Oil Company Case*, 1951 I.C.J. 89 (Interim Protection Order) (interim measures granted), 1952 I.C.J. 93, 102–103 (Jurisdiction) (case dismissed for lack of jurisdiction). Does the prima facie jurisdiction standard strike the right balance between the interests of applicant and respondent?

4. *Denial of Request in Face of Security Council Action.* In 1992, Libya requested that the Court impose provisional measures enjoining the United Kingdom and the United States from taking measures against Libya pursuant to a Security Council decision intended to induce Libya to surrender Libyans accused of terrorist activities to the two respondent countries. In particular, the individuals were accused of planting a bomb on Pan Am Flight No. 103 that caused the plane to crash over Lockerbie, Scotland. Libya based its jurisdictional claim on the compromissory clause in the 1971 Montreal Convention on Suppression of Unlawful Acts Against Safety of Civil Aviation. Libya contended that the Convention recognized its right to prosecute the individuals accused of crimes covered by the Convention and its right not to surrender them to another country. The Court denied the Libyan request by eleven votes to five. The majority considered that Security Council Resolution 745 (1992) requiring Libya to surrender the accused individuals imposed a legal duty on Libya and any indication of provisional measures would run "a serious risk of conflicting with the work of the Security Council." The Court noted that while it was not called on to determine definitively the legal effect of the Security Council resolution, the rights claimed by Libya were not "now" appropriate for protection by provisional measures. 1992 I.C.J. 3, 15.

Libya's cases against the United Kingdom and the United States proceeded through several further preliminary stages before being finally discontinued by agreement of the parties upon achievement of an overall settlement in 2003. See 2003 I.C.J. 149, 152.

5. *Binding Force of Provisional Measures.* For many years, opinion was divided as to whether the Court has power to order binding provisional measures. It was argued that such a power can be inferred from the Charter and Statute taken as a whole, and that an obligation to give effect to an interim order is incumbent upon every party to the Statute, even if that party contests the jurisdiction of the Court over a particular claim. On the other hand, the verbs of Article 4—"indicate" and "ought"—could suggest merely recommendatory authority, and the language used by the Court in its provisional measures orders has often seemed hortatory ("should") rather than compulsory in character. For this reason, some scholars and governments maintained that the obligation of compliance attaches only to a final judgment on the merits and not to preliminary rulings made before the Court has decided challenges to its own jurisdiction. On these issues, see Oxman, Jurisdiction and the Power to Indicate Provisional Measures, in The International Court of Justice at a Crossroads 323 (Damrosch ed. 1987); Rosenne, Provisional Measures in International Law: The International Court of Justice and the International Tribunal for the Law of the Sea (2004).

In the *Case Concerning the Vienna Convention on Consular Relations* (Paraguay v. United States), 1998 I.C.J. 248, also known as the *Breard* case (see Chapter 10), the Court received the application approximately ten days before a death sentence was to be carried out on a Paraguayan national convicted of capital murder by a Virginia court. A few days before the scheduled execution date, the Court entered a provisional measures order, the operative paragraph of which read:

> The United States should take all measures at its disposal to ensure that Angel Francisco Breard is not executed pending the final decision in these proceedings, and should inform the Court of all the measures which it has taken in implementation of this Order.

In an *amicus curiae* submission to the U.S. Supreme Court addressing (*inter alia*) the legal effect of this order in connection with Breard's petition for a stay of execution, the Solicitor–General of the United States said:

> As to the purportedly binding effect of the ICJ's order, there is substantial disagreement among jurists as to whether an ICJ order indicating provisional measures is binding. * * * The better reasoned position is that such an order is not binding. * * * The use of precatory language ("indicate," "ought to be taken," "suggested") instead of stronger language * * * strongly supports a conclusion that ICJ provisional measures are not binding.

> * * *

> Moreover, the ICJ itself has never concluded that provisional measures are binding on the parties to a dispute. That court has indicated provisional measures in seven other cases of which we are aware; in most of those cases, the order indicating provisional measures was not regarded as binding by the respondent. * * * The ICJ did not, in any of the final decisions in those cases, suggest that the failure of the respondent to comply with the indication of provisional measures had violated the court's earlier order.

The Supreme Court denied the stay of execution. On this episode in relation to I.C.J. provisional measures, see documentation and commentary in Agora: *Breard*, 92 A.J.I.L. 666 et seq. (1998), especially the comments by Henkin (Provisional Measures, U.S. Treaty Obligations, and the States, 92 A.J.I.L. 679) and Vázquez (*Breard* and the Federal Power to Require Compliance with I.C.J. Orders of Provisional Measures, 92 A.J.I.L. 683).

Similar issues came to the Court again in Germany's suit under the Vienna Convention on Consular Relations, known as the *LaGrand* case. An order in terms similar to the *Breard* order was entered on Germany's application, without hearing U.S. views. 1999 I.C.J. 9. Judge Schwebel questioned this *ex parte* procedure in his separate opinion. See 1999 I.C.J. at 21. The execution in Arizona took place the next day, without regard to Germany's position or the I.C.J. proceedings. For the point of view that there would have been time to hear both sides even under those urgent circumstances, see Rosenne, Controlling Interlocutory Aspects of Proceedings in the International Court of Justice, 94 A.J.I.L. 307, 310 n. 18 (2000). The legal effect of the provisional measures order was one issue raised by Germany in its pleadings and hearings on the merits held after the execution had occurred.

In its judgment on the merits in *LaGrand*, 2001 I.C.J. 466, at 506, the Court finally resolved this uncertainty in favor of a binding obligation to carry out interim orders. It reaffirmed the binding force of such orders in the *Case Concerning CERD* (Georgia v. Russia), excerpted above (para. 147).

6. *Probability of Success and Safeguards for Respondent's Interests.* In view of the Court's conclusion that provisional measures orders have binding effect, what standard should an applicant state have to satisfy concerning likelihood of eventual success on the merits of the case? By contrast to comparable proceedings in national legal systems, the I.C.J. has not required applicants to demonstrate that they are likely to prevail on the merits. Should applicants be required to post a bond to indemnify respondent against the eventuality that the claim is ultimately determined not to be well-founded? On the existence of such procedures in other international tribunals, see Section 5 below.

7. *Further Reading.* For in-depth treatment of legal issues arising in claims for interim relief, see Rosenne, Provisional Measures in International Law: The International Court of Justice and the International Tribunal for the Law of the Sea (2004); Merrills, Interim Measures of Protection in the Recent Jurisprudence of the International Court of Justice, 44 I.C.L.Q. 90 (1995); see also the commentary on Article 41 in The Statute of the International Court of Justice: A Commentary (Zimmermann et al. eds. 2004).

7. Procedural Problems: Non–Appearance, Third–Party Intervention, and Counter–Claims

Non–Appearance. The Statute of the Court does not provide for entry of judgment by default. In the event that a party fails to appear or does not defend, Article 53 of the Statute requires the Court to satisfy itself that it has jurisdiction and, if so, that the claim of the applicant is well founded in fact and law. The Court has taken the position that it must examine the matter on its own and take "special care" to act with circumspection. Schachter argues that in effect this means that the non-appearing accused state acquires an advantage: it does not have to face questions by the Court, yet the Court takes special care to make sure its views are considered. The applicant state is handicapped since it cannot properly consider and answer arguments of the non-participating state. May the Court take any action against a state that boycotts the proceedings? See Schachter, International Law in Theory and Practice 230–31 (1991); Charney, Disputes Implicating the Institutional Credibility of the Court: Problems of Non–Appearance, Non–Participation, and Non–Performance, in The International Court of Justice at a Crossroads 288–319 (Damrosch ed. 1987); Thirlway, Non–Appearance Before the International Court of Justice (1985); Elkind, Non–Appearance Before the International Court of Justice: Functional and Comparative Analysis (1984); Fitzmaurice, The Problem of the Non–Appearing Defendant Government, 51 Brit. Y.B.I.L. 94–96 (1980).

The United States appeared in the case brought against it by Nicaragua in order to contest jurisdiction and admissibility, but withdrew after the Court found it had jurisdiction. This was the first case of non-appearance after a finding of jurisdiction by the Court. In five prior cases, the respondent had declined to appear at all. These were: Iceland in 1972 (*Fisheries Cases*), India in 1973 (*Case Concerning Prisoners of War*), France in 1974 (*Nuclear Tests Cases*), Turkey in 1976 (*Aegean Sea Continental Shelf Case*), and Iran in 1979 (*Tehran Hostages Case*). All five cases involved objections to jurisdiction at preliminary stages in connection with requests for provisional measures. The non-appearing states brought their objections to the notice of the Court by letters and other communications that did not constitute official memorials or other documents called for by the Court's rules.

Intervention and Other "Third Party" Issues. A state may intervene in a case between other states in two kinds of situations. Under Article 62 of the Statute, a state which considers that "it has an interest of a legal nature in the case" may be permitted to intervene by the Court. The other situation applies when the state requesting intervention is a party to the convention which is before the Court. In that case the state has the right to intervene and if it uses that right, the treaty interpretation given by the Court will be binding on it. Article 63 of the Statute. The case-law on intervention is summarized in the Restatement (Third) § 903, Reporters' Note 7:

> In the Permanent Court of International Justice, there was only one case of intervention, by the Government of Poland in the Wimbledon Case, which involved the interpretation of the Peace Treaty of Versailles of 1919. P.C.I.J., ser. A, No. 1 at 11–13 (1923). In 1951, the International Court of Justice allowed Cuba to intervene in the Haya de la Torre Case between Colombia and Peru, which involved the interpretation of the 1928 Havana Convention on Asylum, to which Cuba was a party. [1951] I.C.J.Rep. 71, 76–77. In later cases involving permissive interventions under Article 62, the Court took a more restrictive attitude and refused to grant permission to intervene. See Nuclear Tests Cases, Reporters' Note 3, [1974] I.C.J.Rep. 530, 535 (Fiji's application to intervene lapsed when the proceedings were terminated because the main case "no longer has any object"); Case Concerning the Continental Shelf (Tunisia/Libyan Arab Jamahiriya) (Application of Malta for Permission to Intervene), [1981] I.C.J.Rep. 3, 19 (Malta's interests were no greater than those of other Mediterranean states, and her application was so restricted by various reservations that the decision in the case could not affect any of her legal interests); Case Concerning the Continental Shelf (Libyan Arab Jamahiriya/Malta) (Application of Italy for Permission to Intervene), [1984] I.C.J.Rep. 3, 18–28 (to permit Italy to intervene would introduce a fresh dispute; Article 62 was not intended as an alternative means of bringing an additional dispute as a case before the Court); Case Concerning Military and Paramilitary Activities in and Against Nicaragua (Nicaragua v. United States) (Declaration of Intervention of the Republic of El Salvador), [1984] I.C.J.Rep. 215, 216 (although El

Salvador's declaration invoked Article 63, this declaration addressed the substance of the dispute and was inadmissible at the stage of proceedings relating only to the Court's jurisdiction). Later, in a decision concluding that it had jurisdiction of the case, the Court noted that if Costa Rica, El Salvador, and Honduras should find that "they might be affected by the future decision of the Court" in the case, they would be free to institute proceedings against Nicaragua or resort to the incidental procedures for intervention under Articles 62 and 63 of the Statute. [1984] I.C.J.Rep. 392, 425. No further action was taken by Costa Rica or Honduras, but proceedings against them were instituted by Nicaragua in 1986. 25 Int'l Leg. Mat. 1290, 1293 (1986) (applications by Nicaragua); [1986] I.C.J.Rep. 548, 551 (procedural orders); [1987] *id.* 182 (order recording the discontinuance by Nicaragua of the proceedings against Costa Rica).

See also Sztucki, Intervention under Article 63 of the I.C.J. Statute in the Phase of Preliminary Proceedings: The Salvadoran Incident, 79 A.J.I.L. 1005 (1985); Damrosch, Multilateral Disputes, in The International Court of Justice at a Crossroads 376–400 (Damrosch ed. 1987); Chinkin, Third Parties in International Law (1993); Ruda, Intervention Before the International Court of Justice, in Fifty Years of the International Court of Justice 487 (Lowe & Fitzmaurice, eds. 1996).

Counter–Claims. Article 80 of the Rules of the Court provides for the filing of counter-claims. Until the 1990s, the International Court had little experience with counter-claims; but recently respondent states have availed themselves of this procedure, and the Court has thus had to consider issues arising under Article 80's requirement that a counter-claim be "directly connected with the subject-matter of the claim of the other party and that it comes within the jurisdiction of the Court."

Counter-claims have been held admissible in various recent cases, including: *Application of the Convention for the Prevention and Punishment of the Crime of Genocide* (Bosnia–Herzegovina v. Yugoslavia), 1997 I.C.J. 243; *Oil Platforms* (Iran v. United States), 1998 I.C.J. 190; and *Land and Maritime Boundary between Cameroon and Nigeria* (Cameroon v. Nigeria), 1999 I.C.J. 983. It is evident that applicant states will have to weigh the possibility of serious counter-claims entailing potentially heavy liabilities as part of the risk of initiating litigation.

NOTES

1. *Non–Appearance.* The Institut de Droit International after some years of study and debate reached the following conclusions in a resolution adopted in 1991:

Article 1

Each State entitled under the Statute to appear before the Court and with respect to which the Court is seized of a case is *ipso facto,* by virtue of the Statute, a party to the proceedings, regardless of whether it appears or not.

Article 2

In considering whether to appear or to continue to appear in any phase of proceedings before the Court, a State should have regard to its duty to co-operate in the fulfillment of the Court's judicial functions.

Article 3

In the event that a State fails to appear in a case instituted against it, the Court should, if circumstances so warrant:

(a) invite argument from the appearing party on specific issues which the Court considers have not been canvassed or have been inadequately canvassed in the written or oral pleadings;

(b) take whatever other steps it may consider necessary, within the scope of its powers under the Statute and the Rules of Court, to maintain equality between the parties.

Article 4

Notwithstanding the non-appearance of a State before the Court in proceedings to which it is a party, that State is, by virtue of the Statute, bound by any decision of the Court in that case, whether on jurisdiction, admissibility, or the merits.

Article 5

A State's non-appearance before the Court is in itself no obstacle to the exercise by the Court of its functions under Article 41 of the Statute.

2. *Third–Party Intervention.* A Chamber of the Court allowed Nicaragua to intervene in a case between El Salvador and Honduras concerning their maritime frontier. The Chamber recognized that Nicaragua had a legal interest in the case by virtue of its co-ownership of the waters of the Gulf of Fonseca which was one area in dispute between the parties. The Chamber made it clear that its permission to Nicaragua to intervene did not make Nicaragua a party to the dispute. *Maritime Frontier Case*, 1990 I.C.J. 92, 133–34. Accordingly, Nicaragua would not be bound by the decision (or protected by it) under the terms of Article 59 of the Statute. It may be asked whether in view of Nicaragua's co-ownership of the waters in litigation, it should not have been treated as a party bound by the decision and protected by it. For a critical view of the Chamber's decision on this point, see Greig, Third Party Rights and Intervention Before the International Court, 32 Va. J. Int'l L. 285, 321–30 (1992). The Chamber's approach was followed by the full Court in addressing the application by Equatorial Guinea for permission to intervene in *Land and Maritime Boundary* (Cameroon v. Nigeria), with respect to the maritime boundary in the Gulf of Guinea. See Order of Oct. 21, 1999, 1999 I.C.J. 1029.

3. *"Necessary" Third Parties?* The issue of third party participation came up before the International Court in a different way when it was argued that two states parties to a treaty at issue were "necessary parties" and therefore their failure to intervene should preclude the Court from adjudicating the case. The case concerned the claim of Nauru that the three states that

were trustees for Nauru under a U.N. trusteeship agreement breached their obligations by marketing Nauru's phosphate resources and failing to restore the property after the phosphate was removed. The Court ruled that the failure of the two trustees (New Zealand and the United Kingdom) to intervene did not bar Nauru from proceeding with its claim against Australia, the third trustee. *Certain Phosphate Lands in Nauru*, 1992 I.C.J. 240 (Preliminary Objection). See generally Weeramantry, Nauru: Environmental Damage Under International Trusteeship (1992). Compare the Court's treatment of the "necessary party" issue in the *East Timor*, 1995 I.C.J. 90, where the Court held that the absence of Indonesia barred Portugal's suit to invalidate a treaty between Australia and Indonesia concerning the offshore resources of the Timor Gap.

    4. *Counter–Claims.* In the *Oil Platforms Case* (Iran v. United States), Iran brought the initial application complaining of U.S. destruction of certain oil platforms in the Persian Gulf in 1987–1988. The United States responded in the first instance by raising threshold objections to jurisdiction. After the Court found that it did have jurisdiction under one aspect of the treaty invoked, 1996 I.C.J. 803, the United States defended on the merits by justifying the destruction of the platforms as a lawful response to Iran's hostile attacks on merchant shipping in the Gulf. The United States also interposed a counter-claim against Iran in respect of those attacks. The parties robustly litigated whether the counter-claim was admissible under the Court's rules: Iran's position was that the United States had impermissibly attempted to widen the scope of the dispute beyond matters "directly connected" with the original claim. The Court allowed the counter-claim to be maintained, reasoning that both the claim and the counter-claim arose out of the same factual complex involving destruction of oil platforms and ships occurring in the Persian Gulf during the same period. 1998 I.C.J. 190. In its final judgment, the Court rejected both Iran's claim and the U.S. counter-claim on the merits. 2003 I.C.J. 161.

8. Compliance With Decisions

    The Court's judgments are binding between the parties under Article 59 of the I.C.J. Statute. Article 94 of the U.N. Charter provides in paragraph 1 that members of the United Nations "undertake to comply" with the judgment of the Court in any case to which they are parties. In the event that a party does not comply, the prevailing party may have recourse under Article 94, paragraph 2 of the Charter to the Security Council, which may make recommendations or decide upon measures to bring about compliance.

    Various scholars have examined the record of compliance with the Court's judgments. The fact that some respondents have ignored the Court's rulings in certain cases, or refused to carry them out for prolonged periods of time if at all, has been the focus of intense commentary and criticism and recommendations aimed at promoting compliance. Over the long run, the compliance record has been generally good and appears to be improving. For a valuable recent analysis, see Schulte, Compliance with Decisions of the International Court of Justice (2004). See also Paulson,

Compliance with Final Judgments of the International Court of Justice Since 1987, 98 A.J.I.L. 434 (2004); Ginsburg & McAdams, Adjudicating in Anarchy: An Expressive Theory of International Dispute Resolution, 45 Wm. & Mary L. Rev. 1229, 1304–29 (2004) (analyzing I.C.J. compliance record from game-theoretic perspective).

It is for each state to take the necessary measures to ensure compliance by its appropriate authorities, which might include executive or judicial action, enactment of legislation, or even constitutional change. Questions of how to bring about compliance with an I.C.J. judgment within a domestic legal system have arisen in the United States in the aftermath of the judgment in *Avena and Other Mexican Nationals* (Mexico v. United States), 2004 I.C.J. 12, as more fully discussed in Chapter 10.

NOTES

1. *Role of the Security Council.* The Security Council has not yet exercised its authority under Article 94(2) of the Charter. An effort by Nicaragua to obtain enforcement of the judgment in its favor in the case of *Military and Paramilitary Activities in and against Nicaragua*, 1986 I.C.J. 14, was vetoed by the United States. The availability of the veto to the United States and other permanent members was one of the factors taken into account by the U.S. Supreme Court in *Medellín v. Texas*, 128 S.Ct. 1346, 1349, 1359–60 (2008), in deciding that an I.C.J. judgment does not have the force of directly applicable federal law in the United States. See Chapter 10. For criticisms of the Supreme Court's understanding of Article 94, see Charnovitz, Revitalizing the U.S. Compliance Power, 102 A.J.I.L. 540, 548–49 (2008); Vázquez, Less Than Zero? 102 A.J.I.L. 563, 571–72 (2008).

2. *Alternative Enforcement Mechanisms?* What other avenues of redress might be available to prevailing parties if voluntary compliance is not forthcoming and if the Security Council does not act? Scholars have pointed to a range of other possibilities, including efforts to obtain execution against assets of the defaulting state in third-country courts. For discussion, see Reisman, The Enforcement of International Judgments, 63 A.J.I.L. 1 (1969); O'Connell The Prospects for Enforcing Monetary Judgments of the International Court of Justice: A Study of Nicaragua's Judgment Against the United States, 30 Va. J. Int'l L. 891 (1990). What might account for the fact that few such efforts have been made?

B. ADVISORY OPINIONS

The Court may give an advisory opinion on "any legal question" requested by a body authorized by or in accordance with the U.N. Charter. See Article 65 of the Statute of the Court. The Charter in Article 96 states that the General Assembly or the Security Council may request advisory opinions. In addition other organs of the United Nations may be so authorized by the General Assembly. Four organs of the United Nations and sixteen specialized agencies have been authorized to request advisory opinions. A state may not request an advisory opinion. It may, however, request an authorized international organization to make such request.

As of 2009, the Court has been asked to render some twenty-five advisory opinions and has done so in almost all cases where requests were made. It found itself without jurisdiction in one instance, where it concluded that the subject-matter of the request—legality of the use or threat of use of nuclear weapons—was not sufficiently connected with the activities of a U.N. specialized agency, the World Health Organization, to meet the requirements of Article 96(2). See p. 628, note 1. Fifteen opinions were in response to requests by the U.N. General Assembly, one (the *Namibia* case) was requested by the Security Council and two by the Economic and Social Council. Three of the specialized agencies (UNESCO, WHO and IMCO) have also requested advisory opinions. Five advisory opinions were given at the request of the U.N. Committee on Applications for Review of Administrative Tribunal Judgments. This U.N. Committee was established in 1955 specifically for the purpose of requesting advisory opinions of the Court to review decisions of the U.N. Administrative Tribunal (UNAT). G.A. Res. 957 (X) (1955). The I.C.J.'s supervisory jurisdiction over UNAT was abolished, by amendment to the UNAT Statute. See G.A. Res. 50/54 (1995); Reisman, The Supervisory Jurisdiction of the International Court of Justice, 258 Rec. des Cours 392 (1996).

Although an advisory opinion has no binding effect in itself, some international agreements provide that disputes relating to the interpretation and application of the agreement shall be submitted to the Court for an opinion that will be accepted as binding by the parties to the dispute. One example is the General Convention on Privileges and Immunities of the United Nations, Feb. 13, 1946 1 U.N.T.S. 15, which provides in Sec. 30 that if a difference arises between the United Nations on the one hand and a U.N. member on the other, "a request shall be made for an advisory opinion on any legal question involved in accordance with Article 96 of the Charter and Article 65 of the Statute of the Court. The opinion given by the Court shall be accepted as decisive by the parties."

The Court's advisory opinions, while typically arising in the context of the fulfillment of functions of U.N. organs, are of interest not only to U.N. specialists but more broadly for their contributions to important substantive issues, such as the law of self-determination (*Western Sahara* Advisory Opinion, 1975 I.C.J. 12) or the law of treaties (*Reservations to the Genocide Convention* Advisory Opinion, 1951 I.C.J. 15, excerpted in Chapter 3). Several of the requests for advisory opinions have arisen in highly political or politicized contexts, which have prompted some states to urge the Court not to answer the questions presented. Two examples—involving nuclear weapons in 1996 and Israel's construction of a wall in the occupied Palestinian territory in 2004—illustrate the Court's view that in general it should not decline to answer a legal question as to which its opinion is requested.

LEGALITY OF THE THREAT OR USE
OF NUCLEAR WEAPONS

International Court of Justice, Advisory Opinion, 1996
1996 I.C.J. 226

[The General Assembly and the World Health Organization (WHO) both asked the I.C.J. for advisory opinions on slightly different questions concerning the legality of the threat or use of nuclear weapons. The Court agreed to give an advisory opinion to the General Assembly but declined to do so for the WHO. Excerpts from the opinion dealing with jurisdiction to reply to the General Assembly's request are reprinted below; for the treatment of the WHO's request, see the notes immediately following. Other aspects of the advisory opinion are considered in Chapters 2 and 15.]

10.   The Court must first consider whether it has the jurisdiction to give a reply to the request of the General Assembly for an Advisory Opinion and whether, should the answer be in the affirmative, there is any reason it should decline to exercise any such jurisdiction.

The Court draws its competence in respect of advisory opinions from Article 65, paragraph 1, of its Statute. Under this Article, the Court

"may give an advisory opinion on any legal question at the request of whatever body may be authorized by or in accordance with the Charter of the United Nations to make such a request".

11.   For the Court to be competent to given an advisory opinion, it is thus necessary at the outset for the body requesting the opinion to be "authorized by or in accordance with the Charter of the United Nations to make such a request". The Charter provides in Article 96, paragraph 1, that:

"The General Assembly or the Security Council may request the International Court of Justice to give an advisory opinion on any legal question." * * *

12.   The question put to the Court has a relevance to many aspects of the activities and concerns of the General Assembly including those relating to the threat or use of force in international relations, the disarmament process, and the progressive development of international law. The General Assembly has a long-standing interest in these matters and in their relation to nuclear weapons. This interest has been manifested in the annual First Committee debates, and the Assembly resolutions on nuclear weapons; in the holding of three special sessions on disarmament (1978, 1982 and 1988) by the General Assembly, and the annual meetings of the Disarmament Commission since 1978; and also in the commissioning of studies on the effects of the use of nuclear weapons. In this context, it does not matter that important recent and current activities relating to nuclear disarmament are being pursued in other fora.
* * *

13. The Court must furthermore satisfy itself that the advisory opinion requested does indeed relate to a "legal question" within the meaning of its Statute and the United Nations Charter. * * *

The question put to the Court by the General Assembly is indeed a legal one, since the Court is asked to rule on the compatibility of the threat or use of nuclear weapons with the relevant principles and rules of international law. To do this, the Court must identify the existing principles and rules, interpret them and apply them to the threat or use of nuclear weapons, thus offering a reply to the question posed based on law.

The fact that this question also has political aspects, as, in the nature of things, is the case with so many questions which arise in international life, does not suffice to deprive it of its character as a "legal question" and to "deprive the Court of a competence expressly conferred on it by its Statute" * * *. Whatever its political aspects, the Court cannot refuse to admit the legal character of a question which invites it to discharge an essentially judicial task, namely, an assessment of the legality of the possible conduct of States with regard to the obligations imposed upon them by international law [citations omitted]. * * *

The Court moreover considers that the political nature of the motives which may be said to have inspired the request and the political implications that the opinion given might have are of no relevance in the establishment of its jurisdiction to give such an opinion.

* * *

14. Article 65, paragraph 1, of the Statute provides: "The Court *may* give an advisory opinion . . ." (Emphasis added.) This is more than an enabling provision. As the Court has repeatedly emphasized, the Statute leaves a discretion as to whether or not it will give an advisory opinion that has been requested of it, once it has established its competence to do so. * * *

The Court has constantly been mindful of its responsibilities as "the principal judicial organ of the United Nations" (Charter, Art. 92). When considering each request, it is mindful that it should not, in principle, refuse to give an advisory opinion. In accordance with the consistent jurisprudence of the Court, only "compelling reasons" could lead it to such a refusal [citations omitted]. There has been no refusal, based on the discretionary power of the Court, to act upon a request for advisory opinion in the history of the present Court; in the case concerning the *Legality of the Use by a State of Nuclear Weapons in Armed Conflict* [Ed.: see note 1 below on WHO request], the refusal to give the World Health Organization the advisory opinion requested by it was justified by the Court's lack of jurisdiction in that case. The Permanent Court of International Justice took the view on only one occasion that it could not reply to a question put to it, having regard to the very particular circumstances of the case, among which were that the question directly concerned an already existing dispute, one of the States parties to which was neither a party to the Statute of the Permanent Court nor a Member of the League of Nations, objected to the proceedings, and refused to take part in any way (*Status of Eastern Carelia, P.C.I.J., Series B, No. 5*).

[The Court next rejected contentions that it should not respond to the request because the question presented was vague and abstract, or because the Assembly had not explained the precise purposes for which it sought the advisory opinion.] * * *

17. It has also been submitted that a reply from the Court in this case might adversely affect disarmament negotiations and would, therefore, be contrary to the interest of the United Nations. The Court is aware that, no matter what might be its conclusions in any opinion it might give, they would have relevance for the continuing debate on the matter in the General Assembly and would present an additional element in the negotiations on the matter. Beyond that, the effect of the opinion is a matter of appreciation. The Court has heard contrary positions advanced and there are no evident criteria by which it can prefer one assessment to another. That being so, the Court cannot regard this factor as a compelling reason to decline to exercise its jurisdiction.

18. Finally, it has been contended by some States that in answering the question posed, the Court would be going beyond its judicial role and would be taking upon itself a law-making capacity. It is clear that the Court cannot legislate, and, in the circumstances of the present case, it is not called upon to do so. Rather its task is to engage in its normal judicial function of ascertaining the existence or otherwise of legal principles and rules applicable to the threat or use of nuclear weapons. The contention that the giving of an answer to the question posed would require the Court to legislate is based on a supposition that the present *corpus juris* is devoid of relevant rules in this matter. The Court could not accede to this argument; it states the existing law and does not legislate. This is so even if, in stating and applying the law, the Court necessarily has to specify its scope and sometimes note its general trend.

19. In view of what is stated above, the Court concludes that it has the authority to deliver an opinion on the question posed by the General Assembly, and that there exist no "compelling reasons" which would lead the Court to exercise its discretion not to do so.

An entirely different question is whether the Court, under the constraints placed upon it as a judicial organ, will be able to give a complete answer to the question asked of it. However, that is a different matter from a refusal to answer at all.

NOTES

1. *Declining a Specialized Agency's Request.* In *Legality of the Use by a State of Nuclear Weapons in Armed Conflict* (Request of the World Health Organization), 1996 I.C.J. 66, the Court determined that it lacked jurisdiction to give the requested opinion. It interpreted Article 65 of its Statute and Article 96(2) of the Charter in the following way:

> Consequently, three conditions must be satisfied in order to found the jurisdiction of the Court when a request for an advisory opinion is submitted to it by a specialized agency: the agency requesting the opinion must be duly authorized, under the Charter, to request opinions from the Court; the opinion requested must be on a legal question; and this question must be one arising with the scope of the activities of the requesting agency * * *.

The Court found "no doubt" that the WHO had been duly authorized under Article 96(2) of the Charter to request advisory opinions. It also concluded (in terms similar to those in paragraph 13 of the advisory opinion excerpted above on the General Assembly request) that the matter involved a "legal question," notwithstanding the presence of political implications. As to the third condition, however, the Court concluded that the question posed did not arise "within the scope of [the] activities" of the WHO:

> 19.   In order to delineate the field of activity or the area of competence of an international organization, one must refer to the relevant rules of the organization and, in the first place, to its constitution. From a formal standpoint, the constituent instruments of international organizations are multilateral treaties, to which the well-established rules of treaty interpretation apply. * * *

The Court examined the 22 subparagraphs of Article 2 of the WHO Constitution attributing functions to the organization, as well as the provisions of the preamble and Article 1 specifying its objectives in the sphere of public health:

> 21.   Interpreted in accordance with their ordinary meaning, in their context and in the light of the object and purpose of the WHO Constitution, as well as of the practice followed by the Organization, the provisions of its Article 2 may be read as authorizing the Organization to deal with the effects on health of the use of nuclear weapons, or of any other hazardous activity, and to take preventive measures aimed at protecting the health of populations in the event of such weapons being used or such activities engaged in.

> The question put to the Court in the present case relates, however, *not to the effects* of the use of nuclear weapons on health, but to the *legality* of the use of such weapons *in view of their health and environmental effects*. Whatever those effects might be, the competence of the WHO to deal with them is not dependent on the legality of the acts that caused them. Accordingly, it does not seem to the Court that the provisions of Article 2 of the WHO Constitution, interpreted in accordance with the criteria referred to above, can be understood as conferring upon the Organization a competence to address the legality of the use of nuclear weapons, and thus in turn a competence to ask the Court about that.

The Court further found that to attribute to the WHO a general competence concerning legality of nuclear weapons would be inconsistent with the "principle of speciality" and the Charter system of specialized agencies:

> 26.   * * * It follows from the various instruments mentioned above that the WHO Constitution can only be interpreted, as far as the powers

conferred upon that Organization are concerned, by taking due account not only of the general principle of speciality, but also of the logic of the overall system contemplated by the Charter. If, according to the rules on which that system is based, the WHO has, by virtue of Article 57 of the Charter, "wide international responsibilities", those responsibilities are necessarily restricted to the sphere of public "health" and cannot encroach on the responsibilities of other parts of the United Nations system. And there is no doubt that questions concerning the use of force, the regulation of armaments and disarmament are within the competence of the United Nations and lie outside that of the specialized agencies. Besides, any other conclusion would render virtually meaningless the notion of a specialized agency; it is difficult to imagine what other meaning that notion could have if such an organization need only show that the use of certain weapons could affect its objectives in order to be empower to concern itself with the legality of such use. It is therefore difficult to maintain that, by authorizing various specialized agencies to request opinions from the Court under Article 96, paragraph 2 of the Charter, the General Assembly intended to allow them to seise the Court of questions belonging within the competence of the United Nations.

For all these reasons, the Court considers that the question raised in the request for an advisory opinion submitted to it by the WHO does not arise "within the scope of [the] activities" of that Organization as defined by its Constitution.

2. *The General Assembly and WHO's Requests Compared.* For commentary on aspects of the two opinions relating to the Court's exercise of its advisory jurisdiction, see Abi–Saab, On Discretion: Reflections on the Nature of the Consultative Function of the International Court of Justice, in International Law, the International Court of Justice and Nuclear Weapons 36–50 (Boisson de Chazournes & Sands eds. 1999); Bothe, The WHO Request, in id., at 103–11; Leary, The WHO Case: Implications for Specialized Agencies, in id., at 112–27; see also Perez, The Passive Virtues and the World Court: Pro–Dialogic Abstention by the International Court of Justice, 18 Mich. J. Int'l L. 399 (1997).

LEGAL CONSEQUENCES OF THE CONSTRUCTION OF A WALL IN THE OCCUPIED PALESTINIAN TERRITORY

International Court of Justice, Advisory Opinion, 2004
2004 I.C.J. 136

[In Resolution ES–10/14 the U.N. General Assembly asked the Court for its opinion on the following question: "What are the legal consequences arising from the construction of the wall being built by Israel, the occupying Power, in the Occupied Palestinian Territory, including in and around East Jerusalem, as described in the report of the Secretary–General, considering the rules and principles of international law, including the Fourth Geneva Convention of 1949, and relevant Security Council and General Assembly resolutions?" The written statements submitted to the Court included the argument from some states (including but not limited to Israel) that the question should not be answered, either for lack of jurisdiction or for prudential reasons. The Court recapitulated its general approach to advisory jurisdiction under Article 65 with reference to the *Nuclear Weapons* advisory opinion and other cases, and then turned to certain specific objections raised by Israel and other states concerning the manner in which this particular request had been presented, in relation to parallel efforts in the Security Council and otherwise to achieve a comprehensive settlement.]

16.   Although [Article 96(1)] states that the General Assembly may seek an advisory opinion "on any legal question", the Court has sometimes in the past given certain indications as to the relationship between the question the subject of a request for an advisory opinion and the activities of the General Assembly (Interpretation of Peace Treaties with Bulgaria, Hungary and Romania, I.C.J. Reports 1950, p. 70; Legality of the Threat or Use of Nuclear Weapons, I.C.J. Reports 1996 (I), pp. 232 and 233, paras. 11 and 12).

17.   The Court will so proceed in the present case. The Court would observe that Article 10 of the Charter has conferred upon the General Assembly a competence relating to "any questions or any matters" within the scope of the Charter, and that Article 11, paragraph 2, has specifically provided it with competence on "questions relating to the maintenance of international peace and security brought before it by any Member of the United Nations ..." and to make recommendations under certain conditions fixed by those Articles. As will be explained below, the question of the construction of the wall in the Occupied Palestinian Territory was brought before the General Assembly by a number of Member States in the context of the Tenth Emergency Special Session of the Assembly, convened to deal with what the Assembly, in its resolution ES–10/2 of 25 April 1997, considered to constitute a threat to international peace and security.

* * *

21.   On 27 October 2003, the General Assembly adopted resolution ES–10/13, by which it demanded that "Israel stop and reverse the construction of the wall in the Occupied Palestinian Territory, including in and around East Jerusalem, which is in departure of the Armistice Line of 1949 and is in contradiction to relevant provisions of international law" (para. 1). In paragraph 3, the Assembly requested the Secretary–General "to report on compliance with the ... resolution periodically, with the first report on compliance with paragraph 1 [of that resolution] to be submitted within one month ...". The Tenth Emergency Special Session was temporarily adjourned and, on 24 November 2003, the report of the Secretary–General prepared pursuant to General Assembly resolution ES–10/13 (hereinafter the "report of the Secretary–General") was issued (A/ES–10/248).

22.   Meanwhile, on 19 November 2003, the Security Council adopted resolution 1515 (2003), by which it "Endorsed the Quartet Performance-based Roadmap to a Permanent Two–State Solution to the Israeli–Palestinian Conflict". The Quartet consists of representatives of the United States of America, the European Union, the Russian Federation and the United Nations. That resolution

> "Called on the parties to fulfil their obligations under the Roadmap in cooperation with the Quartet and to achieve the vision of two States living side by side in peace and security."

Neither the "Roadmap" nor resolution 1515 (2003) contained any specific provision concerning the construction of the wall, which was not discussed by the Security Council in this context.

* * *

24.   Having thus recalled the sequence of events that led to the adoption of resolution ES–10/14, the Court will now turn to the questions of jurisdiction that have been raised in the present proceedings. First, Israel has alleged that, given the active engagement of the Security Council with the situation in the Middle East, including the Palestinian question, the General Assembly acted *ultra vires* under the Charter when it requested an advisory opinion on the legal consequences of the construction of the wall in the Occupied Palestinian Territory.

25.   The Court has already indicated that the subject of the present request for an advisory opinion falls within the competence of the General Assembly under the Charter (see paragraphs 15–17 above). However, Article 12, paragraph 1, of the Charter provides that:

> "While the Security Council is exercising in respect of any dispute or situation the functions assigned to it in the present Charter, the General Assembly shall not make any recommendation with regard to that dispute or situation unless the Security Council so requests."

A request for an advisory opinion is not in itself a "recommendation" by the General Assembly "with regard to [a] dispute or situation". It has however been argued in this case that the adoption by the General Assembly of resolution ES–10/14 was ultra vires as not in accordance with Article 12. The Court thus considers that it is appropriate for it to examine the significance of that Article, having regard to the relevant texts and the practice of the United Nations.

26.   Under Article 24 of the Charter the Security Council has "primary responsibility for the maintenance of international peace and security". In that regard it can impose on States "an explicit obligation of compliance if for example it issues an order or command . . . under Chapter VII" and can, to that end, "require enforcement by coercive action" (*Certain Expenses of the United Nations* (Article 17, paragraph 2, of the Charter), Advisory Opinion of 20 July 1962, I.C.J. Reports 1962, p. 163). However, the Court would emphasize that Article 24 refers to a primary, but not necessarily exclusive, competence. The General Assembly

does have the power, inter alia, under Article 14 of the Charter, to "recommend measures for the peaceful adjustment" of various situations (*Certain Expenses of the United Nations*, ibid., p. 163). "The only limitation which Article 14 imposes on the General Assembly is the restriction found in Article 12, namely, that the Assembly should not recommend measures while the Security Council is dealing with the same matter unless the Council requests it to do so." (Ibid.).

[The Court next traces the evolution of U.N. practice under which the Security Council has addressed peace and security aspects of a situation while the General Assembly has concerned itself with humanitarian, social and economic impacts. In light of that practice, the Court found no contravention of Article 12(1) by virtue of the General Assembly's request for an advisory opinion.]

* * *

36.   The Court now turns to a further issue related to jurisdiction in the present proceedings, namely the contention that the request for an advisory opinion by the General Assembly is not on a "legal question" within the meaning of Article 96, paragraph 1, of the Charter and Article 65, paragraph 1, of the Statute of the Court. It has been contended in this regard that, for a question to constitute a "legal question" for the purposes of these two provisions, it must be reasonably specific, since otherwise it would not be amenable to a response by the Court. * * *

[The Court is satisfied that there is no obstacle to its jurisdiction by virtue of the phrasing of the question and concludes that the question is not an abstract one.]

41.   Furthermore, the Court cannot accept the view, which has also been advanced in the present proceedings, that it has no jurisdiction because of the "political" character of the question posed. [The Court refers here to its previous jurisprudence, including paragraph 13 of the *Nuclear Weapons* advisory opinion excerpted above.]

* * *

43.   It has been contended in the present proceedings, however, that the Court should decline to exercise its jurisdiction because of the presence of specific aspects of the General Assembly's request that would render the exercise of the Court's jurisdiction improper and inconsistent with the Court's judicial function.

* * *

46.   The first such argument is to the effect that the Court should not exercise its jurisdiction in the present case because the request concerns a contentious matter between Israel and Palestine, in respect of which Israel has not consented to the exercise of that jurisdiction. According to this view, the subject-matter of the question posed by the General Assembly "is an integral part of the wider Israeli–Palestinian dispute concerning questions of terrorism, security, borders, settlements, Jerusa-

lem and other related matters". Israel has emphasized that it has never consented to the settlement of this wider dispute by the Court or by any other means of compulsory adjudication; on the contrary, it contends that the parties repeatedly agreed that these issues are to be settled by negotiation, with the possibility of an agreement that recourse could be had to arbitration. It is accordingly contended that the Court should decline to give the present Opinion, on the basis *inter alia* of the precedent of the decision of the Permanent Court of International Justice on the *Status of Eastern Carelia*.

47.   The Court observes that the lack of consent to the Court's contentious jurisdiction by interested States has no bearing on the Court's jurisdiction to give an advisory opinion. [The Court here surveys its previous advisory opinion jurisprudence where states involved in the subject-matter of the request have objected on the grounds of lack of consent and concludes that there is no jurisdictional barrier and no compelling reason to exercise a discretionary power to decline to answer the question.]

* * *

49.   Furthermore, the Court does not consider that the subject-matter of the General Assembly's request can be regarded as only a bilateral matter between Israel and Palestine. Given the powers and responsibilities of the United Nations in questions relating to international peace and security, it is the Court's view that the construction of the wall must be deemed to be directly of concern to the United Nations. The responsibility of the United Nations in this matter also has its origin in the Mandate and the Partition Resolution concerning Palestine (see paragraphs 70 and 71 below). This responsibility has been described by the General Assembly as "a permanent responsibility towards the question of Palestine until the question is resolved in all its aspects in a satisfactory manner in accordance with international legitimacy" (General Assembly resolution 57/107 of 3 December 2002). Within the institutional framework of the Organization, this responsibility has been manifested by the adoption of many Security Council and General Assembly resolutions, and by the creation of several subsidiary bodies specifically established to assist in the realization of the inalienable rights of the Palestinian people.

50.   The object of the request before the Court is to obtain from the Court an opinion which the General Assembly deems of assistance to it for the proper exercise of its functions. The opinion is requested on a question which is of particularly acute concern to the United Nations, and one which is located in a much broader frame of reference than a bilateral dispute. In the circumstances, the Court does not consider that to give an opinion would have the effect of circumventing the principle of consent to judicial settlement, and the Court accordingly cannot, in the exercise of its discretion, decline to give an opinion on that ground.

51.   The Court now turns to another argument raised in the present proceedings in support of the view that it should decline to exercise its

jurisdiction. Some participants have argued that an advisory opinion from the Court on the legality of the wall and the legal consequences of its construction could impede a political, negotiated solution to the Israeli–Palestinian conflict. More particularly, it has been contended that such an opinion could undermine the scheme of the "Roadmap" (see paragraph 22 above), which requires Israel and Palestine to comply with certain obligations in various phases referred to therein. The requested opinion, it has been alleged, could complicate the negotiations envisaged in the "Roadmap", and the Court should therefore exercise its discretion and decline to reply to the question put.

This is a submission of a kind which the Court has already had to consider several times in the past [citing paragraph 17 of *Nuclear Weapons* advisory opinion, above].

53.   The Court is conscious that the "Roadmap", which was endorsed by the Security Council in resolution 1515 (2003) (see paragraph 22 above), constitutes a negotiating framework for the resolution of the Israeli–Palestinian conflict. It is not clear, however, what influence the Court's opinion might have on those negotiations: participants in the present proceedings have expressed differing views in this regard. The Court cannot regard this factor as a compelling reason to decline to exercise its jurisdiction.

54.   It was also put to the Court by certain participants that the question of the construction of the wall was only one aspect of the Israeli–Palestinian conflict, which could not be properly addressed in the present proceedings. The Court does not however consider this a reason for it to decline to reply to the question asked. The Court is indeed aware that the question of the wall is part of a greater whole, and it would take this circumstance carefully into account in any opinion it might give. At the same time, the question that the General Assembly has chosen to ask of the Court is confined to the legal consequences of the construction of the wall, and the Court would only examine other issues to the extent that they might be necessary to its consideration of the question put to it.

55.   Several participants in the proceedings have raised the further argument that the Court should decline to exercise its jurisdiction because it does not have at its disposal the requisite facts and evidence to enable it to reach its conclusions. In particular, Israel has contended, referring to the Advisory Opinion on the Interpretation of Peace Treaties with Bulgaria, Hungary and Romania, that the Court could not give an opinion on issues which raise questions of fact that cannot be elucidated without hearing all parties to the conflict. According to Israel, if the Court decided to give the requested opinion, it would be forced to speculate about essential facts and make assumptions about arguments of law. More specifically, Israel has argued that the Court could not rule on the legal consequences of the construction of the wall without enquiring, first, into the nature and scope of the security threat to which the wall is intended to respond and the effectiveness of that response, and, second, into the

impact of the construction for the Palestinians. This task, which would already be difficult in a contentious case, would be further complicated in an advisory proceeding, particularly since Israel alone possesses much of the necessary information and has stated that it chooses not to address the merits. Israel has concluded that the Court, confronted with factual issues impossible to clarify in the present proceedings, should use its discretion and decline to comply with the request for an advisory opinion.

56. The Court observes that the question whether the evidence available to it is sufficient to give an advisory opinion must be decided in each particular instance. * * *

57. In the present instance, the Court has at its disposal the report of the Secretary–General, as well as a voluminous dossier submitted by him to the Court, comprising not only detailed information on the route of the wall but also on its humanitarian and socio-economic impact on the Palestinian population. The dossier includes several reports based on on-site visits by special rapporteurs and competent organs of the United Nations. The Secretary–General has further submitted to the Court a written statement updating his report, which supplemented the information contained therein. Moreover, numerous other participants have submitted to the Court written statements which contain information relevant to a response to the question put by the General Assembly. The Court notes in particular that Israel's Written Statement, although limited to issues of jurisdiction and judicial propriety, contained observations on other matters, including Israel's concerns in terms of security, and was accompanied by corresponding annexes; many other documents issued by the Israeli Government on those matters are in the public domain.

58. The Court finds that it has before it sufficient information and evidence to enable it to give the advisory opinion requested by the General Assembly. Moreover, the circumstance that others may evaluate and interpret these facts in a subjective or political manner can be no argument for a court of law to abdicate its judicial task. There is therefore in the present case no lack of information such as to constitute a compelling reason for the Court to decline to give the requested opinion.

* * *

63. Lastly, the Court will turn to another argument advanced with regard to the propriety of its giving an advisory opinion in the present proceedings. Israel has contended that Palestine, given its responsibility for acts of violence against Israel and its population which the wall is aimed at addressing, cannot seek from the Court a remedy for a situation resulting from its own wrongdoing. In this context, Israel has invoked the maxim *nullus commodum capere potest de sua injuria propria*, which it considers to be as relevant in advisory proceedings as it is in contentious cases. Therefore, Israel concludes, good faith and the principle of "clean hands" provide a compelling reason that should lead the Court to refuse the General Assembly's request.

no one should profit from their wrong doing

64.   The Court does not consider this argument to be pertinent. As was emphasized earlier, it was the General Assembly which requested the advisory opinion, and the opinion is to be given to the General Assembly, and not to a specific State or entity.

65.   In the light of the foregoing, the Court concludes not only that it has jurisdiction to give an opinion on the question put to it by the General Assembly (see paragraph 42 above), but also that there is no compelling reason for it to use its discretionary power not to give that opinion.

NOTES

1.   *Purpose of Advisory Opinion.* Do you think that advisory judicial opinions on legal questions can be useful in helping to resolve actual disputes? Did the Court properly analyze the relevance of the fact that Israel had not consented to submit this dispute to the Court and the relationship to other pending efforts through the Security Council and the "Quartet"? For differing perspectives, see Agora: ICJ Advisory Opinion on Construction of a Wall in the Occupied Palestinian Territory, 99 A.J.I.L. 1 (2005).

2.   *The Wall Advisory Opinion in Context.* In proceeding to answer the question on the merits, the Court by very large margins (14–1 on three dispositive paragraphs; 13–2 on other paragraphs; all fifteen judges agreed on the Court's jurisdiction to decide the request) found the construction of the wall to be contrary to international law and declared that Israel is under an obligation to cease its construction and dismantle it forthwith. The Court opined on numerous issues of substantive international law interest, including self-determination of the Palestinian people, invocation of self-defense in response to terrorist attacks from non-state actors, application of human rights obligations outside a state's own territory, and specific obligations under international human rights and humanitarian law. The Court's substantive holdings are addressed in the relevant chapters elsewhere in this casebook. Do you think that the Court's elucidation of these legal obligations has assisted in resolving the underlying conflict, or could have the potential to do so?

3.   *Events on the Ground.* In parallel to and also following the advisory proceedings at the I.C.J., litigation in Israel brought on behalf of Palestinian parties also sought to achieve cessation of the wall's construction or its dismantling or rerouting. The Israeli Supreme Court, sitting as the High Court of Justice, determined on the facts before it to require certain changes in the placement of the separation barrier but did not give effect to the I.C.J. opinion as such. Which court was in a better position to appreciate the factual aspects of the matter and to make an authoritative legal analysis? See Watson, The "Wall" Decisions in Legal and Political Context, 99 A.J.I.L. 6 (2005).

4.   *Request Concerning Kosovo's Declaration of Independence.* In October 2008 the U.N. General Assembly asked the Court for an advisory opinion on the following question: "Is the unilateral declaration of independence by the Provisional Institutions of Self–Government of Kosovo in accordance with international law?" The Court fixed a timetable for the United Nations and

its member states to furnish written statements on the question and to make written comments on statements so submitted. The Court also invited "the authors of the above declaration" to make written contributions within the same time limits. This schedule was in progress in 2009. In light of the approach to advisory jurisdiction indicated by the *Wall* case, what objectives might be served by the rendering of such an opinion in the *Kosovo* case?

SECTION 5.   OTHER INTERNATIONAL COURTS AND TRIBUNALS

As indicated at the opening of this chapter, the institutions of international dispute settlement have multiplied rapidly in recent years; and with the creation of new tribunals has come an outpouring of new jurisprudence. Substantive aspects of the work of these bodies are taken up in the chapters to which they pertain—Chapter 13 for human rights, Chapter 14 for claims commissions and other remedies for injury to aliens and foreign investors, Chapter 16 for criminal tribunals, and Chapter 17 for the institutions of the law of the sea. We have also foreshadowed, in Chapters 1–4, some of the jurisprudential questions concerning the sources of law applied by these bodies and the prospects for coherence or inconsistency among their decisions.

The present section introduces the emerging subject of cross-institutional study of international tribunals, with illustrations from the formative years for some of the new bodies. The website of the Project on International Courts and Tribunals, noted at the beginning of this chapter, provides a valuable resource for comparing these bodies from various perspectives. See also Shany, The Competing Jurisdictions of International Courts and Tribunals (2003); Amerasinghe, Jurisdiction of International Tribunals (2003).

A.   "COMPULSORY" DISPUTE SETTLEMENT IN CERTAIN REGIMES

As we have seen, the "compulsory" jurisdiction of the I.C.J. is in reality strictly optional, and only a fraction of potential disputes come with the ambit of this mode of international judicial authority. An alternative possibility, increasingly embraced near the end of the twentieth and the beginning of the twentieth century, is the idea of regimes of compulsory dispute settlement for the subject-matter areas covered by certain general or regional multilateral treaties. The human rights area has become more fully "judicialized," especially in Europe, where acceptance of the competence of the European Court of Human Rights (for both state-to-state and individual petitions) has been made a condition of the inclusion of more states in ever more closely integrated European institutions. The 1982 U.N. Convention on the Law of the Sea (LOS Convention, or UNCLOS), which finally came into force in 1994, contains comprehensive dispute settlement provisions, so that in theory every sea dispute among the now more than 130 parties to this major treaty ought to be covered by one or another form of "compulsory" jurisdiction (with arbitration as the default mechanism). The 1994 agreements creating the World Trade Organization (W.T.O.) and its Dispute Settlement Body (D.S.B.) likewise represented significant progress toward comprehensive dispute settlement among now more than 153 states parties, notably by eliminating the possibility for a losing party to block adoption of a dispute settlement panel's report, so that the outcome of the new process should be conclusive.

These developments have presaged a real shift toward more genuinely "compulsory" forms of jurisdiction. Even so, gaps in compulsory authority have not been eliminated and some unexpected loopholes appear to have opened up. It has always been evident that the dispute settlement provisions of the LOS Convention or the 1994 W.T.O. agreement could not bind parties that remained outside the underlying regime—for example, the United States for the law of the sea. But even among parties to some of these regimes, there has been disagreement over the scope of the undertakings to submit disputes to compulsory settlement.

In the area of trade disputes, the ink was hardly dry on the W.T.O. agreement setting up the D.S.B. before scholars began debating whether its output would be "binding" in a legal sense, as opposed to giving states a choice between compliance and noncompliance (followed by countermeasures). Compare Bello, The WTO Dispute Settlement Understanding: Less is More, 90 A.J.I.L. 416 (1996) (arguing that W.T.O. is a system of voluntary compliance, under which states can elect not to comply with dispute settlement reports and suffer likely retaliation) with Jackson, The W.T.O. Dispute Settlement Understanding–Misunderstandings on the Nature of Legal Obligation, 91 A.J.I.L. 60 (1997) (supporting obligatory character of GATT/W.T.O. rules and dispute settlement procedures). Certain states also intimated reliance on assertedly "self-judging" exceptions to W.T.O. dispute settlement competence, e.g. under the "national security" exemption of GATT Article XXI, thereby arguably jeopardizing the coherence of the third-party dispute settlement system (just as the "domestic jurisdiction" and "vital interests" exceptions had done for I.C.J. compulsory jurisdiction, pp. 593–98). See Schloemann & Ohlhoff, "Constitutionalization" and Dispute Settlement in the W.T.O.: National Security as an Issue of Competence, 93 A.J.I.L. 424 (1999) (analyzing issue of GATT national security exception as a jurisdictional rather than substantive issue). Perhaps most important, several of the early rulings of the D.S.B. Appellate Body, such as the *Shrimp/Turtles* decision (noted in Chapter 18 below), were perceived in many quarters as showing the inadequacy of a trade dispute settlement regime for complex issues involving the intersection of trade law with environmental law or other systems. For diverse contributions to these debates, see Symposium: The Boundaries of the WTO, 96 A.J.I.L. 1 (2002); Jackson, International Law Status of WTO Dispute Settlement Reports: Obligation to Comply or Option to "Buy Out"?, 98 A.J.I.L. 109 (2004).

One of the first cases to be heard under the LOS Convention dispute settlement procedures brought to the fore an unexpected difficulty in realizing what was supposed to have been a comprehensive system of binding dispute settlement. In general, under LOS Convention Part XV, states parties are under an obligation to settle their disputes under the Convention (Article 279). An elaborate system of "compulsory procedures entailing binding decisions" is established, with a variety of mechanisms available among which states may choose an appropriate procedure (Articles 286–96 and Annexes VI, VII, and VIII). Arbitration under Annex VII is the default option if a state has not made another election of if two disputants have not agreed on a procedure. The binding nature of dispute settlement is clearly specified in Article 296 (see Section 5.F below). Notwithstanding the apparently comprehensive and obligatory nature of these provisions, a gaping hole was revealed in the *Southern Bluefin Tuna Cases* of 1999–2000.

In the first phase of the *Southern Bluefin Tuna* procedure, Australia and New Zealand brought a complaint against Japan concerning overfishing of bluefin tuna stocks in the Southern Pacific. The International Tribunal for the Law of the Sea (ITLOS) prescribed provisional measures, ordering Japan to observe the last total allowable catch that had been agreed within the framework of a regional fisheries convention (the 1993 Convention on the Conservation of Southern Bluefin Tuna), pending resolution of the dispute under arbitration. In the second phase, however, Japan contested the jurisdiction of the arbitral tribunal to consider the merits of the claim, on the grounds that the dispute in reality arose not under the LOS Convention but under the regional convention, and that dispute settlement under the LOS Convention was excluded because the parties had agreed to another means of settlement, namely consensual rather than compulsory submission. In a 4–1 decision, the arbitral tribunal agreed with Japan that it lacked jurisdiction to resolve the dispute. The tribunal had to interpret LOS Convention Articles 279–82, which deal with the relationship of dispute settlement under the Convention to other modes of settlement on which the parties may agree. The tribunal reasoned that the regional fisheries convention, which was at the core of the substantive dispute between the parties, contained its own dispute settlement provision, which required the consent of Japan to any arbitral submission. The tribunal's conclusion was that Article 16 of the regional convention "exclude[s] any further procedure" within the contemplation of LOS Convention Article 281(1). As the tribunal stated (at para. 62): "It thus appears to the Tribunal that UNCLOS falls significantly short of establishing a truly comprehensive regime of compulsory jurisdiction entailing binding decisions." *Southern Bluefin Tuna Cases*, Arbitral Award of Aug. 4, 2000, 39 I.L.M.1359 (2000). For analysis, see Oxman, Complementary Agreements and Compulsory Jurisdiction, 95 A.J.I.L. 277 (2001).

Before leaving this topic, we should emphasize a distinction between compulsory jurisdiction—that is, an obligation *to submit* disputes to a stipulated mode of third-party legal settlement—and the binding quality of the decision that may result. Under a genuinely compulsory regime, there would be both an obligation to submit to jurisdiction and an obligation to carry out any eventual ruling. The two questions are, however, analytically different, and one form of obligation may exist without the other. See Section 5.F.

B. STRUCTURE AND COMPOSITION OF THE TRIBUNAL

The I.C.J., as we have seen, has a standing bench of fifteen geographically diverse members serving fixed renewable nine-year terms, supplemented as appropriate by one or more *ad hoc* judges chosen by parties who do not have a judge of their own nationality already on the bench. This system ensures that each litigant has a "voice" in the deliberations, though the judges are required to be independent (I.C.J. Statute, art. 2) and therefore are not to take instruction from their state. Party-appointed arbitrators are likewise a typical feature of international arbitration.

Other international tribunals have made some notable departures from the I.C.J. model of judicial selection, while sometimes borrowing particular features (such as the principle of a representative bench). Instead of the I.C.J. system of nominations by national groups "at one remove" from governments, in general it is states parties to the treaty who make the nominations, and nominations are frequently restricted to the nationals of states parties. The electing authority may be a U.N. organ (as with the two existing ad hoc criminal tribunals; see Chapter 16), but more typically elections are reserved to the states parties to the treaty that establishes the tribunal. The constitutive instrument often specifies the subject-matter expertise required of judges: for example, for ITLOS, "recognized competence in the field of the law of the sea." See Chapter 16 for the specific features of the International Criminal Court. See also The International Judge: An Inquiry Into the Men and Women Who Decide the World's Cases (Terris et al., eds., 2007).

A split has emerged between tribunals that *do* follow the I.C.J. model of allowing national *ad hoc* judges, and those that take the opposite approach of requiring nonparticipation of judges of the nationality of the parties. The ITLOS, for example, has a provision for designation of *ad hoc* members (UNCLOS annex VI, art. 17). The W.T.O., by contrast, constructs its dispute settlement panels so that no member shall have the nationality of any of the disputants (unless the parties to the dispute otherwise agree). W.T.O. Dispute Settlement Understanding, art. 8(3). If a developing country is in a dispute with a developed country, the developing country is entitled to request that the W.T.O. panel include at least one member from a developing country. Id., art. 8(10).

C. STANDING

An important trend is the opening up of some dispute settlement procedures to parties other than states. This possibility has long been available in arbitral institutions (see p. 574), but the recent tendencies are for permanent judicial institutions also to have facilities for disputes between private persons and states (or even between private parties).

The human rights institutions illustrate this trend, as discussed further in Chapter 13. Of particular interest is the availability of the European Court of Human Rights (E.C.H.R.) to the petitions of individuals from any of the member states of the Council of Europe. The European Court of Justice (E.C.J.) also hears cases brought by individuals as well as companies. Although it is outside the scope of this chapter to consider these European institutions or other regional institutions in any detail, it may be noted that individual petitions brought to European tribunals have produced notable judgments addressing questions of interest for the substance of international law in general, as evidenced by the attention to E.C.H.R. cases in Chapter 3 on reservations to multilateral treaties. A claim brought to the E.C.J. by an individual, Yusuf Kadi, has produced a notable judgment on the interaction between Security Council resolutions and the internal legal systems of member states of the European Union, as addressed in Chapter 10.

Judicial institutions in the Western Hemisphere and Africa display a diversity of approaches to problems of standing. On mechanisms for taking up grievances of individuals within the regional human rights bodies, see Chapter 13. A different kind of regional tribunal, the Andean Court of Justice, has become the third most active international court (only the E.C.H.R. and E.C.J. have a larger docket); private individuals and corporations have brought some 1400 cases—mostly intellectual property claims—to this tribunal. See Helfer et al., Islands of Effective International Adjudication, 103 A.J.I.L. 1 (2009).

In the law of the sea field, the ITLOS Statute provides that the tribunal "shall be open to State Parties" and also "open to entities other than States Parties in any case expressly provided for in Part XI (on deep seabed mining) or in any case submitted pursuant to any other agreement conferring jurisdiction on the Tribunal which is accepted by all the parties to that case." (UNCLOS annex VI, art. 30).

The W.T.O. D.S.B. is restricted in its jurisdiction to disputes between states parties. Standing issues have arisen in some of the D.S.B.'s early cases: for example, in the *EC Bananas* dispute, the Appellate Body held that there was no requirement that a member have a "legal interest" in order to be allowed to initiate a complaint. European Communities—Regime for the Importation, Sale and Distribution of Bananas, Report of the Appellate Body, WTO Doc. WT/DS27/AB/R, paras. 132–33 (1997). Third states have been allowed to participate. See, e.g., United States—

Tax Treatment for "Foreign Sales Corporation," Report of the Appellate Body, WTO Doc. WT/DS108/AB/R (2000) (intervention of Canada and Japan in proceeding initiated by European Union against United States).

A few specialized bodies have competence comparable to that of the I.C.J. to render advisory opinions at the request of specified entities, which may include international organizations as well as state. Notable in this regard is the Inter–American Court of Human Rights, which has a vibrant advisory jurisprudence. See Buergenthal, The Advisory Practice of the Inter–American Human Rights Court, 79 A.J.I.L. 1 (1985); Pasqualucci, The Practice and Procedure of the Inter–American Court of Human Rights (2003).

D.   PROVISIONAL MEASURES

The authority of a tribunal to specify urgent measures to preserve the rights of the parties pending the litigation is an important procedural component of a mature dispute settlement system. We have already seen some of the difficulties in I.C.J. provisional measures jurisprudence, stemming from its incomplete patchwork of jurisdiction and from ambiguity prior to the 2001 *LaGrand* decision as to whether parties were required to comply with interim orders. Some of the more recent tribunals benefit from the conferral of broader and clearer competence in this regard. For example, LOS Convention Article 290 and Annex VI Article 25 contain detailed specifications on provisional measures, including on the authority of the ITLOS to prescribe such measures pending the establishment of an arbitral tribunal. Article 290(6) provides that parties "shall comply promptly" with any provisional measures so prescribed.

Under Article 292 of the LOS Convention, the ITLOS can consider applications for prompt release of vessels and crew, subject to the posting of a reasonable bond or other financial security.

The ITLOS has indicated provisional measures and granted applications for prompt release in several cases, including *Southern Bluefin Tuna*, 38 I.L.M. 1624 (1999). As noted above (p. 640, the measures entered by ITLOS in *Southern Bluefin Tuna* were later dissolved by the relevant arbitral tribunal, after that tribunal determined that the dispute did not fall under the compulsory dispute settlement procedures. In *M/V Saiga* (Saint Vincent and the Grenadines v. Guinea), 37 I.L.M. 360 (1998), ITLOS ordered prompt release of an arrested vessel and crew, upon the posting of a reasonable bond. In *Tomimaru* (Japan v. Russian Federation), 46 I.L.M. 1183 (2007), ITLOS ruled on its eighth prompt release case, which arose in the context of parallel proceedings in Russian domestic court. The tribunal denied Japan's application for prompt release of a fishing vessel that had already been confiscated by Russia.

For more on ITLOS provisional measures and related procedures, see Klein, Dispute Settlement in the UN Convention on the Law of the Sea (2005); Rosenne, Provisional Measures in International Law: The International Court of Justice and the International Tribunal for the Law of the Sea (2004).

Regional human rights courts likewise have an active provisional measures jurisprudence. See generally Macdonald, Interim Measures in International Law, with Special Reference to the European System for the Protection of Human Rights, 52 Zeitschrift f. a. ö. R. 703–40 (1992); Pasqualucci, The Practice and Procedure of the Inter–American Court of Human Rights 291–325 (2003).

E. APPELLATE REVIEW

The I.C.J. is a court of both first and last resort; there is no possibility of appeal from its judgments, and it has only a limited competence to act as a supervisory organ with respect to certain administrative or arbitral tribunals. See Reisman, The Supervisory Jurisdiction of the International Court of Justice, 258 Rec. des Cours 9 (1996). With the increasing complexity and sophistication of international litigation, bifurcation of judicial functions between tribunals of first instance and organs of appellate review is becoming ever more necessary. Thus European regional institutions now include panels of first instance and appellate chambers. The two International Criminal Tribunals for Yugoslavia and Rwanda are structured with several trial chambers for each body, and a common appeals chamber to ensure coherence of jurisprudence. The International Criminal Court also has an appeals chamber. See Chapter 16.

The W.T.O. institutional changes have included the creation within the D.S.B. in late 1995 of an Appellate Body, consisting of seven members from different legal systems who serve fixed four-year terms, sitting in divisions of three members on a rotating basis. A set of Working Procedures for Appellate Review, WTO Doc. WT/AB/WP/3 (Feb. 28, 1997) governs the mechanisms for appellate review. A general structural issue addressed in early rulings of the Appellate Body is the appropriate standard of review on appeal. In principle, the Appellate Body has considered that under Article 17 of the Dispute Settlement Understanding, its function is to consider issues of law and legal interpretation rather than new facts. See, e.g., Canada—Aircraft, Report of the Appellate Body, WTO Doc. WT/DS70/AB/R (1999); United States—Tax Treatment for "Foreign Sales Corporations," Report of the Appellate Body, WTO Doc. WT/DS108/AB/R (2000). In the latter proceeding, the Appellate Body also addressed whether new arguments can be raised on appeal (paras. 101–03).

The appellate structure of the W.T.O. dispute settlement system has given rise to several occasions for the Appellate Body to consider the relationship between the rulings of the first-instance panels and its own appellate authority. The following decision crystallizes that issue:

UNITED STATES—FINAL ANTI-DUMPING MEASURES ON STAINLESS STEEL FROM MEXICO

World Trade Organization, Appellate Body, 2008
47 I.L.M. 475 (2008) (some footnotes omitted)

[The dispute concerns the methodology for calculation of margins of dumping by the United States Department of Commerce under Article VI of GATT 1994 and the Anti–Dumping Agreement. The Appellate Body had addressed related issues on several previous occasions in complaints over "zeroing" methodology brought against the United States by the European Community and Japan. The panel convened for the Mexico–U.S. dispute decided not to follow the Appellate Body's prior holdings but instead relied on findings in panel reports that the Appellate Body had reversed. The provisions of the Dispute Settlement Understanding (DSU) cited in the Appellate Body report may be found in the Documents Supplement.]

154.   On appeal, Mexico argues that the Panel acted inconsistently with Article 11 of the DSU by failing to follow well-established Appellate Body jurisprudence. In support of its claim, Mexico refers to Articles 3.2 and 3.3 of the DSU.

155.   We begin our consideration with the text of Article 11 of the DSU, which sets forth the function of panels in the WTO dispute settlement system. The first sentence stipulates that "[t]he function of panels is to assist the DSB in discharging its responsibilities" under the DSU and the covered agreements. The second sentence states that "a panel should make an objective assessment of the matter before it, including an objective assessment of the facts of the case and the applicability of and conformity with the relevant covered agreements, and make such other findings as will assist the DSB in making the recommendations or in giving the rulings provided for in the covered agreements."

* * *

158.   It is well settled that Appellate Body reports are not binding, except with respect to resolving the particular dispute between the parties.[308] This, however, does not mean that subsequent panels are free to disregard the legal interpretations and the *ratio decidendi* contained in previous Appellate Body reports that have been adopted by the DSB. In *Japan–Alcoholic Beverages II*, the Appellate Body found that:

[a]dopted panel reports are an important part of the GATT *acquis*. They are often considered by subsequent panels. They create legiti-

---

308.   See Appellate Body Report, *Japan–Alcoholic Beverages II*, pp. 12–15, DSR 1996:I, 97, at 106–108. In that case, the Appellate Body stated:

It is worth noting that the Statute of the International Court of Justice has an explicit provision, Article 59, to the same effect. This has not inhibited the development by that Court (and its predecessor) of a body of case law in which considerable reliance on the value of previous decisions is readily discernible.

mate expectations among WTO Members, and, therefore, should be taken into account where they are relevant to any dispute.

159. In *US–Shrimp (Article 21.5—Malaysia)*, the Appellate Body clarified that this reasoning applies to adopted Appellate Body reports as well. In *US–Oil Country Tubular Goods Sunset Reviews*, the Appellate Body held that "following the Appellate Body's conclusions in earlier disputes is not only appropriate, but is what would be expected from panels, especially where the issues are the same."

160. Dispute settlement practice demonstrates that WTO members attach significance to reasoning provided in previous panel and Appellate Body reports. Adopted panel and Appellate Body reports are often cited by parties in support of legal arguments in dispute settlement proceedings, and are relied upon by panels and the Appellate Body in subsequent disputes. In addition, when enacting or modifying laws and national regulations pertaining to international trade matters, WTO Members take into account the legal interpretation of the covered agreements developed in adopted panel and Appellate Body reports. Thus, the legal interpretation embodied in adopted panel and Appellate Body reports becomes part and parcel of the *acquis* of the WTO dispute settlement system. Ensuring "security and predictability" in the dispute settlement system, as contemplated in Article 3.2 of the DSU, implies that, absent cogent reasons, an adjudicatory body will resolve the same legal question in the same way in a subsequent case.[313]

161. In the hierarchical structure contemplated in the DSU, panels and the Appellate Body have distinct roles to play. In order to strengthen dispute settlement in the multilateral trading system, the Uruguay Round established the Appellate Body as a standing body. Pursuant to Article 17.6 of the DSU, the Appellate Body is vested with the authority to review "issues of law covered in the panel report and legal interpretations developed by the panel." Accordingly, Article 17.13 provides that the Appellate Body may "uphold, modify or reverse" the legal findings and conclusions of panels. The creation of the Appellate Body by WTO Members to review legal interpretations developed by panels shows that Members recognized the importance of consistency and stability in the

---

313. See H. Lauterpacht, "The so-called Anglo–American and Continental Schools of Thought in International Law" (1931) 12 *British Yearbook of International Law* 53, who points out that adherence to legal decisions "is imperative if the law is to fulfill one of its primary functions, i.e. the maintenance of security and stability." Consistency of jurisprudence is valued also in dispute settlement in other international fora. In this respect we note the Decision of the International Criminal Tribunal for the Former Yugoslavia, Case No. IT–95–14/1–A, *Prosecutor v. Aleksovski*, Judgement of 24 March 2000, para. 113, which states that "the right of appeal is . . . a component of the fair trial requirement, which is itself a rule of customary international law and gives rise to the right of the accused to have like cases treated alike. This will not be achieved if each Trial Chamber is free to disregard decisions of law made by the Appeals Chamber, and decide the law as it sees fit." Furthermore, we note the Decision of 21 March 2007 of the ICSID (International Centre for Settlement of Investment Disputes) Arbitration Tribunal, Case No. ARB/05/07, *Saipem S.p.A. v. The People's Republic of Bangladesh*, ICSID IIC 280 (2007), p. 20, para. 67 [on duty of tribunal to pay due consideration to consistent decisions of other tribunals, in order to contribute to harmonious development of investment law and legitimate expectations toward certainty of the rule of law].

interpretation of their rights and obligations under the covered agreements. This is essential to promote "security and predictability" in the dispute settlement system, and to ensure the "prompt settlement" of disputes. The Panel's failure to follow previously adopted Appellate Body reports addressing the same issues undermines the development of a coherent and predictable body of jurisprudence clarifying Members' rights and obligations under the covered agreements as contemplated under the DSU. Clarification, as envisaged in Article 3.2 of the DSU, elucidates the scope and meaning of the provisions of the covered agreements in accordance with customary rules of interpretation of public international law. While the application of a provision may be regarded as confined to the context in which it takes place, the relevance of clarification contained in adopted Appellate Body reports is not limited to the application of a particular provision in a specific case.

162.   We are deeply concerned about the Panel's decision to depart from well-established Appellate Body jurisprudence clarifying the interpretation of the same legal issues. The Panel's approach has serious implications for the proper functioning of the WTO dispute settlement system, as explained above. Nevertheless, we consider that the Panel's failure flowed, in essence, from its misguided understanding of the legal provisions at issue. Since we have corrected the Panel's erroneous legal interpretation and have reversed all of the Panel's findings and conclusions that have been appealed, we do not, in this case, make an additional finding that the Panel also failed to discharge its duties under Article 11 of the DSU.

F.   COMPLIANCE

Along with the proliferation of international tribunals has come renewed attention to problems of compliance. Some constitutive instruments of international tribunals specify, in terms comparable to those applicable to the I.C.J. (U.N. Charter, art. 94; I.C.J. Statute, art. 59) that parties undertake to comply with the tribunal's decisions and that such decisions are binding on the parties (though not on third parties). See, e.g., LOS Convention Article 296, which provides:

Article 296. Finality and binding force of decisions

1.   Any decision rendered by a court or tribunal having jurisdiction under this section shall be final and shall be complied with by all the parties to the dispute.

2.   Any such decision shall have no binding force except between the parties and in respect of that particulate dispute.

On the other hand, some tribunals, such as the U.N. human rights treaty bodies, may formally have only recommendatory competence even when acting in a quasi-adjudicatory capacity. But this formal shortfall may understate the authority of their decisions, which often enjoy a high degree of respect.

The comparative study of the "compliance pull" of international tribunals is becoming ever more interesting, as their growing output creates larger empirical bases for comparison. For an exploration of a theoretical framework for comparing compliance as between European and U.N. institutions, see Helfer & Slaughter, Toward a Theory of Effective Supranational Adjudication, 107 Yale L.J. 273 (1997). For more recent contributions assessing compliance with decisions of other bodies, see Viljoen & Louw, State Compliance with the Recommendations of the African Commission on Human and People's Rights, 1994–2004, 101 A J.I.L. 1 (2007); Cavallaro & Brewer, Reevaluating Regional Human Rights Litigation in the Twenty–First Century: The Case of the Inter–American Court, 102 A.J.I.L. 768 (2008).

When compliance fails, some (but not many) of the tribunals have at least the theoretical possibility of enlisting assistance in enforcement from treaty parties or a coordinate institution. As noted, the U.N. Charter (Article 94(2)) provides for a prevailing party at the I.C.J. to seek an enforcement order from the Security Council, but this procedure has not yet been successfully invoked. Orders of the criminal tribunals could also theoretically be enforced by the Security Council under Chapter VII authority. Within the framework of the W.T.O., the sanction for noncompliance is authorized retaliation by the prevailing party (i.e., suspending an equivalent value of trade concessions).

NOTES

1. *The Overall System.* For an overview of the multiplicity of new adjudicatory institutions, see Symposium Issue, The Proliferation of International Tribunals: Piecing Together the Puzzle, 31 N.Y.U. J. Int'l L. & Pol. 679–933 (1999). Current information about all international tribunals is maintained on the website of the Project on International Courts and Tribunals, www.pict-pcti.org.

2. *Law of the Sea Dispute Settlement.* On the dispute settlement institutions of the law of the sea, see International Tribunal for the Law of the Sea, Basic Texts (1998). See also Oda, Dispute Settlement Prospects in the Law of the Sea, 44 I.C.L.Q. 863 (1995); Rosenne, Establishing the International Tribunal for the Law of the Sea, 89 A.J.I.L. 806 (1995); Rosenne, International Tribunal for the Law of the Sea, 13 Int'l J. Marine & Coastal L. 487 (1998); Treves, Conflicts Between the International Tribunal for the Law of the Sea and the International Court of Justice, 31 N.Y.U. J. Int'l L. & Pol. 809 (1999); Klein, Dispute Settlement in the UN Convention on the Law of the Sea (2005).

3. *Trade Dispute Settlement.* The GATT/W.T.O. Dispute Settlement Understanding (Understanding on Rules and Procedures Governing the Settlement of Disputes) is reprinted at 33 I.L.M. 1125, 1226 (1994). On W.T.O. dispute settlement, see Palmeter & Mavroidis, Dispute Settlement in the World Trade Organization (1997); Petersmann, The GATT/WTO Dispute Settlement System (1997); presentations by Shoyer, Steger & Van den Bossche, and Cottier at the panel on WTO Dispute Settlement: Three Years in

Review, 92 A.S.I.L. Proc. 75 91 (1998); Jackson, Fragmentation or Unification Among International Institutions: The World Trade Organization, 31 N.Y.U. J. Int'l L. & Pol. 823 (1999); Symposium: The First Five Years of the WTO, Part I: Review of the Dispute Settlement Understanding, 31 L. & Pol'y Int'l Bus. 565 (2000).

For a comprehensive study of dispute settlement under GATT prior to establishment of the W.T.O. D.S.B., see Hudec, Enforcing International Trade Law: The Evolution of the Modern GATT Legal System (1993).

PART 2

INTERFACE OF INTERNATIONAL AND NATIONAL LAW

• • •

CHAPTER 10

INTERNATIONAL LAW IN NATIONAL LAW

■ ■ ■

SECTION 1.   GENERAL CONSIDERATIONS

International law is binding on the state, and the state is obliged to give effect to it, but international law does not replace the national law of states (sometimes referred to as "domestic" or "municipal" law). Indeed international law depends on the governments of states and their constitutional and legal systems for the adherence to and enforcement of international law. The obligation to respect and give effect to international law is upon the state, not upon any particular branch, institution, or member of its government; the state is responsible for violations by any branch of its government or by any official (and in some contexts also for acts and omissions by private individuals). The state is responsible to assure that its constitution and its laws enable its government to carry out its international obligations.

It should go without saying that a state cannot plead its own law as a reason for non-compliance with international law. In 1887, for example, U.S. Secretary of State Bayard declared:

> [I]t is only necessary to say, that if a Government could set up its own municipal laws as the final test of its international rights and obligations, then the rules of international law would be but the shadow of a name and would afford no protection either to States or to individuals. It has been constantly maintained and also admitted by the Government of the United States that a Government can not appeal to its municipal regulations as an answer to demands for the fulfillment of international duties. Such regulations may either exceed or fall short of the requirements of international law, and in either case that law furnishes the test of the nation's liability and not its own municipal rules. * * *

[1887] U.S. Foreign Rel. 751, 753.

Many decisions of international tribunals recognize the principle that every state has the duty to carry out in good faith its obligations arising from international law and that it may not invoke provisions in its constitution or its laws as an excuse for failure to perform this duty. See, e.g., *Rights of Nationals of the United States of America in Morocco*

(France v. United States), 1952 I.C.J. 176; *Norwegian Shipowners' Claims* (Norway v. United States), 1 U.N. Rep. Int'l Arb. Awards 307 (1922); *Shufeldt Claim* (United States v. Guatemala), 1930, 2 U.N. Rep. Int'l Arb. Awards 1079. The same duty is recognized in Article 46 of the Vienna Convention on the Law of Treaties. See Chapter 3, p. 162.

Two principal schools have seen the relation of international law to national law differently. Dualists (or pluralists) regard international law and national law as separate legal systems which operate on different levels. For dualists, international law can be applied by domestic organs only when it has been "transformed" or "incorporated" into national law, such as through enactment of an implementing statute. Further, international law, as incorporated into national law, is subject to constitutional limitations applicable to all domestic law, and may be repealed or superseded by act of the legislature for purposes of national law. Monists, on the other hand, have regarded international law and national law as parts of a single system. In a pure version of monism, national law is seen as ultimately deriving its validity from international law, which stands "higher" in a hierarchy of legal norms. Therefore, international law cannot be subject to national law, not even to constitutional limitations. Particular states have adopted their own variants of one school or the other, not from jurisprudential persuasion but from their own historic, political and constitutional commitments.

International law requires a state to carry out its international obligations but, in general, how a state accomplishes that result is not of concern to international law. In some instances, however, states may commit internationally to carry out their obligations by particular means, for example, by enacting legislation or by taking specified executive or judicial measures. The International Covenant on Civil and Political Rights, December 16, 1966, article 2, 999 U.N.T.S. 171, requires states to "adopt such legislative or other measures as may be necessary to give effect to the rights recognized" in the Covenant, unless such measures already exist. The Genocide Convention, December 9, 1948, articles V & VI, 78 U.N.T.S. 277, requires states parties to make genocide a crime under national law. The Convention Against Torture, December 10, 1984, 1465 U.N.T.S. 85, provides in Article 4(1) that "each state party shall ensure that all acts of torture are offences under its criminal law."

Since a state's responsibility to give effect to international obligations usually does not fall upon any particular institution of its government, international law does not necessarily require that national legislatures or courts be the organ for compliance. (Of course, insofar as international law accords immunity from the jurisdiction of courts, such as to a foreign state or to its diplomats, the exercise of jurisdiction by a national court contrary to the limitations of international law would constitute a violation by the state.) Consequently, states differ as to whether and how international law is incorporated into national law and forms a part of "the law of the land," and whether the executive or the courts will give effect to norms of international law or to treaty provisions in the absence of their implementation by national legislation. Thus a state may have an international obligation that the state fails to uphold due to conflicting or inadequate national implementation; when this occurs, the state may be fully in compliance with its national law, but not in compliance with its international obligation. States generally seek to avoid a gap between their international obligations and national law, either by refraining from adhering to international obligations that cannot be implemented nationally, or by altering national law to meet the international obligations.

The next two sections address the manner in which the United States incorporates international law into U.S. law, focusing first on customary international law and then on treaties. For the approaches of other countries to the relationship between constitutional and international law, see the last section of this chapter.

SECTION 2.   CUSTOMARY INTERNATIONAL LAW IN U.S. LAW

A.   CUSTOMARY INTERNATIONAL LAW AS "LAW OF THE LAND"

THE PAQUETE HABANA

Supreme Court of the United States, 1900
175 U.S. 677

[Reread this case in Chapter 2, p. 61, focusing this time not on the manner in which a rule of customary international law is formed, but on Justice Gray's comment that "international law is a part of our law." Then consider Henkin's views and the Restatement's treatment.]

HENKIN, INTERNATIONAL LAW AS LAW IN THE UNITED STATES

82 Mich. L.Rev. 1555 (1984) (footnotes omitted)

"International law is part of our law." Justice Gray's much-quoted pronouncement in *The Paquete Habana* was neither new nor controversial when made in 1900, since he was merely restating what had been established principle for the fathers of American jurisprudence and for their British legal ancestors.* * * But, after more than two hundred years in our jurisprudence, the import of that principle is still uncertain and disputed. How did, and how does, international law become part of our law? * * *

* * *

International law became part of "our law" with independence in 1776. One view has it that the law of nations came into our law as part of the common law. In the eighteenth century, the law of nations was part of the law of England, and English law, including the law of nations, applied in her colonies. With American independence, the law of England in the colonies (including the law of nations) was "received" as common law in the United States.

A different conception sees the law of nations as coming into our law not by "inheritance" but by implication from our independence, by virtue of international statehood. An entity that becomes a State in the international system is *ipso facto* subject to international law. While the obligations of international law are upon the State as an entity, a State ordinarily finds it necessary or convenient to incorporate international law into its municipal law to be applied by its courts. In the United States, neither state constitutions nor the federal Constitution, nor state or federal legislation, have expressly incorporated international law; from our beginnings, however, following the English tradition, courts have treated international law as incorporated and applied it as domestic law.

The two conceptions, and variations upon them, may bear different consequences. If international law was part of the common law that each state received from England, international law was state law. It would cease to be state law and become federal law only if the U.S. Constitution, or an act of Congress pursuant to the Constitution, so provided. On the other hand, if international law became domestic law by virtue of independence, its status as state or federal law may turn on the international character of our independence and the status of the states between 1776 and 1789. Some have insisted that during those years the states were thirteen independent states (in the international sense), each equal in status to England, France and other nations of the time, each subject to international law. Each state decided for itself whether to incorporate international law, but all of them did so, in the tradition inherited from England. On this view, as on the "common law" view, international law was state law between 1776 and 1789 and remained state law unless the federal Constitution or later federal law pursuant to the Constitution rendered it federal law.

A different view, however, concludes that the thirteen states were never independent States; that for international purposes we were from independence one nation, not thirteen. By virtue of independence and statehood, international law became binding on the United States, not on the individual states. Between 1776 and 1789, there being no national domestic law, international law could not be incorporated into national law, but the national obligations of the United States could be carried out through state law and institutions. In 1789, the obligations of the United States to give effect to international law became effectively the responsibility of the new federal government, to be carried out through federal institutions (including federal courts), through state institutions (including state courts), or both.

RESTATEMENT OF THE LAW (THIRD)
THE FOREIGN RELATIONS LAW OF THE UNITED STATES (1987)

Part I, Chapter 2, Introductory Note.

International law as United States law. International law was part of the law of England and, as such, of the American colonies. With independence, it became part of the law of each of the thirteen States. When the United States became a state it became subject to international law. See § 206. From the beginning, the law of nations, later referred to as international law, was considered to be incorporated into the law of the United States without the need for any action by Congress or the President, and the courts, State and federal, have applied it and given it effect as the courts of England had done. Customary international law as developed to that time was law of the United States when it became a state. Customary law that has developed since the United States became a state is incorporated into United States law as of the time it matures into international law. * * *

* * *

Erie R.R. Co. v. Tompkins, 304 U.S. 64 (1938), held that, in suits based on diversity of citizenship jurisdiction, a federal court was bound to apply the common law as determined by the courts of the State in which the federal court sat. On that basis, some thought that the federal courts must also follow State court determinations of customary international law. However, a different view has prevailed. It is now established that customary international law in the United States is a kind of federal law, and like treaties and other international agreements, it is accorded supremacy over State law by Article VI of the Constitution. Hence, determinations of international law by the Supreme Court of the United States, like its interpretations of international agreements, are binding on the States. See § 111, Comment *d*, § 112(2) and Comment *a* to that section, § 326, Comment *d*. Also, cases "arising under" customary international law arise under "the laws" of the United States. They are within the Judicial Power of the United States (Article III, Section 2) and the jurisdiction of the federal courts (28 U.S.C. §§ 1257, 1331). See § 111(2) and Comment *e* to that section. * * *

SOSA v. ALVAREZ–MACHAIN

Supreme Court of the United States, 2004
542 U.S. 692 (footnotes omitted)

JUSTICE SOUTER delivered the opinion of the Court.

* * *

"When the United States declared their independence, they were bound to receive the law of nations, in its modern state of purity and refinement." *Ware v. Hylton,* 3 U.S. (3 Dall.) 199, 281 (1796) (Wilson, J.).

In the years of the early Republic, this law of nations comprised two principal elements, the first covering the general norms governing the behavior of national states with each other: *"the science which teaches the rights subsisting between nations or states, and the obligations correspondent to those rights,"* E. de Vattel, The Law of Nations, Preliminaries § 3 (J. Chitty et al. transl. and ed. 1883) (hereinafter Vattel) (footnote omitted), or "that code of public instruction which defines the rights and prescribes the duties of nations, in their intercourse with each other," 1 Kent Commentaries on American Law. This aspect of the law of nations thus occupied the executive and legislative domains, not the judicial. *See* 4 W. Blackstone, Commentaries on the Laws of England 68 (1769) (hereinafter Commentaries) ("[O]ffenses against" the law of nations are "principally incident to whole states or nations").

The law of nations included a second, more pedestrian element, however, that did fall within the judicial sphere, as a body of judge-made law regulating the conduct of individuals situated outside domestic boundaries and consequently carrying an international savor. To Blackstone, the law of nations in this sense was implicated "in mercantile questions, such as bills of exchange and the like; in all marine causes, relating to freight, average, demurrage, insurances, bottomry ...; [and] in all disputes relating to prizes, to shipwrecks, to hostages, and ransom bills." *Id.*, at 67. The law merchant emerged from the customary practices of international traders and admiralty required its own transnational regulation. And it was the law of nations in this sense that our precursors spoke about when the Court explained the status of coast fishing vessels in wartime grew from "ancient usage among civilized nations, beginning centuries ago, and gradually ripening into a rule of international law...." *The Paquete Habana,* 175 U.S. 677, 686 (1900).

There was, finally, a sphere in which these rules binding individuals for the benefit of other individuals overlapped with the norms of state relationships. Blackstone referred to it when he mentioned three specific offenses against the law of nations addressed by the criminal law of England: violation of safe conducts, infringement of the rights of ambassadors, and piracy. 4 Commentaries 68. An assault against an ambassador, for example, impinged upon the sovereignty of the foreign nation and if not adequately redressed could rise to an issue of war. *See* Vattel 463–464.
* * *

* * *

* * * *Erie R. Co. v. Tompkins,* 304 U.S. 64 (1938), was the watershed in which we denied the existence of any federal "general" common law, *id.,* at 78, which largely withdrew to havens of specialty, some of them defined by express congressional authorization to devise a body of law directly, *e.g., Textile Workers v. Lincoln Mills of Ala.,* 353 U.S. 448 (1957) (interpretation of collective-bargaining agreements); Fed. Rule Evid. 501 (evidentiary privileges in federal-question cases). Elsewhere, this Court has thought it was in order to create federal common law rules in interstitial areas of particular federal interest. *E.g., United States v. Kimbell Foods, Inc.,* 440 U.S. 715, 726–727 (1979). And although we have even assumed competence to make judicial rules of decision of particular importance to foreign relations, such as the act of state doctrine, *see Banco Nacional de Cuba v. Sabbatino,* 376 U.S. 398, 427 (1964), the general practice has been to look for legislative guidance before exercising innovative authority over substantive law. * * *

* * *

* * * *Erie* did not in terms bar any judicial recognition of new substantive rules, no matter what the circumstances, and post-*Erie* understanding has identified limited enclaves in which federal courts may derive some substantive law in a common law way. For two centuries we have affirmed that the domestic law of the United States recognizes the law of nations. *See, e.g., Sabbatino,* 376 U.S., at 423 ("[I]t is, of course, true that United States courts apply international law as a part of our own in appropriate circumstances"); *The Paquete Habana,* 175 U.S., at 700 ("International law is part of our law, and must be ascertained and administered by the courts of justice of appropriate jurisdiction, as often as questions of right depending upon it are duly presented for their determination"); *The Nereide,* 9 Cranch 388, 423 (1815) (Marshall, C.J.) ("[T]he Court is bound by the law of nations which is a part of the law of the land"); *see also Texas Industries, Inc. v. Radcliff Materials, Inc.,* 451 U.S. 630, 641 (1981) (recognizing that "international disputes implicating . . . our relations with foreign nations" are one of the "narrow areas" in which "federal common law" continues to exist). It would take some explaining to say now that federal courts must avert their gaze entirely from any international norm intended to protect individuals.

NOTES

1. *The Effects of* Erie *on the Law of Nations.* The views expressed by Henkin and the Restatement have been followed in numerous federal cases, and have been recognized as "settled." Those views, however, have been challenged as inconsistent with the teachings of *Erie* by some writers, notably by Professors Bradley and Goldsmith in Customary International Law as Federal Common Law: A Critique of the Modern Position, 110 Harv. L. Rev. 815 (1997). For Bradley and Goldsmith, the standard doctrine "portends a dramatic transfer of constitutional authority from the state to the world community and to the federal judiciary." Id. at 846. Others have responded in defense of the standard position. See, e.g., Koh, Is International Law Really State Law?, 111 Harv. L. Rev. 1824 (1998); Neuman, Sense and Nonsense About Customary International Law: A Response to Professors Bradley and Goldsmith, 66 Fordham L. Rev. 371 (1997).

Judge Friendly maintained that "by leaving to the states what ought to be left to them, *Erie* led to the emergence of a federal decisional law in areas of national concern that is truly uniform because, under the supremacy clause, it is binding in every forum * * * [T]he clarion yet careful pronouncement of *Erie* 'there is no federal common law,' opened the way to what, for want of a better term, we may call a specialized federal common law." Friendly, In Praise of *Erie*—and of the New Federal Common Law, 39 N.Y.U. L. Rev. 381, 405 (1964). See Restatement (Third), Part I, Chapter 2, Introductory Note. See also Jessup, The Doctrine of Erie R.R. v. Tompkins Applied to International Law, 33 A.J.I.L. 740 (1939), and *Banco Nacional de Cuba v. Sabbatino*, 376 U.S. 398, 424–25 (1964) (p. 670 below), in which the Supreme Court said:

> [W]e are constrained to make clear that an issue concerned with a basic choice regarding the competence and function of the Judiciary and the National Executive in ordering our relationships with other members of the international community must be treated exclusively as an aspect of federal law. It seems fair to assume that the Court did not have rules like the act of state doctrine in mind when it decided *Erie R. Co. v. Tompkins*. Soon thereafter, Professor Philip C. Jessup, now a judge of the International Court of Justice, recognized the potential dangers were *Erie* extended to legal problems affecting international relations. He cautioned that rules of international law should not be left to divergent and perhaps parochial state interpretations. His basic rationale is equally applicable to the act of state doctrine.

Reflecting on the *Sabbatino* decision, Henkin has written:

> For long, indeed, the history of international law as part of the common law of the states was a source of confusion and controversy. For many years under the Constitution, states appeared to continue to apply international law as part of their common law. But if for the states customary international law had only the status of their common law, it was presumably subject to modification or repeal by the state legislature. If so, too, state courts could decide for themselves what international law requires, and issues of customary international law, unlike questions arising under treaties, would not raise federal questions and could not be appealed to the Supreme Court for final adjudication. Fifty states could have fifty different views on some issue of international law and the federal courts might have still another view. Indeed, not only would the states be free to disregard the views of the federal courts, but in cases where a federal court is required to apply the law of the state in which it sits, the court would have to apply the state's view on disputed questions of international law.
>
>   *Banco Nacional de Cuba v. Sabbatino*, decided in 1964, supports a better, more orderly view * * *

Henkin, Foreign Affairs and the U.S. Constitution 238 (2d ed. 1996) (footnotes omitted).

In *Sosa* the Supreme Court appears to have accepted the essential features of the standard position by treating customary international law as federal law suitable for judicial application (even while taking a restricted view of the scope of customary law norms that the Court would be prepared to enforce in the contest of the particular statute before it, the Alien Tort Statute, 28 U.S.C. § 1350 (2000)). The debate continues post-*Sosa*. Compare Neuman, The Abiding Significance of Law in Foreign Relations, 2004 Sup. Ct.

Rev. 111, with Bradley, Goldsmith & Moore, *Sosa*, Customary International Law, and the Continuing Relevance of *Erie*, 120 Harv. L. Rev. 869 (2007). See also Bellia & Clark, The Federal Common Law of Nations, 109 Colum. L. Rev. 1 (2009).

2. *Constitutional Provisions.* Although the Constitution addresses treaties in several clauses (including the Supremacy Clause of Article VI, discussed below), the only reference to international law generally is that in Article I, Section 8 giving Congress power to "define and punish * * * Offences against the Law of Nations." Nonetheless, American courts frequently apply customary international law even in the absence of a statute adopted under Article I, as the materials below illustrate.

3. *Define and Punish Clause.* On the "define and punish clause" in Article I, Section 8 of the U.S. Constitution, Henkin has written:

> The rule of law in relations between nations and law at sea loomed large in the minds of the Constitutional Framers, hence the explicit grant to Congress of the power to define and punish piracies, felonies on the high seas and offenses against the law of nations. Congress has made it a federal crime to commit piracy as defined by international law and has prescribed punishment for offenses committed at sea, as on American vessels, and more recently in the air, as on U.S. airplanes.

> The power to define and punish offenses against the law of nations has been little used and its purport has not been wholly clear. * * * Presumably, however, the clause would support laws that would provide punishment of U.S. officials for acts or omissions that constitute violations of international law by the United States, e.g., when they deny fundamental "justice" to an alien, arrest a diplomat, violate an embassy, fail to carry out a treaty obligation (as under human rights covenants or conventions to which the United States is party), or violate the growing customary law of international human rights. The clause would also authorize Congress to enact into U.S. law any international rules designed to govern individual behavior, for example, the humanitarian laws of war relating to the treatment of prisoners of war. Today, when international law or a treaty of the United States may apply directly to acts by individuals, Congress could implement that law by providing for punishment under this clause, as, for example, pursuant to the Genocide Convention or the Convention Against Torture.

But Congress apparently, and the Supreme Court explicitly, gave the clause a broader meaning. In upholding a statute that made it a crime to counterfeit foreign currency, the Supreme Court said:

> A right secured by the law of nations to a nation, or its people, is one the United States as the representatives of this nation are bound to protect. Consequently, a law which is necessary and proper to afford this protection is one that Congress may enact, because it is one that is needed to carry into execution a power conferred by the Constitution on the Government of the United States exclusively. . . .

> This statute defines the offence, and if the thing made punishable is one which the United States are required by their international

obligations to use due diligence to prevent, it is an offence against the law of nations. [*United States v. Arjona*, 120 U.S. 479, 487–88 (1887)]

It is perhaps under such an interpretation of the "Offences clause" that Congress long ago made it a crime to harass diplomats, to impersonate them, to damage the property of foreign governments, or to initiate activities directed against the peace and security of foreign nations. That power, then, would enable Congress also to enforce by criminal penalties any new international obligations the United States might accept, say that U.S. companies shall abide by a new international regime for the sea.

Henkin, Foreign Affairs and the U.S. Constitution 68–70 (2d ed. 1996) (footnotes omitted); see also Kent, Congress's Under–Appreciated Power to Define and Punish Offenses Against the Law of Nations, 85 Tex. L. Rev. 843 (2007).

4. *Civil Remedies for Violations.* The power of Congress to define offenses against the law of nations authorizes Congress to provide remedies in tort for such offenses instead of, or in addition to, criminal penalties. In 1791 Congress gave to U.S. district courts "original jurisdiction of any civil action by an alien for a tort only, committed in violation of the law of nations or a treaty of the United States." See Alien Tort Statute, 28 U.S.C.A. § 1350. The Alien Tort Statute remained largely dormant for almost 200 years, but was successfully resurrected in 1980 in a case by Paraguayan plaintiffs who sought to hold accountable a Paraguayan official for violating the law of nations by committing an act of state-sponsored torture. See *Filartiga v. Pena–Irala*, 630 F.2d 876 (2d Cir.1980), p. 267. The *Filartiga* case unleashed a torrent of human rights litigation in U.S. courts for human rights and other abuses abroad, leading to the Supreme Court's interpretation of the statute in *Sosa v. Alvarez–Machain*, 542 U.S. 692 (2004). In that case (excerpted above, pp. 269, 656), the Court accepted that the Alien Tort Statute allowed for civil remedies for violations of the law of nations, both those defined as of 1789 and those of comparable specificity under the law of nations today. At the same time, the Court rejected the particular claim in that case, finding that the law of nations did not contain a prohibition on arbitrary detention (though it might for some policies of prolonged arbitrary detention).

5. *Congressional Definitions of Torture and War Crimes.* The war on terror subsequent to the attacks of September 11, 2001 has produced new legislation defining crimes related to the law of nations and also establishing rules to govern the treatment of detainees held under U.S. authority. Congressional enactments include the Detainee Treatment Act of 2005, Pub. L. No. 109–148, 119 Stat. 2739 (2005), which prohibited certain coercive interrogation techniques, and the Military Commissions Act of 2006, Pub. L. No. 109–366, 120 Stat. 2600, which codified certain crimes for which "unlawful enemy alien combatants" could be prosecuted outside the ordinary courts-martial system. The latter statute responded in part to the decision in *Hamdan v. Rumsfeld*, 548 U.S. 557 (2006), which had invalidated a presidential military order for a military commissions system on the ground that Congress had not authorized the President to depart from the otherwise applicable laws of war, which has both treaty-based and customary underpinnings. (On treaty aspects of the *Hamdan* ruling, see p. 718.) The constitution-

ality of the Military Commissions Act came before the Supreme Court in *Boumediene v. Bush*, 128 S.Ct. 2229 (2008), which found it unconstitutional in part as exceeding the authority of Congress to suspend the writ of habeas corpus in wartime. Other legal challenges to the Military Commissions Act, including to the exercise of congressional authority to define "offences against the Law of Nations" in a manner at variance with internationally accepted norms, were pending when this casebook went to press.

HENKIN, THE CONSTITUTION AND UNITED STATES SOVEREIGNTY: A CENTURY OF CHINESE EXCLUSION AND ITS PROGENY

100 Harv. L. Rev. 853, 867–78 (1987) (footnotes omitted)

The Constitution * * * explicitly addresses the place of treaties in our jurisprudence. It says little, however, about customary international law. It does not declare expressly whether, and if so how, customary international law is part of our law; it says nothing about how such law relates to the Constitution and to our political institutions; whether customary international law is federal or state law; whether it is supreme over state law; or whether the federal courts have jurisdiction over cases or controversies arising under international law. The Constitution expressly establishes neither the relation of treaties and customary law to each other nor that of either to the Constitution or to laws enacted by Congress. It provides no explicit direction to the courts as to what law should govern a case involving an act of Congress or an action of the President that is inconsistent with a provision in a treaty or with a principle of international law. Nor does it expressly declare that the President is obligated to respect treaties or customary law and to take care that they be faithfully executed.

The [Supreme] Court has yet to declare that the Constitution is * * * supreme over the law of nations and principles of customary law. * * * Nevertheless, it is unlikely that the Court would subordinate the Constitution to the law of nations and give effect to a principle of international law without regard to constitutional constraints. The Court's jurisprudence about treaties inevitably reflects assumptions about the relation between international and United States law and, at least by implication, places the United States outside the strict monist camp. Thus we can assume that, like treaties, customary international law is inferior to the United States Constitution in the hierarchy of our domestic law.

* * * During the Spanish American War, the United States Navy seized fishing vessels belonging to private Spanish citizens and condemned them as prize of war. In *The Paquete Habana*, the owners of those vessels challenged the seizure and sought recovery of the ships, asserting that under international law private fishing vessels, even if belonging to enemy aliens, were not subject to seizure as war prize. The Supreme Court examined the state of international law, found that it indeed exempted

such fishing vessels from seizure, and ordered that the proceeds of the sale of these vessels be paid to the original owners.

In supporting its conclusion, the Court made two oft-quoted statements:

> International law is part of our law, and must be ascertained and administered by the courts of justice of appropriate jurisdiction as often as questions of right depending upon it are duly presented for their determination. For this purpose, where there is no treaty and no controlling executive or legislative act or judicial decision, resort must be had to the customs and usages of civilized nations * * *

And a few pages later:

> This rule of international law is one which prize courts administering the law of nations are bound to take judicial notice of, and to give effect to, in the absence of any treaty or other public act of their own government in relation to the matter.

The statement that international law is law of the land was essential to support the judgment. The qualifying clause "where there is no treaty and no controlling executive or legislative act or judicial decision" was dictum: neither party in the case claimed that there was any relevant treaty, any "controlling executive or legislative act or judicial decision," or any "other public act of their own government" requiring a different result. In the eighty-seven years since *The Paquete Habana,* the Court repeatedly has emphasized that international law is the law of the land, and it has given effect to principles of customary international law as the law of the United States. * * *

Some * * * would construe the *The Paquete Habana* dictum as asserting that customary international law is not equal but rather is inferior to federal law. They argue that unlike treaties, which the Court has held to be equal to acts of Congress, customary international law is subject to "repeal" by subsequent acts of Congress; indeed, it cannot be given effect in the face of even an earlier act of Congress. For support, this view relies on repeated references in legal literature to customary law as "common law" which, it is argued, is inherently inferior to legislation.

I think that this argument is misconceived. * * *

NOTES

1. *The Constitution and Customary International Law.* As indicated by Henkin, neither the President, Congress, nor the courts will give effect to a norm of customary international law or to a treaty provision that is inconsistent with the U.S. Constitution.

2. *Customary Law in Relation to Treaties and Statutes?* At the same time, Henkin presents arguments as to why customary law should be seen, as are treaties (see p. 685 below), as equal in stature with acts of Congress, and arguments why customary law might even be superior to statutes and

treaties, but he concludes: "Despite these arguments, it is unlikely that the Supreme Court will now distinguish customary international law from treaties and declare the former supreme over federal statutory law. I see no basis, however—either in principle, in text, in history, or in contemporary practice— for interpreting *The Paquete Habana* dictum as meaning that customary international law has a status lower than that of treaties. Both treaties and customary law are law of the United States because they constitute binding international obligations of the United States. Like treaties, customary law has now been declared to be United States law within the meaning of both Article III and the Supremacy Clause." 100 Harv. L. Rev. at 877–78.

The Circuit Court of Appeals for the District of Columbia has held that later-in-time statutes supersede customary international law. See *Committee of U.S. Citizens Living in Nicaragua v. Reagan*, 859 F.2d 929, 939 (D.C. Cir.1988); *United States v. Yunis*, 924 F.2d 1086, 1091 (D.C. Cir.1991). For the view that some international law cannot be superseded by an act of Congress, see Paust, Customary International Law and Human Rights Treaties *Are* Law of the United States, 20 Mich. J. Int'l L. 301 (1999); Paust, Van Dyke & Malone, International Law and Litigation in the U.S. 477–82 (2d ed. 2005) (Ch. 2, sec. 2.E.2 on conflicts between federal statutes and customary international law).

3. *Incorporation of Customary International Law.* Customary international law is treated in the United States as automatically "incorporated" from the time that the norm is deemed to have come into existence, without the need of any formal act of incorporation by Congress or the President. See Restatement (Third) § 111(3) and Part I, Chapter I, Introductory Note. Compare the distinction between "self-executing" and "non-self-executing" treaties, p. 692 below.

4. *Conflicts Between Sources of International Law.* Can a later-in-time rule of customary international law supersede a pre-existing statute or treaty? If customary international law is inferior in status, then presumably the statute or treaty still prevails. Yet if customary international law is comparable in status, then perhaps it should prevail. The Restatement (Third) § 115, Comment *d* states:

> *Conflict between successive international agreements or principles of customary law.* * * * It has also not been authoritatively determined whether a rule of customary international law that developed after, and is inconsistent with, an earlier statute or international agreement of the United States should be given effect as the law of the United States. In regard to the law of the sea, the United States has accepted customary law that modifies earlier treaties as well as United States statutes. See Introductory Note to Part V. Compare § 102, Comment *j*.

5. *President's Duty to Comply or Authority to Violate Customary International Law?* It has been noted that customary international law is law for the Executive and the courts to apply, but the Constitution does not forbid the President (or the Congress) to violate international law, and the courts will give effect to acts within the constitutional powers of the political branches without regard to international law. On the other hand, the courts have enforced international law against lower federal officials not directed by the

President to disregard international law. Compare Henkin, Foreign Affairs and the U.S. Constitution 241–42 (2d ed. 1996). The Restatement (Third), § 111, Comment *c* states:

> That international law and agreements of the United States are law of the United States means also that the President has the obligation and the necessary authority to take care that they be faithfully executed. United States Constitution, Article II, Section 2. But under the President's Constitutional authority, as "sole organ of the nation in its external relations" or as Commander in Chief (§ 1, Reporters' Note 2), the President has the power to take various measures including some that might constitute violations of international law by the United States. * * *

The Restatement (Third) § 115, Reporters' Note 3 explains:

> *President's power to supersede international law or agreement.* There is authority for the view that the President has the power, when acting within his constitutional authority, to disregard a rule of international law or an agreement of the United States, notwithstanding that international law and agreements are law of the United States and that it is the President's duty under the Constitution to "take care that the Laws be faithfully executed." Article II, Section 3. Compare the authority of the President to terminate international agreements on behalf of the United States, § 339. That the courts will not compel the President to honor international law may be implied in Supreme Court statements that courts will give effect to international law "where there is no treaty, and no controlling executive or legislative act or judicial decision," and "in the absence of any treaty or other public act of their own government in relation to the matter." The Paquete Habana, 175 U.S. 677, 700 (1900); compare Brown v. United States, 12 U.S. (8 Cranch) 110, 128 (1814). Tag v. Rogers, 267 F.2d 664 (D.C.Cir.1959), certiorari denied, 362 U.S. 904 (1960); and The Over the Top, 5 F.2d 838 (D.Conn.1925) which are sometimes cited, but those cases addressed the power of Congress to act contrary to international law, not the powers of the President.

> In 1986, in Garcia–Mir v. Meese, 788 F.2d 1446 (11th Cir.1986), cert. denied, 479 U.S. 889 (1986), the court, relying on The Paquete Habana, gave effect to an action of the Attorney General authorizing detention of aliens although it accepted that such detention was in violation of international law. Citing this Reporters' Note [in its draft form], the court concluded that "the power of the President to disregard international law in service of domestic needs is reaffirmed." However, the President may have power to act in disregard of international law "when acting within his constitutional authority," but the Court of Appeals failed to find any constitutional authority in the President to detain the aliens in question. See Henkin, "The Constitution and United States Sovereignty: A Century of *Chinese Exclusion* and its Progeny," 100 Harv. L.Rev. 853, 878–86 (1987).

What are the sources and the scope of the President's independent constitutional authority? Can such Presidential constitutional authority provide authority for executive officials other than the President that violate international law?

See generally the discussion in The Authority of the United States Executive to Interpret, Articulate or Violate Customary International Law, 80 A.S.I.L. Proc. 297 (1986); Agora: May the President Violate Customary International Law, 80 A.J.I.L. 913 (1986); Agora: May the President Violate Customary International Law (cont'd), 81 A.J.I.L. 371 (1987). See also Lobel, The Limits of Constitutional Power: Conflicts Between Foreign Policy and International Law, 71 Va. L. Rev. 1071 (1985); Glennon, Raising the *Paquete Habana:* Is Violation of Customary International Law by the Executive Unconstitutional?, 80 Nw. U. L.Rev. 321 (1985); Leigh, Editorial Comment, Is the President Above Customary International Law?, 86 A.J.I.L. 757 (1992); Glennon, Constitutional Diplomacy 232–48 (1990).

If international law is the law of the land and it is the President's duty to "take Care that the Laws be faithfully executed," (U.S. Const. art. II, Sec. 3), should the court refuse to give effect to international law because of a "controlling executive act"? What executive act is "controlling" for this purpose? If, as in *Garcia–Mir,* a violation of international law is not remediable in the circumstances by the courts, are other remedies available?

In the 1990s, U.S. courts considered whether to exercise criminal jurisdiction over an accused who had been kidnapped from foreign territory by agents of the Drug Enforcement Agency. The Court of Appeals for the Ninth Circuit held that such abduction violated an extradition treaty with Mexico and consequently deprived the U.S. courts of jurisdiction. See *United States v. Verdugo–Urquidez*, 939 F.2d 1341 (9th Cir.1991), and *United States v. Alvarez–Machain*, 946 F.2d 1466 (9th Cir.1991). The U.S. Supreme Court reversed in *Alvarez–Machain*, 504 U.S. 655 (1992), and vacated the judgment in *Verdugo–Urquidez*, 505 U.S. 1201 (1992). The majority of the Court found that the abduction did not violate the extradition treaty, and held that the manner in which the defendant had come before the trial court was immaterial, relying on *Ker v. Illinois*, 119 U.S. 436 (1886). See Chapter 11, p. 819. For differing views on *Alvarez–Machain,* see Agora: International Kidnaping, 86 A.J.I.L. 736, 746 (1992); Henkin, Correspondence, 87 A.J.I.L. 100 (1993). For international reactions, see Extradition, 8 Int'l Enforcement L. Rep. 444–51 (1992). See also the compilation of documents by the Mexican Secretaria de Relaciones Exteriores, Limits to National Jurisdiction: Documents and Judicial Resolutions on the Alvarez Machain Case (1992). It has been suggested that by virtue of the posture in which *Alvarez–Machain* was acted on by the Supreme Court, the only issue decided had to do with the extradition treaty and not with the authority of the executive branch to violate customary international law. See Vázquez, Misreading High Court's *Alvarez* ruling, Legal Times, Oct. 5, 1992, at 29–30.

B. JUDICIAL APPLICATION OF CUSTOMARY INTERNATIONAL LAW

RESTATEMENT OF THE LAW (THIRD) THE FOREIGN RELATIONS LAW OF THE UNITED STATES §§ 111–12 (1987)

§ 111. International Law and Agreements as Law of the United States

(1) International law and international agreements of the United States are law of the United States and supreme over the law of the several States.

(2) Cases arising under international law or international agreements of the United States are within the Judicial Power of the United States and, subject to Constitutional and statutory limitations and requirements of justiciability, are within the jurisdiction of the federal courts.

(3) Courts in the United States are bound to give effect to international law and to international agreements of the United States, except that a "non-self-executing" agreement will not be given effect as law in the absence of necessary implementation.

§ 112. Determination and Interpretation of International Law: Law of the United States

* * *

(2) The determination and interpretation of international law present federal questions and their disposition by the United States Supreme Court is conclusive for other courts in the United States.

Nᴏᴛᴇs

1. *Restatement Position.* The Restatement (Third) accepts as established several principles that in the past had been uncertain or debated: that issues of customary law, like those arising under treaties, are matters of federal, not state, law; that matters arising under customary law "arise under the laws of the United States" for purposes of the jurisdiction of the federal courts, U.S. Constitution, Article II, and 28 U.S.C.A. § 1331, and are part of the "laws" of the United States which are supreme to state law under Article VI, clause 2 of the Constitution. See § 111, Comments *c*, *d* and *e* and Reporters' Notes 2–4.

2. *Federal Jurisdiction: "Arising Under" International Law.* The Restatement (Third) § 133, Comment *e* states:

> *Federal jurisdiction over cases "arising under" international law and agreements.* Cases arising under * * * customary international law * * * are "Cases * * * arising under * * * the Laws of the United States * * *," and therefore within the Judicial Power of the United States under Article III, Section 2 of the Constitution. Civil actions arising

under international law * * * are within the jurisdiction of the United States district courts. 28 U.S.C. § 1331 (quoted in Reporters' Note 4). * * * Customary international law, like other federal law, is part of the "laws * * * of the United States."

The jurisprudence implied in the phrase "arising under" is extensive and complex. * * * An action arises under an international agreement of the United States, or under customary international law as part of the law of the United States, if the plaintiff's complaint properly asserts a justiciable claim based upon such international law or agreement. An action does not arise under international law or agreement if the rule of international law or the provision of the agreement enters the case only by way of defense. * * *

If customary international law arises under federal law, does that mean that a claim based on the law of nations may be pursued under the federal question jurisdiction established by 28 U.S.C. § 1331 (2000) ("The district courts shall have original jurisdiction of all civil actions arising under the Constitution, laws, or treaties of the United States.")? In *Sosa v. Alvarez–Machain*, 542 U.S. 692 (2004), the majority in dicta cast doubt on such an application of federal question jurisdiction. Justice Souter wrote in a footnote that not every grant of jurisdiction to a federal court carries with it an opportunity to develop common law and that there was no reason to think that federal-question jurisdiction was extended based on a congressional understanding that courts would exercise jurisdiction by entertaining some common law claims derived from the law of nations. *Id.* at 731 note 19.

3. *Views of Executive Branch.* The Restatement (Third) § 112, Comment *c* states:

Weight given to views of Executive Branch. Courts give particular weight to the position taken by the United States Government on questions of international law because it is deemed desirable that so far as possible the United States speak with one voice on such matters. Compare Baker v. Carr, 369 U.S. 186 (1962), quoted in § 1, Reporters' Note 4. The views of the United States Government, moreover, are also state practice, creating or modifying international law. See § 102 and Comment *b* thereto. Even views expressed by the Executive Branch as a party before the court or as *amicus curiae* will be given substantial respect since the Executive Branch will have to answer to a foreign state for any alleged violation of international law resulting from the action of a court. The degree of respect or deference to Executive Branch views is described variously—"particular weight," "substantial respect," "great weight"—but these various expressions are not used with precision and do not necessarily imply different degrees of deference. Compare the principle that courts will give "great weight" to interpretations by the Executive Branch of international agreements of the United States, § 326 and Reporters' Note 4 thereto.

See also Restatement (Third) § 112, Reporters' Note 1:

Judicial and Executive determinations. Since, in deciding cases, the Supreme Court is the final arbiter of United States law * * *, a determination or interpretation of international law by the Supreme Court would also bind the Executive Branch in a case to which the United States is a party for purposes of that case, and effectively for other purposes of domestic law. The President may, however, be free to take a different view of the law vis-à-vis other nations. See § 326.

4. *Judicial Notice.* The Restatement (Third) § 113, Comment *b* states:

Judicial notice of international law. The determination of international law or the interpretation of an agreement is a question of law for the court, not a question of fact for a jury. As was stated in *The Paquete Habana*, 175 U.S. 677, 708 (1900):

> This rule of international law is one which prize courts, administering the law of nations, are bound to take judicial notice of, and to give effect to, in the absence of any treaty or other public act of their own government in relation to the matter.

State courts take judicial notice of federal law and will therefore take judicial notice of international law as law of the United States. Since it is a question of law, it need neither be pleaded nor proved. But see Comment *c*.

5. *Political Questions.* The Executive Branch has sometimes resisted the adjudication of issues involving international law on the ground that these issues are nonjusticiable political questions. The political question doctrine was restated and guidelines for its application were laid down in *Baker v. Carr*, 369 U.S. 186, 211–12 (1962). The Court stated:

> There are sweeping statements to the effect that all questions touching foreign relations are political questions. Not only does resolution of such issues frequently turn on standards that defy judicial application, or involve the exercise of a discretion demonstrably committed to the executive or legislature; but many such questions uniquely demand single-voiced statements of the Government's views. Yet it is error to suppose that every case or controversy which touches foreign relations lies beyond judicial cognizance.

369 U.S. at 211. Many "foreign affairs" issues are decided by the courts, and since *Baker* no foreign affairs issue has been held to be non-justiciable by the Supreme Court. In 1986, the Supreme Court held that the judicial interpretation of a statute of the United States, even if it involves foreign relations, is not a political question that precludes justiciability. *Japan Whaling Ass'n v. American Cetacean Soc'y*, 478 U.S. 221 (1986). In *Goldwater v. Carter*, 444 U.S. 996 (1979), four justices thought the courts should not adjudicate an issue between the President and the Congress as to who has the authority to terminate treaties, but there was no majority opinion.

The courts have long refused to review some Presidential decisions (e.g., the determination of foreign political boundaries or the recognition of foreign governments) on the ground that they were political questions. *Williams v. Suffolk Ins. Co.*, 38 U.S. (13 Pet.) 415, 420 (1839); *Jones v. United States*, 137 U.S. 202, 212 (1890). See also *Occidental of Umm al Qaywayn, Inc. v. A Certain Cargo of Petroleum*, 577 F.2d 1196, 1201–05 (5th Cir. 1978), cert. denied, 442 U.S. 928 (1979); *Antolok v. United States*, 873 F.2d 369, 379–384 (D.C. Cir. 1989). Henkin suggests that the courts did not say—or need not have said—that the issues were not justiciable, but rather that the decisions were within the President's constitutional authority to make, and therefore should be given effect by the courts. See Henkin, Is There a "Political Question Doctrine?", 85 Yale L.J. 597 (1976). On the political question doctrine generally, see Henkin, Foreign Affairs and the U.S. Constitution 143–48 (2d ed. 1996).

C. THE ACT OF STATE DOCTRINE: WILL COURTS APPLY INTERNATIONAL LAW TO THE ACTS OF FOREIGN STATES?

That international law is part of the law of the United States may mean it is to be given effect as United States law by the Executive Branch and by the courts. Generally, it means that international law will be applied to give effect to limitations that international law imposes upon the United States Government, as in *The Paquete Habana* and in innumerable cases recognizing sovereign or diplomatic immunity. See pp. 658–59 note 1 above. Compare the cases in which the courts give effect to treaty obligations assumed by the United States, p. 692 below.

In a series of cases, the issue arose whether courts in the United States should consider the validity of acts of a foreign state under international law. That question arose as an aspect of the application by U.S. courts of the American "act of state" doctrine. The act of state doctrine developed in those cases is not a rule of international law, but a domestic rule established by the United States Supreme Court. It is a rule of judicial self-restraint, not unlike other prudential rules of judicial self-restraint. It may apply to foreign acts of state that raise no issues under international law. The doctrine became a subject of controversy when it was applied to preclude scrutiny by United States courts of acts of foreign states alleged to be in violation of international law.

BANCO NACIONAL DE CUBA v. SABBATINO
Supreme Court of the United States, 1964
376 U.S. 398

[In retaliation for a U.S. reduction in the import quota for Cuban sugar, the Cuban Government nationalized many companies in which U.S. nationals had interests, including Compañia Azucarera Vertientes—Camaguey de Cuba (CAV). Farr, Whitlock, an American commodities broker, had contracted to buy a shipload of CAV sugar. To obtain the now-nationalized sugar, Farr, Whitlock entered into a new agreement to buy the shipload from the Cuban Government, which assigned the bills of lading to its shipping agent, Banco Nacional. Farr, Whitlock gained possession of the shipping documents and negotiated them to its customers, but protected by CAV's promise of indemnification, Farr, Whitlock turned the proceeds over to CAV instead of Cuba. Banco Nacional sued Farr, Whitlock for conversion of the bills of lading and also sought to enjoin Sabbatino, the temporary receiver of CAV's New York assets, from disposing of the proceeds. Farr, Whitlock defended on the ground that title to the sugar never passed to Cuba because the expropriation violated international law.]

MR. JUSTICE HARLAN delivered the opinion of the Court.

* * * While acknowledging the continuing vitality of the act of state doctrine, the court [i.e., the District Court] believed it inapplicable when the questioned foreign act is in violation of international law. Proceeding on the basis that a taking invalid under international law does not convey good title, the District Court found the Cuban expropriation decree to violate such law in three separate respects: It was motivated by a retaliatory and not a public purpose; it discriminated against American nationals; and it failed to provide adequate compensation. Summary judgment against petitioner was accordingly granted.

The Court of Appeals, 307 F.2d 845, affirming the decision on similar grounds, relied on two letters (not before the District Court) written by State Department officers which it took as evidence that the Executive Branch had no objection to a judicial testing of the Cuban decree's validity. The court was unwilling to declare that any one of the infirmities found by the District Court rendered the taking invalid under international law, but was satisfied that in combination they had that effect. We granted certiorari because the issues involved bear importantly on the conduct of the country's foreign relations and more particularly on the proper role of the Judicial Branch in this sensitive area. * * * For reasons to follow we decide that the judgment below must be reversed.

* * *

The classic American statement of the act of state doctrine * * * is found in *Underhill v. Hernandez*, 168 U.S. 250, where Chief Justice Fuller said for a unanimous Court (p. 252):

"Every sovereign state is bound to respect the independence of every other sovereign state, and the courts of one country will not sit in judgment on the acts of the government of another, done within its own territory. Redress of grievances by reason of such acts must be obtained through the means open to be availed of by sovereign powers as between themselves."

Following this precept the Court in that case refused to inquire into acts of Hernandez, a revolutionary Venezuelan military commander whose government had been later recognized by the United States, which were made the basis of a damage action in this country by Underhill, an American citizen, who claimed that he had been unlawfully assaulted, coerced, and detained in Venezuela by Hernandez.

None of this Court's subsequent cases in which the act of state doctrine was directly or peripherally involved manifest any retreat from *Underhill*. * * *

* * *

The outcome of this case, therefore, turns upon whether any of the contentions urged by respondents against the application of the act of state doctrine in the premises is acceptable: (1) that the doctrine does not apply to acts of state which violate international law; (2) that the doctrine is inapplicable unless the Executive specifically interposes it in a particular case; and (3) that, in any event, the doctrine may not be invoked by a foreign government plaintiff in our courts.

Preliminarily, we discuss the foundations on which we deem the act of state doctrine to rest, and more particularly the question of whether state or federal law governs its application in a federal diversity case.

We do not believe that this doctrine is compelled either by the inherent nature of sovereign authority, as some of the earlier decisions seem to imply, see *Underhill, supra*; *American Banana, supra*; *Oetjen, supra*, 246 U.S. at 303, or by some principle of international law.

That international law does not require application of the doctrine is evidenced by the practice of nations. Most of the countries rendering decisions on the subject fail to follow the rule rigidly. No international arbitral or judicial decision discovered suggests that international law prescribes recognition of sovereign acts of foreign governments, see 1 Oppenheim's International Law, § 115aa (Lauterpacht, 8th ed. 1955), and apparently no claim has ever been raised before an international tribunal that failure to apply the act of state doctrine constitutes a breach of international obligation. If international law does not prescribe use of the doctrine, neither does it forbid application of the rule even if it is claimed that the act of state in question violated international law. The traditional view of international law is that it establishes substantive principles for determining whether one country has wronged another. Because of its peculiar nation-to-nation character the usual method for an individual to seek relief is to exhaust local remedies and then repair to the executive authorities of his own state to persuade them to champion his claim in diplomacy or before an international tribunal. * * * Although it is, of course, true that United States courts apply international law as a part of our own in appropriate circumstances, * * * the public law of nations can hardly dictate to a country which is in theory wronged how to treat that wrong within its domestic borders.

Despite the broad statement in *Oetjen* that "The conduct of the foreign relations of our government is committed by the Constitution to the executive and legislative * * * departments," 246 U.S. at 302, it cannot of course be thought that "every case or controversy which touches foreign relations lies beyond judicial cognizance." *Baker v. Carr*, 369 U.S. 186, 211. The text of the Constitution does not require the act of state doctrine; it does not irrevocably remove from the judiciary the capacity to review the validity of foreign acts of state.

The act of state doctrine does, however, have "constitutional" underpinnings. It arises out of the basic relationships between branches of government in a system of separation of powers. It concerns the competency of dissimilar institutions to make and implement particular kinds of decision in the area of international relations. The doctrine as formulated in past decisions expresses the strong sense of the Judicial Branch that its engagement in the task of passing on the validity of foreign acts of state may hinder rather than further this country's pursuit of goals both for itself and for the community of nations as a whole in the international sphere. Many commentators disagree with this view; they have striven by means of distinguishing and limiting past decisions and by advancing various considerations of policy to stimulate a narrowing of the apparent scope of the rule. Whatever considerations are thought to predominate, it is plain that the problems involved are uniquely federal in nature. If federal authority, in this instance this Court, orders the field of judicial competence in this area for the federal courts, and the state courts are left free to formulate their own rules, the purposes behind the doctrine could be as effectively undermined as if there had been no federal pronouncement on the subject. * * *

[We] are constrained to make it clear that an issue concerned with a basic choice regarding the competence and function of the Judiciary and the National Executive in ordering our relationships with other members of the international community must be treated exclusively as an aspect of federal law. * * * [Passage quoted on p. 659 omitted.]

If the act of state doctrine is a principle of decision binding on federal and state courts alike but compelled by neither international law nor the Constitution, its continuing vitality depends on its capacity to reflect the proper distribution of functions between the judicial and political branches of the Government on matters bearing upon foreign affairs. It should be apparent that the greater the degree of codification or consensus concerning a particular area of international law, the more appropriate it is for the judiciary to render decisions regarding it, since the courts can then focus on the application of an agreed principle to circumstances of fact rather than on the sensitive task of establishing a principle not inconsistent with the national interest or with international justice. It is also evident that some aspects of international law touch much more sharply on national nerves than do others; the less important the implications of an issue are for our foreign relations, the weaker the justification for exclusivity in the political branches. The balance of relevant considerations may also be shifted if the government which perpetrated the challenged act of state is no longer in existence, as in the *Bernstein* case, for the political interest of this country may, as a result, be measurably altered. Therefore, rather than laying down or reaffirming an inflexible and all-encompassing rule in this case, we decide only that the Judicial Branch will not examine the validity of a taking of property within its own territory by a foreign sovereign government, extant and recognized by this country at the time of suit, in the absence of a treaty or other unambiguous agreement regarding controlling legal principles, even if the complaint alleges that the taking violates customary international law.

There are few if any issues in international law today on which opinion seems to be so divided as the limitations on a state's power to expropriate the property of aliens. * * *

The possible adverse consequences of a conclusion to the contrary of that implicit in [our previous act of state] cases is highlighted by contrasting the practices of the political branch with the limitations of the judicial process in matters of this kind. Following an expropriation of any significance, the Executive engages in diplomacy aimed to assure that United States citizens who are harmed are compensated fairly. Representing all claimants of this country, it will often be able, either by bilateral or multilateral talks, by submission to the United Nations, or by the employment of economic and political sanctions, to achieve some degree of general redress. Judicial determinations of invalidity of title can, on the other hand, have only an occasional impact, since they depend on the fortuitous circumstance of the property in question being brought into this country. * * *

* * * If the Executive Branch has undertaken negotiations with an expropriating country, but has refrained from claims of violation of the law of nations, a determination to that effect by a court might be regarded as a serious insult, while a finding of compliance with international law would greatly strengthen the bargaining hand of the other state with consequent detriment to American interests.

* * * Considerably more serious and far-reaching consequences would flow from a judicial finding that international law standards had been met if that determination flew in the face of a State Department proclamation to the contrary. When articulating principles of international law in its relations with other states, the Executive Branch speaks not only as an interpreter of generally accepted and traditional rules, as would the courts, but also as an advocate of standards it believes desirable for the community of nations and protective of national concerns. * * *

Against the force of such considerations, we find respondents' countervailing arguments quite unpersuasive. Their basic contention is that United States courts could make a significant contribution to the growth of international law, a contribution whose importance, it is said, would be magnified by the relative paucity of decisional law by international bodies. But given the fluidity of present world conditions, the effectiveness of such a patchwork approach toward the formulation of an acceptable body of law concerning state responsibility for expropriations is, to say the least, highly conjectural. Moreover, it rests upon the sanguine presupposition that the decisions of the courts of the world's major capital exporting country and principal exponent of the free enterprise system would be accepted as disinterested expressions of sound legal principle by those adhering to widely different ideologies.

* * *

However offensive to the public policy of this country and its constitu ent States an expropriation of this kind may be, we conclude that both the national interest and progress toward the goal of establishing the rule of law among nations are best served by maintaining intact the act of state doctrine in this realm of its application. * * *

MR. JUSTICE WHITE, dissenting.

I am dismayed that the Court has, with one broad stroke, declared the ascertainment and application of international law beyond the competence of the courts of the United States in a large and important category of cases. I am also disappointed in the Court's declaration that the acts of a sovereign state with regard to the property of aliens within its borders are beyond the reach of international law in the courts of this country. * * *

I do not believe that the act of state doctrine, as judicially fashioned in this Court, and the reasons underlying it, require American courts to decide cases in disregard of international law and of the rights of litigants to a full determination on the merits. * * *

The reasons for nonreview, based as they are on traditional concepts of territorial sovereignty, lose much of their force when the foreign act of state is shown to be a violation of international law. * * *

NOTES

1. *Congressional Reaction.* The act of state doctrine as reaffirmed in *Sabbatino* was limited by act of Congress in the "Second Hickenlooper Amendment," Pub. L. No. 89–171, 79 Stat. 653 (1964), 22 U.S.C. § 2370(e)(2), as follows:

> Notwithstanding any other provision of law, no court in the United States shall decline on the ground of the federal act of state doctrine to make a determination on the merits giving effect to the principles of international law in a case in which a claim of title or other right to property is asserted by any party including a foreign state (or a party claiming through such state) based upon (or traced through) a confiscation or other taking after January 1, 1959, by an act of that state in violation of the principles of international law including the principles of compensation and the other standards set out in this subsection: *Provided,* That this subparagraph shall not be applicable (1) in any case in which an act of a foreign state is not contrary to international law or with respect to a claim of title or other right to property acquired pursuant to an irrevocable letter of credit of not more than 180 days duration issued in good faith prior to the time of the confiscation or other taking, or (2) in any case with respect to which the President determines that application of the act of state doctrine is required in that particular case by the foreign policy interests of the United States and a suggestion to this effect is filed on his behalf in that case with the court.

The Senate Foreign Relations Committee's Report on the amendment stated:

> The amendment is intended to reverse in part the recent decision of the Supreme Court in Banco de [sic] Nacional de Cuba v. Sabbatino. The

act-of-state doctrine has been applied by U.S. courts to determine that the actions of a foreign sovereign cannot be challenged in private litigation. The Supreme Court extended this doctrine in the *Sabbatino* decision so as to preclude U.S. courts from inquiring into acts of foreign states, even though these acts had been denounced by the State Department as contrary to international law. * * *

The effect of the amendment is to achieve a reversal of presumptions. Under the *Sabbatino* decision, the courts would presume that any adjudication as to the lawfulness under international law of the act of a foreign state would embarrass the conduct of foreign policy unless the President says it would not. Under the amendment, the Court would presume that it may proceed with an adjudication on the merits unless the President states officially that such an adjudication in the particular case would embarrass the conduct of foreign policy.

S. Rep. No. 1188, at 24 (1964). The ruling in the *Sabbatino* case itself, remanded to the district court, was thereby effectively reversed. *Banco Nacional de Cuba v. Farr*, 243 F.Supp. 957 (S.D.N.Y.1965), affd, 383 F.2d 166 (2d Cir.1967), cert. denied, 390 U.S. 956 (1968).

Congress also sought to abolish the doctrine in respect of Cuba as to matters covered by the Helms–Burton Act. Cuban Liberty and Democracy (Libertád) Act of 1996, Pub. L. No. 104–14, 110 Stat. 785 (1996).

2. *Scope of Doctrine and Exceptions.* Restatement (Third), § 443, Comment *b* states:

Lower courts have been unanimous in holding that the act of state doctrine does not apply to a taking by a foreign state of property outside of its territory at the time of taking, but have been divided as to how the territorial limitations should be applied to intangible property. See Reporters' Note 4. The doctrine has been held inapplicable in the context of a challenge to a taking by a foreign state alleged to be in violation of a treaty between the United States and that state. See Reporters' Note 5. In *Sabbatino,* the Court stressed that the principles of international law on which the challenge to the foreign state's act was based were in sharp dispute, 376 U.S. at 428–30, see § 712, Reporters' Note 1; it has been argued that the doctrine was not intended to preclude review of an act of a foreign state challenged under principles of international law not in dispute * * *. No post-*Sabbatino* case has considered application of the doctrine to acts by an unrecognized state or government. A divided Supreme Court has held that the doctrine would not preclude a counterclaim against the foreign state in certain circumstances.

3. *Extraterritorial Takings.* It is accepted that the act of state doctrine should not apply to a taking by a state of property located outside its territory at the time of the taking. *Republic of Iraq v. First National City Bank*, 353 F.2d 47 (2d Cir.1965), cert. denied, 382 U.S. 1027 (1966). Several cases have attempted to apply that exception to takings of intangibles. See generally Note, The Act of State Doctrine: Resolving Debt Situs Confusion, 86 Colum. L. Rev. 594 (1986). The Restatement Reporters suggest: "In principle, it might be preferable to approach the question of the applicability of the act of state doctrine to intangible assets not by searching for an imaginary situs for

property that has no real situs, but by determining how the act of the foreign state in the particular circumstances fits within the reasons for the act of state doctrine and for the territorial limitation." Restatement (Third) § 443, Reporters' Note 4.

4. *Treaty Exception.* The act of state doctrine was held not to apply in the case of a claim based on an act alleged to be in violation of a treaty between the United States and Ethiopia. *Kalamazoo Spice Extraction Co. v. Provisional Military Government of Socialist Ethiopia,* 729 F.2d 422 (6th Cir.1984). Does the rationale of the doctrine support such a treaty exception? Should it apply where the treaty is one to which the United States is not a party? Compare *Occidental of Umm al Qaywayn, Inc. v. A Certain Cargo of Petroleum,* 577 F.2d 1196 (5th Cir. 1978), cert. denied 442 U.S. 928 (1979).

5. *Commercial Acts.* In *Alfred Dunhill of London, Inc. v. Republic of Cuba,* 425 U.S. 682 (1976), a majority of the Supreme Court found that the mere refusal of a commercial agency of a foreign government to repay funds mistakenly paid to it did not constitute an act of state, since there was no reason to suppose that the agency possessed governmental as distinguished from commercial authority. Four Justices also expressed the view that repudiation by a foreign government of a commercial debt is not entitled to respect as an act of state. "[T]he mere assertion of sovereignty as a defense to a claim arising out of purely commercial acts by a foreign sovereign is no more effective if given the label "act of State" than if it is given the label "sovereign immunity." 425 U.S. at 705.

6. *Validity v. Motivation.* In *W.S. Kirkpatrick & Co., Inc. v. Environmental Tectonics Corp., Int'l,* 493 U.S. 400 (1990), the plaintiff, an unsuccessful bidder for a Nigerian military contract, alleged that the defendants had violated federal antitrust and racketeering statutes by bribing Nigerian officials in order to secure the contract. In holding that the act of state doctrine did not bar the plaintiff's claim, the Supreme Court distinguished between cases that require a court to "declare invalid the official act of a foreign sovereign performed within its own territory," and cases that require a court only to impute an "unlawful motivation" to foreign officials in the performance of official duties. Because the central issue in the case was whether the bribes had occurred, and not whether the Nigerian Government's contracts were valid, the Court ruled the act of state doctrine had no application.

7. *Waning of Expropriation Controversy?.* The act of state doctrine has been less prominent (and less controversial) in U.S. law with the waning of international controversies over expropriation of the properties of foreign nationals. The international legal principles concerning the duty of a state to pay compensation for the taking of alien-owned property are discussed in Chapter 14.

8. *Human Rights Violations.* A restrictive view of the act of state doctrine has been invoked in connection with human rights violations. In *Forti v. Suarez–Mason,* 672 F.Supp. 1531 (N.D. Cal.1987), the court held that the act of state doctrine did not bar an action for torture under the Alien Tort Statute, 28 U.S.C.A. § 1350. Id. at 1544–47. The Torture Victim Protection Act, Pub. L. 102–256, 106 Stat. 73 (1992), provides that an individual who, "under actual or apparent authority or under color of law of any foreign

nation, subjects another individual to torture or extrajudicial killing shall be liable for damages in a civil action * * *." Id., § 2(a). In reporting on the legislation, the Senate Committee on the Judiciary said:

> The committee does not intend the "act of state" doctrine to provide a shield from lawsuit for [individuals]. In Banco Nacional de Cuba v. Sabbatino, 376 U.S. 398 (1964), the Supreme Court held that the "act of state" doctrine is meant to prevent U.S. courts from sitting in judgment of the official public acts of a sovereign foreign government. Since this doctrine applies only to "public" acts, and no state commits torture as a matter of public policy, this doctrine cannot shield [individuals] from liability under this legislation.

S. Rep. No. 249, at 8 (1991). See 138 Cong. Rec. S2667–S2669 (1992). See also *Filartiga v. Pena–Irala*, 630 F.2d 876, 889 (2d Cir.1980) (unauthorized torture by a state official, in violation of the law of the foreign state, could not properly be characterized as an act of state).

9. *Private Acts of Heads of State. Republic of Philippines v. Marcos*, 806 F.2d 344 (2d Cir. 1986), concluded that the act of state doctrine does not apply to "purely private acts" of the head of government as distinguished from his or her "public acts." Id. at 358–59. In a related case, the Ninth Circuit reached the same conclusion. *Republic of Philippines v. Marcos*, 862 F.2d 1355 (9th Cir.1988) (en banc). For the most recent installment in the long-running *Marcos* litigation, see *Republic of the Philippines v. Pimentel*, 128 S.Ct. 2180 (2008).

10. *Executive Positions.* In *First Nat'l City Bank v. Banco Nacional de Cuba*, 406 U.S. 759 (1972), a majority of the Supreme Court held that the act of state doctrine should not apply to bar a counterclaim. There was no opinion of the Court. Three Justices reached the result on the ground that the Executive Branch, by a letter to the Court, had suggested that the act of state doctrine should not apply in such cases and urged that the courts should follow the Executive Branch. Justice Powell, who had joined the Court after *Sabbatino,* concurred in the judgment because he questioned that decision. Justices Brennan, Stewart, Marshall and Blackmun dissented, on the ground that *Sabbatino* applied; like the concurring justices they rejected the view that the courts had to follow direction by the Executive Branch in such cases. See 406 U.S. at 776–77.

11. *The Act of State Doctrine in the Courts of Other States.* Restatement (Third) § 443, Reporter's Note 12, surveys the judicial application of the act of state doctrine in countries other than the United States. See also 1 Oppenheim at 365–71; Benvenisti, Judicial Misgivings Regarding the Application of International Norms: An Analysis of Attitudes of National Courts, 4 E.J.I.L. 159 (1993); Lowenfeld, International Litigation and Arbitration 502–08 (2d ed. 2002).

12. *Further Reading.* On the act of state doctrine generally, see Lowenfeld, International Litigation and Arbitration 501–607 (2d ed. 2002); Born & Rutledge, International Civil Litigation in United States Courts 751–806 (4th ed. 2007).

SECTION 3.   TREATIES IN U.S. LAW
A.   THE CONSTITUTIONAL FRAMEWORK
UNITED STATES CONSTITUTION

ARTICLE II, SECTION 2

He [the President] shall have Power, by and with the Advice and Consent of the Senate, to make Treaties, provided two-thirds of the Senators present concur * * *

ARTICLE VI

This Constitution, and the Laws of the United States which shall be made in Pursuance thereof; and all Treaties made, or which shall be made, under the Authority of the United States, shall be the supreme Law of the Land; and the Judges in every State shall be bound thereby, any Thing in the Constitution or Laws of any State to the Contrary notwithstanding.

NOTES

1. *Senatorial Advice and Consent.* Under international practice, a treaty is often signed subject to later ratification; or, especially in multilateral treaties, a state may accede to a treaty without having signed it. "Ratification" of treaties is not mentioned in the Constitution. In practice, treaties are ratified (or acceded to) by the President after the Senate has given its advice and consent. It is incorrect therefore to refer to the action of the Senate as "ratification." The President is under no duty to proceed with ratification of, or accession to, a treaty after the Senate has given its advice and consent. A number of treaties have remained "unmade" by the President after advice and consent by the Senate.

The Senate may impose conditions to its consent. It may insist that U.S. obligations under the treaty be modified. In such cases the Senate sometimes enters a "reservation" or "amendment"; technically, the Senate can neither amend the treaty nor enter a reservation to it; it can consent to the treaty on condition that the United States (through the President) enter a reservation to it. The Senate has sometimes imposed conditions that sought to control the effect of a treaty in the United States: for example, that it shall not take effect in the United States until implemented by Congress. See the discussion on self-executing treaties, pp. 692–718 below. On the Senate's interpretive understandings of treaty provisions, see p. 722 note 3 below.

2. *Limitations on State Agreements.* The Constitution provides some guidance on what the several states may and may not do with respect to international agreements. Article I, section 10 of the U.S. Constitution provides:

No State shall enter into any Treaty, Alliance, or Confederation. * * *.

No State shall, without the Consent of Congress, * * * enter into any Agreement or Compact with * * * a foreign Power * * *.

Article I, sec. 10, cls. 1, 3.

The Restatement (Third) § 302, Comment f, states:

What distinguishes a treaty, which a State cannot make at all, from an agreement or compact, which it can make with Congressional consent, has not been determined. That would probably be deemed a political decision. Hence, if Congress consented to a State agreement with a foreign power, courts would not be likely to find that it was a "treaty" for which Congressional consent was unavailing.

By analogy with inter-State compacts, a State compact with a foreign power requires Congressional consent only if the compact tends "to the increase of political power in the States which may encroach upon or interfere with the just supremacy of the United States." Virginia v. Tennessee, 148 U.S. 503, 519 (1893). In general, agreements involving local transborder issues, such as agreements to curb a source of pollution, to coordinate police or sewage services, or to share an energy source, have been considered not to require Congressional consent. Such agreements are not international agreements under the criteria stated in § 301(1), but other State compacts might be. See § 301, Comment g; compare Comment d to that section.

B.   CONSTITUTIONAL LIMITATIONS ON THE TREATY POWER

MISSOURI v. HOLLAND

Supreme Court of the United States, 1920
252 U.S. 416

MR. JUSTICE HOLMES delivered the opinion of the Court.

This is a bill in equity brought by the State of Missouri to prevent a game warden of the United States from attempting to enforce the Migratory Bird Treaty Act of July 3, 1918, c. 128, 40 Stat. 755, and the regulations made by the Secretary of Agriculture in pursuance of the same. The ground of the bill is that the statute is an unconstitutional interference with the rights reserved to the States by the Tenth Amendment, and that the acts of the defendant done and threatened under that authority invade the sovereign right of the State and contravene its will manifested in statutes. The State also alleges a pecuniary interest, as owner of the wild birds within its borders and otherwise, admitted by the Government to be sufficient, but it is enough that the bill is a reasonable and proper means to assert the alleged quasi sovereign rights of a State. * * * A motion to dismiss was sustained by the District Court on the ground that the Act of Congress is constitutional. 258 Fed. 479. * * * The State appeals.

On December 8, 1916, a treaty between the United States and Great Britain was proclaimed by the President. It recited that many species of birds in their annual migrations traversed many parts of the United States and of Canada, that they were of great value as a source of food and in destroying insects injurious to vegetation, but were in danger of extermination through lack of adequate protection. It therefore provided for specified closed seasons and protection in other forms, and agreed that the two powers would take or propose to their lawmaking bodies the necessary measures for carrying the treaty out. 39 Stat. 1702. The above mentioned act of July 3, 1918, entitled an act to give effect to the convention, prohibited the killing, capturing or selling any of the migratory birds included in the terms of the treaty except as permitted by regulations compatible with those terms, to be made by the Secretary of Agriculture. Regulations were proclaimed on July 31, and October 25, 1918. 40 Stat. 1812, 1863. * * * [T]he question raised is the general one whether the treaty and statute are void as an interference with the rights reserved to the States.

To answer this question it is not enough to refer to the Tenth Amendment, reserving the powers not delegated to the United States, because by Article 2, Section 2, the power to make treaties is delegated expressly, and by Article 6 treaties made under the authority of the United States, along with the Constitution and laws of the United States made in pursuance thereof, are declared the supreme law of the land. If the treaty is valid there can be no dispute about the validity of the statute under Article 1, Section 8, as a necessary and proper means to execute the powers of the Government. The language of the Constitution as to the supremacy of treaties being general, the question before us is narrowed to an inquiry into the ground upon which the present supposed exception is placed.

It is said that a treaty cannot be valid if it infringes the Constitution, that there are limits, therefore, to the treaty-making power, and that one such limit is that what an act of Congress could not do unaided, in derogation of the powers reserved to the States, a treaty cannot do. An earlier act of Congress that attempted by itself and not in pursuance of a treaty to regulate the killing of migratory birds within the States had been held bad in the District Court. *United States v. Shauver*, 214 F. 154. *United States v. McCullagh*, 221 F. 288. Those decisions were supported by arguments that migratory birds were owned by the States in their sovereign capacity for the benefit of their people, and that under cases like *Geer v. Connecticut*, 161 U.S. 519, this control was one that Congress had no power to displace. The same argument is supposed to apply now with equal force.

Whether the two cases cited were decided rightly or not they cannot be accepted as a test of the treaty power. Acts of Congress are the supreme law of the land only when made in pursuance of the Constitution, while treaties are declared to be so when made under the authority of the United States. It is open to question whether the authority of the United States means more than the formal acts prescribed to make the convention. We do not mean to imply that there are no qualifications to the treaty-making power; but they must be ascertained in a different way. It is obvious that there may be matters of the sharpest exigency for the national well being that an act of Congress could not deal with but that a treaty followed by such an act could, and it is not lightly to be assumed that, in matters requiring national action, "a power which must belong to and somewhere reside in every civilized government" is not to be found. * * * [W]hen we are dealing with words that also are a constituent act, like the Constitution of the United States, we must realize that they have called into life a being the development of which could not have been foreseen completely by the most gifted of its begetters. It was enough for them to realize or to hope that they had created an organism; it has taken a century and has cost their successors much sweat and blood to prove that they created a nation. The case before us must be considered in the light of our whole experience and not merely in that of what was said a hundred years ago. The treaty in question does not contravene any prohibitory words to be found in the Constitution. The only question is whether it is forbidden by some invisible radiation from the general terms of the Tenth Amendment. We must consider what this country has become in deciding what that amendment has reserved.

The State as we have intimated founds its claim of exclusive authority upon an assertion of title to migratory birds, an assertion that is embodied in statute. * * * If we are to be accurate we cannot put the case of the State upon higher ground than that the treaty deals with creatures that for the moment are within the state borders, that it must be carried out by officers of the United States within the same territory, and that but for the treaty the State would be free to regulate this subject itself.

As most of the laws of the United States are carried out within the States and as many of them deal with matters which in the silence of such laws the State might regulate, such general grounds are not enough to support Missouri's claim. * * * No doubt the great body of private relations usually fall within the control of the State, but a treaty may override its power. We do not have to invoke the later developments of constitutional law for this proposition; it was recognized as early as *Hopkirk v. Bell*, 3 Cranch 454, 2 L.Ed. 497 with regard to statutes of limitation, and even earlier, as to confiscation, in *Ware v. Hylton*, 3 Dall. 199. * * *

Here a national interest of very nearly the first magnitude is involved. It can be protected only by national action in concert with that of another power. The subject matter is only transitorily within the State and has no permanent habitat therein. But for the treaty and the statute there soon might be no birds for any powers to deal with. We see nothing in the Constitution that compels the Government to sit by while a food supply is cut off and the protectors of our forests and our crops are destroyed. It is not sufficient to rely upon the States. The reliance is vain, and were it otherwise, the question is whether the United States is forbidden to act. We are of opinion that the treaty and statute must be upheld. * * *

Decree affirmed.

MR. JUSTICE VAN DEVANTER and MR. JUSTICE PITNEY dissent.

NOTES

1. *"Bricker Amendment" Controversy.* Between 1950 and 1955, Senator Bricker of Ohio led a campaign to amend the Constitution so as to "reverse" *Missouri v. Holland.* A principal section would have provided that a treaty could not become law in the United States except by act of Congress which would have been valid in the absence of the treaty. See S.J. Res. 1, 83d Cong. (1953); Treaties and Executive Agreements, Hearings before a Subcommittee on S.J. Res. 1 and S.J. Res. 43, 83d Cong. (1953); S. Rep. No. 412 (1953). For an extensive bibliography on the proposed amendment, see Bishop, International Law 112 n. 39 (3d ed. 1971).

For the suggestion, in regard to the International Covenant on Civil and Political Rights, that reservations and declarations seek to achieve what the failed Bricker Amendment sought to achieve generally by constitutional amendment, see Henkin, U.S. Ratification of Human Rights Conventions: The Ghost of Senator Bricker, 89 A.J.I.L. 341 (1995).

2. *Constitutional Primacy Settled.* In 1957, Justice Black laid to rest the issue of whether a treaty could be concluded that was inconsistent with the Constitution. In *Reid v. Covert*, 354 U.S. 1 (1957), a plurality of the Court stated that

> no agreement with a foreign nation can confer power on the Congress, or on any other branch of Government, which is free from the restraints of the Constitution.... The prohibitions of the Constitution were designed to apply to all branches of the National Government and they cannot be nullified by the Executive or by the Executive and the Senate combined.

Reflecting upon such developments, Henkin has noted:

> The Constitution does not expressly impose prohibitions or prescribe limits on the Treaty Power, nor does it patently imply that there are any. No provision in any treaty has been held unconstitutional by the Supreme Court and few have been seriously challenged there. It is now settled, however, that treaties are subject to the constitutional limitations that apply to all exercises of federal power, principally the prohibitions of the Bill of Rights; numerous statements also assert limitations on the reach and compass of the Treaty Power.

Henkin, Foreign Affairs and the U.S. Constitution 185–88 (2d ed. 1996).

3. *Revival of Federalism Constraints?* In the last years of the twentieth century, the Supreme Court began to find in the Tenth Amendment not merely the "truism" that what was not delegated to the United States was reserved to the states, but a reservation to the states of elements of state sovereignty as a limitation on U.S. powers. See, e.g., *New York v. United States*, 505 U.S. 144 (1992), *Printz v. United States*, 521 U.S. 898 (1997). These cases were held to prohibit federal attempts to command state legislatures, or to co-opt and commandeer state and municipal officials. But Congress could encourage and induce states to act, as by conditional grants of

federal monies. Cf., *South Dakota v. Dole*, 483 U.S. 203 (1987). Similar reinvigoration of states' "sovereign" rights and immunities appeared in the revisiting of the 11th Amendment in *Seminole Tribe of Florida v. Florida*, 517 U.S. 44 (1996), and in new interpretations of the Commerce Clause and the section 5 of Fourteenth Amendment to place limits on the reach of congressional powers in *United States v. Lopez*, 514 U.S. 549 (1995) and *United States v. Morrison*, 529 U.S. 598 (2000). It remains to be seen whether "invisible radiations" from the Tenth Amendment (cf. Holmes, p. 682) will be held to extend to the Treaty Power and to the conduct of U.S. foreign relations.

The revival of constitutional constraints on federal powers in these cases has led to renewed attacks on *Missouri v. Holland*, of a sort that had not been seen since the failure of the Bricker Amendment. Arguments for limiting or overruling *Missouri v. Holland* have been made by Curtis Bradley in a series of articles, including Bradley, The Treaty Power and American Federalism, 97 Mich. L. Rev. 390 (1998), and have been debated in a 1999 symposium issue of the University of Colorado Law Review. Others have risen to defend *Missouri v. Holland* against revisionist attack, showing that nationalist understandings of the treaty power long antedated Justice Holmes's opinion. See, e.g., Golove, Treaty–Making and the Nation: The Historical Foundations of the Nationalist Conception of the Treaty Power, 98 Mich. L. Rev. 1075 (2000). For a recent argument that *Missouri v. Holland* misunderstood the relationship between the treaty power and the Necessary and Proper Clause, see Rosenkranz, Executing the Treaty Power, 118 Harv. L. Rev. 1867 (2005).

Henkin writes:

> Whatever the States retain in regard to foreign affairs as a matter of constitutional right must be found in * * * doctrines [other than the Tenth Amendment]. There are dicta by Justices and by writers asserting hypothetical limitations on federal power, including its foreign affairs powers, in specific constitutional guarantees to the States and in implied state sovereignty and inviolability. Justices have said that a treaty cannot cede State territory without its consent; presumably, the United States could not, by treaty or by statute for international purposes, modify the republican character of state governments or, perhaps, abolish all state militia. Under the Eleventh Amendment foreign governments and their nationals cannot sue a state in the courts of the United States without its consent. There is also something more left, too—how much cannot be said with confidence—of the sovereign immunity of the states, which would presumably limit federal regulation under foreign affairs powers as well. State immunities have shrunk radically and state activities are generally subject to federal regulation, but Mr. Justice Frankfurter said:

> > There are, of course, State activities and State-owned property that partake of uniqueness from the point of view of intergovernmental relations. These inherently constitute a class by themselves. Only a State can own a Statehouse; only a State can get income by taxing. These could not be included for purposes of federal taxation in any abstract category of taxpayers without taxing the State as a State.

Foreign Affairs and the U.S. Constitution 166 (2d ed. 1996) (footnotes omitted).

4. *"International Concern."* For some years, there existed the impression that in order to pass constitutional muster, a treaty had to deal with matters of "international concern." This view had been invoked to suggest that the United States could not constitutionally adhere to human rights treaties because they involved matters of strictly domestic concern. This view has long since been abandoned. See Restatement (Third) § 302, Comment *c* and Reporters' Note 2. Henkin writes:

> If there are reasons in foreign policy why the United States seeks an agreement with a foreign country, it does not matter that the subject is otherwise "internal," that the treaty "makes laws for the people of the United States in their internal concerns", or that—apart from treaty— the matter is "normally and appropriately . . . within the local jurisdiction of the States." Any treaty that has any effect within the United States, including the traditional treaties of friendship and commerce, are specifically designed to change the law of the United States that might otherwise apply, e.g., the rights of aliens here. As other policies and laws of the United States become of interest to other countries, they are equally subject to modification by treaty if the United States has foreign policy reasons for negotiating about them.

> If there were any basis for the [doctrine of "international concern"], and if it barred some hypothetical agreement on some hypothetical subject, surely it is not relevant where some would have invoked it—to prevent adherence by the United States to international human rights covenants and conventions. Human rights had long been of international concern and the subject of international agreements * * *.

Henkin, Foreign Affairs and the U.S. Constitution 197–98 (1996) (footnotes omitted); see also Henkin, The Age of Rights 74–80 (1990). The United States has now adhered to several human rights treaties (see Chapter 13), and the constitutional propriety of such treaties is now accepted.

C. THE LATER-IN-TIME RULE

WHITNEY v. ROBERTSON

Supreme Court of the United States, 1888
124 U.S. 190

[Plaintiff sued to recover amounts paid under protest to the Collector of Customs at New York in satisfaction of duties assessed upon plaintiff's shipments of sugar from the Dominican Republic. Plaintiff alleged that sugar from the Hawaiian Islands was admitted free of duty into the United States, and claimed that a clause of the treaty between the United States and the Dominican Republic guaranteed that no higher duty would be assessed upon goods imported into the United States from the Dominican Republic than was assessed upon goods imported from any other foreign country. Judgment was entered for the Collector of Customs upon the latter's demurrer, and plaintiff appealed. The Supreme Court, in an opinion by Mr. Justice Field, first held that the treaty could not be interpreted to foreclose the extension by the United States of special privileges to countries such as the Hawaiian Islands which were willing in return to extend special privileges to the United States.]

FIELD, J.: * * * But, independently of considerations of this nature, there is another and complete answer to the pretensions of the plaintiffs. The act of Congress under which the duties were collected, authorized their exaction. It is of general application, making no exception in favor of goods of any country. It was passed after the treaty with the Dominican Republic, and, if there be any conflict between the stipulations of the treaty and the requirements of the law, the latter must control. A treaty is primarily a contract between two or more independent nations, and is so regarded by writers on public law. For the infraction of its provisions a remedy must be sought by the injured party through reclamations upon the other. When the stipulations are not self-executing, they can only be enforced pursuant to legislation to carry them into effect, and such legislation is as much subject to modification and repeal by Congress as legislation upon any other subject. If the treaty contains stipulations which are self-executing, that is, require no legislation to make them operative, to that extent they have the force and effect of a legislative enactment. Congress may modify such provisions, so far as they bind the United States, or supersede them altogether. By the Constitution, a treaty is placed on the same footing, and made of like obligation, with an act of legislation. Both are declared by that instrument to be the supreme law of the land, and no superior efficacy is given to either over the other. When the two relate to the same subject, the courts will always endeavor to construe them so as to give effect to both, if that can be done without violating the language of either; but, if the two are inconsistent, the one last in date will control the other: provided, always, the stipulation of the treaty on the subject is self-executing. If the country with which the treaty is made is dissatisfied with the action of the legislative department, it may present its complaint to the executive head of the government, and take such other measures as it may deem essential for the protection of its interests. The courts can afford no redress. Whether the complaining nation has just cause of complaint, or our country was justified in its legislation, are not matters for judicial cognizance. * * *

Judgment affirmed.

BREARD v. GREENE

Supreme Court of the United States, 1998
523 U.S. 371

PER CURIAM.

Angel Francisco Breard is scheduled to be executed by the Common-wealth of Virginia this evening at 9:00 pm. Breard, a citizen of Paraguay, came to the United States in 1986, at the age of 20. In 1992, Breard was charged with the attempted rape and capital murder of Ruth Dickie. * * * Following a jury trial in the Circuit Court of Arlington County, Virginia, Breard was convicted of both charges and sentenced to death. On appeal, the Virginia Supreme Court affirmed Breard's convictions and sentences. State collateral relief was subsequently denied as well.

Breard then filed a motion for habeas relief under 28 U.S.C § 2254 in Federal District Court on August 20, 1996. In that motion, Breard argued for the first time that his conviction and sentence should be overturned because of alleged violations of the Vienna Convention on Consular Relations (Vienna Convention), April 24, 1963, (1970) 21 U.S.T 77, T.I.A.S. No. 6820, at the time of his arrest. Specifically, Breard alleged that the Vienna Convention was violated when the arresting authorities failed to inform him that, as a foreign national, he had the right to contact the Paraguayan Consulate. The District Court rejected this claim, concluding that Breard procedurally defaulted the claim when he failed to raise it in the state court and that Breard could not demonstrate cause and prejudice for this default. * * * The Fourth Circuit affirmed. * * * Breard has petitioned this Court for a writ of certiorari.

In September, 1996, the Republic of Paraguay, the Ambassador of Paraguay to the United States and the Consul General of Paraguay to the United States (collectively Paraguay) brought suit in Federal District Court against certain Virginia officials, alleging that their separate rights under the Vienna Convention had been violated by the Commonwealth's failure to inform Breard of his rights under the treaty and to inform the Paraguayan consulate of Breard's arrest, conviction, and sentence. In addition, the Consul General asserted a parallel claim under 42 U.S.C § 1983, alleging a denial of his rights under the Vienna Convention. The District Court concluded that it lacked subject-matter jurisdiction over these suits because Paraguay was not alleging a "continuing violation of federal law" and therefore could not bring its claims within the exception to Eleventh Amendment immunity established in *Ex parte Young*, 209 U.S. 123 (1908). *Republic of Paraguay v. Allen*, 949 F.Supp. 1269, 1272–1273 (E.D.Va.1996). The Fourth Circuit affirmed on Eleventh Amendment grounds. *Republic of Paraguay v. Allen*, 134 F. 3d 622 (1998). Paraguay has also petitioned this Court for a writ of certiorari.

On April 3, 1998, nearly five years after Breard's conviction became final, the Republic of Paraguay instituted proceedings against the United States in the International Court of Justice (ICJ), alleging that the United States violated the Vienna Convention at the time of Breard's arrest. On April 9, the ICJ noted jurisdiction and issued an order requesting that the United States "take all measures at its disposal to ensure that Angel Francisco Breard is not executed pending the final decision in these proceedings . . ." The ICJ set a briefing schedule for this matter, with oral argument likely to be held this November. Breard then filed a petition for an original writ of habeas corpus and a stay application in this Court in order to "enforce" the ICJ's order. Paraguay filed a motion for leave to file a bill of complaint in this Court, citing this Court's original jurisdiction over cases "affecting Ambassadors . . . and Consuls." U.S. Const., Art. III, § 2.

It is clear that Breard procedurally defaulted his claim, if any, under the Vienna Convention by failing to raise that claim in the state courts. Nevertheless, in their petitions for certiorari, both Breard and Paraguay contend that Breard's Vienna Convention claim may be heard in federal court because the Convention is the "supreme law of the land" and thus trumps the procedural default doctrine. * * * This argument is plainly incorrect for two reasons.

First, while we should give respectful consideration to the interpretation of an international treaty rendered by an international court with jurisdiction to interpret such, it has been recognized in international law that, absent a clear and express statement to the contrary, the procedural rules of the forum State govern the implementation of the treaty in that State. * * * This proposition is embodied in the Vienna Convention itself, which provides that the rights expressed in the Convention "shall be exercised in conformity with the laws and regulations of the receiving State," provided that "said laws and regulations must enable full effect to be given to the purposes for which the rights accorded under this Article are intended." Article 36(2), [1970] 21 U.S.T., at 101. It is the rule in this country that assertions of error in criminal proceedings must first be raised in state court in order to form the basis for relief in habeas. *Wainwright v. Sykes*, 433 U.S. 72 (1977). Claims not so raised are considered defaulted. Ibid. By not asserting his Vienna Convention claim in state court, Breard failed to exercise his rights under the Vienna Convention in conformity with the laws of the United States and Commonwealth of Virginia. Having failed to do so, he cannot raise a claim of violation of those rights now on federal habeas review.

Second, although treaties are recognized by our Constitution as the supreme law of the land, that status is no less true of provisions of the constitution itself, to which rules of procedural default apply. We have held "that an Act of Congress . . . is on a full parity with a treaty, and that when a statute which is subsequent in time is inconsistent with a treaty, the statute to the extent of conflict renders the treaty null." *Reid v. Covert*, 354 U.S. 1, 18 (1957) (plurality opinion); see also *Whitney v. Robertson*, 124 U.S. 190, 194 (1888) (holding that if a treaty and a federal statute conflict, "the one last in date will control the other"). The Vienna Convention—which arguably confers on an individual the right to consular assistance following arrest—has continuously been in effect since 1969. But in 1996, before Breard filed his habeas petition raising claims under the Vienna Convention, Congress enacted the Antiterrorism and Effective Death Penalty Act (AEDPA), which provides that a habeas petitioner alleging that he is held in violation of "treaties of the United States" will, as a general rule, not be afforded an evidentiary hearing if he "has failed to develop the factual basis of [the] claim in State court proceedings." 28 U.S.C.A § 2554(a), (e)(2) (Supp. 1998). Breard's ability to obtain relief based on violations of the Vienna Convention is subject to this subsequently-enacted rule, just as any claim arising under the United States Constitution would be. This rule prevents Breard from establishing that the violation of his Vienna Convention rights prejudiced him. Without a hearing, Breard cannot establish how the Consul would have advised him, how the advice of his attorneys differed from the advice the Consul could have provided, and what factors he considered in electing to reject the plea bargain that the State offered him. That limitation, Breard also argues, is not justified because his Vienna Convention claims were so novel that he could not have discovered them any earlier. Assuming that were true, such novel claims would be barred on habeas review under *Teague v. Lane*, 489 U.S. 288 (1989).

* * *

As for Paraguay's suits (both the original action and the case coming to us on petition for certiorari), neither the text nor the history of the Vienna Convention clearly provides a foreign nation a private right of action in United States' courts to set aside a criminal conviction and sentence for violation of consular notification provisions. The Eleventh Amendment provides a separate reason why Paraguay's suit might not succeed. That Amendment's "fundamental principle" that "the States, in the absence of consent, are immune from suits brought against them ... by a foreign State" was enunciated in *Principality of Monaco v. Mississippi*, 292 U.S. 313, 329–330 (1934). * * *

Insofar as the Consul General seeks to base his claims on § 1983, his suit is not cognizable. Section 1983 provides a cause of action to any "person within the jurisdiction" of the United States for the deprivation "of any rights, privileges, or immunities secured by the Constitution and laws." As an initial matter, it is clear that Paraguay is not authorized to bring suit under § 1983. Paraguay is not a "person" as the term is used in § 1983. * * * Nor is Paraguay "within the jurisdiction" of the United States. And since the Consul General is acting only in his official capacity, he has no greater ability to proceed under § 1983 than does the country he represents. Any rights that the Consul General might have by virtue of the Vienna Convention exist for the benefit of Paraguay, not for him as an individual.

It is unfortunate that this matter comes before us while proceedings are pending before the ICJ that might have been brought to that court earlier. Nonetheless, this Court must decide questions presented to it on the basis of law. The Executive Branch, on the other hand, in exercising its authority over foreign relations may, and in this case did, utilize diplomatic discussion with Paraguay. Last night the Secretary of State sent a letter to the Governor of Virginia requesting that he stay Breard's execution. If the Governor wishes to wait for the decision of the ICJ, that is his prerogative. But nothing in our existing case law allows us to make that choice for him.

For the foregoing reason, we deny the petition for an original writ of habeas corpus, the motion for leave to file a bill of complaint, the petitions for certiorari, and the accompanying stay applications filed by Breard and Paraguay.

[Statement of Justice Souter and dissenting statements of Justices Stevens, Breyer and Ginsburg omitted.]

NOTES

1. *Restatement on Later-in-Time Rule.* The Restatement (Third) § 115 states:

> *Inconsistency Between International Law or Agreements and Domestic Law: Law of the United States*
>
> (1)(a) An act of Congress supersedes an earlier rule of international law or a provision of an international agreement as law of the United States if the purpose of the act to supersede the earlier rule or provision is clear or if the act and the earlier rule or provision cannot be fairly reconciled.
>
> (b) That a rule of international law or a provision of an international agreement is superseded as domestic law does not relieve the United States of its international obligation or of the consequences of a violation of that obligation.
>
> (2) A provision of a treaty of the United States that becomes effective as law of the United States supersedes as domestic law any inconsistent preexisting provision of a law or treaty of the United States.

As to conflict between statutes and customary international law, see pp. 663–64. For the principle of interpretation to avoid conflict between a federal statute and international obligation, see p. 721 note 2.

2. *International Obligation Remains in Force.* In a Memorandum prepared for President Harding, October 8, 1921, Secretary of State Charles Evans Hughes stated, "Congress [by passing inconsistent legislation] has the power to violate treaties, but if they are violated, the Nation will be none the less exposed to all the international consequences of such a violation because the action is taken by the legislative branch of the Government." 5 Hackworth at 324–25. "Where a treaty and an act of Congress are wholly inconsistent with each other and the two cannot be reconciled, the courts have held that the one later in point of time must prevail. While this is necessarily true as a matter of municipal law, it does not follow, as has sometimes been said, that a treaty is repealed or abrogated by a later inconsistent statute. The treaty still subsists as an international obligation although it may not be enforceable by the courts or administrative authorities." Id. at 185–86. See also *The Cherokee Tobacco*, 78 U.S. (11 Wall.) 616, 20 L. Ed. 227 (1871); *Chae Chan Ping v. United States*, 130 U.S. 581 (1889); *Rainey v. United States*, 232 U.S. 310, 316 (1914); and other cases cited in 5 Hackworth at 185–98. For a discussion of the jurisprudence of the Supreme Court on the parity of statutes and treaties, see Henkin, The Constitution and United States Sovereignty: A Century of Chinese Exclusion and Its Progeny, 100 Harv. L. Rev. 853 (1987); Westen, The Place of Foreign Treaties in the Courts of the United States: A Reply to Louis Henkin, 101 Harv. L. Rev. 511 (1987); Henkin, Lexical Priority or "Political Question:" A Response, 101 Harv. L. Rev. 524 (1987).

Sohn has suggested that the United States should adopt the rule of the Netherlands and give effect to a multilateral law-codifying treaty even in the face of a later inconsistent statute. Sohn, Perspectives for International Legal Development: Panel, The Nuremberg Trials and Objection to Military Service in Viet–Nam: Discussion, 63 A.S.I.L. Proc. 180 (1969). Can such a principle be supported by constitutional doctrine? See Henkin, Foreign Affairs and the U.S. Constitution 485 (2d ed. 1996), suggesting that contrary to what the Supreme Court may have implied, the rule announced by *Whitney v. Robertson* is not compelled by the language of the Supremacy Clause, U.S. Const., art. VI.

3. *Presumption in Favor of Treaty Compliance.* "A treaty will not be deemed to have been abrogated or modified by a later statute unless such purpose on the part of Congress has been clearly expressed." *Cook v. United States*, 288 U.S. 102, 120 (1933) (Brandeis, J.). See also Steinhardt, The Role of International Law as a Canon of Domestic Statutory Construction, 43 Vand. L. Rev. 1103 (1990). Do the foregoing principles apply equally to executive agreements? See Restatement (Third) § 114, p. 721 note 2 below. See also Section 4 below.

The interplay between the treaty obligations of the United States and apparently inconsistent legislation was raised in 1987 by the Anti–Terrorism Act (22 U.S.C.A. §§ 5201–5203). The Act was construed by the Attorney General to require the closure of the P.L.O.'s Permanent Observer Mission to the United Nations. Such closure, it was assumed, would have violated U.S. obligations under the United Nations Headquarters Agreement. The dispute led to an advisory opinion of the International Court of Justice, as well as to proceedings in the U.S. federal courts. It was resolved when the District Court ruled that the Act should be interpreted to avoid a conflict with the treaty and thus not to require closure of the mission. See *Applicability of the Obligation to Arbitrate Under Section 21 of the U.N. Headquarters Agreement of June 26, 1947*, 1988 I.C.J. 12; *United States v. Palestine Liberation Organization*, 695 F.Supp. 1456 (S.D.N.Y.1988). See also Quigley, Congress and the P.L.O. and Conflicts between Statutes and Treaties, 35 Wayne L. Rev. 83 (1988).

4. *"Latest Expression" of National Policy.* In *Tag v. Rogers*, 267 F.2d 664 (D.C. Cir. 1959), cert. denied, 362 U.S. 904 (1960), the appellant argued that international practice, formalized in a rule of law, forbids the seizure or confiscation of the property of enemy nationals during time of war, at least where that property had been acquired by enemy nationals before the war and in reliance upon international agreements. In rejecting this argument the court said in part: "Once a policy has been declared in a treaty or statute, it is the duty of the federal courts to accept as law the latest expression of policy made by the constitutionally authorized policy-making authority. If Congress adopts a policy that conflicts with the Constitution of the United States, Congress is then acting beyond its authority and the courts must declare the resulting statute to be null and void. When, however, a constitutional agency adopts a policy contrary to a trend in international law or to a treaty or prior statute, the courts must accept the latest act of that agency." 267 F.2d at 668. See also *The Over the Top*, 5 F.2d 838 (D. Conn. 1925); *Committee of United States Citizens Living in Nicaragua v. Reagan*, 859 F.2d 929 (D.C. Cir. 1988).

As to whether the courts will give effect to executive acts that violate international law, see pp. 664–66.

5. *Breard's Fate and the Case's Aftermath.* The U.S. Supreme Court, in *Breard v. Greene*, wrote: "If the Governor [of Virginia] wishes to wait for the decision of the ICJ, that is his prerogative. *But nothing in our existing case law allows us to make that choice for him.*" (Emphasis added.) The Court's opaque statement appears to conceal more than it declares. Was the court implying that executing Breard did not violate international law? That the State of Virginia was not bound to respect international law? That an issue of international obligation was not a federal question? Or was the Court simply concluding that it was compelled by U.S. law and procedure to acquiesce in the Governor's decision to execute? Compare Henkin, *Breard*: Provisional Measures, U.S. Treaty Obligations, and the States, in Agora: *Breard*, 92 A.J.I.L 679 (1998).

Similar issues were raised at the I.C.J. and again at the U.S. Supreme Court in a case involving application of the death penalty to two German brothers, Karl and Walter LaGrand. See *Vienna Convention on Consular Relations* (Federal Republic of Germany v. United States), 1999 I.C.J. 9 (Provisional Measures Order), discussed at 93 A.J.I.L. 924 (1999). As in *Breard*, the Supreme Court declined to interfere with the state order of execution. For subsequent developments in Vienna Convention cases, see *Medellín v. Texas*, 128 S.Ct. 1346 (2008), excerpted at p. 699 below.

## D.	THE DOCTRINE OF SELF–EXECUTING AND NON–SELF–EXECUTING TREATIES

Although Article VI of the Constitution makes treaties "the supreme Law of the Land," the Supreme Court has not accorded all treaty obligations the status of directly enforceable federal law. The materials below survey various problems in the implementation of treaties in the law of the United States, including the need for legislative action to give certain treaties the force of domestic law; interpretation of treaties in U.S. law; and resolving conflicts between international obligations and statutory law.

FOSTER v. NEILSON
Supreme Court of the United States, 1829
27 U.S. (2 Pet.) 253

[Appellants sued to recover a tract of land in Louisiana which they claimed under a grant made by the Spanish governor. The possessor of the land argued that the grant on which appellants relied was void because it was made subsequent to the transfer to France and the United States of the territory in which the land was situated. The district court upheld the defense, and the case was brought to the Supreme Court by a writ of error. The Court held that it was obliged to conform its decision on the question of sovereignty to that already reached by the executive and legislative branches of government, and that the territory had to be considered as having been part of the United States at the time of the grant. Appellants relied further, however, on Article 8 of a treaty concluded in 1819 between the United States and Spain (Treaty of Amity, Settlements and Limits, Feb. 22, 1819, 8 Stat. 252), which provided that "all the grants of land made before the 24th of January 1818, by his Catholic majesty, or by his lawful authorities, in the said territories ceded by his majesty to the United States, shall be ratified and confirmed to the persons in possession of the lands, to the same extent that the same grants would be valid if the territories had remained under the dominion of his Catholic majesty," arguing that the land in question formed part of the specified ceded territories. The Court found it unnecessary to decide the latter question, holding that the treaty did not operate in itself to ratify or confirm appellants' title.]

MARSHALL, C.J.: * * * Do these words [of Article 8] act directly on the grants, so as to give validity to those not otherwise valid; or do they pledge the faith of the United States to pass acts which shall ratify and confirm them?

A treaty is in its nature a contract between two nations, not a legislative act. It does not generally effect, of itself, the object to be accomplished, especially so far as its operation is infra-territorial; but is carried into execution by the sovereign power of the respective parties to the instrument.

In the United States a different principle is established. Our constitution declares a treaty to be the law of the land. It is, consequently, to be regarded in courts of justice as equivalent to an act of the legislature, whenever it operates of itself without the aid of any legislative provision. But when the terms of the stipulation import a contract, when either of the parties engages to perform a particular act, the treaty addresses itself to the political, not the judicial department; and the legislature must execute the contract before it can become a rule for the Court.

The article under consideration does not declare that all the grants made by his Catholic majesty before the 24th of January 1818, shall be valid to the same extent as if the ceded territories had remained under his dominion. It does not say that those grants are hereby confirmed. Had such been its language, it would have acted directly on the subject, and would have repealed those acts of Congress which were repugnant to it; but its language is that those grants shall be ratified and confirmed to the persons in possession, & c. By whom shall they be ratified and confirmed? This seems to be the language of contract; and if it is, the ratification and confirmation which are promised must be the act of the legislature. Until such act shall be passed, the Court is not at liberty to disregard the existing laws on the subject. Congress appears to have understood this article as it is understood by the Court. * * * [The Court then cited legislation which it construed as inconsistent with an intention on the part of Congress to preserve grants of land made by Spanish authorities.]

[Judgment of the district court affirmed.]

NOTES

1. *Treaties That Tread Upon the Exclusive Powers of Congress.* The Restatement (Third) § 111, Comment *i* states:

> *Constitutional restraints on self-executing character of international agreement.* An international agreement cannot take effect as domestic law without implementation by Congress if the agreement would achieve what lies within the exclusive law-making power of Congress under the Constitution. Thus, an international agreement providing for the payment of money by the United States requires an appropriation of funds by Congress in order to effect the payment required by the agreement. It has been commonly assumed that an international agreement cannot itself bring the United States into a state of war. Similarly, it has been assumed that an international agreement creating an international crime (*e.g.*, genocide) or requiring states parties to punish certain actions (*e.g.*, hijacking) could not itself become part of the criminal law of the United States, but would require Congress to enact an appropriate statute before an individual could be tried or punished for the offense. It has also been suggested that a treaty cannot "raise revenue" by itself imposing a new tax or a new tariff, in view of the provision in Article I, Section 7: "All Bills for raising Revenue shall originate in the House of Representatives." Treaties of friendship, commerce and navigation, however, frequently affect tariffs and trade by "most-favored-nation," "national treatment," and analogous clauses. Compare § 801.

2. *Significance of Treaty–Makers' Intent.* The Restatement (Third) § 111, Comment *h* states:

> *Self-executing and non-self-executing international agreements.* In the absence of special agreement, it is ordinarily for the United States to decide how it will carry out its international obligations. Accordingly, the intention of the United States determines whether an agreement is to be self-executing in the United States or should await implementation by legislation or appropriate executive or administrative action. If the international agreement is silent as to its self-executing character and the intention of the United States is unclear, account must be taken of any statement by the President in concluding the agreement or in submitting it to the Senate for consent or to the Congress as a whole for approval, and of any expression by the Senate or by Congress in dealing with the agreement. See § 314, Comments *b* and *d*; § 303, Comment *d*. After the agreement is concluded, often the President must decide in the first instance whether the agreement is self-executing, *i.e.*, whether existing law is adequate to enable the United States to carry out its obligations, or whether further legislation is required. Congress may also consider whether new legislation is necessary and, if so, what it should provide. Whether an agreement is to be given effect without further legislation is an issue that a court must decide when a party seeks to invoke the agreement as law. Whether an agreement is or is not self-executing in the law of another state party to the agreement is not controlling for the United States.

Some provisions of an international agreement may be self-executing and others non-self-executing. If an international agreement or one of its provisions is non-self-executing, the United States is under an international obligation to adjust its laws and institutions as may be necessary to give effect to the agreement. The United States would have a reasonable time to do so before it could be deemed in default. There can, of course, be instances in which the United States Constitution, or previously enacted legislation, will be fully adequate to give effect to an apparently non-self-executing international agreement, thus obviating the need of adopting new legislation to implement it.

Under Subsection (3), strictly, it is the implementing legislation, rather than the agreement itself, that is given effect as law in the United States. That is true even when a non-self-executing agreement is "enacted" by, or incorporated in, implementing legislation.

Whether a treaty is self-executing is a question distinct from whether the treaty creates private rights or remedies. See Comment *g*.

3. *The Supreme Court Changes Its Mind.* In *United States v. Percheman*, 32 U.S. (7 Pet.) 51 (1833), Chief Justice Marshall relied in part on the Spanish text of Article 8 of the 1819 treaty to support the Court's conclusion that an adverse decision by a board of land commissioners did not foreclose claimant from pursuing judicial remedies to confirm his title to land claimed under a Spanish grant. Emphasizing that "the modern usage of nations, which has become law," demanded that private rights and property be respected upon a transfer of sovereignty over territory, Marshall held that Article 8 merely restated this principle and needed no implementing legislation.

The Spanish has been translated, and we now understand that the article, as expressed in that language, is, that the grants "shall remain ratified and confirmed to the persons in possession of them, to the same extent, & c.,"—thus conforming exactly to the universally received doctrine of the law of nations. * * * No violence is done to the language of the treaty by a construction which conforms the English and Spanish to each other. Although the words "shall be ratified and confirmed" are properly the words of contract, stipulating for some future legislative act; they are not necessarily so. They may import that they "shall be ratified and confirmed" by force of the instrument itself. When we observe that in the counterpart of the same treaty, executed at the same time by the same parties, they are used in this sense, we think the construction proper, if not unavoidable.

In the case of Foster v. Elam [*sic*] 2 Peters 253, this court considered these words as importing contract. The Spanish part of the treaty was not then brought to our view, and we then supposed that there was no variance between them. We did not suppose that there was even a formal difference of expression in the same instrument, drawn up in the language of each party. Had this circumstance been known, we believe it would have produced the construction which we now give to the article.

Id. at 88–89.

4. *Presumptions?* Does the Supremacy Clause (Article VI of the U.S. Constitution) suggest a presumption in favor of the self-executing nature of treaties, in the absence of clear indications to the contrary in a given treaty or the context of its approval? Since ordinarily a treaty creates international obligations for the United States from the date it comes into force for the United States, if a treaty is not self-executing the United States is obligated to act promptly to implement it. If a treaty has been in effect for some time and the Executive has not sought and Congress has not enacted implementing legislation, it may be reasonable to assume that the Executive Branch and Congress had concluded that no implementation was necessary. As to a treaty that has been in effect for some time, a finding that it is not self-executing in effect puts the United States in default on its international obligations. See Restatement (Third) § 111, Reporters' Note 5. See also Iwasawa, The Doctrine of Self–Executing Treaties in the United States: A Critical Analysis, 26 Va. J. Int'l L. 627 (1986); Paust, Self–Executing Treaties, 82 A.J.I.L. 760 (1988); Jackson, Status of Treaties in Domestic Legal Systems: A Policy Analysis, 86 A.J.I.L. 310 (1992).

Recent scholarship has brought out contrasting points of view as to whether Marshall's distinction between self-executing and non-self-executing treaties was well-founded in light of the framers' understanding. Compare Yoo, Globalism and the Constitution: Treaties, Non–Self–Execution, and the Original Understanding, 99 Col. L. Rev. 1955 (1999) with Flaherty, History Right? Historical Scholarship, Original Understanding, and Treaties as "Supreme Law of the Land," 99 Col. L. Rev. 2095 (1999), and Vázquez, Laughing at Treaties, 99 Col. L. Rev. 2154 (1999); see also Yoo, Rejoinder: Treaties and Public Lawmaking: A Textual and Structural Defense of Non–Self–Execution, 99 Col. L. Rev. 2218 (1999).

The Supreme Court returned to questions of self-execution in *Medellín v. Texas*, 128 S.Ct. 1346 (2008), p. 699 below, and that controversial decision has spurred new debate. See notes at 716–18.

5. *Examples.* Many cases have addressed whether given treaties are non-self-executing or self-executing:

a. *Non-self-executing treaties*

● U.N. Charter and I.C.J. Statute. See note 6 below and the *Medellín* case at p. 699.

● Hague Convention Respecting the Laws and Customs of War on Land, Oct. 18, 1907, art. 3, 36 Stat. 2277, 2290. See *Goldstar (Panama) v. United States*, 967 F.2d 965 (4th Cir. 1992), cert. denied, 506 U.S. 955 (1992).

● United Nations Protocol Relating to the Status of Refugees, Jan. 31, 1967, 19 U.S.T. 6223. See *United States v. Aguilar*, 883 F.2d 662 (9th Cir. 1989), cert. denied, 498 U.S. 1046 (1991).

● Geneva Convention Relative to the Protection of Civilian Persons in Time of War, Aug. 12, 1949, 6 U.S.T. 3516, 75 U.N.T.S. 287; Geneva Convention Relative to the Treatment of Prisoners of War, Aug. 12, 1949, 6 U.S.T. 3316; 75 U.N.T.S. 135; Convention to Prevent and Punish the Acts of Terrorism Taking the Forms of Crime Against Persons and Related Extortion That Are of International Significance, Feb. 2, 1971, 27 U.S.T. 3949, 1438

U.N.T.S. 195. See *Tel–Oren v. Libyan Arab Republic*, 726 F.2d 774, 808 09 (D.C. Cir. 1984) (Bork, J., concurring), cert. denied, 470 U.S. 1003 (1985). In *Hamdan v. Rumsfeld*, 548 U.S. 557 (2006), the Supreme Court found Common Article 3 of the Geneva Conventions to be judicially enforceable because Congress in enacting the Uniform Code of Military Justice had conditioned the grant of executive authority to establish military commissions on compliance with treaties on the law of war.

• Geneva Convention on the High Seas, Apr. 29, 1958, 13 U.S.T. 2312, 450 U.N.T.S. 11. See *United States v. Peterson*, 812 F.2d 486 (9th Cir. 1987).

• Geneva Convention on Territorial Sea and Contiguous Zone, Apr. 29, 1958, 15 U.S.T. 1606, 516 U.N.T.S. 205. See *United States v. Thompson*, 928 F.2d 1060 (11th Cir. 1991), cert. denied, 502 U.S. 897 (1991).

• Basel Convention on the Control of Transboundary Movements of Hazardous Wastes, 1989, reprinted in, 28 I.L.M. 657 (1989). See *Greenpeace USA v. Stone*, 748 F.Supp. 749 (D. Haw. 1990), appeal dismissed, 924 F.2d 175 (9th Cir. 1991).

b. Treaties held or assumed to be self-executing/directly applicable in courts

• Treaties of Friendship, Commerce and Navigation with various countries. See *Sumitomo Shoji America, Inc.*, 457 U.S. 176, 180, 189–90 (1982), and other cases cited and discussed by the majority and dissent in *Medellín v. Texas*, p. 699 below.

• Vienna Convention on Consular Relations, Apr. 24, 1963, 21 U.S.T. 77, 596 U.N.T.S. 261. The Supreme Court in *Medellín* assumed without deciding that Article 36 of the Vienna Convention grants an individually enforceable right of self-executing character. See n. 4 of the extract at p. 702 below.

• Convention on Contracts for the International Sale of Goods, Apr. 11, 1980, 1489 U.N.T.S. 3; *Delchi Carrier SpA v. Rotorex Corp.*, 71 F.3d 1024, 1027–28 (2d Cir. 1995); *Filanto, S.p.A. v. Chilewich Int'l Corp.*, 789 F.Supp. 1229, 1237 (S.D.N.Y. 1992), appeal dismissed, 984 F.2d 58 (2d Cir. 1993).

• Convention for the Unification of Certain Rules Relating to International Transportation by Air, 1929, T.S. 876 (1934), reprinted at, 49 U.S.C.A. § 1502 note. See *Trans World Airlines, Inc. v. Franklin Mint Corp.*, 466 U.S. 243 (1984); see also *El Al Israel Airlines, Ltd. v. Tseng*, 525 U.S. 155 (1999).

• Treaty on the Execution of Penal Sentences, Nov. 25, 1976, 20 U.S.T. 7399, 1229 U.N.T.S. 120. See *Cannon v. U.S. Dep't of Justice*, 973 F.2d 1190 (5th Cir. 1992). See also note 7 below.

6. *U.N. Charter.* The United Nations Charter, and in particular its human rights provisions, have been held to be non-self-executing. See *Sei Fujii v. California*, 217 P.2d 481 (Cal. App. 1950), rehearing denied, 218 P.2d 595 (1950), in which the California District Court of Appeal held invalid a state statute forbidding aliens ineligible for citizenship to "acquire, possess, enjoy, use, cultivate, occupy, and transfer" real property, on the ground that the statute conflicted with the United Nations Charter. On appeal, the California Supreme Court held the statute invalid under the Fourteenth Amendment, expressly rejecting the lower court's view that the Charter

provisions on human rights had become the "supreme law of the land." 242 P.2d 617 (1952). Gibson, C.J., stated in part: "The fundamental provisions in the charter pledging cooperation in promoting observance of fundamental freedoms lack the mandatory quality and definiteness which would indicate an intent to create justiciable rights in private persons immediately upon ratification. Instead, they are framed as a promise of future action by the member nations." 242 P.2d at 621–22. What legal obligations, whether or not self-executing, are actually imposed by Articles 1(3), 55 and 56 of the Charter?

In *Weir v. Broadnax*, 56 Empl. Prac. Dec. (CCH) 40,684 (S.D.N.Y.1990), the plaintiff's statement of claim alleging the breach of Articles 55 and 56 of the U.N. Charter, based on a pattern of systematic racial discrimination, was struck on defendant's motion. See also *United States v. Caro–Quintero*, 745 F.Supp. 599 (C.D. Cal.1990), aff'd sub nom. *United States v. Alvarez–Machain*, 946 F.2d 1466 (9th Cir. 1991), rev'd, 504 U.S. 655 (1992); *United States v. Noriega*, 746 F.Supp. 1506 (S.D. Fla. 1990); *Helms v. Secretary of Treasury*, 721 F.Supp. 1354 (D.D.C. 1989).

Medellín v. Texas, 128 S.Ct. 1346 (2008), found the provisions of the U.N. Charter and I.C.J. Statute on compliance with and enforcement of I.C.J. judgments to be non-self-executing. See p. 699.

7. *Non–Self–Executing Declarations.* Marshall did not suggest that treaties (or treaty provisions) of a self-executing character could be rendered non-self-executing by presidential or senatorial declaration. That practice developed largely after World War II in special circumstances, on the basis of arguments for cooperation between the "treaty makers and the law makers." See Henkin, The Treaty Makers and the Law Makers: The Niagara Power Reservation, 56 Colum. L. Rev. 1151 (1956); Foreign Affairs and the U.S. Constitution 198–204, 476–78 (2d ed. 1996); Vázquez, The Four Doctrines of Self-Executing Treaties, 89 A.J.I.L 695 (1995); Damrosch, The Role of the United States Concerning Self–Executing and Non–Self–Executing Treaties, 67 Chi.–Kent L. Rev. 515 (1991).

The practice became more common towards the end of the twentieth century, particularly in ratifying human rights agreements. See the declarations by the Senate in connection with its consent to the United Nations Convention against Torture and Other Cruel, Inhuman or Degrading Treatment or Punishment, and the International Covenant on Civil and Political Rights, discussed in Damrosch, supra, and in Sloss, The Domestication of International Human Rights: Non–Self–Executing Declarations and Human Rights Treaties, 24 Yale. J. Int'l L. 129 (1999).

Declaring a treaty non-self-executing is sometimes justified on the ground that it gives a role in the treaty-making process to the House of Representatives and may make the process more "democratic" insofar as the House is a more representative body than the Senate. It sometimes appears that the President and the Senate may have declared treaties to be non-self-executing from resistance to "law-making by treaty," particularly by multilateral treaties, or in order to delay or even frustrate U.S. implementation of its undertakings. It has been suggested that since other states may have to adopt legislation to give effect to treaties, the United States too, should not enforce its obligations immediately. Compare United States v. Postal, 589 F.2d 862

(5th Cir. 1979), cert. denied, 444 U.S. 832 (1979). But see Restatement (Third) § 111, Reporters' Note 5, declaring that view to be "misconceived."

The practice of the Senate (or the President) to declare non-self-executing a treaty that would otherwise be self-executing has been questioned. See, e.g., Damrosch, The Role of the United States Senate Concerning "Self–Executing" and "Non–Self–Executing" Treaties, 67 Chi.–Kent L. Rev. 515, 516–18 (1991); Riesenfeld & Abbott, The Scope of U.S. Senate Control Over the Conclusion and Operation of Treaties, 67 Chi.–Kent L. Rev. 571, 631 (1991); Vaćzquez, Treaty–Based Rights and Remedies of Individuals, 92 Colum. L. Rev. 1082 (1992). Is it implausible to argue that for the President or the Senate to declare non-self-executing a treaty that could be executed without implementing legislation is contrary to both the letter and spirit of the Constitution, and to the distribution of power between the Senate and the House intended by the Framers? See Henkin, Foreign Affairs and the U.S. Constitution 202 (2d ed. 1996). And compare, generally, the contributions by Damrosch, Glennon, Riesenfeld, & Abbott, and Trimble & Weiss, in Parliamentary Participation in the Making and Operation of Treaties: A Comparative Study 205–382 (Riesenfeld & Abbott eds. 1994). In *Sosa v. Alvarez-Machain*, 542 U.S. 692, 735 (2004), the Supreme Court took note of such a declaration made in connection with ratification of the International Covenant on Civil and Political Rights.

MEDELLIN v. TEXAS

Supreme Court of the United States, 2008
128 S.Ct. 1346 (some citations and footnotes omitted)

[José Ernesto Medellín, a Mexican national, was convicted of murder in the state of Texas and sentenced to death. On appeal and in habeas corpus petitions, he argued that he had not been notified of his right of access to the Mexican consulate as required by Article 36 of the Vienna Convention on Consular Relations and that this treaty violation had prejudiced his defense. The Supreme Court took up his case twice: on the first occasion, certiorari was dismissed in order to allow him to litigate certain new issues in the Texas courts, which in due course denied relief. *Medellín v. Dretke*, 544 U.S. 660 (2005); *Ex parte Medellín*, 223 S.W. 3d 315 (Tex. Crim. App. 2006). Excerpts from the Supreme Court's second ruling follow.]

CHIEF JUSTICE ROBERTS delivered the opinion of the Court.

The International Court of Justice (ICJ), located in The Hague, is a tribunal established pursuant to the United Nations Charter to adjudicate disputes between member states. In the *Case Concerning Avena and Other Mexican Nationals* (*Mex. v. U.S.*), 2004 I.C.J. 12 (Judgment of Mar. 31) (*Avena*), that tribunal considered a claim brought by Mexico against the United States. The ICJ held that, based on violations of the Vienna Convention, 51 named Mexican nationals were entitled to review and reconsideration of their state-court convictions and sentences in the United States. This was so regardless of any forfeiture of the right to raise Vienna Convention claims because of a failure to comply with generally applicable state rules governing challenges to criminal convictions.

In *Sanchez–Llamas v. Oregon*, 548 U.S. 331 (2006)—issued after *Avena* but involving individuals who were not named in the *Avena* judgment—we held that, contrary to the ICJ's determination, the Vienna Convention did not preclude the application of state default rules. After the *Avena* decision, President George W. Bush determined, through a Memorandum to the Attorney General (Feb. 28, 2005) (Memorandum or President's Memorandum), that the United States would "discharge its international obligations" under *Avena* "by having State courts give effect to the decision."

* * * We granted certiorari to decide two questions. *First*, is the ICJ's judgment in *Avena* directly enforceable as domestic law in a state court in the United States? *Second*, does the President's Memorandum independently require the States to provide review and reconsideration of the claims of the 51 Mexican nationals named in *Avena* without regard to state procedural default rules? We conclude that neither *Avena* nor the President's Memorandum constitutes directly enforceable federal law that pre-empts state limitations on the filing of successive habeas petitions. We therefore affirm the decision below.

A

In 1969, the United States, upon the advice and consent of the Senate, ratified the Vienna Convention on Consular Relations (Vienna Convention or Convention), Apr. 24, 1963, [1970] 21 U.S.T. 77, T. I. A. S. No. 6820, and the Optional Protocol Concerning the Compulsory Settlement of Disputes to the Vienna Convention (Optional Protocol or Protocol), Apr. 24, 1963, [1970] 21 U.S.T. 325, T. I. A. S. No. 6820. The preamble to the Convention provides that its purpose is to "contribute to the development of friendly relations among nations." 21 U.S.T., at 79; *Sanchez–Llamas*, supra, at 337. Toward that end, Article 36 of the Convention was drafted to "facilitat[e] the exercise of consular functions." Art. 36(1), 21 U.S.T., at 100. It provides that if a person detained by a foreign country "so requests, the competent authorities of the receiving State shall, without delay, inform the consular post of the sending State" of such detention, and "inform the [detainee] of his righ[t]" to request assistance from the consul of his own state. Art. 36(1)(b), *id.*, at 101.

The Optional Protocol provides a venue for the resolution of disputes arising out of the interpretation or application of the Vienna Convention. Art. I, 21 U.S.T., at 326. Under the Protocol, such disputes "shall lie within the compulsory jurisdiction of the International Court of Justice" and "may accordingly be brought before the [ICJ] . . . by any party to the dispute being a Party to the present Protocol." *Ibid.*

The ICJ is "the principal judicial organ of the United Nations." United Nations Charter, Art. 92, 59 Stat. 1051, T. S. No. 993 (1945). It was established in 1945 pursuant to the United Nations Charter. The ICJ Statute—annexed to the U. N. Charter—provides the organizational framework and governing procedures for cases brought before the ICJ.

Statute of the International Court of Justice (ICJ Statute), 59 Stat. 1055, T. S. No. 993 (1945).

Under Article 94(1) of the U. N. Charter, "[e]ach Member of the United Nations undertakes to comply with the decision of the [ICJ] in any case to which it is a party." 59 Stat. 1051. The ICJ's jurisdiction in any particular case, however, is dependent upon the consent of the parties. See Art. 36, 59 Stat. 1060.* * * By ratifying the Optional Protocol to the Vienna Convention, the United States consented to the specific jurisdiction of the ICJ with respect to claims arising out of the Vienna Convention. On March 7, 2005, subsequent to the ICJ's judgment in *Avena*, the United States gave notice of withdrawal from the Optional Protocol to the Vienna Convention. Letter from Condoleezza Rice, Secretary of State, to Kofi A. Annan, Secretary–General of the United Nations.

* * *

II

Medellín first contends that the ICJ's judgment in *Avena* constitutes a "binding" obligation on the state and federal courts of the United States. He argues that "by virtue of the Supremacy Clause, the treaties requiring compliance with the *Avena* judgment are *already* the 'Law of the Land' by which all state and federal courts in this country are 'bound.'" Accordingly, Medellín argues, *Avena* is a binding federal rule of decision that preempts contrary state limitations on successive habeas petitions.

No one disputes that the *Avena* decision—a decision that flows from the treaties through which the United States submitted to ICJ jurisdiction with respect to Vienna Convention disputes—constitutes an *international* law obligation on the part of the United States. But not all international law obligations automatically constitute binding federal law enforceable in United States courts. The question we confront here is whether the *Avena* judgment has automatic *domestic* legal effect such that the judgment of its own force applies in state and federal courts.

This Court has long recognized the distinction between treaties that automatically have effect as domestic law, and those that—while they constitute international law commitments—do not by themselves function as binding federal law. The distinction was well explained by Chief Justice Marshall's opinion in *Foster v. Neilson*, 27 U.S. 253 (1829), overruled on other grounds, *United States v. Percheman*, 32 U.S. 51 (1833), which held that a treaty is "equivalent to an act of the legislature," and hence self-executing, when it "operates of itself without the aid of any legislative provision." *Foster*, supra, at 314. When, in contrast, "[treaty] stipulations are not self-executing they can only be enforced pursuant to legislation to carry them into effect." *Whitney v. Robertson*, 124 U.S. 190, 194 (1888). In sum, while treaties "may comprise international commitments ... they are not domestic law unless Congress has either enacted implementing statutes or the treaty itself conveys an intention that it be 'self-executing' and is ratified on these terms." *Igartua–De La Rosa v. United States*, 417 F.3d 145, 150 (CA1 2005) (en banc) (Boudin, C. J.).[2]

A treaty is, of course, "primarily a compact between independent nations." *Head Money Cases*, 112 U.S. 580, 598 (1884). It ordinarily "depends for the enforcement of its provisions on the interest and the honor of the governments which are parties to it." *Ibid.*; see also The Federalist No. 33, p 207 (J. Cooke ed. 1961) (A. Hamilton) (comparing laws that individuals are "bound to observe" as "the supreme law of the land" with "a mere treaty, dependent on the good faith of the parties"). "If these [interests] fail, its infraction becomes the subject of international negotiations and reclamations.... It is obvious that with all this the judicial courts have nothing to do and can give no redress." *Head Money Cases*, supra, at 598. Only "[i]f the treaty contains stipulations which are self-executing, that is, require no legislation to make them operative, [will] they have the force and effect of a legislative enactment." *Whitney*, supra, at 194.[3]

Medellín and his *amici* nonetheless contend that the Optional Protocol, United Nations Charter, and ICJ Statute supply the "relevant obligation" to give the *Avena* judgment binding effect in the domestic courts of the United States.[4] Because none of these treaty sources creates binding federal law in the absence of implementing legislation, and because it is uncontested that no such legislation exists, we conclude that the *Avena* judgment is not automatically binding domestic law.

A

The interpretation of a treaty, like the interpretation of a statute, begins with its text. *Air France v. Saks*, 470 U.S. 392, 396–397 (1985). Because a treaty ratified by the United States is "an agreement among sovereign powers," we have also considered as "aids to its interpretation" the negotiation and drafting history of the treaty as well as "the postratification understanding" of signatory nations. *Zicherman v. Korean Air Lines Co.*, 516 U.S. 217, 226 (1996); see also *United States v. Stuart*, 489

---

2. The label "self-executing" has on occasion been used to convey different meanings. What we mean by "self-executing" is that the treaty has automatic domestic effect as federal law upon ratification. Conversely, a "non-self-executing" treaty does not by itself give rise to domestically enforceable federal law. Whether such a treaty has domestic effect depends upon implementing legislation passed by Congress.

3. Even when treaties are self-executing in the sense that they create federal law, the background presumption is that "[i]nternational agreements, even those directly benefiting private persons, generally do not create private rights or provide for a private cause of action in domestic courts." 2 Restatement (Third) of Foreign Relations Law of the United States § 907, Comment *a*, p. 395 (1986) (hereinafter Restatement). Accordingly, a number of the Courts of Appeals have presumed that treaties do not create privately enforceable rights in the absence of express language to the contrary.

4. The question is whether the *Avena* judgment has binding effect in domestic courts under the Optional Protocol, ICJ Statute, and U. N. Charter. Consequently, it is unnecessary to resolve whether the Vienna Convention is itself "self-executing" or whether it grants Medellín individually enforceable rights. As in *Sanchez–Llamas*, 548 U.S., at 342–343, we thus assume, without deciding, that Article 36 grants foreign nationals "an individually enforceable right to request that their consular officers be notified of their detention, and an accompanying right to be informed by authorities of the availability of consular notification."

U.S. 353, 365–366 (1989); *Choctaw Nation v. United States*, 318 U.S. 423, 431–432 (1943).

As a signatory to the Optional Protocol, the United States agreed to submit disputes arising out of the Vienna Convention to the ICJ. * * * Of course, submitting to jurisdiction and agreeing to be bound are two different things. A party could, for example, agree to compulsory nonbinding arbitration. Such an agreement would require the party to appear before the arbitral tribunal without obligating the party to treat the tribunal's decision as binding. See, *e.g.*, North American Free Trade Agreement, U.S.–Can.–Mex., Art. 2018(1), Dec. 17, 1992, 32 I. L. M. 605, 697 (1993) ("On receipt of the final report of [the arbitral panel requested by a Party to the agreement], the disputing Parties shall agree on the resolution of the dispute, which normally shall conform with the determinations and recommendations of the panel").

The most natural reading of the Optional Protocol is as a bare grant of jurisdiction. * * * The Protocol says nothing about the effect of an ICJ decision and does not itself commit signatories to comply with an ICJ judgment. The Protocol is similarly silent as to any enforcement mechanism.

The obligation on the part of signatory nations to comply with ICJ judgments derives not from the Optional Protocol, but rather from Article 94 of the United Nations Charter—the provision that specifically addresses the effect of ICJ decisions. Article 94(1) provides that "[e]ach Member of the United Nations *undertakes to comply* with the decision of the [ICJ] in any case to which it is a party." 59 Stat. 1051 (emphasis added). The Executive Branch contends that the phrase "undertakes to comply" is not "an acknowledgement that an ICJ decision will have immediate legal effect in the courts of U. N. members," but rather "a *commitment* on the part of U. N. Members to take *future* action through their political branches to comply with an ICJ decision."

We agree with this construction of Article 94. The Article is not a directive to domestic courts. It does not provide that the United States "shall" or "must" comply with an ICJ decision, nor indicate that the Senate that ratified the U.N. Charter intended to vest ICJ decisions with immediate legal effect in domestic courts. Instead, "[t]he words of Article 94 . . . call upon governments to take certain action." *Committee of United States Citizens Living in Nicaragua v. Reagan*, 273 U.S. App. D.C. 266, 859 F.2d 929, 938 (CADC 1988) (quoting *Diggs v. Richardson*, 180 U.S. App. D.C. 376, 555 F.2d 848, 851 (CADC 1976); internal quotation marks omitted). See also *Foster*, 27 U.S. 253, at 314 (holding a treaty non-self-executing because its text—" 'all . . . grants of land . . . shall be ratified and confirmed' "—did not "act directly on the grants" but rather "pledge[d] the faith of the United States to pass acts which shall ratify and confirm them"). In other words, the U.N. Charter reads like "a compact between independent nations" that "depends for the enforcement of its provisions on the interest and the honor of the governments which are parties to it." *Head Money Cases*, 112 U.S., at 598.

The remainder of Article 94 confirms that the U.N. Charter does not contemplate the automatic enforceability of ICJ decisions in domestic courts. Article 94(2)—the enforcement provision—provides the sole remedy for noncompliance: referral to the United Nations Security Council by an aggrieved state. 59 Stat. 1051.

The U.N. Charter's provision of an express diplomatic—that is, nonjudicial—remedy is itself evidence that ICJ judgments were not meant to be enforceable in domestic courts. See *Sanchez–Llamas*, 548 U.S., at 347. And even this "quintessentially *international* remed[y]," id., at 355, is not absolute. First, the Security Council must "dee[m] necessary" the issuance of a recommendation or measure to effectuate the judgment. Art. 94(2), 59 Stat. 1051. Second, as the President and Senate were undoubtedly aware in subscribing to the U.N. Charter and Optional Protocol, the United States retained the unqualified right to exercise its veto of any Security Council resolution.

This was the understanding of the Executive Branch when the President agreed to the U.N. Charter and the declaration accepting general compulsory ICJ jurisdiction. [Citations to statements of Executive Branch witnesses omitted.]

If ICJ judgments were instead regarded as automatically enforceable domestic law, they would be immediately and directly binding on state and federal courts pursuant to the Supremacy Clause. Mexico or the ICJ would have no need to proceed to the Security Council to enforce the judgment in this case. Noncompliance with an ICJ judgment through exercise of the Security Council veto—always regarded as an option by the Executive and ratifying Senate during and after consideration of the U.N. Charter, Optional Protocol, and ICJ Statute—would no longer be a viable alternative. There would be nothing to veto. In light of the U.N. Charter's remedial scheme, there is no reason to believe that the President and Senate signed up for such a result.

In sum, Medellín's view that ICJ decisions are automatically enforceable as domestic law is fatally undermined by the enforcement structure established by Article 94. His construction would eliminate the option of noncompliance contemplated by Article 94(2), undermining the ability of the political branches to determine whether and how to comply with an ICJ judgment. Those sensitive foreign policy decisions would instead be transferred to state and federal courts charged with applying an ICJ judgment directly as domestic law. And those courts would not be empowered to decide whether to comply with the judgment—again, always regarded as an option by the political branches—any more than courts may consider whether to comply with any other species of domestic law. This result would be particularly anomalous in light of the principle that "[t]he conduct of the foreign relations of our Government is committed by the Constitution to the Executive and Legislative—'the political'—Depart-ments." *Oetjen v. Central Leather Co.*, 246 U.S. 297, 302 (1918).

The ICJ Statute, incorporated into the U.N. Charter, provides further evidence that the ICJ's judgment in *Avena* does not automatically consti-tute federal law judicially enforceable in United States courts. Art. 59, 59 Stat. 1062. To begin with, the ICJ's "principal purpose" is said to be to "arbitrate particular disputes between national governments." *Sanchez–Llamas*, supra, at 355 (citing 59 Stat. 1055). Accordingly, the ICJ can hear disputes only between nations, not individuals. Art. 34(1), 59 Stat. 1059 ("Only states [*i.e.,* countries] may be parties in cases before the [ICJ]"). More important, Article 59 of the statute provides that "[t]he decision of the [ICJ] has *no binding force* except between the parties and in respect of that particular case." *Id.,* at 1062 (emphasis added).[7] The dissent does not explain how Medellín, an individual, can be a party to the ICJ proceeding.

Medellín argues that because the *Avena* case involves him, it is clear that he—and the 50 other Mexican nationals named in the *Avena* deci-sion—should be regarded as parties to the *Avena* judgment. But cases before the ICJ are often precipitated by disputes involving particular persons or entities, disputes that a nation elects to take up as its own. See, *e.g., Case Concerning the Barcelona Traction, Light & Power Co.* (*Belg.* v. *Spain*), 1970 I. C. J. 3 (Judgment of Feb. 5) (claim brought by Belgium on behalf of Belgian nationals and shareholders); *Case Concerning the Protec-tion of French Nationals and Protected Persons in Egypt* (*Fr.* v. *Egypt*), 1950 I. C. J. 59 (Order of Mar. 29) (claim brought by France on behalf of French nationals and protected persons in Egypt); *Anglo–Iranian Oil Co. Case* (*U. K.* v. *Iran*), 1952 I. C. J. 93, 112 (Judgment of July 22) (claim brought by the United Kingdom on behalf of the Anglo–Iranian Oil Company). That has never been understood to alter the express and established rules that only nation-states may be parties before the ICJ, Art. 34, 59 Stat. 1059, and—contrary to the position of the dissent, *post,*— that ICJ judgments are binding only between those parties, Art. 59, *id.,* at 1062.

It is, moreover, well settled that the United States' interpretation of a treaty "is entitled to great weight." *Sumitomo Shoji America, Inc. v. Avagliano*, 457 U.S. 176, 184–185 (1982); see also *El Al Israel Airlines, Ltd. v. Tsui Yuan Tseng*, 525 U.S. 155, 168 (1999). The Executive Branch has unfailingly adhered to its view that the relevant treaties do not create domestically enforceable federal law. See Brief for United States as *Ami-cus Curiae* 4, 27–29.[9]

---

7. Medellín alters this language in his brief to provide that the ICJ Statute makes the *Avena* judgment binding "in respect of [his] particular case." Medellín does not and cannot have a case before the ICJ under the terms of the ICJ Statute.

9. In interpreting our treaty obligations, we also consider the views of the ICJ itself, "giv[ing] respectful consideration to the interpretation of an international treaty rendered by an interna-tional court with jurisdiction to interpret [the treaty]." *Breard v. Greene*, 523 U.S. 371, 375 (1998) (per curiam); see *Sanchez–Llamas*, supra, at 355–356. It is not clear whether that principle would apply when the question is the binding force of ICJ judgments themselves, rather than the substantive scope of a treaty the ICJ must interpret in resolving disputes. * * * In any event,

The pertinent international agreements, therefore, do not provide for implementation of ICJ judgments through direct enforcement in domestic courts, and "where a treaty does not provide a particular remedy, either expressly or implicitly, it is not for the federal courts to impose one on the States through lawmaking of their own." *Sanchez–Llamas*, 548 U.S., at 347.

B

The dissent faults our analysis because it "looks for the wrong thing (explicit textual expression about self-execution) using the wrong standard (clarity) in the wrong place (the treaty language)." Given our obligation to interpret treaty provisions to determine whether they are self-executing, we have to confess that we do think it rather important to look to the treaty language to see what it has to say about the issue. That is after all what the Senate looks to in deciding whether to approve the treaty.

The interpretive approach employed by the Court today—resorting to the text—is hardly novel. In two early cases involving an 1819 land-grant treaty between Spain and the United States, Chief Justice Marshall found the language of the treaty dispositive. In *Foster*, after distinguishing between self-executing treaties (those "equivalent to an act of the legislature") and non-self-executing treaties (those "the legislature must execute"), Chief Justice Marshall held that the 1819 treaty was non-self-executing. 27 U.S. 253, 2 Pet., at 314. Four years later, the Supreme Court considered another claim under the same treaty, but concluded that the treaty was self-executing. See *Percheman*, 32 U.S. 51, 7 Pet., at 87. The reason was not because the treaty was sometimes self-executing and sometimes not, but because "the language of" the Spanish translation (brought to the Court's attention for the first time) indicated the parties' intent to ratify and confirm the land-grant "by force of the instrument itself." Id., 32 U.S. 51, 7 Pet., at 89.

As against this time-honored textual approach, the dissent proposes a multifactor, judgment-by-judgment analysis that would "jettiso[n] relative predictability for the open-ended rough-and-tumble of factors." * * * The dissent's novel approach to deciding which (or, more accurately, when) treaties give rise to directly enforceable federal law is arrestingly indeterminate. Treaty language is barely probative. * * * Of those committed to the judiciary, the courts pick and choose which shall be binding United States law—trumping not only state but other federal law as well—and which shall not. They do this on the basis of a multifactor, "context-specific" inquiry. Even then, the same treaty sometimes gives rise to United States law and sometimes does not, again depending on an ad hoc judicial assessment.

---

nothing suggests that the ICJ views its judgments as automatically enforceable in the domestic courts of signatory nations. The *Avena* judgment itself directs the United States to provide review and reconsideration of the affected convictions and sentences "by means of its own choosing." 2004 I. C. J., at 72 (emphasis added). This language, as well as the ICJ's mere suggestion that the "judicial process" is best suited to provide such review, id., at 65–66, confirm that domestic enforceability in court is not part and parcel of an ICJ judgment.

Our Framers established a careful set of procedures that must be followed before federal law can be created under the Constitution—vesting that decision in the political branches, subject to checks and balances. U.S. Const., Art. I, § 7. They also recognized that treaties could create federal law, but again through the political branches, with the President making the treaty and the Senate approving it. Art. II, § 2. The dissent's understanding of the treaty route, depending on an ad hoc judgment of the judiciary without looking to the treaty language—the very language negotiated by the President and approved by the Senate—cannot readily be ascribed to those same Framers.

The dissent's approach risks the United States' involvement in international agreements. It is hard to believe that the United States would enter into treaties that are sometimes enforceable and sometimes not. Such a treaty would be the equivalent of writing a blank check to the judiciary. Senators could never be quite sure what the treaties on which they were voting meant. Only a judge could say for sure and only at some future date. This uncertainty could hobble the United States' efforts to negotiate and sign international agreements.

* * *

Nor is it any answer to say that the federal courts will diligently police international agreements and enforce the decisions of international tribunals only when they *should be* enforced. The point of a non-self-executing treaty is that it "addresses itself to the political, *not* the judicial department; and the legislature must execute the contract before it can become a rule for the Court." *Foster*, 27 U.S. 253, 2 Pet., at 314 (emphasis added); *Whitney*, 124 U.S., at 195. See also *Foster*, 27 U.S. 253, 2 Pet., at 307 ("The judiciary is not that department of the government, to which the assertion of its interests against foreign powers is confided"). The dissent's contrary approach would assign to the courts—not the political branches—the primary role in deciding when and how international agreements will be enforced. To read a treaty so that it sometimes has the effect of domestic law and sometimes does not is tantamount to vesting with the judiciary the power not only to interpret but also to create the law.

C

Our conclusion that *Avena* does not by itself constitute binding federal law is confirmed by the "postratification understanding" of signatory nations. See *Zicherman*, 516 U.S., at 226. There are currently 47 nations that are parties to the Optional Protocol and 171 nations that are parties to the Vienna Convention. Yet neither Medellín nor his *amici* have identified a single nation that treats ICJ judgments as binding in domestic courts. In determining that the Vienna Convention did not require certain relief in United States courts in *Sanchez–Llamas*, we found it pertinent that the requested relief would not be available under the treaty in any other signatory country. See 548 U.S., at 343–344. So too here the lack of any basis for supposing that any other country would treat ICJ judgments as directly enforceable as a matter of their domestic law strongly suggests that the treaty should not be so viewed in our courts.

Our conclusion is further supported by general principles of interpretation. To begin with, we reiterated in *Sanchez–Llamas* what we held in *Breard*, that " 'absent a clear and express statement to the contrary, the procedural rules of the forum State govern the implementation of the treaty in that State.' " 548 U.S., at 351 (quoting *Breard*, 523 U.S., at 375). Given that ICJ judgments may interfere with state procedural rules, one would expect the ratifying parties to the relevant treaties to have clearly stated their intent to give those judgments domestic effect, if they had so intended. Here there is no statement in the Optional Protocol, the U. N. Charter, or the ICJ Statute that supports the notion that ICJ judgments displace state procedural rules.

Moreover, the consequences of Medellin's argument give pause. An ICJ judgment, the argument goes, is not only binding domestic law but is also unassailable. As a result, neither Texas nor this Court may look behind a judgment and quarrel with its reasoning or result. (We already know, from *Sanchez–Llamas*, that this Court disagrees with both the reasoning and result in *Avena*.) Medellín's interpretation would allow ICJ judgments to override otherwise binding state law; there is nothing in his logic that would exempt contrary federal law from the same fate. See, e.g., *Cook v. United States*, 288 U.S. 102, 119 (1933) (later-in-time self-executing treaty supersedes a federal statute if there is a conflict). And there is nothing to prevent the ICJ from ordering state courts to annul criminal convictions and sentences, for any reason deemed sufficient by the ICJ. Indeed, that is precisely the relief Mexico requested. *Avena*, 2004 I. C. J., at 58–59.

Even the dissent flinches at reading the relevant treaties to give rise to self-executing ICJ judgments in all cases. It admits that "Congress is unlikely to authorize automatic judicial enforceability of *all* ICJ judgments, for that could include some politically sensitive judgments and others better suited for enforcement by other branches." Our point precisely. But the lesson to draw from that insight is hardly that the judiciary should decide which judgments are politically sensitive and which are not.

In short, and as we observed in *Sanchez–Llamas*, "[n]othing in the structure or purpose of the ICJ suggests that its interpretations were intended to be conclusive on our courts." 548 U.S., at 354. Given that holding, it is difficult to see how that same structure and purpose can establish, as Medellín argues, that *judgments* of the ICJ nonetheless were intended to be conclusive on our courts. A judgment is binding only if there is a rule of law that makes it so. And the question whether ICJ judgments can bind domestic courts depends upon the same analysis undertaken in *Sanchez–Llamas* and set forth above.

* * *

D

Our holding does not call into question the ordinary enforcement of foreign judgments or international arbitral agreements. Indeed, we agree with Medellín that, as a general matter, "an agreement to abide by the result" of an international adjudication—or what he really means, an agreement to give the result of such adjudication domestic legal effect— can be a treaty obligation like any other, so long as the agreement is consistent with the Constitution. The point is that the particular treaty obligations on which Medellín relies do not of their own force create domestic law.

The dissent worries that our decision casts doubt on some 70–odd treaties under which the United States has agreed to submit disputes to the ICJ according to "roughly similar" provisions. Again, under our established precedent, some treaties are self-executing and some are not, depending on the treaty. That the judgment of an international tribunal might not automatically become domestic law hardly means the underlying treaty is "useless." See *post* (describing the British system in which treaties "virtually always requir[e] parliamentary legislation"). Such judgments would still constitute international obligations, the proper subject of political and diplomatic negotiations. See *Head Money Cases*, 112 U.S., at 598. And Congress could elect to give them wholesale effect (rather than the judgment-by-judgment approach hypothesized by the dissent) through implementing legislation, as it regularly has. See, *e.g.*, Foreign Affairs Reform and Restructuring Act of 1998, Pub. L. 105–277, div. G, § 2242, 112 Stat. 2681–822, note following 8 U.S.C. § 1231 (directing the "appropriate agencies" to "prescribe regulations to implement the obligations of the United States under Article 3" of the Convention Against Torture and Other Forms of Cruel, Inhuman or Degrading Treatment or Punishment); see also infra (listing examples of legislation implementing international obligations).

Further, that an ICJ judgment may not be automatically enforceable in domestic courts does not mean the particular underlying treaty is not. Indeed, we have held that a number of the "Friendship, Commerce, and Navigation" Treaties cited by the dissent, see *post,* Appendix B, are self-executing—based on "the language of the[se] Treat[ies]." See *Sumitomo Shoji America, Inc.*, supra, at 180, 189–190. In *Kolovrat v. Oregon*, 366 U.S. 187, 191, 196, for example, the Court found that Yugoslavian claimants denied inheritance under Oregon law were entitled to inherit personal property pursuant to an 1881 Treaty of Friendship, Navigation, and Commerce between the United States and Serbia. See also *Clark v. Allen*, 331 U.S. 503, 507–511, 517–518 (1947) (finding that the right to inherit real property granted German aliens under the Treaty of Friendship, Commerce, and Consular Rights with Germany prevailed over California law). Contrary to the dissent's suggestion, neither our approach nor our cases require that a treaty provide for self-execution in so many talismanic words; that is a caricature of the Court's opinion. Our cases simply require courts to decide whether a treaty's terms reflect a determination by the

President who negotiated it and the Senate that confirmed it that the treaty has domestic effect.

In addition, Congress is up to the task of implementing non-self-executing treaties, even those involving complex commercial disputes. Cf. *post* (Breyer, J., dissenting). The judgments of a number of international tribunals enjoy a different status because of implementing legislation enacted by Congress. See, *e.g.*, 22 U.S.C. § 1650a(a) ("An award of an arbitral tribunal rendered pursuant to chapter IV of the [Convention on the Settlement of Investment Disputes] shall create a right arising under a treaty of the United States. The pecuniary obligations imposed by such an award shall be enforced and shall be given the same full faith and credit as if the award were a final judgment of a court of general jurisdiction of one of the several States"); 9 U. S C. §§ 201–208 ("The [U. N.] Convention on the Recognition and Enforcement of Foreign Arbitral Awards of June 10, 1958, shall be enforced in United States courts in accordance with this chapter," § 201). Such language demonstrates that Congress knows how to accord domestic effect to international obligations when it desires such a result.

* * *

In sum, while the ICJ's judgment in *Avena* creates an international law obligation on the part of the United States, it does not of its own force constitute binding federal law that pre-empts state restrictions on the filing of successive habeas petitions. As we noted in *Sanchez–Llamas*, a contrary conclusion would be extraordinary, given that basic rights guaranteed by our own Constitution do not have the effect of displacing state procedural rules. See 548 U.S., at 360. Nothing in the text, background, negotiating and drafting history, or practice among signatory nations suggests that the President or Senate intended the improbable result of giving the judgments of an international tribunal a higher status than that enjoyed by "many of our most fundamental constitutional protections." *Ibid.*

[In Part III the Court rejected the contention that the President's Memorandum had established a binding federal rule of decision preempting state law. Using the framework of the concurrence of Justice Robert Jackson in *Youngstown Sheet & Tube v. Sawyer*, 343 U.S. 579 (1952), the Court concluded that Congress had neither authorized enforcement of I.C.J. judgments nor acquiesced in presidential enforcement authority but rather had implicitly withheld such authority by approving the U.N. Charter and I.C.J. Statute as non-self-executing treaties. The Court therefore affirmed the judgment of the Texas Court of Criminal Appeals, allowing the conviction and death sentence to stand.]

JUSTICE STEVENS, concurring in the judgment.

* * *

Unlike the text of some other treaties, the terms of the United Nations Charter do not necessarily incorporate international judgments into domestic law. Cf., *e.g.*, United Nations Convention on the Law of the Sea, Annex VI, Art. 39, Dec. 10, 1982, S. Treaty Doc. No. 103–39, 1833 U.N.T.S. 570 ("[D]ecisions of the [Seabed Disputes] Chamber shall be enforceable in the territories of the States Parties in the same manner as judgments or orders of the highest court of the State Party in whose territory the enforcement is sought"). Moreover, Congress has passed implementing legislation to ensure the enforcement of other international judgments, even when the operative treaty provisions use far more mandatory language than "undertakes to comply."[1]

* * *

Absent a presumption one way or the other, the best reading of the words "undertakes to comply" is, in my judgment, one that contemplates future action by the political branches. * * *

* * *

Even though the ICJ's judgment in *Avena* is not "the supreme Law of the Land," U.S. Const., Art. VI, cl. 2, no one disputes that it constitutes an international law obligation on the part of the United States. * * *

Under the express terms of the Supremacy Clause, the United States' obligation to "undertake to comply" with the ICJ's decision falls on each of the States as well as the Federal Government. * * * Texas's duty in this respect is all the greater since it was Texas that—by failing to provide consular notice in accordance with the Vienna Convention—ensnared the United States in the current controversy. Having already put the Nation in breach of one treaty, it is now up to Texas to prevent the breach of another. * * *

* * * The cost to Texas of complying with *Avena* would be minimal, particularly given the remote likelihood that the violation of the Vienna Convention actually prejudiced José Ernesto Medellín. It is a cost that the State of Oklahoma unhesitatingly assumed. [Ed.: See p. 717 note 2 below.]

On the other hand, the costs of refusing to respect the ICJ's judgment are significant. The entire Court and the President agree that breach will jeopardize the United States' "plainly compelling" interests in "ensuring the reciprocal observance of the Vienna Convention, protecting relations with foreign governments, and demonstrating commitment to the role of international law." When the honor of the Nation is balanced against the modest cost of compliance, Texas would do well to recognize that more is at stake than whether judgments of the ICJ, and the principled admoni-

---

1. See, *e.g.*, Convention on the Settlement of Investment Disputes between States and Nationals of Other States (ICSID Convention), Art. 54(1), Mar. 18, 1965, [1966] 17 U.S.T. 1291, T. I. A. S. No. 6090 ("Each Contracting State shall recognize an award rendered pursuant to this Convention as binding and enforce the pecuniary obligations imposed by that award within its territories as if it were a final judgment of a court in that State"); 22 U.S.C. § 1650a ("An award of an arbitral tribunal rendered pursuant to chapter IV of the [ICSID Convention] shall create a right arising under a treaty of the United States. The pecuniary obligations imposed by such an award shall be enforced and shall be given the same full faith and credit as if the award were a final judgment of a court of general jurisdiction of one of the several States").

INTERNATIONAL LAW IN NATIONAL LAW

tions of the President of the United States, trump state procedural rules in the absence of implementing legislation.

The Court's judgment, which I join, does not foreclose further appropriate action by the State of Texas.

Justice Breyer, with whom Justice Souter and Justice Ginsburg join, dissenting.

* * *

The critical question here is whether the Supremacy Clause requires Texas to follow, *i.e.*, to enforce, this ICJ judgment. The Court says "no." And it reaches its negative answer by interpreting the labyrinth of treaty provisions as creating a legal obligation that binds the United States internationally, but which, for Supremacy Clause purposes, is not automatically enforceable as domestic law. In the majority's view, the Optional Protocol simply sends the dispute to the ICJ; the ICJ statute says that the ICJ will subsequently reach a judgment; and the U.N. Charter contains no more than a promise to " 'undertak[e] to comply' " with that judgment. Such a promise, the majority says, does not as a domestic law matter (in Chief Justice Marshall's words) "operat[e] of itself without the aid of any legislative provision." *Foster*, 27 U.S. 253, 2 Pet., at 314. Rather, here (and presumably in any other ICJ judgment rendered pursuant to any of the approximately 70 U.S. treaties in force that contain similar provisions for submitting treaty-based disputes to the ICJ for decisions that bind the parties) Congress must enact specific legislation before ICJ judgments entered pursuant to our consent to compulsory ICJ jurisdiction can become domestic law. See Brief for International Court of Justice Experts as *Amici Curiae* 18 ("Approximately 70 U.S. treaties now in force contain obligations comparable to those in the Optional Protocol for submission of treaty-based disputes to the ICJ"); see also *id.,* at 18, n. 25.

In my view, the President has correctly determined that Congress need not enact additional legislation. The majority places too much weight upon treaty language that says little about the matter. The words "undertak[e] to comply," for example, do not tell us whether an ICJ judgment rendered pursuant to the parties' consent to compulsory ICJ jurisdiction does, or does not, automatically become part of our domestic law. To answer that question we must look instead to our own domestic law, in particular, to the many treaty-related cases interpreting the Supremacy Clause. Those cases, including some written by Justices well aware of the Founders' original intent, lead to the conclusion that the ICJ judgment before us is enforceable as a matter of domestic law without further legislation.

* * *

[The dissent's survey of cases giving self-executing effect to treaty provisions is omitted.] These many Supreme Court cases finding treaty provisions to be self-executing cannot be reconciled with the majority's demand for textual clarity.

Indeed, the majority does not point to a single ratified United States treaty that contains the kind of "clea[r]" or "plai[n]" textual indication for which the majority searches. Justice Stevens' reliance upon one ratified and one *un*-ratified treaty to make the point that a treaty *could* speak clearly on the matter of self-execution does suggest that there are a few such treaties. But that simply highlights how few of them actually *do* speak clearly on the matter. And that is not because the United States never, or hardly ever, has entered into a treaty with self-executing provisions. The case law belies any such conclusion. Rather, it is because the issue whether further legislative action is required before a treaty provision takes domestic effect in a signatory nation is often a matter of how that Nation's domestic law regards the provision's legal status. And that domestic status-determining law differs markedly from one nation to another. See generally Hollis, Comparative Approach to Treaty Law and Practice, in National Treaty Law and Practice 1, 9–50 (D. Hollis, M. Blakeslee, & L. Ederington eds. 2005) (hereinafter Hollis). As Justice Iredell pointed out 200 years ago, Britain, for example, taking the view that the British Crown makes treaties but Parliament makes domestic law, virtually always requires parliamentary legislation. See *Ware [v. Hylton]*, supra, 3 U.S. 199, 3 Dallas, at 274–277; Sinclair, Dickson, & Maciver, United Kingdom, in National Treaty Law and Practice, *supra*, at 727, 733, and n. 9 (citing *Queen* v. *Secretary of State for Foreign and Commonwealth Affairs, ex parte Lord Rees–Mogg*, [1994] Q. B. 552 (1993) (in Britain, " 'treaties are not self-executing' ")). On the other hand, the United States, with its Supremacy Clause, does not take Britain's view. See, *e.g., Ware*, supra, 3 U.S. 199, 3 Dallas, at 277 (opinion of Iredell, J.). And the law of other nations, the Netherlands for example, directly incorporates many treaties concluded by the executive into its domestic law even without explicit parliamentary approval of the treaty. See Brouwer, The Netherlands, in National Treaty Law and Practice, *supra,* at 483, 483–502.

The majority correctly notes that the treaties do not explicitly state that the relevant obligations are self-executing. But given the differences among nations, why would drafters write treaty language stating that a provision about, say, alien property inheritance, is self-executing? How could those drafters achieve agreement when one signatory nation follows one tradition and a second follows another? Why would such a difference matter sufficiently for drafters to try to secure language that would prevent, for example, Britain's following treaty ratification with a further law while (perhaps unnecessarily) insisting that the United States apply a treaty provision without further domestic legislation? Above all, what does the absence of specific language about "self-execution" prove? It may reflect the drafters' awareness of national differences. It may reflect the practical fact that drafters, favoring speedy, effective implementation, conclude they should best leave national legal practices alone. It may reflect the fact that achieving international agreement on *this* point is simply a game not worth the candle.

In a word, for present purposes, the absence or presence of language in a treaty about a provision's self-execution proves nothing at all. At best the Court is hunting the snark. At worst it erects legalistic hurdles that can threaten the application of provisions in many existing commercial and other treaties and make it more difficult to negotiate new ones. * * *

* * *

* * * I would find the relevant treaty provisions self-executing as applied to the ICJ judgment before us (giving that judgment domestic legal effect) for the following reasons, taken together.

First, the language of the relevant treaties strongly supports direct judicial enforceability, at least of judgments of the kind at issue here. The Optional Protocol bears the title "Compulsory Settlement of Disputes," thereby emphasizing the mandatory and binding nature of the procedures it sets forth. 21 U.S.T., at 326. The body of the Protocol says specifically that "any party" that has consented to the ICJ's "compulsory jurisdiction" may bring a "dispute" before the court against any other such party. Art. I, *ibid.* And the Protocol contrasts proceedings of the compulsory kind with an alternative "conciliation procedure," the recommendations of which a party may decide "not" to "accep[t]." Art. III, *id.,* at 327. Thus, the Optional Protocol's basic objective is not just to provide a forum for *settlement* but to provide a forum for *compulsory* settlement.

Moreover, in accepting Article 94(1) of the Charter, "[e]ach Member . . . undertakes to comply with the decision" of the ICJ "in any case to which it is a party." 59 Stat. 1051. And the ICJ Statute (part of the U. N. Charter) makes clear that, a decision of the ICJ between parties that have consented to the ICJ's compulsory jurisdiction has *"binding force . . .* between the parties and in respect of that particular case." Art. 59, *id.,* at 1062 (emphasis added). Enforcement of a court's judgment that has "binding force" involves quintessential judicial activity.

* * *

[T]he United States has ratified approximately 70 treaties with ICJ dispute resolution provisions roughly similar to those contained in the Optional Protocol; many of those treaties contemplate ICJ adjudication of the sort of substantive matters (property, commercial dealings, and the like) that the Court has found self-executing, or otherwise appear addressed to the judicial branch. See Appendix B, *infra* [omitted]. None of the ICJ provisions in these treaties contains stronger language about self-execution than the language at issue here. See, *e.g.,* Treaty of Friendship, Commerce and Navigation between the United States of America and the Kingdom of Denmark, Art. XXIV(2), Oct. 1, 1951, [1961] 12 U.S.T. 935, T. I. A. S. No. 4797 ("Any dispute between the Parties as to the interpretation or application of the present Treaty, not satisfactorily adjusted by diplomacy, shall be submitted to the International Court of Justice, unless the Parties agree to settlement by some other pacific means"). In signing these treaties (in respect to, say, alien land ownership provisions) was the

United States engaging in a near useless act? Does the majority believe the drafters expected Congress to enact further legislation about, say, an alien's inheritance rights, decision by decision?

* * *

Second, the Optional Protocol here applies to a dispute about the meaning of a Vienna Convention provision that is itself self-executing and judicially enforceable. The Convention provision is about an individual's "rights," namely, his right upon being arrested to be informed of his separate right to contact his nation's consul. See Art. 36(1)(b), 21 U.S.T., at 101. The provision['s] language is precise. The dispute arises at the intersection of an individual right with ordinary rules of criminal procedure; it consequently concerns the kind of matter with which judges are familiar. The provisions contain judicially enforceable standards. * * * And the judgment itself requires a further hearing of a sort that is typically judicial. * * *

* * *

Third, logic suggests that a treaty provision providing for "final" and "binding" judgments that "settl[e]" treaty-based disputes is self-executing insofar as the judgment in question concerns the meaning of an underlying treaty provision that is itself self-executing. * * *

* * *

Contrary to the majority's suggestion, that binding force does not disappear by virtue of the fact that Mexico, rather than Medellín himself, presented his claims to the ICJ. Mexico brought the *Avena* case in part in "the exercise of its right of diplomatic protection of its nationals," *e.g.,* 2004 I. C. J., at 21, ¶¶ 13(1), (3), including Medellín, see *id.,* at 25, ¶ 16. Such derivative claims are a well-established feature of international law, and the United States has several times asserted them on behalf of its own citizens. See 2 Restatement (Third) of Foreign Relations, supra, § 713, Comments *a, b,* at 217; *Case Concerning Elettronica Sicula S. p. A. (U. S. v. Italy),* 1989 I. C. J. 15, 20 (Judgment of July 20); *Case Concerning United States Diplomatic and Consular Staff in Tehran (U. S. v. Iran),* 1979 I. C. J. 7, 8 (Judgment of Dec. 15); *Case Concerning Rights of Nationals of the United States of America in Morocco (Fr. v. U. S.),* 1952 I. C. J. 176, 180–181 (Judgment of Aug. 27). They are treated in relevant respects as the claims of the represented individuals themselves. See 2 Restatement (Third) of Foreign Relations, supra, § 713, Comments *a, b.* In particular, they can give rise to remedies, tailored to the individual, that bind the Nation against whom the claims are brought (here, the United States). See *ibid.;* see also, *e.g., Frelinghuysen v. Key,* 110 U.S. 63, 71–72 (1884).

Fourth, the majority's very different approach has seriously negative practical implications. The United States has entered into at least 70 treaties that contain provisions for ICJ dispute settlement similar to the

Protocol before us. Many of these treaties contain provisions similar to those this Court has previously found self-executing—provisions that involve, for example, property rights, contract and commercial rights, trademarks, civil liability for personal injury, rights of foreign diplomats, taxation, domestic-court jurisdiction, and so forth. * * * If the Optional Protocol here, taken together with the U.N. Charter and its annexed ICJ Statute, is insufficient to warrant enforcement of the ICJ judgment before us, it is difficult to see how one could reach a different conclusion in any of these other instances. And the consequence is to undermine longstanding efforts in those treaties to create an effective international system for interpreting and applying many, often commercial, self-executing treaty provisions. I thus doubt that the majority is right when it says, "We do not suggest that treaties can never afford binding domestic effect to international tribunal judgments." In respect to the 70 treaties that currently refer disputes to the ICJ's binding adjudicatory authority, some multilateral, some bilateral, that is just what the majority has done.

Fifth, other factors, related to the particular judgment here at issue, make that judgment well suited to direct judicial enforcement. * * * Courts frequently work with criminal procedure and related prejudice. Legislatures do not. Judicial standards are readily available for working in this technical area. Legislative standards are not readily available. Judges typically determine such matters, deciding, for example, whether further hearings are necessary, after reviewing a record in an individual case. Congress does not normally legislate in respect to individual cases. * * *

Sixth, to find the United States' treaty obligations self-executing as applied to the ICJ judgment (and consequently to find that judgment enforceable) does not threaten constitutional conflict with other branches; it does not require us to engage in nonjudicial activity; and it does not require us to create a new cause of action. * * *

Seventh, neither the President nor Congress has expressed concern about direct judicial enforcement of the ICJ decision. To the contrary, the President favors enforcement of this judgment. Thus, insofar as foreign policy impact, the interrelation of treaty provisions, or any other matter within the President's special treaty, military, and foreign affairs responsibilities might prove relevant, such factors *favor,* rather than militate against, enforcement of the judgment before us. * * *

For these seven reasons, I would find that the United States' treaty obligation to comply with the ICJ judgment in *Avena* is enforceable in court in this case without further congressional action beyond Senate ratification of the relevant treaties. * * *

NOTES

1. *Aftermath of the Supreme Court's Decision.* After the decision in the principal case, Mexico returned to the I.C.J. to seek an interpretation of that Court's previous judgment and renewed its request for provisional measures

to stay the execution of Medellín and four other Mexican nationals covered by *Avena* who were nearing the end of their U.S. appeals. The United States disputed the I.C.J.'s jurisdiction to hear the matter. A divided Court (7–5, with three judges not participating) entered an order directing the United States to take "all measures necessary" to ensure that the five individuals would not be executed pending final judgment, unless they were to receive review and reconsideration required by *Avena*. Request for Interpretation of the Judgment of 31 March 2004 in *Avena and Other Mexican Nationals* (Mexico v. United States), 2008 I.C.J. No 139, Order of July 16, 2008 (Provisional Measures).

Meanwhile, Secretary of State Condoleezza Rice and Attorney General Michael Mukasey wrote to Governor Rick Perry of Texas, calling on Texas to "take the steps necessary to give full effect to the *Avena* decision with respect to the convictions and sentences addressed therein." The Governor declined to do so, referring to the Supreme Court's decision in *Medellín* and maintaining that the federal Executive and Congress should deal with the matter.

A bill was introduced in the House of Representatives in July 2008 in an effort to respond to the Supreme Court's ruling that it was for Congress to decide how to implement the I.C.J.'s judgment, but Congress took no further steps. A few days before his scheduled execution date of August 5, 2008, Medellín again sought a stay from the Supreme Court, which rejected his petition by 5–4 vote. *Medellín v. Texas*, 129 S.Ct. 360 (2008). Texas proceeded to execute him that night. In its briefs filed with the Court, however, Texas represented that if other individuals covered by *Avena* should seek review and reconsideration in a future federal habeas proceeding, "the State of Texas will not only refrain from objecting, but will join the defense in asking the reviewing court to address the claim of prejudice on the merits." See Crook, Contemporary Practice of the United States, 102 A.J.I.L. 860, 863 (2008).

2. *Relief Granted in Oklahoma.* In the case of Osbaldo Torres, a member of the *Avena* group referred to in Justice Stevens' concurrence in *Medellín*, the Oklahoma Court of Criminal Appeals entered a stay of execution and ordered an evidentiary hearing on Torres's claim that he had been prejudiced by the Vienna Convention violation, thereby affording the review and reconsideration required by the I.C.J. judgment. On the same day, the Governor of Oklahoma committed Torres's death sentence to life imprisonment without parole. In the subsequent judicial proceedings, the Oklahoma Court of Criminal Appeals held that Torres had not established prejudice as to his conviction, and that any prejudice with respect to the death sentence was moot by virtue of the commutation. See Crook, Contemporary Practice of the United States, 98 A.J.I.L. 581–84 (2004); 100 A.J.I.L. 462 (2006).

3. *Senate's Evolving Practice.* In the aftermath of the Supreme Court's *Medellín* decision, the Senate Foreign Relations Committee undertook a reexamination of Senatorial practice in order to clarify the views of the political branches concerning the self-executing or non-self-executing status and judicial enforceability of treaties. Beginning with a large batch of treaties approved by the Senate in September 2008, careful attention has been given to including an explicit statement on these matters at the time that the Senate votes on prospective treaties, in the interests of providing guidance to those expected to implement such treaties and ensuring that the necessary

groundwork is laid for full compliance. Also in 2008, a joint Task Force on Treaties convened by the American Bar Association and the American Society of International Law embarked on a study aimed at making recommendations concerning existing treaties as well as future practice in light of *Medellín*. Its report is expected in 2009.

4. *Further Reading.* For commentary from different points of view on the principal case, see Agora: *Medellín*, 100 A.J.I.L. 529–72 (2008) (comments by Bederman, Bradley, Charnovitz and Vazquez). For the approaches of other countries to the implementation of international decisions, see Section 6.

E. INTERPRETING TREATIES; STATUTORY INTERPRETATION IN LIGHT OF INTERNATIONAL OBLIGATIONS

The *Medellín* case reveals differences among the Justices not only over the status of treaty obligations in national law, but also over the significance of various interpretive sources, including text, negotiating history, records from the Senate's deliberations, post-ratification practice, and decisions of international and foreign tribunals interpreting the treaty. The international law of treaty interpretation is addressed in Chapter 3. See also p. 722 note 3, for reference to treaty interpretation controversies in the United States, with attention to the significance of the Senate's understanding of a treaty's meaning.

Medellín also illustrates the general proposition that U.S. courts will give substantial weight to the Executive's views on a treaty's meaning, while also underscoring the Supreme Court's insistence that the Court itself has the final say. The Court rejected an Executive treaty interpretation in the next case.

HAMDAN v. RUMSFELD

Supreme Court of the United States
548 U.S. 557 (2006) (some footnotes omitted)

[Salim Ahmed Hamdan, a Yemeni national who was allegedly Osama bin Laden's bodyguard and personal driver, was captured in November 2001 in Afghanistan and transferred to the U.S. military. From June 2002 onward, he was detained at the U.S. naval base at Guantanamo Bay as an enemy combatant. In 2003 President Bush designated him as eligible for trial by military commission, and in 2004 he was charged with conspiracy to commit offenses connected with the attacks of September 11, 2001, pursuant to a military order issued by President Bush on November 13, 2001 providing for a system of military commissions to try non-citizens affiliated with Al Qaeda. Hamdan filed habeas corpus petitions to challenge the authority of the military commission to try him. The Supreme Court held in a split decision that trial by military commission had not been authorized by Congress and that the military commission's structure and procedures violate the Uniform Code of Military Justice and the four

Geneva Conventions of 1949 to which the United States is party The excerpts below, from Part VI.D of the majority opinion by Justice Stevens, deal with the interpretation of Common Article 3 of the Geneva Conventions.]

* * *

The conflict with al Qaeda is not, according to the Government, a conflict to which the full protections afforded detainees under the 1949 Geneva Conventions apply because Article 2 of those Conventions (which appears in all four Conventions) renders the full protections applicable only to "all cases of declared war or of any other armed conflict which may arise between two or more of the High Contracting Parties." 6 U.S.T., at 3318. Since Hamdan was captured and detained incident to the conflict with al Qaeda and not the conflict with the Taliban, and since al Qaeda, unlike Afghanistan, is not a "High Contracting Party"—*i.e.*, a signatory of the Conventions, the protections of those Conventions are not, it is argued, applicable to Hamdan.

We need not decide the merits of this argument because there is at least one provision of the Geneva Conventions that applies here even if the relevant conflict is not one between signatories. Article 3, often referred to as Common Article 3 because, like Article 2, it appears in all four Geneva Conventions, provides that in a "conflict not of an international character occurring in the territory of one of the High Contracting Parties, each Party to the conflict shall be bound to apply, as a minimum," certain provisions protecting "persons taking no active part in the hostilities, including members of armed forces who have laid down their arms and those placed *hors de combat* by . . . detention." *Id.*, at 3318. One such provision prohibits "the passing of sentences and the carrying out of executions without previous judgment pronounced by a regularly constituted court affording all the judicial guarantees which are recognized as indispensable by civilized peoples." *Ibid.*

The Court of Appeals thought, and the Government asserts, that Common Article 3 does not apply to Hamdan because the conflict with al Qaeda, being " 'international in scope,' " does not qualify as a " 'conflict not of an international character.' " 415 F.3d at 41. That reasoning is erroneous. The term "conflict not of an international character" is used here in contradistinction to a conflict between nations. So much is demonstrated by the "fundamental logic [of] the Convention's provisions on its application." *Id.*, at 44 (Williams, J., concurring). Common Article 2 provides that "the present Convention shall apply to all cases of declared war or of any other armed conflict which may arise between two or more of the High Contracting Parties." 6 U.S.T., at 3318 (Art. 2, ¶ 1). High Contracting Parties (signatories) also must abide by all terms of the Conventions vis-à-vis one another even if one party to the conflict is a nonsignatory "Power," and must so abide vis-à-vis the nonsignatory if "the latter accepts and applies" those terms. *Ibid.* (Art. 2, ¶ 3). Common Article 3, by contrast, affords some minimal protection, falling short of full protection under the Conventions, to individuals associated with neither a signatory nor even a nonsignatory "Power" who are involved in a conflict "in the territory of" a signatory. The latter kind of conflict is distinguishable from the conflict described in Common Article 2 chiefly because it does not involve a clash between nations (whether signatories or not). In context, then, the phrase "not of an international character" bears its literal meaning. See, *e.g.*, J. Bentham, Introduction to the Principles of Morals and Legislation 6, 296 (J. Burns & H. Hart eds. 1970) (using the term "international law" as a "new though not inexpressive appellation" meaning "betwixt nation and nation"; defining "international" to include "mutual transactions between sovereigns as such"); Commentary on the Additional Protocols to the Geneva Conventions of 12 August 1949, p. 1351 (1987) ("[A] non-international armed conflict is distinct from an international armed conflict because of the legal status of the entities opposing each other").

Although the official commentaries accompanying Common Article 3 indicate that an important purpose of the provision was to furnish minimal protection to rebels involved in one kind of "conflict not of an international character," *i.e.*, a civil war, see GCIII Commentary 36–37, the commentaries also make clear "that the scope of the Article must be as wide as possible," *id.*, at 36.[63] In fact, limiting language that would have rendered Common Article 3 applicable "especially [to] cases of civil war, colonial conflicts, or wars of religion," was omitted from the final version of the Article, which coupled broader scope of application with a narrower range of rights than did earlier proposed iterations. See GCIII Commentary 42–43.

iii

Common Article 3, then, is applicable here and, as indicated above, requires that Hamdan be tried by a "regularly constituted court affording all the judicial guarantees which are recognized as indispensable by civilized peoples." 6 U.S.T., at 3320 (Art. 3, ¶ 1(d)). While the term "regularly constituted court" is not specifically defined in either Common Article 3 or its accompanying commentary, other sources disclose its core meaning. The commentary accompanying a provision of the Fourth Geneva Convention, for example, defines " 'regularly constituted' " tribunals to include "ordinary military courts" and "definitely exclude all special tribunals." GCIV Commentary 340 (defining the term "properly constituted" in Article 66, which the commentary treats as identical to "regularly constituted"); see also *Yamashita*, 327 U.S., at 44 (Rutledge, J., dissent-

---

63. See also GCIII Commentary 35 (Common Article 3 "has the merit of being simple and clear.... Its observance does not depend upon preliminary discussions on the nature of the conflict"); GCIV Commentary 51 ("[N]obody in enemy hands can be outside the law"); U.S. Army Judge Advocate General's Legal Center and School, Dept. of the Army, Law of War Handbook 144 (2004) (Common Article 3 "serves as a 'minimum yardstick of protection in all conflicts, not just internal armed conflicts' " (quoting *Nicaragua* v. *United States*, 1986 I.C.J. 14, ¶ 218, 25 I.L.M. 1023)); *Prosecutor* v. *Tadić*, Case No. IT–94–1, Decision on the Defence Motion for Interlocutory Appeal on Jurisdiction, ¶ 102 (ICTY App. Chamber, Oct. 2, 1995) (stating that "the character of the conflict is irrelevant" in deciding whether Common Article 3 applies).

ing) (describing military commission as a court "specially constituted for a particular trial"). And one of the Red Cross' own treatises defines "regularly constituted court" as used in Common Article 3 to mean "established and organized in accordance with the laws and procedures already in force in a country." Int'l Comm. of Red Cross, 1 Customary International Humanitarian Law 355 (2005); see also GCIV Commentary 340 (observing that "ordinary military courts" will "be set up in accordance with the recognized principles governing the administration of justice").

The Government offers only a cursory defense of Hamdan's military commission in light of Common Article 3. See Brief for Respondents 49–50. As Justice Kennedy explains, that defense fails because "the regular military courts in our system are the courts-martial established by congressional statutes." *Post*, at 8 (opinion concurring in part). At a minimum, a military commission "can be 'regularly constituted' by the standards of our military justice system only if some practical need explains deviations from court-martial practice." *Post*, at 10. As we have explained, see Part VI–C, *supra*, no such need has been demonstrated here.

NOTES

1. *Differing Interpretations by Executive and Judicial Branches.* As *Hamdan* indicates, the Supreme Court can autonomously interpret a treaty and reject the Executive's position. For other cases in which it has done so, see, e.g., *Valentine v. Neidecker*, 299 U.S. 5 (1936); *Perkins v. Elg*, 307 U.S. 325 (1939). For discussion of judicial deference to Executive treaty interpretations, see Bederman, Revivalist Canons and Treaty Interpretation, 41 UCLA L. Rev. 953, 1015–19 (1994).

2. *Interpretation of Statute to Enable Compliance With International Obligations.* The Restatement (Third) provides in § 114: "Where fairly possible, a United States statute is to be construed so as not to conflict with international law or with an international agreement of the United States." Reporters' Note 1 to that provision states:

> *Interpretation to avoid violation of international obligation.* Chief Justice Marshall stated that "an Act of Congress ought never to be construed to violate the law of nations if any other possible construction remains * * *" Murray v. Schooner Charming Betsy, 6 U.S. (2 Cranch) 64, 118 (1804). See also Lauritzen v. Larsen, 345 U.S. 571, 578 (1953). On several occasions the Supreme Court has interpreted acts of Congress so as to avoid conflict with earlier treaty provisions. Chew Heong v. United States, 112 U.S. 536, 539–40 (1884) (later immigration law did not affect treaty right of resident Chinese alien to reenter); Weinberger v. Rossi, 456 U.S. 25, 33 (1982); *cf.* Clark v. Allen, 331 U.S. 503 (1947) (Trading with the Enemy Act not incompatible with treaty rights of German aliens to inherit realty which were succeeded to by the United States). See also Cook v. United States, 288 U.S. 102 (1933), in which the Supreme Court found that reenactment, after a series of "liquor treaties" with Great Britain, of prior statutory provisions for boarding vessels did not reflect a purpose of Congress to supersede the effect of the treaties as domestic

law. Construing an international agreement to avoid conflict with a statute is more difficult since the proper interpretation of a treaty is an international question as to which courts of the United States have less leeway. The disposition to seek to construe a treaty to avoid conflict with a State statute is less clear. Compare Nielsen v. Johnson, 279 U.S. 47, 52 (1929), with Guaranty Trust Co. v. United States, 304 U.S. 126, 143 (1938).

One U.S. writer has proposed a reexamination of the presumption of interpreting domestic law consistently with international obligations, on the theory that courts should apply a statute as the legislature enacted it and not as reconstructed to take account of external factors. Bradley, The *Charming Betsy* Canon and Separation of Powers: Rethinking the Interpretive Role of International Law, 86 Geo. L.J. 479 (1998). But U.S. cases continue to invoke the presumption to enable fulfillment of international obligations and to avoid attributing to Congress an intent to violate international law. See, e.g., *United States v. Bin Laden*, 92 F. Supp. 2d 189, 214 (S.D.N.Y. 2000).

The Supreme Court affirmed the continuing vitality of the proposition that Congress is presumed to legislate consistently with international law in *F. Hoffmann–La Roche Ltd. v. Empagran*, 542 U.S. 155 (2004) (excerpted in Chapter 11 at p. 777 note 3), which involved interpretation of an antitrust statute in relation to foreign markets. Recalling that the Court ordinarily construes ambiguous statutes to avoid unreasonable interference with the legitimate interests of other sovereigns and citing *Charming Betsy* and its progeny, Justice Breyer's majority opinion stated that "[t]his rule of construction reflects principles of customary international law—law that (we must assume) Congress ordinarily seeks to follow." 542 U.S. at 164.

3. *Senate's Understanding.* The Senate may express its understanding of a treaty provision that is arguably ambiguous. If the Senate indicates its interpretation of such a provision, the President must honor it: the treaty as so understood is the treaty to which the Senate consents. See *Rainbow Navigation, Inc. v. Department of the Navy*, 699 F.Supp. 339, 343–44 (D.D.C. 1988), rev'd on other grounds, 911 F.2d 797 (D.C. Cir. 1990) ("Any other rule would undermine the authority of the Senate under Article 2 section 2 of the Constitution to concur or to fail to concur in treaties made by the Chief Executive."); *United States v. Stuart*, 489 U.S. 353, 374 (1989) (Scalia, J., concurring) ("Of course the Senate has unquestioned power to enforce its understanding of treaties."). See also ABM Treaty and the Constitution: Joint Hearings Before the Senate Comm. on Foreign Relations and Comm. on the Judiciary, 100th Cong. (1987); Review of ABM Treaty Interpretation Dispute and SDI: Hearing Before the Subcomm. on Arms Control, Int'l Security and Science of the House Comm. on Foreign Relations, 100th Cong. 1st Sess. (1987).

In 1985, controversy erupted when the Reagan Administration sought to give to the Anti–Ballistic Missile (ABM) Treaty an interpretation that was contrary to the Senate's understanding when it gave consent. As a result, when the Intermediate–Range Missiles (INF) Treaty came up for advice and consent in 1988, the Senate attached a condition declaring that "the United States shall interpret the Treaty in accordance with the common understanding of the Treaty shared by the President and the Senate at the time the Senate gave its advice and consent to ratification." See 134 Cong. Rec. S7277–01 (1988). See also Garthoff, Policy Versus the Law: The Reinterpretation of the ABM Treaty (1987); Kennedy, Treaty Interpretation by the Executive Branch: The ABM Treaty and "Star Wars" Testing and Development, 80 A.J.I.L. 854 (1986); Henkin, Constitutionalism, Democracy and Foreign Affairs 51–57 (1990); Glennon, Interpreting "Interpretation:" The President, the Senate, and When Treaty Interpretation Becomes Treaty Making," 20 U.C. Davis L. Rev. 913 (1987).

4. *Legislative History.* Over sharp disagreement by Justice Scalia, the Supreme Court has looked to Senate pre-ratification materials for guidance in the interpretation of treaties. See *United States v. Stuart*, 489 U.S. 353 (1989). See also Vagts, Senate Materials and Treaty Interpretation: Some Research Hints for the Supreme Court, 83 A.J.I.L. 546 (1989); Bederman, *Medellín*'s New Paradigm for Treaty Interpretation, 102 A.J.I.L. 529 (2008).

5. *Interpretations in Foreign Courts.* Other national legal systems generally also accept the principle that, where fairly possible, domestic law should be interpreted to avoid inconsistency with international obligations. See Sorensen, Report Concerning Obligations of a State Party to a Treaty, in Human Rights in National and International Law 13 (Robertson ed. 1968); see also references from various jurisdictions collected in Benvenisti, Exit and Voice in the Age of Globalization, 98 Mich. L. Rev. 167, 191 n. 105 (1999).

6. *From the Outside Looking In.* In a claim brought by the European Community against the United States, a dispute settlement panel of the World Trade Organization referred with favor to the *Charming Betsy* presumption and accepted the U.S. submission that U.S. authorities were required to exercise their administrative discretion in conformity with obligations under the W.T.O. agreements. By virtue of this principle of U.S. domestic law, the panel was able to find that the complaining party had not carried the burden of proving a U.S. violation of international obligations. See *United States—Sections 301–310 of the Trade Act of 1974*, WTO Doc. WT/DS152/R (Dec. 22, 1999), paras. 7.108–7.109 and n. 681.

F. SUSPENSION OR TERMINATION OF TREATIES

HENKIN, FOREIGN AFFAIRS AND THE U.S. CONSTITUTION

211–14 (2d ed. 1996) (footnotes omitted)

The United States sometimes has the right to terminate a treaty by its own terms, at will or at some prescribed time after giving notice of its intention to do so. The international law of treaties permits termination for fraud or coercion in making the treaty or for important breach by the other party; a party may lawfully refuse to carry out its obligation because of a fundamental change in circumstances. International law also recognizes the power—though not the right—of a state party to break a treaty and pay damages or abide other international consequences.

No doubt, the federal government has the constitutional power to terminate treaties on behalf of the United States in all these ways and circumstances: neither the declaration in the Supremacy Clause that treaties are law of the land, nor anything else in the Constitution, denies the United States these powers which countries generally have under international law. But the Constitution tells us only who can make treaties for the United States; it does not say who can unmake them.

At various times, the power to terminate treaties has been claimed for the President, for the President-and-Senate, for President-and-Congress, for Congress. Presidents have claimed authority, presumably under their foreign affairs power, to act for the United States to terminate treaties, whether in accordance with their terms, or in accordance with, or even in violation of, international law. Franklin Roosevelt, for example, denounced an extradition treaty with Greece in 1933 because Greece had refused to extradite the celebrated Mr. Insull; in 1939 he denounced the Treaty of Commerce, Friendship and Navigation with Japan. In 1979, President Carter exercised the right which the United States had reserved to terminate the Defense Treaty with the Republic of China after a period of notice.

In principle, one might argue, if the Framers required the President to obtain the Senate's consent for making a treaty, its consent ought to be required also for terminating it; and there is eminent (if aging) dictum to support that view. But perhaps the Framers were concerned only to check the President in "entangling" the United States; "disentangling" is less risky and may have to be done quickly, and is often done piecemeal, or *ad hoc,* by various means and acts. In any event, since the President acts for the United States internationally he can effectively terminate a treaty; the Senate has not established its authority to join or veto him; it has, however, claimed the right to reserve a voice in the termination of a particular treaty as a condition of its consent.

Congress, we have seen, has some power effectively to breach a treaty. Congress is probably required (morally, constitutionally) to pass legislation necessary and proper to implement treaty obligations, but it could refuse to do so, put the United States in default, perhaps compel the President to terminate the treaty or induce the other party to do so; often Congress can achieve these ends too at a later time, by enacting legislation inconsistent with treaty obligations. Congress can also declare war and terminate or suspend treaty relations with the other belligerent.

In earlier times, Congress purported also to denounce or abrogate treaties for the United States or to direct the President to do so. Those instances, no doubt, reflected the early but recurrent claims of Congress that it has general powers to make foreign policy, supported by arguments that the maintenance or termination of treaties is intimately related to war or peace for which Congress has primary responsibility. But Congressional resolutions have no effect internationally unless the President adopts and communicates them; some Presidents have chosen to comply with Congressional wishes, but others have disregarded them.

* * *

If issues as to who has power to terminate treaties arise again, it seems unlikely that Congress will succeed in establishing a right to terminate a treaty (or to share in the decision to terminate). At the end of the twentieth century, it is apparently accepted that the President has authority under the Constitution to denounce or otherwise terminate a treaty, whether such action on behalf of the United States is permissible under international law or would put the United States in violation. With termination by the President, the treaty no longer exists in international law and ceases to be law in the United States.

The power to terminate a treaty is a political power: courts do not terminate treaties, but they may interpret political acts or even political silences to determine whether they implied or intended termination. Courts do not sit in judgment on the political branches to prevent them from terminating or breaching a treaty. Where fairly possible, the courts will interpret actions of the President or of Congress to render them consistent with the international obligations of the United States, but both President and Congress can exercise their respective constitutional powers regardless of treaty obligations, and the courts will give effect to acts of the political branches within their constitutional powers even if they violate treaty obligations or other international law. If there is a breach of a treaty by the other party, it is the President, not the courts, who will decide whether the United States will denounce the treaty, consider itself liberated from its obligations, or seek other relief, or none at all.

NOTES

1. *Termination of Taiwan Treaty.* In 1979, certain U.S. Senators and other members of Congress challenged the authority of the President to terminate the Mutual Defense Treaty of 1954 with the Republic of China (Taiwan). The District Court held that the power to terminate the treaty was shared between the Congress and the President, but the Court of Appeals, *en banc,* reversed, four judges holding that the President had authority to terminate the treaty in question on his own authority. The Supreme Court vacated the judgment with instructions to dismiss, four of the Justices concluding that the case presented a political question. (See p. 689 note 5 above.) Only one justice, dissenting, reached the merits and upheld the power of the President to terminate the treaty in this case as incidental to his power to recognize governments. *Goldwater v. Carter* (D.D.C. 1979) (Memorandum–Order), reprinted in 125 Cong. Rec. S7050 (daily ed. June 6, 1979), altered and amended, 481 F.Supp. 949 (D.D.C. 1979) (granting injunctive and declaratory relief), rev'd, 617 F.2d 697 (D.C. Cir.), vacated and remanded with instructions to dismiss, 444 U.S. 996 (1979).

2. *Senatorial Conditions on Termination.* The Restatement (Third) § 339, Comment *a* states: "If the United States Senate, in giving consent to a treaty, declares that it does so on condition that the President shall not terminate the treaty without the consent of the Congress or of the Senate, or that he shall do so only in accordance with some other procedure, that

condition presumably would be binding on the President if he proceeded to make the treaty."

3. *Termination in Accordance With Terms of Treaty or Otherwise.* President Carter's termination of the Taiwan mutual defense treaty was carried out in accordance with the provisions of the treaty allowing for such action on one year's notice. In 2002, President George W. Bush gave notice of termination of the Anti–Ballistic Missile Treaty with the former Soviet Union in accordance with its terms. In 2005, Secretary of State Condoleezza Rice gave notice of U.S. withdrawal from the Optional Protocol to the Vienna Convention on Consular Relations which had provided the basis for I.C.J. jurisdiction in the matter considered in *Medellín v. Texas*, p. 699; the Protocol had no termination clause as such. Are these Executive Branch actions of equal constitutional propriety?

4. *Termination for Breach of Agreement.* In *Charlton v. Kelly*, 229 U.S. 447 (1913), petitioner brought a writ of habeas corpus to prevent his extradition as a fugitive from justice in Italy. He argued, *inter alia,* that as a U.S. citizen he was not extraditable under the treaty since Italy had refused to extradite Italian nationals to the United States. On appeal from dismissal of the petition, the Supreme Court affirmed:

4. We come now to the contention that by the refusal of Italy to deliver up fugitives of Italian nationality, the treaty has thereby ceased to be of obligation on the United States. The attitude of Italy is indicated by its Penal Code of 1900 which forbids the extradition of citizens, and by the denial in two or more instances to recognize this obligation of the treaty as extending to its citizens.

* * * If the attitude of Italy was, as contended, a violation of the obligation of the treaty, which, in international law, would have justified the United States in denouncing the treaty as no longer obligatory, it did not automatically have that effect. If the United States elected not to declare its abrogation, or come to a rupture, the treaty would remain in force. It was only voidable, not void; and if the United States should prefer, it might waive any breach which in its judgment had occurred and conform to its own obligation as if there had been no such breach. * * *

That the political branch of the Government recognizes the treaty obligation as still existing is evidenced by its action in this case. In the memorandum giving the reasons of the Department of State for determining to surrender the appellant, after stating the difference between the two governments as to the interpretation of this clause of the treaty, Mr. Secretary Knox said:

"The question is now for the first time presented as to whether or not the United States is under obligation under treaty to surrender to Italy for trial and punishment citizens of the United States fugitive from the justice of Italy, notwithstanding the interpretation placed upon the treaty by Italy with reference to Italian subjects. In this connection it should be observed that the United States, although, as stated above, consistently contending that the Italian interpretation was not the proper one, has not treated the Italian practice as a breach of the treaty obligation necessarily requiring abrogation, has not abrogated the treaty or taken any step looking thereto, and has, on the contrary, constantly regarded the treaty as in full force and effect and has answered the obligations imposed thereby and has invoked the rights therein granted. It should, moreover, be observed that even though the action of the Italian Government be regarded as a breach of the treaty, the treaty is binding until abrogated, and therefore the treaty not having been abrogated, its provisions are operative against us.

"The question would, therefore, appear to reduce itself to one of interpretation of the meaning of the treaty, the Government of the United States being now for the first time called upon to declare whether it regards the treaty as obliging it to surrender its citizens to Italy, notwithstanding Italy has not and insists it can not surrender its citizens to us. It should be observed, in the first place, that we have always insisted not only with reference to the Italian extradition treaty, but with reference to the other extradition treaties similarly phrased that the word 'persons' includes citizens. We are, therefore, committed to that interpretation. The fact that we have for reasons already given ceased generally to make requisition upon the Government of Italy for the surrender of Italian subjects under the treaty, would not require of necessity that we should, as a matter of logic or law, regard ourselves as free from the obligation of surrendering our citizens, we laboring under no such legal inhibition regarding surrender as operates against the government of Italy. Therefore, since extradition treaties need not be reciprocal, even in the matter of the surrendering of citizens, it would seem entirely sound to consider ourselves as bound to surrender our citizens to Italy even though Italy should not, by reason of the provisions of her municipal law be able to surrender its citizens to us."

The executive department having thus elected to waive any right to free itself from the obligation to deliver up its own citizens, it is the plain duty of this court to recognize the obligation to surrender the appellant as one imposed by the treaty as the supreme law of the land and as affording authority for the warrant of extradition.

Judgment affirmed.

On the right of a state to terminate a treaty because of a material breach by the other party, see Chapter 3, Section 6.C, p. 207.

SECTION 4.   OTHER INTERNATIONAL AGREEMENTS IN U.S. LAW

RESTATEMENT OF THE LAW (THIRD) THE FOREIGN RELATIONS LAW OF THE UNITED STATES § 303 (1987)

§ 303.   Authority to Make International Agreements: Law of the United States

* * *

(2) The President, with the authorization or approval of Congress, may make an international agreement dealing with any matter that falls within the powers of Congress and of the President under the Constitution.

* * *

(4) The President, on his own authority, may make an international agreement dealing with any matter that falls within his independent powers under the Constitution.

A. CONGRESSIONAL–EXECUTIVE AGREEMENTS

HENKIN, FOREIGN AFFAIRS AND THE U.S. CONSTITUTION

215–18 (1996) (footnotes omitted)

Since our national beginnings Presidents have made some 1600 treaties with the consent of the Senate; they have made many thousands of other international agreements without seeking Senate consent. Some were "Congressional–Executive agreements", made by the President as authorized in advance or approved afterwards by joint resolution of Congress. Many were made by the President on his own constitutional authority ("sole executive agreements").

The Constitution does not expressly confer authority to make international agreements other than treaties, but such agreements, varying widely in formality and in importance, have been common from our early history. The authority to make such agreements and their permissible scope, and their status as law, continue to be debated. Where do the President and Congress find constitutional authority to join to make international agreements? Can the President, by authority of Congress (acting by majority vote of both houses), conclude as a Congressional–Executive agreement any international agreement he might have made by treaty with the consent of two-thirds of the Senate? Where does the President find constitutional power to make any agreements on his own authority? How does one distinguish an agreement which can be made by the President alone from one requiring Senate consent or the approval of both houses of Congress? * * * Do [agreements other than treaties] have the same quality as law of the land, the same supremacy to state law, the same equality with acts of Congress?

* * *

Agreements made by joint authority of the President and Congress have come about in different ways. Congress has authorized the President to negotiate and conclude international agreements on particular subjects—on postal relations; foreign trade; lend-lease (to allies during the Second World War); foreign assistance; nuclear reactors. During the years following the Second World War, Congress authorized the President to conclude particular agreements already negotiated, as in the case of the

Headquarters Agreement with the United Nations, and various multilater al agreements establishing international organizations, e.g., the International Bank for Reconstruction and Development ("the World Bank"), and the International Monetary Fund. In some instances Congress has approved Presidential agreements already made, by adopting implementing legislation or by appropriating funds to carry out the obligations assumed by the United States.

Constitutional doctrine to justify Congressional–Executive agreements is not clear or agreed. The Constitution expressly prescribes the treaty procedure, and nowhere suggests that another method of making international agreements is available * * *.

Neither Congresses, nor Presidents, nor courts, have been seriously troubled by these conceptual difficulties and differences. Whatever their theoretical merits, it is now widely accepted that the Congressional–Executive agreement is available for wide use, even general use, and is a complete alternative to a treaty: the President can seek approval of any agreement by joint resolution of both houses of Congress rather than by two-thirds of the Senate. Like a treaty, such an agreement is the law of the land, superseding inconsistent state laws, as well as inconsistent provisions in earlier treaties, in other international agreements, or in acts of Congress.

The Congressional–Executive agreement has had strong appeal. By permitting approval of an agreement by simple majority of both houses, it eliminates the veto by one-third-plus-one of the Senators present which in the past had effectively buried important treaties. It gives an equal role to the House of Representatives which has long resented the "undemocratic" anachronism that excludes it from the treaty-making process. Especially since so many treaties require legislative implementation (if only by appropriation of funds), the Congressional–Executive agreement assures cooperation by both houses, virtually eliminating the danger that the House of Representatives might later resist enacting the implementing legislation or appropriating funds. The Congressional–Executive agreement also simplifies the parliamentary process: a treaty goes to the Senate for consent and, often, to the Senate again and to the House for implementation; a Congressional–Executive agreement goes to both Houses in the first instance, and "consent" and implementation can be achieved in a single action. The Congressional–Executive agreement also eliminates issues about self-executing and non-self-executing agreements, and about the consequences of inconsistency between international agreements and statutes: all such agreements are "executed" by Congress, every agreement has Congressional sanction, and clearly the joint resolution approving it can repeal any inconsistent statutes.

[T]he Congressional–Executive agreement has not effectively replaced the treaty. * * * Perhaps the Executive has not pressed this alternative method of making international agreements because the Senate has proved sufficiently responsible and "internationalist" (often more so than the House has been in related contexts); and there have appeared no important agreements which could command a majority but not two-thirds of the Senate and which the President was willing to fight for through both houses. But the constitutionality of the Congressional–Executive agreement seems established, it is used regularly at least for trade and postal agreements, and remains available to Presidents for wide, even general use should the treaty process again prove difficult.

NOTES

1. *Trends in Resort to Congressional–Executive Agreements.* The legislative branch has frequently recognized congressional-executive agreements as alternatives to treaties. After the First World War, a House Committee Report asserted the propriety of adherence to the World Court by Congressional Resolution instead of treaty, citing precedents. H.R. Rep. No. 1569 (1925). See also the joint resolution authorizing conclusion of the Headquarters Agreement with the United Nations, June 26, 1947, ch. 482, 61 Stat. 756 (1947) (text of agreement included in resolution); U.N.R.R.A. Act of March 28, 1944, ch. 135, 58 Stat. 122; Bretton Woods Agreement Act (providing for participation in the International Monetary Fund and the International Bank for Reconstruction and Development), June 31, 1945, ch. 339, 59 Stat. 512 (1945); joint resolutions providing for membership and participation in the International Refugee Organization, July 1, 1947, ch. 185, 61 Stat. 214 (1947); F.A.O., June 31, 1945, ch. 342, 59 Stat. 529 (1945); U.N.E.S.C.O., June 30, 1946, ch. 700, 60 Stat. 712 (1946); W.H.O., June 14, 1948, ch. 469, 62 Stat. 441 (1948). Earlier, Congress had approved United States adherence to that part of the Versailles Treaty which established the International Labor Office, June 19, 1934, ch. 676, 48 Stat. 1182, 1183 (1934).

The U.N. Charter was approved as a treaty, but implementation was left largely to congressional-executive cooperation. See the United Nations Participation Act of 1945, ch. 583, 59 Stat. 619 (1945), as amended, 22 U.S.C.A. §§ 287–287*l*(1990); even "Article 43 agreements" to put forces at the disposal of the Security Council were to be approved by Congress, not consented to by the Senate only. See § 6, 59 Stat. 621, 22 U.S.C.A. 287d. See Chapter 15, p. 1222 *infra* on Article 43 agreements.

When the Executive Branch decided to seek approval of the U.N. Headquarters Agreement by joint resolution, it provided concerned foreign governments with an opinion of the Attorney General assuring them that the congressional-executive agreement would be the equivalent of a treaty and supreme law of the land. 40 Op. Att'y Gen. 469 (1946). While his opinion purported to speak only for the agreement in question, the arguments and authorities cited would seem to apply as well to any agreement.

The courts have approved congressional-executive agreements in a few cases involving matters within the delegated powers of Congress. In 1882 the Supreme Court held that postal conventions have equal status with treaties as part of the law of the land. *Von Cotzhausen v. Nazro*, 107 U.S. 215 (1882). See comments, S. Doc. No. 244, Sen. Misc. Doc., 78th Cong. (1944); 19 Op. Att'y Gen. 513 (1882). See also *B. Altman & Co. v. United States*, 224 U.S. 583

(1912), where the Supreme Court considered a congressional-executive agreement to be a "treaty" within the meaning of a federal statute.

For an early debate over the propriety and scope of congressional-executive and sole executive agreements, see Borchard, Shall the Executive Agreement Replace the Treaty?, 53 Yale L.J. 644 (1944); McDougal & Lans, Treaties and Congressional–Executive or Presidential Agreements: Interchangeable Instruments of National Policy, 54 Yale L.J. 181, 534 (1945); Borchard, Treaties and Executive Agreements—A Reply, id. at 616. The debate has been resolved in their favor. See Restatement (Third) § 303, Comment *e.* For discussion, see Margolis, Executive Agreements and Presidential Power in Foreign Policy (1986). For a revival of the debate in the 1990s, see Note 4 below.

In recent years congressional-executive agreements have been commonly used to establish U.S. military bases in other states, and to accelerate approval of international trade agreements. In 1974 Congress enacted the Trade Act, Pub. L. 93–618, 88 Stat. 1978, 1982, 2001, 19 U.S.C.A. §§ 2101, 2111–2112, 2191, which provided for a "fast track" procedure for congressional approval of trade agreements negotiated by the Executive Branch. The "fast track" seeks to promote executive-congressional cooperation to ensure that trade agreements negotiated by the President will be implemented by Congress with appropriate legislation. This increased cooperation includes notice to Congress of an intention to conclude a trade agreement, and consultation between Executive and Congress on implementing legislation. See Koh, The Fast Track and United States Trade Policy, 18 Brooklyn J. Int'l L. 143 (1992); Holmer & Bello, U.S. Trade and Policy Series No. 20—The Fast Track Debate: A Prescription for Pragmatism, 26 Int'l Law. 183 (1992). Statutory authority for "fast track" trade agreements lapsed in 1994 and was renewed in the Bipartisan Trade Promotion Authority Act of 2002, codified at 19 U.S.C. §§ 3801–3813.

2. *Comparing the Democratic Attributes of Modes of Agreement.* It has been suggested that the congressional-executive agreement might be more consistent with principles of democracy and representative government, but the U.S. Senate is not likely to agree to abandon the treaty process in which it has a special role under the Constitution. See Henkin, Constitutionalism, Democracy and Foreign Affairs 58–62 (1990).

The control of Congress over congressional–executive agreements is at least as strong as that of the Senate over treaties. In 1962, Congress required the inclusion of members of prescribed congressional committees on delegations for trade agreement negotiations. See Trade Expansion Act of 1962, Pub. L. No. 87–794, § 243, 76 Stat. 878, 19 U.S.C.A. § 1873 (1970). In approving agreements by joint resolution Congress has sometimes entered conditions or reservations; see, e.g., the resolution approving U.S. adherence to the International Refugee Organization, ch. 185, 61 Stat. 214 (1947); also the resolution authorizing the U.N. Headquarters Agreement, ch. 482, 61 Stat. 756, 758, 767–68 (1947), Note 1 above.

3. *Termination of Congressional–Executive Agreements.* Who has the power to terminate a congressional-executive agreement is unresolved, but the President's authority seems no weaker than in regard to treaties. In some

cases Congress purported to reserve for itself an equal right to annul authorized arrangements independently of the President. See, e.g., The Postal Service Act of 1960, Pub. L. No. 86–682, § 6103, 74 Stat. 688. The Postal Reorganization Act of 1970 does not contain such a provision. Pub. L. No. 91375, ch. 50, § 5002, 84 Stat. 719, 766, 39 U.S.C.A. § 5002 (1970).

4. *NAFTA and WTO.* In the 1990s, renewed attention was focused on congressional-executive agreements by virtue of their use to conclude the North American Free Trade Agreement (NAFTA) and agreements on the World Trade Organization. Some constitutional scholars, notably Professor Tribe, expressed doubts about the constitutional propriety of undertaking significant obligations in a manner other than the formal Article II treaty, which provides special safeguards for state interests through the requirement for two-thirds approval in the Senate. Professors Ackerman and Golove, on the other hand, explained the evolution of twentieth-century practice in favor of agreements other than Article II treaties: they found that alternative forms of making international agreements had achieved full constitutional equivalence with treaties and were justifiable in terms of constitutional and democratic theory. Compare Ackerman & Golove, Is NAFTA Constitutional?, 108 Harv. L. Rev. 801 (1995), with Tribe, Taking Text and Structure Seriously, 108 Harv. L. Rev. 1221 (1995). For continuation of the debate, see Golove, Treaty–Making and the Nation: The Historical Foundations of the Nationalist Conception of the Treaty Power, 98 Mich. L. Rev. 1075 (2000) and Tribe's rejoinder in his American Constitutional Law 653, n.47 (3d ed. 2000).

5. *Agreements Pursuant to Treaty.* The President has also concluded international agreements based on treaties that appear to envisage follow-on agreements. Henkin has observed: "Presidents have made numerous international agreements contemplated by a treaty, or which they considered appropriate for implementing treaty obligations, and no one seems to have questioned their authority to make them. Perhaps it is assumed that Senate consent to the original treaty implies consent to supplementary agreements; perhaps by such agreements the President takes care that the treaty is faithfully executed." Henkin, Foreign Affairs and the U.S. Constitution 219 (2d ed. 1996). Does the Supreme Court's decision in *Medellín v. Texas* (p. 699) cast doubt on this assumption?

6. *Notification to Congress.* The Case Act of 1972 requires the President to transmit to Congress all international agreements other than treaties within sixty days after their conclusion. If the President deems public disclosure of the agreement prejudicial to national security, he shall transmit it instead to the foreign affairs committees of both houses of Congress under injunction of secrecy to be removed only upon due notice from the President. See 1 U.S.C.A. § 112b.

B.   SOLE EXECUTIVE AGREEMENTS

UNITED STATES v. BELMONT

Supreme Court of the United States, 1937
301 U.S. 324

MR. JUSTICE SUTHERLAND delivered the opinion of the Court.

This is an action at law brought by petitioner against respondents in a federal district court to recover a sum of money deposited by a Russian corporation (Petrograd Metal Works) with August Belmont, a private banker doing business in New York City under the name of August Belmont & Co.

* * * In 1918, the Soviet Government duly enacted a decree by which it dissolved, terminated and liquidated the corporation (together with others), and nationalized and appropriated all of its property and assets of every kind and wherever situated, including the deposit account with Belmont. As a result, the deposit became the property of the Soviet Government, and so remained until November 16, 1933, at which time the Soviet Government released and assigned to petitioner all amounts due to that government from American nationals, including the deposit account of the corporation with Belmont. Respondents failed and refused to pay the amount upon demand duly made by petitioner.

The assignment was effected by an exchange of diplomatic correspondence between the Soviet Government and the United States. The purpose was to bring about a final settlement of the claims and counterclaims between the Soviet Government and the United States; and it was agreed that the Soviet Government would take no steps to enforce claims against American nationals; but all such claims were released and assigned to the United States, with the understanding that the Soviet Government was to be duly notified of all amounts realized by the United States from such release and assignment. The assignment and requirement for notice are parts of the larger plan to bring about a settlement of the rival claims of the high contracting parties. The continuing and definite interest of the Soviet Government in the collection of assigned claims is evident; and the case, therefore, presents a question of public concern, the determination of which well might involve the good faith of the United States in the eyes of a foreign government. The court below held that the assignment thus effected embraced the claim here in question; and with that we agree.

That court, however, took the view that the situs of the bank deposit was within the State of New York; that in no sense could it be regarded as an intangible property right within Soviet territory; and that the nationalization decree, if enforced, would put into effect an act of confiscation. And it held that a judgment for the United States could not be had, because, in view of that result, it would be contrary to the controlling public policy of the State of New York. * * *

First. We do not pause to inquire whether in fact there was any policy of the State of New York to be infringed, since we are of opinion that no state policy can prevail against the international compact here involved. * * *

We take judicial notice of the fact that coincident with the assignment set forth in the complaint, the President recognized the Soviet Government, and normal diplomatic relations were established between that government and the Government of the United States, followed by an exchange of ambassadors. The effect of this was to validate, so far as this country is concerned, all acts of the Soviet Government here involved from the commencement of its existence. The recognition, establishment of diplomatic relations, the assignment, and agreements with respect thereto, were all parts of one transaction, resulting in an international compact between the two governments. That the negotiations, acceptance of the assignment and agreements and understandings in respect thereof were within the competence of the President may not be doubted. Governmental power over internal affairs is distributed between the national government and the several states. Governmental power over external affairs is not distributed, but is vested exclusively in the national government. And in respect of what was done here, the Executive had authority to speak as the sole organ of that government. The assignment and the agreements in connection therewith did not, as in the case of treaties, as that term is used in the treaty making clause of the Constitution (Art. II, § 2), require the advice and consent of the Senate.

A treaty signifies "a compact made between two or more independent nations with a view to the public welfare." *B. Altman & Co. v. United States*, 224 U.S. 583, 600. But an international compact, as this was, is not always a treaty which requires the participation of the Senate. There are many such compacts, of which a protocol, a modus vivendi, a postal convention, and agreements like that now under consideration are illustrations. * * *

* * * And while this rule in respect of treaties is established by the express language of cl. 2, Art. VI, of the Constitution, the same rule would result in the case of all international compacts and agreements from the very fact that complete power over international affairs is in the national government and is not and cannot be subject to any curtailment or interference on the part of the several states. Compare *United States v. Curtiss–Wright Export Corp.*, 299 U.S. 304, 316 et seq. In respect of all international negotiations and compacts, and in respect of our foreign relations generally, state lines disappear. As to such purposes the State of New York does not exist. Within the field of its powers, whatever the United States rightfully undertakes, it necessarily has warrant to consummate. And when judicial authority is invoked in aid of such consummation, state constitutions, state laws, and state policies are irrelevant to the inquiry and decision. It is inconceivable that any of them can be interposed as an obstacle to the effective operation of a federal constitutional power. Cf. *Missouri v. Holland*, 252 U.S. 416; *Asakura v. Seattle*, 265 U.S. 332, 341. * * *

Judgment reversed.

HENKIN, FOREIGN AFFAIRS AND
THE U.S. CONSTITUTION

221–22, 225–26 (2d ed. 1996) (footnotes omitted)

There have indeed been suggestions, claiming support in *Belmont* [p. 732 above], that the President is constitutionally free to make any agreement on any matter involving our relations with another country, but that, for prudential reasons—especially if he will later require Congressional implementation—he will often seek Senate consent (or approval by both houses). As a matter of constitutional construction, however, that view is unacceptable, for it would wholly remove the "check" of Senate consent which the Framers struggled and compromised to write into the Constitution. One is compelled to conclude that there are agreements which the President can make on his sole authority and others which he can make only with the consent of the Senate (or of both houses), but neither Justice Sutherland nor any one else has told us which are which.* * *

NOTES

1. *Agreements Incidental to Recognition.* Henkin writes:

Belmont involved an agreement incidental to recognition of the Soviet Union, and Sutherland's opinion gave some emphasis to that fact. Recognition of a foreign government is indisputably the President's sole responsibility, and for many it is an 'enumerated' power implied in the President's express powers to appoint and receive Ambassadors. *Belmont,* then, might hold only that the President's specific and exclusive powers (principally his power to recognize governments and his authority as Commander in Chief) support agreements on his sole authority. * * * The whole conduct of our foreign relations, we have seen, is the President's, and that authority, too, has been claimed to be expressly 'enumerated' in the clause vesting the 'Executive Power'. Sutherland, in fact, seemed to find authority for the Litvinov Agreement not in the President's exclusive control of recognition policy but in his authority as 'sole organ', his 'foreign affairs power' which supports not only recognition but much if not most other foreign policy.

Henkin, Foreign Affairs and the U.S. Constitution 220–21 (2d ed. 1996).

2. *Claims Settlement with Soviet Union.* In *United States v. Pink*, 315 U.S. 203 (1942), the United States, as assignee, sought to recover the assets in New York of a branch of a Russian corporation which had been nationalized by the Soviet Union. The New York courts held that since, under previously enunciated New York law, the nationalization could not be given extraterritorial effect, the United States as assignee stood no better than did the Russian government and was unable to collect. In reversing the state court, the Supreme Court said in part, 315 U.S. at 222, 224–25, 228–30:

* * * [T]he *Belmont* case is determinative of the present controversy.

* * * [A]s we have seen, the Russian decree in question was intended to have an extraterritorial effect and to embrace funds of the kind which are here involved. Nor can there be any serious doubt that claims of the kind here in question were included in the Litvinov Assignment. It is broad and inclusive. It should be interpreted consonantly with the purpose of the compact to eliminate all possible sources of friction between these two great nations. * * * Strict construction would run counter to that national policy. For, as we shall see, the existence of unpaid claims against Russia and its nationals, which were held in this country, and which the Litvinov Assignment was intended to secure, had long been one impediment to resumption of friendly relations between these two great powers.

* * *

If the priority had been accorded American claims [over foreign claims to the assets] by treaty with Russia, there would be no doubt as to its validity. Cf. *Santovincenzo v. Egan*, [284 U.S. 30 (1931)]. The same result obtains here. The powers of the President in the conduct of foreign relations included the power, without consent of the Senate, to determine the public policy of the United States with respect to the Russian nationalization decrees. * * * That authority is not limited to a determination of the government to be recognized. It includes the power to determine the policy which is to govern the question of recognition. Objections to the underlying policy as well as objections to recognition are to be addressed to the political department and not to the courts. * * * Power to remove such obstacles to full recognition as settlement of claims of our nationals (Levitan, Executive Agreements, 35 Ill. L.Rev. 365, 382–385) certainly is a modest implied power of the President who is the "sole organ of the federal government in the field of international relations." *United States v. Curtiss–Wright Corp.*, [299 U.S. at 320]. Effectiveness in handling the delicate problems of foreign relations requires no less. Unless such a power exists, the power of recognition might be thwarted or seriously diluted. No such obstacle can be placed in the way of rehabilitation of relations between this country and another nation, unless the historic conception of the powers and responsibilities of the President in the conduct of foreign affairs (see Moore, Treaties and Executive Agreements, 20 Pol.Sc.Q. 385, 403–417) is to be drastically revised. It was the judgment of the political department that full recognition of the Soviet Government required the settlement of all outstanding problems including the claims of our nationals. Recognition and the Litvinov Assignment were interdependent. We would usurp the executive function if we held that that decision was not final and conclusive in the courts.

"All constitutional acts of power, whether in the executive or in the judicial department, have as much legal validity and obligation as if they proceeded from the legislature, * * * " The Federalist, No. 64. A treaty is a "Law of the Land" under the supremacy clause (Art. VI, Cl. 2) of the Constitution. Such international compacts and agreements as the Litvinov Assignment have a similar dignity. *United States v. Belmont*, [301 U.S. at 331]. See Corwin, The President, Office & Powers 228–240 (1940).

3. *Claims Settlement Agreements in General.* The President has concluded numerous agreements on his own authority to settle claims between the United States and another state. In *Dames & Moore v. Regan*, 453 U.S. 654 (1981), the Supreme Court upheld the agreement with Iran arising out of the taking of United States hostages, in which the United States agreed, *inter alia,* to terminate numerous cases in the courts of the United States and to have claims resolved by a joint arbitral tribunal. The Supreme Court upheld the validity of the agreement, noting that the power of the President to resolve international claims had been exercised for almost 200 years with Congressional acquiescence. The Court quoted Judge Learned Hand in *Ozanic v. United States*, 188 F.2d 228, 231 (2d Cir.1951):

> The constitutional power of the President extends to the settlement of mutual claims between a foreign government and the United States, at least when it is an incident to the recognition of that government; and it would be unreasonable to circumscribe it to such controversies. The continued mutual amity between the nation and other powers again and again depends upon a satisfactory compromise of mutual claims; the necessary power to make such compromises has existed from the earliest times and been exercised by the foreign offices of all civilized nations.

453 U.S. at 683. The Court postponed consideration of whether the agreement constituted a "taking" requiring compensation under the Fifth Amendment.

4. *Holocaust Claims Settlement.* In *American Ins. Ass'n v. Garamendi*, 539 U.S. 396 (2003), the Supreme Court struck down certain measures of the state of California concerning its dealings with insurance companies that had not fully accounted for obligations owed to victims of the Holocaust. The California act was held to be preempted by federal policy embodied in executive agreements with Germany, Austria, and France concerning Holocaust reparations. The majority opinion by Justice Souter stated: "Generally, * * * valid executive agreements are fit to preempt state law, just as treaties are * * *." After reviewing the history of negotiation of the three settlement agreements, the Court found a consistent national position, "expressed unmistakably in the executive agreements signed by the President with Germany and Austria," governing the matter in question. The Court therefore found the state measures to be incompatible with federal policy.

SECTION 5. INTERNATIONAL LAW IN U.S. CONSTITUTIONAL INTERPRETATION

ROPER v. SIMMONS

Supreme Court of the United States, 2005
543 U.S. 551

[Christopher Simmons was convicted in Missouri of a murder committed when he was 17 years old. The Supreme Court had twice previously considered constitutional challenges to the juvenile death penalty. In *Thompson v. Oklahoma*, 487 U.S. 815 (1988), a divided Court had held the death penalty unconstitutional under the Eighth and Fourteenth Amendments when applied to persons under the age of 16 at the time of commission of the crime. For a four-justice plurality, international trends were relevant to this conclusion. Justice O'Connor concurred on different grounds, while a vigorous dissent written by Justice Scalia and joined by three other justices rejected the relevance of foreign practice or outside opinion on any question of constitutional interpretation. The next year, in *Stanford v. Kentucky*, 492 U.S. 361 (1989), when the issue was the constitutionality of the death penalty for 16– and 17–year–olds, the four dissenters in *Thompson* were joined by Justice O'Connor (again concurring on individual grounds) to uphold the death sentence for a member of this age group.

[Fifteen years later, the Missouri Supreme Court upheld Simmons' contention that a new national consensus against the juvenile death had taken hold after the *Stanford* decision. The U.S. Supreme Court sustained this conclusion. Justice Kennedy's majority opinion (joined by Justices Stevens, Souter, Ginsburg, and Breyer) refers to international practice to confirm the Court's conclusion that national developments subsequent to *Stanford* indicated the overruling of the previous decision. Justice O'Connor dissented, as did Justice Scalia, whose opinion was joined by Chief Justice Rehnquist and Justice Thomas. The aspects of these opinions addressing the relevance of international practice and opinion are excerpted here.]

JUSTICE KENNEDY delivered the opinion of the Court. * * *

* * *

IV

Our determination that the death penalty is disproportionate punishment for offenders under 18 finds confirmation in the stark reality that the United States is the only country in the world that continues to give official sanction to the juvenile death penalty. This reality does not become controlling, for the task of interpreting the Eighth Amendment remains our responsibility. Yet at least from the time of the Court's decision in *Trop* [v. *Dulles*, 356 U.S. 86 (1958)], the Court has referred to the laws of other countries and to international authorities as instructive for its interpretation of the Eighth Amendment's prohibition of "cruel and unusual punishments." 356 U.S., at 102–103 (plurality opinion) ("The civilized nations of the world are in virtual unanimity that statelessness is not to be imposed as punishment for crime"); see also *Atkins* [v. *Virginia*, 536 U.S. 304 (2002)] at 317, n. 21 (recognizing that "within the world community, the imposition of the death penalty for crimes committed by mentally retarded offenders is overwhelmingly disapproved"); *Thompson*, supra, at 830–831, and n. 31 (plurality opinion) (noting the abolition of the juvenile death penalty "by other nations that share our Anglo–American heritage, and by the leading members of the Western European community," and observing that "[w]e have previously recognized the relevance of the views of the international community in determining whether a punishment is cruel and unusual"); *Enmund* [v. *Florida*, 458 U.S. 782 (1982)], at 796797, n. 22 (observing that "the doctrine of felony murder has been abolished in England and India, severely restricted in Canada and a number of other Commonwealth countries, and is unknown in continental Europe"); *Coker* [v. *Georgia*, 433 U.S. 584 (1977)], at 596, n. 10 (plurality opinion) ("It is . . . not irrelevant here that out of 60 major nations in the world surveyed in 1965, only 3 retained the death penalty for rape where death did not ensue").

As respondent and a number of *amici* emphasize, Article 37 of the United Nations Convention on the Rights of the Child, which every country in the world has ratified save for the United States and Somalia, contains an express prohibition on capital punishment for crimes committed by juveniles under 18. United Nations Convention on the Rights of the Child, Art. 37, Nov. 20, 1989, 1577 U.N.T.S. 3, 28 I.L.M. 1448, 1468–1470 (entered into force Sept. 2, 1990); Brief for Respondent 48; Brief for European Union et al. as *Amici Curiae* 12–13; Brief for President James Earl Carter, Jr., et al. as *Amici Curiae* 9; Brief for Former U. S. Diplomats Morton Abramowitz et al. as *Amici Curiae* 7; Brief for Human Rights Committee of the Bar of England and Wales et al. as *Amici Curiae* 13–14. No ratifying country has entered a reservation to the provision prohibiting the execution of juvenile offenders. Parallel prohibitions are contained in other significant international covenants. See ICCPR, Art. 6(5), 999 U.N.T.S., at 175 (prohibiting capital punishment for anyone under 18 at the time of offense) (signed and ratified by the United States subject to a reservation regarding Article 6(5), as noted, supra); American Convention on Human Rights: Pact of San Jose, Costa Rica, Art. 4(5), Nov. 22, 1969, 1144 U.N.T.S. 146 (entered into force July 19, 1978) (same); African Charter on the Rights and Welfare of the Child, Art. 5(3), OAU Doc. CAB/LEG/24.9/49 (1990) (entered into force Nov. 29, 1999) (same).

Respondent and his *amici* have submitted, and petitioner does not contest, that only seven countries other than the United States have executed juvenile offenders since 1990: Iran, Pakistan, Saudi Arabia, Yemen, Nigeria, the Democratic Republic of Congo, and China. Since then each of these countries has either abolished capital punishment for juveniles or made public disavowal of the practice. In sum, it is fair to say that the United States now stands alone in a world that has turned its face against the juvenile death penalty.

Though the international covenants prohibiting the juvenile death penalty are of more recent date, it is instructive to note that the United Kingdom abolished the juvenile death penalty before these covenants came into being. The United Kingdom's experience bears particular relevance here in light of the historic ties between our countries and in light of the Eighth Amendment's own origins. The Amendment was modeled on a parallel provision in the English Declaration of Rights of 1689, which provided: "[E]xcessive Bail ought not to be required nor excessive Fines imposed; nor cruel and unusual Punishments inflicted." 1 W. & M., ch. 2,

§ 10, in 3 Eng. Stat. at Large 441 (1770); see also *Trop*, supra, at 100 (plurality opinion). As of now, the United Kingdom has abolished the death penalty in its entirety; but, decades before it took this step, it recognized the disproportionate nature of the juvenile death penalty; and it abolished that penalty as a separate matter. In 1930 an official committee recommended that the minimum age for execution be raised to 21. House of Commons Report from the Select Committee on Capital Punishment (1930), 193, p 44. Parliament then enacted the Children and Young Person's Act of 1933, 23 Geo. 5, ch. 12, which prevented execution of those aged 18 at the date of the sentence. And in 1948, Parliament enacted the Criminal Justice Act, 11 & 12 Geo. 6, ch. 58, prohibiting the execution of any person under 18 at the time of the offense. In the 56 years that have passed since the United Kingdom abolished the juvenile death penalty, the weight of authority against it there, and in the international community, has become well established.

It is proper that we acknowledge the overwhelming weight of international opinion against the juvenile death penalty, resting in large part on the understanding that the instability and emotional imbalance of young people may often be a factor in the crime. See Brief for Human Rights Committee of the Bar of England and Wales et al. as *Amici Curiae* 10–11. The opinion of the world community, while not controlling our outcome, does provide respected and significant confirmation for our own conclusions.

Over time, from one generation to the next, the Constitution has come to earn the high respect and even, as Madison dared to hope, the veneration of the American people. See The Federalist No. 49, p 314 (C. Rossiter ed. 1961). The document sets forth, and rests upon, innovative principles original to the American experience, such as federalism; a proven balance in political mechanisms through separation of powers; specific guarantees for the accused in criminal cases; and broad provisions to secure individual freedom and preserve human dignity. These doctrines and guarantees are central to the American experience and remain essential to our present-day self-definition and national identity. Not the least of the reasons we honor the Constitution, then, is because we know it to be our own. It does not lessen our fidelity to the Constitution or our pride in its origins to acknowledge that the express affirmation of certain fundamental rights by other nations and peoples simply underscores the centrality of those same rights within our own heritage of freedom.

The Eighth and Fourteenth Amendments forbid imposition of the death penalty on offenders who were under the age of 18 when their crimes were committed. The judgment of the Missouri Supreme Court setting aside the sentence of death imposed upon Christopher Simmons is affirmed.

It is so ordered.

NOTES

1. *Previous Juvenile Death Penalty Cases.* In *Thompson v. Oklahoma*, 487 U.S. 815 (1988), a plurality of the Court had taken account of foreign trends to abolish or restrict the juvenile death penalty and of major human rights treaties (at that time signed but not ratified by the United States), in the course of arriving at the conclusion that "it would offend civilized standards of decency to execute a person who was less than 16 years old at the time of his or her offense" (plurality op. of J.J. Stevens, Brennan, Marshall and Blackmun; Justice O'Connor concurred on a different ground). The next year, in *Stanford v. Kentucky*, 492 U.S. 361 (1989), where the issue was execution of a person who had been over 16 but under 18, Justice Scalia (who had dissented in *Thompson*) wrote an opinion (joined by Chief Justice Rehnquist and Justices White, O'Connor and Kennedy) with the following passage concerning international practice:

> We emphasize that it is *American* conceptions of decency that are dispositive, rejecting the contention of petitioners and their various *amici* * * * that the sentencing practices of other countries are relevant. While "the practices of other nations, particularly other democracies, can be relevant to determining whether a practice uniform among our people is not merely an historical accident, but rather 'so implicit in the concept of ordered liberty' that it occupies a place not merely in our mores, but, text permitting, in our Constitution as well," [citations omitted] they cannot serve to establish the first Eighth Amendment prerequisite, that the practice is accepted among our people.

Justice Scalia (joined by Chief Justice Rehnquist and Justice Thomas) registered a vigorous dissent in *Roper*, reaffirming the position maintained in 1989 in *Stanford* and strongly resisting the Court's resort to "the views of other countries and the so-called international community." Justice O'Connor also dissented because she found insufficient evidence of an established domestic consensus, but she indicated that under at least some circumstances, certain kinds of international authorities could "serve to confirm the reasonableness of a consonant and genuine American consensus."

2. *Same–Sex Relationships.* In *Lawrence v. Texas*, 539 U.S. 558 (2003), the Supreme Court referred to international authorities in deciding to overrule an earlier decision, *Bowers v. Hardwick*, 478 U.S. 186 (1986), which had upheld a state law criminalizing homosexual sodomy. According to the majority opinion in *Lawrence* (written by Justice Kennedy), the *Bowers* Court had erred in failing to take account of the fact that the European Court of Human Rights had found consensual sexual activities between same-sex partners to be protected by the right to privacy under the European Convention on Human Rights. Referring to such decisions, the *Lawrence* Court concluded that "[t]he right the petitioners seek in this case has been accepted as an integral part of human freedom in many other countries."

3. *Division of Views on the Court.* The Supreme Court remains sharply divided between Justices generally sympathetic to the uses of international authorities in constitutional interpretation (Justices Breyer, Ginsburg, Kenne-

dy, Souter, and Stevens) and those strongly opposed (Justices Scalia and Thomas, as well as Chief Justice Roberts and Justice Alito, who joined the Court after the *Lawrence* and *Roper* decisions but who asserted in their confirmation hearings that they would generally disfavor resort to international or foreign law in constitutional interpretation. Several of the Justices . have explained their viewpoints in their extrajudicial writings and speeches.

4. *Further Reading.* A large and growing body of scholarship explores the historical uses of international law to interpret the U.S. Constitution and pursues the debate over the wisdom of judicial reference to international and foreign sources in resolving disputes in this constitutional democracy. For a representative sample of perspectives, see the short pieces by Harold Koh, Roger Alford, Michael Ramsey, Gerald Neuman, and Alexander Aleinikoff in Agora: The United States Constitution and International Law, 98 A.J.I.L. 42 (2004), and the other writings referenced therein. For in-depth treatments supportive of the internationalist perspective, see, e.g., Cleveland, Our International Constitution, 31 Yale J. Int'l L. 1 (2006); Jackson, Constitutional Engagement in a Transnational Era: Interpreting Constitutions in an Expanding Universe of Law (forthcoming); Slaughter, A New World Order 65–103 (2004); see also Jackson & Tushnet, Comparative Constitutional Law 153–90 (2d ed. 2006).

For comparisons to other countries' approaches to the interactions between constitutional and international law, see the next section. For comparative consideration of uses of international and foreign law in constitutional interpretation, see Waters, Creeping Monism: The Judicial Trend Toward Interpretive Incorporation of Human Rights Treaties, 107 Colum. L. Rev. 628 (2007); Benvenisti, Reclaiming Democracy: The Strategic Uses of Foreign and International Law by National Courts, 102 A.J.I.L. 241 (2008).

SECTION 6.   INTERNATIONAL LAW IN THE NATIONAL LAW OF OTHER STATES

Each of the issues addressed in the previous Sections of this Chapter can also be explored from a comparative point of view. Every constitutional democracy—indeed, every domestic legal system—has had to resolve the various questions that inevitably arise in deciding on the priority to be accorded to diverse sources of law, the extent to which international law can give rise to judicially enforceable rights, the procedures for the different steps in the treaty process, the reconciling of conflicts among potentially conflicting rules of decision, and so forth. Most modern constitutions address these questions explicitly and with a level of detail not found in the eighteenth century U.S. Constitution. Many of them—especially those adopted soon after World War II or in successive waves of democratization in the late twentieth and early twenty-first centuries—embrace a consciously internationalist perspective, elevating compliance with international obligations to the level of constitutional rules of decision.

This Section offers only a small sample of comparisons to the U.S. approaches elaborated above. In considering these materials, please reflect on the reasons why countries would adopt more—or less—"international-law-friendly" approaches in light of their own national experiences. Please also consider the relevance of contextual factors—federal or unitary structure; parliamentary or presidential form of government; attitudes toward judicial review of legislative and executive acts; existence of a bill of rights; participation in regional integration systems—in relation to problems of international law.

CONSTITUTION OF THE REPUBLIC OF SOUTH AFRICA

Adopted May 8, 1996; Amended Oct. 11, 1996; In Force Feb. 7, 1997

Chapter 2 Bill of Rights

* * *

Section 39 Interpretation of Bill of Rights

(1) When interpreting the Bill of Rights, a court, tribunal or forum—

(a) must promote the values that underlie an open and democratic society based on human dignity, equality and freedom;

(b) must consider international law; and

(c) may consider foreign law.

* * *

Chapter 14 General Provisions

[Title 1] International Law

Section 231 International agreements

(1) The negotiating and signing of all international agreements is the responsibility of the national executive.

(2) An international agreement binds the Republic only after it has been approved by resolution in both the National Assembly and the National Council of Provinces, unless it is an agreement referred to in subsection (3).

(3) An international agreement of a technical, administrative or executive nature, or an agreement which does not require either ratification or accession, entered into by the national executive, binds the Republic without approval by the National Assembly and the National Council of Provinces, but must be tabled in the Assembly and the Council within a reasonable time.

(4) Any international agreement becomes law in the Republic when it is enacted into law by national legislation; but a self-executing provision of an agreement that has been approved by Parliament is law in the Republic unless it is inconsistent with the Constitution or an Act of Parliament.

(5) The Republic is bound by international agreements which were binding on the Republic when this Constitution took effect.

Section 232 Customary international law

Customary international law is law in the Republic unless it is inconsistent with the Constitution or an Act of Parliament.

Section 233 Application of international law

When interpreting any legislation, every court must prefer any reasonable interpretation of the legislation that is consistent with international law over any alternative interpretation that is inconsistent with international law.

NOTES

1. *Additional Provisions Invoking International Law.* In addition to the above provisions of general character, the South African Constitution makes specific reference to international law in the following sections:

Section 35(3)(1) on arrested, accused and detained persons specifies the right not to be convicted for an act or omission that was not an offense under either national or international law at the time of the act or omission;

Section 37(4)(b)(1) on states of emergency authorizes derogations from the Bill of Rights only under strictly limited conditions, including that legislation so derogating be "consistent with the Republic's obligations under international law applicable to states of emergency;"

Section 198 on governing principles for national security and the security services provides in part:

> (b) The resolve to live in peace and harmony precludes any South African citizen from participating in armed conflict, nationally or internationally, except as provided for in terms of the Constitution or national legislation.

> (c) National security must be pursued in compliance with the law, including international law.

Section 199(5) specifies that the security services "must act, and must teach and require their members to act, in accordance with the Constitution and the law, including customary international law and international agreements binding on the Republic;"

Section 200(2) states that "[t]he primary object of the defence force is to defend and protect the Republic, its territorial integrity and its people in accordance with the Constitution and the principles of international law regulating the use of force."

2. *South African Constitutional Court: Resort to International Law.* The South African Constitutional Court, with now more than a decade of experience in interpreting the Bill of Rights and other constitutional provisions, has engaged in a creative application of international sources of law in order to develop a South African jurisprudence enriched by international law. Among

the interesting instances are its attention to the comments and decisions of human rights treaty bodies as authoritative explications of internationally protected rights.

In *Government of the Republic of South Africa v. Grootboom*, 2001(1) SA 46 (CC), the Constitutional Court ruled on a claim by individuals who had been evicted from informal homes on private land that they had been rendered homeless in violation of a constitutional right of access to adequate housing. Judge Yacoob devoted four pages of reasoning under the heading of the "relevant international law and its impact," observing that according to previous case law, public international law "would include non-binding as well as binding law. They may both be used under the section as tools of interpretation."

> The relevant international law can be a guide to interpretation but the weight to be attached to any particular principle or rule of international law will vary. However, where the relevant principle of international law binds South Africa, it may be directly applicable.

The Court then analyzed the right to housing under the International Covenant on Economic, Social and Cultural Rights, with attention to the general comments issued by the United Nations Committee on Economic, Social and Cultural Rights as a guide to interpretation of both the international and the constitutional right in question. See also the opinion of Judge Mokgoro in *Jaftha v. Schoeman*, 2005 (2) SA 140 (CC), also referring to the International Covenant and the position of the U.N. Committee in elaborating the international law concept of adequate housing.

3. *Unwritten Constitutions; Unwritten Custom.* English courts have applied customary international law since before the American revolution, saying that the law of nations was "part of the law of England." See Lord Mansfield in *Triquet and Others v. Bath*, 97 Eng. Rep. 936, 938, 3 Burr. 1478, 1481 (K.B. 1764). In 1938, the Privy Council said:

> The Courts acknowledge the existence of a body of rules which nations accept amongst themselves. On any judicial issue they seek to ascertain what the relevant rule is, and, having found it, they will treat it as incorporated into the domestic law, so far as it is not inconsistent with rules enacted by statutes or finally declared by their tribunals.

Chung Chi Cheung v. The King, [1939] A.C. 160, 168 (Hong Kong) (1938). In *Mortensen v. Peters*, 8 Sess. Cas. (5th ser.) 93 (1906), the Scottish Court of Justiciary upheld the conviction of a Danish national, master of a Norwegian ship, for fishing in violation of a statute regulating fishing in a part of Moray Firth more than three miles from the nearest land. Appellant argued that the application of British law to foreign nationals in this place would be a violation of international law and that the statute must be presumed not to extend to foreign nationals outside of British territory. The Court expressed doubt whether it was contrary to international law to treat Moray Firth, a bay, as British territory; the following statement was made by Lord Dunedin:

> In this Court we have nothing to do with the question of whether the Legislature has or has not done what foreign powers may consider a usurpation in a question with them. Neither are we a tribunal sitting to

decide whether an Act of the Legislature is ultra vires as in contravention of generally acknowledged principles of international law. For us an Act of Parliament duly passed by Lords and Commons and assented to by the King, is supreme, and we are bound to give effect to its terms.

After this decision, several masters of Norwegian ships were convicted, but eventually released upon Norwegian protest. In Parliament, it was stated on behalf of the British Foreign Office that the Act, as interpreted by the court, was "in conflict with international law." 170 Parl. Deb. (4th ser.) 472 (1907). Subsequently, an Act of Parliament prohibited the landing or selling in the United Kingdom of fish caught by the forbidden methods within the areas specified. 9 Edw. VIII, c. 8 (1909). For the status of international law in British law generally, see Brownlie, Principles of Public International Law 42–47 (5th ed. 1998); Mann, Foreign Affairs in English Courts (1986). Britain's entry into the European Community has had a significant effect on its legal system.

4. *European Constitutions in Regional Context: Custom and General Principles.* Many modern constitutions provide explicitly for application of customary international law or general rules and principles of international law, which others do not. An influential example of an explicit provision is Article 25 of the Basic Law of the Federal Republic of Germany:

> The general rules of public international law shall be an integral part of federal law. They shall take precedence over the laws and shall directly create rights and duties for the inhabitants of the federal territory.

The Federal Constitutional Court of Germany has treated customary international law and the general principles recognized by civilized nations as falling under this article. By contrast, the Dutch Constitution contains no provision on the applicability and priority of customary law, but Dutch courts have regularly applied customary law under a monistic theory. For these and other examples, see generally Wildhaber & Breitenmoser, The Relationship Between Customary International Law and Municipal Law in Western European Countries, 48 ZaöRV 163, 179–204 (1988) (comparing approaches of Germany, Italy, Austria, Greece, France, Switzerland, the Netherlands, and other European countries).

5. *Treaty–Making and Implementation: The Role of Legislatures and Courts.* Constitutional systems display a wide range of variation as regards the role of national parliaments in approving the entry into force of treaty obligations; the need for legislation to implement treaties; the availability of a judicial (or other) procedure for determining the constitutionality of treaties; the extent to which courts may (or may not) apply treaties on a self-executing basis; and the priority given to treaties in relation to other sources of law, including legislation. For valuable comparative reference works, see Riesenfeld & Abbott, Parliamentary Participation in the Making and Implementation of Treaties (1994); Hollis, Comparative Approach to Treaty Law and Practice, in National Treaty Law and Practice 1, 9–50 (Hollis, Blakeslee, & Ederington eds., 2005).

6. *Federal Constitutions and Treaty Implementation.* Like the United States and South Africa, many states in the world today are organized in federal form, with wide variations in their distributions of authority between

the federal and subfederal levels. See Chapter 3, p. 132 note 1 for examples relevant to the treaty-making capacity of subfederal units. By comparison to the U.S. case of *Missouri v. Holland*, p. 680 above, it may be noted that other federations do not necessarily embrace the proposition that the federal level of government enjoys expansive authority to implement treaty obligations; rather, it may be necessary to look to the subunits to carry out treaty obligations within their spheres of domestic competence.

In *Attorney–General for Canada v. Attorney–General for Ontario*, [1937] A.C. 326, the Privy Council was asked to decide whether certain Canadian statutes, enacted in order to fulfill Canada's obligations under a number of International Labor Conventions, were constitutionally effective without the consent of the Canadian provinces to bring the law of those provinces into conformity with the provisions of the conventions. In the course of his opinion holding that the statutes were *ultra vires* of the Parliament of Canada under the British North America Act of 1867, Lord Atkin made the following general observations on the internal effect of treaties:

> * * * It will be essential to keep in mind the distinction between (1.) the formation, and (2.) the performance, of the obligations constituted by a treaty, using that word as comprising any agreement between two or more sovereign States. Within the British Empire there is a well-established rule that the making of a treaty is an executive act, while the performance of its obligations, if they entail alteration of the existing domestic law, requires legislative action. Unlike some other countries, the stipulations of a treaty duly ratified do not within the Empire, by virtue of the treaty alone, have the force of law. If the national executive, the government of the day, decide to incur the obligations of a treaty which involve alteration of law they have to run the risk of obtaining the assent of Parliament to the necessary statute or statutes. To make themselves as secure as possible they will often in such cases before final ratification seek to obtain from Parliament an expression of approval. But it has never been suggested, and it is not the law, that such an expression of approval operates as law, or that in law it precludes the assenting Parliament, or any subsequent Parliament, from refusing to give its sanction to any legislative proposals that may subsequently be brought before it. Parliament, no doubt, as the Chief Justice points out, has a constitutional control over the executive: but it cannot be disputed that the creation of the obligations undertaken in treaties and the assent to their form and quality are the function of the executive alone. Once they are created, while they bind the State as against the other contracting parties, Parliament may refuse to perform them and so leave the State in default. In a unitary State whose Legislature possesses unlimited powers the problem is simple. Parliament will either fulfil or not treaty obligations imposed upon the State by its executive. The nature of the obligations does not affect the complete authority of the Legislature to make them law if it so chooses. But in a State where the Legislature does not possess absolute authority, in a federal State where legislative authority is limited by a constitutional document, or is divided up between different Legislatures in accordance with the classes of subject-matter submitted for legislation, the problem is complex. The obligations im-

posed by treaty may have to be performed, if at all, by several Legislatures; and the executive have the task of obtaining the legislative assent not of the one Parliament to whom they may be responsible, but possibly of several Parliaments to whom they stand in no direct relation. The question is not how is the obligation formed, that is the function of the executive; but how is the obligation to be performed, and that depends upon the authority of the competent Legislature or Legislatures.

[1937] A.C. at 347–48. See the symposium on this case in 15 Can. B. Rev. 393 (1937), and see generally McNair, The Law of Treaties 81–110 (1961). On treaty implementation under the current Canadian Constitution, see International Law[:] Chiefly as Interpreted and Applied in Canada, ch. 3 B (7th ed. 2006).

If difficulties are expected in the process of implementing the provisions of an international agreement, what precautions might the executive of a federal state take in order to avoid international responsibility for defaulting on the obligations imposed by the agreement?

7. *Comparative Approaches to the Implementation of International Judgments.* In *Medellín v. Texas*, p. 699 above, the U.S. Supreme Court took note of the apparent absence of cases from other jurisdictions in which I.C.J. judgments had been given directly enforceable legal effects in domestic law. While the proposition as framed by the Court may be technically correct, it should not obscure the fact that courts in some other countries have taken a relatively "international-law-friendly" approach to implementation of treaty-based obligations reflected in the decisions of international tribunals. Putting to one side the lively interjudicial dialogue between European regional courts on the one hand and the constitutional courts of several European countries on the other (a subject of great jurisprudential interest), national judicial decisions concerning the municipal effects of international decisions display a wide spectrum of approaches. For example, the German Federal Constitutional Court has indicated that in principle, the German legal system should give effect to the I.C.J.'s interpretation of the Vienna Convention on Consular Relations embodied in the I.C.J.'s *LaGrand* and *Avena* decisions. See Gogolin, *Avena* and *Sanchez–Llamas* Come to Germany—The German Constitutional Court Upholds Rights Under the Vienna Convention on Consular Relations, 8 Germ. L.J. 261 (2004).

What do you think is the best approach for a national court to adopt in considering what effects (or deference) to give to an international decision? Should a national court consider itself as an organ or compliance with international law, or an agency for implementing national law—or both or neither? Should it matter whether the international decision in question has the status of formally binding law? To what extent should the respective forums understand themselves to be in an interactive dialogue with each other? For different approaches, see, e.g., Ahdieh, Between Dialogue and Decree: International Review of National Courts, 79 N.Y.U. L. Rev. 2029 (2004); Alford, Federal Courts, International Tribunals, and the Continuum of Deference, 43 Va. J. Int'l L. 675 (2002–03).

8. *International Law in the Municipal Systems of Other States.* For other representative references from the worldwide literature, see, e.g., *Australia—*

International Law in Australia (Ryan, ed. 1984); Byrnes & Charlesworth, Federalism and the International Legal Order: Recent Developments in Australia, 79 A.J.I.L. 622 (1985); McGinley, The Status of Treaties in Australian Municipal Law, 12 Adel. L. Rev. 367 (1990). *Canada*—International Law[:] Chiefly as Interpreted and Applied in Canada, ch. 4 (4th ed. Kindred gen. ed. 1987); Campbell, Federalism and International Relations: The Canadian Experience, 85 A.S.I.L. Proc. 125 (1991); Schwartz, The Charter and the Domestic Enforcement of International Law, 16 Man. L.J. 149 (1986). *China*—Wang, International Law in China, 221 Rec. des Cours 195 (1990—II). *Indonesia*— Hartano, The Interaction Between National Law and International Law in Indonesia, in International Law and Development (de Waart ed. 1988). *Israel*—Lapidoth, International Law Within the Israel Legal System, 24 Isr. L. Rev. 451 (1990). *Japan*—Oda, The Practice of Japan in International Law, 1961–1970 (1982); *Nigeria*—Okeke, The Theory and Practice of International Law in Nigeria (1986).

9. *International Law as a Common Language for Constitutional Courts.* There is growing evidence that courts in many countries are turning to international law as part of a common dialogue over securing shared values in constitutional democracies. On this phenomenon, see Benvenisti, Reclaiming Democracy: The Strategic Uses of Foreign and International Law by National Courts, 102 A.J.I.L. 241 (2008).

To conclude this overview of the place of international law in municipal legal orders, consider a recent case in which the European Court of Justice addressed the enforceability in the member states of the European Union of a regulation promulgated by the European Commission to give effect to a compulsory resolution adopted by the U.N. Security Council in the exercise of its Charter-based power to address the threat to international peace and security from global terrorism.

KADI v. COUNCIL AND COMMISSION
European Court of Justice (Sept. 3, 2008)
2008 E.C.R. ___

[Resolutions of the U.N. Security Council require members of the United Nations to freeze assets of individuals designated by the U.N. Sanctions Committee as being associated with the Al Qaeda network, Osama bin Laden, or the Taliban. Under Article 25 of the U.N. Charter, U.N. members "agree to accept and carry out the decisions of the Security Council in accordance with the present Charter," and by virtue of Article 103 of the Charter, obligations under the Charter prevail over obligations under any other international agreement in the event of a conflict.

[Yassin Abdullah Kadi, a resident of Saudi Arabia, and Al Barakaat International Foundation, established in Sweden, fell within the lists of designated nationals maintained by the U.N. Sanctions Committee. Their assets located within the European Community came within the terms of a regulation adopted by the Council of the European Union aimed at implementing the Security Council directives (Council Regulation (EC) No. 881/2002, May 27, 2002). Kadi and Al Barakaat, along with another individual, Ahmed Ali Yusuf, sought the annulment of this regulation through actions brought to the European Court of First Instance (CFI), which rejected their challenges and upheld the validity of the regulation. *Kadi v. Council and Commission*, Case T–315/01, 2005 ECR II 3649; *Yusuf and Al Barakaat International Foundation v. Council*, Case T–306/01, 2005 ECR II 3533, both decided Sept. 21, 2005. The Court of First Instance ruled that the European Community courts had no jurisdiction in principle to review the validity of a regulation adopted in implementation of a Security Council resolution, except for conformity to overriding rules of *jus cogens*. Kadi and Al Barakaat took appeals from this ruling to the Court of Justice of the European Communities (European Court of Justice). Several member states of the European Union either cross-appealed or urged the Court to overturn the reasoning of the CFI as regards *jus cogens*. The European Commission defended the challenged regulation on reasoning somewhat different from that embraced by the Court of First Instance.

[The excerpts that follow deal with the interrelationship between obligations arising from the U.N. Charter, general international law including *jus cogens*, the internal law of the European Union as an autonomous system, and the domestic legal systems of U.N. members who are also E.U. members.]

248. In the first part of his second ground of appeal, Mr. Kadi maintains that inasmuch as the judgment [of the CFI] in *Kadi* takes a view, first, of the relationships between the United Nations and the members of that organisation and, second, of the procedure for the application of resolutions of the Security Council, it is vitiated by errors of law as regards the interpretation of the principles of international law concerned, which gave rise to other errors of law in the assessment of the pleas in law relating to breach of certain of the applicant's specific fundamental rights.

249. That part contains five claims.

250. By his first claim, Mr. Kadi argues that [the CFI] erred in law in confusing the question of the primacy of the States' obligations under the Charter of the United Nations, enshrined in Article 103 thereof, with the related but separate question of the binding effect of decisions of the Security Council laid down in Article 25 of that Charter.

251. By his second claim, Mr. Kadi complains that [the CFI] erred in law when * * * it took as its premiss that, like obligations under treaty law, resolutions adopted by virtue of Chapter VII of the Charter of the United Nations must automatically form part of the sphere of law and competence of the members of the United Nations.

252. By the third claim, Mr. Kadi alleges that [the CFI] erred in law when it held * * * that it had no power enabling it to review the lawfulness of resolutions of the Security Council adopted by virtue of Chapter VII of the Charter of the United Nations.

253. By the fourth claim, Mr. Kadi maintains that the reasoning of [the CFI] on the subject of *jus cogens* displays considerable incoherence, in so far as, if it must prevail, the principle that resolutions of the Security Council may not be the subject of judicial review and in support of this enjoy immunity from jurisdiction would have to apply generally, and the matters covered by *jus cogens* would not then constitute an exception to that principle.

254. By the fifth claim, Mr. Kadi argues that the fact that the Security Council has not established an independent international court responsible for ruling, in law and on the facts, on actions brought against individual decisions taken by the Sanctions Committee, does not mean that the Member States have no lawful power, by adopting reasonable measures, to improve the finding of facts underlying the imposition of sanctions and the identification of the persons affected by them, or that the Member States are prohibited from creating an appropriate legal remedy by reason of the latitude they enjoy in the performance of their obligations.

[Paraphrase of further arguments made by the parties, and by the four states that intervened on appeal, is omitted.]

281. [In connection with the complaint against the CFI's conclusion that a regulation giving effect to a binding Security Council resolution could not be subject to judicial review except for compatibility with *jus cogens*] it is to be borne in mind that the Community is based on the rule of law, inasmuch as neither its Member States nor its institutions can avoid review of the conformity of their acts with the basic constitutional charter, the EC Treaty, which established a complete system of legal remedies and procedures designed to enable the Court of Justice to review the legality of acts of the institutions (Case 294/83 *Les Verts v. Parliament* [1986] ECR 1339, paragraph 23).

* * *

283. In addition, according to settled case-law, fundamental rights form an integral part of the general principles of law whose observance the Court ensures. For that purpose, the Court draws inspiration from the constitutional traditions common to the Member States and from the guidelines supplied by international instruments for the protection of human rights on which the Member States have collaborated or to which they are signatories. In that regard, the ECHR has special significance (see, inter alia, Case C–305/05 *Ordre des barreaux francophones et germanophone and Others* [2007] ECR I–5305, paragraph 29 and case-law cited).

* * *

286. In this regard it must be emphasised that, in circumstances such as those of these cases, the review of lawfulness thus to be ensured by the Community judicature applies to the Community act intended to give effect to the international agreement at issue, and not to the latter as such.

287. With more particular regard to a Community act which, like the contested regulation, is intended to give effect to a resolution adopted by the Security Council under Chapter VII of the Charter of the United Nations, it is not, therefore, for the Community judicature * * * to review the lawfulness of such a resolution adopted by an international body, even if that review were to be limited to examination of the compatibility of that resolution with *jus cogens*.

288. However, any judgment given by the Community judicature deciding that a Community measure intended to give effect to such a resolution is contrary to a higher rule of law in the Community legal order would not entail any challenge to the primacy of that resolution in international law.

* * *

[291–93. The Court recalls that the European Community must respect international law and must exercise its powers in observance of undertakings given in the context of the United Nations, including when the Community gives effect to resolutions adopted by the Security Council under Chapter VII of the U.N. Charter.]

294. In the exercise of that latter power it is necessary for the Community to attach special importance to the fact that, in accordance with Article 24 of the Charter of the United Nations, the adoption by the Security Council of resolutions under Chapter VII of the Charter constitutes the exercise of the primary responsibility with which that international body is invested for the maintenance of peace and security at the global level, a responsibility which, under Chapter VII, includes the power to determine what and who poses a threat to international peace and security and to take the measures necessary to maintain or restore them.

* * *

298. It must however be noted that the Charter of the United Nations does not impose the choice of a particular model for the implementation of resolutions adopted by the Security Council under Chapter VII of the Charter, since they are to be given effect in accordance with the procedure applicable in that respect in the domestic legal order of each Member of the United Nations. The Charter of the United Nations leaves the Members of the United Nations a free choice among the various possible models for transposition of those resolutions into their domestic legal order.

* * *

[299–304. The Court concludes that judicial review of a Community measure implementing a Security Council resolution is not excluded. It then turns to the provisions of the EC Treaty, which allow Member States to carry out their international obligations for the purpose of maintaining international peace and security, but which cannot be understood to authorize any derogation from the principles of liberty, democracy, and respect for human rights and fundamental freedoms that are enshrined in the Treaty on European Union as a foundation of the Union.]

305.   Nor can an immunity from jurisdiction for the contested regulation with regard to the review of its compatibility with fundamental rights, arising from the alleged absolute primacy of the resolutions of the Security Council to which that measure is designed to give effect, find any basis in the place that obligations under the Charter of the United Nations would occupy in the hierarchy of norms within the Community legal order if those obligations were to be classified in that hierarchy.

* * *

310.   It has however been maintained before the Court * * * that the Community judicature ought, like the European Court of Human Rights, which in several recent decisions has declined jurisdiction to review the compatibility of certain measures taken in the implementing of resolutions adopted by the Security Council under Chapter VII of the Charter of the United Nations, to refrain from reviewing the lawfulness of the contested regulation in the light of fundamental freedoms, because that regulation is also intended to give effect to such resolutions.

[311–15.   The Court distinguishes the ECHR cases declining to review certain actions of Member States taken in the context of their fulfillment of Security Council resolutions because they arose in fundamentally different circumstances. Here, the contested EC regulation cannot be considered directly attributable to the United Nations as an act of one of its subsidiary organs or an action falling under powers lawfully delegated by the Security Council.]

* * *

326.   It follows from the foregoing that the Community judicature must, in accordance with the powers conferred on it by the EC Treaty, ensure the review, in principle the full review, of the lawfulness of all Community acts in the light of the fundamental rights forming an integral part of the general principles of Community law, including review of Community measures which, like the contested regulation, are designed to give effect to the resolutions adopted by the Security Council under Chapter VII of the Charter of the United Nations.

* * *

363.   With reference to an objective of general interest as fundamental to the international community as the fight by all means, in accordance with the Charter of the United Nations, against the threats to international peace and security posed by acts of terrorism, the freezing of the funds, financial assets and other economic resources of the persons identified by the Security Council or the Sanctions Committee as being associated with Usama bin Laden, members of the Al–Qaeda organisation and the Taliban cannot per se be regarded as inappropriate or disproportionate [citations omitted].

[The Court then examines the challenged regulation for conformity to fundamental human rights and finds it deficient. Although the restrictions on appellants' right to property might, in principle, be justified, the applicable procedures must afford the person concerned a reasonable opportunity to put his case to the competent authorities. The regulation must therefore be annulled. The Court however allows a period of three months for the Community to implement a new regulation remedying the defects found in the existing scheme.]

NOTES

1. *"Dualism" in a Multilayered Structure.* Is the conceptual frame of dualism, or pluralism, suitable for understanding the relationship between U.N. Charter obligations and their implementation within the European legal order(s)?

2. *Hierarchy of Norms?* Is it possible to discern an operative hierarchy among the different types of norms mentioned in the Court's opinion—*jus cogens*, U.N. Charter obligations, European treaties, regulations promulgated by European organs, fundamental rights common to the constitutional traditions of European states, or other sources? Which sources do you think should prevail over which other sources?

CHAPTER 11

BASES OF JURISDICTION

■ ■ ■

SECTION 1. OVERVIEW OF JURISDICTION UNDER INTERNATIONAL LAW

A. INTRODUCTION

1. Three Forms of Jurisdiction

The term "jurisdiction" is commonly used to describe authority to affect legal interests. Traditionally, three forms of jurisdiction are distinguished: legislative, judicial, and executive (or enforcement) jurisdiction. Jurisdiction to create rules of general import, however, may be formulated not only by legislatures, but also by other institutions of government, such as administrative agencies, and even courts. For that reason, the Restatement (Third) prefers to use the term "prescriptive jurisdiction" instead of legislative jurisdiction. Similarly, recognizing that adjudicatory functions may be exercised not just by the judiciary, but by other governmental institutions (e.g., administrative tribunals), the Restatement prefers the term "jurisdiction to adjudicate" rather than the term judicial jurisdiction, and defines it as "the authority of a state to subject particular persons or things to its judicial process." By contrast, jurisdiction to enforce is the authority of a state "to use the resources of government to induce or compel compliance with its law." See Restatement (Third), Part IV, Introductory Note. In the materials that follow, the terms legislative, judicial, and executive jurisdiction will be used interchangeably with the terms jurisdiction to prescribe, to adjudicate, and to enforce.

2. Two Levels of Jurisdiction

Jurisdiction should be considered on at least two levels. First, the legislative, judicial or executive powers of particular institutions are established under national law. Within national law, jurisdiction is typically identified and constrained by the states' constitution and then by statutes. For example, in the United States, the legislative, judicial, and executive powers of the federal branches of government are defined first in the U.S. Constitution, which sets limits beyond which the federal government may not go. Federal statutes then identify the scope of the federal government's jurisdiction, leaving to the several states the possibility of exercising their own forms of jurisdiction where there is no conflict with federal law. At the national level, conflict of laws rules also help define the limits of legislative, judicial, and executive jurisdiction, indicating the appropriate choice of law in certain situations, the appropriate forum, and other matters. These limits may, but need not, be the same as those prescribed by constitutional law.

Second, once certain types of jurisdiction are established under international law, the propriety of such jurisdiction can be addressed on the level of international law. Customary international law sets limits upon the exercise of jurisdiction by states and other international legal persons; if those limits are transgressed, then international law is violated (even if national law is not). It is important to note that even though customary international law may allow a state to exercise a form of jurisdiction, that does not mean that the state has in fact done so; reference must be made to the national law to see if the state has exercised jurisdiction to the extent permitted under international law (often, it has not).

Jurisdiction and immunities are related but analytically distinct questions. In *Arrest Warrant* (Democratic Republic of the Congo v. Belgium), 2002 I.C.J. 3, excerpted at p. 929, the D.R.C. complained about the exercise of Belgian criminal jurisdiction over certain conduct of the D.R.C.'s foreign minister that was taken in the D.R.C. The D.R.C. also asserted that the exercise of such jurisdiction infringed the minister's immunity. The Court, in its decision, focused only on the issue of immunity, but certain judges in their separate opinions discussed the extent of national jurisdiction permitted under international law. See p. 811 note 2.

Further, under some treaty regimes, international law *requires* a state to exercise jurisdiction over a person present in its territory accused of a grave offense, so as to either submit the offender to national prosecution or to extradite the person to another state's prosecutorial authorities. For example, in 2009, Belgium sued Senegal before the International Court alleging a *failure* of Senegal to exercise national jurisdiction by not prosecuting a former President of Chad, Hissène Habré, who was living in exile in Senegal. According to Belgium, Senegal is obligated either to prosecute Habré in Senegal or to extradite him to Belgium for prosecution, based on both treaty law for committing acts of torture (the Convention against Torture) and on customary law for committing crimes against humanity.

Sections 1–6 of this Chapter focus on rules of international law governing a state's exercise of national jurisdiction to prescribe. Section 7 considers jurisdiction to adjudicate, while Section 8 addresses jurisdiction to enforce and Section 9 concerns jurisdiction by agreement. Section 10 considers rules relevant when there is a conflict of jurisdiction between two or more states. Section 11 focuses on issues relating to extradition. On jurisdiction under international law generally, see Extraterritorial Jurisdiction in Theory and Practice (Meessen ed. 1996).

3.   Burden of Establishing the Relevant International Rule

International law has not yet developed a comprehensive set of rules defining with precision all forms of jurisdiction that may be exercised by states and other international legal persons. The *Lotus* case, Chapter 2, p. 68, remains the classic international decision addressing the exercise of extraterritorial prescriptive jurisdiction. This classic view asserts that international law allows the exercise of national jurisdiction unless a specific prohibition on doing so is identified in international law; hence, the burden of establishing that an exercise of national jurisdiction violates international law rests upon the state or person asserting the violation. See S.S. *"Lotus"* (France/Turkey), P.C.I.J., (ser. A) No. 10, at 19 ("Restrictions upon the independence of States cannot ... be presumed.").

Yet since the time of the *Lotus* case, many challenges have been made before international tribunals regarding the exercise of national jurisdiction, such as the cases by the D.R.C. and Belgium noted above. Indeed, the view has been espoused that when a states seeks to regulate matters extraterritorially, the burden is upon it to demonstrate the existence of an appropriate basis of jurisdiction. An alternative view is that the exercise of all forms of jurisdiction is subject to an overall limitation of reasonableness. This is the position taken in the Restatement (Third) § 403; see also Schachter, International Law in Theory and Practice 258–61 (1991).

4.   Criminal and Civil Jurisdiction

International law is concerned with the exercise of national jurisdiction in the form of both criminal and civil jurisdiction, but often concerns arise more in the criminal context because that form of national jurisdiction is seen as especially intrusive into the prerogatives of another sovereign. See, e.g., Restatement (Third) § 403, Comment *f* & Reporter's Note 8; id. § 421, Comment *b*. Hence, the possibility that states could object on the grounds of international law to assertions of civil as well as criminal jurisdiction exists and may increase, particularly when civil plaintiffs act as "private attorneys-general" in matters affecting foreign state interests. In recent times, foreign sovereigns have increasingly objected to the exercise of extraterritorial prescriptive jurisdiction through statutes that threaten criminal, administrative, or civil sanctions in the economic sphere. See *infra* Section 2(B)(1) and (2). Administrative and some forms of civil sanctions, such as injunctions and punitive damages, may, of course, affect the person on whom they are imposed as seriously as do criminal sanctions and may therefore be regarded as coming within the realm of criminal jurisdiction for the purposes here discussed. It may well be argued, however, that international law limitations on the exercise of administrative and civil jurisdiction are still in a stage of development and that broad generalizations should be treated with circumspection. By contrast, the exercise of enforcement jurisdiction in any form on the territory of another state is generally regarded as limited by international law, regardless of whether the enforcement measure is of a criminal or civil nature. See Sections 8–9 of this Chapter.

Thus far, international law, in defining the limits of jurisdiction, has concerned itself principally with defining the jurisdiction of states. However, as international entities with varying measures of international legal personality continue to develop, international law will increasingly have to concern itself with their jurisdiction. For example, the European Community has asserted extraterritorial jurisdiction in antitrust matters and in certain maritime areas, claiming the ability to do so derivative from its member states. Likewise, international criminal tribunals are now adjudicating crimes committed across the globe, well outside the territory in which the tribunals sit (see Chapter 16). Such exercises of criminal jurisdiction are justified in some instances on the authority of the Security Council, in other instances on a state's adherence to a treaty regime, and in other instances on the ground that they are applying rules that are embedded in customary international law and therefore applicable to all states in all places at all times. Such developments make clear that international law will play a significant role in defining the jurisdiction of international legal persons other than states.

B. OVERVIEW OF THE PRINCIPLES OF INTERNATIONAL LAW GOVERNING THE EXERCISE OF NATIONAL JURISDICTION

Under international law, the permissible jurisdiction of a state depends on the interest that the state, in view of its nature and purposes, may reasonably have in exercising the particular jurisdiction asserted and on the need to reconcile that interest with the interests of other states in exercising jurisdiction. The nature and significance of the interests of a state in exercising jurisdiction depend on the relation of the transaction, occurrence, or event, and of the person to be affected, to the state's proper concerns.

Whatever happens on the territory of a state is of that state's primary concern (the territorial principle). A state also has a significant interest in exercising jurisdiction over persons or things that possess its nationality (the nationality principle) and in protecting its nationals (the passive personality principle). In addition, a state has an evident interest in protecting itself against acts, even if performed outside of its territory and by persons that owe it no allegiance, that threaten its existence or its proper functioning as a state (the protective principle). And, finally, certain activities are so universally condemned that any state has an interest in exercising jurisdiction to combat them (the universal principle).

RESTATEMENT OF THE LAW (THIRD)
THE FOREIGN RELATIONS LAW OF THE UNITED STATES §§ 402–404 (1987)

§ 402.   Bases of Jurisdiction to Prescribe

Subject to § 403, a state has jurisdiction to prescribe law with respect to

(1) (a) conduct that, wholly or in substantial part, takes place within its territory;

   (b) the status of persons, or interests in things, present within its territory;

   (c) conduct outside its territory that has or is intended to have substantial effect within its territory;

(2) the activities, interests, status, or relations of its nationals outside as well as within its territory; and

(3) certain conduct outside its territory by persons not its nationals that is directed against the security of the state or against a limited class of other state interests.

§ 403.   Limitations on Jurisdiction to Prescribe

(1) Even when one of the bases for jurisdiction under § 402 is present, a state may not exercise jurisdiction to prescribe law with respect to a person or activity having connections with another state when the exercise of such jurisdiction is unreasonable.

(2) Whether exercise of jurisdiction over a person or activity is unreasonable is determined by evaluating all relevant factors, including, where appropriate:

   (a) the link of the activity to the territory of the regulating state, *i.e.*, the extent to which the activity takes place within the territory, or has substantial, direct, and foreseeable effect upon or in the territory;

   (b) the connections, such as nationality, residence, or economic activity, between the regulating state and the person principally responsible for the activity to be regulated, or between that state and those whom the regulation is designed to protect;

   (c) the character of the activity to be regulated, the importance of regulation to the regulating state, the extent to which other states regulate such activities, and the degree to which the desirability of such regulation is generally accepted;

   (d) the existence of justified expectations that might be protected or hurt by the regulation;

    (e) the importance of the regulation to the international political, legal, or economic system;

    (f) the extent to which the regulation is consistent with the traditions of the international system;

    (g) the extent to which another state may have an interest in regulating the activity; and

    (h) the likelihood of conflict with regulation by another state.

(3) When it would not be unreasonable for each of two states to exercise jurisdiction over a person or activity, but the prescriptions by the two states are in conflict, each state has an obligation to evaluate its own as well as the other state's interest in exercising jurisdiction, in light of all the relevant factors, Subsection (2); a state should defer to the other state if that state's interest is clearly greater.

§ 404. Universal Jurisdiction to Define and Punish Certain Offenses

A state has jurisdiction to define and prescribe punishment for certain offenses recognized by the community of nations as of universal concern, such as piracy, slave trade, attacks on or hijacking of aircraft, genocide, war crimes, and perhaps certain acts of terrorism, even where none of the bases of jurisdiction indicated in § 402 is present.

NOTES

1. *Reasonableness as a Limitation Grounded in International Law?* The Restatement (Third) provides in § 403 for an overall limitation on the exercise of jurisdiction. This limitation, it is stated in Comment a, "has emerged as a principle of international law." To what extent is this statement borne out by the materials that follow? Is the imposition of this requirement likely to alleviate the problems that arise in cases of conflicts of jurisdiction? See Section 10 of this Chapter. Should national institutions read this limitation into national law whenever possible? For contrasting views, compare Lowenfeld, International Litigation and the Quest for Reasonableness (1996), with Trimble, The Supreme Court and International Law: The Demise of Restatement § 403, 89 A.J.I.L. 53 (1995).

2. *Reasonableness in Universal Jurisdiction Cases?* Section 403 of the Restatement (Third) does not impose the limitation of reasonableness upon the exercise of jurisdiction on the basis of the universal principle. Is there no room for such a limitation when jurisdiction is exercised on that basis?

The extent to which recognized bases of jurisdiction provide the premises for the exercise of the various forms of jurisdiction will be considered in the sections that follow. Since each state is part of the world community, rules defining jurisdiction must take due account of the needs of that community and, specifically, of the need not to encroach unnecessarily on the interests of other members. This has been a significant consideration in delimiting in different fashion the extraterritorial reach of the various kinds of jurisdiction.

C. HARMONIZING NATIONAL LAW WITH THE PRINCIPLES OF INTERNATIONAL LAW ON JURISDICTION

National courts frequently make reference to certain presumptions or canons of construction aimed at avoiding conflict between international and national law or between the forum's law and the legitimate interests of other states.

One important presumption is that statutes should be construed not to apply extraterritorially unless the legislative intent to do so is clearly expressed. The hallmark statement to this effect for the United States is that of Justice Oliver Wendell Holmes in *American Banana Co. v. United Fruit Co.*, 213 U.S. 347, 357 (1909) ("all legislation is prima facie territorial"); see also *Foley Bros., Inc. v. Filardo*, 336 U.S. 281, 285 (1949). More recently, in *Equal Employment Opportunity Commission v. Arabian American Oil Co.*, 499 U.S. 244 (1991) (*Aramco*), Chief Justice William Rehnquist ruled that Title VII of the Civil Rights Act of 1964 did not apply extraterritorially to reach alleged discrimination (on the ground of race, religion, and national origin) by Aramco, a Delaware corporation, in regard to a U.S. citizen employed in Saudi Arabia.

If, however, Congress expressly indicates in the U.S. law that it should be applied extraterritorially, then U.S. courts will do so. In the aftermath of the *Aramco* case, Congress amended the Civil Rights Act to clarify its applicability to overseas operations of U.S. corporations, thereby overruling the outcome in *Aramco*. See Civil Rights Act of 1991, § 109, Pub. L. No. 102–166, 105 Stat. 1071, codified at 42 U.S.C. § 2000e(f) (2000). Thereafter, U.S. courts applied the statute to conduct occurring abroad. See, e.g., *Davila v. New York Hospital*, 813 F.Supp. 977 (S.D.N.Y. 1993).

Moreover, even if an intent to apply a statute extraterritorially is not expressly stated in the statute, courts may view such intent as implicit in the statute if such application is necessary to achieve the statute's purpose. In *United States v. Bowman*, 260 U.S. 94 (1922), the Supreme Court held that a statute punishing conspiracy to defraud a U.S.-owned corporation was applicable to conduct taking place on the high seas. The Court stated that to limit the statute's scope to "the strictly territorial jurisdiction" would be greatly to curtail its usefulness and to leave open "a large immunity for frauds as easily committed by citizens on the high seas and in foreign countries as at home." In such cases, the Court continued, Congress had not "thought it necessary to make specific provision in the law that the locus shall include the high seas and foreign countries, but allows it to be inferred from the nature of the offense." Id. at 98. The conviction of three United States nationals was accordingly affirmed on the ground that they were "certainly subject to such laws as [the United States] might pass to protect itself and its property." Id. at 102. For more recent examples, see *United States v. Vasquez–Velasco*, 15 F.3d 833 (9th Cir. 1994) (applying anti-racketeering statute to conduct by non-national in Mexico) (see *infra* Section 5); *United States v. Yousef*, 327 F.3d 56 (2d Cir. 2003) (bombing by a foreigner of a foreign aircraft flying between non-U.S. destinations without U.S. citizens aboard reached by U.S. statute implementing treaty).

Assuming that the statute is capable of being interpreted as applying to conduct abroad, a second important presumption becomes relevant. As found by Chief Justice Marshall in *Murray v. Schooner Charming Betsy*, 6 U.S. (2 Cranch) 64 (1804), U.S. statutes are generally interpreted so as to be consistent with international law, unless Congress clearly evinces an intent to do otherwise. In the context of the law of jurisdiction, such judicially fashioned rules help restrict the excessive use of national law, since the courts will not interpret a statute as providing for jurisdiction that runs afoul of the general principles outlined in the prior subsection, unless the legislature has clearly directed them to do so. By adhering to those principles, there is less likelihood of unwarranted intrusion into matters in which other states have greater interests, and can be understood as part of a general system of jurisdictional "reasonableness." See *Lauritzen v. Larsen*, 345 U.S. 571, 577 (1953) (applying a U.S. statute "only to areas and transactions in which American law would be considered operative under prevalent doctrines of international law"); *McCulloch v. Sociedad Nacional de Marineros de Honduras*, 372 U.S. 10, 21–22 (1963) (restricting application of the National Labor Relations Act to foreign-flag vessels).

Where Congress clearly intends to apply U.S. law extraterritorially, however, courts will do so even if it violates international law. See, e.g., *United States v. Yousef*, 327 F.3d 56 (2d Cir. 2003) ("while customary international law may inform the judgment of our courts in an appropriate case, it cannot alter or constrain the making of law by the political branches of the government as ordained by the Constitution"); *United States v. Yunis*, 924 F.2d 1086 (D.C. Cir. 1991) (finding that "Yunis seeks to portray international law as a self-executing code that trumps domestic law whenever the two conflict. That effort misconceives the role of judges as appliers of international law and as participants in the federal system. Our duty is to enforce the Constitution, laws, and treaties of the United States, not to conform the law of the land to norms of customary international law.").

What if national jurisdiction is being used to regulate matters that have occurred in other states *for the purpose of upholding certain rules established by international treaty or custom*? Should not international law be receptive to that use of national jurisdiction, even if it intrudes to an extent into the sovereignty of another state? The following case provides a recent illustration of the tension that may arise in harmonizing national law with principles of international law.

AL–SKEINI v. SECRETARY OF STATE FOR DEFENCE

House of Lords, 2007

[2007] UKHL 26

LORD BINGHAM OF CORNHILL:

1.   These proceedings arise from the deaths of six Iraqi civilians, and the brutal maltreatment of one of them causing his death, in Basra. Each of the deceased was killed (or, in one case, is said to have been killed) and the maltreatment was inflicted by a member or members of the British armed forces. In each case a close relative of the deceased has applied in the High Court in London for an order of judicial review against the Secretary of State for Defence, seeking to challenge his refusal (by a letter of 26 March 2004) to order an independent enquiry into the circumstances of this maltreatment and these deaths, and his rejection of liability to afford the claimants redress for causing them. These six cases have been selected as test cases from a much larger number of claims in order, at this stage, to resolve certain important and far-reaching issues of legal principle.

2.   The claimants found their claims in the English court on the Human Rights Act 1998 ("the HRA" or "the Act"). To succeed each claimant must show that a public authority has acted unlawfully, that is, incompatibly with a Convention right of the claimant or the deceased (section 6(1) of the Act). A Convention right means a right set out in one of the articles of the European Convention on Human Rights reproduced in Schedule 1 to the Act (sections 1(1), 1(3) and 21(1)). * * *

3.   First, the claimant must show that his complaint falls within the scope of the Convention. This is an essential step, since it is clear that a claim cannot fall within the HRA if it does not fall within the Convention. In the ordinary run of claims under the Act, this condition gives rise to no difficulty: the claim relates to conduct within the borders of a contracting state such as the United Kingdom, and the question is whether a claimant's Convention right has been violated and if so by whom. But here the substantial violations alleged did not take place within the borders of a contracting state. They took place in Iraq, which is not part of the UK and not a contracting state. This is an important fact, since the focus of the Convention is primarily on what is done or not done within the borders of contracting states and not outside. To this rule, however, there are certain limited exceptions, recognised in the jurisprudence of the European Court of Human Rights in Strasbourg, the court vested by the Convention with the duty of interpreting and applying it. * * *

4.   Even if the claimants succeed on that first issue, they must satisfy a second condition: of showing that their claims, although falling within the scope of the Convention, also fall within the scope of the HRA. This again is an essential condition, for while a claim cannot succeed under the Act unless it falls within the scope of the Convention, the converse is not true: a claim may in some circumstances fall within the scope of the

Convention but not within the scope of the Act. Here the parties are in radical disagreement. The Secretary of State contends that the HRA has no application to acts of public authorities outside the borders of the UK. The Act has, in legal parlance, no extra-territorial application. * * * The claimants say that the Act does extend to cover the conduct of the British forces in Basra, given the special circumstances in which they were operating and what they did. * * *

* * *

11. In resisting the interpretation, upheld by the courts below, that the HRA has extra-territorial application, the Secretary of State places heavy reliance on what he describes as "a general and well established principle of statutory construction". This is (see Bennion, *Statutory Interpretation,* 4th ed. (2002), p. 282, section 106) that

> "Unless the contrary intention appears, Parliament is taken to intend an Act to extend to each territory of the United Kingdom but not to any territory outside the United Kingdom." * * *

12. In argument before the courts below, the claimants relied on another presumption of statutory interpretation: that, as put by the Divisional Court in paragraph 301 of its judgment, "a domestic statute enacting international treaty obligations will be compatible with those obligations". * * *

* * *

24. In the course of its careful consideration of this question the Divisional Court observed (in paragraph 304 of its judgment): "It is intuitively difficult to think that Parliament intended to legislate for foreign lands". In similar vein, Brooke LJ in the Court of Appeal said (para. 3): "It may seem surprising that an Act of the UK Parliament and a European Convention on Human Rights can arguably be said to confer rights upon citizens of Iraq which are enforceable against a UK governmental authority in the courts of England and Wales". I do not think this sense of surprise, which I share, is irrelevant to the court's task of interpretation. It cannot of course be supposed that in 1997–1998 Parliament foresaw the prospect of British forces being engaged in peacekeeping duties in Iraq. But there can be relatively few, if any, years between 1953 and 1997 in which British forces were not engaged in hostilities or peacekeeping activities in some part of the world, and it must have been appreciated that such involvement would recur. This makes it the more unlikely, in my opinion, that Parliament could, without any express provision to that effect, have intended to rebut the presumption of territorial application so as to authorise the bringing of claims, under the Act, based on the conduct of British forces outside the UK and outside any other contracting state. Differing from the courts below, I regard the statutory presumption of territorial application as a strong one, which has not been rebutted.

* * *

26.   I would accordingly hold that the HRA has no extra-territorial application. A claim under the Act will not lie against the Secretary of State based on acts or omissions of British forces outside the United Kingdom. This does not mean that members of the British armed forces serving abroad are free to murder, rape and pillage with impunity. They are triable and punishable for any crimes they commit under the three service discipline Acts already mentioned, no matter where the crime is committed or who the victim may be. They are triable for genocide, crimes against humanity and war crimes under the International Criminal Court Act 2001. The UK itself is bound, in a situation such as prevailed in Iraq, to comply with the Hague Convention of 1907 and the Regulations made under it [as well as by the 1949 Fourth Geneva Convention and its additional protocol]. * * *

LORD RODGER OF EARLSFERRY

[Lord Rodger surveyed the various presumptions of statutory interpretation, including (in addition to those already noted) the rule applied by U.K. courts to determine whether Parliament has intended to legislate with respect to the overseas conduct of British citizens.]

49.   Again, this rule of construction has to be seen against the background of international law. One state is bound to respect the territorial sovereignty of another state. So, usually, Parliament will not mean to interfere by legislating to regulate the conduct of its citizens in another state. Such legislation would usually be unnecessary and would often be, in any event, ineffective. But sometimes Parliament has a legitimate interest in regulating their conduct and so does indeed intend its legislation to affect the position of British citizens in other states. For example, section 72 of the Sexual Offences Act 2003 makes certain nasty sexual conduct in other countries an offence under English law. So, if the words of a statute are open to more than one interpretation, whether or not it binds British citizens abroad "seems to depend . . . entirely on the nature of the statute": *Maxwell on The Interpretation of Statutes*, p. 169. * * *

* * *

54.   The purpose of the 1998 Act is to provide remedies in our domestic law to those whose human rights are violated by a United Kingdom public authority. Making such remedies available for acts of a United Kingdom authority on the territory of another state would not be offensive to the sovereignty of the other state. There is therefore nothing in the wider context of international law which points to the need to confine sections 6 and 7 of the 1998 Act to the territory of the United Kingdom.

* * *

63.   The European Convention is a treaty under international law. Somewhat unusually, it confers rights on individuals against the contracting parties. While the Geneva Conventions on the Protection of War

Victims 1949 apply "in all circumstances", the geographical scope of the rights under the European Convention is more limited: under article 1, the States Parties are bound to "secure to everyone within their jurisdiction the rights and freedoms defined in Section 1" of the Convention.

64.   It is important therefore to recognise that, when considering the question of jurisdiction under the Convention, the focus has shifted to the victim or, more precisely, to the link between the victim and the contracting state. For the purposes of the extra-territorial effects of section 6 of the 1998 Act, the key question was whether a public authority—in this case the Army in Iraq—was within Parliament's legislative grasp when acting outside the United Kingdom. By contrast, for the purposes of deciding whether the Convention applies outside the territory of the United Kingdom, the key question is whether the deceased were linked to the United Kingdom when they were killed. However reprehensible, however contrary to any common understanding of respect for "human rights", the alleged conduct of the British forces might have been, it had no legal consequences under the Convention, unless there was that link and the deceased were within the jurisdiction of the United Kingdom at the time. For, only then would the United Kingdom have owed them any obligation in international law to secure their rights under article 2 of the Convention and only then would their relatives have had any rights under the 1998 Act.

65.   What is meant by "within their jurisdiction" in article 1 is a question of law and the body whose function it is to answer that question definitively is the European Court of Human Rights.

[Lord Rodger continued with an analysis of the European Court's case law and concluded that with the exception of the claimant who had been mistreated inside a British military detention unit, the claimants were not within U.K. jurisdiction within the meaning of article 1 of the Convention.

Baroness Hale of Richmond, Lord Carswell, and Lord Brown of Eaton–Under–Heywood agreed with Lord Rodger that jurisdiction under the HRA should be coextensive with the interpretation given by the European Court to jurisdiction under the Convention. These four formed the majority; only Lord Bingham took the view that the HRA had a more restrictive jurisdictional scope than the Convention rights it was meant to implement.]

NOTES

1.   *Presumptions in Operation.* U.K. troops were in Basra as part of the deployment of allied forces that invaded and then occupied Iraq starting in March 2003. Do you think the House of Lords properly weighed the manner in which U.K. national law should take account of international law? As you read the cases in this Chapter, consider whether you think they involve presumptions and tensions comparable to those addressed by the House of Lords in *Al–Skeini.*

2. *Jurisdictional Reach of U.S. Habeas Corpus Statute.* Military forces of one state may be present in another state in situations other than as an occupying power; should national jurisdiction of the first state extend to those other places? In *Rasul v. Bush,* 542 U.S. 466 (2004), two Australian citizens and twelve Kuwaiti citizens, who had been captured in Afghanistan by U.S. forces and transferred to the Guantánamo Bay detention facility, sought writs of habeas corpus challenging the lawfulness of their confinement. The U.S. government claimed that the U.S. habeas corpus statute, 28 U.S.C. § 2241 (2000), was not available to foreign nationals outside the territory of the United States. In rejecting this contention, the Supreme Court said:

> [R]espondents contend that we can discern a limit on § 2241 through application of the "longstanding principle of American law" that congressional legislation is presumed not to have extraterritorial application unless such intent is clearly manifested. *EEOC v. Arabian American Oil Co.*, 499 U.S. 244, 248 (1991). Whatever traction the presumption against extraterritoriality might have in other contexts, it certainly has no application to the operation of the habeas statute with respect to persons detained within "the territorial jurisdiction" of the United States. *Foley Bros., Inc. v. Filardo*, 336 U.S. 281, 285 (1949). By the express terms of its agreements with Cuba, the United States exercises "complete jurisdiction and control" over the Guantánamo Bay Naval Base, and may continue to exercise such control permanently if it so chooses. 1903 Lease Agreement, Art. III; 1934 Treaty, Art. III. Respondents themselves concede that the habeas statute would create federal-court jurisdiction over the claims of an American citizen held at the base. * * * Considering that the statute draws no distinction between Americans and aliens held in federal custody, there is little reason to think that Congress intended the geographical coverage of the statute to vary depending on the detainee's citizenship. Aliens held at the base, no less than American citizens, are entitled to invoke the federal courts' authority under § 2241.

For the Court's discussion of why the U.S. *constitutional* right to habeas corpus also applies to aliens detained at Guantánamo Bay, see *Boumediene v. Bush*, 128 S.Ct. 2229 (2008). In that case, the Court advocated a functional approach in determining the extraterritorial reach of the U.S. Constitution that considered several factors, one of which was the likelihood that exercising U.S. jurisdiction would cause friction with the state in which the allegedly wrongful conduct occurred.

SECTION 2. JURISDICTION BASED ON THE TERRITORIAL PRINCIPLE

Subject to the limitation that a state may exercise jurisdiction only in pursuit of purposes that are reasonably within its concern, the territorial principle provides the premise for the exercise by a state of jurisdiction with respect to transactions, persons, or things within its territory (sometimes referred to as the "subjective" territorial principle). The territorial principle in this sense is universally accepted by states.

Yet the territorial principle has also undergone significant development in modern times, so as to acknowledge as well a state's jurisdiction with respect to certain consequences produced within its territory by persons acting *outside* it (the "objective" territorial principle). This development has been a necessary consequence of the increasing complexity of the "act or omission" which constitutes a crime under modern penal legislation. The "act or omission" need not consist of an isolated action or failure to act. Not infrequently it appears as an event consisting of a series of separate acts or omissions. These separate acts or omissions need not be simultaneous with respect to time or restricted to a single state with respect to place. Indeed, with the increasing facility of communication and transportation, the opportunities for committing crimes whose constituent elements take place in more than one state have grown apace. The following sub-sections address these two aspects of the territorial principle.

A. PERSONS AND THINGS WITHIN THE TERRITORY

It is well settled that a state may exercise jurisdiction with respect to all persons or things within its territory. Chief Justice John Marshall stated in *Schooner Exchange v. McFaddon*, 11 U.S. (7 Cranch) 116, 136 (1812) that:

> The jurisdiction of the nation within its own territory is necessarily exclusive and absolute. It is susceptible of no limitation not imposed by itself. Any restriction upon it, deriving validity from an external source, would imply a diminution of its sovereignty to the extent of the restriction, and an investment of that sovereignty to the same extent in that power which could impose such restriction. All exceptions, therefore, to the full and complete power of a nation within its own territories, must be traced up to the consent of the nation itself.

The U.S. Supreme Court recently reaffirmed this principle in *Munaf v. Geren*, 128 S.Ct. 2207 (2008). In that case, two U.S. citizens voluntarily traveled to Iraq, allegedly committed crimes there, and then were captured and detained by U.S. forces participating in the multinational military force in Iraq. Petitioners sought a writ of habeas corpus to prevent the U.S. custodians from turning them over to Iraqi authorities for prosecution. A unanimous Supreme Court held that habeas jurisdiction in U.S. courts was available to test the legality of detention of U.S. citizens under U.S. authority overseas. At the same time, the Court denied any relief, stating there was no basis for a U.S. court to block the transfer of the two men to the authorities of the territorial sovereign in which they allegedly committed wrongful acts. According to the Court:

> [O]ur cases make clear that Iraq has a sovereign right to prosecute Omar and Munaf for crimes committed on its soil. As Chief Justice Marshall explained nearly two centuries ago, "[t]he jurisdiction of the nation within its own territory is necessarily exclusive and absolute."
> * * * See *Wilson* [*v. Girard*, 354 U.S. 524 (1957), p. 830 below] at 529

("A sovereign nation has exclusive jurisdiction to punish offenses against its laws committed within its borders, unless it expressly or impliedly consents to surrender its jurisdiction"); *Reid v. Covert*, 354 U.S. 1, 15, n. 29 (1957) (opinion of Black, J.) ("a foreign nation has plenary criminal jurisdiction ... over all Americans ... who commit offenses against its laws within its territory") * * *.

This is true with respect to American citizens who travel abroad and commit crimes in another nation whether or not the pertinent criminal process comes with all the rights guaranteed by our Constitution.

128 S.Ct. at 2221–22.

B. PERSONS AND THINGS OUTSIDE THE TERRITORY BUT HAVING EFFECTS WITHIN IT

1. Effects Doctrine Illustrated: Application of Antitrust Laws

UNITED STATES v. ALUMINUM CO. OF AMERICA

United States Court of Appeals for the Second Circuit, 1945
148 F.2d 416

Before L. Hand, Swan and A. Hand. Circuit Judges.

[The complaint alleged that defendants Alcoa and Aluminum, Limited (a Canadian corporation formed to take over the properties of Alcoa outside the United States) had illegally conspired in restraint of domestic and foreign commerce with respect to the manufacture and sale of aluminum ingot. The Government's appeal from dismissal of its complaint, 44 F. Supp. 97 (S.D.N.Y. 1941), was referred to the Court of Appeals, because a quorum of six qualified Justices of the Supreme Court was wanting. One of the central issues in the case was whether the participation of Aluminum, Limited, in an "alliance" with a number of foreign producers constituted a violation of the first section of the Sherman Act (15 U.S.C.A. § 1), which provides in relevant part that "every contract, combination * * * or conspiracy, in restraint of trade or commerce among the several States, or with foreign nations, is declared to be illegal." In the course of holding that "Limited" violated the Act, the court (per L. Hand, C.J.) stated:]

Whether "Limited" itself violated that section depends upon the character of the "Alliance." It was a Swiss corporation, created in pursuance of an agreement entered into on July 3, 1931, the signatories to which were a French corporation, two German, one Swiss, a British, and "Limited." The original agreement, or "cartel," provided for the formation of a corporation in Switzerland which should issue shares, to be taken up by the signatories. This corporation was from time to time to fix a quota of production for each share, and each shareholder was to be limited to the quantity measured by the number of shares it held, but was free to sell at any price it chose. The corporation fixed a price every year at which it would take off any shareholder's hands any part of its quota which it did not sell. No shareholder was to "buy, borrow, fabricate or sell" aluminum produced by anyone not a shareholder except with the consent of the board of governors, but that must not be "unreasonably withheld." * * * However, * * * until 1936, when the new arrangement was made, imports into the United States were not included in the quotas. * * *

The agreement of 1936 abandoned the system of unconditional quotas, and substituted a system of royalties. Each shareholder was to have a fixed free quota for every share it held, but as its production exceeded the sum of its quotas, it was to pay a royalty, graduated progressively in proportion to the excess; and these royalties the "Alliance" divided among the shareholders in proportion to their shares. * * * Although this agreement, like its predecessor, was silent as to imports into the United States, when that question arose during its preparation, as it did, all the shareholders agreed that such imports should be included in the quotas. * * *

Did either the agreement of 1931 or that of 1936 violate § 1 of the Act? The answer does not depend upon whether we shall recognize as a source of liability a liability imposed by another state. On the contrary we are concerned only with whether Congress chose to attach liability to the conduct outside the United States of persons not in allegiance to it. That being so, the only question open is whether Congress intended to impose the liability, and whether our own Constitution permitted it to do so: as a court of the United States, we cannot look beyond our own law. Nevertheless, it is quite true that we are not to read general words, such as those in this Act, without regard to the limitations customarily observed by nations upon the exercise of their powers * * *. We should not impute to Congress an intent to punish all whom its courts can catch, for conduct which has no consequences within the United States. * * * On the other hand, it is settled law—as "Limited" itself agrees—that any state may impose liabilities, even upon persons not within its allegiance, for conduct outside its borders that has consequences within its borders which the state reprehends; and these liabilities other states will ordinarily recognize. * * * Restatement of Conflict of Laws § 65. It may be argued that this Act extends further. Two situations are possible. There may be agreements made beyond our borders not intended to affect imports, which do affect them, or which affect exports. Almost any limitation of the supply of goods in Europe, for example, or in South America, may have repercussions in the United States if there is trade between the two. Yet when one considers the international complications likely to arise from an effort in this country to treat such agreements as unlawful, it is safe to assume that Congress certainly did not intend the Act to cover them. Such agreements may on the other hand intend to include imports into the United States, and yet it may appear that they have had no effect upon them. That situation might be thought to fall within the doctrine that intent may be a substitute for performance in the case of a contract made within the United States; or it might be thought to fall within the doctrine that a statute should not be interpreted to cover acts abroad which have no consequence here. We shall not choose between these alternatives; but for argument we shall assume that the Act does not cover agreements, even though intended to affect imports or exports, unless its performance is shown actually to have had some effect upon them. Where both conditions are satisfied, the situation certainly falls within such decisions as United States v. Pacific & Arctic R. & Navigation Co., 228 U.S. 87; Thomsen v. Cayser, 243 U.S. 66, and United States v. Sisal Sales Corporation, 274 U.S. 268. * * * It is true that in those cases the persons held liable had sent agents into the United States to perform part of the agreement; but an agent is merely an animate means of executing his principal's purposes, and, for the purposes of this case, he does not differ from an inanimate means; besides, only human agents can import and sell ingot.

Both agreements would clearly have been unlawful, had they been made within the United States; and it follows from what we have just said that both were unlawful, though made abroad, if they were intended to affect imports and did affect them.

[The Court went on to find that the 1936 agreement intended to set up a quota system for imports and that, absent a showing by "Limited" that imports were not in fact affected, the agreement violated § 1 of the Act.]

NOTES

1. *Objective Territorial Principle.* The objective territorial principle:

> is often said to apply where the offence "takes effect" or "produces its effects" in the territory. In relation to elementary cases of direct physical injury, such as homicide, this is unexceptionable, for here the "effect" which is meant is an essential ingredient of the crime. Once we move out of the sphere of direct physical consequences, however, to employ the formula of "effects" is to enter upon a very slippery slope; for here the effects within the territory may be no more than an element of alleged consequential damage which may be more or less remote. * * * [T]o extend the notion of effects, without qualification, from the simple cases of direct physical injury to cases such as defamation, sedition, and the like, is to introduce a dangerous ambiguity into the basis of the doctrine. If indeed it were permissible to found objective territorial jurisdiction upon the territoriality of more or less remote repercussions of an act wholly performed in another territory, then there would be virtually no limit to a State's territorial jurisdiction.

Jennings, Extraterritorial Jurisdiction and the United States Antitrust Laws, 33 Brit. Y.B.I.L. 146, 159 (1957); see Turley, "When in Rome": Multinational Misconduct and the Presumption Against Extraterritoriality, 84 Nw. U. L.

Rev. 598, 607 (1990); Born, A Reappraisal of the Extraterritorial Reach of United States Law, 24 Law & Pol'y Int'l Bus. 1, 10 (1992).

2. *The Meaning of* Alcoa. Does *Alcoa* stand for the proposition that any anti-competitive agreement abroad that intends to have effects on the United States can be regulated by U.S. law, even if it in fact does not? Does *Alcoa* stand for the proposition that an agreement abroad that had no intention of affecting the United States, but does have some anti-competitive effects on the United States, can be regulated by U.S. law? In short, what kind of conduct abroad in combination with what kind of effects was regarded as within the scope of the objective territorial principle in this case? If you were trying to articulate in a statute or in a Restatement the best standard for courts to follow in cases with different fact patterns, what would you say?

3. *The Rise of Reasonableness.* In the aftermath of *Alcoa,* several courts began applying a "jurisdictional rule of reason" when exercising extraterritorial jurisdiction, in which they balanced the interests of the United States with those of the foreign jurisdiction. See, e.g., *Timberlane Lumber Co. v. Bank of America National Trust & Saving Ass'n,* 549 F.2d 597 (9th Cir. 1976). If the court found that the U.S. connection to the activity was attenuated, while that of the foreign state was strong, then it was seen as unreasonable to apply U.S. antitrust laws to reach the conduct abroad. Do you such cases support imposition of a requirement of reasonableness as a matter of international law?

FOREIGN TRADE ANTITRUST IMPROVEMENTS ACT OF 1982

15 U.S.C. § 6a (2000)

§ 6a. Conduct involving trade or commerce with foreign nations

Sections 1 to 7 of this title [Sherman Antitrust Act and related provisions] shall not apply to conduct involving trade or commerce (other than import trade or import commerce) with foreign nations unless—

(1) such conduct has a direct, substantial, and reasonably foreseeable effect—

    (A) on trade or commerce which is not trade or commerce with foreign nations, or on import trade or import commerce with foreign nations; or

    (B) on export trade or export commerce with foreign nations, of a person engaged in such trade or commerce in the United States; and

(2) such effect gives rise to a claim under the provisions of sections 1 to 7 of this title, other than this section.

RESTATEMENT OF THE LAW (THIRD)
THE FOREIGN RELATIONS LAW OF THE UNITED STATES § 712 (1987)

§ 415. Jurisdiction to Regulate Anti–Competitive Activities

(1) Any agreement in restraint of United States trade made in the United States, and any conduct or agreement in restraint of such trade that is carried out in significant measure in the United States, are subject to the jurisdiction to prescribe of the United States, regardless of the nationality or place of business of the parties to the agreement or of the participants in the conduct.

(2) Any agreement in restraint of United States trade that is made outside of the United States, and any conduct or agreement in restraint of such trade that is carried out predominantly outside of the United States, are subject to the jurisdiction to prescribe of the United States, if a principal purpose of the conduct or agreement is to interfere with the commerce of the United States, and the agreement or conduct has some effect on that commerce.

(3) Other agreements or conduct in restraint of United States trade are subject to the jurisdiction to prescribe of the United States if such agreements or conduct have substantial effect on the commerce of the United States and the exercise of jurisdiction is not unreasonable.

HARTFORD FIRE INSURANCE CO. v. CALIFORNIA

Supreme Court of the United States, 1993
509 U.S. 764 (footnotes omitted)

[The plaintiffs charged that the defendant insurers had violated U.S. antitrust laws by agreeing to restrict the terms of coverage of commercial general liability insurance available in the United States. Foreign defendants who were London insurers, and whose conduct occurred solely in the United Kingdom, raised as one of their defenses that it was unreasonable for U.S. antitrust laws to regulate such conduct. Justice Souter, writing for the Court, stated:]

At the outset, we note that the District Court undoubtedly had jurisdiction of these Sherman Act claims, as the London reinsurers apparently concede. * * * ("Our position is not that the Sherman Act does not apply in the sense that a minimal basis for the exercise of jurisdiction doesn't exist here. Our position is that there are certain circumstances, and that this is one of them, in which the interests of another State are sufficient that the exercise of that jurisdiction should be restrained"). Although the proposition was perhaps not always free from doubt, see *American Banana Co. v. United Fruit Co.*, 213 U.S. 347 (1909), it is well established by now that the Sherman Act applies to foreign conduct that was meant to produce and did in fact produce some substantial effect in the United States. *See* * * * *United States v. Aluminum Co. of America,* 148 F.2d 416, 444 (C.A.2 1945) (L. Hand, J.); Restatement (Third) of Foreign Relations Law of the United States § 415, and Reporters' Note 3 (1987) (hereinafter Restatement (Third) Foreign Relations Law);* * *. Such is the conduct alleged here: that the London reinsurers engaged in unlawful conspiracies to affect the market for insurance in the United States and that their conduct in fact produced substantial effect. * * *

According to the London reinsurers, the District Court should have declined to exercise such jurisdiction under the principle of international comity. The Court of Appeals agreed that courts should look to that principle in deciding whether to exercise jurisdiction under the Sherman Act. * * * This availed the London reinsurers nothing, however. To be sure, the Court of Appeals believed that "application of [American] antitrust laws to the London reinsurance market 'would lead to significant conflict with English law and policy,' " and that "[s]uch a conflict, unless outweighed by other factors, would by itself be reason to decline exercise of jurisdiction." * * * But other factors, in the court's view, including the London reinsurers' express purpose to affect United States commerce and the substantial nature of the effect produced, outweighed the supposed conflict and required the exercise of jurisdiction in this litigation. * * *

When it enacted the Foreign Trade Antitrust Improvements Act of 1982 (FTAIA), 96 Stat. 1246, 15 U.S.C. § 6a, Congress expressed no view on the question whether a court with Sherman Act jurisdiction should ever decline to exercise such jurisdiction on grounds of international comity. See H.R.Rep. No. 97–686, p. 13 (1982) ("If a court determines that the requirements for subject matter jurisdiction are met, [the FTAIA] would have no effect on the court['s] ability to employ notions of comity . . . or otherwise to take account of the international character of the transaction") (citing *Timberlane*). We need not decide that question here, however, for even assuming that in a proper case a court may decline to exercise Sherman Act jurisdiction over foreign conduct (or, as Justice Scalia would put it, may conclude by the employment of comity analysis in the first instance that there is no jurisdiction), international comity would not counsel against exercising jurisdiction in the circumstances alleged here.

The only substantial question in this litigation is whether "there is in fact a true conflict between domestic and foreign law." *Société Nationale Industrielle Aerospatiale v. United States Dist. Court,* 482 U.S. 522, 555 (1987) (Blackmun, J., concurring in part and dissenting in part). The London reinsurers contend that applying the Act to their conduct would conflict significantly with British law, and the British Government, appearing before us as amicus curiae, concurs. * * * They assert that Parliament has established a comprehensive regulatory regime over the London reinsurance market and that the conduct alleged here was perfectly consistent with British law and policy. But this is not to state a conflict. "[T]he fact that conduct is lawful in the state in which it took place will not, of itself, bar application of the United States antitrust laws," even where the foreign state has a strong policy to permit or encourage such conduct. Restatement (Third) Foreign Relations Law § 415, Comment *j*; see *Continental Ore Co., supra*, 370 U.S., at 706–707. No conflict exists, for these purposes, "where a person subject to regulation by two states can comply with the laws of both." Restatement (Third) Foreign Relations Law § 403, Comment *e*.

Since the London reinsurers do not argue that British law requires them to act in some fashion prohibited by the law of the United States, * * * or claim that their compliance with the laws of both countries is otherwise impossible, we see no conflict with British law. See Restatement (Third) Foreign Relations Law § 403, Comment *e*, § 415, Comment *j*. We have no need in this litigation to address other considerations that might inform a decision to refrain from the exercise of jurisdiction on grounds of international comity.

* * *

SCALIA, J. [dissenting, joined by O'Connor, Kennedy, and Thomas, JJ.]:

* * *

* * * [E]ven where the presumption against extraterritoriality does not apply, statutes should not be interpreted to regulate foreign persons or conduct that if that regulation would conflict with principles of international law. * * *

* * *

[Since *Alcoa*,] lower court precedent has * * * tempered the extraterritorial application of the Sherman Act with considerations of "international comity." See *Timberlane Lumber Co. v. Bank of America, N.T. & S.A.*, 549 F.2d 597, 608–15 (CA9 1976) * * *. The "comity" they refer to is not the comity of courts, whereby judges decline to exercise jurisdiction over matters more appropriately adjudged elsewhere, but rather what might be termed "prescriptive comity": the respect sovereign nations afford each other by limiting the reach of their laws. That comity is exercised by legislatures when they enact laws, and courts assume it has been exercised when they come to interpreting the scope of laws their legislatures have enacted. It is a traditional component of choice-of-law theory. * * * Comity in this sense includes the choice-of-law principles that, "in the absence of contrary congressional direction," are assumed to be incorporated into our substantive laws having extraterritorial reach. * * * Considering comity in this way is just part of determining whether the Sherman Act prohibits the conduct at issue.

In sum, the practice of using international law to limit the extraterritorial reach of statutes is firmly established in our jurisprudence. In proceeding to apply that practice to the present cases, I shall rely on the Restatement (Third) for the relevant principles of international law. Its standards appear fairly supported in the decisions of this Court construing international choice-of-law principles * * * and in the decisions of other federal courts, especially *Timberlane*. Whether the Restatement precisely reflects international law in every detail matters little here, as I believe this case would be resolved the same way under virtually any conceivable test that takes account of foreign regulatory interests.

Under the Restatement, a nation having some "basis" for jurisdiction to prescribe law should nonetheless refrain from exercising that jurisdiction "with respect to a person or activity having connections with another state when the exercise of such jurisdiction is unreasonable." Restatement (Third), § 403(1). The "reasonableness" inquiry turns on a number of factors [see Restatement § 403(2), *supra* p. 759]. * * * The activity relevant to the counts at issue here took place primarily in the United Kingdom, and the defendants in these counts are British corporations and British subjects having their principal place of business or residence outside the United States. Great Britain has established a comprehensive regulatory scheme governing the London reinsurance markets, and clearly has a heavy "interest in regulating the activity," *id.*, § 403(2)(g). * * * Finally, § 2(b) of the McCarran–Ferguson Act allows state regulatory statutes to override the Sherman Act in the insurance field, subject only to the narrow "boycott" exception set forth in § 3(b)—suggesting that "the importance of regulation to the [United States]," Restatement (Third) § 403(2)(c), is slight. Considering these factors, I think it unimaginable that an assertion of legislative jurisdiction by the United States would be considered reasonable, and therefore it is inappropriate to assume, in the absence of statutory indication to the contrary, that Congress made such an assertion.

NOTES

1. *Assessing Hartford Fire.* What standard did Justice Souter use in determining whether the U.S. antitrust statute should be applied to conduct occurring outside the United States? Does his standard differ from that of *Alcoa*? What if the United Kingdom had enacted a statute forbidding the English insurers to comply with any antitrust decree issued by an American court? Do you think Justice Souter adequately distinguished between whether the United States *could* properly exercise legislative jurisdiction (under constitutional or international law) and whether the Sherman Act *should* be construed to reach the conduct complained of? As Justice Scalia suggests, should the balancing test of the Restatement (Third) come into play when the latter question is on the table?

2. *Criminal Antitrust Cases. Alcoa* and *Hartford Fire* were civil antitrust actions. Given that civil actions are generally less intrusive into the affairs of foreign sovereigns, should the United States be able to pursue a criminal conviction of a foreign corporation under the federal antitrust statute for alleged price-fixing activities which took place entirely in Japan, simply because they were intended to have, and did in fact have, substantial effects in the United States? In *United States v. Nippon Paper Industries Co. Ltd.*, 109 F.3d 1 (1st Cir. 1997), the First Circuit said yes. According to the Court: "*Hartford Fire* definitively establishes that Section One of the Sherman Act

applies to wholly foreign conduct which has an intended and substantial effect in the United States. We are bound to accept that holding. Under settled principles of statutory construction, we also are bound to apply it by interpreting Section One the same way in a criminal case." For analysis, see Sulcove, The Extraterritorial Reach of the Criminal Provisions of U.S. Antitrust Laws: The Impact of United States v. Nippon Paper Industries, 19 U. Pa. J. Int'l Econ. L. 1067 (1998).

3. *The Return of Reasonableness?* After *Hartford Fire*, what is left of the reasonableness test as formulated in Restatement (Third) §§ 403 and 415(3)? A recent decision interpreting the same antitrust statute involved in *Hartford Fire* is *F. Hoffmann–LaRoche Ltd. v. Empagran, S.A.*, 542 U.S. 155 (2004). In that case, vitamin purchasers filed a class action alleging that vitamin manufacturers and distributors had engaged in a price-fixing conspiracy, which raised vitamin prices in the United States and foreign countries in violation of the Sherman and Clayton Acts. Defendants moved to dismiss the claims as they related to purchases of vitamins by foreign corporations outside the United States. Justice Breyer, writing for a unanimous Court, found the Foreign Trade Antitrust Improvements Act (FTAIA) provides that the Sherman Act "shall not apply to conduct involving trade or commerce * * * with foreign nations," 15 U. S. C. § 6a, unless the conduct significantly harms imports, domestic commerce, or U.S. exporters. In this instance, the latter clause was not satisfied for two reasons. First, the Court recalled that it:

> ordinarily construes ambiguous statutes to avoid unreasonable interference with the sovereign authority of other nations. * * * This rule of construction reflects principles of customary international law—law that (we must assume) Congress ordinarily seeks to follow. See Restatement (Third) of Foreign Relations Law of the United States §§ 403(1), 403(2) (1986) (hereinafter Restatement) (limiting the unreasonable exercise of prescriptive jurisdiction with respect to a person or activity having connections with another State); *Murray v. Schooner Charming Betsy*, 6 U.S. 64, 2 Cranch 64 (1804) ("[A]n act of Congress ought never to be construed to violate the law of nations if any other possible construction remains"); *Hartford Fire Insurance Co. v. California*, 509 U.S. 764, 817 (1993) (Scalia, J., dissenting) (identifying rule of construction as derived from the principle of "prescriptive comity").

> This rule of statutory construction cautions courts to assume that legislators take account of the legitimate sovereign interests of other nations when they write American laws. It thereby helps the potentially conflicting laws of different nations work together in harmony—a harmony particularly needed in today's highly interdependent commercial world.

> No one denies that America's antitrust laws, when applied to foreign conduct, can interfere with a foreign nation's ability independently to regulate its own commercial affairs. But our courts have long held that application of our antitrust laws to foreign anticompetitive conduct is nonetheless reasonable, and hence consistent with principles of prescriptive comity, insofar as they reflect a legislative effort to redress domestic antitrust injury that foreign anticompetitive conduct has caused. See

United States v. Aluminum Co. of America, 148 F.2d 416, 443–444 (CA2 1945) (L. Hand, J.); 1 P. Areeda & D. Turner, Antitrust Law ¶ ;236 (1978).

But why is it reasonable to apply those laws to foreign conduct insofar as that conduct causes independent foreign harm and that foreign harm alone gives rise to the plaintiff's claim? Like the former case, application of those laws creates a serious risk of interference with a foreign nation's ability independently to regulate its own commercial affairs. But, unlike the former case, the justification for that interference seems insubstantial. See Restatement § 403(2) (determining reasonableness on basis of such factors as connections with regulating nation, harm to that nation's interests, extent to which other nations regulate, and the potential for conflict). Why should American law supplant, for example, Canada's or Great Britain's or Japan's own determination about how best to protect Canadian or British or Japanese customers from anticompetitive conduct engaged in significant part by Canadian or British or Japanese or other foreign companies?

We recognize that principles of comity provide Congress greater leeway when it seeks to control through legislation the actions of American companies, see Restatement § 402; and some of the anticompetitive price-fixing conduct alleged here took place in America. But the higher foreign prices of which the foreign plaintiffs here complain are not the consequence of any domestic anticompetitive conduct that Congress sought to forbid, for Congress did not seek to forbid any such conduct insofar as it is here relevant, i.e., insofar as it is intertwined with foreign conduct that causes independent foreign harm. Rather Congress sought to release domestic (and foreign) anticompetitive conduct from Sherman Act constraints when that conduct causes foreign harm. Congress, of course, did make an exception where that conduct also causes domestic harm. See House Report 13 (concerns about American firms' participation in international cartels addressed through "domestic injury" exception). But any independent domestic harm the foreign conduct causes here has, by definition, little or nothing to do with the matter.

We thus repeat the basic question: Why is it reasonable to apply this law to conduct that is significantly foreign insofar as that conduct causes independent foreign harm and that foreign harm alone gives rise to the plaintiff's claim? We can find no good answer to the question.

The Court further noted that the comity concerns remained real as other nations have not in all areas adopted similar antitrust laws and disagreed dramatically about appropriate remedies. Respondents' alternative argument that case-by-case comity analysis is preferable to an across the board exclusion of foreign injury cases was rejected by the Court as too complex to prove workable.

Second, the Court held that the FTAIA's language and history suggested that Congress designed the Act to clarify and perhaps to limit, but not to expand, the Sherman Act's scope as applied to foreign commerce. There was no significant indication that at the time Congress wrote the FTAIA, courts would have thought the Sherman Act applicable to such circumstances. For comments, see Buxbaum, National Courts, Global Cartels: F. Hottmann–LaRoche Ltd. v. Empagran, S.A. (U.S. Supreme Court 2004), 5 German L.J. 1095 (2004); Neuman, The Abiding Significance of Law in Foreign Relations, 2004 Sup. Ct. Rev. 111, 123–27, 133–34.

4. *Foreign Government Objections.* Foreign governments have objected to the extraterritorial application of U.S. antitrust laws, going so far as to adopt national laws that seek to "claw back" their authority. See, e.g., Griffin, Jurisdiction and Enforcement: Foreign Governmental Reactions to U.S. Assertion of Extraterritorial Jurisdiction, 6 Geo. Mason L. Rev. 505 (1998); Kim, The Extraterritorial Application of U.S. Antitrust Law and its Adoption in Korea, 7 Sing. J. Int'l & Comp. L. 386 (2003); Buxbaum, German Legal Culture and the Globalization of Competition Law: A Historical Perspective on the Expansion of Private Antitrust Enforcement, 23 Berkeley J. Int'l L. 474 (2005). Such objections have led to cooperative arrangements whereby, before exercising U.S. extraterritorial antitrust jurisdiction, a foreign government will be notified and given the opportunity to react. For example, the North American Free Trade Agreement, Dec. 17, 1992, ch. 15, 32 I.L.M. 605, 663–64 (1993), requires each nation to cooperate with the authorities of the other members to further the enforcement of their antitrust laws. For U.S. implementation, see the International Antitrust Enforcement Assistance Act of 1994, 15 U.S.C. §§ 6201–6212 (2000).

5. *European Community Position.* Whether the European Community embraced an extraterritorial theory of antitrust jurisdiction was for a long time uncertain. Initially, the European Court of Justice avoided dealing with the problem of extraterritoriality by attributing the conduct of a subsidiary within the European Community to its corporate parent and thereby finding the conduct of the parent to take place within the territory of the Community. The effect of this construction was to apply the EC law extraterritorially in order to reach, among others, U.S. enterprises outside of the Community. See generally 2 Smit & Herzog, The Law of the European Union § 85.19 (2005); Gupta, After *Hartford Fire*: Antitrust and Comity, 84 Geo. L.J. 2287 (1996).

The European Court of Justice's *Wood Pulp* decision, *Ahlstrom Osakeyhtio v. Commission*, [1988] E.C.R 5193, involved the territorial scope of application of Article 85 of the Treaty of Rome concerning practices which have as their object or effect the restriction of competition within the common market. The European Commission charged certain U.S., Finnish, Swedish, and Canadian firms and two of their export associations with fixing the price of wood pulp sold within the Community. The Court found the Commission's decision "not contrary to Article 85 of the Treaty or to the rules of public international law" on jurisdiction. Commentators have debated the extent to which this ruling applied an effects theory to agreements made outside the Community. See Griffin, EC and U.S. Extraterritoriality: Activism and Cooperation, 17 Fordham Int'l L.J. 353 (1994). More recently, the E.C.J. seems to have moved toward a view of the effects doctrine and reasonableness analogous to that of the U.S. Restatement (Third) §§ 402–03, in the *Gencor/Lonrho* case (1999), involving the merger of two South African companies with substantial European business. See Case T–102/96, *Gencor Ltd. v. Commission of the European Communities*, 1999 E.C.R. II–753. Also relevant is the practice of the European Commission as the Community's executive organ. In evaluating the Boeing/McDonnell Douglas merger and the Time Warner/AOL merger, the Commission considered how the amalgamations of these U.S. companies would affect competition within Europe. For commentary, see, e.g., Mavroidis, Some Reflections on the Extraterritorial Application of Laws, in Melanges Waelbroeack 1–14 (1998); Fox, The Competition Law of the European Union in Comparative Perspective (2009).

6. *Conflicts in Application of Antitrust Laws.* Since both the United States and the European Community apply their antitrust laws extraterritorially conflicts may arise. Thus, the European Commission judged violative of its antitrust laws a proposed merged of General Electric with Honeywell that the U.S. Attorney–General had ruled to be not violative of U.S antitrust laws. Similarly, trade conditions imposed by Microsoft that have passed U.S. antitrust scrutiny have been held violative of European Community antitrust laws by the E.C. Court of First Instance. See Commission Decision of Mar. 24, 2004 relating to a proceeding under Article 82 of the E.C. Treaty (Case Comp/C–3/37.792 Microsoft). How can such conflicts be avoided? Would it be appropriate in cases of multinational companies to give precedence to the determination made by the authorities at the principal place of business of the alleged offender, at least on those issues in which the competition laws are as similar as they are in the case of the United States and the European Community? Or should the institutions agree to have an arbitral tribunal render the decision?

2. The Effects Doctrine in Other Areas of Economic Activity

Internet Activity. Notwithstanding their protests about exorbitant exercises of U.S. jurisdiction, some European states have purported to prescribe certain rules of law on a broad extraterritorial basis, affecting U.S. companies acting within U.S. territory in accordance with U.S. law. For example, in November 2000 a French court ruled that French laws barring racist propaganda and sale of Nazi memorabilia would apply to the operations of Yahoo!, a U.S.-based Internet service provider; and it instructed Yahoo! to block access by French nationals to the auction section of its website. Yahoo! contended not only that it would be technologically impossible to prevent French nationals from reaching the website, but also that the First Amendment of the U.S. Constitution would prevent censorship of the content of the site. See "French Court Ruling Hits Yahoo!", Financial Times, Nov. 21, 2000, at 1, and Editorial Comment, id., at 20. See Goldsmith & Wu, Who Controls the Internet? 1–10 (2006); Schultz, Carving Up the Internet: Jurisdiction, Legal Orders and the Private/Public International Law Interface, 19 E.J.I.L. 799 (2008).

Overseas Bribery. In *W.S. Kirkpatrick & Co. v. Environmental Tectonics Corp.*, 493 U.S. 400 (1990), the American plaintiff alleged that the American defendant had violated the Foreign Corrupt Practices Act of 1977 by bribing Nigerian officials in order to obtain a construction contract and that plaintiff had suffered damages as a consequence. The court ruled that the act of state doctrine did not preclude the plaintiff from recovering. See Chapter 10, p. 677 note 6. No question was raised as to whether the 1977 Act could cover conduct and damages suffered in Nigeria. Of course, since the defendant was a U.S. corporation, jurisdiction could be justified on the basis of the nationality principle. See Section 3 *infra*. Along similar lines, see *In Re Grand Jury Subpoena dated August 9, 2000*, 218 F. Supp.2d 544 (S.D.N.Y. 2002).

Securities Litigation. U.S. courts are increasingly asked to apply U.S. securities laws to transactions abroad between foreign corporations and their shareholders in regard to securities registered with the U.S. Securities and Exchange Commission and listed on a New York exchange. These efforts, involving U.S. extraterritorial legislative and judicial jurisdiction, have taken the form of class actions in which the plaintiff class includes the foreign shareholders who engage in the transactions. Defendants in those actions have argued that the U.S. Securities Acts cannot be applied extraterritorially and that inclusion of the foreign shareholders in the class would violate their constitutional and human rights. Thus far, almost all of the U.S. District Courts that have addressed these issues have permitted the class actions to proceed with the inclusion of the foreign shareholders, but in one case, the District Court refused to include the foreign shareholders in the class, and in another case (*AIG*), a Dutch pension fund is requesting to be designated as the lead plaintiff. These cases represent instances in which international (human rights) law has been argued to limit U.S. judicial jurisdiction. Do you judge that the registration with the U.S. Securities and Exchange Commission and the listing on a New York exchange provide an adequate basis for the exercise of U.S. legislative jurisdiction? If so, what is the applicable international law basis? Note that permitting the class action to proceed would extend the protection of U.S. securities law to wherever the U.S.-registered and listed securities are sold.

On transnational securities regulation, see Choi & Guzman, National Laws, International Money: Regulation in a Global Capital Market, 65 Fordham L. Rev. 1855 (1997); Fox, Securities Disclosure in a Globalizing Market: Who Should Regulate Whom, 95 Mich. L. Rev. 696 (1998); Fox, The Political Economy of Statutory Reach: U.S. Disclosure Rules in a Globalizing Market for Securities, 97 Mich. L. Rev. 096 (1998); Patterson, Defining the Reach of the Securities Exchange Act: Extraterritorial Application of the Antifraud Provisions, 74 Fordham L. Rev. 213 (2005); Dammann, A New Approach to Corporate Choice of Law, 38 Vand. J. Transnat'l L. 51 (2005); Dombalagian, Choice of Law and Capital Markets Regulation, 82 Tulane. L. Rev 1903 (2008).

3. "Trafficking" in Property Outside the Territory

The Cuban Liberty and Democratic Solidarity (Libertád) Act of 1996 (also known as the "Helms–Burton Act") and the Iran and Libya Sanctions Act of the same year (ILSA) were adopted to deter persons in third countries from engaging in transactions involving investments or trade with the targeted countries. Both laws have been widely condemned by governments and international bodies as violations of international law because of their assertions of extraterritorial jurisdiction.

Title III of the Helms–Burton Act, Pub. L. No. 104–114, 110 Stat. 785, 22 U.S.C. §§ 6021–6091 (2000), enables United States nationals to recover civil damages in U.S. courts from any person or entity that has "trafficked" in property "confiscated" (i.e., expropriated without payment of compensation) by the Cuban government to which the U.S. national has a claim. "Trafficking" is broadly defined; it includes buying, selling, managing or otherwise benefiting from "confiscated" property. The law also provides that the Act of State doctrine shall not apply to any lawsuit brought under the civil remedy provision (§ 302(a)(6)).

The Iran and Libya Sanctions Act of 1996 (ILSA), Pub. L. No. 104–172, 110 Stat. 1541, required sanctions to be imposed on any person or entity engaging in trade or making investments that contribute to development of petroleum resources in Iran or Libya. These sanctions, in furtherance of counterterrorism and nonproliferation policies, were clearly meant to apply to foreign persons; U.S. nationals had been covered by earlier restrictions. (Sanctions against Libya were lifted following a comprehensive settlement agreement; see Chapter 9, p. 617 note 4. ILSA was thereafter changed to the Iran Freedom Support Act of 2006, Pub. L. No. 109–293, 120 Stat. 1347 (2006), which removes all references to Libya.)

Both acts were criticized by a large number of countries as violations of international law because they imposed penalties for actions outside of the United States that were legal in the countries under the applicable national law. Some states—including close allies of the United States—adopted blocking and clawback statutes to hinder the application of these statutes. The U.N. General Assembly adopted resolutions by a large majority condemning U.S. unilateral economic measures, *inter alia* because of the assertion of extraterritorial jurisdiction. The European Union protested the Helms–Burton Act diplomatically and complained about it at the World Trade Organization. Canada and Mexico raised objections under the North American Free Trade Agreement. A legal body, the Inter–American Juridical Committee (an organ of the Organization of American States), unanimously concluded that the Helms–Burton Act violated the international law of jurisdiction. It declared that "[a] prescribing State does not have the right to exercise jurisdiction over acts of 'trafficking' abroad by aliens under circumstances where neither the alien nor the conduct in question has any connection with its territory and where no apparent connection exists between such acts and the protection of its essential sovereign interests." The U.S. member of the committee, Keith Highet, voted for the declaration. See materials reprinted at 35 I.L.M. 397, 483, 1322, 1333 (1996).

The U.S. government rejected the legal arguments of the European and Latin American states. However, President Clinton issued a series of six-month waivers postponing the right to invoke the remedy under Title III of Helms–Burton, declaring that he would postpone that right as long as the U.S. allies continued their advocacy of democratic change in Cuba. See Statement by the President on Suspending Title III of the Helms–Burton Act, 36 I.L.M. 216 (1997). Such waivers have continued under his successors and thus the right of action has not become operational. Nevertheless, the issue of the international legality of Helms–Burton (as well as ILSA) has remained a lively subject of dispute among governments and international lawyers.

NOTES

1. *"Trafficking."* Supporters of Helms–Burton have argued, citing judicial decisions in national courts, that a state which has taken property without just compensation does not acquire good title and consequently persons acquiring the property (or trafficking in it) are in the same legal position as one who obtains property from a thief. See Clagett, Title III of the Helms–Burton Act Is Consistent with International Law, 90 A.J.I.L. 434, 437 (1996). On the premise that a taking of property without just compensation violates international law, would a state (e.g., the United States) be entitled to give a civil remedy to the original owner (or successor in title) against the person who bought the property in question from the nationalizing state? Would this be justified as adjudicatory jurisdiction to enforce international law? Why have foreign states—even ones that share the U.S. position on legal requirements of compensation for expropriated property—reacted so negatively to Helms–Burton?

2. *Secondary Boycotts.* Should Helms–Burton penalties against traffickers for acts permitted in their countries be regarded as a type of secondary boycott that is (or should be) forbidden by international law? The United States declared its general opposition to secondary boycotts when the Arab states imposed a boycott against persons in other countries who had dealings with Israel. Do such "unfriendly" boycotts violate international law if intended to compel or influence the target state to change its domestic policy? See discussion on intervention in Chapter 15, p. 1192, and Damrosch, Politics Across Borders: Nonintervention and Nonforcible Influence Over Domestic Affairs, 83 A.J.I.L. 1 (1989). On Helms–Burton as a secondary boycott, see Lowenfeld, Congress and Cuba: The Helms–Burton Act, 90 A.J.I.L. 419 (1996); Clagett, A Reply to Professor Lowenfeld, 90 A.J.I.L. 641 (1996); Walker, The Legality of the Secondary Boycott Contained in the Helms–Burton Act Under International Law, 3 DePaul Dig. Int. L. 1134 (1997); Schwartz, Dealing with a "Rogue State": The Libya Precedent, 101 A.J.I.L. 553, 563–64 (2007); Ryngaert, Extraterritorial Export Controls (Secondary Boycotts), 7 Chinese J. Int'l L. 625 (2008).

3. *Protective Principle.* Could Helms–Burton and ILSA be justified on the basis of the "protective principle" of jurisdiction, *infra* p. 798? Both acts refer to protecting the national security of the United States as a purpose of the legislation and its proponents consider the three target states as sources of terrorism against the United States. Is this consideration sufficient to justify measures against individuals in third countries whose economic activities may be beneficial to the target countries?

4. *Russian Objections to U.S. Sanctions.* In October 2008, the United States announced new sanctions pursuant to the Iran, North Korea and Syria Nonproliferation Act, Pub. L. No. 109–353 120 Stat. 2015 (2006), which affected thirteen foreign persons including a Russian company. Russia immediately protested:

> These new sanctions were introduced without any international legal foundation whatsoever * * *. All of our trade and all of our military-technical cooperation with Iran is carried out in strict accordance with current international legal norms * * *. There can be no other explanation here than the rather arrogant extraterritorial implementation of American laws.

See U.S. Penalizes Companies for Selling Arms Technology, N.Y. Times, Oct. 25, 2008, at A6 (quoting Russian foreign minister Sergei Lavrov). Is this objection well-founded? Does your answer depend on the nature of the sanctions imposed? If the sanction in question is the denial of an license to obtain U.S.-origin technology in the hands of a third party, would this be an extraterritorial application of U.S. law?

5. *Further Reading.* For additional readings, see Busby, Jurisdiction to Limit Third–Country Interaction with Sanctioned States: The Iran and Libya Sanctions and Helms–Burton Acts, 36 Colum. J. Transnat'l Law 621 (1998); Gierbolini, The Helms–Burton Act: Inconsistency with International Law and Irrationality at their Maximum, 6 J. Transnat'l L & Pol'y 289 (1997); Fairey, The Helms–Burton Act: The Effect of International Law on Domestic Implementation, 46 Am. U. L. Rev. 1289 (1997); Stern, Vers La Mondialisation Juridique? Les Lois Helms–Burton et D'Amato–Kennedy, 1996 R.G.D.I.P. 4; European Union: Demarches Protesting the Cuban Liberty and Democratic Solidarity Act, 35 I.L.M. 397 (1996); Tramhel, Helms–Burton Invites a Look at Counter–Measures, 30 Geo.Wash. J. Int'l L. & Econ. 317 (1996–97); Damrosch, Enforcing International Law Through Non–Forcible Measures, 269 Rec. des Cours 9, 63–78, 85–91 (1997); Report of the Committee on Inter–American Affairs, Domestic Legal Issues Concerning the Helms–Burton Act, 54 Rec. Ass'n B. City N.Y. 515 (1999).

SECTION 3. JURISDICTION BASED ON THE NATIONALITY PRINCIPLE

A. BASED ON NATIONALITY OF NATURAL PERSONS

BLACKMER v. UNITED STATES

Supreme Court of the United States, 1932
284 U.S. 421 (footnotes omitted)

HUGHES, C.J.: The petitioner, Harry M. Blackmer, a citizen of the United States resident in Paris, France, was adjudged guilty of contempt of the Supreme Court of the District of Columbia for failure to respond to subpoenas served upon him in France and requiring him to appear as a witness on behalf of the United States at a criminal trial in that court.

Two subpoenas were issued, for appearances at different times, and there was a separate proceeding with respect to each. The two cases were heard together, and a fine of $30,000 with costs was imposed in each case, to be satisfied out of the property of the petitioner which had been seized by order of the court. The decrees were affirmed by the Court of Appeals of the District [49 F.2d 523], and this Court granted writs of certiorari * * *.

The subpoenas were issued and served, and the proceedings to punish for contempt were taken, under the provisions of the Act of July 3, 1926, c. 762, 44 Stat. 835, U.S.C., tit. 28, §§ 711–718 (28 U.S.C.A. §§ 711–718). The statute provides that whenever the attendance at the trial of a criminal action of a witness abroad, who is "a citizen of the United States or domiciled therein," is desired by the Attorney General, or any assistant or district attorney acting under him, the judge of the court in which the action is pending may order a subpoena to issue, to be addressed to a consul of the United States and to be served by him personally upon the witness with a tender of traveling expenses. Sections 2, 3 of the act (28 U.S.C.A. §§ 712, 713). Upon proof of such service and of the failure of the witness to appear, the court may make an order requiring the witness to show cause why he should not be punished for contempt, and, upon the issue of such an order, the court may direct that property belonging to the witness and within the United States may be seized and held to satisfy any judgment which may be rendered against him in the proceeding. Sections 4, 5 (28 U.S.C.A. §§ 714, 715). Provision is made for personal service of the order upon the witness and also for its publication in a newspaper of general circulation in the district where the court is sitting. Section 6 (28 U.S.C.A. § 716). If, upon the hearing, the charge is sustained, the court may adjudge the witness guilty of contempt and impose upon him a fine not exceeding $100,000, to be satisfied by a sale of the property seized. Section 7 (28 U.S.C.A. § 717). This statute and the proceedings against the petitioner are assailed as being repugnant to the Constitution of the United States.

First. The principal objections to the statute are that it violates the due process clause of the Fifth Amendment. These contentions are: (1) That the "Congress has no power to authorize United States consuls to serve process except as permitted by treaty;" (2) that the act does not provide "a valid method of acquiring judicial jurisdiction to render personal judgment against defendant and judgment against his property;" (3) that the act "does not require actual or any other notice to defendant of the offense or of the Government's claim against his property;" (4) that the provisions "for hearing and judgment in the entire absence of the accused and without his consent" are invalid; and (5) that the act is "arbitrary, capricious and unreasonable."

While it appears that the petitioner removed his residence to France in the year 1924, it is undisputed that he was, and continued to be, a citizen of the United States. He continued to owe allegiance to the United States. By virtue of the obligations of citizenship, the United States retained its authority over him, and he was bound by its laws made applicable to him in a foreign country. Thus, although resident abroad, the petitioner remained subject to the taxing power of the United States. *Cook v. Tait*, 265 U.S. 47, 54, 56. For disobedience to its laws through conduct abroad, he was subject to punishment in the courts of the United States. *United States v. Bowman*, 260 U.S. 94, 102. With respect to such an exercise of authority, there is no question of international law, but solely of the purport of the municipal law which establishes the duties of the citizen in relation to his own government. While the legislation of the Congress, unless the contrary intent appears, is construed to apply only within the territorial jurisdiction of the United States, the question of its application, so far as citizens of the United States in foreign countries are concerned, is one of construction, not of legislative power. *American Banana Co. v. United Fruit Co.*, 213 U.S. 347, 357; *United States v. Bowman*, supra; *Robertson v. Labor Board*, 268 U.S. 619, 622. Nor can it be doubted that the United States possesses the power inherent in sovereignty to require the return to this country of a citizen, resident elsewhere, whenever the public interest requires it, and to penalize him in case of refusal. Compare *Bartue and the Duchess of Suffolk's Case*, 2 Dyer's Rep. 176b, 73 Eng. Rep. 388; *Knowles v. Luce*, Moore 109, 72 Eng. Rep. 473. What in England was the prerogative of the sovereign in this respect pertains under our constitutional system to the national authority which may be exercised by the Congress by virtue of the legislative power to prescribe the duties of the citizens of the United States. It is also beyond controversy that one of the duties which the citizen owes to his government is to support the administration of justice by attending its courts and giving his testimony whenever he is properly summoned. * * * And the Congress may provide for the performance of this duty and prescribe penalties for disobedience.

In the present instance, the question concerns only the method of enforcing the obligation. The jurisdiction of the United States over its absent citizen, so far as the binding effect of its legislation is concerned, is a jurisdiction in personam, as he is personally bound to take notice of the laws that are applicable to him and to obey them. *United States v. Bowman, supra*. But for the exercise of judicial jurisdiction in personam, there must be due process, which requires appropriate notice of the judicial action and an opportunity to be heard. For this notice and opportunity the statute provides. The authority to require the absent citizen to return and testify necessarily implies the authority to give him notice of the requirement. As his attendance is needed in court, it is appropriate that the Congress should authorize the court to direct the notice to be given, and that it should be in the customary form of a subpoena. Obviously, the requirement would be nugatory, if provision could not be made for its communication to the witness in the foreign country. The efficacy of an attempt to provide constructive service in this country would rest upon the presumption that the notice would be given in a manner calculated to reach the witness abroad. * * *

The question of the validity of the provision for actual service of the subpoena in a foreign country is one that arises solely between the government of the United States and the citizen. The mere giving of such a notice to the citizen in the foreign country of the requirement of his government that he shall return is in no sense an invasion of any right of the foreign government and the citizen has no standing to invoke any such supposed right. While consular privileges in foreign countries are the appropriate subjects of treaties, it does not follow that every act of a consul, as, e.g., in communicating with citizens of his own country, must be predicated upon a specific provision of a treaty. The intercourse of friendly nations, permitting travel and residence of the citizens of each in the territory of the other, presupposes and facilitates such communications. In selecting the consul for the service of the subpoena, the Congress merely prescribed a method deemed to assure the desired result but in no sense essential. The consul was not directed to perform any function involving consular privileges or depending upon any treaty relating to them, but simply to act as any designated person might act for the government in conveying to the citizen the actual notice of the requirement of his attendance. The point raised by the petitioner with respect to the provision for the service of the subpoena abroad is without merit.

As the Congress could define the obligation, it could prescribe a penalty to enforce it. And, as the default lay in disobedience to an authorized direction of the court, it constituted a contempt of court, and the Congress could provide for procedure appropriate in contempt cases. * * *

Decrees affirmed.

NOTES

1. *Exercising Jurisdiction Over Nationals and Residents Abroad.* The statute involved in *Blackmer* is now codified as 28 U.S.C. § 1783 (2000), and is incorporated by reference into Fed. R. Civ. P. 45(b)(2) and Fed. R. Crim. P. 17(e)(2). It provides in relevant part that a United States court may order the issuance of a subpoena requiring the appearance as a witness of a "national or resident of the United States who is in a foreign country" if such testimony is "necessary in the interest of justice." Would the Court in *Blackmer* have reached the same result if Blackmer had been an alien, domiciled in the United States? Is it unreasonable for a state to assert legislative jurisdiction over its domiciliaries when they are abroad? Compare *Milliken v. Meyer*, 311 U.S. 457, 462 (1940) ("Domicile in the state is alone sufficient to bring an absent defendant within the reach of the state's jurisdiction for purposes of a personal judgment by means of appropriate substituted service."). The word "resident" in 28 U.S.C. § 1783 was, in the 1948 revision of the Judicial Code, substituted for "or domiciled therein." Would an alien's residence or domicile in the United States provide a reasonable basis for the assertion of legislative jurisdiction with regard to an act committed outside the United States? See Smit, International Aspects of Federal Civil Procedure, 61 Colum. L. Rev.

1031, 1048–49 (1961). Should a distinction be drawn depending on whether civil or criminal jurisdiction is exercised?

2. *Other U.S. Laws Regulating Overseas Conduct of Nationals.* A number of statutory provisions, in addition to that applied to Blackmer, apply specifically to the conduct or income of United States nationals abroad. See, e.g., Foreign Corrupt Practices Act, 15 U.S.C. § 78dd–2 (2000) (prohibiting bribery of foreign officials abroad); 18 U.S.C. § 953 (2000) (punishing unauthorized attempts by "any citizen of the United States, wherever he may be," to influence a foreign government in its relations with the United States); 18 U.S.C. § 960 (2000) (prohibiting U.S. nationals from fighting in other nations' wars); 18 U.S.C. § 2381 (2000) (proscribing treason by anyone "owing allegiance to the United States" "within the United States or elsewhere"); 18 U.S.C. § 2423 (2000) (prohibiting U.S. nationals from traveling to another country for the purpose of having sex with minors); 50 U.S.C. app. § 453 (2000) (requiring "every male citizen of the United States," *inter alia*, to register for military service).

3. *Discerning Legislative Intent.* Section 1(C) of this Chapter noted the willingness of U.S. courts to apply statutes extraterritorially when Congressional intent can be so implied, as occurred in *United States v. Bowman*, 260 U.S. 94 (1922). *Bowman*, in turn, was relied upon in *Blackmer*. More recently, some lower courts have understood *Bowman* as grounded not only in the power of Congress to regulate the conduct of U.S. nationals, but also in the power to protect state interests (thus relying on the protective principle rather than the nationality principle). In *United States v. Bin Laden*, 92 F. Supp. 2d 189, 193–198 (S.D.N.Y. 2000), the indictment alleged that the defendants (who included foreign nationals) had conspired to bomb American facilities overseas. The court rejected the contention that U.S. statutes making it a crime to destroy property belonging to the United States should be construed as applicable only to U.S. nationals. On other jurisdictional issues in the *Bin Laden* case, see *infra* pp. 797 note 2, 802 note 2.

4. *Exercise by Several States of Nationality Jurisdiction.* In *Skiriotes v. Florida*, 313 U.S. 69, 77 (1941), the Supreme Court affirmed defendant's conviction for violation of a state statute making it criminal to use diving equipment in the taking of sponges off the coast of Florida. Defendant had been arrested in Florida, but argued that the state had no power to try him because he had used the proscribed equipment while six miles from shore. The Court avoided the question of the extent of Florida's territorial waters, and, assuming from the record that Skiriotes was a citizen of the United States and of Florida, concluded that Florida might regulate the conduct of its "citizens" upon the high seas with respect to matters in which it had a legitimate interest and when there was no conflict with acts of Congress.

5. *Practice by Other States.* Many states exercise jurisdiction over their nationals when they travel abroad. In the United Kingdom, statutes provide for the punishment of not only treason, but also homicide, bigamy, perjury, and other crimes, when committed abroad by a British subject. See 10 Halsbury's Laws of England 322–24 (Simonds ed. 1955); see also 2 O'Connell at 898–99; 2 Hackworth at 203–06. India has provided that its criminal law applies to Indian nationals everywhere, no matter how minor the offense.

Indian Penal Code § 4 (3d ed. Raju 1965). Non-common law states also claim comprehensive jurisdiction over crimes committed by nationals abroad. In France, for example, a citizen can be prosecuted in France for any crime (roughly equivalent to a felony) and many *délits* (misdemeanors) committed abroad. See Code de Procédure Pénale, art. 689 (Dalloz 1966); Delaume, Jurisdiction over Crimes Committed Abroad: French and American Law, 21 Geo. Wash. L. Rev. 173 (1952); 1 Travers, Le Droit Pénal International 584–631 (1920). On German law, see German Penal Code (Strafgesetzbuch) § 3 (German criminal law applicable to Germans whether act committed in Germany or abroad), and § 4 (German criminal law applicable to persons acquiring German citizenship after criminal act has been committed).

6. *Further Reading.* For further discussion, see Arnell, The Case for Nationality Based Jurisdiction, 50 I.C.L.Q. 955 (2001); Watson, Offenders Abroad: The Case for Nationality–Based Criminal Jurisdiction, 17 Yale J. Int'l L. 41 (1992).

B. BASED ON NATIONALITY OF LEGAL PERSONS

RESTATEMENT OF THE LAW (THIRD) THE FOREIGN RELATIONS LAW OF THE UNITED STATES § 414 (1987)

§ 414. Jurisdiction with Respect to Activities of Foreign Branches and Subsidiaries

(1) Subject to §§ 403 and 441, a state may exercise jurisdiction to prescribe for limited purposes with respect to activities of foreign branches of corporations organized under its laws.

(2) A state may not ordinarily regulate activities of corporations organized under the laws of a foreign state on the basis that they are owned or controlled by nationals of the regulating state. However, under § 403 and subject to § 441, it may not be unreasonable for a state to exercise jurisdiction for limited purposes with respect to activities of affiliated foreign entities

(a) by direction to the parent corporation in respect of such matters as uniform accounting, disclosure to investors, or preparation of consolidated tax returns of multinational enterprises; or

(b) by direction to either the parent or the subsidiary in exceptional cases, depending on all relevant factors, including the extent to which

(i) the regulation is essential to implementation of a program to further a major national interest of the state exercising jurisdiction;

(ii) the national program of which the regulation is a part can be carried out effectively only if it is applied also to foreign subsidiaries;

(iii) the regulation conflicts or is likely to conflict with the law or policy of the state where the subsidiary is established.

(c) In the exceptional cases referred to in paragraph (b), the burden of establishing reasonableness is heavier when the direction is issued to the foreign subsidiary than when it is issued to the parent corporation.

NOTES

1. *Nationality Jurisdiction Over Multinational Corporations.* The traditional rule is that a state has jurisdiction over legal persons organized under its laws. Many states, in addition, assert jurisdiction over legal persons whose principal place of business or registered office (*siège social*) is located in their territories, without encountering objections assertedly based on international law. States have further sought to regulate activities by legal persons organized or having their principal places of business abroad when these persons are owned or controlled by nationals. All three of these criteria can be found in United States law. See Restatement (Third) § 414, Reporters' Note 4.

2. *Subject Matter Areas.* There are various areas in which the United States has endeavored to extend the extraterritorial reach of its legislation over the conduct of multinational corporations abroad, including shipping, tax, export control, anti-boycott legislation, foreign corrupt practices, and securities law. On such subjects, see Restatement (Third) § 411–14. On the controversial "unitary tax" imposed by many states, see *Barclays Bank PLC v. Franchise Tax Bd. of California*, 512 U.S. 298 (1994) (upholding imposition of California income tax on the part of the worldwide income of a foreign multinational company that was attributed to California under a statutory formula); but see *Japan Line, Ltd. v. County of Los Angeles*, 441 U.S. 434 (1979) (striking down an ad valorem property tax on foreign owned cargo containers used in international commerce).

3. *Jurisdiction Over Licensees to U.S. Legal Persons?* After the Soviet Union's invasion of Afghanistan, the United States sought to prohibit certain pipeline exports to the Soviet Union pursuant to the Export Administration Act of 1979, 50 U.S.C. app. § 2404. That statute extended its reach to "any person subject to the jurisdiction of the United States." In regulations promulgated by the United States, the export prohibition was imposed upon not just U.S. nationals, but also upon foreign persons not owned or controlled by U.S. nationals who had agreed, in licensing contracts with U.S. nationals, to abide by export prohibitions that might be promulgated by the United States. The European Community and several of its member states protested and ordered persons in their territories to perform their contracts and deliver the pipeline materials to their Russian purchasers. See European Communities, Comments on the U.S. Regulations Concerning Trade with the U.S.S.R., 21 I.L.M. 891 (1982); N.Y. Times, Aug. 24, 1982, at D1, col. 3; N.Y. Times, July 23, 1982, at A1, col. 6 (government of France compelling all French companies to honor pipeline-related contracts with the Soviet Union); United Kingdom, Statement and Order Concerning the American Export Embargo with Regard to the Soviet Gas Pipeline, Aug. 2, 1982, 21 I.L.M. 851 (1982)

(British government order to four British companies with the largest pipeline contracts not to comply with the U.S. embargo). Were the European objections based on solid international law grounds? Can it be argued that U.S. technology can be regarded as "national" so as to justify the exercise of jurisdiction on the basis of nationality by the state where it was created? For a statement of the U.S. position, see Dam, Extraterritoriality and Conflicts of Jurisdiction, 1983 A.S.I.L. Proc. 370 (1983); Symposium, 27 Ger. Y.B.I.L. 28 (1984).

C. BASED ON NATIONALITY OF VESSELS, AIRCRAFT, SPACE VEHICLES AND OTHER OBJECTS

Vessels are usually considered to possess the nationality of the state whose flag they fly. But, as in the case of persons, international law requires that there be a "genuine link" between the state and the vessel. To what extent can a state exercise jurisdiction over vessels and other objects as they move from state to state?

Ocean Vessels. In *McCulloch v. Sociedad Nacional de Marineros de Honduras*, 372 U.S. 10 (1963), the Supreme Court refused to apply the National Labor Relations Act to maritime operations of foreign flag vessels employing alien seamen, even though the foreign corporations owning the vessels were wholly owned by American corporations and the vessels were operating in a regular course of trade between foreign and United States ports. The Court referred specifically to complications in international relations that might ensue from the application of the Act to such operations. Compare *McCulloch* with *Spector v. Norwegian Cruise Line Ltd.*, 545 U.S. 119 (2005), in which disabled and non-disabled passengers brought an action against a cruise ship line that operated foreign-flagged ships, alleging violations of Title III of the Americans with Disabilities Act (ADA). The *Spector* Court held:

> It is reasonable to presume Congress intends no interference with matters that are primarily of concern only to the ship and the foreign state in which it is registered. It is also reasonable, however, to presume Congress does intend its statutes to apply to entities in U.S. territory that serve, employ, or otherwise affect American citizens, or that affect the peace and tranquility of the United States, even if those entities happen to be foreign-flag ships. Cruise ships flying foreign flags of convenience but departing from and returning to U.S. ports accommodate and transport over 7 million U.S. residents annually, including large numbers of disabled individuals. To hold there is no Title III protection for the disabled would be a harsh and unexpected interpretation of a statute designed to provide broad protection for them.

Although the Court found that foreign-flagged cruise ships operating in United States waters were places of "public accommodation" and "specified public transportation" within the meaning of the ADA, it nevertheless concluded that the ADA provision requiring the removal of "architectural barriers, and communication barriers that are structural in nature" when such removal is "readily achievable" did not apply if removal would result in noncompliance with the International Convention for the Safety of Life at Sea (SOLAS), Nov. 1, 1974, 32 U.S.T. 47, 1184 U.N.T.S. 276, or any other international legal obligation. For discussion of flag state jurisdiction over acts committed on board ships, see Chapter 17, Section 12.

Aircraft. On nationality of aircraft, see Convention on International Civil Aviation, arts. 17–19, Dec. 7, 1944, 61 Stat. 1180, 15 U.N.T.S. 295, with 185 states parties as of early 2009. Jurisdiction over crimes committed on aircraft is generally regulated by the Tokyo Convention on Offences and Certain Other Acts Committed on Board Aircraft, Sept. 14, 1963, 20 U.S.T. 2941, 704 U.N.T.S. 219, to which more than 150 states are parties as of early 2009. In addition to rules allocating primary jurisdiction to the state of registration of the aircraft and establishing limited exceptions for other interested states, the Tokyo Convention also establishes the powers of the aircraft commander to restrain persons while the aircraft is in flight and to deliver them to the authorities of a contracting state in whose territory the aircraft may land.

Various treaties aim to suppress other unlawful acts against the safety of civil aviation, including terrorist acts, such as the Convention for the Suppression of Unlawful Seizure of Aircraft, Dec. 16, 1970, 22 U.S.T. 1641, 860 U.N.T.S. 105 (Hague Convention), with 173 states parties as of early 2009, and the Convention for the Suppression of Unlawful Acts Against the Safety of Civil Aviation, Sept. 23, 1971, 24 U.S.T. 565, 974 U.N.T.S. 177 (Montreal Convention), with 180 states parties. Under Article 4 of the Hague Convention and Article 5 of the Montreal Convention, several states may have concurrent jurisdiction. May this lead to problems, since the Convention has no provision establishing the priority of their claims? See Abramovsky, Multilateral Conventions for the Suppression of Unlawful Seizures and Interference with Aircraft, Part I: The Hague Convention, 13 Colum. J. Transnat'l L. 381, 396 (1974) (concluding that the state in which the offender is apprehended would enjoy a primary de facto right to exercise jurisdiction).

In the *Lockerbie* cases before the International Court of Justice, Libya argued that it had no obligation under the Montreal Convention to surrender to the United States or the United Kingdom the two Libyan nationals who were suspected in the explosion of a U.S. aircraft en route to the United States over Lockerbie, Scotland. The International Court denied Libya's request for provisional measures to restrain the United States and the United Kingdom from pursuing sanctions against Libya in the U.N. Security Council. *Questions of Interpretation and Application of the 1971 Montreal Convention arising from the Aerial Incident at Lockerbie* (Libyan Arab Jamahiriya v. United Kingdom; Libyan Arab Jamahiriya v. United States), 1992 I.C.J. 3, 114; see also id., 1998 I.C.J. 9, 115 (Jurisdiction). The United States and the United Kingdom maintained, *inter alia*, that the Montreal Convention did not contemplate that a state which may itself have been complicit in terrorist activity could shield its own nationals from prosecution by the states that would otherwise have jurisdiction and that were especially affected by the crime. Although Libya later surrendered the two accused for a special trial in The Hague that concluded in 2000, it did not abandon its legal position on interpretation of the Montreal Convention. Libya's I.C.J. cases were subsequently discontinued pursuant to a comprehensive settlement agreement with the United States, the United Kingdom, and France. See p. 617 note 4.

Space Objects. On jurisdiction over objects launched into outer space and over any personnel thereof while in outer space or on a celestial body, see Treaty on Principles Governing the Activities of States in the Exploration and Use of Outer Space, Including the Moon and Other Celestial Bodies, done at London, Moscow, and Washington, art. 8, Jan. 27, 1967, 18 U.S.T. 2410, 610 U.N.T.S. 205, with 97 states parties as of early 2009.

Other Objects. The notion that inanimate things, like vessels and aircraft, may stand in a sufficiently close relationship to a particular state to provide a basis for the exercise of jurisdiction by that state over the thing and the persons using it naturally leads to the question whether this notion can be extended to other material, and perhaps even immaterial, things. For example, states may seek to exercise jurisdiction over artistic creations and cultural artifacts on the ground that they are part of the national patrimony. See, e.g., Gordon, The UNESCO Convention on the Illicit Movement of Art Treasures, 12 Harv. Int'l J. 537, 543 (1971).

SECTION 4. JURISDICTION BASED ON THE PASSIVE PERSONALITY PRINCIPLE

UNITED STATES v. YOUSEF

United States Court of Appeals for the Second Circuit, 2003
327 F.3d 56 (2d Cir. 2003) (some footnotes omitted)

Introduction

Defendants-appellants Ramzi Yousef, Eyad Ismoil, and Abdul Hakim Murad appeal from judgments of conviction entered in the United States District Court for the Southern District of New York. * * * Yousef, Murad, and Wali Khan Amin Shah were tried on charges relating to a conspiracy to bomb United States commercial airliners in Southeast Asia. * * * Yousef and Ismoil * * * appeal from the District Court's denial of several of their post-judgment motions. * * *

General Background

* * *

* * * Yousef entered Manila, the capital of the Philippines, under an assumed name. By September 1994, Yousef had devised a plan to attack United States airliners. According to the plan, five individuals would place bombs aboard twelve United States-flag aircraft that served routes in

Southeast Asia. The conspirators would board an airliner in Southeast Asia, assemble a bomb on the plane, and then exit the plane during its first layover. As the planes continued on toward their next destinations, the time-bombs would detonate. Eleven of the twelve flights targeted were ultimately destined for cities in the United States.

Yousef and his co-conspirators performed several tests in preparation for the airline bombings. In December 1994, Yousef and Wali Khan Amin Shah placed one of the bombs they had constructed in a Manila movie theater. The bomb exploded, injuring several patrons of the theater. Ten days later, Yousef planted another test bomb under a passenger's seat during the first leg of a Philippine Airlines flight from Manila to Japan. Yousef disembarked from the plane during the stopover and then made his way back to Manila. During the second leg of the flight, the bomb exploded, killing one passenger, a Japanese national, and injuring others.

The plot to bomb the United States-flag airliners was uncovered in January 1995, only two weeks before the conspirators intended to carry it out. Yousef and Murad were burning chemicals in their Manila apartment and accidentally caused a fire. An apartment security guard saw the smoke coming from the apartment and called the fire department. After the firemen left, the Philippine police arrived at the apartment, where they discovered chemicals and bomb components, a laptop computer on which Yousef had set forth the aircraft bombing plans, and other incriminating evidence. Philippine authorities arrested Murad and Shah, though Shah escaped and was not recaptured until nearly a year later. Yousef fled the country, but was captured in Pakistan the next month.

* * *

On February 21, 1996, a grand jury in the Southern District of New York filed a twenty-count superseding indictment against the defendants and others. * * * Counts Twelve through Nineteen charged Yousef, Murad, and Shah with various crimes relating to their conspiracy to bomb United States airliners in Southeast Asia in 1994 and 1995.

The trial of Yousef, Murad, and Shah on the airline bombing charges began on May 29, 1996 and ended on September 5, 1996, when the jury found all three defendants guilty on all counts. * * *

* * *

Discussion

* * *

Yousef contends that the Government exceeded its authority by trying him in the United States for his conduct in the aircraft bombing case. In particular, he asserts that the charges alleged in Counts Twelve, Thirteen, Fourteen and Nineteen should be dismissed because 18 U.S.C. § 32 cannot be applied to conduct outside the United States.[1] He further claims that he cannot be convicted of the charge set forth in Count Nineteen because he was not "found" within the United States as required by 18 U.S.C. § 32(b).[2] Yousef also contends that his prosecution violates customary international law limiting a nation's jurisdiction to proscribe conduct outside its borders * * *.

* * *

3. Count Twelve

In Count Twelve, the defendants were charged with violating 18 U.S.C. § 371 by conspiring to place bombs on board aircraft and destroy aircraft, in violation of 18 U.S.C. § 32(a)(1) and (2). The District Court concluded that, because it had jurisdiction over the substantive crimes charged—including attempted destruction of aircraft in the special aircraft jurisdiction of the United States—it also had derivative jurisdiction over the conspiracy charges. *United States v. Yousef*, 927 F.Supp. 673, 682 (S.D.N.Y. 1996).

We agree. Indeed, this conclusion is a simple application of the rule enunciated by the Supreme Court as long ago as 1922 in *Bowman*, that Congress is presumed to intend extraterritorial application of criminal statutes where the nature of the crime does not depend on the locality of the defendants' acts and where restricting the statute to United States territory would severely diminish the statute's effectiveness. *See Bowman*, 260 U.S. at 98. In the instant case, if Congress intended United States courts to have jurisdiction over the substantive crime of placing bombs on board the aircraft at issue, it is reasonable to conclude that Congress also intended to vest in United States courts the requisite jurisdiction over an extraterritorial conspiracy to commit that crime. * * *

4. Count Nineteen

In Count Nineteen, Yousef alone was charged with violating 18 U.S.C. § 32(b)(3) for placing a bomb on a civil aircraft registered in another country. Specifically, Yousef was charged with planting a bomb on board a Philippine Airlines flight traveling from the Philippines to Japan on

---

1. [Editors' Note: 18 U.S.C. § 32(a) (2000) provides that whoever willfully

(1) sets fire to, damages, destroys, disables, or wrecks any aircraft in the special aircraft jurisdiction of the United States or any civil aircraft used, operated, or employed in interstate, overseas, or foreign air commerce; [or]

(2) places or causes to be placed a destructive device or substance in, upon, or in proximity to, or otherwise makes or causes to be made unworkable or unusable or hazardous to work or use, any such aircraft, or any part or other materials used or intended to be used in connection with the operation of such aircraft, if such placing or causing to be placed or such making or causing to be made is likely to endanger the safety of any such aircraft . . .

shall be fined under this title or imprisoned not more than twenty years or both.]

2. [Editors' Note: 18 U.S.C. § 32(b)(3) (2000) provides that whoever willfully

places or causes to be placed on a civil aircraft registered in a country other than the United States while such aircraft is in service, a device or substance which is likely to destroy that aircraft, or to cause damage to that aircraft which renders that aircraft incapable of flight or which is likely to endanger that aircraft's safety in flight . . . shall be fined under this title or imprisoned not more than twenty years, or both. There is jurisdiction over an offense under this subsection if a national of the United States was on board, or would have been on board, the aircraft; an offender is a national of the United States; or an offender is afterwards found in the United States.]

December 11, 1994. The aircraft was a civil aircraft registered in the Philippines.

There is no dispute that Congress intended § 32(b) to apply to attacks on non-United States-flag aircraft. The statute applies expressly to placing a bomb on aircraft registered in other countries while in flight, no matter where the attack is committed, and provides for jurisdiction over such extraterritorial crimes whenever, inter alia, "an offender is afterwards found in the United States." 18 U.S.C. § 32(b).

* * *

B. Exercise of United States Extraterritorial Jurisdiction and Customary International Law

On appeal, Yousef challenges the District Court's jurisdiction over Counts Twelve through Nineteen of the indictment by arguing that customary international law does not provide a basis for jurisdiction over these counts and that United States law is subordinate to customary international law and therefore cannot provide a basis for jurisdiction. * * *

Yousef's arguments fail. First, irrespective of whether customary international law provides a basis for jurisdiction over Yousef for Counts Twelve through Nineteen, United States law provides a separate and complete basis for jurisdiction over each of these counts and, contrary to Yousef's assertions, United States law is not subordinate to customary international law or necessarily subordinate to treaty-based international law and, in fact, may conflict with both. Further contrary to Yousef's claims, customary international law *does* provide a substantial basis for jurisdiction by the United States over each of these counts, although not (as the District Court held) under the universality principle.

* * *

First, jurisdiction over Counts Twelve through Eighteen is consistent with the "passive personality principle" of customary international jurisdiction because each of these counts involved a plot to bomb United States-flag aircraft that would have been carrying United States citizens and crews and that were destined for cities in the United States. Moreover, assertion of jurisdiction is appropriate under the "objective territorial principle" because the purpose of the attack was to influence United States foreign policy and the defendants intended their actions to have an effect—in this case, a devastating effect—on and within the United States. * * *

* * *

* * * [Second,] we hold that Yousef's conduct charged in Count Nineteen—regardless of whether it is termed "terrorist"—constitutes the core conduct proscribed by the Montreal Convention and its implementing legislation. Accordingly, Yousef's prosecution and conviction on this Count

is both consistent with and required by the United States' treaty obli
gations and domestic laws. We therefore reject Yousef's claim that jurisdiction over Count Nineteen was lacking and affirm the substance of the
District Court's ruling.

* * *

To summarize our conclusions, with respect to the airline bombing
trial we hold: * * * The District Court had jurisdiction over the defendants' extraterritorial conduct pursuant to federal law.

NOTES

1. *Trends in Passive Personality Jurisdiction.* A number of states have
statutes asserting extraterritorial criminal legislative jurisdiction based on the
victim's possessing their nationality. Although it was once disputed whether
this is a permissible basis of jurisdiction, objections to its exercise have
decreased in recent years. See, e.g., O'Connell, International Law 828–29 (2d
ed. 1970) (tentatively accepting it); Watson, The Passive Personality Principle,
28 Tex. Int'l L.J. 1 (1993).

2. *United States Acceptance of the Principle.* The United States was one
of those states that traditionally disfavored the exercise of jurisdiction based
on the victim's nationality, but more recently the United States has moved
toward exercising such jurisdiction itself. See Restatement (Third) § 402,
Comment *g;* see also Kotlarczyk, "The Provision of Material Support and
Resources" and Lawsuits Against State Sponsors of Terrorism, 96 Geo. L.J.
2029 (2008); Tyler, Winning at the Expense of Law: The Ramifications of
Expanding Counter–Terrorism Law Enforcement Jurisdiction Overseas, 14
Am. U. Int'l L. Rev. 1473 (1999); Robinson, United States Practice Penalizing
International Terrorists Needlessly Undercuts Its Opposition to the Passive
Personality Principle, 16 Boston U. Int'l L.J. 487 (1998).

In *United States v. Bin Laden*, 92 F. Supp. 2d 189 (S.D.N.Y. 2000),
concerning the bombings of the U.S. embassies in Kenya and Tanzania in
August 1998 and a broader conspiracy to kill U.S. nationals anywhere in the
world, several of the statutes under which defendants were charged (18 U.S.C.
§§ 2332, 2332a (2000)) were justified under international law, at least in part,
on the passive personality principle. Although defendants challenged the
sufficiency of the indictment on the ground that the United States has
"traditionally rejected" the passive personality theory of jurisdiction, the
district court disagreed, citing the Restatement (Third) § 402, Comment *g* for
the proposition that the passive personality principle is "increasingly accepted
as applied to terrorist and other organized attacks on a state's nationals by
reason of their nationality." 92 F.Supp. at 221; see also *United States v.
Rezaq*, 134 F.3d 1121, 1133 (D.C. Cir. 1998).

3. *Circumscribing the Scope of the Principle.* Is it desirable for a state to
exercise the full extent of possible national jurisdiction over conduct that
victimizes its nationals or should such jurisdiction be more circumscribed? In
the *Achille Lauro* incident of 1985, a U.S. citizen, Leon Klinghoffer, was
murdered by terrorists who seized an Italian-flag vessel in the Mediterranean

and pushed him and his wheelchair into the sea. In the wake of this incident, Congress adopted a new provision for killing or serious bodily injury committed against "a national of the United States while such national is outside the United States." Omnibus Diplomatic Security and Antiterrorism Act of 1986, 18 U.S.C. § 2332 (2000). However, Congress deliberately decided not to extend such homicide jurisdiction to all such extraterritorial murders on a general passive personality theory of jurisdiction, but rather only to those of a specified nature, as follows:

> (e) *Limitation on prosecution.* No prosecution for any offense described in this section shall be undertaken by the United States except on written certification of the Attorney General * * * that, in the judgment of the certifying official, such offense was intended to coerce, intimidate, or retaliate against a government or a civilian population.

Other enactments circumscribe the jurisdiction by focusing on extraordinary types of attacks upon U.S. nationals, such as through the use of weapons of mass destruction or the use of chemical weapons against U.S. nationals abroad. See 18 U.S.C. §§ 2332a, 2332c (2000); see also Damrosch, Enforcing International Law Through Non–Forcible Measures, 269 Rec. des Cours 9, 222 (1997).

SECTION 5.   JURISDICTION BASED ON THE PROTECTIVE PRINCIPLE

Recall that Restatement § 402(3) (p. 759) envisages jurisdiction to prescribe law with respect to "certain conduct outside its territory by persons not its nationals that is directed against the security of the state or against a limited class of other state interests." This form of jurisdiction, known as the protective principle, was involved in the following case.

UNITED STATES v. VASQUEZ–VELASCO

United States Court of Appeals for the Ninth Circuit, 1994
15 F.3d 833 (some footnotes omitted)

FLETCHER, CIRCUIT JUDGE:

Javier Vasquez–Velasco was convicted in a jury trial of committing violent crimes in aid of a racketeering enterprise in violation of 18 U.S.C. § 1959. * * *

Vasquez–Velasco's appeal arises out of the second trial associated with the 1985 kidnapping and murders of Enrique Camarena, an American agent with the Drug Enforcement Agency ("DEA"), and Alfredo Zavala, a DEA informant. The government's theory at trial was that Vasquez–Velasco and his three codefendants all acted to commit violent crimes to further their positions in the "Guadalajara Narcotics Cartel," a drug trafficking enterprise based in Guadalajara. The cartel began distributing large amounts of drugs into the United States in the early 1980's. According to the government, in 1984 and 1985 American DEA enforcement activities resulted in losses to the cartel totalling billions of dollars.

As a result of these losses, the cartel engaged in a series of retaliatory actions against DEA agents in Mexico. The murders with which Vasquez–Velasco and his codefendants were charged were part of these retaliatory activities.

* * *

On the night of January 30, 1985, members of the "Guadalajara Narcotics Cartel" gathered at a Guadalajara restaurant known as "La Langosta." The cartel members at this gathering included Rafael Caro–Quintero, Ernesto Fonseca–Carillo, and Javier Barba–Hernandez, all well-known drug dealers in Guadalajara, the appellant Vasquez–Velasco, and other members of the cartel.

That night [John] Walker [an American citizen writing a novel in Mexico] and [Alberto] Radelat [a photographer who was a U.S. legal resident] went to the La Langosta restaurant at approximately 7:00 p.m. Soon after they entered, they were grabbed by ten to fifteen members of the cartel and beaten with fists and guns. They were subsequently carried to a storage room in the back of the restaurant while the beating continued. Vasquez–Velasco assisted in carrying and beating the two men. The two men were tortured until one of them admitted that they were police. Both were later killed in a field outside of Guadalajara. The next day Vasquez–Velasco informed Barba–Hernandez that both tourists had died. In June 1985, the bodies of Walker and Radelat were found in Primavera Park outside of Guadalajara.

DISCUSSION

I. *Extraterritorial application of 18 U.S.C. § 1959*

Vasquez–Velasco raises four issues on appeal. First, he argues that the district court erred in ruling that § 1959 applies extraterritorially. We review de novo a district court's assumption of jurisdiction.

A. *Extraterritoriality*

"Generally there is no constitutional bar to the extraterritorial application of United States penal laws." *United States v. Felix–Gutierrez*, 940 F.2d 1200, 1204 (9th Cir.1991), cert. denied, 508 U.S. 906 (1993); *Chua Han Mow v. United States*, 730 F.2d 1308, 1311 (9th Cir.1984), cert. denied, 470 U.S. 1031 (1985). To determine whether a given statute should have extraterritorial application in a specific case, courts look to congressional intent. *United States v. Bowman*, 260 U.S. 94, 98 (1922); *Felix–Gutierrez*, 940 F.2d at 1204; *Chua Han Mow*, 730 F.2d at 1311. When faced with a criminal statute such as § 1959, we may infer that extraterritorial application is appropriate from " 'the nature of the offenses and Congress' other legislative efforts to eliminate the type of crime involved.' " *Felix–Gutierrez*, 940 F.2d at 1204 (quoting *United States v. Thomas*, 893 F.2d 1066, 1068 (9th Cir.), cert. denied, 498 U.S. 826 (1990) (quotations omitted)). Where "[t]he locus of the conduct is not relevant to the end sought by the enactment" of the statute, and the statute prohibits conduct that obstructs the functioning of the United States government, it is reasonable to infer congressional intent to reach crimes committed abroad. *United States v. Cotten*, 471 F.2d 744, 751 (9th Cir.), cert. denied, 411 U.S. 936 (1973) (statute that proscribes theft of government property is not logically dependent on the locality of violation for jurisdiction) (emphasis in original); see also *Felix–Gutierrez*, 940 F.2d at 1204.[4]

In determining whether a statute applies extraterritorially, we also presume that Congress does not intend to violate principles of international law. Thus, in the absence of an explicit Congressional directive, courts do not give extraterritorial effect to any statute that violates principles of international law. *McCulloch v. Sociedad Nacional de Marineros de Honduras*, 372 U.S. 10, 21–22 (1963) (quoting *The Charming Betsy*, 2 Cranch 64, 118 (1804) (court will not construe statute to apply extraterritorially where application of National Labor Relations Act to protect foreign seapersons on foreign ships would violate both a Treaty with Honduras and established principles of international law)); *Weinberger v. Rossi*, 456 U.S. 25, 32 (1982) (interpreting statute that prohibits employment discrimination against United States citizens on military bases overseas unless permitted by "treaty" in manner that is consistent with international executive agreements and not just treaties entered into pursuant to Article II of the Constitution); Restatement (Third) of Foreign Relations Law of the United States § 114 (1987) [hereinafter "Restatement"] ("[w]here fairly possible, a United States statute is to be construed so as not to conflict with international law").

In general, international law recognizes several principles whereby the exercise of extraterritorial jurisdiction may be appropriate. These principles include the objective territorial principle, under which jurisdiction is asserted over acts performed outside the United States that produce detrimental effects within the United States, and the protective principle, under which jurisdiction is asserted over foreigners for an act committed outside the United States that may impinge on the territorial integrity, security, or political independence of the United States. See, e.g., *Felix–Gutierrez*, 940 F.2d at 1205–06; *Chua Han Mow*, 730 F.2d at 1311–

---

4. Because jurisdiction is ordinarily exercised on the basis of territorial boundaries, we generally presume that Congress intended the legislation to apply only within the territorial boundaries of the United States absent statutory language or an express statement by Congress to the contrary. Restatement (Third) of Foreign Relations Law of the United States § 402 cmt. *a* (1987); *Foley Bros., Inc. v. Filardo*, 336 U.S. 281, 285 (1949). However, this presumption does not apply to all criminal statutes. In *United States v. Bowman*, 260 U.S. 94, 98 (1922), the Supreme Court stated that "the same rule of interpretation should not be applied to criminal statutes which are, as a class, not logically dependent on their locality for the Government's jurisdiction, but are enacted because of the right of the Government to defend itself against obstruction, or fraud wherever perpetrated. . . ." See also *Felix–Gutierrez*, 940 F.2d at 1205 n. 3. Limiting the jurisdiction of drug smuggling statutes to activities that occur within the United States would severely undermine their scope and effective operation because "drug 'smuggling by its very nature involves foreign countries, and . . . the accomplishment of the crime always requires some action in a foreign country.'" *Felix–Gutierrez*, 940 F.2d at 1204 (citing Brulay v. United States, 383 F.2d 345, 350 (9th Cir.), cert. denied, 389 U.S. 986 (1967)). In the present case § 1959 was applied to violent activities performed overseas to further a drug trafficking enterprise. This application of § 1959 therefore falls within the category of cases described by *Bowman* and *Felix–Gutierrez* for which we do not require an affirmative statement of congressional intent in order to find that the statute applies extraterritorially.

12 (citations omitted); *United States v. King*, 552 F.2d 833, 851–52 (0th Cir.1976), cert. denied, 430 U.S. 966 (1977); Restatement § 402. Nevertheless, an exercise of jurisdiction on one of these bases still violates international principles if it is "unreasonable".[6] Restatement § 403 cmt. *a* (stating that "[t]he principle that an exercise of jurisdiction on one of the bases indicated ... is nonetheless unlawful if it is unreasonable ... has emerged as a principle of international law").

Our circuit has applied this analysis to find that the extraterritorial application of the precursor to § 1959 in circumstances similar to those presented by this case is consistent with Congressional intent. In *Felix–Gutierrez*, the defendant was charged as an accessory after the fact to the commission of a violent crime, the kidnapping and murder of Enrique Camarena, in aid of a racketeering enterprise. The defendant was charged under 18 U.S.C. § 1952B, the predecessor to § 1959. See *United States v. Lopez–Alvarez*, 970 F.2d 583, 586, 596 (9th Cir.), cert. denied, 506 U.S. 989 (1992). We held that because drug trafficking by its nature involves foreign countries and because DEA agents often work overseas, the murder of a DEA agent in retaliation for drug enforcement activities is a crime against the United States regardless of where it occurs. Thus, we found that Congress would have intended that § 1959 be applied extraterritorially to cases involving the murder of DEA agents abroad. *Felix–Gutierrez*, 940 F.2d at 1204; see also, *Lopez–Alvarez*, 970 F.2d at 596 (extraterritorial application of § 1952B is appropriate against defendant who participated in abduction of Camarena).

We have also held that extraterritorial application of a statute such as § 1959 to the murder of a DEA agent is consistent with principles of international law, particularly the objective territorial and the protective principles. Our circuit has repeatedly approved extraterritorial application of statutes that prohibit the importation and distribution of controlled substances in the United States because these activities implicate national security interests and create a detrimental effect in the United States. *Chua Han Mow*, 730 F.2d at 1312; see also *King*, 552 F.2d at 851–52. In *Felix–Gutierrez*, we applied the principle to hold that by acting to prevent the United States from apprehending the murderer of DEA agent Enrique Camarena, the appellants had adversely affected our country's national security interest in eliminating the flow of illegal drugs into the United States. 940 F.2d at 1206.

Finally, we are convinced that extraterritorial application of § 1959 to violent crimes associated with drug trafficking is reasonable under international law principles. Because drug smuggling is a serious and universally condemned offense, no conflict is likely to be created by extraterritorial regulation of drug traffickers. See Restatement § 403, Rptr. n. 8 (1987).

---

6. The Third Restatement identifies a non-exhaustive list of factors that may be relevant to a determination of reasonableness [quotation from Restatement § 403(2), p. 759 *supra*, is omitted].

Although the violent crime in which Vasquez–Velasco participated was the murder of an American citizen, and not the murder of a DEA agent, extraterritorial application of § 1959 is still appropriate in this case. According to the government's theory, the cartel members mistook Walker and Radelat for DEA agents and killed them in retaliation for the losses inflicted on the cartel by the DEA. As in *Felix–Gutierrez*, the violent crime was directed against the United States as a response to its enforcement efforts in Mexico. The murders of Walker and Radelat, like the murder of agent Camarena, were performed to further the cartel's drug smuggling activities by intimidating the DEA from continuing its enforcement activities against the cartel's drug trafficking. Such actions could also intimidate local police and drug agencies, thereby inhibiting them from cooperating with the DEA. In this context, the murder of American citizens has an equally direct and adverse impact on our nation's security interest in combatting the importation and trafficking of illegal narcotics.

* * *

CONCLUSION

We hold that the district court properly found that § 1959 applies extraterritorially to reach the crimes committed by Vasquez–Velasco in Mexico. * * *

NOTES

1. *Protecting Against....* What kinds of conduct abroad may a state "protect" itself against by exercising its national jurisdiction? The case above speaks of the murder of government officials and agents. What about punishing the falsification of a government's documents abroad? See *United States v. Birch*, 470 F.2d 808 (4th Cir. 1972). What about punishing a foreign conspiracy to smuggle drugs into your state? See *United States v. Cardales*, 168 F.3d 548 (1st Cir. 1999). What about punishing perjury abroad before a U.S. government official? In *United States v. Archer*, 51 F.Supp. 708 (S.D. Cal. 1943), the court regarded the federal statute making it a crime for either an alien or a United States citizen to commit perjury before a diplomatic or consular officer, 11 Stat. 61 [now 22 U.S.C. § 4221 (2000)] as resting on the protective principle and convicted thereunder an alien who committed perjury before a vice consul in Mexico in connection with an application for a nonimmigrant visa. See also *United States v. Pizzarusso*, 388 F.2d 8 (2d Cir. 1968); but see *United States v. Corey*, 232 F.3d 1166 (9th Cir. 2000). For a general discussion, see Cameron, The Protective Principle of International Criminal Jurisdiction (1994).

2. *Protecting Embassy Property Abroad.* In *United States v. Bin Laden*, 92 F. Supp. 2d 189 (S.D.N.Y. 2000), the United States returned an indictment charging fifteen defendants (including Bin Laden, who has not yet been apprehended, and six defendants who are in custody in the United States) with offenses under a number of federal statutes for acts committed abroad, including the bombing of the U.S. embassies in Kenya and Tanzania in August 1998. The court referred to the congressional intent that the Antiter-

rorism Act and several other relevant statutes were intended to reach conduct by foreign nationals on foreign soil, and concluded that the Antiterrorism Act was justified by the protective principle under international law. In response to a claim that due process requires minimum contacts with the United States, the court held that "if the extraterritorial application of a statute is justified by the protective principle, such application accords with due process." 92 F. Supp. 2d at 220.

The court also noted that the embassy bombings involved murders of "internationally protected persons" (i.e., diplomats), and referred in this connection to the universality principle of jurisdiction under international law (discussed *infra*). On the status of the embassy premises as relevant to U.S. authority to prescribe and enforce criminal law with respect to acts occurring there, see Chapter 12, pp. 936–37. In *Bin Laden*, the court concluded that the exercise of jurisdiction was sustainable on theories of passive personality, protective, and universal jurisdiction, but not on the subjective territorial principle for acts taking place on embassy premises. 92 F. Supp. 2d at 215 n. 43. Thus the court dismissed certain counts of the indictment under two statutes, upon concluding that Congress did not intend the provisions on murder or maiming on "federal lands" to apply to embassy properties; but it upheld the remaining counts.

In a 2001 amendment to 18 U.S.C. § 7, Congress subsequently expanded the definition of the term "special maritime and territorial jurisdiction of the United States" to cover:

> (A) the premises of United States diplomatic, consular, military or other United States Government missions or entities in foreign States, including the buildings, parts of buildings, and land appurtenant or ancillary thereto or used for purposes of those missions or entities, irrespective of ownership; and

> (B) residences in foreign States and the land appurtenant or ancillary thereto, irrespective of ownership, used for purposes of those missions or entities or used by United States personnel assigned to those missions or entities

with respect to offenses committed by or against a national of the United States.

3. *Other Formulations of the Protective Principle.* How expansive do you think a state can be in exercising its national jurisdiction consistent with the protective principle? Can any form of conduct that harms the state be "protected" against? In 1972, Israel amended its Penal Law to include the following provision:

> The courts in Israel are competent to try under Israeli law a person who has committed abroad an act which would be an offense if it had been committed in Israel and which harmed or was intended to harm the State of Israel, its security, property or economy or its transport or communications links with other countries.

Can this provision be supported by the protective principle? See Note, Extraterritorial Jurisdiction and Jurisdiction Following Forcible Abduction: A New Israeli Precedent in International Law, 72 Mich. L. Rev. 1087 (1974).

SECTION 6.   UNIVERSAL JURISDICTION

The Restatement (Third) expresses in § 404 (p. 760 above) the principle that certain crimes are "recognized by the community of nations as of universal concern," and accepts that any state may define and prescribe punishment for them even without connections of territoriality, nationality or protection of state interest. That principle is referred to as the principle of universal jurisdiction.

The fact that such jurisdiction may be exercised, of course, does not mean that all states do exercise such jurisdiction under their national law. Indeed, relatively few states have enacted laws that assert jurisdiction solely on the basis of a customary law of universal jurisdiction. See Bassiouni, Universal Jurisdiction for International Crimes: Historical Perspectives and Contemporary Practice, 42 Va. J. Int'l L. 81 (2001). For examples of prosecutions that have been justified on the basis of universal jurisdiction, from more than a dozen countries, see a study conducted by the Princeton Project on Universal Jurisdiction, entitled Universal Jurisdiction: National Courts and the Prosecution of Serious Crimes Under International Law (Macedo ed. 2004).

In many instances, jurisdiction is exercised pursuant to a treaty regime that calls for a state to prosecute or extradite an offender, thus making it more difficult to discern what offenses outside the treaty context fall within the scope of universal jurisdiction. Nevertheless, some of the crimes enumerated in the Restatement's formulation have long been accepted as giving rise to universal jurisdiction.

Piracy. Piracy, which typically has been perpetrated on the high seas beyond the jurisdiction of any state, is a classic instance. "It has long been recognized and well settled that persons and vessels engaged in piratical operations on the high seas are entitled to the protection of no nation and may be punished by any nation that may apprehend or capture them. This stern rule of international law refers to piracy in its international-law sense and not to a variety of lesser maritime offenses so designated by municipal law." 2 Hackworth at 681. For the modern expression of the universal jurisdiction principle in this context, see Articles 100–05 of the U.N. Convention on the Law of the Sea, Dec. 10, 1982, 1833 U.N.T.S. 3. For current U.S. law, see 18 U.S.C. §§ 1651–1653, 2280 (2000). In the context of piracy off the coast of Somalia, the Security Council called upon all states, "and in particular flag, port, and coastal States, States of the nationality of victims and perpetrators [of] piracy and armed robbery, and other States with relevant jurisdiction under international law and national legislation," to cooperate in investigating and prosecuting such acts of piracy "consistent with applicable international law including international human rights law." S.C. Res. 1816, para. 11 (June 2, 2008) Does this resolution endorse resort to universal jurisdiction? See Chapter 17, Section 8(B)(2). Contemporary variations on piracy, in the form of aircraft hijacking and other forms of terrorism, are now addressed by various treaties and national implementing legislation.

Slave Trade. Various treaties emerged in the 1800s that required states to enact national laws that would punish acts abroad that further slavery and the slave trade. See General Act of the Conference of Berlin Concerning the Congo, Feb. 26, 1885, 3 A.J.I.L. Supp. 7 (1909); General Act for the Repression of the African Slave Trade, July 2, 1890, 27 Stat. 886. More contemporary versions of such treaties include the International Labor Organization's Convention Concerning the Prohibition and Immediate Action for the Elimination of the Worst Forms of Child Labour, June 17, 1999, I.L.O. No. C182, 38 I.L.M. 1207 (covering the sale and trafficking of children), and the Optional Protocol on the Sale of Children, Child Prostitution and Child Pornography, G.A. Res. 54/263 (May 25, 2000).

Genocide and War Crimes: Eichmann. Genocide and war crimes are likewise among the crimes envisaged by the Restatement as being of universal concern. For example, in part on a universal jurisdiction theory, Israel tried and convicted Adolf Eichmann, who had been captured by Israeli agents in Argentina and brought to Israel for trial. Eichmann was charged under the Nazis and Nazi Collaborators (Punishment) Law with commission of the following crimes in Germany or countries occupied by Germany during World War II—crimes against the Jewish people, crimes against humanity, war crimes, and membership in a hostile organization—in the indictment of February 21, 1961. On December 11, 1961, the District Court of Jerusalem found Eichmann guilty on all counts of the indictment. An appeal was dismissed on May 29, 1962. In the course of its Judgment, the court overruled the defense contention that there was no jurisdiction because the defendant had been captured in a foreign country in violation of international law. The court sustained the exercise of jurisdiction, *inter alia* on the basis of the universality principle. See Cr.C. (Jm.) 20/61, The State of Israel v. Eichmann, 1961, translated in 36 I.L.R. 18, 26 (1968) ("From the point of view of international law, the power of the State of Israel to enact the Law in question . . . is based . . . on a dual foundation: the universal character of the crimes in question and their specific character intended to exterminate the Jewish people.").

More recently, Germany has prosecuted for genocide that occurred in Yugoslavia in the early 1990s based on a theory of universal jurisdiction. See *State Attorney's Office v. Jorgic*, Higher State Court of Dusseldorf, 2 StE 8/96 (1997), applying F.R.G. Penal Code § 220(a) on genocide. A "perfect, but also rare example of universal jurisdiction" is a warrant issued in Belgium "against a Rwandan responsible for massacres of other Rwandans in Rwanda." Meron, International Criminalization of Internal Atrocities, 89 A.J.I.L. 554, 577 (1995).

Universal jurisdiction over "grave breaches" of the four Geneva Conventions on the laws of war is expressed, for example, in Article 146 of the Convention (IV) Relative to the Protection of Civilian Persons in Time of War, Aug. 12, 1949, 6 U.S.T. 3516, 75 U.N.T.S. 287, which provides that each party "shall be under an obligation to search for persons alleged to have committed, or to have ordered to be committed, such grave breaches, and shall bring such persons, regardless of their nationality, before their own courts" or turn them over for trial to another party. Article 129 of the Convention (III) on Prisoners of War, Aug. 12, 1949, 6 U.S.T. 3316, 75 U.N.T.S. 135, is substantially similar. With the advent of the International Criminal Tribunal for the former Yugoslavia (I.C.T.Y.), the International Criminal Tribunal for Rwanda (I.C.T.R.), and the International Criminal Court (I.C.C.), the interest in such offenses of universal concern has grown apace.

The U.S. Congress has enacted several statutes dealing with international crimes, but not all of them have embraced a universal theory of jurisdiction. The War Crimes Act of 1996, 18 U.S.C. § 2441 (2000) stops short of universal jurisdiction. In the Genocide Convention Implementation Act of 1987, 18 U.S.C. § 1091 et seq. (2000), Congress initially chose to assert criminal jurisdiction only if the alleged genocide had been committed in the United States or by a national of the United States. In 2007, Congress expanded the reach of the statute to the full extent of universal jurisdiction by amending § 1091 to add a new paragraph (d)(5), providing for jurisdiction in the following circumstance: "after the conduct required for the offense occurs, the alleged offender is brought into, or found in, the United States, even if that conduct occurred outside the United States." No connection of nationality is required under this new provision. For discussion, see Ratner & Abrams, Accountability for Human Rights Atrocities in International Law (3d ed. 2009).

Other Offenses? Beyond these core areas, the contours of the universal jurisdiction principle are contested, as the materials in this Section illustrate. Should state-sponsored torture that occurs abroad be an offense over which any state may exercise national jurisdiction? A notable U.S. assertion of universal jurisdiction is the Torture Convention Implementation Act of 1994, 18 U.S.C. § 2340 et seq. (2000). In § 2340A(b), Congress has established federal criminal jurisdiction over torture committed or attempted outside the United States if:

(1) the alleged offender is a national of the United States, or

(2) the alleged offender is present in the United States, regardless of the nationality of the victim or alleged offender.

Reasonableness. Note that the Restatement (Third) § 404 does not impose the limitation of reasonableness on the exercise of universal jurisdiction. Should it do so in cases in which there is another state that is better situated effectively to exercise its jurisdiction? On this question, see Schachter, International Law in Theory and Practice 268 (1991). Does the possible absence of any link between the state exercising universal jurisdiction and the person over whom it is exercised require more extensive safeguards for the protection of that person? See id. at 269–70. The

Princeton Principles have endeavored to formulate criteria to guide courts in this regard.

This Section offers perspectives on universality as a jurisdictional principle. Related problems of extradition and alternative methods for obtaining custody of an offender are addressed in this Chapter, Section 11, and immunities questions in Chapter 12.

REGINA v. BARTLE, BOW STREET STIPENDIARY MAGISTRATE & COMMISSIONER OF POLICE, EX PARTE PINOCHET

United Kingdom, House of Lords, March 24, 1999
2 W.L.R. 827, 38 I.L.M. 581 (1999)

[In 1998, at the request of a Spanish investigating judge for extradition, a warrant was issued by an English magistrate for the arrest of Pinochet, a former head of state of Chile. The petition alleged that, while head of state of Chile, Pinochet had conspired with others to take hostage, torture, and kill numerous persons, including Spanish citizens. Pinochet was arrested and contended in the English courts that he was immune from arrest and could not properly be extradited. The House of Lords rendered judgment twice. The first judgment was vacated by the House of Lords itself on the ground that one of the law lords on the panel had failed to disclose his connection with Amnesty International, which had intervened in the case. In its second judgment, the House of Lords ruled that Pinochet could not claim immunity in regard to torture that had been made a universal crime by the International Convention Against Torture and other Cruel, Inhuman or Degrading Treatment or Punishment of 1984. This Convention, incorporated into English law by the Criminal Justice Act of 1988, effective as of September 29, 1988, effected an exception to the otherwise applicable immunity of present and former heads of state from criminal process.

On whether Pinochet was extraditable under the double criminality requirement imposed by the U.K.–Spain Extradition Treaty, the House of Lords ruled that the crime for which extradition was sought had to be a crime under both Spanish and U.K. law at the time of commission of the crime rather than at the time of extradition and that extradition could therefore be sought only for torture committed after 1988. The matter was referred back to the executive authorities and the lower courts for the proper processing of the request for extradition. Subsequently, Pinochet was permitted to return to Chile upon a finding that his poor health did not permit him to stand trial. The decisions rendered at the various stages of this proceedings can be found in 37 I.L.M. 1302 (1998) and 38 I.L.M. 68, 430, 489 and 581 (1999). The part of Lord Browne–Wilkinson's opinion dealing with whether the crimes alleged were crimes under English law follows. For other excerpts in this Chapter, see pp. 843–44. The part of his opinion with the immunity issue is reproduced in Chapter 12, at p. 924 below.]

LORD BROWNE-WILKINSON

* * *

Torture

Apart from the law of piracy, the concept of personal liability under international law for international crimes is of comparatively modern growth. The traditional subjects of international law are states not human beings. But consequent upon the war crime trials after the 1939–45 World War, the international community came to recognise that there could be criminal liability under international law for a class of crimes such as war crimes and crimes against humanity. Although there may be legitimate doubts as to the legality of the Charter of the Nuremberg Tribunal, in my judgment those doubts were stilled by the Affirmation of the Principles of International Law recognised by the Charter of Nuremberg Tribunal adopted by the United Nations General Assembly on 11 December 1946. That Affirmation affirmed the principles of international law recognised by the Charter of the Nuremberg Tribunal and the judgment of the Tribunal and directed the Committee on the codification of international law to treat as a matter of primary importance plans for the formulation of the principles recognised in the Charter of the Nuremberg Tribunal. At least from that date onwards the concept of personal liability for a crime in international law must have been part of international law. In the early years state torture was one of the elements of a war crime. In consequence torture, and various other crimes against humanity, were linked to war or at least to hostilities of some kind. But in the course of time this linkage with war fell away and torture, divorced from war or hostilities, became an international crime on its own: see *Oppenheim's International Law* (Jennings and Watts edition) vol. 1, 996; note 6 to Article 18 of *the I.L.C. Draft Code of Crimes Against Peace*; Prosecutor v. Furundzija, Tribunal for Former Yugoslavia, Case No. 17–95–17/1–T. Ever since 1945, torture on a large scale has featured as one of the crimes against humanity: see, for example, U.N. General Assembly Resolutions 3059, 3452 and 3453 passed in 1973 and 1975; Statutes of the International Criminal Tribunals for former Yugoslavia (Article 5) and Rwanda (Article 3).

Moreover, the Republic of Chile accepted before your Lordships that the international law prohibiting torture has the character of *jus cogens* or a peremptory norm, i.e. one of those rules of international law which have a particular status. In *Furundzija* (supra) at para. 153, the Tribunal said:

"Because of the importance of the values it protects, [the prohibition of torture] has evolved into a peremptory norm or *jus cogens*, that is, a norm that enjoys a higher rank in the international hierarchy than treaty law and even 'ordinary' customary rules. The most conspicuous consequence of this higher rank is that the principle at issue cannot be derogated from by states through international treaties or local or special customs or even general customary rules not endowed with the same normative force. * * * Clearly, the *jus* *cogens* nature of the prohibition against torture articulates the notion that the prohibition has now become one of the most fundamental standards of the international community. Furthermore, this prohibition is designed to produce a deterrent effect, in that it signals to all members of the international community and the individuals over whom they wield authority that the prohibition of torture is an absolute value from which nobody must deviate." (See also the cases cited in Note 170 to the Furundzija case.)

The *jus cogens* nature of the international crime of torture justifies states in taking universal jurisdiction over torture wherever committed. International law provides that offences *jus cogens* may be punished by any state because the offenders are "common enemies of all mankind and all nations have an equal interest in their apprehension and prosecution": *Demjanjuk v. Petrovsky* (1985) 603 F. Supp. 1468; 776 F. 2d. 571.

It was suggested by Miss Montgomery, for Senator Pinochet, that although torture was contrary to international law it was not strictly an international crime in the highest sense. In the light of the authorities to which I have referred (and there are many others) I have no doubt that long before the Torture Convention of 1984 state torture was an international crime in the highest sense. But there was no tribunal or court to punish international crimes of torture. Local courts could take jurisdiction: see *Demjanjuk* (supra); *Attorney–General of Israel v. Eichmann* (1962) 36 I.L.R. 5. But the objective was to ensure a general jurisdiction so that the torturer was not safe wherever he went. For example, in this case it is alleged that during the Pinochet regime torture was an official, although unacknowledged, weapon of government and that, when the regime was about to end, it passed legislation designed to afford an amnesty to those who had engaged in institutionalised torture. If these allegations are true, the fact that the local court had jurisdiction to deal with the international crime of torture was nothing to the point so long as the totalitarian regime remained in power: a totalitarian regime will not permit adjudication by its own courts on its own shortcomings. Hence the demand for some international machinery to repress state torture which is not dependent upon the local courts where the torture was committed. In the event, over 110 states (including Chile, Spain and the United Kingdom) became state parties to the Torture Convention. But it is far from clear that none of them practised state torture. What was needed therefore was an international system which could punish those who were guilty of torture and which did not permit the evasion of punishment by the torturer moving from one state to another. The Torture Convention was agreed not in order to create an international crime which had not previously existed but to provide an international system under which the international criminal—the torturer—could find no safe haven. Burgers and Danelius (respectively the chairman of the United Nations Working Group on the 1984 Torture Convention and the draftsman of its first draft) say, at p. 131, that it was "an essential purpose [of the Convention]

to ensure that a torturer does not escape the consequences of his act by going to another country."

The Torture Convention

Article 1 of the Convention defines torture as the intentional infliction of severe pain and of suffering with a view to achieving a wide range of purposes "when such pain or suffering is inflicted by or at the instigation of or with the consent or acquiescence of a public official or other person acting in an official capacity." Article 2(1) requires each state party to prohibit torture on territory within its own jurisdiction and Article 4 requires each state party to ensure that "all" acts of torture are offences under its criminal law. Article 2(3) outlaws any defence of superior orders. Under Article 5(1) each state party has to establish its jurisdiction over torture (a) when committed within territory under its jurisdiction, (b) when the alleged offender is a national of that state, and (c) in certain circumstances, when the victim is a national of that state. Under Article 5(2) a state party has to take jurisdiction over any alleged offender who is found within its territory. Article 6 contains provisions for a state in whose territory an alleged torturer is found to detain him, inquire into the position and notify the states referred to in Article 5(1) and to indicate whether it intends to exercise jurisdiction. Under Article 7 the state in whose territory the alleged torturer is found shall, if he is not extradited to any of the states mentioned in Article 5(1), submit him to its authorities for the purpose of prosecution. Under Article 8(1) torture is to be treated as an extraditable offence and under Article 8(4) torture shall, for the purposes of extradition, be treated as having been committed not only in the place where it occurred but also in the state mentioned in Article 5(1). * * *

NOTES

1. *Belgian Universal Jurisdiction Law: Applications and Retrenchment.* Belgium's original universal jurisdiction legislation, the "Act concerning Punishment for Grave Breaches of International Humanitarian Law," came into force in 1993 and was amended in 1999 to include universal jurisdiction over crimes against humanity and genocide in addition to war crimes. The Code of Criminal Procedure further granted victims the right to initiate a criminal investigation on the basis of universal jurisdiction. Belgian prosecutions based on universal jurisdiction and leading to a conviction include the "Butare Four" case, and the case of Rwandan businessmen Etienne Nzabonimana and Samuel Ndashykirwa ("The Two Brothers" case), both cases concerning crimes committed in Rwanda during the 1994 genocide.

Following a wave of complaints against high-ranking officials of various foreign states, political pressure led to an amendment of the act in April 2003, removing the right of victims to initiate a universal jurisdiction prosecution, and introducing immunity provisions "in accordance with international law." In June 2003, U.S. Defense Secretary Donald H. Rumsfeld threatened Belgium that it risked losing its status as host to NATO's headquarters if it did not rescind the law. Further pressure led to a new law that entered into force in August 2003. The change in the law required cases against U.S. Gen. Tommy Franks, former Israeli Prime Minister Ariel Sharon and petroleum company TotalFinaElf to be dropped. For arguments against such jurisdiction, see Kissinger, The Pitfalls of Universal Jurisdiction: Risking Judicial Tyranny, Foreign Aff., July–Aug. 2001, at 86.

Under the law now in force, Belgian courts have jurisdiction over international crimes only if the accused is Belgian or has his primary residence in Belgium; if the victim is Belgian or has lived in Belgium for at least three years at the time the crimes were committed; or if Belgium is required by treaty to exercise jurisdiction over the case. The new law also considerably reduces victims' ability to obtain direct access to the courts. Unless the accused is Belgian or has his primary residence in Belgium, the decision whether or not to proceed with any complaint rests entirely with the state prosecutor. Belgium has thus restricted the reach of universal jurisdiction in its courts by adopting a law similar to or more restrictive than those of most European countries.

The 2003 law does, however, preserve a limited number of cases that had already begun to move forward, including those concerning the Rwandan genocide and the killing of two Belgian priests in Guatemala, as well as the complaints filed against ex-Chadian dictator Hissène Habré. In the Habré case, a Belgian investigating judge went to Chad in 2002 to investigate the crimes. Habré is currently under house arrest in Senegal, and in October 2002 the Chadian government waived any immunity which Habré might seek to assert, removing one of the last potential hurdles to his extradition and trial. The groups said that his trial would be important to send a message to tyrants around the world that their impunity is a thing of the past. On the Belgian experience, see Ratner, Belgium's War Crime Statute: A Post Mortem, 97 A.J.I.L. 888 (2003).

2. *Relationship Between Jurisdiction and Immunity*. In the *Arrest Warrant Case* (Democratic Republic of the Congo v. Belgium), 2002 I.C.J. 3, the Congo contested Belgium's jurisdiction to issue an arrest warrant against Congo's foreign minister in connection with crimes that lacked any connection to Belgium, and also claimed that the minister enjoyed immunity under customary international law. The Court ruled only on the immunity question, but Judges Higgins, Kooijmans and Buergenthal addressed the universal jurisdiction issue in a joint separate opinion, concluding that international law has been evolving to allow the exercise of such jurisdiction over exceptionally heinous crimes, at least under certain circumstances. Their opinion devotes some attention to conditions that would make resort to universal jurisdiction proper (such as allowing states that would ordinarily have jurisdiction over the offense the opportunity to demonstrate that they are willing and able to undertake prosecution; if they are not, there is a stronger case for resort to universal jurisdiction in the interests of avoiding impunity). Do you think that states are *obligated* under international law to assert universal jurisdiction when an offender turns up in their territory? See Robertson, Crimes Against Humanity: The Struggle for Global Justice 291, 311 (3d ed. 2006) (finding "there is in international law a duty on state to punish crimes against humanity ... even if this means rejecting or annulling amnesty.").

3. *Further Reading*. For commentary on the *Pinochet* case, see Van Alebeek, The Pinochet Case: International Human Rights Law on Trial, 2000 Brit. Y.B. Int'l L. 29; Wedgwood, International Criminal Law and Augusto Pinochet, 40 Va. J. Int'l L. 829 (2000); Human Rights Watch, The Pinochet Precedent: How Victims Can Pursue Human Rights Criminals Abroad (2000); Bradley & Goldsmith, Pinochet and International Human Rights Litigation, 97 Mich. L. Rev. 2129 (1999); Wilson, Prosecuting Pinochet: International Crimes in Spanish Domestic Law, 2 Hum. Rts. Q. 927 (1999). For a collection of materials concerning proceedings about Pinochet in Spain, the United Kingdom, France, and Belgium, see International Decisions, 93 A.J.I.L. 690–711 (1999), and The Pinochet Papers: The Case of Augusto Pinochet in Spain and Britain (Brody & Ratner eds., 2000).

UNITED STATES v. YOUSEF

United States Court of Appeals for the Second Circuit, 2003
327 F.3d 56 (footnotes omitted)

[Yousef and a co-defendant had been convicted of charges to bomb a Philippine aircraft outside of the United States that carried no U.S. citizens. For additional facts on this Count Nineteen of the indictment, see *supra* p. ___. The District Court had concluded that the principle of universal jurisdiction was applicable, since the defendants' conduct qualified as "terrorist" acts. The Court of Appeals rejected that analysis:]

The class of crimes subject to universal jurisdiction traditionally included only piracy. See, e.g., *Arrest Warrant of 11 Apr. 2000*, 41 I.L.M. at 559 (separate opinion of ICJ President Guillaume) (stating that "universal jurisdiction is accepted in cases of piracy because piracy is carried out on the high seas, outside all State territory"); see also Oppenheim's International Law 753 (Robert Jennings & Arthur Watts, eds., 9th ed. 1996) (discussing universal jurisdiction over acts of piracy); Michael P. Scharf, Symposium: Universal Jurisdiction: Myths, Realities, and Prospects: Application of Treaty–Based Universal Jurisdiction to Nationals of Non–Party States, 35 New Eng. L. Rev. 363, 369 (2001) (same). In modern times, the class of crimes over which States can exercise universal jurisdiction has been extended to include war crimes and acts identified after the Second World War as "crimes against humanity." See, e.g., Demjanjuk v. Petrovsky, 776 F.2d 571, 582–83 (6th Cir. 1985), vacated on other grounds, 10 F.3d 338 (6th Cir. 1993).

The concept of universal jurisdiction has its origins in prosecutions of piracy, which States and legal scholars have acknowledged for at least 500 years as a crime against all nations both because of the threat that piracy poses to orderly transport and commerce between nations and because the crime occurs statelessly on the high seas. See, e.g., *United States v. Smith*, 18 U.S. (5 Wheat) 153, 163 (1820) (Story, J.) (extensively quoting the writings of, among others, the seventeenth-century Dutch legal scholar Hugo Grotius to define piracy as prohibited by the "law of nations" and subject to universal jurisdiction; upholding the defendant's conviction, however, not based upon universal jurisdiction over acts of piracy but under the statute at issue in the case, id. at 153–54, which provided for the exercise of jurisdiction by the United States over those committing acts of piracy, as provided for in the Constitution, which states that Congress may legislate to "define and punish Piracies and Felonies committed on the high Seas, and Offenses against the Law of Nations," U.S. Const. Art. I, § 8, cl. 10); cf. Oscar Schachter, International Law in Theory and Practice 267 (1991) (recounting that Britain during the nineteenth century subjected slave traders apprehended at sea to universal jurisdiction on the view that they were pirates).

Universal jurisdiction over violations of the laws of war was not suggested until the Second World War. See Theodor Meron, International Criminalization of Internal Atrocities, 89 Am. J. Int'l L. 554, 572 (1995) (citing Hersch Lauterpacht, The Law of Nations and the Punishment of War Crimes, 2 Brit. Y.B. Int'l L. 58, 65 (1944), as the first to propose universal jurisdiction over war criminals). Following the Second World War, the United States and other nations recognized "war crimes" and "crimes against humanity," including "genocide," as crimes for which international law permits the exercise of universal jurisdiction. *Demjanjuk*, 776 F.2d at 582.

The historical restriction of universal jurisdiction to piracy, war crimes, and crimes against humanity demonstrates that universal jurisdiction arises under customary international law only where crimes (1) are universally condemned by the community of nations, and (2) by their nature occur either outside of a State or where there is no State capable of punishing, or competent to punish, the crime (as in a time of war).

Unlike those offenses supporting universal jurisdiction under customary international law—that is, piracy, war crimes, and crimes against humanity—that now have fairly precise definitions and that have achieved universal condemnation, "terrorism" is a term as loosely deployed as it is powerfully charged. Judge Harry T. Edwards of the District of Columbia Circuit stated eighteen years ago in *Tel–Oren v. Libyan Arab Republic*, 726 F.2d 774 (D.C. Cir. 1984), that "[w]hile this nation unequivocally condemns all terrorist acts, that sentiment is not universal. Indeed, the nations of the world are so divisively split on the legitimacy of such aggression as to make it impossible to pinpoint an area of harmony or consensus." Id. at 795 (Edwards, J., concurring). Similarly, Judge Robert H. Bork stated in his opinion in *Tel–Oren* that the claim that a defendant "violated customary principles of international law against terrorism[ ] concerns an area of international law in which there is little or no consensus and in which the disagreements concern politically sensitive issues. . . . [N]o consensus has developed on how properly to define 'terrorism' generally." Id. at 806–07 (Bork, J., concurring).

Finally, in a third concurring opinion, Judge Roger Robb found the question of assigning culpability for terrorist acts to be "non-justiciable" and outside of the competency of the courts as inextricably linked with "political question[s]." Id. at 823 (Robb, J., concurring). Judge Robb stated that

> [I]nternational "law", or the absence thereof, renders even the search for the least common denominators of civilized conduct in this area [defining and punishing acts of terrorism] an impossible-to-accomplish judicial task. Courts ought not to engage in it when that search takes us towards a consideration of terrorism's place in the international order. Indeed, when such a review forces us to dignify by judicial notice the most outrageous of the diplomatic charades that attempt to dignify the violence of terrorist atrocities, we corrupt our own understanding of evil.

We regrettably are no closer now than eighteen years ago to an international consensus on the definition of terrorism or even its proscription; the mere existence of the phrase "state-sponsored terrorism" proves the absence of agreement on basic terms among a large number of States that terrorism violates public international law. Moreover, there continues to be strenuous disagreement among States about what actions do or do not constitute terrorism, nor have we shaken ourselves free of the cliché that "one man's terrorist is another man's freedom fighter." We thus conclude that the statements of Judges Edwards, Bork, and Robb remain true today, and that terrorism—unlike piracy, war crimes, and crimes against humanity—does not provide a basis for universal jurisdiction.

[The Court then went on to rule that the requisite extraterritorial jurisdiction could properly be based on the Montreal Convention, which could be implemented by U.S. legislation even without a showing that one of the customary international law bases of jurisdiction covered the case. The Court further concluded that the protective principle of jurisdiction was also applicable, in view of evidence showing that the plot to destroy the aircraft was aimed at influencing the conduct of U.S. foreign policy.]

To summarize, we hold that the District Court erred in holding that jurisdiction over the acts charged in Count Nineteen is proper under the customary international law principle of universal jurisdiction * * *.

NOTES

1. *Next Steps.* In the wake of the *Pinochet* case, some commentators and activists advocated expansive conceptions of the categories of conduct covered by universal jurisdiction to include torture, forced disappearance, and transnational organized crime, among other candidates. For an argument in favor of expanding the universality principle of jurisdiction to terrorism and other offenses the community of nations widely condemns, see Randall, Universal Jurisdiction Under International Law, 66 Tex. L.Rev. 785 (1988). Others are concerned that enthusiasm for universal jurisdiction and compulsory extradition could readily lead to abuse, especially when traditional immunities are not held to cover universal crimes. Do you think such concerns may have animated the court's decision in *Yousef*? In sorting out these issues, particular

attention has been given to determining the crimes covered by universal jurisdiction, designating the courts competent to adjudicate such crimes, extradition, and the effects of immunities and amnesty. For one such effort, see The Princeton Principles on Universal Jurisdiction (Macedo. ed. 2001).

2. *Civil Remedy As Well?* A related issue is the potential expansion of universal jurisdiction to entertain in national courts civil remedies for such crimes. For example, inclusion of torture and the forced disappearance of persons in the categories of universal crimes may expose high officials alleged to have authorized such acts to civil actions in foreign states, especially after their term of office has ended. The threat of such suits may, as a practical matter, not only significantly limit their freedom to travel, but also expose them to suit in their own countries. On civil aspects of universal jurisdiction, see Donovan & Roberts, The Emerging Recognition of Universal Civil Jurisdiction, 100 A.J.I.L. 142 (2006); Fletcher, Tort Liability for Human Rights Abuses (2008); Van Schaack, Justice Without Borders: Universal Civil Jurisdiction, 99 Am. Soc'y Int'l L. Proc. 120 (2005).

3. *Further Reading.* For further discussion, see Kontorovich, The Inefficiency of Universal Jurisdiction, 2008 U. Ill. L. Rev. 389; Colangelo, The Legal Limits of Universal Jurisdiction, 47 Va. J. Int'l L. 149 (2006); Kontorovich, The Piracy Analogy: Modern Universal Jurisdiction's Hollow Foundation, 45 Harv. Int'l L. J 183 (2004); Universal Jurisdiction, National Courts and the Prosecution of Serious Crimes under International Law, 168 (Macedo ed. 2004); Boyd, Universal Jurisdiction and Structural Reasonableness, 40 Tex. Int'l L. J. 1 (2004); Reydams, Universal Jurisdiction: International and Municipal Legal Perspectives (2003); Sadat, Redefining Universal Jurisdiction, 35 New Eng. L. Rev. 241 (2001).

SECTION 7.   JURISDICTION TO ADJUDICATE

A state may not exercise its judicial functions within the territory of another state without the latter's consent. See Section 8 of this Chapter. Conversely, a state may normally exercise its judicial functions in regard to persons or things within its territory. Questions, analogous to those that have arisen in the area of legislative jurisdiction, may arise when a state exercises within its territory judicial authority over persons or things outside of its territory. These questions become particularly acute when the judicial authority is sought to be exercised over persons or things that have no reasonable relation to the state that seeks to exercise judicial jurisdiction.

However, many states have habitually exercised adjudicatory authority over persons outside of their borders in the absence of some contact that would be considered sufficient under due process limitations developed in the United States. Many states permit criminal prosecutions in absentia of the accused. And leading civil law countries exercise adjudicatory authority in civil cases on bases such as the nationality or residence of the plaintiff or the mere presence of unrelated property. For a more detailed discussion, see Rosenberg, Smit & Dreyfuss, Elements of Civil

Procedure 226 (5th ed. 1990) and authorities cited. While these bases have been characterized as exorbitant or extraordinary, they have, thus far, not been asserted, on authoritative grounds, to be violative of international law.

The Restatement (Third) states that "increasingly, they [i.e., states] object to the improper exercise of jurisdiction [i.e. jurisdiction on an extravagant basis] as itself a violation of international principles." Section 421, Introductory Note. Although the Restatement (Third) refers to no source supporting this statement, it would appear that good grounds exist for international law limitations on the exercise of a state's extraterritorial judicial jurisdiction, at least in criminal and administrative matters. For example, in the *Alvarez–Machain* case, p. 819 *infra*, it might be argued that prosecuting in the United States a person abducted in violation of international law constituted itself a violation of international law. See p. 826 note 2. Whether the same is true in civil matters is considerably more doubtful.

The Restatement (Third) has attempted to formulate the proper criteria in the provisions set forth below.

RESTATEMENT OF THE LAW (THIRD)
THE FOREIGN RELATIONS LAW OF THE UNITED STATES § 421 (1987)

§ 421. Jurisdiction to Adjudicate

(1) A state may exercise jurisdiction through its courts to adjudicate with respect to a person or thing if the relationship of the state to the person or thing is such as to make the exercise of jurisdiction reasonable.

(2) In general, a state's exercise of jurisdiction to adjudicate with respect to a person or thing is reasonable if, at the time jurisdiction is asserted:

(a) the person or thing is present in the territory of the state, other than transitorily;

(b) the person, if a natural person, is domiciled in the state;

(c) the person, if a natural person, is resident in the state;

(d) the person, if a natural person, is a national of the state;

(e) the person, if a corporation or comparable juridical person, is organized pursuant to the law of the state;

(f) a ship, aircraft or other vehicle to which the adjudication relates is registered under the laws of the state;

(g) the person, whether natural or juridical, has consented to the exercise of jurisdiction;

(h) the person, whether natural or juridical, regularly carries on business in the state;

(i) the person, whether natural or juridical, had carried on activity in the state, but only in respect of such activity;

(j) the person, whether natural or juridical, had carried on outside the state an activity having a substantial, direct, and foreseeable effect within the state, but only in respect of such activity; or

(k) the thing that is the subject of adjudication is owned, possessed, or used in the state, but only in respect of a claim reasonably connected with that thing.

(3) A defense of lack of jurisdiction is generally waived by any appearance by or on behalf of a person or thing (whether as plaintiff, defendant, or third party), if the appearance is for a purpose that does not include a challenge to the exercise of jurisdiction.

§ 423. Jurisdiction to Adjudicate in Enforcement of Universal and Other Non–Territorial Crimes

A state may exercise jurisdiction through its courts to enforce its criminal laws that punish universal crimes or other non-territorial offenses within the state's jurisdiction to prescribe.

NOTES

1. *Minimum Contacts.* Courts in the United States have consistently ruled that the exercise of adjudicatory power in civil cases is improper unless the defendant had "minimum" contacts with the state purporting the exercise of judicial jurisdiction. The leading decision to that effect is *International Shoe Co. v. Washington*, 326 U.S. 310 (1945). The exercise of judicial power in the absence of such contact is a violation of due process, guaranteed by the Fifth and Fourteenth Amendments to the U.S. Constitution. One might expect that the exercise of judicial jurisdiction in international cases would also be regarded as a violation of international due process. However, a number of civil law countries provide for the exercise of judicial jurisdiction in cases which U.S. courts would regard as violative of due process. For example, in France the French nationality of the plaintiff suffices, in the Netherlands the Dutch domicile of the plaintiff is sufficient, and in Germany the presence of the defendant's property in Germany, although totally unrelated to the claim, is enough. However, EU Regulation No. 44/2001 provides that these bases are not to be recognized as between Member States. This may be regarded as international recognition of the inadequacy of these bases and as providing support for the Restatement (Third)'s unqualified statement that international law forbids the exercise of judicial jurisdiction without an adequate basis. Whether this is so could not be tested in courts of states that do not recognize that international law trumps national legislation. But the ratification of the European Human Rights Convention has opened an avenue for adjudication of the issue, and a number of its provisions are rather analogous to the due process clauses of the U.S. Constitution.

2. *Human Rights Limitations.* It has been argued in both European and U.S. courts that the European Human Rights Convention does impose limita-

tions on the exercise of judicial jurisdiction in civil cases in the context of class actions. In a class action of the type covered by Rule 23(c) of the Federal Rules of Civil Procedure, the members of the class who do not opt out are bound even when there is no other adequate basis for exercising jurisdiction over them. Recently, a number of class actions have been brought in U.S. courts on behalf of foreign shareholders who purchased their shares outside the United States on the ground that the shares have been registered with the SEC and listed on a U.S. Exchange. The defendant argued that the exercise of judicial jurisdiction over foreign members of the class who had not opted out would violate the European Human Rights Convention. See *In re Alstrom SA Securities Litigation*, 253 F.R.D. 266 (2008). While their pleas were not found well-grounded, no one contested that the European Convention did impose limits on the exercise of judicial jurisdiction, at least as regards enforceability of a U.S. class action judgment in Europe.

SECTION 8. JURISDICTION TO ENFORCE

RESTATEMENT OF THE LAW (THIRD)
THE FOREIGN RELATIONS LAW OF THE UNITED STATES §§ 431–32 (1987)

§ 431. Jurisdiction to Enforce

(1) A state may employ judicial or nonjudicial measures to induce or compel compliance or punish noncompliance with its laws or regulations, provided it has jurisdiction to prescribe in accordance with §§ 402 and 403.

(2) Enforcement measures must be reasonably related to the laws or regulations to which they are directed; punishment for noncompliance must be preceded by an appropriate determination of violation and must be proportional to the gravity of the violation.

(3) A state may employ enforcement measures against a person located outside its territory

(a) if the person is given notice of the claims or charges against him that is reasonable in the circumstances;

(b) if the person is given an opportunity to be heard, ordinarily in advance of enforcement, whether in person or by counsel or other representative; and

(c) when enforcement is through the courts, if the state has jurisdiction to adjudicate.

§ 432. Measures in Aid of Enforcement of Criminal Law

(1) A state may enforce its criminal law within its own territory through the use of police, investigative agencies, public prosecutors, courts, and custodial facilities, provided

(a) the law being enforced is within the state's jurisdiction to prescribe;

(b) when enforcement is through the courts, the state has jurisdiction to adjudicate with respect to the person who is the target of enforcement; and

(c) the procedures of investigation, arrest, adjudication, and punishment are consistent with the state's obligations under the law of international human rights.

(2) A state's law enforcement officers may exercise their functions in the territory of another state only with the consent of the other state, given by duly authorized officials of that state.

UNITED STATES v. ALVAREZ–MACHAIN

Supreme Court of the United States, 1992
504 U.S. 655 (some citations and footnotes omitted)

THE CHIEF JUSTICE delivered the opinion of the Court.

The issue in this case is whether a criminal defendant, abducted to the United States from a nation with which it has an extradition treaty, thereby acquires a defense to the jurisdiction of this country's courts. We hold that he does not, and that he may be tried in federal district court for violations of the criminal law of the United States.

Respondent, Humberto Alvarez–Machain, is a citizen and resident of Mexico. He was indicted for participating in the kidnap and murder of United States Drug Enforcement Administration (DEA) special agent Enrique Camarena–Salazar and a Mexican pilot working with Camarena, Alfredo Zavala–Avelar. The DEA believes that respondent, a medical doctor, participated in the murder by prolonging agent Camarena's life so that others could further torture and interrogate him. On April 2, 1990, respondent was forcibly kidnapped from his medical office in Guadalajara, Mexico, to be flown by private plane to El Paso, Texas, where he was arrested by DEA officials. The District Court concluded that DEA agents were responsible for respondent's abduction, although they were not personally involved in it. *United States v. Caro–Quintero*, 745 F.Supp. 599, 602, 604, 609 (C.D.Cal.1990).

Respondent moved to dismiss the indictment, claiming that his abduction constituted outrageous governmental conduct, and that the District Court lacked jurisdiction to try him because he was abducted in violation of the extradition treaty between the United States and Mexico. Extradition Treaty, May 4, 1978, [1979] United States–United Mexican States, 31 U.S.T. 5059, T.I.A.S. No. 9656 (Extradition Treaty or Treaty). The District Court rejected the outrageous governmental conduct claim, but held that it lacked jurisdiction to try respondent because his abduction violated the Extradition Treaty. The district court discharged respondent and ordered that he be repatriated to Mexico. *Caro–Quintero*, supra, at 614.

The Court of Appeals affirmed the dismissal of the indictment and the repatriation of respondent, relying on its decision in *United States v. Verdugo–Urquidez*, 939 F.2d 1341 (C.A.9 1991). In *Verdugo*, the Court of Appeals held that the forcible abduction of a Mexican national with the authorization or participation of the United States violated the Extradition Treaty between the United States and Mexico. Although the Treaty does not expressly prohibit such abductions, the Court of Appeals held that the "purpose" of the Treaty was violated by a forcible abduction, * * * which, along with a formal protest by the offended nation, would give a defendant the right to invoke the Treaty violation to defeat jurisdiction of the district court to try him. The Court of Appeals further held that the proper remedy for such a violation would be dismissal of the indictment and repatriation of the defendant to Mexico.

In the instant case, the Court of Appeals affirmed the district court's finding that the United States had authorized the abduction of respondent, and that letters from the Mexican government to the United States government served as an official protest of the Treaty violation. Therefore, the Court of Appeals ordered that the indictment against respondent be dismissed and that respondent be repatriated to Mexico. 946 F.2d at 1467. We granted certiorari, * * * and now reverse.

Although we have never before addressed the precise issue raised in the present case, we have previously considered proceedings in claimed violation of an extradition treaty, and proceedings against a defendant brought before a court by means of a forcible abduction. We addressed the former issue in *United States v. Rauscher*, 119 U.S. 407 (1886); more precisely, the issue of whether the Webster–Ashburton Treaty of 1842, 8 Stat. 576, which governed extraditions between England and the United States, prohibited the prosecution of defendant Rauscher for a crime other than the crime for which he had been extradited. Whether this prohibition, known as the doctrine of specialty, was an intended part of the treaty had been disputed between the two nations for some time. *Rauscher*, 119 U.S. at 411. Justice Miller delivered the opinion of the Court, which carefully examined the terms and history of the treaty; the practice of nations in regards to extradition treaties; the case law from the states; and the writings of commentators, and reached the following conclusion:

> "[A] person who has been brought within the jurisdiction of the court *by virtue of proceedings under an extradition treaty*, can only be tried for one of the offences described in that treaty, and for the offence with which he is charged in the proceedings for his extradition, until a reasonable time and opportunity have been given him, after his release or trial upon such charge, to return to the country from whose asylum he had been forcibly taken under those proceedings." Id., at 430 (emphasis added).

In addition, Justice Miller's opinion noted that any doubt as to this interpretation was put to rest by two federal statutes which imposed the doctrine of specialty upon extradition treaties to which the United States was a party. * * * Unlike the case before us today, the defendant in *Rauscher* had been brought to the United States by way of an extradition treaty; there was no issue of a forcible abduction.

In *Ker v. Illinois*, 119 U.S. 436 (1886), also written by Justice Miller and decided the same day as *Rauscher*, we addressed the issue of a defendant brought before the court by way of a forcible abduction. Frederick Ker had been tried and convicted in an Illinois court for larceny; his presence before the court was procured by means of forcible abduction from Peru. A messenger was sent to Lima with the proper warrant to demand Ker by virtue of the extradition treaty between Peru and the United States. The messenger, however, disdained reliance on the treaty processes, and instead forcibly kidnapped Ker and brought him to the United States. We distinguished Ker's case from *Rauscher*, on the basis that Ker was not brought into the United States by virtue of the extradition treaty between the United States and Peru, and rejected Ker's argument that he had a right under the extradition treaty to be returned to this country only in accordance with its terms. We rejected Ker's due process argument more broadly, holding in line with "the highest authorities" that "such forcible abduction is no sufficient reason why the party should not answer when brought within the jurisdiction of the court which has the right to try him for such an offence, and presents no valid objection to his trial in such court." * * *

In *Frisbie v. Collins*, 342 U.S. 519, rehearing denied, 343 U.S. 937 (1952), we applied the rule in *Ker* to a case in which the defendant had been kidnapped in Chicago by Michigan officers and brought to trial in Michigan. We upheld the conviction over objections based on the due process clause and the Federal Kidnapping Act. * * *

The only differences between *Ker* and the present case are that *Ker* was decided on the premise that there was no governmental involvement in the abduction, 119 U.S. at 443; and Peru, from which Ker was abducted, did not object to his prosecution. Respondent finds these differences to be dispositive, as did the Court of Appeals in *Verdugo*, 939 F.2d, at 1346, contending that they show that respondent's prosecution, like the prosecution of Rauscher, violates the implied terms of a valid extradition treaty. The Government, on the other hand, argues that *Rauscher* stands as an "exception" to the rule in *Ker* only when an extradition treaty is invoked, and the terms of the treaty provide that its breach will limit the jurisdiction of a court. * * * Therefore, our first inquiry must be whether the abduction of respondent from Mexico violated the extradition treaty between the United States and Mexico. If we conclude that the Treaty does not prohibit respondent's abduction, the rule in *Ker* applies, and the court need not inquire as to how respondent came before it.

* * *

* * * [T]he language of the Treaty, in the context of its history, does not support the proposition that the Treaty prohibits abductions outside of its terms. The remaining question, therefore, is whether the Treaty

should be interpreted so as to include an implied term prohibiting prosecution where the defendant's presence is obtained by means other than those established by the Treaty. See *Valentine*, 299 U.S., at 17 ("Strictly the question is not whether there had been a uniform practical construction denying the power, but whether the power had been so clearly recognized that the grant should be implied").

Respondent contends that the Treaty must be interpreted against the backdrop of customary international law, and that international abductions are "so clearly prohibited in international law" that there was no reason to include such a clause in the Treaty itself. The international censure of international abductions is further evidenced, according to respondent, by the United Nations Charter and the Charter of the Organization of American States. Respondent does not argue that these sources of international law provide an independent basis for the right respondent asserts not to be tried in the United States, but rather that they should inform the interpretation of the Treaty terms.

The Court of Appeals deemed it essential, in order for the individual defendant to assert a right under the Treaty, that the affected foreign government had registered a protest. *Verdugo*, 939 F.2d, at 1357 ("in the kidnapping case there must be a formal protest from the offended government after the kidnapping"). Respondent agrees that the right exercised by the individual is derivative of the nation's right under the Treaty, since nations are authorized, notwithstanding the terms of an extradition treaty, to voluntarily render an individual to the other country on terms completely outside of those provided in the Treaty. The formal protest, therefore, ensures that the "offended" nation actually objects to the abduction and has not in some way voluntarily rendered the individual for prosecution. Thus the Extradition Treaty only prohibits gaining the defendant's presence by means other than those set forth in the Treaty when the nation from which the defendant was abducted objects.

This argument seems to us inconsistent with the remainder of respondent's argument. The Extradition Treaty has the force of law, and if, as respondent asserts, it is self-executing, it would appear that a court must enforce it on behalf of an individual regardless of the offensiveness of the practice of one nation to the other nation. In *Rauscher*, the Court noted that Great Britain had taken the position in other cases that the Webster–Ashburton Treaty included the doctrine of specialty, but no importance was attached to whether or not Great Britain had protested the prosecution of Rauscher for the crime of cruel and unusual punishment as opposed to murder.

More fundamentally, the difficulty with the support respondent garners from international law is that none of it relates to the practice of nations in relation to extradition treaties. In *Rauscher*, we implied a term in the Webster–Ashburton Treaty because of the practice of nations with regard to extradition treaties. In the instant case, respondent would imply terms in the extradition treaty from the practice of nations with regards to international law more generally. Respondent would have us find that the Treaty acts as a prohibition against a violation of the general principle of international law that one government may not "exercise its police power in the territory of another state." There are many actions which could be taken by a nation that would violate this principle, including waging war, but it cannot seriously be contended an invasion of the United States by Mexico would violate the terms of the extradition treaty between the two nations.

In sum, to infer from this Treaty and its terms that it prohibits all means of gaining the presence of an individual outside of its terms goes beyond established precedent and practice. * * * The general principles cited by respondent simply fail to persuade us that we should imply in the United States–Mexico Extradition Treaty a term prohibiting international abductions.

Respondent and his amici may be correct that respondent's abduction was "shocking,"and that it may be in violation of general international law principles. Mexico has protested the abduction of respondent through diplomatic notes, and the decision of whether respondent should be returned to Mexico, as a matter outside of the Treaty, is a matter for the Executive Branch. We conclude, however, that respondent's abduction was not in violation of the Extradition Treaty between the United States and Mexico, and therefore the rule of *Ker v. Illinois* is fully applicable to this case. The fact of respondent's forcible abduction does not therefore prohibit his trial in a court in the United States for violations of the criminal laws of the United States.

The judgment of the Court of Appeals is therefore reversed, and the case is remanded for further proceedings consistent with this opinion.

So ordered.

JUSTICE STEVENS, with whom JUSTICE BLACKMUN and JUSTICE O'CONNOR join, dissenting.

The Court correctly observes that this case raises a question of first impression. The case is unique for several reasons. It does not involve an ordinary abduction by a private kidnaper, or bounty hunter, as in *Ker v. Illinois*, 119 U.S. 436 (1886); nor does it involve the apprehension of an American fugitive who committed a crime in one State and sought asylum in another, as in *Frisbie v. Collins*, 342 U.S. 519 (1952). Rather, it involves this country's abduction of another country's citizen; it also involves a violation of the territorial integrity of that other country, with which this country has signed an extradition treaty.

A Mexican citizen was kidnaped in Mexico and charged with a crime committed in Mexico; his offense allegedly violated both Mexican and American law. Mexico has formally demanded on at least two separate occasions that he be returned to Mexico and has represented that he will be prosecuted and punished for his alleged offense. It is clear that Mexico's demand must be honored if this official abduction violated the

1978 Extradition Treaty between the United States and Mexico. In my opinion, a fair reading of the treaty in light of our decision in *United States v. Rauscher*, 119 U.S. 407 (1886), and applicable principles of international law, leads inexorably to the conclusion that the District Court, *United States v. Caro–Quintero*, 745 F.Supp. 599 (C.D.Cal.1990), and the Court of Appeals for the Ninth Circuit, 946 F.2d 1466 (1991) (per curiam), correctly construed that instrument.

* * *

* * * [T]he Extradition Treaty, as understood in the context of cases that have addressed similar issues, suffices to protect the defendant from prosecution despite the absence of any express language in the Treaty itself purporting to limit this Nation's power to prosecute a defendant over whom it had lawfully acquired jurisdiction.

Although the Court's conclusion in *Rauscher* was supported by a number of judicial precedents, the holdings in these cases were not nearly as uniform as the consensus of international opinion that condemns one Nation's violation of the territorial integrity of a friendly neighbor. It is shocking that a party to an extradition treaty might believe that it has secretly reserved the right to make seizures of citizens in the other party's territory. Justice Story found it shocking enough that the United States would attempt to justify an American seizure of a foreign vessel in a Spanish port:

"But, even supposing, for a moment, that our laws had required an entry of the *Apollon*, in her transit, does it follow, that the power to arrest her was meant to be given, after she had passed into the exclusive territory of a foreign nation? We think not. It would be monstrous to suppose that our revenue officers were authorized to enter into foreign ports and territories, for the purpose of seizing vessels which had offended against our laws. It cannot be presumed that Congress would voluntarily justify such a clear violation of the laws of nations." *The Apollon*, 9 Wheat. 362, 370–371 (1824) (emphasis added).

The law of Nations, as understood by Justice Story in 1824, has not changed. Thus, a leading treatise explains:

"A State must not perform acts of sovereignty in the territory of another State . . . . . It is . . . a breach of International Law for a State to send its agents to the territory of another State to apprehend persons accused of having committed a crime. Apart from other satisfaction, the first duty of the offending State is to hand over the person in question to the State in whose territory he was apprehended." 1 Oppenheim's International Law 295, and n. 1 (H. Lauterpacht 8th ed. 1955).

Commenting on the precise issue raised by this case, the chief reporter for the American Law Institute's Restatement of Foreign Relations used language reminiscent of Justice Story's characterization of an official seizure in a foreign jurisdiction as "monstrous:"

> "When done without consent of the foreign government, abducting a person from a foreign country is a gross violation of international law and gross disrespect for a norm high in the opinion of mankind. It is a blatant violation of the territorial integrity of another state; it eviscerates the extradition system (established by a comprehensive network of treaties involving virtually all states)."

In the *Rauscher* case, the legal background that supported the decision to imply a covenant not to prosecute for an offense different from that for which extradition had been granted was far less clear than the rule against invading the territorial integrity of a treaty partner that supports Mexico's position in this case.[25] If *Rauscher* was correctly decided—and I am convinced that it was—its rationale clearly dictates a comparable result in this case.

* * *

I suspect most courts throughout the civilized world will be deeply disturbed by the "monstrous" decision the Court announces today. For every Nation that has an interest in preserving the Rule of Law is affected, directly or indirectly, by a decision of this character. As Thomas Paine warned, an "avidity to punish is always dangerous to liberty" because it leads a Nation "to stretch, to misinterpret, and to misapply even the best of laws." To counter that tendency, he reminds us:

> "He that would make his own liberty secure must guard even his enemy from oppression; for if he violates this duty he establishes a precedent that will reach to himself."

I respectfully dissent.

NOTES

1. *Male Captus, Bene Detentus.* If a state improperly seizes a person accused of a crime outside of its borders, may it nevertheless properly exercise judicial jurisdiction over this person in the United States? The traditional rule of international law is that of "male captus, bene detentus," i.e., that a person

---

25. Thus, the Restatement of Foreign Relations states in part:

"(2) A state's law enforcement officers may exercise their functions in the territory of another state only with the consent of the other state, given by duly authorized officials of that state.

. . . . .

"c. *Consequences of violation of territorial limits of law enforcement.* If a state's law enforcement officials exercise their functions in the territory of another state without the latter's consent, that state is entitled to protest and, in appropriate cases, to receive reparation from the offending state. If the unauthorized action includes abduction of a person, the state from which the person was abducted may demand return of the person, and international law requires that he be returned. If the state from which the person was abducted does not demand his return, under the prevailing view the abducting state may proceed to prosecute him under its laws."

Restatement § 432, and Comment *c*.

who has been improperly seized may nevertheless properly be tried. This rule has been argued to follow from the principle that, under international law, only the state in the territory of which the person was captured may complain of the improper exercise of executive jurisdiction. However, as the majority decision in *United States v. Alvarez–Machain* demonstrates, U.S. courts have exercised judicial jurisdiction over persons improperly seized even if the state in the territory of which they were seized objected.

2.   *Exercise of Jurisdiction as Violation of International Law.* The Court did not dispute that the forcible abduction of the accused from Mexico violated general international law. Should it also have considered whether the U.S. prosecutor and the Executive had the constitutional power to keep in custody and prosecute a person whose presence they had procured in violation of international law and elementary principles of proper governmental conduct? If they did not, would dismissal of the charges be the appropriate sanction? See Halberstam, In Defense of the Supreme Court Decision in Alvarez–Machain, 86 A.J.I.L. 736, 738–43 (1992).

3.   *Good Faith Interpretation of Extradition Treaty.* Are you persuaded by the majority's analysis of the meaning of the U.S.–Mexico extradition treaty? Recall from Chapter 3 that it is a well-settled rule of international law that international agreements must be construed in accordance with good faith. Good faith is objective good faith; it imposes a standard of objective reasonableness. When a treaty is construed to accord with objective good faith, its provisions are supplemented by reference to the law, not to the subjective intentions of the parties. The pertinent question, in determining what the law requires, is not what the parties actually intended, but, instead, what they would have intended if they had thought of the possibility of including the lacking provision in the treaty. See Smit, Frustration of Contract: A Comparative Attempt at Consolidation, 58 Colum. L. Rev. 287 (1958). Is there any reasonable doubt that, if, at the time of the negotiation and conclusion of the Treaty, the parties had considered the possibility that either party would engage in abduction in violation of international law, they would have included in the Treaty a provision prohibiting this? Does the Court give any consideration to the possible implication of this prohibition on the basis of objective good faith rather than the parties' actual intentions?

4.   *Acquittal on Remand.* Upon remand, the district court granted an acquittal on the ground that the prosecution had failed to produce adequate proof of its charges. Thereafter, Alvarez–Machain brought a civil suit against the United States government and individuals involved in the abduction, including claims for "violation of the law of nations" within the meaning of the Alien Tort Statute, 28 U.S.C. § 1350. For the Supreme Court's eventual ruling that the claim could not be maintained, see *Sosa v. Alvarez–Machain,* 542 U.S. 692 (2004), excerpted and discussed in Chapters 4, 10, and 13.

5.   *International Reactions.* The decision in *United States v. Alvarez–Machain* generated widespread international criticism. On November 23, 1994, the United States and Mexico signed a Treaty to Prohibit Transborder Abductions, Nov. 23, 1994, U.S.–Mex., *reprinted in* Abbell, Extradition to and From the United States, at A–303 (2002). While that agreement would require the prompt return of abducted persons and prohibit the exercise of jurisdic-

tion over them, the treaty is not yet in force because the President has not submitted it to the Senate for its advice and consent. Do you think the Treaty, even though not in force, reflects a rule of customary international law prohibiting the exercise of national jurisdiction over abducted persons? Would it make a difference whether the accused was abducted by private persons or agents of the prosecuting state? On these developments, see Jurisdiction Over Persons Abducted in Violation of International Law in the Aftermath of United States v. Alvarez–Machain, 5 U. Chi. L. Sch. Round Table 205 (1998).

6. *Luring the Target Away from Foreign Territory.* Can a state exercise enforcement jurisdiction in situations where a targeted person was lured away from foreign territory, either to the United States or to a common space, such as the high seas? For example, FBI agents wanted to arrest a person accused of hijacking a Jordanian airplane in Beirut with U.S. passengers aboard. The agents lured the target onto a yacht in the Mediterranean with the promise of a drug deal and then arrested him when the vessel entered international waters. Challenges to the arrest and U.S. jurisdiction were upheld in *United States v. Fawaz Yunis*, 924 F.2d 1086 (D.C. Cir. 1991). If, in the principal case, the U.S. anti-drug enforcement officers had lured the Mexican doctor to the United States, would international law have been violated? Would such a stratagem have been implicitly prohibited by the extradition treaty? On the Yunis arrest and related matters, see the series of articles by Lowenfeld, U.S. Law Enforcement Abroad, 83 A.J.I.L 880 (1989), 84 A.J.I.L. 444 (1990), and 84 A.J.I.L. 712 (1990).

LETTER OF 15 JUNE 1960 FROM THE REPRESENTATIVE OF ARGENTINA TO THE PRESIDENT OF THE SECURITY COUNCIL

U.N. Doc. S/4336

I have the honour, on the instructions of my Government, to request you to call an urgent meeting of the Security Council to consider the violation of the sovereign rights of the Argentine Republic resulting from the illicit and clandestine transfer of Adolf Eichmann from Argentine territory to the territory of the State of Israel, contrary to the rules of international law and the Purposes and Principles of the Charter of the United Nations and creating an atmosphere of insecurity and mistrust incompatible with the preservation of international peace.

An explanatory memorandum is attached. * * *

(Signed) Mario Amadeo
Ambassador

EXPLANATORY MEMORANDUM

In view of the failure of the diplomatic representations made by it to the Government of Israel the Argentine Government is now compelled, in defence of fundamental rights, to request that the case be dealt with by the Security Council, the case being in its view explicitly covered by the provisions of Article 34 and Article 35, paragraph 1, of the United Nations Charter.

The facts which have led to this situation are as follows:

1.   Having learned from reports which had become known to world public opinion that Adolf Eichmann had been captured in Argentine territory by "volunteer groups" which transferred him to the territory of Israel and there delivered him to the authorities of that country, the Argentine Government approached the Government of Israel with a request for information in that connexion.

2.   The Government of Israel, through its Embassy at Buenos Aires, replied to this request in a note of 3 June 1960 in which it stated that Eichmann had in fact been transferred to Israel from Argentine territory. After stating that Eichmann had consented to the transfer, the Government of Israel's note concluded with the statement that "if the volunteer group violated Argentine law or interfered with matters within the sovereignty of Argentina, the Government of Israel wishes to express its regret."

3.   In view of the recognition of the authenticity of the facts reported in connexion with Eichmann's capture, the Argentine Government * * * made the most formal protest against the illegal act committed to the detriment of a fundamental right of the Argentine State, and requested appropriate reparation for the act, namely the return of Eichmann, for which it set a time-limit of one week, and the punishment of those guilty of violating Argentine territory. The Argentine Government stated that, failing compliance with this request, it would refer the matter to the United Nations.* * *

It is unnecessary to adduce further considerations in order to underline the gravity of the resulting situation. The illicit and clandestine transfer of Eichmann from Argentine territory constitutes a flagrant violation of the Argentine State's right of sovereignty, and the Argentine Government is legally justified in requesting reparation. That right cannot be qualified by any other considerations, even those invoked by the Government of Israel with regard to the importance attaching to the trial of a man accused of exterminations in concentration camps, although the Argentine Government and people understand those reasons to the full. Any contrary interpretation would be tantamount to approving the taking of the law into one's own hands and the subjecting of international order to unilateral acts which, if repeated, would involve undeniable dangers for the preservation of peace.

Before appealing to the Security Council, the Argentine Government endeavoured, in accordance with the Charter of the United Nations, to reach a satisfactory solution through the normal diplomatic channels of negotiation. In these endeavours the close friendship between Argentina and the State of Israel played a part. Those endeavours have, however, been without success. In these circumstances, the only remaining recourse is to the Security Council. A political question is involved which, apart from gravely prejudicing Argentine sovereignty, constitutes a precedent dangerous for international peace and security, for the maintenance of which the Security Council bears primary responsibility.

The Argentine Government hopes that the Security Council will attach to this question all the importance which it merits, and will take decisions involving just reparation for the rights violated.

NOTES

1. *Security Council's Treatment of the Incident.* Israel disputed the Council's competence to deal with the incident in a letter of June 21, 1960,U.N. Doc. S/4341, stating that Argentina's unilateral allegations did not suffice to bring the dispute within the terms of Article 34 of the Charter and expressing the conviction that the difficulties between the two countries could best be settled by direct negotiations. At its 865th meeting on June 22, 1960, however, the Council included the matter in its agenda without objection. The Israeli representative was invited to take a seat at the Council table. For the debate, see U.N. Docs. S/P.V. 865–68; see also the summary contained in the Security Council's report to the General Assembly for the year ending July 15, 1960, U.N. Doc. A/4494, at 19–24. On June 23, 1960, the Security Council adopted a resolution by eight votes to none, with two abstentions (Poland and the Soviet Union) and one member (Argentina) not participating in the vote. The operative parts of the resolution, U.N. Doc. S/4349, were as follows:

The Security Council, * * *

1. *Declares* that acts such as that under consideration, which affect the sovereignty of a Member State and therefore cause international friction, may, if repeated, endanger international peace and security;

2. *Requests* the Government of Israel to make appropriate reparation in accordance with the Charter of the United Nations and the rules of international law * * *

2. *Joint Communique Ending the Matter.* On August 3, 1960, the following joint communiqué was published in Jerusalem and Buenos Aires:

The Governments of Israel and the Republic of Argentina, animated by the wish to comply with the resolution of the Security Council of June 23, 1960, in which the hope was expressed that the traditionally friendly relations between the two countries will be advanced, have decided to regard as closed the incident that arose out of the action taken by Israeli nationals which infringed fundamental rights of the State of Argentina.

3. *Enforcement of Universal Jurisdiction.* Should a state's enforcement jurisdiction be more extensive in cases of the exercise of universal legislative jurisdiction than in other cases? May, in such cases, a state exercise enforcement jurisdiction on the territory of another state? Does the propriety of a state's exercising of enforcement jurisdiction in such cases depend on whether the person against whom the jurisdiction is exercised (a) is a national of the state exercising it, (b) performed the acts for which he is called to account within the territory of the state exercising it, (c) did the incriminated acts against a national of the state exercising it, or (d) is not called to account for his conduct by the state on the territory of which the jurisdiction is exercised?

SECTION 9. JURISDICTION BASED ON AGREEMENT

Under international law, a state has jurisdiction to prescribe and enforce law in another state's territory to the extent provided by international agreement with the other state. The principle that jurisdiction may be conferred by agreement also underpins arrangements by which an international organization administers a territory for a temporary or transitional period.

Agreements covering allocation of jurisdictional competences are commonly made when armed forces of one state are present in another state's territory by consent. An example is the Agreement Between the Parties to the North Atlantic Treaty Regarding the Status of Their Forces, signed at London, June 19, 1951, 4 U.S.T. 1792, 199 U.N.T.S. 67, known as the NATO Status of Forces Agreement or NATO SOFA. Similar agreements are in effect with other countries where U.S. troops are based. The following case illustrates the operation of such an agreement between the United States and Japan.

WILSON v. GIRARD

Supreme Court of the United States, 1957
354 U.S. 524

PER CURIAM. Japan and the United States became involved in a controversy whether the respondent Girard should be tried by a Japanese court for causing the death of a Japanese woman. * * *

Girard, a Specialist Third Class in the United States Army, was engaged on January 30, 1957, with members of his cavalry regiment in a small unit exercise at Camp Weir range area, Japan. Japanese civilians were present in the area, retrieving expended cartridge cases. Girard and another Specialist Third Class were ordered to guard a machine gun and some items of clothing that had been left nearby. Girard had a grenade launcher on his rifle. He placed an expended 30–caliber cartridge case in the grenade launcher and projected it by firing a blank. The expended cartridge case penetrated the back of a Japanese woman gathering expended cartridge cases and caused her death.

The United States ultimately notified Japan that Girard would be delivered to the Japanese authorities for trial. Thereafter, Japan indicted him for causing death by wounding. Girard sought a writ of habeas corpus in the United States District Court for the District of Columbia. The writ was denied, but Girard was granted declaratory relief and an injunction against his delivery to the Japanese authorities. 152 F.Supp. 21. The petitioners appealed to the Court of Appeals for the District of Columbia, and, without awaiting action by that court on the appeal, invoked the jurisdiction of this Court under 28 U.S.C. § 1254(1), 28 U.S.C.A. § 1254(1). Girard filed a cross-petition for certiorari to review the denial of the writ of habeas corpus. We granted both petitions. * * *

A Security Treaty between Japan and the United States, signed September 8, 1951, was ratified by the Senate on March 20, 1952, and proclaimed by the President effective April 28, 1952 [3 U.S.T. 3329]. Article III of the Treaty authorized the making of Administrative Agreements between the two Governments concerning "[t]he conditions which shall govern the disposition of armed forces of the United States of America in and about Japan * * *" Expressly acting under this provision, the two Nations, on February 28, 1952, signed an Administrative Agreement covering, among other matters, the jurisdiction of the United States over offenses committed in Japan by members of the United States armed forces, and providing that jurisdiction in any case might be waived by the United States. This Agreement [3 U.S.T. 3341] became effective on the same date as the Security Treaty (April 28, 1952) and was considered by the Senate before consent was given to the Treaty.

Article XVII, paragraph 1, of the Administrative Agreement provided that upon the coming into effect of the "Agreement between the Parties to the North Atlantic Treaty regarding the Status of their Forces," [4 U.S.T. 1792] signed June 19, 1951, the United States would conclude with Japan an agreement on criminal jurisdiction similar to the corresponding provisions of the NATO Agreement. The NATO Agreement became effective August 23, 1953, and the United States and Japan signed on September 29, 1953, effective October 29, 1953, a Protocol Agreement [4 U.S.T. 1846] pursuant to the covenant in paragraph I of Article XVII.

Paragraph 3 of Article XVII, as amended by the Protocol, dealt with criminal offenses in violation of the laws of both Nations and provided:

3. In cases where the right to exercise jurisdiction is concurrent the following rules shall apply:

(a) The military authorities of the United States shall have the primary right to exercise jurisdiction over members of the United States armed forces or the civilian component in relation to

(i) offenses solely against the property or security of the United States, or offenses solely against the person or property of another member of the United States armed forces or the civilian component or of a dependent;

(ii) offenses arising out of any act or omission done in the performance of official duty.

(b) In the case of any other offense the authorities of Japan shall have the primary right to exercise jurisdiction.

(c) If the State having the primary right decides not to exercise jurisdiction, it shall notify the authorities of the other State as soon as practicable. The authorities of the State having the primary right shall give sympathetic consideration to a request from the authorities of the other State for a waiver of its right in cases where that other State considers such waiver to be of particular importance.

Article XXVI of the Administrative Agreement established a Joint Committee of representatives of the United States and Japan to consult on all matters requiring mutual consultation regarding the implementation of the Agreement; and provided that if the Committee " * * * is unable to resolve any matter, it shall refer that matter to the respective governments for further consideration through appropriate channels."

In the light of the Senate's ratification of the Security Treaty after consideration of the Administrative Agreement, which had already been signed, and its subsequent ratification of the NATO Agreement, with knowledge of the commitment to Japan under the Administrative Agreement, we are satisfied that the approval of Article III of the Security Treaty authorized the making of the Administrative Agreement and the subsequent Protocol embodying the NATO Agreement provisions governing jurisdiction to try criminal offenses.

The United States claimed the right to try Girard upon the ground that his act, as certified by his commanding officer, was "done in the performance of official duty" and therefore the United States had primary jurisdiction. Japan insisted that it had proof that Girard's action was without the scope of his official duty and therefore that Japan had the primary right to try him.

The Joint Committee, after prolonged deliberations, was unable to agree. The issue was referred to higher authority, which authorized the United States representatives on the Joint Committee to notify the appropriate Japanese authorities, in accordance with paragraph 3(c) of the Protocol, that the United States had decided not to exercise, but to waive, whatever jurisdiction it might have in the case. The Secretary of State and the Secretary of Defense decided that this determination should be carried out. The President confirmed their joint conclusion.

A sovereign nation has exclusive jurisdiction to punish offenses against its laws committed within its borders, unless it expressly or impliedly consents to surrender its jurisdiction. *The Schooner Exchange v. M'Faddon*, 7 Cranch 116, 136. Japan's cession to the United States of jurisdiction to try American military personnel for conduct constituting an offense against the laws of both countries was conditioned by the covenant of Article XVII, section 3, paragraph (c) of the Protocol that

> " * * *The authorities of the State having the primary right shall give sympathetic consideration to a request from the authorities of the other State for a waiver of its right in cases where that other State considers such waiver to be of particular importance."

The issue for our decision is therefore narrowed to the question whether, upon the record before us, the Constitution or legislation subsequent to the Security Treaty prohibited the carrying out of this provision authorized by the Treaty for waiver of the qualified jurisdiction granted by Japan. We find no constitutional or statutory barrier to the provision as applied here. In the absence of such encroachments, the wisdom of the arrangement is exclusively for the determination of the Executive and Legislative Branches.

The judgment of the District Court in No. 1103 is reversed, and its judgment in No. 1108 is affirmed. * * *

NOTES

1. *Civilians Accompanying Armed Forces.* The United States Supreme Court has, in a series of decisions, sharply limited the power of United States military authorities to try by court martial civilian employees or civilian dependents of members of United States forces. See *Reid v. Covert*, 354 U.S. 1 (1957); *Kinsella v. United States ex rel. Singleton*, 361 U.S. 234 (1960); *Grisham v. Hagan*, 361 U.S. 278 (1960); *Wilson v. Bohlender*, 361 U.S. 281 (1960).

2. *Host State Authority and I.C.C. Jurisdiction.* The decision in *Wilson v. Girard* has received renewed attention in connection with the controversy over potential U.S. participation in the prospective International Criminal Court (see Chapter 16, pp. 1360–71. Although opponents object to the idea that members of the U.S. armed services might conceivably be vulnerable to prosecution by the I.C.C. for crimes committed in other countries, it has been pointed out that they are already subject to jurisdiction of the territorial state for certain crimes under the terms of Status of Forces Agreements and that the Supreme Court upheld constitutional challenges to that jurisdictional scheme in *Wilson v. Girard*. For discussion, see Leigh, The United States and the Statute of Rome, 95 A.J.I.L 124 (2001); Everett, American Servicemembers and the ICC, in The United States and the International Criminal Court 137, 149 nn. 8, 20 (Sewall & Kaysen eds. 2000).

3. *U.S. Forces in Iraq.* The issues raised in *Wilson v. Girard* remain alive in other contexts. In *Munaf v. Geren*, 128 S.Ct. 2207 (2008), the Supreme Court addressed whether federal courts have jurisdiction to consider habeas petitions of U.S. citizen detained by U.S.-led coalition forces in Iraq pending a transfer to Iraqi authorities following a conviction in an Iraqi criminal court. Munaf, a U.S. citizen, was arrested in 2005, on suspicion of kidnapping, by U.S. military officers acting as part of the multinational coalition. Munaf's sister petitioned on his behalf for habeas corpus in the U.S. District Court in the District of Columbia. After the filing of the habeas petition, Munaf was told that he would be tried in an Iraqi court and transferred to Iraqi custody if convicted. Writing for a unanimous Court, Chief Justice Roberts held that the habeas corpus statute extends to American citizens held overseas by American forces operating subject to an American chain of command even if part of a larger multinational force. The Court referred to the habeas statute's application to individuals held in custody "under color of the authority of the United States", 28 U.S.C. § 2241(c)(1). It accordingly held that actual government custody was sufficient to establish habeas jurisdiction in federal courts, but that the petition failed to state a claim on which relief could be granted in light of Iraq's authority as the

territorial sovereign to prosecute crimes committed on its territory. See p. 768.

On November 17, 2008, the United States and the Republic of Iraq entered into an Agreement on the Withdrawal of the United States Forces from Iraq and the Organization of their Activities During their Temporary Presence in Iraq. Article 3 of the Agreement requires U.S. forces conducting military operations in Iraq to respect Iraqi laws, customs, traditions and conventions. Article 12 of the Agreement explicitly recognizes Iraq's sovereign right to determine and enforce the rules of criminal and civil law in its territory. It goes on to state that Iraq shall have the "primary right" over members of the U.S. forces who commit grave felonies outside certain agreed areas. Most significantly, the Agreement vests primary jurisdiction over U.S contractors and contractor employees in Iraq. However, the Agreement recognizes that, when Iraq exercises such jurisdiction, the concerned servicemen or contractors shall be entitled to due process standards consistent with those available under U.S. and Iraqi law. The Agreement provides for the withdrawal of U.S. forces from Iraq by December 31, 2011.

4. *Military Contractors in Iraq.* Other problems of jurisdiction have arisen as a result of the war in Iraq. In that war, the United States has employed under special contracts about as many independent contractors as it has deployed members of its Armed Forces. In many instances, these contractors have performed tasks otherwise performed by the military. However, they are not members of the U.S. armed forces or international institutions and are therefore not subject to military discipline. If they are U.S. nationals, they may be subject to U.S. criminal law, but only if the applicable statutes are given extraterritorial effect. If they are not U.S. nationals, the question arises whether crimes committed by non-U.S. nationals in Iraq employed by the U.S. can be prosecuted under applicable international law and the relevant U.S. statutes (federal or state). Some of these matters are now regulated under the 2008 agreement referred to in the previous Note.

5. *Jurisdiction at Guantánamo.* By an agreement of February 23, 1903, Cuba leased to the United States certain territory in Guantánamo for use by the latter as a naval station. Article III of the agreement recited the United States' recognition of Cuba's continuing "ultimate sovereignty" over the leased territory and Cuba's consent that the United States should exercise "complete jurisdiction and control over and within" the leased areas. 1 Malloy at 358. A later agreement of the same year fixed the conditions of the lease and also provided for the mutual extradition of persons committing offenses against the laws of Cuba or the United States in areas under their respective control. 1 Malloy at 360. Limited jurisdictional rights were granted to the United States when it leased naval and air bases in certain British territories during World War II. Article I of the agreement of March 27, 1941, 55 Stat. 1560, limited United States jurisdiction in the leased areas to "all the rights, power and authority * * * necessary for the establishment, use, operation and defense * * * or appropriate for their control."

The detention of foreign nationals in the Guantánamo Bay Detention Camp following the attacks of September 11th and the conflict in Afghanistan has served to refocus attention on the precise legal status of Guantánamo under international law and the U.S. Constitution. In *Boumediene v. Bush*, 128 S.Ct. 2229 (2008), the Supreme Court reaffirmed the relevant parts of its earlier ruling in *Rasul v. Bush*, 542 U.S. 466 (2004), p. 767, in which the

Court had referred to the 1903 lease agreement and its provision for "complete jurisdiction and control" on the part of the United States. On this basis, the Court ruled that the Guantánamo detainees were entitled to the protections of the Constitution. For a discussion of these cases and the status of Guantánamo, see Extraterritorial Reach of the Writ of Habeas Corpus 122 Harv. L. Rev. 395 (2008); Jurisdiction Over Americans Held Overseas, 122 Harv. L. Rev. 415 (2008); Strauss, Guantánamo Bay: The Global Effects of Wrongful Detention, Torture & Unchecked Executive Power, 10 N.Y. City L. Rev. 479 (2007); de Zayas, The Status of Guantánamo Bay and the Status of the Detainees, 37 U.B.C. L. Rev. 277 (2004); Lazar, International Legal Status of Guantánamo Bay, 62 A.J.I L. 730 (1968); Neuman, Anomalous Zones, 48 Stan. L. Rev. 1197 (1996); Raustiala, The Geography of Justice, 73 Fordham. L. Rev. 2501 (2005).

6. *Jurisdiction Over Peacekeeping Forces.* As discussed in Chapter 15, peacekeepers are now present under authority of U.N. Security Council resolutions in more than a dozen countries, usually but not necessarily by agreement with the territorial state. Issues of jurisdiction to prescribe and enforce law with respect to the peacekeepers' conduct have arisen numerous times, including in relation to crimes of violence committed by members of the peacekeeping contingents against civilians in the territory in question. Generally, the sending state investigates and (if appropriate) prosecutes such allegations. For example, a Canadian court-martial heard charges in 1996 against a Canadian soldier arrested for aiding and abetting the torture of a Somali teenager who had been captured while attempting an intrusion into the Canadian camp during the peacekeeping deployment in Somalia; and an Italian commission investigated allegations of maltreatment and violence against Somali citizens on the part of Italian soldiers. See Young & Molina, International Humanitarian Law and Peace Operations: Sharing Canada's Lessons Learned from Somalia, 1 Y.B. Int'l Humanitarian Law 362–70 (1998); Boustany, Brocklebank: A Questionable Decision of the Court Martial Appeal Court of Canada, id., at 371–74; Lupi, Report by the Enquiry Commission on the Behaviour of Italian Peace–Keeping Troops in Somalia, id., at 375–79. See also Siekmann, The Fall of Srebrenica and the Attitude of Dutchbat from an International Legal Perspective, id., at 301–12.

SECTION 10.   CONFLICTS OF JURISDICTION

Bases of jurisdiction frequently overlap. For example, a state may, on the basis of the nationality principle, reach its nationals abroad, but the conduct of the nationals of that state may, on the basis of the territorial principle, also be within the jurisdiction of the foreign state in which these nationals act. Similarly, one state may have jurisdiction under the subjective territorial principle and another under the objective territorial or the protective principle. These overlaps lead to particularly vexing problems when one of the states having jurisdiction prohibits conduct that the other state having jurisdiction commands. For an example of these problems, see *United States v. Bank of Nova Scotia*, 691 F.2d 1384 (11th Cir.1982).

Further, there may also be conflicts of jurisdiction when one state prohibits conduct that the other state does not command, but permits or encourages. In those cases, the permitting state, if it is sufficiently concerned, may turn the permission into a command. The inclination to do so becomes particularly strong if, as United States courts initially ruled, a United States court would not apply a coercive United States law extraterritorially if the foreign state where the conduct was required forbade it. Many of these so-called "blocking statutes" by other nations were enacted in an effort to accommodate nationals or residents subject to foreign extraterritorial prohibitions and provide them with a proper defense in U.S. courts. As might have been expected, the response of U.S. courts to the emergence of these statutes has been to limit, if not eliminate, the availability of this defense.

The imposition of the limitation of reasonableness recognized by Restatement (Third) § 403 reduces the area of overlap and, as a consequence, the possibility of conflicts of jurisdiction. But that limitation does not eliminate the possibility of conflicts altogether. Indeed, it might aggravate the conflict by giving a state the opportunity to argue that reasonableness, and therefore international law, is on its side.

In an attempt to deal with these conflicts of jurisdiction, the Restatement (Third) provides its suggested solution in Section 441. Do you think its attempt is successful?

RESTATEMENT OF THE LAW (THIRD)
THE FOREIGN RELATIONS LAW OF THE UNITED STATES § 441 (1987)

§ 441. Foreign State Compulsion

(1) In general, a state may not require a person

(a) to do an act in another state that is prohibited by the law of that state or by the law of the state of which he is a national; or

(b) to refrain from doing an act in another state that is required by the law of that state or by the law of the state of which he is a national.

(2) In general, a state may require a person of foreign nationality

(a) to do an act in that state even if it is prohibited by the law of the state of which he is a national; or

(b) to refrain from doing an act in that state even if it is required by the law of the state of which he is a national.

NOTES

1. *Good Faith Efforts to Seek Relief From Prohibition.* Courts have ruled unanimously that the foreign compulsion doctrine cannot be invoked when either the person seeking disclosure or the one opposing it have failed to make good faith efforts to obtain dispensation from the foreign prohibition. For

example, in *Doe v. United States*, 487 U.S. 201 (1988), the prosecution sought disclosure from banks in the Cayman Islands and Bermuda of documents they might have relating to the target. The banks invoked foreign law that prohibited disclosure without the customer's consent. The district court ordered the person who was the target of the grand jury investigation to give his consent to the disclosure of whatever documents the banks might have. The target contended that the order violated his Fifth Amendment privilege against self-incrimination.

The Supreme Court ruled that the particular consent the target had been directed to provide did not constitute testimony by the target that the banks had records relating to him and therefore were not a testimonial statement by him. See also *United States v. Rubin*, 836 F.2d 1096 (8th Cir. 1988) (Rubin could not complain of the district court's having quashed a subpoena seeking Cayman Island bank documents, since he could have obtained the documents by petitioning the Grand Court of the Cayman Islands). For a general discussion, see Browne, Extraterritorial Discovery: An Analysis Based on Good Faith, 83 Colum. L. Rev. 1320 (1983), Feagle, Extraterritorial Discovery: A Social Contract Perspective, 7 Duke J. Comp. & Int'l L. 297 (1996); Brewer, Obtaining Discovery Abroad: The Utility of the Comity Analysis in Determining Whether to Order production of Documents Blocked by Foreign Blocking Statutes, 22 Hous. J. Int'l L. 525 (2000). For a more recent issue, see, Connorton, Tracking Terrorist Financing Through SWIFT: When U.S. Subpoenas and Foreign Privacy Laws Collide, 76 Fordham L. Rev. 283 (2007).

2. *Choice of Law and Choice of Forum Clauses.* Contractual stipulations may seek to avoid a state's exercising its legislative authority. A choice of law clause designating the law of another state as applicable seeks to do this directly. A choice of forum clause achieves this indirectly, when the foreign forum does not apply the local law. In both types of cases, the question arises whether the court of the state addressed will honor the reference to the foreign law or forum. Thus far, this has not been argued to raise a question of public international law. However, states may become gravely concerned when these clauses are used to avoid application of local law that is regarded as mandatory in the sense that its application cannot be affected by contractual stipulations. As global commerce expands and intensifies, this problem is likely to become more acute.

An excellent example is provided by *Allen v. Lloyd's of London*, 94 F.3d 923 (4th Cir. 1996), in which it was contended by participants in Lloyd's insurance projects that the plan to reorganize Lloyd's in the face of claims for injuries caused by asbestos and similarly harmful products violated American securities laws. The court rejected these contentions in upholding choice of forum and choice of law clauses in the participants' (the so–called Names') contracts which designated an exclusive English forum and English law as the applicable law. Eventually, all circuits that addressed the problem ruled the same way. See *Richards v. Lloyd's of London*, 135 F.3d 1289 (9th Cir. 1998). For a general discussion, see Hall, No Way Out: An Argument Against Permitting Parties To Opt Out of U.S. Securities Laws In International Transactions, 97 Colum. L. Rev. 57 (1997).

SECTION 11. EXTRADITION

A. GENERAL CONSIDERATIONS

National jurisdiction over a person may also be exercised so as to transfer that person to the national jurisdiction of a different state. "Extradition" is generally defined as the surrender of an individual by the state within whose territory he is found to the state under whose laws he is alleged to have committed (or already to have been convicted) of a crime. Until the nineteenth century the extradition of fugitives was rare and was a matter of sovereign discretion rather than of obligation. With the dramatic improvements in transportation in the nineteenth century, the number of criminals fleeing to foreign states increased and states began to conclude bilateral treaties providing for their extradition.

In *Factor v. Laubenheimer*, 290 U.S. 276, 287 (1933), the U.S. Supreme Court noted that:

> "[t]he principles of international law recognize no right to extradition apart from treaty. While a government may, if agreeable to its own constitution and laws, voluntarily exercise the power to surrender a fugitive from justice to the country from which he has fled * * * the legal right to demand his extradition and the correlative duty to surrender him to the demanding country exist only when created by treaty.

In fact, the national law of many states prevents arrest and extradition of a fugitive except pursuant to a treaty operating as internal law or a statute providing for extradition. See 2 O'Connell at 793–94; *Valentine v. United States ex rel. Neidecker*, 299 U.S. 5, 9 (1936).

Since most instances of extradition arise under bilateral or multilateral treaties, many of the problems raised by extradition are questions of treaty interpretation. Most bilateral treaties contain a list of acts for which a fugitive may be extradited. Multilateral and some bilateral treaties stipulate merely that the act for which extradition is sought be a crime in both the requested and requesting states punishable by a certain minimum penalty, usually imprisonment for at least one year. For a model extradition treaty developed by the United Nations for the purpose of assisting states in developing such treaties, see G.A. Res. 45/116, annex (Dec. 14, 1990); see also Sambei & Jones, Extradition Law Handbook (2005).

B. EXTRADITION BY THE UNITED STATES

In the United States, international extradition is governed by federal law. See 18 U.S.C. §§ 3181–3196 (2000), leaving the several states with no power to extradite persons to foreign countries. The key provision is § 3184, which states:

> Whenever there is a treaty or convention for extradition between the United States and any foreign government, or in cases arising under

section 3181(b), any justice or judge of the United States, or any magistrate judge authorized so to do by a court of the United States, or any judge of a court of record of general jurisdiction of any State, may, upon complaint made under oath, charging any person found within his jurisdiction, with having committed within the jurisdiction of any such foreign government any of the crimes provided for by such treaty or convention, or provided for under section 3181(b), issue his warrant for the apprehension of the person so charged, that he may be brought before such justice, judge, or magistrate judge, to the end that the evidence of criminality may be heard and considered. Such complaint may be filed before and such warrant may be issued by a judge or magistrate judge of the United States District Court for the District of Columbia if the whereabouts within the United States of the person charged are not known or, if there is reason to believe the person will shortly enter the United States. If, on such hearing, he deems the evidence sufficient to sustain the charge under the provisions of the proper treaty or convention, or under section 3181 (b), he shall certify the same, together with a copy of all the testimony taken before him, to the Secretary of State, that a warrant may issue upon the requisition of the proper authorities of such foreign government, for the surrender of such person, according to the stipulations of the treaty or convention; and he shall issue his warrant for the commitment of the person so charged to the proper jail, there to remain until such surrender shall be made.

Thus, federal law requires a judicial hearing of the evidence against the fugitive to ensure that the proceedings comply with the applicable treaty. If the judge regards the evidence sufficient to sustain the charge under the relevant treaty, the judge so certifies to the U.S. Secretary of State. The Secretary of State then may grant or refuse extradition. The decision of the judge on the sufficiency of the evidence is not subject to correction by appeal. See *Collins v. Miller*, 252 U.S. 364, 369 (1920). However, the fugitive may petition for a writ of habeas corpus to challenge the legality of his detention and may urge upon the Secretary of State that his extradition not be granted. See 4 Hackworth at 174–75; Restatement (Third) §§ 476–79; Bassiouni, International Extradition: United States Law and Practice (4th ed. 2002).

The reference in the statute to section 3181(b)2 was added in 1996. See Antiterrorism and Effective Death Penalty Act of 1996, Pub. L. No. 104–132, 120 Stat. 1280 (1996). That section indicates that it is possible to surrender

persons, other than citizens, nationals, or permanent residents of the United States, who have committed crimes of violence against nationals of the United States in foreign countries *without regard to the existence of any treaty of extradition with such foreign government* if the Attorney General certifies, in writing, that—

(1) evidence has been presented by the foreign government that indicates that had the offenses been committed in the United States, they would constitute crimes of violence as defined under section 16 of this title; and

(2) the offenses charged are not of a political nature.

18 U.S.C. § 3181(b) (emphasis added).

Do you think the federal extradition statute (18 U.S.C. § 3184) is unconstitutional because, in leaving the final decision to extradite to the Secretary of State, it assigns judicial power to the Executive Branch or, in the alternative, improperly assigns to the judiciary a role in making the executive decision to extradite? See *Lo Duca v. United States*, 93 F.3d 1100 (2d Cir. 1996) (rejecting such an argument); see also *United States v. Luna*, 165 F.3d 316 (5th Cir. 1999). How important is it for the judiciary to have a role in the extradition process? In *Parretti v. United States*, 122 F.3d 758 (9th Cir. 1997), defendant raised both Fourth and Fifth Amendment challenges to his arrest on an extradition warrant pursuant to a treaty with France and the denial of bail pending extradition. The court initially held Article IV of the extradition treaty and 18 U.S.C.§ 3184 to be incompatible with the Fourth Amendment, to the extent that they provide for the issuance of "provisional arrest" warrants without independent judicial determinations of probable cause to believe the fugitive committed the offenses charged. The court further found that Parretti's detention without bail prior to the extradition hearing denied him due process of law. While the judicial proceedings were pending, Parretti fled the United States. The Ninth Circuit granted rehearing en banc, withdrew the panel's opinion, and dismissed the appeal. Since Parretti had become a fugitive from justice, the court did not address his constitutional claims in the rehearing en banc.

In 1995, U.S. President Clinton entered into an executive agreement with the International Criminal Tribunal for Rwanda (I.C.T.R.) "to sur-render to the Tribunal * * * persons * * * found in its territory whom the Tribunal has charged with or found guilty of a violation or violations within the competence of the Tribunal." In 1996, Congress enacted Public Law 104–106 to implement the Agreement, Pub. L. 104–106, § 1342, 110 Stat. 486 (1996), by providing that federal extradition statutes are to apply to surrender of persons to the I.C.T.R. Elizaphan Ntakirutimana, a Rwandan pastor indicted on genocide charges by the I.C.T.R., sought to challenge his surrender by writ of habeas corpus, on the grounds that (1) the Constitution of the United States requires an Article II treaty for a surrender tantamount to extradition, (2) the request for surrender does not establish probable cause, (3) the U.N. Charter does not authorize the Security Council to establish the I.C.T.R., and (4) the I.C.T.R. does not protect fundamental rights guaranteed by the U.S. Constitution and international law. Although the first district judge to whom the matter was presented found his arguments persuasive and denied extradition, tho government renewed its request successfully. On appeal, the court rejected all four bases for challenge. *Ntakirutimana v. Reno*, 184 F.3d 419 (5th Cir. 1999). The Secretary of State ordered the surrender and Ntakirutimana was delivered to the custody of the I.C.T.R. in March 2000.

C. EXTRADITION WITHIN EUROPE

The European Arrest Warrant (EAW) Act was adopted by a European Union as a "framework decision"in June 2002—part of a package of measures designed to harmonize E.U. state responses to threats of terrorism and cross-border crime. The EAW Act abolishes the system of extradition among EU members and replaces it with an obligation to mutually recognize arrest warrants issued by judicial authorities of the members. The Act aims to eliminate political obstacles to the transfer of criminals between jurisdictions by providing that the arrest warrant is simply transmitted from one judicial authority to another, outside diplomatic channels. The basic principle underpinning the Act was that a judicial request constitutes a public act by one state which must be recognized and honored as such by another.

On September 16, 2004, the Central Court of Investigation in Criminal Matters in Madrid issued an arrest warrant against Mamoun Darkazanli, who was alleged to be a key Al–Qaeda operative in Europe. German authorities placed Mr. Darkazanli under arrest pending extradition and Hamburg's Higher Regional Court declared his extradition permissible. Before his extradition could be carried out, however, Germany's Constitutional Court declared the EAW Act to be unconstitutional for violating Article 16.2 and 19.4 of Germany's Basic Law. Article 16.2 guarantees German citizens freedom from extradition. The Court also held that the Act infringed the right of judicial review provided in Article 19.4 of the Basic Law since it did not establish effective avenues for the challenge of the grant of extradition. For criticism of this decision, see Nohlen, Germany: The Arrest Warrant Case, 6 Int'l J. Const. L. 153 (2008); Satzger & Pohl, The German Constitutional Court and the European Arrest Warrant: "Cryptic Signals" from Karlsruhe, 4 J. Int'l Crim. Just. 686 (2006). Similar decisions of unconstitutionality were handed down in Poland and Cyprus. See Nussberger, Poland; The Constitutional Tribunal on the Implementation of the European Arrest Warrant, 6 Int'l J. Const. L. 162 (2008). A contrary decision was reached in the Czech Republic.

Following these domestic developments, the European Court of Justice ruled on May 3, 2007, that the European Arrest Warrant Act was valid. For criticism of this decision, see Sarmiento, European Union: The European Arrest Warrant and the Quest for Constitutional Coherence, 6 Int'l J. Const. L. 171 (2008).

D. PRINCIPLES OF SPECIALTY AND DOUBLE CRIMINALITY

According to the "principle of specialty," the state requesting extradition (the requesting state) may not, without the permission of the state in which the offender is present (the requested state), try or punish the fugitive for any crimes committed before the extradition except the crimes for which he was extradited. The permission of the requested state is also required for the requesting state to re-extradite the fugitive to a third state. *United States ex rel. Donnelly v. Mulligan*, 74 F.2d 220 (2d Cir. 1934); *United States v. Rauscher*, 119 U.S. 407 (1886); Restatement (Third) § 478.

Separately, difficult problems arise under the treaties when the act committed by the fugitive is punishable in the requesting state and listed in the treaty, but not punishable in the requested state because the law of the latter defines the crime differently. For an example, see The Eisler Extradition Case, 43 A.J.I.L. 487 (1949). In such a situation, if the requested state applies its own law to define the crime, it may violate its obligations under the treaty since it cannot extradite. See 4 Hackworth at 117–18. If the requested state applies the law of the requesting state, however, it would be extraditing the fugitive for an act that was not an offense under its own law, thereby likely violating its national law.

To avoid such a problem, many treaties contain a requirement of "double criminality," whereby extradition is available only when the act is punishable under the law of both states. The name of the offense and the elements that make it criminal need not be precisely the same, provided that the fugitive could be punished for the act in both states. For example, in *Peters v. Egnor*, 888 F.2d 713 (10th Cir. 1989), the British Theft Act and the U.S. federal securities fraud statute were found "substantially analogous" and therefore to meet the requirement of dual criminality. In *Lo Duca v. United States*, 93 F.3d 1100 (2d Cir. 1996), the court held that an Italian crime concerning an "association of mafia type" was substantially similar to U.S. crimes under the conspiracy statute and the Racketeer Influenced and Corrupt Organizations Act.

The principle of "double criminality" may also require that the act be punishable in both states at the time when it was committed. See the *Pinochet* case, p. 843 note 2; but see *United States ex rel. Oppenheim v. Hecht*, 16 F.2d 955 (2d Cir. 1927) (granting extradition for an act which was made criminal in the United States after it had been committed). Treaties frequently provide that extradition shall not take place if the prosecution of the fugitive is barred by a statute of limitations in either the requesting state or requested state, but that rule can also be set aside. See Extradition Treaty, art. 6, U.S.–U.K., Mar. 31, 2003, S. Treaty Doc. No. 108–23 ("The decision by the Requested State whether to grant the request for extradition shall be made without regard to any statute of limitations in either State").

Special problems may arise when the crime for which extradition is sought was not committed on the territory of the requesting state. In 1977, Abu Daoud—who allegedly participated in the massacre of Israeli athletes at the Munich Olympic Games—was arrested in France. Israel sought his extradition. The Chambre d'Accusation of the Paris Court of Appeals, four days after Daoud's arrest, after a proceeding lasting only twenty minutes, released Daoud, and France expelled him to Algeria where he was accorded a hero's welcome. The ground given for rejection of the Israeli request turned in part on the fact that the alleged crime did not occur in Israel. The Paris Court held that, at the time Daoud allegedly committed the crime, he could not have been prosecuted for it in France even if his victims had been French nationals, and that, therefore, he could not be extradited to Israel, even though Israeli law did permit his prosecution on the ground that the victims were Israeli citizens. The Paris Court also held that, although the French Penal Code was amended in 1975 to give France jurisdiction on the passive personality basis, this amendment could not be given retroactive effect. (The Federal Republic of Germany also requested extradition, but the Paris Court rejected it because it had not been "confirmed at the same time by diplomatic channel.") No reason was given why Daoud was not prosecuted in France for having entered on a false passport. On this case, see Liskofsky, The Abu Daoud Case: Law or Politics, 7 Isr. Y.B. Hum. Rts. 66 (1977).

NOTES

1. *Standing of Individual to Raise Treaty Claim.* In *United States v. Puentes*, 50 F.3d 1567 (11th Cir.), cert. denied, 516 U.S. 933 (1995), the court took note of a split among the federal circuit courts as to whether a defendant has standing to raise a claim of violation of the principle of specialty (i.e., that he was prosecuted for a crime other than the one for which he had been extradited under a treaty), in the absence of affirmative protest from the state party to the treaty. The Eleventh Circuit concluded that the defendant had standing to raise the claim of a treaty violation, but he would lose that right if the state party waived its objection. The court then rejected the challenge on the merits.

2. *Pinochet Case.* The principle of double criminality was involved in the *Pinochet* extradition proceedings in the United Kingdom, pp. 807, 924. Both the requesting state (Spain) and the United Kingdom had ratified the 1984 Convention Against Torture and Other Cruel, Inhuman or Degrading Treatment or Punishment, which had become effective as domestic law in the United Kingdom by enactment of § 134 of the U.K. Criminal Justice Act on September 29, 1988 and had come into force for the United Kingdom with effect from December 8, 1988. Prior to 1988, however, there was no basis in U.K. law for extraterritorial jurisdiction over the crime of torture and thus no dual criminality in relation to Spain's prosecution. (Dual criminality would not have been a concern in respect of extradition to the territory where the torture was alleged to have taken place, namely Chile.) Lord Browne–Wilkinson's opinion stated on this point:

> [T]he principle of double criminality which requires an Act to be a crime under both the law of Spain and of the United Kingdom cannot be satisfied in relation to conduct before that date if the principle of double criminality requires the conduct to be criminal under United Kingdom law at the date it was committed. If, on the other hand, the double criminality rule only requires the conduct to be criminal under U.K. law at the date of extradition the rule was satisfied in relation to all torture alleged against Senator Pinochet whether it took place before or after 1988.

A majority of the House of Lords concluded that Pinochet could be extradited to Spain for crimes committed after the United Kingdom had implemented the Torture Convention, but not for earlier crimes.

The Spanish extradition request was based in part on the allegation that the crimes had been committed against Spanish nationals (passive personality jurisdiction), but also alleged crimes on a universal jurisdiction theory. Should extradition be limited to requests by states relying on the territorial, the subjective nationality, and the protective principle? If it is based on the universality principle, which of the states requesting extradition should be given preference? Should a state be permitted to deny extradition on the ground that it wishes to prosecute itself or has, in the exercise of prosecutorial discretion, decided not to prosecute? If none of these limitations apply, what prevents a single state from prosecuting, and demanding extradition for, crimes based on the universality principle? Note that subsequently to the *Pinochet* case, Spain requested extradition by Mexico for crimes alleged by committed in Argentina by Argentinian officials. See Wide Net in Argentine Torture Case, N.Y. Times, Sept. 11, 2000, at 6, col. 1.

E. EXTRADITION OF A STATE'S OWN NATIONALS

Many extradition treaties contain provisions exempting nationals of the requested state from extradition. A typical provision is that neither party shall be obligated to surrender its nationals, thus leaving the matter in the discretion of the requested state. The policy, which is most commonly reflected in civil law jurisdictions, apparently stems from a feeling that individuals should not be withdrawn from the jurisdiction of their own courts. Consequently, constitutional restrictions on extradition of nationals have regularly featured the decisions of national courts so as to preclude such extradition. For a recent example, see the decision of the German Federal Constitutional Court in the *European Arrest Warrant Case* (2005) discussed *supra* subsection C. However, the courts in many civil law countries have broad jurisdiction to try and punish their nationals for crimes committed in other countries, consistent with the nationality principle discussed *supra* this Chapter, Section 3.

Some states, however, take a different view and allow their nationals to be extradited to other states. The United States surrenders its own nationals (unless exempted by treaty), even in the absence of reciprocity.

See 18 U.S.C. § 3196 ("If the applicable treaty or convention does not obligate the United States to extradite its citizens to a foreign country, the Secretary of State may, nevertheless, order the surrender to that country of a United States citizen whose extradition has been requested by that country if the other requirements of that treaty or convention are met."); see also *Charlton v. Kelly*, 229 U.S. 447 (1913). The United Kingdom generally surrenders nationals. See Extradition Act, 1870, 33 & 34 Vict. c. 52 § 26; 1 Oppenheim at 956. Multilateral extradition conventions which recognize the principle of non-extradition of nationals generally provide that if the sending state refuses to extradite a national it shall itself submit the matter to its own prosecutorial authorities. See e.g., Convention on Extradition, art. 2, Dec. 26, 1933, 49 Stat. 3111, 165 L.N.T.S. 45.

F. "POLITICAL" OFFENSES

In the eighteenth century, extradition was frequently sought and granted for what are now termed "political offenses". By the nineteenth century public opinion in Western Europe turned against the extradition of fugitives accused of only political offenses. Belgium, which enacted the first extradition law in 1833, incorporated the principle of non-extradition for political offenses into the law. Today, most treaties exempt fugitives accused of political offenses from extradition. Though the principle has been almost universally accepted, "political offenses" have never been precisely defined. The first attempt to delineate the principle was the "attentat" clause in many treaties, which provides that the murder of the head of a foreign government or a member of his family is not to be considered a political offense. See, e.g., Treaty of Extradition between the United States and Venezuela, art. 3, Jan. 19, 1922, 43 Stat. 1698, 49 L.N.T.S. 435. Some treaties extend the exclusion to any murder or attempt on life in general. See, e.g., Extradition Treaty between Italy and Finland, art. 3(3), July 10, 1929, 111 L.N.T.S. 295. However, in 1934 in the absence of such a clause in the applicable treaty, the Turin Court of Appeal refused to extradite the assassins of King Alexander of Yugoslavia to France on the ground that the crime was political. *In re Pavelic*, [1933–34] Ann. Dig. No. 158 (Italy).

In 1892, Switzerland adopted a law which provided that a crime was not to be considered political if it was primarily a common offense even though it had a political motivation or purpose. The decision on extradition was left to the highest Swiss Court. See 2 O'Connell at 802; 1 Oppenheim at 967. Some treaties provide that "[c]riminal acts which constitute clear manifestations of anarchism or envisage the overthrow of the bases of all political organizations" shall not be considered political offenses. Treaty of Extradition between the United States and Brazil, art. V(6), Jan. 13, 1961, 15 U.S.T. 2093, 532 U.N.T.S. 177. U.K. and U.S. courts have held that for an offense to be political it must be committed in furtherance of a political movement or in the course of a struggle to control the government of a state. *In re Castioni*, [1891] I Q.B. 149, 156,

166; *In re Ezeta*, 62 F. 972, 999 (D.C. Cal. 1894). However, this strict rule has been relaxed to provide refuge for private individuals fleeing totalitarian states. See *Regina v. Governor of Brixton Prison, Ex parte Kolczynski*, [1955] I Q.B. 540 (1954). Treaties also frequently prohibit extradition for purely military offenses. See Convention on Extradition between the United States and Sweden, art. V(4), 14 U.S.T. 1845, 494 U.N.T.S. 141.

The 2003 U.S.–U.K. Extradition Treaty states in Article 4(2) that the following offenses shall not be considered political offenses:

(a) an offense for which both Parties have the obligation pursuant to a multilateral international agreement to extradite the person sought or to submit the case to their competent authorities for decision as to prosecution;

(b) a murder or other violent crime against the person of a Head of State of one of the Parties, or of a member of the Head of State's family;

(c) murder, manslaughter, malicious wounding, or inflicting grievous bodily harm;

(d) an offense involving kidnaping, abduction, or any form of unlawful detention, including the taking of a hostage;

(e) placing or using, or threatening the placement or use of, an explosive, incendiary, or destructive device or firearm capable of endangering life, of causing grievous bodily harm, or of causing substantial property damage;

(f) possession of an explosive, incendiary, or destructive device capable of endangering life, of causing grievous bodily harm, or of causing substantial property damage;

(g) an attempt or a conspiracy to commit, participation in the commission of, aiding or abetting, counseling or procuring the commission of, or being an accessory before or after the fact to any of the foregoing offenses.

G. HUMAN RIGHTS CHALLENGES

The general rule in most extradition cases has been to reject defendants' efforts to resist extradition on the ground that they would be subjected to standards of procedural due process falling short of those in the requested state or would otherwise suffer unjust treatment following extradition. Courts have typically considered that the treaty obligation to extradite precludes such an inquiry, and that it is the responsibility of the executive branch in negotiating and implementing an extradition treaty (or the legislative branch in approving the treaty) to ensure adequate safeguards for the treatment of extraditees. Thus a "rule of judicial non-inquiry" has been applied under which the court considering an extradition request concerns itself only with whether the treaty standard for extradition is satisfied and does not usually entertain evidence about the quality of the justice system in the requesting state. (The Secretary of State may, however, consider such evidence in making the final discretionary decision whether to go forward with the surrender after the court has certified extraditability.)

Recently, however, some human rights challenges to extradition have proven successful, at least in relation to certain practices in the requesting state that the requested state considers to be contrary to fundamental human rights. There has now been a significant number of cases in which extradition has been withheld (or made subject to conditions) by virtue of differing positions in the requesting and requested state with respect to the death penalty and related practices. Other cases involve concerns about the practice of torture or other forms of cruel, inhuman or degrading treatment or punishment in the requesting state. On these and other human rights challenges, see generally Dugard & Van den Wyngaert, Reconciling Extradition with Human Rights, 92 A.J.I.L 187 (1998) and the notes below.

NOTES

1. *Rule of Non–Inquiry.* In *Ahmad v. Wigen*, 910 F.2d 1063 (2d Cir. 1990), the district court had held a hearing on defendant's habeas corpus petition, in which it took extensive testimony on whether a Palestinian defendant would receive a fair trial in Israel on allegations of a terrorist attack on a bus; after the hearing, the court denied defendant's habeas corpus petition. The Second Circuit affirmed the ruling that defendant was extraditable and confirmed the rationale underlying the "rule of judicial non-inquiry:"

> We have no problem with the district court's rejection of Ahmad's remaining argument to the effect that, if he is returned to Israel, he probably will be mistreated, denied a fair trial, and deprived of his constitutional and human rights. We do, however, question the district court's decision to explore the merits of this contention in the manner that it did. * * * A consideration of the procedures that will or may occur in the requesting country is not within the purview of a habeas corpus judge. * * * Indeed, there is substantial authority for the proposition that this is not a proper matter for consideration by the certifying judicial officer. * * * In *Jhirad v. Ferrandina, supra*, 536 F.2d at 484–85, we said that "[i]t is not the business of our courts to assume the responsibility for supervising the integrity of the judicial system of another sovereign nation." [Other citations omitted.]

> Notwithstanding the above described judicial roadblocks, the district court proceeded to take testimony from both expert and fact witnesses and received extensive reports, affidavits, and other documentation concerning Israel's law enforcement procedures and its treatment of prisoners. This, we think, was improper. The interests of international comity are ill-served by requiring a foreign nation such as Israel to satisfy a United States district judge concerning the fairness of its laws and the manner in which they are enforced. * * *

All the American judge has to find, the Court said, is that the evidence would support a reasonable belief that Ahmad was guilty of the crime charged.

The U.S. Supreme Court most recently reaffirmed the rule of non-inquiry in *Munaf v. Geren*, 128 S.Ct. 2207 (2008). Although *Munaf* involved transfer outside the framework of an extradition treaty (from the U.S. component of a multinational force to Iraq as the territorial sovereign), the Court relied on cases and practice in the extradition context as relevant to its conclusion that challenges to the quality of the justice system of a foreign state are not proper considerations in the context of a habeas petition.

2. *Torture.* Article 3 of the Convention Against Torture and Other Cruel, Inhuman or Degrading Treatment or Punishment, Dec. 10, 1984, 23 I.L.M. 1027 (1984), in force for the United States since 1994, provides:

> 1. No State Party shall expel, return ("refouler") or extradite a person to another State where there are substantial grounds for believing that he would be in danger of being subjected to torture.
>
> 2. For the purpose of determining whether there are such grounds, the competent authorities shall take into account all relevant considerations including, where applicable, the existence in the State concerned of a consistent patter of gross, flagrant or mass violations of human rights.

For discussion of this and comparable treaty provisions and litigation under them, see Dugard & Van den Wyngaert, Reconciling Extradition and Human Rights, 92 A.J.I.L. 187, 197–202 (1998).

Some U.S. courts have treated torture claims as exceptions to the rule of non-inquiry. See, e.g., *Mironescu v. Costner*, 480 F.3d 664 (4th Cir. 2007), holding that an extradition court was competent to answer the "straightforward" question of whether a fugitive would be likely to face torture in the requesting country and noting that American courts routinely answer such questions in other contexts such as asylum proceedings. By contrast, in *Munaf v. Geren*, 128 S.Ct. 2207 (2008), the Supreme Court considered that the determination as to whether a detained person is likely to face torture upon transfer to another state should be made by the political branches rather than the judiciary. There, the U.S. Solicitor–General had informed the Court of the Executive Branch's judgment that Iraq's justice and prison systems generally satisfied international standards. The Court did not think it should second-guess this conclusion.

3. *Extradition to Death Penalty Jurisdictions.* In *Soering v. United Kingdom*, 161 Eur. Ct. H.R. (Ser. A) (1989), the European Court of Human Rights held that the United Kingdom would violate the human rights of a young man by extraditing him to face capital murder charges in the state of Virginia. The court acknowledged that international law does not prohibit the death penalty as such, but it found a serious risk that Soering would be subjected to inhuman or degrading treatment by virtue of what it termed the "death row phenomenon" of prolonged incarceration prior to execution of a death sentence. Soering was later extradited after receipt of assurances that the death penalty would not be applied.

In *Ng v. Canada*, U.N. Doc. CCPR/C/49/D/469/1991 (1993), 98 I.L.R.479, the U.N. Human Rights Committee found that extradition by Canada to the

United States, where petitioner was to be subjected to the death penalty by means of asphyxiation in a gas chamber, was violative of Article 7 of the International Covenant on Civil and Political Rights prohibiting cruel, inhuman or degrading treatment or punishment. Cf. *Kindler v. Canada*, U.N. Doc. CCPR/C/48/D/470/1991 (1993), 98 I.L.R. 426 (since international law does not prohibit the death penalty, there was no obligation on the part of Canada to seek assurances from the United States that the death penalty would not be applied).

In *United States v. Burns*, 2001 S.C.C. 7 (Can.), the Supreme Court of Canada revisited its holdings in *Kindler v. Canada* (Minister of Justice), [1991] 2 S.C.R. 779, and *Reference re Ng Extradition*, [1991] 2 S.C.R. 858, in which it had held that there was no requirement of constitutional or international law to request assurances from the United States against application of the death penalty. In view of international trends toward abolition of the death penalty, and Canada's leadership role in initiatives toward that objective, the Court reinterpreted the Canadian Constitution's provisions on fundamental justice to require the Minister of Justice to obtain such assurances as a condition of extradition.

Meanwhile, an Italian court found that extradition could not be granted to a death penalty jurisdiction even if the executive branch of the requesting state gave assurances that the death penalty would not be sought. The court was apparently concerned that such assurances might not bind an independent branch of government, and interpreted its own fundamental law to preclude any involvement with surrendering the accused to a state where the death penalty was even a possibility. *Venezia v. Ministero di Grazia e Giustizia*, 79 Rivista di Diritto Internazionale 815 (Ital Const. Ct. 1996), discussed in Bianchi, Case Note, 91 A.J.I.L. 727 (1997), and Dugard & Van den Wyngaert, 92 A.J.I.L. 197, 206 n. 143 (1998).

4. *Human Rights Scrutiny of Hong Kong/China.* Several cases have involved challenges to extradition to Hong Kong shortly before or after its incorporation into the People's Republic of China. Although a few courts have been sympathetic to defendants' claims that extradition should not go forward in light of the changeover, appellate courts have found defendants extraditable. See *Lui Kin–Hong v. United States*, 957 F.Supp. 1280 (D. Mass.), reversed, 110 F.3d 103 (1st Cir. 1997), stay denied, 520 U.S. 1206 (1997); *Regina v. Secretary of State for the Home Department, Ex parte Launder*, Nos. C.O. 2480/95, 0018/96 (Q.B. Div'l Ct. 1996), reversed by the House of Lords, [1997] 1 W.L.R. 839. For a survey of U.S. extradition practices with China, see Bloom, A Comparative Analysis of the United States' Response to Extradition Requests from China, 33 Yale. Int'l L.J. 177 (2008).

H. ALTERNATIVES TO TREATY–BASED EXTRADITION: DEPORTATION, EXCLUSION, AND EXTRAORDINARY RENDITION

Where extradition is not possible because of the lack of a treaty or for some other reason, or where extradition is not feasible because of the time and expense involved, states have resorted to other methods of surrendering or recovering fugitives. If the fugitive is not a national of the requested state, it may deport him as an undesirable alien or exclude him (i.e., deny him permission to enter the country). In either case, the fugitive may be turned over directly to the state that desires to prosecute him, or may be sent to a third state from which his extradition is possible. The United States and Mexico, and the United States and Canada, have frequently resorted to exclusion or deportation in order to deliver fugitives to each other without going through the process of extradition. See Divine & Chisam, Immigration Practice (2008–09 ed.).

"Extraordinary rendition" is a term typically used to describe the transfer of a person without any involvement of judicial authorities from the jurisdiction of one state to the jurisdiction of another state, often to take advantage of the second state's ability to interrogate the person. In recent times, the United States has been accused of transferring suspected terrorists and other aliens from U.S. custody to states in which they could be interrogated in a manner that would not be tolerated in the United States. On the cooperation of European governments with the U.S. Central Intelligence Agency in the practice of rendition, see Eur. Parl. Ass. Comm. On Legal Affairs and Human Rights, Alleged Secret Detentions and Unlawful Inter-state Transfers Involving Council of Europe Member States, Draft Report–Part II (Explanatory memorandum), Doc. No. AS/Jur (2006) 16 pt. II (June 7) (report by Swiss rapporteur Dick Marty).

Is such practice permissible under national and international law, including obligations flowing from extradition treaties? See Sadat, Extraordinary Rendition, Torture, And Other Nightmares From The War on Terror, 75 Geo. Wash. L. Rev. 1200 (2007); Sadat, Ghost Prisoners and Black Sites: Extraordinary Rendition Under International Law, 37 Case W. Res. J. Int'l L. 309 (2006) (concluding that such rendition violates both international and U.S. law); Radsan, A More Regular Process for Irregular Rendition, 37 Seton Hall L. Rev. 1 (2006). To what extent can or should victims of this practice seek recourse in U.S. courts? See *El–Masri v. United States*, 479 F.3d 296 (4th Cir. 2007) (dismissing the case due to the state secrets doctrine).

CHAPTER 12

IMMUNITY FROM JURISDICTION

▪ ▪ ▪

Under international law, states and certain other international persons enjoy immunities from the exercise of national jurisdiction. Since jurisdiction may arise in the context of legislative, judicial, and enforcement action, immunities from jurisdiction may also operate in these areas. However, traditionally, primary consideration has been given to immunity from judicial and enforcement jurisdiction. Jurisdictional immunities for states (and their instrumentalities and property) are addressed in Sections 1–3, for persons are addressed in Section 4, and for international organizations are addressed in Section 5.

SECTION 1. JURISDICTIONAL IMMUNITIES OF FOREIGN STATES: FROM ABSOLUTE TO RESTRICTIVE IMMUNITY

A. ABSOLUTE FORM OF SOVEREIGN IMMUNITY

THE SCHOONER EXCHANGE v. McFADDON

Supreme Court of the United States, 1812
11 U.S. (7 Cranch) 116

[A libel was brought against the schooner Exchange by two American citizens who claimed that they owned and were entitled to possession of the ship. They alleged that the vessel had been seized on the high seas in 1810 by forces acting on behalf of the Emperor of France and that no prize court of competent jurisdiction had pronounced judgment against the vessel. No one appeared for the vessel, but the United States Attorney for Pennsylvania appeared on behalf of the United States Government to state that the United States and France were at peace, that the vessel was a public ship (now known as the Balaou) of the Emperor of France, that the vessel had been compelled by bad weather to enter the port of Philadelphia, and that the vessel was prevented from leaving by the process of the court. The United States Attorney stated that, even if the vessel had in fact been wrongfully seized from the libellants, the property therein had passed to the Emperor of France. It was therefore requested that the libel be dismissed with costs and the vessel released. The District Court dismissed the libel, the Circuit Court reversed (4 Hall's L.J. 232), and the United States Attorney appealed to the Supreme Court.]

MARSHALL, C.J.: * * * The jurisdiction of the nation within its own territory is necessarily exclusive and absolute. It is susceptible of no limitation not imposed by itself. * * *

This full and absolute territorial jurisdiction being alike the attribute of every sovereign * * * would not seem to contemplate foreign sovereigns nor their sovereign rights as its objects. One sovereign being in no respect amenable to another; and being bound by obligations of the highest character not to degrade the dignity of his nation, by placing himself or its sovereign rights within the jurisdiction of another, can be supposed to enter a foreign territory only under an express license, or in the confidence that the immunities belonging to his independent sovereign station, though not expressly stipulated, are reserved by implication, and will be extended to him.

This perfect equality and absolute independence of sovereigns, and this common interest impelling them to mutual intercourse, and an interchange of good offices with each other, have given rise to a class of cases in which every sovereign is understood to waive the exercise of a part of that complete exclusive territorial jurisdiction, which has been stated to be the attribute of every nation.

1st. One of these is admitted to be the exemption of the person of the sovereign from arrest or detention within a foreign territory.

* * *

2d. A second case, standing on the same principles with the first, is the immunity which all civilized nations allow to foreign ministers.

* * *

3d. A third case in which a sovereign is understood to cede a portion of his territorial jurisdiction is, where he allows the troops of a foreign prince to pass through his dominions.

* * *

[The Court concluded that the territorial sovereign's license to foreign armies must be express, and not merely implied, but that a different rule applied in the case of foreign ships.] * * * If there be no prohibition, the ports of a friendly nation are considered as open to the public ships of all powers with whom it is at peace, and they are supposed to enter such ports and to remain in them while allowed to remain, under the protection of the government of the place.

* * *

When private individuals of one nation spread themselves through another as business or caprice may direct, mingling indiscriminately with the inhabitants of that other, or when merchant vessels enter for the purposes of trade, it would be obviously inconvenient and dangerous to society, and would subject the laws to continual infraction, and the government to degradation, if such individuals or merchants did not owe temporary and local allegiance, and were not amenable to the jurisdiction of the country. * * *

But in all respects different is the situation of a public armed ship. She constitutes a part of the military force of her nation; acts under the immediate and direct command of the sovereign; is employed by him in national objects. He has many and powerful motives for preventing those objects from being defeated by the interference of a foreign state. Such interference cannot take place without affecting his power and his dignity. The implied license therefore under which such vessel enters a friendly port, may reasonably be construed, and it seems to the Court, ought to be construed, as containing an exemption from the jurisdiction of the sovereign, within whose territory she claims the rights of hospitality.

Upon these principles, by the unanimous consent of nations, a foreigner is amenable to the laws of the place; but certainly in practice, nations have not yet asserted their jurisdiction over the public armed ships of a foreign sovereign entering a port open for their reception.

Bynkershoek, a jurist of great reputation, has indeed maintained that the property of a foreign sovereign is not distinguishable by any legal exemption from the property of an ordinary individual, and has quoted several cases in which courts have exercised jurisdiction over causes in which a foreign sovereign was made a party defendant.

Without indicating any opinion on this question, it may safely be affirmed, that there is a manifest distinction between the private property of the person who happens to be a prince, and that military force which supports the sovereign power, and maintains the dignity and the independence of a nation. A prince, by acquiring private property in a foreign country, may possibly be considered as subjecting that property to the territorial jurisdiction; he may be considered as so far laying down the prince, and assuming the character of a private individual; but this he cannot be presumed to do with respect to any portion of that armed force, which upholds his crown, and the nation he is entrusted to govern.

* * *

It seems then to the Court, to be a principle of public law, that national ships of war, entering the port of a friendly power open for their reception, are to be considered as exempted by the consent of that power from its jurisdiction.

* * *

The arguments in favor of this opinion which have been drawn from the general inability of the judicial power to enforce its decisions in cases of this description, from the consideration, that the sovereign power of the nation is alone competent to avenge wrongs committed by a sovereign, that the questions to which such wrongs give birth are rather questions of policy than of law, that they are for diplomatic, rather than legal discussion, are of great weight, and merit serious attention. But the argument has already been drawn to a length, which forbids a particular examination of these points.

* * *

If the preceding reasoning be correct, the Exchange, being a public armed ship, in the service of a foreign sovereign, with whom the government of the United States is at peace, and having entered an American port open for her reception, on the terms on which ships of war are generally permitted to enter the ports of a friendly power, must be considered as having come into the American territory, under an implied promise, that while necessarily within it, and demeaning herself in a friendly manner, she should be exempt from the jurisdiction of the country.

[Judgment of the Circuit Court reversed, and judgment of the District Court, dismissing the libel, affirmed.]

NOTES

1. *Absolute Form of Immunity*. Originally, jurisdictional immunities of states were regarded as virtually absolute. A state could invoke them, irrespective of the nature of its sovereign activities. Why would it be seen as desirable to accord a foreign state such absolute immunities? Is it based on a conception that all states are equal and that no one state may exercise authority over any other? Is it a pragmatic way of avoiding potentially disruptive conflicts between states, especially for a young nation such as the United States? Is it a vehicle for sovereign elites to privilege themselves?

2. *Relevance of National Law*. Though arising as a part of international law, immunities of this type may be codified by national law, and many countries, including the United States, have enacted statutes on this subject. National law may provide even greater protection than is required under international law. Conversely, national law might grant lesser protection than international law requires; when this happens, the denial of immunity may be effective within states that do not recognize the supremacy of international law, but will likely give rise to a claim for a violation of international law against that state by the state denied immunity. Consequently, in determining the jurisdictional immunities to which an international legal person is entitled, both international and national law must be studied.

B. RESTRICTIVE FORM OF SOVEREIGN IMMUNITY

Though the absolute form of sovereign immunity held sway for centuries, by the first half of the twentieth century pressures emerged pushing many states toward a more restrictive form. One important codification of this development was the Brussels Convention on the Unification of Certain Rules Relating to Immunity of State-owned Vessels, Apr. 10, 1926, 176 L.N.T.S. 199 (concluded in French). The Brussels Convention provides in Article 1 that:

> Sea-going ships owned or operated by States, cargoes owned by them, and cargoes and passengers carried on State-owned ships, and the States owning or operating such vessels, or owning such cargoes, are subject in respect of claims relating to the operation of such vessels or the carriage of such cargoes to the same rules of liability and to the same obligations as those applicable to private vessels, cargoes and equipment.

The same procedures are to be available to enforce such liabilities and obligations as would be available in the case of privately owned merchant vessels and cargoes and their owners. Id. art. 2.

> These provisions do not apply, however, to warships and other vessels "used at the time a cause of action arises exclusively on Governmental and noncommercial service," nor shall such vessels be subject to seizure, attachment or other *in rem* proceedings. Id. art. 3. When such vessels are involved in controversies relating to collision, salvage, general average, repairs, supplies, or other contracts relating to the vessel, the claimant is entitled to institute proceedings in the courts of the state owning or operating the vessel, without that state being permitted to avail itself of its immunity. A supplementary protocol, adopted May 24, 1934, prohibits attachment or seizure of vessels chartered by governments for non-commercial service, without reference to the status of the vessel at the time the cause of action arose. The convention applies only as between parties to it; these were, as of early 2009, Argentina, Belgium, Brazil, Chile, Cyprus, Democratic Republic of the Congo, Denmark, Egypt, Estonia, France, Germany, Greece, Hungary, Italy, Libya, Luxembourg, Madagascar, Netherlands, Norway, Poland, Portugal, Somalia, Suriname, Sweden, Switzerland, Syria, Turkey, United Kingdom, and Uruguay.

Looking upon the practice that had been emerging in the first half of the twentieth century, including the Brussels Convention, the United Kingdom's Lord Maugham in 1938 commented:

> Half a century ago foreign Governments very seldom embarked in trade with ordinary ships, though they not infrequently owned vessels destined for public uses, and in particular hospital vessels, supply ships, and surveying or exploring vessels. There were doubtless very strong reasons for extending the privilege long possessed by ships of war to public ships of the nature mentioned; but there has been a very large development of State-owned commercial ships since the Great War, and the question whether the immunity should continue to be given to ordinary trading ships has become acute. Is it consistent with sovereign dignity to acquire a tramp steamer and to compete with ordinary shippers and ship-owners in the markets of the world? Doing so, is it consistent to set up the immunity of a sovereign

if, owing to the want of skill of captain and crew, serious damage is caused to the ship of another country? Is it also consistent to refuse to permit proceedings to enforce a right of salvage in respect of services rendered, perhaps at great risk, by the vessel of another country? Is there justice or equity, or for that matter is international comity being followed, in permitting a foreign Government, while insisting on its own right of indemnity [sic], to bring actions in rem or in personam against our own nationals?

My Lords, I am far from relying merely on my own opinion as to the absurdity of the position which our Courts are in if they must continue to disclaim jurisdiction in relation to commercial ships owned by foreign Governments. The matter has been considered over and over again of late years by foreign jurists, by English lawyers, and by business men, and with practical unanimity they are of opinion that, if Governments or corporations formed by them choose to navigate and trade as ship-owners, they ought to submit to the same legal remedies and actions as any other shipowner. This was the effect of the various resolutions of the Conference of London of 1922, of the conference of Gothenburg of 1923 and of the Genoa Conference of 1925. Three Conferences not being deemed sufficient, there was yet another in Brussels in the year 1926. It was attended by Great Britain, France, Germany, Italy, Spain, Holland, Belgium, Poland, Japan and a number of other countries. The United States explained their absence by the statement that they had already given effect to the wish for uniformity in the laws relating to State-owned ships by the Public Vessels Act, 1925 (1925, c. 428). The Brussels Conference was unanimously in favour of the view that in times of peace there should be no immunity as regards State-owned ships engaged in commerce; and the resolution was ratified by Germany, Italy, Holland, Belgium, Estonia, Poland, Brazil and other countries, but not so far by Great Britain. (Oppenheim, International Law, 5th ed., vol. i., p. 670.)

Compania Naviera Vascongada v. S.S. Cristina, [1938] A.C. 485, 521–22.

For the United States, early attempts to limit the scope of sovereign immunity came in cases involving claims arising from the operation of commercial vessels by foreign governments. However, in *Berizzi Bros. Co. v. S.S. Pesaro*, 271 U.S. 562 (1926), the Supreme Court rejected the argument, accepted in a prior stage of the case by the District Court, that Italy was not entitled to immunity in an *in rem* proceeding brought to enforce a claim for cargo damage against a merchant vessel owned and operated by Italy. A definitive break in U.S. practice only became apparent in a 1952 letter from the U.S. Department of State (the agency responsible for interpreting immunities to be accorded under international law) to the U.S. Department of Justice (the agency responsible for representing the interests of the U.S. government in U.S. courts).

LETTER OF DEPARTMENT OF STATE ACTING LEGAL ADVISER, JACK B. TATE, TO ACTING ATTORNEY GENERAL OF THE DEPARTMENT OF JUSTICE, PHILIP B. PEARLMAN

Dated May 18, 1952
26 Dep't St. Bull. 984 (1952)

The Department of State has for some time had under consideration the question whether the practice of the Government in granting immunity from suit to foreign governments made parties defendant in the courts of the United States without their consent should not be changed. The Department has now reached the conclusion that such immunity should no longer be granted in certain types of cases. In view of the obvious interest of your Department in this matter I should like to point out briefly some of the facts which influenced the Department's decision.

A study of the law of sovereign immunity reveals the existence of two conflicting concepts of sovereign immunity, each widely held and firmly established. According to the classical or absolute theory of sovereign immunity, a sovereign cannot, without his consent, be made a respondent in the courts of another sovereign. According to the newer or restrictive theory of sovereign immunity, the immunity of the sovereign is recognized with regard to sovereign or public acts *(jure imperii)* of a state, but not with respect to private acts *(jure gestionis)*. There is agreement by proponents of both theories, supported by practice, that sovereign immunity should not be claimed or granted in actions with respect to real property (diplomatic and perhaps consular property excepted) or with respect to the disposition of the property of a deceased person even though a foreign sovereign is the beneficiary.

The classical or virtually absolute theory of sovereign immunity has generally been followed by the courts of the United States, the British Commonwealth, Czechoslovakia, Estonia, and probably Poland.

The decisions of the courts of Brazil, Chile, China, Hungary, Japan, Luxembourg, Norway, and Portugal may be deemed to support the classical theory of immunity if one or at most two old decisions anterior to the development of the restrictive theory may be considered sufficient on which to base a conclusion.

The position of the Netherlands, Sweden, and Argentina is less clear since although immunity has been granted in recent cases coming before the courts of those countries, the facts were such that immunity would have been granted under either the absolute or restrictive theory. However, constant references by the courts of these three countries to the distinction between public and private acts of the state, even though the distinction was not involved in the result of the case, may indicate an intention to leave the way open for a possible application of the restrictive theory of immunity if and when the occasion presents itself.

A trend to the restrictive theory is already evident in the Netherlands where the lower courts have started to apply that theory following a Supreme Court decision to the effect that immunity would have been applicable in the case under consideration under either theory.

The German courts, after a period of hesitation at the end of the nineteenth century have held to the classical theory, but it should be noted that the refusal of the Supreme Court in 1921 to yield to pressure by the lower courts for the newer theory was based on the view that that theory had not yet developed sufficiently to justify a change. In view of the growth of the restrictive theory since that time the German courts might take a different view today.

The newer or restrictive theory of sovereign immunity has always been supported by the courts of Belgium and Italy. It was adopted in turn by the courts of Egypt and of Switzerland. In addition, the courts of France, Austria, and Greece, which were traditionally supporters of the classical theory, reversed their position in the 20's to embrace the restrictive theory. Rumania, Peru, and possibly Denmark also appear to follow this theory.

Furthermore, it should be observed that in most of the countries still following the classical theory there is a school of influential writers favoring the restrictive theory and the views of writers, at least in civil law countries, are a major factor in the development of the law. Moreover, the leanings of the lower courts in civil law countries are more significant in shaping the law than they are in common law countries where the rule of precedent prevails and the trend in these lower courts is to the restrictive theory.

Of related interest to this question is the fact that ten of the thirteen countries which have been classified above as supporters of the classical theory have ratified the Brussels Convention of 1926 under which immunity for government owned merchant vessels is waived. In addition, the United States which is not a party to the Convention, some years ago announced and has since followed, a policy of not claiming immunity for its public owned or operated merchant vessels. Keeping in mind the importance played by cases involving public vessels in the field of sovereign immunity, it is thus noteworthy that these ten countries (Brazil, Chile, Estonia, Germany, Hungary, Netherlands, Norway, Poland, Portugal, Sweden) and the United States have already relinquished by treaty or in practice an important part of the immunity which they claim under the classical theory.

It is thus evident that with the possible exception of the United Kingdom little support has been found except on the part of the Soviet Union and its satellites for continued full acceptance of the absolute theory of sovereign immunity. There are evidences that British authorities are aware of its deficiencies and ready for a change. The reasons which obviously motivate state trading countries in adhering the theory with perhaps increasing rigidity are most persuasive that the United States should change its policy. Furthermore, the granting of sovereign immunity to foreign governments in the courts of the United States is most inconsistent with the action of the Government of the United States in subjecting itself to suit in these same courts in both contract and tort and with its long established policy of not claiming immunity in foreign jurisdictions for its merchant vessels. Finally, the Department feels that the widespread and increasing practice on the part of governments of engaging in commercial activities makes necessary a practice which will enable persons doing business with them to have their rights determined in the courts. For these reasons it will hereafter be the Department's policy to follow the restrictive theory of sovereign immunity in the consideration of requests of foreign governments for a grant of sovereign immunity.

It is realized that a shift in policy by the executive cannot control the courts but it is felt that the courts are less likely to allow a plea of sovereign immunity where the executive has declined to do so. There have been indications that at least some Justices of the Supreme Court feel that in this matter courts should follow the branch of the Government charged with responsibility for the conduct of foreign relations.

In order that your Department, which is charged with representing the interests of the Government before the courts, may be adequately informed it will be the Department's practice to advise you of all requests by foreign governments for the grant of immunity from suit and of the Department's action thereon.

NOTES

1. *The Historical Transition.* For a survey of cases in a variety of jurisdictions showing the movement of many developed states toward the restrictive form of immunity, from the mid-nineteenth to the mid-twentieth century, as well as analysis of treaties and the opinions of scholars, see the decision of the Supreme Court of Austria in *Dralle v. Republic of Czechoslovakia*, [1950] I.L.R. 155. In that case, the Austrian court concluded that the classic (absolute) doctrine of immunity had lost its meaning in view of the growing commercial activities of states. While the clear trend today continues to be toward a more limited concept of immunities in international law and practice, see, Stewart, Immunity and Accountability: More Continuity than Change?, 99 A.S.I.L. Proc. 227 (2005), many countries still adhere to absolute immunity, including many in the developing world.

2. *Coping with Communism.* During the Cold War, the Soviet Union and its allies embraced a doctrine of absolute immunity, which resulted in extremely broad immunity for economic activity within their systems, since the state owned all means of production (private property was not a feature of the communist system). To accommodate the needs of emerging practice, however, the Soviet Union concluded a large number of bilateral treaties under which its trading enterprises in foreign countries were subject to local jurisdiction with respect to their commercial activities. See Setser, The Immunity Waiver for State–Controlled Business Enterprises in United States Commercial Treaties, 55 A.S.I.L. Proc. 89 (1961); see generally Triska & Slusser, The Theory, Law and Policy of Soviet Treaties, 324–33 (1962);

Sucharitkul, State Immunities and Trading Activities in International Law 152–61 (1959). Now that those formerly communist states have opted for a more market-oriented approach, they may be more inclined to the restrictive approach to sovereign immunity, though to date Russia remains an adherent to absolute immunity before its courts.

China also still purports to embrace the absolute theory. See Feinerman, Sovereign Immunity in the Chinese Case and Its Implications for the Future of International Law, in Essays in Honour of Wang Tieya (MacDonald ed. 1993). For an analysis arguing that China may shift to the restrictive immunity doctrine, see Dahai Qi, State Immunity in China and Its Shifting Position, 7 Chinese J. Int'l L. 307 (2008).

SECTION 2.   U.S. FOREIGN SOVEREIGN IMMUNITIES ACT

A.   ADOPTION OF THE FSIA

In the aftermath of the Tate Letter, the U.S. government found itself often called upon to appear in U.S. proceedings to provide its views on whether a particular type of transaction was of the kind that should or should not be granted immunity. While as a general matter, the U.S. government welcomes deference by the courts to its views, the burden of appearing regularly in U.S. court proceedings, the lack of consistency in positions taken by the U.S. government, and the political difficulty presented by taking a position that denied immunity to a foreign ally (or provided immunity to a foe) fomented pressure to enact a statutory scheme that would provide legally defined standards for courts to apply rather than ad hoc interventions by the executive.

In 1976, Congress enacted the Foreign Sovereign Immunities Act (FSIA), Pub. L. No. 94–583, 90 Stat. 2891, codified as amended at 28 U.S.C. §§ 1330, 1332, 1391, 1441, 1602–1611 (West Supp. 2008). The statute accords federal courts jurisdiction over cases against foreign states, but Section 1604 provides those states with immunity unless one of several statutorily defined exceptions applies. Sections 1605 and 1605A then identify a series of exceptions to that immunity that, if established, could allow a case to proceed. While greatest attention was initially focused upon the exception to immunity where the foreign state engages in commercial activity, several other exceptions have also proved of considerable importance. In the years immediately following its passage, U.S. courts grappled with whether the FSIA constituted the *exclusive* basis for suing foreign states in U.S. courts, an issue ultimately addressed by the Supreme Court in the following case.

ARGENTINE REPUBLIC v. AMERADA HESS SHIPPING CORP.

Supreme Court of the United States, 1989
488 U.S. 428 (some footnotes and citations omitted; some footnotes renumbered)

CHIEF JUSTICE REHNQUIST delivered the opinion of the Court.

Two Liberian corporations sued the Argentine Republic in a United States District Court to recover damages for a tort allegedly committed by its armed forces on the high seas in violation of international law We hold that the District Court correctly dismissed the action, because the Foreign Sovereign Immunities Act of 1976 (FSIA), 28 U.S.C. § 1330 *et seq.,* does not authorize jurisdiction over a foreign state in this situation.

Respondents alleged the following facts in their complaints. Respondent United Carriers, Inc., a Liberian corporation, chartered one of its oil tankers, the Hercules, to respondent Amerada Hess Shipping Corporation, also a Liberian corporation. The contract was executed in New York City. Amerada Hess used the Hercules to transport crude oil from the southern terminus of the Trans–Alaska Pipeline in Valdez, Alaska, around Cape Horn in South America, to the Hess refinery in the United States Virgin Islands. On May 25, 1982, the Hercules began a return voyage, without cargo but fully fueled, from the Virgin Islands to Alaska. At that time, Great Britain and petitioner Argentine Republic were at war over an archipelago of some 200 islands—the Falkland Islands to the British, and the Islas Malvinas to the Argentineans—in the South Atlantic off the Argentine coast. On June 3, United States officials informed the two belligerents of the location of United States vessels and Liberian tankers owned by United States interests then traversing the South Atlantic, including the Hercules, to avoid any attacks on neutral shipping.

By June 8, 1982, after a stop in Brazil, the Hercules was in international waters about 600 nautical miles from Argentina and 500 miles from the Falklands; she was outside the "war zones" designated by Britain and Argentina. At 12:15 Greenwich mean time, the ship's master made a routine report by radio to Argentine officials, providing the ship's name, international call sign, registry, position, course, speed, and voyage description. About 45 minutes later, an Argentine military aircraft began to circle the Hercules. The ship's master repeated his earlier message by radio to Argentine officials, who acknowledged receiving it. Six minutes later, without provocation, another Argentine military plane began to bomb the Hercules; the master immediately hoisted a white flag. A second bombing soon followed, and a third attack came about two hours later, when an Argentine jet struck the ship with an air-to-surface rocket. Disabled but not destroyed, the Hercules reversed course and sailed to Rio de Janeiro, the nearest safe port. At Rio de Janeiro, respondent United Carriers determined that the ship had suffered extensive deck and hull damage, and that an undetonated bomb remained lodged in her No. 2 tank. After an investigation by the Brazilian Navy, United Carriers decided that it would be too hazardous to remove the undetonated bomb, and on July 20, 1982, the Hercules was scuttled 250 miles off the Brazilian coast.

Following unsuccessful attempts to obtain relief in Argentina, respondents commenced this action in the United States District Court for the Southern District of New York for the damage that they sustained from the attack. United Carriers sought $10 million in damages for the loss of the ship; Amerada Hess sought $1.9 million in damages for the fuel that went down with the ship. Respondents alleged that petitioner's attack on the neutral Hercules violated international law. They invoked the District Court's jurisdiction under the Alien Tort Statute, 28 U.S.C. § 1350, which provides that "[t]he district courts shall have original jurisdiction of any civil action by an alien for a tort only, committed in violation of the law of nations or a treaty of the United States." Amerada Hess also brought suit under the general admiralty and maritime jurisdiction, 28 U.S.C. § 1333, and "the principle of universal jurisdiction, recognized in customary international law." Complaint of Amerada Hess ¶ 5, App. 20. The District Court dismissed both complaints for lack of subject-matter jurisdiction, 638 F.Supp. 73 (1986), ruling that respondents' suits were barred by the FSIA.

A divided panel of the United States Court of Appeals for the Second Circuit reversed. 830 F.2d 421 (1987). The Court of Appeals held that the District Court had jurisdiction under the Alien Tort Statute, because respondents' consolidated action was brought by Liberian corporations, it sounded in tort ("the bombing of a ship without justification"), and it asserted a violation of international law ("attacking a neutral ship in international waters, without proper cause for suspicion or investigation"). *Id.,* at 424–425. Viewing the Alien Tort Statute as "no more than a jurisdictional grant based on international law," the Court of Appeals said that "who is within" the scope of that grant is governed by "evolving standards of international law." *Id.,* at 425, citing *Filartiga v. Pena–Irala,* 630 F.2d 876, 880 (C.A.2 1980). The Court of Appeals reasoned that Congress' enactment of the FSIA was not meant to eliminate "existing remedies in United States courts for violations of international law" by foreign states under the Alien Tort Statute. 830 F.2d, at 426. The dissenting judge took the view that the FSIA precluded respondents' action. *Id.,* at 431. We granted certiorari, 485 U.S. 1005 (1988), and now reverse.

* * *

We think that the text and structure of the FSIA demonstrate Congress' intention that the FSIA be the sole basis for obtaining jurisdiction over a foreign state in our courts. Sections 1604 and 1330(a) work in tandem: § 1604 bars federal and state courts from exercising jurisdiction when a foreign state *is* entitled to immunity, and § 1330(a) confers jurisdiction on district courts to hear suits brought by United States citizens and by aliens when a foreign state is not entitled to immunity. As we said in *Verlinden,* the FSIA "must be applied by the district courts in every action against a foreign sovereign, since subject-matter jurisdiction in any such action depends on the existence of one of the specified exceptions to foreign sovereign immunity." *Verlinden B.V. v. Central Bank of Nigeria,* 461 U.S. 480, 493 (1983).

The Court of Appeals acknowledged that the FSIA's language and legislative history support the "general rule" that the Act governs the immunity of foreign states in federal court. 830 F.2d, at 426. The Court of Appeals, however, thought that the FSIA's "focus on commercial concerns" and Congress' failure to "repeal" the Alien Tort Statute indicated Congress' intention that federal courts continue to exercise jurisdiction over foreign states in suits alleging violations of international law outside the confines of the FSIA. *Id.*, at 427. The Court of Appeals also believed that to construe the FSIA to bar the instant suit would "fly in the face" of Congress' intention that the FSIA be interpreted pursuant to " 'standards recognized under international law.' " *Ibid.*, quoting H.R.Rep., at 14 * * *.

Taking the last of these points first, Congress had violations of international law by foreign states in mind when it enacted the FSIA. For example, the FSIA specifically denies foreign states immunity in suits "in which rights in property taken in violation of international law are in issue." 28 U.S.C. § 1605(a)(3). Congress also rested the FSIA in part on its power under Art. I, § 8, cl. 10, of the Constitution "[t]o define and punish Piracies and Felonies committed on the high Seas, and Offenses against the Law of Nations." See H.R.Rep., at 12; S.Rep., at 12 * * *. From Congress' decision to deny immunity to foreign states in the class of cases just mentioned, we draw the plain implication that immunity is granted in those cases involving alleged violations of international law that do not come within one of the FSIA's exceptions.

As to the other point made by the Court of Appeals, Congress' failure to enact a *pro tanto* repealer of the Alien Tort Statute when it passed the FSIA in 1976 may be explained at least in part by the lack of certainty as to whether the Alien Tort Statute conferred jurisdiction in suits against foreign states. Enacted by the First Congress in 1789, the Alien Tort Statute provides that "[t]he district courts shall have original jurisdiction of any civil action by an alien for a tort only, committed in violation of the law of nations or a treaty of the United States." 28 U.S.C. § 1350. The Court of Appeals did not cite any decision in which a United States court exercised jurisdiction over a foreign state under the Alien Tort Statute, and only one such case has come to our attention—one which was decided after the enactment of the FSIA.[1]

In this Court, respondents argue that cases were brought under the Alien Tort Statute against foreign states for the unlawful taking of a prize during wartime. The Alien Tort Statute makes no mention of prize jurisdiction, and § 1333(2) now grants federal district courts exclusive jurisdiction over "all proceedings for the condemnation of property taken as a prize." In *The Santissima Trinidad*, 20 U.S. (7 Wheat.) 283, 353–354 (1822), we held that foreign states were not immune from the jurisdiction of United States courts in prize proceedings. That case, however, was not

---

1. *See Von Dardel v. Union of Soviet Socialist Republics,* 623 F.Supp. 246 (DC 1985) (alternative holding). The Court of Appeals did cite its earlier decision in *Filartiga v. Pena–Irala,* 630 F.2d 876 (1980), which involved a suit under the Alien Tort Statute by a Paraguayan national against a Paraguayan police official for torture; the Paraguayan Government was not joined as a defendant.

brought under the Alien Tort Statute but rather as a libel in admiralty. Thus there is a distinctly hypothetical cast to the Court of Appeals' reliance on Congress' failure to repeal the Alien Tort Statute, and respondents' arguments in this Court based on the principle of statutory construction that repeals by implication are disfavored.

We think that Congress' failure in the FSIA to enact an express *pro tanto* repealer of the Alien Tort Statute speaks only faintly, if at all, to the issue involved in this case. In light of the comprehensiveness of the statutory scheme in the FSIA, we doubt that even the most meticulous draftsman would have concluded that Congress also needed to amend *pro tanto* the Alien Tort Statute and presumably such other grants of subject-matter jurisdiction in Title 28 as § 1331 (federal question), § 1333 (admiralty), § 1335 (interpleader), § 1337 (commerce and antitrust), and § 1338 (patents, copyrights, and trademarks). Congress provided in the FSIA that "[c]laims of foreign states to immunity should *henceforth* be decided by courts of the United States in conformity with the principles set forth in this chapter," and very likely it thought that should be sufficient. § 1602 (emphasis added); see also H.R.Rep., at 12; S.Rep., at 11 * * * (FSIA "intended to preempt any other State and Federal law (excluding applicable international agreements) for according immunity to foreign sovereigns").

For similar reasons we are not persuaded by respondents' arguments based upon the rule of statutory construction under which repeals by implication are disfavored. This case does not involve two statutes that readily could be seen as supplementing one another, see *Wood v. United States,* 41 U.S. (16 Pet.) 342, 363 (1842), nor is it a case where a more general statute is claimed to have repealed by implication an earlier statute dealing with a narrower subject. See *Morton v. Mancari,* 417 U.S. 535, 549–551 (1974). We think that Congress' decision to deal comprehensively with the subject of foreign sovereign immunity in the FSIA, and the express provision in § 1604 that "a foreign state shall be immune from the jurisdiction of the courts of the United States and of the States except as provided in sections 1605–1607," preclude a construction of the Alien Tort Statute that permits the instant suit. See *Red Rock v. Henry,* 106 U.S. 596, 601–602 (1883); *United States v. Tynen,* 78 U.S. (11 Wall.) 88, 92 (1871). The Alien Tort Statute by its terms does not distinguish among classes of defendants, and it of course has the same effect after the passage of the FSIA as before with respect to defendants other than foreign states.

AUSTRIA v. ALTMANN

Supreme Court of the United States, 2004
541 U.S. 677 (2004) (footnotes omitted)

JUSTICE STEVENS delivered the opinion of the Court.

In 1998 an Austrian journalist, granted access to the Austrian Gallery's archives, discovered evidence that certain valuable works in the

Gallery's collection had not been donated by their rightful owners but had been seized by the Nazis or expropriated by the Austrian Republic after World War II. The journalist provided some of that evidence to respondent, who in turn filed this action to recover possession of six Gustav Klimt paintings. Prior to the Nazi invasion of Austria, the paintings had hung in the palatial Vienna home of respondent's uncle, Ferdinand Bloch–Bauer, a Czechoslovakian Jew and patron of the arts. Respondent claims ownership of the paintings under a will executed by her uncle after he fled Austria in 1938. She alleges that the Gallery obtained possession of the paintings through wrongful conduct in the years during and after World War II.

The defendants (petitioners here)—the Republic of Austria and the Austrian Gallery (Gallery), an instrumentality of the Republic—filed a motion to dismiss the complaint asserting, among other defenses, a claim of sovereign immunity. The District Court denied the motion, 142 F. Supp. 2d 1187 (CD Cal. 2001), and the Court of Appeals affirmed, 317 F. 3d 954 (CA9 2002), as amended, 327 F. 3d 1246 (2003). We granted certiorari limited to the question whether the Foreign Sovereign Immunities Act of 1976 (FSIA or Act), 28 U.S.C. § 1602 *et seq.*, which grants foreign states immunity from the jurisdiction of federal and state courts but expressly exempts certain cases, including "case[s] . . . in which rights in property taken in violation of international law are in issue," § 1605(a)(3), applies to claims that, like respondent's, are based on conduct that occurred before the Act's enactment, and even before the United States adopted the so-called "restrictive theory" of sovereign immunity in 1952. 539 U. S. 987 (2003).

* * *

Chief Justice Marshall's opinion in *Schooner Exchange v. McFaddon*, 7 Cranch 116 (1812), is generally viewed as the source of our foreign sovereign immunity jurisprudence. In that case, the libellants claimed to be the rightful owners of a French ship that had taken refuge in the port of Philadelphia. The Court first emphasized that the jurisdiction of the United States over persons and property within its territory "is susceptible of no limitation not imposed by itself," and thus foreign sovereigns have no right to immunity in our courts. *Id.*, at 136. Chief Justice Marshall went on to explain, however, that as a matter of comity, members of the international community had implicitly agreed to waive the exercise of jurisdiction over other sovereigns in certain classes of cases, such as those involving foreign ministers or the person of the sovereign. Accepting a suggestion advanced by the Executive Branch, see *id.*, at 134, the Chief Justice concluded that the implied waiver theory also served to exempt the *Schooner Exchange*—"a national armed vessel . . . of the emperor of France"—from United States courts' jurisdiction. *Id.*, at 145–146.

In accordance with Chief Justice Marshall's observation that foreign sovereign immunity is a matter of grace and comity rather than a constitutional requirement, this Court has "consistently ... deferred to the decisions of the political branches—in particular, those of the Executive Branch—on whether to take jurisdiction" over particular actions against foreign sovereigns and their instrumentalities. *Verlinden B.V. v. Central Bank of Nigeria*, 461 U.S. 480, 486 (1983) (citing *Ex parte Peru*, 318 U.S. 578, 586–590 (1943); *Republic of Mexico v. Hoffman*, 324 U.S. 30, 33–36 (1945)). Until 1952 the Executive Branch followed a policy of requesting immunity in all actions against friendly sovereigns. 461 U.S., at 486. In that year, however, the State Department concluded that "immunity should no longer be granted in certain types of cases." * * * In a letter to the Attorney General, the Acting Legal Adviser for the Secretary of State, Jack B. Tate, explained that the Department would thereafter apply the "restrictive theory" of sovereign immunity * * *.

As we explained in our unanimous opinion in *Verlinden*, the change in State Department policy wrought by the "Tate Letter" had little, if any, impact on federal courts' approach to immunity analyses: "As in the past, initial responsibility for deciding questions of sovereign immunity fell primarily upon the Executive acting through the State Department," and courts continued to "abid[e] by" that Department's " 'suggestions of immunity.' " 461 U.S., at 487. The change did, however, throw immunity determinations into some disarray, as "foreign nations often placed diplomatic pressure on the State Department," and political considerations sometimes led the Department to file "suggestions of immunity in cases where immunity would not have been available under the restrictive theory." *Id.*, at 487–488. Complicating matters further, when foreign nations failed to request immunity from the State Department:

> "[T]he responsibility fell to the courts to determine whether sovereign immunity existed, generally by reference to prior State Department decisions.... Thus, sovereign immunity determinations were made in two different branches, subject to a variety of factors, sometimes including diplomatic considerations. Not surprisingly, the governing standards were neither clear nor uniformly applied." *Ibid.*

In 1976 Congress sought to remedy these problems by enacting the FSIA, a comprehensive statute containing a "set of legal standards governing claims of immunity in every civil action against a foreign state or its political subdivisions, agencies, or instrumentalities." *Id.*, at 488. The Act "codifies, as a matter of federal law, the restrictive theory of sovereign immunity," *ibid.*, and transfers primary responsibility for immunity determinations from the Executive to the Judicial Branch. The preamble states that "henceforth" both federal and state courts should decide claims of sovereign immunity in conformity with the Act's principles. 28 U.S.C. § 1602.

The Act itself grants federal courts jurisdiction over civil actions against foreign states, § 1330(a), and over diversity actions in which a foreign state is the plaintiff, § 1332(a)(4); it contains venue and removal provisions, §§ 1391(f), 1441(d); it prescribes the procedures for obtaining personal jurisdiction over a foreign state, § 1330(b); and it governs the extent to which a state's property may be subject to attachment or execution, §§ 1609–1611. Finally, the Act carves out certain exceptions to its general grant of immunity, including the expropriation exception on which respondent's complaint relies. * * * These exceptions are central to the Act's functioning: "At the threshold of every action in a district court against a foreign state, ... the court must satisfy itself that one of the exceptions applies," as "subject-matter jurisdiction in any such action depends" on that application. *Verlinden*, 461 U. S., at 493–494.

* * *

* * * [T]he preamble of the FSIA expresses Congress' understanding that the Act would apply to all postenactment claims of sovereign immunity. That section provides:

> "*Claims* of foreign states to immunity should *henceforth* be decided by courts of the United States and of the States in conformity with the principles set forth in this chapter." 28 U. S. C. § 1602 (emphasis added).

* * * [T]his language is unambiguous: Immunity "claims"—not actions protected by immunity, but assertions of immunity to suits arising from those actions—are the relevant conduct regulated by the Act; those claims are "henceforth" to be decided by the courts. As the District Court observed, * * * this language suggests Congress intended courts to resolve all such claims "in conformity with the principles set forth" in the Act, regardless of when the underlying conduct occurred.

The FSIA's overall structure strongly supports this conclusion. Many of the Act's provisions unquestionably apply to cases arising out of conduct that occurred before 1976. In *Dole Food Co.* v. *Patrickson*, 538 U.S. 468 (2003), for example, we held that whether an entity qualifies as an "instrumentality" of a "foreign state" for purposes of the FSIA's grant of immunity depends on the relationship between the entity and the state at the time suit is brought rather than when the conduct occurred. In addition, *Verlinden*, which upheld against constitutional challenge 28 U.S.C. § 1330's grant of subject-matter jurisdiction, involved a dispute over a contract that predated the Act. 461 U.S., at 482–483, 497. And there has never been any doubt that the Act's procedural provisions relating to venue, removal, execution, and attachment apply to all pending cases. Thus, the FSIA's preamble indicates that it applies "henceforth," and its body includes numerous provisions that unquestionably apply to claims based on pre–1976 conduct. In this context, it would be anomalous to presume that an isolated provision (such as the expropriation exception on which respondent relies) is of purely prospective application absent any statutory language to that effect.

Finally, applying the FSIA to all pending cases regardless of when the underlying conduct occurred is most consistent with two of the Act's principal purposes: clarifying the rules that judges should apply in resolving sovereign immunity claims and eliminating political participation in the resolution of such claims. * * *

* * *

Finally, while we reject the United States' recommendation to bar application of the FSIA to claims based on pre-enactment conduct, * * * nothing in our holding prevents the State Department from filing statements of interest suggesting that courts decline to exercise jurisdiction in particular cases implicating foreign sovereign immunity. The issue now before us * * * concerns interpretation of the FSIA's reach—a "pure question of statutory construction . . . well within the province of the Judiciary." *INS v. Cardoza–Fonseca*, 480 U.S. 421, 446, 448 (1987). While the United States' views on such an issue are of considerable interest to the Court, they merit no special deference. See, *e.g.*, *ibid*. In contrast, should the State Department choose to express its opinion on the implications of exercising jurisdiction over particular petitioners in connection with *their* alleged conduct, that opinion might well be entitled to deference as the considered judgment of the Executive on a particular question of foreign policy. See, e.g., *Verlinden*, 461 U.S., at 486; *American Ins. Assn. v. Garamendi*, 539 U.S. 396, 414 (2003) (discussing the President's " 'vast share of responsibility for the conduct of our foreign relations' "). We express no opinion on the question whether such deference should be granted in cases covered by the FSIA.

The judgment of the Court of Appeals is *affirmed*.

NOTES

1. *Amerada Hess on the Merits*. In the *Amerada Hess* case, the Supreme Court went on to consider whether there was an exception to sovereign immunity within the FSIA that would allow suit against the Argentine Republic. What exception do you think might be relevant? See *infra* p. 890.

2. *Denouement to Altmann*. Austria had hoped that conduct occurring prior to the emergence of the restrictive theory of immunity in U.S. law would continue to be shielded by the absolute theory of immunity. Do you think it should have? After the Court decided that the FSIA was applicable to Altmann's claim, thereby opening the door to invocation of the exception relating to expropriation, Altmann and Austria agreed to submit the claim to binding arbitration. In January 2006, a three-member Austrian arbitration panel found unanimously that the five Klimt paintings must be returned to Altmann. *See* Bernstein, *Austrian Panel Backs Return of Klimt Works*, N.Y. Times, Jan. 17, 2006. The paintings, however, did not remain in the Altmann family, but were auctioned off at record prices. *See* Carol Vogel, *$491 Million Sale at Christie's Shatters Art Auction Record*, N.Y. Times, Nov. 9, 2006.

3. *"Matter of Comity and Grace"*. Given that the law of nations is regarded by the U.S. Supreme Court as a part of U.S. law, and given that international law calls for immunity to be accorded to sovereigns under certain circumstances, do you agree with the Court in *Altmann* that the provision of foreign sovereign immunity in U.S. courts is a "matter of grace

and comity"? For a critique of the Court's reasoning, see Neuman, The Abiding Significance of Law in Foreign Relations, 2004 Sup. Ct. Rev. 111. Further, given that all national court decisions on foreign sovereign immunity are essentially "data points" for assessing the state of international law on immunity, does it serve U.S. interests abroad to regard the provision of such immunity as discretionary?

4. *Deference to the Executive*. In the final paragraph of *Altmann*, the Court draws a distinction concerning deference to executive views. Given that one of the objectives of the FSIA was to remove the executive from the process of deciding whether a foreign entity in a given case should receive sovereign immunity, does it make sense for the Court to invite the executive "to express its opinion on the implications of exercising jurisdiction over particular petitioners in connection with their alleged conduct" since "that opinion might well be entitled to deference as the considered judgment of the Executive on a particular question of foreign policy"?

5. *Finding the Base Line*. Does Section 1604 properly reflect the essential baseline in this area (i.e., overall immunity subject to exceptions)? The 1976 Senate Judiciary Report on the FSIA stated that, "since sovereign immunity is an affirmative defense which must be specially pleaded, the burden will remain on the foreign state to produce evidence in support of its claims of immunity." S. Rep. No. 94–1310, at 17 (1976). Is this statement supported by the text of the FSIA?

6. *Consistency with International Law*. The 1976 Report of the Senate Judiciary Committee also stated that the FSIA codifies "the so-called 'restrictive' principle of sovereign immunity, as formerly recognized in international law." S. Rep. No. 94–1310, at 9 (1976). As you read through the materials in this section on the FSIA exceptions to immunity, as well as the recent development of a global convention on state immunity discussed in Section 3, consider whether you agree with the Senate Committee's statement.

7. *Repeated Amendments*. Since its enactment, the FSIA has been amended repeatedly—in 1988, 1996, 1998, 2000, 2002, 2005 and 2008. The 1988 amendments added provisions dealing with arbitration and admiralty cases, 28 U.S.C. §§ 1605(a)(6), 1605(b)–(d) (2000). In 1996, the FSIA was amended to deny immunity to foreign states that have been formally designated by the U.S. Government as state sponsors of terrorism, when sued for personal injury or death caused by torture, extrajudicial killing, aircraft sabotage, and hostage-taking. Amendments in 1998 and 2000 dealt with execution of judgments under the new 1996 provision. A 2005 amendment excluded U.S. nationals and entities created under the law of a third country from the definition of "an agency or instrumentality of a foreign state" in § 1603(b)(3). The 2008 amendments recodified the exception relating to state sponsors of terrorism, moving it from § 1605(a)(7) to a new § 1605A, and further created a private right of action against such states.

For a comprehensive look at the FSIA by a working group of the American Bar Association, see Reforming the Foreign Sovereign Immunities Act, 40 Colum. J. Transnat'l L. 489 (2002). The recommendations contained in that report may be compared with those proposed in Smit, The Foreign

Sovereign Immunities Act of 1976: A Plea for Drastic Surgery, 1980 A.S.I.L. Proc. 49.

8. *Codification by Other States.* Ironically, most statutory codification of sovereign immunity has occurred in common law countries. The United Kingdom enacted its State Immunity Act in 1978, 26 & 27 Eliz. 2, ch. 33 (Eng.), 17 I.L.M. 1123. Canada enacted its Act to Provide for State Immunity in Canadian courts in 1982, 29, 30 & 31 Eliz. 2, ch. 93 (Can.), 21 I.L.M. 798 (1982). Australia, Pakistan, Singapore, and South Africa have enacted similar statutes. All of the statutes enacted thus far embrace a restrictive view of immunity. On the U.K. State Immunity Act, see Bates, State Immunity for Torture, 7 Hum. Rts. L. Rev. 651 (2007); Seymour, Immunity from Torture: The State and its Representatives Reunited, 65 Cambridge L.J. 479 (2006); Steinerte & Wallace, Jones v. Ministry of Interior of the Kingdom of Saudi Arabia, 100 A.J.I.L. 901 (2006); Mann, The State Immunity Act 1978, 50 Brit. Y.B.I.L. 43 (1981); Shaw, The State Immunity Act of 1978, 128 N.L.J. 1136 (1978). On the Canadian Act, see Prevost, Judging in Splendid Isolation, 56 Am. J. Comp. L. 125 (2008); Ranganathan, Survivors of Torture, Victims of Law: Reforming State Immunity in Canada by Developing Exceptions for Terrorism and Torture, 71 Sask. L. Rev. 343 (2008); Molot & Jewett, The State Immunity Act of Canada, 20 Can. Y.B.I.L. 79 (1982); Jewett & Molot, State Immunity Act—Basic Principles, 61 Can. B. Rev. 843 (1983). On sovereign immunity policy in New Zealand, see Hastings, Sovereign Immunity in New Zealand, 1990 N.Z.L.J. 214 (1990).

B. WAIVER EXCEPTION

The first exception to immunity identified in FSIA Section 1605(a) concerns waiver of the immunity by the foreign state. The FSIA distinguishes between three kinds of waiver: (1) waiver of immunity from jurisdiction (Section 1605(a)(1)); (2) waiver of immunity from attachment in aid of execution or from execution (Section 1610(a)–(c)); and (3) waiver of immunity from attachment prior to the entry of judgment (Section 1610(d)). In addition, counterclaims, regulated in Section 1607, may be regarded as a particular form of waiver. The first two forms of waiver may be effectuated "either explicitly or by implication," while immunity from pre-judgment attachment may be waived only "explicitly." All three forms of waiver are effective "notwithstanding any withdrawal of the waiver which the foreign state may purport to effect except in accordance with the terms of the waiver."

SIDERMAN DE BLAKE v. REPUBLIC OF ARGENTINA

965 F.2d 699 (9th Cir. 1992)

[In this case, the plaintiff sought to recover for torture and wrongful seizure of property by Argentine authorities. In response to Argentina's plea of sovereign immunity, the court ruled, *inter alia,* that Argentina had waived this defense by requesting the assistance of California state courts in proceedings conducted against the plaintiff in Argentina relating to the very conduct that formed the basis for plaintiff's action.]

Here, we confront a situation where Argentina apparently not only envisioned United States court participation in its persecution of the Sidermans, but by its actions deliberately implicated our courts in that persecution. The Sidermans have presented evidence that a year after Jose, Lea and Carlos Siderman fled Argentina in fear for their lives, the Argentine military authorities altered the Tucuman provincial land records to show that they had held title only to 127, as opposed to 127,000 acres of land in the Province, and that in their last-minute efforts to raise cash they had thus sold property which did not belong to them. The Tucuman Public Prosecutor then initiated criminal proceedings against Jose Siderman for this "fraudulent" sale, and had the Tucuman Supreme Court enlist the aid of our courts, via a letter rogatory, in serving him with process. The letter rogatory, dated May 11, 1980, informed the Presiding Judge of the Los Angeles Superior Court that criminal proceedings were pending against Jose Siderman in the Supreme Court of Tucuman. It requested the court's assistance in serving papers on Siderman, who was living in Los Angeles at the time. While the court complied with the request, the record is not clear as to the subsequent course of lawsuit. In their papers in support of jurisdiction, the Sidermans suggest that the Argentine military authorities sought to obtain Jose's return to Argentina in order to further torture and perhaps even to kill him.

* * *

We conclude that the Sidermans have presented evidence sufficient to support a finding that Argentina has implicitly waived its sovereign immunity with respect to their claims for torture. The evidence indicates that Argentina deliberately involved United States courts in its efforts to persecute Jose Siderman. If Argentina has engaged our courts in the very course of activity for which the Sidermans seek redress, it has waived its immunity as to that redress.

NOTES

1. *Express Waiver by Treaty or Contract.* A waiver may be contained in a treaty by the foreign state with the United States. Further, a waiver may also be contained in a contract by the foreign state with a private party. See S. Rep. No. 94–1310, at 17 (1976). If an explicit waiver can also be effectuated by a unilateral act of the foreign state, what law determines the effectiveness of such a waiver? Can an effective waiver be included in a contract that is invalid under the applicable law? The provision that a waiver may not be withdrawn except in accordance with its terms is designed to overrule legislatively decisions such as *Rich v. Naviera Vacuba, S.A.*, 197 F.Supp. 710 (E.D. Va.1961), aff'd, 295 F.2d 24 (4th Cir. 1961). See S. Rep. No. 94–1310, at 18 (1976).

2. *Implicit Waiver.* It is often said that implied waivers are not readily found. See, e.g., *Creighton Ltd. v. Qatar*, 181 F.3d 118 (D.C. Cir.1999). Nevertheless, implicit waiver may be deduced from conduct signifying an intent to waive. A prominent example is the filing of a general appearance

before a court. See *Flota Maritima Browning De Cuba, S.A. v. Motor Vessel Ciudad De La Habana*, 335 F.2d 619 (4th Cir. 1964) (holding ineffective an attempt to raise the plea of immunity at a later stage in the action); see also *Flota Maritima Browning de Cuba, S.A. v. Snobl*, 363 F.2d 733 (4th Cir. 1966). Another example is the signing of a contract that selects U.S. law as the governing law. See, e.g., *Eckert Int'l v. Fiji*, 32 F.3d 77 (4th Cir. 1994); but see *Wasserstein Perella Emerging Markets Finance, LP v. Province of Formosa*, 2000 WL 573231 (S.D.N.Y. 2000) (finding inadequate the mere selection of U.S. law). What about the selection in the contract of a court or tribunal in a third state; does that implicitly waive immunity before U.S. courts? See *Frolova v. Union of Soviet Socialist Republics*, 761 F.2d 370, 377 (7th Cir. 1985) ("[M]ost courts have refused to find an implicit waiver of immunity to suit in American courts from a contract clause providing for arbitration in a country other than the United States").

3. *Failure to Appear*. Can failure to appear be construed as a waiver? In *Von Dardel On Behalf of Raoul Wallenberg v. U.S.S.R.*, 623 F.Supp. 246 (D.D.C. 1985), the court gave an affirmative answer. After a default judgment was entered, the U.S.S.R. filed a special appearance and the court vacated its judgment, 736 F.Supp. 1 (D.D.C. 1990). But see *Frolova v. U.S.S.R.*, 761 F.2d 370 (7th Cir. 1985), in which the court raised the defense of sovereign immunity on its own motion.

4. *Who May Waive the Immunity?* Who is empowered to waive a state's immunity? Assume that a plaintiff makes a loan to a foreign state for renovation of a permanent mission to the United Nations. Assume further that the foreign state's ambassador to the United Nations concludes a promissory note with the plaintiff in which the ambassador waives his state's immunity to an action brought to enforce the note. Was the ambassador empowered to provide the waiver? In *First Fidelity Bank v. Government of Antigua & Barbuda Permanent Mission*, 877 F.2d 189 (2d Cir. 1989), the Second Circuit ruled that the ambassador's authority presented a question of fact to be determined upon a proper hearing. Further, the Second Circuit took the view that, as a matter of law, either actual or apparent authority would suffice to bind the ambassador. Not all other circuits have followed the Second Circuit. In *Velasco v. Government of Indonesia*, 370 F.3d 392 (4th Cir. 2004), the Fourth Circuit held that:

> Whether a third party reasonably perceives that the sovereign has empowered its agent to engage in a transaction * * * is irrelevant if the sovereign's constitution or laws proscribe or do not authorize the agent's conduct and the third party fails to make a proper inquiry. We conclude that a foreign official's manifestation of authority to bind the sovereign is insufficient to bind the sovereign.

Id. at 400.

5. *Nexus to the United States*. Must there be a nexus between the waiver and the United States? Some courts have found that an agreement to arbitrate in a foreign country constitutes a general consent to suit on the award in the United States. See *S.A. Mineraçao da Trindade–Samitri v. Utah Int'l Inc.*, 576 F.Supp. 566 (S.D.N.Y. 1983), aff'd, 745 F.2d 190 (2d Cir. 1984). But other courts have limited the effect of the waiver to the place of

arbitration chosen. See *Ohntrup v. Firearms Center Inc.*, 516 F.Supp. 1281 (E.D. Pa. 1981), aff'd 760 F.2d 259 (3d Cir. 1985). Similarly, even when an agreement provides for the "nonexclusive jurisdiction" of a non-U.S. court, U.S. courts have been reluctant to extend this provision to cover a waiver of immunity in U.S. proceedings, requiring instead that the agreement explicitly waive immunity in the United States. See *Eaglet Corp. Ltd. v. Banco Cent. De Nicaragua*, 839 F.Supp. 232 (S.D.N.Y. 1993).

C.   COMMERCIAL ACTIVITIES EXCEPTION

REPUBLIC OF ARGENTINA v. WELTOVER, INC.

Supreme Court of the United States, 1992
504 U.S. 607 (footnotes omitted)

JUSTICE SCALIA delivered the opinion of the Court.

This case requires us to decide whether the Republic of Argentina's default on certain bonds issued as part of a plan to stabilize its currency was an act taken "in connection with a commercial activity" that had a "direct effect in the United States" so as to subject Argentina to suit in an American court under the Foreign Sovereign Immunities Act of 1976, 28 U.S.C. § 1602 *et seq.*

I

Since Argentina's currency is not one of the mediums of exchange accepted on the international market, Argentine businesses engaging in foreign transactions must pay in U.S. dollars or some other internationally accepted currency. In the recent past, it was difficult for Argentine borrowers to obtain such funds, principally because of the instability of the Argentine currency. To address these problems, petitioners, the Republic of Argentina and its central bank, Banco Central (collectively Argentina), in 1981 instituted a foreign exchange insurance contract program (FEIC), under which Argentina effectively agreed to assume the risk of currency depreciation in cross-border transactions involving Argentine borrowers. This was accomplished by Argentina's agreeing to sell to domestic borrowers, in exchange for a contractually predetermined amount of local currency, the necessary U.S. dollars to repay their foreign debts when they matured, irrespective of intervening devaluations.

Unfortunately, Argentina did not possess sufficient reserves of U.S. dollars to cover the FEIC contracts as they became due in 1982. The Argentine government thereupon adopted certain emergency measures, including refinancing of the FEIC-backed debts by issuing to the creditors government bonds. These bonds, called "Bonods," provide for payment of interest and principal in U.S. dollars; payment may be made through transfer on the London, Frankfurt, Zurich, or New York market, at the election of the creditor. Under this refinancing program, the foreign creditor had the option of either accepting the Bonods in satisfaction of the initial debt, thereby substituting the Argentine government for the private debtor, or maintaining the debtor/creditor relationship with the private borrower and accepting the Argentine government as guarantor.

When the Bonods began to mature in May 1986, Argentina concluded that it lacked sufficient foreign exchange to retire them. Pursuant to a Presidential Decree, Argentina unilaterally extended the time for payment, and offered bondholders substitute instruments as a means of rescheduling the debts. Respondents, two Panamanian corporations and a Swiss bank who hold, collectively, $1.3 million of Bonods, refused to accept the rescheduling, and insisted on full payment, specifying New York as the place where payment should be made. Argentina did not pay, and respondents then brought this breach-of-contract action in the United States District Court for the Southern District of New York, relying on the Foreign Sovereign Immunities Act of 1976 as the basis for jurisdiction. Petitioners moved to dismiss for lack of subject-matter jurisdiction, lack of personal jurisdiction, and *forum non conveniens.* * * *

II

The Foreign Sovereign Immunities Act of 1976, 28 U.S.C. § 1602 *et seq.* (FSIA), establishes a comprehensive framework for determining whether a court in this country, state or federal, may exercise jurisdiction over a foreign state. Under the Act, a "foreign state *shall* be immune from the jurisdiction of the courts of the United States and of the States" unless one of several statutorily defined exceptions applies. § 1604 (emphasis added). The FSIA thus provides the "sole basis" for obtaining jurisdiction over a foreign sovereign in the United States. See *Argentine Republic v. Amerada Hess Shipping Corp.,* 488 U.S. 428, 434–439 (1989). The most significant of the FSIA's exceptions—and the one at issue in this case—is the "commercial" exception of § 1605(a)(2), which provides that a foreign state is not immune from suit in any case

"in which the action is based upon a commercial activity carried on in the United States by the foreign state; or upon an act performed in the United States in connection with a commercial activity of the foreign state elsewhere; or upon an act outside the territory of the United States in connection with a commercial activity of the foreign state elsewhere and that act causes a direct effect in the United States." § 1605(a)(2).

In the proceedings below, respondents relied only on the third clause of § 1605(a)(2) to establish jurisdiction, 941 F.2d, at 149, and our analysis is therefore limited to considering whether this lawsuit is (1) "based ... upon an act outside the territory of the United States"; (2) that was taken "in connection with a commercial activity" of Argentina outside this country; and (3) that "cause[d] a direct effect in the United States." The complaint in this case alleges only one cause of action on behalf of each of the respondents, viz., a breach-of-contract claim based on Argentina's attempt to refinance the Bonods rather than to pay them according to their terms. The fact that the cause of action is in compliance with the first of the three requirements—that it is "based upon an act outside the territory of the United States" (presumably Argentina's unilateral exten sion)—is uncontested. The dispute pertains to whether the unilateral refinancing of the Bonods was taken "in connection with a commercial activity" of Argentina, and whether it had a "direct effect in the United States." We address these issues in turn.

A

Respondents and their *amicus,* the United States, contend that Argentina's issuance of, and continued liability under, the Bonods constitute a "commercial activity" and that the extension of the payment schedules was taken "in connection with" that activity. The latter point is obvious enough, and Argentina does not contest it; the key question is whether the activity is "commercial" under the FSIA.

The FSIA defines "commercial activity" to mean:

"[E]ither a regular course of commercial conduct or a particular commercial transaction or act. The commercial character of an activity shall be determined by reference to the nature of the course of conduct or particular transaction or act, rather than by reference to its purpose." 28 U.S.C. § 1603(d).

This definition, however, leaves the critical term "commercial" largely undefined: The first sentence simply establishes that the commercial nature of an activity does *not* depend upon whether it is a single act or a regular course of conduct, and the second sentence merely specifies what element of the conduct determines commerciality (*i.e.,* nature rather than purpose), but still without saying what "commercial" means. Fortunately, however, the FSIA was not written on a clean slate. As we have noted, see *Verlinden B.V. v. Central Bank of Nigeria,* 461 U.S. 480, 486–489 (1983), the Act (and the commercial exception in particular) largely codifies the so-called "restrictive" theory of foreign sovereign immunity first endorsed by the State Department in 1952. The meaning of "commercial" is the meaning generally attached to that term under the restrictive theory at the time the statute was enacted. * * *

This Court did not have occasion to discuss the scope or validity of the restrictive theory of sovereign immunity until our 1976 decision in *Alfred Dunhill of London, Inc. v. Republic of Cuba,* 425 U.S. 682. Although the Court there was evenly divided on the question whether the "commercial" exception that applied in the foreign-sovereign-immunity context also limited the availability of an act-of-state defense, compare *id.,* at 695–706 (plurality) with *id.,* at 725–730 (Marshall, J., dissenting), there was little disagreement over the general scope of the exception. The plurality noted that, after the State Department endorsed the restrictive theory of foreign sovereign immunity in 1952, the lower courts consistently held that foreign sovereigns were not immune from the jurisdiction of American courts in cases "arising out of purely commercial transactions," *id.,* at 703; citing, *inter alia, Victory Transport, Inc. v. Comisaria General,* 336 F.2d 354 (C.A.2 1964), cert. denied, 381 U.S. 934 (1965), and *Petrol*

Shipping Corp. v. Kingdom of Greece, 360 F.2d 103 (C.A.2), cert. denied, 385 U.S. 931 (1966). The plurality further recognized that the distinction between state sovereign acts, on the one hand, and state commercial and private acts, on the other, was not entirely novel to American law. * * * The plurality stated that the restrictive theory of foreign sovereign immunity would not bar a suit based upon a foreign state's participation in the marketplace in the manner of a private citizen or corporation. 425 U.S., at 698–705. A foreign state engaging in "commercial" activities "do[es] not exercise powers peculiar to sovereigns"; rather, it "exercise[s] only those powers that can also be exercised by private citizens." *Id.,* at 704. The dissenters did not disagree with this general description, see *id.,* at 725. Given that the FSIA was enacted less than six months after our decision in *Alfred Dunhill* was announced, we think the plurality's contemporaneous description of the then-prevailing restrictive theory of sovereign immunity is of significant assistance in construing the scope of the Act.

In accord with that description, we conclude that when a foreign government acts, not as regulator of a market, but in the manner of a private player within it, the foreign sovereign's actions are "commercial" within the meaning of the FSIA. Moreover, because the Act provides that the commercial character of an act is to be determined by reference to its "nature" rather than its "purpose," 28 U.S.C. § 1603(d), the question is not whether the foreign government is acting with a profit motive or instead with the aim of fulfilling uniquely sovereign objectives. Rather, the issue is whether the particular actions that the foreign state performs (whatever the motive behind them) are the *type* of actions by which a private party engages in "trade and traffic or commerce," Black's Law Dictionary 270 (6th ed. 1990). See, *e.g., Rush–Presbyterian–St. Luke's Medical Center v. Hellenic Republic,* 877 F.2d 574, 578 (C.A. 7), cert. denied, 493 U.S. 937, 110 S.Ct. 333, 107 L.Ed.2d 322 (1989). Thus, a foreign government's issuance of regulations limiting foreign currency exchange is a sovereign activity, because such authoritative control of commerce cannot be exercised by a private party; whereas a contract to buy army boots or even bullets is a "commercial" activity, because private companies can similarly use sales contracts to acquire goods, see, *e.g., Stato di Rumania v. Trutta* [1926] Foro It. 1 584, 585–586, 589 (Corte di Cass. del Regno, Italy), translated and reprinted in part in 26 Am.J.Int'l L. 626–629 (Supp. 1932).

* * *

* * * We conclude that Argentina's issuance of the Bonods was a "commercial activity" under the FSIA.

B

The remaining question is whether Argentina's unilateral rescheduling of the Bonods had a "direct effect" in the United States, 28 U.S.C. § 1605(a)(2). * * *

* * *

The Court of Appeals concluded that the rescheduling of the maturity dates obviously had a "direct effect" on respondents. It further concluded that that effect was sufficiently "in the United States" for purposes of the FSIA, in part because "Congress would have wanted an American court to entertain this action" in order to preserve New York City's status as "a preeminent commercial center." *Id.,* at 153. The question, however, is not what Congress "would have wanted" but what Congress enacted in the FSIA. Although we are happy to endorse the Second Circuit's recognition of "New York's status as a world financial leader," the effect of Argentina's rescheduling in diminishing that status (assuming it is not too speculative to be considered an effect at all) is too remote and attenuated to satisfy the "direct effect" requirement of the FSIA. *Ibid.*

We nonetheless have little difficulty concluding that Argentina's unilateral rescheduling of the maturity dates on the Bonods had a "direct effect" in the United States. Respondents had designated their accounts in New York as the place of payment, and Argentina made some interest payments into those accounts before announcing that it was rescheduling the payments. Because New York was thus the place of performance for Argentina's ultimate contractual obligations, the rescheduling of those obligations necessarily had a "direct effect" in the United States: Money that was supposed to have been delivered to a New York bank for deposit was not forthcoming. We reject Argentina's suggestion that the "direct effect" requirement cannot be satisfied where the plaintiffs are all foreign corporations with no other connections to the United States. We expressly stated in *Verlinden* that the FSIA permits "a foreign plaintiff to sue a foreign sovereign in the courts of the United States, provided the substantive requirements of the Act are satisfied," 461 U.S., at 489.

Finally, Argentina argues that a finding of jurisdiction in this case would violate the Due Process Clause of the Fifth Amendment, and that, in order to avoid this difficulty, we must construe the "direct effect" requirement as embodying the "minimum contacts" test of *International Shoe Co. v. Washington,* 326 U.S. 310, 316 (1945). Assuming, without deciding, that a foreign state is a "person" for purposes of the Due Process Clause, cf. *South Carolina v. Katzenbach,* 383 U.S. 301, 323–324 (1966) (States of the Union are not "persons" for purposes of the Due Process Clause), we find that Argentina possessed "minimum contacts" that would satisfy the constitutional test. By issuing negotiable debt instruments denominated in U.S. dollars and payable in New York and by appointing a financial agent in that city, Argentina " 'purposefully avail[ed] itself of the privilege of conducting activities within the [United States],' " *Burger King Corp. v. Rudzewicz,* 471 U.S. 462, 475 (1985), quoting *Hanson v. Denckla,* 357 U.S. 235, 253 (1958).

* * *

We conclude that Argentina's issuance of the Bonods was a "commercial activity" under the FSIA; that its rescheduling of the maturity dates on those instruments was taken in connection with that commercial activity and had a "direct effect" in the United States; and that the District Court therefore properly asserted jurisdiction, under the FSIA, over the breach-of-contract claim based on that rescheduling. Accordingly, the judgment of the Court of Appeals is

Affirmed.

SAUDI ARABIA v. NELSON

Supreme Court of the United States, 1993
507 U.S. 349 (footnotes omitted)

JUSTICE SOUTER delivered the opinion of the Court.

The Foreign Sovereign Immunities Act of 1976 entitles foreign states to immunity from the jurisdiction of courts in the United States, 28 U.S.C. § 1604, subject to certain enumerated exceptions. § 1605. One is that a foreign state shall not be immune in any case "in which the action is based upon a commercial activity carried on in the United States by the foreign state." § 1605(a)(2). We hold that respondents' action alleging personal injury resulting from unlawful detention and torture by the Saudi Government is not "based upon a commercial activity" within the meaning of the Act, which consequently confers no jurisdiction over respondents' suit.

I

Because this case comes to us on a motion to dismiss the complaint, we assume that we have truthful factual allegations before us, see *United States* v. *Gaubert*, 499 U.S. 315, 327, though many of those allegations are subject to dispute * * *. Petitioner Kingdom of Saudi Arabia owns and operates petitioner King Faisal Specialist Hospital in Riyadh, as well as petitioner Royspec Purchasing Services, the hospital's corporate purchasing agent in the United States. * * * The Hospital Corporation of America, Ltd. (HCA), an independent corporation existing under the laws of the Cayman Islands, recruits Americans for employment at the hospital under an agreement signed with Saudi Arabia in 1973. * * *

In its recruitment effort, HCA placed an advertisement in a trade periodical seeking applications for a position as a monitoring systems engineer at the hospital. The advertisement drew the attention of respondent Scott Nelson in September 1983, while Nelson was in the United States. After interviewing for the position in Saudi Arabia, Nelson returned to the United States, where he signed an employment contract with the hospital, * * * satisfied personnel processing requirements, and attended an orientation session that HCA conducted for hospital employees. In the course of that program, HCA identified Royspec as the point of contact in the United States for family members who might wish to reach Nelson in an emergency. * * *

In December 1983, Nelson went to Saudi Arabia and began work at the hospital, monitoring all "facilities, equipment, utilities and mainte-

nance systems to insure the safety of patients, hospital staff, and others."
* * * He did his job without significant incident until March 1984, when
he discovered safety defects in the hospital's oxygen and nitrous oxide
lines that posed fire hazards and otherwise endangered patients' lives.
* * * Over a period of several months, Nelson repeatedly advised hospital
officials of the safety defects and reported the defects to a Saudi Government commission as well. * * * Hospital officials instructed Nelson to
ignore the problems. * * *

The hospital's response to Nelson's reports changed, however, on
September 27, 1984, when certain hospital employees summoned him to
the hospital's security office where agents of the Saudi Government
arrested him. The agents transported Nelson to a jail cell, in which they
"shackled, tortured and bea[t]" him * * * and kept him four days without
food * * * Although Nelson did not understand Arabic, government
agents forced him to sign a statement written in that language, the
content of which he did not know; a hospital employee who was supposed
to act as Nelson's interpreter advised him to sign "anything" the agents
gave him to avoid further beatings. * * * Two days later, government
agents transferred Nelson to the Al Sijan Prison "to await trial on
unknown charges." * * *

At the prison, Nelson was confined in an overcrowded cell area
infested with rats, where he had to fight other prisoners for food and from
which he was taken only once a week for fresh air and exercise. * * *
Although police interrogators repeatedly questioned him in Arabic, Nelson
did not learn the nature of the charges, if any, against him. * * * For
several days, the Saudi Government failed to advise Nelson's family of his
whereabouts, though a Saudi official eventually told Nelson's wife, respondent Vivian Nelson, that he could arrange for her husband's release if she
provided sexual favors.

* * *

The District Court dismissed for lack of subject-matter jurisdiction
under the Foreign Sovereign Immunities Act of 1976, 28 U.S.C. §§ 1330,
1602 *et seq*. * * *

The Court of Appeals reversed. 923 F.2d 1528 (C.A.11 1991). It
concluded that Nelson's recruitment and hiring were commercial activities
of Saudi Arabia and the hospital, carried on in the United States for
purposes of the Act * * *. There was, the court reasoned, a sufficient
nexus between those commercial activities and the wrongful acts that had
allegedly injured the Nelsons: "the detention and torture of Nelson are so
intertwined with his employment at the Hospital," the court explained,
"that they are 'based upon' his recruitment and hiring" in the United
States. * * *

II

The Foreign Sovereign Immunities Act "provides the sole basis for
obtaining jurisdiction over a foreign state in the courts of this country."

Argentine Republic v. *Amerada Hess Shipping Corp.*, 488 U.S. 428, 443 (1989). Under the Act, a foreign state is presumptively immune from the jurisdiction of United States courts; unless a specified exception applies, a federal court lacks subject-matter jurisdiction over a claim against a foreign state. *Verlinden B.V.* v. *Central Bank of Nigeria*, 461 U.S. 480, 488–489 (1983); see 28 U.S.C. § 1604; J. Dellapenna, Suing Foreign Governments and Their Corporations 11, and n. 64 (1988).

Only one such exception is said to apply here. The first clause of § 1605(a)(2) of the Act provides that a foreign state shall not be immune from the jurisdiction of United States courts in any case "in which the action is based upon a commercial activity carried on in the United States by the foreign state." The Act defines such activity as "commercial activity carried on by such state and having substantial contact with the United States," § 1603(e), and provides that a commercial activity may be "either a regular course of commercial conduct or a particular commercial transaction or act," the "commercial character of [which] shall be determined by reference to" its "nature," rather than its "purpose," § 1603(d).

There is no dispute here that Saudi Arabia, the hospital, and Royspec all qualify as "foreign state[s]" within the meaning of the Act. * * * For there to be jurisdiction in this case, therefore, the Nelsons' action must be "based upon" some "commercial activity" by petitioners that had "substantial contact" with the United States within the meaning of the Act. Because we conclude that the suit is not based upon any commercial activity by petitioners, we need not reach the issue of substantial contact with the United States.

* * *

Unlike Argentina's activities that we considered in *Weltover*, the intentional conduct alleged here (the Saudi Government's wrongful arrest, imprisonment, and torture of Nelson) could not qualify as commercial under the restrictive theory. The conduct boils down to abuse of the power of its police by the Saudi Government, and however monstrous such abuse undoubtedly may be, a foreign state's exercise of the power of its police has long been understood for purposes of the restrictive theory as peculiarly sovereign in nature. See *Arango* v. *Guzman Travel Advisors Corp.*, 621 F.2d 1371, 1379 (C.A.5 1980); *Victory Transport Inc.* v. *Comisaria General de Abastecimientos y Transportes*, 336 F.2d 354, 360 (C.A.2 1964) (restrictive theory does extend immunity to a foreign state's "internal administrative acts"), cert. denied, 381 U.S. 934 (1965); *Herbage* v. *Meese*, 747 F. Supp. 60, 67 (D.C. 1990), affirmance order, 292 U.S.App.D.C. 84, 946 F.2d 1564 (1991); K. Randall, Federal Courts and the International Human Rights Paradigm 93 (1990) (the Act's commercial-activity exception is irrelevant to cases alleging that a foreign state has violated human rights). Exercise of the powers of police and penal officers is not the sort of action by which private parties can engage in commerce. "[S]uch acts as legislation, or the expulsion of an alien, or a denial of justice, cannot be performed by an individual acting in his own name. They can be per-

formed only by the state acting as such." Lauterpacht, The Problem of
Jurisdictional Immunities of Foreign States, 28 Brit.Y.B.Int'l L. 220, 225
(1952); see also *id.*, at 237.

* * *

JUSTICE WHITE, with whom JUSTICE BLACKMUN joins, concurring in the
judgment.

* * * The majority concludes that petitioners enjoy sovereign immunity because respondents' action is not "based upon a commercial activity." I disagree. I nonetheless concur in the judgment because in my view
the commercial conduct upon which respondents base their complaint was
not "carried on in the United States."

* * *

* * * That, when the hospital calls in security to get even with a
whistle-blower, it comes clothed in police apparel says more about the
state-owned nature of the commercial enterprise than about the noncommercial nature of its tortious conduct. * * *

[The statements of Justice Kennedy, with whom Justice Blackmun
and Justice Stevens join as to Parts I–B and II, concurring in part and
dissenting in part, and of Justice Blackmun, have been omitted.]

JUSTICE STEVENS, dissenting.

Under the Foreign Sovereign Immunities Act of 1976 (FSIA), a
foreign state is subject to the jurisdiction of American courts if two
conditions are met: The action must be "based upon a commercial
activity" and that activity must have a "substantial contact with the
United States." These two conditions should be separately analyzed because they serve two different purposes. The former excludes commercial
activity from the scope of the foreign sovereign's immunity from suit; the
second identifies the contacts with the United States that support the
assertion of jurisdiction over the defendant.

* * *

Whether the first clause of § 1605(a)(2) broadly authorizes "general"
jurisdiction over foreign entities that engage in substantial commercial
activity in this country, or, more narrowly, authorizes only "specific"
jurisdiction over particular commercial claims that have a substantial
contact with the United States, petitioners' contacts with the United
States in this case are, in my view, plainly sufficient to subject petitioners
to suit in this country on a claim arising out of their nonimmune
commercial activity relating to respondent. If the same activities had been
performed by a private business, I have no doubt jurisdiction would be
upheld. And that, of course, should be a touchstone of our inquiry; for as
JUSTICE WHITE explains, * * * when a foreign nation sheds its uniquely
sovereign status and seeks out the benefits of the private marketplace, it
must, like any private party, bear the burdens and responsibilities im-

posed by that marketplace. I would therefore affirm the judgment of the Court of Appeals.

NOTES

1. *Commercial versus Public Acts.* What criteria determine whether the foreign state's activity or property is "commercial" rather than public? Are they criteria of international law, the law of the forum state, or the law of the foreign state? See, e.g., Decision of April 30, 1963 of the German Constitutional Court, 16 BVerfG 63, 19 L.Z 175 (national law may be used to draw the distinction, but may not deviate from the views of the preponderance of states as to what belongs to the region of state authority in its narrow and proper sense).

2. *Focusing on the FSIA.* Prior to the enactment of the FSIA, some in the United States argued that the *purpose* of the foreign state when engaging in its act was determinative, while others looked at the *nature of the act* without regard to the purpose. For example, the Harvard Research in International Law Project on Competence of Courts in Regard to Foreign States, art. 11, 26 A.J.I.L. Supp. 451, 597 (1932) maintained that a state engages in a commercial activity when it "engages in an * * * enterprise in which private persons may engage." For a discussion, see *Victory Transport, Inc. v. Comisaria General de Abastecimientos y Transportes*, 336 F.2d 354 (2d Cir. 1964). Now, whether a foreign state's act is commercial is determined by reference to the language of the FSIA. FSIA Section 1603(d) provides the following definition:

> A "commercial activity" means either a regular course of commercial conduct or a particular commercial transaction or act. The commercial character of an activity shall be determined by reference to the nature of the course of conduct or particular transaction or act, rather than by reference to its purpose.

The Restatement (Third) § 451 refers to "claims arising out of activities of the kind that may be carried on by private persons." When a foreign state purchases shoes for its army from a U.S. supplier, the purpose of the transaction is public, but the nature of the transaction is of the kind that private persons undertake (e.g., buying shoes). Hence, such a transaction is not entitled to immunity.

3. *Relevance of Reciprocity.* The *Weltover* case demonstrates the difficulty and complexity of some cases that arise under the commercial activity exception and the need to consider prior U.S. case law interpreting the exception. Is it also important to consider foreign case law, since immunities denied within the United States to a foreign state may well be denied to the United States when operating abroad. In 1960, the United States claimed immunity through diplomatic channels in a suit brought in Italy by an Italian company that had built sewers for the U.S. Logistic Command in Italy. The United States argued that the case arose from activity of the U.S. Government in its capacity as a sovereign. The Italian Court of Cassation upheld the decision below denying immunity on the ground that the transaction was of a private law nature even though done for a military purpose. *Governo degli*

Stati Uniti di America c. Soc. I.R.S.A., [1963] Foro Ital. 1405, 47 Revista do Diritto Internazionale 484 (May 13, 1963).

4.   *The Nexus Component.* Why does Section 1605(a)(2) exclude immunity only if the action is based on a commercial activity carried on in, or having a substantial contact with, the United States or on an act performed or having a direct effect there? Should a foreign state, subject to suit in the United States under generally prevailing rules of adjudicatory authority, be allowed a plea of sovereign immunity because the commercial activity or act on which the claim for relief is based occurred abroad and caused no direct effect in, and had no substantial contact with, the United States? Does this provision improperly commingle rules of sovereign immunity and rules of adjudicative competence? Note that Section 1330(a) and (b) of the FSIA provide that, subject to certain qualifications, personal jurisdiction exists as to any claim for relief with regard to which the foreign state is not entitled to immunity under Sections 1605–1607.

5.   *How Direct is "Direct"?* What kinds of commercial activities cause a "direct effect in the United States"? In *Zedan v. Kingdom of Saudi Arabia,* 849 F.2d 1511 (D.C. Cir. 1988), the court found that even if the plaintiff had not received a contractually stipulated payment for work done in Saudi Arabia after his return to the United States, that breach did not produce the statutorily required "effect" in the United States. By contrast, in *Foremost–McKesson, Inc. v. Iran,* 905 F.2d 438 (D.C. Cir. 1990), the U.S. plaintiff sued Iran for allegedly using its majority position in an Iranian corporate joint venture wrongfully to deprive the plaintiff of benefits to which it was entitled. There the Court ruled that Iran's allegedly wrongful conduct caused a direct effect since the complaint alleged a constant flow of capital, management personnel, engineering data, machinery and equipment between the United States and Iran.

6.   *Bonding with the United States.* In what circumstances can a foreign state be sued in the United States on bonds it has issued? In the *Weltover* case, the Court stressed that the bonds were denominated in U.S. dollars and payable in New York. Would a clause in the bond declaring New York law applicable suffice? Would it be sufficient if the bonds were denominated in U.S. dollars and the holders were U.S. citizens or residents, but no place of payment were specified? How can a foreign state avoid being subjected to suit in the United States on bonds it has issued? Would a clause selecting a foreign forum be sufficient? Would the New York court have had *in personam* competence under New York law if the FSIA had not supplied its own basis? If not, is it appropriate for the United States to subject a foreign state to suit in New York if the foreign state would not have been subject to suit if it had been a private entity? In *Wasserstein Perella v. Province of Formosa,* No. 97 Civ. 793, 2000 WL 573231 (S.D.N.Y. May 11, 2000), the court found that a foreign sovereign's use of U.S. banks and securities markets to raise money constituted sufficiently direct effects within the United States to enable the court to exercise jurisdiction.

7.   *Libel in State–Owned Publication as "Commercial Activity"?* In *Yessenin–Volpin v. Novosti Press Agency,* 443 F.Supp. 849 (S.D.N.Y. 1978), the court upheld a claim of immunity in an action alleging a libel in a publication

distributed in the United States on the ground that the libel was not "an act outside of the territory of the United States in connection with a commercial activity of the foreign state elsewhere." Acknowledging that the act had produced a direct effect in the United States, the court held that it had not been performed "in connection with a commercial activity." Although Novosti did engage in commercial activities, the court ruled that the publications in which the alleged libels appeared were official commentary of the Soviet government and therefore could not be regarded as published in the course of a commercial activity. By contrast, commentary by state-owned companies which does not amount to official commentary may be viewed differently. Thus, in *Bryks v. Canadian Broadcasting Corp.*, 906 F.Supp. 204 (S.D.N.Y. 1995), the court noted that, unlike the former Soviet press agencies, the CBC was insulated from political influence and accepted commercial advertising. Nevertheless, the Court found that Congress had intended to provide immunity for all defamation claims under § 1605(a)(5)(B) (discussed *infra*), whether commercial or non-commercial in nature. Accordingly, it held that plaintiffs may not sue a foreign state for defamation under the FSIA's commercial activity exception.

8. *Embassy Employee*. Is a foreign state's employment of a U.S. national to work at its embassy in the United States a "commercial activity" for FSIA purposes (as opposed to employment in the state's civil service), thereby exposing the foreign state to suit in U.S. court by the employee? In *El–Hadad v. United Arab Emirates*, 216 F.3d 29 (2000), the D.C. Circuit Court of Appeals pointed to several factors as relevant when answering that question: (1) how the foreign state's laws defined its civil service and whether the employee's job title and duties came within that definition; (2) whether the employee had a true contractual arrangement with the employer or whether the relationship was based upon the civil service laws; (3) the nature of the employee's work; and (4) whether the employee's status as a non-national would make it unlikely that he or she would be employed in a governmental position by the employer.

9. *Further Reading*. For commentary on the effectiveness of the commercial activity exception in the FSIA, see Mofidi, The Foreign Sovereign Immunities Act and the "Commercial Activity" Exception: The Gulf Between Theory and Practice, 5 J. Int'l Legal Stud. 95 (1999); Donoghue, Taking the "Sovereign" out of the Foreign Sovereign Immunities Act: A Functional Approach To The Commercial Activity Exception, 17 Yale J. Int'l L. 489 (1992); Vazquez, The Relationship Between The FSIA's Commercial Activity Exception And The Due–Process Clause, 1991 A.S.I.L. Proc. 257; Note, Nationalized and Denationalized Commercial Enterprises Under The Foreign Sovereign Immunities Act, 90 Colum. L. Rev. 2278 (1990).

D. EXCEPTION FOR PROPERTY WITHIN THE FORUM STATE

PERMANENT MISSION OF INDIA TO THE UNITED NATIONS v. CITY OF NEW YORK

Supreme Court of the United States, 2007
551 U.S. 193

JUSTICE THOMAS delivered the opinion of the Court.

The Foreign Sovereign Immunities Act of 1976 (FSIA), 28 U.S.C. § 1602 *et seq.*, governs federal courts' jurisdiction in lawsuits against foreign sovereigns. Today, we must decide whether the FSIA provides immunity to a foreign sovereign from a lawsuit to declare the validity of tax liens on property held by the sovereign for the purpose of housing its employees. We hold that the FSIA does not immunize a foreign sovereign from such a suit.

I

The Permanent Mission of India to the United Nations is located in a 26–floor building in New York City that is owned by the Government of India. Several floors are used for diplomatic offices, but approximately 20 floors contain residential units for diplomatic employees of the mission and their families. The employees—all of whom are below the rank of Head of Mission or Ambassador—are Indian citizens who receive housing from the mission rent free.

Similarly, the Ministry for Foreign Affairs of the People's Republic of Mongolia is housed in a six-story building in New York City that is owned by the Mongolian Government. Like the Permanent Mission of India, certain floors of the Ministry Building include residences for lower level employees of the Ministry and their families.

Under New York law, real property owned by a foreign government is exempt from taxation if it is "used exclusively" for diplomatic offices or for the quarters of a diplomat "with the rank of ambassador or minister plenipotentiary" to the United Nations. N. Y. Real Prop. Tax Law Ann. § 418 (West 2000). But "[i]f a portion only of any lot or building ... is used exclusively for the purposes herein described, then such portion only shall be exempt and the remainder shall be subject to taxation...." *Ibid.*

For several years, the City of New York (City) has levied property taxes against petitioners for the portions of their buildings used to house lower level employees. Petitioners, however, refused to pay the taxes. By operation of New York law, the unpaid taxes eventually converted into tax liens held by the City against the two properties. As of February 1, 2003, the Indian Mission owed about $16.4 million in unpaid property taxes and interest, and the Mongolian Ministry owed about $2.1 million.

On April 2, 2003, the City filed complaints in state court seeking declaratory judgments to establish the validity of the tax liens.[1] Petitioners removed their cases to federal court, pursuant to 28 U.S.C. § 1441(d), which provides for removal by a foreign state or its instrumentality. Once there, petitioners argued that they were immune from the suits under the FSIA's general rule of immunity for foreign governments. § 1604. The District Court disagreed, relying on the FSIA's "immovable property" exception, which provides that a foreign state shall not be immune from jurisdiction in any case in which "rights in immovable property situated in the United States are in issue." § 1605(a)(4).

Reviewing the District Court's decision under the collateral order doctrine, a unanimous panel of the Court of Appeals for the Second Circuit affirmed. 446 F.3d 365 (2006). The Court of Appeals held that the text and purpose of the FSIA's immovable property exception confirmed that petitioners' personal property tax obligations involved "rights in immovable property." It therefore held that the District Court had jurisdiction to consider the City's suits. We granted certiorari, 549 U.S. 1177 (2007), and now affirm.

II

"[T]he FSIA provides the sole basis for obtaining jurisdiction over a foreign state in federal court." *Argentine Republic v. Amerada Hess Shipping Corp.*, 488 U.S. 428, 439 (1989). Under the FSIA, a foreign state is presumptively immune from suit unless a specific exception applies. § 1604; *Saudi Arabia v. Nelson*, 507 U.S. 349, 355 (1993). At issue here is the scope of the exception where "rights in immovable property situated in the United States are in issue." § 1605(a)(4). Petitioners contend that the language "rights in immovable property" limits the reach of the exception to actions contesting ownership or possession. The City argues that the exception encompasses additional rights in immovable property, including tax liens. Each party claims international practice at the time of the FSIA's adoption supports its view. We agree with the City.

A

We begin, as always, with the text of the statute. *Limtiaco v. Camacho*, 549 U.S. 483 (2007). The FSIA provides: "A foreign state shall not be immune from the jurisdiction of courts of the United States ... in any case ... in which ... rights in immovable property situated in the United States are in issue." 28 U.S.C. § 1605(a)(4). Contrary to petitioners'

---

1. The City concedes that even if a court of competent jurisdiction declares the liens valid, petitioners are immune from foreclosure proceedings. See Brief for Respondent 40 (noting that there is no FSIA immunity exception for enforcement actions). The City claims, however, that the declarations of validity are necessary for three reasons. First, once a court has declared property tax liens valid, foreign sovereigns traditionally concede and pay. Second, if the foreign sovereign fails to pay in the face of a valid court judgment, that country's foreign aid may be reduced by the United States by 110% of the outstanding debt. See Foreign Operations, Export Financing, and Related Programs Appropriations Act, 2006, § 543(a), 119 Stat. 2214 (hereinafter Foreign Operations); Consolidated Appropriations Act of 2005, § 543(a), 118 Stat. 3011 (hereinafter Consolidated Appropriations). Third, the liens would be enforceable against subsequent purchasers. 5 Restatement of Property § 540 (1944).

position, § 1605(a)(4) does not expressly limit itself to cases in which the specific right at issue is title, ownership, or possession. Neither does it specifically exclude cases in which the validity of a lien is at issue. Rather, the exception focuses more broadly on "rights in" property. Accordingly, we must determine whether an action seeking a declaration of the validity of a tax lien places "rights in immovable property ... in issue."

At the time of the FSIA's adoption in 1976, a "lien" was defined as "[a] charge or security or incumbrance upon property." Black's Law Dictionary 1072 (4th ed. 1951). "Incumbrance," in turn, was defined as "[a]ny right to, or interest in, land which may subsist in another to the diminution of its value...." *Id.*, at 908; see also *id.*, at 941 (8th ed. 2004) (defining "lien" as a "legal right or interest that a creditor has in another's property"). New York law defines "tax lien" in accordance with these general definitions. See N. Y. Real Prop. Tax Law Ann. § 102(21) (West Supp. 2007) (" 'Tax lien' means an unpaid tax ... which is an encumbrance of real property ..."). This Court, interpreting the Bankruptcy Code, has also recognized that a lienholder has a property interest, albeit a "nonpossessory" interest. *United States v. Security Industrial Bank*, 459 U.S. 70, 76 (1982).

The practical effects of a lien bear out these definitions of liens as interests in property. A lien on real property runs with the land and is enforceable against subsequent purchasers. See 5 Restatement of Property § 540 (1944). As such, "a lien has an immediate adverse effect upon the amount which [could be] receive[d] on a sale, ..." constitut[ing] a direct interference with the property...." Republic of Argentina v. New York, 25 N. Y. 2d 252, 262 (1969). A tax lien thus inhibits one of the quintessential rights of property ownership—the right to convey. It is therefore plain that a suit to establish the validity of a lien implicates "rights in immovable property."

B

Our reading of the text is supported by two well-recognized and related purposes of the FSIA: adoption of the restrictive view of sovereign immunity and codification of international law at the time of the FSIA's enactment. * * *

As a threshold matter, property ownership is not an inherently sovereign function. See *Schooner Exchange v. M'Faddon,* 11 U.S. 116 (1812) ("A prince, by acquiring private property in a foreign country, may possibly be considered as subjecting that property to the territorial jurisdiction, he may be considered as so far laying down the prince, and assuming the character of a private individual"). In addition, the FSIA was also meant "to codify ... the pre-existing real property exception to sovereign immunity recognized by international practice." [*Asociacion de Reclamantes v. United Mexican States,* 735 F.2d 1517], at 1521 (Scalia, J.). Therefore, it is useful to note that international practice at the time of the FSIA's enactment also supports the City's view that these sovereigns are not immune. The most recent restatement of foreign relations law at the time of the FSIA's enactment states that a foreign sovereign's immunity does not extend to "an action to obtain possession of or establish a property interest in immovable property located in the territory of the state exercising jurisdiction." Restatement (Second) of Foreign Relations Law of the United States § 68(b), p 205 (1965). As stated above, because an action seeking the declaration of the validity of a tax lien on property is a suit to establish an interest in such property, such an action would be allowed under this rule.

* * *

Because the statutory text and the acknowledged purposes of the FSIA make it clear that a suit to establish the validity of a tax lien places "rights in immovable property . . . in issue," we affirm the judgment of the Court of Appeals and remand the case for further proceedings consistent with this opinion.

It is so ordered.

JUSTICE STEVENS, with whom JUSTICE BREYER joins, dissenting.

* * *

* * * At bottom, this case is not about the validity of the city's title to immovable property, or even the validity of its automatic prejudgment lien. Rather, it is a dispute over a foreign sovereign's tax liability. If Congress had intended the statute to waive sovereign immunity in tax litigation, I think it would have said so.

Accordingly, I respectfully dissent.

NOTES

1. *Immovable Property.* Section 1605(a)(4) of the FSIA provides for denial of immunity in regard to claims to immovable property situated in the United States, irrespective of whether the property is of a commercial nature. This denial extends even to property used for diplomatic or consular purposes. See S. Rep. No. 94–1310, at 20 (1976); see also Restatement (Third) § 455(1) and (2). The reason usually given for this exception to state immunity is that real property, unless it is used for diplomatic or consular purposes, is "so indissolubly connected with the territory of a State that the State of the situs cannot permit the exercise of any other jurisdiction in respect thereof * * *" Harvard Research in International Law, Competence of Courts in Regard to Foreign States, art. 9, 26 A.J.I.L. Supp. 451, 578 (1932). It has also been asserted that a state, by acquiring real property located in the territory of another state, voluntarily submits itself to the jurisdiction of the situs state (i.e., "waives" its immunity) in matters regarding its interests in the property. *Storelli v. Government of the French Republic*, [1923–24] Ann. Dig. 129 (Court of Rome, Italy, 1924); see also Restatement (Third) § 455, Comment *b*.

2. *Tax Liens.* In *Permanent Mission of India*, Justice Thomas, writing for the Court, held that property ownership was not inherently a sovereign function and noted that international practice at the time of the FSIA's

enactment supported the view that sovereigns acquiring foreign property were not immune. Since the effect of a tax lien was to inhibit the right to convey land, a lawsuit to establish the validity of a lien implicated "rights in immovable property." By contrast, Justices Stevens and Breyer dissented, characterizing the suit as one brought to "establish a foreign sovereign's tax liabilities." Who had the better argument? See Shapiro, The Immovable Property Exception to a State's Sovereign Immunity—Permanent Mission of India to the United Nations v. City of New York, 31 Suffolk Transnat'l L. Rev. 719 (2008).

3. *Inherited Property.* According to the 1976 Senate Judiciary Committee Report on the FSIA, "[t]here is general agreement that a foreign state may not claim immunity when the suit against it relates to rights in property, real or personal, obtained by gift or inherited by the foreign state and situated or administered in the country where suit is brought." S. Rep. No. 94–1310, at 20 (1976). What is the basis for this denial of immunity?

4. *Intangible Property.* In *Nemariam v. Republic of Ethiopia*, 491 F.3d 470 (D.C. Cir. 2007), Eritreans brought an action against the Republic of Ethiopia and the Central Bank of Ethiopia claiming the unlawful taking of bank and non-bank accounts in Ethiopia. The defendants pleaded sovereign immunity, whereupon the plaintiffs invoked Section 1605(a)(3) of the FSIA. The D.C. Circuit found that Section 1605(a)(3) applies only to tangible property, a position taken by other courts, and that the freezing of the accounts did not amount to "owning" or "operating" such property. Would the action have failed in any event due to the act-of-state doctrine (see p. 670, since the taking occurred in Ethiopia? Note that the Hickenlooper Amendment, in overriding the act of state doctrine, has been construed to apply only to tangible property. See *Canadian Overseas Ores Ltd. v. Compania de Acero Pacifico S.A.*, 528 F.Supp. 1337 (S.D.N.Y. 1982), aff'd 727 F.2d 274 (2d Cir. 1984).

5. *Eminent Domain.* May a state rely on its immunity in order to resist eminent domain or other proceedings directed against its property by the state in which the property is located? On the expropriation or requisition of a foreign state's chattels, see the position taken by the United States in 1941 in connection with the seizure of eighteen aircraft purchased in the United States by Peru. A memorandum prepared by the U.S. State Department Legal Adviser's Office stated that "[e]very state undoubtedly possesses the right in case of emergency and subject to compensation to seize any foreign property on its territory." [1941] 7 For. Rel. 518. In proceedings before the U.S. Court of Claims, Switzerland did not argue that the United States had violated international law in requisitioning certain property belonging to the Swiss government. *Swiss Confederation v. United States*, 108 Ct.Cl. 388, 70 F.Supp. 235 (1947); *Swiss Fed. Rys. v. United States*, 125 Ct.Cl. 444, 112 F.Supp. 357 (1953).

E.   EXCEPTION FOR TORTS

ARGENTINE REPUBLIC v. AMERADA
HESS SHIPPING CORP.

Supreme Court of the United States, 1989
488 U.S. 428 (some footnotes omitted; some footnotes renumbered)

[For the facts and initial reasoning of the Court in this case, see *supra* p. 860.]

Having determined that the FSIA provides the sole basis for obtaining jurisdiction over a foreign state in federal court, we turn to whether any of the exceptions enumerated in the Act apply here. These exceptions include cases involving the waiver of immunity, § 1605(a)(1), commercial activities occurring in the United States or causing a direct effect in this country, § 1605(a)(2), property expropriated in violation of international law, § 1605(a)(3), inherited, gift, or immovable property located in the United States, § 1605(a)(4), noncommercial torts occurring in the United States, § 1605(a)(5), and maritime liens, § 1605(b). We agree with the District Court that none of the FSIA's exceptions applies on these facts.
* * *

Respondents assert that the FSIA exception for noncommercial torts, § 1605(a)(5), is most in point. * * * Section 1605(a)(5) is limited by its terms, however, to those cases in which the damage to or loss of property occurs *in the United States*. Congress' primary purpose in enacting § 1605(a)(5) was to eliminate a foreign state's immunity for traffic accidents and other torts committed in the United States, for which liability is imposed under domestic tort law. See H.R.Rep., at 14, 20–21; S.Rep., at 14, 20–21.

* * *

The result in this case is not altered by the fact that petitioner's alleged tort may have had effects in the United States. Respondents state, for example, that the Hercules was transporting oil intended for use in this country and that the loss of the ship disrupted contractual payments due in New York. * * * Under the commercial activity exception to the FSIA, § 1605(a)(2), a foreign state may be liable for its commercial activities "outside the territory of the United States" having a "direct effect" inside the United States. But the noncommercial tort exception, § 1605(a)(5), upon which respondents rely, makes no mention of "territory outside the United States" or of "direct effects" in the United States. Congress' decision to use explicit language in § 1605(a)(2), and not to do so in § 1605(a)(5), indicates that the exception in § 1605(a)(5) covers only torts occurring within the territorial jurisdiction of the United States. Respondents do not claim that § 1605(a)(2) covers these facts.

We also disagree with respondents' claim that certain international agreements entered into by petitioner and by the United States create an exception to the FSIA here. * * *

We hold that the FSIA provides the sole basis for obtaining jurisdiction over a foreign state in the courts of this country, and that none of the enumerated exceptions to the Act apply to the facts of this case. The judgment of the Court of Appeals is therefore

Reversed.

NOTES

1. *Scope of the Exception*. Section 1605(a)(5) denies immunity for most non-commercial torts causing "personal injury or death, or damage to or loss of property." As to the basis in international law for this denial of immunity, see S. Rep. No. 94–1310, at 20–21 (1976); see also Restatement (Third) § 454.

2. *Assassination on Embassy Row*. It is commonly stated that this exception provides a basis for circumventing immunity of a foreign state that is responsible for a "slip-and-fall" injury at its embassy or a vehicle collision by an embassy driver. Yet not all cases entail garden-variety torts. A prominent case involving this exception is *Letelier v. Republic of Chile*, 488 F.Supp. 665 (D.D.C. 1980), judgment entered, 502 F.Supp. 259 (D.D.C. 1980). Chile was held not to be immune from suit in respect of an assassination its covert agents undertook in Washington, D.C., by means of a car bombing. For later proceedings involving an unsuccessful effort to execute the judgment against Chile's national airline, see 748 F.2d 790 (2d Cir.1984), cert. denied, 471 U.S. 1125 (1985). The matter was finally settled by intergovernmental agreement. See materials at 30 I.L.M. 421 (1990); 31 I.L.M. 1 (1992). For another case involving allegations of political assassination, see *Liu v. Republic of China*, 892 F.2d 1419 (9th Cir. 1989) (federal choice of law rule points to California law on liability of Republic of China/Taiwan for acts of its agents resulting in a death in California).

3. *Torts outside the United States*. As is apparent in *Amerada Hess*, from the beginning section 1605(a)(5) was generally ruled inapplicable when the tort or injury occurred outside of the United States. See *Persinger v. Islamic Republic of Iran*, 729 F.2d 835 (D.C. Cir. 1984) (detention of hostages in U.S. embassy in Iran held not to have occurred in the United States); *Frolova v. U.S.S.R.*, 761 F.2d 370 (7th Cir. 1985) (alleged violation of human rights did not occur in the United States); *Siderman v. Republic of Argentina*, 965 F.2d 699 (9th Cir. 1992) (torture outside the United States does not confer jurisdiction under the FSIA). Certain torts that arise from the conduct of terrorist-designated states, however, fall within the scope of the terrorist-state exception, discussed *infra* p. 893.

F.   EXCEPTION FOR ENFORCEMENT OF ARBITRAL AGREEMENTS OR AWARDS

In 1988, the FSIA was amended to deal with problems that had arisen in regard to arbitration agreements to which a foreign state was a party. Subsection 6 was added to Section 1605(a) to permit an action to enforce such an arbitration agreement if "(A) the arbitration takes place or is intended to take place in the United States, (B) the agreement or award is or may be governed by a treaty or other international agreement in force for the United States calling for the recognition and enforcement of arbitral awards, (C) the underlying claim, save for the agreement to arbitrate, could have been brought in a United States court under this section or section 1607, or (D) [the waiver provision of § 1605(a)(1)] is otherwise applicable." The 1988 amendment also added subsection 6 to Section 1610(a) providing for execution of a judgment based on an arbitral award rendered against the foreign state, provided such execution is not inconsistent with the arbitration agreement. On the FSIA and arbitration agreements, see Kahale, New Legislation in the United States Facilitates Enforcement of Arbitral Agreements and Awards Against Foreign States, 6 J. Int'l Arb. 57 (1989).

Are the limitations of the amendment desirable? Restatement (Third) § 456(2)(b) provides that an agreement to arbitrate is a waiver of immunity from jurisdiction in an action to compel arbitration or to enforce the award. Is this the preferable rule? On the circumstances in which an arbitration agreement may be regarded as a waiver of immunity, see Restatement (Third) § 456, Reporters' Note 3.

The impact of the FSIA's arbitration provisions was considered in *International Insurance Co. v. Caja Nacional de Ahorro y Seguro*, 293 F.3d 392 (7th Cir. 2002). In that case, a U.S. insurance company contracted with an Argentinean insurance company for the purchase of reinsurance. The contracts contained a clause providing for arbitration in Chicago if a dispute arose. When Caja Nacional breached the contract, International Insurance Co. initiated arbitration in the United States and won a default award after Caja failed to appear. Then, International Insurance Co. sought confirmation of the award in U.S. court. When Caja appeared in U.S. court to plead immunity as an instrumentality of a foreign sovereign (Argentina), the Seventh Circuit stated:

> Section 1605(a)(6)(A) of the FSIA provides that a foreign state or instrumentality is not immune from the jurisdiction of American courts in any proceeding to confirm an arbitral award where that foreign state or instrumentality agreed to submit to arbitration and the arbitration takes place in the United States.... Article XXI of each contract contained a provision that arbitration would occur in Chicago, Illinois, unless some other location was mutually agreed upon by the parties. By agreeing to a contract designating Chicago, Illinois as the site of arbitration, even if it is a foreign instrumentality, Caja waived its immunity in a proceeding to confirm the arbitral award.

293 F.3d at 397. The court also considered whether Caja was entitled to immunity, under FSIA Section 1609, from an order requiring Caja to post a pre-judgment security. Here the court found that any immunity under Section 1609 was waived by virtue of Argentina's adherence to the New York Convention on Recognition and Enforcement of Foreign Arbitral

Awards, June 10, 1958, 21 U.S.T. 2517, 330 U.N.T.S. 38, and the Inter–American Convention on International Commercial Arbitration (Panama Convention), Jan. 30, 1975, 1438 U.N.T.S. 245, OAS T.S. No. 42. According to the court:

> The purpose of the New York Convention, and similarly the Panama Convention, is to "encourage the recognition and enforcement of commercial arbitration agreements in international contracts and to unify the standards by which agreement to arbitrate are observed and arbitral awards are enforced in the signatory countries." *Scherk v. Alberto–Culver Co.,* 417 U.S. 506, 520 n. 15 (1974). Article VI of the New York Convention states, "[i]f an application for the setting aside or suspension of the award has been made to a competent authority ... the authority before which the award is sought to be relied upon may, if it considers it proper, ... on the application of the party claiming enforcement of the award, *order the other party to give suitable security.*"[New York Convention], art. VI (emphasis added). Similarly, Article 6 of the Panama Convention states, "[i]f the competent authority ... has been requested to annul or suspend the arbitral decision, the authority ... at the request of the party requesting execution, *may also instruct the other party to provide appropriate guarantees.*" [Panama Convention], art. 6 (emphasis added). The emphasized language of these Conventions allowing a court to impose a security requirement is very explicit. Thus the court-ordered pre-judgment deposit of security is clearly appropriate.

293 F.3d at 399–400.

Should an arbitration clause in an agreement between two states be treated in the same manner for this purpose as an arbitration clause in an agreement between a state and an individual? Under Article 17 of the Convention on Jurisdictional Immunities of States and their Property, discussed *infra* in Section 3, when a state enters into an agreement to arbitrate disputes arising out of a commercial transaction, that state cannot invoke a defense of immunity in a subsequent arbitration or in proceedings relating to the arbitration and the arbitral award, unless the agreement provides otherwise. An agreement to submit to settlement pursuant to the Convention on the Settlement of Investment Disputes Between States and Nationals of Other States, 17 U.S.T. 1270, raises no question of waiver, since the decision of the tribunal has the force of a judgment in states adhering to the Convention (Article 54(1)).

G. TERRORIST–STATE EXCEPTION

GATES v. SYRIAN ARAB REPUBLIC

District Court for the District of Columbia, 2008
580 F.Supp.2d 53

It was a sunny day somewhere in Iraq and a light wind blew the long curtains into the room through the open door. A group of men clad in total black, faces covered, stood on a Persian rug facing a camera. Before them, a single man knelt. Dressed in an orange jumpsuit, hands bound behind his back, feet similarly bound, with eyes covered and mouth gagged, he rarely moved. One of the standing men began to read a proclamation in Arabic. It continued at length. Suddenly he stopped. The man in the orange jumpsuit tensed. Another of the men in black stepped forward and knocked the kneeling man over onto his side. Brandishing a knife, the man in black began to slice at the neck of the victim lying on the floor. The dying man audibly moaned and gurgled, as it took some time to cut all around his neck and through his bones before the head could be lifted in seeming triumph.

There is no doubt that al-Tawhid wal-Jihad ("al-Qaeda in Iraq") beheaded U.S. civilian contractors Jack Armstrong and Jack Hensley in the manner described, which it videotaped and played on the Internet for all the world, and ultimately this Court, to see. The question raised by this lawsuit is whether the Syrian Arab Republic can be held liable for money damages to the families of the two men pursuant to the Foreign Sovereign Immunities Act (the "FSIA"), 28 U.S.C. § 1602 *et seq.*

I. PROCEDURAL POSTURE

Plaintiffs are Francis Gates and Jan Smith, the mother and sister of Jack Armstrong, and Pati and Sara Hensley, the widow and minor daughter of Jack Hensley. Plaintiffs filed this action on August 25, 2006, against Defendants who include: the Syrian Arab Republic ("Syria"); the president of Syria, Basharal–Assad; the Syrian Military Intelligence, known as the al-Mukhabarat al-Askariya; and the Director of Military Intelligence, General Asif Shawkat. Plaintiffs allege that, acting through these principals, Syria provided material support and resources to the al-Tawhid wal-Jihad ("al-Qaeda in Iraq") and its leader, Abu Mus'ab al-Zarqawi ("Zarqawi"). Plaintiffs assert a cause of action under the FSIA, 28 U.S.C. § 1605A, as well as the following causes of action under state law: battery; assault; false imprisonment; intentional infliction of emotional distress; wrongful death; action for survival damages; conspiracy; and aiding and abetting.

None of the Defendants filed an answer or otherwise appeared. The Court proceeded to a default setting as provided by 28 U.S.C. § 1608(e), which requires a court to enter a default judgment against a non-responding foreign state only where "the claimant establishes his claim or right to relief by evidence satisfactory to the court." Id. The Court held a three-day hearing on liability and damages beginning on January 7, 2008. Plaintiffs presented evidence in the form of live testimony, videotaped testimony, affidavit, and original documentary and video graphic evidence.

[The Court then recounts in detail the facts of the murders and information concerning Syrian support for al-Qaeda in Iraq. On the latter point, the Court concludes: "In this environment, it is clear that support for Zarqawi and his network from Syrian territory or Syrian government actors could not have been accomplished without the authorization of the

Syrian government and Syrian Military Intelligence through President Assad and General Shawkat."]

III.   CONCLUSIONS OF LAW

* * *

* * * Under § 1605A(c), U.S. citizens who are victims of state-sponsored terrorism can sue a responsible foreign state directly. Significantly, state law no longer controls the nature of the liability and damages that may be sought when it is a foreign government that is sued: Congress has provided the "specific source of law" for recovery. See *Acree* [*v. Republic of Iraq*, 370 F.3d 41, 59 (D.C. Cir. 2004).]. By providing for a private right of action and by precisely enumerating the types of damages recoverable, Congress has eliminated the inconsistencies that arise in these cases when they are decided under state law. * * *

* * *

Here, Plaintiffs effectively brought suit only against Syria because they served all Defendants under 28 U.S.C. § 1608(a)(3), claiming that all Defendants in this case should be treated as the foreign state itself. The only cause of action permissible against Syria is a federal cause of action under the FSIA. Thus, Plaintiffs' claims under state law will be dismissed. Plaintiffs have presented evidence satisfactory to the Court in support all elements of a claim under § 1605A. Syria was a state-sponsor of terrorism, and the Plaintiffs are and decedents were U.S. Citizens. The critical issue in this case is whether Syria, and its officials acting within the scope of their employment, provided material support and resources to Zarqawi and to al-Qaeda in Iraq.

* * *

It was the Syrian government's foreign policy to support al-Qaeda in Iraq in order to topple the nascent Iraqi democratic government. In 2003, the foreign minister of Syria stated publicly that it was in Syria's interest to see the U.S. invasion of Iraq fail. The very brutality of Zarqawi's acts against American civilians—broadcast on the Internet for greatest impact—was intended to weaken U.S. resolve to succeed in Iraq. Syria's aid to Zarqawi, from at least 2002 to 2005, was no impetuous or unknowing act. Indeed, not only was it foreseeable that Zarqawi and his terrorist organization would engage in terrorist activities in Iraq to destabilize that country (in concert with Syrian foreign policy), but also Zarqawi had beheaded civilian Nicholas Berg and could be expected to attack civilians again. The murders of Jack Armstrong and Jack Hensley were a foreseeable consequence of Syria's aid and support to Zarqawi and al-Qaeda in Iraq.

In sum, jurisdiction over Syria is consistent with § 1605A(a), the state-sponsored terrorism exception to sovereign immunity, and Plaintiffs have provided evidence satisfactory to the Court in support of their private cause of action for damages under § 1605A(c).

* * *

Damages for a private action for proven acts of terrorism by foreign states under the FSIA § 1605A(c) may include economic damages, solatium, pain and suffering, and punitive damages. 28 U.S.C. § 1605A(c).

* * *

As amended, the FSIA now specifically allows an award of punitive damages for personal injury or death resulting from an act of state-sponsored terrorism. 28 U.S.C. § 1605A(c). Several factors are considered in the analysis of whether to award punitive damages and how substantial an award should be. Those factors include the character of the defendant's acts; the nature and extent of harm to the Plaintiffs that the Defendant caused or intended to cause; the need for deterrence; and the wealth of the Defendant. Restatement (Second) Torts § 908(1)–(2) (1977). The purpose of punitive damages is two-fold: to punish those who engage in outrageous conduct and to deter others from similar conduct in the future. See Eisenfeld v. Islamic Republic of Iran, 172 F. Supp. 2d 1, 9 (D.D.C. 2000). "This cost functions both as a direct deterrent, and also as a disabling mechanism: if several large punitive damage awards issue against a foreign state sponsor of terrorism, the state's financial capacity to provide funding will be curtailed." Flatow [v. Islamic Republic of Iran, 999 F. Supp. 1, 33 (D.D.C. 1998)].

IV. CONCLUSION

Money judgments cannot compensate Jack Armstrong or Jack Hensley for their torture and deaths or compensate their family members for their losses. The law, however, cannot let depraved lawlessness go unremarked and without consequence. Syria provided crucial support to Zarqawi and al-Qaeda in Iraq, without which they could not have entered Iraq or engaged in a long string of terrorist activities under Syrian protection. Default judgment will be entered in favor of Plaintiffs in the following amounts:

Economic Damages to the Estate of Jack Armstrong—$1,051,377.00

Pain and Suffering to the Estate of Jack Armstrong—$50,000,000.00

Punitive Damages to the Estate of Jack Armstrong—$150,000,000.00

Solatium to Francis Gates—$3,000,000.00

Solatium to Jan Smith—$1,500,000.00

Economic Damages to the Estate of Jack Hensley—$1,358,210.00

Pain and Suffering to the Estate of Jack Hensley—$50,000,000.00

Punitive Damages to the Estate of Jack Hensley—$150,000,000.00

Solatium to Pati Hensley—$3,000,000.00

Solatium to Sara Hensley—$3,000,000.00

NOTES

1. *Enactment of the Terrorist–State Exception*. In 1996, the FSIA was amended by the addition of paragraph(a)(7) to Section 1605, which denied a foreign state immunity from jurisdiction in a case of "an act of torture, extrajudicial killing, aircraft sabotage, [or] hostage taking" if the foreign state had been designated as a state sponsor of terrorism, unless (1) the act occurred in that state's territory and that state had not been afforded an opportunity to arbitrate; or (2) neither the claimant nor the victim was a U.S. national. (The text has now been codified at Section 1605A). The text of this provision raised questions: first, whether it also applied to an agent of the foreign state; and second, whether it not only precluded reliance on sovereign immunity, but also created a private right of action.

After passage of the new exception, U.S. courts started handing down large judgments against terrorist-state defendants, who often failed to appear, thus resulting in default judgments. After issuance of such judgments, successive Administrations have intervened to block the judicial attachment of frozen assets to satisfy the judgments, which resulted in repeated amendments of the exception and other measures by Congress designed to assist victims in obtaining compensation. See, e.g., Zaffuto, A "Pirate's Victory": President Clinton's Approach to the New FSIA Exception Leaves the Victors Empty Handed, 74 Tul. L. Rev. 685, 697 (1999). Thus, Congress enacted the Victims of Trafficking and Violence Protection Act of 2000 ("VTVPA"), Pub. L. No. 106–386, 114 Stat. 1464 (2000), in part to liquidate some frozen assets to pay claims and to provide U.S. funds to compensate some victims holding judgments at the time, while the Terrorism Risk Insurance Act of 2002 ("TRIA"), Pub. L. No. 107–297, 116 Stat. 2322 (2002) allowed the attachment of certain blocked assets of terrorist-states.

2. *Cause of Action for the Terrorist–State Exception*. As a general matter, the FSIA provides exceptions to immunity, but does not itself provide a cause of action to plaintiffs; a cause of action must be found elsewhere in federal or state law. However, when Section 1605(a)(7) was adopted, Congress also enacted a statutory cause of action against terrorist-states, which became known as the "Flatow Amendment." See Civil Liability for Acts of State Sponsored Terrorism, Pub. L. 104–208, 110 Stat. 3009 (1996) (previously codified at 28 U.S.C. § 1605 note (2000)). Initially, U.S. courts used the Flatow Amendment to allow actions against the terrorist states themselves, but later courts ruled that the language of the Flatow Amendment was actually rather limited; it did not create a cause of action against terrorist states themselves, but only against their officials, employees, and agents. See *Cicippio–Puleo v. Islamic Republic of Iran*, 353 F.3d 1024 (D.C. Cir. 2004); see also Deutsch, Suing State Sponsors of Terrorism Under the Foreign Sovereign Immunities Act: Giving Life to the Jurisdictional Grant After Cicippio–Puleo, 38 Int'l Law. 891 (2004).

In order to address that limitation, as well as further to assist victims in satisfying their judgments against defendant states' assets, Congress in January 2008 revised and recodified the terrorist-state exception. The National

Defense Authorization Act for Fiscal Year 2008 (NDAA), Pub. L. No. 110–181, 122 Stat. 3, § 1083, recodified the terrorist-state exception by repealing § 1605(a)(7) of Title 28 and adding a new version codified at § 1605A of Title 28. The cause of action, which appears in § 1605A(c), covers foreign terrorist states as well as their agents, officials and employees. Further, the new section indicates the types of damages that may be recovered, including economic damages, solatium, pain and suffering, and punitive damages. For an account of the original enactment of the terrorist-state exception, the early cases construing it, compensatory amounts paid to victims, and the 2008 recodification, see Elsea, Suits Against Terrorist States by Victims of Terrorism, CRS Report No. RL31258 (Aug. 8, 2008).

3. *Listed States.* The State Department classifies a state as a sponsor of terrorism pursuant to § 6(j) of the Export Administration Act of 1979, 50 App. U.S.C. § 2405(j) (2000), § 620A of the Foreign Assistance Act, 22 U.S.C. § 2371 (2000), and § 40(d) of the Arms Export Control Act, 22 U.S.C. § 2780(d) (2000). Published annually, the list contains as of early 2009 the following four states: Cuba (first listed in 1982), Iran (1984), Sudan (1993), and Syria (1979). Afghanistan, Iraq, Libya, North Korea, and South Yemen were previously listed, but are no longer designated as state sponsors of terrorism. The principal effects of being a listed state do not relate to the FSIA, but rather to four categories of sanctions that the designation triggers: restrictions on U.S. foreign assistance; a ban on U.S. defense exports and sales; certain controls over exports of dual use items; and miscellaneous financial and other restrictions. For a discussion of such listings, see Peed, Blacklisting As Foreign Policy: The Politics and Law of Listing Terror States, 54 Duke L.J. 1321 (2005). If a state is not listed, the terrorist-state exception may not be invoked against it. See, e.g., *In re Terrorist Attacks on September 11, 2001*, 538 F.3d 71 (2d Cir. 2008) (effort to sue Saudi government).

4. *Jurisdiction to Prescribe?* Is there a basis under international law for the U.S. exercise of legislative jurisdiction under the terrorist-state exception? Could the universality principle or the passive personality principle (or both) be applicable? See Chapter 11, pp. 793 & 804.

5. *Jurisdiction to Adjudicate?* In *Price v. Libya*, 294 F.3d 82 (D.C. Cir. 2002), two U.S. nationals sued Libya for alleged torture and hostage taking under 28 U.S.C. § 1605(a)(7). Plaintiffs alleged that they had been unlawfully arrested and kicked, beaten, and detained in deplorable conditions by Libyan officials. Libya moved to dismiss, in part on the ground that the court lacked personal jurisdiction under the due process clause. The D.C. Circuit ruled that the foreign state is not a person protected by the Fifth Amendment and therefore rejected the motion. Do you think there is a proper basis for denying a foreign state the due process protection that the Fifth Amendment grants to any "person"? The Court noted that the issue had not been decided by the Supreme Court, but that the Court had ruled in *South Carolina v. Katzenbach*, 383 U.S. 301 (1966) that South Carolina was not a "person" and that it discerned no compelling reason for treating foreign sovereigns more favorably than "States of the Union." Do you agree? See Halverson, Is a Foreign State a "Person"? Does it Matter?: Personal Jurisdiction, Due Process, and the Foreign Sovereign Immunities Act, 34 N.Y.U. J. Int'l L. & Pol. 115 (2001); Damrosch, Foreign States and the Constitution, 73 Va. L. Rev. 483, 520

(1987) ("The most a foreign state can demand is that other states observe international law, not that they enforce provisions of domestic law.").

6. *Miscellaneous Cases.* As of early 2009, the U.S. Supreme Court has not directly addressed the FSIA terrorist-state exception. However, several cases have arisen in lower U.S. courts involving notorious incidents abroad, including hostage-taking in Lebanon, Iran and Iraq, and attacks on Americans in Israel by Hezbollah. In *Rux v. Sudan*, 495 F. Supp. 2d 541 (2007), a U.S. court ruled that, under the terrorist-state exception of the FISA, Sudan was civilly liable for the death of seventeen sailors on board of the *U.S.S. Cole.* For an analysis of this decision, see Bahr, Is the Gavel Mightier Than The Sword? Fighting Terrorism in American Courts: The Problematic Implications of Using the Foreign Sovereign Immunity Act to Compensate Military Victims of America's War of Terror, 15 Geo. Mason L. Rev. 1115 (2008); see also Kotlarczyk, "The Provision of Material Support and Resources" and Lawsuits against State Sponsors of Terrorism, 96 Geo. L.J. 2029 (2008); Taylor, Another Front on the War on Terrorism? Problems with Recent Changes to Foreign Sovereign Immunities Act, 45 Ariz. L. Rev. 533 (2003).

H. IMMUNITY FOR STATE AGENCIES OR INSTRUMENTALITIES

The FSIA accords immunity to a "foreign state," but what entities are considered part of a foreign state? Section 1603(a) defines "foreign state" as including a political subdivision (e.g., both the federal government in Canada and the government of the province of Quebec) and as including any "agency or instrumentality." Section 1603(b) then defines "agency or instrumentality" as an entity which is a separate legal person from the foreign state and yet is either an "organ" of the state or whose majority shares (or other ownership interest) are owned by a foreign state.

In considering what is an "organ" of a foreign state, the Second Circuit Court of Appeals has applied a balancing test. For example, in *In re Terrorist Attacks on September 11, 2001*, 538 F.3d 71 (2d Cir. 2008), the court assessed whether an entity called the Saudi High Commission for Relief to Bosnia and Herzegovina constituted an "organ" of the Saudi government. In finding that it was, the court considered the following facts: the Commission was created by the Saudi government for a national purpose; the Commission was supervised by the government; the government hired and paid many of the employees of the Commission; the Commission was accorded exclusive authority within Saudi Arabia to collect charitable contributions for distribution in Bosnia and Herzegovina; and, like other Saudi government entities, the Commission could be sued in Saudi administrative tribunals.

In considering whether an entity is an agency or instrumentality by virtue of being owned by the foreign state, questions can arise concerning how direct the ownership interest must be and on what dates it must exist. Such questions were explored in the following case.

DOLE FOOD COMPANY v. PATRICKSON

Supreme Court of the United States, 2003
538 U.S. 468

JUSTICE KENNEDY delivered the opinion of the Court.

Foreign states may invoke certain rights and immunities in litigation under the Foreign Sovereign Immunities Act of 1976 (FSIA or Act), Pub. L. 94–583, 90 Stat. 2891. Some of the Act's provisions also may be invoked by a corporate entity that is an "instrumentality" of a foreign state as defined by the Act. *Republic of Argentina v. Weltover, Inc.*, 504 U.S. 607, 611 (1992); *Verlinden B. V. v. Central Bank of Nigeria*, 461 U.S. 480, 488 (1983). The corporate entities in this action claim instrumentality status to invoke the Act's provisions allowing removal of state-court actions to federal court. As the action comes to us, it presents two questions. The first is whether a corporate subsidiary can claim instrumentality status where the foreign state does not own a majority of its shares but does own a majority of the shares of a corporate parent one or more tiers above the subsidiary. The second question is whether a corporation's instrumentality status is defined as of the time an alleged tort or other actionable wrong occurred or, on the other hand, at the time suit is filed. * * *

* * *

The underlying action was filed in a state court in Hawaii in 1997 against Dole Food Company and other companies (Dole petitioners). Plaintiffs in the action were a group of farm workers from Costa Rica, Ecuador, Guatemala, and Panama who alleged injury from exposure to dibromochloropropane, a chemical used as an agricultural pesticide in their home countries. The Dole petitioners impleaded petitioners Dead Sea Bromine Co., Ltd., and Bromine Compounds, Ltd. (collectively, the Dead Sea Companies). The merits of the suit are not before us.

* * *

II

A

Title 28 U.S.C. § 1441(d) governs removal of actions against foreign states. It provides that "any civil action brought in a State court against a foreign state as defined in [28 U.S.C. § 1603(a)] may be removed by the foreign state to the district court of the United States for the district and division embracing the place where such action is pending." See also 28 U.S.C. § 1330 (governing original jurisdiction). Section 1603(a), part of the FSIA, defines "foreign state" to include an "agency or instrumentality of a foreign state." "Agency or instrumentality of a foreign state" is defined, in turn, as:

"[A]ny entity—

(1) which is a separate legal person, corporate or otherwise, and

(2) which is an organ of a foreign state or political subdivision thereof, or a majority of whose shares or other ownership interest is owned by a foreign state or political subdivision thereof, and

(3) which is neither a citizen of a State of the United States ... nor created under the laws of any third country." § 1603(b).

B

The Court of Appeals resolved the question of the FSIA's applicability by holding that a subsidiary of an instrumentality is not itself entitled to instrumentality status. Its holding was correct.

The State of Israel did not have direct ownership of shares in either of the Dead Sea Companies at any time pertinent to this suit. Rather, these companies were, at various times, separated from the State of Israel by one or more intermediate corporate tiers. For example, from 1984–1985, Israel wholly owned a company called Israeli Chemicals, Ltd.; which owned a majority of shares in another company called Dead Sea Works, Ltd.; which owned a majority of shares in Dead Sea Bromine Co., Ltd.; which owned a majority of shares in Bromine Compounds, Ltd.

The Dead Sea Companies, as indirect subsidiaries of the State of Israel, were not instrumentalities of Israel under the FSIA at any time. Those companies cannot come within the statutory language which grants status as an instrumentality of a foreign state to an entity a "majority of whose shares or other ownership interest is owned by a foreign state or political subdivision thereof." § 1603(b)(2). We hold that only direct ownership of a majority of shares by the foreign state satisfies the statutory requirement.

Section 1603(b)(2) speaks of ownership. The Dead Sea Companies urge us to ignore corporate formalities and use the colloquial sense of that term. They ask whether, in common parlance, Israel would be said to own the Dead Sea Companies. We reject this analysis. In issues of corporate law structure often matters. It is evident from the Act's text that Congress was aware of settled principles of corporate law and legislated within that context. The language of § 1603(b)(2) refers to ownership of "shares," showing that Congress intended statutory coverage to turn on formal corporate ownership. Likewise, § 1603(b)(1), another component of the definition of instrumentality, refers to a "separate legal person, corporate or otherwise." In light of these indicia that Congress had corporate formalities in mind, we assess whether Israel owned shares in the Dead Sea Companies as a matter of corporate law, irrespective of whether Israel could be said to have owned the Dead Sea Companies in everyday parlance.

A basic tenet of American corporate law is that the corporation and its shareholders are distinct entities. See, *e.g.*, *First Nat. City Bank v. Banco Para el Comercio Exterior de Cuba*, 462 U.S. 611, 625 (1983) ("Separate legal personality has been described as 'an almost indispensable aspect of the public corporation'"); *Burnet v. Clark*, 287 U.S. 410

(1932) ("A corporation and its stock-holders are generally to be treated as separate entities"). An individual shareholder, by virtue of his ownership of shares, does not own the corporation's assets and, as a result, does not own subsidiary corporations in which the corporation holds an interest. See 1 Fletcher Cyclopedia of the Law of Private Corporations § 31 (rev. ed. 1999). A corporate parent which owns the shares of a subsidiary does not, for that reason alone, own or have legal title to the assets of the subsidiary; and, it follows with even greater force, the parent does not own or have legal title to the subsidiaries of the subsidiary. See *id.*, § 31, at 514 ("The properties of two corporations are distinct, though the same shareholders own or control both. A holding corporation does not own the subsidiary's property"). The fact that the shareholder is a foreign state does not change the analysis. See *First Nat. City Bank, supra,* at 626–627 ("Government instrumentalities established as juridical entities distinct and independent from their sovereign should normally be treated as such").

Applying these principles, it follows that Israel did not own a majority of shares in the Dead Sea Companies. The State of Israel owned a majority of shares, at various times, in companies one or more corporate tiers above the Dead Sea Companies, but at no time did Israel own a majority of shares in the Dead Sea Companies. Those companies were subsidiaries of other corporations.

The veil separating corporations and their shareholders may be pierced in some circumstances, and the Dead Sea Companies essentially urge us to interpret the FSIA as piercing the veil in all cases. The doctrine of piercing the corporate veil, however, is the rare exception, applied in the case of fraud or certain other exceptional circumstances, see, e.g., *Burnet, supra,* at 415; 1 *Fletcher, supra,* §§ 41 to 41.20, and usually determined on a case-by-case basis. The Dead Sea Companies have referred us to no authority for extending the doctrine so far that, as a categorical matter, all subsidiaries are deemed to be the same as the parent corporation. The text of the FSIA gives no indication that Congress intended us to depart from the general rules regarding corporate formalities.

* * *

We now turn to the second question before us, which provides an alternative reason for affirming the Court of Appeals. * * *

C

To be entitled to removal under § 1441(d), the Dead Sea Companies must show that they are entities "a majority of whose shares or other ownership interest is owned by a foreign state." § 1603(b)(2). We think the plain text of this provision, because it is expressed in the present tense, requires that instrumentality status be determined at the time suit is filed.

* * *

Any relationship recognized under the FSIA between the Dead Sea Companies and Israel had been severed before suit was commenced. As a result, the Dead Sea Companies would not be entitled to instrumentality status even if their theory that instrumentality status could be conferred on a subsidiary were accepted.

* * *

For these reasons, we hold first that a foreign state must itself own a majority of the shares of a corporation if the corporation is to be deemed an instrumentality of the state under the provisions of the FSIA; and we hold second that instrumentality status is determined at the time of the filing of the complaint.

I. IMMUNITY FROM EXECUTION AGAINST ASSETS

Before the FSIA, the U.S. State Department took the position that the property of a foreign state was absolutely immune from execution. This position had also been adopted by U.S. courts, the leading case being *Dexter & Carpenter v. Kunglig Jarnvagsstyrelsen*, 43 F.2d 705 (2d Cir. 1930). However, the U.S. position in this regard appeared not to be required by international law. Eminent authority supported the view that, under international law, the restrictive doctrine of immunity could properly be extended to deny immunity from execution against commercial, as distinguished from public, property of a foreign state. See, e.g., Lauterpacht, The Problem of Jurisdictional Immunities of Foreign States, 1951 Brit. Y.B.I.L. 220, 241–43; Restatement (Second) Foreign Relations Law of the United States, § 69, Reporter's Note 2 (1965).

FSIA Section 1610 changed prior U.S. practice and rulings by permitting execution on a foreign state's *commercial* property in the circumstances statutorily specified. It is to be noted that the commercial property upon which execution may be levied need not be used for the activity from which the claims for relief arose. Yet when the claim arises from the conduct of a foreign government, can the claimant execute a judgment in its favor against assets of an *instrumentality* that is owned by the foreign government?

FIRST NATIONAL CITY BANK v. BANCO PARA EL COMERCIO EXTERIOR DE CUBA

Supreme Court of the United States, 1983
462 U.S. 611 (some footnotes omitted; some footnotes renumbered)

JUSTICE O'CONNOR delivered the opinion of the Court.

In 1960 the Government of the Republic of Cuba established respondent Banco Para el Comercio Exterior de Cuba (Bancec) to serve as "[a]n official autonomous credit institution for foreign trade ... with full juridical capacity ... of its own...." Law No. 793, Art. 1 (1960), App. to Pet. for Cert.2d. In September 1960 Bancec sought to collect on a letter of credit issued by petitioner First National City Bank (now Citibank) in its favor in support of a contract for delivery of Cuban sugar to a buyer in the United States. Within days after Citibank received the request for collection, all of its assets in Cuba were seized and nationalized by the Cuban Government. When Bancec brought suit on the letter of credit in United States District Court [Feb. 1, 1961], Citibank counterclaimed [Mar. 8, 1961], asserting a right to set off the value of its seized Cuban assets. The question before us is whether Citibank may obtain such a setoff, notwithstanding the fact that Bancec was established as a separate juridical entity. [On July 7, 1961, Bancec filed a stipulation signed by the parties stating that Bancec had been dissolved and that its claim had been transferred to the Ministry of Foreign Trade, and agreeing that the Republic of Cuba may be substituted as plaintiff.] Applying principles of equity common to international law and federal common law, we conclude that Citibank may apply a setoff.

* * *

II

A

As an initial matter, Bancec contends that the Foreign Sovereign Immunities Act of 1976, 28 U.S.C. §§ 1602–1611 (FSIA), immunizes an instrumentality owned by a foreign government from suit on a counterclaim based on actions taken by that government. * * *

We disagree. The language and history of the FSIA clearly establish that the Act was not intended to affect the substantive law determining the liability of a foreign state or instrumentality, or the attribution of liability among instrumentalities of a foreign state. Section 1606 of the FSIA provides in relevant part that "[a]s to any claim for relief with respect to which a foreign state is not entitled to immunity ..., the foreign state shall be liable in the same manner and to the same extent as a private individual under like circumstances...." The House Report on the FSIA states:

> "The bill is not intended to affect the substantive law of liability. Nor is it intended to affect * * * the attribution of responsibility between or among entities of a foreign state; for example, whether the proper entity of a foreign state has been sued, or whether an entity sued is liable in whole or in part for the claimed wrong." H.R.Rep. No. 941487, p. 12 (1976), U.S.Code Cong. & Admin. News 1976, pp. 6604, 6610.

Thus, we conclude that the FSIA does not control the determination of whether Citibank may set off the value of its seized Cuban assets against Bancec's claim. * * *

B

We must next decide which body of law determines the effect to be given to Bancec's separate juridical status. Bancec contends that internationally recognized conflict-of-law principles require the application of the law of the state that establishes a government instrumentality—here Cuba—to determine whether the instrumentality may be held liable for actions taken by the sovereign.

We cannot agree. As a general matter, the law of the state of incorporation normally determines issues relating to the *internal* affairs of a corporation. Application of that body of law achieves the need for certainty and predictability of result while generally protecting the justified expectations of parties with interests in the corporation. See Restatement (Second) of Conflict of Laws § 302, Comments *a* & *e*, (1971). Cf. *Cort v. Ash*, 422 U.S. 66, 84 (1975). Different conflicts principles apply, however, where the rights of third parties *external* to the corporation are at issue. See Restatement (Second) of Conflict of Laws, *supra*, § 301. To give conclusive effect to the law of the chartering state in determining whether the separate juridical status of its instrumentality should be respected would permit the state to violate with impunity the rights of third parties under international law while effectively insulating itself from liability in foreign courts. We decline to permit such a result.[1]

Bancec contends in the alternative that international law must determine the resolution of the question presented. Citibank, on the other hand, suggests that federal common law governs. The expropriation claim against which Bancec seeks to interpose its separate juridical status arises under international law, which, as we have frequently reiterated, "is part of our law. . . ." *The Paquete Habana*, 175 U.S. 677, 700 (1900). As we set forth below, * * * the principles governing this case are common to both international law and federal common law, which in these circumstances is necessarily informed both by international law principles and by articulated congressional policies.

---

1. Pointing out that 28 U.S.C. § 1606, see *ante*, at 2596–2597, contains language identical to the Federal Tort Claims Act (FTCA), 28 U.S.C. § 2674, Bancec also contends alternatively that the FSIA, like the FTCA, requires application of the law of the forum State—here New York—including its conflicts principles. We disagree. Section 1606 provides that "[a]s to any claim for relief with respect to which a foreign state is not entitled to immunity . . ., the foreign state shall be liable in the same manner and to the same extent as a private individual under like circumstances." Thus, where state law provides a rule of liability governing private individuals, the FSIA requires the application of that rule to foreign states in like circumstances. The statute is silent, however, concerning the rule governing the attribution of liability *among* entities of a foreign state. In *Banco Nacional de Cuba v. Sabbatino*, 376 U.S. 398, 425 (1964), this Court declined to apply the State of New York's act of state doctrine in a diversity action between a United States national and an instrumentality of a foreign state, concluding that matters bearing on the Nation's foreign relations "should not be left to divergent and perhaps parochial state interpretations." When it enacted the FSIA, Congress expressly acknowledged "the importance of developing a uniform body of law" concerning the amenability of a foreign sovereign to suit in United States courts. H.R.Rep. No. 94–1487, p. 32 (1976). See *Verlinden B.V. v. Central Bank of Nigeria*, 461 U.S. 480, 489 (1983). In our view, these same considerations preclude the application of New York law here.

III

A

Before examining the controlling principles, a preliminary observation is appropriate. The parties and *amici* have repeatedly referred to the phrases that have tended to dominate discussion about the independent status of separately constituted juridical entities, debating whether "to pierce the corporate veil," and whether Bancec is an "alter ego" or a "mere instrumentality" of the Cuban Government. In *Berkey v. Third Avenue Ry. Co.*, 244 N.Y. 84, 155 N.E. 58 (1926), Justice (then Judge) Cardozo warned in circumstances similar to those presented here against permitting worn epithets to substitute for rigorous analysis.

> "The whole problem of the relation between parent and subsidiary corporations is one that is still enveloped in the mists of metaphor. Metaphors in law are to be narrowly watched, for starting as devices to liberate thought, they end often by enslaving it." *Id.*, at 94, 155 N.E., at 61.

With this in mind, we examine briefly the nature of government instrumentalities.

Increasingly during this century, governments throughout the world have established separately constituted legal entities to perform a variety of tasks. The organization and control of these entities vary considerably, but many possess a number of common features. A typical government instrumentality, if one can be said to exist, is created by an enabling statute that prescribes the powers and duties of the instrumentality, and specifies that it is to be managed by a board selected by the government in a manner consistent with the enabling law. The instrumentality is typically established as a separate juridical entity, with the powers to hold and sell property and to sue and be sued. Except for appropriations to provide capital or to cover losses, the instrumentality is primarily responsible for its own finances. The instrumentality is run as a distinct economic enterprise; often it is not subject to the same budgetary and personnel requirements with which government agencies must comply.

These distinctive features permit government instrumentalities to manage their operations on an enterprise basis while granting them a greater degree of flexibility and independence from close political control than is generally enjoyed by government agencies. These same features frequently prompt governments in developing countries to establish separate juridical entities as the vehicles through which to obtain the financial resources needed to make large-scale national investments.

> "[P]ublic enterprise, largely in the form of development corporations, has become an essential instrument of economic development in the economically backward countries which have insufficient private venture capital to develop the utilities and industries which are given priority in the national development plan. Not infrequently, these public development corporations * * * directly or through subsidiar-

ies, enter into partnerships with national or foreign private enterprises, or they offer shares to the public." Friedmann, "Government Enterprise: A Comparative Analysis" in Government Enterprise: A Comparative Study 303, 333–334 (W. Friedmann & J. Garner eds. 1970).

Separate legal personality has been described as "an almost indispensable aspect of the public corporation." *Id.*, at 314. Provisions in the corporate charter stating that the instrumentality may sue and be sued have been construed to waive the sovereign immunity accorded to many governmental activities, thereby enabling third parties to deal with the instrumentality knowing that they may seek relief in the courts. Similarly, the instrumentality's assets and liabilities must be treated as distinct from those of its sovereign in order to facilitate credit transactions with third parties. *Id.*, at 315. Thus what the Court stated with respect to private corporations in *Anderson v. Abbott*, 321 U.S. 349 (1944), is true also for governmental corporations:

> "Limited liability is the rule, not the exception; and on that assumption large undertakings are rested, vast enterprises are launched, and huge sums of capital attracted." *Id.*, at 362, 64 S.Ct., at 537.

Freely ignoring the separate status of government instrumentalities would result in substantial uncertainty over whether an instrumentality's assets would be diverted to satisfy a claim against the sovereign, and might thereby cause third parties to hesitate before extending credit to a government instrumentality without the government's guarantee. As a result, the efforts of sovereign nations to structure their governmental activities in a manner deemed necessary to promote economic development and efficient administration would surely be frustrated. Due respect for the actions taken by foreign sovereigns and for principles of comity between nations, see *Hilton v. Guyot*, 159 U.S. 113, 163–164 (1895), leads us to conclude as the courts of Great Britain have concluded in other circumstances[2]—that government instrumentalities established as juridi-

---

2. The British courts, applying principles we have not embraced as universally acceptable, have shown marked reluctance to attribute the acts of a foreign government to an instrumentality owned by that government. In *I Congreso del Partido*, [1983] A.C. 244, a decision discussing the so-called "restrictive" doctrine of sovereign immunity and its application to three Cuban state-owned enterprises, including Cubazucar, Lord Wilberforce described the legal status of government instrumentalities:

"State-controlled enterprises, with legal personality, ability to trade and to enter into contracts of private law, though wholly subject to the control of their state, are a well-known feature of the modern commercial scene. The distinction between them, and their governing state, may appear artificial: but it is an accepted distinction in the law of England and other states. Quite different considerations apply to a state-controlled enterprise acting on government directions on the one hand, and a state, exercising sovereign functions, on the other." *Id.*, at 258 (citation omitted).

Later in his opinion, Lord Wilberforce rejected the contention that commercial transactions entered into by state-owned organizations could be attributed to the Cuban Government. "The status of these organizations is familiar in our courts, and it has never been held that the relevant state is in law answerable for their actions." *Id.*, at 271. See also *Trendtex Trading Corp. v. Central Bank of Nigeria*, [1977] Q.B. 529, in which the Court of Appeal ruled that the Central Bank of Nigeria was not an "alter ego or organ" of the Nigerian Government for the purpose of determining whether it could assert sovereign immunity. *Id.*, at 559.

cal entities distinct and independent from their sovereign should normally be treated as such.

We find support for this conclusion in the legislative history of the FSIA.* * *

Thus, the presumption that a foreign government's determination that its instrumentality is to be accorded separate legal status is buttressed by this congressional determination. We next examine whether this presumption may be overcome in certain circumstances.

B

In discussing the legal status of *private* corporations, courts in the United States[3] and abroad,[4] have recognized that an incorporated entity—described by Chief Justice Marshall as "an artificial being, invisible, intangible, and existing only in contemplation of law"—is not to be regarded as legally separate from its owners in all circumstances. Thus, where a corporate entity is so extensively controlled by its owner that a relationship of principal and agent is created, we have held that one may be held liable for the actions of the other. See *NLRB v. Deena Artware, Inc.*, 361 U.S. 398, 402–404 (1960). In addition, our cases have long recognized "the broader equitable principle that the doctrine of corporate entity, recognized generally and for most purposes, will not be regarded when to do so would work fraud or injustice." *Taylor v. Standard Gas Co.*,

---

In *C. Czarnikow Ltd. v. Rolimpex*, [1979] A.C. 351, the House of Lords affirmed a decision holding that Rolimpex, a Polish state trading enterprise that sold Polish sugar overseas, could successfully assert a defense of *force majeure* in an action for breach of a contract to sell sugar. Rolimpex had defended on the ground that the Polish Government had instituted a ban on the foreign sale of Polish sugar. Lord Wilberforce agreed with the conclusion of the court below that, in the absence of "clear evidence and definite findings" that the foreign government took the action "purely in order to extricate a state enterprise from contractual liability," the enterprise cannot be regarded as an organ of the state. Rolimpex, he concluded, "is not so closely connected with the government of Poland that it is precluded from relying on the ban [on foreign sales] as government intervention. * * * " *Id.*, at 364.

3. See 1 W. Fletcher, Cyclopedia of the Law of Private Corporations § 41 (rev. perm. ed. 1983) * * *.

4. In *Case Concerning The Barcelona Traction, Light & Power Co.*, 1970 I.C.J. 3, the International Court of Justice acknowledged that, as a matter of international law, the separate status of an incorporated entity may be disregarded in certain exceptional circumstances:

"Forms of incorporation and their legal personality have sometimes not been employed for the sole purposes they were originally intended to serve; sometimes the corporate entity has been unable to protect the rights of those who entrusted their financial resources to it; thus inevitably there have arisen dangers of abuse, as in the case of many other institutions of law. Here, then, as elsewhere, the law, confronted with economic realities, has had to provide protective measures and remedies in the interests of those within the corporate entity as well as of those outside who have dealings with it: the law has recognized that the independent existence of the legal entity cannot be treated as an absolute. It is in this context that the process of 'lifting the corporate veil' or 'disregarding the legal entity' has been found justified and equitable in certain circumstances or for certain purposes. The wealth of practice already accumulated on the subject in municipal law indicates that the veil is lifted, for instance, to prevent the misuse of the privileges of legal personality, as in certain cases of fraud or malfeasance, to protect third persons such as a creditor or purchaser, or to prevent the evasion of legal requirements or of obligations.

"In accordance with the principle expounded above, the process of lifting the veil, being an exceptional one admitted by municipal law in respect of an institution of its own making, is equally admissible to play a similar role in international law...." *Id.*, at 38–39. * * *

306 U.S. 307, 322 (1939). See *Pepper v. Litton*, 308 U.S. 295, 310 (1939). In particular, the Court has consistently refused to give effect to the corporate form where it is interposed to defeat legislative policies. E.g., *Anderson v. Abbott*, 321 U.S., at 362–363. * * *

C

We conclude today that similar equitable principles must be applied here. In *National City Bank v. Republic of China*, 348 U.S. 356 (1955), the Court ruled that when a foreign sovereign asserts a claim in a United States court, "the consideration of fair dealing" bars the state from asserting a defense of sovereign immunity to defeat a setoff or counter-claim. *Id.*, at 365. See 28 U.S.C. § 1607(c). As a general matter, therefore, the Cuban Government could not bring suit in a United States court without also subjecting itself to its adversary's counter-claim. Here there is apparently no dispute that, as the District Court found, and the Court of Appeals apparently agreed, see 658 F.2d, at 916, n. 4, "the devolution of [Bancec's] claim, however viewed, brings it into the hands of the Ministry [of Foreign Trade], or Banco Nacional," each a party that may be held liable for the expropriation of Citibank's assets. 505 F.Supp., at 425. See *Banco Nacional de Cuba v. First National City Bank, supra*, 478 F.2d, at 194. Bancec was dissolved even before Citibank filed its answer in this case, apparently in order to effect "the consolidation and operation of the economic and social conquests of the Revolution," particularly the nationalization of the banks ordered by Law No. 891.[5] Thus, the Cuban Government and Banco Nacional, not any third parties that may have relied on Bancec's separate juridical identity, would be the only beneficiaries of any recovery.[6]

In our view, this situation is similar to that in the *Republic of China* case.

> "We have a foreign government invoking our law but resisting a claim against it which fairly would curtail its recovery. It wants our law, like any other litigant, but it wants our law free from the claims of justice." 348 U.S., at 361–362 (footnote omitted).[7]

---

5. Law No. 930, the law dissolving Bancec, contains the following recitations: * * *

"WHEREAS, the consolidation and the operation of the economic and social conquests of the Revolution require the restructuration into a sole and centralized banking system, operated by the State, constituted by the [Banco Nacional], which will foster the development and stimulation of all productive activities of the Nation through the accumulation of the financial resources thereof, and their most economic and reasonable utilization...." * * *

6. The parties agree that, under the Cuban Assets Control Regulations, 31 CFR Part 515 (1982), any judgment entered in favor of an instrumentality of the Cuban Government would be frozen pending settlement of claims between the United States and Cuba.

7. See also *First National City Bank v. Banco Nacional de Cuba, supra*, 406 U.S., at 770–773 (Douglas, J., concurring in result); *Federal Republic of Germany v. Elicofon*, 358 F.Supp. 747 (E.D.N.Y.1970), aff'd, 478 F.2d 231 (C.A.2 1973), cert. denied, 415 U.S. 931 (1974). In *Elicofon*, the District Court held that a separate juridical entity of a foreign state not recognized by the United States may not appear in a United States court. A contrary holding, the court reasoned, "would permit non-recognized governments to use our courts at will by creating 'juridical entities' whenever the need arises." 358 F.Supp., at 757.

Giving effect to Bancec's separate juridical status in these circumstances, even though it has long been dissolved, would permit the real beneficiary of such an action, the Government of the Republic of Cuba, to obtain relief in our courts that it could not obtain in its own right without waiving its sovereign immunity and answering for the seizure of Citibank's assets—a seizure previously held by the Court of Appeals to have violated international law. We decline to adhere blindly to the corporate form where doing so would cause such an injustice. See *Bangor Punta Operations, Inc. v. Bangor & Aroostook R. Co., supra,* 417 U.S., at 713.

Respondent contends, however, that the transfer of Bancec's assets from the Ministry of Foreign Trade or Banco Nacional to Empresa and Cuba Zucar effectively insulates it from Citibank's counterclaim. We disagree. Having dissolved Bancec and transferred its assets to entities that may be held liable on Citibank's counterclaim, Cuba cannot escape liability for acts in violation of international law simply by retransferring the assets to separate juridical entities. To hold otherwise would permit governments to avoid the requirements of international law simply by creating juridical entities whenever the need arises. * * * We therefore hold that Citibank may set off the value of its assets seized by the Cuban Government against the amount sought by Bancec.

IV

Our decision today announces no mechanical formula for determining the circumstances under which the normally separate juridical status of a government instrumentality is to be disregarded.[8] Instead, it is the product of the application of internationally recognized equitable principles to avoid the injustice that would result from permitting a foreign state to reap the benefits of our courts while avoiding the obligations of international law.

NOTES

1. *Attaching and Executing Against State Assets.* FSIA Sections 1604 and 1609 operate in a parallel structure, with each providing immunity to foreign sovereigns when actions are brought in federal courts to pursue the merits of a claim (§ 1604) and then, if the claim is proven meritorious, to seek

---

8. The District Court adopted, and both Citibank and the Solicitor General urge upon the Court, a standard in which the determination whether or not to give effect to the separate juridical status of a government instrumentality turns in part on whether the instrumentality in question performed a "governmental function." We decline to adopt such a standard in this case, as our decision is based on other grounds. We do observe that the concept of a "usual" or a "proper" governmental function changes over time and varies from nation to nation. Cf. *New York v. United States,* 326 U.S. 572, 580 (1946) (opinion of Frankfurter, J.) ("To rest the federal taxing power on what is 'normally' conducted by private enterprise in contradiction to the 'usual' governmental functions is too shifting a basis for determining constitutional power and too entangled in expediency to serve as a dependable legal criterion"); *id.,* at 586, 66 S.Ct., at 316 (Stone, C.J., concurring); *id.,* at 591, 66 S.Ct., at 318 (Douglas, J., dissenting). See also Friedmann, The Legal Status and Organization of the Public Corporation, 16 Law & Contemp. Prob. 576, 589–591 (1951).

attachment of and execute against the assets of the foreign state (§ 1609). FSIA Sections 1605–1607 and Sections 1610–11 also operate in parallel structure, providing certain exceptions to that immunity. Note that after a judgment is won on the merits, the claimant must allow a reasonable time to pass before pursuing execution, so as to allow the foreign sovereign the opportunity to comply with the judgment (§ 1610(c)). See, e.g., *Ned Chartering & Trading, Inc. v. Pakistan*, 130 F.Supp.2d 64 (D.D.C. 2001) (waiting ten days found insufficient). In many instances, foreign sovereigns have a policy of complying with judgments reached on the merits, thus obviating the need to pursue attachment and execution.

2.   *Commercial Assets Only.* If attachment and execution is necessary, a threshold element of Section 1610 is that the property be "used for a commercial activity in the United States." Thus, if a foreign sovereign commits a wrongful act against a claimant, and if that foreign sovereign is receiving royalties or taxes from a U.S. company with whom it has a joint venture, the claimant can try to attach and execute against those payments. See *Connecticut Bank of Commerce v. Congo*, 309 F.3d 240 (5th Cir. 2002); *Ministry of Def. & Support for Armed Serv. of Iran v. Cubic Def. Sys. Inc.*, 385 F.3d 1206 (9th Cir. 2004). Similarly, a claimant could seek to execute against license fees that the foreign sovereign is paid from sources in the United States for the use of certain Internet "domain" names owned by the foreign sovereign. *Lloyd's Underwriters v. AO Gazsnabtranzit*, 2000 WL 1719493 (N.D. Ga. 2000). By contrast, diplomatic and consular properties are generally immune; even if an embassy or mission purchases property commercially (such as buying a home to use as a diplomatic residence), that property will not be regarded as being used for a commercial activity. See *Englewood v. Libya*, 773 F.2d 31 (3d Cir. 1985); *S & S Mach. Co. v. Masinexportimport*, 802 F.Supp. 1109 (S.D.N.Y. 1992); 1976 U.S.C.C.A.N. 6604, 6628 ("embassies and related buildings could not be deemed to be property used for a 'commercial' activity as required by section 1610(a)").

3.   *Secondary Requirement.* Even if the property is used for a commercial activity, the claimant must also show that there is an exception to the foreign sovereign's immunity from attachment and execution, with several exceptions set forth in Section 1610. For instance, if the claimant can show that the foreign sovereign expressly waived its right to immunity from attachment in a contract with the claimant, then the secondary requirement is met. See *Venus Lines Agency v. CVG Industria Venezolana de Aluminio*, 210 F.3d 1309 (11th Cir. 2000).

4.   *The Bancec Doctrine.* The *First National City Bank* case spawned the "Bancec doctrine," whereby if a foreign sovereign acts wrongfully, a claimant may be able to attach and execute against the assets of that foreign sovereign, but usually not the assets of an instrumentality owned by the foreign sovereign. (The doctrine does not apply when the instrumentality itself committed the wrongful act). This is an important hurdle, in that commercial assets of a foreign sovereign may well be held by instrumentalities engaged in commercial activities, rather than by the government itself. As *First National City Bank* itself demonstrates, however, the presumption of juridical separateness can be overcome, allowing the plaintiff to "pierce the corporate veil" in

circumstances where the foreign sovereign exercises extensive economic control over the property at issue or derives profits or benefits from it.

Do you find it odd that the assets of the instrumentality cannot be reached because of its separate juridical status, and yet when the instrumentality itself is accused of wrongdoing, it may claim sovereign immunity because of its connection to the foreign sovereign? In other words, why is the connection between the foreign sovereign and the instrumentality strong enough to accord the latter sovereign immunity, but not strong enough to view the assets of the instrumentality as essentially assets of the foreign sovereign?

5. *Bancec Doctrine and Terrorist–State Actions.* Efforts by claimants in actions based upon the terrorist-state exception to sovereign immunity have encountered considerable difficulty in successfully attaching and executing against assets of those states, in part because of the *Bancec* doctrine. For example, in *Flatow v. Bank Saderat Iran*, 308 F.3d 1065 (9th Cir. 2002), the Flatow family—having won a judgment against Iran for sponsoring a terrorist bombing in Israel—sought to attach assets held by Bank Saderat Iran. Although the government of Iran owned Bank Saderat Iran, the Ninth Circuit held that the assets could not be attached because plaintiffs had not shown that Iran exercised day-to-day managerial control over the bank. Dissatisfaction with this hurdle for these claimants led to the inclusion in Section 1610 of an exception to the *Bancec* doctrine. For claimants who have invoked the terrorist-state exception, it is now sufficient simply to show that the assets are owned by the foreign sovereign or its instrumentality (§ 1610(g)).

6. *Red Light.* Regardless of whether the requirements of Section 1610 are met, Section 1611 sets up a red light for attachment of or execution against particular types of foreign sovereign property, including property held by international organizations that might be disbursed to (or on the order of) a foreign sovereign, property of foreign central banks or monetary authorities, or property intended to be used for a military activity or of a military character. For example, even if a foreign sovereign's central bank has opened a letter of credit in favor of a plaintiff as part of a commercial transaction, when a breach occurs the plaintiff will not be able to execute against funds of the central bank that are "held for its own account." See *Olympic Chartering v. Ministry of Industry and Trade of Jordan*, 134 F.Supp.2d 528 (S.D.N.Y. 2001).

SECTION 3. STATE IMMUNITIES UNDER MULTILATERAL CONVENTIONS

In 1972, the Council of Europe adopted a European Convention on State Immunity and Additional Protocol, May 16, 1972, 11 I.L.M. 470 (1972). This Convention enumerates the specific instances in which a contracting state is not immune from jurisdiction in the courts of another contracting state. These include the case in which a state "has on the territory of the State of the forum an office, agency or other establishment through which it engages, in the same manner as a private person, in an industrial, commercial or financial activity, and the proceedings relate to that activity" (Article 7). On this Convention, see Von Hennigs, European Convention on State Immunity and other International Aspects of State Immunity, 9 Willamette J. Int'l L. & Disp. Resol. 185 (2001); Reinisch, European Court Practice Concerning State Immunity from International Measures, 17 E.J.I.L. 803 (2006); Dellapenna, Foreign State Immunity in Europe, 5 N.Y. Int'l L. Rev. 51 (1992); Sinclair, The European Convention on State Immunity, 22 I.C.L.Q. 254 (1973).

More recently, the United Nations adopted a general multilateral convention on sovereign immunity, called the Convention on Jurisdictional Immunities of States and their Property, G.A. Res. 59/38 (Dec. 2, 2004) (adopted without a vote). The Convention has been described as "the first modern multilateral instrument to articulate a comprehensive approach to issues of state or sovereign immunity from suits in foreign courts." Stewart, The UN Convention on Jurisdictional Immunities of States and Their Property, 99 A.J.I.L. 194 (2005).

The Convention reflects the restrictive theory of sovereign immunity (subject to certain limitations), and provides an exception to immunity in respect of commercial transactions entered into by states. Article 2(1)(b)(i) and (ii) of the Convention define "state" to include the state itself, its various organs of government, as well as the constituent units of a federal state or the political subdivisions of the state if "entitled to perform acts in the exercise of sovereign authority, and ... acting in that capacity." The definition of "state" also encompasses the "agencies and instrumentalities of the State or other entities, to the extent that they are entitled to perform and are actually performing acts in the exercise of sovereign authority of the State." Article 2(b)(i)(iv) extends the definition further to cover individuals who represent the state, acting in their representative capacity.

The Convention expressly excludes from its coverage immunities relating to diplomatic missions, consular posts, special missions, missions to international organizations, or delegations to "organs of international organizations or to international conferences" or any persons connected with such missions or consular posts. This exclusion appears primarily motivated by the fact that these issues are adequately covered in other international instruments. The Convention also excludes the privileges and immunities accorded under international law to heads of state *ratione personae* or with respect to aircraft or space objects owned or operated by a state. Article 4 of the Convention provides another important limitation by specifying that the Convention is not retroactive and therefore does not apply to any question of jurisdictional immunities of states or their property arising in a proceeding instituted against a state before a court of another state prior to the convention's entry into force for the states concerned. The fifth paragraph of the preamble to the Convention notes that matters not covered by the Convention will continue to be governed by customary international law. Article 26 provides a further clarification by stipulating that the Convention does not affect the rights and obligations of state parties to existing international agreements which relate to matters dealt with under the Convention.

Article 5 contains the Convention's general rule on immunity. It specifies that "A State enjoys immunity, in respect of itself and its property, from the jurisdiction of the courts of another State subject to the provisions of the present Convention." Article 6 gives effect to the general rule by requiring each state to refrain from exercising jurisdiction in its courts against another state. Article 6 also requires states to take steps to ensure that their courts respect the immunity of foreign states on their own initiative.

Under Article 7 of the Convention, a state cannot invoke immunity from jurisdiction in a proceeding before a court of another state "with regard to a matter or case" if it has expressly consented to the exercise of jurisdiction by the court with regard to that matter or case by international agreement, in a written contract, by a declaration before the court, or by means of a written communication in a specific proceeding. When, as with choice of law clauses, a state agrees to apply the law of another state, this agreement is not, by itself, consent to the exercise of jurisdiction by the courts of that other state.

Article 8 provides limitations on a state's ability to assert immunity in foreign courts. Thus, a state may not invoke immunity from jurisdiction in a proceeding before a court of another state if it has itself instituted those proceeding, intervened in that proceeding, or taken any other step relating to the merits. However, if the state satisfies the court that it could not have acquired knowledge of facts on which to base a claim to immunity until after it took such a step, the state can nonetheless claim immunity based on those facts, provided that it does so at the earliest possible moment. On the other hand, where a state appears solely to invoke immunity or to assert a right or interest in the property at issue, such a limited appearance will not be considered consent to the exercise of jurisdiction. Similarly, neither the appearance of a state representative as a witness in foreign court proceedings nor a state's failure to make an appearance in foreign proceedings is treated as consent to the exercise of jurisdiction by a foreign court.

The Convention adopts the restrictive view of sovereign immunity by acknowledging an important exception to immunity in the case of commercial transactions. As Article 10(1) of the Convention provides:

> "If a State engages in a commercial transaction with a foreign natural or juridical person and, by virtue of the applicable rules of private international law, differences relating to the commercial transaction fall within the jurisdiction of a court of another State, the State cannot invoke immunity from that jurisdiction in a proceeding arising out of that commercial transaction."

Nevertheless, the absence of immunity for commercial transactions is qualified by several exceptions. For instance, the rule against immunity does not apply when the commercial transaction is exclusively between states or when the parties to the commercial transaction have expressly provided for immunity to apply.

Under Article 12, a state cannot invoke immunity in a foreign court in a proceeding which relates to pecuniary compensation for death or injury to the person, or damage to or loss of tangible property, when such death, injury or damage is caused by an act or omission which is alleged to be attributable to the state. However, Article 12 also requires that the act or omission must have occurred in whole or in part in the territory of the foreign state which seeks to exercise jurisdiction and that the author of the act or omission was present in "that territory at the time of the act or omission." Once again, Article 12 allows the states concerned to contract out of this exception to immunity and thereby to preserve the ability to invoke immunity in each other's courts.

The Convention also provides specific rules regarding the invocation of immunity in proceedings involving employment agreements (Article 11), the ownership, possession or use of property (Article 13), intellectual and industrial property (Article 14), participation in companies and collective bodies (Article 15), ships owned or operated by states (Article 16) and arbitration agreements (Article 17).

The Convention also adopts a restrictive view of state immunity in Articles 18 and 19 which deal with pre- and post-judgment measures respectively. These articles allow attachment of or execution against state property to the extent that the state concerned has allocated or earmarked property for the satisfaction of the claim that is the object of the proceeding, or the state has expressly consented to such measures by international agreement, by an arbitration agreement, in a written contract, by a declaration before the court, or in a written communication after a dispute has arisen.

Through Article 25, the Convention also provides rules for its own interpretation by adopting the understandings provided in Annex 1 to the Convention as an integral part of the Convention. The relevant ILC reports, the reports of the Ad Hoc Committee, and the General Assembly resolution adopting the Convention, together form travaux préparatoires.

The Convention was opened for signature on January 17, 2005 and will enter into force when thirty states have deposited their instruments of ratification, acceptance, approval, or accession with the U.N. Secretary–General. As of January 2009, there were 28 signatories and 6 ratifications. The United States has not yet signed the Convention.

According to Stewart, "[t]he convention's text reflects an emergent global consensus, increasingly demonstrated in doctrine as well as practice, that states and state enterprises can no longer claim absolute immunity from the proper jurisdiction of foreign courts and agencies, especially for their commercial activities." Stewart, *supra*, at 210. However, as Stewart himself notes, the Convention is unlikely to be the final word in the field. Id.

SECTION 4. IMMUNITIES OF STATE REPRESENTATIVES

A. IMMUNITY DERIVED FROM THE FSIA

The FSIA provides for the immunity of foreign states and political subdivisions and agencies and instrumentalities of a foreign state—it does not expressly immunize individuals, such as officials of the foreign state. Moreover, according to the legislative history, an entity that is not comprehended within the definitions of Sections 1603(a) and (b) is not entitled to sovereign immunity. Should foreign officials be protected by the FSIA when the act complained of was done in their official capacity?

CHUIDIAN v. PHILIPPINE NATIONAL BANK
912 F.2d 1095 (9th Cir. 1990)

[Chuidian, a Philippine citizen, sued Daza, a Philippine citizen and an official of the Philippine government, after Daza instructed the Philippine National Bank (Bank) to dishonor a letter of credit issued by the Republic of the Philippines to Chuidian. Daza was a member of the Presidential Commission on Good Government (Commission), an executive agency created after the overthrow of former President Marcos and charged with recovering "ill-gotten wealth" accumulated by Marcos and his associates. According to Daza, the Commission suspected that Marcos and Chuidian had entered into a fraudulent settlement of litigation to pay off Chuidian for not revealing certain facts about Marcos's involvement in Chuidian's business enterprises. As a result, the Commission wished to examine the propriety of the settlement and, in order to secure payment in the event of a decision against Chuidian, needed to prevent payment under the letter of credit. In Chuidian's suit on the letter of credit, Daza moved to dismiss on grounds of sovereign immunity.]

III

The central issue in this appeal is whether Daza is entitled to sovereign immunity for acts committed in his official capacity as a member of the Commission. Daza argues that he qualifies as an "agency or instrumentality of a foreign state," 28 U.S.C. § 1603(b), and hence is entitled to immunity pursuant to the Act, 28 U.S.C. § 1604. Chuidian contends either that Daza is not covered by the Act, or, in the alternative, that this case falls within the exceptions to immunity expressly provided by the Act. See 28 U.S.C. §§ 1605–07. The government, in a "Statement of Interest of the United States," takes a third position. Under the government's view, Daza is not covered by the Act because he is an individual rather than a corporation or an association, but he is nevertheless entitled to immunity under the general principles of sovereign immunity expressed in the Restatement (Second) of Foreign Relations Law § 66(b).

* * *

The government and Chuidian argue that the definition of "agency or instrumentality of a foreign state" in section 1603(b) includes only agencies, ministries, corporations, and other associations, and is not meant to encompass individuals. Such a reading draws some significant support from the legislative history of section 1603(b), which reads in part:

> The first criterion [section 1603(b)(1)] . . . is intended to include a corporation, association, foundation or any other entity which, under the law of the foreign state where it was created, can sue or be sued in its own name. . . .

> The second criterion [section 1603(b)(2)] requires that the entity be either an organ of a foreign state . . . or that a majority of the entity's shares or other ownership interest be owned by a foreign state. . . .

> As a general matter, entities which meet the definition of an "agency or instrumentality of a foreign state" could assume a variety of forms, including a state trading corporation, a mining enterprise, a transport organization such as a shipping line or airline, a steel company, a central bank, an export association, a governmental procurement agency or a department or ministry. . . .

House Report at 6614.

This language from the House Report indicates that Congress was primarily concerned with *organizations* acting for the foreign state, and may not have expressly contemplated the case of *individuals* acting as sovereign instrumentalities. At least one court has so concluded. *Republic of the Philippines v. Marcos,* 665 F.Supp. 793, 797 (N.D.Cal.1987) *(Marcos)* ("The terminology of [section 1603(b)]—'agency', 'instrumentality', 'entity', 'organ'—makes it clear that the statute is not intended to apply to natural persons.").

Chuidian and the United States thus argue that Daza's immunity cannot be evaluated under the provisions of the Act. Chuidian argues that Daza therefore cannot be granted immunity: the Act provides the sole source of sovereign immunity, and Daza does not qualify under its definition of a foreign state. The government, on the other hand, urges us to apply the pre-Act common law of immunity. In its view, the Act replaces common law only in the context of "foreign states" as defined by section 1603(b); elsewhere—i.e., for entities covered by the common law but not covered by the Act—common law principles remain valid. The government further argues that Daza is immune under the common law principles of the Second Restatement [on Foreign Relations Law of the United States]; Chuidian contends that even if the old common law applies, an exception to immunity is applicable.

We are persuaded by neither of these arguments. While section 1603(b) may not explicitly include individuals within its definition of foreign instrumentalities, neither does it expressly exclude them. The terms "agency," "instrumentality," "organ," "entity," and "legal person," while perhaps more readily connoting an organization or collective, do not in their typical legal usage necessarily exclude individuals. Nowhere in the text or legislative history does Congress state that individuals are *not* encompassed within the section 1603(b) definition; indeed, aside from some language which is more commonly associated with the collective, the legislative history does not even hint of an intent to exclude individual officials from the scope of the Act. Such an omission is particularly significant in light of numerous statements that Congress intended the Act to codify the existing common law principles of sovereign immunity. * * * [P]re–1976 common law expressly extended immunity to individual officials acting in their official capacity. If in fact the Act does not include such officials, the Act contains a substantial unannounced departure from prior common law.

The most that can be concluded from the preceding discussion is that the Act is ambiguous as to its extension to individual foreign officials. Under such circumstances, we decline to limit its application as urged by Chuidian and the government. We conclude that the consequences of such a limitation, whether they be the loss of immunity urged by Chuidian or the reversion to pre-Act common law as urged by the government, would be entirely inconsistent with the purposes of the Act.

It is generally recognized that a suit against an individual acting in his official capacity is the practical equivalent of a suit against the sovereign directly. *Monell v. Department of Social Services,* 436 U.S. 658, 690 n. 55 (1978) ("[O]fficial-capacity suits generally represent only another way of pleading an action against an entity of which an officer is an agent."); *Morongo Band of Mission Indians v. California State Board of Equalization,* 858 F.2d 1376, 1382 n. 5 (9th Cir.1988) ("A claim alleged against a state officer acting in his official capacity is treated as a claim against the state itself."), *cert. denied,* 488 U.S. 1006 (1989). Thus, to take Chuidian's argument first, we cannot infer that Congress, in passing the Act, intended to allow unrestricted suits against individual foreign officials acting in their official capacities. Such a result would amount to a blanket abrogation of foreign sovereign immunity by allowing litigants to accomplish indirectly what the Act barred them from doing directly. It would be illogical to conclude that Congress would have enacted such a sweeping alteration of existing law implicitly and without comment. Moreover, such an interpretation would defeat the purposes of the Act: the statute was intended as a comprehensive codification of immunity and its exceptions. The rule that foreign states can be sued only pursuant to the specific provisions of sections 1605–07 would be vitiated if litigants could avoid immunity simply by recasting the form of their pleadings.

Similarly, we disagree with the government that the Act can reasonably be interpreted to leave intact the pre–1976 common law with respect to foreign officials. Admittedly, such a result would not effect the sweeping changes which would accompany the rule suggested by Chuidian: the government merely proposes that immunity of foreign states be evaluated under the Act and immunity of individuals be evaluated under the (substantially similar) provisions of the Second Restatement. Nevertheless, such a rule would also work to undermine the Act.

The principal distinction between pre–1976 common law practice and post–1976 statutory practice is the role of the State Department. If individual immunity is to be determined in accordance with the Second Restatement, presumably we would once again be required to give conclusive weight to the State Department's determination of whether an individual's activities fall within the traditional exceptions to sovereign immunity. *See Ex Parte Peru,* 318 U.S. at 589; Restatement (Second) § 69 note 1. As observed previously, there is little practical difference between a suit against a state and a suit against an individual acting in his official capacity. Adopting the rule urged by the government would promote a peculiar variant of forum shopping, especially when the immunity question is unclear. Litigants who doubted the influence and diplomatic ability of their sovereign adversary would choose to proceed against the official, hoping to secure State Department support, while litigants less favorably positioned would be inclined to proceed against the foreign state directly, confronting the Act as interpreted by the courts without the influence of the State Department.

Absent an explicit direction from the statute, we conclude that such a bifurcated approach to sovereign immunity was not intended by the Act. First, every indication shows that Congress intended the Act to be comprehensive, and courts have consistently so interpreted its provisions. *Amerada Hess,* 109 S.Ct. at 688 ("[T]he text and structure of the [Act] demonstrate Congress' intention that the [Act] be the *sole* basis for obtaining jurisdiction over a foreign state in our courts.") (emphasis added). Yet the rule urged by the government would in effect make the statute optional: by artful pleading, litigants would be able to take advantage of the Act's provisions or, alternatively, choose to proceed under the old common law.

Second, a bifurcated interpretation of the Act would be counter to Congress's stated intent of removing the discretionary role of the State Department. *See* House Report at 6605–06. Under the government's interpretation, the pre–1966 common law would apply, in which the State Department had a discretionary role at the option of the litigant. But the Act is clearly intended as a mandatory rather than an optional procedure. To convert it to the latter by allowing suits against individual officials to proceed under the old common law would substantially undermine the force of the statute. There is no showing that Congress intended such a limited effect in passing a supposedly comprehensive codification of foreign sovereign immunity.

Furthermore, no authority supports the continued validity of the pre–1976 common law in light of the Act. Indeed, the American Law Institute recently issued the Restatement (Third) of Foreign Relations Law, superseding the Second Restatement relied upon by the government in this action. The new restatement deletes in its entirety the discussion of the

United States common law of sovereign immunity, and substitutes a section analyzing such issues exclusively under the Act. Restatement (Third) of Foreign Relations Law, §§ 451 *et seq.* (1986).

For these reasons, we conclude that Chuidian's suit against Daza for acts committed in his official capacity as a member of the Commission must be analyzed under the framework of the Act. We thus join the majority of courts which have similarly concluded that section 1603(b) can fairly be read to include individuals sued in their official capacity. *Kline v. Kaneko,* 685 F.Supp. 386, 389 (S.D.N.Y.1988) ("The [Act] does apply to individual defendants when they are sued in their official capacity."); *American Bonded Warehouse Corp. v. Compagnie Nationale Air France,* 653 F.Supp. 861, 863 (N.D.Ill.1987) ("Defendants Francois Bachelet and Joe Miller, sued in their respective capacities as employees of Air France [an instrumentality of the government of France], are also protected by the [Act]."); *Mueller v. Diggelman,* No. 82 CIV 5513 (S.D.N.Y.1983) (LEXIS, gen-fed library, dist. file) (judges and clerks of foreign court, sued in their official capacities, entitled to immunity under the Act); *Rios v. Marshall,* 530 F.Supp. 351, 371, 374 (S.D.N.Y.1981) (official of British West Indies Central Labour Organization, an instrumentality of the British West Indies, protected under the Act); *but see Marcos,* 665 F.Supp. at 797 (Act not applicable to Philippine solicitor general).

YOUSUF v. SAMANTAR
552 F.3d 371 (4th Cir. 2009)
(footnotes and some citations omitted)

TRAXLER, CIRCUIT JUDGE:

Plaintiffs, all of whom are natives of Somalia, brought this action under the Torture Victim Protection Act of 1991, see Pub. L. 102–256, 106 Stat. 73 (1992), and the Alien Tort Statute, see 28 U.S.C. § 1350, seeking to impose liability against and recover damages from Defendant Mohamed Ali Samantar for alleged acts of torture and human rights violations committed against them by government agents commanded by Samantar during the regime of Mohamed Siad Barre. The district court concluded that Samantar enjoys immunity under the Foreign Sovereign Immunities Act ("FSIA"), see 28 U.S.C. §§ 1602–1611, and dismissed the action for lack of subject matter jurisdiction.

* * *

Plaintiffs, of course, did not bring this action against Somalia or any other foreign state—they brought it against Samantar individually. Under the FSIA, however, the term "foreign state" encompasses more than merely the foreign sovereign itself; "foreign state" includes "a political subdivision of a foreign state or an agency or instrumentality of a foreign state as defined in [§ 1603(b)]." 28 U.S.C. § 1603(a). A majority of the courts considering the scope of "agency or instrumentality" have concluded that an individual foreign official acting within the scope of his official duties qualifies as an "agency or instrumentality of a foreign state." *See, e.g., Chuidian v. Philippine Nat'l Bank*, 912 F.2d 1095, 1103 (9th Cir. 1990).

The district court followed the majority view that individuals are covered under the FSIA and granted Samantar's motion to dismiss because "[t]he allegations in the complaint clearly describe Samantar, at all relevant times, as acting upon the directives of the then-Somali government in an official capacity, and not for personal reasons or motivation." Additionally, the district court found it important that the current government in Somalia has expressly adopted the position that Samantar's alleged actions were taken in his official capacity.

* * *

* * * [T]he majority view clearly is that the FSIA applies to individual officials of a foreign state, as explained in the Ninth Circuit's seminal *Chuidian* decision. See 912 F.2d at 1099–1103. Most of the decisions embracing the view that individuals are covered by the FSIA either expressly adopt *Chuidian*'s reasoning or incorporate substantially similar reasoning. *See, e.g., In re Terrorist Attacks on September 11*, 2001, 538 F.3d 71, 83 (2d Cir. 2008) (explaining that "agency or instrumentality" is broad enough to encompass "senior members of a foreign state's government"); *Keller v. Central Bank of Nigeria*, 277 F.3d 811, 815–16 (6th Cir. 2002) (concluding individual defendants were within "agency or instrumentality" provision); *Byrd v. Corporacion Forestal y Industrial de Olancho*, 182 F.3d 380, 388–89 (5th Cir. 1999) (adopting majority position as articulated in *Chuidian*); *El–Fadl v. Central Bank of Jordan*, 75 F.3d 668, 671 (D.C. Cir. 1996) (same). *Chuidian* holds the definition of an "agency or instrumentality of a foreign state" under § 1603(b) encompasses "individual officials acting in their official capacity." 912 F.2d at 1101. By contrast, the Seventh Circuit stands alone in concluding that the FSIA does not apply to individuals. *See Enahoro v. Abubakar*, 408 F.3d 877, 881–82 (7th Cir. 2005) (rejecting the *Chuidian* approach as inconsistent with the statutory text)

* * *

In determining congressional intent, we focus of course on the language of the provision at issue, but we also consider the overall structure and purpose of the statute. *See Morales v. Trans World Airlines, Inc.*, 504 U.S. 374, 383 (1992). Under the FSIA, an "agency or instrumentality of a foreign state" is defined as an "entity" that "is a separate legal person, corporate or otherwise." 28 U.S.C. § 1603(b)(1). The phrase "separate legal person" is laden with corporate connotations. Generally, courts use this phrase as "a convenient way to capture the essence of the principal of limited liability" that flows from "[t]he fiction of corporate personhood." *Beiser v. Weyler*, 284 F.3d 665, 670 (5th Cir. 2002). "A basic tenet of American corporate law is that the corporation and its share-holders are distinct entities." *Dole Food Co. v. Patrickson*, 538 U.S. 468, 474 (2003).

The idea of a "[s]eparate legal personality has been described as an almost indispensible aspect of the public corporation." *First Nat'l City Bank v. Banco Para El Comercio Exterior de Cuba*, 462 U.S. 611, 625 (1983) (internal quotation marks omitted). We find the Seventh Circuit's view of this passage especially persuasive:

> [I]f it was a natural person Congress intended to refer to, it is hard to see why the phrase "separate legal person" would be used, having as it does the ring of the familiar legal concept that corporations are persons, which are subject to suit. Given that the phrase "corporate or otherwise" follows on the heels of "separate legal person," we are convinced that the latter phrase refers to a legal fiction—a business entity which is a legal person. If Congress meant to include individuals acting in the official capacity in the scope of the FSIA, it would have done so in clear and unmistakable terms.

Enahoro, 408 F.3d at 881–82. Thus, the FSIA's use of the phrase "separate legal person" suggests that corporations or other business entities, but not natural persons, may qualify as agencies or instrumentalities.

Moreover, in order to ensure that an "agency or instrumentality" seeking the benefits of sovereign immunity is actually connected to a "foreign state," the FSIA requires that the "entity" be "neither a citizen of a State of the United States *as defined in section 1332(c) and (e)* of [Title 28], nor created under the laws of any third country." 28 U.S.C. § 1603(b)(3) (emphasis added). Sections 1332(c) and (e), which govern the citizenship of corporations and legal representatives of estates, are inapplicable to individuals, and it is nonsensical to speak of an individual, rather than a corporate entity, being "created" under the laws of a country.

Construing "agency or instrumentality" to refer to a political body or corporate entity, but not an individual, is also consistent with the overall statutory scheme of the FSIA. Section 1608, for example, establishes the exclusive means for service of process on a foreign state or its agencies or instrumentalities. *See* 28 U.S.C. § 1608(a), (b); Fed. R. Civ. P. 4(j)(1). Section 1608(b), which addresses service upon an agency or instrumentality, does not contemplate service on an individual, but instead provides that absent a "special arrangement for service between the plaintiff and the agency or instrumentality," service must be perfected "by delivery of a copy of the summons and complaint either to an *officer, a managing or general agent, or to any other agent authorized by appointment or by law to receive service of process in the United States;* or in accordance with an applicable international convention on service of judicial documents." 28 U.S.C. § 1608(b) (emphasis added). This language is strikingly similar to the general procedural rule for service on a corporation or other business entity. See Fed. R. Civ. P. 4(h)(1)(B). The requirements for serving an individual, by contrast, can be found back in Rule 4(e) ("Serving an Individual Within a Judicial District of the United States"), or even Rule 4(f) ("Serving an Individual in a Foreign Country"). The fact that section 1608 uses language virtually identical to that found in Rule 4(h) for service upon corporate entities and fails to prescribe or refer to service provisions for individual defendants strongly supports our interpretation that "an agency or instrumentality of a foreign state" cannot be an individual.

We also find confirmation for our understanding of the FSIA in the House Committee Report on the FSIA. The House Report explained that "separate legal person" was "intended to include a corporation, association, foundation, or any other entity which, under the law of the foreign state where it was created, can sue or be sued in its own name, contract in its own name or hold property in its own name." H.R. Rep. No. 94–1487, at 15 (1976), *as reprinted* in 1976 U.S.C.C.A.N. 6604, 6614. The House Committee Report provided some examples of entities that would satisfy the prerequisites for an agency or instrumentality under section 1603(b), "including a state trading corporation, a mining enterprise, a transport organization such as a shipping line or airline, a steel company, a central bank, an export association, a governmental procurement agency or a department or ministry which acts and is suable in its own name." H.R. Rep. No. 94–1487, at 16, *as reprinted in* 1976 U.S.C.C.A.N. at 6614.

Accordingly, we conclude, based on the language and structure of the statute, that the FSIA does not apply to individual foreign government agents like Samantar. Accordingly, the district court erred by concluding that Samantar is shielded from suit by the FSIA.

NOTES

1. *Individuals under the FSIA.* Do you find the Ninth Circuit's *Chuidian* approach compelling or do you agree with the Fourth Circuit's reasoning in *Samantar*? As noted in *Samantar*, *Chuidian* appears to have a greater following, but the circuits are split. The U.S. State Department favors the *Samantar* approach. See Statement of Interest of the United States of America as *Amicus Curiae* in *Kensington Int'l Ltd. v. Itoua*, 505 F.3d 147 (2d Cir. 2007); see also Nelson, Does An Individual Foreign Official Qualify As a Foreign State For Purposes of the Foreign Sovereign Immunities Act?, 57 Cath. U. L. Rev. 853 (2008).

2. *Human Rights Cases.* Some courts have denied FSIA immunity to individuals in actions brought under the Alien Tort Statute, 28 U.S.C. § 1350 (2000), for alleged human rights abuses by the official. See, e.g., *Xuncax v. Gramajo*, 886 F.Supp. 162 (D. Mass. 1995); *Granville Gold Trust–Switzerland v. Commissione Del Fallimento/Interchange Bank*, 928 F.Supp. 241 (E.D.N.Y. 1996), aff'd, 111 F.3d 123 (2d Cir. 1997). For commentary, see Fitzpatrick, The Claim to Foreign Sovereign Immunity by Individuals Sued for International Human Rights Violations, 15 Whittier L. Rev. 465 (1994). Further, any immunity can be waived by the government, even if it concerns an official of a predecessor government. For a ruling that the successor government could waive the former Philippines president's immunity, see *In re Doe*, 860 F.2d 40 (2d Cir.1988).

3. *U.S. Officials Abroad.* Should U.S. officials receive protection abroad based on immunities accorded to the U.S. government? One thorny issue that

has arisen is whether persons under contract to the U.S. government should receive immunities accorded to U.S. government personnel. On the legal status of American contractors in Iraq, see Blyth, Minding the Liability Gap: American Contractors, Iraq, And the Outsourcing of Impunity, 62 U. Miami L. Rev. 651 (2008).

B. HEADS AND FORMER HEADS OF STATE

REGINA v. BARTLE AND COMMISSIONER OF POLICE, EX PARTE PINOCHET

United Kingdom, House of Lords, 1999
2 W.L.R. 827, 38 I.L.M. 581 (1999)

[For background on the *Pinochet* case and the House of Lords' treatment of issues of universal jurisdiction and extradition, see p. 807. The following excerpt from the opinion of Lord Browne–Wilkinson relates to the immunity issue. The opinions of the other Law Lords have been omitted.]

LORD BROWNE–WILKINSON:

* * *

STATE IMMUNITY

This is the point around which most of the argument turned. It is of considerable general importance internationally since, if Senator Pinochet is not entitled to immunity in relation to the acts of torture alleged to have occurred after 29 September 1988 [when the Convention Against Torture entered into force for the United Kingdom], it will be the first time so far as counsel have discovered when a local domestic court has refused to afford immunity to a head of state or former head of state on the grounds that there can be no immunity against prosecution for certain international crimes.

Given the importance of the point, it is surprising how narrow is the area of dispute. There is general agreement between the parties as to the rules of statutory immunity and the rationale which underlies them. The issue is whether international law grants state immunity in relation to the international crime of torture and, if so, whether the Republic of Chile is entitled to claim such immunity even though Chile, Spain and the United Kingdom are all parties to the Torture Convention and therefore "contractually" bound to give effect to its provisions from 8 December 1988 at the latest.

It is a basic principle of international law that one sovereign state (the forum state) does not adjudicate on the conduct of a foreign state. The foreign state is entitled to procedural immunity from the processes of the forum state. This immunity extends to both criminal and civil liability. State immunity probably grew from the historical immunity of the person of the monarch. In any event, such personal immunity of the head of state persists to the present day: the head of state is entitled to the same immunity as the state itself. The diplomatic representative of the foreign state in the forum state is also afforded the same immunity in recognition of the dignity of the state which he represents. This immunity enjoyed by a head of state in power and an ambassador in post is a complete immunity attaching to the person of the head of state or ambassador and rendering him immune from all actions or prosecutions whether or not they relate to matters done for the benefit of the state. Such immunity is said to be granted *ratione personae*.

What then when the ambassador leaves his post or the head of state is deposed? The position of the ambassador is covered by the Vienna Convention on Diplomatic Relations, 1961. After providing for immunity from arrest (Article 29) and from criminal and civil jurisdiction (Article 31), Article 39(1) provides that the ambassador's privileges shall be enjoyed from the moment he takes up post; and subsection (2) provides:

> "(2) When the functions of a person enjoying privileges and immunities have come to an end, such privileges and immunities shall normally cease at the moment when he leaves the country, or on expiry of a reasonable period in which to do so, but shall subsist until that time, even in case of armed conflict. However, with respect to acts performed by such a person in the exercise of his functions as a member of the mission, immunity shall continue to subsist."

The continuing partial immunity of the ambassador after leaving post is of a different kind from that enjoyed *ratione personae* while he was in post. Since he is no longer the representative of the foreign state he merits no particular privileges or immunities as a person. However in order to preserve the integrity of the activities of the foreign state during the period when he was ambassador, it is necessary to provide that immunity is afforded to his official acts during his tenure in post. If this were not done the sovereign immunity of the state could be evaded by calling in question acts done during the previous ambassador's time. Accordingly under Article 39(2) the ambassador, like any other official of the state, enjoys immunity in relation to his official acts done while he was an official. This limited immunity, *ratione materiae*, is to be contrasted with the former immunity *ratione personae* which gave complete immunity to all activities whether public or private.

In my judgment at common law a former head of state enjoys similar immunities, *ratione materiae*, once he ceases to be head of state. He too loses immunity *ratione personae* on ceasing to be head of state: see Watts, *The Legal Position in International Law of Heads of States, Heads of Government and Foreign Ministers* p. 88 and the cases there cited. He can be sued on his private obligations: *Ex–King Farouk of Egypt v. Christian Dior* (1957) 24 I.L.R. 228; *Jimenez v. Aristeguieta* (1962) 311 F. 2d 547. As ex head of state he cannot be sued in respect of acts performed whilst head of state in his public capacity: *Hatch v. Baez* [1876] 7 Hun. 596. Thus, at common law, the position of the former ambassador and the former head of state appears to be much the same: both enjoy immunity for acts done in performance of their respective functions whilst in office.

* * *

The question then which has to be answered is whether the alleged organisation of state torture by Senator Pinochet (if proved) would constitute an act committed by Senator Pinochet as part of his official functions as head of state. It is not enough to say that it cannot be part of the functions of the head of state to commit a crime. Actions which are criminal under the local law can still have been done officially and therefore give rise to immunity *ratione materiae*. The case needs to be analysed more closely.

Can it be said that the commission of a crime which is an international crime against humanity and *jus cogens* is an act done in an official capacity on behalf of the state? I believe there to be strong ground for saying that the implementation of torture as defined by the Torture Convention cannot be a state function. This is the view taken by Sir Arthur Watts (*supra*) who said (at p. 82):

> "While generally international law ... does not directly involve obligations on individuals personally, that is not always appropriate, particularly for acts of such seriousness that they constitute not merely international wrongs (in the broad sense of a civil wrong) but rather international crimes which offend against the public order of the international community. States are artificial legal persons: they can only act through the institutions and agencies of the state, which means, ultimately through its officials and other individuals acting on behalf of the state. For international conduct which is so serious as to be tainted with criminality to be regarded as attributable only to the impersonal state and not to the individuals who ordered or perpetrated it is both unrealistic and offensive to common notions of justice.

> "The idea that individuals who commit international crimes are internationally accountable for them has now become an accepted part of international law. Problems in this area—such as the non-existence of any standing international tribunal to have jurisdiction over such crimes, and the lack of agreement as to what acts are internationally criminal for this purpose—have not affected the general acceptance of the principle of individual responsibility for international criminal conduct."

Later, at p. 84, he said:

> "It can no longer be doubted that as a matter of general customary international law a head of state will personally be liable to be called to account if there is sufficient evidence that he authorised or perpetrated such serious international crimes."

It can be objected that Sir Arthur was looking at those cases where the international community has established an international tribunal in relation to which the regulating document *expressly* makes the head of state subject to the tribunal's jurisdiction: see, for example, the Nuremberg Charter Article 7; the Statute of the International Tribunal for former Yugoslavia; the Statute of the International Tribunal for Rwanda and the Statute of the International Criminal Court. It is true that in these cases it is expressly said that the head of state or former head of state is subject to the court's jurisdiction. But those are cases in which a new court with no existing jurisdiction is being established. The jurisdiction being established by the Torture Convention and the Hostages Convention is one where existing domestic courts of all the countries are being authorised and required to take jurisdiction internationally. The question is whether, in this new type of jurisdiction, the only possible view is that those made subject to the jurisdiction of each of the state courts of the world in relation to torture are not entitled to claim immunity.

I have doubts whether, before the coming into force of the Torture Convention, the existence of the international crime of torture as *jus cogens* was enough to justify the conclusion that the organisation of state torture could not rank for immunity purposes as performance of an official function. At that stage there was no international tribunal to punish torture and no general jurisdiction to permit or require its punishment in domestic courts. Not until there was some form of universal jurisdiction for the punishment of the crime of torture could it really be talked about as a fully constituted international crime. But in my judgment the Torture Convention did provide what was missing: a worldwide universal jurisdiction. Further, it required all member states to ban and outlaw torture: Article 2. How can it be for international law purposes an official function to do something which international law itself prohibits and criminalises? Thirdly, an essential feature of the international crime of torture is that it must be committed "by or with the acquiescence of a public official or other person acting in an official capacity." As a result all defendants in torture cases will be state officials. Yet, if the former head of state has immunity, the man most responsible will escape liability while his inferiors (the chiefs of police, junior army officers) who carried out his orders will be liable. I find it impossible to accept that this was the intention.

Finally, and to my mind decisively, if the implementation of a torture regime is a public function giving rise to immunity *ratione materiae*, this produces bizarre results. Immunity *ratione materiae* applies not only to ex-heads of state and ex-ambassadors but to all state officials who have been involved in carrying out the functions of the state. Such immunity is necessary in order to prevent state immunity being circumvented by prosecuting or suing the official who, for example, actually carried out the torture when a claim against the head of state would be precluded by the doctrine of immunity. If that applied to the present case, and if the implementation of the torture regime is to be treated as official business sufficient to found an immunity for the former head of state, it must also be official business sufficient to justify immunity for his inferiors who actually did the torturing. Under the Convention the international crime of torture can only be committed by an official or someone in an official capacity. They would all be entitled to immunity. It would follow that there can be no case outside Chile in which a successful prosecution for torture can be brought unless the State of Chile is prepared to waive its right to its officials' immunity. Therefore the whole elaborate structure of universal jurisdiction over torture committed by officials is rendered abortive and one of the main objectives of the Torture Convention—to provide a system under which there is no safe haven for torturers—will have been frustrated. In my judgment all these factors together demonstrate that the notion of continued immunity for ex-heads of state is inconsistent with the provisions of the Torture Convention.

For these reasons in my judgment if, as alleged, Senator Pinochet organised and authorised torture after 8 December 1988, he was not acting in any capacity which gives rise to immunity *ratione materiae* because such actions were contrary to international law, Chile had agreed to outlaw such conduct and Chile had agreed with the other parties to the Torture Convention that all signatory states should have jurisdiction to try official torture (as defined in the Convention) even if such torture were committed in Chile.

As to the charges of murder and conspiracy to murder, no one has advanced any reason why the ordinary rules of immunity should not apply and Senator Pinochet is entitled to such immunity.

For these reasons, I would allow the appeal so as to permit the extradition proceedings to proceed on the allegation that torture in pursuance of a conspiracy to commit torture, including the single act of torture which is alleged in charge 30, was being committed by Senator Pinochet after 8 December 1988 when he lost his immunity.

NOTES

1. *The Normal Rule.* The House of Lords accepted as a basic premise that both present and past heads of state were immune from criminal process for acts performed in an official capacity while they were in office. Such head-of-state immunity is commonly accepted worldwide. At the same time, the House of Lords ruled that the Convention Against Torture, for the period in which it was in force for the United Kingdom, carved out an exception from the normal rule for alleged acts torture by a former head of state, since otherwise the Convention would be largely illusory. Do you agree that such an exception is appropriate? Should the exception also apply to a sitting head of state? For what other conventions should such an exception be applied? If state-sponsored torture violates customary international law, should not the exception apply even in the absence of a binding convention?

2. *Sauce for the Goose....* Should U.S. courts accord immunity from civil or criminal actions against a former President of Sudan for alleged extrajudicial killings in Darfur? Should foreign courts accord immunity to a former President of the United States for alleged extrajudicial killing of civilians from air strikes ordered in Iraq, Pakistan, or Afghanistan during 2001–2009? Does it serve the needs of the international community to involve

national courts, rather than international ones, in this type of exercise? Or should we recognize that, in the absence of effective international action against this type of misconduct, national courts are unlikely to serve a useful function? For discussion, see Aversano, Can the Pope be a Defendant in American Courts? The Grant of Head of State Immunity and the Judiciary's Role to Answer this Question, 18 Pace Int'l L. Rev. 495 (2006); Tunks, Diplomats or Defendants? Defining the Future of Head of State Immunity, 52 Duke L.J. 651 (2002); George, Head of State Immunity in the United States Courts: Still Confused After All These Years, 64 Ford. L. Rev. 1051 (1999).

3. *Acts Not Performed in Official Capacity.* Suppose the act complained of by the head of state is undertaken while in office, but not undertaken in his or her official capacity. Is it desirable to maintain immunity for such acts by sitting heads of state *ratione personae*, but to deny immunity once the official leaves office? Although not a foreign official case, note that the U.S. Supreme Court held President Clinton subject to civil suit while he was serving as president for acts not taken in his official capacity. *Clinton v. Jones*, 520 U.S. 681 (1997).

4. *Who Benefits?* The Restatement (Second) of the Foreign Relations Law of the United States § 66 (1965) extended immunity to the head of state and members of his official party. The Restatement (Third) does not contain a similar provision. But cf. Restatement (Third) § 464, Comment *i* and Reporters' Note 13. U.S. courts have generally deferred to State Department suggestions of immunity for particular persons, which may be extended to a head of state, a prime minister (head of government), or other high-level officials. See, e.g. *Wei Ye v. Jiang Zemin*, 383 F.3d 620 (7th Cir. 2004) (finding that head of state immunity is governed by general U.S. foreign relations law, which gives exclusive authority to the Executive to determine whether immunity should be recognized). Suggestions of immunity have also been issued in favor of family members of heads of state. See, e.g., *Kilroy v. Windsor*, 81 I.L.R. 127 (1990) (Prince Charles); *Kline v. Kaneko*, 535 N.Y.S.2d 303 (Sup. Ct. 1988) (wife of President of Mexico).

ARREST WARRANT OF 11 APRIL 2000 (DEMOCRATIC REPUBLIC OF THE CONGO v. BELGIUM)

International Court of Justice, 2002
2002 I.C.J. 3

[In October 2000, the Democratic Republic of the Congo (D.R.C.) filed an application against Belgium at the International Court of Justice, concerning an international arrest warrant issued on April 11, 2000 by a Belgian judge against the D.R.C.'s acting minister for foreign affairs, seeking his extradition on allegations of grave violations of international humanitarian law. At that time, Belgian law provided for universal jurisdiction in the case of grave breaches of the Geneva Conventions, crimes against humanity, and other serious offenses. Further, the Belgian statute provided that "the immunity conferred by a person's official capacity does not prevent application of this Law." The Belgian warrant was transmitted to the International Criminal Police Organization (Interpol), and as a result it was circulated internationally.

The D.R.C.'s application claimed, *inter alia*, that Belgium violated international law by purporting to exercise enforcement jurisdiction over another state's foreign minister, and that the foreign minister should enjoy immunity equivalent to that of a diplomat under international law. The D.R.C. also requested the Court to enter an order of provisional measures of protection, on the ground that "the disputed international arrest warrant in effect prevents the Minister from departing that State for any other State where his duties may call him and, accordingly, from accomplishing his duties." In 2002, the Court issued its judgment.]

53. In customary international law, the immunities accorded to Ministers for Foreign Affairs are not granted for their personal benefit, but to ensure the effective performance of their functions on behalf of their respective States. In order to determine the extent of these immunities, the Court must therefore first consider the nature of the functions exercised by a Minister for Foreign Affairs. He or she is in charge of his or her Government's diplomatic activities and generally acts as its representative in international negotiations and intergovernmental meetings. Ambassadors and other diplomatic agents carry out their duties under his or her authority. His or her acts may bind the State represented, and there is a presumption that a Minister for Foreign Affairs, simply by virtue of that office, has full powers to act on behalf of the State (see, for example, Article 7, paragraph 2 *(a)*, of the 1969 Vienna Convention on the Law of Treaties). In the performance of these functions, he or she is frequently required to travel internationally, and thus must be in a position freely to do so whenever the need should arise. He or she must also be in constant communication with the Government, and with its diplomatic missions around the world, and be capable at any time of communicating with representatives of other States. The Court further observes that a Minister for Foreign Affairs, responsible for the conduct of his or her State's relations with all other States, occupies a position such that, like the Head of State or the Head of Government, he or she is recognized under international law as representative of the State solely by virtue of his or her office. He or she does not have to present letters of credence: to the contrary, it is generally the Minister who determines the authority to be conferred upon diplomatic agents and countersigns their letters of credence. Finally, it is to the Minister for Foreign Affairs that chargés d'affaires are accredited.

54. The Court accordingly concludes that the functions of a Minister for Foreign Affairs are such that, throughout the duration of his or her office, he or she when abroad enjoys full immunity from criminal jurisdiction and inviolability. That immunity and that inviolability protect the individual concerned against any act of authority of another State which would hinder him or her in the performance of his or her duties.

55. In this respect, no distinction can be drawn between acts performed by a Minister for Foreign Affairs in an "official" capacity, and those claimed to have been performed in a "private capacity", or, for that matter, between acts performed before the person concerned assumed

office as Minister for Foreign Affairs and acts committed during the period of office. Thus, if a Minister for Foreign Affairs is arrested in another State on a criminal charge, he or she is clearly thereby prevented from exercising the functions of his or her office. The consequences of such impediment to the exercise of those official functions are equally serious, regardless of whether the Minister for Foreign Affairs was, at the time of arrest, present in the territory of the arresting State on an "official" visit or a "private" visit, regardless of whether the arrest relates to acts allegedly performed before the person became the Minister for Foreign Affairs or to acts performed while in office, and regardless of whether the arrest relates to alleged acts performed in an "official" capacity or a "private" capacity. Furthermore, even the mere risk that, by travelling to or transiting another State a Minister for Foreign Affairs might be exposing himself or herself to legal proceedings could deter the Minister from travelling internationally when required to do so for the purposes of the performance of his or her official functions.

56. The Court will now address Belgium's argument that immunities accorded to incumbent Ministers for Foreign Affairs can in no case protect them where they are suspected of having committed war crimes or crimes against humanity. In support of this position, Belgium refers in its Counter–Memorial to various legal instruments creating international criminal tribunals, to examples from national legislation, and to the jurisprudence of national and international courts.

Belgium begins by pointing out that certain provisions of the instruments creating international criminal tribunals state expressly that the official capacity of a person shall not be a bar to the exercise by such tribunals of their jurisdiction.

Belgium also places emphasis on certain decisions of national courts, and in particular on the judgments rendered on 24 March 1999 by the House of Lords in the United Kingdom and on 13 March 2001 by the Court of Cassation in France in the *Pinochet* and *Qaddafi* cases respectively, in which it contends that an exception to the immunity rule was accepted in the case of serious crimes under international law. Thus, according to Belgium, the *Pinochet* decision recognizes an exception to the immunity rule when Lord Millett stated that "[i]nternational law cannot be supposed to have established a crime having the character of a *jus cogens* and at the same time to have provided an immunity which is coextensive with the obligation it seeks to impose", or when Lord Phillips of Worth Matravers said that "no established rule of international law requires state immunity *ratione materiae* to be accorded in respect of prosecution for an international crime". As to the French Court of Cassation, Belgium contends that, in holding that, "under international law as it currently stands, the crime alleged [acts of terrorism], irrespective of its gravity, does not come within the exceptions to the principle of immunity from jurisdiction for incumbent foreign Heads of State", the Court explicitly recognized the existence of such exceptions.

57. The Congo, for its part, states that, under international law as it currently stands, there is no basis for asserting that there is any exception to the principle of absolute immunity from criminal process of an incumbent Minister for Foreign Affairs where he or she is accused of having committed crimes under international law.

In support of this contention, the Congo refers to State practice, giving particular consideration in this regard to the *Pinochet* and *Qaddafi* cases, and concluding that such practice does not correspond to that which Belgium claims but, on the contrary, confirms the absolute nature of the immunity from criminal process of Heads of State and Ministers for Foreign Affairs. Thus, in the *Pinochet* case, the Congo cites Lord Browne–Wilkinson's statement that "[t] his immunity enjoyed by a head of state in power and an ambassador in post is a complete immunity attached to the person of the head of state or ambassador and rendering him immune from all actions or prosecutions ...". According to the Congo, the French Court of Cassation adopted the same position in its *Qaddafi* judgment, in affirming that "international custom bars the prosecution of incumbent Heads of State, in the absence of any contrary international provision binding on the parties concerned, before the criminal courts of a foreign State".

As regards the instruments creating international criminal tribunals and the latter's jurisprudence, these, in the Congo's view, concern only those tribunals, and no inference can be drawn from them in regard to criminal proceedings before national courts against persons enjoying immunity under international law.

58. The Court has carefully examined State practice, including national legislation and those few decisions of national higher courts, such as the House of Lords or the French Court of Cassation. It has been unable to deduce from this practice that there exists under customary international law any form of exception to the rule according immunity from criminal jurisdiction and inviolability to incumbent Ministers for Foreign Affairs, where they are suspected of having committed war crimes or crimes against humanity.

The Court has also examined the rules concerning the immunity or criminal responsibility of persons having an official capacity contained in the legal instruments creating international criminal tribunals, and which are specifically applicable to the latter (see Charter of the International Military Tribunal of Nuremberg, Art. 7; Charter of the International Military Tribunal of Tokyo, Art. 6; Statute of the International Criminal Tribunal for the former Yugoslavia, Art. 7, para. 2; Statute of the International Criminal Tribunal for Rwanda, Art. 6, para. 2; Statute of the International Criminal Court, Art. 27). It finds that these rules likewise do not enable it to conclude that any such an exception exists in customary international law in regard to national courts.

Finally, none of the decisions of the Nuremberg and Tokyo international military tribunals, or of the International Criminal Tribunal for the former Yugoslavia, cited by Belgium deal with the question of the immunities of incumbent Ministers for Foreign Affairs before national courts where they are accused of having committed war crimes or crimes against humanity. The Court accordingly notes that those decisions are in no way at variance with the findings it has reached above.

In view of the foregoing, the Court accordingly cannot accept Belgium's argument in this regard.

59.   It should further be noted that the rules governing the jurisdiction of national courts must be carefully distinguished from those governing jurisdictional immunities: jurisdiction does not imply absence of immunity, while absence of immunity does not imply jurisdiction. Thus, although various international conventions on the prevention and punishment of certain serious crimes impose on States obligations of prosecution or extradition, thereby requiring them to extend their criminal jurisdiction, such extension of jurisdiction in no way affects immunities under customary international law, including those of Ministers for Foreign Affairs. These remain opposable before the courts of a foreign State, even where those courts exercise such a jurisdiction under these conventions.

60.   The Court emphasizes, however, that the *immunity* from jurisdiction enjoyed by incumbent Ministers for Foreign Affairs does not mean that they enjoy *impunity* in respect of any crimes they might have committed, irrespective of their gravity. Immunity from criminal jurisdiction and individual criminal responsibility are quite separate concepts. While jurisdictional immunity is procedural in nature, criminal responsibility is a question of substantive law. Jurisdictional immunity may well bar prosecution for a certain period or for certain offences; it cannot exonerate the person to whom it applies from all criminal responsibility.

61.   Accordingly, the immunities enjoyed under international law by an incumbent or former Minister for Foreign Affairs do not represent a bar to criminal prosecution in certain circumstances.

First, such persons enjoy no criminal immunity under international law in their own countries, and may thus be tried by those countries' courts in accordance with the relevant rules of domestic law.

Secondly, they will cease to enjoy immunity from foreign jurisdiction if the State which they represent or have represented decides to waive that immunity.

Thirdly, after a person ceases to hold the office of Minister for Foreign Affairs, he or she will no longer enjoy all of the immunities accorded by international law in other States. Provided that it has jurisdiction under international law, a court of one State may try a former Minister for Foreign Affairs of another State in respect of acts committed prior or subsequent to his or her period of office, as well as in respect of acts committed during that period of office in a private capacity.

Fourthly, an incumbent or former Minister for Foreign Affairs may be subject to criminal proceedings before certain international criminal courts, where they have jurisdiction. Examples include the International Criminal Tribunal for the former Yugoslavia, and the International Criminal Tribunal for Rwanda, established pursuant to Security Council resolutions under Chapter VII of the United Nations Charter, and the future International Criminal Court created by the 1998 Rome Convention. The latter's Statute expressly provides, in Article 27, paragraph 2, that "[i]mmunities or special procedural rules which may attach to the official capacity of a person, whether under national or international law, shall not bar the Court from exercising its jurisdiction over such a person".

NOTES

1. *Scope of the Immunity.* Should a foreign minister enjoy a level of immunity sufficient to enable him or her to carry on diplomatic relations by traveling to other states? Could a presumption of immunity be overcome in the case of exceptionally serious crimes, such as crimes against humanity?

Some have taken the view that the *Arrest Warrant* case extends immunity *rationae personae* beyond its traditional justification, i.e., protection of the person of a diplomatic representative when abroad from interference by another state. Moreover, this new rule of diplomatic immunity blurs the distinction between immunity *ratione personae* and immunity *ratione materiae*. The former, which attaches to the person of the diplomat entitled to immunity, protects that person only so long as that person is representing her state abroad. The latter protects any state official from being prosecuted for any act, wherever and whenever committed, so long as that act was "official," i.e., one taken on behalf of the state. See Summers: Diplomatic Immunity Rationae Personae: Did the International Court of Justice Create a New Customary Law Rule in Congo v. Belgium? 16 Mich. St. J. Int'l L. 459 (2007); see also Tunks, Diplomats or Defendants? Defining the Future of Head of State Immunity, 52 Duke L.J. 651 (2002).

2. *Arrest Warrant Case and Jurisdiction.* The Court in the *Arrest Warrant* case decided to address the immunity issue without passing upon whether Belgium's statute was permissible under international rules on jurisdiction. In a separate opinion in the *Arrest Warrant* case, Judges Higgins, Kooijmans, and Buergenthal, argued that the Court should have ruled on whether Belgium had jurisdiction in regard to the crimes allegedly committed by non-Belgians against non-Belgians outside of Belgium. The three judges concluded that international law had evolved to recognize universal jurisdiction in regard to the crimes alleged. It referred in this connection to Australian, Belgian, Canadian, Dutch, French, and German legislation (paras. 20–26), and case law in Australia, Austria, Germany, the Netherlands, and the United States (paras. 22–24), as well as certain international conventions (paras. 25–38). The judges observed: "As we have seen, virtually all national legislation envisages links of some sort to the forum State, and no case law exists in which pure universal jurisdiction has formed the basis of jurisdiction," (para. 45). Nevertheless, universal jurisdiction is permitted, though "it is equally necessary that universal criminal jurisdiction be exercised only over those crimes regarded as the most heinous by the international community,"

(para. 60). They referred to a list of such crimes to the 1996 I.L.C. Draft Code of Crimes Against the Peace and Security of Mankind (para. 62).

3. *The Other Congo Sues France.* In 2002, the Republic of the Congo (R.O.C.) filed a case at the I.C.J. against France concerning French proceedings for crimes against humanity and torture commenced, *inter alia*, against the R.O.C. Minister of the Interior, Pierre Oba. In its application, the R.O.C. asserted that in "attributing to itself universal jurisdiction in criminal matters and by arrogating to itself the power to prosecute and try the Minister of the Interior of a foreign State for crimes allegedly committed in connection with the exercise of his powers for the maintenance of public order in his country," France violated "the principle that a State may not, in breach of the principle of sovereign equality among all Members of the United Nations * * * exercise its authority on the territory of another State." Moreover, it maintained that, in issuing a warrant instructing police officers to examine the R.O.C. President as a witness in the case, France violated "the criminal immunity of a foreign Head of State—an international customary rule recognized by the jurisprudence of the Court." As such, the R.O.C. asked the Court to declare that France shall "cause to be annulled the measures of investigation and prosecution taken" by the French judicial officers concerned. See *Certain Criminal Proceedings in France* (R.O.C. v. France) (Application by R.O.C. of Dec. 9, 2002). As of early 2009, the Court had not yet ruled in the case; what do you think the Court should do?

C. DIPLOMATIC REPRESENTATIVES

1. Under the Law of Nations

4 HACKWORTH, DIGEST OF INTERNATIONAL LAW

513–14 (1942)

In a letter of March 16, 1906 to the Secretary of Commerce and Labor, Secretary Root said:

> There are many and various reasons why diplomatic agents, whether accredited or not to the United States, should be exempt from the operation of the municipal law of [*sic*] this country. The first and fundamental reason is the fact that diplomatic agents are universally exempt by well recognized usage incorporated into the Common law of nations, and this nation, bound as it is to observe International Law in its municipal as well as its foreign policy, cannot, if it would, vary a law common to all. * * *

> The reason of the immunity of diplomatic agents is clear, namely: that Governments may not be hampered in their foreign relations by the arrest or forcible prevention of the exercise of a duty in the person of a governmental agent or representative. If such agent be offensive and his conduct is unacceptable to the accredited nation it is proper to request his recall; if the request be not honored he may be in extreme cases escorted to the boundary and thus removed from the country.

And rightly, because self-preservation is a matter peculiarly within the province of the injured state, without which its existence is insecure. Of this fact it must be the sole judge: it cannot delegate this discretion or right to any nation however friendly or competent. It likewise follows from the necessity of the case, that the diplomatic agent must have full access to the accrediting state, else he cannot enter upon the performance of his specific duty, and it is equally clear that he must be permitted to return to the home country in the fulfillment of official duty. As to the means best fitted to fulfil these duties the agent must necessarily judge: and of the time required in entering and departing, as well as in the delay necessary to wind up the duties of office after recall, he must likewise judge.

For these universally accepted principles no authority need be cited.

2. The Concept of Functional Necessity

In its 1958 articles on diplomatic privileges and immunities, which served as the basis for the Vienna Convention on Diplomatic Relations, the International Law Commission noted that diplomatic privileges and immunities had in the past been justified on the basis of the "extraterritoriality" theory or on the basis of the "representative character" theory. According to the former, the premises of the mission represented a sort of extension of the territory of the sending state; according to the latter, privileges and immunities were based on the idea that the diplomatic mission personified the sending state. The Commission then observed that a "third theory" appeared to be gaining ground in modern times; i.e., the "functional necessity" theory, "which justifies privileges and immunities as being necessary to enable the mission to perform its functions." The Commission stated that it had been guided by this third theory "in solving problems on which practice gave no clear pointers, while also bearing in mind the representative character of the head of the mission and of the mission itself." [1958] II Yb.I.L.C. 95.

What is the significance of the "functional necessity" theory to the scope and extent of diplomatic immunities? Does it imply an obligation on the part of the sending state to waive the immunity of one of its diplomatic agents in situations where it can be established that such waiver would not interfere with the functions of the mission? See Kerley, Some Aspects of the Vienna Conference on Diplomatic Intercourse and Immunities, 56 A.J.I.L. 88, 91–93 (1962); Garretson, The Immunities of Representatives of Foreign States, 41 N.Y.U. L. Rev. 67, 71 (1966). For other support for the "functional necessity" theory of diplomatic immunities, see Restatement (Third) § 464, Comments a, c, and Reporters' Note 2; Harvard Research in International Law, Diplomatic Privileges and Immunities, Introductory Comment, 26 A.J.I.L. Supp. 15, 26 (1932). This theory has become increasingly important as nations increase the size of their delegations, and as the number of nations and organizations appointing diplomats has grown. See Ling, A Comparative Study of the Privileges and Immunities of United Nations Member Representatives and Officials with the Traditional Privileges and Immunities of Diplomatic Agents, 33 Wash. & Lee L. Rev. 91 (1976).

The accepted view in recent years is that diplomatic premises and personnel enjoy immunity and inviolability but are not metaphoric extensions of the territory of the sending state. On rejection of the extraterritoriality theory in relation to embassy premises, see *United States v. Bin Laden*, 92 F. Supp. 2d 189 (S.D.N.Y. 2000), discussed at p. 803. See also Paust, Non–Extraterritoriality of "Special Territorial Jurisdiction" of the United States: Forgotten History and the Errors of *Erdos*, 24 Yale J. Int'l L. 305 (1999).

3. Vienna Convention on Diplomatic Relations

The Vienna Convention on Diplomatic Relations, Apr. 18, 1961, 23 U.S.T. 3227, 500 U.N.T.S. 95, entered into force in 1964, after twenty-two states had deposited instruments of ratification. The United States ratified the Convention in 1972. As of early 2009, 179 states were parties. For a full account and analysis of the proceedings in the conference that led to the adoption of the convention, see Kerley, Some Aspects of the Vienna Conference on Diplomatic Intercourse and Immunities, 56 A.J.I.L. 88 (1962).

The Vienna Convention contains an array of articles that address protections for diplomatic property, such as the embassy or the ambassador's residence, as well as protections for diplomats and members of their immediate families, such as immunity from civil and criminal jurisdiction in the host country (Article 31). For example, diplomatic agents are generally free to travel to and from the receiving state (Article 40), and to travel within the receiving state, subject to restrictions for national security reasons (Article 26). By contrast, administrative and technical staff of the embassy are accorded immunity only for acts performed as part of their official duties (Article 37(2)). For recent arbitral awards applying the Vienna Convention to the treatment of diplomats and diplomatic property in time of war, see Eritrea Ethiopia Claims Commission, Partial Award on Ethiopia's Claim No. 8, 135 I.L.R. 544 (2005); Eritrea Ethiopia Claims Commission, Partial Award on Eritrea's Claim No. 20, 135 I.L.R. 519 (2005).

Several issues relating to the scope and applicability of the Vienna Convention on Diplomatic Relations were raised in *Tachiona v. United States*, 386 F.3d 205 (2d Cir. 2004). There, a class action was brought by Zimbabwean nationals who were alleged victims of torture and terror in Zimbabwe against the Zimbabwean president and foreign minister, and their political party, under the Alien Tort Claims Act, the Torture Victim Protection Act and norms of international human rights law. Process was served on the president while speaking at a fund-raiser for his political party and on the foreign minister on the street outside the Zimbabwean Mission during a trip to New York, on the margins of meetings at the

United Nations. The United States Department of State submitted a Suggestion of Immunity on behalf of defendants. The court held that the Vienna Convention's protection of diplomats' "inviolability" of the person (Article 29) protected the president against plaintiffs' service of process and that the president enjoyed the full measure of the Vienna Convention's diplomatic immunity against service of process, even though such service was attempted while the president was engaged in an ancillary activity.

On diplomatic immunity generally, see Restatement (Third) §§ 464–66; Satow, Guide to Diplomatic Practice (5th ed. 1979); Sen, A Diplomat's Handbook on International Law and Practice (3d rev. ed. 1988); Brown, Diplomatic Immunity: State Practice Under the Vienna Convention, 37 I.C.L.Q. 53 (1988); Denza, Diplomatic Law: Commentary on the Vienna Convention on Diplomatic Relations (3d ed. 2008).

4. U.S. Statutory Framework

Until 1978, diplomatic immunity in the United States was provided for by a statute enacted on April 30, 1790. This legislation extended civil and criminal immunity to all diplomats, diplomatic administrators, their family members and staff, resulting in coverage by 1978 of some 30,000 individuals. The Department of State urged that the law be repealed in favor of legislation which would conform to the narrower provisions of the Vienna Convention on Diplomatic Relations. Congress complied, enacting the 1978 Diplomatic Relations Act, Pub. L. 95–393, 92 Stat. 808 (1978), which is codified at 22 U.S.C. § 254a–e & 28 U.S.C. § 1364 (2000). In 1982, Congress adopted the Foreign Missions Act, 22 U.S.C. § 4301 (2000), allocating authority within the U.S. government to the Secretary of State to determine the treatment to be extended to the mission of a foreign state; see also Restatement (Third) § 464, Reporters' Note 5.

In 1973, the U.N. General Assembly adopted the Convention on the Prevention and Punishment of Crimes against Internationally Protected Persons, Including Diplomatic Agents. See U.N. Doc. A/9030 (1973), 28 U.S.T. 1975, 1035 U.N.T.S. 167. As of 2008, the Convention has been ratified by more than a hundred states, including the United States. The United States complies with the convention pursuant to 18 U.S.C. § 112 (2000), which provides, in part, that "[w]hoever assaults, strikes, wounds, imprisons, or offers violence to a foreign official, official guest or internationally protected person or makes any other violent attack upon the person or liberty of such person," shall be subject to fine or imprisonment, or both. In addition, the statute prohibits demonstrations within one hundred feet of foreign government buildings, and makes the destruction or attempted injury to the property of a foreign government or of its officials a felony. The Act extends the jurisdiction of the United States to any offender found within its territory, irrespective of the nationality of the victim or the defendant, or the place where the crime was committed. The constitutionality of restrictions on picketing in the vicinity of an embassy was considered in *Boos v. Barry*, 485 U.S. 312 (1988).

5. Role of the U.S. Department of State

"It is enough that an ambassador has requested immunity, that the State Department has recognized that the person for whom it was requested is entitled to it, and that the Department's recognition has been communicated to the court." *Carrera v. Carrera,* 174 F.2d 496, 497 (1949); see also *United States v. Al–Hamdi,* 356 F.3d 564 (4th Cir. 2004); *Abdulaziz v. Metropolitan Dade County,* 741 F.2d 1328 (11th Cir. 1984). The Diplomatic List maintained by the Department of State (the "Blue List") reflects only a ministerial act and not a determination by the executive of a right to immunity. See *Trost v. Tompkins,* 44 A.2d 226 (D.C. 1945); *Haley v. State,* 88 A.2d 312 (1952) (immunity denied because official notice of defendant's status had not been communicated to Department of State). The State Department also maintains a "White List" of employees of diplomatic missions. See *Carrera v. Carrera, supra*; Restatement (Third) § 464, Reporters' Note 1.

D. CONSULS

In 1963, a U.N. conference adopted the Vienna Convention on Consular Relations, April 24, 1963, 21 U.S.T. 77, 596 U.N.T.S. 261. In addition, the conference adopted two optional protocols, one of which provides for settlement of disputes by the International Court of Justice. The Convention entered into force on March 19, 1967. As of early 2009, the Convention had been ratified by more than 170 states, including the United States.

Article 5 of the Convention contains a list of consular functions. These cover a wide spectrum and include, among others, protecting in the receiving state the interests of the sending state and of its nationals; furthering the development of commercial, economic, cultural and scientific relations; ascertaining conditions and developments in the commercial, economic, cultural and scientific life of the receiving state; issuing passports, visas, and travel documents; helping and assisting nationals of the sending state; serving as a notary or civil registrar; assisting nationals in connection with decedents' estates, guardianships for persons lacking legal capacity and representation and preservation of rights before local tribunals; transmitting documents or executing letters rogatory or commissions to take evidence for courts of the sending state; exercising rights of supervision and inspection of vessels and aircraft of the sending state; and extending assistance to such vessels and aircraft and their crews, including conducting investigations and settling disputes.

Article 17 provides that a consular officer may be authorized to perform diplomatic acts without effect upon his consular status. Articles 3 and 70 deal with the performance of consular functions by diplomatic personnel. Other articles deal, *inter alia,* with the appointment and admission of consular officers, the *exequatur* (authorization from the receiving state admitting the head of a consular post to the exercise of his functions, no longer used by the United States), miscellaneous facilities and privileges to be granted by the receiving state, protocol matters, and the termination of consular functions.

Article 31, on the inviolability of consular premises, provides that authorities of the receiving state shall not enter "that part of the consular premises which is used exclusively for the purpose of the work of the consular post" except by permission, which may be "assumed" in the case of "fire or other disaster requiring prompt protective action." Article 31 of the Vienna Convention further provides that the consular premises and furnishings, as well as other post property, "shall be immune from any form of requisition for purposes of national defense or public utility," but then asserts that "[i]f expropriation is necessary for such purposes," all possible steps shall be taken not to impede consular functions and that "prompt, adequate and effective compensation" shall be paid to the sending state.

For a comprehensive survey of these rules, see Lee & Quigley, Consular Law and Practice (3d ed. 2008). For a comparison of diplomatic and consular immunities, see Restatement (Third) § 466, Comment *a* and Reporters' Note 1. The principal difference is that consular personnel enjoy immunity only in regard to their official acts, while diplomatic personnel enjoy personal immunity for all acts. The State Department normally leaves to the court whether an act was done in the performance of official consular functions. In addition to the Vienna Convention, the United States also has bilateral consular conventions with a large number of countries.

As pointed out by the court in *Arcaya v. Páez*, 145 F.Supp. 464 (S.D.N.Y. 1956), all civil actions and proceedings brought in the United States against consuls or vice consuls of foreign states must be brought in the federal district courts. 28 U.S.C. § 1351 (2000). The Supreme Court has held, however, that divorce proceedings may be brought against consuls in the state courts. *Ohio ex rel. Popovici v. Agler*, 280 U.S. 379 (1930). Until 1978, 28 U.S.C. § 1351 was construed to render only the federal courts competent to hear cases against consular personnel. As a consequence, since the federal courts do not hear cases under state criminal law, consular personnel were in fact immune from prosecution under state law. This situation was changed when Congress, by the Diplomatic Relations Act of 1978, amended § 1351 to make clear that it provided for exclusive federal competence only in civil cases. Further, this statutory provision does not apply to members of the family of consular personnel, who remain subject to normal federal and state rules of judicial competence.

E.   SPECIAL ENVOYS AND MISSIONS

On Dec. 8, 1969, the General Assembly approved a Convention on Special Missions, G.A. Res. 2530 (XXIV), which seeks to regulate more temporary missions or envoys sent from one country to another. The Convention entered into force on June 21, 1985. As of early 2009, there were 31 parties to the Convention. Although the United States has not ratified the Convention, could its provisions be regarded as reflecting general international law? The Restatement (Third), in contrast to its predecessor, does not contain a provision recognizing that an official representative of a foreign state on special mission enjoys immunity to the extent required by the performance of his official duties. This immunity is now covered by the general provision on diplomatic immunity. See Restatement (Third) § 464, Comment *i* and Reporters' Note 13.

The issue is not an academic one. Foutanga Dit Babani Sissoko was designated by Gambia as a special envoy to the United States. The U.S. Embassy in Gambia issued him a diplomatic visa. Subsequently, the United States alleged that Sissoko had tried to bribe a U.S. customs official in a transatlantic phone conversation. The United States requested his extradition from Switzerland and, having obtained his extradition, prosecuted him. Gambia claimed that he was immune as a special envoy. The court rejected the plea on the ground that the State Department had not officially certified him as a special envoy. See *United States v. Sissoko*, 995 F. Supp. 1469 (S.D. Fla. 1997). Under international law, was official certification required? Or was the issuance of a diplomatic visa sufficient acknowledgment of Sissoko's status as a special envoy? If so, what immunities should follow, if any? Would it be advisable for the U.S. Department of State to promulgate rules to clarify situations like this one? See also *Weixum v. Xilai*, 568 F. Supp. 2d 35 (D.D.C. 2008).

SECTION 5. IMMUNITIES OF INTERNATIONAL ORGANIZATIONS

A. EARLY DEVELOPMENTS

The modern law relating to the immunities of international organizations developed initially from the experience of the League of Nations and the International Labor Organization, although some aspects of its origin can be traced back into the nineteenth century. This body of law began as little more than "a general principle resting on the questionable analogy of diplomatic immunities; it has become a complex body of rules set forth in detail in conventions, agreements, statutes and regulations." Jenks, International Immunities XXXV (1961).

The Covenant of the League of Nations provided only for the immunity of League officials (in addition to representatives of members of the League), who were to be entitled to "diplomatic privileges and immunities" when they were "engaged on the business of the League." The only protection intended for the League itself was a provision that League property was to be "inviolable" (Article 7(4), (5)). On the relevance of the experience of the League and the International Labour Organisation to the development of the immunities of the United Nations and other postwar organizations, see Jenks, *supra*, at 12–16. A *modus vivendi* was entered into by the League and the Swiss Federal Government on September 18, 1926, by which Switzerland recognized that the League possessed international personality and legal capacity and that it could not "in principle, according to the rules of international law, be sued before the Swiss Courts without its express consent." The archives and premises of the League were recognized as inviolable, and certain customs and fiscal exemptions were granted. In addition, the League's staff was granted certain immunities from Swiss civil and criminal jurisdiction. See Hill, Immunities and Privileges of Officials of the League of Nations 14–23, 138–98 (1947).

The Permanent Court of International Justice began to sit at The Hague in 1922. In a series of regulations, the government of the Netherlands gave effect to the immunities and privileges of the judges envisaged by Article 19 of the Court's Statute and to the immunities and privileges of Court officials envisaged by Article 7(4) of the Covenant; these regulations were replaced in 1928 by an agreement between the Dutch Foreign Minister and the President of the Court, in which judges and officials continued to be assimilated to corresponding diplomatic representatives and officials. Hill, *supra*, at 21–23; see generally id. at 50–57, and the 1928 Agreement and supplementary rules, id. at 199–202 (Annex III), 1 Hudson, International Legislation 597 (1931).

As the scope and importance of the activities of international organizations have increased over time, so have the extent and significance of their immunities and those of their officials. The bases for their immunities differ in important respects from those for the granting of jurisdictional immunities to foreign states. Like states, international organizations require jurisdictional immunities in order to carry on their functions without interference from national courts and administrators; unlike states, however, international organizations do not enjoy a long history of respect for their authority or the means of taking reciprocal reprisals against infringement of that authority. Consequently, two key questions typically arise: In what essential respects do the immunities of international organizations differ from those of states? To what extent is the trend towards limiting the immunities of states likely to apply to international organizations? As a corollary to the latter question, what procedures and practices can organizations adopt that will forestall abuse and consequent criticism and curtailment of their immunities?

B. THE UNITED NATIONS

Article 105 of the U.N. Charter calls upon member states to accord to the organization such privileges and immunities as are necessary for fulfillment of its purposes and functions. That article, however, does not specify what those privileges and immunities should be. Consequently, a key treaty for immunities relating to the United Nations is the General

Convention on the Privileges and Immunities of the United Nations, Feb. 13, 1946, 21 U.S.T. 1418, 1 U.N.T.S. 15. As of early 2009, 156 states were parties to the Convention, which the United States ratified in 1970.

Does a U.N. member state have to ratify the General Convention before being bound to accord the privileges and immunities that it identifies? U.N. members are a party to the U.N. Charter and are bound to Article 105; arguably, the General Convention simply clarifies the obligation that arises under Article 105. Indeed, before the United States acceded to the Convention in 1970, the U.N. Legal Counsel, speaking as the representative of the Secretary–General of the United Nations, stated:

> With regard to the legal framework of the regime of privileges and immunities of the United Nations, * * * in the first place, Article 105 of the Charter accorded such privileges and immunities as were "necessary." By paragraphs 1 and 2, it imposed an obligation on all Members of the United Nations to accord such privileges and immunities as were necessary for the fulfillment of the purposes of the Organization or for the independent exercise of the functions of representatives and officials, irrespective of whether or not they had acceded to the [General] Convention. In accordance with paragraph 3, the purpose of the Convention was merely to determine the details of the application of the first two paragraphs of the same Article. In the second place, the Convention, in determining the details of certain privileges and immunities, in effect provided the minimum privileges and immunities which the Organization required in all Member States. Additional privileges and immunities necessary for special situations, such as at the Headquarters in New York or for peace-keeping or development missions in various areas of the world, were provided for by special agreements. In the third place, ninety-six Member States had acceded to the [General] Convention while, in most of the remaining Member States as well as in some nonmember States, the provisions of the Convention had been made applicable by special agreements. It could thus be said that in the nearly twenty-two years since the adoption of the Convention by the General Assembly, the standards and principles of the Convention had been so widely accepted that they had now become a part of the general international law governing the relations of States and the United Nations.

Annual Report of the Secretary–General, U.N. Doc. A/7201, at 208–09 (1968).

In addition to the General Convention, 116 States (as of early 2009, not including the United States) had become parties to a companion Convention on the Privileges and Immunities of the Specialized Agencies, Nov. 21, 1947, 33 U.N.T.S. 261. This convention provides in detail for the immunities of organizations related to the United Nations under Articles 57 and 63 of the Charter, known as specialized agencies. Further, the individual constitutions or charters of many of these organizations provide themselves for some degree of immunity, as do the constituent instruments of many organizations not in a relationship with the United Nations. On the status of the International Court of Justice, see Articles 19, 32(8), and 42(3) of the Statute of the Court, the site agreement between the Netherlands and the President of the Court, 8 U.N.T.S. 61, and the recommendations contained in the General Assembly Resolution 90 (I), U.N. Doc. A/64/Add. I at 176–79 (Dec. 11, 1946). The Court as an institution continues to be assimilated to the diplomatic corps. For discussion, see 5 Repertory of Practice of United Nations Organs 362–66 (1955); Jenks, *supra*, at 93–95.

C.   IMMUNITIES OF IO PERSONNEL

The General Convention also accords privileges and immunities to employees of the United Nations. In 1999 the International Court of Justice gave an advisory opinion on the immunity of a special rapporteur of a U.N. body, in relation to national judicial proceedings in his own country. See *Difference Relating to Immunity from Legal Process of a Special Rapporteur of the Commission on Human Rights*, 1999 I.C.J. 62, 38 I.L.M. 873 (1999). In that case, Dato Param Cumaraswamy, a Malaysian lawyer, was appointed by the U.N. Commission on Human Rights (an organ of the U.N. Economic and Social Council (ECOSOC)) to serve as its Special Rapporteur on the Independence of Judges and Lawyers. In an interview with a U.K.-based magazine circulated in Malaysia, he commented on his investigation into complaints that certain business and corporate interests had manipulated the Malaysian courts to influence decisions in their favor. Four defamation lawsuits were then filed in Malaysia by plaintiffs who had been beneficiaries of such favorable rulings. The Malaysian courts from the trial level through two levels of appeals declined to give effect to Cumaraswamy's immunity even though the U.N. Secretary–General had certified that the allegedly defamatory words were spoken in the course of Cumaraswamy's U.N. responsibilities.

In its request for an advisory opinion, ECOSOC asked the I.C.J. to advise on the applicability of the General Convention on the Privileges and Immunities of the United Nations to the circumstances of the case and on Malaysia's legal obligations. The Court observed that Cumaraswamy was an expert on mission, "and that such experts enjoy the privileges and immunities provided for under the General Convention in their relations with States parties, including those of which they are nationals or on the territory of which they reside" (para. 46). The Court further stated:

51.   Article VI, Section 23, of the General Convention provides that "[p]rivileges and immunities are granted to experts in the interests of the United Nations and not for the personal benefit of the individuals themselves." In exercising protection of United Nations

experts, the Secretary–General is therefore protecting the mission with which the expert is entrusted. * * *

52. The determination whether an agent of the Organization has acted in the course of the performance of his mission depends upon the facts of a particular case. In the present case, the Secretary–General, or the Legal Counsel of the United Nations on his behalf, has on numerous occasions informed the Government of Malaysia of his finding that Mr. Cumaraswamy had spoken the words quoted in the article * * * in his capacity as Special Rapporteur of the Commission and that he consequently was entitled to immunity from "every kind" of legal process.

53. * * * [T]he Secretary–General was reinforced in this view by the fact that it has become standard practice of Special Rapporteurs of the Commission to have contact with the media. This practice was confirmed by the High Commissioner for Human Rights who * * * wrote that: "it is more common than not for Special Rapporteurs to speak to the press about matters pertaining to their investigations, thereby keeping the general public informed of their work."

The Court concluded that the Government of Malaysia had an obligation, under Article 105 of the Charter and the General Convention, to inform its courts of the Secretary–General's position; and that the Secretary–General's finding of immunity created a presumption "which can only be set aside for the most compelling reasons and is thus to be given the greatest weight by national courts" (paras. 61–62). On the *Cumaraswamy* advisory opinion, see Bekker, International Decisions 93 A.J.I.L. 913 (1999); Brower, International Immunities: Some Dissident Views on the Role of Municipal Courts, 41 Va. J. Int'l L. 1, 41–57 (2000).

Can an international or national tribunal summon an international peacekeeper to testify about crimes witnessed in the course of his official responsibilities? The International Criminal Tribunal for the former Yugoslavia considered its authority to make binding orders for production of evidence in the *Blaskic* case, I.C.T.Y. Case No. IT–95–14–AR108*bis*, Judgment on Request of Croatia for Review of Subpoena Decision (Oct. 29, 1997); the Appeals Chamber concluded that the Tribunal does have competence to issue such orders to individuals serving under U.N. authority.

In the *Akayesu* case, General Roméo Dallaire, the Canadian head of U.N. peacekeeping forces in Rwanda, testified before the International Criminal Tribunal for Rwanda under a waiver of immunity issued by the U.N. Secretary–General, at defendant's request. *Prosecutor v. Akayesu*, I.C.T.R. Case No. I.T.–96–4–T, Judgment para 1.4.1 (Sept. 2, 1998) (noting decision of Nov. 19, 1997 on motion to subpoena a witness and grant of leave to U.N. Secretariat witness to make a statement on lifting of immunity). General Dallaire's testimony was also requested before national parliamentary bodies and other inquiries in Belgium, Canada, and France. Should the Secretary–General have waived immunity so that the

U.N. commander could testify in national inquiries about the circumstances of the 1994 genocide, in relation to national peacekeeping forces serving under international authority? For immunity of peacekeepers, see Bongiorno, A Culture of Impunity: Applying International Human Rights Law to the United Nations in East Timor, 33 Colum. Hum. Rts. L. Rev. 623 (2002).

On immunities of international organizations and their personnel, see Bekker, The Legal Position of Intergovernmental Organizations (1994); Singer, Jurisdictional Immunity of International Organizations: Human Rights and Functional Necessity Concerns, 36 Va. J. Int'l L. 53 (1995); Schermers & Blokker, International Institutional Law 1016–28 (4th ed. 2004); Amerasinghe, Principles of the Institutional Law of International Organizations 315–51 (2d ed. 2005); Frey & Frey, The History of Diplomatic Immunity 577–78 (1999); Reinisch, International Organizations before National Courts (2000).

D.   HEADQUARTERS AGREEMENTS

Problems concerning the immunities and privileges of international organizations are particularly likely to arise in those states in which the organizations have their headquarters, or in which they carry on extensive activities. The United States-United Nations Headquarters Agreement, June 26, 1947, 61 Stat. 3416, 11 U.N.T.S. 11, was authorized by Congress, 61 Stat. 756, and entered into force in 1947.

Article III of the Agreement (§§ 7–10) deals with "Law and Authority in the Headquarters District." The Headquarters District is itself inviolable, and United States officials may not enter the district in order to perform official duties, nor may legal process be served there, without the consent of the Secretary–General, but the United Nations is obligated to prevent the Headquarters District from becoming a refuge (§ 9). Federal, state and local law apply within the district (§ 7), except insofar as inconsistent with United Nations regulations made "for the purpose of establishing therein conditions in all respects necessary for the full exercise of its [the Organization's] functions" (§ 8). The United Nations is given no enforcement jurisdiction other than that inherent in its power to deny entry to or expel persons from the District (§ 10).

In addition to provisions concerning the privileges and immunities of representatives of members of the United Nations, discussed above, the Headquarters Agreement contains in Article IV certain protections for the communication and transit privileges of the Organization, its officials, and representatives of members:

§ 11.   The federal, state or local authorities of the United States shall not impose any impediments to transit to or from the headquarters district of (1) representatives of Members or officials of the United Nations, or of specialized agencies as defined in Article 57, paragraph 2, of the Charter, or the families of such representatives or officials, (2) experts performing missions for the United Nations or for such specialized agencies, (3) representatives of the press, or of radio, film or other information agencies, who have been accredited by the United Nations (or by such a specialized agency) in its discretion after consultation with the United States, (4) representatives of non-governmental organizations recognized by the United Nations for the purpose of consultation under Article 71 of the Charter, or (5) other persons invited to the headquarters district by the United Nations or by such specialized agency on official business. The appropriate American authorities shall afford any necessary protection to such persons while in transit to or from the headquarters district. This section * * * does not impair the effectiveness of generally applicable laws and regulations as to the operation of means of transportation.

§ 12.   The provisions of Section 11 shall be applicable irrespective of the relations existing between the Governments of the persons referred to in that section and the Government of the United States.

In the joint Congressional resolution that authorized the President to conclude the Headquarters Agreement, it was provided in Section 6, 61 Stat. at 767, that nothing in the agreement should be construed as "in any way diminishing, abridging, or weakening the right of the United States to safeguard its own security and completely to control the entrance of aliens into any territory of the United States other than the headquarters district and its immediate vicinity, * * * and such areas as it is reasonably necessary to traverse in transit between the same and foreign countries."

As a result of negotiations between the Secretary–General and the United States government, it was agreed that the Headquarters Agreement was not to be used as a cover for activities directed against United States security. It was recognized that the United States (1) had a right to grant visas "valid only for transit to and from the Headquarters District and sojourn in its immediate vicinity;" (2) had the authority "to make any reasonable definition, consistent with the purposes of the Agreement, of the 'immediate vicinity' of the Headquarters District, of the necessary routes of transit, and of the time and manner of expiration of the visas following the completion of official functions;" and (3) had a right to deport persons abusing the privileges of residence in activities outside their official capacity. On the other hand, with respect to "aliens in transit to the Headquarters District exclusively on official business of, or before, the United Nations," it was recognized that "the rights of the United States are limited by the Headquarters Agreement to those mentioned." As for borderline cases, i.e., where there might be evidence that a person was coming to the United States for purposes detrimental to United States security, the United States gave assurances that "timely" decisions would be made at "the highest levels," and that the Secretary–General would be kept informed. Report by the Secretary–General to the Economic and Social Council, at 23, U.N. Doc. E/2492 (July 27, 1953). The possibility of submitting future disputes to arbitration, as provided in the Headquarters Agreement, was discussed in the Council as the only alternative to a failure of negotiations. See Liang, The Question of Access to the United Nations Headquarters of Representatives of Non–Governmental Organizations in Consultative Status, 48 A.J.I.L. 434, 445–50 (1954).

The principal U.S. statute regulating the immunities of international organizations in the United States is the International Organizations Immunities Act, 22 U.S.C. § 288a–e (2000) (IOIA). The international organizations designated as entitled to the benefits of the statute are listed in a table following 22 U.S.C. § 288, supplemented by executive orders appearing in the Federal Register and in Title 3 of the Code of Federal Regulations. For an important decision in the United States on the immunity of international organizations under the IOIA, see *Atkinson v. Inter–American Development Bank*, 156 F. 3d 1335 (D.C. Cir. 1998), in which the Court ruled that the Inter–American Development Bank enjoyed "virtually absolute" immunity, thus giving a broad sweep to the notion that an international organization's immunity was to be based on "functional necessity." See also *Mendaro v. World Bank*, 717 F.2d 610 (D.C. Cir. 1983) (finding immunity for the World Bank from suit of former employee); Restatement (Third) § 467, Reporters' Note 4.

Do you think the restrictive immunity doctrine that is now applicable in many states should also apply to international organizations? See Herz, International Organizations in US Courts; Reconsidering the Anachronism of Absolute Immunity, 31 Suffolk Transnat'l L. Rev. 471 (2008); Oparil, Immunity Of International Organizations In United States Courts: Absolute Or Restrictive?, 24 Vand. J. Transnat'l L. 689 (1991); Whiteley, Holding International Organizations Accountable under the Foreign Sovereign Immunities Act: Civil Actions Against the United Nations for Non–Commercial Torts, 7 Wash. U. Global Stud. L. Rev. 619 (2008).

In *Kadic v. Karadzic*, 70 F.3d 232 (2d Cir.1995), the defendant was the political leader of the Bosnian Serb region in Bosnia-Herzegovina. While present in New York City as an invitee of the United Nations, he was personally served with the summons and complaints in two civil actions under the Alien Tort Statute, in which it was alleged that he was responsible for atrocities committed against Bosnian Muslim and Croat women. Karadzic claimed that service of process was defective and that he was immune from suit, inter alia by virtue of his presence in New York to participate in U.N. meetings. In the portion of its opinion dealing with these issues, the court said in part:

> The Headquarters Agreement provides for immunity from suit only in narrowly defined circumstances. * * *

* * *

* * * Counsel for the United Nations has also issued an opinion stating that although the United States must allow United Nations invitees access to the Headquarters District, invitees are not immune from legal process while in the United States at locations outside of the Headquarters District. *See In re Galvao*, [1963] U.N. Jur.Y.B. 164

(opinion of U.N. legal counsel); *see also Restatement (Third)* § 469 reporter's note 8 (U.N. invitee "is not immune from suit or legal process outside the headquarters district during his sojourn in the United States").

* * *

Karadzic nonetheless invites us to fashion a federal common law immunity for those within a judicial district as a United Nations invitee. He contends that such a rule is necessary to prevent private litigants from inhibiting the United Nations in its ability to consult with invited visitors. * * *

Karadzic also endeavors to find support for a common law of immunity in our decision in [Klinghoffer v. S.N.C. Achille Lauro, 937 F.2d 44 (2d Cir.1991)]. Though * * * *Klinghoffer* declined to extend the immunities of the Headquarters Agreement beyond those provided by its express provisions, the decision applied immunity considerations to its construction of New York's long-arm statute * * *.

Despite the considerations that guided *Klinghoffer* in its narrowing construction of the general terminology of New York's long-arm statute as applied to United Nations activities, we decline the invitation to create a federal common law immunity as an extension of the precise terms of a carefully crafted treaty that struck the balance between the interests of the United Nations and those of the United States.

Id. at 247–48.

In *Askir v. Boutros–Ghali*, 933 F. Supp. 368 (S.D.N.Y. 1996), plaintiff sought to sue certain U.N. officials for unlawful possession of his property in Somalia during the peacekeeping and humanitarian operations there. The court found the U.N. defendants to be immune and dismissed the claims for lack of subject-matter jurisdiction. Should the immunity questions have been addressed under an absolute or a restrictive (or functional) theory?

E. ADMINISTRATIVE TRIBUNALS

Since it is often difficult if not impossible to sue an international organization before a national court, such organizations have established administrative tribunals to allow their personnel and other persons to bring claims to an adjudicative body of the organization. The administrative tribunals of the United Nations and of the International Labour Organization are competent "to determine disputes between international organisations and their officials and persons claiming through such officials concerning the terms of appointment and tenure of officials and the rights of officials and pensioners under the applicable staff and pension regulations." Jenks, *supra*, at 161.

The I.L.O. Tribunal was originally established to serve as the administrative tribunal of the I.L.O., but it also served as the League of Nations

Tribunal. Today, the I.L.O. Tribunal has been granted jurisdiction in respect of about 45 international organizations, including the World Health Organization, the Food and Agriculture Organization, UNESCO, the International Telecommunication Union, the World Meteorological Organization, the European Organization for Nuclear Research, the International Atomic Energy Agency, the World Trade Organization, and the International Criminal Court.

The U.N. Administrative Tribunal has jurisdiction over matters relating to the United Nations, but has also been accorded jurisdiction in matters concerning the International Civil Aviation Organization and the International Maritime Organization. In 1954, the International Court of Justice ruled in an advisory opinion that the General Assembly did not have the right to refuse to give effect to a compensation award made by the United Nations Administrative Tribunal. *Effect of Awards of Compensation Made by the United Nations Administrative Tribunal*, Advisory Opinion, 1954 I.C.J. 47. The United Nations has adopted the practice of including arbitration clauses in its commercial contracts.

For recent discussion of the Administrative Tribunals in relation to considerations of immunity from national jurisdiction, see Reinisch, The Immunity of International Organizations and the Jurisdiction of Their Administrative Tribunals, 7 Chinese J. Int'l L. 285 (2008); Reinisch & Weber, The Jurisdictional Immunity of International Organizations, the Individual's Right of Access to the Courts and Administrative Tribunals as Alternative Means of Dispute Settlement, 1 Int'l Org. L. Rev. 59 (2004).

F. REPRESENTATIVES TO INTERNATIONAL ORGANIZATIONS

CONVENTION ON THE PRIVILEGES AND IMMUNITIES OF THE UNITED NATIONS

Adopted by the General Assembly, February 13, 1946
21 U.S.T. 1418, 1 U.N.T.S. 15

Article IV

§ 11. Representatives of Members to the principal and subsidiary organs of the United Nations and to conferences convened by the United Nations, shall, while exercising their functions and during the journey to and from the place of meeting, enjoy the following privileges and immunities:

(a) Immunity from personal arrest or detention and from seizure of their personal baggage, and, in respect of words spoken or written and all acts done by them in their capacity as representatives, immunity from legal process of every kind;

(b) Inviolability for all papers and documents;

(c) The right to use codes and to receive papers or correspondence by courier or in sealed bags;

(d) Exemption in respect of themselves and their spouses from immigration restrictions, aliens registration or national service obligations in the state they are visiting or through which they are passing in the exercise of their functions;

(e) The same facilities in respect of currency or exchange restrictions as are accorded to representatives of foreign governments on temporary official missions;

(f) The same immunities and facilities in respect of their personal baggage as are accorded to diplomatic envoys, and also;

(g) Such other privileges, immunities and facilities not inconsistent with the foregoing as diplomatic envoys enjoy, except that they shall have no right to claim exemption from customs duties on goods imported (otherwise than as part of their personal baggage) or from excise duties or sales taxes.

§ 12.   In order to secure, for the representatives of Members to the principal and subsidiary organs of the United Nations and to conferences convened by the United Nations, complete freedom of speech and independence in the discharge of their duties, the immunity from legal process in respect of words spoken or written and all acts done by them in discharging their duties shall continue to be accorded, notwithstanding that the persons concerned are no longer the representatives of Members.

* * *

§ 14.   Privileges and immunities are accorded to the representatives of Members not for the personal benefit of the individuals themselves, but in order to safeguard the independent exercise of their functions in connection with the United Nations. Consequently a Member not only has the right but is under a duty to waive the immunity of its representative in any case where in the opinion of the Member the immunity would impede the course of justice, and it can be waived without prejudice to the purpose for which the immunity is accorded.

§ 15.   The provisions of Sections 11, 12 * * * are not applicable as between a representative and the authorities of the state of which he is a national or of which he is or has been the representative.

§ 16.   In this article the expression "representatives" shall be deemed to include all delegates, deputy delegates, advisers, technical experts and secretaries of delegations.

AGREEMENT BETWEEN THE UNITED NATIONS AND THE UNITED STATES REGARDING THE HEADQUARTERS OF THE UNITED NATIONS

Signed June 26, 1947
61 Stat. 3416, 11 U.N.T.S. 11

Article V

Section 15

(1) Every person designated by a Member as the principal resident representative to the United Nations of such Member or as a resident representative with the rank of ambassador or minister plenipotentiary,

(2) such resident members of their staffs as may be agreed upon between the Secretary–General, the Government of the United States and the Government of the Member concerned,

(3) every person designated by a Member of a specialized agency, as defined in Article 57, paragraph 2, of the Charter, as its principal resident representative, with the rank of ambassador or minister plenipotentiary, at the headquarters of such agency in the United States, and

(4) such other principal resident representatives of Members to a specialized agency and such resident members of the staffs of representatives of a specialized agency as may be agreed upon between the principal executive officer of the specialized agency, the Government of the United States and the Government of the Member concerned,

shall, whether residing inside or outside the headquarters district, be entitled in the territory of the United States to the same privileges and immunities, subject to corresponding conditions and obligations, as it accords to diplomatic envoys accredited to it. In the case of Members whose governments are not recognized by the United States, such privileges and immunities need be extended to such representatives, or persons on the staffs of such representatives, only within the headquarters district, at their residences and offices outside the district, in transit between the district and such residences and offices, and in transit on official business to or from foreign countries.

NOTES

1. *Vienna Convention.* The privileges and immunities of member representatives to international organizations are also addressed in the Vienna Convention on the Representation of States in Their Relations with International Organizations of a Universal Character, U.N. Doc. A/CONF. 67/16 (Mar. 14, 1975), but as of early 2009 that convention has still not entered into force. The United States abstained on the vote on the final text on the ground that the Convention would unduly expand privileges and immunities; other key states that host international organizations were also unhappy with its provisions. See 1975 Dig. U.S. Prac. 38–40.

2. *Treatment of Representatives to IOs in United States.* Section 7(b) of the International Organizations Immunities Act, 22 U.S.C. § 288d(b) (2000) accords representatives to international organizations, as well as officers and employees of such organizations, immunity "from suit and legal process relating to acts performed by them in their official capacity and falling within their functions as such representatives, officers, or employees." 28 U.S.C. § 1351, as amended by the Diplomatic Relations Act of 1978, gives the district courts exclusive original competence over all civil actions against diplomatic personnel. It is apparently intended also to cover employees of missions to international organizations, such as the United Nations and the Organization of American States. See Restatement (Third) § 470, Reporters' Note 4. A number of decisions by U.S. courts have given effect to the immunity from legal process of representatives to international organizations. See, e.g., *Anonymous v. Anonymous*, 252 N.Y.S.2d 913 (N.Y. Family Ct. 1964) and cases cited in Restatement (Third) § 470, Reporters' Note 2.

3. *Further Reading.* On the immunities of representatives to international organizations, see generally Restatement (Third) § 470; Gross, Immunities and Privileges of Delegations to the United Nations, 16 Int'l Org. 483 (1962); Ling, Comparative Study of The Privileges and Immunities of UN Member Representatives and Officials with the Traditional Privileges and Immunities of Diplomatic Agents, 33 Wash. & Lee L. Rev. 91 (1976); Amerasinghe, Liability To Third Parties Of Member States Of International Organizations: Practice, Principle, and Judicial Precedent, 85 A.J.I.L. 259 (1991).

*

PART 3

SUBJECT MATTER AREAS OF INTERNATIONAL LAW

. . .

CHAPTER 13

HUMAN RIGHTS

∎ ∎ ∎

SECTION 1. FOUNDATIONS OF HUMAN RIGHTS LAW

A. OVERVIEW OF HISTORY AND STRUCTURE

Early in the development of international law there existed some customs and treaties dealing with the condition and treatment of individuals in whom states had an interest—notably their nationals or diplomats. Rules about the rights of aliens (such as discussed in the next chapter), limitations and safeguards in extradition treaties, restrictions on prescriptive jurisdiction, protections under the laws of war, or diplomatic immunities, all afforded significant protections to individuals.

The second half of the 20th century, however, ushered in what has been described as the "Age of Rights." Henkin, The Age of Rights (1990). That characterization reflects the view that, with the end of the Second World War, the idea of human rights became a universal political ideology and a central aspect of an ideology of constitutionalism. The ideology of human rights, of course, is a municipal ideology, to be realized by states within their national societies through national constitutional law and implemented by national institutions. But beginning with the promises made during the Second World War in the plans for a new world order, human rights became a matter of international concern and progressively a subject of international law. Following the Nuremberg Charter and the judgment of the Nuremberg tribunal (and its Tokyo counterpart), the international system, largely under the aegis of the United Nations and of regional bodies in Europe, in the Americas, and in Africa, also promoted new institutions for monitoring and inducing compliance with international norms. In time, with the end of the Cold War, the international system also developed the authority of existing institutions, notably that of the U.N. Security Council, to address human rights violations that threaten international peace and security.

What was once unthinkable became, by the 21st century, wholly normal.

BUERGENTHAL, THE EVOLVING INTERNATIONAL HUMAN RIGHTS SYSTEM

100 A.J.I.L. 783, 784–85 (2006) (footnotes omitted)

I. EARLY INSTITUTIONAL DEVELOPMENTS

The regional human rights machinery in existence today, as well as the plethora of United Nations human rights bodies, traces its antecedents to League of Nations institutions that dealt with minorities' rights and mandated territories. After World War I, the Allied and Associated Powers concluded a series of treaties with Austria, Bulgaria, Czechoslovakia, Greece, Poland, Romania, Turkey, and Yugoslavia for the protection of the rights of the minorities living in those countries. The League agreed to become the guarantor of the obligations the states parties assumed in these treaties. It performed that function by developing special mechanisms, including so-called Committees of Three that reviewed petitions from minorities charging violations of their rights. Serious legal questions that grew out of these reviews were frequently submitted by the Council of the League to the Permanent Court of International Justice, which produced an extensive jurisprudence on the subject.

The League of Nations mandates system applied only to the former colonies of the states that were defeated in World War I. Under Article 22 of the League's Covenant, these colonies were transformed into mandates to be administered by some of the victorious powers in that war. Article 22 further provided that the mandatory states were to administer the mandated territories in accordance with "the principle that the well-being and development of [indigenous] peoples form a sacred trust of civilisation." These states also assumed the obligation to report annually to the League on the discharge of their responsibilities as mandatories. A Mandates Commission, established by the League, was charged with reviewing these reports. Had the League survived, the commission might have been able to transform itself over time into an effective mechanism capable of ensuring that the mandatory powers complied with their obligations. It might also have been able gradually to strengthen these obligations. Although the dissolution of the League of Nations put an end to the work of the commission, some of its functions devolved on the United Nations Trusteeship Council, which was entrusted with powers to supervise the administration of the remaining mandates and other non-self-governing territories. Once most of these territories acquired their independence, the Trusteeship Council itself was abolished.

II. THE UNITED NATIONS CHARTER

International human rights law, as we know it today, begins with the Charter of the United Nations. According to its Article 1(3), one of the purposes of the United Nations is the achievement of "international cooperation in ... promoting and encouraging respect for human rights and for fundamental freedoms for all without distinction as to race, sex, language, or religion." That the UN Charter should have listed this subject among the Organization's purposes is not surprising, considering that it was drafted in the aftermath of World War II, the Holocaust, and the murder of millions of innocent human beings. But contrary to what might have been expected given this background, the Charter did not impose any concrete human rights obligations on the UN member states. Although a group of smaller countries and nongovernmental organizations (NGOs) attending the San Francisco Conference fought for the inclusion of an international bill of rights in the Charter, these efforts failed, principally because they were opposed by the major powers.

Instead of a bill of rights, the San Francisco Conference adopted some intentionally vague Charter provisions on human rights. The two major human rights provisions, in addition to Article 1(3) referred to above, are Articles 55 and 56. * * * The vagueness of these human rights provisions, read together with the nonintervention clause found in Article 2(7) of the Charter, tended for years to hamper serious UN action in confronting human rights violations. State claims based on Article 2(7) were gradually rejected by a majority of the UN membership. But they continued to be regularly made in different UN organs by states that wanted, and in the early days frequently managed, to defeat, or at least weaken, some proposed human rights measures by arguing that how they treated their nationals essentially fell within their domestic jurisdiction, and hence was protected against UN intervention under Article 2(7).

Despite their vagueness, however, the human rights provisions of the Charter did prove to have important consequences. In time, the membership of the United Nations came to accept the proposition that the Charter had internationalized the concept of human rights. This did not mean that as soon as the Charter entered into force, all human rights issues were ipso facto no longer essentially within the domestic jurisdiction of states. It did mean, though, that states were deemed to have assumed some international obligations relating to human rights. Although the full scope of these rights remained to be defined, states could no longer validly claim that human rights as such were essentially domestic in character. Equally important, the obligation imposed by Article 56 on UN member states, which requires them to cooperate with the Organization in the promotion of human rights, provided the United Nations with the requisite legal authority to embark on what became a massive lawmaking effort to define and codify these rights. The centerpiece of this effort was the proclamation in 1948 of the Universal Declaration of Human Rights. The adoption of a large number of human rights conventions followed, including the two International Covenants on Human Rights in 1966. These two treaties, together with the human rights provisions of the Charter and the Universal Declaration, constitute the International Bill of Rights. Although the Universal Declaration was adopted as a nonbinding UN General Assembly resolution and was intended, as its preamble indicates, to provide "a common understanding" of the human rights and fundamental freedoms mentioned in the Charter, it has come to be accepted as a normative instrument in its own right. Together with the Charter, the Universal Declaration is now considered to spell out the general human rights obligations of all UN member states.

Notes

1. *Defining Human Rights*. "Human rights" has been a term in common usage but not authoritatively defined. Such rights were said to include those "moral-political claims which, by contemporary consensus, every human being has or is deemed to have upon his society or government," claims which are recognized "as of right," not by "love, or grace, or charity." Henkin, Rights: American and Human, 79 Colum. L. Rev. 405, 405 (1979); Henkin, The Rights of Man Today 1–3 (1978).

2. *Human Rights versus Rights of Aliens*. International law on state responsibility for injuries to aliens, addressed in Chapter 14, antedated the field of international human rights, and developed certain minimal standards of protection that must be accorded to individuals who travel from their state to another. The existence of that field of state responsibility influenced the emergence of the field of human rights law, which compels states to accord minimum protections to not just aliens but their own nationals as well. Over the past sixty years, the field of international human rights has become more sophisticated and detailed than its predecessor, such that norms now present in the human rights context are often cited to provide content to the standards that must be accorded aliens.

3. *Human Rights versus International Humanitarian Law*. It is common practice to distinguish, and to treat as a separate subject, "international humanitarian law," which is international law applicable during an armed conflict. Many of the rules relating to that body of law may be found in the 1907 Hague Regulations on the law of land warfare, the 1949 Geneva Conventions on protections for the victims of armed conflict, and related instruments. See Chapter 16. The two bodies of law overlap and individuals during armed conflict enjoy rights under both bodies of law. According to the International Court of Justice:

> [T]he Court considers that the protection offered by human rights conventions does not cease in case of armed conflict * * *. As regards, the relationship between international humanitarian law and human rights law, there are thus three possible situations: some rights may be exclusively matters of international humanitarian law; others may be exclusively matters of human rights law; yet others may be matters of both these branches of international law.

Legal Consequences of the Construction of a Wall in the Occupied Palestinian Territory, Advisory Opinion, 2004 I.C.J. 136, para. 106. Where there is a potential conflict between the two systems of law, however, the Court appears to view international humanitarian law as the more appropriate body of law, viewing it in times of armed conflict as the *"lex specialis."* Id.; see also Legality of the Threat or Use of Nuclear Weapons, Advisory Opinion, 1996 I.C.J. 226, para. 25 ("The test of what is an arbitrary deprivation of life * * * falls to be determined by the applicable *lex specialis*, namely, the law applicable in armed conflict which is designed to regulate the conduct of hostilities"); see also Watkin, Controlling the Use of Force: A Role for Human Rights Norms in Contemporary Armed Conflict, 98 A.J.I.L. 1 (2004); Heintze, On the Relationship between Human Rights Law Protection and International Humanitarian Law, 86 Int'l Rev. Red Cross 789 (2004); Meron, The Humanization of Humanitarian Law, 94 A.J.I.L. 239 (2000); Frowein, The Relationship between Human Rights Regimes and Regimes of Belligerent Occupation, 28 Isr. Y.B. Hum. Rts. 1 (1998). International humanitarian law and some human rights law are currently being construed by the various international criminal tribunals. See Chapter 16.

4. *Civil Society and Human Rights.* One key reason the field of human rights has grown dramatically over the past century is the pervasive influence of non-governmental organizations and other elements of "civil society" in promoting, monitoring, and enforcing human rights. Political scientists note that "transnational advocacy networks" have served as important engines in pushing a human rights agenda upon states and international organizations, and once human rights norms are adopted, in monitoring state compliance through investigations and reports. Where human rights can be enforced through national or even international litigation, such groups are at the forefront in developing, funding, and staffing cases, just as has occurred in the area of civil rights. Yet with such influence and power have also arisen questions. Who has anointed these groups to represent "civil society"? Is their agenda truly representative of the "people" given that they have not been elected, nor are accountable to the population at large? See Non-state Actors and Human Rights (Alston ed. 2005); Kennedy, The Dark Sides of Virtue: Reassessing International Humanitarianism (2004).

5. *Protecting Only Natural Persons?* International human rights generally, the Universal Declaration, and, notably, the International Covenant on Civil and Political Rights, Dec. 16, 1966, 999 U.N.T.S. 171, address the rights of natural persons only. (The Covenant on Economic, Social, and Cultural Rights, however, recognizes some rights for trade unions. See art 8(1), Dec. 16, 1966, 993 U.N.T.S. 3). By comparison, some provisions of the European Convention for the Protection of Human Rights and Fundamental Freedoms also apply to juridical persons. For example, Article 25 of that Convention expressly accords a right of petition to "any person, nongovernmental organization or group of individuals claiming to be a victim of a violation." Nov. 4, 1950, 213 U.N.T.S. 221. Article 1 of the First Protocol to the Convention provides: "[e]very natural or legal person is entitled to the peaceful enjoyment of his possessions." Mar. 20, 1952, 213 U.N.T.S. 262.

6. *Obligating Only States?* Do human rights norms only impose obligations upon states in their treatment of persons? Or is it possible to impose human rights obligations upon non-state actors as well, such as corporations or international organizations? In 2003, the U.N. Sub–Commission on the Promotion and Protection of Human Rights adopted a code on the responsibility of transnational corporations, which asserted that such corporations are directly obligated under human rights law. See Norms on the Responsibilities of Transnational Corporations and Other Business Enterprises with Regard to Human Rights, U.N. Doc. E/CN.4/Sub.2/2003/12/Rev.2, pt. A (Aug. 26, 2003); see also Clapham, Human Rights Obligations of Non–State Actors (2006);

Protect, Respect and Remedy: A Framework for Business and Human Rights, U.N. Doc. A/HRC/8/5 (Apr. 7, 2008) (Ruggie Report) (discussing corporate responsibility to respect human rights); Ruggie, Business and Human Rights: The Evolving International Agenda, 101 A.J.I.L. 819 (2007); Knox, Horizontal Human Rights Law, 102 A.J.I.L. 1 (2008) (and sources listed at n. 178).

B. COMPETING INTERESTS

The field of human rights must balance several competing interests. One set are the interests of the individual versus that of the state, where the state may be conceived of as representing the collective interests of the entire community of individuals (at least in a democracy). Central to the field of human rights, of course, is the interest in protecting the dignity of the human person through an array of civil, political, and even economic rights. Yet aligned against this interest is the need for the state to maintain law, order, and stability, which will at times require arresting, incarcerating, and punishing persons, discriminating against persons based on their status as juveniles or felons, or prohibiting speech that threatens persons or offends public morality. With respect to economic rights, while some instruments of international law advance rights to work, education, and shelter, such rights must compete with the lack of resources possessed by many states to provide a robust social safety net.

A second set of competing interests concerns that of a single state versus a broader community (regional or global) of states. There is no inherent reason why a high level of human rights cannot be accorded by a single state to its nationals, without any need for resort to international law. Indeed, some states, such as the United States, tend to view their existing national rights as wholly sufficient, such that there is little need to incorporate international human rights into the existing national legal system as an independent source of law. Yet there are interests in the broader community of states in having states commit to norms by which other states may judge them and by developing appropriate international mechanisms (such as treaty-monitoring committees) that will help to promote implementation and compliance. The tension, then, is the typical tension that permeates international law as a whole—how to balance the sovereignty of the state with the communal interests of a collective of states.

A third set of competing interests concerns allocation of governmental authority within the state. International human rights arises in the context of treaties and customary international law, which is typically the responsibility of national government authorities, such as the Ministry of Foreign Affairs or the Department of State. Yet in states that have federal systems of government, including the United States, rights and obligations of individuals are often addressed at the lowest level of governmental authority, whether it concerns rights to privacy, due process, or physical safety. The field of human rights, then, must find ways to establish and implement effective human rights, yet without trampling on the constitutional structures of states.

A final set of competing interests concerns the aspiration for universal human rights—ones that exist equally in all places at all times—versus the aspiration to preserve cultural and moral differences that exist among states worldwide, a notion sometimes referred to as "cultural relativism." Just as federal systems within national states often laud the ability of difficult cultures and traditions to flourish within a single nation state, the aspiration for cultural relativism lauds the ability of different cultures and traditions to exist worldwide without all being forced to accept the same mores, and especially resists the imposition of Western mores on developing states. Yet the concept of cultural relativism, stated in its strongest terms, goes even further by denying that there are transcendent values that can be agreed upon among all states, and hence challenges a fundamental assumption of the human rights movement. By contrast, those who aspire to universal human rights assert that many rights—such as the right not to be arbitrarily killed—cannot possibly be different in different societies.

As you read the following case, consider the difficulties that arise in trying to balance these disparate interests, including the difficulty of balancing religious freedom with public order. Do you think the majority reached the right conclusion, or are you more persuaded by the dissent?

ŞAHIN v. TURKEY

European Court of Human Rights, 2005
App. No. 44774/98, 44 Eur. H.R. Rep. 99 (2005) (footnotes omitted)

PROCEDURE

1. The case originated in an application against the Republic of Turkey lodged with the European Commission of Human Rights ("the Commission") under * * * the Convention for the Protection of Human Rights and Fundamental Freedoms ("the Convention") by a Turkish national, Ms. Leyla Şahin ("the applicant"), on July, 21 1998.

* * *

3. The applicant alleged that her rights and freedoms under * * * the Convention * * * had been violated by regulations on wearing the Islamic headscarf in institutions of higher education.

* * *

THE FACTS

I. The Circumstances of the Case

14. The applicant was born in 1973 and has lived in Vienna since 1999, when she left Istanbul to pursue her medical studies at the Faculty of Medicine at Vienna University. She comes from a traditional family of

practising Muslims and considers it her religious duty to wear the Islamic headscarf.

A.   Circular of 23 February 1998

15.   On August 26, 1997 the applicant, then in her fifth year at the Faculty of Medicine at Bursa University, enrolled at the *Cerrahpaşa* Faculty of Medicine at Istanbul University. She says that she wore the Islamic headscarf during the four years she spent studying medicine at the University of Bursa and continued to do so until February 1998.

16.   On February, 23 1998 the Vice Chancellor of Istanbul University issued a circular, the relevant part of which provides:

> "* * * [S]tudents whose 'heads are covered' (who wear the Islamic headscarf) and students (including overseas students) with beards must not be admitted to lectures, courses or tutorials. Consequently, the name and number of any student with a beard or wearing the Islamic headscarf must not be added to the lists of registered students. However, students who insist on attending tutorials and entering lecture theatres although their names and numbers are not on the lists must be advised of the position and, should they refuse to leave, their names and numbers must be taken and they must be informed that they are not entitled to attend lectures. If they refuse to leave the lecture theatre, the teacher shall record the incident in a report explaining why it was not possible to give the lecture and shall bring the incident to the attention of the university authorities as a matter of urgency so that disciplinary measures can be taken".

17.   On March 12, 1998, in accordance with the aforementioned circular, the applicant was denied access by invigilators to a written examination on oncology because she was wearing the Islamic headscarf. On March, 20 1998 the secretariat of the chair of orthopaedic traumatology refused to allow her to enroll because she was wearing a headscarf. On April, 16 1998 she was refused admission to a neurology lecture and on June, 10 1998 to a written examination on public health, again for the same reason.

* * *

28.   [O]n September 16, 1999, the applicant abandoned her studies in Turkey and enrolled at Vienna University, where she pursued her university education.

II.   Relevant Law and Practice

* * *

B.   History and Background

1.   Religious Dress and the Principle of Secularism

30.   The Turkish Republic was founded on the principle that the State should be secular [*laik* in Turkish]. Before and after the proclama-

tion of the Republic on October 29, 1923, the public and religious spheres were separated through a series of revolutionary reforms: the abolition of the caliphate on March 3, 1923; the repeal of the constitutional provision declaring Islam the religion of the State on April 10, 1928; and, lastly, on February 5, 1937 a constitutional amendment according constitutional status to the principle of secularism. * * *

31. The principle of secularism was inspired by developments in Ottoman society in the period between the 19th century and the proclamation of the Republic. The idea of creating a modern public society in which equality was guaranteed to all citizens without distinction on grounds of religion, denomination or sex had already been mooted in the Ottoman debates of the nineteenth century.

* * *

33. The first legislation to regulate dress was the Headgear Act of November 28, 1925, which treated dress as a modernity issue. Similarly, a ban was imposed on wearing religious attire other than in places of worship or at religious ceremonies, irrespective of the religion or belief concerned, by the Dress (Regulations) Act of December 3, 1934.

34. Under the Education Services (Merger) Act of March 3, 1924, religious schools were closed and all schools came under the control of the Ministry for Education. * * *

35. In Turkey wearing the Islamic headscarf to school and university is a recent phenomenon which only really began to emerge in the 1980s. There has been extensive discussion on the issue and it continues to be the subject of lively debate in Turkish society. Those in favour of the headscarf see wearing it as a duty and/or a form of expression linked to religious identity. However, the supporters of secularism, who draw a distinction between the başörtüsü (traditional Anatolian headscarf, worn loosely) and the türban (tight, knotted headscarf hiding the hair and the throat), see the Islamic headscarf as a symbol of a political Islam. As a result of the accession to power on June 28, 1996 of a coalition government comprising the *Islamist Refah Partisi*, and the centre-right *Doğru Yol Partisi*, the debate has taken on strong political overtones. The ambivalence displayed by the leaders of the *Refah Partisi*, including the then Prime Minister, over their attachment to democratic values, and their advocacy of a plurality of legal systems functioning according to different religious rules for each religious community was perceived in Turkish society as a genuine threat to republican values and civil peace.

2. The rules on dress in institutions of higher education and the case-law of the Constitutional Court

* * *

39. * * * The Constitutional Court [of Turkey decided on March 7, 1989] that students had to be permitted to work and pursue their education together in a calm, tolerant and mutually supportive atmo-

sphere without being deflected from that goal by signs of religious affiliation. It found that, irrespective of whether the Islamic headscarf was a precept of Islam, granting legal recognition to a religious symbol of that type in institutions of higher education was not compatible with the principle that State education must be neutral, as it would be liable to generate conflicts between students with differing religious convictions or beliefs.

40.   On October 25, 1990 transitional section 17 of Law no. 2547 entered into force. It provides:

"Choice of dress shall be free in institutions of higher education, provided that it does not contravene the laws in force."

41.   In a judgment of April 9, 1991, which was published in the *Official Gazette* of July 31, 1991, the Constitutional Court noted that, in the light of the principles it had established in its judgment of March 7, 1989, the aforementioned provision did not allow headscarves to be worn in institutions of higher education on religious grounds and so was consistent with the Constitution. * * *

3.   Application of the regulations at Istanbul University

42.   Istanbul University was founded in the 15th century and is one of the main centres of State higher education in Turkey. It has 17 faculties (including two faculties of medicine—*Cerrahpaşa* and Çapa) and 12 schools of higher education. It is attended by approximately 50,000 students.

43.   In 1994, following a petitioning campaign launched by female students enrolled on the midwifery course at the University School of Medicine, the Vice Chancellor circulated a memorandum in which he explained the background to the Islamic-headscarf issue and the legal basis for the relevant regulations, noting in particular:

"The ban prohibiting students enrolled on the midwifery course from wearing the headscarf during tutorials is not intended to infringe their freedom of conscience and religion, but to comply with the laws and regulations in force. When doing their work, midwives and nurses wear a uniform. That uniform is described in and identified by regulations issued by the Ministry of Health (. . .). Students who wish to join the profession are aware of this. Imagine a student of midwifery trying to put a baby in or remove it from an incubator, or assisting a doctor in an operating theatre or maternity unit while wearing a long-sleeved coat."

44.   The Vice Chancellor was concerned that the campaign for permission to wear the Islamic headscarf on all university premises had reached the point where there was a risk of its undermining order and causing unrest at the University, the Faculty, the *Cerrahpaşa* Hospital and the School of Medicine. He called on the students to comply with the rules on dress, reminding them, in particular, of the rights of the patients.

* * *

JUDGMENT

I. Alleged Violation of Article 9 of the Convention

70. The applicant submitted that the ban on wearing the Islamic headscarf in institutions of higher education constituted an unjustified interference with her right to freedom of religion, in particular, her right to manifest her religion.

She relied on Article 9 of the [European Convention for the Protection of Human Rights and Fundamental Freedoms], which provides:

> "1. Everyone has the right to freedom of thought, conscience and religion; this right includes freedom to change his religion or belief and freedom, either alone or in community with others and in public or private, to manifest his religion or belief, in worship, teaching, practice and observance.
>
> 2. Freedom to manifest one's religion or beliefs shall be subject only to such limitations as are prescribed by law and are necessary in a democratic society in the interests of public safety, for the protection of public order, health or morals, or for the protection of the rights and freedoms of others."

* * *

75. The Court must consider whether the applicant's right under Article 9 was interfered with and, if so, whether the interference was "prescribed by law," pursued a legitimate aim, and was "necessary in a democratic society" within the meaning of Article 9 § 2 of the Convention.

1. Whether there was interference

* * *

78. As to whether there was interference, the Grand Chamber endorses the following findings of the [2004 decision issued by the European Court's lower] Chamber:

> "The applicant said that, by wearing the headscarf, she was obeying a religious precept and thereby manifesting her desire to comply strictly with the duties imposed by the Islamic faith. Accordingly, her decision to wear the headscarf may be regarded as motivated or inspired by a religion or belief and, without deciding whether such decisions are in every case taken to fulfil a religious duty, the Court proceeds on the assumption that the regulations in issue, which placed restrictions of place and manner on the right to wear the Islamic headscarf in universities, constituted an interference with the applicant's right to manifest her religion".

2. "Prescribed by law"

* * *

84. The Court reiterates its settled case-law that the expression "prescribed by law" requires firstly that the impugned measure should

have a basis in domestic law. It also refers to the quality of the law in question, requiring that it be accessible to the persons concerned and formulated with sufficient precision to enable them—if need be, with appropriate advice—to foresee, to a degree that is reasonable in the circumstances, the consequences which a given action may entail and to regulate their conduct.

* * *

98. In these circumstances, the Court finds that there was a legal basis for the interference in Turkish law, namely transitional section 17 of Law No. 2547 read in the light of the relevant case law of the domestic courts. The law was also accessible and can be considered sufficiently precise in its terms to satisfy the requirement of foreseeability. It would have been clear to the applicant, from the moment she entered Istanbul University, that there were restrictions on wearing the Islamic headscarf on the university premises and, from February 23, 1998, that she was liable to be refused access to lectures and examinations if she continued to do so.

3. Legitimate aim

99. Having regard to the circumstances of the case and the terms of the domestic courts' decisions, the Court is able to accept that the impugned interference primarily pursued the legitimate aims of protecting the rights and freedoms of others and of protecting public order, a point which is not in issue between the parties.

4. "Necessary in a democratic society"

. . .

(i) General principles

104. The Court reiterates that as enshrined in Article 9, freedom of thought, conscience and religion is one of the foundations of a "democratic society" within the meaning of the Convention. This freedom is, in its religious dimension, one of the most vital elements that go to make up the identity of believers and their conception of life, but it is also a precious asset for atheists, agnostics, sceptics and the unconcerned. The pluralism indissociable from a democratic society, which has been dearly won over the centuries, depends on it. That freedom entails, inter alia, freedom to hold or not to hold religious beliefs and to practise or not to practise a religion.

105. While religious freedom is primarily a matter of individual conscience, it also implies, inter alia, freedom to manifest one's religion, alone and in private, or in community with others, in public and within the circle of those whose faith one shares. Article 9 lists the various forms which manifestation of one's religion or belief may take, namely worship, teaching, practice and observance. Article 9 does not protect every act motivated or inspired by a religion or belief.

106.   In democratic societies, in which several religions coexist within one and the same population, it may be necessary to place restrictions on freedom to manifest one's religion or belief in order to reconcile the interests of the various groups and ensure that everyone's beliefs are respected. This follows both from paragraph 2 of Article 9 and the State's positive obligation under Article 1 of the Convention to secure to everyone within its jurisdiction the rights and freedoms defined in the Convention.

107.   The Court has frequently emphasised the State's role as the neutral and impartial organiser of the exercise of various religions, faiths and beliefs, and stated that this role is conducive to public order, religious harmony and tolerance in a democratic society. It also considers that the State's duty of neutrality and impartiality is incompatible with any power on the State's part to assess the legitimacy of religious beliefs or the ways in which those beliefs are expressed and that it requires the State to ensure mutual tolerance between opposing groups. Accordingly, the role of the authorities in such circumstances is not to remove the cause of tension by eliminating pluralism, but to ensure that the competing groups tolerate each other.

108.   Pluralism, tolerance and broadmindedness are hallmarks of a "democratic society". Although individual interests must on occasion be subordinated to those of a group, democracy does not simply mean that the views of a majority must always prevail: a balance must be achieved which ensures the fair and proper treatment of people from minorities and avoids any abuse of a dominant position. Pluralism and democracy must also be based on dialogue and a spirit of compromise necessarily entailing various concessions on the part of individuals or groups of individuals which are justified in order to maintain and promote the ideals and values of a democratic society. Where these "rights and freedoms" are themselves among those guaranteed by the Convention or its Protocols, it must be accepted that the need to protect them may lead States to restrict other rights or freedoms likewise set forth in the Convention. It is precisely this constant search for a balance between the fundamental rights of each individual which constitutes the foundation of a "democratic society".

109.   Where questions concerning the relationship between state and religions are at stake, on which opinion in a democratic society may reasonably differ widely, the role of the national decision-making body must be given special importance . * * * This will notably be the case when it comes to regulating the wearing of religious symbols in educational institutions, especially * * * in view of the diversity of the approaches taken by national authorities on the issue. It is not possible to discern throughout Europe a uniform conception of the significance of religion in society * * * and the meaning or impact of the public expression of a religious belief will differ according to time and context. Rules in this sphere will consequently vary from one country to another according to national traditions and the requirements imposed by the need to protect the rights and freedoms of others and to maintain public order. Accordingly, the choice of the extent and form such regulations should take must

inevitably be left up to a point to the State concerned, as it will depend on the domestic context concerned.

110.   This margin of appreciation goes hand in hand with a European supervision embracing both the law and the decisions applying it. The Court's task is to determine whether the measures taken at national level were justified in principle and proportionate. In delimiting the extent of the margin of appreciation in the present case the Court must have regard to what is at stake, namely the need to protect the rights and freedoms of others, to preserve public order and to secure civil peace and true religious pluralism, which is vital to the survival of a democratic society.

111.   * * * In the *Dahlab* case, which concerned the teacher of a class of small children, the Court stressed among other matters the "powerful external symbol" which her wearing a headscarf represented and questioned whether it might have some kind of proselytising effect, seeing that it appeared to be imposed on women by a religious precept that was hard to reconcile with the principle of gender equality. It also noted that wearing the Islamic headscarf could not easily be reconciled with the message of tolerance, respect for others and, above all, equality and non-discrimination that all teachers in a democratic society should convey to their pupils.

* * *

(ii) Application of the foregoing principles to the present case

112.   The interference in issue caused by the circular of February 23, 1998 imposing restrictions as to place and manner on the rights of students such as Ms Şahin to wear the Islamic headscarf on university premises was, according to the Turkish courts * * * , based in particular on the two principles of secularism and equality.

* * *

115.   After examining the parties' arguments, the Grand Chamber sees no good reason to depart from the approach taken by the Chamber as follows:

"(...) The Court {...} notes the emphasis placed in the Turkish constitutional system on the protection of the rights of women ... Gender equality—recognised by the European Court as one of the key principles underlying the Convention and a goal to be achieved by member States of the Council of Europe * * *—was also found by the Turkish Constitutional Court to be a principle implicit in the values underlying the Constitution (...).

(...) In addition, like the Constitutional Court (...), the Court considers that, when examining the question of the Islamic headscarf in the Turkish context, there must be borne in mind the impact which wearing such a symbol, which is presented or perceived as a compulsory religious duty, may have on those who choose not to wear it. As has already been noted * * *, the issues at stake include the protection of the 'rights and freedoms of others' and the 'maintenance of public order' in a country in which the majority of the population, while professing a strong attachment to the rights of women and a secular way of life, adhere to the Islamic faith. Imposing limitations on freedom in this sphere may, therefore, be regarded as meeting a pressing social need by seeking to achieve those two legitimate aims, especially since, as the Turkish courts stated (...), this religious symbol has taken on political significance in Turkey in recent years.

(...) The Court does not lose sight of the fact that there are extremist political movements in Turkey which seek to impose on society as a whole their religious symbols and conception of a society founded on religious precepts (...). It has previously said that each Contracting State may, in accordance with the Convention provisions, take a stance against such political movements, based on its historical experience * * * . The regulations concerned have to be viewed in that context and constitute a measure intended to achieve the legitimate aims referred to above and thereby to preserve pluralism in the university.''

116. Having regard to the above background, it is the principle of secularism, as elucidated by the Constitutional Court, which is the paramount consideration underlying the ban on the wearing of religious symbols in universities. In such a context, where the values of pluralism, respect for the rights of others * * *, it is understandable that the relevant authorities should wish to preserve the secular nature of the institution concerned and so consider it contrary to such values to allow religious attire, including, as in the present case, the Islamic headscarf, to be worn.

117. The Court must now determine whether in the instant case there was a reasonable relationship of proportionality between the means employed and the legitimate objectives pursued by the interference.

118. Like the Chamber, the Grand Chamber notes at the outset that it is common ground that practising Muslim students in Turkish universities are free, within the limits imposed by educational organisational constraints, to manifest their religion in accordance with habitual forms of Muslim observance. In addition, the resolution adopted by Istanbul University on July 9, 1998 shows that various other forms of religious attire are also forbidden on the university premises.

* * *

121. * * * [I]t is not for the Court to substitute its view for that of the university authorities. By reason of their direct and continuous contact with the education community, the university authorities are in principle better placed than an international court to evaluate local needs and conditions or the requirements of a particular course. Article 9 does not always guarantee the right to behave in a manner governed by a

religious belief and does not confer on people who do so the right to disregard rules that have proved to be justified.

122.   In the light of the foregoing and having regard to the contracting states' margin of appreciation in this sphere, the Court finds that the interference in issue was justified in principle and proportionate to the aim pursued.

123.   Consequently, there has been no breach of Article 9 of the Convention.

* * *

DISSENTING OPINION OF JUDGE TULKENS

* * *

5.   As regards, firstly, *secularism*, * * * [it] is undoubtedly necessary for the protection of the democratic system in Turkey. Religious freedom is, however, also a founding principle of democratic societies. Accordingly, the fact that the Grand Chamber recognised the force of the principle of secularism did not release it from its obligation to establish that the ban on wearing the Islamic headscarf to which the applicant was subject was necessary to secure compliance with that principle and, therefore, met a "pressing social need." * * * Moreover, where there has been interference with a fundamental right, the Court's case law clearly establishes that mere affirmations do not suffice: they must be supported by concrete examples. Such examples do not appear to have been forthcoming in the present case.

6.   Under Article 9 of the Convention, the freedom with which this case is concerned is not freedom to have a religion (the internal conviction) but to manifest one's religion (the expression of that conviction). If the Court has been very protective (perhaps over-protective) of religious sentiment, it has shown itself less willing to intervene in cases concerning religious practices, which only appear to receive a subsidiary form of protection [see paragraph 105 of the judgment]. This is, in fact, an aspect of freedom of religion with which the Court has rarely been confronted up to now and on which it has not yet had an opportunity to form an opinion with regard to external symbols of religious practice, such as particular items of clothing, whose symbolic importance may vary greatly according to the faith concerned.

7.   * * * The majority * * * consider that wearing the headscarf contravenes the principle of secularism. In so doing, they take up position on an issue that has been the subject of much debate, namely the signification of wearing the headscarf and its relationship with the principle of secularism.

In the present case, a generalised assessment of that type gives rise to at least three difficulties. Firstly, the judgment does not address the applicant's argument—which the Government did not dispute—that she had no intention of calling the principle of secularism, a principle with which she agreed, into doubt. Secondly, there is no evidence to show that the applicant, through her attitude, conduct or acts, contravened that principle. This is a test the Court has always applied in its case-law. Lastly, the judgment makes no distinction between teachers and students, whereas in *Dahlab v Switzerland*, which concerned a teacher, the Court expressly noted the role-model aspect which the teacher's wearing the headscarf had. While the principle of secularism requires education to be provided without any manifestation of religion and while it has to be compulsory for teachers and all public servants, as they have voluntarily taken up posts in a neutral environment, the position of * * * students seems to me to be different.

8. Freedom to manifest a religion entails everyone being allowed to exercise that right, whether individually or collectively, in public or in private, subject to the dual condition that they do not infringe the rights and freedoms of others and do not prejudice public order [European Convention Article 9 § 2].

As regards the first condition, this could have been satisfied if the headscarf the applicant wore as a religious symbol had been ostentatious or aggressive or was used to exert pressure, to provoke a reaction, to proselytise or to spread propaganda and undermined—or was liable to undermine—the convictions of others. However, the Government did not argue that this was the case and there was no evidence before the Court to suggest that Ms Şahin had any such intention. As to the second condition, it has been neither suggested nor demonstrated that there was any disruption in teaching or in everyday life at the University, or any disorderly conduct, as a result of the applicant's wearing the headscarf. Indeed, no disciplinary proceedings were taken against her.

* * *

10. In fact, it is the threat posed by "extremist political movements" seeking to "impose on society as a whole their religious symbols and conception of a society founded on religious precepts" which, in the Court's view, serves to justify the regulations in issue, which constitute "a measure intended to ... to preserve pluralism in the university" [see paragraph 115 of the judgment]. The Court had already made this clear in its *Refah Partisi v Turkey* judgment, when it stated:

"In a country like Turkey, where the great majority of the population belong to a particular religion, measures taken in universities to prevent certain fundamentalist religious movements from exerting pressure on students who do not practise that religion or on those who belong to another religion may be justified under Article 9 § 2 of the Convention."

While everyone agrees on the need to prevent radical Islamism, a serious objection may nevertheless be made to such reasoning. Merely wearing the headscarf cannot be associated with fundamentalism and it is vital to distinguish between those who wear the headscarf and "extremists" who seek to impose the headscarf as they do other religious symbols. Not all women who wear the headscarf are fundamentalists and there is nothing to suggest that the applicant held fundamentalist views. * * *

* * *

13.   Since, to my mind, the ban on wearing the Islamic headscarf on the university premises was not based on reasons that were relevant and sufficient, it cannot be considered to be interference that was "necessary in a democratic society" within the meaning of Article 9 § 2 of the Convention. In these circumstances, there has been a violation of the applicant's right to freedom of religion, as guaranteed by the Convention.

NOTES

1.   *Head Scarfs in Europe*. Which do you find more persuasive, the majority's opinion or that of the dissent? Whatever your preference, do you think the same outcome is necessarily called for in a different European country, or will it depend on the particular circumstances in that country? In 2004, France approved a ban on "the wearing of symbols or clothing by which students conspicuously manifest a religious appearance" in public schools, a ban that received political support across the political spectrum. See Law 2004–228 of March 15, 2004, Journal Officiel de la République Française [Official Gazette of France], Mar. 17, 2004, at 5190; Beller, The Headscarf Affair: The Conseil d'Etat on the Role of Religion and Culture in French Society, 39 Tex. Int'l L.J. 581, 581 (2004). Do you think that the French ban would also be upheld by the European Court of Human Rights? For assessment of a hypothetical challenge to the French law, see Boustead, The French Headscarf Law Before the European Court of Human Rights, 16 J. Transnat'l L. & Pol'y 167 (2007); see generally Radacic, Gender Equality Jurisprudence of the European Court of Human Rights, 19 E.J.I.L. 841 (2008); Bennoune, Secularism and Human Rights: A Contextual Analysis of Headscarves, Religious Expression, and Women's Equality Under International Law, 45 Colum. J. Transnat'l L. 367 (2007); McGoldrick, Human Rights and Religion: The Islamic Headscarf Debate in Europe (2006). For further discussion of the European Court of Human Rights, see *infra* this Chapter, Section 3.

2.   *Margin of Appreciation*. The European Court referred in *Şahin v. Turkey* to the "margin of appreciation" doctrine. That doctrine—which has its origins in French and German law—generally may be seen as comprising two elements: (1) an acceptance that certain international norms are open-ended or unsettled (normative flexibility); and (2) a consequent willingness of international courts to exercise restraint when reviewing the decisions of national authorities (judicial deference). Policy reasons supporting the doctrine are: a desire to promote pluralism and diversity in the application of law, within appropriate limits; a preference for empowering decision-makers at the lowest possible level, since they are closest to and most accountable to the persons being governed (often referred to as the principle of subsidiarity); and a concern with the quality, capacity and cost of decision-making at the international level. Does this suggest a technique for balancing of key inter-

ests in the field of human rights? See Shany, Toward a General Margin of Appreciation Doctrine in International Law?, 16 E.J.I.L. 907 (2005); Arai–Takahashi, The Margin of Appreciation Doctrine and the Principle of Proportionality in the Jurisprudence of the ECHR (2002); Gross & Ní Aoláin, From Discretion to Scrutiny: Revisiting the Application of the Margin of Appreciation Doctrine in the Context of Article 15 of the European Convention on Human Rights, 23 Hum. Rts. Q. 625 (2001); Benvenisti, Margin of Appreciation, Consensus, and Universal Standards, 31 N.Y.U. J. Int'l L. & Pol. 843 (1999).

3. *Cultural Relativism.* If you think that the outcome of a head scarf case in Turkey might be different than a similar case in France, then your approach might be taking account of different cultural, political or other traditions in different countries. Should human rights be absolute across states or should they change relative to different national conditions? The former President of the International Court of Justice, Rosalyn Higgins, has written:

> It is sometimes suggested that there can be no fully universal concept of human rights, for it is necessary to take into account the diverse cultures and political systems of the world. In my view this is a point advanced mostly by states, and by liberal scholars anxious not to impose the Western view of things on others. It is rarely advanced by the oppressed, who are only too anxious to benefit from perceived universal standards. * * * Individuals everywhere want the same essential things: to have sufficient food and shelter; to be able to speak freely; to practise their own religion or abstain from religious belief; to feel that their person is not threatened by the state; to know that they will not be tortured, or detained without charge, and that, if charged, they will have a fair trial. I believe there is nothing in these aspirations that is dependent upon culture, or religion, or stage of development. They are as keenly felt by the African tribesman as by the European city-dweller, by the inhabitant of a Latin American shanty-town as by the resident of a Manhattan apartment.

Higgins, Problems and Process: International Law and How We Use It 96–97 (1994) (footnote omitted). Do you agree with Judge Higgins? For citations to scholarship on this issue, see Weston, Human Rights and Nation–Building in Cross–Cultural Settings, 60 Maine L. Rev. 317, 322–24, n. 13 (2008).

4. *Further Reading.* The literature on international human rights is voluminous and continues to grow. See generally Meron, The Humanization of International Law (2006); Meron, International Law in the Age of Human Rights, 301 Rec. des Cours 9 (2003); Marks & Clapham, International Human Rights Lexicon (2005); Guide to International Human Rights Practice (4th ed. Hannum ed. 2004); Tomuschat, Human Rights: Between Realism and Idealism (2d ed. 2008); Steiner, Alston, & Goodman, International Human Rights in Context: Law, Politics, Morals (3d ed. 2008); Realizing Human Rights: Moving from Inspiration to Impact (Power & Allison eds. 2000); The Future of International Human Rights (Weston & Marks eds. 1999); Human Rights: An Agenda for the Next Century (Henkin & Hargrove eds. 1994); Henkin, The Age of Rights (1990).

SECTION 2. GLOBAL NORMS AND INSTITUTIONS

A. GLOBAL NORMS

The international law of human rights includes numerous (and increasing) international agreements and other instruments, as well as a recognized corpus of principles of customary law. Three principal instruments—the Universal Declaration of Human Rights, the International Covenant on Civil and Political Rights (ICCPR), and the International Covenant on Economic, Social and Cultural Rights (ICESCR)—have, together, acquired the designation "The International Bill of Rights."

1. Charter of the United Nations

The excerpt in the prior section by Thomas Buergenthal notes that Articles 55–56 of the U.N. Charter address the promotion of human rights, but only in a vague fashion. Do you agree that these provisions are vague? If so, is it because the rights at issue are unclear? Because the obligations imposed on states are weak? Both? Note that there are other provisions of the U.N. Charter that are also relevant, such as the preamble and Articles 1(3), 13(1)(b), 62(2), 68, and 76(c). As Buergenthal notes, Article 2(7) has limited the effects of the U.N. Charter. Article 2(7) states: "Nothing in the present Charter shall authorize the United Nations to intervene in matters which are essentially within the domestic jurisdiction of any state or shall require the Members to submit such matters to settlement under the present Charter; but this principle shall not prejudice the application of enforcement measures under Chapter VII." What do you think are "matters essentially within the domestic jurisdiction" of U.N. member states?

Are there ways of infusing content into the vague provisions of the U.N. Charter? Historically, it has been suggested that the U.N. Charter should be seen together with the Nuremberg Charter, the latter judging the past, the U.N. Charter prescribing for the future. The Nuremberg Charter applied a customary international law of human rights in charging the Nazi war criminals, with *inter alia,* "crimes against humanity." See Charter of the International Military Tribunal, art. 6(c), Aug. 8, 1945, 58 Stat. 1544, 82 U.N.T.S. 280. Arguably, the U.N. Charter codified that customary law and rendered applicable to all states at least such human rights law as was invoked at Nuremberg. Do you agree?

Further, some argue that the provisions of the Charter can now be interpreted together with later developments, notably the 1948 Universal Declaration of Human Rights, various covenants and conventions, resolutions of the U.N. General Assembly and of other international bodies, and the practices and declarations of states. Arguably those instruments and developments have filled out and made concrete the obligations left inchoate or undefined by the Charter. On this view, all members of the

United Nations are legally bound to at least those rights that are not disputed, for example, those which international law had always included in the concept of "justice" not to be denied to an alien, as well as freedom from slavery, systematic racial discrimination and genocide, perhaps also from systematic patterns of torture and arbitrary detention. For U.N. practice relating to these articles, see 2 The Charter of the United Nations: A Commentary 897–944 (2d ed. Simma ed. 2002); Hannum, Human Rights, in 1 United Nations Legal Order 319 (Schachter & Joyner eds. 1995); see generally Schachter, International Law in Theory and Practice 335–42 (1991); Schwelb, The International Court of Justice and the Human Rights Clause of the Charter, 66 A.J.I.L. 337 (1972); Sohn, Protection of Human Rights through International Legislation, in 1 Cassin, Amicorum Discipulorumque Liber 325 (1969); Lauterpacht, International Law and Human Rights 145–60 (1950).

Do the human rights provisions of the U.N. Charter create binding legal obligations on member States within their national legal systems? Shortly after the Charter entered into force, this issue was tested in national courts. For example, in *Re Drummond Wren*, [1945] O.R. 778 (Ont. Sup. Ct.), [1945] 4 D.L.R. 674 (Ont. High Ct.), a Canadian court declared a restrictive racial covenant void, *inter alia*, as against public policy, citing the Charter provisions on human rights as indicative of public policy. Similarly, in *Sei Fujii v. State*, 217 P.2d 481, rehearing denied, 218 P.2d 595 (Cal. App. 1950), a California state appellate court found the California Alien Land Law invalid in that it conflicted with the human rights provisions of the United Nations Charter. On appeal, however, the California Supreme Court held the statute invalid under the Fourteenth Amendment and expressly rejected the lower court's view that the Charter provisions on human rights had become the "supreme law of the land." 242 P.2d 617, 621–22 (Cal. 1952). The California Supreme Court observed that the Charter provisions lacked the mandatory quality and definiteness that would indicate intent to create enforceable rights. In *Oyama v. California*, the U.S. Supreme Court held a section of the California Alien Land Law unconstitutional as violative of the Fourteenth Amendment. In concurring opinions, Justices Black, Douglas, Rutledge and Murphy referred to the section's inconsistency with the United Nations Charter. 332 U.S. 633, 649–50, 673 (1948) (separate concurring opinions of Justices Black & Murphy). Yet since that time efforts to invoke the human rights provisions of the U.N. Charter in U.S. courts have not been successful, with U.S. courts routinely holding these provisions of the U.N. Charter to be non-self-executing. In light of all the developments in the field of human rights law, should that issue be revisited?

2. Universal Declaration of Human Rights

In 1948 the U.N. General Assembly adopted the Universal Declaration of Human Rights, G.A. Res. 217 (III), pt. A (Dec. 10, 1948), a compendium of thirty articles addressing numerous types of human rights. The United States was a driving force behind the adoption the

Declaration, represented in no small part by the former First Lady, Eleanor Roosevelt. See Glendon, A World Made New: Eleanor Roosevelt and the Universal Declaration of Human Rights (2001).

The Declaration is not a treaty; it was not adopted as a treaty and was never submitted by states to their respective ratification processes. As such, the Declaration originally was not intended to constitute binding law. At the time of its adoption, the U.S. representative, Eleanor Roosevelt, in the General Assembly said: "It is not a treaty; it is not an international agreement. It is not and does not purport to be a statement of law or of legal obligation." 19 Dep't St. Bull. 751 (Dec. 9, 1948); see Lauterpacht, International Law and Human Rights 408–17 (1950); Glendon at 167, 235–38. Nevertheless, there have been efforts to attribute legal character to many of the Declaration's provisions. Proponents of this view note that the Declaration was adopted by a vote of 48 to 0, with 8 abstentions (Byelorussian S.S.R., Czechoslovakia, Poland, Saudi Arabia, Ukrainian S.S.R., U.S.S.R., Union of South Africa, and Yugoslavia). Further, the Communist states of Europe later accepted the Universal Declaration expressly as part of their acceptance of the Final Act of the Conference on Security and Cooperation in Europe, Aug. 1, 1975, 14 I.L.M. 1292 (1975) (Helsinki Final Act). No state or government that has come into existence has questioned or expressed reservations to the Universal Declaration, and it continues to be cited with unanimous approval or acquiescence in resolutions of international bodies. Do you think that virtually uncontested and frequently repeated acceptance of the Declaration means that its provisions have the force of customary law? See Schachter, The Genesis of the Declaration: A Fresh Examination, 11 Pace Int'l L. Rev. 51 (1999); Hannum, The Status of the Universal Declaration of Human Rights in National and International Law, 25 Ga. J. Int'l & Comp. L. 287 (1995–96); Henkin, The Age of Rights 18–19 (1990). The Restatement (Third) concludes: "Few states would agree that any action by a state contrary to any provision of the Declaration is, for that reason alone, a violation of the Charter or of customary international law. On the other hand, almost all states would agree that some infringements of human rights enumerated in the Declaration are violations of the Charter or of customary international law." Restatement (Third), Introductory Note, Part VII, The Law of Human Rights. What do you think?

U.S. courts have declined to accord the Declaration the status of a treaty. In *Sosa v. Alvarez–Machain*, 542 U.S. 692, 735 (2004), the U.S. Supreme Court asserted that because the Universal Declaration was nonbinding at its inception, it could not "establish the relevant and applicable rule of international law," in that instance, whether arbitrary arrest violated the law of nations. Yet some courts have viewed the Declaration as evidence of a rule of customary international law. For example, the Second Circuit in *Filartiga v. Pena–Irala*, 630 F.2d 876, 882 (2d Cir. 1980) (a case cited with approval by the *Sosa* court), referred to the Declaration in finding a customary international law prohibition on state-sponsored torture. See Chapter 2, Section 2(A).

Regardless of its precise legal status, the Universal Declaration is, after the U.N. Charter, probably the most influential instrument in the field of human rights; it helped secure the recognition of human rights by states and instilled the idea and the principles of human rights into the national constitutions and laws of virtually all states. Indeed, the Universal Declaration has been copied or incorporated by reference in numerous constitutions of new states. See Henkin, Human Rights: Ideology and Aspiration, Reality and Prospect, in Realizing Human Rights: Moving From Inspiration to Impact 3, 11–12 (Power & Allison eds. 2000). On the influence of NGOs in the creation of the Declaration, see Korey, NGOs and the Universal Declaration of Human Rights: "A Curious Grapevine" (1998).

3. The Two International Covenants

After adoption of the Universal Declaration, consensus emerged among states to convert its norms into an international human rights covenant that would have the binding force of law. The initial draft provided for a single instrument, focused on political and civil rights, but economic and social rights were added early in the process. Western States then fought for, and obtained, a division into two covenants. They insisted that economic and social rights were essentially aspirations or plans, not rights, since their realization depended on availability of resources and on controversial economic theory and ideology. These, they said, were not appropriate subjects for binding obligations and should not be allowed to dilute the legal character of provisions honoring political-civil rights; states prepared to assume obligations to respect political-civil rights should not be discouraged from doing so by requiring of them impossible social-economic commitments. There was wide agreement and clear recognition that the means required to enforce or induce compliance with social-economic undertakings were different from the means required for civil-political rights. See Henkin, The International Bill of Rights 9–10 (1981).

As it turned out, the International Covenant on Civil and Political Rights (ICCPR) is drafted in terms of the individual's rights, whereas the International Covenant on Economic, Social and Cultural Rights (ICESCR) speaks to the obligations of states. Is that significant? Under the Covenant on Civil and Political Rights, states parties are obligated to respect and ensure the rights recognized in the Covenant without delay or exception. By contrast, a state party to the Covenant on Economic, Social and Cultural Rights undertakes "to take steps to the maximum of its available resources, with a view to achieving progressively the full realization of the rights recognized" (Article 2).

a. *International Covenant on Civil and Political Rights*

The ICCPR entered into force in 1976 and, as of early 2009, there are 162 states that have adhered to it. International Covenant on Civil and

Political Rights, Dec. 16, 1966, 999 U.N.T.S. 171. The rights recognized in the Covenant generally follow the first twenty-one articles of the Universal Declaration, but with greater detail and in some instances qualifications. For example, the ICCPR states that no one shall be arbitrarily deprived of his life (Article 6(1)), no one shall be subject to torture (Article 7), and no one shall be subject to arbitrary arrest or detention (Article 9). By Article 2, states parties undertake to respect and ensure the rights indicated "to all individuals within its territory and subject to its jurisdiction." The obligation of states "to respect and ensure" the rights recognized by the Covenant apparently includes not just an obligation to refrain from direct state action that would violate the right, but also an obligation to protect individuals against violations of their human rights by private persons. Further, the ICCPR creates a Human Rights Committee of experts as its principal monitoring body (discussed *infra* this Chapter in Sections 2(B) and Section 5).

Under a separate protocol to the Covenant, states may opt to submit to "communications"—i.e., complaints—to the Committee lodged against them by or on behalf of private persons claiming to be victims of violation. As of early 2009, 111 states have adhered to this first optional protocol, Dec. 16, 1966, 999 U.N.T.S. 302. A second optional protocol, Dec. 15, 1989, 1642 U.N.T.S. 414, obliges parties to abolish the death penalty. As of early 2009, 66 states have adhered to it. The United States has adhered to neither optional protocol. For further discussion, see Nowak, U.N. Covenant on Civil and Political Rights: CCPR Commentary (2d rev. ed. 2005); Joseph et al., The International Covenant on Civil and Political Rights: Cases, Materials, and Commentary (2d ed. 2004).

b. International Covenant on Economic, Social and Cultural Rights

The ICESCR also entered into force in 1976; as of early 2009, 159 states have adhered to it. Dec. 16, 1966, 993 U.N.T.S. 3. The ICESCR obligates states to recognize and achieve progressively the following rights: the right to work (Article 6); to just and favorable working conditions (Article 7); to form and join trade unions (Article 8); to social security (Article 9); to protection of and assistance to the family, mothers and children (Article 10); to adequate food, clothing and housing (Article 11); to the highest attainable standard of physical and mental health (Article 12); to education (Article 13); and the right to take part in cultural life, to enjoy the benefits of scientific progress and its applications, and to benefit from the protection of the moral and material interests resulting from any scientific, literary, or artistic production of which a person is the author (Article 15). See generally Economic, Social and Cultural Rights in Action (Baderin & McCorquodale eds. 2007); Guide to the Interpretation of the International Covenant on Economic, Social and Cultural Rights (Sohn ed. 1993); Eide, Krause & Rosas, Economic, Social & Cultural Rights (2d rev. ed. 2001).

Article 2(1) obligates states to undertake to realize the rights indicated "individually and through international assistance and cooperation, especially economic and technical." Does this provision create obligations for a state party to assist other states parties to realize the economic and social and cultural rights of their inhabitants? Is it significant that in 1986—twenty years after adoption of the ICESCR—the U.N. General Assembly adopted a Declaration on the Right to Development, which recognized in Article 1 the "right of development" as "an inalienable human right"? That declaration was adopted by a vote of 146 to 1 (the U.S.), with 8 abstentions (including Japan and Great Britain). See G.A. Res. 41/128 (Dec. 4, 1986). For a discussion of the right to development, and of the possible tension between individual and collective rights, see Schachter, International Law in Theory and Practice 331–33 (1991); Henkin, The Age of Rights 191–93 (1990); Crawford, The Rights of Peoples 65–66 (1988); International Law and Development (De Waart, Peters, & Denters eds. 1988); International Law of Development (Snyder & Slinn eds. 1987); Rich, The Right to Development as an Emerging Human Right, 23 Va. J. Int'l L. 287 (1983); Espiell, The Right of Development as a Human Right, 16 Tex. Int'l L.J. 189 (1981).

c. Comparison of the Covenants With the Universal Declaration

The Covenants were designed to transform the provisions of the Universal Declaration into binding treaties, but there are significant differences between the Declaration and the Covenants. Some of the rights set forth in the Declaration, notably Article 14 (asylum) and Article 17 (property), have no counterpart in the Covenants. Failure to include a right to property may have principally reflected international differences, particularly intense at the time, as to the obligation of states to compensate aliens for nationalized properties. See Chapter 14, Section 5. On the other hand, the ICCPR differs from the Declaration by including the right of peoples to self-determination and to freely dispose of their natural resources (Article 1); procedural protections for aliens against expulsion (Article 13); the right not to be compelled to testify against oneself (Article 14(3)(g)); compensation for miscarriage of justice (Article 14(6)); freedom from double jeopardy (Article 14(7)); the prohibition of propaganda for war or advocacy of national, racial or ethnic hatred (Article 20); the right of a child to a name and a nationality (Article 24); and protection for cultural, religious, and linguistic rights of minorities (Article 27). The ICCPR also spells out limitations on rights referred to in the Declaration (art. 29(2)). Similarly, the socio-economic provisions in the Declaration are much expanded in the ICESCR.

Some of the differences between the Declaration and the Covenants reflect differences between a declaration and international agreements, and what states sought to achieve by each. The differences reflect also the changing composition of international society; 58 states were members of the United Nations in 1948, and 122 in 1966 when the Covenants were adopted. Most of the additional members were new states that had recently been colonies, and their admission into the international system changed the balance between traditional and new states, between developed and developing, between "libertarian," "socialist," and various "mixed" societies.

Today, the Covenants serve as major reference points for international and national courts and tribunals confronted with cases that implicate human rights. See generally Jayawickrama, The Judicial Application of Human Rights Law: National, Regional and International Jurisprudence (2002).

4. Other Instruments

The U.N. Charter, Universal Declaration, ICCPR, and ICESCR are not, of course, the only global instruments addressing human rights. A few international human rights agreements were concluded before the Covenants, such as the Slavery Convention, Sept. 25, 1926, 60 L.N.T.S. 253, as amended by Protocol Amending the Slavery Convention, Dec. 7, 1953, 182 U.N.T.S. 51, and the Convention on the Prevention and Punishment of the Crime of Genocide, Dec. 9, 1948, 78 U.N.T.S. 277. An important font of earlier treaties as well as contemporary ones has been the International Labour Organization (originally the International Labour Office), which alone has promulgated more than a hundred conventions dealing with conditions of labor and other social conditions. See generally Valticos & von Potobsky, International Labor Law (2d.rev. ed. 1995).

Since the adoption of the two Covenants, a substantial number of further human rights conventions have been adopted, generally to develop and expand the protections provided in the Covenant on particular subjects. Issues of racial discrimination are addressed in the Convention on the Elimination of All Forms of Discrimination, Dec. 21, 1965, 660 U.N.T.S. 195, 5 I.L.M. 350 (CERD). Concerns with apartheid in Africa led to the Convention on the Suppression and Punishment of the Crime of Apartheid, G.A. Res. 3068 (XXVIII) (Nov. 30, 1973). Key protections for children have been developed in the U.N. Convention on the Rights of the Child, Nov. 20, 1989, 1577 U.N.T.S. 3, and its Optional Protocol on the Involvement of Children in Armed Conflict and Optional Protocol on the Sale of Children, Child Prostitution and Child Pornography. See G.A. Res. 54/263 (May 25, 2000); see also The U.N. Convention on the Rights of the Child: An Analysis of Treaty Provisions and Implications of U.S. Ratification (Todres, Wojcik, & Revaz eds. 2006). Women's rights have also emerged as a significant area of human rights development, especially in the form of the Convention on the Elimination of All Forms of Discrimination Against Women, Dec. 18, 1979, 1249 U.N.T.S. 13 (CEDAW). For a detailed discussion, see *infra* this Section, Part C.

Consequently, today there are numerous instruments, which various Internet cites have helped organize. See, e.g., The Unniversity of Minnesota, Human Rights Library, http://www1.umn.edu/humanrts/treaties.htm, or UN Human Rights Treaty Information Portal, http://www.humanrights info.com/ (not affiliated with the U.N.). With the advent of various types of instruments in successive stages, commentators have sometimes spoken of additional "generations" of rights, e.g., rights to peace, a healthful environment, economic and political development. See, e.g., Buergenthal, The Normative and Institutional Evolution of International Human Rights, 19 Hum. Rts. Q. 703 (1997); Crawford, The Rights of Peoples 159–66 (1988); Alston, A Third Generation of Solidarity Rights: Progressive Development or Obfuscation of International Human Rights Law?, 29 Neth. Int'l L. Rev. 307 (1982); Marks, Emerging Human Rights: A New Generation for the 1980s?, 33 Rutgers L. Rev. 435 (1981). What generations of rights do you think might be yet to come?

5. Do Global Human Rights Treaties Really Make a Difference?

In recent years, several commentators have questioned the effectiveness of human rights instruments, with some even attempting to test empirically whether adherence to human rights instruments has truly altered state compliance with human rights norms. Others have responded pointing to various ways that such treaties might influence states and to deficiencies in the methods and assumptions being used to test causal effects. Do you think adherence to a human rights treaty actually alters future conduct of a state or is it likely that the state is adhering to norms that it already accepts and would abide by anyway? Is it possible that adherence to a human rights treaty might actually shield a state that is engaging in bad behavior, perhaps by defusing or confusing international criticism? Or might adherence to a human rights treaty today by a regime in a particular state "lock in" a normative system, in part through incorporation into national law, thereby making it harder for a different, future regime to walk away from that system without incurring international approbation? Does the treaty at least provide benchmarks by which other states can assess malfeasant conduct?

For discussion, see Hathaway, Do Human Rights Treaties Make a Difference?, 111 Yale L.J. 1935 (2002); Goodman & Jinks, Measuring the Effects of Human Rights Treaties, 14 E.J.I.L. 171 (2003); Hathaway, Testing Conventional Wisdom, 14 E.J.I.L. 185 (2003); Heyns & Viljoen, The Impact of the United Nations Human Rights Treaties on the Domestic Level (2002); Cassel, Does International Human Rights Law Make a Difference?, 2 Chi. J. Int'l L. 121 (2001); Keith, The United Nations International Covenant on Civil and Political Rights: Does It Make a Difference in Human Rights Behaviour?, 36 J. Peace Research 95 (1999).

B. GLOBAL INSTITUTIONS

BUERGENTHAL, THE EVOLVING INTERNATIONAL HUMAN RIGHTS SYSTEM

100 A.J.I.L. 783, 787–91 (2006) (some footnotes omitted)

III. UN HUMAN RIGHTS LAW AND PRACTICE

UN human rights law has evolved over the past sixty years along two parallel paths, one based on the UN Charter, the other on the human rights treaties adopted by the Organization. The Charter-based system comprises the human rights principles and institutional mechanisms that different UN organs have developed in the exercise of their Charter powers. The treaty-based system consists of a large number of human rights treaties drafted under UN auspices that codify much of the international human rights law in existence today. Some of these treaties also establish institutional mechanisms to monitor compliance by the states parties with the obligations imposed by these instruments.

The Charter–Based System

The UN Human Rights Council,[22] the successor to the Human Rights Commission, lies at the center of the Charter-based system, followed by the Commission on the Status of Women and various subsidiary bodies of the Council, such as the Sub–Commission on the Promotion and Protection of Human Rights, formerly the Sub–Commission on the Prevention of Discrimination and Protection of Minorities. Although the Human Rights Commission took the position into the mid–1960s that it lacked the power to act on violations of human rights brought to its attention, that attitude began to change as more and more newly independent states joined the United Nations and campaigned for UN antiapartheid measures. They argued that the United Nations had the requisite authority to take such action because a state that practiced apartheid could not be said to be "promoting" human rights without discrimination, as required by Articles 55 and 56 of the Charter. This argument gradually prevailed, prompting the General Assembly to call on South Africa to end apartheid and on Southern Rhodesia to do away with its racial discrimination policies. The Economic and Social Council followed up with a series of resolutions on the subject. In one of the earliest, ECOSOC authorized the Human Rights Commission "to make a thorough study of situations which reveal a consistent pattern of violations of human rights, as exemplified by the policy of apartheid as practised in the Republic of South Africa . . . , and racial discrimination as practised notably in Southern Rhodesia."[23] This narrow mandate was expanded a few years later when ECOSOC empowered the Commission and its subcommission to act on complaints from groups and individuals that revealed "a consistent pattern of gross and

---

22. *See* GA Res. 60/251 (Mar. 15, 2006) (establishing the Council).

23. ECOSOC Res. 1235 (XLII), para. 3 (June 6, 1967).

reliably attested violations of human rights.''[24] This resolution opened the way for the Commission and subcommission to deal with gross violations of human rights in general, that is, whether or not they involved apartheid or racial discrimination.

These and related ECOSOC resolutions enabled the Human Rights Commission gradually to develop a growing number of UN Charter-based mechanisms for dealing with large-scale human rights violations. Today the system consists of mushrooming rapporteur and special-mission components, as well as the Office of the United Nations High Commissioner for Human Rights with its own bureaucracy. (It is too early to say what changes in this practice, if any, the newly established Human Rights Council will adopt.) These institutions derive their normative legitimacy from the Charter itself and from the Universal Declaration of Human Rights.

The Treaty–Based System

The treaty-based human rights system of the United Nations began with the adoption by the General Assembly of the Convention on the Prevention and Punishment of the Crime of Genocide on December 9, 1948, one day before the proclamation of the Universal Declaration of Human Rights. Since then the United Nations has adopted a large number of human rights treaties. The most important of these are the International Convention on the Elimination of All Forms of Racial Discrimination; the International Covenant on Civil and Political Rights and the International Covenant on Economic, Social and Cultural Rights; the International Convention on the Elimination of All Forms of Discrimination Against Women; the Convention on the Rights of the Child; and the Convention Against Torture and Other Cruel, Inhuman or Degrading Treatment or Punishment. With the exception of the Genocide Convention and the Covenant on Economic, Social and Cultural Rights, each of the foregoing treaties provides for a so-called "treaty body," which consists of a committee of independent experts that monitors compliance by the states parties with the obligations they assumed by ratifying these conventions. Some years after the Covenant on Economic, Social and Cultural Rights entered into force, ECOSOC created a similar body for that Covenant by resolution.

Although the six treaty bodies in existence today are not judicial institutions, they have had to interpret and apply their respective conventions in reviewing and commenting on the periodic reports the states parties must submit to them, and in dealing with the individual complaints that some treaty bodies are authorized to receive. This practice has produced a substantial body of international human rights law. While one can debate the question of the nature of this law and whether or not it is law at all, the fact remains that the normative findings of the treaty

24. ECOSOC Res. 1503 (XLVIII), para. 1 (May 27, 1970).

bodies have legal significance, as evidenced by references to them in international and domestic judicial decisions.

Over the years numerous states have ratified the human rights treaties the United Nations and its specialized agencies have adopted. These conventions not only have internationalized the subject of human rights as between the parties to them, but also to the same extent have internationalized the individual human rights these treaties guarantee. Since some of these treaties have been very widely ratified by member states of the international community, they may be viewed as creating an entire body of customary international human rights law. Nonstates parties may therefore find it increasingly difficult to claim that the human rights guarantees these treaties proclaim, particularly those from which derogation is not permitted, impose no legal obligations on them.

The General Assembly and the Security Council

Even in the days when the power of the General Assembly to deal with charges that member states were engaging in large-scale violations of human rights gave rise to lengthy debates based on Article 2(7) of the Charter, the Assembly was nevertheless able to adopt some resolutions calling on at least some of the states to stop these practices. Its early resolutions, however, tended to be rather mild or timid. But as time went by and it relied increasingly on a more expansive reading of the human rights provisions of the Charter and the normative significance of the Universal Declaration, the General Assembly became more assertive and demanding in its resolutions. In the case of particularly egregious violations, such as those involving apartheid, the General Assembly even invited states to impose sanctions.

The nonbinding character of General Assembly resolutions tended to diminish their effectiveness as a tool for putting an end to large-scale violations of human rights. For many years, the Security Council, while having the power under Chapter VII of the Charter to adopt binding resolutions and to order enforcement measures, including economic sanctions and military action, could rarely agree on taking such measures, even in cases involving egregious human rights violations that could readily be characterized as a threat to the peace within the meaning of Article 39 of the Charter. That situation changed to a large extent with the end of the Cold War, which had prevented unanimity among the Council's permanent members. With increasing frequency, the Security Council has exercised its powers under Chapter VII in situations involving massive violations of human rights. What we are seeing today, despite the Council's ambivalence in dealing forcefully with the human tragedy being played out in Darfur, is the gradual emergence of a modern version of collective humanitarian intervention. This development can be attributed to the convergence of two important factors: the growing assertion of power by the Security Council in the post-Cold War era and the expanding willingness of the international community to confront massive violations of human rights with economic sanctions or force, if necessary.

* * *

It must be recognized, however, that the United Nations and its various human rights institutions are largely ineffectual in dealing with individual human rights violations. Here, the regional human rights systems * * * are more effective. Unfortunately, regional human rights systems have been established in only three regions of the world, even though they are needed in every one. The UN system is better equipped to deal with large-scale violations of human rights, for which it commands the necessary political, military, and public relations resources. The great weakness of the UN system, particularly its Charter-based system, is its susceptibility to politicization. Politicization has resulted in the frequent condemnation of certain violators of human rights while others, some even more blatant, escape criticism. The replacement of the UN Human Rights Commission with the new Human Rights Council was designed to address this problem but is unlikely to resolve it, if only because the United Nations is a political body whose actions are determined by political considerations. The Organization can do only what a majority of its member states want it to do, and many states prefer to do as little as possible about human rights violations, particularly those committed by their friends or allies. This reality is frequently lost sight of when UN human rights action or inaction is criticized.

NOTES

1. *Creation of the Human Rights Council.* As noted by I.C.J. Judge Buergenthal, in April 2006 the General Assembly replaced the Human Rights Commission with a Human Rights Council. G.A. Res. 60/251 (Mar. 15, 2006). Like the Commission, the mandate of the Council is to make recommendations on situations of human rights violations, but in doing so is to be "guided by the principles of universality, impartiality, objectivity and non-selectivity, with a view to enhancing the promotion and protection of all human rights, civil, political, economic, social and cultural rights, including the right to development." Id. at paras. 3–4. The Council consists of forty-seven states elected by the General Assembly and reports directly to the General Assembly annually.

For an assessment of the erstwhile Human Rights Commission, see Tolley, The U.N. Commission on Human Rights (1987). For assessments of the overall success of the U.N. human rights system, see The United Nations and Human Rights: A Critical Appraisal (2d ed. Alston ed. 2002); Bayefsky, The UN Human Rights Treaty System: Universality at the Crossroads (2001); The UN Human Rights Treaty System in the 21st Century (Bayefsky ed. 2000).

2. *Treaty–Monitoring Committees.* The six treaty bodies established under the major human rights treaties and referred to by Judge Buergenthal are: Human Rights Committee (established by the ICCPR); Committee on

Economic, Social and Cultural Rights; Committee on the Elimination of Racial Discrimination; Committee on the Elimination of Discrimination Against Women; Committee on Torture; and Committee on the Rights of the Child. Information on these committees may be found on the website of the Office of the High Commissioner for Human Rights, at http://www2.ohchr.org/english/bodies/treaty/index.htm.

These committees play an important role in monitoring state party compliance, a role that will be discussed further *infra* this chapter, Section 5. The committees will also sometimes issue "general comments" interpreting the provisions of the convention. For a compilation of comments by the major committees, see Compilation of General Comments and General Recommendations Adopted by Human Rights Treaty Bodies, U.N.Doc. HRI/GEN/1/Rev.7 (May 12, 2004). As of early 2009, the ICCPR Human Rights Committee has made thirty-two general comments covering many of the Covenant's substantive guarantees including, *inter alia*, equality between the sexes, the right to life, the right to freedom of thought, conscience and religion, as well as a controversial comment on reservations to the ICCPR which is discussed *infra* this chapter, Section 4(B). For links to the comments, see Human Rights Committee, General Comments, http://www2.ohchr.org/english/bodies/hrc/comments.htm.

For further readings on the treaty-monitoring committees, see O'Flaherty, Human Rights and the UN: Practice Before the Treaty Bodies (2002); Young, The Law and Process of the U.N. Human Rights Committee (2002); Buergenthal, The U.N. Human Rights Committee, 5 Max Planck Y.B. U.N. L. 341 (2001); The Future of UN Human Rights Treaty Monitoring (Alston & Crawford eds. 2000); Ingelse, The Committee Against Torture: One Step Forward, One Step Back, 18 Neth. Q. Hum. Rts. 307 (2000); Wolfrum, The Committee on the Elimination of Racial Discrimination, 3 Max Planck Y.B. U.N. L. 489 (1999); McGoldrick, The Human Rights Committee: Its Role in the Development of the International Covenant on Civil and Political Rights (1991); Cook, State Accountability Under the Convention on the Elimination of All Forms of Discrimination Against Women, in Human Rights of Women: National and International Perspectives 228–56 (Cook ed. 1994).

3. *U.N. High Commissioner for Human Rights.* In 1994, the U.N. General Assembly created the position of U.N. High Commissioner for Human Rights to serve as the U.N. official with principal responsibility for U.N. human rights activities, acting under the direction and authority of the U.N. Secretary–General. The High Commissioner is appointed by the Secretary–General with the approval of the U.N. General Assembly (with due regard to geographical rotation) for a four-year, renewable term, and heads the Office of the High Commissioner of Human Rights (OHCHR), which is based in Geneva. Much in the same way that the Secretary–General is the human "face" of the United Nations, the High Commissioner is the central point person for the U.N. human rights system, and serves as a spokesperson for the general sentiments of the global human rights community. See Ramcharan, The UN High Commissioner for Human Rights: The Challenges of International Protection (2002).

4. *Refugees*. In 1950, the U.N. General Assembly created the position of U.N. High Commissioner for Refugees to monitor whether states are abiding by the U.N. Convention Relating to the Status of Refugees and its associated protocol. The High Commissioner is appointed by the U.N. Secretary–General with the approval of the U.N. General Assembly (with due regard being paid to geographical rotation) for a four-year, renewable term, and heads the U.N. Office of the High Commissioner for Refugees (UNHCR) based in Geneva. For literature on the protection of refugees, see Refugee Protection in International Law: UNHCR's Global Consultations on International Protection (Feller, Türk, & Nicholson eds. 2003); Human Rights Protection for Refugees, Asylum–Seekers, and Internally Displaced Persons: A Guide to International Mechanisms and Procedures (Fitzpatrick ed. 2001).

C. PROBLEMS AND PROSPECTS: A CLOSER LOOK AT THE EMERGENCE OF HUMAN RIGHTS FOR WOMEN

The ideology and the international law of human rights contemplate no distinction between the rights of men and the rights of women: women are human, equally human. And equality (including gender equality) and non-discrimination (including non-discrimination on the basis of gender) are cardinal tenets of the international law of human rights. See the Universal Declaration, Article 2; the International Covenant on Civil and Political Rights, Article 3; and the International Covenant on Economic, Social and Cultural Rights, Article 3.

But societies and their laws continue to distinguish between men and women, and in law and practice equal respect for the equal human rights of women continues to suffer and to demand particular attention. For that reason, feminist approaches have emerged that seek to explain how important aspects of international law disfavor women, and to promote more progressive development. See Chapter 1, Section 3(F). International law includes a global Convention on the Elimination of all Forms of Discrimination Against Women, Dec. 18, 1979, 1249 U.N.T.S. 13 (CEDAW) (not, notably, discrimination on the basis of gender), and a Committee on the same subject (sometimes also referred to as CEDAW), as noted in the prior section. The Convention includes unusual dispositions and obligations, including obligations to modify cultural patterns and eliminate stereotyped concepts that impair women's equality. Both the Convention and the Committee, though modeled upon the Convention on the Elimination of All Forms of Racial Discrimination (CERD) and the CERD Committee, suffer by comparison.

THE HUMAN RIGHTS OF WOMEN
In Human Rights (Henkin, Neuman, Orentlicher & Leebron eds., 1999), p. 358

In the final decade of the twentieth century the human rights of women emerged as a major focus of international advocacy efforts. These efforts have had a significant impact on institutional responses to violations of women's human rights: The subject received prominent attention in the Declaration and Programme of Action adopted at the United Nations' World Conference on Human Rights in Vienna in 1993; the following year the UN Commission on Human Rights appointed a Special Rapporteur on Violence Against Women, and in 1995 the United Nations sponsored a World Conference on Women, in Beijing. During this same period various treaty bodies and international criminal tribunals issued key decisions clarifying gender-specific human rights protections.

* * *

The Universal Declaration expressed the equal human rights of men and women in the plainest possible terms. So, too, did the two Covenants, as well as the United Nations Charter, whose enumeration of Purposes of the Organization includes the following: "To achieve international cooperation in solving international problems of an economic, social, cultural, or humanitarian character, and in promoting and encouraging respect for human rights and for fundamental freedoms for all without distinction as to ... sex...." (Article 1(3).) Like the U.N. Covenants, each of the comprehensive regional human rights treaties guarantees enjoyment of protected rights without discrimination on the basis of sex.

The customary law of human rights protects women and men equally, and it may also be a violation of customary law for any state, as a matter of state policy, to practice, encourage or condone systematic gender discrimination. See Restatement, Third, Foreign Relations Law of the United States, § 702, Comment *l*.

Yet despite these legal guarantees, women have long experienced gross inequalities in the enjoyment of fundamental rights. In many societies women remain subordinate in the home, in the family, in political processes, in social-sexual relations, in the enjoyment of property rights, in matters of employment and in the marketplace. In some countries, these inequalities are enshrined in law; in others, they reflect social, cultural and political resistance to legally-mandated assurances of equality.

Just as in the case of racial discrimination, it was thought necessary to adopt a special treaty dealing specifically with gender-based discrimination. In 1979, the UN General Assembly adopted the Convention on the Elimination of All Forms of Discrimination Against Women ("Women's Convention"), GA Res. 34/180, which entered into force two years later. But unlike the Convention on the Elimination of All Forms of Racial Discrimination, the Women's Convention has attracted numerous reservations, reflecting deeply ingrained historical, cultural and religious attitudes. * * *

Resistance to international protection of women's human rights is reflected also in the comparatively weak powers and procedures of the Committee on the Elimination of Discrimination Against Women (CEDAW), the treaty body that monitors States Parties' compliance with the

Women's Convention.* In larger perspective, until relatively recently the human rights of women scarcely figured in international efforts to secure compliance with established standards. Instead, as many have noted, women's human rights were substantially ignored or marginalized in the principal international fora where human rights are promoted.

* * *

As its name implies, the central aim of the Women's Convention is to eliminate all forms of discrimination against women, which Article 1 defines as "any distinction, exclusion or restriction made on the basis of sex which has the effect or purpose of impairing or nullifying the recognition, enjoyment or exercise by women, irrespective of their marital status, on a basis of equality of men and women, of human rights and fundamental freedoms in the political, economic, social, cultural, civil or any other field."

While the convention's overall thrust is to ensure the enjoyment of rights in every sphere on a basis of equality between men and women, it also requires States Parties to take all appropriate measures "to ensure the full development and advancement of women." (Article 3.) Although this requirement is, to be sure, aimed at assuring the exercise and enjoyment of rights "on a basis of equality with men," it also conveys the distinct and important idea that the full development of women is a goal to be pursued in its own right.

Several other aspects of this convention are noteworthy. First, discrimination against women, which States Parties undertake to eliminate (Article 2), is defined in terms of distinctions, exclusions or restrictions that have the effect *or* purpose of impairing the enjoyment of rights on a basis of equality between men and women. Thus, even when it is not possible to establish discriminatory intent, a State Party might be responsible for a breach of the Women's Convention by virtue of practices that have a discriminatory effect. Second, the Women's Convention authorizes States Parties to undertake "temporary special measures"—measures that would be termed "affirmative action" programs in the United States context—to accelerate the achievement of de facto equality between men and women. (Article 4.)

One of the most distinctive features of the Women's Convention is its requirement that States Parties undertake affirmative steps to modify cultural patterns that impair the enjoyment of rights on a basis of equality of men and women. Article 5(a) requires States Parties "[t]o modify the social and cultural patterns of conduct of men and women, with a view to achieving the elimination of prejudices and customary and all other practices which are based on the idea of the inferiority or the superiority of either of the sexes or on stereotyped roles for men and women." Similarly, Article 10(c) requires States Parties to eliminate discrimination against women in the field of education by, *inter alia*, eliminating "any

---

* * * * [I]n 1999 the UN Commission on the Status of Women adopted an Optional Protocol to the Women's Convention. The protocol will expand CEDAW's supervisory powers * * *.

stereotyped concepts of the roles of men and women at all levels and in all forms of education by encouraging coeducation and other types of education which will help to achieve this aim and, in particular, by the revision of textbooks and school programmes and the adaptation of teaching methods.''

Finally, perhaps more than any other human rights treaty, the Women's Convention embodies a vision of human rights in which the enjoyment of civil and political rights is indivisible from realization of economic, social and cultural rights. For example, Article 13 requires States Parties to take all appropriate measures to eliminate discrimination against women in the areas of economic and social life. To this end, States Parties must take measures to ensure that women enjoy the right to acquire bank loans, mortgages and other forms of financial credit on a basis of equality with men.

Notably, the Women's Convention is textually silent about violence against women, except in its requirement that States Parties take measures to suppress trafficking in women (Article 6). Nonetheless, CEDAW has interpreted the convention to prohibit violence against women and to require States Parties to take affirmative steps to prevent and punish such violence. * * *

CEDAW, GENERAL RECOMMENDATION NO. 19, VIOLENCE AGAINST WOMEN

U.N. Doc. A/47/38 (1992)

8.   The Convention applies to violence perpetrated by public authorities. Such acts of violence may breach that State's obligations under general international human rights law and under other conventions, in addition to breaching this Convention.

9.   It is emphasized, however, that discrimination under the Convention is not restricted to action by or on behalf of Governments. * * * For example, under article 2(e) the Convention calls on States parties to take all appropriate measures to eliminate discrimination against women by any person, organization or enterprise. Under general international law and specific human rights covenants, States may also be responsible for private acts if they fail to act with due diligence to prevent violations of rights or to investigate and punish acts of violence, and for providing compensation. * * *

11.   Traditional attitudes by which women are regarded as subordinate to men or as having stereotyped roles perpetuate widespread practices involving violence or coercion, such as family violence and abuse, forced marriage, dowry deaths, acid attacks and female circumcision. Such prejudices and practices may justify gender-based violence as a form of protection or control of women. The effect of such violence on the physical and mental integrity of women is to deprive them of the equal enjoyment, exercise and knowledge of human rights and fundamental freedoms. While

this comment addresses mainly actual or threatened violence the underlying consequences of these forms of gender-based violence help to maintain women in subordinate roles and contribute to their low level of political participation and to their lower level of education, skills and work opportunities.

12.   These attitudes also contribute to the propagation of pornography and the depiction and other commercial exploitation of women as sexual objects, rather than as individuals. This in turn contributes to gender-based violence. * * *

NOTES

1.   *Adherence to CEDAW.* As of 2009, 185 States have ratified CEDAW. However, the Convention "has attracted the greatest number of reservations with the potential to modify or exclude most, if not all, of the terms of the treaty." Belinda Clark, The Vienna Convention Reservations Regime and the Convention on Discrimination Against Women, 85 A.J.I.L. 281, 317 (1991). For a current listing of reservations by country, see http://www.un.org/womenwatch/daw/cedaw/reservations.htm.

2.   *U.S. Lack of Adherence.* The United States signed CEDAW in 1980 and President Carter sent the treaty to the Senate for advice and consent. Although the Senate Foreign Relations Committee (SFRC) held hearings on CEDAW in 1988 and 1990, the committee did not initially act on the treaty. In 1994, the SFRC recommended that the Senate consent to ratification, subject to a series of reservations, understandings and declarations (RUDs). See 140 Cong. Rec. S13927–04 (1994). Thereafter, the full Senate took no action. In 2002, the SFRC again held hearings and again recommended that the full Senate grant its consent, subject to RUDs. See 148 Cong. Rec. D853 (July 30, 2002). As of early 2009, however, the full Senate still has not acted.

3.   *CEDAW Optional Protocol.* On October 6, 1999, the U.N. General Assembly adopted the text of an Optional Protocol to the Women's Convention, which entered into force on December 22, 2000. See G.A. Res. A/54/4, Oct. 6 1999, 39 I.L.M. 281 (2000). The Protocol provides for two procedures. Under Articles 2–7, the CEDAW Committee can consider communications submitted by individuals or groups of individuals under the jurisdiction of a state party who claim to be victims of a violation of any of the rights set forth in the Convention by that state party. Under Article 8, the Committee can initiate inquiries into situations of grave or systematic violations of women's rights. Only those states that have ratified the Protocol are subject to these procedures. As of early 2009, ninety states are parties to the Protocol.

4.   *Myriad Meanings of Human Rights of Women.* What does the phrase "the human rights of women" mean? Henkin, Neuman, Orentlicher and Leebron suggest the following possibilities:

> *Human rights violations that are peculiar to women,* such as forced pregnancy. Forced pregnancy might violate a number of basic rights, such as the rights to physical integrity, family life, and privacy—*and* it is a type of violation of these rights that is peculiar to women.

Human rights violations to which women are especially—but not exclu-sively—vulnerable by virtue of their gender, such as domestic violence.

Human rights violations that are gender-specific in the sense that they are committed or directed against women at least in part because they are women, such as sexual violence. Unlike forced sterilization, sexual violence is not a violation of physical integrity that only women can experience. Neither, however, is gender beside the point in respect of this offence. Similarly, both boys and girls are potentially subject to genital mutilation, but no one would question that when girls are made to undergo this procedure in cultures where it is commonly practiced, they are subjected to it because they are female.

CEDAW has defined "gender-based violence" in a manner that combines elements of the last two definitions. In its General Recommendation on Violence Against Women, CEDAW defined "gender-based violence" to include "violence that is directed against a woman because she is a woman or that affects women disproportionately." * * *

Human Rights 370 (Henkin, Neuman, Orentlicher & Leebron eds. 1999).

　　5. *Rape as Torture.* The recognition of rape as a form of torture became a focus for many women's human rights activists beginning in the late 1900's. In 1986, the Special Rapporteur on Torture of the U.N. Commission on Human Rights included rape in an enumeration of "methods of physical torture" in his first report to the Commission. Report by the Special Rapporteur, Mr. P. Kooijmans, appointed pursuant to Commission on Human Rights resolution 1985/33, U.N. Doc. E/CN.4/1986/15, p. 29 (1986). In 1995, the Inter–American Commission also concluded that "rape represents not only inhumane treatment that infringes upon physical and moral integrity under Article 5 of the Convention, but also a form of torture in the sense of Article 5(2) of that instrument." See Report on the Situation of Human Rights in Haiti, OEA/Ser.L/V/II.88, Doc. 10 rev. 9 (1995); see also Fernando Mejia Egocheaga and Raquel Martin de Mejia v. Peru, Case 10.970, Inter–Am. Comm'n H.R. 157, OEA/Ser. L/V/II.91, doc. 7 rev. (1996); I.C.T.Y., Prosecutor v. Delalic et al., Judgment, Nov. 16 1998, IT–96–21–T, at paras. 494–496 (finding that rape constitutes torture).

　　6. *Rape as a War Crime.* In 1993, the U.N. Security Council established an international tribunal to prosecute those responsible for serious violations of international humanitarian law committed since 1991 in the territory of the former Yugoslavia (see Chapter 16). The International Criminal Tribunal for the former Yugoslavia (I.C.T.Y.) was created in response to the many reports of mass rapes, killings, and other abuses perpetrated in the course of "ethnic cleansing" in Bosnia and Herzegovina, and there was considerable public pressure to ensure that the rapes were prosecuted as war crimes and the perpetrators punished. The Statute of the I.C.T.Y. confers subject-matter jurisdiction over two categories of war crimes, as well as over genocide and crimes against humanity. Rape is included explicitly only in the provisions relating to crimes against humanity. The I.C.T.Y. judges, however, have interpreted the provisions of the Statute to include rape as both a violation of the laws or customs of war and a grave breach of the Geneva Conventions of 1949 (rape as torture). See Prosecutor v. Delalic et al., Judgment, Nov. 16,

1998, IT–96–21–T, at para. 476, "There can be no doubt that rape and other forms of sexual assault are expressly prohibited under international humanitarian law." In 1994, the Security Council created a second international tribunal, with jurisdiction over crimes relating to the 1994 genocide in Rwanda. The Statute of the International Criminal Tribunal for Rwanda (I.C.T.R.) makes explicit reference to rape as a violation of Common Article 3 of the Geneva Conventions. For a discussion, see Askin, Sexual Violence in Decisions and Indictments of the Yugoslav and Rwandan Tribunals: Current Status, 93 A.J.I.L. 97 (1999).

The Rome Statute for an International Criminal Court (ICC), adopted in July 1998, explicitly includes rape and other forms of sexual violence in its list of war crimes subject to the jurisdiction of the court. See Article 8(2)(b)(xxii) and (c)(vi) (enumerating, in addition to rape, "sexual slavery, enforced prostitution, forced pregnancy * * * [and] enforced sterilization" as war crimes).

7. *The Challenge of Cultural Relativism*. As in other areas of human rights, the denial of women's human rights is often justified in terms of social and/or religious custom. An area where social customs are said to conflict with women's rights is that of female genital mutilation. See, e.g., Lewis, Between Irua and "Female Genital Mutilation": Feminist Human Rights Discourse and the Cultural Divide, 8 Harv. Hum. Rts. J. 1 (1995). An area where religious custom is said to conflict with women's rights concerns the role of women within particular religious doctrines, whether it be the inability to serve as Catholic priests or the inability to exercise certain rights under the tenets of Islam. Henkin, Neuman, Orentlicher and Leebron write,

> some abridgements of women's human rights are justified in terms of religious doctrine mandating separate roles for men and women. In these circumstances, there may be a direct clash between the internationally-protected right to manifest one's religious beliefs in community with others and the right not to be subjected to discrimination on the basis of sex. Even if one accepts in principle the claim that human rights are universal, this situation raises the question of how to resolve conflicts between and among rights each of which is internationally-protected.

> Article 18(3) of the ICCPR provides that "[f]reedom to manifest one's religion or beliefs may be subject only to such limitations as are prescribed by law and are necessary to protect public safety, order, health, or morals or the fundamental rights and freedoms of others." Presumably, then, the Covenant permits some restrictions on religious practice if *necessary* to protect women's fundamental human rights and if those restrictions are prescribed by law. Still, this does not tell us how to determine whether particular forms of religious practice may—or must—be curbed to protect women's human rights.

Human Rights 396 (Henkin, Neuman, Orentlicher & Leebron eds. 1999).

8. *Further Reading*. For further reading, see Parrot & Cummings, Forsaken Females: The Global Brutalization of Women (2006); Merry, Human Rights and Gender Violence: Translating International Law into Local Justice (2006); Gender and Human Rights (Knop ed. 2004); Women and International Human Rights Law (Askin & Koenig eds. 1999).

D. U.S. ADHERENCE TO GLOBAL HUMAN RIGHTS TREATIES

The United States was a major player in the promulgation of the Universal Declaration of Human Rights and in transforming the Declaration into the principal human rights Covenants. As of early 2009, however, the United States is a party to only one of the two Covenants and to a few other international human rights conventions. Some conventions which the President of the United States has signed have not been ratified. The instruments which have been ratified were subjected to extensive reservations, understandings and declarations. See Roth, The Charade of US Ratification of International Human Rights Treaties 1 Chi. J. Int'l L. 347 (2000); Kaufman, Human Rights Treaties and the Senate: A History of Opposition (1990); Tananbaum, The Bricker Amendment Controversy: A Test of Eisenhower's Political Leadership (1988).

HENKIN, THE AGE OF RIGHTS

74, 76–77 (1990) (footnotes omitted)

From the beginning, the international human rights movement was conceived by the United States as designed to improve the condition of human rights in countries other than the United States (and a very few like-minded liberal states). United States participation in the movement was also to serve the cause of human rights in other countries. To that end, the United States promoted and actively engaged in establishing international standards and machinery. It did not strongly favor but it also did not resist the move to develop international agreements and international law, but, again, it saw them as designed for other states.

* * *

The reasons why the United States has maintained its distance from the international human rights agreements are not obvious. At one time, some lawyers in the United States questioned the constitutional authority of the treaty makers to adhere to such agreements: it was said that the agreements dealt with matters that under the United States Constitution were reserved to the States; or were delegated exclusively to Congress; or were not a proper subject for a treaty because they were only of "domestic concern." Each of these legal objections was long ago refuted. Thirty-five years ago some feared that United States adherence to international human rights agreements would threaten then-existing institutions and practices, such as racial segregation; now, Americans are happy to say, those practices are outlawed, independently of international agreements. Thirty-five years ago Senator Bricker's proposed constitutional amendment sought to prevent the use of treaties to "nationalize" human rights matters and to give Congress authority to deal with them. Today, as a result of new constitutional interpretations, individual rights are already national, Congress already has power to legislate about them.

And yet, resistance to United States adherence remains strong. In some measure, resistance to United States participation builds on differences between constitutional rights and international human rights. In particular, American constitutional rights are individualistic and deeply democratic in their eighteenth-century conception. Self-government is the basic right on which all others depend: *Representative government is freedom,* Thomas Paine said. In contemporary international human rights, on the other hand, popular sovereignty does not imply any particular system of government; individual participation in government is only one right among others, and the form of participation is not defined. * * *

But the resistance in the United States is deeper. There is resistance to imposing national standards on some matters that have long been deemed "local"; even more, there is resistance to accepting international standards, and international scrutiny, on matters that have been for the United States to decide. A deep isolationism continues to motivate many Americans, even some who are eager to judge others as by interceding on behalf of human rights in other countries.

NOTES

1. *Source of U.S. Resistance.* What do you think is the principal source of U.S. resistance to ratification of major human rights treaties. A sense that existing U.S. constitutional and statutory norms are wholly sufficient? An general aversion to governance "from abroad"? An historical vision of the United States as standing apart from the world on issues of democracy and political rights? A preference for governance on individual rights at the most local level possible? A concern that unelected judges will use open-ended norms to subvert U.S. democratic decision-making? A simple inability to push important treaties through the U.S. Senate, absent some obvious benefit to the United States?

2. *Further Reading.* See Bradley, Unratified Treaties, Domestic Politics, and the U.S. Constitution, 48 Harv. Int'l L.J. 307 (2007); Koh, Restoring America's Human Rights Reputation, 40 Cornell Int'l L.J. 635 (2007); Waters, Creeping Monism: The Judicial Trend Towards Interpretive Incorporation of Human Rights Treaties, 107 Colum. L. Rev. 628 (2007); Koh, On American Exceptionalism, 55 Stan. L. Rev. 1479 (2003).

E. CUSTOMARY INTERNATIONAL LAW OF HUMAN RIGHTS

The international law of human rights consists primarily of multilateral conventions, covenants and other international agreements largely concluded in the aftermath of the Second World War. Was there customary international law on human rights that predated these agreements? Recall that customary law was the foundation for "crimes against humanity" under the Nuremberg Charter. Since that time, has the emergence of numerous treaties had a collateral effect on developing customary international law on human rights? If so, which human rights are now embedded in customary international law? Which human rights are not? Note that the existence of such law is extremely important if it binds those states who have not yet joined a particular treaty.

RESTATEMENT OF THE LAW (THIRD) THE FOREIGN RELATIONS LAW OF THE UNITED STATES § 702 (1987)

§ 702. Customary International Law of Human Rights

A state violates international law if, as a matter of state policy, it practices, encourages or condones

(a) genocide,

(b) slavery or slave trade,

(c) the murder or causing the disappearance of individuals,

(d) torture or other cruel, inhuman or degrading treatment or punishment,

(e) prolonged arbitrary detention,

(f) systematic racial discrimination, or

(g) a consistent pattern of gross violations of internationally recognized human rights.

Comments:

a. Scope of customary law of human rights. This section includes as customary law only those human rights whose status as customary law is generally accepted * * * and whose scope and content are generally agreed. * * * The list is not necessarily complete, and is not closed: human rights not listed in this section may have achieved the status of customary law, and some rights might achieve that status in the future. * * *

* * *

j. Systematic religious discrimination. The United Nations Charter (Articles 1, 13, 55) links religious discrimination with racial discrimination and treats them alike; to the extent that racial discrimination violates the Charter religious discrimination does also. Religious discrimination is also treated identically with racial discrimination in the principal covenants and in the constitutions and laws of many states. There is as yet no convention on the elimination of religious discrimination, and there has been no concerted attack on such discrimination comparable to that on *apartheid,* but there is a strong case that systematic discrimination on grounds of religion as a matter of state policy is also a violation of customary law. See Reporters' Note 8.

* * *

l. Gender discrimination. The United Nations Charter (Article 1(3)) and the Universal Declaration of Human Rights (Article 2) prohibit discrimination in respect of human rights on various grounds, including sex. Discrimination on the basis of sex in respect of recognized rights is prohibited by a number of international agreements, including the Covenant on Civil and Political Rights, the Covenant on Economic, Social and Cultural Rights, and more generally by the Convention on the Elimination of All Forms of Discrimination Against Women, which, as of May 1987, had been ratified by 91 states and signed by a number of others. The United States had signed the Convention but had not yet ratified it. See Introductory Note to this Part. The domestic laws of a number of states, including those of the United States, mandate equality for, or prohibit discrimination against, women generally or in various respects. Gender-based discrimination is still practiced in many states in varying degrees, but freedom from gender discrimination as state policy, in many matters, may already be a principle of customary international law. Discrimination by a state that does not constitute a violation of customary law may violate a particular international agreement if practiced by a state party.

m. Consistent pattern of gross violations of human rights. The acts enumerated in clauses (a) to (f) are violations of customary law even if the practice is not consistent, or not part of a "pattern," and those acts are inherently "gross" violations of human rights. Clause (g) includes other infringements of recognized human rights that are not violations of customary law when committed singly or sporadically (although they may be forbidden to states parties to the International Covenants or other particular agreements); they become violations of customary law if the state is guilty of a "consistent pattern of gross violations" as state policy.

NOTES

1. *Assessing State Practice.* Does the practice of states support § 702 of the Restatement? If so, what types of practice is relevant in making that assessment? Is it relevant that some states violate international human rights with some regularity?

2. *Human Rights and* Jus Cogens. The Vienna Convention on the Law of Treaties (VCLT) defines *jus cogens* as a norm "accepted and recognised by the international community of States as a whole as a norm from which no derogation is permitted and which can be modified only by a subsequent norm of general international law having the same character." VCLT, art. 53. As discussed in Chapter 2, Section 2(D), while *jus cogens* might be viewed as a form of customary international law, the concept appears driven in part by state practice and in part by natural law reasoning concerning first principles of morality or ethics. See Simma & Alston, The Sources of Human Rights Law: Custom, Jus Cogens, and General Principles, 12 Australian Y.B.I.L. 82 (1988–89). Certain human rights norms are regarded by some tribunals as having now qualified as a norm of *jus cogens*. For instance, the Inter–American Court of Human Rights has advised that the prohibition against racial discrimination is *jus cogens*. See *Juridical Condition and Rights of*

Undocumented Migrants, *Advisory Opinion OC–18/03, Inter–Am. Ct. Hum. Rts. (ser. A) No. 18, paras. 98–101 (2003). The International Criminal Tribunal for the former Yugoslavia has declared that the prohibition against state-sponsored torture "has evolved into a peremptory norm or jus cogens, that is, a norm that enjoys a higher rank in the international hierarchy than treaty law and even 'ordinary' customary rules." Prosecutor v. Furundžija, I.C.T.Y. Case No. I–95–17/1–T, Judgment, para. 153 (1998). Similarly, the European Court of Human Rights declared that the prohibition against state-sponsored torture is a peremptory norm of international law, though in that instance the Court found that the norm did not override state immunity, at least in the context of a civil claim brought before a national court. See Al–Adsani v. United Kingdom, 2001–XI Eur. Ct. H.R. 79 (2002). Various decisions of the Inter–American Commission on Human Rights have also declared norms as jus cogens. See, e.g., Domingues v. United States, Case 12.285, Inter–Am. C.H.R., Report No. 62/02, OEA/Ser.L./V/II.116 doc. 33, paras. 45–46, 64 (2002) (regarding death penalty for juvenile offenders).*

SECTION 3. REGIONAL NORMS AND INSTITUTIONS

The Council of Europe and the Organization of American States have established comprehensive human rights regimes for those regions parallel to, and in important respects more effective than, that of the United Nations. In 1981, African states moved toward a regional human rights system when the Organization of African Unity adopted the African (Banjul) Charter of Human and Peoples' Rights. The League of Arab States established a Commission on Human Rights in 1968, but as of early 2009 it has been inactive in assessing human rights in Arab states.

A. THE EUROPEAN HUMAN RIGHTS SYSTEM

1. Birth of the European Convention System

Western European states were prominent in the development of international human rights under the auspices of the United Nations. Simultaneously, Western Europe saw the growth of European human rights as an important element in the political and economic rebirth of Western Europe after the Second World War. Western European governments saw in human rights the core of a common ideology that would promote European unity. Trust and friendly relations among the states of the region permitted the growth of institutions that helped promote and support respect for rights within these states. With the Cold War, respect for human rights in the West also served to distinguish conditions there from totalitarian repression in the East. Human rights in Europe drew on the burgeoning international human rights law and institutions, and on constitutional traditions and developments within European countries (and the United States). Rights in Europe inspired and contributed to the development of human rights norms and institutions in the larger U.N.

human rights universe. See Greer, The European Convention on Human Rights: Achievements, Problems and Prospects (2006); Fundamental Rights in Europe: The European Convention on Human Rights and Its Member States, 1950–2000 (Blackburn & Polakiewicz eds. 2001).

The European Convention for the Protection of Human Rights and Fundamental Freedoms, Nov. 4, 1950, 213 U.N.T.S. 221, entered into force on September 3, 1953. It was drafted under the sponsorship of the Council of Europe (not to be confused with the European Union) and is open to accession by the member states of the Council. While the Convention has been ratified by all Council members, some states have ratified subject to reservations or declarations of interpretation, and not all have ratified its various protocols.

Protocols have added protection for property, the right to an education, and an obligation on states to hold free elections (Protocols 1–3); a prohibition on the deprivation of liberty for inability to fulfill a contractual obligation, freedom of movement and residence, the right to leave any country (including one's own), freedom of expulsion from the country of one's nationality, and a prohibition on the collective expulsion of aliens (Protocol 4); abolition of capital punishment in time of peace (Protocol 6); restrictions on the expulsion of aliens, the right to review of a criminal conviction by a higher tribunal, the right of a victim of a miscarriage of justice to be compensated, freedom from double jeopardy, and the equality of spouses in respect of marriage (Protocol 7); expedited implementation procedures (Protocol 8); and new procedures for bringing individual complaints before an expanded European Court of Human Rights, along with the termination of a previously-used European Commission on Human Rights (Protocol 11).

At the beginning of the 21st century, the European Convention continues to differ from the International Covenant on Civil and Political Rights (ICCPR), Dec. 16, 1966, 999 U.N.T.S. 171, in some respects. Unlike the ICCPR (Article 1), the Convention contains no reference to a right of peoples to self-determination, or to "economic self-determination"; to the rights of persons belonging to ethnic, religious or linguistic minorities to enjoy their own culture, profess and practice their own religion, or use their own language (Article 27); the right to recognition everywhere as a person before the law (Article 16); and the right to equality before the law and equal protection of the law (Article 26). There is also no European counterpart to the ICCPR's requirement that parties prohibit war propaganda, or advocacy of national, racial, or religious hatred that constitutes incitement to discrimination (Article 20), nor is there explicit mention of the rights of the child (Article 24). Unlike the ICCPR, the European Convention protects property (Protocol 1, Article 1). The Convention provides that no one shall be deprived of the right to enter his own country (Protocol 4, Article 3), whereas the ICCPR provides that no one shall be *arbitrarily* deprived of that right (ICCPR, Article 12(4)). The Convention provides explicitly that no one may be expelled from the territory of the state of which he is a national (Protocol 4, Article 3).

2. European Court of Human Rights Jurisprudence

The new system established in Protocol 11 was put in place in November 1998, after a one-year preparatory period following its ratification by all states parties to the European Convention. Cases such as *Şahin v. Turkey* (*supra* this chapter, Section 1) are decided under the new system, but the revised European Court of Human Rights still draws upon the practice and jurisprudence of the European Commission and the old Court, and the decisions of these bodies will continue to form part of the case-law interpreting the provisions of the Convention and Protocols. These include:

- *Fair Trials*. The guarantees of Article 6 to—a fair public trial and the presumption of innocence, as well as the right to legal counsel— have generated numerous cases. The Court has ruled on the reasonableness of time spent by prisoners in detention before trial, on the appropriate length of judicial proceedings, and on the right to counsel. See, e.g., *Golder v. United Kingdom*, 18 Eur. Ct. H.R. (ser. A) (1975).

- *Speedy Trials*. In several cases the Court has looked with ill favor on lengthy trial proceedings and concluded that any unreasonable delay, not the fault of the defendant, violates Article 6(1). See, e.g. *Laino v. Italy*, 1999–I Eur. Ct. H.R. 361; *Bottazzi v. Italy*, 1999–V Eur. Ct. H.R. 1.

- *Disappearances/Torture*. In several cases brought against Turkey, the Court considered violations of Articles 2, 3 and 5 in relation to disappearances, torture and ill-treatment in detention. See, e.g., *Kurt v. Turkey*, 1998–III Eur. Ct. H.R. 1152; *Aydin v. Turkey*, 1997– VI Eur. Ct. H.R. 1866.

- *Death Penalty*. In the *Soering* case the Court prohibited the extradition by the United Kingdom to the United States of a suspect charged with a capital offence because, if convicted, he might be sent to "death row." The Court found that, in the circumstances of the case, being held on "death row" for a significant period of time, awaiting execution, would violate the prohibition on torture, inhuman or degrading treatment or punishment contained in Article 3 of the European Convention. Eventually, Soering was extradited when the U.S. agreed that he would be tried for a non-capital offence only. See Britain Extradites Soering, 6 Int'l Enforcement Rep. 26 (1990).

The cases coming before the Court have continued to increase in number and variety, and include cases concerning the prohibition of forced labor, the right to respect for private and family life, home and correspondence, the right to marry, freedom of expression, the right to peaceful assembly, the right to trade union freedom, the right to effective remedy, the right to education, and the right to free elections. For discussion of the case-law, see Ovey & White, Jacobs & White: The

European Convention on Human Rights (4th ed. 2006); Theory and Practice of the European Convention on Human Rights (4th ed. Van Dijk et al. eds. 2006);. Harris et al., Law of the European Convention on Human Rights (2d rev. ed. 2005); European Court of Human Rights: Remedies and Execution of Judgments (Christou & Raymond eds. 2005); Mowbray, The Development of Positive Obligations under the European Convention on Human Rights by the European Court of Human Rights (2004) Merrills & Robertson, Human Rights in Europe: A Study of the European Convention on Human Rights (4th ed. 2001).

3. The European Social Charter

Separate from the European Convention, which addresses civil and political rights, the Council of Europe concluded in 1961 an instrument on economic, social and cultural rights, known as the European Social Charter, Oct. 18, 1961, 529 U.N.T.S. 89, which entered into force in 1965. The following states have become parties as of early 2009: Albania, Andorra, Armenia, Austria, Azerbaijan, Belgium, Bulgaria, Croatia, Cyprus, the Czech Republic, Denmark, Estonia, Finland, France, Georgia, Germany, Greece, Hungary, Iceland, Ireland, Italy, Latvia, Lithuania, Luxembourg, Macedonia, Malta, Moldova, Montengro, the Netherlands, Norway, Poland, Portugal, Romania, Slovakia, Slovenia, Spain, Sweden, Turkey, Ukraine, and the United Kingdom.

The original Charter expresses the resolution of the parties "to make every effort in common to improve the standard of living and to promote the social well-being of both their urban and rural populations by means of appropriate institutions and action." In Part I, the parties "accept as the aim of their policy, to be pursued by all appropriate means, both national and international in character, the attainment of conditions in which the following rights and principles may be effectively realized." Part II lists undertakings in various categories, e.g., the right to work, the right to a fair remuneration, the right to bargain collectively, the rights of children, the right of employed women to protection, the right to social security, the right to social and medical assistance. Parties are required to submit reports on their implementation of the Charter, which are reviewed by an independent Committee of Experts, specialists on social questions, joined by a representative from the International Labor Organization. The Charter was revised in 1996, principally to strengthen the role and independence of the Committee of Experts. See generally Harris & Darcy, The European Social Charter (2d ed. 2001); Samuel, Fundamental Social Rights: Case Law of the European Social Charter (2d ed. 2002); Council of Europe, Revised European Social Charter and Explanatory Report (1996).

4. European Union Charter of Fundamental Rights

In December 2000, the Presidents of the European Union Parliament, Council, and Commission signed and proclaimed the Charter of Fundamental Rights of the European Union, Dec. 7, 2000, 40 I.L.M. 2GG (2001) This non-binding Charter purports to set out in a single text the whole range of civil, political, economic and social rights of EU citizens and residents, divided into six sections on dignity, freedoms, equality, solidarity, citizens' rights, and justice. Among other things, the Charter is based upon the European Convention on Human Rights, the European Social Charter, the constitutional traditions of EU member states, and the 1989 European Community Charter of Fundamental Social Rights of Workers. See de Búrca, The Drafting of the European Union Charter of Fundamental Rights, 26 Eur. L. Rev. 126 (2001); see also Ahmed & de Jesús Butler, The European Union and Human Rights: An International Law Perspective, 17 E.J.I.L. 771 (2006); von Bogdandy, The European Union as a Human Rights Organization?, 37 Common Mkt. L. Rev. 1307 (2000); The EU and Human Rights (Alston, Bustello, & Heenan eds. 1999); Alston & Weiler, An 'Ever Closer Union" in Need of a Human Rights Policy, 9 E.J.I.L. 658 (1998); The European Union and Human Rights (Neuwahl & Rosas eds. 1995); Weiler & Lockhart, "Taking Rights Seriously" Seriously: The European Court and Its Fundamental Rights Jurisprudence (Parts I & II), 32 Comm. Mkt. L. Rev. 51, 579 (1995).

5. The Helsinki System

A series of human rights norms were enunciated in the Final Act of the Conference on Security and Cooperation in Europe, Aug. 1, 1975, 14 I.L.M. 1292 (1975), commonly known as the "Helsinki Final Act" or "Helsinki Accord." These norms are not, strictly speaking, regional human rights law, since the Helsinki Final Act is not limited to Europe and is not law (since all agreed that the Act was not legally binding). The result of a period of Cold War detente, the Act was signed by the leaders of thirty-three Eastern and Western European states, as well as the United States and Canada. Many view the Final Act as an important political bargain, in which Western states accepted the political *status quo* in Europe and the Communist states made human rights commitments. Specifically, they agreed that:

> In the field of human rights and fundamental freedoms, the participating States will act in conformity with the purposes and principles of the Charter of the United Nations and with the Universal Declaration of Human Rights. They will also fulfil their obligations as set forth in the international declarations and agreements in this field, including inter alia the International Covenants on Human Rights, by which they may be bound.

Id. at para. 1(a)(VII); see Henkin, The Age of Rights 57–58 (1990); Human Rights, International Law, and the Helsinki Accord (Buergenthal & Hall eds. 1977).

After 1975, the Conference on Security and Cooperation (CSCE) met several times to promote implementation of the Final Act, with the meetings often becoming arenas for charges that members of the Soviet bloc were violating human rights. After the Cold War ended the OSCE changed in character and focus. First, in 1995, the CSCE was renamed the Organization for Security and Co-operation in Europe (OSCE). Second, successive meetings in 1989–1991 at Paris, Vienna, Bonn, Copenhagen, and Moscow produced important documents on the "Human Dimension of the CSCE," which elaborated the commitment to human rights in important detail and gave prominent emphasis to democracy as a major human right and as a foundation for other human rights. See The Conference on Security and Co-operation in Europe: Basic Documents, 1993–1995 (Bloed ed. 1997).

The OSCE began as a conference of states, without an institutional structure, but, since 1991, has "become operational rather than serv[ing] simply as a forum for discussion, dialogue, verbal confrontation, and adoption of documents." Brett, Human Rights and the OSCE, 18 Hum. Rts. Q. 668, 670 (1996). A High Commissioner for National Minorities was created in 1992 and an OSCE Office for Democratic Institutions and Human Rights has been instrumental in election, human rights, and related monitoring functions. For example, in 1998, OSCE monitors were established in Kosovo, to verify withdrawal of Yugoslav military forces, and again in 1999 with the lead role in matters relating to institution-building, democratization and monitoring, protecting and promoting human rights. See The OSCE in the Maintenance of Peace and Security: Conflict Prevention, Crisis Management, and Peaceful Settlement of Disputes (Bothe, Ronzitti, & Rosas eds. 1997).

B. THE INTER–AMERICAN HUMAN RIGHTS SYSTEM

1. American Declaration on the Rights and Duties of Man

The American Declaration on the Rights and Duties of Man was adopted in 1948, seven months before the Universal Declaration. It is generally understood that the American Declaration was not intended to have legally binding character and has not acquired such character since. See LeBlanc, The OAS and the Promotion and Protection of Human Rights 13–17 (1977). Substantively, the American Declaration parallels the Universal Declaration, though the former also includes a chapter containing ten articles setting forth the individual's duties. American Declaration on the Rights and Duties of Man, arts. XXIX–XXXVIII, OAS Res. XXX (1948).

2. American Convention on Human Rights

The American Convention on Human Rights, sometimes referred to as the "Pact of San José," was signed in San José, Costa Rica on November 22, 1969, and came into force in June of 1978, 444 U.N.T.S. 123, OAS T.S. No. 36. As of early 2009, twenty-four states are parties to the Convention. Substantively, the American Convention parallels the International Covenant on Civil and Political Rights (ICCPR). The protected rights include: the right to life, freedom from torture and inhuman treatment, freedom from slavery and servitude, the right to liberty and security, the right to a fair trial, freedom from retroactivity of the criminal law, the right to respect for private and family life, freedom of conscience and religion, freedom of thought and expression, freedom of assembly, freedom of association, freedom to marry and found a family, the right to property, freedom of movement, freedom from exile, prohibition of the collective expulsion of aliens, the right to participate in free elections, the right to an effective remedy if one's rights are violated, the right to recognition as a person before the law, the right to compensation for miscarriage of justice, the right of reply, the right to a name, the rights of the child, the right to a nationality, the right to equality before the law, and the right of asylum.

The American Convention protects generally-accepted political and civil rights, but does so for some in terms significantly different from the ICCPR. For example, under Article 4(1) the American Convention the right to life "shall be protected by law and, in general, from the moment of conception." Like the European Convention but unlike the ICCPR, the American Convention includes protection for property, and freedom from exile and collective expulsion for aliens. Unlike both the ICCPR and the European Convention, the American Convention recognizes a right of reply (to anyone injured by inaccurate or offensive statements or ideas) and the right of asylum.

Unlike the European Convention, which anticipated amendment of and addition to its provisions by way of subsequent protocols, the OAS did not contemplate that the American Convention would be continually altered. Nonetheless, two additional protocols have been adopted by the General Assembly of the OAS, one on economic, social and cultural rights, Additional Protocol to the American Convention on Human Rights in the Area of Economic, Social, and Cultural Rights (Protocol of San Salvador), Nov. 17, 1988, OAS T.S. No. 69, and the other on prohibiting the death penalty, Protocol to the American Convention on Human Rights to Abolish the Death Penalty, June 8, 1990, OAS T.S. No. 73.

3. Inter–American Commission on Human Rights

The Inter–American Commission of Human Rights was created in 1960, before the creation of the Inter–American Court (see next subSection). The Commission was elevated to the status of an organ of the OAS in 1970. As such, its competence has been to "further respect" for human rights; the quoted words were interpreted to grant authority "to promote" but not "to protect" human rights. Almost immediately, however, an activist Commission read its mandate very broadly, acting as a controversial investigative body and advocate for human rights. See Padilla, The Inter–American Commission on Human Rights of the Organization of American States: A Case Study, 9 Am. U. J. Int'l L. & Pol'y 95 (Fall 1993); Norris, Observations in Loco: Practice and Procedure of the Inter–

American Commission on Human Rights, 1979–1983, 19 Tex. Int'l L.J. 285 (1984).

In 1965, it was granted authority "to examine" private communications alleging violation of rights. The Commission has exercised its authority with mixed success, high in the Dominican Republic in 1965–1966, least notable as regards Cuba (which refused to cooperate with the Commission). Regardless of its success, the Commission itself is a source of jurisprudence interpreting the American Declaration, the American Convention, and other sources, whether or not complaints are later referred to the Court. For example, the Commission interpreted and applied not only the American Convention, but also provisions of international humanitarian law and determined that common Article 3 of the Geneva Conventions of 1949 was applicable to combat between Argentinean military forces and a group of armed attackers, which lasted for a period of thirty hours. See *Abella v. Argentina*, Case 11.137, Inter–Am. C.H.R., Report No. 55/95 OEA/Ser.L./V/II.98, doc. 6 rev. (1997).

With the coming into force of the American Convention, the Inter–American Commission acquired a second judicial character and function not unlike that of the erstwhile European Commission, whereby it could refer cases to the American Court with respect to those states who have accepted the Court's jurisdiction. The 2001 Rules of Procedure provide that virtually all cases of non-compliance by such states must be referred to the Court with the Commission's recommendations. Inter–Am. Court of Human Rights, Rules of Procedure, Inter–Am. C.H.R. (ser. A) No. 17 (2003); see Shelton, New Rules of Procedure for the Inter–American Commission on Human Rights, 22 Hum. Rts. L.J. 169 (2001).

The two functions of the Commission (as an overall advocate of human rights in the Americas and as a screening mechanism for judicial cases under the Convention) have sometimes appeared in tension—a tension which may affect the respect given the Commission's judgments. By contrast, the European Commission was formed solely as an enforcement arm of the European Convention and given only quasi-judicial functions, and its past role in the European human rights system is widely appreciated.

Since 1980, the Inter–American Commission has heard several complaints against the United States alleging violations of the American Declaration of the Rights and Duties of Man and of the customary law of human rights. See, e.g., *White v. United States ("Baby Boy Case")*, Case No. 2141, Inter–Am. C.H.R., Report No. 23/81, OEA/Ser.L./V/II.54, doc. 9 rev. 1 (1981) *(Roe v. Wade* does not violate the right to life granted by American Declaration and the American Convention); *Roach v. United States*, Case No. 9647, Inter–Am.C.H.R., Report No. 3/87, OEA/Ser.L./V/II.71, doc. 9 rev. 1 (1987) (U.S. death sentence for crime committed by juvenile under 18 is not a violation of a customary norm, although such a norm may be emerging); *Beazley v. United States,* Case 12.412, Inter–Am. C.H.R., Report No. 101/03, OEA/Ser.L./V/II.114 doc. 70 rev. 2

(2003) (execution of juvenile under 18 does violate Article 1 of the American Declaration); *Celestine v. United States*, Case No. 10.031, Inter–Am.C.H.R. Report No. 23/89, OEA/Ser. L./V/II.77, doc. 7 rev. 1 (1989) (facts did not establish that U.S. applied death penalty in racially discriminatory manner); *Statehood Solidarity Committee v. United States*, Case 11.204, Inter–Am. C.H.R., Report No. 98/03, OEA/Ser.L./V/II.118 doc. 5 rev. 2 (2003) (violation of right to equality before the law and right to vote by denying residents of the District of Columbia the opportunity to vote for members of the U.S. Congress). There have also been charges before the Commission that the United States violated the Declaration and customary law when it invaded Panama in 1989, and when it interdicted vessels carrying Haitian asylum seekers on the high seas. See *Haitian Centre for Human Rights v. United States*, Case 10.675, Inter–Am. C.H.R., Report No. 51/96, OEA/Ser.L./V/II.95, doc. 7 rev. (1997).

4. Inter–American Court of Human Rights

The Inter–American Court of Human Rights was established in 1979. Twenty-two OAS states have recognized the jurisdiction of the Court as binding and twenty-one are currently so bound: Argentina, Barbados, Bolivia, Brazil, Chile, Colombia, Costa Rica, the Dominican Republic, Ecuador, El Salvador, Guatemala, Haiti, Honduras, Mexico, Nicaragua, Panama, Paraguay, Peru, Suriname, Uruguay, and Venezuela. According to Article 62 of the American Convention on the Rights and Duties of Man, *supra*, any state party may accept the jurisdiction of the Court in a specific case. Contentious cases come to the Court by referral from the Inter–American Commission. See Pasqualucci, The Practice and Procedure of the Inter–American Court of Human Rights (2003). Unlike the new European system under Protocol 11, individuals remain unable to bring a complaint to the Inter–American Court, a subject of criticism of the inter–American system. See Trindade, The Consolidation of the Procedural Capacity of Individuals in the Evolution of the International Protection of Human Rights, 30 Colum. Hum. Rts. L. Rev. 1 (1998).

Elections to the Inter–American Court of Human Rights first took place in May 1979. Terms are for six years and are staggered. Article 52 of the American Convention permits nationals of all OAS member states to serve on the Court, whether or not the member state is a party to the Convention. For example, Judge Thomas Buergenthal, a national of the United States—which is not a party to the Convention—served on the Court from 1979 to 1991, including as its Vice–President and President. See Buergenthal, Remembering the Early Years of the Inter–American Court of Human Rights, 37 N.Y.U. J. Int'l L. & Pol. 259 (2005).

The Inter–American Court issues both advisory opinions and decisions in contentious cases. Much of the jurisprudence of the Inter–American Court has been generated through advisory opinions, which may be rendered at the request of the Commission, or of any OAS member state. The Court's advisory opinions may provide interpretations not only of the Convention, but also of "other treaties concerning the protection of human rights in the American states." American Convention, *supra*, art. 64.

The Court's advisory opinions address important issues for the functioning of the inter–American human rights system, including the role of the Court, such as:

- *Adoption of Non–Compliant National Law*. In 1993, the Commission requested an advisory opinion on the legal effects of a law promulgated by a state party to the Convention which manifestly violates the obligations of that state party under the Convention. This question was raised in light of Peru's re-introduction of the death penalty for the crime of terrorism, which ran contrary to Article 4 of the Convention. The Court found that the promulgation of such a law is a violation of the Convention and its enforcement by agents or officials of the state would give rise to international responsibility. See *International Responsibility for the Promulgation and Enforcement of Laws in Violation of the Convention (Arts. 1 and 2 of the American Convention on Human Rights)*, Advisory Opinion OC–14/94, 1995 Inter–Am. Ct. H.R. (ser. A) No. 14 (1994).

- *Scope of Court's Advisory Jurisdiction*. In response to a series of questions posed by the government of Peru relating to the Court's jurisdiction to issue advisory opinions, the Court found that it had advisory jurisdiction "with regard to any provision dealing with the protection of human rights set forth in any international treaty applicable in the American states, regardless of whether it be bilateral or multilateral, whatever be the principal purpose of such a treaty, and whether or not non-member states of the inter-American system are or have a right to become parties thereto." *"Other Treaties" Subject to the Advisory Jurisdiction of the Court (Art. 64 American Convention on Human Rights)*, Advisory Opinion OC–1/82, 1981–84 Inter–Am. Ct. H.R. (ser. A) No. 1, at 55 (1982).

- *Legal Status of American Declaration*. In 1989, the Inter–American Court issued an advisory opinion on the legal effect to be given to the American Declaration on the Rights and Duties of Man. Colombia requested the Court to determine whether the Court had the authority under the Inter–American Convention on Human Rights to render advisory opinions interpreting the Declaration. The Court decided that it had such authority provided that the interpretation of the Declaration was necessary to resolve a question related to either the American Convention or one of the "other treaties" over which the Court has advisory jurisdiction. The Court noted that the American Declaration is an authoritative interpretation of the OAS Charter. *Interpretation of the American Declaration of the Rights and Duties of Man in the Context of Article 64 of the American Convention on Human Rights*, Advisory Opinion OC–10/89, 1990 Inter–Am. Ct. H.R. (ser. A) No. 10 (1989).

What are the implications of the Court's advisory opinion in respect of the American Declaration on the Rights and Duties of Man? Has the Court in effect expanded its advisory jurisdiction to include the customary international law of human rights? Does the advisory opinion on "other treaties", together with the Court's opinion on the American Declaration support the conclusion that the Court can also issue advisory opinions concerning other "non-binding resolutions," such as the Universal Declaration of Human Rights?

The Court's decisions in contentious cases have been quite substantial. For example, beginning in 1987, the Court considered a series of cases submitted by the Inter–American Commission concerning disappearances in Honduras. The Court awarded compensation to the next of kin in two of the cases. *Velasquez Rodriguez Case*, 1989–90 Inter–Am. Ct. H.R. (ser. C) No. 7 (1989) (compensatory damages); *Godinez Cruz Case*, 1989–90 Inter–Am. Ct. H.R. (ser. C) No. 8 (1990) (compensatory damages). In another case, the Court held that the responsibility of the Government of Honduras for the deaths of two Costa Rican citizens who had allegedly entered Honduras and disappeared had not been proved. *Fairen Garbi & Solis Corrales Case*, 1989–90 Inter–Am. Ct. H.R. (ser. C) No. 6 (1989) (compensatory damages). In all three cases, the Court dealt with harassment and assassination of witnesses, finally indicating provisional measures ordering the Honduran government to do everything within its power to stop the harassment. The Court also considered a number of preliminary objections by Honduras, including failure to exhaust local remedies, and ruled that where a pattern of disappearances was proven, local remedies such as habeas corpus were non-existent or ineffective because of the failure of government officials to reveal the whereabouts of the victims and because of persistent harassment of persons trying to invoke local remedies. See, e.g., *Godinez Cruz Case*, 1989–90 Inter–Am. Ct. H.R. (ser. C) No. 5, at 116 (1989). The Court also made strong statements on the burden and standard of proof to be applied in cases of wide-scale disappearances where the state subject of the complaint has most control over the evidence. See *Godinez Cruz Case*, *supra*, and *Velasquez Rodriguez Case*, 1987–89 Inter–Am. Ct. H.R. (ser. C) No. 4 (1988).

For the jurisprudence of the Inter–American Court, see Davidson, The Inter–American Court of Human Rights (1992); Ventura Robles, Systematization of the Contentious Jurisprudence of the Inter–American Court of Human Rights 1981–1991 (1996); Shelton, The Jurisprudence of the Inter–American Court of Human Rights, 10 Am. U. J. Int'l L. & Pol'y 333 (1994); Frost, The Evolution of the Inter American Court of Human Rights: Reflections of Present and Former Judges, 14 Hum. Rts. Q. 171 (1992).

For further reading on the Inter–American system, see Harris & Livingstone, The Inter–American System of Human Rights (1998); Davidson, The Inter–American Human Rights System (1997); Buergenthal & Shelton, Protecting Human Rights in the Americas (4th ed. 1995); Mower,

Regional Human Rights: A Comparative Study of the West European and Inter–American Systems, (1991).

C. THE AFRICAN HUMAN RIGHTS SYSTEM

1. The Banjul Charter

For most of its existence, the Organization of African Unity (OAU) was concerned with colonialism and its vestiges, with apartheid in South Africa, Namibia, and Rhodesia (now Zimbabwe), and the economic development of post-colonial African states. In 1981, the OAU adopted the African Charter on Human and Peoples' Rights, officially named the "Banjul Charter." June 27, 1981, 1520 U.N.T.S. 217. The Charter entered into force on October 21, 1986, after it was ratified by a majority of OAU member states. When the African Union (AU) succeeded the OAU in 2002, its constituent instrument did not indicate the African Union's relationship to the African Charter, but the African Commission, discussed below, was retained, and the functions with respect to it previously performed by the OAU Assembly of Heads of State and Government were taken over by the AU Assembly. See Murray, Human Rights in Africa: From the OAU to the African Union (2004).

The Banjul Charter speaks to both rights of individuals and of peoples, which states must recognize, as well as to the duties which every individual has "towards his family and society, the state and other legally recognized communities and the international community" (Article 27). For individuals, the Charter protects the right to equal protection of the law; the right to life; freedom from slavery, torture and cruel, inhuman or degrading punishment and treatment; the right to liberty and freedom from arbitrary arrest or detention; the presumption of innocence in a criminal trial, and the right to counsel; freedom of conscience, profession, religion, expression, association, assembly and movement; the right to leave and return to one's own country; the right to seek and obtain asylum when persecuted; the right to participate freely in government; the right to property; the right to work under equitable and satisfactory conditions; the right to enjoy the best attainable state of physical and mental health; the right to an education; freedom from discrimination; and the prohibition of mass expulsion of aliens. The Charter also lists duties owed by a citizen to his state. They include the duty not to discriminate against others; to protect the family and respect and maintain parents; to serve the state and contribute to its defense; and to pay taxes in the interest of society.

The Charter guarantees the right of "peoples" to existence and to self-determination. It specifically reserves to "colonized" or "oppressed" peoples the right to free themselves by resorting to any means recognized by the international community, and declares that all such peoples shall have the right to receive assistance from states parties to the Charter (Article 20). Also included is the right of peoples to economic, social and cultural development and the right to freely dispose of their wealth and natural resources. States parties are required to eliminate all forms of foreign economic exploitation. Peoples have the right to a "general satisfactory environment favorable to their development" (Article 24). See generally Ouguergouz, The African Charter on Human and Peoples' Rights: A Comprehensive Agenda for Human Dignity and Sustainable Democracy in Africa (2003); Udombana, Between Promise and Performance: Revisiting States' Obligations Under the African Human Rights Charter, 40 Stan. J. Int'l L. 105 (2004); Umozurike, The African Charter on Human and Peoples' Rights (1997).

2. African Commission on Human and Peoples' Rights

The Banjul Charter establishes an African Commission on Human and Peoples' Rights to promote and ensure protection of human rights in Africa. The Commission is a body of independent experts whose mandate is generally three-fold: to promote respect for human rights through studies, seminars, conferences, the dissemination of information, and cooperation with local agencies; to "ensure" the protection of human rights under conditions laid down by the Banjul Charter; and to interpret the provisions of the Charter (Article 45). Article 55 of the Charter has been interpreted to permit individuals and groups to petition the Commission concerning violations of its provisions by a state party. In addition, the Commission can consider whether communications reveal a series of serious or massive violations of Charter rights and bring this to the attention of the African Union (Article 58).

The Commission is therefore quasi-judicial in character, but only renders reports to the states concerned with a particular case and to the AU Assembly of Heads of State and Government. It is up to the states concerned, or the Assembly, to take any action in response to violations described in the reports. In these respects, the Commission is not unlike the human rights commission of the American Convention. A study of state compliance with the recommendations of the African Commission from 1987 to 2003 found that, of the 122 communications sent to the Commission, 63 were declared inadmissible, 5 were settled, and 8 were withdrawn. Of the remaining 46 admissible communications, states were found to have violated the Banjul Charter in 44 of the communications. Thereafter, the study found that the relevant states fully complied with the Commission's recommendations in six cases (14%), did not comply in thirteen cases (30%), partially complied in fourteen (32%), complied but likely due to a regime change in seven cases (15%), and could not be assessed due to lack of information in four cases (9%). See Viljoen & Louw, State Compliance with the Recommendations of the African Commission on Human and Peoples' Rights, 1994–2004, 101 A.J.I.L. 1, 2, 5–7 (2007).

Information on the work of the Commission may be found in its annual reports, available at http://www.achpr.org; see also Österdahl, Implementing Human Rights in Africa–The African Commission on Human and Peoples' Rights and Individual Communications (2002); Murray, The African Commission on Human and Peoples' Rights and International Law (2000); Odinkalu, The Individual Complaints Procedures of the African Commission on Human and Peoples' Rights: A Preliminary Assessment, 8 Transnat'l L. & Contemp. Probs. 359 (1998); Ankumah, The African Commission on Human and Peoples' Rights: Practices and Procedures (1996).

3. African Court on Human Rights

The lack of an African Court on Human Rights was considered a significant failure in the system of implementation and enforcement of Banjul Charter rights and the subject of a sustained advocacy campaign by many individuals and non-governmental organizations up until the 1990s. On June 10, 1998, the OAU Assembly adopted a Protocol to the Charter on Human and People's Rights on the Establishment of an African Court on Human and Peoples' Rights, available at http://www.africa-union.org/root/au/Documents/Treaties/Text/africancourt-humanrights.pdf. The court was established in January 2004, and operates in a manner similar to that of its European and American counter-parts, with both contentious and advisory jurisdiction.

NOTES

1. *Further Reading on Human Rights in Africa.* See The African Charter on Human and Peoples' Rights: The System in Practice, 1986–2006 (2d ed. Evans & Murray eds. 2005); Nmehielle, The African Human Rights System: Its Laws, Practice, and Institutions (2001); see also Naldi & Magliveras, Reinforcing the African System of Human Rights: The Protocol on the Establishment of a Regional Court of Human and Peoples' Rights, 16 Neth. Q. Hum. Rts. 431 (1998); Protecting Human Rights in Africa: Roles and Strategies of Non–Governmental Organizations (1995); Salem, The African System for the Protection of Human and Peoples' Rights, 8 Interights Bull. 55 (1994); Amoah, The African Charter on Human and Peoples' Rights—An Effective Weapon for Human Rights?, 4 Afr. J. Int'l & Comp. L. 226 (1992): Mbaye, Les Droits de L'Homme en Afrique (1992); Human Rights in Africa: Cross–Cultural Perspectives (An–Na'im & Deng eds. 1990).

2. *Human Rights in the Arab World.* The Arab League, founded in 1945, decided in 1968 to establish a Permanent Arab Commission on Human Rights. Arab League Res. 2443 (Sept. 3, 1968). Its essential aim is to promote respect for human rights, but provides no measures and creates no institutions to protect them. The Commission has focused on alleged human rights abuses by Israel in the occupied territories but not on human rights problems within the Arab States. See Boutros–Ghali, The League of Arab States, in 2 Vasak, The International Dimensions of Human Rights 575 (1982); Rembe, Human Rights in Africa: Some Selected Problems (1984).

In 1994, the Council of the League of Arab States adopted the Arab Charter on Human Rights, which was revised in May 2004, and entered into force in 2008. The text of the Charter is set forth in 12 Int'l Hum. Rts. Rep.

893 (2005). Upon its entry into force, the U.N. High Commissioner for Human Rights, Louise Arbour, stated:

> Throughout the development of the Arab Charter, my office shared concerns with the drafters about the incompatibility of some of its provisions with international norms and standards. These concerns included the approach to death penalty for children and the rights of women and non-citizens. Moreover, to the extent that it equates Zionism with racism, we reiterated that the Arab Charter is not in conformity with General Assembly Resolution 46/86, which rejects that Zionism is a form of racism and racial discrimination. OHCHR does not endorse these inconsistencies. We continue to work with all stakeholders in the region to ensure the implementation of universal human rights norms.

Statement by U.N. High Commissioner for Human Rights on the Entry into Force of the Arab Charter on Human Rights, Press Release (Jan. 30, 2008), http://www.unhchr.ch.

3. *Human Rights in Asia*. An Asian system for human rights protection does not exist as of early 2009. The vast diversity of Asian countries, and differing attitudes about human rights as a general matter, did not conduce toward agreement on a regional system. See generally The East Asian Challenge for Human Rights (Bauer & Bell eds. 1999).

SECTION 4. DEVIATING FROM THE NORMS

A. LIMITATIONS WITHIN THE NORMS THEMSELVES

HENKIN, THE INTERNATIONAL BILL OF RIGHTS: THE COVENANT ON CIVIL AND POLITICAL RIGHTS

Introduction, 21–22 (Henkin ed. 1981)

As in even the most enlightened and libertarian national rights systems, most of the rights in the Covenant [on Civil and Political Rights] are not absolute. The freedom of expression, in the classic reference, does not permit one falsely to cry "fire" in a crowded theater; the most libertarian societies do not permit slander, all countries impose some limits on freedom of movement in some circumstances to protect national security or public order. In the rights jurisprudence of the United States these permissible limitations are not expressed in the Constitution, although sometimes read into general phrases: search and seizure is forbidden only if "unreasonable," punishment only if "cruel and unusual," infringements on liberty only if they deny "due process of law."

The Framers of the Covenant sought to define the permissible scope of limitations as strictly as possible, although inevitably in general phrases. For example, the freedom of movement within a country or the right to leave it "shall not be subject to any restrictions except those which are provided by law, are necessary to protect national security, public order (*ordre public),* public health or morals, or the rights and freedoms of others, and are consistent with the other rights recognized" in the Covenant (Article 12(3)). Or, "the Press and the public may be excluded from all or part of a trial for reasons of morals, public order (*ordre public*) or national security in a democratic society, or when the interest of the private lives of the parties so requires, or to the extent strictly necessary in the opinion of the court in special circumstances where publicity would prejudice the interests of justice" (Article 14(1)). One can debate the merits of these and other limitations or their particular formulations, but few would question that in principle some such limitations are inevitable and probably desirable. The limitations themselves, however, are governed by law, not by the whim of the state. Whether a particular limitation on a right is permissible under the Covenant is a question of international law, and the state's action can be scrutinized and challenged as a violation of the Covenant * * *.

NOTES

1. *Limiting Human Rights.* Do you think human rights should be absolute or do you agree that express or implicit limitations, as a practical matter, must exist? Are those limitations driven by the need to protect the rights not just of one person but of other persons as well? By the need of the state to function effectively and peaceably? Even if limitations are admitted, how broadly should they be construed? Note that Article 29(2) of the Universal Declaration states:

> In the exercise of his rights and freedoms, everyone shall be subject only to such limitations as are determined by law solely for the purpose of securing due recognition and respect for the rights and freedoms of others and of meeting the just requirements of morality, public order and the general welfare in a democratic society.

2. *Further Reading.* See Kiss, Permissible Limitations on Rights, in The International Bill of Rights: The Covenant on Civil and Political Rights 290 (Henkin ed. 1981).

B. RESERVATIONS

UNITED STATES RESERVATIONS, UNDERSTANDINGS AND DECLARATIONS TO ITS RATIFICATION OF THE INTERNATIONAL COVENANT ON CIVIL AND POLITICAL RIGHTS

138 Cong. Rec. 8070–71 (1992)

Resolved (two-thirds of the Senators present concurring therein), That the Senate advise and consent to the ratification of the International Covenant on Civil and Political Rights, adopted by the United Nations General Assembly on December 16, 1966, and signed on behalf of the United States on October 5, 1977 (Executive E, 95–2), subject to the following Reservations, Understandings, Declarations and Proviso:

I. The Senate's advice and consent is subject to the following reservations:

(1) That Article 20 does not authorize or require legislation or other action by the United States that would restrict the right of free speech and association protected by the Constitution and laws of the United States.

(2) That the United States reserves the right, subject to its Constitutional constraints, to impose capital punishment on any person (other than a pregnant woman) duly convicted under existing or future laws permitting the imposition of capital punishment, including such punishment for crimes committed by persons below eighteen years of age.

(3) That the United States considers itself bound by Article 7 to the extent that "cruel, inhuman or degrading treatment or punishment" means the cruel and unusual treatment or punishment prohibited by the Fifth, Eighth and/or Fourteenth Amendments to the Constitution of the United States.

(4) That because U.S. law generally applies to an offender the penalty in force at the time the offense was committed, the United States does not adhere to the third clause of paragraph 1 of Article 15.

(5) That the policy and practice of the United States are generally in compliance with and supportive of the Covenant's provisions regarding treatment of juveniles in the criminal justice system. Nevertheless, the United States reserves the right, in exceptional circumstances, to treat juveniles as adults, notwithstanding paragraphs 2(b) and 3 of Article 10 and paragraph 4 of Article 14. The United States further reserves to these provisions with respect to individuals who volunteer for military service prior to age 18.

II. The Senate's advice and consent is subject to the following understandings, which shall apply to the obligations of the United States under this Covenant:

(1) That the Constitution and laws of the United States guarantee all persons equal protection of the law and provide extensive protections against discrimination. The United States understands distinctions based upon race, color, sex, language, religion, political or other opinion, national or social origin, property, birth or any other status—as those terms are used in Article 2, paragraph I and Article 26—to be permitted when such distinctions are, at minimum, rationally related to a legitimate governmental objective. The United States further understands the prohibition in paragraph I of Article 4 upon discrimination, in time of public emergency, based "solely" on the status of race, color, sex, language, religion or social origin not to bar distinctions that may have a disproportionate effect upon persons of a particular status.

(2) That the United States understands the right to compensation referred to in Articles 9(5) and 14(6) to require the provision of effective and enforceable mechanisms by which a victim of an unlawful arrest or

detention or a miscarriage of justice may seek and, where justified, obtain compensation from either the responsible individual or the appropriate governmental entity. Entitlement to compensation may be subject to the reasonable requirements of domestic law.

(3) That the United States understands the reference to "exceptional circumstances" in paragraph 2(a) of Article 10 to permit the imprisonment of an accused person with convicted persons where appropriate in light of an individual's overall dangerousness, and to permit accused persons to waive their right to segregation from convicted persons. The United States further understands that paragraph 3 of Article 10 does not diminish the goals of punishment, deterrence, and incapacitation as additional legitimate purposes for a penitentiary system.

(4) That the United States understands that subparagraphs 3(b) and (d) of Article 14 do not require the provision of a criminal defendant's counsel of choice when the defendant is provided with court-appointed counsel on grounds of indigence, when the defendant is financially able to retain alternative counsel, or when imprisonment is not imposed. The United States further understands that paragraph 3(e) does not prohibit a requirement that the defendant make a showing that any witness whose attendance he seeks to compel is necessary for his defense. The United States understands the prohibition upon double jeopardy in paragraph 7 to apply only when the judgment of acquittal has been rendered by a court of the same governmental unit, whether the Federal Government or a constituent unit, and is seeking a new trial for the same cause.

(5) That the United States understands that this Convention shall be implemented by the Federal Government to the extent that it exercises legislative and judicial jurisdiction over the matters covered therein, and otherwise by the state and local governments; to the extent that state and local governments exercise jurisdiction over such matters, the Federal Government shall take measures appropriate to the Federal system to the end that the competent authorities of the state or local governments may take appropriate measures for the fulfillment of the Convention.

III. The Senate's advice and consent is subject to the following declarations:

(1) That the United States declares that the provisions of Articles 1 through 27 of the Covenant are not self-executing.

(2) That it is the view of the United States that States Party to the Covenant should wherever possible refrain from imposing any restrictions or limitations on the exercise of the rights recognized and protected by the Covenant, even when such restrictions and limitations are permissible under the terms of the Covenant. For the United States, Article 5, paragraph 2, which provides that fundamental human rights existing in any State Party may not be diminished on the pretext that the Covenant recognizes them to a lesser extent, has particular relevance to Article 19, paragraph 3, which would permit certain restrictions on the freedom of expression. The United States declares that it will continue to adhere to

the requirements and constraints of its Constitution in respect to all such restrictions and limitations.

(3) That the United States declares that it accepts the competence of the Human Rights Committee to receive and consider communications under Article 41 in which a State Party claims that another State Party is not fulfilling its obligations under the Covenant.

(4) That the United States declares that the right referred to in Article 47 may be exercised only in accordance with international law.

IV. The Senate's advice and consent is subject to the following proviso, which shall not be included in the instrument of ratification to be deposited by the President:

Nothing in this Covenant requires or authorizes legislation, or other action, by the United States of America prohibited by the Constitution of the United States as interpreted by the United States.

UNITED NATIONS HUMAN RIGHTS COMMITTEE, GENERAL COMMENT 24

U.N. Doc. CCPR/C/21/Rev.1/Add.6 (Nov. 11, 1994)
reprinted in 34 I.L.M. 839 (1995) (footnotes omitted)

General Comment on Issues Relating to Reservations Made upon Ratification or Accession to the Covenant or the Optional Protocol thereto, or in Relation to Declarations under Article 41 of the Covenant

[See pp. 155–58, for more extensive extracts from the Human Rights Committee's General Comment 24. In addition to the material reproduced there, the Committee stated:]

8. Reservations that offend peremptory norms would not be compatible with the object and purpose of the Covenant. Although treaties that are mere exchanges of obligations between States allow them to reserve *inter se* application of rules of general international law, it is otherwise in human rights treaties, which are for the benefit of persons within their jurisdiction. Accordingly, provisions in the Covenant that represent customary international law (and *a fortiori* when they have the character of peremptory norms) may not be the subject of reservations. Accordingly, a State may not reserve the right to engage in slavery, to torture, to subject persons to cruel, inhuman or degrading treatment or punishment, to arbitrarily deprive persons of their lives, to arbitrarily arrest and detain persons, to deny freedom of thought, conscience and religion, to presume a person guilty unless he proves his innocence, to execute pregnant women or children, to permit the advocacy of national, racial or religious hatred, to deny to persons of marriageable age the right to marry, or to deny to minorities the right to enjoy their own culture, profess their own religion, or use their own language. And while reservations to particular clauses of Article 14 may be acceptable, a general reservation to the right to a fair trial would not be.

* * *

11.   The Covenant consists of not just the specified rights, but of important supportive guarantees. These guarantees provide the necessary framework for securing the rights in the Covenant and are thus essential to its object and purpose. Some operate at the national level and some at the international level. Reservations designed to remove these guarantees are thus not acceptable. Thus, a State could not make a reservation to article 2, paragraph 3, of the Covenant, indicating that it intends to provide no remedies for human rights violations. Guarantees such as these are an integral part of the structure of the Covenant and underpin its efficacy. The Covenant also envisages, for the better attainment of its stated objectives, a monitoring role for the Committee. Reservations that purport to evade that essential element in the design of the Covenant, which is also directed to securing the enjoyment of the rights, are also incompatible with its object and purpose. A State may not reserve the right not to present a report and have it considered by the Committee. The Committee's role under the Covenant, whether under article 40 or under the Optional Protocols, necessarily entails interpreting the provisions of the Covenant and the development of a jurisprudence. Accordingly, a reservation that rejects the Committee's competence to interpret the requirements of any provisions of the Covenant would also be contrary to the object and purpose of that treaty.

12.   The intention of the Covenant is that the rights contained therein should be ensured to all those under a State party's jurisdiction. To this end certain attendant requirements are likely to be necessary. Domestic laws may need to be altered properly to reflect the requirements of the Covenant; and mechanisms at the domestic level will be needed to allow the Covenant rights to be enforceable at the local level. Reservations often reveal a tendency of States not to want to change a particular law. And sometimes that tendency is elevated to a general policy. Of particular concern are widely formulated reservations which essentially render ineffective all Covenant rights which would require any change in national law to ensure compliance with Covenant obligations. No real international rights or obligations have thus been accepted. And when there is an absence of provisions to ensure that Covenant rights may be sued on in domestic courts, and, further, a failure to allow individual complaints to be brought to the Committee under the first Optional Protocol, all the essential elements of the Covenant guarantees have been removed.

UNITED STATES, OBSERVATIONS ON GENERAL COMMENT NO. 24

U.N. Doc. A/50/40, annex 6(A)
reprinted in 3 Int'l Hum. Rts. Rep. 265 (1996)

[See pp. 158–59, for more extracts from the U.S. Observations on the Human Rights Committee's General Comment 24. In addition to the material reproduced there, the United States asserted:]

1. *Role of the Committee*

The last sentence of paragraph 11 states that "a reservation that rejects the Committee's competence to interpret the requirements of any provisions of the Covenant would also be contrary to the object and purpose of that treaty".

This statement can be read to present the rather surprising assertion that it is contrary to the object and purpose of the Covenant not to accept the Committee's views on the interpretation of the Covenant. This would be a rather significant departure from the Covenant scheme, which does not impose on States Parties an obligation to give effect to the Committee's interpretations or confer on the Committee the power to render definitive or binding interpretations of the Covenant. The drafters of the Covenant could have given the Committee this role but chose not to do so.

In this respect, it is unnecessary for a State to reserve as to the Committee's power or interpretative competence since the Committee lacks the authority to render binding interpretations or judgments. The quoted sentence can, however, be read more naturally and narrowly in the context of the paragraph as a whole, to assert simply that a reservation may not be taken to the reporting requirement. This narrower view would be consistent with the clear intention of the Convention.

* * *

4. *Domestic Implementation*

The discussion in paragraph 12, as it stands, is very likely to give rise to misunderstandings in at least two respects. The Committee here states, with regard to implementing the Covenant in domestic law, that such laws "may need to be altered properly to reflect the requirements of the Covenant; and mechanisms at the domestic level *will be needed to allow the Covenant rights to be enforceable at the local level*". (Emphasis added)

First, this statement may be cited as an assertion that States Parties *must* allow suits in domestic courts based directly on the provisions of the Covenant. Some countries do in fact have such a scheme of "self-executing" treaties. In other countries, however, existing domestic law already provides the substantive rights reflected in the Covenant as well as multiple possibilities for suit to enforce those rights. Where these existing rights and mechanisms are in fact adequate to the purpose of the Covenant, it seems most unlikely that the Committee intends to insist that the Covenant be directly actionable in court or that States must adopt legislation to implement the Covenant.

As a general matter, deciding on the most appropriate means of domestic implementation of treaty obligations is * * * left to the internal law and processes of each State Party. Rather, the Committee may properly be concerned about the case in which a State has joined the Covenant but lacks any means under its domestic law by which Covenant rights may be enforced. The State could even have similar constitutional guarantees which are simply ignored or non-enforceable. Such an approach would not, of course, be consistent with the fundamental principle of *pacta sunt servanda*.

Second, paragraph 12 states that "[r]eservations often reveal a tendency of States not to want to change a particular law". Some may view this statement as sweepingly critical of any reservation whatsoever which is made to conform to existing law. Of course, since this is the motive for a large majority of the reservations made by the States in all cases, it is difficult to say that this is inappropriate in principle. Indeed, one might say that the more seriously a State Party takes into account the necessity of providing strictly for domestic implementation of its international obligations, the more likely it is that some reservations may be taken along these lines.

It appears that the Comment is not intended to make such a criticism, but rather is aimed at the particular category of "widely formulated reservations" which preserve complete freedom of action and render uncertain a State Party's obligations as a whole, e.g., that the Covenant is generally subordinated to the full unspecified range of national law. This, of course, would be neither appropriate nor lawful. The same is not true, however, when by means of a discrete reservation, a State party declines for sufficient reasons to accept a particular provision of the Covenant in preference for existing domestic law.

NOTES

1. *U.S. Ratification of the ICCPR.* In seeking Senate consent to ratification of the ICCPR, the administration of George H.W. Bush indicated that it would not seek implementing legislation because none was necessary. Do you think that position was legally defensible? Professor Henkin writes:

> By adhering to human rights conventions subject to these reservations, the United States, it is charged, is pretending to assume international obligations but in fact is undertaking nothing. It is seen as seeking the benefits of participation in the convention (e.g., having a U.S. national sit on the Human Rights Committee established pursuant to the Covenant) without assuming any obligations or burdens. The United States, it is said, seeks to sit in judgment on others but will not submit its human rights behavior to international judgment. To many, the attitude reflected in such reservations is offensive: the conventions are only for other states, not for the United States.

Henkin, U.S. Ratification of Human Rights Conventions: The Ghost of Senator Bricker, 89 A.J.I.L. 341, 344 (1995) (footnote omitted). By contrast, Professor Neuman writes:

> Human rights experts critical of the United States' reservations to the CCPR have described them as designed to ensure that the U.S. was taking on no new obligations, beyond what its constitution and laws already required. * * * This rhetoric should not be misunderstood. The U.S. certainly identified a series of respects in which the CCPR would

have imposed new obligations, and sought to avoid them. But the reservations contain no systematic exclusion of new obligations, and the U.S. did not explicitly reserve against every aspect of the CCPR that went beyond existing law.

Neuman, The Global Dimension of RFRA, 14 Const. Comment. 33, 43–44 n. 58 (1997); see also Reservations to Human Rights Treaties and the Vienna Convention Regime: Conflict, Harmony, or Reconciliation (Ziemele ed. 2004); Goodman, Human Rights Treaties, Invalid Reservations, and State Consent, 96 A.J.I.L. 531 (2002); Korkelia, New Challenges to the Regime of Reservations under the International Covenant on Civil and Political Rights, 13 E.J.I.L. 437 (2002); Bradley & Goldsmith, Treaties, Human Rights, and Conditional Consent, 149 U. Pa. L. Rev. 399 (2000).

2. *The ICCPR Human Rights Committee's Reaction to the U.S. RUDs.* In its Consideration of Reports Submitted by States Parties Under Article 40 of the Covenant: Comments of the Human Rights Committee, U.N. Doc. CCPR/C/79/Add.50 (Apr. 7, 1995), the Human Rights Committee criticized the extent of the U.S. reservations, understandings, and declarations (RUDs) to the ICCPR, and asserted that some of them were incompatible with the object and purpose of the Covenant. It stated:

> 14. The Committee regrets the extent of the State party's reservations, declarations, and understandings to the Covenant. It believes that, taken together, they intended to ensure that the United States has accepted what is already the law of the United States. The Committee is also particularly concerned at reservations to article 6, paragraph 5, and article 7 of the Covenant, which it believes to be incompatible with the object and purpose of the Covenant. * * *

> 27. The Committee recommends that the State party review its reservations, declarations and understandings with a view to withdrawing them * * *.

3. *General Comment No. 24.* Do you think the Human Rights Committee is correct that certain reservations simply cannot be made to the ICCPR? Where in the ICCPR does the Human Rights Committee have the authority to make such determinations? For the United Kingdom's reaction to General Comment 24, see The Human Rights Committee, Observations on General Comment No. 24, U.N. Doc. A/50/40, annex 6(B), 3 Int'l Hum. Rts. Rep. 261 (1996); see also Redgwell, Reservations to Treaties and Human Rights Committee General Comment No. 24(52), 46 I.C.L.Q. 390, 393 (1997).

4. *Revisiting Customary International Law.* In paragraph 8 of General Comment No. 24, the Human Rights Committee enumerated "provisions in the Covenant that represent customary international law." Compare those rights with the rights identified in the Restatement (Third), which were reprinted in Section 2(E) above. What could account for the differences in the two catalogues of rights?

C. DEROGATIONS IN EMERGENCIES

LAWLESS CASE

[1961] European Court of Human Rights, Ser. A. no. 1

[Beginning in December 1956, members of the non-governmental group called the Irish Republican Army (IRA), operating out of the Republic of Ireland, staged a series of cross-border attacks into Northern Ireland against U.K. police and radio stations, and courthouses. The IRA's objective was to foment popular support for an independent and unified Irish Republic covering the entire island. Under pressure from the United Kingdom, the government of the Republic of Ireland arrested some 130 known IRA activists, including Gerard Lawless, who were placed in an internment camp. An Irish statute, known as the Offences against the State (Amendment) Act of 1940, allowed such detentions without trial, if necessary for preservation of public peace or for the security of the state, so long as the government issued a proclamation to that effect. The statute provided for some safeguards, such as the creation of a Detention Commission to investigate each person's circumstances to see if they could be released.

Lawless filed a case first before the Irish courts and then before the newly-established European Court of Human Rights, claiming a violation of his rights under Articles 5 and 6 of the European Convention for the Protection of Human Rights and Fundamental Freedoms, Nov. 4, 1950, 213 U.N.T.S. 221, Europ. T.S. No. 5. Those articles guarantee certain fundamental liberties, including the right to a fair trial if detained. Article 15 of the Convention, however, allows a government to derogate from those rights in time of war or public emergency. The European Commission on Human Rights (which no longer exists) investigated the matter and concurred with the Republic of Ireland that a public emergency existed warranting derogation under the Convention. The matter then went before the European Court, which addressed in a section on "The Law" whether the derogation was proper and what standards should be applied when so determining.]

As to whether, despite Articles 5 and 6 of the [European Convention for the Protection of Human Rights and Fundamental Freedoms], the detention of G.R. Lawless was justified by the right of derogation allowed to ·the High Contracting Parties in certain exceptional circumstances under Article 15 of the Convention.

20. *Whereas* the Court is called upon to decide whether the detention of G.R. Lawless from 13th July to 11th December 1957 under the Offences against the State (Amendment) Act, 1940, was justified by the right of derogation * * *;

21. *Whereas* Article 15 reads as follows:

"(1) In time of war or other public emergency threatening the life of the nation any High Contracting Party may take measures derogating from its obligations under this Convention to the extent strictly required by the exigencies of the situation, provided that such measures are not inconsistent with its other obligations under international law.

(2) No derogation from Article 2, except in respect of deaths resulting from lawful acts of war, or from Articles 3, 4 (paragraph 1) and 7 shall be made under this provision.

(3) Any High Contracting Party availing itself of this right of derogation shall keep the Secretary–General of the Council of Europe fully informed of the measures which it has taken and the reasons therefor. It shall also inform the Secretary–General of the Council of Europe when such measures have ceased to operate and the provisions of the Convention are again being fully executed.'';

22. *Whereas* it follows from these provisions that, without being released from all its undertakings assumed in the Convention, the Government of any High Contracting Party has the right, in case of war or public emergency threatening the life of the nation, to take measures derogating from its obligations under the Convention other than those named in Article 15, paragraph 2, provided that such measures are strictly limited to what is required by the exigencies of the situation and also that they do not conflict with other obligations under international law; whereas it is for the Court to determine whether the conditions laid down in Article 15 for the exercise of the exceptional right of derogation have been fulfilled in the present case;

(a) *As to the existence of a public emergency threatening the life of the nation.*

23. *Whereas* the Irish Government, by a Proclamation dated 5th July 1957 and published in the Official Gazette on 8th July 1957, brought into force the extraordinary powers conferred upon it by Part II of the Offences against the State (Amendment) Act, 1940, ''to secure the preservation of public peace and order'';

24. *Whereas,* by letter dated 20th July 1957 addressed to the Secretary–General of the Council of Europe, the Irish Government expressly stated that ''the detention of persons under the Act is considered necessary, to prevent the commission of offences against public peace and order and to prevent the maintaining of military or armed forces other than those authorized by the Constitution''; * * *

* * *

27. *Whereas* the Commission, following the investigation carried out by it in accordance with Article 28 of the Convention, expressed a majority opinion in its Report that in ''July 1957 there existed in Ireland a public emergency threatening the life of the nation within the meaning of Article 15, paragraph 1, of the Convention'';

28. *Whereas,* in the general context of Article 15 of the Convention, the natural and customary meaning of the words ''other public emergency

threatening the life of the nation" is sufficiently clear; whereas they refer to an exceptional situation of crisis or emergency which affects the whole population and constitutes a threat to the organised life of the community of which the State is composed; whereas, having thus established the natural and customary meaning of this conception, the Court must determine whether the facts and circumstances which led the Irish Government to make their Proclamation of 5th July 1957 come within this conception; whereas the Court, after an examination, find this to be the case; whereas the existence at the time of a "public emergency threatening the life of the nation," was reasonably deduced by the Irish Government from a combination of several factors, namely: in the first place, the existence in the territory of the Republic of Ireland of a secret army engaged in unconstitutional activities and using violence to attain its purposes; secondly, the fact that this army was also operating outside the territory of the State, thus seriously jeopardising the relations of the Republic of Ireland with its neighbour; thirdly the steady and alarming increase in terrorist activities from the autumn of 1956 and throughout the first half of 1957;

29. *Whereas,* despite the gravity of the situation, the Government had succeeded, by using means available under ordinary legislation, in keeping public institutions functioning more or less normally, but whereas the homicidal ambush on the night of 3rd to 4th July 1957 in the territory of Northern Ireland near the border had brought to light, just before 12th July—a date, which, for historical reasons is particularly critical for the preservation of public peace and order—the imminent danger to the nation caused by the continuance of unlawful activities in Northern Ireland by the IRA and various associated groups, operating from the territory of the Republic of Ireland;

30. *Whereas,* in conclusion, the Irish Government were justified in declaring that there was a public emergency in the Republic of Ireland threatening the life of the nation and were hence entitled, applying the provisions of Article 15, paragraph 1, of the Convention for the purposes for which those provisions were made, to take measures derogating from their obligations under the Convention;

(b) *As to whether the measures taken in derogation from obligations under the Convention were "strictly required by the exigencies of the situation".*

31. *Whereas* Article 15, paragraph 1, provides that a High Contracting Party may derogate from its obligations under the Convention only "to the extent strictly required by the exigencies of the situation;" whereas it is therefore necessary, in the present case, to examine whether the bringing into force of Part II of the 1940 Act was a measure strictly required by the emergency existing in 1957; * * *

* * *

35. *Whereas* it was submitted that in view of the means available to the Irish Government in 1957 for controlling the activities of the IRA and its splinter groups the Irish Government could have taken measures which would have rendered superfluous so grave a measure as detention without trial; whereas, in this connection, mention was made of the application of the ordinary criminal law, the institution of special criminal courts of the type provided for by the Offences against the State Act, 1939, or of military courts; whereas it would have been possible to consider other measures such as the sealing of the border between the Republic of Ireland and Northern Ireland;

36. *Whereas,* however, considering, in the judgment of the Court, that in 1957 the application of the ordinary law had proved unable to check the growing danger which threatened the Republic of Ireland; whereas the ordinary criminal courts, or even the special criminal courts or military courts, could not suffice to restore peace and order; whereas, in particular, the amassing of the necessary evidence to convict persons involved in activities of the IRA and its splinter groups was meeting with great difficulties caused by the military, secret and terrorist character of those groups and the fear they created among the population; whereas the fact that these groups operated mainly in Northern Ireland, their activities in the Republic of Ireland being virtually limited to the preparation of armed raids across the border was an additional impediment to the gathering of sufficient evidence; whereas the sealing of the border would have had extremely serious repercussions on the population as a whole, beyond the extent required by the exigencies of the emergency;

Whereas it follows from the foregoing that none of the above-mentioned means would have made it possible to deal with the situation existing in Ireland in 1957; whereas, therefore, the administrative detention—as instituted under the Act (Amendment) of 1940—of individuals suspected of intending to take part in terrorist activities, appeared, despite its gravity, to be a measure required by the circumstances;

37. *Whereas,* moreover, the Offences against the State (Amendment) Act of 1940, was subject to a number of safeguards designed to prevent abuses in the operation of the system of administrative detention; whereas the application of the Act was thus subject to constant supervision by Parliament, which not only received precise details of its enforcement at regular intervals but could also at any time, by a Resolution, annul the Government's Proclamation which had brought the Act into force; whereas the Offences against the State (Amendment) Act 1940, provided for the establishment of a "Detention Commission" made up of three members, which the Government did in fact set up, the members being an officer of the Defense Forces and two judges; whereas any person detained under this Act could refer his case to that Commission whose opinion, if favourable to the release of the person concerned, was binding upon the Government; whereas, moreover, the ordinary courts could themselves compel the Detention Commission to carry out its functions;

Whereas, in conclusion, immediately after the Proclamation which brought the power of detention into force, the Government publicly announced that it would release any person detained who gave an undertaking to respect the Constitution and the Law and not to engage in any illegal activity, and that the wording of this undertaking was later altered to one which merely required that the person detained would undertake to observe the law and refrain from activities contrary to the 1940 Act; whereas the persons arrested were informed immediately after their arrest that they would be released following the undertaking in question; whereas in a democratic country such as Ireland the existence of this guarantee of release given publicly by the Government constituted a legal obligation on the Government to release all persons who gave the undertaking;

Whereas, therefore, it follows from the foregoing that the detention without trial provided for by the 1940 Act, subject to the above-mentioned safeguards, appears to be a measure strictly required by the exigencies of the situation within the meaning of Article 15 of the Convention;

38. *Whereas,* in the particular case of G.R. Lawless, there is nothing to show that the powers of detention conferred upon the Irish Government by the Offences against the State (Amendment) Act 1940, were employed against him, either within the meaning of Article 18 of the Convention, for a purpose other than that for which they were granted, or within the meaning of Article 15 of the Convention, by virtue of a measure going beyond what was strictly required by the situation at that time;
* * *

Notes

1. *A Timeless Lawless.* The *Lawless Case*, although not successful in upholding a claimed violation of human rights, remains an important legal precedent concerning when European governments may intern their citizens in times of crisis. Moreover, the *Lawless Case* was the first case to be heard by the European Court of Human Rights and the first time an individual sued his own government before an international tribunal.

2. *Why Allow Derogations?* Should derogations from human rights treaties be permitted? Would states ratify the treaties if derogations were not permitted? What is the effect of continuous or repeated derogations? Henkin writes:

The relation of rights to remedies to enjoyment raises other questions for the international law of human rights. In principle, whether the human rights agreements are being honored, whether the individuals are in fact enjoying the human rights promised, is not immediately legally (or philosophically) relevant. For the short term, at least, failure of one or more states to carry out their international human rights undertakings does not vitiate the character of the undertakings as legal obligations, or the rights and duties they create. But if international human rights obligations fail to make any difference in fact over an extended time; if the states that undertook these obligations act continuously and consistently as though they had not, or as if they were not legal obligations; if the promisee-states do not seek to have the undertakings enforced, and otherwise acquiesce in violations and act as though no obligations exist— then one would have to consider whether there are legal obligations and consequent rights and duties.

Henkin, International Human Rights as "Rights," 1 Cardozo L. Rev. 425, 446 (1979). Does the availability of derogations from human rights obligations render the agreements that embody them ineffectual? Henkin asserts that "derogation clauses are not destructive of the obligations (or the rights) so long as they are in fact interpreted and applied as written and intended, and the other states and the international bodies scrutinize their interpretation and application." Id. at 446–47. Do you agree?

3. *Comparing the European Convention and ICCPR.* The substantive provisions of the European Convention on derogation are similar to those in the International Covenant on Civil and Political Rights (ICCPR), Dec. 16, 1966, 999 U.N.T.S. 171. ICCPR Article 4 provides for derogation, but prohibits it in certain situations, such as derogations from guarantees to the right to life (Article 6), against torture (Article 7), and against slavery and servitude (Article 8).

4. *Justifying the Derogation.* Must a state notify other states concerning its intent to derogate? What must such notification say? In *Silva v. Uruguay*, the Human Rights Committee expressed its views on the derogation clause of ICCPR, stating:

> 8.1   According to article 4(1) of the Covenant, the States Parties may take measures derogating from their obligations under that instrument in a situation of public emergency which threatens the life of the nation and the existence of which has been formally proclaimed * * *.

* * *

> 8.3   Although the sovereign right of a State party to declare a state of emergency is not questioned * * * the Human Rights Committee is of the opinion that a State, by merely invoking the existence of exceptional circumstances, cannot evade the obligations which it has undertaken by ratifying the Covenant. Although the substantive right to take derogatory measures may not depend on a formal notification being made pursuant to article 4(3) of the Covenant, the State Party concerned is duty-bound to give a sufficiently detailed account of the relevant facts when it invokes article 4(1) of the Covenant in proceedings under the Optional Protocol. * * * If the respondent Government does not furnish the required justification itself, as it is required to do under article 4(2) of the Optional Protocol and article 4(3) of the Covenant, the Human Rights Committee cannot conclude that valid reasons exist to legitimize a departure from the normal legal regime prescribed by the Covenant.

Silva v. Uruguay, U.N. Doc. CCPR/C/OP/1, at 65 (1981); see also General Comment 5, in Report of the Human Rights Committee, U.N. Doc. A/36/40, annex VII, at 110 (1981). For derogations in the Inter–American System, see *Habeas Corpus in Emergency Situations (Arts. 27(2), 25(1), and 7(6) of the*

American Convention on Human Rights), Advisory Opinion OC–8/87, Inter–Am. Ct. H.R. (ser. A) No. 8 (1987).

5. *Further Reading.* See Fitzpatrick, Human Rights in Crisis: The International System for Protecting Human Rights during States of Emergency (1994); Oraa, Human Rights in States of Emergency in International Law (1992); Despouy, The Administration of Justice and the Human Rights of Detainees: Question of Human Rights and States of Emergency, U.N.Doc. E/CN.4/Sub. 2/1992/23/Rev.1 (Nov. 2, 1992); International Commission of Jurists, States of Emergency: Their Impact on Human Rights (1983); Higgins, Derogations Under Human Rights Treaties, 48 Brit. Y.B.I.L. 281 (1975–76); Buergenthal, To Respect and to Ensure: State Obligations and Permissible Derogations, in The International Bill of Rights: The Covenant on Civil and Poltical Rights 72 (Henkin ed. 1981); Grossman, States of Emergency: Latin America and the United States, in Constitutionalism and Rights 176 (Henkin & Rosenthal eds. 1990); Chowdhury, Rule of Law in a State of Emergency: The Paris Minimum Standards of Human Rights Norms in a State of Emergency (1989). In 1984 at Siracusa, Italy, a colloquium sponsored by the American Association of the International Commission of Jurists (a nongovernmental body) produced the Siracusa Principles on the Limitation and Derogation Provisions in the International Covenant on Civil and Political Rights. 7 Hum. Rts. Q. 3 (1985).

D. EXTRATERRITORIAL APPLICATION

LEGAL CONSEQUENCES OF THE CONSTRUCTION OF A WALL IN THE OCCUPIED PALESTINIAN TERRITORY

International Court of Justice, Advisory Opinion, 2004
2004 I.C.J. 136

107. It remains to be determined whether the two international Covenants and the Convention on the Rights of the Child are applicable only on the territories of the States parties thereto or whether they are also applicable outside those territories and, if so, in what circumstances.

108. The scope of application of the International Covenant on Civil and Political Rights is defined by Article 2, paragraph 1, thereof, which provides:

> "Each State Party to the present Covenant undertakes to respect and to ensure to all individuals within its territory and subject to its jurisdiction the rights recognized in the present Covenant, without distinction of any kind, such as race, colour, sex, language, religion, political or other opinion, national or social origin, property, birth or other status."

This provision can be interpreted as covering only individuals who are both present within a State's territory and subject to that State's jurisdiction. It can also be construed as covering both individuals present within a State's territory and those outside that territory but subject to that

State's jurisdiction. The Court will thus seek to determine the meaning to be given to this text.

109.   The Court would observe that, while the jurisdiction of States is primarily territorial, it may sometimes be exercised outside the national territory. Considering the object and purpose of the International Covenant on Civil and Political Rights, it would seem natural that, even when such is the case, States parties to the Covenant should be bound to comply with its provisions.

The constant practice of the Human Rights Committee is consistent with this. Thus, the Committee has found the Covenant applicable where the State exercises its jurisdiction on foreign territory. It has ruled on the legality of acts by Uruguay in cases of arrests carried out by Uruguayan agents in Brazil or Argentina (case No. 52/79, *López Burgos v. Uruguay*; case No. 56/79, *Lilian Celiberti de Casariego v. Uruguay*). It decided to the same effect in the case of the confiscation of a passport by a Uruguayan consulate in Germany (case No. 106/81, *Montero v. Uruguay*).

The *travaux préparatoires* of the Covenant confirm the Committee's interpretation of Article 2 of that instrument. These show that, in adopting the wording chosen, the drafters of the Covenant did not intend to allow States to escape from their obligations when they exercise jurisdiction outside their national territory. They only intended to prevent persons residing abroad from asserting, vis-à-vis their State of origin, rights that do not fall within the competence of that State, but of that of the State of residence (see the discussion of the preliminary draft in the Commission on Human Rights, E/CN.4/SR.194, para. 46; and United Nations, *Official Records of the General Assembly, Tenth Session, Annexes*, A/2929, Part II, Chap. V, para. 4 (1955)).

* * *

111.   In conclusion, the Court considers that the International Covenant on Civil and Political Rights is applicable in respect of acts done by a State in the exercise of its jurisdiction outside its own territory.

DENNIS, APPLICATION OF HUMAN RIGHTS TREATIES EXTRATERRITORIALLY DURING TIMES OF ARMED CONFLICT

100 A.S.I.L. Proc. 86, 86–90 (2006) (some footnotes omitted)

[S]tates generally do not appear to apply the international human rights treaties extraterritorially during times of armed conflict and military occupation. For example, during the recent military occupation of Iraq, the Commission on Human Rights called upon parties only "to abide strictly by their obligations under *international humanitarian law*, in particular the Geneva Conventions and the Hague Regulations including those relating to essential civilian needs of the people of Iraq."[3] Similarly,

---

3. CHR Res. 2003/84 (Apr. 25) (emphasis added).

in resolutions 1511 and 1546, acting under Chapter VII of the Charter, the Security Council authorized the [Multi–National Force (MNF)] "to take all necessary measures to contribute to the maintenance of security and stability in Iraq."[4] Moreover, this week the United Kingdom's Court of Appeal issued an important decision that specifically addresses the relationship between the authority of MNF in Iraq to intern civilians under UNSCR 1546 and existing human rights law. The Court in *Al Jedda* concluded that even though "the very essence of internment is inconsistent with the 'due process' requirements of ECHR Article 5(1) or Article 9 of the ICCPR," UNSCR 1546 "unquestionably gave the MNF the power to intern people for imperative reasons of security."[5]

* * *

SCOPE OF APPLICATION PROVISIONS

I will start with the ordinary meaning of the scope of application clauses of both the ECHR and the ICCPR. While both instruments reflect a territorial notion of jurisdiction, their specific scope of application clauses are different. Article 1 of the European Convention states that "the High Contracting Party shall secure to everyone *within their jurisdiction* the rights and freedoms defined in section 1 of the Convention." On the other hand, Article 2(1) of the ICCPR stipulates that "[e]ach State Party to the present Covenant undertakes to respect and to ensure to all individuals *within its territory* and *subject to its jurisdiction* the rights recognized in the present Covenant without discrimination of any kind."

A plain reading of the texts would indicate that to enjoy the protections of the European Convention a person must only be within the jurisdiction of the High Contracting Party. On the other hand, to enjoy the protections of the ICCPR, a person must be *both* within the territory of a State Party *and* subject to the jurisdiction of that State Party.

SUBSEQUENT PRACTICE

The leading case in the European Court of Human Rights on the extraterritorial application of the ECHR during periods of armed conflict and military occupation continues to be *Bankovic v. Belgium*.[6] In that case, the Grand Chamber of the Court found that victims of the extraterritorial acts by NATO forces in bombing the headquarters of Radio Television Serbia were not "within the jurisdiction" of the member states for purposes of Article 1 of the ECHR. The Court stated that "Article 1 of the Convention must be considered to reflect this ordinary and essentially territorial notion of jurisdiction, other bases of jurisdiction being exceptional and requiring special justification in the particular circumstances of each case."[7] Perhaps most significant for present purposes, the Court

---

4. SC Res. 1511 (Oct. 16, 2003); SC Res. 1546 (June 8, 2004).

5. The decision is available at <http://www.bailii.org/dw/cases/EWCA/Civ/2006/327.html>.

6. 2001—XII Eur. Ct. H.R. 333 (Grand Chamber), 123 ILR 94 (emphasis added).

7. *Id*. para. 37.

described the territorial scope of Article 2 of the ICCPR as having been "definitively and specifically confined" by the drafters. "[I]t is difficult to suggest," the Court observed, "that exceptional recognition by the Human Rights Committee of certain instances of extra-territorial jurisdiction (and the applicants give one example only) displaces in any way the territorial jurisdiction expressly conferred by" Article 2(1).[8]

The European Court also relied on the fact that although various overseas military missions involving states parties had been undertaken since the adoption of the ECHR, not one contracting state had indicated, by making a derogation from those rights as provided under Article 15 of the ECHR, a belief that its actions abroad constituted an exercise of jurisdiction. All derogations under Article 15 have been lodged with respect to internal conflicts only.[9]

More recently, several courts have struggled with the issue of whether the ECHR applies in Iraq. For example, a British court in *Al Skeini & Others v. Secretary of State for Defence*, found that it did not have extra-territorial personal jurisdiction over the case of deaths as a result of military operations by British occupation forces in the southern Basra area of Iraq because the coalition did not have effective control over these areas during its occupation of Iraq.[10] The British Court did find that it had jurisdiction over the case of an individual who had been arrested by British forces on charges of terrorism and was being held in a British military prison because the individual was in the custody and control of British state agents.[11]

* * *

Turning to the ICCPR, it would appear that State practice has for the most part been to assume that the ICCPR does not have extraterritorial application. Consistent with state practice under the ECHR, not one state has made a derogation from the extraterritorial application of Covenant rights. All derogations under Article 4 have been lodged with respect to internal emergencies only.

Some states have also informed the Human Rights Committee during its review of state party reports that the provisions of the Covenant do not have an extraterritorial application. For example, in 1995, Conrad Harper, then the Legal Adviser of the US Department of State, told the Committee that the: "dual requirement [of Article 2(1)] restricted the scope of the Covenant to persons under United States jurisdiction and within United States territory."[12] Similarly, the Netherlands challenged a request by the Committee on Human Rights to provide information about the fall of Srebrenica. The Netherlands told the Committee that:

---

8. *Id*. para. 54.

9. *Id*. para. 38.

10. [2005] EWCA 1609, paras. 108, 124.

11. *Id*. paras. 286–87.

12. UN Doc. CCPR/C/SR. 1405 para. 20 (1995).

[t]he Government disagrees with the Committee's suggestion that the provisions of the International Covenant on Civil and Political Rights are applicable to the conduct of Dutch blue helmets in Srebrenica. . . . It goes without saying that the citizens of Srebrenica, *vis-à-vis* the Netherlands, do not come within the scope of [Article 2(1)].[13]

Initially, commentators endorsed a literal reading of Article 2(1), and further argued that Covenant obligations applied, in the context of armed conflict, only with respect to acts of a state's armed forces executed within that territory. The Human Rights Committee first departed from this literal reading of Article 2(1) in several early decisions on individual communications (cited with approval by the International Court of Justice in its *Wall* opinion),[14] where it found that it had jurisdiction in "exceptional circumstances" when state agents had taken unlawful action against *citizens* of that state living abroad.

More recently, the Human Rights Committee in its General Comment No. 31 (May 2004), abandoned the literal reading altogether, taking the position that "the enjoyment of Covenant rights is not limited to citizens of States Parties but must also be available to all individuals . . . who may find themselves *in the territory* or *subject to the jurisdiction of the State Party*."[15]

The Committee does not explain why it turned the "and" in Article 2(1) into an "or," but one can assume that it was influenced by the arguments of several distinguished commentators who argue that the phrase "within its territory and subject to its jurisdiction" should be read as a disjunctive conjunction. Other commentators, including Manfred Nowak in his CCPR Commentary and Professor Christian Tomuschat have challenged this view.[16]

It is not without significance that the ICJ's advisory opinion in the *Wall* case, in concluding that the provisions of the Covenant applied extraterritorially, did not cite General Comment No. 31 in its opinion. Instead, it relied upon earlier concluding observations of the Committee concerning "the long-standing presence of Israel in [the occupied] territories, Israel's ambiguous attitude toward their future status, *as well as the exercise of effective jurisdiction by Israeli forces therein*."[17] Indeed, the Court's specific holding was founded on ICCPR Article 12(1),[18] which contains an express territorial limitation: "Everyone lawfully within the territory of a State shall, within that territory, have the right to liberty of movement and freedom to choose his residence." Thus, arguably, the most

---

13. UN Doc. CCPR/CO/72/NET/Add.1, para. 19 (2003).

14. Wall Opinion, * * * para. 109.

15. UN Doc. CCPR/C/21/Rev.I/Add.13 para. 10 (2004) (emphasis added).

16. Manfred Nowak, *U.N. Covenant on Civil and Political Rights*, CCPR Commentary 43 (2d rev. ed. 2005); Christian Tomuschat, Human Rights: Between Idealism and Realism 109–11 (2003).

17. *Wall* Opinion, . . . para. 110 (emphasis added) (quoting UN Docs. CCPR/C/79/Add.93, para. 10 (1998) and CCPR/CO/78/ISR, para. 11 (2003)).

18. *Wall* Opinion, . . . para. 134.

logical reading of the Court's advisory opinion is that it was based only on the view that the West Bank and Gaza were part of the "territory" of Israel for purposes of the application of the Covenant.

Preparatory Work

* * *

The ICJ decision in the *Wall* case refers to the preparatory work, but oddly it fails to discuss the relevant portions. The key point in the preparatory work is that, in 1950, the draft text of Article 2 of the ICCPR then under consideration by the Commission on Human Rights, like Article 1 of the European Convention, would have required that each state ensure Covenant rights to everyone "within its jurisdiction." The United States, however, proposed the addition of "within its territory." Eleanor Roosevelt, the U.S. representative and then-chair of the Commission, emphasized that the United States was "particularly anxious" that it not assume "an obligation to ensure the rights recognized in it to the citizens of countries under United States occupation" or in what she characterized as "leased territory."[19] She explained:

> An illustration would be the occupied territories of Germany, Austria and Japan: persons within those countries were subject to the jurisdiction of the occupying States in certain respects, but were outside the scope of legislation of those States. Another illustration would be leased territories.[20]

Several delegations spoke against the U.S. amendment, including René Cassin (France) and Charles Malik (Lebanon), arguing that a nation should guarantee fundamental rights to its citizens abroad as well as at home, but the amendment was ultimately adopted at the 1950 session by a vote of 8–2 with 5 abstentions. Subsequently, after similar debates, the United States and others defeated French proposals to delete the phrase "within its territory" at both the 1952 session of the Commission and the 1963 session of the General Assembly.

Hence the preparatory work confirms the ordinary meaning of Article 2(1)—i.e., to enjoy the protections of the ICCPR, a person must be both within the territory of a State Party and subject to the jurisdiction of that State Party. The Human Rights Committee will no doubt face an uphill struggle in seeking to implement its views on the extraterritorial application of the ICCPR, even after the ICJ decision. Unlike judgments of the European Court of Human Rights, the views of the Human Rights Committee under the First Optional Protocol to the ICCPR are not considered to be legally binding. In all events, as this discussion has shown, the Committee's position in its General Comment No. 31 is at odds with the plain meaning of Article 2(1), the practice of states that have ratified the Covenant, and the original intent of the negotiators.

---

19. UN Doc. E/CN.4/SR.193 at 13, 18 (1950); UN Doc. E/CN.4/SR.194, at 5, 9 (1950).

20. UN Doc. E/CN.4/SR.138, at 10 (1950).

BEN–NAFTALI, THE EXTRATERRITORIAL APPLICATION OF HUMAN RIGHTS TO OCCUPIED TERRITORIES

100 A.S.I.L. Proc. 90, 92–94 (2006) (some footnotes omitted)

I propose that the term "jurisdiction," which appears in four of the six major [international human rights (IHR)] treaties, but is defined in none, signifies the ability to rule, to exercise the powers of government vis-á-vis individuals who are affected by these powers. This reading gives expression to the object and purpose of the HR Conventions which is to protect individuals from the improper exercise of power, whereas a narrower, territorially-based meaning, would exclude certain individuals from protection, but not from power.

Reading the jurisdictional formula used in the ICCPR—which applies the Convention to individuals within a state territory and subject to its jurisdiction—in the light of the above interpretation, generates the conclusion that the terms "territory" and "jurisdiction" are disjunctive. The following considerations further support this reading: (1) it avoids redundancy of terms; (2) it coheres with the jurisdictional clauses of the [Convention Against Torture] and the [Convention on the Elimination of Racial Discrimination], many of the obligations of which overlap with the ICCPR, thus generating the sensible subjection of all major HR treaties to the same jurisdictional regime; (3) it coheres with Article 1 of the first Optional Protocol [of the ICCPR] which authorizes the [Human Rights Committee (HRC)] to review communications from individuals subject to the jurisdiction of state parties, dispensing with the term "territory" altogether; (4) it advances the object and purpose of the treaty—a method of interpretation that, under Art. 31 of the Vienna Convention, carries more weight than the drafters' intent;[6] and (5) it is highly supported by practice. * * *

* * *

There is overwhelming jurisprudence—of diverse [human rights] bodies such as the HRC,[7] the [Inter–American Human Rights Commission],[8] the ICJ,[9] the [International Criminal Tribunal for the former Yugo-

---

6. Even if the U.S. reading of the *travaux préparatoires* is the only possible reading, and it is not, the *travaux* indicate that the reference to "within its territory" was designed to clarify that states would not be obliged to interfere coercively abroad to comply with their obligations under the ICCPR. *See* UN Doc. E/CN.4/SR.194 (1950) paras. 15, 16, 31, 32.

7. *E.g.,* Comm. R.12/52 Lopez–Burgos v. Uruguay, UN Doc. A/36/40 (1981). (Note that Professor Tomuschat, who agreed with the majority that wilful and deliberate attacks by a state against its own nationals abroad are covered by the ICCPR, was in a minority when opting for a stricter interpretation of the scope of jurisdiction of the ICCPR.)

8. *E.g.,* Report No. 109/99 Coard v. U.S., Sept. 29, 1999, *available at* <http://www.cidh.oas.org/annualrep/99eng/Merits/UnitedStates10.951.htm>.

9. Legality of the Use by a State of Nuclear Weapons in Armed Conflict, Advisory Opinion, 1996 ICJ Rep. 226 para. 25; Legal Consequences of the Construction of a Wall in the Occupied Palestinian Territory, Advisory Opinion (Int'l Ct. Justice July 9, 2004), 43 ILM 1009 (2004) paras. 104–06.

slavia][10] and the [European Court of Human Rights][11] in support of the extra-territorial application of IHR to areas under the effective control of a state. It is true, however, that there are some areas of debate about particular aspects of this application. The debate seems to revolve around the issue of "effective control": can one talk about "effective control" in an occupied territory where significant hostilities are still occurring?[12] What, indeed, constitutes "effective control"?[13]

These are important questions. They may indeed rise to debate.[14] Far from generating the conclusion that IHR does not apply extra-territorially, however, by shifting the debate from "territory" to "effective control", they underscore the opposite conclusion. Indeed, it is important to note that in the *Bankovic* decision, while the court did not think that NATO exercised effective control, it did not forsake the test of "effective control" and specifically said that military occupations do entail the extra-territorial application of IHR. The problematic aspect of the decision is the Court's position that "effective control" cannot be divided into various aspects of control. The logic of this conclusion seems faulty as it would seem more sensible to think about control in relative terms, wherein the scope of the obligations is relative to actual control: control over space generating obligations that are more limited than full-fledged military occupation. Indeed, the decision in *Ocalan*[15] seems to have adopted this approach: states, and states' agents are bound to respect those HR obligations that they have the power to effect.

NOTES

1. *Application of ICCPR outside Territory.* Do you think the ICCPR is violated if a state party fails to respect or ensure the rights of persons when they are in the territory of another state? Does it matter if the foreign territory is being occupied? If the foreign territory is subject to a long-term lease (e.g., Guantanomo Bay naval base in Cuba)? What about when the conduct at issue is on the high seas or in Antarctica?

2. *Distinguishing among Conventions.* As the readings indicate, not all human rights conventions are crafted the same in terms of their scope. For example, the Convention Against Torture requires in Article 2(1) "each State Party to take effective legislative, administrative, judicial or other measures to

---

10. *E.g.*, Prosecutor v. Furundzija, No. IT–95–17/I–T, para. 183 (Dec. 10, 1999), 121 ILR 214.

11. *E.g.*, Loizidou v. Turkey, 1996–VI, Eur. Ct. H.R. 2216, paras. 62, 72–75.

12. Al Skeini v. Secretary of State for Defence, [2004] EWHC 2911 * * *.

13. Bankovic v. Belgium, Admissibility, App. No. 52207/99 (Eur. Ct. H.R. Dec. 12, 2001), 213 ILR (2003) 94.

14. Note that the degree—indeed, the existence—of effective control exercised by Israel over the Gaza Strip following the withdrawal (disengagement) is pending before the HCJ. The state maintains that it has none, and thus no obligations under IHL or IHR. The petitioners maintain that the control Israel exercises over Gaza's air, water, and land borders; the transfer of goods and people; Gaza's residents' registry; custom, and thereby the ability of public institutions to receive foreign donations and salaries of civil servants through taxation indicate such control.

15. Ocalan v. Turkey, [2003] ECHR 125 (Mar. 12, 2003). It should be noted that the decision retreated from *Bankovic* regarding the ECHR zone of application.

prevent acts of torture in any territory under its jurisdiction." Convention Against Torture and Other Cruel, Inhuman or Degrading Treatment or Punishment, art. 2(1), Dec. 10, 1984, S. Treaty Doc. No. 100–20 (1988), 1465 U.N.T.S. 85. Given the contrast, does such language suggest that the ICCPR should be read not to apply extraterritorially? Or do you think that the conventions should be read more holistically, in which case should they all be viewed as applying extraterritorially?

3. *Background Rule from the Law of Treaties?* Article 29 of the Vienna Convention on the Law of Treaties, May 23, 1969, 1155 U.N.T.S. 331, states: "Unless a different intention appears from the treaty or is otherwise established, a treaty is binding upon each party in respect of its entire territory." Does this mean that as a general matter, human rights treaties only apply within a state's territory, unless some other intention can be definitively established? Or is this provision simply clarifying that treaties apply throughout a state's territory and not to just a portion of it? The I.L.C. Commentary to the draft article that became Article 29 (then Article 25) states that "the law regarding the extra-territorial application of treaties could not be stated simply in terms of the intention of the parties or of a presumption as to their intention; and it considered that to attempt to deal with all the delicate problems of extra-territorial competence in the present article would be inappropriate and inadvisable." [1966] II Yb.I.L.C. 214.

4. *Extraterritorial Application of Refugee Convention.* While the United States is not a party to the U.N. Convention Relating to the Status of Refugees, July 28, 1951, 19 U.S.T. 6259, 189 U.N.T.S. 150, it is derivatively bound to the convention's core provisions through its adherence to the Protocol Relating to the Status of Refugees, Jan. 31, 1967, 19 U.S.T. 6223, 606 U.N.T.S. 267. In *Sale v. Haitian Centers Council Inc.*, 509 U.S. 155 (1993), the U.S. Supreme Court held that Article 33 of the Convention, which provides that no state shall expel or return ("*refouler*") a refugee to a state where his or her life or freedom is threatened because of race, religion, nationality or political beliefs, was not intended to have extraterritorial effect. As such, a U.S. interdiction program designed to stop persons fleeing by boat from Haiti was not in violation of Article 33 because it took place outside U.S. territorial waters. The Court stated the interdiction program may "violate the spirit of Article 33," but because " * * * the text of Article 33 cannot reasonably be read to say anything at all about a nation's actions toward aliens outside its own territory, it does not prohibit such actions." Id. at 157.

The U.N. High Commissioner for Refugees issued a statement critical of the *Sale* decision, expressing the opinion that the *non-refoulement* obligation of Article 33 applied also outside a state's own borders. See U.N. High Commissioner for Refugees Responds to U.S. Supreme Court Decision in *Sale v. Haitian Centers Council*, 32 I.L.M 1215 (1993). The Inter–American Commission on Human Rights later expressed its conclusion that the interdiction program upheld in *Sale* violated Article 33 of the Refugee Convention, as well as several provisions of the American Declaration of the Rights and Duties of Man. See *Haitian Centre for Human Rights v. United States*, Case 10.675, Inter–Am. C.H.R., Report No. 51/96, OEA/Ser.L/V/II.95 doc. 7 rev. (1997). The United States Government has continued to assert that Article 33 does not apply extraterritorially.

In 1998, however, Congress enacted a rider forbidding the use of appropriated funds for extraterritorial *refoulement* of refugees, and also establishing a policy of applying *non-refoulement* as required by the Torture Convention without regard to geographical location. See Pub. L. No. 105–277, §§ 2241, 2242, 112 Stat. 2681–821 (1998).

5. *Further Reading.* See Ben–Naftali & Shany, Living in Denial: The Application of Human Rights in the Occupied Territories, 37 Isr. L. Rev. 17 (2003–04); Dennis, Application of Human Rights Treaties Extraterritorially in Times of Armed Conflict and Military Occupation, 99 A.J.I.L. 119 (2005); Extraterritorial Application of Human Rights Treaties (Coomans & Kamminga eds. 2004); Neuman, Extraterritorial Violations of Human Rights by the United States, 9 Am. U. J. Int'l L. & Pol. 213 (1994); Buergenthal, To Respect and Ensure: State Obligations and Permissible Derogations, in The International Bill of Rights 72, 73–77 (Henkin ed. 1981).

SECTION 5. MECHANISMS FOR PROMOTING COMPLIANCE

Compliance and enforcement have long been seen as the weak link in the international legal system, and they are surely the weak link of international human rights law. As a subject mainly concerned with relations between the state and the individual, rather than with inter-state relations, human rights have presented special problems. For example, in respect of remedies for violations of international law generally, it has been traditionally posited that only states with a legal interest to bring a claim for a breach of international norms have standing to seek enforcement. By contrast, the interests directly affected by human rights violations are those of individual victims, not of states, and moreover of individuals under the "sovereign" control of the state committing the breach. Hence, in the case of human rights, the injury suffered by a state and, by implication, the legal interest to bring a claim, necessitates a variation in traditional conceptions of injury, remedy and implementation. Because the victims of violations are the violating state's own inhabitants, traditional "horizontal enforcement" must be reconsidered if inter-state claims are to be used.

Are inter-state claims the only appropriate mechanism to promote compliance? International human rights conventions typically provide for the establishment and operation of treaty bodies to monitor compliance by states parties. In some instances, petitions by individuals are made available, as can be seen in the regional human rights systems discussed *supra* in Section 3. Further, the major global human rights treaties require states parties not only to respect human rights, but also to ensure that those rights are protected through national law. See The Future of UN Human Rights Treaty Monitoring (Alston & Crawford eds. 2000).

Is it necessary that there be remedies of some kind when human rights are violated? Rights, it is commonly assumed, imply remedies. If human rights are claims upon society, do you think society is required to provide means to realize them, to assure that they are respected, and to provide compensation and other remedies to individuals whose rights are violated? See generally Shelton, Remedies in International Human Rights Law (2d ed. 2005).

A. REPORTING REQUIREMENTS

HENKIN, INTERNATIONAL LAW: POLITICS AND VALUES

210–11 (1995) (footnotes omitted)

State reporting is the least "intrusive" enforcement machinery, reflecting the international system's strong commitment to values of state autonomy and impermeability. (It reflects too some abiding feeling that a "sovereign state" is not to be accused or adjudged, surely not without its consent.) State values are respected also in the limitations on committee consideration of the reports. The Human Rights Committee "shall study the report." It may make only "general comments" and its comments (and the "observations" of the state party) are reported to the Economic and Social Council, a political body. State values and inter-state political forces have been reflected also in various aspects of the Committee's operations: in the rules of procedure adopted by the Committee; in the kind and degree of attention given to reports by Committee members. The Committee members serve in their personal capacity and solemnly declare their impartiality, yet the kind and amount of "cross-examination" of state representatives about the reports often differs with the degree of independence which the member enjoys from his (her) own government in fact, and with relations between that government and the reporting state. The process is inevitably influenced by the disposition of political forces in the system generally—"Cold War" or "détente," considerations of "Third World solidarity" and "non-alignment."

Political forces have moved enforcement small steps beyond reporting, in different measure for different conventions. Differences reflect the degree of the international system's commitment to the particular rights involved in a particular convention, and corresponding political pressures to accept more intrusive monitoring. The time at which a convention was adopted may be significant, as later draftsmen learned from experience under earlier bodies, and states were reassured (or habituated) by that experience. Thus, the Covenant on Civil and Political Rights, applying to all rights, had to settle for the reporting system as the lowest common denominator of agreement.

NOTES

1. *ICCPR Human Rights Committee.* As discussed *supra* in Section 2, Article 28 of the International Covenant on Civil and Political Rights (ICCPR) provides for the establishment of the Human Rights Committee, the ICCPR's principal organ of implementation. Dec. 16, 1966, 999 U.N.T.S. 171. The

Committee consists of eighteen members, nationals of states parties, who serve in their personal capacities. The Committee considers the reports submitted by states parties under Article 40. See Rules of Procedure of the Human Rights Committee, Rules 66–73, U.N. Doc. CCPR/C/3/Rev.8 (Sept. 22, 2005). Most of the other major human rights treaties have similar committees, though some (such as the Genocide Convention) do not.

2. *Guidelines for Reporting.* In 1995, the U.N. General Assembly called upon the leading institutions of the U.N. human rights system to update a manual on how states should prepare their reports for the major human rights conventions. Effective Implementation of International Instruments on Human Rights, G.A. Res. 50/170 (Dec. 22, 1995). The revised manual, which was completed in 1997, provides that the first part of the report should describe the general legal framework within which civil and political rights in the state are protected. The second part is to deal with the legislative, administrative and other measures in force to protect each of the rights under the relevant convention, and include information about limitations or restrictions on their exercise. See Office of the High Commissioner for Human Rights/United Nations Institute for Training and Research/United Nations Staff College Project, Manual on Human Rights Reporting under Six Major International Human Rights Instruments, U.N.Doc. HR/PUB/91/1 (Rev. 1) (1997). The manual covers reporting under the ICCPR, the International Covenant on Economic, Social and Cultural Rights (ICESCR), the Convention on the Elimination of All Forms of Racial Discrimination (CERD), the Convention on the Suppression and Punishment of the Crime of Apartheid, the Convention on the Elimination of All Forms of Discrimination Against Women (CEDAW), and the Convention Against Torture and Other Cruel, Inhuman or Degrading Treatment or Punishment.

3. *Meeting to Discuss Reports.* The relevant committee typically invites states to send representatives to discuss their reports with the committee and to answer questions at a meeting in Geneva. The committee also considers information from other sources. During the Cold War there had been controversy within the ICCPR Human Rights Committee as to what additional sources of information should be consulted.

4. *Reactions to the Reports.* The ICCPR Human Right Committee is authorized only to make general comments on reports. For the Committee's comments on the U.S. second and third ICCPR reports, see Human Rights Committee, Consideration of Reports Submitted by States Parties Under Article 40 of the Covenant: United States of America, UN Doc. CCPR/C/USA/CO/3/Rev.1/Add.1 (Feb. 12, 2008), reprinted in 47 I.L.M. 589 (2008). The states concerned are not required to take any action on the Committee's comments, nor are the Committee's conclusions submitted to an authoritative political organ empowered to make formal and specific recommendations to the government concerned. Pursuant to Article 45, the Committee submits to the General Assembly an annual report on its activities. In these reports, the Committee has not restricted itself to reporting compliance of states, but has included general comments on the substance of particular articles of the Covenant, such as General Comment No. 24, excerpted in Chapter 3, Section 3(F), and *supra* this chapter, Section 4(B).

5. *Emergency Reports*. Since 1991, the ICCPR Human Rights Committee has sometimes requested States to submit "emergency" reports when events indicated that the enjoyment of Covenant rights had been seriously affected. See Joseph, New Procedures Concerning the Human Rights Committees Examination of State Reports, 13 Neth. Q. Hum. Rts. 5 (1995).

6. *Mobilization of Shame*. Does simple reporting and publicization of human rights malfeasance help in "shaming" a recalcitrant state into compliant behavior? Presumably a "rogue state" may not be influenced by such action, but what about states that are trying to establish alliances, open up economic relations, and otherwise be regarded as upstanding members of the community of states? See Drinan, The Mobilization of Shame: A World View of Human Rights (2001).

B. INTER–STATE COMPLAINTS

INTERNATIONAL COVENANT ON CIVIL AND POLITICAL RIGHTS ARTICLE 41(1)

General Assembly of the United Nations, December 16, 1966
999 U.N.T.S. 171, 6 I.L.M. 368 (1967)

A State Party to the present Covenant may at any time declare under this article that it recognizes the competence of the Committee to receive and consider communications to the effect that a State Party claims that another State Party is not fulfilling its obligations under the present Covenant. Communications under this article may be received and considered only if submitted by a State Party which has made a declaration recognizing in regard to itself the competence of the Committee. No communication shall be received by the Committee if it concerns a State Party which has not made such a declaration.

NOTES

1. *ICCPR Opt–In Approach*. The ICCPR does not compel states to expose themselves to the inter-state complaint procedure. Instead, pursuant to Article 41, it is left to the discretion of the state whether to affirmatively declare its acceptance. In the section on "declarations" submitted by the United States when it joined the ICCPR, excerpted *supra* this chapter, Section 4, the United States accepted this procedure. As of early 2009, forty-eight states (including the United States) have elected to declare recognition of the Committee's competence under Article 41. After reading Article 41 closely, why do you think a state would decide to expose itself to complaints from other states about the treatment of its own nationals? Why do you think exposure is not mandatory under the convention?

2. *ICCPR Inter-state Complaint Process*. The ICCPR procedure assumes that bilateral negotiations have failed and domestic remedies exhausted. Under procedures contained in Article 41 (but not excerpted above), as well as developed by the ICCPR Human Rights Committee under its Rules of Proce-

dure, the Committee is to make available its "good offices" to help settle the dispute. If a settlement is not achieved, the Committee is required to consider the matter, with the States parties having the right to be represented through written and oral submissions. The Committee must then submit a report within twelve months, which is to be confined to a brief statement of the facts and the Committee's view on the possibilities of an amicable solution. The parties then have three months to decide whether to accept the Committee's report. See ICCPR, art. 41; Rules of Procedure of the Human Rights Committee, Rules 74–83, U.N. Doc. CCPR/C/3/Rev.8 (Sept. 22, 2005).

3.   *Dormancy.* Although it would provide for the "horizontal" implementation and enforcement of the convention, through 2008 *no* parties have made use of this inter-state complaint mechanism in *any* of the major human rights treaties. Why do you think that is the case?

4.   *Traditional Approach: Sue at the I.C.J.* The Convention on the Prevention and Punishment of the Crime of Genocide, Dec. 9, 1948, 78 U.N.T.S. 277, provides in Article IX that: "Disputes between the Contracting Parties relating to the interpretation, application or fulfillment of the present Convention, including those relating to the responsibility of a State for genocide or for any of the other acts enumerated in article III, shall be submitted to the International Court of Justice at the request of any of the parties to the dispute." When ratifying the Convention, a state may file a reservation opting out of Article IX, as was done by the United States.

Various efforts were made during the 1970s to persuade one or more states to bring a proceeding to the International Court against Cambodia in respect of genocide by the Khmer Rouge under the leadership of Pol Pot. Similar efforts were made in the 1990s with respect to Iraq on account of its actions towards the Kurds. In the 1990s, both Bosnia–Herzegovina and Croatia brought cases to the I.C.J. charging genocide by the Federal Republic of Yugoslavia (F.R.Y.) (later Serbia). See *Application of the Convention on the Prevention and Punishment of the Crime of Genocide* (Bosnia–Herzegovina v. Serbia & Montenegro), 2007 I.C.J. 191; see also Symposium: Genocide, Human Rights and the I.C.J., 18 E.J.I.L. 591 (2007). What do you think generally deters states from instituting proceedings at the I.C.J. charging genocide?

C.   PETITIONS BY INDIVIDUALS

HENKIN, INTERNATIONAL LAW: POLITICS AND VALUES

213–14 (1995)

It had been anticipated that states would be reluctant to submit to complaints that they were violating their obligations under the [ICCPR] and other conventions, but that they would be less reluctant to submit to state complaints than to private complaints. Therefore, the Convention on the Elimination of Racial Discrimination provided for inter-state complaints but made submission to private complaint optional. The [ICCPR] made both procedures optional, but relegated State submissions to private complaint to a separate protocol so as not to discourage adherence to the Covenant.

* * *

Many states, we must conclude, remain reluctant to submit to individual complaints—because they resist penetration of the state veil, are unwilling to have their citizens act independently in the international arena, and fear they might be embarrassed by accusations. But slowly an increasing number of states are becoming less unwilling to submit to the possibility of such complaints before a respected international body in a discreet process before an international body that has earned respect. On the other hand, states remain unwilling to expend political capital and to jeopardize their friendly relations by complaining of human rights violations by another state; states are unwilling to invite such complaints against themselves. States have made significant steps towards accepting third party resolution of disputes involving traditional state interests; they have not yet recognized that human rights everywhere are every state's proper interest.

NOTES

1. *Numbers of ICCPR Individual Petitions.* In the thirty years since the Committee began its work under the Optional Protocol at its second session in 1977, 1777 communications have been placed before it. See Office of the High Commissioner for Human Rights, Statistical Survey of Individual Complaints Dealt with by the Human Rights Committee under the Optional Protocol to the International Covenant on Civil and Political Rights (Apr. 9, 2008), http://www2.ohchr.org/english/bodies/hrc/stat2.htm. Of the 1777 communications, 617 were concluded by Committee views expressed under Article 5(4) of the Optional Protocol (of those, 489 were determined to be state violations of the ICCPR); 494 were declared inadmissible; 250 were discontinued or withdrawn; 15 were declared admissible but have not yet been concluded; and 401 were pending at the pre-admissibility stage.

2. *Representative Actions.* Although the Protocol to the International Covenant on Civil and Political Rights speaks of "communications from individuals * * * claiming to be victims of a violation," the Human Rights Committee early concluded that it may receive communications on behalf of such individuals from other persons. See Report of the Human Rights Committee, U.N. Doc. A/32/44, at i (1977). That is now reflected in Rule 96(b) of the Committee's Rules of Procedure. See Rules of Procedure of the Human Rights Committee, Rule 96(b), U.N. Doc. CCPR/C/3/Rev.8 (Sept. 22, 2005) ("Normally, the communication should be submitted by the individual personally or by that individual's representative; a communication submitted on behalf of an alleged victim may, however, be accepted when it appears that the individual in question is unable to submit the communication personally").

3. *Subsequent Interpretations.* The Committee defines and clarifies the Optional Protocol as it presents its views on the cases it finds admissible. For

example, the Committee has required authors of communications to justify their authority to act on behalf of an alleged victim. It has declared that only individuals, not organizations, may submit communications. The Committee has also explained its understanding of many of the substantive provisions of the Covenant on Civil and Political Rights, including the right to life (Article 6), the right not to be subjected to torture (Article 7), the right to liberty and security of person (Article 9), the rights to family life and protection of the family (Articles 17 and 23), and others. See generally Compilation of General Comments and General Recommendations Adopted by Human Rights Treaty Bodies, U.N. Doc. HRI/GEN/1/Rev.7 (May 12, 2004).

D. INTERNATIONAL ECONOMIC SANCTIONS

As is the case with international law generally, states can impose sanctions upon other states for their failure to abide by their obligations under international human rights laws. Such sanctions may be imposed bilaterally or multilaterally through the United Nations or regional organizations.

For example, in late 2007 the United States adopted the Sudan Accountability and Divestment Act of 2007, Pub. L. No. 110–174, 121 Stat. 2516 (2007). The law permits state and local governments to divest from, and prohibit the investment in, business operations in Sudan in a variety of sectors including power production, mineral extraction, and the fabrication of military equipment (§ 3). Certain businesses may be exempted from such restrictions, however, if they have a license from the federal government and are providing goods or services to marginalized persons in Sudan, peacekeeping forces, or humanitarian organizations. Further, the law permits the heads of executive branch agencies to suspend or debar contractors from eligibility for federal contracts for up to three years for a false certification that they are complying with the law.

Rather than target a specific country, some U.S. statutes target any country that the President determines is committing human rights violations. For example, U.S. law requires cutting off economic aid and military sales to "any country which engages in a consistent pattern of gross violations of internationally recognized human rights, including torture or cruel, inhuman, or degrading treatment or punishment, prolonged detention without charges, or other flagrant denial of the right to life, liberty, and the security of the person." 22 U.S.C. § 2151n(a) (2000); see also 22 U.S.C. § 2304 (2000). The Jackson–Vanik Amendment conditions trade benefits for communist countries on their permitting emigration. 19 U.S.C. § 2432(1)(a) (2000).

E. INTERNATIONAL CRIMINAL SANCTIONS

Ordinarily, when violations of international human rights obligations have been established, the responsible actor is the state that failed to meet its obligations. But international law also imposes some human rights obligations directly on individuals, making them liable for criminal punishment. The principle of individual responsibility was first recognized and enforced in the aftermath of World War II, when Allied countries established tribunals in Nuremberg and Tokyo to prosecute major war criminals. The work of these tribunals provided the foundation for two *ad hoc* international tribunals established by the U.N. Security Council in 1993 and 1994 for the former Yugoslavia and Rwanda, respectively, and for the recently-established International Criminal Court. See generally Zappalà, Human Rights in International Criminal Proceedings (2003); see also Chapter 16.

F. MILITARY ACTION

UNITED NATIONS GENERAL ASSEMBLY, 2005 WORLD SUMMIT OUTCOME

G.A. Res. 60/1 (Oct. 24, 2005)

138.   Each individual State has the responsibility to protect its populations from genocide, war crimes, ethnic cleansing and crimes against humanity. This responsibility entails the prevention of such crimes, including their incitement, through appropriate and necessary means. We accept that responsibility and will act in accordance with it. The international community should, as appropriate, encourage and help States to exercise this responsibility and support the United Nations in establishing an early warning capability.

139.   The international community, through the United Nations, also has the responsibility to use appropriate diplomatic, humanitarian and other peaceful means, in accordance with Chapters VI and VIII of the Charter, to help to protect populations from genocide, war crimes, ethnic cleansing and crimes against humanity. In this context, we are prepared to take collective action, in a timely and decisive manner, through the Security Council, in accordance with the Charter, Chapter VII, on a case-by-case basis and in cooperation with relevant regional organizations as appropriate, should peaceful means be inadequate and national authorities are manifestly failing to protect their populations from genocide, war crimes, ethnic cleansing and crimes against humanity.

NOTES

1. *The Responsibility to Protect: Trigger for Unilateral Military Action?* The 2005 World Summit Outcome document adopted by consensus of the General Assembly, in paragraphs 138–39, addressed the responsibility of states to protect their own people, a concept that clearly intrudes into an expansive notion of "sovereignty." As background, it should be noted that shortly after the 1999 NATO intervention in Serbia to protect Kosovar Albanians, an International Commission on Intervention and State Sovereignty (ICISS) (established by the Government of Canada) issued a December 2001 report entitled The Responsibility to Protect. ICISS, The Responsibility

to Protect (Dec. 2001), available at http://www.iciss.ca/report2-en.asp. The report asserted that a responsibility to protect (or "R2P") exists under international law and that, in a "conscience-shocking" situation when both the state concerned and the Security Council fail to discharge that responsibility, then it "is a real question in these circumstances where lies the most harm: in the damage to international order if the Security Council is bypassed or in the damage to that order if human beings are slaughtered while the Security Council stands by." Id. at para. 6.37. For a discussion of the emergence of this concept, see Stahn, Responsibility to Protect: Political Rhetoric or Emerging Legal Norm?, 101 A.J.I.L. 99 (2007).

2. *High–Level Panel Report: Leave it to the Security Council.* A 2004 U.N. high-level panel of experts appointed by the Secretary–General, writing in the wake of the 2003 U.S. intervention in Iraq, agreed with the ICISS that there existed an "emerging norm that there is a collective international responsibility to protect," but concluded that armed force may be used to fulfill the responsibility only if so authorized by the Security Council. See U.N. Secretary–General, Report of the High-level Panel on Threats, Challenges and Change, para. 203, U.N. Doc. A/59/565 (Dec. 2, 2004); see also id. at paras. 196, 272. The U.N. Secretary–General thereafter generally endorsed the high-level panel's approach, as did the General Assembly in its 2005 World Summit Outcome document, though neither expressly ruled out the unilateral use of force. See In Larger Freedom: Towards Development, Security and Human Rights for All, Report of the Secretary–General, U.N. Doc. A/59/2005, para. 135 (Mar. 21, 2005). For further discussion of unilateral and collective military action, see Chapter 15.

G. NATIONAL ENFORCEMENT: THE UNITED STATES

The machinery established by human rights conventions is designed, above all, to secure compliance through the effective operation of national law and procedures. Many states that adhere to human rights treaties either allow the treaty to operate directly within their national legal systems or enact implementing statutes to the same effect. Further, the national criminal and civil laws of most states prohibit conduct that assist in implementing conventional and customary human rights law. See generally The Protection Role of National Human Rights Institutions (Ramcharan ed. 2005). The following touches upon human rights enforcement mechanisms in the United States.

1. Human Rights Treaties in U.S. Law

Whether U.S obligations under treaty obligations can be enforced in U.S. courts may depend on whether the treaties are viewed as self-executing, as discussed in Chapter 10, Section 3(D). For a case holding that the human rights provisions of the U.N. Charter are not self-executing, see *Frolova v. Union of Soviet Socialist Republics*, 761 F.2d 370 (7th Cir. 1985). The United States is a party to the Protocol Relating to the Status of Refugees, Jan. 31, 1967, 19 U.S.T. 6223, 606 U.N.T.S. 267, and this Protocol has been invoked as a source of law many times in United States courts. See, e.g., *INS v. Stevic*, 467 U.S. 407 (1984). Whether the Protocol is self-executing and whether some of its provisions were violated, was argued extensively in the challenge to the U.S. program for interdicting at sea Haitian refugees. See *Haitian Refugee Center, Inc. v. Gracey*, 600 F.Supp. 1396 (D.D.C. 1985), affirmed, 809 F.2d 794 (D.C. Cir. 1987); *Haitian Refugee Center, Inc. v. Baker*, 953 F.2d 1498 (11th Cir. 1992), cert. denied, 502 U.S. 1122 (1992) (interdiction program was consistent with the legislation); *Haitian Centers Council, Inc. v. McNary*, 969 F.2d 1350 (2d Cir. 1992).

In 1998, on the fiftieth anniversary of the Universal Declaration, President Clinton issued an Executive Order on Implementation of Human Rights Treaties. Exec. Order No. 13107, 63 Fed. Reg. 68,991 (1998). The order declares it to be the "policy and practice of the Government of the United States * * * fully to respect and implement its obligations under the international human rights treaties to which it is a party, including the ICCPR, the CAT [Convention Against Torture], and the CERD." The Executive Order directs executive departments and agencies to perform their functions in a manner that respects relevant human rights obligations. It also creates an Interagency Working Group on Human Rights Treaties to provide guidance, oversight and coordination in such matters. The significance of the Interagency Group remains to be seen. The Order expressly states that it does not create any rights or benefits enforceable by any party, or create any justiciable obligations.

2. Customary Human Rights Law in U.S. Law

Human rights norms recognized as customary international law are law in the United States and can be enforced in appropriate proceedings. For the suggestion that such cases arise under U.S. law and are therefore within the general jurisdiction of U.S. federal courts under 28 U.S.C. § 1331, see Restatement (Third) § 703, Reporters' Note 7. For the view that the courts will not compel the President to respect customary international law, however, see *supra* Chapter 10, Section 2(A).

3. Implementation Through Criminal Jurisdiction

A wide variety of U.S. federal and state criminal statutes allow for punishment of conduct that occurs in the United States that, if unaddressed, could constitute a violation of U.S. human rights obligations, such as torture by a U.S. prison official of a prisoner. From the internal U.S. perspective, such statutes are simply designed to punish undesirable behavior, but from the international perspective they provide a basis for the United States to promote and implement its obligations under human rights treaties and customary law.

Some U.S. statutes also criminalize conduct that occurs abroad in violation of international human rights. For example, in late 2007 President George W. Bush signed the Genocide Accountability Act, which permits prosecution of a person for committing an act of genocide if the alleged offender (1) is an alien who was lawfully admitted for permanent residence in the United States; (2) is a stateless person whose habitual residence is in the United States, or; (3) after the offending conduct transpires, the alleged offender is brought into, or found in the United States. See 18 U.S.C.A. § 1091(d) (West Supp. 2008). Prior to enactment of this Act, a non-U.S. national accused of committing genocide abroad could only be tried for lesser crimes under U.S. law (often visa fraud). Similarly, the United States recently criminalized torture committed abroad irrespective of the nationality of the victim or the alleged offender, so long as the alleged offender turns up in the United States. See 18 U.S.C. § 2340A (2000). In December of 2001, Charles Taylor, Jr., the son of the former Liberian president Charles Taylor, became the first person indicted under this law for acts he committed in Liberia.

Of course, human rights can also be invoked by defendants in criminal proceedings, such as to support a claim that due process has been denied or that a sentence is arbitrary. See Trechsel & Summers, Human Rights in Criminal Proceedings (2005).

4. Implementation Through Civil Jurisdiction

a. Alien Tort Statute

Under the Alien Tort Statute (ATS), U.S. courts have civil jurisdiction to provide a remedy to aliens for torts in violation of either treaties or the law of nations, including human rights violations. The statute reads: "The district courts shall have original jurisdiction of any civil action by an alien for a tort only, committed in violation of the law of nations or a treaty of the United States." 28 U.S.C. § 1350 (2000).

In the principal case that launched the era of ATS litigation, Dr. Joel Filártiga and his daughter, Dolly—both Paraguayan nationals residing in the United States—brought suit in the Eastern District of New York against Américo Peña–Irala. Peña–Irala, a former police official in Paraguay, was in New York on an expired visa. Dr. Filártiga claimed that Peña–Irala had kidnapped and tortured his son to death in retaliation for the father's political opposition to the Paraguayan government. Alleging that such torture was a violation of international law, the plaintiffs invoked the jurisdiction of the district court under the Alien Tort Statute, which gives the district court jurisdiction over a civil action by an alien for a tort only, committed in violation of the law of nations or a treaty of the United States. The district court dismissed the claim for lack of jurisdiction. On appeal, the Court of Appeals for the Second Circuit reversed, stating that "[a]lthough the Alien Tort Statute has rarely been the basis for jurisdiction during its long history, there can be little doubt that this action is properly brought in federal court. This is undeniably an action by an alien, for a tort only, committed in violation of the law of nations." See *Filártiga v. Peña–Irala*, 630 F.2d 876, 887–90 (2d Cir. 1980). For other seminal cases, see *Kadic v. Karadžić*, 70 F.3d 232 (2d. Cir. 1995) (concerning genocide); *Doe I v. Unocal Corp.*, 395 F.3d 932 (9th Cir. 2002), vacated, 395 F.3d 978 (9th Cir. 2003) (concerning slavery or forced labor); *Abebe–Jira v. Negewo*, 72 F.3d 844 (11th Cir. 1996) (concerning cruel, degrading, or inhuman treatment); *Flores v. Southern Peru Copper Corp.*, 343 F.3d 140 (2d Cir. 2003) (rejecting claim based on alleged environmental tort).

In 2004, the U.S. Supreme Court for the first time construed the ATS in a case concerning an individual who alleged he had been arbitrarily arrested in Mexico by an agent of the United States, in violation of international law, whether arising from treaties (such as the ICCPR) or from customary international law. The Court affirmed that the ATS provides a jurisdictional basis in U.S. courts for such actions and further that the torts at issue are not just ones that existed when the statute was first drafted in 1789; other, more modern torts are included so long as they reflect a "specific, universal, and obligatory" norm of international law. *Sosa v. Alvarez–Machain*, 542 U.S. 692, 732 (2004). In that particular case, however, the Court found that there was no relevant treaty obligation enforceable in U.S. courts. Rather, the Court found that "a single illegal detention of less than a day, followed by the transfer of custody to lawful authorities and a prompt arraignment, violates no norm of customary international law so well defined as to support the creation of a federal remedy." Id. at 738. For further discussion, see Chapter 10, Section 2(A). In the wake of Sosa, U.S. courts apply its standards in construing ATS claims. See, e.g., *Taveras v. Taveraz*, 477 F.3d 767 (6th Cir. 2007) (rejecting claim based on cross-border parental child abduction).

One confusing aspect of ATS litigation concerns sovereign immunity. The ATS does not supersede the Foreign Sovereign Immunities Act, 28 U.S.C. §§ 1330, 1332, 1391(f), 1441(d), 1602–11 (2000) (FSIA) (see Chapter 12). Therefore, efforts under the ATS to sue a foreign *government* have usually been frustrated by the principle of sovereign immunity, since the FSIA tort exception only applies to torts occurring in the United States. See, e.g., *Argentina v. Amerada Hess Shipping Corp.*, 488 U.S. 428 (1989). For this reason, most ATS cases involve claims against individuals. Yet in order for a tort to be in violation of the "law of nations or a treaty," usually a government official or someone in a close relationship with a government must have performed the conduct at issue, not a person operating in a private capacity. For example, if one person tortures another person, that alone is not regarded as a violation of international law; rather, both the Convention against Torture and customary international law prohibits only *state-sponsored* torture (only a handful of torts, such as genocide, would be considered in violation of international law even when committed by a private actor). Consequently, while most ATS cases do not involve a government as defendant, they do involve a government official as the defendant, or at least a person acting under the actual or apparent authority of a government (U.S. jurisprudence refers to the latter concept as acting under "color of law"). The tricky part is that if the individual was acting within the scope of his authority as a government official, then the conduct will likely be regarded as conduct of the government and hence immune. Only if the individual was acting outside a valid grant of authority by the government (e.g., a government official who uses his position of authority to torture a prisoner, but was not ordered or authorized by his government to do so), or if the government waives any immunity that might benefit the individual, will the ATS claim be able to proceed. See, e.g., *In re Estate of Marcos Litigation,* 978 F.2d 493, 498 (9th Cir. 1992) (involving government official who acted on her own authority, not the government's); *In re Estate of Marcos Human Rights Litigation*, 25 F.3d 1467 (9th Cir. 1994) (involving permission by the government for the litigation to proceed).

A key area of controversy about the ATS concerns its use against corporate defendants, based on a theory of complicity with foreign governments who commit human rights violations. A leading decision by a three-judge panel of the Ninth Circuit opined that plaintiffs needed to show that the corporation "provided knowing practical assistance or encouragement" to the foreign government in perpetrating the abuses. See *Doe v. Unocal Corp.*, 395 F.3d 932, 947 (9th Cir. 2002). That decision was vacated in anticipation of a rehearing by the Ninth Circuit *en banc*, *Doe I v. Unocal Corp.,* 395 F.3d 978 (9th Cir. 2003), but the case was settled before any further decision was reached. Do you think corporations, including U.S. corporations, should be within the ambit of claims brought under the ATS? See Herz, The Liberalizing Effects of Tort: How Corporate Complicity Liability Under the Alien Tort Statute Advances Constructive Engagement, 21 Harv. Hum. Rts. J. 207 (2008); Hoffman & Zaheer, The Rules of the Road: Aiding and Abetting Under the Alien Tort Claims Act, 26 Loy. L.A. Int'l & Comp. L. Rev. 47 (2003).

b. *Torture Victim Protection Act*

In 1992, Congress enacted the Torture Victim Protection Act, 28 U.S.C. § 1350 note (2000) (TVPA), providing a remedy in damages for victims of torture, whether the victim is an alien or a U.S. national (hence, aliens will often plead their case using both the ATS and TVPA if possible). Section 2(a) of the TVPA provides that an "individual who, under actual or apparent authority, or color of law, of any foreign nation * * * subjects an individual to torture shall, in a civil action, be liable for damages to that individual; or * * * subjects an individual to extrajudicial killing shall, in a civil action, be liable for damages to the individual's legal representative, or to any person who may be a claimant in an action for wrongful death."

Various U.S. courts have applied this statute in cases where U.S. nationals abroad have been allegedly harmed. See, e.g., *Ford v. Garcia*, 289 F.3d 1283 (11th Cir. 2002). The same issue noted above with respect to the ATS and sovereign immunity applies for the TVPA, since the TVPA is not construed as creating a new exception to sovereign immunity under the FSIA. See *Belhas v. Ya'alon*, 515 F.3d 1279, 1288–89 (D.C. Cir. 2008). Hence, most TVPA cases do not involve claims against foreign governments but do involve claims against foreign government officials.

The TVPA does not expressly indicate the constitutional basis for the jurisdiction of the federal courts, but presumably it confers jurisdiction pursuant to Article III, Section 2 of the Constitution, on the basis that the cases at issue arise "under the laws" of the United States. Does this confirm that U.S. government considers torture (and by implication other violations of customary international law) to be violations of U.S. law and therefore within 28 U.S.C. § 1331 (2000)? In other words, is it possible to bring such cases even in the absence of the ATS or TVPA?

CHAPTER 14

INJURY TO ALIENS AND FOREIGN INVESTORS

▪ ▪ ▪

SECTION 1. INTRODUCTION

Under ordinary circumstances, and in the absence of an international agreement to the contrary, a state is not obligated under international law to admit nationals of another state into its territory, and it incurs no international responsibility if it deports them. If aliens are admitted, they may be subjected to restrictions on the duration of their stay, where they may travel, and the activities in which they may engage. Similarly, a state may generally exclude a juridical entity (e.g., a corporation) organized under the laws of, or headquartered in, another state, or, if it is admitted, the state may regulate its activities.

Moreover, a national (whether an individual or juridical entity) of one state that comes within the territorial jurisdiction of another generally becomes subject to the legal regime applicable to nationals of that state, except to the extent that a special regime is applicable to aliens. For example, foreign nationals or foreign juridical entities may be excluded from engaging in various commercial or other gainful activities, from owning real property, from enjoying certain civil and political rights such as the right to vote or to hold public office, and from certain duties such as fulfilling a military service obligation. Generally, aliens' substantive and procedural rights are neither better nor worse than those of local nationals, and they do not carry with them to the host state the rights and protections they may enjoy under the law of the state of their nationality.

Yet international law provides certain important protections to aliens and foreign juridical entities. International agreements, including treaties of friendship, commerce and navigation and bilateral investment treaties, often guarantee the right of persons of one contracting party to do business in the other state, subject to some restrictions. The standards accorded to aliens by such agreements are often either the national treatment standard (according the alien the same protections accorded to local nationals) or the most-favored-nation standard (according the alien the most favorable protections accorded to other aliens). Even in the absence of an applicable international agreement, customary international law affords certain minimal or absolute protections to alien individuals and foreign juridical entities, regardless of how the host state treats its own nationals or other aliens.

If those substantive standards of protection are not met by the host state, international agreements and customary international law have developed procedural rules for the vindication of claims. Generally speaking, if the alien or entity has suffered an injury as a result of a violation of a substantive rule of international law attributable to the host state, the state of the alien's nationality may "espouse" the claim and assert it on the state-to-state level against the offending state. Various procedural rules must be met; for example, the injured alien or foreign entity normally must first exhaust remedies under the legal system of the host state before the claim of the private party can be elevated to the international plane.

The core substantive and procedural rules on the protection of aliens and foreign investors are the subject of this chapter. The student should keep in mind the general rules on state responsibility addressed in Chapter 8, which serve as a backdrop to these rules on injury to aliens.

SECTION 2. SOURCES OF LAW ON INJURY TO ALIENS

A. CUSTOMARY INTERNATIONAL LAW

As in other areas of international law, the treatment by states of aliens over the centuries has resulted in patterns of state practice, in which states accord certain protections to those aliens out of a sense of legal obligation. To ascertain the content of those standards, states, tribunals, and non-state actors regularly consult relevant sources of information, including: statements by governments, digests of state practice, decisions of international tribunals and national courts, and the writings of learned scholars. Further, the emergence of the extensive treaty practice noted below has had an effect on the development of customary international law in this area, as states increasingly conform their practice to their treaty obligations, and in doing so rely upon broad standards that tend to transcend any single treaty instrument.

B. BILATERAL TREATIES

A large number of bilateral treaties have been entered into between industrialized, capital-exporting countries and developing countries that have as one of their objectives, or as their sole objective, increasing the legal protection to private parties of one of the contracting states that invest or engage in other business transactions in the other contracting state against non-commercial risks. These bilateral treaties may be divided into three categories: (1) treaties of friendship, commerce, and navigation (FCN treaties) which, as the title implies, cover a wide range of trade relations; (2) bilateral investment treaties (BITs) that focus specifically on protection of the foreign investor against specified non-commercial risks, such as the taking of the investor's property without compensation, discriminatory treatment, and, in some cases, breach or repudiation by a contracting state of contracts with nationals of the other contracting state; and (3) free trade agreements, which contain as one portion of the agreement protections for foreign businesses and investors. The United Nations estimates that, as of 2006, 2,573 BITs had been concluded worldwide, along with 241 other agreements (e.g., trade agreements) containing investment provisions. See United Nations Conference on Trade and Development (UNCTAD), World Investment Report 2007, at 16 (2007).

1. Friendship, Commerce, and Navigation (FCN) Treaties

Since its inception, the United States has concluded bilateral treaties of "amity and commerce" or "friendship, commerce and navigation" (FCN treaties), which prior to World War II were principally focused on issues of trade and navigation. The first FCN was concluded with France after the signing of the Declaration of Independence. See Treaty of Amity and Commerce, Feb. 6, 1778, U.S.–France, 8 Stat. 12, T.S. No. 83. During the 1950s and 1960s, the United States negotiated a new network of FCN treaties designed primarily for the protection and encouragement of U.S. private trade and investment abroad. The basic thrust of these agreements is to obligate each contracting state to grant at least national and most-favored-nation treatment to citizens and companies of the other contracting state. With respect to some activities, however, such as those related to national security, transport, utilities, and exploitation of national resources, most-favored-nation treatment may be all that is guaranteed. In evaluating the significance of the FCN treaties, one must consider not only their substantive coverage or lack of coverage but also the fact that the very existence of the treaty may reflect a favorable climate for U.S. trade and investment in the other contracting state. One must also keep in mind that the United States has concluded relatively few FCN treaties with developing countries (and particularly few with Africa and Asia), where the protections they afford are often needed. All such treaties, moreover, are terminable by either party on notice.

While the FCN program focused principally on developed countries, the United States did succeed in negotiating several FCNs with third world states. In total, from 1946 to 1966, the United States concluded more than forty FCN agreements, with Argentina, Austria, Belgium, Bolivia, Brazil, Canada, Chile, Colombia, Denmark, Ecuador, Finland, Germany, Greece, Guatemala, Honduras, Iran, Ireland, Israel, Italy, Korea, Latvia, Liberia, Luxembourg, Nepal, the Netherlands, Nicaragua, Norway, Oman, Pakistan, Paraguay, Spain, Suriname, Switzerland, Thailand, Togo, Tonga, Turkey, the United Kingdom, Venezuela, Vietnam, and Yemen. See U.S. Department of State, Treaties in Force 2007 passim (2007). A treaty with the Republic of China remains applicable with

Taiwan, while the United States in 1985 terminated the treaty with Nicaragua after Nicaragua used the treaty to sue the United States before the International Court of Justice.

After the 1960s, the United States ceased negotiating FCN treaties with developing countries and shifted its efforts to negotiating reciprocal bilateral investment treaties, which focus principally on providing the nationals of each contracting state with liberalized access to the market of the other contracting state, and on providing enhanced legal protection against non-commercial risks.

For commentary, see American Bar Association, Commercial Treaty Index (2d ed. 1976); Wilson, United States Commercial Treaties and International Law (1960); Walker, Modern Treaties of Friendship, Commerce, and Navigation, 42 Minn. L. Rev. 805 (1958); American Bar Association, The Protection of Private Property Invested Abroad Law 39–58 (1963); Fatouros, Government Guarantees to Foreign Investors 218 (1962).

2.   Bilateral Investment Treaties (BITS)

Hundreds of bilateral investment treaties (BITs) have entered into force since the first such treaty was concluded by the Federal Republic of Germany and Pakistan in 1959. All the major capital-exporting states, led by Germany, and more than eighty developing countries have become parties to BITs. The treaties normally encompass such matters as general standards of treatment of foreign investment, protection against expropriation, compensation for losses from armed conflict or internal disorder, currency transfers and convertibility, and settlement of disputes. Recent treaties for the protection of foreign private investors in Kazakhstan, Romania, and Russia represent radical departures from the past and reflect the dramatic change in the legal climate for foreign investment in those economies. Many of these investment treaties have their roots in the Draft Convention on the Protection of Foreign Property, prepared under the auspices of the Organization for Economic Cooperation and Development (OECD) and adopted in 1967 by the OECD Council, stating the belief that the Draft Convention would be useful in the preparation of bilateral agreements for the protection of foreign property. Protection of Foreign Property: Draft Convention and Resolution of the Council, C(67)102 (Oct. 12, 1967), available at http://www.oecd.org.

The United States has placed considerable reliance on BITs, usually denominated Treaties Concerning the Reciprocal Encouragement and Protection of Investments. The 2004 "Model United States BIT" may be found at http://www.ustr.gov. As of 2008, there were BITs in force between the United States and about forty countries. The U.S. treaties differ from many entered into by European countries in that their purpose is not merely protection of investments but also ensuring free access (with limited exceptions) of investors of each contracting state to the markets of the other contracting state.

For background, see UNCTAD, International Investment Arrangements: Trends and Emerging Issues (2006); Vandevelde, The Economics of Bilateral Investment Treaties, 41 Harv. J. Int'l L. 469 (2000); Guzman, Why LDCs Sign Treaties That Hurt Them: Explaining the Popularity of Bilateral Investment Treaties, 38 Va. J. Int'l L. 639 (1998); Kishoiyian, The Utility of Bilateral Investment Treaties in the Formulation of Customary International Law, 14 Nw. J. Int'l L. & Bus. 327 (1994); Vandevelde, The Political Economy of a Bilateral Investment Treaty, 92 A.J.I.L. 621 (1998); Dolzer & Stevens, Bilateral Investment Treaties (1995); Vandevelde, United States Investment Treaties: Policy and Practice (1992); Salacuse, BIT by BIT: The Growth of Bilateral Investment Treaties and Their Impact on Foreign Investment in Developing Countries, 24 Int'l Law. 655 (1990); Gann, The U.S. Bilateral Investment Treaty Program, 21 Stan. J. Int'l L. 373 (1985); see also UNCTAD, Investment Provisions in Economic Integration Agreements (2006).

3. Bilateral Free Trade Agreements

Some countries, including the United States, have developed extensive bilateral "free trade" agreements that contain not only obligations to reduce or eliminate tariffs on trade, but also obligations on host states that allow foreign nationals to gain access to local industry, to obtain intellectual property protections, and otherwise to secure protections for their investments.

For example, the United States and Chile completed a lengthy bilateral free trade agreement in December 2002, which entered into force in 2003. See Free Trade Agreement, United States–Chile, June 6, 2003, available at http://www.ustr.gov (U.S.–Chile FTA). The first comprehensive trade agreement between the United States and a South American country, the U.S.–Chile FTA provides for the elimination over time of tariffs on bilateral trade in consumer, industrial products and farm goods, and provides for bilateral access by services industries, such as banks, insurance and telecommunications companies, express-delivery companies, and professional firms. Various protections and obligations for nondiscriminatory treatment are included with respect to intellectual property rights, covering products such as software, music, and videos. For the purpose of providing a secure, predictable legal environment for investors, the agreement's chapter 10 on investment provides detailed provisions that define investment interests and the protections to be accorded to them. Moreover, the agreement's core obligations are subject to dispute settlement provisions, which initially call for compliance through consultation and then, as necessary, for submission of the dispute to a panel of experts for binding arbitration.

C. MULTILATERAL TREATIES

The same types of rules embedded in bilateral treaties can and have been included in multilateral treaties among like-minded states. Examples include: Convention Establishing the Multilateral Investment Guarantee Agency, Oct. 11, 1985, 24 I.L.M. 1598 (1985) (MIGA Convention); Association of Southeast Asian Nations (ASEAN), Agreement for the Promotion and Protection of Investments, Dec. 15, 1987, 27 I.L.M. 612 (1988); North American Free Trade Agreement, Dec. 17, 1992, 32 I.L.M. 289 & 605 (1993) (NAFTA); Energy Charter Treaty, Dec. 12, 1994, 34 I.L.M. 381 (1995); Mercado Común del Sur (MERCOSUR), Protocol of Colonia for the Promotion and Reciprocal Protection of Investments, Jan. 17, 1994, http://www.sice.oas.org/Trade/MRCSR/colonia/pcolonia_s.asp (Spanish); Central America–Dominican Republic–United States Free Trade Agreement, Aug. 5, 2004 (CAFTA), available at http://www.ustr.gov.

D. CONTRACTS OR CONCESSION AGREEMENTS

If a foreign national or juridical entity is engaging in a business activity in a host state, it is common for there to be a contract or concession agreement between that national and the state. That contract may contain commitments by the host state to provide certain protections or benefits to the foreign investor, as well as clauses that "internationalize" the contract by establishing international law as the applicable law governing the contract and by creating jurisdiction in an international arbitral tribunal in the event that a dispute arises under the contract. Various institutions have assisted in the development of such contracts by crafting "model clauses" for inclusion in the contract, such as the model clauses developed by the World Bank's International Centre for the Settlement of Investment Disputes (ICSID). See Baker, Foreign Direct Investment in Less Developed Countries: The Role of ICSID and MIGA 62 (1999).

E. NATIONAL LAW

As noted in the Introduction to this chapter, when a national or juridical entity travels to a foreign country, the national is exposed to the laws of that country. International law can provide certain protections, but national law always operates in tandem with those protections and is the default source of law if no other source is deemed applicable. For example, when a dispute concerning a foreign investor is referred to an ICSID arbitration tribunal, unless a different choice of law has been specified by the parties, "the Tribunal shall apply the law of the Contracting State party to the dispute (including its rules on the conflict of laws) and such rules of international law as may be applicable." Convention on the Settlement of Investment Disputes between States and Nationals of Other States, art. 42(1), Mar. 18, 1965, 17 U.S.T. 1270, 575 U.N.T.S. 159.

Moreover, even when international law is the principal choice of law, national law still serves as an important reference for certain aspects of the international law analysis. For example, in considering whether a foreign national has "exhausted" all available local remedies (discussed further in Section 3), one must analyze the rules and procedures of the national legal system for pursuing claims before local courts and tribunals. Or, when considering whether the property of a foreign national has been expropriated, one must analyze the specific legal effects under the national law of steps taken by the host government with respect to that property. Hence, national law is an inescapable source of law whenever the rights of foreign nationals are at stake.

F.   HUMAN RIGHTS LAW

The rules on injury to aliens developed prior to the international law of human rights, which was examined in Chapter 13. Notwithstanding differences in the development and origins of the customary law of responsibility for injury to aliens and the law of human rights, there is a substantial overlap and a growing interrelationship between them. As stated by the Reporters of the Restatement (Third):

> The difference in history and in jurisprudential origins between the older law of responsibility for injury to aliens and the newer law of human rights should not conceal their essential affinity and their increasing convergence. The law of responsibility to aliens posited and invoked an international standard of justice for individuals, even if dogmas of the international system limited the application of that standard to foreign nationals. That standard of justice, like contemporary human rights law, derived from historic conceptions of natural law, as reflected in the conscience of contemporary mankind and the major cultures and legal systems of the world. As the law of human rights developed, the law of responsibility for injury to aliens, as applied to natural persons, began to refer to violation of their "fundamental human rights," and states began to invoke contemporary human rights norms as the basis for claims for injury to their nationals.

Restatement (Third), Part VII, Introductory Note. By way of example, Article 6 of the African Charter on Human and Peoples' Rights, June 27, 1981, 21 I.L.M. 59 (1982) (Banjul Charter), states: "Every individual shall have the right to liberty and to the security of his person. No one may be deprived of his freedom except for reasons and conditions laid down by law. In particular, no one may be arbitrarily arrested or detained." With respect to economic rights, Article 14 of the Banjul Charter provides: "The right to property shall be guaranteed. It may only be encroached upon in the interest of public need or in the general interest of the community and in accordance with the provisions of appropriate laws." Id. at 61.

For that reason, the materials discussed in this chapter will sometimes make reference to instruments and case law in the field of human rights law. Nevertheless, it should be kept in mind that the law on injury to aliens retains independent vitality in providing protection against injuries to individual aliens that do not rise to the level of violations of human rights and against injuries to juridical entities (such as privately owned corporations) that have no "human" rights.

For background, see Mountfield, Regulatory Expropriation in Europe: The Approach of the European Court of Human Rights, 11 N.Y.U. Envtl. L.J. 136 (2002); Anderson, Compensation for Interference with Property, [1999] Eur. Hum. Rts. L. Rev. 543; Antinori, Note, Does Lochner Live in Luxembourg?: An Analysis of the Property Rights Jurisprudence of the European Court of Justice, 18 Fordham Int'l L.J. 1778 (1995).

SECTION 3.   SUBSTANTIVE RULES ON INJURY TO ALIENS

A.   RELATIVE STANDARDS OF TREATMENT

Relative standards of treatment can be accorded by a host country to a foreign national at its discretion (international law does not compel a host state to accord such protections). Such treatment might be extended on the basis of a provision of national law or by means of an international agreement or contract. The standards are "relative" because they are not fixed but, rather, depend upon the treatment that is separately being accorded to persons other than the foreign national.

1.   National Treatment Standard

The "national treatment" standard is commonly used by a host state for protecting a foreign national. Under this standard, the host state agrees to extend to the foreign national treatment no less favorable than that accorded to its own nationals. In other words, the standard aspires to an equality of treatment as between the foreign national and the local national. In some ways, this standard is the easiest for a host state to apply, for it simply requires that the foreign national receive the same benefits and protections that are accorded in the normal course of events to nationals living in the host state. In another way, however, the standard is never fully met, in that the host state will not wish to accord to foreign nationals all the benefits and burdens of its own nationals (e.g., a right to vote in elections or a requirement to serve in the military). Consequently, when the national treatment standard is extended, it typically must be conditioned in some fashion. See UNCTAD, National Treatment (2000).

For example, Article 10.2(1), of the U.S.–Chile Free Trade Agreement, *supra* Section 2(B)(3), provides: "Each Party shall accord to investors of the other Party treatment no less favorable than that it accords, in like circumstances, to its own investors with respect to the establishment, acquisition, expansion, management, conduct, operation, and sale or other disposition of investments in its territory." Note how such a provision does not accord the foreign investor an absolute right to establish or acquire an investment; if local nationals are not provided a particular ability to engage in investments (e.g., in a particular sector of the economy), then the foreign investor does not have that ability as well. Hence, the right is relative in nature, not absolute.

2. Most–Favored–Nation Standard

Under the "most-favored-nation" standard, the host state agrees to extend to the foreign national treatment no less favorable than the most preferential treatment it accords to other foreign nationals. In other words, if a host State A has accorded certain benefits or protections to the foreign nationals of State B, and if State C's nationals are entitled to receive MFN treatment from State A, then State C's nationals are entitled to receive the same benefits or protections that are accorded to State B's nationals.

For example, Article 10.3(1), of the U.S.–Chile Free Trade Agreement provides: "Each Party shall accord to investors of the other Party treatment no less favorable than that it accords, in like circumstances, to investors of any non-Party with respect to the establishment, acquisition, expansion, management, conduct, operation, and sale or other disposition of investments in its territory." Again, note how the protection accorded to the foreign nationals is not absolute; it turns upon the highest level of protection that has been granted to third-country nationals.

B. ABSOLUTE OR NON–CONTINGENT STANDARDS OF TREATMENT

1. Minimum Standard of Treatment

While the relative standards of treatment noted *supra* Section A are commonly used in the course of establishing rights for foreign nationals, international law has also developed over time a concept of a "minimum standard" of treatment that a host state must accord to a foreign national. This standard is absolute, meaning that the standard must be accorded to the foreign national without regard to how the host state treats it own nationals or nationals from third countries. As former Secretary of State and Senator Elihu Root said in 1910:

> There is a standard of justice, very simple, very fundamental, and of such general acceptance by all civilized countries as to form a part of the international law of the world. The condition upon which any country is entitled to measure the justice due from it to an alien by the justice which it accords to its own citizens is that its system of law and administration shall conform to this general standard. If any country's system of law and administration does not conform to that standard, although the people of the country may be content or compelled to live under it, no other country can be compelled to accept it as furnishing a satisfactory measure of treatment to its citizens.

4 A.S.I.L. Proc. 13, 21 (1910); see also Roth, The Minimum Standard of International Law Applied to Aliens 127 (1949) ("the international stan-

dard is nothing else than a set of rules, correlated to each other and deriving from one particular norm of general international law, namely that the treatment of an alien is regulated by the law of nations'').

The 1926 decision of the United States–Mexico General Claims Commission in the *Neer Claim* has become a classic general articulation of the standard. Paul Neer had been killed in Mexico under obscure circumstances, such that it was difficult to conclude that the Mexican government had failed to diligently apprehend and prosecute those responsible. In articulating the kind of conduct that is necessary to violate this standard, the Commission stated:

> [T]he propriety of governmental acts should be put to the test of international standards, and * * * the treatment of an alien, in order to constitute an international delinquency, should amount to an outrage, to bad faith, to wilful neglect of duty, or to an insufficiency of governmental action so far short of international standards that every reasonable and impartial man would readily recognize its insufficiency. Whether the insufficiency proceeds from the deficient execution of an intelligent law or from the fact that the laws of the country do not empower the authorities to measure up to international standards is immaterial.

Neer Claim (United States v. Mexico), 4 U.N. Rep. Int'l Arb. Awards 60, 61–62 (1926). Case law and treaty provisions have helped to flesh out the precise meaning of this minimum standard of treatment; there appear to be a few different ways in which the standard might be breached.

a. *Denial of Procedural Justice*

One aspect of the minimum standard of treatment focuses on the requirement that an alien receive certain procedural justice before the courts and tribunals of the host state. The Restatement (Third) Reporters' Notes cite several examples of injuries that would be treated under traditional customary international law as unlawful failures to afford a minimum standard of justice to an alien and further that, under contemporary law, would be accepted as a human rights violation: (1) denials of due process in criminal proceedings (e.g., arbitrary arrest; unlawful or prolonged detention; unreasonably delayed or unfair trial; being tried twice for the same offense; denial of the right to defend oneself and confront witnesses or to communicate with representatives of one's government); and (2) arbitrary and unreasonable use of force by governmental representatives (e.g., excessive use of force by state officials; inhuman treatment and torture to elicit ''confession''). See Restatement (Third) § 711, Reporters' Note 2.

In considering the minimum standard of due process required in the context of an alien's investment, a NAFTA arbitral dispute panel stated:

> The test is not whether a particular result is surprising, but whether the shock or surprise occasioned to an impartial tribunal leads, on reflection, to justified concerns as to the judicial propriety of the

outcome * * *. In the end, the question is whether, at an international level and having regard to generally accepted standards of the administration of justice, a tribunal can conclude in light of all the available facts that the impugned decision was clearly improper and discreditable, with the result that the investment has been subject to unfair and inequitable treatment. This is admittedly a somewhat open-ended standard, but it may be that in practice no more precise formulation can be offered to cover the range of possibilities.

Mondev Int'l, Ltd. v. United States, ICSID Case No. ARB (AF)/99/2, Award, 42 I.L.M. 85, para. 127 (2003).

It is well settled that mere error in a decision or relatively minor procedural irregularities do not constitute unlawful denials of procedural justice. The injustice must be egregious. The decision must be so obviously wrong that it cannot have been made in good faith and with reasonable care, or a serious miscarriage of justice must otherwise be clear. See, e.g., *Herrera v. Canevaro & Co.*, [1927–28] Ann. Dig. Pub. Int'l L. Cases (McNair & Lauterpacht) 219 (Sup. Ct. Peru 1927). Examples of procedural insufficiencies or mistakes for which states have not been held responsible under international law include failure of a witness to take an oath, incorrect but good faith misapplication or misinterpretation of the law, and improper dismissal of a case for lack of jurisdiction (when another forum was available). Restatement (Third) § 711, Reporters' Note 2(C). In the *Elettronica Sicula S.p.A. (ELSI)* case, the International Court declined to find that the "minimum international standard" was transgressed by a sixteen month delay in a municipal judicial proceeding. *Elettronica Sicula S.p.A. (ELSI)* (United States v. Italy), 1989 I.C.J. 15, para. 111. Moreover, there are denials of procedural justice that would be unlawful under customary international law, but that would not rise to the level of human rights violations. An example would be denial of access to domestic courts in civil proceedings for the determination of an alien's rights. *Van Bokkelen Case* (United States v. Haiti), 2 Moore, Int'l Arbitrations to which the United States Has Been a Party 1807 (1898).

Note that there may be a link to the national treatment standard, in that the assessment of the procedural justice owed is sometimes made by reference to the process available to the nationals of the host state. Hence, international agreements commonly guarantee reasonable access to a court or other tribunal on the same basis as nationals. See, e.g., Friendship, Commerce and Navigation Treaty, United States–Netherlands, art. V(1), Mar. 27, 1956, 8 U.S.T. 2043, 285 U.N.T.S. 231; European Convention for the Protection of Human Rights and Fundamental Freedoms, art. 6(1), Nov. 4, 1950, 213 U.N.T.S. 221; Universal Declaration of Human Rights, arts. 6–9, [1948] U.N.Y.B. Hum. Rts 458; American Declaration of The Rights and Duties of Man, art. XVIII (1948), 43 A.J.I.L. Supp. 133, 136 (1949); International Covenant on Civil and Political Rights, arts. 9(3) & 14, Dec. 16, 1966, 999 U.N.T.S. 171.

b. Failure to Protect Aliens

In several cases, a state has been found responsible for failing to take reasonable steps to prevent a criminal act that harms an alien or, once the act occurs, for failing to take reasonable steps to detect, prosecute, and impose an appropriate penalty on the person responsible for the act. For example, in the *Chapman Claim*, the United States–Mexico General Claims Commission held Mexico liable for failure of Mexican authorities (1) to take appropriate steps to protect a U.S. Consul who was shot and seriously wounded in Puerto Mexico after threats to U.S. diplomatic and consular representatives had been communicated to Mexican authorities and (2) to take proper steps to apprehend and punish the person who did the shooting. *William E. Chapman Claim* (United States v. Mexico), 4 U.N. Rep. Int'l Arb. Awards 632 (1930). Similarly in the *Laura M.B. Janes Claim*, the General Claims Commission made an award based on the failure of the Mexican authorities to take prompt and effective action to apprehend and punish the killer of the claimant's husband. (United States v. Mexico), 4 U.N. Rep. Int'l Arb. Awards 82 (1926).

In *United States Diplomatic and Consular Staff in Tehran* (United States v. Iran), 1980 I.C.J. 3, para. 74, the International Court held that after the U.S. Embassy was seized and diplomatic and consular officials had been held as hostages by the militants, the Iranian Government had a duty to make every effort to bring the hostage situation to a prompt end, which it clearly failed to fulfill. However, in *Elettronica Sicula S.p.A. (ELSI)*, the International Court declined to find that a bilateral treaty provision requiring "constant protection and security" protected a U.S. investor from any disturbance under any circumstance that might adversely affect the investment. *Elettronica Sicula S.p.A. (ELSI)* (United States v. Italy), 1989 I.C.J. 15, para. 108.

c. Fair and Equitable Treatment

Since the mid-twentieth century, bilateral and multilateral treaties concerned with protection of foreign investment have articulated a version of the minimum standard of treatment using the formulation "fair and equitable treatment." For example, Article 1105 of the North American Free Trade Agreement (NAFTA), entitled "Minimum Standard of Treatment," provides in paragraph 1: "Each Party shall accord to investments of investors of another Party treatment in accordance with international law, including fair and equitable treatment and full protection and security." North American Free Trade Agreement, art. 1105(1), Dec. 17, 1992, http://www.sice.oas.org/trade/nafta/chap–111.asp.

Various tribunals have adjudicated the meaning of the "fair and equitable" treatment standard. For example, Zaire's failure to prevent widespread looting that harmed a U.S. investor was found by an ICSID tribunal to have violated the standards of fair and equitable treatment, and full protection and security, contained in a U.S.–Zaire bilateral investment treaty. See *American Mfg & Trading, Inc. v. Zaire*, ICSID Case No. ARB/93/1, 36 I.L.M. 1531 (1997). By contrast, a foreign steel producer failed to show a denial of fair and equitable treatment when faced with host state legislation that required government-funded highway projects to use only domestically-produced steel. See *ADF, Int'l v. United States*, ICSID Case No. ARB(AF)/00/1, Award (2003), http://www.state.gov/documents/organization/16586.pdf. Further, the meaning of "fair and equitable treatment" is not infinitely elastic in covering all types of conduct. When Iran sought to charge that U.S. military attacks on Iranian oil platforms in the Persian Gulf constituted a failure to provide "fair and equitable treatment" to Iran under a bilateral treaty of amity, the International Court declined to view the standard as covering such action. See *Oil Platforms* (Iran v. United States), 1996 I.C.J. 803, paras. 32–36.

One issue that has arisen in contemporary practice is whether the "fair and equitable treatment" standard is to be regarded as referring to the minimum standard that existed back at the time of the *Neer Claim* (i.e., the early twentieth century), as referring to the standard that existed at the time the relevant bilateral or multilateral treaty was adopted, or as referring to an evolving standard that is influenced by new treaties, case law, and state practice. A NAFTA arbitration tribunal, in considering the "fair and equitable treatment" standard set forth in NAFTA Article 1105(1), stated:

> [T]here can be no doubt that, by interpreting Article 1105(1) to prescribe the customary international law minimum standard of treatment of aliens as the minimum standard to be afforded to investments of investors of another Party under NAFTA, the term "customary international law" refers to customary international law as it stood no earlier than the time at which NAFTA came into force. It is not limited to the international law of the 19th century or even the first half of the 20th century, although decisions from that period remain relevant. In holding that Article 1105(1) refers to customary international law, the [NAFTA-created Free Trade Commission's] interpretations incorporate current international law, whose content is shaped by the conclusion of more than two thousand bilateral investment treaties and many treaties of friendship and commerce. Those treaties largely and concordantly provide for "fair and equitable" treatment of, and for "full protection and security" for, the foreign investor and his investments.

Mondev Int'l, Ltd. v. United States, ICSID Case No. ARB(AF)/99/2, Award, para. 125, 42 I.L.M. 85 (2003). Commenting on whether arbitrators are free to interpret the standard as they wish, the same tribunal stated:

> Article 1105(1) did not give a NAFTA Tribunal an unfettered discretion to decide for itself, on a subjective basis, what was "fair" or "equitable" in the circumstances of each particular case. * * * [T]he Tribunal is bound by the minimum standard as established in State practice and in the jurisprudence of arbitral tribunals. It may not simply adopt its own idiosyncratic standard of what is "fair" or "equitable" without reference to established sources of law.

Id. at para. 119.

For discussion of "fair and equitable" treatment, see Mayeda, Playing Fair: The Meaning of Fair and Equitable Treatment in Bilateral Investment Treaties, 41 J. World Trade 273 (2007); Dolzer, Fair and Equitable Treatment: A Key Standard in Investment Treaties, 39 Int'l Law. 87 (2005); Organisation for Economic Co-operation and Development (OECD), Fair and Equitable Treatment Standard in International Investment Law (Working Paper on International Investment No. 2004/3, 2004); Vasciannie, The Fair and Equitable Treatment Standard in International Investment Law and Practice, 70 Brit. Y.I.L. 99 (2000).

2. Expropriation and Nationalization

FIREMAN'S FUND INSURANCE CO. v. MEXICO

ICSID Case No. ARB(AF)/02/1, Award, July 17, 2006

[Fireman's Fund Insurance Company is a U.S. insurance company that pursued an arbitration against Mexico for violation of the NAFTA, including in the form of expropriation of property. Fireman's claimed that Mexico helped facilitate the purchase of debentures denominated in Mexican pesos and owned by Mexican investors, but did not facilitate the purchase of debentures denominated in U.S. dollars and owned by Fireman's Fund (both series of debentures had been issued at the same time, in the same amount, and by the same Mexican financial services corporation). Although the tribunal ultimately decided that none of the acts taken by Mexico, individually or collectively, constituted an expropriation (para. 217), the tribunal provided in paragraph 176 the following definition of what "expropriation" means.]

NAFTA does not give a definition for the word "expropriation." In some ten cases in which Article 1110(1) of the NAFTA was considered to date, the definitions appear to vary. Considering those cases and customary international law in general, the present Tribunal retains the following elements.

(a) Expropriation requires a taking (which may include destruction) by a government-type authority of an investment by an investor covered by the NAFTA.[155]

(b) The covered investment may include intangible as well as tangible property.[156]

---

155. A failure to act (an "omission") by a host State may also constitute a State measure tantamount to expropriation under particular circumstances, although those cases will be rare and seldom concern the omission alone. *See Draft Articles on Responsibility of States for International Wrongful Acts*, adopted by the International Law Commission at its fifty-third session (2001), Article 2....

156. *Mondev International Ltd. v. United States*, ICSID Case No. ARB(AF)/99/2, Award, 11 October 2002, at 98.... The tribunal in *Methanex* observed: "[I]n *Pope & Talbot Inc. v. Canada*, the tribunal held 'the Investor's access to the U.S. market is a property interest subject to protection under Article 1110 [n. 159 *infra*, at ¶ 96]. Certainly, the restrictive notion of property as a material 'thing' is obsolete and has ceded its place to a contemporary conception which

(c) The taking must be a substantially[157] complete deprivation of the economic use and enjoyment of the rights to the property, or of identifiable distinct parts thereof (i.e., it approaches total impairment).

(d) The taking must be permanent, and not ephemeral or temporary.

(e) The taking usually involves a transfer of ownership to another person (frequently the government authority concerned), but that need not necessarily be so in certain cases (e.g., total destruction of an investment due to measures by a government authority without transfer of rights).[158]

(f) The effects of the host State's measures are dispositive, not the underlying intent, for determining whether there is expropriation.

(g) The taking may be *de jure* or *de facto*.

(h) The taking may be "direct" or "indirect."[159]

(i) The taking may have the form of a single measure or a series of related or unrelated measures over a period of time (the so-called "creeping" expropriation).

(j) To distinguish between a compensable expropriation and a non-compensable regulation by a host State,[160] the following factors (usually in combination) may be taken into account: whether the measure is within the recognized police powers of the host State; the (public) purpose and effect of the measure; whether the measure is discriminatory; the proportionality between the means

---

includes managerial control over components of a process that is wealth producing. In the view of the Tribunal, items such as goodwill and market share may, as Professor White wrote, 'constitute [ ] an element of value of an enterprise and as such may have been covered by some of the compensation payments' [Gillian White, Nationalisation of Foreign Property, 49 (1961)]. Hence, in a comprehensive taking, these items may figure in the valuation." *Methanex Corp. v. United States of America*, Final Award, 3 August 2005, at ¶ 17....

157. A number of tribunals employ the adjective "significant," "fundamental," "radical" or "serious."

158. "A deprivation or taking of property may occur under international law through interference by a state in the use of that property or the enjoyment of its benefits, *even where legal title to that property is not affected*" (emphasis added), *Tippets, Abbett, McCarthy, Stratton v. TAMS–AFFA Consulting Engineers of Iran*, Award No. 141–7–2, *reprinted in* 6 Iran–United States Cl. Trib. 219 (1984).

159. "Indirect" expropriation is contemplated by Article 1110(1) of the NAFTA: "No Party may directly or *indirectly* nationalize or expropriate ... or take a *measure tantamount to* nationalization or expropriation ..." (emphasis added). According to certain case law, the expression "a measure tantamount to nationalization or expropriation" in Article 1110 of the NAFTA means nothing more than "a measure equivalent to nationalization or expropriation." *Pope & Talbot Inc. v. The Government of Canada*, Interim Award, 26 June 2000, at ¶ ¶ 96 and 104 ...; *S.D. Myers Inc. v. The Government of Canada*, Partial Award, 13 November 2000, at ¶ ¶ 285– 286 ...; *Marvin Roy Feldman Kappa v. United Mexican States*, ICSID Case No. ARB(AF)/99/1, Award, 16 December 2002, at ¶ 100....

160. *S.D. Myers Inc. v. The Government of Canada*, Partial Award, 13 November 2000, at ¶ 281 ... observed that regulatory action by public authorities is unlikely to be the subject of legitimate complaint under Article 1110 of the NAFTA, although the possibility cannot be ruled out. The present Tribunal believes that the issue is more subtle than the proposition of "unlikely" in *S.D. Myers*.

employed and the aim sought to be realized;[161] and the bona fide nature of the measure.

(k) The investor's reasonable "investment-backed expectations" may be a relevant factor whether (indirect) expropriation has occurred.[162]

RESTATEMENT OF THE LAW (THIRD) THE FOREIGN RELATIONS LAW OF THE UNITED STATES § 712 (1987)

§ 712. State Responsibility for Economic Injury to Nationals of Other States

A state is responsible under international law for injury resulting from:

(1) a taking by the state of the property of a national of another state that

(a) is not for a public purpose, or

(b) is discriminatory, or

(c) is not accompanied by provision for just compensation;

For compensation to be just under this Subsection, it must, in the absence of exceptional circumstances, be in an amount equivalent to the value of the property taken and be paid at the time of taking, or within a reasonable time thereafter with interest from the date of taking, and in a form economically usable by the foreign national;

(2) a repudiation or breach by the state of a contract with a national of another state * * *; or

(3) other arbitrary or discriminatory acts or omissions by the state that impair property or other economic interests of a national of another state.

---

161. The Tribunal notes that this factor was relied upon in *Técnicas Medioambientales Tecmed S.A. v. United Mexican States*, ICSID Case No. ARB(AF)/00/2, Award, 29 May 2003, at ¶ 122 *et seq*..... The factor is used by the European Court of Human Rights ... and it may be questioned whether it is a viable source of interpreting Article 1110 of the NAFTA.

162. The factors attempt to close the perceived "gaping loophole" of a "blanket exception for regulatory measures" as articulated in *Pope & Talbot, supra* n. 159, at ¶ 99. For a useful overview, *see* Jack Coe, Jr., and Noah Rubins, *Regulatory Expropriation and the Tecmed Case: Context and Contributions*, in Todd Weiler, Ed., International Investment Law and Arbitration: Leading Cases from the ICSID, NAFTA, Bilateral Treaties and Customary International Law (2005) 597 at 632–643; *see also* L. Yves Fortier and Stephen L. Drymer, *Indirect Expropriation in the Law of International Investment: I Know It When I See It, or Caveat Investor*, Vol. 19, No. 2, ICSID Rev.–FILJ (2004) 293–327. *See also Saluka Investments BV (The Netherlands) v. The Czech Republic*, Partial Award, 17 March 2006, at ¶ ¶ 253–265....

C. CONTEMPORARY CASE LAW

As the materials above suggest, the substantive standards on protections for aliens derive much of their content from prior case law. One example of such case law is the 2003 *Tecmed v. Mexico* arbitral decision, reproduced in part below, which involves an investment by a Spanish national in Mexico. As you read that decision and the relevant provisions of the associated treaty, consider the following questions:

- In cases of injury to aliens, does the substantive standard being applied largely turn on the specific language of a relevant treaty or on broader norms present in customary international law?

- Can it be "unfair or inequitable treatment" of an alien if a host state fails to discuss openly and transparently the investment climate within the host country?

- If citizens within a host country become upset with a foreign investment, and are allowed to engage in protest operations against the investment, does that breach the host state's obligation to provide "full protection" to the investment?

- When an "expropriation" is alleged, must the claimant establish that the host government physically seized control of property or can other forms of interference in the property be expropriatory?

- When a state exercises police powers with respect to an alien's property (e.g., refusal to grant a permit), can that constitute an "expropriation"? If so, under what circumstances?

- Do you think there has developed a substantial overlap between state responsibility for failure to accord a minimum standard of justice to aliens and state responsibility for violations of human rights?

- If so, to what extent does the development of human rights law have the potential for facilitating a deeper understanding of the rules on state responsibility for injury to aliens?

AGREEMENT ON THE PROMOTION AND RECIPROCAL PROTECTION OF INVESTMENTS BETWEEN SPAIN AND MEXICO

June 23, 1995, 1965 U.N.T.S. 171 (translation)

The Kingdom of Spain and the United Mexican States, hereinafter referred to as the "Contracting Parties",

Desiring to intensify their economic cooperation for the mutual benefit of both countries,

Intending to create favourable conditions for investments made by investors of each Contracting Party in the territory of the other Contracting Party, and

Recognizing that the promotion and protection of investments under this Agreement stimulates initiatives in this field,

Have agreed as follows:

* * *

Article III

Protection

1.   Each Contracting Party shall grant full protection and security to investments made by investors of the other Contracting Party, in accordance with international law, and shall not hamper, by means of illegal or discriminatory measures, the management, maintenance, development, use, enjoyment, expansion, sale or, as the case may be, liquidation of such investments.

2.   Each Contracting Party, within the framework of its law, shall grant the necessary permits relating to these investments and shall allow the execution of employment contracts, manufacturing licences, and technical, commercial, financial and administrative assistance.

3.   Each Contracting Party shall grant, within the framework of its law, and whenever necessary, the permits required in connection with the activities of consultants or experts engaged by investors of the other Contracting Party.

Article IV

Treatment

1.   Each Contracting Party shall guarantee in its territory fair and equitable treatment, in accordance with international law, for the investments made by investors of the other Contracting Party.

2.   This treatment shall be no less favourable than that which is extended in similar circumstances by each Contracting Party to the investments made in its territory by investors of a third State.

Article V

Nationalization and Expropriation

1.   The nationalization, expropriation or any other measure of similar characteristics or effects (hereinafter referred to as "expropriation") that may be applied by the authorities of one Contracting Party against the investments in its territory of investors of the other Contracting Party must be applied exclusively for reasons of public interest pursuant to the law, shall in no case be discriminatory and shall require the payment of compensation to the investor or his assign or legal successor in accordance with paragraphs 2 and 3 of this article.

2.   Such compensation shall be equivalent to the market value of the expropriated investment immediately before the expropriation occurred or before it was announced or made public, whichever occurs first. The criteria for calculating that value shall be determined in accordance with

the applicable legislation in force in the territory of the Contracting Party in which the investment has been made.

3.   Such compensation shall be paid without delay, in convertible and freely transferable currency.

TECNICAS MEDIOAMBIENTALES TECMED S.A. ("TECMED") v. MEXICO

ICSID Case No. ARB(AF)/00/2, Award, 43 I.L.M. 133 (2004) (some footnotes omitted)

4.   On July 28, 2000, the Claimant filed with the Secretariat of the International Centre for Settlement of Investment Disputes ("ICSID") * * * a request for arbitration against the Respondent in accordance with the Additional Facility Rules for the Administration of Proceedings by the Secretariat of the International Centre for Settlement of Investment Disputes (hereinafter referred to as the "Rules") and under the provisions of the Agreement on the Reciprocal Promotion and Protection of Investments signed by the Kingdom of Spain and the United Mexican States (hereinafter referred to as the "Agreement"). The Agreement entered into force for both countries on December 18, 1996. The Claimant is the parent company in Spain of TECMED, TECNICAS MEDIOAMBIENTALES DE MEXICO, S.A. de C:V. ("Tecmed"), a company incorporated under Mexican law, and holds over 99% of the shares of such company. Additionally, Tecmed holds over 99% of the shares of CYTRAR, S.A. DE C.V. ("Cytrar"), a company incorporated under Mexican law through which the investment giving rise to the disputes leading to these arbitration proceedings was made.

* * *

C.   Summary of Facts and Allegations Presented by the Parties

35.   The Claimant's claims are related to an investment in land, buildings and other assets in connection with a public auction called by Promotora Inmobiliaria del Ayuntamiento de Hermosillo (hereinafter referred to as "Promotora"), a decentralized municipal agency of the Municipality of Hermosillo, located in the State of Sonora, Mexico. The purpose of the auction was the sale of real property, buildings and facilities and other assets relating to "Cytrar", a controlled landfill of hazardous industrial waste [in the locality of Las Víboras]. Tecmed was the awardee, pursuant to a decision adopted by the Management Board of Promotora on February 16, 1996. Later on, the holder of Tecmed's rights and obligations under the tender came to be Cytrar, a company organized by Tecmed for such purpose and to run the landfill operations.

* * *

38.   In a letter dated April 16, 1996, confirmed by letters of June 5, August 26 and September 5, 1996, Tecmed made a request to [the Mexican Government's agency for hazardous waste management, INE] for the operating license of the landfill—then in the name of Confinamiento Controlado Parque Industrial de Hermosillo O.P.D.—to be issued in the name of Cytrar. The Municipality of Hermosillo supported this request in its note to INE dated March 28, 1996, requesting INE to provide all possible assistance in connection with the name change procedure in the operating license in favor of Tecmed or of the company organized by it. In an official letter of September 24, 1996, INE notified Cytrar, in connection with the application to change the name of the entity from Promotora to Cytrar, that Cytrar had been registered with INE. The official letter was then returned by Cytrar to INE as requested by INE after having been issued, and replaced by another one of the same date to which the authorization relating to the landfill was attached, dated November 11, 1996, stating the new name of the entity. Such authorization could be extended every year at the applicant's request 30 days prior to expiration. It was so extended for an additional year, until November 19, 1998.

39.   The arbitration claim seeks damages, including compensation for damage to reputation, and interests in connection with damage alleged to have accrued as of November 25, 1998, on which date INE rejected the application for renewal of the authorization to operate the landfill, expiring on November 19, 1998, pursuant to an INE resolution on the same date, whereby INE further requested Cytrar to submit a program for the closure of the landfill. Subsidiarily, the Claimant has requested restitution in kind through the granting of permits to the Claimant enabling it to operate the Las Víboras landfill until the end of its useful life, in addition to compensation for damages.

* * *

42.   * * * The Claimant claims that such modifications, with detrimental effects for its investment and which allegedly led to the denial by the Federal Government of an extension to operate the landfill, are, to a large extent, due to political circumstances essentially associated to the change of administration in the Municipality of Hermosillo, in which the landfill is physically situated, rather than to legal considerations. * * * According to the Claimant's allegations, the new authorities of Hermosillo encouraged a movement of citizens against the landfill, which sought the withdrawal or non-renewal of the landfill's operating permit and its closedown, and which also led to confrontation with the community, even leading to blocking access to the landfill. * * *

* * *

E.   The Merits of the Dispute

* * *

I.   Expropriation

95.   The Claimant alleges that, when the INE did not renew the permit to operate the Las Víboras Landfill (the "Landfill") through its resolution dated November 25, 1998 (hereinafter the "Resolution"), it expropriated the Claimant's investment and that such expropriation has caused damage to the Claimant. The Claimant relates the expropriation—which according to the Claimant is the exclusive cause of the damage—to the prior actions of a number of organizations and entities at the federal, state and municipal levels, and also states that those actions are attributable to the Respondent and that they are adverse to the Claimant's rights under the Agreement and to the protection awarded to its investment thereunder. The Claimant further alleges that those actions objectively facilitated or prepared the subsequent expropriatory action carried out by INE.

96.   The Claimant alleges that the Agreement protects foreign investors and their investments from direct and indirect expropriation; i.e. not only expropriation aimed at real or tangible personal property whereby the owner thereof is deprived of interests over such property, but also actions consisting of measures tantamount to an expropriation with respect to such property and also to intangible property. The Claimant states that, as the resolution deprived Cytrar of its rights to use and enjoy the real and personal property forming the Landfill in accordance with its sole intended purpose, the Resolution put an end to the operation of the Landfill as an on going business exclusively engaged in the landfill of hazardous waste, an activity that is only feasible under a permit, the renewal of which was denied. Therefore, Cytrar alleges that it was deprived of the benefits and economic use of its investment. The Claimant highlights that without such permit the personal and real property had no individual or aggregate market value and that the existence of the Landfill as an on going business, as well as its value as such, were completely destroyed due to such Resolution which, in addition, ordered the closing of the Landfill.

97.   The Respondent alleges that INE had the discretionary powers required to grant and deny permits, and that such issues, except in special cases, are exclusively governed by domestic and not international law. On the other hand, the Respondent states that there was no progressive taking of the rights related to the permit to operate the Las Víboras landfill by means of a legislative change that could have destroyed the *status quo*, and that the Resolution was neither arbitrary nor discriminatory. It also states that the Resolution was a regulatory measure issued in compliance with the State's police power within the highly regulated and extremely sensitive framework of environmental protection and public health. In those circumstances, the Respondent alleges that the Resolution

is a legitimate action of the State that does not amount to an expropriation under international law.

* * *

113.   The Agreement does not define the term "expropriation", nor does it establish the measures, actions or behaviors that would be equivalent to an expropriation or that would have similar characteristics. Although formally an expropriation means a forcible taking by the Government of tangible or intangible property owned by private persons by means of administrative or legislative action to that effect, the term also covers a number of situations defined as *de facto* expropriation, where such actions or laws transfer assets to third parties different from the expropriating State or where such laws or actions deprive persons of their ownership over such assets, without allocating such assets to third parties or to the Government.[125]

114.   Generally, it is understood that the term "... equivalent to expropriation ..." or "tantamount to expropriation" included in the Agreement and in other international treaties related to the protection of foreign investors refers to the so-called "indirect expropriation" or "creeping expropriation", as well as to the above-mentioned *de facto* expropriation.[126] Although these forms of expropriation do not have a clear or unequivocal definition, it is generally understood that they materialize through actions or conduct, which do not explicitly express the purpose of depriving one of rights or assets, but actually have that effect. This type of expropriation does not necessarily take place gradually or stealthily—the term "creeping" refers only to a type of indirect expropriation—and may be carried out through a single action, through a series of actions in a short period of time or through simultaneous actions. Therefore, a difference should be made between creeping expropriation and *de facto* expropriation,[127] although they are usually included within the broader concept of "indirect expropriation" and although both expropriation methods may take place by means of a broad number of actions that have to be examined on a case-by-case basis to conclude if one of such expropriation methods has taken place.[128]

115.   To establish whether the Resolution is a measure equivalent to an expropriation under the terms of section 5(1) of the Agreement, it must be first determined if the Claimant, due to the Resolution, was radically

---

125.   Award dated August 30, 2000, in ICSID case No. ARB(AF)/97/1 *Metalclad v. United Mexican States*, 16 Mealey's International Arbitration Report (2000), pp. A–I *et seq.*; p. A–13 (p. 33 of the award, 103): <<Thus, expropriation [. . .] includes not only open, deliberate and acknowledged takings of property, such as outright seizure or formal or obligatory transfer of title in favor of the host State, but also covert or incidental interference with the use of property which has the effect of depriving the owner, in whole or in significant part, of the use or reasonably-to-be expected economic benefit of property even if not necessarily to the obvious benefit of the host State.>>

126.   G. Sacerdoti, Bilateral Treaties and Multilateral Instruments on Investment Protection, 269 Recueil des cours, Académie de droit international de La Haye, 255, 285–386 (1997).

127.   *Ibid.* p. 383.

128.   R. Dolzer & M. Stevens, Bilateral Investment Treaties, pp. 99–100 (1995).

deprived of the economical use and enjoyment of its investments, as if the rights related thereto—such as the income or benefits related to the Landfill or to its exploitation—had ceased to exist. In other words, if due to the actions of the Respondent, the assets involved have lost their value or economic use for their holder and the extent of the loss.[129] This determination is important because it is one of the main elements to distinguish, from the point of view of an international tribunal, between a regulatory measure, which is an ordinary expression of the exercise of the state's police power that entails a decrease in assets or rights, and a *de facto* expropriation that deprives those assets and rights of any real substance. Upon determining the degree to which the investor is deprived of its goods or rights, whether such deprivation should be compensated and whether it amounts or not to a *de facto* expropriation is also determined. Thus, the effects of the actions or behavior under analysis are not irrelevant to determine whether the action or behavior is an expropriation. Section 5(1) of the Agreement confirms the above, as it covers expropriations, nationalizations or

> ... any other measure with similar characteristics or *effects* ...[130]

The following has been stated in that respect:

> In determining whether a taking constitutes an "indirect expropriation", it is particularly important to examine the effect that such taking may have had on the investor's rights. Where the effect is similar to what might have occurred under an outright expropriation, the investor could in all likelihood be covered under most BIT provisions.[131]

116. In addition to the provisions of the Agreement, the Arbitral Tribunal has to resolve any dispute submitted to it by applying international law provisions * * *, for which purpose the Arbitral Tribunal understands that disputes are to be resolved by resorting to the sources described in Article 38 of the Statute of the International Court of Justice[132] considered, also in the case of customary international law, not as frozen in time, but in their evolution.[133] Therefore, it is understood that the measures adopted by a State, whether regulatory or not, are an indirect *de facto* expropriation if they are irreversible and permanent and if the assets or rights subject to such measure have been affected in such a way that "... any form of exploitation thereof ..." has disappeared; i.e. the economic value of the use, enjoyment or disposition of the assets or

---

129. Partial Award in the case *Pope & Talbot Inc v. Government of Canada*, 102–104, pp. 36–38, <www.naftalaw.org>; and II Restatement of the Law (Third) Restatement of the Foreign Relations Law of the Untied States § 712, pp. 200–201; notes 6–7, pp. 211–212 (1987).

130. Emphasis added by the Arbitral Tribunal.

131. R. Dolzer & M. Stevens, Bilateral Investment Treaties, p. 100 (1995).

132. I. Brownlie, Principles of International Law (5th Edition, 1998) p.3: <<These provisions [...] represent the previous practice of arbitral tribunals, and Article 38 is generally regarded as a complete statement of the sources of international law>>.

133. *Mondev International Ltd v. United States of America* award, October 11, 2002, ICSID case No. ARB(AF)/99/2, p. 40, 116.

rights affected by the administrative action or decision have been neutral-ized or destroyed.[134] Under international law, the owner is also deprived of property where the use or enjoyment of benefits related thereto is exacted or interfered with to a similar extent, even where legal ownership over the assets in question is not affected, and so long as the deprivation is not temporary. The government's intention is less important than the effects of the measures on the owner of the assets or on the benefits arising from such assets affected by the measures; and the form of the deprivation measure is less important than its actual effects.[135] To deter-mine whether such an expropriation has taken place, the Arbitral Tribu-nal should not

> ... restrict itself to evaluating whether a formal dispossession or expropriation took place, but should look beyond mere appearances and establish the real situation behind the situation that was de-nounced.[136]

117. The Resolution meets the characteristics mentioned above: undoubtedly it has provided for the non-renewal of the Permit and the closing of the Landfill permanently and irrevocably, not only due to the imperative, affirmative and irrevocable terms under which the INE's decision included in the Resolution is formulated, which constitutes an action—and not a mere omission—attributable to the Respondent, with negative effects on the Claimant's investment and its rights to obtain the benefits arising therefrom, but also because after the non-renewal of the Permit, the Mexican regulations issued by INE become fully applicable. Such regulations prevent the use of the site where the Landfill is located to confine hazardous waste due to the proximity to the urban center of Hermosillo. Since it has been proved in this case that one of the essential causes for which the renewal of the Permit was denied was its proximity and the community pressure related thereto, there is no doubt that in the future the Landfill may not be used for the activity for which it has been used in the past and that Cytrar's economic and commercial operations in the Landfill after such denial have been fully and irrevocably destroyed, just as the benefits and profits expected or projected by the Claimant as a result of the operation of the Landfill. Moreover, the Landfill could not be used for a different purpose since hazardous waste has accumulated and been confined there for ten years. Undoubtedly, this reason would rule out any possible sale of the premises in the real estate market. Finally, the destruction of the economic value of the site should be assessed from the investor's point of view at the time it made such an investment. In consideration of the activities carried out, of its corporate purpose and of

---

134. European Court of Human Rights, *In the case of Matos e Silva, Lda., and Others v. Portugal*, judgment of September 16, 1996, 85, p. 18, <http://hudoc.echr.coe.int>.

135. *See* Iran–USA Claims Tribunal, *Tippetts, Abbet, McCarthy, Stratton v.TAMS/Affa Con-sulting Engineers of Iran et al.*, decision of June 29, 1984; 6 Iran–United States Rep., p. 219 *et seq.*; p. 225 (1984–I1); of the same Tribunal, *Phelps Dodge Corp. et al. v. Iran*, 10 Iran–U.S.Cl. Trib. Rep. p. 121 *et seq.*.; esp. 22, p. 130 (1986–I).

136. Interamerican Court of Human Rights, *Ivcher Bronstein Case (Baruch Ivcher Bronstein vs. Peru)*, judgment of February 6, 2001, 124, p. 56; <www.corteidh.or.cr>.

the terms and conditions under which assets related to the Landfill were acquired from Promotora, the Claimant, through Tecmed and Cytrar, invested in such assets only to engage in hazardous waste landfill activities and to profit from such activities. * * *

118.   However, the Arbitral Tribunal deems it appropriate to examine, in light of Article 5(1) of the Agreement, whether the Resolution, due to its characteristics and considering not only its effects, is an expropriatory decision.

* * *

121.   After reading Article 5(1) of the Agreement and interpreting its terms according to the ordinary meaning to be given to them (Article 31(1) of the Vienna Convention), we find no principle stating that regulatory administrative actions are *per se* excluded from the scope of the Agreement, even if they are beneficial to society as a whole—such as environmental protection—, particularly if the negative economic impact of such actions on the financial position of the investor is sufficient to neutralize in full the value, or economic or commercial use of its investment without receiving any compensation whatsoever. It has been stated that:

> Expropriatory environmental measures—no matter how laudable and beneficial to society as a whole—are, in this respect, similar to any other expropriatory measures that a state may take in order to implement its policies: where property is expropriated, even for environmental purposes, whether domestic or international, the state's obligation to pay compensation remains.[139]

122.   After establishing that regulatory actions and measures will not be initially excluded from the definition of expropriatory acts, in addition to the negative financial impact of such actions or measures, the Arbitral Tribunal will consider, in order to determine if they are to be characterized as expropriatory, whether such actions or measures are proportional to the public interest presumably protected thereby and to the protection legally granted to investments, taking into account that the significance of such impact has a key role upon deciding the proportionality.[140] * * *

The European Court of Human Rights has defined such circumstances as follows:

> Not only must a measure depriving a person of his property pursue, on the facts as well as in principle, a legitimate aim "in the public interest", but there must also be a reasonable relationship of proportionality between the means employed and the aim sought to be realised ... [...]. The requisite balance will not be found if the person concerned has had to bear "an individual and excessive bur-

---

139. Award: *Compañía del Desarrollo de Santa Elena, S.A. v. Republic of Costa Rica*, ICSID case No. ARB/96/1, 15 ICSID Review–Foreign Investment Law Journal, 72, p. 192 (2000).

140. European Court of Human Rights, *In the case of Matos e Silva, Lda., and Others v. Portugal*, judgment of September 16, 1996, 92, p. 19, <http://hudoc.echr.coe.int>.

den" [. . .] The Court considers that a measure must be both appropriate for achieving its aim and not disproportionate thereto.[143]

... non-nationals are more vulnerable to domestic legislation: unlike nationals, they will generally have played no part in the election or designation of its authors nor have been consulted on its adoption. Secondly, although a taking of property must always be effected in the public interest, different considerations may apply to nationals and non-nationals and there may well be legitimate reason for requiring nationals to bear a greater burden in the public interest than non-nationals.[144]

[The arbitral tribunal then determined that the factors that drove INE to decline to renew the claimant's permit were political in nature—a response to "community pressure"—not reasons relating to the protection of human health or the environment. In considering whether INE's adoption of its Resolution was proportionate to the deprivation of rights sustained by the claimant, the tribunal found that the "community pressure" was not "so great as to lead to a serious emergency situation, social crisis or public unrest" that outweighed the loss of economic value to the claimant (paras. 133 & 139).]

151.   Based on the above; and furthermore considering that INE's actions * * * are attributable to the Respondent under international law and have caused damage to the Claimant, * * * the Arbitral Tribunal finds and resolves that the Resolution and its effects amount to an expropriation in violation of Article 5 of the Agreement and international law.

II.   Fair and Equitable Treatment

* * *

153.   The Arbitral Tribunal finds that the commitment of fair and equitable treatment included in Article 4(1) of the Agreement is an expression and part of the *bona fide* principle recognized in international law,[189] although bad faith from the State is not required for its violation:

To the modern eye, what is unfair or inequitable need not equate with the outrageous or the egregious. In particular, a State may treat foreign investment unfairly and inequitably without necessarily acting in bad faith.[190]

---

143. European Court of Human Rights, *In the case of James and Others*, judgment of February 21, 1986, 50, pp. 19–20 <http://hudoc.echr.coe.int>.

144. *ibid.*, 63, pp. 24.

189. I. Brownlie, Principles of Public International law, Oxford, 5th. Edition (1989), p. 19. It is understood that the fair and equitable treatment principle included in international agreements for the protection of foreign investments expresses ". . . the international requirements of due process, economic rights, obligations of good faith and natural justice"; arbitration case *S.D. Myers, Inc. v. Government of Canada*, partial award of November 13, 2000; 134, p. 29; <www.naftalaw.org>.

190. ICSID Arbitration no. ARB(AF)/99/2, *Mondev International Ltd v United States of America*, p. 40, 116, October 11, 2002, <www.naftalaw.org>.

154. The Arbitral Tribunal considers that this provision of the Agreement, in light of the good faith principle established by international law, requires the Contracting Parties to provide to international investments treatment that does not affect the basic expectations that were taken into account by the foreign investor to make the investment. The foreign investor expects the host State to act in a consistent manner, free from ambiguity and totally transparently in its relations with the foreign investor, so that it may know beforehand any and all rules and regulations that will govern its investments, as well as the goals of the relevant policies and administrative practices or directives, to be able to plan its investment and comply with such regulations. Any and all State actions conforming to such criteria should relate not only to the guidelines, directives or requirements issued, or the resolutions approved thereunder, but also to the goals underlying such regulations. The foreign investor also expects the host State to act consistently, i.e. without arbitrarily revoking any preexisting decisions or permits issued by the State that were relied upon by the investor to assume its commitments as well as to plan and launch its commercial and business activities. The investor also expects the State to use the legal instruments that govern the actions of the investor or the investment in conformity with the function usually assigned to such instruments, and not to deprive the investor of its investment without the required compensation. In fact, failure by the host State to comply with such pattern of conduct with respect to the foreign investor or its investments affects the investor's ability to measure the treatment and protection awarded by the host State and to determine whether the actions of the host State conform to the fair and equitable treatment principle. Therefore, compliance by the host State with such pattern of conduct is closely related to the above-mentioned principle, to the actual chances of enforcing such principle, and to excluding the possibility that state action be characterized as arbitrary; i.e. as presenting insufficiencies that would be recognized "... by any reasonable and impartial man,"[191] or, although not in violation of specific regulations, as being contrary to the law because:

> ... (it) shocks, or at least surprises, a sense of juridical propriety.[192]

155. The Arbitral Tribunal understands that the scope of the undertaking of fair and equitable treatment under Article 4(1) of the Agreement described above is that resulting from an autonomous interpretation, taking into account the text of Article 4(1) of the Agreement according to its ordinary meaning (Article 31(1) of the Vienna Convention), or from international law and the good faith principle, on the basis of which the scope of the obligation assumed under the Agreement and the actions related to compliance therewith are to be assessed.

* * *

191. *Neer v. México* case, (1926) R.I.A.A. iv. 60.

192. International Court of Justice Case: *Elettronica Sicula S.p.A. (ELSI) (United States of America v. Italy)*, 128, p. 65, July 20, 1989, ICJ, General List No. 76.

173.   Briefly, INE's described behavior frustrated Cytrar's fair expectations upon which Cytrar's actions were based and upon the basis of which the Claimant's investment was made, or negatively affected the generation of clear guidelines that would allow the Claimant or Cytrar to direct its actions or behavior to prevent the non-renewal of the Permit, or weakened its position to enforce rights or explore ways to maintain the Permit. During the term immediately preceding the Resolution, INE did not enter into any form of dialogue through which Cytrar or Tecmed would become aware of INE's position with regard to the possible non-renewal of the Permit and the deficiencies attributed to Cytrar's behavior—including those attributed in the process of relocation of operations—which would be the grounds for such a drastic measure and, thus, Cytrar or Tecmed did not have the opportunity, prior to the Resolution, to inform of, in turn, their position or provide an explanation with respect to such deficiencies, or the way to solve such deficiencies to avoid the denial of renewal and, ultimately, the deprivation of the Claimant's investment. Despite Cytrar's good faith expectation that the Permit's total or partial renewal would be granted to maintain Cytrar's operation of the Landfill effective until the relocation to a new site had been completed, INE did not consider Cytrar's proposals in that regard and not only did it deny the renewal of the Permit although the relocation had not yet taken place, but it also did so in the understanding that this would lead Cytrar to relocate.

174.   Such behavior on the part of INE, which is attributable to the Respondent, results in losses and damage[217] for the investor and the investment * * * coinciding both as to essence and time with those derived from the Resolution, whether such behavior is considered generically or only as to the stages mentioned and analyzed by the Arbitral Tribunal * * *. The Respondent's behavior in such stages amounts, in itself, to a violation of the duty to accord fair and equitable treatment to the Claimant's investment as set forth in Article 4(1) of the Agreement * * *.

III.   Full Protection and Security and Other Guarantees under the Agreement

175.   The Claimant alleges that Mexican municipal and state authorities encouraged the community's adverse movements against the Landfill and its operation by Tecmed or Cytrar * * *. Further, the Claimant alleges that Mexican authorities, including the police and the judicial authorities, did not act as quickly, efficiently and thoroughly as they should have to avoid, prevent or put an end to the adverse social demonstrations expressed through disturbances in the operation of the Landfill or access thereto, or the personal security or freedom to move about of the members of Cytrar's staff related to the Landfill. It is the opinion of the Claimant that such behavior of the Mexican authorities,

---

217. "Damage" is not limited to the economic loss or detriment and shall be interpreted in a broad sense (J. Crawford, The International Law Commission's Articles on State Responsibility, 29–31) (Cambridge University Press, 2002).

attributable to the Respondent, amounts to a violation of Article 3(1) of the Agreement * * *.

176. The Arbitral Tribunal considers that the Claimant has not furnished evidence to prove that the Mexican authorities, regardless of their level, have encouraged, fostered, or contributed their support to the people or groups that conducted the community and political movements against the Landfill, or that such authorities have participated in such movement. Also, there is not sufficient evidence to attribute the activity or behavior of such people or groups to the Respondent pursuant to international law.

177. The Arbitral Tribunal agrees with the Respondent, and with the case law quoted by it, in that the guarantee of full protection and security is not absolute and does not impose strict liability upon the State that grants it. At any rate, the Arbitral Tribunal holds that there is not sufficient evidence supporting the allegation that the Mexican authorities, whether municipal, state, or federal, have not reacted reasonably, in accordance with the parameters inherent in a democratic state, to the direct action movements conducted by those who were against the Landfill. This conclusion is also applicable to the judicial system, in relation to the efforts made to take action against the community's opposing demonstrations or to the attempt to reverse administrative measures which were deemed inconsistent with the legal rules applicable to the Landfill, such as the withdrawal by the Hermosillo's Municipal authorities of the license to use the Landfill's site.

NOTES

1. *Minimum Standard of Protection.* While bilateral or multilateral treaties are sometimes the central reference point in according the minimum standard of protection, they will often simply cross-reference to general international law for ascertaining what it is that standard requires. For example, the investment chapter of the U.S.–Chile Free Trade Agreement, in calling for a "minimum standard of treatment" for investors, provides that:

   (a) "fair and equitable treatment" includes the obligation not to deny justice in criminal, civil, or administrative adjudicatory proceedings in accordance with the principle of due process embodied in the principal legal systems of the world; and

   (b) "full protection and security" requires each Party to provide the level of police protection required under customary international law.

U.S.–Chile FTA, *supra* Section 2(B)(3), art. 10.4(2). Consequently, states and tribunals are often left analyzing the outcomes in prior situations, such as the *Tecmed* dispute, to determine what kinds of conduct do and do not run afoul of the standard.

2. *Expropriation of Property.* A central feature of all contemporary investment treaties, like the Spain–Mexico treaty, is the provisions relating to expropriation. All call for payment of full compensation, and many go beyond the usual provisions of the FCN treaties by covering indirect takings of

property of nationals of the other contracting state. Further, some treaties cover violation of contractual undertakings given by a contracting state to a national of the other contracting state.

The United States has long maintained that a taking of property for public purposes is contrary to international law unless it is accompanied by "prompt, adequate and effective compensation," a formulation often attributed to U.S. Secretary of State Cordell Hull. See Letter of Secretary of State Cordell Hull to Mexican Ambassador to the United States Francisco Castillo Nájera (July 21, 1938), *reprinted in* Mexico–United States: Expropriation by Mexico of Agrarian Properties Owned by American Citizens, 32 A.J.I.L. Supp. 131 (1938). In contrast, during the twentieth century many developing states maintained that the obligation to compensate under international law involved nothing more than a duty of the host state to compensate aliens at the same level it compensated its own nationals. See *infra* Note on Historical Attitudes Concerning Expropriation.

3. *Requirement of a Public Purpose When Expropriating.* The public "purpose" or "interest" requirement is usually included in treaties of friendship, commerce, and navigation and bilateral investment treaties, such as the treaty between Spain and Mexico in the *Tecmed* case. In theory, an expropriation that is not for a public purpose is unlawful, even if full compensation is paid to the injured alien. Yet because "public purpose" is a broad and undefined concept, challenges to expropriations on the ground that they are not for a public purpose have been rare; instead, the challenge usually concerns the failure of the expropriating state to pay compensation. See Pellonpää, Compensable Claims Before the Tribunal: Expropriation Claims, in The Iran–United States Claims Tribunal: Its Contribution to the Law of State Responsibility 185, 201–02 (Lillich, Magraw, & Bederman eds. 1998). The few decisions applying the rule have also involved a denial of compensation by the taking state. See, e.g., *Walter Fletcher Smith Claim*, 2 U.N. Rep. Int'l Arb. Awards 913 (1929); *Banco Nacional De Cuba v. Sabbatino*, 193 F.Supp. 375, 384 (S.D.N.Y. 1961), aff'd, 307 F.2d 845 (2d Cir. 1962), rev'd on other grounds, 376 U.S. 398 (1964).

Does it matter if an expropriation occurs without a public purpose? Arguably, whether a public purpose exists or not, the alien is entitled to full compensation for the loss. Does the lack of a public purpose make it easier to argue that the appropriate remedy is restitution-in-kind (i.e., return of the property)? Does it make it easier to argue for a higher level of compensation than would otherwise be warranted?

4. *Requirement of Non–Discrimination When Expropriating.* Similarly, it is often maintained that an expropriation that discriminates as between aliens is unlawful, even if full compensation is paid to the injured alien. The Restatement (Third) states that "[d]iscrimination implies unreasonable distinction. Takings that invidiously single out property of persons of a particular nationality would be unreasonable; classifications, even if based on nationality, that are rationally related to the state's security or economic policies might not be unreasonable." Restatement (Third) § 712, Comment *f*; see Maniruzzaman, Expropriation of Alien Property and the Principle of Non–

Discrimination in International Law of Foreign Investments: An Overview, 8 J. Transnat'l L. & Pol'y 57 (1998).

5. *Indirect Expropriation*. As demonstrated in *Tecmed*, under certain circumstances, an interference with an alien's property rights that falls short of an outright expropriation may constitute an effective or constructive taking of property that gives rise to an obligation to compensate the alien. On the other hand, although conduct attributable to the state interferes with or impairs the alien's property rights, it may be deemed not to constitute a taking of his property because the conduct represents a reasonable exercise of the state's power to regulate matters related to public order, safety or health, its currency, foreign exchange resources, balance of payments, or emergency situations. See Restatement (Third) § 712(1). The extensive jurisprudence of the Iran–U.S. Claims Tribunal on when a compensable taking of property has occurred is discussed in Aldrich, The Jurisprudence of the Iran–United States Claims Tribunal 171–218 (1996).

Article 10.9(1) of the U.S.–Chile FTA prohibits expropriation or nationalization of an investment, "directly or indirectly through measures equivalent to expropriation or nationalization," except for a public purpose, in a nondiscriminatory manner, on payment of prompt adequate and effective compensation, and in accordance with due process of law. An annex to the chapter interprets what is meant by "direct" and "indirect" expropriation:

3.   Article 10.9(1) addresses two situations. The first is direct expropriation, where an investment is nationalized or otherwise directly expropriated through formal transfer of title or outright seizure.

4.   The second situation addressed by Article 10.9(1) is indirect expropriation, where an action or series of actions by a Party has an effect equivalent to direct expropriation without formal transfer of title or outright seizure.

   (a) The determination of whether an action or series of actions by a Party, in a specific fact situation, constitutes an indirect expropriation, requires a case-by-case, fact-based inquiry that considers, among other factors:

      (i) the economic impact of the government action, although the fact that an action or series of actions by a Party has an adverse effect on the economic value of an investment, standing alone, does not establish that an indirect expropriation has occurred;

      (ii) the extent to which the government action interferes with distinct, reasonable investment-backed expectations; and

      (iii) the character of the government action.

   (b) Except in rare circumstances, nondiscriminatory regulatory actions by a Party that are designed and applied to protect legitimate public welfare objectives, such as public health, safety, and the environment, do not constitute indirect expropriations.

U.S.–Chile FTA, *supra* Section 2(B)(3), annex 10–D (3)–(4).

For further discussion of indirect expropriation, see Ratner, Regulatory Takings in Institutional Context: Beyond the Fear of Fragmented International Law, 102 A.J.I.L. 475 (2008); Reisman & Sloane, Indirect Expropriation and Its Valuation in the BIT Generation, 74 Brit. Y.B.I.L. 115 (2004); Weston, "Constructive Takings" under International Law: A Modest Foray into the Problem of "Creeping Expropriation", 16 Va. J. Int'l L. 101 (1975); Christie, What Constitutes a Taking of Property Under International Law, 38 Brit. Y.B.I.L. 307 (1962).

6.   *Seizure of Enemy Property in Time of War.* Customary and conventional international law allows a belligerent to take control of enemy property, both public and private, subject to certain safeguards. The Eritrea Ethiopia Claims Commission recently characterized the law as follows:

> 126.   The modern *jus in bello* * * * contains important protections of aliens' property, beginning with the fundamental rules of discrimination and proportionality in combat operations, which protect both lives and property. Article 23, paragraph (g), of the Hague Regulations similarly forbids destruction or seizure of the enemy's property unless "imperatively demanded by the necessities of war." Article 33 of Geneva Convention IV prohibits pillage and reprisals against protected persons' property, both in occupied territory and in the Parties' territory. Article 38 of Geneva Convention IV is also relevant. It establishes that, except for measures of internment and assigned residence or other exceptional measures authorized by Article 27, "the situation of protected persons shall continue to be regulated, in principle, by the provisions governing aliens in time of peace."

> 127.   However, these safeguards operate in the context of another broad and sometimes competing body of belligerent rights to freeze or otherwise control or restrict the resources of enemy nationals so as to deny them to the enemy State. Throughout the twentieth century, important States including France, Germany, the United Kingdom, and the United States have frozen "enemy" property, including property of civilians, sometimes vesting it for the vesting State's benefit. * * * Such control measures have been judged necessary to deny the enemy access to economic resources otherwise potentially available to support its conduct of the war.

> 128.   States have not consistently frozen and vested enemy private property. In practice, States vesting the assets of enemy nationals have done so under controlled conditions, and for reasons directly tied to higher state interests; commentators emphasize these limitations. The post-war disposition of controlled property has often been the subject of agreements between the former belligerents. These authorize the use of controlled or vested assets for post-war reparations or claims settlements, thereby maintaining at least the appearance of consent for the taking. This occurred both in the Versailles Treaty after World War I and in peace treaties after World War II.

Partial Award, Civilian Claims, Eritrea's Claims 15, 16, 23 & 27–32, Dec. 17, 2004, 44 I.L.M. 601, paras. 126–28 (2005) (footnotes omitted); see Carnahan,

Lincoln, Lieber, and the Laws of War: The Origins and Limits of the Principle of Military Necessity, 92 A.J.I.L. 213 (1998).

NOTE ON HISTORICAL ATTITUDES CONCERNING EXPROPRIATION

During the twentieth century, criticisms based on a variety of conceptual foundations were leveled at the traditional customary international law of state responsibility by representatives of many Latin American states, socialist states and states newly emerged from colonial domination in Africa and Asia. The clashing views between the developed and developing world over compensation for expropriation may be seen in the diplomatic correspondence between the United States (represented by Secretary of State Cordell Hull) and Mexico on the obligation of Mexico under international law to compensate U.S. owners of agrarian properties expropriated by the Mexican government.

On March 18, 1938, the Mexican Government expropriated the properties in Mexico of certain foreign-owned oil companies operating there, including a number of U.S. companies. By a 1941 agreement, Mexico agreed to pay $40 million in settlement of all prior agrarian and other claims exclusive of those arising out of the petroleum seizures. See Convention Providing for the Final Adjustment and Settlement of Certain Unsettled Claims, United States–Mexico, Nov. 19, 1941, 56 Stat. 1347, 4 U.N. Rep. Int'l Arb. Awards 767. After voluminous diplomatic exchanges concerning the appropriate level of compensation, in 1942 Mexico agreed to pay $24 million in settlement of all claims arising out of the expropriation of oil properties, an amount that was a fraction of the losses claimed. See Agreement Respecting Payment for Expropriated Petroleum Properties, United States–Mexico, Sept. 29, 1943, 58 Stat. 1408. Some excerpts that capture the substance and the flavor of the U.S.–Mexico debate follow:

> [*Secretary of State Hull to the Mexican Ambassador, July 21, 1938:*] During recent years the Government of the United States has upon repeated occasions made representations to the Government of Mexico with regard to the continuing expropriation by Your Excellency's Government of agrarian properties owned by American citizens, without adequate, effective and prompt compensation being made therefor.
>
> * * *
>
> If it were permissible for a government to take the private property of the citizens of other countries and pay for it as and when, in the judgment of the government, its economic circumstances and its local legislation may perhaps permit, the safeguards which the constitutions of most countries and established international law have sought to provide would be illusory. Governments would be free to take property far beyond their ability or willingness to pay, and the owners thereof would be without recourse. We cannot question the right of a foreign government to treat its own nationals in this fashion if it so desires. This is a matter of domestic concern. But we cannot admit that a foreign government may take the property of American nationals in disregard of the rule of compensation under international law. * * *

[*The Mexican Minister for Foreign Affairs to the American Ambassador, August 3, 1938:*] * * * My Government maintains, on the contrary, that there is in international law no rule universally accepted in theory nor carried out in practice which makes obligatory the payment of immediate compensation, nor even of deferred compensation, for expropriations of a general and impersonal character like those which Mexico has carried out for the purpose of redistribution of the land.

* * *

* * * Nevertheless Mexico admits, in obedience to her own laws, that she is indeed under obligation to indemnify in an adequate manner; but the doctrine which she maintains on the subject, is that the time and manner of such payment must be determined by her own laws.

The republics of our continent have let their voice be heard since the first Pan American Conference, vigorously maintaining the principle of equality between nationals and foreigners, considering that the foreigner who voluntarily moves to a country which is not his own, in search of a personal benefit, accepts in advance, together with the advantages which he is going to enjoy, the risks to which he may find himself exposed. It would be unjust that he should aspire to a privileged position, safe from any risk * * *.

[*Secretary of State Hull to the Mexican Ambassador, August 22, 1938*]: * * * The Government of the United States merely adverts to a self-evident fact when it notes that the applicable and recognized authorities on international law support its declaration that, under every rule of law and equity, no government is entitled to expropriate private property, for whatever purpose, without provision for prompt, adequate, and effective payment therefor. * * *

* * *

The doctrine of equality of treatment, like that of just compensation, is of ancient origin. It appears in many constitutions, bills of rights and documents of international validity. The word has invariably referred to equality in lawful rights of the person and to protection in exercising such lawful rights. There is now announced by your Government the astonishing theory that this treasured and cherished principle of equality, designed to protect both human and property rights, is to be invoked, not in the protection of personal rights and liberties, but as a chief ground of depriving and stripping individuals of their conceded rights. It is contended, in a word, that it is wholly justifiable to deprive an individual of his rights if all other persons are equally deprived.

19 Dep't St. Press Releases 50–52, 135–37, 139–44 (1938).

The issue framed during the 1930s in this United States–Mexico correspondence was echoed in a series of debates and resolutions at the United Nations during the 1960s and 1970s. First, in 1962 the U.N. General Assembly adopted a Resolution on Permanent Sovereignty over Natural Resources, G.A. Res. 1803 (XVII) (Dec. 14, 1962), by 87 votes to 2, with 12 abstentions. That resolution provided that, in case of nationalization, the alien owner shall be paid "appropriate compensation, in accordance with the rules in force in the State taking such measures in the exercise of its sovereignty and in accordance with international law," and that "[f]oreign investment agreements freely entered into by or between sovereign States shall be observed in good faith." The United States interpreted "appropriate" compensation to mean "prompt, adequate and effective." See Schwebel, The Story of the U.N. Declaration on Permanent Sovereignty over Natural Resources, 49 A.B.A. J. 463 (1963).

Second, in 1972, the Trade and Development Board of the U.N. Conference on Trade and Development (UNCTAD) adopted a resolution stating, in part, that it

> 2. *Reiterates* that * * * such measures of nationalization as States may adopt in order to recover their natural resources are the expression of a sovereign power in virtue of which it is for each State to fix the amount of compensation and the procedure for these measures, and any dispute which may arise in that connection falls within the sole jurisdiction of its courts, without prejudice to what is set forth in General Assembly resolution 1803 (XVII)* * *.

UNCTAD Res. 88 (XII), U.N. Doc. TD/B/423 (1972), reprinted at 11 I.L.M. 1472 (1972).

Third, in 1973 the U.N. General Assembly adopted a Resolution on Permanent Sovereignty over Natural Resources, G.A. Res. 3171 (XXVIII) (Dec. 17, 1973), which, after recalling G.A. Res. 1803 (XVII) (Dec. 14, 1962), affirmed "that the application of the principle of nationalization carried out by States, as an expression of their sovereignty in order to safeguard their natural resources, implies that each State is entitled to determine the amount of possible compensation and the mode of payment, and that any disputes which might arise should be settled in accordance with the national legislation of each State carrying out such measures * * *." The vote for this resolution was 108 in favor, 1 against (United Kingdom), and 17 abstaining (including the United States and most developed countries).

Finally, in 1974, the U.N. General Assembly adopted a Charter of Economic Rights and Duties of States, G.A. Res. 3281(XXIX) (Dec. 12, 1974). Chapter II, Article 2(2)(c) asserted that every state has the right to:

> [N]ationalize, expropriate or transfer ownership of foreign property, in which case appropriate compensation should be paid by the State adopting such measures, taking into account its relevant laws and regulations and all circumstances that the State considers pertinent. In any case where the question of compensation gives rise to a controversy, it shall be settled under the domestic law of the nationalizing State and by its tribunals, unless it is freely and mutually agreed by all States concerned that other peaceful means be sought on the basis of the sovereign equality of States and in accordance with the principle of free choice of means.

The vote on this subsection was 104 in favor, 16 against (including the United States and many developed states), and 6 abstentions.

In recent years the sharp edge of the debate over the basic principles of state responsibility for injury to aliens has been blunted as a result of pressures from a number of quarters. First, the states that emerged from the former U.S.S.R. and Eastern Europe moved away from principles of communism and socialism and toward instead privatization and market economies. Second, states in the developing world similarly recognized that the movement toward freer markets and privatization of business was more likely to encourage economic development than would continued reliance on government-owned enterprises and government-managed economies. Third, many of these countries concomitantly have acknowledged that foreign private investment plays an essential role in fostering economic development, and that in order to encourage foreign investment and associated technical and managerial know-how, it is necessary to enhance the legal security of foreign investment. Fourth, the needs for capital in the developing world, the republics of the former U.S.S.R. and the states of Eastern Europe far exceed the available supply. The developing world and the states of Eastern Europe must therefore compete for scarce capital, and the competition has become all the keener as a result of the economic woes experienced worldwide during the early twenty-first century. Consequently, the compelling need in emerging economies of the world to attract foreign private capital has been accompanied by a widespread willingness to move beyond acerbic debates over doctrinal differences on rules of state responsibility to aliens and to consider more specific substantive and procedural arrangements to enhance the investment climate and legal security for foreign private investment. See Lauterpacht, International Law and Private Foreign Investment, 4 Ind. J. Global Legal Stud. 259 (1997).

Even so, the prior doctrinal positions of the Latin American states, states tending toward socialism, and the developing states in Africa and Asia have not completely dissipated and, in some situations, reappear in strength. Partly for that reason, it has been impossible to fashion in a global multilateral treaty the basic rules of state responsibility concerning the protection of aliens. For example, the 1993 Uruguay Round Agreement on Trade Related Investment Measures (TRIMS) failed to establish strong protections for foreign investors in part due to resistance by developing states. Similarly, when members of the Organisation for Economic Co-operation and Development (OECD) beginning in 1995 sought to negotiate a Multilateral Agreement on Investment (MAI), the effort foundered in part due to widespread criticism from developing countries. The effort was abandoned by 1998. See Geiger, Regulatory Expropriations in International Law: Lessons from the Multilateral Agreement on Investment, 11 N.Y.U. Envtl L.J. 94, 94–96 (2002). For the MAI drafts, see http://www1.oecd.org/daf/mai/htm/2.htm.

The failure of these initiatives, however, was also due to resistance by civil society groups, who have expressed concern about creating international rules that make it more difficult for host countries to impose environmental, labor and other regulations on foreign investors. In light of such resistance to a global convention, states have instead emphasized the development of protections through bilateral treaties (and regional treaties among like-minded states), with a continuing reliance on customary rules of state responsibility.

D. BREACH BY A STATE OF ITS CONTRACTUAL UNDERTAKING TO AN ALIEN

Contractual agreements between states and aliens are a common phenomenon in international society and may cover a great variety of matters. Some agreements are similar to agreements between private parties in a purely commercial context. A private supplier may sell goods or services to a foreign government or grant to it rights to patents or know-how under a licensing arrangement, in the same way it would any other buyer. Alternatively, the contract may involve special features related to the fact that the agreement is between an alien investor and a foreign government. For instance, a private company may enter into a concession agreement with a foreign government calling for the exploitation, development and marketing by the private company of a major source of mineral resources owned by the foreign government. Or the private investor may enter into the contract pursuant to an investment incentive program, under which various special guarantees and incentives are provided by the foreign government to promote investment in a particular geographic region. The undertakings made by the state under such varied arrangements differ widely, and these differences may be relevant to the question of whether state responsibility under international law attaches as a result of its breach of a particular undertaking.

When does a breach of a contractual undertaking by a state to an alien constitute a violation of international law? On the one hand, one might argue that since only states have rights and obligations under international law, a state can limit its exercise of sovereignty only by international agreement with another state or international organization, and consequently a state cannot limit its exercise of sovereignty by agreement with an alien. On the other hand, as the other chapters in this book demonstrate, non-state actors play an important role in the formation, interpretation, and implementation of international law, and are in many situations accorded a status under international law where they have rights and obligations. As such, perhaps a state's breach of a contractual undertaking to an alien should be treated just like a breach of a treaty. Or is the breach of such a contract best conceptualized as an "expropriation" of a property right, bringing into play the concepts discussed in the prior section? See Choharis, U.S. Courts and the International Law of Expropriation: Toward a New Model for Breach of Contract, 80 S. Cal. L. Rev. 1 (2006).

1. Choice and Effect of Governing Law

A necessary first step in determining whether a breach or repudiation of a contractual obligation gives rise to state responsibility is to ascertain, in accordance with the principles of conflict of laws (or private international law), what body of law (or bodies of law) governs questions of the validity, interpretation, and performance of the contract. As pointed out in the *Saudi Arabia v. Arabian Am. Oil Co. (Aramco)*, 27 I.L.R. 117, 165 (1958) (footnote omitted):

> It is obvious that no contract can exist *in vacuo, i.e.*, without being based on a legal system. The conclusion of a contract is not left to the unfettered discretion of the Parties. It is necessarily related to some positive law which gives legal effects to the reciprocal and concordant manifestations of intent made by the parties. The contract cannot even be conceived without a system of law under which it is created. Human will can only create a contractual relationship if the applicable system of law has first recognized its power to do so.

Determining the "applicable system of law" can be quite complex in relation to an agreement between a state and an alien. In negotiating such an agreement, the parties are free under principles of conflict of laws to designate the body or bodies of law that will govern the validity, interpretation and performance of the agreement and, if they so choose, to withdraw the agreement from the exclusive application of the law of the contracting state or any other domestic legal system. National and international tribunals generally accept the choice by the contracting parties of governing law as binding, and it is only in the rare case that the parties, by design or inadvertence, fail to choose what law is to govern a significant contract. In connection with the materials that follow, consider what factors are likely to influence the negotiations on this issue.

In the absence of an explicit choice by a state and a foreign private party of the law or laws to govern their contract, the determination of governing law may be complicated by questions such as whether there should be a presumption in favor of the municipal law of the contracting state or whether reference of disputes under the agreement to an international arbitral tribunal implies a choice as to governing law or at least, as found by Arbitrator Cavin in the *Sapphire Int'l Petroleums, Ltd. v. Nat'l Iranian Oil Co.* arbitration, a rejection of municipal law of the contracting state as controlling. See Lalive, Contracts Between a State or a State Agency and a Foreign Company, 13 I.C.L.Q. 987, 1011–15 (1964). Determining the governing law or the "proper law" of the contract may swing the door open to problems concerning the content of that law. For example, if municipal law of the contracting state is selected, does it encompass the municipal law relating to public or administrative contracts under which, in certain circumstances, the contracting state may not be bound if the public interest otherwise requires? Is it municipal law as it existed on the date of the agreement or as it may be amended from time to time? The parties may include a so-called "stabilization clause," stating that the agreement will be governed throughout its term by municipal or international law in force at the time the agreement is concluded. The purpose of a stabilization clause is to protect the foreign investor from risk of changes in municipal law detrimental to its interests.

The 1933 concession granted by Persia to the Anglo–Persian Oil Company provided that differences between the parties were to be settled by arbitration and that an award of the arbitrators was to be based on the judicial principles contained in Article 38 of the Statute of the Permanent Court of International Justice. Does such a choice of law provision render international law directly applicable to the agreement? Does it follow that the agreement could not be altered or terminated by the application of municipal law? See *Anglo–Iranian Oil Co.* (United Kingdom v. Iran), 1952 I.C.J. 93. Would such an agreement be subject to adjustment in accordance with fundamentally changed circumstances to the same extent that a treaty would?

TEXACO OVERSEAS PETROLEUM CO. v. LIBYA
104 J. Droit Int'l 350 (1977)
translated in, 17 I.L.M. 1 (1978) (footnotes omitted)

[On September 1, 1973 and February 11, 1974, Libya promulgated decrees purporting to nationalize all of the rights, interests, and property of Texaco Overseas Petroleum Company (TOPCO) and California Asiatic Oil Company (CAOC) in Libya that had been granted to them jointly by the Government of Libya under 14 deeds of concession.

TOPCO and CAOC requested arbitration and appointed an arbitrator. The Libyan Government refused to accept arbitration and did not appoint an arbitrator. Pursuant to the arbitration provision in their deeds of concession, TOPCO and CAOC requested the President of the International Court of Justice to appoint a sole arbitrator to hear and determine the disputes. The Libyan Government opposed such request and filed a memorandum with the President contending, *inter alia*, that the disputes were not subject to arbitration because the nationalizations were sovereign acts.

After considering the Libyan Government's objections, the President of the International Court of Justice appointed René-Jean Dupuy, Secretary General of The Hague Academy of International Law and Professor of Law at the University of Nice, as the sole arbitrator. The Libyan Government did not participate in the subsequent proceedings.

On January 19, 1977, Professor Dupuy delivered an Award on the Merits in favor of TOPCO and CAOC. He held that (1) the deeds of concession were binding on the parties, (2) by adopting the measures of nationalization the Libyan Government breached its obligations under the deeds of concession, and (3) the Libyan Government was legally bound to perform the deeds of concession in accordance with their terms. The award on the merits stated, in part, as follows:]

22.   * * * [T]he juridical value and, consequently, the binding nature of the Deeds of Concession in dispute can only be judged on the basis of the law which is applicable to them because it is obvious that, if— assuming arguendo—these contracts were governed by Libyan law, the result would have been that their binding nature could be affected *a priori*

by legislative or regulatory measures taken within the Libyan national legal order * * *.

But the Deeds of Concession in dispute are not controlled by Libyan law or, more exactly, are not controlled by Libyan law alone. It is incontestable that these contracts were international contracts, both in the economic sense because they involved the interests of international trade and in the strict legal sense because they included factors connecting them to different States * * *.

23.   What was the law applicable to these contracts? It is this particular question that the parties intended to resolve in adopting Clause 28 of the Deeds of Concession in a form which must be recalled here:

"This concession shall be governed by and interpreted in accordance with the principles of the law of Libya common to the principles of international law and in the absence of such common principles then by and in accordance with the general principles of law, including such of those principles as may have been applied by international tribunals."

* * *

24.   Two questions must therefore be decided by the Tribunal in order to rule on the binding nature of the Deeds of Concession which are in dispute:

— first question: Did the parties have the right to select the law which was to govern their contract?

— second question: Under what circumstances was the choice of law applicable and what consequence should be derived from the international character of the contracts?

25.   The answer to this first question is beyond any doubt: all legal systems, whatever they are, apply the principle of the autonomy of the will of the parties to international contracts. * * *

* * *

36.   Under what circumstances was the choice of applicable law made and what consequences should be derived therefrom as to the internationalization of the Deeds of Concession in dispute?

* * *

40.   * * * [T]he internationalization of contracts entered into between States and foreign private persons can result in various ways which it is now time to examine.

41.   (a) At the outset, it is accepted that the reference made by the contract, in the clause concerning the governing law, to the general principles of law leads to this result. These general principles, being those which are mentioned in Article 38 of the Statute of the International Court of Justice, are one of the sources of international law: they may

appear alone in the clause or jointly with a national law, particularly with the law of the contracting State.

* * *

42.   International arbitration case law confirms that the reference to the general principles of law is always regarded to be a sufficient criterion for the internationalization of a contract. * * *

* * * The recourse to general principles is to be explained not only by the lack of adequate legislation in the State considered (which might have been the case, at one time, in certain oil Emirates). It is also justified by the need for the private contracting party to be protected against unilateral and abrupt modifications of the legislation in the contracting State: it plays, therefore, an important role in the contractual equilibrium intended by the parties.

* * *

44.   (b) Another process for the internationalization of a contract consists in inserting a clause providing that possible differences which may arise in respect of the interpretation and the performance of the contract shall be submitted to arbitration.

* * *

Even if one considers that the choice of international arbitration proceedings cannot by itself lead to the exclusive application of international law, it is one of the elements which makes it possible to detect a certain internationalization of the contract. The *Sapphire International Petroleum Ltd.* award is quite explicit: "If no positive implication can be made from the arbitral clause, it is possible to find there a negative intention, namely to reject the exclusive application of Iranian law" (35 Int'l L.R. 136 (1963), at 172); this is what led the arbitrator in that case, in the absence of any explicit reference to the law applicable, not to apply automatically Iranian law, thus dismissing any presumption in its favor. It is therefore unquestionable that the reference to international arbitration is sufficient to internationalize a contract, in other words, to situate it within a specific legal order—the order of the international law of contracts.

45.   (c) A third element of the internationalization of the contracts in dispute results from the fact that it takes on a dimension of a new category of agreements between States and private persons: economic development agreements * * *.

Several elements characterize these agreements: in the first place, their subject matter is particularly broad: they are not concerned only with an isolated purchase or performance, but tend to bring to developing countries investments and technical assistance, particularly in the field of research and exploitation of mineral resources, or in the construction of factories on a turnkey basis. Thus, they assume a real importance in the development of the country where they are performed: it will suffice to mention here the importance of the obligations assumed in the case under consideration by the concession holders in the field of road and port infrastructures and the training on the spot of qualified personnel. The party contracting with the State was thus associated with the realization of the economic and social progress of the host country.

In the second place, the long duration of these contracts implies close cooperation between the State and the contracting party and requires permanent installations as well as the acceptance of extensive responsibilities by the investor.

Finally, because of the purpose of the cooperation in which the contracting party must participate with the State and the magnitude of the investments to which it agreed, the contractual nature of this type of agreement is reinforced: the emphasis on the contractual nature of the legal relation between the host State and the investor is intended to bring about an equilibrium between the goal of the general interest sought by such relation and the profitability which is necessary for the pursuit of the task entrusted to the private enterprise. The effect is also to ensure to the private contracting party a certain stability which is justified by the considerable investments which it makes in the country concerned. The investor must in particular be protected against legislative uncertainties, that is to say the risks of the municipal law of the host country being modified, or against any government measures which would lead to an abrogation or rescission of the contract. Hence, the insertion, as in the present case, of so-called stabilization clauses: these clauses tend to remove all or part of the agreement from the internal law and to provide for its correlative submission to *sui generis* rules as stated in the *Aramco* award, or to a system which is properly an international law system. * * *

* * *

46.   The Tribunal must specify the meaning and the exact scope of internationalization of a contractual relationship so as to avoid any misunderstanding: indeed to say that international law governs contractual relations between a State and a foreign private party neither means that the latter is assimilated to a State nor that the contract entered into with it is assimilated to a treaty.

47.   This Tribunal * * * shall * * * consider as established today the concept that legal international capacity is not solely attributable to a State and that international law encompasses subjects of a diversified nature. If States, the original subjects of the international legal order, enjoy all the capacities offered by the latter, other subjects enjoy only limited capacities which are assigned to specific purposes. * * * In other words, stating that a contract between a State and a private person falls within the international legal order means that for the purposes of interpretation and performance of the contract, it should be recognized that a private contracting party has specific international capacities. But, unlike a State, the private person has only a limited capacity and his quality as a subject of international law does enable him only to invoke, in

the field of international law, the rights which he derives from the contract.

* * *

49. * * * It is significant * * * that, in a formula in which it must be assumed that each term has been weighed, the parties concerned referred not to Libyan law itself, but to "the principles of Libyan law." Indeed, the parties thereby wanted to demonstrate that they intended the Arbitral Tribunal to base itself on the spirit of the Libyan law as expressed in the fundamental principles of that law, rather than by its rules which may be contingent and variable since these rules depended, in the last instance, on the unilateral will—even arbitrariness—of one of the contracting parties: hence, the reference which is also made to the principles of international law.

It follows that the reference made by the contracts under dispute to the principles of Libyan law does not nullify the effect of internationalization of the contracts which has already resulted from their nature as economic development agreements and recourse to international arbitration for the settlement of disputes. The application of the principles of Libyan law does not have the effect of ruling out the application of the principles of international law, but quite the contrary: it simply requires us to combine the two in verifying the conformity of the first with the second.

* * *

51. Applying the principles stated above, the Arbitral Tribunal will refer:

(1) On the one hand, as regards the principles of Libyan law: regardless of the source of Libyan law taken into consideration, whether we refer to the Sharia, the Sacred Law of Islam (a special reference should be made to Surah 5 of the Koran which begins with the verse: "O ye believers, perform your contracts!") or to the Libyan Civil Code which includes on this point two basic articles illustrating the value which Libyan law attaches to the principle of the respect for the word given:

— Article 147, under which "The contract makes the law of the parties. It can be revoked or altered only by mutual consent of the parties or for reasons provided by the law;"

— Article 148, under which "A contract must be performed in accordance with its contents and in compliance with the requirements of good faith,"

one is led to the same conclusion, that is: that Libyan law recognizes and sanctions the principle of the binding force of contracts.

(2) On the other hand, as regards the principles of international law: from this second point of view, it is unquestionable, as written by Professor Jessup * * * that the maxim " 'pacta sunt servanda' is a

general principle of law; it is an essential foundation of international law."

* * *

52. The conformity, on this essential point, of the principles of Libyan law with the principles of international law relieves the Tribunal from discussing the matter further * * *. * * *

[The arbitrator then considered whether the Deeds of Concession could be regarded as administrative contracts under civil law which the State would be entitled, under certain circumstances, to amend unilaterally or even abrogate in the public interest. The arbitrator concluded this position was untenable for two reasons. First, the Deeds of Concession did not meet the definition of administrative contracts under Libyan law. One element of this definition was that the contract confer upon the government rights and powers not usually found in a civil contract, such as the power to amend or abrogate the contract unilaterally if the public interest requires, or—in the terminology of French law—rights and powers going beyond the ambit of ordinary law (clauses exorbitantes du droit commun). The second reason cited by the arbitrator was that the distinction between administrative contracts and civil contracts was a creature of the French legal system (and others based upon it) and it could not be regarded as a "principle of international law" or as a "general principle of law."]

61. * * * It is clear from an international point of view that it is not possible to criticize a nationalization measure concerning nationals of the State concerned, or any measure affecting aliens in respect of whom the State concerned has made no particular commitment to guarantee and maintain their position. On the assumption that the nationalizing State has concluded with a foreign company a contract which stems from the municipal law of that State and is completely governed by that law the resolution of the new situation created by nationalization will be subject to the legal and administrative provisions then in force.

62. But the case is totally different where the State has concluded with a foreign contracting party an internationalized agreement, either because the contract has been subjected to the municipal law of the host country, * * * applicable as of the effective date of the contract, and "stabilized" on that same date by specific clauses, or because it has been placed directly under the aegis of international law. Under these two assumptions, the State has placed itself within the international legal order in order to guarantee vis-à-vis its foreign contracting party a certain legal and economic status over a certain period of time. In consideration for this commitment, the partner is under an obligation to make a certain amount of investments in the country concerned and to explore and exploit at its own risks the petroleum resources which have been conceded to it.

Thus, the decision of a State to take nationalizing measures constitutes the exercise of an internal legal jurisdiction but carries international consequences when such measures affect international legal relationships in which the nationalizing State is involved.

* * *

67. * * * [T]he State, by entering into an international agreement with any partner whatsoever, exercises its sovereignty whenever the State is not subject to duress and where the State has freely committed itself through an untainted consent.

* * *

70. * * * Clause 16 of the Deeds of Concession contains a stabilization clause with respect to the rights of the concession holder. As consideration for the economic risks to which the foreign contracting parties were subjected, the Libyan State granted them a concession of a minimum duration of 50 years and, more specifically, containing a non-aggravation clause, Clause 16, which provided:

"The Government of Libya will take all steps necessary to ensure that the company enjoys all the rights conferred by this concession. The contractual rights expressly created by this concession shall not be altered except by mutual consent of the parties."

Another paragraph was added to this provision under the Royal Decree of December 1961 and became an integral part of the contract on the basis of the Agreement of 1963. It provides:

"This Concession shall throughout the period of its validity be construed in accordance with the Petroleum Law and the Regulations in force on the date of execution of the agreement of amendment by which this paragraph (2) was incorporated into the concession agreement. Any amendment to or repeal of such Regulations shall not affect the contractual rights of the Company without its consent."

71. Such a provision, the effect of which is to stabilize the position of the contracting party, does not, in principle, impair the sovereignty of the Libyan State. Not only has the Libyan State freely undertaken commitments but also the fact that this clause stabilizes the petroleum legislation and regulations as of the date of the execution of the agreement does not affect in principle the legislative and regulatory sovereignty of Libya. Libya reserves all its prerogatives to issue laws and regulations in the field of petroleum activities in respect of national or foreign persons with which it has not undertaken such a commitment. * * *

* * *

73. Thus, in respect of the international law of contracts, a nationalization cannot prevail over an internationalized contract, containing stabilization clauses, entered into between a State and a foreign private company. The situation could be different only if one were to conclude that the exercise by a State of its right to nationalize places that State on a level outside of and superior to the contract and also to the international legal order itself, and constitutes an "act of government" ("acte de gouvernement") which is beyond the scope of any judicial redress or any criticism.

* * *

91. * * * One should conclude that a sovereign State which nationalizes cannot disregard the commitment undertaken by the contracting State: to decide otherwise would in fact recognize that all contractual commitments undertaken by a State have been undertaken under a purely permissive condition on its part and are therefore lacking of any legal force and any binding effect. From the point of view of its advisability, such a solution would gravely harm the credibility of States since it would mean that contracts signed by them did not bind them; it would introduce in such contracts a fundamental imbalance because in these contracts only one party—the party contracting with the State—would be bound. In law, such an outcome would go directly against the most elementary principle of good faith and for this reason it cannot be accepted.

[The arbitrator then analyzed at length Libyan law and international law relating to remedies for breach of contractual obligations and held that the injured complainants were entitled to *restitutio in integrum*, and that Libya was required to perform specifically its contractual obligations with respect to the complainants, stating that " * * * this Tribunal must hold that *restitutio in integrum* is, both under the principles of Libyan law and under the principles of international law, the normal sanction for non-performance of contractual obligations and that it is inapplicable only to the extent that restoration of the *status quo ante* is impossible" (para. 109).]

NOTES

1. *Post–Script.* Following the rendering of the Award on the Merits, Libya agreed to provide TOPCO and CAOC with $152 million of Libyan crude oil in exchange for ending the arbitral proceedings.

2. *"Internationalizing" a Contract.* Consider the bases for what Professor Dupuy refers to as "internationalization" of the contract. What, if anything, does "internationalization" connote beyond the specific features on which the characterization is based? Does it imply that international remedies would be available to the private party for breach by the state that would not be available for violation by the state of other contracts? What, if anything, does the concept of internationalization contribute to the analysis of what law governs the contract? Dupuy makes clear that "internationalization" does not

imply that the private party is assimilated to a state or the contract to a treaty. Is it more than just a label for a contract between an alien and a state that is explicitly to be governed by international law (or general principles of law)?

3. *Are Contracts for "Development" Special?* Dupuy suggests that in the case of international development contracts, the contract may be "internationalized," whether or not there is an international arbitration clause or a clause selecting as the governing law a body of law other than that of the contracting state. Is there any basis for concluding that an international development contract involves obligations on the international level different from other contracts? See Fatouros, International Law and the Internationalized Contract, 74 A.J.I.L. 134–41 (1980). Consider the position of Professor Schachter:

> State practice confirms the role of the home states in extending diplomatic protection to private companies in cases of development agreements of a certain magnitude and salience. Host states tend to accept such "protection" as legitimate. In this sense, it may be said that the development agreements are "internationalized." But this is not the same as saying that they have become directly subject to international law or that their alleged breach by the state in itself involves a violation of international law.

> In sum, we need to be cautious in employing the phrase "internationalized" contracts. We may use the term in a descriptive sense for contracts which have the transnational features we have discussed— namely, non-national governing law, non-national arbitration, or international economic and political significance. However, we cannot infer from these features that the contracts have been transposed to another "legal order" or that they have become subject to international law in the same way as a treaty between two States.

> To be sure, the international law of State responsibility applies to these so-called international contracts just as it does to all other contracts and transactions between states and foreign nationals. The application of the rules of state responsibility will have to take cognizance of the special contractual provisions for non-national law and arbitration and also, when appropriate, the interest of the state to which the private party belongs. But these special features do not alter the basic principles of State responsibility applicable to injury to non-nationals resulting from contractual violations.

Schachter, International Law in Theory and Practice 310–11 (1991) (footnotes omitted).

2. Breach of Undertaking as a Violation of International Law

It is apparent from the foregoing that, under the applicable principles of conflict of laws (or private international law), the law governing the interpretation, validity, and performance of the contract may be determined to be the municipal law of the contracting state, principles of law applied in common by two or more municipal law systems, principles of public international law, general principles of law, some other body of law, or some combination of these. Indeed, various aspects of the contractual relationship may be governed by different bodies of law.

Having determined the governing law, the problem shifts to seeking the content of that law as applied to the particular contractual undertaking involved. To what extent under the governing principles are contracting parties held to their undertakings under an inflexible application of *pacta sunt servanda?* To what extent, if at all, is either party afforded leeway in meeting its obligations? To what extent can the rights and duties of the parties be adjusted to meet changing conditions?

Then, assuming that a breach of a contractual obligation by the contracting state is established under the law governing the agreement, when, in the absence of a treaty violation or a denial of procedural justice, will such a breach constitute a violation of international law thereby providing the substantive basis for a claim of state responsibility?

**RESTATEMENT OF THE LAW (THIRD)
THE FOREIGN RELATIONS LAW OF THE
UNITED STATES § 712(2) (1987)**

§ 712. State Responsibility for Economic Injury to Nationals of Other States

A state is responsible under international law for injury resulting from:

* * *

(2) a repudiation or breach by the state of a contract with a national of another state

(a) where the repudiation or breach is (i) discriminatory; or (ii) motivated by non-commercial considerations, and compensatory damages are not paid; or

(b) where the foreign national is not given an adequate forum to determine his claim of repudiation or breach, or is not compensated for any repudiation or breach determined to have occurred;
* * *.

NOTES

1. *Restatement Commentary.* Restatement (Third) § 712(2), Comment *h* states as follows:

> *h. Repudiation or breach of contract by state.* A state party to a contract with a foreign national is liable for a repudiation or breach of that contract under applicable national law, but not every repudiation or breach by a state of a contract with a foreign national constitutes a

violation of international law. Under Subsection (2), a state is responsible for such a repudiation or breach only if it is discriminatory * * * or if it is akin to an expropriation in that the contract is repudiated or breached for governmental rather than commercial reasons and the state is not prepared to pay damages. A state's repudiation or failure to perform is not a violation of international law under this section if it is based on a bona fide dispute about the obligation or its performance, if it is due to the state's inability to perform, or if nonperformance is motivated by commercial considerations and the state is prepared to pay damages or to submit to adjudication or arbitration and to abide by the judgment or award.

With respect to any repudiation or breach of a contract with a foreign national, a state may be responsible for a denial of justice under international law if it denies to the alien an effective domestic forum to resolve the dispute and has not agreed to any other forum; or if, having committed itself to a special forum for dispute settlement, such as arbitration, it fails to honor such commitment; or if it fails to carry out a judgment or award rendered by such domestic or special forum. * * *

A breach of contract by a state may sometimes constitute "creeping expropriation," * * * for example, if the breach makes impossible the continued operation of the project that is the subject of the contract. For discussion of the treatment under international law of breaches by a state of different types of contracts, see Restatement (Third) § 712, Reporters' Notes 9 and 10.

2. *World Bank Guidelines.* The Guidelines on the Treatment of Foreign Direct Investment published by the World Bank Group and the IMF on September 25, 1992, 31 I.L.M. 1379 (1992), take the position that only under limited conditions may a state unilaterally terminate, amend or otherwise disclaim liability under a contract with a foreign private investor for other than commercial reasons. These conditions are that the action be taken (a) in accordance with applicable legal procedures, (b) in pursuance in good faith of a public purpose, (c) without discrimination on the basis of nationality, and (d) against the payment of appropriate compensation. The appropriateness of compensation will be determined under the standards applicable to instances of expropriation. Guideline IV, Section 11, at 1383–84.

3. *Stabilization Clauses.* Agreements between states and foreign investors sometimes contain "stabilization clauses" stating that the law in force at the time of execution of the agreement will govern (an example was considered in the *TOPCO* Arbitration in the prior sub-section). In addition to freezing tax laws and customs laws and other regulatory regimes that might adversely affect profitability of the project, these clauses are often intended to prevent repudiation of the contract or expropriation of the project.

It has been argued that a state cannot be bound by such a clause because it would be inconsistent with its sovereignty. See *Saudi Arabia v. Arabian Am. Oil Co. (Aramco)*, 27 I.L.R. 117 (1958); *Kuwait v. American Indep. Oil Co. (Aminoil)*, 21 I.L.M. 976 (1982). The better view, however, seems to be that expressed by Professor Dupuy, namely that entering into such an undertaking is itself an exercise of sovereignty that is binding on the state. In the *Kuwait v. Aminol* decision, the tribunal concluded that the contract before it had such a long duration (i.e., sixty years) that the tribunal would not presume that the stabilization clause was intended to preclude nationalization unless that were expressly so stipulated (paras. 94–95), but decided that the stabilization clause had a legal effect in respect of nationalization by reinforcing requirements for proper indemnification as a condition of the taking (para. 96). Under the formulation of the Restatement (Third), if a state breaches a stabilization clause in an economic development agreement with a foreign private investor, for example, by imposing on the project exchange controls or tax increases that otherwise apply to nationals and aliens alike, would such a breach without more be a violation of international law? See Restatement (Third) § 712, Reporters' Note 10, where the view is expressed that "[i]f coupled with an arbitration clause, such a stabilization clause will be given effect by the arbitrator."

Liberian E. Timber Corp. (LETCO) v. Liberia, 26 I.L.M. 647 (1987), an arbitration under the rules of the International Centre for the Settlement of Investment Disputes (ICSID), involved a timber concession agreement governed by Liberian law with a stabilization clause. The tribunal expressed the view that the stabilization clause must be respected. "Otherwise, the contracting state may easily avoid its contractual obligations by legislation. Such legislation action could only be justified by nationalization which [is for a *bona fide* public purpose, is nondiscriminatory and is accompanied by payment of appropriate compensation]." Id. at 667.

4. *Unilateral Instruments of Approval.* Often under the investment incentive program of developing countries, instruments of approval are issued. Under a typical procedure:

[T]he prospective investor must apply to the competent state agency, designated and quite often created by the basic investment law, in order to have its investment approved or "registered." * * * The final instrument of approval is very often the product of extensive negotiations. By that instrument, the state grants to the investor some or all of the assurances and privileges provided for in the original investment law, while the investor undertakes certain obligations with respect to the form, amount, and other elements of the investment. The precise form of the instrument varies in the different countries. It is usually an act of the executive branch of government: an administrative decree, a decision of the cabinet or of certain ministers, or some other administrative act.

Fatouros, Government Guarantees to Foreign Investors, 122–23 (1962) (footnotes omitted). Do such unilateral undertakings by a state fall outside the area of "contract?" Fatouros concludes that such instruments "are of a mixed character, both contractual and noncontractual." Id. at 196. If an undertaking constitutes no more than a unilateral act by the state, can a breach thereof constitute a breach of international law? To what extent are contractual principles applicable? Should general principles of estoppel come into play? See, e.g., MacGibbon, Estoppel in International Law, 7 I.C.L.Q. 468 (1958); Friedmann, Some Impacts of Social Organization on International Law, 50 A.J.I.L. 475, 506 (1956).

SECTION 4.　PROCEDURAL RULES ON INJURY TO ALIENS

As noted in Chapter 8, Section 7(D), the International Law Commission is currently drafting a set of "Articles" on the topic of "diplomatic protection of nationals," which refers to efforts by a state, through the exercise of international diplomacy, to protect the interests of its nationals when they are harmed by a foreign state. See Report of the International Law Commission, Fifty-eighth Session, U.N. Doc. A/61/10, at 13 (2006). This section addresses some of the core procedural rules that arise in the area of diplomatic protection of nationals.

A.　STATE ESPOUSAL OF CLAIMS OF NATIONALS

Under international law, a state is entitled to exercise diplomatic protection on behalf of one of its nationals by advancing a claim against another state that injured the national. International law, however, traditionally has imposed no duty on a state to "espouse" the claim of its national. Under the law of the United States, as well as most other states, the injured national has no legally enforceable right to compel his or her government to espouse the claim. See Borchard, The Diplomatic Protection of Citizens Abroad 355–98 (1915); *Chytil v. Powell*, 15 F. App'x 515, 517 (9th Cir. 2001) ("Espousal seems particularly unsusceptible to resolution in the judicial branch. * * * The judiciary has no experience in espousal and has no way of considering the many other factors that espousal decisions would affect * * *)"; *Marik v. Powell*, 15 F. App'x 517, 519 (9th Cir. 2001) (the same). In light of recent developments favoring the ability of individuals to bring claims before certain international fora, do you think the traditional rule should change?

If the national's claim is espoused by the state, it becomes a claim of the state and, as such, is addressed through negotiations between the espousing state and the state that has allegedly caused the injury. From the time it espouses the claim, it has traditionally been thought that the espousing state enjoys exclusive control over the handling and disposition of it. In *Administrative Decision No. V* (United States v. Germany), Mixed Claims Commission, Administrative Decisions and Opinions to June 30, 1925, 145, 190, 7 U.N. Rep. Int'l Arb. Awards 119, 152 (1924), Umpire Parker stated:

> In exercising such control [the nation] is governed not only by the interest of the particular claimant but by the larger interests of the whole people of the nation and must exercise an untrammeled discretion in determining when and how the claim will be presented and pressed, or withdrawn or compromised, and the private owner will be bound by the action taken. Even if payment is made to the espousing nation in pursuance of an award, it has complete control over the fund so paid to and held by it and may, to prevent fraud, correct a

mistake, or protect the national honor, at its election return the fund
to the nation paying it or otherwise dispose of it.

Thus, it is assumed that the Executive may waive or settle a claim by the
United States against a foreign state concerning an injury to a U.S.
national despite the latter's objection. See Kelso, Espousal: Its Use in
International Law, 1 Ariz. J. Int'l & Comp. L. 233, 245 (1982) ("By
espousing an international claim on behalf of one of its nationals, the
claiming nation has in effect received an assignment of the claim from its
nationals. * * * The claiming nation, through ownership of the claim, is
able to determine how the claim will be presented, what amount will be
sought and whether any settlement, compromise or release will be accepted."); Pipko & Sack, Rediscovering Executive Authority: Claims Settlement and Foreign Sovereign Immunity, 10 Yale J. Int'l L. 295, 303 (1985)
("The state, with binding effect on a claimant, may waive the claim
entirely or settle it for an amount substantially less than its fair value
* * *."); *Meade v. United States*, 76 U.S. (9 Wall.) 691, 724–25 (1869)
(finding that regardless of the attitude of the private claimant to the U.S.
government's espousal of the claim, the claimant lacked the power to
deprive the government of settlement authority by resorting to a private
remedy); *Asociacion de Reclamantes v. Mexico*, 735 F.2d 1517, 1523 (D.C.
Cir. 1984) ("the fact that a claim has been espoused provides a complete
defense for the defendant sovereign in any action by the private individual
* * *."). Given contemporary developments in favor of the rights of
individuals under international law, should the traditional rule on exclusive state control of the claim evolve?

A state's claim based on an injury to its national is derivative in a
number of respects. See Restatement (Third) § 713, Comment *a*. For
example, the injured national enjoys broad rights to settle its claim
against the foreign state *before* it is espoused by the national's state and,
by such private settlement, preclude any claim by the national's state.
Moreover, as discussed below, the injured national is generally required to
exhaust possible remedies under the local law of the foreign state before
the national's state may assert a claim. In addition, the measure of
compensation that may be recovered by the national's state is based on
the injury to its national; reparation normally does not encompass any
element of recompense for injury to the state itself.

B. RULE ON EXHAUSTION OF LOCAL REMEDIES

AHMADOU SADIO DIALLO (GUINEA v. DEMOCRATIC REPUBLIC OF THE CONGO)

International Court of Justice, 2007
2007 I.C.J. ____

[On December 28, 1998, the Republic of Guinea filed a state responsibility case against the Democratic Republic of Congo (DRC) in the International Court of Justice. Guinea alleged that Ahmadou Sadio Diallo, a

national of Guinea who had resided in the D.R.C. for thirty-two years, was unlawfully imprisoned, without a trial, by the authorities of that state. Moreover, Guinea claimed that Diallo's investments, businesses, and property were unlawfully expropriated. After Diallo attempted unsuccessfully, in local proceedings, to recover sums owed to him by companies owned by the government of the Congo and companies in which it was a shareholder, Guinea claimed that, without judicial process, Diallo was expelled from the Republic of Congo. Before the International Court, the DRC objected to the admissibility of the claims, in part based on a failure to exhaust local remedies].

40.   In the present case Guinea seeks to exercise its diplomatic protection on behalf of Mr. Diallo in respect of the DRC's alleged violations of his rights as a result of his arrest, detention and expulsion, that violation allegedly constituting an internationally wrongful act by the DRC giving rise to its responsibility. It therefore falls to the Court to ascertain whether the Applicant has met the requirements for the exercise of diplomatic protection, that is to say whether Mr. Diallo is a national of Guinea and whether he has exhausted the local remedies available in the DRC.

41.   To begin with, the Court observes that it is not disputed by the DRC that Mr. Diallo's sole nationality is that of Guinea and that he has continuously held that nationality from the date of the alleged injury to the date the proceedings were initiated. The parties have however devoted much argument to the issue of exhaustion of local remedies.

42.   As the Court stated in the *Interhandel (Switzerland v. United States of America)* case,

> "[t]he rule that local remedies must be exhausted before international proceedings may be instituted is a well-established rule of customary international law; the rule has been generally observed in cases in which a State has adopted the cause of its national whose rights are claimed to have been disregarded in another State in violation of international law. Before resort may be had to an international court in such a situation, it has been considered necessary that the State where the violation occurred should have an opportunity to redress it by its own means, within the framework of its own domestic legal system." (*I.C.J. Reports 1959*, p.27.)

43.   The parties do not question the legal remedies rule; they do however differ as to whether the Congolese legal system actually offered local remedies which Mr. Diallo should have exhausted before his cause could be espoused by Guinea before the Court.

44.   In matters of diplomatic protection, it is incumbent on the applicant to prove that local remedies were indeed exhausted or to establish that exceptional circumstances relieved the allegedly injured person whom the applicant seeks to protect of the obligation to exhaust available local remedies (see *Elettronica Sicula S.p.A. (ELSI) (United States of America v. Italy), I.C.J. Reports 1989*, pp. 43–44, para. 53). It is

for the respondent to convince the Court that there were effective remedies in its domestic legal system that were not exhausted (see *ibid.*, p. 46, para. 59). Thus, in the present case, Guinea must establish that Mr. Diallo exhausted any available local remedies or, if not, must show that exceptional circumstances justified the fact that he did not do so; it is, on the other hand, for the DRC to prove that there were available and effective remedies in its domestic legal system against the decision to remove Mr. Diallo from the territory and that he did not exhaust them.

45.   The Court will recall at this stage that, in its Memorial on the merits, Guinea described in detail the violations of international law allegedly committed by the DRC against Mr. Diallo. Among those cited is the claim that Mr. Diallo was arbitrarily arrested and detained on two occasions, first in 1988 and then in 1995. It states that he suffered inhuman and degrading treatment during those periods in detention and adds that his rights under the 1963 Vienna Convention on Consular Relations were not respected. The Court observes however that Guinea has not, in any way, developed the question of the admissibility of the claims concerning this inhuman and degrading treatment or relating to the 1963 Vienna Convention on Consular Relations. * * * [T]he DRC has for its part endeavoured in the present proceedings to show that remedies to challenge the decision to remove Mr. Diallo from Zaire are institutionally provided for in its domestic legal system. By contrast, the DRC did not address the issue of exhaustion of local remedies in respect of Mr. Diallo's arrest, his detention or the alleged violations of his other rights, as an individual, said to have resulted from those measures, and from his expulsion, or to have accompanied them. In view of the above, the Court will address the question of local remedies solely in respect of Mr. Diallo's expulsion.

46.   The Court notes that the expulsion was characterized as a "refusal of entry" when it was carried out, as both Parties have acknowledged and as is confirmed by the notice drawn up on 31 January 1996 by the national immigration service of Zaire. It is apparent that refusals of entry are not appealable under Congolese law. Article 13 of Legislative Order No. 83–033 of 12 September 1983, concerning immigration control, expressly states the "measure [refusing entry] shall not be subject to appeal". The Court considers that the DRC cannot now rely on an error allegedly made by its administrative agencies at the time Mr. Diallo was "refused entry" to claim that he should have treated the measure as an expulsion. Mr. Diallo, as the subject of the refusal of entry, was justified in relying on the consequences of the legal characterization thus given by the Zairean authorities, including for purpose of the local remedies rule.

47.   The Court further observes that, even if this was a case of expulsion and not refusal of entry, as the DRC maintains, the DRC has also failed to show that means of redress against expulsion decisions are available under its domestic law. The DRC did, it is true, cite the possibility of requesting reconsideration by the competent administrative authority * * *. The Court nevertheless recalls that, while the local

remedies that must be exhausted include all remedies of a legal nature, judicial redress as well as redress before administrative bodies, administrative remedies can only be taken into consideration for purposes of the local remedies rule if they are aimed at vindicating a right and not at obtaining a favour, unless they constitute an essential prerequisite for the admissibility of subsequent contentious proceedings. Thus, the possibility open to Mr. Diallo of submitting a request for reconsideration of the expulsion decision to the administrative authority having taken it—that is to say the Prime Minister—in the hope that he would retract his decision as a matter of grace cannot be deemed a local remedy to be exhausted.

48.   Having established that the DRC has not proven the existence in its domestic legal system of available and effective remedies allowing Mr. Diallo to challenge his expulsion, the Court concludes that the DRC's objection to admissibility based on the failure to exhaust local remedies cannot be upheld in respect of that expulsion.

NOTES

1.   *The Basic Rule.* A well-established rule of customary international law is that before a state can institute international proceedings for denial of rights to its nationals, remedies in local courts or administrative agencies must first have been exhausted. See Draft Articles 14–15, Report of the International Law Commission, Fifty-eighth Session, U.N. Doc. A/61/10, at 13, 20 (2006). Although originally confined to the context of diplomatic protection of aliens, today international tribunals apply the "rule of local remedies" to the field of human rights as well. The rule confers on the host or respondent state an important initial role in the international dispute settlement process. C.F. Amerasinghe explains the justification for the rule as follows:

> The rule sprang up primarily as an instrument designed to ensure respect for the sovereignty of host states in a particular area of international dispute settlement. Basically, this is the principal reason for its survival today and also for its projection into international systems of human rights protection. Whether in the modern law of diplomatic protection or in the conventional law of human rights protection, the *raison d'être* of the rule is the recognition given by members of the international community to the interest of the host state, flowing from its sovereignty, in settling international disputes of a certain kind by its own means before international mechanisms are invoked.

Amerasinghe, Local Remedies in International Law 425–26 (2d ed. 2004). Thus, the rule ensures that "the State where the violation occurred should have an opportunity to redress it by its own means, within the framework of its own domestic legal system." *Interhandel Case* (Switzerland v. United States), 1959 I.C.J. 6. This requirement means that a remedy must be sought until the highest court rules on the issue. See generally Trindade, The Application of the Rule of Exhaustion of Local Remedies in International Law (1983). The I.L.C. Articles on State Responsibility provide in Article 44(b) that "[t]he responsibility of a State may not be invoked if [t]he claim is one to which the rule of exhaustion of local remedies applies and any available and effective local remedy has not been exhausted." U.N. Doc. A/56/10, at 304 (2001).

2. *Non–Application When State Rights Also at Issue*. The local remedies rule does not apply if the injury at issue is wholly or preponderantly to the state itself rather than to one of its nationals. For example, in the *Avena* case, the International Court of Justice found exhaustion of local remedies within the United States unnecessary, since Mexico was requesting the Court to rule on the violation of Mexico's own rights under the Vienna Convention on Consular Relations, though Mexico also sought a ruling on the violation of individual rights conferred on Mexican nationals. According to the Court:

> In these special circumstances of interdependence of the rights of the State and of individual rights, Mexico may, in submitting a claim in its own name, request the Court to rule on the violation of rights which it claims to have suffered both directly and through the violation of individual rights conferred on Mexican nationals * * *. The duty to exhaust local remedies does not apply to such a request.

Avena and Other Mexican Nationals (Mexico v. United States of America), 2004 I.C.J. 12, 36, para. 40. Can a state, then, avoid application of the rule by simply asserting a concomitant direct violation of the state's rights? Efforts by the United States to formulate its claim in the *ELSI* case as concerning injury directly to the United States were not successful; the Court found that the claim was essentially one seeking to vindicate injury to two U.S. companies. For an analysis if the Court's treatment of the rule and other aspects of the *ELSI* case, see Murphy, The ELSI Case: An Investment Dispute at the International Court of Justice, 16 Yale J. Int'l L. 391 (1991).

3. *Burden of Proof*. Is it incumbent upon the applicant state to prove that local remedies were exhausted? Or must the defendant state convince the Court that there were effective remedies that were not exhausted?

4. *Futile Efforts Unnecessary*. In *Finnish Shipowners against Great Britain* (Finland v. Great Britain), 3 U.N. Rep. Int'l Arb. Awards 1479 (1934) (*Finnish Shipowners Case*), thirteen ships belonging to Finnish nationals had been requisitioned and used by the British government in wartime during 1916–1917. The Finnish shipowners sought, and were denied, compensation under British law. The Finnish Government, believing the shipowners had exhausted all local remedies, brought a claim on their behalf. The British Government, however, contended that the shipowners had not exhausted all local remedies, failing to appeal the decision of the Admiralty Transport Arbitration Board to the Court of Appeal. Sole Arbitrator Bagge disagreed, holding an attempted appeal would have been ineffective and unrealistic because the applicable law only allowed an appeal on points of law, not on findings of fact, such as the finding in this case that the ships had been requisitioned by Russia, not Great Britain. In sum, the Arbitrator held that there is no need to exhaust local remedies if it is established that such resort would be futile or that such remedies are nonexistent. Does the *Ahmadou Sadio Diallo* case echo that outcome?

If an alien claimant loses on a point of law before a court of first instance, is there an obligation to appeal even if the appellate courts regard the applicable point of law as well settled? See *Panevezys–Saldutiskis Ry. Case*

(Estonia v. Lithuania), 1939 P.C.I.J. (ser. A/B) No. 76, in which the Court stated that if it could be substantiated that the highest Lithuanian court had already given a decision in a previous case adverse to the Estonian company's claim, there would be no need to appeal in order to satisfy the local remedies rule. Id. at 18. The Court held, however, that the highest Lithuanian court had not yet pronounced upon the applicable point of law, and the Estonian claim was rejected. Id. at 20–21. See Restatement (Third) § 713, Comment *f*, § 902, Comment *k*.

If it were shown that the Finnish shipowners had lost before the Arbitration Board because they had failed to call an available witness, would the Arbitrator have held that local remedies had been exhausted? See *Ambatielos Claim* (Greece v. United Kingdom), 12 U.N. Rep. Int'l Arb. Awards 83 (1956), decided in 1956 by a special arbitral commission, which held that failure to call an essential witness in a British proceeding necessitated the rejection of a Greek national's claim. See also Bagge, Intervention on the Ground of Damage Caused to Nationals, with Particular Reference to Exhaustion of Local Remedies and the Rights of Shareholders, 34 Brit. Y.B.I.L. 162, 167–68 (1958).

5. *Waiver of the Rule by Defendant State.* A state may waive the requirement of exhaustion of local remedies, allowing claims against it to be brought by another state directly to an international tribunal. See, e.g., Convention for the Reciprocal Settlement of Claims, Sept. 8, 1923, art. V, 43 Stat. 1730, 4 Malloy at 4441 (establishing the Mexico–United States General Claims Commission and providing that no claim should be "disallowed or rejected by the Commission by the application of the general principle of international law that the legal remedies must be exhausted as a condition precedent to the validity or allowance of any claim.") Where two states have agreed to arbitrate existing disputes, will they be held impliedly to have waived the local remedies rule? Authority on this point is not uniform. Amerasinghe concludes that "it is clear that, whether such treaties are signed before or after the disputes arise, no waiver of the local remedies may be generally applied," citing, *inter alia*, the *ELSI* case. Amerasinghe, Local Remedies in International Law 252 (2d ed. 2004). An example involving an implied waiver is the Claims Settlement Declaration establishing the Iran–United States Claims Tribunal. The Declaration called for submission of claims by nationals of either party to arbitration "whether or not filed with any court" and stated that claims referred to the arbitration tribunal shall "be considered excluded from the jurisdiction of the courts of Iran or of the United States, or of any other court." Declaration of Algeria Concerning the Settlement of Claims by the United States and Iran (Algiers Declaration), art. 1, Jan. 19, 1981, 20 I.L.M. 230 (1981); see also *Am. Int'l Group v. Iran*, Award No. 93–2–3 [1983], 4 Iran–U.S. Cl. Trib. Rep. 102 (1983–III).

C.　RULE ON CONTINUOUS NATIONALITY

A state may generally assert a claim against another state arising out of an injury to an individual or a juridical entity, such as a corporation, only if the injured party has the nationality of the claimant state. The I.L.C. Articles on State Responsibility provide in Article 44 (a) that "[t]he responsibility of a State may not be invoked if * * * the claim is not brought in accordance with any applicable rule relating to the nationality of claims." One of the difficult issues is how to handle changes of the injured person's nationality that might arise before, during, or after a claim is espoused by the person's state, a matter the International Law Commission is currently studying as part of its work on diplomatic protection of nationals.

Establishing Nationality. The principles governing the circumstances under which an individual or a corporation may be treated as a national of the claimant state for various purposes, including the law of state responsibility, have been examined in Chapter 7. As discussed there, a state allegedly responsible for an injury to an alien with multiple nationalities may refuse a claim or intercession by another state if the injured person (1) is also a national of the respondent state or (2) is also a national of both a third state and the respondent state and the respondent state treats the person as its national for purposes of the conduct causing the injury. A state claim or intercession may not be refused, however, if the "dominant and effective" nationality is that of the claimant state, as a result of the injured alien's stronger ties to that state based on all relevant factors, such as extended residence, family relationships and the like. Generally, no state may assert a claim or intercede diplomatically on behalf of a stateless person, but the human rights of a stateless person are protected under international human rights law, which applies to all persons subject to a state's jurisdiction regardless of their nationality. See Chapter 13; see also Restatement (Third) § 713, Comments *c* and *d*.

Continuous Nationality Required. If the nationality of a claimant changes after the injury on which the claim is based has occurred, or the claim is assigned to a person of another nationality, or the claimant dies and leaves heirs of a different nationality, can the claim still be espoused? The International Law Commission has tentatively formulated the rule, along with certain exceptions, as follows:

1.   A State is entitled to exercise diplomatic protection in respect of a person who was a national of that State continuously from the date of injury to the date of the official presentation of the claim. Continuity is presumed if that nationality existed at both of these dates.

2.   Notwithstanding paragraph 1, a State may exercise diplomatic protection in respect of a person who is its national at the date of the official presentation of the claim but was not a national at the date of injury, provided that the person had the nationality of a predecessor State or lost his or her previous nationality and acquired, for a reason unrelated to the bringing of the claim, the nationality of the former State in a manner not inconsistent with international law.

3.   Diplomatic protection shall not be exercised by the present State of nationality in respect of a person against a former State of nationality of that person for an injury caused when that person was

a national of the former State of nationality and not of the present State of nationality.

Draft Article 10, Report of the International Law Commission, Fifty-eighth Session, U.N. Doc. A/61/10, at 13, 19 (2006). See also 8 Whiteman at 1243; 5 Hackworth at 804–08; 1 Oppenheim at 512–13; Brownlie, Principles of Public International Law 460 (6th ed. 2003) (quoting Oppenheim); Duchesne, Continuous–Nationality–of–Claims Principle: Its Historical Development and Current Relevance to Investor-state Investment Disputes, 36 Geo. Wash. Int'l L. Rev. 783 (2004). In explaining the source of the general rule, a NAFTA arbitral tribunal explained:

> As with most hoary international rules of law, the requirement of continuous nationality was grounded in comity. It was not normally the business of one nation to be interfering into the manner in which another nation handled its internal commerce. Such interference would be justified only to protect the interests of one of its own nationals. If that tie were ended, so was the justification.

Loewen Group v. United States, ICSID Case No. ARB(AF)/98/3, Award, para. 230 (2003) http://www.state.gov/documents/organization/22094.pdf.

Contracting Around the Rule. The rule may be modified by agreement between the governments of the claimant and respondent states. For example, the agreement establishing the Eritrea Ethiopia Claims Commission provided that: "In appropriate cases, each party may file claims on behalf of persons of Ethiopian or Eritrean origin who may not be its nationals. Such claims shall be considered by the Commission on the same basis as claims submitted on behalf of that party's nationals." Peace Agreement, Ethiopia–Eritrea, art. 5(9), Dec. 12, 2001, 40 I.L.M. 260 (2001). Thereafter, Eritrea sought to file a claim against Ethiopia before the Commission for injuries to certain Ethiopian nationals, but made the mistake of styling the claim as a claim of Eritrea itself, rather than as claims of the Ethiopian nationals that were being submitted on their behalf by Eritrea. Because of the improper method of filing, the Commission dismissed Eritrea's claim for any damage directly sustained by those Ethiopian nationals. As the Commission explained:

> Article 5, paragraph 9, creates an exceptional procedure empowering the Commission to decide claims for the benefit of persons of Eritrean origin who are not Eritrean nationals. The wording "on behalf of" indicates that the claim remains the property of the individual and that any eventual recovery of damages should accrue to that person. However, Eritrea's Statements of Claim 15, 16 and 23 present the injuries and losses suffered by its nationals and by Ethiopians of Eritrean origin as its own. Such claims based on injuries to non-nationals made for Eritrea's own account, and not on behalf of the affected individuals, are outside the Commission's jurisdiction.

Partial Award, Civilian Claims, Eritrea's Claims 15, 16, 23 & 27–32, Dec. 17, 2004, 44 I.L.M. 601, para. 19 (2005); see also id. at para. 90 ("the State of Eritrea could not claim for injuries to itself based on injuries suffered by persons who were solely Ethiopian nationals when they were injured").

The Problem of the Corporate Form. In *Barcelona Traction, Light and Power Company* (Belgium v. Spain), 1970 I.C.J. 3, the International Court found that Belgium could not pursue an international claim against Spain for injury to a Canadian corporation, even though there were Belgian shareholders in that corporation. Excerpts of that case appear at p. 482 (with respect to identifying corporate nationality) and p. 516 (with respect to identifying some norms as *erga omnes* obligations). That rule is developed and codified in the recent work of the International Law Commission as follows:

> A State of nationality of shareholders in a corporation shall not be entitled to exercise diplomatic protection in respect of such shareholders in the case of an injury to the corporation unless:
>
> (a) The corporation has ceased to exist according to the law of the State of incorporation for a reason unrelated to the injury; or
>
> (b) The corporation had, at the date of injury, the nationality of the State alleged to be responsible for causing the injury, and incorporation in that State was required by it as a precondition for doing business there.

Draft Article 11, Report of the International Law Commission, Fifty-eighth Session, U.N. Doc. A/61/10, at 13, 19 (2006). Notwithstanding this rule, is it possible for a claim to be brought on behalf of shareholders for direct injury to them? Consider the following excerpt.

AHMADOU SADIO DIALLO (GUINEA v. DEMOCRATIC REPUBLIC OF THE CONGO)

International Court of Justice, 2007
2007 I.C.J. ___

54. In support of its diplomatic protection claim on behalf of Mr. Diallo as *associé*, Guinea refers to the Judgement in the *Barcelona Traction* case, where, having ruled that "an act directed against and infringing only the company's rights does not involve responsibility towards the shareholders, even if their interests are affected" (*I.C.J. Reports 1970*, p. 36, para. 46), the Court added that "[t]he situation is different if the act complained of is aimed at the direct rights of the shareholders as such" (*ibid.*, p. 36, para. 47). Guinea further claims that this position of the Court was taken up in Article 12 of the ILC's draft Articles on Diplomatic Protection, which provides that:

> "To the extent that an internationally wrongful act of a State causes direct injury to the rights of shareholders as such, as distinct from those of the corporation itself, the State of nationality of any such shareholders is entitled to exercise diplomatic protection in respect of its nationals."

55.   According to Guinea, the direct rights of Mr. Diallo as a shareholder of Africom–Zaire and Africontainers–Zaire are essentially determined by the Decree of 27 February 1887 on commercial corporations. This text is said to confer on him firstly a series of "property rights", including the right to dividends from these companies, and secondly a series of "functional rights", including the right to control, supervise and manage the companies. Guinea claims that the Congolese investment code also affords Mr. Diallo certain additional rights as shareholder, for example "the right to share of the profits of his companies" and "a right of ownership in his companies, in particular in respect of his shares". Guinea thus takes the view that it is confining itself, in its claim, to the violation of the rights enjoyed by Mr. Diallo in respect of the companies, including his rights of supervision, control and management, and that it is therefore not confusing his rights with those of the company.

* * *

64.   The exercise by a State of diplomatic protection on behalf of a natural or legal person, who is *associé* or shareholder, having its nationality, seeks to engage the responsibility of another State for an injury caused to that person by an internationally wrongful act committed by that State. Ultimately, this is no more than the diplomatic protection of a natural or legal person as defined by Article 1 of the ILC draft Articles; what amounts to the internationally wrongful act, in the case of *associés* or shareholders, is the violation by the respondent State of their direct rights in relation to a legal person, direct rights that are defined by the domestic law of that State, as accepted by both Parties, moreover. On this basis, diplomatic protection of the direct rights of *associés* of a [*sociétés privées à responsabilité limitée* (SPRL)] or shareholders of a public limited company is not to be regarded as an exception to the general legal régime of diplomatic protection for natural or legal persons, as derived from customary international law.

65.   Having considered all of the arguments advanced by the Parties, the Court finds that Guinea does indeed have standing in this case in so far as its action involves a person of its nationality, Mr. Diallo, and is directed against the allegedly unlawful acts of the DRC which are said to have infringed his rights, particularly his direct rights as *associé* of the two companies Africom–Zaire and Africontainers–Zaire.

66.   The Court notes that Mr. Diallo, who was *associé* in Africom–Zaire and Africontainers–Zaire, also held the position of *gérant* in each of them. An *associé* of an SPRL holds *parts sociales* in its capital, while the *gérant* is an organ of the company acting on its behalf. It is not for the Court to determine, at this stage in the proceedings, which specific rights appertain to the status of *associé* and which to the position of *gérant* of an SPRL under Congolese law. It is at the merits stage, as appropriate, that the Court will have to define the precise nature, content and limits of these rights. It is also at that stage of the proceedings that it will be for the Court, if need be, to assess the effects on these various rights of the

action against Mr. Diallo. There is no need for the Court to rule on these substantive matters in order to be able to dispose of the preliminary objections raised by the Respondent.

67. In view of the foregoing, the Court concludes that the objection of inadmissibility raised by the DRC due to Guinea's lack of standing to protect Mr. Diallo cannot be upheld in so far as it concerns his direct rights as *associé* of Africom–Zaire and Africontainers–Zaire.

[The Court then considered whether Guinea might advance a claim encompassing harms to the company itself based on a "theory of substitution," which would allow for a deviation from the normal rule of state responsibility in exceptional circumstances. The Court had hinted that such an exception might exist in paragraph 93 of its 1970 *Barcelona Traction* decision. See p. 489].

87. Since its dictum in the *Barcelona Traction* case * * *, the Court has not had occasion to rule on whether, in international law, there is indeed an exception to the general rule "that the right of diplomatic protection of a company belongs to its national State" * * *, which allows for protection of the shareholders by their own national State "by substitution", and on the reach of any such exception. It is true that in the case concerning *Elettronica Sicula S.p.A. (ELSI) (United States of America v. Italy)*, the Chamber of the Court allowed a claim by the United States of America on behalf of two United States corporations (who held 100 per cent of the shares in an Italian company), in relation to alleged acts by the Italian authorities injuring the rights of latter company. However, in doing so, the Chamber based itself not on customary international law but on a Treaty of Friendship, Commerce and Navigation between the two countries directly granting to their nationals, corporations and associations certain rights in relation to their participation in corporations and associations having the nationality of the other State. The Court will now examine whether the exception invoked by Guinea is part of customary international law, as claimed by the latter.

88. The Court is bound to note that, in contemporary international law, the protection of the rights of companies and the rights of their shareholders, and the settlement of the associated disputes, are essentially governed by bilateral or multilateral agreements for the protection of foreign investments, such as treaties for the promotion and protection of foreign investments, and the Washington Convention of 18 March 1965 on the Settlement of Investment Disputes between States and Nationals of Other States, which created an International Centre for Settlement of Investment Disputes (ICSID), and also by contracts between States and foreign investors. In that context, the role of diplomatic protection somewhat faded, as in practice recourse is only made to it in rare cases where treaty régimes do not exist or have proved inoperative. It is in this particular and relatively limited context that the question of protection by substitution might be raised. The theory of protection by substitution seeks indeed to offer protection to the foreign shareholders of a company

who could not rely on the benefit of an international treaty and to whom no other remedy is available, the allegedly unlawful acts having been committed against the company by the State of its nationality. Protection by "substitution" would therefore appear to constitute the very last resort for the protection of foreign investments.

89. The Court, having carefully examined State practice and decisions of international courts and tribunals in respect of diplomatic protection of *associés* and shareholders, is of the opinion that these do not reveal—at least at the present time—an exception in customary international law allowing for protection by substitution, such as is relied on by Guinea.

D. WAIVER BY ALIEN OF CLAIM OR RIGHT TO DIPLOMATIC PROTECTION

It is generally agreed that if an alien injured by a state in a manner wrongful under international law waives or settles the claim prior to diplomatic intervention by the state of which the alien is a national, then the waiver or settlement is effective as a defense on behalf of the respondent state, provided the waiver or settlement is not made under duress. The result appears to be different if the waiver or purported settlement is made by the alien after the alien's state has espoused the claim because that state enjoys exclusive control once it has asserted a claim against the respondent state. See Restatement (Third) § 713, Reporters' Note 6.

More troublesome problems arose in the twentieth century from the widespread adoption by Latin American states of statutory and constitutional provisions embodying the "Calvo Doctrine," named after Argentine jurist Carlos Calvo. This doctrine essentially asserted that jurisdiction over disputes involving aliens lies solely within the country in which the alien was harmed under that country's laws. To that end, a number of states not only enacted national laws embodying the Calvo Doctrine, but additionally obligated aliens doing business under contract with the state to agree to a so-called "Calvo clause." Under this clause, the alien was required to submit all disputes to the courts of the host state and renounce all claims to diplomatic intercession by the state of which the alien was a national. See Shea, The Calvo Clause 24 (1955); Graham, Note, The Calvo Clause: Its Current Status as a Contractual Renunciation of Diplomatic Protection, 6 Tex. Int'l L.F. 289 (1971).

Are Calvo clauses effective as a matter of international law? An agreement between the North American Dredging Company and the Government of Mexico contained a Calvo clause requiring the contractor to submit any contractual dispute solely to the laws of Mexico and to waive all rights of diplomatic intercession by the United States. The United States–Mexico General Claims Commission, however, held that the contractor had only waived his right to protection by the United States in matters connected with the fulfillment, execution, or enforcement of the contract, thereby retaining the right of his Government to extend protection to him against violations of international law. *North American Dredging Co. Case* (United States v. Mexico), [1927] Opinions of Commissioners 21, 22, 4 U.N. Rep. Int'l Arb. Awards 26, 26–27 (1926); see also *Mexican Union Ry, Ltd. Case* (Great Britain v. Mexico), Mexico–Great Britain Claims Commission, 5 U.N. Rep. Int'l Arb. Awards 115, 120 (1930) (finding that no person could "deprive the Government of his country of its undoubted right to apply international remedies to violations of international law committed to his hurt. * * * For the Government the contract is *res inter alios acta*, by which its liberty of action can not be prejudiced.").

The United States and certain other states deny the validity of the Calvo Doctrine and the Calvo clause on the ground that the right of diplomatic protection is not the injured national's to waive. In recent years, many Latin American states have departed from their adherence to the Calvo doctrine, and entered into bilateral investment agreements that incorporate international law standards of treatment and that require settlement of disputes through international arbitration. See Manning–Cabrol, Note, The Imminent Death of the Calvo Clause and the Rebirth of the Calvo Principle: Equality of Foreign and National Investors, 26 Law & Pol'y Int'l Bus. 1169 (1995); Wiesner, ANCOM: A New Attitude Toward Foreign Investment?, 24 U. Miami Inter–Am. L. Rev. 435 (1993). For example, in the United States–Argentina bilateral investment treaty, Nov. 14, 1991, 31 I.L.M. 124 (1992), Argentina itself abandoned the Calvo Doctrine and accepted binding international dispute settlement between the investor and the host government under the rules of ICSID or UNCITRAL or other institution agreed to by the parties, with no requirement for prior exhaustion of remedies in the host country. See id. art. VII. Moreover, the treaty embodies the rule that expropriation must be accompanied by "prompt, adequate and effective compensation"—the Hull formula (discussed *supra* Section 3)—which had been an anathema to most Latin American countries since the 1930s. See id. art. IV(1).

E.   INVESTOR–STATE DISPUTE SETTLEMENT

So as to be effective, treaties protective of aliens and juridical entities typically contain dispute settlement clauses. The earlier FCN treaties usually provided for inter-state dispute settlement at the International Court of Justice. The more recent BITs, as well as the North American Free Trade Agreement (NAFTA), provide for inter-state dispute settlement on certain matters, but also provide for dispute settlement directly between an injured investor and the state in which the investment was made (investor-state disputes). Such agreements typically provide that the investor claimant may not be of the nationality of the defendant state. See UNCTAD, Investor–State Disputes Arising from Investment Treaties (2005).

Many BITs provide for resolution of investor-state disputes under the rules and procedures of the International Centre for Settlement of Investment Disputes (ICSID). The ICSID Centre is available whenever the investor's state and the defendant state have ratified the ICSID Convention. If either has not ratified the ICSID Convention, then resort is made to the "Additional Facility" of the Centre. Though panels are formed under ICSID on an *ad hoc* basis, and may be construing a range of legal sources (such as a specific BIT, customary international law, or national law), empirical analysis of some 100 cases over a ten year period suggests that there is considerable convergence in the methodological approach taken by ISCID tribunals, such as on how treaties should be interpreted and what sources are important in determining customary international law. See Fauchald, The Legal Reasoning of ICSID Tribunals—An Empirical Analysis, 19 E.J.I.L. 301 (2008). As such, it would appear that ICSID dispute settlement is providing a relatively predictable legal framework for the resolution of investment disputes.

Nevertheless, the jurisprudence of these tribunals has occasioned criticism. For example, decisions rendered by ICSID tribunals typically are not appealable; should they be? See Gantz, An Appellate Mechanism for Review of Arbitral Decisions in Investor–State Disputes: Prospects and Challenges, 39 Vand. J. Transnat'l L. 39 (2006); see also Franck, The Legitimacy Crisis in Investment Treaty Arbitration: Privatizing Public International Law Through Inconsistent Decisions, 73 Fordham L. Rev. 1521 (2005).

One issue of contemporary interest relates to the *Nottebohm Case* (Liechtenstein v. Guatemala), 1955 I.C.J. 4. See Chapter 8, Section 2(C). In that case, the International Court of Justice found that Liechtenstein could not bring a claim against Guatemala on behalf of Nottebohm because, while he had obtained Liechtenstein nationality, Nottebohm had very few contacts with Liechtenstein, such that the Court said there was no "genuine link" between Liechtenstein and Nottebohm. That decision in turn influenced the emergence of the doctrine on "dominant and effective" nationality, which has been applied in the context of a claim brought on behalf of a dual national by one of the national's state against the other. See Chapter 8, Section 2(D). Should concepts such as "genuine link" and "dominant" nationality, which arose in the context of state-to-state claims, apply to investor-state claims as well?

Nottebohm and its progeny could potentially apply in two contexts. First, the *claimant investor* might argue that, although under the nationality law of the respondent state the claimant technically has the nationality of the respondent, the claimant also possesses a different nationality that is more dominant and that allows the claimant to qualify as a "foreign" investor. Second, the *respondent state* might argue that, although the claimant formally has a foreign nationality, the relationship of the investor to that state of nationality is so ephemeral that such nationality cannot be asserted as against the respondent. Although such arguments have been made before international tribunals, to date no clear precedent has emerged indicating whether and how the *Nottebohm* line of reasoning applies to investor-state claims. See Champion Trading Co. v.

Arab Republic of Egypt, 19 ICSID Rev.-F.I.J.J. 275, 288 (2004) (discussing the concept but dismissing the claim because the underlying treaty explicitly excluded claims by dual nationals); Soufraki v. United Arab Emirates, ICSID Case. No. ARB/02/7, Award of July 7, 2004, para. 84 (discussing the concept, but dismissing the claim because the claimant did not possess the asserted Italian nationality on the relevant dates). In two cases, the tribunal declined to apply the "genuine link" test on grounds that the underlying treaty provided that the nationality of an investor be determined in accordance with the law of the investor's state (not international law), and further that the concept was only relevant in situations involving dual nationality. See Siag v. Egypt, 46 I.L.M. 863 (2007); Micula v. Romania, ICSID Case No. ARB/05/20, Award of Sept. 24, 2008, paras 101–104. Do you think the *Nottebohm* principle should be available to assist claimants in establishing a foreign nationality in investor-state disputes? Or do you think that the *Nottebohm* principle is designed only to protect a respondent state? Should the principle be viewed as in conflict with the national law of the investor's state, or is it better seen as accepting the application of that law but disallowing invocation of nationality against the respondent state in certain circumstances? Why should the principle only apply in situations of dual nationality?

SECTION 5. REPARATION FOR INJURY TO ALIENS

INTERNATIONAL LAW COMMISSION COMMENTARY ON ARTICLE 36 OF THE I.L.C. ARTICLES ON STATE RESPONSIBILITY

[2001] II(2) Yb.I.L.C. 101–05 (footnotes omitted)

(16) Within the field of diplomatic protection, a good deal of guidance is available as to appropriate compensation standards and methods of valuation, especially as concerns personal injury and takings of, or damage to, tangible property. It is well-established that a State may seek compensation in respect of personal injuries suffered by its officials or nationals, over and above any direct injury it may itself have suffered in relation to the same event. Compensable personal injury encompasses not only associated material losses, such as loss of earnings and earning capacity, medical expenses and the like, but also non-material damage suffered by the individual (sometimes, though not universally, referred to as "moral damage" in national legal systems). Non-material damage is generally understood to encompass loss of loved ones, pain and suffering as well as the affront to sensibilities associated with an intrusion on the person, home or private life. No less than material injury sustained by the injured State, non-material damage is financially assessable and may be the subject of a claim of compensation, as stressed in the *"Lusitania"* case. The umpire considered that international law provides compensation for mental suffering, injury to feelings, humiliation, shame, degradation, loss

of social position or injury to credit and reputation, such injuries being "very real, and the mere fact that they are difficult to measure or estimate by money standards make them none the less real and affords no reason why the injured person should not be compensated ...".

(17) International courts and tribunals have undertaken the assessment of compensation for personal injury on numerous occasions. For example, in the *M/V "Saiga"* case, the tribunal held that Saint Vincent and the Grenadines' entitlement to compensation included damages for injury to the crew, their unlawful arrest, detention and other forms of ill-treatment.

(18) Historically, compensation for personal injury suffered by nationals or officials of a State arose mainly in the context of mixed claims commissions dealing with State responsibility for injury to aliens. Claims commissions awarded compensation for personal injury both in cases of wrongful death and deprivation of liberty. Where claims were made in respect of wrongful death, damages were generally based on an evaluation of the losses of the surviving heirs or successors, calculated in accordance with the well-known formula of Umpire Parker in the *"Lusitania"* case:

> Estimate the amounts (*a*) which the decedent, had he not been killed, would probably have contributed to the claimant, add thereto (*b*) the pecuniary value to such claimant of the deceased's personal services in claimant's care, education, or supervision, and also add (*c*) reasonable compensation for such mental suffering or shock, if any, caused by the violent severing of family ties, as claimant may actually have sustained by reason of such death. The sum of these estimates reduced to its present cash value, will generally represent the loss sustained by claimant.

In cases of deprivation of liberty, arbitrators sometimes awarded a set amount for each day spent in detention. Awards were often increased when abusive conditions of confinement accompanied the wrongful arrest and imprisonment, resulting in particularly serious physical or psychological injury.

(19) Compensation for personal injury has also been dealt with by human rights bodies, in particular the European Court of Human Rights and the Inter–American Court of Human Rights. Awards of compensation encompass material losses (loss of earnings, pensions, medical expenses, etc.) and non-material damage (pain and suffering, mental anguish, humiliation, loss of enjoyment of life and loss of companionship or consortium), the latter usually quantified on the basis of an equitable assessment. Hitherto, amounts of compensation or damages awarded or recommended by these bodies have been modest. Nonetheless, the decisions of human rights bodies on compensation draw on principles of reparation under general international law.

(20) In addition to a large number of lump-sum compensation agreements covering multiple claims, property claims of nationals arising out of an internationally wrongful act have been adjudicated by a wide range of

ad hoc and standing tribunals and commissions, with reported cases spanning two centuries. Given the diversity of adjudicating bodies, the awards exhibit considerable variability. Nevertheless, they provide useful principles to guide the determination of compensation under this head of damage.

(21) The reference point for valuation purposes is the loss suffered by the claimant whose property rights have been infringed. This loss is usually assessed by reference to specific heads of damage relating to (i) compensation for capital value; (ii) compensation for loss of profits; and (iii) incidental expenses.

(22) Compensation reflecting the capital value of property taken or destroyed as the result of an internationally wrongful act is generally assessed on the basis of the "fair market value" of the property lost. The method used to assess "fair market value", however, depends on the nature of the asset concerned. Where the property in question or comparable property is freely traded on an open market, value is more readily determined. In such cases, the choice and application of asset-based valuation methods based on market data and the physical properties of the assets is relatively unproblematic, apart from evidentiary difficulties associated with long outstanding claims. Where the property interests in question are unique or unusual, for example, art works or other cultural property, or are not the subject of frequent or recent market transactions, the determination of value is more difficult. This may be true, for example, in respect of certain business entities in the nature of a going concern, especially if shares are not regularly traded.

(23) Decisions of various *ad hoc* tribunals since 1945 have been dominated by claims in respect of nationalized business entities. The preferred approach in these cases has been to examine the assets of the business, making allowance for goodwill and profitability, as appropriate. This method has the advantage of grounding compensation as much as possible in some objective assessment of value linked to the tangible asset backing of the business. The value of goodwill and other indicators of profitability may be uncertain, unless derived from information provided by a recent sale or acceptable arms-length offer. Yet, for profitable business entities where the whole is greater than the sum of the parts, compensation would be incomplete without paying due regard to such factors.

(24) An alternative valuation method for capital loss is the determination of net book value, i.e. the difference between the total assets of the business and total liabilities as shown on its books. Its advantages are that the figures can be determined by reference to market costs, they are normally drawn from a contemporaneous record, and they are based on data generated for some other purpose than supporting the claim. Accordingly, net book value (or some variant of this method) has been employed to assess the value of businesses. The limitations of the method lie in the reliance on historical figures, the use of accounting principles which tend

to undervalue assets, especially in periods of inflation, and the fact that the purpose for which figures were produced does not take account of the compensation context and any rules specific to it. The balance sheet may contain an entry for goodwill, but the reliability of such figures depends upon their proximity to the moment of an actual sale.

(25) In cases where a business is not a going concern, so-called "break-up", "liquidation" or "dissolution" value is generally employed. In such cases, no provision is made for value over and above the market value of the individual assets. Techniques have been developed to construct, in the absence of actual transactions, hypothetical values representing what a willing buyer and willing seller might agree.

(26) Since 1945, valuation techniques have been developed to factor in different elements of risk and probability. The discounted cash flow (DCF) method has gained some favour, especially in the context of calculations involving income over a limited duration, as in the case of wasting assets. Although developed as a tool for assessing commercial value, it can also be useful in the context of calculating value for compensation purposes. But difficulties can arise in the application of the DCF method to establish capital value in the compensation context. The method analyses a wide range of inherently speculative elements, some of which have a significant impact upon the outcome (e.g. discount rates, currency fluctuations, inflation figures, commodity prices, interest rates and other commercial risks). This has led tribunals to adopt a cautious approach to the use of the method. Hence, although income-based methods have been accepted in principle, there has been a decided preference for asset-based methods. A particular concern is the risk of double-counting which arises from the relationship between the capital value of an enterprise and its contractually based profits.

(27) * * * [I]n certain cases compensation for loss of profits may be appropriate. International tribunals have included an award for loss of profits in assessing compensation: for example, the decisions in the *Cape Horn Pigeon* case and *Sapphire International Petroleums Ltd.* v. *National Iranian Oil Company*. Loss of profits played a role in the *Factory at Chorzów* case itself, the Permanent Court deciding that the injured party should receive the value of property by the way of damages not as it stood at the time expropriation but at the time of indemnification. Awards for loss of profits have also been made in respect of contract-based lost profits in *Libyan American Oil Company (LIAMCO)* and in some ICSID arbitrations. Nevertheless, lost profits have not been as commonly awarded in practice as compensation for accrued losses. Tribunals have been reluctant to provide compensation for claims with inherently speculative elements. When compared with tangible assets, profits (and intangible assets which are income-based) are relatively vulnerable to commercial and political risks, and increasingly so the further into the future projections are made. In cases where lost future profits have been awarded, it has been where an anticipated income stream has attained sufficient attributes to be considered a legally protected interest of sufficient certainty to be compensable.

This has normally been achieved by virtue of contractual arrangements or, in some cases, a well-established history of dealings.

(28) Three categories of loss of profits may be distinguished: first, lost profits from income-producing property during a period when there has been no interference with title as distinct from temporary loss of use; secondly, lost profits from income-producing property between the date of taking of title and adjudication; and thirdly, lost future profits in which profits anticipated after the date of adjudication are awarded.

(29) The first category involves claims for loss of profits due to the temporary loss of use and enjoyment of the income-producing asset. In these cases there is no interference with title and hence in the relevant period the loss compensated is the income to which the claimant was entitled by virtue of undisturbed ownership.

(30) The second category of claims relates to the unlawful taking of income-producing property. In such cases lost profits have been awarded for the period up to the time adjudication. In the *Factory at Chorzów* case, this took the form of re-invested income, representing profits from the time of taking to the time of adjudication. In the *Norwegian Shipowners' Claims* case, lost profits were similarly not awarded for any period beyond the date of adjudication. Once the capital value of income-produced property has been restored through the mechanism of compensation, funds paid by way of compensation can once again be invested to re-establish an income stream. Although the rationale for the award of lost profits in these cases is less clearly articulated, it may be attributed to a recognition of the claimant's continuing beneficial interest in the property up to the moment when potential restitution is converted to a compensation payment.

(31) The third category of claims for loss of profits arises in the context of concessions and other contractually protected interests. Again, in such cases, lost future income has sometimes been awarded. In the case of contracts, it is the future income stream which is compensated, up to the time when the legal recognition of entitlement ends. In some contracts this is immediate, e.g. where the contract is determinable at the instance of the State, or where some other basis for contractual termination exists. Or it may arise from some future date dictated by the terms of the contract itself.

(32) In other cases, lost profits have been excluded on the basis that they were not sufficiently established as a legally protected interest. In the *Oscar Chinn* case a monopoly was not accorded the status of an acquired right. In the *Asian Agriculture Products* case, a claim for lost profits by a newly established business was rejected for lack of evidence of established earnings. Claims for lost profits are also subject to the usual range of limitations on the recovery of damages, such as causation, remoteness, evidentiary requirements and accounting principles, which seek to discount speculative elements from projected figures.

TECNICAS MEDIOAMBIENTALES TECMED S.A. ("TECMED") v. MEXICO

ICSID Case No. ARB(AF)/00/2, Award, 43 I.L.M. 133 (2004) (some footnotes omitted)

[For the facts of this case, and the arbitral tribunal's findings of substantive violations of the U.S.–Spain Agreement on the Promotion and Reciprocal Protection of Investments Between Spain and Mexico (Agreement), see *supra* this Chapter, p. 1069.]

F. Compensation. Restitution in kind.

183. The Claimant's claim for compensation or restitution in kind is based upon the provisions of Title VII(I) of the Appendix to the Agreement, which contemplates those two options. The Claimant requests restitution in kind—which the Claimant considers "absolutely impossible"—only secondarily, as the Claimant primarily seeks monetary damages. The Arbitral Tribunal considers that monetary damages paid to the Claimant as compensation for the loss of the investment constitutes an adequate satisfaction of the Claimant's claim under the Agreement. Therefore, and taking into account that the Claimant primarily seeks monetary damages, the Arbitral Tribunal will not consider the admissibility or inadmissibility of the restitution in kind in this case.

* * *

195. On the basis of its own valuation, taking into account the Landfill's market value of US$4,028,788 upon its acquisition and adding the investments made thereafter according to Cytrar's financial statements for 1996, 1997 and 1998, and the profits for two years of operation following the Resolution date, the Arbitral Tribunal finds that such market value as of November 25, 1998, was US $5,553,017.12. Although the Claimant's expert witness assessed the value of such additional investments at US$1,951,473,237, no documentary evidence has been filed to support such amount, and such evidence has not been alleged by the Claimant in its closing statement. The Respondent challenges such amount in its closing statement on the basis of accounting data by comparing the fiscal years mentioned above, and estimates such amount to be US$439,000. This amount has been accepted by the Arbitral Tribunal. Regarding the profits for the two additional years of operation, the Arbitral Tribunal has calculated such profits at the amount of US$1,085,-229.12. For this, the Arbitral Tribunal has considered that an informed buyer of the Landfill would have assumed that it had to be relocated due to the community pressure and that such relocation might take about two years. In such calculation, the Arbitral Tribunal has further considered that the projections clearly stated that Cytrar was increasing its revenues, the value of its clientele and goodwill as an on going business related to the Landfill exploitation, and the other considerations * * * which, in the opinion of the Arbitral Tribunal, cannot be ignored upon establishing the economic compensation owed to the Claimant for the loss of the market

value of its investment. The Arbitral Tribunal finds that it is not appropriate to deduct from such amount, which also reflects the principle that compensation of such loss must amount to an integral compensation for the damage suffered, including lost profits,[239] the cost of closing down the Landfill due to a decision attributable to the Respondent that the Arbitral Tribunal has found to be in violation of the Agreement.

196.   The Claimant requests that any compensation awarded to it accrue compound interest at a rate of 6%. The Arbitral Tribunal has not found any specific allegation by the Respondent regarding this point. The application of compound interest has been accepted in a number of awards, and it has been stated that:

> ... compound (as opposed to simple) interest is at present deemed appropriate as the standard of international law in [...] expropriation cases.[241]

In connection with this case, in the opinion of the Arbitral Tribunal, application of compound interest is justified as part of the integral compensation owed to the Claimant as a result of the loss of its investment.

197.   Therefore, the amount of US $5,533,017.12 will accrue interest at an annual rate of 6%, compounded annually, commencing on November 25, 1998, until the effective and full payment by the Respondent of all amounts payable by the Respondent to the Claimant under this award.[36]

198.   The Arbitral Tribunal finds no reason to award compensation for moral damage, as requested by the Claimant, due to the absence of evidence proving that the actions attributable to the Respondent that the Arbitral Tribunal has found to be in violation of the Agreement have also affected the Claimant's reputation and therefore caused the loss of business opportunities for the Claimant. In addition, the Arbitral Tribunal has not found that the adverse press coverage for Tecmed or Cytrar of the events regarding the Landfill, was fostered by the Respondent or that it was the result of actions attributable to the Respondent.

199.   Promptly after effective payment to the Claimant of all sums payable to it by the Respondent under this award, the Claimant shall take all the necessary steps to transfer, or cause to be transferred, to the Respondent, or to a nominee designated by the Respondent, the assets forming the Landfill.

---

239.   P.C.I.J. *Chorzów Factory* case, (1938) P.C.I.J., Ser. A, 17, p. 29, 47.

241.   Award in ICSID case ARB/99/6 *Middle East Cement Shipping and Handling Co. S.A v Arab Republic of Egypt*, April 12, 2002, 174, p. 42. *See also*: award of December 8, 2000, in ICSID case ARB/98/4, *Wena Hotels Ltd. v Arab Republic of Egypt*, 41 I.L.M. 896 (2002), specially 128–129, p. 919; award in ICSID case No. ARB/96/1 *Compañia del Desarrollo de Santa Elena S.A. v Republic of Costa Rica*, 15 ICSID Law Review–Foreign Investment Law Journal, p. 167; specially 96–106, p. 200–202 (2000); award in ICSID case no. ARB(AF)/97/1 *Metalclad Corporation v United Mexican States*, 16 Mealey's International Arbitration Report, A–1; specially 128, pp. 41–42 (A–16) (2000).

36.   Award in ICSID case No. ARB/84/3 *Southern Pacific Properties (Middle East) Limited v Arab Republic of Egypt*, 8 Foreign Investment Law Journal–ICSID Law Review, p[.] 328, specially 234–235, p. 393 (1993).

200. Taking into account that the Claimant has been successful only with respect to some of its claims and that the challenges or defenses filed by the Respondent were also admitted partially, each Party will bear its own costs, expenses and legal counsel fees. The costs incurred by the Arbitral Tribunal and ICSID will be shared equally between the Claimant and the Respondent.

G. Decision

201. Therefore, the Arbitral Tribunal finds as follows:

1. The Respondent has breached its obligations under the Agreement set forth in Articles 4(1) and 5(1).

2. The Respondent will pay the Claimant the amount of US$5,533,-017.12, plus a compound interest on such amount at an annual rate of 6%, commencing on November 25, 1998, until the effective and full payment by the Respondent of all amounts payable by the Respondent to the Claimant under this award.

3. Promptly after effective and full payment to the Claimant of all sums payable to it by the Respondent under this award, the Claimant shall take all the necessary steps to transfer, or cause to be transferred, to the Respondent, or to a nominee designated by the Respondent, the assets forming the Landfill.

4. Each Party will bear its own costs, expenses and legal counsel fees. The costs incurred by the Arbitral Tribunal and ICSID will be shared equally between the Claimant and the Respondent.

5. Any claim or petition filed in this arbitration and not admitted herein will be considered rejected.

NOTES

1. *Relevance of Rules on Inter–State Remedies.* When an act or omission attributed to a state causes injury to an alien in violation of international law, the state of which the injured alien is a national has, as against the responsible state, the same remedies generally available between states for violation of customary international law, as discussed in Chapter 8, Section 5. The information set forth in this section is supplemental to those remedies.

2. *Measuring Derivative Harm.* When a state asserts a claim based on responsibility of another state for an injury to one of its nationals, the state's claim is essentially derivative in nature. As such, when a state's claim arises from an injury to one of its nationals, reparation often takes the form of a monetary payment measured by the damages suffered by its national; the injury to the dignity or sovereignty of the state is frequently treated as having only theoretical or symbolic significance. The Permanent Court of International Justice observed in *Factory at Chorzów,* 1928 P.C.I.J. (ser. A) No. 17, at 28:

Rights or interests of an individual the violation of which rights causes damage are always in a different plane to rights belonging to a State, which rights may also be infringed by the same act. The damage suffered by an individual is never therefore identical in kind with that which will be suffered by a State; it can only afford a convenient scale for the calculation of the reparation due to the State.

In unusual circumstances, reparation might also include additional monetary damages for the injury to the claimant state. For discussion of the relationship between the injury to an individual and to a state of which he is a national in fixing the measure of reparation, see *Laura M.B. Janes Claim* (United States v. Mexico), 4 U.N. Rep. Int'l Arb. Awards 82 (1926).

3. *The Harm Must Be Caused by the Wrongful Act*. Difficulties sometimes arise in attributing responsibility to the delinquent state for the damages suffered by an individual claimant. A state is ordinarily responsible only for the damages caused by its delinquency. Where the delinquency is a failure to apprehend and punish a private person who has injured an alien or his property, the offending state has not damaged the claimant except in so far as the state's delinquency prevents the claimant from bringing a claim against the responsible person. If, as is often the case, an action against the private wrongdoer would be fruitless, the delinquent state has not caused any damage to the claimant. International tribunals have sometimes avoided such a result by finding that the delinquent state's lack of diligence in apprehending or punishing the private wrongdoer amounted to condoning the injury and imposed derivative liability on the state, or by finding that the claimant suffered grief, mistrust, and lack of safety resulting from the state's failure to apprehend or punish the wrongdoer. See *Poggioli Case* (Italy v. Venezuela), 10 U.N. Rep. Int'l Arb. Awards 669, 689 (1903); *Laura M.B. Janes Claim* (United States v. Mexico), 4 U.N. Rep. Int'l Arb. Awards 82 (1926). Under either theory, damages have usually been measured by the loss suffered by the individual claimant rather than by the gravity of the state's delinquency. See 1 Whiteman, Damages in International Law 39, 721–44, 788 (1937); Brierly, The Theory of Implied State Complicity in International Claims, 9 Brit. Y.B.I.L. 42 (1928); Freeman, The International Responsibility of States for Denial of Justice 367–69 (1938). But cf. *William T. Way Claim* (United States v. Mexico), 4 U.N. Rep. Int'l Arb. Awards 391 (1928); *S.S. "I'm Alone" Case* (Canada v. United States), 3 U.N. Rep. Int'l Arb. Awards 1609 (1935).

4. *Scope of Attributable Harm*. Even where the wrongful act has caused harm in a "but for" sense of causation, there are limits within international law on the scope of harm that will be compensated. Tribunals generally speak of "proximate cause" and tend to disallow damages which are "remote," "indirect," or not proximately caused by the delinquency. See *Administrative Decision No. II* (United States v. Germany), Mixed Claims Commission, Administrative Decisions and Opinions to June 30, 1925, 5, 12–13, 7 U.N. Rep. Int'l Arb. Awards 23, 29–30 (1923). Whatever particular damages will be allowed depends on the particular circumstances of each case, including the specific mandate of the commission or tribunal deciding the case. See 3 Whiteman, Damages in International Law 1765–1874 (1937). The Eritrea Ethiopia Claims Commission, in the course of its proceedings on damages for violations of international law during the 1998–2000 Eritrea–Ethiopia war, decided that "[c]ompensation can only be awarded in respect of damages

having a sufficient causal connection with conduct violating international law," that historically the use of causation standards by tribunals have been vague and uneven, and that:

> Given this ambiguous terrain, the Commission concludes that the necessary connection is best characterized through the commonly used nomenclature of "proximate cause." In assessing whether this test is met, and whether the chain of causation is sufficiently close in a particular situation, the Commission will give weight to whether particular damage reasonably should have been foreseeable to an actor committing the international delict in question. The element of foreseeability although not without its own difficulties, provides some discipline and predictability in assessing proximity. Accordingly, it will be given considerable weight in assessing whether particular damages are compensable.

Eritrea Ethiopia Claims Commission Decision No. 7, paras. 7, 13 (2007), available at http://www.pca-cpa.org. For additional commentary on the issue of causation, see Borek, Other State Responsibility Issues, in The Iran–United States Claims Tribunal: Its Contribution to the Law of State Responsibility 317, 330 (1998).

5.   *Material Damage from Death or Personal Injury.* In claims for personal injuries, the measure of reparation is the loss to the individual claimant. Damages have included medical expenses and loss of earnings, *George Henry Clapham Claim* (Great Britain v. Mexico), 5 U.N. Rep. Int'l Arb. Awards 201, 203–04 (1931), pain and suffering, 1 Whiteman, Damages in International Law 588–89 (1937), and mental anguish, *Lusitania Cases* (United States v. Germany), Mixed Claims Commission, Administrative Decisions and Opinions to June 30, 1925, 17, 21–22, 7 U.N. Rep. Int'l Arb. Awards 32, 36–37 (1923). Damages may be reduced where the claimant has contributed to the injury. *Lillie S. Kling Claim* (United States v. Mexico), [1931] Opinions of Commissioners 36, 49–50, 4 U.N. Rep. Int'l Arb. Awards 575, 585 (1930); Bederman, Contributory Fault and State Responsibility, 30 Va. J. Int'l L. 335 (1990).

Contemporary treaties and other instruments provide guidance on such compensation. For example, the U.N. General Assembly in 2005 adopted a resolution entitled "Basic Principles and Guidelines on the Right to Reparation for Victims of Gross Violations of Human Rights and Humanitarian Law." Paragraph 20 of those basic principles states:

> *Compensation* should be provided for any economically assessable damage, as appropriate and proportional to the gravity of the violation and the circumstances of each case, resulting from gross violations of international human rights law and serious violations of international humanitarian law, such as:
>
> (a) Physical or mental harm;
>
> (b) Lost opportunities, including employment, education and social benefits;
>
> (c) Material damages and loss of earnings, including loss of earning potential;
>
> (d) Moral damage;

(e) Costs required for legal or expert assistance, medicine and medical services, and psychological and social services.

G.A. Res. 60/147, annex, para. 20 (Dec. 16, 2005).

6. *Moral or Non–Material Damage*. Case law, publicists, and instruments such as the General Assembly resolution in the prior note are all in accord that the traditional theory of state responsibility fully recognizes moral injury as an element of damages. See, e.g., Gray, Judicial Remedies in International Law 42–43 (1987). As one reviews these instruments, case law, and commentary, there are three kinds of moral damage that are typically recognized: (1) physical pain and suffering, since common human experience recognizes the reality of such suffering; (2) mental anguish independent of physical injury (including humiliation and loss of enjoyment of life); and (3) more generally losing the ability to enjoy life and to function normally in the world, including the loss of consortium. Professor Shelton notes: "In the European system, moral damages have been awarded for anxiety, distress, 'isolation, confusion and neglect', abandonment, feelings of injustice, impaired way of life, 'harassment and humiliation' and other suffering. * * * In some cases, due to the nature of the violation, the Court has presumed moral injury." Shelton, Remedies in International Human Rights Law 307 (2d ed. 2005) (footnotes omitted). Indeed, given the nature of moral damages, typically tribunals recognize the difficulty of proving with precision the harm suffered. See, e.g., *König v. Germany*, 36 Eur. Ct. H.R. (ser. A), para. 19 (1980).

7. *Damage to Property*. Reparation has been held to include compensation for lost profits when the violation of international law consists in tortious conduct resulting in loss or destruction of property if the profits were reasonably certain and not speculative. See 3 Whiteman, Damages in International Law 1840–58 (1937). If the profits were speculative in view of the circumstances, they have generally not been included in the measure of reparation. In cases involving contract claims, lost profits may be allowed where they are reasonable and within the contemplation of the parties. See 3 Whiteman, Damages in International Law 1858–66 (1937). When an arbitral tribunal is not permitted by the *compromis* to grant reparation for anticipated profits, or when it feels that the profits are too speculative to measure, it can normally grant interest in lieu of profits.

What criteria are or should be relevant when valuing expropriated facilities for purposes of determining appropriate or just compensation? Consider use of book value, replacement value or fair market value of the expropriated assets or fair market value of the "going concern." To what extent should the value reflect lost future profits of the enterprise and other intangibles such as "good will" or managerial and technical know-how? To what extent, if at all, should adequacy of compensation be affected by other factors not bearing directly on current value of the expropriated business, such as the unavailability of foreign exchange with which to pay compensation in convertible currency, a history of large profits to the alien owners without commensurate benefits to the local economy, past environmental damage caused by the project and the ability of the expropriating state to pay? See Iran–United States Claims Tribunal, *Aryeh v. Iran*, Award No. 583–266–3, 33

Iran–U.S. Cl. Trib. Rep. 368 (1997); *Ebrahimi v. Iran*, Award No. 560–44/46/47–3, 30 Iran–U.S. Cl. Trib. Rep. 170 (1994); *Amoco Int'l Finance Corp. v. Iran*, Award No. 310–56–3, 15 Iran–U.S. Cl. Trib. Rep. 189 (1987–II). For further commentary see Leigh, Expropriation, 82 A.J.I.L. 358 (1988); Lillich, The Valuation of Nationalized Property by the Foreign Claims Settlement Commission, in 1 The Valuation of Nationalized Property in International Law 95 (Lillich ed. 1972).

8. *World Bank/IMF Guidelines*. On September 25, 1992, the World Bank Group and the International Monetary Fund (IMF) published the Report to the Development Committee and Guidelines on the Treatment of Foreign Direct Investment, which is set forth at 31 I.L.M. 1366 (1992). The Development Committee is a Joint Ministerial Committee of the Boards of Governors of the IMF and the World Bank. Its approval and publication of the Report and Guidelines were particularly significant because of the almost universal membership of the sponsoring institutions and their central role in international development. In a foreword to the publication, the President of the World Bank Group indicated that the Development Committee agreed "without reservation" to call the guidelines to the attention of the member states. He further stated that the guidelines may "assist in the progressive development of international law in this important area." Id.

With respect to expropriation, Part IV of the Guidelines provides, in part, that "[a] State may not expropriate or otherwise take in whole or in part a foreign private investment in its territory, or take measures which have similar effects, except where this is done in accordance with applicable legal procedures, in pursuance in good faith of a public purpose, without discrimination on the basis of nationality and against the payment of appropriate compensation." Id. at 1382. The Guidelines go on to state that compensation will be deemed "appropriate" if it is "adequate, effective and prompt." Id. Adequacy is generally to be based on the fair market value of the asset taken. Fair market value may be determined by a method agreed to by the expropriating state and the foreign investor or by a tribunal designated by them. In the event that such agreement is not achieved, the Guidelines set forth in detail the circumstances under which compensation will be deemed to be adequate, effective and prompt.

9. *Payment Using Host State Bonds*. In some situations, the host state may find it financially difficult to compensate for injury to an alien using "hard" (i.e., convertible) currency. Should international law allow payment to the alien using bonds issued by the host state, even if the fair market value of those bonds is lower?

10. *Interest and Costs*. International tribunals generally award interest either from the date of the obligation to make reparation or from the date of the award. The rate varies depending on the nature of the claim and on the rate of interest generally prevailing at the time and place of the injury. See O'Connell at 1122–23; 3 Whiteman, Damages in International Law 1913–2006 (1937). In the absence of an agreement to the contrary, usually the two parties involved bear their own costs in preparing or defending their claims and share the cost of the tribunal equally. 3 Whiteman, Damages in International Law at 2024–30 (1937).

11. *Compensating the Injured Alien.* As a matter of international law, any compensation is paid to the claimant state and then only disbursed to its national claimants at the state's discretion. United States policy as regards claims on behalf of U.S. nationals who invest abroad is as follows:

> The decision to espouse [the alien's claim] is wholly within the discretion of the Executive branch and is not subject to judicial review; since espousal represents only a final stage in the resolution of the claim, it is often unnecessary. Once espoused, the U.S. investor's claim is considered, under both U.S. law and international law, to become the U.S. Government's own claim. This means the Executive branch may settle the claim without the consent of the injured investor or may waive it altogether. Once the espoused claim is settled, the U.S. investor's claim is extinguished. In practice, formal espousal is normally at the request of the investor, or with his consent, and the proceeds received by the U.S. Government are turned over to the investor, sometimes with a small deduction to cover U.S. Government administrative expenses.

2 Department of State, Cumulative Digest of United States Practice in International Law, 1981–88, at 2308–09 (1994); see also Legal Aspects Regarding the Ownership and Distribution of Awards, Opinion of Joshua Reuben Clark, Jr., Solicitor for the Department of State, 7 A.J.I.L. 382 (1913); 3 Whiteman, Damages in International Law 2035–59 (1937).

CHAPTER 15

USE OF FORCE

■ ■ ■

In principle, the international (interstate) system implies the autonomy and independence of every state, both its freedom from coercion and the integrity of its territory. Section 1 of this Chapter considers the progression from the nineteenth into the twenty-first century of efforts to prohibit transboundary attacks by one state against another, while nevertheless allowing states to act in self-defense, a body of law referred to as the *jus ad bellum* (the law of going to war). Section 2 then turns to the difficult issues that arise from transboundary uses of force in the form of intervention in civil wars or humanitarian intervention. Section 3 considers collective uses of force undertaken through the United Nations, either in the form of forcible action or peacekeeping operations, or through regional or sub-regional organizations. Section 4 takes up efforts to mitigate the devastation of war through restraints on weapons and on the conduct of warfare: that body of law is often referred to as the *jus in bello* (law in wartime).

SECTION 1. USE OF FORCE BETWEEN STATES

The U.N. Charter radically transformed the law governing use of force and resort to war. In particular respects, however, the traditional law may have survived or been incorporated into the Charter. The traditional law is presented first (Section A), followed by a review of efforts to prohibit war immediately prior to the U.N. era (Section B). The changes effected by the Charter are discussed in Section C.

A. CUSTOMARY INTERNATIONAL LAW ON FORCE PRIOR TO THE TWENTIETH CENTURY

1. Non–Regulation of the Resort to War

The concern of states to regulate the conduct and the impact of war was an early impetus to the development of international law. The first systematic international law treatise, that of Grotius, was entitled *De Jure*

Belli Ac Pacis (Of the Law of War and Peace). International law writers postulated a dichotomy between war and peace and distinguished laws for nations at peace from laws for nations at war. "Belligerent" states, those at war, had the duty to observe the rules of war, and to respect the neutrality of non-belligerent states. These rules were designed to limit the spread of armed conflict and to promote a modicum of humanity in battle. Neutral states were expected to follow the relevant rules if they were to avoid the conflict. See Eagleton, The Duty of Impartiality on the Part of a Neutral, 34 A.J.I.L. 99 (1940).

In order to determine whether the rules of war (or of neutrality) applied, it was necessary to determine whether a state of war existed between states. Such a determination was not always easy to make. State practice during the nineteenth century suggests that a state of war resulted when one party declared war or intended a state of war to exist. Yet if a state of war did not exist unless war was declared or intended, a state could refrain from declaring war so as to avoid the necessity of complying with the laws of war (other nations also could not then invoke the laws of neutrality.) Some writers argued for an objective test, notably evidence of large-scale fighting. This view seemed more realistic as states began to initiate and engage in hostilities without formal declarations of war.

Yet while the existence of a state of war might trigger certain sets of rules about the conduct of warfare or the status of belligerents/neutrals, was there any prohibition on the resort to war?

2 OPPENHEIM, INTERNATIONAL LAW
177–78 (7th ed. Lauterpacht ed. 1952)

Prior to the General Treaty for the Renunciation of War the institution of war fulfilled in International Law two contradictory functions. In the absence of an international organ for enforcing the law, war was a means of self-help for giving effect to claims based or alleged to be based on International Law. Such was the legal and moral authority of this notion of war as an arm of the law that in most cases in which war was in fact resorted to in order to increase the power and the possessions of a State at the expense of others, it was described by the States in question as undertaken for the defence of a legal right. This conception of war was intimately connected with the distinction, which was established in the formative period of International Law and which never became entirely extinct, between just and unjust wars. At the same time, however, that distinction was clearly rejected in the conception of war as a legally recognised instrument for challenging and changing rights based on existing International Law. In the absence of an international legislature it fulfilled the function of adapting the law to changed conditions. Moreover, quite apart from thus supplying a crude substitute for a deficiency in international organisation, war was recognised as a legally admissible instrument for attacking and altering existing rights of States independently of the objective merits of the attempted change. As Hyde, writing in 1922, said: "It always lies within the power of a State * * * to gain political or other advantages over another, not merely by the employment of force, but also by direct recourse to war." International Law did not consider as illegal a war admittedly waged for such purposes. It rejected, to that extent, the distinction between just and unjust wars. War was in law a natural function of the State and a prerogative of its uncontrolled sovereignty.

NOTES

1. *Peace and War.* Why do you think for hundreds of years international law did not prohibit the resort to war? Did international law nevertheless encourage states to refrain from doing so? Henkin writes:

> It was not a cynic who once suggested that international law establishes order in unimportant matters but not in important ones. Doubtless, the comment referred in particular to the anomaly of international law before our times, which set up rules about international conduct in time of peace but did not forbid nations to commit the ultimate "aggression" against international order, the resort to war. That incongruity had its explanations, principally in the failure of early attempts to distinguish just wars (to be permitted, even encouraged) from unjust wars (to be outlawed). Third nations also wished to avoid becoming involved in the wars of others and wished to go their way in relation to both belligerent sides without having to decide which was in "the right." And, in fact, one cannot say that the anomaly nullified international law. Indeed, nations were more likely to observe the international law of peace, knowing that if their interests were too gravely jeopardized they could go to war to vindicate them and establish a new basis for new relations in a revised international order with different international obligations.

Henkin, How Nations Behave 135–36 (2d ed. 1979). Do you agree?

2. *Is It "War"?* On the difficulty of determining when armed hostilities constituted war under customary international law prior to the twentieth century, see Brownlie, International Law and the Use of Force by States 38–40 (1963). In recent times, the practice of formally recognizing a state of belligerency has fallen into disuse. See 2 Oppenheim, International Law 653–54 (7th ed. Lauterpacht ed. 1952).

3. *Qualifying as Neutral.* Neutrality was a legal status accorded to certain non-belligerents. In order to qualify for treatment as a neutral, a state had to assume an attitude of impartiality toward the belligerents. Policies adopted by the neutral state had to be applied equally to all parties at war. In return for assuming the duty of impartiality toward belligerents, the neutral was guaranteed the inviolability of its territory and freedom from belligerent acts. The Hague Peace Conferences of 1899 and 1907 led to two conventions defining the rights of neutrals. See Convention Respecting the Rights and Duties of Neutral Powers and Persons in Case of War on Land, Oct. 18, 1907, 36 Stat. 2310, T.S. No. 540; Convention Concerning the Rights and Duties of Neutral Powers in Naval War, Oct. 18, 1907, 36 Stat. 2415, T.S. No. 545. (As

of 2009, about thirty states were parties to these conventions.) On the early development of the law of neutrality, see Jessup & Deák, Neutrality, Volume I: The Origins (1935); 2 Oppenheim at 623–42; Örvik, The Decline of Neutrality 1914–1941, at 11–37 (1953).

2. Coercive Measures Short of War: Retorsion and Reprisals

As discussed in Chapter 8, states have traditionally utilized coercive measures short of resorting to "war" in disputes with other states, which are characterized as either "retorsion" or "reprisal." Retorsion refers to measures that are "unfriendly" but are not prohibited by international law, such as severance of diplomatic relations, shutting of ports to vessels of an unfriendly state, imposition of travel restrictions or denial of visas for its nationals, suspension of foreign aid, trade restrictions not contrary to treaty obligations, or the display of naval forces near the waters of an unfriendly state. See Restatement (Third) § 203(3), § 905, Comment *a*; Stone, Legal Controls of International Conflict 288 (rev. ed. 1959); von Glahn, Law Among Nations 637–40 (6th ed. 1992).

Reprisal refers to measures otherwise prohibited by international law that are nevertheless justified as responses to prior violations. Since under customary international law prior to the twentieth century there was no prohibition on the resort to war, did that mean that there were no legal restraints on forcible reprisals?

NAULILAA INCIDENT
6 Hackworth, Digest of International Law 154–55 (1943)

On October 19, 1914 a German official and two German officers from German Southwest Africa were killed at the Portuguese post of Naulilaa in Angola under the following circumstances: A party of Germans had crossed into Angola to discuss with the Portuguese authorities the importation of food supplies into German Southwest Africa. Due to difficulties in interpreting, misunderstandings arose between the parties. In the course of a discussion a Portuguese officer seized the bridle of a German official's horse and the official struck him. At that time a German officer drew his pistol. The Portuguese officer ordered his men to fire and the official and two officers were killed. Portuguese authorities subsequently interned the German interpreter and a German soldier. The authorities of German Southwest Africa did not communicate with the Portuguese authorities, but in alleged reprisal for the incident German troops attacked and destroyed certain forts and posts in Angola. These events took place prior to the entry of Portugal into the World War.

After the war, the Portuguese Government claimed damages on account of the incident. Alois de Meuron, a Swiss lawyer, was designated on August 15, 1920 as arbitrator to determine in conformance with paragraph 4 of the annex to articles 297–298 of the Treaty of Versailles the amount of the Portuguese claims. On February 9, 1928 two other arbitrators, both Swiss nationals, Robert Guex and Robert Fazy, were added to the tribunal. In an award rendered July 31, 1928 the arbitrators stated that the death of the German official and of the two German officers was not the consequence of an act contrary to the law of nations on the part of the Portuguese authorities. They declared that the *sine qua non* of the right to exercise reprisals is a motive furnished by a preliminary act contrary to the law of nations and that, even had such an act on the part of the Portuguese authorities been established, the German argument that the reprisals were justified would have been rejected because reprisals are only permissible when they have been preceded by an unsatisfied demand. The use of force, they stated, is only justified by necessity. They also stated that, even if it were admitted that the law of nations does not demand that reprisals be in approximate proportion to the offense, it would, nevertheless, certainly be necessary to consider as excessive and illegal reprisals out of all proportion to the act motivating them. They found that there was obvious disproportion between the incident at Naulilaa and the reprisals which followed, and defined reprisals as follows:

> Reprisals are an act of self-help (Selbsthilfehandlung) on the part of the injured state, an act corresponding *after an unsatisfied demand* to an act contrary to the law of nations on the part of the offending state. They have the effect of momentarily suspending, in the relations between the two states, the observance of such or such a rule of the law of nations. They are limited by the experiences of humanity and the rules of good faith applicable in relations between state and state. They would be illegal if a preliminary act contrary to the law of nations had not furnished a reason for them. * * * [Translation.]

For the tribunal's full opinion, see 2 U.N. Rep. Int'l Arb. Awards 1011 (1949).

Notes

1. *Reprisals Under Customary International Law.* If states were not prepared to go to "war" in its legal sense, whether for reasons given by Henkin or for other reasons, they remained bound by the legal restraints on resort to force expressed in rules such as those on non-intervention, reprisal, and self-defense. See Waldock, The Regulation of the Use of Force by Individual States, 81 Rec. des Cours 457 (1952); Brownlie, International Law and the Use of Force by States 21 (1963).

2. *Gunboat Diplomacy.* Compare the Joint Resolution of April 22, 1914, relating to the U.S. occupation of Veracruz, which stated that "the President is justified in the employment of the armed forces of the United States to enforce his demands for unequivocal amends for certain affronts and indignities committed against the United States" by Mexico. The Resolution further stated that "the United States disclaims any hostility to the Mexican people or any purpose to make war upon Mexico." 38 Stat. 770. See 1 Hackworth at 151; 6 Hackworth at 152.

3. Self–Defense

Suppose a state prior to the twentieth century used force against another state, but wished to argue that it was not resorting to "war," but was merely defending itself from a threat by that other state. By doing so, the state would avoid characterizing its conduct as initiating a formal state of war. Did traditional international law acknowledge a right of self-defense and, if so, what were the characteristics of such a right?

THE CAROLINE

2 Moore, Digest of International Law 412 (1906)
Hyde, International Law 239 (1945)

[During an insurrection in Canada in 1837, the insurgents secured recruits and supplies from the American side of the border. There was an encampment of one thousand armed men organized at Buffalo, and located at Navy Island in Upper Canada; there was another encampment of insurgents at Black Rock, on the American side. The *Caroline* was a small steamer employed by these encampments. On December 29, 1837, while moored at Schlosser, on the American side of the Niagara River, and while occupied by some thirty-three American citizens, the steamer was boarded by an armed body of men from the Canadian side, who attacked the occupants. The latter merely endeavored to escape. Several were wounded; one was killed on the dock; only twenty-one were afterwards accounted for. The attacking party fired the steamer and set her adrift over Niagara Falls. In 1841, upon the arrest and detention of one Alexander McLeod, in New York, on account of his alleged participation in the destruction of the vessel, Lord Palmerston avowed responsibility for the destruction of the *Caroline* as a public act of force in self-defense, by persons in the British service. He therefore demanded McLeod's release. McLeod was, however, tried in New York, and acquitted. In 1842 the two Governments agreed in principle that the requirements of self-defense might necessitate the use of force. Daniel Webster, the U.S. Secretary of State, denied that the necessity existed in this particular case, while Lord Ashburton, the British Minister, apologized for the invasion of American territory. Said Mr. Webster in the course of a communication to the British Minister, August 6, 1842:]

The President sees with pleasure that your Lordship fully admits those great principles of public law, applicable to cases of this kind, which this government has expressed; and that on your part, as on ours, respect for the inviolable character of the territory of independent states is the most essential foundation of civilization. And while it is admitted on both sides that there are exceptions to this rule, he is gratified to find that your Lordship admits that such exceptions must come within the limitations stated and the terms used in a former communication from this department to the British plenipotentiary here. Undoubtedly it is just, that, while it is admitted that exceptions growing out of the great law of self-defense do exist, those exceptions should be confined to cases in which the "necessity of that self-defence is instant, overwhelming, and leaving no choice of means, and no moment for deliberation."

NOTES

1. *The* Caroline *Standard*. Do you view the *Caroline* standard articulated by Secretary Webster as allowing a broad or narrow scope for self-defense? How would you relate the standard to the facts in the case?

2. *Proportionality.* In an earlier letter to the British authorities, Secretary Webster included a requirement of proportionality:

> It will be for [Her Majesty's Government] to show, also, that the local authorities of Canada, even supposing the necessity of the moment authorized them to enter the territories of the United States at all, did nothing unreasonable or excessive; since the act, justified by the necessity of self-defence, must be limited by that necessity, and kept clearly within it.

Mr. Webster to Mr. Fox (April 24, 1841), 29 Brit. & For. St. Papers 1129, 1138 (1857).

3. *Self–Defense Under the U.N. Charter.* Why is it important to understand the law on self-defense as it operated prior to the twentieth century, such as the concept of necessity and proportionality? Note that U.N. Charter Article 51, discussed *infra* p. 1165, states that nothing in the Charter "shall impair the inherent right of individual or collective self-defense".

B. PRE–UNITED NATIONS EFFORTS TO DISCOURAGE OR OUTLAW WAR

CONVENTION RESPECTING THE LIMITATION OF THE EMPLOYMENT OF FORCE FOR THE RECOVERY OF CONTRACT DEBTS

Signed at the Hague, October 18, 1907
36 Stat. 2241, T.S. No. 537

ARTICLE 1

The contracting Powers agree not to have recourse to armed force for the recovery of contract debts claimed from the Government of one country by the Government of another country as being due to its nationals.

This undertaking is, however, not applicable when the debtor State refuses or neglects to reply to an offer of arbitration, or, after accepting the offer, prevents any *compromis* from being agreed on, or, after the arbitration, fails to submit to the award. * * *

BOWETT, THE LAW OF INTERNATIONAL INSTITUTIONS

17–18 (4th ed. 1982)

The creation of a league of States, dedicated to the maintenance of peace, had long been advocated in philosophical and juristic writings and in the aims of private organisations. The immediate source of the League of Nations was, however, a proposal introduced at the Peace Conference of Paris in 1919. In the drafting of the Covenant of the League the major powers played the decisive role; it emerged as a fusion of President Wilson's third draft and the British proposals emanating from the Phillimore Committee.

The League's objective was "to promote international co-operation and to achieve international peace and security." The system of collective security envisaged in the Covenant rested, essentially, on the notions of disarmament (Art. 8), pacific settlement of disputes and the outlawry of war (Arts. 11–15), a collective guarantee of the independence of each member (Art. 10), and sanctions (Arts. 16 and 17). The League's disarmament programme failed dismally. As envisaged in the Covenant, the pacific settlement of disputes likely to lead to a rupture of the peace was obligatory; parties to the dispute could choose to go to arbitration, judicial settlement or to the Council of the League. It was obligatory to accept the award or a unanimous report of the Council and an obligation on all members not to go to war with any State so accepting. The members agreed to respect and preserve the "territorial integrity and existing political independence" of all members against external aggression. War, as such, was not made illegal but only where begun without complying with the requirements of the Covenant with regard to prior resort to pacific settlement of the dispute. A State resorting to war in violation of its undertaking with regard to pacific settlement was deemed to have committed an act of war against all other members. Yet it was left to each member to decide whether a breach had occurred or an act of war had been committed, so that even the obligation to apply economic sanctions under Article 16(1) was dependent on the member's own view of the situation. Military sanctions could be recommended by the Council, but the decision on whether to apply them rested with each member.

Such was the system; in itself a not unworkable one. After an initial success in dealing with the Graeco–Bulgarian crisis of 1925, and a less spectacular achievement in the Chaco dispute of 1928, the League witnessed the invasion of Manchuria in 1931, the Italo–Abyssinian War of 1934–35, the German march into the Rhineland in 1936, into Austria in 1938, into Czechoslovakia in 1939, the Soviet Union's invasion of Finland in 1939 and, finally, the German invasion of Poland in 1939. Apart from half-hearted economic sanctions against Italy in 1935, no sanctions were ever really applied by the League. To this extent the failure of the League was due, not to the inadequacies of the Covenant, but to the apathy and reluctance of the member States to discharge their obligations.

COVENANT OF THE LEAGUE OF NATIONS

Signed June 28, 1919
1 Hudson International Legislation 1 (1931)

ARTICLE XVI

Should any Member of the League resort to war in disregard of its covenants under Articles 12, 13 or 15, it shall *ipso facto* be deemed to have committed an act of war against all other Members of the League, which hereby undertake immediately to subject it to the severance of all trade or financial relations, the prohibition of all intercourse between their nationals and the nationals of the covenant-breaking State, and the prevention of all financial, commercial or personal intercourse between the nationals of the covenant-breaking State and the nationals of any other State, whether a Member of the League or not.

It shall be the duty of the Council in such case to recommend to the several Governments concerned what effective military, naval or air force the Members of the League shall severally contribute to the armed forces to be used to protect the covenants of the League.

The Members of the League agree, further, that they will mutually support one another in the financial and economic measures which are taken under this Article, in order to minimise the loss and inconvenience resulting from the above measures, and that they will mutually support one another in resisting any special measures aimed at one of their number by the covenant-breaking State, and that they will take the necessary steps to afford passage through their territory to the forces of any of the Members of the League which are co-operating to protect the covenants of the League.

GENERAL TREATY FOR THE RENUNCIATION OF WAR (KELLOGG–BRIAND PACT)

August 27, 1928, 46 Stat. 2343, 94 L.N.T.S. 57

Art. I. The High Contracting Parties solemnly declare in the names of their respective peoples that they condemn recourse to war for the solution of international controversies, and renounce it as an instrument of national policy in their relations with one another.

Art. II. The High Contracting Parties agree that the settlement or solution of all disputes or conflicts of whatever nature or of whatever origin they may be, which may arise among them, shall never be sought except by pacific means.

NOTES

1. *Small Steps.* Why do you think the 1907 Hague Convention prohibited the use of force when employed to recover contract debts? Why do you think attitudes began to change about whether international law should prohibit the use of force in certain circumstances?

2. *The Rise of Collective Security.* The League of Nations was founded as a result of the Treaty of Versailles in 1919 and at one time had fifty-eight members. As noted by Bowett, the goals of the League included promoting the pacific settlement of disputes and preventing war through collective security. Did the Covenant ban the use of military force in international relations or simply establish procedures that might inhibit the resort to war? Which features of the Covenant's approach to collective security do you see as useful and which do you find ineffective?

3. *Failure of the Covenant.* The provisions of Article 16 of the Covenant were given their decisive test in the war between Italy and Abyssinia (Ethiopia). Italy invaded Abyssinia on October 3, 1935. Despite the absence of any procedural provisions in the Covenant, machinery for the implementation of Article 16 was swiftly devised. The League Council, after hearing the plea of Abyssinia, appointed a Committee of Six to draw up a report. On October 11, the Council adopted the report of the Committee which had found that the Italian Government had resorted to war in violation of the Covenant. Within sixteen days of the outbreak of war the League drew up a series of proposals suggesting to its members the implementation of embargoes extending to arms, financial credit, exports and imports and calling for mutual economic help to those innocent countries adversely affected by the embargo. The sanctions, however, fell short in many ways of those prescribed in Article 16 of the Covenant. Due to weakness and vacillation on the part of Britain and France, the export embargo did not extend to coal, steel and oil, the commodities most vital to Italy. The subsequent refusal of the League to take further measures when the initial sanctions proved inadequate exposed its impotence. In the face of British, French and Russian fears of war with Italy, the controversial oil embargo was never adopted.

The failure of the League to prevent the obvious aggression of Italy and to deal effectively with the aggressor undermined the credibility of a regime of international law under which war was to be abolished as an instrument of national policy. See Wright, The Test of Aggression in the Italo–Ethiopian War, 30 A.J.I.L. 45 (1936). For a description of the League actions, see Spencer, The Italian–Ethiopian Dispute and the League of Nations, 31 A.J.I.L. 614 (1937). The relevant documents are set forth in League of Nations—Dispute Between Ethiopia and Italy, 30 A.J.I.L. Supp. 1 (1936). On the League of Nations generally, see Walters, A History of the League of Nations (1960); Scott, The Rise and Fall of the League of Nations (1973); Joyce, Broken Star: The Story of the League of Nations, 1919–1939 (1978); Ostrower, Collective Insecurity: The United States and the League of Nations During the Early Thirties (1979); The League of Nations in Retrospect: Proceedings of the Symposium (1983); Northedge, The League of Nations: Its Life and Times, 1920–1946 (1986).

4. *The Kellogg–Briand Pact.* The Kellogg–Briand Pact (also known as the Pact of Paris) was named after its drafters, U.S. Secretary of State Frank Kellogg and French Foreign Minister Aristide Briand, and is regarded as the first effort under international law to ban broadly the resort to war as an instrument of national policy. The Pact entered into force on July 24, 1929 and remains in force today. Some new states (e.g., Barbados and Fiji) have adhered to it, and some of the new states of the former Yugoslavia (e.g.,

Bosnia–Herzegovina and Slovenia) have specifically registered acceptance. (All the states of the former Soviet Union and former Yugoslavia could be considered bound on an automatic continuity theory of succession; see Chapter 19, p. 1534 note 2.) As of early 2009, more than seventy states are parties.

5. *Inter–American Renunciation of War.* The "Saavedra Lamas Treaty," signed by certain American states at Rio de Janeiro on October 10, 1933, and by the United States in 1934, condemns wars of aggression and provides in Article 1 that "the settlement of disputes or controversies of any kind * * * shall be effected only by the pacific means which shall have the sanction of international law." 6 Hackworth at 9.

1. CRIMINALIZING AGGRESSION: THE NUREMBERG CHARTER AND TRIALS

An International Military Tribunal was established at the end of World War II by the London Agreement among the United States, France, the United Kingdom, and the U.S.S.R. "for the trial of war criminals whose offenses have no particular geographical location whether they be accused individually or in their capacity as members of organizations or groups or in both capacities." The original indictment presented to the Tribunal on October 6, 1945, charged the German defendants under Article VI of the Charter of the International Military Tribunal with committing Crimes against the Peace, War Crimes and Crimes against Humanity. An additional charge which merged with the others alleged that the defendants had planned and conspired to commit these same acts.

Crimes against the Peace were defined by Article VI as:

planning, preparation, initiation, or waging of a war of aggression, or a war in violation of international treaties, agreements, assurances, or participation in a common plan or conspiracy for the accomplishment of any of the foregoing.

The Charter and the subsequent judgment never adopted a definition of aggressive war. Although the United States representative tried to have such a definition included in the Charter, his efforts were rebuffed. In the end, the Tribunal apparently accepted the argument that the acts perpetrated by Germany speak for themselves, and that under any seriously propounded definition of aggression the German leaders were guilty.

Since one of the central concerns of the Nuremberg Tribunal was the imputation of individual criminal responsibility, its use of the concept of aggressive war was influenced by the notion of a criminal conspiracy. Both the proof by the prosecution and the judgment of the Tribunal detail how the Nazi leaders in deliberate fashion planned the Second World War. The judgment describes the seizure of power by the Nazi Party, the intentions of its leaders, and finally the specific aggressive acts of the government. Aggressive war in these terms was the pursuit of an expansionist policy through deliberate criminal acts.

JUDGMENT OF THE INTERNATIONAL MILITARY TRIBUNAL

Nuremberg, Sept. 30, 1946
Reprinted in 41 A.J.I.L. 186–218 (1946)

The charges in the Indictment that the defendants planned and waged aggressive wars are charges of the utmost gravity. War is essentially an evil thing. Its consequences are not confined to the belligerent states alone, but affect the whole world.

To initiate a war of aggression, therefore, is not only an international crime; it is the supreme international crime differing only from other war crimes in that it contains within itself the accumulated evil of the whole.

The first acts of aggression referred to in the Indictment are the seizure of Austria and Czechoslovakia; and the first war of aggression charged in the Indictment is the war against Poland begun on the 1st September 1939.

Before examining that charge it is necessary to look more closely at some of the events which preceded these acts of aggression. The war against Poland did not come suddenly out of an otherwise clear sky; the evidence has made it plain that this war of aggression, as well as the seizure of Austria and Czechoslovakia, was premeditated and carefully prepared, and was not undertaken until the moment was thought opportune for it to be carried through as a definite part of the preordained scheme and plan.

For the aggressive designs of the Nazi Government were not accidents arising out of the immediate political situation in Europe and the world; they were a deliberate and essential part of Nazi foreign policy.

From the beginning, the National Socialist movement claimed that its object was to unite the German people in the consciousness of their mission and destiny, based on inherent qualities of race, and under the guidance of the Fuehrer.

For its achievement, two things were deemed to be essential: The disruption of the European order as it has existed since the Treaty of Versailles, and the creation of a Greater Germany beyond the frontiers of 1914. This necessarily involved the seizure of foreign territories.

War was seen to be inevitable, or at the very least, highly probable, if these purposes were to be accomplished. The German people, therefore, with all their resources, were to be organized as a great political-military army, schooled to obey without question any policy decreed by the State.* * *

The Charter [of the Tribunal] defines as a crime the planning or waging of war that is a war of aggression or a war in violation of international treaties. The Tribunal has decided that certain of the defendants planned and waged aggressive wars against 12 nations, and were therefore guilty of this series of crimes. This makes it unnecessary to discuss the subject in further detail, or even to consider at any length the extent to which these aggressive wars were also "wars in violation of international treaties, agreements, or assurances." * * *

The jurisdiction of the Tribunal is defined in the [London] Agreement and [Nuremberg] Charter, and the crimes coming within the jurisdiction of the Tribunal, for which there shall be individual responsibility, are set out in Article 6. The law of the Charter is decisive, and binding upon the Tribunal. * * *

The [Nuremberg] Charter makes the planning or waging of a war of aggression or a war in violation of international treaties a crime; and it is therefore not strictly necessary to consider whether and to what extent aggressive war was a crime before the execution of the London Agreement. * * *

The question is, what was the legal effect of this [the Kellogg–Briand] Pact? The nations who signed the pact or adhered to it unconditionally condemned recourse to war for the future as an instrument of policy, and expressly renounced it. After the signing of the Pact, any nation resorting to war as an instrument of national policy breaks the Pact. In the opinion of the Tribunal, the solemn renunciation of war as an instrument of national policy necessarily involves the proposition that such a war is illegal in international law; and that those who plan and wage such a war, with its inevitable and terrible consequences, are committing a crime in so doing. War for the solution of international controversies undertaken as an instrument of national policy certainly includes a war of aggression, and such a war is therefore outlawed by the Pact. * * *

NOTES

1. *Aggressive Wars.* The Tribunal, following its Charter, distinguishes a war of aggression from one in breach of international agreements, but deals only briefly with the latter. Appendix C to the indictment sets out the various agreements which Germany was charged with having breached. The defense argued on behalf of the German defendants that although a nation could not wage aggressive war without transgressing international law, it could use war as an instrument of self-defense, and that the nation itself must be the sole judge of whether its actions were in self-defense. If action in self-defense is permissible, who is to judge when a nation is an aggressor? Is it realistic to outlaw aggressive war without providing for a tribunal to arbitrate whether a particular course of conduct is aggressive? In rejecting the plea of self-defense, the Tribunal adopted the test stated in the *Caroline* case, p. 1134.

2. *Political Domain?* The International Military Tribunal was criticized as necessarily biased since the victors could not impartially judge their adversaries. For example, it was pointed out that although the German "invasion" of Poland was found to be aggressive, this action by the Germans was executed in concert with the Union of Soviet Socialist Republics, which was never accused of aggressive conduct before the International Military

Tribunal. For a survey of the "aggressive" acts of the various governments, see Hankey, Politics, Trials and Errors 10–16 (1950).

It has also been argued that the question of aggression is so predominantly a political question that it should be settled through political means, not by a court. Before the decision was taken to establish an international judicial tribunal, the alternative of summary execution of the top Nazi figures was advocated at the highest levels in several of the Allied governments, including the United Kingdom and the United States. On the counsels that overcame this advocacy, see Bass, Stay the Hand of Vengeance: The Politics of International War Crimes Tribunals 147–95 (2000).

Do you think a defeated nation could ever hope to punish the leaders of a victorious aggressor nation? Would a victorious aggressor, or nations involved in wars where there is no clear victor, ever submit to the jurisdiction of an international tribunal with the possibility that their leaders might be declared perpetrators of crimes against the peace? See Chapter 16, p. 1352.

3. *Tokyo Tribunal.* A similar Tribunal was established in the Far East. For discussion of the Tokyo war crimes trials, in which several major Japanese leaders were found guilty and sentenced to death, see Keenan & Brown, Crimes against International Law (1950); Röling & Cassese, The Tokyo Trial and Beyond (1993). For an alternative perspective, see Kopelman, Ideology and International Law: The Dissent of the Indian Justice at the Tokyo War Crimes Trial, 23 N.Y.U. J. Int'l L. & Pol. 373 (1991).

4. *Nuremberg Principles and Vietnam.* A key Nuremberg principle, as endorsed by the U.N. General Assembly in 1946, is individual responsibility for the kinds of violations of international law at stake in the Nuremberg trials. There were several attempts to invoke the Nuremberg principles in relation to U.S. involvement in the Vietnam war. In *United States v. Mitchell*, 246 F.Supp. 874 (D. Conn.1965), the defendant, charged with having failed to report for induction as ordered, defended on the ground, *inter alia,* that the war in Vietnam was a war of aggression within the meaning of the London Agreement, and that he would be responsible for participating even though ordered to do so. The trial court charged the jury that the agreement did not interfere "in any manner in respect to this defendant fulfilling his duty under this order." He was convicted and his conviction was affirmed, 369 F.2d 323 (2d Cir.1966); the Supreme Court denied certiorari, Douglas J. dissenting with a brief opinion, 386 U.S. 972 (1967). See also the dissenting opinion of Justices Stewart and Douglas from the denial of certiorari in *Mora v. McNamara*, 389 U.S. 934 (1967). Compare Taylor, Nuremberg and Vietnam: An American Tragedy (1970).

C. USE OF FORCE UNDER THE UNITED NATIONS CHARTER

1. Overview of the Law of the Charter

The U.N. Charter laid the foundation of a "new world order" after the Allied victory in the Second World War. Originally an international agreement open only to states that had declared war against the Axis powers, it has become a universal agreement open to all states. Membership in the United Nations and adherence to the Charter have been the aim of virtually every entity that aspired to and achieved statehood.

Importantly, the Charter prescribes international norms directed at states that outlaw the threat or use of force, the principal norms on which the new order stands, and now universally recognized as *jus cogens.* Article 2(3) commits members to settle their disputes by peaceful means. By Article 2(4) member states undertake to refrain from the "threat or use of force," broader concepts than "aggression." See p. 1146. At the same time, Article 51 provides that "[n]othing in the present Charter shall impair the inherent right of individual or collective self-defence if an armed attack occurs * * *." See p. 1165.

The Charter also sets forth machinery for states to react collectively to threats or uses of force. Indeed, the principal purpose of the United Nations Organization is "[t]o maintain international peace and security, and to that end: to take effective collective measures for the prevention and removal of threats to the peace, and for the suppression of acts of aggression or other breaches of the peace, and to bring about by peaceful means, and in conformity with the principles of justice and international law, adjustment or settlement of international disputes or situations which might lead to the breach of the peace * * *." U.N. Charter, Article 1(1). Authority is allocated among different actors:

The Security Council. The Security Council's principal task is to ensure international peace and security. The authority of the fifteen-member Council is set forth in Chapters V through VII of the Charter. Members delegate to the Security Council "primary responsibility for the maintenance of international peace and security" (Article 24) and "agree to accept and carry out the decisions of the Security Council" (Article 25). Chapter VII of the Charter gives the U.N. Security Council authority to determine the existence of any threat to the peace, breach of peace or act of aggression, and to make recommendations or decide what measures shall be taken to maintain or restore international peace or security. See p. 1222.

The General Assembly. The General Assembly, consisting of all U.N. members, may discuss and make recommendations on any matters within the scope of the Charter (Article 10), but it may make recommendations on disputes or situations with regard to which the Security Council is exercising its powers only upon the Security Council's request (Article 12(1)). On the role of the General Assembly in peacekeeping, see pp. 1250–51.

Regional Arrangements. Article 52 of the Charter authorizes regional arrangements and agencies for dealing with matters relating to the maintenance of international peace and security. The Security Council may utilize regional arrangements for enforcement action under its authority (Article 53). See p. 1265.

At the same time, a general limitation on the purposes and powers of the United Nations is laid down in Article 2(7) of the Charter: "Nothing contained in the present Charter shall authorize the United Nations to intervene in matters which are essentially within the domestic jurisdiction of any state * * *;" this provision, however, "shall not prejudice the application of enforcement measures under Chapter VII."

For some forty years, however, the collective security mechanism of the United Nations was hampered, and often thwarted, by the Cold War. The Security Council was largely incapacitated by lack of agreement (and by veto) of the permanent members. The Council did develop the concept of peacekeeping operations, deployed at the consent of the host state, but agreement among the permanent members on such operations was often elusive. As a consequence, the General Assembly sought to assume part of the Security Council's responsibility (see, e.g., the Uniting for Peace Resolution, G.A. Res. 373(V) (Nov. 3, 1950)), discussed at p. 1229 *infra*, but it too was hampered by the Cold War and by the enlarged membership dominated by new, developing states.

The Cold War doubtless influenced the interpretation of the normative principles of the Charter and weakened compliance with those norms, but there was never a serious suggestion that the inability of the United Nations to maintain peace invalidated or impaired the Charter norms proscribing the threat or use of force.

HENKIN, HOW NATIONS BEHAVE
137–38 (2d ed. 1979)

Unlike the limited restraints in the Covenant of the League and the provisions of the Kellogg–Briand Pact, the Charter's prohibition on unilateral force was to apply universally: members were bound by it; they were to see to it that nonmembers also complied. For the first time, nations tried to bring within the realm of law those ultimate political tensions and interests that had long been deemed beyond control by law. They determined that even sincere concern for national "security" or "vital interests" should no longer warrant any nation to initiate war. They agreed, in effect, to forgo the use of external force to change the political status quo. Nations would be assured their fundamental independence, the enjoyment of their territory, their freedom—a kind of right to be let alone. With it, of course, came the corresponding obligation to let others alone, not to use force to resolve disputes, or even to vindicate one's "rights." Change—other than internal change through internal forces—would have to be achieved peacefully, by agreement. Henceforth there would be order, and international society could concentrate on meeting better the needs of justice and welfare.

This most political of norms has been the target of "realists" from the beginning. They have questioned whether it is viable, even whether it is clearly desirable. Some who approved the norm in 1945 began to ask later whether it was acceptable. A "realist" would suggest that the law could have worked only if the United States and the Soviet Union had been prepared to cooperate to enforce peace. A lawyer might ask whether the law remains law, according to the principle of *rebus sic stantibus,* when the assumptions on which it was based have failed, when the circumstances in which it was made and those for which it was contemplated have radically changed.

For me, the changing facts and faces of international law have not detracted from the validity of the law of the Charter and have only reinforced its desirability. Consider, first, the argument based on the failure of the original conception of the United Nations: it has not established an effective international police system; it has not developed and maintained machinery for peaceful settlement of disputes (making self-help unnecessary and undesirable). But the draftsmen of the Charter were not seeking merely to replace "balance of power" by "collective security"; they were determined, according to the Preamble, to abolish "the scourge of war." All the evidence is persuasive that they sought to outlaw war, whether or not the U.N. organization succeeded in enforcing the law or in establishing peace and justice. And none of the original members, nor any one of the many new members, has ever claimed that the law against the use of force is undesirable now that the United Nations is not what had been intended.

NOTES

1. *The Charter During the Cold War.* Henkin argues also that the other "changed circumstances"—the failure of Allied cooperation that gave way to the ideological confrontation of the Cold War, the development and proliferation of terrible weapons of mass destruction, and the transformation of the political system by the emergence of new nations and the "Third World"—did not render Article 2(4) less valid or less desirable. Henkin, How Nations Behave 138–39 (2d ed. 1979). U.S. actions, e.g., in Grenada, Nicaragua, and Panama, gave rise to charges that for the United States the law of the Charter was inapplicable when important national interests were at stake. Official U.S. representatives, however, continued to insist on the validity of the law of the Charter, and sought to justify U.S. actions under that law and to judge the actions of other states by that standard. The revival of the Security Council deflected arguments that the Charter norms against the use of force (Articles 2(3) and 2(4)) may have been voided under the doctrine of *rebus sic stantibus,* but its long dormant state encouraged arguments for inferring exceptions, for example to permit the use of force for humanitarian purposes or to defend or promote democracy. See pp. 1201, 1214.

Henkin concludes that even during the Cold War there were fewer violations of the Charter than was commonly assumed. The principal "wars" were civil wars with external involvement, as to which the law of the Charter did not speak clearly. See p. 1196. The Cold War may have encouraged violations by smaller developing powers who expected that ideological conflict between the superpowers would incapacitate the Security Council and provide them immunity from other adverse consequences (e.g., the Iran–Iraq War 1980–1988 and wars between Ethiopia and its neighbors). See Henkin, How Nations Behave 112–18 (2d ed. 1979).

On the continuing validity and viability of Article 2(4) during the Cold War, compare Franck, Who Killed Article 2(4)? or: Changing Norms Governing the Use of Force by States, 64 A.J.I.L. 809 (1970), with Henkin, The Reports of the Death of Article 2(4) Are Greatly Exaggerated, 65 A.J.I.L. 544 (1971). See also Schachter, In Defense of International Rules on the Use of Force, 53 U. Chi. L. Rev. 113 (1986); Henkin, The Use of Force: Law and U.S. Policy, in Right v. Might: International Law and the Use of Force 37, 38–41 (2d ed. 1991); Macdonald, The Use of Force by States in International Law, in International Law: Achievements and Prospects 715, 719–31 (Bedjaoui ed. 1991).

2. *The Charter After the Cold War.* The end of the Cold War led to different patterns of conflict and new types of external intervention, as in the former Yugoslavia. These have left their mark on international law. See pp. 1261–64. After the attacks of September 11, 2001, some questioned whether the U.N. Charter system had been rendered irrelevant or would require major change, in light of the kinds of threats from non-state actors that the attacks exemplified. The U.N. Secretary–General convened a high-level panel to consider these and other questions concerning twenty-first century threats. For its report, see A More Secure World: Report of the Secretary–General's High–Level Panel on Threats, Challenges and Change (2004); for the substance of some of its major recommendations, see p. 1213.

In the World Summit Outcome Document, G.A. Res. 60/1 (Sept. 16, 2005), under the heading "Use of force under the Charter of the United Nations," U.N. members at the level of heads of state and government in 2005 endorsed the following propositions by consensus:

> 78. We reiterate the importance of promoting and strengthening the multilateral process and of addressing international challenges and problems by strictly abiding by the Charter and the principles of international law, and further stress our commitment to multilateralism.

> 79. We reaffirm that the relevant provisions of the Charter are sufficient to address the full range of threats to international peace and security. We further reaffirm the authority of the Security Council to mandate coercive action to maintain and restore international peace and security. We stress the importance of acting in accordance with the purposes and principles of the United Nations.

After you have completed the readings in this Chapter, consider whether you think the Charter-based system is sufficient to meet contemporary threats.

2. The Prohibition of the Use of Force

a. *General Considerations*

CHARTER OF THE UNITED NATIONS, ARTICLE 2(4)
Signed in San Francisco, June 26, 1945

All Members shall refrain in their international relations from the threat or use of force against the territorial integrity or political independence of any state, or in any other manner inconsistent with the Purposes of the United Nations.

SCHACHTER, INTERNATIONAL LAW IN THEORY AND PRACTICE

110–13 (1991) (footnotes omitted)

The basic provision restricting the use of force (or its threat) in international relations is Article 2, paragraph 4, of the Charter. * * *

The paragraph is complex in its structure and nearly all of its key terms raise questions of interpretation. We know that the principle was intended to outlaw war in its classic sense, that is, the use of military force to acquire territory or other benefits from another State. Actually the term "war" is not used in Article 2(4). It had been used in the League of Nations Covenant and the Kellogg–Briand Pact of 1928, but it had become evident in the 1930s that States engaged in hostilities without declaring war or calling it war. The term "force" was chosen as a more factual and wider word to embrace military action.

"Force" has its own ambiguities. It is sometimes used in a wide sense to embrace all types of coercion: economic, political and psychological as well as physical. Governments in the United Nations have from time to time sought to give the prohibition in Article 2(4) the wider meaning particularly to include economic measures that were said to be coercive. Although support was expressed by a great many states in the Third World for this wider notion, it was strongly resisted by the Western States. * * *

Even limited to armed force, the term raises questions of interpretation. Some center on the notion of "indirect" force. Does a State indirectly employ force when it allows its territory to be used by troops fighting in another country? Does a State use force when it provides arms to insurgents or to one side in a war? Does troop training as expert advice amount to indirect force? These questions have tended to be treated under the rubric of "intervention", a concept which has often been dealt with independently of Article 2(4) and defined as dictatorial interference by a State in the affairs of another State. However, Article 2(4) remains the most explicit Charter rule against intervention through armed force, indirect and direct, and it is pertinent to consider such actions as falling within the scope of the prohibition. * * *

* * *

A * * * basic question of interpretation is presented by the peculiar structure of the article. It is generally presumed that the prohibition was intended to preclude all use of force except that allowed as self-defence or authorized by the Security Council under Chapter VII. Yet the article is not drafted that way. The last 23 words contain qualifications. The article requires States to refrain from force or threat of force when that is "against the territorial integrity or political independence of any State" or "inconsistent with the purposes of the United Nations". If these words are not redundant, they must qualify that all-inclusive prohibition against force. Just how far they do qualify the prohibition is difficult to determine from a textual analysis alone.

The problem of interpretation has arisen in regard to two types of justification for the use of force. One such justification concerns the use of force solely to vindicate or secure a legal right. Thus it has been claimed that a State is allowed to use force to secure its lawful passage through waters of an international strait or to compel compliance with an arbitral or judicial award. One may extend this to other cases where a State considers that its rights have been violated. The textual argument based on the qualifying clause of Article 2(4) is that such force is not directed against the territorial integrity or political independence of the target state nor is it inconsistent with United Nations purposes. In its simplest form, it is the argument that force for a benign end does not fall within the qualifying language of Article 2(4). The argument, if accepted, would go a long way to cut down on the scope of Article 2(4). * * *

One answer to this argument is that the Charter itself requires that disputes be settled by peaceful means (Article 2, para. 3) and that the first declared purpose of the Charter is to remove threats to the peace and to suppress breaches of the peace. Consequently any use of force in international relations would be inconsistent with a Charter purpose. The only exceptions would be self-defense under Article 51 and military enforcement measures under Chapter VII.

A second answer is that any coercive incursion of armed troops into a foreign State without its consent impairs that State's territorial integrity, and any use of force to coerce a State to adopt a particular policy or action must be considered as an impairment of that State's political independence. On these premises it does not matter that the coercive action may have only a short-term effect nor does it matter that the end sought by the use of force is consistent with a stated purpose of the Charter. As long as the act of force involves a non-consensual use of a State's territory or compels a State to take a decision it would not otherwise take, Article 2(4) has been violated.

This position has been taken by the great majority of States and by most international lawyers. It finds support in the two decisions of the International Court of Justice concerned with the legality of the use of force[: *The Corfu Channel* case and the *Nicaragua* case].

NOTES

1. *Obligation of Peaceful Settlement.* Article 2(3) provides: "All Members shall settle their international disputes by peaceful means in such a manner that international peace and security, and justice, are not endangered." This is also a legal undertaking, but in practice it has been subordinated to Article 2(4). As long as a state does not resort to force, there has been no disposition

to find a violation of law in failure to settle disputes peacefully, as by leaving them unsettled. Compare Chapter 9, p. 558.

2. *Terminology.* Unlike earlier efforts to outlaw "war" or "aggression," Article 2(4) does not mention either term. The framers avoided them because these terms lend themselves to circumvention. There could be hostilities without a declared war, and uses of force that did not acquire the character of war. Aggression had long resisted definition, and who was the aggressor could be falsified and might not always be easy to determine. The framers also sought to outlaw even war as a "duel" by mutual consent, when neither side could properly be seen as aggressor.

3. *What "Force" Is Prohibited?* The Charter was intended to outlaw war as well as all lesser uses of force, but the language used was not without ambiguity. Is only military force forbidden or does the prohibition include the use of "economic" force and other coercive measures? Is the threat of force forbidden only if a threat is expressed or clearly implied, or is it forbidden also to create threatening situations, as when one state builds up armed forces and armaments that could threaten another? Does the prohibition of the threat or use of force against the territorial integrity of another state forbid only force designed permanently to deprive another state of any part of its territory or does it also forbid any forcible invasion of another's territory however temporary? Does the prohibition of force against the "political independence" of another state forbid only force designed to end the latter's independence and render it a "puppet," or does it also bar force designed to coerce a state to act against its will, even once, in any circumstances? Is force forbidden even if its purpose is humanitarian, to save human lives, or to help a people achieve "self-determination?" Is the use of force permissible to install a legitimate, democratic government? Does Article 2(4) forbid a state to give military support to insurgents? to the incumbent government battling insurgents? to either side in a civil war? The relation of the prohibition in Article 2(4) to the right of self-defense (Article 51) is considered at p. 1165 *infra*.

For a discussion of the meaning of Article 2(4), including many of the issues addressed in the following pages, see Schachter, The Right of States to Use Armed Force, 82 Mich. L. Rev. 1620 (1984). Schachter concludes (at 1633):

> Admittedly, the article does not provide clear and precise answers to all the questions raised. Concepts such as "force," "threat of force" or "political independence" embrace a wide range of possible meanings. Their application to diverse circumstances involves choices as to these meanings and assessments of the behavior and intentions of various actors. Differences of opinion are often likely even among "disinterested" observers; they are even more likely among those involved or interested. But such divergences are not significantly different from those that arise with respect to almost all general legal principles.

> The foregoing analysis shows that article 2(4) has a reasonably clear core meaning. That core meaning has been spelled out in interpretive documents such as the Declaration of Principles of International Law, adopted unanimously by the General Assembly in 1970. The International Court and the writings of scholars reflect the wide area of agreement

on its meaning. It is therefore unwarranted to suggest that article 2(4) lacks the determinate content necessary to enable it to function as a legal rule of restraint.

4. *Intervention.* The U.N. Charter does not speak to "intervention" by states in the domestic affairs of other states. Insofar as intervention is used strictly to refer to "dictatorial interference" by use or threat of force, it is to be considered in the light of the prohibition of Article 2(4). Other international instruments have inveighed against intervention, and several attempts have been made to define it with respect to nonforcible as well as forcible techniques (e.g., "economic coercion"). See, e.g., Declaration on the Inadmissibility of Intervention into the Domestic Affairs, of States, G.A. Res. 2131 (XX) (Dec. 21, 1965); Declaration on Principles of International Law Concerning Friendly Relations and Co-operation Among States in Accordance with the Charter of the United Nations, G.A. Res. 2625 (XXV) (Oct. 24, 1970) (Friendly Relations Declaration). See generally Damrosch, Politics Across Borders: Nonintervention and Nonforcible Influence Over Domestic Affairs, 83 A.J.I.L. 1 (1989). Intervention in civil conflicts and intervention for asserted "humanitarian" purposes will be addressed in Section 2 below.

5. *Economic Coercion.* During the drafting of Article 2(4), Brazil proposed including a prohibition against the use of "economic measures" against a state. See 6 Docs. of the U.N. Conf. on Int'l Org. 335. The proposal was rejected, but it is not clear whether the rejection reflected a belief that economic aggression was not included within the term "force" or whether "force" was a broad enough term to cover it without specific mention. Goodrich, Hambro and Simons state:

> It seems reasonable to conclude that while various forms of economic and political coercion may be treated as threats to the peace, as contrary to certain of the declared purposes and principles of the Organisation, or as violating agreements entered into or recognised principles of international law, they are not to be regarded as coming necessarily under the prohibition of Article 2(4), which is to be understood as directed against the use of armed force.

Goodrich, Hambro & Simons, Charter of the United Nations 49 (3d ed. 1969). See p. 1152 on the definition of aggression.

6. *Charter and Custom: Jus Cogens and Erga Omnes.* It is commonly accepted that in substance Article 2(4) has become a principle of customary law binding on all states, and has acquired the character of *jus cogens.* See Restatement (Third) § 102, Comment *k* and Reporters' Note 6. A violation of Article 2(4) is clearly a breach of international obligations to the victim of the threat or use of force. The International Court of Justice has said, moreover, that the principles of international law outlawing acts of aggression are obligations *erga omnes,* to the international community as a whole. See *Barcelona Traction, Light and Power Company, Ltd.,* 1970 I.C.J. 3. See also *Military and Paramilitary Activities in and against Nicaragua* (Nicaragua v. United States) (Dissenting Opinion of Judge Schwebel), 1984 I.C.J. 169, 190. On the invalidity of agreements procured by the use or threat of force, see Article 52 of the 1969 Vienna Convention on the Law of Treaties, discussed in Chapter 3, p. 189.

In the *Nicaragua* case, p. 1166 *infra*, the I.C.J., after ruling that limitations on the Court's exercise of jurisdiction in the case precluded it from considering Nicaragua's claim under the U.N. Charter, went on to consider the claim under customary law which the Court held to be virtually identical to the law of the Charter as regards the use of force and the right of self-defense. See also *Armed Activities on the Territory of the Congo* (Democratic Republic of the Congo v. Uganda), 2005 I.C.J. 168, paras. 148, 162. On justiciability of such questions, see Chapter 9, p. 598.

7. *Further Reading.* On the Charter-based prohibition, see Gray, International Law and the Use of Force (3d ed. 2008); Walzer, Just and Unjust Wars (4th ed. 2006); Dinstein, War, Aggression and Self–Defence (4th ed. 2005); O'Connell, International Law and the Use of Force: Cases and Materials (2005); Franck, Recourse to Force: State Action Against Threats and Armed Attacks (2002); Law and Force in the New International Order (Damrosch & Scheffer eds. 1991); Henkin, The Use of Force: Law and U.S. Policy, in Right v. Might: International Law and the Use of Force 37–69 (2d ed. 1991). Earlier works include Falk, Legal Order in a Violent World (1968); Brownlie, International Law and the Use of Force by States (1961); McDougal & Feliciano, Law and Minimum World Public Order (1961); Stone, Legal Controls of International Conflict (1959).

8. *Belligerency and Neutrality.* Given that the U.N. Charter prohibits any threat or use of force, it presumably was designed also to abolish the traditional state of "war" in which states were expected to be neutral as to the conduct of the aggressor. If so, the concepts of both belligerency and neutrality were overtaken by the Charter. Instead, it should be expected that the Security Council would identify an aggressor when aggression occurs, and member states may then be obliged to assist the victim state rather than remain neutral. See Henkin, How Nations Behave 140 (2d ed. 1979).

Unfortunately, the Charter did not put an end to large scale hostilities, however denominated, nor trigger in all instances an authoritative determination as to which state was the aggressor. Consequently, issues about the rights and duties of both the participants in hostilities and of nonparticipants have continued to arise. For example, the Iran–Iraq war in the 1980s saw frequent invocation of the neutral-belligerent distinction, particularly as it relates to states that shipped oil from Iran. Compare Henkin, Force, Intervention and Neutrality in Contemporary International Law, 57 A.S.I.L. Proc. 147, 159–61 (1963) with Deak, Neutrality Revisited, in Transnational Law in a Changing Society 137 (Friedmann, Henkin & Lissitzyn eds., 1972). See also Norton, Between the Ideology and the Reality: The Shadow of the Law of Neutrality, 17 Harv. Int'l L.J. 249 (1976).

b. Efforts to Define Aggression

FRIEDMANN, THE CHANGING STRUCTURE OF INTERNATIONAL LAW
254–55 (1964)

* * * There is no reason to believe that the nations of the world could not theoretically agree on the concepts of "invasion," "armed attacks" or

"blockade." Differences are primarily ones of objectives; they are essentially of a political and ideological, not of a logical, character. * * *

Basic disagreements can be reflected either in definitions so vague and ambiguous as to give effective liberty of action, or in a reluctance to entrust the decision to an impartial authority. The unwillingness of the nations, up to date, to entrust full authority over war and peace to the United Nations or to any international body, may be attributed to three major factors: (a) the continuing struggle between the conflicting demands of national sovereignty and international order, expressed in the claims and limitations of the national right of self-defence; (b) the development of means of destruction so swift and devastating that the traditional time lag between the development of an armed attack and the organisation of defence has become largely obsolete; (c) the enormously increased importance of political and ideological warfare, which has created new forms of "indirect" aggression, not amenable to the established criteria and definitions of aggression.

RESOLUTION ON THE DEFINITION OF AGGRESSION

G.A. Res. 3314 (XXIX) (Dec. 14, 1974)

Article 1

Aggression is the use of armed force by a State against the sovereignty, territorial integrity or political independence of another State, or in any other manner inconsistent with the Charter of the United Nations, as set out in this Definition.

Article 2

The first use of armed force by a State in contravention of the Charter shall constitute *prima facie* evidence of an act of aggression although the Security Council may, in conformity with the Charter, conclude that a determination that an act of aggression has been committed would not be justified in the light of other relevant circumstances, including the fact that the acts concerned or their consequences are not of sufficient gravity.

Article 3

Any of the following acts, regardless of a declaration of war, shall, subject to and in accordance with the provisions of article 2, qualify as an act of aggression:

(a) The invasion or attack by the armed forces of a State of the territory of another State, or any military occupation, however temporary, resulting from such invasion or attack, or any annexation by the use of force of the territory of another State or part thereof,

(b) Bombardment by the armed forces of a State against the territory of another State or the use of any weapons by a State against the territory of another State;

(c) The blockade of the ports or coasts of a State by the armed forces of another State;

(d) An attack by the armed forces of a State on the land, sea or air forces, or marine and air fleets of another State;

(e) The use of armed forces of one State which are within the territory of another State with the agreement of the receiving State, in contravention of the conditions provided for in the agreement or any extension of their presence in such territory beyond the termination of the agreement;

(f) The action of a State in allowing its territory, which it has placed at the disposal of another State, to be used by that other State for perpetrating an act of aggression against a third State;

(g) The sending by or on behalf of a State of armed bands, groups, irregulars or mercenaries, which carry out acts of armed force against another State of such gravity as to amount to the acts listed above, or its substantial involvement therein.

Article 4

The acts enumerated above are not exhaustive and the Security Council may determine that other acts constitute aggression under the provisions of the Charter.

NOTES

1. *U.S. Concerns.* At the San Francisco Conference, and for many years thereafter, the United States opposed the elaboration of a definition of aggression. President Truman summarized the United States position in his annual report to Congress, 1950:

> At the San Francisco Conference on International Organization (1945) there was a movement to insert a definition of aggression in the United Nations Charter. The United States opposed this proposal. It took the position that a definition of aggression cannot be so comprehensive as to include all cases of aggression and cannot take into account the various circumstances which might enter into the determination of aggression in a particular case. Any definition of aggression is a trap for the innocent and an invitation to the guilty. The United States position prevailed at San Francisco, and the Charter adopted a system whereby the appropriate U.N. organ, in the first instance the Security Council, would determine on the basis of the facts of a particular case whether aggression has taken place.

5 Whiteman, Digest of International Law 740 (1965).

2. *Mixed Views on the Definition of Aggression Resolution.* The United States acquiesced in the adoption of the 1974 Definition of Aggression Resolution. For its comments on the definition and on each of its articles, see the statement of Robert Rosenstock, the U.S. Representative to the Special Committee, 70 Dep't St. Bull. 498 (1974). Have the fears the United States

previously expressed in opposition to defining aggression been realized? Has the U.N. definition served any useful purpose?

The 1974 Resolution has had mixed reviews (among other reasons because it glosses over or avoids many disputed issues), but it has influenced subsequent developments, including the cases discussed in this Chapter. See generally Nyiri, The United Nations Search for a Definition of Aggression (1989); Stone, Conflict Through Consensus: UN Approaches to Aggression (1977); Ferencz, Defining Aggression (1975) (2 vols.); Bennett, A Linguistic Critique of the Definition of Aggression, 31 Germ. Y.B.I.L. 481 (1988); Brown–John, The 1974 Definition of Aggression: A Query, 15 Can. Y.B.I. L. 301 (1977); Garvey, The U.N. Definition of "Aggression": Law and Illusion in the Context of Collective Security, 17 Va. J. Int'l L. 177 (1977); Stone, Hopes and Loopholes in the 1974 Definition of Aggression, 71 A.J.I.L. 224 (1977); Ferencz, Can Aggression be Deterred by Law?, 11 Pace Int'l L. Rev. 341 (1999).

3. *"Enumerative" versus General Approaches.* There were two approaches to the definition of aggression during the years of debate in the United Nations. Some favored an "enumerative" definition that would include a list of the acts that constitute aggression; others favored a general definition similar to that of Article 2(4) of the Charter. The 1974 Resolution contains elements of both. Article 1 follows the general definition of the Charter, and limits the definition of aggression to armed force, despite the suggestion by a number of states that aggression includes other forms of hostile acts. Article 3, however, sets out a number of acts that constitute aggression and Article 4 indicates that the list is not exhaustive. The threat of force was not included in Article 1, and "[t]he economic, ideological and other modes of aggression were carefully considered * * * but the result was an interpretation that they did not fall within the term 'aggression' as it had been used in the Charter." Broms, The Definition of Aggression, 154 Rec. des Cours 299, 386 (1977–I).

Under the resolution's definition, would any first attack in strength across an international boundary constitute a *prima facie* case of aggression? Compare the difficulties in developing a workable and meaningful test of the "initiator" of war in political science and other disciplines. See Damrosch, Use of Force and Constitutionalism, 36 Colum. J. Transnat'l. L. 449, 460–65 (1997).

4. *Economic Aggression.* A 1952 U.N. Report on the Question of Defining Aggression suggested that "unilateral action to deprive a State of the economic resources derived from the fair practice of international trade, or to endanger its economy" may be an act of aggression. U.N. Doc. A/2211 at 58 (Oct. 3, 1952). The concept of economic aggression was criticized by others as "liable to extend the concept of aggression almost indefinitely." Id. Economic coercion was not included in the 1974 Definition of Aggression but several resolutions have denounced such coercion as subverting sovereign rights. See, e.g., Article 32 of the Charter of Economic Rights and Duties of States, G.A. Res. 3281 (XXIX) (Dec. 12, 1974), reprinted in 14 I.L.M. 251 (1975); Declaration of the Principles of International Law Concerning Friendly Relations and Co-operation among States, G.A. Res. 2625 (XXV) (Oct. 24, 1970); Declaration

on the Inadmissibility of Intervention in Domestic Affairs of States and the Protection of their Independence and Sovereignty, G.A. Res. 2131 (XX) (Dec. 21, 1965). Compare Article 16 of the Charter of the Organization of American States: "No State may use or encourage the use of coercive measures of an economic or political character in order to force the sovereign will of another State and obtain from it advantages of any kind." Apr. 30, 1948, 2 U.S.T. 2394, 119 U.N.T.S. 3.

5. *Individual Criminal Responsibility.* On efforts to formulate a definition of aggression for applicability in criminal prosecutions against individuals at the International Criminal Court, see Chapter 16 at p. 1352.

c. Indirect Aggression

FRIEDMANN, THE CHANGING STRUCTURE
OF INTERNATIONAL LAW

262 (1964)

It is the increasingly numerous and important forms of attack upon the integrity of a state by other than the traditional means of military attack, usually styled "indirect" or "ideological" aggression, that give rise to problems of altogether different dimensions and that affect some of the foundations of traditional international law. These attacks range from many types of ideological and political propaganda and psychological warfare, by radio, by aerial leaflets, etc., to the organisation of subversive, political movements inside another country, the systematic infiltration of political agents, and the systematic economic strangulation of a regime by comprehensive trade boycott.

The legal problems arising from these important but often highly elusive forms of interference with the integrity of a state are further complicated by the fact that they are often intertwined with civil strife and the ensuing question whether assistance to one or both sides in a civil conflict, ranging from military assistance to the supply of arms, political and economic help, is permitted or prohibited by international law. In modern civil wars, military assistance to one or the other side may often be a means of deliberately supporting one political or social order as against another.

NOTES

1. *Aid to Rebel Forces in Civil War.* Brownlie writes:

Charges of "aggression" are frequently based on allegations of military aid to, and control over, rebels in a civil war. If rebels are effectively supported *and controlled* by another state that state is responsible for a "use of force" as a consequence of the agency. Thus aid to rebels by foreign states has been held by the General Assembly to be inconsistent with the principles of the United Nations Charter, with implicit reference to Article 2, paragraphs 3 and 4. However, in cases in which aid is given but there is no agency established, and there is no exercise of control over the rebels by the foreign government, it is very doubtful if it is correct to describe the responsibility of that government in terms of a use of force or armed attack. Unfortunately the resolutions referred to above and the other relevant materials do not draw this distinction. The illegality of aid to rebel groups has been established in a variety of ways. It has been described as "intervention in the internal affairs of a state" and as "indirect aggression." In resolution 380(V) of 17 November 1950, the General Assembly included "fomenting civil strife" in its strong condemnation of aggression.

Brownlie, International Law and the Use of Force 370 (1963).

2. *Defining Aggression in Respect of Indirect Acts.* The 1952 Report of the Secretary–General on the Question of Defining Aggression, U.N. Doc. A/2211 (Oct. 3, 1952), included extended discussion of "indirect aggression." See Section VII at 55.

The characteristic of indirect aggression appears to be that the aggressor state, without itself committing hostile acts as a State, operates through third parties who are either foreigners or nationals seemingly acting on their own initiative. * * * The concept of indirect aggression has been construed to include certain hostile acts or certain forms of complicity in hostilities in progress.

Id. at 56. The report also considered "cases of indirect aggression which do not constitute acts of participation in hostilities in progress, but which are designed to prepare such acts, to undermine a country's power of resistance, or to bring about a change in its political or social system." Id. at 55. Among examples proposed by spokesmen of various countries were: intervention in another state's internal or foreign affairs; violation of the political integrity of a country by subversive action; incitement to civil war; maintenance of a fifth column; ideological aggression and propaganda. Id. at 55–56.

The term "indirect aggression" is not included in the definition of aggression adopted by the General Assembly, but some elements in the definition may be deemed indirect, e.g., Article 3(g). Note that Article 4 states that the acts enumerated in Article 3 are not exhaustive.

3. *What Degree of Control, With What Legal Consequence?* In the *Nicaragua* case, 1986 I.C.J. 14 at 106–10, the International Court of Justice considered whether U.S. assistance to rebels seeking to overthrow the government of Nicaragua violated the rules of customary international law which it found to be essentially parallel to Article 2(4). Although the Court concluded that the U.S. actions were indeed violations of the prohibitions on use of force and intervention, it did not find a basis for attributing all the actions of the rebels to the U.S. government, since Nicaragua had not proved that the United States directly and effectively controlled their actions.

Some years later, the International Criminal Tribunal for the Former Yugoslavia expressed its disagreement with the *Nicaragua* court's "effective control" test and applied a different (lower) standard for attributing the conduct of a paramilitary group to a foreign government that had given it substantial support. *Prosecutor v. Tadic,* I.C.T.Y. Case No IT–94–1–A, 38

I.L.M. 1518, Judgment on Appeal from Conviction (July 15, 1999). However, the I.C.T.Y. was not considering "aggression" (or armed attack or intervention) but rather the different question of whether the conflict in Bosnia–Herzegovina was an "international" or "non-international" conflict for purposes of prosecution of an individual for war crimes. See p. 1284 note 2. The I.C.J. addressed this disagreement and reaffirmed its *Nicaragua* conclusion when it returned to a related question in the *Bosnian Genocide Case* (Bosnia–Herzegovina v. Serbia), 2007 I.C.J. 191. See p. 503.

4. *Irregular Forces: Congo v. Uganda.* In *Armed Activities on the Territory of the Congo* (Democratic Republic of the Congo v. Uganda), 2005 I.C.J. 168, the Court reached the following disposition:

> THE COURT,
>
> (1) By sixteen votes to one,
>
> *Finds* that the Republic of Uganda, * * * by actively extending military, logistic, economic and final support to irregular forces having operated on the territory of the DRC, violated the principle of non-use of force in international relations and the principle of non-intervention.

Uganda had claimed its activities to be justified as lawful self-defense, in part as a response to military and logistical support allegedly provided by the Congolese authorities to anti-Ugandan insurgents who were engaging in cross-border attacks from Congo into Uganda. The Court rejected Uganda's self-defense plea. See further pp. 1177–78 note 4 below.

3. Threat of Force

Professor Schachter writes:

> What is meant by a "threat of force" has received rather less consideration [than what is meant by "the use of force"]. Clearly a threat to use military action to coerce a State to make concessions is forbidden. But in many situations the deployment of military forces or missiles has unstated aims and its effect is equivocal. However, the preponderance of military strength in some States and their political relations with potential target States may justifiably lead to an inference of a threat of force against the political independence of the target State. An examination of the particular circumstances is necessary to reach that conclusion, but the applicability of Article 2(4) in principle can hardly be denied. Curiously, it has not been invoked much as an explicit prohibition of such implied threats. The explanation may lie in the subtleties of power relations and the difficulty of demonstrating coercive intent. Or perhaps more realistically, it may be a manifestation of the general recognition and tolerance of disparities of power and their effect in maintaining dominant and subordinate relationships between unequal States. However, such toleration, wide as it may be, is not without limits. A blatant and direct threat of force to compel another State to yield territory or make substantial political concessions (not required by law) would have to

be seen as illegal under Article 2(4), if the words "threat of force" are to have any meaning.

Schachter, International Law in Theory and Practice 111 (1991) (footnotes omitted). See also Sadurska, Threats of Force, 82 A.J.I.L. 239 (1988). For the first book-length treatment (compiling 443 threats of force between 1945 and 2003 and analyzing several dozen of them), see Stürchler, The Threat of Force in International Law (2007), critically reviewed by Dinstein at 102 A.J.I.L. 918 (2008).

NOTES

1. *Nuclear Weapons.* In the Advisory Opinion on the Legality of the Threat or Use of Nuclear Weapons, 1996 I.C.J. 226, the Court addressed the "threat" aspect as follows:

47. In order to lessen or eliminate the risk of unlawful attack, States sometimes signal that they possess certain weapons to use in self-defence against any State violating their territorial integrity or political independence. Whether a signalled intention to use force if certain events occur is or is not a "threat" within Article 2, paragraph 4, of the Charter depends upon various factors. If the envisaged use of force is itself unlawful, the stated readiness to use it would be a threat prohibited under Article 2, paragraph 4. Thus it would be illegal for a State to threaten force to secure territory from another State, or to cause it to follow or not follow certain political or economic paths. The notions of "threat" and "use" of force under Article 2, paragraph 4, of the Charter stand together in the sense that if the use of force itself in a given case is illegal—for whatever reason—the threat to use such force will likewise be illegal. In short, if it is to be lawful, the declared readiness of a State to use force must be a use of force that is in conformity with the Charter. For the rest, no State—whether or not it defended the policy of deterrence—suggested to the Court that it would be lawful to threaten to use force if the use of force contemplated would be illegal.

48. Some States put forward the argument that possession of nuclear weapons is itself an unlawful threat to use force. Possession of nuclear weapons may indeed justify an inference of preparedness to use them. In order to be effective, the policy of deterrence, by which those States possessing or under the umbrella of nuclear weapons seek to discourage military aggression by demonstrating that it will serve no purpose, necessitates that the intention to use nuclear weapons be credible. Whether this is a "threat" contrary to Article 2, paragraph 4, depends upon whether the particular use of force envisaged would be directed against the territorial integrity or political independence of a State, or against the Purposes of the United Nations, or whether, in the event that it were intended as a means of defence, it would necessarily violate the principles of necessity and proportionality. In any of these circumstances the use of force, and the threat to use it, would be unlawful under the law of the Charter.

2. *Ultimatum.* One criticism of the 1999 NATO intervention in Kosovo was that the United States and other NATO powers effectively gave the Yugoslav leadership an ultimatum that military force would be used against the Federal Republic of Yugoslavia unless the negotiators agreed without delay to the terms of a peace settlement offered at Rambouillet, France, in February 1999. Would such "threat diplomacy" constitute a prohibited "threat of force" under Article 2(4)? See discussion by the Independent International Commission on Kosovo in its Kosovo Report (2000). For more on the Kosovo intervention, see pp. 1206–12.

3. *Maritime Enforcement in Disputed Area.* Guyana and Suriname had a longstanding dispute over their maritime boundary. In 1998, Guyana granted a concession to a Canadian company, CGX, for oil exploration of the continental shelf in the disputed area. In May 2000, CGX moved an oil rig into the disputed area and began extending the rig's "legs" onto the continental shelf in preparation for exploratory drilling. Suriname demanded that Guyana cease oil exploration activities in the disputed area and ordered CGX to cease all activities there. Then, on June 3, 2000, a Surinamese patrol boat approached the CGX oil rig in the middle of the night and ordered it to depart from the disputed area within twelve hours "or the consequences will be yours."

In an arbitration convened under Annex VII of the U.N. Convention on the Law of the Sea (see Chapters 9 and 17), the parties requested the tribunal to determine their maritime boundary. Guyana also asked the tribunal to find Suriname responsible for violating Article 2(4) of the Charter, which Guyana asserted was incorporated into the Convention. In its pleadings, Guyana characterized Suriname's actions as an unlawful threat or use of force, while Suriname argued that it had merely engaged in a law enforcement measure within the area of its territorial claim. The tribunal found no actual use of force but, as regards the claim of a threat of force, the tribunal said:

> 439. The testimony of those involved in the incident clearly reveals that the rig was ordered to leave the area and if this demand was not fulfilled, responsibility for unspecified consequences would be theirs. There was no unanimity as to what these "consequences" might have been. The Tribunal is of the view that the order given by Major Jones to the rig constituted an explicit threat that force might be used if the order was not complied with. The question now arises whether this threat of the use of force breaches the terms of the Convention, the UN Charter and general international law. The ICJ has thrown some light on the circumstances, where a threat of force can be considered illegal. [Quoting part of para. 47 of the *Nuclear Weapons* advisory opinion, Note 1 above.]

> * * *

> 445. The Tribunal accepts the argument that in international law force may be used in law enforcement activities provided that such force is unavoidable, reasonable and necessary. However in the circumstances of the present case, this Tribunal is of the view that the action mounted by Suriname on 3 June 2000 seemed more akin to a threat of military action rather than a mere law enforcement activity. * * * Suriname's

action therefore constituted a threat of the use of force in contravention of the Convention, the UN Charter and general international law.

The Tribunal rejected Suriname's plea that its action was a lawful response to a wrongful act by Guyana in granting a concession in the disputed area, on the ground that a measure involving the threat of force cannot have been a lawful countermeasure. The Tribunal concluded that a declaratory judgment in Guyana's favor on this point was sufficient given the lack of evidence of any damage, and hence did not order Suriname to pay monetary compensation. Permanent Court of Arbitration, In the Matter of an Arbitration Between Guyana and Suriname, Award of the Arbitral Tribunal, Sept. 17, 2007, 47 I.L.M. 166 (2008).

4. Threat or Use of Limited Force

THE CUBAN MISSILE CRISIS, 1962
4 Whiteman, Digest of International Law 523–24 (1965)

On the evening of October 22, 1962, President John F. Kennedy announced that "This Government, as promised, has maintained the closest surveillance of the Soviet military buildup on the island of Cuba. Within the past week unmistakeable evidence has established the fact that a series of offensive missile sites is now in preparation on that imprisoned island." He added that "This urgent transformation of Cuba into an important strategic base—by the presence of these large, long-range, and clearly offensive weapons of sudden mass destruction—constitutes an explicit threat to the peace and security of all the Americas, in flagrant and deliberate defiance of the Rio Pact of 1947, the traditions of this nation and hemisphere, the Joint Resolution of the 87th Congress, the Charter of the United Nations, and my own public warnings to the Soviets on September 4 and 13 [1962]." On the following day, October 23, the Council of the Organization of American States, meeting as the Provisional Organ of Consultation, called for "the immediate dismantling and withdrawal from Cuba of all missiles and other weapons with any offensive capability" and recommended that "the member states, in accordance with Articles 6 and 8 of the Inter–American Treaty of Reciprocal Assistance [1947], take all measures, individually and collectively, including the use of armed force, which they may deem necessary to ensure that the Government of Cuba cannot continue to receive supplies which may threaten the peace and security of the Continent and to prevent the missiles in Cuba with offensive capability from ever becoming an active threat to the peace and security of the Continent."

On that same day—October 23, 1962—President Kennedy by Proclamation ordered the interdiction by U.S. forces of the delivery of offensive weapons to Cuba. The substantive portions of the Proclamation provided that in accordance with the resolution of the Organ of Consultation of the American Republics of October 23, 1962, "and to defend the security of the United States," the forces under the President's command were ordered, beginning at 2 p.m. Greenwich time October 24, 1962, to interdict the delivery of offensive weapons and associated matériel to Cuba. To enforce this order, the Secretary of Defense was ordered to take appropriate measures to prevent the delivery of the prohibited matériel to Cuba, "employing the land, sea and air forces of the United States in cooperation with any forces that may be made available by other American States." The Secretary of Defense was authorized to make designations "within a reasonable distance of Cuba, of prohibited or restricted zones and of prescribed routes." Further, the Proclamation specified:

> Any vessel or craft, which may be proceeding toward Cuba may be intercepted and may be directed to identify itself, its cargo, equipment and stores and its ports of call, to stop, to lie to, to submit to visit and search, or to proceed as directed. Any vessel or craft which fails or refuses to respond to or comply with directions shall be subject to being taken into custody. Any vessel or craft which it is believed is en route to Cuba and may be carrying prohibited matériel or may itself constitute such matériel shall, wherever possible, be directed to proceed to another destination of its own choice and shall be taken into custody if it fails or refuses to obey such directions. All vessels or craft taken into custody shall be sent into a port of the United States for appropriate disposition.

> In carrying out this order, force shall not be used except in case of failure or refusal to comply with directions, or with regulations or directives of the Secretary of Defense, issued hereunder, after reasonable efforts have been made to communicate them to the vessel or craft, or in case of self-defense. In any case, force shall be used only to the extent necessary.

Proclamation No. 3504, 47 Dep't St. Bull. 717 (1962), 27 Fed. Reg. 10401 (1962).

NOTE

Evaluating the Quarantine. Was the U.S. action to impose a quarantine of Cuba a threat or use of force? against the territorial integrity or political independence of Cuba? of the Soviet Union? of states whose ships were prevented from going to Cuba? Was it "in any other manner inconsistent with the purposes of the United Nations?" See MacChesney, Some Comments on the "Quarantine" of Cuba, 57 A.J.I.L. 592, 596 (1963); Henkin, The UN and Its Supporters, 78 Pol. Sci. Q. 504, 527, 528 (1963). But see Wright, The Cuban Quarantine, 57 A.J.I.L. 546 (1963). Wright rejected the positions that the U.S. action was a "pacific blockade" under traditional international law, that it was permissible in self-defense under Article 51 (quoted below), and that it was justified under the authority of the Organization of American States, as officially argued by the State Department. (Note that the United States did not invoke a self-defense justification for the quarantine, but rather based its position on the O.A.S. authorization. See p. 1268 note 2.)

For the suggestion that international law was not "relevant" in the Cuban Missile Crisis, see Dean Acheson's statement at p. 19 *supra*. For defense of its relevance, see Henkin, How Nations Behave 279–302 (2d ed. 1979); Chayes, The Cuban Missile Crisis: International Crises and the Role of Law (1974, 1987).

5. Consent to Military Intervention

SCHACHTER, THE RIGHT OF STATES TO USE ARMED FORCE

82 Mich. L. Rev. 1620, 1644–45 (1984) (footnotes omitted)

A separate comment is called for by the kind of case presented by the request of the Governor–General of Grenada for military intervention by the United States and neighboring states [in 1983]. That request was premised on the "vacuum of authority" resulting from an attempted coup d'état and a danger of foreign intervention. A factual question was raised as to whether the Governor–General made his request prior to the intervention or whether it was "concocted" after the invasion had been agreed upon and set in motion. Another question was raised as to whether the Governor–General had the constitutional authority to make such a request. On both these points, there was reason to doubt that the Governor–General's "request" constituted an adequate legal justification for the armed intervention. However, apart from these questions specifically related to Grenada, there is the broader issue of principle concerning intervention on invitation of the government. * * * [I]n the absence of a civil war, recognized governments have a right to receive external military assistance and outside states are free to furnish such aid. But a problem arises if such outside military force is used to impose restrictions on the "political independence" of the country, as, for example, by limiting the choice of the population in regard to the composition of the government or the policies it should follow. In such cases, we would conclude that the foreign armies, though invited by the government, are using military force to curtail the political independence of the state, and therefore it is an action that contravenes article 2(4). A different conclusion may be reached when a foreign force is invited by the government to help put down an attempted coup or to assist in restoring law and order. This would not violate article 2(4). Recent examples include French and British military support of African governments facing internal disorder. The line between the two situations may not always be easy to draw. An initial intervention of a limited character may evolve into a more protracted use of foreign forces to repress internal democracy and political expression. There is good reason therefore to place a heavy burden on any foreign government which intervenes with armed forces even at the invitation of the constitutional authority to demonstrate convincingly that its use of force has not infringed the right of the people to determine their political system and the composition of their government. It cannot be assumed that governments will, as a rule, invite foreign interventions that leave the people entirely free to make their own political determinations, though on occasion this may be the case.

NOTES

1. *Who Can Give Consent?* The U.S. action in Grenada implicated not only the issue of whether an appropriate Grenadian authority had consented to the intervention, but also whether military intervention might have been justified to protect U.S. nationals who were asserted to be in danger there. See p. 1188 below. A similar combination of arguments was invoked concerning the U.S. intervention in Panama a few years later. Among the justifications claimed by the United States for the invasion of Panama in 1989, President Bush included the following:

> In the early morning of December 20, 1989, the democratically elected Panamanian leadership announced the formation of a government, assumed power in a formal swearing-in ceremony, and welcomed the assistance of the U.S. Armed Forces in removing the illegitimate Noriega regime.

Communication from the President of the United States Transmitting a Report on the Development Concerning the Deployment of United States Forces to Panama on December 20, 1989, House Doc. 101–127, at 1 (1990). In summing up the justifications for the invasion the President repeated that the deployment of U.S. forces "was welcomed by the democratically elected government of Panama." Id. at 2. See the President's letter to Congress, p. 1180 *infra*.

It appears that several hours before the invasion began, a U.S. representative in Panama informed Guillermo Endara, who had apparently been the majority's choice in a recent election, that the invasion was about to take place. Endara was then taken to a U.S. military base in the Panama Canal Zone where the oath of office was administered to him. The United States did not claim that Endara invited the invasion or was asked to consent to it, or that if he had not done so the invasion would not have taken place. Did Endara's "welcome" of the invasion constitute an invitation by a government, justifying it under international law? Was it justified as a use of force to give effect to the wishes of the Panamanian people? See the discussion of the invasion of Panama, p. 1180 *infra*. See also Hargrove, Intervention by Invitation and the Politics of the New World Order; Müllerson, Intervention by Invitation; Wedgwood, Commentary on Intervention by Invitation; and Ferencz, Commentary on What International Law Demands and How States Respond, all in Law and Force in the New International Order 111–85 (Damrosch & Scheffer eds. 1991).

2. *Requests from Opposition.* In the *Nicaragua Case* (Merits), the International Court of Justice said:

> As the Court has stated, the principle of non-intervention derives from customary international law. It would certainly lose its effectiveness as a principle of law if intervention were to be justified by a mere request for assistance made by an opposition group in another State—supposing such a request to have actually been made by an opposition to the régime in Nicaragua in this instance. Indeed, it is difficult to see what would remain of the principle of non-intervention in international law if inter-

vention, which is already allowable at the request of the government of a State, were also to be allowed at the request of the opposition. This would permit any State to intervene at any moment in the internal affairs of another State, whether at the request of the government or at the request of its opposition. Such a situation does not in the Court's view correspond to the present state of international law.

Military and Paramilitary Activities in and Against Nicaragua (Nicaragua v. United States), 1986 I.C.J. 14, 126.

3. *Advance Consent?* If an incumbent government has the right under international law to invite foreign troops into the country to help repel external or internal threats (compare pp. 1170–72 and 1196–1201 below), may it also consent *in advance* to foreign intervention? Could it grant an irrevocable consent to future entry of foreign troops? Consider the following examples:

a. As a condition of ratification of the Panama Canal Treaties of 1977 (which provided *inter alia* for the return to Panama of full control over the Canal as of December 31, 1999), the United States insisted on reserving the right to take necessary steps, including by means of military force, to reopen the Canal if it should ever be closed in the future. Assuming that the government of Panama did properly agree to this condition (compare Chapter 3, pp. 151, 184 on challenges to validity of treaties and treaty reservations), could such agreement authorize the United States to take actions that would otherwise violate Article 2(4)'s prohibition on use of force? Could such consent endure in perpetuity?

b. Proposals have been made for an agreement among democratic governments that each would come to the aid of any other treaty partner, with military force if necessary, to resist or reverse any forcible attempt to overthrow such a government. It has also been suggested that consent to future external intervention to protect minorities or quell ethnic strife could be an important element in bringing about settlement of intractable ethnic conflicts. If a foreign military intervention would violate Article 2(4) in the absence of effective consent, may political leaders at a given time commit the country to receive a prospective intervention upon the occurrence of specified contingencies in the future? How might such consent thereafter be rescinded? For discussion of these and related problems, see, e.g., Farer, a Paradigm of Legitimate Intervention, in Enforcing Restraint: Collective Intervention in Internal Conflicts 316, 332 (Damrosch ed. 1993); Wippman, Treaty–Based Intervention: Who Can Say No?, 62 U. Chi. L. Rev. 607 (1995).

c. Upon intervening with military force in the Republic of Cyprus in 1974 (assertedly to protect the Turkish Cypriot minority on the island in the aftermath of a Greek-instigated coup), Turkey referred to a Treaty of Guarantee concluded when Cyprus attained independence in 1960. Under the Turkish interpretation, the treaty allowed the three guarantor powers—the United Kingdom, Greece, or Turkey—to intervene in the event of developments disrupting the agreed constitutional balance between the Greek and Turkish communities in Cyprus. Many governments and scholars have rejected the Turkish position that the Treaty of Guarantee could be interpreted to authorize unilateral forcible intervention, and have also considered that prospective consent to a use of force that would otherwise violate Article 2(4) could not validly be given in international law. Should Article 2(4) be understood as precluding any form of prospective consent? See discussion in Wippman, 62 U. Chi. L. Rev. at 635–48 (1995).

d. Could a potential settlement of the Israel–Palestinian conflict include a reservation to Israel of rights to send military forces into (or in airspace over) a future Palestinian state? Would the compatibility of such a provision with Article 2(4) depend on the contingencies in which such rights might be invoked, and/or on the purposes for which such forces might be used? See below on self-defense and anticipatory self-defense.

4. *Withdrawal of Consent.* In *Armed Activities on the Territory of the Congo* (Democratic Republic of the Congo v. Uganda), 2005 I.C.J. 168, Congo complained that Uganda had sent its military forces into Congolese territory and engaged in military activities there in violation of the prohibition on use of force. Uganda maintained that its forces were present with the consent of Congolese authorities (in part to prevent crossborder incursions) and that renewal of consent had been given. The Court addressed the factual dispute between the parties as to whether consent had ever been granted, renewed, or withdrawn as of the several time frames relevant to the legal issues. Part of the dispute concerned the significance of ceasefire agreements aimed at settling the civil war in Congo and setting a timetable for an orderly withdrawal of all foreign forces. The Court rejected Uganda's contention that the setting of a deadline for all foreign troops to leave Congo constituted consent to their presence up to that deadline. It stated that Congo's acceptance of a *modus operandi* for orderly withdrawal merely acknowledged realities on the ground; Congo did not thereby recognize the situation on the ground as legal. The Court therefore denied Uganda's plea of consent in general (with one limited exception in a specific border region in a given time period). See 2005 I.C.J. 168, paras. 42–54, 92–105. Would it be appropriate in such circumstances to require a fairly high degree of clarity in communications purporting to authorize a foreign military presence? Should withdrawal of consent entail any particular formality? (The Court suggested that "no particular formalities" would in principle be required but also observed that one statement invoked by Congo as terminating consent was textually ambiguous.)

6. The Self–Defense Exception: Article 51 and Customary Law

The materials presented here on lawful self-defense under Article 51 of the Charter begin with the terms of that provision, which are framed in terms of "armed attack," and then turn to the application of the customary law of self-defense (parallel to the Charter-based law) in the context of such attacks. Self-defense against an actual armed attack needs to be distinguished from self-defense against an attack that is imminent but has not yet commenced, as well as from measures to prevent more remote threats of future attacks and from self-defense against non-state actors. After a review of general considerations, we turn to problems of anticipatory self-defense and preemption or prevention, and then to defense against non-state actors.

a. General Requirements

CHARTER OF THE UNITED NATIONS

Signed at San Francisco, June 26, 1945

ARTICLE 51

Nothing in the present Charter shall impair the inherent right of individual or collective self-defence if an armed attack occurs against a Member of the United Nations, until the Security Council has taken measures necessary to maintain international peace and security. Measures taken by Members in the exercise of this right of self-defence shall be immediately reported to the Security Council and shall not in any way affect the authority and responsibility of the Security Council under the present Charter to take at any time such action as it deems necessary in order to maintain or restore international peace and security.

MILITARY AND PARAMILITARY ACTIVITIES IN AND AGAINST NICARAGUA (NICARAGUA v. UNITED STATES)

1986 I.C.J. 14, 103–23

[In 1984 the Republic of Nicaragua brought a case charging the United States with violations of customary and treaty law by military and paramilitary activities against Nicaragua. Nicaragua accused the United States of attacks on oil pipelines, storage and port facilities, and Nicaraguan naval patrol boats; the mining of Nicaraguan ports; violation of Nicaraguan air space; as well as training, arming, equipping, financing and supplying counter-revolutionary forces (known as the *contras*) seeking to overthrow the government of Nicaragua. Nicaragua claimed that these acts constituted violations of Article 2(4) of the U.N. Charter and corresponding principles of customary law. The United States withdrew from participation in the proceedings after the Court's adverse ruling on jurisdiction (see Chapter 9, p. 609), but it made known its position that Nicaragua had supplied arms and given other support from its territory to armed opposition to the Government of El Salvador, and that U.S. actions were designed to interdict that support. The United States justified its activities against Nicaragua as acts in collective self-defense of El Salvador and of other Central American states allegedly threatened by Nicaraguan subversion.

Because of reservations in the U.S. declaration accepting the compulsory jurisdiction of the Court (see Chapter 9), the Court concluded that it could not consider the Nicaraguan claims under the U.N. Charter, but that the principles as to the use of force incorporated in the Charter "correspond, in essentials, to those found in customary international law." The Court proceeded to adjudicate Nicaragua's customary law claims accordingly (in effect construing Articles 2(4) and 51 of the Charter). The

Court (by twelve votes to three) decided that by the actions in question the U.S. had breached its obligations under customary law not to use force against another state, not to intervene in the affairs of another state, and not to interrupt peaceful maritime commerce, and had breached its obligations under the Treaty of Friendship, Commerce and Navigation between the two states. The Court rejected claims that the Acts were justified as being in collective self-defense with the Government of El Salvador.

In its judgment the Court said:]

195. In the case of individual self-defence, the exercise of this right is subject to the State concerned having been the victim of an armed attack. Reliance on collective self-defence of course does not remove the need for this. There appears now to be general agreement on the nature of the acts which can be treated as constituting armed attacks. In particular, it may be considered to be agreed that an armed attack must be understood as including not merely action by regular armed forces across an international border, but also "the sending by or on behalf of a State of armed bands, groups, irregulars or mercenaries, which carry out acts of armed force against another State of such gravity as to amount to" *(inter alia)* an actual armed attack conducted by regular forces, "or its substantial involvement therein". This description, contained in Article 3, paragraph *(g)*, of the Definition of Aggression annexed to General Assembly resolution 3314 (XXIX), may be taken to reflect customary international law. The Court sees no reason to deny that, in customary law, the prohibition of armed attacks may apply to the sending by a State of armed bands to the territory of another State, if such an operation, because of its scale and effects, would have been classified as an armed attack rather than as a mere frontier incident had it been carried out by regular armed forces. But the Court does not believe that the concept of "armed attack" includes not only acts by armed bands where such acts occur on a significant scale but also assistance to rebels in the form of the provision of weapons or logistical or other support. Such assistance may be regarded as a threat or use of force, or amount to intervention in the internal or external affairs of other States. It is also clear that it is the State which is the victim of an armed attack which must form and declare the view that it has been so attacked. There is no rule in customary international law permitting another State to exercise the right of collective self-defence on the basis of its own assessment of the situation. Where collective self-defence is invoked, it is to be expected that the State for whose benefit this right is used will have declared itself to be the victim of an armed attack.

* * *

199. At all events, the Court finds that in customary international law, whether of a general kind or that particular to the inter-American legal system, there is no rule permitting the exercise of collective self-defence in the absence of a request by the State which regards itself as the

victim of an armed attack. The Court concludes that the requirement of a request by the State which is the victim of the alleged attack is additional to the requirement that such a State should have declared itself to have been attacked.

* * *

201. To justify certain activities involving the use of force, the United States has relied solely on the exercise of its right of collective self-defence. However the Court, having regard particularly to the non-participation of the United States in the merits phase, considers that it should enquire whether customary international law, applicable to the present dispute, may contain other rules which may exclude the unlawfulness of such activities. * * * [T]he Court must enquire whether there is any justification for the activities in question, to be found not in the right of collective self-defence against an armed attack, but in the right to take counter-measures in response to conduct of Nicaragua which is not alleged to constitute an armed attack. It will examine this point in connection with an analysis of the principle of non-intervention in customary international law.

* * *

211. The Court has recalled above (paragraphs 193 to 195) that for one State to use force against another, on the ground that that State has committed a wrongful act of force against a third State, is regarded as lawful, by way of exception, only when the wrongful act provoking the response was an armed attack. Thus the lawfulness of the use of force by a State in response to a wrongful act of which it has not itself been the victim is not admitted when this wrongful act is not an armed attack. In the view of the Court, under international law in force today—whether customary international law or that of the United Nations system—States do not have a right of "collective" armed response to acts which do not constitute an "armed attack". Furthermore, the Court has to recall that the United States itself is relying on the "inherent right of self-defence" (paragraph 126 above), but apparently does not claim that any such right exists as would, in respect of intervention, operate in the same way as the right of collective self-defence in respect of an armed attack. In the discharge of its duty under Article 53 of the Statute, the Court has nevertheless had to consider whether such a right might exist; but in doing so it may take note of the absence of any such claim by the United States as an indication of *opinio juris*.

* * *

227. The Court will first appraise the facts in the light of the principle of the non-use of force, examined in paragraphs 187 to 200 above. What is unlawful, in accordance with that principle, is recourse to either the threat or the use of force against the territorial integrity or political independence of any State. For the most part, the complaints by Nicaragua are of the actual use of force against it by the United States. Of

the acts which the Court has found imputable to the Government of the United States, the following are relevant in this respect:

– the laying of mines in Nicaraguan internal or territorial waters in early 1984 (paragraph 80 above);

– certain attacks on Nicaraguan ports, oil installations and a naval base (paragraphs 81 and 86 above).

These activities constitute infringements of the principle of the prohibition of the use of force, defined earlier, unless they are justified by circumstances which exclude their unlawfulness, a question now to be examined. The Court has also found (paragraph 92) the existence of military manoeuvres held by the United States near the Nicaraguan borders; and Nicaragua has made some suggestion that this constituted a "threat of force," which is equally forbidden by the principle of non-use of force. The Court is however not satisfied that the manoeuvres complained of, in the circumstances in which they were held, constituted on the part of the United States a breach, as against Nicaragua, of the principle forbidding recourse to the threat or use of force.

* * *

229.   The Court must thus consider whether, as the Respondent claims, the acts in question of the United States are justified by the exercise of its right of collective self-defence against an armed attack. The Court must therefore establish whether the circumstances required for the exercise of this right of self-defence are present and, if so, whether the steps taken by the United States actually correspond to the requirements of international law. For the Court to conclude that the United States was lawfully exercising its right of collective self-defence, it must first find that Nicaragua engaged in an armed attack against El Salvador, Honduras or Costa Rica.

230.   As regards El Salvador, the Court has found (paragraph 160 above) that it is satisfied that between July 1979 and the early months of 1981, an intermittent flow of arms was routed via the territory of Nicaragua to the armed opposition in that country. The Court was not however satisfied that assistance has reached the Salvadorian armed opposition, on a scale of any significance, since the early months of 1981, or that the Government of Nicaragua was responsible for any flow of arms at either period. Even assuming that the supply of arms to the opposition in El Salvador could be treated as imputable to the Government of Nicaragua, to justify invocation of the right of collective self-defence in customary international law, it would have to be equated with an armed attack by Nicaragua on El Salvador. As stated above, the Court is unable to consider that, in customary international law, the provision of arms to the opposition in another State constitutes an armed attack on that State. Even at a time when the arms flow was at its peak, and again assuming the participation of the Nicaraguan Government, that would not constitute such armed attack.

231.   Turning to Honduras and Costa Rica, the Court has also stated (paragraph 164 above) that it should find established that certain transborder incursions into the territory of those two States, in 1982, 1983 and 1984, were imputable to the Government of Nicaragua. Very little information is however available to the Court as to the circumstances of these incursions or their possible motivations, which renders it difficult to decide whether they may be treated for legal purposes as amounting, singly or collectively, to an "armed attack" by Nicaragua on either or both States. The Court notes that during the Security Council debate in March/April 1984, the representative of Costa Rica made no accusation of an armed attack, emphasizing merely his country's neutrality and support for the Contadora process (S/PV.2529, pp. 13–23); the representative of Honduras however stated that "my country is the object of aggression made manifest through a number of incidents by Nicaragua against our territorial integrity and civilian population" (ibid., p. 37). There are however other considerations which justify the Court in finding that neither these incursions, nor the alleged supply of arms to the opposition in El Salvador, may be relied on as justifying the exercise of the right of collective self-defence.

232.   The exercise of the right of collective self-defence presupposes that an armed attack has occurred; and it is evident that it is the victim State, being the most directly aware of that fact, which is likely to draw general attention to its plight. It is also evident that if the victim State wishes another State to come to its help in the exercise of the right of collective self-defence, it will normally make an express request to that effect. Thus in the present instance, the Court is entitled to take account, in judging the asserted justification of the exercise of collective self-defence by the United States, of the actual conduct of El Salvador, Honduras and Costa Rica at the relevant time, as indicative of a belief by the State in question that it was the victim of an armed attack by Nicaragua, and of the making of a request by the victim State to the United States for help in the exercise of collective self-defence.

233.   The Court has seen no evidence that the conduct of those States was consistent with such a situation, either at the time when the United States first embarked on the activities which were allegedly justified by self-defence, or indeed for a long period subsequently. So far as El Salvador is concerned, it appears to the Court that while El Salvador did in fact officially declare itself the victim of an armed attack, and did ask for the United States to exercise its right of collective self-defence, this occurred only on a date much later than the commencement of the United States activities which were allegedly justified by this request. The Court notes that on 3 April 1984, the representative of El Salvador before the United Nations Security Council, while complaining of the "open foreign intervention practised by Nicaragua in our internal affairs" (S/PV.2528, p. 58), refrained from stating that El Salvador had been subjected to armed attack, and made no mention of the right of collective self-defence which it had supposedly asked the United States to exercise. Nor was this men-

tioned when El Salvador addressed a letter to the Court in April 1984, in connection with Nicaragua's complaint against the United States. It was only in its Declaration of Intervention filed on 15 August 1984, that El Salvador referred to requests addressed at various dates to the United States for the latter to exercise its right of collective self-defence (para. XII), asserting on this occasion that it had been the victim of aggression from Nicaragua "since at least 1980". In that Declaration, El Salvador affirmed that initially it had "not wanted to present any accusation or allegation [against Nicaragua] to any of the jurisdictions to which we have a right to apply", since it sought "a solution of understanding and mutual respect" (para. III).

234.   As to Honduras and Costa Rica, they also were prompted by the institution of proceedings in this case to address communications to the Court; in neither of these is there mention of armed attack or collective self-defence. As has already been noted (paragraph 231 above), Honduras in the Security Council in 1984 asserted that Nicaragua had engaged in aggression against it, but did not mention that a request had consequently been made to the United States for assistance by way of collective self-defence. On the contrary, the representative of Honduras emphasized that the matter before the Security Council "is a Central American problem, without exception, and it must be solved regionally" (S/PV.2529, p. 38), i.e., through the Contadora process. The representative of Costa Rica also made no reference to collective self-defence. Nor, it may be noted, did the representative of the United States assert during that debate that it had acted in response to requests for assistance in that context.

235.   There is also an aspect of the conduct of the United States which the Court is entitled to take into account as indicative of the view of that State on the question of the existence of an armed attack. At no time, up to the present, has the United States Government addressed to the Security Council, in connection with the matters the subject of the present case, the report which is required by Article 51 of the United Nations Charter in respect of measures which a State believes itself bound to take when it exercises the right of individual or collective self-defence. The Court, whose decision has to be made on the basis of customary international law, has already observed that in context of that law, the reporting obligation enshrined in Article 51 of the Charter of the United Nations does not exist. It does not therefore treat the absence of a report on the part of the United States as the breach of an undertaking forming part of the customary international law applicable to the present dispute. But the Court is justified in observing that this conduct of the United States hardly conforms with the latter's avowed conviction that it was acting in the context of collective self-defence as consecrated by Article 51 of the Charter. This fact is all the more noteworthy because, in the Security Council, the United States has itself taken the view that failure to observe the requirement to make a report contradicted a State's claim to be acting on the basis of collective self-defence (S/PV.2187).

236.   Similarly, while no strict legal conclusion may be drawn from the date of El Salvador's announcement that it was the victim of an armed attack, and the date of its official request addressed to the United States concerning the exercise of collective self-defence, those dates have a significance as evidence of El Salvador's view of the situation. The declaration and the request of El Salvador, made publicly for the first time in August 1984, do not support the contention that in 1981 there was an armed attack capable of serving as a legal foundation for United States activities which began in the second half of that year. The States concerned did not behave as though there were an armed attack at the time when the activities attributed by the United States to Nicaragua, without actually constituting such an attack, were nevertheless the most accentuated; they did so behave only at a time when these facts fell furthest short of what would be required for the Court to take the view that an armed attack existed on the part of Nicaragua against El Salvador.

237.   Since the Court has found that the condition *sine qua non* required for the exercise of the right of collective self-defence by the United States is not fulfilled in this case, the appraisal of the United States activities in relation to the criteria of necessity and proportionality takes on a different significance. As a result of this conclusion of the Court, even if the United States activities in question had been carried on in strict compliance with the canons of necessity and proportionality, they would not thereby become lawful. If however they were not, this may constitute an additional ground of wrongfulness. On the question of necessity, the Court observes that the United States measures taken in December 1981 (or, at the earliest, March of that year—paragraph 93 above) cannot be said to correspond to a "necessity" justifying the United States action against Nicaragua on the basis of assistance given by Nicaragua to the armed opposition in El Salvador. First, these measures were only taken, and began to produce their effects, several months after the major offensive of the armed opposition against the Government of El Salvador had been completely repulsed (January 1981), and the actions of the opposition considerably reduced in consequence. Thus it was possible to eliminate the main danger to the Salvadorian Government without the United States embarking on activities in and against Nicaragua. Accordingly, it cannot be held that these activities were undertaken in the light of necessity. Whether or not the assistance to the *contras* might meet the criterion of proportionality, the Court cannot regard the United States activities summarised in paragraphs 80, 81 and 86, i.e., those relating to the mining of the Nicaraguan ports and the attacks on ports, oil installations, etc., as satisfying that criterion. Whatever uncertainty may exist as to the exact scale of the aid received by the Salvadorian armed opposition from Nicaragua, it is clear that these latter United States activities in question could not have been proportionate to that aid. Finally on this point, the Court must also observe that the reaction of the United States in the context of what it regarded as self-defence was continued long after

the period in which any presumed armed attack by Nicaragua could reasonably be contemplated.

238.   Accordingly, the Court concludes that the plea of collective self-defence against an alleged armed attack on El Salvador, Honduras or Costa Rica, advanced by the United States to justify its conduct toward Nicaragua, cannot be upheld; and accordingly that the United States has violated the principle prohibiting recourse to the threat or use of force by the acts listed in paragraph 227 above, and by its assistance to the *contras* to the extent that this assistance "involve[s] a threat or use of force" (paragraph 228 above).

NOTE

Dissenting and Separate Opinions. Judge Schwebel's dissent was based largely on his conclusion that Nicaragua's support of the insurgency in El Salvador was so extensive and persistent as to amount to an armed attack justifying collective self-defense by the United States, and that this warranted military activities not only in El Salvador but against Nicaraguan territory as well. Moreover, in his view, judgment for Nicaragua was unwarranted because it had pressed false testimony on the Court in a deliberate effort to conceal its wrongs. Schwebel voted with the majority holding that the United States violated customary law by failing to make known the existence and location of the mines it had laid.

Judge Oda objected to the Court's consideration of the Nicaraguan claim as arising under customary law. In his view, the U.S. reservation denied the Court jurisdiction of any proceeding based on a multilateral treaty, and even if the treaty and customary law could be disentangled, the Court could not entertain the case and decide it on principles of customary law. Moreover, the claim presented a political dispute, not a legal dispute under Article 36(2) of the Court's Statute.

Judge Jennings agreed with Oda that the U.S. multilateral treaty reservation must be respected and the Court could not exercise jurisdiction and apply customary law in lieu of the multilateral treaties. Therefore, he voted against the Court's decisions on the use of force, on intervention and on self-defense. However Jennings and Oda both joined the majority in holding that the laying of mines by the United States breached United States obligations under a bilateral treaty.

Seven of the judges who voted with the majority appended separate opinions dealing with various aspects of the judgment.

SCHACHTER, INTERNATIONAL LAW
IN THEORY AND PRACTICE

141–46 (1991) (footnotes omitted)

A critical question affecting both law and policy on self-defense concerns the degree of uncertainty or indeterminacy that inheres in the proclaimed legal limits. Some indeterminacy results from the key standards of necessity and proportionality, concepts that leave ample room for diverse opinions in particular cases. Other sources of uncertainty can be traced to differing interpretations of the events that would permit forcible defensive action. Varying views have been advanced by governments and scholars relating to the kinds of illegal force that would trigger the right of an armed defensive response. While strong positions have been taken by nearly all States against "preventive" or "preemptive" war, some uncertainty remains as to threats of force that credibly appear as likely to result in imminent attack. Other issues, highlighted by the *Nicaragua* case, concern the illegal use of force through subversion, supply of arms, and logistic support of armed forces as sufficient ground for defensive response. It is not entirely clear to what extent self-defense responding to an armed attack embraces the use of force as a deterrent to future attacks. Nor is there agreement on the circumstances that would permit a State to intervene (or "counterintervene") in an internal conflict under the principle of collective self-defense. Even more unsettling is the uncertainty about the first use of nuclear weapons, the targeting of civilian centers and the proportionality of retaliatory action.

These controversial issues indicate that the rules of self-defense fall far short of a code of conduct that would provide precise "hard law" for many cases likely to arise. * * *

* * *

Notwithstanding its relative indeterminacy, self-defense as a legal norm can have an ascertainable relationship to the policies and actions of governments. The "defensist" principle namely, that self-defense is the only legitimate reason to use force against another State has been expressed as the strategic policy of most States. Evidence for this is not only found in governmental statements to international bodies, where they may be expected. Recent studies by political scientists and students of military strategy confirm the practical implication of defensist doctrine. When States proclaim the principle of self-defense as governing the use of force, they have a stake in its credibility to other States and to their own citizens. For such States to be credible, their weapons, training and contingent planning must reflect a defensist strategy. Their good faith can be tested by their willingness to consider ways to reduce threats and resolve conflicts without using force. Hence, a defensist posture is not merely one of restraint but a source of policy that goes beyond the essentially negative rules of the law. It has obvious implications for such protective activities as monitoring and inspection. It calls for limitations on weaponry and balance among adversaries. The danger that systems which purport to be defensive may be perceived as offensive and therefore "destabilizing" becomes a matter of central concern. The most obvious consequence of defensist doctrine is that States no longer consider that they may invade other States for objectives that were considered in prior periods as legitimate and appropriate. Thus, the naked use of force for economic gain, or to avenge past injustices, or civilize "inferior" people, or vindicate honor, or achieve "manifest destiny", is no longer asserted as national policy. Seen in the perspective of history, this is a profound change in the relations of States.

* * *

The more controversial questions of self-defense have been raised by actions and claims that would expand a State's right to use force beyond the archetypical case of an armed attack on the territory or instrumentality of that State. Such expanded conceptions of self-defense are exemplified by the following uses of force by States claiming self-defense:

(1) the use of force to rescue political hostages believed to face imminent danger of death or injury;

(2) the use of force against officials or installations in a foreign State believed to support terrorists acts directed against nationals of the State claiming the right of defense;

(3) the use of force against troops, planes, vessels or installations believed to threaten imminent attack by a State with declared hostile intent;

(4) the use of retaliatory force against a government or military force so as to deter renewed attacks on the State taking such action;

(5) the use of force against a government that has provided arms or technical support to insurgents in a third State;

(6) the use of force against a government that has allowed its territory to be used by military forces of a third State considered to be a threat to the State claiming self-defense;

(7) the use of force in the name of collective defense (or counterintervention) against a government imposed by foreign forces and faced with large-scale military resistance by many of its people.

* * * Nearly all the cases have been discussed in U.N. bodies and, although opinions have been divided, it is clear that most governments have been reluctant to legitimize expanded self-defense actions that go beyond the paradigmatic case. Thus, no U.N. resolution has approved the use of force in any of the cases that I have listed. In the few cases where resolutions were adopted that passed judgment on the legality of the action, they denied the validity of the self-defense claim. In many cases, resolutions were not adopted, but the majority of States that addressed the issue of lawfulness criticized the actions as contrary to the Charter. Few ventured to defend the legality of the self-defense claims. * * *

* * * [T]he general reluctance to approve uses of force under expanded conceptions of self-defense is itself significant. Such reluctance is evidence of a widespread perception that widening the scope of self-defense will erode the basic rule against unilateral recourse to force. The absence of binding judicial or other third-party determinations relating to the use of force adds to the apprehension that a more permissive rule of self-defense will open the way to further disregard of the limits on force.

The refusal of the United States to take part in the proceedings of the International Court on the merits in the *Nicaragua* case and by its non-compliance with the judgment against it has given new emphasis to this point.

It is true that some international lawyers believe that legitimate self-defense should be construed more liberally. They argue that the absence of effective collective remedies against illegal force makes it necessary, indeed inevitable, that States take defensive action on the basis of their own perceptions of national interest and capabilities. In addition to the imperatives of national security, they cite the responsibility of powerful States to maintain international order. They call for a liberal construction of self-defense, stressing that the words of the Charter should be interpreted "in context" so as to yield "reasonable" meanings required by the "purpose and object" of the text. Unilateral acts that stretch the meaning of self-defense are treated as "State practice", although there is no general *opinio juris* to support their "acceptance as law". Conduct that violates text and earlier interpretations may be viewed as new or emerging law based on the efficacy of accomplished facts in shaping the law. Some of these arguments, if accepted, would extend the concept of self-defense so broadly as to allow almost any unilateral use of force taken in the name of law and order. There is no evidence that governments by and large would favor this result. On the contrary, the records of the United Nations, as already mentioned, show strong resistance to widening self-defense to permit force except where there has been an armed attack or threat of imminent attack. It does not seem likely that this resistance will disappear in the foreseeable future.

This does not mean, of course, that the law of self-defense will remain static. The kaleidoscopic events of our era will continue to create new pressures for resort to force. The role of international law cannot be limited to repeating the old maxims. What its role should be calls for further consideration.

NOTES

1. *Scope of Self-Defense.* During the years when the Security Council was largely neutralized, victims of an armed attack had to defend themselves indefinitely, alone or with the assistance of allies. In such circumstances, does the right of self-defense under Article 51 justify only such action as necessary to beat back the attack? Does it justify retaliation, limited perhaps by the principle of proportionality? Does it remove all the prohibitions of Article 2(4), so that the victim of an armed attack is in effect warranted in engaging in a "just war" against the aggressor, limited only by the traditional rules of war? May the victim carry the war to the territory of the aggressor? To the territories of allies of the aggressor? Are other states forbidden to help the aggressor? Obligated to help the victim?

If the victim of an armed attack, acting in lawful self-defense under Article 51, succeeds in conquering territory of the aggressor, is annexation of such territory lawful? See Chapter 5, p. 381 note 4.

2. *Threshold of "Attack" Justifying Self-Defense.* Do you agree with the *Nicaragua* Court that Nicaragua's conduct in providing arms to opposition forces in neighboring countries did not constitute "armed attack" for purposes of the U.S. claim that it was engaged in legitimate defense of those countries? What different proof of facts might have changed the result?

3. *Border Disputes.* The question of the nature or level of an armed incursion sufficient to qualify as an "armed attack" also arises in other contexts. An arbitration commission convened in the aftermath of a border war between Eritrea and Ethiopia addressed Ethiopia's claim that Eritrea had unlawfully invaded Ethiopian territory in May 1998 and occupied the town of Badme, which Ethiopia was then peacefully administering, as well as other Ethiopian territory. Eritrea claimed self-defense, saying that it was merely reoccupying its own territory and defending itself against forcible incursions carried out by Ethiopian armed militia into Eritrea. The tribunal rejected Eritrea's argument that its resort to force could have been lawful self-defense under the circumstances. Acknowledging that the boundary was disputed, the tribunal continued:

> However, the practice of States and the writings of eminent publicists show that self-defense cannot be invoked to settle territorial disputes. In that connection, the Commission notes that border disputes between States are so frequent that any exception to the prohibition of the threat or use of force for territory that is allegedly occupied unlawfully would create a large and dangerous hole in a fundamental rule of international law.
>
> * * * Localized border encounters between small infantry units, even those involving the loss of life, do not constitute an armed attack for purposes of the Charter. * * *

The Commission further found that it did not need to resolve a factual dispute between the parties over events in the vicinity of Badme leading up to Eritrea's invasion,

> because it is clear from the evidence that these incidents involved geographically limited clashes between small Eritrean and Ethiopian patrols along a remote, unmarked, and disputed border. The Commission is satisfied that these relatively minor incidents were not of a magnitude to constitute an armed attack by either State against the other within the meaning of Article 51 of the UN Charter.

Eritrea Ethiopia Claims Commission, Partial Award—*Jus ad Bellum*, Ethiopia's Claims 1–8 (Dec. 19, 2005), 45 I.L.M. 430, 432–33, paras. 10–15 (2006).

4. *Necessity and Proportionality of Defensive Response.* The International Court of Justice and arbitral tribunals apply exacting standards of necessity and proportionality in evaluating states' claims of justification for their resort to allegedly defensive force, not only as regards substantive criteria but also in allocating the burden of factual proof to the party invoking self-defense. In addition to the *Nicaragua* case, the I.C.J. was unpersuaded by the U.S. plea in the *Oil Platforms Case* (Iran v. United States), 2003 I.C.J. 161, paras. 72–78, finding that the U.S. actions were neither necessary nor proportional under the circumstances as they appeared to the Court. In *Armed Activities on the*

Territory of the Congo (Democratic Republic of the Congo v. Uganda), 2005 I.C.J. 168, para. 147, the Court found that the preconditions for the exercise of self-defense were unsatisfied (see p. 1157 above) and thus did not have to resolve whether Uganda's actions were necessary or proportionate, adding:

> The Court cannot fail to observe, however, that the taking of airports and towns many hundreds of kilometres from Uganda's border would not seem proportionate to the series of transborder attacks it claimed had given rise to the right of self-defence, nor to be necessary to that end.

In its advisory opinion on *Legal Consequences of Construction of a Wall in the Occupied Palestinian Territory*, 2004 I.C.J. 136, 195 para. 140, the Court was "not convinced" that the wall was "the only means" to safeguard Israel against the peril to its security which it claimed as justification for its construction. On other aspects of the *Wall* advisory opinion, see p. 630. For discussion of the cases in which tribunals have ruled (or been asked to rule) on proportionality of forcible defensive responses in the *jus ad bellum*, see Franck, On Proportionality of Countermeasures in International Law, 102 A.J.I.L. 715, 719–22 (2008); see also Gardam, Necessity, Proportionality and the Use of Force by States (2004). On proportionality in *jus in bello*, see Section 4, p. 1296.

To what extent does evaluation of these criteria turn on ascertaining disputed facts? In the war that broke out between Georgia and Russia in 2008, for example, each side claimed to be responding to provocations of the other in a defensive way: Georgia claimed that Russia was fomenting separatist activity in parts of Georgian territory, while Russia claimed to be defending Russians and other non-Georgians from Georgia's first resort to military force. How is it possible to know which is correct? Even if the facts were as claimed by Russia, could its ensuing invasion and occupation of parts of Georgian territory have been proportionate under the *jus ad bellum*? For excerpts from the decision on Georgia's case against Russia brought to the I.C.J. in 2008, see Chapter 9.

5. *Relation to Security Council Authority.* The end of the Cold War and the revival of the Security Council raised additional questions about the relation of the right of self-defense to the authority of the Security Council and about the implications of the "until" clause of Article 51. How does the availability of the Security Council affect the right of self-defense? Apart from the reporting requirement of Article 51, is the victim of an armed attack expected to enlist the involvement of the Security Council (together with whatever steps the state may take in the exercise of its own "inherent right")? Can states continue to use armed force in self-defense after the Security Council is seized of the matter or after it has begun taking measures aimed at (but not yet successful in) restoring peace and security? Does the Article 51 right persist (or perhaps revive after a period of suspension) if the Security Council cannot definitively resolve the situation? See Section 3, pp. 1229–44 on these issues in relation to Iraq's attack on Kuwait in 1990s and the continuation of Security Council measures against Iraq through 2003.

6. *Defense Against State–Sponsored Terrorism and Other Hostile Acts.* On April 14, 1986, the United States bombed targets in Libyan territory, killing both military and civilian persons and inflicting substantial damage.

President Reagan announced that the United States had "launched a series of strikes against the headquarters, terrorist facilities, and military assets that support Muammar Qadhafi's subversive activities." The President's statement justified the action as being in response, in particular, to a bombing of a Berlin nightclub frequented by U.S. servicemen in which one was killed and many wounded. Reagan described the attack as "a mission fully consistent with Article 51 of the UN Charter. We believe that this preemptive action against terrorist installations will not only diminish Colonel Qadhafi's capacity to export terror, it will provide him with incentives and reasons to alter his criminal behavior." Presidential Statement of April 14, 1986, U.S. Dept. of State, Selected Documents No. 24.

Was the action of the United States justified as a use of force in self-defense under Article 51? Was it in response to an "armed attack against a member of the United Nations" within the meaning of that article? Note the reference to the bombing as a "preemptive action." (See further p. 1181 on anticipatory self-defense and p. 1190 on threats from non-state actors.)

In October 1985 Israel launched an air attack on the Headquarters of the Palestine Liberation Organization (PLO) in Tunisia, in response to terrorist activities attributed to the PLO. The Security Council condemned the action as an "act of armed aggression * * * against Tunisian territory in flagrant violation of the Charter." S.C. Res. 573 (Oct. 4, 1985). The United States abstained. See Leich, Resort to War and Armed Force, 80 A.J.I.L. 165 (1986).

Compare the use or threat of force to apprehend alleged terrorists who are in another state's jurisdiction or control. In 1985, four United States military planes intercepted an Egyptian aircraft over the Mediterranean Sea, compelling it to land in Italy so that alleged terrorists aboard the aircraft could be prosecuted for seizing a vessel, taking hostages, and murder. Was the action lawful under the Charter? See Schachter, In Defense of International Rules on the Use of Force, 53 U. Chi. L. Rev. 113, 139–40 (1986); Cassese, Terrorism, Politics and Law: The Achille Lauro Affair (1989).

On April 14, 1993, it was reported that Kuwaiti authorities had thwarted a terrorist plot to assassinate former President George Bush while on a visit to Kuwait. An investigation by U.S. intelligence agencies concluded that the highest levels of the Iraqi government had directed its agents to carry out the assassination. On June 26, 1993, United States forces fired twenty-three Tomahawk missiles at Iraqi intelligence headquarters, from war ships stationed in the Persian Gulf and the Red Sea. At a special session of the Security Council, the U.S. representative said:

> [T]his was a direct attack on the United States, an attack that required a direct United States response. Consequently, President Clinton yesterday instructed the United States armed forces to carry out a military operation against the headquarters of the Iraqi Intelligence Service in Baghdad. We responded directly, as we were entitled to do, under Article 51 of the United Nations Charter, which provides for the exercise of self defense in such cases.

Assuming the facts as reported, was the U.S. action justified under Article 51 as a response to an armed attack? Was it necessary? proportional? Was the

U.S. action justifiable under Security Council resolutions relating to Iraq, p. 1230 (discussed in Section 3)?

On self-defense against non-state terrorism, see p. 1190.

7. *Response to Attacks on Troops.* On December 20, 1989 the United States initiated military operations in Panama, with a deployment of 11,000 troops additional to 13,000 U.S. forces already present. The background to the invasion included a declaration by the Panamanian National Assembly on December 15, 1989 that a state of war existed between Panama and the United States; an inflammatory anti-American speech given by Manuel Noriega (Panama's *de facto* president, who had refused to relinquish power after losing an election earlier in the year); and a series of violent attacks by Panama Defense Forces on U.S. military personnel and dependents in Panama, including the killing of a U.S. Marine officer and the beating of a U.S. naval officer on December 16, 1989.

President George Bush reported to the U.S. Congress that the "deployment of U.S. Forces is an exercise of the right of self-defense recognized in Article 51 of the United Nations Charter and was necessary to protect American lives in imminent danger and to fulfill our responsibilities under the Panama Canal Treaties. It was welcomed by the democratically elected government of Panama." See Report on the Development Concerning the Deployment of United States Forces to Panama, House Doc. 101–127 (1990).

Critics of the Panama invasion have concluded that the alleged justifications were not the real reasons for U.S. intervention and that its main purpose was to bring General Noriega to trial in the U.S. for conspiracy to smuggle drugs into the United States. However, assuming the facts and characterizations as alleged, was the Panama invasion justified under international law? Compare the article by the then Legal Adviser to the U.S. Department of State, Sofaer, The Legality of the United States Actions in Panama, 29 Colum. J. Transnat'l L. 281 (1991) and the letter to the President of the U.N. Security Council from the U.S. Permanent Representative to the United Nations. U.N. Doc. S/21035 (Dec. 20, 1989), with Henkin, The Invasion of Panama Under International Law: A Gross Violation, 29 Colum. J. Transnat'l L. 293 (1991). See also Agora: U.S. Forces in Panama: Defenders, Aggressors or Human Rights Activists, 84 A.J.I.L. 494 (1990).

One of the principal justifications invoked by President Bush appears to be the right of self-defense under Article 51. Do you agree? Was the invasion necessary? proportional? Are the U.S. justifications consistent with the opinion of the International Court of Justice in the *Nicaragua* case (Merits), p. 1166 *supra*? In a detailed report, a committee of the Association of the Bar of the City of New York concluded that the legality of the intervention under existing standards of the law of self-defense was not established on the facts, as the existence of an "armed attack" (or anticipation of an imminent attack) and satisfaction of the requirements of necessity and proportionality were all in doubt. See Report, The Use of Armed Force in International Affairs: The Case of Panama, 47 Record A.B.C.N.Y. 604–738 (1992)

8. *Responses in Diverse Theaters.* In August 1998, terrorist bombs exploded at U.S. embassy buildings in Nairobi, Kenya and Dar-es-Salaam, Tanzania, resulting in large loss of life. U.S. intelligence attributed the

bombings to a terrorist network sustained by Osama bin Laden, then living in Afghanistan. About two weeks after the embassy explosions, U.S. cruise missiles struck facilities in Afghanistan and Sudan that were said to be part of bin Laden's network. Some of the targets were alleged to be training camps for terrorists; in Sudan, one of the targets was supposedly a factory for chemicals to be used in chemical weapons (later reports identified it as a pharmaceutical plant). In justifying the cruise missile strikes, President Clinton invoked U.S. rights of self-defense; and the U.S. government notified the Security Council of the missile attacks, referring to Article 51. Does the action withstand scrutiny under Article 51? See Murphy, Contemporary Practice of the United States Relating to International Law, 93 A.J.I.L. 161–67 (1999).

After the attacks of September 11, 2001, the United States launched major military action in Afghanistan against Taliban and Al Qaeda forces, in order to eradicate the training camps in which the attacks had been prepared and to prevent a recurrence. This large-scale intervention is discussed further below (p. 1190) under the heading of Self-Defense Against Non–State Actors.

b. *Anticipatory Self–Defense and "Preemption"*

SCHACHTER, THE RIGHT OF STATES TO USE ARMED FORCE

82 Mich. L. Rev. 1620, 1633–35 (1984) (footnotes omitted)

Our first question—whether self-defense requires an armed attack or whether it is permissible in anticipation of an attack—has given rise to much controversy among international lawyers. The text of article 51 does not answer the question directly. It declares that "[n]othing in the present Charter shall impair the inherent right of individual or collective self-defense if an armed attack occurs." On one reading this means that self-defense is limited to cases of armed attack. An alternative reading holds that since the article is silent as to the right of self-defense under customary law (which goes beyond cases of armed attack), it should not be construed by implication to eliminate that right. The drafting history shows that article 51 was intended to safeguard the Chapultepec Treaty which provided for collective defense in case of armed attack. The relevant commission report of the San Francisco Conference declared "the use of arms in legitimate self-defense remains admitted and unimpaired." It is therefore not implausible to interpret article 51 as leaving unimpaired the right of self-defense as it existed prior to the Charter. The main interpretive difficulty with this is that the words "if an armed attack occurs" then become redundant, a conclusion which should not be reached without convincing evidence that such redundant use was in keeping with the drafters' intention. The link with the Chapultepec Treaty provides a reason for the inclusion of the words "if an armed attack occurs" and explains why it was not said that self-defense is limited to cases of armed attack.

Much of the debate in recent years has focused on the consequences of adopting one or the other interpretation, especially in the light of the apprehension over nuclear missiles. Even as far back as 1946, the U.S. Government stated that the term "armed attack" should be defined to include not merely the dropping of a bomb but "certain steps in themselves preliminary to such action." In recent years, the fear that nuclear missiles, could, on the first strike, destroy the capability for defense and allow virtually no time for defense has appeared to many to render a requirement of armed attack unreasonable. States faced with a perceived danger of immediate attack, it is argued, cannot be expected to await the attack like sitting ducks. In response to this line of reasoning, others argue that the existence of nuclear missiles has made it even more important to maintain a legal barrier against preemptive strikes and anticipatory defense. It is conceded by them that states facing an imminent threat of attack will take defensive measures irrespective of the law, but it is preferable to have states make that choice governed by necessity than to adopt a principle that would make it easier for a state to launch an attack on the pretext of anticipatory defense.

Both of the foregoing positions express apprehensions that are reasonable. It is important that the right of self-defense should not freely allow the use of force in anticipation of an attack or in response to a threat. At the same time, we must recognize that there may well be situations in which the imminence of an attack is so clear and the danger so great that defensive action is essential for self-preservation. It does not seem to me that the law should leave such defense to a decision *contra legem*. Nor does it appear necessary to read article 51 in that way—that is, to exclude completely legitimate self-defense in advance of an actual attack. In my view it is not clear that article 51 was intended to eliminate the customary law right of self-defense and it should not be given that effect. But we should avoid interpreting the customary law as if it broadly authorized preemptive strikes and anticipatory defense in response to threats.

The conditions of the right of anticipatory defense under customary law were expressed generally in an eloquent formulation by the U.S. Secretary of State Daniel Webster in a diplomatic note to the British in 1842 * * * [on the *Caroline* episode, p. 1134 above, in which he asserted] that self-defense must be confined to cases in which "the necessity of that self-defense is instant, overwhelming, and leaving no choice of means, and no moment for deliberation."

The Webster formulation of self-defense is often cited as authoritative customary law. It cannot be said that the formulation reflects state practice (which was understandably murky on this point when war was legal), but it is safe to say it reflects a widespread desire to restrict the right of self-defense when no attack has actually occurred. A recent case in point concerns the Israeli bombing of a nuclear reactor in Iraq in 1981, which the Israeli government sought to justify on the ground of self-defense. Israel cited the Iraqi position that it was at war with Israel and claimed that the reactor was intended for a nuclear strike. Many governments and the UN Security Council rejected the Israeli position. In the debates in the Security Council on this question, several delegates referred to the *Caroline* Case formulation of the right of anticipatory defense as an accepted statement of customary law. We may infer from these official statements recognition of the continued validity of an "inherent" right to use armed force in self-defense prior to an actual attack but only where such an attack is imminent "leaving no moment for deliberation."

NOTES

1.   *A Spectrum of Approaches.* Compare the following views:

(a) Under the Charter, alarming military preparations by a neighboring state would justify a resort to the Security Council, but would not justify resort to anticipatory force by the state which believed itself threatened.

The documentary record of the discussions at San Francisco does not afford conclusive evidence that the suggested interpretation of the words "armed attack" in Article 51 is correct, but the general tenor of the discussions, as well as the careful choice of words throughout Chapters VI and VII of the Charter relative to various stages of aggravation of dangers to the peace, support the view stated.

Jessup, A Modern Law of Nations 166–67 (1948) (footnotes omitted).

(b) It was to avoid and eliminate the political and military dangers of letting the nations judge by themselves the vital issues of attack and defence that the relevant provisions of the United Nations Charter were formulated. But the inability of the UN, as at present organised, to act swiftly has handed the power of decision back to the national states. * * * But while this immensely increases the necessity for a reliable international detection organisation and mechanism, in the absence of effective international machinery the right of self-defense must probably now be extended to the defence against a clearly imminent aggression, despite the apparently contrary language of Article 51 of the Charter. The dangers of such an interpretation should not be underestimated. It means that the United States or the Soviet Union may, on the basis of plausible but inaccurate information, send a bomber or missile force to the other country to destroy the force believed to be poised for aggression.

Friedmann, The Changing Structure of International Law 259–60 (1964) (footnotes omitted).

(c) If there were clear evidence of an attack so imminent that there was no time for political action to prevent it, the only meaningful defense for the potential victim might indeed be the pre-emptive attack and—it may be argued—the scheme of Article 2(4) together with Article 51 was not intended to bar such attack. But this argument would claim a small and special exception for the special case of the surprise nuclear attack; today, and one hopes for a time longer, it is meaningful and relevant principally only as between the Soviet Union and the United States * * * But such a reading of the Charter, it should be clear, would not permit (and encourage) anticipatory self-defense in other, more likely situations between nations generally.

Henkin, How Nations Behave 143–45 (2d ed. 1979) (footnotes omitted).

> (d) The United States was right in the Cuban Missile crisis not to say that the deployment of missiles in Cuba by the Soviet Union constituted an "armed attack" that would give rise to the right of self-defense. I agree that it would be too dangerous for the world community to allow unilateral uses of force simply because there were some deployments of weapons or modernization of weapons. On the other hand, to say that a nation has to be a sitting duck (to use Professor Myres McDougal's phrase) and wait until the bombs are actually dropping on its soil—that cannot be right either. When attack is initiated and is underway, even though the attacker has not actually arrived in the victim state, measures can be taken. There should be agreement on that principle.

> But there are hard cases. Egyptian President Gamal Abdel Nasser announced the blockade of the Gulf of Aqaba in 1967; Israel attacked. I think most people felt that was justified self-defense. But when Israel attacked the nuclear reactor in Iraq in 1981, most people—maybe with the exception of McDougal and one or two others—argued that that went too far. And yet, if anticipatory self-defense cannot cover the Iraqi reactor case (and I have no doubt that nuclear reactor was not for peaceful purposes only), how are we going to deal with a Saddam Hussein who may be preparing to use weapons of mass destruction against his neighbors?

Gardner, Commentary on the Law of Self–Defense, in Law and Force in the New International Order 51–52 (Damrosch & Scheffer eds. 1991).

A distinction has been suggested between "interceptive" and "anticipatory" self-defense: "interceptive, unlike anticipatory, self-defence takes place after the other side has committed itself to an armed attack in an ostensibly irrevocable way." Dinstein, War, Aggression and Self–Defense [190] (4th ed. 2005). Is this distinction helpful in clarifying the scope of legitimate self-defense?

2. *Cuban Missile Crisis.* The official justification of United States action in the 1962 Cuban missile crisis (p. 1160 *supra*) did not invoke anticipatory self-defense, but some writers sought to justify the quarantine on that basis. See, e.g., MacChesney, Some Comments on the "Quarantine" of Cuba, 57 A.J.I.L. 592 (1963). For an opposing view, see Henkin, How Nations Behave 295–96 (2d ed. 1979). Some who argued against limiting the right to self-defense to cases where an armed attack occurs may have had in mind particularly a right to anticipate a nuclear attack. See, e.g., McDougal, The Soviet Cuban Quarantine and Self–Defense, 57 A.J.I.L. 597, 599–601 (1963). For a revisiting of the Cuban missile crisis in light of new assertions of expansive claims of "preemptive" self-defense, see Gardner, Neither Bush Nor the "Jurisprudes," 97 A.J.I.L. 585 (2003) (in Agora on Future Implications of the Iraq Conflict, p. 1187 note 6); Doyle, Striking First: Preemption and Prevention in International Conflict 70–77 (2008) (calling the quarantine "a case of justifiable, *legitimate* (though illegal) preventive force").

3. *Arms Buildup.* In the *Nicaragua* case, 1986 I.C.J. 14, 135, para. 269, the United States had based part of its collective self-defense claim on the proposition that Nicaragua had engaged in alarming conduct, including a massive build-up of armaments far in excess of what it needed for its own defense, which its neighbors could perceive as a threat to attack them. In addressing this contention (with the United States absent at the merits stage), the Court observed that in the absence of any limitations agreed upon by the states concerned, international law places no restrictions on the right of states to decide for themselves what level of weapons to maintain for their own security, and that this principle "is valid for all States without exception." Should this principle apply equally to weapons of mass destruction as well as conventional weapons? See the following two notes on nuclear threats and self-defense.

4. *Preventing Future Threats.* In 1981, Israel bombed a nuclear reactor under construction in Iraq and sought to justify its action by claiming a right of "anticipatory" self-defense. Was the threat to Israel such as to bring it within a "liberal" reading of Article 51? Was the alleged Iraqi threat "immediate" within the formula or the spirit of *The Caroline?* Was it relevant that Iraq had continued to maintain that Iraq was in a state of war with Israel? See D'Amato, Israel's Air Strike Upon the Iraqi Nuclear Reactor, 77 A.J.I.L. 584 (1983); Fischer, Le bombardement par Israël d'un réacteur nucléaire irakien, 1981 Annuaire Français de Droit International 147. For discussion of this action in the Security Council, see U.N. Docs. S/PV.2285–88 (June 16–19, 1981), and S.C. Res. 487 (June 19, 1981). Compare Alexandrov, Self–Defense Against the Use of Force in International Law 159–65, 296 (1996) (Israel's raid not justified on self-defense grounds) with McCormack, Self–Defense in International Law: The Israeli Raid on the Iraqi Nuclear Reactor 122–24, 238–39, 253–84 (1996).

Does the evidence developed in the 1990s of persistent Iraqi efforts to develop weapons of mass destruction cast the legal issues concerning anticipatory self-defense in any different light? On variations of self-defense arguments raised in connection with subsequent military action against Iraq, see pp. 1236–37 note 4, 1239–43.

5. *Self–Defense And Nuclear Weapons.* When, if ever, might the use or threat of nuclear weapons be justified as a self-defensive measure? Strategic doctrine during and after the Cold War maintained that a credible threat of nuclear retaliation was the linchpin of deterrence, and that a posture of nuclear readiness had dissuaded any party from mounting a destabilizing attack with conventional or any other weapons. As part of the policy of deterrence, NATO has kept open the option of nuclear response to a large-scale attack with conventional weapons, as well as possibilities for certain uses of tactical nuclear weapons.

In *Legality of the Threat or Use of Nuclear Weapons*, 1996 I.C.J. 226, the International Court of Justice was asked by the General Assembly for an advisory opinion on the following question: "Is the threat or use of nuclear weapons in any circumstance permitted under international law?" In its opinion, the Court referred to certain constraints applicable to self-defense under Article 51 of the Charter and customary international law, including the requirements of necessity and proportionality (paras. 40–42), and observed:

> 96.   Furthermore, the Court cannot lose sight of the fundamental right of every State to survival, and thus its right to resort to self-defence, in accordance with Article 51 of the Charter, when its survival is at stake.
>
> Nor can it ignore the practice referred to as "policy of deterrence", to which an appreciable section of the international community adhered for many years. * * *

In the dispositive provisions of its ruling, the Court unanimously agreed (para. 105(2)C) that

> A threat or use of force by means of nuclear weapons that is contrary to Article 2, paragraph 4, of the United Nations Charter and that fails to meet all the requirements of Article 51, is unlawful.

The judgment also contained the following paragraph, adopted by an equally divided Court (seven votes to seven, by President Bedjaoui's casting vote) (para. 105(2)E):

> However, in view of the current state of international law, and of the elements of fact at its disposal, the Court cannot conclude definitively whether the threat or use of nuclear weapons would be lawful or unlawful in an extreme circumstance of self-defence, in which the very survival of a State would be at stake.

In dissent, Judge Schwebel (United States) referred to evidence suggesting that Iraq may have been deterred from using chemical weapons against coalition forces in the 1991 Gulf War because of a belief that the United States might respond with nuclear weapons. He criticized the Court for a disposition which left unanswered the ultimate question of permissibility of nuclear self-defense. See also pp. 79–90.

On this aspect of the I.C.J. opinion, see Kohen, The Notion of "State Survival" in International Law, in International Law, the International Court of Justice and Nuclear Weapons 293–314 (Boisson de Chazournes & Sands eds. 1999). For other references, see p. 90 note 9.

6.   *Preemption Doctrine as Element of U.S. National Security Strategy.* After the attacks of September 11, 2001, President George W. Bush made several speeches announcing a broad doctrine of preemptive defense against terrorist networks and states harboring terrorists; in 2002, the Bush administration published a National Security Strategy document explaining the doctrine in the following terms:

> For centuries, international law recognized that nations need not suffer an attack before they can lawfully take action to defend themselves against forces that present an imminent danger of attack. Legal scholars and international jurists often conditioned the legitimacy of preemption on the existence of an imminent threat—most often a visible mobilization of armies, navies, and air forces preparing to attack.
>
> We must adapt the concept of imminent threat to the capabilities and objectives of today's adversaries. * * *

The United States has long maintained the option of preemptive actions to counter a sufficient threat to our national security. The greater the threat, the greater is the risk of inaction—and the more compelling the case for taking anticipatory action to defend ourselves, even if uncertainty remains as to the time and place of the enemy's attack. To forestall or prevent such hostile acts by our adversaries, the United States will, if necessary, act preemptively.

The United States will not use force in all cases to preempt emerging threats, nor should nations use preemption as a pretext for aggression. Yet in an age where the enemies of civilization openly and actively seek the world's most destructive technologies, the United States cannot remain idle while dangers gather.

The National Security Strategy of the United States of America 15 (Sept. 2002).

This doctrine of preemptive use of force (sometimes identified as the "Bush Doctrine") has been widely debated in the literature of international law. After the renewal of military conflict against Iraq in March 2003 (discussed further in Section 3, p. 1239, different views emerged as to whether the U.S.-led invasion of Iraq was an instance of preemption (and if so, whether a claim of preemptive self-defense was justifiable) or should be analyzed in another way. For a range of perspectives addressing preemption in particular, see Agora: Future Implications of the Iraq Conflict, 97 A.J.I.L. 553–642 (2003), including contributions by Taft & Buchwald, Preemption, Iraq and International Law. at 557; Wedgwood, The Fall of Saddam Hussein: Security Council Mandates and Preemptive Self–Defense, at 576; and Sapiro, Iraq: The Shifting Sands of Preemptive Self–Defense, at 599. On other legal issues in the Iraq conflict, see pp. 1229–44.

7. *Other Assessments of Preemptive and Preventive Self–Defense*. In recent lectures, Michael Doyle has proposed evaluation of preemptive or preventive self-defense claims in light of four criteria:

– lethality (the likely loss of life from the threat);

– likelihood (probability that the threat will occur);

– legitimacy (necessity, proportionality, and deliberativeness)

– legality (whether the threat is produced by legal or illegal actions, and whether the proposed remedy is more or less legal).

Doyle, Striking First: Preemption and Prevention in International Conflict 46–64 (2008). Doyle also attaches high importance to attempting to obtain multilateral support through the U.N. Security Council; see further Section 3, p. 1221. Do you think such criteria are well-grounded in the international law materials presented in this chapter, or if not, would they be a desirable advance over existing law?

Scholarly discussions of the Bush Doctrine and other assertions of preemptive self-defense have pointed out that such a doctrine, if claimed by one state, could equally be invoked by others. For evidence concerning the statements and actions of the United States and other states, see Reisman & Armstrong, The Past and Future of the Claim of Preemptive Self–Defense,

100 A.J.I.L. 525 (2006). How do you evaluate the possibility that adherence to such a doctrine on the part of a multiplicity of states could put states on a "hair trigger," with an increased likelihood of escalation to armed conflict?

c. Protection of Nationals; Rescue of Hostages

Intervention by a state to protect its nationals and ensure their humane treatment in another state was traditionally justified on the grounds of self-defense. Bowett, writing in 1958, took the position that such intervention to protect nationals had been lawful before the U.N. Charter as self-defense and remained lawful thereafter under Article 51. Bowett, Self–Defence in International Law 87–90 (1958). See also his later essay, The Use of Force for the Protection of Nationals Abroad, in The Current Legal Regulation of the Use of Force 39 (Cassese ed. 1986). Friedmann wrote that:

> The conditions under which a state may be entitled, as an aspect of self-defense, to intervene in another state to protect its nationals from injury, were formulated by Professor Waldock in 1952 as follows: "There must be (1) an imminent threat of injury to nationals, (2) a failure or inability on the part of the territorial sovereign to protect them and (3) measures of protection strictly confined to the object of protecting them against injury" * * * This was invoked, among other reasons, by the British Government in support of its armed intervention in Egypt during the Suez Canal crisis of 1956. Since, unlike in the Dominican Republic in April, 1965, there was no breakdown of organized government in Egypt nor any physical threat to foreign nationals, the United States had much greater legal justification for its original, limited intervention in protection of its nationals in the Dominican crisis than did Great Britain in the Suez crisis.

Friedmann, United States Policy and the Crisis of International Law, 59 A.J.I.L. 857, 867 n. 10 (1965). See generally, 1 Oppenheim's International Law 440–42 (9th ed. Jennings & Watts, eds. 1992). For the law prior to the Charter, see the opinion of Judge Huber in *The Spanish Zones of Morocco Claims,* 2 U.N. Rep. Int'l Arb. Awards 615 (1925).

The right to intervene to protect nationals was one of the grounds invoked by the United States for its invasion of Grenada in 1983. See p. 1163. See also Joyner, The United States Action in Grenada, 78 A.J.I.L. 131 (1984). It was also used as a justification by the U.S. for the invasion of Panama in 1989. See p. 1163; see also Use of Force, Protection of Nationals—Deployment of U.S. Forces to Panama (U.S. Digest, Ch. 14, § 1), reprinted in 84 A.J.I.L. 545 (1990). Schachter suggests:

> Reliance on self-defence as a legal ground for protecting nationals in emergency situations of peril probably reflects a reluctance to rely solely on the argument of humanitarian intervention as an exception to Article 2(4) or on the related point that such intervention is not "against the territorial integrity or political independence" of the territorial State and that it is not inconsistent with the Charter. Many

governments attach importance to the principle that any forcible incursion into the territory of another State is a derogation of that State's territorial sovereignty and political independence, irrespective of the motive for such intervention or its long term consequences. Accordingly, they tend to hold to the sweeping prohibition of Article 2(4) against the use or threat of force except where self-defence or Security Council enforcement action is involved.

Schachter, International Law in Theory and Practice 166–67 (1991) (footnotes omitted).

By no means have all writers agreed that the right to intervene to protect nationals survived the U.N. Charter. Professor Brownlie, for example, argues:

> * * *[I]t is very doubtful if * * * intervention [to protect nationals] has any basis in the modern law. The instances in which states have purported to exercise it, and the terms in which it is delimited, show that it provides infinite opportunities for abuse. Forcible intervention is now unlawful. It is true that the protection of nationals presents particular difficulties and that a government faced with a deliberate massacre of a considerable number of nationals in a foreign state would have cogent reasons of humanity for acting, and would also be under very great political pressure. The possible risks of denying the legality of action in a case of such urgency, an exceptional circumstance, must be weighed against the more calculable dangers of providing legal pretexts for the commission of breaches of the peace in the pursuit of national rather than humanitarian interest.

Brownlie, International Law and the Use of Force by States 301 (1963). See also Ronzitti, Rescuing Nationals Abroad through Military Coercion and Intervention on Grounds of Humanity 64 (1985). As regards the U.S. invasion of Panama in 1989, Henkin argues, *inter alia,* that the alleged protection of U.S. nationals could not be justified under Article 51 as a use of force in self-defense since no "armed attack" had occurred. Henkin, The Invasion of Panama Under International Law: A Gross Violation, 29 Colum. J. Transnat'l L. 293, 305–06 (1991). On Panama, see p. 1163.

A special case of protection of nationals is intervention to rescue nationals being held hostage and in mortal peril. Because this is a narrower category than intervention to protect nationals from situations of general instability or insecurity, the use of force in such circumstances seems more likely to be viewed as acceptable (or tolerable).

Consider the intervention by Israel in Uganda to release Israeli hostages from a hijacked plane at Entebbe, and the U.S. attempt to rescue U.S. hostages in Iran after the U.S. embassy was seized. Henkin maintains that in hostage situations there may be a limited right to intervene "to liberate hostages if the territorial state cannot or will not do so." Henkin, Use of Force: Law and U.S. Policy, in Right v. Might: International Law and the Use of Force 37, 41–42 (2d ed. 1991). Henkin would not limit this protection to hostages that are nationals of the intervening state. Provided the "use of force is strictly limited to what is necessary to save lives," an intervening state could act to rescue its own nationals, the territorial state's nationals, or the nationals of a third state. Id. But see the Security Council debate on the Entebbe Incident, where the Israeli (and U.S.) representatives defended Israel's action as self-defense because the hostages were its nationals. U.N. Doc. S/PV.1939, at 5159 (July 9, 1976), reprinted in 15 I.L.M. 1224 (1976).

d. Self–Defense Against Non–State Actors

In the wake of the attacks of September 11, 2001, much attention has focused on evaluation of the lawfulness of use of force in defense against actors who are not states. Beginning long before those events, governments frequently drew on concepts from international law to justify their responses to insurgencies, terrorist attacks, or other non-state threats. The 1837 *Caroline* incident, p. 1134, entailed legal arguments about forcible action across an international boundary to suppress insurrectionary activity. In the U.N. Charter period, Article 51 has been invoked in justification of forcible responses to various sorts of non-state threats, including transnational terrorism. See p. 1179.

The day after the 9/11 attacks, the U.N. Security Council adopted Resolution 1368 (Sept. 12, 2001) which condemned the attacks, characterized them "like any act of international terrorism, as a threat to international peace and security," and called for increased international cooperation to suppress terrorist acts. At the same time, in the preamble of the resolution, the Council recognized "the inherent right of individual or collective self-defence in accordance with the Charter." Later the same month, the Council reaffirmed the inherent right of individual or collective self-defense in the preamble to Resolution 1373 (Sept. 28, 2001) adopting a range of new counterterrorist measures (see Chapter 4, p. 274), which also reaffirmed previous statements by the Council that "every State has the duty to refrain from organizing, instigating, assisting or participating in terrorist acts in another State or acquiescing in organized activities within its territory directed toward the commission of such acts."

Meanwhile, on September 12, 2001, within the framework of the NATO alliance, the North Atlantic Council met to consider action under Article 5 of the North Atlantic Treaty, April 4, 1949, 63 Stat. 2241, 34 U.N.T.S. 243, which provides:

> that an armed attack against one or more of [the parties] in Europe or North America shall be considered an attack against them all; and consequently they agree that, if such an armed attack occurs, each of them, in exercise of the right of individual or collective self-defense recognized by Article 51 of the Charter of the United Nations, will assist that Party or Parties so attacked by taking forthwith, individually and in concert with the other Parties, such action as it deems necessary, including the use of armed force, to restore and maintain the security of the North Atlantic area.

The North Atlantic Council issued a statement that "If it is determined that this attack was directed from abroad against the United States, it shall be regarded as an action covered by Article 5." On October 2, 2001, following a briefing from the United States concerning its investigation, which had "clearly determined that the individuals who carried out the attacks belonged to the worldwide terrorist network of Al–Qaida, headed by Osama bin Laden and protected by the Taliban regime in Afghanistan," NATO Secretary–General Lord Robertson announced that it had been determined that the attacks had been directed from abroad and were therefore covered by Article 5. Similar action was taken under the Inter-American Treaty of Reciprocal Assistance (Rio Pact), art. 3, Sept. 2, 1947, 62 Stat. 1681, 21 U.N.T.S. 77, which embodies a comparable collective self-defense commitment within the American hemisphere.

In October 2001, the United States and its alliance partners launched major military action in the territory of Afghanistan, with the objective of eradicating the bases of terrorist activity within Afghanistan and removing the Taliban regime which had sheltered Osama bin Laden and his affiliates. Military operations continued after the overthrow of the Taliban government and as of 2009 are still in progress. Military and paramilitary activities (such as attacks by unmanned U.S. aircraft and missiles or raids on terrorist targets in Pakistan, Syria, and Yemen, and covert actions in various countries) have also been undertaken in other countries where Al–Qaida is believed to be active.

While the principle of lawful self-defense against terrorist attacks is not in doubt, the expansion of counterterrorist operations to diverse theaters and the open-ended nature of the global conflict have given rise to a variety of legal issues. Some of these involve the *jus in bello* and will be considered in that context in Section 4.

NOTES

1. *Defense Against Attacks on Israel from the Occupied Palestinian Territory.* In *Legal Consequences of the Construction of a Wall in the Occupied Palestinian Territory*, Advisory Opinion, 2004 I.C.J. 136, the International Court of Justice addressed itself to Israel's position that the erection of a barrier to protect its territory and people from terrorist attacks emanating from the Palestinian territory was lawful self-defense. In a brief passage (para. 139), the Court stated:

> Article 51 of the Charter thus recognizes the existence of an inherent right of self-defence in the case of armed attack by one State against another State. However, Israel does not claim that the attacks against it are imputable to a foreign State.

> The Court also notes that Israel exercises control in the Occupied Palestinian Territory and that, as Israel itself states, the threat which it regards as justifying the construction of the wall originates within, and not outside, that territory. The situation is thus different from that contemplated by Security Council resolutions 1368 (2001) and 1373

(2001), and therefore Israel could not in any event invoke those resolutions in support of its claim to be exercising a right of self-defence.

Consequently, the Court concludes that Article 51 of the Charter has no relevance in this case.

Commentators have criticized the Court for its handling of the self-defense issue. See, e.g., Wedgwood, The ICJ Advisory Opinion on the Israeli Security Fence and the Limits of Self–Defense, 99 A.J.I.L. 52 (2005); Murphy, Self–Defense and the Israeli *Wall* Advisory Opinion: An *Ipse Dixit* from the ICJ?, 99 A.J.I.L. 62 (2005). For a response, see Scobbie, Words My Mother Never Taught Me—"In Defense of the International Court," 99 A.J.I.L. 76 (2005).

2. *Military Action Against Hostile Groups.* In *Armed Activities on the Territory of the Congo* (Democratic Republic of the Congo v. Uganda), 2005 I.C.J. 168, the I.C.J. rejected Uganda's claim that it had engaged in lawful military activity in Congo's territory to protect itself against insurgents who had organized there. Is the I.C.J.'s approach adequate in light of contemporary threats? Consider the large number of incidents in recent years in which states have sent military forces or aircraft into foreign territory in order to address transborder threats from non-state actors, including the United States into Pakistan (against Taliban and Al Qaeda forces operating across the border from Afghanistan), a U.S. raid into Syrian territory in 2008, Turkey in its recurrent incursions into Iraq against Kurdish separatists, Colombia into Ecuador in pursuit of insurgents, and other examples. Do you think the Charter-based law on self-defense is sufficiently responsive to the concerns of states who face transborder threats from groups that the territorial sovereign is not able to control?

SECTION 2.   INTERVENTION IN INTERNAL CONFLICTS

A notable feature of the post-Cold War era is the shift in conflict patterns away from interstate violence toward struggles taking place mainly within the borders of states. Of course, civil wars, revolutions, and ethnic strife are not new phenomena; and international law has long grappled with their implications for international order. Prior to the U.N. Charter, international law sought to constrain external involvement in civil wars, by limiting the support that outsiders could give to participants in an internal struggle. The doctrine of non-intervention was the principal heading under which such restraints were found (or claimed). The Charter period reaffirmed legal constraints on intervention in internal affairs, but there have been substantial pressures for change in the traditional law. With the savagery of some recent conflicts, claims favoring intervention to protect populations from atrocities have been given new urgency. The emergent concept of "responsibility to protect" offers a framework for addressing some such situations. In this Section, we review these developments and consider the prospects for future evolution of the law. Our emphasis here is on interventions by states acting unilaterally; collective interventions (including for protective purposes) will be addressed in Section 3.

A. THE TRADITIONAL LAW

Even before the U.N. Charter, intervention by foreign powers in civil war or other domestic strife was, for international law, a particularly troublesome form of intervention. Henkin writes:

> Not surprisingly, revolutionary movements sought external assistance for themselves, but condemned as intervention any assistance to the governments against which they were rebelling. Not surprisingly, governments (including those which themselves came to power by revolution) saw objectionable "intervention" when other nations supported rebellion, whether by financial, political, or military means. Not surprisingly, governments saw no objectionable "intervention" in financial, military, or political support for themselves, even to shore them up against possible rebellion.

> The result was that international society struggled to achieve consensus and law on such questions as: What kinds of assistance may be given to legitimate governments? At what point does such assistance cease to be permissible because the government's right and power to rule are being challenged? At what stage may nations begin to accord rebels limited rights as "insurgents"? When may they decide to accord them belligerent rights equal to those of the government previously in power? When may they recognize them as the legitimate government? What are the rights and duties of states in regard to one side or the other in full-blown civil war? * * *

How Nations Behave 155 (2d ed. 1979).

The Spanish Civil War was a watershed for international law on intervention in civil war. In February of 1936, the Spanish Popular Front came to power in Spain through an electoral victory. Influential members of several rightist parties attempted to seize power without bloodshed, but when this effort failed, they started a revolt in Morocco headed by General Franco. From the start of hostilities, Germany and Italy intervened by transporting the rebel troops of General Franco to the mainland. The incumbent Republican government appealed for assistance. After initial vacillation, the French Cabinet decided not to intervene, but it did permit the private sale of arms to the Republican government. France's non-intervention policy appears to have been influenced by a fear of provoking Germany into more open intervention, leading to a world war. If France had been willing to provide the guns and ammunition sought by the Republican government, the rebellion might have been crushed.

At the initiative of Great Britain and France, an attempt was made to end intervention in the Spanish Civil War through the exchange of unilateral pledges by twenty-seven European governments. The agreements to prevent shipments of arms, ammunition and implements of war were to be supervised by the International Committee for the Application of the Agreement Regarding Non–Intervention in Spain. From its first meeting on September 9, 1936, until the middle of November, 1936, the Committee heard charges of intervention by the various powers. It is generally recognized that Germany and Italy violated the agreements on a major scale from the beginning. Although the Soviet Union maintained neutrality in the first stages of the war, it began to intervene in October, 1936, by sending significant quantities of equipment to the Republican Government.

The United States was not a party to the Non–Intervention Agreements, but it maintained a policy of strict neutrality, including an absolute embargo against the shipment of arms to Spain. The refusal of the United States to sell arms, combined with the non-intervention policy of the British and French, deprived the Spanish Republic of adequate armaments while the rebels received supplies from Germany and Italy.

The Non–Intervention Pact departed from the traditional doctrine that, in a civil war, the government but not the rebels may receive outside assistance, at least until the rebels have been granted belligerent status. This status was never accorded to the Franco forces, who moved directly from rebels to full recognition as the government of Spain. Germany and Italy, while nominally parties to this Pact, not only violated it by providing massive supplies and armed contingents—of which the German bombing squadron that obliterated Guernica is the most notorious example—but they also circumvented the problem of inequality of status between government and rebels by recognizing the Franco rebels as the Government of Spain in November, 1936. This recognition came when the fall of Madrid was anticipated by many observers, but it has been criticized as premature recognition, forbidden by international law. (Compare p. 369 in Chapter 5.)

NOTES

1. *Which Foreign Interventions Ought to Have Been Permitted?* The classic analysis of the international law implications of the Spanish Civil War is Padelford, International Law and Diplomacy in the Spanish Civil Strife (1939). Friedmann has commented as follows:

> A distinction has often been made between support for the incumbent government and support for insurgents, on the ground "that a foreign state commits an international delinquency by assisting insurgents in spite of being at peace with the legitimate government." But since there is a very wide measure of discretion in the speed and manner in which any individual state may recognize insurgents in another state either as belligerents or as the legitimate government, the value of this distinction is highly doubtful. At most it may be said that, in extreme cases of foreign assistance to rebels in the guise of their immediate recognition as the legitimate government, at a time when they had no substantial control of the country, as was notably the case in the almost immediate recognition of the Franco government by Germany and Italy after the rebellion, is a thinly disguised interference in the affairs of another state, utterly at

variance with established principles of recognition. Apart from such extreme cases, the parties in a civil strife seriously contesting the control of the country, must probably be taken as equals. Any, reasonably precise, definition of the rights and duties of other states with regards to the parties in a civil war is made extremely difficult by the fact that civil war usually arises from clashes of political philosophy and bitter social tensions, and that therefore the sympathies of governments and political groups outside the state torn by civil war are usually deeply engaged on one side or the other. This tends to mould legal interpretations of rights of intervention and duties of abstention even more in the direction of political sympathies, than in other situations. Thus, in the Spanish Civil War from 1936–38, which deeply stirred official and non-official political opinion abroad, those favoring the cause of the incumbent Republican Government of Spain affirmed the widely supported doctrine that in the case of civil war, the legal government but not the insurgents are entitled to assistance, at least up to the point when the insurgents have become sufficiently established to attain the status of belligerency. This attitude was strengthened by the blatant intervention of Nazi Germany and Fascist Italy on the side of Franco, from the very outbreak of revolution. For reasons of policy rather than law, the Western governments came to treat both sides as equals, by concluding a non-intervention pact to which the Fascist Powers, as well as the Soviet Union, were also parties. This pact, based on the principle of abstention from assistance to either side proved a complete failure, not because of the underlying principle but because the Fascist Powers, and to a lesser extent the Soviet Union, ignored the obligations undertaken in the pact so that the disparity between the assistance granted to the Franco faction by states in league with him and the failure of the Republican Government to obtain aid from the Western Powers, became even greater. Legally, however, a case can be made for the theory underlying the nonintervention pact, provided, of course, that it is genuinely observed by all sides. Quincy Wright has contended, with powerful support in the legal literature, that "in a situation of civil strife, the state is temporarily inhibited from acting. A government beset by civil strife is not in a position to invite assistance in the name of the state." * * *

Friedmann, The Changing Structure of International Law 265–66 (1964) (footnotes omitted).

Does the history of the Spanish Civil War illustrate the obsolescence of the traditional rule under which neutral governments are enjoined from assisting either side in a war by military supplies, but private manufacturers and traders are permitted to do so? Compare Friedmann, The Growth of State Control over the Individual and its Effect upon the Rules of International State Responsibility, 19 Brit. Y.B.I.L. 118 (1938). Can a government disclaim responsibility for the movement of arms from its territory to any other power, or disclaim the power to regulate or interdict such supplies?

2. *Supporting Insurgencies.* Supplying arms to a belligerent is one example of an act that may violate the neutral duty of impartiality. See pp. 1130–32 *supra.* The recruitment and training of troops in one state to launch

an attack against another state is another example. Title 18 U.S.C. § 960 (2000) provides:

> Whoever, within the United States, knowingly begins or sets on foot or provides or prepares a means for or furnishes the money for, or takes part in, any military or naval expedition or enterprise to be carried on from thence against the territory or dominion of any foreign prince or state, or of any colony, district, or people with whom the United States is at peace, shall be fined under this title or imprisoned not more than three years, or both.

In 1959, the Department of Justice asked the Department of State for its opinion whether an organization formed in California and called the "Tibetan Brigade," which reportedly intended to go into Tibet in order to "aid the Tibetans in their revolt against the Chinese Communist tyranny," might be acting in violation of 18 U.S.C.A. § 960. The Department of State replied that Communist China should not be considered a state within the meaning of the statute, since at the time the Communist régime was not recognized by the United States as the legitimate government. Furthermore the United States could not be considered at peace with Communist China. See 5 Whiteman at 254–55.

Following the abortive action against the Castro régime by Cuban refugees and their sympathizers at the Bay of Pigs on April 15, 1961, the Attorney General of the United States stated that none of their activities had violated the neutrality laws of the United States. While conceding that the laws prohibit the departure from the United States of a group organized as a military expedition against a nation with whom the United States is at peace, he contended that the departure of several persons at the same time with the intent of joining an insurgent group was not criminal. 5 Whiteman at 275–76.

The applicability of U.S. neutrality laws also became an issue with respect to private assistance for the Nicaraguan *contras* in the 1980s. See generally *Dellums v. Smith*, 573 F.Supp. 1489 (N.D. Cal. 1983).

3. *Mercenaries*. In 1989, the United Nations General Assembly adopted an International Convention against the Recruitment Use, Financing and Training of Mercenaries. See U.N. Doc. A/RES/44/34 (Dec. 4, 1989), reprinted in 29 I.L.M. 89 (1990). The Convention entered into force in October 2001 and in 2009 has thirty-two parties.

B.   CIVIL STRIFE AND THE UNITED NATIONS CHARTER

HENKIN, HOW NATIONS BEHAVE

155–57 (2d ed. 1979) (footnotes omitted)

When, in the U.N. Charter, the nations decided to outlaw wars and the use of force, they said nothing explicit about internal wars; clearly, they did not intend to prohibit revolution or civil war. The Charter, too, though it enshrines principles of "independence," "sovereign equality," and "self-determination," says nothing explicit about outside intervention in internal struggles. It is not commonly insisted that the Charter itself forbids intervention in internal wars by political and economic means. The question that has divided lawyers is whether the Charter provision that members shall not use or threaten force against the political independence or territorial integrity of another member forbids also intervention by force in a civil war.

* * *

Some lawyers have argued that, when nations come to the support of one side or the other in cases of independent insurrection or *bona fide* civil war, it is not a violation of the norms of the U.N. Charter but only of some customary rule against such intervention which, if it was ever sound, may not have recovered from the wounds it suffered in the Spanish Civil War. Many believed that there is no agreed norm forbidding active military support for the recognized government of a country, at least before rebellion has made great headway. The United States has invoked the right to give such aid to Greece, Lebanon, Nationalist China, and South Vietnam. The Soviet Union claimed a similar justification in Hungary. Some may even assert the right to recognize and support rebel causes, as in Angola (against Portugal), and even in the Congo in 1964–65. * * *

In our time, some forces for intervention have been particularly strong and unlikely to heed an uncertain law. The difficulties of defining and preventing "unlawful intervention" have been multiplied where domestic and international interests are entangled and internal conflicts have special international significance. There were interventions to help end colonialism, as when Tunisia actively supported the Algerian rebels, and when other nations supported rebels against Portuguese rule in Angola. The major interventions involved, of course, Communist expansionism and Western efforts to contain it.

SCHACHTER, THE RIGHT OF STATES TO USE ARMED FORCE

82 Mich. L. Rev. 1620, 1641–45 (1984) (footnotes omitted)

Foreign military interventions in civil wars have been so common in our day that the proclaimed rule of nonintervention may seem to have been stood on its head. Talleyrand's cynical quip comes to mind: "nonintervention is a word that has the same meaning as intervention." Indeed, virtually all the interventions that occur today are carried out in the name of nonintervention; they are justified as responses to prior interventions by the other side. No state today would deny the basic principle that the people of a nation have the right, under international law, to decide for themselves what kind of government they want, and that this includes the right to revolt and to carry on armed conflict between competing groups. For a foreign state to support, with "force," one side or the other in an internal conflict, is to deprive the people in some measure of their right to decide the issue by themselves. It is, in terms of article 2(4), a use of force against the political independence of the state engaged in civil war.

The states that intervene do not challenge this legal principle; they generally proclaim it as the basis for their "counter-intervention." They are often able to do so with some plausibility, because in almost every civil war the parties have sought and received some outside military support. A preeminent difficulty in applying the rule of nonintervention in these circumstances arises from the equivocal position of the established government. Other states are free as a general rule (in the absence of contrary treaties) to furnish arms, military training and even combat forces to that government at its request. On the other hand, they may not do the same for an opposing force; that would clearly violate the sovereignty and independence of the state.

Consequently, governments commonly receive foreign military aid and they may request more such aid when faced with an armed insurrection. At that point two questions arise: (1) is there an obligation to cease aid to the established regime because that now involves taking sides in an internal conflict? And (2) if such aid to the government constitutes foreign intervention, does it permit counter-intervention to support the other side? Concretely, if the Nicaraguan Sandinista regime receives Cuban and Soviet military supplies and advisors, is the United States free to support the armed opposition by training, arms and technical advice? An answer to the first question involves an assessment of the particular circumstances and of the presumption that the government is entitled to continued aid. The relevant general principle, in keeping with the concept of political independence and non-intervention, would be that when an organized insurgency occurs on a large scale involving a substantial number of people or control over significant areas of the country, neither side, government or insurgency, should receive outside military aid. Such outside support would be contrary to the right of the people to decide the issue by their own means. It would be immaterial whether the insurgency was directed at overthrow of the government or at secession (or autonomy) of a territorial unit.

The second and more difficult question is whether an illegal intervention on one side permits outside states to give military aid to the other party (whether government or insurrectionists). Such counter-intervention may be justified as a defense of the independence of the state against foreign intervention; it may then be viewed as "collective self-defense" in response to armed attack. True, it may also further "internationalize" a local conflict and increase the threat to international peace. The Vietnam War is the outstanding example. Despite the danger, the law does not proscribe such counter-intervention. It is not that two wrongs make a right but that the grave violation of one right allows a defensive response. The political solution is to avoid its necessity by a strict application of a nonintervention rule applied to both sides. To achieve this it is probably essential in most cases to have international mechanisms (peacekeeping forces or observer teams) to monitor compliance with a *cordon sanitaire* and a ban on assistance.

NOTES

1. *Aid to Rebels as Unlawful Intervention.* In *Military and Paramilitary Activities in and Against Nicaragua*, 1986 I.C.J. 14, 123–26, paras. 239–49, the International Court of Justice found that the United States was in violation of the prohibition on intervention in customary international law by its provision of material support to the counterrevolutionary forces (*contras*) seeking to overthrow the Sandinista government of Nicaragua, saying (para. 241):

> The Court considers that in international law, if one State, with a view to the coercion of another State, supports and assists armed bands in that State whose purpose is to overthrow the government of that State, that amounts to an intervention by the one State in the internal affairs of the other, whether or not the political objective of the State giving such support and assistance is equally far-reaching.

The Court did not accept the U.S. contention that its measures were merely aimed at interdicting Nicaragua's supply of arms to the armed opposition in El Salvador and also found that U.S. aid to the *contras* could not be viewed as the legitimate provision of humanitarian assistance, since such aid was offered only to the *contra* faction and not on a non-discriminatory basis to all in need. See excerpts at p. 1166.

2. *Cold War Instances.* During the Cold War there were many instances of external participation in situations of internal disorder, strife or civil war: U.S. support for Greek and Turkish governments fighting Communist guerrilla bands (1947); the Soviet Union's interventions in Hungary (1956); Czechoslovakia (1968); and Afghanistan (1979); India in Bangladesh (1971); civil war in Lebanon (1958 and 1982); the sending of U.S. marines to the Dominican Republic (1965); internal and interstate war in the Horn of Africa; interventions in civil war in Angola and Southern Africa; Vietnam's invasion of Kampuchea to depose the Pol Pot regime (1979); external roles in civil war in El Salvador and Nicaragua (during most of the 1980s); French and Libyan involvement in civil war in Chad (1980s); and various other situations.

As to whether intervention in a state by one outside power justifies counter-intervention by another, see Cutler, The Right to Intervene, 64 Foreign Affairs 96 (1985). Compare Schachter, The Right of States to Use Armed Force, 82 Mich. L. Rev. at 1641–45; Schachter, In Defense of International Rules on the Use of Force, 53 U. Chi. L. Rev. 113, 120–21, 137–38 (1986); Henkin, The Use of Force: Law and U.S. Policy, in Right v. Might: International Law and the Use of Force 37, 50–65 (2d ed. 1991).

3. *Vietnam.* The most extensive involvement by the United States in foreign civil strife since World War II was in Vietnam. As Henkin has written:

> There are at least three possible models to characterize the Vietnam War and the U.S. role in it, and the judgment of international law will largely depend on which characterization it accepts.

Model A saw the war as civil war within an independent South Vietnam, with North Vietnam an outside state helping one side, the United States another outside state helping the other. Military intervention in civil war was not acceptable under traditional international law, but that law may never have recovered from the wounds it suffered at many hands during the Spanish Civil War. On its face at least, such external intervention is not obviously a violation of Article 2(4) of the U.N. Charter as a use of force against the political independence or territorial integrity of another state, if the support was bona fide and the intervenor was not seeking to dominate the side it supported and establish a puppet regime. * * *

A second view (Model B) also saw the war as civil war, not between the Vietcong and the Saigon Government in a separate independent South Vietnam, but within the single state of Vietnam, between North Vietnam and the Vietcong on one hand and Saigon forces on the other. In such a war, U.S. intervention, even bombing North Vietnam, was—again—perhaps a violation of traditional international norms against intervention in civil war, but not clearly of the U.N. Charter. * * *

Officially, the United States saw the war in Vietnam in yet a third perspective (Model C). North Vietnam launched an armed attack against the territorial integrity and political independence of an independent country, the Republic of South Vietnam, using the Vietcong as its agent. This was a use of force in clear violation of Article 2(4) of the Charter. In the face of this armed attack, the Republic of South Vietnam had its inherent right of self-defense under Article 51 of the Charter, and the United States could come to its aid in collective self-defense—as indeed, it had obligated itself to do in the South East Asian Collective Defense Treaty. The United States and the Republic of South Vietnam had every right to carry the war to the territory of the aggressor in order to defeat the aggression; they could carry the war to the territory of any other countries that involved themselves in the aggression, or permitted the aggressor to use their territory for its aggressive purposes, *i.e.*, Laos and Cambodia.

Henkin, How Nations Behave 306–08 (2d ed. 1979) (footnotes omitted). See The Vietnam War and International Law (Falk ed. 1968–1974); see also Falk, International Law and the United States Role in the Vietnam War, 75 Yale L.J. 1122 (1966); Moore, The Lawfulness of Military Assistance to the Republic of Vietnam, 61 A.J.I.L. 1 (1967); Falk's response at 76 Yale L.J. 1095 (1967); Falk, The Six Legal Dimensions of the Vietnam War (1968); Moore, Law and the Indo–China War (1972); Symposium on U.S. Military Action in Cambodia, 65 A.J.I.L. 1 (1971).

4. *Post–Cold War Internal Conflicts.* Civil wars have claimed millions of lives in the decade spanning the turn of the century. More than two dozen such wars were in progress when the Carnegie Commission on Prevention of Deadly Conflict issued its Final Report in December 1997 (for illustrative figures, see the Final Report at 11–22). A large portion of these wars involved the residue of arms transfers dating from the period of U.S.–Soviet confrontation, as well as the remnants of armies that had been proxies for one or the

other superpower at an earlier time. Conflicts between ethnic groups likewise produced bloodshed on a staggering scale. On efforts to deploy techniques of international law to quell ethnic strife, see International Law and Ethnic Conflict (Wippman ed. 1998); Ratner, Does International Law Matter in Preventing Ethnic Conflict?, 32 N.Y.U. J. Int'l L. & Pol. 591 (2000).

C. HUMANITARIAN INTERVENTION; RESPONSIBILITY TO PROTECT

The legality of intervention for humanitarian reasons has been debated for decades. In the sense used here, humanitarian intervention refers to uses of force by one state to protect persons within another state from massive atrocities such as genocide. There were various examples of such interventions in state practice in the nineteenth century, before a prohibition on the use of force had crystallized in international law. The lawfulness of humanitarian intervention in the U.N. Charter period has been much disputed, because it is difficult to reconcile such claims with the text of Article 2(4), with its negotiating history, or with subsequent U.N. efforts to clarify its meaning (as in the Friendly Relations Declaration or the Definition of Aggression Resolution). Similarly, it has not been clear that state practice or *opinio juris* could establish the existence of a customary law right of humanitarian intervention in the post-World War II period.

Developments near the end of the twentieth century brought renewed attention to the humanitarian intervention controversy. As hundreds of thousands lost their lives in brutal ethnic conflict in the former Yugoslavia, in Hutu-against-Tutsi massacres in Rwanda, in suppression of the self-determination movement in East Timor, and similar savagery in too many parts of the globe, there were growing demands for the outside world to become involved. Media attention—the so-called "CNN factor"—drew the spotlight to such situations and underscored the moral urgency of doing whatever could be done to stop the slaughter of innocents. Humanitarian aid to victims of manmade as well as natural disasters was delivered on several occasions in the 1990s with the help of outside military forces, as in Somalia (see p. 1252). It began to seem possible that external military interventions might be able to prevent or interrupt vast human tragedies, and if so, that international law should be interpreted (or reinterpreted, or revised) to permit rather than prohibit such uses of force.

The debates over humanitarian intervention took on a new dimension with the Rwandan genocide of 1994 and the Kosovo crisis of 1999 (pp. 1206, 1256, 1263). Some political leaders and international lawyers explicitly embraced a humanitarian intervention rationale, in more expansive terms than had previously been acceptable under the dominant views of previous decades. Others, however, were reluctant to embrace a theory that could loosen the Charter's constraints on transboundary uses of force and provide a pretext for abusive interventions.

The materials that follow trace developments up to and after the Kosovo intervention. We will return to related questions in Section 3 on collective uses of force, since several recent interventions have had explicit Security Council authorization (and implicit multilateral approval was one of the claims proffered to justify NATO's action in Kosovo).

1. Humanitarian Intervention Under the U.N. Charter and Customary International Law

SCHACHTER, INTERNATIONAL LAW IN THEORY AND PRACTICE

123–25 (1991) (footnotes omitted)

Apart from self-defense, the strongest claim to allowing an exception to the prohibition on armed force would appear to be the use of force to save the lives of innocent human beings threatened by massacres, atrocities, widespread brutality and destruction. * * *

In support, it has been argued that the renunciation of armed force could not have been intended to prevent such humanitarian interventions when other means, short of force, were proven ineffective. The interventions, if limited to humanitarian ends under conditions of necessity and proportionality, could not be against the territorial integrity or political independence of the State in question, nor could they be inconsistent with the purposes of the Charter. If the U.N. failed to take effective action and no other international body did, elementary humanitarian principles impose an obligation on States capable of taking protective measures to do so, including, if necessary the employment of armed forces in the troubled countries.

These arguments, appealing as they seem to be, have failed to win the explicit support of the international community of States or of any significant segment of that community. No United Nations resolution has supported the right of a State to intervene on humanitarian grounds with armed troops in a State that has not consented to such intervention. Nor is there evidence of State practice and related *opinio juris* on a scale sufficient to support a humanitarian exception to the general prohibition against non-defensive use of force.

It is true that, in a few cases, the action of an intervening army outside of its borders was seen as serving a humanitarian end because it saved innocent lives from death or injury. Whether these cases can be considered as precedents accepted as law is dubious, especially as no intervening state claimed a legal right based on that ground. Thus, when Indian troops acted to protect Bengalis in East Pakistan in 1971 from Pakistani troops, India asserted the action was necessary to protect its borders. * * * Despite much sympathy for the East Pakistan Bengalis, the great majority of States were clearly unwilling to legitimize India's armed action as a permissible exception to Article 2(4).

A second case that some lawyers have viewed as humanitarian intervention occurred when Tanzanian troops moved into Uganda following a Ugandan frontier incursion repulsed by Tanzania. Actually, Tanzania claimed self-defense rather than a right of humanitarian intervention. * * * Some African leaders criticized Tanzania's action but, understandably, many governments were not disposed to challenge its relatively benign occupation. It is hard to regard such non-action as accepting a right of unilateral intervention for humanitarian ends. What it does show is that governments hesitate to condemn a short-term military move against an egregious régime. * * *

A claim of humanitarian intent was used by Vietnam to support its armed action in Cambodia in 1978 against the Pol Pot forces. * * * The majority of States in the United Nations have rejected the Vietnamese contentions and called for the withdrawal of its troops.

* * *

Our sympathy for victims of atrocities should not obscure the lessons of past invasions claimed to be humanitarian. Past armed interventions, going back to 19th century incursions by imperial powers, have shown that intervening States have invariably had their own political agenda. They imposed conditions that were not freely chosen by the people of the country in question. They often obtained special advantages and exacerbated internal conflicts. It is hardly surprising that governments have refrained from adopting a general rule for humanitarian intervention. Indeed, I believe no government has actually declared itself as favoring so broad an exception to the rule against force.

NOTES

1. *Humanitarian Intervention in Historical Context.* For a treatment relating current controversies about intervention to historical practices over several centuries, see Bass, Freedom's Battle: The Origins of Humanitarian Intervention (2008). See also Roberts, The So–Called "Right" of Humanitarian Intervention, 2000 Y.B. Int'l Humanitarian L. 3. Philosophical and political treatments include Rawls, The Law of Peoples 89–94 (1999); Wheeler, Saving Strangers: Humanitarian Intervention in International Society (2000); Walzer, Just and Unjust Wars at 21–34, 51–73, 86–109 (4th ed. 2006).

2. *Scholars' Differing Views in the Charter Era.* For a pointed debate on whether the law of the Charter could or should be understood to allow humanitarian intervention, compare Brownlie, Humanitarian Intervention, in Law and Civil War in the Modern World 218–19 (Moore ed. 1974) (finding no basis for the doctrine), with Lillich, Humanitarian Intervention: A Reply to Dr. Brownlie and a Plea for Constructive Alternatives, in id. at 229, 247–48 (arguing in favor). For other discussions, see the essays by Farer, Kartashkin, Meron and Damrosch, in Law and Force in the New International Order 185–223 (Damrosch & Scheffer eds. 1991). See also Tesón, Humanitarian Intervention: An Inquiry into Law and Morality (2d ed. 1997); Murphy, Humanitarian Intervention (1996); Hoffmann et al., The Ethics and Politics of Humanitari-

an Intervention (1996); Müllerson & Scheffer, Legal Regulation of the Use of Force, in Beyond Confrontation: International Law for the Post–Cold War Era 93, 117–24 (Damrosch, Danilenko, & Müllerson eds. 1995). For earlier treatments, see Humanitarian Intervention and the United Nations (Lillich ed. 1973); Akehurst, Humanitarian Intervention, in Intervention in World Politics (Bull ed. 1984); Franck & Rodley, After Bangladesh: The Law of Humanitarian Intervention by Military Force, 67 A.J.I.L. 275 (1973); Jhabvala, Unilateral Humanitarian Intervention and International Law, 21 Indian J. Int'l L. 208 (1981); Rodley, Human Rights and Humanitarian Intervention: The Case Law of the World Court, 38 I.C. L.Q. 321 (1989); Scheffer, Toward a Modern Doctrine of Humanitarian Intervention, 4 Fla. Int'l L.J. 435 (1989). See also Restatement (Third) § 703, Comment e.

For a recent interdisciplinary inquiry, see Humanitarian Intervention: Ethical, Legal, and Political Dilemmas (Holzgrefe & Keohane eds. 2003). For an argument that the U.N. Charter could be construed to authorize intervention to defend persons from violent attacks in their own country, see Fletcher & Ohlin, Defending Humanity: When Force Is Justified and Why (2008). See also Human Rights, Intervention and the Use of Force (Alston & Macdonald eds. 2008).

2. Efforts to Formulate Criteria for Legitimate Intervention

Writers supporting the legitimacy of humanitarian intervention generally agree that the scope for any such exception to the prohibition on use of force would have to be carefully circumscribed. Various sets of criteria have been formulated. Though they differ in their specifics, most would embody some or all of the following conditions:

—The violation of human rights would have to be extremely grave, e.g., genocide or similar atrocities on a mass scale, rather than lower-level breaches.

—There must be no other means of rectifying the violations: military force should be a last resort.

—The intervention should be supported (or at least not actively opposed) by those who would be its putative beneficiaries.

—The intervention should be conducted in full compliance with the laws of war (see Section 4) and with the least destructive means to achieve the objective of terminating the violations.

—The intervention should be calculated to cause less harm to the target state than would occur in the absence of intervention. (If the costs would outweigh the benefits, or if the probability of success is low, then there is probably not a good case for intervention on policy grounds. Some such considerations may also be relevant to legal and moral appraisal.)

—The intervenors should withdraw upon achieving termination of the violations.

Many writers would add that humanitarian intervention should preferably be carried out under the auspices of the United Nations or another appropriate multilateral institution; but if organizational capacity is lacking and international authorization cannot be obtained, unilateral intervention might be necessary. Some would also require the intervener to be willing to allow its actions to be scrutinized by an international body after the fact for conformity to international law. As to these considerations, see below on the Kosovo crisis and further discussion on multilateral authority for intervention in Section 3 at p. 1244.

NOTES

1. *Pretextual Interventions.* Critics of humanitarian intervention point out that many interventions undertaken with a purportedly humanitarian rationale have involved an ulterior motive on the intervener's part. For example, Vietnam's 1979 intervention in Cambodia did not end with the ouster of the Khmer Rouge regime and persisted into the 1990s. The likelihood of disingenuous or abusive invocations of a humanitarian rationale is one reason why many scholars reject the theory of humanitarian intervention in general, but others disagree:

> The fact that humanitarian intervention can serve as a pretext for achieving political objectives in another states argues strongly for invalidating multinational or unilateral missions altogether. But most norms of international law can be abused. Professor Higgins has aptly observed that "so have there been countless abusive claims of the right to self-defence." That does not mean that the right to self-defence has ceased to exist.

Müllerson & Scheffer, Legal Regulation of the Use of Force, in Beyond Confrontation: International Law for the Post–Cold War Era 93, 124 (Damrosch, Danilenko, & Müllerson eds. 1995), citing Higgins, Problems and Process: International Law and How We Use It 247 (1994). Does it matter that self-defense is a well-established doctrine of international law, while humanitarian intervention is hotly contested? For an argument drawing on social science literature to suggest that the "pretext" objection is not well-founded, see Goodman, Humanitarian Intervention and Pretexts for War, 100 A.J.I.L. 107 (2006).

2. *Altruism v. Interest.* Could humanitarian intervention ever be wholly altruistic? Mixed motives and some degree of self-interest on the part of the intervener would seem inevitable. On the difficulties in devising a "principled" approach to humanitarian intervention, see Damrosch, The Inevitability of Selective Response? Principles to Guide Urgent International Action, in Kosovo and the Challenge of Humanitarian Intervention 405–19 (Schnabel & Thakur eds. 2000).

3. *Temporary Presence.* Should an intervener be expected to withdraw promptly? An intervening force may have to remain in place for a considerable period of time while the underlying causes of the humanitarian violations are being addressed. Precipitous withdrawal could quite likely lead to a renewal of genocide or other conditions that led to the intervention in the first place. On the prolonged presence of international forces in former Yugoslavia, see p. 1261.

4. *Humane Methods.* Adam Roberts has commented that in "the long history of legal debates about humanitarian intervention, there has been a consistent failure to address directly the question of the methods used in such interventions." Roberts, NATO's Humanitarian War Over Kosovo, 41 Survival, No. 3, 102, 110 (1999). It has recently been suggested that perhaps humanitarian interveners should be held to *higher* standards (e.g., of avoiding inadvertent civilian casualties) than would be required under the generally applicable laws of war (discussed in Section 4). On this point in relation to the intervention in Kosovo, see p. 1212.

3. The Kosovo Intervention, 1999

Controversy over the international law of humanitarian intervention came to the fore with the multinational military intervention mounted by NATO countries against the Federal Republic of Yugoslavia (Serbia–Montenegro) concerning Kosovo in spring 1999. The intervention needs to be understood against the background of almost a decade of international efforts to alleviate the bloody ethnic conflicts in former Yugoslavia. Aspects of these efforts will be addressed in Section 3 below, under the heading of collective uses of force. Although the Kosovo intervention had multinational participation, formal Security Council authorization was not conferred in advance. (On the Security Council's role in the Yugoslav conflict and arguments that the Security Council implicitly or retroactively authorized the NATO intervention in Kosovo, see pp. 1263–64 note 4.) Given the lack of explicit Security Council imprimatur and doubts about the authority of NATO to act non-defensively within the territory of a non-member, the legal analysis of the military operation can begin by considering the Kosovo operation under the rubric of unilateral humanitarian intervention (in other words, with the unilateral intervener being thirteen NATO states acting jointly).

Kosovo had been an autonomous region within Serbia. A large majority of the population living in Kosovo (some 90%) was ethnic Albanian, and a small minority (perhaps 10%) was ethnic Serb. With the collapse of the socialist economic system of the former Yugoslavia at the end of the 1980s came increasing ethnic tensions (whipped up by nationalist politicians including the Serbian leader Slobodan Milosěvic), revocation of Kosovo's autonomous status, and growing discrimination against the Albanians who were a minority within Serbia. The outbreak of ethnic violence in various parts of former Yugoslavia in the early 1990s was accompanied by increased repression of the Kosovar Albanians in Serbia. Although the conclusion of the Dayton Agreement for Peace in Bosnia–Herzegovina of December 1995 largely stabilized the ethnic conflicts among Serbs, Croats, and Bosnian Muslims, the situation of the Kosovar Albanians grew increasingly bleak in the late 1990s. The formation of the Kosovo Liberation Army (with a separatist agenda) led to an escalation of violence as Yugoslav forces cracked down on the KLA insurgency. In 1998 more than 230,000 Kosovar Albanians fled their villages to escape what the Security Council soon condemned as "the excessive and indiscriminate use of force by Serbian security forces and the Yugoslav Army." S.C. Res. 1199 (Sept. 23, 1998).

Despite the presence of an international verification force stationed in Kosovo with Security Council authorization from fall 1998, S.C. Res. 1203 (Oct. 24, 1998), Serb elements perpetrated an "ethnic cleansing" campaign aimed at driving Albanians out of Kosovo. Meanwhile, in January 1999, a "contact group" consisting of the United States, the United Kingdom, France, Germany, Italy and the Russian Federation convened talks at Rambouillet, France, with the participation of the Kosovar Albanians and the Yugoslav government, in an effort to reach a negotiated political settlement of the conflict. The Albanian side reluctantly agreed to the Rambouillet proposals (which were presented on a take-it-or-leave-it basis), but the Yugoslav side found them unacceptable. (Objectionable features included, among other things, provision for NATO implementation within Yugoslav territory.) Even as the talks foundered, a massacre of dozens of Albanian civilians in the Kosovo village of Rajak in early 1999 convinced NATO to move toward military intervention.

The apparent haste of the decision to proceed to a major military action is best understood in light of the desire of NATO leaders not to allow a replay of the tragedy of Bosnia–Herzegovina earlier in the 1990s, where "ethnic cleansing" went on for several years, with tremendous loss of life and civilian hardship, while the outside world weighed and adjusted the options. Thus, although the precise number of Albanians already killed in the first months of 1999 may not have reached a high toll, the record of the recent past gave reason to suspect that a massive humanitarian catastrophe would unfold if Milosĕvic's forces were left to their own devices.

On March 24, 1999, NATO began a bombing campaign against Serbia, with the proclaimed objective of protecting the Kosovar Albanians from further attacks at the hands of the Serbian forces. In the short term, however, the humanitarian disaster worsened as Serbs accelerated the "ethnic cleansing" of Albanians. The air war, which lasted for seventy-eight days, was conducted from a height that kept NATO warplanes out of reach of ground fire but also made it difficult to carry out precision attacks on military targets; the results included several hundred civilian casualties (of Albanians as well as Serbs). Some blatant errors—such as the inadvertent bombing of the Chinese embassy in Belgrade, which had been misidentified as an intelligence facility for the Yugoslav military—compounded the perception of a flawed military operation.

Efforts to obtain an authoritative appraisal of the legal aspects of the NATO intervention were inconclusive at the time and afterwards. In the first days of the campaign, Russia introduced a Security Council resolution to condemn the NATO action as a "flagrant violation" of the U.N. Charter, but the resolution was defeated with only three votes in favor (Russia, China, and Namibia) and twelve against. U.N. Doc. S/PV.3989, at 6 (Mar. 26, 1999). While the bombing campaign was in progress, the

Federal Republic of Yugoslavia (Serbia–Montenegro) brought separate suits at the International Court of Justice against ten of the NATO members involved in the military action (Belgium, Canada, France, Germany, Italy, the Netherlands, Portugal, Spain, the United Kingdom, and the United States), in which Yugoslavia alleged:

> The Government of [the Kingdom of Belgium, and others *mutatis mutandis*], together with the Governments of other Member States of NATO, took part in the acts of use of force against the Federal Republic of Yugoslavia by taking part in bombing targets in the Federal Republic of Yugoslavia. In bombing the Federal Republic of Yugoslavia military and civilian targets were attacked. Great number of people were killed, including a great many civilians. Residential houses came under attack. Numerous dwellings were destroyed. Enormous damage was caused to schools, hospitals, radio and television stations, cultural and health institutions and to places of worship. * * *

> [B]y taking part in the bombing of the territory of the Federal Republic of Yugoslavia, the Kingdom of Belgium has acted against the Federal Republic of Yugoslavia in breach of its obligation not to use force against another State * * *.

Yugoslavia also sought provisional measures, which the Court denied in orders of June 2, 1999. (See discussion of jurisdictional and other aspects in Chapter 9, p. 598.)

The various NATO states took different approaches to the legal issues involved in the military intervention. The United States did not issue a formal legal opinion, but U.S. leaders pointed to a variety of factors as supportive of the lawfulness of the NATO action. A few days before the commencement of the military action, the U.S. Department of State's spokesman said:

> There has been extensive consideration of the international legal issue with our NATO allies. We and our NATO allies have looked to numerous factors in concluding that such action, if necessary, would be justified—including the fact that Yugoslav military and police forces have committed serious and widespread violations of international law, and have used excessive and indiscriminate force in violation of international law. * * *

> * * * With Belgrade giving every indication that it will prepare a new offensive against Kosovar Albanians, we face the prospect of a new explosion of violence if the international community doesn't take preventative action. * * * Serb actions also constitute a threat to the region, particularly Albania and Macedonia and potentially NATO allies, including Greece and Turkey. In addition, these actions constitute a threat to the safety of international observers in Kosovo.

> On the basis of such considerations, we and our NATO allies believe there are legitimate grounds to threaten and, if necessary, use military force.

Murphy, Contemporary Practice of the United States Relating to International Law, 93 A.J.I.L. 628, 631 (1999).

The United Kingdom's Secretary of State for Defence, George Robertson, said: "We are in no doubt that NATO is acting within international law and our legal justification rests upon the accepted principle that force may be used in extreme circumstances to avert a humanitarian catastrophe." An earlier U.K. note of October 1998 had specified the position that "as matters now stand and if action through the Security Council is not possible, military intervention by NATO is lawful on grounds of overwhelming humanitarian necessity." Quoted in Duke, Ehrhart, & Karadi, The Major European Allies: France, Germany and the United Kingdom, in Kosovo and the Challenge of Humanitarian Intervention (Schnabel & Thakur eds. 2000, at 128, 137.) For the positions of other states, see the related chapters in the same volume (covering Italy, Greece and Turkey; Portugal, Belgium, Canada, and Spain; as well as Hungary, Poland and the Czech Republic which were new entrants to NATO; the Nordic countries in and out of NATO; Russia, China and India which were adamantly opposed to NATO's action; and others).

By early June 1999 the Milosĕvic´government of Yugoslavia was ready to accept NATO's terms. A resolution formalizing the settlement of the conflict was soon adopted by the Security Council under Chapter VII of the U.N. Charter. S.C. Res. 1244 (June 10, 1999). The resolution demanded that the Federal Republic of Yugoslavia "put an immediate and verifiable end to violence and repression in Kosovo, and begin and complete verifiable phased withdrawal from Kosovo of all military, police and paramilitary forces according to a rapid timetable, with which the deployment of the international security presence in Kosovo will be synchronized." Significantly, Russia was willing to participate along with NATO military forces in the international security presence, known as KFOR. For more on the Security Council's role in the Kosovo crisis, see pp. 1263–64.

NOTES

1. *Diverse Views of Scholars.* On legal aspects of the Kosovo intervention, see editorial comments by Henkin, Wedgwood, Charney, Chinkin, Falk, Franck, and Reisman, in 93 A.J.I.L. 824–62 (1999); Simma, NATO, the UN and the Use of Force: Legal Aspects, 10 E.J.I.L. 1 (1999); Cassese, *Ex iniuria ius oritur*: Are We Moving Towards International Legitimation of Forcible Humanitarian Countermeasures in the World Community?, 10 E.J.I.L. 23 (1999); Guicherd, International Law and the War in Kosovo, 41 Survival, No. 2, 19–34 (1999); Roberts, NATO's "Humanitarian War" Over Kosovo, 41 Survival, No. 3, 102–23 (1999); Charney, Anticipatory Humanitarian Intervention in Kosovo, 32 Vand. J. Transnat'l L. 1231 (1999); and the contributions by Brownlie & Apperley, Chinkin, Greenwood, and Lowe, in 49 I.C.L.Q. 878–941 (2000). A valuable collection of essays, including legal perspectives, is Kosovo and the Challenge of Humanitarian Intervention (Schnabel & Thakur eds. 2000). See also the Report of the Independent International Commission on Kosovo, Note 3 *infra*.

2. *Secretary–General's Position.* In his annual address to the U.N. General Assembly in September 1999, Secretary–General Kofi Annan said:

> While the genocide in Rwanda will define for our generation the consequences of inaction in the face of mass murder, the more recent conflict in Kosovo has prompted important questions about the consequences of action in the absence of complete unity on the part of the international community. * * * And to each side in this critical debate, difficult questions can be posed.

> To those for whom the greatest threat to the future of international order is the use of force in the absence of a Security Council mandate, one might ask—not in the context of Kosovo—but in the context of Rwanda: If, in those dark days and hours leading up to the genocide, a coalition of States had been prepared to act in defence of the Tutsi population, but did not receive prompt Council authorization, should such a coalition have stood aside and allowed the horror to unfold?

> To those for whom the Kosovo action heralded a new era when States and groups of States can take military action outside the established mechanisms for enforcing international law, one might ask: Is there not a danger of such interventions undermining the imperfect, yet resilient, security system created after the Second World War, and of setting dangerous precedents for future interventions without a clear criterion to decide who might invoke these precedents, and in what circumstances?

Report of the Secretary–General, U.N. Doc. A/54/PV.4 (Sept. 20, 1999). See also U.N. Secretary–General Kofi Annan, The Question of Intervention: Statements by the Secretary–General (1999).

3. *Independent Commission on Kosovo.* Following the Kosovo intervention, an independent international commission co-chaired by Richard Goldstone and Carl Tham prepared a comprehensive analysis of the situation. A chapter on "International Law and Humanitarian Intervention," puts forward an interpretation of the evolution of humanitarian intervention doctrine:

> This interpretation is situated in a gray zone of ambiguity between an extension of international law and a proposal for an international moral consensus. In essence, this gray zone goes beyond strict ideas of legality to incorporate more flexible views of legitimacy

> * * *

> One way to analyze the international law status of the NATO campaign is to consider legality a matter of degree. This approach acknowledges the current fluidity of international law on humanitarian intervention, caught between strict Charter prohibitions of non-defensive uses of force and more permissive patterns of state practice with respect to humanitarian interventions and counter-terrorist use of force. * * *

> NATO and its supporters have wisely avoided staking out any doctrinal claims for its action either prior to or after the war. Rather than defining the Kosovo intervention as a precedent, most NATO supporters

among international jurists presented the intervention as an unfortunate but necessary and reasonable exception. Nevertheless, NATO cannot hope to preclude states, and especially other regional organizations, from referring to its claims of intervention in Kosovo as a precedent. * * *

The Kosovo "exception" now exists, for better and worse, as a contested precedent that must be assessed in relation to a wide range of international effects and undertakings. Chief among these is that NATO * * * was widely viewed by many non-NATO countries as having independently waged a non-defensive war without having made sufficient effort to obtain proper authorization or to achieve a peaceful settlement. * * *

* * *

This situation supports the general conclusion that the NATO campaign was illegal, yet legitimate. Such a conclusion is related to the controversial idea that a "right" of humanitarian intervention is not consistent with the UN Charter if conceived as a legal text, but that it may, depending on context, nevertheless, reflect the spirit of the Charter as it relates to the overall protection of people against gross abuse. Humanitarian intervention may also thus be legitimately authorized by the UN, but will often be challenged legally from the perspective of Charter obligations to respect the sovereignty of states.

Allowing this gap between legality and legitimacy to persist is not healthy, for several reasons. Acknowledging the tension with most interpretations of international law either inhibits solidarity with civilian victims of severe abuse by territorial governments, or seriously erodes the prohibition on the use of force that the World Court and other authorities have deemed valid. * * * Therefore, although the Commission's finding is that the use of force by NATO in intervening in Kosovo is validated from the perspective of the legitimacy of the undertaking and its overall societal effects, the Commission feels that it would be most beneficial to work diligently to close the gap between legality and legitimacy in a convincing manner for the future.

The Commission is of the opinion that the best way to do this is to conceive of an emergent doctrine of humanitarian intervention that consists of a process of three phases:

● a recommended framework of principles useful in a setting where humanitarian intervention is proposed as an international response and where it actually occurs;

● the formal adoption of such a framework by the General Assembly of the United Nations in the form of a Declaration on the Right and Responsibility of Humanitarian Intervention, accompanied by UNSC interpretations of the UN Charter that reconciles such practice with the balance between respect for sovereign rights, implementation of human rights, and prevention of humanitarian catastrophe;

● the amendment of the Charter to incorporate these changes in the role and responsibility of the United Nations and other collective actors in international society to implement the Declaration on the Right and Responsibility of Humanitarian Intervention.

Independent International Commission on Kosovo, Kosovo Report: Conflict, International Response, Lessons Learned, ch. 6 (2000) (footnotes omitted). The Commission then went on to elaborate a set of criteria for legitimacy, which overlap in large measure with those indicated at p. 1204 above. A new and controversial idea, however, would be that

> There must be even stricter adherence to the laws of war and international humanitarian law than in standard military operations. This applies to all aspects of the military operation, including any post cease-fire occupation.

Elsewhere, the Commission observed:

> In effect, the Commission believes that a greater obligation is imposed on the intervening side to take care of the civilian population in a humanitarian campaign. The specific modalities of this higher standard of "military necessity" do not yet exist in any international agreement or United Nations declaration, but the Commission envisages this standard to be a flexible notion that complements the adaptation of legal constraints on the use of force to the realities of the early twenty-first century. The Commission believes that this proposal should be formalized in international law, perhaps in the form of a "Protocol III" to the Geneva Conventions.

On issues of application of the laws of war in the Kosovo conflict, see pp. 1282, 1286 in Section 4.

4. *Codification of Criteria?* Would formal codification of criteria for humanitarian intervention be desirable? Some believe that such codification would help clarify the legitimacy of such operations and discourage pretextual claims. Others fear that giving humanitarian intervention formal legal blessing would be more likely to encourage questionable military adventures. Compare Damrosch, Concluding Reflections, in Enforcing Restraint: Collective Intervention in Internal Conflicts 358–60 (Damrosch ed. 1993) (contending that it would be premature and perhaps counterproductive to attempt to codify criteria for intervention), with the Kosovo Commission's initiative outlined in the preceding note.

4. Responsibility to Protect

In the wake of the Kosovo intervention, governments, scholars, and opinion leaders searched for new ways of thinking about protection of vulnerable populations, in order to establish a framework for concrete actions that could be widely embraced as both legitimate and lawful. With a view to reframing the debate and proposing practical solutions, the Canadian government in September 2000 launched an International Commission on Intervention and State Sovereignty (ICISS), which presented its findings to the U.N. General Assembly in late 2001 under the title "The Responsibility to Protect." For the text of the report and accompanying materials, see http://www.iciss.ca. The ICISS's report, which gave rise to the coinage "R2P," emphasizes a range of obligations incumbent on all states: to *prevent* manmade catastrophes from arising, to *react* when they do, and to *rebuild* after any intrusive intervention. Its recommendations have attracted significant attention, notably in the report of the Secretary–General's High–Level Panel on Threats, Challenges, and Change, A More Secure World: Our Shared Responsibility (2004); in Secretary–General Kofi Annan's report, In Larger Freedom: Towards Development, Security and Human Rights for All (2005); and in the World Summit Outcome Document adopted in 2005 (excerpted below).

R2P envisages five criteria relevant to resort to military force, which may be compared to those distilled from the humanitarian intervention literature at p. 1204:

(1) Seriousness of harm: Does the threatened harm involve genocide and other large-scale killing, ethnic cleansing, or serious violations of international humanitarian law (actual or imminent)?

(2) Proper purpose: Is it clear that the primary purpose of the proposed military action is to avert such a threat (even if there are other motives as well)?

(3) Last resort: Have all nonmilitary options been explored and found unavailing?

(4) Proportional means: Are the scale, duration, and intensity of proposed military action the minimum necessary for the protective purpose?

(5) Balance of consequences: Is there a reasonable prospect of success, with the consequences of inaction likely to be worse than undertaking military action?

See generally Evans, The Responsibility to Protect: From an Idea to an International Norm 15, 23–24, in Responsibility to Protect: The Global Moral Compact for the 21st Century (Cooper & Kohler eds. 2009), and other contributions in the same volume.

In the ensuing debates over the ideas underlying R2P and applications in particular contexts (such as the Darfur crisis in Sudan), one line of cleavage has been over the extent to which R2P should be understood as a framework for collective action through multilateral institutions, as contrasted to a justification for unilateral military intervention. The 2005 World Summit adopted the following statement: how would you understand its position on this question?

WORLD SUMMIT OUTCOME
G.A. Res. 60/1 (Sept. 16, 2005)

Responsibility to protect populations from genocide, war crimes, ethnic cleansing and crimes against humanity.

138.   Each individual State has the responsibility to protect its populations from genocide, war crimes, ethnic cleansing and crimes against humanity. This responsibility entails the prevention of such crimes, in-

cluding their incitement, through appropriate and necessary means. We accept that responsibility and will act in accordance with it. The international community should, as appropriate, encourage and help States to exercise this responsibility and support the United Nations in establishing an early warning capability.

139.   The international community, through the United Nations, also has the responsibility to use appropriate diplomatic, humanitarian and other peaceful means, in accordance with Chapters VI and VIII of the Charter, to help to protect populations from genocide, war crimes, ethnic cleansing and crimes against humanity. In this context, we are prepared to take collective action, in a timely and decisive manner, through the Security Council, in accordance with the Charter, including Chapter VII, on a case-by-case basis and in cooperation with relevant regional organizations as appropriate, should peaceful means be inadequate and national authorities are manifestly failing to protect their populations from genocide, war crimes, ethnic cleansing and crimes against humanity. We stress the need for the General Assembly to continue consideration of the responsibility to protect populations from genocide, war crimes, ethnic cleansing and crimes against humanity and its implications, bearing in mind the principles of the Charter and international law. We also intend to commit ourselves, as necessary and appropriate, to helping States build capacity to protect their populations from genocide, war crimes, ethnic cleansing and crimes against humanity and to assisting those which are under stress before crises and conflicts break out.

NOTES

1.   *R2P and Unilateral Action?* Do you find any support in the foregoing excerpt for justified unilateral military intervention for protective purposes?

2.   *Further Reading.* U.N. Secretary–General Ban Ki–Moon has appointed a special adviser on R2P, Edward Luck. Drawing on Luck's work under the mandate, the Secretary–General issued a report on "Implementing the Responsibility to Protect" U.N. Doc. A/63/677 (Jan. 12, 2009), which represents the latest contribution to the debate.

D.   INTERVENTION IN SUPPORT OF DEMOCRATIC GOVERNANCE OR SELF–DETERMINATION

REISMAN, COERCION AND SELF–DETERMINATION: CONSTRUING CHARTER ARTICLE 2(4)

78 A.J.I.L. 642, 643–45 (1984) (footnotes omitted)

A sine qua non for any action—coercive or otherwise—I submit, is the maintenance of minimum order in a precarious international system. Will a particular use of force enhance or undermine world order? When this requirement is met, attention may be directed to the fundamental principle of political legitimacy in contemporary international politics: the enhancement of the ongoing right of peoples to determine their own political destinies. That obvious point bears renewed emphasis for it is the main purpose of contemporary international law: Article 2(4) is the means. The basic policy of contemporary international law has been to maintain the political independence of territorial communities so that they can continue to express their desire for political community in a form appropriate to them.

Article 2(4), like so much in the Charter and in contemporary international politics, rests on and must be interpreted in terms of this key postulate of political legitimacy in the 20th century. Each application of Article 2(4) must enhance opportunities for ongoing self-determination. Though all interventions are lamentable, the fact is that some may serve, in terms of aggregate consequences, to increase the probability of the free choice of peoples about their government and political structure. Others have the manifest objective and consequence of doing exactly the opposite. There is neither need nor justification for treating in a mechanically equal fashion Tanzania's intervention in Uganda to overthrow Amin's despotism, on the one hand, and Soviet intervention in Hungary in 1956 or Czechoslovakia in 196[8] to overthrow popular governments and to impose an undesired regime on a coerced population, on the other. Here, as in all other areas of law, it is important to remember that norms are instruments devised by human beings to precipitate desired social consequences. One should not seek point-for-point conformity to a rule without constant regard for the policy or principle that animated its prescription, and with appropriate regard for the factual constellation in the minds of the drafters.

Coercion should not be glorified, but it is naive and indeed subversive of public order to insist that it never be used, for coercion is a ubiquitous feature of all social life and a characteristic and indispensable component of law. The critical question in a decentralized system is not whether coercion has been applied, but whether it has been applied in support of or against community order and basic policies, and whether it was applied in ways whose net consequences include increased congruence with community goals and minimum order.

SCHACHTER, THE LEGALITY OF PRO–DEMOCRATIC INVASION

78 A.J.I.L. 645, 649–50 (1984)

The difficulty with Reisman's argument is not merely that it lacks support in the text of the Charter or in the interpretation that states have given Article 2(4) in the past decades. It would introduce a new normative basis for recourse to war that would give powerful states an almost unlimited right to overthrow governments alleged to be unresponsive to the popular will or to the goal of self-determination. The implications of this for interstate violence in a period of superpower confrontation and obscurantist rhetoric are ominous. That invasions may at times serve democratic values must be weighed against the dangerous consequences of legitimizing armed attacks against peaceful governments. It will be recalled that the International Court of Justice in the *Corfu Channel* case rejected the defense of the United Kingdom that it had used armed force in the cause of international justice. The Court's pronouncement on this bears repetition:

> The Court cannot accept such a line of defence. The Court can only regard the alleged right of intervention as the manifestation of a policy of force, such as cannot, whatever be the present defects in international organization, find a place in international law. Intervention is perhaps still less admissible in the particular form it would take here; for, from the nature of things, it would be reserved for the most powerful States, and might easily lead to perverting the administration of international justice itself.

The Court's measured phrases remind us of the historic realities of abuse by powerful states for supposedly good causes. It is no answer to say that invasions should be allowed where there is no abuse and only for the higher good of self-determination. In the absence of an effective international mechanism to restrain force, individual governments would have the latitude to decide on the "reality" of democracy and self-determination in various countries. The test one side would favor would not be acceptable to others. Ideological confrontations would sooner or later become clashes of power.

These considerations are so evident that we can be quite sure that governments will not adopt the suggested reinterpretation of Article 2(4) as law. Not even its espousal by a powerful state would make it law. In short, it is not, will not, and should not be law. Yet there is a reason for concern that the thesis has been put forward by an international lawyer of standing. In this period of tension and unilateral action, arguments such as those presented may influence policy in favor of armed intervention. The fragility of international organization enhances the danger. This is surely not the time for international lawyers to weaken the principal normative restraint against the use of force. The world will not be made safe for democracy through new wars or invasions of the weak by the strong.

NOTES

1. *The "Reagan Doctrine."* In a speech on March 1, 1985, President Reagan said: "freedom movements arise and assert themselves. They're doing so on almost every continent populated by man—in the hills of Afghanistan, in Angola, in Kampuchea, in Central America * * * They're our brothers, these freedom fighters, and we owe them our help." See Reisman, Allocating Competences to Use Coercion in the Post–Cold War World: Practices, Conditions, and Prospects, in Law and Force in the New International Order 26, 34 n. 13 (Damrosch & Scheffer eds. 1991). This and subsequent statements were

interpreted as asserting the right of the United States (or any other state) to intervene by force to defend, maintain, restore or impose democratic government. See Kirkpatrick & Gerson, The Reagan Doctrine, Human Rights, and International Law, in Right v. Might: International Law and the Use of Force 19 (2d ed. 1991); but see Henkin, The Use of Force: Law and U.S. Policy, in Right v. Might at 37, 44 (contending that the use of force for democracy could not be reconciled with Article 2(4)).

Support for democracy was implied by President Bush among his justifications for the 1989 invasion of Panama. See p. 1180.

2. *The "Brezhnev Doctrine."* During the Cold War, the Reagan doctrine's counterpart was the Soviet Union's Brezhnev doctrine, which had its genesis in the Soviet invasion of Czechoslovakia on September 25, 1968; it asserted the right of socialist states to intervene in another socialist state when socialism there was threatened. See the reported statement of Leonid Brezhnev on the occasion of the invasion of Czechoslovakia, reprinted in 7 I.L.M. 1323 (1968). The doctrine was unequivocally repudiated under Mikhail Gorbachev in the twilight of the Soviet period. See Müllerson & Scheffer, Legal Regulation of the Use of Force, in Beyond Confrontation: International Law for the Post–Cold War Era 93, 95–96 (Damrosch, Danilenko, & Müllerson eds. 1995).

3. *Freedom to Choose Political System.* The International Court of Justice stated in the *Nicaragua* case (Merits):

> The finding of the United States Congress also expressed the view that the Nicaraguan Government had taken "significant steps towards establishing a totalitarian Communist dictatorship". However the régime in Nicaragua be defined, adherence by a State to any particular doctrine does not constitute a violation of customary international law; to hold otherwise would make nonsense of the fundamental principle of State sovereignty, on which the whole of international law rests, and the freedom of choice of the political, social, economic and cultural system of a State. Consequently, Nicaragua's domestic policy options, even assuming that they correspond to the description given of them by the Congress finding, cannot justify on the legal plane the various actions of the [U.S.] complained of. The Court cannot contemplate the creation of a new rule opening up a right of intervention by one State against another on the ground that the latter has opted for some particular ideology or political system.

Military and Paramilitary Activities in and Against Nicaragua (Nicaragua v. United States), 1986 I.C.J. 14, 133.

4. *Forcible Support for Self–Determination Movements.* During the years of decolonization there was some support for the view that states may intervene to promote the process of self-determination, as well as substantial criticism of that view. See Article 7 of the Resolution on the Definition of Aggression, p. 1152 *supra*, which provides that nothing in the definition is intended to prejudice the "right to self-determination" and the right of "peoples forcibly deprived of that right * * * to struggle to that end and to seek and receive support, in accordance with the principles of the Charter and in conformity with the [Declaration on Friendly Relations]." G.A. Res. 3314

(XXIX) (Dec. 14, 1974). See also The Principle of Equal Rights and Self–Determination of Peoples in the Declaration on Principles of International Law Concerning Friendly Relations and Co-operation Among States in Accordance with the Charter of the United Nations, G.A. Res. 2625 (XXXV) (Oct. 24, 1970). Compare Reisman, Allocating Competences to Use Coercion in the Post–Cold War World, in Law and Force in the New International Order (Damrosch & Scheffer eds. 1991), at 26, 30–34, with Henkin's position:

> Self-determination as a justification for the use of force to end colonialism has lost its raison d'être, but some have invoked a people's right to "internal self-determination" to support the use of force by one state to preserve or impose democracy in another * * * Like the use of force to impose or maintain socialism or any other ideology, the use of force for democracy clearly would be contrary to the language of Article 2(4), to the intent of the framers, and to the construction long given to that article by the United States.
>
> At bottom, all suggestions for exceptions to article 2(4) imply that, contrary to the assumptions of the Charter's framers, there are universally recognized values higher than peace and the autonomy of states. In general, the claims of peace and state autonomy have prevailed.

Henkin, The Use of Force: Law and U.S. Policy, in Right v. Might: International Law and the Use of Force 37, 44 (2d ed. 1991).

5. *Consent to Pro–Democratic Intervention.* Could democratic states agree among themselves to support their respective governments against any forcible *coup d'état*? For such a proposal, see Farer, A Paradigm of Legitimate Intervention, in Enforcing Restraint: Collective Intervention in Internal Conflicts 316, 332–33 (Damrosch ed. 1993). See also Wippman, Treaty–Based Intervention: Who Can Say No?, 62 U. Chi. L. Rev. 607, 667–78 (1995).

6. *Collective Intervention Distinguished.* After the end of the Cold War, issues of intervention to support democratic government took on a substantially different character, notably in the Haitian crisis of 1991–1994, which began with the overthrow of a democratically elected president and continued until the U.N. Security Council approved a multilateral military operation to bring about his restoration. This episode will be dealt with in Section 3 at p. 1259, together with other instances where the Security Council has identified a "threat to peace" emanating from internal conflicts. Collective economic sanctions to counter antidemocratic coups or to bring pressure on abusive dictators to yield power had been organized in a variety of instances. See generally Damrosch, Enforcing International Law Through Non–Forcible Measures, 269 Rec. des Cours 9, 150–53 (1997).

7. *"Regime Change."* The U.S.-led intervention in Iraq in 2003 is one of the most controversial recent uses of force from the legal point of view. It will be considered in Section 3 in relation to issues of collective security and the authority of the Security Council. We may observe here that the broad context of that conflict included U.S. objectives of removing from power a repressive regime headed by Saddam Hussein, cultivating in its stead a new government chosen through democratic processes, and encouraging the inculcation of democratic values. These objectives—whatever their merits from the policy

perspective—have not been considered as giving rise to well-founded legal justifications for military intervention. On other justifications, see p. 1239.

8. *Further Reading.* See generally the essays on intervention against illegitimate regimes by Lukashuk, Franck, Burley, and Nanda, in Law and Force in the New International Order 143–84 (Damrosch & Scheffer eds. 1991); Schachter, Is There a Right to Overthrow an Illegitimate Regime, in Le Droit international au service de la justice et du développement: mélanges Michel Virally 423 (1991); Reisman, Old Wine in New Bottles: The Reagan and Brezhnev Doctrines in Contemporary International Law and Practice, 13 Yale J. Int'l L. 171 (1988); Henkin, The Use of Force: Law and U.S. Policy, in Right v. Might: International Law and the Use of Force 37 (2d ed. 1991). See also Wippman, Defending Democracy Through Foreign Intervention, 19 Houston J. Int'l L. 659 (1997); Byers & Chesterman, "You the People:" Pro–Democratic Intervention in International Law, in Democratic Governance and International Law 259–92 (Fox & Roth eds. 2000).

E. THE CHARTER'S CONTINUING RESTRAINTS ON THE UNILATERAL USE OF FORCE

SCHACHTER, THE RIGHT OF STATES TO USE ARMED FORCE

82 Mich. L. Rev. 1620–21, 1623–24, 1645–46 (1984)

When the United Nations (UN) Charter was adopted, it was generally considered to have outlawed war. States accepted the obligation to settle all disputes by peaceful means and to refrain from the use or threat of use of force in their international relations. Only two exceptions were expressly allowed: force used in self-defense when an armed attack occurs, and armed action authorized by the UN Security Council as an enforcement measure. These provisions were seen by most observers as the heart of the Charter and the most important principles of contemporary international law. They have been reaffirmed over and over again in unanimous declarations of the United Nations, in treaties and in statements of political leaders.

Yet as we are all acutely aware, there is widespread cynicism about their effect. Reality seems to mock them. Wars take place, countries are invaded, armed force is used to topple governments, to seize territory, to avenge past injustice, to impose settlements. Threats of force, open or implicit, pervade the relations of states. The menace of a nuclear holocaust hangs over all nations, great or small. Collective security, as envisaged in the Charter, has had little practical effect. Our personal lives are deeply affected by the expectation of violence, by the vast resources devoted to armaments, and perhaps most insidiously, by the belief that little can be done to replace force as the ultimate arbiter in conflicts between nations.

It is no wonder that the obligations of the Charter are widely seen as mere rhetoric, at best idealistic aspirations, or worse as providing a pretext or "cover" for aggression. This evaluation, devastating as it may appear for international law, cannot be dismissed or minimized. But there is the other aspect of reality. * * *

* * *

If we take the realistic view that governments deciding on the use of force take into account the diverse considerations referred to earlier—the probable costs and benefits, the responses of other states and the public, the effect on future claims by other states, the value of law-compliance to international order—we may conclude that the issue of permissibility under the law is a factor that would normally be considered. That this is often the case is shown, at least in some degree, by the fact that in virtually every case the use of force is sought to be justified by reference to the accepted Charter rules. While such justification may be no more than a rationalization of an action chosen solely on grounds of interest and power, the felt need to issue a legal justification is not without importance. It demonstrates that states require a basis of legitimacy to justify their actions to their own citizens and, even more, to other states whose cooperation or acquiescence is desired. The fact that claims of legitimacy are also self-serving does not mean that they do not influence conduct by the actors or by those to whom they are addressed. Even if we label those claims as hypocritical ("the tribute that vice pays to virtue"), they require credibility and for that reason must be confirmed by action. We need not treat this as a categorical imperative that holds good in every case in order to recognize that in a great many situations there is a link between conduct and the perceived restraints of law. Power and interest are not superseded by law, but law cannot be excluded from the significant factors influencing the uses of power and the perception of interests.

* * *

It would be a mistake to conclude that the international law of force is so vague and fragmentary as to allow governments almost unlimited latitude to use force. International texts and the legal positions taken by governments reveal a coherent body of principles that apply to a wide range of conduct involving armed force. These principles are grounded in two major interests, both widely accepted as basic to our international system. The first is the paramount interest in the sovereignty and independence of nation-states. The second is the common interest in restraints on the unbridled exercise of power. Such restraints are no longer seen as "mere" ideals. The fear of nuclear war and mass destruction has made them a prime necessity for survival.

It is true that the efficacy of law is limited because the system lacks effective central authority and is characterized by vast discrepancies in the power of states. Fear of nuclear devastation has not eliminated the Hobbesian element in that system. Powerful states may violate international obligations; they may do so with relative impunity or they may pay a price. But they also have a stake in stability and an acute sense of countervailing power. A decentralized legal system can operate because of these factors of self-interest and reciprocal reactions.

Moreover, the system is not wholly decentralized. As we have indicated, collective judgments are continuously being made both within and outside of formal institutions. Decisions of international bodies add both to the specificity and density of agreed law and affect the costs that result from illegitimate conduct. However inadequate this may seem in comparison to a mature national legal system, it should not be scorned as an element in maintaining peace. To consider its inadequacy a reason for ignoring the restraints can only add to the present insecurity. A world in which power and self-interest alone are expected to restrain force would not be a safer world. We may move dangerously in that direction by weakening existing law on the ground that it lacks impartial organs of application and enforcement. The best would then become the enemy of the good.

SECTION 3.   COLLECTIVE USE OF FORCE

The League of Nations, the first "universal" organization established for the purpose of maintaining international peace, failed and effectively died in the Second World War. The reason for its failure was the unwillingness or inability of the principal world powers to resist Nazi–Fascist aggression, with subsidiary reasons commonly cited: the dominance of narrow nationalism among the Big Powers over their willingness to cooperate, the failure of the United States to participate, the unwillingness of France and Great Britain to act decisively to make the League work, suspicious hostility between them and the U.S.S.R. preventing cooperation against aggressive fascism.

The creation of the United Nations in 1945 embodied aspirations for a system that would effectively keep peace between nations. Since the end of the Cold War, it has been asked to take on increasingly ambitious tasks, including enforcement operations in internal conflicts and post-conflict peace-building. Alongside the United Nations (Section 3.A) are a variety of regional organizations and arrangements with the potential for carrying out complementary functions (Section 3.B).

A.   THE UNITED NATIONS

According to Article 1(1) of the U.N. Charter, the principal purpose of the United Nations is:

> To maintain international peace and security, and to that end: to take effective collective measures for the prevention and removal of threats to the peace, and for the suppression of acts of aggression or other breaches of the peace, and to bring about by peaceful means, and in conformity with the principles of justice and international law, adjustment or settlement of international disputes or situations which might lead to a breach of the peace.

The primary responsibility for achieving that purpose was lodged in the Security Council (Article 24). The Security Council was given the authority to pursue that purpose by peaceful means (Chapter VI) and also if necessary by collective enforcement action (non-forcible or military) (Chapter VII). Additionally, the General Assembly as well as the Secretary–General were given authority which might be used for keeping the peace. See arts. 10–15 & 99.

1. The Collective Use of Force Under the Charter

The fifty-one states that signed the Charter of the United Nations in San Francisco on June 26, 1945, believed that the new Organization's principal function would be to maintain peace and security through an authoritative institution and process, including, if necessary, the use of collective force against an aggressor. To that end, the Charter entrusted executive authority and "primary responsibility" to the Security Council, and within the Council, to the five Permanent Members, whose unanimity is required for non-procedural decisions. By design, enforcement action under Chapter VII of the Charter cannot be taken against any Permanent Member, or against any state without the consent (or acquiescence) of all Permanent Members. Four of the five Permanent Members were the major Allied powers of World War II. Their collaboration was expected to lay the foundation for German and European reconstruction and for world-wide security from aggression. The fifth Permanent Member was China, the "awakening giant," expected to play a major role in the post-war world. Two of the world's great powers, Germany and Japan, were excluded as the recently defeated enemies.

By 1947, the Cold War had split the former Allies into opposing ideological blocs. West Germany became a major ally of the United States and East Germany a satellite of the Soviet Union, and the mutual exercise of the veto in the Security Council long prevented either Germany from becoming a U.N. member. After the Communist takeover in China, the United States opposed the seating of the Communist government in any organ of the United Nations, so that the more than 700 million inhabitants of mainland China remained for more than two decades without effective representation in the United Nations. The incapacitation of one of the major pillars of the new organization—a security system built on the unified action of the world's five leading powers—shattered a second pillar: the Permanent Military Force envisaged in Articles 43–47 of the Charter could not be established because the major powers could not agree on the essentials of composition, command structure, territorial facilities, and conditions of action. The Korean War which began in 1950 evoked a response from U.N. organs, but not in the mode contemplated by U.N.'s founders. See pp. 1227–29.

The void left by the absence of an international security system was temporarily, but only partly, filled by a "second phase" of U.N. collective security. After the collapse of the Charter's plan for a Security Council guided by the major powers acting in concert, an activist Secretary General and a more engaged General Assembly gave the United Nations a general "watchdog" function in international conflicts and the power to undertake a "peacekeeping" role on an *ad hoc* basis (at least in some conflicts). The composition and function of these peacekeeping forces, however, were different from those of military forces envisaged under Chapter VII of the Charter. The peacekeeping forces were made up in the main of units from smaller states and they operated with the consent of the member states concerned. Their function was—and still is—to discourage hostilities, not to restore or maintain peace.

The "second phase" of United Nations collective security changed radically during the 1960s and 1970s. The principal reason was the explosive rate at which colonial and dependent territories attained statehood and membership in the United Nations. This accentuated the discrepancy between power and responsibility. Under the original scheme of the Charter, the proliferation of new states would not have affected the predominance of the Security Council and the privileged position within the Council of the Permanent Members. But as the Security Council remained paralyzed, and as the functions and power of the General Assembly—in which each member has one vote—increased, a change in attitude of the major powers occurred as control slipped from their hands. This change was reflected in the crisis provoked by French and Soviet resistance to the advisory opinion of the International Court of Justice in *Certain Expenses of the United Nations,* see p. 1250 *infra,* a reaction against the increasing domination of the General Assembly by smaller and poorer states.

The policy of the United States also shifted in light of these trends. When, in 1950, the United States sponsored the "Uniting for Peace" resolution (p. 1229), which purports to confer on (or recognize in) the General Assembly powers to "recommend" collective measures when the Security Council is unable to act, the U.S. was still certain of a comfortable two-thirds majority in the General Assembly for action that it strongly sponsored. But that situation changed. In the aftermath of the Arab–Israeli war of June 1967, it was the Soviet Union—which had bitterly opposed the Uniting for Peace Resolution as usurping the functions of the Security Council—that invoked the Resolution when it failed to obtain a Security Council resolution condemning Israel as the aggressor, and it was the United States that opposed the convocation of the Assembly. In the General Assembly, neither the United States nor the U.S.S.R. thought it advisable to pursue its own draft resolution, and threw their support to conflicting resolutions introduced by smaller powers. The voting showed an almost even division among the members and it was not possible to obtain the required two-thirds majority.

Further political change brought further change to the United Nations. The continued proliferation of new states and the emergence of the "Third World" with substantial political solidarity; the acceptance of the People's Republic of China as the government of China to be represented in the U.N. and its aspirations to be the Big Power representative of the developing nations; conflict between the Soviet Union and China and improved relations between China and the United States—all further modified the U.N. peacekeeping system. It became possible for a combination of smaller members, sometimes with the support of one or both of the Communist powers, to authorize a United Nations operation to which the United States (and the United Kingdom) were opposed. In time, despite the stand earlier taken by the United States as to peacekeeping expenses, the U.S. and the U.K. began to see their interest in a voluntary rather than compulsory assessment for the cost of all but basic administrative expenses for U.N. operations. That would help contain the power of the majority of non-Western and economically underdeveloped states in the General Assembly. At the same time, the U.N. majority was unwilling or unable to use the U.N. effectively. The U.N. played no role in the Vietnam War. It had little role in restoring or maintaining peace between African states such as Ethiopia and Somalia. It remained virtually irrelevant to the resolution of civil wars and other internal conflicts, even where they spilled out of national borders, and the result was largely determined by outsiders (e.g. Bangladesh in 1971; Angola in 1974; Western Sahara in 1975; Afghanistan in 1980; Chad in 1984).

A "third phase" of collective security in the United Nations began as the Cold War ended, with increased cooperation by the Permanent Members of the Security Council from the late 1980s into the 1990s and (with some qualifications) into the twenty-first century as well. This phase included a new willingness and ability by the Security Council to fulfill its primary responsibility under the Charter for the maintenance of international peace and security, as seen in the Gulf War of 1990–1991 and its aftermath, in modest but assertive measures in connection with the conflict in the former Yugoslavia throughout the 1990s, in the 1992–1993 relief effort in Somalia, in authorizations from the Security Council to willing states to take military action in support of internationally approved purposes in Rwanda (1994), Haiti (1994), East Timor (1999), and elsewhere, and other actions presaging genuine enforcement of community interests.

In the 1990s, the Security Council moved well beyond the Charter's original understanding of "international" peace to a conception of "threats to peace" embracing some kinds of internal conflicts. When acting in its Chapter VII mode, the Council can overcome Article 2(7)'s constraint on intervention in "matters which are essentially within the domestic jurisdiction of any state," as that article continues with the proviso that "this principle shall not prejudice the application of enforcement measures under Chapter VII." The Council has lent multilateral imprimatur to certain forcible interventions (e.g., for humanitarian purposes), thereby conferring legitimacy and legality that might otherwise have been lacking under the doctrines for evaluation of unilateral uses of force addressed in Section 2. In other instances where the Permanent Members have been unable to agree to grant specific authority (e.g., the

Kosovo crisis of 1999), action has sometimes gone forward on a claim of implicit authorization flowing from previous resolutions.

After the attacks of September 11, 2001, the Security Council asserted its Chapter VII authority with respect to various aspects of the struggle against terrorism and also to control weapons of mass destruction. See Chapter 4, p. 274, and p. 1304. It also took significant steps relevant to the situation in Iraq, both before and after the resumption of military conflict in spring 2003, as discussed more fully below. Substantial differences of position among the Permanent Members on Iraq and on other conflicts and threats have complicated the prospects for taking collective decisions.

The future of collective security and enforcement actions under Chapter VII of the Charter remains to be seen. Will cooperation continue? Will the Council's decision-making process avoid bias and the appearance of bias? Will the Security Council's structure, composition, and procedures, be reformed to reflect the world of the new century, with more (or different) permanent members? Will the authority and mandate of the Security Council expand or retrench? Will the U.N. mobilize the resources to enable it to meet the challenges that clamor for collective action, perhaps even use of force, against massive violations of human rights, ethnic strife, and floods of refugees?

CHARTER OF THE UNITED NATIONS
Signed at San Francisco, June 26, 1945

Chapter VII
Action With Respect to Threats to the Peace, Breaches of the Peace, and Acts of Aggression

Article 39

The Security Council shall determine the existence of any threat to the peace, breach of the peace, or act of aggression and shall make recommendations, or decide what measures shall be taken in accordance with Articles 41 and 42, to maintain or restore international peace and security.

Article 40

In order to prevent an aggravation of the situation, the Security Council may, before making the recommendations or deciding upon the measures provided for in Article 39, call upon the parties concerned to comply with such provisional measures as it deems necessary or desirable. Such provisional measures shall be without prejudice to the rights, claims, or position of the parties concerned. The Security Council shall duly take account of failure to comply with such provisional measures.

Article 41

The Security Council may decide what measures not involving the use of armed force are to be employed to give effect to its decisions, and it may call upon the Members of the United Nations to apply such measures. These may include complete or partial interruption of economic relations and of rail, sea, air, postal, telegraphic, radio, and other means of communication, and the severance of diplomatic relations.

Article 42

Should the Security Council consider that measures provided for in Article 41 would be inadequate or have proved to be inadequate, it may take such action by air, sea, or land forces as may be necessary to maintain or restore international peace and security. Such action may include demonstrations, blockade, and other operations by air, sea, or land forces of Members of the United Nations.

Article 43

1.   All Members of the United Nations, in order to contribute to the maintenance of international peace and security, undertake to make available to the Security Council, on its call and in accordance with a special agreement or agreements, armed forces, assistance, and facilities, including rights of passage, necessary for the purpose of maintaining international peace and security.

2.   Such agreement or agreements shall govern the numbers and types of forces, their degree of readiness and general location, and the nature of the facilities and assistance to be provided.

3.   The agreement or agreements shall be negotiated as soon as possible on the initiative of the Security Council. They shall be concluded between the Security Council and Members or between the Security Council and groups of Members and shall be subject to ratification by the signatory states in accordance with their respective constitutional processes.

NOTES

1.   *Other Charter Provisions.* See also Articles 2(6), 2(7), 9–12, 18, 23–25, 27, 34, 44–50, 103, 107 of the Charter.

2.   *Chapter VII During the Cold War.* The Security Council found threats to the peace, breaches of the peace or acts of aggression only rarely between 1945 and 1990, and only twice in that period did it act to impose compulsory measures under Chapter VII of the Charter: those were the cases of Southern Rhodesia and South Africa. Concerning Southern Rhodesia, see S.C. Res. 217 (Nov. 20, 1965) (calling on the United Kingdom to quell the rebellion of the racist minority regime, using "appropriate measures which would prove effective"); S.C. Res. 221 (Apr. 9, 1966) (authorizing the United Kingdom "to prevent by the use of force if necessary" the arrival, in a third-country port, of vessels reasonably believed to be carrying contraband oil destined for Rhodesia); S.C. Res. 232 (Dec. 16, 1966) (imposing selective mandatory sanctions, including an arms embargo); S.C. Res. 253 (May 29, 1968) (expanding sanctions). Concerning South Africa, see S.C. Res. 418 (Nov. 4, 1977) (imposing a

mandatory arms embargo), On these measures, see Gowland–Dobban, Collec
tive Responses to Illegal Acts in International Law: United Nations Action in
the Question of Southern Rhodesia (1990); How Sanctions Work: Lessons
from South Africa (Crawford & Klotz eds. 1999).

On the by now numerous determinations and actions under Chapter VII
since 1990, see pp. 1229 44, 1253–64.

2. Collective Actions to Maintain or Restore International Peace and Security

The two major actions in which the Security Council has authorized
the use of collective force in response to a transboundary attack are the
Korean War beginning in 1950 and the Persian Gulf War of 1990–1991.
Additionally, both the Security Council and the General Assembly have
approved the formation of peacekeeping forces under U.N. authority.
Before the 1990s these forces mainly functioned with the consent of
affected parties, but they have increasingly been placed on a Chapter VII
footing as more and more ambitious tasks have been entrusted to them, as
in former Yugoslavia in the 1990s and Congo, Liberia and Sudan in the
2000s. The Council has also approved military enforcement actions to be
carried out by states, on newly expansive theories of "threats to peace"
which have come to embrace humanitarian considerations in internal
crises (with transboundary impacts being merely secondary effects of
principally domestic conflicts).

a. Korea

On June 25, 1950 North Korean forces invaded South Korea. A
resolution adopted at an emergency meeting of the Security Council
determined that the North Korean action constituted a breach of the
peace and called for the immediate cessation of hostilities and the withdrawal of the North Korean units. S.C. Res. 82 (June 25, 1950). There
were no negative votes on the Council. (The Soviet delegate had been
absent since January of 1950 because of a dispute over the representation
of China.)

The Security Council met on June 27, 1950, and, having noted that
"urgent military measures are required to restore international peace and
security," recommended "that the Members of the United Nations furnish
such assistance to the Republic of Korea as may be necessary to repel the
armed attack and to restore international peace and security in the area."
S.C. Res. 83 (June 27, 1950). This resolution was the first collective
security effort authorized under the Charter. Again, the Soviet delegate
was absent and thus did not exercise a veto.

A Security Council resolution of July 7, 1950, requested the United
States to appoint the commander of a unified command to which all
Members were urged to provide assistance, including forces. The unified
command was authorized to use the U.N. flag. S.C. Res. 84 (July 7, 1950).
The Soviet delegate returned to the Security Council on August 1, 1950,
and blocked any further action by the Council. On October 7, 1950 the

General Assembly, noting that the objectives of the Security Council had not yet been attained, established the United Nations Commission for the Unification and Rehabilitation of Korea. G.A. Res. 376 (V) (Oct. 7, 1950). In view of the impasse in the Security Council produced by the threat of Soviet veto, the General Assembly also adopted the "Uniting for Peace" Resolution, note 3 below.

The Korean conflict continued until the conclusion of an armistice agreement, T.I.A.S. No. 2782, at Panmunjom on July 27, 1953, between the Commander-in-Chief, United Nations Command, and the respective commanders of the North Korean and Communist Chinese forces. Although some of the principal provisions in the armistice agreement were not carried out and there were several incidents, hostilities did not resume. See Henkin, How Nations Behave 77–79; Hoyt, The United States Reaction to the Korean Attack, 55 A.J.I.L. 45 (1961); Goodrich, Korea (1950); 5 Whiteman at 102–09, 789–95, 1113–18 (1965).

NOTES

1. *Abstention by a Permanent Member.* The U.S.S.R. long maintained that the Council's resolution recommending that states assist South Korea was illegal because it did not have the affirmative vote of all the permanent members of the Security Council. The practice of the Security Council since that time has rejected the Soviet position and established that abstention (or absence) does not constitute a veto. For example, in 1990, China, a permanent member, abstained from voting on Resolution 678, authorizing the use of force to expel Iraq from Kuwait, but the legality of the resolution or of the subsequent use of force has not been questioned. (China has also abstained on various other occasions, notably when the Council since the 1990s has taken decisions on an expansive conception of "threats to peace" under Chapter VII; see below.) For the practice of the Council in respect of the veto, see Bailey, The Procedure of the U.N. Security Council 224–25 (2d ed. 1988); Kirgis, The Security Council's First Fifty Years, 89 A.J.I.L. 506, 510–11 (1995).

2. *Collective Action or Collective Self–Defense.* The resolutions adopted by the Council in June and July of 1950 make no mention of Chapter VII of the Charter or of any specific Charter articles. Does that matter? Does the Security Council have power to make any recommendation whatsoever for the maintenance of international peace and security, or is it restricted to the specific measures set out in Chapter VII? See Dinstein, War, Aggression and Self–Defence 283–89 (4th ed. 2005); Bowett, U.N. Forces 32–59 (1964); Goodrich, Korea 102–21 (1956). See also the advisory opinion of the International Court of Justice in *Certain Expenses of the United Nations,* p. 1250 *infra.* Some commentators have argued that the action taken in Korea is more appropriately characterized as an action taken in collective self-defense rather than an enforcement action under the Charter. See Stone, Legal Controls of International Conflict 234–37 (2d ed. 1959). Was Article 51 of the Charter applicable even though neither North Korea nor South Korea was a member of the United Nations?

3. *Uniting for Peace Resolution.* In the Uniting for Peace Resolution, G.A. Res. 377, U.N. Doc. A/1775 (Nov. 3, 1950), the General Assembly asserted authority to act in matters relating to international peace and security if the Security Council could not discharge its "primary" responsibility because of lack of unanimity among the permanent members. The resolution provides that in the event of a threat to the peace, breach of the peace, or act of aggression to which the Security Council cannot respond,

> the General Assembly shall consider the matter immediately with a view to making appropriate recommendations to Members for collective measures, including in the case of a breach of the peace or act of aggression the use of armed force when necessary, to maintain or restore international peace and security.

After the Korean case, the resolution has had limited but significant application, having been invoked a total of eleven times between 1950 and 2009. One of the most important instances was the creation of the United Nations Emergency Force in the wake of the Suez crisis of 1956, pp. 1247–48 below. In the aftermath of the Kosovo events of 1999 (p. 1206), some urged a revival of the Uniting for Peace framework when the Security Council is immobilized.

On the Uniting for Peace Resolution, see The Charter of the United Nations: A Commentary [235, 260–61] (2d ed. Simma et al. eds. 2002). See also Zaum, The Security Council, the General Assembly and War: The Uniting for Peace Resolution, in The United Nations Security Council and War: The Evolution of Thought and Practice Since 1945, at 154–74 (Lowe et al. eds. 2008)

b. *Iraq*

The end of the Cold War and the thaw in relations between the United States and the Soviet Union resulted in a revitalized Security Council that faced its first major test when Iraq invaded Kuwait on August 2, 1990. The Security Council unanimously condemned the invasion, determined the existence of a "breach of international peace and security" and demanded that Iraq "withdraw immediately and unconditionally all its armed forces." S.C. Res. 660 (1990). On August 6, 1990, the Security Council acted under its compulsory powers to require comprehensive sanctions against Iraq. S.C. Res. 661 (1990). Despite the economic and military embargo established by Resolution 661, some Iraqi ships were reported to be sailing in and out of Iraqi ports apparently carrying embargoed goods. The United States took the position that Resolution 661 authorized the use of military force to stop Iraqi ships suspected of carrying prohibited cargo, but other states, including the Soviet Union, disputed that view. The United States took no action to enforce the sanctions until, after intensive negotiations, the Security Council adopted Resolution 665 authorizing the use of "measures commensurate to the specific circumstances as may be necessary * * * to halt all inward and outward maritime shipping in order to inspect and verify their cargoes and destinations and to ensure strict implementation of * * * resolution 661 * * *." S.C. Res. 665 (Aug. 6, 1991).

Later, the Security Council adopted Resolution 666 to ensure that permissible food shipments went to those most in need and not to the Iraqi military. The Council also adopted Resolution 670, directing states to take steps to ensure that their aircraft, and aircraft flying over their territory, were in compliance with Resolution 661.

During the time the Security Council was engaged in implementing Resolution 661, there was a dramatic military buildup in the Persian Gulf. U.S. forces were rushed early to the Gulf area and entered Saudi Arabia pursuant to agreement between the two countries to deter and help defend Saudi Arabia against possible attack by Iraq. Other states, including Egypt, Saudi Arabia, Britain, France, Argentina and Canada, also deployed forces, resulting in a substantial presence. When Iraq remained adamant in refusing to withdraw from Kuwait, the Security Council adopted Resolution 678 to authorize the use of military force to eject Iraq from Kuwait.

SECURITY COUNCIL RESOLUTION 678
Adopted November 29, 1990

The Security Council * * *

Noting that, despite all efforts by the United Nations, Iraq refuses to comply with its obligation to implement resolution 660 (1990) * * * in flagrant contempt of the Security Council,

Mindful of its duties and responsibilities under the Charter of the United Nations for the maintenance and preservation of international peace and security,

Determined to secure full compliance with its decisions,

Acting under Chapter VII of the Charter,

1. *Demands* that Iraq comply fully with resolution 660 (1990) and all subsequent relevant resolutions, and decides, while maintaining all its decisions, to allow Iraq one final opportunity, as a pause of goodwill, to do so;

2. *Authorizes* Member States co-operating with the Government of Kuwait, unless Iraq on or before 15 January 1991 fully implements, as set forth in paragraph 1 above, the foregoing resolutions, to use all necessary means to uphold and implement resolution 660 (1990) and all subsequent relevant resolutions and to restore international peace and security in the area;

3. *Requests* all States to provide appropriate support for the actions undertaken in pursuance of paragraph 2 of the present resolution;

4. *Requests* the States concerned to keep the Security Council regularly informed on the progress of actions undertaken pursuant to paragraphs 2 and 3 of the present resolution * * *.

As Iraq did not withdraw from Kuwait by the January 15, 1001 deadline set in Resolution 678, the military coalition supporting Kuwait began air strikes at that time. After an air war of several weeks and a ground war lasting a few more weeks, hostilities were suspended as noted in Resolution 686 (March 2, 1991), followed by terms for comprehensive settlement of the conflict in Resolution 687 (April 3, 1991). The latter resolution—the Council's most ambitious to date—maintained economic sanctions on Iraq and detailed the conditions that Iraq would have to meet in order for sanctions to be lifted. It is excerpted and discussed below.

NOTES

1. *Collective Self–Defense or Collective Security?* Schachter states that the action taken in the Gulf can be characterized either as one of collective self-defense authorized by the Security Council or as an action taken under Article 42. Does the characterization have legal or practical consequences? See generally Schachter, United Nations Law in the Gulf Conflict, 85 A.J.I.L. 452–463 (1991).

For compilations of documents and references, see The Kuwait Crisis: Basic Documents (Lauterpacht, Greenwood, Weller, & Bethlehem eds. 1991); Bibliography, The International Legal Implications of Iraq's Invasion of Kuwait: A Research Guide, 23 N.Y.U. J. Int'l L. & Pol. 231 (1991). See also Moore, The Gulf Crisis: Enforcing the Rule of Law (1992); Agora: The Gulf Crisis in International and Foreign Relations Law, 85 A.J.I.L. 63–109, 506–35 (1991); Malone, The International Struggle Over Iraq: Politics in the UN Security Council 1980–2005 (2006).

2. *Until the Security Council Acts?* The Gulf War raised long dormant issues under Article 51 of the Charter, which provides that states may exercise the "inherent" right of individual or collective self-defense "until the Security Council has taken measures necessary to maintain international peace and security." Would action by the Council suspend the right to self-defense, or would that right come to an end only when the measures taken by the Security Council are successful and peace and security are restored? Who determines whether the measures taken have been effective? Once the Council has taken necessary measures, does the right of self-defense cease, or is it merely suspended, possibly to be revived at a later date? Professor Chayes has commented:

> In the larger scheme of the Charter, it is the Security Council that has "primary responsibility for the maintenance of international peace and security," which is recognized as primarily a political rather than a legal task. To carry out that responsibility, the Council, once seized of a matter under Chapter VII, must have the authority to make the political judgments as to the requirements of the situation and the measures necessary to deal with it. Security Council preemption, moreover, reinforces the fundamental objective of Article 2(4) and Article 51 to confine the permissible occasions for the unilateral use of force to the narrowest possible range, where it is immediately and universally apparent that armed response is required.

* * *

From the beginning of the Iraq–Kuwait crisis, as has been widely acknowledged, the Security Council worked "as it was supposed to work" according to the design of its framers. It cannot be argued that the Council failed to address the situation with appropriate gravity or to adopt measures with real impact or to strengthen those measures as the need became apparent. If the United Nations works as intended, judgments as to the ultimate objectives of U.N. action, the sufficiency of the measures to be taken, how long to wait for the sanctions to take effect, and the like are consigned to the Council, which acts by a majority of nine out of fifteen members, including the concurring or abstaining votes of the permanent members. * * *

Chayes, The Use of Force in the Persian Gulf, in Law and Force in the New International Order 3–7 (Damrosch & Scheffer eds. 1991) (footnotes omitted). Compare Schachter's view:

A Council decision that calls on an invader to withdraw and to cease hostilities is certainly a necessary measure, but it could not be intended to deprive the victim state of its right to defend itself when the invader has not complied with the Council's order. A reasonable construction of the provision in Article 51 would recognize that the Council has the authority to adopt a measure that would require armed action to cease even if that action was undertaken in self-defense. However, this would not mean that *any* measure would preempt self-defense. The intent of the Council as expressed in its decision would determine whether the right to use force in self-defense had been suspended by the Council.

Schachter, United Nations Law in the Gulf Conflict, 85 A.J.I.L. 452, 458 (1991). See also Greig, Self–Defence and the Security Council: What Does Article 51 Require?, 40 I.C.L.Q. 366 (1991); Gardner, Commentary on the Law of Self–Defense, in Law and Force in the New International Order (Damrosch & Scheffer eds. 1991); Müllerson, Self–Defense in the Contemporary World, in Law and Force in the New International Order (Damrosch & Scheffer eds. 1991).

3. *U.N. Command versus Ad Hoc Coalition.* In Korea the Security Council recommended a Unified Command controlled by the United States and authorized the use of the U.N. flag, while the Gulf War proceeded as an ad hoc coalition. The Security Council did not seek to exercise any control over the actions either in Korea or in the Gulf. Schachter states that "the problems of authority and control are almost certain to complicate any future large scale enforcement action." Schachter, International Law in Theory and Practice 398 (1991). This prediction has proven accurate, e.g. in Somalia in 1993 (p. 1252).

SECURITY COUNCIL RESOLUTION 687

Adopted April 3, 1991

The Security Council * * *

Affirming the commitment of all Member States to the sovereignty, territorial integrity and political independence of Kuwait and Iraq, * * *

Conscious of the need to take the following measures acting under Chapter VII of the Charter, * * *

A

2. *Demands* that Iraq and Kuwait respect the inviolability of the international boundary * * *;

3. *Calls upon* the Secretary–General to lend his assistance to make arrangements with Iraq and Kuwait to demarcate the boundary between Iraq and Kuwait * * *;

B

5. *Requests* the Secretary–General, after consulting with Iraq and Kuwait, to submit within three days to the Security Council for its approval a plan for the immediate deployment of a United Nations observer unit to monitor the Khor Abdullah and a demilitarized zone, which is hereby established, extending ten kilometres into Iraq and five kilometres into Kuwait from the boundary * * *;

6. *Notes* that as soon as the Secretary–General notifies the Security Council of the completion of the deployment of the United Nations observer unit, the conditions will be established for the Member States cooperating with Kuwait in accordance with resolution 678 (1990) to bring their military presence in Iraq to an end consistent with resolution 686 (1991);

C

7. *Invites* Iraq to reaffirm unconditionally its obligations under the Geneva Protocol for the Prohibition of the Use in War of Asphyxiating, Poisonous or Other Gases, and of Bacteriological Methods of Warfare, signed at Geneva on 17 June 1925, and to ratify the Convention on the Prohibition of the Development, Production and Stockpiling of Bacteriological (Biological) and Toxin Weapons and on Their Destruction, of 10 April 1972;

8. *Decides* that Iraq shall unconditionally accept the destruction, removal, or rendering harmless, under international supervision of:

(a) All chemical and biological weapons and all stocks of agents and all related subsystems and components and all research, development, support and manufacturing facilities;

(b) All ballistic missiles with a range greater than 150 kilometres and related major parts, and repair and production facilities;

9. *Decides*, for the implementation of paragraph 8 above, the following:

(a) Iraq shall submit to the Secretary–General, within fifteen days of the adoption of the present resolution, a declaration of the locations, amounts and types of all items specified in paragraph 8 and agree to urgent, on-site inspection as specified below;

(b) The Secretary–General [shall develop a plan for a Special Commission to carry out immediate on-site inspection of Iraq's biological, chemical and missile capabilities, and for their destruction, removal or rendering harmless];

10. *Decides* that Iraq shall unconditionally undertake not to use, develop, construct or acquire any of the items specified in paragraphs 8 and 9 above and requests the Secretary–General, in consultation with the Special Commission, to develop a plan for the future ongoing monitoring and verification of Iraq's compliance with this paragraph * * *;

11. *Invites* Iraq to reaffirm unconditionally its obligations under the Treaty on the Non–Proliferation of Nuclear Weapons of 1 July 1968;

12. *Decides* that Iraq shall unconditionally agree not to acquire or develop nuclear weapons or nuclear-weapons-usable material or any subsystems or components or any research, development, support or manufacturing facilities related to the above; * * * to place all of its nuclear-weapons-usable materials under the exclusive control, for custody and removal, of the International Atomic Energy Agency, with the assistance and cooperation of the Special Commission * * *; to accept * * * urgent on-site inspection and the destruction, removal or rendering harmless as appropriate of all items specified above; and to accept the plan discussed in paragraph 13 below for the future ongoing monitoring and verification of its compliance with these undertakings;

13. *Requests* the Director–General of the International Atomic Energy Agency * * * to carry out immediate on-site inspection of Iraq's nuclear capabilities * * *; to develop a plan * * * for the destruction, removal, or rendering harmless as appropriate of all items listed in paragraph 12 above; * * *

F

22. *Decides* that * * * upon Council agreement that Iraq has completed all actions contemplated in paragraphs 8, 9, 10, 11, 12 and 13 above, the prohibitions against the import of commodities and products originating in Iraq and the prohibitions against financial transactions related thereto contained in resolution 661 (1990) shall have no further force or effect; * * *

24. *Decides* that, in accordance with resolution 661 (1990) and subsequent related resolutions and until a further decision is taken by the Security Council, all States shall continue to prevent the sale or supply * * * to Iraq by their nationals, or from their territories or using their flag vessels or aircraft, of:

(*a*) Arms and related *matériel* of all types * * *;

(*b*) Items specified and defined in paragraphs 8 and 12 above * * *;

I

33. *Declares* that, upon official notification by Iraq to the Secretary–General and to the Security Council of its acceptance of the provisions above, a formal cease-fire is effective between Iraq and Kuwait and the

Member States cooperating with Kuwait in accordance with resolution 678 (1990);

34. *Decides* to remain seized of the matter and to take such further steps as may be required for the implementation of the present resolution and to secure peace and security in the area.

NOTES

1. *Other Aspects of Resolution 687.* In addition to the provisions excerpted above, Resolution 687 dealt with steps to facilitate the return of Kuwaiti property seized by Iraq (Part D, para. 15); to create a fund to pay compensation for claims for direct loss or injury resulting from Iraq's unlawful invasion and occupation of Kuwait, including environmental damage (Part E, paras. 16–19); to facilitate repatriation of all Kuwaiti and third-country nationals with the assistance of the International Committee of the Red Cross (Part G, paras. 30–31); and to renounce terrorism (Part H, para. 32). On the U.N. Compensation Commission established pursuant to Part E, see p. 550.

2. *Protection of Kurds and Shiites.* After the cease-fire in March 1991, there were reports of widespread attacks by Iraqi forces against Iraq's Kurdish and Shiite populations, causing nearly two million refugees to flee towards the Turkish and Iranian borders. On April 5, 1991, the Security Council adopted Resolution 688, which, while recalling Article 2(7) of the Charter and reaffirming commitment to the sovereignty, territorial integrity and political independence of Iraq, condemned "the repression of the Iraqi civilian population in many parts of Iraq, including most recently in Kurdish populated areas, the consequences of which threaten international peace and security in the region," and demanded that Iraq cease the repression and allow "immediate access by international humanitarian organizations to all those in need of assistance in all parts of Iraq." Resolution 688 authorized the Secretary–General to pursue humanitarian efforts through U.N. agencies and to send a mission to the region, but did not explicitly authorize use of force to protect the refugees. See S.C. Res. 688 (Apr. 5, 1991). See generally Iraq and Kuwait: The Hostilities and Their Aftermath (Weller ed. 1993); U.N. Dep't of Public Information, The United Nations and the Iraq–Kuwait Conflict, 1990–1996 (1996).

In April, 1991, Britain, France and the United States sent forces into northern Iraq to create "safe havens" to which the Iraqi Kurdish refugee population could return. The United States stressed the humanitarian nature of the operation and invoked Resolution 688 "to establish several encampments in northern Iraq, where relief supplies * * * [would] be made available in large quantities and distributed in an orderly way." See Adelman, Humanitarian Intervention: The Case of the Kurds, 4 Int'l J. Refugee L. 4, 4–5 n. 1 (1992). The United States declared that "[a]dequate security [would] be provided at those sites by U.S., British and French ground forces, consistent with United Nations Resolution 688." Id. The United States, the United Kingdom and France and Britain also unilaterally declared a "no-fly zone" north of the 36th parallel in Iraq; and in August 1992, after renewed Iraqi attacks on Shiites in the southern marshes, they proclaimed another no-fly zone south of the 32nd parallel. No U.N. Security Council resolution specifically refers to such no-fly zones or explicitly confers authority to enforce them with military force.

Does Resolution 688 support these measures taken inside Iraq? See Stromseth, Iraq's Repression of Its Civilian Population: Collective Responses and Continuing Challenges, in Damrosch (ed.), Enforcing Restraint: Collective Intervention in Internal Conflicts 77–117 (1993); Murphy, Humanitarian Intervention: The United Nations in an Evolving World Order 165–98 (1996).

3. *Policing of Ceasefire and No–Fly Zones.* After the 1991 ceasefire and continuing through the 1990s and into the 2000s, the United States and other states took recurrent military action in and over Iraqi territory. The no-fly zones were regularly policed by coalition aircraft using a Turkish base at Incirlik in proximity to northern Iraq, and from aircraft carriers in the Persian Gulf. Iraq repeatedly tested the coalition forces' willingness to enforce the flight ban, thereby provoking numerous military confrontations. The U.S. and other states mounted air strikes or other military actions when Iraq violated the terms of the cease-fire resolution, trespassed into Kuwait, renewed attacks on its Kurdish or Shiite populations, or otherwise acted in a hostile manner. In January 1993, U.S., British and French forces carried out air strikes in response to cease-fire violations, including unauthorized incursions into Kuwaiti territory and refusal to guarantee the safety and free movement of the Special Commission established under Resolution 687 (UNSCOM). The allies reiterated this stance frequently thereafter (though by the late 1990s, France had dissociated itself from military enforcement of the no-fly zones).

4. *Forcible Responses to Cease-fire Violations.* Tensions over Iraq's refusal to allow UNSCOM to carry out its mandate to inspect and verify destruction of all capability for weapons of mass destruction escalated over the 1990s, culminating with the departure of the UNSCOM inspectors in 1998 and Iraq's refusal to permit them or a successor team to resume their functions. See generally Butler, The Greatest Threat: Iraq, Weapons of Mass Destruction, and the Crisis of Global Security (2000). In response to these provocations, the United States and the United Kingdom undertook a series of air strikes in December 1998, and in the first eight months of 1999 they had flown more than 10,000 sorties and used more than 1000 bombs and missiles against more than 400 Iraqi targets. See Murphy, Contemporary Practice of the United States Relating to International Law: Continuation of Air Attacks and Sanctions Against Iraq, 94 A.J.I.L. 102–04 (2000); see also Murphy, Contemporary Practice, 93 A.J.I.L. 471 (1999).

Legal authority for use of military force in the post-cease-fire phase was disputed. The United States and its allies relied on arguments derived from a combination of Resolutions 678, 687, 688 and other resolutions. For use of force to enforce Resolution 687 (which does not specify forcible enforcement or use terms such as "all necessary means" to confer such authority), one line of argument was that the authority granted in Resolution 678 never lapsed, or if that authority had been provisionally suspended upon conclusion of the cease-fire, it was revived by virtue of Iraq's violation of the conditions of

Resolution 687 (or, alternatively, that Kuwait's inherent rights of collective self-defense in cooperation with other states revived). These arguments rested in part on the position that Iraq was in material breach of the cease-fire resolution. (Compare p. 212 on issues of "material breach" in connection with armistice agreements.) For findings of "unacceptable and material breach," or "flagrant violation" of Resolution 687, see U.N. Doc. S/25081 (Jan. 8, 1993); U.N. Doc. S/25091 (Jan. 11, 1993); S.C. Res. 1134 (Oct. 23, 1997); S.C. Res. 1137 (Nov. 12, 1997); see also S.C. Res. 1154 (Mar. 2, 1998) (warning of "the severest consequences" should Iraq impede the inspectors) and accompanying statements. In Resolution 1205 (Nov. 5, 1998), the Council condemned Iraq's decision not to cooperate with UNSCOM but did not mention use of force.

For differing legal positions, compare Wedgwood, The Enforcement of Security Council Resolution 687: The Threat of Force Against Iraq's Weapons of Mass Destruction, 92 A.J.I.L. 724 (1998), with Lobel & Ratner, Bypassing the Security Council: Ambiguous Authorizations to Use Force, Cease–Fires and the Iraqi Inspection Regime, 93 A.J.I.L. 124 (1999). Lobel and Ratner argue that a valid claim of Security Council authorization to use force must be based on a resolution that is explicit, that clearly articulates the objectives and puts the Council in control, and that terminates with the establishment of a durable cease-fire unless explicitly extended by the Council.

5. *Sanctions and Civilian Harm.* The sanctions regime remained in effect for more than a decade, with dire effects on Iraq's civilian population, because Iraq did not meet the conditions set by paragraph 22 of Resolution 687 for the lifting of sanctions. With the objective of alleviating the humanitarian impact of the sanctions, the Security Council approved an "oil-for-food" program, under which Iraq was permitted to sell specified quantities of oil, with the proceeds earmarked for food, medicines, and other internationally approved purposes. See S.C. Res. 706 (Aug. 15, 1991); S.C. Res. 712 (Sept. 19, 1991); S.C. Res. 986 (Apr. 14, 1995). The program was periodically reauthorized. See, e.g., S.C. Res. 1111 (June 4, 1997); S.C. Res. 1153 (Feb. 20, 1998); S.C. Res. 1210 (Nov. 24, 1998); S.C. Res. 1284 (Dec. 17, 1999). During its lifespan, as later investigations revealed, the program was manipulated so that resources intended for civilian relief were diverted to the pockets of Iraqi officials and other unauthorized persons.

On humanitarian and other issues concerning sanctions, and the relationship of the Iraq sanctions to uses of force, see, e.g., Damrosch, The Civilian Impact of Economic Sanctions, in Enforcing Restraint: Collective Intervention in Internal Conflicts 274–315 (Damrosch ed. 1993); Damrosch, Enforcing International Law Through Non–Forcible Measures, 269 Rec. des Cours 9, 108–21 (1997); Cortwright & Lopez, The Sanctions Decade: Assessing UN Strategies in the 1990s 37–61 (2000). On the oil-for-food program and its mismanagement, see Independent Inquiry Committee into the United Nations Oil-for-Food Programme (chaired by Paul Volcker), Report on the Management of the Oil-for-Food Programme (2005) and Report on the Manipulation of the Oil-for-Food Programme (2005), available at http://www.iic-offp.org.

SECURITY COUNCIL RESOLUTION 1441

Adopted November 8, 2002

The Security Council,

Recalling all its previous relevant resolutions, * * *

Recognizing the threat Iraq's non-compliance with Council resolutions and proliferation of weapons of mass destruction and long-range missiles poses to international peace and security,

Recalling that its resolution 678 (1990) authorized Member States to use all necessary means to uphold and implement its resolution 660 (1990) of 2 August 1990 and all relevant resolutions subsequent to resolution 660 (1990) and to restore international peace and security in the area,

* * *

Deploring the fact that Iraq has not provided an accurate, full, final, and complete disclosure, as required by resolution 687 (1991), of all aspects of its programmes to develop weapons of mass destruction and ballistic missiles * * *,

Deploring further that Iraq repeatedly obstructed immediate, unconditional, and unrestricted access to sites designated by the United Nations Special Commission (UNSCOM) and the International Atomic Energy Agency (IAEA), failed to cooperate fully and unconditionally with UNSCOM and IAEA weapons inspectors, as required by resolution 687 (1991), and ultimately ceased all cooperation with UNSCOM and the IAEA in 1998,

* * *

Determined to secure full compliance with its decisions,

Acting under Chapter VII of the Charter of the United Nations,

1. *Decides* that Iraq has been and remains in material breach of its obligations under relevant resolutions, including resolution 687 (1991), in particular through Iraq's failure to cooperate with United Nations inspectors and the IAEA, and to complete the actions required under paragraphs 8 to 13 of resolution 687 (1991);

2. *Decides*, while acknowledging paragraph 1 above, to afford Iraq, by this resolution, a final opportunity to comply with its disarmament obligations under relevant resolutions of the Council; and accordingly decides to set up an enhanced inspection regime with the aim of bringing to full and verified completion the disarmament process established by resolution 687 (1991) and subsequent resolutions of the Council;

3. *Decides* that, in order to begin to comply with its disarmament obligations, in addition to submitting the required biannual declarations, the Government of Iraq shall provide to UNMOVIC [the United Nations Monitoring, Verification and Inspection Commission, established in reso-

lution 1284 (1999) as the successor organization to UNSCOM], the IAEA, and the Council, not later than 30 days from the date of this resolution, a currently accurate, full, and complete declaration of all aspects of its programmes to develop chemical, biological, and nuclear weapons, ballistic missiles, and other delivery systems * * *;

4. *Decides* that false statements or omissions in the declarations submitted by Iraq pursuant to this resolution and failure by Iraq at any time to comply with, and cooperate fully in the implementation of, this resolution shall constitute a further material breach of Iraq's obligations and will be reported to the Council for assessment in accordance with paragraphs 11 and 12 below;

* * *

[Provisions on access of UNMOVIC and IAEA inspectors and procedures for their work in Iraq are omitted.]

11. *Directs* the Executive Chairman of UNMOVIC and the Director–General of the IAEA to report immediately to the Council any interference by Iraq with inspection activities, as well as any failure by Iraq to comply with its disarmament obligations, including its obligations regarding inspections under this resolution;

12. *Decides* to convene immediately upon receipt of a report in accordance with paragraphs 4 or 11 above, in order to consider the situation and the need for full compliance with the relevant Council resolutions in order to secure international peace and security;

13. *Recalls*, in that context, that the Council has repeatedly warned Iraq that it will face serious consequences as a result of its continued violations of its obligations;

14. *Decides* to remain seized of the matter.

TAFT & BUCHWALD, PREEMPTION, IRAQ, AND INTERNATIONAL LAW

97 A.J.I.L. 557 (2003) (some footnotes omitted)

Operation Iraqi Freedom [the U.S.-led military action in Iraq which began on March 20, 2003] has been criticized as unlawful because it constitutes preemption. This criticism is unfounded. Operation Iraqi Freedom was and is lawful. An otherwise lawful use of force does not become unlawful because it can be characterized as preemption. Operation Iraqi Freedom was conducted in a specific context that frames the way it should be analyzed. This context included the naked aggression by Iraq against its neighbors, its efforts to obtain weapons of mass destruction, its record of having used such weapons, Security Council action under Chapter VII of the United Nations Charter, and continuing Iraqi defiance of the Council's requirements.

* * *

On April 3, 1991, the Council adopted Resolution 687. That resolution did not return the situation to the status quo ante, the situation that might have existed if Iraq had never invaded Kuwait or if the Council had never acted. Rather, Resolution 687 declared that, upon official Iraqi acceptance of its provisions, a formal cease-fire would take effect, and it imposed several conditions on Iraq, including extensive obligations related to the regime's possession of weapons of mass destruction (WMD). As the Council itself subsequently described it, Resolution 687 provided the "conditions essential to the restoration of peace and security."[7]

The Council's conclusion that these WMD-related conditions were essential is neither surprising in the wake of the history of aggression by the Iraqi regime against its neighbors nor irrelevant to the legal situation faced by the coalition when Operation Iraqi Freedom began in March 2003. The Iraqi regime had demonstrated a willingness to use weapons of mass destruction, including by inflicting massive deaths against civilians in large-scale chemical weapons attacks against its own Kurdish population in the late 1980s, killing thousands. On at least ten occasions, the regime's forces had attacked Iranian and Kurdish targets with combinations of mustard gas and nerve agents through the use of aerial bombs, rockets, and conventional artillery shells. There was no question that such weapons in the hands of such a regime posed dangers to the countries in the region and elsewhere, including the United States, because of the possibility both of their use by Iraq and of their transfer for use by others. After considering the nature of the threat posed by Iraq, the Council, acting under its Chapter VII authority, established a special set of rules to protect against it.

As a legal matter, a material breach of the conditions that had been essential to the establishment of the cease-fire left the responsibility to member states to enforce those conditions, operating consistently with Resolution 678 to use all necessary means to restore international peace and security in the area. On numerous occasions in response to Iraqi violations of WMD obligations, the Council, through either a formal resolution or a statement by its president, determined that Iraq's actions constituted material breaches, understanding that such a determination authorized resort to force. Indeed, when coalition forces—American, British, and French—used force following such a presidential statement in January 1993, then Secretary–General Boutros–Ghali stated that the

> raid was carried out in accordance with a mandate from the Security Council under resolution 678 (1991), and the motive for the raid was Iraq's violation of that resolution, which concerns the cease-fire. As Secretary–General of the United Nations, I can tell you that the

---

7. *See, e.g.*, SC Res. 707 (Aug. 15, 1991). The use of the term "cease-fire" itself carries the connotation that one party is not bound to observe it in the face of violations by the other. Even a more formal armistice is subject to the same qualification, as specifically reflected in Article 40 of the 1907 Hague Regulations Respecting the Laws and Customs of War on Land, annexed to Convention Respecting the Laws and Customs of War on Land, Oct. 18, 1907, 36 Stat. 2277, 1 Bevans 631, which states that "any serious violation of the armistice by one of the parties gives the other party the right of denouncing it."

action taken was in accordance with the resolutions of the Security Council and the Charter of the United Nations.

* * *

* * * The U.S. view [in 1998, see pp. 1236–37 note 4] was that whether there had been a material breach was an objective fact, and it was not necessary for the Council to so determine or state. The debate about whether a material breach had occurred and who should determine this, however, should not obscure a more important point: all agreed that a Council determination that Iraq had committed a material breach would authorize individual member states to use force to secure compliance with the Council's resolutions.

This was well understood in the negotiations leading to the adoption of Resolution 1441 on November 8, 2002, and, indeed, the importance attached to the use of the phrase "material breach" was the subject of wide public discussion. The understanding of the meaning of the phrase was also reflected in the structure of Resolution 1441 itself. Thus, the preamble contained specific language recognizing the threat that Iraq's noncompliance and proliferation posed to international peace and security, recalling that Resolution 678 had authorized member states to use "all necessary means" to uphold the relevant resolutions and restore international peace and security, and further recalling that Resolution 687 had imposed obligations on Iraq as a necessary step for achieving the stated objective of restoring international peace and security.

After recounting and deploring Iraq's violations at some length, the resolution in operative paragraph 1 removed any doubt that Iraq's actions had constituted material breaches. Specifically, paragraph 1 stated that "Iraq has been and remains in material breach of its obligations under relevant resolutions, including resolution 687 (1991), in particular through Iraq's failure to cooperate with United Nations inspectors and the IAEA, and to complete the actions required under [the WMD and missile provisions] of resolution 687." In adopting the "material breach" language, the resolution established that Iraq's violations of its obligations had crossed the threshold that earlier practice had established for coalition forces to use force consistently with Resolution 678.

* * *

No serious argument was put forward in the period following the adoption of Resolution 1441 either that the declaration submitted by Iraq was "currently accurate, full, and complete" or that Iraq had complied with and cooperated fully in the implementation of the resolution. Under Resolution 1441, the Council had already decided that any such failure to cooperate would constitute a further material breach by Iraq.

* * *

The Council held numerous formal sessions on this issue. However, nothing in Resolution 1441 required the Council to adopt any further resolution, or other form of approval, to establish the occurrence of the material breach that was the predicate for coalition forces to resort to force. The very careful wording of paragraph 12 reflected this fact clearly. Paragraph 12 contemplated that the Council would "consider" the matter, but specifically stopped short of suggesting a requirement for a further decision. As the British attorney general stated on this point, "Resolution 1441 would in terms have provided that a further decision of the Security Council to sanction force was required if that had been intended. Thus, all that resolution 1441 requires is reporting to and discussion by the Security Council of Iraq's failures, but not an express further decision to authorise force."[22]

* * *

What does all this tell us about Iraq and the preemptive use of force? Was Operation Iraqi Freedom an example of preemptive use of force? Viewed as the final episode in a conflict initiated more than a dozen years earlier by Iraq's invasion of Kuwait, it may not seem so. However, in the context of the Security Council's resolutions, preemption of Iraq's possession and use of weapons of mass destruction was a principal objective of the coalition forces. A central consideration, at least from the U.S. point of view, was the risk embodied in allowing the Iraqi regime to defy the international community by pursuing weapons of mass destruction. But do U.S. actions show a disregard for international law? The answer here is clearly no. Both the United States and the international community had a firm basis for using preemptive force in the face of the past actions by Iraq and the threat that it posed, as seen over a protracted period of time. Preemptive use of force is certainly lawful where, as here, it represents an episode in an ongoing broader conflict initiated—without question—by the opponent and where, as here, it is consistent with the resolutions of the Security Council.

Notes

1. *Divergent Legal Views.* The authors of the foregoing extract were Legal Adviser and Assistant Legal Adviser of the U.S. Department of State at the time of the 2003 operation and wrote their article in official capacity. The U.S. legal position was sharply contested and indeed rejected in many quarters. For a range of differing perspectives on legality of the resumption of combat in 2003 (some supportive, some strongly critical), see the collection of pieces in Agora: Future Implications of the Iraq Conflict, 97 A.J.I.L. 553–642 (2003) (with editors' introduction by Damrosch & Oxman, and contributions by Yoo, Wedgwood, Gardner, Falk, Sapiro, Franck, Farer and Stromseth). See also Murphy, Assessing the Legality of Invading Iraq, 92 Geo. L. Rev. 173 (2004). In this connection, please return to the materials earlier in this Chapter (p. 1186) on the U.S. strategic doctrine of preemptive self-defense. Do

---

22. Lord Goldsmith, *Legal Basis for Use of Force Against Iraq* (Mar. 17, 2003) (statement by UK attorney general in answer to a parliamentary question), *available at* <http://www.labour.org. uk/legalbasis>.

you think that the U.S. action in Iraq was an application of that doctrine? How do you evaluate the self-defense arguments (individual or collective, as the case may be)? Are you persuaded by the legal views advanced by the United States? If you had been asked to prepare a legal memorandum on the question at the time, what position would you have taken? What significance (if any) do you attribute to the subsequent inability of the United States and its coalition partners to locate any active programs for weapons of mass destruction in Iraq in 2003?

2. *Deliberations and Decisions at National and International Levels.* In the United States, both the 1991 and the 2003 uses of force were authorized by the U.S. Congress. See Authorization for Use of Military Force Against Iraq Resolution, Pub. L. No. 102–1, 105 Stat. 3 (1991); Authorization for Use of Military Force Against Iraq Resolution of 2002, Pub. L. No. 107–243, 116 Stat. 1498 (2002) ("AUMF").

The 2002 AUMF authorized the President to use U.S. armed forces in order to

> (1) defend the national security of the United States against the continuing threat posed by Iraq; and

> (2) enforce all relevant United Nations Security Council resolutions regarding Iraq.

The President was instructed to (and did) make available to Congress his determination that

> (1) reliance by the United States on further diplomatic or other peaceful means alone either (A) will not adequately protect the national security of the United States against the continuing threat posed by Iraq or (B) is not likely to lead to enforcement of all relevant United Nations Security Council resolutions regarding Iraq; and

> (2) acting pursuant to this joint resolution is consistent with the United States and other countries continuing to take the necessary actions against international terrorist and terrorist organizations, including those nations, organizations, or persons who planned, authorized, committed or aided the terrorist attacks that occurred on September 11, 2001.

In relation to the parallel U.N. deliberations, the sequence of events was different in the two instances. In the earlier case, the administration of President George H.W. Bush first made its case to the United Nations and received the Security Council's endorsement in Resolution 678 in November 1990; the congressional action came later, just days before the expiration of the January 15, 1991 deadline set by that resolution. By contrast, in fall 2002 President George W. Bush first secured the approval of Congress in October and then pursued the U.N. negotiations which produced Resolution 1441 in November. Which sequence do you think better reflects the optimal relationship between national and international decision-making, for the United States and for other potential participants in multinational military action?

3. *Aftermath.* In Resolution 1483, adopted May 22, 2003, the Security Council addressed the situation on the ground in Iraq:

Noting the letter of 8 May 2003 from the Permanent Representatives of the United States of America and the United Kingdom of Great Britain and Northern Ireland to the President of the Security Council (S/2003/538) and recognizing the specific authorities, responsibilities, and obligations under applicable international law of these states as occupying powers under unified command (the "Authority"),

Noting further that other States that are not occupying powers are working now or in the future may work under the Authority,

* * *

Determining that the situation in Iraq, although improved, continues to constitute a threat to international peace and security,

Acting under Chapter VII of the Charter of the United Nations,

1. *Appeals* to Member States and concerned organizations to assist the people of Iraq in their efforts to reform their institutions and rebuild their country, and to contribute to conditions of stability and security in Iraq in accordance with this resolution;

* * *

10. *Decides* that, with the exception of prohibitions related to the sale or supply to Iraq of arms and related materiel other than those arms and related material required by the Authority to serve the purposes of this and other related resolutions, all prohibitions related to trade with Iraq and the provision of financial or economic resources to Iraq established by resolution 661 (1990) and subsequent relevant resolutions * * * shall no longer apply;

11. *Reaffirms* that Iraq must meet its disarmament obligations, *encourages* the [U.K. and U.S.] to keep the Council informed of their activities in this regard, and *underlines* the intention of the Council to revisit the mandates of [UNMOVIC and the IAEA]; * * *.

Resolution 1483 took no position on the lawfulness of the military operation up to that point. In provisions not excerpted here, it addressed various aspects of post-conflict reconstruction, including creation of a Development Fund for Iraq and decisions concerning Iraqi debts, assets, and petroleum revenues. Subsequent resolutions dealt with political and constitutional processes in Iraq, e.g. Resolutions 1500 (Aug. 14, 2003) and 1511 (Oct. 16, 2003). On these and related developments, see Agora (Continued), Future Implications of the Iraq Conflict, 97 A.J.I.L. 803–72 (2003). As envisaged in Security Council Resolution 1546 (June 8, 2004), the Interim Government of Iraq assumed full authority and the occupation formally ended in late June of 2004. A Transitional National Assembly was elected in January 2005 and a draft constitution was approved by the Iraqi people in a referendum held in October 2005. See S.C. Res. 1637 (Nov. 11, 2005).

3. U.N. Peace Operations and "Coalitions of Willing States"

During the Cold War and the frustration of the Security Council, the principal U.N. contribution to international peace and security consisted of various forms of "peacekeeping"—efforts to prevent hostilities from erupting or resuming. The Security Council established some peacekeeping arrangements pursuant to its authority under Chapter VI. The General Assembly also exercised authority to recommend peacekeeping arrangements under Article 14. All the organs of the United Nations, including the Secretary–General, have contributed to peacekeeping by various forms of "preventive diplomacy."

The model of peacekeeping that evolved through innovations and improvisations of the U.N.'s early decades took on several salient features. In traditional peacekeeping, U.N. troops carry only light arms and are allowed to use force only in self-defense from attack or from armed interference with their mandate. They take up positions along a "thin blue line" between forces that have already agreed to stop fighting, and are present with the consent of the territorial state and the agreement of the parties to the conflict. They are expected to maintain strict neutrality and impartiality. Between 1945 and 1990, the United Nations initiated some fifteen operations on this traditional model, as well as ten missions involving unarmed observers.

Beginning in 1990, U.N. peace operations took on increasingly complex mandates of a qualitatively different character. Some operations in this "second generation" have involved the implementation of a comprehensive peace settlement in the aftermath of years or even decades of armed conflict; in these instances, U.N. forces have maintained order for a transitional period, administered elections, and supervised the inauguration of new institutions. In other cases, U.N. troops have entered in the absence of a firm peace settlement, with difficult and perhaps unachievable mandates and unintended "mission creep." The most ambitious of these undertakings have entailed as many as 20,000 troops, contributed by member states but serving under U.N. command. The following table presents summary information about both first-and second-generation operations:

U.N. PEACEKEEPING OPERATIONS (AS OF EARLY 2009)[1]

Year launched	Location	Name of Mission	Size[2]
1948	MIDDLE EAST	UNTSO—UN Truce Supervision Organization	379
1949	INDIA/PAKISTAN	UNMOGIP—UN Military Observer Group in India and Pakistan	113
1964	CYPRUS	UNFICYP—UN Peacekeeping Force in Cyprus	1,072
1974	SYRIA	UNDOF—UN Disengagement Observer Force	1,176
1978	LEBANON	UNIFIL—UN Interim Force in Lebanon	13,392

1. Source: United Nations, Dept. of Peacekeeping Operations, www.un.org./Depts/dpko.

2. Includes military observers, troops, police, and international and local civilian personnel as of late 2008.

Year launched	Location	Name of Mission	Size[2]
1991	WESTERN SAHARA	MINURSO—UN Mission for the Referendum in Western Sahara	491
1993	GEORGIA	UNOMIG—UN Observer Mission in Georgia	455
1999	KOSOVO	UNMIK—UN Interim Administration Mission in Kosovo	2,990[3]
1999	DEMOCRATIC REP. OF CONGO	MONUC—UN Organization Mission in the Democratic Republic of the Congo	22,174
2003	LIBERIA	UNMIL—UN Mission in Liberia	13,562
2004	CÔTE D'IVOIRE	UNOCI—UN Operation in Côte d'Ivoire	10,572
2004	HAITI	MINUSTAH—UN Stabilization Mission in Haiti	11,002
2005	SUDAN	UNMIS—UN Mission in the Sudan	13,545
2006	TIMOR–LESTE	UNMIT—UN Integrated Mission in Timor–Leste	2,915
2007	DARFUR (Sudan)	UNAMID—AU–UN Hybrid Operation in Darfur	17,593
2007	CENTRAL AFRICAN REP/ CHAD	MINURCAT—UN Mission in the Central African Republic and Chad	876

For legal purposes it is important to distinguish between operations organized and run by the United Nations (whether as classic or as complex peace operations), and operations undertaken by "coalitions of the willing" with Security Council approval. The 1991 enforcement operation against Iraq, as discussed above, was a "coalition of the willing" in support of Kuwait. Other "coalitions of the willing" include the Unified Task Force led by the United States in Somalia, the multinational intervention in Haiti (1994), *Opération Turquoise* led by France in Rwanda (1994), the NATO implementation force in Bosnia–Herzegovina (1995–2002), and the intervention led by Australia in East Timor in 1999. Each of these had an authorizing resolution from the Security Council, but the United Nations did not control the national operations. In certain theaters, the parallel existence of U.N. peacekeeping forces and national forces operating as part of a "coalition of the willing" has led to confusion about their respective mandates and lines of authority and control. An example is the overlapping roles for the U.N. forces and U.N.-led Unified Task Force in Somalia, which came to an unhappy end. See pp. 1254–55.

The materials that follow highlight some of the essential features of the most important U.N. peace operations, beginning with ones from the "first generation" whose mandate was to separate forces along an agreed cease-fire line, and then proceeding to the complex "second generation" operations of more recent years. Thereafter (Section 3B) we turn to regional organizations and arrangements, which have assumed a significant share of responsibility for collective security and self-defense.

---

3. UNMIK was in the process of reconfiguration in early 2009, with an anticipated reduction in staff of 70%, in light of the transfer of certain of its functions to a European Union rule-of-law mission.

NOTE

Bibliography. Among the many works on U.N. peacekeeping, a good introduction is published by the United Nations as The Blue Helmets: A Review of United Nations Peace–Keeping (3d ed. 1996). A series of U.N. "blue books" addresses specific conflicts, e.g., The United Nations and Rwanda, 1990–1996 (1996). A journal of International Peacekeeping has been published since 1994. Earlier references include: The Evolution of U.N. Peacekeeping: Case Studies and Comparative Analysis (Durch ed. 1993); James, Peacekeeping and International Politics (1990); Higgins, United Nations Peacekeeping 1946–79: Documents and Commentary (1981) (4 vols.); United Nations Peace–Keeping (Cassese ed. 1978); Rikhye, Harbottle, & Egge, The Thin Blue Line: International Peacekeeping and Its Future (1974); Bowett, United Nations Forces (1964); Goodrich & Simons, The United Nations and the Maintenance of International Peace and Security (1955).

On "second-generation" peace operations, see Ratner, The New U.N. Peacekeeping: Building Peace in Lands of Conflict After the Cold War (1994). See also Carnegie Commission on the Prevention of Deadly Conflict, Final Report 63–67 (1997) and bibliography at 222–42. For up-to-date as well as historical information, the website of the U.N. Department of Peacekeeping Operations (http://www.un.org/Depts/dpko) is a valuable resource.

On delegations of Security Council authorities to coalitions of states, see Sarooshi, The United Nations and the Development of Collective Security: The Delegation by the U.N. Security Council of Its Chapter VII Powers (1999). See also Sarooshi, International Organizations and Their Exercise of Sovereign Powers (2005).

The following materials survey some of the most important peacekeeping operations from early in the U.N. experience to the current period. Since it is not possible to be comprehensive, we highlight here certain instances that have raised salient legal problems.

a.   The Arab–Israeli Conflict

After the cessation of fighting between Israel and the Arab states that followed the Israeli declaration of independence on May 14, 1948, friction with Egypt continued. The Egyptians had obstructed Israeli commerce through the Gulf of Aqaba and through the Suez Canal; Israeli complaints to the Security Council on four occasions between 1950 and 1955 failed to achieve results. President Nasser then announced, on July 26, 1956, the nationalization of the Suez Canal Company. The principal shareholders of the latter were the United Kingdom and various private interests in the United Kingdom and in France.

On October 29, 1956, Israeli forces invaded Egypt, in concert with forces from the United Kingdom and France. On October 31, the Security Council approved by a vote of 7–2–2 a resolution introduced by Yugoslavia that placed the question before the General Assembly. As a procedural matter, the resolution was not defeated by the negative votes of France and the United Kingdom. See Article 27(2) of the Charter. The resolution, S.C. Res. 119 (Oct. 31, 1956), noted the grave situation created by the action against Egypt and called for the convocation of an emergency special session of the General Assembly pursuant to the "Uniting for Peace" Resolution.

On November 5, 1956, the General Assembly passed a resolution establishing "a United Nations Command for an emergency international Force to secure and supervise the cessation of hostilities." G.A. Res. 1000. By November 7, the fighting had stopped. On November 8, Major–General E.L.M. Burns of Canada was appointed Chief of the United Nations Command of the United Nations Emergency Force (UNEF). See U.N. Doc. A/3317. With Egyptian approval the UNEF was established on Egyptian territory. Israel indicated that "on no account" would she "agree to the stationing of a foreign force, no matter how called, in her territory or in any of the areas occupied by her." See U.N. Docs. A/3313 and A/3314; see generally Friedmann & Collins, The Suez Canal Crisis of 1956, in Scheinman & Wilkinson, International Law and Political Crisis: An Analytic Casebook 91 (1968). After some delay and further resolutions of the U.N. General Assembly, on March 8, 1957, the Secretary–General confirmed full Israeli withdrawal behind the armistice lines.

Ten years later, on May 18, 1967, Egypt (then known as the United Arab Republic, or UAR) decided to terminate the presence of UNEF from the territory of the UAR and the Gaza Strip. The U.N. Secretary General U Thant accepted the authority of the UAR to take this action and instructed UNEF to withdraw. See Special Report of the Secretary–General, U.N. Doc. A/6669 (May 18, 1967). The United States announced that it viewed with dismay the withdrawal of UNEF without action by either the General Assembly or the Security Council. See the letter of Ernest A. Gross challenging the legal right of the UAR to withdraw UNEF unilaterally and the propriety of the Secretary General's compliance. N.Y. Times, May 26, 1967, at 44.

As the UNEF troops withdrew, large UAR units took their place. Tension in the Middle East increased rapidly. Israeli Premier Eshkol warned that any interference with the freedom of Israeli shipping would be taken as an act of aggression. The efforts of the major powers to avert the outbreak of war were unavailing. On June 5, 1967, Israel, claiming attacks by its Arab neighbors, launched a major invasion of Arab territory. See U.N. Doc. S/PV.1347 at 3, 17–20 (June 5, 1967); U.N. Doc. S/PV.1348 at 73–75 (June 6, 1967). Within a week the Israeli troops were completely victorious and a large portion of Arab territory had been occupied. The Security Council's demand for an immediate cease-fire was eventually honored by the parties. Resolution 242 (Nov. 22, 1967), among other things, called for the withdrawal of Israeli forces "from territories" occupied by them. The efforts of the Soviet Union to have a resolution adopted requiring the withdrawal of Israeli troops were unsuccessful. See generally Bowie, The Suez Crisis 1956 (1974).

Despite Resolution 242, there was no progress towards a peaceful settlement, and Israel remained in control of the territories seized in the 1967 war. On October 6, 1973, Egyptian, Syrian and Iraqi forces launched a surprise attack on Israel, but after some initial successes they were repelled. Under pressure from the United States and the U.S.S.R., Israel agreed to withdraw its forces from Egyptian soil and disengagement agreements were signed between Israel–Egypt and Israel–Syria. The Security Council established another U.N. Emergency Force (UNEF II) to monitor disengagement between Egypt and Israel, S.C. Res. 340 (1973), and the U.N. Disengagement Observer Force (UNDOF), S.C. Res. 350 (May 31, 1974), for the buffer zone between Israel and Syria.

Israel also occupied southern Lebanon in retaliation for raids launched from bases of the Palestine Liberation Organization in that area. In 1978, the United Nations Interim Force in Lebanon (UNIFIL) was established to oversee the withdrawal of Israeli forces and assist the government of Lebanon in ensuring the return of its effective authority in the area. See S.C. Res. 425 and 426 (Mar. 19, 1978). UNIFIL was unable to fulfill its mandate completely but managed to reduce the level of violence and the risk of wider conflict between Israeli and Arab forces. In 1982 the Lebanese government asked France, Britain and the United States to send troops to bolster U.N. forces attempting to police a fragile cease-fire in Lebanon's civil war. Frequent attacks by the various militias culminated in a bomb attack on the U.S. troop barracks, killing 250 marines. Soon all Western troops were withdrawn and only the U.N. force remained.

In 1978–1979, with U.S. support and intermediation, Israel and Egypt negotiated a peace treaty under which Israel agreed to withdraw from the Sinai, and Egypt agreed to end the state of war and to establish normal relations with Israel. The treaty was signed at Camp David on March 26, 1979. See 28 I.L.M. 362 (1979). Other Arab states rejected it, and a plan to have the agreement monitored by U.N. forces was abandoned because of Soviet opposition. Instead, a Multinational Force and Observers led by the United States has assisted in implementation of the Camp David agreement.

As of 2009, UNDOF and UNIFIL were still in place in the Middle East. The Security Council has extended their mandates for successive six-month or one-year periods. See, e.g., S.C. Res. 1832 (Aug. 27, 2008); S.C. Res. 1848 (Dec. 12, 2008).

b. The Congo

The Security Council and the General Assembly were both involved in authorizing peacekeeping in the Congo in 1960–1964. Within a week of Congo's attaining independence from Belgium in 1960, there were mutinies in the Congolese army and attacks on Belgians and other Europeans. On July 8, Belgium dispatched troops to the Congo for the announced purpose of protecting its nationals. On July 11, the mineral-rich province of Katanga announced its secession. On July 12, President Kasavubu and Prime Minister Lumumba of the Republic of the Congo requested U.N. assistance in a telegram to the Secretary–General. See U.N. Doc. S/4382 (July 13, 1960). On July 14, the Security Council approved a resolution authorizing the Secretary–General "to provide the Government of the Republic of the Congo with such military assistance as may be necessary until, through the efforts of the Congolese Government with the technical assistance of the United Nations, the national security forces may be able, in the opinion of the Government, to fully meet their tasks." S.C. Res. 143 (July 17, 1960). The U.N. force is known by its French acronym, ONUC.

The Security Council became embroiled in a debate on the right of U.N. forces to enter Katanga. See the Secretary–General's memorandum of August 12, 1960, U.N. Doc. S/4417/Add.6 (Aug. 12, 1960). During September, the Soviet Union vetoed several resolutions that would have reaffirmed the power of the U.N. forces to maintain law and order. An impasse developed and continued until the adoption on September 17 of a U.S.-sponsored resolution (S.C. Res. 157) that called for an emergency meeting of the General Assembly as provided for in the "Uniting for Peace" Resolution. On September 20, the General Assembly passed a resolution confirming the functions of the U.N. forces and requesting the Secretary–General to continue his support of the Central Government of the Congo. G.A. Res. 1474.

Despite the presence of U.N. forces, civil strife in the Congo continued. On February 21, 1961, the Security Council reaffirmed its previous resolutions and urged that the United Nations act to prevent the occurrence of a civil war in the Congo. It called for the withdrawal of all foreign military personnel and called upon all states to take measures to prevent persons from joining the civil strife. The Council also urged the restoration of order through the convening of the Parliament and the reorganization of Congolese armed units. See S.C. Res. 161. Further resolutions of the Security Council were necessary before foreign mercenaries were removed, the secession of Katanga ended, and law and order restored. See U.N. Secretary–General, Report on the Withdrawal of the United Nations Force in the Congo and on other aspects of the United Nations operation, U.N. Doc. S/5784 (June 29, 1964). Compare the withdrawal of the United Nations forces from the Congo with the withdrawal of forces from Egypt in 1967. Was the withdrawal of the forces in either case required by international law?

NOTES

1. *Relevance of Law.* On the role of law in the crisis in the Congo, see Abi–Saab, The United Nations Operation in the Congo 1960–64 (1978). See also Miller (pseudonym for Schachter), Legal Aspects of the United Nations Action in the Congo, 55 A.J.I.L. 1 (1961).

2. *Peacekeeping Expenses.* As noted (p. 1223), France and the Soviet Union questioned the legality of U.N. assessments to pay for peacekeeping operations authorized by the General Assembly rather than by the Security Council. In *Certain Expenses of the United Nations*, Advisory Opinion, 1962 I.C.J. 151, the International Court of Justice concluded that the General Assembly had acted within the scope of its authority in recommending

establishment of a peacekeeping force and approving its expenses. The opinion states in part (after quoting U.N. Charter Article 24 on the Security Council's primary—but not exclusive—responsibility for peace and security):

The Charter makes it abundantly clear, however, that the General Assembly is also to be concerned with international peace and security. Article 14 authorizes the General Assembly to "recommend measures for the peaceful adjustment of any situation, regardless of origin, which it deems likely to impair the general welfare or friendly relations among nations, including situations resulting from a violation of the provisions of the present Charter setting forth the purposes and principles of the United Nations." The word "measures" implies some kind of action, and the only limitation which Article 14 imposes on the General Assembly is the restriction found in Article 12, namely, that the Assembly should not recommend measures while the Security Council is dealing with the same matter unless the Council requests it to do so. Thus while it is the Security Council which, exclusively, may order coercive action, the functions and powers conferred by the Charter on the General Assembly are not confined to discussion, consideration, the initiation of studies and the making of recommendations; they are not merely hortatory. Article 18 deals with *"decisions"* of the General Assembly "on important questions". These "decisions" do indeed include certain recommendations, but others have dispositive force and effect. Among these latter decisions, Article 18 includes suspension of rights and privileges of membership, expulsion of Members, "and budgetary questions". * * *

By Article 17, paragraph 1, the General Assembly is given the power not only to "consider" the budget of the Organization, but also to "approve" it. The decision to "approve" the budget has a close connection with paragraph 2 of Article 17, since thereunder the General Assembly is also given the power to apportion the expenses among the Members and the exercise of the power of apportionment creates the obligation, specifically stated in Article 17, paragraph 2, of each Member to bear that part of the expenses which is apportioned to it by the General Assembly. When those expenses include expenditures for the maintenance of peace and security, which are not otherwise provided for, it is the General Assembly which has the authority to apportion the latter amounts among the Members. The provisions of the Charter which distribute functions and powers to the Security Council and to the General Assembly give no support to the view that such distribution excludes from the powers of the General Assembly the power to provide for the financing of measures designed to maintain peace and security.

c. Second–Generation Peacekeeping: Cambodia

For many years, Cambodia suffered from civil war, interventions, genocide and other gross violations of human rights, and massive dislocations of its population. In 1975, the Khmer Rouge gained control of Cambodia, renaming it Democratic Kampuchea, and attempted a total restructuring of Cambodian society, committing mass state-sponsored killing and other violations of human rights. In 1979, Vietnam invaded Cambodia and installed a régime known as the People's Republic of

Kampuchea, which controlled most of Cambodia during the 1980s. After the Vietnamese invasion, four factions conducted a guerrilla war in an attempt to gain control of Cambodia.

In 1991, the four Cambodian warring factions endorsed a U.N. plan designed to help rebuild Cambodia and signed a number of agreements aimed at a comprehensive settlement. See Paris Conference on Cambodian Agreements Elaborating the Framework for a Comprehensive Political Settlement of the Cambodian Conflict, U.N. Doc. A/46/608 (Oct. 30, 1991) and S/23177, reprinted in 31 I.L.M. 174 (1992). Under the 1991 Paris Agreements the four factions agreed to create a Supreme National Council (SNC), composed of representatives of the factions, to act as the "unique * * * source of authority" and embody Cambodian sovereignty. The SNC delegated to the United Nations all authority necessary to ensure the implementation of the comprehensive settlement. In 1992, the United Nations set up the U.N. Transitional Authority (UNTAC) to monitor the disarmament of the four Cambodian factions and supervise free elections. UNTAC was comprised of over 20,000 personnel and was given substantial authority within Cambodia, including aspects of civil administration. In order to create a neutral environment for elections, the factions delegated to UNTAC control of five ministries and supervision of others, access to all governmental documents, and power to issue binding directives and replace personnel.

Cambodia's first free and fair elections took place under UNTAC's supervision in May of 1993. Despite considerable violence in the preceding months, the elections unfolded without significant violence, disruptions or irregularities. After the election UNTAC worked to train the Cambodian army and other national institutions and assisted the constituent assembly in drafting a constitution compatible with human rights principles. UNTAC withdrew on schedule by the end of 1993, having successfully discharged its mandate.

NOTE

See generally Ratner, The Cambodian Settlement Agreements, 87 A.J.I.L. 1 (1993); Ratner, The United Nations in Cambodia: A Model for Resolution of Internal Conflicts?, in Enforcing Restraint: Collective Intervention in Internal Conflicts 241–73 (Damrosch ed. 1993); Ratner, The New U.N. Peacekeeping (1994).

d. Somalia

In 1992, the Security Council authorized a United Nations Operation in Somalia (UNOSOM) to alleviate hunger and starvation there. S.C. Res. 733 (Jan 23, 1992). On November 24 and November 30, 1992, the Secretary–General transmitted letters to the President of the Security Council reporting on the continuing deterioration of humanitarian conditions in Somalia, and on the civil strife between various factions and clans preventing UNOSOM from implementing the earlier Security Council mandate to provide relief assistance. See U.N. Docs. S/24859 and S/24868; S.C. Res. 733 (Jan. 23, 1992), S.C. Res. 746 (Mar. 17, 1992), S.C. Res. 751 (Apr. 24, 1992), S.C. Res. 767 (July 24, 1992), and S.C. Res. 775 (Aug. 28, 1992). The Secretary–General urged military action pursuant to Article 39 of the Charter, to ensure that UNOSOM succeeded in its relief mission; in his opinion "no government exist[ed] in Somalia that could request and allow such use of force." U.N. Doc. S/24868, at 3 (Nov. 30, 1992). He emphasized that the purpose of the force would be to bring the violence against the international relief effort to an end and that in order to achieve this goal it would be necessary to disarm the various warring factions, irregular forces and gangs. On December 3, 1992 the Security Council adopted a resolution authorizing the use of "military forces" to establish "a secure environment for humanitarian relief operations in Somalia:"

SECURITY COUNCIL RESOLUTION 794

Adopted December 3, 1992

The Security Council * * *

Recognizing the unique character of the present situation in Somalia and *mindful* of its deteriorating, complex and extraordinary nature, requiring an immediate and exceptional response;

Determining that the magnitude of the human tragedy caused by the conflict in Somalia, further exacerbated by the obstacles being created to the distribution of humanitarian assistance, constitutes a threat to international peace and security * * *

* * *

Determined * * * to restore peace, stability and law and order with a view to facilitating the process of a political settlement under the auspices of the United Nations, aimed at national reconciliation in Somalia * * *

* * *

2. *Demands* that all parties, movements and factions in Somalia take all measures necessary to facilitate the efforts of the United Nations * * * and humanitarian organizations to provide humanitarian assistance to the affected population in Somalia;

* * *

7. *Endorses* the recommendation by the Secretary–General * * * that action under Chapter VII of the Charter * * * should be taken in order to establish a secure environment for humanitarian relief operations in Somalia as soon as possible;

8. *Welcomes* the offer by a Member State * * * concerning the establishment of an operation to create such a secure environment;

9. *Welcomes also* offers by other Member States to participate in that operation;

10. *Acting* under Chapter VII of the Charter of the United Nations, *authorizes* the Secretary–General and Member States cooperating to implement the offer referred to in paragraph 8 above to use all necessary means to establish as soon as possible a secure environment for humanitarian relief operations in Somalia;

11. *Calls* on all Member States which are in a position to do so to provide military forces and to make additional contributions, in cash or in kind, in accordance with paragraph 10 * * *;

12. *Authorizes* the Secretary–General and the Member States concerned to make the necessary arrangements for the unified command and control of the forces involved, which will reflect the offer referred to in paragraph 8 above;

13. *Requests* the Secretary–General and the Member States acting under paragraph 10 above to establish appropriate mechanisms for coordination between the United Nations and their military forces * * *.

NOTES

1. *Attitudes in Somalia.* There was little initial Somali resistance to the military intervention authorized by the Security Council for the protection of humanitarian aid. Would the authorization of force be within the authority of the Security Council under Chapter VII if taken in the face of active objection by a government in control of its territory? Would it be consistent with Article 2(7)? Did it matter that Somalia was perceived to be in a state of anarchy without an effective government? Was there a threat to the peace or a breach of the peace in Somalia within the meaning of Article 39 of the Charter? Is a determination of threat to international peace and security a prerequisite to Security Council action on humanitarian grounds? Is there any other legal basis for such action?

2. *Confusion Over Lines of Authority and "Mission Creep."* The "Member State" to which the cryptic paragraph 8 of Resolution 794 refers is the United States. The "necessary arrangements for the unified command and control of the forces involved" (para. 12) and "appropriate mechanisms for coordination between the United Nations and their military forces" (para. 13) led to confusion about the lines of authority between, on the one-hand, the U.S.-led Unified Task Force (which despite its acronym of UNITAF was independent of U.N. command and control), and on the other hand, UNOSOM II which was authorized by the Security Council in Resolution 814 (Mar. 26, 1993) and operated under the control of the U.N. Secretary–General. There was also considerable disagreement about the respective mandates of the parallel endeavors. While the purpose of UNITAF was "to establish a secure environment for humanitarian relief operations," the resolution establishing UNOSOM II demanded that the Somali factions comply with undertakings on disarmament and also called for U.N. assistance to the people of Somalia in "the re-establishment of national and regional institutions and civil administration in the entire country" and in "the restoration and maintenance of peace, stability and law and order."

On June 5, 1993, twenty-four Pakistani peacekeepers serving under UNOSOM command were ambushed and killed. In response, the Security Council called on the Secretary–General "to take all necessary measures against all those responsible for the armed attacks * * * including to secure the investigation of their actions and their arrest and detention for prosecution, trial and punishment." S.C. Res. 837, para. 5 (June 6, 1993). A U.N. investigation subsequently found clear and convincing evidence that the leader of one of the Somali clans, General Mohammed Farah Aideed, had authorized the attack. The ensuing manhunt for General Aideed intensified the confrontation between his faction and U.S. and U.N. forces, culminating on October 3, 1993 with a devastating clash resulting in the deaths of 18 U.S. Army Rangers and at least seventy other U.S. casualties—and an even higher toll among Somali civilians. See Enforcing Restraint 378–82 (Damrosch ed. 1993); Bowden, Black Hawk Down: A Story of Modern War (1999).

3. *U.S. Policy Changes.* The backlash to the deaths of the U.S. Army Rangers in Somalia prompted the U.S. Congress to set a time-limit on the U.S. deployment. See Pub. L. 103–139, § 8151, 107 Stat. 1418, 1475 (1993). The limitation on funding the mission past March 31, 1994 contained the further proviso that "United States combat forces in Somalia shall be under the command and control of United States commanders under the ultimate direction of the President of the United States." 107 Stat. 1418, 1476. In fact, the U.S. forces had never been under U.N. command and were under U.S. control at all times, including when the fatal clashes occurred. The other participants in the U.S.-led multinational force withdrew their troops at approximately the same time as the United States.

Shortly after the completion of the U.S. withdrawal from Somalia, the Clinton Administration announced a set of guidelines for U.S. participation in U.N. peace operations, which became known as Presidential Decision Directive (PDD) 25. See United States; Administration Policy on Reforming Multilateral Peace Operations, 33 I.L.M. 705 (1994). The directive stated that the President would necessarily retain ultimate command authority, but that he could delegate operational control if appropriate to foreign commanders. The conditions for U.S. participation in any U.N. operation under PDD 25 include that the operation should enjoy support in Congress and among the public. Later, the Congress required that the President should give at least fifteen days' advance notice before any Security Council vote to approve a peacekeeping operation.

4. *Criminalizing Attacks on Peacekeepers.* Following the attacks on U.N. and U.S. forces in Somalia, the United Nations elaborated a Convention on the Safety of United Nations and Associated Personnel, 34 I.L.M. 482 (1995), which entered into force in 1999. The Rome Statute of the International Criminal Court, art. 8(2)(b)(iii), provides for the war crime of "[i]ntentionally directing attacks against personnel, installations, material, units or vehicles involved in a humanitarian assistance or peacekeeping mission in accordance with the Charter of the United Nations, as long as they are entitled to the protection given to civilians or civilian objects under the international law of armed conflict."

5. *Further Reading.* On UNITAF's accomplishments, see Hirsch & Oakley, Somalia and Operation Restore Hope: Reflections on Peacemaking and Peacekeeping (1995). The U.N. role is described in the U.N. bluebook series, U.N. Dep't of Public Information, The United Nations and Somalia, 1992–1996 (1996). On disagreements between the United States and the U.N. Secretary–General, see Boutros–Ghali, Unvanquished 92–103 (1999). On U.S. domestic legal aspects, see Stromseth, Collective Force and Constitutional Responsibility: War Powers in the Post–Cold War Era, 50 U. Miami L. Rev. 145, 168–72 (1995); Damrosch, The Clinton Administration and War Powers, 63 L. & Contemp. Problems 125, 132–33 (2000).

e. *Rwanda*

In a paroxysm of genocidal violence in spring 1994, approximately 800,000 people died in Rwanda. Most of the victims were of the Tutsi ethnic group, and most of the perpetrators were Hutu extremists, though some moderate Hutus were also killed at the outbreak of the genocide. The genocide took place despite the presence in Rwanda of a small U.N. peacekeeping force, UNAMIR, which the Security Council had authorized to assist in the implementation of a peace agreement between the Government of Rwanda (Hutu-dominated) and the Rwandese Patriotic Front (mainly but not exclusively Tutsis, with an exile base in Uganda). See S.C. Res. 872 (Oct. 5, 1993). UNAMIR had begun deployment in late 1993 in difficult conditions, against a backdrop of increasing violence, with inadequate troop strength for the tasks at hand. The United States, still smarting from the debacle in Somalia in October 1993, was unwilling to commit significant resources to Rwanda and reluctant to exert leverage on others to do so. The Secretary–General had requested authority for a force of 5000 troops but the Security Council did not approve this request. Military experts later confirmed that a force of that size, with a proper mandate and adequately armed and trained, could have prevented the genocide. Nonetheless, UNAMIR's troop strength never exceeded 550. Included in that number was a battalion from Belgium, the former colonial power in Rwanda.

On April 6, 1994, a plane carrying Rwandan President Juvenal Habyarimana and the President of Burundi was shot down over Kigali, Rwanda while returning from a subregional summit. Almost immediately, Hutu extremists began executing a carefully-prepared plan for extermination of Tutsis and moderate Hutus who supported the peace process. Later investigations revealed that as early as January 11, 1994, UNAMIR's commander had urgently cabled U.N. headquarters with a warning from a government informant of a strategy to provoke the killing of Belgian peacekeepers and the Belgian battalion's withdrawal, to be followed by rapid extermination of Tutsi in Kigali. This warning elicited only a tepid response from New York at the time. In the event, on April 7, ten Belgian peacekeepers who were guarding Rwandan Prime Minister Agathe Uwilingiyimana were killed, as was the Prime Minister herself. Thereafter, the Belgian government proceeded with a swift evacuation of the remainder of the Belgian contingent and indeed urged that UNAMIR should collectively withdraw. Hutu-on-Tutsi violence unfolded with staggering rapidity and intensity in the following weeks.

On May 17, 1994, the Security Council adopted Resolution 918, which increased UNAMIR's authorized troop strength and imposed an arms embargo on Rwanda. Rwanda, which was sitting as a non-permanent member of the Security Council at the time, voted against the resolution. As late as July 25, UNAMIR still had only 550 troops (one-tenth of the authorized strength), and the Secretary–General was unable to induce states to contribute to the peacekeeping force.

Meanwhile, in late June 1994, France proposed to lead a multinational military operation in parallel to that of UNAMIR, in an effort to reestablish security and "safe humanitarian areas" in Rwanda. France requested that the Security Council authorize such an intervention under Chapter VII of the Charter, which was done in Resolution 929 (June 22, 1994), by a vote of 10 in favor with 5 abstentions (Brazil, China, New Zealand, Nigeria, and Pakistan). The intervention, known as *Opération Turquoise*, was authorized only for a two-month period. At the end of that time, with the situation largely stabilized, the participating countries withdrew their troops.

NOTES

1. *Post–Mortem.* In 1999, U.N. Secretary–General Kofi Annan, who had been head of the U.N. Department of Peacekeeping Operations in 1994, requested an independent inquiry into U.N. actions in Rwanda in 1994. Ingvar Carlsson, former Prime Minister of Sweden, led this inquiry. The inquiry's report (available on the U.N. website) concludes in part:

> The overriding failure in the response of the United Nations before and during the genocide in Rwanda can be summarized as a lack of resources and a lack of will to take on the commitment which would have been necessary to prevent or to stop the genocide. UNAMIR, the main component of the United Nations presence in Rwanda, was not planned, dimensioned, deployed or instructed in a way which provided for a proactive and assertive role in dealing with a peace process in serious trouble. The mission was smaller than the original recommendations from the field suggested. It was slow in being set up, and was beset by debilitating administrative difficulties. It lacked well-trained troops and functioning materiel. The mission's mandate was based on an analysis of the peace process which proved erroneous, and which was never corrected despite the significant warning signs that the original mandate had become inadequate. By the time the genocide started, the mission was not functioning as a cohesive whole: in the real hours and days of deepest crisis, consistent testimony points to a lack of political leadership, lack of military capacity, severe problems of command and control and lack of coordination and discipline.

* * *

[I]t *is incomprehensible to the Inquiry that not more was done to follow-up on the information provided by the informant.* * * * Information received by a United Nations mission that plans are being made to exterminate any group of people requires an immediate and determined response * * *.

* * *

[T]he *threat against the Belgian contingent should have been followed up* more clearly, not only in relation to the security of that particular contingent, but equally as part of the strategic discussions within the Secretariat and with the Security Council on the role of UNAMIR in Rwanda. The United Nations knew that extremists on one side hoped to achieve the withdrawal of the mission. * * *

Questions have been raised as to the wisdom of inviting Belgium, a former colonial power, to participate in UNAMIR. The threats against the Belgian contingent described in the Dallaire cable as well as on the radio and through other forms of propaganda, show the difficulties inherent in that participation. In the case of UNAMIR it must be said, however, that Belgium was providing well-equipped troops which were not being offered by others, and that both parties had accepted that they participate in the mission.

* * *

The Inquiry believes that it is essential to preserve the unity of United Nations command and control, and that troop contributing countries, despite the domestic political pressures which may argue the reverse, should refrain from unilateral withdrawal to the detriment and even risk of ongoing peacekeeping operations.

The loss of ten peacekeepers is a terrible blow to any troop contributing country. However, even if the Belgian Government felt that the brutal murder of its para-commandos and the anti-Belgian rhetoric in Rwanda at the time made a continued presence of its own contingent impossible, *the Inquiry finds the campaign to secure the complete withdrawal of UNAMIR difficult to understand.* * * * [T]he focus seems to have been solely on withdrawal rather than on the possibilities for the United Nations to act, with or without Belgium.

* * *

A general point about the need for political will is that such will must be mobilised equally in response to conflicts across the globe. *It has been stated repeatedly during the course of the interviews conducted by the Inquiry* * * * *that Rwanda was not of strategic interest to third countries and that the international community exercised double standards when faced with the risk of a catastrophe there compared to action taken elsewhere.*

* * *

Faced in Rwanda with the risk of genocide, and later the systematic implementation of a genocide, the United Nations had an obligation to act which transcended traditional principles of peacekeeping. In effect, there can be no neutrality in the face of genocide, no impartiality in the face of a campaign to exterminate part of a population. *While the presence of United Nations peacekeepers in Rwanda may have begun as a traditional peacekeeping operation to monitor the implementation of an existing peace agreement, the onslaught of the genocide should have led decision-makers in the United Nations * * * to realize that the original mandate, and indeed the neutral mediating role of the United Nations, was no longer adequate and required a different, more assertive response, combined with the means necessary to take such action.*

2. *Further Reading.* On the events in Rwanda, see Prunier, The Rwanda Crisis: History of a Genocide (1995); Murphy, Humanitarian Intervention: The United Nations in an Evolving World Order 243–60 (1996); Gourevitch, We Wish to Inform You that Tomorrow We Will Be Killed with Our Families (1998).

f. *Haiti*

As described in Chapter 5, p. 350, President Jean–Bertrand Aristide took office in Haiti in early 1991 after an election that had been certified by U.N. and other international monitors as free and fair. On September 30, 1991, he was overthrown in a military coup. In addition to the diplomatic pressures from October 1991 forward (noted in Chapter 5), which included collective non-recognition of the usurping government by the Organization of American States and its members, the OAS recommended economic sanctions to bring about the isolation of those who had illegally seized power in Haiti. The U.N. General Assembly likewise recommended measures supportive of the OAS actions. When the regional, voluntary embargo had not achieved its objective as of June 1993, the locus of activity shifted to the U.N. Security Council, which imposed a mandatory embargo on oil and petroleum products and on arms and police equipment, as well as a freeze of the assets of the Haitian Government and *de facto* authorities. S.C. Res. 841 (June 16, 1993).

These measures went farther than any before in applying universal, mandatory and severe sanctions to influence a domestic political crisis over democratic governance. Initially, they seemed to have the desired effect of inducing the military rulers to begin serious negotiations over a transfer of power. On July 3, 1993, an agreement was reached at Governors Island, New York, according to which the Aristide government should have returned to power by October 30, 1993; a U.N. peacekeeping mission would have supervised the transition and assisted in reconstruction of the shattered nation. Following Resolution 841's formula, the Council suspended the compulsory sanctions in late August 1993, after the U.N. Secretary–General reported that the *de facto* authorities had begun implementing the Governors Island agreement. The illusion of good-faith compliance dissolved when the *de facto* rulers orchestrated a demonstration which blocked the disembarcation of the troop ship carrying the first deployment of the peacekeeping mission. On October 13, 1993, the Security Council reimposed the suspended sanctions. S.C. Res. 873. Unfortunately, this enforcement decision did not produce the desired results, nor did a series of supplementary measures adopted pursuant to further Security Council decisions in the first half of 1994, which expanded the sanctions to cover trade and financial assets. S.C. Res. 905 (Mar. 23, 1994); S.C. Res. 917 (May 6, 1994); S.C. Res. 933 (June 30, 1994).

The sanctions took a dire toll on Haiti's desperately poor people, prompting many of them to set sail in leaky boats for the United States and other neighboring countries. On July 31, 1994, the Security Council moved toward still more decisive action—the authorization of a "multinational force under unified command and control" which was empowered:

> to use all necessary means to facilitate the departure from Haiti of the military leadership, consistent with the Governors Island Agreement, the prompt return of the legitimately elected President and the restoration of the legitimate authorities of the Government of Haiti, and to establish and maintain a secure and stable environment that will permit implementation of the Governors Island Agreement * * *.

S.C. Res. 940 (July 31, 1994). On September 19, 1994, as the initial units of this multinational force were on their way to Haiti from the United States, the *de facto* authorities finally allowed the transfer of power to the Aristide government to proceed.

NOTES

1. *Non–Forcible versus Forcible Measures.* Does the international law of the use of force require that non-forcible options be exhausted before the Security Council could authorize military force? See Damrosch, The Civilian Impact of Economic Sanctions, in Enforcing Restraint: Collective Intervention in Internal Conflicts 274, 299–301 (Damrosch ed. 1993); Damrosch, Enforcing International Law Through Non–Forcible Measures, 269 Rec. des Cours 9, 139–53 (1997).

2. *Precedent or Not?* The Security Council resolutions stress the "unique and exceptional" nature of the Haitian crisis and draw attention to its regional context. How relevant were the regional treaties such as the OAS Charter, which establish commitments to representative democracy? Do they provide grounds for limiting the Haitian "precedent" to the American region? (Note that several members of the Security Council denied that the episode could constitute a precedent for the future.) Could the OAS have authorized a military intervention? Compare Acevedo, The Haitian Crisis and the OAS Response, in Enforcing Restraint, at 119, 138–40 (Damrosch ed. 1993).

3. *Consent?* Did the Security Council need President Aristide's approval to authorize a military intervention to restore his government to power? Compare Malone, Decision–Making in the U.N. Security Council: The Case of Haiti, 1990–1997 (1998). See also Murphy, Humanitarian Intervention 260–81 (1996).

g. Former Yugoslavia

The former Socialist Federal Republic of Yugoslavia had been composed of six republics (Slovenia, Croatia, Serbia, Montenegro, Bosnia–Herzegovina, and Macedonia) with ethnic populations of Serbs, Croats, Muslims, Slovenes, Albanians, Macedonians and other groups. Negotiations among the republics in the early 1990s to achieve a loose federation of fully or semi-sovereign states failed, and further attempts to negotiate the political future and territorial integrity of the former Yugoslavia were unsuccessful. On June 25, 1991 Slovenia and Croatia declared their independence. On June 27, 1991, armed forces controlled by Serbia attacked the provisional Slovenian militia, which appealed for international assistance from the European Community (EC), the Conference on Security and Cooperation in Europe (CSCE), and the United Nations. By July 1991, Serbia had initiated hostilities in Croatia.

On September 25, 1991, the Security Council unanimously adopted Resolution 713 expressing support for the collective efforts of the EC and CSCE to bring about peace. The Council then decided under Chapter VII of the Charter "that all States shall, for the purposes of establishing peace and stability in Yugoslavia, immediately implement a general and complete embargo on all deliveries of weapons and military equipment to Yugoslavia until the Security Council decides otherwise * * *." S.C. Res. 713. The Security Council did not invoke Article 2(4) and there was no suggestion that an international act of aggression had taken place. As noted in Chapter 5, pp. 314–20, most of the former Yugoslav republics attained general international recognition in early 1992, so that what had begun as an internal conflict soon acquired transboundary character.

As ethnic fighting worsened during 1992–1993, spilling over into Bosnia–Herzegovina, U.N. action remained modest and largely ineffective. The fighting continued to worsen in Croatia and Bosnia–Herzegovina, with atrocities and "ethnic cleansing." On May 30, 1992 the Security Council tightened its embargo with respect to Serbia and Montenegro, by prohibiting the import and export of commodities to or from these states. The Council also ordered that all air links with Serbia and Montenegro be severed. S.C. Res. 757. The Council had authorized creation of a U.N. Protection Force (UNPROFOR), initially as an interposition force between the Serbian and Croatian groups that had been fighting in Croatia, as one step within the framework of negotiations for an overall settlement. S.C. Res. 743 (Feb. 21, 1992); UNPROFOR's mandate was later extended to Bosnia–Herzegovina. On October 6, 1992, the Security Council banned military flights over Bosnia–Herzegovina. S.C. Res. 781 (1992). On November 16, 1992, in order to combat wide-spread violations of the Security Council's economic sanctions, the Council decided to impose a naval blockade in the Adriatic Sea and on the Danube River. S.C. Res. 787.

On December 11, 1992, the Security Council approved a deployment of 700 U.N. personnel to the former Yugoslavian republic of Macedonia. S.C. Res. 795. This was the first time that United Nations peacekeepers had been deployed in support of "preventive diplomacy" as called for by Secretary–General Boutros–Ghali in his Agenda for Peace, U.N. Doc. A/47/277, S/24111 (June 17, 1992).

The series of Security Council resolutions adopted in 1992–1993 provided explicit legitimacy for a limited range of unilateral military activities on the part of states acting in support of the international efforts to promote peace in Yugoslavia, as well as for concerted multilateral force alongside UNPROFOR's peacekeeping objectives. These included: "all measures necessary" to ensure the delivery of humanitarian assistance, S.C. Res. 770 (Aug. 13, 1992); forcible measures of enforcement of the economic sanctions, including forcible interdiction of vessels bound to or from the Federal Republic of Yugoslavia, S.C. Res. 820 (Apr. 17, 1993); measures to enforce the no-fly zone in Bosnia–Herzegovina, through operations toward that end in Bosnian airspace, S.C. Res. 816 (Mar. 31, 1993); and the use of air power to support UNPROFOR in protecting the "safe areas" in Bosnia–Herzegovina, S.C. Res. 836 (June 4, 1993).

In late spring and summer of 1995, an escalating series of events dramatically changed the dynamics of the conflict. NATO forces, acting to protect the U.N.-designated "safe areas" in Bosnia–Herzegovina, carried out air strikes against Bosnian Serb positions. In response, the Bosnian Serbs shelled the safe areas and seized more than 300 UNPROFOR troops as hostages. On July 11, 1995, Bosnian Serbs overran the Srebrenica "safe area," trapping some 430 Dutch members of UNPROFOR. The ensuing massacre of Muslim civilians at Srebrenica (see Chapter 16, p. 1329) is said to be the worst atrocity in Europe since World War II.

In August 1995, Croatian government forces began a new offensive in the Krajina region of Croatia, displacing as many as 200,000 Serbs from the Krajina who fled into Serbia–Montenegro and Bosnia–Herzegovina. This offensive, together with renewed NATO airstrikes against the Bosnian Serb forces, motivated the Serbian side to agree to new peace talks. A cease-fire was reached on October 6, 1995, followed by several weeks of intensive peace negotiations under U.S. auspices at a military base near Dayton, Ohio. The result was the General Framework Agreement for Peace in Bosnia and Herzegovina, U.N. Doc. S/1995/999 (Nov. 30, 1995), which was initialed at Dayton and formally signed at Paris on December 14, 1995. See 35 I.L.M. 75 (1996). It was approved by the Security Council and placed on a Chapter VII footing in Resolution 1031 (Dec. 15, 1995).

The Dayton Agreement replaced UNPROFOR with a new force under NATO auspices, known as the Implementation Force or IFOR. IFOR was both substantially larger (up to 60,000 troops) and more robust in its mandate than UNPROFOR. In a scaled-down version known as the Stability Force (SFOR), the NATO force remained in Bosnia–Herzegovina until December 2004, when its functions were taken over by the European Union.

NATO's recognition as an enforcement organ of the Security Council, in the series of resolutions referred to above, was one basis for the contention that NATO had implicit authority to use force against the Federal Republic of Yugoslavia in the Kosovo crisis of spring 1999. See pp. 1206–12 and note 4 below.

NOTES

1. *Further Reading.* See generally Weller, The International Response to the Dissolution of the Socialist Federal Republic of Yugoslavia, 86 A.J.I.L. 569 (1992); Steinberg, International Involvement in the Yugoslavia Conflict, in Enforcing Restraint: Collective Intervention in Internal Conflicts 27–75 (Damrosch ed. 1993); Murphy, Humanitarian Intervention: The United Nations in an Evolving World Order 198–217 (1996); The World and Yugoslavia's Wars (Ullman ed. 1996). On the negotiations for the Dayton Agreement, see Holbrooke, To End a War (1998). For references on the Kosovo conflict, see p. 1209.

2. *Srebrenica Massacre.* A U.N. report on the fall of Srebrenica contains pointed criticisms of U.N. actions leading up to the disaster. In language cited and approved by the inquiry on Rwanda (p. 1237 above), the report concluded that "a deliberate and systematic attempt to terrorize, expel or murder an entire people must be met decisively with all necessary means, and with the political will to carry the policy through to its logical conclusion." Report of the Secretary–General Pursuant to General Assembly Resolution 53/55 (1998), U.N. Doc. A/54/549, sec. 502 (Nov. 15, 1999).

3. *Impartiality in the Face of Evil?* In a document known as the "Brahimi Report" (formally, the Comprehensive Review of the Whole Question of Peacekeeping Operations in All Their Aspects), U.N. Doc. A/55/305, S/2000/809 (Aug. 21, 2000), a panel chaired by the former foreign minister of Algeria made recommendations aimed at improving the U.N.'s capacity to respond to complex situations. A key paragraph addresses the need to rethink the rationale for certain of the hallmarks of "classical" peacekeeping (at ix; see also at 9, para. 50):

> The Panel concurs that consent of the local parties, impartiality and the use of force only in self-defence should remain the bedrock principles of peacekeeping. Experience shows, however, that in the context of intra-State/transnational conflicts, consent may be manipulated in many ways. Impartiality for United Nations operations must therefore mean adherence to the principles of the Charter: where one party to a peace agreement clearly and incontrovertibly is violating its terms, continued equal treatment of all parties by the United Nations can in the best case result in ineffectiveness and in the worst may amount to complicity with evil. No failure did more to damage the standing and credibility of United Nations peacekeeping in the 1990s than its reluctance to distinguish victim from aggressor.

On follow-through to the Brahimi Report, see Security Council Res. 1327 (Nov. 13, 2000) ("On the Implementation of the Report of the Panel on United Nations Peace Operations").

4. *Kosovo.* As indicated at pp. 1207–09, the Security Council did not adopt a resolution explicitly authorizing "all necessary means" to enforce its

previous resolutions with respect to Kosovo. Cf. S.C. Res. 1160 (March 31, 1998); S.C. Res. 1199 (Sept. 23, 1998); S.C. Res. 1203 (Oct. 24, 1998) (on arms embargo; deployment of Kosovo Verification Mission). Indeed, the language of those resolutions was crafted in awareness that Russia and China would not have approved use of force and were prepared to use their veto accordingly. Nonetheless, some governments and scholars have contended that those resolutions could be understood to convey implicit authority for use of force. See Murphy, Contemporary Practice of the United States Relating to International Law, 93 A.J.I.L. 628, 631–32 (1999). For commentary supportive of this line of argument, see, e.g., Wedgwood, NATO's Campaign in Kosovo, 93 A.J.I.L. 835–37 (1999). Others have found implicit Security Council approval in the decisive rejection (by 3–12 vote) of Russia's draft resolution to condemn NATO's action. Some believe that the Council, in Resolution 1244 adopted at the end of the conflict (June 10, 1999), in effect retroactively validated the operation. See Henkin, Kosovo and the Law of "Humanitarian Intervention," 93 A.J.I.L. 824 (1999).

By contrast, other commentators see great difficulties with the argument for implicit authority derived from resolutions that not only do not specify authority for military action, but in context reflect an intent to approve non-forcible rather than forcible means. They observe that such a line of reasoning could have the detrimental effect of making permanent members less willing to approve non-forcible measures in the first place. On this point, see Independent International Commission, Kosovo Report, Chapter 6 (2000).

Could NATO have asked the General Assembly to authorize the Kosovo intervention, possibly by invoking the "Uniting for Peace" Resolution, p. 1229? On this question, the Independent Commission observed:

> the NATO states chose not to utilize the residual role of the General Assembly under the Uniting for Peace Resolution, because, even though there is no veto in the General Assembly, the sensitivity of non-Western states to interventionary claims of any sort made it unlikely that an authorization of force would have been endorsed by the required two-thirds majority.

Under the framework established by Resolution 1244 (1999), security and other public functions have been carried out in Kosovo by means of an overlapping set of international arrangements, one of which is an "international security presence with substantial North Atlantic Treaty Organization participation" (S.C. Res. 1244, annex, para. 4). This force, known as KFOR, remains in Kosovo as of early 2009, with a troop strength of approximately 14,000 (at its peak, 47,000 troops were deployed). Alongside KFOR, a significant U.N. peacekeeping operation known as UNMIK served for a decade as the interim administration in Kosovo. Following Kosovo's declaration of independence in February 2008 (see Chapter 5, p. 320), UNMIK adjusted its functions (many of which were to be assumed by a European Union rule-of-law mission known as EULEX) and reduced its size. See generally de Wet, The Governance of Kosovo: Security Council Resolution 1244 and the Establishment and Functioning of EULEX, 103 A.J.I.L. 83 (2009).

h. African Conflicts

As the chart on pp. 1245–46 indicates, the most substantial U.N. peacekeeping commitments as of early 2009 are in Africa, with major operations in place in the Democratic Republic of the Congo, Liberia, Côte d'Ivoire, Sudan/Darfur, and the Central African Republic and Chad. In addition, previous African operations involving Sierra Leone and Ethiopia–Eritrea have now been wrapped up. (In the case of the U.N. Mission in Ethiopia and Eritrea (UNMEE), the Security Council terminated its mandate in Resolution 1827 (2008) because of restrictions imposed by Eritrea on its operations, which made it impossible for it to carry out its tasks.)

In several of the African conflicts, the U.N. efforts have been undertaken in conjunction with African regional or subregional organizations. Illustrations will be given in the next subsection.

B. REGIONAL ORGANIZATIONS

CHARTER OF THE UNITED NATIONS

Signed at San Francisco, June 26, 1945

CHAPTER VIII. REGIONAL ARRANGEMENTS

Article 52

1. Nothing in the present Charter precludes the existence of regional arrangements or agencies for dealing with such matters relating to the maintenance of international peace and security as are appropriate for regional action, provided that such arrangements or agencies and their activities are consistent with the Purposes and Principles of the United Nations.

2. The Members of the United Nations entering into such arrangements or constituting such agencies shall make every effort to achieve pacific settlement of local disputes through such regional arrangements or by such regional agencies before referring them to the Security Council.

3. The Security Council shall encourage the development of pacific settlement of local disputes through such regional arrangements or by such regional agencies either on the initiative of the states concerned or by reference from the Security Council.

* * *

Article 53

1. The Security Council shall, where appropriate, utilize such regional arrangements or agencies for enforcement action under its authority. But no enforcement action shall be taken under regional arrangements or by regional agencies without the authorization of the Security Council * * * provided for pursuant to Article 107 or in regional arrangements directed against renewal of aggressive policy on the part of any such state, until such time as the Organization may, on request of the Governments

concerned, be charged with the responsibility for preventing further aggression by such a state.

SCHACHTER, AUTHORIZED USES OF FORCE BY THE UNITED NATIONS AND REGIONAL ORGANIZATIONS

Law and Force in the New International Order, 65, 86–88
(Damrosch & Scheffer eds. 1991) (footnotes omitted)

The U.N. Charter recognizes in its Chapter VIII that regional arrangements and agencies are appropriate means for maintaining peace and security, provided that their activities are consistent with the purposes and principles of the Charter. Indeed, Article 52 of the Charter requires states to make every effort to achieve peaceful settlement of "local disputes" through regional arrangements or agencies before referring such disputes to the U.N. Security Council. The idea that disputes and threats to the peace involving states within a region should preferably be dealt with primarily by regional bodies has been an early and persistent influence. At San Francisco the Security Council was perceived as a forum of last resort when states were unable to resolve conflicts between them through the peaceful means listed in Chapter VI or through regional instrumentalities.

The Charter in Article 53 expressly directs the Security Council to utilize the regional arrangements or agencies covered by Chapter VIII for enforcement action where appropriate. The regional bodies are indirectly authorized to undertake enforcement action inasmuch as Article 53 states that they may not do so without the authorization of the Security Council. Thus the failure of the Council to grant permission for enforcement action would bar such action. A permanent member could therefore prevent enforcement action by a regional organization. Cases have come before the Security Council involving decisions of the Organization of American States (OAS) to apply diplomatic and economic measures that were in the nature of sanctions as envisaged in Article 41 of the U.N. Charter. In these cases, the Council did not decide that those measures were covered by Article 53. The majority of members maintained that such non-forcible coercive measures were within the competence of individual states. Since states were free to sever trade or diplomatic relations, they could do so by concerted action under the aegis of a regional organization. The reasoning is not wholly compelling since concerted action by a regional body to impose sanctions of the kind contemplated in Chapter VII (Article 41) would appear to be within the meaning of enforcement action in Article 53.

* * *

Apart from collective self-defense, regional organizations may institute peacekeeping operations that do not involve coercive measures against a state. This has been done in a number of cases. However, it has not always been agreed that the regional peacekeeping operation has actually received the consent of the territorial sovereign. Questions of this kind have come up where it was uncertain who, if anyone, may legitimately grant such consent in the absence of effective and recognized governmental authority. This emerged as a problem when U.S. forces together with troops from several Caribbean countries intervened in Grenada, claiming *inter alia* that they had been authorized to do so by a regional body (the Organization of Eastern Caribbean States) to bring peace and order to a country in a condition of anarchy. The General Assembly condemned the intervention as a violation of the Charter. However, there was no international criticism of a regional peacekeeping force of West African states that sought to bring an end to a bloody internal conflict in Liberia in 1990. This was clearly not an enforcement action or collective defense, nor was there an invitation from a government enjoying international recognition. A case of this kind would suggest an interpretation of peacekeeping by regional bodies that allows for a collective military intervention to help end an internal conflict when a government has been deposed or no longer has effective authority.

1.   The Inter–American System

The Inter–American system of collective security includes two principal international agreements: the 1947 Inter–American Treaty of Reciprocal Assistance (The Rio Treaty), Sept. 2, 1947, 62 Stat. 1681, 21 U.N.T.S. 77, and the Charter of the Organization of American States (OAS Charter), Apr. 30, 1948, 2 U.S.T. 2394, 119 U.N.T.S. 3. See in particular Articles 1, 3, 6, 8 & 9 of the Rio Treaty, and Articles 14–19, 24 & 25 of the OAS Charter. Also relevant are the 1933 Convention on the Rights and Duties of States (the Montevideo Convention) and the 1926 Convention for the Maintenance, Preservation, and Reestablishment of Peace. See 1 Garcia–Amador, The Inter–American System: Treaties, Conventions & Other Documents, pt. 2, at 261–326 (1983).

The Rio Treaty was an outgrowth of the Act of Chapultepec (Resolution on "Reciprocal Assistance and American Solidarity"), Mar. 8, 1945, T.I.A.S. No. 1543 (1945). The Act contained a provision recognizing that aggression or the threat of aggression would warrant consultation among the American Republics with a view to collective measures of defense. The Charter of the Organization of American States entered into force for the United States on December 13, 1951. As of 2009, there were thirty-five member states in the Organization.

Notes

1.   *Relationship with the United Nations.* A former legal adviser of the State Department described the relation as follows, in relation to an operation in the Dominican Republic:

> The appropriate relationship between the United Nations and regional organizations such as this one, the OAS, can be summarized in terms I think of six principles.

One, the members of the United Nations pursuant to articles 33 and 52 of the charter should seek to deal with threats to the peace within a geographical region through regional arrangements before coming to the United Nations. This is precisely what the members of the OAS have done in the Dominican case.

Second, regional organizations should not of course take enforcement action without the authorization of the Security Council. But in the Dominican Republic the Organization of American States did not take the kind of action that would require Security Council approval.

Third, action taken by regional organizations must be consistent with the purposes and principles of the United Nations. This is obviously the case with the actions of the OAS in the Dominican Republic case.

Fourth, the Security Council should at all times be kept fully informed of actions undertaken by regional organizations. The OAS is keeping the Security Council fully informed; witness the report you have just had from Dr. Mora through Mr. Mayobre this afternoon. And the Council has also arranged to keep itself informed through a representative of the Secretary–General.

Fifth, the Security Council has the competence to deal with any situation which might threaten international peace and security. This competence is not at issue here.

But sixth, the Security Council should not seek to duplicate or interfere with action through regional arrangements so long as those actions remain effective and are consistent with our charter. The purposes of the United Nations Charter will hardly be served if two international organizations are seeking to do things in the same place with the same people at the same time.

As a matter of sound practice and the wise use of discretion, the Security Council under present conditions should keep itself fully informed but not undertake any activity, either diplomatic or on the ground, which would hinder the efforts and the responsibilities of the competent organization. It will serve the purposes of the United Nations Charter best if the OAS achieves what it has set out to accomplish, and that is to restore peace and achieve reconciliation so that the Dominican people can develop their own democratic institutions.

Stevenson, Principles of U.N.–OAS Relationship in the Dominican Republic, 52 Dep't St. Bull. 975, 976–77 (1965). See also Scheffer, Commentary on Collective Security, in Law and Force in the New International Order 101, 107–08 (Damrosch & Scheffer eds. 1991).

2. *OAS Approval of Cuban Quarantine.* Meeker suggests that the Cuban quarantine of 1962 was justified under the Charter as an action taken by a "regional organization":

It is clear that collective action for peace and security which the Security Council may take under Chapter VII does not contravene Article 2, paragraph 4. It is also clear that individual or collective self-defense against armed attack, in accordance with Article 51, does not violate the Charter. Here it may be noted that the United States, in adopting the defensive quarantine of Cuba, did not seek to justify it as a measure required to meet an "armed attack" within the meaning of Article 51. Nor did the United States seek to sustain its action on the ground that Article 51 is not an all-inclusive statement of the right of self-defense and that the quarantine was a measure of self-defense open to any country to take individually for its own defense in a case other than "armed attack." Indeed, as shown by President Kennedy's television address of October 22 and by other statements of the Government, reliance was not placed on either contention, and the United States took no position on either of these issues.

> The quarantine was based on a collective judgment and recommendation of the American Republics made under the Rio Treaty. It was considered not to contravene Article 2, paragraph 4, because it was a measure adopted by a regional organization in conformity with the provisions of Chapter VIII of the Charter. The purposes of the Organization and its activities were considered to be consistent with the purposes and principles of the United Nations as provided in Article 52. This being the case, the quarantine would no more violate Article 2, paragraph 4, than measures voted by the Council under Chapter VII, by the General Assembly under Articles 10 and 11, or taken by United Nations Members in conformity with Article 51.

Meeker, Defensive Quarantine and the Law, 57 A.J.I.L. 523, 524 (1963).

For other expressions of this argument in support of the United States action, see Chayes, The Legal Case for U.S. Action in Cuba, 47 Dept. St. Bull. 763 (1962); Chayes, The Cuban Missile Crisis (1974). Henkin expressed doubts about this justification. See Comment, in Chayes, The Cuban Missile Crisis 150–53 (1974); see also How Nations Behave 291–92 (2d ed. 1979).

3. *Subregional Organization.* The 1983 U.S. intervention in Grenada was said to be in response to a request for help from a group of Caribbean states called the Organization of Eastern Caribbean States (OECS). Is this group a regional organization within Article 52? Was the invasion of Grenada in 1983 by the United States and several Caribbean states a lawful "regional action" under the U.N. Charter? John Norton Moore argues:

> The Grenada mission by the OECS countries and Barbados, Jamaica and the United States is a paradigm of a lawful regional peacekeeping action under Article 52. It was undertaken in a context of civil strife and breakdown of government following the brutal murder of Maurice Bishop and members of his cabinet in an attempted coup. It was in response to a request for assistance in restoring human rights and self-determination from the only constitutional authority on the island, Governor–General Sir Paul Scoon. * * *

> Jointly requested or participated in by almost one-third of the membership of the Organization of American States, the Grenada mission is also consistent with the OAS Charter. * * * Articles 22 and 28 of the OAS Charter make clear that regional peacekeeping or defensive actions in accordance with special regional treaties do not violate the noninterventionist provisions. * * *

Moore, Grenada and the International Double Standard, 78 A.J.I.L. 145, 154–59 (1984) (footnotes omitted).

Christopher Joyner disagrees:

Several reasons rebut the use of [the OECS] Treaty to legitimize U.S. intervention in Grenada. First, the United States is not a party to the Treaty and therefore legally lies outside the ambit of its concerns. (Interestingly enough, neither are Barbados and Jamaica, which also participated in the invasion.) Second, Article 8 specifically deals with "collective defence and the preservation of peace and security against external aggression." No external aggressor existed: Grenada, the state in question, was a Treaty member. In addition, the OECS Treaty makes no mention of any collective security or defensive measures to be taken against a member of the organization, should such an occasion arise. There is, in short, no provision for military action in instances other than those involving "external aggression, including mercenary aggression," and such a case was absent in the October 1983 Grenada episode.

Joyner, Reflections on the Lawfulness of Invasion, 78 A.J.I.L. 131, 135–37, 142 (1984) (footnotes omitted). See also the editorial comment, Vagts, International Law Under Time Pressure, 78 A.J.I.L. 169 (1984), and the communication by Boyle et al., International Lawlessness—Grenada, 78 A.J.I.L. 172 (1984).

4. *Haiti and Dominican Republic.* On October 3, 1991, in response to the overthrow of the President of Haiti by military coup, the OAS unanimously recommended that its member states take "action to bring about the diplomatic isolation of those who hold power illegally in Haiti" and "suspend their economic, financial, and commercial ties * * * "OAS Doc. OEA/Ser. F/V.1/MRE/ RES. 1/91, corr. 1, paras. 5, 6 (1991). The trade embargo was strengthened on May 17, 1992. OAS Doc. OEA/Ser. F/V.1/MRE/RES.3/92 (1992), reprinted in 86 A.J.I.L. 667 (1992). As discussed above (p. ___), these measures were insufficient to end the crisis, and the U.N. Security Council authorized a military intervention in 1994. Some experts on the OAS consider it doubtful that the OAS could itself have authorized use of military force in the context of a strictly domestic political crisis. See Acevedo, The Haitian Crisis and the OAS Response, in Enforcing Restraint: Collective Intervention in Internal Conflicts 119, 138–40 (Damrosch ed., 1993).

However, in the Dominican Republic crisis, the OAS had adopted the following resolution on May 6, 1965:

1. To request governments of member states that are willing and capable of doing so to make contingents of their land, naval, air or police forces available to the Organization of American States, within their capabilities, and to the extent that they can do so, to form an inter-American force that will operate under the authority of this Tenth Meeting of Consultation.

2. That this Force will have as its sole purpose, in a spirit of democratic impartiality, that of cooperating in the restoration of normal conditions in the Dominican Republic, in maintaining the security of its inhabitants and the inviolability of human rights, and in the establish-

> mont of an atmosphere of peace and conciliation that will permit the
> functioning of democratic institutions.

4 I.L.M. 594 (1965), 59 A.J.I.L. 986 (1965), 52 Dep't St. Bull. 862 (1965). Argentina, Bolivia, Brazil, Colombia, Costa Rica, Dominican Republic, El Salvador, Guatemala, Haiti, Honduras, Nicaragua, Panama, Paraguay, and the United States voted for the resolution. Chile, Ecuador, Mexico, Peru, and Uruguay voted against it, and Venezuela abstained.

5. *Further Reading.* On the OAS generally, see Thomas & Thomas, The Organization of American States (1963); Levin, The Organization of American States and the United Nations: Relations in the Peace and Security Field (1974); Lima, Intervention in International Law with Reference to the Organization of American States (1971); The Inter–American System: Treaties, Conventions and Other Documents: A Compilation (1983); The Organization of American States and International Law, 80 A.S.I.L. Proc. 1 (1986); cf., Acevedo, The Right of Members of the Organization of American States to Refer Their "Local Disputes Directly to the United Nations Security Council," 4 Am. U. J. Int'l L. & Pol'y 25 (1989); Caminos & Lavalie, New Departures in the Exercise of Inherent Powers by the UN and OAS Secretaries–General: The Central American Situation, 83 A.J.I.L. 395 (1989).

2.   African Union (AU)

The African Union came into existence in 2002 as the successor to the former Organization of African Unity (OAU). The Charter of the OAU, May 25, 1963, 479 U.N.T.S. 39, had provided in Article 2 that the promotion of the unity and solidarity of the African states and the defense of the sovereignty, territorial integrity, and independence of these states shall be among the purposes of the Organization. The states agreed to coordinate and harmonize their policies in several fields, among which was "defense and security." Article 3 set forth the following principles:

1.   the sovereign equality of all Member States;

2.   non-interference in the internal affairs of States;

3.   respect for the sovereignty and territorial integrity of each State and for its inalienable right to independent existence;

4.   peaceful settlement of disputes by negotiation, mediation, conciliation or arbitration;

5.   unreserved condemnation, in all its forms, of political assassination as well as of subversive activities on the part of neighboring States or any other State; * * *

These principles may be compared to the Constitutive Act of the African Union, July 11, 2000 (in Documents Supplement), which contains remarkable changes in the direction of greater protection for the peoples of African states. Of special note is the new provision in Article 4(h) of the AU Constitutive Act, which provides for "[t]he right of the Union to intervene in a Member State pursuant to a decision of the Assembly in respect of grave circumstances, namely war crimes, genocide and crimes against humanity."

During its almost four decades of existence, the OAU had some opportunity to play a role in peacekeeping, beginning with a 1963 border dispute between Algeria and Morocco over mineral-rich land, which flared up following Algerian independence in July 1962. By October 1963 small skirmishes had yielded to military occupation of border towns and a general mobilization in Algeria. First attempts to arrange a cease-fire were not successful. The parties were induced, however, to seek an all-African rather than a United Nations settlement as the result of a meeting arranged in Mali by Emperor Haile Selassie and President Modibo Keita. An extraordinary session of the OAU was convened, at which the Council of Ministers appointed an *ad hoc* commission and charged it with the tasks of ascertaining responsibility for the hostilities and of recommending a settlement. The commission met in Mali and in the Ivory Coast, receiving documents from both sides. On February 20, 1964, the two governments announced that an agreement had been reached. Withdrawal of forces was to take place, and a demilitarized zone was to be established. In April, prisoners were exchanged. The two states had reestablished diplomatic relations by May 1965, and the respective heads of state had met at the border.

The OAU was less successful in dealing with subsequent problems. It did not play an effective role in the dispute over the Western Sahara, in efforts to curtail the atrocities of the Idi Amin regime in Uganda, or in resolving the long Rhodesian crisis before the creation of the State of Zimbabwe. Nor did the OAU play a role in the civil war in Chad. Peacekeeping troops were sent by individual African states.

The African Union, by contrast, has been striving since its establishment to contribute constructively to the resolution of African conflicts. The most significant initiative has been the AU's contribution to peacekeeping in Darfur (Sudan), initially through a force known as the African Union Mission in Sudan (AMIS), which was transformed as of December 31, 2007 to a hybrid force known as UNAMID–AU–U.N. Hybrid Operation in Darfur. As of early 2009, UNAMID was seeking to achieve its authorized strength of 19,555 military personnel and was struggling in dire circumstances to help quell the violence in that intractable conflict.

NOTES

1. *Moral Support.* In 1992, the OAU welcomed the United Nations military presence in Somalia to establish a secure environment for the distribution of relief aid but the Organization did not contribute to the military forces. By contrast, in 2009 an African Union Mission to Somalia (AMISOM) was in place there and had been authorized by the U.N. Security Council to provide security. See S.C. Resolution 1772 (2007) and S.C. Resolution 1863 (2009).

In 1990, the OAU endorsed the peacekeeping efforts of the Economic Community of West African States (ECOWAS) in Liberia. On ECOWAS as a subregional organization and its role in African peacekeeping, see p. 1274.

2. *Further Reading.* On the OAU generally, see Documents of the Organization of African Unity (Naldi ed. 1992); The Organization of African Unity, 1963–1988 (Akindele ed. 1988); Andemicael, The OAU and the UN: Relations Between the Organization of African Unity and the United Nations (1976); El Ayouty, The OAU After 10 Years: Comparative Perspectives (1975); Naldi, Peacekeeping Attempts by the Organization of African Unity, 34 I.C.L.Q. 593 (1985); Ramphul, The Role of International and Regional Organizations in the Peaceful Settlement of Internal Disputes (With Special Emphasis on the Organization of African Unity), 13 Georgia J. Int'l & Comp. L. 371 (1983); M'Baye & Ndiaye, The Organization of African Unity, in The International Dimensions of Human Rights (Vasak ed. 1982). On the African Union, see materials on its website at http://www.africa-union.org.

3. Other Regional and Subregional Bodies

a. *The Arab League*

The Arab League is a regional, political organisation of comprehensive aims. * * *

* * *

Under Article V [of the League Pact] the League Members renounce recourse to force to resolve disputes between them and, whilst they do not accept the jurisdiction of the Council of the League to mediate or arbitrate as compulsory over such disputes, if they do have recourse to the Council its decision is binding. In practice the League Council has used the more informal processes of conciliation on many occasions in dealing with inter-regional disputes, without any formal acceptance of the Council's jurisdiction under Article V. Indeed, in the Kuwait crisis in 1961, the Council established an Inter–Arab Force as a "peace-keeping" operation in view of the dispute between Kuwait and Iraq. The Council did the same in June 1976 in Lebanon.

Under Article VI each Member has a right to summon the Council immediately in the event of aggression, whether by another League Member or an outside State. The Council may then, by unanimous vote (excepting the aggressor State), decide upon measures to check the aggression. This collective security function is further specified in a separate collective security pact, based upon Article 51 of the UN Charter and on the notion that aggression against any League Member is aggression against all; the pact entered into force on August 23, 1952, and established a Permanent Joint Defence Council and Permanent Military Commission. On the occasion of the Anglo–French aggression against Egypt in 1956, involving the landing of troops in Suez, the collective security machinery failed to bring assistance to Egypt. Prior to the Arab/Israeli war of June 1967, Egypt, Jordan and the PLA (Palestine Liberation Army) instituted a joint military command, although it is clear that no integration of armed forces comparable to that which has occurred in NATO and the Warsaw Pact has yet happened.

Bowett, The Law of International Institutions 229–31 (4th ed. 1982) (footnote omitted).

During the early days of the 1990 Persian Gulf crisis, the Arab League, in a bitterly divided vote, urged its members to participate in the military deployment approved by the Security Council to protect Saudi Arabia and other Arab states against Iraqi aggression. On the Arab League generally, see Pogany, The Arab League and Peacemaking in Lebanon (1987); Pogany, The League of Arab States: An Overview, 21 Bracton L.J. 41 (1989). For earlier works see Hassouna, League of Arab States and Regional Disputes (1975); MacDonald, League of Arab States (1965); Khalil, The Arab States and the Arab League (1962) (2 vols).

b.   Association of South–East Asian Nations (ASEAN)

ASEAN is an organization comprised of rapidly developing nations in Southeast Asia; it includes Brunei, Cambodia, Indonesia, Laos, Malaysia, Myanmar (Burma), the Philippines, Singapore, Thailand, and Vietnam. The 1967 Bangkok Declaration that brought the organization into existence declared that ASEAN was designed to improve the economic well-being of its members, but ASEAN has also a regional security component. The 1969 declaration provided that one of the purposes of the Association is to "promote regional peace and stability." It has been noted that all the members face threats from internal insurgency movements supported by external assistance and fear the power of Mainland China and Japan. See Krause, U.S. Economic Policy Toward ASEAN 5–6 (1982). See also Unger, ASEAN, in Negotiating World Order: The Artisanship and Architecture of Global Diplomacy, chap. 11 (1986).

Does either the Arab League or ASEAN qualify as a regional organizations within the meaning of Article 52? Compare generally Bowett, The Law of International Institutions 229 (4th ed. 1982), with Goodrich, Hambro & Simons, Charter of the United Nations 351 (3d ed. 1969).

c.   Economic Community of West African States (ECOWAS)

The Economic Community of West African States, as the name implies, was established largely to promote the economic well-being of the states in its subregion. However, it took an active part in attempting to stabilize the chaotic situations in Liberia in the 1990s, and later in Sierra Leone, in the absence of any other institution willing to carry out peacekeeping there. Although the U.N. Security Council did not explicitly authorize ECOWAS to take "enforcement action" in Liberia under Article 53 of the Charter, approval could arguably be inferred from certain resolutions and statements issued by or on behalf of the Council. See Wippman, Enforcing the Peace: ECOWAS and the Liberian Civil War, in

Enforcing Restraint: Collective Intervention in Internal Conflicts 157, 184–87 (Damrosch ed. 1993).

On the role of ECOWAS in Sierra Leone, see S.C. Res. 1132, para 8 (Oct. 8, 1997), which refers to Chapter VIII of the Charter in authorizing ECOWAS to carry out implementing action.

4. NATO: New Tasks for a Collective Self–Defense Arrangement

During the decades of the Cold War, groups of states established organizations principally for collective self-defense, but some had additional cooperative purposes. The most important politically was the North Atlantic Treaty Organization (NATO); the Communist bloc responded by establishing the Warsaw Pact (now defunct). In other parts of the world groups of states established the Southeast Asia Treaty Organization (SEATO), the Central Treaty Organization (CENTO), and the ANZUS Council. Some of these organizations withered early; others lost their raison d'être with the end of the Cold War. NATO, however, metamorphosed in the 1990s from a defense alliance against the Soviet threat to an organ of enforcement, acting under U.N. authority to enforce Security Council resolutions in Bosnia–Herzegovina and to police the agreements reached at Dayton. In the Kosovo crisis of 1999, NATO claimed authority to act even without an explicit U.N. mandate, partly on the basis of inference from previous U.N. actions, but more generally to maintain security and advance humanitarian objectives in the European region.

The North Atlantic Treaty was signed in Washington on April 4, 1949, 63 Stat. 2241, T.I.A.S. No. 1964, 34 U.N.T.S. 243, and entered into force on August 24, 1949. The original parties were Belgium, Canada, Denmark, France, Iceland, Italy, Luxembourg, the Netherlands, Norway, Portugal, the United Kingdom, and the United States. Greece and Turkey acceded in 1951, 3 U.S.T. 43, 126 U.N.T.S. 350, and the Federal Republic of Germany in 1955, 6 U.S.T. 5707, 243 U.N.T.S. 308. France withdrew its military contingents from the NATO commands in 1966, but continued to be a member of NATO. (As of early 2009, France was preparing to return to NATO's military structure.) Further decisions extended NATO membership to Spain (1982); the Czech Republic, Hungary, and Poland (1999); Bulgaria, Estonia, Latvia, Lithuania, Romania, Slovakia, and Slovenia (2004); and Albania and Croatia (effective April 1, 2009).

The Treaty does not obligate a member to come to the aid of any other member when an armed attack occurs. A member need take only "such action as it deems necessary" to restore and maintain the security of the North Atlantic area (Article 5). The treaty also recognizes that each state's response must be in accord with its own constitutional processes (Article 11). Unified commands (Supreme Allied Commander in Europe and Supreme Commander for the North Atlantic) were formed with regional planning groups. Within the system of cooperation developed, there has been a substantial measure of integration. While there is no legal obstacle to a member state's withdrawing its forces from NATO commitments, in practice such withdrawal is difficult. Nevertheless, the absence of a legal obligation to come to a member state's defense kept alive concern about U.S. response in case of an armed attack in Europe.

1. *Further Reading.* On NATO generally, see Stromseth, The North Atlantic Treaty and European Security after the Cold War, 24 Cornell Int'l L.J. 479 (1991). For earlier analysis, see Stein & Hay, Law and Institutions in the Atlantic Area, 1031–1108 (1967). For current as well as historical resources, see NATO website at www.nato.int.

2. *Fish or Fowl?* Standard treatises on international law and organization have traditionally treated NATO not as a regional organization under Chapter VIII of the U.N. Charter but as a defense alliance. Indeed, NATO did not typically act as a regional arrangement under Security Council authority within the meaning of Articles 52–54 (e.g., by making the kinds of reports expected under Article 54). Do the developments in former Yugoslavia suggest that NATO has become, in effect, a regional arrangement in Chapter VIII's terms? Or is it *sui generis?*

SECTION 4. THE LAW OF WAR AND THE CONTROL OF WEAPONS

A. THE LAWS OF WAR: INTERNATIONAL HUMANITARIAN LAW

The traditional rules of war addressed three subjects: the definition of war; the conduct of war (regulation of weapons, treatment of prisoners and injured participants, treatment of enemy nationals and their property, treatment of the populations of occupied territories, and protection for nonmilitary ships); and the relations between neutral states and belligerent states. Although war and acts of war, *per se,* were not unlawful, deviations from the laws of war (the *jus in bello*) were violations of international law. The adoption of the U.N. Charter and its provisions outlawing the use of force cast doubt on whether the state of war has remained part of international law and raised questions about the continued validity of conceptions of belligerency and neutrality. See p. 1151 above. However, there has been universal agreement that "humanitarian law"—governing the conduct of war—remains part of international law and is applicable in hostilities, lawful or unlawful under the Charter, and to both attackers and defenders against attack.

In describing the content of the laws of war one must consider the rationale of each rule, since the weapons and conditions addressed in the nineteenth and twentieth centuries have markedly changed. The originators could not foresee the sophisticated lethal and non-lethal technologies of the twenty-first century. However, old norms, interpreted in light of the values they were designed to promote, may be applicable to modern

wartare. Guerrilla wars, undeclared wars, and ethnic conflicts raise perti
nent issues under these bodies of law as well. Indeed, rules which were not
scrupulously observed in the total wars of the twentieth century may find
application in today's more limited conflicts.

The interaction between the customary international law of war and
formally codified treaties has been complex. Much of the law of war was
codified at the Hague Peace Conferences of 1899 and 1907, then strengthened after the World Wars—notably through the four Geneva Conventions
of 1949 (cited and discussed at p. 1283)—and in 1977 with two additional
protocols to the 1949 Geneva Conventions. These treaties have all received
widespread multilateral adherence, and in most aspects—with some notable qualifications—they reflect contemporary customary international law.
As of 2009, there were 194 parties to the four 1949 Conventions (including
all U.N. member states, as well as the Holy See), making them among the
most widely-ratified international treaties. The 1977 additional protocols
have also received impressive (although not universal) international support, with 168 parties to Protocol I and 164 to Protocol II as of 2009.
Although the United States had not ratified either of the 1977 protocols as
of 2009, it does view many of their articles as reflecting customary
international law or acceptable practice.

Increasingly sophisticated weaponry, as seen in the Iraq war of 1991,
the Kosovo conflict of 1999, in Afghanistan since 2001 and the renewed
Iraq conflict since 2003, has placed new demands on the laws of war. How
do the rules apply in the era of so-called "smart bombs"? Are the
distinctions between military and civilian targets meaningful? Can they be
articulated with greater precision for stronger protection of civilians? Will
they be observed? Can the "revolution in military affairs" and the
"information warfare" of the computer age be addressed under the
existing laws of war, or will new instruments be necessary?

NOTE

On the evolution of the laws of war from the 1899 Hague Conference
through the end of the twentieth century, see the Symposium: The Hague
Peace Conferences, 94 A.J.I.L. 1 (2000) (essays by Aldrich, Chinkin, Caron,
Vagts, Roach and Meron). On the customary status of the laws of war and
their interaction with treaty norms, see generally Meron, Human Rights and
Humanitarian Norms as Customary Law (1989); Meron, The Continuing Role
of Custom in the Formation of International Humanitarian Law, 90 A.J.I.L.
238 (1996). For the U.S. position on aspects of unratified treaties that are
considered customary law, see U.S. Army, Operational Law Handbook 2007,
Chapter 5. On the issues dissuading the United States and other states from
ratification of Protocols I and II, see p. 1287 note 7.

1. Regulation of Weapons

a. General Principles

Classic conceptions of the use of weapons in war began with the
proposition that the amount of force required to overpower the enemy

may be used, but kinds and degrees of force that were not necessary for that military purpose were restricted by humanitarian principles. Nineteenth- and twentieth-century agreements to limit the use of weapons focused on four types: (1) bullets; (2) poisons and poisoned weapons; (3) gases; and (4) aerial bombardment. These sought to limit the introduction of new techniques that appeared to be particularly destructive or inhumane. Generally, international agreements (such as the 1868 Declaration of St. Petersburg) attempted to eliminate weapons that cause unnecessary suffering. For example, mustard gas incapacitated soldiers but also burned flesh and internal organs; the dum-dum bullet expanded on impact, tearing great wounds in its victims. For the earliest treaty regulating bullets, see Declaration Renouncing the Use, in Time of War, of Explosive Projectiles under 400 Grammes Weight, Dec. 11, 1868, Hertslet, Treaties and Conventions between Great Britain and Foreign Powers 79 (1877). See also Declaration Respecting Expanding Bullets, July 29, 1899, [1907] Gr. Brit. T.S. No. 32; The Hague Conventions and Declarations of 1899 and 1907, at 227 (3d ed. Scott ed. 1918).

Concentrated aerial bombardment, introduced by Germany during the First World War and condemned by the Allies as inhumane, became the accepted practice of both sides during World War II. For an early but unsuccessful attempt to regulate aerial bombardment, see Declaration Prohibiting the Discharge of Projectiles and Explosives from Balloons, Oct. 18, 1907, 36 Stat. 2439, T.S. No. 546. The use of incendiary and explosive shells and bombs was another hazard that developed along with air power. Though they were widely condemned when used, attempts to eliminate them (and later, flamethrowers, fire and napalm) failed. Efforts to eliminate concentration bombing as practiced in World War II did not succeed at the time, and controversy about the applicability of legal constraints to strategic bombardment of populated areas continued through the era of the Vietnam war. Compare Spaight, Air Power and War Rights 259–95 (3d ed. 1947); Stone, Legal Controls of Armed Conflict 629–31 (3d. rev. ed. 1959); Bush, Review Essay, Nuremberg: The Modern Law of War and Its Limitations, 93 Colum. L. Rev. 2022, 2032 n. 34, 2085 (1993).

With the arrival of the nuclear age, the traditional international law of weapons regulation came under pressure for the development of new approaches. Efforts to restrain weapons of mass destruction—nuclear, chemical, biological, or other—will be dealt with in Section 4.B below. In parallel to these efforts, many international lawyers advocated the application to nuclear weapons of doctrines rooted in the Hague and Geneva streams of humanitarian law. These issues were addressed, though not fully resolved, by the International Court of Justice in its Advisory Opinion on Nuclear Weapons, 1996 I.C.J. 226, at paras 74–95. In its opinion the Court distilled the essence of humanitarian law in terms which it envisioned as applicable to nuclear as well as conventional weapons:

78. The cardinal principles contained in the texts constituting the fabric of humanitarian law are the following. The first is aimed at the protection of the civilian population and civilian objects and establishes the distinction between combatants and non-combatants; States must never make civilians the object of attack and must consequently never use weapons that are incapable of distinguishing between civilian and military targets. According to the second principle, it is prohibited to cause unnecessary suffering to combatants: it is accordingly prohibited to use weapons causing them such harm or uselessly aggravating their suffering. In application of that second principle, States do not have unlimited freedom of choice of means in the weapons they use.

The Court would likewise refer, in relation to these principles, to the Martens Clause, which was first included in the Hague Convention II with Respect to the Law and Customs of War on Land of 1899 and which has proved to be an effective means of addressing the rapid evolution of military technology. A modern version of that clause is to be found in Article 1, paragraph 2, of Additional Protocol I of 1977, which reads as follows:

> "In cases not covered by this Protocol or by other international agreements, civilians and combatants remain under the protection and authority of the principles of international law derived from established custom, from the principles of humanity and from the dictates of public conscience."

In conformity with the aforementioned principles, humanitarian law, at a very early stage, prohibited certain types of weapons either because of their indiscriminate effect on combatants and civilians or because of the unnecessary suffering caused to combatants, that is to say, a harm greater than that unavoidable to achieve legitimate military objectives. * * *

79. It is undoubtedly because a great many rules of humanitarian law applicable in armed conflict are so fundamental to the respect of the human person and "elementary considerations of humanity" as the Court put it in its Judgment of 9 April 1949 in the *Corfu Channel* case (*I.C.J. Reports 1949*, p. 22) that the Hague and Geneva Conventions have enjoyed a broad accession. Further these fundamental rules are to be observed by all States whether or not they have ratified the conventions that contain them, because they constitute intransgressible principles of international customary law.

* * *

82. The extensive codification of humanitarian law and the extent of the accession to the resultant treaties, as well as the fact that the denunciation clauses that existed in the codification instruments have never been used, have provided the international community with a corpus of treaty rules the great majority of which had

already become customary and which reflected the most universally recognized humanitarian principles. These rules indicate the normal conduct and behavior expected of States.

The Court did not, however, find it necessary to pronounce on whether these rules had attained the status of *jus cogens*. Id., para. 83. In the dispositive portion of its judgment, para. 105(2)D, the Court unanimously found that a threat or use of nuclear weapons "should * * * be compatible with the requirements of the international law applicable in armed conflict, particularly those of the principles and rules of international humanitarian law * * *." For discussion of the aspects of the Court's opinion dealing with humanitarian law, see Matheson, The Opinions of the International Court of Justice on the Threat or Use of Nuclear Weapons, 91 A.J.I.L. 417, 427–34 (1997) and other references at p. 90. On the history of the Martens Clause (para. 78), see Meron, The Martens Clause, Principles of Humanity and Dictates of Public Conscience, 94 A.J.I.L. 78 (2000).

The destructive capabilities even of "conventional" weapons in the late twentieth and early twenty-first centuries have led to new developments in the legal regulation of weaponry, along with attempts to strength the implementation of traditional doctrines. The initiative to ban anti-personnel landmines is a notable contemporary manifestation of the drive begun in the nineteenth century to eradicate weapons that cannot discriminate between civilians and combatants or that cause unnecessary suffering. For other examples concerning weapons of mass destruction (nuclear, chemical or biological), see Section 4.B.

b. New Law–Making: The Landmines Convention and Other Recent Developments

The Landmines Convention of 1997—formally, the Convention on the Prohibition of the Use, Stockpiling, Production, and Transfer of Anti–Personnel Mines and on Their Destruction, December 3, 1997, 2056 U.N.T.S. 211—is notable both for its substance and for the law-making process that brought it into being. Non-governmental organizations played an exceedingly influential role in the design of the Convention (also known as the Mine Ban Treaty), in the mustering of political pressure in support of the diplomatic conference that produced the final text in 1997, and thereafter for ratification and implementation. An unusually brisk pace of ratifications brought the treaty into force with effect from March 1, 1999. As of 2009, 156 states were parties.

The substantive obligations under the Landmines Convention include an international ban on the use, production, stockpiling and sale of anti-personnel mines, and the destruction of stockpiles and of mines in the ground in territories under the jurisdiction of states parties on specified timetables. No reservations to these obligations are permitted. Parties are required to report to the U.N. Secretary–General on their implementation measures (Article 7). Non-governmental organizations and civil society are also vigilantly monitoring the steps being taken (or not taken) by states parties, as well as by non-signatories and non-parties, in support of the Convention's objectives.

As of 2009, the United States had neither signed nor ratified the Landmines Convention; Russia and China also remained outside the treaty framework, as did several other important states. However, the United States has accepted a more limited treaty commitment restricting certain kinds of mines. See Convention on Prohibitions or Restrictions on the Use of Certain Weapons Which May Be Deemed to be Excessively Injurious or to Have Indiscriminate Effects, and its Protocol on Prohibitions or Restrictions on the Use of Mines, Booby–Traps and Other Devices (entered into force for the United States Sept. 24, 1995) and Amended Protocol II (ratified by the United States May 24, 1999); see also Matheson, The Revision of the Mines Protocol, 91 A.J.I.L. 158 (1997). The United States has also maintained a self-imposed restriction on exports of landmines since 1993 (extended by legislation through 2003) and has contributed significant resources (said to be as much as $1 billion) and expertise to demining activities around the world. The United States has said it would consider eventually joining the Landmines Convention, provided that alternatives could be found to address specific military needs, especially on the Korean peninsula.

According to the International Campaign to Ban Landmines (a coalition of non-governmental organizations working for complete elimination of landmines), there has been a sharp drop in the number of new mines being laid and a sharp drop in exports of mines since the conclusion of the Mine Ban Treaty. NATO did not use anti-personnel mines as such in the Kosovo war of 1999 (but see note 4 below on cluster bombs), though landmines had been laid in many areas of former Yugoslavia between 1991 and 1999. Even so, millions of mines remain in the ground, not only in several dozen areas of ongoing armed conflict, but also in many countries where wars have ended. The practical problems of eliminating these stealthy killers are enormous and expensive.

NOTES

1. *Customary Law?* Does the information above concerning the Landmines Convention support the position that a norm of customary international law has already come into existence to ban these weapons? Would the "persistent objector" rule apply in the case of the United States or other states that have declined to support the treaty-based norm?

2. *Obligations Pending Ratification.* The International Campaign to Ban Landmines has found that three signatories (Angola, Guinea–Bissau and Senegal) used landmines in 1998, after signing the treaty but before ratification. Would such use defeat the object and purpose of the treaty within the meaning of Article 18 of the Vienna Convention on the Law of Treaties?

3. *Further Reading.* For a compendium of current materials on landmines, including status of ratifications and implementation measures, see

International Campaign to Ban Landmines, Landmine Monitor Report (annual volumes beginning in 1999). On the preparation of the Landmines Convention and the influence of non-governmental organizations, see Thakur & Maley, The Ottawa Convention on Landmines: A Landmark Humanitarian Treaty in Arms Control?, 5 Global Governance 273 (1999); Anderson, The Ottawa Convention Banning Landmines, the Role of Non–Governmental Organizations and the Idea of International Civil Society, 11 E.J.I.L. 91 (2000). For analysis and critique of the positions of the United States and other countries, see Human Rights Watch, Clinton's Landmine Legacy (2000), and the respective country chapters of the Landmine Monitor Report.

4. *Cluster Munitions.* The high dud rate of cluster bombs can turn these weapons into the equivalent of antipersonnel landmines, which lie in the ground until detonated on contact. Cluster bombs were dropped from high-flying aircraft in the 1999 Kosovo war and were also used with several kinds of delivery systems in the 1991 Gulf War. See, e.g., Human Rights Watch, Ticking Time Bombs: NATO's Use of Cluster Munitions in Yugoslavia (1999). A report prepared for the Prosecutor of the International Criminal Tribunal for the Former Yugoslavia found no legal basis for accusations that NATO's use of cluster bombs in the Kosovo campaign could constitute a criminal violation of the laws of war. See ICTY: Final Report to the Prosecutor by the Committee Established to Review the NATO Bombing Campaign Against the Federal Republic of Yugoslavia, 39 I.L.M. 1257, 1264–65 (2000). The Independent Commission on Kosovo (p. 1210 *supra*) did not dispute this conclusion, "but nevertheless recommend[ed] that cluster bombs should never be used in any future undertaking under UN auspices or claiming to be a 'humanitarian intervention'." Kosovo Report, Chapter 6, text at n. 34 (2000).

In order to address this problem, a new Convention on Cluster Munitions was concluded at a diplomatic conference in Dublin on May 30, 2008 and was opened for signature at Oslo December 3, 2008. Upon entry into force (with the deposit of thirty ratifications), states parties undertake never under any circumstances to use cluster munitions; to develop, produce, otherwise acquire, stockpile, retain or transfer such munitions to anyone, directly or indirectly; or to assist, encourage, or induce anyone to engage in those prohibited activities. Its text is available at http://www.icrc.org/ihl.nsf. For a recent statement of U.S. policy on cluster munitions, see Crook, Contemporary Practice of the United States, 101 A.J.I.L. 501 (2007).

5. *Other Prohibitions on Weaponry; Recent U.S. Ratifications.* For other recent treaty prohibitions on particularly harmful kinds of weapons, see Protocol on Prohibitions or Restrictions on the Use of Incendiary Weapons (Protocol III to the Convention on Prohibitions or Restrictions on the Use of Certain Conventional Weapons (CCW)); Protocol on Blinding Laser Weapons (Protocol IV to the CCW Convention); and Protocol on Explosive Remnants of War (Protocol V to the CCW Convention). The U.S. Senate gave advice and consent to these protocols, along with several other treaties regulating warfare and dangerous weaponry, in September 2008. See Crook, Contemporary Practice of the United States, 103 A.J.I.L. 135, 137–38 (2009).

2. International Humanitarian Law Concerning Combatants and Non–Combatants

a. *Geneva Conventions, Protocols, and Customary Law*

Alongside the norms restricting weaponry is the body of law governing treatment of combatants and non-combatants. The four Geneva Conventions of 1949 and their additional protocols provide detailed codes in this regard. They are:

— Geneva Convention for the Amelioration of the Condition of the Wounded and Sick in Armed Forces in the Field, Aug. 12, 1949, 6 U.S.T. 3114, 75 U.N.T.S. 31 (Geneva Convention No. I)

— Geneva Convention for the Amelioration of the Condition of the Wounded, Sick, and Shipwrecked Members of the Armed Forces at Sea, Aug. 12, 1949, 6 U.S.T. 3217, 75 U.N.T.S. 85 (Geneva Convention No. II)

— Geneva Convention Relative to the Treatment of Prisoners of War, Aug. 12, 1949, 6 U.S.T. 3316, 75 U.N.T.S. 135 (Geneva Convention No. III)

— Geneva Convention Relative to the Protection of Civilian Persons in Time of War, Aug. 12, 1949, 6 U.S.T. 3516, 75 U.N.T.S. 287 (Geneva Convention No. IV)

— Additional Protocol Relating to the Protection of Victims of International Armed Conflicts, June 8, 1977, 1125 U.N.T.S. 3 (Protocol I)

— Additional Protocol Relating to the Protection of Victims of Non–International Armed Conflicts, June 8, 1977, 1125 U.N.T.S. 609 (Protocol II)

— Additional Protocol Relating to the Adoption of an Additional Distinctive Emblem, December 8, 2005, 2404 U.N.T.S. ___ (Protocol III)

This set of rules applies differentially, depending on whether the conflict in question is "international" or "non-international." In general, stricter standards apply to conflicts of an international character. In the case of non-international (internal) conflicts, Article 3 common to all four Geneva Conventions ("Common Article 3") requires humane treatment of all persons not taking an active part in hostilities and prohibits various acts, including murder, torture, hostage-taking, and non-judicial punishments. (See Document Supplement.) Protocol II (1977) establishes rules for non-international conflicts expanding upon Common Article 3; but a number of states (including the United States) have not ratified Protocol II, and its status as customary international law is uncertain.

The newest protocol, Protocol III, adds a "red crystal" emblem to the traditional red cross and red crescent. It has forty parties as of 2009 (including the United States, which ratified it in 2007).

For authoritative interpretations of the International Committee of the Red Cross on the Geneva Conventions and Protocols, see Commentaries on the Geneva Conventions (Pictet ed. 1994); Sandoz et al., Commentary on the Additional Protocols of 8 June 1977 to the Geneva Conventions (1987). See also Best, War and Law Since 1945 (1994).

NOTES

1. *"Armed Conflict."* On what basis must the existence of an "armed conflict" be established, as a precondition to the applicability of the 1949 Geneva Conventions or the 1977 Protocols? What level of violence should such a requirement entail? What should be the scope of applicability in relation to hostilities that flare up, die down, recur, and perhaps subside again? What factors should be relevant in internal (as contrasted to international) armed conflicts? For the reasons why the states that drafted the Conventions and Protocols were relatively cautious in setting the thresholds for applicability (to exclude low-level disturbances or isolated incidents) and distinguishing between international and non-international conflicts, see Aldrich, The Laws of War on Land, 94 A.J.I.L. 42, 58–62 (2000).

In the 1995 *Tadic* Appeal on Jurisdiction, I.C.T.Y. Case No. IT–94–1–AR72 (Oct. 2, 1995), the International Criminal Tribunal for the Former Yugoslavia discussed the preliminary issue of the existence of an armed conflict, in a context where defendant disputed whether there had been active hostilities in the area of the alleged crimes at the relevant time:

> 70. * * * [W]e find that an armed conflict exists whenever there is a resort to armed force between States or protracted armed violence between governmental authorities and organized armed groups or between such groups with a State. International humanitarian law applies from the initiation of such armed conflicts and extends beyond the cessation of hostilities until a general conclusion of peace is reached; or, in the case of internal conflicts, a peaceful settlement is achieved. Until that moment, international humanitarian law continues to apply in the whole territory of the warring States or, in the case of internal conflicts, the whole territory under the control of a party, whether or not actual combat takes place there.

> Applying the foregoing concept of armed conflicts to this case, we hold that the alleged crimes were committed in the context of an armed conflict. * * * Even if substantial clashes were not occurring in the Prijedor region at the time and place the crimes allegedly were committed—a factual issue on which the Appeals Chamber does not pronounce—international humanitarian law applies. It is sufficient that the alleged crimes were closely related to the hostilities occurring in other parts of the territories controlled by the parties to the conflict. * * *

2. *International versus Non–International Armed Conflicts: Tribunal Case Law.* The jurisprudence of the I.C.T.Y. deals in depth with the distinction between international and non-international conflicts and the determination of which set of rules applies to the facts of the conflicts in former Yugoslavia. The 1995 *Tadic* appeal on jurisdiction, and the 1999 decision on

Tadic's appeal of his conviction, both examine these issues at length. In the 1995 ruling, the I.C.T.Y.'s Appeals Chamber found that certain aspects of humanitarian law, notably the "grave breaches" system of the Geneva Conventions, would apply only to offenses committed in international armed conflicts, while other aspects could apply as well to internal conflicts. I.C.T.Y. Case No. IT–94–1–AR72, paras. 79–85, 95–137 (Oct. 2, 1995). In the 1999 decision, the Appeals Chamber found that the conflict entailed sufficient involvement of the Federal Republic of Yugoslavia in Bosnia–Herzegovina to bring into play the provisions of Geneva Convention No. IV on protecting civilians in times of international armed conflict, and likewise found that Bosnian Muslims in the hands of Bosnian Serbs were "protected persons" in the hands of a party of which they were not nationals under the Convention. The Appeals Chamber therefore found Tadic guilty of grave breaches of the Geneva Conventions. See *Prosecutor v. Tadic*, I.C.T.Y. Case No. IT–94–1–A, Judgment on Appeal from Conviction, paras. 68–171 (July 15, 1999).

The jurisdiction of the International Criminal Tribunal for Rwanda is differently formulated. On the apparent assumption that the conflict was non-international in character, the Security Council specified that the I.C.T.R.'s jurisdiction over war crimes would be based on Common Article 3 of the 1949 Geneva Conventions and 1977 Protocol II (the "grave breaches" regime is thus not applicable). See *Prosecutor v. Akayesu*, I.C.T.R. Case No. ICTR–96–4–T, Judgment, sec. 6.5 (Sept. 2, 1998). *Akayesu* also held (Section 7.1) that civilians can in principle be criminally responsible for violations of the laws of war; but the trial chamber held that defendant's individual responsibility under Common Article 3 and Protocol II was not proved, although it did convict Akayesu (who had held the civilian post of *bourgmestre*) on charges of genocide and crimes against humanity.

3. *International versus Non–International Armed Conflicts: U.S. Supreme Court.* In *Hamdan v. Rumsfeld*, 548 U.S. 557 (2006), excerpted in Chapter 10, the U.S. government argued that the conflict with Al Qaeda was not an armed conflict "between two or more of the High Contracting Parties" within the meaning of Common Article 2 of the Geneva Conventions and thus the full protections of the Conventions could not apply. The government also insisted that the global scope of the conflict meant that it could not be considered a conflict "not of an international character" within the meaning of Common Article 3. The Supreme Court disagreed, interpreting Common Article 3 to reach conflicts other than those between nation and nation and finding its protections (minimal though they may be) applicable to the situation of a detainee held as an "enemy combatant" in that conflict. (The Court did not reach the Common Article 2 argument.) See p. 718.

4. *Toward a Common Standard?* It has been said that there "is no moral justification, and no truly persuasive legal reason, for treating perpetrators of atrocities in internal conflicts more leniently than those engaged in international wars." Meron, War Crimes Law Comes of Age 238 (1998). Similarly, there are strong arguments for establishing standards of protection that would apply in all situations, including those of internal violence falling short of "armed conflict." On the progress toward promulgation of such a declaration of minimum humanitarian standards ("fundamental standards of humanity,") see Meron, International Criminalization of Internal Atrocities,

89 A.J.I.L. 554 (1995); Meron, The Humanization of Humanitarian Law, 94 A.J.I.L. 239, 274–75 (2000).

5. *Standards for "Humanitarian" Intervention?* The Independent International Commission on Kosovo (p. 1210 *supra*) suggested that standards for the conduct of armed conflict should be more exacting in the case of a war carried out for "humanitarian" purposes than in other kinds of conflicts. The Commission recommended that the International Committee of the Red Cross or another body should prepare a new legal convention to this effect, for applicability to U.N. peacekeeping or to humanitarian interventions.

On applicability of humanitarian law to U.N. operations, see U.N. Secretary–General, Bulletin on the Observance by U.N. Forces of International Humanitarian Law, U.N. Doc. ST/SGB/1999/13 (Aug. 6, 1999), reprinted in 38 I.L.M. 1656 (1999). See also Greenwood, International Humanitarian Law and United Nations Military Operations, 1 Y.B. Int'l Humanitarian L. 3 (1998); Shraga, UN Peacekeeping Operations: Applicability of International Humanitarian Law and Responsibility for Operations–Related Damage, 94 A.J.I.L. 406 (2000).

6. *Peacetime.* Some aspects of humanitarian law apply in peacetime as well as in wartime. See, e.g., the Genocide Convention, Art. 1. In respect of crimes against humanity, it is important to distinguish between the substantive law, which is now generally understood to apply irrespective of the existence of armed conflict, and particular jurisdictional instruments which may be limited to such crimes committed in the course of armed conflict. For example, Article 5 of the I.C.T.Y Statute confers jurisdiction over crimes against humanity "when committed in armed conflict, whether international or internal in character." The Appeals Chamber of the I.C.T.Y. has explained that it is "a settled rule of customary international law that crimes against humanity do not require a connection to internal armed conflict * * * and may not require a connection between crimes against humanity and any conflict at all." Thus the Security Council "may have defined [crimes against humanity] more narrowly than necessary under customary international law." *Prosecutor v. Tadic*, I.C.T.Y. Case No. IT–94–1–AR72, Appeal on Jurisdiction, para. 141 (Oct. 2, 1995); see also Appeal from Conviction, para. 251 (July 15, 1999). Compare Rome Statute for the International Criminal Court, art. 7 (defining crimes against humanity without reference to armed conflict).

In the *Nicaragua* case (Merits), the Court observed that the laying of mines in the waters of another state without any warning or notification is ·not only an unlawful act but also a breach of the principles of humanitarian law applicable in peacetime as well as wartime. The Court stated:

> [I]f a State lays mines in any waters whatever in which the vessels of another State have right of access or passage, and fails to give any warning or notification whatsoever, in disregard of the security of peaceful shipping, it commits a breach of the principles of humanitarian law underlying the specific provisions [Articles 3 and 4] of [Hague] Convention No. VIII of 1907. Those principles were expressed in the *Corfu Channel* case as follows:

"certain general and well recognized principles namely: elementary considerations of humanity, even more exacting in peace than in war" (I.C.J. Reports 1949, p. 22).

1986 I.C.J. 14, 112.

7. *U.S. Position.* As of 2009, the United States had not ratified either Protocol I or Protocol II. Issues of concern to the United States (and other states) include provisions on wars of national liberation; application of rules on combatants and prisoner-of-war status to non-uniformed fighters; and prohibitions on belligerent reprisals. See generally Meron, The Time Has Come for the United States to Ratify Geneva Protocol I, 88 A.J.I.L. 678 (1994); Aldrich, The Laws of War on Land, 94 A.J.I.L. 42, 45–48, 57–58 (2000) and references therein. On the objection concerning belligerent reprisals and the debate over whether that prohibition might be (or become) customary international law, see Meron, The Humanization of Humanitarian Law, 94 A.J.I.L. 239, 249–51 (2000). On other aspects of the controversy, see Reisman, Holding the Center of the Law of Armed Conflict, 100 A.J.I.L. 852, 857–58 (2006).

8. *I.C.R.C. Study.* In 2005 the International Committee of the Red Cross published a major study on the customary laws of war, representing the culmination of more than a decade of empirical research into the practice of states and other actors in both international and non-international armed conflicts. See International Committee of the Red Cross, Customary International Humanitarian Law (Henckaerts & Doswald–Beck eds. 2005) (I.C.R.C. study); see also references and discussion of the I.C.R.C. study in Chapter 2, pp. 67–68, notes 5–6. A salient contribution of this vast research effort (more than 5,000 pages in two volumes) is the compilation of empirical data tending to show which of the rules formulated as treaty rules in Protocols I and II can be considered on the basis of practice and *opinio juris* to have attained the status of customary international law. The I.C.R.C. study has attracted considerable attention and commentary (both favorable and critical). See, e.g., Perspectives on the ICRC Study on Customary International Humanitarian Law (Wilmshurst & Breau eds. 2007). For governmental reactions questioning some aspects of the study's methodology (particularly as regards the practice of non-state actors), see Joint Letter from Legal Adviser of U.S. Department of State and General Counsel of U.S. Department of Defense, reprinted at 46 I.L.M. 511, 513 (2007), and the response by one of the study's lead authors, reprinted at 46 I.L.M. 957 (2007).

b. Treatment of Prisoners of War and the Sick and Wounded on Land and at Sea

Humanitarian treatment of prisoners of war was not emphasized until the second half of the nineteenth century. See 2 Oppenheim, International Law 367–96 (7th ed., Lauterpacht ed., 1952); Stone, Legal Controls of Armed Conflict 651–79 (1959). The Hague Regulations did not prevent many of the hardships that prisoners suffered during World War I, but they did provide an enlightened basis for regulation. After the First World War, a conference at Geneva adopted new, more elaborate rules. See Convention Relating to the Treatment of Prisoners of War, July 27,

1929, 47 Stat. 2021, 118 L.N.T.S. 343. Like the prior rules, the new rules did not anticipate the new modes of warfare adopted in the world war that followed their acceptance.

The Third Geneva Convention is now the authoritative statement on prisoners of war. An innovation of the Convention, beyond its application to all declared war, is its partial application to all other armed conflicts, including internal wars. The Convention defines prisoners in a way that was thought to include every person likely to be captured in hostilities (though difficulties in application have arisen in conflicts of the post–9/11 period). Full and primary responsibility for the treatment of prisoners of war falls upon the Detaining Power, which is under a general obligation to treat prisoners humanely. They must receive maintenance and medical attention. Medical and scientific experiments are prohibited, as are reprisals for breaches of the laws of war other than breaches of the Convention itself. See Stone, *supra*, at 656 n. 21 (1959); 2 Oppenheim, *supra*, at 562 n. 3. Prisoners are to be treated alike, regardless of race, nationality, religious beliefs, or political opinions.

At the time of detention, the prisoner is required to give a minimum of information and may retain his personal effects. He is not to be subjected to torture. Conditions at detention camps must meet standards provided in the Convention. The work that the prisoner is required to perform must not be inherently dangerous, humiliating, or directly connected with the operations of the war. The prisoner must be permitted contact with his family and correspondence privileges. Procedures must be established for registering complaints against the administration of the detention camp. Penal and disciplinary sanctions, including procedures for determining guilt, are prescribed. Additional articles regulate repatriation and information to the outside regarding prisoners. Each party undertakes to provide penal sanctions against persons who violate the established norms. Parties to the conventions are obligated to search out those persons alleged to have committed such breaches.

NOTES

1. *"Unlawful Enemy Combatants."* In the course of the global conflict following the attacks of September 11, 2001, the United States detained several hundred fighters who were said to be affiliated with Al Qaeda and other terrorist groups. The Bush administration promulgated a military order and related directives under which persons designated as "unlawful enemy combatants" were not to be treated as prisoners of war (though they were supposed to be treated "humanely" as a matter of policy). Many of them were transferred to a naval facility at Guantánamo Bay and detained there for long periods. The Supreme Court has had several occasions to consider legal challenges on behalf of these detainees, including in *Hamdan v. Rumsfeld*, 548 U.S. 557 (2006), p. 718; more such litigation was pending as this casebook went to press. (The Obama administration announced certain policy changes in early 2009 but left other decisions for later determination.). Within interna-

tional legal circles since 9/11, intense debate has focused on the criteria for prisoner of war status as enunciated in Articles 4–5 of the Third Geneva Convention and related issues, including the criteria for detention of persons who do not qualify as combatants in the traditional sense. See, e.g., Goodman, The Detention of Civilians in Armed Conflict, 103 A.J.I.L. 48 (2009) and references therein. Do you think the Third Geneva Convention is clear in defining the persons entitled to claim its protection? Would new law-making be desirable?

2. *Armed Conflict at Sea.* The laws of war have also included limitations in favor of merchant shipping. Unlike armed ships and other public vessels, an enemy merchant ship was not to be attacked unless it refused to submit to visit and capture. See generally 2 Oppenheim, *supra,* at 465–97; Stone, *supra,* at 571–607. These rules were widely disregarded in both World Wars, notably by submarines. Prohibitions on submarine warfare against merchant ships were made explicit between the wars. See Treaty for the Limitation and Reduction of Naval Armaments (London Naval Treaty of 1930), April 22, 1930, pt. IV, art. 22, 46 Stat. 2858, 2881, 112 L.N.T.S. 65, 88; 2 Hackworth at 690–95; 6 Hackworth at 466. After visit, a merchant vessel could be taken to port and adjudicated a prize, and thereafter its disposition was governed by municipal law. For a description of American prize practice, see Gilmore & Black, The Law of Admirality 40 (2d ed. 1975). Immunities have been granted to hospital ships, to vessels with religious, scientific, or philanthropic missions and also to coastal fishing boats. On the legal regime for naval conflicts, see San Remo Manual on International Law Applicable to Armed Conflicts at Sea (Doswald–Beck ed., 1995); see also Roach, The Law of Naval Warfare at the Turn of Two Centuries, 94 A.J.I.L. 64 (2000).

c. *Protection of Civilians in Wartime*

The Fourth Geneva Convention governs protection of civilians in time of war. It comes into play during armed conflict when civilians ("protected persons") are in the hands of a party of which they are not a national. It prohibits violence to life and person and allows no distinction based on race, religion, or political opinion. It defines situations in which an alien may leave the territory of the belligerent and provides that the regulation of aliens who remain may deviate from the provisions regulating such aliens in peacetime only to the extent required by wartime control and security. Civilians must be allowed to receive relief, necessary medical care and religious comfort. They must be allowed to move from exposed areas. They may not be compelled to work on any task related to military operations and when working they must be accorded working conditions equal to those of the belligerent's nationals. There is also an elaborate set of rules regulating treatment of internees. See Stone, Legal Controls of Armed Conflict 684–92 (1959).

When belligerent occupation has been established in accordance with the requirements of international law, the occupying power assumes broad legal powers that it would not have merely as a belligerent. These powers and reciprocal duties reflect the divergent and common interests of the occupying power and the local inhabitants. Both have a common interest in the maintenance of law and order. The occupying power desires to minimize the diversion of its resources from other war operations, while the local inhabitants want to conduct their lives without violence and undue coercion. Humane treatment of the inhabitants not only serves the values of decency, but is a precondition of administering the territory with a minimal expenditure of force. See McDougal & Feliciano, Law and Minimum World Public Order 790–808 (1961).

Belligerent occupation creates a complicated scheme of legal relations involving not only the occupant and the inhabitants, but also the temporarily ousted sovereign. Customary rules governing these relationships have been strongly influenced by the Hague Regulations and the Fourth Geneva Convention. For the purposes of the latter instrument, the fact that one of the parties to the conflict had violated a norm of international law in initiating hostilities would not affect the applicability of the Convention. The occupant is empowered to maintain order and utilize the resources of the country for its own military needs. The occupying power may not force the people to swear allegiance to it. The precise extent of its power is uncertain, particularly with respect to effecting changes in fundamental institutions. See Stone, *supra*, at 688–89, 723–32.

Ordinarily, an occupying power is expected to rely on the organs of the subservient government, such as the courts, for maintaining law and order. When these institutions prove inadequate, the belligerent may replace them with institutions of a military nature. In punishing war crimes or activity directed against the occupying power, the courts are forbidden to apply any retroactive law or to depart from the principle of proportionality in punishment. Death penalties are permissible in certain types of cases only. Collective penalties, intimidation, terrorism, taking of hostages and acts of reprisal against the civilian population are prohibited. Since, in reaction to a recalcitrant civilian population, an occupying power might well adopt penal measures without regard to these niceties, the practicality of such rules has been questioned. See McDougal & Feliciano at 797. Discrimination on the grounds of race, religion or political opinion is also forbidden. In general, all forcible mass transfers of population are prohibited, except where required by security or military necessity. The occupying power is also required to provide certain welfare services.

NOTES

1. *Alien Internment and Property Seizure in Wartime.* Alien enemy control during the First and Second World Wars included internment of dangerous foreign nationals. Based on the experience at the outbreak of the First World War, the government increased the efficiency and incidence of internment at the beginning of the Second World War. On December 7, 1941, a presidential proclamation provided for the internment of Japanese nationals. Subsequent decrees applied to German, Italian, Hungarian, Bulgarian and Rumanian nationals. By October 5, 1943, 14,807 aliens had been taken into custody. See Hoover, Alien Enemy Control, 29 Iowa L. Rev. 398 (1944).

Presidential authority for the supervision of enemy aliens is contained in 50 U.S.C.A. § 21. Habeas corpus was available to these persons, although the only justiciable question was whether they belonged to the category of persons designated by legislation as liable to seizure. See Brandon, Legal Control Over Resident Enemy Aliens in Time of War in the United States and in the United Kingdom, 44 A.J.I.L. 382 (1950).

Customary law permits the seizure of public enemy property and the prohibition of the withdrawal of private enemy property. At one time, belligerents were permitted to confiscate private as well as public enemy property, movable and immovable, including debts. This practice was reversed in respect of private property through treaties that provided that enemy subjects and private property could be withdrawn at the outbreak of war. The last case of outright confiscation of private property occurred in 1793. See 2 Oppenheim at 326. As to whether such confiscation today would violate customary international law, compare the treatment of private fishing vessels, *The Paquete Habana*, p. 61 *supra*.

In the early stages of the First World War, states scrupulously avoided confiscatory acts against enemy states, but most states eventually adopted exceptional war measures which, though not amounting to confiscation, inflicted great loss and injury. Regulation of enemy property has been recognized in the United States as within the war power of the federal government. See Hays, Enemy Property in America (1923); Gathings, International Law and American Treatment of Alien Enemy Property (1940); Council on Foreign Relations, The Postwar Settlement of Property Rights 16–22 (1945). Eight months after the United States entered the First World War, Congress enacted the Trading with the Enemy Act, 40 Stat. 411 (1917). See 50 U.S.C.A. App. §§ 1–44 for the current authority. The Trading with the Enemy Act prohibited all trade with persons or firms resident within enemy territory or resident outside the United States and doing business within such territory or with nationals of an ally of an enemy state unless authorized by license. All business enterprises whose stock was held by enemies or allies of enemies, and all persons holding property of or indebted to enemies, were required to register with the Alien Property Custodian.

At the end of both the First and Second World Wars, the peace treaties included provisions giving nationals of the victorious states recourse against the vanquished states for loss of property. Nationals of the vanquished country, however, could apply only to their own states for compensation. See, e.g., Article 79 of the 1947 Peace Treaty with Italy, 61 Stat. 1245, 49 U.N.T.S. 1; Chapter 6, [Bonn] Convention on the Settlement of Matters Arising Out of the War and Occupation, 1952, 6 U.S.T. 4411, 332 U.N.T.S. 219; *Tag v. Rogers*, 267 F.2d 664 (D.C. Cir. 1959); DeVries, The International Responsibility of the United States for Vested German Assets, 51 A.J.I.L. 18 (1957). On the treatment of enemy property, see generally Stone at 434–36; 2 Oppenheim at 326–32. On the practice during and after World War II, see Domke, Trading with the Enemy in World War II (1943); Domke, The Control of Alien Property (1947); Mann, Enemy Property and the Paris Peace Treaties, 64 L.Q. Rev. 492 (1948); Martin, The Treatment of Enemy Property under the Peace Treaties of 1947, 34 Grotius Soc. Trans. 77 (1948). The United States never recognized any obligation to compensate for the seizure of enemy property. In accordance with principles enunciated in the Potsdam and Paris agreements, the United States enacted the War Claims Act of 1948, 62 Stat. 1240, which provided that owners of alien property seized during the Second World War would not be compensated.

2. *Occupied Territory.* On the treatment of the population of occupied territory, see Stone, *supra*, at 697–706, 723–26, 727–32; 2 Oppenheim, *supra*, at 438–56; McDougal & Feliciano, *supra*, at 732; Von Glahn, The Occupation of Enemy Territory (1957); Gutteridge, The Protection of Civilians in Occupied Territory, 5 Y.B. World Aff. 290 (1951). See also Benvenisti, The International Law of Occupation (1993).

3. *Israel and the Occupied Palestinian Territory.* The extended occupation by Israel since the 1967 war of territories previously in Arab hands has raised difficult problems. See Roberts, Prolonged Military Occupation: The Israeli–Occupied Territories Since 1967, 84 A.J.I.L. 44 (1990). Israel has not acknowledged applicability of the Fourth Geneva Convention, claiming that the Convention applies only to territories that belonged to another sovereign state, and that in view of the termination of the British Mandate and the failure of the U.N. Partition Plan of 1947 which the Arab states rejected, the Geneva Convention does not formally apply. A discussion of the Israeli position is found in Blum, The Missing Reversioner: Reflections on the Status of Judea and Samaria, 3 Israel L. Rev. 279, 281–95 (1968). The U.N. called on Israel to cancel an order expelling a number of Palestinians from the West Bank in 1988 and from Gaza in 1992. See S.C. Res. 607 (Jan. 5, 1988) and S.C. Res. 799 (Dec. 18, 1992). U.N. organs, including the Security Council, General Assembly, and Commission on Human Rights, have frequently insisted that the Fourth Geneva Convention does apply to the territories occupied by Israel and have called upon Israel to comply with its provisions. Cf. S.C. Res. 1322 (Oct. 7, 2000.) See discussion in Benvenisti & Zamir, Private Claims to Property Rights in the Future Israeli–Palestinian Settlement, 89 A.J.I.L. 295, 305–07 (1995). The International Court of Justice confirmed the applicability of the Fourth Geneva Convention in its advisory opinion on the *Wall in the Occupied Palestinian Territory*, 2004 I.C.J. 136, p. 630.

4. *Forcible Population Transfers.* The 1998 Rome Statute of the International Criminal Court includes in the definition of "crimes against humanity" the following provisions (Article 7(1), 7(2)(d)):

> 1. For the purpose of this Statute, "crime against humanity" means any of the following acts, when committed as part of a widespread or systematic attack directed against any civilian population, with knowledge of the attack: * * *
>
> (d) Deportation or forcible transfer or population; * * *
>
> 2. For the purpose of paragraph 1: * * *
>
> (d) "Deportation or forcible transfer of population" means forced displacement of the persons concerned by expulsion or other coercive acts from the area in which they are lawfully present, without grounds permitted under international law; * * *

and in the enumeration of "war crimes" the following provision (Article 8(2)(b)(viii)):

The transfer, directly or indirectly, by the Occupying Power of parts of its own civilian population into the territory it occupies, or the deportation or transfer of all or parts of the population of the occupied territory within or outside this territory.

How might these provisions apply to expulsions of Palestinians from the occupied territories, or to Israeli settlements in the occupied territories?

5. *Iraq Occupation: "Transformative"?* As noted in Section 3 at p. 1244, the United States and the United Kingdom accepted responsibilities and obligations as occupying powers in Iraq between spring 2003 and June 2004, as recognized by the U.N. Security Council in Resolutions 1483 (2003) and subsequent resolutions, until the termination of the legal status of occupation in June 2004 pursuant to Resolution 1546 (2004). Under the traditional law of occupation reflected in Article 43 of the 1907 Hague Regulations and Article 64 of the Fourth Geneva Convention, the occupying power would ordinarily be expected to restore order while also generally maintaining the laws in force in the country. In a variety of occupations subsequent to World War II, however, the occupying powers have engaged in a more or less thoroughgoing transformation of the political system of the occupied country, notably to bring its legal system into conformity with contemporary human rights norms. Are the actions of the United States and United Kingdom in Iraq justifiable under a human-rights-centered conception of the role of occupying powers? See Roberts, Transformative Military Occupation: Applying the Laws of War and Human Rights, 100 A.J.I.L. 580, 604–18 (2006).

6. *Cultural Property.* The problem of protection of cultural property in wartime has received increasing attention, with the prominence in recent conflicts of wanton destruction of mosques, churches, statues, and other indicia of group identity and heritage. A 1954 Hague Convention for the Protection of Cultural Property in the Event of Armed Conflict, 249 U.N.T.S. 215, had 122 parties in 2009 and its first protocol approximately 100 parties. To strengthen existing protections, a Second Protocol to the 1954 Convention was adopted under the auspices of the United Nations Educational, Scientific and Cultural Organization (UNESCO) at The Hague in March 1999. See 38 I.L.M. 769 (1999). The U.S. Senate gave advice and consent to the 1954 Convention in late 2008; formal ratification was pending in early 2009.

d. Sexual Violence and Abuse of Children in Wartime

The rape of women by belligerent or occupying forces has been a perennial atrocity addressed by international law in only general terms and not yet effectively deterred or punished. See Khushalani, Dignity and Honour of Women as Basic and Fundamental Human Rights 63–64 (1982); Meron, Rape as a Crime under International Humanitarian Law, 87 A.J.I.L. 424 (1993). An analogous atrocity has been the forced enrollment of women into brothels, as was done to Korean and other Asian women by Japan in the Second World War—a grievance remaining essentially unredressed through the end of the twentieth century. During the hostilities in the former Yugoslavia, it was reported that there had been as many as 20,000 cases of rape committed as a matter of state policy and strategy of war. The pattern continued with the use of rape against Kosovar Albanians in 1998–1999. See Human Rights Watch, Kosovo: Rape as a Weapon of "Ethnic Cleansing" (2000).

The Geneva Conventions contain provisions relevant to wartime sexual violence, e.g. in Article 27 of the Fourth Convention, which provides that "[w]omen shall be especially protected against any attack on their honour, in particular against rape, enforced prostitution, or any form of indecent assault," and in Common Article 3 (applicable in non-international conflicts) which prohibits "(a) violence to life and person, in particular murder of all kinds, mutilation, cruel treatment and torture * * * [and] (c) outrages upon personal dignity, in particular humiliating and degrading treatment * * *." Protocol II (applicable in non-international conflicts) specifies in Article 4(2)(e) that "outrages upon personal dignity, in particular humiliating and degrading treatment, rape, enforced prostitution and any form of indecent assault" are prohibited at any time and in any place. These formulations have been criticized for being insufficiently explicit or comprehensive, as well as for the references to "honour" and "dignity" which might seem to reflect patriarchal attitudes or to ignore the violent quality of rape. Another criticism is the omission of specific reference to sexual violence from the "grave breaches" provisions of the Geneva Conventions, thus leaving it a matter of inference that rape and other sexual offenses could be punishable as grave breaches by interpretation of the clauses on torture, "wilfully causing great suffering or serious injury to body or health," "unlawful confinement of a civilian," or another enumerated grave breach.

The jurisprudence of the International Criminal Tribunals for the Former Yugoslavia and for Rwanda affirms that rape and other forms of sexual violence can indeed be prosecuted as grave breaches of the Geneva Conventions, as torture, as crimes against humanity, and even as genocide. In reaching these conclusions, the Tribunals have given specific readings to the general provisions of humanitarian law over which they have jurisdiction. In interpreting their statutory provisions, the Tribunals have clarified the prohibition of the crime of rape in humanitarian law and have convicted many defendants for perpetrating or being complicit in crimes of sexual violence.

The 1998 Rome Statute of the International Criminal Court is the most detailed codification to date of sexual and gender-based atrocities. Article 7(1) on crimes against humanity defines the crime to include "any of the following acts when committed as part of a widespread or systematic attack directed against any civilian population * * *:"

> (g) Rape, sexual slavery, enforced prostitution, forced pregnancy, enforced sterilization, or any other form of sexual violence of comparable gravity;

and subparagraph (h) also includes persecution on gender grounds (paragraph 3 states that the term " 'gender' refers to the two sexes, male and female, within the context of society"). The term "forced pregnancy is defined as

> * * * the unlawful confinement, of a woman forcibly made pregnant, with the intent of affecting the ethnic composition of any population or carrying out other grave violations of international law. This definition shall not in any way be interpreted as affecting national laws relating to pregnancy. (Art. 7(2)(f))"

The provisions on war crimes (Article 8(2)(b)) likewise specify as "serious violations" in international conflicts

> (xxii) Committing rape, sexual slavery, enforced prostitution, forced pregnancy, as defined in article 7, paragraph 2(f), enforced sterilization, or any other form of sexual violence also constituting a grave breach of the Geneva Conventions;

and a substantially similar provision is adopted for non-international conflicts (Article 8(2)(e)(vi)) (substituting the term "serious violation of article 3 common to the four Geneva Conventions" in place of "grave breach of the Geneva Conventions").

NOTES

1. *International Tribunal Convictions.* For convictions of crimes of sexual violence, see, e.g., *Prosecutor v. Akayesu*, I.C.T.R. Case. No. ICTR–96–4–T, Judgment (Sept. 2, 1998); *Prosecutor v. Delalic,* et al. (*Celebici* case), I.C.T.Y. Case No. IT–96–21–T (Judgment, Nov. 16, 1998, affirmed on appeal, Feb. 20, 2001); *Prosecutor v. Furundžija*, I.C.T.Y. Case No. IT–95–17/1–A, Judgment on Appeal from Conviction (July 21, 2000); *Prosecutor v. Kunarac* (*Focá* case), I.C.T.Y. Case No. IT–96–23–T, Judgment (Feb. 22, 2001). For commentary, see, e.g., Askin, War Crimes Against Women, Prosecution in International War Crimes Tribunals (1997); Askin, Sexual Violence in Decisions and Indictments of the Yugoslav and Rwandan Tribunals: Current Status, 93 A.J.I.L. 97 (1999); Oosterveld, Sexual Slavery and the International Criminal Court: Advancing International Law, 25 Mich. J Int'l. 605 (2004); Oosterveld, The Definition of "Gender" in the Rome Statute of the International Criminal Court: A Step Forward or Back for International Criminal Justice?, 18 Harv. Hum. Rts. J. 55 (2005).

The practical problems of prosecuting these crimes have been enormous, entailing not only all the obstacles familiar in domestic contexts (traumatized victims who may be reluctant to testify, defendants' efforts to put the victim's sexual history in issue or to insist that the victim's lack of consent must be affirmatively proved, and so on), but also the additional problems of securing evidence at great distance from the forum in the context of what may still be ongoing violence.

2. *"Comfort Women."* On the plight of the Korean comfort women, see Boling Mass Rape, Enforced Prostitution, and the Japanese Imperial Army: Japan Eschews International Legal Responsibility?, 32 Colum. J. Transnat'l L. 533 (1995). In December 2000, a nonofficial trial was held to focus attention on the continuing wrong of failure to acknowledge and make redress

for their grievance. For discussion, see Chinkin, The Prosecutor and People of the Asian Pacific Region v. Emperor Hirohito and the Government of Japan, forthcoming in 95 A.J.I.L. (2001).

3. *Children in War.* The Convention on the Rights of the Child, 1577 U.N.T.S. 3, deals in Article 38 with international humanitarian law as relevant to children and provides (Article 38, paras. 2 and 3) for restrictions on participation in hostilities by, and recruitment into armed forces of, children who have not attained the age of fifteen years. The 1998 Rome Statute of the International Criminal Court includes in the enumeration of war crimes "[c]onscripting or enlisting children under the age of fifteen years into the national armed forces or using them to participate actively in hostilities." Article 8(2)(b)(xxvi). The provision applicable to non-international armed conflicts, Article 8(2)(e)(vii), is substantially similar, with application to "armed forces or groups" in lieu of "national armed forces." See also S.C. Res. 1261 (Aug. 25, 1999); Convention Concerning the Prohibition and Immediate Action for the Elimination of the Worst Forms of Child Labour, June 17, 1999, 38 I.L.M. 1207 (1999) (prohibiting compulsory recruitment of children in armed conflicts).

An Optional Protocol to the Convention on the Rights of the Child on the Involvement of Children in Armed Conflict, U.N. Doc. A/54/L.84 (May 16, 2000), 39 I.L.M. 1285 (2000), raises the minimum age for children's participation from fifteen to eighteen years. It enjoins states parties to take all feasible measures to ensure that those under age eighteen do not take direct part in hostilities, and to ensure that they are not compulsorily recruited into a state's armed forces. States parties are also expected to raise the minimum age for voluntary recruitment, by means of a binding declaration setting forth a minimum age. The Protocol has 122 parties as of 2009 (including the United States, which ratified in 2002).

3. The Law of War and Environmental Protection

Article 35(3) of Additional Protocol I to the Geneva Conventions prohibits "methods or means of warfare which are intended, or may be expected, to cause widespread, long-term and severe damage to the natural environment." See also Article 55 (prohibiting methods or means which are intended or may be expected to cause such damage "and thereby to prejudice the health or survival of the population"). In the *Advisory Opinion on Nuclear Weapons*, 1996 I.C.J. 226, at paras. 27–33, the International Court of Justice discussed Articles 35(3) and 55 of Protocol I, as well as other environmental treaties. The Court considered that these treaties could not have been intended to deprive states of their rights of self-defense, but that respect for the environment is "one of the elements that go to assessing whether an action is in conformity with the principles of necessity and proportionality" (para. 30). As for whether these obligations are embodied in customary law, the Court referred to Articles 35(3) and 55 of Protocol I as "powerful constraints for all the States having subscribed to these provisions" (para. 31), thereby apparently treating them only as treaty commitments rather than as obligations under customary international law.

Another important instrument is the Convention on the Prohibition of Military or Any Other Hostile Use of Environmental Modification Techniques, 31 U.S.T. 333, 1108 U.N.T.S. 151 (ENMOD Convention), which prohibits military or any other hostile use of environmental modification techniques having widespread, long-lasting or severe effects. This prohibition is defined with reference to "any technique for changing—through the deliberate manipulation of natural processes—the dynamics, composition or structure of the Earth, including its biota, lithosphere, hydrosphere and atmosphere, or of outer space." The Conference of the Committee on Disarmament, which drafted the ENMOD Convention, appended four nonbinding "Understandings" in explanation of certain provisions. As of 2009, the ENMOD Convention had seventy-three parties, including the United States, United Kingdom, and the Russian Federation.

NOTES

1. *Environmental Damage in Iraq–Kuwait War.* During the 1991 Gulf War Iraqi forces opened valves at the Mina al-Ahamadi and Mina al-Gakr oil terminals and pumped large quantities of crude oil into the Persian Gulf. Toward the end of the conflict Iraq set massive fires in Kuwaiti oil fields. After the cease-fire, the Security Council adopted a resolution that declared Iraq was "liable under international law for any direct loss, damage, including environmental damage and the depletion of natural resources, or injury * * * as a result of Iraq's unlawful invasion and occupation of Kuwait." S.C. Res. 687, at ¶ 16 (Apr. 3, 1991). Would Protocol I or the ENMOD Convention apply to Iraq's actions? See Oxman, Environmental Warfare, 22 Ocean Dev. & Int'l L. 433, 433–36 (1991); Robinson, International Law and the Destruction of Nature in the Gulf War, 21 Env'l Pol'y & L. 216 (1991); Szasz, Environmental Destruction as a Method of Warfare: International Law Applicable to the Gulf War, 15 Disarmament 128 (1992).

2. *Environmental Damage as War Crime.* Article 8(2)(b)(iv) of the Rome Statute of the International Criminal Court provides for the war crime of "intentionally launching an attack in the knowledge that such attack will cause * * * widespread, long-term and severe damage to the natural environment which would be clearly excessive in relation to the concrete and direct overall military advantage anticipated." The terms "widespread," "long-term," and "severe" correspond to terms in Protocol I and the ENMOD Convention, and the interpretations and understandings of those instruments may be relevant to the Rome Statute.

B. ARMS CONTROL AND DISARMAMENT

After the First World War, disarmament was high on the international agenda. The victorious nations imposed limitations on German rearmament and sought also to regulate their own armaments. The emphasis was on the weapons of the previous war. For example, revulsion at the use of mustard gas led to the Protocol for the Prohibition of the Use in War of

Asphyxiating, Poisonous or Other Gases and of Bacteriological Methods of Warfare, June 17, 1925, 94 L.N.T.S. 65 (Geneva Gas Protocol). Disarmament conferences at Washington and London reached agreements establishing ratios on battleships for the major powers. See Washington Treaty for the Limitation of Naval Armament (1922), 43 Stat. 1655, 25 L.N.T.S. 201; Treaty for the Limitation and Reduction of Naval Armaments (London Naval Treaty of 1930), April 22, 1930, 46 Stat. 2858, 112 L.N.T.S. 65.

The emergence of nuclear weapons at the end of the Second World War gave urgency to the quest for means of eliminating or controlling them, along with other weapons of mass destruction. Arms control negotiations have never been long in abeyance, and a number of agreements to limit or regulate nuclear and other weaponry are in force. Many of these are multilateral treaties concluded within the framework of the United Nations. The most important ones are excerpted in the Documents Supplement.

1. Chemical and Biological Weapons

The ban on poisonous weapons embodied in the 1925 Geneva Gas Protocol was generally observed during World War II. Prohibitions were extended to biological weapons in the Convention on the Prohibition of the Development, Production and Stockpiling of Bacteriological (Biological) and Toxin Weapons and on Their Destruction, 26 U.S.T. 583, 1015 U.N.T.S. 163, which was signed at Washington, London, and Moscow April 10, 1972 and entered into force in 1975.

In the 1980s and 1990s, however, disturbing evidence mounted of chemical weapons use during the Iran–Iraq War, both on a cross-boundary basis and by Iraq against its own Kurdish population. See reports of experts appointed by the U.N. Secretary–General, U.N. Docs. S/16433 (Mar. 26, 1984), S/17127 (Apr. 24, 1985), S/17130 (Apr. 25, 1985); U.N. Chronicle, at 3 (March 1984); id., at 24 (March 1985); Human Rights Watch, Iraq's Crime of Genocide: The Anfal Campaign Against the Kurds 262–65 and Appendix C (1995) (documenting chemical attacks against at least 60 Kurdish villages and the town of Halabja). By the 1990s (in the wake of further disclosures concerning Iraq's non-compliance with international obligations concerning weapons of mass destruction), the need for a stricter international regime with verification and sanctions had become clear.

On January 13, 1993, a new Convention on the Prohibition of the Development, Production, Stockpiling and Use of Chemical Weapons and on Their Destruction (Chemical Weapons Convention), 1974 U.N.T.S. 45 (1993), was opened for signature and promptly signed by more than 120 states. It quickly garnered the ratifications necessary to bring it into force in April 1997. As of 2009, it has more than 187 states parties, including the United States. Iraq became a party by accession in January 2009.

Under the terms of the Chemical Weapons Convention, states parties are prohibited from using, producing or stockpiling poison gas or lethal chemical weapons, and are obliged to dispose of existing chemical weapons by the year 2010. The treaty creates rigorous verification procedures implemented through an Organization for the Prohibition of Chemical Weapons which has been established at The Hague and functioning since 1997. The implementation mechanisms include routine inspections at facilities that are declared to possess or use chemicals that may be precursors to weapons agents, and "challenge inspections" to guard against cheating.

NOTES

1. *National Constitutional Questions.* Some concerns were expressed in the United States, prior to the Senate's advice and consent to ratification given in April 1997, that the inspection regime under the Chemical Weapons Convention (especially the system for challenge inspections) might pose constitutional problems, e.g. in light of the Fourth Amendment's requirements for searches and seizures or Fifth Amendment protections of private property. Another objection, based on a view of the original understanding of the Constitution's structural provisions, was that the treaty power should not be used to transfer enforcement powers to an international organization whose officials would not be accountable through constitutional processes. See Rotunda, The Chemical Warfare Convention: Political and Constitutional Issues, 15 Const. Comment. 131 (1998); Yoo, The New Sovereignty and the Old Constitution: The Chemical Weapons Convention and the Appointments Clause, 15 Const. Comment. 87 (1998). The Senate approved the treaty on the basis that there were no insuperable constitutional obstacles.

2. *Customary Law.* Does the almost universal ratification of the Chemical Weapons Convention indicate emergence of a customary norm coextensive with the normative provisions of the treaty? To what extent could implementation provisions be mobilized to press a non-party to comply with the normative provisions? On the treaty system in general, see The New Chemical Weapons Convention: Implementation and Prospects (Bothe, Ronzitti, & Rosas eds. 1998).

3. *Reprisals for Violation?* Could retaliation for chemical weapons use in kind, or with other weapons of mass destruction, ever be permissible? Compare Judge Schwebel's dissent in the Advisory Opinion on Legality of Use of Nuclear Weapons, p. 87. See also Müllerson, Missiles with Non–Conventional Warheads and International Law, 27 Isr. Y.B. Hum. Rts. 225, 226 n. 3 (1998). Compare Vienna Convention on the Law of Treaties, art. 60(5), discussed at p. 210; and U.S. concerns about the prohibition on belligerent reprisals in Geneva Protocol I, p. 1287 note 7 *supra*.

4. *Biological Weapons.* The ban on use of bacteriological weapons found in the 1925 Geneva Gas Protocol did not cover development, production and stockpiling. Those aspects are addressed in the Convention on the Prohibition of the Development, Production and Stockpiling of Bacteriological (Biological) and Toxin Weapons and on Their Destruction (Biological Weapons Convention), April 10, 1972, 26 U.S.T. 583, 1015 U.N.T.S. 163, which has 163 parties as of 2009. It has no counterpart to the institutional regime created by the

Chemical Weapons Convention. On efforts to devise such a regime and reasons for their failure, see Kellman, Bioviolence (2007); Fidler & Gostin, Biosecurity in the Global Age: Biological Weapons, Public Health, and the Rule of Law (2008).

5. *Delivery Systems.* The Missile Technology Control Regime, 26 I.L.M. 599 (1987), discussed in Müllerson, Missiles with Non–Conventional Warheads and International Law, 27 Isr. Y.B. Hum. Rts. 225, 243–49 (1998), covers not only nuclear weapons delivery systems but also chemical and biological weapons delivery systems, and any surface-to-surface missile with a range over 150 km. See also Angelova, Note, Compelling Compliance with International Regimes: China and the Missile Technology Control Regime, 38 Colum. J. Transnat'l L. 419 (1999).

2. Nuclear Weapons: Possession, Testing, Use

In 1961, the U.N. General Assembly adopted a resolution declaring that the use of nuclear weapons is a violation of the U.N. Charter and of international law. Declaration on the Prohibition of the Use of Nuclear and Thermonuclear Weapons, G.A. Res. 1653 (XVI) (Nov. 24, 1961). The resolution was adopted by a vote of 55 to 20, with 26 abstentions. The United States, United Kingdom, France, Australia, Canada, China, and Italy were among the states voting no. The United States has strongly and repeatedly reiterated its view that the resolution does not reflect the state of international law.

The major powers recognized a shared interest in preventing the spread of nuclear weapons capability to other states. A significant milestone in this regard has been the Nuclear Non–Proliferation Treaty ("N.P.T."), 21 U.S.T. 483, 729 U.N.T.S. 161, which was signed in 1968 and entered into force in 1970. Under the N.P.T., the nuclear-weapon state parties undertake not to transfer to any recipient any nuclear weapons or or nuclear explosive devices or assist any non-nuclear-weapon state in acquiring them; and the non-nuclear-weapon states undertake not to acquire such weapons or devices. A safeguards system is established under the auspices of the International Atomic Energy Agency (I.A.E.A.) to verify that fissionable material is not diverted from peaceful uses to nuclear weapons or explosive devices. At the time, the nuclear-weapon states were the five declared nuclear powers: the United States, the Soviet Union, the United Kingdom, France, and China. A few threshold-nuclear states (notably India, Pakistan, and Israel) remained outside the N.P.T. framework. Others—Iraq, North Korea, and Iran—undertook N.P.T. obligations, including I.A.E.A. safeguards, but came under strong suspicion of violating those undertakings. See pp. 201–02, 782–84, 1232–34.

The initial duration of the N.P.T. was twenty-five years from entry into force. At a review conference held in May 1995, an indefinite extension was agreed.

NOTES

1. *Succession to Soviet Treaties.* The fragmentation of the Soviet Union into fifteen independent republics has raised issues regarding succession to arms control treaties binding on the former Soviet Union. Bunn and Rhinelander discuss the application of a "continuity" theory of succession to the Soviet Union's arms control obligations, as contrasted to the "clean slate" rule frequently applied in decolonization situations (see Chapter 19, p. 1525):

> * * * Application of the continuity rule would not make each former republic a nuclear-weapon state party to the NPT [Non–Proliferation Treaty] just because the Soviet Union was such a party and the treaty applied throughout Soviet territory. Such a result would mean each could control nuclear weapons, which would be wholly inconsistent with the purpose of the treaty. The NPT was intended to hold the line at the number of nuclear-weapon states that had "manufactured and exploded a nuclear weapon or other nuclear explosive device prior to January 1, 1967." That was five: Britain, China and France as well as the Soviet Union and the United States.

> The 1978 Vienna Convention [on Succession of States in respect of Treaties] contains an exception to the continuity rule if "it appears from the treaty or is otherwise established that the application of the treaty in respect of the successor State would be incompatible with the object and purpose of the treaty * * *." Clearly, this exception is applicable to succession to the NPT by republics other than Russia. That means they are non-nuclear-weapon states under the NPT, and must join it in that capacity if they wish to become members.

> What has happened in the former republics so far is consistent with this view. Tactical nuclear weapons from all the republics that had them other than Russia have been moved to Russia, except for some remaining in Belarus and Ukraine, and removal of these is promised before July 1, 1992. Strategic nuclear weapons exist only in Belarus, Kazakhstan and Ukraine besides Russia, and removal of the last of these from Kazakhstan is promised by 1999. Both Belarus and Ukraine have promised to join the NPT as non-nuclear-weapon states and to become nuclear-free zones. While Kazakhstan's position is more ambiguous, U.S. representatives are negotiating with it as well as with Belarus, Russia and Ukraine about further removal of nuclear weapons.

Bunn & Rhinelander, Who Inherited the Former Soviet Union's Obligations Under Arms Control Treaties with the United States? Memorandum to the Committee on Foreign Relations (Mar. 10, 1992). See also Chapter 19, p. 1530.

2. *Hiroshima and Nagasaki.* In an action against the Japanese government, Japanese citizens argued that the Japanese government had unlawfully waived their claims for damages resulting from the atomic bombs dropped at Hiroshima and Nagasaki by the United States in 1945. The court stated:

> [T]here is not an established theory among international jurists in connection with the difference of poison, poison gas, bacterium, etc. from atomic bombs. However, judging from the fact that the St. Petersburg

Declaration declares that " * * * considering that the use of a weapon which increases uselessly the pain of people who are already placed out of battle and causes their death necessarily is beyond the scope of this purpose, and considering that the use of such a weapon is thus contrary to humanity * * * " and that article 23(e) of the Hague Regulations respecting War on Land prohibits "the employment of such arms, projectiles, and material as cause unnecessary injury," we can safely see that besides poison, poison-gas and bacterium the use of the means of injuring the enemy which causes at least the same or more injury is prohibited by international law. The destructive power of the atomic bomb is tremendous, but it is doubtful whether atomic bombing really had an appropriate military effect at that time and whether it was necessary. It is a deeply sorrowful reality that the atomic bombing on both cities of Hiroshima and Nagasaki took the lives of many civilians, and that among the survivors there are people whose lives are still imperilled owing to the radial rays, even today 18 years later. In this sense, it is not too much to say that the pain brought by the atomic bombs is severer than that from poison and poison-gas, and we can say that the act of dropping such a cruel bomb is contrary to the fundamental principle of the laws of war that unnecessary pain must not be given.

The Shimoda Case, Judgment of the Tokyo District Court (7 Dec. 1963), reprinted in 8 Japanese Ann. Int'l L. 212, 241–42 (1964). See discussion of the Shimoda Case in the dissenting opinion of Judge Shahabuddeen in, *Legality of the Threat or Use of Nuclear Weapons*, Advisory Opinion, 1996 I.C.J., 375, 397, 400–02.

3. *U.S. Cases.* The illegality of nuclear weapons under international law was raised in U.S. courts, without success, as a defense to criminal charges stemming from civil protests against such weapons. See *United States v. Kabat*, 797 F.2d 580 (8th Cir. 1986), cert. denied, 481 U.S. 1030 (1987); *United States v. Montgomery*, 772 F.2d 733 (11th Cir. 1985); *United States v. Brodhead*, 714 F.Supp. 593 (D. Mass. 1989). See also Boyle, Defending Civil Resistance Under International Law (1987); Lippman, Civil Resistance: Revitalizing International Law in the Nuclear Age, 13 Whittier L. Rev. 17 (1992). The illegality of such weapons was also asserted as a ground for challenging production and deployment of nuclear weapons. See *United States v. Thompson*, disposition (unpublished) tabled at, 931 F.2d 898 (9th Cir. 1991); *United States v. Allen*, 760 F.2d 447 (2d Cir.1985). See also *Pauling v. McElroy*, 164 F.Supp. 390 (D.D.C. 1958), aff'd, 278 F.2d 252 (D.C. Cir. 1960), cert. denied, 364 U.S. 835 (1960); *Greenham Women Against Cruise Missiles v. Reagan*, 591 F.Supp. 1332 (S.D.N.Y. 1984), aff'd, 755 F.2d 34 (2d Cir. 1985).

4. *Limitations on Testing; Comprehensive Test Ban Treaty.* Efforts to control the spread of nuclear weapons have long focused on restricting the conditions for testing such weapons, with a view toward an ultimate ban on all forms of testing. Treaties and other instruments over some four decades established several kinds of limitations, either on a general multilateral basis with widespread ratification or by special agreement among some or all of the declared nuclear powers. (See the Documents Supplement for the most significant of these undertakings.) Atmospheric testing was restricted under the Limited (Partial) Test Ban Treaty of 1963 which has been widely ratified

(more than 125 adherences as of 2009). France did not become a party, however. As noted in earlier chapters, litigation at the International Court of Justice seeking a determination of unlawfulness of French atmospheric testing was dismissed in 1974, after France unilaterally announced an end to such testing. *Nuclear Tests Cases* (Australia and New Zealand v. France), 1974 I.C.J. 253, 457. See pp. ___, ___.

On September 24, 1996 a Comprehensive Test Ban Treaty (CTBT) was opened for signature at the United Nations and was promptly signed by more than 135 states, including all five permanent members of the Security Council (who were at that time the only declared nuclear powers). Significantly, India and Pakistan did not sign; see below. The basic obligation of the CTBT is embodied in Article I, which provides:

> 1. Each State Party undertakes not to carry out any nuclear weapon test explosion or any other nuclear explosion, and to prohibit and prevent any such nuclear explosion at any place under its jurisdiction or control.

> 2. Each State Party undertakes, furthermore, to refrain from causing, encouraging, or in any way participating in the carrying out of any nuclear weapon test explosion or any other nuclear explosion.

The CTBT would also create a Comprehensive Nuclear Test–Ban Treaty Organization headquartered in Vienna, which would carry out verification activities under the treaty (Article II). Verification mechanisms include international monitoring, consultation and clarification, on-site inspections, and confidence-building measures (Article IV). States parties are also to implement the treaty through national measures, including adoption of prohibitions on nuclear testing anywhere on its territory or in any other place under its jurisdiction or control, or by any of its nationals (Article III).

By its terms (Article XIV), the CTBT can only enter into force after all forty-four states listed in its Annex 2 have ratified: they include all states with nuclear reactors. As of 2009, nine of the required forty-four ratifications were still outstanding. The United States, China and Israel have signed but not ratified; and India, Pakistan, and North Korea have neither signed nor ratified.

In October 1999, the U.S. Senate cast a negative vote (48–51) on a resolution to give advice and consent to ratification of the CTBT. The main objections expressed by opponents of the treaty included concerns about its verifiability and about whether a total test ban could impair the integrity of the U.S. nuclear deterrent. President Clinton insisted that the defeat in the Senate was only a temporary setback and that the treaty could be brought forward again at a more auspicious time. See Murphy, Contemporary Practice of the United States, Senate Rejection of the Comprehensive Test Ban Treaty, 94 A.J.I.L. 137 (2000). In April 2009, President Barack Obama announced that he would give priority to securing ratification of the CTBT.

Meanwhile, in spring 1998, first India and then Pakistan exploded nuclear weapons devices, thereby becoming the first states to do so since the CTBT had been opened for signature. They are also the first states—apart from the five permanent members of the Security Council—to have demonstrated overt nuclear weapons capability. On the motivations for the Indian and Pakistani tests in relation to the CTBT, see Thakur, Envisioning Nuclear Futures, 31 Security Dialogue 25 (2000). North Korea carried out a nuclear test in October 2006 and was sanctioned by the U.N. Security Council in Resolution 1718 (2006).

5. *Security Council Resolution 1540*. In 2004 the U.N. Security Council embarked on a new initiative to prevent weapons of mass destruction from falling into the hands of terrorists. See S.C. Resolution 1540 (2004) (in Documents Supplement) and discussion of Security Council "legislation" in Chapter 4, p. 274. Are such measures a suitable supplement to ordinary treaty-making?

C. THE LAWS OF WAR IN THE INTERNET ERA

It is an open question how the laws of war will apply to techniques of warfare in the age of cyberspace and "virtual war." The recent "revolution in military affairs" has produced a wide range of new technologies which could either exacerbate or alleviate the destructiveness of war. Potentially, more precise weapons could make it possible to discriminate more carefully between military and civilian objects, so that collateral damage to civilians might be minimized. "Non-lethal" military technologies—e.g, slippery foam to impede traffic, microwaves to disable electronic devices, pungent gases to disperse crowds—can assist combatants to direct their lethal fire against military forces and other military objectives, while avoiding civilian casualties. The legal issues surrounding such technologies are just beginning to be explored. See generally Council on Foreign Relations, Non–Lethal Technologies: Military Options and Implications xi, 11–13 (1995), and Nonlethal Technologies: Progress and Prospects 35 (1999) (noting possible concerns under treaties such as the Chemical Weapons Convention about certain non-lethal weapons). The possibilities for conducting remote warfare by computer, or using computer technologies to disable enemy capabilities while protecting one's own systems and infrastructure from comparable attacks, have opened up new avenues for legal inquiry.

The term "information warfare" (or "information operations") has come into use with respect to military techniques that target the opponent's information systems and infrastructure, including communications, weapons systems, command and control systems, intelligence systems, and civil infrastructure such as power grids and banking, as well as comparable defensive techniques. It has been suggested that some "information operations"—physical attacks on information systems, psychological operations, and jamming of radar and radio signals—are by now "traditional," and the application to them of the international laws of war is "reasonably well settled." See U.S. Department of Defense, Office of General Counsel, An Assessment of International Legal Issues in Information Operations 4 (1999). On the other hand, "[i]t will not be as easy to apply existing international law principles to *information attack*, a term used to describe the use of electronic means to gain access to or change information in a targeted information system without necessarily damaging its physical components," as by computer network attack, popularly known as "hacking". Ibid.

The difficulty in pinpointing the origin of computer network attack is one complication in seeking to apply traditional legal concepts to this new kind of activity. An attack emanating from a foreign state and targeting another state's military or other governmental computers could bring into play rights of self-defense under international law and principles of the humanitarian laws of war. On the other hand, "hacking" could be done by domestic as well as foreign actors and might have merely private rather than governmental objectives. To the extent that information operations techniques are understood as weapons, aspects of the laws of war that regulate weaponry could come into play. More to the point, if a belligerent uses information techniques to cause injury, death and destruction to another belligerent, its actions could be evaluated under the humanitarian principles of the laws of war, including the principle of distinguishing between combatants and non-combatants, and the requirements of necessity and proportionality and of refraining from causing superfluous injury.

NOTES

1. *Further Reading.* The 1999 Department of Defense legal study, cited above, has "Notes for Further Research" with bibliographic references at 48–54. Other sources include: Kanuck, Information Warfare: New Challenges for Public International Law, 37 Harv. Int'l L.J. 272 (1996); Greenberg, et al., Information Warfare and International Law (1997); Sharp, Cyberspace and the Use of Force (1999); Schmitt, Computer Network Attack and the Use of Force in International Law: Thoughts on a Normative Framework, 37 Colum. J. Transnat'l L. 885 (1999); Shulman, Discrimination in the Laws of Information Warfare, 37 Colum. J. Transnat'l L. 939 (1999); Ignatieff, Virtual War: Kosovo and Beyond (2000); Walker, Information Warfare and Neutrality, 33 Vand. J. Transnat'l L. 1079 (2000); Schmitt & O'Donnell, Computer Network Attack and International Law (forthcoming in U.S. Naval War College, 76 International Law Studies, 2001).

2. *Further Regulation?* Would a new instrument to address legal regulation of information warfare be desirable? In 1998 the Russian Federation proposed a resolution inviting views on the "advisability of elaborating international legal regimes to ban the development, production, and use of particularly dangerous information weapons." The General Assembly thereafter adopted a resolution on "developments in the field of information and telecommunications in the context of international security," inviting multilateral consideration of information security issues. U.N. Doc. A/RES/53/70 (Jan. 4, 1999). The United States and the United Kingdom took the position that it is premature to consider international regulation of information operations as a security matter, and that the priority should be on measures against computer crime and terrorism. See U.N. Doc. A/54/213 (Aug. 1, 1999).

CHAPTER 16

INTERNATIONAL CRIMINAL LAW

■ ■ ■

SECTION 1. INTRODUCTION

If a state violates international law, thereby causing injury to another state or that state's nationals, claims for such violation are properly addressed by the government of the injured state to that of the state responsible for the violation, as discussed in Chapters 8–9. Ordinarily, the officials, or other persons, who committed the act constituting the violation are not held personally responsible for it under international law.

Yet in a growing number of circumstances, international law has recognized *individual responsibility* for conduct labeled as criminal under international law. The field of international criminal law encompasses serious crimes under customary international law or treaty for which an individual may be prosecuted and punished, as well as the institutions that may be involved in enforcement and prosecution of these crimes. Some crimes, such as piracy and slave trading, have long been recognized under customary international law. Many more now have been defined in multilateral treaties, and some of these treaty crimes enjoy such widespread acceptance and *opinio juris* that they are considered to be a part of customary law binding on all states, even those not party to the treaty concerned. Examples would include war crimes constituting grave breaches of the 1949 Geneva Conventions, genocide and state-sponsored torture. (The term "international humanitarian law" is often used to encompass the law relating to protecting persons from genocide, crimes against humanity, and war crimes. It might also be used to cover the crime relating to aggression and other crimes under international law committed during international or internal conflict.) Many other crimes, including various acts of terrorism, are defined in multilateral treaties but may not have met the threshold requirements to qualify as crimes under customary international law.

The areas of international criminal law identified above often intersect and implicate the international law of human rights discussed in Chapter 13. First, crimes under international law for which an individual may be held responsible will often constitute a violation of internationally protected human rights. In this sense, international human rights are the normative foundation for an important part of international criminal law.

International criminal law and the institutions that enforce it have, as their control thrust, the vindication and protection of internationally protected human rights. Genocide, crimes against humanity, state-sponsored torture, and serious war crimes represent egregious violations of human rights recognized and protected under international law. It is the importance of basic human rights, such as the right to life and security of the person, and the right to be free from slavery, torture and other inhuman or degrading treatment, that is the moral imperative that underlies the legitimacy of criminalizing their violation. Second, in investigating, arresting, detaining and prosecuting an individual for international conduct made criminal under international law, national and international law enforcement officials and tribunals must respect and uphold the human rights of the accused to due process, a public trial, the presumption of innocence and a right to appeal.

The institutions involved in enforcement and prosecution of crimes under international law may include national or international institutions or both. But at present it is *national* institutions that play the dominant role in enforcing international criminal law. In many cases in which conduct is a crime under international law, it is also a crime under national law, and it may be investigated and prosecuted by national enforcement authorities and adjudicated in national courts. Section 2 of this Chapter discusses the role of national laws and courts in defining, prosecuting, and punishing international crimes. Section 2 also notes that the subject of international criminal law also extends to transnational cooperation in investigating and prosecuting persons for violations of crimes arising purely under national criminal law, such as corruption, bribery, money laundering, tax evasion, or fraud. Although this area is analytically distinct from the international criminal law that involves crimes under customary international law or international treaty, there is a some overlap given that international crimes are often prosecuted in national legal systems.

In a very limited category of cases, alleged crimes under international law may be investigated and prosecuted before an *ad hoc* international criminal tribunals, which are temporary in nature and limited in the temporal and geographic range of their jurisdiction, as discussed in Section 3. In such cases, if delivered to the custody of the tribunal, the accused will be tried and, in the event of conviction, will be punished by that international tribunal composed of judges and prosecutors that have an international character. Further, as discussed in Section 4, there now exists a *permanent* International Criminal Court based on a multilateral treaty known as the Rome Statute, which was adopted in 1998 and entered into force in 2002. A little over a hundred states are a party to that statute, not including important states such as China, India, Russia, and the United States.

SECTION 2.   PROSECUTION OF INTERNATIONAL CRIMES IN NATIONAL COURTS AND TRANSNATIONAL CRIMINAL COOPERATION

For hundreds of years there have been some crimes under customary international law for which individuals could be tried and, if convicted, punished in national courts. Because of such crimes, there are many references in national constitutions, statutes, and judicial decisions worldwide, as well as in treatises by scholars, to individuals committing "an offense against the law of nations." See, e.g., U.S. Const. art. 1, § 8(10). A prominent historical example is individual responsibility for acts of piracy, which, although crimes under customary international law, have been prosecuted in national courts in the absence of an international court with jurisdiction. In *United States v. Smith,* 18 U.S. (5 Wheat.) 153 (1820), the Supreme Court held that Smith had properly been convicted under an act of Congress that criminalized "piracy, as defined by the law of nations;" according to the Court, Congress had adequately defined the crime by incorporating by reference the definition of piracy under customary international law. 18 U.S. at 158.

Another example of crimes arising under customary international law is war crimes under the laws of war. In *Ex parte Quirin*, 317 U.S. 1 (1942), the Supreme Court held that Congress had, by enacting a statute referred to as the Articles of War, explicitly provided that U.S. military tribunals have jurisdiction to try individuals for offenses against the laws of war. The case involved the trial and conviction of a group of spies (one, a U.S. national, and the others, German nationals) who were put ashore with explosives in the United States by German submarines during World War II. The Court stated:

> * * * Similarly by the reference in the 15th Article of War to "offenders or offenses that . . . by the law of war may be triable by such military commissions", Congress has incorporated by reference, as within the jurisdiction of military commissions, all offenses which are defined as such by the law of war * * * and which may constitutionally be included within that jurisdiction. Congress had the choice of crystallizing in permanent form and in minute detail every offense against the law of war, or of adopting the system of common law applied by military tribunals so far as it should be recognized and deemed applicable by the courts. It chose the latter course.

> * * * The spy who secretly and without uniform passes the military lines of a belligerent in time of war, seeking to gather military information and communicate it to the enemy, or an enemy combatant who without uniform comes secretly through the lines for the purpose of waging war by destruction of life or property, are familiar examples of belligerents who are generally deemed not to be

entitled to the status of prisoners of war, but to be offenders against the law of war subject to trial and punishment by military tribunals. * * *

Such was the practice of our own military authorities before the adopting of the Constitution, and during the Mexican and Civil Wars. 317 U.S. at 30–31.

A more recent prosecution was of former Peruvian President Alberto Fujimori, who was convicted by a Peruvian court in April of 2009 of crimes against humanity, for his role in the killings and kidnapings by Peruvian security forces in operations against leftist guerrillas (the Shining Path) in the 1990s. Fujimori was sentenced to twenty-five years in prison. The case was unusual in that Fujimori, an elected head of state, fled his country after leaving office to live in another country (Japan), traveled to a third country (Chile) where he was arrested, and then was extradited back to his home country for trial.

While customary law is regarded as identifying certain acts as crimes under international law, the past fifty years has seen many such crimes identified in multilateral treaties, along with obligations upon the states parties to prosecute offenders who turn up in their territory. For example, the Convention on the Prevention and Punishment of the Crime of Genocide, Dec. 9, 1948, 78 U.N.T.S. 277, provides that persons committing genocide and related enumerated offenses "shall be punished, whether they are constitutionally responsible rulers, public officials or private individuals" (Article IV). Moreover, the contracting parties undertake to enact the necessary legislation to provide effective penalties for guilty persons (Articles V). Further, the Convention provides that "[p]ersons charged with genocide * * * shall be tried by a competent tribunal of the State in the territory of which the act was committed, or by such international penal tribunal as may have jurisdiction * * *" (Article VI). The United States ratified the Convention in 1988 and has enacted legislation rendering genocide a crime for which individuals may be tried and punished in U.S. courts. Genocide Convention Implementation Act of 1988, 18 U.S.C. § 1091 (2000); Genocide Accountability Act of 2007, Pub. L. No. 110–151, 121 Stat. 1821 (2007); see also LeBlanc, The United States and the Genocide Convention (1991).

Similarly, the four Geneva Conventions of 1949 on the laws of war require any state party (including a belligerent state) to try individuals (including members of enemy forces) who are alleged to have committed grave breaches specified in the conventions. Geneva Convention for the Amelioration of the Condition of the Wounded and Sick in Armed Forces in the Field, art. 49, Aug. 12, 1949, 6 U.S.T. 3114, 75 U.N.T.S. 31; Geneva Convention for the Amelioration of the Condition of Wounded, Sick and Shipwrecked Members of Armed Forces at Sea, art. 50, Aug. 12, 1949, 6 U.S.T. 3114, 75 U.N.T.S. 85; Geneva Convention Relative to the Treatment of Prisoners of War, art. 129, Aug. 12, 1949, 6 U.S.T. 3316, 75 U.N.T.S. 135; Geneva Convention Relative to the Protection of Civilian

Persons in Time of War, art. 146, Aug. 12, 1949, 6 U.S.T. 3516, 75 U.N.T.S. 287. An individual member of a belligerent's own military force who violates the laws of war may also be tried by a military tribunal of that state. Yet such rules also may inhibit states from pursuing certain kinds of prosecutions. In *Hamdan v. Rumsfeld*, 548 U.S. 557 (2006), the Supreme Court struck down the President's creation of certain military commissions to prosecute "unlawful combatants" being held at Guantánamo Bay Naval Base in the "war on terrorism," because those commissions deviated from common Article 3 of the 1949 Geneva Conventions and in so doing so were inconsistent with Congress' incorporation of those rules by statute.

The Convention Against Torture and Other Cruel, Inhuman or Degrading Treatment or Punishment, Dec. 10, 1984, S. Treaty Doc. No. 100–20, 1465 U.N.T.S. 85, which entered into force for the United States in 1994, requires all parties to "take effective legislative, administrative, judicial or other measures to prevent acts of torture in any territory under its jurisdiction," where torture is defined as state-sponsored torture (Articles 1 & 2(1)). Moreover, the Convention provides that if a party obtains custody of an alleged perpetrator (no matter where the act occurred), it must either (1) investigate, and, if the facts warrant, prosecute the suspect; or (2) extradite the suspect to another state that has a basis for exercising jurisdiction and that has requested extradition (Articles 6 & 7). This requirement is referred to as the principle of *aut dedere aut judicare* (Latin for extradite or prosecute). See Bassiouni & Wise, Aut Dedere Aut Judicare: The Duty to Extradite or Prosecute in International Law (1995). Such treaties are often considered to embody an application of the universality principle as among the state parties, because custody of the suspect is the only relevant nexus; there is no requirement that the offence be committed within the state's territory, by its national or against its national.

One Convention Against Torture case that produced considerable international furor in recent years was the attempt by the Government of Spain to have Augusto Pinochet, former dictator of Chile, extradited from the United Kingdom, where he had traveled for medical treatment, for crimes under international law committed in Chile. The Law Lords of the U.K. House of Lords held that Pinochet could be extradited to be tried for the crime of state-sponsored torture, as defined in the Convention Against Torture, though only for acts occurring after enactment of the U.K. Criminal Justice Act of 1988, which implemented that Convention within the United Kingdom. However, the U.K. Home Secretary ultimately declined to extradite because of Pinochet's failing health and Pinochet was allowed to return to Chile. See Chapter 11, Section 6. Similarly efforts at extradition by both Spain and Germany have arisen in 2008–2009 with respect to U.S. government officials involved in authorizing harsh interrogation techniques of alien detainees at Guantánamo Bay Naval Base. See Simons, Spanish Court Weighs Inquiry on Torture for 6 Bush–Era Officials, Mar. 28, 2009, at A1. Do you favor national courts pursuing such prosecutions? Does it matter whether the victims were nationals of the prosecuting state? What limits, if any, should exist?

Provisions in the anti-terrorism conventions, such as the conventions relating to the suppression of aircraft hijacking and sabotage, frequently require any state party to make the offense punishable by severe penalties and either to investigate and prosecute, if appropriate, an alleged offender in its custody or to extradite the individual to another party having jurisdiction under the convention. See, e.g., Hague Convention for the Suppression of Unlawful Seizure of Aircraft, art. 2, Dec. 16, 1970, 22 U.S.T. 1641, 860 U.N.T.S. 105; Montreal Convention for Suppression of Unlawful Acts Against the Safety of Civilian Aviation, arts. 3 & 7, Sept. 23, 1971, 24 U.S.T. 564, 974 U.N.T.S. 177; International Convention for the Suppression of Terrorist Bombings, G.A. Res. 52/164, annex (Dec. 15, 1997); International Convention for the Suppression of the Financing of Terrorism, Dec. 9, 1999, S. Treaty Doc. No. 106–49 (2000), G.A. Res. 54/109, annex (Dec. 9, 1999). Other crimes that have been established under multinational treaty include apartheid and crimes against internationally protected persons, such as diplomats and officials of international organizations.

In the absence of international tribunals with broad jurisdiction over crimes under international law, it is left to national courts to try individuals who have committed such crimes. There is ample authority within international law for the proposition that a national court may try an individual who has committed a crime under customary international law or international treaty, as long as there is a jurisdictional basis under international law for doing so (see Chapter 11). Within the national legal system, the conduct is considered criminal if the international criminal law is automatically incorporated as part of national law or, as is required in the case of the United States, legislation has been enacted which identifies the conduct as a crime under national law.

There is also a conceptually distinct branch of "international criminal law" that is focused on transnational cooperation by states in the investigation and prosecution of conduct that only violates *national* criminal law. While there is sometimes overlap between these two areas of international criminal law, most national prosecutors, to the extent that they encounter a criminal matter with transnational dimensions, are faced with conduct that violates only national criminal law, and yet involves evidence or a prospective defendant in another country.

Elaborate bilateral and multilateral arrangements have been adopted by states to enable and promote mutual assistance in national criminal investigations and prosecutions. Mutual legal assistance treaties (MLATs) require a "requested state" to assist a "requesting state's" law enforcement efforts by sharing with the requesting state useful information in the requested state's possession, searching for and seizing evidence located in the requested state, serving summons on and tracing suspects or witnesses located in the requested state, and taking written testimony from such persons. In 1959, the Council of Europe adopted a Convention on Mutual Legal Assistance in Criminal Matters, Apr. 20, 1959, E.T.S. No. 30, as amended by protocol, which has had a significant influence on the development of MLATs by European Union member states. Since many countries (particularly in the developing world) do not have MLATs with one another, the United Nations in 1990 adopted a model MLAT. See G.A. Res. 45/117, annex (Dec. 14, 1990), *reprinted in* 30 I.L.M. 1419 (1991). In June 2003, the European Union and United States signed an MLAT which provides for cooperation between the United States and all twenty-seven E.U. member states. *See* Agreement on Mutual Legal Assistance in Criminal Matters, U.S.–E.U., June 25, 2003, 2003 O.J. (L 181) 34, 43 I.L.M. 758.

Further, a variety of treaties have also been developed that seek to harmonize national criminal laws in particular areas, as well as promote cooperation among states in investigating and prosecuting those laws. Often the impetus for such treaties is that states realize that the area in question cannot adequate be addressed by each state acting individually; that cooperation is necessary to combat transnational criminal networks. For example, the 1961 Single Convention on Narcotic Drugs, Mar. 30, 1961, 18 U.S.T. 1407, 520 U.N.T.S. 204, seeks to limit the use of narcotics with cannabis, coca, and opium-like effects solely to scientific and medical purposes. To that end, it obligates parties to restrict to licensed persons the cultivation, manufacture, and distribution of such narcotics. Further, the convention created an International Narcotics Control Board, to which the parties must report the amount of narcotics produced, consumed, or seized in their territory. The 1971 Convention on Psychotropic Substances, Feb. 21, 1971, 32 U.S.T. 543, 1019 U.N.T.S. 175, was developed in response to the diversification and expansion of the spectrum of drugs beyond those addressed in the 1961 Single Convention. It introduced controls over mind-altering and synthetic drugs, including import and export restrictions, based on the risk of abuse and therapeutic value of the drug. The 1988 U.N. Convention Against the Illicit Traffic in Narcotic Drugs and Psychotropic Substances, Dec. 20, 1988, S. Treaty Doc. No. 101–4, 1582 U.N.T.S. 95, regulates the precursor chemicals to drugs controlled by the Single Convention and the Convention on Psychotropic Substances. It also contains important provisions related to money laundering and other drug-related crimes. Similar regimes exist in other areas, such as corruption, organized crime, money laundering, tax evasion, and even cyber-crime.

Once an offender is located abroad whom a state wishes to apprehend, various bilateral and multilateral treaties provide a basis for pursuing extradition, as discussed in Chapter 11, Section 11. As was the case with MLATs, the European Union and United States signed an extradition treaty in June 2003. *See* Agreement on Extradition, U.S.–E.U., June 25, 2003, 2003 O.J. (L 181) 27, 43 I.L.M. 749. The treaty does not eliminate bilateral extradition agreements between the United States and E.U. member states; rather, it supplements and selectively amends them. So as to conform to that treaty, for example, the United States and the United

Kingdom negotiated a new Extradition Treaty in 2003, See Extradition Treaty, U.S.–U.K., Mar. 31, 2003, S. Treaty Doc. No. 108 23, at 1, 4 (2003). Various cases have arisen in recent years by which the United States has used both MLATs and extradition treaties in pursuit of investigations and prosecutions of U.S. criminal law.

SECTION 3. PROSECUTION OF INTERNATIONAL CRIMES BEFORE *AD HOC* INTERNATIONAL CRIMINAL TRIBUNALS

A. NUREMBERG AND TOKYO INTERNATIONAL MILITARY TRIBUNALS

As noted in the prior Section, individuals have long been tried and punished for commission of crimes under customary international law and international treaty in national courts, usually on the basis of national legislation criminalizing the conduct and imposing penalties. However, in the mid-twentieth century individuals were tried for crimes under customary international law by two multinational tribunals created specially for the purpose of trying German and Japanese war criminals after World War II. Although the Nuremberg and Tokyo international military tribunals (IMTs) were established by the victorious nations, the trials established important precedents for prosecuting individuals in international fora for crimes against peace, crimes against humanity and war crimes. Chapter 15, Section 1(B) focused on the issue of crimes against the peace at Nuremberg, whereas this section focuses on prosecution of war crimes and crimes against humanity.

CHARTER OF THE INTERNATIONAL MILITARY TRIBUNAL

Annex to the Agreement for the Prosecution and Punishment of the Major War Criminals of the European Axis (London Agreement), Aug. 8, 1945
59 Stat. 1544, 82 U.N.T.S. 279

I. CONSTITUTION OF THE INTERNATIONAL MILITARY TRIBUNAL

Article 1.

In pursuance of the Agreement signed on the 8th day of August 1945 by the Government of the United States of America, the Provisional Government of the French Republic, the Government of the United Kingdom of Great Britain and Northern Ireland and the Government of the Union of Soviet Socialist Republics, there shall be established an International Military Tribunal (hereinafter called "the Tribunal") for the just and prompt trial and punishment of the major war criminals of the European Axis.

Article 2.

The Tribunal shall consist of four members, each with an alternate. One member and one alternate shall be appointed by each of the Signatories. The alternates shall, so far as they are able, be present at all sessions of the Tribunal. In case of illness of any member of the Tribunal or his incapacity for some other reason to fulfill his functions, his alternate shall take his place.

* * *

II. JURISDICTION AND GENERAL PRINCIPLES

Article 6.

The Tribunal established by the Agreement referred to in Article 1 hereof for the trial and punishment of the major war criminals of the European Axis countries shall have the power to try and punish persons who, acting in the interests of the European Axis countries, whether as individuals or as members of organizations, committed any of the following crimes:

The following acts, or any of them, are crimes coming within the jurisdiction of the Tribunal for which there shall be individual responsibility:

(a) CRIMES AGAINST PEACE: namely, planning, preparation, initiation or waging of a war of aggression, or a war in violation of international treaties, agreements or assurances, or participation in a common plan or conspiracy for the accomplishment of any of the foregoing;

(b) WAR CRIMES: namely, violations of the laws or customs of war. Such violations shall include, but not be limited to, murder, ill-treatment or deportation to slave labor or for any other purposes of civilian population of or in occupied territory, murder or ill-treatment of prisoners of war or persons on the seas, killing of hostages, plunder of public or private property, wanton destruction of cities, towns or villages, or devastation not justified by military necessity;

(c) CRIMES AGAINST HUMANITY: namely, murder, extermination, enslavement, deportation, and other inhumane acts committed against any civilian population, before or during the war; or persecutions on political, racial or religious grounds in execution of or in connection with any crime within the jurisdiction of the Tribunal, whether or not in violation of the domestic law of the country where perpetrated.

Leaders, organizations, instigators, and accomplices participating in the formulation or execution of a common plan or conspiracy to commit any of the foregoing crimes are responsible for all acts performed by any persons in execution of such plan.

Article 7.

The official position of defendants, whether as Heads of State or responsible officials in Government Departments, shall not be considered as freeing them from responsibility or mitigating punishment.

Article 8.

The fact that the Defendant acted pursuant to order of his Government or of a superior shall not free him from responsibility, but may be considered in mitigation of punishment if the Tribunal determines that justice so requires.

Article 9.

At the trial of any individual member of any group or organization the Tribunal may declare (in connection with any act of which the individual may be convicted) that the group or organization of which the individual was a member was a criminal organization.

After the receipt of the Indictment the Tribunal shall give such notice as it thinks fit that the prosecution intends to ask the Tribunal to make such declaration and any member of the organization will be entitled to apply to the Tribunal for leave to be heard by the Tribunal upon the question of the criminal character of the organization. The Tribunal shall have power to allow or reject the application. If the application is allowed, the Tribunal may direct in what manner the applicants shall be represented and heard.

Article 10.

In cases where a group or organization is declared criminal by the Tribunal, the competent national authority of any Signatory shall have the right to bring individuals to trial for membership therein before national, military or occupation courts. In any such case the criminal nature of the group or organization is considered proved and shall not be questioned.

Article 11.

Any person convicted by the Tribunal may be charged before a national, military or occupation court, referred to in Article 10 of this Charter, with a crime other than of membership in a criminal group or organization and such court may, after convicting him, impose upon him punishment independent of and additional to the punishment imposed by the Tribunal for participation in the criminal activities of such group or organization.

* * *

IV. FAIR TRIAL FOR DEFENDANTS

Article 16.

In order to ensure fair trial for the Defendants, the following procedure shall be followed:

    (a) The Indictment shall include full particulars specifying in detail the charges against the Defendants. A copy of the Indictment and of all the documents lodged with the Indictment, translated into a language which he understands, shall be furnished to the Defendant at a reasonable time before the Trial.

(b) During any preliminary examination or trial of a Defendant he shall have the right to give any explanation relevant to the charges made against him.

(c) A preliminary examination of a Defendant and his Trial shall be conducted in, or translated into, a language which the Defendant understands.

(d) A Defendant shall have the right to conduct his own defense before the Tribunal or to have the assistance of Counsel.

(e) A Defendant shall have the right through himself or through his Counsel to present evidence at the Trial in support of his defense, and to cross-examine any witness called by the Prosecution.

REPORT OF JUSTICE ROBERT JACKSON TO PRESIDENT HARRY TRUMAN ON THE MILITARY TRIAL OF THE MAJOR NAZI LEADERS AT NUREMBERG

Oct. 7, 1946

MY DEAR MR. PRESIDENT:

I have the honor to report as to the duties which you delegated to me on May 2, 1945 in connection with the prosecution of major Nazi war criminals.

The International Military Tribunal sitting at Nurnberg, Germany on 30 September and 1 October, 1946 rendered judgment in the first international criminal assizes in history. It found 19 of the 22 defendants guilty on one or more of the counts of the Indictment, and acquitted 3. It sentenced 12 to death by hanging, 3 to imprisonment for life, and the four others to terms of 10 to 20 years imprisonment.

The Tribunal also declared 4 Nazi organizations to have been criminal in character. These are: The Leadership Corps of the Nazi Party; Die Schutzstaffel, known as the SS; Die Sicherheitsdienst, known as the SD; and Die Geheimstaatspolizie, known as the Gestapo, or Secret State Police. It declined to make that finding as to Die Sturmabteilungen, known as the SA; the Reichscabinet; and the General Staff and High Command. The latter was solely because the structure of the particular group was considered by the Tribunal to be too loose to constitute a coherent "group" or "organization," and was not because of any doubt of its criminality in war plotting. In its judgment the Tribunal condemned the officers who performed General Staff and High Command functions as "a ruthless military caste" and said they were "responsible in large measure for the miseries and suffering that have fallen on millions of men, women and children. They have been a disgrace to the honorable profession of arms." This finding should dispose of any fear that we were prosecuting soldiers just because they fought for their country and lost, but the failure to hold the General Staff to be a criminal organization is regrettable.

The magnitude of the task which, with this judgment, has been brought to conclusion may be suggested statistically: The trial began on November 20, 1945 and occupied 216 days of trial time. 33 witnesses were called and examined for the prosecution. 61 witnesses and 19 defendants testified for the defense; 143 additional witnesses gave testimony by interrogatories for the defense. The proceedings were conducted and recorded in four languages—English, German, French, and Russian—and daily transcripts in the language of his choice was provided for each prosecuting staff and all counsel for defendants. The English transcript of the proceedings covers over 17,000 pages. All proceedings were sound-reported in the original language used.

In preparation for the trial over 100,000 captured German documents were screened or examined and about 10,000 were selected for intensive examination as having probable evidentiary value. Of these, about 4,000 were translated into four languages and used, in whole or in part, in the trial as exhibits. Millions of feet of captured moving picture film were examined and over 100,000 feet brought to Nurnberg. Relevant sections were prepared and introduced as exhibits. Over 25,000 captured still photographs were brought to Nurnberg, together with Hitler's personal photographer who took most of them. More than 1,800 were selected and prepared for use as exhibits. The Tribunal, in its judgment, states: "The case, therefore, against the defendants rests in large measure on documents of their own making, the authenticity of which has not been challenged except in one or two cases." * * *

As authorized by your Executive Order, it was my policy to borrow professional help from Government Departments and agencies so far as possible. The War Department was the heaviest contributor, but many loans were also made by the State, Justice, and Navy Departments and, early, by the Office of Strategic Services. * * * The United States staff directly engaged on the case at Nurnberg, including lawyers, secretaries, interpreters, translators, and clerical help numbered at its peak 654, 365 being civilians and 289 military personnel. British, Soviet and French delegations aggregated approximately the same number. Nineteen adhering nations also sent representatives, which added thirty to fifty persons to those actively interested in the case. The press and radio had a maximum of 249 accredited representatives who reported the proceedings to all parts of the world. During the trial over 60,000 visitors' permits were issued * * *. Guests included leading statesmen, jurists, and lawyers, military and naval officers, writers, and invited representative Germans.

On the United States fell the obligations of host nation at Nurnberg. The staffs of all nations, the press, and visitors were provided for by the United States Army. It was done in a ruined city and among an enemy population. Utilities, communications, transport, and housing had been destroyed. The Courthouse was untenantable until extensively repaired. The Army provided air and rail transportation, operated a motor pool for local transportation, set up local and long distance communications service for all delegations and the press, and billeted all engaged in the work. It operated messes and furnished food for all, the Courthouse cafeteria often serving as many as 1,500 lunches on Court days. The United States also provided security for prisoners, judges, and prosecution, furnished administrative services, and provided such facilities as photostat, mimeograph, and sound recording. Over 30,000 photostats, about fifty million pages of typed matter, and more than 4,000 record discs were produced. The Army also met indirect requirements such as dispensary and hospital, shipping, postal, post exchange, and other servicing. It was necessary to set up for this personnel every facility not only for working, but for living as well, for the community itself afforded nothing. The Theatre Commander and his staff, Military Government officials, area commanders and their staffs, and troops were cordially and tirelessly cooperative in meeting our heavy requirements under unusual difficulties and had the commendation, not only of the American staff, but of all others.

It is safe to say that no litigation approaching this in magnitude has ever been attempted. * * *

NOTES

1. *Jackson at Nuremberg*. Those who negotiated the IMT Charter, including Justice Robert H. Jackson of the U.S. Supreme Court, who became Chief U.S. Prosecutor, and U.S. Secretary of War Henry Stimson, had three principal objectives: to treat wars of aggression as crimes under international law, to treat atrocities against civilians as "crimes against humanity," and to achieve these ends through a trial that would uphold the rule of law by protecting the rights of the defendants to due process. Official Records of the General Assembly, Forty-ninth Session, Supplement No. 10 (A/49/10), para. 90–91. By its existence and the manner in which it was conducted, the trial had to exemplify the hope that at long last the conscience of mankind might hold those individuals responsible for aggression and atrocities to account under the rule of law. As stated by Justice Jackson in his opening statement to the International Military Tribunal (IMT):

> The privilege of opening the first trial in history for crimes against the peace of the world imposes a grave responsibility. The wrongs which we seek to condemn and punish have been so calculated, so malignant, and so devastating, that civilization cannot tolerate their being ignored, because it cannot survive their being repeated. That four great nations, flushed with victory and stung with injury, stay the hand of vengeance and voluntarily submit their captive enemies to the judgment of the law is one of the most significant tributes that power has ever paid to reason.

2 Trial of the Major War Criminals 99 (1947).

2. *The Tribunal and its Defendants*. The IMT consisted of four judges, one representing each of France, United Kingdom, United States, and

U.S.S.R. The Tribunal indicted and tried twenty-four top Nazis, not including Adolf Hitler, Joseph Goebbels and Heinrich Himmler, who had committed suicide when Soviet troops entered Berlin. Those convicted included, among others, Hermann Goering (Hitler's designated successor); Rudolf Hess (Hitler's Deputy for Nazi Party Affairs); Joachim von Ribbentrop (Foreign Minister); Julius Streicher (editor of the anti-Semitic paper, Der Stuermer); and Admiral Karl Doenitz (chief of the Navy). Martin Bormann (Hess's successor who played a key role in the Holocaust) was convicted in absentia and sentenced to death (but his whereabouts and fate remain shrouded in mystery). International Military Tribunal (Nuremberg), Judgment and Sentences, Oct. 1, 1946, 41 A.J.I.L. 172, 331–33 (1947).

3. *Defense of Superior Orders.* Among the important principles relating to individual responsibility for crimes under international law addressed by the Judgment of the IMT were those dealing with the accused's official position and obedience to law or to orders of a superior. On those issues, the IMT's Judgment stated, in part, as follows:

> The principle of international law, which under certain circumstances protects the representatives of a state, cannot be applied to acts which are condemned as criminal by international law. The authors of these acts cannot shelter themselves behind their official position in order to be freed from punishment in appropriate proceedings. Article 7 of the Charter expressly declares:
>
> > The official position of Defendants, whether as heads of State, or responsible officials in Government departments, shall not be considered as freeing them from responsibility, or mitigating punishment.
>
> On the other hand, the very essence of the Charter is that individuals have international duties which transcend the national obligations of obedience imposed by the individual state. He who violates the laws of war cannot obtain immunity while acting in pursuance of the authority of the state if the state, in authorizing action, moves outside its competence under international law.
>
> It was also submitted on behalf of most of these defendants that in doing what they did they were acting under the orders of Hitler, and therefore cannot be held responsible for the acts committed by them in carrying out these orders. The Charter specifically provides in Article 8:
>
> > The fact that the Defendant acted pursuant to order of his Government or of a superior shall not free him from responsibility, but may be considered in mitigation of punishment.
>
> The provisions of this article are in conformity with the law of all nations. That a soldier was ordered to kill or torture in violation of the international law of war has never been recognized as a defense to such acts of brutality, though, as the Charter here provides, the order may be urged in mitigation of the punishment. The true test, which is found in varying degrees in the criminal law of most nations, is not the existence of the order, but whether moral choice was in fact possible.

International Military Tribunal (Nuremberg) Judgment and Sentences, 41 A.J.I.L. 172, 221 (1947). For further discussion of individual responsibility under international law before the Nuremberg tribunal, see Tomuschat, International Criminal Prosecution: The Precedent of Nuremberg Confirmed, in Clark & Sann, The Prosecution of International Crimes 18 (1996); Sunga, Individual Responsibility in International Law for Serious Human Rights Violations (1992).

4. *Criminal Organizations*. As Justice Jackson indicated, and as contemplated in the IMT Charter, the prosecution pursued indictments against several alleged criminal organizations. Whether to find such organizations as criminal, and what effects if any that had on individual responsibility, proved contentious among the prosecutors and among the IMT judges. Ultimately, the judgment found:

> A criminal organization is analogous to a criminal conspiracy in that the essence of both is cooperation for criminal purposes. There must be a group bound together and organized for a common purpose. The group must be formed or used in connection with the commission of crimes denounced by the [IMT] Charter. Since the declaration with respect to the organizations and groups will * * * fix the criminality of its members, that definition should exclude persons who had no knowledge of the criminal purposes or acts of the organization and those who were drafted by the State for membership, unless they were personally implicated in the commission of the acts declared criminal by Article 6 of the Charter as members of the organization. Membership alone is not enough to come within the scope of these declarations.

1 Trial of the Major War Criminals Before the International Military Tribunal 256 (1947). Given this finding, many have concluded that the "whole scheme for streamlined mass trials envisaged by Articles 9 and 10 was nullified. Obviously, having a choice between considerations of expedience, on the one hand, and fundamental principles of criminal law, on the other, the Tribunal decided to sacrifice the former for the sake of the latter." Pomorski, Conspiracy and Criminal Organizations, in The Nuremberg Trial and International Law 243 (Ginsburgs & Kudriavtsev eds. 1990).

5. *The Tokyo Tribunal*. In the Tokyo trials before the International Military Tribunal for the Far East (IMTFE), twenty-five Japanese leaders were tried and twenty-three were convicted. Seven, including Prime Minister Tojo and Admiral Yamashita (chief of the Navy), were executed; sixteen were sentenced to life in prison. For documents related the tribunal, see Documents on the Tokyo International Military Tribunal: Charter, Indictment, and Judgments (Boister & Cryer eds. 2008). For commentary, see Boister & Cryer, The Tokyo International Military Tribunal: A Reappraisal (2008); Maga, Judgment at Tokyo: The Japanese War Crimes Trials (2001); Brackman, The Other Nuremberg: The Untold Story of the Tokyo War Crimes Trial (1987); Minear, Victor's Justice: The Tokyo War Crimes Trial (1971).

6. *Further Reading*. For further readings on Nuremberg, see Perspectives on the Nuremberg Trial (Mettraux ed. 2008); Taylor, The Anatomy of the Nuremberg Trials: A Personal Memoire (1992); Davidson, The Trial of the Germans (1966). For accounts more contemporary to the trial, see Taylor,

Nuremberg Trials, [1949] Int'l Conciliation No. 450, at 243; Memorandum Submitted by the Secretary–General, The Charter and Judgment of the Nurnberg Tribunal, U.N. Doc. A/ACN. 4/5 (1949), Hankey, Politics, Trials and Errors (1950); Taylor, The Nuremberg Trials, 55 Colum. L. Rev. 488 (1955); Jackson, The Nurnberg Case (1947); Wright, The Law of the Nuremberg Trial, 41 A.J.I.L. 38 (1947); Finch, The Nuremberg Trial and International Law, 41 A.J.I.L. 20 (1947); Jessup, Crime of Aggression, 62 Pol. Sci. Q. 1 (1947); Schick, Crimes Against the Peace, 38 J. Crim. L. & Crim. 445 (1948). For a convenient collection of materials concerning the trials, see Marrus, The Nuremberg War Crimes Trial 1945–46: A Documentary History (1997).

"THE JUSTICE CASE" (CASE 3), UNITED STATES v. JOSEF ALTSTOETTER, ET AL.

Trials of Individuals Before the Nuremberg Military Tribunals Under
Control Council Law No. 10, 1946–1949, Vol. III (1951)
Opinion and Judgment, at 954–84

[A series of subsequent trials involving less prominent figures also took place at Nuremberg and elsewhere in Germany between 1946 and 1949. Those trials were conducted under Control Council Law No. 10 (C.C. Law 10). The Control Council was the body, comprised of representatives of France, the United Kingdom, the United States, and the U.S.S.R., that governed occupied Germany. In the U.S. occupation zone of Germany, trials were conducted before U.S. judges.

In February 1947, the U.S. Military Government for Germany created Military Tribunal III to try the "Justice Case", which involved sixteen important German judges and legal officials, nine whom were officials in the Reich Ministry of Justice (the others were members of the People's and Special Courts). The indictment charged all the defendants with "judicial murder and other atrocities, which they committed by destroying law and justice in Germany, and then utilizing the emptied forms of legal process for the persecution, enslavement and extermination on a large scale." Specifically, the defendants were charged with conspiracy to commit war crimes against civilians in territories occupied by Germany and against soldiers of countries at war with Germany; and crimes against humanity against German civilians and nationals of occupied territories. Some of the defendants were also charged with a fourth count of membership in the SS, SD, or the leadership corps of the Nazi Party, all of which had been declared criminal organizations a year before by the International Military Tribunal.

All the defendants pled not guilty. Military Tribunal III returned its judgment on December 3 and 4, 1947. The case raised interesting questions about the nature of the law such tribunals apply, whether defendants are aware of that law, the role of lawyers and judges in assisting policy-makers in the commission of criminal acts, and whether lower-level officials could excuse their behavior because it had been ordered by superiors.]

* * * We sit as a Tribunal drawing its sole power and jurisdiction from the will and command of the Four occupying Powers. * * *

* * * As to the punishment of persons guilty of violating the laws and customs of war (war crimes in the narrow sense), it has always been recognized that tribunals may be established and punishment imposed by the state into whose hands the perpetrators fall. These rules of international law were recognized as paramount, and jurisdiction to enforce them by the injured belligerent government, whether within the territorial boundaries of the state or in occupied territory, has been unquestioned. (Ex parte Quirin, [317 U.S. 1 (1942)]; In re Yamashita, 327 U.S. 1, [(1946)].) However, enforcement of international law has been traditionally subject to practical limitations. Within the territorial boundaries of a state having a recognized, functioning government presently in the exercise of sovereign power throughout its territory, a violator of the rules of international law could be punished only by the authority of the officials of that state. The law is universal, but such a state reserves unto itself the exclusive power within its boundaries to apply or withhold sanctions. Thus, notwithstanding the paramount authority of the substantive rules of common international law, the doctrines of national sovereignty have been preserved through the control of enforcement machinery. It must be admitted that Germans were not the only ones who were guilty of committing war crimes; other violators of international law could, no doubt, be tried and punished by the state of which they were nationals, by the offended state if it can secure jurisdiction of the person, or by an international tribunal if of competent authorized jurisdiction.

Applying these principles, it appears that the power to punish violators of international law in Germany is not solely dependent on the enactment of rules of substantive penal law applicable only in Germany. Nor is the apparent immunity from prosecution of criminals in other states based on the absence there of the rules of international law which we enforce here. Only by giving consideration to the extraordinary and temporary situation in Germany can the procedure here be harmonized with established principles of national sovereignty. In Germany an international body (the Control Council) has assumed and exercised the power to establish judicial machinery for the punishment of those who have violated the rules of the common international law, a power which no international authority without consent could assume or exercise within a state having a national government presently in the exercise of its sovereign powers.

* * *

C.C. Law 10 is not limited to the punishment of persons guilty of violating the laws and customs of war in the narrow sense; furthermore, it can no longer be said that violations of the laws and customs of war are the only offenses recognized by common international law. The force of circumstance, the grim fact of worldwide interdependence, and the moral pressure of public opinion have resulted in international recognition that certain crimes against humanity committed by Nazi authority against German nationals constituted violations not alone of statute but also of common international law. * * *

As the prime illustration of a crime against humanity under C.C.Law 10, which by reason of its magnitude and its international repercussions has been recognized as a violation of common international law, we cite "genocide" * * *. A resolution recently adopted by the General Assembly of the United Nations is in part as follows:

"The General Assembly therefore

Affirms that genocide is a crime under international law which the civilized world condemns, and for the commission of which principals and accomplices—whether private individuals, public officials, or statesmen, and whether the crime is committed on religious, racial, political or any other grounds—are punishable * * *."

The General Assembly is not an international legislature, but it is the most authoritative organ in existence for the interpretation of world opinion. Its recognition of genocide as an international crime is persuasive evidence of the fact. We approve and adopt its conclusions. Whether the crime against humanity is the product of statute or of common international law, or, as we believe, of both, we find no injustice to persons tried for such crimes. They are chargeable with knowledge that such acts were wrong and were punishable when committed.

The defendants contend that they should not be found guilty because they acted within the authority and by the command of German laws and decrees. Concerning crimes against humanity, C.C.Law 10 provides for punishment whether or not the acts were in violation of the domestic laws of the country where perpetrated (C.C.Law 10, art. II, par. 1(c)) * * *.

* * * The Nuremberg Tribunals are not German courts. They are not enforcing German law. The charges are not based on violation by the defendants of German law. On the contrary, the jurisdiction of this Tribunal rests on international authority. It enforces the law as declared by the IMT Charter and C.C.Law 10, and within the limitations on the power conferred, it enforces international law as superior in authority to any German statute or decree. It is true, as defendants contend, that German courts under the Third Reich were required to follow German law (i.e., the expressed will of Hitler) even when it was contrary to international law. But no such limitation can be applied to this Tribunal. Here we have the paramount substantive law, plus a Tribunal authorized and required to apply it notwithstanding the inconsistent provisions of German local law. The very essence of the prosecution case is that the laws, the Hitlerian decrees and the Draconic, corrupt, and perverted Nazi judicial system themselves constituted the substance of war crimes and crimes against humanity and that participation in the enactment and enforcement of them amounts to complicity in crime. We have pointed out that governmental participation is a material element of the crime against humanity. Only when official organs of sovereignty participated in atroci-

ties and persecutions did those crimes assume international proportions. It can scarcely be said that governmental participation, the proof of which is necessary for conviction, can also be a defense to the charge.

* * *

The defendants claim protection under the principle *nullum crimen sine lege,* though they withheld from others the benefit of that rule during the Hitler regime. Obviously the principle in question constitutes no limitation upon the power or right of the Tribunal to punish acts which can properly be held to have been violations of international law when committed. By way of illustration, we observe the C.C.Law 10, article II, paragraph 1(b), "War Crimes," has by reference incorporated the rules by which war crimes are to be identified. In all such cases it remains only for the Tribunal, after the manner of the common law, to determine the content of those rules under the impact of changing conditions.

Whatever view may be held as to the nature and source of our authority under C.C.Law 10 and under common international law, the *ex post facto* rule, properly understood, constitutes no legal nor moral barrier to prosecution in this case.

Under written constitutions the *ex post facto* rule condemns statutes which define as criminal, acts committed before the law was passed, but the *ex post facto* rule cannot apply in the international field as it does under constitutional mandate in the domestic field. Even in the domestic field the prohibition of the rule does not apply to the decisions of common law courts, though the question at issue be novel. International law is not the product of statute for the simple reason that there is as yet no world authority empowered to enact statutes of universal application. International law is the product of multipartite treaties, conventions, judicial decisions and customs which have received international acceptance or acquiescence. It would be sheer absurdity to suggest that the *ex post facto* rule, as known to constitutional states, could be applied to a treaty, a custom, or a common law decision of an international tribunal, or to the international acquiescence which follows the event. To have attempted to apply the *ex post facto* principle to judicial decisions of common international law would have been to strangle that law at birth. As applied in the field of international law, the principle *nullum crimen sine lege* received its true interpretation in the opinion of the IMT in the case versus Goering, et al. The question arose with reference to crimes against the peace, but the opinion expressed is equally applicable to war crimes and crimes against humanity. The Tribunal said:

> In the first place, it is to be observed that the maxim *nullum crimen sine lege* is not a limitation of sovereignty, but is in general a principle of justice. To assert that it is unjust to punish those who in defiance of treaties and assurances have attacked neighboring states without warning is obviously untrue, for in such circumstances the attacker must know that he is doing wrong, and so far from it being

unjust to punish him, it would be unjust if his wrong were allowed to go unpunished. * * *

NOTES

1. *Justice Accused*. The tribunal found ten of the defendants guilty and acquitted four. Two defendants were not included in the judgment: one died before the trial began while the other's case was declared a mistrial because he was too sick to attend much of the trial. The court sentenced four of the guilty to life imprisonment and the remainder to prison terms ranging from five to ten years. The proceedings spawned both riveting literature, see Müller, Hitler's Justice: The Courts of the Third Reich (Schneider trans. 1991), and an award-winning 1961 movie, *Judgment at Nuremberg*. What standards do you think should apply to lawyers and judges who facilitate or allow others to perpetrate war crimes, crimes against humanity, or genocide?

2. *Victors' Justice?* Although the Nuremberg and Tokyo trials formed the foundation for development of much of the contemporary rules on individual responsibility for crimes under international law, they have not escaped criticism. A bias was built into the IMT Charter itself, given that it authorized only prosecution of war criminals of the "European Axis countries." The murder of thousands of Polish officers by Soviet forces in the Katyn Forest near Smolensk, the allied fire bombing of Dresden, and the dropping of the atomic bombs on Hiroshima and Nagasaki, Japan, are among the events that suggest that the victors may not have been free of culpability. The IMT convicted Germans for invading Poland, but refused to admit evidence of the Soviet Union's secret agreement with Hitler to divide Poland. Admiral Doenitz was convicted on different and lesser charges after evidence was adduced that one of the charges against him, sinking nonmilitary ships without warning, was essentially similar to the practice of the U.S. Navy in the Pacific. Does the partiality inherent in a tribunal established by the victors impugn the legal validity of the IMT's judgment and sentences? Does it undercut the moral legitimacy of the Tribunal?

3. *Ex Post Facto Prosecutions*. To what extent did the goal of the framers of the IMT Charter to establish crimes against peace and crimes against humanity as crimes under international law conflict with the basic principle of criminal justice prohibiting *ex post facto* prosecutions (*nullum crimen sine lege; nulla poena sine lege*)? In the case of acts labeled crimes against humanity, such as mass murder, the acts concerned were crimes under every legal system. They were "internationalized" by the IMT Charter, but it hardly seems unfair to the defendants to be prosecuted and punished for such acts. Could the same be said for crimes against peace or aggression? Soldiers had not been prosecuted for the act of planning, initiating or participating in an act of aggression from the Peace of Westphalia in 1648 to the Nuremberg trials. Aggression had not been characterized as a crime under international law until the IMT Charter did so. Does the IMT Judgment quoted in *The Justice Case* deal persuasively with this issue?

AFFIRMATION OF THE PRINCIPLES OF INTERNATIONAL LAW RECOGNIZED BY THE CHARTER OF THE NUREMBERG TRIBUNAL

Adopted by the U.N. General Assembly, Dec. 11, 1946
G.A. Res. 95(I), U.N. Doc. A/236 (1946), at 1144

The General Assembly,

Recognizes the obligation laid upon it by Article 13, paragraph 1, subparagraph a, of the [U.N.] Charter, to initiate studies and make recommendations for the purpose of encouraging the progressive development of international law and its codification;

Takes note of the Agreement for the establishment of an International Military Tribunal for the prosecution and punishment of the major war criminals of the European Axis signed in London on 8 August 1945, and of the [IMT] Charter annexed thereto, and of the fact that similar principles have been adopted in the Charter of the International Military Tribunal for the trial of the major war criminals in the Far East, proclaimed at Tokyo on 19 January 1946;

Therefore,

Affirms the principles of international law recognized by the Charter of the Nürnberg Tribunal and the judgment of the Tribunal;

Directs the Committee on the Codification of International Law established by the resolution of the General Assembly of 11 December 1946, to treat as a matter of primary importance plans for the formulation, in the context of a general codification of offences against the peace and security of mankind, or of an International Criminal Code, of the principles recognized in the Charter of the Nürnberg Tribunal and in the judgment of the Tribunal.

NOTES

1. *Stalled Progress.* In 1948, the General Assembly asked the International Law Commission to study the desirability and possibility of establishing an international judicial organ for the trial of persons charged with genocide or other crimes over which jurisdiction would be conferred upon that organ by international conventions. Report of the International Law Commission on the Work of its First Session, U.N. Doc. A/925 (1949). The Commission was further requested to consider the possibility of establishing a Criminal Chamber of the International Court of Justice. The Cold War, however, effectively precluded any real progress toward creation of an international criminal tribunal. It took an end to the Cold War and inhuman atrocities in the former Yugoslavia, beginning in 1991, to bring about the creation of the first truly international tribunal to try individuals accused of crimes under international law (see next Section).

2. *National Court Prosecutions.* A number of prosecutions concerning atrocities committed by prominent Nazis and collaborators during the World

War II period were carried out by national courts subsequent to the Nuremberg trials. Most celebrated was the trial in Israel in 1961 of Adolf Eichmann, who played an important role in implementing the Holocaust. Eichmann was kidnapped by Israeli agents in Argentina, brought to Israel and convicted for the crimes under Israeli law, including crimes against the Jewish people, crimes against humanity and war crimes. 36 I.L.R. 5 (1968). For discussion, see Chapter 11, Sections 6 & 8. Similarly, Klaus Barbie in 1987, Paul Touvier in 1994, and Maurice Papon in 1998, were convicted by French courts of crimes against humanity committed during World War II.

3. *Vietnam and War Crimes.* Questions of individual responsibility for violations of the laws of war received widespread public attention during the Vietnam war. The U.S. killing of prisoners in custody and the massacre of Vietnamese civilians (most notoriously in the Son My–My Lai cases) resulted in the court martial of some U.S. soldiers and stimulated demands for punishment of higher officials in both military and civilian positions. There was ample evidence that higher-ranking military commanders knew or were in a position to know that the laws of war in respect of the treatment of the civilian population and of prisoners of war in Vietnam were being violated in numerous situations. See Taylor, Nuremberg and Vietnam, ch. 5–7 (1970). Although no punitive action was taken against the senior military commanders, the issue of their individual responsibility was widely discussed and the precedent of Nuremberg invoked. Civilian officials, including the President and the Secretary of State, were also the targets of allegations of complicity in war crimes, most notably the bombing of civilian populations in Vietnam and Cambodia. On the My–Lai massacre prosecutions, see United States v. Calley, 46 C.M.R. 1131 (A.C.M.R. 1973), aff'd, 22 C.M.A. 534, 48 C.M.R. 19 (1973), petition for writ of habeas corpus granted sub nom., Calley v. Callaway, 382 F.Supp. 650 (M.D. Ga.1974), rev'd, 519 F.2d 184 (5th Cir.1975).

B. INTERNATIONAL CRIMINAL TRIBUNAL FOR THE FORMER YUGOSLAVIA

Creation. Widespread atrocities, including mass killings and other forms of what came to be called "ethnic cleansing," committed within the territory of the former Yugoslavia, and especially in Bosnia and Herzegovina, in the early 1990s, prompted the creation of an *ad hoc* international criminal tribunal by the U.N. Security Council for the prosecution of responsible individuals. On May 25, 1993, the Security Council unanimously adopted Resolution 827, to establish "an international tribunal for the sole purpose of prosecuting persons responsible for serious violations of international humanitarian law committed in the territory of the former Yugoslavia between 1 January 1991 and a date to be determined by the Security Council upon the restoration of peace * * *." S.C. Res 827 (1993). The Security Council took this action under Chapter VII of the Charter, having found that the situation in the former Yugoslavia constituted a threat to the peace. Annexed to Resolution 827 was a Statute for the International Criminal Tribunal for the Former Yugoslavia (I.C.T.Y.). The I.C.T.Y., which is located in the Hague, the Netherlands, has been granted jurisdiction with respect to grave breaches of the Geneva Conventions of 1949 (Article 2); violations of the laws or customs of war (Article 3); genocide (Article 4); and crimes against humanity (Article 5).

The Three Organs. The Statute provides that the I.C.T.Y. will be comprised of three organs: the judges, the prosecutor's office, and the registry. The Tribunal's fourteen permanent judges are elected by the U.N. General Assembly; they sit in three trial chambers of three judges and one appeals chamber of five judges. The permanent judges are assisted by temporary *ad litem* judges who are also elected by the General Assembly. The permanent judges select one of their members to serve as the President of the I.C.T.Y. The I.C.T.Y. judges have adopted Rules of Procedure and Evidence, which have been amended several times since their inception. (For the latest version, see the I.C.T.Y. website at www. un.org/icty.)

The Office of the Prosecutor is charged with investigating, indicting, and prosecuting persons who fall within the jurisdiction of the I.C.T.Y. It is headed by a chief prosecutor, who is appointed by the Security Council for a renewable four-year term. The prosecutor acts independently, neither seeking nor receiving instructions from governments or international organizations (nor from either of the Tribunal's other two organs). Pursuant to the Statute, U.N. members are under an obligation to cooperate with the prosecutor's investigations and prosecutions.

The registry provides all the administrative support for the tribunal, including the staffing of the courtroom reporters and interpreters, the bringing of witnesses to the tribunal, the provision of defense counsel for indigent defendants, and oversight of the U.N. detention unit where the accused are housed during trials.

Obtaining Indictees. Security Council Resolution 827 requires all states to cooperate fully with the Tribunal and to take "any measures necessary under their domestic law to implement" the resolution and the I.C.T.Y.'s Statute. All member states of the United Nations are obligated under Article 25 of the Charter to accept and carry out decisions of the Security Council. Consequently, a number of countries, including the France, Germany, Italy, Netherlands, Spain, and the United States have enacted legislation that permits surrender of individuals indicted for serious crimes against humanitarian law to an international tribunal with jurisdiction. Indictees may also voluntarily surrender themselves to the I.C.T.Y. and many have done so. Rarely, indictees have been captured by military or civilian forces present in the former Yugoslavia, such as NATO forces. Some defendants have raised challenges to the legality of the manner of their apprehension in unsuccessful efforts to defeat the Tribunal's jurisdiction. See Prosecutor v. Dokmanović, I.C.T.Y. Case No. IT–95– 13a–PT, Decision on Motion for Release by the Accused (1997); Scharf, The Prosecutor v. Dokmanović: Irregular Rendition and the ICTY, 11 Leiden J.I.L. 369 (1998).

The First Case: Dusko Tadić. The first indictee taken into custody by the I.C.T.Y. (based on a transfer by Germany) was Dusko Tadić, a Bosnian Serb accused of war crimes and crimes against humanity. After resolution of certain important jurisdictional issues by the decision of the Appeals Chamber (see Chapter 4, Section 1), the Trial Chamber proceeded to hear the Tadić case on the merits. In May 1997, following seven months of hearings, Tadić was found guilty in a 300–page judgment of 11 counts of war crimes and crimes against humanity, including taking part in Serb attacks on his home town of Kozarac and other villages, and herding the inhabitants into camps, where they were beaten and kept in inhuman conditions. Prosecutor v. Dusko Tadić, I.C.T.Y. Case No. IT–94–1–T, Opinion and Judgment (May 7, 1997). Tadić was sentenced to twenty years in prison. Tadić appealed his conviction to the Appeals Chamber, as did the prosecutor for separate reasons. The Appeals Chamber found Tadić guilty of additional crimes and increased his sentence to twenty-five years. Id., Appeals Judgment, July 15, 1999, 38 I.L.M. 1518 (1999) and Sentencing Judgment, Nov. 11, 1999, 39 I.L.M. 117 (2000). The Tribunal subsequently adjusted this to twenty years because Tadić had spent five years in investigative custody. Tadić's case, which began on May 7, 1996, was finally concluded on January 26, 2000, and Tadić is serving out his sentence in Germany, one of several countries that have agreements with the I.C.T.Y. for incarceration of persons who have been convicted. For a narrative of the case through the trial, see Scharf, Balkan Justice: The Story Behind the First International War Crimes Trial Since Nuremberg (1997). For critical legal commentary, see Alvarez, Rush to Closure: Lessons of the Tadić Judgment, 96 Mich. L. Rev. 2031 (1998).

Karadžić and Mladić. On July 25, 1995, the Tribunal handed down public indictments involving 24 individuals. Most of these were members of the Bosnian Serb military and police forces as well as politicians and detention camp commanders accused of atrocities. Of particular note were Dr. Radovan Karadžić, the leader of the Bosnian Serbs, and General Ratko Mladić, the commander of the Bosnian Serb military. Karadžić and Mladić are alleged to be responsible for the internment of thousands of Bosnian Muslims and Croats in detention facilities where they were subjected to widespread acts of physical and psychological abuse and to inhuman conditions. Karadžić and Mladić were charged with genocide committed with intent to destroy, in whole or in part, a national, ethnic or religious group. In early November 1995, the Tribunal amended the indictments against Karadžić and Mladić to include genocide for allegedly orchestrating the slaughter in July of up to 8,000 Bosnian Muslims in the town of Srebrenica, which had been designated a U.N.-protected safe area under the protection of a lightly armed Dutch contingent of the peacekeeping force known as UNPROFOR. Karadžić was arrested in Belgrade in July, 2008 and extradited to the Netherlands for trial at the I.C.T.Y., where his trial is expected to start in late 2009. By contrast, Mladić remains at large as of early 2009.

Not Just Serbs. Most indictees at the I.C.T.Y. have been Serbs. However, on November 16, 1998, the I.C.T.Y. convicted two Bosnian Muslims and one Bosnian Croat for crimes of murder, torture and rape committed while they were running the Čelebići prison camp in 1992. This was the first time Bosnian Muslims had been convicted of atrocities against Serbs. The two Bosnian Muslims, Hazim Delić and Esad Landzo, were sentenced to prison terms of twenty years and fifteen years, respectively. The Bosnian Croat, Zdravco Mucić, was sentenced to seven years. Delić was found guilty of committing two murders and "calculated cruelty," including rape, against prisoners. The tribunal found Landzo guilty of three murders, and cited his "perverse pleasure in the infliction of pain and suffering." The I.C.T.Y. found Mucić responsible for nine murders and for allowing guards "to commit the most heinous of offenses without taking any disciplinary action." The I.C.T.Y. set an important precedent in holding that acts of rape may constitute torture under customary law. Also, the conviction of Mucić marked the first time since the Nuremberg and Tokyo trials following World War II that anyone had been found guilty by an international tribunal for the actions of subordinates.

Overall Record. As of early 2009, the Tribunal has indicted a total of 161 individuals, and completed proceedings with regard to 116 of them: ten have been acquitted, fifty-seven sentenced, and thirteen have had their cases transferred to local courts. Another thirty-six cases have been terminated (either because indictments were withdrawn or because the accused died, before or after transfer to the Tribunal). Proceedings remain on-going with regard to forty-five accused: ten are at the appeals stage, six are awaiting the Trial Chamber's judgment, twenty-one are currently on trial, and six are at the pre-trial stage. Two fugitives are still at large. A further twenty-nine individuals have been or are the subject of contempt proceedings. For a thematic review of the Tribunal's jurisprudence mid-way through its life, see Murphy, Progress and Jurisprudence of the International Criminal Tribunal for the Former Yugoslavia, 93 A.J.I.L. 57 (1999).

Atrocities in Kosovo. Atrocities in the former Yugoslavia entered a new phase in January 1999 when the Serbs initiated an ethnic cleansing campaign directed against ethnic Albanians in Kosovo. The massacre of more than forty-five ethnic Albanians in Račak in mid-January drew international condemnation. In February, peace talks were initiated in Rambouillet, France. In mid-March, after the Kosovar–Albanian delegation agreed to accept the limited autonomy proposed in the negotiations but the Serbs refused, the peace talks were adjourned. Serbian forces then massed in and around Kosovo and began an offensive against ethnic Albanians and the Kosovo Liberation Army (KLA). On March 24, 1999, NATO initiated airstrikes against Serb targets, and the Serbs promptly launched a military and police assault against the ethnic Albanians in almost every city and town in Kosovo. Over 10,000 ethnic Albanians are estimated to have been killed and hundreds of thousands were displaced from their homes, most of which were pillaged and destroyed. The NATO bombing campaign lasted 78 days before Serbian officials accepted the NATO peace plan on June 3, 1999, and, on June 9, Serb forces began their withdrawal from Kosovo. On June 12, 1999, NATO troops arrived. Thereafter, more than 100,000 Serbs and Gypsies fled Kosovo amid reprisal killings by ethnic Albanians.

On May 27, 1999, the I.C.T.Y. Prosecutor announced the indictment of Slobodan Milošević (President of the Federal Republic of Yugoslavia) and other Serbian leaders for crimes against humanity—more specifically, murder of over 340 identified individuals, forced deportation and persecution of 740,000 Kosovo Albanians—and violations of the laws and customs of war in Kosovo. The 42–page indictment encompassed only crimes allegedly committed in Kosovo beginning in 1999, but was later expanded with respect to Milošević to cover crimes allegedly committed earlier in Bosnia–Herzegovina and Croatia.

This was the first instance in modern times of an indictment by an international criminal tribunal of a sitting head of state. After Milošević resigned as President of the Federal Republic of Yugoslavia in 2000, he was arrested by Yugoslav federal authorities and then extradited to the Netherlands for trial at the I.C.T.Y. The trial of Milošević ended without a verdict because he died during the proceedings, after nearly five years in the I.C.T.Y. detention unit in the Hague. Milošević' suffered from heart ailments and high blood pressure, and apparently died of a heart attack. Thereafter, the trial of the other senior Serbian leaders for their conduct in Kosovo was completed, leading to a judgment issued in February 2009.

PROSECUTOR v. MILUTINOVIC ET AL.

I.C.T.Y. Case No. IT–05–87–T, Summary of Trial Chamber Judgment (Feb. 26, 2009)
International Criminal Tribunal for the former Yugoslavia

JUDGE BONOMY:

The Trial Chamber is sitting today to deliver its Judgement in the case of Prosecutor v. Milan Milutinović, Nikola Šainović, Dragoljub Ojdanić, Nebojša Pavković, Vladimir Lazarević, and Sreten Lukić. What I am about to read is a summary of the Chamber's findings in that Judgement.
* * *

* * *

The length of the trial, and volume of evidence, as well as the size of the Judgement, are in large part a consequence of the number and nature of the charges in the Indictment. The Accused are charged under every form of responsibility set out in Articles 7(1) and 7(3) of the Statute of the Tribunal for their alleged role in crimes said to have been committed between 1 January and 20 June 1999 in Kosovo by forces of the Federal Republic of Yugoslavia and the Republic of Serbia, referred to as the forces of the FRY and Serbia.

Specifically, the Accused are alleged to be responsible for deportation, a crime against humanity (count 1); forcible transfer as "other inhumane acts," a crime against humanity (count 2); murder, a crime against humanity and a violation of the laws or customs of war (counts 3 and 4); and persecution, a crime against humanity (count 5). According to the Indictment, the Accused participated, along with others, in a joint criminal enterprise to modify the ethnic balance in Kosovo in order to ensure continued control by the FRY and Serbian authorities over the province. The Prosecution further alleges that the purpose of the joint criminal enterprise was to be achieved through a widespread or systematic campaign of terror or violence against the Kosovo Albanian population, including the various crimes specified in each of the counts of the Indictment.

Under count 1, the Indictment sets out how the deportation of Kosovo Albanians was carried out in early 1999 from 13 municipalities across Kosovo, and particular towns and villages in those municipalities. It should be noted that these descriptions also contain information about killings, property destruction, theft, sexual assaults, beatings, and other forms of violence, which the Prosecution alleges contributed to an atmosphere of fear and oppression created by the FRY and Serbian forces to facilitate the expulsion of the Kosovo Albanian population. Under counts 3 and 4, a number of killings are alleged in various locations in Kosovo. Finally, under the fifth count, the Indictment avers that the forces of the FRY and Serbia executed a campaign of persecution against the Kosovo Albanian population, including by way of murder, sexual assault, and wanton destruction or damage of religious sites. * * *

At the time of the alleged crimes, Milan Milutinović was the President of the Republic of Serbia; Nikola Šainović was a Deputy Prime Minister of the Federal Republic of Yugoslavia, or FRY; Dragoljub Ojdanić was the Chief of the General Staff of the Yugoslav Army, or VJ; Nebojša Pavković was the Commander of the VJ 3rd Army; Vladimir Lazarević was the Commander of the VJ Priština Corps; and Sreten Lukić was the Head of the Serbian Ministry of Interior Staff for Kosovo, referred to as the MUP Staff. The Indictment alleges that each of the Accused participated in the joint criminal enterprise, and that in these roles they exercised command authority and/or effective control over VJ and MUP forces involved in the commission of the alleged crimes. They are also said to have planned, instigated, ordered, or otherwise to have aided and abetted these crimes.

* * *

The Chamber finds that a political crisis developed in Kosovo in the late 1980s and through the 1990s, culminating in an armed conflict involving forces of the FRY and Serbia and forces of the Kosovo Liberation Army, or KLA, from mid–1998. During that armed conflict, there were incidents where excessive and indiscriminate force was used by the VJ and MUP, resulting in damage to civilian property, population displacement, and civilian deaths. Despite efforts to bring the crisis to an end, which included the introduction into Kosovo of an international verification mission, the conflict continued through to and beyond 24 March 1999, when NATO forces began an aerial bombardment campaign against targets in the FRY. That campaign ended on 10 June 1999, and the forces of the FRY and Serbia were withdrawn from Kosovo. * * *

It is largely uncontested that significant numbers of people from Kosovo left their homes during the NATO bombing, many of whom crossed the borders into Albania and Macedonia. Documentary evidence and witnesses brought by both the Prosecution and Defence confirmed this swift movement, primarily of Kosovo Albanians. * * *

The Prosecution case is that these hundreds of thousands of Kosovo Albanians fled the province because of the violent and coercive actions of the forces of the FRY and Serbia, which engaged in a campaign of terror and violence against the Kosovo Albanian population in order to expel them from their homes and force them across the borders. This case was supported by the consistent evidence of many Kosovo Albanian witnesses, along with some of the former VJ and MUP personnel brought by the Prosecution. However, witnesses brought by the Defence consistently denied that there was any organised expulsion of Kosovo Albanians from their homes, and many of them gave other reasons for the mass movement of Kosovo Albanians across the borders into Albania and Macedonia, including the NATO bombing itself, and the actions of the KLA.

The Trial Chamber is mindful of the fact that in some parts of Kosovo, both within the 13 municipalities discussed in this Judgement and elsewhere, people may have left their homes for different reasons, such as instructions from the KLA, the desire to avoid being present while combat between the KLA and forces of the FRY and Serbia was taking place, or indeed the fact that NATO was bombing targets close to where they lived. However, despite the arguments by the Defence that these were the primary reasons for the massive movement of people within Kosovo and across the borders with Albania and Macedonia, none of the Kosovo Albanians who testified cited the NATO bombing as among the reasons for their departure, and in only one area of Vučitrn municipality and another area of Suva Reka municipality did the Chamber find that people were moving as a consequence of the actions of the KLA. * * *

Furthermore, NATO bombs struck targets across the FRY, with Belgrade suffering the most destruction, according to the former Commander of the VJ Air Force and Air Defence, and yet people did not leave Belgrade, or other parts of the FRY, in the massive numbers which fled Kosovo. The Chamber finds, therefore, that the NATO bombing was not the reason for the mass displacement of Kosovo Albanians from Kosovo.

While there was a continuing armed conflict between the KLA and the forces of the FRY and Serbia, at the same time as the NATO air campaign, the Chamber also does not consider that this conflict was the cause of the flight of hundreds of thousands of Kosovo Albanians from late March to early June 1999. * * *

The Trial Chamber therefore finds that there was a broad campaign of violence directed against the Kosovo Albanian civilian population during the course of the NATO air-strikes, conducted by forces under the control of the FRY and Serbian authorities, during which there were incidents of killing, sexual assault, and the intentional destruction of mosques. It was the deliberate actions of these forces during this campaign that caused the departure of at least 700,000 Kosovo Albanians from Kosovo in the short period of time between the end of March and beginning of June 1999. Efforts by the MUP to conceal the killing of Kosovo Albanians, by transporting the bodies to other areas of Serbia, as discussed in detail in the Judgement, also suggest that such killings were criminal in nature.

I will briefly mention some of the Chamber's factual findings in relation to the various crime sites. At the end of March 1999 an extremely threatening and violent environment was created in Peć town, in western Kosovo, by police and military forces burning houses, firing weapons, and abusing the local Kosovo Albanian population. A significant number of the town's residents thus fled or were ordered out of their homes, some of them being directed to go to Montenegro and others being sent to the centre of the town where they were put on buses and driven to the Albanian border. When these Kosovo Albanians returned to Peć after the conflict, they found that many of their houses had been burned, although the houses belonging to Serb residents of the town were undamaged.

In Dečani municipality, immediately to the south of Peć, similar events transpired in the village of Beleg at the end of March 1999. There the Kosovo Albanian residents were rounded up by police and VJ personnel, including reservists, in the course of which some men were killed. A large group of predominantly Kosovo Albanian women and children was detained and mistreated: some of the women were sexually assaulted; and some men were physically abused. The next day most of the people from the group were ordered to go to Albania, and those who remained have not been heard from since.

[The Trial Chamber continued to recount a long series of such events, which are omitted here.]

In addition to the evidence pertaining to the specific crime sites set out in the Indictment, the Chamber heard evidence going to the broad pattern of violence and intimidation of the Kosovo Albanian population from witnesses who were members of the VJ and MUP forces in Kosovo at that time. For example, three former members of the VJ, who testified under protective measures, admitted that they were involved in the expulsion of Kosovo Albanians from their homes during the NATO campaign. Other witnesses from the VJ and MUP described their own participation in the killing of Kosovo Albanian civilians and other criminal acts.

Applying the legal elements of the crimes charged in the Indictment to the facts found proved in relation to each of the 13 municipalities, the Trial Chamber finds that the crimes of: deportation, a crime against humanity; other inhumane acts (forcible transfer), a crime against humanity; murder, a violation of the laws or customs of war, and a crime against humanity; and murder, sexual assault, and wanton destruction of or damage to religious property, as forms of persecution on ethnic grounds, were committed by VJ and MUP forces in many of the locations alleged in the Indictment. However, there were a number of allegations that were not proved on the facts, or did not satisfy one or more of the requisite legal elements, such as the execution of at least 17 people in Kotlina on or about 24 March 1999, and the deliberate destruction of several mosques, and these charges are dismissed. The Chamber also notes that, for some crime sites where there was a large number of murder charges and the Indictment listed the alleged victims by name in a Schedule, the Prosecution did not provide convincing evidence that all the particular named victims were in fact among the dead, although the Chamber was satisfied that the killing of a significant group of people by VJ and/or MUP forces took place as alleged.

I will now briefly set out the Chamber's findings in respect of each of the Accused. Milan Milutinović' was the President of Serbia throughout 1998 and 1999, and much of the evidence brought by the Prosecution and his Defence concerned the nature and extent of his powers in that position. The Judgement sets out the Chamber's analysis of the pertinent provisions of the Serbian Constitution, and other relevant legislation, as well as of the witness testimony in relation to those provisions. The Chamber finds that, as President of Serbia, Milutinović did not have direct individual control over the VJ, a federal institution. His formal role in relation to the VJ was as an ex officio member of the Supreme Defence Council, or SDC, which comprised FRY President Slobodan Milošević, along with the Presidents of Serbia and Montenegro, and which made strategic decisions with respect to the VJ. However, analysis of the records of SDC sessions in evidence does not indicate the formulation or implementation of the common plan alleged in the Indictment.

* * *

The Chamber finds that, as the President of Serbia, Milutinović had powers that potentially could allow for significant oversight of the work of the Serbian Government Ministries, most importantly the Ministry of Interior. But the evidence does not establish extensive interaction between Milutinović and the MUP in the relevant period, and his de facto powers over the MUP were not significant. He issued several decrees during the state of emergency that came into force on 23 March 1999. However, * * * the Chamber is unable to draw any inferences adverse to him from the evidence surrounding these decrees.

In addition to being a Deputy Prime Minister of the FRY, Nikola Šainović was the Chairman of the FRY Commission for Co-operation with the OSCE Kosovo Verification Mission, a body set up following the various agreements concluded in October 1998 by the FRY and Serbian authorities and the international community. The Indictment alleges that he was FRY President Milošević's personal representative for Kosovo, and that he was the head of a body called the Joint Command, which had authority over the VJ and MUP forces deployed in Kosovo in 1998 and early 1999 until the end of the NATO air campaign. A significant amount of time during the trial proceedings was devoted by the Prosecution and the Šainović Defence to the issue of the existence, powers, and functioning of the Joint Command. * * * The Chamber finds that a body known by some as the Joint Command did come into existence in mid–1998, in order to co-ordinate the activities of the VJ and MUP and other state bodies involved in the Kosovo conflict. Notes of meetings of the Joint Command held between July and October 1998, taken by one of the participants, were entered into evidence, and gave insight into the nature of the body. These Notes reveal that Šainović was an active participant in Joint Command meetings, as were the Accused Pavković and Lukić, and, on occasion, Lazarević. Indeed, Šainović issued instructions at the meetings, including in relation to matters concerning the activities of the VJ and MUP. There is direct evidence of only one Joint Command meeting in 1999, in June, but military orders were issued with a Joint Command heading, in order to ensure the co-operation and co-ordination of MUP forces with the VJ.

* * *

The Chamber also finds that Šainović was very well informed about events in Kosovo, both in 1998 and 1999, and that he was aware that criminal acts had been committed by VJ and MUP forces in Kosovo both in 1998 and 1999, including during the NATO air strikes. Šainović failed to use his extensive authority in Kosovo, and his own initiative, to ensure the cessation of such criminal conduct.

Dragoljub Ojdanić became the Chief of the General Staff, the highest position within the VJ, at the end of 1998, replacing Momčilo Perišić who was removed by Milošević. Prior to this elevation, he had been the Deputy Chief of the General Staff. As Chief of the General Staff, Ojdanić was only subordinate to the civilian authorities in which overall command of the VJ was vested, namely the Supreme Defence Council. The Chamber is convinced that, as Chief of the General Staff, Ojdanić exercised command and control over all units and organs of the VJ. He worked closely with the FRY President before and during the NATO air campaign, and exercised de facto, as well as de jure, authority over the VJ. He did not, however, have direct control over MUP forces engaged in Kosovo, despite orders for the resubordination of the MUP to the VJ issued in April 1999. As Chief of the General Staff, Ojdanić attended SDC meetings and was an active participant in the discussions held. The evidence does not establish that he participated in the body known as the Joint Command, but he was aware of it and accepted its operation.

* * *

Leading up to and during the NATO air campaign, Ojdanić issued orders for the VJ to carry out operations throughout Kosovo, including in support of the MUP. He also mobilised extra VJ units for deployment in Kosovo during the time-period when the majority of crimes found by the

Chamber to have been committed took place. Through the VJ reporting system, Ojdanić was kept well-informed on a daily basis of the situation on the ground in Kosovo both before and during the NATO air strikes. Specific information about the use of excessive or indiscriminate force by VJ and MUP units was conveyed to him in 1998 and 1999. He was also aware that volunteers incorporated into the ranks of the VJ during the NATO bombing had been involved in the commission of criminal acts. He did take some action in response to the reports that he was receiving, such as issuing orders for adherence to international humanitarian law, mobilising the military justice system, and dispatching senior officers from the Security Administration to investigate. Nonetheless, he continued to order the VJ to participate in military operations with the MUP in Kosovo.

In 1998 Nebojša Pavković was the Commander of the VJ Priština Corps, which had responsibility for the territory of Kosovo. At the end of that year he was made Commander of the 3rd Army, which encompassed both the Priština Corps and the Niš Corps. In both positions he had de jure and de facto control over the units subordinated to him, and a central role in the planning and implementation of the activities of the VJ in Kosovo, in coordination with the MUP. * * *

The Chamber finds that in 1998 Pavković was involved in the arming of the non-Albanian civilian population in Kosovo, and simultaneous disarming of the Kosovo Albanians, despite his knowledge of the divisions and animosity in Kosovo along ethnic lines. As Commander of the Priština Corps in 1998, Pavković issued numerous orders for the deployment of VJ units, often in joint operations with the MUP. He was informed of allegations of excessive or indiscriminate force by the VJ and MUP in Kosovo, including through his frequent participation in Joint Command meetings where the situation in Kosovo was discussed in detail, and yet continued to engage his units. * * *

In 1998 and 1999, Pavković was present in Kosovo the majority of the time. Through his presence in Joint Command and other meetings in 1998, the regular VJ reporting system, and his tours of VJ units deployed across Kosovo, he had a detailed knowledge and understanding of the situation on the ground and the activities of his and the MUP forces. This knowledge extended to the commission of crimes by both the VJ and MUP, including the forcible displacement of Kosovo Albanians, murder, and sexual assaults. Indeed, the Chamber finds that, while Pavković knew about criminal acts committed by VJ members in Kosovo, he sometimes under-reported and minimised the serious criminal wrongdoing in his reports sent up to the Supreme Command Staff. Although he issued some orders calling for adherence to international humanitarian law in the course of these operations, the Chamber does not consider these to have been genuine measures to limit the commission of crimes in Kosovo.

When Pavković became the 3rd Army Commander at the end of 1998, his former Chief of Staff in the Priština Corps, Vladimir Lazarević, was appointed to replace him as Commander of the Priština Corps. * * *

The Chamber finds that, in 1998, Lazarević was aware of the fact that criminal acts were being committed against civilians and civilian property during VJ and MUP operations in Kosovo. He also knew that this had resulted in the displacement of a significant number of civilians.

* * * The evidence proves that Lazarević significantly participated in the planning and execution of joint VJ and MUP operations conducted from March to June 1999 in Kosovo, including in places where the Chamber has found that crimes were committed. He continued to do so, despite his knowledge of the commission of such crimes. However, unlike Pavković, Lazarević was not involved in or necessarily aware of all the political decision-making that generally took place in Belgrade, and did not participate in high-level meetings there.

The central issue of contention during the trial concerning the alleged criminal responsibility of Sreten Lukić related to the nature and powers of the body called the MUP Staff for Kosovo, of which Lukić was the head. The Lukić Defence brought a number of witnesses who testified that the MUP Staff was a body with logistical functions, and no real power or authority over MUP forces deployed in Kosovo in 1998 and 1999. This evidence starkly contrasted [with] both the content of the decisions establishing the body, which set out its tasks, and many other documents in evidence which revealed the role played by the MUP Staff in 1998 and the first half of 1999. Some witnesses also ascribed a greater degree of responsibility for the various MUP forces in Kosovo to the MUP Staff and to Lukić as its head, than suggested by the Lukić Defence.

* * * [The Chamber] finds that [the MUP staff] indeed had a significant role in the planning, organising, controlling, and directing of actions by various MUP forces in Kosovo. The Chamber is convinced that the MUP Staff was a key body in both 1998 and 1999, with substantial authority over units falling under the MUP Public Security Department, including special police units when they were deployed to Kosovo, although it did not replace the chains of command within the various MUP units and secretariats. The MUP Staff liaised with the VJ to ensure full co-ordination of MUP and VJ activities in Kosovo, and had an important role in the planning of joint VJ and MUP operations. It also provided a link to the MUP headquarters in Belgrade, to which it regularly reported.

The Chamber is satisfied that, as head of the MUP Staff, Lukić was endowed with significant authority over the MUP forces answering to the MUP Staff. Indeed, he was understood to be the commander of MUP forces in Kosovo by the foreign diplomats and observers with whom he interacted in Kosovo, and he attended meetings with them on behalf of the MUP. He also regularly attended and participated in meetings of the Joint Command. and other high-level meetings, including in Belgrade. The Chamber finds, therefore, that Lukić was a de facto commander of MUP forces in Kosovo from mid–1998 to mid–1999, as well as being the bridge between the actions of the MUP on the ground in Kosovo and the overarching policies and plans decided in Belgrade. The evidence establishes that Lukić had detailed knowledge of events in Kosovo, as they developed, as well as being informed of allegations of criminal conduct by MUP personnel there. However, the Chamber is not convinced by the evidence brought that Lukić was involved in the concealment of these crimes through the clandestine transportation of civilian bodies from Kosovo to other parts of Serbia.

Having briefly described the Chamber's conclusions concerning each of the Accused, I shall now turn to our findings in relation to the joint criminal enterprise set out in the Indictment, and the Accused's alleged participation therein. The most compelling evidence in support of the allegation that there was a common purpose to modify the ethnic balance in Kosovo in order to ensure continued control by the FRY and Serbian authorities over the province is the evidence establishing the widespread campaign of violence that was directed against the Kosovo Albanian population between March and June 1999, and the resulting massive displacement of that population. This campaign was conducted in an organised manner, utilising significant state resources, and the Chamber heard evidence from numerous witnesses about the fact that they were directed to leave Kosovo for Albania or Macedonia, and that they were forced to relinquish their personal identity documents, either as they began their departure, en route, or at the border. These documents were never returned to them.

Other factors which the Chamber has taken into account in reaching the conclusion that there was indeed a common purpose to use violence and terror to force a significant number of Kosovo Albanians from their homes and across the borders, in order for the state authorities to maintain control over Kosovo, are: the events leading up to the conflict; the arming of non-Albanian civilians in Kosovo and simultaneous disarming of Kosovo Albanians; the breakdown of negotiations to end the Kosovo crisis at the same time as the October Agreements were being breached by the FRY and Serbian authorities; and the concealment of bodies of Kosovo Albanians killed by VJ and MUP forces. The Chamber is not, however, convinced that murder, sexual assault, or the destruction or damage of religious property was within the common purpose, and only considers whether these crimes were reasonably foreseeable in the execution of the common purpose when addressing each of the Accused. Being satisfied that there was such a common purpose among high-level officials in the FRY and Serbia who were in a position to execute it through the various forces under their control, the Chamber has analysed whether or not each of the Accused participated voluntarily in the joint criminal enterprise, made a significant contribution to it, and shared the intent to commit the crimes or underlying offences that were the object of the enterprise.

[The Trial Chamber concluded by finding Milutinović not guilty and therefore ordering his release. By contrast, Šainović, Lukić, and Pavković were each found guilty under all five counts of the indictment, by committing acts as members of a joint criminal enterprise that fell within the scope of Article 7(1) of the Statute. They were each sentenced to twenty-two years of imprisonment, with credit for time served. Ojdanić and Lazarević were both found guilty of counts 1 and 2, by aiding and abetting acts falling under Article 7(1), but not guilty of counts 3 to 5. Both were sentenced to fifteen years of imprisonment, with credit for time served.]

NOTES

1. *Prosecuting Massive Atrocities.* What kinds of evidence were necessary for the prosecution to present in successfully convicting the defendants in the Milutinović case? Why was Milutinović himself acquitted? How would you analyze the difference drawn between direct involvement in the commission or failure to stop atrocities, and being a part of a criminal conspiracy during which atrocities are committed? Recall the Nuremberg Tribunal's treatment of the concept of criminal organizations.

2. *Victims and Witnesses.* Given that atrocities are often inflicted on persons who feel vulnerable long after the injury has occurred, what protections, if any, should be provided to them when appearing to testify against their alleged assailants? Several cases at the I.C.T.Y. have involved a weighing of defendant's fair trial rights in relation to the interests of victims and witnesses. The Statute and Rules provide for measures to protect victims and witnesses, and the Tribunal has applied these to safeguard witness identities from the public and, in exceptional cases, even from the defendant. These measures have provoked intense debate between those who see them as appropriate to prevent retraumatization of victims and perhaps even additional harm to them or their families, and those who question whether they are compatible with due process for defendants. For different perspectives, see Chinkin, International Tribunal for the Former Yugoslavia: Amicus Curiae Brief on Protective Measures for Victims and Witnesses, 7 Crim. L.F. 179 (1996); Chinkin, Due Process and Witness Anonymity, 91 A.J.I.L. 75 (1997); Leigh, Witness Anonymity Is Inconsistent with Due Process, 91 A.J.I.L. 80 (1997).

The Trial Chambers and Appeals Chamber have considered these matters in, among others, the *Tadic* case (discussed above); the so-called "Foca" case (Prosecutor v. Kunarac, Decision Granting Protective Measures for Witness FWS–191); and the *Furundzija* case (I.C.T.Y. Case No. IT–95–17/1–A, Appeals Chamber, Judgment (July 21, 2000)). In the latter case, a dispute arose over whether the Prosecutor should have disclosed to the defense certain materials concerning counseling that a witness had received at a treatment center in Bosnia–Herzegovina; the defense sought to impugn her testimony as arguably affected by post-traumatic stress disorder. On this and related matters, see Kelly Dawn Askin, Sexual Violence in Decisions and Indictments of the Yugoslav and Rwandan Tribunals: Current Status, 93 A.J.I.L. 97, 110–115 (1999).

3. *Completion Strategy.* Since the I.C.T.Y. was established as a temporary institution, in 2003 the Tribunal's judges devised a plan which became known as the "completion strategy" for winding down the I.C.T.Y.'s work. The plan was endorsed by the U.N. Security Council in Resolutions 1503 and

1534, and it consists of three phases and target dates. The first date called for completion of all investigations by 31 December 2004. The second date called for completion of all trials by the end of 2008, but that has slipped such that, as of early 2009, it was expected that all trials would be completed by 2010. The third date called for completion of all proceedings, including appeals, by 2012. For links to the I.C.T.Y.'s completion strategy reports to the Security Council, see http://www.icty.org/tabs/14/2.

4.   *Further Reading*. For further discussion of the I.C.T.Y., see Kerr, The International Criminal Tribunal for the Former Yugoslavia: An Exercise in Law, Politics and Diplomacy (2004); Mettraux, International Crimes and the Ad–Hoc Tribunals (2006); Bass, Stay the Hand of Vengeance: The Politics of War Crimes Tribunals 206–75 (2000); Goldstone, For Humanity: Reflections of a War Crimes Investigator (2000); Meron, War Crimes Law Comes of Age 210–27 (1998); Morris & Scharf, An Insider's Guide to the International Criminal Tribunal for the Former Yugoslavia: Documentary History and Analysis (2 vols., 1995).

C.   INTERNATIONAL CRIMINAL TRIBUNAL FOR RWANDA

Creation. Rwanda has experienced recurrent outbreaks of ethnic conflict between the Hutus (who have comprised approximately 85% of the population) and the Tutsis (less than 15%). In April 1994, shortly after the assassination of Hutu President Juvenal Habyarimana of Rwanda, Hutu extremist troops, militia and mobs launched a genocidal wave of murder and rape against the Tutsi minority and Hutu moderates. Between April and July 1994, some 800,000 or more Tutsis and moderate Hutus were killed. For background on the conflict, see Prunier, The Rwanda Crisis: History of a Genocide (1997); Gourevitch, We Wish to Inform You That Tomorrow We Will Be Killed with Our Families: Stories from Rwanda (1998); Power, "A Problem from Hell": America and the Age of Genocide (2003).

On November 8, 1994, the U.N. Security Council established an *ad hoc* tribunal similar to the I.C.T.Y. to prosecute individuals responsible for genocide and other serious violations of international humanitarian law in the territory of Rwanda during 1994. See S.C. Res. 955 (1994). Known as the International Criminal Tribunal for Rwanda (I.C.T.R.), the Tribunal is based in Arusha, Tanzania, though the prosecutor's office is also based in Kigali, Rwanda. Interestingly, while the Government of Rwanda had requested the creation of an international tribunal, Rwanda (which happened to occupy a non-permanent seat on the Security Council in 1994) voted against the final formulation of Resolution 955, partly because the resolution did not authorize use of the death penalty.

Structure. The Statute of the I.C.T.R., which was annexed to Resolution 955, mirrors closely the I.C.T.Y. Statute. Differences between the subject matter jurisdiction of the two tribunals derive largely from the fact that the conflict in Rwanda was essentially internal, whereas the conflict in the former Yugoslavia was in part international. Thus, the competence of the I.C.T.R. encompasses genocide, crimes against humanity, and serious violations of common article 3 of the Geneva Conventions of August 12, 1949 and Additional Protocol II thereto of June 8, 1977, but not grave breaches of the Geneva Conventions or war crimes under the 1907 Hague Convention, because the latter are implicated only in international conflict.

Like the I.C.T.Y., the organs of the I.C.T.R. include the judges (including a President), a prosecutor's office, and a registrar. There are nine permanent judges divided into three trial chambers and assisted by nine *ad litem* judges. The I.C.T.R. and the I.C.T.Y. have the same five-judge Appeals Chamber based in the Hague. While at one time both tribunals were served by a single prosecutor, the tribunals now have separate prosecutors.

Case Law. A wide variety of persons have been indicted and prosecuted by the I.C.T.R. For example, in February 1999, two former Rwandan ministers, Eliezer Niyitegeka (Information Minister) and Casimir Bizimungu (Minister of Health) were arrested in Kenya and transferred to the custody of the I.C.T.R. In August 1999, a woman, Pauline Nyiramasuhuko (former Rwandan Minister of Family and Women's Affairs) was indicted by the I.C.T.R. and charged with genocide and with rape as a crime against humanity. The rape charge is based on allegations that she knew her subordinates were raping Tutsi women and failed to take reasonable and necessary measures to stop or punish them. Her indictment was the first for a woman by an international tribunal involving a charge of rape in violation of international humanitarian law.

On July 23, 1999, Kenyan authorities arrested Georges Ruggiu, a Belgian journalist whose broadcasts had urged Hutus to kill Tutsis and Hutu moderates. Ruggiu, the first non-Rwandan to be indicted by the I.C.T.R., pleaded guilty to the crime of direct and public incitement to commit genocide and a crime against humanity (persecution). He was sentenced in June 2000 to two concurrent twelve-year sentences. See Prosecutor v. Ruggiu, Case No. ICTR–97–32–1, Judgement and Sentence (June 1, 2000), 39 I.L.M. 1338 (2000). Similarly, three media leaders were convicted for crimes of speech through radio broadcasts and newspaper publications, a judgment upheld by the Appeals Chamber in November 2007. See MacKinnon, International Decision: Prosecutor v. Nahimana, Barayagwiza & Ngeze, Case No. ICTR 99–92–A, 103 A.J.I.L. 97 (2009).

As of early 2009, the I.C.T.R. had arrested more than seventy individuals accused of involvement in the 1994 genocide in Rwanda. Among those arrested were the former Prime Minister and several other members of the interim Government of Rwanda during the genocide, as well as senior military leaders and high ranking government officials. Further, it had completed trials of several of those arrested, including that of the former Prime Minister, Jean Kambanda. Kambanda's trial was the first time that a Head of Government had been convicted for genocide. For discussion of the I.C.T.R.'s successes and failures, see Akhavan, Justice and Reconciliation in the Great Lakes Region of Africa. The Contribution of the International Criminal Tribunal for Rwanda, 7 Duke J. Comp. & Int'l L. 325 (1997); Schabas, Justice, Democracy and Impunity in Post–Genocide Rwanda: Searching for Solutions to Impossible Problems, 7 Crim. L.F. 523 (1996); Morris & Scharf, The International Criminal Tribunal for Rwanda (1998).

Rwandan National Proceedings. In parallel to the international proceedings, Rwanda went forward with a wholesale program under its national law of arrest and detention of genocide suspects: indeed, approximately 125,000 (roughly 10% of the adult male Hutu population) had been detained through the late 1990s. In 1996, Rwanda enacted legislation to facilitate the processing of this overwhelming number of cases. National trials have gone forward, and in some genocide cases the death penalty has been imposed and carried out. Ironically, the most senior alleged perpetrators have been indicted by the I.C.T.R., where they cannot face the death penalty, while more junior persons are exposed to the Rwandan national system where such punishment is available. On the relationship between the international and national proceedings in respect of Rwanda, see Dubois, Rwanda's National Criminal Courts and the International Tribunal, 321 Int'l Rev. Red Cross 717 (1997); Alvarez, Crimes of State/ Crimes of Hate: Lessons from Rwanda, 24 Yale J. Int'l L. 365 (1999); Drumbl, Rule of Law Amid Lawlessness: Counseling the Accused in Rwanda's Domestic Genocide Trials, 29 Colum. Hum. Rts. L. Rev. 545 (1998); Drumbl, Punishment, Postgenocide: From Guilt to Shame to *Civis* in Rwanda, 75 N.Y.U. L. Rev. 1221 (2000).

Surrender by the United States. A Rwandan (Hutu) clergyman, Elizaphan Ntakirutimana, who had been indicted by the I.C.T.R., was arrested in 1996 in Texas by federal marshals. A 1996 agreement between the United States and the two *ad hoc* U.N. Tribunals, incorporated in legislation by Congress, provides for rendition by the United States of indicted individuals to the Tribunal issuing the indictment. Ntakirutimana was alleged to have urged men, women and children to take refuge in a church and hospital to escape the ethnic slaughter in progress. He then allegedly returned with a band of Rwandan soldiers who murdered hundreds of people who had sought sanctuary at his urging. N.Y. Times, Dec. 12, 1997, at 1. A divided Court of Appeals affirmed the denial of Ntakirutimana's petition for a writ of habeas corpus and cleared the way for his rendition. Ntakirutimana v. Reno, 184 F.3d 419 (5th Cir.1999). The Secretary of State approved the rendition in March 2000, marking the first instance of transfer of an indicted criminal by the United States to an international criminal tribunal. Ntakirutimana pled not guilty, but was convicted and sentenced to ten years' imprisonment.

Completion Strategy. Like the I.C.T.Y., the I.C.T.R. is a temporary institution that is expected to complete its work in the near term. As of early 2009, its "completion strategy" called for finishing its work by 2010, although many observers think that further time will be needed. For links to the I.C.T.Y.'s completion strategy reports to the Security Council, see http://69.94.11.53/ENGLISH/completionstrat/index.htm.

D. OTHER *AD HOC* TRIBUNALS

In the wake of the establishment of the I.C.T.Y. and I.C.T.R., recurrent demands arose for the creation of new tribunals to address atrocities that occurred in other contexts. Yet the costs of operating the Yugoslavia and Rwanda tribunals led some to see "tribunal fatigue" at the Security Council, and hence a preference for greater reliance on national processes. Further, often the state where the atrocities occurred wished to maintain greater control and involvement in the tribunal, sometimes for internal political reasons, sometimes to have justice dispensed "closer to home," and sometimes due to a distrust of fully internationalized processes. Such circumstances led to the creation of a variety of *ad hoc* tribunals that had greater or lesser degrees of "internationalization." The defining feature of all these tribunals is some level of international oversight or involvement, but with a heavy dose of national control by the state in which the atrocities occurred. How would you assess the advantages and disadvantages of using such "hybrid" *ad hoc* tribunals?

MURPHY, PRINCIPLES OF INTERNATIONAL LAW 430–36 (2006)

In addition to the ICTY, ICTR, and ICC, various smaller tribunals or courts have been established to address serious violations of international humanitarian law. Such tribunals or courts are not international in the sense of being independent of a national legal system, yet they have certain design features that allow international participation as a means of promoting meaningful accountability.[104]

Cambodia Extraordinary Chambers

The Khmer Rouge, a communist organization that governed Cambodia from 1975 to 1979, murdered, starved, and exposed Cambodians to forced labor resulting in the death of an estimated 1.7 million people. (When these deaths are taken as a proportion of the total population, the Khmer Rouge was the most lethal regime of the twentieth century). In December 1978, Vietnamese troops invaded Cambodia and deposed the Khmer Rouge. The Vietnamese, however, were assisted by defections from the Khmer Rouge, while other Khmer Rouge members retreated to the west where they continued to control a portion of Cambodia. Consequently, no members of the Khmer Rouge regime were brought to justice. Vietnam ultimately left Cambodia after installing a government, but civil strife continued for more than a decade. In 1991, the Cambodian political

---

104. *See generally* Laura Dickinson, *The Promise of Hybrid Courts*, 97 AM. J. INT'L L. 295 (2003).

factions signed an agreement calling for elections and disarmament. The remaining Khmer Rouge members fought against the elections and the result, yet most members had surrendered or been captured by 1999.

In 2003, Cambodia enacted a law creating "extraordinary chambers" in its courts to try former leaders of the Khmer Rouge, which the U.N. General Assembly welcomed.[105] Further, after more than five years of negotiations, the United Nations and Cambodia in 2003 signed an agreement on U.N. involvement with these extraordinary chambers.[106] The chambers have jurisdiction over serious violations of Cambodian criminal law and international humanitarian law committed from April 1975 to January 1979. The trial chamber consists of three Cambodian judges and two international judges, while the appeals chamber consists of four Cambodian judges and three international judges. The foreign judges are appointed by Cambodia's Supreme Council of the Magistracy upon nomination by the U.N. secretary-general. A decision of the trial chamber requires an affirmative vote of at least four judges, while the appeals chamber requires an affirmative vote of at least five judges. There are foreign and Cambodian "co-prosecutors" who appear in the cases, and foreign and Cambodian "co-investigating judges" who investigate cases. The chamber's office of administration is headed by a Cambodian director and a foreign deputy director appointed by the U.N. secretary-general. The maximum penalty that can be issued is life imprisonment.

Since the U.N.–Cambodia agreement only entered into force in April 2005, it is not yet clear whether the trials will succeed. The cost of the trials, however, will be substantial. The three-year budget is approximately U.S. $56.3 million, of which U.S. $43 million is to be paid by the United Nations and U.S. $13.3 million by the government of Cambodia. Moreover, many significant Khmer Rouge leaders have died, included its leader during 1975–79, Pol Pot.

East Timor Special Panels

In August 1999, the people of East Timor opted by referendum for independence from Indonesian rule. Immediately after the vote, extensive violence broke out in which East Timorese militias who were opposed to independence attacked East Timorese civilians, unchecked (and sometimes assisted) by Indonesian military and police. Some estimates indicated that 2,000 people were murdered and 500,000 were forced to flee their homes, alongside widespread destruction and looting of property. A U.N. Transitional Administration in East Timor (UNTAET) was then established to administer East Timor until it became stable enough to function as a fully independent nation.[107]

---

105. *See* G.A. Res. 57/228B (May 13, 2003).

106. *See* Agreement Concerning the Prosecution Under Cambodian Law of Crimes Committed During the Period of Democratic Kampuchea, Cambodia–U.N., June 6, 2003, *at* <http://www.cambodia.gov.kh/krt/english/draft% 20agreement.htm>.

107. *See* S.C. Res. 1272 (Oct. 25, 1999).

UNTAET determined that it was important to bring the perpetrators of the atrocities to justice, but the East Timor judicial system was very weak, with few experienced judges and lawyers, and poor facilities. Consequently, UNTAET, in conjunction with a national consultative council of East Timorese, issued regulations that created a system of district courts for East Timor. The Dili District Court was granted exclusive jurisdiction over war crimes, crimes against humanity, genocide and other serious crimes (murder, sexual offenses, and torture), so long as they were committed between January 1 and October 25, 1999. The regulations also created special panels within the Dili District Court to exercise this jurisdiction, composed of both East Timorese and international judges.[108] Thus, although the panels are part of the East Timor national court system (*e.g.*, appeals from the panels are made to East Timor courts), each panel consists of one Timorese and two foreign judges. Further, a serious crimes unit was created to conduct investigations and indict persons for prosecution before the special panels. Finally, the regulations called for foreign prosecutors and judges to assist local lawyers. When East Timor became an independent country in May 2002, UNTAET and the consultative council ceased to exist, but the system for the special panels was maintained.

Although hampered by shortages of resources and staff, from 2000 to 2005 the serious crimes unit filed 95 indictments with the special panels covering 391 persons. The special panels convicted dozens of individuals for the commission of atrocities in proceedings that were generally regarded as conforming to international standards. At the same time, critics noted that the special panels were unable to bring to justice persons located outside East Timor, including high-level Indonesian indictees, such as the former Indonesian Minister of Defence and Commander of the Indonesian National Military (TNI), several high-ranking TNI commanders, and the former Governor of East Timor.[109]

Iraqi Special Tribunal

After the 2003 U.S.-led intervention in Iraq, coalition authorities appointed an Iraqi Governing Council consisting of local Iraqi leaders. Shortly after its creation, the council decided to establish a special criminal tribunal to try high-level officials of former Iraqi President Saddam Hussein's Baath Party for crimes committed under his reign. In December 2003, the Governing Council issued a "Statute of the Iraqi Special Tribunal."[110] The statute establishes a tribunal with jurisdiction over any Iraqi national or resident who, from July 1968 to May 2003, committed genocide, crimes against humanity, or serious war crimes, or

---

108. *See* UNTAET Regulation No. 2000/11 on the Organization of Courts in East Timor (Mar. 6, 2000), *at* <http://www.un.org/peace/etimor/untaetR/Reg11.pdf>.

109. *See* Report to the Secretary–General of the Commission of Experts to Review the Prosecution of Serious Violations of Human Rights in Timor–Leste (the then East Timor) in 1999 (May 26, 2005), U.N. Doc. S/2005/458, annex II (July 15, 2005).

110. Statute of the Iraqi Special Tribunal, Dec. 10, 2003, *reprinted in* 43 I.L.M. 231 (2004) [hereinafter Iraqi Special Tribunal Statute].

who violated specified Iraqi laws (*e.g.*, using military force against an Arab country). The tribunal consists of one or more trial chambers (five judges each), an appeals chamber (nine judges), investigative judges, a prosecutor's department, and an administrative department.[111]

As a general matter, the personnel of the tribunal are to be Iraqi nationals. Yet the statute provides that the Iraqi Governing Council[112] may appoint non-Iraqi judges. Further, the tribunal president must appoint non-Iraqi nationals to act in an advisory capacity to (or as observers of) the trial and appeals chambers, and provide assistance and monitor the tribunal's due process standards. The chief tribunal investigative judge must also appoint non-Iraqi nationals to act in an advisory capacity or as observers with respect to the investigation and prosecution of cases (for the same purposes as above).[113]

The statute provides various rights to defendants, including the presumption of innocence, access to counsel, a public trial, adequate time to prepare a defense, the opportunity to present evidence and cross-examine prosecution witnesses, and a prohibition against self-incrimination. Penalties that may be imposed on defendants are set forth in the Iraqi criminal code of 1969, which includes life imprisonment and the death penalty.[114]

Kosovar Special Panels

In March/April 1999, NATO states conducted an extensive bombing campaign against the Federal Republic of Yugoslavia (Serbia & Montenegro) to prevent its government from engaging in ethnic cleansing and atrocities in the autonomous province of Kosovo. The intervention led to the deployment of a U.N. Interim Administration in Kosovo (UNMIK) to administer the province until the situation could be stabilized. Years of civil conflict, however, had left the local judicial system in disarray; resources were scarce and trained judges or lawyers were inexperienced. At the same time, numerous persons were being held in custody on suspicion of having committed atrocities.

Consequently, U.N. administrators promulgated regulations allowing foreign judges to sit with Kosovar judges on special panels within the Kosovar court system, and allowing foreign lawyers to participate in the criminal proceedings.[115] The regulations provide that the courts apply local law so long as it does not conflict with human rights standards present in international law.[116] Thereafter, Kosovar courts conducted numerous trials for war crimes.

---

111. *Id.*, arts. 1, 3–4, & 10–14.

112. The Iraqi Governing Council was created during the coalition occupation of Iraq. It has since been disbanded and replaced by the current Iraqi government.

113. Iraqi Special Tribunal Statute, *supra* note 110, arts. 4(d), 6(b), 6(c), 7(n), 7(o), & 28.

114. *Id.*, arts. 20 & 24.

115. *See, e.g.*, UNMIK Regulation No. 2000/64 on Assignment of International Judges/Prosecutors and/or Change of Venue (Dec. 15, 2000).

116. *See* UNMIK Regulation No. 1999/24 on the Law Applicable in Kosovo (Dec. 2, 1999).

Sierra Leone Special Court

After extensive efforts by the Economic Community of West African States, the Organization of African Unity, the United Nations, and interested states, the government of Sierra Leone and the Revolutionary United Front (RUF) signed a peace agreement in July 1999 to end the country's civil war.[117] In addition to providing for a cease-fire between the parties and for disarmament of the RUF, the agreement granted an "absolute and free pardon and reprieve to all combatants and collaborators in respect of anything done by them in pursuit of their objectives...."[118] The special representative of the U.N. secretary-general, however, appended to his signature a statement that the United Nations understood the amnesty provisions of the agreement as not applying to international crimes of genocide, crimes against humanity, war crimes, and other serious violations of international humanitarian law.

In May 2000, the RUF began resisting disarmament and resumed hostilities, taking hostage some 500 members of the U.N. Mission in Sierra Leone.[119] In August 2000, the U.N. Security Council requested that the secretary-general negotiate with the Sierra Leone government for the establishment of a special court that would combine elements of Sierra Leonean and international law to try Sierra Leone nationals accused of atrocities during the course of the conflict.[120] Given the extensive atrocities that had occurred, the Sierra Leone government wished to provide for a system of accountability. Yet the local justice system had been severely damaged by years of civil war and associated corruption, such that it could not handle large-scale atrocity trials. Moreover, the new government did not want full responsibility for the politically-charged trial of RUF leader Foday Sankoh. Consequently, the Sierra Leone government agreed to the creation of a special court charged with hearing cases concerning war crimes, crimes against humanity, and other serious violations of international humanitarian law, as well as certain violations of local law, such as child abuse and arson (the crime of genocide was not included since it did not occur in Sierra Leone).[121]

Unlike the other courts and tribunals referred to in this section, the Special Court of Sierra Leone is not part of a national legal system. Rather, it is a product of an international agreement between the United Nations and the Sierra Leone government.[122] The chief prosecutor is appointed by the U.N. secretary-general and the deputy prosecutor is

---

117. *See* Peace Agreement Between the Government of Sierra Leone and the Revolutionary United Front of Sierra Leone, July 7, 1999, *reprinted in* Letter Dated 12 July 1999 from the Chargé d'Affaires ad interim of the Permanent Mission of Togo to the United Nations Addressed to the President of the Security Council, U.N. Doc. S/1999/777, annex (1999).

118. *Id.*, art. IX(2).

119. *See* Steven Mufson, *Sierra Leone's Peace Succumbs to Its Flaws*, WASH. POST, May 8, 2000, at A1.

120. *See* SC Res. 1315 (Aug. 14, 2000).

121. *See generally* <http://www.sc-sl.org>.

122. *See* Agreement on the Establishment of a Special Court for Sierra Leone, Sierra Leone–U.N., Jan. 16, 2002, U.N. Doc. S/2002/246, app. II, attach. (2002).

appointed by the Sierra Leone government. The two trial chambers each consist of two foreign judges appointed by the secretary-general and one local judge appointed by the Sierra Leone government. The appellate chamber consists of three foreign judges and two local judges, similarly appointed. A registry provides administrative support, while a defense office is responsible for ensuring that all indictees are represented by qualified attorneys, who are appointed in the event the indictee is indigent.

As of 2005, the special court has indicted thirteen individuals for war crimes, crimes against humanity, and other serious violations of international humanitarian law, of whom nine are being tried. Once convicted, defendants can be sentenced to as much as life imprisonment, but not to the death penalty.

NOTES

1. *Special Court for Lebanon.* In addition to the special tribunals discussed above, in December 2005 Lebanese Prime Minister Fouad Siniora, asked the United Nations to create a tribunal with an "international character" to try those charged with the terrorist attacks perpetrated in Lebanon since October 2004, especially a massive car bombing in Beirut in February 2005 that killed twenty-one people, including the former Prime Minister Rafik Hariri. Once the nature and the scope of the international assistance needed by the Lebanese government was determined, the U.N. Security Council unanimously passed a resolution in March 2006 authorizing creation of an international tribunal to try persons implicated in the assassination of Hariri. See S.C. Res. 1664 (2006). That resolution requested the Secretary–General to negotiate an agreement with the Lebanese Government.

While the Secretary–General successfully concluded and signed such an agreement with the Lebanese Government, the agreement could not enter into force due to the lack of approval by Lebanon's Parliament, where certain factions opposed creation of the tribunal. Consequently, in May 2007 the U.N. Security Council, acting under Chapter VII of the Charter, adopted Resolution 1757 (May 30, 2007) imposing the creation of the Special Tribunal for Lebanon (by a vote of ten in favor, none against, and five abstentions, including China and Russia). The resolution provided for automatic entry into force of the 2007 agreement.

The tribunal is unique not just because of its origins. It also marks the first time that a U.N.-based international criminal court will be trying a "terrorist" crime committed against a specific person. Moreover, it will not apply international criminal law but, rather, Lebanese law. The chambers will be composed of both Lebanese and international judges, though with a majority of international judges. The tribunal officially opened in March 2009 and is based in Leidschendam, the Netherlands.

2. *Trial and Execution of Saddam Hussein.* Since publication of the excerpt above, former Iraqi President Saddam Hussein and other senior Iraqi leaders have been tried by what is now known as the Supreme Iraqi Criminal Tribunal. Saddam Hussein was convicted and executed in December 2006. See

Newton & Scharf, Enemy of the State: The Trial and Execution of Saddam Hussein (2008).

3. *Trial of Charles Taylor.* In June 2003, the Special Court for Sierra Leone made public an indictment against Liberian President Charles Taylor, whose military forces were implicated in cross-border raids and human rights abuses in neighboring states, including Sierra Leone. Taylor agreed to step down as president and left Liberia for Nigeria, where he remained for three years. In March 2006, Taylor was arrested by Nigerian police, transported to Liberia, and taken into custody by the Special Court. Taylor's trial, however, was considered so politically sensitive that it was transferred to the Hague, where the Special Court is using the facilities of the International Criminal Court. See S.C. Res. 1688 (June 16, 2006). Taylor is charged with war crimes, crimes against humanity and other serious violations of international humanitarian law committed in Sierra Leone, relating to murdering and mutilating civilians (including cutting off their limbs), using women and girls as sex slaves, abducting adults and children, and forcing them to perform forced labor or become fighters during Sierra Leone's civil war.

4. *Further Information.* See Internationalized Criminal Courts and Tribunals: Sierra Leone, East Timor, Kosovo, and Cambodia (Romano et al. eds. 2004). For up-to-date information on the work of these tribunals, reference may be made to their or other web sites. For the Cambodia Extraordinary Chambers, see http://www.eccc.gov.kh. For the Sierra Leone Special Court, see http://www.sc-sl.org. For the Iraqi Special Tribunal (now known as the Supreme Iraqi Criminal Tribunal), see http://www.iraq-iht.org. For the East Timor Special Panels, see a web site maintained by the University of California, http://socrates.berkeley.edu/?warcrime/ET-special-panels-docs.htm.

SECTION 4. THE INTERNATIONAL CRIMINAL COURT

A. BACKGROUND, STRUCTURE AND JURISDICTION

After years of groundwork by the International Law Commission and more than a year of meetings by special preparatory committees under the auspices of the U.N. General Assembly, a U.N.-sponsored conference of plenipotentiaries was convened in Rome on June 15, 1998. More than 160 countries participated with input from scores of non-governmental organizations. After five weeks of difficult negotiations, the conference adopted the Rome Statute of the International Criminal Court, July 17, 1998, 2187 U.N.T.S. 3, by a vote of 120 states in favor and seven opposed. The United States voted against approval, as did China, Israel, and four other states. The Rome Statute entered into force on July 1, 2002, sixty days after ten states simultaneously filed their instruments of ratification, which made for a total of sixty ratifications. As of early 2009, 108 states had ratified the Rome Statute, not including China, India, Russia, and the United States.

Under Article 1 of the Rome Statute, the International Criminal Court (I.C.C.) is a permanent institution vested with competence to try individuals indicted for the "most serious crimes of international concern" specified in Article 5. Further, Article 1 provides that the Court "shall be complementary to national criminal jurisdictions." The I.C.C. is based in the Hague, the Netherlands and, though a treaty-based institution, has a relationship with the United Nations established by agreement approved by the Assembly of states parties to the Statute. See http://www.icc-cpi.int/menus/icc/home.

The Rome Statute provides that the I.C.C. may exercise jurisdiction over only certain specified crimes. Article 5 of the Statute provides:

1. The jurisdiction of the Court shall be limited to the most serious crimes of concern to the international community as a whole. The Court has jurisdiction in accordance with this Statute with respect to the following crimes:

(a) The crime of genocide;

(b) Crimes against humanity;

(c) War crimes;

(d) The crime of aggression.

2. The Court shall exercise jurisdiction over the crime of aggression once a provision is adopted in accordance with articles 121 and 123 defining the crime and setting out the conditions under which the Court shall exercise jurisdiction with respect to this crime. Such a provision shall be consistent with the relevant provisions of the Charter of the United Nations.

Separate articles in the Rome Statute define what is meant by these crimes: genocide (Article 6); crimes against humanity (Article 7); and war crimes (Article 8). In order to clarify further those definitions, Article 9(1) provides that "Elements of Crimes" shall be prepared to assist the Court in interpreting these crimes. The Elements of Crimes were adopted and entered into force in 2002. See I.C.C. Doc. ICC–ASP/1/3, part II–B (2002). The Elements of Crimes deal with such matters as the perpetrator's knowledge and intent in relation to the acts in question, the connection of the perpetrator's actions to the actions of others (e.g., to interpret the term "widespread or systematic attack directed against any civilian population" in Article 7's definition of crimes against humanity), and the meaning of terms such as "forcibly" (which is not restricted to physical force, but may include threat of force or coercion). The elements of the crime of rape and other sexual crimes are defined in detail, drawing on the jurisprudence of the I.C.T.Y. and I.C.T.R.

A series of other rules have also been developed to govern the operations of the I.C.C., including Rules of Procedure and Evidence; Regulations of the Court; Regulations of the Registry; Code of Professional Conduct for Counsel; and Code of Judicial Ethics. The I.C.C.'s expenses are funded primarily by its states parties, though it also receives voluntary contributions from governments, international organizations, individuals, corporations and other entities.

As implied by Article 5(2), the I.C.C. will have jurisdiction to try individuals for the crime of aggression only if the state parties are able to agree on a definition of the crime and on the conditions that would have to be fulfilled before the I.C.C. could exercise jurisdiction over it for any given situation. As of early 2009, it was expected that the states parties to the Rome Statute would consider at their Review Conference in 2010 whether to adopt the crime of aggression. Among the issues that must be considered is whether there should first be a finding by the U.N. Security Council that an act of aggression has occurred before the exercise of the Court's jurisdiction over this crime. See Report of the Special Working Group on the Crime of Aggression, I.C.C. Doc. ICC–ASP/7/SWGCA/2 (Feb. 20, 2009). Do you think Security Council action should first be required or not? What repercussions may flow from having an international court that is capable of declaring on its own that a crime of aggression has occurred? See, e.g., Murphy, Criminalizing Humanitarian Intervention, 40 Case W. Res. J. Int'l L. (forthcoming 2009).

Other crimes, such as terrorism or drug trafficking, were not included in the Rome Statute, since some states believed the I.C.C. should remain narrowly focused in order to succeed. Do you think that once the I.C.C. has been fully operational for a few years the states parties should revisit including additional crimes in its jurisdiction?

There are additional limitations to the I.C.C's jurisdiction beyond subject matter. First, the I.C.C. only has jurisdiction over crimes committed after the Rome Statute entered into force; crimes committed prior to July 1, 2002 do not fall within its ambit. States who ratify or accede to the Rome Statute after July 1, 2002, are only exposed to the I.C.C.'s jurisdiction after that point, unless they grant the I.C.C. jurisdiction retroactively to July 1, 2002 (Rome Statute, art. 11).

Second, under Articles 12–14 of the Rome Statute, the I.C.C. may only investigate and prosecute acts when one of several situations arises: (1) the state where the alleged crime was committed is a party to the Rome Statute (including where the crime was committed on an aircraft or vessel of the state); (2) the person suspected of committing the crime is a national of a party to the Rome Statute; (3) the state where the alleged crime was committed, or whose national is suspected of committing the crime, consents *ad hoc* to the jurisdiction of the I.C.C.; or (4) the crime is referred to the I.C.C. by the Security Council under Chapter VII of the U.N. Charter.

No matter the nature of the situation, the Rome Statute accords the Security Council the ability, by a resolution adopted under Chapter VII, to request that an investigation or prosecution be delayed for a period of one year (Article 16). Even without that provision, do you think the Security Council could order that an I.C.C. case be delayed or even terminated?

Third, under the principle of "complementarity," the I.C.C. is to regard a case as inadmissible if there is a state with jurisdiction that is willing and genuinely able to carry out an investigation or prosecution (Rome Statute, Articles 1 & 17). The fact that a state has investigated a matter and decided against prosecution is not a basis for the I.C.C. to exercise jurisdiction, unless there is something disingenuous about the state's conduct.

The prosecutor can initiate an investigation on the basis of a referral from any state party or from the U.N. Security Council, unless she determines that there is no reasonable basis to proceed under the Rome Statute (Article 53). In addition, the prosecutor can initiate investigations *proprio motu* on the basis of information on crimes within the jurisdiction of the Court received from individuals or organizations, but she must first conclude that there is a reasonable basis to proceed (Article 15). During an investigation, each situation is assigned to a pre-trial chamber. If the prosecutor requests, the pre-trial chamber may issue a warrant of arrest or a summons to appear if there are reasonable grounds to believe a person has committed a crime within the jurisdiction of the Court. Once a wanted person has been surrendered to or voluntarily appears before the Court, the pre-trial chamber holds a hearing to confirm the charges that will be the basis of the trial.

Once the charges are confirmed, the case is assigned to a trial chamber of three judges, which conducts the trial. Under the Rome Statute, the defendant has a right to be present during the trial (Article 63) and is presumed innocent until proven guilty by the prosecutor beyond reasonable doubt (Article 66). The accused has the right to a public trial without undue delay, and to conduct his or her defense in person or through counsel of his or her choosing (Article 67). Victims may also participate in proceedings directly or through their legal representatives. Upon conclusion of the trial, the trial chamber issues its decision, acquitting or convicting the accused by at least a majority vote (Article 74). If the accused is convicted, the trial chamber issues a sentence for a specified term of up to thirty years or, when justified by the extreme gravity of the crime and the individual circumstances of the convicted person, life imprisonment (Article 77). The trial chamber may also order reparations to victims (Article 75). Throughout the proceedings, either the accused or the prosecutor (or even a concerned state) may appeal decisions of the chambers as specified by the statute (Articles 81–83). All appeals are decided by the appeals chamber of five judges.

As of early 2009, three states parties to the Rome Statute—Central African Republic, Democratic Republic of the Congo, and Uganda—have referred situations occurring on their territories to the Court for investigation and prosecution. With respect to the Central African Republic, one case is underway against the alleged President and Commander-in-chief of the Mouvement de libération du Congo, who is in I.C.C. custody. With respect to the D.R.C., three cases have been opened, with three of the accused in I.C.C. custody while one remains at large. With respect to

Uganda, warrants of arrest have been issued against the top members of the Lords Resistance Army, but they all remain at large. In addition, the Security Council has referred one situation to the I.C.C. arising in a non-state party—the atrocities in Darfur, Sudan. Two cases have been opened relating to that situation, with all three suspects still at large (see next Section). Some supporters have expressed concern (and some opponents have expressed criticism) that all the initial situations before the I.C.C. relate solely to Africa.

On the Rome conference and its outcome, see generally The International Criminal Court: The Making of the Rome Statute: Issues, Negotiations, Results (Lee ed. 1999); Kirsch & Holmes, The Rome Conference on an International Criminal Court: The Negotiating Process, 93 A.J.I.L. 2 (1999); Arsanjani, The Rome Statute of the International Criminal Court, 93 A.J.I.L. 22 (1999). For a collection of documents, see The Statute of the International Criminal Court and Related Instruments: Legislative History 1994–2000 (Bassiouni ed. 2005) (3 vols.). For broader discussions, see Sadat, The International Criminal Court and the Transformation of International Law: Justice for the New Millennium (2002); Schabas, An Introduction to the International Criminal Court (3d ed. 2004).

B.   CASE STUDY: WAR CRIMES
IN DARFUR, SUDAN

SECURITY COUNCIL RESOLUTION 1593

S/RES/1593 (Mar. 31, 2005)

The Security Council,

Taking note of the report of the International Commission of Inquiry on violations of international humanitarian law and human rights law in Darfur (S/2005/60),

Recalling article 16 of the Rome Statute under which no investigation or prosecution may be commenced or proceeded with by the International Criminal Court for a period of 12 months after a Security Council request to that effect,

Also recalling articles 75 and 79 of the Rome Statute and encouraging States to contribute to the ICC Trust Fund for Victims,

Taking note of the existence of agreements referred to in Article 98(2) of the Rome Statute,

Determining that the situation in Sudan continues to constitute a threat to international peace and security,

Acting under Chapter VII of the Charter of the United Nations,

1. *Decides* to refer the situation in Darfur since 1 July 2002 to the Prosecutor of the International Criminal Court;

2. *Decides* that the Government of Sudan and all other parties to the conflict in Darfur shall cooperate fully with and provide any necessary

assistance to the Court and the Prosecutor pursuant to this resolution and, while recognizing that States not party to the Rome Statute have no obligation under the Statute, urges all States and concerned regional and other international organizations to cooperate fully;

3. *Invites* the Court and the African Union to discuss practical arrangements that will facilitate the work of the Prosecutor and of the Court, including the possibility of conducting proceedings in the region, which would contribute to regional efforts in the fight against impunity;

4. *Also encourages* the Court, as appropriate and in accordance with the Rome Statute, to support international cooperation with domestic efforts to promote the rule of law, protect human rights and combat impunity in Darfur;

5. *Also emphasizes* the need to promote healing and reconciliation and encourages in this respect the creation of institutions, involving all sectors of Sudanese society, such as truth and/or reconciliation commissions, in order to complement judicial processes and thereby reinforce the efforts to restore long-lasting peace, with African Union and international support as necessary;

6. *Decides* that nationals, current or former officials or personnel from a contributing State outside Sudan which is not a party to the Rome Statute of the International Criminal Court shall be subject to the exclusive jurisdiction of that contributing State for all alleged acts or omissions arising out of or related to operations in Sudan established or authorized by the Council or the African Union, unless such exclusive jurisdiction has been expressly waived by that contributing State;

7. *Recognizes* that none of the expenses incurred in connection with the referral, including expenses related to investigations or prosecutions in connection with that referral, shall be borne by the United Nations and that such costs shall be borne by the parties to the Rome Statute and those States that wish to contribute voluntarily;

8. *Invites* the Prosecutor to address the Council within three months of the date of adoption of this resolution and every six months thereafter on actions taken pursuant to this resolution;

9. *Decides* to remain seized of the matter.

[The resolution was adopted by a vote of 11 in favor and 4 abstentions (Algeria, Brazil, China, United States).]

WARRANT OF ARREST FOR OMAR HASSAN AHMAD AL BASHIR

No. ICC–02/05–01/09 (Mar. 4, 2009), http://www.icc-cpi.int (footnotes omitted)

Pre-trial Chamber I of the International Criminal Court ("the Chamber" and "the Court" respectively);

Having Examined the "Prosecution's Application under Article 58" ("the Prosecution Application"), filed by the Prosecution on 14 July 2008 in the record of the situation in Darfur, Sudan ("the Darfur situation") requesting the issuance of a warrant for the arrest of Omar Hassan Ahmad Al Bashir (hereinafter referred to as "Omar Al Bashir") for genocide, crimes against humanity and war crimes;

Having Examined the supporting material and other information submitted by the Prosecution;

Noting the "Decision on the Prosecution's Request for a Warrant of Arrest against Omar Hassan Ahmad Al Bashir" in which the Chamber held that it was satisfied that there are reasonable grounds to believe that Omar Al Bashir is criminally responsible under article 25(3)(a) of the Statute as an indirect perpetrator, or as an indirect co-perpetrator, for war crimes and crimes against humanity and that his arrest appears to be necessary under article 58(1)(b) of the Rome Statute ("the Statute");

Noting articles 19 and 58 of the Statute;

Considering that, on the basis of the material provided by the Prosecution in support of the Prosecution Application and without prejudice to any subsequent determination that may be made under article 19 of the Statute, the case against Omar Al Bashir falls within the jurisdiction of the Court;

Considering that, on the basis of the material provided by the Prosecution in support of the Prosecution Application, there is no ostensible cause or self-evident factor to impel the Chamber to exercise its discretion under article 19(1) of the Statute to determine at this stage the admissibility of the case against Omar Al Bashir;

Considering that there are reasonable grounds to believe that from March 2003 to at least 14 July 2008, a protracted armed conflict not of an international character within the meaning of article 8(2)(f) of the Statute existed in Darfur between the Government of Sudan ("the GoS") and several organised armed groups, in particular the Sudanese Liberation Movement/Army ("the SLM/A") and the Justice and Equality Movement ("the JEM");

Considering that there are reasonable grounds to believe: (i) that soon after the attack on El Fasher airport in April 2003, the GoS issued a general call for the mobilisation of the Janjaweed Militia in response to the activities of the SLM/A, the JEM and other armed opposition groups in Darfur, and thereafter conducted, through GoS forces, including the Sudanese Armed Forces and their allied Janjaweed Militia, the Sudanese Police Force, the National Intelligence and Security Service ("the NISS") and the Humanitarian Aid Commission ("the HAC"), a counterinsurgency campaign throughout the Darfur region against the said armed opposition groups; and (ii) that the counter-insurgency campaign continued until the date of the filing of the Prosecution Application on 14 July 2008;

Considering that there are reasonable grounds to believe: (i) that a core component of the GoS counter-insurgency campaign was the unlawful attack on that part of the civilian population of Darfur—belonging largely to the Fur, Masalit and Zaghawa groups—perceived by the GoS as being close to the SLM/A, the JEM and the other armed groups opposing the GoS in the ongoing armed conflict in Darfur; and (ii) that, as part of this core component of the counter-insurgency campaign, GoS forces systematically committed acts of pillaging after the seizure of the towns and villages that were subject to their attacks;

Considering, therefore, that there are reasonable grounds to believe that from soon after the April 2003 attack in El Fasher airport until 14 July 2008, war crimes within the meaning of articles 8(2)(e)(i) and 8(2)(e)(v) of the Statute were committed by GoS forces, including the Sudanese Armed Forces and their allied Janjaweed Militia, the Sudanese Police Force, the NISS and the HAC, as part of the abovementioned GoS counter-insurgency campaign;

Considering, further, that there are reasonable grounds to believe that, insofar as it was a core component of the GoS counter-insurgency campaign, there was a GoS policy to unlawfully attack that part of the civilian population of Darfur—belonging largely to the Fur, Masalit and Zaghawa groups—perceived by the GoS as being close to the SLM/A, the JEM and other armed groups opposing the GoS in the ongoing armed conflict in Darfur;

Considering that there are reasonable grounds to believe that the unlawful attack on the above-mentioned part of the civilian population of Darfur was (i) widespread, as it affected, at least, hundreds of thousands of individuals and took place across large swathes of the territory of the Darfur region; and (ii) systematic, as the acts of violence involved followed, to a considerable extent, a similar pattern;

Considering that there are reasonable grounds to believe that, as part of the GoS's unlawful attack on the above-mentioned part of the civilian population of Darfur and with knowledge of such attack, GoS forces subjected, throughout the Darfur region, thousands of civilians, belonging primarily to the Fur, Masalit and Zaghawa groups, to acts of murder and extermination;

Considering that there are also reasonable grounds to believe that, as part of the GoS's unlawful attack on the above-mentioned part of the civilian population of Darfur and with knowledge of such attack, GoS forces subjected, throughout the Darfur region, (i) hundreds of thousands of civilians, belonging primarily to the Fur, Masalit and Zaghawa groups, to acts of forcible transfer; (ii) thousands of civilian women, belonging primarily to these groups, to acts of rape; and (iii) civilians, belonging primarily to the same groups, to acts of torture;

Considering therefore that there are reasonable grounds to believe that, from soon after the April 2003 attack on El Fasher airport until 14 July 2008, GoS forces, including the Sudanese Armed Forces and their allied Janjaweed Militia, the Sudanese Police Force, the NISS and the HAC, committed crimes against humanity consisting of murder, extermination, forcible transfer, torture and rape, within the meaning of articles

7(1)(a), (b), (d), (f) and (g) respectively of the Statute, throughout the Darfur region;

Considering that there are reasonable grounds to believe that Omar Al Bashir has been the de jure and de facto President of the State of Sudan and Commander-in-Chief of the Sudanese Armed Forces from March 2003 to 14 July 2008, and that, in that position, he played an essential role in coordinating, with other high-ranking Sudanese political and military leaders, the design and implementation of the abovementioned GoS counter-insurgency campaign;

Considering, further, that the Chamber finds, in the alternative, that there are reasonable grounds to believe: (i) that the role of Omar Al Bashir went beyond coordinating the design and implementation of the common plan; (ii) that he was in full control of all branches of the "apparatus" of the State of Sudan, including the Sudanese Armed Forces and their allied Janjaweed Militia, the Sudanese Police Force, the NISS and the HAC; and (iii) that he used such control to secure the implementation of the common plan;

Considering that, for the above reasons, there are reasonable grounds to believe that Omar Al Bashir is criminally responsible as an indirect perpetrator, or as an indirect co-perpetrator, under article 25(3)(a) of the Statute, for:

i.   intentionally directing attacks against a civilian population as such or against individual civilians not taking direct part in hostilities as a war crime, within the meaning of article 8(2)(e)(i) of the Statute;

ii.   pillage as a war crime, within the meaning of article 8(2)(e)(v) of the Statute;

iii.   murder as a crime against humanity, within the meaning of article 7(1)(a) of the Statute;

iv.   extermination as a crime against humanity, within the meaning of article 7(1)(b) of the Statute;

v.   forcible transfer as a crime against humanity, within the meaning of article 7(1)(d) of the Statute;

vi.   torture as a crime against humanity, within the meaning of article 7(1)(f) of the Statute; and

vii.   rape as a crime against humanity, within the meaning of article 7(1)(g) of the Statute;

Considering that, under article 58(1) of the Statute, the arrest of Omar Al Bashir appears necessary at this stage to ensure (i) that he will appear before the Court; (ii) that he will not obstruct or endanger the ongoing investigation into the crimes for which he is allegedly responsible under the Statute; and (iii) that he will not continue with the commission of the above-mentioned crimes;

For These Reasons, Hereby Issues:

A Warrant of Arrest for Omar Al Bashir, a male, who is a national of the State of Sudan, born on 1 January 1944 in Hoshe Bannaga, Shendi Governorate, in the Sudan, member of the Jaàli tribe of Northern Sudan, President of the Republic of the Sudan since his appointment by the RCC–NS on 16 October 1993 and elected as such successively since 1 April 1996 and whose name is also spelt Omar al-Bashir, Omer Hassan Ahmed El Bashire, Omar al-Bashir, Omar al-Beshir, Omar el-Bashir, Omer Albasheer, Omar Elbashir and Omar Hassan Ahmad el-Beshir.

Done in English, Arabic and French, the English version being authoritative.

Judge Akua Kuenyehia, Presiding Judge

Judge Anita Usarka

Judge Sylvia Steiner

NOTES

1. *Indicting a Sitting Head of State.* The indictment and warrant issued against President Bashir was the first issued by the International Criminal Court against a sitting head of state, but not the first by an international criminal tribunal. Recall that the I.C.T.Y. indicted President Slobodan Milošević of the Federal Republic of Yugoslavia in 1999. Further, the Special Court for Sierra Leone indicted Liberia's President Charles Taylor in 2003. Both of the latter two presidents were ultimately arrested and brought to trial, but only after they had fallen from power. Should international criminal tribunals indict sitting heads of state? What peril or promise lies in such a course of action?

2. *Bashir's Reaction.* The *New York Times* reported that in the wake of the warrant for his arrest, President Bashir denounced the International Criminal Court as "a hangover from the worst days of colonialism and its indictment of him a naked grab for Sudanese resources like oil." Moreover, the Sudanese government shut down numerous relief agencies that were providing aid to millions of Sudanese, because Sudan accused them of conspiring in the I.C.C. case. See MacFarquhar & Simons, Bashir Defies War Crimes Arrest Order, N.Y. Times, Mar. 5, 2009, at A1.

3. *Have Arrest Warrant, Will Travel?* Article 59 of the Rome Statute provides that all parties "shall immediately take steps to arrest the person in question in accordance with [their] laws...." In the aftermath of his indictment, President Bashir traveled to Egypt, Eritrea, and Libya, none of which are parties to the Rome Statute. Moreover, President Bashir attended an Arab League summit in Qatar (also not a party). See Unity of a Kind, Economist, Apr. 2, 2009 ("Delegates denounced the court for picking on Arab and Muslim leaders while ignoring the alleged crimes of Israel. Syria's president, Bashar Assad, said the court had no right to interfere in countries' sovereign affairs— an understandable complaint, as a UN tribunal is investigating Syria's likely involvement in a series of political murders in Lebanon.").

4. *Complicating Peace Efforts.* One difficulty with indicting a sitting head of state is that it may complicate ongoing political efforts to bring about

a peaceful resolution to an ongoing conflict. In the wake of President Bashir's indictment, the African Union decided to lobby for the Security Council to request a one-year suspension (pursuant to Rome Statute, Article 16) of the case against President Bashir, on grounds that a trial at the I.C.C. could threaten Sudan's fledgling peace process. If they were to conflict, how would you weigh the values of pursuing international criminal justice and pursuing the restoration of peace?

5. *Sudan and Complementarity.* In considering whether to investigate the possibility of crimes in Sudan, the I.C.C. prosecutor conducted an assessment in 2004–2005 of Sudan's laws, institutions, and procedures, and interviewed numerous Sudanese government officials. Based on this assessment, the prosecutor determined that possible atrocities in Sudan fell within the jurisdiction of the I.C.C. notwithstanding the principle of complementarity, given the absence of criminal proceedings in Sudan relating to cases on which the prosecutor was likely to focus. The prosecutor noted that the assessment was part of an ongoing process and that it was possible at a later time that the I.C.C. would be precluded from pursuing cases if there were "genuine national investigations or prosecutions." See Report of the Prosecutor of the International Criminal Court, Mr. Luis Moreno Ocampo, to the Security Council Pursuant to UNSCR 1593, at 4 (June 29, 2005), http://www.icc-cpi.int.

C. THE UNITED STATES AND THE INTERNATIONAL CRIMINAL COURT

The United States voted against the adoption of the Rome Statute in 1998. Under President Bill Clinton, the United States then signed the Rome Statute in December 2000, during the last few days that it was open for signature. Even President Clinton, however, expressed concerns about the Rome Statute, indicating that he would not submit it to the U.S. Senate for advice and consent unless further changes were made. See Statement on the Rome Treaty on the International Criminal Court (Dec. 31, 2000), 37 Weekly Comp. Pres. Doc. 4 (Jan. 8, 2001).

Under President George W. Bush, the United States in 2002 notified the Secretary–General that the United States would not pursue steps to ratify the Rome Statute. See Chapter 3, Section 2(C). Further, the United States took various steps to insulate U.S. personnel from the jurisdiction of the Court. Is there a legal reason why President Bush decided to send such a notice? Looking toward the future, do you think the United States should ratify the Rome Statute? Even if the United States does not ratify, should it take steps to support the work of the Court? What constitutional or statutory impediments are there to U.S. ratification or cooperation?

The following extract is from a report of a task force that included former Supreme Court Justice Sandra Day O'Connor, former State Department Legal Adviser William H. Taft, IV, and former I.C.T.Y. Judge (and D.C. Circuit Court of Appeals Judge) Patricia Wald.

U.S. POLICY TOWARD THE INTERNATIONAL CRIMINAL COURT: FURTHERING POSITIVE ENGAGEMENT

Report of an Independent Task Force Convened by the
American Society of International Law, at 26–46
http://www.asil.org/files/ASIL–08–DiscPaper2.pdf (March 2009) (footnotes omitted)

LEGAL ISSUES AFFECTING U.S. COOPERATION WITH THE COURT

The Task Force finds that short of joining the Court, there is much that the United States can do to support this institution in its pursuit of accountability for the worst offenders against the laws of nations. It is consistent with longstanding U.S. interests that it engage the Court in this manner, and the Task Force recommends that a number of legal issues be addressed to clear the way for such engagement.

Legal Effect of the U.S. Signature and the 2002 Letter to the U.N. Secretary General

Upon signing the Rome Statute on December 31, 2000—though with singular qualifications—the United States became eligible to consent to the Treaty by ratification. Signature ordinarily obligates the Signatory State "to refrain from acts which would defeat the object and purpose of [the] treaty." However, in his signing statement President Clinton expressed continuing concerns about the Court and recommended that the Treaty not be submitted for ratification until these concerns are satisfied. Two years later, the United States submitted a letter to Kofi Annan, U.N. Secretary General, declaring:

> This is to inform you, in connection with the Rome Statute of the International Criminal Court adopted on July 17, 1998, that the United States does not intend to become a party to the treaty. Accordingly the United States has no legal obligations arising from its signature on December 31, 2000. The United States requests that its intention not to become a party, as expressed in this letter, be reflected in the depositary's status lists relating to this treaty.

This letter, inaccurately characterized as "unsigning," raised questions about the current state of U.S. rights and obligations vis-à-vis the Court, the Treaty's object and purpose, and whether the United States remains capable of joining through ratification.

Article 18 of the Vienna Convention on the Law of Treaties (VCLT), establishes the obligations of a Signatory State to a treaty. It provides:

> A State is obliged to refrain from acts which would defeat the object and purpose when: (a) it has signed the treaty or has exchanged instruments constituting the treaty subject to ratification, acceptance or approval, until it shall have made its intention clear not to become a party to the treaty; or (b) it has expressed its consent to be bound by the treaty pending the entry into force of the treaty and provided that such entry into force is not unduly delayed.

Although the 2002 letter of the United States to the U.N. Secretary General does not mention Article 18, it is cast in Article 18's terms, giving direct notification of the U.S. intention not to become a party and thereby relieving the United States of its Article 18 obligations to refrain from acts that defeat the Rome Statute's object and purpose.

The letter relieved the United States of its Signatory obligations, but contrary to popular understanding, the letter did not result in the United States "unsigning" the Rome Statute. Neither the VCLT nor State practice provides any support for such a possibility. This is not a case where the U.S. signatory lacked authority to sign for the United States. Nor do the provisions for invalidating treaties or withdrawing ratification instruments apply; these only operate with respect to a State's consent to be bound by the treaty. And Article 18 itself speaks in terms of indications of intent not to ratify; it says nothing about a State's original signature. Indeed, there appears to exist no support for the proposition that declaring an intent not to ratify voids or otherwise undoes a State's earlier signature. On the contrary, the practice of depositaries—who are charged by VCLT Article 77 with receiving treaty signatures and related texts— favors continuing Signatory status even after a State indicates an intent not to ratify. The International Committee of the Red Cross still lists the United States as a Signatory to Protocol I to the Geneva Conventions notwithstanding President Reagan's disavowal of that treaty. Similarly, the United Nations Treaty Collection continues to list the United States as a Signatory to the Rome Statute, albeit with a footnote reproducing the text of the 2002 letter.

Thus, although the United States no longer has any obligation to refrain from acts that would defeat the Rome Statute's object and purpose, it remains a Signatory to that treaty. As a Signatory, the United States could proceed to ratify the treaty, if it so decided. Reembracing Signatory rights and responsibilities requires only that the United States make a clear articulation of its current policy. The Task Force accordingly believes that, as part of its articulation of a policy of positive engagement with the Court, the President should announce the U.S. Government's intention, notwithstanding its prior letter of May 6, 2002 to the U.N. Secretary–General, to support the object and purpose of the Rome Statute of the Court.

Constraints of the American Service–Members' Protection Act on U.S. Policy Toward the Court

The American Service–Members' Protection Act of 2002 (ASPA)[, P.L. 107–206, 16 Stat. 899 (2002) (codified at 22 U.S.C. §§ 7421 et seq.),] places restrictions on U.S. interaction with the ICC. ASPA prohibits cooperation with the ICC and mandates that funds not be used to support, directly or indirectly, the ICC. ASPA prohibits cooperation by any U.S. court or agency—federal, state or local—with the ICC. Forms of prohibited cooperation include responding to requests of cooperation from the Court, provision of support, extraditing any person from the United States to the

ICC or transferring any U.S. citizen or permanent resident alien to the ICC, restrictions on funds to assist the Court, and permitting ICC investigations on U.S. territory. ASPA also prohibits direct or indirect transfer of classified national security information and law enforcement information to the Court. Finally, ASPA authorizes the President to use "all means necessary and appropriate" to free its service-members and others, including "allied persons," detained or imprisoned by or on behalf of the ICC.

Section 2003(c) of ASPA provides for the possibility of presidential waiver of these restrictions and prohibitions established under the Act "to the degree such prohibitions and requirements would prevent United States cooperation with an investigation or prosecution of a *named* individual by the International Criminal Court." ASPA also explicitly reiterates that it does not apply to actions taken by the President under his authority as Commander in Chief of the Armed Forces with regard to cooperation with the Court and providing information to the Court, in specific instances. Finally, Section 2015, the so-called Dodd Amendment, appears to grant leeway for cooperation with the Court; it states that "*[n]othing in this title shall prohibit the United States from rendering assistance to international efforts* to bring to justice Saddam Hussein, Slobodan Milosovic, Osama bin Laden, other members of Al Qaeda, leaders of Islamic Jihad, *and other foreign nationals* accused of genocide, war crimes or crimes against humanity."

The 2006 and 2008 amendments to ASPA only addressed restrictions on aid to States Parties. They left in place the broad ASPA prohibitions and restrictions on cooperation with and support to the Court.

Particularly with regard to Darfur, the United States has indicated that it will review requests by the Court to cooperate with it. If it decides to cooperate, the President will have to provide a waiver under Section 2003(c) or employ section 2015 in order do so. While both options appear to grant significant latitude—at least in relation to "named individuals"—the extent of this latitude is, as yet, untested. Even if the waiver authority under ASPA permits cooperation with the ICC in specific cases, ASPA remains an impediment to a more systematic or institutionalized program of cooperation with or support of the Court. The development of U.S. relations with the Court along these lines would thus require further amendment or repeal of ASPA.

It would also appear that the United States could not become a State Party to the Rome Statute without significant amendment or repeal of ASPA, given States Parties obligations to cooperate with and provide judicial assistance to the Court. Even if the United States could become party to the treaty, ASPA restrictions would hinder it from fulfilling its obligations as a State Party, particularly to "cooperate fully with the Court in its investigation and prosecution of crimes within the jurisdiction of the Court." Also ASPA required "Article 98 agreements," but, as discussed below, the overbreadth of some them may also be contrary to a

State Party's obligations under the Rome Statute, as well as a Signatory's obligations under the Vienna Convention on the Law of Treaties.

Thus, the Task Force recommends that in furtherance of a policy of continued positive engagement with the ICC, the President issue any presidential waivers in the interests of the United States that address restrictions on assistance to and cooperation with the Court contained in the American Service–Members' Protection Act of 2002 and advise the Congress on the need for further amendments or repeal of ASPA. To the fullest extent possible the President should make use of waivers permitted by ASPA to by-pass its restrictions. However, to enable the development of more systematic institutional ties to and cooperation with the Court, rather than addressing discreet cases individually, the President should propose amendment or repeal of ASPA eliminating these restrictions. Elimination of these prohibitions and restrictions would also ensure that, if at a later date the United States decides to become a Party to the Statute, ASPA would not prevent it from carrying out its obligations under the Statute. For the reasons mentioned above, it is further recommended that Congress pursue a legislative agenda on the Court that includes amendment or repeal of the American Service–Members' Protection Act and other applicable laws to the extent necessary to enhance flexibility in the U.S. Government's engagement with the Court and allies that are State Parties to the Rome Statute.

"Article 98 Agreements"

In 2002, the United States began concluding agreements with States to protect U.S. nationals from the assertion of ICC jurisdiction by prohibiting the Signatory State from surrendering U.S. nationals to the ICC. These agreements are often referred to as "Article 98 agreements," as they made use of Article 98(2) of the Rome Statute. Article 98(2) states:

> The Court may not proceed with a request for surrender which would require the requested State to act inconsistently with its obligations under international agreements pursuant to which the consent of a sending State is required to surrender a person of that State to the Court, unless the Court can first obtain the cooperation of the sending State for the giving of consent of the surrender.

The U.S. Government's "Article 98 agreements" have been assailed as contrary to the Rome Statute and as evidence of an effort to undermine the ICC. Opposition to the U.S. agreements became particularly acute when pursuant to ASPA and the Nethercutt Amendment the United States conditioned military and economic assistance on conclusion of "Article 98 agreements."

These "Article 98 agreements" have been considered by some to be inconsistent in two ways with the text of Article 98(2). Some have declared "Article 98 agreements" *per se* contrary to the Rome Statute and, thus, inconsistent with States Parties' obligations under the Statute. Others have accepted "Article 98 agreements" but only under limited conditions.

First, it is disputed that Article 98(2) of the Rome Statute permits the conclusion of *new* agreements. Rather, opponents of the U.S. Government's "Article 98 agreements" argue that Article 98(2) was included in the Statute to avoid possible legal conflicts that might arise with agreements existing at the time the Statute came into force or renewals of them; critics contend that reading this Article to permit new agreements insulating individuals from ICC jurisdiction would place it in direct contradiction to Article 27 of the Rome Statute which stipulates that no one is immune from crimes under the ICC's jurisdiction. The Task Force does not find this argument persuasive. In 2002, the nineteen-member International Security Assistance Force (ISAF)—consisting of numerous European States party to the Rome Statute—proceeded to conclude such an agreement with the Interim Administration of Afghanistan. The Military Technical Agreement provided that "ISAF and supporting personnel, including associated liaison personnel, may not be surrendered to, or otherwise transferred to the custody of, an international tribunal or any other entity or State without the express consent of the contributing nation."

A second objection to the U.S. "Article 98 agreements" rests on the use of the term "sending State" in Article 98(2). It is argued on this basis that Article 98 is only intended to cover agreements, such as the fairly routine status-of-forces-agreements (SOFAs) concluded with States where the United States stations troops. These SOFAs reallocate jurisdiction for U.S. service-members from foreign to U.S. courts. Some of the U.S. Government's "Article 98 agreements" generated the criticism that they go beyond the typical SOFA, which covers a limited class of persons deliberately sent from one country to another. The scope of some "Article 98 agreements" extends not only to U.S. nationals on official business but also to U.S. citizens present in that State for business or personal reasons, as well as employees, including contractors regardless of nationality. Guidelines issued by the European Union to its member countries on acceptable terms for "Article 98 agreements" set parameters in order to "preserve the integrity of the Rome Statute ... and ... ensure respect for the obligations of States Parties under the Statute." The guidelines provide that the scope be limited to government representatives on official business; that they do not contain a reciprocal promise to prevent the surrender of nationals of an ICC State Party; and that the United States expressly pledge to investigate, and, where appropriate, prosecute its nationals for ICC crimes.

The President should examine U.S. policy concerning the scope, applicability, and implementation of "Article 98 Agreements" concerning the protections afforded to U.S. personnel and others in the territory of States that have joined the Court. As opposition to "Article 98 agreements" arose in large part due to the connection between concluding "Article 98 agreements" and a State's receipt of certain U.S. assistance (as per ASPA and the Nethercutt Amendment), the receipt of such assistance should be further de-linked from any such agreements.

Domestic Primacy—Safeguarding State Sovereignty Through Complementarity

The complementary jurisdiction established by the Rome Statute affords domestic courts the primary authority to try the crimes under the jurisdiction of the ICC. The relevant provision of the Rome Statute provides:

> An International Criminal Court ... is hereby established, it shall be a permanent institution and shall have the power to exercise its jurisdiction over persons for the most serious crimes of international concern, as referred to in this Statute, *and shall be complementary to national criminal jurisdictions.*

Coupled with the Rome Statute's other jurisdictional and admissibility requirements (particularly the gravity threshold), complementarity is intended to place a check on the power of the ICC and the prosecutor and protect the sovereignty of States—whether party or not to the Treaty.

The complementarity principle is layered throughout the procedural structure of the Rome Statute, including provisions on jurisdictional competence. However, Article 17 "provides the most direct implementation of the complementarity principle in the Rome Statute" by stipulating the criteria for evaluating whether domestic authority over a particular case limits ICC authority over the same. These provisions indicate that the ICC is a court of last resort. The Court has no jurisdiction to act if a case is investigated or prosecuted by a national judicial system unless the national proceedings are not genuine, due to the State's unwillingness or inability to carry out the investigation or prosecution, for example, if proceedings were undertaken only to shield a person from criminal responsibility.

The Statute's procedures to obtain preliminary rulings on admissibility and to challenge the prosecutorial assertions of admissibility provide the means to enforce the complementarity principle. The Rules of Procedure contain explicit guidance for the Court on implementing complementarity, albeit they are "subordinate in all cases" to the Rome Statute. The Court's role vis-à-vis national proceedings is also limited by the *ne bis in idem* principle, "which protects perpetrators from repetitive trials, with some caveats based on the complementarity principle."

While the Rome Statute and Rules of Procedure provide significant guidance, how the Court functions in practice will determine the effectiveness of its complementarity regime in ensuring domestic primacy of jurisdiction, as interpretation and application of these provisions is left solely to the ICC. The prosecutor is accountable to the trial chambers and to the appeals chamber, but "any dispute concerning the judicial functions of the Court shall be settled by the decision of the Court." The one exception, of course, is the Security Council's authority under Article 16 of the Rome Statute to defer an investigation or prosecution for twelve months. To implement complementarity, the Rome Statute requires a Court decision on, for example, a State's "unwillingness" to carry out an investigation or prosecution. How the prosecutor and Court address amnesties and pardons, interpret the law of armed conflict (*inter alia*, such issues as the definition of military objective, proportionality, and military necessity), and evaluate differences in charges for particular conduct between domestic law and the ICC will also affect the extent of the Court's jurisdiction in the face of complementary domestic proceedings. As noted above, these issues have not been tested yet in the Court's jurisprudence. It should be noted, however, that the current Prosecutor has generally exercised his authority judiciously, with his stated policy, at this initial phase of operations, being "to take action only where there is a clear case of failure to take national action."

Of course, as a preliminary manner, States must have in place the appropriate domestic, implementing legislation, in order to take advantage of the complementarity regime of the Rome Statute. Therefore, the United States must be able to try the crimes within the Court's jurisdiction—genocide, crimes against humanity, and war crimes. Concern has been raised that current U.S. criminal and military law is not sufficient to ensure, in all cases, the primacy of U.S. jurisdiction. That is, as the United States does not have the criminal laws on the books that parallel ICC crimes, the ICC could find U.S. domestic proceedings inadequate to bar ICC proceedings. Regardless of whether the United States eventually decides to join the Court, it makes sense to review the law in order to ensure that the United States is able to investigate and try the criminal acts that have been described in the Rome Statute. * * *

The Genocide Accountability Act of 2007[, Pub. L. No. 110–151, 121 Stat. 1821 (2007,)] closed a key jurisdictional loophole in the Genocide Implementation Act of 1987 by granting the United States authority to prosecute alleged perpetrators of genocide committed anywhere in the world, so long as the suspect is physically present in the United States. The Child Soldiers Accountability Act of 2008[, Pub. L. No. 110–340, 122 Stat. 3735 (2008),] makes it a federal crime to recruit knowingly or to use soldiers under the age of fifteen and permits the United States to prosecute any individual on U.S. soil for the offense, even if the children were recruited or served as soldiers outside the United States. However, without appropriate domestic criminal law on all ICC crimes, the United States cannot benefit in all cases from the complementarity regime, regardless of the Court's implementation of it.

Congress should consider amendments to U.S. law to permit full domestic U.S. prosecution of crimes within the jurisdiction of the Court so as to ensure the primacy of U.S. jurisdiction over the Court's jurisdiction under the complementarity regime. The Genocide Accountability Act of 2007 and The Child Soldiers Accountability Act of 2008 were important steps, and Congress should continue its efforts to close any gaps in U.S. criminal and military law with regard to ICC crimes. No doubt should remain as to whether U.S. federal or military courts can exercise subject matter jurisdiction over these crimes. * * *

* * *

U.S. CONSTITUTIONAL ISSUES RAISED WITH RESPECT TO JOINING THE COURT

* * * [T]he Task Force does not recommend U.S. ratification of the ICC Statute at this time. Rather, it suggests that both the executive and legislative branches monitor closely developments at the ICC to inform future consideration of whether the United States should join, particularly in light of developments at the 2010 Review Conference. In that connection, policy makers will want to consider compatibility of the ICC Statute with the U.S. Constitution. While the Task Force's initial analysis suggests that these concerns do not present any insurmountable obstacles to joining the Court, such concerns should be further analyzed if the United States were to consider becoming a member of the Court in the future. They certainly do not prevent the United States from cooperating with or supporting the Court today.

It has been asked whether U.S. ratification of the Rome Statute would be consistent with the requirements of the U.S. Constitution. Two main objections are raised: 1) the ICC does not offer the same due process rights, particularly trial by jury and protection against double jeopardy, guaranteed under the U.S. Constitution; and 2) ratification would contravene Article 1, Section 8 and Article III, Section 1 of the Constitution, dealing with the establishment of domestic courts.

Some legal experts assert that the Rome Statute contains "the most comprehensive list of due process protections which has so far been promulgated." Others maintain that the procedures still fall short of U.S. constitutional standards of due process. The due process rights found in the Rome Statute and implemented through the Rules of Procedure and Evidence are: the right to remain silent and the guarantee against compulsory self-incrimination, the presumption of innocence, the right to confront accusers and cross-examine witnesses, the right to have compulsory process to obtain witnesses, the obligation on the prosecutor to disclose exculpatory evidence, the right to a speedy and public trial, the right to assistance of counsel of one's own choosing, the right to a written statement of charges, the prohibition of *ex post facto* crimes, protection against double jeopardy, freedom from warrantless arrests and searches, the right to be present at trial and the prohibition of trials *in absentia*, exclusion of illegally obtained evidence, and the right to a "Miranda" warning. [See Rome Statute, Articles 20, 22, 54–55, 57–58, 61, 63, 66–67, & 69.]

Given that the due process rights in the Rome Statute significantly parallel those in the U.S. Constitution, concern has focused on the lack of a jury trial before the ICC. The ICC follows the tradition of many countries as well as the International Tribunals for the former Yugoslavia and Rwanda, as well as those at Nuremberg and Tokyo, empanelling judges to decide questions of law and fact. A second area of concern has been the ICC's divergence from a common-law understanding of protection against double jeopardy.

The U.S. constitutional right to trial by jury is not unlimited. The United States extradites Americans, who committed crimes outside U.S. territory, to non-jury criminal trials before foreign courts in situations analogous to those where the ICC would likely claim jurisdiction. And, with regard to international courts, the United States has already participated, without raising concerns about constitutionality, in courts that could try—without jury—American citizens, such as the International Criminal Tribunals for the former Yugoslavia and Rwanda. It must not be forgotten that a properly functioning complementarity regime ensures that the ICC only has jurisdiction to try Americans if the United States does not or cannot exercise its primary jurisdiction.

The Rome Statute explicitly provides for the protection against double jeopardy, prohibiting trying a person before the ICC for conduct for which the person has been convicted or acquitted by the ICC or by another court. [Rome Statute, Article 20.] As in the case of other international tribunals and many other countries, the understanding of when the ICC has reached a final judgment for purposes of double jeopardy differs from that in U.S. jurisprudence. In the ICC and other international tribunals as well as other countries, evidence may be adduced during the appellate proceedings, and the judgment at trial is not viewed as an end to the criminal proceedings. Thus, appeals by the prosecution are allowed, as they are simply seen as another step in the criminal proceedings, not as a challenge to a final judgment. Once a final judgment has been rendered (generally by the Appeals Chamber), the person cannot be tried again for crimes for which he/she has been charged.

The question has been raised as to whether this approach is inconsistent with the U.S. interpretation of the scope of the protection against double jeopardy. However, as noted above, the legal regime of the ICC, as well as the other international tribunals, differs significantly from that of the United States, as the Appeals Chamber can consider new evidence, including hearing testimony. Thus, it can be argued that, if the verdict is appealed, the criminal proceeding is not complete until the Appeals Chamber issues a judgment and, therefore, that the prohibition of double jeopardy does not come into play until that judgment is rendered. Moreover, the United States frequently extradites its citizens to countries, such as Germany, that take the same approach to the principle of double jeopardy as that taken by the ICC, and this has passed constitutional muster.

The important issue is whether the fundamental principles of a fair trial are present. The Task Force concludes that the ICC is compliant with the fundamental elements in established international norms, such as those set out in the International Covenant on Civil and Political Rights to which the United States is party.

In addition to the right to a jury trial and double jeopardy, a further constitutional objection has been made to the ICC that, since Congress neither created the ICC nor promulgated its rules, ratification of the Rome

Statute would be inconsistent with the provisions of the Constitution vesting in Congress the sole role of establishing federal courts. The Constitutional provisions at issue here are Article I, Section 8, empowering Congress with the authority to "constitute tribunals inferior to the Supreme Court," and Article III, Section 1, which states that "judicial power of the United States, shall be vested in one Supreme Court, and in such inferior courts as the Congress may from time to time ordain and establish." This concern is based on a conception of the ICC as an extension of U.S. jurisdiction, requiring the ICC to be established in a manner consistent with the jurisdiction contemplated under the U.S. Constitution. However, the ICC is an independent international court separate from U.S. courts and exercises jurisdiction distinct from that enjoyed by U.S. courts.

In practice, the existence of constitutional concerns need not necessarily preclude ratification of a treaty. For example, the Senate gave its advice and consent to ratification of the International Covenant of Civil and Political Rights subject to the *proviso* that "[n]othing in this Covenant requires or authorizes legislation, or other action, by the United States of America prohibited by the Constitution of the United States as interpreted by the United States." The United States could employ such a *proviso* accompanying ratification to underscore that in joining the Court it does not undertake any obligations contrary to the Constitution. Although the Rome Statute does not permit reservations to the treaty, other States have relied on such declarations. The Task Force recommends that the executive and legislative branches consider *provisos*, understandings, and declarations similar to those adopted by other States Parties that may be deemed necessary, in connection with any future consideration of whether to join the Court.

NOTES

1. *Nethercutt Amendment*. The excerpt above refers to the "Nethercutt Amendment" to the U.S. Department of State operations appropriations law. That amendment was introduced starting in 2004 by Representative George Nethercutt as a means of suspending U.S. economic support funds (ESF) to parties of the Rome Statute who did not conclude bilateral immunity agreements (BIAs) with the United States. See, e.g., Consolidated Appropriations Act, 2005, Pub. L. No. 108–447, § 574, 118 Stat. 2809, 3037–38 (2004). The amendment was dropped in the omnibus appropriations law adopted in early 2009.

2. *Exposure of U.S. Nationals*. If U.S. military personnel involved in a U.N. peace-keeping mission abroad were accused of committing a crime covered by the Rome Statute in a state that is party to the Statute, under what circumstances, if any, could those personnel be prosecuted before the I.C.C.? What if the crime were committed within a state that is not a party? Does it matter that the United States is not a party to the Statute? During the negotiations at the Rome Conference, the United States pressed hard to make prosecution before the I.C.C. contingent on a referral to the Court by

the U.N. Security Council (where the United States wields the veto), but failed to persuade other states.

Article 16 of the Statute does allow the Security Council to obtain a one-year, renewable delay of any investigation or prosecution. In Resolution 1422 (July 12, 2002), the Security Council unanimously requested

> consistent with the provisions of Article 16 of the Rome Statute, that the ICC, if a case arises involving current or former officials or personnel from a contributing State not a Party to the Rome Statute over acts or omissions relating to a United Nations established or authorized [peace-keeping] operation, shall for a twelve-month period starting 1 July 2002 not commence or proceed with investigation or prosecution of any such case, unless the Security Council decides otherwise.

The United States had threatened to veto the renewal of all U.N. peacekeeping missions unless this resolution was adopted. In 2003, the resolution was renewed for an additional twelve months. See S.C. Res. 1487 (June 12, 2003). Yet in 2004, the Security Council declined to renew the resolution, after photographs emerged of U.S. troops abusing Iraqi prisoners in Abu Ghraib Prison, Iraq. See Murphy, United States Practice in International Law: 2002–2004, at 312–17 (2005).

3. *Rome Statute As a Treaty.* A key principle of international law is that only states that are party to a treaty should be bound by its terms. See Vienna Convention on the Law of Treaties, arts. 34–38 1155 U.N.T.S. 331; see also Scheffer, The United States and the International Criminal Court, 93 A.J.I.L. 12, 16 (1999). Yet under Article 12 of the Rome Statute, the I.C.C. may exercise jurisdiction over anyone (even non-nationals of a party) anywhere in the world if either the state in which the crime was committed or the state of the accused's nationality consents. Does the theory of universal jurisdiction for genocide, crimes against humanity and war crimes justify such an exercise of jurisdiction by the I.C.C.? Do procedural safeguards, such as the requirement for a determination of admissibility, the primacy accorded to national jurisdictions, and possible deferral of I.C.C. jurisdiction at the behest of the Security Council, adequately protect U.S. military or civilian personnel from unwarranted prosecution before the I.C.C.?

4. *Thinking Through Due Process Objections.* As indicated in the report of the Task Force, some opponents of the I.C.C. argue that the Rome Statute contains inadequate safeguards for defendants' rights, in comparison to the U.S. Bill of Rights. One example is the absence of provisions for jury trial; another is the fact that the prosecution as well as the defense could appeal from adverse rulings. Supporters point out, however, that although there may be some differences between U.S. procedural protections and those embodied in the Rome Statute, the latter fully satisfies modern human rights standards and is at least as protective of defendants' rights as the U.S. Constitution. See, e.g., Leigh, The United States and the Statute of Rome, 95 A.J.I.L. 124, 130–31 (2001) ("the list of due-process rights guaranteed by the Rome Statute is, if anything, somewhat more detailed and comprehensive than those in the American Bill of Rights. Not better, but more detailed.").

CHAPTER 17

THE LAW OF THE SEA

∎ ∎ ∎

SECTION 1. HISTORY AND SOURCES OF THE LAW OF THE SEA

A. CODIFICATION OF THE LAW OF THE SEA: UNCLOS I, II, AND III

For hundreds of years after Hugo Grotius prevailed in his famous controversy with John Selden (see Historical Introduction), international law saw the seas as belonging to everyone or to no one, with *mare liberum* as the fundamental principle (except in times of war). In tandem with that principle of freedom has been the concept of commonage; unlike land, the sea could not be acquired by nations and made subject to national sovereignty.

Exceptions to this concept of commonage, principally in favor of coastal states, developed slowly, and historically were seen—and resisted— as derogations from freedom. Zones of "national jurisdiction" for the coastal states—the territorial sea, the continental shelf, the exclusive economic zone—are later developments, some very recent, creating distinctions between them and the "high seas." Thus, at the most abstract level, the history of the law of the sea reflects a continuing struggle between coastal states that asserted special rights in areas of the sea adjacent to their territory and other states that insisted on the freedom to navigate and fish in all the ocean spaces.

From the time of Grotius to the mid–20th century, the law of the sea was largely customary law, built upon the practice of seafaring nations. The *Paquete Habana* case, extracted in Chapter 2, Section 2(A), is a good example of customary law of the sea, in that instance on the practice of states over the centuries in handling small fishing vessels in time of war. Some treaties were crafted at this time, but they were typically limited to two or a few states within a particular region, such as the Anglo–French Fisheries Convention of 1839 or the North Sea Fisheries Convention of 1882. By the mid–20th century, however, the number of states and the number of vessels engaged in maritime activities, including long-range fishing activities and off-shore oil extraction, made regulation of the seas through custom no longer feasible. Consequently, in 1958 the United Nations convened the first Conference on the Law of the Sea (UNCLOS I), which codified and developed the law in this area through the adoption of four conventions:

- Convention on the Territorial Sea and the Contiguous Zone, Apr. 29, 1958, 15 U.S.T. 1606, 516 U.N.T.S. 205 (as of early 2009, fifty-two parties)

- Convention on the High Seas, Apr. 29, 1958, 13 U.S.T. 2312, 450 U.N.T.S. 11 (sixty-three parties)

- Convention on the Continental Shelf, Apr. 29, 1958, 15 U.S.T. 471, 499 U.N.T.S. 311 (fifty-eight parties)

- Convention on Fishing and Conservation of the Living Resources of the High Seas, Apr. 29, 1958, 17 U.S.T. 138, 559 U.N.T.S. 285 (thirty-eight parties)

The United States signed and ratified all four 1958 conventions. Insofar as the 1958 Conventions codify customary law, then they reflect law binding even upon states that have not adhered to them. Yet the 1958 conventions also have contributed to the development of customary law, as discussed in the *North Sea Continental Shelf Cases*. See Chapter 2, Section 2(B).

In 1960, the United Nations convened a second Conference on the Law of the Sea to address unresolved issues, but insufficient time had passed, and UNCLOS II resulted in no further treaty instruments. See generally Dean, The Second Geneva Conference on the Law of the Sea, 54 A.J.I.L. 751 (1960). Yet times continued to change; technological, economic, and political developments in the 1960s built pressure for substantive changes in the law of the sea and prompted repeated calls for a new recodification. Among other things, those calls were inspired by the proliferation of new states that did not participate in the earlier codifications and by a desire to respond to the promises of technological developments. Such developments led Professor Henkin to observe:

A law of the sea is as old as nations, and the modern law of the sea is virtually as old as modern international law. For three hundred years it was probably the most stable and least controversial branch of international law. It was essentially reaffirmed and codified as recently * * * as 1958. By 1970 it was in disarray.

Henkin, How Nations Behave 212 (2d ed. 1979).

The result was commencement in 1973 of a third Law of the Sea Conference (UNCLOS III), which entailed nine years of negotiations, and the adoption in 1982 of a new, comprehensive convention—the U.N. Convention on the Law of the Sea of 1982 (LOS Convention). The new convention, containing 320 articles and nine annexes (with 125 additional articles), was signed in Jamaica, December 10, 1982, by 115 states. 1833 U.N.T.S. 3, reprinted in 21 I.L.M. 1245 (1982).

B. U.S. RESISTANCE TO THE LOS CONVENTION

From 1973 to 1980, the United States was actively engaged in the negotiations at UNCLOS III that resulted in an initial draft convention. See Draft Convention on the Law of the Sea, U.N. Doc. A/CONF.62/WP.10/Rev.3 (1980). However, the Reagan Administration, which had taken office in the United States in 1981, proposed a number of changes to the draft convention, particularly with regard to the deep sea-bed mining provisions, which were viewed as "socialist" in nature. These U.S. proposals were largely rejected by the Conference and the final draft of the Convention was approved on April 30, 1982, by a vote of 130 states in favor, 4 against, and 17 abstentions. The four states voting against adopting the Convention were Israel, Turkey, the United States, and Venezuela.

After the Convention was finalized, the United States accepted many of its provisions as authoritative, but maintained its opposition to certain aspects and insisted that until those problems were solved the United States would not be able to join the Convention. In 1983 President Reagan announced:

> [T]he convention * * * contains provisions with respect to traditional uses of the oceans which generally confirm existing maritime law and practice and fairly balance the interests of all states.

> Today I am announcing three decisions to promote and protect the oceans interests of the United States in a manner consistent with those fair and balanced results in the convention and international law.

> First, the United States is prepared to accept and act in accordance with the balance of interests relating to traditional uses of the oceans—such as navigation and overflight. In this respect, the United States will recognize the rights of other states in the waters off their coasts, as reflected in the convention, so long as the rights and freedoms of the United States and others under international law are recognized by such coastal states.

> Second, the United States will exercise and assert its navigation and overflight rights and freedoms on a worldwide basis in a manner that is consistent with the balance of interests reflected in the convention. The United States will not, however, acquiesce in unilateral acts of other states designed to restrict the rights and freedoms of the international community in navigation and overflight and other related high seas uses.

> Third, I am proclaiming today an exclusive economic zone in which the United States will exercise sovereign rights in living and nonliving resources within 200 nautical miles of its coast.

83 Dep't St. Bull. 70 (June 1983).

The failure of the United States to support the final text of the Convention resulted in uncertainty as to the status of the Convention before it went into force, and as to the status of the law of the sea in relation to states that do not become parties to the Convention. The United States appeared ready to accept as customary law virtually all the provisions except those relating to mining in the deep sea-bed. Many states, however, especially developing states, argued that the Convention was a "package deal" reflecting not only compromises as to the terms of particular articles, but "trade-offs" between articles and subjects. In particular, they insisted that they had agreed to provisions favorable to the interests of developed states (notably the United States) in some sections of the treaty, in order to achieve agreement on the provisions of interest to developing states, notably the regime for deep sea-bed mining. Consequently, they argued, sections desired by the developed states could not be treated as reflecting agreed customary law unless the entire treaty—including the deep sea-bed regime—was recognized as customary law. Nevertheless, all agreed that many provisions of the 1982 Convention duplicate provisions in the 1958 conventions, and many other provisions are clearly established customary law of the sea.

The number of states that adhered to the 1982 Convention grew steadily throughout the 1980s, though a number of states saw no reason to adhere to the Convention as long as the United States (and other industrialized states) did not join, especially since the implementation of key sections of the Convention depended on the financial and technological commitment of those states. The 1990s brought radical changes in the political context of the Convention and in underlying economic assumptions. In particular, it became clear that deep sea-bed mining would not be economical for a long time, perhaps for decades, and that no country had any economic reason (and few had political reasons) for proceeding with sea-bed mining. Doubt as to the economic viability of deep sea-bed mining muted the debate about its legality. The changed world order following the end of the Cold War also largely overtook the ideological differences that underlay some of the compromises of the "package deal" behind important provisions of the Convention; the general commitment to "privatization" and free market principles, and democracy, also may have outdated some of the provisions to which the United States objected.

C. THE 1994 IMPLEMENTING AGREEMENT

In the early 1990s, with the approaching entry-into-force of the LOS Convention, the U.N. Secretary–General undertook informal negotiations with a view to removing the obstacles to widespread ratification of the Convention. These efforts bore fruit in 1994 with the adoption by the U.N. General Assembly of the Agreement Relating to the Implementation of Part XI of the United Nations Convention on the Law of the Sea of 10 December 1982, July 28, 1994, S. Treaty Doc. No. 103–39 (1994), at 263 (1994), 1836 U.N.T.S. 3. After the General Assembly's vote, which was

121 in favor, none against, and 7 abstentions, most industrialized states ratified the LOS Convention, which entered into force in November 1994. Further, the 1994 implementing agreement was signed promptly by many states, including the United States.

The United States then announced that it would seek to accede to the 1982 Convention and to ratify the 1994 agreement modifying it, and President Clinton requested the consent of the U.S. Senate. The Senate did not consent prior to the end of the Clinton Administration. After George W. Bush assumed office, a review process was undertaken involving a wide range of executive agencies, after which the Bush Administration decided to support U.S. accession. According to the U.S. Department of State Legal Adviser, the United States concluded that there were several important benefits to joining the Convention:

> First, the Convention strongly advances U.S. national security interests because it guarantees our military and commercial vessels— both ships and aircraft—navigational rights and freedoms throughout the world's oceans, including the right of innocent passage through and over foreign territorial seas and international straits. We concluded that these protections are particularly important at a time when the U.S. military is conducting military operations in Iraq and Afghanistan and new initiatives like the Proliferation Security Initiative, but faces increasing challenges to its activities around the globe. The navigational rights guaranteed by the Convention led all branches of our military to strongly support accession.

> Second, the Convention advances U.S. economic interests. It would codify U.S. sovereign rights over all the resources in the ocean, and on and under the ocean floor, in a 200–nautical mile Exclusive Economic Zone off our coastline. The United States has one of the longest coastlines and the largest Exclusive Economic Zone of all the countries in the world and stands to gain greatly from these provisions. The Convention also codifies sovereign rights over resources on and under the ocean floor beyond 200 nautical miles, if the area meets certain geological criteria set out in the Convention. The Convention establishes an institution—the Commission on the Limits of the Continental Shelf—that offers a coastal State the opportunity to maximize international recognition and legal certainty with respect to the continental shelf beyond 200 nautical miles offshore. This is an especially valuable feature of the Convention right now, as it would maximize legal certainty regarding U.S. rights to energy resources in vast offshore areas, including in areas that are likely to extend at least 600 miles north of Alaska.

> The third principal benefit of the Convention is that it sets forth a comprehensive legal framework and establishes basic obligations for protecting the marine environment from all sources of pollution. This framework allocates regulatory and enforcement authority so as to balance a coastal State's interests in protecting the marine environ-

ment and its natural resources with the rights and freedoms of navigation of all States.

Apart from the benefits of these substantive provisions, joining the Convention would give the United States a "seat at the table" in the interpretation and development of the law of the sea. As a leading maritime power and a country with one of the longest coastlines in the world, the United States has an enormous stake in that project, and we need to ensure a level of influence commensurate with our interests. Although the Convention's first several years were fairly quiet on this score, its provisions are now being actively applied and developed. The Continental Shelf Commission and the International Seabed Authority, for example, are up and running, and we—the country with perhaps the most to gain, and lose, on law of the sea issues—should not be sitting on the sidelines. Our status as a non-Party puts us in a far weaker position to advance U.S. interests.

U.S. Dep't of State Legal Adviser John B. Bellinger III, The United States and the Law of the Sea Convention, Remarks at the Law of the Sea Institute, Berkeley, California (Nov. 3, 2008). Similarly, an expert commission convened by the U.S. government advanced 212 recommendations for U.S. oceans policy, placing U.S. accession to the LOS Convention on its list of thirteen "critical actions," since doing so would "provide the foundation for a comprehensive national ocean policy." U.S. Commission on Ocean Policy, An Ocean Blueprint for the 21st Century 63 (2004).

Yet while there are many supporters of U.S. adherence to the LOS Convention, some critics remain unmoved, saying that it impairs U.S. sovereignty and national security. See, e.g., Bandow, Don't Resurrect the Law of the Sea Treaty, CATO Institute Policy Analysis No. 552 (2005); Leitner, A Bad Treaty Returns: The Case of the Law of the Sea Treaty, 160 World Affairs 134 (1998). In October 2007, the Senate Foreign Relations Committee voted 17 to 4 to recommend that the full Senate consent to ratification. As of early 2009, however, the Senate had still not given its consent.

Even so, as of early 2009, 156 states have become party to the LOS Convention, and 133 of these states have become party to the 1994 Implementing Agreement. Moreover, additional efforts to codify the law of the sea have continued apace. Some agreements are global in nature, such as an agreement reached in 1995 to handle the vexing problem of fish that move between or "straddle" areas under the jurisdiction of two or more states. See Agreement for the Implementation of the Provisions of the United Nations Convention on the Law of the Sea of 10 December 1982 Relating to the Conservation and Management of Straddling Fish Stocks and Highly Migratory Fish Stocks, Aug. 4, 1995, 2167 U.N.T.S. 3, 34 I.L.M. 1542 (1995). Other agreements are regional in nature, sometimes targeting specific issues, such as management of a particular species of fish. See, e.g., Treaty Concerning Pacific Salmon, United States–Canada, Jan. 28, 1985, T.I.A.S. 11,091, 1469 U.N.T.S. 357 (further amended in

June 1999). Some agreements tackle unusual issues, such as how to handle ancient shipwrecks discovered on the floor of the ocean. See Convention on the Protection of the Underwater Cultural Heritage, Nov. 6, 2001, 41 I.L.M. 40 (2002). Consequently, the law of the sea today is a complicated series of global, regional, and even bilateral agreements, with a backdrop of well-established customary rules.

D. ZONES AND USES OF THE SEA

The best approach for studying the law of the sea is to conceive of it, in the first instance, as a series of zones that are measured outwards from the coastal states. In the zones closest to the coastal state, that state has increasing levels of jurisdiction, while other states engaged in maritime activities have decreasing levels of rights. In zones further away from the coastal state, the converse is true; the coastal state's levels of jurisdiction decrease and the freedoms of other states engaged in maritime activities become increasingly stronger. At the same time, there are some regimes— such as on the regulation of ships transporting oil—that remain constant as the vessel traverses the oceans.

This chapter proceeds with sections on the various laws of the sea zones, commencing with the areas closest to the coastal state and moving outward toward the high seas and deep seabed. Further sections explore regimes that remain constant as between the zones, as well as the important topic of dispute settlement under the LOS Convention.

NOTES

1. *Continuing Relevance of the 1958 Conventions.* Understandably, the negotiation, adoption, and entry into force of the LOS Convention discouraged additional adherence to the 1958 conventions, but did not render them moot or unimportant. The 1958 conventions continue to govern states parties who have not acceded to the 1982 Convention (notably the United States, which did not sign the 1982 Convention and, as of early 2009, has not acceded to it). The 1958 conventions also continue to govern states parties to them who are also parties to the later Convention, except insofar as a provision in the latter is inconsistent with and supersedes the earlier provision. The 1958 conventions are also guides to the customary law of the sea governing states not parties to any convention.

2. *Admiralty Law Distinguished.* The law of the sea is commonly used to describe that part of international law that deals with the relations, activities, and interests of states involving the sea. It is distinct from other branches of sea-related law. Admiralty or maritime law, for example, deals primarily with relations, activities, and interests of private persons involved in the transport by sea of passengers or goods. Those relations are generally governed by the domestic law of states, but various aspects are now regulated by international agreement. The International Maritime Organization (IMO) has included among its concerns maritime safety and marine pollution, and

the Law of the Sea Convention contains some rules of maritime law as well—for example, those relating to penal jurisdiction in the event of collision.

3. *Further Reading.* For wide-ranging discussions of the contemporary law of the sea, see The Law of the Sea: Progress and Prospects (Freestone, Barnes, & Ong eds. 2006); Oxman, The Territorial Temptation: A Siren Song at Sea, 100 A.J.I.L. 830 (2006); Unresolved Issues and New Challenges to the Law of the Sea (Strati, Gavouneli, & Skourtos eds. 2006); Stability and Change in the Law of the Sea: The Role of the LOS Convention (Elferink ed. 2005); Bringing New Law to Ocean Waters (Caron & Scheiber eds. 2004); Law of the Sea: The Common Heritage and Emerging Challenges (Scheiber ed. 2000); Symposium, The Law of the Sea in the New Millennium: Neglected and Unresolved Issues, 31 Ocean Dev. & Int'l L. 3 (2000).

SECTION 2. BASELINES AND INTERNAL WATERS

The starting point for considering the zones of the law of the sea is the "baseline" drawn along the coast of the coastal state. LOS Convention Article 5 states that except where otherwise provided in the LOS Convention, "the normal baseline for measuring the breadth of the territorial sea is the low-water line along the coast as marked on large-scale charts officially recognized by the coastal state." Thus, where the coastline of a state is straight or smooth, drawing of the baseline is a relatively simple task.

Unfortunately, the coastlines of most states are neither straight nor smooth; there are indentations, bays, river mouths, peninsulas, and outright changes in direction. Consequently, the LOS Convention has sought to establish certain rules for handling such anomalies, some of which are noted below, as well as important rules that arise with respect to islands.

A. DEEP INDENTATIONS

LOS Convention Article 7(1) provides that "[i]n localities where the coastline is deeply indented and cut into, or if there is a fringe of islands along the coast in its immediate vicinity, the method of straight baselines joining appropriate points may be employed in drawing the baseline." That provision obviously gives the coastal state discretion in drawing lines that allow for a "smoother" baseline than would otherwise exist. However, the LOS Convention is also designed to prevent the coastal state in overreaching when it draws those baselines. Article 7(3) states that the "drawing of straight baselines must not depart to any appreciable extent from the general direction of the coast, and the sea areas lying within the lines must be sufficiently closely linked to the land domain to be subject to the régime of internal waters." Article 7(4) states that the baselines "shall not be drawn to and from low-tide elevations, unless lighthouses or similar installations which are permanently above the sea level have been built upon them or except in instances where the drawing of baselines to and from such elevations has received general international recognition." Can you see how Article 7 is seeking to balance the interests of the coastal state against the interest of other maritime nations, as well as take account of prior historical practice? That theme runs throughout the law of the sea.

An important case that preceded and heavily influenced codification of the law of the sea concerning the drawing of baselines was the 1951 *Fisheries Case* between the United Kingdom and Norway. In response to intensified exploitation of Norwegian coastal waters by U.K. fishing vessels, the Norwegian government had issued a decree in 1935 which delimited Norway's northern territorial waters on the basis of straight baselines drawn along the most seaward points on the islands ("skjærgaard") which line the coast. Contending that international law required the baseline to be solely the low-water mark of the actual coast (except in the case of bays), the United Kingdom instituted proceedings in the International Court of Justice after its negotiations with Norway had failed. (There was no objection to Norway's use of four miles as the breadth of its territorial sea, in view of Norway's historic claim to a four-mile territorial sea, so the dispute turned on the baselines from which that breadth was measured.) The Court prefaced its decision with a discussion of the geographic and economic characteristics of the coastal regions of the Norwegian mainland, as well as of the "skjærgaard" of some 120,000 islands, rocks, and reefs, in the course of which it stressed the pronounced indentations and convolution of the coast and the dependence of the local population on fishing as a means of survival. The Court found, by a vote of ten to two, that the method of drawing baselines used by Norway was not contrary to international law, and, by a vote of eight to four, that the baselines drawn by the 1935 decree did not violate international law. *Fisheries Case* (United Kingdom v. Norway), 1951 I.C.J. 116.

Among other things, the Court stated that "while such a State must be allowed the latitude necessary in order to be able to adapt its delimitation to practical needs and local requirements, the drawing of base-lines must not depart to any appreciable extent from the general direction of the coast." 1951 I.C.J. 116, 133. Comparison of such language to LOS Convention Article 7(3) demonstrates the influence of international jurisprudence on the development of treaties. Moreover, when coastal states today seek to justify their baselines, such prior case law, which is rendered in the context of specific geographic circumstances, can be useful when seeking to apply Article 7(1) to a comparable coastline. This is sometimes necessary, since the method of establishing the baselines can involve highly technical and controversial geographical considerations.

The *Fisheries Case* often has been cited as denying to coastal states a role as sole judge of where their baselines exist. The Court said: "The delimitation of the sea areas has always an international aspect; it cannot be dependent merely upon the will of the coastal State as expressed in its municipal law." See 1951 I.C.J. at 132.

B. RIVERS AND BAYS

For a state with a river that flows into the sea, Article 9 of the LOS Convention provides that "the baseline shall be a straight line across the mouth of the river between points on the low-water line of its banks." Yet what if there exists a wide body of water with land on both sides before reaching the sea? Should the baseline cut across the mouth of such a bay (an outcome favorable to the coastal state) or should it run along the inside low-water line of the bay (an outcome favorable to other maritime states)?

Attempts to establish, for international legal purposes, a geographic definition for bays occurred with some frequency during the 19th century, especially in the Anglo–French Fisheries Convention of 1839 and in the North Sea Fisheries Convention of 1882 (both of which provided that the mouth of a "bay" might be no more than ten miles wide in order for the coastal state to claim exclusive fishing rights therein). See Johnston, The International Law of Fisheries 361 (1987). At the same time, however, a number of states claimed, on historic or other grounds, bays the openings of which were of greater width.

A twenty-four-mile closing line was adopted in Article 7 of the 1958 Convention on the Territorial Sea and the Contiguous Zone, and was retained in Article 10(4) of the LOS Convention. Further, the LOS Convention defines a bay in Article 10(2) as:

> [A] well-marked indentation whose penetration is in such proportion to the width of its mouth as to contain land-locked waters and constitute more than a mere curvature of the coast. An indentation shall not, however, be regarded as a bay unless its area is as large as, or larger than, that of the semi-circle whose diameter is a line drawn across the mouth of that indentation.

While the rules noted above focus on simple geography, the LOS Convention also takes into account prior historical practice. Article 10(6) provides that the "foregoing provisions do not apply to so-called 'historic' bays." In *Continental Shelf* (Tunisia/Libya), 1982 I.C.J. 18, the Court noted that historic bays had been purposefully left for later consideration when Article 7 of the 1958 Convention was drafted and that the 1982 Convention had failed to address the issue. The Court concluded:

> It seems clear that the matter continues to be governed by general international law which does not provide for a *single* "régime" for "historic waters" or "historic bays," but only for a particular régime for each of the concrete, recognised cases of "historic waters" or "historic bays".

1982 I.C.J. 18, para. 100.

The United States has long characterized its "bays" according to two principles: a geographic test, based on a maximum closing line of ten miles, or a "historic" test. Examples of historic bays claimed by the United States are the Delaware Bay and the Chesapeake Bay. See 1 Moore, Digest of International Law 735–39, 741–42 (1906). Important "historic" bays claimed by Canada are the Bay of Chaleurs, Conception Bay, and Miramichi Bay. Canada also claims all of Hudson's Bay as an "historic bay," but this claim has been disputed by the United States. See 4 Whiteman at 233–58. It should be noted that some "historic" bays may now be able to qualify as geographic bays under the liberalized criteria adopted in Article 7 of the 1958 Convention and Article 10 of the 1982 Convention.

Another controversial claim to an historic bay is Libya's claim to the Gulf of Sidra. That claim and its rejection by the United States played a role in a 1981 incident in the Gulf where United States jets shot down two Libyan fighters that were challenging the presence of United States ships in Gulf waters and United States jets in the airspace above. In 1986, the United States again engaged Libyan forces in the Gulf when a naval fleet crossed the Libyan-set baseline for the bay, so as to assert the right to innocent passage. See Blum, The Gulf of Sidra Incident, 80 A.J.I.L. 668 (1986). On bays generally, see Westerman, The Juridical Bay (1987).

C. INTERNAL WATERS

It is important to note that once the baselines are drawn, they demarcate not only the zones of the law of the sea that span outward from the coastal state, but also help define the "internal waters," which include all sea waters on the landward side of the baseline. LOS Convention Article 8(1) states that, "waters on the landward side of the baseline of the territorial sea form part of the internal waters of the State." Under international law, the coastal state's sovereignty over its land territory extends to all its internal waters, including bays and areas of water wholly enclosed by its land territory (such as lakes).

The law of the sea does not seek to regulate a state's internal waters, with the narrow exception of granting a right of innocent passage (discussed further below) through waters enclosed by a straight baseline that previously had not been considered internal waters. See LOS Convention, art. 8(2). Thus, international law provides no general right for foreign vessels to enter a state's internal waters, though a state's international ports are presumed to be open to international, non-military vessels absent any contrary statement by the coastal state. For further discussion of rights and obligations of a port state with respect to foreign-flagged vessels, see this Chapter, Section 12(D).

For federal states, important issues can arise regarding the allocation of authority in maritime areas as between the federal and state governments, which are sometimes influenced by the law of the sea. In the 1965 case of *United States v. California*, the U.S. Supreme Court resolved a dispute between the federal government and the State of California over the definition of "inland waters" on the California coast. The United

States had ceded various submerged lands to coastal states under the Submerged Lands Act of 1953, but retained ownership of lands "lying seaward of the ordinary low-water mark on the coast of California, and outside of the inland waters, extending seaward three nautical miles." 381 U.S. 139, 142 (1965). In upholding the statute, the Court applied the recently "settled" international rule defining inland waters, contained in the 1958 Convention on the Territorial Sea and the Contiguous Zone, which was carried over as LOS Convention Article 8. Id. at 163–64.

In *United States v. Alaska*, the Supreme Court considered whether Alaska could build an artificial extension to the Alaskan coastline. The Court pointed out that, in *United States v. California*, it had held that "international law recognized the seaward expansion of sovereignty through artificial additions to the coastline." 503 U.S. 569, 586 (1992). As between the U.S. federal and state governments, however, the Court upheld the power of the U.S. Secretary of the Army to require that Alaska agree that any extension would not alter the location of the existing internal federal-state boundary. See also *United States v. Alaska*, 521 U.S. 1 (1997).

D. ISLANDS

Suppose a state has as part of its territory an island, such as Hawaii. Can baselines be drawn around such islands and can the various zones of the law of the sea then be applied to that island? What if it is a very small island, consisting of just a few rocks?

LOS Convention Article 121 sets forth the following three rules:

    1. An island is a naturally formed area of land, surrounded by water, which is above water at high tide.

    2. Except as provided for in paragraph 3, the territorial sea, the contiguous zone, the exclusive economic zone and the continental shelf of an island are determined in accordance with the provisions of this Convention applicable to other land territory.

    3. Rocks which cannot sustain human habitation or economic life of their own shall have no exclusive economic zone or continental shelf.

The first two provisions repeat that of the 1958 Convention, but the third restricts the conditions under which an island may have an exclusive economic zone and continental shelf. According to the Conciliation Commission in the *Jan Mayen* case, the 1982 Convention "reflects the present status of international law," with respect to islands. See Conciliation Commission on the Continental Shelf between Iceland and Jan Mayen, Report and Recommendations, 20 I.L.M. 797, 803 (1981); see also Jayewardene, The Regime of Islands in International Law (1990); Charney, Rocks That Cannot Sustain Human Habitation, 93 A.J.I.L. 863 (1999).

Small islands have become increasingly important because of the possibility of exploiting gas and oil resources in the sea-bed of their adjacent waters. In the South China Sea, for example, China, Taiwan, Vietnam, the Philippines, and Malaysia have been in dispute over the Paracel Islands and Spratly Islands for many years for this reason. China and Vietnam have engaged in hostilities over their competing claims to the Spratly Islands and, in 1992, China reportedly stationed military forces on the islands over the protests of the other claimants. See generally Johnston, Pacific Ocean Boundary Problems: Status and Solutions (1991); Bennett, The People's Republic of China and the Use of International Law in the Spratly Islands Dispute, 28 Stan. J. Int'l L. 425 (1992).

For this reason, international litigation over the status of islands has been quite lively. In *Land, Island and Maritime Frontier Dispute* (El Salvador/Honduras: Nicaragua intervening), 1992 I.C.J. 351, the Court put an end to a century-old territorial dispute between El Salvador and Honduras. The Court held, among other things, that El Salvador is entitled to possession of the islands in the Gulf of Fonseca. In *Maritime Delimitation and Territorial Questions* (Qatar v. Bahrain), 2001 I.C.J. 40, the Court found that Bahrain has sovereignty over the Hawar Islands and the island of Qit'at Jaradah, while Qatar has sovereignty over Janan Island. In *Sovereignty over Pulau Ligitan and Sipadan* (Indonesia/Malaysia), 2001 I.C.J. 575, the Court found that Malaysia was sovereign over two very small islands located in the Celebes Sea. In *Territorial and Maritime Dispute in the Caribbean Sea* (Nicaragua v. Honduras), 2007 I.C.J. ___, the Court determined that Honduras has sovereignty over Bobel Cay, Savanna Cay, Port Royal Cay, and South Cay in the Caribbean Sea (the Court noted that these cays remain above high tide and thus fall within the definition of "islands" under LOS Convention Article 121). In *Sovereignty over Pedra Branca/Palau Batus Peteh, Middle Rocks and South Ledge* (Malaysia/Singapore), 2008 I.C.J. ___, the Court recognized Singapore's sovereignty over Pedra Branca/Paul Batu Peteh, but accorded to Malaysia sovereignty over Middle Rocks. The Court concluded that South Ledge would belong to the "state in the territorial waters of which it is located" but, since the Court had no jurisdiction to draw a line delimiting territorial waters, South Ledge's sovereignty could not be determined.

LOS Convention Article 6 provides that, for islands situated on atolls or having fringed reefs, the baseline is the seaward low-water line of the reef. Where the coastline is highly unstable, Article 7(2) permits the coastal state to select the appropriate points along such baselines which remain effective until changed by the coastal state. Article 11 adds that "[o]ff-shore installations and artificial islands shall not be considered as permanent harbour works" to be regarded as part of the coast. Article 14 adds that, "[t]he coastal State may determine baselines in turn by any of the methods provided for in the foregoing articles to suit different conditions."

E. ARCHIPELAGOS

What about states, such as the Philippines or Indonesia, that are really a collection of islands? Is it expected that they should simply draw baselines around each of their islands (an outcome favorable to maritime nations seeking to navigate between the islands) or can they draw special baselines that encompass the outer perimeter of the islands as a collective unit? In other words, should the problems of security, communications and fishing faced by the Philippines and Indonesia outweigh the interests of other states in the use of the intervening waters and their airspace for international transport (and, to a lesser extent, for fishing)?

In a note of December 12, 1955 to the United Nations, the Philippine government declared its position that "all waters around, between and connecting the different islands belonging to the Philippine Archipelago irrespective of their widths or dimensions, are necessary appurtenances of its land territory, forming an integral part of the national or inland waters, subject to the exclusive sovereignty of the Philippines," and that other water areas (specified in the Spanish cession of 1898 to the United States, and in other United States agreements) were considered as territorial waters. See 4 Whiteman at 282–83; see Dellapenna, The Philippines Territorial Water Claim in International Law, 5 J.L. & Econ. Dev. 45 (1970).

On December 14, 1957, the Indonesian government stated that the "Indonesian archipelago" had historically been considered as an "entity," and that all waters "around, between and connecting" the islands of the archipelago were consequently to be considered as "inland or national waters subject to the absolute sovereignty of Indonesia." The peaceful passage of foreign vessels was guaranteed to the extent they did not infringe Indonesian sovereignty or security. See 4 Whiteman at 284.

The United States refused to recognize the validity of the Philippine and Indonesian claims and Australia and Japan refused to recognize the validity of the Indonesian claim. Id. at 283–85. Yet, the claims of archipelagic states were largely accepted in the LOS Convention which, in Articles 46 and 47, defines archipelagoes and permits the drawing of straight "archipelagic baselines" under specified terms. The territorial sea, contiguous zone, exclusive economic zone, and the continental shelf (discussed below) of an archipelagic state are measured from these baselines (Article 48). The archipelagic state has sovereignty over all the waters enclosed by these baselines as well as over the airspace, seabed and subsoil (Article 49). But archipelagic states also agree to respect existing agreements with other states and traditional fishery rights and other activities of immediately adjacent neighboring states and submarine cables laid by other states (Article 51). There is a right to innocent passage within archipelagic waters (Article 52). The archipelagic state may designate sea lanes and air routes suitable for continuous and expeditious passage, analogous to those established by states bordering international straits. All ships and aircraft have the right of "archipelagic sea lane passage" (Article 53).

A state does not have to draw archipelagic baselines around its islands if it does not wish to do so. In *Civil Aeronautics Bd. v. Island Airlines, Inc.*, 235 F.Supp. 990 (D. Haw. 1964), aff'd sub nom. *Island Airlines, Inc. v. Civil Aeronautics Bd.*, 352 F.2d 735 (9th Cir. 1965), it was held that each island of the Hawaiian archipelago had its own territorial sea and that the intervening waters were high seas. For the State Department position in *Island Airlines*, see 4 Whiteman at 281.

On archipelagoes generally, see United Nations, Analytical Studies on the Law of the Sea Convention–Archipelagic States (1990); Rajan, The Legal Regime of Archipelagos, 29 German Y.B.I.L. 137 (1986); Herman, The Modern Concept of the Off–Lying Archipelago in International Law, 23 Canadian Y.B.I.L. 172 (1985); Tolentino, Archipelagoes under the Convention on the Law of the Sea, 28 Far E. L.Rev. 1 (1984); Coquia, Development of the Archipelagic Doctrine as a Recognized Principle of International Law, 58 Philippine L.J. 143 (1983).

F. EFFECTS OF GLOBAL CLIMATE CHANGE

Global climate change is causing a rise in sea levels due to the expansion of ocean water and the melting of glaciers on land. That rise in sea levels, in turn, is causing shifts in coastlines, with the potential for greater uncertainty in the location of baselines and the seaward maritime zones. Should steps be taken to "lock in" maritime boundaries as these shifts occur, or to accommodate them? For an analysis of this phenomenon and recommendations for next steps, see DiLeva & Morita, Maritime Rights of Coastal States and Climate Change: Should States Adapt to Submerged Boundaries? (2008) (World Bank law and development working paper series).

SECTION 3. THE TERRITORIAL SEA

A. HISTORIC DEVELOPMENT

After state claims to vast expanses of ocean had ceased, during the 17th century, to obtain international respect in law or in practice, there remained the idea that a coastal state might properly claim special interests in at least certain areas of adjacent waters, the inviolability of which was necessary to its safety and protection. The doctrine of the "territorial sea" is traditionally regarded as having been based on the maxim laid down by the Dutch jurist Bynkershoek in the early 18th century, that a state's dominion extended only so far out to sea as its cannon would reach; this, in turn, is regarded as having given rise to the doctrine of a three-mile belt of territorial waters, three miles supposedly being the approximate range of 18th-century, shore-based cannons. See Walker, Territorial Waters: The Cannon Shot Rule, 22 Brit. Y.B.I.L. 210,

213–23 (1945); Jessup, The Law of Territorial Waters and Maritime Jurisdiction (1927).

This rule did not involve a continuous belt of waters, but merely constructed zones or "pockets" of adjacent sea from which, prizes could not be taken during war without violating a duty owed to the neutral state. Yet the German jurist Pufendorf envisaged as early as 1672 a maritime belt for defensive purposes and Denmark (which had at various times claimed the whole ocean between Iceland and Norway, as well as the Baltic Sea) claimed, for certain purposes, a belt of waters adjacent to her territories and measured in leagues. Under pressure from other states, Denmark was forced in 1745 to reduce her jurisdiction for neutrality purposes to one league, but this was the Scandinavian league of four nautical miles and not the three-mile league used in the rest of Europe. Kent, The Historical Origins of the Three–Mile Limit, 48 A.J.I.L. 537, 538–44 (1954).

The doctrine of a continuous belt of territorial sea, one league or three marine miles wide, received its first explicit statement in 1782, on the basis of the Italian writer Galiani's conclusion that it would be unreasonable for the neutrality of particular waters to depend on whether or not forts were built on the adjacent shores, and on the range of the guns which might be mounted therein. Walker, *supra*, at 228–29. Galiani's proposal of a standard three-mile limit probably had no relation to the actual or supposed range of contemporary cannons, but simply represented a convenient standard measure, just as had the league in northern Europe. The cannon shot tradition, however, was to linger for many years in diplomatic practice and in writings on international law.

The first acceptance in state practice of the three-mile belt of territorial sea occurred in 1793, when the United States, forced to define its neutral waters in the war between France and Great Britain, proposed that the belligerents should respect United States neutrality up to "*the utmost range of a cannon ball*, usually stated at one sea league," this being the smallest breadth claimed by any state. 1 Moore, Digest of International Law 702–03 (1906) (emphasis in original). France and Great Britain agreed, and the three-mile limit was subsequently applied in British and United States prize courts. Walker, *supra*, at 230. Thereafter, the three-mile limit was applied for a number of purposes, and states came to rely on the comprehensive notion of the territorial sea as a basis for the exercise of, *inter alia*, fishing, police, and revenue jurisdiction. After its inclusion in a number of European treaties regulating fishing rights, and after its adoption by a number of Asian and South American states, the three-mile limit was world-wide by the end of the 19th century, with comparatively few exceptions.

In time, the traditional association of the three-mile limit with the cannon shot doctrine was rendered obsolete. But state practice remained fairly constant up to and during the first three decades of the 20th century, though there was considerable, deep-rooted dissatisfaction with the three-mile territorial sea. With the emergence of many states from colonial rule, those states sought to seize control of any available economic resources, including offshore fishing and minerals. To do so, many of those states extended their territorial sea claims to six or twelve miles, and some to even 200 miles or more.

B. CODIFICATION OF THE TERRITORIAL SEA

UNCLOS I developed the 1958 Convention on the Territorial Sea and Contiguous Zone, but failed to reach agreement on the two most important problems before it—the breadth of the territorial sea and the extent of fishing rights in the contiguous zone. Those lacunae prompted the convening of UNCLOS II, which resulted in no further agreement. After 1960, with the continuing proliferation of states, the drive for a twelve-mile territorial sea became stronger and the opposition to it eroded. The United States indicated its readiness to accept the twelve-mile zone, provided passage through international straits was assured. Developing states no longer saw widening their territorial sea beyond twelve miles as the way to extend their exclusive jurisdiction over economic resources, so long as additional zones were created providing such authority (discussed below). Consequently, UNCLOS III succeeded in resolving key elements of the territorial sea. LOS Convention Article 2 provides:

> 1. The sovereignty of a coastal State extends, beyond its land territory and internal waters and, in the case of an archipelagic State, its archipelagic waters, to an adjacent belt of sea, described as the territorial sea.
>
> 2. This sovereignty extends to the air space over the territorial sea as well as to its bed and subsoil.
>
> 3. The sovereignty over the territorial sea is exercised subject to this Convention and to other rules of international law.

LOS Convention Article 3 resolved the issue of the breadth of the territorial sea, providing: "Every State has the right to establish the breadth of its territorial sea up to a limit not exceeding 12 nautical miles, measured from baselines determined in accordance with this Convention." Article 15 provides that delimitation of the territorial sea as between states with adjacent or opposite coasts should be done by agreement. If the states cannot agree, neither state may "extend its territorial sea beyond the median line every point of which is equidistant from the nearest points on the baselines from which the breadth of the territorial seas of each of the two States is measured." Such a line is commonly referred to as an "equidistance line."

As of the early 21st century, the basic principles of the territorial sea are well-settled. The Restatement (Third) § 512 asserts that, except for the right of innocent passage (discussed below), "the coastal state has the same sovereignty over its territorial sea, and over the air space, sea-bed, and subsoil thereof, as it has in respect of its land territory." Further, state practice has now taken a marked swing from three miles to twelve miles as the width most commonly claimed. The LOS Convention probably states the present customary law and coastal state claims beyond twelve miles are habitually challenged.

Under the 1982 Convention a state "has the right" to establish a territorial sea "to a limit not exceeding" 12 miles, but is not required to do so. The United States initially refrained from extending its own territorial sea beyond three miles, perhaps in the hope of inducing others to exercise similar restraint. In 1988, however, President Reagan issued a Proclamation declaring that, "[t]he territorial sea of the United States henceforth extends to 12 nautical miles from the baselines of the United States determined in accordance with international law." Presidential Proclamation on the Territorial Sea of the United States No. 5928 of Dec. 27, 1988, 54 Fed. Reg. 777 (Jan. 9, 1988).

C. THE RIGHT OF INNOCENT PASSAGE

The LOS Convention characterizes the coastal state's sovereignty as extending beyond its land territory to the territorial sea. The coastal state's rights in the territorial sea, however, are not absolute; the law of the sea qualifies those rights significantly through the concept of the right of innocent passage for vessels of other states. Philip Jessup, prior to becoming a judge on the International Court of Justice, wrote: "The right of innocent passage seems to be the result of an attempt to reconcile the freedom of ocean navigation with the theory of territorial waters. While recognizing the necessity of granting to littoral states a zone of waters along the coast, the family of nations was unwilling to prejudice the newly gained freedom of the seas. As a general principle, the right of innocent passage requires no supporting argument or citation of authority; it is firmly established in international law." Jessup, The Law of Territorial Waters and Maritime Jurisdiction 120 (1927).

Why is it important for states to be able to pass through the territorial sea? Can they not simply travel along the coast but further out at sea? The United States representative at the 1958 Geneva Conference, in the context of discussing whether there should be a three-mile or twelve-mile territorial sea, pointed out:

> One of the merits of the three mile limit was that it was safest for shipping. Many landmarks still used for visual plotting by small craft were not visible at a range of twelve miles; only 20% of the world's lighthouses had a range that exceeded that distance; radar navigation was of only marginal utility beyond twelve miles; and many vessels (which frequently did not want to enter the territorial sea) did not carry sufficient cable or appropriate equipment to anchor at the depths normally found outside the twelve mile-limit.

* * *

One further objection to extending the territorial sea was that, in time of war, a neutral state would have greater difficulty in safeguarding the broader belt of territorial waters against the incursions of ships of belligerents.

3 United Nations Conference on the Law of the Sea Official Records 26 (1958). Hence, as consensus developed in favor of a twelve-mile territorial sea, many states were concerned with preserving and clarifying the right of vessels to navigate through that sea.

LOCS Article 17 provides that, "ships of all States, whether coastal or land-locked, enjoy the right of innocent passage through the territorial sea." Note that aircraft are not included and that there are two important concepts embedded in this provision: the concept of "passage" and the concept of "innocent." The first concept, "passage," is defined in LOS Convention Article 18(1) as "traversing that sea without entering internal waters or calling at a roadstead or port facility outside internal waters" or "proceeding to or from internal waters or a call at such roadstead or port facility." Further, Article 18(2) makes clear that passage "shall be continuous and expeditious," though it may include "stopping and anchoring, but only in so far as the same are incidental to ordinary navigation or are rendered necessary by *force majeure* or distress or for the purpose of rendering assistance to persons, ships or aircraft in danger or distress."

LOS Convention Article 19 indicates what is meant by the second concept, "innocent" passage. Article 19(1) sets forth a general definition: "Passage is innocent so long as it is not prejudicial to the peace, good order or security of the coastal State." Article 19(2) then provides a series of specific illustrations of non-innocent passage, such as acts that threaten or use military force, weapons exercises, intelligence collection, fishing activities, or any other activities "not having a direct bearing on passage." Further, LOS Convention Article 20 states that: "In the territorial sea, submarines and other underwater vehicles are required to navigate on the surface and to show their flag."

Does the right of innocent passage mean that the coastal state may not regulate in any fashion the passage of foreign vessels through its territorial sea, since that might interfere with the passage? The LOS Convention spells out in detail the kinds of laws and regulations relating to innocent passage that the coastal state may adopt. Article 21(1) states that the "coastal State may adopt laws and regulations * * * relating to innocent passage" on various issues, such as safety of navigation, conservation of living resources, and prevention of infringement of its customs or immigration laws. However, Article 21(2) states that such "laws and regulations shall not apply to the design, construction, manning or equipment of foreign ships unless they are giving effect to generally accepted international rules or standards." This reference to generally accepted international rules and standards is a technique used throughout the LOS Convention to cross-reference to myriad other treaties and non-binding instruments, often produced by relevant international organizations such as the International Maritime Organization, which reflect global consensus on navigational safety, environmental protection, and other maritime matters. Similarly, Article 22 authorizes the coastal state to establish sea lanes and traffic separation schemes, especially for ships carrying nuclear or other dangerous or toxic substances.

At the same time, the LOS Convention imposes duties upon the coastal state within the territorial sea (imposition of such duties explains in part why some states do not claim the entire twelve nautical mile territorial sea to which they are entitled). Under LOS Convention Article 22(4), the coastal state must "clearly indicate sea lanes and traffic separation schemes on charts to which due publicity shall be given." Under LOS Convention Article 24(2), the coastal state "shall give appropriate publicity to any danger to navigation, of which it has knowledge, within its territorial sea." See also *Fisheries Jurisdiction Case*, United Kingdom v. Iceland, 1973 I.C.J. 3, 28 n. 8 (Separate Opinion of Judge Fitzmaurice) (noting the duty of states to discharge in their territorial sea obligations of policing; marking channels, reefs and, other obstacles; giving notice of dangers to navigation; and providing rescue services). Further, as a part of its basic duty not to hamper innocent passage, the coastal state may not discriminate against the ships of any state or against ships carrying cargoes to, from or on behalf of any state (Article 24(1)(b)), and may not levy charges for passage, except for any specific service rendered the ship, and without discrimination (Article 26).

Is a foreign state's warship entitled to a right of innocent passage through a state's territorial waters? For example, if a Cuban naval vessel wanted to travel from Nova Scotia to Havana, could it do so by traveling south just a few miles off the coast of the U.S. Eastern seaboard? Under customary international law, a warship's right of innocent passage was unclear. Jessup concluded in 1927 that "the sound rule seems to be that they [warships] should not enjoy an absolute legal right to pass through a state's territorial waters any more than an army may cross the land territory." The Law of Territorial Waters and Maritime Jurisdiction 120 (1927); see also 4 Whiteman at 404–17.

Part II, Section 3, of the LOS Convention does not expressly state that warships are entitled to a right of innocent passage. Yet Section 3, which is entitled "Innocent Passage in the Territorial Sea," contains references to warships. LOS Convention Article 20 provides that "submarines and other underwater vehicles are required to navigate on the surface and to show their flag." LOS Convention Article 30 provides: "If any warship does not comply with the laws and regulations of the coastal State concerning passage through the territorial sea and disregards any request for compliance which is made to it, the coastal State may require the warship to leave the territorial sea immediately." Do such provisions imply that warships have a right of innocent passage through a foreign state's territorial sea? See Delupis, Foreign Warships and Immunity for Espionage, 78 A.J.I.L. 53 (1984); Oxman, The Regime of Warships Under the United Nations Convention on the Law of the Sea, 24 Va. J. Int'l L. 809 (1984).

D. PASSAGE THROUGH INTERNATIONAL STRAITS (TRANSIT PASSAGE)

1. Customary International Law

CORFU CHANNEL CASE
(UNITED KINGDOM v. ALBANIA)

International Court of Justice, 1949
1949 I.C.J. 4

[The United Kingdom sought to hold Albania responsible for damage caused to British warships by mines moored in the Corfu Channel in Albanian territorial waters. Albania, in turn, charged that, on another occasion, British warships had passed through the channel without the permission of Albanian authorities, and sought satisfaction as reparation.]

To begin with, the foundation for Albania's responsibility, as alleged by the United Kingdom, must be considered. On this subject, the main position of the United Kingdom is to be found in its submission No. 2: that the minefield which caused the explosions was laid between May 15th, 1946, and October 22nd, 1946, by or with the connivance or knowledge of the Albanian Government.

* * *

The obligations incumbent upon the Albanian authorities consisted in notifying, for the benefit of shipping in general, the existence of a minefield in Albanian territorial waters and in warning the approaching British warships of the imminent danger to which the minefield exposed them. Such obligations are based, not on the Hague Convention of 1907, No. VIII, which is applicable in time of war, but on certain general and well-recognized principles, namely: elementary considerations of humanity, even more exacting in peace than in war; the principle of the freedom of maritime communication; and every State's obligation not to allow knowingly its territory to be used for acts contrary to the rights of other States.

In fact, Albania neither notified the existence of the minefield, nor warned the British warships of the danger they were approaching.

* * *

In fact, nothing was attempted by the Albanian authorities to prevent the disaster. These grave omissions involve the international responsibility of Albania.

The Court therefore reaches the conclusion that Albania is responsible under international law for the explosions which occurred on October 22nd, 1946, in Albanian waters, and for the damage and loss of human life which resulted from them, and that there is a duty upon Albania to pay compensation to the United Kingdom.

* * *

In the second part of the Special Agreement, the following question is submitted to the Court:

"(2) Has the United Kingdom under international law violated the sovereignty of the Albanian People's Republic by reason of the acts of the Royal Navy in Albanian waters on the 22nd October and on the 12th and 13th November 1946 and is there any duty to give satisfaction?"

The Court will first consider whether the sovereignty of Albania was violated by reason of the acts of the British Navy in Albanian waters on October 22nd, 1946.

On May 15th, 1946, the British cruisers *Orion* and *Superb*, while passing southward through the North Corfu Channel, were fired at by an Albanian battery in the vicinity of Saranda. It appears from the report of the commanding naval officer dated May 29th, 1946, that the firing started when the ships had already passed the battery and were moving away from it; that from 12 to 20 rounds were fired; that the firing lasted 12 minutes and ceased only when the ships were out of range; but that the ships were not hit although there were a number of "shorts" and of "overs". An Albanian note of May 21st states that the Coastal Commander ordered a few shots to be fired in the direction of the ships "in accordance with a General Order founded on international law."

The United Kingdom Government at once protested to the Albanian Government, stating that innocent passage through straits is a right recognized by international law. There ensued a diplomatic correspondence in which the Albanian Government asserted that foreign warships and merchant vessels had no right to pass through Albanian territorial waters without prior notification to, and the permission of, the Albanian authorities. This view was put into effect by a communication of the Albanian Chief of Staff, dated May 17th, 1946, which purported to subject the passage of foreign warships and merchant vessels in Albanian territorial waters to previous notification to and authorization by the Albanian Government. The diplomatic correspondence continued, and culminated in a United Kingdom note of August 2nd, 1946, in which the United Kingdom Government maintained its view with regard to the right of innocent passage through straits forming routes for international maritime traffic between two parts of the high seas. The note ended with the warning that if Albanian coastal batteries in the future opened fire on any British warship passing through the Corfu Channel, the fire would be returned.

* * *

It is, in the opinion of the Court, generally recognized and in accordance with international custom that States in time of peace have a right to send their warships through straits used for international navigation between two parts of the high seas without the previous authorization of a coastal State, provided that the passage is *innocent*. Unless otherwise prescribed in an international convention, there is no right for a coastal State to prohibit such passage through straits in time of peace.

The Albanian Government does not dispute that the North Corfu Channel is a strait in the geographical sense; but it denies that this Channel belongs to the class of international highways through which a right of passage exists, on the grounds that it is only of secondary importance and not even a necessary route between two parts of the high seas, and that it is used almost exclusively for local traffic to and from the ports of Corfu and Saranda.

It may be asked whether the test is to be found in the volume of traffic passing through the Strait or in its greater or lesser importance for international navigation. But in the opinion of the Court the decisive criterion is rather its geographical situation as connecting two parts of the high seas and the fact of its being used for international navigation. Nor can it be decisive that this Strait is not a necessary route between two parts of the high seas, but only an alternative passage between the Ægean and the Adriatic Seas. It has nevertheless been a useful route for international maritime traffic. * * *

* * *

Having regard to these various considerations, the Court has arrived at the conclusion that the North Corfu Channel should be considered as belonging to the class of international highways through which passage cannot be prohibited by a coastal State in time of peace.

On the other hand, it is a fact that the two coastal States did not maintain normal relations, that Greece had made territorial claims precisely with regard to a part of Albanian territory bordering on the Channel, that Greece had declared that she considered herself technically in a state of war with Albania, and that Albania, invoking the danger of Greek incursions, had considered it necessary to take certain measures of vigilance in this region. The Court is of opinion that Albania, in view of these exceptional circumstances, would have been justified in issuing regulations in respect of the passage of warships through the Strait, but not in prohibiting such passage or in subjecting it to the requirement of special authorization.

2. Codification in the LOS Convention

In response to pressures to widen the territorial sea, the United States and several other powers indicated a willingness to accept a twelve-mile territorial sea provided they were assured passage through international straits. They were not content with mere rights of "innocent passage" through such straits, since there had been disagreement as to whether warships were entitled to innocent passage, and submarines were explicitly required to surface in the territorial sea. Further, the exact meaning of innocent passage had been disputed and, in any event, left passing vessels substantially at the mercy of the coastal state. The result was a new regime in the LOS Convention for international straits with a right of "transit passage."

LOS Convention Article 37 states that the transit passage regime "applies to straits which are used for international navigation between one part of the high seas or an exclusive economic zone and another part of the high seas or an exclusive economic zone." Article 38 then sets forth the following right of transit passage:

> 1. In straits referred to in article 37, all ships and aircraft enjoy the right of transit passage, which shall not be impeded; except that, if the strait is formed by an island of a State bordering the strait and its mainland, transit passage shall not apply if there exists seaward of the island a route through the high seas or through an exclusive economic zone of similar convenience with respect to navigational and hydrographical characteristics.
>
> 2. Transit passage means the exercise in accordance with this Part of the freedom of navigation and overflight solely for the purpose of continuous and expeditious transit of the strait between one part of the high seas or an exclusive economic zone and another part of the high seas or an exclusive economic zone. However, the requirement of continuous and expeditious transit does not preclude passage through the strait for the purpose of entering, leaving or returning from a State bordering the strait, subject to the conditions of entry to that State.
>
> 3. Any activity which is not an exercise of the right of transit passage through a strait remains subject to the other applicable provisions of this Convention.

While the LOS Convention establishes this right of transit passage, it also sets forth in Article 39 a series of duties that vessels (and aircraft) exercising this passage must observe. Ships and aircraft engaged in transit passage shall "proceed without delay through or over the strait," shall "refrain from any threat or use of force," and shall "refrain from any activities other than those incident to their normal modes of continuous and expeditious transit unless rendered necessary by *force majeure*, or by distress."(Article 39(1)(a)(b)(c)). Moreover, vessels shall "comply with generally accepted international regulations, procedures and practices for safety at sea" and with respect to pollution from ships. (Article 39(2)). Aircraft must "observe the Rules of the Air established by the International Civil Aviation Organisation as they apply to civil aircraft; state aircraft will normally comply with such safety measures and will at all times operate with due regard for the safety of navigation." (Article 39(3)(a)). Moreover, aircraft shall "at all times monitor the radio frequency assigned by the competent internationally designated air traffic control authority or the appropriate international distress radio frequency." (Article 39(3)(b)). Again, note how the LOS Convention cross-references to other sources of international law in establishing the rights and obligations of vessels and aircraft in transit passage.

Coastal states may designate sea lanes and prescribe traffic separation schemes where necessary to promote safe passage (Article 41), and may make laws and regulations for safety, regulation of traffic, prevention of pollution and fishing, enforcing customs, immigration, fiscal and sanitary laws (Article 42). User states and border states shall by agreement cooperate in navigation and safety aids and prevention of pollution from ships (Article 43). International straits not covered by this regime (see Article 36) shall be governed by "innocent passage" which shall not be suspended (Article 45). See generally Jia, The Regime of Straits in International Law (1998).

NOTES

1. *Corfu Channel Aftermath.* The *Corfu Channel* decision has been criticized for giving insufficient weight to functional considerations, i.e., failing to balance the interest which the coastal state has in its own territorial sea against that which the international maritime community has in using the strait. Does the language in LOS Convention Article 38(1) about "transit passage shall not apply if there exists seaward of the island a route through the high seas or through an exclusive economic zone of similar convenience" mean that the *Corfu Channel* decision would be decided differently today?

2. *The 1958 Convention and the Gulf of Aqaba.* The Straits of Tiran, which are controlled by Egypt and Saudi Arabia, connect the high seas to the Gulf of Aqaba, on which Israel has several miles of frontage. When the International Law Commission was drafting the provision on straits for the 1958 Convention on the Territorial Sea and Contiguous Zone, it initially limited the right of passage through straits to those which are "normally used for international navigation between two parts of the high seas." Report of the International Law Commission on the Work of Its Eighth Session, U.N. Doc. A/3159, art. 17(14) (1956). In the First Committee, however, the word "normally" was deleted and the article was further amended so as to read: "There shall be no suspension of the innocent passage of foreign ships through straits which are used for international navigation between one part of the high seas and another part of the high seas or the territorial sea of a foreign state." See Convention on the Territorial Sea and Contiguous Zone, art. 16(4) Apr. 29, 1958, 15 U.S.T. 1606, 516 U.N.T.S. 205. Adoption of that language, by a vote of 31 in favor, 30 against, and 10 abstaining, only occurred over the vigorous objection by the Arab states. 3 United Nations Conference on the Law of the Sea, Official Records 93–96, 100 (1958). Thereafter, several Arab states entered reservations to the final provision. For materials on the problem of the Gulf of Aqaba, see 4 Whiteman at 465–80. The 1979 Israeli–Egypt Peace Treaty helped overcome this problem with Egypt's commitment to freedom of navigation in the Straits of Tiran, an obligation still monitored today by an international peacekeeping force known as the Multinational

Force and Observers (MFO). See Multinational Force and Observers, http://www.mfo.org/.

3. *The Dardanelles and Bosphorus Straits.* By the terms of the Treaty of Lausanne (Convention relating to the Régime of the Straits, July 24, 1923, 28 L.N.T.S. 115), the Dardanelles and the Bosphorus came under the supervision of an international "Straits Commission," the only one of its type ever to function. Vessels of commerce were to be allowed free passage in time of war and in peace, but limits were placed on the number of naval vessels permitted to transit the Straits into the Black Sea. Turkey was permitted to take defensive measures against enemy ships in time of war (Annex to Article 2 of the Treaty of Lausanne), but the Straits were demilitarized (Article 4). The Straits Commission functioned as a supervisor of transit, assuring that warships could pass through the Straits without undue hindrance, upon occasion making representations to Turkey on this subject.

The Straits Commission was terminated upon conclusion of the Montreux Convention of 1936 (Convention Concerning the Régime of the Straits, July 20, 1936, 173 L.N.T.S. 213). The Montreux Convention transferred the functions of the Straits Commission to Turkey (Article 24), the littoral state, which thus reasserted its sovereignty. Turkey was granted the right to remilitarize the Straits, but several restrictions were maintained on non-Turkish warships transiting the Straits into the Black Sea: they cannot exceed a certain size, they cannot possess certain armaments, they cannot be aircraft carriers, there cannot be more than nine in the Black Sea at once, and only one foreign warship is allowed in the Straits at any one time (some restrictions are lessened for non-Turkish "Black Sea states," which were effectively concessions to the Soviet Union). Separately, Turkey assumed responsibility under the Convention for the free and unlimited navigation through the Straits for merchant vessels (Articles 2–7).

During the early years of the Cold War, the Soviet Union sought to exploit limitations within the Montreaux Convention, such as by keeping one of its warships in the Straits at all times as a means of blocking non-Turkish warships from being able to enter the Straits. The Soviet Union and now the Russian Federation have sought to evade the ban on aircraft carriers passing through the Straits, by designating certain vessels as "heavy aircraft carrying cruisers" rather than "aircraft carriers." In 1976 the Soviet Union, and in 1991 the Russian Federation, sent actual aircraft carriers through the Straits, notwithstanding the Convention's prohibition. The United States has also sought to stretch the rules, sending vessels through the Straits equipped with "guided missiles" even though the Convention bans vessels with "guns" of larger than eight inches (203 mm). See generally Rozakis & Stagos, The Turkish Straits (1987).

In January 1994, Turkey adopted new "Maritime Traffic Regulations for the Turkish Straits and the Marmara Region," designed to allow free passage but to promote "safety of navigation, life and property and to protect the environment in the region." Ünlü, The Legal Regime of the Turkish Straits (2002). After the August 2008 Russia–Georgia war concerning South Ossetia and Abkhazia, Russia called upon all states to comply with the Montreux Convention, including the restrictions on transit by non-Turkish military shipping, in an effort to limit NATO vessels from entering the Black Sea in support of Georgia.

4. *Further Reading.* For further reading, see de Yturriaga, Straits Used for International Navigation: A Spanish Perspective (1991); Mahmoudi, Customary International Law and Transit Passage, 20 Ocean Dev. & Int'l L. 157 (1989); Caminos, The Legal Régime of Straits in the 1982 United Nations Convention on the Law of the Sea, 205 Rec. des Cours 9 (1987–V); Valencia & Marsh, Access to Straits and Sealanes in Southeast Asian Seas: Legal, Economic and Strategic Considerations, 16 J. Mar. L. & Com. 513 (1985).

E. INTERNATIONAL CANALS

In considering the status of international canals in international law, Richard Baxter wrote:

> The right of free passage through international straits is a product of state practice hardening into customary international law and thence into treaty. The right of free passage through interoceanic canals is a consequence of the opening of each waterway to usage by the international community. It is the origin of the right in a series of individual grants which distinguishes the law relating to canals from the law of straits. The privilege of free passage through the three major interoceanic canals, Suez, Panama, and Kiel, has been created in each case by a treaty to which the territorial sovereign, acting freely or under the pressure of other powers, has been a party.

Baxter, The Law of International Waterways 168–69 (1964). Consequently, in assessing the precise status of rights and obligations with respect to canals used by international traffic, the particular legal regime established by custom or treaty with respect to any given canal must be considered.

Suez Canal. The right of free passage through the Suez Canal is usually said to be founded on the Convention of Constantinople, Oct. 29, 1888, 79 B.S.P. 18, reprinted in 3 A.J.I.L. Supp. 123 (1909), although some writers maintain that the international character of the canal had already been established by concessions of 1854 and 1866. The Convention was signed by Great Britain, Germany, France, Austria–Hungary, Italy, the Netherlands, Russia, Spain, and the Ottoman Empire (then holding sovereignty over Egypt). After the Canal's nationalization in 1956, Egypt reaffirmed its obligations under the Convention. See Declaration on the Suez Canal, Apr. 24, 1957, 265 U.N.T.S. 299; Declaration of the Government of Egypt of 24 April 1957 on the Suez Canal, July 18, 1957, 272 U.N.T.S. 225. The Convention provides in Article 1 that the Canal "shall always be free and open, in time of war as in time of peace, to every vessel of commerce or of war, without distinction of flag," and in Article 4 that "no right of war, no act of hostility, nor any act having for its object the obstruction of the free navigation of the canal, shall be committed in the canal and its ports of access, as well as within a radius of three marine miles from those ports, even though the Ottoman Empire should be one of the belligerent powers." The Convention also includes restrictions on warships and fortifications. In practice, rights under Article 1 have usually been regarded as granted to all states whether or not they adhere to the Convention. See 1 O'Connell, International Law 645–48 (1965); Baxter, *supra*, at 89–91, 169–70, 183 n. 162. During the two World Wars, the United Kingdom justified measures inconsistent with the Convention as necessary to prevent the Canal's destruction. After 1948, Egypt justified anti-Israeli restrictions on the basis of its "inherent right of self-defense." See 1 O'Connell, *supra*, at 647–48; Gross, Passage Through the Suez Canal of Israel-bound Cargo and Israel Ships, 51 A.J.I.L. 530 (1957). The Suez Canal was opened to Israel-bound cargoes pursuant to the Treaty of Peace, Egypt–Israel, art. 5, Mar. 26, 1979, 18 I.L.M. 362 (1979).

Panama Canal. The regime of the Panama Canal was governed by the Hay–Pauncefote Treaty of 1901 between the United States and Great Britain, art. III, Nov. 18, 1901, 32 Stat. 1903, the rules of which were expressly stated to be "substantially as embodied in the Convention of Constantinople." The agreement provided in Article III that: "The canal shall be free and open to the vessels of commerce and of war of all nations observing these Rules, on terms of entire equality, so that there shall be no discrimination against any such nation, or its citizens or subjects, in respect of the conditions or charges of traffic, or otherwise." The foregoing language was substantially reproduced in the 1903 treaty by which the United States acquired the Canal Zone from Panama. See Baxter, *supra*, at 170–71.

The Panama Canal treaties were replaced by new ones concluded in 1977. See Panama Canal Treaty, United States–Panama, Sept. 7, 1977, 33 U.S.T. 39; Treaty Concerning the Permanent Neutrality and Operation of the Panama Canal, United States–Panama, Sept. 7, 1977, 33 U.S.T. 1 (Neutrality Treaty). By Article 2 of the Panama Canal Treaty, the United States returned control of the Canal to Panama at noon, Panama time, on December 31, 1999. The Neutrality Treaty, which is of unlimited duration, commits both the United States and Panama to maintain the permanent neutrality of the Canal and access to it for vessels of all flags.

Kiel Canal. The 61–mile (98–kilometer) Kiel Canal links the North Sea to the Baltic Sea, saving vessels a 280 nautical mile (519 kilometer) journey around the Jutland Peninsula, an area sometimes prone to dangerous storms. Completed in 1895, the Canal had not, prior to the Treaty of Versailles of 1919, been operated by Germany as an international waterway open without restriction to all states. Article 380 of the Treaty of Versailles, June 28, 1919, T.S. No. 4, 2 Bevans 43, however, provided that "the Kiel Canal and its approaches shall be maintained free and open to the vessels of commerce and of war of all nations at peace with Germany on terms of entire equality." The Permanent Court of International Justice, in the case of *S.S. "Wimbledon"*, 1923 P.C.I.J. (ser. A) No. 1, at 22, referred to the Canal as "an international waterway * * * for the benefit of all nations of the world," even though only twenty-eight states were parties to Article 380. In 1936, Germany denounced Article 380 without effective protest from other states.

After the Second World War, the Federal Republic of Germany regarded the provisions of the Treaty of Versailles as null and void, returning the Canal to unlimited German control. Several Warsaw Pact states maintained, however, that in the absence of a final peace treaty with Germany, the Canal's "internationalized" status remained intact. After German reunification in 1989, claims of such international status have diminished and, in any event, Germany has allowed foreign vessels to use the Canal on a non-preferential basis, so long as prior notification is given to the German government (unless other arrangements are made). See Lampe, The Kiel Canal, in The Baltic Sea: New Developments in National Policies and International Cooperation 133 (Platzöder & Verlaan eds., 1996). Today, the Canal is the world's most heavily used artificial seaway, with more than 43,000 ships passing through it in 2007 alone. See http://www.kiel-canal.org/english.htm.

Third–Party Beneficiaries. The legal position of states that are not parties to treaties guaranteeing passage through international canals has been rationalized by the doctrine of "international servitudes," by the "third-party beneficiary" concepts drawn from national law, by the theory that certain treaties are "dispositive" in nature in the sense that they create "real rights" that attach to a territory and are therefore not dependent on the treaty which created them, and by analogy to treaties, such as the United Nations Charter, that have an objective, legislative character, in that they create international status that must be recognized by all states, whether contracting parties or not. Baxter states that:

> The preferable theory concerning the rights of nonsignatories is that a state may, in whole or in part, dedicate a waterway to international use, which dedication, if relied upon, creates legally enforceable rights in favor of the shipping of the international community. A treaty, a unilateral declaration—perhaps even a concession—may be the instrument whereby the dedication is effected. Its form is not important; what is important is that it speaks to the entire world or to a group of states who are to be the beneficiaries of the right of free passage.

Baxter, *supra*, at 182–83. See generally 2 Hackworth at 769–829; 3 Whiteman at 1076–1261; 1 O'Connell, International Law 640–51 (1965).

F. ARCHIPELAGIC SEA LANES PASSAGE

As noted above in Section 2, the LOS Convention allows baselines to be drawn around archipelagic islands, in which case the waters within those baselines and between the islands become "archipelagic waters." The major maritime states, however, were unwilling to accept such baselines in the LOS Convention, unless provisions were included that protected rights of navigation through the archipelagic waters. Hence, in such waters all vessels have the right of innocent passage, just as they would in the territorial sea (Article 52), but not in internal waters delimited by straight lines drawn across mouths of rivers, bays, and entrances to ports of the islands themselves. (Articles 50 and 52(1)). Moreover, all vessels and aircraft enjoy a right of "archipelagic sea lanes passage" in sea lanes and air routes designated by the archipelagic state (Article 53). The sea lanes and air routes are to be designated by agreement between the archipelagic state and the competent international organization (principally the International Maritime Organization) and such passage is generally subject to the same standards as transit passage through straits (Article 54). If the archipelagic state has not designated archipelagic sea lanes or routes, "the right of archipelagic sea lanes passage may be exercised through the routes normally used for international navigation." (Article 53(12)). Since the LOS Convention expressly states that archipelagic sea lanes passage is allowed in the "normal" mode (Article 53(2)), submarines may transit under water.

SECTION 4.   THE CONTIGUOUS ZONE

The law of the sea provides for a further zone just outside the territorial sea called the "contiguous zone," in which coastal states may elect to exercise control, as necessary, to prevent and punish infringements of its customs, sanitary, fiscal, and immigration regulations. Though it originally emerged in customary international law from the practice of states, the zone was codified in the 1958 Convention on Territorial Sea, Article 24, and again in 1982 LOS Convention Article 33, which provides:

>   1.   In a zone contiguous to its territorial sea, described as the contiguous zone, the coastal State may exercise the control necessary to:

>>   (a) prevent infringement of its customs, fiscal, immigration or sanitary laws and regulations within its territory or territorial sea;

>>   (b) punish infringement of the above laws and regulations committed within its territory or territorial sea.

>   2.   The contiguous zone may not extend beyond 24 nautical miles from the baselines from which the breadth of the territorial sea is measured.

NOTES

1.   *Coastal State Enforcement Outside the Territorial Sea Under Customary International Law.* From the early part of the 18th century, the United Kingdom enforced laws, sometimes referred to as "hovering acts", which authorized the search and seizure on the high seas at varying distances (up to eight or even 100 leagues) from the coast of U.K. and foreign ships suspected of having an intention to smuggle goods ashore. See Masterson, Jurisdiction in Marginal Seas with Special Reference to Smuggling 1–162 (1929); Jessup,

The Law of Territorial Waters and Maritime Jurisdiction 77–79 (1927). No state protested these acts, and Sir William Scott defended them in the case of *Le Louis*, 2 Dodson Adm. Rep. 210, 245 (1817), as founded on the "common courtesy" and "common convenience" of nations. The United States and a number of Latin American countries, upon becoming independent, adopted similar customs zones, usually of twelve miles, and some European states also authorized seizures outside territorial waters. Jessup, *supra*, at 80–91; Masterson, *supra*, at 175–206. In 1876, however, the United Kingdom reversed its policy and, in repealing the "hovering acts," took the position that a state could not, under international law, exercise jurisdiction on the high seas against vessels of other states. Jessup, *supra*, at 79. The new British doctrine gained the adherence of some other states, notably Germany and Japan, but the United States and a number of other countries continued to regard contiguous zone jurisdiction in customs matters as a right sanctioned by state practice. Brierly, The Law of Nations 205 (6th ed. Waldock ed. 1963).

Prior to the advent of Prohibition—the laws implementing the 18th Amendment to the U.S. Constitution prohibiting "the manufacture, sale, or transportation of intoxicating liquors within, the importation thereof into, or the exportation thereof from the United States," U.S. Const. amend. VXIII—the United States did not attempt to board foreign vessels beyond the three-mile territorial sea except when the vessel was bound for the United States, or when it had been caught violating United States laws in the territorial sea and was then "hotly pursued." See *Cook v. United States*, 288 U.S. 102, 112–13 (1933). The widespread smuggling of liquor after 1920 by British and other ships led Congress to provide, in the Tariff Act of 1922, Pub. L. No. 67–318, 42 Stat. 858, that even foreign vessels not bound for the United States might be boarded, searched, and seized beyond the three-mile limit. Hyde at 780–82.

It nevertheless continued to be consistent United States policy to release vessels seized beyond this limit that had not been bound for the United States, except in cases where it appeared that the vessel had already been in contact with the shore. See *Cook v. United States*, *supra*. The "shore contact" rule was applied in *The Grace and Ruby*, 283 F. 475 (D. Mass. 1922), to justify forfeiture of a British schooner seized outside the three-mile limit but which had used its boat and members of its crew to assist in ferrying liquor ashore. In *The Henry L. Marshall*, 286 F. 260 (S.D.N.Y. 1922), aff'd, 292 F. 486 (2d Cir. 1923), cert. denied, 263 U.S. 712 (1923), the "shore contact" rule was applied even though contact was made through shore-based boats, rather than the ship's own. The United States and the United Kingdom finally entered into a treaty in 1924, Convention for the Prevention of Smuggling of Intoxicating Liquors, United States–United Kingdom, Jan. 23, 1924, 43 Stat. 1761, under which the United Kingdom agreed not to protest restrictions imposed on British vessels by the United States within an hour's sailing distance from the latter's coast, and the United States agreed that it would not enforce the Prohibition laws against liquor carried by British vessels in United States waters as sealed cargo destined for foreign ports or as sea stores.

2. *The Contiguous Zone under the Law of the Sea*. The International Law Commission's commentary on Article 24 of the Convention of the Territorial Sea and the Contiguous Zone provided:

1   International law accords States the right to exercise preventive or protective control for certain purposes over a belt of the high seas contiguous to their territorial sea. It is, of course, understood that this power of control does not change the legal status of the waters over which it is exercised. These waters are and remain a part of the high seas and are not subject to the sovereignty of the coastal State, which can exercise over them only such rights as are conferred on it by the present draft or are derived from international treaties.

2.   Many States have adopted the principle that in the contiguous zone the coastal State may exercise customs control in order to prevent attempted infringements of its customs and fiscal regulations within its territory or territorial sea, and to punish infringements of those regulations committed within its territory or territorial sea. The Commission considered that it would be impossible to deny to States the exercise of such rights.

3.   Although the number of States which claim rights over the contiguous zone for the purpose of applying sanitary regulations is fairly small, the Commission considers that, in view of the connexion between customs and sanitary regulations, such rights should also be recognized for sanitary regulations.

4.   The Commission did not recognize special security rights in the contiguous zone. It considered that the extreme vagueness of the term "security" would open the way for abuses and that the granting of such rights was not necessary. The enforcement of customs and sanitary regulations will be sufficient in most cases to safeguard the security of the State. In so far as measures of self-defence against an imminent and direct threat to the security of the State are concerned, the Commission refers to the general principles of international law and the Charter of the United Nations.

5.   Nor was the Commission willing to recognize any exclusive right of the coastal State to engage in fishing in the contiguous zone.

Report of the International Law Commission on the Work of Its Eighth Session, U.N. Doc. A/3159 (1956). The Commission's decision not to include "immigration" as one of the matters over which a coastal state could exercise jurisdiction outside its territorial waters was overruled at the Geneva Conference. 3 United Nations Conference on the Law of the Sea, Official Records 181–82, 198–99 (1958).

3.   *Scope of Coastal State Authority in the Zone.* Given the brevity of LOS Convention Article 33 (and its 1958 counterpart), what do you think is the scope of the authority permitted to the coastal state in the contiguous zone? From the language, it seems clear that a coastal state may prescribe rules concerning customs, fiscal, immigration, or sanitary (i.e., environmental) matters that apply within its territory and territorial waters, and may further enforce those rules against vessels located in the contiguous zone. May a coastal state also prescribe other rules with which foreign vessels in the contiguous zone must comply, such as using a particular route? May a coastal state engage in enforcement action against foreign vessels for violations of the rules that occur only in the contiguous zone (e.g., violation of a sanitary law

by a vessel that is transiting through the contiguous zone)? What is the scope of jurisdiction to "prevent" violations within the coastal state's territory or territorial sea? Is it only to stop the activity occurring at that time or might legitimate "preventive" measures include the arrest of a smuggling vessel or the confiscation of contraband? See Churchill & Lowe, The Law of the Sea 137–49 (3d ed. 1999); Symonides, Origin and Legal Essence of the Contiguous Zone, 20 Ocean Dev. & Int'l L. 203 (1989); Mason, Alien Stowaways, the Immigration and Naturalization Service, and Shipowners, 12 Tul. Mar. L.J. 361 (1988); Varghese, Territorial Sea and Contiguous Zone–Concept and Development, 9 Cochin U. L. Rev. 436 (1985); Lowe, The Development of the Concept of the Contiguous Zone, 52 Brit. Y.B.I.L. 109 (1981).

4. *U.S. Adoption of a Contiguous Zone.* The United States adopted a contiguous zone in 1999 by proclamation of President Clinton. That proclamation states in part: "The contiguous zone of the United States extends to 24 nautical miles from the baselines of the United States determined in accordance with international law, but in no case within the territorial sea of another nation." Contiguous Zone of the United States, Proclamation No. 7219, 64 Fed. Reg. 48,701 (Aug. 2, 1999). Given that the United States *is* a party to the 1958 conventions, but *is not* a party to the LOS Convention, how is it possible for the President to extend the contiguous zone to 24 nautical miles from the U.S. baselines, when the 1958 Convention only allows such a zone to an extent of 12 nautical miles? Under international law, is this an example of a customary international law norm overtaking an earlier-in-time treaty norm? Under U.S. constitutional law, is this an example of a presidential determination supported by customary international law superseding an earlier-in-time treaty to which the Senate has given advice-and-consent? Or do you think the President's action is unconstitutional?

5. *Regulation for Reasons of National Security or Armed Conflict?* Does coastal state jurisdiction in the contiguous zone include measures to prevent threats to national security, even though it is not listed in LOS Convention Article 33? One study lists eighteen states that have made such claims, including: China, Egypt, India, Iran, Pakistan, Saudi Arabia, and Venezuela, all of which elicited protests from the United States. See Roach & Smith, United States Responses to Excessive Maritime Claims 172 (2d ed. 1996). What is the effect of war, or armed conflict not labeled "war," on the jurisdiction which a state may exercise in adjacent waters? During the Algerian war, French forces intercepted a number of vessels outside its territorial sea that were suspected of carrying arms destined for Algerian revolutionaries. Germany protested the interception of its vessels as a violation of international law. 4 Whiteman at 513–14. Did the United States have the right in meeting the threat posed by the installing of Soviet missiles in Cuba in October, 1962 to intercept outside its territorial sea vessels bound for Cuba?

6. *Contemporary Significance.* As discussed further below, the LOS Convention now accords to the coastal state certain rights in a 200 nautical mile exclusive economic zone and a continental shelf extending at least that far and, in some cases, even beyond. Given that, do you think the significance of the contiguous zone has changed?

SECTION 5. THE CONTINENTAL SHELF

A. EMERGENCE OF THE CONTINENTAL SHELF REGIME

SCHACHTER, INTERNATIONAL LAW IN THEORY AND PRACTICE

275–77 (1991) (footnotes omitted)

Viewed from a lawyer's perspective, the first notable action in derogation of the *res communis* was the claim by the United States in 1945 to full sovereignty over the continental shelf. That claim expressed in the Truman Proclamation has been generally seen as the start of the process of territorial expansion in ocean space. The shelf was claimed by the United States as an extension of the land-mass of the adjacent State and thus naturally appurtenant to it. Over a decade or so, the United States position was adopted by others and then embodied in the 1958 Geneva Convention on the Continental Shelf. It did not give rise to controversy since the extension of national authority over the shelf did not impinge very much on the traditional uses of the seas—fishing and navigation. * * * What was important as technology developed were the hydrocarbon resources, oil and gas, that were found and exploited on the shelf. These resources are still the most valuable of the resources of the sea. * * *

Although the appropriation of the shelf by coastal States did not appear to challenge the freedom of the seas, it had an influence on the claims made in the 1940s and 1950s by some coastal States to exclusive rights to fish or to engage in whaling in a 200–mile zone off their coasts * * *. In due course, the demands for preferential and exclusive fishing zones spread to other coastal countries and were more vigorously expressed.

POLICY OF THE UNITED STATES WITH RESPECT TO THE NATURAL RESOURCES OF THE SUBSOIL AND SEA BED OF THE CONTINENTAL SHELF

Presidential Proclamation 2667
10 Fed. Reg. 12303 (Sept. 28, 1945)

WHEREAS the Government of the United States of America, aware of the long range world-wide need for new sources of petroleum and other minerals, holds the view that efforts to discover and make available new supplies of these resources should be encouraged; and

WHEREAS its competent experts are of the opinion that such resources underlie many parts of the continental shelf off the coasts of the United States of America, and that with modern technological progress their utilization is already practicable or will become so at an early date; and

WHEREAS recognized jurisdiction over these resources is required in the interest of their conservation and prudent utilization when and as development is undertaken; and

WHEREAS it is the view of the Government of the United States that the exercise of jurisdiction over the natural resources of the subsoil and sea bed of the continental shelf by the contiguous nation is reasonable and just, since the effectiveness of measures to utilize or conserve these resources would be contingent upon cooperation and protection from the shore, since the continental shelf may be regarded as an extension of the land-mass of the coastal nation and thus naturally appurtenant to it, since these resources frequently form a seaward extension of a pool or deposit lying within the territory, and since self-protection compels the coastal nation to keep close watch over activities off its shores which are of the nature necessary for utilization of these resources;

NOW, THEREFORE, I, HARRY S. TRUMAN, President of the United States of America, do hereby proclaim the following policy of the United States of America with respect to the natural resources of the subsoil and sea bed of the continental shelf.

Having concern for the urgency of conserving and prudently utilizing its natural resources, the Government of the United States regards the natural resources of the subsoil and sea bed of the continental shelf beneath the high seas but contiguous to the coasts of the United States as appertaining to the United States, subject to its jurisdiction and control. In cases where the continental shelf extends to the shores of another State, or is shared with an adjacent State, the boundary shall be determined by the United States and the State concerned in accordance with equitable principles. The character as high seas of the waters above the continental shelf and the right to their free and unimpeded navigation are in no way thus affected.

UNITED NATIONS CONVENTION ON THE LAW OF THE SEA, ARTICLE 76

Adopted Dec. 10, 1982
1833 U.N.T.S. 3

Article 76

Definition of the continental shelf

1. The continental shelf of a coastal State comprises the sea-bed and subsoil of the submarine areas that extend beyond its territorial sea throughout the natural prolongation of its land territory to the outer edge of the continental margin, or to a distance of 200 nautical miles from the baselines from which the breadth of the territorial sea is measured where the outer edge of the continental margin does not extend up to that distance.

* * *

3. The continental margin comprises the submerged prolongation of the land mass of the coastal State, and consists of the sea-bed and subsoil

of the shelf, the slope and the rise. It does not include the deep ocean floor with its oceanic ridges or the subsoil thereof.

* * *

5. The fixed points comprising the line of the outer limits of the continental shelf on the sea-bed * * * either shall not exceed 350 nautical miles from the baselines * * * or shall not exceed 100 nautical miles from the 2,500 metre isobath, which is a line connecting the depth of 2,500 metres.

* * *

10. The provisions of this article are without prejudice to the question of delimitation of the continental shelf between States with opposite or adjacent coasts.

NOTES

1. *Changing Custom.* The Truman Proclamation itself did not set the seaward limit of the continental shelf. A White House press release issued on the same day, however, noted that: "Generally, submerged land which is contiguous to the continent and which is covered by no more than 100 fathoms (600 feet) of water is considered as the continental shelf." 4 Whiteman at 758. When the Truman Proclamation was made, did the United States violate customary international law? In 1951, in the *Abu Dhabi* case, Lord Asquith of Bishopstone concluded that the doctrine of the continental shelf was unknown to international law in 1939 and had not yet become part of the corpus of international law in 1951. See Award of Lord Asquith of Bishopstone, 1 I.C.L.Q. 247 (1952). Yet by 1958, UNCLOS I saw the adoption of the Convention on the Continental Shelf, Apr. 29, 1958, 15 U.S.T. 471, 499 U.N.T.S. 311, much of which is now regarded as reflecting customary international law. Is this an example of a state having to "violate" custom in order to help make it evolve? See Kunz, Continental Shelf and International Law: Confusion and Abuse, 50 A.J.I.L. 828, 829–32 (1956).

2. *Defining the Continental Shelf.* Having read portions of LOS Convention Article 76, would you say that all states can claim at least a 200 nautical mile continental shelf, even if their coast is cliff that drops straight down to what a geologist would consider the deep ocean floor or sea-bed? On what basis could a state argue that it is entitled to a continental shelf greater than 200 nautical miles?

3. *Comparison to the 1958 Convention.* The 1958 Convention on the Continental Shelf contained in Article 1 a much more restrictive definition of the continental shelf. The wide expansion of the definition in the LOS Convention is related to the acceptance of the exclusive economic zone of 200 miles, discussed in the next section.

4. *The Continental Shelf Commission.* The LOS Convention also establishes a Commission on the Limits of the Continental Shelf which makes recommendations to coastal states about the limits of their continental shelves beyond 200 nautical miles. The limits established by the coastal state

taking into account these recommendations shall be final and binding (Article 76(8)). Do states not party to the LOS Convention need to take into account recommendations of the Commission? See Continental Shelf Limits: The Scientific and Legal Interface (Cook & Carleton eds. 2000).

B. RIGHTS OF THE COASTAL STATE TO ITS CONTINENTAL SHELF

What rights does the coastal state have with respect to its continental shelf? LOS Convention Article 77 provides that the "coastal State exercises over the continental shelf sovereign rights for the purpose of exploring it and exploiting its natural resources" and that such rights "are exclusive in the sense that if the coastal State does not explore the continental shelf or exploit its natural resources, no one may undertake these activities without the express consent of the coastal State." LOS Convention art. 77(1) & (2). "[N]atural resources" means "the mineral and other non-living resources of the sea-bed and subsoil together with living organisms belonging to sedentary species, that is to say, organisms which, at the harvestable stage, either are immobile on or under the sea-bed or are unable to move except in constant physical contact with the sea-bed or the subsoil." Id. art. 77(3). The coastal state has "the exclusive right to authorize and regulate drilling on the continental shelf for all purposes." Id. art. 81. For a discussion of situations where offshore resources of adjacent states are shared, see Ong, Joint Development of Common Offshore Oil and Gas Deposits: "Mere" State Practice or Customary International Law?, 93 A.J.I.L. 771 (1999).

What rights does the coastal state not have? Article 78 indicates that such rights "do not affect the legal status of the superjacent waters or of the air space above those waters," and "must not infringe, or result in any unjustifiable interference with navigation and other rights and freedoms of other States as provided for in this Convention." Article 79 recognizes the rights of other states to lay and maintain cables and pipelines subject to reasonable measures of the coastal state for the exploration of the continental shelf. The LOS Convention also permits the coastal state to take reasonable measures to control pollution from pipelines, and requires the consent of the coastal state to the delineation of the course for laying pipelines. States laying pipelines shall pay due regard to cables or pipelines already in position.

While the coastal state has exclusive rights to exploitation of the continental shelf, the LOS Convention imposes a special obligation with respect to any exploitation of the shelf beyond 200 nautical miles from the baselines. Article 82 provides:

> 1. The coastal State shall make payments or contributions in kind in respect of the exploitation of the non-living resources of the continental shelf beyond 200 nautical miles from the baselines from which the breadth of the territorial sea is measured.

2.   The payments and contributions shall be made annually with respect to all production at a site after the first five years of production at that site. For the sixth year, the rate of payment or contribution shall be 1 per cent of the value or volume of production at the site. The rate shall increase by 1 per cent for each subsequent year until the twelfth year and shall remain at 7 per cent thereafter. Production does not include resources used in connection with exploitation.

3.   A developing State which is a net importer of a mineral resource produced from its continental shelf is exempt from making such payments or contributions in respect of that mineral resource.

4.   The payments or contributions shall be made through the Authority, which shall distribute them to States Parties to this Convention, on the basis of equitable sharing criteria, taking into account the interests and needs of developing States, particularly the least developed and the landlocked among them.

Do you think that a state not party to the Convention can exploit its continental shelf beyond 200 nautical miles if it does not accept also the obligations of Article 82? See generally Jewett, The Evolution of the Legal Regime of the Continental Shelf, 22 Canadian Y.B.I.L. 153 (1984) and 23 Canadian Y.B.I.L. 201 (1985).

Are there collateral consequences to a state's possession of rights in its continental shelf? In *United States v. Ray*, 423 F.2d 16, 18 (5th Cir. 1970), the Fifth Circuit Court of Appeals granted the United States a decree enjoining U.S. nationals from establishing a "new sovereign country" on two coral reefs on the U.S. continental shelf (outside the U.S. territorial sea) without finding that these reefs were the property of the United States. The Court held that the structures interfered with the exclusive rights of the United States to exploit the reefs under the 1958 Convention on the Continental Shelf, as well as the Outer Continental Shelf Lands Act, 43 U.S.C. §§ 1331–1346 (2000). In *Treasure Salvors, Inc. v. Unidentified Wrecked and Abandoned Sailing Vessel*, 569 F.2d 330, 339–40 (5th Cir. 1978), however, the same Court of Appeals denied the United States sovereign rights to an abandoned vessel found by a private person on the continental shelf, since U.S. interests in the shelf were only for the purpose of exploring it and exploiting its natural resources.

C.   DELIMITATION OF THE CONTINENTAL SHELF BETWEEN STATES

LOS Convention Article 83(1) provides: "The delimitation of the continental shelf between States with opposite or adjacent coasts shall be effected by agreement on the basis of international law, as referred to in Article 38 of the Statute of the International Court of Justice, in order to achieve an equitable solution." If states cannot reach such agreement "within a reasonable period of time," they may resort to LOS Convention dispute settlement procedures. LOS Convention Article 83(2); see *infra* Section 11. In the meantime, the states "shall make every effort to enter into provisional arrangements of a practical nature and, during this transitional period, not to jeopardize or hamper the reaching of the final agreement. Such arrangements shall be without prejudice to the final delimitation." Id. art. 83(3).

Article 83 (and the analogous Article 74 dealing with delimitation of exclusive economic zones) reflect the inability of states to achieve a formula for maritime boundary delimitation between continental shelves or exclusive economic zones of different states. The article does not adopt a pure "equidistance line" approach, which was defined in the 1958 conventions as the line every point of which is equidistance from the nearest points of the baselines of the two adjacent or opposite states. See Convention on the Territorial Sea and Contiguous Zone, art. 12(1), Apr. 29, 1958, 15 U.S.T. 1606, 516 U.N.T.S. 205; Convention on the Continental Shelf, art. 6(1), Apr. 29, 1958, 15 U.S.T. 471, 499 U.N.T.S. 311. Those conventions adopted an equidistance line approach, but allowed for deviations in special circumstances. Nor does the LOS Convention reject the equidistance line approach in favor of some other method.

Sometimes states are able to agree on delimitation of their maritime areas, including the continental shelf. For example, consider the progressive steps taken by Mexico and the United States to delimit their maritime boundary. In 1970, the United States and Mexico negotiated and signed an agreement based on the equidistance method establishing maritime boundaries out to 12 nautical miles off their Pacific coasts and the mouth of the Rio Grande into the Gulf of Mexico. In 1978, a second treaty extended both of these boundaries seaward to the limit of their respective 200–mile zones. In the Gulf of Mexico, this resulted in the creation of two boundary segments where their 200–mile exclusive economic zones (EEZ) overlapped (as discussed in the next Section, the EEZ is a zone permitted under the law of the sea in which coastal states can exercise certain rights over the living resources). In 2000, a third treaty was completed delimiting the continental shelf area in this "western gap" again using an equidistance line method. See Treaty to Resolve Pending Boundary Differences and Maintain the Rio Grande and Colorado River as the International Boundary, United States–Mexico, Nov. 23, 1970, 23 U.S.T. 371; Treaty of Maritime Boundaries, United States–Mexico, May 4, 1978, S. Exec. Doc. F., 96–6 (1979); Treaty on Delimitation of Continental Shelf, United States–Mexico, June 9, 2000, S. Treaty Doc. No. 106–39 (2000).

Yet often states cannot reach agreement. When this happens, the maritime area remains disputed or the matter is placed before a tribunal for adjudication, with the disputing states advancing whatever method they view as maximizing their maritime area. The International Court of Justice has heard numerous maritime boundary cases of wide-ranging geographical diversity, including: *North Sea Continental Shelf Cases* (F.R.G./Denmark; F.R.G./Netherlands), 1969 I.C.J. 3; *Continental Shelf* (Tunisia/Libya), 1982 I.C.J. 18; 1985 I.C.J. 192; *Continental Shelf* (Libya/Malta), 1985 I.C.J. 13; *Delimitation of the Maritime Boundary in the Gulf of Maine Area* (Canada/United States), 1984 I.C.J. 246; *Arbitral Award of 31 July 1989* (Guinea–Bissau v. Senegal), 1991 I.C.J. 53; *Land, Island and Maritime Frontier Dispute* (El Salvador/Honduras: Nicaragua intervening), 1992 I.C.J. 351 (an attempt to revise this judgment in 2003 failed); *Maritime Delimitation in the Area Between Greenland and Jan Mayen* (Denmark v. Norway), 1993 I.C.J. 38; *Maritime Delimitation and Territorial Questions* (Qatar v. Bahrain), 1995 I.C.J. 6; *Land and Maritime Boundary* (Cameroon v. Nigeria: Equatorial Guinea intervening), 1998 I.C.J. 275; *Territorial and Maritime Delimitation between Nicaragua and Honduras in the Caribbean Sea* (Nicaragua v. Honduras), 2007 I.C.J. ___; Maritime Delimitation in the Black Sea, 2009 I.C.J. ___. Cases on the Court's docket as of early 2009 that are still to be decided include disputes between Chile and Peru and between Nicaragua and Colombia. Moreover, arbitral tribunals have also issued delimitation decisions, including tribunals convened under the LOS Convention. See, e.g., *Arbitral Award* (Barbados/Trinidad & Tobago) (Apr. 11, 2006), available at http://www.pca-cpa.org; *Arbitral Award* (Guyana v. Suriname) (Sept. 17, 2007), available at http://www.pca-cpa.org.

The earliest of these decisions—the *North Sea Continental Shelf Cases* and the *Continental Shelf* case between Libya and Tunisia—relied on "equitable principles" to divide a shelf where there was no interruption in the natural prolongation of the coasts. Yet these decisions gave no clear guidelines as to exactly what those principles entailed and whether they could be generalized across different cases. The Court did provide a few general statements, such as that a delimitation should not refashion nature and that special effects or circumstances could be taken into account. In the *Gulf of Maine Case*, a Chamber of the Court seemed to abandon any quest for general principles to apply to delimitation cases generally. *Delimitation of the Maritime Boundary in the Gulf of Maine Area* (Canada/United States), 1984 I.C.J. 246. The Chamber said:

> 111.   A body of detailed rules is not to be looked for in customary international law * * * and not [to be tested] by deduction from preconceived ideas. It is therefore unrewarding, especially in a new and still unconsolidated field like that involving the quite recent extension of the claims of States to areas which were until yesterday zones of the high seas, to look to general international law to provide a ready-made set of rules that can be used for solving any delimitation problems that arise. A more useful course is to seek a better formulation of the fundamental norm, on which the Parties were fortunate enough to be agreed, and whose existence in the legal convictions not only of the Parties to the present dispute, but of all States, is apparent from an examination of the realities of international legal relations.

> 112.   The Chamber therefore wishes to conclude this review * * * by attempting a more complete and, in its opinion, more precise reformulation of the "fundamental norm" already mentioned. For

this purpose it will, *inter alia*, draw also upon the definition of the "actual rules of law... which govern the delimitation of adjacent continental shelves—that is to say, rules binding upon States for all delimitations" which was given by the Court in its 1969 Judgment in the *North Sea Continental Shelf* cases (*I.C.J Reports 1969*, pp. 46–47, para. 85). What general international law prescribes in every maritime delimitation between neighbouring States could therefore be defined as follows:

(1) No maritime delimitation between States with opposite or adjacent coasts may be effected unilaterally by one of those States. Such delimitation must be sought and effected by means of an agreement, following negotiations conducted in good faith and with the genuine intention of achieving a positive result. Where, however, such agreement cannot be achieved, delimitation should be effected by recourse to a third party possessing the necessary competence.

(2) In either case, delimitation is to be effected by the application of equitable criteria and by the use of practical methods capable of ensuring, with regard to the geographic configuration of the area and other relevant circumstances, an equitable result.

The Chamber concluded that, in the absence of agreement, states will have to seek third party determination of maritime boundaries. No principle applies in the absence of agreement. (The equidistance line, for example, cannot be applied in the absence of agreement.)

As for the principles that should guide the third party, the Chamber said:

157. There has been no systematic definition of the equitable criteria that may be taken into consideration for an international maritime delimitation, and this would in any event be difficult *a priori* because of their highly variable adaptability to different concrete situations.

* * *

162. Here again the essential consideration is that none of the potential methods has intrinsic merits which would make it preferable to another in the abstract.

163. * * * Above all there must be willingness to adopt a combination of different methods whenever that * * * may be relevant in the different phases of the operation and with reference to different segments of the line.

More recent cases have continued to demonstrate that no one approach is dictated by international law, although typically a tribunal will commence its analysis by drawing a provisional equidistance line and then consider whether any special circumstances require adjusting that line to achieve an equitable solution. That was the approach in the 2007 *Guyana v. Suriname* case, where the arbitral tribunal developed a line that largely tracked an equidistance line. The only portion that deviated from an equidistance line arose in the territorial sea, where the tribunal found that for thirty years the two countries had, by their conduct, regarded a particular line along an azimuth from a specific point on the coast as the boundary of their three-mile territorial seas—a line that accorded to Suriname appropriate access to the western channel of the Corentyne River. *Arbitral Award* (Guyana v. Suriname), paras. 299, 306 (Sept. 17, 2007), available at http://www.pca-cpa.org. Interestingly, after using that line for a distance of three nautical miles, the tribunal then drew a connecting line between that line's seaward terminus and the point of the equidistance line that lay *twelve* nautical miles off the coast (rather than the point of the equidistance line that lay *three* nautical miles off the coast). Doing so, according to the tribunal, "avoids a sudden crossing of the area of access to the Corentyne River, and interposes a gradual transition from the 3 nm to the 12 nm point. It also ensures that the line is convenient for navigational purposes." *Id.*, para. 324.

By contrast, in the 2007 *Territorial and Maritime Dispute* case between Nicaragua and Honduras, the International Court rejected the equidistance line approach in favor of an angle bisector approach. According to the Court, drawing an equidistance line was problematic because of the difficulty in fixing base points along the coast, given the instability of the mouth of the River Coco due to sediment accretion, the uncertain nature of small offshore islands and cays, and disagreements between the parties about geographic coordinates. *Territorial and Maritime Delimitation between Nicaragua and Honduras in the Caribbean Sea* (Nicaragua v. Honduras), 2007 I.C.J. ___, paras. 277–81. Instead, the Court explained that it was appropriate to "consider whether in principle some form of bisector of the angle created by lines representing the relevant mainland coasts could be a basis for the delimitation. * * * In instances where, as in the present case, any base points that could be determined by the Court are inherently unstable, the bisector method may be seen as an approximation of the equidistance method." *Id.* para. 287. The Court proceeded to draw two lines that reflected the overall frontal projections of the two relevant coasts, which formed an angle that was bisected to establish the delimitation line. (The Court also rejected an approach that would rely upon evidence of prior Nicaraguan and Honduran oil concessions in the disputed area, mainly because such concessions did not reveal any form of tacit agreement between the two states as to the existence of a boundary. *Id.*, paras. 247, 254.)

All these cases indicate that in applying equitable principles, geography is the primary concern; economic conditions and environmental concerns are excluded. Nevertheless, geography was often "modified" to some extent to achieve a more equitable result. A concavity of the Federal Republic of Germany's coast was taken into account in the *North Sea Cases.* A line dictated by the general direction of the coasts was modified by the presence of islands in the *Continental Shelf* case between Libya and Tunisia. The proportionality of the coasts was considered in the *Gulf of Maine* case.

The International Court of Justice Chamber in *Gulf of Maine* also looked for the first time at a unitary boundary for both the shelf and the water column above. While it reiterated the dual character of its task throughout the opinion, the Chamber did not indicate how the line it drew would be different if it were delimiting the shelf only. It seemed to imply that in the absence of a clear, natural division in the continental shelf between adjacent states, it will be possible to divide both water column and shelf using the same principles. Again, the exact nature of those principles remains unclear, but many subsequent tribunals have also been asked to delimit a unitary maritime boundary.

NOTES

1. *U.S. Maritime Delimitation Agreements.* The United States has concluded numerous agreements with foreign states delimiting its maritime boundaries, including the continental shelf and exclusive economic zone. Such agreements have been concluded not just with Canada and Mexico, but also with various other states, such as Cuba, Venezuela (relating to Puerto Rico and the U.S. Virgin Islands), the Cook Islands (relating to Hawaii), Russia (with respect to Alaska), and the United Kingdom (with respect to the U.S. and U.K. Virgin Islands and Anguilla). Boundary lines are typically drawn based on a series of points that reflect a specific latitude and longitude.

2. *U.S. Federal/State Allocation of Authority.* Within the United States, controversy over the continental shelf has sometimes erupted concerning the rights of the federal government as opposed to those of the coastal states. In 1947, the Supreme Court held that the United States was "possessed of paramount rights in and power over, the lands, minerals and other things of value underlying the Pacific Ocean, lying seaward of the ordinary low water mark on the coast of California and outside of inland waters," to the extent of three nautical miles, and that California had no title thereto or property interest therein. *United States v. California*, 332 U.S. 19, 22 (1947). In *United States v. Louisiana*, 339 U.S. 699 (1950), the Court followed the *California* decision and held that the United States possessed identical rights over areas underlying the Gulf of Mexico, to the extent (27 miles from the coast) claimed by Louisiana. Noting that the one difference between Louisiana's claim and the earlier claim of California was that the former state claimed rights "twenty-four miles seaward of the three-mile belt," the Court (per Douglas, J.) stated: "If, as we held in California's case, the three-mile belt is in the domain of the Nation rather than that of the separate States, it follows *a fortiori* that the ocean beyond that limit also is. The ocean seaward of the marginal belt is perhaps even more directly related to the national defense, the conduct of foreign affairs, and world commerce than is the marginal sea." 339 U.S. at 705. On the same day as the *Louisiana* decision, the Court held that Texas had no interest in the undersea areas contiguous to its coast, even though Texas argued that it had acquired both proprietary and sovereign rights in a nine-mile marginal belt prior to annexation by the United States. *United States v. Texas*, 339 U.S. 707 (1950). Rather, the United States was held to be possessed of paramount rights in, and full dominion and power over, the undersea areas extending to the edge of the continental shelf in the

Gulf of Mexico first claimed by Texas in 1947. 339 U.S. at 715–20; see also *United States v. Texas*, 340 U.S. 900, 900–01 (1950).

On May 22, 1953, Congress passed the Submerged Lands Act, 43 U.S.C. §§ 1301–1315 (2000), by which the United States relinquished to the coastal states all of its rights in submerged lands within certain geographical limits, and confirmed the rights of the United States beyond those limits. The Act defined the areas relinquished to the states in terms of state boundaries as they existed at the time a state became a member of the Union, but not extending beyond three geographic miles in the Atlantic and Pacific Oceans or beyond three marine leagues (nine miles) in the Gulf of Mexico. On August 7, 1953, Congress approved the Outer Continental Shelf Lands Act, 43 U.S.C. §§ 1331–1346 (2000), which provided for the jurisdiction of the United States over the "outer Continental Shelf," defined as areas seaward of those relinquished to the states by the Submerged Lands Act. Moreover, the statute authorized the Secretary of the Interior to lease such areas for exploitation purposes.

In *United States v. States of Louisiana, Texas, Mississippi, Alabama & Florida*, 363 U.S. 1 (1960), the United States sought a declaration that it was entitled to full dominion and power over the undersea areas underlying the Gulf of Mexico that were more than three geographic miles seaward from the coast, notwithstanding the language of the Submerged Lands Act. The State Department took the position that it could not accept an interpretation of the Submerged Lands Act that would result in recognition of state claims to "marginal seas of a greater breadth than 3 marine miles." 4 Whiteman at 62. The Court rejected that contention, finding that the allocation of authority between the federal government and the states in the statute was for "purely domestic purposes." 363 U.S. at 33. Turning to the historic claims of the coastal states, the Court concluded that Texas was entitled, as against the United States, to the areas underlying the Gulf of Mexico to a distance of three leagues from her coast. Id. at 64. Florida was also held, on other grounds, to be entitled to a three-marine-league belt of land under the Gulf of Mexico, seaward from its coast. *United States v. Florida, et al.*, 363 U.S. 121 (1960). The other Gulf states were held not to be entitled to rights in submerged lands lying beyond three geographic miles from their respective coasts. *United States v. Louisiana, et. al.*, 363 U.S. at 79, 82; see also *United States v. Louisiana*, 394 U.S. 1, 11 (1969); 420 U.S. 529 (1975) (Special Masters Report; accepted and decree issued); 422 U.S. 13 (1975) (supplemental decision); *United States v. Maine*, 420 U.S. 515 (1975) (finding that the right to explore and exploit the sea bed beyond three miles belonged to the federal government, not to the defendants, the original states of the Union that had claimed these rights by succession to Great Britain).

3. *Further Reading.* See generally Maritime Delimitation (Lagoni & Vignes eds. 2006); Tanaka, Predictability and Flexibility in the Law of Maritime Delimitation (2006); Oxman, The Territorial Temptation: A Siren Song at Sea, 100 A.J.I.L. 830 (2006); Brilmayer & Klein, Land and Sea: Two Sovereignty Regimes in Search of a Common Denominator, 33 N.Y.U. J. Int'l L. & Pol. 703 (2001); Charney, Progress in International Maritime Boundary Delimitation, 88 A.J.I.L. 227 (1994); International Maritime Boundaries (Charney & Alexander eds. 1993).

SECTION 6.   THE EXCLUSIVE
ECONOMIC ZONE

A.   CUSTOMARY INTERNATIONAL LAW

Long before the law of the sea conventions, coastal states pursued exceptions to the rule of *mare liberum*. Coastal state claims that led to the development of the territorial sea were inspired, in significant part, by the desire for exclusive rights in the resources of that part of the sea, principally its fish. Coastal states also asserted a right to enforce measures of conservation outside their territorial sea that were designed to maintain the supply of fish for the benefit of national fisheries.

A series of new claims by coastal states to fishing zones arose between 1945 and 1958, some under the guise of expanded territorial seas and some based on a new type of fishing zone located outside those seas. (In support of their expanded claims, such states would sometimes note the customs laws of the United States, which projected coastal authority out past the territorial sea, as well the Truman Proclamation asserting the exclusive jurisdiction of the coastal state to the mineral resources of the continental shelf beyond the territorial sea.) Expanded claims by coastal states were the product of myriad factors: the emergence of sophisticated technology, including sonar, that allowed for increasing amounts of fish to be found; the development of non-traditional methods for large-scale catching of fish, such as the lengthy driftnets that could be deployed once nylon was invented; the increased use of refrigeration on vessels, allowing them to travel further distances from their markets in search of catch; and the concomitant decline in fisheries as stocks became depleted from these developments.

For years the United States resisted claims by other coastal states to large exclusive fishing zones, and strenuously supported claims by its nationals to fish in distant waters outside the territory of other states. On September 28, 1945, President Truman issued a proclamation asserting that the United States would consider it proper "to establish conservation zones in those areas of the high seas contiguous to the coasts of the United States." The United States would regulate fishing activities of its own nationals unilaterally, and those of foreign nationals by agreement with their states. Policy of the United States with Respect to Coastal Fisheries in Certain Areas of the High Seas, Presidential Proclamation No. 2664, 10 Fed. Reg. 12,304 (Oct. 1, 1945), 4 Whiteman at 945–62. Thus, rather than establish a fishing zone exclusively for its own use, the United States claimed only a more limited "conservation zone" that would be shared.

Hence, by the time of UNCLOS I in 1958, insufficient consensus existed on the creation of exclusive fishing zones outside the territorial sea. Instead, states adopted the Convention on Fishing and Conservation of the Living Resources of the High Seas, Apr. 29, 1958, 17 U.S.T. 138,

559 U.N.T.S. 285, which only went so far as to acknowledge that a coastal state has a "special interest in the maintenance of the productivity of the living resources in any area of the high seas adjacent to its territorial sea" Id. art. 6. As such, the convention envisaged that coastal states would take the initiative in prescribing measures of conservation, which must be non-discriminatory, based on "appropriate" scientific findings, and in situations where the need was "urgent." Id.; see also Bishop, The 1958 Geneva Convention on Fishing and Conservation of the Living Resources of the High Seas, 62 Colum. L. Rev. 1206 (1962).

During the 1960s, Iceland attempted to extend its exclusive fisheries jurisdiction from twelve to fifty miles nautical miles from its baselines. That effort was opposed in the International Court of Justice by the United Kingdom, whose vessels had fished off the Icelandic coast for centuries. In the *Fisheries Jurisdiction Case* (United Kingdom v. Iceland), 1974 I.C.J. 3, the Court acknowledged an increasing and widespread acceptance of preferential fishing rights for coastal states. The Court said, however, that such rights are not absolute and could not imply the extinction of the concurrent rights of other states, particularly states that had historic claims to fish in particular waters. The Court concluded that Iceland could not unilaterally exclude the United Kingdom from its historic fishing grounds. The Court declared also that the two countries had an obligation to resolve their dispute by negotiation.

In time, however, the clamor for exclusive fishing zones became ever greater. Even the United States, in 1966, adopted a "Contiguous Fishery Zone" of twelve miles (nine miles beyond its territorial sea). See Act to Establish a Contiguous Fishery Zone beyond the Territorial Sea of the United States, Pub. L. No. 89–658, 80 Stat. 908 (1966). The stage was set for the establishment of a new type of zone when UNCLOS III was launched in 1973. Professor Henkin writes:

> Developed maritime states early resisted coastal-state expansion. As distant fishing states, they rejected the notion that a coastal state might exclude them from wide coastal zones in which they had long fished. They feared, too, "creeping jurisdiction." Already they had seen how exclusive mining rights for coastal states on the continental shelf (beyond their territorial sea) had created pressures for exclusive fishing rights for coastal states in wide zones beyond the territorial sea. Developed maritime states feared that if the coastal state acquired exclusive fishing rights, its jurisdiction would continue to expand to other uses and would interfere also with navigation, scientific research, and military uses in wide coastal zones.

> But developed maritime states are also coastal states and have important national interests that stood to gain from coastal-state expansion. They had some sympathy with the economic needs of poor coastal states. They were reluctant to confront developing coastal states (supported by the rest of the Third World), especially since the latter had effective "possession" of the coastal areas and could seize

them (or threaten to seize them) unilaterally. Pressed from without and by national interests from within, they acquiesced in the concept of an exclusive economic zone. (This, in fact, unleashed domestic forces that pressed unilateral expansion. While the conference was in process, the United States Congress declared a 200–mile fishing zone for the United States.)

Henkin, How Nations Behave 217 (2d ed. 1979) (footnotes omitted); see also Hollick, The Origins of 200–Mile Offshore Zones, 71 A.J.I.L. 494 (1977); Henkin, Politics and the Changing Law of the Sea, 89 Pol. Sci. Q. 46 (1974).

B. LOS CONVENTION EXCLUSIVE ECONOMIC ZONE (EEZ)

LOS Convention Article 55 provides: "The exclusive economic zone is an area beyond and adjacent to the territorial sea * * * under which the rights and jurisdictions of the coastal State and the rights and freedoms of other States are governed by the relevant provisions of this Convention." Article 57 provides: "The exclusive economic zone shall not extend beyond 200 nautical miles from the baselines from which the breadth of the territorial sea is measured." Article 56(1) indicates that the coastal State has the following rights, jurisdiction, and duties in this EEZ:

(a) sovereign rights for the purpose of exploring and exploiting, conserving and managing the natural resources, whether living or non-living, of the waters superadjacent to the seabed and of the sea-bed and subsoil, and with regard to other activities for the economic exploitation and exploration of the zone, such as the production of energy from the water, currents and winds;

(b) jurisdiction as provided for in the relevant provisions of this Convention with regard to:

(i) the establishment and use of artificial islands, installations and structures;

(ii) marine scientific research;

(iii) the protection and preservation of the marine environment;

(c) other rights and duties provided for in this Convention.

At the same time, other States have certain rights and duties in the EEZ as well. LOS Convention Article 58 provides as follows:

1. In the exclusive economic zone, all States, whether coastal or land-locked, enjoy, subject to the relevant provisions of this Convention, the freedoms referred to in article 87 of navigation and over-flight and of the laying of submarine cables and pipelines, and other internationally lawful uses of the sea related to these freedoms, such as those associated with the operation of ships, aircraft and subma-

rine cables and pipelines, and compatible with the other provisions of this Convention.

* * *

3.   In exercising their rights and performing their duties under this Convention in the exclusive economic zone, States shall have due regard to the rights and duties of the coastal State and shall comply with the laws and regulations adopted by the coastal State in accordance with the provisions of this Convention and other rules of international law in so far as they are not incompatible with this Part.

As indicated above, an important component of the coastal State's rights concerns managing the living resources of the EEZ. In that regard, the LOS Convention accords to the coastal state important rights and responsibilities for determining the allowable catch of living resources in the EEZ, which it can then harvest itself if it so chooses. If it does not have the capacity to harvest the entire allowable catch, however, it is obligated to allow other States access to its EEZ for the purpose of doing so. See LOS Convention, arts. 61 & 62.

NOTES

1.   *Nature of Coastal State Interest in the EEZ.* How does having "sovereign rights" in the EEZ differ from having "sovereignty" over the EEZ? In *Mayaguezanos por la Salud y el Ambiente v. United States*, 198 F.3d 297 (1st Cir. 1999), the First Circuit found that there was no U.S. authority to regulate a foreign vessel transiting through the U.S. EEZ carrying nuclear waste. The court stated:

> The interests of the coastal state in its EEZ largely have to do with development of natural resources and the availability of scientific research. A coastal state has limited powers in the EEZ under customary international law. * * * [T]here is no platform from which to begin to construct an argument that such circumstances could give rise to federal action. Foreign ships do not require the permission of the United States to pass through its EEZ.

Id. at 305; see also Restatement (Third) § 514, Comment *c.* Though not included in the LOS Convention provisions extracted above, the coastal state is given exclusive rights in the EEZ with regard to artificial islands, installations and structures (Article 60).

2.   *Nature of Other States' Interest in the EEZ.* Is the EEZ a part of the "high seas"? On the one hand, the EEZ is located outside any state's territorial sea. On the other hand, the LOS Convention does not expressly designate the EEZ as part of the high seas. All other states may exercise most high seas freedoms in the EEZ, such as those of navigation, overflight, and laying of submarine cables and pipelines, yet their fishing rights are subjugated to those of the coastal state. Does it matter if the EEZ is regarded as "high seas" or not?

3. *Comparing the EEZ and Continental Shelf Regimes.* Do you agree with the following assessment? The continental shelf regime has a rather complicated method of determining the geographic limits of the regime but, once determined, the rights of coastal states and other states in that regime are fairly clear. By contrast, the EEZ regime has a fairly clear method of determining the geographic limits of the regime, but has a somewhat complicated method of determining the rights of the coastal and other states in that regime. With respect to the latter, can the coastal state decide to catch every single fish in its EEZ? Does the coastal state have unfettered discretion in determining what constitutes an "optimum yield"? Once an optimum yield is determined, can the coastal state reserve solely to its fishing vessels access to those fish, or must it be shared with other states?

4. *Guidelines for Sharing.* Article 62(1) of the LOS Convention provides that if the coastal state does not have the capacity to harvest the entire allowable catch, it shall give access to other states. When doing so, the LOS Convention directs the coastal state to take into account the "need to minimize economic dislocation in States whose nationals have habitually fished in the zone or which have made substantial efforts in research and identification of stocks" (Article 62(3)). In particular, there is a right to participate by land-locked states in the region (Article 69), and states with special "geographical disadvantages," having no zone of their own or one unable to supply the needs of their population (Article 70). But developed land-locked states are entitled to participate only in the economic zones of developed coastal states of the region (Articles 69(4), 70(5)). Articles 69–70 do not apply when the coastal state's economy is "overwhelmingly dependent" on the exploitation of the living resources of its exclusive economic zone (Article 71).

5. *Delimitation of the EEZ.* Article 74 of the 1982 Convention, dealing with delimitation of exclusive economic zones between states with opposite or adjacent coasts, is identical with Article 83 which deals with delimitation of the continental shelf. See, *supra*, Section 5(C). Delimitation problems in the exclusive economic zone and the shelf are generally the same, and are sometimes considered together.

6. *U.S. Establishment of an EEZ.* In the midst of UNCLOS III, Congress adopted the Fishery Conservation and Management Act of 1976, 16 U.S.C. § 1801 et seq. (1982) (also known as the Magnuson Act), which provided:

> There is established a zone contiguous to the territorial sea of the United States to be known as the fishery conservation zone. The inner boundary of the fishery conservation zone is a line coterminous with the seaward boundary of each of the coastal States, and the outer boundary of such zone is a line drawn in such manner that each point on it is 200 nautical miles from the baseline from which the territorial sea is measured.

Id. § 1811. After adoption of the LOS Convention, President Reagan in 1983 established an exclusive economic zone for the United States by proclamation, asserting rights over living and nonliving resources in accordance with the LOS Convention. Proclamation 5030–Exclusive Economic Zone of the United States of America, 1 Pub. Papers 380, 383 (Mar. 10, 1983), 22 I.L.M. 464

(1983). Congress then dropped the concept of a "fishery conservation zone" from the Magnuson Act by amendment, in favor of a U.S. "exclusive economic zone," with the inner boundary being the seaward boundary of the coastal U.S. states. Among other things, the statute provides for management of fish and other species in the EEZ under plans drawn up by Regional Fishery Management Councils, which are comprised of federal and state officials. The plans are then reviewed and approved by the U.S. Secretary of Commerce. Further, the statute provides for regulation of foreign fishing in the EEZ under "governing international fishing agreements" (GIFAs) and vessel fishing permits.

7. Further Reading. See Hannesson, The Privatization of the Oceans (2004); Orrego Vicuña, The Exclusive Economic Zone: Regime and Legal Nature under International Law (1989); Kwiatkowska, The 200 Mile Exclusive Economic Zone in the New Law of the Sea (1989); Attard, The Exclusive Economic Zone in International Law (1987); Charney, The Exclusive Economic Zone and Public International Law, 15 Ocean Dev. & Int'l L. 233 (1985).

THE "HOSHINMARU" CASE
(JAPAN v. RUSSIAN FEDERATION)

International Tribunal for the Law of the Sea, 2007
ITLOS Case No. 14, Judgment

Factual background

27. The *Hoshinmaru* is a fishing vessel flying the flag of Japan. Its owner is Ikeda Suisan, a company incorporated in Japan. The Master of the *Hoshinmaru* is Mr Shoji Takahashi. The 17 crew members of the *Hoshinmaru* including the Master are of Japanese nationality.

28. According to the Certificate of Registration, the *Hoshinmaru* was entered in the State Ship's Registry of Nyuzen-machi, Shimoniikawa-gun, Toyama Prefecture, in Japan on 24 March 2004. On 14 May 2007, the Russian Federation provided the *Hoshinmaru* with a fishing licence for drift net salmon and trout fishing in three different areas of the exclusive economic zone of the Russian Federation. According to the fishing licence, the *Hoshinmaru* was authorized to fish, from 15 May until 31 July 2007, the following: 101.8 tons of sockeye salmon; 161.8 tons of chum salmon; 7 tons of sakhalin trout; 1.7 tons of silver salmon; and 2.7 tons of spring salmon.

29. On 1 June 2007, the *Hoshinmaru* was fishing in the exclusive economic zone of the Russian Federation off the eastern coast of the Kamchatka Peninsula when it was ordered to stop by a Russian patrol boat. Subsequently, the *Hoshinmaru* was boarded by an inspection team of the State Sea Inspection of the Northeast Border Coast Guard Directorate of the Federal Security Service of the Russian Federation (hereinafter the "State Sea Inspection"). According to the Applicant, at the time of boarding, the *Hoshinmaru* was at the position 56°09′N, 165°28′E, which is a point located within the exclusive economic zone of the Russian Federation and where the vessel was licensed to fish.

30.   After boarding the vessel, an inspection team of the State Sea Inspection examined it. A protocol of inspection No. 003483 drawn up on 1 June 2007 by a senior state coastguard inspector recorded the following:

[Translation from Russian provided by the Respondent]

During the inspection of holds No 10 and No 11 the inspectors of the State [Sea] Inspection found out that under the upper layer of chum salmon sockeye salmon is kept.

Therefore an offence is detected: substitution of output of one kind (*chum salmon*) with the other kind (*sockeye salmon*) and, thus, concealment of part of sockeye salmon catch in the Exploitation area No 1; misrepresentation of data in a fishing log and daily vessel report (*SSD*).

31.   On 2 June 2007, a protocol of detention was drawn up by an officer of the Frontier Service of the Federal Security Service of the Russian Federation which recorded the detention of the *Hoshinmaru* on the basis of the following reasons:

[Translation from Russian provided by the Respondent]

transmitting of untrue inadequate operational accounts in the form of SSD [daily vessel report], creating in the course of checking a difference between the amount permitted for catching by the license and the actual catch on board, incorrect reflecting of inadequate information on catching in the vessel's logbook, substitution of biological resources species.

* * *

Amount and form of the bond or other financial security

95.   The Tribunal must now determine the amount, nature and form of the bond or other financial security to be posted [by Japan to obtain a release of the *Hoshinmaru* from Russian custody], as laid down in article 113, paragraph 2, of the Rules. In accordance with article 293 of the Convention, the Tribunal must apply the provisions of this Convention and other rules of international law not incompatible with the Convention.

96.   The Tribunal notes that the Respondent considers the offence committed by the Master of the *Hoshinmaru* to be a grave one. The Respondent maintains that the Master of the *Hoshinmaru* had declared 20 tons of raw sockeye salmon as the cheaper chum salmon. If the substitution of the species on the *Hoshinmaru* had not been revealed by the competent authorities of the Russian Federation, the 20 tons of sockeye salmon would simply have been stolen and taken illegally out of the exclusive economic zone of the Russian Federation. This amount of marine living resources could not have been accounted for by the competent bodies of the Russian Federation in exercising control over the percentage of total allowable catch of the species, i.e. sockeye salmon. In the view of the Respondent this was a classic manifestation of illegal,

unreported and unregulated fishing. In the view of the Respondent, the gravity of the offence justifies the bond of 22,000,000 roubles.

97.   The Applicant maintains that the alleged offence is not fishing without a licence or overfishing but falsely recording a catch that the vessel was entitled to take under its licence. Further, the Applicant argues that, since the amount of sockeye salmon on board the *Hoshinmaru* was well within the limit the vessel was licensed to fish, the sockeye salmon stock could not be considered to have been damaged or endangered.

98.   The Tribunal notes that the present case is different from cases it has previously dealt with, since this case does not entail fishing without a licence. The *Hoshinmaru* held a valid fishing licence and was authorized to be present and to fish in the Russian exclusive economic zone. The Tribunal further notes that Russia and Japan cooperate closely in respect of fishing activities in the area in question. They have even established an institutional framework for consultations concerning the management and conservation of fish stocks which also deals with the enforcement of the applicable rules on the management and conservation of fish stocks in the exclusive economic zone of the Russian Federation in the Pacific. They have been cooperating in order to promote the conservation and reproduction of salmon and trout of Russian origin in the exclusive economic zone of the Russian Federation. The Tribunal notes that Japan expresses the wish to continue to endeavour ensuring that the crews of fishing vessels flying its flag respect local laws and regulations.

99.   The offences considered here may be seen as transgressions within a broadly satisfactory cooperative framework. At the same time, the Tribunal is of the view that the offence committed by the Master of the *Hoshinmaru* should not be considered as a minor offence or an offence of a purely technical nature. Monitoring of catches, which requires accurate reporting, is one of the most essential means of managing marine living resources. Not only is it the right of the Russian Federation to apply and implement such measures but the provisions of article 61, paragraph 2, of the Convention should also be taken into consideration to ensure through proper conservation and management measures that the maintenance of the living resources in the exclusive economic zone is not endangered by over-exploitation.

100.   On the basis of these considerations, the Tribunal is of the view that the security should be in the total amount of 10,000,000 roubles. The security should take the form either of a payment made to the bank account indicated by the Respondent, or of a bank guarantee, if the Applicant prefers this alternative.

NOTES

1.   *Prompt Release of Detained Vessel and Crew*. LOS Convention Article 73(1) provides: "The coastal State may, in the exercise of its sovereign rights to explore, exploit, conserve and manage the living resources in the exclusive

economic zone, take such measures, including boarding, inspection, arrest and judicial proceedings, as may be necessary to ensure compliance with the laws and regulations enacted by it in conformity with this Convention." However, LOS Convention Article 73(2) provides: "Arrested vessels and their crews shall be promptly released upon the posting of reasonable bond or other security." Article 292(1) provides that when a detention occurs, and it is alleged that the detaining state has not complied with the prompt release requirement, then the flag state may submit the matter to any court or tribunal agreed upon by the two states or, failing that, to the International Tribunal for the Law of the Sea (ITLOS). The decision on such release is without prejudice to the merits of any case concerning violation of the rules of the detaining state in its maritime jurisdiction. See Article 292(3).

2. *ITLOS Jurisprudence.* Dispute resolution procedures under the LOS Convention are discussed *infra* this chapter in Section 11. For now, it is simply noted that most of the cases handled by ITLOS to date have involved efforts to secure prompt release of vessels and crew that have been detained for fishing or other violations. The ITLOS Rules of Procedure call for the tribunal to determine whether an application for prompt release is well-founded and, if so, to "determine the amount, nature and form of the bond or financial security to be posted for the release of the vessel or the crew." ITLOS Rules of Procedure, art. 113(2), ITLOS Doc. ITLOS/8 (Sept. 28, 2001). In doing so, the Tribunal "considers that a number of factors are relevant in an assessment of the reasonableness of bonds or other financial security. They include the gravity of the alleged offences, the penalties imposed or imposable under the laws of the detaining State, the value of the detained vessel and of the cargo seized, the amount of the bond imposed by the detaining State and its form." See *"Camouco" Case* (Panama v. France), ITLOS Case No. 5, para. 67 (2000). In the *"Monte Confurco" Case*, the Tribunal clarified that this "is by no means a complete list of factors. Nor does the Tribunal intend to lay down rigid rules as to the exact weight to be attached to each of them." *"Monte Confurco"* (Seychelles v. France), ITLOS Case No. 6, para. 109 (2000).

3. *Weighing the Reasonableness of Coastal State Action.* What does it mean for the Tribunal to weigh the "gravity of the alleged offences" when considering the reasonableness of the detaining state's bond requirement and what non-financial conditions might be imposed (such as installation of a satellite tracking device on the detained vessel)? Consider the following statement by a judge appointed *ad hoc* to the Tribunal:

> In the short period since the conclusion of the Convention in 1982, and in the even shorter period since its entry into force in 1994, there have been catastrophic declines in the stocks of many fish species throughout the world. The words "bond" and "financial security" should be given a liberal and purposive interpretation in order to enable the Tribunal to take full account of the measures—including those made possible by modern technology—found necessary by many coastal States (and mandated by regional and sub-regional fisheries organizations) to deter by way of judicial and administrative orders the plundering of the living resources of the sea.

"Volga" Case (Russia v. Australia), ITLOS Case No. 11, para. 17 (2002) (Dissenting Opinion of Judge *ad hoc* Shearer).

4. *Confiscation of a Detained Vessel.* A prompt release case may only be submitted to the Tribunal by the flag state. See, e.g., *"Grand Prince" Case* (Belize v. France), ITLOS Case. No. 8, para. 93 (2001) (finding that "documentary evidence submitted by the Applicant fails to establish that Belize was the flag State of the vessel when the Application was made"). Suppose the detaining state confiscates the vessel (i.e., transfers ownership to itself) before the flag state is able to bring a claim before the Tribunal. Does that confiscation defeat the flag state's ability to present a claim? In the *Juno Trader* case, the Tribunal allowed the claim to proceed, finding that "whatever may be the effect of a definitive change in the ownership of a vessel upon its nationality, the Tribunal considers that there is no legal basis in the particular circumstances of this case for holding that there has been a definitive change in the nationality of the *Juno Trader*." *"Juno Trader" Case* (St. Vincent & The Grenadines v. Guinea–Bissau), ITLOS Case No. 13, para. 63 (2004).

5. *Have Fins, Will Roam.* Different species of fish present different kinds of problems and are hence addressed differently under the LOS Convention. Salmon, the fish at issue in the *"Hoshinmaru" Case*, are anadromous fish, which are fish that live mostly at sea, but ascend rivers to spawn. Other fish, such as European eels, are catadromous fish; they live in freshwater but migrate to the sea to spawn. Hence, these are fish that have a close connection to a coastal state, but that during their lifespan will go to sea and, in doing so, possibly migrate into waters under the jurisdiction of another state. When that happens, conservation of the species may require coordination among two or more states. Other species of fish are likely to stay in EEZs, but to migrate or "straddle" between them, while other highly migratory species are likely to traverse the entire ocean, moving from EEZs out to the highs and back. Hence, the LOS Convention contains special provisions on coastal state regulation of stocks occurring within two or more economic zones (Article 63), highly migratory species (Article 64), anadromous stocks (Article 66), and catadromous species (Article 67). Exploitation of marine mammals is left to regulation by the coastal state (or an international organization) (Article 65). Sedentary species are governed by the regime of the continental shelf (Article 77(4)).

6. *Highly Migratory Species.* Tuna, a commercially valuable fish, is found both on the high seas and in the exclusive economic zones of many states. As a "highly migratory species," it is covered by LOS Convention Article 64, as well as LOS Convention Annex 1. The United States maintains that under Article 64, and under customary law, a coastal state does *not* have exclusive rights over tuna in its exclusive economic zones. The Fishery Conservation and Management Act of 1976, 16 U.S.C. § 1801 et seq. (2000), excludes highly migratory species, such as tuna, but not other migratory species. However, other coastal states have asserted exclusive authority over tuna within their EEZ and have seized U.S. vessels fishing for tuna within their zones without their authorization. In retaliation the United States has imposed embargos on the import of fish from these countries. Several South Pacific island states and Mexico have been seriously affected.

Is it plausible to regard tuna and other highly migratory species as "non-residents" and therefore not a resource of the EEZ? Is the United States correct in construing the obligation to cooperate in LOS Convention Article 64 as precluding exclusive rights of the coastal state in respect of highly migratory species? See Munro, Extended Jurisdiction and the Management of Pacific Highly Migratory Species, 21 Ocean Dev. & Int'l L. 289 (1990); Kelly, The Law of the Sea: The Jurisdictional Dispute Over Highly Migratory Species of Tuna, 26 Colum. J. Transnat'l L. 475 (1988). Assuming that the law recognizes an exclusive right to tuna in the EEZ, is the United States a "persistent objector" entitled to an exception from that principle? Is it relevant that the United States has not asserted an exception in its law for highly migratory species other than tuna? To a certain extent, this issue is now being addressed through regional fisheries agreements. See, e.g., Convention on the Conservation and Management of Highly Migratory Fish Stocks in the Western and Central Pacific Ocean, Sept. 5, 2000, S. Treaty Doc. No. 109–1 (2005), 40 I.L.M. 278 (2001) (agreement covering region from which comes two-thirds of the world's tuna catch).

7. *Marine Scientific Research.* Under the 1958 Conventions, marine scientific research was unrestricted on the high seas but subject to the control of the coastal state in its territorial sea. Research on the continental shelf also required coastal state consent, but the Convention on the Continental Shelf, arts. 5(1) & 5(8), Apr. 29, 1958, 15 U.S.T. 471, 499 U.N.T.S. 311, provided that consent should not normally be withheld. In practice, coastal states withheld their consent despite the latter provision. Some states further restricted research by applying the consent requirement to the superadjacent waters as well.

At UNCLOS III, scientific research was the subject of intense negotiation, with the United States taking the lead in challenging coastal state control both on the continental shelf and in the exclusive economic zone. The LOS Convention does not change the status of research in the territorial sea or on the high seas. (See Article 143 on marine scientific research in the area beyond national jurisdiction, and Part XIII, especially Articles 245, 256–57). As to the EEZ, the United States sought in the negotiations a regime that would not subject research to coastal state constraints. The developing states, however, viewed control of scientific research as crucial for protecting their interests in resources of the EEZ and the continental shelf. The views of the developing states prevailed. Coastal state consent is required for research in the EEZ and on the continental shelf (Article 246). The coastal state shall normally grant consent unless the research falls into certain categories, e.g., is related to resource use (Article 246(5)). See also Article 297(2)(a)(i), whereby the coastal state is not obliged to submit to settlement under Part XV, section 2, disputes arising out of the exercise by the coastal state of its discretion under Article 246 or of its right to suspend research under Article 253. Compare also Article 297(2)(b), providing for conciliation in these two cases. See Wegelein, Marine Scientific Research: The Operation and Status of Research Vessels and Other Platforms in International Law (2005); Gorina–Ysern, An International Regime for Marine Scientific Research (2003).

8. *Success Story?* Should the creation of the LOS Convention regime of EEZs be regarded as a success story in helping preserve global fisheries? What

management regimes have states actually developed to take advantage of their EEZs? Consider the following assessment.

WYMAN, THE PROPERTY RIGHTS CHALLENGE IN MARINE FISHERIES

50 Ariz. L. Rev. 511, 515–20 (2008) (footnotes omitted)

Most commercial fisheries are under national jurisdiction because they are within national EEZs. In many countries, the national or federal government regulates marine fisheries in the EEZ. In contrast, the U.S. regime for regulating EEZ fisheries is heavily regionalized. States regulate wild and farmed fisheries up to and including three nautical miles from the shore. Federal wild fisheries, which are 3–200 miles from the shore, are regulated primarily by regional fishery management councils. Established under the Magnuson–Stevens Fishery Conservation and Management Act, the councils include substantial representation of state interests since many of the councils' voting members are selected by the federal Secretary of Commerce from nominees submitted by state governors. Furthermore, the councils are overseen by a federal agency, the National Marine Fisheries Service ("NMFS"), that itself is heavily regionalized, with offices throughout the country. * * *

* * *

Most countries, including the United States, continue to regulate capture fisheries in their EEZs using conventional management techniques. These include overall catch limits (often called total allowable catches), restrictions on the length of the fishing season and the gear fishers are allowed to use, closed areas, and sometimes limits on the numbers of fishers allowed to fish.

Some countries, however, have also established property rights in wild fisheries. For instance, in some countries inshore fisheries in the territorial sea are the subject of territorial use rights ("TURFs"), which give fishers ownership of the stock of the fish in designated areas. Fish covered by TURFs generally are sedentary species that do not migrate much because these fish can be allocated territorially. An increasing number of countries, including the United States, are establishing ITQs. These are individual rights-based instruments which allocate fishers shares of the allowable catch that they can buy and sell. Migratory fisheries are amenable to individual transferable quotas because, unlike TURFs, ITQs provide exclusive rights to shares of the flow of fish, not to fish in geographically determined areas of the sea.

Many countries also have long-established communally-run fisheries in which community norms often substitute for state regulation. For instance, in Japan, fishing cooperatives—not individuals—have TURF rights to fish in "specific territories extending as far as five and a half miles seaward." The premier example of a communal property regime in United States fisheries, the lobster gangs of Maine, may be slowly giving way to a formal regulatory apparatus established by the state of Maine. Interestingly, there are recent efforts in the U.S. and elsewhere to create new communal regimes to manage fisheries, sometimes from above by government regulators and sometimes from below by fishers. For instance, in Alaska, the Pacific, and New England, fisheries regulators have allocated shares of the total allowable catch of certain species to groups of fishers. Some of these groups have formed cooperatives that in turn allocate the group share among their members, establishing by contract or by custom an individual quota program. Other groups—such as the Native American communities holding community development quotas in Alaska—lease their shares of the total allowable catch to other fishing interests.

Several categories of fisheries remain outside the control of a single state: fisheries that cross the EEZs of more than one country (transboundary fisheries), fisheries that straddle the EEZs of one or more countries and the high seas outside of areas of national jurisdiction (straddling or highly migratory species), and fisheries exclusively on the high seas (discrete high seas fisheries). Many of these fisheries are regulated by regional fisheries management organizations ("RFMOs") established by conventions and dominated by nation states. Currently, 16 RFMOs are authorized "to establish conservation and management measures." Notably, 75% of the high seas are not regulated by any RFMO. The gap in regulation reflects the fact that the high seas account for a relatively small share of world fish catches. Estimates vary, but perhaps 90% of fisheries are in national EEZs, meaning that the high seas account for perhaps only 10% of fisheries.

RFMOs generally are weak and ineffective regulators. RFMOs are governed by commissions comprised of representatives of the countries whose vessels fish the species that the RFMOs regulate. RFMOs tend to operate by setting total allowable catches and then allocating these among their member states in the form of country quotas. Some RFMOs also establish gear and other kinds of restrictions. No RFMO seems to have established individual transferable quotas. RFMOs depend on their member states to enforce their regulations. Nation states may fail to do so, however, because enforcement is too costly, for example because of political pressures from domestic fishing industries to allow higher catch levels. An RFMO also may be hobbled by the refusal of some countries to join even though the countries' vessels are harvesting fisheries the RFMO regulates. Historically there has been an incentive not to join an RFMO because vessels flying the flags of nonparty states are not bound by the RFMO's regulations.

In sum, over two decades after the negotiation of the Law of the Sea Convention, countries have developed a range of approaches for regulating fisheries within and outside of their EEZs. But wild fisheries are declining notwithstanding the governance regimes established in the wake of the Law of the Sea Convention. To date, the regulatory infrastructure countries have built has yet to yield much improvement in the status of fish stocks.

SECTION 7.   THE RIGHT OF HOT PURSUIT

Suppose a foreign vessel present in a state's territorial sea commits a violation of a law or regulation relating to that zone. The coastal state sends a patrol boat to impose a fine or other sanction upon the foreign vessel, but before it can stop and board the vessel, the vessel flees out of the territorial sea. Suppose a similar scenario unfolds with respect to a foreign vessel present in the contiguous zone, the EEZ, or on the continental shelf; a violation of coastal state laws applicable in those zones occurs, but the foreign vessel flees before it can be stopped. Can the coastal patrol boat give chase, even if it means stopping, boarding, and perhaps seizing the foreign vessel on the high seas without the consent of the flag state?

LOS Convention Article 111(1) states:

> The hot pursuit of a foreign ship may be undertaken when the competent authorities of the coastal State have good reason to believe that the ship has violated the laws and regulations of that State. Such pursuit must be commenced when the foreign ship or one of its boats is within the internal waters, the archipelagic waters, the territorial sea or the contiguous zone of the pursuing State, and may only be continued outside the territorial sea or the contiguous zone if the pursuit has not been interrupted. * * * If the foreign ship is within a contiguous zone, as defined in article 33, the pursuit may only be undertaken if there has been a violation of the rights for the protection of which the zone was established.

If a suspected violation occurred in the EEZ or the continental shelf zones with respect to coastal state laws that apply to those zones, Article 111(2) states that the "right of hot pursuit shall apply *mutatis mutandis*" in those zones as well. As for how the pursuit may be conducted, it "may only be commenced after a visual or auditory signal to stop has been given at a distance which enables it to be seen or heard by the foreign ship" (Article 111(4)); it "may be exercised only by warships or military aircraft, or other ships or aircraft clearly marked and identifiable as being on government service and specially authorized to that effect" (Article 111(5)); and it must cease "as soon as the ship pursued enters the territorial sea of its own country or of a third State" (Article 111(3)).

NOTES

1. *To the Ends of the Earth.* The Patagonian toothfish (also known as Chilean sea-bass) is in strong commercial demand, yet is endangered because it is a slow-growing deep sea species. Vessels can be licensed to catch the Patagonian toothfish pursuant to the regime set up under the Convention on the Conservation of Antarctic Marine Living Resources, May 20, 1980, 33 U.S.T. 3476, 1329 U.N.T.S. 47 (CCAMLR), yet there are many vessels illegally

doing so. In August 2003, Australian patrol boats detected a Uruguayan-flagged vessel named the *Viarsa 1* illegally catching Patagonian toothfish in the Australian EEZ. The *Viarsa 1* fled and was pursued by Australian patrol boats more than 3,900 nautical miles—one of the longest "hot pursuits" in maritime history. The pursuit, which lasted twenty-one days, only ended with the detention of the *Viarsa 1* in the South Atlantic, off the coast of South Africa. The vessel was seized and brought back to Australia, where the crew was tried and civil proceedings were brought against the vessel. See Knecht, Hooked: Pirates, Poaching, and the Perfect Fish (2006).

2. *Application in the Contiguous Zone.* Is it clear from Article 111 how the right of "hot pursuit" relates to a coastal state's rights in the contiguous zone? See generally Allen, Doctrine of Hot Pursuit: A Functional Interpretation Adaptable to Emerging Maritime Law Enforcement Technology and Practices, 20 Ocean Dev. & Int'l L. 309 (1989).

3. *U.S. Hot Pursuit.* Though not a party to the LOS Convention, U.S. courts have upheld the right of hot pursuit by U.S. patrol boats. In *United States v. F/V Taiyo Maru*, 395 F.Supp. 413 (D. Me. 1975), the U.S. district court upheld the right of hot pursuit from the U.S. contiguous fisheries zone. The court decided that Articles 23 and 24 of the 1958 Convention on the High Seas do not forbid a coastal state from establishing a contiguous fisheries zone (up to twelve miles), nor from conducting hot pursuit from such a zone. See Ciobanu, Hot Pursuit From a Fisheries Zone: A Further Comment on United States v. Fishing Vessel Taiyo Maru No. 28; United States v. Kawaguchi, 70 A.J.I.L. 549 (1976); Fidell, Hot Pursuit from a Fisheries Zone, 70 A.J.I.L. 95 (1976).

4. *Further Reading.* See Poulantzas, The Right of Hot Pursuit in International Law (2d ed. 2002); Gilmore, Hot Pursuit: The Case of R. v. Mills and Others, 44 I.C.L.Q. 949 (1995); Korolera, The Right to Hot Pursuit from the Exclusive Economic Zone, 14 Mar. Pol'y 137 (1990).

SECTION 8. THE HIGH SEAS

A. THE BASIC FREEDOMS

Once, all the seas were governed by a regime characterized by principles of commonage and freedom. The emergence of the concept of the territorial sea, followed by other special zones and privileges for coastal states, reduced the areas subject to that regime (now distinctively called the "high seas") and created additional exceptions to its principles of commonage and freedom. Under the LOS Convention, the extent of the "high seas" is reduced further still, such as by recognition of archipelagic states, emergence of the exclusive economic zone, new regimes for pollution control and scientific research, and solidification of a continental shelf regime that can extend even beyond the 200 nautical miles (hence, "underneath" the high seas). Subject to these limitations, the regime of the high seas continues to be characterized by commonage and freedom, though further limitations, such as relating to mining of the deep seabed, have also emerged.

LOS Convention Article 86 states that Part VII of the Convention on "High Seas" applies to "all parts of the sea that are not included in the exclusive economic zone, in the territorial sea or in the internal waters of a State, or in the archipelagic waters of an archipelagic State," but does not impair "the freedoms enjoyed by all States in the exclusive economic zone." Article 87(1) then states that the "high seas are open to all States, whether coastal or land-locked," for the "[f]reedom of the high seas," which comprises, *inter alia*, the following: (a) freedom of navigation; (b) freedom of overflight; (c) freedom to lay submarine cables and pipelines; (d) freedom to construct artificial islands and other installations permitted under international law; (e) freedom of fishing; and (f) freedom of scientific research. Such freedoms are to be exercised "with due regard for the interests of other States." LOS Convention, art. 87(2).

The freedom to fish is the oldest freedom of the sea and remains an essential freedom in the regime of the high seas. LOS Convention Article 116 confirms the freedom of fishing for all states and their nationals, but also recognizes the need to regulate and conserve living marine resources. Article 117 provides: "All States have the duty to take, or to co-operate with other States in taking, such measures for their respective nationals as may be necessary for the conservation of the living resources of the high seas." Article 118 provides, in part, that: "States whose nationals exploit identical living resources, or different living resources in the same area, shall enter into negotiations with a view to taking the measures necessary for the conservation of the living resources concerned. They shall, as appropriate, co-operate to establish subregional or regional fisheries organizations to this end."

Because the LOS Convention contains only these very general provisions on the conservation of fish stocks in the high seas, two avenues of further regulation exist. First, there are some global agreements or codes of conduct on fishing that both pre-date and post-date the LOS Convention. For example, the International Convention for the Regulation of Whaling (ICRW), Dec. 2, 1946, 62 Stat. 1716, 161 U.N.T.S. 72, established a schedule of regulations that lists particular species covered by the ICRW, as well as the controls on each of those species, and created an International Whaling Commission (IWC). In 1982, the IWC voted to amend the schedule in order to phase out commercial whaling, leading to a complete moratorium in 1986—except for aboriginal whaling and scientific research. For a comprehensive review of the law and politics of international whaling, see Gillespie, Whaling Diplomacy (2005).

Important conventions post-dating the adoption of the LOS Convention include the Agreement to Promote Compliance with International Conservation and Management Measures by Fishing Vessels on the High Seas, Nov. 24, 1993, S. Treaty Doc. No. 103–24 (1994), 2221 U.N.T.S. 91 (also known as the FAO Compliance Agreement) and the Agreement for the Implementation of the Provisions of the United Nations Convention on the Law of the Sea of 10 December 1982 Relating to the Conservation and Management of Straddling Fish Stocks, Aug. 4, 1995, 2167 U.N.T.S. 3,

34 I.L.M. 1542 (1995) (Straddling Fish Stocks Convention). The Straddling Fish Stocks Convention promotes compatibility between conservation and management measures established for the high seas and those adopted by coastal states in their areas of national jurisdiction. Further, it requires also that regional cooperation measures be observed by all states parties. Some non-binding instruments also help encourage responsible high seas fishing, such as the FAO Code of Conduct for Responsible Fisheries, (1995), http://www.fao.org/DOCREP/005/v9878e/v9878e00.htm, and in the International Plan of Action to Prevent, Deter and Eliminate Illegal, Unreported and Unregulated Fishing (IPOA–IUU), (2001), http://www.fao.org/DOCREP/003/y1224e/y1224e00.htm.

Second, about forty regional fishery organizations have been established by treaty, including the Northwest Atlantic Fisheries Organization (NAFO); the International Commission for the Conservation of Alaska Tunas (ICCAT); Inter–American Tropical Tuna Commission (IATTC); the North Pacific Anadromous Fish Commission (NPAFC); and the Commission for the Conservation of Antarctic Living Marine Resources (CCALMR). The exact powers and responsibilities of these organizations vary, but they encompass a process for establishing an appropriate amount of fish to be harvested on the high seas in that region and allocate to each state an equitable portion of that amount. See Internet Guide to International Fisheries Law, http://www.intfish.net/netpath/page1–rfo.htm.

NOTES

1. *Driftnets.* Starting in the late 1980s, the use of "driftnets" by some East Asian countries in the South Pacific, such as Japan and the Republic of Korea, caused controversy. Driftnets are gillnets or other combinations of nets that can stretch as much as forty kilometers in length. Many states charged that the use of driftnets seriously depletes stocks of commercial fish and indiscriminately traps and kills porpoises, seabirds, and a wide variety of fish not sought by fishermen. International efforts to ban the use of driftnets in the South Pacific resulted in the Convention for the Prohibition of Fishing with Long Driftnets in the South Pacific, Nov. 24, 1989, S. Treaty Doc. No. 102–7 (1991), 1899 U.N.T.S. 3, (also known as the Wellington Convention). The convention requires state parties to prohibit their nationals from engaging in driftnet fishing in the South Pacific. Id. art. 3(1)(a). Further, state parties "must also undertake measures consistent with international law against other driftnet fishing activities within the Convention area, including * * * the transhipment of driftnet catches." Id. art. 3(1)(b); see Hewison, The Convention for the Prohibition of Fishing With Long Driftnets in the South Pacific 25 Case W. Res. J. Int'l L. 449 (1993). Thereafter, the General Assembly adopted a resolution recommending a global moratorium on all highs seas use of driftnets. See G.A. Res. 44/225 (Dec. 22, 1989). Many states, under their national laws, have either prohibited or heavily regulated driftnet fishing. See, e.g., 16 U.S.C. § 1826(c) (2000) ("It is declared to be the policy of the Congress in this section that the United States should implement the

moratorium called for by the United Nations General Assembly in Resolution Numbered 44–225; * * * and secure a permanent ban on the use of destructive fishing practices, and in particular large-scale driftnets, by persons or vessels fishing beyond the exclusive economic zone of any nation'').

2. *National Regulation of High Seas Fishing?* On March 9, 1995, Canadian coast guard authorities boarded and seized on the high seas the fishing vessel *Estai*, which was flying the flag of Spain, as a means of enforcing regulations promulgated under Canada's Coastal Fisheries Protection Act. Spain maintained that such action constituted an unlawful exercise of national jurisdiction over a ship flying a foreign flag on the high seas, outside the exclusive economic zone of Canada. After Spain sued Canada at the International Court of Justice, the Court decided that it lacked jurisdiction over the dispute, since Canada's acceptance of the Court's compulsory jurisdiction expressly excluded disputes arising from "conservation and management measures." See *Fisheries Jurisdiction Case* (Spain v. Canada), 1998 I.C.J. 432, 439. If the Court had found jurisdiction over the case, which state do you think had the better position on the merits? For the perspective of the Director of the U.N. Legal Affairs Office's Division on Ocean Affairs and Law of the Sea, see Hayashi, Enforcement by Non–Flag States on the High Seas Under the 1995 Agreement on Straddling and Highly Migratory Fish Stocks, 9 Geo. Int'l Envtl. L. Rev. 1 (1996). While the case was pending, Canada and the European Community signed an Agreed Minute on the Conservation and Management of Fish Stocks, which resolved some (but not all) of the underlying dispute. See Oxman, International Decisions, Fisheries Jurisdiction, 93 A.J.I.L. 502, 505 (1999).

3. *Problems with Fishing Dispute Settlement.* The Spain/Canada case highlights the difficulty in resolving fisheries disputes through international courts or tribunals. Although the LOS Convention now establishes a process for compulsory dispute settlement, it is still the case that jurisdiction might be defeated when a fishing dispute arises, even as among parties to the LOS Convention. For example, in the late 1990s, a dispute arose between Australia and New Zealand on one side and Japan on the other (all parties to the LOS Convention), concerning the conservation of the population of southern bluefin tuna. To address a request for immediate and provisional measures of protection, the matter was placed before the International Tribunal for the Law of the Sea (ITLOS). In August 1999, ITLOS issued several provisional orders to prevent damage to joint fisheries. The Tribunal noted that there was no disagreement between the parties that the stock of southern bluefin tuna was severely depleted. It recognized that there is scientific uncertainty regarding measures to be taken to conserve the stock, but considered that, in the circumstances, the parties should act prudently and cautiously to ensure that serious harm to the stock of southern bluefin tuna is prevented. The Tribunal ordered that the parties ensure that their annual catches did not exceed the levels to which they had last agreed, and that the parties refrain from conducting an experimental fishing program until the dispute was arbitrated. See *Southern Bluefin Tuna Cases* (New Zealand v. Japan; Australia v. Japan), ITLOS Cases Nos. 3 and 4, Order on Provisional Measures (Aug. 27, 1999). Yet when the case was placed before an arbitral tribunal constituted under the LOS Convention to address jurisdiction and the merits, the arbitral

tribunal dismissed the case for lack of jurisdiction and vacated the provisional measures. The arbitral tribunal essentially found that, while the LOS Convention created a compulsory dispute settlement process, it also allowed states to craft their own preference for dispute settlement, and that in the relevant agreement relating to southern bluefin tuna, these states had opted for a process that was not compulsory in nature. See Morgan, Implications of the Proliferation of International Legal Fora: The Example of the Southern Bluefin Tuna Cases, 43 Harv. Int'l L.J. 541 (2002); Oxman, Complementary Agreements and Compulsory Jurisdiction, 95 A.J.I.L. 277 (2001); see also Chapter 9, Section 5(A).

4. *Further Reading.* See Carr & Scheiber, Dealing with a Resource Crisis: Regulatory Regimes for Managing the World's Marine Fisheries, 21 Stan. Envtl. L.J. 45 (2002); Stokke, Governing High Seas Fisheries: The Interplay of Global and Regional Regimes (2001); Orrego Vicuña, The Changing International Law of High Seas Fisheries (1999).

B. LIMITATIONS ON HIGH SEAS FREEDOMS

Freedom of navigation on the high seas normally provides that vessels of one state may not stop, board, or otherwise interfere with vessels flagged to another state, absent consent from that other state. Only in very limited circumstances could such action be taken in the absence of consent. LOS Convention Article 110(1) says that a "warship" of a state may board a foreign vessel, provided that vessel is not otherwise immune (such as vessels owned or operated by a foreign government), and provided there is reasonable ground for suspecting that the foreign vessel: (a) is engaged in piracy; (b) is engaged in the slave trade; (c) is engaged in unauthorized broadcasting; (d) is without nationality; or (e) is, despite flying a foreign flag or no flag, of the same nationality as the warship. The following materials explore these bases for enforcement action on the high seas.

1. Consent to Board

Consent by the foreign state to the stopping and boarding of one of its flagged vessels on the high seas might be given *ad hoc*, at the time that the vessel is identified. See, e.g., *United States v. Cardales*, 168 F.3d 548 (1st Cir. 1999) (U.S. interception of narcotics trafficker after obtaining consent from Venezuelan government). Some states, such as the United States, have developed speedy channels of communications with certain countries to obtain consent in "real time," with U.S. coast guard vessels keeping the suspected vessel in sight until consent is communicated. Yet it is also possible to negotiate bilateral or multilateral agreements or arrangements by which consent is granted in advance under certain conditions, perhaps providing simply that notification be given to the flag state and that no objection is made by the flag state for a certain period of time before the boarding can occur.

Suppose you are a government official and you want to promote the ability of your coast guard to stop and board vessels on the high seas that

you think are engaged in narcotics smuggling, smuggling of illegal immi-
grants, or even the transport of weapons of mass destruction (WMD).
What strategy would you follow to try to maximize your ability to address
those problems, staying within the confines of international law? In May
2003, President George W. Bush launched a "proliferation security initiative" (PSI) designed to promote cooperation among states on the interdiction of shipments of WMD, their delivery systems, and related materials,
whether on land, at sea, or in the air. That program, in turn, has led to
the conclusion by the United States in recent years of a series of bilateral
agreements with various states, including those that are very liberal in
allowing vessels to fly their flags (known as "flags of convenience"). How
should such agreements be crafted so as to achieve U.S. policy objectives,
while still respecting the core rights of the flag state? See Hodgkinson et
al., Challenges to Maritime Interception Operations in the War on Terror:
Bridging the Gap, 22 Am. U. Int'l L. Rev. 583 (2007); Shulman, The
Proliferation Security Initiative and the Evolution of the Law on the Use
of Force, 28 Houston J. Int'l L. 771 (2006); Joyner, The Proliferation
Security Initiative: Nonproliferation, Counterproliferation, and Interna-
tional Law, 30 Yale J. Int'l L. 507 (2005); Becker, The Shifting Public
Order of the Ocean: Freedom of Navigation and Interdiction of Ships at
Sea, 46 Harv. Int'l L.J. 131 (2005); Byers, Policing the High Seas: The
Proliferation Security Initiative, 98 A.J.I.L. 526 (2004).

AGREEMENT CONCERNING COOPERATION TO SUPPRESS THE PROLIFERATION OF WEAPONS OF MASS DESTRUCTION, THEIR DELIVERY SYSTEMS, AND RELATED MATERIALS BY SEA (UNITED STATES–LIBERIA)

Signed Feb. 11, 2004, entered into force Dec. 9, 2004
Available at http://www.state.gov/t/isn/trty/32403.htm

Article 1

Definitions

In this Agreement, unless the context otherwise requires:

1.   "Proliferation by sea" means the transportation by ship of weapons of mass destruction, their delivery systems, and related materials to or
from States or non-state actors of proliferation concern.

2.   "Weapons of mass destruction" (WMD) means nuclear, chemical,
biological and radiological weapons.

3.   "Related materials" means materials, equipment and technology,
of whatever nature or type, that are related to and destined for use in the
development, production, utilization or delivery of WMD.

* * *

6.   "Security Force Officials" means:

a. for the United States, uniformed or otherwise clearly identifiable members of the United States Coast Guard and the United States Navy, who may be accompanied by clearly identifiable law enforcement officials of the Departments of Homeland Security and Justice, and other clearly identifiable officials duly authorized by the Government of the United States of America and notified to the Competent Authority of the Republic of Liberia; and

b. for Liberia, uniformed or otherwise clearly identifiable members of the armed forces or law enforcement authorities of Liberia, duly authorized by the Government of the Republic of Liberia and notified to the Competent Authority of the United States.

* * *

8. "Suspect vessel" means a vessel used for commercial or private purposes in respect of which there are reasonable grounds to suspect it is engaged in proliferation by sea.

9. "International waters" means all parts of the sea not included in the territorial sea, internal waters and archipelagic waters of a State, consistent with international law.

10. "Competent Authority" means for the United States, the Commandant of the United States Coast Guard (including any officer designated by the Commandant to perform such functions), and for Liberia, the Agent of the Commissioner of Maritime Affairs appointed under section 13 of Title 21 (the Maritime Law) of the Laws of the Republic of Liberia.

* * *

Article 4

Operations in International Waters

1. *Authority to Board Suspect Ships.* Whenever the Security Force Officials of one Party ("the requesting Party") encounter a suspect vessel claiming nationality in the other Party ("the requested Party") located seaward of any State's territorial sea, the requesting Party may request through the Competent Authority of the requested Party that it:

a. confirm the claim of nationality of the suspect ship; and

b. if such claim is confirmed:

i. authorize the boarding and search of the suspect ship, cargo and the persons found on board by Security Force Officials of the requesting Party; and

ii. if evidence of proliferation is found, authorize the Security Force Officials of the requesting Party to detain the vessel, as well as items and persons on board, pending instructions conveyed through the Competent Authority of the requested Party as to the actions the requesting Party is permitted to take concerning such items, persons and vessels.

2. *Contents of Requests.* Each request should contain the name of the suspect vessel, the basis for the suspicion, the geographic position of the vessel, the IMO number if available, the homeport, the port of origin and destination, and any other identifying information. If a request is conveyed orally, the requesting Party shall confirm the request in writing by facsimile or e-mail as soon as possible. The requested Party shall acknowledge to the Competent Authority of the requesting Party in writing by e-mail or facsimile its receipt of any written or oral request immediately upon receiving it.

3. *Responding to Requests.*

a. If the nationality is verified, the requested Party may:

    i.   decide to conduct the boarding and search with its own Security Force Officials;

    ii. authorize the boarding and search by the Security Force Officials of the requesting Party;

    iii. decide to conduct the boarding and search together with the requesting Party; or

    iv. deny permission to board and search.

b. The requested Party shall answer through its Competent Authority requests made for the verification of nationality within two hours of its acknowledgment of the receipt of such requests.

c. If the nationality is not verified within the two hours, the requested Party may, through its Competent Authority:

    i. nevertheless authorize the boarding and search by the Security Force Officials of the requesting Party; or

    ii. refute the claim of the suspect vessel to its nationality.

d. If there is no response from the Competent Authority of the requested Party within two hours of its acknowledgment of receipt of the request, the requesting Party will be deemed to have been authorized to board the suspect vessel for the purpose of inspecting the vessel's documents, questioning the persons on board, and searching the vessel to determine if it is engaged in proliferation by sea.

2. Suppression of Piracy

Piracy is one of the bases under LOS Convention Article 110(1) for which a state may board and visit a vessel on the high seas, even without the consent of the flag state. As Hackworth noted in the years leading up to codification of the law of the sea: "It has long been recognized and well settled that persons and vessels engaged in piratical operations on the high seas are entitled to the protection of no nation and may be punished by any nation that may apprehend or capture them. This stern rule of international law refers to piracy in its international-law sense and not to a variety of lesser maritime offenses so designated by municipal law." 2 Hackworth at 681. Indeed, piracy was a key problem identified by the framers of the U.S. Constitution, when they crafted the clause empowering Congress to "define and punish Piracies and Felonies committed on the high Seas, and Offences against the Law of Nations." U.S. Const. art. I, § 8, cl. 10.

LOS Convention Article 100 provides: "All States shall co-operate to the fullest possible extent in the repression of piracy on the high seas or in any other place outside the jurisdiction of any State." Piracy is defined in Article 101(a) as consisting of any "illegal acts of violence, detention or any act of depredation, committed for private ends by the crew or the passengers of a private ship or a private aircraft, and directed * * * against another ship or aircraft, or against persons or property on board such ship or aircraft," either on the high seas or in a place outside the jurisdiction of any state. When a pirate ship or aircraft is identified, the state may seize it and arrest the persons on board, and its courts may decide upon the penalties to be imposed. See LOS Convention, art. 105; see also Rubin, The Law of Piracy (2d ed. 1998); McWhinney, Aerial Piracy and International Terrorism: The Illegal Diversion of Aircraft and International Law (2d rev. ed. 1987).

An increasing number of cases of piracy have been reported in recent years in the waters of Southeast Asia and Africa. In Southeast Asia, a variety of incidents have occurred in the Gulf of Thailand, the Malacca Straits, and the Sulu and Celebes Seas. See Johnson, Piracy in Southeast Asia: Status, Issues, and Responses (2005). In Africa, many incidents of piracy have occurred in recent years off the coasts of Nigeria and Somalia. For instance, during 2008, "Somali pirates plying the Gulf of Aden in speedboats equipped with grenade launchers and scaling ladders have launched what the maritime industry calls the biggest surge of piracy in modern times, sending shipping costs soaring and the world's navies scrambling to protect the main water route from Asia and the Middle East to Europe." Knickmeyer, On a Vital Route, a Boom in Piracy, Wash. Post, Sept. 27, 2008, at A1. In response, the U.N. Security Council authorized those states cooperating with the Somali Transitional Federal Government (TFG), upon advance notice, to "enter the territorial waters of Somalia for the purpose of repressing acts of piracy and armed robbery at sea" and to use "all necessary means to repress acts of piracy and armed robbery." S.C. Res. 1816, para. 7 (June 2, 2008). After pirates hijacked a Ukrainian vessel containing weapons (such as tanks) almost 200 miles off the coast of Somalia and then demanded a $20 million ransom, the Security Council called upon U.N. member states "whose naval vessels and military aircraft operate on the high seas and airspace off the coast of Somalia to use * * * the necessary means, in conformity with international law, as reflected in the [LOS] Convention, for the repression of acts of piracy in a manner consistent with the 1982 United Nations Convention on the Law of the Sea." S.C. Res. 1838, para. 3 (Oct. 7, 2008). Moreover, in light of a request received from the TFG, the Security Council decided that states may even take action in Somalia territory and airspace to suproos piracy. See S.C. Res. 1851, pmbl. & para. 6 (Dec. 16, 2008). For an overview of the piracy phenomenon, see Burnett, Dangerous Waters. Modern Piracy and Terror on the High Seas (2002).

3. Suppression of Unauthorized Broadcasting

Suppression of unauthorized broadcasting is also one of the bases under LOS Convention Article 110(1) for which a state may board and visit a vessel on the high seas, even without the consent of the flag state. In the late 1950s, a number of unauthorized radio and television stations operated in international waters in the North, Baltic, and Irish Seas. These stations, situated on fixed platforms or on ships flying foreign "flags of convenience," were a multiple source of irritation to the governments of the coastal states to which their broadcasts were directed: they used unauthorized wave lengths, evaded the payment of royalties due to holders of copyright on the material used (largely popular music), evaded income and other taxes, and either broke the monopoly of the coastal state's government on broadcasting or violated its prohibition on commercial broadcasting.

In 1962, Belgium and the four continental Scandinavian countries enacted legislation directed at nationals of those states engaged in or assisting offshore broadcasting. See Hunnings, Pirate Broadcasting in European Waters, 14 I.C.L.Q. 410, 417–21 (1965). In view of the insufficiency of such laws to deal with stations owned and manned by foreigners, and because of the reluctance of some states to take direct unilateral action against stations operating off their shores, the Council of Europe adopted a convention intended to deal with the problem. In brief, the European Agreement for the Prevention of Broadcasts Transmitted from Stations Outside National Territories, Jan. 22, 1965, E.T.S. No. 53, requires contracting states to make punishable under domestic law the operation of, or collaboration with, unauthorized broadcasting stations located outside national territories, and to apply such legislation to nationals and to foreigners otherwise within their jurisdiction. The Agreement applies only to stations situated "on board ships, aircraft, or any other floating or airborne objects" and thus does not cover stations installed on fixed platforms; it expressly provided, however, that nothing in the agreement prevents a party from applying the provisions thereof to such platforms. Id. art. 1.

LOS Convention Article 109 provides that: "All States shall cooperate in the suppression of unauthorized broadcasting from the high seas," which it defines as "the transmission of sound radio or television broadcasts from a ship or installation on the high seas intended for reception by the general public contrary to international regulations, but excluding the transmission of distress calls." Further, Article 109 states that a person engaged in such broadcasting may be prosecuted before courts of: "(a) the flag State of the ship; (b) the State of registry of the installation; (c) the State of which the person is a national; (d) any State where the transmissions can be received; or (e) any State where authorized radio communication is suffering interference." Any state whose courts have jurisdiction is authorized, on the high seas, to "arrest any person or ship engaged in unauthorized broadcasting and seize the broadcasting apparatus." See generally Robertson, The Suppression of Pirate Radio Broadcasting: A Test Case of the International System for Control of Activities outside National Territory, 45 L. & Contemp. Probs. 71 (Winter 1982).

4. Suppression of Smuggling of Persons

Suppression of smuggling of persons is *not* one of the bases under LOS Convention Article 110(1) for which a state may board and visit a vessel on the high seas. In 1981, President Reagan issued a proclamation addressing "the continuing problem of migrants coming to the United States, by sea, without necessary entry documents * * *." The Proclamation instructed the Secretary of State "to enter into, on behalf of the United States, cooperative arrangements with appropriate foreign governments for the purpose of preventing illegal migration to the United States by sea." The Coast Guard was to be instructed to "enforce the suspension of the entry of undocumented aliens and the interdiction of any vessel carrying such aliens in waters beyond the territorial sea of the United States." The order applied to vessels of the United States, vessels without nationality, and vessels of foreign nations with whom the United States has entered into arrangements authorizing the United States to stop and board such vessels. The Attorney General, in consultation with other departments, was instructed to "take whatever steps are necessary to ensure the fair enforcement of our laws relating to immigration" and "the strict observance of our international obligations concerning those who genuinely flee persecution in their homeland." High Seas Interdiction of Illegal Aliens, Presidential Proclamation No. 4865, 46 Fed. Reg. 48,107 (Sept. 29, 1981), reprinted at 8 U.S.C. § 1182.

By an exchange of letters the week before the proclamation issued, the United States entered into a cooperative arrangement with the government of Haiti. In effect, the parties agreed that the United States may do what the President's Proclamation instructed the Coast Guard to do, including to board Haitian vessels, investigate, detain the vessel and the persons aboard it, and return the vessel and the persons aboard it to Haiti. Challenges to the program on the ground that it violated the obligations of the United States under the Protocol to the Refugee Convention, and the rights of individuals under the U.S. Constitution and laws, were rejected in *Haitian Refugee Center, Inc. v. Gracey*, 600 F. Supp. 1396 (D.D.C. 1985), aff'd, 809 F.2d 794 (D.C.Cir. 1987).

The United States policy of interdiction on the high seas was continued after the Haitian government was overthrown by military coup in 1991 and a large number of Haitians attempted to seek asylum in the United States. On May 24, 1992, President Bush issued Executive Order 12807 requiring the Coast Guard to "enforce the suspension of entry of undocumented aliens by sea and the interdiction of any defined vessel carrying such aliens" in waters "beyond the territorial sea of the United

States." Interdiction of Illegal Aliens, Ex. Order 12807, §§ 2(a) and 2(d), 57 Fed. Reg. 23,133 (May 24, 1992). Pursuant to that order, the Coast Guard intercepted boatloads of Haitian asylum seekers and returned them to Haiti without making a determination as to whether they were refugees under Article 33 of the Refugee Convention. See Chapter 13, Section 4(D) for discussion of *Sale v. Haitian Centers Council*, 509 U.S. 155 (1993), which rejected the Haitians' challenges to the interdiction program.

Does international law permit the United States to protect against illegal immigration by boarding any vessels on the high seas suspected of smuggling persons? Can the United States establish a ring of military vessels on the high seas to keep vessels suspected of carrying asylum seekers from leaving their home state's territorial waters or from entering U.S. territorial waters? For one recent case, see *United States v. de León*, 270 F.3d 90 (1st Cir. 2001) (finding that coast guard interception outside the U.S. contiguous zone was permissible in a situation where the defendant had previously been deported from the United States as an aggravated felon and had not been given permission to return).

C. MILITARY USES OF THE HIGH SEAS

The seas have never been far from military strategy and planning and from concern for national security in war, and even in peace. With advancing technology, the seas became a locus also for new weapons and new uses. Even during the Cold War, the antagonists were concerned to seek advantage and support in international law, in customary law or in applicable treaties; they were also willing to explore the possibility of agreement on arms control, even on some disarmament. To what purposes today do military forces seek to use the seas? Does the LOS Convention advance or hinder those purposes?

TESTIMONY OF U.S. DEPUTY SECRETARY OF DEFENSE GORDON ENGLAND BEFORE THE SENATE FOREIGN RELATIONS COMMITTEE ON U.S. ACCESSION TO THE LAW OF THE SEA CONVENTION

The U.N. Convention on the Law of the Sea: Hearing on S. Treaty Doc. No. 103–39
Before the S. Comm. on Foreign Relations, 110th Cong. (2007)
Available at http://www.senate.gov/?foreign/testimony/2007/EnglandTestimony070927.pdf

As the world's foremost maritime power, our security interests are intrinsically linked to freedom of navigation. America has more to gain from legal certainty and public order in the world's oceans than any other country. By joining the Convention, we provide the firmest possible legal foundation for the rights and freedoms needed to project power, reassure friends and deter adversaries, respond to crises, sustain combat forces in the field, and secure sea and air lines of communication that underpin international trade and our own economic prosperity. Specifically, the legal foundation of this Convention:

- Defines the Right of Innocent Passage, whereby ships may continuously and expeditiously transit the territorial seas of foreign States without having to provide advance notification or seek permission from such States.

- Establishes the Right of Transit Passage through, under, and over international straits and the approaches to those straits. This right, which may not be suspended, hampered or infringed upon by coastal States, is absolutely critical to our national security. This is the right that underpins free transit through the critical choke-points of the world, such as the Strait of Hormuz, the Straits of Singapore and Malacca, and the Strait of Gibraltar.

- Establishes the Right of Archipelagic Sealane Passage, which, like Transit Passage, helps ensure free transit through, under, and over the sealanes of archipelagic nations, such as Indonesia.

- Secures the right to exercise High Seas Freedoms in exclusive economic zones, the 200 nautical mile-wide bands of ocean off coastal shores. The Department's ability to position, patrol, and operate forces freely in, below, and above those littoral waters is critical to our national security.

- Secures the right of U.S. warships, including Coast Guard cutters, to board stateless vessels on the high seas, which is a critically important element of maritime security operations, counter-narcotic operations, and anti-proliferation efforts, including the Proliferation Security Initiative.

If the United States is not a Party to the Convention, then our current legal position is reduced to President Reagan's oceans policy statement of March 1983 and several 1958 Conventions on the seas that remain in force but are, in our judgment, no longer adequate. President Reagan accepted that the navigation and overflight provisions of the Convention—as well as those relating to other traditional uses of the oceans—reflected customary international law and state practice. Further, President Reagan directed the United States Government to adhere to those provisions of the Convention while he, and successive Presidents, worked to fix the Deep Seabed Mining provisions of the Convention.

* * *

Although reliance on customary international law has been relatively effective for us as an interim measure, neither customary international law nor the 1958 Conventions are adequate in the long-term. U.S. assertions of rights under customary international law carry less weight to States than do binding treaty obligations. By its very nature, customary international law is less certain than convention law, as it is subject to the influence of changing State practice. In addition, the 1958 Conventions are inadequate for many reasons, including their failure to establish a fixed limit to the breadth of territorial seas, silence regarding transit passage and archipelagic sea lanes passage, and absence of well-defined limits on the jurisdictional reach of coastal states in waters we now recognize as exclusive economic zones. If the United States remains outside the Convention, it will not be best positioned to interpret, apply, and protect the rights and freedoms contained in the Convention.

* * *

* * * Critics of the Convention argue that an international tribunal will have jurisdiction over our Navy and that our intelligence and counter-proliferation activities will be adversely affected. In the judgment of the Department, these concerns have been more than adequately addressed within the terms of the Convention.

- Our intelligence activities will not be hampered by the Convention. * * *.

- The Senate can ensure that international tribunals do not gain jurisdiction over our military activities when we join this Convention. In 2003, the Administration worked closely with the Committee [on Foreign Relations] to develop a proposed Resolution of Advice and Consent—which we continue to support—that contains a declaration regarding choice of procedure for dispute resolution. The United States rejected the International Court of Justice and the International Tribunal for the Law of the Sea and instead chose arbitration. That choice-of-procedure election is expressly provided for in the Convention itself. In addition, and again in accordance with the express terms of the Convention, the draft Resolution of Advice and Consent completely removes our military activities from the dispute resolution process. Furthermore, each State Party, including the United States, has the exclusive right to determine which of its activities constitutes a military activity, and that determination is not subject to review.

- Regarding our counter-proliferation efforts, which include interdiction activities at sea and in international airspace, * * * not only does the Convention enhance our interdiction authorities, but not joining the Convention is detrimental to our efforts to expand the number of countries that support the Proliferation Security Initiative.

- And, as all recognize, this Convention does not affect the United States' inherent right and obligation of self defense. Further, * * * joining the Convention gives us the opportunity to extend our sovereign rights dramatically and advance our energy security interests by maximizing legal certainty and international recognition for our extended continental shelf off Alaska and elsewhere.

* * * President Bush, Secretary Gates, the Joint Chiefs of Staff, the Military Department Secretaries, the Combatant Commanders, the Commandant of the Coast Guard and I urge the Committee to give its approval for U.S. accession to the Law of the Sea Convention and ratification of the 1994 Agreement [altering the deep sea-bed mining regime]. The United States needs to join the Law of the Sea Convention, and join it now, to take full advantage of the many benefits it offers, to mitigate the increas-

ing costs of being on the outside, and to support the global mobility of our armed forces and the sustainment of our combat forces overseas.

NOTES

1. *Testing Weapons at Sea.* The testing of nuclear weapons on the high seas during the Cold War gave rise to substantial debate. In 1963, the United Kingdom, the United States, the Soviet Union, and others adhered to the Treaty Banning Nuclear Weapon Tests in the Atmosphere, in Outer Space and Under Water, Aug. 5, 1953, 14 U.S.T. 1313, 480 U.N.T.S. 43; see also the Treaty on the Prohibition of the Emplacement of Nuclear Weapons and Other Weapons of Mass Destruction on the Seabed and the Ocean Floor and in the Subsoil Thereof, Feb. 11, 1971, 23 U.S.T. 701, 955 U.N.T.S. 115. Can states test other types of weapons on the high seas? Note that LOS Convention Article 88 provides that the "high seas shall be reserved for peaceful purposes." What about testing of military equipment, such as long-range sonar on the high seas; does that run afoul of LOS Convention Article 88? At present, efforts to stop such testing have not focused on their non-peaceable nature but, rather, on alleged harm caused to marine mammals. See Winter v. Natural Res. Def. Council 129 S.Ct. 365 (2008) (finding that the public interest in conducting naval training exercises, for national security, outweighed even irreparable harm to marine life.).

2. *Military Incidents at Sea.* In the 1960s, there were several incidents between U.S. and Soviet naval forces at sea involving both vessels and aircraft, some involving threatening movements ("mock attacks"), others involving very close encounters, and some even involving bumping of each other. In 1972, the two states concluded an Agreement on the Prevention of Incidents On and Over the High Seas, United States–U.S.S.R., May 25, 1972, 23 U.S.T. 1168. The agreement obligates the two states to: (1) take steps to avoid collisions; (2) not interfere with the "formations" of the other party; (3) avoid maneuvers in areas of heavy sea traffic; (4) only engage in surveillance from a safe distance from the object of investigation; (5) use accepted international signals when ships maneuver near one another; (6) not simulate attacks at, launching objects toward, or illuminating the bridges of the other state's vessels; etc. Id. art. 3. The agreement does not directly regulate the size, weaponry, or force structure of the states.

Subsequently, the U.S.S.R. concluded comparable agreements with other nations, including Germany and the United Kingdom. Agreements such as these have remained in force with respect to Russia, the successor state to the U.S.S.R. Further, other states with naval forces that are likely to encounter each other have concluded such agreements. See, e.g., Agreement Concerning the Prevention of Incidents at Sea Beyond the Territorial Sea, Germany–Poland, Nov. 27, 1990, 1910 U.N.T.S. 39; see also Winkler, The Evolution and Significance of the 1972 Incidents at Sea Agreement, 28 J. Strategic Stud. 361 (2005).

In 1989, the United States and the U.S.S.R. concluded an Agreement on the Prevention of Dangerous Military Activities, United States–U.S.S.R., June 12, 1989, 28 I.L.M. 77 (1989) (PDMA Agreement), which includes naval forces and activities. The agreement basically applies the principles of the earlier agreement to all military activities in four situations that are considered to have unique risk. Those situations are whenever the armed forces of one party: (1) enter the territory of the other, due to *force majeure* or unintentionally; (2) use a laser in such a manner that its radiation could cause harm to personnel or damage to equipment of the armed forces of the other party; (3) hamper the activities of the personnel and equipment of the armed forces of the other Party in a designated "Special Caution area"; and (4) interfere with command and control networks of the other party. Id. art. II(1). If an incident occurs, both sides agree to resolve the matter peacefully, without resort to the use of force. Id. art. II(2).

In January 1998, China and the United States signed an Agreement on Establishing a Consultation Mechanism to Strengthen Military Maritime Safety, United States–China, Jan. 19, 1998, T.I.A.S. 12,924. Under that agreement, senior military officials meet annually to discuss issues of Sino–U.S. military maritime safety.

3. *Further Reading.* See Pirtle, Military Uses of Ocean Space and the Law of the Sea in the New Millennium, 31 Ocean Dev. & Int'l L. 7 (2000); Stephens, The Impact of the 1982 Law of the Sea Convention on the Conduct of Peacetime Naval/Military Operations, 29 Cal. W. Int'l L.J. 283 (1999); Fieldhouse, Security at Sea: Naval Forces and Arms Control (1990).

SECTION 9.   THE DEEP SEA–BED

A.   VIEWS OF DEVELOPED VERSUS DEVELOPING STATES PRIOR TO THE LOS CONVENTION

After World War II, technologically-advanced coastal states, such as the United States, became extremely interested in exploring and exploiting the resources of the deep sea-bed by mining its mineral resources. These states were content with *laissez-faire,* the freedom to exploit the commonage. Developing states, however, sought to establish the sea-bed beyond national jurisdiction as "the common heritage of mankind," to be developed by all states together, through institutions governed by "democratic principles" (generally one state, one vote). They wished also that the "haves" contribute generously to the costs of exploitation by "mankind," and provide mankind with access to the relevant technology, even technology that is privately owned. See Henkin, Law for the Sea's Mineral Resources 49–51, 58–59 (1968); Borgese, The Mines of Neptune: Minerals and Metals from the Sea (1985).

The developing states pressed their views at the principal global forum that they dominated starting in the 1960s—the U.N. General Assembly. First, they engineered a resolution at the U.N. General Assembly in 1969 purporting to establish a moratorium on exploitation of resources of the deep sea-bed. See G.A. Res. 2574, pt. D (XXIV) (Dec. 15, 1969). The resolution declared that, pending the establishment of international treaty regime, "States and persons, physical or juridical, are bound to refrain from all activities of exploitation of the resources of the area of the seabed and ocean floor, and the subsoil thereof, beyond the limits of national jurisdiction," and "[n]o claim to any part of that area or its resources shall be recognized." The vote on this resolution was 62 in favor, 28 against, with 28 abstentions; the United States challenged the statement as not reflecting international law and the authority of the Assembly to declare such a "moratorium."

Second, the General Assembly passed a further resolution in 1970 declaring that the "sea-bed and ocean floor, and the subsoil thereof, beyond the limits of national jurisdiction * * * as well as the resources of the area, are the common heritage of mankind." Declaration of Principles Governing the Sea–Bed and the Ocean Floor, and Subsoil Thereof, Beyond the Limits of National Jurisdiction, G.A. Res. 2749 (XXV), para. 1 (Dec. 17, 1970). This concept of the "common heritage of mankind" is usually attributed to Ambassador Arvid Pardo of Malta, who, in 1967, proposed the subject of sea-bed mining for consideration by the General Assembly. See de Marffy, The Pardo Declaration and the Six Years of the Sea–Bed Committee, in 1 A Handbook on the New Law of the Sea 141 (Dupuy & Vignes eds. 1991). Yet the concept was expressed even earlier, including a statement by U.S. President Lyndon Johnson: "We must ensure that the deep seas and the ocean bottoms are, and remain, the legacy of all human beings." Remarks at the Commissioning if the Research Ship Oceanographer, 2 Pub. Papers 722, 724 (July 13, 1966).

In the meantime, the technologically-advanced states began laying the groundwork for unilateral exploitation. Beginning in 1972, bills were introduced in the U.S. Congress which would authorize the licensing of U.S. nationals to mine the deep sea-bed in areas beyond national jurisdiction, and recognize the rights of nationals of other states on the basis of reciprocity. Initially, the Executive Branch opposed passage of such legislation on the ground that it would prejudice the negotiation of an acceptable international regime at UNCLOS III. However, as the Conference dragged on, the U.S. Administration in 1977 endorsed passage of "interim" legislation which would authorize licensing pending the conclusion of a comprehensive law of the sea treaty. Ultimately, The Deep Seabed Hard Mineral Resources Act, Pub. L. No. 96–283, 94 Stat. 553 (1980), explicitly adopted the U.S. position that, in the absence of a treaty, states had the right to mine the sea-bed as an aspect of the freedom of the seas, and that national licensing would not be an assertion of sovereignty of ownership over any part of the sea-bed. The Act recognizes the character of sea-bed resources as the common heritage of mankind, and provides for the establishment of an international revenue-sharing fund. Congress's declared purpose in adopting the Act was to provide "assured and nondiscriminatory access" as well as "security of tenure" to U.S. nationals seeking to exploit deep sea-bed resources. Id. at §§ 3, 201. While the act was declared to be transitional pending U.S. adherence to a treaty resulting from UNCLOS I, it establishes that any regulation issuing as a result of its passage not inconsistent with subsequent treaties shall remain valid. Other states enacted similar interim legislation. Further, a Provisional Understanding Regarding Deep Seabed Mining, Aug. 3, 1984, 23 I.L.M. 1354 (1984), was signed by the United States and seven other parties to establish a preliminary scheme for resolving overlapping claims to deep sea-bed mining areas.

The legality of unilateral legislation, "interim" or otherwise, was challenged by developing states as inconsistent with the moratorium resolution. See Letter dated 23 April 1979 from the Chairman of the Group of 77 to the President of the Conference, U.N. Doc. A/CONF. 62/77.

B. THE ORIGINAL 1982 LOS CONVENTION SCHEME

At UNCLOS III, the developed states sought essentially an international licensing system: an international authority would issue licenses to governments (or to their nationals) for mining of specific locations, and would collect fees or royalties that might go to international development purposes. The international authority would be organized to reflect the dominant interests of the states that had the capital and the technology necessary to support exploitation, and to assure the authority's limited function. The developing states, represented by the "Group of 77" (which actually included more than one hundred developing states), sought a regime whereby the exclusive right to mine the sea-bed beyond national jurisdiction would be vested in an international Sea–Bed Authority which would establish an Enterprise for that purpose. They sought an authority organized principally on the basis of majority-rule by states of equal voting authority. Some developing states also sought to assure that sea-bed minerals would not compete with land-based minerals which they produced and exported.

In 1976, a compromise was proposed which would establish a "parallel" system, one set of mining sites to be exploited by states (or their corporations), the other by an operating arm of the Authority—the Enterprise. The developed states would also provide the Enterprise with capital and technology to enable the Enterprise to carry out its exploitation. Differences continued, however, as to the organization of the Sea–Bed Authority. There was agreement in principle on a Council (with weighted representation) and an Assembly (with equal representation), as in the United Nations. The developed states, however, insisted on "assured access" to their part of the system, and wished to allocate authority to make certain that the Assembly, which they could not control, could not interfere with such access. The developing states continued to press for effective control by the majority through the Assembly. In 1980, a compromise was reached on the decision-making powers of the organs of the Authority; methods for insuring, and the terms for, transfer of capital and technology to the Enterprise; the criteria for licensing and taxing of state-owned and private mining companies; and limitations on sea-bed mining to protect land-based sources. The parties agreed to review the system in fifteen to twenty-five years.

By 1981 the new Convention was all but complete, and a vote on the final version was scheduled for April 1982. However, in 1981 the new Reagan Administration in the United States said it wanted major changes in the treaty before it would sign it. Though some changes were made, the controversial sea-mining provisions were largely retained. See LOS Convention, pt. XI (arts. 133–85); annex III, & annex IV. The United States and other industrialized states announced that they would not sign or ratify the Convention because of Part XI.

C.   THE REVISED 1994 LOS CONVENTION SCHEME

In 1994, consultations under the auspices of the U.N. Secretary–General sought agreement to modify LOS Convention Part XI to meet the principal objections of the industrialized nations. The consultations proceeded with urgency, in view of the fact that the LOS Convention was about to enter into force following the deposit of the sixtieth instrument of ratification. The result was the 1994 Agreement Relating to the Implementation of Part XI of the United Nations Convention on the Law of the Sea of 10 December 1982, July 28, 1994, S. Treaty Doc. No. 103–39 (1994), 1836 U.N.T.S. 3, endorsed as an annex to a resolution of the U.N. General Assembly. See G.A. Res. 48/263 (July 28, 1994) (adopted with 121 states in favor, 0 opposed, and 7 abstentions).

The 1994 Implementing Agreement entered in force on July 28, 1996. By its terms, it is to be interpreted and applied together with Part XI of the LOS Convention as a single instrument. In case of conflict with the provisions of Part XI, the 1994 Implementing Agreement prevails. States ratifying the LOS Convention after July 1994 are bound by the 1994 Implementing Agreement. States that had ratified the LOS Convention prior to the adoption of the 1994 Implementing Agreement have to establish their consent to be bound by the Agreement separately. As of early 2009, 136 parties to the LOS Convention, including the European Community, are bound by the 1994 Implementing Agreement.

OXMAN, THE 1994 AGREEMENT AND THE CONVENTION
88 A.J.I.L. 687, 688–95 (1994) (footnotes omitted)

It may be instructive to consider how the 1994 Agreement responds to the problems identified and the concerns expressed by the United States when it sought, without success, to change Part XI in 1982.

U.S. policy regarding the 1982 Convention, as enunciated by the Reagan administration, may be summarized as follows. "While most provisions of the draft convention are acceptable and consistent with U.S.

Interests, some major elements of the deep seabed mining regime are not acceptable." The United States "has a strong interest in an effective and fair Law of the Sea treaty which includes a viable seabed mining regime." It was "not seeking to change the basic structure of the treaty" or "to destroy the system" "but to make it work for the benefit of all nations to enhance, not resist, seabed resource development." If negotiations could fulfill six key objectives with respect to the deep seabed mining regime, the "Administration will support ratification" of the Convention. It was the administration's "judgement that, if the Presidents' objectives as outlined are satisfied, the Senate would approve the Law of the Sea Treaty."

The six objectives identified by President Reagan required a deep seabed mining regime that would:

● Not deter development of any deep seabed mineral resources to meet national and international demand;

● Assure national access to these resources by current and future qualified entities to enhance U.S. security of supply, to avoid monopolization of the resources by the operating arm of the international authority, and to promote the economic development of these resources;

● Provide a decision making role in the deep seabed regime that fairly reflects and effectively protects the political and economic interests and financial contributions of participating states;

● Not allow for amendments to come into force without approval of the participating states, including, in our case, the advice and consent of the Senate;

● Not set other undesirable precedents for international organizations; and

● Be likely to receive the advice and consent of the Senate. In this regard, the convention should not contain provisions for the mandatory transfer of private technology and participation by and funding for national liberation movements.

How the 1994 Agreement responds to U.S. objections and U.S. requirements may be considered under several headings.

Decision Making

Like many international organizations, the International Sea–Bed Authority established by the Convention will have an Assembly in which all parties are represented, a Council of limited membership, and specialized elected organs also of limited membership.

1982 text: While all specific regulatory powers with regard to deep seabed mining are reposed exclusively or concurrently in the Council, Article 160 gives the Assembly "the power to establish general policies."

Problem: "Policymaking in the seabed authority would be carried out by a one-nation, one-vote assembly."

Response: The 1994 Agreement qualifies the general policy-making powers of the Assembly by requiring the collaboration of the Council. It also provides: "Decisions of the Assembly on any matter for which the Council also has competence or on any administrative, budgetary or financial matter shall be based on the recommendations of the Council." The Assembly may either approve the recommendations or return them.

Problem: "The executive council which would make the day-to-day decisions affecting access of U.S. miners to deep seabed minerals would not have permanent or guaranteed representation by the United States."

Response: The new Agreement guarantees a seat on the Council for "the State, on the date of entry into force of the Convention, having the largest economy in terms of gross domestic product." That state is the United States.

1982 text: Consensus on the thirty-six-member Council is required for such matters as proposing treaty amendments; adopting rules, regulations and procedures; and distributing financial benefits and economic adjustment assistance. Other substantive Council decisions require either a two-thirds or three-quarters vote.

Problem: The "United States would not have influence on the council commensurate with its economic and political interests." * * *

Response: The new Agreement establishes "chambers" of states with particular interests. Two four-member chambers of the Council are likely to be effectively controlled by major industrial states, including the United States (which is guaranteed a seat in one of those chambers). The Agreement provides that "decisions on questions of substance, except where the Convention provides for decisions by consensus in the Council, shall be taken by a two-thirds majority of members present and voting, provided that such decisions are not opposed by a majority of any one of the chambers." Any three states in either four-member chamber may therefore block a substantive decision for which consensus is not required.

The Agreement further specifies: "Decisions by the Assembly or the Council having financial or budgetary implications shall be based on the recommendations of the Finance Committee." The United States and other major contributors to the administrative budget are guaranteed seats on the Finance Committee, and the committee functions by consensus.

This approach to voting enables interested states (including the United States) to block undesirable decisions. Because blocking power encourages negotiation of decisions desired by and acceptable to the states principally affected, it enhances affirmative as well as negative influence.

Production Limitation

Problem: "The United States believes that its interests ... will best be served by developing the resources of the deep seabed as market conditions warrant. We have a consumer-oriented philosophy. The draft treaty, in our judgment, reflects a protectionist bias which would deter the development of deep seabed mineral resources." Specifically, the "treaty would impose artificial limitations on seabed mineral production" and "would permit discretionary and discriminatory decisions by the Authority if there is competition for limited production allocations." The production ceiling is undesirable as a matter of principle and precedent, and the process for allocating production authorizations is a significant source of uncertainty and discriminatory treatment impeding guaranteed access to minerals by qualified miners.

Response: The new Agreement specifies that the provisions regarding the production ceiling, production limitations, participation in commodity agreements, production authorizations and selection among applicants "shall not apply." In their place, the Agreement incorporates the market-oriented GATT restrictions on subsidies. It prohibits "discrimination between minerals derived from the [deep seabed] and from other sources," and specifies that the rates of payments by miners to the Authority "shall be within the range of those prevailing in respect of land-based mining of the same or similar minerals in order to avoid giving deep seabed miners an artificial competitive advantage or imposing on them a competitive disadvantage."

Technology Transfer

Problem: "Private deep seabed miners would be subject to a mandatory requirement for the transfer of technology to the Enterprise and to developing countries." This provision was considered burdensome, prejudicial to intellectual property rights, and objectionable as a matter of principle and precedent.

Response: The new Agreement declares that the provisions on mandatory transfer of technology "shall not apply." It substitutes a general duty of cooperation by sponsoring states to facilitate the acquisition of deep seabed mining technology, "consistent with the effective protection of intellectual property rights," if the Enterprise (the operating arm of the Sea–Bed Authority) or developing countries are unable to obtain such technology on the open market or through joint-venture arrangements.

Access

Problem: "The draft treaty provides no assurance that qualified private applicants sponsored by the U.S. Government will be awarded contracts. It is our strong view that all qualified applicants should be granted contracts and that the decision whether to grant a contract should be tied exclusively to the question of whether an applicant has satisfied objective qualification standards."

Response: The new Agreement eliminates the provisions for choice among qualified applicants. Access will be on a first-come, first-served basis. The qualification standards for mining applicants are to be set forth in rules, regulations and procedures adopted by the Council by consensus and "shall relate to the financial and technical capabilities of the applicant and his performance under any previous contracts." If the applicant is qualified; if the application fee is paid; if procedural and environmental requirements are met; if the area applied for is not the subject of a prior contract or application; and if the sponsoring state would not thereby exceed maximum limits in the Convention, "the Authority shall approve" the application. Its failure to do so will be subject to arbitration or adjudication.

* * *

The new Agreement accords important "grandfather" rights to the U.S. consortia that already have made investments under the U.S. Deep Seabed Hard Mineral Resources Act. They are deemed to have met the necessary financial and technical qualifications if the U.S. Government, as the sponsoring state, certifies that they have made the necessary expenditures. They are also entitled to arrangements "similar to and no less favourable than" those accorded investors of other countries that registered as pioneers with the Preparatory Commission prior to entry into force of the Convention.

Problem: U.S. objectives "would not be satisfied if minerals other than manganese nodules could be developed only after a decision was taken to promulgate rules and regulations to allow the exploitation of such minerals."

Response: The new Agreement requires the Council of the Authority to adopt necessary rules, regulations and procedures within two years of a request by a state whose national intends to apply for the right to exploit a mine site. This applies to manganese nodules or any other mineral resource. If the Council fails to complete the work on time, it must give provisional approval to an application based on the Convention and the new Agreement, notwithstanding the fact that the rules and regulations have not been adopted.

The Enterprise

Problem: "The treaty would give substantial competitive advantages to a supra-national mining company—the Enterprise." It "creates a system of privileges which discriminates against the private side of the parallel system. Rational private companies would, therefore, have little option but to enter joint ventures or other similar ventures with the operating arm of the Authority, the Enterprise, or with developing countries. Not only would this deny the United States access to deep seabed minerals through its private companies because the private access system would be uncompetitive but, under some scenarios, the Enterprise could establish a monopoly over deep seabed mineral resources."

Response: The new Agreement provides: "The obligations applicable to contractors [private miners] shall apply to the Enterprise." It requires the Enterprise to conduct its initial operations through joint ventures "that accord with sound commercial principles," and delays the independent functioning of the Enterprise until the Council decides that those criteria have been met. The Agreement does not exclude the Enterprise either from the principle that mining "shall take place in accordance with sound commercial principles" or from its prohibitions on subsidies. It specifies that the "obligation of States Parties to fund one mine site of the Enterprise ... shall not apply and States Parties shall be under no obligation to finance any of the operations in any mine site of the Enterprise or under its joint-venture arrangements." The Agreement also eliminates mandatory transfer of technology to the Enterprise and the potentially discriminatory system for issuing production authorizations.

The Agreement makes clear that a private miner may contribute the requisite "reserved area" to the Enterprise at the time the miner receives its own exclusive exploration rights to a specific area (thus minimizing its risk and investment). That miner has "the right of first refusal to enter into a joint-venture arrangement with the Enterprise for exploration and exploitation of" the reserved area, and has priority rights to the reserved area if the Enterprise itself does not apply for exploration or exploitation rights to the reserved area within a specified period.

Finance

Problem: "The treaty would impose large financial burdens on industrialized countries whose nationals are engaged in deep seabed mining and financial terms and conditions which would significantly increase the costs of mineral production."

Response: The new Agreement halves the application fees for either exploration or exploitation to $250,000 (subject to refund to the extent the fee exceeds the actual costs of processing an application), and eliminates the detailed financial obligations of miners set forth in the 1982 text, including the million-dollar annual fee. Financial details would be supplied, when needed, by rules, regulations and procedures adopted by the Council by consensus, on the basis of general criteria that, for example, would link the rates to those prevailing for mining on land, and prohibit discrimination or rate increases for existing contracts.

With respect to state parties, in addition to eliminating any requirement that states contribute funds to finance the Enterprise or provide economic adjustment assistance to developing countries, the new Agreement provides for streamlining and phasing in the organs and functions of the Authority as needed, and for minimizing costs and meetings. Budgets and assessments for administrative expenses are subject to consensus procedures in the Finance Committee and approval by both the Council and the Assembly.

Regulatory Burdens

Problem: "The new international organization would have discretion to interfere unreasonably with the conduct of mining operations, and it could impose potentially burdensome regulations on an infant industry."

Response: The substantive changes set forth in the new Agreement, including the elimination of production limitations, production authorizations and forced transfer of technology, and the relaxation of diligence requirements, substantially narrow the area of potential abuse. The new procedural provisions, including voting arrangements in the Council of the Finance Committee, and restrictions on the Assembly, decrease the risk of unreasonable regulatory decisions. As indicated in its Preamble and in the General Assembly resolution adopting it, the new Agreement is the product of a marked shift, throughout the world, from statist and interventionist economic philosophies toward more market-oriented policies. Taken together, the new provisions and new attitudes give reason to expect the system to operate in accordance with the provisions of the Convention and the Agreement guaranteeing the miner exclusive rights to a mine site, security of tenure, stability of expectations and title to minerals extracted, and according the miner and its sponsoring state extensive judicial and arbitral remedies to protect those rights.

What cannot be supplied in advance by any blueprint for a deep seabed mining regime is the measure of confidence born of experience with a system in operation.

Distribution of Revenues

1982 text: The Convention authorizes the equitable sharing of surplus revenues from mining, "taking into particular consideration the interests and needs of the developing States and peoples who have not attained full independence or other self-governing status."

Problem: "The convention would allow funding for national liberation groups, such as the Palestine Liberation Organization and the South West Africa People's Organization."

Response: Political developments in Africa and the Middle East have mitigated this problem. Moreover, distribution to such groups would be a practical impossibility unless the Sea–Bed Authority's revenues from miners and from the Enterprise exceeded both its administrative expenses and its assistance to adversely affected land-based producers, and would be possible then only if the Council decided by consensus to include such groups in the distribution of surplus revenues. A decision on distribution of surplus funds would also be subject, under the new Agreement, to a consensus in the Finance Committee.

Review Conference

Problem: "A review conference would have the power to impose treaty amendments on the United States without its consent."

Response: The new Agreement declares that the provisions in Part XI relating to the review conference "shall not apply." Amendments to the deep seabed mining could not be adopted without U.S. consent.

NOTE

After conducting its review of the LOS Convention in light of the 1994 Agreement, the Administration of George W. Bush concluded that "the 1994 Agreement overcomes each one of the U.S. objections to the Convention and meets President Reagan's goal of guaranteed access by U.S. industry to deep seabed minerals on the basis of reasonable terms and conditions." U.S. Dep't of State Legal Adviser John B. Bellinger III, The United States and the Law of the Sea Convention, Remarks at the Law of the Sea Institute, Berkeley, California (Nov. 3, 2008).

SECTION 10. POLLUTION OF THE MARINE ENVIRONMENT

Marine pollution has received special attention in international law. This is readily understandable, since pollution of the marine environment, and especially the oceans, affects all users. The rapid growth of maritime traffic since World War II has increased pollution of the marine environment. In addition, dumping of noxious and harmful substances, including radioactive materials, oil spills from wells in maritime areas, and tanker disasters have added substantially to marine pollution. All of these developments have enhanced concern for the marine environment and produced international and national measures for its protection.

The 1958 Convention on the High Seas contains a number of provisions seeking to ensure safety at sea and to prevent pollution by discharges of oil and radioactive waste. Id. arts. 10, 24–25, Apr. 29, 1958, 13 U.S.T. 2312, 450 U.N.T.S. 11. The LOS Convention includes provisions that deal not only with the types of pollution addressed in the 1958 Convention, but also with pollution from land-based sources, pollution through the atmosphere, pollution from continental shelf activities and from deep sea-bed mining, and dumping at sea. LOS Convention, arts. 207–12. Most significantly, the 1982 Convention on the Law of the Sea gave coastal states, particularly port states, power to enforce international rules and to do so against foreign vessels, but made special provision for the settlement of disputes that might result. Id. arts. 218, 220. The protection of the marine environment has been addressed not only as part of the law of the sea, but also in the context of environmental protection generally. Problems of pollution by ships have been treated specially by the International Maritime Consultative Organization (IMCO), now the International Maritime Organization (IMO).

As you read the following provisions, consider the following questions. Suppose that states are concerned about massive oil spills off their coast, which can cause extensive damage to the marine environment, as well as cripple land-based activities, including tourism. What measures of regulation or enforcement can a *coastal state* take with respect oil tankers that engage in innocent passage through its territorial sea? That transit through its EEZ? Is there a way that the LOS Convention grants the coastal state greater authority for greater threats to its marine environment and lesser authority for lesser threats? What measures of regulation or enforcement can be taken by the *flag states* of oil tankers? Suppose the oil tanker, after committing an unlawful discharge in a coastal state's territorial sea or EEZ, or on the high seas, makes its way to the port of different state. What measures of regulation or enforcement can be undertaken by that *port state*? Why grant that port state any authority to regulate or enforce against the oil tanker, if the port state was never directly affected by the oil spill? Overall, is the LOS Convention creating a minimum standard of rules that must be adopted by states to protect the marine environment, but allowing adoption of more stringent national standards in certain situations as well as enforcement of those standards?

UNITED NATIONS CONVENTION ON THE LAW OF THE SEA, ARTICLES 194, 217–18, 220

Adopted Dec. 10, 1982
1833 U.N.T.S. 3

Article 194

Measures to prevent, reduce and control pollution of the marine environment

1. States shall take, individually or jointly as appropriate, all measures consistent with this Convention that are necessary to prevent, reduce and control pollution of the marine environment from any source, using for this purpose the best practicable means at their disposal and in accordance with their capabilities, and they shall endeavour to harmonize their policies in this connection.

2. States shall take all measures necessary to ensure that activities under their jurisdiction or control are so conducted as not to cause damage by pollution to other States and their environment, and that pollution arising from incidents or activities under their jurisdiction or control does not spread beyond the areas where they exercise sovereign rights in accordance with this Convention.

3. The measures taken pursuant to this Part shall deal with all sources of pollution of the marine environment. * * *

* * *

Article 211

Pollution from vessels

1. States, acting through the competent international organization or general diplomatic conference, shall establish international rules and standards to prevent, reduce and control pollution of the marine environment from vessels and promote the adoption, in the same manner, wherever appropriate, of routing systems designed to minimize the threat

of accidents which might cause pollution of the marine environment, including the coastline, and pollution damage to the related interests of coastal States. Such rules and standards shall, in the same manner, be re-examined from time to time as necessary.

2.   States shall adopt laws and regulations for the prevention, reduction and control of pollution of the marine environment from vessels flying their flag or of their registry. Such laws and regulations shall at least have the same effect as that of generally accepted international rules and standards established through the competent international organization or general diplomatic conference.

3.   States which establish particular requirements for the prevention, reduction and control of pollution of the marine environment as a condition for the entry of foreign vessels into their ports or internal waters or for a call at their off-shore terminals shall give due publicity to such requirements and shall communicate them to the competent international organization. * * * This article is without prejudice to the continued exercise by a vessel of its right of innocent passage * * *.

4.   Coastal States may, in the exercise of their sovereignty within their territorial sea, adopt laws and regulations for the prevention, reduction and control of marine pollution from foreign vessels, including vessels exercising the right of innocent passage. Such laws and regulations shall, in accordance with Part II section 3,[1] not hamper innocent passage of foreign vessels.

5.   Coastal States * * * may in respect of their exclusive economic zones adopt laws and regulations for the prevention, reduction and control of pollution from vessels conforming to and giving effect to generally accepted international rules and standards established through the competent international organization or general diplomatic conference.

Article 217

Enforcement by flag States

1.   States shall ensure compliance by vessels flying their flag or of their registry with applicable international rules and standards, established through the competent international organization or general diplomatic conference, and with their laws and regulations adopted in accordance with this Convention for the prevention, reduction and control of pollution of the marine environment from vessels and shall accordingly adopt laws and regulations and take other measures necessary for their implementation. Flag States shall provide for the effective enforcement of such rules, standards, laws and regulations, irrespective of where a violation occurs.

---

1.   [Editors' Note: LOS Convention Part II, Section 3, includes in Article 21(2) a requirement that coastal state laws and regulations, "shall not apply to the design, construction, manning or equipment of foreign ships unless they are giving effect to generally accepted international rules or standards."]

2. States shall, in particular, take appropriate measures in order to ensure that vessels flying their flag or of their registry are prohibited from sailing, until they can proceed to sea in compliance with the requirements of the international rules and standards referred to in paragraph I, including requirements in respect of design, construction, equipment and manning of vessels.

Article 218

Enforcement by port States

1. When a vessel is voluntarily within a port or at an off-shore terminal of a State, that State may undertake investigations and, where the evidence so warrants, institute proceedings in respect of any discharge from that vessel outside the internal waters, territorial sea or exclusive economic zone of that State in violation of applicable international rules and standards established through the competent international organization or general diplomatic conference.

2. No proceedings pursuant to paragraph 1 shall be instituted in respect of a discharge violation in the internal waters, territorial sea or exclusive economic zone of another State unless requested by that State, the flag State, or a State damaged or threatened by the discharge violation, or unless the violation has caused or is likely to cause pollution in the internal waters, territorial sea or exclusive economic zone of the State instituting the proceedings.

Article 220

Enforcement by coastal States

1. When a vessel is voluntarily within a port or at an off-shore terminal of a State, that State may, subject to section 7, institute proceedings in respect of any violation of its laws and regulations adopted in accordance with this Convention or applicable international rules and standards for the prevention, reduction and control of pollution from vessels when the violation has occurred within the territorial sea or the exclusive economic zone of that State.

2. Where there are clear grounds for believing that a vessel navigating in the territorial sea of a State has, during its passage therein, violated laws and regulations of that State adopted in accordance with this Convention or applicable international rules and standards for the prevention, reduction and control of pollution from vessels, that State, without prejudice to the application of the relevant provisions of Part II, section 3, may undertake physical inspection of the vessel relating to the violation and may, where the evidence so warrants institute proceedings, including detention of the vessel, in accordance with its laws, subject to the provisions of section 7.

3. Where there are clear grounds for believing that a vessel navigating in the exclusive economic zone or the territorial sea of a State has, in the exclusive economic zone, committed a violation of applicable interna-

tional rules and standards for the prevention, reduction and control of pollution from vessels or laws and regulations of that State conforming and giving effect to such rules and standards, that State may require the vessel to give information regarding its identity and port of registry, its last and its next port of call and other relevant information required to establish whether a violation has occurred.

4.   States shall adopt laws and regulations and take other measures so that vessels flying their flag comply with requests for information pursuant to paragraph 3.

5.   Where there are clear grounds for believing that a vessel navigating in the exclusive economic zone or the territorial sea of a State has, in the exclusive economic zone, committed a violation referred to in paragraph 3 resulting in a substantial discharge causing or threatening significant pollution of the marine environment, that State may undertake physical inspection of the vessel for matters relating to the violation if the vessel has refused to give information or if the information supplied by the vessel is manifestly at variance with the evident factual situation and if the circumstances of the case justify such inspection.

6.   Where there is clear objective evidence that a vessel navigating in the exclusive economic zone or the territorial sea of a State has, in the exclusive economic zone, committed a violation referred to in paragraph 3 resulting in a discharge causing major damage or threat of major damage to the coastline or related interests of the coastal State, or to any resources of its territorial sea or exclusive economic zone, that State may, subject to section 7, provided that the evidence so warrants, institute proceedings, including detention of the vessel, in accordance with its laws.

7.   Notwithstanding the provisions of paragraph 6, whenever appropriate procedures have been established, either through the competent international organization or as otherwise agreed, whereby compliance with requirements for bonding or other appropriate financial security has been assured, the coastal State if bound by such procedures shall allow the vessel to proceed.

NOTES

1.   *National Rules versus International Rules.* The articles above reflect various balancing acts, including an effort to balance the application of rules developed unilaterally by a single state against rules developed multilaterally through treaties or international organizations. Alternatively, why not allow states to apply their national laws in all areas of the oceans, including the high seas? Why not require all states to only apply multilaterally agreed rules in all areas of the oceans, including territorial seas and even internal waters. What interests are at stake here?

2.   *"Applicable International Rules and Standards."* The LOS Convention articles above refer in several places to "applicable international rules and standards" (or a similar formulation) and sometimes indicate that they

are to be "established through the competent international organization or general diplomatic conference." No single international organization or treaty serves as the font for such rules and standards, although certain sources are of particular importance. The International Maritime Organization (IMO), based in London, traditionally has been responsible for developing rules relating to maritime safety, and the prevention of marine pollution from vessels and by dumping. The United Nations Environment Programme (UNEP), based in Nairobi, Kenya, has been responsible for the development of rules on the protection and preservation of the marine environment from land-based sources, and for the development of regional rules and standards through its Regional Seas Programme. The International Atomic Energy Agency (IAEA), based in Vienna, has been responsible for the development of rules relating to nuclear safety and radioactive waste management. The International Seabed Authority (ISA), established under the LOS Convention and based in Kingston, Jamaica, is now responsible for the development of the international rules and standards with regard to pollution from seabed activities.

3. *Pollution from Any Source.* LOS Convention Article 194 calls upon states to use "the best practicable means at their disposal" to regulate pollution from "all sources." Subsequent articles address not only pollution from vessels, but also from land-based sources (Article 207), from sea-bed activities (Article 208), from dumping (Article 210), from noxious emissions by aircraft (Article 212), and from the use of technologies or the introduction of alien or new species (Article 196). Note, however, that the LOS Convention provisions dealing with the environment do not apply to state-owned or state-operated vessels or aircraft used on noncommercial service (Article 236). The most significant source of marine pollution is from land-based activities, but while several regional treaties are focused on this issue, there is as yet no global convention that does so. See Hassan, International Conventions Relating to Land–Based Sources of Marine Pollution Control: Applications and Shortcomings, 16 Geo. Int'l Envtl. L. Rev. 657 (2004).

4. *Port State Authority.* Granting jurisdiction to a flag state to regulate its vessel is not surprising, nor is doing so for a coastal state whose marine environment is directly at risk. Granting "port state jurisdiction" in Article 218—meaning authority to a state in whose port a malfeasant vessel happens to dock—was considered an important component of the LOS Convention. Bear in mind that the port state may have no connection whatsoever to the vessel or the pollution, other than the fact that the vessel showed up in its port. For purposes of developing a harmonized system of port state control, regional memoranda of understanding have been developed. For example, to address the waters between Europe and North America, twenty-seven states have developed the Paris Memorandum of Understanding on Port State Control, Jan. 26, 1982, as amended, http://www.parismou.org/ (Paris MOU). Each year, more than 20,000 inspections occur on foreign vessels in the ports of Paris MOU states, for purposes of checking international safety, security and environmental standards, See generally The Paris Memorandum of Understanding on Port State Control, Port State Control: Steady as She Goes, Annual Report (2006). Such inspections also seek to ensure that crew members have adequate living and working conditions, an issue regulated in part

by International Labour Organization Convention (No. 147) Concerning Minimum Standards in Merchant Ships, Oct. 29, 1976, 1259 U.N.T.S. 334.

5. *Safety at Sea*. Collisions involving large tankers led to revisions in 1960 and 1974 of international conventions dealing with safety at sea, see International Convention for the Safety of Life at Sea (SOLAS), June 17, 1960, 16 U.S.T. 185, 536 U.N.T.S. 27, as amended, Nov. 1, 1974, 32 U.S.T. 47, 1184 U.N.T.S. 2, as well as the development of the International Convention on Load Lines, Apr. 5, 1966, 18 U.S.T. 1857, 640 U.N.T.S. 133 (and its protocol), and the International Convention on Standards of Training, Certification and Watchkeeping for Seafarers (STCW), July 7, 1978, S. Exec. Doc. EE, 96–1 (1979), 1361 U.N.T.S. 2. Such instruments are principally designed to avoid human error, the principal cause of accidents at sea.

6. *Dumping of Wastes at Sea*. The Convention on the Prevention of Marine Pollution by Dumping of Wastes and Other Matter, Dec. 29, 1972, 26 U.S.T. 2403, 1046 U.N.T.S. 120, prohibits the deliberate disposal of waste at sea. Originally referred to as the "London Dumping Convention," the convention has been revised or amended several times, and is now generally termed the "London Convention." In general, the convention establishes conditions for states to grant permits to dump in waters subject their national jurisdiction. Further, Annex I establishes a list of substances that may never be dumped at sea, such as high-level radioactive wastes, persistent plastics, and mercury (collectively known as the "black list"). Annex II establishes a list of substances that may be dumped, but only subject to strict controls and a special permit (the "grey list"). Annex III sets forth criteria for determining whether other substances may be dumped at sea pursuant to a general permit. A 1996 Protocol to the London Convention, Nov. 7, 1996, S. Treaty Doc. 110–5 (2007), 36 I.L.M. 1 (1997), which entered into force in March 2006, replaces the prior Convention for states party to the Protocol. Taking a much more restrictive approach, the protocol drops the "black" and "grey" lists in favor of prohibiting the dumping of *any* wastes or other matter, with the exception of the seven categories listed in its Annex 1, for which a permit issued by states parties is required.

7. *MARPOL Convention*. Discharges other than dumping are the subject of the International Convention for the Prevention of Pollution from Ships (MARPOL), Nov. 2, 1973, S. Exec. Doc. C, 95–1 (1977), 1340 U.N.T.S. 184. The Protocol of 1978 Relating to the International Convention for the Prevention of Pollution from Ships, 1973 (MARPOL Protocol of 1978), Feb. 17, 1978, S. Exec. Doc. C, 96–1 (1979), 1340 U.N.T.S. 61, incorporates with modifications the provisions of the 1973 Convention, including its annexes and protocol. The annexes address specific types of pollution: Annex I (prevention of pollution by oil); Annex II (pollution by noxious liquid substances in bulk); Annex III (pollution by harmful substances carried by sea in packaged forms); Annex IV (pollution by sewage from ships); Annex V (pollution by garbage from ships); and Annex VI (air pollution from ships). See Mitchell, Intentional Oil Pollution at Sea: Environmental Policy and Treaty Compliance (1994). The United States implements its obligations under MARPOL through the Act to Prevent Pollution from Ships, 33 U.S.C. § 1901 (2000), which provides for both civil and criminal penalties. For an example of a U.S. prosecution for failure to maintain properly an oil record

book, which includes a log of a vessel's discharge and disposal of oil and certain oil-water mixtures, see United States v. Jho, 534 F.3d 398 (5th Cir. 2008) (finding that each time the ship called on a U.S. port with the falsely maintained record book, it constituted a separate criminal offense).

8. *Emergency Response to Spills.* In the 1967 *Torrey Canyon* disaster, the United Kingdom bombed a super-tanker after it had run aground off Lands End in the English Channel, and was leaking crude oil. The United Kingdom acted without the consent of the flag state in an effort to set fire to the oil, in the hope that it would minimize environmental damage. The incident prompted adoption of the International Convention Relating to Intervention on the High Seas in Cases of Oil Pollution Casualties, Nov. 29, 1969, 26 U.S.T. 765, 970 U.N.T.S. 211. In 1973, the Convention was broadened to extend coverage to specific substances other than oil. See Protocol Relating to Intervention on the High Seas in Cases of Pollution by Substances Other than Oil, Nov. 2, 1973, 34 U.S.T. 3407, 1313 U.N.T.S. 3. Further relevant conventions are the International Convention on Salvage, Apr. 28, 1989, S. Treaty Doc. No. 102–12 (1991), 1953 U.N.T.S. 165, and the International Convention on Oil Pollution Preparedness, Response and Cooperation, Nov. 30, 1990, S. Treaty Doc. No. 102–11 (1991), 1891 U.N.T.S. 51 (and its 2000 Protocol, which extended its coverage to hazardous and noxious substances).

9. *Compensation for Oil Spills.* After an oil spill occurs, a further international treaty regime provides that the owner of the oil tanker is liable to pay compensation up to a certain limit. See Convention on Civil Liability for Oil Pollution Damage from Offshore Operations, art. 11, Dec. 17, 1976, 16 I.L.M. 1450 (1977). Pursuant to a 1992 protocol to the convention, if the damage exceeds that limit, further compensation is available from an oil fund if the damage occurs in a state which is a member of that fund. Additional compensation may also be available from a supplementary fund, created in 2000, provided the state is a member of that fund.

10. *Further Reading.* See Tan, Vessel–Source Marine Pollution: The Law and Politics of International Regulation (2006); Craig, Protecting International Marine Biodiversity: International Treaties and National Systems of Marine Protected Areas, 20 J. Land Use & Envtl. L. 333 (2005); Charney, The Marine Environment and the 1982 United Nations Convention on the Law of the Sea, 28 Int'l Law. 879 (1994).

SECTION 11. PACIFIC SETTLEMENT OF DISPUTES

The LOS Convention includes a complex set of provisions for resolving various disputes under the Convention. In several instances, agreement on a means of resolving disputes was indispensable to achieving agreement on the underlying substantive principles. The dispute settlement provisions are found in Part XV (Articles 279–99) and Annex VI, which contains the Statute for the International Tribunal for the Law of the Sea (ITLOS), as well as in Annex V on conciliation, Annex VII on arbitration, and Annex VIII on special arbitration.

LOS Convention Part XV, Section 1, Article 279, contains a general obligation for parties to settle disputes arising under the convention by peaceful means. Article 284 provides an optional conciliation procedure that may be used if both parties agree to do so. If non-compulsory methods under Section 1 cannot resolve the dispute, then either party may under Section 2 submit the dispute to compulsory dispute settlement. When a state joins the convention, the state can declare its acceptance of compulsory dispute settlement at one of four possible fora:

(a) the International Tribunal for the Law of the Sea established in accordance with LOSC Convention Annex VI;

(b) the International Court of Justice;

(c) an arbitral tribunal constituted in accordance with Annex VII;

(d) a special arbitral tribunal constituted in accordance with Annex VIII for one or more of the categories of disputes specified therein.

LOS Convention, art. 287(1). If when a state joins the LOS Convention no declaration is made in favor of one of these fora, the state "shall be deemed to have accepted arbitration in accordance with Annex VII." LOS Convention, art. 287(3). If, once a dispute arises, the two parties have selected the same forum, then that forum has jurisdiction over the dispute, unless the parties agree otherwise. LOS Convention, art. 287(4). However, if "the parties to a dispute have not accepted the same procedure for the settlement of the dispute, it may be submitted only to arbitration in accordance with Annex VII, unless the parties otherwise agree." LOS Convention, art. 287(5). Do such provisions suggest that there is considerable flexibility in the method of dispute settlement under the LOS Convention, even if the procedures are ultimately compulsory in nature?

NOTES

1. *Promoting Dispute Settlement without Litigation.* Section 1 of Part XV is designed to promote settlement of disputes without resort to litigation. The conciliation procedure envisaged in Article 284 entails each party choosing two conciliators (of which one may be its national) from a list established by LOS Convention parties. The four conciliators would then select a fifth to serve as chairperson. After considering the views of both parties, the panel would issue a report in which it makes non-binding recommendations.

2. *Compulsory Dispute Settlement.* If the opportunities available under Section 1 fail to resolve the dispute, the LOS Convention contemplates compulsory dispute settlement under Section 2. Four possible fora are identified; why do you think there are so many options? Why not just insist that all states go to the International Court of Justice?

3. *Automatic Carve-outs.* Various limitations on compulsory dispute settlement are contained in Section 3 of Part XV. Consequently, for any given dispute that might arise, one must check Section 3 to see if that kind of

dispute has been carved out from Part XV. For example, Article 297(3)(a) states:

> Disputes concerning the interpretation or application of the provisions of this Convention with regard to fisheries shall be settled in accordance with section 2, except that the coastal State shall not be obliged to accept the submission to such settlement of any dispute relating to its sovereign rights with respect to the living resources in the exclusive economic zone or their exercise, including its discretionary powers for determining the allowable catch, its harvesting capacity, the allocation of surpluses to other States and the terms and conditions established in its conservation and management laws and regulations.

Can you imagine why such matters were carved out from LOS Convention compulsory dispute settlement, either for political or practical reasons?

4. *Optional Carve-outs.* In addition to the automatic carve-outs, states may under Article 298 opt to carve out certain additional types of disputes when they join the LOS Convention. For instance, under Article 298(1)(a)(i), a state may reject compulsory dispute settlement over "disputes concerning the interpretation or application of articles 15, 74 and 83 relating to sea boundary delimitations, or those involving historic bays or titles * * * ." Moreover, Article 298(1)(b) allows a state to carve-out from compulsory dispute settlement "disputes concerning military activities, including military activities by government vessels and aircraft engaged in non-commercial service, and disputes concerning law enforcement activities in regard to the exercise of sovereign rights or jurisdiction excluded from the jurisdiction of a court or tribunal under" the automatic carve-outs contained in Article 297(2) or (3).

5. *U.S. Proposed Approach to Compulsory Dispute Settlement.* When the Senate Foreign Relations Committee recommended, in October 2007, that the full Senate consent to U.S. ratification of the LOS Convention, it proposed that a resolution be adopted that stated in part:

> The advice and consent of the Senate * * * is subject to the following declarations:
>
> (1) The Government of the United States of America declares, in accordance with article 287(1), that it chooses the following means for the settlement of disputes concerning the interpretation or application of the Convention:
>
> > (A) a special arbitral tribunal constituted in accordance with Annex VIII for the settlement of disputes concerning the interpretation or application of the articles of the Convention relating to (1) fisheries, (2) protection and preservation of the marine environment, (3) marine scientific research, and (4) navigation, including pollution from vessels and by dumping; and
> >
> > (B) an arbitral tribunal constituted in accordance with Annex VII for the settlement of disputes not covered by the declaration in subparagraph (A).
>
> (2) The Government of the United States of America declares, in accordance with article 298(1), that it does not accept any of the procedures provided for in section 2 of Part XV (including, inter alia, the Sea–Bed Disputes Chamber procedure referred to in article 287(2)) with respect to the categories of disputes set forth in subparagraphs (a), (b),

and (c) of article 298(1). The United States further declares that its consent to accession to the Convention is conditioned upon the understanding that, under article 298(1)(b), each State Party has the exclusive right to determine whether its activities are or were military activities and that such determinations are not subject to review.

S. Exec. Rep. No. 110–9, § 2 (2007). What is the effect of the final portion of this language? Can the United States declare that it alone may determine whether particular activities are "military" in nature or is such a self-judging acceptance of dispute settlement voidable? If voidable, would it result in a tribunal being able to interpret the meaning of "military" or would it eviscerate the U.S. consent to ratification, resulting in the United States not being a party to the LOS Convention?

6. *Establishment of ITLOS.* After entry into force of the LOS Convention, the International Tribunal for the Law of the Sea (ITLOS) was established, based on Hamburg, Germany. ITLOS consists of twenty-one judges elected by secret ballot by the parties to the LOS Convention. Each State Party may nominate up to two candidates, no two judges may be nationals of the same state. Moreover, to preserve an equitable geographical distribution, there are no fewer than three members from the following geographical groups: African States, Asian States, Eastern European States, Latin American and Caribbean States, and Western European and Other States. Members are elected for nine years and may be re-elected; the terms of one third of the members expire every three years. See Rosenne, Establishing the International Tribunal on the Law of the Sea, 89 A.J.I.L. 806 (1995); ITLOS, http://www.itlos.org.

ITLOS has established two special seven-member chambers, one a Chamber for Fisheries Disputes and the other a Chamber for Marine Environment Disputes. The Chamber for Fisheries Disputes is available to hear any disputes which parties agree to submit to it concerning the conservation and management of marine living resources. The Chamber for Marine Environment Disputes was established to provide a forum to settle disputes relating to the protection and preservation of the marine environment.

7. *ITLOS's Jurisprudence.* Despite the sophistication of the dispute resolution process, litigation under the LOS Convention has been modest, with only fifteen cases been filed at ITLOS as of early 2009, mostly related to requests for prompt release of vessels or crew. The first case was filed in November 1997 by Saint Vincent and the Grenadines against the Government of Guinea with regard to the arrest of the oil tanker *M/V Saiga* off the coast of West Africa. *M/V "SAIGA" Case* (Saint Vincent and the Grenadines v. Guinea), ITLOS Case No. 1, Prompt Release (1997). In 1997, the *M/V Saiga* was serving as a bunkering vessel off the coast of West Africa, supplying gas oil to three fishing vessels licensed by Guinea to fish in its 200–mile exclusive economic zone (EEZ). After a refueling within Guinea's EEZ about twenty-two miles off the island of Alcatraz, the *M/V Saiga* departed Guinea's EEZ. The next day, Guinean patrol boats fired on, boarded, and arrested the *M/V Saiga* off the coast of Sierra Leone, beyond the southern limit of Guinea's EEZ. Two persons on board suffered gunshot wounds. The *M/V Saiga* was brought to Conakry, Guinea, where the ship and crew were detained, the

cargo of gas oil was removed, and the master was prosecuted for customs violations.

Saint Vincent and the Grenadines requested the Tribunal to order the prompt release of the *M/V Saiga*, its cargo and crew. The application, based on LOS Convention Article 292, alleged that Guinea did not comply with the requirements of the Convention for prompt release of the vessel or its crew and that the parties, both of whom are party to the Convention, did not agree within ten days from the time of detention to submit the case to another court or tribunal. On December 4, 1997 the full Tribunal ruled unanimously that the Court had jurisdiction and, by a vote of twelve to nine, the court ordered Guinea to release the vessel and the crew with the deposit of U.S. $400,000 as security. See Oxman & Bantz, Judgment of the International Tribunal for the Law of the Sea on Legality of Seizure of a Bunkering Ship at Sea and Prosecution of its Master for Customs Violations, 94 A.J.I.L. 140 (2000). For discussions of other ITLOS cases, see, e.g., Churchill & Scott, The MOX Plant Litigation: The First Half–Life, 53 I.C.L.Q. 643 (2004); Oxman, The "Grand Prince" (Belize v. France), 96 A.J.I.L. 219 (2002).

8. *Further Reading*. See Klein, Dispute Settlement in the UN Convention on the Law of the Sea (2005); The International Tribunal for the Law of the Sea: Law and Practice (Rao & Khan eds. 2001); The Rules of the International Tribunal for the Law of the Sea: A Commentary (Rao & Gautier eds. 2006); Eiriksson, The International Tribunal for the Law of the Sea (2000).

SECTION 12.   THE LAW OF OCEAN VESSELS

A.   NATIONALITY OF VESSELS: THE GENUINE LINK REQUIREMENT

The principal uses of the sea have required vessels. At one time, very small vessels were private property, while larger vessels tended to be public property and enjoyed privileges and immunities. In time, all vessels that plied the seas came to enjoy the protection of the state whose flag they flew (the flag state) by having registered with that state. LOS Convention Article 90 provides: "Every State, whether coastal or land-locked, has the right to sail ships flying its flag on the high seas." Further, Article 91 states:

1.   Every State shall fix the conditions for the grant of its nationality to ships, for the registration of ships in its territory, and for the right to fly its flag. Ships have the nationality of the State whose flag they are entitled to fly. There must exist a genuine link between the State and the ship.

2.   Every State shall issue to ships to which it has granted the right to fly its flag documents to that effect.

Some states, such as Liberia and Panama, permit vessel registry with few requirements, except the payment of a fee. These "flags of convenience" have been challenged on the grounds that a "genuine link" must exist between the ship and the state whose flag it flies, given the language of Article 91(1) above. But what exactly is meant by a "genuine link" between the flag state and the flag vessel? Is a ship owned by a national or domiciliary of the flag state bound to the flag state by a "genuine link"? What if the shipowner is a corporation created under the law of the state of registry, but whose shares are held by foreign interests, or if the ship is owned in part by foreign interests and in part by domestic interests? Is a ship that is required by the law of the state of registry to carry a crew made up in whole or in part of nationals of that state connected to the latter by a "genuine link"? If only the officers are required to be nationals? See Treves, Flags of Convenience Before the Law of the Sea Tribunal, 6 San Diego Int'l L.J. 179 (2004).

The report of the Senate Committee on Foreign Relations explaining the same clause in the 1958 Convention on the High Seas said:

> The International Law Commission did not decide upon a definition of the term "genuine link." This article as originally drafted by the Commission would have authorized other states to determine whether there was a "genuine link" between a ship and the flag state for purposes of recognition of the nationality of the ship.

> It was felt by some states attending the Conference on the Law of the Sea that the term "genuine link" could, depending upon how it was defined, limit the discretion of a state to decide which ships it would permit to fly its flag. Some states, which felt their flag vessels were at a competitive disadvantage with vessels sailing under the flags of other states, such as Panama and Liberia, were anxious to adopt a definition which states like Panama and Liberia could not meet.

> By a vote of 30 states, including the United States, against 15 states for, and 17 states abstaining, the provision was eliminated which would have enabled states other than the flag state to withhold recognition of the national character of a ship if they considered that there was no "genuine link" between the state and the ship.

> Thus, under the Convention on the High Seas, it is for each state to determine how it shall exercise jurisdiction and control in administrative, technical and social matters over ships flying its flag. The "genuine link" requirement need not have any effect upon the practice of registering American built or owned vessels in such countries as Panama or Liberia. The existence of a "genuine link" between the state and the ship is not a condition of recognition of the nationality of a ship; that is, no state can claim the right to determine unilaterally that no genuine link exists between a ship and the flag state. Nevertheless, there is a possibility that a state, with respect to a particular ship, may assert before an agreed tribunal, such as the International Court of Justice, that no genuine link exists. In such event, it would be for the Court to decide whether or not a "genuine link" existed.

Executive Report No. 5, Law of the Sea Conventions, 106 Cong. Rec. 11189, 11190; see Restatement (Third) § 501, Comment *b*; Boczek, Flags of Convenience 39–53 (1962).

B. FLAG STATE JURISDICTION OVER VESSELS

Once flagged to a state, that vessel *while on the high seas* is subject exclusively to the jurisdiction of the flag state, absent exceptional circumstances provided for in the LOS Convention or other international agreements. See *supra* Section 8(B). Various duties of the flag state are set forth under Article 94; the flag state must "effectively exercise its jurisdiction and control in administrative, technical and social matters over ships flying its flag," and in particular, shall (1) maintain a register of ships containing the names and particulars of ships flying its flag; (2) assume jurisdiction under its internal law over each ship flying its flag and its master, officers and crew; and (3) take measures necessary for ensuring safety at sea, including with respect the construction, equipment and seaworthiness of ships, and the training of its crews.

What happens, however, when the flag vessel enters the territorial or internal waters of a foreign state? Does the flag state still have jurisdiction to prosecute a crime committed on board the vessel while in those waters?

UNITED STATES v. FLORES

Supreme Court of the United States, 1933
289 U.S. 137 (footnotes omitted)

JUSTICE STONE: By indictment found in the District Court for Eastern Pennsylvania it was charged that appellee, a citizen of the United States, murdered another citizen of the United States upon the S.S. "Padnsay," an American vessel, while at anchor in the Port of Matadi, in the Belgian Congo, a place subject to the sovereignty of the Kingdom of Belgium, and that appellee, after the commission of the crime, was first brought into the Port of Philadelphia, a place within the territorial jurisdiction of the District Court. * * * [T]he "Padnsay," at the time of the offense charged, was unloading, being attached to the shore by cables, at a point 250 miles inland from the mouth of the Congo river.

The District Court * * * sustained a demurrer to the indictment and discharged the prisoner on the ground that the court was without jurisdiction to try the offense charged. *United States v. Flores* [3 F. Supp. 134 (E.D. Pa. 1932)]. The case comes here by direct appeal * * *.

Sections 273 and 275 of the Criminal Code, 18 U.S.C. §§ 452, 454, define murder and fix its punishment. Section 272, upon the construction of which the court below rested its decision, makes punishable offenses defined by other sections of the Criminal Code, among other cases, "when committed within the admiralty and maritime jurisdiction of the United States and out of the jurisdiction of any particular State on board any vessel belonging in whole or in part to the United States" or any of its nationals. And by § 41 of the Judicial Code, 28 U.S.C. § 102, venue to try offenses "committed upon the high seas, or elsewhere out of the jurisdiction of any particular State or district," is "in the district where the offender is found, or into which he is first brought." As the offense charged here was committed on board a vessel lying outside the territorial jurisdiction of a state * * * , and within that of a foreign sovereignty, the court below was without jurisdiction to try and punish the offense unless it was within the admiralty and maritime jurisdiction of the United States.

Two questions are presented on this appeal, first, whether the extension of the judicial power of the federal government "to all cases of admiralty and maritime jurisdiction," by Art. 3, § 2, of the Constitution confers on Congress power to define and punish offenses perpetrated by a citizen of the United States on board one of its merchant vessels lying in navigable waters within the territorial limits of another sovereignty; and second, whether Congress has exercised that power by the enactment of § 272 of the Criminal Code under which the indictment was found.

[The Court held that Congress had the constitutional power to define and punish crimes on American vessels in foreign waters, and that the language of the statute making it applicable to offenses committed on an American vessel outside the jurisdiction of a state "within the admiralty and maritime jurisdiction of the United States" was broad enough to include crimes in the "territorial waters" of a foreign country. Id. at 146, 150. Mr. Justice Stone continued:]

It is true that the criminal jurisdiction of the United States is in general based on the territorial principle, and criminal statutes of the United States are not by implication given an extraterritorial effect. *United States v. Bowman*, 260 U.S. 94, 98; compare *Blackmer v. United States*, 284 U.S. 421. But that principle has never been thought to be applicable to a merchant vessel which, for purposes of the jurisdiction of the courts of the sovereignty whose flag it flies to punish crimes committed upon it, is deemed to be a part of the territory of that sovereignty, and not to lose that character when in navigable waters within the territorial limits of another sovereignty. * * * Subject to the right of the territorial sovereignty to assert jurisdiction over offenses disturbing the peace of the port, it has been supported by writers on international law, and has been recognized by France, Belgium, and other continental countries, as well as by England and the United States. * * *

* * *

A related but different question, not presented here, may arise when jurisdiction over an offense committed on a foreign vessel is asserted by the sovereignty in whose waters it was lying at the time of its commission, since for some purposes, the jurisdiction may be regarded as concurrent, in that the courts of either sovereignty may try the offense.

There is not entire agreement among nations or the writers on international law as to which sovereignty should yield to the other when the jurisdiction is asserted by both. See Jessup, the Law of Territorial Waters, 144–93. The position of the United States exemplified in *Wildenhus's Case*, 120 U.S. 1, has been that at least in the case of major crimes, affecting the peace and tranquillity of the port, the jurisdiction asserted by the sovereignty of the port must prevail over that of the vessel. * * *

This doctrine does not impinge on that laid down in *United States v. Rodgers* [150 U.S. 249 (1893)], that the United States may define and punish offenses committed by its own citizens on its own vessels while within foreign waters where the local sovereign has not asserted its jurisdiction. In the absence of any controlling treaty provision, and any assertion of jurisdiction by the territorial sovereign, it is the duty of the courts of the United States to apply to offenses committed by its citizens on vessels flying its flag, its own statutes, interpreted in the light of recognized principles of international law. So applied the indictment here sufficiently charges an offense within the admiralty and maritime jurisdiction of the United States and the judgment below must be reversed.

NOTES

1. *Flag State "Floating Territory"?* Because of the flag state's ability to apply its law to a vessel as it travels around the world, it is sometimes said that the vessel is "floating territory" of the flag state, a characterization that, strictly speaking, is not accurate. There are various ways in which the vessel does not have the status of "territory" of the flag state, especially as it becomes subject to the jurisdiction of coastal or port states in the course of its journey. Nevertheless, the near-assimilation of vessels to the flag-state's territory is apparent in various cases, old and new. For example, *Regina v. Leslie*, 8 Cox's Criminal Law Cases 269, 277 (Ct. Crim. App. 1860), involved the question of whether a conviction for false imprisonment could be sustained against the master of an English merchant ship who, under contract with the Chilean Government, transported to England a group of persons who had been banished from Chile and who were placed aboard the ship by Chilean Government officials while the ship was in Chilean waters. After indicating that the conviction could not be sustained for what was done in Chilean waters because the Chilean Government could "justify all that it did within its own territory" and the defendant merely acted as its agent, the Court sustained the conviction for acts committed on the high seas, stating:

> It is clear that an English ship on the high seas, out of any foreign territory, is subject to the laws of England, and persons, whether foreign or English, on board such ship are as much amenable to English law as they would be on English soil. In *Reg. v. Sattler* (7 Cox Crim. Cas. 431), this principle was acted on so as to make the prisoner, a foreigner, responsible for murder on board an English ship at sea. The same principle has been laid down by foreign writers on international law * * *.

2. *Exercising Flag State Enforcement in Foreign Waters.* In March 1920, Charles Vincenti, a citizen of the United States, was arrested while on an American motorboat in British territorial waters off North and South Bimini,

Bahama Islands, British West Indies, by a special officer of the Department of Justice and by two internal-revenue agents holding a warrant against him for unlawful sale of liquor in Maryland. Vincenti was taken to the United States, although the motorboat was fired upon and pursued by British officials. Subsequently, the Department of State informed the British Ambassador that,

> [Y]ou will observe that the persons who arrested Vincenti and forcibly removed him from the Biminis Islands, acted on their own initiative and without the knowledge or approval of this Government in any way, and have been reprimanded and indefinitely suspended for their participation in the affair. Furthermore, it appears that Vincenti's bail has been exonerated and all proceedings subsequent to his unlawful arrest have been revoked. The incident is greatly regretted by this Government and I trust that the steps taken to make amends for it are entirely satisfactory to your Government.

The British Ambassador replied that the action taken by the United States was satisfactory. 1 Hackworth at 624. What circumstances distinguish the jurisdiction exercised by the United States in the Vincenti affair from that exercised in *United States v. Flores*? In *United States v. Conroy*, 589 F.2d 1258 (5th Cir. 1979), the court held that the United States Coast Guard had the authority to search an American vessel in foreign territorial waters. In that case the local government had agreed to the search but the court suggested that permission of the local government was not required. Id. at 1268. Do you think the court was correct?

3. *High Seas Collisions: Who Can Prosecute?* What if on the high seas a flag state's vessel collides with a vessel flying a different flag; which state or states have jurisdiction to over the matter? LOS Convention Article 97(1) provides:

> In the event of a collision or any other incident of navigation concerning a ship on the high seas, involving the penal or disciplinary responsibility of the master or of any other person in the service of the ship, no penal or disciplinary proceedings may be instituted against such person except before the judicial or administrative authorities either of the flag State or of the State of which such person is a national.

This provision, which also appears in Article 11 of the 1958 Convention on the High Seas, overturns in part the holding of the Permanent Court of International Justice in the *Lotus Case, supra* Chapter 2, Section 2(A), which allowed Turkey to pursue penal sections against a person who was neither its national nor part of the crew of its flag vessel. To some extent, this result had already been achieved by the parties to the International Convention for the Unification of Certain Rules Relating to Penal Jurisdiction in Matters of Collisions and Other Incidents of Navigation, May 10, 1952, 439 U.N.T.S. 233.

4. *Exercising Jurisdiction Based on Ownership Interests*. What if, rather than jurisdiction being exercised by a flag state, it is exercised by a state whose nationals own the vessel? Is that permissible when the vessel is on the high seas? When it is in the territorial or internal waters of a foreign state? The "special maritime and territorial jurisdiction of the United States," which triggers the application of a range of federal statutes, encompasses:

The high seas, any other waters within the admiralty and maritime jurisdiction of the United States and out of the jurisdiction of any particular State, *and any vessel belonging in whole or in part to the United States or any citizen thereof,* or to any corporation created by or under the laws of the United States, or of any State, Territory, District, or possession thereof, when such vessel is within the admiralty and maritime jurisdiction of the United States and out of the jurisdiction of any particular State.

18 U.S.C. § 7(1) (2000) (emphasis added). Does § 7(1) purport to assert U.S. jurisdiction over acts committed on foreign-flag vessels whenever they are owned in whole or in part by a U.S. citizen? Does it matter where the vessel is located? Do you think § 7(1) is permissible as a matter of international law? See Restatement (Third) § 403, Reporters' Note 9; Id. § 502, Reporters' Note 4.

C. COASTAL STATE JURISDICTION OVER VESSELS

Coastal (and port) state jurisdiction over vessels whose activities pose a threat to the marine environment are discussed *supra* this Chapter, Section 10. What about coastal or port state jurisdiction in other situations? One likely circumstance where such jurisdiction might be exercised is with respect to a vessel that is transiting through a coastal state's territorial waters. For example, suppose a Canadian-flagged vessel is traveling through U.S. territorial waters from Vancouver en route to Puerto Vallarta, Mexico. A passenger calls the Los Angeles police department to report a suspected murder on board the vessel committed during the passage. Can the Los Angeles police stop and board the vessel to investigate the alleged crime? Alternatively, suppose the owner of the vessel owes you money; can you get an order from a Los Angeles court that allows for seizure and attachment of the vessel?

UNITED NATIONS CONVENTION ON THE LAW OF THE SEA, ARTICLES 27–28

Adopted Dec. 10, 1982
1833 U.N.T.S. 3

Article 27

Criminal jurisdiction on board a foreign ship

1. The criminal jurisdiction of the coastal State should not be exercised on board a foreign ship passing through the territorial sea to arrest any person or to conduct any investigation in connection with any crime committed on board the ship during its passage, save only in the following cases:

(a) if the consequences of the crime extend to the coastal State;

(b) if the crime is of a kind to disturb the peace of the country or the good order of the territorial sea;

(E.D. La. 1998); *United States v. Pizdrint*, 983 F.Supp. 1110 (M.D. Fl. 1997). For application of a state criminal statute in similar circumstances, see *State v. Stepansky*, 761 So.2d 1027 (Sup. Ct. Fla. 2000).

D. PORT STATE JURISDICTION OVER VESSELS

WILDENHUS' CASE

Supreme Court of the United States, 1887
120 U.S. 1

[Wildenhus, a Belgian national, killed another Belgian national below the deck of the Belgian vessel of which they were both crew members, which was, at the time of the slaying, moored to a dock in Jersey City. The local police authorities arrested Wildenhus, charging him with the killing, and held two other crew members as witnesses. The Belgian consul applied for a writ of *habeas corpus*, citing Article 11 of the Convention Concerning the Rights, Privileges and Immunities of Consular Officers, art. XI, Mar. 9, 1880, 21 Stat. 776, between Belgium and the United States, which provided: "The consuls-general, consuls, vice-consuls and consular agents shall have exclusive charge of the internal order of the merchant vessels of their nation, and shall alone take cognizance of all differences which may arise, either at sea or in port, between the captains, officers and crews, without exception, particularly with reference to the adjustment of wages and the execution of contracts. The local authorities shall not interfere except when the disorder that has arisen is of such a nature as to disturb tranquility and public order on shore, or in the port, or when a person of the country or not belonging to the crew shall be concerned therein." The Circuit Court refused to order the release of the prisoners, and the consul appealed to the Supreme Court.]

Waite, C.J. * * * §§ 751 and 753 of the Revised Statutes the courts of the United States have power to issue writs of *habeas corpus* which shall extend to prisoners in jail when they are in "custody in violation of the constitution or a law or treaty of the United States," and the question we have to consider is whether these prisoners are held in violation of the provisions of the existing treaty between the United States and Belgium.

It is part of the law of civilized nations that, when a merchant vessel of one country enters the ports of another for the purposes of trade, it subjects itself to the law of the place to which it goes, unless by treaty or otherwise the two countries have come to some different understanding or agreement; for, as was said by Chief Justice Marshall in *The Exchange*, 7 Cranch, 144: "It would be obviously inconvenient and dangerous to society, and would subject the laws to continual infraction, and the government to degradation, if such ... merchants did not owe temporary and local allegiance, and were not amenable to the jurisdiction of the country." * * * And the English judges have uniformly recognized the rights of the courts of the country of which the port is part to punish crimes committed by one foreigner on another in a foreign merchant ship.

Regina v. Cunningham, Bell, C.C. 72; *S.C.* 8 Cox, C.C. 104; *Regina v. Anderson*, 11 Cox, C.C. 198, 204; *S.C.L.R.* 1 C.C. 161, 165; *Regina v. Keyn*, 13 Cox, C.C. 403, 486, 525; *S.C.* 2 Ex. Div. 63, 161, 213. As the owner has voluntarily taken his vessel for his own private purposes to a place within the dominion of a government other than his own, and from which he seeks protection during his stay, he owes that government such allegiance for the time being as is due for the protection to which he becomes entitled.

From experience, however, it was found long ago that it would be beneficial to commerce if the local government would abstain from interfering with the internal discipline of the ship, and the general regulation of the rights and duties of the officers and crew towards the vessel or among themselves. And so by comity it came to be generally understood among civilized nations that all matters of discipline and all things done on board which affected only the vessel or those belonging to her, and did not involve the peace or dignity of the country, or the tranquility of the port, should be left by the local government to be dealt with by the authorities of the nation to which the vessel belonged as the laws of that nation or the interests of its commerce should require. But if crimes are committed on board of a character to disturb the peace and tranquility of the country to which the vessel has been brought, the offenders have never by comity or usage been entitled to any exemption from the operation of the local laws for their punishment, if the local tribunals see fit to assert their authority. Such being the general public law on this subject, treaties and conventions have been entered into by nations having commercial intercourse, the purpose of which was to settle and define the rights and duties of the contracting parties with respect to each other in these particulars, and thus prevent the inconvenience that might arise from attempts to exercise conflicting jurisdictions.

The first of these conventions entered into by the United States after the adoption of the Constitution was with France, on the 14th of November, 1788, 8 Stat. 106, "for the purpose of defining and establishing the functions and privileges of their respective consuls and vice-consuls," Art. VIII of which is as follows:

"The consuls or vice-consuls shall exercise police [power] over all the vessels of their respective nations, and shall have on board the said vessels all power and jurisdiction in civil matters in all the disputes which may there arise. They shall have entire inspection over the said vessels, their crew, and the changes and substitutions there to be made, for which purpose they may go on board the said vessels whenever they may judge it necessary. Well understood that the functions hereby allowed shall be confined to the interior of the vessels, and that they shall not take place in any case which shall have any interference with the police of the ports where the said vessels shall be."

It was when this convention was in force that the cases of *The Sally* and *The Newton* arose * * *. *The Sally* was an American merchant vessel in the port of Marseilles, and *The Newton* a vessel of a similar character in the port of Antwerp, then under the dominion of France. In the case of *The Sally,* the mate, in the alleged exercise of discipline over the crew, had inflicted a severe wound on one of the seamen, and, in that of *The Newton,* one seaman had made an assault on another seaman in the vessel's boat. In each case the proper consul of the United States claimed exclusive jurisdiction of the offense, and so did the local authorities of the port; but the council of state, a branch of the political department of the government of France to which the matter was referred, pronounced against the local tribunals, "considering that one of these cases was that of an assault committed in the boat of the American ship *Newton* by one of the crew upon another, and the other was that of a severe wound inflicted by the mate of the American ship *Sally* upon one of the seamen for having made use of the boat without leave." This was clearly because the things done were not such as to disturb "the peace or tranquility of the port." Wheaton's Elements Int. Law, 3d ed. 154. The case of *The Sally* was simply a quarrel between certain of the crew while constructively on board the vessel, and that of *The Newton* grew out of a punishment inflicted by an officer on one of the crew for disobedience of orders. Both were evidently of a character to affect only the police of the vessel, and thus within the authority expressly granted to the consul by the treaty.

[The Court then analyzed a number of treaties subsequently entered into by the United States, and concluded that these treaties either impliedly, or as in the case of the Belgian treaty under consideration explicitly] gave the consuls authority to cause proper order to be maintained on board, and to decide disputes between the officers and crew, but allowed the local authorities to interfere if the disorders taking place on board were of such a nature as to disturb the public tranquility, and that is substantially all there is in the convention with Belgium which we have now to consider. This treaty is the law which now governs the conduct of the United States and Belgium towards each other in this particular. Each nation has granted to the other such local jurisdiction within its own dominion as may be necessary to maintain order on board a merchant vessel, but has reserved to itself the right to interfere if the disorder on board is of a nature to disturb the public tranquility.

* * * [T]he only important question left for our determination is whether the thing which has been done—the disorder that has arisen—on board this vessel is of a nature to disturb the public peace, or, as some writers term it, the "public repose" of the people who look to the state of New Jersey for their protection. If the thing done—"the disorder," as it is called in the treaty—is of a character to affect those on shore or in the port when it becomes known, the fact that only those on the ship saw it when it was done is a matter of no moment. Those who are not on the vessel pay no special attention to the mere disputes or quarrels of the seamen while on board, whether they occur under deck or above. Neither

do they as a rule care for anything done on board which relates only to the discipline of the ship, or to the preservation of order and authority. Not so, however, with crimes which from their gravity awaken a public interest as soon as they become known, and especially those of a character which every civilized nation considers itself bound to provide a severe punishment for when committed within its own jurisdiction. In such cases inquiry is certain to be instituted at once to ascertain how or why the thing was done, and the popular excitement rises or falls as the news spreads, and the facts become known. It is not alone the publicity of the act, or the noise and clamor which attends it, that fixes the nature of the crime, but the act, itself. If that is of a character to awaken public interest when it becomes known, it is a "disorder," the nature of which is to affect the community at large, and consequently to invoke the power of the local government whose people have been disturbed by what was done. The very nature of such an act is to disturb the quiet of a peaceful community, and to create, in the language of the treaty, a "disorder" which will "disturb tranquility and public order on shore or in the port." The principle which governs the whole matter is this: Disorders which disturb only the peace of the ship or those on board are to be dealt with exclusively by the sovereignty of the home of the ship, but those which disturb the public peace may be suppressed, and, if need be, the offenders punished, by the proper authorities of the local jurisdiction. It may not be easy at all times to determine to which of the two jurisdictions a particular act of disorder belongs. Much will undoubtedly depend on the attending circumstances of the particular case, but all must concede that felonious homicide is a subject for the local jurisdiction; and that, if the proper authorities are proceeding with the case in a regular way the consul has no right to interfere to prevent it.

* * *

The judgment of the circuit court is affirmed.

SPECTOR v. NORWEGIAN CRUISE LINE LTD.

Supreme Court of the United States, 2005
545 U.S. 119

JUSTICE KENNEDY announced the judgment of the Court * * *.

The respondent Norwegian Cruise Line Ltd. (NCL), a Bermuda Corporation with a principal place of business in Miami, Florida, operates cruise ships that depart from, and return to, ports in the United States. The ships are essentially floating resorts. They provide passengers with staterooms or cabins, food, and entertainment. The cruise ships stop at different ports of call where passengers may disembark. Most of the passengers on these cruises are United States residents; under the terms and conditions of the tickets, disputes between passengers and NCL are to be governed by United States law; and NCL relies upon extensive advertising in the United States to promote its cruises and increase its revenues.

Despite the fact that the cruises are operated by a company based in the United States, serve predominately United States residents, and are in most other respects United States-centered ventures, almost all of NCL's cruise ships are registered in other countries, flying so-called flags of convenience. The two NCL cruise ships that are the subject of the present litigation, the Norwegian Sea and the Norwegian Star, are both registered in the Bahamas.

The petitioners are disabled individuals and their companions who purchased tickets in 1998 or 1999 for round-trip cruises on the Norwegian Sea or the Norwegian Star, with departures from Houston, Texas. Naming NCL as the defendant, the petitioners filed a class action in the United States District Court for the Southern District of Texas on behalf of all persons similarly situated. They sought declaratory and injunctive relief under Title III of the ADA, which prohibits discrimination on the basis of disability. * * *

[The Court of Appeals for the Fifth Circuit dismissed the claim, finding that general statutes do not apply to foreign-flag vessels in United States territory absent a clear indication of congressional intent. *Spector v. Norwegian Cruise Line Ltd.*, 356 F.3d 641, 644 (5th Cir. 2004).]

* * *

This Court has long held that general statutes are presumed to apply to conduct that takes place aboard a foreign-flag vessel in United States territory if the interests of the United States or its citizens, rather than interests internal to the ship, are at stake. See *Cunard S. S. Co. v. Mellon*, 262 U.S. 100, 127 (1923) (holding that the general terms of the National Prohibition Act apply to foreign-flag ships in United States waters because "[t]here is in the act no provision making it [in]applicable" to such ships); *Uravic v. F. Jarka Co.*, 282 U.S. 234, 240 (1931) (holding that "general words" should be "generally applied" and that therefore there is "no reason for limiting the liability for torts committed [aboard foreign-flag ships in United States territory] when they go beyond the scope of discipline and private matters that do not interest the territorial power"). The general rule that United States statutes apply to foreign-flag ships in United States territory is subject only to a narrow exception. Absent a clear statement of congressional intent, general statutes may not apply to foreign-flag vessels insofar as they regulate matters that involve only the internal order and discipline of the vessel, rather than the peace of the port. This qualification derives from the understanding that, as a matter of international comity, "all matters of discipline and all things done on board which affec[t] only the vessel or those belonging to her, and [do] not involve the peace or dignity of the country, or the tranquility of the port, should be left by the local government to be dealt with by the authorities of the nation to which the vessel belonged." *Wildenhus's Case*, 120 U.S. 1, 12 (1887). This exception to the usual presumption, however, does not extend beyond matters of internal order and discipline. "[I]f crimes are committed on board [a foreign-flag vessel] of a character to disturb the peace and tranquility of the country to which the vessel has been brought, the offenders have never by comity or usage been entitled to any exemption from the operation of the local laws." *Ibid.*

* * *

The precise content of the category "internal affairs" (or, as it is variously denoted in the case law, "internal order" or "internal operations") is difficult to define with precision. There is, moreover, some ambiguity in our cases as to whether the relevant category of activities is restricted to matters that affect only the internal order of the ship when there is no effect on United States interests, or whether the clear statement rule further comes into play if the predominant effect of a statutory requirement is on a foreign ship's internal affairs but the requirement also promotes the welfare of United States residents or territory. We need not attempt to define the relevant protected category with precision. It suffices to observe that the guiding principles in determining whether the clear statement rule is triggered are the desire for international comity and the presumed lack of interest by the territorial sovereign in matters that bear no substantial relation to the peace and tranquility of the port.

It is plain that Title III might impose any number of duties on cruise ships that have nothing to do with a ship's internal affairs. The pleadings and briefs in this case illustrate, but do not exhaust, the ways a cruise ship might offend such a duty. The petitioners allege the respondent charged disabled passengers higher fares and required disabled passengers to pay special surcharges, * * *; maintained evacuation programs and equipment in locations not accessible to disabled individuals * * *; required disabled individuals, but not other passengers, to waive any potential medical liability and to travel with a companion * * *; and reserved the right to remove from the ship any disabled individual whose presence endangers the "comfort" of other passengers * * * . The petitioners also allege more generally that respondent "failed to make reasonable modifications in policies, practices, and procedures" necessary to ensure the petitioners' full enjoyment of the services respondent offered. * * * These are bare allegations, and their truth is not conceded. We express no opinion on the factual support for those claims. We can say, however, that none of these alleged Title III violations implicate any requirement that would interfere with the internal affairs and management of a vessel as our cases have employed that term.

At least one subset of the petitioners' allegations, however, would appear to involve requirements that might be construed as relating to the internal affairs of foreign-flag cruise ships. These allegations concern physical barriers to access on board. For example, according to the petitioners, most of the cabins on the respondent's cruise ships, including the most attractive cabins in the most desirable locations, are not accessible to disabled passengers. * * *

* * *

Title III requires barrier removal if it is "readily achievable" * * *.

Surely a barrier removal requirement under Title III that would bring a vessel into noncompliance with the International Convention for the Safety of Life at Sea (SOLAS), Nov. 1, 1974, [1979–1980], 32 U.S.T. 47, T.I.A.S. No. 9700, or any other international legal obligation, would create serious difficulties for the vessel and would have a substantial impact on its operation, and thus would not be "readily achievable." This understanding of the statute, urged by the United States, is eminently reasonable. * * * If, moreover, Title III's "readily achievable" exemption were not to take conflicts with international law into account, it would lead to the anomalous result that American cruise ships are obligated to comply with Title III even if doing so brings them into noncompliance with SOLAS, whereas foreign ships—which unlike American ships have the benefit of the internal affairs clear statement rule—would not be so obligated. Congress could not have intended this result.

* * *

Title III's own limitations and qualifications prevent the statute from imposing requirements that would conflict with international obligations or threaten shipboard safety. These limitations and qualifications, though framed in general terms, employ a conventional vocabulary for instructing courts in the interpretation and application of the statute. If, on remand, it becomes clear that even after these limitations are taken into account Title III nonetheless imposes certain requirements that would interfere with the internal affairs of foreign ships—perhaps, for example, by requiring permanent and substantial structural modifications—the clear statement rule would come into play. It is also open to the court on remand to consider application of the clear statement rule at the outset if, as a prudential matter, that appears to be the more appropriate course.

We reverse the judgment of the Court of Appeals and remand the case for further proceedings.

JUSTICE SCALIA, with whom THE CHIEF JUSTICE and JUSTICE O'CONNOR join, and with whom JUSTICE THOMAS joins * * * dissenting.

* * *

As the plurality explains, where a law would interfere with the regulation of a ship's internal order, we require a clear statement that Congress intended such a result. * * * This rule is predicated on the "rule of international law that the law of the flag ship ordinarily governs the internal affairs of a ship," *McCulloch v. Sociedad Nacional de Marineros de Honduras*, 372 U.S. 10, 21 (1963), and is designed to avoid "the possibilit[y] of international discord," *Benz v. Compania Naviera Hidalgo, S.A.*, 353 U.S. 138, 147 (1957); see also *McCulloch, supra*, at 19.

The clear-statement rule finds support not only in *Benz* and *McCulloch*, but in cases like *Cunard S.S. Co. v. Mellon*, 262 U.S. 100, 128–29 (1923), where we held that the National Prohibition Act, 41 Stat. 305, forbade foreign-flag ships from carrying or serving alcohol in United States territorial waters. Though we did not say so expressly in that case, prohibiting the carrying and serving of alcohol in United States waters cannot be said to affect the "internal order" of the ship, because it does not in any way affect the operation or functioning of the craft. Similarly, in *Lauritzen v. Larsen*, 345 U.S. 571 (1953), and *Hellenic Lines Ltd. v. Rhoditis*, 398 U.S. 306 (1970), we did *not* employ a clear-statement rule in determining whether foreign seamen injured aboard foreign-flag ships could recover under the Jones Act, 41 Stat. 1007, 46 U.S.C. App. § 688. We distinguished these cases in *McCulloch*, explaining that a clear statement is not required "in different contexts, such as the Jones Act ... where *the pervasive regulation of the internal order of a ship may not be present*." 372 U.S., at 19, n. 9 (emphasis added).

As the plurality concedes, * * * the structural modifications that Title III of the ADA requires under its barrier-removal provisions, * * * would plainly affect the ship's "internal order." Rendering exterior cabins handicapped-accessible, changing the levels of coamings, and adding public restrooms—the types of modifications petitioners request—would require alteration of core physical aspects of the ship, some of which relate to safety. (Safety has, under international law, traditionally been the province of a ship's flag state.) This is quite different from prohibiting alcohol in United States waters or imposing tort liability for injuries sustained on foreign ships in port—the laws at issue in *Cunard* and the Jones Act cases. * * *

* * *

The purpose of the "internal order" clear-statement requirement is to avoid casually subjecting oceangoing vessels to laws that pose obvious risks of conflict with the laws of the ship's flag state, the laws of other nations, and international obligations to which the vessels are subject. That structural modifications required under Title III qualify as matters of "internal order" is confirmed by the fact that they may already conflict with the International Convention for the Safety of Life at Sea (SOLAS), Nov. 1, 1974, [1979–1980] 32 U.S.T. 47, T.I.A.S. No. 9700. That treaty, which establishes the safety standards governing the design and maintenance of oceangoing ships, has been ratified by 155 countries. * * * The ADA Accessibility Guidelines (ADAAG) Review Advisory Committee—the Government body Congress has charged with formulating the Title III barrier-removal guidelines—has promulgated rules requiring at least one accessible means of egress to be an elevator, whereas SOLAS, which requires at least two means of escape, does not allow elevators to be one of them.

* * *

Similar inconsistencies may exist between Title III's structural requirements and the disability laws of other countries. * * *

* * *

I would therefore affirm the Fifth Circuit's judgment that Title III of the ADA does not apply to foreign-flag cruise ships in United States territorial waters.

NOTES

1. *The Power of the Port.* If the local police and judicial authorities may decide for themselves whether a particular incident "disturbs the peace of the port," even though there is no actual disturbance, can it be said that the "peace of the port" doctrine ever allows the foreign vessel to claim immunity as of right? The British view is that "the subjection of the ship to the local criminal jurisdiction is * * * complete and that any derogation from it is a matter of comity in the discretion of the coastal state." Brierly, The Law of Nations 223 (6th ed. Waldock ed. 1963). When the United States prohibition laws were held, in *Cunard S.S. Co. v. Mellon*, 262 U.S. 100 (1923), to be applicable to foreign vessels temporarily in United States ports, the protests of foreign governments were based almost entirely on appeals to comity. Jessup, The Law of Territorial Waters and Maritime Jurisdiction 221–28 (1927). For general discussions of criminal jurisdiction over visiting foreign vessels, see id. at 144–94; Stanger, Criminal Jurisdiction over Visiting Armed Forces, 52 Int'l L. Stud. v, 43–54 (1957–58).

2. *Handling Concurrent Jurisdiction.* Obviously, if both the port (or coastal) state and the flag state have jurisdiction over acts occurring on board the vessel, there is the potential for competing jurisdiction, as was recognized in the *Flores* case *infra* this Section. Should the flag state defer to the port state? A threshold issue is whether, in fact, the two states both wish to exercise jurisdiction. In *United States v. Reagan*, 453 F.2d 165 (6th Cir. 1971), the defendant was accused of killing a fellow seaman on a U.S. vessel in a German harbor. The Court said in part:

> Since there is no "controlling treaty provision" the resolution of the question before us turns upon whether there has been "any assertion of jurisdiction by the territorial sovereign." It is our view that there was no "assertion of jurisdiction" by Germany and, therefore, that the district court was not without jurisdiction.

> The record shows that Reagan was taken into custody by German authorities on December 16, 1966, and judicially committed to a German mental institution on December 17, 1966, when his ship went to sea. He was subsequently released (after the return of the *SS Thunderbird* to port) and on April 5, 1967 the appropriate local court refused to issue a warrant for Reagan's arrest requested by the local prosecutor, finding that there was no probable cause for the issuance of such a warrant. The German court had before it the results of a rather extensive police investigation.

> We do not believe that this preliminary proceeding constituted an "assertion of jurisdiction" by the local sovereign which would operate to oust the jurisdiction of the flag sovereign. It would appear that for whatever its reasons, the German court declined to "assert jurisdiction" within the meaning of *Flores, supra*. The application of the doctrine of

"concurrent jurisdiction" is based on principles of comity. Assertion by the court below of its own jurisdiction in no way infringed upon the jurisdiction of the German court. The appropriate German authorities carefully scrutinized the matter and no formal charges were ever brought. There was no determination of Reagan's guilt or innocence. A different case would be presented if Reagan had been brought to trial in Germany or perhaps even if he had been indicted in Germany. We hold that the district court did have proper subject matter jurisdiction.

Id. at 171. Assuming that both states do wish to exercise jurisdiction, the advantage may lie with the state where the act occurred, assuming the vessel is still present there. Hyde notes:

It may be doubted whether in the absence of a concession by treaty, the territorial sovereign is deterred by the operation of any rule of international law from exercising through its local courts jurisdiction over civil controversies between masters and members of a crew, when the judicial aid of its tribunals is invoked by the latter, and notably when a libel *in rem* is filed against the ship. It is to be observed, however, that American courts exercise discretion in taking or withholding jurisdiction according to the circumstances of the particular case. Their action in so doing is not to be regarded as indicative of any requirement of public international law.

Hyde at 742–43. On the application of the doctrine of *forum non conveniens* in litigation involving foreign merchant vessels and seamen, see *The Ester*, 190 F. 216 (E.D.S.C. 1911) (summary of United States practice); Bickel, The Doctrine of Forum Non Conveniens as Applied in the Federal Courts in Matters of Admiralty, 35 Cornell L.Q. 12 (1949).

As the Chief Justice indicates in *Wildenhus' Case,* states customarily resort to international agreements in order to reconcile potential conflicts of jurisdiction that might arise from the presence of merchantmen in foreign ports. The Convention Relating to Consular Officers, United States–United Kingdom, June 6, 1951, 3 U.S.T. 3426, 165 U.N.T.S. 121, provides in Article 22:

(2) Without prejudice to the right of the administrative and judicial authorities of the territory to take cognizance of crimes or offenses committed on board the vessel when she is in the ports or in the territorial waters of the territory and which are cognizable under the local law or to enforce local laws applicable to vessels in ports and territorial waters or persons and property thereon, it is the common intention of the High Contracting Parties that the administrative and police authorities of the territory should not, except at the request or with the consent of the consular officer,

(a) concern themselves with any matter taking place on board the vessel unless for the preservation of peace and order or in the interests of public health or safety, or

(b) institute prosecutions in respect of crimes or offenses committed on board the vessel unless they are of a serious character or involve the tranquillity of the port or unless they are committed by or against persons other than the crew.

3. *U.S. Practice in Port State Jurisdiction.* The United States has not ordinarily applied its law to events and transactions aboard foreign vessels. In *Lauritzen v. Larsen*, the U.S. Supreme Court rejected the applicability to a foreign vessel of the Jones Act, providing for compensation to seamen for injury suffered in the course of their employment. "By usage as old as the Nation, such statutes have been construed to apply only to areas and transactions in which American law would be considered operative under prevalent doctrines of international law." *Lauritzen v. Larsen*, 345 U.S. 571, 577 (1953).

> International or maritime law in such matters as this does not seek uniformity and does not purport to restrict any nation from making and altering its laws to govern its own shipping and territory. However, it aims at stability and order through usages which considerations of comity, reciprocity and long-range interest have developed to define the domain which each nation will claim as its own. Maritime law, like our municipal law, has attempted to avoid or resolve conflicts between competing laws by ascertaining and valuing points of contact between the transaction and the states or governments whose competing laws are involved. The criteria, in general, appear to be arrived at from weighing of the significance of one or more connecting factors between the shipping transaction regulated and the national interest served by the assertion of authority. It would not be candid to claim that our courts have arrived at satisfactory standards or apply those that they profess with perfect consistency. But in dealing with international commerce we cannot be unmindful of the necessity for mutual forbearance if retaliations are to be avoided; nor should we forget that any contact which we hold sufficient to warrant application of our law to a foreign transaction will logically be as strong a warrant for a foreign country to apply its law to an American transaction.

Id. at 582. In listing and weighing the various factors connecting a particular incident to different states, the Court said: "[The law of the flag] must prevail unless some heavy counterweight appears." Id. at 585–86. Do you think a "heavy counterweight" existed in *Spector v. Norwegian Cruise Line*? Or do you find Justice Scalia's dissent more persuasive? See Symeonides, Cruising in American Waters: Spector, Maritime Conflicts, and Choice of Law, 37 J. Mar. L. & Comm. 491 (2006).

4. *Vessels in Distress.* Vessels in distress that enter the territorial waters of a state in search of refuge, or as a result of *force majeure* or other necessity, are generally exempt from the jurisdiction of the port state. See *Kate A. Hoff Claim* (United States v. Mexico), 4 U.N. Rep. Int'l Arb. Awards 444 (1929). However, "if the vessel or those on board commit an offense against the local law subsequent to the entry in distress, the littoral state's power to punish is undiminished." Harvard Research in International Law, Draft Convention on the Law of Territorial Waters, 23 A.J.I.L. Spec. Supp. 241, 299 (1929). On the right of entry in distress, see generally Jessup, The Law of Territorial Waters and Maritime Jurisdiction 194–208 (1927); 2 Hackworth at 277–82. On the right of entry into ports in general, see Lowe, The Right of Entry into Maritime Ports in International Law, 14 San Diego L. Rev. 597 (1977). See also Restatement (Third) § 512, Comment *c*, Reporters' Note 3.

CHAPTER 18

INTERNATIONAL ENVIRONMENTAL LAW

■ ■ ■

Like the field of human rights law, international environmental law has principally developed over the past half-century, largely through the conclusion of hundreds of bilateral and multilateral treaties, but also through key non-binding instruments and important rules and principles present in customary law. These instruments and rules seek to develop protections for, or to resolve problems that have arisen in, the lithosphere, hydrosphere, and atmosphere, usually from anthropogenic (i.e., human-source) activities. This chapter introduces this field of international law through a brief historical section, followed by a look at three important and paradigmatic threats: transborder environmental harm, typically through transfrontier air or water pollution; broader environmental harm to collective goods, such as the global atmosphere; and global trade in hazardous or endangered goods.

SECTION 1. HISTORIC DEVELOPMENT

A. PRE–STOCKHOLM CONFERENCE

International legal measures of one kind or another have long existed to prevent or alleviate pollution or accidents affecting more than one state. Treaties on sharing of water resources along a boundary have existed for centuries, such as the Treaty Relating to Boundary Waters, United States–United Kingdom, Jan. 11, 1909, 36 Stat. 2448, which regulates water resources between the United States and Canada. Treaties regulating the catch of fish, whales, or birds developed as soon as those resources became threatened by excessive exploitation. See, e.g., Interim Convention on Conservation of North Pacific Fur Seals, Feb. 9, 1957, 8 U.S.T. 2283, 314 U.N.T.S. 105; Convention for the Regulation of Whaling, Sept. 24, 1931, 49 Stat. 3079, 161 U.N.T.S. 72. Regional conventions addressing wildlife protection were also concluded, with a strong focus on the promotion of national wildlife parks. See, e.g., Convention on Nature Protection and Wildlife Preservation in the Western Hemisphere, Oct. 2, 1940, 56 Stat. 1354, 161 U.N.T.S. 193; African Convention on the Conservation of Nature and Natural Resources, Sept. 15, 1968, 1001 U.N.T.S. 3. Certain non-legally binding instruments that sought to less formally coordinate the conduct of states were also concluded, such as the Agreed Measures for the Conservation of Antarctic Fauna and Flora, June 13, 1964, 17 U.S.T. 991. Yet such measures tended to be bilateral or regional in nature, and often focused on particular species rather than broader problems of global biodiversity loss or pollution.

B. 1972 STOCKHOLM CONFERENCE AND ITS SUCCESSORS

Only after the emergence in the 1960s of extensive concern with pollution, and of national movements in favor of stronger environmental protections, did the international community begin to appreciate the benefits of greater collaborative efforts on the global level. Popular movements and scientific bodies pressed governments to take remedial measures over a wide range of human activity. Hence, international environmental law, as a distinctive legal regime, resulted from a heightened awareness of the degradation of air, water, and natural resources throughout the world, and concomitant efforts to promote sub-regional, regional, and global cooperation to address that degradation.

Stockholm. Following years of study and discussion on a global basis, the United Nations responded to these changes in 1972 by convening in Stockholm a conference of 113 states, along with representatives of international and non-governmental organizations. The conference unanimously adopted a political-binding action plan targeting various areas for future work and adopted a non-binding declaration of principles to guide that work. Stockholm Declaration on the Human Environment, June 16, 1972, 11 I.L.M. 1416 (1972). Famously, Principle 21 of the Stockholm Declaration declared that all states are responsible for ensuring "that the activities within their jurisdiction and control do not cause damage to the environment of other States or areas beyond the limits of national jurisdiction." At the same time and in the same provision, the declaration recognized the "sovereign right [of States] to exploit their own resources pursuant to their own environmental policies" in accordance with the Charter and principles of international law. Thus, typically of U.N. resolutions, this provision embraced the competing principles of international responsibility and national sovereignty. Decisions at Stockholm also led to the founding of the U.N. Environment Programme (UNEP), based in Nairobi, Kenya, to coordinate the development of environmental policy consensus within the U.N. system. See G.A. Res. 2997 (XXVII) (Dec. 15, 1972); see also United Nations Environment Programme, http://www.unep.org.

After Stockholm, numerous negotiations occurred on global and regional treaties addressing environmental problems, ranging from treaties on trade in endangered species, on long-range air pollution, on conservation of wetlands, and on protection of common spaces, such as the seas (as discussed in Chapter 17) or the Antarctic. See Protocol on Environmental Protection to the Antarctic Treaty, Oct. 4, 1991, 30 I.L.M. 1455 (1991).

Various regional treaties were also adopted, including extensive regulation within the system of the European Community. Non-binding instruments also emerged, such as the General Assembly's 1982 World Charter for Nature, which called for the integration of nature conservation into national law. G.A. Res. 37/7 (Oct. 28, 1982). Important scholarship and expert studies focused on this field. For example, the concept of "sustainable development" was articulated in a report entitled Our Common Future, produced by the World Commission on Environment and Development (the so-called Brundtland Commission), and defined as "development that meets the needs of the present without compromising the ability of future generations to meet their own needs." World Commission on Environment and Development, Our Common Future 8–9, 43 (1987).

Rio. Twenty years after Stockholm, states met again for the U.N. Conference on Environment and Development (UNCED), this time in Rio de Janeiro (often called the Rio Earth Summit). UNCED recognized that the environment and development must be addressed in their mutual relationship, and that many internal development projects can significantly affect the global environment. Population growth, the depletion of the ozone layer, deforestation, desertification, and preservation of biological diversity all provided ready examples. At UNCED, two politically-binding instruments were approved: The Rio Declaration on Environment and Development, June 14, 1992, U.N. Doc. A/CONF.151/26, annex I (Aug. 12, 1992), 31 I.L.M. 874 (1992), a series of twenty-seven principles; and an action program for the twenty-first century, known as "Agenda 21." U.N. Doc. A/CONF.151/26, annex II (Aug. 12, 1992). UNCED also adopted two important treaties discussed later in this chapter, the Framework Convention on Climate Change and the Convention on Biological Diversity. On the Earth Summit and the preparatory work that preceded it, see Gardner, Negotiating Survival: Four Priorities after Rio (1992).

Decisions at UNCED led to the creation of the U.N. Commission on Sustainable Development (CSD) based in New York, as a focal point for U.N. work in coordinating developmental and environmental initiatives. See U.N. Commission on Sustainable Development, http://www.un.org/esa/sustdev/csd/review.htm. Various treaties also emerged from initiatives discussed at UNCED, including the Convention to Combat Desertification, Oct. 14, 1999, Treaty Doc. No. 104–29, 1954 U.N.T.S. 3, 33 I.L.M. 1328 (1994), and the 2000 Cartegena Protocol on Biosafety, discussed this chapter in Section 4.

Johannesburg. The high hopes that emerged from Stockholm and Rio were not fully met; despite the creation of new institutions and new treaties, throughout the 1990s there existed considerable concern that progress in implementing sustainable development was slow, and that in many respects both poverty and environmental degradation were growing worse. In 2002, the General Assembly convened yet another summit, the World Summit on Sustainable Development (WSSD), this time in Johannesburg, where again a political declaration and plan of action were adopted. Yet the principal legacy of the Johannesburg summit would appear to be its emphasis on the need for states and international organizations to engage in meaningful and effective partnerships with non-state actors in order to achieve the objectives of sustainable development. See Johannesburg Summit 2002, http://www.un.org/jsummit/index. html; see also Green Planet Blues: Environmental Politics from Stockholm to Johannesburg (Conca & Dabelko eds. 2004).

C. WORK OF THE INTERNATIONAL LAW COMMISSION

The International Law Commission has undertaken studies of relevance to the field of international environmental law. The I.L.C.'s work on the rules of state responsibility (see Chapter 8) focused exclusively on the consequences of internationally wrongful acts, but the I.L.C. believed that even where an act was not internationally wrongful (e.g., building and operating a nuclear power plant), it might nonetheless cause serious damage to a neighboring state if an accident occurs. Consequently, in 1978 the I.L.C. launched a study on the topic of "international liability for injurious consequences arising out of acts not prohibited by international law," which, over time, generated a series of draft articles. For many, however, the scope and content of the topic was unclear, leading to considerable conceptual and theoretical difficulties, and even skepticism about the appropriateness of the topic's title.

Consequently, in 1997, the I.L.C. sub-divided the topic into issues concerning prevention and issues concerning liability. The I.L.C.'s work on "prevention" resulted in the adoption in 2001 of Draft Articles on Prevention of Transboundary Damage from Hazardous Activities. See Report of the International Law Commission, Fifty-third Session, U.N. Doc. A/56/10 (2001). While those articles were submitted to the General Assembly with a recommendation that they form the basis of a new treaty, the General Assembly simply expressed its appreciation for the articles without taking any further action. See G.A. Res. 56/82 (Dec. 12, 2001). The I.L.C.'s work on "liability" remains unfinished as of publication of this casebook, as are separate studies relating shared natural resources and on the protection of persons in the event of disasters.

D. LOOKING FORWARD

Today, international environmental law is an extensive field involving hundreds of multilateral and bilateral treaties, spanning the full array of environmental concerns. While significant progress has been made, many states and non-state actors see insufficient implementation of existing treaty regimes, as well as the need to find solutions to critical outstanding problems (such as global climate change). For useful surveys of the field, see The Oxford Handbook of International Environmental Law (Bodansky, Brunée, & Hey eds. 2007); Kiss & Shelton, International Environmental Law (3d ed. 2004); Birnie & Boyle, International Law and the Environment (2d ed. 2002).

Moreover, there are important conceptual issues that remain outstanding. First, what should be the scope of the field of international environmental law? Governments have justified their environmental law mainly as protective of human health and well-being, yet many environmentalists see this as unjustifiably anthropocentric (i.e., overly concerned with human welfare). They favor extending the concept of environmental harm to include injury or interference with the natural order whether or not harmful to humans. Protection of other species and the physical aspects of the earth, and/or extra-terrestrial objects, should also be protected regardless of injury to human beings. Sometimes referred to as "deep ecology," or the "holistic approach," this conception has found international legal recognition in conventions that protect other species and works of nature. It has even been proposed that natural objects such as trees or mountains should have "standing" to obtain legal protection. A number of treaties do extend protection to natural features and non-human species, though for political reasons they may be justified as benefits to human beings. For example, the 1992 Convention on Biological Diversity, discussed in Section 3(C), is justified both for its protection of the natural order and for its indirect benefits to human beings.

Second, is the manner in which international environmental law is developing "legitimate"? Many global environmental issues, such as climate change, have become divisive and political. Some have questioned the legitimacy of international environmental rules that lack general consensus of states and approval of the peoples affected. As Daniel Bodansky has written:

> First, the coming generation of environmental problems will probably require more expeditious and flexible lawmaking approaches, which do not depend on consensus among states. Second, to the extent that international environmental law is beginning to have significant implications for non- or substate actors (who have not consented to it directly), rather than just for the relations among states, state consent may for them have little legitimating effect.* * * Its lack of transparency and accountability will become increasingly problematic.

Bodansky, The Legitimacy of International Governance: A Coming Challenge for International Environmental Law?, 93 A.J.I.L. 596, 606 (1999).

Third, does or should international law encompass a human right to a safe environment? No legally binding international instrument deals specifically with the nexus between environmental protection and human rights, though certain non-binding instruments make that link. See, e.g., Popović, In Pursuit of Environmental Human Rights: Commentary on the Draft Declaration of Principles on Human Rights and the Environment, 27 Colum. Hum. Rts. L. Rev. 487 (1996). Article 2 of the Institut de Droit International's Resolution on Environment, adopted in Strasbourg in 1997, states: "Every human being has the right to live in a healthy environment." Résolutions adoptées par l'Institut, 67–II Ann. de l'Institut de Droit Int. 477, 479 (1998). Judge Weeramantry, in his separate opinion to the 1997 I.C.J. *Gabčíkovo* decision, stated. "The protection of the environment is likewise a vital part of contemporary human rights doctrine, for it is a *sine qua non* for numerous human rights such as the right to health and the right to life itself. It is scarcely necessary to elaborate on this, as damage to the environment can impair and undermine all the human rights spoken of in the Universal Declaration and other human rights instruments." *Gabčíkovo–Nagymaros Project* (Hungary v. Slovakia), 1997 I.C.J. 88, 91–92 (Separate Opinion of Vice–President Weeramantry).

The relationship between human rights and environmental protection has been recognized by the European Court of Human Rights. In *Guerra v. Italy*, 1998–I Eur. Ct. H.R. 210, the plaintiffs, who lived close to a chemical factory, claimed, firstly, that the Italian Government had failed to provide them with information about the risks of the factory, and secondly, that the state had violated its alleged obligation to prevent the effects of toxic emissions. The Court rebuffed the first contention, but upheld the second one, holding that "severe environmental pollution may affect individuals' well-being and prevent them from enjoying their homes in such a way as to affect their private and family life adversely." Id. at para. 60. Therefore, the Court found that the Italian Government had not fulfilled its obligation to secure plaintiff's right to respect for private and family life under Article 8 of the Convention.

In U.S. jurisprudence, the Alien Tort Statute, 28 U.S.C. § 1350 (2000) has been a vehicle for efforts to litigate major environmental torts abroad, in situations that often link the alleged environmental tort with a deprivation of human rights (and that link major corporations with alleged governmental abuses). See Chapter 10, Section 2(A), and Chapter 13, Section 5. In the wake of *Sosa v. Alvarez–Machain*, 542 U.S. 692, 732 (2004), where the Supreme Court stated that ATS causes of action (whether by treaty or customary international law) must reflect a "specific, universal, and obligatory" norm of international law, some speculate that such environmental actions under the ATS will face considerable hurdles. What environmental torts do you think would be regarded universally as a violation of international law and how would you go about proving it? See Boeving, Half Full ... or Completely Empty?: Environmental Alien Tort Claims Post Sosa v. Alvarez–Machain, 18 Geo. Int'l Envtl. L. Rev. 109 (2005). Even before the *Sosa* decision, environmental claims under the ATS had faced considerable difficulties. See, e.g., *Flores v. Southern Peru Copper*, 343 F.3d 140 (2d Cir. 2003) (dismissing claims by Peruvian nationals against a U.S. mining company for violation of rights to life, health, and sustainable development, both as falling outside the scope of the ATS and due to *forum non conveniens*).

SECTION 2. TRANSBORDER ENVIRONMENTAL HARM

Although the term "environmental law" was rarely used until recently, international law had long taken cognizance of environmental injuries in the context of transborder or transfrontier injuries. Pollution of shared rivers or lakes, marine oil spills, and transfrontier fumes were among the environmental problems dealt with through international agreements and principles of international state responsibility.

Consider two cases recently filed before the International Court of Justice, both of which remain pending as of the publication of this casebook. In May 2006, Argentina filed a case against Uruguay alleging breach of a bilateral agreement concerning the use of the River Uruguay, a waterway that runs along their common border. According to Argentina, Uruguay commenced operation of two pulp mills on the river without engaging in prior notification and consultation with Argentina, as required by the bilateral agreement. In its application to the Court, Argentina claimed that the pulp mills will "damage the environment of the River Uruguay and its area," affecting more than 300,000 persons, through "significant risks of pollution of the river, deterioration of biodiversity, harmful effects on health and damage to fisheries resources," and "extremely serious consequences for tourism and other economic interests." Application of Argentina, *Pulp Mills on the River Uruguay* (Argentina v. Uruguay) (2006), http://www.icj-cij.org/docket/files/135/10779.pdf (in French). How should two states, or a court, resolve such a complaint, where the two states share a common waterway that one seeks to use for economic development, but in a manner the other fears will cause environmental harm?

In March 2008, Ecuador filed a case against Colombia concerning the latter's aerial spraying of herbicides at locations near its border with Ecuador, purportedly to stop illicit coca and poppy plantations in the frontier area. According the Ecuador, the spraying "has already caused serious damage to people, to crops, to animals, and to the natural environment on the Ecuadorian side of the frontier, and poses a grave risk of further damage over time." Application of Ecuador, *Aerial Herbicide Spraying* (Ecuador v. Colombia), para. 2 (2008), http://www.icj-cij.org/docket/files/138/14474.pdf. How are two states, or a court, to resolve such an issue, where the two states may have differing views as to the danger of such plantations as weighed against the danger of environmental harm? Is Ecuador entitled to prior notice and consultation? Can Ecuador insist upon cessation of the spraying? (To check on the current status of either case, see International Court of Justice, http://www.icj-cij.org).

As you read the following materials, consider what elements of treaty, custom, general principles, or prior jurisprudence would be relevant in resolving such disputes. Bear in mind as well instruments such as the 1992 Rio Declaration on Environment and Development, which appears in the Documents Supplement, especially Principles 2 and 13–19.

TRAIL SMELTER ARBITRATION
(UNITED STATES v. CANADA)
3 U.N. Rep. Int'l Arb. Awards 1905 (1941)

[The case was decided by a Special Arbitral Tribunal under a convention which required the application of the "law and practice followed in dealing with cognate questions in the United States of America as well as international law and practice." Id. at 1908. The arbitration grew out of air pollution from sulfur dioxide fumes emitted by a smelter plant at Trail, British Columbia, owned by a Canadian corporation. In a previous decision, the Special Arbitral Tribunal had found that the fumes caused damage in the State of Washington during the period from 1925 to 1937. In holding Canada responsible and directing injunctive relief and payment of an indemnity, the Tribunal stated:]

As Professor Eagleton puts it (*Responsibility of States in International Law*, 1928, p. 80): "A State owes at all times a duty to protect other States against injurious acts by individuals from within its jurisdiction." * * * These and many others have been carefully examined. International decisions, in various matters, from the Alabama case onward, and also earlier ones, are based on the same general principle, and, indeed, this principle, as such, has not been questioned by Canada. But the real difficulty often arises rather when it comes to determine what, *pro subjecta materie*, is deemed to constitute an injurious act.

* * *

No case of air pollution dealt with by an international tribunal has been brought to the attention of the Tribunal nor does the Tribunal know of any such case. The nearest analogy is that of water pollution. But, here also, no decision of an international tribunal has been cited or has been found.

There are, however, as regards both air pollution and water pollution, certain decisions of the Supreme Court of the United States which may legitimately be taken as a guide in this field of international law, for it is reasonable to follow by analogy, in international cases, precedents established by that court in dealing with controversies between States of the Union or with other controversies concerning the quasi-sovereign rights of such States, where no contrary rule prevails in international law and no reason for rejecting such precedents can be adduced from the limitations of sovereignty inherent in the Constitution of the United States.

[The Tribunal then discussed *Missouri v. Illinois*, 200 U.S. 496 (1906), *New York v. New Jersey*, 256 U.S. 296 (1921), and *New Jersey v. New York*, 283 U.S. 473 (1931), dealing with water pollution, and *Georgia v. Tennessee Copper Co.*, 206 U.S. 230 (1907) and *Georgia v. Tennessee Copper Co.*, 237 U.S. 474 (1915), dealing with air pollution, and concluded: "[U]nder the principles of international law, as well as of the law of the United States, no State has the right to use or permit the use of its territory in such a manner as to cause injury by fumes in or to the territory of another or the properties or persons therein, when the case is of serious consequence and the injury is established by clear and convincing evidence." Id. at 1965. In light of this finding, the Tribunal described in detail the measures of control to be imposed upon the Trail Smelter. These measures included the maintenance of meteorological and sulfur emission records and the specification of maximum hourly emission of sulfur dioxide under various conditions.]

LEGALITY OF THE THREAT OR USE OF NUCLEAR WEAPONS

International Court of Justice, Advisory Opinion, 1996
1996 I.C.J. 226

[In this advisory opinion, the Court was asked whether international law prohibited the use, or threat to use, nuclear weapons. In reaching its conclusion (addressed in greater detail *supra* Chapter 2, Section 2(A)) the Court considered whether treaties relating to environmental law were relevant.]

29.   The Court recognizes that the environment is under daily threat and that the use of nuclear weapons could constitute a catastrophe for the environment. The Court also recognizes that the environment is not an abstraction but represents the living space, the quality of life and the very health of human beings, including generations unborn. The existence of the general obligation of States to ensure that activities within their jurisdiction and control respect the environment of other States or of areas beyond national control is now part of the corpus of international law relating to the environment.

30.   However, the Court is of the view that the issue is not whether the treaties relating to the protection of the environment are or are not applicable during an armed conflict, but rather whether the obligations stemming from these treaties were intended to be obligations of total restraint during military conflict.

The Court does not consider that the treaties in question could have intended to deprive a State of the exercise of its right of self-defence under international law because of its obligations to protect the environment. Nonetheless, States must take environmental considerations into account when assessing what is necessary and proportionate in the pursuit of legitimate military objectives. Respect for the environment is one of the elements that go to assessing whether an action is in conformity with the principles of necessity and proportionality.

GABČÍKOVO–NAGYMAROS PROJECT
(HUNGARY/SLOVAKIA)
International Court of Justice, 1997
1997 I.C.J. 7

[Hungary and Slovakia entered into a treaty in 1977 for construction of a system of dams and other works on the Danube River in their territories and to reroute waters of the river by way of a canal. After disputes arose, Hungary in 1992 notified Slovakia that it was terminating the treaty, citing in part environmental concerns. The two states submitted the case to the International Court of Justice. Hungary argued that it rightfully terminated the treaty because of fundamentally changed circumstances and "ecological necessity." While the Court acknowledged Hungary's "basic right to an equitable and reasonable sharing of the resources of an international watercourse" (para. 78), the Court rejected Hungary's arguments that changed circumstances and necessity warranted termination of the treaty (see Chapter 3, Section 6(D), and Chapter 7, Sections 4 and 5). The Court then turned to Hungary's argument that it was entitled to terminate because of new requirements of international law on the protection of the environment, especially given certain provisions in the 1977 treaty that called upon the parties to implement the project with an eye to environmental effects.]

112.   Neither of the Parties contended that new peremptory norms of environmental law had emerged since the conclusion of the 1977 Treaty, and the Court will consequently not be required to examine the scope of Article 64 of the Vienna Convention on the Law of Treaties [on *jus cogens*]. On the other hand, the Court wishes to point out that newly developed norms of international law are relevant for the implementation of the Treaty and that the parties could, by agreement, incorporate them through the application of Articles 15, 19 and 20 of the Treaty. These articles do not contain specific obligations of performance but require the parties, in carrying out their obligations to ensure that the quality of the Danube is not impaired and that nature is protected, to take new environmental norms into consideration when agreeing upon the means to be specified in the Joint Contractual Plan.

By inserting these evolving provisions in the Treaty, the parties recognized the potential necessity to adapt the Project. Consequently, the treaty is not static, and is open to adapt to emerging norms of international law.* * *

The responsibility to do this was a joint responsibility. The obligations contained in Articles 15, 19 and 20 are, by definition, general and have to be transformed into specific obligations of performance through a process of consultation and negotiation. Their implementation thus requires a mutual willingness to discuss in good faith actual and potential environmental risks.

It is all the more important to do this because as the Court recalled in its Advisory Opinion on the *Legality of the Threat or Use of Nuclear Weapons*, "the environment is not an abstraction but represents the living space, the quality of life and the very health of human beings, including generations unborn" * * *.

The awareness of the vulnerability of the environment and the recognition that environmental risks have to be assessed on a continuous basis have become much stronger in the years since the Treaty's conclusion. * * *

113.   The Court recognizes that both Parties agree on the need to take environmental concerns seriously and to take the required precautionary measures, but they fundamentally disagree on the consequences this has for the joint Project. In such a case, third-party involvement may be helpful and instrumental in finding a solution, provided each of the Parties is flexible in its position.

* * *

115.   In the light of the conclusions it has reached above, the Court * * * finds that the notification of termination by Hungary of 19 May 1992 did not have the legal effect of terminating the 1977 Treaty and related instruments.

[After finding that the treaty was not in fact terminated, the Court held that the parties were obliged to negotiate further on implementation of the treaty in accordance with its terms, balancing environmental and developmental concerns.]

140.   It is clear that the Project's impact upon, and its implications for, the environment are of necessity a key issue. The numerous scientific reports which have been presented to the Court by the Parties—even if their conclusions are often contradictory—provide abundant evidence that this impact and these implications are considerable.

In order to evaluate the environmental risks, current standards must be taken into consideration. This is not only allowed by the wording of Articles 15 and 19, but even prescribed, to the extent that these articles impose a continuing—and thus necessarily evolving—obligations on the parties to maintain the quality of the Danube and to protect nature.

The Court is mindful that, in the field of environmental protection, vigilance and prevention are required on account of the often irreversible character of damage to the environment and of the limitations inherent in the very mechanism of reparation of this type of damage.

Throughout the ages, mankind has, for economic and other reasons, constantly interfered with nature. In the past, this was often done without consideration of the effects upon the environment. Owing to new scientific insights and to a growing awareness of the risks for mankind—for present and future generations—of pursuit of such interventions at an unconsidered and unabated pace, new norms and standards have been developed, set forth in a great number of instruments during the last two decades. Such new norms have to be taken into consideration, and such new standards given proper weight, not only when States contemplate new activities but also when continuing with activities begun in the past. This need to reconcile economic development with protection of the environment is aptly expressed in the concept of sustainable development.

NOTES

1. *Sic Utere Tuo Maxim*. In the *Trail Smelter* case, the arbitral tribunal imposed liability for the harm resulting to the United States from fumes of a plant in Canada. In situations such as this, the international law concept of "abuse of rights" has sometimes been invoked to condemn state behavior harmful to the environment of neighboring states. The same idea has been expressed in the maxim *sic utere tuo ut alienum non laedas* (usually simply referred to as *sic utere tuo*). Its literal meaning is "use your own so as not to injure another." The maxim has often been applied to situations of pollution or drainage of a shared waterway. See Transboundary Harm in International Law: Lessons from the Trail Smelter Arbitration (Bratspies & Miller eds. 2006); Hanqin, Transboundary Damage in International Law (2003). In advancing this concept, reference is sometimes made to *Corfu Channel* (United Kingdom v. Albania), 1949 I.C.J. 4, where the United Kingdom sought to hold Albania responsible for damage caused to British warships by mines moored in the Corfu Channel in Albanian territorial waters. Among other things, the Court stated that Albania should have warned the United Kingdom about the mines because of "every State's obligation not to allow knowingly its territory to be used for acts contrary to the rights of other States."

The basic principle of territorial integrity has also been invoked as a legal ground for condemning activities that caused injurious substances to enter other states. Other principles have been cited as legal grounds for preventing or reducing transboundary pollution. A Dutch scholar, Johan Lammers, listed eleven such principles and concepts bearing on transboundary pollution. Lammers, Pollution of International Watercourses 556–80 (1984). The main non-official bodies of international lawyers have adopted resolutions that broadly assert state obligations to prevent or abate transboundary environmental damage. See, for example, Institut de Droit International, Resolution on Responsibility and Liability under International Law for Environmental Damage, 67–II Ann. de l'Institut de Droit Int. 487 (1998); Restatement (Third) § 601. Yet the *sic utere tuo* principle leaves many questions unanswered. What exactly is meant by "harm"? Is a state strictly liable or does it matter whether the harm was unanticipated? Does it matter whether the activity in question provides significant economic benefits, perhaps even ones that outweigh the environmental harm? Do customary rules or general principles of law fully govern in this area or are treaty regimes necessary to provide the necessary guidance?

2. *Nature and Quantum of "Harm" Required*. A wide range of situations fall within the concept of transborder environmental harm, yet not every interference or detrimental impact on the environment can be regarded as

"harm" in its international law meaning. What conditions do you think are or should be required? Must the harm result solely from human activity? Floods or storms would seem not to fall within the legal concept of environmental harm. Must the environmental injury result from a *physical* consequence of a human activity? Declines or increases in the price of commodities would seem not to be regarded as environmental harm, even if they are caused by human activity, and even if they adversely affect crops or indirectly impact on land or water management. Must the physical environmental impact extend beyond the national boundaries of the source state? Destruction of a forest entirely within national territory presumably would not be an *international* environmental harm, unless it could be shown somehow to be harmful to another state or states. Is any quantum of harm sufficient or must the environmental harm be "substantial" or at least "significant"—the latter a term that has been used in the work of the International Law Commission? See, e.g., Draft Articles on Prevention of Transboundary Harm from Hazardous Activities, arts. 3–4, U.N. Doc. A/56/10 (2001).

3. *Taking Account of the Risk of Harm.* Attempts to formulate treaty regimes or general rules for transborder environmental harm usually link harm and risk. To the extent that states are enjoined to take steps to prevent appreciable (or substantial or significant) harm, they are also called upon to minimize the risk of such harm occurring. Proposed measures tend to distinguish two different types of situations. The first is one in which a disaster of great magnitude could occur, though the probability of such occurrence is low. The meltdown of a nuclear plant or an oil tanker running aground are examples where the risk of occurrence is not high, but the harm that results is great, perhaps catastrophic. In such situations, international efforts to regulate tends to be high. In the second type of situation, such as automobile exhaust, the overall probability of harm occurring is high, but the transboundary effects are relatively minor and often undetected. In this situation, the diffuse nature of the harmful effects, together with the recognized benefits to the population as a whole, tend to reduce the felt need for international restrictions and precautionary measures. The International Law Commission defined "risk of causing significant transboundary harm" as meaning "risks taking the form of a high probability of causing significant transboundary harm and a low probability of causing disastrous transboundary harm." See Draft Articles on Prevention of Transboundary Harm from Hazardous Activities, art. 2(a), U.N. Doc. A/56/10 (2001).

In its opinion in the *Gabčíkovo–Nagymaros Project* case, the International Court stated that "The awareness of the vulnerability of the environment and the recognition that environmental risks have to be assessed on a continuous basis have become much stronger in the years since the Treaty's conclusion" (para. 112). Does this suggest that, apart from any existing treaty obligation, there is a general obligation to conduct environmental risk assessments of potentially significant transboundary harms? See Rio Declaration, principle 17; Draft Articles on Prevention of Transboundary Harm from Hazardous Activities, art. 7, U.N. Doc. A/56/10 (2001) ("Any decision in respect of the authorization of an activity within the scope of the present articles shall, in particular, be based on an assessment of the possible transboundary harm caused by that activity, including any environmental impact assessment.");

Knox, The Myth and Reality of Transboundary Environmental Impact Assessment, 96 A.J.I.L. 291 (2002).

4. *Sustainable Development.* Economic and social factors generally have a substantial effect on judgments of risk and harm. A poor community faced by food shortages and lack of economic opportunities will tend to minimize the harm to the environment from measures taken to stimulate the economy. In fact, the great divide in present international environmental debates is between the developed countries that emphasize the need to reduce environmental dangers and the developing countries concerned about meeting food and health necessities, along with overall economic development, even if environmental harm occurs. Does either side—environmental protection or development—carry a trump card?

The notion of sustainable development attempts to fuse these two competing concepts. Note the balancing of both concepts in Principle 2 of the Rio Declaration, and the Court's reliance on the concept at the end of the *Gabčíkovo–Nagymaros Project* case. Judge Weeramantry, in a separate opinion in that case, expounded upon the principle of sustainable development as a part of modern international law, citing to various instruments. See *Gabčíkovo–Nagymaros Project* (Hungary v. Slovakia), 1997 I.C.J. 7, 92–95 (Separate Opinion of Vice–President Weeramantry); see also International Law and Sustainable Development (Schrijver & Weiss eds. 2004); see also Draft Articles on Prevention of Transboundary Harm from Hazardous Activities, art. 10, U.N. Doc. A/56/10 (2001) (listing factors to be balanced).

5. *Obligation to Prevent Harm or to Exercise Due Care to Prevent?* Are states strictly obligated to prevent harm (however "harm" may be defined) or are they obligated to exercise due care to prevent harm, such that if sufficient care is taken, the responsibility is met even if harm occurs? International environmental law seems to provide for at least the latter form of obligation. The Restatement (Third) § 601(1)(b) asserts that a state is legally obligated to "take such measures as may be necessary, to the extent practicable under the circumstances, to ensure that activities within its jurisdiction or control are conducted so as not to cause significant injury to the environment of another state or of areas beyond the limits of national jurisdiction." Similarly, the International Law Commission's draft articles on prevention of transboundary harm require states to "take all appropriate measures to prevent significant transboundary harm *or at any event to minimize the risk thereof.*" Draft Articles on Prevention of Transboundary Harm from Hazardous Activities, art. 3, U.N. Doc. A/56/10 (2001) (emphasis added). Do you think international environmental law does or should go further?

6. *Precautionary Principle.* In recent years, the "precautionary principle" or "precautionary approach" has been a recurrent feature in international environmental treaties. As Principle 15 of the 1992 Rio Declaration suggests, this concept requires states in certain circumstances to take preventive measures even before there exists convincing scientific evidence that the failure to do so will cause appreciable harm of an environmental character. In some contexts, the precautionary principle or approach operates by placing the burden of proof on a state to show that its activity or product would not cause significant harm. Do you think precaution is appropriate where the

overall cost of such measures would exceed the benefit that the preventive action would produce in the long run? For in-depth treatment of the concept and its application, see The Precautionary Principle and International Law: The Challenge of Implementation (Freestone & Hey eds. 1996).

7. *Duty to Inform and Consult.* Is there a duty of a source state to inform others of impending harm to them or of the risk of harm from a planned activity, perhaps as a corollary of the obligation to exercise due care to prevent harm? See Rio Declaration, Principles 18 & 19; Draft Articles on Prevention of Transboundary Harm from Hazardous Activities, arts. 8–9, U.N. Doc. A/56/10 (2001). If so, the duty to inform and consult would presumably apply to situations that have a fair probability of causing serious damage. For example, the transport of dangerous materials would require notification to the governments of states that could be injured by accidents or operational difficulties. Normal development activities, such as hydroelectric projects or oil drilling near a border, may have potential extraterritorial environmental consequences that should be discussed with neighboring states. For more than just *ad hoc* consultations, a joint commission might be created as a practical means for surveying and consulting with respect to ongoing situations, such as pollution along a shared waterway. On the International Joint Commission set up by Canada and the United States in 1909 to address shared water resources, see International Joint Commission, http://www.ijc. org; see also Francis, Binational Cooperation for Great Lakes Water Quality: A Framework for the Groundwater Connection, 65 Chi.–Kent L. Rev. 359 (1989).

8. *Chernobyl Nuclear Plant Explosion.* On April 26, 1986, an explosion occurred at the Chernobyl atomic power plant near Kiev in the Union of Soviet Socialist Republics (U.S.S.R.). The explosion caused radioactive substances to be released into the atmosphere. It was not until three days later, when significantly higher levels of radioactivity were found in Scandinavian countries, that the U.S.S.R. acknowledged that an explosion had occurred. Did the U.S.S.R. have an international obligation to inform potentially affected countries of the occurrence of the accident and its potential effects? Soon after Chernobyl, the International Atomic Energy Agency (IAEA) adopted two conventions, the Convention on Assistance in Case of a Nuclear Accident or Radiological Emergency, Sept. 26, 1986, S. Treaty Doc. No. 100–4, 1457 U.N.T.S. 133, and the Convention on Early Notification of a Nuclear Accident, Sept. 26, 1986, S. Treaty Doc. No. 100–4, 1439 U.N.T.S. 275. See also Draft Articles on Prevention of Transboundary Harm from Hazardous Activities, art. 17, U.N. Doc. A/56/10 (2001).

9. *Using the Treaty Device.* Transboundary environmental harm might be addressed through reliance just on customary rules or principles of international environmental law of the type discussed above, but where the harm is significant or ongoing, states will often resort to treaties as a means of identifying the specific rules they wish to apply. For example, by the 1970s it was readily apparent that national laws on controlling air pollution could be undermined if neighboring states were not taking comparable regulatory measures. Consequently, North American and European states adopted the Convention on Long–Range Transboundary Air Pollution, Nov. 13, 1979, 34 U.S.T. 3043, 1302 U.N.T.S. 267 (LRTAP), so as "to limit, and, as far as

possible, gradually reduce and prevent air pollution including long-range air pollution." As of early 2009, twenty-four states are party to LRTAP, including the United States, though lesser numbers are party to the LRTAP protocols where some of the most important obligations appear. For example, protocols developed in 1985 and 1994 require states to reduce their national annual sulfur emissions, using certain baseline years and certain percentage reductions to be reached by certain dates. Other protocols address controls of emissions of nitrogen oxides, volatile organic compounds, heavy metals, persistent organic pollutants, and ozone. See United Nations Economic Commission for Europe, Convention on Long–Range Transboundary Air Pollution, http://www.unece.org/env/lrtap/.

Some states have concluded further, bilateral agreements with even greater commitments, such as the Agreement on Air Quality, United States–Canada, Mar. 13, 1991, T.I.A.S. No. 11,783, 1852 U.N.T.S. 79, and the Agreement on Cooperation for the Protection and Improvement of the Environment in the Border Area, United States–Mexico, Aug. 14, 1983, 35 U.S.T. 2916, 1987 U.N.T.S. 346 (La Paz Agreement) (on air pollution, see annexes IV & V).

10. *U.S. National Law.* The principal United States statutes dealing with transfrontier pollution are the Clean Water Act, 33 U.S.C. §§ 1251–1387 (2000) and the Clean Air Act, 42 U.S.C. §§ 7401–7442 (2000), both of which apply to transfrontier pollution on condition of reciprocity. See generally Hall, Transboundary Pollution: Harmonizing International and Domestic Law, 40 U. Mich. J.L. Reform 681 (2007). Ironically, the United States is still attempting to address pollution from the Trail Smelter, now in the form of transboundary groundwater pollution. See Robinson–Dorn, The Trail Smelter: Is What's Past Prologue? EPA Blazes a New Trail for CERCLA, 14 N.Y.U. Envtl. L.J. 233 (2006); Parrish, Trail Smelter Déjà Vu: Extraterritoriality, International Environmental Law, and the Search for Solutions to Canadian–U.S. Transboundary Water Pollution Disputes, 85 B.U. L. Rev. 363 (2005).

11. *International Responsibility and Civil Liability.* International responsibility and civil liability have been basic concepts in the formation of international environmental law, but usage has varied as to their meaning and application. In keeping with general international law usage, *international responsibility* (i.e. state responsibility) arises as a consequence of a state's breach of an obligation established under international law and of its duty to re-establish the original position or pay compensation. An international obligation to compensate may also arise from violation of a rule of international law imposing strict responsibility for harm, irrespective of fault. The concept of *civil liability* is applicable to operators (whether private or governmental) who are assigned liability under national law or governing rules of international law. Both concepts are present in international environmental law though, as Rio Declaration Principle 13 makes clear, they are not fully developed.

Why pursue such concepts? State responsibility and operator liability each serve corrective justice by shifting loss from an innocent victim to the causal agent. They also give teeth to rules of prevention and mitigation. From an economist's point of view, liability internalizes the costs of environmental damage, thus tending to promote more efficient use of resources. The "polluter pays" principle (see Rio Declaration Principle 16) has been widely supported by governments and environmentalists on the double ground of fairness and efficiency. The principle has also been cited to support the contention that the richer developed countries should pay a major share of cleaning up the global environment since they were the source of most of the pollution.

Should liability be strict or only when negligence is found? As noted in Chapter 8, the "secondary rules" of state responsibility in international law do not automatically impose strict liability on states, but leave to the "primary rules" in a particular subject matter area or regime the possibility of imposing such liability. Do you think the *Trail Smelter* case endorsed a standard of strict liability for transboundary environmental harm?

SECTION 3. PRESERVING COLLECTIVE GOODS

Not all environmental harm is in the form of transborder environmental harm, at least not in the sense of pollution from one state crossing a border and causing harm in an adjacent state. A quite different set of issues arises from the activities of all states worldwide that, collectively, cause harm to goods held in common by all states. No single state is the cause of such harm, though the activities of some may be of greater concern than those of others. Regulating a solution to such problems can be difficult; multiple states must be persuaded to act together collectively and efficiently, and some states will have incentives not to cooperate since they can "free ride" on the restraint of others (i.e., benefit from the regime without bearing its costs). Further, such problems usually arise not from the direct activities of governments but, rather, the activities of widely-dispersed private entities, such that any regulation must take account of the variety of ways national legal systems control private behavior.

A. PROTECTING AGAINST OZONE DEPLETION

Scientific reports in the 1970s and 1980s showed that certain chemicals, such as the chlorofluorocarbons (CFCs) used in refrigerators and air conditioners, when released into the atmosphere, migrated to the upper atmosphere (stratosphere), where they initiate a chemical process that depletes the ozone molecules present in the "ozone layer." That layer is important for inhibiting ultraviolet radiation from reaching the earth's surface, where it can have various deleterious effects, including causing skin cancer and damage crops.

Responding to such findings, states began to take legal action to address the problem of ozone depletion. First, in 1985 states adopted the Vienna Convention for the Protection of the Ozone Layer, Mar. 22, 1985, T.I.A.S. No. 11,097, 1513 U.N.T.S. 293. The Convention created a framework for international cooperation in research, monitoring and exchange of information with respect to ozone depletion, but did not proscribe any concrete obligation for the member states to curb their production or use of ozone depleting chemicals. Two years later, with increasing public awareness of the dangers of ozone depletion, there was sufficient political will for the adoption of the Montreal Protocol on Substances that Deplete the Ozone Layer, Sept. 16, 1987, S. Treaty Doc. No. 100–10, 1522 U.N.T.S. 3. The Montreal Protocol imposed quantitative limits on the production and consumption of CFCs as well as another ozone-depleting chemical, halons.

The Montreal Protocol uses a standard approach for quantitative limitations on air emissions. A base year of ozone emissions is used to establish a benchmark for emissions by each party and then quantitative limits are set for particular target dates. The quantitative limit can simply call for emissions to remain stable (i.e., maintain emissions during the target year at no more than 100% of the base year) or can call for reductions below that of the base year (e.g., produce emissions during the target year of no more than 75%, 50%, or 25% of the base year). The Montreal Protocol creates a mechanism for adding new ozone-depleting chemicals to the regime and for adjusting the targets and timetables for the emissions of those chemicals, as has been done many times since 1987. Id. art. 2. For chemicals to be added to the regime, the treaty must actually be amended, requiring states to pursue their normal treaty ratification processes. Once a chemical is added to the treaty, however, the target date for reducing or eliminating the chemical can be changed by an "adjustment" which, under the Montreal Protocol, can be done with just a two-thirds vote of the meeting of the parties (MOP) (though consensus is preferred), so long as that two-thirds represents at least half of global consumption of the chemical in question. Id. art. 11.

The regime contains certain innovative components that have now been used in other regimes as well. For instance, to attract developing states to the regime, the second MOP held at Copenhagen established a multilateral fund to provide financial and technical aid to developing states that joined the regime. Further, the Protocol allowss for differential treatment for developing states, such as providing them with a longer period of time to achieve compliance. See Rajamani, Differential Treatment in International Environmental Law 176–250 (2006).

Moreover, at the Copenhagen meeting a procedure was adopted for handling noncompliance by a member state. Under this non-compliance procedure, an implementation committee is charged with examining complaints against member states that are allegedly in violation of the Protocol. The committee's reports are studied by the MOP, which has the authority to decide whether measures shall be taken. The possible measures are "appropriate assistance," "issuing cautions," and "suspension * * * of specific rights and privileges, * * * including those concerned with industrial rationalization, production, consumption, trade, transfer of technology, financial mechanism and institutional arrangements." Report of the Fourth Meeting of the Parties to the Montreal Convention on Substances that Deplete the Ozone Layer, U.N. Doc. UNEP/OzL.Pro.4/15, annex V (Nov. 28, 1992); see also Bankobeza, Ozone Protection: The International Legal Regime 256–84 (2005).

For further discussion on the ozone protection regime and its implementation, see Andersen & Sarma, Protecting the Ozone Layer: The United Nations History (2002); Yoshida, The International Legal Régime for the Protection of the Stratospheric Ozone Layer (2001); Benedick, Ozone Diplomacy: New Directions in Safeguarding the Planet (2d ed. 1998).

B. PROTECTING AGAINST GLOBAL CLIMATE CHANGE

Perhaps the most challenging contemporary threat to the global environment is that of climate change. Building upon the experience of the ozone-depletion regime, states developed an initial framework convention, which was then supplemented by a protocol that sets specific targets and timetables concerning emission of "greenhouse gases." To date, the United States has not joined this regime, and some doubt its overall likelihood of success. Do you think that the current approach to addressing the threat of climate change is the most feasible? Can it be improved? Are there any credible alternatives for a legal regime that might be superior?

CONGRESSIONAL RESEARCH SERVICE, GLOBAL CLIMATE CHANGE: MAJOR SCIENTIFIC AND POLICY ISSUES

CRS Report RL33602 (Aug. 11, 2006) (footnotes omitted)

Global Climate Change Science

A preponderance of the world's scientists have concluded that human activities have contributed to increased atmospheric concentrations of carbon dioxide (CO_2) by 36% from pre-industrial values of 280 parts per million (ppm) to 380 ppm over the past 150 years, leading to an increase in global average temperatures. Global temperatures have already risen 0.6° (0.9°F) in the last 100 years, and, according to model projections, might rise anywhere from as little as 1.8°C to as much as 7.1°C (2.7°F to 10.7°F) over the next 100 years. However, the science of climate change is not without challengers, who argue that scientific proof is incomplete or contradictory, and that there remain many uncertainties about the nature and direction of Earth's future climate state. Nevertheless, there is significant concern that human activities, such as the burning of fossil fuels, industrial production, deforestation, and certain land-use practices, are increasing atmospheric concentrations of carbon dioxide (CO_2) that, along with increasing concentrations of other trace gases such as methane

(CH_4), nitrous oxide (N_2O), hydrofluorocarbons (HFCs), perfluorocarbons (PFCs), and sulfur hexafluoride (SF_6), may be leading to changes in the chemical composition and physical dynamics of Earth's atmosphere, including how heat/energy is distributed between land, ocean, atmosphere, and space.

* * *

U.N. Framework Convention on Climate Change (UNFCCC)

The United Nations Framework Convention on Climate Change (UNFCCC) was opened for signature at the 1992 United Nations Conference on Environment and Development (UNCED) conference in Rio de Janeiro (known by its popular title, the Earth Summit). On June 12, 1992, the United States, along with 153 other nations, signed the UNFCCC, that upon ratification committed signatories' governments to a voluntary "non-binding aim" to reduce atmospheric concentrations of greenhouse gases with the goal of "preventing dangerous anthropogenic interference with Earth's climate system." These actions were aimed primarily at industrialized countries, with the intention of stabilizing their emissions of greenhouse gases at 1990 levels by the year 2000; and other responsibilities would be incumbent upon all UNFCCC parties. The parties agreed in general that they would recognize "common but differentiated responsibilities," with greater responsibility for reducing greenhouse gas emissions in the near term on the part of developed/industrialized countries, which were listed and identified in Annex I of the UNFCCC and thereafter referred to as "Annex I" countries.

On September 8, 1992, then-President George H. W. Bush transmitted the UNFCCC for advice and consent of the U.S. Senate to ratification. The Foreign Relations Committee approved the treaty and reported it (Senate Exec. Rept. 102–55) October 1, 1992. The Senate consented to ratification on October 7, 1992, with a two-thirds majority vote. President Bush signed the instrument of ratification October 13, 1992, and deposited it with the U.N. Secretary General. According to terms of the UNFCCC, having received over 50 countries' instruments of ratification, it entered into force March 24, 1994.

Since the UNFCCC entered into force, the parties have been meeting annually in conferences of the parties (COP) to assess progress in dealing with climate change, and beginning in the mid–1990's, to negotiate the Kyoto Protocol to establish legally binding obligations for developed countries to reduce their greenhouse gas emissions. After completion of the Protocol in 1997, COP meetings focused on formulating the operational rules that would prevail as nations attempted to meet their obligations to reduce emissions. These rules were essentially agreed upon at COP–7 (see below) in 2001. A number of difficult issues were under discussion at these annual meetings, including how emissions trading rules would be set, how to count elements in a nation that absorb carbon (carbon "sinks") such as forests, and the continuing question of "next steps" that might focus on how to proceed in the period following the year 2012, which concludes the "commitment period" during which emissions reductions were to be achieved by those countries with reduction obligations. * * *

[Note: The Kyoto Protocol, Dec. 10, 1997, U.N. Doc. FCCC/ CP/1997/L.7/Add.1, 37 I.L.M 22 (1998), only sets emissions targets for developed states (e.g., the United States) or states regarded as undergoing a transition to a market economy (e.g., Bulgaria). Those targets are set forth in Annex B to the Kyoto Protocol, which overall would result in about a 5.2% reduction in emission levels from 1990 during a five-year period 2008–2012. Targets are not uniform; they vary among states owing to differences in energy production and consumption profiles. Thus, the targets range from an 8% reduction for most developed European states to a 10% increase in the emission levels allowed for Iceland.]

On February 16, 2005, the Kyoto Protocol entered into force. At that time, 141 nations had ratified it, including 35 of the 38 Annex B industrialized countries. Those Annex B parties to the UNFCCC that have ratified the Kyoto Protocol continue to express hope that the United States will re-engage in international efforts to reduce greenhouse gas emissions. As of July 10, 2006, some 164 nations had ratified or accepted the Kyoto Protocol.

* * *

COP–4, Buenos Aires

COP–4 took place in Buenos Aires in November 1998. It had been expected that the remaining issues unresolved in Kyoto would be finalized at this meeting. However, the complexity and difficulty of finding agreement on these issues proved insurmountable, and instead the parties adopted a two-year "Plan of Action" to advance efforts and to devise mechanisms for implementing the Kyoto Protocol, to be completed by 2000.

* * *

COP–6 "bis," Bonn, Germany

[The COP–6 negotiations in Bonn, Germany] took place after President George Bush had become the U.S. President and had rejected the Kyoto Protocol in March. As a result, the U.S. delegation to this meeting declined to participate in the negotiations related to the Protocol, and chose to act as observers. As the other parties negotiated the key issues, agreement was reached on most of the major political issues, to the surprise of most observers given the low level of expectations that preceded the meeting. The agreements included:

(1) Mechanisms—the "flexibility" mechanisms which the United States had strongly favored as the Protocol was initially put together, including emissions trading; joint implementation; and the Clean Development Mechanism (CDM), which provides fund-

ing from developed countries for emissions reduction activities in developing countries, with credit for the donor countries. One of the key elements of this agreement was that there would be no quantitative limit on the credit a country could claim from use of these mechanisms, but that domestic action must constitute a significant element of the efforts of each Annex B country to meet their targets.

(2) Carbon sinks—credit was agreed to for broad activities that absorb carbon (carbon sinks) from the atmosphere or store it, including existing forest and crop land management, and revegetation, with no overall cap on the amount of credit a country could claim for sinks activities. In the case of forest management, an Appendix Z establishes country-specific caps for each Annex I country; for example, a cap of 13 million tons could be credited to Japan (which represents about 4% of its base-year emissions). For crop land management, countries could receive credit only for carbon sequestration increases above 1990 levels.

(3) Compliance—final action on compliance procedures and mechanisms that would address noncompliance with Protocol provisions was deferred to COP–7, but broad outlines of consequences for failing to meet emissions targets would include a requirement to "make up" shortfalls at 1.3 tons to 1; suspension of the right to sell credits for surplus emissions reductions; and a required compliance action plan for those not meeting their targets.

(4) Financing—* * * new funds were agreed upon to provide assistance for needs associated with climate change; a least-developed-country fund to support National Adaptation Programs of Action; and a Kyoto Protocol adaptation fund supported by a CDM levy and voluntary contributions.

A number of operational details attendant upon these decisions remained to be negotiated and agreed upon; these were the major issues of the COP–7 meeting that followed.

* * *

COP–7, Marrakesh, Morocco

At the COP–7 meeting in Marrakech, Morocco, October 29–November 10, 2001, negotiators in effect completed the work of the Buenos Aires Plan of Action, finalizing most of the operational details and setting the stage for nations to ratify the Protocol. The United States delegation continued to act as observers, declining to participate in active negotiations. Other parties continued to express their hope that the United States would re-engage in the process at some point, but indicated their intention to seek ratification of the requisite number of countries to bring the Protocol into force (55 countries representing 55% of developed country emissions of carbon dioxide in 1990). A target date for bringing the Protocol into force was put forward—the August–September 2002 World

Summit on Sustainable Development (WSSD) to be held in Johannesburg, South Africa—but this target was not met. The main decisions at COP–7 included operational rules for international emissions trading among parties to the Protocol and for the CDM and joint implementation; a compliance regime that outlines consequences for failure to meet emissions targets but defers to the parties to the Protocol after it is in force to decide whether these consequences are legally binding; accounting procedures for the flexibility mechanisms; and a decision to consider at COP–8 how to achieve a review of the adequacy of commitments that might move toward discussions of future developing country commitments.

DERNBACH & KAKADE, CLIMATE CHANGE LAW: AN INTRODUCTION

29 Energy L.J. 1, 8–9, 29–30 (2008) (footnotes omitted)

Virtually all options for addressing climate change fall into one of four categories. The first is emissions control, which involves direct reductions in greenhouse gas emissions. The first is the option that is most like traditional pollution control. The second is energy efficiency and conservation, which indirectly reduces greenhouse gas emissions from fossil fuels because it reduces the amount of energy that is used. The third is long-term carbon storage or carbon sequestration. In this option, carbon dioxide is stored in soil, bedrock, or other places so that it is no longer in the atmosphere and cannot return to the atmosphere. Some of these places, or sinks, work naturally (e.g., carbon dioxide storage in trees), but there is also considerable discussion about creating them to store carbon on a massive basis. This option, for example, might enable the carbon dioxide emissions from a coal-fired power plant to be captured and then placed permanently underground. The final option is adaptation. This option is based on the recognition that climate change is already under-way—as indicated by the [Intergovernmental Panel on Climate Change (IPCC)] reports. The object of adaptation is to anticipate and minimize the negative consequences of climate change.

Most observers believe that all four of these approaches will be needed to effectively address climate change. * * *

* * *

A significant number of comprehensive climate change bills were introduced [in the U.S. Congress] in 2007. These bills are comprehensive because they address all six greenhouse gases that are subject to reduction under the Kyoto Protocol, not just carbon dioxide. They also apply to all sectors of the economy, not just, for example, electrical generation or transportation. The bills tend to cover the largest emitters of greenhouse gases and those entities indirectly responsible for the largest share of emissions. The bills would also establish a national goal of reducing greenhouse gas emissions to one-quarter or one-third of existing levels by 2050. If Congress decides to adopt comprehensive regulation of greenhouse gas omissions, it has three basic options. These are a cap-and-trade approach, a greenhouse gas tax, and a "sectoral hybrid" approach. As indicated by the bills introduced in 2007, the sectoral hybrid approach is the direction in which U.S. policy is most likely to evolve.

The cap-and-trade approach builds on U.S. experience with the acid rain provisions of the 1990 Clean Air Act amendments, which imposed emissions reduction on many electric power plants. Within that approach, there are "downstream" and "upstream" options. A "downstream" approach involves the direct regulation of emitters. The 1990 Clean Air Act amendments, for instance, represent "downstream" regulation of power plants. A pure "downstream" approach in the U.S. would be impossible because it would include direct regulation of millions of cars and buildings. An "upstream" approach, by contrast, would capture such sources through direct regulation of, for example, upstream gasoline and home heating, fuel refiners or suppliers. Still another cap-and-trade would establish a "downstream" cap-and-trade system that would apply only to large stationary sources such as power plants or industrial facilities. * * *

A greenhouse gas tax, the preferred approach for most economists, is attractive because it would be comprehensive and because it would reach all sources regardless of size. It is not clear in advance, however, how much greenhouse gas emissions reduction would be achieved. The public reaction to recent high oil prices indicates that the effect may be easier to measure afterwards than it is to predict in advance. An additional problem, of course, is political acceptability. Still, there are indications that policy makers may be taking a carbon tax more seriously.

The "sectoral hybrid" approach employs both a large-source cap-and-trade program and product efficiency standards such as those for automobiles and appliances. This approach would build on existing experience and would, if designed properly, reach most of the economy. Many of the bills now before Congress would cap overall emissions and emissions from covered entities at declining levels in accordance with emissions reduction goals, and authorize regulated entities to purchase and use allowances (equal to one ton of carbon dioxide equivalent) to meet required reductions. They also combine a cap-and-trade approach with renewable energy portfolio standards and similar requirements. * * *

There are, of course, other issues. One is how to most effectively maintain and enhance the considerable state and local efforts that already exist. A second is how to most effectively engage individuals in a national effort to address climate change. A third is whether we can effectively address climate change without addressing energy demand in the United States and the rest of the world.

NOTES

1. *IPCC.* The Intergovernmental Panel on Climate Change (IPCC) is a scientific, intergovernmental body of experts set up in 1988 by the World

Meteorological Organization (WMO) and the United Nations Environment Programme (UNEP) for the purpose of surveying existing research on climate change and providing objective assessments of the projected impact of climate change, as well as options for adaptation and mitigation. Its reports are widely publicized and have served as catalysts for development of the climate change treaties. See Intergovernmental Panel on Climate Change, http://www.ipcc.ch/index.htm.

2. *Further Reading*. For further reading, see Yamin & Depledge, The International Climate Change Regime: A Guide to Rules, Institutions and Procedures (2004); Climate Change Policy: A Survey (Schneider, Rosencranz, & Niles eds. 2002); Victor, The Collapse of the Kyoto Protocol, and the Struggle to Slow Global Warming (2001); Bodansky, The United Nations Framework Convention on Climate Change: A Commentary, 18 Yale J. Int'l L. 451 (1993).

C. PROTECTING AGAINST LOSS OF BIOLOGICAL DIVERSITY

Traditionally, international environmental law dealt only with the protection of particular endangered species, not with the conservation of the entire global ecosystem. Yet over the past twenty years, many have become alarmed at the rapid and accelerating loss of "biological diversity" (or "biodiversity") from the extensive human encroachment upon virtually all areas of the planet, some of which is attributable to ozone depletion and climate change.

Why worry about loss of biodiversity? Apart from any inherent concern about the rights of non-human species to exist, scientists warn that loss of biodiversity can upset the balance of the ecosystem in which humans live, creating adverse consequences for human health and well-being. Less plant species means less potential variety of crops. Less genetic materials in plants means less possible new drugs from extraction of those materials. While maintaining a spectrum of bacteria may not seem relevant to daily life, it becomes so when we appreciate that bacteria are critical in the breakdown and absorption of pollution, nutrient storage and recycling, and soil formation.

At the 1992 UNCED, states adopted the Convention on Biological Diversity, June 5, 1992, 1760 U.N.T.S. 79. Under this Convention, "biological diversity" is defined as "the variability among living organisms from all sources including, *inter alia*, terrestrial, marine and other aquatic ecosystems and the ecological complexes of which they are part: this includes diversity within species, between species and of ecosystems." Id. art 2. The Convention establishes a monitoring system for biodiversity and provides for national *in situ* and *ex situ* conservation measures. Id. arts. 8 & 9. Each Party is obliged to set up a system of protected areas "where special measures need to be taken to conserve biological diversity." Id. art. 8(a). For the purpose of complementing these *in situ* measures, each Party must adopt measures for *ex situ* conservation of components of biodiversity outside their natural habitat. Furthermore, the Convention provides for national reports on implementing measures and their effectiveness, national strategies, plans or programs to protect biodiversity, and environmental impact assessments of projects for adverse effects on biodiversity.

A central dynamic in the negotiation of the Convention involved concerns by developing states that their biodiversity not only be preserved, but be protected from exploitation by companies from developed states (e.g., pharmaceutical companies), who might seize unique biological specimens, develop a marketable product from those specimens, and then reap the economic rewards without any equitable sharing with the developing state. Consequently, various provisions of the Convention speak to access to genetic resources within states, access to technology developed from those resources, and sharing of any benefits derived from those resources. See id. arts. 15–19. The United States has signed, but not ratified the Convention, apparently due to continuing concerns that these provisions fail to protect adequately private intellectual property rights.

For further discussion of the Convention and protection of biodiversity, see Biodiversity and the Precautionary Principle: Risk and Uncertainty in Conservation and Sustainable Use (Cooney & Dickson eds. 2005); Kunich, Ark of the Broken Covenant: Protecting the World's Biodiversity Hotspots (2003); McConnell, The Biodiversity Convention: A Negotiating History (1996); Perlman & Adelson, Biodiversity: Exploring Values and Priorities in Conservation (1997).

SECTION 4. TRADE IN HAZARDOUS AND ENDANGERED GOODS

A third important and recurring paradigm in international environmental law concerns trade in hazardous or endangered goods. Here there is a conscious decision by states (or private actors within states) to send the goods across frontiers for use or disposal, and the concern is that such transboundary movements may have adverse effects on human or animal health or the environment. Legal regimes have tended to focus on a notice-and-consent process, whereby the exporting and important states have obligations to maintain transparency in the trade and to restrict trade that is deemed to have deleterious effects.

A. KEY REGIMES

1. Trade in Endangered Species

Long before adoption of the Convention on Biological Diversity, states realized that many species of animals or plants had become, or were on the verge of becoming, extinct due to human demand for them or their body parts, such as tortoise shells or ivory for jewelry, whale oil for energy, rhinoceros horns and tiger bones for medicines, leopard skins for coats, mahogany for furniture, or orangutans as pets. In 1973, shortly after the Stockholm Conference, states adopted the Convention on International Trade in Endangered Species of Wild Fauna and Flora, Mar. 3, 1973, 27 U.S.T. 1087, 993 U.N.T.S. 243 (CITES). CITES establishes a global system for strictly regulating trade in species threatened with extinction.

While it contains various provisions designed to protect endangered species, at the heart of CITES are three lists that trigger differing levels of protection for any given proposed transboundary movement of a species or specimen. Appendix I species are those "threatened with extinction which are or may be affected by trade." See id. art. II(1). Giant pandas, gorillas, and Asian elephants, for example, are on this list. For such species, both the exporting state and the importing state must first issue permits authorizing the shipment, after both states consider whether the export will be detrimental to the survival of the species and whether the shipment is suitable in terms of safety and care of the animal. If either permit has not been issued, the shipment may not go forward.

Appendix II species are generally those who "although not necessarily now threatened with extinction may become so unless trade in specimens of such species is subject to strict regulation in order to avoid utilization incompatible with their survival." Id. art II(2)(a). The American black bear and African grey parrot are examples of Appendix II species. For these species, only the exporting state must issue a permit upon satisfying itself that the export will not be detrimental to the species and that the shipment will be safe; the importing state must simply check to be sure an export permit has been issued. If no export permit has been issued, the shipment may not go forward.

Appendix III species are those that any particular party identifies as ones that they wish to subject to regulation. Id. art. II(3). For instance, the United States has placed the alligator and snapping turtle on this list. For those species, all importing states must require their importers of that species to present a certificate of origin for their shipment; if that certificate shows that the animal (or specimen) came from the state that listed the species on Appendix III, then the importer must also present an export permit from the state that listed the species. If this is not done, the shipment may not go forward. Id. art. 5.

For an assessment that the convention is generally effective, but has several weaknesses, see Reeve, Policing International Trade in Endangered Species: The CITES Treaty and Compliance (2002); see also Endangered Species, Threatened Convention (Hutton & Dickson eds. 2000).

2. Trade in Hazardous Wastes

Endangered species are regarded as positive goods; we seek to protect and preserve them. By contrast, there can also be trade in negative goods, such as hazardous wastes from industrial or other processes, that can cause adverse effects if released into the environment during their shipment or after their disposal.

In 1989, states adopted the Basel Convention on the Control of Transboundary Movements of Hazardous Wastes and their Disposal, Mar. 22, 1989, S. Treaty Doc. No. 102–5, 1673 U.N.T.S. 57. The convention provides for environmentally sound management and disposal of hazardous wastes transported across borders principally through use of a notice-and-consent regime. Wastes falling within the scope of the convention are defined; those wastes cannot be exported until notice is sent to and consent is received from the importing state. Both states must satisfy themselves that both the shipment and the disposal or recycling process is conducted in a manner that will protect human health and the environment. Id. art. 4; see Belenky, Cradle to Border: U.S. Hazardous Waste Export Regulations and International Law, 17 Berkeley J. Int'l L. 95, 120–24 (1999).

Similar conventions have also been adopted with respect to trade in chemicals and persistent organic pollutants. See Rotterdam Convention on the Prior Informed Consent Procedure for Certain Hazardous Chemicals and Pesticides in International Trade, Sept. 10, 1998, 2244 U.N.T.S. 337; Stockholm Convention on Persistent Organic Pollutants, May 22, 2001, S. Treaty Doc. No. 107–5, U.N. Doc. UNEP/POPS/CONF/2.

3. Trade in Genetically Modified Organisms

The Convention on Biological Diversity contemplated the possibility of a protocol that would address risks concerning the release of genetically modified organisms (GMOs) into the environment. In 2000, states adopted the Cartagena Protocol on Biosafety to the Convention on Biological Diversity, Jan. 29, 2000, 39 I.L.M. 1027, which establishes a notice-and-consent regime for the export of living, genetically-modified organisms (LMOs) that are to be introduced into the environment of the importing state (e.g., genetically-modified seeds for planting or fish for stocking a lake). Hence, the Protocol requires exporting states to obtain advance permission from the importing country before shipping the LMO. The protocol does not regulate trade in non-living genetically altered products, such as bread made from genetically engineered wheat that is intended for consumption, nor does the Protocol apply to pharmaceuticals.

Once an LMO has been approved for commercial use in one country, that country is obliged to send information about it to an Internet-based biosafety clearinghouse. Other countries are then free to decide whether or not they are willing to accept the imports. The aim is to ensure that recipient countries have both the opportunity and the capacity to assess risks involving the products of genetic modification. This may be viewed as an application of the precautionary principle allowing a state to take action to protect itself even if there is no scientific certainty that the import of an LMO would be dangerous.

A state that has not become a party to the Convention on Biological Diversity (such as the United States) cannot become a party to the Protocol. Nevertheless, a state not party to the Protocol likely will have to comply with its provisions when exporting to states parties to the Protocol, since the latter otherwise may not allow the shipment to enter its territory. For commentary, see Biotechnology and International Law (Francioni & Scovazzi eds. 2006); Murphy, Biotechnology and International Law, 42 Harv. Int'l L.J. 47 (2001).

B. BALANCING TRADE AND ENVIRONMENT RULES

The regimes discussed above, and other international environmental regimes, seek to restrict the trade in goods in certain circumstances so as to achieve environmental objectives. As a general matter, however, international trade law seeks to reduce or eliminate barriers to trade in order to promote open markets and economic development. Consequently, there is a tension between the fields of trade law and international environmental law that has led to conflicts between states and, in some instances, resort international dispute resolution. Moreover, this tension has a North/South dimension, with developing states quite wary that developed states are using environmental concerns essentially as a non-tariff barrier to imports from the developing world. How should international agreements and principles of international law resolve such conflicts?

One avenue is to include within treaties some mechanism for resolving conflicts. For example, in the Biosafety Protocol, the parties stated in the preamble that "trade and environment agreements should be mutually supportive with a view to achieving sustainable development," suggesting a need for trade obligations to account for environmental objectives. At the same time, that preamble states "that this Protocol shall not be interpreted as implying a change in the rights and obligations of a Party under any existing international agreements," suggesting that existing trade law obligations are unaffected by the Protocol. Cartagena Protocol, 39 I.L.M. 1027, preamble. How would you interpret such language? See Rivera–Torres, The Biosafety Protocol and the WTO, 26 B.C. Int'l & Comp. L. Rev. 263 (2003); Safrin, Treaties in Collision? The Biosafety Protocol and the World Trade Organization Agreements, 96 A.J.I.L. 606 (2002).

The principal agreement in world trade law is the General Agreement on Tariffs and Trade, Oct. 30, 1947, 61 Stat. A–11, 55 U.N.T.S. 194 (GATT), which was first adopted in 1947, but revised as part of the Uruguay Round of trade negotiations, so as to create a "GATT 1994." See Marrakesh Agreement Establishing the World Trade Organization, Apr. 15, 1994, 108 Stat. 4809, 1867 U.N.T.S 3 (GATT 1994). GATT Article XX contains important exceptions to its trade rules, including two especially relevant to international environmental law. It states:

Subject to the requirement that such measures are not applied in a manner which would constitute a means of arbitrary or unjustifiable discrimination between countries where the same conditions prevail, or a disguised restriction on international trade, nothing in this Agreement shall be construed to prevent the adoption or enforcement by any contracting party of measures:

* * *

(b) necessary to protect human, animal or plant life or health; [or]

* * *

(g) relating to the conservation of exhaustible natural resources if such measures are made effective in conjunction with restrictions on domestic production or consumption; * * *.

One well-known example of the trade/environment tension arose in the so-called *Tuna/Dolphin* and *Shrimp/Turtle* cases before GATT or World Trade Organization dispute panels. In the *Tuna/Dolphin* dispute, the United States had banned the import of tuna caught by Mexican fisherman, which was being done without proper regard for the incidental catch and killing of dolphins. In 1991, the U.S. ban was ruled incompatible with U.S. obligations under the GATT. See Report of the Panel, United States—Restrictions on Imports of Tuna, (Sept. 3, 1991), GATT B.I.S.D. (39th Supp.) at 155 (1993). That decision caused an outcry among environmentalists, who saw global trade rules as a potential vehicle for striking down national laws worldwide that were protective of the environment. These facts are an example of a ''process and production method'' (PPM) dispute; the issue is not whether the imported goods themselves are unsafe or harmful (the tuna), but rather whether the method by which they were produced had adverse environmental effects—effects not even directly felt in the importing state.

In the *Shrimp/Turtle* case seven years later, a WTO panel came to the same result with regard to the U.S. import ban on shrimp from India, Malaysia, Pakistan and Thailand, which were being harvested without regard to the incidental, harmful effects on sea turtles. The WTO Appellate Body, however, partially overturned that finding. See Appellate Body Report, United States—Import Prohibition of Certain Shrimp and Shrimp Products, WTO Doc. WT/DS58/AB/R (Oct. 12, 1998). In part through references to major international environmental conventions (especially to the Convention on Trade in Endangered Species and the Convention on the Conservation of Migratory Species of Wild Animals), the Appellate Body held that the trade restraints imposed by the U.S. regime served a legitimate environmental objective and were not incompatible with the GATT. However, the Appellate Body found that, while the environmentally based trade restraints were not themselves contrary to the GATT, the United States had contravened the GATT by applying those restraints unilaterally in a discriminatory manner. When concluding its decision, the Appellate Body highlighted the following:

> 185.   * * * [W]e wish to underscore what we have *not* decided in this case. We have *not* decided that the protection and preservation of the environment is of no significance to Members of the WTO. Clearly it is. We have *not* decided that the sovereign nations that are Members of the WTO cannot adopt effective measures to protect endangered species, such as sea turtles. Clearly they can and should. And we have *not* decided that sovereign states should not act together bilaterally, plurilaterally or multilaterally, either within the WTO or in other international fora, to protect endangered species or to otherwise protect the environment. Clearly they should and do.

> 186.   What we *have* decided in this appeal is simply this: although the measure of the United States in dispute in this appeal serves an environmental objective that is recognized as legitimate under paragraph (g) of Article XX of the GATT 1994, this measure has been applied by the United States in a manner which constitutes arbitrary and unjustifiable discrimination between Members of the WTO, contrary to the requirements of the chapeau of Article XX. For all of the specific reasons outlined in this Report, this measure does not qualify for the exemption that Article XX of the GATT 1994 affords to measures which serve certain recognized, legitimate environmental purposes but which, at the same time, are not applied in a manner that constitutes a means of arbitrary or unjustifiable discrimination between countries where the same conditions prevail or a disguised restriction on international trade. As we emphasized in *United States—Gasoline*, WTO Members are free to adopt their own policies aimed at protecting the environment as long as, in so doing, they fulfill their obligations and respect the rights of other Members under the *WTO Agreement*.

Id. (footnotes omitted).

Part of the discrimination identified by the Appellate Body derived from the U.S. ban on imports of shrimp harvested by the commercial shrimp trawlers from any country not certified by the United States, even when those vessels were using turtle-excluder devices (TEDs) comparable to those considered acceptable for U.S. vessels. After the Appellate Body's decision, the United States instituted a broad range of procedural changes to the U.S. import regime, including greater flexibility for the importation of shrimp harvested by vessels using TEDs in uncertified nations. A WTO panel determined that with these changes the U.S. regime was fully compatible with WTO rules, a decision upheld by the WTO Appellate Body. Appellate Body Report, United States—Import Prohibition of Certain Shrimp and Shrimp Products: Recourse to Article 21.5 by Malaysia, WTO Doc. WT/DS58/AB/RW (Oct. 22, 2001).

For further discussion, see Sustainable Development in World Trade Law (Gehring & Segger eds. 2005); Knox, The Judicial Resolution of Conflicts Between Trade and the Environment, 28 Harv. Envtl L. Rev. 1 (2004); Charnovitz, The Law of Environmental "PPMs" in the WTO: Debunking the Myth of Illegality, 27 Yale J. Int'l L. 59 (2002); Driesen, What is Free Trade? The Real Issue Lurking Behind the Trade and Environment Debate, 41 Va. J. Int'l L. 279 (2001).

CHAPTER 19

STATE SUCCESSION

∎ ∎ ∎

SECTION 1. INTRODUCTION

The rights, capacities, and obligations of a state appertain to the state and are not affected by changes in its government. Yet if a state becomes independent of another state of which it had formed a part, or a predecessor state has separated into a number of states, important issues arise relating to the extent to which the resulting states succeed to the rights, capacities, and obligations of their predecessor. For instance, do the predecessor state's treaty obligations continue? Do the new states succeed to the predecessor state's membership in international organizations? Which state or states should have access to funds of the predecessor state held abroad, such as reserves held with the New York Federal Reserve Bank? Which state or states should have access to the predecessor state's diplomatic properties abroad? Which should be viewed as responsible for paying the debts of the prior state?

Most successions in the twentieth century resulted from peace treaties or from decolonization. At the end of the Cold War in the 1990s, major successions took place with the disintegration of the Soviet Union and the political changes that swept Eastern and Central Europe. These included the unification of Germany in 1990 (which involved an absorption by the Federal Republic of Germany of all of the territory of the German Democratic Republic without creating a new state), the dissolution of the U.S.S.R. at the end of 1991 and the emergence of fifteen states in its former territory, the peaceful separation of the Czech Republic and Slovakia effective in 1993, and the violent breakup of the Socialist Federal Republic of Yugoslavia that has given rise to half a dozen states in its former territory.

What rules should apply when these changes occur? Should there be a rule in international law that the new state succeeds to no rights or obligations of its predecessor, but instead begins with a *tabula rasa* (blank slate)? Or should such a rule be reserved to situations of decolonization, where there is a sense that the new state should not be bound by an oppressor's prior decisions? Instead of a blank slate, should a new state be responsible for all the obligations of, and enjoy all rights of, its predecessor? Would that rule make sense in a situation where the predecessor state fragments into multiple new states? In that instance, should the rule provide for some form of equitable allocation of the rights and responsibilities? If so, what standards should determine equitability? Should it depend upon the circumstances of the succession and the specific rights and obligations that are at issue?

There is no single, comprehensive treaty, nor fully consistent state practice, setting forth the rules in this area of international law. Three major efforts at international law-making initiated by the U.N. International Law Commission have sought to resolve some of the uncertainties:

- In 1978, a Convention on Succession of States in Respect of Treaties was adopted in Vienna, Aug. 23, 1978, 1946 U.N.T.S 3 [1978 Treaty Succession Convention]. This convention finally entered into force in 1996, but has garnered only a relatively small number of ratifications (twenty-two as of early 2009).

- In 1983, a Convention on the Succession of States in Respect of State Property, Archives and Debts was adopted in Vienna, Apr. 6, 1983, U.N. Doc. A/CONF. 117/14, 22 I.L.M. 306 (1983) [1983 Succession Convention]. This convention was still not yet in force as of early 2009. See generally Nathan, The Vienna Convention on Succession of States in Respect of State Property, Archives and Debts, in International Law at a Time of Perplexity 489 (Dinstein ed. 1989).

- In 1999, the I.L.C. completed work on a third succession topic and recommended to the General Assembly the adoption, in the form of a declaration, of Articles on Nationality in Relation to the Succession of States. See U.N. Doc. A/CN.4/L.573 (May 27, 1999). The General Assembly took note of the articles and invited states to take them into account when faced with such an issue. G.A. Res. 55/153 (Dec. 12, 2000).

Some of the rules expressed in these three instruments may be codifying general international law, but for two reasons it cannot be assumed that this is true of the documents overall. First, the I.L.C.'s work was aimed in some respects at progressive development in controversial spheres. Second, the I.L.C.'s results have been skeptically received and have not yet achieved general acceptance through treaty ratifications. Consequently, the law must be divined by carefully analyzing the practice of states and the conditions under which certain precedents occurred. For a classic discussion, see O'Connell, State Succession in Municipal Law and International Law (1967); see also Menon, The Succession of States in Respect to Treaties, State Property, Archives, and Debts (1991).

The United States has ratified neither of the two conventions. Nonetheless, the U.S. State Department Legal Adviser stated that the rules of the 1978 Vienna Convention were "generally regarded as declarative of existing customary international law by the United States." Roberts Owen quoted in Leich, Digest of US Practice 1041 n. 43 (1980). In at least some aspects, international courts have treated that convention as codificatory of customary law. See the 1997 *Gabčíkovo–Nagymaros* case, *infra* this chapter, Section 3(b). In other respects, however, the existence of state practice to validate the claim that it reflects custom is questionable.

This chapter surveys the effect of state succession in a variety of contexts, including membership in international organizations, treaty relations, the internal legal system of the successor state, public debt and other contracts, property rights, obligations arising from violations of international law, and nationality of natural persons.

SECTION 2. DEVOLUTION, DISSOLUTION, AND SECESSION

As discussed in Chapter 5, pp. 300–301, an entity may become an independent state from a predecessor state in different ways: by operation of national law allowing separation (devolution), sometimes occurring as part of the process of decolonization; by dismemberment of a predecessor state, resulting in the establishment of possibly multiple new states (dissolution); or by departure of the entity from the parent state without the latter's consent (secession).

In situations of dissolution, an important theoretical starting point is whether a complete dissolution has occurred, or whether there is a new state that can properly claim to be the "continuator" of the predecessor state, with other new states simply being pieces of the predecessor that have broken away. In other words, has the predecessor state dissolved into two or more successor states leaving nothing of the original state, or have just fragments of the predecessor state broken off to form new states, leaving behind a state that is best regarded as a "continuator state" or "continuity of the predecessor state"? The theoretical framework chosen has important implications when considering succession of treaty obligations, of membership in international organizations, or of debts and assets.

Chapter 5 recounted how the former Socialist Federal Republic of Yugoslavia (S.F.R.Y.) ended in the early 1990s when several of its constituent units declared independence (Bosnia–Herzegovina, Croatia, Macedonia, Slovenia). Should those declarations of independence be regarded as decisions by parts of the S.F.R.Y. to break away, leaving intact a reduced "mother" state? Or did the declarations of independence signify the disappearance of the S.F.R.Y., thereby requiring all the sub-units (including those left behind, Serbia and Montenegro) to seek admission to the United Nations and other international organizations as new members? If the latter, what should be done with all the assets and debts of the S.F.R.Y.?

CONFERENCE ON YUGOSLAVIA ARBITRATION
COMMISSION OPINION NO. 8

Issued July 4, 1992
31 I.L.M. 1521 (1992), 4 E.J.I.L. 87 (1993)

[On May 18, 1992, the Chairman of the Badinter Commission received a letter from Lord Carrington, Chairman of the Conference for Peace in Yugoslavia, asking for the Commission's opinion on the following question:

> "In its Opinion No 1 of 29 November 1991 the Arbitration Commission was of the opinion 'that the SFRY (was) in the process of dissolution'. Can this dissolution now be regarded as complete?"

The Commission responded in part as follows:]

2. The dissolution of a state means that it no longer has legal personality, something which has major repercussions in international law. It therefore calls for the greatest caution.

The Commission finds that the existence of a federal state, which is made up of a number of separate entities, is seriously compromised when a majority of these entities, embracing a greater part of the territory and population, constitute themselves as sovereign states with the result that federal authority may no longer be effectively exercised.

By the same token, while recognition of a state by other states has only declarative value, such recognition, along with membership of international organizations, bears witness to these states' conviction that the political entity so recognized is a reality and confers on it certain rights and obligations under international law.

3. The Arbitration Commission notes that since adopting Opinion No 1:

— the referendum proposed in Opinion No 4 was held in Bosnia–Herzegovina on 29 February and 1 March: a large majority of the population voted in favour of the Republic's independence;

— Serbia and Montenegro, as Republics with equal standing in law, have constituted a new state, the "Federal Republic of Yugoslavia", and on 27 April adopted a new constitution;

— most of the new states formed from the former Yugoslav Republics have recognized each other's independence, thus demonstrating that the authority of the federal state no longer held sway on the territory of the newly constituted states;

— the common federal bodies on which all the Yugoslav republics were represented no longer exist: no body of that type has functioned since;

— the former national territory and population of the SFRY are now entirely under the sovereign authority of the new states;

— Bosnia–Herzegovina, Croatia and Slovenia have been recognized by all the Member States of the European Community and by numerous other states, and were admitted to membership of the United Nations on 22 May 1992;

— UN Security Council Resolutions Nos 752 and 757 (1992) contain a number of references to the "former SFRY";

— what is more, Resolution No 757 (1992) notes that "the claim by the Federal Republic of Yugoslavia (Serbia and Montenegro) to continue automatically (the membership) of the former Socialist Federal Republic of Yugoslavia (in the United Nations) has not been generally accepted";

— the declaration adopted by the Lisbon European Council on 27 June makes express reference to "the former Yugoslavia".

4.   The Arbitration Commission is therefore of the opinion:

— that the process of dissolution of the SFRY referred to in Opinion No 1 of 29 November 1991 is now complete and that the SFRY no longer exists.

CONFERENCE ON YUGOSLAVIA ARBITRATION COMMISSION OPINION NO. 9

Issued July 4, 1992
31 I.L.M. 1523 (1992), 4 E.J.I.L. 88 (1993)

[If the S.F.R.Y. dissolution was now complete, Lord Carrington also asked "on what basis and by what means should the problems of the succession of states arising between the different states emerging from the S.F.R.Y. be settled?" The Commission responded in part as follows:]

1.   * * * In Opinion No. 8, the Arbitration Commission concluded that the dissolution of the Socialist Republic of Yugoslavia (SFRY) had been completed and that the state no longer existed. New states have been created on the territory of the former SFRY and replaced it. All are successor states to the former SFRY.

2.   As the Arbitration Commission pointed out in its first Opinion, the succession of states is governed by the principles of international law embodied in the Vienna Conventions of 23 August 1978 and 8 April 1983, which all Republics have agreed should be the foundation for discussions between them on the succession of states at the Conference for Peace in Yugoslavia.

The chief concern is that the solution adopted should lead to an equitable outcome, with the states concerned agreeing on procedures subject to compliance with the imperatives of general international law and, more particularly, the fundamental rights of the individual and of peoples and minorities.

3.   In the declaration on former Yugoslavia adopted in Lisbon on 27 June 1992, the European Council stated that:

"the Community will not recognize the new federal entity comprising Serbia and Montenegro as the successor State of the former Yugoslavia until the moment that decision has been taken by the qualified international institutions. They have decided to demand the suspension of the delegation of Yugoslavia at the CSCE and other international fora and organizations."

The Council thereby demonstrated its conviction that the Federal Republic of Yugoslavia (Serbia and Montenegro) has no right to consider itself the SFRY's sole successor.

4.   The Arbitration Commission is therefore of the opinion that:

— the successor states to the SFRY must together settle all aspects of the succession by agreement;

— in the resulting negotiations, the successor states must try to achieve an equitable solution by drawing on the principles embodied in the 1978 and 1983 Vienna Conventions and, where appropriate, general international law;

— furthermore full account must be taken of the principle of equality of rights and duties between states in respect of international law;

— the SFRY's membership of international organizations must be terminated according to their statutes and that none of the successor states may thereupon claim for itself alone the membership rights previously enjoyed by the former SFRY;

— property of the SFRY located in third countries must be divided equitably between the successor states;

— the SFRY's assets and debts must likewise be shared equitably between the successor states;

— the states concerned must peacefully settle all disputes relating to succession to the SFRY which could not be resolved by agreement in line with the principle laid down in the United Nations Charter;

— they must moreover seek a solution by means of inquiry, mediation, conciliation, arbitration or judicial settlement;

— since, however, no specific question has been put to it, the Commission cannot at this stage venture an opinion on the difficulties that could arise from the very real problems associated with the succession to the former Yugoslavia.

NOTES

1. *The Pursuit of Continuity.* Why do you think the F.R.Y. (Serbia and Montenegro) saw it as desirable to be regarded as the continuator of the S.F.R.Y.? To maintain existing memberships in international organizations? To obtain exclusive control over S.F.R.Y. assets abroad, including bank accounts and embassies? To preserve a measure of prestige and authority in the region? See Buhler, State Succession and Membership in International Organizations: Legal Theories versus Political Pragmatism (2001).

2. *A Pursuit that Failed.* In various international bodies, the F.R.Y. claimed continuity with the former S.F.R.Y. At the United Nations, this would have meant keeping the S.F.R.Y.'s U.N. membership, including its seat at the U.N. General Assembly. As it turned out, the F.R.Y.'s claim in this regard was not accepted. On the recommendation of the U.N. Security Council, S.C. Res. 757, (May 30, 1992), the General Assembly denied the F.R.Y. the right to succeed automatically to the U.N. membership of the S.F.R.Y. See G.A. Res. 47/1 (Sept. 22, 1992). Other U.N. organs and agencies followed suit. After the F.R.Y. election in 2000 resulting in the fall of Slobodan Milošević, the F.R.Y. applied for U.N. membership and was admitted by the General Assembly upon the Security Council's favorable recommendation. See G.A. Res. 55/12 (Nov. 1, 2000). See Blum, UN Membership of the "New" Yugoslavia: Continuity or Break?, 86 A.J.I.L. 830 (1992); Blum, Was Yugoslavia a Member of the United Nations in the Years 1992–2000?, 101 A.J.I.L. 800 (2007).

3. *A Pursuit that Succeeded.* By contrast, the claim of the Russian Federation to assume the U.N. membership of the former Union of Soviet Socialist Republics, including the permanent seat on the Security Council, was generally accepted, including by the other permanent members and by the new states that had formerly formed part of the Soviet Union. When the U.S.S.R. began collapsing, a Commonwealth of Independent States (C.I.S.) was formed consisting of the former Soviet republics, with the exception of the three Baltic states of Estonia, Latvia, and Lithuania. The C.I.S. founding agreement provided that the states of the C.I.S. "support Russia's continuance of the membership of the Union of Soviet Socialist Republics in the United Nations, including permanent membership of the Security Council, and other international organizations." See Agreements Establishing the Commonwealth of Independent States, Dec. 8 & 21, 1991, 31 I.L.M. 138, 151 (1992). Note that Article 23 of the U.N. Charter still provides that a permanent seat is held by "the Union of Soviet Socialist Republics".

Hence, there was an essential continuity of the Russian Federation with the U.S.S.R., albeit with alterations in territory, population, and government, rather than a wholesale dissolution of the U.S.S.R. On this and related points, see Müllerson, The Continuity and Succession of States, by Reference to the Former USSR and Yugoslavia, 42 I.C.L.Q. 473 (1993); Shaw, State Succession Revisited, 5 Finnish Y.B.I.L. 34 (1994).

SECTION 3. STATE SUCCESSION IN RESPECT OF TREATIES

A. GENERAL STATE PRACTICE ON TREATY SUCCESSION

In situations of devolution, the predecessor and the new state often conclude agreements concerning the "devolution" of rights and obligations under treaties. For example, such agreements were generally used by the United Kingdom when transferring sovereignty to former colonial territories. Such agreements provide a clear and convenient means for ascertaining which agreements that previously bound the predecessor state are now viewed as also binding the new state, at least in the eyes of the predecessor state and the new state.

Yet, by their terms, such agreements do not bind other states, including states that are parties to the treaties in question. Can a devolution agreement have an effect of third parties? The International Law Commission has commented on such agreements as follows:

> The practice of States does not admit, therefore, the conclusion that a devolution agreement should be considered as by itself creating a legal nexus between the successor State and third States parties, in relation to treaties applicable to the successor State's territory prior to its independence. Some successor States and some third States parties to one of those treaties have undoubtedly tended to regard a devolution agreement as creating a certain presumption of the continuance in force of certain types of treaties. But neither successor States nor third States nor depositaries have as a general rule attributed automatic effects to devolution agreements. Accordingly, State practice as well as the relevant principles of the law of treaties would seem to indicate that devolution agreements, however important as general manifestations of the attitude of successor States to the treaties of their predecessors, should be considered as *res inter alios acta* for the purposes of their relations with third States.

International Law Commission Report on Succession of States, [1974] II(1) Yb.I.L.C. 186.

To address the situation of the relationship to third states, the International Law Commission distinguished the situation of a "newly independent state" in the 1978 Vienna Convention. Article 2, paragraph 1(f) defines a "newly independent State" as "a successor State the territory of which immediately before the date of the succession * * * was a dependent territory for the international relations of which the predecessor State was responsible." In these essentially decolonization situations, the drafters of the Vienna Convention favored a "clean slate" approach, in which the newly independent state would be able to pick and choose which treaties of the colonial power it wished to retain. By contrast, in non-colonial situations, a new state generally would be expected to continue all the predecessor state's treaty obligations, unless for any given treaty there was a particular reason why it should not be continued (e.g., a new state that was land-locked would not be expected to continue certain maritime agreements). Does such a distinction make sense? Is it still relevant given that the process of decolonization (of significance in the 1970s) is now essentially over?

Further complications may arise in circumstances where there are no agreements even between a predecessor state and the new state(s), which may occur in the context of dissolution (in which there may be no agreement among the various units that emerge as new states) or in the situation of unilateral secession. Are those new states bound to the treaties of the predecessor state? Should they be entitled to a "blank slate"? The 1978 Treaty Succession Convention attempted to answer such questions; do you think the answers are the right ones?

VIENNA CONVENTION ON SUCCESSION OF STATES IN RESPECT OF TREATIES

Signed in Vienna, Aug. 23, 1978
1946 U.N.T.S. 3

Article 11

Boundary regimes

A succession of States does not as such affect:

(a) a boundary established by a treaty; or

(b) obligations and rights established by a treaty and relating to the regime of a boundary.

Article 12

Other territorial regimes

1. A succession of States does not as such affect:

(a) obligations relating to the use of any territory, or to restrictions upon its use, established by a treaty for the benefit of any territory of a foreign State and considered as attaching to the territories in question;

(b) rights established by a treaty for the benefit of any territory and relating to the use, or to restrictions upon the use, of any territory of a foreign State and considered as attaching to the territories in question.

2. A succession of States does not as such affect:

(a) obligations relating to the use of any territory, or to restrictions upon its use, established by a treaty for the benefit of a group of States or of all States and considered as attaching to that territory;

(b) rights established by a treaty for the benefit of a group of States or of all States and relating to the use of any territory, or to restrictions upon its use, and considered as attaching to that territory.

3. The provisions of the present article do not apply to treaty obligations of the predecessor State providing for the establishment of foreign military bases on the territory to which the succession of States relates.

* * *

Article 22: Notification of succession

1. A notification of succession in respect of a multilateral treaty [by a newly independent state] shall be made in writing.

2.   If the notification of succession is not signed by the Head of State, Head of Government or Minister for Foreign Affairs, the representative of the State communicating it may be called upon to produce full powers.

3.   Unless the treaty otherwise provides, the notification of succession shall:

(a) be transmitted by the newly independent State to the depositary, or, if there is no depositary, to the parties or the contracting States;

(b) be considered to be made by the newly independent State on the date on which it is received by the depositary or, if there is no depositary, on the date on which it is received by all the parties or, as the case may be, by all the contracting States.

* * *

Article 31

Effects of a uniting of States in respect of treaties in force at the date of the succession of States

1.   When two or more States unite and so form one successor State, any treaty in force at the date of the succession of States in respect of any of them continues in force in respect of the successor State unless:

(a) the successor State and the other State party or States Parties otherwise agree; or

(b) it appears from the treaty or is otherwise established that the application of the treaty in respect of the successor State would be incompatible with the object and purpose of the treaty or would radically change the conditions for its operation.

* * *

Article 34: Succession of States in cases of separation of parts of a State

1.   When a part or parts of the territory of a State separate to form one or more States, whether or not the predecessor State continues to exist:

(a) any treaty in force at the date of the succession of States in respect of the entire territory of the predecessor State continues in force in respect of each successor State so formed;

(b) any treaty in force at the date of the succession of States in respect only of that part of the territory of the predecessor State which has become a successor State continues in force in respect of that successor State alone.

2.   Paragraph 1 does not apply if:

(a) the States concerned otherwise agree; or

(b) it appears from the treaty or is otherwise established that the application of the treaty in respect of the successor State would be incompatible with the object and purpose of the treaty or would radically change the conditions for its operation.

REPORT OF THE INTERNATIONAL LAW ASSOCIATION COMMITTEE ON ASPECTS OF THE LAW OF STATE SUCCESSION

Promulgated at the 73rd Conference, Rio De Janeiro
Res. 3/2008, annex (Aug. 17–21, 2008)

5.   Recent State practice shows different approaches of the successor States with regard to treaties in cases of secession and dissolution. Although in their vast majority, successor States considered themselves as successor to the multilateral treaties, some of them adopted the clean slate rule, rendering that succession merely optional. Yet other States decided to accede to some multilateral treaties to which the predecessor State was a party. In principle, Article 34 of the 1978 Vienna Convention was referred to by most of the successor States, whereas for some others that Article does not reflect customary law.

6.   The UN Secretary–General has requested to every successor State—no matter the type of State succession concerned—to produce specific declarations of succession to each multilateral treaty to which the UN is the depositary. This practice is also being followed by other depositaries, either States or international organizations. Remarkably, this practice corresponds to that set up by Article 22 to the 1978 Vienna Convention, [which] only related to newly independent States. According to UN practice, the successor State must satisfy the conditions provided for by the treaty for becoming party to it.

7.   In the case of incorporation of a State to another existing one, international practice departs from the partial spatial succession established by Article 31 of the 1978 Vienna Convention. Succession to the treaties concluded by the predecessor States seems to be the general rule in case of unification, whereas in the case of incorporation the trend is the termination of the treaties to which the predecessor State was a party, unless otherwise decided by the successor State or agreed between the parties.

8.   With regard to bilateral treaties concluded by the predecessor State, practice shows that the fate of these treaties is generally decided through negotiation between the successor State and the other party, no matter the category of State succession involved. The *rebus sic stantibus* rule is sometimes invoked as a way to obtain the renegotiation of the treaty.

9.   Case law and practice show that the rule of Article 11 related to succession to boundaries established by a treaty is largely followed. The same can be stated in relation with the rule upon other territorial regimes set up by Article 12 of the same Convention. The general rule of succession is particularly followed in relation to the successor State whose territory is directly concerned by the relevant territorial regime.

10. Succession with regard to disarmament treaties is governed by the object and purpose thereof. In some cases, this has lead to the application of the non-succession rule to the successor States.

11. Treaties related to the protection of human rights are generally perceived by the doctrine as governed by the succession rule. However, international practice is not homogeneous. Some successor States opted to accede to those treaties. It seems that no specific rule has emerged thereon. Hence, general rules on State succession with regard to treaties remain applicable.

12. Treaties constituting international organizations are governed by what they establish in relation to membership. With the exception of the uniting of States and incorporation of existing member States, international practice shows a general application of the non-succession rule, although some particular international organizations—in particular those having a financial character—adopted the succession rule. Article 4 of the 1978 Vienna Convention proceeds to a conciliation of interests leading in practice to the exclusion of succession, unless explicitly admitted by the treaties constituting international organizations themselves.

13. Treaties adopted within international organizations follow the general rules related to succession, with the exception of those treaties which require membership as a condition to be parties to them. In the latter case, no automatic succession is permitted.

NOTES

1. *Parsing the Practice.* If the I.L.A. report is correct, is state practice following the dichotomy established by the I.L.C. for the treatment of "newly independent states"? How would you explain the direction that state practice is taking?

2. *Unilateral Declarations Concerning Continuation.* A number of newly independent states have made unilateral declarations of a general character regarding the continuation of treaties of their predecessor states. Such declarations have varied in form but have generally provided for the provisional application of such treaties during a period in which the new state would examine the treaties and determine which would be adopted and which terminated. Such declarations were designed to avoid sudden discontinuity and also to avoid an assumption of universal succession; they came to be known as "pick and choose" declarations. For examples of such declarations, see International Law Commission Report on Succession of States, [1974] II(1) Yb.I.L.C. 188–92. The International Law Commission described the legal effect of such agreements, as follows:

> Accordingly, the legal effect of the declarations seems to be that they furnish bases for a *collateral* agreement in simplified form between the newly independent State and the individual parties to its predecessor's treaties for the provisional application of the treaties after independence. The agreement may be express but may equally arise from the conduct of any individual State party to any treaty covered by the declaration, in

particular from acts showing that it regards the treaty as still having application with respect to the territory.

International Law Commission Report on Succession of States, [1974] II(1) Yb.I.L.C. 192; see also Zimmermann, Secession and the Law of State Succession, in Secession: International Law Perspectives 208, 213–21 (Kohen ed. 2006) ("Seceding States have traditionally—at least as a matter of principle—claimed not to be automatically bound by treaties concluded by their respective predecessor States.")

3. *German Reunification*. Article 31 of the 1978 Treaty Succession Convention addresses the issuing of the uniting of states. While such occurrences are rare, they do occur. In the case of the reunification of Germany, two treaties entered into by the two German states helped address problems of treaty succession. First, the two German states entered into a Treaty Covering the Establishment of German Unity, Aug. 31, 1990, 30 I.L.M. 457 (1991), which established a single, democratic, federal state upon entry into force on October 3, 1990. Among other things, the treaty (also known as the "Unification Treaty") recognized that the treaties in force for the Federal Republic of Germany (i.e., West Germany) before unification would extend to the territory of the German Democratic Republic (i.e., East Germany). With respect to treaties of the former G.D.R., the Unification Treaty called for consultation with the other parties to settle the questions of continuity, adjustment or termination. Second, the Treaty on the Final Settlement with Respect to Germany, Sept. 12, 1990, 29 I.L.M. 1186 (1990), which was also signed by the four main allies of World War II (France, U.S., U.S.S.R., and U.K.), terminated the rights and responsibilities of the four powers and the quadripartite treaties relating to Germany. This treaty (also known as the "Two Plus Four" treaty) provided that the prior external borders of the two German states would remain final, that all Soviet troops would be withdrawn from Germany by the end of 1994, and that Germany had the right to belong to alliances. As indicated, these treaties left open for consultation which treaties of the former G.D.R. would continue in force for that territory, but it was understood that "GDR treaties with ideological-political contents inconsistent with the attitude of the unified state are no longer valid." Steinberger, Germany Reunified: International and Constitutional Problems, 1992 B.Y.U. L. Rev. 23.

4. *Treaty Succession for the former Soviet Republics*. In the case of the dissolution of the U.S.S.R., several instruments were concluded just before and shortly after dissolution among the republics, which included a memorandum of understanding on issues of succession to treaties. See 32 I.L.M. 138 (1992); see also Müllerson, The Continuity and Succession of States, by Reference to the Former USSR and Yugoslavia, 42 I.C.L.Q. 473, 479–80 (1993).

5. *Treaty Succession for the former Yugoslavia*. In the case of the dissolution of the Socialist Federal Republic of Yugoslavia (S.F.R.Y.), no one of the resulting republics was accepted as the "continuator" state; rather, they were all viewed as successor states. Some of them affirmed continuity of the treaties of the S.F.R.Y., while in other cases new instruments of accession were registered. This issue held very important practical consequences for a

region beset with ethnic turmoil and armed conflict: for example, were the successor states bound to major human rights treaties to which the S.F.R.Y. was a party? Could they be held accountable before the committees and tribunals involved in monitoring implementation of such treaties? What degree of specificity must exist in a unilateral declaration to make clear whether succession to a treaty has occurred?

APPLICATION OF THE CONVENTION ON THE PREVENTION AND PUNISHMENT OF THE CRIME OF GENOCIDE (CROATIA v. SERBIA)

International Court of Justice, 2008
www.icj-cij.org

[In 1999, Croatia sued the Federal Republic of Yugoslavia (F.R.Y.)—which in 2003 became "Serbia and Montenegro" and then in 2006 just "Serbia"—before the International Court of Justice. According to Croatia, Serbia was responsible for committing violations of the 1948 Genocide Convention from 1991 to 1995 by directly engaging in or encouraging acts of "ethnic cleansing" of Croats in certain parts of Croatia. Further, Croatia argued that pursuant to Article IX of the Convention, the Court has jurisdiction over disputes relating to the responsibility of a state under the Convention.

Serbia responded by raising certain preliminary objections to the Court's jurisdiction, one of which concerned whether the F.R.Y. was a party to the Genocide Convention. While its predecessor state (the Socialist Federal Republic of Yugoslavia or S.F.R.Y.) had adhered to the Genocide Convention, Serbia argued that the F.R.Y. did not become bound upon dissolution of the S.F.R.Y. since the F.R.Y. was not the continuator state. Croatia responded that the F.R.Y. had made a declaration on April 27, 1992 that the F.R.Y. was the continuator state and "shall strictly abide by all the commitments that the [S.F.R.Y.] had assumed" (a similar statement was made by the Permanent Mission of Yugoslavia to the United Nations by a Diplomatic Note of April 27, 1992). To this, Serbia responded that a much more specific notification is required to bring about secession of a treaty, one that specifies which treaty the notification covers.]

109.　In the view of the Court, there is a distinction between the legal nature of ratification of, or accession to a treaty, on the one hand, and on the other, the process by which a State becomes bound by a treaty as a successor State or remains bound as a continuing State. Accession or ratification is a simple act of will on the part of the State manifesting an intention to undertake new obligations and to acquire new rights in terms of the treaty, effected in writing in the formal manner set out in the Treaty (cf. Arts. 15 and 16 of the Vienna Convention on the Law of Treaties). In the case of succession or continuation on the other hand, the act of will of the State relates to an already existing set of circumstances, and amounts to a recognition by that State of certain legal consequences flowing from those circumstances, so that any document issued by the State concerned, being essentially confirmatory, may be subject to less rigid requirements of form. Article 2 *(g)* of the 1978 Vienna Convention on Succession of States in respect of Treaties reflects this idea, defining a "notification of succession" as meaning "in relation to a multilateral treaty, any notification, however framed or named, made by a successor State expressing its consent to be considered as bound by the treaty". Nor does international law prescribe any specific form for a State to express a claim of continuity.

* * *

111.   For the purposes of the present case, the Court points out first and foremost that the FRY in 1992 clearly expressed an intention to be bound—or, consistently with the view of the legal situation it then held, to continue to be bound—by the obligations of the Genocide Convention. The FRY was then claiming to be the continuator State of the SFRY, but it did not repudiate its status as a party to the Convention even when it became apparent that that claim would not prevail, and that the FRY was regarded by other States, particularly by those that had emerged from the dissolution of the former Yugoslavia, as simply one of the successor States of the SFRY. In the particular context of the case, the Court is of the view that the 1992 declaration must be considered as having had the effects of a notification of succession to treaties, notwithstanding that its political premise was different. It is clear that the operative part of the 1992 declaration, the acceptance of "all the commitments that the Socialist Federal Republic of Yugoslavia assumed internationally", had been drawn up in the light of its assertion, made in the declaration and in the Note of the Permanent Mission, of "the continuity of the international personality of Yugoslavia", and this was linked with the claim of the FRY to continue the membership of the SFRY in the United Nations. There was however no indication that the commitment undertaken would be conditional on acceptance of the claim of continuity. That claim did not in fact prevail. Nonetheless, the conduct of Serbia after the transmission of the declaration made it clear that it regarded itself bound by the Genocide Convention.

* * *

114.   * * * As early as 1993, in the context of the first request for the indication of provisional measures in the proceedings brought against it by Bosnia and Herzegovina, the FRY, while questioning whether the applicant State was a party to the Genocide Convention at the relevant dates, did not challenge the claim that it was itself a party, and itself presented a request for the indication of provisional measures, referring to Article IX of the Convention. On this basis, the Court in its Order found that "both Bosnia–Herzegovina and Yugoslavia are parties" to the Convention (*Application of the Convention on the Prevention and Punishment of the Crime of Genocide (Bosnia and Herzegovina* v. *Yugoslavia (Serbia and Montenegro)), Provisional Measures, Order of 8 April 1993, I.C.J.*

Reports 1993, p. 16, para. 26), and cited the 1992 declaration and Note (*ibid.*, p. 15, paras. 22–23). Moreover, in the same case, at the preliminary objections stage, the FRY argued that the Genocide Convention had begun to apply to relations between the two Parties on 14 December 1995, * * * having itself continued the rights and duties, under *(inter alia)* that Convention, established by the SFRY. Furthermore, on 29 April 1999 the FRY filed in the Registry of the Court Applications instituting proceedings against ten States Members of NATO, citing *(inter alia)* the Genocide Convention as title of jurisdiction (see for example *Legality of Use of Force (Serbia and Montenegro v. Belgium), Preliminary Objections, Judgment, I.C.J. Reports 2004*, p. 284, para. 1).

115.   This was still the situation when on 2 July 1999 Croatia filed the Application instituting the present proceedings. During the period between the making of the 1992 declaration and that date, neither the FRY nor any other State for which the issue might have had significance questioned that the FRY was a party to the Genocide Convention, without reservations; and no other event occurring during that period had any impact on the legal situation arising from the 1992 declaration. On 1 November 2000, the FRY was admitted as a new Member of the United Nations, as it had requested * * *. As the Court observed in its Judgments in the cases concerning the *Legality of Use of Force*, "[t]his new development effectively put an end to the *sui generis* position of the Federal Republic of Yugoslavia within the United Nations . . ." (*Legality of Use of Force (Serbia and Montenegro v. Belgium), Preliminary Objections, Judgment, I.C.J. Reports 2004*, p. 310, para. 78). Nevertheless, the FRY did not at that time withdraw, or purport to withdraw, the declaration and Note of 1992, which had been drawn up in the light of the contention that the FRY was continuing the legal personality of the SFRY. It did not, for example, suggest that the failure of that contention to gain acceptance had entailed the nullity of the declaration, or cessation of the commitment to the international obligations contemplated by it.

* * *

117.   In sum, in the present case the Court, taking into account both the text of the declaration and Note of 27 April 1992, and the consistent conduct of the FRY at the time of its making and throughout the years 1992–2001, considers that it should attribute to those documents precisely the effect that they were, in the view of the Court, intended to have on the face of their terms: namely, that from that date onwards the FRY would be bound by the obligations of a party in respect of all the multilateral conventions to which the SFRY had been a party at the time of its dissolution, subject of course to any reservations lawfully made by the SFRY limiting its obligations. It is common ground that the Genocide Convention was one of these conventions, and that the SFRY had made no reservation to it; thus the FRY in 1992 accepted the obligations of that Convention, including Article IX providing for the jurisdiction of the Court

and that jurisdictional commitment was binding on the Respondent at the date the present proceedings were instituted.

NOTES

1. *Genocide Cases Against Serbia.* The International Court of Justice has confirmed the essential continuity of obligations under the human rights treaties of the S.F.R.Y. throughout the territories of all the successor states. See *Application of the Genocide Convention* (Bosnia and Herzegovina v. Yugoslavia (Serbia–Montenegro)), 1996 I.C.J. 595, 610–12 (Jurisdiction). For a critique of the Court's disposition of Serbia's preliminary objections in the Croatia case, see Blum, Consistently Inconsistent: The ICJ and the Former Yugoslavia (Croatia v. Serbia Judgment), 103 A.J.I.L. (forthcoming 2009).

On the merits in the *Bosnia–Herzegovina v. Yugoslavia* case, the Court found unproven that Serbia was directly involved in genocide during the armed conflict in Bosnia in 1993–95, but found that Serbia did violate the Convention by failing to prevent the 1995 massacre at the town of Srebrenica. Further, the Court found that Serbia violated the Convention by failing to try or transfer persons accused of genocide to the International Criminal Tribunal for the former Yugoslavia (ICTY). *Application of the Convention on the Prevention and Punishment of the Crime of Genocide* (Bosnia & Herzegovina v. Serbia & Montenegro), 2007 I.C.J. 191. Croatia's case before the Court against Serbia remains pending as of the publication of this casebook.

2. *Automatic Succession of Human Rights Treaties?* Do you think that global human rights and humanitarian law treaties should generally be seen as continuing given their fundamental importance, especially in times of turmoil (such as occurs in cases of dissolution or secession), regardless of any declaration by the successor state? In the *Čelebići Case* before the International Criminal Tribunal for the former Yugoslavia, the Appeals Chamber considered whether Bosnia–Herzegovina was a party to the 1949 Geneva Conventions on the protection of persons in times of armed conflict, during the period between its independence as a state on March 6, 1992 and its deposit of an instrument of succession to the Conventions with the International Committee of the Red Cross (ICRC) on December 31, 1992. The Appeals Chamber stated:

> 111.   Although Article 23(2) of the [1978 Treaty Succession] Convention * * * provides that pending notification of succession, the operation of the treaty in question shall be considered "suspended" between the new State and other parties to the treaty, the Appeals Chamber finds that in the case of this type of treaty, this provision is not applicable. This is because, for the following reasons, the Appeals Chamber confirms that the provisions applicable are binding on a State from creation. The Appeals Chamber is of the view that irrespective of any findings as to formal succession, Bosnia and Herzegovina would in any event have succeeded to the Geneva Conventions under customary law, as this type of convention entails automatic succession, *i.e.*, without the need for any formal confirmation of adherence by the successor State. It may now be

considered in international law that there is automatic State succession to multilateral humanitarian treaties in the broad sense, *i.e.*, treaties of universal character which express fundamental human rights. * * *

112. It is indisputable that the Geneva Conventions fall within this category of universal multilateral treaties which reflect rules accepted and recognized by the international community as a whole. The Geneva Conventions enjoy nearly universal participation.

113. In light of the object and purpose of the Geneva Conventions, which is to guarantee the protection of certain fundamental values common to mankind in times of armed conflict, and of the customary nature of their provisions, the Appeals Chamber is in no doubt that State succession has no impact on obligations arising out from these fundamental humanitarian conventions. * * *

Čelebići Case (Prosecutor v. Delalic et al.), I.C.T.Y. Case No. IT–96–21–A, paras. 111–13 (2001).

3. *Overcoming a Presumption of Automatic Continuity.* If there is automatic continuity for some types of treaties, it this a fixed rule of international law or only a presumption that the successor state can overcome? In 1969, Ethiopia ratified the 1949 Geneva Conventions. In 1993, Eritrea separated from Ethiopia to form a new country. In 1998, war broke out between Ethiopia and Eritrea. Eritrea eventually acceded to the Geneva Conventions in August 2000; before that date, was Eritrea bound to the 1949 Geneva Conventions, including Geneva Convention III on the protection of prisoners of war? The Eritrea Ethiopia Claims Commission analyzed the issue as follows:

24. * * * Successor States often seek to maintain stability of treaty relationships after emerging from within the borders of another State by announcing their succession to some or all of the treaties applicable prior to independence. Indeed, treaty succession may happen automatically for certain types of treaties [citing to *Gabcíkovo–Nagymaros Project*, 1997, I.C.J. 7, para. 123]. However, the Commission has not been shown evidence that would permit it to find that such automatic secession to the Geneva Conventions occurred in the exceptional circumstances here, desirable though such secession would be as a general matter. From the time of its independence from Ethiopia in 1993, senior Eritrean officials made clear that Eritrea did not consider itself bound by the Geneva Conventions.

25. During the period of the armed conflict and prior to these proceedings, Ethiopia likewise consistently maintained that Eritrea was not a party to the Geneva Conventions. The ICRC, which has a special interest and responsibility for promoting compliance with the Geneva Conventions, likewise did not at that time regard Eritrea as a party to the Conventions.

26. Thus, it is evident that when Eritrea separated from Ethiopia in 1993 it had a clear opportunity to make a statement of its succession

to the Conventions, but the evidence shows it refused to do so. It consistently refused to do so subsequently, and in 2000, when it decided to become a party to the Conventions, it did so by accession, not by succession. While it may be that continuity of treaty relationships often can be presumed absent facts to the contrary, no such presumption could properly be made in the present case in view of these facts. These unusual circumstances render the present situation very different from that addressed in the Judgement by the Appeals Chamber of the International Tribunal for the Former Yugoslavia in the *Čelebići Case*. * * * Thus, from the outbreak of the conflict in May 1998 until August 14, 2000, Eritrea was not a party to Geneva Convention III. Ethiopia's argument to the contrary, in reliance upon Article 34 of the Vienna Convention on Succession of States in Respect of Treaties, cannot prevail over these facts.

Eritrea Ethiopia Claims Commission, Partial Award on Prisoners of War, Ethiopia's Claim No. 4 (July 1, 2003), 135 I.L.R. 251 (footnotes omitted). Interestingly, although the 1978 Treaty Succession Convention referred to by the Commission has garnered only a relatively small number of ratifications, Ethiopia is among them, having ratified the treaty in 1980. How should one analyze whether Eritrea was bound to the 1978 Treaty Succession Convention as a matter of treaty succession?

B. SUCCESSION OF BOUNDARY AND TERRITORIAL TREATIES

Paragraph 9 of the I.L.A. Committee report (excerpted above) indicates that states generally follow Vienna Convention Articles 11 and 12's approach to succession of treaties relating to boundaries and territorial regimes. Why do you think that is the case?

INTERNATIONAL LAW COMMISSION REPORT ON SUCCESSION OF STATES

[1974] II(1) Yb.I.L.C. 157, 196, 201, 206

(1) Both in the writings of jurists and in State practice frequent reference is made to certain categories of treaties, variously described as of a "territorial," "dispositive," "real" or "localized" character, as binding upon the territory affected notwithstanding any succession of States. The question of what will for convenience be called in this commentary "territorial treaties" is at once important, complex and controversial. In order to underline its importance the Commission need only mention that it touches such major matters as international boundaries, rights of transit on international waterways or over another State, the use of international rivers, demilitarization or neutralization of particular localities, etc.

* * *

(17) The weight of the evidence of State practice and of legal opinion in favour of the view that in principle a boundary settlement is unaffected by the occurrence of a succession of States is strong and powerfully reinforced by the decision of the United Nations Conference on the Law of Treaties to except from the fundamental change of circumstances rule a treaty which establishes a boundary. Consequently, the Commission considered that the present draft must state that boundary settlements are not affected by the occurrence of a succession of States as such. Such a provision would relate exclusively to the effect of the succession of States on the boundary settlement. It would leave untouched any other ground of claiming the revision or setting aside of the boundary settlement, whether self-determination or the invalidity or termination of the treaty. Equally, of course, it would leave untouched any legal ground of defence to such a claim that might exist. In short, the mere occurrence of a succession of States would neither consecrate the existing boundary if it was open to challenge nor deprive it of its character as legally established boundary, if such it was at the date of the succession of States.

* * *

Running through the precedents and the opinions of writers are strong indications of a belief that certain treaties attach a régime to territory which continues to bind it in the hands of any successor State. Not infrequently other elements enter into the picture, such as an allegation of fundamental change of circumstances or the allegedly limited competence of the predecessor State, and the successor State in fact claims to be free of the obligation to respect the régime. Nevertheless, the indications of the general acceptance of such a principle remain. * * * The evidence does not, however, suggest that this category of treaties should embrace a very wide range of so-called territorial treaties. On the contrary, this category seems to be limited to cases where a State by a treaty grants a right to use territory, or to restrict its own use of territory, which is intended to attach to territory of a foreign State or, alternatively, to be for the benefit of a group of States or of all States generally. There must in short be something in the nature of a territorial régime.

GABČÍKOVO–NAGYMAROS PROJECT (HUNGARY/SLOVAKIA)

International Court of Justice, 1997
1997 I.C.J. 7

[For the factual background of this case, see p. 225.]

117.   The Court must first turn to the question whether Slovakia became a party to the 1977 Treaty as successor to Czechoslovakia. As an alternative argument, Hungary contended that, even if the Treaty survived the notification of termination, in any event it ceased to be in force as a treaty on 31 December 1992, as a result of the "disappearance of one

of the parties". On that date Czechoslovakia ceased to exist as a legal entity, and on 1 January 1993 the Czech Republic and the Slovak Republic came into existence.

118.   According to Hungary, "There is no rule of international law which provides for automatic succession to bilateral treaties on the disappearance of a party" and such a treaty will not survive unless another State succeeds to it by express agreement between that State and the remaining party. * * * It contended that it had never agreed to accept Slovakia as successor to the 1977 Treaty. Hungary referred to diplomatic exchanges in which the two Parties had each submitted to the other lists of those bilateral treaties which they respectively wished should continue in force between them, for negotiation on a case-by-case basis; and Hungary emphasized that no agreement was ever reached with regard to the 1977 Treaty.

119.   Hungary claimed that there was no rule of succession which could operate in the present case to override the absence of consent. Referring to Article 34 of the Vienna Convention of 23 August 1978 on Succession of States in respect of Treaties, in which "a rule of automatic succession to all treaties is provided for", based on the principle of continuity, Hungary argued not only that it never signed or ratified the Convention, but that the "concept of automatic succession" contained in that Article was not and is not, and has never been accepted as, a statement of general international law.

Hungary further submitted that the 1977 Treaty did not create "obligations and rights ... relating to the regime of a boundary" within the meaning of Article 11 of that Convention, and noted that the existing course of the boundary was unaffected by the Treaty. It also denied that the treaty was a "localized" treaty, or that it created rights "considered as attaching to [the] territory" within the meaning of Article 12 of the 1978 Convention, which would, as such, be unaffected by a succession of States. The 1977 Treaty was, Hungary insisted, simply a joint investment. * * *

120.   According to Slovakia, the 1977 Treaty * * * remains in force between itself, as successor State, and Hungary. * * * It relied * * * on the "general rule of continuity which applies in the case of dissolution"; it argued, secondly, that the Treaty is one "attaching to [the] territory" within the meaning of Article 12 of the 1978 Vienna Convention, and that it contains provisions relating to a boundary.

* * *

122.   * * * According to Slovakia, [Article 12] can be considered to be one of those provisions of the Vienna Convention that represent the codification of customary international law". The 1977 Treaty is said to fall within its scope because of its "specific characteristics ... which place it in the category of treaties of a localized or territorial character". Slovakia also described the Treaty as one "which contains boundary provisions and lays down a specific territorial régime" which operates in

the interest of all Danube riparian States, and as "a dispositive treaty, creating rights *in rem*, independently of the legal personality of its original signatories". * * *

123. The Court does not find it necessary for the purposes of the present case to enter into a discussion of whether or not Article 34 of the 1978 Convention reflects the state of customary international law. More relevant to its present analysis is the particular nature and character of the 1977 Treaty. An examination of the Treaty confirms that, aside from its undoubted nature as a joint investment, its major elements were the proposed construction and joint operation of a large, integrated and indivisible complex of structures and installations on specific parts of the respective territories of Hungary and Czechoslovakia along the Danube. The Treaty also established the navigational régime for an important sector of an international waterway, in particular the relocation of the main international shipping lane to the bypass canal. In so doing, it inescapably created a situation in which the interests of other users of the Danube were affected. Furthermore, the interests of third States were expressly acknowledged in Article 18, whereby the parties undertook to ensure "uninterrupted and safe navigation on the international fairway" in accordance with their obligations under the Convention of 18 August 1948 concerning the Régime of Navigation on the Danube.

In its Commentary on the Draft Articles on Succession of States in respect of Treaties, adopted at its twenty-sixth session, the International Law Commission identified "treaties of a territorial character" as having been regarded both in traditional doctrine and in modern opinion as unaffected by a succession of States [citation omitted]. The draft text of Article 12, which reflects this principle, was subsequently adopted unchanged in the 1978 Vienna Convention. The Court considers that Article 12 reflects a rule of customary international law; it notes that neither of the Parties disputed this. Moreover, the Commission indicated that "treaties concerning water rights or navigation on rivers are commonly regarded as candidates for inclusion in the category of territorial treaties" (*ibid.*, p. 33, para. 26). The Court observes that Article 12, in providing only, without reference to the treaty itself, that rights and obligations of a territorial character established by a treaty are unaffected by a succession of States, appears to lend support to the position of Hungary rather than of Slovakia. However the Court concludes that this formulation was devised rather to take account of the fact that, in many cases, treaties which had established boundaries or territorial régimes were no longer in force (*ibid.*, pp. 26–37). Those that remained in force would nonetheless bind a successor State.

Taking all these factors into account, the Court finds that the content of the 1977 Treaty indicates that it must be regarded as establishing a territorial régime within the meaning of Article 12 of the 1978 Vienna Convention. It created rights and obligations "attaching to" the parts of the Danube to which it relates; thus the Treaty itself cannot be affected by a succession of States. The Court therefore concludes that the 1977 Treaty became binding upon Slovakia on 1 January 1993.

NOTES

1. *The Ties That Bind*. Why should there be a rule favoring the ability of "newly independent states" (or any new state) to terminate treaties of predecessor states, but at the same preclude them doing so with respect to treaties on boundaries or territorial regimes? Recall the discussion in Chapter 3, Section 5(B) on the principle of *uti possidetis juris* ("as you possess"). Even when boundary disputes have arisen between a new state and another state, the new state has not claimed that it was free from the obligation to respect boundaries made in treaties of their predecessor state, whether colonial rulers or not. See Constitutive Act of the African Union, July 11, 2000, Art. 4 ("The Union shall function in accordance with the following principles: * * * (b) Respect of borders existing on achievement of independence").

2. *Parsing the Vienna Convention*. Does 1978 Vienna Convention Article 11 bar a new state from challenging an existing boundary based on a treaty? What grounds might be advanced for such challenge? Article 12 relates to "other territorial régimes" not affected by succession. Why did not this Article (and Article 11) simply provide for succession, i.e., continuity of rights and obligations, instead of declaring that the territorial régime is not affected by succession? In either case, there would be a rule of continuity. Is it not artificial to separate succession in respect of the territorial régime from succession in respect of the treaty establishing that régime? On the other hand, does it favor stability if the territorial régime (or boundary régime) is regarded as established by an executed treaty and that this legal situation rather than the treaty passed to the successor state? For discussion see International Law Commission Report on Succession of States, [1974] II(1) Yb.I.L.C. 201 (paras. 18–20), & 206 (para. 36.).

3. *Military Bases*. Article 12(3) excludes from that article treaties for the establishment of foreign military bases. Would such treaties otherwise have been binding on successor states? The United Kingdom had in 1941 granted to the United States military bases in British colonies in the West Indies. When these colonies were approaching independence, the United States declared that the future of the bases must be a matter of agreement with the newly independent states. Would the United States have had legal grounds to insist on the retention of the bases irrespective of the successor's consent? See Esgain, Military Servitudes and the New Nations, in The New Nations in International Law and Diplomacy 42–97 (O'Brien ed. 1963).

SECTION 4.   SUCCESSION IN RESPECT OF STATE ASSETS AND DEBTS

The general rules relating to succession in respect of the predecessor state's assets or debts often turn on whether the relevant assets or debts relate to the predecessor state as a whole, or relate to identifiable parts of its territory. As noted below, these general rules guide states in reaching concrete agreements about succession to assets and debts.

A. STATE ASSETS

State assets are generally "property, rights and interests which, at the date of the succession of States, were, according to the internal law of the predecessor State, owned by that State." 1983 Succession Convention, art. 8. According to the 1983 Succession Convention, a distinction should be drawn between national state assets, which are assets identifiable with the state as a whole, and territorial or local state assets, which are assets identifiable with a specific territory or owned by a political subdivision (e.g., a city or province). National assets might include gold reserves or diplomatic property held abroad, while territorial assets might include such things as power plants, dams, or mineral deposits.

1. Continuity

In a situation of continuity, and in the absence of some alternative agreement, immovable national property located outside the predecessor state (such as an embassy) remains within the ownership of the continuator state. Similarly, immovable national property located within the continuator state remains with that state. By contrast, immovable or movable state property of the predecessor state situated in, or associated with, the territory of a new state that breaks away shall pass to that new successor state. 1983 Succession Convention, art. 17(1)(a) & (b). Although state practice on the issue is scant, movable state property of the predecessor state not covered above arguably passes to the successor states in an "equitable proportion." See 1983 Succession Convention, art. 17(1)(c); but see Restatement (Third) § 209, Reporters' Note 3 (stating that all property located outside the predecessor state, including intangibles, such as bank accounts, generally remains with the predecessor state).

2. Dissolution

In a situation of dissolution, and in the absence of some alternative agreement, immovable national property located outside the predecessor state passes to the successor states in equitable proportions. 1983 Succession Convention, art. 18(1)(b). Immovable or movable state property of the predecessor state situated in or associated with the territory of a successor state shall pass to that successor state. 1983 Succession Convention, art. 18(1)(a) & (c). Movable state property of the predecessor state not covered above passes to the successor states in an equitable proportion. 1983 Succession Convention, art. 18(1)(d).

B. STATE DEBT

State debts are debts that are not attributable to private individuals or entities. This public debt may be owed to another state, to an international organization, to a publicly or privately owned financial institution, or to a private person. Here, too, a distinction is drawn between the national public debt, which is owed by the state as a whole, and territorial or local public debt, which includes debts owed by the state in respect of a specific territory or specific assets, revenues, and debts contracted by a political subdivision (e.g., a city or province). See generally Cheng, State Succession and Commercial Obligations (2006); 1 O'Connell, State Succession 369–453; Feilchenfeld, Public Debts and State Succession (1931).

1. National Public Debt

In the case of national public debt, the 1983 Succession Convention provides that, in the absence of an agreement governing succession, if there is a transfer of part of the territory of a state, a separation of part of the territory of a state or a dissolution of a state, the public debt of the predecessor shall pass to the successor state "in an equitable proportion, taking into account, in particular, the property, rights and interests which pass to the successor State in relation to that * * * debt." Articles 37, 40, & 41, 22 I.L.M. 306, 323–24 (1983). See *Ottoman Public Debt Case*, 1 U.N. Rep. Int'l Arb. Awards 529 (1925); Zemanek, State Succession after Decolonization, 116 Rec. des Cours 180, 258–69 (1965–III).

If two or more states unite, the public debt of the predecessors passes to the successor. 1983 Succession Convention, Article 39. 22 I.L.M. 322 (1983). The result is the same if a state is absorbed by another state. Restatement (Third) § 209(2)(b). If the successor state were not responsible for the public debt of the predecessor(s), the creditors would have no source of payment and the successor state might be unjustly enriched by acquiring territory or assets without having to assume the debtor entity's obligations. Restatement (Third) § 209, Comment *c*.

Article 33 of the 1983 Succession Convention takes the position that the rules relating to public debt do not apply to public debt of a state held by creditors other than states and international institutions such as the World Bank. 22 I.L.M. 306, 322 (1983). The Restatement (Third) § 209, Comment *b*, rejects this view and adopts the position that the rules also apply to public debt held by private creditors, citing the prevailing position in the International Law Commission.

When Austria was made part of the German Reich in 1938, the United States delivered notes to the German Government indicating that the United States believed it was a general doctrine of international law that the substituted sovereign assumed the debts and obligations of the absorbed state. 1 Hackworth at 545. The German Government replied that the law of state succession did not apply in this particular case because Austria had liquidated herself, the debts were "political" in character, and, moreover, that in the past the United States had failed to assume responsibility for the payment of debts. Garner, Questions of State Succession Raised by the German Annexation of Austria, 32 A.J.I.L. 421 (1938). The United States rejected these contentions. Hyde at 419.

2. Territorial or Local Public Debt

Local public debts frequently take the form of obligations incurred for funds expended on a particular project in the territory that is directly affected by separation or absorption. An example of this would be loans contracted with the International Bank for Reconstruction and Development. The Bank during the colonial era required that if the loans were extended to dependent territories, a separate Guarantee Agreement between the Bank and the colonial power be concluded. Today, debts contracted by, or on behalf of, the separating territory are assigned to the successor state by agreement between the predecessor state and the new state. If no agreement is concluded, the new state nevertheless usually assumes the debts related to its territory which were incurred before the separation or absorption. See Zemanek, *supra*, at 261–66; Feilchenfeld, *supra*, at 417–22.

Local debts may be obligations that were incurred by a fiscally autonomous governmental subdivision in the territory of the successor state before the creation of the new state. The general rule with regard to such local debts is that the change in sovereignty does not affect the local debts if the subdivision incurring those debts is unaffected by the change. If, moreover, the successor state impairs the repayment of the obligation, or causes the demise of the autonomy of the local authority which contracted the debt, the new state must assume repayment of the debt. See 1 O'Connell, State Succession, at 452–54.

3. Odious Debts

There was discussion in the International Law Commission about whether the convention on state succession to debts should include articles dealing with "odious" debts, meaning (1) debts contracted by the predecessor State with a view to attaining objectives contrary to the major interests of the successor state or of the transferred territory; or (2) all debts contracted by the predecessor State with an aim and for a purpose not in conformity with international law and, in particular, the principles of international law embodied in the Charter of the United Nations. See Report of the International Law Commission on the Work of Its Thirty–Third Session, [1981] II(2) Yb.I.L.C. 1, 78–79. Ultimately, the 1983 Succession Convention did not, in fact, deal with the issue of the non-transferability of odious debts. For a discussion of the issues and authorities relating to odious debt issues see the Ninth Report of the Special Rapporteur in [1977] II(1) Yb.I.L.C. 45, U.N. Doc. A/CN.4/301 & add. I.

C. AGREEMENTS AMONG THE SUCCESSOR STATES

While the rules above provide a framework for considering the treatment of assets and debts in a situation of succession, the specific treatment of specific assets and debts must be reduced to agreements among the relevant states. In principle, the succession of states does not affect the rights and obligations of creditors with respect to public debts. 1983 Succession Convention, art. 36, 22 I.L.M. 306, 323 (1983). However, the issue of succession to obligations in the form of public debts is often resolved by agreement between the predecessor and successor states, albeit at times under pressure from creditor states.

After the fall of Slobodan Milošević in 2000, agreement was reached among the then-five successors to the former Yugoslavia on the allocation of various assets and liabilities. See Agreement on Succession Issues Between the Five Successor States of the Former State of Yugoslavia, June 29, 2001, 41 I.L.M. 1 (2002). Annexes to the agreement address: moveable and immovable properties (Annex A); diplomatic and consular properties (Annex B); financial assets and liabilities (Annex C); archives (Annex D); pensions (Annex E); other rights, interests and liabilities (Annex G). For intricate issues faced by the International Monetary Fund and World Bank from the Yugoslav break-up, as well as that of Czechoslovakia, see Williams, State Succession and the International Financial Institutions: Political Criteria v. Protection of Outstanding Financial Obligations, 43 I.C.L.Q. 780 (1994).

Similarly, under a Memorandum of Understanding on the Debt to Foreign Creditors of the Union of Soviet Socialist Republics and Its Successors, Oct. 28, 1991, the republics declared themselves jointly and severally liable for the U.S.S.R.'s debt. Then the Treaty on Succession with Respect to the State Foreign Debts and Assets of the Soviet Union, Dec. 4, 1991, which was concluded between Armenia, Belarus, Georgia, Kazakhstan, Kyrgyzstan, Russia, Tajikistan, and Ukraine, proportionally divided the assets and debts of the former Soviet Union among the successor republics. Russia ultimately agreed to assume the debt of the U.S.S.R. and, while the other republics received certain shares in diplomatic and other properties abroad, Russia largely assumed the assets of the U.S.S.R. as well. For a discussion of these and related agreements, see Williams & Harris, State Succession to Debts and Assets: The Modern Law and Policy, 42 Harv. Int'l L.J. 355, 366–83 (2001); Antonowitcz, The Disintegration of the U.S.S.R. from the Point of View of International Law, 19 Polish Y.B.I.L. 7 (1991–92); Müllerson, The Continuity and Succession of States, by Reference to the Former USSR and Yugoslavia, 42 I.C.L.Q. 473, 475–80 (1993); Dronova, The Division of State Property in the Case of State Succession in the Former Soviet Union, in La Succession d'Etats: La Codification á L'épreuve des Faits/State Succession: Codification Tested against the Facts 781, 787–821 (Eisemann & Koskenniemi eds. 2000).

For other examples, see Treaty Covering the Establishment of German Unity, Aug. 31, 1990, 30 I.L.M. 457, 478–80 (1991); Financial and Economic Agreement, Indonesia–Netherlands, art. 25, Dec. 27, 1949, 69 U.N.T.S. 3, 252–57. For older examples, see 1 O'Connell, *supra*, at 220–32.

D.   EQUITABLE PROPORTION

What standards should guide the concept of "equitable proportion" as among successor states? Consider the following possibilities for dividing up a predecessor state's assets or debts among several successor states: (1)

distribution based on the per capita distribution among the successor states; (2) distribution based on the distribution of gross domestic product among the successor states; or (3) distribution among the successor states based on their historical contribution to the creation of the assets or the benefits they received from the debts. Regardless of which possibility is chosen, should the proportion used for distribution of assets always be the same for the distribution of the debts? For a discussion, see Blum, The Apportionment of Public Debt and Assets During State Secession, 29 Case W. Res. J. Int'l L. 263 (1997).

E. OTHER CONTRACTUAL OBLIGATIONS

When the predecessor state is a party to contracts, these contracts are often governed by national law, and if the predecessor state remains in being (as was the case where a colony became independent), the contract between the predecessor state and a private party would remain valid, unless it was so connected with the territory of the new state that it would be impossible for the predecessor state to continue to perform the contract, in which case the successor state might be considered bound. If the private party has performed only part of the contract, but is prevented from completing performance because of the change in sovereignty, national law doctrines of frustration, *quantum meruit,* unjust enrichment, or restitution may become applicable. See 1 O'Connell, *supra,* 266–67, 298.

If a contract between a private party and the state requires the construction and operation of public works or the extraction of minerals, it is clear that the contract is closely linked with the territory affected by change of sovereignty. However, it is also true that the successor state is not a party to the contract. Although the traditional law on this subject was unclear, compare *West Rand Central Gold Mining Co., Ltd. v. The King,* [1905] 2 K.B. 391, with *Sopron–Köszeg Railway Co. v. Austria & Hungary,* 2 U.N. Rep. Int'l Arb. Awards 961 (1929), economic development and concession agreements involving substantial investments by a foreign investor should be binding on the successor state. Restatement (Third) § 209, Comment *f.* Succession agreements may provide for the assumption of obligations under such agreements by the successor state.

SECTION 5. STATE SUCCESSION IN RESPECT OF DELICTUAL RESPONSIBILITY

It has been held that the successor state has no responsibility in international law for the international delicts of its predecessor. In *Robert E. Brown Claim* (United States v. Great Britain), American & British Claims Arbitration, Claim No. 30; 6 U.N. Rep. Int'l Arb. Awards 120 (1923), the claimant sought compensation for the refusal of local officials of the Boer Republics to issue licenses to exploit a goldfield. The United Kingdom contended that this was a delictual claim, and that it did not succeed to responsibility from the Boer Republics. The United States asserted that the claimant's acquired rights were infringed and that Britain did succeed to the obligation to compensate Brown. The tribunal held that Brown had acquired a property right and that he had been injured by a denial of justice, but that this was a delict responsibility that did not devolve on Britain. Similarly, in *Frederick Henry Redward Claim* (Hawaiian Claims) (Great Britain v. United States), American & British Claims Arbitration, Claim No. 85, 160–61; 6 U.N. Rep. Int'l Arb. Awards 157, 158 (1925), the claimants had been wrongfully imprisoned by the Government of the Hawaiian Republic, which was subsequently annexed by the United States. The tribunal held that "legal liability for the wrong has been extinguished" with the disappearance of the Hawaiian Republic. Note, however, that if the claim has been reduced to a money judgment, which may be considered a debt, or an interest on the part of the claimant in assets of fixed value, there will be an acquired right in the claimant, and an obligation to which the successor state has succeeded. See 1 O'Connell, State Succession 482, 485–86.

Why should the successor state not be responsible for an international wrong if it has been enriched by the wrongful action of its predecessor? With respect to the *Brown* and *Redward* awards, it has been observed: "These cases date from the age of colonialism when colonial powers resisted any rule that would make them responsible for the delicts of states which they regarded as uncivilized. The authority of those cases a century later is doubtful. At least in some cases, it would be unfair to deny the claim of an injured party because the state that committed the wrong was absorbed by another state." Restatement (Third) § 209; Reporters' Note 7. See generally Demberry, State Succession to International Responsibility (2007).

SECTION 6. STATE SUCCESSION AND A STATE'S INTERNAL LEGAL SYSTEM

With respect to the question of succession to the internal legal system of a territory, a distinction has traditionally been drawn between public law and private law. Public law, broadly, is that body of laws promulgated by the government for the effective administration of the country; it is political in character, concerns the relation of the population to the state, and pertains to the prerogatives of sovereignty. Private law, on the other hand, governs the relations between individual citizens and need not be directly affected by the administration of the country. See 1 O'Connell, *supra*, at 101–41. The traditional view held that although private law survives a state succession and the rights of private parties are not affected by the change in sovereignty, public law does not survive. Id. at 104. This view, however, does not accord with state practice.

An alternative approach, which seems closer to actual practice, is that if the public law of the new state and the public law of the predecessor state are consistent, succession takes place, but that if the laws are inconsistent, no succession occurs. In this view, succession is, in effect, a presumption, which can be rebutted by positive legislation of the new state. Id. at 107. State practice indicates that new states generally make legislative provision for continuity of the internal legal order, with the qualification that continuity must be consistent with the change in sovereignty. Id. at 118–41. Sometimes, both the predecessor state and the new state make legislative provision for succession with respect to the legal system. For instance, in the case of India, Britain provided for continuity of the legal system in the India Independence Act, 1947, 10 & 11 Geo. 6, c. 30, § 18. India provided for continuity in the Indian Constitution, art. 372(2).

With the disintegration of the U.S.S.R., some of the successor states revived aspects of municipal law predating incorporation into the Soviet Union, notably the citizenship laws of Baltic republics. On this problem, see Müllerson, The Continuity and Succession of States, by Reference to the Former USSR and Yugoslavia, 42 I.C.L.Q. 473, 484 (1993).

SECTION 7. STATE SUCCESSION IN RESPECT OF NATIONALITY

Issues involving nationality of natural persons in the context of succession have notably arisen in connection with efforts of the post-Soviet and Eastern European entities to define the categories of persons entitled to exercise rights of citizenship or to reside in their territories upon the emergence (or reemergence) of new states.

In the case of the Baltic republics, which reassumed their former sovereignty in 1991 after a half-century of forcible incorporation into the Soviet Union, one approach was to revive their pre-incorporation citizenship laws dating from the 1930s. Such measures had the effect of conferring automatic nationality on those who had been citizens prior to World War II or who were descended from such persons, and the corresponding intent of putatively denationalizing very large segments of the population (principally ethnic Russians) who had taken up residence in those republics during the Soviet period and who were now expected to meet stringent conditions for naturalization (including mastery of the local language). These nationality policies of Estonia, Latvia, and Lithuania beginning in the early 1990s came under close scrutiny and criticism from human rights groups and international organizations, on the ground of unjustifiable discrimination on the basis of ethnicity and unfair hardship to individuals and families with longstanding ties to the territory. See Müllerson, Human Rights Diplomacy 53–57, 132 (1997); Orentlicher, Citizenship and National Identity, in International Law and Ethnic Conflict 296 (Wippman ed. 1998).

The I.L.C. Articles on Nationality in Relation to Succession of States, U.N. Doc. A/CN.4/L.573 (May 27, 1999), are notable for a much greater sensitivity to human rights considerations than most earlier treatments, either of nationality or of succession. The preamble affirms, for example, that "due account should be taken both of the legitimate interests of States and those of individuals," and the I.L.C.'s commentary stresses that it is "important to safeguard basic rights and fundamental freedoms of all persons whose nationality may be affected by a succession." See Report of the International Law Commission on the work of its fifty-first session, U.N. Doc. A/54/10 (1999), [1999] II(2) Yb.I.L.C. 1. Substantively, the I.L.C. Articles would establish presumptions and default rules so that no person would be left stateless by succession, and would affirm principles of respect for the will of persons concerned, family unity, and non-discrimination.

INDEX

References are to Pages